Current Biography Yearbook 2011

EDITOR
Clifford Thompson

SENIOR EDITORS
Miriam Helbok
Mari Rich

PRODUCTION EDITOR
Bertha Muteba

ASSISTANT EDITOR
Margaret R. Mead

STAFF WRITERS
Christopher Cullen
William Dvorak
Molly M. Hagan
Dmitry Kiper
Joanna Padovano
Hallie Rose Waxman

CONTRIBUTING WRITERS
Matt Broadus
In-Young Chang
Forrest Cole
Nicholas W. Malinowski
Majid Mozaffari
Margaret R. Mead
Tracy O'Neill
Kenneth J. Partridge
Jamie E. Peck
Claire Stanford
Maria A. Suarez

EDITORIAL ASSISTANT
Carolyn Ellis

H. W. WILSON
A Division of EBSCO Publishing, Inc.
IPSWICH, MASSACHUSETTS

SEVENTY-SECOND ANNUAL CUMULATION—2011

PRINTED IN THE UNITED STATES OF AMERICA

International Standard Serial No. (0084-9499)

International Standard Book No. – 978-0-8242-1121-9

Library of Congress Catalog Card No. (40-27432)

Table of Contents

PREFACE

The aim of *Current Biography Yearbook 2011*, like that of the preceding volumes in this series of annual dictionaries of contemporary biography, now in its eighth decade of publication, is to provide reference librarians, students, and researchers with objective, accurate, and well documented biographical articles about living leaders in all fields of human accomplishment. Whenever feasible, obituary notices appear for persons whose biographies have been published in *Current Biography*.

Current Biography Yearbook 2011 carries on the policy of including new and updated biographical profiles that supersede earlier articles. Profiles have been made as accurate and objective as possible through careful researching of newspapers, magazines, the World Wide Web, authoritative reference books, and news releases of both government and private agencies. Immediately after they are published in the 11 monthly issues, articles are submitted to biographees to give them an opportunity to suggest additions and corrections in time for publication of the *Current Biography Yearbook*.

Classification by Profession–2011 and *2011 Index* are at the end of this volume. *Current Biography Cumulated Index 1940–2005* cumulates and supersedes all previous indexes. For the index to the 2006–2010 articles, see *Current Biography Yearbook 2010*.

For their assistance in preparing *Current Biography Yearbook 2011*, I thank the staff of *Current Biography* and also the staffs of the company's Computer and Manufacturing departments.

Clifford Thompson

List of Biographical Sketches

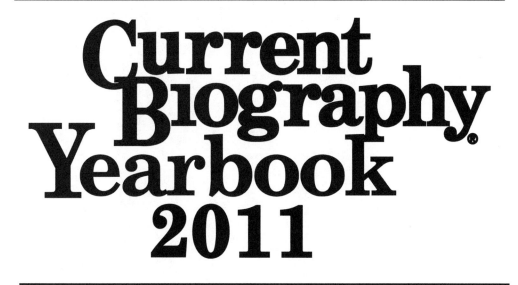

Current Biography Yearbook 2011

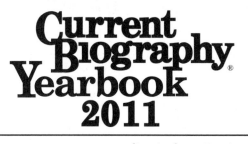

Abagnale, Frank

(AB-ig-nale)

Apr. 27, 1948– Document-security expert; lecturer; educator; writer

Address: 66 Church St., Charleston, SC 29401

As a world-renowned expert on the prevention of forgery, counterfeiting, and embezzlement, Frank Abagnale has aided the Federal Bureau of Investigation (FBI) for more than 35 years, as a consultant and educator. Abagnale serves the FBI free of charge, partly as compensation for his criminal activities in the 1960s. For nearly five years beginning when he was 16, Abagnale conned banks and other businesses out of millions of dollars by means of counterfeited and forged checks. "It started out as a means of survival, it turned into an adventure, then it became a chase," he told Stephanie Hunt for *CharlestonMag.com* (September 2010). "Despite blatant wrongdoing," Hunt noted, "Abagnale always abided by a certain code of ethics: he never swindled an individual or someone who might lose their job because of his cons"—though he feared that bank tellers might suffer that fate—and "he only bilked large institutions." In addition, he never physically injured anyone. While disguised as a Pan American Airlines pilot, Abagnale traveled, at the airline's expense, more than two million miles on Pan Am planes. Later, the false claim that he had earned an M.D. degree landed him a job as a pediatrician, and fabricated documents enabled him to join the teaching staff of a university and work in a state attorney-general's office. "I'd be a liar to say that there wasn't some parts of [that life of crime] that were glamorous . . . ," Abagnale told Anthony Breznican for the Associated Press State and Local Wire (December 24, 2002). "It was wonderful and I'll never say it wasn't. I got to go all over the world. But . . . I do understand that it was immoral, it was illegal, it was unethical, and it's not something I'm proud of." "There was no real satisfaction in walking out of a bank or situation when I had deceived someone," he told Hunt. "If anything, I felt guilt. I always knew I was wrong and that I'd get caught. Toward the end, I almost wanted to be caught. It was a very, very lonely way for a teenage boy to live."

Abagnale's career as a con artist ended in 1970, when he was captured by French police. He spent months in French and Swedish prisons and more than four years in a federal prison in the U.S. After his release, in 1976, he established Abagnale & Associates, a company that advises on the most effective methods of making documents secure against theft. On his firm's Web site, he maintains that "because punishment for fraud and recovery of stolen funds are so rare, prevention is the only viable course of action." According to that site, "More than 14,000 financial institutions, corporations and law enforcement agencies use his fraud prevention programs." His entrepreneurial success enabled Abagnale to pay back in full the airlines, hotels, and other businesses he victimized.

With Stan Redding, Abagnale wrote the book *Catch Me If You Can* (1980). The preface of the first edition stated, "This book is based on the true-life exploits of Frank Abagnale. To protect the rights of those whose paths have crossed the author's, all of the characters and some of the events have been altered, and all names, dates and places have been changed." *Catch Me If You Can* inspired the Hollywood film of the same name; released in 2002, it was directed by Steven Spielberg and starred Leonardo DiCaprio as Abagnale, Christopher Walken as his father, and Tom Hanks as an FBI agent. A Broadway adaptation of the book was scheduled to open in April 2011. Abagnale has also written several how-to books about fraud and identify-theft prevention and has lectured worldwide on those topics. "People ask me what was the most incredible thing I did in my life," he told Peter Ross for the *Sunday Herald* (January 26, 2003), a Scottish newspaper. "Was it being the pilot? Was it doing this scam? Was it being the doctor? The most incredible thing to me is that I've done all those things then come out of prison and turned my life around. I took all those negatives and made them positives. I think that's the most incredible thing about my life. It's not what I did, but what I did with it."

The second of the four children of Frank William Abagnale Sr. and the former Paulette Noel Anton, Frank William Abagnale Jr. was born on April 27, 1948. He grew up in an affluent Roman Catholic family in Bronxville, a New York City suburb, with his two brothers and a disabled sister. His father met his wife, who is of French-Algerian descent, while serving in North Africa during World War II; after his marriage he owned and managed a stationery store in Manhattan.

As a teenager and new driver, the charismatic and creative Frank Abagnale Jr. concocted a scheme involving his father's Mobil credit card to get money to spend on girls. In cahoots with a gas-station attendant, he would pretend to buy new tires or batteries with the card, which he was supposed to use only to buy gas. The credit-card company would pay the station for the purchase and bill his father, while the attendant would keep the merchandise (and the money from its sale at full price later on) and give Abagnale cash amounting to half the purchase price. The $3,400 in gas-station purchases that appeared on the credit-card statement alerted his father to Abagnale's shenanigans. Abagnale was reprimanded and briefly attended a school for delinquent boys.

Earlier, when Abagnale was 14, his parents had separated; his mother had moved out, and Abagnale had remained with his father. Two years later his parents divorced. During the divorce proceedings a judge asked Frank Jr. to decide which parent he preferred to live with. Rather than choose, he left home and found lodgings in New York City. Seven years passed before he saw his mother again; he never again saw his father, who died in 1974, while Abagnale was in prison. "There isn't a man who can look me in the eye and say he ever got over his parents' divorce," Abagnale told Jan Galletta for the Chattanooga, Tennessee, *Free Press* (September 27, 1998). "You never get over it." His mother remarried in the 1980s.

In New York Abagnale held a series of minimum-wage jobs. Unwilling to be limited by his meager earnings, he hatched a plan to acquire a lot more money. "I was very much an opportunist . . . ," he told Norman Swan for *Life Matters* (March 17, 2000). "I didn't really sit there and premeditate these things. I didn't have a genius mind and say, 'I'll do this,' but things would come to me." First, he changed the birth date on his driver's license to read 1938 (licenses did not have photo IDs back then and could be altered easily, Abagnale told Swan). At six feet in height and with premature streaks of gray in his hair, he began to pass as a 26-year-old. When he opened a checking account, he was told that until the bank issued him a checkbook containing his personalized deposit slips, he must write his account number on the bank's blank deposit slips. He then took a batch of deposit slips, printed his account number on them with magnetic ink, and returned them to the lobby for use by others. "Everyone who came in put their check right in my bank account," he told Swan. In that way, within days, his account had grown by thousands of dollars. Once his personalized checks arrived, Abagnale began cashing checks at stores, hotels, and banks, often flirting with female tellers to induce them to ignore normal security precautions.

Seeking a way to cash checks in larger amounts, Abagnale realized that a pilot's uniform would give him an air of respectability. Identifying himself as a pilot, he called Pan American Airlines' purchasing department and said that his uniform had been lost by a cleaning establishment and that he needed a replacement for an early-morning flight. He was instructed to visit the airline's vendor in New York City, where he acquired a new uniform, charging it to an employee number that he had selected randomly. Next, in the guise of an airline executive inquiring about prices, Abagnale obtained a sample Pan Am identification card from the card manufacturer and authenticated it with a decal of Pan Am's logo from a model-airplane kit. He then memorized air-industry and flight terminology. With his uniform, faked accessories, and insider's jargon, Abagnale flew free of charge all over the world as a Pan Am deadheader—an off-duty pilot who is traveling to reach a specific destination for his next assigned flight. He logged more than two million miles, visiting all 50 states and several dozen countries; he also stayed in hotels and ate in restaurants at Pan Am's expense and cashed forged Pan Am paychecks. His bogus checks acquired a more authentic look after he met an Air France stewardess whose father, a printer in France, helped him produce them. "What people see is what they believe," he told Duncan Campbell for the London *Guardian* (January 23, 2003). "When I started writing those checks, if you had used common sense and looked at them you would have laughed in my face. But they just looked at the pilot in front of them saying, 'Will you cash this check for me?'" Abagnale also adopted a series of aliases, by acquiring from government departments of vital records information concerning infants who had died soon after birth in the late 1930s. He dated many women but lost touch with all of them, in part because, to avoid the notice of police, he never stayed at any location for long. "It was a very lonely life," he told Bob Baker for the *Ottawa (Ontario, Canada) Citizen* (December 23, 2002). "Even though I met all those girls, they all thought I was someone I wasn't."

After two years Abagnale moved to Atlanta, Georgia, where he masqueraded as a pediatrician who, while on leave from a job elsewhere, was seeking to invest in real estate. Through the intervention of a neighbor of his, a physician, that deception led to his filling the temporarily vacant position of chief resident pediatrician at a local hospital. For a year, in what he described to Galletta as one of his "easiest deceptions," Abagnale worked in the largely administrative post, without ever having to diagnose or treat patients by himself. He told Anthony Breznican, "If I had applied [for the job], they'd have run all kinds of background checks, but they were saying to me, 'Can't you do this?' They were asking me to do it."

After his stint as a pediatrician, Abagnale forged a Harvard University Law School transcript, studied Louisiana state law for a few weeks, and passed the Louisiana bar examination. He practiced law for one year, for part of that time as an assistant to the state attorney general. Later, he forged a Columbia University degree and transcript and worked as a lecturer in sociology at Brigham Young University, in Salt Lake City, Utah. "He was very good at being bad at a very young age," Joseph Shea, an FBI agent who pursued Abagnale during the latter's crime spree, told Breznican. "He never hurt anybody, never physically harmed anyone. He mostly used his brain in pretending." Contrary to some sources, Abagnale was never on the FBI's "10 Most Wanted" list.

A few weeks before Abagnale's 21st birthday, a police officer in Montpellier, France, recognized and arrested him. Abagnale spent five months in a prison in Perpignon, France, in a five-by-five-foot room with stone floors and walls. According to his book *Catch Me If You Can*, the cell had no light, electricity, plumbing, or bedding; he had nothing to wear and nothing with which to brush his teeth, shave, cut his hair, or trim his nails; he had no water with which to wash except what he was given to drink with his meals; a bucket served as his toilet, and his only nourishment was bread, thin chicken soup once a day, and a daily cup of coffee. He emerged from the Perpignon prison emaciated, ill with pneumonia, and covered with lice and scabs. He then served several months in far more humane penal facilities in Sweden, from which, thanks to a sympathetic judge, he was sent not to Italy—the next on a long list of countries waiting to try him for criminal offenses—but to the U.S. As his plane landed on American soil, he escaped by removing a toilet bowl and slipping onto the runway through a hole in the plane's underside. He was soon recaptured, then escaped and was apprehended once more. He was convicted of seven counts of fraud and, in April 1971, sentenced to 12 years in a federal penitentiary in Petersburg, Virginia. There, he told Campbell, "we had movies on weekends, a miniature golf course, tennis, air conditioning. There were many people living better there than they lived on the street. The French have a shorter sentence and it's much more effective. The sentences here are long and accomplish nothing."

Abagnale was released after less than five years, "on the condition that he would help the federal government, without remuneration, by teaching and assisting federal law enforcement agencies," according to his firm's Web site. "Egotistical and self-centered" at that time, as he told Breznican, he boasted of his escapades as a guest on *The Tonight Show with Johnny Carson* and other TV talk shows and appeared in an installment of the TV game show *To Tell the Truth*, on which panelists had to guess which of three guests was "the real Frank Abagnale." He sold his story to the TV and film producers Norman Lear and Bud Yorkin for a modest sum; subsequently, the rights to the story changed hands a half-dozen times. With the help of Stan Redding, he wrote *Catch Me If You Can: The Amazing True Story of the Youngest and Most Daring Con Man in the History of Fun and Profit*, which was published in 1980. Abagnale has acknowledged that the "comically sensationalized" book, as Breznican described it, frequently stretches and embellishes the truth and sometimes departs from it altogether; although categorized as autobiography, it was written as a tale to attract readers. Bob Baker reported on his Web site Newsthinking (December 28, 2002) that his attempts to corroborate Abagnale's activities and associations through extensive investigations proved to be fruitless. Baker wrote that as early as 1978, when a *San Francisco Chronicle* reporter questioned Abagnale's assertions, the latter responded, "Due to the embarrassment involved, I doubt if anyone would confirm the information." *Catch Me If You Can* was reissued, with the subtitle *The True Story of a Real Fake*, in 2000. A musical based on the book was scheduled to open on Broadway in April 2011.

Meanwhile, Abagnale held a series of dead-end jobs, some of which he lost when his employers discovered his criminal history. Then, at the suggestion of his parole officer and with the help of an FBI agent, he launched a career as a paid security consultant, charging small sums for lectures to bank officers. Thanks to his firsthand experiences with counterfeiting and forgery and his natural talent as a public speaker, his reputation grew through word of mouth, and his income soared. He settled in Tulsa, Oklahoma, and in 1976 founded Abagnale & Associates, a firm that helps law-enforcement agencies and other government departments, financial institutions, and other businesses combat document fraud and theft. Phillip Desing, a staff member of the FBI Academy's Investigative Training Division, told Baker for the *Ottawa Citizen* that Abagnale has an "uncanny ability" to figure out criminal tactics and come up with steps to prevent their successful use in given situations. "He's about as close to brilliant as you can get," Desing declared. Abignale developed procedures, manuals, and educational programs for thousands of enterprises ranging from high-security printing companies to Australian government officials worried about fraud during the 2000 Summer Olympic Games, in Sydney. He published

Abagnale's Document Verification and Currency Transactions Manual in 1991. A multimillionaire, Abagnale paid back years ago the money he stole from airlines, hotels, and other businesses. He stopped accepting new clients in 1998; currently, he works mostly for the FBI and other U.S. government agencies.

Abagnale has often noted that tremendous advances in technology have made check fraud far easier than it was in the past. "To replicate a check 35 years ago I would have needed a printing press, color separation, plates and skill," he told Peter Sheridan for the London *Express* (May 3, 2001). "Today a PC [personal computer], color copier, scanner and ink jet printer have made this task elementary." Among other measures, he advises companies to eliminate signatures from their annual reports, so that they cannot be photocopied; to use specially watermarked or chemically treated papers for checks, to increase the difficulty of alteration; and to adopt a variety of check sizes and colors for different types of payments. He has patented the SuperBusinessCheck, which is touted as "the most secure business check in the world," its 16 safety features rendering it "virtually impossible to replicate or alter without the fraud being evident." Abagnale has also become an expert on identity theft and ways to avoid it. He has shared his expertise in lectures, seminars, and in his books *Art of the Steal: How to Protect Yourself and Your Business from Fraud—America's #1 Crime* (2001), *Real U Guide to Identity Theft* (written with Johanna Bodnyk, 2004), and *Stealing Your Life: The Ultimate Identity Theft Prevention Plan* (2007).

Abagnale and his wife, the former Kelly Anne Welbes, married in 1976. The couple lived in Tulsa until 2009, when they moved to Charleston, South Carolina. Their eldest son, Scott, is an FBI agent; the second son, Chris, owns a boutique in Charleston; and the youngest, Sean, who is fluent in Mandarin, lives and works in China. Abagnale told Peter Ross that his wife "changed my life. She gave me everything that I was always looking for in life. . . . I am the man I am today because of Kelly and my children."

—M.R.M.

Suggested Reading: Abagnale & Associates Web site; *Anchorage (Alaska) Daily News* Money p1 Apr. 19, 2004; Associated Press State and Local Wire Dec. 24, 2002; *CharlestonMag.com* Sep. 2010; *Chattanooga (Tennessee) Free Press* Lifestyle p17 Sep. 27, 1998; *Life Matters* (on-line) Mar. 17, 2000; *Ottawa (Ontario, Canada) Citizen* C p1 Dec. 23, 2002; (Scotland) *Sunday Herald* p3 Jan. 26, 2003; Abagnale, Frank, and Stan Redding. *Catch Me If You Can: The True Story of a Real Fake*, 2000; Barton, Chris. *Can I See Your I.D.?: True Stories of False Identities*, 2011

Selected Books: *Catch Me If You Can* (with Stan Redding), 1980; *The Art of the Steal: How to Protect Yourself and Your Business from Fraud—America's #1 Crime*, 2001; *Real U Guide to Identity Theft* (with Johanna Bodnyk), 2004; *Stealing Your Life: The Ultimate Identity Theft Prevention Plan*, 2007

Matthew Peyton/Getty Images

Abramson, Jill

Mar. 19, 1954– Executive editor of the New York Times

Address: New York Times, *620 Eighth Ave., New York, NY 10018*

On June 2, 2011 Jill Abramson was named executive editor of the *New York Times*, becoming the first woman to hold that post in the paper's 160-year history. After cutting her teeth as an investigative reporter in Washington, D.C., for the *Wall Street Journal* and the *Times*, Abramson became the *Times*'s Washington bureau chief in 2000 and managing editor of the paper in 2003. She was the first woman to occupy either position in what many consider to be a male-dominated institution. Upon accepting her new post—which she was to assume officially in September 2011—Abramson told the newsroom, as quoted by Jeremy W. Peters for the *New York Times* (June 2, 2011), that the appointment is "the honor of my life." "Every executive stands on the shoulders of others," she said, mentioning in particular and thanking her "sisters"—her female colleagues at the newspaper, including its chief executive, Janet L. Robinson, and the columnist Maureen Dowd, as well as the women who came before her there. Abramson told Ed Pilkington for the London *Guardian* (June 7, 2011), "I know I didn't get this job because I'm a woman; I got it because I'm the best qualified person. But nonetheless what it means to me is that the executive editor of the *New York Times* is such an important position in our society, the *Times* itself is indispensable to society, and a woman gets to run the newsroom, which is meaningful." Abramson will replace Bill Keller, who will step down to become a contributing writer for the *Times*. As the executive editor Abramson will be charged with balancing the interests of the business side of the newspaper and its publisher, Arthur Sulzberger, with those of the newsroom. Abramson will also seek, as she has already begun to do, to reconcile the printed newspaper's production, marketing, and advertising with those of the coexisting—and to some extent competitive—Web version of the *Times*. In addition to her newspaper career, Abramson is the author or co-author of books including *Strange Justice: The Selling of Clarence Thomas* (1994). "There is no one I'd rather be in a foxhole with," Abramson's friend Jane Mayer, the co-author of *Strange Justice*, told Keach Hagey for *Politico.com* (June 2, 2011). "She is tough as nails. . . . She's a vigorous defender of the truth, and she's fearless."

The second of two daughters, Jill Ellen Abramson was born on March 19, 1954 and raised in an upper-middle-class Jewish home on the Upper West Side of Manhattan, in New York City. Her father, Norman Abramson, ran a textile-importing firm called Irish Looms Associates, and her mother, Dovie, was a homemaker; like their children, the Abramsons were Manhattanites by birth. Abramson's sister, Jane Abramson O'Connor, born in 1947, is the editor at large for Penguin USA Books for Young Readers. She is also the author of 46 books for young people, including the popular series *Fancy Nancy*, about a precocious girl with a fondness for things she considers "fancy," such as French words and feather boas; O'Connor has said that the character is based on herself and her sister during their younger years. The Abramsons were avid readers of the *New York Times*. Abramson told Pilkington that while she was growing up, her family's attitude toward the paper was that "what the *New York Times* said was absolute truth."

Abramson was educated at Ethical Culture schools: the Midtown School, in Manhattan, from kindergarten through sixth grade, and from seventh through 12th grades, the Fieldston School, an elite, private preparatory school in the New York City borough of the Bronx. Students at the schools received lessons in ethics in every grade. Abramson remembers her third-grade ethics teacher, Florence Klaber, posing the question, "Do the ends justify the means?" "We were constantly being pitched moral dilemmas by her and trying to separate the ends and the means, and answer that question, which for a small child is powerful," she told

Josh Nathan-Kazis for the *Forward* (June 1, 2011, on-line).

Abramson graduated from Fieldston in 1972 and enrolled at Harvard University, in Cambridge, Massachusetts. During her college years she became a stringer for *Time* magazine. She graduated magna cum laude with a B.A. degree in history and literature in 1976, the same year she covered the presidential-election campaign for *Time*. In an op-ed piece for the *New York Times* (March 21, 2010), Abramson recalled both the excitement and apprehension she felt at the time. "I remember being in the bar of the Sheraton Wayfarer [hotel] on the night of the New Hampshire primary, so proud of the press credentials dangling from my neck. I gazed at all the famous 'boys on the bus,' including [*Washington Star* and *Baltimore Sun* reporter] Jack Germond and ['Gonzo' journalist and *Rolling Stone* reporter] Hunter Thompson. But as a very young woman, I didn't dare belly up to the bar. Those days are over."

Abramson next worked at NBC News and then became an editorial consultant and staff reporter for the *American Lawyer*. That publication's editor, Steven Brill, hired her along with a handful of other young journalists, including the future Reuters editor in chief Stephen Adler; James B. Stewart, later of the *New Yorker*; the future *Businessweek* editor Ellen Pollack; and Jim Cramer, later the host of the TV show *Mad Money*. Brill, a demanding editor, was impressed by Abramson's journalistic zeal. In 1986 he named Abramson, then 32, editor in chief of his Washington, D.C., legal-trade weekly the *Legal Times*. Two years later she met Al Hunt, who was then the Washington editor of the *Wall Street Journal*. Even though the *Journal* had put a freeze on hiring, Hunt interviewed Abramson in 1988. "It was the most dazzling interview I've ever had in my life," Hunt told Hagey. "She rattled off stories that she thought we should be doing right away. So I hired her. I've never made a better hire." For the *Journal* Abramson covered politics with her fellow Fieldston graduate and childhood friend Jane Mayer, who is currently a staff writer at the *New Yorker*. Abramson was named deputy to then–bureau chief Alan S. Murray in 1993.

Meanwhile, Abramson had published her first book, *Where They Are Now: The Story of the Women of Harvard Law, 1974* (1986), written with the former *American Lawyer* staff reporter Barbara Franklin. The 1974 class at Harvard University School of Law was the first at the school in which women had constituted more than 10 percent of the entering students. Of the 70 women Abramson and Franklin interviewed, less than a quarter had made partner in their respective firms, while over half of their male counterparts had; others had left the profession altogether to start families. The authors had looked for women who "had it all," or who they felt had managed to balance their professional and personal lives successfully, but they had been unable to find any; perhaps for that reason Linda Greenhouse, in her review of *Where They Are Now* for the *New York Times* (February 23, 1988), found the book to be "ultimately unsatisfying." "What remains unclear is the authors' stance toward their material," Greenhouse wrote. "The book is scarcely a celebration of the range of choices in women's lives. Rather, the emphasis is on the degree to which the women have strayed from the Harvard (male) model of success. . . . Are the women who left the partnership track victims? Failures? By whose standard?"

Where They Are Now reflected Abramson's interest in the plight of professional women looking to strike a balance between their personal and work lives while trying to navigate male-dominated fields. She was the editor of the *Legal Times* when, in 1988, she wrote a feature for the *New York Times Magazine* (March 6, 1988) profiling Peggy Kerr and Nancy Lieberman, who were among the first women to be named partners at one of the country's most prestigious law firms, Skadden, Arps, Slate, Meagher & Flom, in New York City. (Kerr was the firm's very first, in 1981.) "During the 1980's the overall progress of women at private law firms has been slow," Abramson wrote, "but dramatic gains have come in the last two years." At Skadden, Arps in 1988, she noted, women accounted for 184 of the 651 associates employed; 14 of the firm's 158 partners were women.

Abramson was also interested in another gender-related issue, one that would become a common refrain in her reportage—most notably in an April 9, 2006 *Times* article titled (ironically, given future events), "When Will We Stop Saying 'First Woman to ____ '?." Abramson noted that in the 1980s, when law firms were looking to diversify while bringing in more revenue, more lawyers were making partner than ever before, but she wondered if the increase in the number of female partners was a by-product of expanding business rather than a breakthrough for women. In the article Abramson also discussed varied reactions to Katie Couric's becoming the first solo female anchor of a network primetime news program, the *CBS Evening News.* "Surprisingly to me, in the immense coverage of [Couric's taking the job] . . . many stories did not lead with the 'first woman' angle," Abramson wrote, arguing that that perhaps indicated progress for women; on the other hand, she also noted, the anchor position had been devalued: "The network news shows are all suffering from declining, aging audiences. . . . With the fragmentation of television audiences and the advent of cable and on-demand services . . . the prestige of being an anchor is not what it was in the days of Walter Cronkite." Abramson concluded the article by writing, "This is yet another transitional moment for professional women. . . . But there are still few women successfully leading the cornerstone institutions of our society."

Abramson and Mayer's *Strange Justice: The Selling of Clarence Thomas* (1994) addressed events in 1991, after President George H. W. Bush

nominated Clarence Thomas to serve on the U.S. Supreme Court. During the Senate confirmation hearings, Thomas's former colleague Anita Hill, a 35-year-old lawyer, testified under oath that he had sexually harassed her while he was her supervisor at the Equal Employment Opportunity Commission. Thomas also testified under oath, refuting Hill's claim. Due to the seriousness of the charge and the explicit nature of Hill's accusations, the story consumed headlines for months. Meanwhile, a smear campaign was mounted against Hill: David Brock wrote a scathing indictment of her called *The Real Anita Hill* (1993), which famously declared Hill to be "a little bit nutty and a little bit slutty." (The book was praised in conservative circles, but Brock later completely retracted its claims, admitting that he had worked with Thomas's supporters to skew information and threaten witnesses who would have supported Hill. Brock detailed those events in another book, *Blinded by the Right*, published in 2003.) Abramson and Mayer's book, researched over the course of three years, represented an attempt to set the record straight. "Clarence Thomas said that if he had ever behaved in the manner that Anita Hill had accused him of in the hearings . . . , 'You would think that there would be bits and pieces of this elsewhere in my life that would have suggested some sort of pattern,'" Mayer told Nina Totenberg for the National Public Radio program *Morning Edition* (November 3, 1994). "And what we were able to do was to find the bits and pieces and put together the pattern." The two journalists found numerous women who supported Hill's claim and had stories of their own to share about Thomas. Abramson and Mayer also raised troubling questions about the inner workings of the confirmation process itself, and they blamed then–Senator Joseph R. Biden for refusing to call women who he knew had raised similar claims against Thomas to testify and corroborate Hill's story. In a review of *Strange Justice*, Richard Lacayo wrote for *Time* (November 14, 1994): "The authors conclude that 'the preponderance of the evidence suggests' that Thomas lied under oath when he told the committee he had not harassed Hill. Their book doesn't quite nail that conclusion. Yet its portrait of Thomas as an id suffering in the role of a Republican superego is more detailed and convincing than anything that has appeared so far." (Thomas was narrowly confirmed by the Senate.) *Strange Justice* was nominated for a National Book Award.

On April 5, 1997 the *National Journal* featured Abramson on its cover, naming her one of the 25 most influential journalists in Washington. The magazine called her a "triple threat," adding about her work at the *Wall Street Journal*, where she was then deputy Washington bureau chief: "Abramson not only has a say in hiring decisions (she's pushed for more women) and a hand in shaping the bureau's coverage of Washington, but also weighs in with her own investigative reports on the money-in-politics front." That same year Abramson met the *New York Times* columnist Maureen Dowd (the two would become close friends); Dowd asked Abramson if she knew a female journalist who would be interested in working for the *Times*. Abramson suggested herself. By September of that year, Abramson was working for the Washington bureau of the *New York Times* as the new editor of investigative-reporting projects. Michael Oreskes, the *Times*'s incoming Washington bureau chief, told Paul Starobin for the *National Journal* (September 6, 1997) that Abramson's name was "at the top of everyone's list" of investigative reporters in Washington, thanks to *Strange Justice* and her illuminating reporting on the intersection of money and politics in the nation's capital. As for Abramson, she was very happy to join the *Times*, the newspaper that she had revered as a child, telling Starobin: "I had always harbored a desire to work there at some point." Abramson quickly rose through the ranks, becoming Washington editor in 1999 and bureau chief, in charge of a staff of 60, in 2000—a position she was the first female to hold.

Abramson's years at the helm of the *Times*'s Washington bureau coincided with several historic events. The year 2000 saw the Republican George W. Bush—following a protracted vote recount and a 5–4 Supreme Court decision—defeat the Democrat Al Gore for the U.S. presidency. Abramson had many run-ins with the Bush administration. "I'm a battle-scarred veteran in that regard," she recalled to Pilkington. "There were several national security stories that they asked us not to publish that we ended up publishing." In New York the reporter and former foreign correspondent Howell Raines was named the executive editor of the *Times* five days before the September 11, 2001 terrorist attacks on the U.S. The *Times* and Raines were praised for their in-depth coverage in the immediate aftermath of the tragedy; the *Times* won several Pulitzer Prizes.

Raines encouraged competition among his staff, including the Washington bureau, and continually pushed for bigger stories; "Hunt big game, not rabbits," he would say, as sources told Ken Auletta for the *New Yorker* (June 10, 2002). Many at the *Times* accused Raines of becoming too aggressive and of micro-managing the paper after his initial success, and he and Abramson often butted heads. She felt that he was trying to edge her out of her job (in fact, he tried to move her to the paper's Book Review section); he would try to tell her, rather than ask her, what the Washington reports would include. "It was humiliating," one reporter told Auletta. "It wasn't, 'Jill, what do you have in the Washington report?' It was, 'Jill, this is what we think should be in the Washington report.'" It was not until Abramson threatened to quit that relations between the New York and Washington offices improved.

Meanwhile, Raines's competitive attitude began to cause larger problems for the paper. Between 2001 and 2003 the *Times* reporter Judith Miller, citing unnamed sources, published many articles detailing the Iraqi leader Saddam Hussein's supposed production of weapons of mass destruction (WMD). That information, much of it cited by the Bush administration as justification for the 2003 invasion of Iraq, later proved to be false. Abramson revealed little publicly about the matter until 2008, when she assessed Bob Woodward's book *The War Within*, the fourth volume of his inside look at the Bush administration, for the *Times Book Review* (September 28, 2008). She wrote that in his second volume, *Plan of Attack*, Woodward "acknowledges an error of his own: he admits he should have pushed the *Washington Post* to publish a front-page article about the flimsiness of the intelligence on W.M.D. I was Washington bureau chief for the *Times* while this was happening, and I failed to push hard enough for an almost identical, skeptical article, written by [investigative reporter] James Risen. This was a period when there were too many credulous accounts of the administration's claims about Iraq's W.M.D. (including some published in the *Times* and the *Post*)."

Raines stepped down as executive editor in 2003, after Jayson Blair, a *Times* reporter, was discovered to have fabricated many of his stories, precipitating a scandal that was deeply embarrassing for the newspaper. When Bill Keller assumed the post of executive editor at the *Times*, he appointed an unprecedented two managing editors to address the complexities of a newsroom beginning to grapple with competition from the Internet. One of the editors was John M. Geddes, who dealt specifically with news operations; the other was Abramson, who dealt with news gathering. (At the age of 49, Abramson got a small tattoo of a New York subway token on her right shoulder to commemorate her return to the city.) Keller told Gabriel Sherman for *New York* magazine (September 26, 2010) that he (Keller) and Abramson were a perfect match. "She's an investigative reporter by temperament. The investigative reporter in you makes you alert to hidden agendas. I tend to see the good in people. Jill is more wary and suspicious—she's the perfect person to have my back." The two editors grew close as they worked hard to become, as Sherman wrote, "a stabilizing force after the tumultuous Raines era."

Tumult of another sort soon developed, however, as the *Times*, facing the worldwide economic recession that began in December 2007, fell victim to one of the most extensive cutbacks in advertising ever to hit the newspaper industry. Sales declined steadily, and in 2009 the *Times* was forced to eliminate more than 100 newsroom jobs. Still, as of 2011 the *Times* had maintained the largest newsroom in the country, with more than 1,200 reporters, photographers, and digital journalists. Many believe that digital journalism will mark the defining challenge of Abramson's tenure as executive editor, the post she was to assume in September 2011. "She's going to be dealing with all the problems [Keller] dealt with but at an accelerated pace and with less resources . . . ," the media business blogger Alan Mutter told Jason Horowitz and Paul Farhi for the *Washington Post* (June 3, 2011). "He had the problem of rebuilding morale and credibility. . . . She has the problem of a broken business model."

Abramson became familiar with such challenges in 2010, during a six-month stint of overseeing the *Times*'s on-line operation and researching and visiting other on-line news organizations, including the *Huffington Post* and *Politico*. "Her aim is to push our integration to the next level," Keller wrote to the *Times* staff in 2010, as quoted by Dylan Byers in *Adweek* (June 2, 2011, on-line), "which means mastering all aspects of our digital operation, not only the newsroom digital pipeline but also the company's digital strategy in all its ramifications." Abramson was one of the architects of the *New York Times* Web site "paywall," which was implemented in March 2011. Capitalizing on the popularity of the site, which draws nearly 33 million unique visitors per month, the *Times* began to allow readers to view 20 articles each month for free; to view more, readers pay subscription fees of between $15 and $35 per month. After almost three months the *Times* paywall had garnered 100,000 on-line subscribers, which is, Horowitz and Farhi reported, "a promising start to a business model that could fundamentally change the news industry's financial base."

Abramson told Sherman that digital revenues alone would not be enough to support the *Times*: "If you were digital only, you'd be talking about a smaller news organization." She added that the *Times* is different from on-line news sites such as the ones she visited, which, "with a few exceptions, [offer] surprisingly little original reporting of consequence," she told Sherman. "I don't want to belittle what *Politico* and others do. They do break real news, and they're quite enterprising. But they're not doing the Pentagon Papers"—a reference to the classified Vietnam War–era government documents made public in 1971 by the *New York Times*. Ideally, Abramson suggested, digital media will provide a new forum for long-form investigative journalism. "The long-form article isn't only alive, it's actually dancing to new music," she told Boston University students at a conference on June 9, 2011, alluding to the advent of personal electronic reading devices such as the Kindle and the iPhone.

Abramson has taught a course in narrative journalism at Yale University, in New Haven, Connecticut, since 2006. She has also been a visiting professor at Princeton University, in New Jersey.

In 2009 Abramson brought home a nine-week-old Golden Retriever. She then began writing "The Puppy Diaries," a popular series in the *Times*'s House & Garden section, in which she described raising her family's new pet. In the fall of 2011, she will publish a compilation of the articles, called *The Puppy Diaries: Raising a Dog Named Scout*.

When asked to describe Abramson, most friends and colleagues use the word "tough," in both a mental and physical sense. In 2007 Abramson was hit by a refrigerated truck while walking across West 44th Street in New York. She lost a great deal of blood and suffered a fractured leg; police told her that her life had been spared by inches. From her hospital bed, where she remained for three weeks, Abramson led the *Times* investigation of the media mogul Rupert Murdoch as he was finalizing the purchase of the *Wall Street Journal*. "Long before she got run over by the truck, people knew she had a lot of strength," Keller told Gabriel Sherman.

Abramson met her husband, Henry Little Griggs III, at Harvard University. They were married on March 14, 1981. The couple have a son, Will, who is the founder of the indie-rock label Cantor Records, and a daughter, Cornelia, a resident surgeon at New York–Presbyterian Hospital. Abramson and her husband live in the Tribeca neighborhood of New York City.

—M.M.H.

Suggested Reading: *Adweek* (on-line) June 2, 2011; *Forward* (on-line) June 1, 2011; *(London) Guardian* (on-line) June 7, 2011; *National Journal* p650 Apr. 5, 1997, p1722 Sep. 6, 1997; National Public Radio *Morning Edition* (on-line transcript) Nov. 3, 1994; *New York* (on-line) Sep. 26, 2010; *New York Times* (on-line) Feb. 23, 1986, June 2, 2011; *New York Times Book Review* p6 Mar. 21, 2010; *New Yorker* p48 June 10, 2002; *Politico.com* June 2, 2011; *Time* (on-line) Nov. 14, 1994; *Washington Post* C p1 June 3, 2011

Selected Books: *Where They Are Now: The Story of the Women of Harvard Law, 1974* (with Barbara Franklin), 1986; *Strange Justice: The Selling of Clarence Thomas* (with Jane Mayer), 1994; *The Puppy Diaries: Raising a Dog Named Scout*, 2011

Achatz, Grant

(AK-ets)

Apr. 25, 1974– Chef; restaurateur; writer

Address: Alinea, 1723 N. Halsted, Chicago, IL 60614

Grant Achatz "is something new on the national culinary landscape: a chef as ambitious and disciplined as Thomas Keller who wants to make his mark not with perfection but with constant innovation," Corby Kummer wrote for *Technology Review* (January 1, 2007). "Where Keller marries ironclad French technique with American ingredients, Achatz plays with every new way to change the

Joe Corrigan/Getty Images

Grant Achatz

art kind of things. Not everyone really gets it. Which might just be a large part of its appeal." Achatz is among the leaders of the so-called progressive food movement. According to the restaurant critic Frank Bruni, writing for the *New York Times* (May 11, 2005) one week after Alinea's debut, "The movement or mindset to which [its members] belong has been described as avant-garde. It has been labeled molecular gastronomy, because some practitioners deconstruct and reconstruct food with the tools and temperament of biochemists. It has been dubbed shock cuisine but could also be called mock cuisine, because much of it sets out to flout widely held values. In this realm, centrifuges, dehydrators and chemical and technological transmogrification of food are not reviled methods of corporate kitchens but paths to discovery."

Three months later, after dining at Alinea, another *New York Times* (September 25, 2005) critic, Jonathan Hayes, wrote that each of Achatz's dishes served as a "validation" of the chef's methods. "And we're talking a lot of dishes," Hayes continued: "a tasting menu can run to 24 courses. After the second course (a tiny sorrel leaf poking out of a frozen lozenge of sour cream with a layer of shaved salmon, the shoot to be used as a handle), I was bracing for an orgy of preciousness. But the next hours were some of the most exhilarating I've spent in a restaurant. The food requires a small leap of faith; specifically, a belief that the chef is sincere. And Achatz convinces early on. A bowl of dried freesia blossoms held a smaller bowl of rich seafood custard and trout fillets. Boiling water poured into the larger bowl released a half-herbal, half-floral fume. The smell of the flower tea, the texture and flavor of the custard and steamed fish: it all was heaven. This kind of cooking walks a fine line between gimmicky and revolutionary, but Achatz is on the right side. Astonishingly self-assured at 31, he will be, I believe, the next great American chef." Three years later, in 2008, the James Beard Foundation named Achatz among the nation's three outstanding chefs, and in 2010 Alinea won the foundation's Outstanding Service Award. Achatz's cookbook, *Alinea* (2008), won the foundation's book award in the category of cooking from a professional point of view. The book *Life, on the Line: A Chef's Story of Chasing Greatness, Facing Death, and Redefining the Way We Eat*, by Achatz and his business partner, Nick Kokonas, contains an account of Achatz's successful battle with a potentially fatal case of oral cancer. It was scheduled in early 2011, soon after the opening of Achatz's second restaurant.

An only child, Grant Sherman Achatz Jr. was born in Michigan on April 25, 1974 to Grant Sherman Achatz Sr. and Barbara Jean Achatz. He grew up in St. Clair, in eastern Michigan. His paternal grandparents ran a restaurant, and an aunt of his runs the Achatz Pie Co., which supplies restaurants and also sells through retail stores in parts of the Midwest. In 1982 his parents opened the

viscosity, texture, form, moistness, and even color of food, applying food-industry methods to haute cuisine." A third-generation restaurateur and a graduate of the Culinary Institute of America, Achatz is the executive chef and managing partner of Alinea (ah-LIN-ee-uh), which opened in Chicago, Illinois, on May 4, 2005. The very next year *Gourmet* magazine named Alinea the best restaurant in the United States. The year after that Alinea ranked 36th among the S. Pellegrino World's 50 Best Restaurants, according to a poll of chefs, restaurant critics, and others conducted by *Restaurant Magazine*, an influential British trade journal. In 2010 Alinea ranked seventh on the same list, higher than any other restaurant in North America, including such renowned restaurants as Daniel Boulud's Daniel and Keller's Per Se and French Laundry. Earlier in his career, Achatz worked at the French Laundry (1996–2000), the last two years as sous chef. He was serving as the executive chef at Trio, a restaurant in Evanston, Illinois, when, in 2002, *Food & Wine* magazine named him among the best new chefs in the nation. In 2003 the James Beard Foundation named him "rising star chef of the year."

"We're trying to break the monotony of not only food technique, presentation and preparation, but the emotional response that you have," Achatz told *Art Culinaire* magazine (June 22, 2007). "If we can make it more interactive, or more entertaining, or make it intimidating, or make it fun—then we create something that's not just about eating and filling your stomach. It's an event, you know?" "Basically, it's art. Food as art . . . ," Debra Pickett wrote for the *Chicago Sun-Times* (June 1, 2003), "like one of those video installation, performance

Achatz Family Restaurant, which served standard American fare. Achatz's father was in charge of the kitchen; his mother made pies and managed the dining area. When Grant Jr. was around seven years old, his parents recruited him to wash dishes. He became a prep cook by the age of 12. During high school Achatz worked in the restaurant as a line cook. "I could leave him with more responsibility than the chefs or line cooks," his father told Craig Davison for the Port Huron, Michigan, *Times Herald* (December 23, 2006). "He just had a focus. He always wanted to make it better." Even as a teenager Achatz was eager to add new flavors or garnishes to existing dishes. His father dissuaded him, telling him that their only requirements were to make sure that the food was well prepared, hot, and affordable.

Although his father advised him to avoid the restaurant business, after high school Achatz enrolled at the Culinary Institute of America (CIA), in Hyde Park, New York. There, he told William Rice for the *Chicago Tribune* (January 11, 2002), "I developed a new attitude. What I was learning went way beyond burgers. I realized there was no ceiling on what I could do, that I had to work within perimeters and learn a lot of details, but in time I could tailor them to myself and my personal vision." After he completed the CIA course, Achatz worked for a short time in the kitchen of the Amway Grand Plaza Hotel, in Grand Rapids, Michigan. He then landed a position at Charlie Trotter's, a world-renowned Chicago restaurant. After working 17-hour days for six months, he quit. "A year out of culinary school, and I was at arguably the best restaurant in the country. I was in way over my head. And it was an enormous amount of work and I freaked out," he told Emily B. Hunt for *Newcity Chicago* (April 30, 2003, on-line).

Achatz spent the next three months traveling in Europe with a girlfriend. When he returned to the U.S., he sent letters to six restaurants that he admired, asking for a job. The two that responded failed to impress him when he visited them, so for seven straight days, he sent letters with his résumé to the owner and chef of his top choice—Thomas Keller, of the French Laundry. His tactic led Keller to invite him for a two-day trial and then hire him as a chef. The first food Achatz ate at the French Laundry was Keller's signature dish, oysters and pearls, which contains warm tapioca pudding, oysters, and caviar. Achatz described it to a *Chicago Tribune* (April 29, 2007) reporter as "very complex. It is sweet and savory and, texturally, it is amazing. You have the tapioca rolling around and the textures of the oysters and then the caviar." The creation "basically embodied the philosophy I would soon learn working there . . . ," he continued. "Eating that course . . . was the starting point of thinking about food in this manner, beyond just flavor. I started thinking about the texture and the mingling of sweet and savory."

In 1996, when Achatz began working at the then-two-year-old French Laundry, Keller won the James Beard Foundation Award for best chef in California; the next year the foundation named Keller the best chef in the U.S. Achatz has credited Keller not only with vastly increasing his knowledge of food and the culinary arts, and greatly broadening the ways in which he thought about food and its preparation, but also providing him with a model of a chef/restaurant owner worthy of emulation. "The first thing I saw when I walked into The French Laundry was Thomas sweeping the floor. So, it was eye-opening," he told Jeff Houck for the *Tampa Tribune* (May 16, 2007). "He wasn't afraid to get his hands dirty. I thought that was great, so I kind of fell in love with the whole thing. The work ethic. The integrity. The passion. The kitchen, that whole thing."

The divorce of his parents, in 1998, led Achatz to reexamine his career path. "Since I went to culinary school, it was: go work here, go work there, we'll help you buy a restaurant someday," Achatz told Emily B. Hunt. "But then all of a sudden, my parents weren't together anymore and I wasn't even talking to my dad. All of a sudden, the opportunity for me to own my own restaurant vanished." Soon after his parents' marriage ended, Achatz left the French Laundry to work as an assistant winemaker at La Jota Vineyards, a Napa Valley, California, winery. Before long he found that he missed the hectic atmosphere of the French Laundry's kitchen, and in 1999 he returned to that restaurant as a sous chef—assistant to the executive chef.

Some months into Achatz's second stint at the French Laundry, Keller arranged for him to work with other well-known chefs, among them Alan Wong in Honolulu, Hawaii; Daniel Boulud in New York City; Nobu Matsuhisa in Los Angeles, California; and Martin Berasategui in San Sebastián, Spain. In 2000 Achatz spent a week with the Catalan chef Ferran Adrià at his restaurant, El Bulli, in Roses, Spain. Adrià is known for his invention of culinary foam, which involves blending natural flavors with gelling agents and forcing the mixture through the nozzle of a pressurized container (as is done with shaving cream and whipped cream). At El Bulli Achatz witnessed Adriá's use of aroma to enhance taste: diners were asked to sniff vanilla beans or rosemary, for example, before they ate particular dishes. Writing 10 years later of his visit to El Bulli for the *New York Times* (February 16, 2010), Achatz recalled that the cooks "us[ed] tools as if they were jewelers," and he described a 40-course, five-and-a-half-hour meal he had there as "the stuff of magic."

Achatz returned from Spain convinced that "after that many years, I needed to move on to develop my own style and build my own platform," he told Carolyn Walkup for *Nation's Restaurant News* (April 15, 2002). "I began to conceptualize dishes that didn't fit into the framework of a restaurant that has been established under a super chef. It's the drive to always move forward. At some point you have to move away from home." In 2001 Achatz responded to a "chef-wanted" notice posted on the Internet by Henry Adaniya, the owner of Trio, a popular restaurant in Evanston, Illinois. After an audition, in which Achatz prepared a seven-course meal, Adaniya hired him as Trio's executive chef. Beginning that July, Trio offered four-, eight-, and 24-course tasting menus (priced from $75 to $175) with new dishes containing highly imaginative combinations of ingredients, served at unusual temperatures and presented in original ways. Dishes included a watermelon ball spiked with chili sauce; a small wafer of dehydrated vegetable paper, served on the head of a pin, that tasted like pepperoni pizza; and a granita (a granular frozen dessert) made with arugula, watercress, and black pepper. "The first six months were very turbulent," Achatz told Debra Pickett. "[Trio's] name was the same, but it was a new restaurant. We had clientele that had been coming to Trio for years and years, expecting a certain thing, and they were just like, 'What is this?'"

While Trio lost some of its longtime clients, it attracted new ones, lured by word of mouth and restaurant critics' descriptions. Laura Levy, for one, wrote for the *Chicago Reader* (August 24, 2001), "Achatz is classically trained, with a refined style and a skillful hand that speaks of disciplined experience, but he's also playful and daring, creating flavor and texture combinations not seen before in these parts." On January 11, 2002 the *Chicago Tribune*'s restaurant critic Phil Vettel awarded Trio four stars, writing, "Grant Achatz is the most dynamic, boundary-stretching chef to hit town in a long, long time." "His food speaks with a global assertion and a visual elegance translated from his experiences around the world," Adaniya told Bob Krummert for *Restaurant Hospitality* (March 2002). "You cannot help but feel his far-reaching vision and tireless commitment, in both his personality and his food."

Achatz's "black truffle explosion"—ravioli filled with black-truffle sauce and garlic chips—soon became his signature dish. Like Ferran Adrià, he added a separate, olfactory component to some of his dishes, but by different means: a small bag would be filled with smoke from burning oak leaves, for example; then tiny holes would be punched in the bag, which would then be covered with a small pillowcase. The pressure from a plate of food resting on top of the bag forced tiny amounts of the trapped smoke to emerge as the diners ate. "We try to find unusual flavor combinations or techniques. We try to involve more senses than just taste, even hearing," Achatz told Carolyn Walkup. To maintain diners' interest, Achatz changed the tasting menus each season. In 2002 *Food & Wine* named Achatz among the best new chefs in the U.S., and he won the "rising star chef" award from the James Beard Foundation in 2003. According to the foundation's Web site, that award recognizes "a chef age 30 or younger who displays an impressive talent and who is likely to have a significant impact on the industry in years to come."

In January 2004 Nick Kokonas, a retired derivatives trader who ate at Trio regularly, suggested to Achatz that they open a restaurant together. Achatz responded enthusiastically, and within a few days, he and Kokonas had come up with a basic plan. Achatz left Trio a half-year later to devote himself full-time to the new restaurant, every aspect of which, from the entranceway to the table settings, was designed to evoke an emotional response. Achatz collaborated with the industrial designer Martin Kastner to create the special utensils and other tableware necessary to serve the chef's new creations in the ways he envisioned. They include the "bow," a U-shaped device that suspends food on a thin wire. Achatz also worked with the laboratory-equipment maker PolyScience to develop the "anti-griddle"; remaining at 30 degrees Fahrenheit below zero, it freezes the exterior of a dish, creating a crunchy shell, while leaving the food's soft center warm.

Located in Chicago's Lincoln Park neighborhood, Achatz and Kokonas's restaurant opened on May 4, 2005. The partners named it Alinea, an obscure name for the proofreader's symbol that indicates the start of a new paragraph—that is, the introduction of something new or different. Alinea, which serves only dinner, from Wednesday through Sunday, immediately earned outstanding reviews from local and national restaurant critics, and patrons soon competed for reservations. In 2006 *Gourmet* magazine named Alinea the best restaurant in the U.S., and it won the Zagat Survey's Top Service Award. The next year it won the Jean Banchet Award for best fine dining (a Chicago-area honor, named for a renowned chef who worked at the famous restaurant Le Français, in a Chicago suburb). Also in 2007 Alinea was ranked 36th among the S. Pellegrino World's 50 Best Restaurants. Achatz himself won the 2007 Jean Banchet Award in the category of best celebrity chef and the 2007 James Beard Foundation Award—regarded as the Oscar of the culinary world—as the best chef in the Great Lakes region. Both Achatz and Alinea have continued to collect honors and earn laudatory reviews ever year since then. In November 2010 Alinea's 21-course meal cost $195.

Earlier, during the planning stages of Alinea, Achatz had noticed a small lesion on the left side of his tongue that had begun to cause discomfort when he ate. For over three years beginning in early 2004, the lesion was misdiagnosed as simply a sign of stress-related tongue-biting. By the spring of 2007, when he was diagnosed with stage-four oral cancer, the lesion had become a tumor so large that Achatz could talk only with difficulty. Doctors told him that he was likely to die within four months unless he underwent treatment—the surgical removal of three-quarters of his tongue. After a desperate search, Achatz and Kokonas learned of an alternative treatment, offered by the University of Chicago Medical Center, where Achatz underwent a combination of chemotherapy and radiation. Although during treatment he lost the ability to taste, he continued to work at Alinea, relying on his memory and the help of his sous chefs. "People don't realize that 90 percent of what I do is up here," he told Steven Gray for *People* (October 22, 2007), tapping his head. The treatments, along with surgical removal of infected lymph nodes from his neck, was successful; to date there has been no recurrence of the cancer, and to a large extent Achatz has regained his sense of taste.

Achatz and Kokonas opened their second restaurant, named Next, in early 2011. To make reservations at Next, patrons must pay on-line in advance. Achatz and Agnela Snell, a former events coordinator at the French Laundry, are the parents of two sons. Achatz and Snell's marriage ended in divorce.

—M.A.S.

Suggested Reading: Alinea-restaurant.com; *Chicago Sun-Times* S p5 Sep. 12, 2007; *Chicago Tribune* C p1 Jan. 11, 2002; *Food and Wine* p66+ Mar. 2005; *New York Times* (on-line) May 5, 2010; *New Yorker* p84 May 12, 2008; *Newcity Chicago* (on-line) Apr. 30, 2003; (Port Huron, Michigan) *Times Herald* A p1 Dec. 23, 2006; *Restaurant Hospitality* p16+ Mar. 2006, p42 Sep. 2010; (Toronto) *Globe and Mail* L p1 June 13, 2008

Selected Books: *Alinea*, 2008; with Nick Kokonas—*Life, on the Line: A Chef's Story of Chasing Greatness, Facing Death, and Redefining the Way We Eat* (2011)

Joerg Koch/AFP/Getty Images

Ai Weiwei

(eye way-way)

1957– Artist; architect; photographer; writer; blogger; activist

Address: China Art Archives & Warehouse, P.O. Box 100102-43, Beijing 100102, China

"Art is about social change," Ai Weiwei has said. A native of China now in his mid-50s, Ai is an internationally respected sculptor, painter, installation artist, photographer, filmmaker, and architect; in the last-named role, he contributed to the celebrated design of the National Stadium in Beijing,

China—nicknamed the Bird's Nest—the site of many of the 2008 Summer Olympic Games. Ai is also an outspoken critic of the Chinese government. He told John Sunyer for the *New Statesman* (October 12, 2010) that as a teenager in the late 1970s, he "decided to become an artist . . . to try to escape the totalitarian conditions in China." "Art and politics are fragments of the same thing—they're about an understanding of our surroundings," he continued. "Sometimes my work is political, sometimes it is architectural, sometimes it is artistic. I don't think I am a dissident artist; I see them as a dissident government." He also said, "My art works best when there is an underlying political theme. I want all of my political efforts to become art. I also feel a responsibility to speak out for people around me who are afraid and who have totally given up hope."

On his blog, from 2005 to 2009—when it was shut down, almost certainly by government agents—Ai sent some 3,000 electronic messages to thousands of people expressing his complaints about the government. Also in 2009, in order to prevent him from serving as a witness in the trial of another fierce opponent of the government, Chinese police officers punched Ai's head so viciously that he suffered a neurological bleed and nearly died. In April 2011 Ai was arrested, allegedly for economic crimes, although his opposition to the government was widely assumed to be the real reason. On June 22, 2011 he was released on bail after reportedly having confessed to the crime of tax evasion.

A son of Ai Qing and his wife, Gao Ying, Ai Weiwei was born in Beijing in 1957. (In Chinese, surnames precede given names.) According to an obituary of his father written by Lee Ruru for the London *Independent* (May 20, 1996, on-line), Ai Qing's name at birth was Jiang Haicheng, and he and his wife were the parents of five sons and three daughters. In the 1930s Ai Qing, an artist and a renowned poet, endured torture and a prison sentence after officials in China's ruling Kuomintang government accused him of being a leftist. Ai Qing joined the Communist Party in 1941, and in some of his poetry, according to Lee Ruru, he praised Mao Zedong, the leader of China's Communist Party and the dictator of China from 1949 until his death, in 1976. Nevertheless, during the Anti-Rightist Movement in China in the late 1950s, Ai Qing was denounced as a rightist; according to Michael Wines, writing for the *New York Times* (November 28, 2009), "He ran afoul of the Communist Party for subtly criticizing its suppression of free speech." The family were banished from Beijing and sent to live in Xinjiang, in northwestern China. Ai Weiwei was then a year old.

In 1966, at the start of the Chinese Cultural Revolution, Ai and his family were forced to move to a "reeducation camp" in north-central China, near the Gobi Desert—a region analogous to Siberia in Russia. Ai Qing was not allowed to read or write, and he was assigned to clean public toilets. The family lived in poverty in an underground hut whose roof was made of branches and mud. "To me, it was fine," Ai told Rachel Cooke for the London *Observer* (July 6, 2008). "But for my father it must have been difficult. He had been to Paris in the 1930s; he loved art; he was a poet. But the worst thing was not the living conditions, not that we had no meat or even a drop of oil, and only one kind of vegetable: potatoes, or onions. The worst is when you are accused of a crime that isn't a crime: to be hated and insulted. You can't imagine the insults. Everybody wanted to join in. Children threw stones at him, their parents poured ink on his face. He was the enemy. He hadn't done anything to those people. His writing was not even political. But you cannot give an excuse if you are deemed an enemy of the people. So we felt ashamed, even though we had nothing to be ashamed of." He also told Cooke, "It was terrible but life at that time was terrible for everyone. There was no humanity and no wisdom."

When Ai was 14 he and his family were permitted to return to Xinjiang, and after the Cultural Revolution ended, in 1976, they were allowed to go back to Beijing. His father was exonerated in 1978. That year Ai enrolled at the Beijing Film Institute, where his classmates included the future filmmakers Chen Kaige and Zhang Yimou. During that period he helped to establish the Stars Group, a collective of avant-garde artists and writers. "With the Stars' open-air shows and other activities largely (though not completely) thwarted," David Coggins wrote for *Art in America* (September 2007), Ai decided to leave China. According to Rachel Cooke, a friend of his whose relatives lived in the U.S. helped him get the proper papers, which proved to be "surprisingly easy." "I went to the American embassy and I told them I was going to study. The man asked if I wanted to go to Disneyland, and [then he] said, yes, OK," Ai told Cooke.

In 1981 Ai moved to New York, where he studied at the Parsons School of Design and the Art Students League. While living in New York City's East Village, he pursued his career as a conceptual artist and earned money by working as a cleaner and a carpenter. In his new environment, after having endured the restrictions and regimentation of life in China for nearly 25 years, he felt liberated. "It was almost like gravity disappeared, as if I was just floating," he told Christopher Hawthorne for the *New York Times* (October 28, 2004), "that's how much I enjoyed New York."

In 1993 Ai learned that his father was sick, and he returned to China; his father died three years later. "My relatives all told me just to come back and visit him," he told Hawthorne, "but I knew that it was either go back to China for good or stay in New York for good." Back in Beijing Ai worked as an independent artist. He established a studio called East Village and co-founded the China Art Archives and Warehouse, a gallery in which art from around the world is displayed. In 1999, in the Chaoyang District of Beijing, he set up a studio called Beijing Fake Cultural Development Ltd. (known as Fake), which specializes in architecture, interior design, and landscape architecture.

In 1995 Ai created a controversial piece called *Dropping a Han Dynasty Urn*, a series of three photographs that show him doing exactly that: destroying what appears to be a ceramic vessel some 2,000 years old. "For me, it is about exploring possibilities, understanding values of so-called construction and destruction," he explained to Steve Meacham for the *Sydney (Australia) Morning Herald* (April 24, 2008). "It's merely a gesture without political intentions, although people always want to associate it with political intentions." Around that time he also began to produce works that reflected his feelings about the Tiananmen Square massacre of 1989, when army troops killed hundreds of demonstrators urging the government to initiate democratic reforms. One of Ai's pieces, produced in June 1994, is a black-and-white photograph of his wife lifting up her skirt in the square.

During the 1990s Ai published three books on Chinese avant-garde art and artists; their names translated into English are "The Black Cover Book" (1994), "The White Cover Book" (1995), and "The Grey Cover Book" (1997). His work *Table with Three Legs* (1997–98) is an original piece of furniture made during the Qing Dynasty (1644–1911) altered so that each of the three remaining legs is perpendicular to the others; thus, when it stands on one leg in a corner of a room, the bottom of each of the other two legs rests on one or the other of the walls that meet there at right angles.

During the late 1990s Ai leased some land outside Beijing. "I asked the owner if I could build on the land," he recalled to Christopher Hawthorne. "He said, 'I can't say yes, but if you don't ask, it's O.K.' In China there are lots of situations like this." Ai then hired local farmers who helped to construct a residence and workspace that included a studio, an office for his staff, a living room, a library, and three bedrooms. By that time he had become involved in architectural projects designed for the public. One of Ai's projects, dating from 2002, was the Jinhua Architecture Park, which honors the memory of Ai Qing, who was born in Jinhua, a city near Shanghai, in eastern China. In addition to overseeing all the construction in the new park, which stretches for over a mile along the Yiwu River, Ai designed a small museum for ancient Chinese pottery. At Ai's invitation 16 other architects, from North America and Europe as well as China, designed other structures, such as a welcome center, eateries, and a newspaper stand.

Later in the 2000s the Swiss architects Jacques Herzog and Pierre de Meuron (who contributed a design to the Jinhua Architecture Park) consulted with Ai on a proposal for a design for a national stadium in Beijing, where the 2008 Olympic Games were scheduled to take place. Ai came up with the idea for the stadium's "bird's-nest" shape, which came to symbolize the Olympics. He later downplayed his contribution to the design (which won a national competition), because of his disapproval of the Chinese government and what he denounced as its glossy Olympics propaganda, which struck him as attempts to cover up or disregard widespread human-rights abuses. "They don't believe in liberty. They don't believe in China before the Communists," Ai said to Michael Wines. "There is only one simple, clear task: to protect their control, to maintain their governing. Which is such a pity." To underline his position Ai refused to attend any of the Olympic events.

Earlier, in 2006, Ai had created a series of flowered dresses made entirely of porcelain. In 2007 he designed a work called *Fairytale* for the group exhibition Documenta, held in Kassel, Germany. For that project he turned a warehouse into a living space, installed 1,001 chairs, and brought 1,001 people from China to inhabit the space for the duration of the exhibition. The next year Ai held a solo exhibition in Seoul, South Korea, at the Gallery Hyundai. That show included *6.3.2006*, a series of photographs he had taken of the Beijing National Stadium during its construction, as well as a series of photographs of Ai giving the middle finger to Tiananmen Square, the White House, and other famous landmarks.

On the afternoon of May 12, 2008, a devastating earthquake struck China's Sichuan Province, killing well over 70,000 people. At least 10,000 of the victims were children trapped in schools that, as subsequent investigations soon revealed, had been shoddily constructed, because strict building codes had been widely ignored. The national government refused to release the names of the students who had died in the disaster, and in July, according to the *New York Times* (May 6, 2009, online), "reports emerged . . . that local governments in the province had begun a coordinated campaign to buy the silence of angry parents whose children died." Along with dozens of volunteers, Ai learned

from parents who refused to remain silent the names of about 5,000 children who had perished in their schools, and he posted their names on his blog. "The picture became clear," Ai told Michael Wines. "All of them belonged to about 20 schools, and those schools, the buildings collapsed to dust. Why did those buildings collapse, and the ones next to it are standing?" Ai later created for a show mounted in 2009 at the Haus der Kunst, in Munich, Germany, a work entitled *Remembering.* The piece consisted of 9,000 specially made children's backpacks, differing only in color, afixed to a frame mounted on a façade of the building. On a background of blue backpacks, backpacks in four other colors spelled out in Chinese characters the statement, "She lived happily for seven years in this world," words that a mother of one of the deceased schoolchildren had uttered.

In August 2009 Ai was preparing to testify at the trial of Tan Zuoren, a Chinese activist and writer who had investigated the deaths of schoolchildren in the Sichuan earthquake. While Ai was in a hotel in Chengdu, Chinese police officers broke into his room in the middle of the night. "They kicked open the door," Ai recalled to Wines. "I said, 'How do I know you are the police?' They said, 'I'll show you,' and punched me. . . . It was a very solid punch." He was then detained for several hours, making it impossible for him to attend Zuoren's trial. (Zuoren was later imprisoned.) Ai subsequently began to suffer from frequent headaches, which he disregarded due to his busy schedule. A month after the assault, while in Germany for an art exhibition, he went to a hospital, where he underwent emergency surgery to drain blood from his brain. "The attack almost ended my life, but this work will always be worth the effort if I can make a strong voice and readjust living conditions for the people around me," he told John Sunyer. "I will always feel sad when students are killed and nobody takes responsibility."

In late 2010 Chinese authorities announced that sometime after the Chinese New Year, in early February 2011, they were going to demolish Ai's newly built studio in Shanghai, on the grounds that he had not acquired the proper building permits. Ai's plan to stage a protest attended by hundreds of others was aborted when he was placed under house arrest for two days. "They put you under house arrest, or they make you disappear," he said of the Chinese government to Michael Wines for the *New York Times* (November 6, 2010). "That's all they can do. There's no facing the issue and discussing it; it's all a very simple treatment." In January 2011 Ai's Shanghai studio was destroyed.

On April 3, 2011 government agents took Ai into custody as he was about to board a plane to Hong Kong. Ai was arrested and his studio was raided by the police. He was one of many artists to be detained by Chinese authorities, who likely fear that dissidents such as Ai will contribute to a "jasmine revolution" in China, much like the recent political uprisings that have occurred in Egypt and other parts of the world. For a while no reason was given for Ai's arrest; then it was reported that Ai was under investigation for tax evasion and the destruction of financial documents. His detainment, in an undisclosed location, was protested by many people, including fellow artists and human-rights activists in China and overseas. Official calls for his release came from the United States and several European nations. In mid-May, after having had no contact with his family for over a month, Ai was permitted to have a brief, supervised visit with his wife.

In early June 2011 curators of the Incidental Arts Festival in Beijing were forced to cancel their show, which included a label with Ai's name under an empty space on a gallery wall. On June 22 Ai was released on bail. "This is a technique that the public security authorities sometimes use as a face-saving device to end controversial cases that are unwise or unnecessary for them to prosecute," Jerome A. Cohen, an expert on China's legal system, told Edward Wong for the *New York Times* (June 22, 2011). "Often in such cases a compromise has been reached in negotiation with the subject, as apparently it has been here." According to the terms of Ai's bail, he is not permitted to be interviewed, cannot travel freely outside of Beijing, and cannot post anything on social networking Web sites for the next 12 months. Although he reportedly confessed to tax evasion, his family members maintain that he is innocent.

A documentary entitled "Ai Weiwei: Never Sorry" is expected to be released before the end of 2011. The feature-length film, made by the freelance journalist and filmmaker Alison Klayman, will show footage of Ai from 2008 to 2010.

In the *New York Times* (November 28, 2009), Michael Wines described Ai as a "beefy, bearded man with an air of almost monastic composure." His wife, Lu Qing, is an artist. According to the London *Guardian* (April 15, 2011), artlyst.com (May 16, 2011), and other sources, the Chinese government has accused Ai of fathering a child with another, unnamed woman.

—J.P.

Suggested Reading: aiweiwei.com; *Art in America* p118+ Sep. 2007; (Canada) *National Post* A p22 May 21, 2011; *Christian Science Monitor* (on-line) May 4, 2011; (London) *Observer* Review Features p8 July 6, 2008; *Los Angeles Times* A p4 Apr. 22, 2011; *New Statesman* (on-line) Oct. 12, 2010; *New York Times* A p6 Nov. 28, 2009, (on-line) June 22, 2011

Selected Works: *Dropping a Han Dynasty Urn*, 1995; *Table with Three Legs*, 1997–98; *Fairytale*, 2007; *Remembering*, 2009

Amalric, Mathieu

Oct. 25, 1965– Film director; actor; screenwriter

Address: c/o Zelig Talent Agency, 57 rue Réaumur, 75002 Paris, France

For his work in *Diary of a Seducer*, *My Sex Life . . . or How I Got into an Argument*, *Kings and Queen*, and *The Diving Bell and the Butterfly*—four of more than 60 films in which he has appeared—the actor Mathieu Amalric won eight of the most prestigious awards in the French movie industry. Amalric has also directed five feature-length films—*Eat Your Soup*, *Wimbledon Stadium*, *On Tour* (all of which he also wrote), and two made for French television—and six shorts, and it is as a director that he would prefer to be best known. "I think my nightmare would be that maybe I'm just a good actor," he told Elizabeth Day for the London *Observer* (May 11, 2008). "But I love directing. I think about that all the time, but sometimes, maybe, you're better at something you don't care about."

Eight years elapsed between Amalric's first appearance in a film, in *Favourites of the Moon*, in 1984, when he was 19, and his second, in *The Sentinelle*. Two years later Amalric was seen in a supporting role in *Diary of a Seducer* and as the star

Miguel Medina/AFP/Getty Images

of *My Sex Life . . . .* In a review of the latter film for the *Village Voice* (September 23, 1997), Amy Taubin wrote, "Fine as the supporting actors are,"

My Sex Life . . . "would be inconceivable without Amalric's performance. He seems to wear his nervous system outside his skin, and his remarkable eyes can look simultaneously evasive, mischievous, defensive, seductive, and besotted." A decade later another film critic, Lynn Hirschberg, wrote for the *New York Times* (September 17, 2006) that Amalric's face "seems to register at least five emotions at once." In an assessment of his portrayal in *The Diving Bell and the Butterfly* of the French journalist Jean-Dominique Bauby, who, as the result of a stroke, lost the ability to move any part of his body except his left eye, Stephen Whitty wrote for the Newark, New Jersey *Star-Ledger* (November 30, 2007), "Amalric . . . uses his performance to give real meaning to 'minimalist.' He's not some handsome if immobile hunk but an afflicted man, his mouth twisted in a fishy grimace, his one good eye wide and staring like some slippery oyster. And yet, with that one eye, he acts entire pages." "He's got this chimeric sensitivity . . . ," Nicolas Klotz, who directed Amalric in *The Heartbeat Detector* (2007), told Elizabeth Day. "I think he's obsessive but also very lucid, very precise and he also allows himself to be directed. He's child-like in that way: he has the confidence just to let himself go." When James Mottram interviewed him for the London *Sunday Times* (October 18, 2007, on-line), Amalric, who by then had more than 50 acting credits, said that with each role he still thought, "People will see I'm not an actor and it will stop." But he also insisted, "I don't want to be a star!"

Mathieu Amalric was born on October 25, 1965 in Neuilly-sur-Seine, a suburb of Paris, France, to Nicole Zand and Jacques Amalric. His father is a native Frenchman. His mother moved with her immediate family to France from Poland at the start of World War II; most of her other relatives perished in the Holocaust. Although his mother is Jewish, Amalric "had no religious education, nothing," he told Day, adding, "I feel Jewish sometimes when I watch a Woody Allen film." Nicole Zand is a longtime literary critic for the French afternoon daily *Le Monde*; Amalric's father (now retired) joined *Le Monde*'s staff in 1963. When Amalric was five his father was named *Le Monde*'s foreign-affairs editor and was assigned to report from Washington, D.C., where the Amalrics lived for the next three years. During that time Mathieu attended American schools and learned English. The Amalrics next spent four years in Moscow, Russia, then part of the Soviet Union. They returned to Paris in 1977. Jacques Amalric was *Le Monde*'s editor in chief when he left that paper, in 1993, to work for the French daily newspaper *Libération*; as *Libération*'s editor in chief, he wrote editorials. Tobias Grey wrote for the *Financial Times* (December 3, 2010, on-line) that Mathieu Amalric had one brother, who committed suicide, and one sister, who "struggled with drugs." His parents separated after Amalric left home, when he was 17.

That same year, according to Grey, Amalric got work as a production assistant. During many of the following years, when he could not find a job in the film industry, he supported himself as a truck driver, a food-stall attendant, or at other odd jobs. His first on-screen appearance came in *Favourites of the Moon* (1984), the first French-language film by the Georgian-born filmmaker Otar Iosseliani, who called it an "abstract comedy." As Amalric watched Iosseliani at work, the seed of his desire to direct took root. In 1987 a family friend recommended Amalric to the French director Louis Malle, and he was hired as a trainee assistant director during the filming of Malle's critically acclaimed, much-honored film *Au Revoir les enfants* ("Goodbye, Children"). Amalric was cast in small roles in *La Sentinelle* (*The Sentinel*, 1992) and several other films and served as an assistant director on five others between 1992 and 1995. In 1996, at the age of 30, he won his first major role, in Arnaud Desplechin's comedy-drama *Comment je me suis dispute . . . (ma vie sexuelle)* (*My Sex Life . . .*). He played Paul Dedalus, a graduate student unsure about both his professional life and his 10-year relationship with his girlfriend. Amalric has credited Desplechin with persuading him to take his acting career seriously, which he had not done until then. *My Sex Life . . .* became a cult classic in France and earned Amalric the 1997 César Award (equivalent to an Oscar) for most promising actor. That same year, after directing two shorts, Amalric directed, co-wrote, and starred in his first feature film, *Mange ta soupe* (*Eat Your Soup*). A semiautobiographical comedy, it depicted its protagonist's strained relationship with his literary mother and journalist father during a visit home following a years-long absence. In a review for the *International al Herald Tribune* (November 21, 1997), Joan Dupont wrote, "Amalric . . . was irresistible as a waif lost in a world of intellectuals. In this hilarious first film as director, he touches on the sources of that world—displaced people who cannot stay together, but cannot make it on their own. A minimalist portrait, drawn with devastating special effects." Amalric's response to the completed *Eat Your Soup* differed radically from Dupont's; he told Day that though he had tried to make a comedy, the film was "pure tragedy."

Amalric's plan to focus on directing got sidetracked by offers of film roles from directors he admired. "Each time, I say, 'Okay, this one is the last one, then I do my film'—but each time I get an irresistible offer," he told Matthew Campbell for the London *Sunday Times* (January 27, 2008). He earned praise for his complex and emotionally honest performances, including his starring roles in André Téchiné's *Alice et Martin* (*Alice and Martin*, 1998) and Olivier Assayas's *Fin août, début septembre* (*Late August, Early September*, 1998). In 2001 the actress Jeanne Balibar (whom he had married in the mid-1990s) starred in his second feature film as a director, *Le Stade de Wimbledon* (*Wimbledon Stadium*), an adaptation of a novel by the Italian writer Daniele del Giudice that was screened at the Cannes Film Festival. Catherine Shoard, writing for the London *Guardian* (May 17, 2010, on-line), called *Wimbledon Stadium* "a slow-burn thriller" in which Amalric's "passion for his lead pulses from the screen."

In 2003 Amalric directed and co-wrote the made-for-television movie *La chose publique (Public Affairs)*, a comedy about a television director working on a documentary about local politics while his marriage is crumbling. Amalric was cast as the star of Desplechin's *Rois et reine (Kings and Queen,* 2004), a mix of comedy and drama about a single mother and her ex-husband. For that performance Amalric won the 2005 César Award as well as that year's Lumière Award (equivalent to a Golden Globe) and the French film critics' Étoil d'Or Award. He next appeared in Steven Spielberg's *Munich* (2005), a film based on the murder of Israeli athletes by a Palestinian terrorist group at the 1972 Olympic Games. Describing Amalric's portrayal of Louis, a devious informant, Lynn Hirschberg wrote, "Amalric brought layers of complication to that performance—his character was never wholly trustworthy and, yet, canny enough to become indispensable to the Israelis. It was all in his eyes, which are quick and knowing and which reflect even tiny shifts in mood."

Lavish praise greeted Amalric for his work in Julian Schnabel's *Le Scaphandre et le papillon (The Diving Bell and the Butterfly,* 2007). The film—which earned virtually universal acclaim—was adapted by Ronald Harwood from the same-titled best-selling memoir by Jean-Dominique Bauby, a well-known French journalist and bon vivant. Bauby was the editor of the French *Elle* when, in 1995, at age 43, he suffered a brain-stem stroke that left his body—except for his left eye—completely paralyzed (a rare disorder known as locked-in syndrome); his mind, however, remained intact, and his hearing and vision were only mildly impaired. (His unblinking right eye was stitched closed to prevent infection.) Bauby composed his memoir mentally, memorizing what he had written in his mind each morning. Later in the day, while Claude Mendibil, a freelance editor and ghostwriter, recited the alphabet, organized according to each letter's frequency in French (it began "e-s-a-r-i-n-t-u"), Bauby would blink once for "yes" whenever she uttered a letter in the word he wanted spelled out. In that way Bauby wrote his 130-page book and approved its light editing. He died of heart failure in 1997, a few days after *The Diving Bell and the Butterfly* was published.

Amalric had initially felt reluctant to accept the role of Bauby, because the film was to be directed by an American, Julian Schnabel, and he thought, as he recalled to Philippa Hawker for the Melbourne, Australia, *Age* (February 8, 2008), that it "would be a Hollywood thing. To take a sad, true story and turn it into a movie about a guy who is an arsehole and an ordinary man and who overcomes obstacles and becomes a saint . . . that's

what 95% of Hollywood movies are all about." Schnabel, however, had no intention of making a stereotypically Hollywood film and agreed to shoot the film in French, as Amalric had requested.

In his portrayal of Bauby, Amalric was seen in flashbacks, as he had been before the stroke; for most of the film, though, he remained motionless, conveying emotions only with his left eye and his interior monologue; he also tried to refrain from moving and to stay silent between takes. "It's very, very hard not to move. . . . You have to move your muscles not to move. You're always contracted, so it's exhausting," he told James Mottram for the London *Times* (October 18, 2007). "At the end of each day I couldn't do anything. It's as if I'd done an action film!" Amalric also improvised many of the interior monologues, recorded as voiceovers. "The first few days I read the script, but after a bit I started to invent what I imagined [Bauby] to be," he told Sheila Johnston for the London *Daily Telegraph* (February 1, 2008). For his performance in *The Diving Bell and the Butterfly*, Amalric won the 2008 César, Lumière, and Étoiles d'Or best-actor awards.

Later that year, Amalric won the Golden Swan at the Copenhagen International Film Festival, in Denmark, and a best-actor award at the Gijón International Film Festival, in Spain, for his work in Nicolas Klotz's *La question humaine (The Heartbeat Detector)*. Amalric portrayed an industrial psychologist working for the French branch of a German-owned petrochemical company; while surreptitiously watching an executive (played by Michael Lonsdale) seemingly on the brink of a nervous breakdown, the psychologist finds what appears to be evidence of the firm's involvement with Nazis during World War II. His realization that he himself has voiced Nazi-like euphemisms during downsizing maneuvers undermines his own mental stability. After identifying Amalric and Lonsdale as "two of France's best actors," a London *Evening Standard* (May 15, 2008) reviewer declared, "The sparring between them is alone worth the price of admission."

Amalric played a villainous tycoon in the 22d James Bond film—*Quantum of Solace* (2008)—starring Daniel Craig as British secret agent 007 and directed by Marc Forster. "I couldn't resist it," Amalric told Campbell. "My two boys, who are 8 and 10—I can't tell them one day that I refused to be the villain in a Bond movie." "Now that the Bonds are more realistic, you don't know who the villain is anymore—they don't have a metal jaw, they don't have a scar, they don't have an eye that bleeds," he told Day. "In this film, I don't have anything to help me be a villain; I just have my face." *Quantum of Solace* did not impress most reviewers. Kenneth Turan, who offered his assessment on the National Public Radio program *Morning Edition* (November 14, 2008), said, "To watch Amalric struggle to add some life to a hapless part is to understand how much even fine actors are dependent on the words written for them." By contrast, Turan enjoyed Amalric's performance in Desplechin's *Un Conte de Noël (A Christmas Tale*, 2008), in which three generations of the Vuillard family (headed by its matriarch, portrayed by Catherine Deneuve) have gathered to celebrate the holiday. In Desplechin's hands, Turan said, "this familiar conception comes to vivid and astonishing life. Part of the credit for this goes to . . . Amalric, who's given one of the juiciest roles of his career and runs with it." Amalric, Turan continued, "plays the family's ne'er-do-well brother, a sibling so irritating his words cause dinner table riots. The difference between Amalric's two performances is so great it's like we're watching two completely different actors."

In 2009 Amalric appeared in movies including Ming-liang Tsai's *Visage (Face)*; Alain Resnais's *Les Herbes folles (Wild Grass)*; and Arnaud Larrieu's *Les Derniers jours du monde (Happy End)*. In 2010 he appeared in *Tournée (On Tour)*, which he co-wrote as well as directed. Amalric told Joan Dupont for the *New York Times* (May 12, 2010) that his inspiration for *On Tour* was a reminiscence by the French novelist Colette (1873–1954) of her experiences as a music-hall entertainer; his character, whom he named Joachim Zand, to honor his mother's murdered relatives, mimics Cosmo Vitelli, the hero of the John Cassavetes film *The Killing of a Chinese Bookie*. Amalric recruited several American neo-burlesque artists to perform in the film, much as they had in real life in the U.S., as part of a troupe that Joachim, a washed-up French producer, manages in gigs in small French towns. "I wanted the girls to become characters in a fiction, not just to be playing themselves," he told Dennis Lim for the *New York Times* (May 16, 2010, on-line). "But I also wanted the pleasure and the force of documentary to be included in the fiction." Amalric's direction of *On Tour* earned him the prize for best director at the 2010 Cannes Film Festival and a Lumière Award nomination in the same category.

The five-foot six-inch Amalric has taught introductory directing courses at the National Film School of France, known as La Fémis, in Paris. He and Jeanne Balibar separated in around 2003. Their two sons are Antoine and Pierre. Amalric also has a three-year-old son with his current girlfriend, a playwright and writer, with whom he lives in the Belleville section of Paris.

—M.A.S.

Suggested Reading: *Anthem Magazine* (on-line) Mar. 17, 2008; *Financial Times* (on-line) Dec. 3, 2010; imdb.com; (London) *Daily Telegraph* p31 Feb. 1, 2008; (London) *Guardian* (on-line) May 17, 2010; (London) *Observer* p8 May 11, 2008; (London) *Sunday Times* p11 Jan. 27, 2008; Mathieu Amalric's Web site; *New York Times* (on-line) May 16, 2010

Selected Films: as actor—*Favourites of the Moon*, 1984; *The Sentinel*, 1992; *My Sex Life . . . or How I Got into an Argument*, 1996; *Alice and Martin*, 1998; *Late August, Early September*, 1998; *Kings and Queens*, 2004; *Munich*, 2005; *The Diving Bell and the Butterfly*, 2007; *The Heartbeat Detector*, 2007; *Quantum of Solace*, 2008; *A Christmas Tale*, 2008; *Face*, 2009; *Wild Grass*, 2009; *Happy End*, 2009; as actor, writer, and director—*Eat Your Soup*, 1997; *Wimbledon Stadium*, 2001; *On Tour*, 2010

Tammy Woodard, courtesy of Clark University

Arnett, Jeffrey Jensen

July 30, 1957– Psychologist; writer; educator

Address: Dept. of Psychology, Clark University, 950 Main St., Worcester, MA 01610

On August 22, 2010 the *New York Times Magazine* published a story, "What Is It about 20-Somethings?," that dominated the *Times* Web site's list of "most-emailed" articles for weeks. The piece, written by Robin Marantz Henig, focused on Jeffrey Jensen Arnett—a professor of psychology at Clark University—and his proposed recognition of a stage of life he calls "emerging adulthood." That stage, according to Arnett, has come about in industrialized countries over the last 50 years and includes people aged roughly 18 to 29; the stage is defined in part by self-exploration and a willingness to delay commitments in favor of making the best possible choices. Arnett has devoted years of study to the subject and has written extensively on emerging adults, in works including his 2004 book,

Emerging Adulthood: The Winding Road from the Late Teens through the Twenties.

In support of his theory, in his widely quoted article "Emerging Adulthood: A Theory of Development from the Late Teens through the Twenties," published in *American Psychologist* in May 2000, Arnett cited research concerning current and previous generations of emerging adults. "Sweeping demographic shifts have taken place over the past half century," he wrote, "that have made the late teens and early twenties not simply a brief period of transition into adult roles but a distinct period of the life course, characterized by change and exploration of possible life directions. As recently as 1970, the median age of marriage in the United States was about 21 for women and 23 for men; by 1996, it had risen to 25 for women and 27 for men." According to Henig, those figures have climbed to age 26 for women and 28 for men. The age at which people first become parents has followed suit. Also, the portion of young Americans obtaining higher education has risen from 14 percent in 1940 to over 60 percent in the mid-1990s, according to Arnett, and for those who graduate, about one-third are enrolled in postgraduate education the following year. Further support for Arnett's theories can be found in residential status. "Emerging adults have the highest rates of residential change of any age group," Arnett wrote, adding: "For about 40% of the current generation of emerging adults, residential changes include moving back into their parents' home and then out again at least once in the course of their late teens and twenties." In a survey administered by Arnett, when participants were asked whether they felt they had reached adulthood, the majority of respondents in their late teens and early twenties chose the answer, "In some respects yes, in some respects no." Arnett believes that the ambiguity of that response is justified. "They have no name for the period they are in—because the society they live in has no name for it," Arnett wrote, "so they regard themselves as being neither adolescents not adults, in between the two but not really one or the other." It appeared, he observed, that recent generations of people in their twenties—due to factors including extended education and prolonged periods of exploration—were taking significantly longer to show the traditional signs of maturity.

Arnett has found that his research sometimes sparks negative feedback from parents and other adults. He told the *Boston Globe* (August 9, 2008) that he often gets such responses as, "'What's the matter with [people in their twenties]?' 'Why don't they grow up?'" Such reactions spring largely from traditional definitions of adulthood, which sociologists have long seen as encompassing five milestones: completing school, leaving home, becoming financially independent, marrying, and having children. When asked by Bella DePaulo for *Psychology Today* (August 20, 2010) what today's young people view as signs of adulthood, Arnett argued that such criteria now vary according to the

individual, but he specified three: "accepting responsibility for yourself, making independent decisions, and becoming financially independent."

The psychologist and educator was born Jeffrey Arnett (he added "Jensen" after his marriage) in Detroit, Michigan, on July 30, 1957, the fourth of five children. His mother, Marjorie Littlefield Arnett, was a homemaker, and his father, Calvin Arnett, was an engineer and personnel executive at Ford Motor Co. Arnett attended Bentley High School in Livonia, Michigan, and graduated in 1975. He told *Current Biography* that he would describe his own "emerging adulthood" as "long and colorful." The summer before his senior year at Michigan State University, when he was 22, he hitchhiked 8,000 miles from his home in Detroit to Seattle, Washington, then from Seattle to Los Angeles, California, and back to Detroit. "It was a tremendous adventure," he told *Current Biography*, "and I still remember a lot of it vividly. This one kind old couple I met, we still exchange Christmas cards 30 years later. Of course, it seems insane to me now! My mom was horrified at the prospect."

Arnett graduated from Michigan State University in 1980. Afterward, he told *Current Biography*, "I worked for two years as a musician, playing and singing in small bars and restaurants, [doing covers of] James Taylor [songs] and that kind of thing. . . . I never intended to go into music as a career—I wasn't good enough, and in any case I had other dreams—but it was a great way to enjoy those two years." Arnett then attended the University of Virginia and received a doctoral degree in developmental psychology. By 1986 he had begun teaching introductory psychology at Oglethorpe University, in Atlanta, Georgia.

At Oglethorpe a student of Arnett's, Henry, inspired him to explore the attraction that heavy-metal music holds for some young people. Arnett observed that heavy metal, through its almost violent loudness and the rebellion against mainstream musical forms that it represents, offers catharsis for alienated teens. His research led to his 1996 book, *Metalheads: Heavy Metal and Adolescent Alienation.* Through his interviews (he spoke with more than 100 "metalheads" for the book), Arnett discovered a profound sense of isolation among the teens. Thus, as he wrote in the book's preface, "soon the focus of my interest had changed from the effects of heavy metal music on adolescents to what their love for the music reflects about their alienation and, more generally, about adolescent alienation in the United States. . . . My primary interest [in writing the book] is not the music but the fans: what the music means to them and what it reflects about their lives."

Arnett completed his postdoctoral work at the University of Chicago. In 1992 he became an associate professor in the Department of Human Development and Family Studies at the University of Missouri at Columbia, where he remained until 1998. Beginning in 1997 he served as an expert witness against tobacco companies in numerous court cases. In 1998, after 46 states brought a suit against the tobacco industry, charging in part that it had long targeted minors in ad campaigns, Arnett testified in a trial that led to the largest civil settlement in U.S. history. Having studied adolescents and their responses to cigarette ads, Arnett concluded—and testified—that cigarette companies had been targeting minors consistently for 40 years, knowing that nearly all who smoke begin doing so as minors. Arnett has written seven articles on the subject, which include discussions of several major ad campaigns, among them the Joe Camel ads promoting Camel cigarettes and Winston's "No Additives . . . No Bull" campaign, which suggested that Winston's products were healthier than other cigarettes. The terms of the settlement included banning cartoon characters in advertising, restricting brand-name sponsorship of events with large youth audiences, and banning youth access to free samples. The settlement also required the tobacco industry to make a commitment to the reduction of youth access to and consumption of cigarettes.

Arnett's position at the University of Missouri, which he accepted in his mid-thirties, "seemed to me like my first real career job . . . ," he told *Current Biography*. "Perhaps that's the way it is for many of us who choose academia, it takes a long time to reach full adulthood because our education lasts so long and then it takes still more years to find a stable place in the academic world." It was at the University of Missouri that Arnett noticed something about his students that surprised him: while they had matured physically, in other ways they were different from those somewhat older than themselves. "I was in my . . . mid-30s myself, and I remember thinking, 'They're not a thing like me,'" Arnett told Henig. "I realized there was something special going on." Recalling the experiences of his own twenties and early thirties, Arnett told *Current Biography*, "It took me a long time to 'emerge' into adulthood. I've found that most people feel adult by their late twenties, but for me it wasn't until I was about 35 that I felt that way. . . . When I did finally feel like I had reached adulthood, I became curious about how and when other people felt adult, and that's the question that started me on the road to what eventually became emerging adulthood."

Arnett first presented the theory of emerging adulthood, and coined that term, in "Emerging Adulthood: A Theory of Development from the Late Teens through the Twenties," in 2000. The article opens with a quote from a 22-year-old, Kristen, whom Arnett had interviewed as part of his research. "When our mothers were our age, they were engaged [to be married] . . . ," she said. "They at least had some idea what they were going to do with their lives. . . . I, on the other hand, will have a dual degree in majors that are ambiguous at best and impractical at worst (English and political science), no ring on my finger and no idea who I am, much less what I want to do. . . . Under duress, I will admit that this is a pretty exciting time. Sometimes, when I look out across the wide expanse that is my future, I can see beyond the void. I realize that having nothing ahead to count on means I now have to count on myself; that having no direction means forging one of my own."

Arnett found that the feelings expressed by Kristen were representative of those of many people her age. He asserted that in the U.S., a collision of economic and cultural forces had fundamentally changed life and opportunity for people in their twenties, rendering previous criteria for adulthood problematic. Many people in their twenties are acquiring greater levels of education than their counterparts in previous generations, taking their time to decide on career paths that they hope will be not only financially rewarding but emotionally satisfying as well. In other words, emerging adults (among the 60 percent of Americans who go to college) are taking time to find what makes them happy, which Arnett thinks is wise, if not always lucrative; many 20-somethings are still partially supported by their parents as they explore unpaid internships or travel abroad, which Lev Grossman, writing for *Time* (January 16, 2005), cited as "reaping the fruit of decades of American affluence and social liberalism." Conversely, Grossman also acknowledged that mounting debt from school loans and the poor job market of late have left other 20-somethings—many highly educated—in an emerging-adulthood limbo, working at jobs for which they are overqualified as they struggle to make the next step. "Cultural influences structure and sometimes limit the extent to which emerging adults are able to use their late teens and early twenties in this way," Arnett wrote, "and not all young people in this age period are able to use these years for independent exploration. Like adolescence, emerging adulthood is a period of the life course that is culturally constructed, not universal and immutable."

Kenneth Keniston, a Yale University psychologist who studied adulthood in the 1960s, was a proponent of the view that a previously unnamed stage of development existed; while Arnett used the term "emerging adulthood," Keniston called the stage "youth." As quoted by Henig, Keniston believed that while adulthood had traditionally suggested the ability to answer "questions of relationship to the existing society, questions of vocation, questions of social role and lifestyle," more and more postadolescents found that they were unable to define themselves in those terms. Instead, as quoted by Henig, Keniston found that those in the "youth" category felt "pervasive ambivalence toward self and society," experienced "the feeling of absolute freedom, of living in a world of pure possibilities," and placed "enormous value" on "change, transformation and movement." Arnett, who "readily acknowledges his debt to Keniston," in Henig's words, has identified those same traits in emerging adults.

Hundreds of factors have emerged to contribute to a shift in our perception of how and when people grow up, though there is much debate over whether emerging adulthood is truly a new stage of human development on par with adolescence (which was recognized at the turn of the 20th century, when some aspects of American society had to be restructured to accommodate it). Not the least of those factors, Arnett has pointed out, is recent evidence of continuing brain-cell development. "Neuroscientists once thought the brain stops growing shortly after puberty," Henig wrote, "but now they know it keeps maturing well into the 20s." Through a study sponsored by the National Institutes of Health that followed nearly 5,000 children and young adults ages three to 16, scientists were surprised to find that the brain does not fully mature until at least age 25. Those scientists also found what Henig called a "time lag between the growth of the limbic system, where emotions originate, and of the prefrontal cortex, which manages those emotions." Jay Giedd, the director of the study, explained to Henig, "The prefrontal part is the part that allows you to control your impulses, come up with a long-range strategy, answer the question, 'What am I going to do with my life?' That weighing of the future keeps changing into the 20s and 30s."

Some of the neurological findings indicating a previously unacknowledged stage of development are borne out in the characteristics Arnett has identified in emerging adults. Arnett told Henig that like adolescence, emerging adulthood has a "particular psychological profile," which in this case includes identity exploration, feelings of being unsettled in life, self-focus, feelings of being between childhood and adulthood, and, Henig wrote, "a rather poetic characteristic [Arnett] calls 'a sense of possibilities,'" or an optimism independent of economic or other circumstances. That optimism does not anticipate fates that befall many adults—including what Arnett described to Henig as "dreary, dead-end jobs, bitter divorces . . . disappointing and disrespectful children." He added, "None of them imagine that this is what the future holds for them." Further, according to Arnett's study, when asked if they agreed with the statement, "I am very sure that someday I will get to where I want to be in life," 96 percent of emerging adults surveyed said yes. Arnett told Bella DePaulo, "Never in human history have we had such a long gap between the time people reach the end of puberty and the time they feel fully adult and have taken on the full range of adult responsibilities."

In 2004 Arnett published *Emerging Adulthood: The Winding Road from the Late Teens through the Twenties*. Frank Furstenberg wrote for the *Washington Post* (October 5, 2004) that the book "charts a new terrain that is only likely to grow in the 21st century. [Arnett's] sense of optimism and advocacy for young adults in infectious. This work is likely to help build a field of scholarship that is urgently needed to renovate policies, programs and general public understanding of the lengthy and arduous process of becoming an adult in American society." Ann S. Masten, director of the Institute of Child Development at the University of Minnesota, as quoted by CollegeParentCentral.com, took a more global perspective, writing, "This engaging account of emerging adulthood in American society provides an optimistic perspective on a rapidly spreading global phenomenon that is transforming societies as well as individual lives and families in our time."

In 2005 Arnett was named a Fulbright scholar and traveled to Denmark to interview emerging adults. His research there led to many of the same findings he had reached in the United States. In an article for the Institute of Foreign Culture Relations (IFA) in Denmark, Arnett cited the larger forces that had contributed to the new stage he calls emerging adulthood. He wrote, "The economy in Europe and similar countries has changed from a base in manufacturing and industry to a base in information and technology. The new economy rewards education and training, which led to the boom in participation in university education." He also noted that "sexual mores" have changed due to more-effective contraceptive methods, such as the birth-control pill, and that having "a regular sex life was no longer an inducement to marriage, and becoming pregnant unintentionally no longer resulted in forced marriages." Arnett wrote that most young Europeans of today are the heirs of peace and prosperity brought by Europe's growth from "rubble in the aftermath of the most violent and destructive war in human history [World War II]" to "the most affluent, peaceful, humane region in the world." Arnett asserted in the same article, "Emerging adulthood should rightfully be seen as one of the fruits of affluence. Emerging adults now seek work that is not just a way to put food on the table but a form of self-fulfillment. In love, too, their hopes for an ideal mate are high, probably too high. But here, too, how could this not be seen as an improvement over the old way of having few hopes and few options and everything settled forever by the early twenties?"

Arnett admitted to Henig that not every person goes through a period of emerging adulthood. He pointed to the developing world, where children take on responsibility quickly by necessity, and to some young people in industrialized countries, such as young mothers or those forced to find jobs right out of high school. Those exceptions have led some scholars, including Richard Lerner of Tufts University, who is a close friend of Arnett's, to express doubts about the concept of emerging adulthood. "The core idea of classical stage theory is that all people—underscore 'all'—pass through a series of qualitatively different periods in an invariant and universal sequence in stages that can't be skipped or reordered," Lerner told Henig. Essentially, Lerner said, if it possible to avoid the phase of emerging adulthood then it is not, according to classical theory, a true developmental stage.

Arnett's most recent book, *Debating Emerging Adulthood: Stage or Process?* (2011), co-written with the developmental psychologists Marion Kloep, Leo B. Hendry, and Jennifer L. Tanner, explores some of the issues raised by the theory. The book's primary debate focuses on the acceptance of emerging adulthood: whether it should be considered a developmental stage, as adolescence is. Arnett and Tanner argued that around the world, people between the ages of 18 and 25 share characteristics associated with emerging adulthood, but that, because the experiences of those young people vary widely—due to culture, education, and social class—it is possible to experience emerging adulthood in different ways. By contrast, Kloep and Hendry argued that such theories about life stages have never been able to describe individuals' developmental transitions accurately over a lifetime and should be disregarded altogether.

Arnett's other books include *Emerging Adults in America: Coming of Age in the 21st Century* (2005), co-edited with Tanner, which grew out of the first Conference on Emerging Adulthood, held at Harvard University in 2003; the textbook *Adolescence and Emerging Adulthood: A Cultural Approach*, whose most recent edition was published in 2010; and two encyclopedias he edited: the *International Encyclopedia of Adolescence* and the *Encyclopedia of Children, Adolescents, and the Media*, both published in 2007. Since 2002 he has been the editor of the bimonthly *Journal of Adolescent Research*.

Currently, Arnett is interviewing the parents of emerging adults for an advice book for parents due to be published in 2012. "I've really enjoyed those interviews," he told *Current Biography*, "because most of the parents are about my age, their late forties to their early sixties. So far what's most interesting to me about the interviews is the way parents describe the delicate dance of their relationships with their emerging-adult children. Their emerging adults want their support, emotional and financial, and yet don't want them to intrude, and where support becomes intrusion is often difficult to specify. . . . There's often a lot of ambiguity to the relationship, but the good news is that for the most part they really enjoy each other." He added, "Emerging adults appreciate being treated more like an adult by their parents, and having adult conversations with them, while parents savor the love and respect their emerging adults give them much more freely than in adolescence. For a lot of parents, emerging adulthood is the big payoff for all the years of struggle and sacrifice involved in raising children."

Arnett taught as a visiting professor at the University of Maryland until 2006, when he became a research professor in the Department of Psychology at Clark University, in Worcester, Massachusetts. (The university's first president, G. Stanley Hall, also the founding president of the American Psychological Association, published a groundbreaking study in 1904 that identified adolescence as a distinct life stage.) Arnett has also been a visiting scholar at Stanford University. He met his wife, Lene Jensen, at Oglethorpe University in 1986. The couple have twins—a boy and a girl, Miles and Paris, who were born in 1999. Jensen, too, is a developmental psychologist at Clark University. She specializes in moral development and the development of cultural identity among immigrants.

—M.M.H.

Suggested Reading: AFI Health Committee (on-line) Mar. 1999; *American Psychologist* (on-line) May 2000; *Boston Globe* G p26 Aug. 8, 2009; JeffreyArnett.com; *New York Times* (on-line) Aug. 22, 2010; *Psychology Today* (on-line) Dec. 7, 2008, Aug. 20, 2010; *Time* (on-line) Jan. 16, 2005; *Washington Post* C p2 Oct. 5, 2004

Selected Books: *Metalheads: Heavy Metal and Adolescent Alienation*, 1996; *Emerging Adulthood: The Winding Road from the Late Teens through the Twenties*, 2004; *Emerging Adults in America: Coming of Age in the 21st Century* (with Jennifer L. Tanner), 2005; *Debating Emerging Adulthood: Stage or Process?* (with Marion Kloep, Leo B. Hendry, and Jennifer L. Tanner), 2011

Aronson, Jane

Nov. 10, 1951– Pediatrician; international adoption consultant; founder of the Worldwide Orphans Foundation

Address: International Pediatric Health Services, 338 E. 30th St., #1R, New York, NY 10016

Known worldwide as the "orphan doctor," Jane Aronson is a pediatrician specializing in adoption medicine: the evaluation from afar (through medical records, photos, and videos) of the physical and developmental health of orphans selected for possible adoption. The vast majority of those orphans are infants and toddlers born in China, Vietnam, Russia, and a handful of other nations overseas; abandoned by caregivers who cannot look after them, they live in institutions that, with few exceptions, are underfunded and understaffed. In 1993 Aronson founded International Adoption Medical Consultation Services, to advise would-be adoptive parents regarding the physical and developmental condition of their prospective children and also to assist parents in obtaining proper medical care for their adopted children after they are brought to the U.S. "I'm helping children find parents and helping families be created," Aronson told Sylvia Adcock for a 2000 *Newsday* interview posted on her Web site, orphandoctor.com. "What drives me is that thought, *Another family. How wonderful for them.*" To date Aronson has assessed

Michael Loccisano/Getty Images
Jane Aronson

cluding the Babies & Children's Hospital of Columbia Presbyterian Medical Center, which is affiliated with the Columbia University Medical School, in New York (1990–91); the Albert Einstein College of Medicine, in the Bronx, New York (1991–92); the School of Medicine at the Stony Brook University Medical Center, on Long Island (1992–2000); and the Weill Cornell Medical College, in New York City (2000–08). Among other honors, in 2000 she was named an Angel in Adoption by the Congressional Coalition on Adoption Institutes, and in 2006 she won the Humanitarian Award from the World of Children, for helping "the most vulnerable children in their societies and making profound changes in these children's lives," according to the organization's Web site.

A descendant of Russian Jews, Jane Ellen Aronson was born on November 10, 1951 in the New York City borough of Brooklyn to Selma Aronson, a high-school and college accounting teacher, and Harold Aronson, a college-educated grocery owner who often extended credit to his poor customers. Shortly after Aronson's birth the family moved to Franklin Square, a small town on Long Island, New York, where she and her brother, Barry, grew up. (Some sources state that she was raised in nearby Valley Stream.) From early on Aronson would charm adults by telling them of her plan to become a doctor and live in a big Manhattan brownstone with her many children. A natural athlete, she worked hard to keep her grades up and was especially fond of science. She now believes that she studied with unusual diligence to compensate for an undiagnosed learning disability. Her favorite television show was *The Lone Ranger*. "I scheduled everything around *The Lone Ranger*," Aronson told Lauren Foster for the *Financial Times* (October 21, 2008, on-line), describing the nameless title character as "an unsung hero, doing good for those who were downtrodden." Another powerful influence was her great-uncle Joseph Aronson, a pioneering tuberculosis researcher and physician for the Armed Forces Institute of Pathology, who captivated her with accounts of his experiences in treating midwestern Native Americans suffering from tuberculosis in the 1930s. Also influential was her family's rabbi, Harold Saperstein, "who spoke of his travels and the plight of the Jews and other oppressed people all over the world, inspiring Aronson's global mind set," Jessica Remo wrote. Perhaps the biggest impetus for Aronson's early determination to pursue a career in medicine was her fondness for her own pediatrician. "He saved lives," she told Janine di Giovanni for the London *Times* (December 12, 2009, on-line). "He saved kids from having polio. I grew up thinking, 'I want to do that.'"

upwards of 7,000 foreign-born children adopted by Americans, and she has continued to monitor the progress of many of those youngsters in her practice as a primary-care pediatrician in New York City. She herself is the mother of two adopted boys, one from Vietnam and the other from Ethiopia.

Aronson's visits to many ill-equipped and overcrowded orphanages overseas—including some in which conditions verged on medieval—led her, in 1997, to establish the Worldwide Orphans Foundation (WWO). Aronson is the chief executive officer of the WWO, whose mission is to improve the lives of some of the millions of orphans who will never be adopted and will grow up in group homes or institutions. "Kids can have a fantastic life in their own countries if there are proper services," she told Jessica Remo for *Park Place* magazine (November/December 2010, on-line). To help provide those services, "orphan rangers"—WWO-supported health-care professionals and others—assist orphanage employees in addressing the medical, developmental, and educational needs of the children in their care. "That's what my foundation, Worldwide Orphans, is about . . . ," Aronson said to Lisa Henricksson for *Marie Claire* (January 1, 2007, on-line), "trying to do something for kids who are rotting in an orphanage. That'll be my main legacy—trying to help those left behind, because they are the most disenfranchised, the most unentitled, the most victimized. That's what keeps me up at night: trying to make a dent in it."

Aronson is a specialist in pediatric HIV/AIDS and other infectious diseases that strike children, among them diseases rarely if ever seen by most pediatricians in the U.S., such as diphtheria, tuberculosis, and polio. She has taught at schools in-

Aronson ranked 11th in her class of 310 students when she graduated from Valley Stream North High School, in 1969. She next enrolled at Hunter College, a division of the City University of New York in Manhattan, attending classes part-time while working as a photographer. During her undergraduate years she came out as a lesbian. She earned a B.A. degree in psychology and biology in 1976. Deeply disappointed when she failed to gain admission to Yale Medical School, she spent the next 10 years working occasionally as a photographer, carpenter, or bartender but mostly as a teacher. At the Sagamore Children's Center, in Melville, New York, she worked with autistic and other emotionally handicapped children. She then taught math and science at public and private schools in Manhattan, sometimes coaching the schools' cross-country and girls' basketball teams. One day, while she was teaching at a public middle school, Aronson found out that one of her students had a gun in his lunch bag. She soon concluded that she would be safer and perhaps more effective working with children in a different capacity. After reconsidering her goal of becoming a doctor, she enrolled in a course to prepare for the medical-schools admission test. A year later she won acceptance to the School of Osteopathic Medicine at the University of Medicine and Dentistry of New Jersey, a state school in Stratford. She graduated with a D.O. (doctor of osteopathic medicine) degree in 1986. (According to Medline, a Web site maintained by the National Institutes of Health, a D.O. degree is equivalent to an M.D. degree, except that "osteopathic physicians receive an additional 300–500 hours in the study of hands-on manual medicine and the body's musculoskeletal system.")

Aronson completed four years of pediatric residencies in New Jersey, at Monmouth Medical, in Long Branch (1986–87), Newark Beth Israel Medical Center (1987–89), and Morristown Memorial Hospital (1989–90), at the last of which she was the chief resident in pediatrics. In 1990–91 she gained expertise in pediatric infectious diseases as a fellow at Columbia Presbyterian Babies Hospital (now the Morgan Stanley Children's Hospital), in New York City, and in 1991–92 she worked at four Bronx hospitals. From 1992 to 2000 Aronson served as the chief of pediatric infectious diseases at Winthrop-University Hospital in Mineola, on Long Island, New York.

In the early 1990s Aronson began to become known among adoptive parents for her expertise in infectious diseases and certain other problems seldom if ever seen by most pediatricians working in the U.S. They include tuberculosis, diphtheria, polio, hepatitis B, syphilis, and some other diseases caused by bacteria and viruses; maladies caused by parasites such as roundworms and tapeworms; and conditions caused by malnutrition, such as rickets, anemia, failure to grow, abnormally small stature, and delays in mental development. Retardation in language acquisition and other aspects of intellectual development are also symptoms of a prolonged absence of stimulation (that is, minimal contact with other humans), as are apathy, depression, muscle weakness, lack of small or large muscle control, and social problems ranging from unwillingness to make eye contact to uncontrollable violent tantrums. Some babies showed evidence of alcohol-associated birth defects, and others displayed symptoms of having ingested dangerously high amounts of lead.

Often, symptoms displayed by the growing numbers of children adopted from abroad mystified or escaped the notice of the pediatricians whom the children's adoptive parents consulted. Moreover, many U.S. pediatricians were unaware that the medical reports prepared in the children's native countries for use by U.S. physicians were often misleading or erroneous. In some cases the reports' preparers had been incompetent or lacked the equipment necessary for an adequate examination, or they had knowingly tried to hide medical problems that they knew might jeopardize the adoption process; in others, the inadequacy or virtual uselessness of the reports stemmed from huge differences between the cultures of medicine in those countries and medical standards and customs in the U.S. Russian physicians, for example, sometimes described abnormal conditions in terms completely unknown in the American medical community. The parents of many children adopted from abroad struck Aronson as "desperate for information," she recalled to Melissa Fay Greene for the New Yorker (July 17, 2000). She told David Tuller for the New York Times (September 4, 2001, on-line), "It became clear to me that this was a big population that had nowhere to go for information." To begin to address such problems, in 1993 Aronson founded the International Adoption Medical Consultation Services clinic at Winthrop-University Hospital.

As an international adoption consultant in the early and mid-1990s, Aronson witnessed firsthand the dire conditions that prevailed in some institutions. The terrible conditions in many Romanian orphanages stemmed from policies of the ruthless Communist dictator Nicolae Ceauşescu, who ruled Romania from early 1965 until the end of 1989. Determined to increase the nation's population, Ceauşescu had banned abortion and contraception for women under 40 and offered incentives for families with five or more children. Unable to afford the costs of their growing families, impoverished parents turned over their children to the state. In addition, within their first three years, children whom state doctors deemed disabled— even for minor learning disabilities—were institutionalized. Most orphanages were unable to take proper care of the rapidly increasing numbers of resident children. Many children died of disease or malnutrition; some suffered fatal cases of frostbite. Others languished in filthy cribs, where they had virtually no visual or tactile stimulation and had contact with people only a few minutes a day; they drank from bottles propped up so that the nipples remained in their mouths for hours at a time. Even with sufficient nourishment, the almost total lack of human touch and interaction led to failure to thrive and, in many cases, death. While adoption was a possibility for a few of those children, the vast majority would remain institutionalized until they turned 18. At that point they were expected to fend for themselves, a task for which they were woefully unprepared. Many of them, incapacitated by physical and/or psychiatric illness and developmentally stunted, would remain wards of the state indefinitely.

After the fall of the Iron Curtain, the conditions in such institutions—"child gulags," as some American observers labeled them—became public knowledge outside the Soviet Union and other formerly Communist nations in Europe. International pressure for reform erupted, and the adoption rate of Eastern-bloc orphans by families abroad increased significantly. Since many former Soviet-bloc nations had extremely limited resources for improving conditions in orphanages, Aronson realized that help had to come from the West. "Work with orphans is for and with the local community," she told Jim Luce for the *Huffington Post* (February 8, 2009, on-line). "Adoption is not the solution, community support is." That conviction led Aronson in 1997 to establish the Worldwide Orphans Foundation, or WWO. The foundation's mission, as stated on its Web site, is "to transform the lives of orphaned children by taking them out of anonymity and helping them to become healthy, independent, productive members of their communities and the world." The WWO is active in Azerbaijan, Bulgaria, China, Ecuador, Ethiopia, Haiti, Kenya, Serbia, and Vietnam. In the organization's Orphan Ranger Program, a sort of Peace Corps for orphanages, health-care professionals and graduate students work directly with institutionalized children and also help orphanage staff members develop procedures to ensure that higher standards of care can be maintained.

Other WWO initiatives include medical programs for children suffering from HIV/AIDS in Vietnam and Ethiopia and the Early Intervention Program (also known as the "granny program"), in which retired local schoolteachers, medical professionals, and other volunteers are recruited to interact with institutionalized children one on one. WWO also operates health clinics and, in collaboration with the Paul Newman Foundation's Hole in the Wall program, summer camps. The programs are funded in part by grants from companies and agencies including Bristol-Myers Squibb, USAID/PEPFAR (the President's Emergency Plan for AIDS), Catholic Relief Services, and UNICEF.

In 2000 Aronson left Winthrop-University Hospital and set up a private practice, known as International Pediatric Health Services, in New York City. She devotes a lot of time to reviewing medical records and any available photos and video footage of potential adoptees, to determine—to the extent that she can with such limited materials—the presence of physical or other developmental problems. The faces of babies suffering from fetal alcohol syndrome, for example, show characteristic abnormalities. Other developmentally stunted babies, who based on their ages would be expected to show in-

terest in and grab toys within their reach, may retain sad or apathetic expressions and fail to unclench their fists when toys are presented to them. "It's hard," Aronson said to Sylvia Adcock. "I'm making a judgment about a child, putting them in a category where they may not get adopted. And I feel guilty. . . . I don't tell people whether to adopt a kid or not. I leave that to the families. There are some people who are more ready for risks than others."

In 2000 Aronson began the process that led to her adoption of her first son, Ben, four months after his birth, in Vietnam. Shortly before Ben's arrival in the U.S., she and Diana Leo, who was then a professional fundraiser and director of development at New York Law School, became romantically involved. She and Leo, who is currently WWO's director of development and communications, live in Maplewood, New Jersey, where they are raising Ben and his brother, the Ethiopian-born Desalegn (called Des), whom Aronson adopted in 2004, when he was six years old. Leo's daughter, Hillary, adopted as a child in the U.S., is now an adult. Aronson and her previous partner split up after 18 years together, in part because Aronson wanted a child and her partner did not. "Being a mom definitely influenced my practice of medicine," Aronson told Tina Kelley for the *New York Times*'s Maplewood, New Jersey, blog (May 6, 2009). "I think I was probably afraid before. You have a baby, and then you really know how to listen to other mothers. I was good and hard-working before, but after becoming a parent I knew more about being compassionate, and about what was practical. . . . I learned so much about being a better listener, how hard it is to implement change in a family setting, and the many challenges you have with an infant from an orphanage. . . . Now, with adoptive parents, I can say I'm one of you."

—H.R.W.

Suggested Reading: *Babble.com* Sep. 24, 2007; *Financial Times* (on-line) Oct. 21, 2008; *Huffington Post* (on-line) Feb. 8, 2009; (London) *Times* (on-line) Dec. 12, 2009; *Marie Claire* (on-line) Jan. 1, 2007; *New York Times* (on-line) May 4, 1997, Sep. 4, 2001; *New Yorker* p38+ July 17, 2000; *Park Place* (on-line) Nov./Dec. 2010; *People* p13+ Nov. 12, 2001

Dan Kitwood/Getty Images

Assange, Julian

July 3, 1971– Founder of WikiLeaks.org

Address: WikiLeaks, Box 4080, Australian Post Office—University Melbourne Branch, Victoria 3052, Australia

The Australian-born computer hacker and activist Julian Assange is the founder and editor in chief of the whistle-blowing Web site WikiLeaks.org. Since its inception, in 2006, WikiLeaks has posted more than one million confidential documents, offering unprecedented glimpses into the inner workings of national governments, the military, religious organizations, corporations, and other institutions. As the public face of an organization that exposes secrets and operates based on the promise of anonymity for its sources, Assange has become the object of both admiration and scorn. Some have called Assange a welcome agent of governmental transparency and accountability, and he was the readers' choice for *Time* magazine's 2010 Person of the Year; meanwhile, others have accused him of disrupting sensitive diplomatic relations and endangering lives, U.S. federal prosecutors have weighed building a legal case against him based on the Espionage Act, and he is undergoing hearings in Britain that could get him extradited to Sweden for questioning on allegations of sexual molestation. (Assange and his supporters have maintained that he has done nothing illegal. Rather, they claim, the allegations are meant to distract the public from facts revealed by WikiLeaks and sow doubts about the legitimacy of the group's work.) With Assange portrayed in the media as everything from a paranoid megalomaniac to a force for truth,

debate continues over whether he is a hero or a villain—and over the function and value of an organization such as WikiLeaks.

Julian Paul Assange was born on July 3, 1971 in Townsville, in the state of Queensland, on the northeastern coast of Australia. He was raised primarily by his mother, Christine; little is known about Assange's father, whom Assange never knew, other than that Christine met the man at a rally held to protest the Vietnam War. Shortly after Julian's first birthday, Christine married Brett Assange, the director of a touring theater company. In an interview with Raffi Khatchadourian for the *New Yorker* (June 7, 2010, on-line), Assange described his early childhood with his mother and stepfather as being "pretty Tom Sawyer. I had my own horse. I built my own raft. I went fishing. I was going down mine shafts and tunnels." Due to the nature of their work, the family moved often, making Julian's enrollment within the Australian school system haphazard. That, combined with Christine's feelings of distrust toward formalized education in general ("I didn't want [my children's] spirits broken," she told Khatchadourian), led her to favor a home-schooling curriculum for Julian that included occasional correspondence courses or informal tutoring sessions with a friend of the family who was a university professor. As Assange grew older his education was styled around his love of reading. "I spent a lot of time in libraries going from one thing to another, looking closely at the books I found in citations, and followed that trail," Assange told Khatchadourian. In his reading Assange found himself especially drawn to science and technology.

When Assange was eight years old, his mother's relationship with Brett Assange dissolved. She started seeing a musician, and the two had a son together. Soon the musician began to abuse Assange's mother, and the couple separated. Fearing that her second son would be taken away, Christine told Julian that they needed to "disappear," and Assange spent the next five years, from age 11 to 16, on the run with his mother and half-brother. For a brief period the family rented a house across the street from an electronics store, where Assange spent much of his time teaching himself to write programs on a Commodore 64 computer that the store owner let him use. When Christine learned about her son's aptitude for computers, she moved the family into a cheaper dwelling while she saved money to buy Julian the Commodore 64 he had been using. In 1987, at the age of 16, Assange acquired a modem. While the Internet as we know it today had not yet been developed, computer and telecom systems formed a network that a person with the necessary hardware and technical knowledge could explore. "The austerity of one's interaction with a computer is something that appealed to me," Assange told Khatchadourian. "It is like chess—chess is very austere, in that you don't have many rules, there is no randomness, and the problem is very hard." Before long Assange had become a skilled hacker and programmer.

Assange soon adopted the on-line name "Mendax" (derived from the Latin phrase "splendide mendax," used by the Roman lyric poet Horace and translated as "nobly untruthful") and collaborated with two other hackers to form the collective known as the International Subversives. The Subversives are known to have broken into computer networks belonging to the U.S. Department of Defense, the Los Alamos National Laboratory, and a number of Australian and Canadian organizations and corporations. While there is no question that the Subversives were breaking the law by entering those systems without permission, they claimed to operate according to a strict code of conduct, outlined by Assange for the book *Underground: Tales of Hacking, Madness and Obsession on the Electronic Frontier* (1997), by Suelette Dreyfus: "Don't damage computer systems you break into (including crashing them); don't change the information in those systems (except for altering logs to cover your tracks); and share information."

At 17 Assange became romantically involved with a girl a year younger than himself and moved out of his mother's home to live with her. Soon the girl became pregnant, and the couple's son, Daniel, was born when Assange was 18. Soon afterward Assange and the child's mother, who had married in an unofficial ceremony before the birth, separated.

One night in September 1991, Assange hacked into the master terminal of the Canadian telecom company Nortel, maintained in Melbourne, Australia, and was shocked to find that he was not alone there; a Nortel administrator was signed on as well. Aware of the likelihood that he would be discovered, Assange tried to engage the administrator by sending him a message: "I have taken control. For years, I have been struggling in this grayness. But now I have finally seen the light." When the administrator failed to respond, Assange sent one more message ("It's been nice playing with your system. We didn't do any damage and we even improved a few things. Please don't call the Australian Federal Police") before logging off.

In the weeks that followed, Assange lived with the fear that he would be caught—eating little, sleeping badly, and worried that his phone had been tapped. As it turned out, his fears were not unfounded, and in late October he was arrested by the Australian federal police unit that had been monitoring the Subversives. Charged with 31 counts of hacking and related offenses and facing a maximum of 10 years in prison, Assange pleaded guilty to 25 of the charges and was ordered to pay the Australian government a small sum in damages. Ken Day, the lead investigator in the pursuit of the Subversives, told Khatchadourian that he felt Assange had "some altruistic motive. I think he acted on the belief that everyone should have access to everything."

After the case came to a close, Assange took various jobs to help support his son. (He shared custody of Daniel with the boy's mother.) He studied math and physics at the University of Melbourne but left when he suspected that the work of other students in one of its labs was being used by defense contractors and the military. Khatchadourian wrote that by that time, Assange "had come to understand the defining human struggle not as left versus right, or faith versus reason, but as individual versus institution. As a student of [the writers Franz] Kafka, [Arthur] Koestler, and [Aleksandr] Solzhenitsyn, he believed that truth, creativity, love, and compassion are corrupted by institutional hierarchies, and by 'patronage networks' . . . that contort the human spirit." In 2006 he wrote a kind of manifesto, entitled "Conspiracy as Governance," applying graph theory to political networks. Around that same time Assange cloistered himself in a house near the University of Melbourne to begin work on what would become WikiLeaks.

According to its Web site, WikiLeaks is a not-for-profit media organization with the goal of bringing "important news and information to the public" by providing an "innovative, secure and anonymous way for sources to leak information to our journalists" via an "electronic drop box." Original source material is then posted on-line alongside WikiLeaks news stories and commentary "so readers and historians alike can see evidence of the truth." The group has about 40 core members and hundreds of volunteers. Like the Web-based encyclopedia Wikipedia and other projects of the Wikimedia Foundation, WikiLeaks takes its name from "wiki," a category of Web site that allows for user collaboration. WikiLeaks is not connected to Wikipedia or the Wikimedia Foundation in any way.

Although Assange registered the organization's domain name in 1999, WikiLeaks did not make public its first document until December 2006, when it posted a secret order allegedly penned by Sheikh Hassan Dahir Aweys of Somalia, the leader of the militia group Conservative Council of Islamic Courts, calling for the assassination of other Somali officials. WikiLeaks next made headlines in August 2007, when the London *Guardian* (August 31, 2007) ran a front-page article detailing corruption on the part of the former Kenyan president Daniel Arap Moi and named WikiLeaks as its information source. In November 2007 WikiLeaks published a highly sensitive, 238-page manual from 2003 called "Camp Delta Standard Operating Procedures," which detailed day-to-day operations at the U.S. military's detention facility in Guantánamo Bay, Cuba.

In January 2008 WikiLeaks released upwards of 600 internal United Nations reports, more than 70 of which were classified. The following month the site posted 6,780 Congressional Research Service reports concerning a number of sensitive political issues relating to U.S. social policy, defense, and foreign affairs. The research-service reports were commissioned by the U.S. Congress at an estimated cost of $1 billion; generally, such material is read only by members of Congress and their staffs.

In early February 2008 officials at the Swiss bank Julius Baer, incensed by WikiLeaks's publication of some of the bank's confidential financial records, won an injunction in a U.S. district court forcing Dynadot, the domain-name registrar of WikiLeaks, to disable the domain, preventing use of the domain name to reach the site. (The records, which the bank claimed were falsified, pointed to money-laundering schemes and other illegal practices.) The existence of WikiLeaks mirror sites allowed for continued access to the leaked documents despite the injunction; meanwhile, the suit had the unintended effect of increasing media scrutiny of the financial documents in question and strengthening public support for WikiLeaks's rights under the First Amendment. At the end of the month, the court reversed its decision, ruling that the order to shut down the site amounted to unconstitutional prior restraint and possible violations of the First Amendment. Also in 2008 WikiLeaks published the contents of a Yahoo! e-mail account belonging to Sarah Palin, a former Alaska governor and the 2008 Republican vice-presidential candidate; a British National Party membership list; and the secret "bibles" of the Church of Scientology, including eccentric writings by the Church's founder, L. Ron Hubbard. When the Church of Scientology's lawyers threatened legal action on the basis of copyright infringement if the documents were not removed from the site, WikiLeaks responded the following week by uploading approximately 1,000 pages of additional material relating to the Church of Scientology.

In November 2009 WikiLeaks published a number of documents obtained from the University of East Anglia's Climatic Research Unit, including e-mail correspondence among climate scientists that appeared to undermine some research data related to global warming. The documents were immediately cited by those skeptical of climate change as evidence that the threat of global warming had been largely exaggerated, if not completely fabricated. The same year also saw the release of 570,000 intercepts of pager messages sent on September 11, 2001 in response to that day's terrorist attacks and the lists of Web sites forbidden within countries including China, Thailand, and Iran, all three of which, in response, added WikiLeaks to their lists of banned Web sites. Since it went "live," WikiLeaks.org has experienced several interruptions of service, some for extended periods, for reasons ranging from legal injunction to server overloads resulting from cyber attacks. The contents of the site, however, have remained accessible through multiple mirror sites hosted on servers in several countries. Assange was honored by the human-rights organization Amnesty International with the 2009 U.K. Media Award for new media for running a series of reports, called *Kenya: The Cry of Blood—Extra Judicial Killings and Disappearances*, exposing hundreds of extrajudicial assassinations in Kenya. In March 2010 WikiLeaks published a 32-page report from the U.S. Department of Defense naming WikiLeaks as a threat to U.S. security interests and suggesting possible methods of marginalizing the organization, including deterring potential whistleblowers with threats of termination of employment and/or criminal prosecution.

The April 2010 leak of classified U.S. military video footage documenting a series of July 2007 helicopter attacks in Baghdad, Iraq, followed by the release of hundreds of thousands of documents relating to the U.S. wars in Afghanistan and Iraq, drew international attention to the conduct of the U.S. military in those countries and to the methods of WikiLeaks. As a result of those leaks, the organization and Assange became the focus of an investigation by the U.S. government into how, and from whom, the released documents and footage had been obtained. The grainy, black-and-white footage, shot from the cockpit of an army helicopter, is accompanied by radio communications between the crews on the air and the ground and shows gunfire and missiles aimed at groups of people apparently assumed to be Iraqi insurgents. The strikes resulted in the deaths of 12 people, some of whose supposed ties to the insurgency later came into question, including two who were later determined to be Reuters news-staff members (their cameras were mistaken for weapons). A shorter (17-minute) version of the footage, which ran for 38 minutes in its original form, was released under the name "Collateral Murder" for on-line use by media outlets worldwide. Portions of a cache of more than 91,000 military logs relating to the U.S. war in Afghanistan from January 2004 to December 2009, known commonly as the Afghan War Diaries, were made available to the *Guardian*, the *New York Times*, and *Der Spiegel* newspapers before being posted to the WikiLeaks site on July 25, 2010. WikiLeaks provided those newspapers with similar previews of material prior to the October 22, 2010 posting of the Iraq War Logs, purported to be the largest leak of classified documents in American military history.

In late May 2010 a 22-year-old U.S. Army intelligence analyst, Private First Class Bradley Manning, was arrested and held at a military base in Kuwait, near Iraq, while the army investigated allegations that he was responsible for supplying WikiLeaks with classified documents and footage; those included the video footage of the July 2007 Baghdad airstrikes seen in "Collateral Murder" and some 260,000 diplomatic communications, or cables. The allegations came after a former hacker turned government informer and journalist, Adrian Lamo, turned over to authorities logs of instant messages between him and Manning in which the army analyst allegedly confessed to being the source of the leaks. On July 5, 2010 the army filed two misconduct charges against Manning. Following those allegations Assange released several statements explaining that it is not the organization's policy to collect personal information about its sources, making it impossible to confirm Manning's involvement. Nevertheless, he went on to announce that WikiLeaks would be arranging for Manning's legal defense, writing on the social-networking Web site Twitter (June 7, 2010), "We do not know if Mr. Manning is our source, but the U.S. military is claiming he is so we will defend [him]." As of January 2011 Manning was being held at a military base in Virginia while awaiting a court martial.

In August 2010 Swedish authorities opened an investigation into allegations that Assange had had inappropriate sexual contact (one act of unlawful coercion, two acts of sexual molestation, and one instance of rape) with two women while in Sweden earlier in the month. Shortly afterward the investigation was closed due to insufficient evidence that crimes had been committed. While Assange admitted to having had consensual sex with both women, he and his supporters claimed that he had been the target of a smear campaign and was innocent of any wrongdoing. (Both women said they had had consensual sex with Assange on occasions other than those under discussion.) Sweden reopened the case in September, citing new but as yet unspecified information that had come into evidence, and issued a warrant for Assange's arrest. An attempt by Assange's legal defense to quash the warrant was unsuccessful. After an application that Assange filed with Sweden earlier in the year for a work and residency permit was rejected, he went into hiding; he cited his concern that there were opponents of WikiLeaks in positions of power who might want him in custody, if not dead.

On November 28, 2010 WikiLeaks published the first installment of about 220 documents from a collection of more than 130,000 diplomatic cables said to be in the organization's possession. The release of the documents, described by the *New York Times* (November 28, 2010, on-line) as providing "an unprecedented look at back-room bargaining by embassies around the world" that could "strain relations with some countries, influencing international affairs in ways that are impossible to predict," also had the effect of uniting WikiLeaks's critics, ranging from U.S. secretary of state Hillary Rodham Clinton to Australian prime minister Julia Gillard. While many people consider Assange a hero, others argue that his decision to publish documents that are essentially stolen in a manner that could potentially put innocent lives in jeopardy is not only irresponsible but possibly illegal. U.S. federal prosecutors have been trying to put together a case against Assange based on the Espionage Act.

In an interview with Steve Kroft for the television newsmagazine *60 Minutes* (January 30, 2011), Assange was given an opportunity to defend WikiLeaks's actions and explain his position. "We don't say that the State Department should have no secrets," he said. "That's not what we're saying. Rather, we say that if there are people in the State Department who say that there is some abuse going on, and there's not a proper mechanism for internal accountability and external accountability, they

must have a conduit to get that out to the public. And we are the conduit. . . . We are free press activists. It's not about saving the whales. It's about giving people the information they need to support whaling or not support whaling. Why? That is the raw [ingredient] that is needed to make a just and civil society. And without that you're just sailing in the dark."

WikiLeaks has drawn comparisons to the Pentagon Papers, a highly classified history of the United States' political and military involvement in Vietnam from 1945 to 1967 that was prepared by the U.S. Department of Defense and leaked to the *New York Times* by the former military analyst Daniel Ellsberg in 1971. Ellsberg has been vocal in his support of Assange, Private Manning, and the WikiLeaks movement.

Two days after the first batch of diplomatic cables were published, the law-enforcement agency Interpol issued a "red notice" for Assange. A red notice is meant to notify the international community that a valid arrest warrant exists for a particular person and that, should the person be taken into custody, the country that issued the warrant will seek to have him or her extradited. On December 7, 2010 Assange was arrested by British authorities after turning himself in for a meeting with police. He remained in custody until December 16, 2010, when he was granted bail and placed under house arrest at a friend's home in Ellingham Hall, Norfolk, England. Assange and his lawyers appeared at a 10-minute hearing at the Belmarsh Magistrates' Court in east London on January 11, 2011; a two-day extradition hearing was held on February 7 and 8, 2011. Additional arguments in the hearing took place on February 11, with a ruling expected on February 24.

The white-haired Assange has been described as brilliant, scatterbrained, and, with regard to his running of WikiLeaks, imperious. In an interview with Carole Cadwalladr for the London *Observer* (August 1, 2010, on-line), David Leigh, the London *Guardian* editor who oversaw the publication of information made available to the paper by WikiLeaks, explained why he thinks WikiLeaks has initiated a movement toward a higher standard of information transparency that cannot be reversed, regardless of Assange's legal status or future level of involvement with the Web site: "He's a function of technological change. It's because the technology exists to create these enormous databases, and because it exists it can be leaked. And if it can be leaked, it will be leaked."

—H.R.W.

Suggested Reading: (London) *Guardian* (on-line) Aug. 31, 2007, Aug. 1, 2010; *Mother Jones* (on-line) Apr. 6, 2010; *New York Times* A p1 Nov. 28, 2010, A p18 Dec. 1, 2010; *New York Times Magazine* (on-line) Jan. 26, 2011; *New Yorker* (on-line) June 7, 2010; Reuters (on-line) Feb. 29, 2008; *Sydney (Australia) Morning Herald* (on-line) Apr. 10, 2010, May 22, 2010; *Time* (on-line)

July 26, 2010, July 27, 2010; *Utne Reader* (online) Nov./Dec. 2010; Dreyfus, Suelette. *Underground: Tales of Hacking, Madness and Obsession on the Electronic Frontier*, 1997

Bad Plus

Music group

Iverson, Ethan
Feb. 11, 1973– Jazz and rock pianist; composer

Anderson, Reid
Oct. 15, 1970– Jazz bassist; composer

King, David
1972– Jazz and rock drummer; composer

Address: c/o Depth of Field Management, 1501 Broadway, Suite 1304, New York, NY 10036; c/o Big Hassle, 44 Wall St., 22d Fl., New York, NY 10005

For the Bad Plus, playing popular songs in an acoustic-jazz style alongside original jazz compositions has proven to be a winning approach to crossover success. The group attracts mainstream audiences with its covers—or "deconstructions," as the band calls them—of classical, country, and film music, works by the pop group Abba and the rock bands Black Sabbath and Nirvana, and songs by other acts, while also earning kudos from jazz aficionados for its original material. Within four years of the trio's arrival on the music scene, in 2000, as Marke Andrews wrote for the *Vancouver (Canada) Sun* (June 25, 2004), fans of the Bad Plus had "made the band a best-seller among jazz artists, outselling all contemporary instrumental groups." In April 2004 the Bad Plus was the subject of the cover article of *Jazz Times*. The band's members—the bassist Reid Anderson, the pianist Ethan Iverson, and the drummer David King—are composers as well as instrumentalists, and all of them made recordings with others before they organized their trio. The albums they have released as the Bad Plus include their eponymous debut album (also known as *Motel*); *These Are the Vistas*; *Give*; *Suspicious Activity?*; *Blunt Object: Live in Tokyo*; *Prog*; *For All I Care*; and *Never Stop*. Only the last of those offers all original material, and only one—*For All I Care*—contains vocals.

When the Bad Plus began to perform in public, some critics derided the band as a novelty act or as "ironic jesters," as David Hill put it in a post for the blog *JazzHotHouse.com* (February 2009), and dismissed its music as "fake jazz." The trio's continuing success has silenced all but a few such detractors. In an article headlined "Together for 10 Years and Still Totally Committed," Nate Chinen wrote for the *New York Times* (September 18, 2010), "Ten years ago the Bad Plus came together in a warm rush of camaraderie and with a clear grasp of novelty. Here was a jazz piano trio with the heart and gall of a stadium rock band, grappling wryly but directly with anthemic covers and its own scarcely less anthemic originals. The group was brash and clever, its crooked sincerity often mistaken for smug acidity. A debate arose in jazz circles over the entitlements of such a group, what it meant and whether it deserved what it got. The band outlasted the debate; outsmarted it besides. Over the last decade, its fraternal order of contributors"—Iverson, Anderson, and King—"have held fast, patiently refining their brand of superhero jazz. Their habit of addressing pop tunes has settled into something like a continuing art project, a thing unto itself. Meanwhile their discernment and rapport have only deepened." An undated, unsigned post on nextbop.com declared, "For the better part of a decade, the progressive jazz trio known as The Bad Plus have been stirring up a musical stew that defies easy description. Drawing on sources as diverse as classical, jazz, rock, pop and beyond, they have created a singular esthetic that forces even the most skeptical listener to rethink the commonly held notions of what differentiates one style of music from another."

Discussing the Bad Plus's merging of rock and jazz, King told Steve Greenlee for the *Boston Globe* (August 8, 2003), "One of the main things that I think separates us from some of the other [jazz] groups that do rock music is that Reid and I have spent a lot of time in rock bands. A lot of times when a jazz guy does a rock piece of music, they approach it very much like a jazz musician. Once you've toured in a van and slept on the floor and played in really crappy rock clubs, there's an appreciation of the rock aesthetic." He also said, "It's the type of thing that's always been going on. Jazz musicians always look at the music of the day. But we have a unique trinity where one of us, Ethan, has never heard rock music—it's kind of astounding how little he knows about pop music. And then you have two guys who have actually played a lot of rock music and a lot of jazz. So we're very interested in retaining the dirty energy that rock music carries with it. We're not trying to clean it up and jazzify it."

The birthdates of the members of the Bad Plus are all within three years of one another, and all three men are originally from the Midwest. Reid H. Anderson was born on October 15, 1970 in Minneapolis, Minnesota. In his teens he grew interested in rock music and learned to play the electric upright bass. Later, inspired by the jazz double bassist Charlie Haden, he began to play jazz and switched to the acoustic bass. He attended the University of Wisconsin at Eau Claire and then the Curtis Institute of Music, in Philadelphia, Pennsylvania, earning a music degree from the latter school in 1993. He played jazz in the Philadelphia area before moving to New York City, in 1994. David R. Adler wrote for the All Music Guide Web site that during that time, Anderson "emerged as one of the most

Cameron Wittig, courtesy of International Music Network
The Bad Plus (l. to r.): Reid Anderson, Ethan Iverson, David King

promising bassists and composers on the New York jazz scene." In New York Anderson adapted his electric upright bass to suit himself and began to perform with the jazz guitarist Kurt Rosenwinkel, the tenor saxophonists Mark Turner and Bill McHenry, and the drummer Jorge Rossy, among others. He released several albums on the Fresh Sound New Talent label: *Dirty Show Tunes* (1997), for which he had formed a quartet with Iverson, Turner, and Rossy; *Abolish Bad Architecture* (1999), with Iverson, Turner, and the drummer Jeff Ballard; and *The Vastness of Space* (2000), with McHenry, the alto saxophonist Andrew D'Angelo, the guitarist Ben Monder, and the drummer Marlon Browden. "There isn't a weak track on Reid Anderson's remarkable debut CD . . . ," David R. Adler wrote of *Dirty Show Tunes* for the All Music Guide. "Anderson constructs a universe of staggering complexity and lofty melodicism. The shape-shifting tempos of 'Dirty Showtune,' the sizzling grooves and winding melodies of 'Kafka,' and the sheer difficulty of 'Imagination Is Important'—all make it clear that Anderson will go far as a composer and bandleader." Commenting on the same album for the *New York Times* (January 14, 1999), Ben Ratliff described Anderson's compositions as "witty, thoughtful, sweet-and-sour small-group music." In a later *New York Times* (January 3, 2001) article, Ratliff listed *The Vastness of Space* among his choices of the 10 best "obscure" or "underdog" pop and jazz albums of 2000; Reid, he wrote, "is a careful composer with good ideas about what jazz can do now; he sets it up with backbeats and two saxophones with lines gently intertwining, an art-pop mistiness. It's full of bal-

lads that don't sound anything like the old kind of jazz ballads." Two songs from that album, "Prehensile Dream" and "Silence Is the Question," later became part of the Bad Plus repertoire.

Ethan A. Iverson was born on February 11, 1973 in Menomonie, Wisconsin, and raised in nearby Eau Claire. He began playing piano early and took classical-music lessons. His influences ranged from the Russian-born composer Igor Stravinsky (1882–1971) to the free-jazz innovator Ornette Coleman (who is now 81). He attended the University of Wisconsin at Eau Claire, where he met Anderson. Once, in 1990, Iverson, Anderson, and King played together in a jam session.

In 1993 Iverson quit school and moved to New York City to take private lessons with the influential jazz pianists and educators Fred Hersch and Sofia Rosoff. There, at the age of 20, he made his debut recording, *School Work*, backed by the bassist Johannes Weidenmuller and the drummer Falk Willis, with the tenor-saxophone player Dewey Redman contributing to several tracks. The album contained covers, includings Coleman's "School Work" and Duke Ellington's "I Got It Bad," and several Iverson originals. Scott Yanow wrote of *School Work* for the All Music Guide Web site, "The free bop music is often quite exciting without getting too radical for straight-ahead fans. Ethan Iverson shows a lot of talent." Around that time Iverson became the musical director of the choreographer Mark Morris's dance troupe. While working with that company, Iverson collaborated with the dancer and choreographer Mikhail Baryshnikov and the cellist Yo Yo Ma. He also fronted the Ethan Iverson Trio, with Reid Anderson on bass and Jorge Rossy on drums. In 1998 the Iverson Trio released *Construction Zone (Originals)* and *Deconstruction (Standards)*. Iverson recorded a live session called *Minor Passions* (1999), with Anderson and the drummer Billy Hart.

David King was born in 1972 in Minneapolis and raised in Golden Valley, one of that city's suburbs. From birth he was exposed to the music in his parents' eclectic record collection. He began playing the piano on his own at age four and started lessons the next year. "He just sat for hours, sounding things out on the piano," his father, Dwayne King, a retired IBM systems engineer, told Megan Wiley for *MSPMag* (January 2007, on-line). "And he began making things up." King took up drums in fifth grade, when he played with the student band. He met Anderson in junior high school, and the two soon became friends. While attending Robbinsdale Cooper High School, in the Minneapolis suburb of New Hope, King resolved to perform music that combined his passions for rock and jazz. He told Megan Wiley, "I started realizing what was coming out of me was a combination of all this stuff. I'm into Devo and Rush and John Coltrane and Led Zeppelin. What does that sound like? And I like them all the same. And I like Stravinsky and Charlie Parker." After graduating from high school, in about 1990, and taking classes at the McPhail Center for Music, in Minneapolis, King moved to Los Angeles, California, where he supported himself as a studio session musician. After five years, eager to get his creative juices flowing, he returned to Minneapolis. "I was living in LA when Nirvana took off," he told Wiley. "All of a sudden, you saw 300 bands trying to sound like Nirvana instead of trying to make their own stuff." In 1996, with the saxophonist Michael Lewis and the electric bassist Erik Fratzke, King formed the jazz/rock band Happy Apple, which released an album in each of the next three years. He also joined several other bands—12 Rods, Love-Cars, and Rhea Valentine—all of which he later left in order to focus on the Bad Plus and Happy Apple.

After a one-off performance in Minneapolis in 2000, Anderson, Iverson, and King formed the Bad Plus. The name is a combination of "words that are very simple and sounded like they mean something, but they don't," King told Wiley. Their first gig was in December 2000, at the Dakota, a Minneapolis jazz club. Several more followed before they recorded their self-titled debut album (also known as *Motel*), released in 2001 on the Fresh Sound New Talent label. The disk included covers of Abba's "Knowing Me, Knowing You," the Richard Rodgers and Lorenz Hart ballad "Blue Moon," and Nirvana's "Smells Like Teen Spirit." It also offered several original songs. Ben Ratliff included *The Bad Plus* in an end-of-the-year list of critics' choices that appeared in the *New York Times* (December 23, 2001) with the subtitle "The Value of Humor and Recklessness." "There's some kitsch-surprise here . . . ," Ratliff wrote, noting that that was "rare in the sobersided jazz world. All the music, including originals by all three members . . . is arranged to be actual songs, rather than vessels for improvisation; Mr. King's frenzied drumming with a rock-funk thump kicks it along."

The Bad Plus self-released the six-track, 38-minute CD *Authorized Bootleg* (currently out of print) around the beginning of 2002. After a performance at New York's Village Vanguard in June 2002, the Bad Plus signed a recording contract with Columbia Records. Yves Beauvais, a Columbia representative, "had actually seen us once before, and he had a mixed reaction," Iverson told Marke Andrews. "But that night the Vanguard was packed and it went really well, and we met with him the next day." Most critics hailed the group's Columbia debut, *These Are the Vistas* (2003), as a triumph. Steve Greenlee declared it to be "a groundbreaking work, discarding any neotraditionalist notions about what acoustic jazz ought to be. This jazz doesn't merely swing, it rocks. It is melodious but steeped in the avant-garde. It is full of serious improvisation, and it is also full of swagger." Noting the way in which the group straddled the line between the improvisational and complex playing associated with jazz and the bombastic showmanship of rock, Chris Willman described the group for *Entertainment Weekly* (May 2, 2003, on-line) as "a piano-bass-drums power trio who's forged a fairly traditionalist jazz sound any rocker could recognize as spiritually akin."

National Public Radio (NPR) listed *These Are the Vistas* among the 50 most important records of the 2000s. Patrick Jarenwattananon wrote for the NPR Web site (November 16, 2009), "The real coup lies in the fact that it got people outside jazz to listen. That'll happen when you play covers of Nirvana, Aphex Twin and Blondie as an acoustic piano trio. But there's far more than novelty appeal at work here: The Bad Plus . . . used the tunes as frameworks for distinct, original improvisation, aided by knottily textured originals, nutso percussion and bass that would challenge a car's Alpine subwoofer. Love it or hate it, it was impossible to ignore—and the musical ideas had staying power, too."

The Bad Plus's next two albums, *Give* (2004) and *Suspicious Activity?* (2005), also carry the Columbia label. *Give* included both original pieces and covers of such pieces as Black Sabbath's "Iron Man" and Ornette Coleman's "Street Woman." *Suspicious Activity?* offered original compositions by each member of the trio and only one cover, built around the theme to the 1981 movie *Chariots of Fire*. In a review of the latter album, Elias Ravin wrote for the *L Magazine* (August 31, 2005, online), "Although their arrangements are invariably spirited and clever, the jazz-trio-playing-rock thing has always smacked of gimmickry and aroused suspicions that the group is basically a cynical novelty act. . . . Ironically, it's the Bad Plus' *Suspicious Activity?* that should ultimately put those suspicions to rest. *Suspicious Activity?* is a surprisingly reflective affair for the Bad Plus, but the quiet, bittersweet strain that ties the album together serves to make the group's signature sweeping crescendos all the more cathartic. The new originals are improbably catchy and emotive for their complexity, and the trio's spontaneous interplay now borders on what Miles Davis used to call E.S.P." In a four-star review of *Suspicious Activity?* for *Rolling Stone* (November 3, 2005), David Fricke wrote that the Bad Plus "deserve to be better known for the romantic detail and addictive gallop of their originals."

In 2007 the Bad Plus parted ways with Columbia and released the album *Prog* on the independent jazz label Heads Up. A collection of originals and covers, *Prog* was generally well received. It was followed the next year by *For All I Care*, the first Bad Plus album with vocals, delivered by the singer Wendy Lewis and, to a much lesser extent, Anderson and King. Released through Heads Up, *For All I Care* consisted entirely of covers, ranging from Nirvana's "Lithium" and songs by Pink Floyd, the Bee Gees, Flaming Lips, Wilco, and Yes to Stravinsky's "Variation d'Apollon," Milton Babbitt's "Semi-Simple Variations," and Gyorgy Ligeti's "Fem (Étude No. 8)." In a representative review Jeff Tamarkin wrote for the Boston *Phoenix* (January 27, 2009, on-line), "Though it inches the Bad Plus closer to the pop mainstream, it never loses the particular rhythmic and harmonic quirks that have defined them so far." Thom Jurek, an All Music Guide critic, wrote, "Perhaps the most compelling, shocking, and wonderful thing about this collaboration is how much Lewis' presence becomes part of the trio's landscape. . . . The emotional intensity and reverence Lewis offers the material only intensify their approach." By contrast, Evan Sawdey complained on Popmatters.com (February 19, 2009) that Lewis's "mere presence . . . destroys what made the Plus so special. . . . By adding a vocalist, the Plus can no longer be as loose with their interpretations, making *For All I Care* a frightfully straightforward affair for a band that doesn't do well with conventional methodology."

The group's most recent album, *Never Stop*, released on the E1 label in 2010, is a collection of entirely original material. Patrick Jarenwattananon wrote for the NPR Web site (September 5, 2010), "The band's compositions, which come from all three members, have a sophisticated architecture; they also have an impish, understated glee that can be mistaken for irony ('Beryl Loves to Dance,' 'My Friend Metatron'). There are big, throbbing beats ('Never Stop'), free-improv spasms ('2 p.m.'), non-bluesy but harmonically intriguing chord voicings (like, everything). It's an improvising piano-bass-drums group—a celebrated jazz layout, with musicians fluent in the standard tongues of jazz—which probably wouldn't mind if you called it a weirdo instrumental rock band." Peter Hum wrote for the *Ottawa (Canada) Citizen* (January 15, 2011) that on *Never Stop* the Bad Plus "make a glorious mishmash of things, never descending into mere parody or pastiche. . . . *Never Stop* demonstrates that Iverson, Anderson and King are much more than their covers of Nirvana, Rush, David Bowie and the like might have suggested. They never sound so good as when they are left to their own devices."

In 2010 and 2011 the Bad Plus were artists in residence at Duke University, in Durham, North Carolina. In March 2011, at Duke's Reynolds Industries Theatre, the trio introduced *On Sacred Ground*, their adaptation of Stravinsky's *The Rite of Spring*; created on a commission from Duke Performances and Lincoln Center, in New York City, it was the product of eight months of work. In a review of that world premiere for CVNC.org (March 26, 2011), Kate Dobbs Ariall wrote, "It was really fantastic how each of [the] three used his instrument for both rhythm and melody as the moment demanded. To hear the unforgettable motif central to *The Rite* conveyed by the various tones of King's percussion set was amazing, and when it came from Anderson's bass, it just slayed me. But then, here came Iverson picking it out on the piano, sounding like a nightingale . . . ravishing. The whole was so rich and engrossing and *alive* that it seemed to pass in a much shorter time than its actual 40 minutes." The sold-out audience gave the trio a standing ovation.

The Bad Plus tours regularly and performs about 160 shows a year, in the U.S. and overseas. Iverson and King are also members of the improvisational group Buffalo Collision, which released the album *Duck* as a digital download in 2008. King can be heard on the album *Gang Font Featuring Interloper* (2007). For his solo album *Indelicate* (2010), he played piano as well as drums. He has also performed with his group the Dave King Trucking Company; their album, *Good Old Light*, was released in 2011. Anderson leads the rock band the Sun, for which he provides vocals and plays guitar. Iverson has taught at the School for Improvised Music, in Brooklyn, New York City. *Live at Small's* (2010) is a recording of a gig at Small's Jazz Club, in New York City, in which Iverson performed with the drummer Albert "Tootie" Heath and the double bassist Ben Street.

King lives in Minneapolis with his wife, Laura, and their two children. Anderson and Iverson live near each other in Brooklyn.

—W.D.

Suggested Reading:All About Jazz Web site; All Music Guide Web site; *Boston Globe* C p12 Aug. 8, 2003; *MSPMag* (on-line) Jan. 2007; *New York Times* C p4 Sep. 18, 2010; thebadplus.com; *Vancouver (British Columbia, Canada) Sun* D p2 June 25, 2004

Selected Recordings: *The Bad Plus* (also known as *Motel*), 2001; *These Are the Vistas*, 2003; *Give*, 2004; *Suspicious Activity?*, 2005; *Blunt Object: Live in Tokyo*, 2005; *Prog*, 2007; *For All I Care*, 2008, *Never Stop*, 2010

Badinter, Elisabeth

Mar. 5, 1944– Philosopher; writer; former educator

Address: c/o Henry Holt and Co. Inc., 175 Fifth Ave., New York, NY 10010

The French writer and *philosophe* (thinker) Elisabeth Badinter, one of the most prominent intellectuals in her native country, writes primarily about feminism, gender identity, and the role of women (especially as mothers) in French society. A household name and a best-selling author in France, she is also known in the English-speaking world, where she first made her mark in 1981 with the English translation of her work *Mother Love: Myth and Reality*, in which she argued that maternal instinct is not a scientifically proven fact but a cultural construct. Her latest book, *Le Conflit: La Femme et la Mère* (2010), has been translated into nine languages; the English translation, *The Conflict: The Woman and the Mother*, scheduled to appear in January 2012, has already been reviewed in

Eric Feferberg/AFP/Getty Images

Elisabeth Badinter

mainstream publications in both the U.K. and the U.S. In *The Conflict* Badinter attacks trends—particularly those supporting the concept of the "perfect" mother—that she considers to be steps backward for feminism, including "fundamentalist" notions that every mother should breast-feed, use cloth diapers, serve homemade baby food, and otherwise reject practices aimed at making women's lives easier. While those and others of her views have drawn the ire of many on the political right, Badinter has also clashed with some of her fellow feminists, opposing, for example, legislation based on distinctions between men and women—even measures designed to benefit the latter. She told Jane Kramer in an interview for the *New Yorker* (July 25, 2011), "I get a great deal of pleasure in expressing ideas . . . that go against the current. I love to throw out a contrary point of view, and I do it with, perhaps, a certain lack of subtlety. . . . I am a fanatic of clarity."

The second of three daughters, Elisabeth Badinter was born on March 5, 1944 in Hauts-de-Seine, outside Paris, France, during World War II, when the country was still occupied by Germany. (Allied forces liberated France later that year.) Her father, Marcel Bleustein-Blanchet, who was of Russian-Jewish origin, did intelligence work for the French Resistance; he went on to found Publicis, one of the world's largest advertising agencies. Because any sign of Jewish ancestry was a potential death sentence during Germany's occupation of France, Badinter was identified on her birth certificate as Elisabeth Vaillant; "Vaillant" was the surname of her mother, Sophie, who worked for *Elle* magazine during Badinter's youth. Badinter told Jane Kramer that her relationship with her mother was "compli-

cated" but recalled her father with a great deal of affection. "His sense of family was very strong," Badinter told Kramer, "and I got the benefit of that. He and I were the early risers. We'd wake up every morning at five or six, and I would go into his room and sit at the foot of his bed, and we'd talk for hours. He would ask me, What do you want to do in life? And he would answer for me: he said that if I made the effort there was nothing I couldn't do." Kramer paraphrased her as theorizing that "most strong women have fathers like hers." In her teens Badinter read the writing of the French philosopher Simone de Beauvoir, who is best known for her groundbreaking work *The Second Sex* (1949), the book that Badinter credits with sparking her feminist views. Badinter attended the prestigious private school l'École Alsacienne, in Paris, and went on to study psychology and sociology at the Sorbonne, officially known as Paris Sorbonne University. During those years she spent summers in London, England, where she improved her English, and lived for a year in New York City, studying at Columbia University and serving an internship with the *New York Times*.

At the age of 22, around the time that Badinter received her undergraduate degrees, she married Robert Badinter, a well-known lawyer and government official 16 years her senior. Badinter continued her education, pursuing philosophy at the graduate level and receiving an *agrégation*, a predoctoral degree, in 1972. By that point she had given birth to three children. In an interview with Britta Sandberg for *Der Spiegel* (August 26, 2010), Badinter said, "Truth be told, like most other moms, I was a very mediocre one. I always tried to do as much as I could for my children. But, from a present-day perspective, I also did a lot of things wrong. So, I'd describe myself as a completely average mother."

At the age of 35, Badinter published *L'Amour en plus: histoire de l'amour maternal* (1980), her first best-seller, translated the following year as *Mother Love: Myth and Reality*. By the time of its publication in English (among 12 other languages), the book had sold more than 220,000 copies in France and aroused considerable controversy. Badinter had challenged the notion that the maternal instinct is innate and universal; instead, she argued, it is a cultural construct. Speaking to Nan Robertson for the *New York Times* (November 16, 1981), she said, "Maternal love is not a given but a gift. It is a human feeling, and like any feeling, it is uncertain, fragile and imperfect. Contrary to many assumptions, it is not a deeply rooted given in women's natures. When we observe the historical changes in maternal behavior, we notice that interest in and devotion to the child are sometimes in evidence, sometimes not." Badinter told Jill Forbes for the London *Guardian* (May 16, 1989), "I have longstanding memories of going to the Bois de Boulogne [a park in Paris] as a child and seeing the mothers sitting round the sand pit, while their children played, with an expression of utter boredom on their faces. I began the book because I realised it was a lie to say the mothers love their children spontaneously. I wanted to show that the concept of the maternal instinct is very convenient for society and for men but that it makes women feel guilty. . . . All I did was to say out loud something that many women were almost conscious of but dared not allow themselves to think."

In her examination of the concept of French motherhood over the previous four centuries, Badinter focused on one particular, widespread practice of the 18th century: the tendency of mothers in urban areas to send their newborns to wet nurses, with whom the children would remain for up to four years. In his review of the book for the *New York Times* (October 4, 1981), Paul Robinson pointed out that the urban population of France was only about 20 percent of its total number of people and questioned the sources of Badinter's information even for city dwellers. He then added: "Of course, the thesis of maternal indifference doesn't require that wet-nursing was universal in the early modern period. It is sufficient to establish that the practice was widespread, and for this the evidence will do. But Professor Badinter's clumsy and deceitful handling of the question of incidence is characteristic of her book's intellectual manner. This is popular social history of the rudest variety. . . . To conclude from the prevalence of wet-nursing that 18th-century mothers didn't love their children involves the sort of intellectual leap that historians approach with the greatest possible caution. It means drawing inferential connections between what people do and what they feel—moving, in other words, from things that are visible to those that are not. It is effected, if at all, primarily by a careful examination and rejection of alternative explanations, a delicate process of intellectual winnowing of which Professor Badinter's book is entirely innocent."

Badinter's *Un est l'autre: des relations entre hommes et femmes* (1986) was published in English in 1989 as *The Unopposite Sex: The End of the Gender Battle*. That book also became a bestseller in France. Drawing on ethnology, sociology, psychology, paleontology, history, and literature, Badinter argued that patriarchy and inequality between the sexes has ended. She offered three reasons: women no longer need men to support them; they no longer have to be homemakers; and they can control their fertility. Whereas Jill Forbes, in her *Guardian* article, called Badinter "one of the most lucid and penetrating observers of the way we live now," most reviewers in the U.S. and England attacked her for what they perceived as intellectual sloppiness. "Elisabeth Badinter's book, described as 'drawing on the latest research' in ethnology, sociology and psychology, is actually a jumbled digest of texts, using the languages of various sciences but dispensing with their rigour," Adam Mars-Jones wrote for the London *Independent* (June 22, 1989). He added: "But Elisabeth Badinter's most remarkable characteristic, over and

above her sloppiness and her incuriosity, is her naïveté. She believes absolutely that patriarchy is dead: 'Two decades have been sufficient to put an end to the system of representations that for several thousand years allowed men to wield power over women.' In another passage she expresses the same conviction with stereotypical Gaelic gush: 'The violent spasms of this moribund system did not prevent its end. This took place yesterday . . . but no one has yet gone out into the streets to celebrate the event, perhaps because people were afraid that if they made too much noise they would bring the dead back to life, perhaps too because men's disarray touches women to the heart.' Perhaps too because it hasn't happened. For these resonant statements, naturally, Elisabeth Badinter offers not a scrap of evidence." In her next book, *XY, de l'identité masculine* (1992), translated as *XY: On Masculine Identity* (1995), Badinter focused on men, arguing that notions of manhood and masculinity are a kind of negation, a reaction against the concept of femininity—I am not my mother; I am not a girl; I am not a woman—rather than an embrace of positive traits. The book, Sally Abrahms wrote for the *New York Times* (February 4, 1996), is "well researched and skillfully presented."

The title of Badinter's volume *Fausse Route* (2003) means "wrong way," a reference to what Badinter considers the misguided path of feminists who consider all women to be victims of male oppression. The book was translated into English as *Dead End Feminism* (2006).

With her most recent work, *The Conflict: The Woman and the Mother*, Badinter again succeeded in gaining attention and rousing debate. In *The Conflict* she attacked those in the back-to-nature movement and what she terms the "essentialist" feminism camp, who call for what she sees as an unreasonable standard of motherhood—for example, the notion that all women should breast-feed, experience natural childbirth, and forsake epidurals and birth-control pills. Badinter argued that those standards represent a step backward for female liberation and a rebuke of successful, ambitious women. She wrote, as quoted in the *New York Times* (June 6, 2010), "The specter of the bad mother imposes itself on [women] even more cruelly insofar as [they have] unconsciously internalized the ideal of the good mother."

Although the book was widely discussed in the French mainstream press, many French feminists did not feel that its themes applied to their country. Sylvie Kauffmann, the editor-at-large of *Le Monde*, told Kramer: "Women here? They don't see this return to the house that she talks about. I don't see it. Women here want to be good mothers *and* to succeed at a job." Badinter's argument, Kramer wrote, is aimed at France but is in fact more apt for the U.S. and European countries such as Germany. In France women have twice as many children, on average, as those in most other European Union countries (the birthrate in France is the highest in Europe); they also stop breast-feeding earlier, go back to work sooner after childbirth and in larger numbers, and leave their children in well-staffed nurseries. While acknowledging that French women balance full-time employment and motherhood well, Badinter offered cautionary notes, wondering how long French women will be able to resist the so-called back-to-nature trend; and she argued that failure to meet the expectations imposed by those trends could bring about feelings of guilt in mothers. Some feminists, such as Cécile Duflot, the leader of France's Green Party, argued that Badinter had confused ecology with "naturalism," that ecology involves protecting the planet and does not oppose but in fact supports—by being gender neutral—the notion that men should be full partners in children's upbringing. Mary Elizabeth Williams wrote in a review for *Salon.com* (March 22, 2010): "Badinter is spot on to advocate that women keep on being women when they become mothers—women who can move comfortably between sex, work and a nicely chilled glass of sauvignon blanc. . . . But where Badinter starts to go off the rails is when she says that she doesn't buy the '1001 claims in favor of breast-feeding' or shrugs that the French have 'always been mediocre mothers, but we've tended to have happier lives.' Plenty of devoted mothers actually do have happy lives. Badinter seems to have overlooked the possibility that nurturing may not be an instinct all women share, but for many, the challenge is still a joy. She also ignores the possibility that fathers can parent, too." In her profile of Badinter, Kramer pointed out that *The Conflict* was produced "perhaps with more conviction than reflection." With a few exceptions, most publications reviewing *The Conflict* did not mention that Badinter has been, since her father's death, a major shareholder and chairperson of the supervisory board of Publicis, an advertising and communications company that represents many firms, including Nestlé (which makes powdered milk) and Procter & Gamble (which manufactures Pampers diapers). Badinter told Kramer that her business holdings have no relation to her work as a social critic.

In addition to the books by Badinter mentioned above, she has written several that have not been translated into English, among them *Emilie, Emilie: l'ambition féminine au XVIIIe siècle* (1984), about two gifted, ambitious women in 18th-century France, the philosopher Émilie du Châtelet and the writer Louise d'Épinay (who adopted the name Émilie); *Les Passions intellectuelles*, a three-volume history of the French Enlightenment; a work she co-wrote about Simone de Beauvoir; and a children's book, *Voyage en Laponie de Monsieur de Maupertuis* (2003). With her husband she wrote *Condorcet, 1743–1794* (1988), a biography of the 18th-century philosopher Nicolas de Condorcet.

Badinter has been outspoken about several hot-button issues that directly affect women and overlap with the worlds of religion or politics. With regard to the latter, Badinter opposed the 1990s pari-ty campaign, a movement aimed at increasing the number of women in political office via the requirement that half of all political candidates be female. Badinter is in favor of the so-called "burqa law," which made it illegal for women to wear full-face veils in public, a practice advocated by some followers of Islam. She testified in the National Assembly and the Senate in support of the law.

Starting in the late 1970s, Badinter taught philosophy at l'École Polytechnique, a prestigious university in Paris, a position she held for approximately 30 years. Badinter and her husband live in Paris. The couple have three grown children: two sons, Robert and Benjamin, who work in advertising, and a daughter, Judith, a psychoanalyst. They also have three grandchildren.

—D.K.

Suggested Reading: *Der Spiegel* (on-line) Aug. 26, 2010; *Los Angeles Times* Book Review p6 July 23, 1989; *New York Times* B p16 Nov. 16, 1981; *New Yorker* p44 July 25, 2011; *Salon.com* Mar. 22, 2010

Selected Books in English Translation: *Mother Love: Myth and Reality*, 1981; *The Unopposite Sex: The End of the Gender Battle*, 1989; *XY: On Masculine Identity*, 1995; *Dead End Feminism*, 2006

Ball, Alan

May 13, 1957– Playwright; film and TV writer, director, and producer

Address: c/o United Talent Agency, 9560 Wilshire Blvd., Suite 500, Beverly Hills, CA 90212-2401

"I hate those arbitrary distinctions between comedy and drama," Alan Ball, who writes scripts for television, film, and the stage, told Marc Peyser for *Newsweek* (March 18, 2002). "My life seems to have a mixture of both, and I respond to entertainment that has both. Also, I think humor is a necessary tool for survival." A sometime director and producer as well, Ball served as a writer for the TV sitcoms *Grace Under Fire* and *Sybill* before he rose to national prominence in 1999, with his screenplay for the widely admired feature film *American Beauty*. A tale of a dysfunctional suburban family, *American Beauty* won dozens of honors, among them five Academy Awards, including those for best picture and best screenplay. Ball next produced, wrote the scripts for, and occasionally directed *Six Feet Under*, a critically acclaimed HBO TV series about a distinctive family of morticians. During its five-year run, each episode of *Six Feet Under* involved a death; the family's husband and father died in Episode One, then returned in ghost-

Francois Guillot/AFP/Getty Images

Alan Ball

ly fashion to comment on the behavior of his wife and children. "What grief can do for us is teach us that the ability to feel tremendous pain increases our capacity to feel joy," Ball commented to Sharon Waxman for the *Washington Post* (May 26, 2002). "You can't just have it one way. Life is filled with both." *Six Feet Under*, like *American Beauty*, blended tragic and comedic elements and won multiple awards. Ball also wrote the scripts for the TV series *Oh, Grow Up,* the feature film *Towelhead*, the full-length plays *Five Women Wearing the Same Dress*, *All That I Will Ever Be*, and the one-acters *Made for a Woman, Bachelor Holiday, Power Lunch, The M Word*, and *Your Mother's Butt*. He is the writer and executive producer of the TV series *True Blood*, which premiered in 2008 and which, according to Gina Piccalo, writing for the *Los Angeles Times* (July 18, 2010), "has cemented Ball as the creative hero of HBO."

Alan Ball was born on May 13, 1957 in Atlanta, Georgia, and grew up in Marietta, an Atlanta suburb. His father, Frank Ball, was a quality-control manager for Lockheed Aircraft; his earlier, unsuccessful experience as a carpenter had left him permanently demoralized. Alan, the family's fourth and last child, was born when his mother, Mary Ball, a homemaker, was 44. His birth came about 20 years after those of his brothers and about nine years after that of his sister, Mary Ann, whom as a child he considered to be his best friend. Ball wrote his first play at age six, and he "constantly directed the kids in the neighborhood in little productions," according to Waxman. One of his favorite activities—playing with other children in nearby woods—ended when all the trees were cleared to make way for construction of a four-lane highway;

many homes were bulldozed, too, though not that of the Balls. "That was probably my first experience with a profound sense of loss," Ball told Bob Longino for the *Atlanta Journal-Constitution* (March 26, 2000). "You know, of something being really important that was suddenly gone. And it was weird and never the same after that."

When Ball was about eight, he became dimly aware of his homosexuality; for the next 25 years, he remained largely in denial about it. Nearly everyone he knew in his home town regarded homosexuality with hostility, so the idea of being gay was "terrifying" to him as a child and young adult, he told Waxman; he added, in reference to a popular sitcom (1998–2006) whose male title character was gay, "I didn't grow up watching *Will & Grace*." He told Bernard Weinraub for the *New York Times* (March 4, 2001), "The only images of gay people I saw on the screen were either villains or noble martyrs who usually died." Recognition of his homosexuality "threatened something in me," he said to Waxman. "I knew it was something I couldn't let anybody know." Ball came out of the closet when he was 33. Shedding the burden of his long-held secret, he told Waxman, "was the biggest step I ever took toward emotional well-being."

Earlier, when he was 13, on the day his sister turned 22, she was killed instantly when, while driving Ball to his piano lesson, she crashed into an oncoming car while rounding a blind curve. "That was like death just stuck its face right in mine and said, 'Uh, helloooo,' and I've been living with that ever since," Ball (who was unhurt in the collision) told Phil Rosenthal for the *Chicago Sun-Times* (May 31, 2001). His sister's death "separated my life into 'the life before' and 'the life after,'" Ball told Paul Clinton for the *Advocate* (July 3, 2001). After the accident, Ball recalled to Weinraub, sometimes—"at the worst of it"—he felt as if he was living "in a house with ghosts." "My mother got into a gothic end-of-the-world religion thing," he said, and his father became severely depressed. When Ball was 19 his father died of lung cancer. "It wasn't so much that I was unhappy [after those losses]," Ball told Waxman. "I was painfully aware of the ephemeral nature of life. No matter what you have, you can lose it in an instant, without warning. What that did for me for many, many years was, it kept me from committing to anything. It kept me from committing to myself, even, from really fully taking risks emotionally. From going after things."

Ball attended Marietta High School, where he served as senior-class president, editor of the student newspaper, and a drum major in the band. He told Bob Longino that he invented "this persona for myself of really being an overachiever, kind of an All-American guy that really wasn't me." With the goal of pursuing a career as an actor, Ball enrolled at the University of Georgia, then transferred to the School of Theatre at Florida State University, in Tallahassee. After he earned a bachelor's degree, in 1980, Ball moved to Sarasota, Florida, where he helped to set up a theater company called General Nonsense. In his late 20s he moved to New York City, and with several friends he formed the Alarm Dog Repertory Company. Between 1986 and 1994 the group performed at such New York venues as the Public Theater, the Westbeth Theater Center, and the West Bank Cafe. To support his acting and writing, Ball worked as an art director at the magazines *Inside PR* and *Adweek*.

During that period several of Ball's plays were mounted Off-Off-Broadway, including *Five Women Wearing the Same Dress*. That snarky comedy, whose title refers to five gossipy bridesmaids (one of them portrayed by Allison Janney), debuted at the Manhattan Class Company in early 1993; it struck Mel Gussow, writing for the *New York Times* (February 18, 1993), as "frothy and frivolous," with the sorts of "one-liners and comebacks" characteristic of TV sitcoms. Those qualities impressed Tom Werner and Marcy Carsey, two of the executive producers of the sitcom *Grace Under Fire*, and won for Ball a position as a writer for that show. The title character of *Grace Under Fire* was a single mother who, after leaving her abusive husband, becomes a hard-hat-wearing oil-refinery worker. Ball accepted the job, he told Weinraub, because "my theater company was sort of spinning its wheels," and his colleagues' "day jobs were turning into careers. People were starting to have kids." In addition, Brett Butler, the actress chosen to play Grace, was a native of Marietta. "I thought, 'How many times will this happen in my life?' I flew out on a Friday and began working Monday."

Ball wrote for *Grace Under Fire* during its highly rated first year (1993–94), then left to write for the sitcom *Cybill*, with Cybill Shepherd in the role of a twice-divorced mother who yearns to build a flourishing acting career. During *Cybill*'s three-year run (1995–98), Ball became the show's executive producer. "I had a meteoric rise at *Cybill*," he told Weinraub. "[Shepherd] would have a big meltdown in the middle of every season and fire half the staff. And those of us who stuck around got big promotions." With both *Grace Under Fire* and *Cybill*, Ball was frustrated by his bosses' seemingly never-ending demands for script changes. He told Rosenthal, "One of the things I've heard network executives say in a meeting is: 'Let's assume I'm the stupidest person in America. Am I going to get this?' And, you know, frankly I'm thinking: 'If you're the stupidest person in America, I don't care if you get it. I'm not writing for you.'" Furthermore, as he told Weinraub, "[Butler and Shepherd] looked on the shows as basically p.r. for their lives. It was like taking dictation. You'd hear, 'I have a bad haircut, so let's do a show about that.' It taught me a valuable lesson about television: not to be too proprietary about the material. Let it go. Find something else."

While working overtime on *Cybill* virtually every day, Ball would spend a couple of hours around midnight writing the story that became *American Beauty*. He told an Amazon.com (1999)

interviewer that he "channeled" into its script the "anger and rage" his working situation provoked in him. "It's no mistake that *American Beauty* was about a man who was beaten down and lost interest in his life rediscovering his passion for living," he told Weinraub. The completed script was sold to DreamWorks, Steven Spielberg's studio, for $400,000; Sam Mendes, who previously had worked only in theater, signed on to direct.

The focus of *American Beauty*—"a tale of pain and dysfunction beneath the surface of suburban life, told through the eyes of a dead man," in Waxman's words—is a well-to-do couple, Lester Burnham (Kevin Spacey) and his wife, Carolyn (Annette Bening), and their teenage daughter, Janie (Thora Birch). As the film opens Lester speaks from beyond the grave; he is then shown several months before his death, when, feeling depressed, cynical, and burned-out over his profession and his home life, he quits his lucrative job in the advertising industry, finds work with a fast-food outlet, and becomes infatuated with Janie's friend Angela (Mena Suvari), a would-be femme fatale. Lester then undergoes a transformation, passing up a chance to have sex with Angela and growing aware of the world's nonmonetary, mundane treasures. Carolyn, meanwhile, in a singleminded quest to succeed as a real-estate agent, has lost interest in her husband and daughter; in her drive to get ahead, she begins an affair with one of her competitors. The morose Janie, who seems to despise her parents, becomes friendly with her teenage neighbor, Ricky Fitts (Wes Bentley), a Peeping Tom often seen with a video camera. Circumventing the cold, rigid discipline of his father, Ricky uses and sells marijuana—to Lester, among others. Ricky's father, a retired Marine colonel, hides his attraction to men behind a fierce homophobia; his wife, Barbara (Allison Janney), has become nearly catatonic.

A plastic bag wafting in the breeze is a recurring image in *American Beauty*. The image was inspired by an experience Ball had years earlier, in which a plastic bag floating in the air seemed to circle him, triggering in him a "completely unexpected sense of peace and wonder," he recalled to Longino. He told the Amazon.com (1999) interviewer, "When you first see the title [of the film] you think 'American Beauty + rose,' and then you see the movie and you think that Angela's the American Beauty—the blond cheerleader that is the secretive object of lust. But it's not Angela—it's that plastic bag. It's the way of looking at the world and seeing what incredible beauty there is in the world. And I think that's something that we're born with that gets ironed out of us by our culture and by experience and by conformity. I think there's a part of everybody that yearns to get that back."

American Beauty earned virtually unanimous praise. In a representative review for *TV Guide* (1999, on-line), Maitland McDonagh described the film as "black comedy of the deepest, richest darkness laid over an aching meditation on the atrophy of dreams not so much deferred as unformed, unarticulated and lost in the shuffle." "This chronicle of suburban families imploding in slow motion contains genuine laughs," he continued, "but they escape through clenched teeth. . . . First-time screenwriter Alan Ball . . . pulls off his satirical jibes with pitch-perfect aplomb, weaving them into a plot that oozes menace" and "keeps you spellbound." "As a thumbnail analysis of the middle-class American psyche, Alan Ball's script is a devastating attack," Angus Wolfe Murray wrote for the British Web site Eye for Film (1999). "It is also extremely funny. . . . The movie astonishes with its breadth of scope, covering every aspect of dysfunction—from voyeurism to stalking to homophobic rage to role playing to unlawful killing. . . . Films like this save Hollywood from atrophy."

Ball did not expect *American Beauty* to become a hit, and shortly before its release he had agreed to write a sitcom for ABC. The show, *Oh, Grow Up*, about a gay man and his two straight roommates, was partly autobiographical. "The [final product] was not at all what I intended when I pitched it," Ball told Waxman. "But you talk yourself into believing it's good. Otherwise how do you justify going to work every day?" The series was canceled after 11 episodes.

By then Ball had become much sought-after in Hollywood and had received many lucrative film proposals. "I was offered everything, but I didn't want to become a hired gun, I didn't want to be hired to write other people's ideas," he told Weinraub. A suggestion from the HBO executive Caroline Strauss that Ball create a show about a family of undertakers drew him back to TV. "What interested me is what it would be like to live with death on a daily basis," Ball told Drew Jubera for the *Atlanta Journal-Constitution* (June 3, 2001). "What do these people do: Embalm somebody and then go to their Little League game? Well, yes. That's what they do." *Six Feet Under* revolved around the Fishers—three siblings, Nate, David, and Claire, and their mother, Ruth—who own a Los Angeles, California, mortuary. "Like the characters in [*American Beauty*], the Fishers . . . are sardonic and screwed up," Tad Friend wrote for the *New Yorker* (May 14, 2001). "Nate is a soulful social dropout who sees marriage as the enemy; Claire spends much of the first episode high on crystal meth; and David, the middle child, is chalky-faced and remote, seemingly the ideal funeral-home director—but he's also a closeted gay man who is about to plunge into a night life of clubs, drugs, and one-night stands." The father, Nathaniel, is killed in a car crash in the first episode and reappears, in surreal sequences, to offer the family members "advice, support or, just as often, a sarcastic gibe," Sharon Waxman wrote. Ball told Waxman, "The show is about the loss I've felt in my life. The grief I've felt over loss, the people I've lost. . . . About greeting grief, and being able to move past it." *Six Feet Under* ran for five seasons (2001–05) and attracted a sizable following; it became "one of the flagship components, along with *The Sopranos*,

Sex and the City, and *Curb Your Enthusiasm*, that have made [HBO] a critical favorite and powerhouse," Greg Braxton wrote for the *Los Angeles Times* (August 15, 2005). *Six Feet Under* won a Golden Globe Award for best dramatic series in 2001; the cast won the Screen Actors Guild Award for outstanding ensemble in a drama series in 2002 and 2003; and the series and those associated with it garnered a total of nine Emmy Awards, including one, in 2002, for Ball as outstanding director of a drama series.

"Some critics have derided Ball's vision of the world as a cynical one, in which desperate people fail themselves and their loved ones," Sharon Waxman wrote. Ball does not dispute that description, but he has maintained that his work reflects real life more accurately than most other popular works for TV and Hollywood. "It's hard to have a brain in your head, keep your eyes open to the culture, and not be cynical," he told Waxman. "People who are the most cynical are the most romantic at heart. That's definitely true of me." Still, he said, "I'm completely not cynical about the characters in [*Six Feet Under*]. I believe in them as thinking beings struggling to find meaning in their lives. Failing sometimes. Succeeding sometimes. What's necessary, what's important, is not failing or succeeding, it's the struggle that's important. Our culture is so much about success, which I think is very—very—shallow. You learn more from failure."

Ball both wrote and directed *Towelhead* (2008), a feature film based on a novel by Alicia Erian, about the coming-of-age and identity struggles of 13-year-old Jasira, the daughter of a Lebanese-American father and his former wife, an American. The film starred Summer Bishil as Jasira; Peter Macdissi as her father; Maria Bello as her mother; and Toni Collette and Aaron Eckhart as neighbors. The story was set in Houston, Texas, during the first Persian Gulf War (1990–91), which triggered some anti-Muslim sentiment but far less, and of far less virulence, than the sort that followed the 9/11 terrorist attacks. The film generated mixed reviews. Its admirers included Carrie Rickey, who described it for the *Philadelphia Inquirer* (September 19, 2008) as a "brutally honest and edgily funny story" about "the many forms of social and sexual abuse that does not make the abusee a victim but victor." "Not since [the 1961 film] *Splendor in the Grass* has there been such a candid and sympathetic account of the mixed messages, double-standards, giddy highs and hormonal free falls experienced by teenage girls," Rickey asserted. By contrast, *Towelhead* struck Ruthe Stein, the reviewer for *SFGate.com* (September 19, 2008), as "so disturbing it makes you uncomfortable watching it. For the price of admission, you become an unwilling voyeur." "Towelhead" is a derogatory label derived from the fabric headwear traditional among many Arab men. According to Stein, "An Islamic civil rights group wanted the film's title to be changed because it is insulting to Arab Americans," and then added, "There is much else in *Towelhead* to take exception to."

Ball came up with the idea for the HBO show *True Blood* after he happened upon the first four novels in Charlaine Harris's best-selling Southern Vampire series in a Barnes and Noble outlet in 2005. (In 2011 Harris published the 11th volume in the series, each title of which contains the word "dead.") The heroine of the book and HBO series is Sookie Stackhouse (played by Anna Paquin), a waitress who has telepathic powers; its hero—and Stackhouse's love interest—is the nearly 200-year-old vampire Bill Compton (Stephen Moyer). (Moyer and Paquin married in 2010.) "True Blood" refers to the synthetic blood marketed by a Japanese soft-drink company, which enables vampires to enter civilized society. Ball told Ed Potton for the London *Times* (April 1, 2006) that *True Blood*—which he has often described as "popcorn for smart people"—is "very raucous, more entertaining, much, much funnier" than *Six Feet Under*, adding, "I'm done peering into the abyss for a while." Michael Lombardo, HBO's president of programming, told Gina Piccalo for the *Los Angeles Times* (July 18, 2010) that *True Blood* won the approval of HBO executives solely "because of [Ball's] creative vision." In a conversation with Dave Itzkoff for the *New York Times* (July 17, 2011, on-line), Ball recalled that when he was "called upon to give a one-sentence thematic pitch to the higher-ups at HBO as to what the show was about," he told them, "Well, ultimately at its heart, it's about the terrors of intimacy." "From the beginning, Ball has used *True Blood* vampires as stand-ins for every genre of the disenfranchised," according to Piccalo. "Nearly all the characters grapple with shame and struggle against their instincts." She added, "Occasionally, remnants of Ball's own Buddhist faith influence the plot." Ball commented to her, "Certainly, people's desires get them in trouble on the show. That's definitely a Buddhist concept." *True Blood* debuted in 2008; its fourth season began in June 2011. Among its many honors, the show won the Television Critics Association Award for outstanding new program of 2008–09.

Alan Ball lives in Los Angeles. The book *Considering Alan Ball: Essays on Sexuality, Death and America in the Television and Film Writings* (2006), edited by Thomas Fahy, contains essays by Fahy and nine others. The subtitle notwithstanding, it includes discussions of Ball's works for the theater.

—M.B.

Suggested Reading: *Advocate* p50+ July 3, 2001; *Atlanta Journal-Constitution* L p1+ Mar. 26, 2000, L p1+ June 3, 2001; *Chicago Sun-Times* p49 May 31, 2001; *Los Angeles Times* E p1+ Aug. 15, 2005; *New York Times* II p21 Mar. 4, 2001, (on-line) June 17, 2011; *New Yorker* p80+ May 14, 2001; *Utne* p51+ Sep./Oct. 2005; *Washington Post* G p1+ May 26, 2002

Selected Films: *American Beauty*, 1999; *Towelhead*, 2008

Selected Television Programs: *Cybill*, 1995–98; *Six Feet Under*, 2001–05; *True Blood*, 2008–

Banerjee, Mamata

Jan. 5, 1955– Chief minister of West Bengal, India; founder and chair of the All India Trinamool Congress

Address: Home: 30B, Harish Chatterjee St., Kolkata-700 026, West Bengal, India

On May 20, 2011 56-year-old Mamata Banerjee was formally sworn in as the chief minister of the Indian state of West Bengal, whose population—approximately 91 million—is larger than those of all but 12 of the world's nations. The first woman to hold that post, Banerjee is the chair of the All India Trinamool ("Grassroots") Congress (TMC), the political party that she founded in 1998. In the West Bengal elections held in phases between April 18 and May 10, 2011, the TMC won 184 of the 294 elected seats in the Legislative Assembly—a clear majority, and 154 more seats than TMC candidates had won in the previous election, five years earlier. With those impressive victories the TMC ended the 34-year rule in West Bengal of the Communist Party of India (Marxist) (CPI–M), which, as the majority in an alliance known as the Left Front, had formed the longest-serving democratically elected Communist government in the world. "Mamata doesn't promise anything radical—more industry, investment, clean government," Sandip Roy noted on the National Public Radio program *Morning Edition* (May 11, 2011, on-line). "She's really about change."

Called Didi ("elder sister" or "big sister") by her supporters, Banerjee became familiar with local politics during her childhood in Kolkata (formerly Calcutta). While in college she became politically active as a member of the Indian National Congress (INC), which was founded in 1885 and is one of the country's main political parties. Since 1976 Banerjee has held a series of more than 30 elective offices or appointed jobs (sometimes concurrently), among them general secretary of the Mahila Congress (the women's wing of the INC); seven-term member of the Lok Sabha ("House of the People"), the lower house of India's bicameral Parliament; member of national government committees, including those on home affairs and public accounts; and, twice, head of the Ministry of Railways, a national cabinet position.

Raveendran/AFP/Getty Images

Mamata Banerjee

Early on Banerjee became known as a political street fighter who inspired supporters with her passionate rhetoric. Barely five feet tall, she was dubbed the "Bengal tigress" by the Indian media for her unpredictable rages and sometimes over-the-top behavior. While her determination and dynamism remain as strong as ever, over the years she has tamped down her impulsiveness and recklessness and strengthened her reputation as an effective, responsible leader. "She is a shrewd politician," the sociologist Anjan Ghosh told Damayanti Datta for *India Today* (August 7, 2009), "who has decided to move from street drama mode to cool, calculated politics." Banerjee responded powerfully in 2006 and 2007 to widely condemned actions by West Bengal's ruling Left Front regarding the acquisition of land for industrial development; as a result a large number of intellectuals and business-people joined the many among the rural and urban poor who had long supported her.

A major factor in Banerjee's allure among the poor and working class is that she identifies with them: she wears plain white saris, rubber flip-flops, no makeup, and minimal jewelry, carries a traditional cotton shoulder bag, lives in the tiny house in which she grew up, and usually travels in a non-air-conditioned car. "All these make Mamata a picture of plain living," a *Times of India* (May 14, 2011) reporter wrote in an article headlined "Mamata Banerjee: Hysterics to History." The prominent Bengali writer and social activist Mahasweta Devi told Ajitha Menon for the *Navhind Times* (May 14, 2011, on-line), "No one can question her struggle or the transparent honesty with which she has fought her battles," adding that Banerjee is "someone who truly feels for the people and works toward their well-being."

The job of chief minister in West Bengal is equivalent to that of governor of a U.S. state. (West Bengal has a governor, too, but that person serves as a figurehead.) Banerjee's success as chief minister will hinge largely on her ability to attract investors and businesses to her state, which currently has an enormous debt and whose residents include an estimated 30 million people living in poverty. According to information gathered in India's 2001 national census, as posted on the Web site Census-India.gov.in, millions of families in West Bengal live in single rooms with mud walls and floors; have no nearby sources of water; have no toilet facilities except outdoor latrines; use kerosene for lighting; and rely on cowdung cakes, crop residues, or firewood as fuel for cooking in outdoor kitchens.

Lying along the Bay of Bengal in eastern India, West Bengal is India's fourth-largest state in population and the 13th in area. About 70 percent of its inhabitants depend on agriculture for their livelihoods. Nevertheless, West Bengal "was once seen as an industrial model for the rest of the nation," Vikas Bajaj wrote for the *New York Times* (June 10, 2011, on-line). "Fifty years ago, the state had India's highest per-capita income, and its biggest city, Kolkata, . . . was the nation's de facto business capital. But in recent decades, the city's and state's growth rates have lagged behind the rest of the country's. The communist government's restrictive economic policies, authoritarian rule and penchant for strikes prompted many businesses to leave. The country's largest bank, the State Bank of India, moved its headquarters to Mumbai [formerly Bombay], the current financial capital. In a 2009 World Bank report, Kolkata ranked last among 18 Indian cities based on ease of doing business." The finance minister in Banerjee's cabinet is Amit Mitra, a businessman and TMC member, who in the 2011 elections won by a landslide the seat in the Assembly held for 24 years by a Communist; Mitra predicted, as quoted by a reporter in the *Jagran Post* (May 14, 2011, on-line), "Mamata Banerjee will breathe life into the moribund economy by a people-centric programme which will be a win-win for all strata of society."

The second of four children and the only girl, Mamata Banerjee was born on January 5, 1955 to Promileswar Banerjee and his wife, Gayetri (also spelled "Gayatri"), in Kalighat, a lower-middle-class neighborhood in Kolkata, West Bengal's capital. (A few sources report that she has six brothers, not three.) Banerjee still lives with her mother in the house in which her parents raised her and her siblings—a modest structure that stands near an open sewer. Her father, described variously as a small-business owner or a schoolteacher, was active in local INC politics, and as a child Banerjee would accompany him to rallies and make paper flags for participants. Her father, who died when she was 17 (some sources give earlier ages), remains "the most important influence of my life . . . ," Banerjee told Arnab Mitra for the *Hindu-*

stan Times (April 23, 2011). "He inspired me to retain a humanitarian outlook."

Banerjee earned four degrees, all from institutions in Kolkata: a B.A. degree in history from Jogamaya Devi College, a women's school that is affiliated with the University of Calcutta; an M.A. degree in Islamic history from the University of Calcutta; a B.Ed. degree from Shiri Shishayatan College; and an LL.B. degree from the Jogesh Chandra Chaudhuri College of Law. (Banerjee once reportedly maintained that she had received a Ph.D. degree from East Georgia University, a fictitious institution in the U.S.) On the West Bengal government Web site, she described her "educational qualifications" as "trained in work education"; on a parliamentary Web site, she listed her professions as "political and social worker" and "trade unionist."

While at Jogamaya Devi College, Banerjee joined the Chhatra Parishad, the student wing of the INC. According to a several sources, as an undergraduate she once danced on the hood of the distinguished politician Jayaprakash Narayan's car during a protest. From 1976 to 1980 she served as general secretary of the West Bengal Mahila Congress, the INC's women's wing. In 1984 she won election to the Lok Sabha, the lower house of India's Parliament, defeating the veteran CPI–M politician Somnath Chatterjee for the seat representing the Jadavpur constituency in Kolkata. (From 1971 to 2004 that was the only election that Chatterjee ever lost.) At 29 she was one of the youngest members of the Parliament. Also in 1984 she was named the general secretary of the All India Youth Congress, a branch of the INC.

In the national elections of 1989, charges of widespread political corruption and disillusionment with the policies of the INC, which had ruled India for all but two-and-a-half of the previous 42 years, led to the downfall of the government of Rajiv Gandhi, a member of an INC family dynasty with whom Banerjee later became close. (Rajiv was a son of the earlier prime minister Indira Gandhi and a grandson of Jawaharlal Nehru, the first prime minister of India after it gained independence from Great Britain, in 1947). In the same elections Banerjee lost her seat in the Lok Sabha to Malini Bhattacharya, a CPI–M member.

Banerjee was serving as the president of the West Bengal Youth Congress when an incident occurred, on April 16, 1990, that greatly increased her political profile. The INC had organized a *bandh*, or general strike, to take place that day in Kolkata to protest an increase in bus fare. Many violent clashes between INC and CPI–M members erupted, including one at the intersection where Banerjee was holding a rally. Ignoring the warnings of her colleagues, Banerjee rushed into the melee, where CPI–M goons beat her with batons and fractured her skull. She spent at least a month in the hospital recuperating. "The disillusioned youths in the [INC] saw in her a determination that was missing among senior leaders," an INC worker, Anil Kumar Mukherjee, told a *Times of India*

(May 14, 2011) reporter for an article headlined "A Blow that Made Mamata an Icon of Resistance."

Although the Indian constitution specifies that national elections be held every five years, new elections have occurred more frequently in certain circumstances. The resignations of Prime Minister Manmohan Singh and his council of ministers in 1991 resulted in national elections only two years after the previous one. (The voting, which began in May, was halted temporarily after the assassination of Rajiv Gandhi and resumed in June.) Banerjee was returned to the Lok Sabha, this time winning the seat for Kolkata South, and the new prime minister, P. V. Narasimha Rao, appointed her minister of state for human resource development, youth affairs and sports, and women and child development. She held that cabinet post until 1993.

Banerjee became involved in another violent incident on July 21, 1993, when she led a West Bengal Youth Congress march to the building that housed the offices of Jyoti Basu, a CPI–M leader who served as West Bengal's chief minister from 1977 to 2000. The marchers were protesting a new requirement that voters identify themselves at the polls not only with their state-issued ID cards but with additional documents. Police officers dragged Banerjee from the building; other officers opened fire on the crowd, killing 13 protesters. On every July 21 since then, Banerjee has held a rally to commemorate what has become known as "Martyrs Day." (It is one of several such days in West Bengal.)

Several other events that occurred in the 1990s contributed to the widespread impression that Banerjee was intemporate and imprudent. One occurred in April 1996, during a rally to protest government corruption, when Banerjee wrapped her black shawl around her neck and threatened to hang herself. Another took place in February 1997, when, to protest the neglect of West Bengal's needs in the newly announced Railway Ministry budget, she threw her shawl at the railway minister. In December 1998 she and a male Lok Sabha member came to blows in the house chamber, with Banerjee accusing him of kicking her and the man claiming that she had punched him in addition to grabbing his collar in an attempt to drag him away.

Earlier, in the national elections held in April and May 1996, Banerjee (as an INC candidate) had won a third term in the Lok Sabha. Candidates from more than two dozen parties also claimed seats in the 545-member lower house, and no party had a majority. The formations of shaky coalitions led to two years of political instability in which a succession of three prime ministers headed the government.

Meanwhile, in the mid-1990s Banerjee had begun to publicly express her displeasure with INC leaders who, she charged, had become overly friendly with Communist officials and, in some cases, had become their puppets. In December 1997 Banerjee renounced the INC and resigned from Parliament (or was forced out, according to some sources) and announced that she was forming a new party. The All India Trinamool Congress was officially registered with the state in early 1998, and Banerjee was named its chair. (The TMC is also referred to as the AITMC and sometimes as the Trinamool Congress.) The party has branches for youths, students, women, workers, and farmers. In the general elections held in February 1998, more than three dozen parties captured seats in the Lok Sabha, with the top two, the Bharatiya Janata Party (BJP) and the INC, securing 182 and 141, respectively. Banerjee and six other TMC members won the seats in their districts; all of them joined representatives from a dozen other parties to form the BJP-led National Democratic Alliance, with Atal Bihari Vajpayee as prime minister. In 1999 the coalition disintegrated, and new elections were held in September and October of that year. Banerjee and the 11 other TMC members who won seats again joined the BJP-led National Democratic Alliance government, a coalition of 14 parties that constituted a majority in the Lok Sabha. That government, headed by Vajpayee, survived for a full five years.

In addition to representing her constituency, Kolkata South, in the Lok Sabha, from October 13, 1999 to March 16, 2001 Banerjee served in the cabinet as the minister of railways. Her achievements in that post included the addition of track and express trains and the introduction of train cars set aside for women, to free them from physical and verbal harassment by men, which had become increasingly common during rush hours as more women entered the workplace. From September 3, 2003 to January 8, 2004, Banerjee served as a minister without portfolio, and for the next four months, as the minister for coal and mines.

Earlier in the 2000s internal ideological battles had weakened the TMC. In the 2001 elections for the West Bengal Assembly, the party fared poorly; in the 2004 national elections, Banerjee was the only TMC candidate to win a seat from West Bengal in the Lok Sabha. At times Banerjee complained publicly that her voice was being ignored. "Ms. Banerjee's career is going nowhere," an editorial writer for the *Hindu* (August 8, 2005) declared. "The rabble-rousing 'Mamatadi,' who once had a considerable popular base, is today a marginal force in West Bengal politics."

That situation changed in 2006, because of fierce controversies triggered when West Bengal's Communist government started to take steps to bring two industrial companies to Singur and Nandigram, so-called census towns composed of many villages in areas of the state with particularly rich soils and many small farms. Buddhadeb Bhattacharjee, the CPI–M chief minister, announced that the state had set up special economic zones on about 1,000 acres in Singur for use by the Tata Group, one of India's largest industrial conglomerates, and about 10,000 acres in Nandigram, for use by the Salim Group, Indonesia's largest conglomer-

ate. The Tata Motor Co. intended to build an automobile factory, while Salim planned to construct a complex devoted to the production of chemicals. The controversies stemmed from both the powerlessness of peasants to decide their own fates and the ways in which the acreage had changed, or was to change, hands. According to the government, peasants had willingly agreed to sell their land and had received reasonable compensation for it; according to many of those peasants and various observers—among them Banerjee and other TMC members—the government had virtually forced the sellers to agree to the transactions and to accept far less than what their land was worth. Moreover, the government was offering no provisions for sharecroppers or day laborers, few of whom had skills transferable to factory work.

In the face of mounting protests, including general strikes in Kolkata, the government "fenced off the land, deployed hundreds of state police officers and private guards on its perimeter, and . . . banned assemblies of five or more people in villages nearby," Somini Sengupta reported for the *New York Times* (December 29, 2006, on-line). Clashes between the police and protesters sometimes became violent; in the worst single instance, in Nandigram on March 14, 2007, the police killed 14 villagers. Although no official figures are available, various sources have suggested that the protests on that day and others led to many more deaths, as well as large numbers of injuries and police-organized gang rapes. Additional clashes occurred between those opposed to the Bhattacharjee government's policies and the not insignificant numbers of peasants who had sold or wanted to sell their land and hoped that some among their family members would become factory workers.

In speaking out against the Bhattacharjee government's tactics in Singur and Nandigram, Banerjee emphasized that West Bengal needed an influx of industries, but that the state's industrial development must not entail forced acquisition of land. On December 4, 2006, in an expression of solidarity with the farmers and in an attempt to reverse the West Bengal government's actions, Banerjee embarked on a hunger strike—a tactic used repeatedly by Mohandas Gandhi, the leader of the nonviolent movement that led to India's independence from Great Britain, in 1947. (He was not related to Indira Gandhi.) Banerjee held the strike in public in downtown Kolkata, and by the time she ended it, 25 days later (reportedly at the request of Prime Minister Manmohan Singh and President P. J. Abdul Kalam), she had become the face of the protest. Tata later abandoned its partially built factory in Singur in favor of a site in Gujarat, a state in western India, and Salim abandoned its plans to build a chemical complex in West Bengal. Likening the situations in Singur and Nandigram to those in myriad other places throughout India, Somini Sengupta wrote for the *New York Times* (September 16, 2008), "At the heart of the challenge, one of the most important facing the Indian government, is not only how to compensate peasants who make way for India's industrial future, but also how to prepare them—in great numbers—for the new economy India wants to enter."

Banerjee won a seventh term in the Lok Sabha in 2009; 18 other TMC members from West Bengal also won seats. Banerjee was again appointed head of the Ministry of Railways; she has since given up that post.

Banerjee's achievements during the Singur and Nandigram conflicts enormously influenced the campaign that preceded the elections held for the West Bengal Legislative Assembly, which took place in six phases in April and May 2011. Banerjee campaigned with the slogan "Ma, Mati, Manush," which refers to India and means "Mother, Motherland, People." ("Mati" has also been translated as "land," "soil," or "earth.") She repeatedly said at rallies, "I am against CPM, but I am not against communists," according to the *Times of India*'s "Hysterics to History" article. "There are good people among Left sympathizers, but they should leave the company of CPM which has lost its moorings and deviated from the path of socialism." In the days leading up to the balloting, many journalists and commentators predicted that Banerjee and the TMC would prevail over the Communists. Their predictions proved to be correct: the TMC won 184 seats, more than six times as many as they had in 2006 and an absolute majority of the Assembly's 294 elected seats. (An appointed seat is reserved for an Anglo-Indian.) The CPI–M won only 40 seats, down from 136 seats five years earlier. On May 13 Buddhadeb Bhattacharjee stepped down; two days later the TMC legislators unanimously elected Banerjee as their leader.

Banerjee herself had not run for a seat in the Assembly in the April/May election. However, according to state law she was required to do so within six months of her assumption of the post of chief minister. On September 28, 2011, in a contest against the CPI-M nominee, Nandini Mukherjee, she won the seat for the Bhabanipur constituency (also called Bhowanipore), in Kolkata. That seat had been held by Subrata Bakshi, a TMC party official, who, according to the Web site BengalInformation.org (August 19, 2011), had resigned from the Assembly after having "insisted" that Banerjee run for his seat. On October 8, 2011 Banerjee resigned from the Lok Sabha, so as to devote herself entirely to her work in West Bengal.

Banerjee, who has never married, is close to her mother and her brothers and their families. A writer and poet, she has written many books in Bengali and several in English. She enjoys cooking and painting.

—M.M.H.

Suggested Reading: BBC News South Asia (on-line) Apr. 14, 2011; *Hindu* (on-line) Aug. 8, 2005; *Hindustan Times* (on-line) Apr. 23, 2011; *India Today* (on-line) Mar. 10, 1996, Aug. 7,

2009, May 12, 2011; National Public Radio (on-line) May 11, 2011; *Navhind Times* (on-line) May 14, 2011; *New York Times* (on-line) May 2, 2009, Jan. 14, 2011, June 10, 2011; *Times of India* (on-line) May 14, 2011; West Bengal government Web site

Selected Books: *Struggle for Existence*, 1998; *Slaughter of Democracy*, 2006

Warren Little/Getty Images

Barbosa, Leandro

(BAR-boh-suh, lee-AN-droh)

Nov. 28, 1982– Basketball player

Address: Toronto Raptors, US Air Canada Centre, 40 Bay St., Suite 400, Ontario M5J 2X2, Canada

Growing up in a country where the game of choice is soccer, Leandro Barbosa earned the nickname "the Brazilian Blur" for the speed he displays in a different sport: basketball. Barbosa—who is six feet three inches tall with a six-foot 10-inch wingspan—honed his skills in the Brazilian Basketball League, where he quickly became one of the nation's most dominant players. In 2002, at age 19, he was the youngest player to join the Brazilian men's national basketball team, which participated in that year's World Championships. After two seasons with the professional Brazilian basketball team Bauru Tilibra, during which he was named the league's Rookie of the Year, Barbosa was selected as the 28th overall pick in the 2003 National

Basketball Association (NBA) draft by the San Antonio Spurs; he was then traded to the Phoenix Suns, where over the next seven seasons he made significant contributions in a backup role. His breakthrough came during the 2005–06 season, when he garnered 101 out of a possible 127 first-place votes to win the NBA's Sixth Man of the Year Award, which recognizes the league's top reserve player. Following the 2009–10 season Barbosa was traded to Toronto, where, despite injuries, he has continued to combine unusual speed with a stoic, competitive, upbeat spirit.

Leandro Mateus Barbosa was born on November 28, 1982 in São Paulo, Brazil, to Vicente Barbosa, a hospital worker and onetime boxer, and Ivete Barbosa. He lived in poverty in a two-room house with his parents and four older siblings—two brothers and two sisters. As a four-year-old he helped to support his family by selling fruits and vegetables alongside his two brothers at a neighborhood market. His brother Arturo, who was 21 years his senior and a first sergeant and paratrooper in the Brazilian Special Forces, sparked his interest in basketball. "My brother . . . used to play basketball back in the day and I was with him all the time," Barbosa told Tracy Graven for *Swish Magazine* (February 2007, on-line). "I decided to play basketball because it was too hard to get on a [soccer] team in Brazil, with so many people wanting to play the same sport. I decided to play [basketball] and my brother was the deciding factor for me to change sports." His brother, who had begun to watch NBA games on satellite television in the early 1980s, recognized that the young Barbosa possessed considerable athletic talent. He began training him in basketball, using a series of routine drills, which included dribbling a ball through and around a course of folding chairs and bouncing a tennis ball. Another exercise involved a three-foot stick. "[Arturo] would have me hold out my hands and he would hold the stick," Barbosa told Norm Frauenheim and Debora Britz for the Phoenix *Arizona Republic* (October 26, 2003), as translated by an interpreter, Michel Fernandes. "It was for agility. He'd move the stick, and if the hands didn't move, that stick would hit [me] really hard. Sometimes, I almost couldn't play in organized games because my hands were so sore." The brothers would often perform those drills in back alleys and in the rain.

Barbosa joined the Brazilian Junior National Team when he was 15 years old. Two years later he became a member of the Palmeiras professional basketball team, averaging 14.2 points per game under the tutelage of Coach Aluísio "Lula" Ferreira, before moving in January 2001 to the Bauru Tilibra team in the Campeonato Brasileiro de Basquete (Brazilian Basketball League). In his first full season with that squad (2001–02), Barbosa scored an average of 15.8 points per game with 6.4 assists and 1.7 steals to earn the nod as the Rookie of the Year. He finished the season ranked fourth in three-point percentage, sixth in assists, and 11th in two-point field-goal percentage. At age 19 he made his first visit to the U.S., as the youngest member of the Brazilian National Team, which competed at the 2002 FIBA World Championship, held in Indianapolis, Indiana. (The International Basketball Federation, or FIBA, the world governing body for basketball, organizes the international basketball tournaments for men and women, which take place every four years.) The Brazilian team, ranked eighth out of 16 teams, advanced to the quarterfinals, where they lost to the squad from Argentina, 78–67, to finish in eighth place overall with a tournament record of four wins and five losses. Barbosa appeared in four of the nine games, during which he had nine points, five assists, and five rebounds while playing a total of 21 minutes.

During his second full season (2002–03) with the Bauru Tilibra team, Barbosa scored an average of 28.2 points per game—second-best in the league—and ended the season as one of the league leaders in assists (with an average of seven per game) and in rebounds (with an average of four per game). He was part of the national team that represented Brazil in the 2003 FIBA Americas Men's Olympic Tournament in San Juan, Puerto Rico, during which he averaged 12 points and a .493 field-goal percentage in eight games. Barbosa was among the international players who applied to the NBA for early entry into the June 2003 draft. Slowed by a hip-flexor injury, he was able to work out for only a few teams prior to the draft. Selected 28th overall by the San Antonio Spurs, he was one of a record 21 international players chosen in that year's draft. The Phoenix Suns' president, Bryan Colangelo, at the urging of the team's head coach, Frank Johnson, acquired Barbosa's draft rights from the Spurs in exchange for a future protected first-round pick, following a private workout on the eve of the draft. Barbosa, at 20, signed a three-year, $2.6 million contract. Thereafter, he began supporting his family in Brazil.

In his rookie NBA season, Barbosa was initially expected to fill the role of backup to the Suns' starting point guard, Stephon Marbury. Johnson told Steven Koek in an interview posted on the NBA Web site (June 27, 2003), "There were times when we were playing Stephon 45 minutes. Hopefully [Barbosa] will be able to come in and give us a boost off the bench from a point guard standpoint. Defensively, he can come up and put some defensive pressure on their guards. We're very, very excited." Barbosa was promoted to starting point guard on January 5, 2004, after Marbury was traded, along with the guard/forward Anfernee Hardaway and the center Cezary Trybanski, to the New York Knicks.

Despite his limited grasp of English, Barbosa quickly adjusted to his new role on the team. In his first NBA start, he scored a then-career-best 27 points, setting a franchise record for the most points ever scored by a rookie in his first start and tying the mark for most points scored by an international player in his first start. His streak of 10 consecutive games with one or more three-pointers in January 2004 also set a franchise rookie record. After the Marbury trade he averaged 10 points per game along with per-game averages of 2.4 rebounds, 3.3 assists, and 1.6 steals. By the end of the 2003–04 season, Barbosa had appeared in 70 games and scored an average of 7.9 points per game with 1.7 rebounds and 2.4 assists; the Suns finished sixth in the Pacific Division of the Western Conference with a 29–53 record and failed to make the play-offs. Barbosa led all rookies in three-point field-goal percentage and was among the league leaders in scoring, assists, field-goal percentage, steals, and three-point field goals made.

During the 2004–05 season Barbosa returned to the backup point-guard role, following the free-agent signing of Steve Nash, a former Suns player, in July 2004. He thrived, appearing in 63 games and coming off the bench to average seven points, two assists, and 2.1 rebounds per game. He made six starts in place of Nash, averaging 14.2 points and four rebounds despite an injury-plagued season that saw him miss 14 games, including nine in which he sat out with a sprained left ankle. In a dramatic improvement during Mike D'Antoni's first full season as the Suns' head coach, the team ended the regular season with a record of 62 wins and 20 losses to clinch the Western Conference division title and earn a berth in the 2005 NBA play-offs. Following a four-game sweep of the Memphis Grizzlies in the first round, the Suns advanced past the Dallas Mavericks in the conference semifinals, then lost to the Spurs, who went on to win the NBA championship that year. Barbosa was more successful at the 2005 FIBA Americas Championship in Santo Domingo, Dominican Republic, where the Brazilian men's national team won a gold medal.

Despite battling injuries to his left knee and undergoing a spinal tap to test for meningitis (he was ultimately diagnosed as having the flu), Barbosa had arguably the best season of his career during the 2005–06 NBA campaign. He achieved career-best per-game averages in points (13.1), rebounds (2.6), assists (2.8), field-goal percentage (.481), three-point field-goal percentage (.444), three-pointers made (87), and minutes played (27.9 minutes). With a regular-season record of 54 wins and 28 losses, the Suns clinched the Pacific Division title and advanced to the play-offs for the second consecutive year. Barbosa performed well in his first play-off appearance against the Suns' first-round opponents, the Los Angeles Lakers, coming off the bench to score 15 points in Game One. He made his first NBA play-off start in Game Six, replacing the suspended Raja Bell; Barbosa scored 22 points in a 126–118, series-tying overtime victory for the Suns, who had rallied from a 3–1 deficit. In the seventh and deciding game of the series, Barbosa recorded a play-off career-high 26 points in the Suns' 121–90 win. He also played a crucial role in the Western Conference semifinal series against the Los Angeles Clippers, coming off the bench and scoring in the double digits in six of the seven

games. The Suns advanced to the Western Conference finals before losing to the Dallas Mavericks in six games. In August 2006 Barbosa signed a five-year, $33 million contract extension to remain with the Suns.

During the 2006–07 season Barbosa appeared in 80 games, starting in 18, while averaging 18.1 points, 2.7 rebounds, four assists, and 1.2 steals per game. He was among the league leaders in three-point field-goal percentage for the second season in a row. With a record of 61 wins and 21 losses, the Suns claimed the Western Conference's Pacific Division title and made the play-offs for the third consecutive season. In the first round Barbosa scored an average of 21.2 points in five games against the Los Angeles Lakers, also their first-round opponent in the 2006 NBA play-offs, to help the Suns advance to the Western Conference semifinals, in which they lost to the Spurs. Barbosa was voted the NBA Sixth Man of the Year, becoming only the fourth player in the history of the franchise to win that honor.

Barbosa continued to shine in the 2007–08 season. He had four games with 30 or more points scored and 22 contests in which he scored at least 20; he averaged 15.6 points per game for a greater number of total points off the bench than any other player in the NBA. That season the Suns lost to the Spurs in five games in the first round of the play-offs.

The following year was a difficult one for Barbosa and his family in Brazil; the athlete missed two weeks of training camp prior to the 2008–09 season to be with his ailing mother, who succumbed to pneumonia in November 2008. (His father had died of cancer in late 2004.) Despite that hardship Barbosa had a good season, the highlight of which was a game against Oklahoma City, on February 20, 2009, in which he made 41 points—joining the all-time greats Michael Jordan, Julius "Dr. J" Erving, Walt Frazier, and Larry Bird as the only players to have at least 40 points, seven rebounds, seven assists, and six steals in a single game. With a 46–36 record the Suns finished second in the Pacific Division and missed the play-offs. The 2009–10 season was a challenging one for Barbosa, who suffered a sprained ankle and then missed several weeks of play after having a cyst removed from his right wrist in January 2010; in a career-low 44 games, he averaged 9.5 points, 1.6 rebounds, and 1.5 assists. On the positive side, he became only the third player to amass 700 three-pointers as a member of the Suns. For their part, the Suns made it past the Portland Trail Blazers and the Spurs before losing in six games to the Lakers in the Western Conference Finals. Also that year Barbosa played in the FIBA championship series for Brazil, which lost in the preliminary round to the U.S., 70–68, when Barbosa failed to sink a basket at the buzzer.

Following that season Barbosa was traded to the Toronto Raptors. As an off-the-bench player for that squad in the 2010–11 season, Barbosa—despite an often painful injured right wrist—has shown his speed and skills to be undiminished. As of late April 2011, he had maintained a double-digit points-per-game average, and on March 11, in a game against the Indiana Pacers, he scored a season-high 29 points. An injured finger caused him to miss several games late in the season.

Barbosa is said to be a genial man who plays without complaint even when he is in pain. With the Brazilian actress Samara Felippo, Barbosa has a daughter, Alicia, born in June 2009.

—B.M.

Suggested Reading:*Arizona Republic* C p16 Oct. 26, 2003; *Canadian Press* General Sports Mar. 11, 2011; nba.com; *New York Times* VIII p2 Mar. 6, 2005; (Ontario, Canada) *Woodstock Sentinel–Review* Sports p11 Sep. 29, 2010; *Swish Magazine* (on-line) Feb. 2007; *Toronto Star* Sports p5 Sep. 29, 2010

Courtesy of the Gersh Agency

Barfield, Tanya

1969(?)– Playwright

Address: c/o Seth Glewen, Gersh Agency, 41 Madison Ave., 33d Fl., New York, NY 10010

"I've written plays with all-white casts, I've written plays with all-black casts," the playwright Tanya Barfield, who is biracial, told Jim Catalano for the *Ithaca (New York) Journal* (March 4, 2004). "I prefer not to be seen as an African American playwright because I try to address a variety of human experiences in my work. I think of myself as an 'American Playwright' because I write about the is-

sues and situations affecting people in this country." Barfield's plays pose complex questions about race and identity. From her first work, a solo performance piece called *Without Skin, or Breathlessness*, about a young biracial girl and her white mother, to her more recent, acclaimed play *Blue Door*, which examines the modern-day implications of African-American history through the lens of the scholar W.E.B. DuBois's concept of "double consciousness," Barfield has developed a reputation for refusing to shy away from weighty subjects. The playwright, a former actress, has garnered prestigious theater awards, including the Helen Merrill Award for Emerging Playwrights (2003) and honorable mention for the Kesselring Prize for Drama (2005). She was awarded a Lark Play Development/NYSCA grant in 2006 and has twice been a finalist for the prestigious Princess Grace Award.

Tanya Barfield was born in about 1969 in San Francisco, California, and was raised in Portland, Oregon. She has often talked about growing up as the only child of a black father and white mother; she spent most of her childhood with her mother, after her parents' divorce, and grew up in a predominantly white community. Barfield has described her upbringing as working-class. She discovered her love of theater in elementary school, when she saw a performance of Shakespeare's *Macbeth* by the school's advanced English class. "Perhaps I was the only youngster in the audience that watched the show," Barfield said in an interview with Jacqueline E. Lawton for the Web site of the Arden Theatre Company, in Philadelphia, Pennsylvania (January 15, 2010). "I was riveted. It was storytelling and poetry like I had never heard." Barfield was so influenced by *Macbeth* that in her high school, which had no theater department, she staged a production of the play. "Everyone that auditioned was cast and Macduff was played by a girl because not enough boys tried out," she recalled to Lawton. Barfield saw her first professional theater production at age 17, at the Oregon Shakespeare Festival, and decided to pursue a career in acting. "Looking back on it," Barfield said to Lawton, "I think the only reason I studied acting instead of playwriting was because I didn't know that there was such a thing as a living playwright."

Barfield studied acting at Tisch School of the Arts at New York University (NYU), where she played a wide range of roles. After she graduated, in 1991, as she told Jeff Rivers for the *Hartford (Connecticut) Courant* (March 3, 2003), "nobody told me I wouldn't be playing the roles I'd played in college." In her essay "A Meditation on 'Blackness,'" posted on broadway.com (October 2, 2006), Barfield wrote that after studying at NYU, she encountered racial stereotypes in theater and film and was "submitted to a myriad of [roles as] prostitutes and drug addicts." One particularly disheartening experience helped push her toward playwriting. "I remember one time," she wrote, "sandwiched between hip-hop auditions, I went in for a household paper product commercial. I even got a callback. But then the producer asked me to bring a little more of 'the hood' to my acting. Try as I might, I just could not manage to make the line 'This toilet paper is so soft' as bland as it is sound inner-city." In her essay Barfield expressed her weariness of stereotypes portrayed by African-Americans in the entertainment industry and the seemingly endless depictions of "ghetto culture." "In reality," she wrote, "a vast number of African-Americans are part of an underrepresented group: We're middle-class."

In an interview with Misha Berson for the *Seattle Times* (February 2, 2007), Barfield listed many jobs she held as a young woman to support her theater career, including working in hotels and grocery stores, waitressing, and her oddest job, "spelunking through Oregon caves, monitoring the number of bats in them for the state." Barfield told Emily DeVoti for the *Brooklyn Rail* (2006) that such work has affected her career as well as her character: "[I] worked really hard in day jobs. I've always worked. The Lucrative Day Job. And the money I got from that, got me access to things. . . . It's had a big impact on my identity, although I don't know that I can articulate how. Maybe I'm a little prouder of that history. And I'm a little more knowledgeable." Her complex relationships to race and class—she told DeVoti that she has had "many different relationships to money throughout my life"—have informed her writing and the characters she chooses to portray.

In 1996 Barfield wrote and performed a one-woman show, *Without Skin Or Breathlessness*, which was presented at P.S. 122 in New York City in May of that year. The play is narrated by a young biracial girl; its title refers to the colorless apparition of the protagonist's white mother. For the New York *Daily News* (May 8, 1996), Nick Charles wrote, "The play, about racial identity and coming of age, features pointed incidents that make the girl aware of her status. Barfield does this by portraying a wide range of characters including a grizzled black father, an Asian playmate and a tart-tongued black classmate with a riveting physicality." Charles added, "The play focuses not just on the girl's coming-of-consciousness concerning her racial identity but on the fallout from that realization and the steps she takes to claim her heritage and humanity." In the same year, along with Andrea Kline and Aaron Landsman, Barfield created and performed the piece *Hand to Mouth's Cakewalk*—a deconstruction of Shakespeare's *Othello*—for the Red Eye Theater's Isolated Acts Festival in Minneapolis, Minnesota. They performed the show again at P.S. 122.

As a result of her solo performance work, Barfield won a Van Lier Fellowship from the New York Theatre Workshop. As a fellow she began work on her first traditional play, *The Houdini Act* (1999). The play was presented in the fall of 1999 as part of the Just Add Water Festival; there, Barfield met the director Leigh Silverman, one of her future collaborators, who was an intern at the time. Silverman and Barfield participated in a workshop in which Barfield wrote 10 pages of material every night and Silverman staged her work the next day with actors. After a week Barfield had written the first act of a play, *Dent*, whose second act she completed over the course of the next few months. The play was featured in 2003 as part of "Voices!," a showcase of African-American playwrights at the Hartford Stage, in Connecticut. *Dent* tells the story of two white college freshmen, Jack and Ted; Ted comes from a wealthy family while Jack's family is poor. After the boys are accused of committing a hate crime, the women in their families must come together to discover the truth and deal with their own feelings of guilt. Barfield told Chris Heneghan for the *Hartford Courant* (February 27, 2003), "I chose to tell the story of Jack and Ted because I was searching for humanity within inhumanity."

After Barfield's two years at the New York Theatre Workshop, Silverman suggested that she apply to the prestigious Juilliard School, in New York; she did so and was accepted, studying with the playwrights Christopher Durang and the Pulitzer Prize–winner Marsha Norman, the co-directors of Juilliard's Lila Acheson Wallace American Playwrights Program (where she earned the school's artist's diploma). While there Barfield ventured into historical territory with her 10-minute play *Wanting North*, about two young sisters who are slaves. The piece was presented as part of a series of short works by the Echo Theater Company, in Los Angeles, California. Paul Birchall wrote for *L.A. Weekly* (June 12, 2003), "Tanya Barfield's *Wanting North*—in which two 1840 Southern slaves . . . share experiences over who is actually the most free—is an emotionally nuanced and intimate vignette." Barfield followed *Wanting North* with another 10-minute play, *Medallion* (2004), as a part of the Antigone Project at the Women's Project in New York City, for which writers were commissioned to create their own versions of Sophocles's *Antigone*. In *Antigone*, the daughter of the fallen King Oedipus fights for a proper burial for her brother even though he is considered to be a traitor to the city of Thebes. A CurtainUp.com (October 23, 2004) review by Elyse Sommer called Barfield's reimagining—about a woman who demands a Purple Heart for her brother, a soldier in World War I—to be one of the most "moving and satisfying" of the Antigone Project's five plays.

Barfield has credited Durang—famous for his outrageous and absurd style—for bringing out the comedy in her own work, an aspect she emphasized in her play *Pecan Tan* (2004), which received preview readings at the Actors Theatre of Louisville, in Kentucky, and Hartford Stage. "Most of my other work is quite serious in subject matter, often about dysfunctional families," Barfield told Jim Catalano. "When I started *Pecan Tan* . . . I was ready for a break from my typical gloom-and-doom stories which is why this play is much lighter, more playful and optimistic in tone than some of my other work." The play, which premiered at the Kitchen Theatre Company, in Ithaca, New York, and went on to be produced by the African Continuum Theatre Company, in Washington, D.C., in 2005, is a comedy about a South Carolina African-American family whose lives are thrown into chaos by the appearance of a biracial "secret daughter." Catalano wrote that the play "uses sharply written, sweet-and-sour dialogue to turn stereotypes of all kinds on their heads." The play received mixed reviews, the most positive comparing Barfield to the comedian Richard Pryor or to Durang, and the least favorable likening the comedic style to that of a bad sitcom. A reviewer for the *Washington City Paper* (February 11, 2005) wrote of the African Continuum Theatre Company performance, "If Barfield doesn't have anything terribly profound to say about how families go along and get along, she's got a deft enough touch for capturing the ways we all irritate the life out of each other, and there's a kind of humanity in the amusement with which she showcases them."

In 2005 Barfield and the composer Eric Schorr received a commission from Theatre Works USA to write a children's musical about the Civil War. "We wanted to find a fresh, emotional story that hadn't been told before, and we didn't want it too preachy or educational," Schorr told Ellyce Field for the *Detroit News* (January 14, 2005). The result of their efforts was *The Civil War: The South Carolina Black Regiment*, which premiered at the Youtheatre at the Millennium Centre, in Detroit, Michigan, in January 2005. The story is set off the coast of Charleston, South Carolina, where the first regiment of black former slaves was formed for the Union Army. The musical chronicles the coming of age of a young boy, Kofi. In her essay Barfield wrote about the experience of mounting the play, "At first I was surprised that several young actors refused to audition—or even read the script. 'I won't play a slave,' was the reason. I was discouraged, to say the least. It goes without saying that one would not want to play a one-dimensional stereotype. But why refuse to play a heroic, intelligent boy who joins the Union Army? 'Black people are just tired of playing slaves and maids' was the answer. In a way, I understood. Being light-skinned, I got tired of 'tragic mulatto' roles, too."

In her next play Barfield took on the themes of shame about the past and what she referred to in "A Meditation on 'Blackness'" as "the complicated problem of success and assimilation." *Blue Door* (2006), set in 1995, finds Lewis, a black mathematician, facing the ghosts of his ancestors over the course of a sleepless night. Lewis's wife, a white woman, has just left him because he refused to attend the Million Man March, a real-life 1995 gathering on the National Mall of African-American men seeking to unite and atone for their past failures. In his solitude Lewis confronts ghosts including a distant and abusive father, a grandfather who died at the hands of a lynch mob, and a brother—a veteran of the Black Power movement of the 1960s—who even in death continues to accuse Lewis of turning his back on his heritage. Lewis, who has distanced himself from his family's history, listens to their stories for the first time as he takes stock of his life. Barfield has insisted that the themes explored in *Blue Door* are universal. "Every culture has a legacy from which it's birthed," she told Lawton. "I think it is part of human nature to be pulled by our ancestors, to feel their watchful spirits, to wish we knew their stories, to both scorn and adore them. In times of crisis (when our own self threatens to fragment), we might wonder if our ancestors could answer the basic question of identity. In this vast and complicated universe: who am I? It is only through memory that the soul of an ancestor is kept alive. If we forget out past, do we in some way forget ourselves?"

Blue Door, Barfield wrote in her essay, is about "what part of the self a person carves away to get ahead" and the repercussions of that division, including what the writer and intellectual leader W.E.B. DuBois referred to in his landmark 1903 book, *The Souls of Black Folk*, as "double-consciousness." Barfield used the full quotation in the epigraph of the play: "One ever feels his twoness," DuBois wrote, "an American, a Negro; two souls, two thoughts, two unreconciled strivings; two warring ideals in one dark body, whose dogged strength alone keeps it from being torn asunder." In her essay Barfield wrote of the play and what inspired it, "Ultimately, I see *Blue Door* as a theatrical meditation on 'blackness'—a dialogue between *then* and *now,* between cultural amnesia and memory. I believe it's a universal story: Is my present determined by my familial past?"

In representing the concept of "double-consciousness," Barfield created roles for two actors in *Blue Door*—the actor playing Lewis and a second performer, who portrays more than 20 characters. She also researched subjects ranging from the West African Yoruba language to African folktales to Euclidean mathematics (in which, in keeping with Barfield's theme, two parallel lines can never meet). Barfield read troves of slave narratives and manuscripts from the Library of Congress, catalogued during the Great Depression, when the Works Progress Administration (WPA) dispatched reporters to the American South to record the oral histories of former slaves. The research, Barfield has said, led to constant discovery—making for a personal as well as theatrical journey and revealing a relationship between her and the past that Barfield had never considered. She recounted to DeVoti reading about "the story of friends who went to visit Africa, and how Africans they met felt that black Americans have suffered the worst thing possible . . . separation from their ancestors," in DeVoti's words. "And I feel in some ways that I have felt that way in my own life," Barfield added. "Because of the separation from ancestral heritage. Writing *Blue Door* made me feel a connection."

Blue Door had its world premiere at South Coast Repertory, in Costa Mesa, California, in May 2006. Paul Hodgins wrote for the *Orange County (California) Register* (May 1, 2006) that Barfield was a "young playwright of immense promise" who "is already writing with the assurance and fine-tuned emotional control of an established playwright." After the play's New York premiere, at Playwrights Horizons, in October 2006, Barfield garnered more positive reviews, which praised the intimacy of the play despite its grand themes and the 144-year time span of its plot. Critics found that the play inspired comparisons to the work of the poet and playwright August Wilson. "Ms. Barfield's thoughtful play deals with themes central to the work of August Wilson, but the dramatic format she has chosen for *Blue Door* is strikingly different," Charles Isherwood wrote for the *New York Times* (October 9, 2006). "Mr. Wilson examined the African-American experience through a wide-angle lens. . . . Ms. Barfield concentrates on the same battle but locates it in a single man's soul."

Barfield's next play was inspired by a story she came across while researching *Medallion*, involving blacks in President Woodrow Wilson's administration during World War I. The play, *Of Equal Measure* (2008), follows the fictional character Jade, an African-American White House stenographer who has access to important information. As the presidential Cabinet begins to trample civil rights at home while fighting for freedom abroad, Jade questions her civic responsibilities. *Of Equal Measure* received its world premiere at the Kirk Douglas Theatre in Culver City, California, to lukewarm reviews. "The trouble with historical fiction," Charles McNulty wrote for the *Los Angeles Times* (July 14, 2008), "is that there often isn't a satisfying amount of either element." McNulty added, "Barfield has thought deeply about her material, but she keeps imposing her insights onto her narrative rather than allowing them to emerge freely. It's as though she has interpreted her world before constructing it." The play was criticized for its penchant for melodrama and Barfield's attempt to relate the material to the then-present-day George W. Bush administration.

Barfield's latest play, *The Call*, was to receive its world premiere in May 2011 at the Intiman Theatre, in Seattle, Washington, but was canceled when the theater closed. *The Call* examines interracial and international adoption and, according to the theater's Web site, what it means to be responsible for a child from another culture. Her other works include *The Quick* (2002), *121 Degrees West* (2004), and *The Wolves* (2004).

Since 2009 Barfield has worked as the literary manager of the Juilliard School Drama Division, overseeing the administrative and dramaturgical needs of staff and students. She is on the faculty of the Department of English at Barnard College, in New York. She has a son, Tez, and a daughter, Zeri. Barfield and her family live in the Crown Heights neighborhood of Brooklyn, New York.

—M.M.H.

Suggested Reading: ardentheatre.org Jan. 15, 2010; broadway.com Oct. 2, 2006; *Brooklyn Rail* (on-line) 2006; CurtainUp.com Oct. 23, 2004; *Detroit News* E p12 Jan. 14, 2005; *Hartford (Connecticut) Courant* p35 Feb 27, 2003, D p1 Mar. 3, 2003; *Ithaca (New York) Journal* C p12 Mar. 4, 2004, C p13 Mar. 4, 2004; *L.A. Weekly* (on-line) June 12, 2003; *Los Angeles Times* E p3 July 14, 2008; (New York) *Daily News* p38 May 8, 1996; *New York Times* E p5 Oct. 9, 2006; *Seattle Times* H p39 Feb. 2, 2007; *Washington City Paper* p40 Feb. 11, 2005

Selected Plays: *Without Skin Or Breathlessness*, 1996; *The Houdini Act*, 1999; *Wanting North*, 2003; *Dent*, 2003; *Pecan Tan*, 2004; *The Civil War: The South Carolina Black Regiment*, 2005; *Blue Door*, 2006; *Of Equal Measure*, 2008; *The Call*, 2011

Toby Canham/Getty Images

Bastianich, Joseph

(bass-TYAN-itch)

Sep. 17, 1968– Restaurateur; winemaker

Address: Becco, 355 W. 46th St., New York, NY 10036

In a manner contrasting with that of his more widely known business partner, the boisterous celebrity chef and television personality Mario Batali, Joseph Bastianich has become one of the most successful restaurateurs in the country without any fanfare. Bastianich, who was described by Julia

Sexton for *Westchester* magazine (July 2008, online) as "a force of restaurant-world nature," has founded nearly two dozen restaurants across the country within the last several years; he opened his first, Becco, in 1993, in partnership with his mother, the award-winning chef, cookbook author, and public-television host Lidia Bastianich. Becco, located in New York City's theater district, quickly became known for its innovative prix-fixe wine list and traditional pasta dishes. In 1998 Bastianich teamed up with Batali to found Babbo, which was named the best new restaurant in America by the James Beard Foundation and was widely credited with revitalizing Italian cuisine in New York City. "Among the restaurants that make my stomach do a special jig, Babbo ranks near the top," the esteemed restaurant critic Frank Bruni wrote in his three-star review for the *New York Times* (June 9, 2004, on-line). (According to the paper's rating system, three stars indicates an "excellent" restaurant, while the rare four-star establishment is considered "extraordinary." Bruni withheld a fourth star from Babbo because of the hard-rock music blaring from its sound system and the "slightly ragtag quality" of its ambience.) Bastianich and Batali have since co-founded other establishments, including Lupa, Esca, Otto, Casa Mono, and Del Posto, in New York City; Osteria Mozza and Pizzeria Mozza, in Los Angeles, California, and Singapore; B&B Ristorante, Enoteca Otto Pizzeria, and Carnevino, in Las Vegas, Nevada; and Tarry Lodge, in Port Chester, New York.

Bastianich, who has been heralded for his extensive knowledge of wine, is also the owner of three wineries in Italy. "Wine has been the driving force in my life—it's how I met my wife, how I've gotten work, how I've maintained a physical and emotional connection to my heritage and my family," he wrote on his Web site. "[My mother] taught me that all of her values were somehow captured in the spirit and essence of wine. She really drove it home—from the vineyard to the bottle, the wine we drink has a rich history, it is part of a deep-rooted tradition, and often it travels the whole world to get to our table. It reaches across all levels of society. It was a happy metaphor."

Among Bastianich's latest ventures is Eataly, a massive Italian food and wine marketplace that opened in New York City's Flatiron District in 2010. He is reportedly scouting locations for an Eataly in Los Angeles as well. For those not living in New York or one of the other cities to which Bastianich's empire has spread, he is perhaps best known as a judge on the televised cooking competition *MasterChef*, which debuted on the Fox network in 2010.

Joseph Bastianich was born on September 17, 1968 in the New York City borough of Queens. His parents, Felice Bastianich and the former Lidia Matticchio, had both come to New York in the late 1950s from Istria, which was described by David Savona for *Cigar Aficionado* (February 2007, on-line) as "a part of northeastern Italy lost to the car-

tographers who reworked the maps of Europe after the Second World War." Savona explained, "Istria became part of Yugoslavia, and many of the region's ethnic Italians found themselves in the strange, unwelcome world of Tito's communist Yugoslavia." After fleeing to the U.S., Felice and Lidia met and married. They raised Joe and his younger sister, Tanya, in Bayside, Queens. In the early 1970s they opened Buonavia, an Italian restaurant, on Queens Boulevard, in the nearby neighborhood of Forest Hills. On his Web site Bastianich described Buonavia as a "typical . . . red-sauce joint, with velvet wallpaper and fake paintings of Venice." The family later opened a second restaurant, Villa Seconda. Bastianich began working with his parents at an early age, washing dishes, hosing down the sidewalk in front of the restaurants, and accompanying his father to wholesale-meat markets. "I learned the business the old fashioned way. Full immersion. That's the Harvard MBA in restaurants. You learn from the ground up," he wrote.

The family visited Italy regularly, and those trips heightened Bastianich's passion for Italian food, wine, and culture. He became determined to follow in his parents' footsteps, a plan his mother and father did not encourage. Bastianich told Richard Bienstock for *Guitar Aficionado* (December 2008, on-line), "Their idea of success was to be something like an accountant or a dentist." (Bastianich was interviewed for that magazine because of his large collection of vintage guitars.)

In 1981 Bastianich's parents sold both of their Queens restaurants and launched their first Manhattan-based venture, Felidia. The restaurant, located not far from the U.N. building, in an expensive East Side neighborhood, quickly earned acclaim around the city. Lidia, who still runs Felidia, subsequently became a best-selling cookbook author and has hosted public-television cooking shows since the late 1990s. (Bastianich's parents divorced in 1997, at which point his father left the family business.) Bastianich worked at Felidia throughout his teens before enrolling at Boston College, in Massachusetts.

After graduating, in 1989, with a degree in political science and philosophy, Bastianich began to work on Wall Street as a corporate bond trader. He remained there for only a short time before returning to his family's restaurant business. He explained to Amy Zuber for *Nation's Restaurant News* (January 25, 1999), "The [Wall Street] work was interesting and rewarding, but at the same time it didn't offer the satisfaction that I got growing up in the restaurant environment. Working in the financial world, I felt a void without the interaction of making people happy through food and hospitality. So one day I just up and left."

At his mother's urging, after leaving Wall Street Bastianich spent a year in Italy. He wrote on his Web site, "I was a cellar rat, grape picker, waiter, cook, private driver—you name it. I met and worked with the people who embodied the very essence of Italian food and wine culture." The experience solidified his decision to become a restaurateur. He told Zuber, "At that point I realized that I had a natural affinity and love for wine and food and the culture of the Italian table as it relates to products and hospitality. But I didn't abandon the experience of Wall Street and how money is made in the world. I thought that ultimately if I could marry the two in some reasonable way, it could be the greatest fulfillment."

In 1991 Lidia lent Bastianich half of the $80,000 he needed to lease a brownstone on a then-unfashionable stretch of West 46th Street in Manhattan. He opened Becco, his first restaurant, in one part of the building and lived in another part. The 140-seat restaurant offered pasta served tableside and a prix-fixe wine list containing more than 100 selections, each costing $15 per bottle. Bastianich explained to Zuber, "What I found from my experience is that people would read wine lists from right to left and first find a price parameter before selecting a bottle. My goal was to take the price point out of the wine-making decision and therefore allow the customer to be able to freely choose wines that really pair with what they are eating." The idea for the wine list was considered groundbreaking, and it quickly won Becco a large following.

With the success of Becco, which has remained popular—thanks in part to its wine offerings, still reasonable at $25 per bottle—Bastianich was able to launch his second venture, Frico Bar, which opened in 1995. The 75-seat restaurant, located a few blocks from Becco, specializes in cuisine from the Friulian region of northwest Italy. In a review for the *New York Times* (January 5, 1996, on-line), Eric Asimov, who assessed inexpensive restaurants for the paper, wrote: "Becco, [Bastianich's] first restaurant, is a solid value with its offbeat prix fixe menu. Frico is an even better bargain. The name Frico refers to the house specialty, a torte from the Friulian region . . . , made of grilled Montasio, a cow's milk cheese, with stuffings like sausage, mushrooms and potatoes and onions. As a diet food, the frico . . . is a disaster. But it's delicious, rich and filling enough to be a small meal with a salad or plate of grilled vegetables. It's also typical of the casual delights of Frico Bar, where meals can range from informal soups and panini, or sandwiches, to small pizzas to complete meals."

In 1998 Bastianich teamed up with Mario Batali—then an up-and-coming chef and the founder of the acclaimed Italian restaurant Po—to open Babbo, an Italian restaurant in New York City's Greenwich Village. Bastianich told Richard Bienstock, "Babbo was about creating the restaurant of our dreams. We wanted to take what's good and right about the Italian table and transform it into a user-friendly format." Featuring a wide array of dishes made with offal, such as tripe alla parmigiana and beef-cheek ravioli, and an all-Italian wine list of more than 1,200 selections, Babbo opened to rave reviews and instantly became one of the most popular restaurants in New York City. It has been awarded three stars by the *New York Times* twice—first by Ruth Reichl in 1998 and then by Frank Bruni in 2004—and is one of the few Italian establishments in the city ever to garner that rating. Bruni wrote in his review, "Some restaurants revel in exquisite subtleties, while others simply go for the gut. Babbo, blessedly, hangs with the latter crowd." Babbo was named the best new restaurant of the year at the James Beard Awards ceremony in 1999, and it has since been credited with redefining Italian cuisine in New York City. Bastianich told Erica Duecy for *Nation's Restaurant News* (May 22, 2006, on-line) that Babbo had also "become the definitive place for Italian wines in America. It has kind of led the revolution of Italy both in the bottle and on the table." In 2006, a year in which Babbo brought in $8 million in revenue, it became one of the few Italian restaurants in the city to receive a star in the prestigious *Michelin Guide*.

Bastianich, who was concurrently helping his mother open restaurants in other cities, teamed with Batali again in 1999 to open Lupa Osteria Romana on Irving Place, a tony street in the Gramercy Park section of Manhattan. The following year they opened Esca ("bait" in Italian), a 70-seat restaurant in Midtown Manhattan that specializes in *crudo*, Italian-style raw fish. In 2003 the two opened both Otto Enoteca Pizzeria, a gourmet pizza parlor near Washington Square Park, and Casa Mono, a 35-seat taverna on Irving Place. Casa Mono, which marked their embrace of Spanish cuisine, received a two-star rating from the *New York Times* and was the highest-rated Spanish restaurant in the 2006 and 2007 editions of the *Zagat Guide*. It has also won acclaim for its wine list, which includes nearly 600 Spanish wines and has been honored with awards from *Wine Enthusiast* and *Wine Spectator* magazines. Next door to Casa Mono, Bastianich and Batali later opened Bar Jambon, which serves the flavorful appetizers and snacks known as tapas.

In early 2004 Bastianich became a partner in the Spotted Pig, a highly popular gastropub in Greenwich Village. He made a foray into French cuisine in 2005 with Bistro du Vent, but the restaurant, which was co-owned by Batali and David Pasternack, the chef at Esca, failed to take off and closed after 15 months. In a posting for the culinary Web site SlashFood.com (April 26, 2006), Nicole Weston wrote, "[The bistro] received reviews ranging from 'not bad' to 'deeply satisfying' and Frank Bruni gave it two stars, so the food isn't what is causing the [closure]." Quoting a *New York Post* piece, she theorized, "Its downfall was probably helped by the scandal that occurred last year, in which 'four employees—including a chef—were caught on [security] videotape in a steamy after-hours sex romp' in the restaurant. Though the employees were subsequently fired, it's not the sort of thing that necessarily enhances a restaurant's reputation." In late 2005 Bastianich, his mother, and Batali teamed up to open Del Posto ("of the place" in Italian), a 24,000-square-foot, 180-seat restaurant in the Chelsea section of New York City. According to David Savona, "Del Posto boasts one of the most opulent dining rooms in Manhattan, a grandiose main space with balconies overlooking the dining floor and a wide staircase in the middle. Marble and black mahogany are virtually everywhere." Awarding the restaurant three stars, Frank Bruni wrote for the *New York Times* (March 1, 2006, on-line), "Much has been said about the marble, mahogany and millions of dollars poured into Del Posto, but the risk that Mario Batali and Joseph Bastianich have taken with this grand Italian restaurant is best measured in the gutsy way they have defied what their fans expect. They have crumpled up page after page of the script that made their previous ventures so beloved and written a new libretto, emphasizing refined notes over rustic ones, sacrificing hip on the altar of elegant." Bruni continued, "Teaming for the first time with Mr. Bastianich's mother, Lidia, whose restaurant Felidia is a more relevant point of reference, the two men have challenged New Yorkers to accept Italian cuisine presented with fastidious rituals and opulent trappings usually reserved for French fare. . . . [Del Posto] has ample ethnic grounding in Italy's fancier restaurants. It also has something more important: mostly terrific food, distinguished by first-rate ingredients (the arugula here makes arugula at many other restaurants seem like iceberg in drag), clear flavors and, more often than not, superior cooking." Bruni's successor, Sam Sifton, awarded Del Posto four stars in 2010, making it the highest-rated Italian restaurant in the city in over three decades. Sifton wrote for the *New York Times* (September 29, 2010), "Del Posto's is a pleasure that lasts, offering memories of flavors that may return later in a dream." In 2007 Del Posto earned two stars in the *Michelin Guide*, making it the only Italian restaurant in New York City to earn more than one star.

In November 2006 Bastianich, Batali, and the chef Nancy Silverton opened Pizzeria Mozza in Los Angeles, and the following year the trio added a free-standing mozzarella bar, Osteria Mozza, to the upscale pizzeria; the two-part venture was nominated by the James Beard Foundation in 2007 as the best new restaurant. Also that year Bastianich and Batali opened B&B Ristorante and Enoteca Otto Pizzeria at the Venetian Hotel in Las Vegas. In a review of B&B for the travel section of the *Los Angeles Times* (July 25, 2007, on-line), S. Irene Virbila wrote, "In a city where ersatz is celebrated, in a hotel and casino where gondoliers float revelers down 'canals' filled with chlorine-puffing water, Batali and Bastianich have installed a restaurant that exudes Italian soul."

In 2008 Bastaniach and Batali opened their first steakhouse, Carnevino, at the Palazzo Hotel in Las Vegas. In the fall of that year, the two launched their first suburban venture, Tarry Lodge, in Port Chester, New York. Pointing out that Bastaniach and Batali were among "a few prominent New York chefs and restaurateurs [who] have been looking toward the northeastern suburbs lately," Colman Andrews wrote for *Gourmet* magazine (October 13, 2008, on-line), "The menu will remind Batali–Bastianich fans of the one at Otto. There's a large selection of cured meats and unusual seafood and vegetable antipasti (cuttlefish with chickpeas; shrimp with watermelon; an unusual and fairly addictive combination of *farro*, grilled corn, and pickled onions), a few other cold appetizers (like a wonderfully delicate *vitello tonnato*), pizzas both conventional and otherwise (from a classic Margherita to a delightful one with grilled scallions, *piquillo* peppers, and white anchovies), hearty pastas (the soupy *spaghetti alla carbonara*, missing the ample dusting of black pepper that defines the dish, needs work), and some serious main courses—among them a pyramid of mahogany-dark little lamb chops and a juicy grilled guinea hen with braised radicchio and oranges (described on the menu as chicken because, well, as our waitress said, 'This is Port Chester')."

In 2010 Bastianich joined his mother, Batali, and other partners to open the first U.S. branch of Eataly. (The original is in Torino, Italy.) The 50,000-square-foot marketplace, which includes an espresso bar, a cheese store, a wine shop, and a cooking school, among other amenities, caused considerable buzz even before it opened and has continued to be a source of excitement for the city's food enthusiasts. "Upon walking into Eataly," Jaya Saxena wrote for the *Gothamist* (August 25, 2010, on-line), "you might actually think you were in Italy. Besides the produce, nearly everything is imported, and the 50,000 sq. ft. bi-level space is filled with rows upon rows of dried pasta, nougat, olive oils and anchovies piled 12 feet high. You're welcomed with a smart espresso bar as the space opens into seven 'restaurants,' 14 food stations and a full 'piazza' with a raw bar, fresh-cut prosciutto and marble-top tables." Sam Sifton wrote for the *New York Times* (October 19, 2010, on-line), "It is giant and amazing, on its face, a circus maximus."

In addition to his restaurant ventures, Bastianich owns an upscale wine shop, Italian Wine Merchants, in New York, and he now owns three wineries in Italy. He purchased his first winery, which bears his family name, in the region of Friuli-Venezia Giulia in 1997, and his second, La Mozza, in southwest Tuscany in 2000. He purchased a third winery, Agricola Brandini, in the Piedmont region. He has emerged in recent years as a leading expert on Italian wines, co-authoring *Vino Italiano: The Regional Wines of Italy* (2002) and a companion volume, *Vino Italiano Buying Guide* (2004), with the food and wine writer David Lynch, who has worked at Babbo. (The buying guide was revised and updated in 2008.) Bastianich's third book, *Grandi Vini: An Opinionated Tour of Italy's 89 Finest Wines*, was published in 2010. That year he became a judge on the U.S. version of the televised cooking competition *MasterChef*, hosted by the celebrity chef Gordon Ramsay, which has been renewed for a second season.

Bastianich has received several honors; in 2005 he was named one of the world's most respected wine and spirits professionals by both the James Beard Foundation and *Bon Appetit* magazine, and in 2008 he and Batali shared the James Beard Foundation's award for outstanding restaurateur. Those accolades notwithstanding, Bastianich prefers to remain in the background of his food and wine empire. He explained to Edward Lewine for the *New York Times* (September 23, 2010, on-line), "I am Lidia's son and Mario's partner and Gordon Ramsay's judge, and I am good with that."

Bastianich lives in Greenwich, Connecticut, with his wife, Deanna, and their three children: Olivia, Miles, and Ethan. He is an avid guitar player and amateur opera singer. After being diagnosed several years ago with sleep apnea caused by being overweight, Bastianich dropped 45 pounds and began running seriously. When he was preparing to run the 2008 New York City Marathon, Christine Yi quipped for the *New York Times* (October 27, 2008, on-line), "As a first-time marathoner with modest goals, he will not be in contention [to win the race]. But if he completes [the full] 26.2 miles . . . perhaps Bastianich should win something for defying the usual culinary doldrums of marathon training and instead finding his way to the finish line on a diet of rib-eyes, cured pig jowl and even Dom Perignon."

—C.C.

Suggested Reading: *Cigar Aficionado* (on-line) Feb. 2007; *Food & Wine* (on-line) July 2004; *Gothamist* (on-line) Aug. 25, 2010; *Gourmet* (on-line) Oct. 13, 2008; *Guitar Aficionado* (on-line) Dec. 2008; *Los Angeles Times* (on-line) July 25, 2007, July 27, 2010; *Nation's Restaurant News* p14 Jan. 25, 1999, (on-line) May 22, 2006; *New York Times* F p1+ Dec. 7, 2005, D p1+ Sep. 29, 2010, (on-line) Jan. 5, 1996, June 9, 2004, Mar. 1, 2006, Oct. 27, 2008, Sep. 23, 2010, Oct. 19, 2010; *Westchester* (on-line) July 2008

Selected Books: *Vino Italiano: The Regional Wines of Italy* (with David Lynch), 2002; *Vino Italiano Buying Guide* (with David Lynch), 2004; *Grandi Vini: An Opinionated Tour of Italy's 89 Finest Wines*, 2010

Batali, Mario

Sep. 19, 1960– Chef; restaurateur; television personality; cookbook writer

Address: Babbo Ristorante e Enoteca, 110 Waverly Pl., New York, NY 10011-9109

Mario Batali joined the pantheon of celebrity chefs in 1996, when he became the host of *Molto Mario*, a cooking show that aired on the Food Network for eight years. "Molto" is Italian for "very" or "very much," and since his television debut, Batali has remained very much in the public eye. He has done so as one of the winningest chefs on the TV cooking series *Iron Chef America*; as a restaurateur who founded such award-winning eating places as Babbo and Esca, in New York City, and now co-owns 18 restaurants and counting; and as the author of nine cookbooks, including one—*Molto Italiano: 327 Simple Italian Recipes to Cook at Home*—that the James Beard Foundation named the best international cookbook of 2005. *Spain . . . A Culinary Road Trip* (2008) was published in association with his most recent television series, *Spain . . . On the Road Again*, which aired on PBS as a 13-part record of his travels with the American actress Gwyneth Paltrow, who co-authored the book, the food writer Mark Bittman, and the Spanish actress Claudia Bassols.

Usually dressed in his signature orange clogs and khaki shorts, with his thinning, carrot-colored hair pulled back in a ponytail, Batali "became a rock-star chef by pushing modern Italian food to the three-star level," Christine Muhlke wrote for

Stephen Lovekin/Getty Images

the *New York Times Book Review* (June 6, 2010), in an assessment of *Molto Gusto: Easy Italian Cooking*. (The book's co-author, Mark Ladner, is the executive chef of Batali's restaurant Del Posto.) Although Batali visits each of his New York restaurants several times a week, he no longer works hands-on in the kitchens of any of them; according to a statement posted on his Web site, "A great chef is a great cook who can also organize and operate a business or kitchen." "The chef is the guy who directs the cooks, and who also knows how much the toilet paper costs and how to calculate when you need to repaint," he explained to John Heilemann for *New York* (September 21, 2008). In New York City in mid-2010, in partnership with the restaurateur and wine expert Joseph Bastianich, the television chef, writer, and restaurateur Lidia Matticchio Bastianich, and the Turin, Italy–based entrepreneur Oscar Farinetti, Batali opened the 50,000-square-foot Eataly, billed by the Batali-Bastianich Hospitality Group as "the largest artisanal Italian food and wine marketplace in the world." "My restaurants are always full," Batali remarked to Heilemann, "my businesses do well, my books sell well, the events I do are well attended. And there's very little downside. No one chases me down the street." He also said, "When people ask, 'How are you, man?,' I say, 'Life is a constant source of joy, every breath a gift!' . . . It sounds like crap. But it isn't crap. It's my life."

The first of the three children of Armandino and Marilyn Batali, the chef was born Mario Francis Batali on September 19, 1960 in Yakima, Washington. (He has changed his middle name to "Francesco.") His mother is of French-Canadian and English descent; his father's ancestors were Italian. A store opened by his paternal great-grandparents in Seattle, Washington, in 1903 that sold imported Italian foods remained in the family for six decades. Batali's father, a Boeing Co. engineer, enjoyed hunting, butchering meat, and cooking. "Our idea of a rainy-day event was making 200 pounds of sausage," Mario Batali recalled to Kate Krader for *Food & Wine* (June 1998, on-line). He told Andy Battaglia for *Nation's Restaurant News* (September 6, 1999), "When blackberries were in season, we would go . . . and pick for seven or eight hours and then come home and make jam and pies. We'd freeze enough to last a whole year." Batali's father and mother, a nurse, raised Mario and his brother, Dana (born in 1961), and sister, Gina (born in 1965), in a Seattle suburb until about 1974, when Boeing transferred his father to Madrid, Spain; the whole family followed him there, and Mario attended a Madrid high school. After Armandino Batali retired from Boeing, he studied the science of curing meat and in 1999 opened a shop and restaurant, Salumi Artisan Cured Meats, in Seattle; currently, Gina Batali and her husband run Salumi. Dana Batali is a software engineer with Pixar Animation Studios.

In 1978 Mario Batali enrolled at Rutgers College, a division of the State University of New Jersey. He concentrated in both Spanish theater and economics (or finance or business management, according to various sources). As an undergraduate he found a job as a dishwasher at Stuff Yer Face, a popular off-campus restaurant, where he was soon promoted from prep cook to line cook. During his junior year he abandoned his idea of entering the banking industry and began to consider pursuing a career as a chef. After his graduation, in 1982, he enrolled at the branch of the famous cooking school Le Cordon Bleu in London, England, where his father was then posted. He attended classes during the day; at night he worked as a bartender at the Six Bells, a London pub. In 1983, when the pub owner opened an upscale restaurant on the premises, Batali left Le Cordon Bleu—"It just wasn't as intensive as I would have liked," he told Battaglia—and got a job as the assistant to the Six Bells' chef, the British up-and-comer Marco Pierre White. White "really looked at preparing food from outside the box," he told Bill Buford for the *New Yorker* (August 19–26, 2002). "He was a genius on the plate. I'd never worked on presentation. I just put s[tuff] on the plate." (Buford's account of his experiences as an assistant in one of Batali's restaurants appears in both the *New Yorker* article and his 2007 book, *Heat*.) The fiercely demanding, volatile White often lashed out at Batali; once, infuriated by the consistency of some hot risotto, he threw a plate of it at him. Batali left Six Bells after four months.

Next, having decided—despite his conflicts with White—that cooking is best learned in the kitchens of experts rather than in the classroom, Batali secured a series of jobs in well-respected British and continental European restaurants. Among other establishments, he worked at the Waterside Inn, in Bray, near London; in France he worked at La Tour d'Argent, in Paris, and Le Moulin de Mougins, in a Côte d'Azur hotel. At each he stayed only a month or two. After he returned to the U.S., in 1985, he settled in San Francisco, California, and began working with a catering firm. Within six months Batali was hired as sous chef at the restaurant of the venerable Clift Hotel, in San Francisco's Union Square. After work he and his kitchen mates discussed culinary philosophies at the upscale restaurant Stars, which the chef Jeremiah Tower had opened in 1984. Tower had worked with Alice Waters, the founder of Chez Panisse, and he and Waters became known as originators of so-called California cuisine, which emphasizes the use of fresh, locally grown or produced foods and their artful preparation and presentation. Batali has cited Stars as a major influence in his development as a chef.

After two years at the Clift, Batali accepted an offer to oversee La Marina, the restaurant of the Biltmore Hotel in Santa Barbara, California, which Four Seasons Hotels Ltd. had acquired in 1987. Despite his exceptionally high salary, he soon felt "restless," he has said, and he left within a year. Eager to learn how to cook the sorts of dishes he had enjoyed at the table of his paternal grandmother, he resolved to continue his culinary education in Italy. In exchange for room and board, he became an apprentice at La Volta, in Borgo Capanne, an Appenine Mountain village in northern Italy. La Volta was managed by Gianni Valdiserri, who co-owned it with his brother Roberto, an engineer whom Batali's father knew. Its chef, Gianni's wife, Betta, used produce grown by her father and wild edibles that her father found in local woods. "I knew that first week, once I saw the food, that I'd made the right move," Batali told Buford. "The food was traditional. Very simple. No sauces, no steam tables, no pans of stock, none of the things I'd learned to do. This was exactly what I'd hoped for." He told Andy Battaglia that at La Volta he learned "what not to put on the plate. Italian food is about two or three textures or flavors coming together . . . not putting together a symphony of nine very strange ingredients, but two or three separate things and allowing them to sing." Although he often felt painfully lonely in Borgo Capanne, Batali remained at La Volta for about three years.

Back in the U.S. Batali formed a partnership with Arturo Sighinolfi, a close friend of his from Rutgers, and became the co-owner of Rocco, a 70-year-old Italian-American restaurant in the Greenwich Village section of Manhattan. The restaurant had been run for many years by Sighinolfi's father, who was retiring. After a modest renovation Rocco reopened in 1992, with Batali as chef and Arturo Sighinolfi as front man. Batali's cooking differed from what Rocco's longtime customers had grown to expect, and many of them stopped coming. As business declined, relations between Batali and Sighinolfi grew increasingly acrimonious, and after nine months the partnership ended.

In late 1993, with the help of a loan from his future wife, Batali and his friend Steven Crane opened Pó, an Italian restaurant in Greenwich Village. Crane, a chef, served as Pó's dining-room manager, while Batali presided over the kitchen. Through admiring reviews and word of mouth, the restaurant gained an enthusiastic clientele. Batali, meanwhile, had attracted the attention of representatives of the recently launched Food Network. His first show, *Molto Mario*, debuted on that network in 1996 and soon attracted a loyal following; it remained on the air until 2004. "*Molto Mario* was probably the most intelligent cooking show on the network," the pseudonymous Anaximenes wrote for his blog Greek Notion (June 30, 2009), "and took the viewer through a vast realm of new, exciting foods from Italy, light years beyond that which most Americans even understood as Italian food." In his second show, *Mediterranean Mario*, which ran for only one season, in 1998, Batali combined cooking with geography lessons, using a huge map to point out areas famous for particular dishes. By that time, William Grimes wrote for the *New York Times* (December 6, 1998), viewers regarded him as "the Bob Vila of chefs"—a reference to a television expert on house renovation.

Also in 1998 Batali published his first cookbook, *Simple Italian Food: Recipes from My Two Villages* ("villages" referring to Borgo Capanne and Greenwich Village). "In true Italian fashion," Grimes wrote, "Batali blends rigor and insouciance. He describes his food as 'Italian in sensibility, but made of local ingredients—some never used in classical Italian cooking.' He likes big flavors. He dislikes fuss and bother. If he can get away with using three ingredients, he won't tack on a fourth. This pared-down, workmanlike approach to Italian food . . . makes *Simple Italian Food* immensely appealing and endlessly useful." After describing one recipe as "ridiculously easy to make and almost impossible to stop eating," Grimes wrote, "That's the way it goes throughout the book" and concluded, "No tricks here, just brilliance."

By that time, in partnership with Joe Bastianich, Batali had opened a second Italian restaurant in Greenwich Village, called Babbo Ristorante e Enoteca ("babbo" meaning "daddy," and "enoteca" meaning "wine bar"). In a highly laudatory assessment for the *New York Times* (June 26, 1998), Ruth Reichl, after acknowledging that she was "not a big fan of Pó," wrote that Babbo's decor and menu were "simple and appealing." "Still, I was not prepared for the sheer deliciousness of the first dish I tasted," she continued: "warm house-cured anchovies in a vinaigrette. The flavors were deep, the tang of the vinegar edged with the taste of lemon peel. It was wonderful. So was a special pasta with sheep's milk cheese and broccoli [rabe] that had just the right degree of bitterness. But the big event of the evening was two-minute spicy squid, a big, robust bowl of tomato-drenched seafood that is supposedly eaten by Italian lifeguards. Lucky them. Much of the food is rustic. Desserts, on the other hand, move in the opposite direction. Who would imagine that a tiny portion of saffron panna cotta topped with peaches, served in a tiny portion, could be so deeply satisfying?" Reichl awarded Babbo three stars—the *Times*'s designation for "excellent"—and the James Beard Foundation named it the best new restaurant of 1998.

In 1999 *GQ* magazine named Batali Man of the Year in the chef category. That year he and Bastianich opened Lupa Osteria Romana, a Roman-style trattoria, in Greenwich Village. In 2000, in partnership with David Pasternack, the men launched Esca ("bait"), which specializes in fish dishes from southern Italy; Esca is located in Midtown Manhattan, with Pasternack as chef. In that capacity Pasternack was honored as the best chef in the U.S. by the James Beard Foundation in 2004, and in 2007 the *New York Times* restaurant critic Frank Bruni awarded Esca three stars. "After eating at Esca repeatedly" for three years, Bruni wrote for the *Times* (April 18, 2007), it seemed to him that the restaurant "keeps getting better." Does Pasternack "enjoy some preternatural rapport with the sea's creatures, an extrasensory insight into which [ones] might benefit from a raw appointment with coarse salt and which are fated for frying? Can he tease out their greatest performances? On the evidence of Esca, I'd have to say yes," Bruni wrote, and he added that the restaurant's "straightforwardness," "air of conviviality," and "Mediterranean orientation" "link it to other Batali-Bastianich productions."

In addition to Babbo and Lupa Osteria Romana, those other "productions" are Casa Mono, Bar Jamón, Del Posto (in partnership with Bastianich's mother, Lidia Matticchio Bastianich), Otto Enoteca

Pizzeria, and Eataly, in New York City; Tarry Lodge, in Port Chester, a New York City suburb; B&B Ristorante, Carnevino Italian Steakhouse, and Otto Enoteca Pizzeria, in Las Vegas, Nevada; and Pizzeria Mozza, Osteria Mozza, and Mozza2Go (all with the multi-award-winning baker and restaurateur Nancy Silverton as partner), in Los Angeles, California. Batali has maintained that he spends at least one hour at each of his New York City restaurants two or three times weekly, and that all the items on their menus are prepared according to recipes and techniques agreed upon at meetings he holds regularly with their chefs and other staff members. Batali's association with Pó ended in 2000, after years of conflict, when Crane, presented with the choice of selling his share in Pó to Batali or buying Batali's share, agreed to the latter. "It was like someone putting his name on your first baby," Batali told Buford with seemingly still-fresh chagrin.

In an interview with Andrea Chang for the *Los Angeles Times* (September 20, 2009), Batali said that he and his partners try to make sure that meals in their restaurants are "fairly priced." He and Joe Bastianich have been working to make all their properties "green," by composting and using energy-efficient lights and appliances and products sold by entrepreneurs who adhere to sustainable ways of farming; their restaurants do not offer bottled water. On the June 14, 2010 installment of the *Charlie Rose Show*, Batali—who suffered a brain aneurism and underwent emergency surgery in 1999—advocated eating not only natural rather than processed foods and maintaining a balanced diet but also eating smaller portions. The five-foot 11-inch Batali weighed 240 pounds a decade ago; according to Joyce Wadler, writing for the *New York Times* (December 27, 2000), he told Rose that one day he decided, "I don't want to look like that next week." He then began to reduce his portions to half of what he had previously consumed.

Widely described as unusually unpretentious, Batali married Susan Cahn in 1994. The couple live with their sons, Benno and Leo, in Greenwich Village, and they vacation in their house on a Lake Michigan bay. The boys' births, in the late 1990s, inspired the name of the restaurant Babbo. The Batalis spend all day every Sunday together. In New York City Batali travels everywhere on one of his several Vespa scooters. The Mario Batali Foundation, founded in 2008, is dedicated to hunger relief and children's charities.

—H.R.W.

Suggested Reading: *Crain's New York Business* Special Issue A p84+ June 6–12, 2005; *Esquire* p130+ May 2004; *Harvard Business Review* p132 May 2010; *Los Angeles Times* (on-line) Sep. 20, 2009; Mario Batali Web site; *Nation's Restaurant News* p36 Sep. 6, 1999, p10+ Jan. 27, 2003; *New York* (on-line) Sep. 21, 2008; *New Yorker* p122+ Aug. 19–26, 2002; *People* p85+ Nov, 2, 1998; *Time* p66+ Apr. 10, 2006; Buford, Bill. *Heat: An*

Amateur's Adventures as Kitchen Slave, Line Cook, Pasta-Maker, and Apprentice to a Dante-Quoting Butcher in Tuscany, 2007

Selected Books: *Simple Italian Food: Recipes from My Two Villages*, 1998; *Mario Batali Holiday Food*, 2000; *The Babbo Cookbook*, 2002; *Vino Italiano: The Regional Wines of Italy* (with Joseph Bastianich, David Lynch, and Lidia Bastianich), 2002; *Molto Italiano: 327 Simple Italian Recipes to Cook at Home*, 2005; *Mario Tailgates NASCAR Style*, 2006; *Italian Grill* (with Judith Sutton), 2008; *Spain . . . a Culinary Road Trip* (with Gwyneth Paltrow), 2008; *Molto Gusto: Easy Italian Cooking at Home* (with Mark Ladner), 2010

Selected Television Shows: *Molto Mario*, 1996–2004; *Mediterranean Mario*, 1998; *Iron Chef America: The Series*, 2005–10; *Spain . . . On the Road Again*, 2008

Frederick M. Brown/Getty Images

Bautista, Jose

Oct. 19, 1980– Baseball player

Address: Toronto Blue Jays, Rogers Centre, 1 Blue Jays Way, Suite 3200, Toronto, Ontario M5V 1J1, Canada

The Toronto Blue Jays' outfielder Jose Bautista, Bruce Arthur wrote for the Toronto *National Post* (September 11, 2010), is "baseball's equivalent of Kurt Warner." "He's been discarded and dismissed," Arthur noted, "Rule 5-ed and waived, purchased and traded and thrown away by such disreputable and desperate outfits as the Baltimore Orioles, the Kansas City Royals, the New York Mets, and the Pittsburgh Pirates. Twice. And now, he's a star." Like Warner, a former professional quarterback who famously stocked shelves at an Iowa grocery store and toiled in the Arena Football League for several years before making his mark in the National Football League, where he won two league Most Valuable Player (MVP) awards and played in three Super Bowls, the Dominican-born Bautista is a highly celebrated late bloomer. He was drafted by the Pittsburgh Pirates in the 2000 Major League Baseball (MLB) amateur draft and then spent three seasons in the Pirates' farm system before being claimed by the Baltimore Orioles in the 2003 Rule 5 draft, which protects talented players from languishing in farm systems. Bautista made his MLB debut with the Orioles in 2004 but was waived from the team shortly afterward, and in the space of a year he served brief stints with the Tampa Bay Rays, the Kansas City Royals, and the New York Mets before finishing his rollercoaster rookie campaign back with the Pirates; he is the only player in history to be a member of five major-league organizations in a single season. After spending four seasons with the Pirates, during which he posted modest numbers while playing positions in both the outfield and infield, Bautista was traded to the Toronto Blue Jays. He has since transformed himself from an obscure utility player to one of baseball's most feared home-run hitters. He overhauled his swing and overall approach at the plate during the 2009 season, which saw him bat just .235 with 13 home runs, 10 of them in the final 27 games of the season. He then carried his late-season home-run barrage into 2010, when he led the majors with 54 home runs—setting a new Blue Jays' single-season home-run benchmark, breaking a major-league record for the highest single-season home-run increase (among players with at least 400 at-bats in previous years), and becoming the first player to top the 50-home-run mark since 2007. Also in 2010 he was named to the All-Star team for the first time in his career and finished fourth in the American League (AL) MVP voting. He earned his second consecutive All-Star selection in 2011, when he broke the record for All-Star votes for a single player with 7.4 million, after going into the midseason break leading the majors in several statistical categories. Commenting on his career renaissance in Toronto, Bautista told Robert Mac-Leod for the Toronto *Globe and Mail* (September 24, 2010), "It's been a long journey. But I think the most important thing was that I came to this organization in the critical point of my career. I needed another chance and I found it here." Cito Gaston, who retired as the Blue Jays' manager after the 2010 season, told Seth Livingstone for *USA Today* (September 17, 2010) about Bautista, "I believed in him because he showed me he believed in himself."

Named for his mother's father, Jose Antonio Bautista was born on October 19, 1980 in Santo Domingo, the capital of and largest city in the Dominican Republic. He has a younger brother, Luis, with whom he has always been very close. Unlike many Dominican-born ballplayers, who were raised in poverty and played baseball on makeshift fields with homemade gloves, Bautista grew up in a middle-class family that stressed the importance of education. Both of his parents, Americo and Sandra, held master's degrees and enjoyed successful careers in business; his father ran a large poultry farm, and his mother was an accountant. Bautista attended private schools as a child and adolescent, excelling in math and the sciences, and during after-school hours he helped his father with various tasks on the farm.

Bautista, like most of his peers, developed a love of baseball early on, and he started playing the game at the age of five. He told a writer for the *Toronto Star* (June 18, 2011) that playing baseball "was the only thing [he] wanted" as a boy. By the age of eight, Bautista had reportedly memorized the stats of every active major-league player. He developed his baseball skills by spending hours each day playing with his brother and a group of friends; they also played soccer, basketball, and other sports. Despite his small size he quickly stood out among his peers not only for his talent but also for his tireless work ethic. Bautista recalled for another *Toronto Star* (August 17, 2010) article, "I wasn't a power-hitting guy. I was a leadoff hitter and speedy."

Bautista began to fill out physically in his teens. During that time he started sending to U.S. major-league scouts VHS tapes of himself playing baseball. While that approach brought no attractive offers from the pros, he won a scholarship to Chipola Community College, in Marianna, Florida, where he studied business. In his time there he became a standout on the baseball team, and following an impressive 2000 campaign, he was selected by the Pittsburgh Pirates in the 20th round of that year's MLB draft, with a signing bonus of $50,000, which increased to $600,000 the following year. In 2001 he began his professional career with the Williamsport Crosscutters, the Pirates' short-season affiliate in the single-A New York–Penn League, finishing third on the team in home runs (with five) and tied for fourth in runs batted in, or RBIs, with 30. Bautista then spent all of the 2002 season with the organization's single-A affiliate in Hickory, North Carolina, the Hickory Crawdads of the South Atlantic League, with whom he made appearances at multiple positions, including third base, shortstop, and designated hitter. That year he finished 10th in the South Atlantic League in batting average (.301) and was selected to participate in the league's midseason All-Star Game; he also ranked eighth among Pirates' farm prospects in extra base hits (43), tenth in homers (14), and fourth in on-base percentage (.402). Tony Beasley, who managed Bautista in his first two minor-league seasons and later became the Pirates' third-base coach, described him to Charlie Gillis for *Maclean's* (April 11, 2011) as "a perfectionist among perfectionists," with a tendency to get upset over insignificant things, adding, "There were times I had to take him out of games and sit with him on the bench and say, dude, you got three hits today and lined out in your fourth at-bat."

Bautista began the 2003 season playing with the rookie-level Gulf Coast League Pirates, batting .348 in seven games before being promoted to the Lynchburg Hillcats of the Carolina League, in Lynchburg, Virginia, the organization's advanced single-A affiliate. He appeared in only 51 games, batting .242 with four home runs, before breaking his hand. After being sidelined for two months, Bautista returned for the Carolina League play-offs, in which he batted an impressive .375. Nonetheless, because of the Pirates' large number of talented prospects, he was left off the organization's 40-man roster after the season, and in December 2003 he was acquired by the Baltimore Orioles in the annual Rule 5 draft. (Players picked in the draft not only become members of their new teams' 40-man rosters in extended spring training but also must be kept on the teams' 25-man active rosters all season; otherwise they must be returned to the teams from which they were acquired.)

After reporting to the Orioles in 2004 for spring training, the 23-year-old Bautista earned a roster spot as backup to the team's starting third baseman, the All-Star Melvin Mora. He made his MLB debut on April 4, 2004, in a game against the Boston Red Sox, appearing as a pinch runner in the game and scoring his first career run. On April 7 Bautista made his first big-league plate appearance, in another contest against the Red Sox, and singled off the pitcher Ramiro Mendoza for his first major-league hit. He appeared in just 16 games with the Orioles, batting .273 with no home runs or RBIs in 11 at-bats, before being waived by the team. (According to Charlie Gillis, Bautista was waived at the urging of the Orioles' temperamental owner, Peter Angelos, after making an error while playing right field.) The next day Bautista was picked up by the Tampa Bay Rays, with whom he remained for less than a month before being traded to the Kansas City Royals. Then, after appearing in 13 games with the Royals, he was traded to the New York Mets, who dealt him back to the Pirates on the same day. Bautista finished out his whirlwind rookie year with the Pirates, hitting only .200 with 18 strikeouts in 40 at-bats; in 64 games overall that year, he posted a paltry .205 batting average with no home runs and two RBIs. Commenting on his rookie-year odyssey, Bautista, who earned the dubious distinction of becoming the first player in history to appear on five different major-league rosters in one season, told Jeff Blair for the *Globe and Mail* (September 18, 2010), "For somebody in A-ball like I was, without a lot of experience, the Rule 5 experience can be hard. The results weren't there for me, but I learned a lot of things. I got to

see how guys went about their business, and how they really trusted their coaches and each other—how they used reports, video and all that stuff. They don't have video in the minors."

Bautista spent most of the 2005 season in the minors. He began the year with the Pirates' double-A affiliate in Altoona, Pennsylvania, the Altoona Curve of the Eastern League, a move that reunited him with the manager Tony Beasley. Equipped with a better grasp of the game, Bautista enjoyed a breakout year with the club, batting .283 with 23 home runs and 90 RBIs, before being promoted to the Indianapolis Indians, in the triple-A International League. After 13 games with the Indians, he earned a late-season call-up to the Pirates, with whom he saw limited action, appearing in 11 games and hitting .143 in 28 at-bats. Bautista returned to the Indians to start the 2006 season but was recalled to the Pirates after 29 games. He remained in Pittsburgh for the rest of the year and finished his first full season in the majors with a .235 batting average, 16 home runs, and 51 RBIs in 117 games. Throughout the year Bautista was mainly a utility player, appearing at five different positions for the Pirates: center field, designated hitter, left field, third base, and second base. To date, Bautista has made big-league appearances at every position except shortstop, catcher, and pitcher. He is known for having one of the strongest arms among position players, with the ability to throw base runners out from all parts of the outfield; in addition, if he were needed in an emergency pitching situation, he could throw consistently in the 90-mile-per-hour range.

Bautista expected to serve again as the Pirates' utility man during the 2007 season, mainly as a backup to the team's starting third baseman, Freddy Sanchez, who had earned his first career All-Star selection and had led the National League (NL) in batting (.344) in 2006. However, Sanchez replaced Jose Castillo at second base in spring training, and Bautista became the Pirates' starter at third. In his first year as an everyday player, he set personal bests in most statistical categories, batting .254 with 15 home runs and 63 RBIs in 142 games. In 122 starts at third that year, he had a .958 fielding percentage, which was good for fifth among NL third basemen; he also made 13 starts in right field, four in center field, and one in left field. Prior to the 2008 season, Bautista signed a one-year, $1.8 million contract with the Pirates to avoid arbitration.

In 2008 Bautista hoped to solidify his role as an everyday player for the Pirates, but he was inconsistent and eventually gave up his starting job to Andy LaRoche, who had been acquired from the Los Angeles Dodgers at the 2008 trade deadline. That year Bautista appeared in 107 games for the Pirates, batting .242 with 12 home runs and 44 RBIs, before being optioned down to triple-A Indianapolis. After performing well in five games with the Indians, in which he batted .300 in 20 at-bats, Bautista was traded to the Toronto Blue Jays for the catching prospect Robinson Diaz. In 21 games with the Blue Jays, he batted .214 with three home runs and 10 RBIs, while playing at several infield positions and making several starts as designated hitter.

During the 2009 season Bautista began working with the Jays' hitting coach, Dwayne Murphy, on his swing mechanics and approach to the plate. "I had some holes in my swing," he told Seth Livingstone. "I was getting ready too late, and the ball was beating me in the zone. I kept fouling off fastballs and I was too early on breaking balls. I was a more vulnerable hitter, and pitchers took advantage." Under Murphy's instruction Bautista went into action earlier with his hands, during the pitcher's delivery, rather than relying on his shoulders, an approach that had made him swing late routinely. He also devoted more time to studying the tendencies of opposing pitchers. Bautista, who during his first five seasons in the majors was almost exclusively a guess hitter—one who goes to the plate with the intention of guessing what the pitcher will throw given the situation—explained to the *Toronto Star* writer (June 18, 2011), "I don't have enough ability to just go up there and naturally hit without having this information [about pitchers' tendencies] in my head. I need all of this in order to be successful." Bautista did not see the effects of his adjustments until the second half of the 2009 season. At that point the Blue Jays traded Scott Rolen to the Cincinnati Reds, and then, shortly afterward, the Jays' All-Star right fielder Alex Rios went to the Chicago White Sox. Those vacancies allowed Bautista to become a regular starter for the Jays, and in the final 27 games of the season, he hit 10 home runs—tying for the major-league lead in homers for the month of September, with eight, before adding two more in October—with 21 RBIs. He finished the year batting .235 with 13 home runs and 40 RBIs.

Following his late-season power surge in 2009, Bautista entered the 2010 season with a great deal expected of him. He responded by putting up some of the best offensive numbers in Blue Jays history. Bautista led the majors and set a franchise record with 54 home runs (surpassing George Bell's 47 homers of 1987) and also led the majors in extra base hits (92) and tied for first in total bases (351). In addition, he finished among the AL leaders in other offensive categories, ranking second in walks (100) and third in RBIs (125), slugging percentage (.617), and on-base plus slugging percentage, or OPS (.995). Bautista became the 26th player in history to belt 50 or more home runs in a season and the first player to accomplish that feat since Alex Rodriguez and Prince Fielder in 2007; moreover, he set the MLB record for biggest single-season increase in home runs (among players with at least 400 at-bats in past years) with 41, passing Davey Johnson's increase of 38 in 1973. He earned his first career All-Star selection and won consecutive AL Player of the Month awards, in July and August. Serving mostly in right field, where he made 113 of his 161 starts, Bautista performed solidly on defense and finished in a tie for second in outfield assists, with 12. While his unexpected power output immediately drew speculation about possible steroid use, Bautista denied using performance-enhancing drugs. "I understand [the question] because of . . . what happened in the past," he told reporters after hitting his 50th home run of the season, as quoted by Jon Krawczynski for the Associated Press (October 2, 2010). "Those days are gone. It's been six years since we have a new [drug-testing] program in place. It seems to be working. It's the most strict in all of professional sports. I don't see why those questions really come up. The only reason why is the history of what happened in the past." That speculation notwithstanding, Bautista was recognized for his record-breaking accomplishments, finishing fourth in the AL MVP voting and winning the AL Hank Aaron Award as the most outstanding offensive performer in the league. He also won an AL Silver Slugger Award as an outfielder, becoming the 22d Blue Jay to claim that honor.

Bautista, who signed a five-year, $65 million contract extension with the Blue Jays during the 2011 off-season, has continued to silence his detractors. He began the 2011 season by winning consecutive Player of the Month awards, for April and May, after hitting a combined 20 home runs with 38 RBIs. He was then selected as one of the starting outfielders for the AL at the 2011 All-Star Game after receiving an MLB-record 7.4 million votes, shattering Ken Griffey Jr.'s record of six million votes in 1994; he also participated in the 2011 MLB Home Run Derby. As of early September 2011, Bautista was leading the majors in home runs (40), walks (110), slugging percentage (.632), and OPS (1.076) and ranked fourth in runs (96).

In addition to his hitting power, Bautista has drawn attention for his beard. "He can grow it back in two days, a full beard in two days, it's unreal," his former teammate Vernon Wells, now a member of the Los Angeles Angels of Anaheim, told the *Toronto Star* writer (August 17, 2010). Bautista is fluent in Spanish and English and enjoys shopping for clothes in his spare time. He spends his off-seasons in Santo Domingo, where he trains and catches up with friends and family members. On April 6, 2011 Bautista and his longtime girlfriend, Neisha Croyle, became the parents of a daughter, Estela Marie.

—C.C.

Suggested Reading: *Maclean's* p56+ Apr. 11, 2011; *New York Times* D p1 Apr. 30, 2011; (Ottawa, Ontario, Canada) *Citizen* C p1 Sep. 5, 2010; (Toronto, Ontario, Canada) *Globe and Mail* S p1 Sep. 18, 2010, S p1 Sep. 24, 2010; (Toronto, Ontario, Canada) *National Post* S p1 Sep. 11, 2010, S p1 Mar. 31, 2011; (Toronto, Ontario, Canada) *Star* S p1 Aug. 17, 2010, S p1 Apr. 21, 2011, S p1 June 18, 2011; *USA Today* C p4 Sep. 17, 2010

Elsa/Getty Images

Beckett, Josh

May 15, 1980– Baseball player

Address: Boston Red Sox, 4 Yawkey Way, Boston, MA 02215-3496

Josh Beckett is one of a long line of Texas-born pitchers who have become big names in Major League Baseball (MLB). Many rookie players might consider following in the footsteps of such Texas natives as the Hall of Famer Nolan Ryan, the celebrated Roger Clemens, and the former high-school sensations Todd Van Poppel and Kerry Wood a daunting challenge, but since Beckett was a teenager, he has exhibited confidence well beyond his years. Shortly after being selected in the first round of the 1999 draft by the Florida Marlins, Beckett made many grand claims about his future, including a prediction that he would play in the 2001 All-Star Game. "I ain't done nothing yet, but hopefully I'll join [Ryan and Clemens] maybe in the Hall [of Fame] one day," he told Mike Berardino for the Fort Lauderdale, Florida, *Sun Sentinel* (June 3, 1999). "I think one day I will be able to live up to all that, I really do. . . . I'm a confident guy. You've got to have some arrogance to be a professional pitcher." Though Beckett did not appear in the 2001 All-Star Game (he made his first All-Star appearance in 2007 and his second in 2009), he has not disappointed fans and teammates. Despite suffering from numerous injuries—including shoulder tendonitis and recurring, disabling blisters on the middle finger of his pitching hand—Beckett is one of the most valuable pitchers in professional baseball. During more than eight full seasons in the major leagues, he has wowed coaches and opposing batters with a pitching repertoire that includes an almost three-digit-mile-per-hour (mph) fastball, a hard-breaking curveball with mph speeds in the mid-80s, a sinker clocked in the mid-90s, and a speedy changeup that has consistently frustrated batters. In 2003 he helped the Marlins win their second World Series championship since the franchise's inception, and in 2007 Beckett—who was traded to the Boston Red Sox in 2006—helped that team win its second World Series title in four years.

The second of three sons, Joshua Patrick Beckett was born on May 15, 1980 in Spring, a town in southeastern Texas, to John and Lynn Beckett. He excelled as a pitcher in Little League, and as early as his freshman year at Spring High School, he was already considered a major contender for the big leagues. Beckett had an immature attitude, however, which, along with poor grades, kept him on the bench of the junior-varsity team for most of his freshman season. In an effort to motivate him to take his future seriously, the school's varsity baseball coach, Kenny Humphreys, who had recognized Beckett's talent, told the young player that he was suspended indefinitely. Beckett, actually suspended for only three days, was affected by Humphreys's scare tactic. His attitude and grades soon improved, and as a result, Humphreys thrust him into a leadership role. At the end of Beckett's freshman year, Humphreys wrote for an MLB scouting report, as quoted by Al Carter in the *Dallas Morning News* (March 31, 1999): "If you don't know about this kid by now, you ought to be fired." As a junior Beckett had a 13–2 record with a .39 earned-run average (ERA). Because he had started school a year late, Beckett was eligible for the MLB draft at the end of his junior year. Had he entered the draft at that point, Beckett would likely have been picked relatively early, but he decided to stay in high school for his senior year. John Beckett explained to Carter: "This way he gets another year to mature, and that's going to help him reach his goals. He wants to be drafted No. 1. And he wants to play in the major leagues."

As a high-school senior, Beckett continued to dominate, often intimidating opposing players with pitches that reached mph speeds in the mid-80s. Though his attitude had improved, he was still given to the occasional outburst. For example, once when Beckett was on the mound, he noticed the father of an opposing player communicating Beckett's upcoming pitches to the batter. Beckett promptly threw a pitch 20 feet wide of the plate, directly at the man, who was saved from potential injury by the batting cage. During his senior year Beckett notched a 10–1 record with a .46 ERA and 155 strikeouts in $75^1/_3$ innings. He was named *USA Today*'s High School Pitcher of the Year and was identified as a top draft pick by *Baseball America*. Though confident he would be drafted into MLB, Beckett sought out college scholarships, in an effort to gain some bargaining power with major-league teams. Because of his immense pitching talent, however, most college coaches refused to commit scholarship money to the young star, saying that that "would be a waste of our time and yours," as Beckett recalled to Carter. He was offered a partial scholarship by Texas A&M University, in College Station, and he also signed a letter of intent with Blinn Junior College, in Brenham, Texas.

In the run-up to the 1999 MLB draft, many observers predicted that Beckett would be the number-one pick, which would have guaranteed him a large signing bonus. Beckett was drafted second overall, by the Marlins, behind the outfielder Josh Hamilton, who was chosen by the Tampa Bay Devil Rays. The Marlins initially hesitated to sign Beckett, because their executives were reluctant to furnish the large salary he demanded; when the deadline approached, however, Beckett threatened to enroll at Blinn Junior College if the Marlins did not sign him, which would have resulted in a wasted first-round draft pick. The Marlins gave Beckett a $7 million contract, with a $3.6 million signing bonus.

The Marlins' coaches were impressed with Beckett's early performances. He pitched well in two spring-training appearances, in games against the Kansas City Royals and the Atlanta Braves. The franchise, however, did not want to rush Beckett through the minor leagues. He began his professional career playing for the Cougars, the Marlins' single-A affiliate in the Midwest League, based in Kane County, Illinois. Despite being instructed to relax and being given a 100-pitch limit, Beckett was sidelined with tendonitis and other injuries to his shoulder by the middle of the season. He told Richard Justice for the *Houston Chronicle* (July 15, 2000), "I was trying to prove too much. When you think about the outcome, you corrupt the whole process. I know it's a cliché, but you've got to take it one pitch at a time." Beckett ended his first professional season with a 2–3 record, a 2.12 ERA, and 61 strikeouts in $59^{1}/_{3}$ innings.

Beckett began his second minor-league season with the single-A Brevard County Manatees, in the Florida State League (FSL). One reason he was moved to Florida was to allow him to pitch in warmer weather, which appeared to benefit his performance. After beginning the season with a 6–0 record—including $38^{2}/_{3}$ innings without a single earned run—and a 1.23 ERA, Beckett moved to the double-A Portland Sea Dogs, in the Eastern League. He struck out the first eight batters he faced while playing with the Sea Dogs. Later in the season he pitched a no-hitter, and in four of his last five starts, he allowed no runs. He compiled an impressive 14–1 record that season, with a cumulative 1.54 ERA and a total of 203 strikeouts in 140 innings, and was named 2001 Minor League Player of the Year by *Baseball America* and *USA Today*.

Beckett made his major-league debut on September 4, 2001, in a game against the Chicago Cubs. In six innings he allowed just one hit and no runs; out of 85 pitches that night, he threw 54 strikes. Beckett received a standing ovation after throwing

the last two outs of the sixth inning. He also hit a double and scored a run. When Eric Owens was brought in to pinch-hit for Beckett, in the bottom of the seventh inning, the crowd, upon realizing that Beckett was not returning, booed Owens. The Marlins beat the Cubs 8–1, marking only their fifth win in 22 games. The Marlins' manager, Tony Perez, said of Beckett, as quoted by Mark Long for the Associated Press (September 4, 2001): "He was in control. Nothing bothers him. He knows what he's doing. He knows how to pitch. He looked like he's been there a long time. He looked like a veteran." Beckett finished the 2001 season with a 2–2 record, with 24 strikeouts in 24 innings.

At the beginning of the 2002 season, Beckett's performance was erratic. In a May 29 game against the Cincinnati Reds, Beckett gave up seven runs on eight hits, and as a result, his ERA shot up from 2.9 to 4.09. (Prior to that game Beckett had never given up more than five runs in a single game.) That month he had begun suffering from severe blisters on his right middle finger, caused by friction between that finger and the seam of the ball. For weeks he tried to pitch despite the discomfort caused by the blisters, but by June it had become obvious that they were affecting his pitching, and he was placed on the disabled list. After he received treatment the blister problems appeared to subside, and Beckett began pitching for the Jupiter Hammerheads in the single-A FSL, in order to prepare for his return to the Marlins. By mid-July Beckett was back in the Marlins' lineup. On July 21 he notched his first major-league win since May, in a shutout of the Montreal Expos, in which he threw a career-high 12 strikeouts. Beckett began suffering from blisters once again in August. After a period spent on the disabled list, he was reactivated in mid-September and returned to pitch 13 innings over five games. He finished the season with 23 appearances, 113 strikeouts in 107 innings, a 6–7 record, and a 4.10 ERA.

In 2003 Beckett was slotted to become the youngest starting pitcher on opening day since the Mets' Dwight Gooden in 1986, before the Baltimore Orioles decided to have C. C. Sabathia, who is two months younger than Beckett, start their season. The opening-day game was an unfortunate one for Beckett, who struggled to communicate with the Marlins' newly acquired catcher, Ivan "Pudge" Rodriguez. In May, after it became apparent that Beckett was having mechanical difficulties, he admitted that his elbow was causing him a great deal of pain. Doctors discovered an elbow sprain and deemed surgery unnecessary; Beckett was placed on the disabled list for a week.

The Marlins started the season with a disappointing 16–22 record, and as a result, the team's owner, Jeffrey Loria, hired Jack McKeon to replace Jeff Torborg as the Marlins' general manager. McKeon, in his 70s, was thought to be an unusual choice. His advice to the players included the suggestion that they relax and enjoy themselves. From May 23 to the end of the season, the Marlins held

Josh Beckett

Jim Rogash/Getty Images

the best record in baseball, finishing the year with a win–loss record of 91–71, second-best in the National League (NL) East. The turnaround performance helped the Marlins secure the NL wildcard play-off berth. The Marlins were considered underdogs when they faced the San Francisco Giants in the NL Division Series (NLDS) but proceeded to win, 3–1. In the NL Championship Series (NLCS), the Marlins fell behind the Chicago Cubs, 3–1, before a late-series surge brought a victory over the Cubs, 4–3. In Game Five Beckett pitched a complete game, allowing just two hits and striking out 11 batters. As a relief pitcher in Game Seven, he helped the Marlins secure their come-from-behind pennant win. Tim Marchman wrote about Beckett's performance in that series for the *New York Sun* (October 22, 2003), "Smoothly angling his elbows above his head and then whipping the ball with seemingly no more exertion than he would need to close a door, Beckett became a star last week. He didn't win the series MVP award, but Beckett was probably more responsible for the Marlins' victory than any other player." Marchman, along with others in the media, also observed that Beckett's victories had affected his demeanor, noting, "Certainly the Beckett I saw pitch in Chicago has no resemblance to the profane and arrogant young man who's been built up in the press over the last few days. The one I saw was friendly, articulate, eager to talk to reporters, quick to joke with teammates, and, I thought, clearly destined to lead them."

The 2003 World Series pitted the Marlins against the New York Yankees, who had won four championships in the previous seven years and were highly favored. Entering Game Three, the Marlins and the Yankees had won one game apiece. The Marlins lost that match (6–1) despite a stellar performance by Beckett, who allowed just three hits and two runs in 7.1 innings. The Marlins rebounded, winning the next two games. It is standard MLB practice that pitchers receive four days' rest between games, so McKeon's decision to start Beckett in Game Six—after just three days of rest—sparked significant debate. McKeon was vindicated: Beckett pitched a complete game, allowing only five hits on 107 pitches and shutting out the Yankees, 2–0. Having contributed greatly to the Marlins' second World Series win in the 11 years since the franchise was founded, Beckett was named the World Series MVP. McKeon, who was named NL Manager of the Year, said of Beckett, as quoted on National Public Radio's *Weekend Edition* (October 26, 2003), "He's special. I told you that. . . . The guy has got the guts of a burglar, he's mentally tough and I knew that he had the confidence to go out there and do the job that he did tonight." Beckett responded to the win with a touch of incredulity, telling T. R. Sullivan for the Fort Worth, Texas, *Star Telegram* (October 26, 2003): "It's kind of a relief. I can't believe we don't have a game tomorrow. That's kind of the weird thing. I get to go deer hunting now. I'm looking forward to that."

The 2004 and 2005 seasons were relatively unsuccessful for Beckett, due primarily to injuries. In 2004 he made three trips to the disabled list because of recurring blisters and a strained back muscle. He ended the season with a 9–9 record and a 3.79 ERA, as well as 152 strikeouts in 156 innings. In 2005 his record improved to 15–8 with a 3.38 ERA and 166 strikeouts in 178 innings. Beckett suffered more blister problems and a left oblique strain, however, which placed him on the disabled list for nearly a month. The Marlins finished both of those seasons third in the National League East, failing to advance to the play-offs.

In 2006 Beckett was traded to the Boston Red Sox. In July of that year, he signed a three-year, $30 million contract extension. He ended the year with a 16–11 record, a 5.01 ERA, and 158 strikeouts in 204 innings. Beckett also became the first Red Sox pitcher in 35 years to hit a home run, in a game against the Philadelphia Phillies on May 20. The team finished third in the American League (AL) East division, with a record of 86–76. In 2007 Beckett had his most successful season to date. In the first half of the season, he notched a 12–2 record, with a 3.44 ERA, and was selected to play in an All-Star Game for the first time. He ended the regular season with an AL–leading 20 wins, along with 194 strikeouts in 200 innings, and a 3.27 ERA. His performance led him to finish second in voting for the AL Cy Young Award, behind C. C. Sabathia. The Red Sox returned to the postseason hoping for a second World Series championship in four years—and only their second in nearly nine decades. In Game One of the AL Division Series (ALDS), against the Los Angeles

Angels of Anaheim, Beckett once again demonstrated his pitching dominance. He helped the Red Sox shut out the Angels, holding them to four hits and striking out eight batters. After sweeping the Angels, the Red Sox beat the Cleveland Indians, 4–3, to win the ALCS, with Beckett winning two games in the series. Beckett's 1.93 ERA during that series helped him win the ALCS MVP Award. He also opened the World Series against the Colorado Rockies, securing a win after allowing just one run in seven innings. The Red Sox went on to sweep the Rockies in four games.

On May 8, 2008, in a win over the Detroit Tigers, Beckett recorded his 1,000th career strikeout. He finished the 2008 season with a 12–10 record and a 4.03 ERA, though he had struggled that year with injuries and was on the disabled list twice, with elbow and back problems. The Red Sox finished second in the AL East, with 95 wins and 67 losses, and advanced to the play-offs as a wildcard team. After defeating the Los Angeles Angels, 3–1, in the ALDS, they lost the ALCS, 4–3, to the Tampa Bay Rays. Beckett performed poorly in the postseason, recording a dismal 11.61 ERA, which many speculated was due to lingering injuries. The team finished with the same win–loss record the next season, advancing again to the play-offs as a wildcard team. This time they lost 3–0 in the ALDS to the Angels. Beckett's performance, however, was much improved. He finished the season with a 17–6 record, a 3.86 ERA, and a career-high 199 strikeouts. His 17 wins marked the fourth-highest total in the AL, and his two shutouts were good for third-best in the league. Beckett's solid performance in 2009 led to his second appearance at the MLB All-Star Game.

In April 2010 Beckett signed a four-year, $68 million contract extension with the Red Sox. He struggled with a back injury during the 2010 season and was placed on the disabled list several times. He finished with a 6–6 record and an unimpressive 5.78 ERA. The team notched a 89–73 record in 2010, failing to advance to the play-offs. As of early June Beckett had turned in stellar performances in the 2011 season, notching four wins and two losses and a league-leading 1.80 ERA. The Red Sox had a 30–24 record, placing the team first in the AL East division.

Beckett became a celebrity after his 2003 World Series win and was offered product-endorsement deals. For a while he dated Leeann Tweeden, a model for the lingerie retailer Frederick's of Hollywood. Beckett owns a nearly 2,000-acre ranch outside San Antonio, Texas, which he purchased with his signing bonus. His main hobby is deer hunting. In January 2011 he married Holly Fisher, a space-engineering consultant with whom he went to high school.

—F.C.

Suggested Reading: *Dallas Morning News* B p1 Mar. 31, 1999; (Fort Lauderdale, Florida) *Sun Sentinel* C p1 June 3, 1999, C p1 May 8, 2003;

Fort Worth (Texas) Star Telegram C p1 Oct. 26, 2003; *Houston Chronicle* p1 July 15, 2000; *Miami Herald* D p2 Mar. 7, 2000; National Public Radio *Weekend Edition* (Transcript) Oct. 26, 2003; *Palm Beach (Florida) Post* C p1 May 17, 2001; (Quincy, Massachusetts) *Patriot Ledger* Sports p15 Mar. 28, 2011; (Saskatoon, Saskatchewan, Canada) *Star Phoenix* C p5 Mar. 25, 2002

Courtesy of Ben Zweig Photography

Bernard, Michelle

July 30, 1963– Journalist; political commentator; writer; lawyer; organization official

Address: Bernard Center for Women, Politics & Public Policy, P.O. Box 59410, Potomac, MD 20859

Michelle Bernard, a lawyer, journalist, and political commentator, is the founder, chairman, president, and chief executive officer (CEO) of the Bernard Center for Women, Politics & Public Policy. The mission of the Bernard Center, according to its Web site, is to "promote, advance, and support individual rights, free markets, comprehensive education reform and parental choice, personal responsibility, self-reliance, and smart government as the keys to achieving the American dream." From 2006 to early 2011, Bernard was the president and CEO of the Independent Women's Forum, which, its Web site states, is "dedicated to building support for free markets, limited government, and individual responsibility," seeks to "combat the too-common presumption that women want and benefit from big government," and aims to "build awareness of the ways that women are better served by greater economic freedom." For several years after she passed the Washington, D.C., bar exam, Bernard worked for private law firms. She left one firm after her appointment as chairman of the board of the District of Columbia Redevelopment Land Agency (RLA). An MSNBC political analyst, Bernard has appeared regularly as a guest on such television shows as *The McLaughlin Group*, *Hardball with Chris Matthews*, and the *Dylan Ratigan Show*. She is the national spokesperson for National School Choice, whose goal is to raise awareness regarding effective education options for all children. She is the author of *Women's Progress: How Women Are Wealthier, Healthier and More Independent Than Ever Before* (2007).

When asked about her political beliefs, Bernard told Bill Steigerwald, writing for the *Anderson (Indiana) Free Press* (August 29, 2008, on-line), "I think the best way to describe me is as an independent. I am without a party affiliation. I am definitely right of center. I have a very, very deep belief in individualism rather than group thought. I believe in personal responsibility. I believe in free markets. I believe in equality under the law rather than equal outcomes. My preference is equal opportunity." She added, "I don't know where [my beliefs] come from, other than this is just the way I was raised. . . . I was raised with very American and Jamaican values. In our culture, we have a very strong sense of pride and of family honor and of self-reliance."

The oldest of the four children of Milton Desmond Bernard and Nesta Hyacinth Grant Bernard, Michelle Denise Bernard was born on July 30, 1963 in Washington, D.C., and raised in Potomac, Maryland. Her parents immigrated to the U.S. from Jamaica, in the West Indies. Bernard's birth occurred nearly a decade after the U.S. Supreme Court, in *Brown v. Board of Education*, ruled that officially enforced segregation in public schools is unconstitutional. "As a young child, I most certainly had little appreciation of the political discourse and civil rights struggles that followed Brown," she said to Tony Cox in an interview for National Public Radio (May 21, 2004). "However, as a result of the many biographies my parents introduced me to, I not only gained a strong appreciation for the fact that I could read, but for those I read about. I read biographies about Sojourner Truth, Harriet Tubman and Shirley Chisholm, Frederick Douglass and Marcus Garvey, Martin Luther King and Malcolm X, Thurgood Marshall and Charles Hamilton Houston. As a young black child, I recognized the wisdom of these great black women and men. I learned that education is necessary to achieve true equality."

Bernard graduated from Wootton High School, in Rockville, Maryland. She then enrolled at Howard University, in Washington, D.C. "I started off being a science major thinking that I was going to go to medical school," she recalled in an interview with Andrew Belonsky for the Web site wowOwow.com (April 9, 2009), which is geared toward and written by women. In her junior year, she continued, "I took a class called Philosophy of the Law as an elective and on the very first day of the course I absolutely fell in love with philosophy of the law. . . . I just remember thinking, 'Wow, I finally found my place.' And I knew that I wanted to go to law school; I knew that I wanted to fight against injustice." In order to concentrate in philosophy and political science rather than science, she said, "I had to go to summer school and take an outrageous number of credits every semester so that I could still graduate on time. My parents were really not very happy with my decision, to put it mildly." Bernard earned a B.A. degree in philosophy and political science in 1985. Three years later she earned a J.D. degree from the Georgetown University Law Center, also in Washington, D.C.

From 1988 to 1991 Bernard worked as an associate for the law firm Washington, Perito & Dubuc. She had left that firm and was working for another law firm, Shaw, Pittman, Potts & Trowbridge, when, in 1994, she was appointed to the District of Columbia Redevelopment Land Agency board. (The agency is now called the National Capital Revitalization Corp.) As chairperson, beginning in 1995, she participated in the negotiation of the financing package for the construction of a new sports arena in the nation's capital. (The arena was known as the MCI Center when it opened, in 1997; in 2006 it was renamed the Verizon Center. It is the home of two professional sports teams, the Washington Wizards basketball team and the Washington Capitals hockey team.) "Financing for the project was supposed to be a done deal until Ms. Bernard got involved," Adrienne T. Washington wrote for the *Washington Times* (July 24, 1995), noting that the mayor, the D.C. City Council, the Federal City Council, the D.C. Chamber of Commerce, other organizations, "and even some members of Congress" had approved it. Nevertheless, Washington wrote, "Ms. Bernard has doggedly raised red flags when she felt proposals offered for the arena were lacking. She grabbed headlines by characterizing the arena's financing package as 'preposterous' and once likened a supporter's testimony to 'verbal garbage,'" while she herself was labeled "a loose cannon" and "politically naive" and was accused of acting at the behest of others. In order to avoid charges of a conflict of interest, Bernard left her position at Shaw, Pittman, Potts & Trowbridge. "I never thought I'd be criticized for trying to save the District $70 million," Bernard told Washington. Bernard's term on the RLA board ended in 1997. From 1996 to 2000 Bernard was a partner with the law firm Patton Boggs.

When Andrew Belonsky asked her whether she had ever experienced on-the-job sexism, Bernard said, "I can tell you of instances when, coming up as a junior lawyer, I was working with one male partner who would not work with women attorneys who had not played a team sport in high school or college. He thought that if you criticized a woman litigator who had not been involved in sports, she might cry. That was sexist and absolutely ridiculous." Belonsky also asked Bernard if, in her opinion, racism or sexism is more prevalent in America, to which she responded, "I know a lot of my peers will disagree with me, but I feel that racism is still a lot stronger than sexism. And maybe that is based on my personal experiences. I have had people say nastier things to me about my race than I have about me being a woman."

In 2004 Bernard became a senior fellow with the Independent Women's Forum (IWF). That nonprofit think tank had grown out of an ad hoc organization called Women for Clarence Thomas, which was set up in 1991 to ensure that the U.S. Senate would approve President George H. W. Bush's nomination of Thomas for a seat on the U.S. Supreme Court. Less than a year later she was named IWF's senior vice president. "We have a philosophical belief that women are not victims," Bernard told Andrew Belonsky. "We believe in limited government, free markets and personal responsibility. And we believe that free markets are really the great equalizer, and will allow women to become truly equal with men in areas where we still may be unequal." In 2006 Bernard was promoted to president and CEO of the IWF. In that post she founded the IWF's Iraqi Women's Democracy Initiative, which provides leadership training to Iraqi women.

In 2008 the cable news channel MSNBC hired Bernard to provide conservative political analysis. When Bill Steigerwald asked her if she thought that she had gotten that job because of her race, gender, or political views, she responded, "I would say probably a little bit of all of the above. I think a lot of the networks realized that the American people wanted to hear more than one voice and one type of viewpoint. I guess I'm a 'three-fer' as a black person and as a woman and as a conservative." Bernard created, co-produced, and hosted a two-hour MSNBC program called *About Our Children*, which aired on September 20, 2009 and in which, in a town-meeting format held in front of a live studio audience, she discussed poverty and education reform with the comedian and activist Bill Cosby.

Bernard is the founder (in 2010), president, chairman, and CEO of the Bernard Center for Women, Politics & Public Policy, which, according to its Web site, is "a research and educational institution—a think tank—whose mission is to fundamentally change the terms of the nation's most critical domestic and foreign policy debates and challenge the American public, policymakers, and the media to discuss those issues." Posted in the Events section of the center's Web site in early 2011 was an invitation to the public to join Bernard and Kent B. Amos, a Washington, D.C., businessman, on February 9, 2011 at a screening of the film *The Boys of Baraka*, "in honor of National School Choice Week and Black History Month," held at a Washington, D.C., public charter school. A panel discussion about underserved communities, school choice, and education reform was held after the movie.

Bernard's book *Women's Progress: How Women Are Wealthier, Healthier and More Independent Than Ever Before*, was published in 2007 under the Spence imprint. "Women are thriving in our country," Bernard wrote in its introduction. "That's often not the story you hear in the media. The drumbeat from liberal women's groups is that women are falling behind in our society. . . . The facts tell a different story. It's a story of women's progress. Women in the United States are excelling in our educational system and playing increasingly prominent roles in our workforce and government. Women are enjoying a higher standard of living and living longer and healthier than their mothers and grandmothers. Of course, we expect continued improvements and more groundbreaking achievements from our daughters' generation, but women's progress to date deserves celebration." Critics of Bernard's argument noted that she gave short shrift to the facts that on average, women's pay is significantly less than what men are paid for doing exactly the same jobs; that the responsibilities of caring for home and children still fall preponderantly on working women rather than their husbands; and that among heads of *Fortune* 500 companies, only a tiny minority are women. Critics also accused her of failing to address the problems of millions of mothers who hold low-paying jobs—for example, difficulties in finding adequate childcare facilities and convenient public transportation to those jobs.

Bernard's essays have appeared in publications including *U.S. News & World Report*, *Fast Company*, *Legal Times*, the New York *Daily News*, and the *Washington Business Journal*. Representative essays include "Protect Freedom of Speech: Bury the Misnamed 'Fairness Doctrine,'" which appeared in the *Washington Examiner* (December 1, 2008, online), and "Teachers Unions Are Real Roadblock to Education Reform," published in the *Grio.com* (August 10, 2010), an NBCUniversal e-magazine. In "40 Years Later, Revisiting the Kerner Commission," for the *Washington Times* (February 29, 2008), Bernard wrote about the report issued by a committee appointed by President Lyndon B. Johnson after the widespread race riots in the U.S. in 1967; the report discussed long-term and immediate causes for the riots and made recommendations to prevent such disasters. In that essay Bernard declared, "The Kerner Commission recommended new welfare programs, and the federal government has spent more to fight poverty than it spent to win World War II. Unfortunately, bigger social programs backfired, encouraging family and community break-up, discouraging education and employment, and creating pervasive dependency. We know more government social engineering will not work. The 1996 welfare reform, agreed to by a Republican Congress and Democratic president, freed many of the nation's poor from the fetters of dependency and encourages self-sufficiency. To-day, we must improve education and generate economic opportunity for those still stuck in poverty. To do so we must empower people rather than bureaucracies. For instance, pouring more money into failing public schools won't improve student achievement. Giving parents improved options and forcing public institutions to compete will help kids learn. Poor people are poor, not stupid, which is why so many black Baptists work so hard to place their children in parochial schools. Similarly, policies like the minimum wage may sound 'progressive,' but actually destroy jobs. We need to clear away regulations that make it hard to start a small business and enter a profession. Entrepreneurs, not politicians, create real jobs with the potential for advancement. Although people are focused on the subprime lending crisis, and its negative impact on minority homeownership, building codes, rent controls and zoning restrictions do far more to limit good housing. Better policing is also necessary to provide safe neighborhoods for poor as well as rich."

Bernard assisted briefly with the 2000 Bush-Cheney Presidential Inaugural Committee. She contributed to the National Urban League's book *State of Black America* (2009). She has served as the director of the American Board for Certification of Teacher Excellence. In 2008 she was named one of three "Fast Trackers" on *Newsmax* magazine's list of the nation's top opinion leaders.

In 1996 Bernard married Joe Johns, a CNN correspondent who formerly reported for NBC News. (As of 2009 the couple were said to be separated.) She and Johns are the parents of a son, Logan Christopher, and a daughter, Avery Michelle.

—J.P.

Suggested Reading: *Anderson Free Press* (online) Aug. 29, 2008; Bernard Center for Women, Politics & Public Policy Web site; *Washington Times* C p6 July 24, 1995; wowOwow.com Apr. 9, 2009

Selected Books: *Women's Progress: How Women Are Wealthier, Healthier and More Independent Than Ever Before,* 2007

Billups, Chauncey

Sep. 25, 1976– Basketball player

Address: Denver Nuggets, 1000 Chopper Cir., Denver, CO 80204

In 13 seasons with the National Basketball Association (NBA), the Denver Nuggets' point guard Chauncey Billups has entered the ranks of professional basketball's most proficient floor leaders—one who "shares the characteristics of some of the greats," Joshua Duplechian wrote for the Denver, Colorado, *Rocky Mountain News* (January 9, 2009). "His passion for winning . . . is taken straight from Vince Lombardi's playbook. His ability to command respect from his peers, teammates and subordinates is reminiscent of Gen. George S. Patton. His ability to orchestrate an offense in the manner of a finely tuned symphony conjures images of Leonard Bernstein." Billups was a standout high-school player and was credited with reviving the basketball program at the University of Colorado at Boulder (CU–Boulder) before making the jump to the NBA's Boston Celtics in 1997, after his sophomore year. After being traded to the Toronto Raptors midway through his rookie season, he played with the Denver Nuggets, the Orlando Magic, and the Minnesota Timberwolves during the next four years. "People just gave up on me," he told Mark J. Spears for the *Denver Post* (June 6, 2004). "They thought because teams kept trading me, I wasn't good enough. I took that all in and it was motivation for me."

Christian Petersen/Getty Images

Billups blossomed after he joined the Detroit Pistons, prior to the 2002–03 season. Under the legendary Larry Brown, who coached the Pistons during the next two seasons, Billups developed into an all-around point guard. Earning the nickname "Mr. Big Shot" for his tendency to make clutch shots, he helped transform the Pistons into perennial playoff contenders—they reached six consecutive Eastern Conference finals—and led them to their third

NBA championship, in 2004, when he was named the NBA Finals Most Valuable Player (MVP). Upon returning to the Denver Nuggets several games into the 2008–09 season, Billups immediately filled a leadership void and was credited with "lifting an unappealing and underachieving collection of basketball parts into a frenzy-inducing title contender," John Branch wrote for the *New York Times* (May 24, 2009). With Billups at point guard, the Nuggets tied a franchise record for most regular-season wins (54) during the 2008–09 season, and the squad advanced to the Western Conference finals for the first time since 1985. (They lost to the Los Angeles Lakers in six games.) In 2009–10 the then-33-year-old Billups posted a career-high average of 19.5 points per game, becoming the first player in NBA history to accomplish such a feat in his 13th season. The Nuggets, meanwhile, recorded their third consecutive 50-win season, then were upset in the first round of the play-offs by the Utah Jazz. Billups has been named to five consecutive All-Star teams and has also earned All-NBA and All-Defensive honors. In the summer of 2010, he played for the U.S. national basketball team, which took home the gold medal at the FIBA World Championship, in Turkey. The Nuggets' head coach, George Karl, told Benjamin Hochman for the *Denver Post* (October 3, 2010) that Billups "knows how to win games, he can do it playing well and he can do it playing poorly, which is very unusual. He just kind of feels the game as it happens. He understands what is going right and wrong on the court. And the combination with me, we do a good job at figuring out how to win down the stretch and winning in the fourth quarter."

The eldest of the three children of Ray and Faye Billups, Chauncey Billups was born on September 25, 1976 in Denver, Colorado. He was raised in the city's rough Park Hill neighborhood with his brother, Rodney, and sister, Maria. As a child he was a fan of the Nuggets and idolized the Denver Broncos quarterback John Elway. His parents bought him his first basketball when he was five. His father, whom he used to watch play in local basketball-league games, "was definitely my biggest influence," he told Marc. J. Spears. He was also close to his maternal grandmother, Florence Gresham, who taught him important life values. (Gresham died in the mid-1990s.) Faye Billups recalled to Roscoe Nance for *USA Today* (May 31, 2006), "He was always mature beyond his years. . . . He listened to my mother better than I did."

When Billups was in fifth grade, his recreation-league basketball coach, the former NBA player Bobby Wilkerson, gave him the nickname "Smooth" for his seemingly effortless skills on the court. During the next three years, Billups played in leagues with older children. At Denver's George Washington High School, "he was a gym rat," the former NBA All-Star Micheal Ray Richardson told Chris Tomasson for the Denver *Rocky Mountain News* (February 13, 2009). "You could tell that he . . . had natural basketball ability." In his sopho-

more, junior, and senior years, the *Denver Post* named him Colorado's "Mr. Basketball"—the state's top honor for players on preparatory-school teams. He led George Washington to two high-school state championships and earned McDonald's All-American honors as a senior. Regarded as one of the nation's top prospects, Billups was heavily recruited by college-basketball powerhouses including the Universities of California, Michigan, and Oklahoma. He chose to enroll at the University of Colorado at Boulder, although its team, the Buffaloes, had not earned a berth in the National Collegiate Athletic Association (NCAA) tournament since the 1960s.

Billups arrived during a major rebuilding project led by the Buffaloes' coach, Joe Harrington. As point guard in the 1995–96 season, he averaged 17.9 points, 6.3 rebounds, and 5.5 assists per game and scored more than 30 points on four occasions. Billups was named the Big 12 Conference Co-Freshman of the Year after becoming the only player in the league to rank in the top 10 in eight statistical categories. The Buffaloes, however, finished with a 9–18 record. Following a series of mishaps and what turned out to be unwise personnel decisions, Harrington was forced to resign early in the 1996–97 season. He was replaced by his assistant Ricardo Patton, who immediately renewed efforts to revive Colorado's basketball program. At the center of those efforts was the six-foot-three, 202-pound Billups, who teamed up with the newly recruited Martice Moore to form one of the best guard duos in the nation. During his sophomore season Billups started 29 games and led the Buffaloes in points per game (an average of 19.1), assists per game (an average of 4.9), three-pointers made (75), and free-throw percentage (.854), and helped the team finish the year with a school-record 22 victories. Billups then led the Buffaloes to their first NCAA tournament victory in more than 30 years, when they upset the Indiana University Hoosiers in the first round, 80–62; with their loss to the University of North Carolina Tar Heels, they were eliminated from the tournament. At the end of that season, Billups earned All-Conference and second-team All-America honors. "The thing that stood out to me about Chauncey was that he focused on going to the NBA and being a real player," Ricardo Patton told Marc J. Spears. "Some players want to get the cars, the jewels, the glitter. But Chauncey didn't want to just get there; he wanted to be a real player in the league. . . . He really tried to be a student of the game. . . . Some of his teammates were a little critical at times because he didn't go to the parties. He was focused."

After his sophomore season Billups decided to turn professional. The Boston Celtics chose him as the third overall pick in the first round of the 1997 NBA draft. His failure to adjust to the system imposed by the Celtics' head coach, Rick Pitino, led to his being traded to the Toronto Raptors in his rookie season, after 51 games. Billups later recalled to Roscoe Nance that that "was my first, real humbling experience." In a total of 80 games with the Celtics and Raptors that year, Billups averaged 11.2 points and 3.9 assists per game. His stint with Toronto ended prior to the 1997–98 season, when he was traded to the Denver Nuggets. Playing in a reserve role behind the point guard Nick Van Exel and the shooting guard Ron Mercer, Billups averaged 13.9 points and 3.8 assists per game in 45 games. (Due to a lockout, the 1998–99 NBA season did not start until February 1999, when only 50 games remained in the regular season.)

After 13 games in the 1999–2000 season, Billups was forced to undergo season-ending surgery. He was traded to the Orlando Magic in a multi-player deal while he was recuperating. He spent the next several months rehabilitating his shoulder and then was let go. Doc Rivers, the head coach of the Magic then, told Liz Robbins for the *New York Times* (January 19, 2006) years later, "The one thing that stood out was that he made every practice, every game and in every team meeting he spoke up. And he never put on a Magic uniform."

As a free agent Billups signed with the Minnesota Timberwolves. Under the team's head coach, Flip Saunders, he served mostly as a fill-in for the injured All-Star point guard Terrell Brandon. In 2000–01 Billups made 33 starts in 77 games and averaged 9.3 points and 3.4 assists per game. The next season those averages rose to 12.5 and 5.5, respectively. In the first round of the 2001–02 play-offs, Billups averaged 22 points, five rebounds, and 5.7 assists in three games, all of which the Timberwolves lost to the Dallas Mavericks.

After the postseason Minnesota's general manager, Kevin McHale, made a series of cuts to the roster that included Billups. On July 17, 2002 the Detroit Pistons' president, Joe Dumars, signed him to a six-year, $33.7 million contract. Dumars told Liz Robbins, "I thought he had N.B.A. talent, but more so than that, he never gave up. When you see that in a person, you know that there's something special there. People keep telling him he can't get it done, that he's not a true point guard. I like guys like that. He's a nonstop fighter." With the Pistons Billups soon emerged as one of the league's best point guards. During the 2002–03 regular season, he appeared in 74 games (all starts) and averaged 16.2 points, a career-high 3.7 rebounds, and 3.9 assists per game. He solidified his reputation as a clutch performer and led the league in game-tying or lead-changing field goals in the final two minutes. His six game-winning shots, the most in the league, earned him the nickname "Mr. Big Shot." The Pistons achieved a regular-season record of 50–32 and advanced to the Eastern Conference finals, where they were swept by the New Jersey Nets in four games. In the 2002–03 play-offs, Billups averaged 18 points and 4.7 assists in 14 games.

Before the 2003–04 season, the Pistons' head coach, Rick Carlisle, was fired and replaced by Larry Brown, who had coached the Philadelphia 76ers during the previous six seasons. Under Brown, who implemented a system that relied heavily on constant ball-sharing and movement, Billups developed further at the point-guard position. He told Robbins, "The biggest thing with Larry, I learned I could dominate a game without scoring 25 points. I learned how to feel good about that." During the regular season, as the Pistons' floor leader, Billups brought Brown's concepts to the court and helped lead the team to a 54–28 record. In 78 starts that year, he averaged 16.9 points and 5.7 assists per game. In the first round of the play-offs, the Eastern Conference semifinals, and the Eastern Conference finals, the Pistons defeated the Milwaukee Bucks, the New Jersey Nets, and the Indiana Pacers, respectively, to secure their first NBA Finals appearance since 1990. They entered that competition as heavy underdogs against the Los Angeles Lakers, who were then anchored by the superstars Kobe Bryant and Shaquille O'Neal. Nevertheless, the Pistons won the series in six games to capture the NBA championship. Billups, who averaged 21 points, 3.2 rebounds, 5.2 assists, and 1.2 steals per game in the series, was named the NBA Finals MVP.

In 2004–05 Billups averaged 16.5 points and 5.8 assists in 80 starts and led the Pistons to their second consecutive 54-win season, helping them earn the number-two seed in the Eastern Conference play-offs. After defeating the Philadelphia 76ers, the Indiana Pacers, and the Miami Heat, the Pistons squared off against the Western Conference champion San Antonio Spurs in the 2005 NBA Finals. They lost the hard-fought series in seven games, as the Spurs took home their third title in seven years. At the end of the year, Billups was named to the NBA All-Defensive Second Team. (He was named to the team again in 2006.)

During the summer of 2005, Flip Saunders replaced Brown as the Pistons' head coach. That season Billups was named co-captain of the team and helped lead the Pistons to a franchise-best 64–18 record, while averaging 18.5 points and a career-high 8.6 assists per game in a career-high 81 starts. He earned his first career All-Star selection as a reserve for the Eastern Conference squad. In the 2005–06 play-offs, the Pistons were victorious against the Milwaukee Bucks and the Cleveland Cavaliers before losing to the Miami Heat in six games in the Eastern Conference finals. Billups led the Pistons to their fifth and sixth consecutive Eastern Conference finals appearances in the 2006–07 and 2007–08 seasons; in both years he was named to the All-Star team. He was named to the All-NBA second team in 2006 and the All-NBA third team in 2007.

After losing in the Eastern Conference finals for the third consecutive year, the Pistons replaced Saunders with the first-year assistant coach Michael Curry and traded away several players. Although he had signed a five-year, $60 million contract extension with the Pistons during the summer of 2007—and was a fan favorite in Detroit—Billups was traded to the Denver Nuggets two games into the 2008–09 season in return for the point guard Allen Iverson. The trade paid immediate dividends for the Nuggets, who reached several franchise milestones in 2008–09 with Billups as point guard: with a 54–28 record, they tied a franchise record for most regular-season wins, and they earned a franchise-best number-two seed in the Western Conference play-offs, while recording back-to-back 50-win seasons for the first time in franchise history. Billups, meanwhile, helped the Nuggets, perennial first-round losers, make their first Western Conference finals appearance since 1985; they lost the series to the Los Angeles Lakers in six games. That year Billups earned his fourth career All-Star selection and was named to the All-NBA third team for the second time, after averaging 17.9 points and 6.4 assists per game during the regular season. He led the Nuggets to the play-offs again in 2009–10, when he made the All-Star team for the fifth consecutive year. With an average of 19.5 points per game, he became the first NBA player to achieve a career high in that category in his 13th season. During the summer of 2010, Billups was a member of the gold-medal-winning U.S. national basketball team at the FIBA World Championship, in Turkey. Billups entered the 2010–11 season as the Nuggets' starting point guard. In December 2010 he missed three games due to a partially torn ligament in his right wrist. After he returned to the

lineup, Billups scored 20 points or more in four of his next five games. On December 29 he scored a team- and season-high 36 points in a come-from-behind victory over the Minnesota Timberwolves. As of early January 2011, Billups was averaging 16.6 points and 5.3 assists per game.

Billups has been married to his high-school sweetheart, the former Piper Riley, since 2001. The couple have three daughters: Cydney, Ciara, and Cenaya. Billups has been involved in many charitable activities, including the Porter-Billups Leadership Academy of Regis University in Denver, which helps prepare at-risk Denver youths for college. He has also had a longstanding association with the Children's Center, an organization dedicated to enriching the lives of youngsters in the Detroit area. In 2008 Billups won the NBA's J. Walter Kennedy Citizenship Award for his charity work.

—C.C.

Suggested Reading: *Denver (Colorado) Post* B p1+ June 6, 2004, C p16 Oct. 3, 2010; (Denver, Colorado) *Rocky Mountain News* C p1+ Nov. 9, 1997; (Detroit, Michigan) *Free Press* Sports p1 May 20, 2007, Jan. 9, 2009; *New York Times* D p5 Jan. 19, 2006, Sports p6 May 24, 2009; *Sports Illustrated* p54 May 12, 2003, p40 May 23, 2005, p52+ Feb. 20, 2006, p60+ May 11, 2009, (on-line) Nov. 3, 2008; *USA Today* C p6 May 31, 2006

Blankfein, Lloyd

Sep. 20, 1954– Chairman and CEO of Goldman Sachs

Address: Goldman Sachs Group Inc., 85 Broad St., New York, NY 10004

"At some point, I can't say that I had a disadvantaged background," Lloyd Blankfein, the chairman and CEO of Goldman Sachs, one of the world's leading financial-services companies, told William D. Cohan for *Time* (August 31, 2009). "After a while, I kind of evolved into having an advantaged background." A product of a poor New York City neighborhood and the first person in his family to graduate from college, Blankfein worked as a lawyer in the 1970s and early 1980s before entering the field of finance. He assumed the presidency of Goldman Sachs in 2004 and then became chairman and CEO two years later; in part through his willingness to embrace great risk, he has steered the company to unprecedented success—which has brought him and Goldman a great deal of criticism during the recent global economic recession. The sizeable bonuses given to employees at Goldman and other financial firms in a time of widespread unemployment have reinforced the perception that Wall Street is, at best, out of touch with the suffering of average citizens. Taking a different

Chip Somodevilla/Getty Images

view, Robert Steel, a former partner at Goldman, told Cohan, "You can never forget that Lloyd came from a pretty significantly challenging environment. That's at the root of Lloyd."

Lloyd Craig Blankfein was born on September 20, 1954 in the South Bronx section of New York City. His father worked for the U.S. Postal Service, sorting mail on the night shift, after he lost his job as a truck driver; his mother was a receptionist at a burglar-alarm company. His parents raised him in the Jewish faith. At the age of three, Blankfein moved with his family to the East New York neighborhood in the city's borough of Brooklyn—one of the poorest and most crime-ridden neighborhoods in New York. There, he grew up in a public-housing complex called the Linden Houses. Blankfein landed his first job when he was 13 years old, working on commission as a drinks vendor at New York Yankees baseball games. Extremely studious, he graduated from the predominantly African-American Thomas Jefferson High School in 1971 as valedictorian of his class. Steel told Cohan that Blankfein said about his high-school years, "You survive by either one of two things. You were either a great athlete or funny and entertaining, and I decided to go with funny and entertaining." After representatives from Harvard University, in Cambridge, Massachusetts, recruited at Thomas Jefferson, Blankfein applied successfully to the Ivy League school, enrolling when he was only 16. With the help of scholarships and financial aid, he earned a B.A. degree from the prestigious university in 1975 and went on to receive a law degree there in 1978.

Blankfein next became a corporate tax lawyer for the now-defunct law firm Donovan, Leisure, Newton & Irvine, where he worked from 1978 to 1981. Then, having what he described to Cohan as a "pre-midlife crisis," he decided that he no longer wanted to pursue a career in law and switched his professional path to the financial industry. He applied for jobs with companies such as Dean Witter and Morgan Stanley. He was considered for employment by Goldman Sachs—which sometimes interviews a prospective employee more than a dozen times to ensure that the candidate is right for the position—but was rejected. In 1982 he was hired as a gold salesman for J. Aron & Co., a commodity-trading firm that had recently been acquired by Goldman Sachs. In his new field he initially "had trouble with the language, with the speed and the pacing," Blankfein admitted in his interview with William D. Cohan. He improved with time, however, soon designing a $100 million trade that generated massive profits for the firm. Building on that success, he began to work his way up the ranks of J. Aron's parent company. In 1994 he became co-head of Goldman's Currency and Commodities Division, and in 1997 he was made co-head of a new division, known as FICC, that combined Goldman's Fixed-Income operation with J. Aron's Currency and Commodities Division.

Goldman Sachs was founded in 1869 by Marcus Goldman, a German immigrant, who established a one-room office on Pine Street in New York City, from which he purchased promissory notes and sold them at a profit. In 1882 Samuel Sachs, Goldman's son-in-law, joined the company. As of 2010 Goldman Sachs had approximately 30,000 employees in more than 30 countries; the company's services include investment management, investment banking, and securities. In 2002 Blankfein was named a vice chairman of Goldman Sachs. In that post he was responsible for managing FICC as well as the Equities Division. He became the president and chief operating officer (COO) of the firm in 2004, after the former COO John Thain left to become the CEO of the New York Stock Exchange. Two years later Blankfein became the chairman of the board and the 11th CEO of Goldman Sachs, following the resignation of Henry Paulson, who went on to become the 74th U.S. treasury secretary, during the George W. Bush administration. In an interview with the *New York Times* (June 10, 2007), Blankfein—who has called himself "a worrier, not a warrior"—told Jenny Anderson, "When I joined the firm I thought, 'How will I ever survive here?' Then I worried about whether I'd be able to make the area I was responsible for important for the firm." He added, "When I was made partner, I had all the statistics and I knew how long partners lasted and I asked myself, 'Can I last as long as an average partner lasts in the firm?'"

Over the years Blankfein has proved himself to be a more than competent chief executive of the company, greatly boosting Goldman Sachs's position within the financial-services industry. As Blankfein mentioned to Anderson, "We went from being a firm with a small balance sheet which was considered to be too advice-oriented and lacking the financial muscle to be taken seriously, to an organization which generates articles with headlines like 'Too Big? Too Powerful? Too Bad!'" Goldman's growth was due in part to the 1999 repeal of the Glass-Steagall Act, which eliminated the separation between commercial and investment banking—allowing Goldman to serve as both financial adviser, its former specialty, and investor. Blankfein encouraged the company to take more risks and carry out more principal transactions, such as proprietary trading and private-equity investing, in addition to providing investment advice. "Lloyd understands risk taking," Citadel Investment Group's CEO, Kenneth C. Griffin, said to Anderson. "In a sense, it's his most fundamental skill." Blankfein said to Bethany McLean for CNN-Money.com (March 2008), "The best traders are not right more than they are wrong. They are quick adjusters. They are better at getting right when they are wrong." Although he was successful at his job, many disliked Blankfein; some high-level employees left the firm after he became the CEO. He had become known for a biting sense of humor and aggressively stated opinions. "Even on the management committee, I was aggressive in expressing my views," Blankfein said to McLean. "You have to be aggressive if you're trying to move a big concrete block." He has also been accused of putting his friends at Goldman in high positions. "I promote the people who do well and make them my friends," he explained to McLean. "I gravitate to the people who are talented."

With Blankfein's rise at Goldman came some cosmetic changes. When he worked for J. Aron & Co., the image he projected was that of an overweight man with a poor sense of style. He was also an excessive smoker and a gambler—he used to enjoy going to Las Vegas, Nevada, with a friend to play blackjack. Jenny Anderson wrote in 2007, "Blankfein's makeover from frumpy gold salesman to chief executive has a bit of a reality-TV feel to it. Less than a decade ago, he could be seen in shorts at a golf outing, tube socks stretched to his knees, 50 pounds heavier, and toting his BlackBerry in the same plastic bag as his bagel with cream cheese. Today, he dons navy pinstripes and a power tie."

In 2007 the U.S. economy took a dramatic turn for the worse, following the "mortgage meltdown"—a crisis brought on by financial institutions' widespread practice of making mortgage loans to individuals who proved unable to keep up with payments. Goldman Sachs, meanwhile, had its best year to date: that year Blankfein earned $68.7 million (a combination of his salary, bonus, restricted stock awards, and other compensation), a record among Wall Street CEOs, according to McLean. When asked by Clair Shipman and Huma Khan for ABC News (April 28, 2010) whether or not Goldman Sachs bears any responsibility for the financial meltdown, Blankfein responded, "It embarrasses me to say it. But of course we do. The financial system failed and Goldman Sachs is a very influential member of the financial system. We have our share of the burden of that." In 2008 Goldman Sachs earned $2.3 billion and distributed among its workers $4.82 billion in bonuses, giving more than 900 employees at least $1 million each and nearly 80 executives at least $5 million each, although Goldman's top five executives (including Blankfein) declined bonuses. Many outsiders were angry about the amount of money Goldman Sachs employees made during the financial crisis, but Blankfein felt that his workers deserved the money because they had performed their jobs well. He told John Arlidge in an interview for the London *Sunday Times* (November 8, 2009), "If you examine our practices on compensation, you will see a complete correlation throughout our history of having remuneration match performance." When asked by Arlidge if it was possible to have too much ambition or to be too successful, Blankfein replied, "I don't want people in this firm to think they have accomplished as much for themselves as they can and go on vacation. As the guardian of the interests of the shareholders and, by the way, for the purposes of society, I'd like them to continue to do what they are doing. I don't want to put a cap on their ambition. It's hard for me to argue for a cap on their compensation."

Although Goldman Sachs did not seem to be struggling financially, it received a $10 billion bailout from the federal government, a portion of the $700 billion Troubled Asset Relief Program of 2008. The company was eligible for the money because it had converted from an investment bank to a bank holding company after acquiring securities from American International Group (AIG), an ailing insurance company. Goldman Sachs has since paid back all of the money with interest. Because Goldman continued to be profitable during a time of economic crisis, the company experienced a lot of animosity from its competitors, Congress, the public, and the media. In a much-discussed article for *Rolling Stone* (July 2009), Matt Taibbi described the firm as "a great vampire squid wrapped around the face of humanity, relentlessly jamming its blood funnel into anything that smells like money." Among other things, Taibbi accused Goldman Sachs of "helping $5 trillion in wealth disappear from NASDAQ . . . pawning off thousands of toxic mortgages on pensioners and cities . . . helping to drive the price of gas up to $4 a gallon and to push 100 million people around the world into hunger, after securing tens of billions of taxpayer dollars through a series of bailouts overseen by its former CEO." In a *New Yorker* article (November 29, 2010), John Cassidy accused big Wall Street companies—including Goldman Sachs—of being "socially worthless" and unable to "design, build, or sell a single tangible thing." In the interview with William D. Cohan, Blankfein said, "There's clearly some resentment." He continued, "There are people who are disposed to think that because we were careful and successfully avoided many of the pitfalls, it should be thought of as some kind of conspiracy." In the face of the extensive negative publicity, Blankfein was determined to defend his company as well as the investment-banking industry as a whole. "We help companies grow by helping them to raise capital," he told John Arlidge. "Companies that grow create wealth. This, in turn, allows people to have jobs that create more growth and more wealth. It's a virtuous cycle." He added, "We have a social purpose." For the same article, Blankfein made a comment that brought him even more criticism and ridicule, describing himself to Arlidge as simply a banker "doing God's work." He later said that he regretted the statement and that it was not intended to be taken seriously.

Goldman Sachs was sued by the Securities and Exchange Commission in April 2010 for fraud. The company was accused of misleading investors who were involved in the purchase of collateralized debt obligations (CDOs)—asset-backed securities—that were linked to subprime mortgages. As a result of the controversy surrounding the firm, there was speculation that Blankfein might have to step down. For the *Wall Street Journal* (May 6, 2010), David Weidner penned an article entitled "Lloyd Blankfein Should Resign from Goldman Sachs," in which he wrote, "Under Mr. Blankfein, Goldman's reputation has gone from Teflon to Velcro. Criticism that used to [harm] other firms without nicking . . . Goldman now seem to only stick to Goldman." Blankfein did not resign, however, and in July 2010 Goldman Sachs agreed to pay $550 million to settle the case—one of the largest settlements in financial history.

In 2009 Blankfein was named number one on *Vanity Fair*'s "New Establishment" list, which profiled the top 100 people of the Information Age. That same year he was ranked 18th on *Forbes*'s list of the world's most powerful people and 45th on the *Forbes* executive-pay list. Also in 2009 Blankfein was chosen as the *Financial Times* person of the year, which led the bank analyst Christopher Whalen to cancel his subscription to the newspaper and write a disapproving letter to its editors.

Blankfein, who is five feet eight inches tall, is known for being knowledgeable about history. He is a member of the dean's advisory board at Harvard Law School, the Harvard University Committee on University Resources, and the advisory board of Tsinghua University School of Economics

and Management, and he is on the board of overseers for the Weill Medical College of Cornell University. He is also a co-chairman of the Partnership for New York City and a member of the Robin Hood Foundation. Blankfein has been married to Laura Susan Jacobs, a former corporate lawyer, since June 1983. The couple have three adult children. In 2008 Blankfein bought a $26.5 million apartment on Central Park West in Manhattan, in one of the most fashionable buildings in New York City. As of 2009 he also owned a home near the ocean in Sagaponack, New York. A Democrat, Blankfein contributed heavily to U.S. senator John Kerry's 2004 presidential campaign.

—J.P.

Suggested Reading: CNNMoney.com Mar. 2010; (London) *Independent* (on-line) Apr. 24, 2010; (London) *Sunday Times* (on-line) Nov. 8, 2009; *New York Times* (on-line) June 10, 2007; *Time* (on-line) Aug. 31, 2009

Boxx, Shannon

June 29, 1977– Soccer player

Address: c/o U.S. Soccer Federation, 1801 S. Prairie Ave., Chicago, IL 60616

"You might not be the star that gets all the notice, but if you work hard, someone is eventually going to notice it," the soccer player Shannon Boxx said, as quoted on DigSoccer.com. Boxx began her international career in 2003, at the relatively late age of 26, when the impressive results of her hard work led April Heinrichs, then the coach of the U.S. Women's National Soccer Team (WNT), to recruit her. She was the first U.S. player in women's soccer history to be named to a World Cup roster without ever having played for the national team, and she was the first American to score in each of the first three games she played with the U.S. team. She went on to become one of the WNT's central and most recognizable figures as well as one of the most versatile female defensive midfielders in the world. She has played in two World Cups, won gold medals at the 2004 and 2008 Olympic Games, and helped the U.S. women's team finish in first place six times at the Algarve Cup, a prestigious global event held in Portugal every February since 1994. In addition, she has been nominated three times for the World Player of the Year Award (in 2004, 2005, and 2008) by the International Federation of Soccer Associations (FIFA, an acronym derived from its name in French). "I never get sick of soccer," Boxx told Ned Barnett for the Raleigh, North Carolina, *News & Observer* (June 19, 2003). "It's a great game, especially when you understand it."

Stephen Dunn/Getty Images

Boxx excelled as a member of the Notre Dame University women's soccer team and played for three years with Women's United Soccer Association teams during that league's three-year lifetime (2001–03). Currently she is a member of the Washington Freedom, with the Women's Professional Soccer league. She has been described as physically aggressive, tenacious, and consistent and has been called a fiercely competitive workhorse and a "leader by example." "Fight, grunt, battle: That's my personality," she once said, as quoted by Scott

M. Reid in the *Orange County (California) Register* (August 24, 2007). Julie Foudy, the WNT captain from 1992 to 2004, told Mike Jensen for the *Philadelphia Inquirer* (September 28, 2008) that Boxx is "like a Viking. She's diving into tackles and knocking people over. Your ball-winner. She's perfect for that." "Not only is she a great defender in the midfield, but she's also great with the ball and has a calming influence on the team," Greg Ryan, who coached the WNT from 2005 to 2007, told an Associated Press reporter, as posted on *USA Today* (August 24, 2007, on-line). "On top of that, she's great in scoring goals. It's rare to find all those qualities wrapped up in one player." "She's got power and grace, and she's balancing those two," Boxx's WNT colleague Brandi Chastain told Grahame L. Jones for the *Los Angeles Times* (September 1, 2003). "You don't find too many players who can do that."

The daughter of a white mother and an African-American father, Shannon Leigh Boxx was born on June 29, 1977 in Fontana, California. (Some sources erroneously list the month as July.) Her parents' union ended when Boxx was very young; afterward her mother, Julie Boxx, an administrator for the City of Los Angeles Department of Recreation and Parks, raised Boxx and her sister, Gillian, as a single parent in Torrance, Los Angeles County, California. Boxx told an interviewer for *Girl Talk* (on-line) that Gillian, who is almost four years her senior, "has always been my one role model that I have tried to emulate. . . . She taught me how to take care of myself, be independent, and believe in myself." Gillian Boxx became a world-class softball player; she was a catcher on the gold-medal-winning U.S. women's softball team at the 1996 Olympic Games. "I definitely wasn't as good as my sister" in softball, Boxx told John Powers for the *Boston Globe* (September 25, 2003). "I decided: 'I have to find a sport where I'm better than you.'" She told John Philip Wyllie for *Soccer Digest* (December 2003) that she and her sister "have this little game going that we are always fighting for our Mom's acceptance as the number one daughter. I think we go by who is doing better in sports." The girls' mother, meanwhile, Boxx told an interviewer for Women's Professional Soccer (WPS, January 30, 2008, on-line), "allowed us to spread our wings and choose what we wanted to do. . . . She put us in sports right away. We loved it. She never held us back." Boxx and her sister spent much of their free time playing athletic games at a local park. "I was in such a great area to be able to run outside. It was safe," she told the WPS interviewer. Usually she was the only girl among a group of boys. "When you play on all-boys teams you have to prove yourself. You can't be weak," she told Scott M. Reid. From 1988 to 1994 Boxx played youth-league soccer with what was known as the Torrance United Waves Soccer Club; her team won regional titles in 1993 and 1994, and Boxx won Most Valuable Player (MVP) honors after both tournaments.

From 1991 to 1995 Boxx attended South Torrance High School, where she played soccer, volleyball, basketball, and softball and was named to the *Parade* All-American girls' soccer team in her senior year. As a student at Notre Dame University, in Indiana, she played with the Fighting Irish women's soccer team, a member of the Big East Conference in National Collegiate Athletic Association (NCAA) Division I soccer. During her freshman year she helped the team win its first NCAA women's championship. She was named to Soccer America's All-Freshman team, as well as to the All–Big East team, and earned the same honors in each of the next three years. Also each year during her tenure, the women's team won their conference's championships. Boxx finished her college career by winning the Big East Scholar-Athlete Award and tying the school's record for career games played—101—on her way to amassing 39 goals, 57 assists, and 135 points. She graduated in 1999 with a B.A. degree in psychology and African-American studies. In 2010 *Sports Illustrated* (on-line) ranked her third among Notre Dame's all-time top-10 athletes.

In 1999 there was no professional women's soccer league in the U.S. Boxx—"labelled as something of a nomad after her college days," according to FIFA.com (November 30, 2005)—played briefly with the Boston Renegades of the amateur W-League before moving to Germany to play for FC Saarbrücken in the women's Bundesliga. She left Germany after six months, because she knew little German, the coach knew no English, she missed the U.S., and the experience "just wasn't fun," as she recalled to Scott M. Reid for the *Orange County Register* (September 25, 2003). After she returned to the U.S., she trained for a while with the soccer team at Saddleback College, a community college in Mission Viejo, California, and played with Ajax America, an amateur team; she supported herself as a hostess at a California Pizza Kitchen outlet.

On July 10, 1999 the more than 90,000 spectators at the Rose Bowl, in Pasadena, California—a record audience for a women's sports competition—watched the U.S. Women's National Soccer Team beat China at that year's FIFA Women's World Cup. The members of the U.S. team included such outstanding athletes as Mia Hamm, Brandi Chastain, Kristine Lilly, and Joy Fawcett. In 2000, in the wake of that triumph, the Women's United Soccer Association (WUSA) was set up, as the first professional women's soccer league in the U.S. in which all players earned salaries. In the inaugural draft, in April 2001, Boxx was selected by the San Diego Spirit as the 19th pick overall. Boxx missed only 20 minutes of the WUSA's first, 21-game season and was named to the All-USA team for 2001. Nevertheless, in 2002 her playing time was greatly reduced—"for reasons she can't explain," Tom Timmermann wrote for the *St. Louis (Missouri) Post-Dispatch* (April 9, 2010)—and in September of that year, she was traded to the New York Power in exchange for the superstar prospect Aly Wagner.

"By then, her confidence was as diminished as her time on the field," Jeré Longman wrote for the *New York Times* (September 25, 2003). Initially unhappy about having to leave California (and her then-fiancé, Sean Taketa), she spent the off-season improving her fitness. "Once I found out that it was Power coach Tom Sermanni that wanted me, I became gung ho about it and I was ready to go out and prove myself again," Boxx told Wyllie. "That extra level of fitness allowed Tom to let me go wherever I wanted to go on the field. In San Diego, they wanted me to defend, defend, defend. In New York I was told that if I could go forward that I should do it." At the end of the 2003 season, Boxx was named to the All-WUSA First Team (the league's top 11 players) and was awarded First Team MVP honors. "Shannon is the best in our league at that position"—midfield—"physical, strong, technical," Tony DiCicco, the WUSA commissioner from 2000 to 2003 and a former WNT coach, said after the 2003 season, according to Longman.

Ned Barnett reported that at a WUSA press conference held two days after the league's 2003 All-Star Game, he was the only journalist who came to Boxx's table to talk with her. "In the world of professional sports, Boxx is an endangered species—an athlete in love with her game, undemanding about money and grateful for her fans," he wrote. "If the world was a better place and we had better priorities, there would be a line out the door to meet her." The WUSA, meanwhile, had been suffering from insufficient attendance at games and low TV ratings and was falling ever more deeply in debt. In a bid to keep the league from going bankrupt, "top players agreed this year to take salary cuts of 40 percent," Barnett wrote, noting that the average player earned $37,235 annually. "We make enough to have this as our only job, let's just say that," Boxx told him. "We're not really in it for the money though. . . . I play because I love this sport." She also told him, "This is the greatest job you can have. If it takes a pay cut so we can continue playing and have this entire year to make [the WUSA] better so that next year it's around and growing and expanding . . . I'm going to do it." (In a 2007 article about the inequalities between the salaries of male and female professional athletes in the U.S., a writer for the Women's Sports Foundation Web site pointed out, "For finishing in third place in the 2003 Women's World Cup, each U.S. women's national soccer team member was awarded $25,000. They would have received $58,000 if they had won the Cup. For reaching the quarterfinal of the World Cup in 2002, the U.S. men's national soccer team members received $200,000 each." The bonuses reflect the fact that while the U.S. Soccer Federation receives millions of dollars from corporations and other sources for the American men's World Cup team, the organization gets no money when the women's team qualifies for the World Cup.) The WUSA folded on September 15, 2003.

In anticipation of the WUSA's demise, Boxx planned to matriculate at Pepperdine University, in Malibu, California, in the fall term, to pursue a master's degree in clinical psychology; she was also committed to working as assistant coach of women's soccer at California State University–Dominguez Hills, in Carson. Earlier during the 2003 WUSA season, April Heinrichs, the WNT coach, had spoken with Boxx. "She told me that she had been watching me and that I was playing great," Boxx told Wyllie. "She said that I would get my chance, but she didn't know if it would be before or after the World Cup." On the assumption that Heinrichs would contact her again after the World Cup, Boxx bought tickets to attend the final competition of that event, scheduled for October 12 at the Home Depot Center in Carson. But during the summer Heinrichs invited Boxx to attend the WNT training camp, in August. Later that month she told Boxx that she had chosen her for the national team. "I think what she likes about me is my hardness, my toughness, my strength, my size," Boxx told Grahame L. Jones. Boxx was 26 when she joined the WNT—far older than most players: Hamm, Lilly, and Foudy, for example, had come on board at ages 15, 16, and 17, respectively.

Boxx scored a goal in each of the U.S. team's warm-up games, thus earning a place on the starting lineup for the first game of the World Cup. In each of her first three games, she scored once. Heinrichs told interviewers that Boxx had adapted to international play faster than any athlete she had ever seen. "Shannon is playing brilliantly . . . ," she said, as quoted by Andy Gardiner for *USA Today* (September 22, 2003). "Having her on our team has freed Julie Foudy up a little bit, it's freed up Kristine Lilly and allowed us to play a three-[person] midfield. And when you can do that, you can play three up top"—that is, in the front line. In the semifinals the U.S. lost to the eventual World Cup winner, Germany. At the end of the tournament, Boxx was named to the women's World Cup All-star team. In May 2004 she was named captain of the All-Star World XI team, which played an exhibition match against Germany as part of FIFA's centennial celebrations in Paris, France. She started in all but one of the 32 games she played with the WNT in 2004, including all six matches at the 2004 Summer Olympic Games, held in Athens, Greece. The U.S. team beat Brazil in extra time in those Games to win the gold medal. That year Boxx scored eight goals and set up five—a remarkable achievement for a defensive midfielder. Boxx came in seventh in votes for the 2004 FIFA World Player of the Year Award.

In 2005 Boxx started in the nine matches in which the WNT took part. To train competitively between international games, she played with Ajax Southern California of the Women's Premier Soccer League—"an independent national league whose main focus is on the development of highly competitive amateur women's soccer teams," according to its Web site. She was again nominated for the World Player of the Year Award, coming in third behind the Brazilian player Marta, in first place, and the German player Birgit Prinz.

In the spring of 2006, Boxx underwent surgery to repair damaged cartilage in her right hip. In July, after two months of physical therapy, she returned to train with the WNT. A collision with a player during her first practice session resulted in two torn ligaments in her right knee. Each tear required a separate operation, and her rehabilitation lasted for eight months. "I had to learn how to sprint all over again. My therapist had to explain it to me step by step," Boxx told Sal Ruibal for *USA Today* (August 24, 2007). She told the Associated Press reporter, "The biggest part for me that was hard was just that doubt of, 'Am I going to come back the same?' I got hurt at a time where I felt like I was going on a high. I was a leader on this team and I was playing at my peak." Boxx resumed playing competitively in early 2007 and quickly reestablished herself as a team leader. The WNT were unbeaten that year and ranked first in the world before the World Cup. They reached the semifinals of that tournament, where Brazil defeated them, 4–0. "It is difficult to imagine a more complete collapse than the one the United States suffered," Longman wrote for the *New York Times* (September 29, 2007). "Almost everything that could have gone wrong did." Boxx played a central role in the loss, because she was ejected just before halftime, after she had been cautioned twice for fouls; the team had to finish the match one player short.

The U.S. Women's National Soccer Team, coached by Pia Sundhage, was among 12 teams that competed in women's soccer at the 2008 Olympics, held in Beijing, China. In the gold-medal match, held on August 21, the U.S. triumphed over Brazil, 1–0. The next year marked the debut of a new league, Women's Professional Soccer, with seven teams. Boxx played for the Los Angeles Sol and served that squad as captain. The Sol ended the season in first place, with 12 wins, three losses, five ties, and 41 points. In 2010 the Sol disbanded, and Boxx, a free agent, moved to the St. Louis, Missouri, Athletica. At the end of May 2010, the Athletica, too, ended its run, for financial reasons. Again a free agent, Boxx joined the FC Gold Pride, in the San Francisco Bay area. That team ceased operations, also for monetary reasons, in November 2010. Boxx is currently a member of the Washington Freedom, along with her WNT teammates Hope Solo, Christie Rampone, and Lindsay Tarpley.

On March 9, 2011 the WNT won the Algarve Cup for the eighth time, defeating Iceland 4–2. Earlier, on March 7, in a 4–2 victory against Finland, Boxx scored one goal. The WNT will be competing in the FIFA Women's World Cup this summer.

Greg Ryan described Boxx to the Associated Press reporter as invariably "straight-up, good, and honest." Boxx has coached many girls' soccer teams and for some years ran soccer camps. She lives in Hermosa Beach, California. (She and Tekata never married and ended their relationship years ago.) Boxx has said that after she retires from soccer, she may follow in the footsteps of her sister, who has built a second career as a firefighter.

—M.M., M.H.

Suggested Reading: *Boston Globe* Sports C p2 Sep. 25, 2003; FIFA.com Nov. 30, 2005; *Los Angeles Times* Sports D p3 Sep. 1, 2003; *New York Times* D p8 Sep. 25, 2003; *Orange County Register* Sports Sep. 25, 2003, Aug. 24, 2007; *Oregonian* Sports D p1 Sep. 23, 2005; (Raleigh, North Carolina) *News & Observer* Sports C p1 June 19, 2003; *Soccer Digest* p52+ Dec. 2003; U.S. Soccer (on-line) Sep. 20, 2003; *USA Today* Sports C p10 Sep. 22, 2003, (on-line) Aug. 24, 2007; *Zimbio.com* July 3, 2008

Courtesy of WellPoint Inc.

Braly, Angela F.

(BRAH-lee)

July 2, 1961– Health-insurance company executive

Address: WellPoint Inc., 120 Monument Cir., Indianapolis, IN 46204

As chair, president, and chief executive officer (CEO) of the commercial health-insurance company WellPoint Inc., Angela Braly is widely regarded as the most powerful woman in the health-care industry. In terms of numbers of people covered, WellPoint is the largest health insurer in the United States. When Braly succeeded Larry Glasscock as WellPoint's president and CEO, on June 1, 2007, she joined the exclusive ranks of female heads of *Fortune* 500 companies and also became the first woman to head a *Fortune* 50 company. She replaced Glasscock as WellPoint's chair in 2010. The Indianapolis, Indiana–based WellPoint, which provides coverage to nearly 35 million people (one in nine Americans) and operates Blue Cross–Blue Shield companies in 14 states, brings in roughly $60 billion in annual revenue. Prior to stepping into her current role, Braly, who has a degree in law, spent two years as WellPoint's general counsel and government-affairs strategist, during which she ran the company's Medicare contracting business—the largest of its kind in the nation. Prior to that she served as president and chief executive of WellPoint's Missouri division from 2003 to 2005. Known for her charm and deal-making abilities, Braly has used her expertise in public policy and experience in negotiating with government agencies to guide WellPoint as it faces challenges posed by the recent global economic recession (such as loss of customers due to mass layoffs) and sweeping national health-care reforms. The administration of President Barack Obama has cited WellPoint's practices as representative of injustices perpetrated by the health-insurance industry, such as canceling the policies of very sick patients. Braly does not apologize for such actions. She told Reed Abelson for the *New York Times* (May 16, 2010), "I'm not a politician. I'm a businessperson."

Braly was born Angela Frick on July 2, 1961 in Dallas, Texas. After she graduated from Richardson High School, in a Dallas suburb, in 1979, Braly attended Texas Tech University (TTU), in Lubbock, where she studied finance. Braly's father, an electrical engineer, died in a car accident when she was 18, and her mother subsequently worked as a secretary to support Braly's siblings and help pay Braly's tuition. Braly received a bachelor's of business administration (BBA) degree from TTU in 1983. She then enrolled at the Dedman School of Law, at Southern Methodist University (SMU), in University Park, a Dallas suburb. Braly earned a J.D. degree from SMU in 1985.

After she completed law school, Braly moved to St. Louis, Missouri, where she worked as an attorney for the law firm Lewis, Rice & Fingersh; her husband, Douglas Braly, an accountant, became the treasurer of his family's trucking business. At Lewis, Rice & Fingersh, Braly became known for her drive, dedication, and energy. John Riffle, a partner at the law firm and one of her mentors, recalled to Daniel Lee for the *Indianapolis Star* (February 27, 2007) that she "was often seen carrying around an overstuffed briefcase, papers hanging out of the sides, as she ran from place to place hand[ling] her duties as a lawyer and a working mother." Braly was named a partner in corporate finance at the law firm, and in the 1990s she made a name for herself after helping the firm's client Anthem Blue Cross and Blue Shield of Missouri convert from a nonprofit into a publicly traded

company called RightChoice. She tackled an array of legal problems for RightChoice before taking on the job of interim general counsel, in 1997. Two years later she became an executive vice president and official general counsel for RightChoice and left Lewis, Rice & Fingersh.

As general counsel Braly brokered a deal with Missouri state regulators and community groups that established the Missouri Foundation of Health, which was to pay for health care for uninsured Missourians. At Braly's urging the foundation allocated grant money for various projects neglected by the state. Braly, whose negotiating style had won over lawmakers and other officials, recalled to Vanessa Fuhrmans for the *Wall Street Journal* (November 19, 2007, on-line) that she became completely "invested" in RightChoice's legal concerns, adding, "I felt we were really striving to do the right thing." Braly's association with the health insurer WellPoint began in 2002, when WellPoint acquired RightChoice, for $1.3 billion. In August 2003 Braly was appointed president and CEO of WellPoint's Missouri enterprises, responsible for overseeing all facets of those businesses and for devising new ways to satisfy customers' needs. Braly's expertise in overcoming political and regulatory hurdles was called upon in 2004, when she served as a key adviser during the merger of WellPoint and Anthem Blue Cross and Blue Shield; with that merger WellPoint became the largest health insurer in the U.S. Braly moved to WellPoint's Indianapolis headquarters in 2005, when the company's CEO, Larry Glasscock, named her executive vice president, general counsel, and chief public-affairs officer.

In late 2005 Braly served as a primary strategist during WellPoint's $6.5 billion acquisition of WellChoice, the parent company of the Empire Blue Cross–Blue Shield plans in New York and New Jersey. The deal marked the last of a string of major acquisitions by WellPoint under Glasscock. During Braly's two-year tenure as WellPoint's general counsel, she was responsible for leading the company's government-affairs efforts and its National Government Services division, which handles Medicare claims—a greater number than any other company. Her knowledge of public policy and experience in dealing with the government led WellPoint's board to name her as Glasscock's successor when he unexpectedly announced his resignation, in 2007, choosing her from among 200 others under consideration. The selection of Braly came as a surprise to many analysts and investors, most of whom had pegged David Colby, WellPoint's chief financial officer, or John Watts, president of the company's consumer and commercial businesses, as Glasscock's most likely successor. Glasscock, who stayed on as WellPoint's chairman until 2010, said of Braly, as quoted by Daniel Lee, "She's got an incredible combination of business experience, vision, the right operational experience and finally, and very importantly for the future, very good experience in the area of public policy." Randy Brown, WellPoint's chief human-resources officer, told Vanessa Fuhrmans that Braly was "not afraid to deal with tough challenges" and that she "deals with the reality that she has, not the reality that she'd like."

On June 1, 2007 Braly officially succeeded Glasscock as WellPoint's CEO and joined the company's board of directors. Braly oversees a firm that has 40,000 employees and insures nearly 35 million individuals. With upwards of $60 billion in annual revenue, the company is among the most profitable health insurers in the U.S. Remaining in that position requires constant maneuvering in a health-care landscape that is continuously changing. Almost immediately after Braly became WellPoint's head, she assembled a new management team, led extensive restructuring and reorganization moves, and increased her public profile by traveling to each of the 14 states where WellPoint operates Blue Cross and Blue Shield health plans.

One of Braly's main goals has been to "help stabilize health care costs and premiums," David Whelan wrote. Braly told Daniel Lee for the *Indianapolis Star* (March 15, 2008), "We're looking at the many different ways that we can have a positive impact on the question of what the cost and quality of health care is, and what it needs to be." In 2009 falling stock prices forced Braly to cut more than 2,000 jobs at WellPoint.

Barack Obama singled out WellPoint during his push for health-care reform early in his presidency, citing the company's practices of raising premiums on policies already deemed too expensive (the increases were significantly higher than those proposed by most of its competitors) and cancelling the policies of patients with unusually large medical expenses. Braly testified before a congressional committee in February 2010 in defense of WellPoint's premium increases. "Raising our premiums was not something we wanted to do," she said, as quoted by Robert Pear in the *New York Times* (February 25, 2010, on-line). "But we believe this was the most prudent choice, given the rising cost of care and the problems caused by many younger and healthier policyholders dropping or reducing their coverage during tough economic times. By law, premiums must be reasonable in relationship to benefits provided, which means they need to reflect the known and anticipated costs they will cover."

With the passage of President Obama's two health-care-reform bills, the Patient Protection and Affordable Care Act and the Health Care and Education Reconciliation Act, both of which were signed into law in March 2010, WellPoint and other health insurers have been forced to reevaluate the way they do business. The new legislation will extend health-care coverage to the 32 million Americans who are currently uninsured and will ultimately make health care more accessible and affordable for customers through a new, regulated marketplace. Under the new reforms WellPoint and its competitors are no longer allowed to deny coverage to children based on preexisting conditions, and beginning in 2014 they will not be able to deny coverage to anyone because of a preexisting condition. In addition, insurance companies are now required to allow all dependents to stay on their parents' or guardians' plans until age 26. Braly has described government-run health care as a "blunt instrument," according to Patrick Howington, writing for the Lousiville, Kentucky, *Courier-Journal* (September 11, 2007), and she has criticized the stipulation in federal law that will force most Americans to get health insurance coverage or pay a penalty, an approach that she believes will prove to be ineffective in the long run. (In 2014, as per the individual mandate clause in the law, every American—with some exceptions in the cases of those with particularly low incomes—will be required to acquire health insurance or face an annual fine.) Braly has instead placed her focus on the individual consumer and favors a combination of public and private initiatives (heavily weighted toward the latter) to expand health-care coverage. "A politician once told me, 'Know who you are, because a lot of people will tell you what you should be,'" she told Vanessa Fuhrmans. "We need to know who we are as a company, and we need to be a company that delivers value and can prove it." She told Howington, "The private sector creates competition. With competition you get innovation."

Vanessa Fuhrmans described Braly as having "a personable nature that belies her steeliness and skill as a tough-minded negotiator." Braly is a member of the board of Procter and Gamble. A registered Republican who has contributed to the campaigns of Republican candidates, she is a member of America's Health Insurance Plans Political Action Committee. She has served as a volunteer for the United Way Foundation. Braly was named one of the 25 most influential women in business by the *St. Louis Business Journal* in 2000 and was listed among *Modern Healthcare* magazine's top 25 women in business in 2007. *Forbes* magazine ranked her 16th, fourth, eighth, and 12th among the world's most powerful women in 2007, 2008, 2009, and 2010, respectively. Braly lives in Indianapolis with her husband, Douglas, who retired from his job to become the full-time caretaker of their three children; he now sells and invests in real estate and serves as an adjunct instructor of business administration at an Indianapolis community college. "I don't have a great system," Braly told David Whelan, referring to her hectic schedule. "I just have a great husband."

—C.C.

Suggested Reading: *American* p102+ Sep./Oct. 2007; *Forbes* p116 Sep. 17, 2007; *Indianapolis Star* p1 Feb. 27, 2007, p1 June 3, 2007, p1 Mar. 15, 2008; (Louisville, Kentucky) *Courier-Journal* D p1 Sep. 11, 2007; *New York Times* p1 May 16, 2010, (on-line) Feb. 27, 2007; *St. Louis Business*

Journal p30 Aug. 14, 2000; *Wall Street Journal* (on-line) Nov. 19, 2007; WellPoint Web site

Frederick M. Brown/Getty Images

Brand, Russell

June 4, 1975– Comedian; actor; television and radio host

Address: c/o John Noel Management, Block B, Imperial Works, Perren St., London NW5 3ED, England

The British actor and comedian Russell Brand seems never to have doubted that he was going to be famous. As a 16-year-old he wrote in the high-school yearbook of a friend, "You might be as famous as me one day. If so, see you at the top." Today Brand is one of the best-known comics in Britain. His scene-stealing appearance as a rock star in the 2008 film *Forgetting Sarah Marshall* introduced him to American audiences, who have since been fascinated by the tall, lanky, flamboyant, articulate, hyperenergetic Brit often seen in eyeliner and women's pants. Brand's rise to fame, however, did not progress as smoothly as his initial confidence might suggest. His career started in 2000, when he was hired by MTV to present music videos for the show *Dance Floor Chart*; his charisma brought him additional television and radio work, but scandal, substance abuse, and self-doubt threatened to destroy his career almost before it took off. Brand had to decide which was stronger—his tendency toward self-destruction or his dreams of stardom. In the last few years, he appears to have chosen the latter, kicking his drug habit, writing

two successful memoirs, and giving critically acclaimed performances in movies including *Get Him to the Greek* (2010).

Russell Edward Brand was born on June 4, 1975 in Grays, Essex, England, the only child of Barbara Brand, a secretary, and Ronald Henry Brand, a photographer. Raised primarily by his mother following his parents' separation when he was six months old, Brand remembers his childhood and teen years as being difficult; he was sexually abused by a tutor at the age of seven, and the following year, after Brand's mother developed uterine cancer, he was sent to live with relatives while she underwent treatment. (Brand's mother had two more bouts with cancer before he was 18.) In an interview with Ria Higgins for the London *Times Online* (December 23, 2007), Brand's mother described him as having been a sensitive, precocious child. Brand also developed his offbeat sense of style early on. "Before he was two, Russell was already talking; he was also a very affectionate child," she told Higgins. "One of his favourite books was *Pinocchio*, and one Christmas I bought him a Pinocchio puppet. But he didn't have it more than five minutes when he cut the strings off. I didn't tell him off but I asked him why he'd done it, and he told me it was because he couldn't cuddle him properly. I mean, my heart just melted. To be honest, although he could be willful, it was hard for me to be angry with him and the problem with sending him up to his room was that he didn't see it as a punishment at all. He'd go up and play or sit on his bed and start reading. . . . He loved books. I remember when he was 11, he'd been reading about Oscar Wilde"—an Irish-born writer and flamboyant figure whose behavior outraged many in 19th-century England—"and he asked me if I'd buy him a paisley dressing gown for Christmas." Brand told Chrissy Iley for the London *Sunday Times* (November 1, 2009), "I'm an only child of a single mother—it probably meant that I'm demanding and have high expectations of women. I look for salvation and redemption, to be utterly embraced."

A chubby adolescent, Brand developed an eating disorder in an effort to gain control over his body—and as a way of acting on the self-destructive impulses he felt. In an interview with a writer for the London *Daily Mail* (June 23, 2006, on-line), Brand described his battle with the eating disorder as his first experience with addiction: "I was bulimic when I was 14. I had problems with food and self-harming. I've always had these odd compulsive traits looking for an outlet." Speaking with Erik Hedegaard for *Rolling Stone* (June 10, 2010), Brand referred to his teenage self as "tubby and unlovely and odd and obscure and bland." At 16 Brand, who did not get along with his mother's live-in partner and felt unable to cope with her illness, left home. By then he had begun experimenting with drugs.

Brand's first acting role, meanwhile, came when he was a 15-year-old student at the Grays School, where he played Fat Sam in a production of *Bugsy Malone*. He described the experience to Barbara Allen for the London *Observer* (June 18, 2006, on-line) as "a blissful epiphany." According to National Public Radio (March 14, 2009, on-line), Brand said that performing led him to realize that "life doesn't have to be the maudlin trudge through misery . . . it can be a right laugh. Being able to make people laugh . . . imbues you with power." Soon afterward Brand applied successfully to the Italia Conti Academy of Theatre Arts, in London, from which he was expelled before the end of the year for poor attendance. In 1995 Brand was accepted at the Drama Centre, also in London. By that point he had become a full-fledged heroin addict and alcoholic, and in the final term of his last year at the Drama Centre, despite having impressed teachers with his ability, he was asked to leave. (According to one source, he left on his own after being taken out of a play in which he had the lead role.)

Brand next decided to focus on comedy. In 2000 he finished fourth in the Hackney Empire New Act of the Year stand-up comedy competition. Also in 2000 his stand-up act was well-received at the Edinburgh Fringe Festival, and on the strength of that, he was hired that year as a video deejay by the music channel MTV, touring nightclubs in Britain and the Spanish island of Ibiza to present videos for the show *Dance Floor Chart*. Brand also hosted an afternoon music-request show called *Select* and was hired to co-host a Sunday-afternoon talk show with another English comedian, Matt Morgan, on the London indie-rock radio station XFM. With a regular paycheck, Brand could afford to buy harder drugs, and his substance abuse escalated, which did not escape the notice of his employers. His judgment clouded by heroin and crack, Brand was fired by MTV after coming to work on the day after the September 11, 2001 terrorist attacks dressed as the Al Qaeda leader Osama bin Laden. A year later he lost his job at XFM for, among other actions, bringing homeless people into the studio and reading pornographic letters aloud on the air. He told the *Daily Mail* writer about that period that he "was basically ill at the time."

In 2002 Brand conceived, wrote, and starred in the short-lived documentary-style television comedy series *RE:Brand*, which aired on the now-defunct digital-satellite channel UK Play. The content of the show—which Tanith Carey, writing for the *Daily Mail* (January 29, 2007, on-line), called "an excuse to sink to new levels of depravity"—often involved sex. In one often-mentioned installment, Brand participated in a boxing match with his father, during which he vented his long-held anger at the older man.

During that period Brand's agent abandoned him. When his new agent, John Noel, caught him using heroin in a restroom during a Christmas party in 2002, Noel promised he would continue to represent Brand, but only if he checked into rehab and kicked alcohol and drugs for good. After three months in rehab, Brand emerged sober and eager to get his career back on track. Brand, who has remained drug-free ever since, has said that giving up drugs was not easy and even that he misses drugs from time to time. As quoted by National Public Radio, Brand said, "One feels enshrouded and comforted by substance abuse, but then you realize that it wasn't making you any better at what you did, it just makes you care less about being rubbish."

In 2004 Brand was hired by Endemol, the producers of the *Big Brother* series of reality television shows, to host *Big Brother's Efourum*; he later hosted a similar show, called *Big Brother's Big Mouth*, described by Carey as "a verbal free-for-all that could have descended into chaos had it not been for Brand's quick-thinking repartee." Also in 2004 Brand performed his confessional, one-man show *Better Now* to sold-out audiences at the Edinburgh Festival, in Scotland. The show received four- and five-star reviews from the London newspapers the *Times,* the *Guardian*, and the *Metro* as well as the *Scotsman*. Brand had similar success with his stand-up shows at the festival in 2005 and 2006.

In the spring of 2006, MTV tapped Brand to host a new talk show, *1 Leicester Square*, focusing on celebrity guests and musical entertainment. The show was widely viewed as a comeback vehicle for Brand, who slowly regained MTV's trust and was thus awarded more freedom. Later in 2006 the debate show *Russell Brand's Got Issues* debuted on E4. Sluggish ratings led the network to rework the program as the *Russell Brand Show*, which aired on E4's parent station, Channel 4. The *Russell Brand Show* ran for only five weeks after its first broadcast, in November 2006. That year Brand headlined a national comedy tour, called "Shame"; much of his material was confessional, concerning his childhood, his time as a struggling actor/comedian, and his rise to fame, drug addiction, and rehabilitation. He hosted the 2006 English NME (National Music Express) Awards, during which he engaged in a well-publicized name-calling match with the Irish singer-songwriter and activist Bob Geldof. Also in 2006 Brand was offered the chance to host his own talk show on BBC Radio. Despite its popularity, the *Russell Brand Show* went into hiatus in late October 2008, when Brand was forced to resign after an on-air prank in which he and a guest left a series of lewd messages on the answering machine of the popular British actor Andy Sachs (who played Manuel on the sitcom *Fawlty Towers*); the airing of the episode sparked a national outcry and cost the network a considerable sum in fines. After nearly two years the *Russell Brand Show* resurfaced in a slightly different incarnation on the BBC radio station Talk-Sport.

The year 2007 proved to be Brand's busiest up until that time. He hosted the BRIT Awards and appeared in two new shows: *Russell Brand On the*

Road, a documentary about the writer Jack Kerouac, and *Russell Brand's Ponderland*, on which the comedian discussed a range of topics in a series of standup-style monologues interspersed with footage from old television shows and movies. *Ponderland* was nominated for an award from the British Academy of Film and Television Arts (BAFTA). That year also saw Brand's second national stand-up tour, "Russell Brand: Only Joking." (Footage from that tour, "Shame," and other live performances was included on his 2009 DVD release, *Russell Brand: Doing Life Live*.) In 2007 Brand's *My Booky Wook: A Memoir of Sex, Drugs, and Stand-Up* was published by Hodder & Stoughton in the U.K. *My Booky Wook* was named biography of the year at the British Book Awards ceremony in 2008. In June of that year, Brand signed a £1.8 million contract with the publisher Harper-Collins. The first of his books to be published by that company, *Articles of Faith*, a collection of articles from the football column Brand wrote for the London *Guardian* starting in 2006, appeared in 2008, and the following year the company published *My Booky Wook* in the U.S. Bill Scheft, writing for the *New York Times* (March 27, 2009), called it "a child's garden of vices" and "a relentless ride with a comic mind clearly at the wheel." A second memoir, *My Booky Wook 2: This Time It's Personal*, was published in 2010.

Meanwhile, Brand, who had acted in small roles in a handful of mostly comic British television series and made-for-TV movies, made his breakthrough as a comedic actor in the 2008 film *Forgetting Sarah Marshall*. In the movie a man's friends take him on a Hawaiian vacation to help him get over his recent break-up with the title character; complications ensue when the group discover they are staying at the same resort as Sarah and her new boyfriend. Brand played the boyfriend, the rock star Aldous Snow. Kristen Bell, who played Sarah Marshall, recalled to Hedegaard her first meeting with her future co-star: "When I walked in the room to test with [Brand], I saw a man wearing more makeup than I was, in tighter jeans than I was, and who was prettier than I was. I said, 'Guys, no way.' And then he went into the bathroom for 10 minutes to primp his hair a little higher . . . , came back and gave the most amazing audition I've ever seen. His brain is so expeditious, oftentimes I'm quite certain he's an alien." *Forgetting Sarah Marshall* represented many Americans' first exposure to the English comedian, who was still relatively unknown in the U.S. when it was announced that he would host the 2008 MTV Video Music Awards. During the ceremony some of Brand's jokes offended viewers (he facetiously called the singer Britney Spears "the female Christ" and referred to President George W. Bush as "that retard . . . cowboy fella"). Still, when the ratings for the awards show proved to be 20 percent higher than those of the previous year, MTV invited Brand to host the program again in 2009—a year that brought the show the highest ratings it had seen

since 2004. Brand himself won the Best Live Stand-Up Award at the 2008 British Comedy Awards ceremony.

In early 2009 Brand returned to stand-up, traveling the United Kingdom, Australia and the U.S. on a tour called "Russell Brand: Scandalous." Additional dates were added to the tour in November to raise money for the substance-abuse rehabilitation charity Focus 12, of which Brand has been a supporter since he gave up drugs. In March of that year, Brand again made his way into American homes with an hour-long stand-up special for Comedy Central, *Russell Brand in New York City*. The year 2009 also marked Brand's return to radio, when he and his close friend Noel Gallagher, the guitarist for the band Oasis, hosted a once-only football talk show, the *Russell Brand and Noel Gallagher Football Show*, for TalkSport.

Brand revived his *Forgetting Sarah Marshall* character, Aldous Snow, for the 2010 buddy comedy *Get Him to the Greek*. In that film a record-company intern (played by Jonah Hill) is assigned to escort the out-of-control rock star Snow from London to the Greek Theater in Los Angeles for a show that is meant to save his failing career. Although the film received mixed reviews, Brand won praise from critics, among them Roger Ebert, who wrote for the *Chicago Sun-Times* (June 2, 2010), "Russell Brand is convincing as a rock star, imperious, self-destructive, smarter than he seems, calculating, measuring out wretched excess in survivable portions."

Brand's other film work includes the movies *Bedtime Stories* (2008), *Despicable Me* (2010), and Julie Taymor's 2010 film version of Shakespeare's *The Tempest*, in which Brand took the role of Trinculo. His upcoming projects include remakes of the 1981 film *Arthur* and the 1991 movie *Drop Dead Fred*. Brand is also collaborating with Oliver Stone on a documentary. Stone told Hedegaard about Brand, "He's different, unique, a sweetheart, a rogue, a bad boy, he's completely honest, and I think he lives in another dimension." Stone added about the comedian's manic energy, "He's burning at a very high level, and you have to wonder how long he can keep it up without burning out."

Brand, a notorious ladies' man who in the past described himself as a sex addict, has told interviewers that he is ready to leave his bed-hopping days behind. In the fall of 2010, he married the American pop-music star Katy Perry. He and his wife recently bought a home in Los Angeles.

—H.R.W.

Suggested Reading: *Chicago Sun-Times* (on-line) June 2, 2010; (London) *Daily Mail* (on-line) June 23, 2006, Jan. 29, 2007; (London) *Guardian* (on-line) Nov. 13, 2007, Apr. 6, 2010; (London) *Observer* (on-line) June 18, 2006; (London) *Sunday Times* (on-line) Nov. 1, 2009; (London) *Times Online* Dec. 23, 2007, Oct. 16, 2008; *New York Times* (on-line) Mar. 27, 2009; *Rolling Stone* (on-line) June 10, 2010

Selected Books: *My Booky Wook: A Memoir of Sex, Drugs, and Stand-Up*, 2007; *My Booky Wook 2: This Time It's Personal*, 2010

Selected Films: *Forgetting Sarah Marshall*, 2008; *Get Him to the Greek*, 2010; *The Tempest*, 2010

Jemal Countess/Getty Images

Brannaman, Buck

Jan. 29, 1962– Horse trainer; writer; motivational speaker

Address: c/o Premiere Speakers Bureau, 109 International Dr., Suite 300, Franklin, TN 37067

Buck Brannaman was one of the horse trainers who provided the inspiration for the best-selling book *The Horse Whisperer* (1995), by Nicholas Evans. When the book was made into a Hollywood film, in 1998, Brannaman served as a technical adviser and doubled for the picture's star, Robert Redford, who also directed. Brannaman and his compatriots practice a type of training called "natural horsemanship," which calls for communicating with the animal through body language, understanding its behavior, and treating it gently and respectfully, thus earning its trust. Brannaman, who overcame the effects of an abusive childhood by working with horses, wrote on his Web site, "I've started horses"—or acclimated them to the process of being saddled and ridden—"since I was 12 years old and have been bit, kicked, bucked off and run over. I've tried every physical means to contain my horse in an effort to keep from getting myself killed. I started to realize that things would come much eas-

ier for me once I learned why a horse does what he does. This method works well for me because of the kinship that develops between horse and rider."

In equestrian circles Brannaman is widely revered. The Olympic show-jumper George Morris told Carol Schmidt for the University of Montana publication *Mountains and Minds* (Spring 2007, on-line) that Brannaman is "a horseman's horseman." Morris continued, "He is a world-class rider, trainer and teacher. The horse world, in general, cannot say enough about this man." "When it comes to horses, [he] is part guru, part psychologist, and all cowboy," the broadcast journalist Tom Brokaw once said, as quoted on the Web site of Lyons Press, which published *The Faraway Horses: The Adventures and Wisdom of One of America's Most Renowned Horsemen* (2001) and *Believe: A Horseman's Journey* (2004), memoirs by Brannaman. "He's a 19th-century man in a 21st-century world, and his life is at once inspirational and instructive." Brannaman's life is the focus of *Buck*, an acclaimed 2011 documentary film.

Thousands of riders sign up for the horse-training clinics that Brannaman holds each year in the U.S. and elsewhere. He has told many of the attendees that they themselves are the sources of their horses' behavioral problems. "So often people start horses with a sort of caveman mentality," he told Paul Trachtman for *Smithsonian* magazine (May 1998). "For some people, working with the horse is just a way of stroking their own egos. Sometimes they have a lot of emotional baggage. Sometimes they lack awareness of their surroundings. That's why horses have so many problems with humans." At one clinic, according to Kathleen McFarren, writing for *Ride* magazine (August 28, 2009, on-line), a woman tried to explain to Brannaman that her horse threw tantrums. "No he doesn't," Brannaman asserted. "He [just] doesn't know what's to be expected of him. . . . I'm dealing with people problems here, not horse problems." He admitted to Trachtman that he sometimes prefers equine company to that of humans, saying, "I've run across some people I don't like, but [never] a horse."

Dan "Buck" Brannaman was born on January 29, 1962 in Sheboygan, Wisconsin. After a brief period in California during his infancy, his family moved to Coeur d'Alene, Idaho, when Brannaman was a toddler. There, his father, Ace, worked as a cable splicer and construction worker. (He also performed black-market veterinary services when called upon, suturing lacerations on local farm animals, for example, and helping to birth calves.) Brannaman's mother, Carol, worked for a utility company. Brannaman, who began riding horses at the age of three, has an older brother, Bill, who was known as "Smokie." In *The Faraway Horses* Brannaman explained why he and his brother were given nicknames: "As a young man, my father admired the famous trick roper Montie Montana, and he became infatuated with Montana's life. After returning from World War II, he realized that he would never be a Montie Montana, but he decided that his boys would be. He would live vicariously through Smokie and me—Dad figured 'Buckshot' and 'Smokie' would sell better than Dan and Bill."

The family ultimately settled in Whitehall, a tiny town in Montana, where Ace ran a saddle shop; Carol commuted some 50 miles to her job as a waitress. Determined that his sons would be young rodeo stars, Ace became a tough taskmaster. Buck Brannaman wrote in *The Faraway Horses*, "Dad pushed us real hard. My brother and I practiced for hours each day. We had the choice of practicing rope tricks or getting whipped. After just a few whippings, we sorted out pretty quick that practicing our rope tricks was the wise choice to make." Buck, then five years old, and Smokie, then about seven, made their first public appearances as trick ropers on a local TV talent show called *Starlit Stairway*, sponsored by Boyle Heating Oil. Soon the boys were traveling the rodeo circuit, performing to enthusiastic crowds. "Although I enjoyed the audience's applause and attention, there were days when we would've given anything to go out and play baseball," Brannaman wrote. "We did a bit, but most days consisted of getting on a horse and practicing roping." Once, they were featured on a nationally aired commercial for Sugar Pops cereal.

Ace Brannaman's physical and psychological abuse continued. Buck Brannaman told Trachtman, "I remember from about [the time I was] eight or nine years old, I would beg [my mother] not to go to work every day, 'cause I was terrified of being at home alone with my dad for the four or five hours after school, before she'd get home. I feel terrible . . . now, 'cause every day I made her cry." Carol, who had long suffered from diabetes, died when her younger son was 11. Ace began drinking heavily, and the abuse intensified. "He moved us to Ennis, Montana," Brannaman recalled to Trachtman. "We ended up on a little ranch where my dad was putting up hay for a fellow, and he really started getting rough on us boys. . . . Some nights he'd knock the hell out of you and some nights he'd just holler at you all night long, and you'd rather get beat up and go to bed and get some sleep than listen to him all night." Brannaman continued, "I remember one night, he got to chasing us around the house. There was a sort of little island in the middle of the house, so you could kind of work in a circle when he was real drunk, and stay ahead of him. I was in the lead and my older brother, Smokie, was right behind me, and just as my brother came around a corner in the kitchen he jerked a drawer open and grabbed a knife. And I told him real quietly, 'Put it back!' And he did. If my dad saw it, Smokie would've had to use it. It was one of those moments that define a person's life."

One winter night Ace locked Buck, who was dressed only in underwear, outside the house, where he huddled until morning with the family dog in an attempt to keep warm. Eventually the situation got so bad that the boys were removed from Ace's home, thanks to the intervention of a woman named Norma, who has been described in various sources as either the family housekeeper or Ace's girlfriend; one of Smokie's teachers, Bob Cleverly; and Johnny France, a Madison County deputy sheriff who had been in foster care as a child. France had been raised by Forrest and Betsy Shirley, a couple who owned a ranch just outside Ennis. The Shirleys agreed to house the Brannaman brothers temporarily. Brannaman told Trachtman that he instantly felt comfortable when he met Forrest for the first time. "He got out of [his] truck, walked over to me, and said, 'You must be Buck,' and I just kind of nodded my head, and he said, 'Well, I'm Forrest,' and he handed me a brand-new pair of leather gloves, real nice deerskin leather gloves for work," Brannaman recalled. The older man spent hours with Brannaman that day—talking little but companionably repairing fences with him on the expansive property. "That's where his influence really began with me," Brannaman told Trachtman. "He was a good old cowboy." After a month the couple agreed that the boys could remain on the ranch permanently. "Dad was very bitter to us after we left, and we had to go to court to get the few things that we owned: a couple of horses, a saddle or two, and our clothing," Brannaman wrote in *The Faraway Horses*.

Brannaman began riding colts with Forrest, and as a teenager he earned pocket money by starting the young, male horses on neighboring ranches. "If I wrecked the horse, they just sent it to the sale ring," he admitted to Trachtman. "It wasn't pretty, but I could get it done after a fashion." Brannaman also began competing in rodeo events, trying his luck as a bronc rider, an act that required him to stay atop a wildly bucking horse for several seconds. "None of [my friends] could afford a horse trailer or roping horses, so we'd throw a bronc saddle in the trunk of my car and take off for the weekend," he wrote in *The Faraway Horses*. "We didn't have much money, but we could live pretty cheap, and like a lot of kids in those days, we'd figure out a way to get someone to buy us a bottle of Boone's Farm or Annie Green Springs. If not, we'd forgo eating so we could afford a couple bottles of that two-dollar wine. And away we'd go riding bucking horses, chewing tobacco, and chasing girls. . . . We never hurt anybody, and it was a pretty harmless kind of fun."

Brannaman also started to practice his trick roping once more, and he reinstated his lapsed membership in the Professional Rodeo Cowboys Association. (He has held two Guinness world records, one for a move called the Texas Skip, in which he hopped in and out of a twirling loop of rope 980 times in quick succession, and another for jumping through the world's smallest "butterfly loop," with a diameter of about three feet.) At age 18 Brannaman was recruited by the U.S. State Department for its Friendship Force, which traveled the world to promote U.S. culture and tourism. He was excited to be sent to Japan. "The Japanese loved cowboys, and there I was, now over six feet tall, with blond hair, surrounded by beautiful Japanese girls and keeping company with Miss Montana," who was also on the tour, he reminisced in *The Faraway Horses*.

Despite Brannaman's showmanship and skills, it was often difficult for him to find work as a trick roper on the professional rodeo circuit, and the few available jobs did not pay as well as ranch work. For those reasons he joined a large outfit called the Madison River Cattle Co., based in Three Forks, Montana. "It was there that my life as a horseman truly began," he told Schmidt.

One day Brannaman wandered into a clinic run by Ray Hunt, a pioneering trainer who was popularizing the natural-horsemanship method. "I heard about this Ray Hunt in high school," Brannaman told Trachtman, "but I was a cocky teenager and said I don't need any of that!" Despite his initial skepticism, Brannaman was transfixed by Hunt's skill and vowed to learn all he could from the older man. "I still tell people that if I do something that looks pretty good with horses, then I probably learned it from Ray Hunt," he told Carol Schmidt. "If it doesn't look pretty good to you, then I probably learned it on my own." Brannaman also met and learned from Tom and Bill Dorrance, who were considered, like Hunt, to be among the foremost practitioners of the method.

Brannaman regularly attended Hunt's clinics and applied the teachings to his own work at Madison River, despite ridicule from some of his fellow cowboys. One day, after watching a group of co-workers try to make a filly stand up by beating it and pouring water in its ears, he quit. In 1983 he began running his own clinics, holding his first in a small arena near Bozeman, Montana.

Concurrently, Brannaman enrolled at Montana State University, where he studied accounting. Attending classes during the day and working with horses until three or four in the morning proved to be nearly impossible, and he reluctantly quit school before earning a degree to focus on his equine business. Married at the time to his first wife, Adrian, the daughter of a famous rodeo announcer, he struggled to make ends meet. "We stumbled along," he wrote in *The Faraway Horses*. "Adrian liked riding colts and helping me out, and the business was [slowly] starting to grow. I was settled into doing some clinics, and I was riding a lot of colts. We bought twenty acres and a double wide trailer in a pretty spot. . . . It was the first time I ever owned anything substantial in my life. Granted, it was just a trailer house, but it was brand new, and it beat the hell out of the bunkhouses I had been living in. For the next several months, I rode colts like crazy. I rode fifteen a day, every day, until I had our little place paid for."

Soon after the trailer was paid for, Adrian had a riding accident that left her temporarily in a coma. Her parents, who had never been particularly welcoming to Brannaman, blamed him and used the incident to drive a wedge between the couple, whose marriage had already been on shaky ground; Brannaman and Adrian ultimately divorced. In 1986 a student named Mary Swenson caught Brannaman's eye at a clinic he was running in Colorado. "I had a policy about dating any clinic student," he recalled to Jane E. B. Simmons for *Saddle and Bridle* magazine (June 2011, on-line), "so if I were ever going to break that rule I'd have to marry her." However, Mary, a former model, was married at the time to a pro football player and had two daughters, Loren and Kristen. She later divorced her husband, and she and Brannaman wed in 1992. Their daughter, Reata, who is named after a type of braided rope used for lassos, was born two years later.

During the late 1980s and early 1990s, Brannaman, his reputation in equine circles well established, began to travel to Florida, where he worked with polo ponies, meeting such figures as Prince Charles of England and the writer George Plimpton. (He has admitted to journalists that when he first drove through the exclusive areas there, he thought that some of the large, private homes he passed were hotels.)

In 1995 the British writer Nicholas Evans was moved by the work of Brannaman, Hunt (who died in 2009), and Tom Dorrance (who died in 2003) to write *The Horse Whisperer*, a best-selling book that follows the composite character Tom Booker as he works with Grace, a traumatized young rider, and her injured horse, Pilgrim. Although many other trainers have claimed that Booker is based on them, Evans has asserted that the aforementioned trio provided his inspiration, and he traveled widely in the U.S. to meet them. "I realized how sincere [Evans] was," Brannaman told Trachtman, "and I gave him quite a bit of my time over those few days. Then he went on his way. Next thing I know, he's sold about a bazillion books."

The Horse Whisperer was made into a film of the same name, directed by and starring Robert Redford, in 1998. Redford hired Brannaman to serve as his coach, technical adviser, and stand-in. (So closely do the two resemble each other in build and coloring that Reata occasionally mistook Redford for her father.) One of Brannaman's own horses played Pilgrim. Although some critics felt the plot to be contrived or saccharine, the movie was a hit, grossing more than $75 million in domestic box-office receipts. Brannaman told Trachtman, "In the beginning, I was a bridge between what was real and what was a movie. I think [the filmmakers] believed that it's really just fiction, just a story they were trying to create. . . . But there [was] nothing phony or made up about the horsemanship in this book."

Thanks in part to the visibility afforded him by the movie, Brannaman has since been in constant demand, traveling around the country from March to November each year, with two horses and a Cimarron custom trailer that he tows with a Freightliner truck. Sometimes Mary or Reata accompany him. In addition to conducting horse-training clinics, he is often called upon as a motivational speaker and has spoken at corporate gatherings for such companies as Sprint and Wells Fargo. "Buck Brannaman eats double whoppers with cheese. He likes his coffee black. He says he like two kinds of music—that'd be country and western—and he likes to joke around. On the surface that places him squarely in the category of being a 'regular guy.' But he isn't," the Web site of the Premiere Speakers Bureau asserts. "To the people who attend his colt starting and horsemanship clinics each year, Buck Brannaman is a mix of mentor, living legend and folk hero."

In his motivational speeches Brannaman draws largely on his experiences with horses and their owners. "Fear is something I deal with a lot in my work with horses," he wrote in *Believe: A Horseman's Journey*. "I've found that frightened horse owners can overcome their fear of doing the wrong thing by doing something else that is safe. Just be proactive and do *something*. Don't be locked up by fear." He continued, "Horses can be scary animals to work with because of their size and apparent skittishness, but often fear of an animal is just covering up other personal issues that the person is trying to deal with. I've never seen a situation where a person was just simply afraid of their horse, and didn't have that same characteristic fear permeating the fabric of their entire life. . . . Around horses, it all comes to the surface." He draws on his childhood frequently as well, writing, "I was afraid of being hurt [by my father], and that fear of pain is an amazing force that's very hard to shake off."

In 2011 *Buck*, a documentary film about Brannaman's life, was released to great acclaim. "A not-so-simple story simply told, *Buck* was directed by Cindy Meehl, a fashion designer turned artist who, after meeting Mr. Brannaman in 2003 at one of his clinics, decided to make a movie about him, her first," Manohla Dargis wrote for the *New York Times* (June 16, 2011, on-line). "Finding a great subject can be half the battle in documentary, and in Mr. Brannaman she discovered one who holds your attention and heart for a tight 88 minutes. From the moment he gets on his horse ('Well, I'm off to the office') and through the hushed interludes and excursions down highways and into the past, he keeps you rapt." Some critics felt disappointed that the film did not reveal what happened to Smokie Brannaman as an adult; Buck Brannaman told Zorianna Kit for the *Huffington Post* (July 14, 2011, on-line), "His life took a different route than mine did. . . . Right out of high school, he joined the Coast Guard where he spent 25 years and had a very distinguished career. He got married, had kids and he lives a comfortable life in Wisconsin."

Although much of his success can arguably be traced back to Evans's book, which has been published in more than 30 languages, Brannaman does not call himself a horse whisperer. Explaining to

John Biewen for the National Public Radio show *Morning Edition* (December 8, 1997) that the phrase was first used in the British Isles hundreds of years ago, he said, "'To whisper' is a metaphor for being subtle and discreet. That's all fine horsemanship is. These ancient horse whisperers or horsemen—all they were is people that were very handy at what they did, and they were so good at what they did that to the average laymen watching them, it looked like magic." Brannaman told Trachtman, "There's a horse whisperer behind every bush these days. [But] I don't think of myself as a horse whisperer." He concluded, "If you want to give me a label, just call me a cowboy and leave it at that."

When he is not on the road teaching and giving speeches, Brannaman lives on a 1,200-acre ranch in Sheridan, Wyoming. In addition to his memoirs, he is the author of the how-to books *Groundwork: The First Impression* (1997) and *Ranch Roping: The Complete Guide to a Classic Cowboy Skill* (2009). Brannaman, who holds conservative Republican views, has told journalists that he may one day run for a seat in the U.S. Senate.

—M.R.

Suggested Reading: *Huffington Post* (on-line) July 14, 2011; *Mountains and Minds* (on-line) Spring 2007; *New York Times* (on-line) June 16, 2011; *Ride* (on-line) Aug. 28, 2009; *Saddle and Bridle* (on-line) June 2011; *Smithsonian* p56+ May 1998; Brannagan, Buck. *The Faraway Horses: The Adventures and Wisdom of One of America's Most Renowned Horsemen*, 2011, *Believe: A Horseman's Journey*, 2004

Selected Books: *Groundwork: The First Impression*, 1997; *The Faraway Horses: The Adventures and Wisdom of One of America's Most Renowned Horsemen*, 2001; *Believe: A Horseman's Journey* (with Bill Reynolds), 2004; *Ranch Roping: The Complete Guide to a Classic Cowboy Skill*, 2009

Brantley, Ben

Oct. 26, 1954– Theater critic

Address: New York Times, *620 Eighth Ave., New York, NY 10018*

When the *New York Times* chief theater critic Ben Brantley writes a review, he tries to evoke the excitement that comes with watching the show in person. People who love the theater, he wrote for the *New York Times* Web site (September 9, 2008), are a "fierce and passionate lot," so "theater criticism should be visceral, an articulation of that fierceness and passion." Brantley recognizes what he calls "the critic as seducer," he told *Current Bi-*

Courtesy of Ben Brantley

Ben Brantley

ography, the source of all quotes in this article unless otherwise noted. He named the notoriously brash film critic Pauline Kael, who wrote for the *New Yorker* from 1968 to 1991, as an example. "Even though I don't often agree with her," he said, her writing contains "the rush of her conviction, [as if she's] co-opting you, and making you—while you're reading—glow with the rush of her writing. . . . I think the goal of criticism is to create a dialogue in the minds of other people. That's what I try to do while I'm writing, but also when I read criticism. I want to participate in that dialogue."

A longstanding complaint regarding Brantley and his predecessors at the *Times* is that they have held too much sway over which productions succeed on Broadway and—more recently, as Brantley has expanded his base—in Off-Broadway, regional, and London theaters as well. A former chief *Times* theater critic, Frank Rich, was known as the "Butcher of Broadway," and Brantley has sometimes been similarly demonized. "A bad review from the chief theatre critic of the *New York Times* . . . is enough to strike fear into show investors," a reporter for the London *Evening Standard* (May 5, 2010) noted. While Brantley has admitted that his position affords him a tremendous amount of power, especially when it comes to new work, he told Jennifer Baker for *Mediabistro.com* (June 17, 2003), "You can't think in those terms. I realized that early on. You do have to be respectful, of course. . . . You can't just hurl abuse or gush unconditionally about something. As a critic, I try to catch my most base instincts before they emerge. On the other hand, I don't want to muzzle myself altogether, because, if I do, who is going to read what I have to say?" Brantley also said that he does

not read what others have written about him, adding, "I hope the people I review avoid reading what I write about them."

Brantley, who reviews three or four shows a week, is the co-editor, with the *Washington Post* critic Peter Marks, of the anthology *The New York Times Book of Broadway: On the Aisle for the Unforgettable Plays of the Last Century* (2001). He told *Current Biography* of his job, "It amazes me that after all these years it appeals. I love it. I'm never bored. I feel incredibly privileged and lucky to be able to do it."

The youngest of the three children of Russell H. Brantley Jr. and his wife, the former Elizabeth Jones, Benjamin D. Brantley was born on October 26, 1954 in Durham, North Carolina. He and his siblings were raised in Winston-Salem, about 100 miles west, near the campus of Wake Forest University. His sister, Robin, was an editor at the *New Yorker* and the *New York Times*; she is now an assistant to Wake Forest's president. His brother, William Russell "Russ" Brantley, a writer, died of melanoma at age 33, in 1983. Brantley's mother was one of the first women to attend Wake Forest, which became co-ed in 1942. Her father, Henry Broadus Jones, had headed the school's English Department and also taught courses in Shakespeare there; Ben Brantley has attributed his love of the Bard to reading Shakespeare's plays aloud with his family when he was a boy. Both of Brantley's parents worked as journalists, his father as managing editor of the *Durham Morning Herald* until 1953, when he joined Wake Forest's staff. He served as the director of communications at the university for many years. He also published one novel and a book of poetry. (Both of Brantley's parents are now deceased.) Brantley said that during his childhood, the Wake Forest campus "was basically my playground." He also said that the school "was a great place for a cultural education": "They had a terrific movie program during the time I was really sort of coming of age. From 11 on I remember they would have silent movies one night, foreign movies another night, black and white Hollywood movies."

As a boy Brantley was often recruited for Wake Forest and community theatrical productions, and he even appeared in a few local television commercials. Acting "was the first thing I really fell in love with," he said, adding, "I was a shy kid and acting is often a great refuge for shy kids." Brantley has also recalled his first foray into journalism: an article that he wrote at age nine for the *Winston-Salem Journal*, about what he had worn for Halloween that year. By the time he entered high school, he was acting less and writing more, as the teen correspondent for the *Journal*. He graduated from R. J. Reynolds High School in 1973 and then enrolled at Swarthmore College, outside Philadelphia, Pennsylvania. About a year earlier Brantley had seen a Broadway musical for the first time: the original production of Stephen Sondheim's *Follies*, choreographed by Michael Bennett and directed by

Bennett and Harold Prince. Brantley recalled the experience as "thrilling." "It was an amazing introduction to Broadway because it's a very complex musical, very sophisticated musical that went places no musical had gone before," he said. "But it was essentially about the end of a tradition in show business—an elegy to the old-fashioned musical and sort of about letting go of the past. I think it was the last production that could have been done on that kind of scale." Brantley has since reviewed five other mountings of *Follies*.

At Swarthmore Brantley majored in English and studied what he called "intellectual history"— "how the culture of the times is born of the society." (At the time he and Swarthmore faculty members regarded intellectual history as Brantley's own creation; it has since come to be widely recognized as a legitimate field of study.) Brantley worked for the local Swarthmore town newspaper, reviewing movies and occasionally tryouts of theater productions in Philadelphia before their arrival on Broadway. He took one semester off in 1975 to intern at the New York City weekly the *Village Voice*. "It was a gopher job," Brantley said. "I answered telephones and sorted though mail, and so forth, did some photo research, but New York was—well, it was the other thing I fell in love with growing up, long before I ever came here." Brantley earned a B.A. degree with high honors in 1977; he also won election to the honor society Phi Beta Kappa.

In 1978, through a contact at Wake Forest, Brantley landed a job as a reporter with the trade journal *Women's Wear Daily* (*WWD*). (When its publisher, John Fairchild, interviewed him, he asked Brantley to name his ideal New York job. Brantley replied that he would like to be a theater critic at the *New York Times*.) Brantley was assigned to cover sportswear news. His first headline read "Trend Is Toward Long Skirts and More of Them." Although he had had no experience in the fashion industry, in time Brantley was promoted to chief fashion critic. Fairchild was interested in the narrative aspects of fashion, Brantley said, and he liked the way Brantley wrote. "He wanted fashion covered as if it were a Balzac novel or something— with characters and how the clothes reflected the people who wore them or would buy them." From January 1983 to June 1985, Brantley worked at the *WWD*'s offices in Paris, France; his titles were European editor, publisher, and bureau chief. Shortly before his 30th birthday, in 1984, he resigned from his job, because, he explained jokingly, "I'd close my eyes and see women in high heels walking towards me one after another." He has said that leaving *WWD* was the bravest thing he has ever done, because when he quit he had no prospects for another job.

In 1987 Brantley joined the magazine *Vanity Fair* as a staff writer; he wrote profiles about such people as the actresses Michelle Pfeiffer, Goldie Hawn, and Angelica Huston, the film director Barbet Schroeder, and the designers Giorgio Armani and Gianni Versace. When *Vanity Fair*'s editor, Tina Brown, left for the *New Yorker* magazine, in 1992, Brantley went with her. During his time with Condé Nast (which publishes *Vanity Fair* and the *New Yorker*), his friend Marian McEvoy, a former *WWD* writer, became the editor in chief of *Elle* and invited Brantley to write movie reviews for that magazine. Brantley's editor at *Elle* was Alex Witchel, the wife of Frank Rich, the chief theater critic of the *New York Times* from 1980 to 1994. Brantley's *Elle* reviews came to Rich's attention, and when the *Times* was looking for a second-string theatre critic, Rich recommended Brantley. *Times* editors "auditioned" Brantley by having him write reviews of several plays, including the musical *Kiss of the Spider Woman*; *Playboy of the Caribbean*, an adaptation of the 1907 comedy/drama *The Playboy of the Western World*; and *Three Hotels*, a series of three monologues by Jon Robin Baitz. Brantley won the position and began writing for the *Times* in 1993.

Brantley took to his new job immediately. "I was used to agonizing over writing, as one does, especially at *Vanity Fair* because you had so much time between stories," he said. But writing theater reviews "was just like breathing, almost, from the beginning." At the same time, Brantley knew that he would be closely judged in his new high-profile position. "I was aware that the scalpels were out," he said, "so I wasn't going to be caught looking uninformed." He spent a lot of time researching previous productions, actors, directors, and playwrights in the Theatre on Film and Tape Archive of the New York Public Library for the Performing Arts, at Lincoln Center, in Manhattan. The first play Brantley reviewed for the *Times* was *Annie Warbucks*, the much-anticipated sequel to the 1977 hit *Annie*. *Annie Warbucks*, like *Annie*, was directed by Martin Charnin, but with less successful results, in Brantley's view. Referring to Charnin's production team, Brantley wrote (August 10, 1993), "They have slavishly upped the ante on much of what made the first production a hit. Its little-girl star is younger, the slap-stick is broader, the jokes hoarier, and the can-do optimism more intense." He added, "Indeed, the show seems as eager to be liked as Liza Minnelli on a comeback tour."

From 1993 to 1996 Brantley worked under the chief theater critic David Richards (who had succeeded Frank Rich) and then Vincent Canby. In 1996, when Canby began writing criticism for the Sunday editions only, Brantley was promoted. One of the first shows he reviewed as chief theater critic was the New York Theater Workshop production of the rock opera *Rent*. The show was an adaptation of Puccini's opera *La Bohème* set in the East Village of Manhattan. *Rent* went on to be a phenomenal success, its music an anthem for a city and generation ravaged by AIDS. On January 25, 1996, one day before the show's first preview performance, *Rent*'s 35-year-old creator, Jonathan Larson, died of a tear in his aorta. Brantley recalled the "raw emotion" in the house on February 13, 1996, the opening night of the show. He wrote in his review (February 14, 1996), "[Rent] rushes forward on an electric current of emotion. . . . Puccini's ravishingly melancholy work seemed, like many operas of its time, to romance death; Mr. Larson's spirited score and lyrics defy it." Brantley told Current Biography that Rent was one of the most memorable productions he had covered in his career.

The collective horror, fear, and sorrow that followed the destruction of the World Trade Center in New York City on September 11, 2001 colored Brantley's writing in the following months. An example is his review (October 19, 2001) of Mamma Mia!, which opened on Broadway less than six weeks after the tragedy. One of the first "jukebox musicals" to arrive on Broadway, Mamma Mia! (which currently is still running on Broadway) features songs by the Swedish pop group Abba. Brantley famously called the show "the theatrical equivalent of comfort food," opening his review (in a takeoff of the opening sentence of Jane Austen's novel Pride and Prejudice) with the declaration, "It is a widely known if seldom spoken truth that when the going gets tough, the tough want cupcakes." He continued, "Mamma Mia! manipulates you, for sure, but it creates the feeling that you're somehow a part of the manipulative process. And while it may be widely described as a hoot by most theatergoers embarrassed at having enjoyed it, it gives off a moist-eyes sincerity that is beyond camp."

"It was such a singular moment," Brantley said of the time. "But there were a couple shows like that." Among them was Mary Zimmerman's production of Ovid's Metamorphosis. After the show transferred to the Circle on the Square, on Broadway, Brantley reflected (March 5, 2002) about its opening Off-Broadway, at the Second Stage Theater, "It was then less than a month after the terrorist attacks of Sept. 11, and the show's ritualistic portrayal of love, death and transformation somehow seemed to flow directly from the collective unconscious of a stunned city. Metamorphosis became a sold-out hit, and every night you could hear the sounds of men and women openly crying."

Brantley has reserved some of his harshest criticism for Broadway's more commercial tactics. At a time when box-office numbers are dwindling, Broadway producers have increasingly turned to jukebox musicals, musical adaptations of popular movies, and Hollywood celebrities to attract ticket buyers. Brantley wrote (January 11, 2008) of the Broadway production of Disney's The Little Mermaid (which was based on the 1989 film), "In a perverse process of devolution The Little Mermaid arrives on Broadway stripped of the movie's generation-crossing appeal. Coherence of plot, endearing quirks of character, even the melodious wit of the original score (supplemented by new, substandard songs by [Alan] Mencken and the lyricist Glenn Slater) have been swallowed by an unfocused spectacle, more parade than narrative, that achieves the dubious miracle of translating an animated cartoon into something that feels like less than two dimensions." Regarding the casting of Hollywood celebrities in theatrical productions, Brantley told Elizabeth Vargas for ABC News (November 24, 2008), "I think there is a sense on the part of a lot of people in Hollywood that the stage is 'legitimate stage' still. That's where you go to prove your chops as as an actor." Brantley has praised many film stars' stage performances; in his review of December 3, 2009, he called Cate Blanchett's portrayal of Blanche DuBois in a production of Tennessee Williams's A Streetcar Named Desire—directed by Liv Ullmann and mounted at the Brooklyn Academy of Music, in New York City—one of the best portrayals of that character that he had ever seen. But he has been unkind to others. His review (April 20, 2006) of the premiere of Richard Greenberg's drama Three Days of Rain was headlined "Enough Said About Three Days of Rain. Let's Talk About Julia Roberts!"—the film star who was making her Broadway debut. He wrote that Roberts was the only reason for the show's being sold-out, adding, "The only emotion that his production generates arises not from any interaction onstage, but from the relationship between Ms. Roberts and her fans." (Brantley, who wrote that Roberts was "stiff with self-consciousness [especially in the first act]" and "only glancingly acquainted with the two characters she plays," acknowledged that he counts himself among those fans.)

Unsurprisingly, some of Brantley's reviews have angered producers. "When producers blame critics for a bad season, they're just killing the messenger," Brantley told Melissa Block for the National Public Radio program All Things Considered (November 20, 2003). "It's not the critics; it's the shows."

In his interview with Current Biography, Brantley said that "for a number of reasons," the current Broadway season has been "very vital." He cited the success of such original works as Jerusalem, a comedy by the British playwright Jez Butterworth, and The Book of Mormon, a musical by Trey Parker and Matt Stone, the creators of the adult animated cartoon South Park. "Usually, you're lucky to have one show anywhere near that level and here you have four or five of them," he said, adding, "I don't know if it's going to change the course of Broadway, but it may make Broadway more receptive to new work and things that are a little more experimental. The form of all the plays I mentioned . . . is fairly conventional [yet] they go unconventional places."

Brantley received the 1996–97 George Jean Nathan Award for Dramatic Criticism, whose winners are selected by the heads of the English Departments of Cornell, Princeton, and Yale Universities. He is gay and single and lives in Columbia County, New York, in a town near the border with Connecticut, about 90 miles north of New York City.

—M.M.H.

Suggested Reading: *ABC News* (transcript) Nov. 24, 2008; *Advocate* p66+ Jan. 22, 2002; *All Things Considered* (National Public Radio transcript) Nov. 20, 2003; (London) *Evening Standard* (on-line) May 5, 2010; *Mediabistro.com* (June 17, 2003); *New York Times* Knowledge Network (on-line) Aug. 10, 1993, (on-line) Feb. 14, 1996, Mar. 5, 2002, Apr. 20, 2006, Jan. 11, 2008, Sep. 9, 2008

Selected Books: as co-editor—*The New York Times Book of Broadway: On the Aisle for the Unforgettable Plays of the Last Century* (with Peter Marks), 2001

Courtesy of MIT Media Lab

Breazeal, Cynthia

(bruh-ZIL)

Nov. 15, 1967– Roboticist; engineer; educator; writer

Address: Personal Robots Group, MIT Media Lab, E15468, 20 Ames St., Cambridge, MA 02139

"The process of building robots is a quest of self-understanding," the roboticist Cynthia Breazeal told Karlin Lillington for the *Irish Times* (November 28, 2008). Breazeal directs the Personal Robots Group at the Massachusetts Institute of Technology (MIT), where she is an associate professor of media arts and sciences. She is a world leader in the design, construction, and programming of so-called social robots, which not only communicate with humans but also learn from them, reflect-

ing the way human babies learn from adult caregivers, who respond in turn to signals from the babies. Kismet, the robot Breazeal created as a doctoral student at MIT's Artificial Intelligence Lab in the 1990s, was designed to "engage in meaningful social exchanges with humans," according to the MIT Web site ai.mit.edu, through movements of its head, eyes, lips, and babbling "speech." "Kismet's big triumph was that he was able to communicate a kind of emotion and sociability that humans did indeed respond to, in kind," Breazeal told Claudia Dreifus for the *New York Times* (June 10, 2003, on-line). Breazeal's book *Designing Sociable Robots* (2002) grew out of her doctoral dissertation. In it she wrote, "Kismet connects to people on a physical level, on a social level, and on an emotional level. It is jarring for people to play with Kismet and then see it turned off, suddenly becoming an inanimate object. For this reason, I do not see Kismet as being a purely scientific or engineering endeavor. It is an artistic endeavor as well. It is my masterpiece." Breazeal's next robot, the furry Leonardo, who was assigned the male gender, was made in collaboration with the Stan Winston Studio; he can move his head, ears, eyes, arms, and hands to mimic such emotions as happiness, sadness, surprise, anger, and disgust in response to human voices and various objects placed near him. Nexi, a "female," is a member of a more advanced class of robots, known as "MDS," for "Mobile/Dexterous/Social." Nexi's facial features mimic a greater range of emotions than those of her predecessors; she also has wheels that enable her to move and jointed arms and hands that can pick objects up.

"Today we know that robots can push our social buttons," Breazeal told Ellen Shakespear for central New Jersey's *Times of Trenton* (March 27, 2011). "Given that, can we imagine applications of robots that use their social abilities to manipulate our own experiences?" "Robots have already been to the moon, to Mars, and to the deep oceans," Breazeal told Annie Vernick for *Scholastic News* (October 20, 2006, on-line). "Where they really haven't been is in our homes. For robots, the final frontier isn't space; it's your living room. I dream of a future where robots are a beneficial part of everyday life for everyone—helping people, being companions for people, enriching our lives." In a piece for CNN.com (February 13, 2011), Breazeal wrote, "I want a future where our technology deeply supports our ability to attain our highest and best selves for each other and our planet. Information and decision making are wonderful. I want to design personal technologies that also have 'heart' so that we become the kind of people we truly aspire to be."

The daughter of Norman Lee Breazeal and Juliette Breazeal, Cynthia Lynn Breazeal was born on November 15, 1967 in Albuquerque, New Mexico, about two years after the birth of her brother, William (called Bill). In 1970 the Breazeals moved to Livermore, California, where her father worked as a mathematician and systems research analyst at Sandia National Laboratories; her mother, who is of Korean ancestry, was a computer scientist with Lawrence Livermore National Laboratory. As children Breazeal and her brother climbed trees and played sports and other games together; Bill also helped her learn to ignore other children who teased her about her somewhat exotic looks.

When Breazeal was in third grade, the TV series *Star Trek* inspired her to write a composition for school about a machine with computerized "feelings" that would find blueberry pies on Earth and take them to hungry Klingons. When she saw George Lucas's film *Star Wars* (1977), at age 10, she "fell in love" with its robot characters C-3PO and R2-D2, she told an interviewer for a 2008 video created by Discover Science and Engineering (DSE, an initiative of the government of Ireland) and posted on youtube.com. "I think the thing that was so captivating to me," she said, was that "these robots were full-fledged characters in their own right. They had personalities, they had emotions, they had a relationship with one another, they had relationships with the humans that they interacted with; they were more like friends than just tools that people used." The "indelible impression" their behavior made, she added, strongly influenced "how I aspire to what robots could be in the future."

Breazeal's imagination was also sparked by visits with her family to places including the Exploratorium, a San Francisco, California, museum; Dinosaur National Monument, which straddles Utah and Colorado; and the Disneyland exhibit Tomorrowland, in Anaheim, California. At Women in Science conferences sponsored by her parents' workplaces, which she attended with her mother, she learned about vocations that women had begun to pursue in recent years. She told Jordan D. Brown for his book *Robo World: The Story of Robot Designer Cynthia Breazeal* (2005) that her parents and her fifth- and sixth-grade teacher, Ben Green, encouraged her to excel at both academics and sports. Her mother and father often advised her, "Don't be afraid to toot your own horn." As a student at Mendenhall Middle School and Granada High School, both in Livermore, she won dozens of awards in tennis, track (including hurdles), and soccer. As a high-school senior, she won a Livermore-Granada Boosters Olympian Award for her scholastic and athletic achievements, and when she graduated, in 1985, she ranked seventh in her class of 328.

In an interview for the PBS series *Scientific American Frontiers* (March 1, 2005, on-line), Breazeal noted that her family was "very science and technology oriented." She recalled that "growing up I was more interested in medicine, being a doctor, and that lasted pretty much through high school. My parents had encouraged me to major in engineering, and their argument was that it keeps your doors open." Breazeal accepted that advice as "very practical" and "very sound," she said. As an undergraduate at the University of California at Santa Barbara, she studied electrical and computer engineering. She worked part-time at the school's robotics center, and during the summer after her sophomore year, she had a job testing microchips at a nearby Xerox facility. She earned a B.S. degree magna cum laude in 1989.

In considering where she would pursue graduate research, Breazeal learned that the MIT professor and robotics pioneer Rodney Brooks had recently started a planetary rover project. "When I visited MIT," she told the *Scientific American Frontiers* interviewer, "I saw the autonomous robots in Rod Brooks' group; at the time a lot of them were modeled on insect intelligence. They would do things like follow walls and use simple image processing sensor techniques to find things like soda cans and pick them up and try to find a trash can." She decided, she recalled, that "if we're ever going to see robots like R2-D2, this lab is the place where that's going to start."

Breazeal gained admission to MIT, in Cambridge, Massachusetts, where she pursued graduate degrees in engineering and computer science. Working under Brooks in the Computer Science and Artificial Intelligence Laboratory, she developed two insect-like micro-rovers, named Hannibal and Attila. She designed each of them to traverse rough terrain, by means of 60 sensors and six legs, each with three motors; also called actuators, the motors enabled each leg to move up and down and back and forth and bend like an elbow. Breazeal also designed software that alerted the rovers to malfunctions and offered them ways to "figure out how to function with the remaining parts," in Brown's words. Breazeal earned an M.S. degree in 1993; her thesis was entitled "Robust Agent Control of an Autonomous Robot with Many Sensors and Actuators."

That year Brooks embarked on a project to build humanoid robots. The first, named Cog, had a head, a torso, and arms, all approximately the size of an adult human's, but no legs, because Brooks wanted to concentrate on making it aware of its environment, through "sight" and "hearing," rather than having it move from place to place like the micro-rovers. Breazeal became the chief architect of Cog's "eyes"—cameras with either wide-angle or close-up lenses—and the visual elements of its "brain": software that enabled Cog to respond to what it was "seeing" by moving its head and arms. One day Cog touched a whiteboard eraser repeatedly, whenever Breazeal shook it near its face. When she saw a video of Cog's responses, she began to think about creating a "sociable" robot that could "learn" the way human infants do. Breazeal explained to Claudia Dreifus, "I was curious to see if benevolent interactions with people could accelerate and enrich the learning process of machines. In short, I wanted to see if I could build a robot that could learn from people and actually could learn how to be more socially sophisticated. It was that thinking that led to Kismet."

The robot Kismet (a Turkish word meaning "fate" or "destiny") has real-looking blue eyes (designed by a special-effects expert); eyelids; eyebrows; and lips (curved metal bands affixed with red rubbery surgical tubes). Kismet—now on permanent display in the MIT museum—"saw" by means of four cameras and software that enabled it to recognize familiar faces, gauge distances, and focus on colorful objects or other visual stimuli. With its rudimentary facial features, Kismet responded to stimuli and voices with expressions that seemed to indicate fear, anger, joy, surprise, or sadness. "According to psychologists, these expressions are automatic, unconscious and universally understood," Robin Marantz Henig wrote for the *New York Times Magazine* (July 29, 2007). "So when the drivers on Kismet's motors were set to make surprise look like raised eyebrows, wide-open eyes and a rounded mouth, the human observer knew exactly what was going on. Kismet's responses to stimulation were so socially appropriate that some people found themselves thinking that the robot was actually feeling the emotions it was displaying."

Making use of findings in developmental psychology, Breazeal also provided Kismet with motivational "drives": one for social interaction, a second for stimulation, and a third for rest after too much activity. Those drives, as well as the robot's "brain," derived from a network of 15 programmed computers. Breazeal told Dreifus, "I intentionally created [Kismet] to provoke the kind of interactions a human adult and a baby might have. My insight for Kismet was that human babies learn because adults treat them as social creatures who can learn; also babies are raised in a friendly environment with people. I hoped that if I built an expressive robot that responded to people, they might treat it in a similar way to babies and the robot would learn from that. So, if you spoke to Kismet in a praising tone, it would smile and perk up. If you spoke to it in a scolding tone, it was designed to frown." Breazeal also told Dreifus, "As we continued to add more abilities to the robot, it could interact with people in richer ways. And so, we learned a lot about how you could design a robot that communicated and responded to nonlinguistic cues; we learned how critical it got for more than language in an interaction—body language, gaze, physical responses, facial expressions. But I think we learned mostly about people from Kismet. . . . The robot and the humans were in a kind of partnership for learning." The construction and programming of Kismet, which took four years, was a team effort to which other MIT students contributed; Breazeal, who served, in effect, as the project's lead investigator, made use of skills she had developed as a member of her middle-school and high-school sports teams. She earned an Sc.D. degree (equivalent to a Ph.D.) in 2000; her dissertation was entitled "Sociable Machines: Expressive Social Exchange Between Humans and Robots." She remained at MIT to engage in postgraduate work.

In 2001 Breazeal was hired as a consultant for the filmmaker Steven Spielberg and the producers Brad Ball and Kathleen Kennedy in connection with their motion picture *A.I. Artificial Intelligence*, about a robotic boy who has been programmed to feel love. Her job was to prepare them for questions they expected to get regarding robotics at events arranged for members of the press in anticipation of the film's release. In 2002 she was appointed an assistant professor at MIT and became the founding director of the school's Robotic Life Group, later renamed the Personal Robots Group. The students enrolled in the first class she taught designed a semi-autonomous robotic sea anemone that "lived" in a large terrarium. Christened Public Anemone, it drew enthusiastic audiences at the 2002 SIGGRAPH (Special Interest Group for Graphics) conference, held in San Francisco. Breazeal's students' Cyberflora installation, in which four robotic "flowers" responded to humans' physical warmth and movements, was exhibited in 2003 at the National Design Triennial, held at the Cooper-Hewitt National Design Museum, a division of the Smithsonian Institution, in New York City.

Breazeal designed the robot Leonardo with the help of the Stan Winston Studio, a famed Hollywood special-effects and animatronics studio, which also provided the funds for its construction. Leonardo—named for Leonardo da Vinci (1452–1519), whose ideas for a humanoid robot appear in one of his many notebooks—is about three feet high; he has an oversize head, large brown eyes, huge ears, arms, hands, a bulbous belly, and thick brown fur made of goat and yak hair (but not movable legs). His coat covers his internal equipment and is removable to allow easy access for repairs. "We wanted to make a robot with more of a body to push our experiments to the next level," Breazeal told Dreifus. "Leonardo has the ability to shrug its shoulders and sway its hips. It has 32 motors in the face, so it can do near-human facial expression and near-human lip synchronization. It's just an incredibly rich platform for social interaction, and that's what it's designed for. It can manipulate objects, which is very different from the armless Kismet." Leonardo was programmed to remember faces, track the movements of humans and objects, and follow people's gazes to ascertain what they are looking at. He can also learn and repeat simple actions and infer "from observable behavior (e.g., their gestures, facial expressions, speech, actions, etc.)" some human mental states and goals and thereby provide "appropriate assistance in a collaborative task," according to the Personal Robots Group Web site. The robot Nexi is more expressive, more dexterous, and more mobile than Leonardo; she is part of a generation of robots that Breazeal envisions as potential learning tools for children. Breazeal is currently working with Nexi and similar robots, testing their interactions with humans and recording the results, which are then uploaded to a robot at the Boston Museum of

Science with the goal of building a social memory for future robots to tap into. She told Tom Cheshire for *Wired* (March 3, 2011, on-line), "If we're going to make personal robots a reality, we need to get them out into the wild and see what happens."

Breazeal's lab has developed about three dozen robots. Notable among them is Autom, the brainchild of Cory Kidd, who completed his doctoral degree at MIT in 2007. Autom is a robotic weight-loss and fitness coach; it has a human-like head that makes eye contact with the user and sits atop a touch-screen "body." The would-be dieter inputs information about meals, snacks, and exercise and then receives encouragement and support or reminders to try harder—spoken in a female voice. Amy Harmon wrote for the *New York Times* (July 4, 2010) that one user "found particularly helpful" the "blend of the machine's dispassion with its personal attention." The user told Harmon, "It would say, 'You did not fulfill your goal today; how about 15 minutes of extra walking tomorrow?' It was always ready with a Plan B."

Breazeal's honors include the National Academy of Engineering's Gilbreth Lecture Award, *Technology Review*'s TR35 Award, and the Office of Naval Research Young Investigator Award. In 2003 she was a finalist for a National Design Award, given by the National Design Museum. She often gives lectures on robotics. A talk she presented at the TED (Technology, Entertainment, and Design) Conference in December 2010 has been posted on the Web. She appears interacting with C-3PO in a video made for the touring exhibition "Star Wars: Where Science Meets Imagination," made by the Boston Museum of Science. With Yoseph Bar-Cohen, she co-edited the book *Biologically Inspired Intelligent Robots* (2003).

In 2003 Breazeal married Robert D. "Bobby" Blumofe, an executive with Akamai Technologies, a computer-services firm. The couple live in Cambridge with their three sons, the oldest of whom was born in 2004.

—W.D.

Suggested Reading: CNN.com Feb. 13, 2011; *New York Times* (on-line) June 10, 2003; *New York Times Magazine* p28 July 29, 2007; pbs.org Mar. 1, 2005; robotic.media.mit.edu; *Time* (on-line) Dec. 3, 2000; *Times of Trenton* (New Jersey) A p3 Mar. 27, 2011; web.media.mit.edu; Brown, Jordan D. *Robo World: The Story of Robot Designer Cynthia Breazeal*, 2005

Selected Books: *Designing Sociable Robots*, 2002; co-editor (with Yoseph Bar-Cohen)—*Biologically Inspired Intelligent Robots*, 2003

Brewer, Jan

Sep. 26, 1944– Governor of Arizona (Republican)

Address: Governor of Arizona, 1700 W. Washington, Phoenix, AZ 85007

In April 2010, when Republican Arizona governor Jan Brewer signed into law what is considered to be the strictest immigration policy currently on the books in the U.S., her profile quickly grew from that of a relatively unknown state leader to a national figure championed by conservatives and vilified by liberals. The controversial law, the Support Our Law Enforcement and Safe Neighborhoods Act (known earlier as Arizona Senate Bill 1070, or SB 1070), requires noncitizens to carry immigration documents and allows law-enforcement officials to check those documents to determine individuals' legal status; the signing of SB 1070 sparked a nationwide debate about immigration reform, states' rights, and civil rights. Although Brewer did not write the bill, her endorsement and subsequent defense of it made her its public face. "The immigration issue has pushed the fast-forward button on the once congenial conservative, forcing her to evolve more quickly than any high-profile politician in recent memory," Adam Klawonn wrote for *Time* (August 24, 2010, on-line). Klawonn also wrote, "Once more [of] a fiscal conservative than a social one, she has decoded Ar-

Ethan Miller/Getty Images

izona's political landscape and is riding the immigration issue, even though it came to her almost by accident."

In January 2009 Brewer, then Arizona's secretary of state and first in line to succeed the governor, replaced Janet Napolitano, who vacated the governor's post to become the U.S. secretary of homeland security. A veteran of Arizona politics, Brewer served as a representative of District 19 in Arizona's House of Representatives from 1983 to 1986, as a state senator from 1987 to 1996, and as the chairman of the Maricopa County board of supervisors from 1997 to 2002. In the fall of 2010, she was elected to her first full term as governor. Brewer supports gun-ownership rights, opposes abortion except in cases of rape or incest, and is opposed to tax hikes, although in 2010 she raised Arizona's sales tax to help reduce a massive budget deficit.

The once relatively obscure Brewer has emerged as a key Republican figure on the national political landscape, and her vows to defend the immigration bill against a lawsuit filed by the U.S. Department of Justice have made her a hero among those who support stronger states' rights. J. R. Dunn wrote for the conservative publication *American Thinker* (May 23, 2010, on-line), "Brewer is a serious conservative, and one who . . . actually is doing things." He added, "Governor Brewer has, in a matter of weeks, gone from being the accidental governor of a second-tier state to standing as an exemplar of the activist conservative politician."

Brewer was born Janice Kay Drinkwine on September 26, 1944 in Hollywood, California. Her father, Perry Wilford Drinkwine, was a civilian supervisor stationed at a navy munitions depot in Hawthorne, Nevada. "There wasn't a night we didn't go to sleep singing, God Bless the Soldiers," Brewer recalled to Doug MacEachern for the Phoenix *Arizona Republic* (December 7, 2008). Brewer lived on the base with her mother, Edna Clarice (Bakken) Drinkwine, and her older brother, Paul, until she was 10 years old, when her father's lung disease (resulting from exposure to chemicals at work) worsened. The family then relocated to the healthier climate of Tujunga, California, but Brewer's father died within a year. "It was a terrible ordeal," Brewer told MacEachern. "Mom had never worked. And government workers at the time didn't pay into Social Security, so we got minimal help." Left to raise her two children on her own, Brewer's mother opened a small dress shop. Brewer spent her time after school working there, cleaning dressing rooms, operating the cash register, and keeping track of inventory. She told Daniel Scarpinato for the Tucson *Arizona Daily Star* (January 22, 2009) that her mother "taught me that you always had to be honest, you always had to be loyal, and you always had to work hard."

After high school Brewer attended Glendale Community College, in California (some sources say Valley College, in Burbank, California), earning a certificate as a practical radiological technician in 1963. She married John Brewer that year and moved with him to Glendale, California, where she found work as an office manager. During that time she supported her husband while he studied to become a chiropractor. When he finished his studies, the couple moved to Phoenix and then Glendale, Arizona, where John Brewer opened a profitable chiropractic business and began to develop commercial real estate.

In 1981 Brewer—who by then had three children—became concerned about the way her children's school was being run and began attending local school-board meetings. She considered running for a seat on the board of education but instead jumped at the chance to run for the state legislature after a seat became vacant. She told Scarpinato, "I thought, 'Well, maybe I could have bigger a impact on education by going to the Legislature.'" Despite her lack of political experience, Brewer won the seat, one of two representing the state's District 19, serving from 1983 to 1986. In 1987 she became the state senator from the district, a post she held until 1996; she was majority whip during her last three years as a senator. During that time she earned a reputation as a conservative who worked well with others regardless of political persuasion. Alberto Gutier, who worked for Arizona governor Evan Mecham in the 1980s, told Scarpinato, "I remember [Brewer] and her very cheery, positive attitude toward getting things done. Everybody liked her because she got along with people and she had a 'we can get things done together' attitude."

In 1996 Brewer ran for chair of the Maricopa County board of supervisors, beating the incumbent, Ed King, in the primary. She took office in 1997, inheriting the oversight of a county named by *Governing* magazine then as one of the most mismanaged in the country. According to MacEachern, when her term in office ended, in 2002, Brewer left the county "with a sparkling reputation as one of the best" in the country. (A November 2001 article in *Governing* largely credits the "fiscal turnaround specialist" David Smith, who then served as county manager, for that achievement.)

In 2002 Brewer ran successfully to replace the outgoing Arizona secretary of state, Betsey Bayless. Soon after taking office, in January 2003, Brewer implemented a program to allow U.S. troops stationed overseas to vote via the Internet or fax machine—a successful initiative other states adopted. She also worked to reduce the state's budget deficit. According to her Web site, as secretary of state she "had legislation introduced to update antiquated laws and remove unnecessary and expensive publication requirements. She consolidated her workforce assignments, eliminated staff overtime, and eliminated various other non-essential expenditures." She courted controversy, however, with her involvement in the creation of Proposition 200, a ballot initiative passed in 2004 that requires state citizens to provide proof of citizenship before they can vote. Proposition 200 was labeled "anti-immigrant" and became the subject of a drawn-out legal battle. In 2006 several Latino advocacy groups filed a suit over the bill and asked for a preliminary injunction, which a federal district judge denied. A panel of the U.S. Court of Appeals for the Ninth Circuit unanimously upheld the judge's decision in 2007. In a 2008 trial the district judge upheld the bill in its entirety, but in October 2010 a Ninth Circuit panel in San Francisco struck down the portion of the bill that required proof of citizenship to register to vote, as it was found to be in violation of the National Voting Rights Act of 1993. (The court left in place a provision requiring voters to show proof of citizenship at the polls.) Arizona is expected to attempt to have the ruling overturned.

In late 2008 President Barack Obama selected then–Arizona governor Janet Napolitano to serve as the U.S. secretary of homeland security. Brewer, who as secretary of state was first in line to succeed Napolitano, became Arizona's governor in January 2009. As Brewer prepared to take office, Arizona political analysts noted that she was vastly different from her Democrat predecessor. Mary Jo Pitzl observed for the *Arizona Republic* (November 23, 2008), "Her backers laud her as conservative but pragmatic, while others see her as a politician without a strong internal compass. Fans cheer the prospect of the return of a conservative government; detractors worry who will be pulling the strings." She also noted, "Napolitano has overseen an expansion of state government and the state budget; Brewer earned a reputation during her 14 years in the Legislature as a fiscal and social conservative. Napolitano is comfortable speaking off the cuff, and her confident, sometimes gruff, manner conveys that she is in charge. Brewer is a less-assured public speaker and doesn't display the same easy command of facts and statistics as do more polished officeholders."

In her inaugural speech as governor, Brewer promised to lower taxes to encourage economic growth and lure new businesses to the state. Only two months later, however, she shocked observers by proposing a tax increase as a means to combat the state's $2.6 billion budget deficit, brought on by the recession that had begun in 2007. In June 2009 she unveiled a budget proposal that called for increasing the sales tax by one percent for three years, enacting spending cuts, selling state assets, and taking other actions aimed at closing the deficit. The proposal riled some Republicans and led to a long battle over the budget in which few of Brewer's goals were realized.

Brewer was more successful in 2010, when—despite the objections of many in her party—the one-percent sales-tax increase was approved by voters in a public ballot. She also exceeded her 2009 goal of cutting $1 billion from general-fund spending in 2010: as of November, Brewer had achieved more than $2.2 billion in spending cuts since taking office, according to Ginger Rough in an article for the *Arizona Republic* (November 22, 2010, on-line). Nonetheless, her efforts got a mixed response. Rough observed, "Democrats acknowledge that Brewer has had some success in pushing her agenda but remain critical of the overall direction she is leading Arizona." She noted that many criticized the governor for cutting money needed by the "most vulnerable" state residents and for failing to create new jobs. The Democratic Arizona House minority leader David Lujan said to Rough, "When you are seeing massive cuts to education, public safety, mental health . . . is that really the direction the state should be heading?" "Given the circumstances and the climate I have been operating under, I think overall, we have been successful," Brewer said in her defense, as quoted by Rough. "But we haven't completed everything I would have liked to complete."

Brewer entered the national spotlight on April 23, 2010, when she signed the Support Our Law Enforcement and Safe Neighborhoods Act. (Some analysts speculated that she signed the bill—which is popular with a majority of Arizona residents—as a way to increase her popularity before pushing for the one-cent sales-tax hike.) The legislation, introduced by Arizona state senator Russell Pearce, makes it a crime under state law to be in the country illegally, requires aliens in Arizona to carry documentation, and allows law-enforcement officials to question the legal status of suspects during lawful detention or stop-and-frisk operations. The officers are required to arrest those without documentation and bring them to the attention of federal immigration officers. The law also tightens restrictions on the hiring and transportation of so-called day laborers and allows for lawsuits against government agencies thwarting the enforcement of immigration laws. Republican legislators in Arizona had supported the bill because of "a perception that the federal government wasn't taking action on the issue," as Dan Nowicki wrote for the *Arizona Republic* (July 25, 2010, on-line); many feared that illegal immigrants would take jobs from U.S. citizens and that drug-related violence in Mexico would spill across the U.S. border. "Border violence and crime due to illegal immigration are critically important issues to the people of our state," Brewer said at the signing of the bill, as quoted by Mariano Castillo for CNN.com (April 29, 2010). "There is no higher priority than protecting the citizens of Arizona. We cannot sacrifice our safety to the murderous greed of the drug cartels."

The bill prompted an outcry from numerous civil rights groups, who argued that those who appear to be Hispanic could be subject to racial profiling whether or not they are in the country illegally. It also drew rebuke from liberal politicians and President Barack Obama, who described the bill as "misguided." In response to claims that the bill would lead to racial profiling, Brewer and her supporters explained that the law specifically prohibits law-enforcement officers from using race or nationality as the sole reason for a legal-status check, and argued that the legislation simply reinforced existing federal law. Brewer also ordered that a training program be developed to educate officers about what constitutes reasonable cause for an immigration-status check.

Media reports of the immigration bill and, later, its signing into law led to numerous protests in Arizona and the rest of the country, and economic boycotts were mounted by celebrities, businesses, school districts, professional associations, and the city councils of cities including Boston, Massachusetts, and Los Angeles, California. (Despite those actions, polls indicated that a majority of Americans supported Arizona's law.) A number of lawsuits have since been filed challenging the constitutionality of the law, including one by the U.S. Justice Department. The law was scheduled to go into effect in June 2010, but the Justice Department persuaded a district-court judge to issue an injunction against several of its most controversial measures. Brewer appealed that decision in the Ninth Circuit Court of Appeals in San Francisco, where a decision was pending as of early December 2010. Many predict that the legal battle will reach the U.S. Supreme Court. Brewer has vowed to continue to fight for the law, and she has become popular among conservatives and many in her state for her willingness to stand up to the federal government. She told Sean Hannity in an interview available on Foxnews.com (September 7, 2010), "It's just unbelievable that we as a state, a small state at that, that we have to sit here and defend ourselves from the violence coming across the border and from the statements that are being made by our federal government [that the border is secure]. Not only don't they protect us, but they sue us."

In November 2010 Brewer was elected to a full term as governor of Arizona, winning 56 percent of the vote in her race against the Democrat Terry Goddard, who received 41 percent. Her victory was thought to be due in part to the support she received after signing the immigration bill.

In her short time as governor, Brewer has also taken up a number of other major conservative causes. She repealed a measure, backed by Napolitano, that gave gay couples many of the same legal rights as married heterosexuals. She instituted a 24-hour waiting period for abortions and required that minors provide written and notarized permission from their parents or guardians before undergoing the procedure. A proponent of gun-owners' rights and a member of the National Rifle Association, Brewer signed a controversial bill allowing individuals with concealed-weapon permits to bring firearms into establishments that serve alcohol. (Bar owners are allowed to post signs forbidding weapons.) She signed into law a measure that removed the license requirement for people without criminal records to carry concealed firearms. She is opposed to the Patient Protection and Affordable Care Act, the health-care-reform legislation enacted by Congress and the Obama administration, and has brought Arizona into a multi-state lawsuit challenging the constitutionality of the act. In October 2010 Arizona courted more controversy by cutting Medicaid for those urgently needing certain life-saving organ transplants. As of December 2010 it was the only state to cut such funding. The decision was made by Brewer and the state's Republican-controlled legislature after an assessment of survival and success rates for transplants. "It seems inappropriate that life-saving care has the potential to be withheld based solely on budgetary issues and the bureaucratic determination of relative benefits," Robert S. Gaston, the president-elect of the American Society of Transplantation, told Kevin Sack for the *New York Times* (December 4, 2010).

Brewer and her husband have three sons, one of whom died of cancer in 2007. She is an active member of the Life in Christ Lutheran Church, in Peoria, Arizona.

—W.D.

Suggested Reading: janbrewer.com; *New York Times* A p14 Apr. 25, 2010; (Phoenix) *Arizona Republic* p1 Dec. 7, 2008; *Time* (on-line) Aug. 24, 2010; (Tucson) *Arizona Daily Star* A p8 Aug. 30, 2002, Jan. 22, 2009

Brûlé, Tyler

(broo-LAY)

Nov. 25, 1968– Media entrepreneur; founder of Wallpaper* *and* Monocle *magazines*

Address: Monocle, *20 Boston Pl., Marylebone, London NW1 6ER, England*

"In many ways," Amy Larocca wrote for *New York* (December 5, 2010), the media entrepreneur and journalist Tyler Brûlé "has become the gold standard of what is currently considered modern 'good taste,' a Martha Stewart for the global elite." Brûlé's influence in the worlds of high-end fashion, interior and architectural design, travel, and leisure stems largely from the contents and look of *Wallpaper**, the lifestyle magazine that he launched in 1996. The idea for *Wallpaper** came to the Canadian-born Brûlé after he sustained serious injuries as a 25-year-old freelance journalist in Afghanistan in 1994 and was forced to take a months-long break from work. None of the dozens of fashion, design, and food magazines that he read while recuperating at his home in London, England, "talked to me," he recalled to Janet Izatt for *PR Week* (September 13, 1996), and they contained "very little that appealed. There were a lot of gaps in the market, but I thought I could fill them with one magazine." Still feeling the "lure of the road" but unwilling to put his life in jeopardy again, he told Izatt, "I thought, why not take foreign reportage, fashion and trends, art and great travel and turn it into a magazine?" In 1997, after the publication of only four issues of *Wallpaper**, Time Warner bought an 85 percent share in the magazine, mak-

Sean Gallup/Getty Images for Burda Media

Tyler Brûlé

ing Brûlé a millionaire. Brûlé remained editor in chief of *Wallpaper**, and in 2001, when he was only 32 years old, he earned a Lifetime Achievement Award from the British Society of Magazine Editors.

By that time Brûlé had started two other magazines, *Spruce* and *Line*, which did not survive, and the company Wink Media (later renamed Winkreative), which was set up to produce print ads that appeared in *Wallpaper**. Since his departure from *Wallpaper**, in 2002, Brûlé has hosted two television shows and expanded his reputation as an arbiter of good taste, as a design consultant for firms including Prada, BMW, Adidas, and Switzerland's national airline. In 2007 he founded the upscale magazine *Monocle*, whose Web site identifies it as "a global briefing on current affairs, business, culture, and design." According to Chris Daniels, writing for *Marketing Magazine* (July 30, 2007), Brûlé applied the same approach to *Monocle* as he had to *Wallpaper**: "Treat the planet as one massive marketplace." Brûlé is the chairman and editor in chief of *Monocle*, which has spawned radio and TV shows and a half-dozen retail shops around the world. An extremely frequent flyer, he also writes a column, "Fast Lane," for the *Financial Times*. According to James Silver, writing for the London *Guardian* (February 12, 2007, on-line), Brûlé is "one of a very few media personalities to have excelled in both the creative and business sides of the industry, as well as inspiring a generation of loft-dwelling, interiors-obsessed metrosexuals, who think nothing of popping over to Lisbon [Portugal] at the weekend to go trousers-shopping." Writing for *Bloomberg BusinessWeek* (July 5, 2010), Tim Adams described Brûlé as

"combin[ing] no-holds-barred career momentum with an aesthete's playfulness, stubborn business judgment with an entrenched place on *The Independent on Sunday*'s annual Pink List of the most influential gay people in Britain."

An only child, Jayson Tyler Brûlé was born in Winnipeg, Manitoba, Canada, on November 25, 1968. His parents, Paul Brule and Virge Brule (who spell their surname without accent marks and are now divorced), raised him in a series of Canadian cities. His mother, who is of Estonian descent, is an artist; his father, who is of French-Canadian and Irish descent, played with Canadian Football League teams (the Ottawa Rough Riders, the Winnipeg Blue Bombers, and the Montreal Alouettes) from 1968 to 1972, then built a career in marketing. At a young age, Brûlé recalled to Sholto Byrnes for the London *Independent* (January 10, 2005), "I was quite clear that I wanted to go to New York and take Peter Jennings' job as the main anchor on ABC." When he was a ninth-grader in Quebec, a threatened teachers' strike led his parents to send him to live with his grandmother in Ottawa. He completed the ninth and 10th grades at Nepean High School, where he felt very happy. "I really found my groove there and it carries all my fondest school memories," he told Richard Starnes for the *Ottawa Citizen* (July 30, 1997). He later attended Humberside Collegiate and Etobicoke Collegiate, in Toronto, Ontario. "I became a delinquent when I went to Toronto and I hated all the schools I went to," he told Richard Starnes for the *Ottawa Citizen* (July 30, 1997).

After he graduated from high school, Brûlé studied journalism and political science at Ryerson University, in Toronto; he worked as a waiter part-time as well. (James Silver reported that he also took classes at Bennington College, in Vermont.) Brûlé dropped out of college in 1989 and then moved to England, where he landed a job as a researcher for the BBC2 television show *Reportage*. During the next few years, he held various positions with the TV show *Good Morning America*, Fox Television, and *Elle* magazine. "It was an amazing time to network," he told Janet Izatt. As a freelance writer, he also contributed pieces to publications including *Esquire*, *Vanity Fair*, the London *Sunday Times*, the German magazine *Stern*, and the *Globe and Mail*'s now-defunct *Destinations* magazine.

In 1994, while in Afghanistan preparing to write a story for *Focus*, a German newsmagazine, Brûlé was shot in both of his arms during an ambush on the vehicle in which he was riding. (According to various sources, he was in Afghanistan under the auspices of the organization Doctors without Frontiers, the vehicle had a United Nations emblem on it, and he was shot in a shoulder as well.) "It looked like someone had thrown a bucket of blood across his chest," Zed Nelson, a photojournalist who was in the car with Brûlé and accompanied him to a hospital, told Fiona McClymont for the London *Independent on Sunday* (July 15, 2001). After medics removed Brûlé's shirt, jewelry, and watch, Brûlé called Nelson to come close to him. "I thought he was going to say his last words. I said, 'What is it, Tyler?' and he said, 'Get my Rolex!' . . . Within an hour of that we were laughing. I was taking photos of him and he was saying, 'Check my hair.'"

Following his evacuation from Afghanistan, Brûlé spent about half a year recuperating in London. (Despite treatment, his left arm and hand have remained severely impaired.) "I recovered through a great, hot London summer, with cocktails in the garden all the time and cooking," he told Richard Starnes. He also read scores of magazines. "This is what life's about, I thought," he recalled to Starnes. "It's about living in a great house, wearing good clothes and seeing the world." He added, "The more I thought about it, the more I thought that's what everyone wants at the end of the day. These are primal needs. But traditionally magazines that deal with those primal pursuits are always aimed at people who are pushing 50 and the market never addresses younger readers. I want to go for younger readers." In January 1996 Brûlé visited the headquarters of the clothing and accessories company the Gap, in San Francisco, California, and signed the firm on as the first advertiser for his proposed magazine. He then secured a small business loan from the British government, backing from an Australian publisher, and funds from friends and family, including his mother (the last of whom he thanked in *Wallpaper*'s masthead in every issue).

Bearing the slogan "The stuff that surrounds you," *Wallpaper* debuted in September 1996 as a bimonthly. In 1997, after the fourth issue appeared, Time Warner paid Brûlé a rumored $1.63 million for 85 percent ownership of *Wallpaper*. In addition to holding the remaining 15 percent, Brûlé retained editorial control. "He's taken *Martha Stewart Living* and made it hip," Bronwyn Cosgrove, a former beauty editor for the British edition of *Cosmopolitan*, told Caroline Byrne for the Toronto, Canada, *Globe and Mail* (November 1, 1997). Sam Whiting wrote for the *San Francisco Chronicle* (July 2, 1998), "With retro graphics reminiscent of the '60s, Brûlé's creation has become a style reference for the urbane." Through news accounts of *Wallpaper*'s sale, Brûlé's father deduced that his son was homosexual. "He called me up in a rage and said I was a disgrace, and he disowned me," Brûlé recalled to Jan Wong for the *Globe and Mail* (October 13, 1998). The long period of estrangement between father and son ended a few years ago.

After Time Warner bought *Wallpaper*—its first European acquisition—the company conducted a marketing campaign to introduce the brand to U.S. advertisers and readers. The magazine won the Art Direction Award from the New York division of the Society of Publication Designers and was declared the "best international launch" by the International Press Distributors. "Where the magazine is completely brilliant is that it's multi-dimensional," Mike Moore, a furniture-store owner who adver-

tised in the magazine, said to Sam Whiting. "It talks about travel, it talks about home. It talks about architecture, food." The magazine did not please all its readers. "Tyler's definitely got a voice. But whether you like the sound of Tyler's voice or not is another thing," Bronwyn Cosgrove told Caroline Byrne, condemning the style of *Wallpaper* as "elitist, nauseating, grotesque." In response to such criticism, Brûlé told Byrne, "Look, this [magazine] is not going to change governments. This is about escaping and getting away."

In 2001 Brûlé became the youngest-ever recipient of the British Society of Magazine Editors Lifetime Achievement Award. The next year Time Warner fired him—reportedly over unauthorized expenses involving use of a London taxi, according to Brûlé, or use of a chartered plane, according to others—and he sold his share of *Wallpaper*. He also signed a noncompete agreement stipulating that he would not establish another magazine for two and a half years. (Now published 11 times a year, *Wallpaper* had a circulation of 105,000 in 2009, with 90 percent of its buyers in Europe, including Great Britain, and the U.S.) Brûlé then devoted himself to developing Wink Media, a full-service design and branding agency that he had established in 1998. Later renamed Winkreative, it is now a subsidiary of Winkorp AG ("AG" being equivalent to "Inc."), which Brûlé set up in 2002. Headquartered in Zürich, Switzerland, Winkreative has worked with clients including Swiss International Air Lines (which, as Brûlé suggested, changed its stewards' uniforms, airport lounges, and logo to simply "Swiss"), Sky One, Marks & Spencer, BMW, Nokia, Adidas, Bally, B&B Italia, Spanair, James Perse, Pottery Barn, Stella McCartney, and Prada. Brûlé told Chris Daniels that at that time Winkreative's annual billings totaled $20 million.

In 2004 Brûlé began writing a column for the Weekend section of the *Financial Times*, an internationally distributed newspaper published in London. His column, "Fast Lane," discusses architecture, travel, fashion, and style, as observed by Brûlé during his extensive global travels. "We wanted an expert on trends and we decided he would be a very good trend-spotter," Richard Addis, a *Financial Times* editor, told Tony Lofaro for the *Ottawa Citizen* (January 15, 2004). In 2005–06, through Winkontent, Winkorp's editorial and TV-production division, Brûlé produced and hosted a new show about the media, called *The Desk*, which aired on BBC4; its failure to attract many viewers led to its being canceled after one season. "I loved the show and curiously if another [program about the media] had replaced it, then maybe I'd say something went wrong, but nothing has," Brûlé told James Silver. "We were never promised a second series. . . . I don't know whether the BBC really knew what they wanted from the programme." Concurrently, in another Winkontent project, he produced and hosted *Counter Culture*, a BBC4 series in which he investigated consumerism in Russia, Sweden, Italy, Libya, Japan, and the U.S. According to one on-line blurb for the series, he aimed to examine "the cultures of six very different countries through their attitudes to retail."

Toward the end of 2006, Brûlé announced his intention to launch a magazine called *Monocle*. "I noticed a gap in the global market from watching consumer behaviour at airports," he explained to Justin Pearse for the British publication *New Media Age* (June 28, 2007). "I saw people buying a business news monthly and an interiors magazine, like *The Economist* and *Wallpaper**. . . . So I thought, why do you have to divorce business and lifestyle?" He recruited investors from Spain, Sweden, Switzerland, Japan, and Australia, each of whom owns a flourishing family business and a 10 percent stake in *Monocle*. In publicity material released before its debut, according to Chris Daniels, *Monocle*'s prospective readers were described as people "who probably don't live in their country of birth, whose work takes them to several different countries a week and who thought they had outgrown news and business magazines as we currently know them"—"in other words," Daniels commented, "a reader like Brûlé." The first issue of *Monocle* reached newsstands in February 2007. "There is page after page of dense yet enticing text, laced with savvy argument and writerly panache," Matthew DeBord wrote about *Monocle* for the *Los Angeles Times* (September 29, 2007). "By and large, the writers are not big names but rather versatile journalists who can get the job done." DeBord added, "Brûlé has managed to create—twice now—something of absorbing visual elegance that's also worth reading."

Monocle is published 10 times a year in London, where it is headquartered, and maintains bureaus in New York, Zürich, Hong Kong, China, and Tokyo, Japan. Several different high-quality types of paper are used in each issue. "It's part of our mantra," Brûlé explained to Amy Larocca for *New York*. "If you deliver something that has an improved quality of paper and is collectible, it shouldn't come as a surprise that people want to pick it up, hold on to it, pay a premium on it." The magazine currently sells about 150,000 copies of each issue in more than 80 countries; the 16,000 subscribers pay 50 percent more for their copies than those who pay the $10 newsstand price. "The editorial tone is the opposite of jaded, with a relentless optimism that suggests we can build a better world if we just think creatively about intractable global problems and buy the right stuff along the way," David Carr wrote for the *New York Times* (August 24, 2009). Fred Pawle wrote for the *Australian* (April 16, 2009), "While print publications around the world turn to technology to retain their readers, Tyler Brûlé has created a magazine with a distinctly old-fashioned tone and built it into a global phenomenon. . . . In a world of tightly defined demographic niches, *Monocle* is boldly diverse." *Monocle* has retail stores in Tokyo, Los Angeles, London, New York, and Hong Kong; each

sells merchandise, including *Monocle* tie-ins (a *Monocle* Blackberry, for example) as well as the magazine and maintains bureau offices in back rooms. The brand also includes *Monocle Radio* and *Monocle TV*, which began airing on the Bloomberg Network in December 2010. In the summer of 2010, Brûlé published a one-off newspaper called *Monocle Meditarraneo*, offering news, interviews, essays, and fashion spreads.

"Tyler is a man with a brain that goes a mile a minute," Ben Boehm, an executive with Bombardier Aerospace, one of Winkreative's clients, told Chris Daniels. Brûlé is said to have a bone-crushing handshake and, in Larocca's words, a "deep, modulated, reassuring" voice. He lives in London, where he works on each of *Monocle*'s issues for about two weeks. He spends the other 32 weeks of the year traveling.

—J.P.

Suggested Reading: *Bloomberg BusinessWeek* p64+ July 5, 2010; (London) *Guardian* (on-line) Feb. 12, 2007; (London) *Independent* Features p4+ Jan. 10, 2005; *Marketing Magazine* p10+ July 30, 2007; *New York* (on-line) Dec. 5, 2010; *New York Times* B p1+ Aug. 24, 2009; *Ottawa (Canada) Citizen* B p1 July 30, 1997; (Toronto, Canada) *Globe and Mail* C p1 Nov. 1, 1997

Buckley, George W.

Feb. 23, 1947– President, chairman, and CEO of 3M

Address: 3M Corporate Headquarters, 3M Center, St. Paul, MN 55144

As a native-born citizen of Great Britain, the president, chairman, and chief executive officer (CEO) of the highly diversified conglomerate 3M became Sir George W. Buckley when he was knighted by Queen Elizabeth II in June 2011. The queen honored Buckley for his decades-long contributions to the business community, not only in England but also in the U.S., where he has held a series of executive positions since 1993. The 64-year-old Buckley—who is also a naturalized U.S. citizen—began his working life as a 15-year-old apprentice electrician. Ten years later he earned a bachelor's degree in electrical engineering, and three years after that he received a doctoral degree in the same field. He conducted research for a British government electricity board for three years, then came in 1978 to the U.S., where he managed an arm of the utility Detroit Edison, in Michigan, until 1986. For the next seven years, he was employed in England; between 1989 and 1993 he worked for the United Kingdom's government-run railroad. Back in the U.S. he held multiple high-level positions with Emerson Electric Co., in St. Louis, Missouri, and

Kazuhiro Nogi/AFP/Getty Images
George W. Buckley

then secured a series of promotions at the Bruns-wick Corp., in Lake Forest, Illinois, rising to the posts of chairman and CEO. By the time he left Brunswick, in December 2005, he had transformed the company into the world's biggest manufacturer of recreational boats.

Buckley "has a mantra: cost is the ultimate competitive weapon; however, you cannot save yourself into prosperity. You have to take some of your cost savings, [and] redeploy them into new products," Timothy Conder, a Wells Fargo financial analyst, told Eric Dash for the *New York Times* (December 8, 2005, on-line) when 3M announced that Buckley had been chosen as the company's new head. Buckley was two months into his sixth year as 3M's leader when Leslie P. Norton wrote for the *Wall Street Journal* (March 6, 2011, on-line), "Shares of 3M . . . are entering a sweet spot, thanks to a blizzard of new products and the rising popularity of the company's wares outside the U.S." "The main hand behind 3M's revival," Norton continued, was that of Buckley. Referring to the global recession that started in December 2007, he added, "Even in the Great Recession, [Buckley] pushed to boost sales abroad and broaden 3M's product lines, without stanching its lifeblood—research and development."

3M maintains its headquarters in St. Paul, Minnesota. As of the end of 2010, according to an on-line 3M fact sheet, the company employed about 80,000 people globally, including 47,102 (about 59 percent) overseas. Its workforce included 7,350 researchers, among them 3,700 in the U.S. In 2010 3M spent $1.091 billion for research and development. In December of that year, 3M was operating factories and laboratories in 28 states and upwards of 65 countries. Its products—some 55,000 of them, when different sizes or varieties of particular items are counted individually—are sold in close to 200 countries. Its worldwide sales in 2010 amounted to $26.662 billion, with overseas markets accounting for $17.452 billion (65 percent) of that total. The company's revenues and profits increased in four of the five years beginning in 2006, the first full year of Buckley's leadership.

George William Buckley was born on February 23, 1947 to a steelworker and his wife and spent the first part of his childhood in Pitsmoor, a downtrodden section of Sheffield, England. As a child he was conscious that his family occupied "the lowest end of the social strata," he told Charles S. Lauer for *Modern Healthcare* (September 20, 2004). "All my life I have been compensating for that perceived disadvantage." He also told Lauer that when he was four months old, his parents separated; although they reunited from time to time, for the most part his father remained a stranger to him. At age four he went to live with a grandmother and a friend of hers. Several dozen "itinerants" rented rooms in his grandmother's house, he told Lauer, and one of them "abused me countless times." After his grandmother's friend died, when he was seven, "I essentially raised myself until I was 11, at which point I went to live with my mother and her new husband."

By his own account, four of Buckley's six siblings died from childhood illnesses. His remaining siblings are his sisters, Jean and Susan. As a boy he himself suffered a host of ailments, including chronic bronchitis, kidney disease, and pernicious anemia. He attended a school for disabled children until age 15. According to Eric Dash, Buckley "was raised by Catholic nuns." In the *Star* (July 25, 2011), which covers Sheffield and surrounding communities, an article reported that Buckley attended the Springvale School, in Penistone, near Pitsmoor, and then the Southey Green School, in North Sheffield, "the area to which his family was moved after slum clearance."

In 1962 Buckley began training as an electrician's apprentice; sources differ as to whether the company where he apprenticed was N. G. Bailey, a building-services firm, or Samuel Osborn, which produced steel and engineering tools, or both. Later in the 1960s he took courses at Granville College, the *Star* reported, and though he never earned a high-school diploma, in 1969 he gained admission to the University of Huddersfield, near Sheffield. (The first of his five children from his first marriage was born around that time.) He earned a B.S. degree in electrical engineering from that school in 1972. He told Lauer that the idea of studying electrical engineering had remained with him since the age of three, when he had heard his grandmother tell a visitor that he would become an electrical engineer someday. "Once she suggested it and I learned what an electrical engineer did, I thought it would be really great," he recalled. In 1976 Buckley earned a Ph.D. degree in electrical engineering through a joint program administered by the University of Huddersfield and the University of Southampton.

Earlier, in 1975, Buckley had been hired as a researcher with Great Britain's now-defunct Central Electricity Generating Board. In 1978 he moved to the U.S. to become the general manager of a subsidiary of the utility Detroit Edison, which serves southeastern Michigan. He found a mentor there in Harry Tauber, who was then a Detroit Edison vice president of engineering and construction. Tauber "knocked me into shape and took risks with me," Buckley told Lauer.

In 1986 Buckley returned to England, to serve as president of a division of GEC (General Electric Co. of the United Kingdom) called Turbine Generators, in Stafford. In 1989 he joined British Railways—a government-run operation then—as the director of the Central Services unit. In that post he managed the railroad's 14 manufacturing plants, new projects, and research efforts, among other responsibilities. In 1993 British Railways was privatized; unhappy with the new regime, Buckley quit. He told Hal Weitzman for the *Financial Times* (February 27, 2011), "I wouldn't have left otherwise. . . . It was a wonderful place to work, stuffed with hugely intelligent and dedicated people."

Buckley returned to the U.S. to work for the St. Louis, Missouri–based Emerson Electric Co., a multinational *Fortune* 500 manufacturer that also offers engineering and technology services in the commercial, industrial, and consumer sectors. He held the post of president of Emerson's electrical-motors and automotive- and precision-motors divisions as well as chief technology officer for the company's international motor and appliance businesses. "When I came to America," he told Weitzman, "there was an impression that if we were building a railway line 100 miles long in Britain, they were building one 1,000 miles long," he said. "Everything seemed to be bigger, better, faster, more complicated and more impressive. I wanted a part of that, to see if I could live, survive and succeed in that world." At Emerson Electric Buckley worked under Charles F. "Chuck" Knight, the company's CEO from 1973 to 2000. "The two best things I did in my career were joining Emerson and leaving Emerson," Buckley told Weitzman. "It was the ultimate business finishing school. Very different from British Rail, which was gentle and polite. Working for Chuck Knight was like working for Genghis Khan." He told A. T. Palmer for the *Chicago Tribune* (September 13, 2004), "Emerson inculcated in me a love of planning. . . . They forced you to quantifiably justify everything you normally think instinctively."

In 1997 Buckley resigned from Emerson and joined the Brunswick Corp., a *Fortune* 500 company, headquartered in Lake Forest, Illinois, that manufactures boats and boat engines and equipment for billiards, bowling, and physical fitness. His title was president of Brunswick's Mercury Marine Group, which produces marine-propulsion

devices, primarily outboard motors. Under Buckley the group's sales increased by 14 percent and operating earnings by 31 percent. In 1998 he was promoted to vice president of Brunswick, and the next year to senior vice president. In 2000 he was named executive vice president and director, and in May 2000 he rose to become president and chief operating officer. The next month he was made Brunswick's chairman and CEO. As the company's head he sold underperforming units, cut costs, increased sales and profits, and saw Brunswick's stock price rise almost 150 percent. Buckley also invested in leadership training for some of Brunswick's 26,000 employees. He told Del Jones for *USA Today* (May 17, 2009, on-line), "I was asked, 'George, it's a tough time right now. Should we be spending money on training? What if these people leave the company?' My answer was, 'What if we don't, and they stay?'" Alfred Marcus, a faculty member of the University of Minnesota's Carlson School of Management, told Tony Randolph for Minnesota Public Radio (December 7, 2005, on-line) that Buckley "stressed all the things an executive should be stressing. That is, at the same time he's talking about product development and growth, he's also talked a lot and made a lot [of] changes with regard to efficiency and leanness of the company. [He was] working both sides of it, increasing revenues and also lowering costs."

Propelling Brunswick's growth were its purchases of more than 20 companies, most of them firms that manufactured boats and engines. Largely by means of those acquisitions, Buckley turned Brunswick into the fastest-growing company in the boating business. In 2004 boats and engines accounted for 80 percent of the company's $5.2 billion in sales. "What's really drawing attention lately . . . is Brunswick's aggressive strategy as it tries to reshape an industry that has seen millions of boaters quit the pastime since the 1990s," David Carpenter wrote for the Associated Press State & Local Wire (March 6, 2005). By early 2005 Brunswick had become the world's biggest manufacturer of recreational boats. Its market value had reached $4 billion, and Buckley's total annual compensation, according to *Forbes* (2005, on-line), had risen to $19.1 million.

On December 7, 2005 3M announced that Buckley had been appointed the company's chairman, president, and CEO. He succeeded W. James McNerney Jr., who had left suddenly five months earlier to head Boeing. (Robert Morrison had served as 3M's interim CEO.) Earlier, during McNerney's three years at the helm of G.E. Aircraft Engines, he had turned that company into the largest manufacturer of jet engines on Earth and had doubled its profits. He had gained the reputation of a corporate star when, in 2001, 3M's board recruited him as the first leader of 3M to come from outside the company. 3M's choice of Buckley to fill McNerney's shoes led Eric Dash to observe, "The replacement of a General Electric golden boy with a brass-tacks executive is emblematic of a larger shift in the executive suite," as indicated by "a greater willingness to hire . . . a proven leader of a smaller company."

3M—the company's official name since 1959—came into existence in 1902, when five partners launched the Minnesota Mining and Manufacturing Co., with the idea of mining a particular mineral they had found and using it to make grinding-wheel abrasives. That plan came to naught. With different minerals and the introduction of abrasive cloths and sandpaper, the company began to turn a profit; stockholders earned their first dividend—six cents per share—in 1916. The invention of the first waterproof sandpaper, in the early 1920s, and masking tape, in 1925, boosted the company's fortunes tremendously. The firm also became recognized for fostering inventiveness and experimentation. 3M employees have created dozens of types of tape, for example—among them the original Scotch cellophane tape, electrical tapes, fire-retardent tapes, corrosion- and impact-resistant tapes, aluminum-foil tapes, duct tapes, urethane-foam tapes, surgical tapes, and vinyl-coated cloth tape with rubber adhesive for use by entertainment-industry gaffers. Currently 3M manufactures about 55,000 products, in the categories of electronics, electricity, and communications; health care; safety and security; transportation; manufacturing and other industries; and graphics and displays for computers and other purposes. In addition to such well-known items as Scotch-Brite cleaning pads, Thinsulate, Post-It notes, Scotch-gard fabric protector, and Scotchlite reflective materials, 3M manufactures such diverse items as fuel-cell components; materials for energy conduction; antimicrobial cleaners; skin patches for drug delivery; a dentistry line including composites, cements, implants, materials for making impressions, tools for finishing and polishing, and teeth-whitening products; coatings that provide barriers to moisture, oxygen, other types of corrosion, and graffiti; optical films including liquid crystal displays (LCDs) for laptop computers, flat-screen televisions, cockpit instrument panels, and other devices; concrete-repair urethane; aircraft sealants; anti-slip materials; goggles and other protective devices; and fishing lines, among myriad other products. 3M subsidiaries also make such varied products as stethoscopes and pet foods.

3M prospered under McNerney, and it has continued to do so with Buckley at the helm. Within a year of Buckley's arrival, 3M's sales had grown, and the company had earned $3.9 billion on revenues of $23 billion. The number of employees had risen by 6 percent, to 75,000; the total currently stands at about 80,000. At the behest of the board of directors, Buckley led the company through 19 relatively modest acquisitions, costing a total of $900 million. According to the Minnesota Public Radio's business reporter Martin Moylin (February 28, 2007, on-line), the purchases ranged from those of "a German firm that makes personalized passports to a Brazilian company that provides ear-

plugs, eyewear and hand cream." The Morningstar analyst Scott Burns told Moylin, "When you take them in aggregate, [Buckley] has done a good job—he and his team have done a good job—of finding high-margin, high-growth businesses that really tuck in well with what 3M already has."

Continuing an approach introduced by McNerney, Buckley cut costs by focusing more on the improvement of existing products than on the creation of completely new ones (though he did not neglect the latter). Despite the recession he reduced spending for research and development only slightly, because, he told Dana Mattioli and Kris Maher for the Wall Street Journal (March 1, 2010), "if you don't invest in the future, there isn't going to be one. A lot of the stuff we spend on may not deliver a product for two or three years. There may be no return. But the alternative—not doing—is worse." Citing as an example a newly designed respirator mask that cost less to manufacture than previous models, Buckley told Mattioli and Maher, "I didn't drive the invention of this, but I said the invention of this is necessary. You have to drive out costs to defend yourself against competition." He also said, "It was finding ways to simplify how you make the lowest-cost high-performance respirator possible. We often think innovation is making a breakthrough at the top of the pyramid. That's often not where the hardest challenges are. The hardest challenges are often: How do I make a breakthrough for next to nothing?"

Except for one 12-month period, 3M's profits have climbed steadily in the years since Buckley came to the company, according to Fortune magazine's rankings (in terms of gross revenues) of the top 500 American publicly or privately held firms. (Fortune publishes that list annually at the end of April or beginning of May, with rankings indicating revenues as of December 31 of the previous year.) On the 2006 list, which was based on information from 2005, for most of which McNerney headed the company, 3M ranked 101st, with gross revenues of $21.167 billion and a profit of $3.199 billion. On the 2007 Fortune 500 list, 3M ranked 97th, with revenues of $22.923 billion and a profit of $3.851 billion. The corresponding figures on the next four annual lists are as follows: 2008—100th, $24.462 billlion, $4.069 billion; 2009—95th, $25.269 billion, $3.460 billion; 2010—106th, $23.123 billion, $3.193 billion; 2011—97th, $26.662 billion, $4.085 billion. The last figures show that revenues rose about 15 percent in 2010, and profits that year climbed about 13 percent.

According to the Wall Street Journal (May 8, 2011, on-line), a survey of CEO compensation derived from the "definitive proxy statements" of 350 U.S. public companies between May 1, 2010 and April 30, 2011 showed Buckley in 24th place, with his direct compensation totaling $20.379 million, an increase of 53.8 percent over the previous year. (According to the same survey, the highest-paid CEO, Philippe P. Dauman of Viacom, accrued

$84.328 million in total direct compensation; David N. Farr of Emerson Electric received $22.469 million; and W. James McNerney Jr. of Boeing, $17.370 million.) In May 2011 3M reported that, following a prearranged trading plan, Buckley would sell up to 350,272 shares of his stock in 3M (out of a total of about 1.2 million shares) within the following two months. According to RTTnews.com (May 18, 2011), at the time of the announcement, those 350,272 shares were worth about $32.9 million.

Buckley has been praised for his emphasis on training employees for future leadership positions. In January 2009 the magazine *Chief Executive* and the Hay Group ranked 3M as the number-one company in leadership development. Buckley told Del Jones, "The absolutely best way for me to be successful is to have people working for me who are better. Having that kind of emotional self-confidence is vital to leaders. The people I work with are my friends. How can you possibly be objective if you work with your friends? You build respect in those people because you admire what they do. Having once built respect, you build trust. However hokey it sounds, it works."

In his conversation with Weitzman, Buckley criticized President Barack Obama as being "anti-business" and "Robin Hood-esque." "There is a sense among companies that this is a difficult place to do business," Buckley asserted. "It is about regulation, taxation, seemingly anti-business policies in Washington, attitudes towards science." He added, "Politicians forget that business has choice. We're not indentured servants and we will do business where it's good and friendly. If it's hostile, incrementally, things will slip away. We've got a real choice between manufacturing in Canada and Mexico—which tend to be pro-business—or America." In response, Obama's chief of staff, William Daley, in an op-ed piece for the *Financial Times* (March 1, 2011, on-line) entitled "Why Obama Is a Pro-Business President," wrote, "Obama has always believed that America succeeds when business succeeds. He has a deep, abiding commitment to doing what is necessary to strengthen our economy and make America more competitive. That is why, having spent decades in government and business myself, I was amazed to see the critical comments [of] George Buckley. . . . There is plenty of work to do. But the stakes are too high to give credence to the kind of comments Mr Buckley made this week, or to believe those who would question Mr Obama's commitment to our economic recovery."

Traditionally, 3M's heads have retired at age 65. Buckley will turn 65 in 2012. He told Nick Zieminski for Reuters (March 31, 2011, on-line), "I love being the CEO of 3M. I'm not the guy that has the choice on whether I stay or not. If the opportunity were there, I would stay." "He's done a very good job," Oliver Pursche, a portfolio manager and the president of Gary Goldberg Financial Services, told Zieminski. "If I were to speculate, I would say he's going to stay on a little longer. It certainly wouldn't hurt the stock."

Buckley serves on the boards of Stanley Black & Decker Inc. and Archer Daniels Midland, and he is a member of the boards of trustees of the University of St. Thomas and Minnesota Public Radio. His interests include history, gardening, fishing, and woodworking. He holds more than a dozen patents. With his second wife, Carol, he has twin daughters. The couple live in Minnesota and also own a home in England.

—W.D.

Suggested Reading: 3M Web site; *Chicago Tribune* p5 Sep. 3, 2004; *Chief Executive* Jan. 2009; *Huddersfield (England) Daily Examiner* p7 May 27, 2009; (London) *Financial Times* (on-line) Feb. 7, 2011; *Modern Healthcare* p20 Sep. 20, 2004

Emmanuel Dunand/AFP/Getty Images

Cain, Herman

Dec. 13, 1945– Businessman; radio host; writer; presidential candidate (Republican)

Address: Herman Cain Campaign Headquarters, P.O. Box 2158, Stockbridge, GA 30281

On May 21, 2011 the businessman, talk-radio host, Baptist minister, and noted inspirational speaker Herman Cain announced that he was seeking the 2012 Republican presidential nomination. A self-proclaimed "dark horse" candidate, Cain—who has never held elective office—worked for the Coca-Cola and Pillsbury companies before making a name for himself during the 1990s as the chief executive officer (CEO) of a midwestern franchise, Godfather's Pizza, which he steered from the edge of bankruptcy to profitability in 14 months. Since he declared his longshot candidacy, Cain has surprised pundits and voters alike: with nearly zero percent name recognition when his campaign began, he soon became one of the race's more popular candidates, winning followers at an astonishing rate with his charisma and compelling, rags-to-riches personal story. Charles Henderson, a former director of marketing at Godfather's Pizza, told Angie Drobnic Holan for the *St. Petersburg (Florida) Times* (June 10, 2011) that Cain is "probably the most inspiring person I've ever met in my life." "He can be mesmerizing . . . ," Henderson said. "He is without a doubt the most dynamic speaker I've ever heard." A grandson of sharecroppers, Cain grew up in the Jim Crow South. Though he graduated from high school near the top of his class, he was, because of being an African-American, refused admission to the University of Georgia; he nonetheless completed undergraduate and graduate degrees and went on to become not only a successful businessman but an adviser to major Republican presidential candidates, a path for which he was honored in 1996 by the Horatio Alger Association of Distinguished Americans.

Cain has endeared himself to the conservative Tea Party movement, which has fielded accusations of racism. In a recent campaign video, Cain is shown with his arms around a group of white supporters. "To anyone who says the Tea Party is racist," he says to the camera, "eat your words." When Brian Montopoli asked him in an interview for *CBS News* (June 9, 2011) about the video, Cain said that the Tea Party movement "has been getting a bad rap." "The fact that I happen to be American, black, Conservative, is just coincidental to this whole discussion," he said of the attention being paid to his race. His strongest asset, Cain has said, is the experience he has gained from his 40-year business career. That experience, he told Montopoli, "basically represents the business skills that I have developed about how you fix problems. . . . Those skills work. I've used them all my life. And I believe they will work [when I am] President of the United States of America."

One of two sons, Herman Cain was born on December 13, 1945 in Memphis, Tennessee, and raised Atlanta, Georgia. His parents were both children of sharecroppers; his mother, Lenora, was a domestic worker, and his father, Luther Cain Jr., worked as a barber and janitor and as the chauffeur to Robert Woodruff, president of the Coca-Cola Co. from 1923 to 1955. In his 1999 book, *Speak as a Leader*, as paraphrased by the *Atlanta Tribune* (November 2002), Cain wrote that his father's "first job paid the rent, the second put food on the table, and the third helped purchase a home." Cain told Andrew Goldman for the *New York Times* (June 30, 2011) that his father "didn't have a lot of formal education, but he had a Ph.D. in common sense."

Growing up, Cain and his younger brother, Thurman, shared a roll-away bed in the kitchen of the section of a house their family occupied. When Cain was in eighth grade, his father surprised the family by purchasing a small brick house on Albert Street in Atlanta. "My brother and I just about went crazy," he recalled to Jason Horowitz for the *Washington Post* (May 31, 2011).

Cain's parents held high expectations for their sons and enforced strict rules. "The rules of the house were simple and direct," Cain said of his childhood, as quoted by Conor Friedersdorf for the *Atlantic* (June 30, 2011). "Don't get into trouble. Don't talk back to your mother. Go to church. Study hard and finish school." On the subject of growing up in segregated Atlanta, Cain has often told the story of when he and his brother asked their mother for permission to get a drink of water at a department store. She warned them to use the fountain marked "colored"; they complied, but then, in act of defiance when no one else was looking, took sips from the fountain labeled "white" as well. "We looked at each other," Cain recalled, as quoted by Friedersdorf, "[and said], 'The water tastes the same. What's the big deal?'" He added, "We were never taught discrimination. We had to live in a segregated society. But we hadn't fully grasped the significance of those public differences." Friedersdorf noted that Cain's depiction of the incident is typical of his inspirational narrative, at once capturing the "abhorrent" nature of segregation, "the absurdity at its core," and Cain's refusal to feel victimized by it. "There's also," Friedersdorf added, "the implicit idea that a good upbringing and being inculcated with sound values can trump even the worst sorts of influences from the outside world."

Cain graduated from high school second in his class and attended Morehouse College, in Atlanta, where he earned a degree in mathematics in 1967. (He was the first in his family to graduate from college.) While pursuing a master's degree in computer science from Purdue University, in Indiana, which he received in 1971, Cain developed fire-control systems for ships and fighter planes as a civilian with the Department of the Navy. After earning his degree he returned to Atlanta and began working for the Coca-Cola Co. as a computer-systems analyst. In 1977 he joined the Pillsbury Co., where within five years he rose through the ranks to become vice president of corporate systems and services.

At the age of 36, wanting to run a company, Cain resigned his position to join Pillsbury's Burger King division, where he learned all aspects of the business, beginning with flipping burgers and cleaning bathrooms. After nine months he was overseeing 400 Burger King restaurants in the Philadelphia, Pennsylvania, area—the company's poorest-performing region in the country. When Cain arrived he set out to make those restaurants the company's most profitable, a goal he accomplished after three years, though the odds were against him. "That first restaurant that I had was at the end of the street," Cain recalled to a writer for the *Atlanta Tribune* (November 2002), "not even in a cul de sac, and they told me to increase sales." He conceived what he called the "Happy Bee" program for the Burger King employees, with "Bee" standing for the Bad attitudes they were to leave at home, the Eye contact they were to maintain with customers, and the Everyday basis of those actions. "Service is everything," Cain said to the *Atlanta Tribune* writer. "Hospitality is spelled s-m-i-l-e." After the "Happy Bee" program was introduced, sales in the region increased by 20 percent.

Cain was still with Burger King when, in 1986, Pillsbury purchased Diversifoods Inc. That conglomerate included 300 Burger King outlets, which had inspired the acquisition; Godfather's Pizza was also a part of the conglomerate, which is how, almost incidentally, Pillsbury acquired more than 800 Godfather's restaurants. Holan quoted John McMillin, an industry analyst, as saying about the deal at the time: "Pillsbury got Godfather's for nothing, and some say they got what they paid for." Due to less-than-inspired advertising campaigns and dwindling sales, Godfather's appeared to be nearing its demise, and Cain was installed as president and CEO seemingly to oversee its closure. (He was the company's fourth head in just over a year.) Instead, when he arrived at the Omaha, Nebraska, headquarters, he began an aggressive campaign to turn the company around. He brought the advertising account up for review; trimmed the restaurants' extensive menu and focused on boosting the quality of the remaining offerings; pushed restaurants to offer delivery services; and closed franchises that were not performing up to his standards. To rally his staff around the new and improved Godfather's, Cain employed his "get on the wagon" speech, which he now uses at political events. The heart of the speech was inspired by Cain's grandfather, a potato farmer, who would offer rides on his wagon to his grandchildren on his weekly trips into town. Echoing the booming voice of his grandfather, Cain concluded his speech by saying, "Them that's going, get on the wagon! Them that ain't, get out of the way!" As with his tenure at Burger King, Cain was eager to learn every aspect of the business; once a week he would gather his executive staff to make pizzas at the nearby test store. Cain also introduced the successful "Pizza Emergency" advertising campaign to promote Godfather's new "hot slice"—a single slice of pizza available to boost lunch sales. The TV ads depicted businesspeople facing "pizza emergencies" during their lunch breaks; the only solution, the ad advised, was Godfather's pizza. Within 14 months Godfather's had turned a profit, and soon after that, in 1988, Cain and his management team bought the company from Pillsbury for an undisclosed sum. In 1989 Cain appeared in a Godfather's commercial as part of a campaign that *Advertising Age* named the best of that year. He remained with the company until 1995. During his tenure

Cain was one of a small handful of African-American CEOs of major U.S. companies.

Cain was elected to the board of directors of the National Restaurant Association (NRA) in 1988. He was elected president and CEO of the NRA in 1995. Meanwhile, Cain was becoming a vocal political advocate for business owners. In 1994, in a televised town-hall meeting, he famously challenged President Bill Clinton on his proposal for health-care reform, specifically the stipulation that employers would be forced to pay for health insurance for all their employees. "On behalf of all of those business owners that are in a situation similar to mine," Cain said, as quoted by a reporter for FoxNews.com, "my question is, quite simply, if I'm forced to do this, what will I tell those people whose jobs I will have to eliminate?" Clinton responded that there would be subsidies for small businesses, but Cain countered, as quoted by Steven Waldman and Bob Cohn for *Newsweek* (September 19, 1994): "Quite honestly, your calculation is inaccurate. In the competitive marketplace it simply doesn't work that way." According to Kate O'Beirne, writing for the *National Review* (July 14, 2003), Cain traveled to 19 states to campaign against the proposed reform, arguing that the plan would kill jobs. His actions were effective; Larry Neal, an aide to U.S. senator Phil Gramm of Texas, called Cain "the lightning rod" for the anti-reform camp. "Cain transformed the debate," Waldman and Cohn wrote. (Unsurprisingly, Cain has become one of the most outspoken critics of the health-care reform signed into law in 2010 by President Barack Obama.)

Cain's effectiveness was not lost on the Republican Party; he became a significant player in Washington politics, even dubbing himself the "Herminator," after the unstoppable title character played by Arnold Schwarzenegger in the *Terminator* films. (Cain officially trademarked the nickname in 1995.) He was appointed by Newt Gingrich, then Speaker of the House, to serve on the Economic Growth and Tax Reform Commission, and in 1996 he was a senior adviser to the campaign of that year's Republican presidential nominee, Bob Dole—though at the time he was still registered as an Independent. He told Goldman the story of how his party affiliation changed: Dole's running mate, Jack Kemp, "took me and as many other big black guys as he could to Sylvia's [restaurant] in the heart of Harlem. As we were walking into the restaurant, a very large black guy yelled out: 'Black Republicans? There's no such thing.' When I got back to Omaha, I registered as a Republican. It haunted me for three days that someone would dare tell me what party affiliation I should have." Cain said to an *Atlanta Tribune* (July 2004) writer that he was a Republican because, "until [African-Americans] get inside the GOP to be able to influence the leadership of the GOP, it's never going to change. And we can never assume that one party is always going to be in power."

Cain served from 1992 to 1996 as a director of the Federal Reserve Bank of Kansas City, one of a dozen local institutions that advise the nation's Federal Reserve Board—which sets monetary policy in the U.S. and regulates banks. As quoted by Robin Abcarian for the *Los Angeles Times* (July 7, 2011), Cain has expressed his views on the Fed; he asked those who might agree with one of his fellow Republican presidential candidates, the limited-government advocate Ron Paul, "People who want to eliminate the Federal Reserve, what would you replace it with? They don't have an answer to that." In 2000 Cain was co-chairman of the publishing executive Steve Forbes's presidential campaign, and in turn Forbes supported Cain's 2004 run for the Republican nomination in an election to fill the U.S. Senate seat being vacated by Zell Miller of Georgia. Cain campaigned on much the same platform he would adopt for the 2012 presidential race. "I'm talking about fixing problems and not just putting band-aids on the problems," he told a group of Georgia voters, as quoted by the *Atlanta Tribune* (July 2004). "I'm not a professional politician, I'm a professional problem solver." Though Cain lost the nomination to Congressman Johnny Isakson by 27 percentage points, with 26 percent of the vote to Isakson's 53 percent, he performed better than many expected. The columnist Jim Wooten of the *Atlanta Journal-Constitution* wrote, as quoted by the *Tribune* reporter, "Cain may be the best first-time candidate Georgia has ever seen." In 2006 Cain was diagnosed with Stage 4 cancer that had spread from his colon to his liver. According to Abcarian, Cain underwent chemotherapy, and surgeons removed 30 percent of his colon and 70 percent of his liver, an organ that can regenerate. He has been cancer-free since that time.

Cain is the author of the books *Speak as a Leader: Develop the Better Speaker in You* (1999), *Leadership Is Common Sense* (2000), *CEO of Self: You're in Charge* (2001), and *They Think You're Stupid: Why Democrats Lost Your Vote and What Republicans Must Do to Keep It* (2005). In 2005 he began appearing at speaking engagements, billing himself not only as an inspirational guru but as the "new voice" of conservative politics. He later formed T.H.E. New Voice Inc. along with the grassroots organization Herman's Intelligent Thinkers' Movement, or HITM. (It appears that "T.H.E." is an aesthetic decision, not an acronym. HITM, in addition to being a community of Cain's supporters, embodies his idea for involving voters in the legislative process if he is elected president.) Cain also became a frequent guest on the nationally broadcast *Neal Boortz Show*, hosted by that libertarian, author, and commentator. Cain began filling in for Boortz and became so popular that he got his own radio talk show, *The Herman Cain Show*, in 2008. He ended its run shortly before announcing his bid for the presidency.

Since he announced his bid, in May 2011, Cain has won a large number of supporters but has also made a fair number of political gaffes. In a record-ing made at one of his speaking engagements, Cain is heard confusing the Declaration of Independence and Constitution after admonishing his political opponents to "reread" the latter. In an interview with Chris Wallace for Fox News in May 2011, Cain showed a lack of familiarity with foreign policy, appearing not to understand the concept of the Palestinian right of return and telling Wallace, when asked about his policy on the U.S. war in Afghanistan, that if elected he would devise a plan of action between Election Day and his inauguration. However, Cain drew the most ire for saying that he did not want any Muslims to serve in his administration. Expressing his differences with and perhaps some confusion over the nature of Sharia law, the code of conduct in Islam, Cain told the talk-radio host Laura Ingram in April 2011, "I want people in my administration that are committed to the Declaration of Independence and the Constitution of the United States. I don't want any inkling of anybody in my administration who would put Sharia law over American law. I have not found a Muslim that has said that they will denounce Sharia law, you know, in order to support the Constitution of the United States." Cain's words, and subsequent comments of a similar nature, drew sharp criticisms from the Muslim community and the media. He has since revised his statements, telling Mark Anthony Green for *GQ* magazine (July 15, 2011) that he is against Islamic terrorists, not the general Muslim population. "If I had to say it all over again, I'd say it again. I'm just Herman being Herman! I know a Muslim that I would put in my cabinet, OK? I'm not going to tell you his name. I know a guy that I would put in my cabinet because he does not believe in the terrorist aspect of the Muslim religion."

Early in his campaign Cain supported the so-called Fair Tax policy, which would eliminate income taxes in favor of a 30 percent sales tax. Cain defended the Fair Tax to Paul Gigot for *Journal Editorial Report* (June 11, 2011), arguing that "the fair tax moves taxation from a decision by the government on your income to a decision made by the consumer based upon that purchased behavior." As of mid-September 2011, Cain had participated in six debates among the Republican presidential contenders for 2012. He gave perhaps his strongest performance in the first, held in May 2011, during which he characterized himself as a Washington outsider. While the debate of September 7 was dominated by exchanges between former Massachusetts governor Mitt Romney and Texas governor Rick Perry, Cain received applause for proposing his "9-9-9" plan, which would replace the federal income tax with a 9 percent sales tax, a 9 percent personal-income tax, and a 9 percent corporate-income tax, to "level the playing field," in his words.

Cain's newest book, *This Is Herman Cain!: My Journey to the White House*, was due to be published in October 2011. His many awards include seven honorary doctoral degrees.

A devoted Baptist, Cain often preaches at his local church. A baritone, he released a gospel album called *Sunday Morning* in 1996. He opposes abortion and gay marriage and has called homosexuality "a sin."

Cain met his wife, Gloria, shortly after graduating from college. They have been married for nearly 43 years and have two children, Melanie and Vincent, and three grandchildren. Cain and his wife live in Georgia.

—M.M.H.

Suggested Reading: *Atlantic* (on-line) June 30, 2011; *Atlanta Tribune* p10+ Nov. 2002, p57 July 2004; *CBS News* (transcript) June 9, 2011; *Los Angeles Times* (on-line) July 7, 2011; *National Review* (on-line) July 14, 2003; *Newsweek* p73 Sep. 19, 1994; *New York Times* (on-line) June 30, 2011; *St. Petersburg (Florida) Times* (on-line) June 10, 2011; *Washington Post* C p2 May 31, 2011

Selected Books: *Speak as a Leader: Develop the Better Speaker in You*, 1999; *Leadership Is Common Sense*, 2000; *CEO of Self: You're in Charge*, 2001; *They Think You're Stupid: Why Democrats Lost Your Vote and What Republicans Must Do to Keep It*, 2005

Chris Trotman/Getty Images

Calhoun, Jim

May 10, 1942– College basketball coach

Address: University of Connecticut, 2095 Hillside Rd., Mansfield, CT 06269

In 25 seasons as head coach of the University of Connecticut (UConn) men's basketball team, Jim Calhoun has led the Huskies to 17 National Collegiate Athletic Association (NCAA) tournament appearances and three national championships. Prior to his taking over, in 1986, UConn had been little more than a regional power—a team not capable of competing with Big East Conference rivals such as Georgetown, Syracuse, and St. John's. Calhoun has been credited with revitalizing the program, and in 1990, in his fourth year at the helm, the Huskies ad-vanced to the Elite 8 round of the NCAA tournament, where the squad came within one shot of making its first Final Four appearance. Though the Huskies continued to qualify for the NCAA tournament throughout the 1990s, Calhoun had to wait nine years before making the Final Four. The team capped its 1998–99 season with a win over Duke University in the tournament championship game, capturing the first national title in UConn history. Five years later Calhoun led the team to another championship, and he repeated that feat in April 2011, becoming the oldest coach ever to win the NCAA title. In 2005, in recognition of his success at UConn, as well as at Northeastern University, where he began his NCAA coaching career, Calhoun was inducted into the Naismith Memorial Basketball Hall of Fame.

The older son in an Irish Catholic family of six children, Jim Calhoun was born on May 10, 1942 in Braintree, Massachusetts, a suburb of Boston. Before Jim was born his father, James Calhoun, served in the Merchant Marine. His first wife died while giving birth to a daughter, Rose, and James was so distraught that he asked for and received sea duty. James later married Jim Calhoun's mother, Kathleen, and took an engineering job with the Boston Gas Co. As a young boy Jim idolized his father, a well-respected man who was president of the local chapter of the Knights of Columbus lodge. "He was my hero, a silent leader," Calhoun told Bob Snyder for the Syracuse, New York, *Post-Standard* (January 23, 1998). One day when Jim was 15 years old and about to play in a Babe Ruth League all-star baseball game, his father complained of what he thought was indigestion and told his son he would see him at the game later. During the game a man walked to center field and told Jim Calhoun, "Your father's dead." James Calhoun, at 53, had had a fatal heart attack. Though he was devastated by the loss, Jim Calhoun vowed to take care of his family. "One of the gifts my father gave to me was that he always told me, 'The oldest son takes responsibility,'" Calhoun told Mark Blaudschun for the *Boston Globe* (September 9,

2005). After high school he studied for three months at the American International College (AIC), in Springfield, Massachusetts, before returning home to help his mother support the family. (According to some sources Calhoun began his college career at the University of Massachusetts, not AIC.) He spent 18 months carving gravestones in Quincy, Massachusetts, before his former high-school basketball coach, Fred Herget, who had stepped in as a father figure after James's death, persuaded him to return to college.

Calhoun, who stands six feet four inches tall, played basketball for AIC, scoring 922 career points and earning Little All-American honors in 1966, his final year of college eligibility. Two years later he graduated from AIC with a B.A. degree in sociology; from 1966 to 1968 he had served as an assistant coach. He later tried out successfully for the Boston Celtics, but soon afterward he was cut from the team and decided to pursue coaching. He began his career in 1969 at Old Lyme High School, in Old Lyme, Connecticut, where, in addition to coaching for one season, he served as the local constable. The following year he took a job at Westport High School, in Westport, Massachusetts, where he stayed for a single season. His third coaching stint, at Dedham High School, in Dedham, Massachusetts, was his most successful up to that time: under his leadership the school's 1971–72 team was undefeated in the regular season. In 1968 Calhoun was a volunteer for U.S. senator Robert F. Kennedy's presidential campaign.

In 1972 Calhoun was offered the head-coaching job at Northeastern University, in Boston, a school then known more for hockey than basketball. The men's basketball team was making the jump from Division II to Division I, and though leaving Dedham for Boston entailed taking a pay cut, Calhoun signed on. Calhoun revitalized the Northeastern program, amassing a 250–137 record over 14 seasons. During Calhoun's tenure the team made five NCAA tournament appearances, advancing past the first round in three of those seasons.

In 1986 Calhoun left Boston for Storrs, Connecticut, home of the UConn Huskies. Though UConn played in the Big East, one of the NCAA's premier conferences, Calhoun's move to Connecticut was something of a gamble, as UConn had struggled in recent seasons. The team played its home games at the dilapidated Storrs Field House, notorious for its leaky roof. "Anybody who knows me understands that if you appeal to my competitive aspect, it's hard for me to resist," Calhoun told Rich Cimini for New York Newsday (March 5, 1990), explaining that UConn's then–athletic director, John Toner, persuaded him to take the position. While the team was popular within the state, it was more a regional threat than a national one. Calhoun set out to change that, citing the success of other Big East teams—Georgetown, Syracuse, and St. John's—as a means of recruiting top players. "We'd say, 'Come to a place where you're not going to be the next something. Come to a place where you can

be the first. This can be your stage,'" Calhoun told Leigh Montville for Sports Illustrated (April 14, 2004).

Calhoun struggled in his first season, posting a 9–19 record, the worst of his collegiate career. "He vowed that we, and he, would never, ever, ever, go through another season of losses like that again," Calhoun's assistant coach then, Howie Dickenman, told Malcolm Moran for the New York Times (February 27, 1995). Calhoun fared better during the team's 1987–88 season, and the Huskies defeated Ohio State to win the National Invitational Tournament (NIT), a postseason competition for teams that fail to make the more prestigious NCAA tournament. The following year the Huskies again made the NIT, this time advancing as far as the quarterfinal round and finishing the year with an 18–13 record.

It was not until UConn's 1989–90 "dream season," however, that Calhoun became known for transforming UConn's program. The Huskies finished the year with a 31–6 record, its most memorable victory coming in the Sweet 16 round of the NCAA tournament, when the guard Tate George made a buzzer-beating shot against Clemson. In the Elite 8 round, UConn lost in overtime to Duke University, as the forward Christian Laettner, capitalizing on a play in which George lost the ball out of bounds, made a last-second game-winning jumper. Despite falling short of the Final Four, Calhoun was voted national coach of the year. "I'll always remember that team," Calhoun told Bob Ryan for the Boston Globe (April 5, 2005). "They captured the hearts of everyone who saw them play." The following season UConn again had its hopes dashed by Duke, losing to the Blue Devils in the Sweet 16 round.

UConn made the NCAA tournament in four of its next five seasons, twice advancing to the Sweet 16, once to the Elite 8. The Elite 8 appearance came in 1994–95, when UConn fell to the University of California–Los Angeles Bruins, who went on to win the national championship. Calhoun, a former marathon runner, had always pushed his players to be fast, and in UCLA he found "the only team that could match us up and down the floor," he told Snyder. In the 1996–97 season UConn ended its streak of three consecutive NCAA tournament appearances, qualifying instead for the NIT. The Huskies made it to the tournament's consolation game. "It was for third place and Jimmy was coaching like it was for the NCAA title," the former UConn coach Dee Rowe told Blaudschun. "The fire, the passion, the competitiveness in his eye was amazing." The Huskies defeated Arkansas and finished the year with an 18–15 record.

The team returned to the NCAA tournament in the 1997–98 season, making it as far as the Elite 8, where it lost to the University of North Carolina, 75–64. The following year Calhoun realized his dream of reaching the Final Four, as the Huskies—who had been ranked first in the nation for 10 weeks during the regular season—captured its first national title. The team finished the season with a 77–74 victory over Duke, outrunning its top-seeded archrival. "We're a great basketball team," Calhoun told Paul McMullen for the *Baltimore Sun* (March 31, 1999), following the championship game. "We beat another great basketball team, the best team we've played all year." UConn returned to the NCAA tournament the following season but was eliminated in the second round. In 2000–01 the team failed to make the tournament and lost to Detroit in the second round of the NIT. The Huskies qualified for the NCAA tournament in each of its next five seasons. (Between 1991 and 2011 the UConn women's basketball team reached the Final Four 12 times and the Elite 8 16 times and won the NCAA tournament seven times.)

In January 2003 Calhoun was diagnosed with prostate cancer; he underwent surgery in early February. He was back in his office days after being released from the hospital, and in under three weeks, he was on the sideline, coaching a home game against St. John's. When he took the floor at Gampel Pavilion, which replaced the Field House in 1990, Calhoun received a three-minute standing ovation. "It was really chilling and reaffirmed what I felt," Calhoun told Dick Weiss for the New York *Daily News* (November 9, 2003). "I was really a lucky person." Calhoun received treatment for skin cancer in 2007 and had a cancerous growth removed from his neck the following year.

In 2003–04 UConn won its second national title, defeating Georgia Tech, 82–73, in the final game of the NCAA tournament. The next season, with a victory against Georgetown on March 2, 2005, Calhoun became the 19th coach in NCAA Division I history to reach 700 career wins. (He is also the only coach in NCAA history to have at least 250 wins at each of two schools.) In April 2005, after the Huskies lost to North Carolina State University in the second round of the NCAA tournament, Calhoun was among those voted into the Hall of Fame. "This is the greatest honor I could ever receive," Calhoun said in his induction speech, according to the *Connecticut Post* (January 1, 2006). "This has been a game that's consumed me. It's taken me from east to west, north to south, and along the way, it's blessed me." For Calhoun the honor marked a homecoming, as the Hall of Fame is located in Springfield, Massachusetts, where he attended college.

The Huskies returned to the NCAA tournament in the 2005–06 season. The year ended with disappointment, as the top-seeded squad was upset by 11th-seed George Mason University in the Elite 8 round. The Huskies finished the year 30–4, and in the summer of 2006, a record five UConn players were selected in the first two rounds of the National Basketball Association (NBA) draft. (To date Calhoun has coached 26 players who have gone on to play in the NBA.) The following year UConn ended its streak of 19 straight postseason appearances, failing to make either the NCAA tournament or the NIT. "I told our guys this won't happen again," Cal-

houn told Paul Schwarz for the *New York Post* (March 8, 2007), following his team's season-ending loss to Syracuse in the Big East tournament. "As long as I'm coaching at UConn, this won't happen again." The Huskies rebounded in 2007–08, finishing the regular season ranked 16th out of 64 in the Associated Press poll. The team fell to San Diego in the first round of the NCAA tournament, losing 70–69. In 2008–09 it achieved a stellar 31–5 record and reached the Final Four, where it lost to Michigan State, 82–73. In February 2009 Calhoun notched his 800th win, in a game against Marquette University.

That season brought Calhoun some negative attention. In February, at a press conference after a game, a political blogger questioned the coach about his salary, which was upwards of $1.5 million, implying that that figure was unjustified in a time of economic crisis. Calhoun replied, in part, "We make $12 million a year for this university. Get some facts, and come back and see me," also calling the blogger stupid and telling him to shut up. Members of the Connecticut General Assembly, among others, criticized the coach, arguing that his comments were unbecoming of one who serves as a role model for students and other young people. In a statement soon afterward, Calhoun said that his comments had been "misinterpreted" to suggest that he was not sensitive to others' economic struggles, and he added, as quoted by the Associated Press (February 27, 2009), "I believe I have a duty, responsibility and obligation to support the state I love and the many people and organizations of Connecticut that are in need. I look forward to continuing with the same amount of passion and commitment to assist people and causes that are important to me and my family." An article in the March 4, 2009 edition of the *Hartford (Connecticut) Courant* noted that the newspaper had received many letters in support of Calhoun.

In a more serious matter, in March 2009 Yahoo.com published a report that the UConn men's basketball program had violated recruiting standards. The report alleged that a player UConn sought to recruit, Nate Miles, had been provided with transportation and lodging from a sports agent, Josh Nochimson, who as a former student manager at UConn was seen as representing the school's interests and should have been barred from the recruiting process; Yahoo.com also reported that Calhoun and other members of the coaching staff had exchanged more than 1,500 phone calls and text messages with Miles. The report led to a lengthy investigation by the NCAA, which ruled in February 2011 that Calhoun was guilty of "failing to promote an atmosphere of compliance," as the *Hartford Courant* (February 23, 2011) noted; the NCAA suspended Calhoun from the first three Big East games of the 2011–12 season. The same newspaper (February 26, 2011) quoted the coach as saying in response, "I fully acknowledge that we, as a staff, made mistakes and would like to apologize to the University and all associated with UConn on behalf of myself and the men's basketball program."

In the meantime the Huskies had had a comparatively tough 2009–10 season, compiling a record of 18–16 and losing in the first round of the Big East tournament. Missing the NCAA tournament, the team fell to Virginia Tech in the second round of the NIT. UConn rebounded the next season, winning five games in five days in the Big East tournament and going on to defeat Butler University to claim the NCAA championship. Calhoun, at 68, became the oldest coach ever to win the championship and only the fifth to win three or more NCAA titles.

Calhoun has been voted Big East Coach of the Year four times: 1990, 1994, 1996, and 1998. He is notorious for his tough treatment of his players and his fiery, profanity-laden sideline tirades. According to Moran, Dee Rowe calls Calhoun "Bobby Knight East," a reference to the former Indiana University coach who once threw a chair during a game. In 1992 one player, Toraino Walker, left UConn due to Calhoun's penchant for berating his squads. "I'm the reality check, every single day," Calhoun told Moran. "I've always said that coaches should be able to earn the right to criticize their players, to make them the best they can be. And how you earn that right is you let them know you do it because you care about them. And that takes nurturing." Kevin Ollie, a former player under Calhoun, told William C. Rhoden for the *New York Times* (March 28, 2011), "You come in as a freshman, you're going to get screamed at . . . but it's all out of love. It's all about getting you tougher because situations in life are going to come when you're going to have to fall back on what you believe in and your core convictions. That's all [Calhoun is] doing, he's putting a demand on your potential."

Leigh Montville wrote that Calhoun "has a tendency to talk fast, 78 rpm in a 33 1/3-rpm world, all the words bent by his Boston accent." Calhoun married his wife, Pat, in 1966. In 1998 the couple, through a donation of $125,000, established the Pat and Jim Calhoun Cardiology Center at the University of Connecticut Health Center. Off the court Calhoun is a warm family man, and whenever he sees his two sons, Jim and Jeff, he prefers kisses to handshakes. "Some people ask me if my father smiles," Jeff told Jack Curry for the *New York Times* (March 19, 1998). "People see him on TV and don't think he's a caring, sensitive man. They'll never understand that [he is]." Calhoun is a film and theater buff; Curry noted that he "loves blaring songs from *Les Miserables* or *The Phantom of the Opera*." Calhoun runs a summer basketball camp in Connecticut for children. He has co-written two books—*Dare to Dream: Connecticut Basketball's Remarkable March to the National Championship* (with Leigh Montville, 1999) and *A Passion to Lead: Seven Leadership Secrets for Success in Business, Sports, and Life* (with Richard

Ernsberger Jr., 2007). "I like the challenge, every year, of taking a group of individual kids—many of them still teens—and trying to mold them into a smart, tough-minded *team*," he wrote in *A Passion to Lead*. "It's not an easy thing to do. . . . But when you succeed, there's nothing more gratifying."

—K.J.P.

Suggested Reading: *Boston Globe* E p1 Sep. 9, 2005; (Cleveland, Ohio) *Plain Dealer* D p1 Apr. 3, 2004; *Hartford (Connecticut) Courant* C p1 Sep. 10, 2005, A p17 Mar. 4, 2009, A p1 Feb. 23, 2011; *New York Times* C p1 Feb. 27, 1995, C p1 Mar. 19, 1998, (on-line) Apr. 5, 2011; *Seattle (Washington) Times* F p1 Mar. 30, 1999; *Sports Illustrated* p56 Apr. 14, 2004; *USA Today* C p1 Aug. 26, 2008

Selected Books: *Dare to Dream: Connecticut Basketball's Remarkable March to the National Championship* (with Leigh Montville), 1999; *A Passion to Lead: Seven Leadership Secrets for Success in Business, Sports, and Life* (with Richard Ernsberger, Jr.), 2007

Cam'ron

Feb. 4, 1976– Hip-hop artist; filmmaker

Address: c/o Asylum Records, 1906 Acklen Ave., Nashville, TN 37212-3700

"As a rapper, Cam'ron is great at many things," Jon Caramanica wrote for *Vibe* magazine (May 2009), about the Grammy Award–nominated hip-hop artist. "He's a detailed reporter, his verses filled with weights, dates, calibers, places, even a name or two. He's a searing wit, regarding everything from the mundanities of the corner to the politics of romantic relationships; even his vulgarity is hilarious. He's one of the greatest technicians in the history of the genre, capable of staggering feats of rhyme, both compressed into tiny spaces and drawn out over whole verses." One of the most prominent rappers to emerge from New York City's storied Harlem neighborhood, Cam'ron, also known as "Killa Cam," has achieved cult status in rap circles for his brash and flamboyant style; he has become "famous for a sort of avant-garde gangster rap that is dense with polysyllabic rhyme schemes and fashion references," Caramanica noted in an earlier article for the *New York Times* (October 17, 2004). Cam'ron launched his career in the late 1990s, after meeting the New York rap icon Notorious B.I.G. (also known as Biggie Smalls), who helped him land a deal with Lance "Un" Rivera's Epic Records subsidiary Untertainment. Following the releases of two albums for Epic, *Confessions of Fire* (1998) and *S.D.E.* (2000), Cam'ron

Scott Gries/Getty Images

Cam'ron

moved to his childhood friend Damon Dash's label, Roc-A-Fella Records, in 2001. He then overhauled his image, projecting the persona of a flashy, macho, hardcore hip-hop artist—one so masculine and cool that he not only got away with wearing pink but turned the color into a hip-hop fashion trend; meanwhile, he won both critical acclaim and commercial success with his third studio effort, *Come Home with Me* (2002), which included the chart-topping singles "Oh Boy" and "Hey Ma." He also formed his own record label, Diplomatic Man Records, and began heading a rap group called the Diplomats, or the Dipset, which included the rappers Jim Jones, Juelz Santana, and Freekey Zekey. Cam'ron released the Diplomats' debut, *Diplomatic Immunity* (2003), and one more solo album on the Roc-A-Fella label, *Purple Haze* (2004), before joining the Warner Music Group in 2005 under the Asylum Records imprint. In 2006 he released his fifth studio album, *Killa Season*, in conjunction with a film of the same name, starring Cam'ron, which he also wrote and directed. Cam'ron next took a hiatus from the music industry to care for his mother, who had suffered a series of debilitating strokes. He released new material in 2009 with *Crime Pays*, on the Asylum label, and formed a new duo, the U.N., with the Harlem-based rapper Vado. Their album *Heat in Here, Volume 1* appeared in 2010.

Cam'ron was born Cameron Giles on February 4, 1976 in Harlem, in the New York City borough of Manhattan. He was raised by his mother, Fredericka, until age 13, when he was put in the care of his maternal grandmother due to his mother's substance-abuse problems. The rapper has refused to discuss his father, who abandoned him and his mother shortly after Cam'ron was born. (In 2000 Cam'ron's father died of AIDS-related complications.) Before embarking on a music career, Cam'ron aspired to become a professional basketball player. He was a standout, All-American point guard at Manhattan Central High School, described by his coach, Charles Johnson, as a "very feisty and temperamental" player, as noted by Del Quentin Wilber and Stephen A. Crockett Jr. for the *Washington Post* (November 18, 2005). (Wilber and Crockett wrote that even then, Cam'ron "was often jotting rap lyrics into notebooks.") Cam'ron drew the attention of a number of college-basketball powerhouses, including the University of North Carolina, Syracuse University, and the University of Miami, but he was ultimately denied admission to those schools due to low SAT scores and a poor overall academic record.

After dropping out of high school, in 1994, Cam'ron sold illegal drugs for some time before earning his General Equivalency Diploma (GED), which allowed him to play basketball at Navarro College, a small junior college in Corsicana, Texas. (In April 2010 Cam'ron claimed in a Twitter post to have paid $600 to obtain his GED, in order to please his mother.) He was expelled from the school for selling marijuana (or, according to some sources, carrying a gun). After he returned to Harlem, Cam'ron went back to dealing drugs but soon turned to rap, after becoming reunited with one of his high-school basketball teammates, Mason "Mase" Betha, then a fledgling rapper and protégé of the Bad Boy Entertainment music mogul P. Diddy. Along with Mase and his cousin, known as Bloodshed, Cam'ron—who adopted the name "Killa Cam"—formed a rap group called Children of the Corn. The group was overseen by the underground New York City rapper Big L; it dissolved in 1996, after Bloodshed was killed in a car accident. (Big L was murdered in Harlem in 1999.)

Cam'ron's rap career took off after Mase introduced him to Notorious B.I.G. Impressed with Cam'ron's talent for improvised rap, Notorious B.I.G. introduced the young hip-hop performer to Lance "Un" Rivera, who signed him to his Untertainment label. Cam'ron penned several songs for Untertainment/Epic, including Lil' Kim's 1997 platinum-selling single "Crush on You," before making his solo debut in 1998 with *Confessions of Fire*. (It was then that he became known as "Cam'ron.") That album showcased his pop-rap style and storytelling abilities and boasted the singles "Horse & Carriage," "3-5-7" (included in the 1998 film *Woo*), and "Feels Good," songs that featured Cam'ron's collaborations with Mase, DMX, and Usher, respectively. Another song, "Me, My Moms & Jimmy," was recorded with the future Diplomats member Jim Jones and Cam'ron's mother. *Confessions of Fire* attained gold-record status, selling 600,000 copies, and reached number two on *Billboard*'s top R&B/hip-hop albums chart; it peaked at number six on the *Billboard* 200 album chart. It also earned positive reviews from critics.

Stephen Thomas Erlewine, in a review for the All Music Guide (on-line), wrote that the album "created an accessible fusion of rap and pop that manages to keep some sort of street edge."

Cam'ron's sophomore album, *S.D.E.* (an acronym for "Sex, Drugs, and Entertainment," or, as some sources have it, "Sports, Drugs, and Entertainment"), was released by Epic Records in September 2000. The album's songs chronicle Cam'ron's life and include his collaborations with such acts as Destiny's Child, Prodigy of the group Mobb Deep, and Noreaga. Propelled by the hits "Let Me Know" and "What Means the World to You," the album reached number two on *Billboard*'s R&B/hip-hop-albums chart and number 14 on the *Billboard* 200 chart. Charles E. Rogers, writing for *New York Amsterdam News* (July 14, 1999), called the album a "concrete, hard cacophony of gritty beats, lethal lyrics and real-life-inspired scenarios" and added that it reflected Cam'ron's "advancement at all levels, personal and professional." Lines in the song "Let Me Know" include, "Yo I get dough any way / I can flow any way / Yo you rap about money, man, who are you anyway? / C'mon, all my jewels ice and gray / And n**** might I say / I'm Mister Rogers status, change twice a day / Any beef you let me know, I'll be there right away / And when I'm rhyming, I've always got the right of way / I got some cats that'll come down here right away / To take your a** right away / Believe me you could die today / We explode and bullets we reload and killers speak in code / So please let me know."

Following the release of *S.D.E.*, Cam'ron moved to Roc-A-Fella Records, the label founded by Jay-Z, Damon Dash, and Kareem Burke. Dash, one of his childhood friends, helped negotiate the release from his contract at Epic and signed him to a $4.5 million record deal. (Cam'ron has said that he switched record labels in order to work in a more hip-hop-friendly environment.) Cam'ron's Roc-A-Fella debut and third studio album, *Come Home with Me*, was released in May 2002. The album—whose 15 tracks Cam'ron wrote or co-wrote—marked the introduction of his rap crew the Diplomats, also known as Dipset, whose other members were Jim Jones, Juelz Santana, and Freekey Zekey. Santana performed alone on six tracks, including the hit single "Oh Boy," which held the top spot on the *Billboard* R&B/hip-hop singles chart for five consecutive weeks and earned a Grammy nomination for best rap song; it reached number four on the *Billboard* 200 chart. The second single from the album, "Hey Ma," showcased Santana, Zekey, and DJ Kay Slay and became Cam'ron's biggest hit, peaking at number three on the *Billboard* Hot 100 singles chart. *Come Home with Me*, meanwhile, earned widespread praise from critics and became his most commercially successful album to date, reaching number two on the *Billboard* 200 chart and achieving platinum status, with sales of more than one million copies. The *Vibe* writer declared about the album, "*Come Home with Me* is far from

a perfect album, but the unbridled, at times absurd braggadocio makes for marvelous music."

The success of *Come Home with Me* allowed Cam'ron to pursue other ventures. He established his own record label, Diplomatic Man Records, and made a foray into acting with a supporting role in the 2002 crime drama *Paid in Full*, which was directed by Charles Stone III and distributed through Roc-A-Fella's film division. Cam'ron also launched his own cologne, Oh Boy, through Roc-A-Wear, Roc-A-Fella's clothing division, and introduced Sizzurp Purple Punch Liqueur, in a partnership with the company Harbrew Imports. In 2003, after striking a deal with Roc-A-Fella, the Diplomats released their debut album, *Diplomatic Immunity*, which featured the lead single "Dipset Anthem" and production work from such artists as Kanye West, Just Blaze, and the Heatmakerz; the album quickly achieved gold status. The following year the Diplomats released their second album, *Diplomatic Immunity 2* (2004), which was also certified gold by the Recording Industry Association of America (RIAA). It was around that time that Cam'ron became known for his flamboyant fashions, often appearing in videos and at events wearing flashy jewelry and expensive fur coats. He is credited as the rapper who popularized the color pink among the hip-hop crowd; he went so far as to purchase an all-pink Range Rover. "When I did pink, I did it so I wouldn't be dressing like everybody else," Cam'ron told Jon Caramanica for the *New York Times* (December 17, 2004).

Along with praise for Cam'ron's musical achievements came publicity for other matters, including his July 2002 arrest for drug and gun possession and a 2003 shooting in Boston, Massachusetts. The latter incident stemmed from a dispute between members of Cam'ron's entourage and several fans while the Diplomats were promoting their debut album at a nightclub in Washington, D.C.'s theater district. Following that dispute, someone on Cam'ron's tour bus fired shots at a car carrying three women on Boston's Southeast Expressway. (None of the women were hurt.) While neither Cam'ron nor any members of the Diplomats were arrested, two people on the tour bus were taken into custody for handgun possession and assault, and two others traveling in a black Ford Excursion—also said to be part of Cam'ron's entourage—were charged with unlawful possession of a firearm.

Those incidents notwithstanding, Cam'ron's fourth studio album, *Purple Haze* (2004), was a critical and commercial success and achieved gold-record status. The album included tracks sampled from the work of such artists and groups as Cyndi Lauper, Earth, Wind and Fire, Smokey Robinson, and Marvin Gaye, as well as contributions by Jaheim, Twista, Psycho, and Kanye West. In a review of the album posted on the Web site thesituation.co.uk, Dapo Ogunjana wrote that it was "a signature album from Cam'ron" with "almost an equal representation of strong, upbeat tracks and weak tracks." The writer for *Vibe*, on the other hand, called it a "cult classic" and "an album better heard than described."

Dissatisfied with the way Roc-A-Fella had handled *Purple Haze*'s promotion, Cam'ron left the label in 2005 to sign with Asylum Records, a subsidiary of Warner Music Group. The rapper made headlines in October of that year, when he was attacked in his car after leaving a nightclub in Washington, D.C.; whether the attackers were simply robbers or rivals of Cam'ron's in the notoriously factional and violent world of hip-hop was never publicly revealed. Cam'ron was shot in both arms and underwent surgery at Howard University Hospital, in Washington, which released him after 12 hours. He frustrated local police when he refused to cooperate in the investigation of the shooting, unwilling to violate the macho codes of rap and street life. Santana told Wilber and Crockett, "[Cam'ron] isn't going to stand up and point out a guy in a witness line and say, 'That is the dude who shot me.' We all came from the street." Wilber and Crockett wrote, "One thing seems sure: Getting shot means more street cred for Cam, more aggravation for the cops."

That "street cred" may have fueled the anticipation of Cam'ron's return in 2006, with the release of *Killa Season*, his fifth studio album and first on the Asylum label. *Killa Season* debuted at number two on the *Billboard* 200 chart. Cam'ron served as executive producer of the album, which included collaborations with the HeatMakerz, Charlemagne, Ty Fyff, Alchemist, and I.N.F.O. In conjunction with the album, Cam'ron wrote, directed, and starred in a direct-to-DVD film of the same name. The film, which tells the story of an aspiring basketball player who leads the life of a street hustler, received mostly tepid reviews from critics. Jim Farber wrote in an assessment for the New York *Daily News* (May 15, 2006), "No one will mistake *Killa Season* for *Citizen Kane*, but there is a certain honesty and refreshing candor to its low-budget presentation."

After the release of *Killa Season*, whose sales disappointed expectations, Cam'ron took a hiatus from the music industry to take care of his mother, who suffered three strokes in one day in the spring of 2007. For over a year he shared a home with her in Fort Lauderdale, Florida, where he transported her back and forth to a rehabilitation center. Cam'ron recalled to Jon Caramanica for *Vibe*, "My mom couldn't walk or nothing. It was like, putting her in the car, get her out the car, in the wheelchair, out the wheelchair." He added, "You only get one mother." Following his mother's recovery, he released *Harlem's Greatest* (2008), a collection of his greatest hits, and returned to the studio to record his sixth studio album, *Crime Pays*, which was released in May 2009. With the singles "My Job" and "Cookies-n-Apple Juice," the album was described by Caramanica as having "the combination of brash street talk and dazzling, absurdist wordplay that has made Cam'ron a cult figure, if not quite a superstar." Also that year Cam'ron formed a rap duo, the U.N., with the Harlem-based rapper Vado. The two released the album, *Heat in Here, Vol. 1*, in 2010. The leadoff single from the album, "Speaking in Tungs," reached number 82 on the *Billboard* R&B/hip-hop singles chart, and the album received generally positive reviews. David Jeffries, in a review for the All Music Guide (online), wrote that the collaboration with Cam'ron's protégé Vado "offers a level-headed gangsta alternative to Cam's oddball, attitude-filled rhymes" and called the album "another fan-aimed success."

Despite having falling-outs with Diplomat members Jim Jones, Juelz Santana, and Freekey Zekey, all of whom have had moderately successful solo careers, Cam'ron announced in 2010 that the Diplomats had reunited. They are currently working on their next album, which will be produced by the hip-hop legend Dr. Dre and released by Interscope Records.

Cam'ron has homes in Lodi, New Jersey, and Fort Lee, New Jersey. He has a son, who is pictured on the cover of his album *Come Home with Me*. The boy is currently in the fourth grade.

—C.C.

Suggested Reading: *Blender* magazine (on-line) Aug. 15, 2002; *Boston Globe* D p1 Mar. 1, 2003; (New York) *Amsterdam News* p22 July 14, 1999; (New York) *Daily News* p46 Aug. 11, 1998; *New York Times* p8+ Oct. 17, 2004; *USA Today* E p9 Nov. 1, 2002; *Vibe* (on-line) May 2009

Selected Recordings: as solo artist—*Confessions of Fire*, 1998; *G.D.E.*, 2000; *Come Home with Me*, 2002; *Purple Haze*, 2004; *Killa Season*, 2006; *Crime Pays*, 2009; with the Diplomats— *Diplomatic Immunity*, 2003; *Diplomatic Immunity 2*, 2004; with the U.N.—*Heat in Here, Volume 1*, 2010

Carroll, Cynthia

Nov. 13, 1956– Mining executive

Address: Anglo American PLC, 20 Carlton House Terrace, London SW1Y 5AN, England

On March 1, 2007 Cynthia Carroll succeeded Tony Trahar as chief executive officer (CEO) of the London, England–based Anglo American PLC, one of the world's largest mining companies. In the process she became the first woman, first person recruited from outside the company, and first person from outside South Africa (Anglo's headquarters until 1999) to head the 94-year-old mining giant, which was founded by the German-born industrialist Sir Ernest Oppenheimer in 1917. With her appointment Carroll also broke the proverbial glass ceiling for women in the historically male-

Courtesy of Anglo American

Cynthia Carroll

dominated mining industry, becoming the first female ever to lead a mining company and one of only three women to head a FTSE 100 company. (The FTSE 100 Index, compiled by the *Financial Times* and the London Stock Exchange, is a compendium of the largest publicly traded businesses in England.) Carroll began her career on the gas-and-exploration side of the mining business, working as a petroleum geologist for the oil company Amoco (now part of the British oil conglomerate BP) in the early 1980s before moving to the business side of the industry later in the decade. After earning an M.B.A. degree from Harvard University, in 1989, Carroll started working for the Canadian aluminum company Alcan (now part of Rio Tinto Alcan Inc.), where she enjoyed a rapid rise, culminating in her tenure as head of the company's primary-metals group, from 2002 to 2006. As president and CEO of that division, Carroll was credited with lowering costs, improving operations, and leading Alcan's efforts to expand business all over the world, resulting in some of the highest returns in the company's history; during her tenure the division accounted for $12 billion in annual sales and 75 percent of Alcan's total profit. Carroll was hired as Anglo American's sixth CEO in October 2006 and joined the company's board in January 2007. Known for her even-tempered demeanor and no-nonsense management style, Carroll has used a progressive approach in revamping Anglo American's staid corporate culture. One of her main goals at Anglo, as she explained to Sylvia Pfeifer for the London *Sunday Telegraph* (August 5, 2007), has been "to create one Anglo, one organisation, one that has common standards, with ambitious targets," in hopes of turning it into the leading mining

company in the world. On the subject of her status as a woman in the multibillion-dollar industry, Carroll noted to the same writer, "I have always worked in a male-dominated environment. . . . At the end of the day it comes down to performance, what you stand for and leadership capabilities." Nicky Oppenheimer, Sir Ernest Oppenheimer's grandson, proclaimed in an article for *Time* (April 30, 2009, on-line), "Nobody symbolizes the changing face of world mining more than Cynthia Carroll."

Carroll was born Cynthia Blum on November 13, 1956 and grew up in Princeton, New Jersey. (Some sources say that Carroll grew up in Philadelphia, Pennsylvania.) Her father, Frederick, worked as an investment banker and stockbroker, and her mother, Britta, was a homemaker. Carroll's interest in business and finance was sparked at an early age by her father, who brought home articles from the *Wall Street Journal* for her to read each night. During her youth she also developed interests in art and history and in learning French. After graduating from the Stuart Country Day School of the Sacred Heart, an independent, all-girls Catholic school in Princeton, Carroll attended Skidmore College, in Saratoga Springs, New York. During the first semester of her freshman year, Carroll, intending to become a liberal-arts major, took a geology course. "Geology was a complete fluke," she recalled to Louise Armitstead for the London *Sunday Times* (October 29, 2006). "At college I had to do a science requirement. Someone said do geology, so I did and I was hooked."

After earning a B.S. degree in geology from Skidmore, in 1978, Carroll enrolled at the University of Kansas (KU) in Lawrence. She received an M.S. degree in geology from KU in 1982. She then started working as a petroleum geologist for the oil company Amoco, based in Denver, Colorado. (Amoco merged with BP in 1998.) She held that position for about a half-dozen years, during which she traveled all over the western U.S., overseeing oil drilling and exploration in such places as Wyoming, Utah, Montana, and Alaska. During those excursions Carroll "used willpower and lots of chewing gum to overcome childhood motion sickness and tolerate bumpy helicopter rides over the Rockies," Phyllis Berman wrote for *Forbes* (June 16, 2008). Later with Amoco she moved into the business side of the industry and held both management and deal-making responsibilities. Commenting on the initial difficulties she faced as a woman working in the oil industry, Carroll told Sarah Dougherty for the *Edmonton (Canada) Journal* (June 14, 2003), "I had to deal with some tough and rough oil types. Early on, I had to learn how to defend a position in circumstances where I was being challenged."

In 1988 Carroll returned to school, enrolling at Harvard University's prestigious graduate school of business, in Cambridge, Massachusetts. "People told me I was out of my mind to be interrupting my career," she told Dougherty, referring to her decision to leave a comfortable home in Colorado for a modest Harvard dorm room. Between academic years at Harvard, Carroll landed a summer job with the aluminum producer Alcan. Upon receiving her M.B.A. degree, in 1989, she moved to Cleveland, Ohio, to work full-time as a business analyst in Alcan's rolled-products division. (Rolled products include sheets, plates, and foil.) At Alcan Carroll was appointed to a succession of positions of increasing responsibility. In 1991 she was named vice president and general manager of Alcan's foil division, a position she held for the next five years. Then, in 1996, Carroll moved overseas to become the managing director of the Alcan subsidiary Aughinish Alumina Ltd., an alumina refinery located on the west coast of Ireland. (Aughinish Alumina is now owned by RUSAL, a subsidiary of the Russia-based United Company RUSAL.) In 1998 Carroll earned another promotion and returned to Montreal to head Alcan's bauxite, alumina, and specialty-chemicals group; she served as president of that division until 2002. In those posts Carroll developed a reputation as a cost-cutter and became known for optimizing operational performance and negotiating effectively in groups. Daniel Gagnier, a senior executive at Alcan, told Dougherty, "She is not intimidated by what is at stake, is a good negotiator and manages and motivates her teams well."

In January 2002 Carroll was appointed president and CEO of Alcan's primary-metals group. As head of that division, which has 18,000 employees and operations in 20 countries, she helped transform Alcan from one of the highest-cost producers of aluminum to one of the lowest, making it one of the top-performing aluminum companies in the world. Carroll also broadened Alcan's international presence by initiating projects worth more than $10 billion, including deals to develop new facilities in France, South Africa, and China. She served as one of the main forces behind the successful integration of the French aluminum producer Pechiney, which Alcan purchased in 2003, and then played a vital role in Alcan's first acquisition in the Middle East—a stake in a smelter project in Oman in 2005. Due in large part to Carroll's efforts, Alcan achieved the highest earnings in the history of the company, with the primary-metals group's sales tripling during her five years as the unit's leader. By the end of her tenure, Alcan's primary-metals group had accounted for 75 percent of the company's total profit, bringing in approximately $12 billion in annual sales. (In 2007 Alcan Inc. merged with Rio Tinto Aluminum to form Rio Tinto Alcan Inc., making it the second-largest aluminum company in the world.)

Carroll's relationship with the London-based mining company Anglo American began at the 2006 World Economic Forum in Davos, Switzerland, when she happened to sit next to Sir Mark Moody-Stuart, the company's non-executive chairman, at a breakfast meeting. Impressed with her charm, jovial spirit, and operational expertise, he immediately considered her as a possible successor to Tony Trahar, who was retiring as Anglo's CEO. In October of that year, it was announced that Carroll would become Anglo's first female chief executive and the sixth CEO in the company's history. As the first woman, outsider, and non–South African to be named to the post, Carroll initially faced resistance from members of the mining community, who questioned her ability to run a global mining conglomerate. Because of such sentiments Anglo's market capitalization fell considerably (by approximately $1.1 billion) the day her appointment was announced. (Market capitalization is the total estimated value of a company, calculated by multiplying its total number of issued or purchased shares by its current share price.) Carroll had nonetheless become the highest-ranking female executive in England and the first woman ever to lead a mining group, while joining a group of only three women to head FTSE 100 companies. Commenting on Anglo's exhaustive, months-long search for a CEO, Moody-Stuart later told Phyllis Berman, "We had been looking for someone with international exposure and experience in a capital-intensive long-cycle business—and not necessarily someone from the mining industry. You balance internal talents with external talents. When you are looking for change, an external appointment has its merits."

In mid-January 2007 Carroll became an executive member of Anglo's board of directors. She officially succeeded Trahar as Anglo's CEO on March 1, 2007. Since she stepped into that role, Carroll has been charged with overhauling the company, described by Sylvia Pfeifer as "one of the most conservative companies in a famously traditional industry," by spinning off unrelated assets in order to focus on its core mining operations. Prior to moving its headquarters to London, in 1999, Anglo American was based in South Africa, where it was long known as a producer of gold, diamonds, and platinum and later diversified into other areas, such as banking, paper, packaging, steel, media, and brewing. Those diversifications, and their exclusive focus in South Africa, were a result of the company's inability to invest in overseas markets because of international sanctions in response to the country's brutal system of apartheid, or government-enforced racial segregation, which lasted from 1948 to 1994. Carroll's predecessor, Trahar, who had served as Anglo's CEO since 2000, had spent much of his tenure trying to unload nonmining assets in efforts to restructure the company. Those efforts notwithstanding, Anglo was lagging behind its mining competitors, such as Australia's BHP Billiton PLC and Brazil's Vale SA, and had been the subject of several takeover rumors at the time of Carroll's hiring. At that time Carroll explained, as quoted in *Africa News* (October 29, 2006), "The restructuring moves have been the right ones. My challenge is to really get in and understand where we can further develop, to ensure operational excellence and organic growth." She added, "I want to see a strong Anglo—a stronger Anglo—not another company, going forward. And that's the way to do it—ensure we're better than everyone else in all aspects of our business."

Carroll was brought on not only to continue with Trahar's restructuring initiatives but also to transform Anglo's culture, with a primary emphasis on improving safety. "There was a mindset that it was inevitable that people would be killed in deep-level mining," she explained in an interview posted on the Skidmore University Web site. "In the years before I joined Anglo, hundreds of people had died in accidents. For me, it was completely unacceptable." In June 2007, after a string of mining-related deaths, Carroll shut down the largest platinum mine in South Africa, leading to the retraining of some 28,000 workers. That was followed by the firing of several high-level Anglo executives who had poor safety records. "This had never been done before and it was not a popular decision, but it sent a clear message that safety was fundamental and it was not to be negotiated," Carroll said in the same interview. "So it was the first major step in altering the mindset of the business and in sending a clear signal to the South African mining industry and to Anglo American that things were changing." As a result of Carroll's focus on safety, Anglo has seen a 60 percent drop in fatalities since 2007.

Another one of Carroll's priorities has been to repair Anglo's relationship with South Africa, which has long served as the company's main source of revenue. Because Anglo had done little to forge stronger ties with the country's government ministers and mining officials since the end of the apartheid era, the company had been in danger of losing its lucrative mining assets in the region. Carroll has worked closely with South African ministers and officials in efforts to retain Anglo's presence in the country. Her attempts to salvage those relations have included a series of deals through South Africa's Black Economic Empowerment (BEE) program, including the sale of a portion of Anglo's assets to the country's predominantly black population. In other actions as CEO, Carroll has spurned strong takeover advances by the Switzerland-based mining company Xstrata and suspended Anglo's shareholder dividend in the wake of sweeping cost-cutting measures. (In 2010 the dividend was restored thanks to rising commodity prices.)

Along with the implementation of new safety measures and the fostering of stronger relations with South Africa, Carroll has set in motion a number of cost-cutting initiatives while leading efforts to broaden Anglo's global presence. Not long after becoming CEO, she launched a project to survey and improve operations at Anglo's mines, with the goal of saving the company approximately $2 billion by 2011. Carroll's other moves have included spinning off Anglo's paper and packaging business, Mondi, and selling off its remaining stake in the gold-mining company AngloGold

Ashanti. Carroll has also made several acquisitions, buying stakes in the Michiquillay copper mine project in northern Peru, the MMX Minas-Rio iron-ore project in Brazil, the Pebble copper project in Alaska, and the Foxleigh coal mine in Australia.

As head of Anglo American, Carroll oversees more than 100,000 employees on six continents and in more than 40 countries. Anglo ranks among the top five mining companies in the world in market capitalization and is the world's largest producer of platinum, through its 45 percent stake in the South Africa–based company De Beers. Carroll has been credited with steering Anglo through the global economic crisis that began in 2008 and that had a major impact on the mining industry; she has helped the company almost triple its sales over the last two years, thanks to higher productivity and commodity prices. In 2010 Anglo achieved pre-tax earnings of $10.9 billion, up from $4.02 billion the previous year.

Phyllis Berman described the blond, blue-eyed Carroll as "petite" and as having a "bubbly voice" and "a remarkable lack of ego or pretension." She serves as chairman of the board of Anglo Platinum Ltd. and is a member of the boards of the American Aluminum Association and the International Aluminum Institute. Formerly a director of the Sara Lee Corp. and AngloGold Ashanti Ltd., she also serves as a director of the De Beers Group and as a non-executive director of BP PLC. In 2008 Carroll was named by *Time* magazine as one of the world's 100 most influential people, and she has frequently been listed by *Forbes* magazine in its annual survey of the world's most powerful women, ranking fifth, fourth, and 14th in 2008, 2009, and 2010, respectively. Carroll lives in Surrey, England, with her husband, David, who has an accounting background, and their four children (three daughters and a son). Carroll's husband is now a full-time homemaker. "I have a wonderful husband," she told Sylvia Pfeifer. "He is highly supportive and we work as a team."

—C.C.

Suggested Reading: *Africa News* Oct. 29, 2006; *The Business* Mar. 3, 2007; (Edmonton, Alberta, Canada) *Journal* J p1 June 14, 2003; *Forbes* p100 June 16, 2008; (London) *Sunday Telegraph* p5 Oct. 29, 2006, p8 Aug. 5, 2007; (London) *Sunday Times* p6+ Oct. 29, 2006; *New York Times* p10 Oct. 25, 2006

Chris Jackson/Getty Images

Catherine, Duchess of Cambridge

Jan. 9, 1982–

Address: St. James's Palace, Chapel Royal, Cleveland Row, London, SW1A 1DH, England

In April 2011, when Catherine Middleton—known as Kate—married Prince William, a grandson of Queen Elizabeth II of Great Britain, she became the first commoner since the 17th century to wed a member of the British royal family close to the throne. Prince William is second in line (after his father, Prince Charles) to become king of the Commonwealth realms, which are the United Kingdom, Canada, Australia, New Zealand, Jamaica, Barbados, the Bahamas, Grenada, Papua New Guinea, the Solomon Islands, Tuvalu, Saint Lucia, St. Vincent and the Grenadines, Belize, Antigua and Barbuda, and St. Kitts and Nevis. As a result of the union, Catherine is officially known as Her Royal Highness the Duchess of Cambridge; in the event that Prince William becomes king, she will become the queen consort. (Although the media has referred to her as Princess Catherine, that title is not technically correct, as she was not born into royalty.)

The royal couple began dating a decade ago, while they were both attending the University of St. Andrew's, in Scotland, and Catherine has been in the public eye ever since. "Kate Middleton is intelligent, good looking, kind and fun, and she is remarkably normal . . . ," Penny Junor, who has penned biographies of other members of the royal family, wrote for the London *Daily Telegraph* (November 17, 2010). "Kate has proved to be discreet, loyal and trustworthy, despite the greatest provo-

cation. She has also proved to be a lot tougher than she looks." Although Catherine has been followed by the paparazzi for several years, she has managed to keep some aspects of her life private. "We have a lot to learn about our future queen," Robert Finch, Dominion chairman of the Monarchist League of Canada, said to Daniel Drolet for the Victoria, British Columbia, Canada, *Times Colonist* (May 1, 2011). "Part of the interest and excitement surrounding Miss Middleton is the mystery, quite frankly."

The oldest of three children, Catherine Elizabeth Middleton was born on January 9, 1982 in Reading, England. She has a brother, James, and sister, Philippa, who is better known as Pippa. Catherine's parents, Michael and Carole, are former British Airways employees who in 1987 established a lucrative mail-order company called Party Pieces, which sells children's party toys and paraphernalia. When Catherine was two she and her family moved to Amman, Jordan, where her father's work had taken him. In 1986 the family returned to England, where they lived in a five-bedroom house in Berkshire. Around that time Catherine enrolled at St. Andrew's School, a private institution in Pangbourne. She remained there until the mid-1990s, then attended Downe House School for a short period before transferring at 14 to Marlborough College, in Wiltshire. As quoted in a London *Telegraph* (April 29, 2011) profile of Catherine, Nicholas Sampson, a master at Marlborough, described the future Duchess of Cambridge as a "bright, popular and extremely capable pupil." By contrast, the London *Independent* (April 23, 2011) quoted a former classmate as saying that "you barely noticed" Catherine, who "very sweetly just slipped in and out of class," and reported that a former tutor of Catherine's "barely remembered her at all."

After leaving Marlborough College, in 2000, Catherine attended the British Institute in Florence, where she studied art history and Italian. She also went to Chile to participate in a program run by Raleigh International, which recruits young people of different backgrounds for the purpose of serving others and developing leadership skills. In 2001 she enrolled at Scotland's University of St. Andrews, where she majored in art history and played for the school's hockey team. During her freshman year she became acquainted with Prince William, the older son of Charles, Prince of Wales, and Diana, Princess of Wales. (Following a much-publicized divorce from Charles, Princess Diana died in a 1997 car crash after being chased by paparazzi.) Prince William was also studying art history when he met Catherine; he later switched his major to geography. Catherine and Prince William became friends, but, according to many reports, his attraction to her began later, when he saw her model a revealing dress during a student fashion show. The pair subsequently shared housing with two other students. After their respective relationships with others ended, they became romantically involved.

In 2004 Catherine went on a ski trip in Switzerland with Prince William. At that point it became clear that the two were a couple, and the media began to speculate about when they would become engaged. In 2005 both graduated from St. Andrews and moved to London, England. The following year Catherine began working as a part-time assistant accessories buyer for Jigsaw, a British clothing chain owned by friends of her parents. Due to her frequent encounters with paparazzi, she hired lawyers to help protect her privacy.

Catherine's relationship with Prince William came to a temporary halt in April 2007. Some sources suggested that the constant media attention may have caused problems for the couple; others reported that Prince William was not ready to commit to marriage, quoting him as saying that he did not want to do so until he was at least in his late twenties. "Maybe the relationship had to end anyway, but the intrusion and the pressure of the press must have been a factor," Robert Lacey, an author who has written about the royal family, told Kevin Sullivan for the *Washington Post* (April 15, 2007). "It is hard enough to be young and decide if something is right for you without that." Catherine rekindled her romance with Prince William over the summer of 2007. "At the time I wasn't very happy about [the breakup], but actually it made me a stronger person," Catherine said, according to Christina Boyle, writing for the New York *Daily News* (April 24, 2011). "I think you can get quite consumed by a relationship when you're younger. I really valued that time [away from Prince William] . . . although I didn't think it at the time." During the latter part of the year, she resigned from her job and was able to spend more time accompanying Prince William on foreign holidays and attending his family events and polo matches. She later began to work for Party Pieces, the company owned by her parents. Meanwhile the British press, alluding to Catherine's supposedly having spent years hoping for a marriage proposal from Prince William, nicknamed her "Waity Katie."

In November 2010 the couple announced that they had become engaged. While on vacation in Kenya the previous month, Prince William had proposed to Catherine with the sapphire-and-diamond engagement ring that once belonged to his mother. The general public was reportedly pleased by the announcement, which many viewed as a pleasant distraction from economic crises and other worldwide problems. In early 2011 Catherine resigned from Party Pieces so she could devote more time to planning the wedding.

On April 29, 2011 Catherine married Prince William in Westminster Abbey, in London. Prior to the royal union, Queen Elizabeth II selected for her the official title Her Royal Highness the Duchess of Cambridge, and Prince William officially became His Royal Highness the Duke of Cambridge. For the wedding Catherine wore a dress designed by Sarah Burton of the fashion house Alexander McQueen; it was rumored to have cost between $66,500 and $200,000. The ivory and lace dress had a V-neck satin bodice and a train that was almost nine feet long. "It's got a touch of vintage, a classic 1950s ball gown, so timeless that her daughter would look gorgeous in this gown 30 years from now," the fashion designer Mark Badgley said to Catherine Saint Louis for the *New York Times* (May 1, 2011). "She had a perfect dress, a very traditional dress for a very traditional wedding," the famed designer Oscar de la Renta told Saint Louis.

Following the televised ceremony, which was viewed by many millions of people around the world, Catherine and Prince William stood on a balcony at Buckingham Palace, where they kissed in front of photographers and a cheering crowd of onlookers. Nearly two weeks later the royal couple embarked on their honeymoon; they attempted to keep the destination hidden from the public, but it was later reported that they spent 10 days in the Seychelles, an archipelago of 115 islands in the Indian Ocean.

Catherine, who is five months older than her husband, is the first commoner in over three centuries to marry a prince who will most likely become king. Over the years marriages to ordinary citizens have become more frequent among European royalty; the heirs to the thrones of Belgium, Spain, Norway, Sweden, Denmark, and the Netherlands have all wed commoners. "The big difference between her and the other women who have married into royalty recently is that she's never really had a job," Regine Salens, editor of the blog *Noblesse et Royautés*, said to Daniel Drolet. "She did a brief stint as a buyer for fashion accessories, but that's about it. The other women who became princesses had jobs before they got married—and some of those jobs involved quite a lot of responsibility." Salens added that Catherine "faces a problem the other women never did: She has been in the media spotlight ever since she graduated from university, and as a result it has probably been very difficult for her to find a job in which she could really flourish." Offering another perspective on the royal marriage—in particular, on Catherine's being frequently identified as a commoner—Anthony Failoa wrote for the Norfolk *Virginian-Pilot* (December 20, 2010) that some were "wincing at the notion that a young woman whose family's self-made fortune is larger than many in the landed gentry is being so strongly defined by her bloodline in 21st century Britain. It shows, observers say, that despite the rise of mega-rich commoners such as [the entrepreneur] Richard Branson and [the novelist] J.K. Rowling, this is still very much a society where status is measured in birthright and breeding."

Since she became involved with the royal family, Catherine has been frequently compared with Diana, Prince William's mother. Diana was often referred to as the People's Princess, because she connected with the public more than other members of the royal family did, and because she performed a lot of philanthropic work. "Miss Middleton will inevitably be compared to Diana," Robert Finch told Daniel Drolet. "But I think Miss Middleton should not pay too much attention to it and concentrate on building her own personality and creating her own image. She surely doesn't want to be cast in Diana's shadow, and I think in time people will realize that she is her own person."

As the Duchess of Cambridge, Catherine will be expected to learn royal protocol, travel, become involved in charities, and assist her husband in his public role. Prince William is currently serving as an RAF (Royal Air Force) Search and Rescue pilot; he also attends royal events and is involved in several charities. "The best thing Miss Middleton can do is be loyal," Finch said to Drolet. "When I say loyal, I don't mean remaining monogamous—although that's obviously important, too. I'm talking about loyalty in the true sense. A consort needs to stand by her spouse no matter what, always present a united face, and be there to listen and advise when the spouse needs it." He added, "It's also very important that the consort act and be seen as a complementary figure rather than a competitive figure. You don't want to run the risk of overshadowing your partner."

Claudia Joseph wrote for the London *Mail on Sunday* (December 30, 2007) that Catherine, who stands at five feet eight inches tall, has a "glossy mane of brown hair, classic English-rose looks and natural, unforced elegance." "There is something quintessentially English and modest about her, which echoes Diana in 1981 [the year she married Prince Charles]," Geordie Greig, the editor of *Tatler*, told David Smith for the London *Observer* (December 31, 2006). "She's elegant and beautiful and a million miles from Hollywood glamour. It is a very particular English rose bearing which cannot be crafted by cosmetics companies."

In June 2011 Catherine and Prince William were in the process of acquiring an apartment in Kensington Palace, in London. (In London they had previously stayed at Prince William's bachelor apartment in Clarence House, the residence of his father, Prince Charles; stepmother, Camilla; and brother, Prince Harry.) The royal couple will continue to live primarily in their house on Anglesey, a Welsh island. Their administrative office is in St. James's Palace, in London. Catherine and Prince William traveled to Canada in July 2011 for their first royal tour of the country, and that same month they appeared before cheering crowds in Los Angeles, California.

—J.P.

Suggested Reading: (London) *Daily Telegraph* Features p27 Nov. 17, 2010; (London) *Independent* Comment p40 Apr. 23, 2011; (London) *Observer* Home Pages p11 Dec. 31, 2006; (New York) *Daily News* Special p4 Apr. 24, 2011; (Victoria, British Columbia, Canada) *Times Colonist* D p7 May 1, 2011; Andersen, Christopher. *William and Kate: A Royal Love Story*, 2011

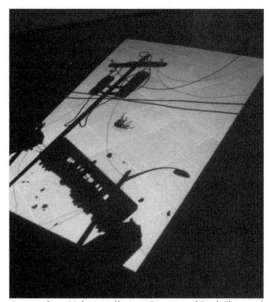

Image of 1st Light installation. Courtesy of Paul Chan and Greene Naftali Gallery, New York.

Chan, Paul

1973– Video artist; activist

Address: c/o Greene Naftali, 508 W. 26th St., New York, NY 10001

As an artist Paul Chan, whose primary medium is video, has created works that encompass worlds—whether fantastical, such as the utopian hermaphrodite community in *Happiness (Finally) After 35,000 Years of Civilization (after Henry Darger and Charles Fourier)*, or semi-abstract, as in the falling and ascending objects in his series *The 7 Lights*. (The word "Lights" in the name of the series and each of its parts should have a line through it, as if crossed out.) The eclectic interests of the extremely well-read Chan are reflected in his work, which has alluded, sometimes simultaneously, to subjects and individuals as seemingly unrelated as rappers, Italian film, religion, and Spanish painting; he is often more concerned with the aesthetics than with the messages in his art, which has been shown in prestigious museums and galleries around the world. Chan's art thus contrasts sharply with his work as an outspoken protester of globalization, the Iraq war, and other forms of what he considers to be injustice. He has said that he prefers to keep those two realms of his life separate, so that, as he told Nell McClister for *Bomb* magazine (Summer 2005), he can "keep his allegiances clear."

Paul Chan was born in 1973 in Hong Kong, then a British crown colony and now part of China. He lived in the city's industrial district of Kwun Tong until he was eight years old; he and his family then immigrated to Omaha, Nebraska, where they had relatives, in part to help reduce the severity of Chan's asthma symptoms. As a child Chan liked to draw and aspired to become an artist, although his mother wanted him to "go to the Massachusetts Institute of Technology and be a rocket scientist," as he told Carrie Chan for the *South China Morning Post* (July 5, 2006). Describing the artist as having been "an unruly youngster," Carrie Chan quoted him as saying about his mother, "She always reminded me that I shouldn't be ashamed of my own anger and I have to articulate it." During high school Paul Chan studied photography and considered pursuing a career in photojournalism. "I was doing some writing too," he told Nell McClister. "But journalism wasn't free enough, so I went to art school." He attended the Art Institute of Chicago, where he received a B.F.A. degree in video and digital arts in 1996.

For the next two years, Chan served as an adjunct professor in the Academic Computing Department at Columbia College, in Chicago, and was a lecturer in the Video Department at the Art Institute of Chicago. He next taught in the Communications Department at Fordham University, in New York City, from 1998 until 2001. In 2001 and 2002 Chan was an adjunct professor of film and media studies at Hunter College, in New York, and a lecturer in the Graduate School of Fine Arts at the University of Pennsylvania. In 2002 he earned an M.F.A. degree in film, video, and new media from Bard College, in Annandale-on-Hudson, New York.

Meanwhile, Chan had become politically active. As an undergraduate he supported part-time teachers at the Art Institute of Chicago in their struggle for better pay, and he participated in 1999 anti-globalization protests (though not in Seattle, Washington, the epicenter of the protests). Just before the United States invaded Iraq, in 2003, Chan went to Baghdad, that nation's capital city, as a volunteer with Voices in the Wilderness, a Chicago-based organization that opposed the anticipated war. (In 2005 Voices in the Wilderness was fined $20,000 for violating sanctions against Iraq by smuggling food and medication into the country.) "There is nothing more tragic, funny, absurd, and therefore more pleasurable, than activism," Chan told Andrea Bellini in an interview for *Flash Art* (March/April 2005). "Its orthodoxy seduces you in a kind of myopic hope that is hard to resist. So I don't." While in Baghdad Chan documented the lives of ordinary Iraqi citizens and shot video journals and hundreds of photographs of local residents. During his trip, Chan recalled in the interview with McClister, "people wouldn't talk to me sincerely unless I told them I was religious. The idea was if I didn't have a religion, my words were not connected to a higher order that would punish me if I didn't speak the truth. . . . Religion provided a passport for an honest exchange. Even if we didn't agree, at least I was speaking a particular form of truth. It's beyond fascinating. It's a survival

instinct and a kind of thinking that I hadn't thought about in a long, long time."

After one month in Baghdad, Chan returned to the U.S. with footage that he presented during talks at schools and other institutions. He also helped to organize hundreds of people who posted around Manhattan thousands of copies of pictures of Iraqi citizens. "I felt like I did what I could to stop an unjust and illegal war," Chan explained to Doug Mac-Cash and David Cuthbert for the New Orleans, Louisiana, *Times-Picayune* (November 2, 2007). He added, referring to the terrorist group responsible for the 2001 attacks on the U.S., "We knew there was no connection between al-Qaeda and Iraq, no WMDs [weapons of mass destruction]. The invasion and occupation of Iraq as a part of the war on terror was a tragedy." One of the videos that came out of Chan's time in Iraq is *RE: The Operation* (2002), a satire of the George W. Bush administration's response to the 2001 terrorist attacks. He then created *Baghdad in No Particular Order* (2003), a video essay that depicts him interacting with Iraqi people prior to the U.S. invasion of their country. The video, which was made in collaboration with Voices in the Wilderness, contains very little dialogue. "I didn't want to make anti-war pornography or war pornography," Chan said in the interview with McClister. "You realize that in both of those, from CNN to documentaries, there are always voice-overs telling you what you are seeing onscreen." (Chan explained to McClister that he called pro-war or antiwar propaganda "pornography" because "it's very voyeuristic, almost sexual. . . . We watch because there's a perverse pleasure in it.") His next video, *Now Promise Now Threat* (2005), made shortly after the 2004 presidential election, comprises footage of and interviews with people in Nebraska and explores the cultural attitudes of "red state"—or conservative Republican—America. Those three videos were exhibited at various museums, among them the Barbican Gallery in London, England, and RedCat in Los Angeles, California, and were released as a compilation DVD, *Tin Drum Trilogy*, in 2009. In 2004 Chan took part in a demonstration at the Republican National Convention in New York City. (Contrary to accounts in some sources, he was not arrested there.) He and members of a group called Friends of William Blake had designed and distributed *The People's Guide to the Republican National Convention*, a free map for protesters, which highlighted the hotels where delegates were staying as well as locations of convention events and restrooms.

In 2003, meanwhile, Chan's video *Happiness (Finally) After 35,000 Years of Civilization* was shown at the New York gallery Greene Naftali's summer group exhibition, entitled Regarding Amy. The 18-minute animated video shows a community of young hermaphrodites who live peacefully in a utopia before being brutally attacked by an army of men, whom they ultimately defeat. The video, which garnered Chan a lot of attention, was influenced by the work of the American "outsider" artist Henry Darger (1892–1973) and the French philosopher Charles Fourier (1772–1837). Merrily Kerr wrote about the show for *Flash Art* (May/June 2004), "We're asked to imagine abandoning our inhibitions and letting our passions lead us to fight against injustice. We don't know how the girls recover their autonomy, but Chan's insistence on dreaming of a better life is clear." The next year Chan had his solo debut, at Greene Naftali, where he presented *My Birds . . . Trash . . . The Future* (2004), whose centerpiece was a 17-minute apocalypse-themed digital animation shown on two sides of a hanging screen. The video referenced subjects as disparate as the rapper Biggie Smalls, the Italian filmmaker Pier Paolo Pasolini, the Bible, Samuel Beckett's absurdist, existentialist play *Waiting for Godot*, and the Spanish painter Francisco de Goya's series *The Disasters of War*; the show also included a series of charcoal drawings, prints, and a toy gun with a radio inside, which could be heard by pointing the gun at one's head. "I read too much," the artist conceded to Carrie Chan, referring to the eclecticism of the references in *Happiness* and *My Birds*. "But my view is we should think without boundaries." He also said to Carrie Chan that he is driven more to produce interesting forms in his art than to make a central point. "The moving images could be [a form of] music," he said, "but not a message." Andrea Bellini commented about *My Birds . . . Trash . . . The Future*, "Using digital animation techniques so basic as to awaken memories of video games from the late '80s, Chan manages to say something new. The work's originality lies precisely in its ability to combine a relatively unsophisticated technique with an astounding sensibility for the moving image. The narration thus assumes a highly poetic and surreal tone, such as when sheets of paper are lifted into the air by a gust of wind, transforming the entire screen into a large, abstract composition."

In a major development in Chan's career, his work *1st Light* (2005), the first project in a seven-part series, was shown at the 2006 Whitney Biennial, an exhibition of contemporary American art held at the Whitney Museum in New York City. *1st Light* was a silent, 14-minute digital video projection on a floor, in which the silhouettes of various man-made objects (such as cell phones, tires, and laptops) float up to the sky, while the shadows of human bodies fall from above—or the objects fall as the bodies rise, depending on the viewer's perspective. *1st Light* was followed by *2nd Light*, *3rd Light*, and *4th Light* in 2006; and then *5th Light*, *6th Light*, and *Score for 7th Light* in 2007. The series, collectively titled *The 7 Lights*, was displayed in its entirety for the first time at London's Serpentine Gallery in 2007. In an article for *Artnet* magazine (2007, on-line), Ben Street wrote that in *The 7 Lights*, "Chan has made a comprehensive imaginative world with a specific iconography of suburban ephemera, entropic nature and fallen humans.

Gravity, the force that ties us to the world, has disappeared, a loss that marks a passage into a spiritual world." Also in 2007 Chan held his first major European show, at the Stedelijk Museum in Amsterdam, the Netherlands, where he presented his exhibit Lights and Drawings, which centered on his creation of *The 7 Lights* and included digital studies, projections, charcoal drawings, and collages.

Chan had been invited to lecture at Tulane University, in New Orleans, Louisiana, in November 2006, a little over a year after the devastation brought to that city by Hurricane Katrina. While visiting the city's Lower Ninth Ward, where flooding caused by the hurricane was especially destructive, he noticed an eerie similarity between his surroundings and those depicted in Beckett's *Waiting for Godot*. "It was unmistakable," Chan wrote in an artist's statement that appears on *Creativetime.org* (June 2007) and was later published in the book *Waiting for Godot in New Orleans: A Field Guide*, which he edited. "The empty road. The bare tree leaning precariously to one side with just enough leaves to make it respectable. The silence. What's more, there was a terrible symmetry between the reality of New Orleans post-Katrina and the essence of this play, which expresses in stark eloquence the cruel and funny things people do while they wait: for help, for food, for tomorrow. It was uncanny. Standing there at the intersection of North Prieur and Reynes, I suddenly found myself in the middle of Samuel Beckett's *Waiting for Godot*." Chan then decided to mount a production of the tragicomedy that would be staged outdoors in New Orleans.

After much planning and preparation, *Waiting for Godot in New Orleans* had five performances in November 2007, with Chan serving as artistic director and Christopher McElroen as director; the production starred Wendell Pierce as Vladimir and J. Kyle Manzay as Estragon. Staged in the Lower Ninth Ward and the Gentilly neighborhood, it was produced in association with the Classical Theatre of Harlem and was presented by the nonprofit organization Creative Time. *Waiting for Godot in New Orleans*, which offered free admission, was attended by thousands of people. Around the same time that he was coordinating the project, Chan also taught a practicum workshop in the city at Xavier University as well as a contemporary-art seminar at the University of New Orleans. He also helped to set up the Shadow Fund, which collected over $45,000 in donations for the rebuilding of New Orleans neighborhoods.

In 2009 Chan's exhibit My Laws Are My Whores was held at the Renaissance Society at the University of Chicago. Combining animation, sculpture, drawing, and video, My Laws Are My Whores examined the connections between power and pleasure. The exhibit consisted of five separate but related sections: charcoal portraits of nine U.S. Supreme Court justices; ink drawings based on the work of the French writer Marquis de Sade (1740–

1814), famous for his promotion of sexual abandon; a digital projection of human shadows in different sexual positions; a TV playing a muted episode of the crime drama *Law and Order*—with original subtitles by Chan; and a keyboard with tombstones for keys. Writing for the *Chicago Maroon* (March 3, 2009), Rob Underwood noted, "Paul Chan fuses sexual discourse and legal politics in ways that, though at times stilted, are ultimately very powerful and affecting. His artwork breaks down the distinctions between politics and aesthetics with remarkable economy and alacrity." Also in 2009 Chan's exhibit Sade for Sade's Sake premiered at the Venice Biennale; it was the centerpiece of a show carrying the same name at Green Naftali Gallery in October 2009. In addition to drawings and sex-themed videos, Sade for Sade's Sake featured 21 types of fonts on large drawings, with each letter of the alphabet transformed into sexual phrases. The fonts are included on the DVD *Sade for Fonts Sake* (2009).

Solo screenings and exhibitions of Chan's work have been held by the Museum of Modern Art (MoMA) Film at the Gramercy Theater, in New York; the Hammer Museum of the University of California in Los Angeles; the Institute of Contemporary Art in Boston, Massachusetts; the Blanton Museum of Art, in Austin, Texas; and the Portikus, in Frankfurt, Germany, among other museums. His work has also been displayed as part of group exhibitions at venues such as the Carnegie International, at the Carnegie Museum of Art, in Pittsburgh, Pennsylvania; the Dogmatic Gallery, in Chicago; the Istanbul Biennale; the Shanghai Museum of Contemporary Art; the Biennale of Sydney; and the Venice Biennale. Honors Chan has received include a National Endowment for the Arts Development Fellowship from the College Art Association (2001); a Lower East Side Printshop Van Lier Fellowship from the Andy Warhol Foundation (2001); a new-media-arts fellowship from the Rockefeller Foundation (2003); a Wexnter Center Residency Award (2005–06); and the Alpert Award in the Arts (2009). He has penned articles on art and other matters for many publications and has authored, among other volumes, the children's book *The Shadow and Her Wanda* (2008); *Between Artists* (2006, a conversation between Chan and Martha Rosler about art and politics); and *Phaedrus Pron* (2010), an electronic book (or ebook) that uses Chan's invented fonts.

In 2010 Chan founded the art-publishing house Badlands Unlimited, which publishes ebooks, limited-edition print books, and both digital and print forms of artwork. His stated aim in founding Badlands Unlimited, he told *Current Biography*, was to publish "books in an expanded field."

"In person quiet, good-humored and self-contained," Chan is "an unlikely firebrand," Holland Carter wrote for the *New York Times* (December 2, 2007, on-line). Chan said during an interview for *F Newsmagazine* (January 29, 2010, on-line), when asked "What's next for you?," that he

was planning to retire as an artist. (As of November 2010 he had not done so.) When asked why, he told the interviewer, Beth Capper, "Real beginnings demand real ends. I think the world is big, and I can do a lot of different things. I want to believe that we are not beholden to certain things." At the time of the interview, he worked in a studio in the Sunset Park section of Brooklyn, New York.

—J.P.

Suggested Reading: *Bomb* p22+ Summer 2005; *Boston Globe* G p24 Dec. 19, 2008; *Flash Art* p68+ Mar./Apr. 2005; *Frieze* (on-line) Mar. 3, 2005; *South China Morning Post* p5 July 5, 2006

Selected Works: as artist—*RE: The Operation*, 2002; *Baghdad in No Particular Order*, 2003; *My Birds . . . Trash . . . The Future*, 2004; *Now Promise Now Threat*, 2005; *The 7 Lights*, 2005–07; as theater director—*Waiting for Godot in New Orleans*, 2007

Selected Books: *Between Artists* (with Martha Rosler), 2006; *The Shadow and Her Wanda*, 2008; *Phaedrus Pron*, 2010

Chang Díaz, Franklin

Apr. 5, 1950– Astronaut; physicist; rocket scientist; entrepreneur

Address: Ad Astra Rocket Co., 141 W. Bay Area Blvd., Webster, TX 77598

Recently, thanks to the controversy stirred up by the so-called Tea Partyers regarding President Barack Obama's place of birth and the authenticity of his birth certificate, newscasters repeatedly noted that United States law requires that candidates for the American presidency must either have been born within the territorial limits of the U.S. or, if outside those limits, born to parents who are or (if deceased) were U.S. citizens. Like U.S. presidents, astronauts employed by the National Aeronautics and Space Administration (NASA) must be U.S. citizens, but unlike presidential candidates, they can be naturalized U.S. citizens. Franklin Chang Díaz is the first naturalized American citizen to become an astronaut; he is also the first Hispanic-American astronaut and the first native Costa Rican to join the U.S. space program. When Chang Díaz arrived in the U.S. from Costa Rica, in 1967, at age 17, he came with minimal knowledge of English but with the determination to become an astronaut—an ambition that had gripped him since the dawn of the space age, in 1957, when the Soviet Union launched the first man-made satellite to orbit Earth. In the U.S. he became fluent in English, earned a bachelor's degree in mechanical engineering and a doctorate in plasma physics, and con-

Tony Ranze/AFP/Getty Images

Franklin Chang Díaz

ducted scientific research at the Massachusetts Institute of Technology (MIT). During his quarter-century career as an astronaut, which began in 1981, he completed a record seven missions (only one other astronaut has flown that many); he spent a total of 1,601 hours in space, including 19 hours and 31 minutes on three spacewalks.

After his retirement from NASA, in 2005, Chang Díaz founded the Ad Astra Rocket Co., to continue his work in plasma physics and nuclear fusion. His goal is to develop a new kind of rocket engine that, he has predicted, "will revolutionize space travel, putting our entire solar system at our disposal," in the words of an on-line Public Broadcasting System (PBS) blurb publicizing a documentary about Chang Díaz that aired on its series *Nova* on July 14, 2009. Chang Díaz told Erica Naone for *Technology Review* (September 25, 2007, on-line), "In order for us to conduct a serious space-exploration program, we need to develop two things: power and propulsion. Power in space is still severely limited. Mainly, we use solar power. This is fine as long as we stay near the sun, but . . . far and beyond, we will need to develop nuclear electric power. If we don't, we might as well quit. We're not going to get anywhere without it." He also said, "Space is a vast void, and you're really going to have to travel fast if you're going to have any chance of surviving. I . . . would not want to send people to Mars on a fragile and power-limited ship. If you send people that far, you have to give them a fighting chance to survive, and the only way you can do that is if you have ample supplies of power. Power is life in space."

One of the six children of María Eugenia Dìaz and Ramón A. Chang Morales, Franklin Ramón Chang Díaz was born on April 5, 1950 in San José, Costa Rica. (In some sources, including NASA Web sites, his surname is hyphenated.) His paternal grandfather immigrated to Costa Rica from Guangzhou (Canton), in southern China, and married a descendant of Spanish settlers. "I still have a large number of family members" in China, Chang Díaz told Julie D. Soo for *AsianWeek* (December 22, 2004.) His father was half-Chinese, his mother Costa Rican, making him one-quarter Chinese. "To define me only as Hispanic is too narrow," he told Peggy Hernandez for the *Boston Globe* (January 3, 1986). During the early years of his childhood, Chang Díaz lived with his family in Venezuela, where his father worked in the oil industry as a construction foreman. "I wanted to be just like my father," Chang Díaz told Soo. "He taught me about a strong work ethic: to be honest and to be on time."

Chang Díaz recalled to the astrophysicist Neil deGrasse Tyson on *Nova* that when he was "about four or five, . . . I took my sister, at 2:00 or 3:00 in the morning, and we climbed to the roof of our house. And we sat on the roof, eating grapefruits with sugar and looking at the stars. The sky was absolutely beautiful. I knew that among those stars there were other worlds, other places, and I wanted to be there." Using cardboard boxes as spaceships, he and his young cousins would pretend to be astronauts. The news that the Soviet Union had successfully launched *Sputnik 1*—the first Earth-orbiting satellite—on October 4, 1957 made a lasting impression on him. "I can remember standing outside as a boy of 7 one night in 1957, looking up at the night sky, straining for my first glimpse of this thing they called *Sputnik*," he told Mike Toner for the *Miami Herald* (November 15, 1983). "I decided then and there that I wanted to be an astronaut."

As a student at the Colegio De La Salle, a private San José secondary school, Chang Díaz wrote a letter to NASA about his dream of becoming an astronaut. He was crushed to learn that all prospective astronauts had to be American citizens. "It drove me crazy," he recalled to Joseph D'Agnese for *Discover* (November 2003). "Even today it does. Why would they encourage us to be rocket scientists if we couldn't be? Space exploration is a worldwide endeavor, and the fact that the United States is on top doesn't mean they should be the only ones in it." Chang Díaz resolved to learn English and become a U.S. citizen. After his high-school graduation, in 1967, he flew to the U.S. with a one-way ticket his father had bought for him and $50 that he had earned from a part-time job. While living with relatives in Hartford, Connecticut, he enrolled at Hartford High School. There, he became fluent in English, and when he graduated, in 1969, he ranked at the top of his class. He also won a full scholarship to the University of Connecticut. In his interview with D'Agnese, Chang Díaz said that that particular scholarship was for U.S. citizens only, but university administrators had mistakenly thought he was Puerto Rican, and they let him keep the scholarship to avoid the embarrassment that re-scinding it might bring to the school.

Chang Díaz entered the University of Connecti-cut at Storrs a few weeks after the American astro-nauts Neil Armstrong, Edwin "Buzz" Aldrin Jr., and Michael Collins traveled to the moon in *Apollo 11*. The momentous voyage, during which humans first walked on the moon, "was a reaffirmation of something that at the time was kind of still elusive" for Chang Díaz, as he remarked to Wendy Pedrero for *Latino Leaders* (October 1, 2004). During his undergraduate years Chang Díaz worked as a re-search assistant in the university's Physics Depart-ment. In 1973 he earned a B.S. degree in mechani-cal engineering. He then entered the Massachusetts Institute of Technology, in Cambridge, where his research centered on fusion technology and plas-ma-based rocket propulsion. "Fusion" refers to nu-clear fusion, in which the nuclei of two or more atoms merge, with the release of a great deal of en-ergy; plasma in this context is defined as ionized gas—superhot gas (with temperatures as high as 180 million degrees) whose constituent particles are negatively or positively charged and respond to electromagnetic fields. Considered a fourth state of matter, ionized gas is more common in the uni-verse than the other three states of matter (solids, liquids, and ordinary gases); the sun, for example, is composed of plasma. Chang Díaz's ideas about plasma-based rocket propulsion "began as a result of my Ph.D. thesis," he recalled to Tyson. "It was clear to me that chemical rockets, the conventional rockets that we had been using all along, were not really going to give us the capability to travel far, to Mars, to Jupiter." According to the Ad Astra Rocket Co. Web site, his doctoral research involved "the controlling and ducting of million degree plasmas, in magnetic structures called magnetic mirrors." Chang Díaz received an Sc.D. degree in applied plasma physics and fusion technology in 1977.

That same year Chang Díaz became a natural-ized U.S. citizen and joined the Charles Stark Dra-per Laboratory (formerly the Instrumentation Lab-oratory) at MIT. During the next three years, he worked on the development of plasma and fusion technology. In 1980 Chang Díaz successfully ap-plied to NASA's space-shuttle program, along with only 14 others among the 3,500 applicants. As part of his training, he worked in the Shuttle Avionics Integration Laboratory (SAIL) and participated in early studies for space-station design. In August 1981 he officially earned the title of astronaut. No-tice of that achievement came to him in a tele-phone call that he received while he was in the of-fice of his superior at the Draper Lab. "I was so ex-cited that I started pacing in circles and wrapped the phone cord around my superior's neck," he re-called to D'Agnese.

Chang Díaz served as a member of the Earth-bound support crew preparing for the first mission of Spacelab, a multi-use scientific laboratory that joined 22 flights of one or another of the space shuttles between November 1983 and April 1998. Between October 1984 and August 1985, Chang Díaz led the astronaut-support team at the Kenne-dy Space Center, on Cape Canaveral, near Orlando, Florida.

Chang Díaz's first space flight—mission STS-61-C on the space shuttle *Columbia*—extended from January 12 to January 18, 1986. ("STS" is the acronym for Space Transportation System, the offi-cial name of the space-shuttle program.) STS-61-C was the 24th mission of the program and the sev-enth for the *Columbia*, which on that mission was piloted by Charles F. Bolden Jr. (who was named NASA's administrator in mid-2009). During the flight Chang Díaz helped to deploy a communica-tions satellite, performed astrophysics experi-ments, and operated a materials-processing device. Ten days after he and the other members of the STS-61-C crew returned to Earth, the space shuttle *Challenger* broke apart 73 seconds after liftoff, kill-ing all seven crew members. "By luck my crew was shifted to the earlier shuttle," Chang Díaz recalled to Soo. "It was a realization of fragility that I didn't recognize my first time in space. The first time felt fun, indestructible. I approached my second flight with a scar. I was no longer a rookie; I had battle scars that hurt."

On his second space mission, STS-34 (October 18–23, 1989), Chang Díaz flew aboard the space shuttle *Atlantis*. The crew on that mission de-ployed the satellite *Galileo*, which on December 7, 1995, after traveling 2.3 billion miles over more than six years, began orbiting the planet Jupiter. (*Galileo* continued to relay a huge amount of infor-mation about the Jovian atmosphere and surface for eight years.) Chang Díaz took part in STS-46 (July 31–August 8, 1992), an eight-day mission during which the crew deployed the unmanned Earth-orbiting satellite European Retrievable Carri-er, which was designed to conduct a dozen experi-ments; called EURECA, the satellite returned to Earth unharmed one year later. Also during that mission Chang Díaz and his crewmates, in a collab-orative effort between NASA and the Italian Space Agency, conducted the first Tethered Satellite Sys-tem test flight, in which a satellite was extended from the *Atlantis* by means of a thin Kevlar cord. Because of equipment problems, the tether extend-ed 6.1 miles rather than the intended 12.5 miles, but it still enabled the astronauts to gather informa-tion about the electrodynamics of such a tether sys-tem.

Chang Díaz's fourth mission, STS-60 (February 3–11, 1994) was the first one in which a U.S. space shuttle (*Discovery*) rendezvoused with the Russian space station *Mir* and the first in which a Russian cosmonaut, Sergei K. Krikalev, visited an orbiting shuttle. STS-75, Chang Díaz's fifth mission, on board the *Columbia*, took close to 16 days (February 22 to March 9, 1996). It marked the third flight of the United States Microgravity Payload, an array of scientific devices that were controlled remotely from the Spacelab Mission Operations Control Center at the Marshall Space Flight Center, in Huntsville, Alabama. STS-91 (June 2–12, 1998), again on the *Discovery*, marked Chang Díaz's sixth space mission and the final one in which a U.S. shuttle docked with the Soviet *Mir*. The final space mission in which Chang Díaz participated was STS-111 (June 5–19, 2002), on the *Endeavour*. That mission took a new crew (Expedition Five) to the International Space Station (which is approximately as big as a football field) and supplied a Canadian mobile base for the space station's robotic arm. During that mission Chang Díaz performed three spacewalks to assist in the installation of the mobile base. At the end of STS-111, the *Discovery* brought to Earth the Expedition Four crew, who had spent 196 days aboard the International Space Station.

Earlier, in 1983, while a NASA employee, Chang Díaz had returned to MIT as a visiting scientist; he worked at the school's Plasma Fusion Center, where he ran the plasma propulsion program for the next 10 years. From 1993 to 2005 he directed the Advanced Space Propulsion Laboratory at the Johnson Space Center, in Houston, Texas, where he continued his work with plasma propulsion using a magnetic mirror moved there from MIT. In conducting plasma experiments Chang Díaz collaborated with scientists associated with the University of Houston, the University of Texas at Austin, Rice University, and other academic institutions.

In 2005 Chang Díaz retired from NASA and set up the Ad Astra Rocket Co., with himself as chairman and chief executive officer. That year Ad Astra and NASA signed a Space Act Agreement, which specified that, while the space agency and the company would work together, Chang Díaz's rocket technology was a private pursuit. Chang Dìaz holds patents in his own name for several of the techniques and devices he has created.

Ad Astra's headquarters are in Webster, Texas, near Houston, and it also has a laboratory at EARTH University (La Escuela de Agricultura de la Región Tropical Húmeda, or School of Agriculture of the Humid Tropical Region), in Liberia, Costa Rica. Funded by private investors, the firm is developing plasma rocket-propulsion technology, specifically the Variable Specific Impulse Magnetoplasma Rocket (VASIMR), which grew out of the research Chang Díaz began as a graduate student. The rocket uses electromagnetic waves and radio waves to heat gases such as argon and hydrogen to temperatures high enough to transform them into plasma, whose expulsion provides the rocket's thrust. Chang Díaz explained to Neil deGrasse Tyson, "Typically, a conventional rocket runs at temperatures of a few thousand degrees. Sounds pretty hot, but we would like to run at temperatures of a few million degrees, temperatures like

the sun. . . . At those temperatures, the stuff that you're shooting is going so fast that you only need little, tiny amounts of it." Plasma rockets would not only be far less expensive but also far faster than conventional rockets, thus reducing significantly the estimated time of travel to destinations in space.

"The VASIMR isn't any use for getting into space in the first place as its power-to-weight ratio is small: the VX-200, the size of a small car, can only produce enough thrust to lift half a kilogramme or so off the ground," Billy Ozks wrote for *TheTechJournal.com* (April 29, 2011). "Once in orbit, however, a VASIMR comes into its own. A normal rocket will burn up any practical amount of fuel very quickly: thus it can be used only in brief bursts. A spacecraft driven by such means must spend almost all its time coasting along unpowered. Thus a journey to Mars, for instance, would take 6 months for a conventional spacecraft. A VASIMR, however, can keep on exerting its relatively tiny push for weeks on end without using any more juice, gradually boosting a ship up to terrific speeds that would never be possible with a chemical rocket."

In the near future VASIMR rockets might be used for in-space refueling and repair, for removing space trash (commercially owned inoperative satellites) from Earth's orbit, and for transporting cargo to the moon and robots into deep space. In 2009 Ad Astra successfully tested the VX-200, a small-scale prototype of the VASIMR engine, in a vacuum chamber at NASA facilities. NASA and Ad Astra hope to substitute Ad Astra engines for the fuel-hungry device that currently provides thrust for the International Space Station and the massive solar arrays that generate its electricity.

According to his biography on the NASA Web site, Chang Díaz was "instrumental in implementing closer ties between the astronaut corps and the scientific community," through the Astronaut Science Colloquium Program, which he formed in 1987, and the Astronaut Science Support Group, which he directed for several years. He has organized conferences in several Central and South American countries to promote the possibilities for space-related industries there. On two of his space-shuttle missions, he conducted experiments aimed at identifying "potential natural inhibitors to Chagas disease in the microgravity of space," according to the Ad Astra Web site. For two years he managed a residence for formerly institutionalized mental patients, and he has also served as an instructor at a drug rehabilitation program for Hispanic-Americans in Massachusetts. He helped to draft and implement "The Strategy for the 21st Century," described on the Ad Astra Web site as "a master plan designed to transform Costa Rica into a fully developed country before 2050." Since 1993 he has taught as an adjunct professor in the Physics Departments of both the University of Houston and Rice University, also in Houston.

Chang Diaz's honors include, from NASA, two Distinguished Service Medals (1995, 1997) and three Exceptional Service Medals (1988, 1990, 1993), four honorary doctoral degrees, and a Medal of Excellence from the Congressional Hispanic Caucus (1987). From his first marriage, to Canoce Buker, which ended in divorce, Chang Díaz has two daughters: Jean Elizabeth Chang Díaz, a teacher, and Sonia Chang Díaz, the first Latina to win election to the Massachusetts state Senate, in 2008. With his second wife, identified variously as the former Peggy Marguerite Doncaster or Peggy Marguerite Stafford, he has two daughters, Lidia Aurora and Miranda Karina. In Costa Rica, where he is considered a hero, his image has appeared on a postage stamp. His recreational interests include playing soccer, scuba diving, hiking, and flying gliders. His book *Los Primeros Años: Mis Promeros*

Aventuras en el Planeta Tierra ("The First Years: My First Adventures on Planet Earth"), the first in a planned autobiographical trilogy, covers his life until he left Costa Rica for the U.S. "I always tell the kids I meet to follow your dreams; it's the first thing I tell them, to not let anyone tell you that you can't do something, until you find out for yourself," he told Tyson. "I'm talking about the ability of a child to say, 'Look, I want to change the world.' Go do it."

—W.D.

Suggested Reading: adastrarocket.com; *AsianWeek* p8 Dec. 22, 2004; *Discover* (on-line) Nov. 8, 2003; jsc.nasa.gov; *Latino Leaders* p22 Oct. 1, 2004; *Miami Herald* B p1 Nov. 15, 1983; pbs.org July 14, 2009; *TheTechJournal.com* Apr. 29, 2011

Frazer Harrison/Getty Images

Cora, Cat

Apr. 3, 1967– Chef; television personality; cookbook writer

Address: c/o Fifteen Minutes Public Relations, 8436 W. Third St., Suite 650, Los Angeles, CA 90048

Cat Cora began to appear on the popular Food Network show *Iron Chef America* in 2005. She has won fame as the first—and thus far only—female Iron Chef, competing alongside such high-profile males as Bobby Flay, Mario Batali, and Masaharu Morimoto. Each installment of the show pits one

of the Iron Chefs against a culinary newcomer in a contest to create five dishes that must be based on a "secret" ingredient, which is unveiled at the start of the show. The dishes are then judged by a panel of experts for taste, visual appeal, and creativity. "Cora has not only stood the heat [on *Iron Chef America*], she's turned it up, bottled it and repurposed it for several sizzling careers," Chris Mann wrote for *WellBella* magazine (May 2011). In addition to her work on television, Cora serves in an advisory role as executive chef for *Bon Appetit* magazine. She founded the philanthropic organization Chefs for Humanity, which provides nutrition education and humanitarian food aid around the world. Referring to the distinctive toques often donned by professional chefs, the group's motto is, "The good guys still wear white hats." Cora is the co-author of three cookbooks.

One of the three children of Spiro and Virginia Cora, Catherine Cora was born on April 3, 1967 in Jackson, Mississippi, where her family was part of a small, close-knit Greek community. (Some sources mistakenly give the year of her birth as 1968 and the date as January 1.) Her father, a high-school history teacher, was born in the Mississippi Delta shortly after his parents emigrated from Skopelos, a Greek island. In her book *Cat Cora's Kitchen: Favorite Meals for Family and Friends* (2004), Cora wrote that he possessed "the warmth and fun-loving appetite of a Greek and the humor and charm of a Southern gentleman." She told Mann, "For me, food was really all about our family. Being Greek and also being from the South, I had all of these very rich cultures all around me. We were eating great Greek food and then great Southern food. So it was really rewarding learning about these different cuisines. But also just being around the cultures together—they're such strong food cultures. . . . It made a huge impact on me." Cora wrote in *Favorite Meals* that her father was a natural cook. "In my earliest memories of my dad cooking, he's sitting by the fire, checking the smoke occasionally and happily reading a book. No matter how hectic my surroundings [now], if I want to lower my blood pressure by ten points, I just envision my father smoking a brisket."

Cora's mother, Virginia, is a nurse. (She had originally wanted to become a veterinarian, but her father, an army physician, told her that that was not a suitable career for a woman.) Currently, she teaches at the School of Nursing of the University of Mississippi Medical Center. When Cora was in junior high school, her mother returned to school and earned a D.S.N. (doctor of science in nursing) degree. Cora's maternal grandmother, Alma, who was an accomplished cook, moved into the family home to help care for Cora and her two brothers.

Cora told Kara Kimbrough for GetFitMississippi.com, "Ever since I was little I was involved in some way with food. I loved to host tea parties and bake cookies or roll grape leaves for church events. Most of my childhood memories growing up in Jackson center around food, family gatherings and all the warmth and excitement that comes with gathering around the dinner table." Cora recalled in an article she wrote for O, The Oprah Magazine (September 2011, on-line), "When I was growing up . . . there was always that time between 5 and 6 in the evening when my two brothers and I would storm the house, famished from school and sports and wanting to eat *right now*. My mom would be at the stove, and the smell of browning onions or searing chicken would only make us hungrier. My grandmother, who lived with us, came up with the idea of turning that restless interlude into family happy hour. . . . She'd put out Kalamata olives and nuts, along with Feta cheese or sharp Cheddar and crackers. Then she and my mom would pour themselves a glass of wine, my dad would pop open a beer, and we kids would get juice or milk in grown-up glasses. We'd all sit together in the kitchen and talk about what had happened at school or work that day. The ritual allowed my mom a few extra minutes to finish cooking dinner. And it taught me that happy hour doesn't have to involve prowling around bars and drinking 100-proof rum—it can be just as fun to gather as a family."

Cora's godfather, Peter "Taki" Costas, too, was a major influence on her. "Taki owned several restaurants in Jackson," Cora wrote in *Favorite Meals*. "The fanciest was the Continental, an old-style restaurant with big leather booths that you sank into when you sat down. The continental was my favorite place in the world to eat because Taki would come out to the dining room, take me by the hand into the kitchen, and lift me up onto the counter where I'd sit talking to the cooks. I remember them asking me, 'What do you want to eat; we'll cook you anything you like.' When you're five years old, sitting in an enormous kitchen with three people asking what they can cook for you, of course you develop a fondness for restaurant kitchens."

"When I was about 13, I really became interested in cooking, and Peter Costas taught me how to make roast chicken," she recalled to Kimbrough. "I invited my godparents over and prepared dinner for them." Virginia Cora confirmed for Kimbrough, "It was a delicious chicken dinner served with root vegetables that were cooked to perfection. We knew right then that she was going to be a great cook." By the time she was 15, Cora had drawn up a business plan for the restaurant she dreamed of opening one day.

Rather than diving into a culinary career immediately after high school, Cora attended the University of Southern Mississippi, in Hattiesburg, where she studied exercise physiology and biology. She graduated with honors in 1990. "College taught me to be articulate, helped me be well read and shaped me as a businesswoman. Studying wellness plays into my platform today, which is healthy cooking," she told Suzanne Riss for *Working Mother* magazine (August/September 2010). Intrigued by the idea of continuing her education at a formal culinary school, Cora attended a book signing in Natchez by the legendary chef Julia Child. Determined to speak to Child, she lingered at the end of the line until the other autograph seekers had gone. "She spent 45 minutes with me," Cora recalled to Riss. "We discussed where I'd go to culinary school, and she suggested the Culinary [Institute] of America. I applied the next day."

The Culinary Institute of America, often referred to as the CIA, is a renowned institution with campuses in Hyde Park, New York; St. Helena, California; San Antonio, Texas; and Singapore. Widely characterized as the "Harvard of cooking schools," it boasts alumni from recent decades including such luminaries as Anthony Bourdain, Rocco DiSpirito, and Todd English. "Women were just starting to go [to the CIA], so there were only about six of us in a class of 60," Cora told Riss. "There were still some old-school professors who gave us trouble. . . . I was told I should be barefoot and pregnant in the kitchen, things like that. If you let yourself feel inspired rather than discouraged when you hear comments like that, it can be a very powerful motivator. Instead of making me insecure or shrink against a challenge, it made me step up even more."

Cora excelled at the CIA, and upon completing her studies in Hyde Park, she found work at the New York City restaurant Arcadia, run by the chef Anne Rosenzweig, with whom she had apprenticed as a student. "At Arcadia," the food critic Ruth Reichl wrote for the *New York Times* (April 22, 1994, on-line), "the food does not allow itself to be ignored. This is a place where a Caesar salad is made with peppery arugula instead of wimpy romaine lettuce and the croutons are made of buttery brioche instead of plain old bread. . . . What [really] sets Ms. Rosenzweig apart from many chefs is the elegance with which she puts her plates together. She is not satisfied to serve a piece of fish with a random vegetable and a starch, but offers a careful composition, each element complementing the others." Cora also worked under the chef Larry Forgione at the Beekman 1776 Tavern, in Rhinebeck, New York. Forgione was already a legend in the food world. Matt DeLucia wrote for *Restaurant Insider* (January 1, 2008, on-line), "Since the mid-1980's, Larry Forgione's name has rarely been mentioned in the press without 'The Godfather of American Cuisine' tacked onto the end of it."

Cora subsequently traveled to Europe, where she completed apprenticeships under George Blanc and Roger Verge, both Michelin three-star chefs. (Under the Michelin system, a chef may earn one to three stars; a three-star ranking, which is very rarely awarded, indicates that a chef is creating exceptional cuisine that is worth a special journey for diners.) After she returned to the U.S., Cora became a sous chef (second in command) at the now-closed Old Chatham Shepherding Company Inn, working under chef Melissa Kelly, whom she had originally met at the Beekman.

Cora next moved to California and began working at the Bistro Don Giovanni, long considered one of the finest restaurants in Napa Valley. She served as the chef de cuisine—the chef in charge of running the kitchen. She also began writing a food column, "Cooking from the Hip," for a local newspaper, the *Contra Costa Times*. (The column later provided the title for Cora's second cookbook, published in 2007.)

In 1999 Cora made her television debut, as one of a rotating roster of co-hosts on the Food Network show *Melting Pot*, which explored various ethnic cuisines. The Food Network, which was launched in 1993, was not yet the ratings powerhouse that it is today, but it was attracting loyal viewers with its mix of instructional cooking programs, food-related travel shows, and culinary competitions. Cora quickly proved to be a network favorite, and she went on to appear on such shows as *Kitchen Accomplished* and *Celebrity Cooking Showdown*. When she cooked a dinner in April 2002 at the James Beard House, at the invitation of the James Beard Foundation (whose self-described mission is "to celebrate, nurture, and preserve America's diverse culinary heritage and future"), the network aired a special documentary, *Cat's in the Kitchen*, about the event.

In 1993 a televised culinary competition called *Ryōri no Tetsujin* ("Ironmen of Cooking") premiered in Japan. Broadcast on the Fuji Television Network, the campy show included an elaborate backstory involving a wealthy gourmand known as Chairman Kaga, who retains a team of "Iron Chefs." For his own entertainment he has built a "kitchen stadium," to which he invites cooks from all over the world to compete with his team. In each installment a challenger and a chosen Iron Chef must each prepare a multi-course meal, prominently featuring a secret ingredient that has just been revealed to them. One journalist described the show by asking readers to imagine that Julia Child had joined the World Wrestling Federation and moved to Asia. (The wrestling comparison was apt: on occasion the *Ryōri no Tetsujin* chefs were injured during the filming. Once, for example, Masaharu Morimoto was bitten by a monkfish, and Hiroyuki Sakai was bitten by a squid.)

Ryōri no Tetsujin attracted a passionate cult following in Japan, and in 1999 the Food Network began airing Japanese episodes dubbed in English. In 2004 the network presented an English-language miniseries called *Iron Chef America: Battle of the Masters*, in which American chefs, including Bobby Flay and Mario Batali, were pitted against Sakai and Morimoto. The premise of the miniseries was that Chairman Kaga had dispatched his nephew, played by the martial artist Mark Dacascos, to build a kitchen stadium in the U.S. The miniseries proved to be popular, and the Food Network began broadcasting *Iron Chef America* the following year as a regular series. (*Iron Chef America* is not to be confused with *Iron Chef USA*, an ill-fated series starring William Shatner that aired for just two episodes on UPN in 2001.) "The faces have changed, but the mythology remains the same," William Grimes wrote for the *New York Times* (January 14, 2005, on-line). Stephen Kroopnick, the executive producer of the series, told Grimes, "The goal was to preserve what the die-hards love, and also to make it exciting for people just coming to it. You don't have to know Episode 121, Battle Octopus."

Cora made her debut as the first-ever female Iron Chef in late 2005, in a match against Alex Lee, the executive chef at the exclusive New York City restaurant Daniel. The secret ingredient was potato, and Cora triumphed over Lee in the competition by one point. Since then Cora has faced such challengers as Kerry Simon, Sam Choy, Michael Psilakis, Elizabeth Falkner, and Paul Miranda. To date she has won the majority of her matches on the show, which is taped in the Chelsea section of New York City.

Cora owns three restaurants: CCQ, in Costa Mesa, California, which she opened in 2008 and which features barbeque from around the world; Kouzzina by Cat, a Mediterranean-themed establishment at Disney World, in Florida, which opened in 2009; and an eponymous lounge at the San Francisco International Airport that was launched in early 2011. (The restaurants all serve her own wines, bottled under the label Coranation.)

All three of Cora's cookbooks were co-authored by Ann Krueger Spivack. In addition to *Cat Cora's Kitchen*, they are *Cooking from the Hip: Fast, Easy, Phenomenal Meals* (2007), which offers recipes that can be prepared quickly, and *Fresh Takes on Favorite Dishes: Cat Cora's Classics with a Twist* (2010), which contains simpler, more healthful versions of such dishes as nachos, stroganoff, and fried calamari. Of her sophomore effort, a reviewer for *Publishers Weekly* (January 15, 2007, on-line) wrote, "Cora . . . aims to translate the fast, flashy style of that high-pressure [*Iron Chef America*] kitchen into recipes that home cooks who have similar time constraints but comparatively modest gadgets and pantries can enjoy. The results are generally pleasing and more accessible than many of the concoctions presented on TV by battling chefs." Cora has also written a children's book, *A Suitcase Surprise for Mommy* (2011), aimed at youngsters (like her own) whose parents' jobs require them to travel a lot.

In 2005 Cora founded Chefs for Humanity, modeled on the organization Doctors Without Borders. Its aim, according to the Chefs for Humanity Web site, is "providing nutrition education, hunger relief, and emergency and humanitarian aid to reduce hunger across the world." Additionally, Cora serves as a spokesperson for UNICEF. In 2010 she accepted an invitation from the White House to prepare a meal in honor of Greek Independence Day.

Cora is a member of the Macy's Culinary Council, a group of chefs who endorse the store's culinary and houseware products, and since 2006 she has served as *Bon Appetit*'s executive chef, advising the editorial staff and representing the magazine at various media events. Cora has recently lent her name to a line of cookware and a line of gourmet products, including olive oils, prepared cooking sauces, and packaged olives. She is preparing a cooking-and-lifestyle show that is scheduled to debut on the Oprah Winfrey Network (OWN) in 2012.

Openly gay, Cora has been married to her partner, Jennifer Johnson Cora, a former nanny, since 2001. "I remember as a child of 4 or 5 having crushes on babysitters," Cora told Suzanne Riss. "Of course, a little girl can have crushes, and that doesn't mean she's gay. I didn't know what it meant. But it's who I was, just like when you have brown hair or blue eyes." She continued, "All through high school and college I dated boys, but by then I knew I was gay. I had a girlfriend in high school while I was dating a guy. I couldn't tell anybody. My first love. My first kiss. And I couldn't tell my mom. It was a lonely place. I came out to my parents when I was 19. . . . I was tired of hiding my pain or my happiness. . . . My parents had always told us that it was okay to be different, that they'd always love us. They were open-minded. But it was hard for them. That was in the '80s at the height of the AIDS epidemic. Then they talked to people. They [eventually] accepted it."

Together, Cat and Jennifer Cora have four sons, ranging in age from seven to two: Zoran, Caje, Thatcher, and Nash. Employing the same sperm donor and in-vitro fertilization, Jennifer carried the first three, and Cat gave birth to Nash, three months after Thatcher was born. The family live in Santa Barbara, California. Cora told Meredith Bryan for *O, The Oprah Magazine* (July 2011, on-line) that in 2012 she plans to reduce the number of days she is away from home from 200 to 50.

—M.R.

Suggested Reading: *Advocate* p24 Dec. 18, 2007; *New York Times* (on-line) Apr. 22, 1994, Jan. 14, 2005; *O, The Oprah Magazine* (on-line) July 2011, Sep. 2011; *Publishers Weekly* (on-line) Jan. 15, 2007; *WellBella* p22 May 2011; *Working Mother* p50 Aug./Sep. 2010

Selected Books: with Ann Krueger Spivack—*Cat Cora's Kitchen: Favorite Meals for Family and Friends*, 2004; *Cooking from the Hip: Fast, Easy, Phenomenal Meals*, 2007; *Fresh Takes on Favorite Dishes: Cat Cora's Classics with a Twist*, 2010; *A Suitcase Surprise for Mommy*, 2011

Jonathan Ferrey/Getty Images

Creamer, Paula

Aug. 5, 1986– Golfer

Address: c/o Ladies Professional Golf Association, 100 International Golf Dr., Daytona Beach, FL 32124

"There is so much I want to do in women's golf and I'm living my dream," Paula Creamer told Matt Ginella for *Golf Digest* (March 1, 2010, on-line). The 24-year-old Creamer has been playing golf since the age of 10. She was named Player of the Year by the American Junior Golf Association in 2003. In 2004 she became the youngest person and the first amateur to win the Ladies Professional Golf Association (LPGA) Final Qualifying Tournament, and both *Golf Digest* and *Golfweek* named her Amateur of the Year. Creamer then turned professional, and in 2005 she earned the LPGA Louise Suggs Rolex Rookie of the Year Award. By 2007, Curtis Pashelka wrote for the *Contra Costa (California) Times* (October 2, 2007), thanks to her "success, attitude and girl-next-door appearance," Creamer had "evolved into one of the biggest and most marketable stars in women's professional golf." In 2008 she became the first American to log four first-place finishes on an LPGA tour since Juli Inkster in 1999. Despite a stomach ailment that plagued her for much of 2009, that year she qualified for the third time for the biennial Solheim Cup, in which professional women golfers from Europe and the U.S. compete individually, in pairs, and in teams. As in 2005 and 2007, the U.S. team won the cup, and Creamer led her team in number of points earned.

While not noted for her form or grace, Creamer is known for her fiercely competitive spirit. Inkster, one of Creamer's 2009 Solheim Cup teammates, told Ron Kroichick for the *San Francisco Chronicle* (September 22, 2009), "Paula's got the will, and you can't teach that. She might not hit the ball great or putt it the best that day, but she'll find a way to be in contention." Natalie Gulbis, another of her teammates, told Pashelka, "She's not only a great individual player, but she's a great team player. . . . She's one of those players that wants it really bad and it always shows in her performances." In May 2010, competing with a noticeably swollen left thumb not long after having undergone surgery on it, Creamer won the U.S. Women's Open—her first major LPGA victory. "I was in pain, but I was trying to do everything to not think about it," Creamer told an Associated Press reporter, as quoted on *Golf.com* (July 11, 2010). "It shows you how much the mental side of golf can really take over." As of March 14, 2011, Creamer was listed 12th in the LPGA/Rolex women's world golf rankings.

The only child of Paul and Karen Creamer, Paula Creamer was born on August 5, 1986 in Mountain View, California. Her father is an airline pilot. The Pleasanton, California, home where the Creamers lived overlooked the Castlewood Country Club Golf Course, and as a youngster Creamer would sometimes tag along while her father, an avid recreational golfer, played a round or two. Her primary athletic interest in her early years was acrobatic dancing; for several years she belonged to a team that competed in acrobatic-dance contests nationally. At age 10 she tried her hand at golf and liked it so much that she began accompanying her father on his frequent visits to the Castlewood course with her own bag of clubs in tow. In an interview with Ryan Herrington for *Golf World* (December 2, 2004, on-line), Paul Creamer described his daughter as "competitive to the hilt, been like that since she was little. It's not mean-spirited . . . it's just at times it's like there are two Paulas. She's never been satisfied just doing something. She wants to do it better than anyone else."

At the age of 11, Creamer "had to decide whether to be a cheerleader or on the golf team," she recalled in an interview for ABC *World News* (May 27, 2005, on-line). "[My school] wouldn't let me do

both." Creamer chose golf and quickly developed into a top player at the junior level, winning 18 tournaments in a row. In 2000, at Paula's urging, the Creamers moved to Bradenton, Florida, so that the young golfer could train with the British coach David Whelan at the IMG Leadbetter Golf Academy while attending the Pendleton School, an IMG-affiliated college-preparatory institution designed for athletes in training. "When we started, everybody said, 'Oh, you've got to work with this girl; she's such a great prospect,'" Whelan told Dave Scheiber for the *St. Petersburg (Florida) Times* (September 18, 2005). "And when I watched her hit the ball, I thought, well she must be very determined and a great competitor, because she didn't particularly swing the club that well. But she could hit it straight." Creamer still trains with Whelan.

As an amateur Creamer participated in the Ping Junior Solheim Cup in 2002 and 2003. She was a member of the victorious 2003 Spirit International team and the 2004 U.S. Curtis Cup team, which also included Michelle Wie. Wie had entered the international spotlight in 2000 when, at age 10, she became the youngest-ever player to qualify for the Women's U.S. Amateur Public Links Championship. When Creamer and Wie began to face each other regularly on the amateur circuit, the media were quick to draw comparisons between the two. In a conversation with Brian Murphy for the *San Francisco Chronicle* (July 3, 2003), Creamer said, "I play against the best juniors in the world, and [Wie is] just another junior. I don't place her on a higher plateau."

In 2003 the American Junior Golf Association named Creamer Player of the Year. She took part in the 2004 LPGA Tour's Shoprite Classic on a sponsor's exemption (an event's sponsor may pick several contestants regardless of their status), held at the Marriott Seaview Resort in Galloway Township, New Jersey, and finished only one stroke behind the winner, Cristie Kerr. That same year Creamer tied for 13th place at the U.S. Women's Open, held at the Orchards Golf Club in South Hadley, Massachusetts, and became the youngest person and first amateur player to win the LPGA Final Qualifying Tournament, in Daytona Beach, Florida; her five-shot victory earned her exempt status for the 2005 season (that is, she did not have to qualify for most events). Creamer turned professional immediately after she completed the tournament's final round. In 2004 *Golfweek* and *Golf Digest* named her Amateur of the Year.

Creamer decided against attending college right after high school. She told Mike Baldwin for the *Oklahoman* (June 10, 2007), "I always thought I'd go to college. But given the opportunity I wanted to be the best professional player, not the best college player. I've been very lucky. I'm living a dream." In 2010, when Mike Ginella asked her, "Do you regret not going to college?," she responded, "No. I can honestly say that. These have been the best five years of my life." She added, "I will go back and get my degree, there's not a doubt in my mind. But when you have opportunities like I did, you have to take advantage of them."

Creamer performed well during her rookie season with the LPGA. On May 22, 2005, four days before her high-school graduation and at the age of 18 years, nine months, and 17 days, Creamer made a 17-foot birdie putt on the 18th hole to win the Sybase Classic in New Rochelle, New York, which took place in rain. Her victory made her the youngest winner of a multi-round event in LPGA history. (Marlene Hagge, one of the original 13 founders of the LPGA, was slightly younger when she won two single-round events.) "I've always played in the rain," Creamer told Damon Hack for the *New York Times* (May 23, 2005). "I like it. It shows what kind of person you are. You have to fight through it. You have to be a tough person and go through adversity." Paul Creamer told Hack that his daughter "was always a good mudder. We worked hard on playing in weather when she was growing up. I knew that Paula was not one to complain of wind, temperature. She's always found a way."

Two months later Creamer achieved a record-breaking eight-shot win at the 2005 Evian Masters in Evian-les-Bains, France, making her the youngest player to pass the $1 million mark in total earnings on a LPGA tour; she also earned that amount faster than any others had. Creamer easily qualified for the 2005 U.S. Solheim Cup team, which she led to victory as the team's top point-earner. "Anytime you get to wear red, white and blue and go out and play for your country, there's nothing better than that," Creamer told Joe Fleming for *USA Today* (May 7, 2008). After tying for second at the 2005 Wendy's Championship for Children, Creamer was named the Louise Suggs Rolex Rookie of the Year and, with a total of $1,531,780, set an LPGA record for most money earned by a rookie. (That record was broken by Julieta Granada the next year.) During the final round of the Jamie Farr Owens Corning Classic at the Highland Meadows Golf Club in Sylvania, Ohio, Creamer shot 64—a career low for her then. She finished the season by winning the NEC Karuizawa and the Master GC Ladies, two events on the LPGA of Japan tour.

Despite being hampered by wrist and foot injuries and fatigue through much of the 2006 season, Creamer logged 14 top-10 finishes, including a tie for second place at the Mitchell Co. LPGA Tournament of Champions at the Magnolia Grove Golf Course in Mobile, Alabama. At the HSBC Women's World Match Play Championship, held at the Hamilton Farm Golf Club in Far Hills, New Jersey, Creamer's career earnings surpassed $2 million. By season's end she had set the LPGA record for most money earned in a single season without a win ($1,076,183).

For almost a month at the beginning of 2007, Creamer gave up golf and rested. In resuming competition she won the season-opening SBS Open at Turtle Bay, held at the Arnold Palmer Course in Turtle Bay, Hawaii, where she sank a 40-foot birdie on the 17th hole to defeat Julieta Granada by one

stroke; she also won the Mitchell Co. LPGA Tournament of Champions. She recorded an additional 11 top-10 finishes, among them second place at the CN Canadian Women's Open, a tie for second at the LPGA Corning Classic, and third place at both the Honda LPGA Thailand and the ADT Championship at the Trump International Golf Club in West Palm Beach, Florida. She set an LPGA record for speed when she crossed the $3 million mark in career earnings, at the Michelob Ultra Open at Kingsmill Golf Club in West Virginia. She was one of four players to compete in all five matches at the 2007 Solheim Cup. At that event, Pashelka wrote, she "was the catalyst for the American team's win over Europe" and earned more points than any of her teammates. "I just felt really rested and ready to come out strong," Creamer told Pashelka, referring to her brief sabbatical from golf. "That's all learning experiences. That's all figuring out what works best for you."

In 2008 Creamer won the Fields Open in Hawaii, the SemGroup Championship at the Cedar Ridge Country Club in Broken Arrow, Oklahoma, the Samsung World Championship at the Ocean Course at Half Moon Bay Golf Links in Half Moon Bay, California, and the Jamie Farr Owens Corning Classic, where she set a new career low (and tournament record) of 60 strokes in the first round. Those victories made Creamer the first American to finish first four times on an LPGA tour since Juli Inkster in 1999. Also in 2008 Creamer's career earnings topped $4 million in record time (at the SBS Open at Turtle Bay) and set the record for topping $5 million (at the U.S. Women's Open, where she tied for sixth place).

During most of 2009 a stomach ailment that resisted diagnosis plagued Creamer. She told Kroichick, "Getting sick constantly on the road was the most difficult thing I've ever had to go through." Although Creamer went winless on the LPGA tour that year, she qualified once again for the U.S. Solheim Cup team and again led the victorious team in points. She crossed the $6 million mark in career earnings at the HSBC Women's Championship at the Tanah Merah Country Club in Singapore, where she tied for third place, and finished the season in first place in the category of percentage of greens reached (74.7).

In the first round of the first event of the 2010 season—the Honda-PTT (Petroleum Authority of Thailand) LPGA Thailand—a left-thumb injury forced Creamer to withdraw. She underwent surgery in March after noninvasive rehabilitative efforts proved futile. During the operation Creamer's surgeon discovered that the damage to Creamer's thumb included two torn ligaments, a torn volar plate, and an injured tendon—impairments far more extensive than had been expected. After the operation the surgeon asked her father, "How in the world did she play golf with that thumb?," as Paul Creamer told Karen Crouse for the *New York Times* (July 11, 2010). For weeks afterward Creamer had a cast on her hand and then a splint. Her thumb had not completely healed when she returned to golf in June for the ShopRite LPGA Classic, where she finished in seventh place with 10 under par.

The continuing trouble with her thumb led Creamer to limit herself to only 40 practice swings before each of the three rounds at the 2010 U.S. Women's Open, held in July at the notoriously difficult Oakmont Country Club course in Oakmont, Pennsylvania. Despite that precaution the condition of Creamer's hyperextended thumb deteriorated, and it became extremely swollen. Nevertheless, Karen Crouse reported, Creamer's game "improved with each round. . . . She has shown a steeliness and patience beyond what she exhibited before her injury-induced hiatus from golf." That year's U.S. Open ended with Creamer's triumphant win, in a three-under-par 281 victory. She finished four strokes ahead of Suzann Pettersen and Na Yeon Choi, who tied for second place. With that accomplishment Creamer no longer had to endure, as she had for years, hearing herself described as the best female golfer never to win a major event. At the beginning of the 2011 season, she ranked 12th in the world among professional women golfers. Thus far in the year she has played in the Honda LPGA

Thailand, in which she came in fifth; the HSBC Women's Champions, in which she tied for 24th, and the RR Donnelley LPGA Founders Cup, in which she tied for second place.

Creamer, who stands five feet nine inches, has endorsement deals with major companies including the TaylorMade-Adidas Golf Co. and the Citizen Watch Co. She lives with her dog, Tank, near her parents' home in a gated community adjoining the Isleworth Golf and Country Club in Windermere, Florida. Her fondness for pink clothing, tees, and balls has earned her the nickname "Pink Panther." She told Mike Aitken for the *Scotsman* (August 2, 2007) that pink "shows the softer side of me. . . . Pink helps me bridge the gap between tough on-course competitor to my softer, feminine off-course side." She also told Aitken, "If my love for the game inspires other young junior girls to take up golf, there is nothing more pleasing to me than that."

—H.R.W.

Suggested Reading: *New York Times* D p7 May 23, 2005; *Oklahoman* B p2 June 10, 2007; *San Francisco Chronicle* B p1 Sep. 22, 2009; *St. Petersburg (Florida) Times* C p1 Sep. 18, 2005

Crenshaw, Kimberlé Williams

May 5, 1959– Legal scholar; activist; writer

Address: UCLA School of Law, 385 Charles E. Young Dr., 1242 Law Bldg., Los Angeles, CA 90095

The legal scholar and activist Kimberlé Williams Crenshaw, a professor of law at both the University of California–Los Angeles (UCLA) and Columbia University, has been an influential thinker in matters of minority and women's rights for nearly three decades. Starting in the early 1980s, Crenshaw was one of the early advocates of Critical Race Theory, a scholarly approach to civil rights that focuses on the real-world implications of laws. Unlike approaches that emphasize the championing of individual rights as the best means of achieving liberty for all, Critical Race Theory seeks to examine and expose the oppression of minorities (particularly African-Americans) by systematic forces, such as the free market and the court system, and to advocate solutions that focus on the needs of groups. Crenshaw also developed the concept of "intersectionality," according to which minority women are discriminated against on the basis of both race and gender, in ways that are not addressed sufficiently—if at all—by either feminist or antiracist groups. In 1996 Crenshaw co-founded the African American Policy Forum (AAPF) to highlight the importance of gender in racial-justice discourse. Crenshaw is a co-author of the book

Peter Kramer/Getty Images For V-Day

Words That Wound: Critical Race Theory, Assaultive Speech, and the First Amendment (1993) and a co-editor of *Critical Race Theory: The Key Writings That Formed the Movement* (1995), which includes one of her essays. Her articles have appeared in legal journals including *Harvard Law Review*, *National Black Law Journal*, *Stanford Law*

Review, and *Southern California Law Review* as well as in such mainstream publications as *Essence*, the *Los Angeles Times*, and the *Wall Street Journal*. She has lent her opinions and expertise to programs on National Public Radio (NPR), PBS, NBC, C-Span, ABC, and other stations. In addition, for about a decade, Crenshaw has been a regular commentator on NPR's *Tavis Smiley* show.

Kimberlé Williams Crenshaw was born on May 5, 1959 and grew up in Canton, Ohio. From a young age she followed the course of the civil rights movement, watching some of its key events unfold on television. On April 4, 1968, the day Martin Luther King Jr. was assassinated, parents and leaders in Crenshaw's community gathered local black children to talk about the slain civil rights leader. "What they weren't anticipating," Crenshaw told Denise B. Hawkins for *Black Issues in Higher Education* (August 10, 1995), "was that a lot of kids didn't know who Martin Luther King was. They kept trying to get somebody to say something." So Crenshaw spoke out. "By the time I had gotten home from the King assembly, neighbors had already called my mother saying, 'Your daughter was talking up a storm today.'" Crenshaw added: "My mother likes to say that's where it really began for me, but it was really with my parents and their parents who shaped our family's tradition of thinking politically about being African American."

Crenshaw attended Cornell University, in Ithaca, New York, earning a B.A. degree in 1981, then enrolled as a law student at Harvard University, in Cambridge, Massachusetts, where she received a J.D. degree in 1984. In the following year she was awarded an LL.M. degree from the University of Wisconsin. In college and law school, Crenshaw's studies and activism were influenced by her sense of what was lacking in the schools' curricula. "In the Africana studies program at Cornell, the gender aspect of race was woefully underdeveloped," Crenshaw told Sheila Thomas in an interview for *Perspectives* magazine that appears on the American Bar Association Web site. "When women were discussed, it was not in political or economic contexts but rather those of literature and poetry. The serious political discourses were framed by men, and women came in at the periphery." As a student she was also influenced by the work of the legal scholar and fiction writer Derrick Bell and the U.S. Court of Appeals judge A. Leon Higginbotham. Speaking to Hawkins about Bell and Higginbotham, Crenshaw said, "They are people who represented some of the earliest attempts to think about the relationship between law and race as an ongoing phenomenon, not something that was limited to some historical period in the past. And to think about how the law affects the lives of Black people, real people, rather than just talking about race in abstract terms or talking about civil rights laws in terms of balancing civil rights laws with other values in society like privacy, federalism or any other number of interests that traditional (by traditional I mean white) civil rights scholars used to think about."

Although the presence of Bell, who had begun teaching law at Harvard in 1971, was one of the factors leading Crenshaw to apply to Harvard Law School, she was unable to study with him: by the time she entered the program, he had resigned from the university to protest what he alleged to be Harvard's racially unjust hiring practices. Bell had taught a class on the relationship between race and law—the only such class offered at the university. With Bell gone from the faculty, Crenshaw, along with several other African-American students, actively campaigned for such a class. They encountered resistance. "The administration's response to us," Crenshaw told Hawkins, "was the lightning rod and in some ways the focal point for the actual genesis of critical race theory." Crenshaw and her fellow black law students succeeded in getting a dozen law scholars to come to campus to teach an "alternative course" that used Bell's book *Race, Racism and American Law* as a basis for discussion. The Critical Race Theory movement was underway.

Although Crenshaw often worked with fellow black students toward a common cause, she, as a black woman, found herself at what she called an intersection. As part of her concept of intersectionality, Crenshaw argued that women of color—a designation she uses to include black, Asian, and Latino women—face discrimination both for their race and their sex, sometimes (in the case of sex) on the part of members of their own race. While Crenshaw was at Harvard, for example, she and a black male friend went to visit a member of their study group, a black man who had recently joined a club that was formerly reserved for whites. When the man opened the club's door, he stepped out rather than letting them in, saying that he had forgotten to tell them something. Upon hearing that, Crenshaw's friend protested, saying that if he and Crenshaw—because they were black—were expected to enter through the back door, he would leave instead. The club member then informed Crenshaw's friend that *he* could enter through the front door, but that women had to go in through the back. To Crenshaw's surprise, the man who had accompanied her to the club did not object to that arrangement. Speaking to Thomas, Crenshaw elaborated on what she learned from the incident: "I understood that we can all stand together as long as we think that we are all equally affected by a particular discrimination, but the moment where a different barrier affects a subset of us, our solidarity often falls apart. I began to look at all the other ways that not only the race and civil rights agenda but the gender agenda are sometimes uninformed by and inattentive to the ways that subgroups experience discrimination. There are institutional elisions as well. For example, at Harvard, when we were struggling to get the law school to interview and perhaps hire women and people of color, the school responded with two committees. One was a gender committee that studied women candidates; the other was a committee that studied candidates of color. Not too surprisingly, women of color seemed to fall through the cracks."

After receiving her LL.M. degree, Crenshaw served from 1985 to 1986 as a law clerk for a judge on the Wisconsin Supreme Court. In the latter year she joined the faculty at UCLA, where, after serving as an acting professor for five years, she earned the title of professor of law. In 1995 she also became a professor of law at Columbia University, in New York City. In 1991 Crenshaw had served on the legal team for Anita Hill, a black law professor who had served as an assistant to Clarence Thomas when Thomas worked at the Department of Education and then at the Equal Employment Opportunity Commission. Now a federal judge, Thomas, an African-American, had been nominated to serve on the U.S. Supreme Court. Crenshaw was among those who represented Hill—who alleged that as her supervisor Thomas had sexually harassed her—during U.S. Senate confirmation hearings. Despite the allegations and the resulting controversy, which dominated the news media for a time, Thomas was (narrowly) confirmed by the Senate in October of that year.

Discussing and writing about the concept of intersectionality proved to be a motif in Crenshaw's career. The year 1993 saw the publication of *Words That Wound: Critical Race Theory, Assaultive Speech, and the First Amendment* (1993), to which Crenshaw and other Critical Race Theory scholars contributed previously published essays about the intersection of free speech and so-called hate speech; two years later Crenshaw contributed to *Critical Race Theory: The Key Writings that Formed the Movement* (1995), a collection of previously published essays by Bell, Crenshaw, and others. Speaking to Hawkins, Crenshaw elaborated on why she thought such a book was necessary: "Cultural studies people, historians, economists, sociologists . . . all of them are starting to look increasingly to legal scholarship to get some sense of how race has traditionally been debated and critiqued. Unfortunately most of these materials are contained in law review articles, and a lot of scholars who aren't in the law don't have access to these publications." Crenshaw is listed as the book's co-editor and contributed a previously published essay from 1994, "Mapping the Margins: Intersectionality, Identity Politics, and Violence Against Women of Color," which examines the relationship between intersectionality and domestic violence. (The essay is posted on the Web site of the Washington Coalition of Sexual Assault Programs.)

The introduction to the essay states that it will explore "the various ways in which race and gender intersect in shaping structural and political aspects of violence against women of color." Crenshaw acknowledged that she would barely, if at all, address other intersections for women of color, such as class and sexuality. In the paper's first section, "Structural Intersectionality," Crenshaw explored how the experiences of women of color

with domestic violence, sexual assault, and related legal reform differ from those of white women. She argued that although class—along with correlated factors such as lack of education, job skills, and employment—is an important factor in the disempowerment of many women of color, it is not deeply intertwined with race and gender. Furthermore, immigrant women, especially women of color, can face further challenges: if a woman who needs to be married for at least two years before applying for permanent U.S. resident status is married to someone who is physically abusive, she might not go to the authorities for fear of eventual deportation. Although some legal protections exist that would offer the woman a waiver, she might still choose not to file charges if she feels she cannot get proper legal representation or conclusive evidence of abuse. Adding to those challenges is the potential language barrier: the already difficult process is made that much more difficult for non-English-speaking women. In the paper's second section, "Political Intersectionality," Crenshaw elaborated on the "conflicting political agendas" frequently pursued by antiracist activists, who focus mainly on discrimination against men, and women's-rights activists, who concentrate chiefly on discrimination against white women. Crenshaw wrote, "The problem is not simply that both discourses fail women of color by not acknowledging the 'additional' burden of patriarchy or of racism, but that the discourses are often inadequate even to the discrete tasks of articulating the full dimensions of racism and sexism. Because women of color experience racism in ways not always the same as those experienced by men of color, and sexism in ways not always parallel to experiences of white women, dominant conceptions of antiracism and feminism are limited, even on their own terms."

In gathering information for the essay, Crenshaw could not get statistics on domestic-violence intervention in Los Angeles by district; the reason, she was told by the Los Angeles Police Department, had to do with concerns that the statistics would be "misused" to argue that domestic violence is a problem mainly in minority communities—which, some activists feared, could reinforce negative stereotypes about black and Latino men. Furthermore, Crenshaw noted, various antiracist and community activists "fail" women of color by making an effort to prevent or discourage the politicization of domestic violence by arguing that "gender issues are internally divisive, and that raising such issues within nonwhite communities represents the migration of white women's concerns into a context in which they are not only irrelevant but also harmful. At their most extreme, critics who seek to defend their communities against this feminist assault deny that gender violence is a problem in their community, and characterize any effort to politicize gender subordination as itself a community problem." Further cultural factors, such as the reluctance of many minority communities to subject their private lives to the scrutiny of the police, contribute to a lack of reporting and intervention. "In this sense," Crenshaw added, "the home is not simply a man's castle in patriarchal terms, but it is also a safe haven from the indignities of life in a racist society. In many cases, the desire to protect the home as a safe haven against assaults outside the home may make it more difficult for women of color to seek protection against assaults from within the home."

Throughout her career Crenshaw has also been an active proponent of affirmative action. In 1996 voters in California passed Proposition 209, a measure that banned public institutions from considering race, gender, or ethnicity in hiring or admissions, which effectively ended the practice of affirmative action in state universities and other public institutions. In an essay for *Essence* magazine (July 1998), Crenshaw argued that opponents of affirmative action misrepresent Martin Luther King's vision of an America where people are judged not, in his famous phrase, "by the color of their skin but by the content of their character." King, she averred, would not have opposed affirmative action, an argument she defended by quoting from his book *Where Do We Go From Here? Chaos or Community* (1967): "A society that has done something special against the Negro for hundreds of years must now do something special for him." King, Crenshaw argued, found "a significant moral distinction between using race as a welcome mat and using it as a No Trespass sign." California's Proposition 209, she concluded, is an example of the latter. Crenshaw noted that the number of black students admitted to UCLA dropped 80 percent after the passage of the measure. "Affirmative action," she wrote, "is not a preference; it is a modest effort to recognize the ways that standardized tests don't measure the potential of entire groups of people, particularly those who were not represented when these tests were developed." She went on to argue that in admitting undergraduates, colleges over-rely on standardized testing—particularly the SAT—and that those tests are not very reliable in predicting academic and professional potential. She stressed the latter point with regard to the LSAT, the standardized test required to enter law school.

In the following decade, when a similar debate about affirmative action was taking place in Michigan, Crenshaw, in an essay for the *Michigan Law Review* (2007), again attacked what she regarded as the misleading notion of colorblindness in admittance policies. In 1965 President Lyndon B. Johnson, in his famous commencement address at Howard University, said: "You do not wipe away the scars of centuries by saying: Now you are free to go where you want, and do as you desire, and choose the leaders you please. You do not take a person who, for years, has been hobbled by chains and liberate him, bring him up to the starting line of a race and then say, 'you are free to compete with all the others,' and still justly believe that you have been completely fair. Thus it is not enough just to open the gates of opportunity. All our citizens must have the ability to walk through those gates." Opponents of affirmative action would later use the starting-line-of-a-race analogy to make the point that those who stand to benefit from affirmative action actually get a head start. It is precisely that "idea of preference," Crenshaw argued, that supporters of affirmative action must fight. In an approach consistent with Critical Race Theory's emphasis on systematic discrimination, Crenshaw reformulated the race-track analogy: "There is an alternative narrative that can be presented, one that actually throws light on the conditions that affirmative action is designed to address. This alternative frame suggests that the problem affirmative action seeks to address is not damaged runners, but damaged lanes that make the race more difficult for some competitors to run in than others. Rethinking affirmative action so as to account for the unequal conditions of the lanes on the track—the debris that some runners must avoid, the craters over which some must climb, the crevices that some must jump and the detours that some must maneuver—suggests that affirmative action is not about providing preferences at all. Rather it is about removing and neutralizing the obstacles and conditions that compromise the fair running of the race."

Crenshaw's concerns with regard to civil rights extend beyond American borders. According to the Web site of the African American Policy Forum, Crenshaw has "facilitated workshops for human rights activists in Brazil and in India, and for constitutional court judges in South Africa. Her groundbreaking work on 'Intersectionality' has traveled globally and was influential in the drafting of the equality clause in the South African Constitution. Crenshaw authored the background paper on Race and Gender Discrimination for the United Nations' World Conference on Racism, served as the Rapporteur for the conference's Expert Group on Gender and Race Discrimination, and coordinated NGO [nongovernmental organization] efforts to ensure the inclusion of gender in the WCAR [World Conference Against Racism] Conference Declaration." In the United States she has served as a member of the National Science Foundation's committee to research violence against women and "has consulted with leading foundations, social justice organizations and corporations to advance their race and gender equity initiatives."

Crenshaw has received the Lucy Terry Prince Unsung Heroine Award, presented by the Lawyers' Committee on Civil Rights Under Law, and was an Ira Glasser Racial Justice Fellow of the American Civil Liberties Union from 2005 to 2007. She has also served as the Fulbright Distinguished Chair for Latin America and received the Alphonse Fletcher Fellowship as well as fellowships to the Center for Advanced Study in the Behavioral Sciences at Stanford University (2008–09) and to the European University Institute in Florence, Italy (2010). She is currently the faculty director of the

Critical Race Studies program at the UCLA Law School.

—D.K.

Suggested Reading: aapf.org; *Black Issues in Higher Education* p13 Aug. 10, 1995; law.columbia.edu; law.ucla.edu; wcsap.org

Selected Books: as co-author—*Words That Wound: Critical Race Theory, Assaultive Speech, and the First Amendment*, 1993; as co-editor—*Critical Race Theory: The Key Writings That Formed the Movement*, 1995

Henry S. Dziekan III/Getty Images

Cromer, David

Oct. 17, 1964– Theater director; actor

Address: c/o William Morris Agency, 1325 Ave. of the Americas, New York, NY 10019

In 2010, when the theater director and occasional actor David Cromer won a John D. and Catherine T. MacArthur Foundation fellowship, commonly known as a "genius grant," the organization cited his efforts in "reinvigorating classic American plays and illuminating their relationship to the present." The citation continued, "His incisive interpretations of the twentieth-century repertoire honor the original intention of each work while providing audiences with more psychologically complex performances than previous renderings. . . . From venues in Chicago to the theaters of New York, Cromer is re-staging earlier plays with a spirit and urgency that resonates with con-

temporary audiences." Over the course of his career Cromer has directed such plays as William Inge's *Picnic* and *Come Back, Little Sheba*, Thornton Wilder's *Our Town*, Tennessee Williams's *A Streetcar Named Desire*, and Neil Simon's *Brighton Beach Memoirs*. "His productions are marked by a delicate touch and an emotional intricacy that are best served by a seat in the front row," Charles Isherwood wrote for the *New York Times* (November 9, 2008, on-line). "But the remarkable thing about his work is that you always seem to have a prime view, even if you're up against the back wall."

David Cromer was born on October 17, 1964 in Skokie, Illinois, a suburb of Chicago. He was the third of four sons born to Louise Cromer, a public-school teacher, and Richard Cromer, who worked variously as a TV writer, encyclopedia researcher, and human-resources consultant. Cromer was not a happy child. "I suffered from depression as a kid even though I wasn't diagnosed," he told Alex Witchel for the *New York Times* (February 14, 2010, on-line). "I was easily defeated, easily shut down, easily insulted. If the train door closes right before you get into it, you go, 'Oh, I missed the train.' What I would do was, 'The train hates me, I don't deserve to get on the train.'" He continued, "And I was a hugely loud, talkative kid. . . . [My parents] were always mortified by me. Everything was, 'Will you be quiet?' 'Will you stop doing that?'" Noting that he was also "a particularly flamey little kid," Cromer quipped to Witchel, "I think the fact that I was gay was visible from space."

When Cromer was 12 years old, his father fell in love with another woman and moved to California. His parents subsequently divorced, and his maternal grandparents moved into the family home to help his mother, who was struggling to work and raise four boys by herself. Not receiving much parental supervision, Cromer dropped out of high school during his junior year and began experimenting with sex and drugs. He also became obsessed with attending *The Rocky Horror Picture Show*, a cult film that regularly screened at midnight at the Biograph Theater in Chicago, finding in its devotees a group of artistically minded outsiders like himself.

After two years Cromer decided to get a General Educational Development (GED) certificate, and he later enrolled at Columbia College in Chicago to study acting. (His father had once taught a screenwriting class at the school.) He soon dropped out. Cromer explained to Alan Bird for the *New York Theater Guide* (August 23, 2010, on-line), "The school's design is that your teachers are working professionals in a very vibrant theatre scene. So if you were halfway decent (and I was exactly halfway decent) you made some professional connections and you could start working fairly early. I never really finished, though. I think I may have four general studies credits. Not four left to obtain. Four total."

Cromer told Robert Simonson for *Playbill* (February 25, 2009, on-line), "I took a single directing class that was required when I was a student and it was such a disaster that I didn't consider directing for several years after that." He joked to Bird, "Maybe I thought [directing] would distract me from my destiny of playing [the very minor part of] Brutus' boy Lucius in the Oak Park Festival Theatre's production [of] *Julius Caesar.*"

Despite such self-deprecation, which many journalists have noted is characteristic of him, Cromer found relatively steady work, acting at various Chicago-area venues and teaching courses at Columbia College even though he had not obtained a degree. In 1995 he appeared in Brian Friel's *Dancing at Lughnasa* at the Bog Theatre, directing the production as well. Three years later he acted in and directed Tony Kushner's *Angels in America* at the Journeymen Theater, which won him the 1998 Joseph Jefferson Award for best director. (Casually known as the Jeff Award, that honor recognizes excellence in the Chicago-area theater world.) In 2000 Cromer directed Austin Pendleton's *Orson's Shadow*, which premiered at Chicago's famed Steppenwolf Theatre and later moved to the Barrow Street Theatre in New York, marking his Off-Broadway directorial debut.

Comer was nominated for Jeff Awards in the category of best director for his work on Ann Noble's *And Neither Have I Wings to Fly* in 2001 and Arthur Miller's *The Price* in 2002. In 2002 he was also nominated in the category of best supporting actor for his appearance in Eugene O'Neill's *Long Day's Journey Into Night.* The following year he and Marc Grapey shared the director's prize for their work on Peter Parnell's *Cider House Rules*—a two-part, six-hour play based on a novel by John Irving and mounted at Chicago's Famous Door Theatre.

Among Cromer's other high-profile productions in Chicago over the next few years were William Inge's *Come Back, Little Sheba*, which was mounted to great acclaim at the Shattered Globe Theatre in 2006, earning him a Jeff Award nomination. He followed that with *Adding Machine*, a musical adaptation of Elmer Rice's 1923 anti-capitalist screed about a worker, Mr. Zero, who is being replaced by automation. The musical, with a score by the young composer Joshua Schmidt and book by Schmidt and Jason Loewith, was staged by the Next Theater Company in 2007 before moving to the Off-Broadway Minetta Lane Theatre in 2008. "The stylish production, directed by David Cromer, honors the dark, acrid flavor of Mr. Schmidt's score and the play's grimly comic vision of life on the lower rungs of American society," Charles Isherwood wrote for the *New York Times* (February 28, 2007), while the show was still in Chicago. "A candidate for a brisk march to Broadway this adventurous musical certainly isn't . . . but its uncompromising artistry and imaginative scope suggest that Mr. Schmidt is a composer to watch. And Mr. Cromer, whose credits include the Steppenwolf-born *Orson's Shadow*, later seen in New York,

is unquestionably a talent of significance too. Either one could prove to be the next important artist to emerge from the little streams that feed the fertile theatrical landscape here." *Adding Machine* garnered Cromer both a Lucille Lortel Award and an Obie Award for his directing.

Isherwood's intuition about Cromer seemed to be correct. In 2008 Cromer directed a critically acclaimed version of William Inge's three-act play *Picnic* at the Writers' Theatre, in Chicago, that earned him a Jeff Award nomination, and also that year he directed a revival of *Our Town*, Thornton Wilder's look at small-town life in Grover's Corners, New Hampshire, in the early 20th century. (The play was first produced in 1938 and has gone on to become one of the most frequently mounted shows in the U.S., thanks in some part to its minimal sets and props.) Cromer's version opened at Chicago's Chopin Theatre before moving to Barrow Street in New York. In addition to directing Cromer starred as the Stage Manager, a character who introduces the play, provides background information during the story, and sometimes joins the action to talk with the other characters.

Reviews in both cities were ecstatic. In his assessment for the *Chicago Tribune* (May 2, 2008), Chris Jones wrote, "David Cromer has directed some distinguished Chicago productions in his career . . . but I think [his] brilliantly revisionist and generally astounding new production of Thornton Wilder's *Our Town . . .* is his masterwork to date." Jones continued, "In the jaw-dropping third act, which makes some truly shocking and inspired conceptual choices that are best experienced without foreknowledge, I found myself speaking the words 'Oh, my God' to no one. And despite eccentricities, I'm not that given to inappropriate interjections. It's just that this *Our Town* hit me that hard. If your tastes run to shows that make you stare right in the face of your own mortality and inability to prioritize what and who really matters in life, your own petty obsessions and jealousies, then cancel whatever you're doing tonight and go and see this show. . . . 'He's going on like this about Thornton Wilder's *Our Town*?' you must be thinking. 'That hoary small-town staple of the high school repertory?' Ah, but you've never seen it done like this before." In her *New York Times* profile of Cromer, Alex Witchel called the play "imaginatively staged [and] emotionally transcendent," and in a review for the same paper (February 27, 2009, on-line), Charles Isherwood called it a "modest but highly rewarding production." The MacArthur Foundation Web site stated, "Every element of [Cromer's] production of Thornton Wilder's *Our Town*—from set design, to costumes, to music, to the choice of actors—converges into a cohesive whole that evokes an immediate and powerful experience for viewers." Cromer won Lucille Lortel and Obie Awards for his direction of the production, which ran in New York until September 2010.

Following the success of *Our Town*, Cromer moved to New York to direct his Broadway debut, a revival of Neil Simon's *Brighton Beach Memoirs*, a nostalgic look at a Jewish family living in Brooklyn, New York, during the late 1930s. The show was staged at the Nederlander Theatre in 2009. "There are definitely moments in Mr. Cromer's gentle production—particularly in intimate, tightly focused scenes between two characters—that are genuinely, freshly stirring. On other occasions, text and performance seem to be tugging in different directions," Ben Brantley wrote for the *New York Times* (October 26, 2009, on-line), echoing other critics' mixed reactions. After only nine performances the production was canceled due to low ticket sales. Most theater insiders blamed Simon's kitschy, dated dialogue and the sitcom star Laurie Metcalf's unsympathetic portrayal of her character, rather than Cromer's direction, for the closure.

Although Simon's *Broadway Bound*, the sequel to *Brighton Beach Memoirs*, was scheduled to be mounted as well, that plan was scrapped. "I wish we had opened both plays. It was like leaving at intermission," Cromer told Witchel. "I felt like we delivered an honest, heartfelt, explored version of that play, and there's nothing more you can do. . . . Look, these things can close in a week no matter what you do. That's the nature of it."

In 2010 Cromer directed the Australian playwright Andrew Bovell's *When the Rain Stops Falling*, which premiered at the Mitzi E. Newhouse Theater, at New York City's Lincoln Center. "Cromer tries to carry *When the Rain Stops Falling* beyond its flawed script by constantly shifting and reshifting our focus, but, in the midst of all these leaps, we lose the story's thread," Hilton Als wrote for the *New Yorker* (March 22, 2010, on-line). "Still, in this age of ready-made drama, confusion can be a positive thing; we are forced to rethink our relationship to the play, to become engaged spectators. In a theatre that's mired in fashionability, Cromer offers us its timeless opposite: style." For his work on *When the Rain Stops Falling*, Cromer won a Lucille Lortel Award as outstanding director. That same year he directed a well-received revival of Tennessee Williams's *A Streetcar Named Desire* in Chicago, at the Writers' Theatre. "The revelation of Mr. Cromer's meticulously detailed *Streetcar*—the most uniformly well-acted production I've yet seen, right down to the smallest roles," Charles Isherwood wrote for the *New York Times* (June 19, 2010, on-line), "is in presenting the play not as a hyper-intense lyric tragedy or a vehicle for a dominant star turn but as an intimate domestic drama that achieves its power through the exposure of the complicated and conflicting humanity of all its characters." Isherwood added, "Mr. Cromer's production underscores the humanity of Williams's vision, dark though it may be, allowing us to feel our way deeply into the play's painful beauty." Also in 2010 Cromer directed Kirk Lynn's innovative play *Cherrywood: The Modern Comparable* at the Angel Island Theater in Chicago. *Cherrywood*

is "a virtual reality party experience without the pressure to mingle or the aid of a cocktail," Katy Walsh wrote for the Chicago Theater Beat Web site (June 25, 2010). "In a large living-room-like space, the audience seats encircle the action. Closely matched in numbers, the 50+ wallflowers watch the 49 performers party. . . . David Cromer has gone fire-code-capacity to create an authentic party."

Cromer next directed a revival of John Guare's *The House of Blue Leaves*, which opened at the Walter Kerr Theater on Broadway in April 2011 and closed two months later. Featuring an all-star cast that included Ben Stiller, Edie Falco and Jennifer Jason Leigh, the production drew good notices from major critics. Terry Teachout, for example, wrote for the *Wall Street Journal* (April 26, 2011, on-line), "It's dauntingly difficult to bring off John Guare's *The House of Blue Leaves*, which may explain why this modern masterpiece, first performed in 1966, hasn't been seen on Broadway since 1987. The trick is in the tone. *The House of Blue Leaves* is a comedy about hopelessness, and it plays like *You Can't Take It With You* rewritten by Eugène Ionesco: It won't work if it isn't zany, and it won't work if it isn't horrifically disturbing. Fortunately, David Cromer has cracked Mr. Guare's complex code with the effortless understanding that he brings to every show he stages." Marilyn Stasio wrote for *Variety* (April 25, 2011, on-line), "Helmer David Cromer knows the secret to a good revival: Keep it faithful and don't comment from on high. The year is 1965 and America is looking for miracles in Cromer's transporting revival of *The House of Blue Leaves*, John Guare's insanely funny comedy about the impact of a historic Papal visit on a troubled Queens household. Topliners Ben Stiller, Edie Falco and Jennifer Jason Leigh should get more bottoms on seats; but the starry casting was no desperation measure. Guare's iconic play not only holds up, it still sets the bar for smart comic lunacy."

In the fall of 2011, Cromer is scheduled to work with a star of even greater wattage: he will direct Nicole Kidman, as the female lead, in a Broadway revival of Tennessee Williams's *Sweet Bird of Youth*. In the near future he will also direct Joe and David Zellnik's musical *Yank! A WWII Love Story* and a new Broadway production of Inge's *Picnic*.

"I really assumed that I would spend my life wandering the wilderness directing the four major Chekhov plays . . . over and over again and then be buried at sea sewn up in a clean white sack and pitched overboard—at noon—in the blaze of summer—and into an ocean as blue as my first lover's eyes," Cromer told Alan Bird. "But no one has ever, ever, ever asked me to direct any Chekhov."

—J.P.

Suggested Reading: *Chicago Tribune* C p6 May 9, 2008; *New York Theater Guide* (on-line) Aug. 23, 2010; *New York Times* (on-line) Feb. 28, 2007, Nov. 9, 2008, Feb. 27, 2009, Oct. 26, 2009, Feb.

14, 2010, June 19, 2010; *New Yorker* (on-line) Mar. 22, 2010; *Playbill* (on-line) Feb. 25, 2009; *Variety* (on-line) Apr. 25, 2011; *Wall Street Journal* W p7 Feb. 27, 2009, (on-line) Apr. 26, 2011

Selected Productions: *Dancing at Lughnasa*, 1995; *Angels in America*, 1998; *Orson's Shadow*, 2000, *Cider House Rules* (with Marc Grapey), 2003; *Come Back, Little Sheba*, 2006; *Adding Machine*, 2007; *Picnic*, 2008; *Our Town*, 2008; *Brighton Beach Memoirs*, 2009; *When the Rain Stops Falling*, 2010; *A Streetcar Named Desire*, 2010; *Cherrywood: The Modern Comparable*, 2010, *The House of Blue Leaves*, 2011

Courtesy of HarperOne

Crossan, John Dominic

Feb. 17, 1934– Theologian; biblical scholar; writer

Address: c/o HarperCollins Publishers, 10 E. 53d St., New York, NY 10022

"Saying something didn't happen, that's not interesting. Saying something didn't happen but someone made up a story to say it did, *that's* interesting," the Irish-American biblical scholar and former Catholic priest John Dominic Crossan told Stephanie Nolen for the Toronto, Canada, *Globe and Mail* (June 26, 1999). "The question is not, 'What do you believe' but, 'What did someone in the first century want to communicate when they said this?'" That question has been the crux of Crossan's career as a theologian, and he has written

extensively about the factual life of Jesus Christ as it relates to the stories in the New Testament of the Christian Bible. In his often controversial work, Crossan employs archaeological and anthropological findings as well as analyses of biblical texts in order to better grasp what is called the "historical Jesus"—Jesus Christ as understood through the historical, fact-based research of biblical scholars.

From his research Crossan has concluded that the historical Jesus was a first-century Jewish peasant who gained a following through his teachings of equality, kindness, and helping the poor, which challenged the hierarchical order of both the Roman Empire and the Jewish faith. Crossan refutes the many accounts of miracles and supernatural events ascribed to Jesus; those accounts, he says, are not rooted in fact but are derived from the stories Jesus's followers told in order to communicate his philosophies—"dramatic visualizations," Peter Steinfels wrote for the *New York Times* (December 23, 1991), "created by the early Christians to make concrete their experiences of the continued presence of Jesus after His death." Crossan's belief is that Jesus was, as John Blake put it for CNN (February 27, 2011, on-line), "an exploited 'peasant with an attitude'" who did not perform miracles, did not physically rise from the grave, and did not die to atone for the sins of mankind.

Crossan, who considers himself a Christian, was educated in the Roman Catholic seminary system and was ordained as a priest in 1957. His interest in pursuing a relationship with a woman and his devotion to scholarly research—even when its findings refuted aspects of Catholic dogma—led him to abandon the priesthood, in 1969. He then began teaching religion at DePaul University, in Chicago, Illinois, of which he is now a professor emeritus. He has published more than 20 books on the historical Jesus and the Bible, four of which have been best-sellers; his 1991 book, the best-selling *The Historical Jesus: The Life of a Mediterranean Jewish Peasant*, has been credited with helping to bring awareness of the historical Jesus into the mainstream. Crossan is also the co-founder of the Jesus Seminar, a group of scholars who work to maintain a collective view of the historical Jesus. Criticized sharply by some religious leaders, Crossan has been praised by others for shedding light on the history of a religious figure long shrouded in mystery. "He's changed the way we look [at] and think about Jesus," Byron McCane, an archaeologist and professor of religion at Wofford College, in South Carolina, told Blake. "He's important in a way that few scholars are."

The scholar was born John Michael Edmund Crossan on February 17, 1934 in Nenagh, in Tipperary County, Ireland. His father, Daniel Crossan, was a banker, and his mother, Elizabeth Farry Crossan, a homemaker. (Upon becoming a member of the Servite order, he took the name Brother Dominic; later, after he left the priesthood, he began to refer to himself as John Dominic Crossan.) Crossan's family also included his brother, Daniel, and sister, Aileen. In his interview with Blake, Crossan said that religion was never forced on him while he was growing up; in his family's home the subject was "undiscussed, uninvestigated and uncriticized," he explained. Nonetheless, he became an altar boy at the age of eight, writing in his memoir, *A Long Way from Tipperary* (2000), "Was I particularly pious as a boy? No, at least not in any sense of that word I knew then or have come to recognize since. . . . It may have been piety, but I thought of it as fun, as adventure, as seeing the inside of something mysterious, and maybe even, at eight and after, as a sort of instant adulthood."

Crossan graduated from St. Eunan's College, an all-male secondary school in the town of Letterkenny, in 1950. Then, at the age of 16, he traveled to the U.S. to join the Roman Catholic monastic order known as the Servites, which had a monastery in Chicago. There, he studied at Stonebridge Seminary, in nearby Lake Bluff, Illinois; having already taken courses in Latin and Greek for five years, he was encouraged to become a scholar. In 1957 Crossan, at 23, was ordained a priest. He then returned to Ireland and studied at St. Patrick's College, in Maynooth (often referred to as Maynooth College), receiving a doctorate in theology in 1959. From that year until 1961 he conducted postdoctoral research at the Pontifical Biblical Institute in Rome, Italy, and from 1961 to 1965, he served as assistant professor of biblical studies at Stonebridge Seminary. He then studied at the École Biblique et Archéologique Française de Jérusalem (French Institute of Bible and Archaeology in Jerusalem), in Israel, from 1965 to 1967. By that time he had established himself as a New Testament scholar and an expert on the parables of Jesus.

Returning to the U.S. in 1967, Crossan served for a year as assistant professor of biblical studies at St. Mary of the Lake Seminary, in Mundelein, Illinois. He then joined the faculty at the newly formed Chicago Catholic Theological Union, in Illinois, as assistant professor of biblical studies. Around that time he began to have doubts about his decision to become a priest; in his memoir he wrote, "For me, by the 1960s, the monastic priesthood had become less important than biblical scholarship, and clerical celibacy had become much less important than female relationship." He often questioned why church officials encouraged him to orient his research toward conclusions that were in line with church doctrine. He said in his interview with Blake, "It's like you're a scientist in research and development, and you say that this drug is lethal, and they say, 'Find something good in it.'"

Crossan recounted in his memoir that it was the reaction to his appearance as part of a panel on a Chicago PBS television program, in which he criticized Pope Paul VI's 1968 encyclical forbidding artificial birth control, that helped trigger his exit from the priesthood, in 1969. During that program, he wrote, "I repeatedly made a simple comparison. There were many Americans who deeply loved their country and respected their legitimate leaders but considered them totally, irresponsibly, and immorally wrong about Vietnam. . . . There were similarly many Roman Catholics who deeply loved their church and respected their legitimate leaders, but considered them totally, irresponsibly, and immorally wrong about birth control." His statements on the show angered church leaders. Another factor in his decision to leave the priesthood was his desire to marry Margaret Dagenais, a professor at Loyola University in Chicago. The two were wed in 1969.

Late in that same year, Crossan accepted a post as associate professor of religious studies at DePaul University. He remained with the school for the rest of his teaching career, becoming a full professor in 1973 and retiring as emeritus professor of religious studies in 1995. In the fall of 1996, Crossan was the Croghan bicentennial visiting professor of religion at Williams College, in Williamstown, Massachusetts. During his time as a professor and afterward, he wrote the many books on the historical Jesus that established his reputation.

Crossan's first books were *Scanning the Sunday Gospel* (1966) and *The Gospel of Eternal Life* (1967). *In Parables: The Challenge of the Historical Jesus* (1973, reprinted in 1992) was his first foray into the subject with which he is most closely identified. In that book Crossan examined the parables of Jesus—the stories attributed to Jesus found in the three Synoptic Gospels (Matthew, Mark, and Luke) of the New Testament. That work was followed by *The Dark Interval: Towards a Theology of Story* (1975, reprinted in 1988), which further expounded on biblical parable. According to a description of the book on the Westar Institute Web site, "From myth to parable, Crossan identifies five types of stories. Among these types it is parable that subverts the world and undercuts the safe shelter we build. Using literary theory, philosophy, theology and biblical studies, he demonstrates the subversive power of the parable."

Crossan's subsequent books include *Raid on the Articulate: Comic Eschatology in Jesus and Borges* (1976), about the religious themes in the work of the Argentine writer Jorge Luis Borges, and *Finding Is the First Act: Trove Folktales and Jesus' Treasure Parable* (1979), which, according to the book's preface, "places historical thinking in creative tension with literary appreciation. The structures of Jesus's parable of the hidden treasure (Matt 13:44) are examined by mapping its plot options (finding, acting, buying) in view of other Jewish treasure stories and the vast array of treasure plots in world folklore. Startling differences emerge in the plot options chosen by Jesus that point to a new understanding of the directive to give up all one has for the Kingdom of God."

That book was followed by *Cliffs of Fall: Paradox and Polyvalence in the Parables of Jesus* (1980); *A Fragile Craft: The Work of Amos Niven Wilder* (1981), about that 20th-century New Testament scholar; *In Fragments: The Aphorisms of Jesus* (1983); and *Four Other Gospels: Shadows on* the Contours of Canon (1985, reprinted in 1992), which discusses the noncanonical gospels, or gospel literature not included in the New Testament. (The canonical gospels are those of Matthew, Mark, Luke, and John; the others include the Gospel of Thomas, the Secret Gospel of Mark, the Gospel of Peter, and Papyrus Egerton 2.) In that book Crossan examined the ways in which the noncanonical gospels influenced those in the canon. A synopsis from the publisher, posted on the Barnes and Noble Web site, reads, "These four other gospels have generally been regarded as mere digests or collages of the canonical gospels, whereas in fact, as Professor Crossan persuasively shows, the four others hold within their mutilated fragments independent or earlier traditions than those tradition has canonized. . . . Four Other Gospels does not propose a new or alternative canon. The canon is a fact both of history and of theology. But the thesis of this book is that anyone who takes the four other gospels seriously and thoughtfully will never again be able to read the four canonical gospels in quite the same way. A new light has been shed." Crossan next wrote Sayings Parallels: A Workbook for the Jesus Tradition (1986) and The Cross that Spoke: The Origins of the Passion Narrative (1988).

In 1991 Crossan's The Historical Jesus: The Life of a Mediterranean Jewish Peasant was published, becoming his most successful work and propelling its author to the forefront of religious scholarship and debate. The initial attention given the book was due in part to the page-one New York Times article (December 23, 1991) by Peter Steinfels, which mentioned Crossan's work in discussing research into the historical Jesus. In writing The Historical Jesus, Crossan used historical fact, literary analysis, and the findings of various anthropological studies to reach his conclusion that Jesus was a peasant and a subversive, revolutionary figure who wanted to effect social change through his teachings about God. "Professor Crossan's book reflects a shift away from the depiction of Jesus as proclaiming an imminent end of the world and coming of God's kingdom," Steinfels wrote. "The professor argues that although Jesus was originally a follower of the apocalyptic prophet, John the Baptist, he became a wisdom teacher using Zen-like aphorisms and puzzling parables to challenge social conventions. By His parables, miraculous healings performed without reward, itinerant lifestyle and insistence that meals be shared with all and sundry, Jesus challenged the Mediterranean codes of honor and patronage, the professor says, as well as all the hierarchical and patriarchal assumptions of Jewish religion and Roman imperial power."

Crossan's methodology involved setting the historical information available about Jesus in the context of the social and political atmosphere of Jesus's time. He told Rose Simone for the Kitchener-Waterloo, Ontario, Canada, Record (April 10, 1993), "We have four Gospel accounts of the life of Jesus written 40 to 60 years after he died from the point of view of people who believed Jesus was, for them, a manifestation of God. It's sort of like having a biography of a presidential candidate written by his adoring daughter—it's not lies, but it's not exactly history either. The historical problem is how do you get back, through the screen of interpretation, to what was there when the interpretation began." Simone wrote that what Crossan "ends up with is a picture of Jesus as a Jewish peasant who became a social revolutionary, and who lived his ideas by example." "He didn't just have an idea about how life should be if God were really in charge, but he also had a program. Without that program, he probably wouldn't have gotten himself killed," Crossan told Simone.

Crossan's subsequent books on Jesus include The Essential Jesus: Original Sayings and Earliest Images (1994); Jesus: A Revolutionary Biography (1994), a volume for laypeople addressing the themes of The Historical Jesus; Who Killed Jesus? Exposing the Roots of Anti-Semitism in the Gospel Story of the Death of Jesus (1995); The Birth of Christianity: Discovering What Happened in the Years Immediately After the Execution of Jesus (1998); Excavating Jesus: Beneath the Stones, Behind the Texts (with Jonathan L. Reed, 2001), a book that examines the archaeological evidence backing many of Crossan's assertions; In Search of Paul: How Jesus's Apostle Opposed Rome's Empire with God's Kingdom (with Jonathan L. Reed, 2004); and The Last Week: What the Gospels Really Teach About Jesus's Final Days in Jerusalem (with Marcus J. Borg, 2006). The last-named book was also published with the subtitle A Day-by-Day Account of Jesus's Final Week in Jerusalem.

Crossan's 2007 book, God and Empire: Jesus Against Rome, Then and Now, examines Jesus's nonviolent attempt to usurp Roman authority through his teachings about the kingdom of God; the book compares the Roman Empire to the U.S. According to a description from the book's publisher, "Crossan reveals what the Bible has to say about land and economy, violence and retribution, justice and peace, and, ultimately, redemption. In contrast to the oppressive Roman military occupation of the first century, he examines the meaning of the non-violent Kingdom of God prophesized by Jesus and the equality advocated by [the apostle] Paul to the early Christian churches. Crossan contrasts these messages of peace with the misinterpreted apocalyptic vision from the Book of Revelation, which has been misrepresented by modern right-wing theologians and televangelists to justify U.S. military actions in the Middle East." In the 2009 book The First Paul: Reclaiming the Radical Visionary Behind the Church's Conservative Icon, which Crossan wrote with Marcus J. Borg, he turned his attention again to Paul, arguing that letters attributed to the apostle that condemn homosexuality and condone slavery and the subordination of women were, in fact, written by members of the early church in order to render Paul's philosophies less radical.

Crossan's most recent book, *The Greatest Prayer: Rediscovering the Revolutionary Message of the Lord's Prayer*, was published in 2010. In it he examined the history and meaning behind the Lord's Prayer (also known as the "Our Father" and the "Abba Prayer") and analyzed the words of the prayer in the context of the Bible. He concluded that the prayer is a manifesto reinforcing Jesus's themes of justice, equality, and nonviolence. According to a *Booklist* description posted on cathedralbookstore.org, "This seemingly radical exegesis will be as welcome to some as it is disconcerting to others. Even if one disagrees with the author's conclusions, it will be difficult to dislike his book, as one of Crossan's gifts is his ability to challenge his readers in a gentle, respectful, and nonconfrontational manner."

Crossan's views on the life of Jesus, informed by his research, have often brought criticism from those who believe the Gospel stories should be taken literally and that supernatural events were part of the life of Jesus. He believes that Jesus did not physically rise from the dead—that the resurrection story is, rather, a parable. He has also argued that stories of the many miracles associated with Jesus in the minds of Christians, such as the virgin birth and the predicted Rapture—during which Christians will rise to heaven—are not rooted in fact. Crossan believes that Jesus did not die on the cross for the sins of humanity according to God's plan, but was crucified—and thus martyred—by Roman leaders because he was a peasant rebel who posed a threat to their authority. In defense of his arguments and statements about the historical Jesus, which some have condemned as anti-Christian, Crossan explained to Blake that he has only sought the truth and that he is "trying to understand the stories of Jesus, not refute them." In his memoir he recalled that his interest in the historical Jesus was shaped by the Roman Catholic leaders who put him on course, during his years of study, to become a biblical scholar. The role of biblical scholar "was thrust upon me by others," he wrote, "but I accepted the role with enthusiasm. . . . Since it was neither my idea nor my plan, I have been quite comfortable with the controversies accompanying that role."

Criticism of Crossan's work has continued, with some claiming that the scholar has weakened the importance of Jesus to the detriment of the Christian faith. Ben Witherington, a New Testament scholar, told Blake that Crossan's work has made it easier for some to question whether Jesus was actually God's son and what importance, if any, he has for their lives. Witherington said that Crossan had put forth the idea of "a user-friendly Jesus that doesn't make demands on someone." The stories about Jesus, Witherington said, "are inherently theological. They all suggest that God intervenes in history. If you have a problem with the supernatural, you have a problem with the Bible. It's on every page."

After the publication of *The Historical Jesus*, Crossan discovered that he and his fellow historical-Jesus scholars were not alone, as the concept they embraced was finding greater acceptance among modern Christians. In his memoir he wrote that "those centrist Christians demanded both reason *and* revelation, both history *and* faith, both mind *and* heart. They knew that history was not just history anymore and that Jesus research opened up all the theological and religious questions worth asking." As a result of the growing interest in the topic, over the past two decades Crossan has appeared on television programs and lectured at parish seminars about the historical Jesus. He told Blake that when historical-Jesus scholars "started out, people thought we were out on the left wing. Now, I'm talking in about 30 churches a year. . . . A lot of this is becoming mainstream."

In 1985, along with Robert Funk, a fellow biblical scholar, Crossan founded the Jesus Seminar, whose members study the historical Jesus, vote on which information they consider historically accurate, and work to spread awareness of the historical Jesus to the public. The seminar is supported by the nonprofit Westar Institute. Crossan is a former co-chair of the seminar. He is also a former chair of the Historical Jesus Section of the Society of Biblical Literature. He has received many honors, including the Award for Excellence in Religious Studies from the American Academy of Religion (1989), the Cortelyou-Lowery Award for Excellence and the Via Sapientiae Award from DePaul University (1991 and 1995, respectively), and an honorary doctorate from Stetson University (2003). He has lectured around the world, and his books have been translated into many languages. Crossan is now a U.S. citizen and lives in Orlando, Florida, with his wife, Sarah, a yoga instructor. His first wife, Margaret Dagenais, died of a heart attack in 1983.

Crossan, despite his religious faith, has not joined a church since he left the priesthood. "If I attend a local Roman Catholic Church, I would get sucked back into all the debates," he told Blake. "I don't want to spend my life fighting Roman Catholicism."

—W.D.

Suggested Reading: CNN (on-line) Feb. 27, 2011; johndominiccrossan.com; (Kitchener-Waterloo, Ontario, Canada) *Record* A p11 Apr. 10, 1991; *New York Times* A p1+ Dec. 23, 1991; (Toronto, Canada) *Globe and Mail* C p17 June 26, 1999; westarinstitute.org; Crossan, John Dominic. *A Long Way from Tipperary*, 2000

Selected Books: *In Parables: The Challenge of the Historical Jesus*, 1973, reprinted in 1992; *The Dark Interval: Towards a Theology of Story*, 1975, reprinted in 1988; *Raid on the Articulate: Comic Eschatology in Jesus and Borges*,1976; *Finding Is the First Act: Trove Folktales and Jesus' Treasure Parable*, 1979; *Cliffs of Fall:*

Paradox and Polyvalence in the Parables of
Jesus, 1980; A Fragile Craft: The Work of Amos
Niven Wilder, 1981; In Fragments: The
Aphorisms of Jesus, 1983; Four Other Gospels:
Shadows on the Contours of Canon, 1985,
reprinted in 1992; Sayings Parallels: A Workbook
for the Jesus Tradition, 1986; The Cross that
Spoke: The Origins of the Passion Narrative,
1988; The Historical Jesus: The Life of a
Mediterranean Jewish Peasant, 1991; The
Essential Jesus: Original Sayings and Earliest
Images, 1994; Jesus: A Revolutionary Biography,
1994; Who Killed Jesus? Exposing the Roots of
AntiSemitism in the Gospel Story of the Death of
Jesus, 1995; The Birth of Christianity:
Discovering What Happened in the Years

Immediately After the Execution of Jesus, 1998;
Excavating Jesus: Beneath the Stones, Behind the
Texts (with Jonathan L. Reed), 2001; In Search of
Paul: How Jesus's Apostle Opposed Rome's
Empire with God's Kingdom (with Reed), 2004;
The Last Week: What the Gospels Really Teach
About Jesus's Final Days in Jerusalem (with
Marcus J. Borg, also published with the subtitle
A Day-by-Day Account of Jesus's Final Week in
Jerusalem), 2006; God and Empire: Jesus Against
Rome, Then and Now, 2007; The First Paul:
Reclaiming the Radical Visionary Behind the
Church's Conservative Icon (with Borg), 2009;
The Greatest Prayer: Rediscovering the
Revolutionary Message of The Lord's Prayer,
2010

Evan Agostini/Getty Images

Crowley, Candy

Dec. 26, 1948– Television journalist

Address: State of the Union, CNN, 820 First St.,
N.E., Washington, DC 20002-4243

Until Sunday, February 7, 2010 the veteran broadcast journalist Candy Crowley was the "perennial
smart lady some well-lit anchor would conjure via
satellite to explain Washington," Ellen McCarthy
wrote for the Washington Post (August 24, 2010,
on-line). "She'd talk, he'd nod. Then the cameras
would turn away; he'd move on to a hurricane
watch or pop-star update, and she'd blink back to
political Neverland." At 9:00 a.m. Eastern Standard Time on that day, at the age of 61, Crowley

made her debut as the host of State of the Union,
the Cable News Network's Sunday-morning news-
and-interview program. During the previous 28
years, Crowley had reported on national and world
events for, in succession, a Washington, D.C., radio
station, the Associated Press (in two stints separated by seven years), the Mutual Broadcasting System (a radio network), NBC-TV News, and, since
1987, CNN, as that network's White House and
Capitol Hill correspondent and then as its senior
political correspondent. Crowley's profile on
CNN's Web site offers a sample of the wide range
of events she has covered: "Among her most vivid
memories as a reporter, Crowley counts the aftermath of Hurricane Katrina in the Gulf Coast; the
impeachment trial of President Clinton; Election
Night 2000; ceremonies marking the 40th anniversary of D-Day on the beaches of Normandy; Ronald
Reagan's trips to China, Bitburg and Bergen-
Belsen; the night the United States bombed Libya;
and the terrorist bombing of the U.S. Marine barracks in Beirut."

Crowley has reported from all 50 states and
many countries overseas; attended all but one of
the Democratic and Republican National Conventions beginning with those of 1976; and accompanied 10 major-party candidates during their presidential campaigns, from the Republican Ronald
Reagan's run, in 1980, to the Democrat Barack Obama's, in 2008. The documentary filmmaker Alexandra Pelosi, who traveled with Crowley during
two of those campaigns, told McCarthy, "She's like
the CliffNotes for all other reporters. They talk
about those things that nobody reads—nobody
reads bills. But Candy does. She reads all of that
stuff. She reads everything. On the [campaign] bus,
everyone would just go to her and ask her, 'Candy,
so what's this bill about?'" Molly Boyle, a former
CNN colleague of Crowley's, told McCarthy, "She
has a very logical mind, so when she's covering a
story or an issue, she's able to cut through all this
stuff and get to what's at the core of it. And then,
because she's such an incredible writer, she's able

to take that and explain it to you in a way that not only makes sense, but is beautiful to hear." The current senior executive producer of *State of the Union*, Tom Bettag, who executive-produced both *CBS Evening News with Dan Rather* and ABC's *Nightline* when it was anchored by Ted Koppel, said to McCarthy, "What [Crowley] brings is a real humanity. She's got that mix of, 'You would absolutely believe her and go to her in a crisis, but you would also enjoy having dinner with her.'"

The daughter of Richard Casper Alt, a furniture salesman, and Nadine Lois (Webster) Alt, a homemaker, Crowley was born Candy Alt on December 26, 1948 in Kalamazoo, Michigan. Her brother, Howard, works in the furniture business. Her family moved to St. Louis, Missouri, when she was six months old, and she grew up in Creve Coeur, a St. Louis suburb. From kindergarten through 12th grade, Crowley attended the Principia School, whose Web site describes it as a community based on the principles of Christian Science, though the school is not affiliated with the Christian Science church and does not offer instruction in Christian Science. She graduated in 1966 and then entered Randolph-Macon Women's College, in Lynchburg, Virginia (known as Randolph College since 2007, when it became co-educational). She earned an A.B. degree in English there in 1970. At that time, she told McCarthy, "I was wildly in love with this guy. I thought I would marry him, move to California, have five kids, iron his shirts and write the Great American Novel." When her relationship with her college boyfriend ended, Crowley moved to Washington, D.C., and looked for work. She found a job as a writer for the newsletter of a chemical-manufacturers trade association and, as a freelancer, wrote for the National Education Association's magazine.

At age 22 Crowley married a television producer. When her husband heard about an opening at Metromedia's WASH-FM, a local radio station, he suggested that Crowley apply for the position. In 1972 WASH-FM hired her as a newsroom assistant, a job that entailed "basic gopher work, calling around to find out what happened the night before," Crowley told Brian Stelter for *Mediabistro.com* (February 5, 2007). According to Ellen McCarthy, Crowley "worked a split shift producing traffic and crime reports during morning and evening drive times." In 1974 Crowley landed a job as a general-assignment reporter for Associated Press (AP) Radio. From 1975 to 1977 she worked as a reporter for the Mutual Broadcasting System, a radio network that operated nationally. She became the mother of two boys around the time her family moved to Iowa, where her husband had taken a job. For several years Crowley was a full-time homemaker. She has expressed thankfulness for being able to remain at home when her sons were small. "I'm not sure you always appreciate those times when you're in them," she told McCarthy. "But I look back and say to everybody, 'Take it off—your career will find you. Trust me, when you go back, it'll find you.'"

By the time her younger son was ready to enter kindergarten, the Crowleys had moved back to Washington. Crowley rejoined the AP in 1981, and during the next few years, she became a White House correspondent for the agency. At a press conference in the spring of 1986 in which President Ronald Reagan discussed plans to respond in kind to Libyan aggression against U.S. aircraft in the Gulf of Sidra, she asked Reagan, "How does a show of force show that we're against force?" The next day an NBC representative invited her to take a screen test, as a prelude to a possible job on TV. She was hired as an NBC News correspondent almost immediately, but within a year, after a series of corporate cutbacks, she lost her job. By that time Crowley and her husband had divorced, and Crowley had assumed most of the day-to-day and financial responsibility for raising her children. In 1987 she found steady work as a White House and Capitol Hill correspondent for CNN, at first as a freelancer and then as a full-time employee. In the early 1990s CNN promoted her to national political correspondent.

Until her sons were both in college, Crowley never accepted assignments that required her to be away from home for more than five days at a time. Afterward, while reporting on presidential campaigns, she was often on the road for weeks at a stretch. Presidential hopefuls (both successful and unsuccessful) whose campaigns she covered include the Republicans Pat Buchanan, Ronald Reagan, George H. W. Bush, Bob Dole, and George W. Bush and the Democrats Jesse Jackson, Bill Clinton, Howard Dean, John Kerry, and Barack Obama. Karen Hughes, who served in 2001 and 2002 as an adviser to President George W. Bush and as a public-affairs official in the U.S. State Department (2005–07) later in Bush's administration, said of Crowley to McCarthy, "I think everyone enjoyed her. She has that great laugh and is just a lot of fun. And some of the interviews I've done with her are some of the best interviews that I can remember doing. She's probing and difficult and tough . . . but there's not the air of confrontation that you get from some interviewers."

At the end of 2008, Crowley, feeling run-down after nearly 18 months on the road, resolved to improve her health during the next 12 months by working out with a personal trainer and maintaining a proper diet. "I just wanted to be a better person. I wanted to feel better," she told McCarthy. "And if at the end of the year I just hated it, then I'd go do whatever I want." In addition to exercising and eating well, she trained with a Transcendental Meditation instructor. She now meditates for 20 minutes every morning and night. "I find that my thought is clearer," she told McCarthy. "I still get mad. I still get upset. But I let it go more quickly." During that year of more-healthful living, Crowley thought about leaving journalism and writing a novel.

On November 12, 2009, the day after the commentator Lou Dobbs abruptly left CNN, the network announced that in early 2010, John King would end his stint as host of the Sunday-morning program *State of the Union* to fill the time slot vacated by Dobbs. At the urging of a friend, Crowley expressed to CNN executives her interest in taking King's place on *State of the Union*. Crowley explained to McCarthy that having her own show had long been a dream that she never allowed herself to think about seriously. "People always used to say to me, 'Don't you want your own show? That'd be so cool if you had your own show.' I said, 'You know, it's not gonna happen. So—no.'" Crowley had just returned from a trip to New Zealand with her sons when Jon Klein, CNN's president, offered her King's job. "I think Candy's got a disarming approach," Klein told McCarthy. "She's never looking to snooker anybody. She's just talking to you. And I think that because she is so real in the conversations, the people she's interviewing become very real, too."

After CNN announced in January 2010 that on February 7 Crowley would make her debut as the host of *State of the Union*, Crowley received many e-mail messages and letters of congratulations. A large portion of them came from women who expressed their admiration for her accomplishments and their happiness that CNN had recognized her value. Crowley's promotion would make her the first woman to anchor a Sunday-morning public-affairs show since Cokie Roberts, who, with Sam Donaldson, co-hosted ABC's *This Week* from 1996 to 2002. (The only other women who hosted Sunday-morning public-affairs interview shows before Crowley were the pioneering newscaster Martha Rountree, the first host of NBC's *Meet the Press*, who held that position from 1947 to 1953, and Lesley Stahl, who hosted CBS's *Face the Nation* from 1983 to 1991. On August 1, 2010 Christiane Amanpour became the host of ABC's *This Week*.) In an interview with Chris Rovzar for *New York* (March 5, 2010, on-line), Crowley said, "When Jon offered me the job I just thought, 'What a good journalistic opportunity. This is gonna be really fun.' . . . I didn't really think about the whole female part of it until I started getting all these e-mails." The news of Crowley's promotion also triggered many discussions in blogs and elsewhere about Crowley's recent weight loss and whether it might have influenced CNN's decision to make her King's successor. "Would I have gotten the job without having lost the weight? I don't know. That's an X factor," Crowley told Stelter. She also said to him, "I'm not the most obvious pick, from a purely cosmetic point of view. I'm not going to argue that when you turn on the TV, you basically get young, blonde, thin women. This is changing."

Regarding the format and content of *State of the Union*, Crowley planned no major changes. "I don't think the core of the Sunday genre changes," she told Rovzar. "I think you want to have people on to either explain last week, or to look into next week. Still, one of the things that Jon Klein told me when I got the job was, 'I don't want Candy Crowley to do John King's show, I want Candy Crowley to do Candy Crowley's show.' And I wish that I could delineate for you what that is. For instance—and this is a small thing—last week we got a smaller table. And it made for a more intimate discussion, which I liked. I have topics that I've written out that I think would be nice to cover, but I don't have specific questions, because I like to listen to the answers and just see where it's going." She also told him, "I'm not by nature an interrupter; it may be my Midwest background. But there comes a time when someone goes on and on, and you have to say: 'Yes, but let me just . . .' I try to do it in a way that I'm comfortable with it. It's hard." "My Dad always used to say, 'Never criticize a man unless you've walked a mile in his shoes,'" Crowley said during an on-line chat for *All Things Anderson* (May 7, 2009, on-line). "It's how I approach my interviews. The interviewee has something to say, born of experiences I haven't had. I am so curious to know what they think that my opinions just don't pop into my head. No interview is about me or what I think."

On February 7, 2010, her first morning as host of *State of the Union*, Crowley interviewed Secretary of State Hillary Clinton about U.S. relations with Iran and North Korea. Her guest the next week was National Security Adviser James Jones, who talked about military and political conditions in Afghanistan. On February 21, 2010 she discussed with House Speaker Nancy Pelosi the status of the Obama administration's proposed comprehensive health-care bill. On November 28, 2010 Crowley spoke with Arizona senator John McCain about North Korea, financial regulatory reform, and relations between Democratic and Republican politicians. On other fronts, Crowley also discussed the redecoration of the Oval Office; the U.S. Senate's unanimous passage of the Commercial Advertisement Loudness Mitigation Act; and the second birthday of Bo, the Obama family's dog.

In her free time Crowley enjoys playing bridge and, weather permitting, swimming daily in the lap pool in her Bethseda, Maryland, backyard. In her interview with McCarthy, she offered one piece of advice for young people: "Don't plan too hard, because something much better might be out there." Crowley's older son, Richard Webster Crowley, is a surgeon. Her second son, Jonathan Milligan Crowley, is a rock musician; his band, Vinyette, released its debut album, *Hawkins Sessions*, in 2010. Crowley also has a stepdaughter and a stepson and several step-grandchildren.

—H.R.W.

Suggested Reading: allthingscnn.com June 7, 2009; CNN.com; *Los Angeles Times* (on-line) Nov. 18, 2009; *Mediabistro.com* Feb. 5, 2007; *New York* (on-line) Mar. 5, 2010; *Washington Post* (on-line) Aug. 24, 2010

Scott Wintrow/Getty Images

Cunningham, Bill

Mar. 13, 1929– Photographer; writer

Address: New York Times, *620 Eighth Ave., New York, NY 10018*

The photographer Bill Cunningham has been documenting fashion—what people wear day to day—in New York City since the 1960s. His subjects are ordinary New Yorkers and visitors to the city as well as celebrities and other newsmakers, but only people whose apparel strikes him as fascinating or beautiful. To the general public Cunningham is best known as the man behind the "On the Street" and "Evening Hours" columns, which have appeared in the Style section of the Sunday *New York Times* every week since the early 1990s. For "On the Street" Cunningham—whose primary means of transportation and frequent perch is his bicycle—occasionally takes photos in Central Park, Madison Square Park, Governors Island, Union Square, and, during Fashion Week, all over Midtown Manhattan; but his usual location, where he often spends hours a day, is the intersection of Fifth Avenue and 57th Street. Cunningham "seeks out and captures humanity amid the maelstrom of life . . . ," Carina Chocano wrote for the *New York Times* (March 15, 2011). "In these fleeting and otherwise unseen or unremarked moments, Mr. Cunningham finds something creative, life-affirming and free, and preserves it forever." "He'll do anything for the shot," Kim Hastreiter, the co-founder and co-editor of *Paper* magazine, told Richard Press, whose documentary about the photographer's life and work, *Bill Cunningham New York*, premiered in 2011. "I've been in deep conversations with him where

he'll just run from me because he sees someone"—that is, someone wearing an interesting outfit whom he has spied out of the corner of his eye. Cunningham does not hold preconceived ideas about fashion trends. "I don't decide anything [in advance]," he told Richard Press, "I let the street speak to me; and in order for the street to speak to you, you've got to stay out there and see what it is."

For the first dozen years of his professional life, starting in about 1949 (except for the two years he served in the U.S. Army), Cunningham made hats of his own design. His creations attracted a *New York Times* fashion reporter and purchasers including the rich and famous—Ginger Rogers and other actresses and members of the Vanderbilt and Kennedy families, for example. During the 1960s and '70s, he wrote about fashion for *Women's Wear Daily* and the *Chicago Tribune*. He later contributed fashion photos to the *SoHo News*, *Details*, and, starting in 1978, the *New York Times*. The text that accompanies his photos in "On the Street" reflects his journalistic sense for storytelling. For "Evening Hours" Cunningham attends fund-raising events for museums, hospitals, schools, libraries, and other nonprofit enterprises, but only those whose missions and methods meet his approval.

Writing for the *New Yorker* (March 16, 2009), Lauren Collins likened "On the Street" and "Evening Hours" to a series of New York City high-school yearbooks, "an exuberant, sometimes retroactively embarrassing chronicle of the way we looked. Class of 1992: velvet neck ribbons, leopard prints, black jeans, catsuits, knotted shirts, tote bags. . . . Class of 2000: clamdiggers, beaded fringe, postcard prints, jean jackets, fish-net stockings, flower brooches (this was the height of *Sex and the City*). The column, in its way, is as much a portrait of New York at a given moment in time as any sociological tract or census—a snapshot of the city." Cunningham's "weekly roundups of sidewalk and nightlife shots beloved by fashion doyens and people-watchers alike . . . have gained an avid, almost cultish following," Nathan Heller wrote for *Slate.com* (March 18, 2011). Kenneth Turan wrote for the *Los Angeles Times* (March 28, 2011), "Because Cunningham's interest is so undeniably pure, and because he doesn't believe in mocking or unkind photographs, he has legions of devoted readers, including society types."

According to Cunningham, "Fashion is the armor to survive the reality of every day life." Since the spring of 2008, in addition to his *Times* print-edition columns, he has provided a weekly photo slideshow with voiceover commentary for the *New York Times* Web site. As his photos slide by, Cunningham, in his cheery, old-fashioned Boston accent—pronouncing "marvelous" as MAAH-vah-lous—talks about trends and how they relate to the season, weather conditions, and even the economy. "It's more than mere picture taking," Philip Gefter, the producer of *Bill Cunningham New York*, told Richard Press for *New York* (March 6, 2011), "it's cultural anthropology—the intersection of fashion and society in New York City."

The second of four children, William J. Cunningham was born into an Irish Catholic family on March 13, 1929 in Boston, Massachusetts. According to "Bill on Bill," a 2,100-word autobiography he wrote for the *New York Times* (October 27, 2002), as a child Cunningham would sometimes photograph people at parties and ski resorts. But his first true passion was fashion. "I could never concentrate on Sunday church services because I'd be concentrating on women's hats," he wrote in "Bill on Bill." At the Bonwit Teller department store in Boston, where the teenage Cunningham worked as a stock boy, an executive noticed that Cunningham's lunch-break pastime was watching passersby. In "Bill on Bill," Cunningham recalled her telling him, "If you think what they're wearing is wrong, why don't you redo them in your mind's eye." That, he wrote, was "the first professional direction I received." Cunningham attended Harvard University, in Cambridge, Massachusetts, for one term, then dropped out, at age 19, in 1948. "Harvard," he wrote, "wasn't for me at all."

Cunningham then moved in with an aunt and uncle in New York City and got a job in the advertising department at Bonwit Teller. "Advertising was also my uncle's profession," he wrote. "That's why my family allowed me to come here and encouraged me to go into the business. I think they were worried I was becoming too interested in women's dresses. But it's been my hobby all my life." A year later, after some pressure from his family to pick a career path, Cunningham decided to become a milliner (a hat maker). He ruled out designing other apparel because of the expense. Lacking the funds to rent his own apartment, he found a single room in a building on East 57th Street near Park Avenue, up several flights of narrow stairs, and set up his hat shop and living quarters there. He supplemented his income by working at a drugstore during lunchtime and at a hotel at night. To protect his family's privacy, Cunningham named his business "William J." Among his early patrons were socialite clients of the very expensive nearby dress shop Chez Ninon, who included members of the Vanderbilt, Astor, and Kennedy families, including First Lady Jacqueline Kennedy and President John F. Kennedy's sisters and sisters-in-law. Chez Ninon's owners—whom Cunningham had met during his time at Bonwit's—directed those and other wealthy women to William J.

A brief item that appeared in the February 9, 1951 edition of the *New York Times* mentioned the "diversity of silhouette and material" and "individuality" of the hats Cunningham had brought to display at a Plaza Hotel luncheon. Several paragraphs devoted exclusively to his creations were published in the *Times* on April 5, 1951, after the fashion journalist Virginia Pope came to his first fashion show, held in the garden behind his building. Cunningham's hat business was thriving when, later in 1951, during the Korean War, he was drafted into the U.S. Army. After his military discharge, two years later, he returned to New York

and opened a salon in a brownstone on West 54th Street. In an article for the *New York Times* (January 29, 1954) headlined "Sculptural Theme Marks First Showing By Young Milliner Back From Army Duty," he was described as having "his own ideas about millinery" and "a fresh approach." His designs ranged from the elegant and "irresistibly pretty," in the words of the *Times* reporter, to the outrageous and bizarre. "I remember he had this hat in the window with fringe hanging from the brim to the ground," the illustrator Joe Eula told Cathy Horyn for the *New York Times* (October 27, 2002). "It was a bathing suit hat, and you were supposed to change your clothes behind the fringe. I called up Sally Kirkland, who was the fashion editor at *Life*, and I said, 'You've got to see this!' She put it in *Life*. Bill was an absolute innovator right from the get-go." Thanks to word of mouth, such film stars as Marilyn Monroe, Joan Crawford, and Ginger Rogers came to Cunningham to buy hats. During Fashion Week in 1956, most of the cast of the Broadway musical *My Fair Lady* attended Cunningham's late-night fashion show.

In the early 1960s, around the time when women's fashion designers started to drop hats from their collections, Cunningham received an offer to write for the trade journal *Women's Wear Daily* (now called *WWD*), widely considered to be the bible of the fashion industry. He had never written for a newspaper or a magazine, and he suspected that *WWD*'s publisher, John Fairchild, had recruited him because Fairchild thought he would have the inside scoop on the clients at Chez Ninon. (In actuality, Chez Ninon's owners maintained strict confidentiality regarding their clients.) In any event, Cunningham proved to have a talent for writing. Mort Sheinman, *WWD*'s managing editor at the time, told Horyn that Cunningham "looked wide-eyed and dazzled. I don't think he was prepared for the environment of a newsroom . . . the unbelievable noise, the pounding of the manual typewriters, the clattering of the teletype machines, people shouting across the room. . . . In comes this hat designer, and Fairchild is giving him a column. I mean, a column! Immediately everybody resented him. . . . But once you met Bill, you stopped resenting him. He sure knew the fashion business, and he was a terrific reporter."

Cunningham continued to work at *Women's Wear Daily* until Fairchild killed his story about the designer Courrèges. "No, no, Saint Laurent is the one," Cunningham recalled Fairchild saying. The documentary *Bill Cunningham New York*, however, makes the case, via the testimony of many people in the know, that Cunningham left for another reason: He had taken photos of women on the street wearing that year's fashions and written accompanying text indicating the contrast between how fashions look on the runway and their appearance in real life. Instead of presenting a nonjudgmental juxtaposition, the magazine's editors changed Cunningham's layout and text to make fun of the women on the street. Furious, Cunningham quit *WWD* and went to work for the New York bureau of the *Chicago Tribune*, which had an office in the *New York Times* building.

In the mid-1960s the photographer David Montgomery, having learned that Cunningham's interest in taking pictures had deepened, gave him an Olympus Pen-D half-frame camera and advised him to "use it like a notebook," as Cunningham recalled in "Bill on Bill." "I had just the most marvelous time with that camera," Cunningham recalled. "Everybody I saw I was able to record, and that's what it's all about. I realized that you didn't know anything unless you photographed the shows and the street, to see how people interpreted what designers hoped they would buy. I realized that the street was the missing ingredient." In the late 1960s Cunningham started photographing young people—"the flower children," as he and others called them—hanging out at Sheep Meadow, in Central Park. "All these kids dressed in everything from their mother's and grandmother's trunks, lying on the grass,"Cunningham wrote. "It was unbelievable. It was all about the fashion revolution."

By the early 1970s the *New York Times* had started to buy Cunningham's photos. His pictures also appeared in the *SoHo Weekly News* and the New York *Daily News*. After the *SoHo Weekly News* folded, in the spring of 1982, some of its employees went on to found *Paper* magazine, and others founded *Details*. For the latter Cunningham took a great number of fashion photos, and the magazine sometimes dedicated more than 100 pages in a single issue to his photographs. Cunningham refused to take any money from *Details*, and in 1988, when the giant magazine-publishing company Condé Nast bought that publication, Cunningham refused a hefty payment for all his work. In *Bill Cunningham New York*, Cunningham said, "If you don't take money, they can't tell you what to do."

Cunningham's primary goal is to document clothes he finds interesting, regardless of who is wearing them; if someone is not dressed in a way that strikes him as "marvelous," he has no interest in photographing her or him. Nevertheless, his first major spread in the *New York Times* Style section (December 30, 1978)—his entry into what would soon become a weekly column—was a layout with photos of the rich and famous. (The former included Stanley Marcus, of the department-store chain Neiman Marcus; the latter, the actress Greta Garbo, John F. Kennedy's sister Patricia Kennedy Lawford, and the clothing and jewelry designer Paloma Picasso.)

Since then Cunningham has documented in his "On the Street" column New York City fashions of the 1980s, '90s, and the first decade of the new millennium. His first "Evening Hours" spread, which contained images of young adults at a benefit for the New York City Ballet, appeared in the *New York Times* on May 3, 1992.

During the last few summers, Cunningham has observed loose-fitting dresses, slim skirts, straw fedora hats, scarves, and even black clothing. In late fall and winter, he has noticed men wearing gloves with suit jackets, men in dress shoes and women in high heels jumping over huge melted-snow puddles (and women in fancy boots and galoshes stepping into them), people wearing bright colors such as red, orange, and purple in the middle of February, extremely high, "picture-frame" collars, and women wearing their old coats from seasons past—a trend Cunningham attributed to the poor economy. (The relationship between the economy and street fashion has been an occasional theme in his column.) Other trends include men and women wearing vests (often casually or semiformally), men wearing suits in nontraditional ways (with no tie or with pants slightly rolled up or with jacket and shirt sleeves unbuttoned), and women wearing "saucy" skirts that fit snugly at the hips but swing side-to-side at the hem. "I think fashion is as vital and as interesting today as ever," Cunningham wrote in "Bill on Bill." "I know what people with a more formal attitude mean when they say they're horrified by what they see on the street. But fashion is doing its job. It's mirroring exactly our times."

In the 1950s Cunningham moved into one of the tiny rent-controlled studio apartments located above the venerated New York City concert venue Carnegie Hall, on the corner of West 57th Street and Seventh Avenue, two blocks south of Central Park. The studios (there were once 170 of them) served as a kind of bohemian live/work space for artists, writers, musicians, singers, designers, photographers, and dancers. Cunningham's apartment had no kitchen; his bathroom was a communally shared facility in the hall. In May 2010 Cunningham was among the last five residents forced to vacate their apartments, after the Carnegie Hall Corp. decided to turn the residential area into educational and rehearsal spaces. The corporation resettled Cunningham in a small apartment a few blocks away. Like his former studio, his new apartment is jammed with the filing cabinets in which he keeps decades' worth of photo negatives. His other possessions amount to little more than a cot, a few articles of clothing, his camera, and his bicycle—his 29th. (Its 28 predecessors were all stolen.)

Bill Cunningham New York shows that "Cunningham's honesty, kindness and integrity . . . are what truly set him apart," Katie Fischer wrote for her blog thefischnette.com in 2011. His fascination with fashion notwithstanding, while at work he invariably wears the $20 royal-blue smock that comprises part of the uniform of Paris street cleaners, and when it rains a large plastic trash bag often serves to keep him dry. (He has said that he particularly enjoys photographing in the rain, because in inclement weather people are apt to take the least notice of him and to be the least self-conscious.) Carina Chocano described him as "an aesthete and an ascetic, a member of the establishment and a bohemian, and among the last of his kind."

In addition to his New York photography, Cunningham has photographed people on the streets of Paris, France, and models on the runway during that city's Fashion Week. In 2008 the French government honored Cunningham as an officer of the Order of Arts and Letters. In the same year Cunningham was among six people recognized by the Citizens Committee for New York City for making the city's communities "better, safer and more beautiful," according to panachemag.com.

Cunningham lives alone. In *Bill Cunningham New York*, he confessed to having never had a romantic relationship. He attends church services every Sunday.

—D.K.

Suggested Reading: *Esquire* (on-line) Mar. 25, 2010; *Los Angeles Times* D p6 Mar. 27, 2011; *New York* (on-line) Mar. 6, 2011; *New Yorker* (on-line) Mar. 16, 2009; *New York Times* Style p5, p13 Oct. 27, 2002

Dardenne, Jean-Pierre and Luc

Film directors and screenwriters

Dardenne, Jean-Pierre
Apr. 21, 1951–

Dardenne, Luc
Mar. 10, 1954–

Address: Les Films du Fleuve, 13 Quai de Gaulle, 4020 Liège, Belgium

The Belgian film writers and directors Jean-Pierre and Luc Dardenne, Xan Brooks wrote for the London *Guardian* (February 9, 2006), "are cinema's 'brothers grim,' professional gloom-mongers who trade in harsh, social-realist studies of the Belgian underclass." The Dardenne brothers—who share writing and directing credits on all of their films—are among the most critically respected filmmakers working in European cinema today; they are known for their gritty, cinema-verité style, which involves the use of hand-held cameras, natural lighting, and on-location sets and the eschewing of traditional musical scores and soundtracks. The Dardennes entered the film industry in the early 1970s as documentary filmmakers and branched out to fiction features in the late 1980s. They rose to prominence in 1996, with their third feature, *La Promesse* (The Promise), about a father and son involved in illegal operations involving immigrants. After earning rave reviews on the festival circuit, the film was picked up for distribution in the U.S., where it took home several awards as an international art-house release. The Dardennes won even more acclaim for their next feature, *Rosetta* (1999), which centers on a desperate, unemployed 17-

year-old Belgian girl; the film won the highly coveted Palme d'Or at the 1999 Cannes Film Festival. The Dardennes followed that up with *Le Fils* (*The Son*, 2002), which was also entered into Cannes's main competition, winning the festival's Ecumenical Jury Prize. In 2005 they garnered their second Palme d'Or—a rare feat—for *L'Enfant* (*The Child*, 2005), which tells the story of a financially struggling young couple who make a drastic decision. Their most recently released feature film, *Le Silence de Lorna* (*Lorna's Silence*, 2008), focuses on a young Albanian woman involved in a sham marriage with a drug addict as part of a scheme to open a business; the film won the award for best screenplay at the 2008 Cannes Film Festival. Commenting on the films that brought the brothers prominence, all of which deal with characters living on the margins of society in Belgium, Mark Jenkins wrote for the *Washington City Paper* (April 27, 2006), "Dardennes films are driven, fidgety, and wholly unsweetened, whether by music or sentimentality. Avoiding any hint of the picturesque— no one will ever consider arranging a tour of the brothers' Belgium—the movies seem naturalistic and yet supercharged, despite the fact that the scenes usually play in real time. Whether inspired or simply intimidated, their casts are equally intent, giving performances of unparalleled urgency and tenacious focus. The result is far from conventional entertainment but still thrilling to experience." Lance Goldenberg wrote for *Creative Loafing* (May 30, 2006), "The Dardennes' films . . . are like no one else's, although they are clearly extensions of an earlier time, an unfashionably serious auteur-cinema that's much admired abroad and anathema in the land of the multiplex." The Dardennes' next film, *Le Gamin au velo* (The Kid with a Bike), is scheduled to be released in 2011.

The Dardenne brothers were born in Engis, a town on the Meuse River in the French-speaking Wallonia region of southeast Belgium—Jean-Pierre on April 21, 1951 and Luc on March 10, 1954. They grew up and attended school in Seraing, a neighboring, working-class city known for its steel industry; during the years of the brothers' boyhood, the city saw strikes and public demonstrations that resulted from the government's decision to raise taxes while slashing pensions and unemployment benefits. The pollution-ridden area would influence, and serve as the main setting of, the Dardennes' work. The brothers' interest in film was sparked by a French teacher at Saint-Martin, the Catholic grade school they attended in Seraing. The teacher often used the school's chapel to screen works by such European master filmmakers as Jean-Luc Godard, François Truffaut, Bernardo Bertolucci, and Robert Bresson. While the Dardennes have seldom spoken to reporters about their family life, it is known that they enjoyed a more privileged upbringing than most of Seraing's inhabitants. In the book *Jean-Pierre and Luc Dardenne* (2010), Joseph Mai wrote that the Dardennes' "father stuck out from the local communi-

Jean-Pierre (left) and Luc Dardenne

ty as a white-collar employee of one of the [steel] companies. Later this state of things represented a slight disconnect between the Dardennes and their film subjects, as if they were watching everything from close by, but 'through a window.'"

Jean-Pierre Dardenne studied drama at the Institut National Súperieur des Arts du Spectacle (Institute for Performing Arts), in Brussels, Belgium, and his brother majored in philosophy at the University of Louvain, the country's oldest and most prestigious university. At the Institute for Performing Arts, Jean-Pierre studied under the acclaimed French playwright and filmmaker Armand Gatti. A member of the French Resistance who escaped from a German prison camp during World War II, Gatti was known for his radical efforts to remove the separation between actors and audiences and for such films as *Enclosure* (1961) and *El otro Cristóbal* (1963); he would play a key role in the Dardennes' move into filmmaking. In the 1970s the Dardennes worked with Gatti on two theater productions, *La Colonne Durutti* and *L'Arche d'Adelin*. Their experience working with video on those projects inspired them to return to their home region of Liège, where they began shooting videos of strikes, union meetings, and local housing developments. (To make ends meet and finance their work, they held jobs in a cement factory.) Those early video works chronicled the effects on Liège of the devastating economic recession that occurred during that time; the films came to be known as *documentaires d'animation* or *documentaires d'intervention*, which were screened in schools and other local venues. For the Dardennes, Joseph Mai wrote, "filmmaking was seen as a practical means of pursuing a larger, 'on-the-ground

militantism.' Starting with a political desire, the brothers themselves slowly 'wandered' into filmmaking from the outside."

In 1975 the Dardennes formed their own production company, Collectif Dérivés, and made nonfiction films and videos for Belgian television—approximately 60 in all—the bulk of them dealing with politically charged subject matter. The brothers made extensive use of such stylistic devices as dramatic reenactments and studio-filmed interviews. The Dardennes' first documentary, *Le Chant du rossignol* (Song of the Nightingale, 1978), focuses on the Belgian Resistance against the Nazis during World War II. For the documentaries *Lorsque le bateau de Léon M. descendit la Meuse pour la première fois* (When Leon M's Boat Descended the Meuse for the First Time, 1979) and *Pour que la guerre s'acheve, les murs devaient s'écrouter* (For the War to Be Finished the Walls Must Have Fallen, 1980), they focused on subjects who had participated in the Belgian labor strike of 1960. Commenting on the latter work, which includes the post-strike recollections of a worker named Edmond, who helped found an underground newspaper called *La Voix Ouvrière* (The Worker's Voice), Manohla Dargis observed for the *New York Times* (May 24, 2009), "With its emphasis on an isolated human figure moving through an urban landscape, the documentary points to [the Dardennes'] later fictions. Yet also bridges the early and later work is, as the emphasis on workers' own voices suggests, the problem of enunciation. One of the crucial questions in documentary is who speaks for whom, particularly when filmmakers are separated from their subjects by critical differences like class and race. The Dardennes don't so much . . . speak for Edmond but through him as he guides them across the city and into the past. At one point the narrator suggests that cinema is inadequate to the historical task with the comment-question 'The eye of the camera always opens too late?'"

In 1981 the Dardennes teamed up with Gatti again to work on the documentary *Nous étions tous des noms d'arbre* (We Were All Names of Trees, 1982). That film centers on a community workshop for young people that was held in Northern Ireland at the time of the 1981 hunger strikes by paramilitary prisoners who had fought against British rule there. (Jean-Pierre served as the film's chief camera assistant, and Luc served as an assistant director.) After that collaboration, the brothers made the documentaries *R . . . ne répond plus* (R . . . No Longer Answers, 1981), about the Radio Free movement in Europe during the early 1980s, and *Leçons d'une université volante* (Lessons from a Floating University, 1982), comprising five vignettes about informal "universities" set up in private homes in Poland during times of governmental oppression. Those were followed by the documentary *Regarde Jonathan* (Look at Jonathan, 1983), which explores the life and work of the influential Belgian playwright Jean Louvet, who co-founded the Proletarian Theater of La Louvière after the general strike of 1960.

Afterward, the Dardennes set their sights on fictional narrative. Joseph Mai noted that the brothers ultimately felt limited by "the understandably reserved attitude that many subjects of their documentaries took to their prying questions and imposing camera" and had become frustrated with the "problem of access to the historical event in the documentary, as if the camera, forced to come after the event, could only film indirect *témoignages* [evidence or testimony], or the effects of history on individual identities." Mai wrote, "In a sense, by moving out of documentary, they were hoping to step outside and stop observing others through a window, as they had since they were children." Jean-Pierre Dardenne told Dave Kehr for the *New York Times* (January 5, 2003), "We decided that fiction allowed us to push the potential of the human being, and that documentary didn't."

The Dardennes' debut narrative feature, *Falsch* (1987), was an adaptation of the Belgian writer René Kalisky's 1983 autobiographical play of the same name. Set in a deserted yet brightly lit airport, the film follows a Jewish man, Joe, the lone survivor of a family lost in the Holocaust, as he encounters the ghosts of his family and reflects on his past. (In Kalisky's play Joe sees his family's ghosts at a disco in 1970s New York.) Manohla Dargis noted about the surreal film, "With its steady framing, smooth camerawork and self-conscious artificiality (a white actor in blackface, among other touches), it bears little resemblance to [the Dardennes'] more famous titles." The Dardennes next made the 12-minute film *Il court, il court, le monde* (He Runs, He Runs, the World, 1987), which chronicles a day in the life of a television news producer. That short film enabled the brothers to secure funding for their second feature, *Je Pense à Vous* (I Think of You), which was released in 1992. With a script by the renowned French screenwriter Jean Gruault, the film is about the effect of a factory closure on a working-class family in Seraing. Scott Foundas, writing for *LA Weekly* (March 24, 2006), described *Je Pense à Vous* as "everything the Dardennes would soon come to reject—a conventional melodrama made in the 'tradition of quality,' with beautiful sun-drenched vistas and a relentlessly uplifting musical score." Although the film earned positive reviews, the Dardennes were unhappy with it, as well as with the industry practices to which they had to adhere in order to make it; those included working with an assigned team of technicians and actors, an arrangement that compromised the brothers' vision. Jean-Pierre explained to Foundas, "We were video artists first, and people in the film industry always thought that video artists were ne'er-do-wells. So when we made *Je Pense à Vous*, we announced that we were now entering the film world. We weren't going to be bulls in the china shop anymore. It was a big mistake. We were surrounded by people who were protecting that china, who were telling us what we should do to keep each piece intact, and we ended up saving the porcelain at the expense of the film. We were paralyzed with fear. And that was the greatest lesson: You should be afraid when you're making a film, but the fright that you should have shouldn't paralyze you. After that experience, we became people who were not only against the work that we did in that film, but against the whole film industry."

In 1994 the Dardennes formed another production company, Les Films du Fleuve, to finance their next fiction feature. Doing so allowed them to have creative control over all aspects of their subsequent feature films—from casting to costume design to cinematography. (The Dardennes have continued to produce documentaries through Collectif Dérivés.) The Dardennes' third feature, *La Promesse* (The Promise, 1996), marked a major shift in their style as well as a major breakthrough in their career. Shot on location in Seraing, the film has no musical score and features natural lighting, handheld camera work, long sequential takes, and mostly nonprofessional actors—all of which would become hallmarks of the Dardennes' style. *La Promesse* tells the story of a teenage boy, Igor (played by Jérémie Renier), who helps his father, Roger (Olivier Gourmet), operate a tenement building that houses, employs, and exploits illegal immigrants. When a Burkina Faso man, Hamidou, dies while working at his father's building site, Igor promises to look after the man's wife and son, a decision that forces him to choose between his morally reprehensible father and the fulfillment of his pledge. Premiering at the Directors' Fortnight Program of the 1996 Cannes International Film Festival, *La Promesse* was widely praised by critics. James Berardinelli, in a review for the Web site reelviews.net, described the film as "a variation of that motion picture staple, the 'coming of age' story. The difference here, however, is that the choices faced by Igor are more complex than is the norm." In another review, for *Boxoffice* magazine (December 18, 2009, on-line), Alex Albanese called the film "a work of great emotional depth and impact that ironically draws much of its power from low-key, naturalistic performances captured with a shooting style that is more often associated with traditional documentary making." Joseph Mai noted, "The greatest stylistic difference between *La Promesse* and the fictional works that preceded it is the film's impressive power to elicit an audience's empathy and belief, as if the film were taking place in our own world." *La Promesse* won several awards, including the prizes for best foreign film at the 1997 Los Angeles Film Critics Association Awards ceremony and best foreign-language film from the National Society of Film Critics in 1998.

The Dardennes' next film, *Rosetta* (1999), brought them even more international recognition. The title character is a young and desperate 17-year-old girl (played by Émilie Dequenne) who lives in a trailer park in Seraing with her alcoholic mother. The film follows Rosetta on her warlike campaign to obtain work after her trial period at a factory ends badly. Screened in competition at the 1999 Cannes Film Festival, *Rosetta* became the first Belgian film to win the prestigious Palme d'Or—the highest prize awarded to films at the festival; Dequenne won the festival's best-actress prize, despite having had no previous acting experience. As quoted by Karen Durbin in the *New York Times* (November 7, 1999), the Canadian director David Cronenberg, the head juror at Cannes that year, called the film "a fantastic portrayal of a primal life force—so unsentimental, so uncompromising and yet in the end so moving. . . . The film has such a physical, tactile understanding of this girl's life. It's beyond desperation, her determination to live and to survive. Making the character sympathetic is a rule of thumb of all popular filmmaking. And they didn't do that. She does shocking things in the movie. Yet by the end you love her; you're so with her by then." In addition to its impact on the film cognoscenti, *Rosetta* struck a chord with the Belgian Parliament, which passed a law (known as "the Rosetta law") shortly after the film's release to protect the rights of teenage workers.

Instead of using their international success to take on bigger projects, the Dardennes continued to make small-scale films that focused on working-class lives in Seraing. In an interview with Howie Movshovitz for the National Public Radio (NPR) program *All Things Considered* (April 1, 2006), Luc Dardenne explained, "Seraing is partly imaginary and partly real. It's the town that represents, if you like, the town that we see that represents life after the cataclysm, after the catastrophe." Seraing served as the setting for the Dardennes' next two films: *Le Fils* (The Son, 2002) and *L'Enfant* (The Child, 2005). In the former, a man named Olivier (played by Olivier Gourmet), who works as a carpentry instructor at a rehabilitation center for youthful offenders, takes on a teenager as an apprentice; Olivier knows, as the apprentice does not, that the boy killed Olivier's son. As a bond develops between the two, Olivier is torn between revenge for his son's murder and acceptance of the troubled teenager. Like *La Promesse* and *Rosetta*, *Le Fils* was well received by critics. At the 2002 Cannes Film Festival, it was awarded the Ecumenical Jury Prize, and Gourmet took home best-actor honors. Many critics pointed out the film's daring cinematography: for much of it the Dardennes shot Gourmet from behind. Jean-Pierre explained to Dave Kehr, "We're always behind Olivier because, for him, the story has already begun. The knowledge of his son's death is something he already carries on his back. To film him mainly from behind, and then, at a certain moment, to film his face, gives the spectator the sense of being in Olivier's head, as if that's where the film was really taking place."

The Dardennes' sixth feature film, *L'Enfant*, chronicles several days in the life of a young petty thief, Bruno (played by Jérémie Renier), his teen-age girlfriend, Sonia (Deborah François), and their newborn baby. The family live mostly off Sonia's welfare checks and the meager funds from Bruno's money-making scams; their situation comes to a head when Bruno sells their baby on the black market. After buying the baby back, Bruno faces the consequences of his act. Unanimously praised by critics, *L'Enfant* earned the Dardennes their second Palme d'Or, at the 2005 Cannes Film Festival; only five other directors have won the coveted award more than once (the others are Alf Sjöberg, 1946, 1951; Francis Ford Coppola, 1974, 1979; Shohei Imamura, 1983, 1997; Emir Kusturica, 1985, 1995; and Bille August, 1988, 1992). The film also received several other honors, including the awards for best foreign-language film and best director at the 2006 Toronto Film Critics Association Awards. In a review for the Toronto, Canada, *Globe and Mail* (April 13, 2006), Mark Peranson called *L'Enfant* "gripping, concise, and flawless" and "clearly the work of masters of narration. Each scene begins and ends at the perfect moment; each scene fits into the whole. It's a masterpiece."

The Dardennes' most recently released film, *Le Silence de Lorna* (Lorna's Silence), appeared in 2008. Set on the outskirts of Seraing in Liège, the film deals with a series of scams involving a young Albanian woman, Lorna (played by Arta Dobroshi), who dreams of opening a snack bar in Belgium with her boyfriend. After attaining Belgian citizenship in an arranged marriage with a hopeless drug addict, Claudy (Jérémie Renier), Lorna becomes ensnared in a plot by her Russian sponsor (Fabrizio Rongione), who wants to murder Claudy so that Lorna can marry a Russian immigrant who needs citizenship papers. Though not as well received as the Dardennes' previous features, *Le Silence de Lorna* won the best-screenplay award at the 2008 Cannes Film Festival and the 2008 LUX Prize from the European Parliament. The Dardennes' next film, *Le Gamin au velo* (The Kid with a Bike), about an 11-year-old boy deserted by his father, will star the Belgian actress Cécile De France and the frequent Dardenne collaborator Jérémie Renier. The film is scheduled to receive its world premiere in the main competition of the 2011 Cannes Film Festival.

The Dardenne brothers live in Belgium. Both are married and have been said to resemble each other in appearance. Luc is reportedly the more talkative of the two. Regarding their similarities as filmmakers, Jean-Pierre told Xan Brooks, "We are the same: one person, four eyes. We have to be, otherwise we could not make the same film. There is no secret."

—C.C.

Suggested Reading: All Movie Guide Web site; *Film Criticism* p64+ Sep. 22, 2005; *LA (California) Weekly* p86+ Mar. 24, 2006; (London) *Guardian* p18 Feb. 9, 2006; *New York Times* p29 Jan. 5, 2003, E p1 May 18, 2005, AR p9 May 24, 2009; *Village Voice* (on-line) Aug. 5,

2008; Mai, Joseph. *Jean-Pierre and Luc Dardenne*, 2010

Selected Films: *La Promesse*, (The Promise), 1996; *Rosetta*, 1999; *Le Fils*, (*The Son*), 2002; *L'Enfant*, (*The Child*, 2005); *Le silence de Lorna* (*Lorna's Silence*), 2008

Frederick M. Brown/Getty Images

DeBarge, El

June 4, 1961– Singer

Address: c/o Geffen Records, 2220 Colorado Ave., Santa Monica, CA 90404

"Before there was Usher, Ne-Yo, Chris Brown, Justin Timberlake, there was El DeBarge," Sarah Rodman wrote for the *Boston Globe* (November 29, 2010, on-line). "Fronting his family group with his silken croon, the slinky Michigan vocalist was among the finest to cop the moves of Prince and Michael Jackson and even Barry Gibb in hopes of making the ladies swoon." From the early to mid-1980s, the singer and four of his siblings, under the group name DeBarge, released such hits as "I Like It," "All This Love," "Love Me in a Special Way," and "You Wear It Well." Later, as a solo performer, El DeBarge had a measure of success with songs including "Who's Johnny?" before his career and personal life were derailed by his increasingly out-of-control addictions to heroin and crack cocaine; he virtually disappeared from the music scene after 1994, even as his music was being covered and sampled by such R&B and hip-hop artists as Tupac Shakur, Notorious B.I.G, Mary J. Blige, Blackstreet,

Mariah Carey, Ashanti, and Patti LaBelle. A year-long stint in prison led DeBarge to quit drugs and get back to making music. After signing with Geffen Records, he released the appropriately titled album *Second Chance* (2010), which led to two Grammy Award nominations. "On his luscious new album, his first in a decade and a half," Rodman wrote, "DeBarge simply soars, his feather-light vocals still in top form following years of personal struggles."

The sixth of 10 children, Eldra Patrick DeBarge was born on June 4, 1961 in Grand Rapids, Michigan, to an African-American mother, Etterlene (Abney) DeBarge, a gospel singer, and a white father, Robert DeBarge Sr. After marrying in 1953, when interracial unions were illegal in some states, DeBarge's parents often faced discrimination and hostility; Robert's mother was so opposed to the marriage that she disowned him. Music was one of the uniting forces for the family. The two oldest children, Bobby and his sister Bunny, taught their younger siblings to sing harmonies. Eldra, nicknamed El, began playing piano at home at age seven—strongly encouraged by his mother—and by age 11 was playing organ at the Bethel Pentecostal Church. He and his siblings sang at the church, where his uncle, a bishop, led the choir. Robert Sr., a truck driver for the U.S. Postal Service who had served in the U.S. Army during the Korean War, would sometimes sing country songs by the likes of Johnny Cash and Hank Williams, accompanying himself on the family piano. Years later some of the children would allege that their father abused them, physically and sexually; their mother claimed that she, too, was physically abused. (The father has denied all accusations.) In an interview with Margena A. Christian for *Ebony* (October 2010), DeBarge said that he had never been abused by his father but added: "I stayed out of [my father's] way growing up. My daddy had problems. I was so young when it all started. I was born into it. I didn't know the difference. My father gave all of us love. That was the disturbing thing about it. [He] was like Jekyll and Hyde. He would hug us and play games with us. The next thing you know, it was on and popping! Then he'd apologize. 'I love you. I'm sorry, and pray for your daddy.' He would always win our sympathy and our empathy. Always. You could tell he was dead serious. He would cry. He wasn't faking. That man had some issues." DeBarge's parents divorced in the mid-1970s. At the age of 16, DeBarge became a first-time father, and during his senior year, he dropped out of high school. (DeBarge would go on to father at least 10 more children—sources differ as to the number—and have three marriages, all of which ended in divorce.)

In 1978, at the age of 17, DeBarge moved to California with Bunny and his brothers Mark (called Marty), James, and Randy. By that time the two oldest brothers, Tommy and Bobby, had achieved relative success as part of the pop-soul group Switch, which was managed on the Motown label by Jermaine Jackson—a brother of the megastar singer Michael Jackson and a member of the supremely successful group the Jackson 5. In 1980, because of that family connection to the label and the siblings' obvious talent, Motown signed El, Marty, James, Randy, and Bunny, who the following year brought out their largely unnoticed debut album, *The DeBarges* (1981). Their sophomore effort, which they released as DeBarge, was much more successful: *All This Love* (1982) became a gold record (indicating sales of a half-million or more copies) and reached number three on the R&B album chart. Observers made enthusiastic comparisons between DeBarge and the Jackson 5—which was clearly the intention of Motown's founder, Berry Gordy, who in 1975 had lost the latter act to another label and sought another successful family group. Gordy also intended to highlight the talents of El DeBarge, whose vocals were prominently featured on the singles "Stop! Don't Tease Me" and "All This Love"; DeBarge shared the spotlight with his brother Randy on the hit single "I Like It." The group's third album, *In a Special Way* (1983), was another gold record and made it to number four on the R&B album chart. The record, to which DeBarge lent not only his vocals but also his writing and producing skills, was widely considered the group's best effort up to that time. "You can just imagine how Motown Records is kicking itself for letting the Jacksons slip out of its grasp," Geoffrey Himes wrote for the *Washington Post* (March 16, 1984). "Though nothing can compensate for the loss of [Michael Jackson], Motown can console itself somewhat with the success of DeBarge, an extremely likable family quintet, not at all unlike the Jackson 5. The four brothers and one sister write and sing a familiar brand of bubble-gum soul: innocent clichés about teenage romance sung to jingly melodies and a simple, bouncy beat. What makes it all special is the way they blend their high, giddy voices. Only siblings can match tone, phrasing and intervals so naturally that it sounds like one voice singing five different parts. The DeBarge sound has ripened on *In a Special Way*. . . . Gone is the clutter of too many horns and guitars; instead Eldra DeBarge's production keeps the instrumentation light and crisp so that the voices stand out front. Four members contribute compositions; three share lead vocals. Eldra is the balladeer; his 'Love in a Special Way' recalls Stevie Wonder's slow, sweet love songs." *Rhythm of the Night* (1985), DeBarge's last album as a group, had two hit singles: the title track, which was featured in the Berry Gordy–produced film *The Last Dragon* (1985), went to number three on the *Billboard* pop chart and number one on the *Billboard* R&B chart; and the mellow, mid-tempo "Who's Holding Donna Now," with El DeBarge on vocals, reached number six on the *Billboard* Hot 100 chart.

That year El DeBarge quit the group to pursue a solo career. His first solo effort for Motown, *El DeBarge* (1986), for which he did not write or produce any of the songs, did not make much of an impact

with critics or fans. His second album, *Gemini* (1989), was a better showcase for his talent, in large part because he had a significant role in writing and producing the songs, including "Broken Dreams," "Somebody Loves You," and "Love Life." That year, along with Barry White and James Ingram, he contributed vocals to the hit song "The Secret Garden (Sweet Seduction Suite)," a track on the star-packed Quincy Jones album *Back on the Block* (1989). DeBarge was subsequently released from his contract with Motown, where he felt his creativity and potential as a solo artist had not been allowed to flourish. In an interview with Janine McAdams for *Billboard* (April 11, 1992), he said, "I was made to feel insecure because every time I would do something [musically], it would end up being changed. . . . It kinda made me shell up, made me to the point where I didn't want to create anymore."

After signing with Warner Bros., in 1991, DeBarge released *In the Storm* (1992), which he co-produced with Maurice White of the highly popular soul group Earth, Wind and Fire. The album, for which he also wrote or co-wrote most of the songs, was a tribute of sorts to Marvin Gaye's 1977 album *I Want You*—although it did not feature any covers except that of Gaye's "After the Dance," on which DeBarge was accompanied by the jazz quartet Fourplay. The album also included the bass-heavy "My Heart Belongs to You," the funky "Fast Lane," the smooth "Another Chance," and the catchy "Tip O' My Tongue," which DeBarge co-wrote with Prince—who, along with Sly and the Family Stone, was another influence on DeBarge. That year DeBarge toured with Chaka Khan, opening for the soul/funk singer. DeBarge co-wrote and co-produced the songs on his album *Heart, Mind & Soul* (1994) with Kenneth "Babyface" Edmonds, who sang a duet with DeBarge on the ballad "Where Is My Love?" and backup vocals on "Where You Are." Reviewing the album for the *Washington Post* (July 20, 1994), Geoffrey Himes observed that it "dwells on idealized romanticism, claiming true love is 'all I ever wanted, baby.' Sex is included in that love, but the emphasis is clearly on the emotions, and the unwavering intensity of DeBarge's voice, even in the highest octaves, gives his claims of tender devotion a rare credibility. When he croons 'I'll Be There' to a woman abandoned by men in the past, there's no macho swagger or implied wink to spoil the aura of sincerity. When Babyface adds a lovely counter-harmony on the chorus, the dizzying effect recalls old-fashioned soul music at its sweetest. The pop spotlight has swung in the direction of the bragging, grunting baritones of rappers and new-jack Casanovas, but the tradition of romantic soul survives in the shadows. DeBarge pays tribute to that tradition by having Stevie Wonder play a harmonica solo on 'Where You Are' and by unabashedly imitating Marvin Gaye on the title track." The album was generally well-received, but the singles did not stay on the charts for long, and DeBarge would not be heard from again for 16 years.

DeBARGE

The singer spent much of that time struggling with addictions to crack cocaine and heroin. Even during periods when he was performing with his brothers and sister, he spoke about feeling troubled, telling Dennis Hunt for the *Los Angeles Times* (April 21, 1985), "I'm a nice guy, but not all the time. There are these personalities in me, so many of them. They come out at strange times. I can be one way, then five minutes later I'm another way." Speaking of those "personalities," he added: "Nothing I do determines what comes out. They come out as they want to. I fight some of them. I don't enjoy some of them and I know other people don't enjoy them either." DeBarge, who was 23 years old at the time, confessed that his least favorite personality was "the depressed one." Music, he said, helped him fight his loneliness and depression. His consumption of hard drugs and run-ins with the law began around that time. In 1985 he was accused by a college student of hitting her after she refused his sexual advances; DeBarge, who denied the accusation, was convicted the following year of creating a disturbance and ordered to perform community service, then was jailed for contempt of court in 1987 after he failed to comply. In 1988 his brothers Bobby and Chico were convicted on drug-conspiracy charges and sentenced to five years in prison. In 1995, at the age of 39, Bobby died of AIDS; the family was devastated, and El DeBarge took the loss especially hard. By the late 1980s, meanwhile, DeBarge was regularly using heroin and cocaine—he would snort the heroin because of his fear of needles—and he soon moved on to smoking crack cocaine. (DeBarge would later talk about drug dealers who refused to sell to him because they knew who he was and did not want him to waste his life.) In 1996 he was arrested for drug possession, vandalism, and disturbing the peace. Five years later he was charged with domestic violence (he has said he was attacked) and received a suspended sentence. In the fall of 2008, he was again arrested for vandalism and drug possession, which was a violation of his probation. As a result he was sentenced to two years in prison, where he initially suffered intense drug-withdrawal symptoms. Withdrawal is "worse than what you see on TV or in movies. . . . It's nastier than that," he told Christian. "It's bad, bad. You hurt past your body. You hurt from the inside out. Your hair hurts." The other inmates knew who he was and would often ask him to sing and play the one piano in the prison; sometimes he did. In January 2009, after serving 13 months, DeBarge was released.

"I picked up a crack pipe when I was 25 years old because I wanted to try it, and it took me 22 years to un-try it," DeBarge told Steve Jones for *USA Today* (October 1, 2010). "But it's a wrap now. I lost all that time with a pipe in my mouth. Now it's a mike to my mouth." He got in touch with a veteran music executive, Peter Farmer, who later became his manager. Farmer persuaded executives at Geffen Records to give DeBarge another chance.

At an audition for Geffen, to prove that his voice was still pristine, DeBarge sang a capella; he soon landed a record deal. In June 2010 he made his re-entry into the music world, giving a surprise performance at the 10th annual BET Awards ceremony, during which he won the audience's attention and adoration by performing a medley of his old hits. Later that year he toured as an opening act for the singer Mary J. Blige and gave concerts of his own as well. His first album for Geffen, *Second Chance*, came out in November 2010. Consisting mostly of R&B love songs, the album was co-produced by James "Jimmy Jam" Harris, Terry Lewis, and Babyface. The title track received two Grammy Award nominations—for best male R&B vocal performance and best R&B song—and positive reviews. "The acrobatic falsetto and supple harmonies are as present as ever," Andy Kellman wrote for allmusic.com. "While the first ten songs would have made for a strong return on their own, the final three put *Second Chance* over the top as one of the year's best R&B albums. The rippling 'Sad Songs' and the sparse 'The Other Side,' two of the three songs written with Jam & Lewis, illustrate heartbreak while tapping into a vivid anguish that El had never before approached. They are both exceptionally poignant; anyone with the vaguest idea about the singer's struggles will hear them as more than just remorseful breakup songs. In this context, the closing 'Second Chance'—issued as the album's lead single—sounds nothing short of triumphant."

On February 14, 2011 DeBarge announced that he had checked into a rehabilitation center and canceled his upcoming concerts. He is currently scheduled to give performances in the summer of 2011.

—D.K.

Suggested Reading: allmusic.com; *Billboard* p13 Apr. 11, 1992; *Ebony* p76 Oct. 2010; *New York Times* II p27 Apr. 1, 1984; *Vibe* Oct. 2007; *USA Today* D p5 Oct. 1, 2010; *Washington Post* T p1 Jan. 30, 2011

Selected Recordings: with DeBarge—*The DeBarges*, 1981; *All This Love*, 1982; *In A Special Way*, 1983; *Rhythm of the Night*, 1985; as solo artist—*El DeBarge*, 1986; *Gemini*, 1989; *In The Storm*, 1992; *Heart, Mind & Soul*, 1994; *Second Chance*, 2010

Photo by Matt Haughey

Denton, Nick

Aug. 24, 1966– Founder of Gawker Media and Gawker.com; journalist; entrepreneur

Address: Gawker Media, 210 Elizabeth St., Fourth Fl., New York, NY 10012

"The barrier to entry in Internet media is low," the publishing executive Nick Denton told David Carr for the *New York Times* (July 3, 2006, on-line). "The barrier to success is high." Described on CNNMoney.com (June 1, 2004) as "the smartest publisher in the blogosphere" and in Michael Idov's portrait of him for *New York* (October 4, 2010) as "the most powerful" to emerge in it, Denton is the founder of Gawker Media, an exemplar of nanopublishing, so-called because startup and operating costs on the Internet amount to a tiny fraction of those for print publications. When Denton entered the world of nanopublishing, in 2002, blogs, with few exceptions, served as outlets for the personal observations or opinions of individuals unknown to the general public, and many regarded them as merely "non-revenue-generating megaphones for online bloviators," in the words of Steven Levy, writing for *Wired.com* (December 2006). To Denton, though, the content and presentation of blogs offered a refreshing contrast to the writings of traditional journalists, who usually censored not only their own points of view but information that, while factually correct, they deemed unpublishable for one reason or another. Blogs, by contrast, Denton told Edward Helmore for the London *Independent* (November 29, 2004), "have the characteristics of honesty and humour and they speak to audiences at their level, not from on high." By creat-

ing Gawker Media and thereby "professionalizing" blogs, Denton "bestowed instant credibility" on them, Levy wrote; he "hadn't merely created a blog, he'd created a brand." The Gawker brand—especially its flagship title, the gossipmonger Gawker.com—is known not only for its honesty and humor but for what many have described as irreverence, nastiness, rudeness, and audacity. "Like all gossip merchants," Ben McGrath wrote for a *New Yorker* (October 18, 2010) profile of him, "Denton fancies himself a truth-teller who relishes flouting the conventions of good taste and privilege."

Gawker Media made its debut in 2002, with Gawker.com and the consumer-electronics blog Gizmodo.com. In addition to those blogs, the company's nine current titles include Jezebel.com, "a smart, feisty antidote to traditional women's magazines," Lauren Lipton wrote for the *New York Times* (May 4, 2008); Kotaku.com, a gamers' site; Jalopnik.com, for automobile enthusiasts; Lifehacker.com, which offers suggestions for increasing productivity at the computer; and io9.com, for science-fiction aficionados. On February 23, 2011 Technorati.com, which according to its Web site measures blogs' "standing and influence in the blogosphere" daily, named Gizmodo.com, Gawker.com, Kotaku.com, Lifehacker.com, and Jezebel.com in its list of the top 50 blogs.

Ideally, revenues from on-site advertisers cover Gawker Media's main expense—salaries for its editors, writers, and software engineers; blogs that have failed to generate sufficient advertising dollars have been folded into other Gawker Media blogs, terminated, or sold. Denton-introduced blogs now owned by others include Wonkette.com, which focuses on political issues and the activities of movers and shakers in Washington, D.C., and Consumerist.com, which offers advice and warnings regarding everyday products and services. "The one common theme is to take an obsession, say a gadget obsession, and feed it—produce more content than the people could ever dream of having or consuming," Denton, a self-described Internet addict, told Helmore. He added, "Everybody likes to read about themselves, about their worlds. As with addicts, the more you give them, the more they want."

For a decade after he graduated from college, in 1988, Denton worked as a journalist. While on the staff of the *Financial Times*, he co-wrote a book about events leading to the collapse of the British bank Barings, in 1995. After he ended his career in print news media, he co-founded the news aggregator Moreover.com, whose subscribers included international companies, and the social-networking firm First Tuesday, which organized get-togethers for like-minded businesspeople and job hunters in cities around the world. The sales of those enterprises made him a multimillionaire. According to Michael Idov, "From the moment of Gawker Media's inception, the common wisdom dictated that Denton was going to flip it"—that is, sell it. In 2010 *Business Insider* (on-line) estimated Gawker Media's worth to be $150 million and ranked it 77th among the world's most valuable startups. Denton has repeatedly told questioners that he has no plans to relinquish ownership or management of Gawker Media. His company, he told Idov, is "embryonic. This is at most a midsize media group that might, in twenty years, be something a bit more." Gawker's modest size notwithstanding, Idov declared that Denton "isn't just an heir" to such publishing-world bigwigs as "Rupert Murdoch, Anna Wintour, Harry Evans, Tina Brown, and other ostensible Gawker targets; he's become their peer."

The first of the two children of Geoffrey Denton and the former Marika Marton, Nicholas Denton was born in London, England, on August 24, 1966. His father taught university-level economics and published widely, on topics ranging from conditions in post-apartheid South Africa to the effects on international commerce of government subsidies for private industries. One of his students at the University of Southampton was his future wife, Marika Marton; a Jewish native of Hungary, she fled that country in 1956, after the Soviet Union crushed an attempt by Hungarians to rid themselves of Communist rule. After her marriage she worked as a psychotherapist at the Institute for Group Analysis, in London; she died of cancer in 2001. The Dentons raised Nick and his younger sister, Rebecca (born in 1969), in the Hampstead section of London, a "citadel of the moneyed liberal intelligentisia, posh but not stuffy," Idov wrote. Denton attended a private day school, the University College School (for boys only then), in Hampstead, and then University College at Oxford University, about 55 miles from London, where he studied economics, politics, and philosophy. While at Oxford he edited the prestigious campus magazine *Isis*, which was published by a private firm that granted the student journalists complete editorial freedom. His college friends included several future Labour Party politicians and members of Parliament, among them David Milibrand, Ed Balls, and Yvette Cooper. As an undergraduate he worked as an intern for several periodicals; he spent one summer at the Woodrow Wilson International Center for Scholars, in Washington, D.C., and for a few weeks another summer, he worked on a kibbutz in Israel. He graduated from University College in 1988.

Denton next got a job as an editor with the Economist Group, whose publications include the *Economist*. He found his work monotonous and soon left. Fluent in Hungarian, he was living in Hungary in November 1989 when the Berlin Wall fell, in Germany, and he wrote for a few small newspapers about the repercussions of that event in Hungary. Before long the London *Telegraph* hired him; on assignment, he wrote a front-page report on the revolution in Romania, which toppled that nation's Communist government in late December 1989. He next joined the staff of the *Financial Times*, as a foreign correspondent, investment reporter, and media specialist. He covered the collapse of the 233-year-old Barings Bank of London, in 1995, which stemmed from the machinations of Nick Leeson, a so-called rogue trader. Under the name Nicholas Denton, he co-wrote, with John Gapper, his editor at the *Financial Times*, *All That Glitters: The Fall of Barings* (1997). The book attracted few reviewers or buyers.

Earlier, in 1996, at Denton's request, the *Financial Times* had sent him to the San Francisco Bay Area of California, to write about the semiconductor market and technological innovations emanating from Silicon Valley. "The deadlines were horrible and the *Financial Times* had no prestige there," he recalled to a London *Observer* (March 9, 2008) reporter. Denton quit the *Financial Times* in 1998 and, with two friends with computer-software expertise—David Galbraith and Angus Bankes—launched Moreover.com, an on-line news service, with funding from Atlas Venture and other British enterprises. Under the umbrella of Moreover Technologies, Moreover.com collected news from many sources and sent it to its clients four times per hour via electronic mail. "If you want to be courageous and create fantastic content," Denton told *Editor & Publisher* (June 19, 2000), "do an online content site. But if you want to build a company that will make a huge amount of money, aggregation is the way to go." McGraw Hill, Wells Fargo, Ernst & Young, British Telecom, and other companies paid up to $200,000 a year for Moreover.com's services. Moreover Technologies soon developed a search tool, the Business Intelligence Solution, which could be customized to target particular topics from its database of news sources.

Also in 1998 Denton co-founded First Tuesday, with Julie Meyer, who had just received her master's degree; John Browning of *Wired*; and Adam Gold, an investment banker. Originating in a pub as a small congregation of Denton's technology-savvy friends, it became a huge social-networking business, organizing gatherings for people working in technology. In 1999 Denton began hosting First Tuesday parties in big cities in the U.S. By mid-2000 First Tuesday had acquired more than 70,000 members and was operating in more than 100 cities. That year Denton and his partners sold the company to Yazam, an Israeli investment company, for about $50 million in cash and stock. In 2001 Denton ended his day-to-day management of Moreover.com; four years later he sold Moreover Technologies to the Virginia-based corporation VeriSign for a reported $30 million. Earlier, in 2002, he had joined Peter Molnar, a former member of the Hungarian Parliament, to teach a course called "Freedom of the Press: Political Change and the Media in Hungary" at the University of California–Berkeley Graduate School of Journalism. Finding Molnar to be "inflexibly idealistic" and therefore "hugely annoying," he told McGrath, he left California halfway through the term and moved to New York.

That same year he founded Gawker Media and launched two blogs: Gizmodo.com, edited by the journalist Pete Rojas, and Gawker.com, written by Elizabeth Spiers, a former hedge-funds analyst in her mid-20s who had already started several adult-oriented Web sites. Early on the Gawker Web site described itself as "a live review of city news, and . . . among other things, urban dating rituals, no-ropes social climbing, Condé Nastiness, downwardly mobile i-bankers, real estate porn—the serious stuff"; Spiers described its focus as "the darker Manhattan-centric themes: class warfare as recreational sport; pathological status obsession; and the complete, total, and wholly unapologetic embrace of decadence." "Don't bother accusing Ms. Spiers's site of being small-minded or superficial; she says so herself," Warren St. John wrote for the *New York Times* (May 18, 2003, on-line), calling Spiers "the ringleader of a sort of New York School of bloggers . . . who use the city as a backdrop for their musings" and characterizing Gawker.com as "voyeuristic," "media-obsessed," and "occasionally creepy." "It's a catty, hilarious internet gossip column that skewers the elites of New York," Andy Pemberton wrote for the London *Observer* (December 5, 2004). "Celebrities, PRs [personal representatives], magazine editors, restaurateurs—anyone attempting to slither up the greasy pole [of success] is fair game." In 2003 Spiers left Gawker.com; her replacement was Choire Sicha, whose "appeal was in being almost impersonally sharp and cruel and correct," Carla Blumenkranz wrote for *n+1* (December 3, 2007). The sixth of Sicha's successors was Gabriel Snyder, whose tenure lasted 18 months. When, in February 2010, Gawker Media bought Cityfile.com (its first and thus far only acquisition), Cityfile's founder and editor, Remy Stern, replaced Snyder. According to Ben McGrath, "Gawker's writers will hint at [one's] incompetent thievery with parenthetical wit, or by employing an exclamation point or a question mark where a period would suffice, but the real insults come from an extremely dedicated clique of anonymous readers [in the blog's comments section], after the fact."

Posts on Gawker.com have often incurred the wrath of their individual subjects or of executives at corporations it has targeted, sometimes making headlines in the process. In 2006, for example, Gawker posted pictures of *People* and *Hello!* magazine covers bearing images of Brad Pitt, Angelina Jolie, and their infant daughter Shiloh—photos for which *People* and *Hello!* had each paid millions of dollars—before those magazines reached newsstands. In another instance, in 2008 Gawker.com posted an internal Church of Scientology video showing Tom Cruise extolling that religion at a church event; despite demands by church leaders, Denton refused to remove the video, which was viewed more than 2.3 million times. In 2010 Denton paid $5,000 to a bar patron for an iPhone prototype that an Apple engineer had inadvertently left at the bar and that Apple had not yet displayed

publicly; a post on Gizmodo.com displaying photos of the device and a second Gizmodo post that revealed the identity of the engineer generated a total of about 20 million page views. "In the morning, we're outlaw journalists, taking on Apple, and by the afternoon we were the ***holes who made fun of a helpless engineer," Joel Johnson, a longtime Gizmodo writer, said to McGrath. "It does really typify what it's like working for Nick. You're always going to push it a little too far." Although Gawker's targets have often threatened to sue, Denton has never had to appear in a courtroom and has rarely paid damages.

In early 2011 Gawker Media had a stable of nine blogs: in addition to Gawker.com, whose tagline is "Today's gossip is tomorrow's news," they were Gizmodo.com, "The gadget guide"; Lifehacker.com—"Tips and downloads for getting things done"; Jalopnik—"Obsessed with the cult of cars"; Kotaku—"The Gamer's Guide"; io9—"We come from the future"; Deadspin.com—"Sports news without access, favor, or discretion"; Jezebel.com—"Celebrity, sex, fashion for women, without airbrushing"; and Fleshbot.com—"Pure filth." According to Andrew Ross Sorkin, writing for the *New York Times* (November 17, 2003), Fleshbot.com, which Denton launched in 2003, "might best be described as an erudite pornography site, with the same kind of catty writing and timely links that have made Gawker a must-read for New York's gossip crowd." Matthew Patin wrote for *Gelf Magazine* (December 4, 2008, on-line) that Fleshbot "isn't the usual porn dump. . . . It's a mindful collection of links and articles, chosen by bloggers who don't seem to be interested in porn as a five-free-minutes, means-to-an-end affair, but interested in sex itself, and all the joys, humor, and absurdities that accompany it." The main Gawker Media site does not list Fleshbot.com among its titles, and while the eight other current titles refer to one another, they do not mention it, either, because, according to Ben McGrath, Fleshbot is "a drag on the reputable kind of advertising that Denton now covets." Enormously popular in its early years, Fleshbot.com is now "the worst-performing" of Denton's current titles, McGrath noted.

Two once-independent Gawker Media blogs have been absorbed by Gawker.com: Valleywag.com, which offered Silicon Valley news and rumors, and Defamer.com, which was devoted to Hollywood gossip. Denton tried without success to sell the now-defunct Sploid.com, which David Carr, writing for the *New York Times* (July 3, 2006, on-line), called "a tabloid-infested site built on screen shots." Gawker's gambling site, Oddjack.com, ceased operations in 2005. Kinja.com, a portal to a huge number of other blogs, failed to generate much interest and was discontinued. Blogs launched by Gawker that Denton has sold and that were available elsewhere on the Internet in early 2011 include Wonkette.com; Consumerist.com, purchased by Consumers Union, the publisher of *Consumer Reports*; Screenhead.com, a pay-per-view movie site; Gridskipper.com, an "urban travel" site; and Idolator.com, a music-industry news and gossip site. "We are becoming a lot more like a traditional media company," Denton told Carr in 2006, the year he placed Sploid and Screenhead on the market. "You launch a site, you have great hopes for it and it does not grow as much as you wanted. You have to have the discipline to recognize what isn't working and put your money and efforts into those sites that are."

Gawker Media is incorporated in Budapest, Hungary, where a small group of its programmers work. For the company's first six years, its offices were housed in Denton's apartment—a loft in the Soho section of Manhattan. In 2008 Denton set up office space in a nearby loft. In late 2010 the company had about 120 employees, half of whom worked with Denton at the Manhattan office. Each Gawker Media title has its own editor and writers; Denton himself has written several thousand pieces over the years. Until recently Denton was reputed to be "a kind of digital-sweatshop operator," Ben McGrath wrote; Elizabeth Spiers, for example, was paid $24,000 a year, and for some time Denton paid writers $12 per piece, with bonuses correlated to numbers of hits. Currently, according to McGrath, Gawker workers "make good money."

According to Gawker Media figures posted online on October 1, 2008, in the previous month 22 million unique visitors worldwide had visited the 12 Gawker blogs then being published; the company had recorded some 274 million page views—69 percent more than in September 2007 and a Gawker all-time high—and a total of about 500,000 reader comments. In late 2010, according to Ben McGrath, the number of monthly page views was more than 450 million, with about 17 million unique visitors. "The 'geek' sites, as Gizmodo, Lifehacker, Kotaku, io9, and Jalopnik are known internally, bring in twice the traffic of the 'gossip' sites," he noted. In a major redesign unveiled in early 2011, Gawker sites highlighted major stories rather than up-to-the-minute items and in general adopted the appearance of on-line versions of many print magazines and newspapers. "Denton is intending to showcase writers who do deeper, original reporting," Jesse Baker said on the National Public Radio show *Morning Edition* (January 3, 2011, on-line). Denton told Baker, "I would like to show the full range of content, from scurrilous and sensationalist through to beautiful and uplifting, because people can't live on snark and vicious gossip alone." In the readers' comments sections of Gawker Media blogs, initial reactions to the changes were overwhelmingly unfavorable.

McGrath described Denton as "tall and rangy," as having "a famously large head that sits precariously on a thin neck and narrow shoulders," and as "someone who likes and knows how to have fun." At the parties he frequently attends or hosts, Michael Idov wrote, Denton projects a "mix of aloofness and approachability." Friends and associates of Denton's told Idov that his reputation for being unfeeling and unkind is based on firsthand experiences of many people; McGrath wrote, "From reading Gawker, I had learned that Denton is not just a terrible employer but one of 'New York's worst,' as well as an unapologetic liar and the kind of person who leaves his own party early in search of a better one." Nevertheless, Idov was told that Denton has become much more cheerful and warm than he was when he lived in London or San Francisco. Denton, who is gay, travels around New York by bicycle.

—T.O.

Suggested Reading: *Editor & Publisher* p86 June 19, 2000; (London) *Guardian* p30 Aug. 20, 1999, p50 Apr. 19, 2004; (London) *Independent* p18 Nov. 29, 2004; (London) *Observer* p32 Dec. 5, 2004; *New York* p58+ Oct. 4, 2010, (on-line) Oct. 22, 2007; *New York Times* C p5 Oct. 4, 2004, p1 Jan. 13, 2008; *New Yorker* (on-line) Oct. 18, 2010; nickdenton.org; *Topeka (Kansas) Capital-Journal* p2 Jan. 19, 2008

Selected Books: *All That Glitters: The Fall of Barings* (with John Glapper), 1997

Desplat, Alexandre

Aug. 23, 1961– Film composer

Address: c/o Robert M. Urband, 8981 Sunset Blvd., Suite 311, West Hollywood, CA 90069

"The trouble with Hollywood film scores these days is that so many sound as if you have heard them before," Jon Burlingame wrote for the *New York Times* (January 7, 2007). "So originality, when it occurs, can be startling, as when American audiences first heard the enchanting waltzes of *Girl with a Pearl Earring* in 2003, or the fairy-tale flutes and surging orchestral drama of *Birth* in 2004." The composer who created the scores for those films is Alexandre Desplat, now widely considered one of the top practitioners in his field. Jake Coyle wrote for the Associated Press (February 17, 2011, on-line), "[Desplat's] scores are remarkably varied, veering from grandly epic to minimalist and intimate, from 80-piece orchestras to lone whistling." Desplat has been widely praised for his ability to create music that enhances a film's themes without distracting the viewer. He explained to Burlingame, "The first moment I see a movie, I don't think melodies, I think colors. . . . I think about what the orchestra will play. What texture does this movie need?'" Among other notable films that Desplat has scored are *Syriana* (2005), *The Painted Veil* (2006), *The Queen* (2006), *The Golden Compass* (2007), *The Curious Case of Benjamin Button* (2008), *Fantastic Mr. Fox* (2009),

Frazer Harrison/Getty Images For BAFTA Los Angeles
Alexandre Desplat

New Moon (2009), *Harry Potter and the Deathly Hallows: Part 1* (2010), and *The King's Speech* (2010).

Alexandre Michel Gérard Desplat was born on August 23, 1961. His Greek mother and French father had met in the U.S. while attending the University of California, Berkeley. They were married in San Francisco and subsequently moved to Paris, France, where their son was born. Desplat began taking piano lessons at the age of five and later studied trumpet and flute. He told Burlingame, "When I was a child, I was raised almost as a little American. I've been listening to American composers and watching American films since I was 14 or 15. [Francis Ford] Coppola, [Martin] Scorsese, [Alfred] Hitchcock, [Steven] Spielberg, all these masters. So writing for American movies is part of the dream."

Desplat first became intensely interested in film scores when he saw the Stanley Kubrick picture *Spartacus* (released in the U.S. in 1960), which featured a soundtrack composed by Alex North. He later became fascinated with the work of such film composers as Bernard Herrmann (*Psycho* and *Citizen Kane*), Nino Rota (*The Godfather* and *The Godfather Part II*), and Maurice Jarre (*Lawrence of Arabia* and *Doctor Zhivago*). After he saw *Star Wars* (1977), which featured an epic, sprawling soundtrack by John Williams that was voted the best score of all time by the American Film Institute, Desplat became determined to follow a similar career path. He told Coyle, "I remember saying to my friends: 'That's what I want to do.'" He asserted, "I never dreamed of writing for concert or opera. I always dreamed, if I was a composer, to write music for films."

Desplat did not listen only to film soundtracks. "Between the ages of 13 and 20, I would listen to everything I could, day and night," he recalled to Charlotte Smith for the classical-music magazine *Gramophone* (January 25, 2011, on-line). "I was dripping in music—from jazz to bossa nova, to [Maurice] Ravel, [Claude] Debussy, [Dmitri] Shostakovich, [Olivier] Messiaen and [Pierre] Boulez. Every kind of music was rich and different and exciting. In this way I started to discover a musical vocabulary of my own."

After studying at the Paris Conservatory of Music, Desplat found work performing and writing music with a traveling theater group. The first full-length film he scored was *Ki Lo Sa?*, directed by Robert Guédiguian and released in 1985 in France. From 1989 to 1990 Desplat scored the animated French television series *Pif et Hercule*, and for the next decade he composed music for various television shows, commercials, and films. Describing those early works, William Ruhlmann wrote for the All Music Guide Web site, "[Desplat] developed a contemplative style that did not attempt to respond on a point-by-point basis to the action on-screen, but rather set its own complementary mood."

In 1991 Desplat, increasingly in demand throughout Europe, scored the English-language picture *Family Express*, about an orphaned boy who travels from Milan to Zurich while hiding on a tour bus. The following year he scored the thriller *Lapse of Memory* (also released as *Mémoire traquée*), a French and Canadian production that starred John Hurt. Desplat's subsequent films included *Sexes Faibles!* (1992); the comedy *Le tronc* (1993); *The Advocate* (1993), an English-language drama produced in the U.K. and France that featured Colin Firth; *Innocent Lies* (1995), a British detective thriller; *Les Milles* (1995), a World War II drama; *Love, etc.* (1996), a romantic comedy that starred Charlotte Gainsbourg; *Sweet Revenge* (1998), a British comedy with Helena Bonham Carter and Kristin Scott Thomas; and *The Luzhin Defence* (2000), based on a novel by Vladimir Nabokov about a chess master and starring John Turturro and Emily Watson.

In certain quarters Desplat was particularly recognized for his work with the filmmaker Jacques Audiard, whose pictures, while not widely seen by American audiences, were favorites with both critics and other filmmakers. Desplat scored Audiard's *Regarde les hommes tomber* (1994, released in the U.S. as *See How They Fall*); *Un héros très discret* (*A Self-Made Hero*, 1996); *Sur mes lèvres* (2001, released in the U.S. the following year as *Read My Lips*); *De battre mon coeur s'est arrêté* (*The Beat That My Heart Skipped*, 2005); and *Un prophète* (*A Prophet*, 2009). Desplat won a César Award, often referred to as the French equivalent of the Oscar, for his *De battre mon coeur s'est arêté* score.

When the director Peter Webber saw one of Audiard's earlier films, he was struck by the music and asked Desplat to score *Girl with a Pearl Earring*

(2003), a film based on the popular novel of the same title by Tracy Chevalier. The film starred Colin Firth as the Dutch painter Johannes Vermeer and Scarlett Johansson as Griet, the young servant girl who inspired his famous 1665 painting. Webber told Burlingame, "[Desplat] had a sense of restraint and a sense of lyricism that I liked. I remember the first time I saw the cue where Griet opens the shutters. He was really describing what the light was doing, articulating that in a musical sphere." The score for *Girl with a Pearl Earring* was nominated for a Golden Globe Award, a British Academy of Film and Television Arts (BAFTA) Award, and a European Film Award. In a review for Soundtrack.net (April 28, 2004), Andrew Granade wrote, "Although Desplat, a Frenchman, has been writing music for films in Europe quite successfully for some time and received some recognition in the United States for his score to *The Luzhin Defence*, his name is unknown to the general public. This score should change that situation. . . . [It] is a stunning work both in terms of structure and power and is easily one of the year's best." Granade concluded, "Do yourself a favor and become acquainted with Desplat's work; it's a name you'll be seeing a lot more in coming years."

The following year Desplat scored Jonathan Glazer's controversial thriller *Birth*, about a woman (played by Nicole Kidman) who believes that a young boy may be her reincarnated husband. In his review of the film for *Variety* (September 7, 2004, on-line), David Rooney observed, "Ranging from a sustained electronic hum to delicate harps to thundering, full-bodied orchestrations . . . Desplat's rich score accentuates the film's troubling mood." Granade quipped for Soundtrack.net (February 2, 2005), "When I reviewed *Girl With a Pearl Earring* last year, I encouraged you to seek out Desplat's work, as you would not only enjoy it, but could then feel smug as all your friends caught up with your taste [while] Desplat became better and better known. So, did you follow my advice? Unfortunately, it may be too late now as Desplat seems to have firmly arrived and be making a distinctive mark on Hollywood."

In 2005 Desplat contributed scores to a number of Hollywood films, including *The Upside of Anger*, a romantic comedy starring Kevin Costner; the action film *Hostage*, starring Bruce Willis; *Casanova*, in which Heath Ledger played the titular lover; and *Syriana*, a political thriller starring George Clooney and Matt Damon. Desplat's *Syriana* score was nominated for a Golden Globe Award. In a review of the film for the *New York Times* (November 23, 2005, on-line), A. O. Scott praised the way in which the "anxious, irregular heartbeat of Alexandre Desplat's score" linked *Syriana*'s multiple storylines—"each one subject to enough twists and reversals to make plot summary a treacherous exercise."

The following year was a busy one for Desplat, who continued to be in demand in Europe, even as his popularity in the U.S. soared. Among his 2006

films were the romantic comedy *Lies and Alibis*; the Harrison Ford thriller *Firewall*; the comedy *La doublure* (released in the U.S. the same year as *The Valet*); and *Quand j'étais chanteur*, which starred Gerard Depardieu. He also provided the score for *The Queen*, which starred Helen Mirren as Queen Elizabeth II. The film, whose events take place during the tumultuous days following the death of Diana, Princess of Wales, earned Desplat his first Oscar nomination. A review of the soundtrack posted on IGN.com (February 21, 2007) stated, "Considering the haughty melodramatic nature of the subject matter, the score to [director] Stephen Frears' *The Queen* is wonderfully sprightly and inventive, with composer Alexandre Desplat eschewing the requisite pomp and circumstance for an overwhelmingly surprising sense of whimsy."

In 2006 Desplat also scored *The Painted Veil*, a period picture set in 1920s China. In a review for *Variety* (December 14, 2006), Todd McCarthy called the film "a pleasure to look at and listen to, thanks to [its] fine, supple score," and Elisabeth Vincentelli, in a review posted on Amazon.com, wrote, "Desplat set out to evoke 1920s romanticism with a series of brief vignettes, usually greatly enhanced by the sensitive playing of pianist Lang Lang. And considering that most of the movie takes place in China, Desplat has refrained from easy orientalism: 'Walter's Mission' is one of the few tracks to allude to Asian sounds. The only non-original track on the CD is Erik Satie's well-known 'Gnossienne No. 1,' a slow piece that evidently served as inspiration for Desplat's own 'River Waltz.' But who's complaining? There are worse people to emulate than Satie." The film garnered Desplat a Golden Globe Award for best original score.

Desplat's work in 2007 included scores for the adventure epic *The Golden Compass*, based on a novel by Philip Pullman; *Mr. Magorium's Wonder Emporium*, a poorly received comedy starring Dustin Hoffman and Natalie Portman; *Ségo et Sarko sont dans un bateau . . .*, a documentary about French presidential elections; *L'ennemi intime*, an Algerian war drama that was released in the U.S. two years later as *Intimate Enemies*; and *Se, jie*, (released in the U.S. that year as *Lust, Caution*), Ang Lee's erotic spy thriller set in World War II–era Shanghai.

Desplat was nominated for multiple awards, including an Oscar and a Golden Globe, for his highest-profile project of 2008: David Fincher's *The Curious Case of Benjamin Button*, which starred Brad Pitt as a man who ages in reverse. For the score, Desplat created musical palindromes—themes that sound the same when played in reverse—to mirror the plight of Pitt's character. Desplat told a reporter for WBUR.org (January 9, 2009) that he had tried to keep his use of the device subtle: "If I were to show off too much about my reverse thing, it would be disconnected from the picture and the story, and we have to be really, completely overwhelmed by the story before [anything else]." In his review of the score for *Patrol Magazine* (January 26, 2009, on-line), David Sessions wrote, "Subtlety doesn't preclude elaborate texture, which Desplat's score is always hiding beneath its glassy surface. The intensity of his details and their flawless relationship to the picture are his most deadly weapon." Sessions continued, "Every bit the invisible 'glue' Desplat says he aimed for, the gentle score only announces itself after Brad Pitt has uttered his final line, . . . the screen has gone black, and the full weight of the past three hours hits. As the main theme gets its most defined iteration under the closing credits, it becomes clear that every second of *Benjamin Button*'s effectiveness was resting in its powerful hands." In 2008 Desplat also scored *Largo Winch*, which was based on a popular Belgian comic-book series, and *Afterwards*, a thriller starring John Malkovich.

In 2009 Desplat provided the scores for the French biographical film *Coco avant Chanel* (released as *Coco Before Chanel* in the U.S.) and Stephen Frears's drama *Chéri*, which starred Michelle Pfeiffer as a seductive woman who carries on an affair with a much younger man. More widely seen that year were the big-budget films *Julie & Julia*, which starred Meryl Streep as the iconic chef Julia Child and Amy Adams as a young woman who idolizes her, and Wes Anderson's animated *Fantastic Mr. Fox*, which was based on a tale by Roald Dahl about a sophisticated fox defending his family from farmers. The score for the latter movie, which featured original music by Desplat as well as a variety of pop songs picked by the filmmaker, was nominated for an Academy Award. That year Desplat also wrote the music for *New Moon*, the highly anticipated sequel to *Twilight*. The films were based on the wildly popular series of young-adult novels by Stephenie Meyer, about lustful teen vampires. Like *Twilight*, *New Moon* was a massive hit at the box office, and its soundtrack, which consisted of original music by Desplat and several songs by contemporary pop artists, debuted at number two on the *Billboard* 200 chart. (It later reached the number-one spot.)

The following year Desplat wrote the score for another fantasy blockbuster, *Harry Potter and The Deathly Hallows: Part 1*, the penultimate film in the series—based on J. K. Rowling's novels—about young students at Hogwarts School of Witchcraft and Wizardry. John Williams, who had so enchanted Desplat with his *Star Wars* score decades before, had written the music for the first picture, *Harry Potter and the Sorcerer's Stone* (2001). "Since a grand musical wizard named John Williams established the sound of Harry Potter nine years ago with *The Sorcerer's Stone*, new composing students at Hogwarts School of Witchcraft and Wizardry have capably added on to its ever-evolving foundations. These acolytes have ranged from William Ross to Patrick Doyle and Nicholas Hooper, each bringing their distinctive touch of fantastical wonder and darkness during their sojourns," Daniel Schweiger wrote for *Film Music Magazine* (November 9, 2010, on-line). "*Hallows* [boasts a] terrif-

ic score by Alexandre Desplat. No stranger to gracing such fantastical sagas, Desplat has mixed the emotions of age and fantasy with *Birth* and *Benjamin Button*, not to mention brought in the symphonic thunder in the supernatural battles of . . . *New Moon* and *The Golden Compass*. Now Desplat enters Hogwarts with an inimitably lush score that could be described as being more Williams than Williams, while more than retaining Desplat's own thematically rich voice that has made him Hollywood's most in-demand French musical import since the days of such master melodicists as Maurice Jarre." Desplat composed the music for the upcoming final film in the series, *Harry Potter and The Deathly Hallows: Part 2*.

In 2010 Desplat also scored *The King's Speech*, which starred Colin Firth as King George VI of Great Britain, who reigned from 1936 to 1952. The film, based on true incidents, follows the beloved monarch as he struggles to overcome a stutter through the unorthodox methods of the speech therapist Lionel Logue, played by Geoffrey Rush. The score, recorded in part with vintage microphones actually used by George VI and the royal family, earned Desplat Academy Award and Golden Globe nominations, and he took home BAFTA's Anthony Asquith Award for Film Music. Jake Coyle wrote, "In a film where sound is central, Alexandre Desplat's score to *The King's Speech* enters subtly. A simple melody slinks in, a soft, demure line of hopeful piano notes, fittingly repetitive, like the stuttering speech of the film's main character." "It's a film where the music is not here to shine," Desplat told Lisa Zhito for BMI.com (February 23, 2011). "But I think if you take the music I wrote out there will be [a] huge hole, because the music is conveying what the character cannot express. . . . For example how do you express stuttering in music? Well you can't just repeat the same chord. I found the idea of repeated notes, this thing that can't evolve because it's like it's stuck. . . . The music is an echo of the king's difficulties. And I'm certain this [gets] under the skin of the audience and emphasizes all of the emotions and suffering that the king has." Desplat's other 2010 projects included Roman Polanski's *The Ghost Writer* and the Stephen Frears comedy *Tamara Drewe*.

In early 2011 Desplat's music could be heard in *The Burma Conspiracy* (a sequel to *Largo Winch*) and *La Fille du puisatier*, a romantic drama directed by and starring Daniel Auteuil. (The title translates as "The Well-Digger's Daughter.") In addition to *Harry Potter and the Deathly Hallows: Part 2*, which will be released in July 2011, Desplat's compositions will be featured in the mid-2011 releases *A Better Life*, about a struggling Mexican immigrant trying to keep his son safe on the streets of L.A., and Terrence Malick's long-awaited new picture, *The Tree of Life*. At Malick's request, Desplat wrote the score for the latter film, which stars Brad Pitt and Sean Penn, before seeing footage from it. Explaining that the soundtrack uses "musical cues from 19th century romantic composer Hector Berlioz and modern composer György Ligeti," Desplat told Kevin Jagernauth for IndieWire.com (December 13, 2010), "[Malick] always told me that the music should be like a river flowing through the film, and that's what I tried to achieve—something that flows and never stops, very alive and fluid."

Desplat, who is married to the French musician Dominique Lemonnier, was named film composer of the year by the International Film Music Critics Association in 2007, and in both 2009 and 2010 he was honored with the same title at the World Soundtrack Awards ceremony.

In his interview with Charlotte Smith, the composer said, "Most important [to my job] is finding the balance between function and fiction. Function will ensure that the music fits well into the mechanics of the film but fiction enables you to tap into the invisible—the deep psychology, pain and notions of the characters."

—W.D.

Suggested Reading: Associated Press (on-line) Feb. 17, 2011; BMI.com Feb. 23, 2011; *Film Music Magazine* (on-line) Nov. 9, 2010; *Gramophone* (on-line) Jan. 25, 2011; IGN.com Feb. 21, 2007; IndieWire.com Dec. 13, 2010; *New York Times* A p12 Jan. 7, 2007, (on-line) Nov. 23, 2005; *Patrol Magazine* (on-line) Jan. 26, 2009; *Variety* (on-line) Sep. 7, 2004; WBUR.org Jan. 9, 2009

Selected Films: *Girl with a Pearl Earring*, 2003; *Birth*, 2004; *The Upside of Anger*, 2005; *Hostage*, 2005; *Casanova*, 2005; *Syriana*, 2005; *The Queen*, 2006; *Firewall*; 2006 *Lies and Alibis*; 2006; *The Valet*, 2006; *The Painted Veil*, 2006; *The Golden Compass*, 2007; *Mr. Magorium's Wonder Emporium*, 2007; *Largo Winch*, 2008; *Afterwards*, 2008; *The Curious Case of Benjamin Button*, 2008; *Coco Before Chanel*, 2009; *Fantastic Mr. Fox*, 2009; *Julie & Julia*, 2009; *New Moon*, 2009; *Che@ri*, 2009; *The Ghost Writer*, 2010; *Tamara Drewe*, 2010; *Harry Potter and the Deathly Hallows: Part 1*, 2010; *The King's Speech*, 2010; *The Burma Conspiracy*, 2011; *A Better Life*, 2011; *The Tree of Life*, 2011; *Harry Potter and the Deathly Hallows: Part 2*, 2011

Diggs, Taye

Jan. 2, 1971(?)– Actor

Address: c/o Burton Goldstein Co., 156 W. 56th St., Suite 1803, New York, NY 10019

Writing for *Vanity Fair* (February 2011), Cortney Pellettieri declared that Taye Diggs "is a throwback to the days when movie stars were all-around entertainers." "I want to dance and sing and act. There aren't that many actors out there who can do all of that, straight up," Diggs told Jennifer Frey for the *Washington Post* (October 27, 2004). Diggs honed his skills in acting, singing, and dancing at a specialized public middle school/high school in Rochester, New York, and at Syracuse University, where he studied musical theater. Within months of his college graduation, in 1993, he had won a role in a critically acclaimed 1994 Broadway revival of the musical *Carousel*. In 1996, after working for nearly two years as a performer at the Tokyo Disney Resort, in Japan, he appeared in the original Off-Broadway production of *Rent*, which made a tremendous splash and soon opened on Broadway to rave reviews. In his cinematic debut, in 1998, Diggs starred with the celebrated actress Angela Bassett in the feature film *How Stella Got Her Groove Back*; his megawatt smile, charm, and buff physique—displayed to full advantage from the back in a shower scene—turned him overnight into a heartthrob and a sex symbol. Diggs told Jack Garner for the *Rochester Democrat and Chronicle* (October 22, 1999) that during his student days, "I

Pascal Le Segretain/Getty Images

knew I wanted to be an actor for the rest of my life, and that I'd be successful at it. But all this has happened a lot sooner than I'd planned."

Diggs has since appeared in films including *Go*, *The Wood*, *The Best Man*, *House on Haunted Hill*, *Brown Sugar*, *Equilibrium*, *Chicago*, *Days of Wrath*, and the screen version of *Rent*; onstage in the Broadway musicals *Chicago* and *Wicked* and

Off-Broadway productions of *The Wild Party* and *A Soldier's Play*; and on television in series including *Guiding Light, Ally McBeal, The West Wing, Kevin Hill, Will & Grace, Day Break,* and *Grey's Anatomy* and its spin-off, *Private Practice*, which completed its fourth season on ABC in May 2011. His character in *Private Practice*, the doctor Sam Bennett, has appeared in each of the 76 episodes that have aired since the show's debut, in 2009. With Andrew Palermo Diggs co-founded the dance troupe dre.dance, in 2004; the two men serve as choreographers and as the group's co–artistic directors. In 2010 Diggs and his wife, the actress and singer Idina Menzel, launched the foundation A Broader Way, which sponsors theater workshops, a 10-day summer camp, and other programs that provide performance opportunities for young people.

The first of the five children of Marcia Ann Berry-Diggs and Jeffries L. Diggs, Taye Diggs was born Scott Leo Diggs on January 2, 1971 (or 1972, according to some sources) in Newark, New Jersey. "Taye" comes from "Scot*taye*," a childhood nickname. Diggs has two brothers, Gabriel and Michael, and two sisters, Shalom and Christian. "My mother raised [my siblings and me] with songs about brushing our teeth," he told Cortney Pellettieri. Various accounts report that Diggs's mother, a teacher and avocational actress, singer, and dancer, was widowed when all her children were in their teens or younger, but in the May 14, 2001 issue of *People* magazine, when Diggs was 29 or 30, Jeffries Diggs was said to be 60 years old, and according to Jennifer Frey, writing for the *Washington Post* (October 27, 2004), Diggs "grew up in a traditional two-parent family." During Diggs's childhood his family moved to Rochester, New York, where his mother took courses toward a Ph.D. in the social sciences at the State University of New York at Brockport while running a medical-transcription service. In 1993 Marcia Berry-Diggs earned an M.F.A. degree in theater from the University of Mississippi; her thesis was entitled "An Examination of the Preparation and Performance of Three Major Roles, 1990–1993." That same year she relocated with her children to Bloomington, Indiana, where later in that decade she pursued a doctorate in drama and theater at Indiana University.

On the Web site of Diggs and Menzel's organization, A Broader Way, Diggs wrote that "as a youth, I was small, insecure and didn't have a real community of friends outside of my family." "I was a dweeb," he told Frey. "I had glasses, and because I always played sports, the glasses were always broken. I was kind of insecure. Not romantically inclined. I saw that there was a definite difference between me and the cool people." In hopes of building his strength and physique, Diggs enrolled in modern-dance classes and began lifting weights. His mother—who taught acting then at a community theater—encouraged him to nurture his artistic talents. With some effort she persuaded him to transfer from an ordinary public school to the School of the Arts, a specialized Rochester facility for seventh- through 12th-graders. "At that time I was interested in sports, but I finally let [my mother] convince me to give acting a shot. I did and now I feel that I have finally found my niche, and I thank my mother everyday for her insight," Diggs told Don Thomas for the *New York Beacon* (September 16, 1998). Diggs excelled at the School of the Arts. He wrote for A Broader Way (on-line), "My life was transformed permanently. I was surrounded by students with similar interests and I finally had a peer group to call my own. I built up my courage to take risks and express myself. I am convinced that my being exposed to the arts at that age set the stage for the rest of my life."

After his high-school graduation, Diggs studied dance, singing, and acting at Syracuse University, in New York State; he earned a B.F.A. degree in musical theater there in 1993. As an undergraduate he performed in productions mounted at the Lakes Region Summer Theatre, in Meredith, New Hampshire. During his senior year Diggs and a handful of other students were chosen to participate in a New York showcase—an event designed to introduce aspiring performers to artists' representatives—and he succeeded in signing with his first agent. When he completed college Diggs moved to New York City to launch his career as a professional actor. He quickly landed understudy roles for three characters as well as an ensemble part in Nicholas Hytner's triumphant Broadway revival of the musical *Carousel* (1994). He contributed to the revival's cast album, recorded that year.

In 1995 Diggs moved to Japan to serve as the emcee in a faux cabaret show called Sebastian's Caribbean Carnival at the Tokyo Disney Resort. "People thought I was silly, to go from Broadway to a theme park," Diggs told Bob Ivry for the Bergen County, New Jersey, *Record* (July 17, 1999). "But I stayed . . . and learned the language."

When Diggs returned to the States, in 1996, after close to two years overseas, he was determined to seek only nonmusical acting jobs. But prodded by his agent, and short of money, he auditioned for a role in an upcoming Off-Broadway musical called *Rent*, with words and music by Jonathan Larson (who died of an undiagnosed heart abnormality a few hours after the final dress rehearsal). Loosely based on the Giacomo Puccini opera *La Bohème*, which was adapted from a book of stories by the French writer Henri Murger (1822–61), Larson's rock opera revolves around a group of struggling artists who live in New York City's East Village neighborhood and deal with issues of money, love, AIDS, and death. Diggs landed the role of the hated landlord Benjamin Coffin III, a onetime bohemian who turns on his friends in the process of gaining financial stability. Set to run for only a few months, the musical was an instant hit and quickly moved to Broadway, greatly boosting the careers of the show's previously little-known cast members. "Sparked by a young, intensely vibrant cast . . .

and sustained by a glittering, inventive score, the work finds a transfixing brightness in characters living in the shadow of AIDS," Ben Brantley wrote in a *New York Times* (February 14, 1996) review of *Rent*. "The cast . . . is terrific, right down to the last ensemble member, and blessed with voices of remarkable flexibility and strength." The musical won the Pulitzer Prize for drama in 1996 as well as multiple Tony Awards, including one for best musical. "I needed a credit on my resume," Diggs told Bob Ivry. "I hadn't even heard the whole thing when I took the part. We had no idea it would catapult like it did, the Pulitzer Prize, the magazine covers, the move uptown to Broadway. It was an amazing period in all our lives, the whole cast. No matter what we do in the future, we'll have that incredible experience in common." In 2004 Diggs married another *Rent* original cast member—Idina Menzel, with whom he had lived for more than five years. He and Menzel reprised their *Rent* roles in the adaptation for film, also called *Rent* (2005), directed by Chris Columbus.

Concurrently while he performed in *Rent* on Broadway, Diggs appeared in guest spots on television shows including *Law and Order*, *New York Undercover*, *Guiding Light*, and, most notably, as the attorney Jackson Duper in *Ally McBeal*. In 1998, in a major coup for the relatively untried young actor, Diggs auditioned successfully for the leading male role opposite Angela Bassett in the film adaptation of Terry McMillan's novel *How Stella Got Her Groove Back*. Thanks to the box-office success of the 1995 film based on McMillan's previous novel *Waiting to Exhale*, the new film was expected to become a blockbuster hit. Diggs was cast as Winston Shakespeare, a 20-year-old Jamaican who becomes the love interest of Stella (Bassett), a divorced 40-year-old San Francisco stockbroker and mother. Diggs, like the film, earned mostly middling reviews.

Diggs won leading roles in the romance-driven, black-centered drama/comedies *The Wood* (1999), directed by Rick Famuyiwa and co-starring Omar Epps and Richard T. Jones; *The Best Man* (1999), co-starring Morris Chestnut and Nia Long and directed by Malcolm D. Lee; and *Brown Sugar* (2002), directed by Famuyiwa and co-starring Sanaa Latham and Mos Def. His pleasure in that work was marred by the belief that he was being passed over for parts in top-quality racially integrated films. "I rose to the top of the list, but I rose to the top of the black people list, which is always going to be below the white people's list," he told Frey in 2004. "And I didn't think that existed because of the way I was raised. My high school was integrated. I always dated all different types of girls; the parts [at school] were not black or white."

Diggs had supporting roles in the films *The House on Haunted Hill* (1999), a remake of a 1958 horror film; Doug Liman's *Go* (1999), a trio of tales; and Christopher McQuarrie's *The Way of the Gun* (2000), starring Ryan Philippe and Benicio Del Toro. He returned briefly to the Off-Broadway stage in 2000, to play Mr. Black in *The Wild Party*, a musical set during the 1920s Jazz Age. Andrew Lippa wrote the book, lyrics, and music for *The Wild Party*, based on a long narrative poem by Joseph Moncure March that was widely banned when it was published, in 1928. In an article about Diggs and Menzel for the *New York Times Magazine* (February 13, 2000), Jesse Green wrote that in light of Diggs's reputation as "something of an established heartthrob," *The Wild Party* audiences "may be surprised to discover (again) what a beautiful voice he has, what natural, un-Hollywood presence." *The Wild Party*, which ran for two months, won the Outer Critics Circle Award for outstanding Off-Broadway musical. The same group nominated Diggs for the award in the category of outstanding actor in a musical.

Although Diggs appeared in the blockbuster film *Chicago* (2002) and two films in 2003— *Malibu's Most Wanted* and *Basic*—it seemed his movie career was at a standstill. "The roles were becoming a bit stale, and artistically there was not much I could really dig into," Diggs told Lola Ogunnaike for the *New York Times* (September 26, 2004). "I wanted to go to the next level in film, and that wasn't happening."

Hoping to give his career a boost, in 2004 Diggs signed with the now-defunct United Paramount Network (UPN) to take the leading role in its new TV show *Kevin Hill*. He was also one of its producers. Hill, Diggs's character, is a 28-year-old entertainment lawyer who, not by choice, becomes the guardian of Sarah, the 10-month-old daughter of a deceased cousin. A womanizing, club-hopping workaholic, Hill leaves his high-paying job, joins a smaller, all-female law firm, and hires a homosexual male nanny to help raise the baby. "I knew it would be difficult to find a guy who could be the Casanova without being obnoxious," the show's creator, Jorge Reyes, told Marc Peyser for *Newsweek* (August 30, 2004). "With a lesser actor than Taye," the show would go "off the rails." The weekly one-hour series appealed to a wide spectrum of viewers, crossing color lines with its racially diverse cast and humorously exploring sexual-identity issues through the mildly chauvinistic and homophobic tendencies of Diggs's character. "There were so many different relationships to bite into," Diggs told *Jet* magazine (November 22, 2004). "That was the most attractive element of the whole situation—the relationship with the gay nanny, the relationship with Sarah, . . . the relationship with the women in the law firm and continuing the relationship with his best friend." Through the genuinely caring—though sometimes shallow—Hill, *Kevin Hill* avoided the stereotypical image of the absent black father. Echoing the general sentiments of critics, Peyser praised the show as "one of the most promising new programs of the season. . . . And Diggs is delightful—funny, charming and warm." But *Kevin Hill*'s novelty soon waned, and UPN dropped it after one season. "When I agreed to do the show, I thought it was a brilliant premise," Diggs told Ogunnaike. "But it turned out to be a fixer-upper. By the end, I was beat down. It takes a lot of energy fixing and up-ping."

Also in 2004, with his fellow School of the Arts alumnus Andrew Palermo, Diggs co-founded dre.dance, a contemporary-dance troupe based in New York City. "Nobody knows that between sing-ing, acting and dancing, I enjoy dance the most," he told Ogunnaike. As the principal choreogra-pher, Diggs made use of his years of study with such internationally renowned dance teachers as Timothy Draper and Garth Fagan. Together or sep-arately Diggs and Palermo have choreographed five long works that last from 40 minutes to one hour and 10 short works that range from three to 10 min-utes. One of the longer works, *beyond.words*, was choreographed by both Diggs and Palermo—dre.dance's artistic directors—and accompanied music by Nico Muhly and the band TV on the Ra-dio. The work is an attempt "to translate the inner and outer experience of autism into dance," Robert Abrams wrote for ExploreDance.com (April 4, 2009), after seeing it performed at the Tribeca Per-forming Arts Center, in New York City. According to Abrams, Diggs and Palermo had succeeded: the piece "proved to be a well-executed, beautiful and thought-provoking work of abstract dance." As of mid-2011 six female dancers and three males com-prised the company.

Earlier, in 2005, Diggs had returned to the stage to star in a revival of Charles Fuller's Pulitzer Prize–winning *A Soldier's Play*. Diggs portrayed Captain Richard Davenport, the arrogant lawyer who investigates the murder of a black sergeant at a Louisiana army base during World War II. Wres-tling with the racial prejudices of the white com-manding officers and the expectations of the black community, Davenport walks a fine racial line in the tension-filled story. "I think it's one of the greatest pieces of literature dealing with African-American men," Diggs told Ogunnaike for the *New York Times* (November 13, 2005). "Davenport has to stay one step ahead of the white people so he'll be seen as equal, and he has all this pressure from the African-American community because he's the one who broke through; he represents the race." In a review for the Associated Press (October 17, 2005), Michael Kuchwara wrote, "Diggs gives a controlled, laid-back performance." Ben Brantley wrote for the *New York Times* (October 18, 2005), "Diggs is a lucid and commanding center of atten-tion."

On television Diggs joined the cast of the series *Will & Grace* four times in 2006, and he starred in the show *Day Break* (2006–07) before rapidly dwindling viewership led to its cancellation, after 13 episodes. In *Day Break* Diggs's character, a Los Angeles, California, police detective named Brett Hopper, has been falsely accused of killing an as-sistant district attorney. Desperate to find the real culprit, he repeatedly relives the day of the mur-der—much as Phil (played by Bill Murray), the

lead character in Harold Ramis's comedy *Ground-hog Day* (1993), wakes up on February 2 many times in succession.

Diggs was cast as internist Sam Bennett in a two-part episode of Shonda Rhimes's series *Grey's Anatomy* in 2007; in the spin-off from that show, *Private Practice*, which premiered later that year, Bennett and two other *Grey's Anatomy* physicians have formed a new group medical practice, called the Oceanside Wellness Group. One of Bennett's partners is his former wife, Naomi (played by Au-dra McDonald), with whom he has a teenage daughter, Maya. During Season Four of *Private Practice*, the unmarried Maya becomes pregnant and gives birth to a daughter. During a few of the 76 episodes of *Private Practice* that have aired to date, Bennett has been seen reconnecting, tempo-rarily, with his former wife in intimate settings and becoming romantically involved with two other doctors, portrayed by Chandra Wilson and Kate Walsh. Diggs, as Bennett, was included in a short list of actors described in *Cosmopolitan* (December 2008) as "TV's most bedable dads." Some critics have complained that *Private Practice* is often tainted by the over-the-top emotionality and com-plex tangled relationships associated with tradi-tional soap operas. Nevertheless, for the most part Diggs and the others in the ensemble cast have earned praise for the high quality of their acting. *Private Practice* has been renewed for a fifth sea-son.

Diggs's honors include the award for best acting ensemble (in *Chicago*) from the Broadcast Film Critics Association and the Screen Actors Guild (both in 2003); Image Awards from the NAACP (National Association for the Advancement of Col-ored People), for outstanding actor in a drama se-ries (in *Kevin Hill*, 2004) and outstanding support-ing actor in a drama series (in *Private Practice*, 2007); nominations for five other Image Awards; and nominations for Black Reel Awards, from the Foundation for the Advancement of African Amer-icans in Film, for best actor (in *The Best Man*, 2000) and best ensemble (in *Rent*, 2005).

Diggs and his wife, Idina Menzel, became the parents of a son, Walker, in September 2009. The couple maintain homes in New York City and Los Angeles.

—I.C.

Suggested Reading: ABC Studios Medianet (on-line); abroaderway.org; dredance.com; *Ebony* p100+ Jan. 2000, p161+ May 2005; imdb.com; *New York Beacon* p27 Sep. 16, 1998; *New York Times* II p9 Nov. 13, 2005, (on-line) Feb. 13, 2000; *Newsweek* 58+ Aug. 24, 1998, p50+ Aug. 30, 2004; *People* p172 May 14, 2001; (Syracuse, New York) *Post-Standard* C p1+ Aug. 13, 1998; *Washington Post* C p1+ Oct. 27, 2004

Selected Films: *How Stella Got Her Groove Back*, 1998; *Go*, 1999; *The Wood*, 1999; *The Best Man*, 1999; *The House on Haunted Hill*, 1999; *The*

Way of the Gun, 2000; New Best Friend, 2002; Brown Sugar, 2002; Equilibrium, 2002; Chicago, 2002; Basic, 2003; Malibu's Most Wanted, 2003; Drum, 2004; Rent, 2005

Selected Plays: A Soldier's Play, 2005

Selected Musicals: Carousel, 1994; Rent, 1996; The Wild Party, 2000; Chicago, 2002; Wicked, 2003

Selected Television Shows: Kevin Hill, 2004; Will & Grace, 2006; Day Break, 2006–07; Private Practice, 2007–

Hal Eastman, courtesy of the Wendy Weil Agency

Doerr, Anthony

(dore)

Oct. 27, 1973– Novelist; short-story writer

Address: c/o Wendy Weil Agency, 232 Madison Ave., Suite 1300, New York, NY 10016

The writer Anthony Doerr has won admiration and awards for his skill in incorporating scientific information and observations in tales that illuminate the human condition. In an assessment of Doerr's first book, the short-story collection The Shell Collector, Gail Caldwell wrote for the Boston Globe (January 27, 2002), "Obsessed with our own existence, we tend to be far more enamored with stories about people—about wounded soldiers or heartbroken lovers or alienated souls—than we are with the vibrant theater beyond the human heart.

Particularly in the English-speaking order of things, the natural world is afforded a place on the second tier in literature, somewhere below fiction and history. . . . All kinds of writers have defied this tenet over time, so that we have Hemingway's trout streams and Willa Cather's prairies and the rocky desolation of Annie Proulx's landscapes to remind us of our size. . . . Anthony Doerr seems to grasp this relativism as well." Dana Oland wrote for the Idaho Statesman (February 18, 2011, on-line) that Doerr "examines his subjects with the scrupulous attention of a naturalist of an early era, drawing every detail of an exotic gnat's wing. He studies scientific theories and human behavior from every angle. He thinks through his characters from the inside out, then shapes their experiences in meticulous detail." In addition to The Shell Collector (2002), Doerr is the author of the novel About Grace (2004); the travel memoir Four Seasons in Rome (2007); and a second short-story collection, Memory Wall (2010). His honors include the Rome Prize from the American Academy of Arts and Letters, a Guggenheim fellowship, a National Endowment for the Arts literature fellowship, and three O. Henry Prizes. His story "Memory Wall," along with tales by two other writers, earned McSweeney's Quarterly a 2010 National Magazine Award for excellence in fiction.

Nicknamed Tony, Anthony Doerr was born on October 27, 1973 in Cleveland, Ohio, and raised about 20 miles east, in the town of Novelty. He has two older brothers. His father, Richard Doerr, owns a printing and graphic-design company. His mother, Marilyn N. Doerr, is a curriculum consultant and science and math teacher; Doerr was a student in some of her classes. In her book Currere and the Environmental Autobiography: A Phenomenological Approach to the Teaching of Ecology (2004), his mother described a course that she taught according to a method espoused in the 1970s by the educator William Pinar.

In a Washington Post Q&A with readers (October 14, 2004, on-line), Anthony Doerr recalled, "I guess you could say I've been writing all my life. When I was nine I was writing . . . but you never think you're going to become a writer. I always told my dad I'd play professional football. You don't say, I'm going to be a writer when I grow up—at least I didn't. I guess whatever maturity is there may be there because I've been keeping a journal forever. . . . I was always trying to translate experience into words." Doerr's interest in science was inspired by his mother, who "always had us examining caterpillars, snails, frogs," he recalled to Martha Liebrum for Sun Valley Magazine (Winter 2009, on-line). His interest grew during the family's annual trips to Sanibel Island, in the Gulf of Mexico near Fort Myers, Florida. The island, half of which consists of wildlife refuges, is famous for its seashells, the remains of an unusually large variety of mollusks. In the Washington Post Q&A, Doerr recalled, "Every time we found anything, any mollusk, my mom would bring out the guidebook and quiz us on what it was, so that stuff was built in early." At home the family maintained a large salt-water aquarium.

From kindergarten through eighth grade, Doerr attended the Ruffing Montessori School, in Cleveland Heights. In an undated statement posted on the Web site of the Montessori-based Post Oak School, in Texas, he wrote, "Of all the skills nine years of Montessori education gave me . . . the most lasting has been a sense of my place in deep geologic time. We were making twenty-foot-long timelines as early as first grade. . . . You're six or seven years old and you're being asked to measure the brief, warm, intensely complicated fingersnap of your life against the absolutely incomprehensible vastness of time. The sense of luck that made me feel—to be here at all!—has never left me. It permeates my writing, my attitudes toward natural resources, and my relationship with my sons." As a boy, he told Martha Liebrum, he pinned to his bedroom walls "dozens" of maps and pictures of landscapes cut from magazines.

Doerr spent grades nine through 12 at the private, all-boys University School, whose high-school campus is in Hunting Valley, a Cleveland suburb. His friends would tease him when they saw him writing in what they called his "man diary," he recalled for the *Washington Post*. During his teens he became deeply interested in rock climbing. After his graduation, in 1991, he enrolled at Bowdoin College, in Brunswick, Maine, where he earned a B.A. degree in history and English in 1995 and met his future wife. During the next few years, he traveled and worked at a fish-processing plant in Alaska and at a ski resort in Telluride, Colorado. He told Karen Sandstrom for the Cleveland *Plain Dealer* (April 2, 2002) that with time he felt the need to do more with his life. He recalled, "I was reading a ton, and I thought, 'If I'm not careful, I could spend the rest of my life doing this—reading and drinking beer.'"

To avoid that fate Doerr enrolled in the master's-degree program in writing at Bowling Green State University (BGSU), in Ohio. While he was studying there, his story "Only So Many Chances" appeared in the Winter/Spring 1999 issue of the *Sycamore Review*. (In *The Shell Collector* that tale is entitled "So Many Chances.") Another, called "For a Long Time, This Was Griselda's Story," appeared in the November/December 1999 issue of the *North American Review*. After earning an M.F.A. degree, in 1999, Doerr embarked on a yearlong fellowship at the University of Wisconsin, then returned to Ohio to teach at BGSU. In 2001 he moved to Boise, Idaho, the hometown of his wife. That same year saw the publication of his stories "River Run," in the *Sewanee Review* (July/September issue), and "The Caretaker," in the *Paris Review* (Fall issue). The Winter 2001/Spring 2002 issue of the *Chicago Review* included his story "The Shell Collector," in which a blind, retired professor and malacologist (mollusk expert) who lives reclusively in Kenya and collects shells along its coast stumbles upon the curative powers of the venom of a species of cone snail. After his discovery becomes public, his self-imposed exile from family and the outside world ends. "I think the character of the shell collector started . . . with the tactile pleasure of holding shells and the associations and memories they fired in me," Doerr told Martha Liebrun. "Then I did some research and found out that there is, actually, a real-life malacologist who happens to be blind. So the story came out of research and personal interest. It took a lot of drafts before I learned how to explore the metaphor of making the shell collector's life like a shell itself, how he tries to retreat into it but cannot."

Named for that story, Doerr's first book, *The Shell Collector* (2002), offers tales about characters interacting with nature through such activities as gardening, fishing, and hunting. A writer for the Web site of the Penguin Group, which published the book, noted that in his stories Doerr "demonstrates how immersion in the natural world, far from limiting the scope of these lives, allows them to be truly free individuals, to be themselves in the purest sense. His characters seem to find comfort in necessity, in simplicity, and in isolation. . . . Yet even as Doerr evokes the lure of the natural world and seems to espouse its virtues over those of civilization, he also subtly advocates for the irreplaceable value of human relations, however fragile and ephemeral those might be."

The Shell Collector earned much critical praise, with Doerr's being compared to such literary luminaries as Ernest Hemingway and Don DeLillo. Gail Caldwell described the book as "a paean to the exquisite universe outside ourselves. Perilously beautiful, as precise and elegant as calculus, that wider place of Doerr's imagination is so commanding, so poetically rendered, that it informs and even defines the characters who wander across its stage." In an assessment for the *New York Times Book Review* (March 3, 2002, on-line), Nancy Willard wrote, "Doerr's prose dazzles, his sinewy sentences blending the naturalist's unswerving gaze with the poet's gift for metaphor." *The Shell Collector* was listed on various periodicals' "notable books" lists and won the Barnes & Noble Discover Prize, the New York Public Library's Young Lions Award, and the Ohioana Book Award for fiction.

The main character of Doerr's novel *About Grace* (2004) is an Alaskan hydrologist, David Winkler, who loves to study snowflakes and has an uncanny ability to dream about future events that come to pass. (Doerr told Liebrum that Wilson Bentley, a Vermont farmer who made thousands of photomicrographs of snowflakes around the turn of the 19th–20th century, was "the little grain of dust at the nucleus, around which the whole structure of *About Grace* precipitated.") After marrying and becoming a father, Winkler dreams that he will be responsible for the death of his little daughter, Grace. Terrified, he abandons his family and ekes out a hand-to-mouth existence on a Caribbean island. After 25 years he returns to the U.S. and embarks on a search for Grace. Critics extolled the beauty of Doerr's writing in *About Grace* but most found its storyline tedious. An unnamed writer for *Kirkus Reviews* (on-line), for example, reported that *"About Grace* possesses a seductive symbolic intensity, and abounds with gorgeous descriptions and metaphors. . . . But it's much too long, and is significantly marred by its climactic momentum toward a reconciliation that simply isn't very credible. Its protagonist's loneliness, regret, and guilt are painfully palpable, and go a long way toward making this risky book work—but, in the end, aren't enough. A bold attempt, nevertheless, by a gifted writer." Nicholas Fonseca wrote for *Entertainment Weekly* (September 24, 2004, on-line), "Doerr nearly drowns beneath an annoying surfeit of drippy water metaphors, but *About Grace* remains grounded because he keeps a steady grasp on Winkler's roiling emotions, never allowing the reluctant antihero to become a simpering, aimless fool." The Book of the Month Club included *About Grace* in its choices of the five best books of 2004, and the novel was a finalist for the PEN USA Fiction Award.

A nomination by the American Academy of Arts and Letters led the American Academy in Rome to award Doerr a fellowship, known as a Rome Prize, that enabled him and his family to spend nearly a year in Rome, Italy, starting in the fall of 2004. *Four Seasons in Rome: On Twins, Insomnia, and the Biggest Funeral in the History of the World* (2007) describes sites that Doerr visited, his experiences as a new father of twin sons living in a foreign city, and the massive vigil held during the last days of Pope John Paul II, in late March and early April 2005, and the pope's funeral. "I wanted to write it for the boys," Doerr told Dana Oland for the *Idaho Statesman* (June 7, 2007). "They won't remember. Now, they can read about it when they're 30 and they'll know this was the first year of their life. I found myself falling in love with that city, just like I fell in love with my kids."

In a review of *Four Seasons in Rome*, Boyd Tonkin wrote for the London *Guardian* (July 18, 2009, on-line), "Two qualities lift this book above the herd of American-abroad travelogues. First, his writing is fleet and sharp, fixing monuments, neighbours, dishes and Popes . . . with a radiant image, not a purple passage. Second, it's a book about the foreign country of fatherhood. Twin baby sons ease his path through Roman life and mock his 'hopelessly hilarious' ambitions. While the 'city of always' bewitches him, parenthood demands 'a kind of love that has no conclusions.'" Rosemary Mahoney Little wrote for *Salon.com* (June 18, 2007), "Doerr has composed a bittersweet and artful meditation on the craft of writing and a celebration of the city and the senses."

Doerr wrote the novella "Memory Wall" for the 32d issue of *McSweeney's Quarterly* (2009), which was devoted to stories set in the year 2024. The inspiration for "Memory Wall" came from an essay in the book *What We Believe but Cannot Prove* (2006), edited by John Brockman, in which computational neuroscientist Terrence J. Sejnowski "speculates that someday soon we might be able to locate specific memories in the 'extracellular machinery' of our heads and stain them," according to Doerr, writing for an Amazon.com Q&A. Doerr continued, "I had been fascinated by that idea for months, primarily because it reminded me of hunting fossils: looking for one record in a world that generally does not allow such records. I had simultaneously been writing some (lousy) essays about my own memories of my grandmother's descent into dementia. It wasn't until *McSweeney's* came calling that I gave myself permission to try to braid together a story [of] all these enthusiasms: Alzheimer's and grandma and fossils and South Africa." The old, white South African woman in "Memory Wall" has had a special port installed in her head—a device that accepts and "plays" cartridges in which some of her memories have been stored. The characters include a man determined to get ahold of a cartridge that contains a description of a secret, potentially lucrative scientific discovery made by the woman's now-deceased husband. "Memory Wall," the title story in Doerr's latest collection, helped to earn *McSweeney's Quarterly* a National Magazine Award for fiction in 2010. Another tale in *Memory Wall*, "Village 113," originally appeared in the Summer 2006 issue of the magazine *Tin House* and was included in the anthology *The O. Henry Prize Stories 2008*; "The River Nemunas," which originally appeared in the Summer 2009 issue of *Tin House*, earned a 2011 Pushcart Prize.

In a review of *Memory Wall* for the *New York Times* (July 30, 2010, on-line), Terrence Rafferty wrote, "The impetus of a Doerr story is always a movement toward transcendence, and the process is what matters, not the vehicles: not the metaphors, not the tricky plots, not the local color, not the occasional bursts of melodrama. It's the flow of experience toward something resembling meaning, a sense of one's place in time. And if that seems impossibly lofty—these stories are very difficult to talk about without sounding grandiose or woolly-headed—it's also winningly blunt. Doerr writes about the big questions, the imponderables, the major metaphysical dreads, and he does it fearlessly. The stories in *Memory Wall* shouldn't work at all, and yet they do, spectacularly. They're about time and memory, and they move to a rhythm that suggests something pulsing under their calm surfaces, the steady breaking of old blood, old memories, the oldest waves of human feeling. When you keep time as well as Anthony Doerr, you can get away with anything."

Doerr's short story "The Deep," which appeared in *Zoetrope* (Fall 2010), was reprinted in the London *Sunday Times* after winning that newspaper's EFG Private Bank Short Story Award in 2011. Doerr won the 2010 Story Prize for *Memory Wall*. In addition to *The Best American Short Stories*, his work has been included in *The Anchor Book of*

New American Short Stories and *The Scribner Anthology of Contemporary Fiction*. With the writers A. S. Byatt and Tim O'Brien, he was a jurist for the PEN/O. Henry Prize Stories 2009. Doerr writes a bimonthly column for the *Boston Globe* in which he recommends books by lesser-known science authors. He teaches in the low-residency M.F.A. program at Warren Wilson College, in Swannanoa, North Carolina, near Asheville.

Doerr told Martha Liebrum, "As I write any piece of fiction, I look back through my journals, which were written while I was in the grips of a place, and all its whirling details. That's my raw material. Then I quarantine myself in some quiet place, a library or my office, and I'll look at photos, or Web sites, or travel brochures, or naturalists' accounts, or whatever else I can use to help me evoke the setting. In the end, my settings are products of memory and research, buttressed by imagination, and tinted by the psyche of the point-of-view character. They are places you could find in an atlas, sure, but they are as much products of imagination as anything else." He also told her, "I read and write a lot and I wander around outside a lot, which means I'm alone a lot. One nice thing, among many, about being a writer of literary fiction is that your ego can never get very large. It's similar to being a parent, actually: both endeavors are pretty humbling. You never know, really, if you're doing a good job as a dad, and you never know if you're doing a good job as a writer. When you spend three years working on a few thousand sentences and they still somehow only approximate the truths you're trying to represent, it's hard to get too full of yourself."

Doerr writes in a small rented office a short bicycle ride from his home, in Boise. He lives with his wife, Shauna Doerr, an independent market researcher, and their seven-year-old sons, Henry and Owen.

—W.D.

Suggested Reading: American Academy in Rome, Society of Fellows (on-line) Mar. 6, 2009; anthonydoerr.com; (Cleveland, Ohio) *Plain Dealer* E p1 Apr. 2, 2002; *Fiction Writers Review* (on-line) Aug. 4, 2010; *Idaho Statesman* (on-line) Feb. 18, 2011; *Sun Valley Magazine* (on-line) Winter 2009; *Washington Post* (on-line) Oct. 14, 2004

Selected Books: *The Shell Collector*, 2002; *About Grace*, 2004; *Four Seasons in Rome: On Twins, Insomnia, and the Biggest Funeral in the History of the World*, 2007; *Memory Wall*, 2010

Doig, Ivan

June 27, 1939– Writer

Address: c/o Harcourt Trade Publishers, 525 B St., Suite 1900, San Diego, CA 92101

Although he has lived in Seattle, Washington, for many years, the award-winning author Ivan Doig is best known for writing about his native Montana. His work, which includes 10 novels, two memoirs, a handful of other nonfiction books, and more than 100 articles, often draws comparisons to that of Wallace Stegner, the "dean of western writers." With his descriptions of Rocky Mountain Front landscapes and elegies for bygone eras, Doig, too, is often referred to as a western writer. In a note to his readers on his Web site, Doig responded to the grouping of writers such as himself and Stegner, writing, "I don't think of myself as a 'Western' writer. To me, language—the substance on the page, that poetry under the prose—is the ultimate 'region,' the true home, for a writer."

Ivan Doig was born on June 27, 1939 in White Sulphur Springs, Montana, the only child of Charles "Charlie" Doig, a ranch hand, and Berneta (Ringer) Doig, a ranch cook. Doig's love of language developed early on, in part because his mother and other relatives often read aloud to him. On Doig's sixth birthday his mother, a chronic asthmatic, died of heart failure. In the years immediately fol-

Courtesy of A. Wayne Arnst

lowing her death, Charlie—except for a brief second marriage—struggled to raise Ivan as a single parent. When his son turned 11, Charlie's unpredictable health prompted him to ask Ivan's maternal grandmother, Elizabeth "Bessie" Ringer, to help raise the boy. Bessie agreed, and for the rest of Ivan's childhood, he was raised by his father and grandmother, first in White Sulphur Springs and then in Dupuyer, Montana. Ivan Doig attended high school in nearby Valier.

The summer after his sophomore year of high school, Doig helped his father and grandmother to care for some 2,000 sheep on the Blackfoot Indian reservation near Glacier National Park. Because it is dangerous for sheep to be exposed to snow or cold rain within the first week or so of being sheared, the family was careful to wait until early July, when the temperature is relatively mild, to shear them. "The day after we sheared, a cold rainstorm blew out to the Rockies," Doig recalled in an interview with Peter Gorner for the *Chicago Tribune* (December 10, 1987). "The sheep all broke in panic and scattered. Some froze, others jumped over the cliffs along the Two Medicine [Lake]. That whole year's profit went with them, the third year in a row that something disastrous had happened. We lost 500 animals." It was then that Doig decided he would seek a life different from that of his parents and grandparents. "I didn't exactly hate sheep," he told Gorner. "But I hated the economic uncertainties of running sheep on shares—sort of sharecropping for rich ranchers who owned all the land—and being perpetually at the mercy of the weather and market prices."

With the encouragement of his high-school Latin and English teacher, Doig applied successfully to study journalism at Northwestern University, in Evanston, Illinois, on an academic scholarship. "I was an economic casualty of Montana," he said in his interview with Gorner. "That scholarship was my ticket out. I came to Evanston [Illinois] in the fall of 1957 and stepped off a train onto Davis Street, which was a brick street. I'd never seen a brick street before." It was difficult for Doig to adapt to life at the university. "All the way through school, I washed dishes at the Northwestern Apartments. I had very little social life, no money and was Montana bashful. I also was a grind. My goal," he said to Gorner, referring to a pioneering television journalist, "was to become another Edward R. Murrow." Upon receiving a B.S. degree, in 1961, Doig was awarded a scholarship for one year of graduate study, and in 1962 he earned a master's degree in journalism from Northwestern.

Doig then spent one year in Texas, on active duty with the U.S. Air Force Reserve. Soon afterward he found a job in Decatur, Illinois, composing editorials for a chain of newspapers. He left his job in Decatur in 1964, when he was offered an assistant-editor position at *Rotarian* magazine, whose offices were a couple of blocks from Northwestern. In 1965 he married Carol Dean Muller, and the following year the couple moved to Seattle, where Doig enrolled in a graduate program in U.S. history at the University of Washington. Doig earned money as a freelance writer while he worked toward his doctorate; he has said that he credits his early experiences as a journalist with developing his skills

as a novelist. He received a Ph.D. in 1969. While he might have pursued a career in academia, "what graduate school taught me . . . was that I wanted to write more than I wanted to teach," he wrote for his Web site.

During the mid-1970s Doig published four nonfiction books. With the first, *News, a Consumer's Guide* (co-written with his wife), he sought to teach readers to be critical of how news is presented—to detect bias and spot omissions. Next, Doig edited two anthologies—*The Streets We Have Come Down: Literature of the City* (1975) and *Utopian America: Dreams and Realities* (1976)—and wrote *Early Forestry Research: A History of the Pacific Northwest Forest and Range Experiment Station, 1925–1975.*

The deaths of his father and grandmother, in 1971 and 1974, respectively, prompted Doig to begin work on a memoir. In an interview with Eric S. Elkins for the *Denver Post* (April 23, 2003), Doig explained: "Part of the impetus behind my writing of the book was to try and fix permanently into book form my father's generation; what the story of that generation was. And by memory and everything, I was able to retrieve much about that way of life by going out journalistically with tape recorder and my wife's camera, and going to all the places where I had lived; where my dad and grandmother had lived. I went to Montana for a couple of months and just did that. I did things like, we carried water from the neighbor's house and I paced off how far it was—how far we carried those buckets of water. And measured the size of rooms in every house and did diagrams and looked at the artifacts that people had. So, it really was a feeling on my part that, hey, this is a really sizable, notable, and in some ways, kind of noble effort that these people's lives added up to: to try and find a distinctive way of life on this big, unrolled carpet of land." In contrast to his earlier journalistic work, Doig found it liberating to write on a subject he already knew so much about. "You don't have to do the long archaeological digs on your own family or people you grew up around," he told Elkins. "And you are not confined as you are by the journalistic efforts of reporting accuracy." The memoir, *This House of Sky: Landscapes of a Western Mind* (1978), focuses primarily on Doig's life in the years after his mother's death, from first grade through high school. It was a finalist for the 1979 National Book Award.

For his next book, *Winter Brothers: A Season at the Edge of America* (1980), Doig retraced the footsteps of James Gilchrist Swan, a man who left his family in Massachusetts to start a new life in California in 1850, eventually settling on the Olympic Peninsula. Referring to Swan's diaries, Doig juxtaposed Swan's journey with his own experiences during the course of a winter on the same tract of land over a century later. Doig first encountered Swan's diaries while doing research in the libraries of the University of Washington, when he was a student there. In a review of the book for the *Chris-*

tian *Science Monitor* (March 9, 1981), James Kaufmann wrote, "The interchange between Swan and Doig is musical. Their moods dip up and down, sometimes in tandem, sometimes in counterpoint. They remark on the weather, on their personal lives, and they watch—with eyes alert to its wonders—the world that surrounds them." Other critics, however, faulted Doig for presuming an intimacy with Swan that they felt he had not quite earned.

Doig found the historical inspiration for his first novel, *The Sea Runners* (1982), in a letter to the editor printed in a contemporary issue of the *Oregon Weekly Times* referring to a group of Swedes who escaped from indentured servitude in Alaska by canoe in the winter of 1952–53. To flesh out the Swedes' story, Doig drew on his extensive research skills and powers of imagination, as he explained to Mary Ann Gwinn for the *Seattle Times* (July 18, 2010, on-line): "The research is the necessary spadework . . . there are historical laws of gravity in historical fiction; big things are happening in the world, and my characters are affected by those."

Doig's 1984 novel, *English Creek*, is the first book in a trilogy about a Montana family. *English Creek* is narrated by the 14-year-old Jick McCaskill; the story is set in the summer of 1939, when Jick looks on, perplexed, as his older brother, Alec, intent on marrying a local girl and becoming a cowhand, resists his parents' pleas for him to go to college. In his review for the *Washington Post* (November 4, 1984), Reid Beddow wrote, "What sustains this unexceptional plot is some very exceptional writing. Indeed this is not a conventional western novel at all. . . . The new novel is full of good writing and the sweat and tears and laughter of hardworking plain people—people whose lives are shaped by a land which as it grows more scenic becomes more hostile to human habitation, the incomparable Big Sky country of western Montana."

Dancing at the Rascal Fair (1987) is the second in Doig's McCaskill family trilogy. Instead of moving forward, however, the novel follows the family back in time, to 1889, when Angus McCaskill (Jick's grandfather) and a group of other Scotsmen arrive in Montana. The trilogy's final installment, *Ride with Me, Mariah Montana* (1990), takes place in 1989, Montana's centennial year. Now 65 years old, Jick McCaskill recounts his travels around the state with his adult daughter Mariah and her ex-husband, both journalists searching for subjects to feature in a Missoula newspaper's series of articles celebrating the centennial.

Following the death of Doig's maternal uncle, Wallace Ringer, in 1986, Doig received a packet of letters his mother had written to Wallace while he was stationed on a U.S. destroyer in the Pacific toward the end of World War II. The letters, written over a period of about six months from 1944 until Berneta's death, in 1945, inspired Doig to revisit his memories of his mother and reconstruct what life was like for his family during the last months of her life. The resulting memoir was *Heart Earth*

(1993). As with Doig's previous works, the book received mostly favorable reviews. According to Nancy Pearl, writing for *Library Journal* (June 1, 2002), through Doig's rendering in *Heart Earth*, Berneta Ringer emerges "a true Western heroine."

Doig opened his 1996 novel, *Bucking the Sun*, with a Montana community's discovery of two naked bodies, one male, one female, in the cab of a truck submerged in a lake formed by the town's new dam. Although *Bucking the Sun* initially piques readers' interest with the promise of scandal, it soon becomes clear that Doig's primary interest is in providing a historically accurate account of the building of the Fort Peck Dam across the Missoula River, as a writer for the *Virginia Quarterly Review* (Fall 2006) noted: "*Bucking the Sun* opens with a murder and ends with its solution, but this novel is anything but a fast-paced thriller. . . . Doig's concentration on detail and historical accuracy, as well as his large cast of characters, demands the slow delivery. But what the novel lacks in pulse-pounding plot twists it gains in rich prose, human insight, and character development."

Doig's sixth novel, *Mountain Time* (1999), picks up with the McCaskill family where *Ride with Me, Mariah Montana* left off, focusing in part on Jick's daughters, Mariah and Lexa. The book's central character is Lexa's lover, Mitch Rozier, a Seattle resident who visits his native Montana to deal with family matters. Both Lexa and Mariah accompany Mitch on the trip, during which he confronts the difficult past, and father, he left behind. The novel has "a lot of balls to keep in the air," Jonathan Yardley wrote for the *Washington Post* (August 22, 1999, on-line), "but by and large Doig is up to the challenge. If human speech presents formidable obstacles for him—the phrase 'wooden dialogue' has rarely been more apt—human emotions do not; he understands his characters well, and manages to make them all the more interesting not in spite for their flaws but because of them."

In Doig's novel *Prairie Nocturne* (2003), Wes, the scion of a wealthy ranching family, enlists his mistress, Susan, in his effort to launch the singing career of Monty, his African-American chauffeur. Doig has said that Monty is based on the real-life Taylor Gordon, a native of Doig's hometown (and the only black man the writer can remember living there while Doig was growing up), who enjoyed a brief but brilliant career as a singer and vaudeville performer in the Harlem section of New York City during the 1920s. *The Whistling Season* (2006), set in the early 1900s, introduces readers to Oliver Milliron, the recently widowed father of three boys in Montana. Struggling to raise his sons on his own, Oliver responds to a posting in the local newspaper advertising the services of a housekeeper who "can't cook but doesn't bite." The ever-whistling housekeeper, Rose Llewellyn, arrives from Minneapolis with an unexpected guest—introduced as her brother, Morris—in tow; matters become even more complicated when homesteaders, drawn by the jobs promised by a large-scale irrigation project called the Big Ditch, begin to arrive in droves. In his review of the novel for the *New York Times* (July 2, 2006, on-line), Sven Birkerts wrote, "*The Whistling Season* is quiet and unassuming throughout. If the novel carries any shock it is of contrast with the past. Could people have ever been that . . . unmodern? That straight-up, or straight-on, or at least compounded of such seemingly simple ingredients? Even where we find chicanery and vile behavior—there is a bit—it's chicanery and vileness of the old sort; we almost pine for it."

Doig's next book, *The Eleventh Man* (2008), follows Ben Reinking, a former football star who, as a military correspondent during World War II, is ordered by his superiors to write a series of articles about his former teammates at the fictional Treasure State University, all of whom have enlisted. (Doig was inspired by the true story of 11 starting players on Montana State College's football team, all of whom died in World War II.) Some reviewers criticized Doig for his use of dialogue in *The Eleventh Man*; Mike Peed, for example, wrote in his review for the *New York Times* (November 21, 2008, on-line), "The members of Doig's cast speak an easygoing 1940s vernacular, more imagined, one hopes, than real. Soldiers drink 'skunk juice,' receive the 'galoot salute' and look forward to a 'rub a dub dub'. . . . These incessant wisecracks overwhelm, yielding characters who become less individuals than accomplices in parody." On the other hand, most critics applauded Doig's powers of description, especially when it came to the Montana landscape. As quoted on *BookPage* (October 2008, on-line), Doig said that he tries in his writing to produce "an interior rhyme or chime of language, something in a sentence which you hope will surprise and delight the reader, at least a little bit."

Doig's most recent book, *Work Song* (2010), focuses on the character Morris ("Morrie") Morgan from *The Whistling Season*, who, a decade later, in the aftermath of World War I, is back in Montana to cash in on the copper-mining boom. Although Morrie initially comes to town intent on selling his bookkeeping services to the behemoth Anaconda Mining Co., he quickly learns of the company's suspect business practices and takes a job at the town's public library instead. When one of Morrie's former students reenters his life, he discovers that she is engaged to the charismatic leader of the miners' union; soon Morrie's life becomes intertwined with those of Anaconda's maltreated workers. In his review for the *Los Angeles Times* (July 15, 2010, on-line), Tim Rutten wrote that *Work Song* is "a book that can be appreciated just for the quality of the prose and the author's adherence to the sturdy conventions of old-fashioned narrative or for Doig's sly gloss on Western genre fiction and unforced evocation of our current condition—or, better yet, for all those things." In a minority view, Jonathan Yardley of the *Washington Post* (July 18, 2010, on-line) described *Work Song* as "the worst

work of fiction to cross my desk in years," one he found to be "mawkish, corny, clumsy and uninviting" and to contain "characters so quaint 'n' cute you want to execute them on the spot."

Doig and his wife, Carol, a college English teacher, live outside Seattle, in the community of Innis Arden. Doig, who tries to write a thousand words a day, not including revisions, has said that he considers himself more of a craftsman than an artist, but that through honing his craft he hopes to approach the level of art. He is currently working on a novel about a bachelor saloonkeeper, "the best bartender that ever lived." When asked in an interview for Powell's Books (on-line) why he writes, Doig responded, "A lifetime of reasons, but here's one: for the love of language and that daily tryst of the pair of us, it and me, creating something that did not exist before."

—H.R.W.

Suggested Reading: *Chicago Tribune* (on-line) Dec. 10, 1987; *New York Times* (on-line) July 9, 2010; *Seattle Times* (on-line) July 18, 2010; Simpson, Elizabeth. *Earthlight, Wordfire: The Work of Ivan Doig*, 1992

Selected Books: nonfiction—*This House of Sky: Landscapes of a Western Mind*, 1978; *Winter Brothers: a Season at the Edge of America*, 1980; *Heart Earth*, 1993; fiction—*The Sea Runners*, 1982; *English Creek*, 1984; *Dancing at the Rascal Fair*, 1987; *Ride with Me, Mariah Montana*, 1990; *Bucking the Sun*, 1996; *Mountain Time*, 1999; *Prairie Nocturne*, 2003; *The Whistling Season*, 2006; *The Eleventh Man*, 2008; *Work Song*, 2010

Dolan, Timothy

Feb. 6, 1950– Archbishop of New York

Address: Archdiocese of New York, 1011 First Ave., New York, NY 10022

In February 2009 Timothy Dolan succeeded Edward Egan as the archbishop of New York, becoming the leader of the second-largest Catholic archdiocese in the U.S. (after that of Los Angeles, California) and occupying perhaps the most prominent religious post in the nation, one that Pope John Paul II called "archbishop of the capital of the world." The transition in leadership "represented not only a generational changing of the guard but also a kind of personality transplant for the office of archbishop," according to a biography of Dolan posted on the *New York Times* Web site (November 16, 2010). Whereas Egan acquired a reputation for being distant and had a difficult relationship with the priests under his charge, Dolan is known for his warmth, exuberance, and sense of humor and for his tendency to persuade rather than con-

Lucas Jackson-Pool/Getty Images

Timothy Dolan

front. His congenial manner notwithstanding, Dolan has taken a doctrinaire approach to matters including abortion and gay marriage—positions in line with those of John Paul II and his successor, Pope Benedict XVI, who has sought to reaffirm the Catholic Church's traditionally conservative stance on such controversial issues. The church's push for strong conservative leadership was further affirmed in November 2010, when Dolan was elected president of the U.S. Conference of Catholic Bishops.

Dolan, who was ordained as a priest in 1976, is an expert on American Catholic church history and has held several important leadership positions in the Catholic hierarchy and seminary system. After occupying several minor posts in the Midwest, where he was raised, in 1987 Dolan served in Washington, D.C., as secretary to representatives of the Vatican. That assignment was followed by appointments as vice rector of Kenrick-Glennon Seminary, in St. Louis, Missouri, from 1992 to 1994, and then as rector of the Pontifical North American College, in Rome, Italy. In 2001 he became the auxiliary bishop of St. Louis, and a year later he was named the archbishop of Milwaukee, Wisconsin. In Milwaukee Dolan had to respond to charges of sexual abuse by priests under his jurisdiction—part of a phenomenon that, increasingly starting in about 2001, rocked the Catholic Church nationwide, with many parishioners coming forward to claim that they were molested as minors by priests. Although his handling of the crisis received mixed assessments from sex-abuse victims, Dolan dealt ably with the media during that time. He was also credited with addressing the archdiocese's budget woes successfully.

The New York archdiocese includes three New York City boroughs (Manhattan, the Bronx, and Staten Island—each its own county) and seven other New York State counties for a total of about 480 parishes, 400 churches, 2.5 million worshipers, and an annual budget of roughly a half-billion dollars. Referring to John Joseph O'Connor, the outspoken eighth archbishop of the New York archdiocese, Robert Kolker observed for *New York Magazine* (April 23, 2009), "In choosing Timothy Dolan for the critical New York post, Rome has picked someone who is, if nothing else, an expert message-deliverer, blending the spotlight-loving tendencies of an O'Connor with all of the warmth and approachability that Egan lacked."

The oldest of five children, Timothy Michael Dolan was born on February 6, 1950 in St. Louis to Matthew Dolan, an aircraft engineer, and Shirley Radcliffe Dolan. He has two brothers and two sisters. Dolan was baptized at Immaculate Conception Parish in Maplewood, Missouri, a St. Louis suburb. In 1955 his family relocated to Ballwin, Missouri, another St. Louis suburb, where they attended the recently formed Holy Infant Parish church. In a video interview for the Web site saltandlighttv.org (August 3, 2010), Dolan told Thomas Rosica that he and his siblings "grew up with the parish . . . . It was sort of the center of life in so many ways. Not just prayer and worship and devotion, but also my schooling—socially, athletically—it was a real cohesive, formative experience for me."

Dolan told Patricia Rice for the *St. Louis Beacon* (February 22, 2009, on-line), "I can never remember a time I didn't want to be a priest." As a boy he pretended to be a priest, using sheets and cardboard boxes to make an altar. His parents enrolled him in Holy Infant Grade School, after which he attended St. Louis Preparatory Seminary South in Shrewsbury, Missouri. In 1972 he earned a B.A. degree in philosophy from Cardinal Glennon College of the Kenrick-Glennon Seminary, in St. Louis. Cardinal John Joseph Carberry, then archbishop of St. Louis, invited Dolan to study at the Pontifical North American College, in Rome; he completed his priestly formation at the Pontifical University of St. Thomas Aquinas (also referred to as the Angelicum), also in Rome, where he earned a licentiate of sacred theology. At the Pontifical North American College, he studied under Monsignor John Tracy Ellis, a Catholic Church historian, who inspired in Dolan an interest in the history of the Catholic Church in the U.S.

Dolan was ordained as a priest on June 19, 1976 at his home parish by then–Auxiliary Bishop Edward T. O'Meara. He then became associate pastor at Immacolata Parish in Richmond Heights, Missouri. In 1979 he left to attend the Catholic University of America, in Washington, D.C., where, on a scholarship, he studied church history. He spent a year researching his doctoral dissertation, which concerned the life and ministry of the late Kansas City, Missouri, archbishop Edwin O'Hara, a founder of the Catholic Biblical Association of America and a social activist. Of his fascination with church history, Dolan told Rosica, "You can find an example of every problem, you can find an example of every virtue, you can find something in church history to exemplify what we're going through now."

After earning his doctorate Dolan returned to the St. Louis area, where he served as associate pastor of Cure of Ars Parish in Shrewsbury from 1983 to 1985. He next served as associate pastor, from 1985 to 1987, at Little Flower Parish in Richmond Heights, Missouri. Around that time he also worked as liaison with St. Louis archbishop John L. May to restructure the educational programs of the local seminary system. In 1987 Dolan found himself back in the nation's capital, serving for five years as secretary of the Apostolic Nunciature, an office of the U.S. Roman Catholic Church; in that post Dolan was essentially the secretary to the Pope's ambassador to the U.S.

In 1992 Dolan was appointed to the post of vice rector of Kenrick-Glennon Seminary. He also served as its director of spiritual formation and as a professor of church history, and he held the position of adjunct professor of theology at Saint Louis University. In 1994 Dolan left the U.S. for Rome, where he had been appointed rector of the Pontifical North American College. He also served as a visiting professor of church history at the Pontifical Gregorian University and as a faculty member in the Department of Ecumenical Theology at the Pontifical University of St. Thomas Aquinas. A collection of Dolan's lectures from his time as rector of the Pontifical North American College was published in 2000 as *Priests for the Third Millennium*. The book has since become influential among clergy and has been used as a textbook at seminaries. Dolan has also published the book *Called to Be Holy* (2005).

In 2001—25 years after he was ordained as a priest—Dolan was named the auxiliary bishop of St. Louis by Pope John Paul II. His appointment came not long after a national explosion of reports of sex abuse in the Catholic Church, and he quickly became involved in organizing a response to accusations of abuse in his archdiocese. He spoke candidly to the media about the church's responsibilities, invited victims to come forward, and ousted eight clergymen who had been accused of abuse—including two from his own rectory. Speaking of the accusers, he told a reporter for the *Milwaukee Journal Sentinel* (September 14, 2002), "These people, they're my people. They're still Catholics, they're still believers. If they're hurting, we've got to respond." He also created a fund—supported by the sale of some church assets—to pay for victim compensation and disclosed the names of predatory priests (a move some Catholics did not support). Through independent mediators the archdiocese arrived at resolutions with 170 victims, paying a total of $10.2 million in settlements. "I've learned some very hard-won lessons," Dolan told Laurie Goodstein for the *New York Times* (June 26, 2002,

on-line). "One of them would be that it is impossible to exaggerate the gravity of the situation, and the suffering that victims feel, because I've spent the last four months being with them, crying with them, having them express their anger to me."

In 2002 Pope John Paul II named Dolan the archbishop of Milwaukee. His appointment came after the resignation of Archbishop Rembert Weakland, which followed reports that the church had paid $450,000 to a man who claimed to have been molested by Weakland in 1979. Serge F. Kovaleski wrote for the *New York Times* (May 16, 2010), "One of a generation of bishops who came to the job after many of their predecessors were discredited, Archbishop Dolan faced a daunting set of challenges: assuaging not only abuse victims but also a church hierarchy worried about ruinous damages awards, parishioners angry over payments to victims, and his own priests, some perhaps falsely accused. It was a diplomatic gantlet many recent bishops have had to walk, and Archbishop Dolan trod it with particular care."

Dolan received praise initially for having his archdiocese hold meetings and listening sessions with victims and community groups, some of which were open to other members of the public. However, Dolan was also the subject of criticism for asking lawyers to seek the dismissal of five lawsuits against the church and for declining to reveal the names of allegedly abusive priests who belonged to religious orders—for example, the Jesuits or Capuchins. (Dolan has said church law forbids him to do so.) He also opposed state legislation that would have extended the statute of limitations for victims of abuse to sue the church. In a rare move he appeared before a Wisconsin Senate committee to argue against the legislation, saying, as quoted by Kovaleski, "There is no Catholic Superfund that can provide the monies this legislation will require of the church."

During his time in Milwaukee, Dolan struggled to placate both sides of the sex-abuse scandal—victims of priest abuse and their advocacy groups, such as the Survivors Network for those Abused by Priests (SNAP), and the Catholic Church and his fellow clergy. Victims accused of him of not doing enough and of breaking his promises to help them seek justice; some clergymen and churchgoers accused him of going too far in his efforts to address the abuse. In defense of his handling of the crisis, Dolan told Kovaleski that the church had made great strides in working to prevent future sex-abuse incidents, but he conceded that mistakes had been made in dealing with the scandal because of its unexpectedness and size. "This is a work in progress, and we're learning as we go along," he said. "That's why perhaps you've heard me say, go ahead and criticize. We are just like everybody else that's dealing with this painful issue—families, Boy Scouts, every other religion."

Dolan was commended for his handling of the financial affairs of the Milwaukee archdiocese, which some worried might have to declare bankruptcy due to the sex-abuse lawsuits and settlements. Dolan responded by laying off one-third of the 150 workers in the archdiocese, consolidating more than 20 parishes with dwindling attendance, and shuttering about eight schools. He launched a successful fund-raising initiative and, by 2008, had closed a $3 million deficit in the budget. In addition, he recruited new seminarians. He endeared himself to the Milwaukee public through his "regular guy" demeanor; for example, he wore the iconic "cheesehead" hat of Green Bay Packers football fans at an outdoor Mass, and he joked about switching his beer of choice to Miller, whose manufacturing headquarters are in Milwaukee. (He was not joking, however, about liking beer, and he also enjoys drinking whiskey.)

On February 23, 2009 Dolan was appointed the 10th archbishop of New York by Pope Benedict XVI. His appointment ended several years of speculation that began after Egan offered to retire in 2007, when he turned 75 (the age at which a bishop is required to submit his offer of resignation). Dolan was installed in a ceremony on April 15. When he took the post, he became the first archbishop in the history of the New York archdiocese to replace a living predecessor, and he added another link to a long chain of Irish-American New York archbishops broken only once, by the French-born John Dubois, who served from 1826 to 1842.

Dolan is a theological conservative who adheres to doctrine on matters of gay marriage, abortion, birth control, and the celibacy of priests. A little more than a week after his installation, he came out against New York governor David Paterson's plans to push for gay-marriage legislation. He told Dan Mangan for the *New York Post* (April 23, 2009), "There's an in-built code of right and wrong that's embedded in the human DNA. Hard-wired into us is a dictionary, and the dictionary defines marriage as between one man, one woman for life, please God, leading to the procreation of human life. And if we begin to tamper with the very definition of marriage, then we're going to be in big trouble. We're not anti-gay—we're pro the most basic definition of marriage." In May 2009 he criticized the University of Notre Dame, the nation's best-known Catholic University, for inviting President Barack Obama, a supporter of abortion rights, to speak at a graduation ceremony. Later in the year Dolan hosted the meetings that led to the creation of the "Manhattan Declaration," a document signed by Eastern Orthodox Christians and many Catholic leaders affirming their opposition to abortion and gay marriage.

Clarifying his and the Catholic Church's stance on gay marriage, Dolan told Kolker, "We're more into the defense of marriage itself, so that even though people [of the same sex] would have the right to companionship, the right to marriage would only be, by its very definition, between a man and a woman. . . . There are ways to ameliorate some of the disadvantages that same-sex couples feel without tampering with the very defini-

tion of marriage." When asked by Kolker what he would tell a woman considering abortion, he explained, "I wouldn't get argumentative. But I would say, 'Well, you're kind enough to ask me. So what I think I hear you say is what guidance and enlightenment can I give.' Would I be a bully about it? In no way whatsoever. I would hope I would come across as tender, as compassionate as possible, but that wouldn't lessen the cogency of my saying 'Please don't do this. We're talking about an innocent life here. What can I do to help you make the decision to keep your baby?'" Dolan explained to Mangan that his pro-life stance went beyond opposing abortion to helping to care for the young; he cited the work of the archdiocese's Catholic Charities group in running a nursery for children born to female prison inmates in Westchester County, New York. "That's pro-life at its best . . . [a] creative, life-giving alternative to what we call the 'culture of death,'" he said.

In 2009, while generally popular among parishioners and his fellow church leaders, Dolan received some criticism for failing to tackle the financial issues plaguing the archdiocese in the firm manner of his predecessor. In 2010 he became more active in financial and organizational efforts; in December he announced that about 30 Catholic schools in New York City and the surrounding counties would likely be shuttered as part of an effort to close schools with low attendance, rent those spaces to others, and use some of the revenue to offset the high cost of Catholic-school tuition for struggling parents.

In November 2010 the United States Conference of Catholic Bishops elected Dolan as its president, a "surprise move that reaffirmed the conservative direction of the Roman Catholic Church in America," Laurie Goodstein wrote for the *New York Times* (November 16, 2010, on-line). She explained that the vote "makes Archbishop Dolan the most visible face of the church in the United States. It also suggested that the bishops were seeking a powerful and reliably orthodox voice to reassert the church's teaching in the court of public opinion and to disarm critics who insist that the bishops have lost their moral authority as a result of their role in the sexual abuse scandals." "It's a doubling down on efforts like opposing same-sex marriage," Rocco Palmo, a blogger who follows the Catholic Church, told William Wan and Michelle Boorstein for the *Washington Post* (November 17, 2010). "With Dolan, just by his personality and by his position in New York, he's going to be able to multiply that kind of outspokenness by a factor of 10." In a news conference after the announcement of his election to the presidency, Dolan said that he would continue the efforts of his predecessor, Cardinal Francis George of Chicago, Illinois, to oppose the health-care-reform legislation passed by the Obama administration, because church officials believe it would expand abortion funding. Dolan was elected with 128 votes over the 111 received by the incumbent vice president, Bishop Gerald

Kicanas of Tucson, Arizona, a more moderate figure who had defeated Dolan in his bid for the vice presidency in 2007. In response to the media's take on his election, Dolan told Wan and Boorstein that his winning the presidency had not been for political reasons, arguing that the "bishops of the United States are not partisans, they're pastors."

Dolan was the chairman of Catholic Relief Services from January 2009 to November 2010 and is a member of the board of trustees of the Catholic University of America. In 2009 he was named an apostolic visitor to seminaries in Ireland, where he has been assigned by Pope Benedict XVI to investigate sex-abuse claims. As the archbishop of New York, Dolan will spend much of his time working to win parishioners back to the Catholic Church; according to recent studies, one-third of American adults raised as Catholics have abandoned the faith. "The bishops are saying we need to make sure our house is in order as a church. We need to recover our vigor," he said, as quoted by Goodstein in the *New York Times* (November 22, 2010, on-line). "Then we can be of better service to the world and to our culture."

—W.D.

Suggested Reading: archny.org; *Milwaukee Journal Sentinel* A p10 Sep. 14, 2002; *New York* (on-line) Sep. 28, 2009; *New York Post* p23 Apr. 23, 2009; *New York Times* (on-line) Feb. 24, 2009, June 26, 2002; saltandlighttv.org Aug. 3, 2010; *St. Louis (Missouri) Beacon* (on-line) Feb. 22, 2009; *Washington Post* A p2 Nov. 17, 2010

Selected Books: *Priests for the Third Millennium*, 2000; *Called to Be Holy*, 2005

Gareth Cattermole/Getty Images

Drogba, Didier

Mar. 11, 1978– Soccer player

Address: The Didier Drogba Foundation, Villa 353 Ilot B4, Riviera les Jardins, BP 755 Cidex 3, Cocody, Abidjan, Côte d'Ivoire

The Ivorian soccer star Didier Drogba is a striker for the English Premier League's Chelsea Football Club (better known as Chelsea FC), the captain and all-time leading scorer of the Ivory Coast national team, and one of Africa's best-known and most beloved soccer players. Described by Eben Harrell for *Time* (April 29, 2010, on-line) as having "the body of an NBA star with feet as nimble as a prima ballerina's," Drogba emerged from an impoverished upbringing in a war-ravaged country to become a transformative figure in his sport. He joined Chelsea FC in 2004, at age 26, signing a contract—worth £24 million—that made him the highest-paid Ivorian player in history. After leading Chelsea to consecutive Premier League championships, during the 2004–05 and 2005–06 seasons, Drogba served as captain of the Ivorian national team and helped them qualify for the 2006 FIFA World Cup, in Germany. There, he played a vital role in bringing peace to his birth country, appearing on television with a message of nonviolence to warring factions in the Ivory Coast. While his team failed to progress beyond the first round of that tournament, Drogba's peace efforts won widespread notice: he was appointed by the United Nations Development Program (UNDP) as a goodwill ambassador in 2007 and was named as one of the world's 100 most influential people by *Time* magazine in 2010. Alex Hayes wrote for the London *Telegraph* (August 8, 2007, on-line), "Many footballers have used their influence to great effect in recent years, whether by putting their name to an inner city project or sponsoring a charity, but none has ever stopped a country tearing itself apart. Truth be told, no other player could. Drogba is a god to the Ivorian people, not just because he is a famous footballer, but also because he is someone who speaks for the masses. He is in tune with the average Ivorian."

Drogba is widely considered to be one of the best strikers in the world. He was named African Footballer of the Year in 2006 and 2009, and in 2007 and 2010 he won the Golden Boot Award, given to the English Premier League's leading scorer. In 2010 Drogba led Chelsea FC to its third Premier League title in six years and helped the Ivory Coast team make its second straight World Cup appearance, in South Africa.

The eldest of six children, Didier Yves Drogba Tébily was born on March 11, 1978 in Abidjan, the former capital of the Ivory Coast. (The city of Yamoussoukro is now the capital.) Drogba was given the nickname "Tito" as a child, after the Yugoslav president Josip Broz Tito, whom his mother admired. Ravaged by years of civil war and extreme poverty, the Ivory Coast had a male life expectancy of 46 years and an adult-literacy rate of just 50 percent. When Drogba was five his parents, Clotilde and Albert, sent him to France to live with an uncle, Michel Goba, a professional soccer player. Goba had convinced the boy's parents that the move to Europe would give him "a real chance to succeed in life," as Sebastian Hassett noted for the *Sydney (Australia) Morning Herald* (June 7, 2010). While being sent to live with relatives in Europe was common among Africans his age, Drogba recalled to Brian Oliver for the London *Observer Sport Monthly* (February 4, 2007, on-line), "I had to travel alone, I was only five. I remember having this thing hanging around my neck, a label saying what my name was, and the stewardess looking after me. It was very, very difficult." He added, "When I arrived in France, I cried every day. Not because I was in France—I could have been anywhere—but because I was so far, far away from my parents. I missed them so much."

Drogba's uncle lived in the city of Brest, in the northwestern region of Brittany. Drogba traveled with Goba for the next three years, as his uncle played successively for teams in Brest, Angoulême, and Dunkerque ("Dunkirk," in English). Drogba told Joe Lovejoy for the London *Sunday Times* (December 31, 2006), "My uncle is like my father because he took care of me for such a long time. Whatever I am today is because of the role he has played in my life." Drogba was still homesick, however, and moved back to the Ivory Coast at the age of eight to be with his parents. There, he began honing his soccer skills with friends in a car park that had been converted into a soccer pitch. After a severe financial crisis struck the country, in 1989, his parents, both bank workers, lost their jobs. As a result Drogba, now 11, went again to live with his uncle, this time in Dunkerque. Under his uncle's guidance Drogba continued his education and joined a soccer team. He initially played the position of right-back, or defender, which annoyed his uncle. Drogba noted to Lovejoy that Goba "told me it was better to play up front," adding, "He knew I could score goals, and once I started I scored a lot."

In 1991 Drogba moved back to Brittany, settling in the commune of Vannes. That year his parents and siblings joined him in France, immigrating to the outskirts of Paris. By that time Drogba's studies had taken a backseat to soccer, with the result that he repeated a year of school. His parents banned him from soccer for a year, and he was sent to live with his cousin Kriza in the city of Poitiers, in central France. Drogba returned to live with his family in 1993, in the Paris suburb of Antony, where he resumed his soccer career. At 15 he joined Levallois-Perret, a semiprofessional club in the northern suburbs of Paris. Drogba—who was then living with another cousin, Olivier Tébily, a professional soccer player with a team in Chateauroux—was put under the supervision of Srebencko Repcic, from the former Yugoslavia, a onetime international player who served as technical director of Levallois-Perret. Repcic said about Drogba, as quoted on Drogba's Web site, "He didn't go out to nightclubs on the nights before matches like his mates. He was a very sensible lad." Drogba first made a name for himself on the club's under-17 squad, under Coach Christian Pornin. After scoring 30 goals as a center-forward, or striker, during the 1994–95 and 1995–96 seasons, he was promoted to the club's first team, coached by Jacques Loncar, and played in the French second division. His coach did not trust his abilities, and Drogba played in that division for only 10 minutes—long enough to score a goal, evening the score in a match against a team from Fontainebleau.

After completing high school Drogba attended college in Le Mans, where he studied accounting. He joined the professional soccer club there, becoming an apprentice under Coach Marc Westerloppe. In 1999, at the relatively advanced age of 21, Drogba signed his first professional contract, with the Le Mans club, after becoming a member of its first team. "At 21 I knew it was my last chance," he recalled to Joe Lovejoy. "Everybody told me, 'If this doesn't work out, you'll have to earn a living doing something else.' I could have been an accountant—I had the qualifications." Over four seasons with the club, Drogba scored a less-than-stellar 12 goals in 64 appearances in the French second division. He suffered several minor injuries during that time, which slowed his development as a player. Injuries notwithstanding, Drogba made numerous changes to his game at the suggestion of Westerloppe, whom he has called the biggest influence on his playing. Drogba told Lovejoy, "He gave me everything I needed to be where I am today. He changed so many things in my game and in my life. Before he signed me I used to train once or twice a week, but with him it was every day. He taught me everything he knew about [soccer]."

In 2002 Drogba signed a contract to play in France's first division for the club En Avant de Guingamp, which had initially scouted him four years earlier. (The contract was worth £80,000.) He soon realized his potential under Coach Guy Lacombe, scoring in his first game and helping Guingamp rise from the depths of its division. During the 2002–03 season, his only full year with the club, Drogba scored a remarkable 17 goals in 34 appearances and guided Guingamp to a club-best seventh-place finish in its division. Also during that season he made his international debut for Ivory Coast, in September, and notched his first goal in international play the following February. By that time Drogba had drawn the attention of more prominent clubs. In 2003 he signed a contract worth £3.3 million with one of France's biggest clubs, Olympique de Marseille, which also played in France's first division. Drogba continued his prolific scoring there, with 19 goals in 35 appearances during the 2003–04 season. He finished third in the league in scoring and led Marseille to the final of the Union of European Football Associations (UEFA) Cup, where the team lost to Valencia. (As of the 2009–10 soccer season, the UEFA Cup has been known as the UEFA Europa League.) After netting 11 more goals in European competition that season, which in addition to the UEFA Cup included the UEFA Champions League, Drogba was named Foreign Player of the Year for the French first division. Recalling his single season with Marseille, he told Lovejoy, "I had a great time there. Their warm welcome and the patience they showed is something I will never forget. I only had one season with Marseille, but it felt like I'd been there for ages. Playing for such a big club improved me because I had to maintain my standards. When people say how good you are, you cannot afford to be bad."

In July 2004 Drogba moved to Chelsea FC of the English Premier League, signing a then-club-record contract worth £24 million, which made him the highest-paid Ivorian player in history. (Considered the highest level of the English football league, the Premier League consists of the top 20 clubs in England, with every team playing each of the others twice during the course of a 38-game season. In addition to Premier League competition, Chelsea participates in the UEFA Champions League, the FA Cup competition, and the Worthington Cup.) In his first season with Chelsea, under the management of Jose Mourinho, Drogba scored 16 goals in 30 games and posted the second-best goals-to-minutes ratio in the Premier League, despite having missed over two months due to injury. Chelsea, meanwhile, won the Premier League title for the second time in club history and the first since 1955; the team also won the Carling Cup, defeating Liverpool in the final on an extra-time goal by Drogba. The club also reached the semifinals of the Champions League competition but lost to Liverpool. Despite his impressive play that season, Drogba initially struggled to adapt to the more physical nature of English soccer and was often accused of diving—that is, diving to the ground and feigning injury in an attempt to draw a foul during a particular play. He explained to Joe Lovejoy, "People think I'm big and strong, so I shouldn't fall over, but I wasn't used to the English style and at first I didn't use my arms to protect myself. I played exactly as I had in France. In England you can use your body more. I had to learn to fight for the ball, to be more physical, and while I was doing that, people misunderstood me. Part of the problem is that challenges that are penalized as fouls in France are seen as okay here [in England]."

During the 2005–06 season Drogba played in 31 games, scoring 17 goals, including 12 in the Premier League. In addition, he led the Premier League in assists that season, with 11. Chelsea successfully defended the premiership title, becoming just the fifth English team to win back-to-back league championships since World War II, and also won the FA Community Shield in 2005. Also that season Drogba captained the Ivory Coast national team for the first time and helped it qualify for its first World Cup, in October 2005. After the team did so, with a 3–1 victory over Sudan, he rounded up his team in the locker room and—after falling to his knees—made a plea on live national television for the warring factions in his country to cease the fighting that had gone on for five years. "It was just something I did instinctively," Drogba explained to Alex Hayes. "All the players hated what was happening to our country and reaching the World Cup was the perfect emotional wave on which to ride." The fighting stopped after a week. Drogba said to Hayes, "I have won many trophies in my time but nothing will ever top helping win the battle for peace in my country. I am so proud because today in the Ivory Coast we do not need a piece of silverware to celebrate." In February 2006 he led the Ivory Coast to the final of the Africa Cup of Nations, where the team lost to Egypt in a penalty shootout. Then, at the 2006 World Cup that summer, Drogba scored Ivory Coast's first-ever goal of the competition in an opening-round loss to Argentina. The Ivory Coast was eliminated from the tournament after losing its second game, against the Netherlands.

Drogba enjoyed a breakthrough year in 2006–07, leading the Premier League in goals with 20 in 32 games and winning the Golden Boot Award for being the league's highest scorer. Chelsea failed to win a third straight premiership but claimed victory in both the Carling Cup and FA Cup in 2007, on winning goals by Drogba. At the end of the season, Drogba was named Ivorian Player of the Year and African Footballer of the Year, and he finished as the runner-up to Real Madrid's Cristiano Ronaldo in the voting for the Professional Football Association (PFA) Footballer of the Year Award. He was also named a goodwill ambassador by the United Nations Development Program for helping to raise awareness of African issues. Drogba's peace efforts culminated during the summer of 2007, when he arranged to move an Africa Cup of Nations qualifying match between the Ivory Coast and Madagascar to Bouaké, a rebel stronghold 220 miles north of Abidjan. As noted by Austin Merrill for *Vanity Fair* (July 10, 2007, on-line), around the time of the match, in which the Ivory Coast defeated Madagascar, 5–0, the Ivorian rebel leader turned prime minister Guillaume Soro called Drogba "a national hero," adding, "From north to south, from east to west, all Ivorians are proud of him. I'd even say that all of Africa is proud of him. This game is taking place because Drogba came to Bouaké to consecrate reconciliation and reinforce peace." Commenting on the historic game, Drogba recalled to Hayes, "Seeing both leaders side by side for the national anthems was very special. I felt then that the Ivory Coast was born again."

Mike Hewitt/Getty Images

Didier Drogba

Drogba battled a recurring knee problem throughout the 2007–08 season, in which he played in 28 games and scored 16 goals. Under Avram Grant, who replaced Mourinho as head coach at the beginning of the season, Chelsea reached its first UEFA Champions League final but lost to Manchester United on penalty kicks. In February 2008 Drogba led the Ivory Coast to a fourth-place finish in the Africa Cup of Nations. During the 2008–09 season he appeared in 29 games for Chelsea, scoring five goals in the Premier League, five in the Champions League, three in FA Cup competition, and one in Carling Cup play. In 2009 Chelsea won its second FA Cup in three years, defeating Everton Football Club, 2–1. In that game Drogba scored the equalizing shot before his teammate Frank Lampard came through with the game-winning point. (Luiz Felipe Scolari served as Chelsea's manager at the start of the season but was replaced by an interim manager, Guus Hiddink, after only seven months.)

Prior to the start of the 2009–10 season, former Milan coach Carlo Ancelotti was named Chelsea's new manager, replacing Hiddink. That season Drogba returned to top form and led the Premier League with 29 goals, earning him his second Golden Boot Award. Under Ancelotti Chelsea won both the premiership and the FA Cup in 2010, marking the first "double" in club history. In the latter tournament Drogba scored the team's only goal in a 1–0 victory over Portsmouth Football Club. In international competition that season, he scored six goals in five qualification games to help the Ivory Coast qualify for the 2010 World Cup, in South Africa, and helped his national team reach the quarterfinals of the 2010 Africa Cup of Nations,

where it was defeated by Algeria, 3–2. Drogba was subsequently named African Footballer of the Year for the second time. In June 2010 he injured his arm in a World Cup warm-up match against Japan, which the Ivory Coast won, 2–0. Despite the injury Drogba participated in the World Cup, after undergoing emergency surgery on his arm. The Ivory Coast, however, failed to make it past the group stage, finishing behind Brazil and Portugal. In August 2010 Drogba announced that he was withdrawing from Ivory Coast's national team in order to rest and focus on his club commitment with Chelsea. He holds the record for most goals scored by a foreign player for Chelsea and is currently ranked sixth all-time among the club's highest scorers. Dispelling rumors that he had permanently left the team, Drogba said during an Africa Cup of Nations qualifying match in September 2010 (in which he did not play), as posted on goal.com, "I've always been part of this team and we've done some great things together. I wanted to let everyone know my heart is still here and I throw my full support behind the team. Every time I'm called up I'll be here to play my role."

During the 2010–11 season, Drogba scored 12 goals in 36 games for Chelsea and finished second in the Premier League in assists, with 15. Chelsea, however, failed to defend its Premier League and FA Cup titles, finishing as runner-up behind Manchester United for the Premier League championship and losing in the fourth round of the FA Cup competition to Everton. The team also reached the quarterfinals of the Champions League competition but again lost to Manchester United. Carlo Ancelotti was fired after failing to secure any trophies during the year. As of early June 2011, the managerial position at Chelsea remained vacant.

Despite his many accomplishments on and off the field, Drogba has often found himself in the midst of controversy due to his sometimes quick temper. One of the most infamous incidents involving Drogba occurred in May 2008, when he became only the second player ever to receive a red card in a Champions League final, after slapping the Manchester United defenseman Nemanja Vidic in the face minutes before the end of extra time. Drogba was immediately ejected from the game, and his departure almost certainly cost Chelsea the victory; they lost to Manchester United in a subsequent shootout. In November 2008 Drogba was involved in another controversy: during a game against Burnley Football Club, after having a coin thrown at him by a fan during a goal-scoring celebration, he threw the coin back into the stands while showing Burnley fans his middle finger. Four months later he was cautioned for common assault by the Metropolitan Police and received a three-game suspension from the FA for violent conduct. In May 2009 Drogba received a four-match ban and was fined £8,000 following an expletive-laden rant at a referee that was caught by television cameras during a Champions League semifinal. (The ban was reduced by a game after an appeal.) Most recently, in March 2010, Drogba was red-carded after committing an aggressive foul on the Inter Milan midfielder Thiago Motta. He received a two-match ban and had his period of probation extended for two years, to July 2013.

Austin Merrill described Drogba as having "classic runway looks," with "broad shoulders," "high cheekbones," and a "sculpted jaw." Drogba and his wife, Alla (born Lalla Diakité), who hails from the western African country of Mali, have four children. The eldest of their three sons, Isaac (born in 1999), plays soccer in Chelsea's academy system. As a United Nations Goodwill Ambassador, Drogba has done extensive charity work and has founded an eponymous foundation to help build an all-purpose hospital in his home city of Abidjan, which will accommodate upwards of 200 people and serve as an orphanage. In 2010 he was named one of the world's most influential people by *Time* magazine for his involvement in the Ivory Coast peace process.

—C.C.

Suggested Reading: *Africa News* Mar. 2, 2007, May 22, 2010; (London) *Independent* p54+ May 8, 2009; (London) *Mail on Sunday* p14+ Apr. 29, 2007; (London) *Observer Sport Monthly* (on-line) Feb. 4, 2007; (London) *Sunday Times* p9+ Dec. 31, 2006; (London) *Telegraph* (on-line) Aug. 8, 2007; *Sydney (Australia) Morning Herald* p34+ June 7, 2010; *Time* (on-line) Apr. 29, 2010; *Vanity Fair* (on-line) July 10, 2007

Courtesy of Eric Drooker

Drooker, Eric

Oct. 25, 1958– Artist; graphic novelist

Address: HarperCollins Publishers, 1350 Ave. of the Americas, New York, NY 10019-4703

The artist Eric Drooker is probably best known for paintings that have appeared on many *New Yorker* magazine covers since 1994. Those covers, which often portray Drooker's native Manhattan in all its wonder, humor, and menace, reflect his deep love of the city he began exploring as a boy. Inspired by social-realist art of the first half of the 20th century, Drooker is also the creator of two graphic novels: *Flood! A Novel in Pictures* (1992) and *Blood Song: A Silent Ballad* (2002). His friendship with the late poet Allen Ginsberg led to several projects, including, most recently, Drooker's animation for the 2010 film *Howl*, starring James Franco.

A third-generation New Yorker, Eric Drooker was born in New York City on October 25, 1958. He grew up on Manhattan's Lower East Side, historically a working-class neighborhood that was home to many Jews and immigrants from Eastern Europe and, by the 1950s, migrants from Puerto Rico. Drooker grew up in the neighborhood's northwest section, which would, in large part through the marketing efforts of real-estate agents in the 1960s, become known as the East Village. Growing up on 14th Street, the dividing line between lower and midtown Manhattan, Drooker was constantly exposed to contrasts. "I would see homeless people—or bag ladies as we called them in those days—on the street, and I would see Cadillacs going by," Drooker told Rob Walker for *World Art* (Autumn 1998). "I would see these social discrepancies at a pretty early age, before I was able to understand what it all meant. But I'm convinced that it must have affected me." Drooker's mother, Nina, was a public-school teacher (and a painter and musician on the side), and his father, Harold, was a computer programmer. They both loved art and would often take the young Eric to art museums, such as the Museum of Modern Art. Drooker's maternal grandparents, Eastern European Jewish immigrants, had become Socialists in the 1930s; when Drooker was a boy, his grandfather showed him books by the Belgian artist Frans Masereel, a pacifist who had created several politically informed, social-realist, wordless novels composed entirely of woodcut prints, and Lynd Ward, who was best-known for his woodcuts and is considered today to be one of the pioneers of the American graphic novel. While the influence of Masereel's work on Drooker's art would manifest itself later, at the time Drooker was more interested in the counterculture-comics artist R. Crumb, whose work was then featured in *Zap Comix*. Drooker would also be influenced by the work of Francisco Goya and Diego Rivera; the work of pre–World War II social-realist artists such as John Sloan of the Ashcan School, an American art movement that sought to portray the physical reality of city life; that school's follower Edward Hopper, who focused on the psychological theme of urban loneliness; and German Expressionists such as Otto Dix and George Grosz, whose realistic/cartoonish drawings and paintings unromantically portrayed the after-effects of World War I on Germany's people and urban life.

The look of New York City, especially from above, also had a profound effect on Drooker. Growing up, he had to share a room with his brother, so he would often go to the roof of his building to be alone with his thoughts. He saw the city's skyline at all hours and under different lighting conditions. During his high-school years, he went to the roof almost every day before sunset to see the sun disappear beyond the Hudson River and then watch thousands of windows light up at dusk. Starting in the late 1960s, he watched the World Trade Center being built. After it was completed, in 1973, Drooker went there with his brother and saw New York City from a height of more than 100 stories. With a few exceptions—when he went to summer camp—Drooker spent his free time soaking up sights and sounds in the metropolis, which he understood to be entirely man-made. "But it occurred to me one day on the rooftop that, of course, this [man-made city] too is part of nature, because people are just animals, and it's part of nature the way a beehive is part of nature," Drooker recalled to Current Biography. Since then Drooker has continued to hold a paradoxical view of cities: that they are on the one hand a "cancerous growth" threatening the planet and on the other hand a "natural growth" that has evolved as humans have evolved. (The idea of the city as jungle would later be a prevalent theme in his New Yorker covers.)

Starting in 1979 Drooker attended Cooper Union, a very selective, private college in Lower Manhattan, where all students get full-tuition scholarships. He majored in sculpture. On the side he created political comic strips and posters, which he distributed and posted around the Lower East Side, where he was living. After he graduated Drooker continued to create and distribute his political art—black-and-white works that urged people in the neighborhood to fight unfair landlord practices and protest other injustices. He supported himself by making and selling lapel buttons on the street, which became illegal in the early 1980s; he told Chris Lanier for the Comics Journal (June 2008, on-line) that the police arrested him and confiscated his materials during that period. Around that time Drooker began contributing caricatures to such radical-left publications as the Daily World and the humorous porn magazine Screw. He also sold political comic magazines he made himself, which he titled Communicomix.

In 1988, on a hot August night, Drooker and many other Lower East Side residents gathered to protest a curfew placed on the neighborhood's main outdoor-recreation and meeting area, Tompkins Square Park. The demonstration turned chaotic, with some police officers taking violent action against the protesters, riding on horseback through the crowd and hovering in helicopters overhead. Those events, which lasted for hours, made a strong impression on Drooker. As the violence seemed about to escalate, Drooker saw the poet Allen Ginsberg getting out of a taxi. He filled Ginsberg in on what had happened and warned him that the situation was getting worse. (Ginsberg had been living in the Lower East Side on and off since the early 1960s. Drooker became aware of him at age nine, while on a bus with his mother, who pointed out the "famous poet.") The two talked briefly before losing each other in the crowd. The following year they spotted each other near Drooker's apartment on East 10th Street. It was then that Ginsberg discovered Drooker to be the artist whose posters he had been collecting. The artist and poet formed a friendship that years later yielded a collaborative work, Illuminated Poems (1996). Ginsberg wrote in the introduction to that volume, "I first glimpsed Eric Drooker's odd name on posters pasted on fire-alarm sides, construction walls checkered with advertisements, & lamppost junction boxes in the vortex of Lower East Side Avenues leading to Tompkins Square Park. . . . I began collecting Drooker's posters soon after overcoming shock, seeing in contemporary images the same dangerous class conflict I'd remembered from childhood, pre-Hitler block print wordless novels by Frans Masereel and Lynd Ward. Ward's images of the solitary artist dwarfed by the canyons of a Wall Street Megalopolis lay shadowed behind my own vision of Moloch [the malevolent presence in Ginsberg's most famous poem, 'Howl']. What 'shocked' me in Drooker's scratchboard prints was his graphic illustration of economic crisis similar to Weimar-American 1930's Depressions." Drooker and Ginsberg had planned to collaborate again, but Ginsberg died in 1997. The following year saw the publication of Drooker's Street Posters & Ballads, an anthology of the sociopolitical posters he put up around the Lower East Side in the 1980s. He decided to publish the poster anthology after realizing that the issues he was addressing in the flyers—police brutality, real-estate speculation, and the need for protest—were not only local but also universal. Part of his aim was to let nonprofit activist groups use the posters for free. "Drooker documents contemporary events, but renders them as part of the tragic continuum of human history," Sara Ferguson wrote in a review for the Village Voice (September 21, 1999). A decade later Drooker published another anthology of sociopolitical poster art, Slingshot (2008), a collection of 32 postcards. In the early 1990s, meanwhile, Drooker's political cartoons had begun to appear in the Village Voice, the Nation, and other publications.

Drooker's graphic novel *Flood! A Novel in Pictures*, on which he worked for six years, was published in 1992. *Flood!* is divided into three chapters, "Home," "L," and "Flood." "Home" depicts a man who, after losing his job at a plant, goes home to find out he has been evicted. He then walks the city streets, rummages through a trash can, visits the zoo, gets arrested for pickpocketing, and eventually ends up homeless. The work's "tragic theme was informed by my experiences on the Lower East Side," Drooker told Lanier. "I'd literally climb over [homeless] people to enter my apartment each night. After Ronald Reagan was elected president in 1980, a tidal wave of homelessness overflowed onto city streets, on a scale unseen since the Great Depression of the 1930s." ("Home" was originally self-published as a stand-alone work and sold in bookstores in Lower Manhattan.) "L," named for the 14th Street subway line, shows one man's subway ride, which turns into a fantastical dream involving primitive jungle visions. "Flood," longer than the first two chapters, is mostly autobiographical. It starts with the hero, an artist, emerging from a subway station; he walks the rainy streets of New York, draws in his studio, and attends a carnival, where he sees a man whose tattoos tell a version of American history, from Columbus's journey to modern-day capitalism. One of the book's major themes is existential alienation in a bustling metropolis. In an assessment of Drooker's book, Art Spiegelman—best known for his Pulitzer Prize–winning graphic novel *Maus: A Survivor's Tale*—wrote for the *New York Times Book Review* (December 27, 1992), "Like his forebears, Mr. Drooker has discovered the magic of pulling light and life out of an inky sea of darkness. If a picture is indeed worth a thousand words, this is one heck of a hefty novel."

Around that time, Spiegelman—who had recently joined the *New Yorker* as a contributing artist—encouraged Drooker to submit his art to the magazine. "The fact that I was born and raised in New York," Drooker said to *Current Biography*, "gave me a sense that it was somehow my birthright to be on the cover." Drooker's first *New Yorker* cover appeared on the magazine's September 12, 1994 issue, which depicted men in suits walking to work through the streets of New York on giant stilts. His second cover, the following year, was a painting of two homeless men warming themselves at a trashcan fire under the Brooklyn Bridge on a dark, snowy New York night. A cover he created the following year showed a man wearing a fedora, suit, and tie staring up at a bright-blue sky through a maze of skyscrapers at a bird in flight. "One thing I appreciate about the *New Yorker* is it's pretty much the only mainstream publication that still has art—paintings or drawing—on the cover," Drooker said to *Current Biography*. One of his favorites among his covers for the magazine is a painting of a businessman walking and talking on his cell phone on Wall Street, oblivious to the manhole he is about to fall into. The cover suggested a coming financial collapse; when Drooker submitted it, in 2005, three years before the global financial crisis, the cover was rejected. Still, Drooker asked the editors to hold onto it, and in September 2008, about a week after "Black Monday"—the day the Dow Jones average fell 778 points, signaling the impending financial collapse—that painting made the cover. His latest cover, for the October 25, 2010 issue, shows a couple holding hands at night on a rooftop, silhouetted by buildings with hundreds of lit windows.

During the mid-1990s Drooker underwent a personal transformation, which was also reflected in his art. "As I look back over the stylistic change," Drooker told Walker in 1998, "you can see this trajectory: I was coming out of this very monochromatic, very black and white, kind of doctrinaire, stark, propagandistic, heavy-handed view of the world, to a more subtle, kind of nuanced expression of the range, the colorful range of experience. It's not just the politics. Over the years, I've consciously tried to be more subtle in the work, to not make the work look like propaganda [though] I'm still very concerned with trying to persuade people of certain ideas, educate them." A subtle, effective way to slip in a sociopolitical message on a *New Yorker* cover, Drooker said, is to make the painting beautiful or funny.

Following the appearance of a second edition of *Flood!*, in 2002, Drooker published his second graphic novel, *Blood Song: A Silent Ballad* (2002), a wordless fable. The work's heroine, first seen as a girl, lives in a jungle with her dog. One day, as a young woman, she returns home after getting water and sees her family killed and her village destroyed by faceless, heavily armed soldiers. With her dog by her side, the young woman flees and ends up in a modern metropolis, where she sees homelessness, police brutality, corporate logos, mannequins, and large TV screens with commercial messages. She then meets a street musician; he is later arrested, but not before impregnating the young woman, who then has to care for her newborn. In the opinions of various reviewers, there is depth behind the story's seeming simplicity. "I made the mistake of reading *Blood Song* before noticing the sub-title, *A Silent Ballad*," Andrew D. Arnold wrote for *Time* (November 2002, on-line). "That is, I read it like a graphic novel, with a novel-reader's interest in character and story. . . . But taken as a ballad—a narrative poem—*Blood Song* becomes beautiful and expansive. . . . The two big themes of Eric Drooker's work have always been the individual vs. the state and nature vs. technology. . . . In *Blood Song*, often these themes will overlap."

It was not until he was in his early 30s, only a few years prior to his work on *Illuminated Poems*, that Drooker read Ginsberg's poem "Howl" in its entirety. "It really hit me," he said to *Current Biography*. "It snuck up on me. The second chapter, the Moloch chapter, really got to me." In the poem Moloch is the embodiment of a chaotic, materialistic metropolis. "I started crying when I read the line 'Moloch whose eyes are a thousand blind windows.' I'll never forget it because he was really describing where I grew up—that was my natural landscape. So that's when I really got hooked on his poetry." Years later, after seeing his art in *Illuminated Poems*, the filmmakers Rob Epstein and Jeffrey Friedman contacted Drooker; after meeting him and seeing his graphic novels, they asked if he would like to provide animation based on "Howl" for their film about the poem. "Howl" is a nonlinear poem, and Drooker had never done animation before, so he knew the project would present a challenge. "The only reason I wasn't completely intimidated by the project," he said, "was because I had already worked with Ginsberg and was friends with him and had the rabbi's blessing, if you will." For the next two years, with the official title of animation designer, Drooker led a computer-animation team. The feature-length film *Howl* (2010), which starred James Franco as Ginsberg, mixed Drooker's animation of the poem with re-created scenes of an interview Ginsberg gave at his home, a reading he did of "Howl" in San Francisco, California, and the trial of the poem's publisher, the poet Lawrence Ferlinghetti, for "obscenity." In a review for the *New York Times* (September 23, 2010), A. O. Scott wrote: "Not quite a biopic, not really a documentary and only loosely an adaptation, *Howl* does something that sounds simple until you consider how rarely it occurs in films of any kind. It takes a familiar, celebrated piece of writing and makes it come alive." The film received many positive reviews, although many critics felt differently about the 3D animation. Scott observed that "both *Howl* the poem and *Howl* the movie are strong enough to overcome the weakness of the cartoons, which come to seem less like offenses against art than like charming, fumbling tributes to its power." Drooker himself was not entirely pleased with the cartoon sequence. It was animated by a studio in Asia, to which Drooker did not travel (he had to communicate his ideas electronically) because of the film's tiny budget. For the book *Howl: A Graphic Novel* (2010), Drooker selected his favorite animated images from the film.

In 1998, after living in the same New York neighborhood for 40 years, Drooker left the city for a calmer life in Berkeley, California. Despite leaving New York, he has become even "more obsessed" with the city in his art, and he comes back often. "New York is still my favorite place to be," he said. "My heart is there."

—D.K.

Suggested Reading: *Boston Globe* Books p6 Sep. 26, 2010; drooker.com; *East Bay Express* July 23, 2008; *New York Times* C p6 Sep. 24, 2010; *Time* (on-line) Nov. 2002

Selected Books: *Flood! A Novel in Pictures*, 1992; *Illuminated Poems*, 1996; *Street Posters & Ballads*, 1998; *Blood Song: A Silent Ballad*, 2002; *Slingshot*, 2008; *Howl: A Graphic Novel*, 2010

Selected Films: *Howl*, 2010

Dudley, Bob

Sep. 14, 1955– Executive director of BP

Address: BP International Headquarters, 1 St. James's Sq., London SW1Y 4PD, England

On October 1, 2010 Bob Dudley became the first American executive director of BP, the global oil and gas corporation formerly known as British Petroleum. (His title is equivalent to that of chief executive officer, or CEO.) Dudley's appointment came five months after an explosion on a BP-operated oil rig in the Gulf of Mexico off the coast of Louisiana; that accident killed 11 workers and led to a spill of millions of gallons of crude oil that continued for nearly three months, polluting vast areas of the gulf and the coast and killing enormous numbers of seabirds and other animals. Unlike Tony Hayward, his predecessor as head of BP, Dudley has been praised for his ability to remain calm, levelheaded, and productive in stressful situations. "He has, to use oil rig drilling terms, superb dynamic positioning," a friend of Dudley's said to Terry Macalister for the London *Guardian* (October 1, 2010). "That is where a rig remains on station no matter how much the sea swirls and swells by using special 'thrusters' in all directions. Bob can keep focused on the issue in hand even when mayhem is breaking out all around." Dudley lived near the Gulf of Mexico during his elementary- and middle-school years, and he can empathize with people whose lives were adversely affected by the spill. "I know what it's like to jump off and swim off a boat in the gulf," he told Clifford Krauss and Andrew E. Kramer for the *New York Times* (June 22, 2010, on-line). "I know what crabbing, shrimping and fishing is all about." In an article for the *Vancouver (British Columbia) Sun* (July 28, 2010), Rowena Mason wrote of Dudley, "The slow-walking, slow-talking new boss appears to strike the right tone of caution and reflection aimed at softening up a hostile American public." Prior to his recent promotion, Dudley was in charge of BP's Gulf Coast Restoration Organization, where he helped to organize attempts to cap the well at which the 2010 spill originated. Before that he was the president and CEO of TNK-BP, an oil company owned by BP and a group of Russian businessmen. "He's not the stereotypical aggressive, know-it-all CEO type of guy," Ángel Cabrera, the president of the Thunderbird School of Global Management,

Ki Price/AFP/Getty Images

Bob Dudley

one of Dudley's alma maters, said to Matthew Bigg and Nick Carey for Reuters (July 29, 2010). "He's a humble man."

Robert Warren Dudley was born in a U.S. Navy hospital in the New York City borough of Queens on September 14, 1955, while his father, a physicist, was serving as a naval officer. At the age of five, he moved with his family to Hattiesburg, Mississippi, where his father taught at the University of Southern Mississippi. Dudley spent his childhood in Hattiesburg, a small city in the southern part of the state, about 70 miles from the Gulf of Mexico; during summers he and his family would fish and swim in the gulf. In the 1960s Hattiesburg was the site of a lot of activity connected with the civil rights movement, including major voter-registration drives among the area's African-Americans. On January 10, 1966 members of the Ku Klux Klan firebombed the house of Vernon Dahmer, a local official of the National Association for the Advancement of Colored People (NAACP), who had made his store available for voter registration; Dahmer was fatally burned in the attack, but another 33 years passed before anyone was found guilty and punished for the crime. When Dudley attended Hattiesburg's Thames Middle School, it was in the process of becoming integrated. (Five boys were the first blacks to attend the school, in 1966.) Dudley was a member of the Boy Scouts and a YMCA swim team and shone academically. "He was a chess player in a checkers playing town," Joel Johnson, one of Dudley's former swim teammates, told Bigg and Carey. "He didn't lord it over anyone but he was certainly very smart," Charles Brent, a school friend of Dudley's, told Andrew Clark for the London *Guardian* (July 28, 2010). "He

was very intelligent and very unflappable. Nothing, nobody, could get him angry."

When Dudley was a teenager, his family moved to Chicago, Illinois, where he attended high school. After he graduated he enrolled at the United States Naval Academy, in Annapolis, Maryland. According to John Stepek, writing for *MoneyWeek* (January 21, 2011, on-line), a "chronic shoulder injury" led him to leave the academy and transfer to the University of Illinois, where he graduated with a B.S. degree in chemical engineering in 1978. In 1979 he earned an M.B.A. degree from Southern Methodist University, in Dallas, Texas, and a master's degree in international management at the Thunderbird School of Global Management, in Glendale, Arizona.

In 1979 Dudley was hired by the Amoco Corp., an American oil company based in Chicago. He held a series of commercial and engineering positions in the U.S. and the United Kingdom until 1987, when he began working on projects in the South China Sea. In 1994 Dudley relocated to Moscow, Russia, where he managed Amoco's Russian Corporate Development division for the next three years. In 1997 he was named Amoco's general manager of strategic planning. The following year Amoco was acquired by British Petroleum, one of the leading producers of oil and natural gas in the United States as well as overseas. In 1999 Dudley became the executive assistant to the executive director (also known as the group chief executive), a position he held until 2000, when he became BP's vice president of renewable and alternate energy activities. He was named in 2001 as vice president of the company's businesses in Russia, Angola, Algeria, Egypt, and a portion of the region surrounding the Caspian Sea, whose coastline forms parts of the borders of Russia and four other nations. In 2003 he was appointed president and CEO of TNK-BP, an oil company owned by BP and Russian business partners.

"In Russia, [Dudley] was working in a very high-pressure environment, and he demonstrated his ability to stay focused," Daniel Yergin, an oil historian and the founder and chairman of IHS CERA (formerly Information Handling Services/Cambridge Energy Research Associates), told Jad Mouawad and Clifford Krauss for the *New York Times* (July 25, 2010, on-line). "People thought he wouldn't last," Ángel Cabrera said to Ronald D. White and P. J. Huffstutter for the *Los Angeles Times* (July 27, 2010). "But he just stayed and stayed and kept working." According to BP Dudley helped TNK-BP improve its safety record and increase production by 26 percent. "Under his leadership, TNK-BP became the best-run energy company in Russia, operationally and financially," Fadel Gheit, a senior energy analyst for Oppenheimer, said to White and Huffstutter.

Dudley served as the head of TNK-BP until 2008, when a conflict arose among the company's shareholders. "I became a lightning rod between BP and the Russian owners," he told Clifford

Krauss and Andrew E. Kramer. "You learn in that kind of fast-paced, unpredictable environment to stay calm, get organized quickly and make sure you can communicate across an organization so everyone knows the direction and remains committed." As a result of the dispute, Russia refused to renew Dudley's visa, and he was forced to leave the country. In the same year he became the executive vice president of BP. In 2009 he was seated on BP's board and assumed responsibility for the company's activities in Asia and the Americas.

On April 20, 2010 an explosion occurred on the Deepwater Horizon, a leased, BP-operated oil-drilling rig situated above the Macondo well in the Gulf of Mexico. The explosion killed 11 crewmen and led to the worst oil spill in history. Dudley investigated the response to the disaster, talking to politicians, reporters, and Gulf Coast residents who were affected by the spill. That June—when the oil was still gushing from the Macondo well—Dudley was appointed president and CEO of BP's Gulf Coast Restoration Organization in the U.S. In that post he oversaw the daily response to the leaking oil, the cleanup efforts, and management of the company's image—tasks previously under the purview of Tony Hayward, BP's then-CEO, who had received a great deal of criticism for the way he handled the disaster. On July 15, 2010, after 86 days, the well was capped. By that time nearly five million barrels, or more than 200 million gallons, of crude oil had spewed into the Gulf of Mexico. That same month it was announced that Hayward was stepping down as CEO and that Dudley would replace him later in the year.

Dudley officially became the new CEO of BP on October 1, 2010. "In order to stay in the Gulf of Mexico, what BP needed more than anything was an American to take over as CEO," Malcolm Graham-Wood, a director at Westhouse Securities, said to Sarah Arnott for the London *Independent* (July 27, 2010). One of Dudley's first tasks was to deal with the financial and legal consequences of the oil spill; the company had set aside $20 billion to compensate people and businesses harmed by the disaster. He is also striving to improve safety measures and salvage BP's reputation in the United States. "He's clearly got strong emotional connections with the south of the US in general and that's a big part of him," Ángel Cabrera said in the interview with Andrew Clark. "When he shows empathy in terms of the oil spill in the Gulf, he doesn't need to fake it." "Inside the company, he has to be forceful in changing the way this company has been run," Phil Weiss, an energy analyst at Argus Research, told Ronald D. White and P. J. Huffstutter. "Outside of it, he has to assuage an angry Congress, make all of the spill's victims economically whole again and restore his company's tarnished image. And that's a lot to ask of anyone."

As CEO Dudley has sold billions of dollars' worth of BP's assets to pay for damage from the oil spill; as of March 2011 the company had spent over $40 billion toward that end. He established a new global safety division as well as a new exploration and production division. In May 2010 President Barack Obama established the National Commission on the BP Deepwater Horizon Oil Spill and Offshore Drilling; the commission was co-chaired by Bob Graham, a former governor and U.S. senator from Florida, and William K. Reilly, a former administrator of the Environmental Protection Agency. The group concluded that the Deepwater Horizon explosion and subsequent oil spill were due to the negligence of BP, the contractor Halliburton (which handled cement work on the rig shortly before the explosion), and Transocean, the company that owned the rig.

In January 2011 BP concluded a $7.8 billion deal with Rosneft, a Russian oil company, to drill in the Arctic. Oil experts suggested that the deal will give Dudley and Russia an opportunity to improve their relationship and that BP is pursuing business in Russia because it will take a long time for Americans to trust the company again. Dudley has also organized projects in nations including Canada and India. In March 2011 Dudley offered an apology on behalf of BP at the CERAWeek energy conference and declared that the company was going to make safety its number-one priority. In May 2011 BP was fined $25 million for its failure to prevent corrosion on the Alaska pipeline, which led to two oil spills in 2006. Federal regulators and an outside monitor will keep tabs on the company's maintenance of the pipeline. According to John M. Broder, writing for the *New York Times* (May 3, 2011), BP could be fined more than $20 billion if it is determined that the firm was grossly negligent before the 2010 Gulf of Mexico oil spill.

Andrew Clark described Dudley as "a softly spoken figure with wispy blond hair and an easy-going southern drawl." Dudley is a member of the Society of Petroleum Engineers and the Thunderbird School of Global Management board of fellows. In 2009 he was named an honorary Commander of the Order of the British Empire (CBE) for his services to global energy security and industry.

Dudley and his wife, Mary, married in 1980 and have two children. They own homes in London, England, and Houston, Texas.

—J.P.

Suggested Reading: BP Web site; (London) *Guardian* Financial Pages p31 Oct. 1, 2010; *Los Angeles Times* B p1 July 27, 2010; *MoneyWeek.com* Jan. 21, 2011; *New York Times* (on-line) June 22, 2010; nndb.com; Reuters (on-line) July 29, 2010; *Washington Post* G p5 June 27, 2010

Patrick Kovarik/AFP/Getty Images

Duflo, Esther

(dew-FLOH)

Oct. 25, 1972– Economist; educator; writer; organization official

Address: Dept. of Economics, 50 Memorial Dr., Bldg. E52, Rm. 252G, MIT, Cambridge, MA 02139

Esther Duflo is a developmental economist who has dedicated herself to understanding and combating poverty in the world's poorest countries, where hundreds of millions of people each survive on less than 99 cents a day. For the past 10 years, the 38-year-old Duflo has been conducting field experiments in India and Africa to identify which antipoverty measures have improved people's lives and which have failed to do so—results that could not have been discovered through theories alone. Much of what she has learned has surprised her. Duflo's main tool is the randomized trial—the kind used to test the effectiveness of prescription drugs—in which people are randomly divided into two groups, only one of which, the "treatment" group, is introduced to a new procedure, product, or activity; the other group is called the control group. At the end of the study, Duflo and her team compare the groups to see what has changed, if anything, since the start of their project. For example, in India she found that parents are much more likely to have their children immunized against deadly diseases if they have received a two-pound bag of lentils (a relatively tiny reward) as an incentive. In Kenya she found that farmers are much more likely to use fertilizer for their crops if it is delivered to them at no cost. Duflo, a professor at the

Massachusetts Institute of Technology (MIT), in Cambridge, is a pioneer in the use of randomized trials in the field of economics. In 2003 she co-founded the Abdul Latif Jameel Poverty Action Lab (J-PAL), which is now a network of more than 50 professors around the world who are united in their use of randomized trials to answer crucial questions about reducing poverty.

Duflo, along with the MIT economics professor and J-PAL co-founder Abhijit Banerjee, is the author of *Poor Economics: A Radical Rethinking of the Way to Fight Global Poverty* (2011), which describes some of the authors' hundreds of randomized trials and reveals some aspects of poverty previously undetected by economists or other specialists. *Poor Economics* "draws on a variety of evidence, not limiting itself to the results of randomised trials, as if they are the only route to truth," a reviewer wrote for the *Economist* (April 23, 2011). "And the authors' interest is not confined to 'what works', but also to how and why it works. Indeed, Ms Duflo and Mr Banerjee, perhaps more than some of their disciples, are able theorists as well as thoroughgoing empiricists. They are fascinated by the way the poor think and make decisions. Poor people are not stupid, but they can be misinformed or overwhelmed by circumstance, struggling to do what even they recognise is in their best interests."

In the past few years, recognition of Duflo's work has skyrocketed. An article about her in the London *Independent* (January 13, 2009) by John Lichfield, referring to the Nobel Prize–winning French philosopher Jean-Paul Sartre, was headlined, "Step aside, Sartre: this is the new face of French intellectualism." It continued, "While the West threw billions at global poverty, Esther Duflo tried to solve the problem with science. It has made her France's most fêted thinker." Lichfield called Duflo "one of the world's greatest experts—perhaps the greatest—on why development programmes in poor countries often fail and why they sometimes succeed." In a poll in which the *Economist* (April 23, 2011) asked some of the world's leading authorities in economics whom they believed to be the best young economists in the world, Duflo ranked first. *Time* (April 21, 2011) listed her among the 100 "most influential people in the world," and *Foreign Policy* (November 11, 2010) included her on its list of the top 100 global thinkers. In 2009 she won a so-called genius grant from the MacArthur Foundation, and in 2010 she received from the American Economic Association (AEA) its annual John Bates Clark Medal, awarded to the person it deems the nation's most promising economist under the age of 40.

The second of three children, Esther Duflo was born on October 25, 1972 and raised in Asnières-sur-Seine, a suburb of Paris, France. Her mother was a pediatrician; "generous . . . to the point where it's unnerving for the rest of us," as Duflo described her to Ian Parker for the *New Yorker* (May 17, 2010), she spent a few weeks each year in Africa or Central America, under the auspices of a nongovernmental organization, treating children who had been affected by war. Duflo's father was a math professor. From the age of five—after her father showed her how—Duflo rode the train by herself to go to a nearby town to visit a relative. She was a serious, responsible, determined child. "I can't really remember a time where I didn't do whatever I wanted to do," Duflo told Parker. "Partly because my parents are laid-back, and partly because I was not very willing to let anybody interfere with my plans."

Even before high school Duflo knew that she wanted to study history. She completed her undergraduate degree in history and economics at the prestigious École Normale Supérieure, in Paris. During her last year of college (1992–93), she conducted research as an exchange student in Moscow, Russia, gathering material on Soviet-era propaganda. She also served as a research assistant to the American economist Jeffrey Sachs, whose work convinced her that economics could be used to make positive changes in the real world. By the time she returned to France, her interests had shifted toward politics and helping the poor. She then enrolled in a graduate-level program run jointly by the École Normale Supérieure and the École Polytechnique (known jointly with the acronym ENSAE in France and as DELTA in English). She earned an M.A. degree in history in 1995.

Duflo next enrolled at MIT. Although she was very interested in issues facing the developing world, she knew very little about development economics. But after a month in Abhijit Banerjee's course in that subject, "I was sold. It was clear that this was my path," she told Parker. Banerjee questioned the dominant economic view that poor people's decision-making is no different from wealthier individuals': he argued instead that being poor changes one's priorities and limits one's thinking. Banerjee, who became one of Duflo's dissertation advisers, told Parker that Duflo was "extraordinarily bright, but not like your average pushy student. She didn't speak unless she had something to say." Her other dissertation adviser was Joshua Angrist. Duflo's dissertation was entitled "Three Essays in Empirical Development Economics." In an interview with Judith Chevalier for the *Newsletter of the Committee on the Status of Women in the Economics Profession* (Spring/Summer 2004), a group affiliated with the AEA, she named as "very influential" in her early career, in addition to Banerjee and Angrist, the economists Thomas Piketty of MIT, Angus Deaton of Princeton University, Duncan Thomas of Duke University, Marc Rosenzweig of Yale University, and two Nobel Prize winners in economics: Amartya Sen and Joseph Stiglitz.

After she earned a Ph.D. in economics, in 1999, Duflo got job offers from many of the nation's top university economics departments. Although MIT traditionally did not hire its own graduates, she joined that school's faculty as an assistant professor of economics.

In the papers she published in professional journals at that time, Duflo would typically describe what she felt was the ideal way to test her hypotheses. After a while, she recalled to Parker, "I just got fed up writing about what the ideal experiment would be. Why don't we just do it?" It was then that she began creating experiments to be carried out in the real world. One quintessential experiment asked the question, Why are most maize farmers in Kenya not using fertilizer, even though doing so would produce greater yields for a relatively small investment? Duflo learned that when farmers had the most money, after a harvest, they did not buy fertilizer because they did not need it immediately; then, when the next growing season arrived, they were usually low on funds and could no longer afford it. In a string of experiments, Duflo and her colleagues demonstrated that a free fertilizer delivery after the harvest makes farmers much more likely to use the product.

In one of the first significant profiles of Duflo to appear in an American publication, Daniel Altman wrote for the *New York Times* (August 20, 2002) that Duflo, then 29, "epitomizes the new development economics with her broad use of theoretical and statistical tools and her willingness to conduct research in the field." Because of her experiments to get to the roots of poverty, Duflo was already being considered for lifetime tenure positions at major universities. The following year she rejected tenure-position offers from both Princeton and Yale Universities and accepted one at MIT, as a professor of economics. In 2005 she was promoted to the post of Abdul Latif Jameel Professor of Poverty Alleviation and Development Economics. (The professorship, as well as the Poverty Action Lab, is named in honor of the father of an MIT alumnus, Mohammed Abdul Latif Jameel, who also endowed two fellowships and a research and teaching fund.)

In 2003 Duflo, Banerjee, and Sendhil Mullainathan (an MIT professor of economics who joined the faculty of Harvard University in 2004) founded J-PAL. Their stated goal was to reduce poverty in the developing world by recommending only policies that have been tested empirically, by randomized trials, and were found to promise success. (Duflo is aware of the limitations of that approach. Sometimes the populations of the treatment and control groups become mixed, for example; in addition, splitting a population into treatment and control groups might in some cases—for instance, after a major national disaster such as a hurricane—be unethical, because it would deprive one group of a new, potentially better treatment.)

One experiment addressed the high rates of absenteeism among teachers in parts of India. In an experiment that aimed to find a way to ensure greater teacher attendance, Duflo had teachers in 60 schools take photographs of themselves with their pupils every day, using a camera that dated each photo with an incorruptible time stamp. The teachers were informed that those with better attendance records would be rewarded with higher salaries. No cameras were given to teachers in 60 other schools, who served as the control group; they were not promised higher salaries for better attendance. The teachers in the first group had a higher attendance record, and as a result their pupils did better in school. The teachers did not resent having to take the pictures, Parker wrote, but even if they had, Duflo would not have changed her methodology. In her typically direct manner, Duflo told Parker, "Who do you care about? Lazy teachers who show up sixty per cent of the time, or the kids? O.K., I care about the kids."

In another experiment Duflo investigated whether incentives for parents might motivate them to get their children immunized against potentially deadly diseases, such as measles and tuberculosis. The problem, as Duflo saw it, was that very poor people in developing countries spend little time or money on preventive care, even when it is available. Particularly perplexing to her was that parents in the northern India district of Udaipur—which has a very high rate of child mortality—did not even take their children to receive free immunizations. Among two-year-olds only 2 percent had received any immunizations. In the experiment Duflo, Banerjee, and others devised, residents of some villages who took their children to get immunized each got a free two-pound bag of lentils (worth $1); in the control group of villagers, parents who took their children to get vaccinated did not receive any reward. In the villages where lentils were offered as an incentive, the rate of immunization increased to 38 percent; in the other villages the rate stayed around 2 percent. The findings were surprising, because lentils are cheap and easily available in India. "The standard theory of human capital accumulation cannot explain why you go from a few percent to 38 percent," Duflo told Peter Dizikes for *Technology Review* (January/February 2010). "The fact that there is huge responsiveness to such a small thing is contrary to theory." That is precisely why, Duflo has said many times, researchers and aid workers must allow themselves to be surprised. She has maintained that she has never refused to accept the results of any of her studies, however counterintuitive, strange, or unpalatable they may be.

The failure of others to accept data that she considers solid, however, does arouse Duflo's displeasure. One such instance involved her tests of the effectiveness of microcredit, the giving of very small loans to very poor people—usually women, and usually for entrepreneurial purposes—an idea pioneered by the economist Muhammad Yunus, who in 2006 received the Nobel Peace Prize for his efforts. For that experiment J-PAL, in a collaborative project with Spandana, a microfinance provider, found 104 neighborhoods in Hyderabad, India, that had not been introduced to microcredit. Fifty-two neighborhoods served as the control group—receiving no loans from Spandana, though some received loans from microfinance companies not affiliated with the study—while people in the other 52 neighborhoods were free (though not required) to borrow from Spandana. After more than a year of measuring business income, buying patterns, health, and other factors, Duflo and her colleagues published their initial findings in a 2009 paper titled "The Miracle of Microfinance?" The paper argues that although microcredit increased available funds in the form of loans, it did not lead to noticeable increases in poor people's purchases of goods or services (which would indicate an improved standard of living) or improvements in their health. Most microfinance organizations did not welcome the data and reacted defensively. Duflo told Parker, "Here is what I think: We tried to help [the microcredit companies]. They don't want to be helped. Too bad."

Many of Duflo's studies have been carried out in several phases or over the course of several years. One such study began in India in 2000 to measure differences between villages governed by men and those led by women. (In the early 1990s the Indian constitution was amended to require that a third of the country's local-council seats be reserved for women.) In her study Duflo found, among other results, that female leaders invested more in drinking water than their male counterparts, so their villages had 30 percent more taps and hand pumps. Female leaders were also less likely to take bribes. Yet female leaders were less appreciated than their male counterparts: both male and female voters expressed more dissatisfaction with their female leaders. Six years later Duflo returned with a follow-up experiment: She took two randomly chosen groups and played for one an audio recording of a political speech read by a man and for the other the same speech read by a woman. Duflo found that, based on that single speech, men and women in villages that had never had female leaders considered the female speaker to be less capable than the man. By contrast, people in villages that had had female leaders showed no prejudice. "The findings were the first credible evidence Duflo had seen for the idea that public policy"—in that case, the one-third rule regarding the female/male composition of local councils—"can influence voter prejudice," Parker wrote. Years later, in around 2010, J-PAL added another goal to its agenda: aside from measuring the effectiveness of programs and ideas, it started trying to persuade organizations and political leaders to adopt programs and ideas that J-PAL experiments have proven to be effective.

Duflo and Banerjee wrote *Poor Economics: A Radical Rethinking of the Way to Fight Global Poverty* (2011) for policy makers, philanthropists, activists, and anyone else interested in significantly reducing poverty. The book analyzes a great deal of evidence, including hundreds of J-PAL studies, to show how the world's poor live and why most of those people—the 865 million individuals who subsist on less than 99 cents a day—stay poor. The poor often make impulsive purchases and fail to save even the money they could save; for example, they often spend money on cigarettes, alcohol, and festivals even when they do not have enough food. With regard to health care, poor people usually do not give up their money or time to acquire inexpensive medicine, food, mosquito nets, or other items that could prevent illness or death. However, it would be a mistake to think that poor people do not care about their families' health; evidence shows that they do. Indeed, occasionally the poor will exchange hard-earned cash for costly or ostensible cures. Most people need incentives to do the wise thing, the authors wrote, but because of their circumstances, poor people need them even more. (As an example, consider the experiment in which a gift of lentils led parents to have their children immunized.) The lives of the poor, Duflo and Banerjee asserted, are in many ways—beyond the obvious ones—far more difficult than those of wealthier people: they are often searching for work or operating small businesses in ultra-competitive markets, all with extremely limited resources. The authors proposed solutions apparent from J-PAL studies and other experiments and data, and they criticized views on the extreme sides of the solution spectrum. At one extreme is William Easterly, who opposes aid as a solution to poverty and believes that markets, local action, and democracy will conquer it; at the other is Jeffrey Sachs, who believes that more Western aid, properly distributed, is the best way to help the world's poorest people.

One of the most significant findings in the book shows ways in which stress, insecurity, and hopelessness about the future affect decision-making by poor people. The authors demonstrate that when people have increased opportunity and a consequent sense of hope, their decision-making improves. Some reviewers criticized the authors' focus on the micro level and their assertion that "it is possible to improve governance and policy without changing the existing social and political structures." Madeleine Bunting, in a review for the London Guardian (April 11, 2011), wrote, "There will be plenty of politicians and development agencies who will like such claims; they seem to offer hope to development—don't worry about the really difficult political issues, you can just tweak a few policies and hey presto, major social change is possible without anyone minding. It's this lack of understanding of power and how it works at every level that I found glaringly absent in [Duflo and Banerjee's] analysis: how power works in families, in local economies and in political systems. But they are clearly very clever economists and are doing a grand job to enrich their discipline's grasp of complex issues of poverty—so often misunderstood by people who have never been poor."

Duflo is the founding editor of American Economic Journal: Applied Economics and the author of three books in French on the struggle against poverty. She is a research associate at the National Bureau for Economic Research, in Cambridge, and a member of the board of directors of the Bureau for Research and Economic Analysis of Development (BREAD).

In addition to the above-mentioned honors, Duflo received the American Economic Association's Elaine Bennett Prize for Research, in 2003, and in 2005 she earned both a bronze medal from the Centre National de la Recherche Scientifique and the Best Young French Economist Prize, from Le Cercle des Économistes and the periodical Le Monde. In 2009 she was elected a fellow of the American Academy of Arts and Sciences.

Duflo, who is small and short, has described herself as having "a pretty strong French accent." She has retained her French citizenship. During one of her interviews for the New Yorker, Parker wrote, "her manner mixed intellectual assurance with slight social impatience. (A favorite English phrase: 'Give me a break.')" Duflo told Judith Chevalier, "I much prefer being in the field than in Cambridge." Nevertheless, she said to Chevalier, "teaching and advising students who are going to become development economists is very important." She also said, "I consider it to be a very important part of my job to be giving undergraduate or graduate students who will do something else a glimpse of the problems in the developing world." Duflo's frequent travels include at least two trips to India and one to Kenya every year as well as visits to conferences and other events in many other countries. Every winter she spends four to six weeks overseas; in the summer, eight to 10 weeks. Duflo lives alone in an apartment in Cambridge. She enjoys rock climbing, cooking Indian food, and listening to classical music.

—D.K.

Suggested Reading: econ-www.mit.edu; Economist Apr. 23, 2011; (London) Independent p24 Jan. 13, 2009; New York Times C p2 Aug. 20, 2002; New Yorker p79 May 17, 2010; Newsletter of the Committee on the Status of Women in the Economics Profession p1+ Spring/Summer 2004; pooreconomics.com; povertyactionlab.org; Technology Review Jan./Feb. 2010;

Selected Books: Poor Economics: A Radical Rethinking of the Way to Fight Global Poverty (with Abhijit Banerjee), 2011

Anita Cochrane, courtesy of Paul Dunmall

Dunmall, Paul

May 6, 1953– Jazz saxophonist

Address: c/o Wayside Music, 8905 Fairview Rd., Silver Spring, MD 20910

Some critics of free jazz have argued, among other complaints, that the term itself is redundant—since jazz, a style of music characterized in part by improvisation, is already free. Proponents of the form, though, celebrate the musicians' freedom to improvise and express their ideas without the restrictions of prearranged chord patterns, standard time signatures, and other elements of traditional or "straight-ahead" jazz. Some credit the pianist Lennie Tristano with making the first free-jazz recordings, in the late 1940s; all agree, however, that the form was given its strongest push in the late 1950s and early 1960s, by the recordings of Ornette Coleman, with Albert Ayler, Cecil Taylor, and John Coltrane soon making important contributions to the new sound. Among the musicians carrying free jazz forward on the contemporary scene is the British saxophonist Paul Dunmall. Early in his career Dunmall played with rock and soul bands in the U.S. before returning to his native England, where he has co-founded several improvisation-based groups—most notably, perhaps, Mujician. Dunmall is recognized today as a leading figure in free jazz. A writer for the London *Guardian* (February 18, 2011) called him "a force-of-nature performer"; the *New York Times* (June 13, 2008) referred to him as "an eminence of British free jazz"; the *Evesham (England) Journal* (February 26, 2009) pronounced him to be "one of the most talented reed players on the international scene"; and the

Birmingham (England) Post (January 7, 2008) identified Dunmall, in the context of free jazz, as "the man himself."

Paul Dunmall was born on May 6, 1953 in Welling, a suburb of London, England. He grew up in a working-class, musical family; his father played the drums semiprofessionally, and his mother loved to sing. Dunmall received drum lessons from his father as a child and started taking clarinet lessons through his school's music program at age 12. About a year later, at a jazz concert, he first encountered the instrument he would play professionally. "[My father] took me to a gig where the tenor player in the band gave me his sax to hold, and I remember thinking 'wow, what an incredible thing that is,'" he told Phillip Gibbs for mindyourownmusic.co.uk (September 27, 2000). At age 14 he took a job delivering newspapers in order to purchase his first saxophone, an alto. He traded that instrument for a larger, lower-pitched tenor sax when the soul group he wanted to join, Element of Truth, told him they wanted a tenor player. Dunmall joined the group, also taking music lessons on the weekends at the Blackheath Conservatoire of Music.

At age 15 Dunmall left school to work at Bill Lewington's music shop in London. He learned to repair various instruments, including saxophones, and was introduced to many great jazz musicians of the day, among them Ben Webster and Stan Getz, when they came into the shop to get their instruments fixed or try out new ones. He listened voraciously to jazz. "I think the first guy[s] who really turned me on [were] Junior Walker and King Curtis," he told Gibbs. Dunmall also learned from the older musicians with whom he played. "I was doing lots of soul gigs at that time . . . ," he recalled to Gibbs, "and I met a lot of great sax players, older guys playing in Bluebeat/Soul bands, with [the British jazz/R&B singer] Georgie Fame or whatever, and of course I was so enthusiastic I would pick up everything I could from these guys—fantastic experience." After working in the music shop for about two years, Dunmall auditioned successfully for the progressive rock band Marsupilami and moved with the band's other members to a farmhouse in Somerset, England, to practice and record before touring Europe for two years. During that time the singer of the band introduced him to the later recordings of the jazz innovator John Coltrane. Coltrane's music had a profound effect on Dunmall and led to his interest in free jazz. "I really loved the energy of free music," Dunmall told Gibbs. "For me it was similar to [Jimi] Hendrix and the rock scene at that time. Energy! . . . listen to Albert Ayler or Pharoah Sanders—wow, that's the saxophone—powerful!"

When the members of Marsupilami parted ways, in 1972, Dunmall returned to London and experienced what he described to Gibbs as "a spiritual awakening, or a moment of expanded consciousness . . . the peace that passeth all understanding." Having already delved into Indian philosophy, he discovered a spiritual music collective called the Divine Light Mission; he decided in 1973 that a move to its ashram in California would be the best way to combine his spiritual and musical pursuits. He told Andy Isham for *Avant*, as quoted on mindyourownmusic.co.uk, that the Divine Light Mission "gave me a spiritual understanding through meditation, Coltrane's music, and all the rest of it, led me to that, and that's been a fundament in my life ever since—that I can actually sit down and meditate and forget my body."

Dunmall played original music with the Divine Light Mission; that jazz/soul/rock group worked with such well-known musicians as Alice Coltrane (the widow of John Coltrane) and the blues guitarist Johnny "Guitar" Watson. After a couple of years, the Divine Light Mission experienced financial problems and "started to go weird," as Dunmall said to Gibbs, and its members dispersed. Dunmall remained in the United States, touring as part of Watson's band. "I was on the road with him 1975/'76," Dunmall told Gibbs, "during which time I practiced my a** off, really getting my technique together, listening to everyone and seeing loads of gigs—[the jazz musicians] Roland Kirk, Elvin [Jones], McCoy Tyner, Freddie Hubbard, et al." Dunmall played saxophone on *Ain't That a Bitch* (1976), Watson's first successful funk record and Dunmall's first major-label recording, before returning to England.

The late 1970s saw Dunmall participate in a wide variety of projects. He formed an Oxford-based trio with Nigel Morris and Tony Moore that represented his first true foray into free jazz. In 1979 he moved to Bristol and helped found the group Spirit Level, with the pianist Tim Richards, the bassist Paul Ansley, and the drummer Tony Orrell, a group with which he played for the next 10 years and released four original albums: *Mice in the Wallet* (1982), *Proud Owners* (1984), *Killer Bunnies* (1986), and *Swiss Radio Tapes* (1989). In 1999 the band released a two-disk "best of" album titled *Great Spirit*. The German magazine *Jazz Podium*, as quoted by timrichards.co.uk, called Spirit Level "one of the few glimpses of hope in the currently overflowing post-bop scene."

In 1985 Dunmall joined Tenor Tonic, fronting the group with his fellow tenor saxophonist Alan Skidmore. In 1986 Dunmall played with Dave Alexander and Tony Moore in the DAM trio. The following year he joined the London Jazz Composers Orchestra, an improvisational jazz collective, and has performed on many of their recordings since, including *Zurich Concerts* (1988), the EPs *Harmos* (1989) and *Theoria* (1991), and *Portraits* (1993). "Riding over the Orchestra, you needed plenty of stamina and energy," Dunmall told Fred Jung for jazzweekly.com (2003). "I think what I learned from a composing point of view was try to keep the music simple. It always brings the best results. Let the music [breathe] and be flexible." Dunmall released his first solo album, *Soliloquy*, in 1986 to good reviews. Richard Williams, writing for the

London *Times* (June 17, 1989), called it "an engaging demonstration of multi-tracking," going on to say that "the vigorous passages of fervent, Ayler-inspired wailing suggest that Dunmall may be in the early stages of worthwhile discoveries."

In 1988 Dunmall formed a quartet called Mujician, with the trumpeter Keith Tippett, the bassist Paul Rogers, and the drummer Tony Levin, and began playing mainly in improvisational settings. "With Mujician, the rule is we never talk about what we are going to play," he told Allen J. Huotari for allaboutjazz.com (March 1999). "We walk on stage and—away we go and trust to the music." The still-active band has released seven albums to date: *The Journey* (1992), *Poem About the Hero* (1994), *Birdman* (1996), *Colours Fulfilled* (1998), *The Bristol Concert* (2000), *Spacetime* (2002), and *There's No Going Back Now* (2006).

Dunmall has also been quite prolific outside the framework of Mujician. He played for a time in a trio with Keith and Julie Tippett and in Keith Tippett's big band, Tapestry. He also formed separate duos with members of Mujician, recording two improvisational records with Tony Levin (*Spiritual Empathy*, 1994, and *Essential Expressions*, 1996) as well as a more folk-influenced record with Paul Rogers (*Folks*, 1993). When performing live Dunmall and Rogers took liberties with the folk-music form. "We call it Folks, but more and more the last few gigs we've done have been totally improvised," Dunmall told Martin Longley for the *Birmingham Post* (February 26, 1999). "Gradually, we took the melodies apart, dismantled them so much that we just decided, if you play one note of that melody, then that's enough. We've actually dispensed with it, so we just improvise, which is what we're all about anyway."

In 1995 Dunmall formed two new trios: one with Oren Marshall on tuba and Steve Noble on percussion, and one with John Adams on guitar and Mark Sanders on percussion. The two trios occasionally combined to form a sextet. He also continued to play with his longtime collaborator and fellow saxophonist Elton Dean; the two have released eight recordings together, including *Twos and Threes* (1988), *Silent Knowledge* (1995), and *If Dubois Only Knew* (1996).

In 1996 Dunmall founded the Paul Dunmall Octet, featuring collaborators both old and new. The group was composed of the members of Mujician plus four other jazz musicians: Simon Picard on tenor sax, Paul Rutherford and Hilary Jeffery on trombone, and Gethin Liddington on trumpet. Unlike the work of Mujician, which was purely an improvisational group, the octet's songs had many written passages. Of the group's second release, *Bebop Starhurst* (1999), Glenn Astarita wrote for allaboutjazz.com (February 1999) that Dunmall "summons his Be-Bop roots with a vengeance" and "effectively illustrates the boundless concepts that could be derived from Be-Bop as a musical art form." The octet, Astarita wrote, "aggressively takes on its own identity from the onset. Dunmall

. . . maintains the patented swift pace and 'free-style' approach yet explores crafty and fertile brass arrangements with this adventurous and captivating effort."

The octet's third album, *The Great Divide* (2000), was equally inventive. Frank-John Hadley, writing for *Down Beat* (September 2001), found *The Great Divide* to be "as dazzling as liquid mercury." "Unlike related bands on the Continent," he wrote, "the members of Dunmall's octet delve into abstraction without succumbing to self-absorbed rambling and over-cerebral dryness. Their displays of personal expression, whether in unisons, in collective improvisations or in solos, are infused with life and vivacity." Dunmall has recorded two other albums with the octet: *Desire and Liberation* (1996) and *Bridging: The Great Divide Live* (2002). When questioned by Huotari about the ways in which the octet was different from Mujician, despite including all of its members, Dunmall responded, "As soon as you add or take away a musician from an ensemble, especially improvising groups, it changes quite dramatically. The chemistry between the musicians changes! A musician becomes super-sensitive when performing—listening to all the musicians' contributions around him and that makes him respond accordingly."

In 1998 Dunmall began playing with the Belfast, Ireland–based Brian Irvine Ensemble. "I was interested in letting [Dunmall] work away as a free improviser," Irvine told Martin Longley for the *Birmingham Post* (February 14, 2002), "superimposing him on the band situation. Everything [the Brian Irvine Ensemble] play is written, although there are moments where we can break away from that and get into a wee bit of improv. I write very strict stuff for my band to play, but I do like the idea of superimposing two extremes." "Irvine's music was suitably clanky, crammed with outrageously spiky detail and dense invention," Longley wrote about the fruits of the collaboration, describing the album *Bersudsky's Machines* (1999). "Its electric rock core was trimmed by cello, violin, flute and horns. . . . The music's heavy mass is subject to some quite nimble, dynamic leaps, with Dunmall's solos ranging from flying rage to reverberant lyricism."

Also in 1999 Dunmall started his own record label, Duns. His original reason for doing so was to release *Solo Bagpipes* (1999); as it was difficult to find a label willing to put out a jazz album performed entirely on the instrument of the title, he undertook that job himself. The label has released most of Dunmall's albums recorded since then, as well as work by fellow musicians including Keith Tippet and Satoko Fujii. Dunmall has enjoyed the flexibility his own label offered him, as well as its production speed. "Record for a 'real' label and you might wait 18 months to two years for your work to see the light of day—by which time you would certainly have moved on as a player," Steve Lake wrote for mindyourownmusic.co.uk. "With [Duns, Dunmall] could record in July and have fin-ished copies for sale in August. It was possible to think of the discs almost as newspapers: This is the latest news, this is what we're doing now. Without any limits imposed by another label's agenda."

In 2003 the British Broadcasting Corp. (BBC) commissioned Dunmall to create a program-length piece in commemoration of his 50th birthday. He enlisted members of Mujician and other collaborators to form the 14-piece Moksha Big Band, named for the Hindi word for the final liberation of the soul. Informed by the wars currently being fought in the Middle East and the death of his fellow saxophonist Jerry Underwood, Dunmall composed "I Wish You Peace," a work in three parts. Describing the 2004 recording of the work, Bill Shoemaker wrote for *Down Beat* (February 2005): "Garden-variety descriptions of intensity fall flat as passages of the piece blur the difference between exhilaration and terror. So too do facile reductions of the piece's structure, as it's both wide open and tight as a snare's head. This is the type of music for which clichés like 'challenging music that requires and rewards committed listening' were coined."

Dunmall's albums of recent years include *Go Forth Duck* (2004), *Awareness Response* (a 2004 collaboration with Paul Rogers), *In Your Shell Like* (2005), and *Identical Sunsets* (2010). *In Your Shell Like* found Dunmall alternating between saxophone and bagpipes in a series of duets and trios with Paul Lytton on drums and Stevie Wishart on hurdy-gurdy (a stringed instrument). Reviewing the record for allmusic.com, François Couture wrote that it "may not be a key Dunmall recording, but it represents a rare quieter outing, rich in surprises and unique in sound." Another writer for allmusic.com, Phil Freeman, wrote about *Identical Sunsets*—on which Dunmall is paired with the drummer Chris Corsano—that it is "a unique meeting of two men who are legends within their own spheres."

Dunmall lives in Worcester, England, and continues to record and release music through Duns. Though he is no longer actively involved with any spiritual group, he sees his improvisational approach to music as being parallel to his spirituality. "I try not to think if I can help it, more an attitude of 'anything can happen'—I love that," he told Gibbs. "It's a bit like meditation, the idea is to quieten the mind, almost as if something is taking over, tuning into an energy where a second can last forever. Of course, there is also the chaos of it, when you're not listening to what's going on. But if you are listening, and the playing is happening, you can get to that magical point, and for me this can only happen when I'm freely improvising. *That's* what I am after in music."

—J.E.P.

Suggested Reading: AllAboutJazz (on-line) Mar. 1999, Dec. 14, 2006; allmusic.com; Mind Your Own Music (on-line) Sep. 27, 2000, June 23, 2002; pauldunmall.com

Selected Recordings: *Soliloquy*, 1986; *In Your Shell Like*, 2005; *Identical Sunsets*, 2010; with Mujician—*The Journey*, 1992; *Poem About the Hero*, 1994; *Birdman*, 1996; *Colours Fulfilled*, 1998; *The Bristol Concert*, 2000; *Spacetime*, 2002; *There's No Going Back Now*, 2006; with the Paul Dunmall Octet—*Bebop Stardust*, 1999; *The Great Divide*, 2000

Courtesy of Sunoco, Inc.

Elsenhans, Lynn

May 6, 1956– President, CEO, and chair of Sunoco

Address: Sunoco Inc., 1735 Market St., Suite LL, Philadelphia, PA 19103

In 2008 the oil-industry veteran Lynn Elsenhans became the first female chief executive officer (CEO) and president of Sunoco, a *Fortune* 500 company that is one of the biggest independent oil refiners and marketers in the United States. Based in Philadelphia, Pennsylvania, Sunoco has nearly 15,000 employees and 4,700 gas stations in 26 states, and its annual earnings currently top $54 billion. Before she was named the head of Sunoco, Elsenhans spent 28 years with Royal Dutch Shell, a global oil and gas company, where she held various executive positions and gained international experience in manufacturing, marketing, and planning.

"Refining is not normally viewed as a woman's area of expertise or business," Malcolm Turner, an engineering consultant, told Kate Galbraith for the *New York Times* (July 17, 2008). Elsenhans re-

called to Christopher Dow for *Rice Magazine* (Fall 2008), "When I first started, there weren't many women in the industry, and women's credibility was very much questioned." Later in the same interview she noted, "Women in all kinds of fields have opportunities for leadership that didn't exist when I started working. . . . As society gets more comfortable with the notion that women can be tough when there's a reason to get tough, as well as taking the more traditional supportive role, it will tend to make it easier for women to have top jobs and break that glass ceiling."

Elsenhans was born Lynn Laverty on May 6, 1956. Her father worked for Exxon USA in the areas of marketing and research, and his assignments led the family to move repeatedly back and forth between New York and Texas. During her youth Elsenhans developed an interest in mathematics. "When I was in the sixth grade," she recalled in an interview for *Pathways Magazine* (Fall 2009), "I had a math teacher who told me 'Don't let anybody tell you that girls can't do math. You are very good in this subject. You can do this.'" She attended a series of several high schools, according to Christopher Dow. She next enrolled at Rice University, in Houston, Texas, where she played on the school's first women's intercollegiate basketball team. "I've participated in sports throughout my life, and it's a big part of who I am," she told Dow. "In fact, one thing I tell anyone—women, especially—who is interested in going into business and being in leadership is to play a team sport. You learn a lot about yourself and what it means to interrelate with people and to work toward a common objective at the highest levels when you play on a good sports team."

Also during college Elsenhans was elected to the student government; served as a student representative on the Examinations and Standings Committee; worked as a sports editor for the *Thresher*, the school's weekly student newspaper; and was a member of the Marching Owl Band—actually, an orchestra that never marched. "For me, [college] was the total experience, both inside and outside the classroom," she told Dow. "It was absolutely excellent for me." In 1978 Elsenhans earned a B.A. degree in applied mathematics from Rice. When one of her former professors learned that she intended to pursue a graduate degree at the Harvard Business School, he told her that she would be wasting her time and money. During an awards-ceremony acceptance speech, Elsenhans quoted him as saying, "You're not smart enough, you are not tough enough, and besides, you are a woman," as Mike Armstrong reported for *Philly.com* (March 18, 2011). "Believe it or not, this guy did me a big favor," she told the audience. "He helped strengthen my resolve to prove him wrong and succeed. I was more determined than ever to push ahead and give it my best efforts."

At the Harvard Business School, in Cambridge, Massachusetts, Elsenhans earned an M.B.A. degree in 1980. She resolved to build a career in the energy industry. "It sounds corny, but it really mattered to me to work for something that made a difference," she recalled to Christopher Dow. "I couldn't think of anything that had more of an impact on our society than energy." Elsenhans was hired by Royal Dutch Shell in 1980. She worked first at Shell's U.S. headquarters, in Houston, then transferred to Shell's Deer Park refinery, 20 miles east of Houston, where she handled assignments in the company's so-called downstream business. In the petroleum industry downstream business includes crude-oil refineries, transportation networks, petrochemical plants, gasoline-processing plants, natural-gas distribution companies, and retail gas stations. It also involves the marketing and sale of refined petroleum products.

In 1999 Elsenhans became the president and CEO of Shell Oil Products East, which is based in Singapore, a city-state on the southern tip of the Malay Peninsula, in Southeast Asia. Three years later she was named the director of strategic planning, sustainable development, and external affairs at Shell International Ltd. in London, England. In that post she had responsibility for the operation and financial performance of the corporation's refining sector. She held that title until 2003, when she was named the president of Shell Oil Co. (a subsidiary of Royal Dutch Shell) as well as the CEO and president of Shell Oil Products U.S. (a subsidiary of Shell Oil Co.). Also in 2003 she became the chairperson of the U.S. operations of Royal Dutch Shell. Next, from 2005 to 2008 Elsenhans served as the executive vice president of global manufacturing for Shell Downstream Inc. and Shell Oil Co. In that position she was responsible for the company's refining business and chemical manufacturing worldwide.

After spending nearly three decades with Royal Dutch Shell, Elsenhans could have chosen to retire or work out of the company's European headquarters. Instead, in August 2008 she left Shell to become the president, CEO, and director of Sunoco Inc., a leading manufacturer and marketer of petroleum and petrochemical products. She also became the chairman of Sunoco Logistics Partners L.P., a subsidiary of Sunoco Inc. that, according to its Web site, is "in the business of transporting, terminalling, and storing refined products and crude oil." Elsenhans replaced John G. Drosdick, who was retiring from those positions after eight years. As CEO Elsenhans restructured the top management team and introduced a cost-reduction program. "We had to get clear about a competitive cost structure so we could position ourselves well," she told Dustin S. Klein for *Smart Business Cleveland* (May 2010). "We invested more in our people for leadership development and addressed gaps in our leadership pipeline. We also invested in our brand to position us for the future in our industry, and then looked for ways to turn weaknesses into opportunities. It was a chance to look back and decide what's really important."

As CEO Elsenhans has worked toward turning Sunoco into a "pull" company—that is, one that lures customers to it instead of pushing products toward them. "We were looking to raise our brand as a pull point and then use our company to be in transportation and energy markets and meet the demands of those future markets," she explained to Dustin S. Klein. In January 2009 Elsenhans was given the additional title of chairwoman of Sunoco. Since she became the head of the company, Elsenhans has laid off hundreds of workers, sold Sunoco's chemicals businesses, and closed or sold three of its five refineries.

When Christopher Dow asked her to describe the qualities of an effective leader, Elsenhans responded, "The critical thing I tell people is to be yourself. Authenticity is incredibly important, and if you're trying to be someone you're not, people see that, and it's the kiss of death. Being self-aware also is important. Understanding the impact you have on others and being open to feedback. One of the hardest lessons for me to learn as a leader was the need to give up being right. If you're always advocating your position, you aren't being open to the ideas of others." She added, "Beyond that, a leader has to be more positive than negative and have a vision for the future and a belief that things can be better. People need a reason to believe and hope, and they will not follow a leader who doesn't have the view that tomorrow will be better than today." In the interview with Dustin S. Klein, Elsenhans said that it is essential for CEOs to have the ability to adapt during hard times. "If you don't innovate, you're going to die," she told Klein. "If you are not attuned to the disruptive forces in your marketplace and reacting to those through innovation, you're going to be left behind."

Elsenhans was named one of the World's 100 Most Powerful Women by *Forbes* magazine in 2008 and 2009. She was listed among the 50 Women to Watch by the *Wall Street Journal* in 2008 and the 50 Most Powerful Women in Business by *Fortune* magazine in 2009 and 2010. Elsenhans has been a director of the International Paper Co. since 2007. A former trustee of Rice University, she is a member of the council of overseers for Rice's Jones Graduate School of Business. She has served on the board of directors of United Way of Southeastern Pennsylvania, the World Golf Foundation, the American Petroleum Institute, the Greater Houston Partnership, the National Urban League, the Texas Medical Center, and the Greater Philadelphia Chamber of Commerce. On March 17, 2011 Elsenhans received the Paradigm Award from the last-named group, in recognition of her accomplishments as a businesswoman in the Greater Philadelphia region. The chamber of commerce also gave her $25,000 in charitable gifts, which she donated to nonprofit organizations. That same month Sunoco earned the U.S. Environmental Protection Agency's Energy Star Sustained Excellence Award, for "its continued efforts to protect the environment through energy efficiency," according to *Business Wire* (March 16, 2011, on-line).

Elsenhans lives in Philadelphia and is married to John W. Elsenhans, who is described on various Web sites as "a consultant"; he is also the chief financial officer of the Pogo Producing Co., a Houston-based oil and gas business.

—J.P.

Suggested Reading: *Houston Chronicle* Business p1 Mar. 7, 2003; *Pathways Magazine* (on-line) Fall 2009; *Philadelphia Inquirer* C p1 July 17, 2008; *Rice Magazine* (on-line) Fall 2008; *Smart Business Cleveland* p20 May 2010

Eric Cabanis/AFP/Getty Images

Enders, Thomas

Dec. 21, 1958– President and CEO of Airbus

Address: Airbus, 1 Rond Point Maurice Bellonte, Toulouse-Blagnac, F-31707 France

In August 2007 Thomas Enders, a native of Germany, was named the president and chief executive officer of Airbus, which in recent years has manufactured about half of the world's commercial airliners and is the Boeing Co.'s biggest competitor. Airbus was launched in 1970 as a cooperative endeavor of the British, French, German, and Spanish governments, all of which wanted to end domination of the aerospace industry by Boeing and other American companies. In 2000 Airbus became a subsidiary of the European Aeronautics Defence and Space Co. (EADS); at present, a total of 50.5 percent of Airbus is controlled by French, German, and Spanish private and/or public owners and the rest by holders of shares traded on European stock exchanges. Nearly all of the firm's 52,000 employees work at sites in France, Germany, Spain, or Great Britain; the governments of those countries strive "to optimise their national gains," a goal that is "at odds with a company that is transnationally organised and trying to optimise" its efficiency and profits, Enders told an *Economist* (July 17, 2008, on-line) interviewer. Those competing interests, Sarah Arnott noted for the London *Independent* (July 15, 2010, on-line), are "emblematic of a company that is much like a commercial incarnation of the EU [European Union] itself: an impossible mix of soaring vision, competing factions and stultifying political compromise." Enders told the *Economist* interviewer that his mission is "to drive this company as far and as fast as possible in the direction of being a normal company. Aerospace is a political and strategic industry, but we need to make as much room as possible for business thinking and entrepreneurial decisions."

"Paradoxically," the *Economist* reporter noted, "Mr. Enders is himself a product of the nexus between politics and aerospace." The son of a shepherd, Enders became a paratrooper while fulfilling his military service, in the late 1970s. He began his professional life as an assistant with the West German legislature in 1982, before his college graduation. Starting in 1985 he worked for a series of prestigious research institutes and then for the West German Defense Ministry. During that period he earned a doctoral degree in political science. For the past two decades, he has worked in the aerospace industry, beginning in the marketing department of an arm of DaimlerChrysler Aerospace AG ("AG" being equivalent to "Inc."). He held executive positions with EADS from 2000 to 2007. His accession to the top post at Airbus followed several rocky years for the firm, marked by significant delays in production of several aircraft—most notably, the A380 passenger jet, the world's largest commercial aircraft—and administrative turmoil. Under his leadership Airbus has largely recovered, and it has suffered relatively little during the current worldwide recession; according to Sarah Arnott, "Three years on" since Enders's arrival at the firm, "there has been enough progress for him to claim that the benefits of cross-border creative rivalry outweigh the difficulties of different language and culture." Nevertheless, Enders told Arnott, "We are dancing on a volcano. The volcano may be silent for a long time, and you don't know when it will erupt again." In an illustration of his unusual versatility, on November 15, 2010 Enders (along with nine other sports parachutists) jumped from the rear-cargo ramp of an Airbus A400M military plane at an altitude of 12,000 feet, in a test of the suitability of that aircraft (which is still under development) for paratroopers.

Thomas Enders was born on December 21, 1958 in Neuschlade, in the eastern part of what was then West Germany. He grew up in a rural area, where his father raised and herded sheep, some of them for other farmers. "It was tough. We were not rich people, obviously," Enders told Rupert Steiner for the London *Sunday Times* (December 31, 2000). After he completed high school, Enders served in the elite Airborne Division of the Bundeswehr (German Federal Defense Forces), in 1977 and 1978. He then studied economics, political science, and history at the University of Bonn, Germany, which awarded him a B.A. degree in 1983. "I wanted to raise my social status," he told Steiner. "I didn't want to work as a shepherd, although it's not such a bad thing and many people dream of it."

For about three years beginning in 1982, Enders worked as an assistant for the West German Parliament. In 1985 he became a research associate with the institute of the Konrad Adenauer Foundation in Sankt Augustin, near Bonn; the institute is among the foundation's many education centers in eight countries, all of which promote democracy, the unification of Europe, and cooperation among all nations. The institute published Enders's monograph *Missile Defense as Part of an Extended NATO Air Defense* in 1986. Also during the 1980s, according to various sources, Enders took courses at the University of California at Los Angeles (UCLA). In 1987 he earned a Ph.D. in political science from the University of Bonn. (Reports that he received his doctorate from UCLA are erroneous.) His doctoral dissertation focused on changes in the ideas of Germany's Social Democratic Party during the period 1966 to 1982, when it was the ruling party. In 1988 Enders was hired by the German Council on Foreign Relations, in Bonn, as a research associate, and also by the International Institute for Strategic Studies, in London, England, as a senior research associate; he held both positions until 1990. Concurrently, in 1989 he became a member of the planning staff of the German minister of defense, Gerhard Stoltenberg, under Chancellor Helmut Kohl, during the period when the Berlin Wall, separating East and West Berlin, fell, and East and West Germany were reunited, in October 1990.

In 1991 Enders joined the marketing division of Messerschmitt-Boelkow-Blohm, a manufacturer of helicopter and airplane parts that had been acquired by Deutsche Aerospace AG (DASA) in 1989. He held various marketing posts until 1995, by which year the corporation had been renamed Daimler-Benz Aerospace (also known as DASA), the German industrial giant Daimler-Benz having acquired Deutsche Aerospace, Deutsche Airbus, and several other firms. Enders was promoted in 1995 to corporate secretary in DASA's chairman's office (in effect, becoming the chairman's chief of staff). In 1996 he became director of corporate strategy and technology. With the 1998 merger of Daimler-Benz and the Chrysler Corp., the aerospace division was renamed DaimlerChrysler Aerospace AG. In November 1999 DASA merged with Aerospatiale-Matra of France, and in 2000 the new entity merged with Construcciones Aeronáuticas SA (CASA) of Spain to form the European Aeronautic Defence and Space Co. That year Enders was named the CEO of EADS's defense and security-system division; he also gained the titles of EADS executive vice president and member of the EADS board of management.

In early 2001 EADS became a joint stock company (which combines elements of a corporation and a partnership), led by two executives—one from France and the other from Germany (at first, Philippe Camus and Rainer Hertrich). The French government held a 15 percent interest, the French media group Lagardère held an additional 15 percent, DaimlerChrysler held 30 percent, and Spain 5.5 percent. The rest was owned by shareholders. Enders was named CEO of the EADS Defence and Security Systems Division and a member of the EADS executive committee. With the encouragement of Hertrich and Camus, Enders expanded EADS's production of military aircraft, to enable the firm to be less dependent on the frequent fluctuations in the civil-aviation market. During his time in that post, the United States purchased maritime patrol aircraft, helicopters, and radar components for the U.S. Coast Guard.

When Hertrich retired, in June 2005, Enders assumed the role of co-CEO alongside Noel Forgeard, after a protracted power struggle in which Forgeard fought to be EADS's sole CEO. According to Mark Landler, writing for the *New York Times* (December 18, 2004), the squabble was "only the latest power struggle between France and Germany." Within a year the public learned that delivery of Airbus's A380 twin-deck jet, the world's largest passenger plane, would be delayed by six months. That news led to a 26 percent drop in the value of EADS stock on June 14, 2006. "When a company screws up the way . . . EADS admitted yesterday," Gordon Pitts wrote for the Toronto, Canada, *Globe and Mail* (June 15, 2006), "it is natural to think about firing the chief executive officer. But which CEO?" Enders asserted, as quoted in the London *Daily Telegraph* (June 19, 2006), "Every crisis brings opportunities with it. Because of this we should not act too hastily." That July Forgeard and Gustav Humbert, the CEO of Airbus, resigned after it was revealed that the two had sold millions of dollars' worth of EADS stock shortly before the announcement about the A380 production delays. Forgeard was replaced by Louis Gallois.

Later in 2006 EADS announced a restructuring and cost-cutting plan called Power8, which aimed to reduce overhead expenses by 30 percent (in part by selling several factories) and increase productivity by 20 percent. Some 10,000 workers learned that their jobs were to be eliminated. Although, in an attempt to placate employees, Enders and Gallois announced that 5,000 of them would be rehired as temporary workers and subcontractors, workers in France held a strike on March 6, 2007 to protest the restructuring plan. The French Socialist presidential candidate, Ségolène Royal, urged the French government to increase its stake in EADS to protect the interests of workers, but to no avail. (She also failed to win the presidency.)

In July 2007 EADS named Gallois to the newly created single-CEO post and announced that the position would alternate every five years between a French and a German citizen. Enders became the CEO of Airbus. Some observers, according to the *Economist* writer, viewed Enders's move "as a demotion, because he was stepping down as co-chief executive of the parent company," but Enders told that reporter, "It was the first time in my life that I was really prepared to fight to get a job. I wanted it so much." In October of that year, Airbus finally delivered its first A380, to Singapore Airlines. The jet—which can carry a maximum of 853 passengers—is 80 feet high at its tallest and, at 240 feet long, is about two-thirds the length of a football field. It is not only the largest commercial airplane ever built but also one of the quietest and most fuel efficient.

The A380 is one of the eight models currently being manufactured for Airbus's line of commercial passenger aircraft. (Variations in the sizes of fuselages bring the total number of models in that line to 13.) Airbus also produces corporate jets, freight aircraft, and military planes. In the four years beginning in January 2007, it surpassed Boeing in total number of planes ordered (2,963 for Airbus, 2,747 for Boeing) and in total number of planes delivered (1,944 versus 1,759). In recent years, in complaints brought before the World Trade Organization (WTO), the U.S. government, on behalf of Boeing, charged that Airbus had benefited unfairly from below-market-rate-interest loans made by the European Union and individual governments within the union. At the same time the European Union, on behalf of Airbus, also lodged complaints with the WTO, charging that Boeing has benefited unfairly from federal aid, from the National Aeronautics and Space Administration (NASA) and the U.S. Defense Department, and state and local tax breaks. The WTO has backed the U.S. government with regard to some complaints and supported the European Union in connection with others; both sides have appealed some of the WTO's decisions.

In October 2007 the French financial-markets authority AMF, a stock-market watchdog, accused Enders and 16 other senior EADS executives, along with the company itself and Lagardère and Daimler, its two principal private shareholders, of illegal insider trading in early 2006—in particular, the 17 officials' sales of some of their stock before the public learned that production of the Airbus A380 would be significantly delayed. Enders and all the others denied any wrongdoing, and in late 2010 all the charges were dismissed.

On February 1, 2008 an Airbus craft completed the world's first commercial jet flight powered by liquid fuel processed from natural gas (known as GTL, "gas to liquid"), which produces significantly smaller quantities of greenhouse-gas emissions than petroleum-based fuels. Four days later the Clean Sky Joint Technology Initiative (commonly known as Clean Sky) was launched, with Airbus among the 86 participating companies, research centers, and universities from 16 European Union countries. Funded by the European Union and private firms and scheduled to extend until 2014, the project aims to reduce aircraft-emitted carbon dioxide by 50 percent, nitrous oxide by 80 percent, and external noise by 50 percent (all as measured in 2000) by 2020. "The environmental challenges facing aviation today are global and will require multinational collaboration for the best solutions," Enders said, according to a Clean Sky news release posted on GreenAirOnline.com (February 5, 2008). "Innovation, alternative fuels, research and technology are some key enablers and air traffic management is another. Being an eco-efficient company is key to Airbus's vision to help the industry prosper responsibly with less and less impact on the environment."

Toward the end of 2008, Airbus opened its first factory in China. The plant, in Tianjin, on a gulf of the Yellow Sea not far from Beijing, handles the final assembly of A320 planes. With its opening, Enders said, according to *Tooling & Production* (November/December 2008, on-line), "we deepen and expand our industrial relationship [with non-European countries], which is a key pillar of the internationalization strategy of Airbus." In Enders's view, that strategy must not be derailed by conflicts arising from the self-interests of governments within the European Union. "Could we really renationalise and fragment our industry in the face of globalisation and rising competition from Asia? No way," he declared to Sarah Arnott. Like all other European businesses, Airbus has been affected by financial instabilities stemming from the European Union's adoption of a single monetary unit, the euro, which is used as currency in 17 of the 27 E.U. nations and five non-E.U. European countries. According to the Adelaide, Australia, *Advertiser* (January 17, 2008), "Airbus sells its jets in dollars, though many of its costs remain in euros."

Since 2005 Enders has served as president of the German Aerospace Industries Association BDLI and as chair of Atlantik-Brucke ("Atlantic Bridge"), a nonprofit organization that aims to promote a reciprocal understanding between German citizens and Americans, Canadians, and other Europeans. The Library of Congress lists four publications by Enders in German in addition to his 1986 monograph.

According to Sarah Arnott, Enders "is not the flashy chief executive type. Dressed with German precision, he looks more like a soldier than a businessman, with short blond hair, chiselled looks and a rather piercing, blue stare. He has a reputation for sternness. . . . But there are flashes of humour, although often so dry that they could easily be missed." Arnott also wrote that he speaks "clipped but flawless English." Enders and his wife have four sons. His recreational interests include skiing, mountaineering, and skydiving.

—T.O.

Suggested Reading: airbus.com; *BusinessWeek* (on-line) Jan. 13, 2011; *Economist* (on-line) July 17, 2008; *Financial Times* p5 Nov. 19, 2003; (London) *Daily Mail* p67 July 17, 2007; (London) *Independent* (on-line) July 15, 2010; (London) *Times* p42 June 27, 2005; *Marquis Who's Who* (on-line); *New York Times* A p6 Dec. 18, 2004, C p3 Mar. 25, 2006, (on-line) July 1, 2010; *Who's Who in European Business and Industry*; *Who's Who in France*

Courtesy of Wayne Escoffery

Escoffery, Wayne

Feb. 23, 1975– Jazz saxophonist

Address: c/o Scott Global Music Group, 36 Plaza St. East, Suite 1F, Brooklyn, NY 11238

"Wayne Escoffery clearly has arrived. . . . His name deserves mention in any discussion of upper echelon tenor players," Edward Zucker wrote for *All About Jazz* (2007, on-line) in a review of the jazz saxophonist Escoffery's 2007 album *Veneration: Live at Smoke*. A master of both the tenor and soprano saxophones, Escoffery has released several albums over the past decade, including *Times Change* (2001), *Intuition* (2004), *If Dreams Come True* (2007), *Hopes and Dreams* (2008), *Uptown* (2009), and *Tides of Yesterday* (2010). He is also a noted sideman: in addition to leading his own band, Veneration, he has played and recorded albums with such groups as the Mingus Big Band, the Tom Harrell Quintet, the Lonnie Plaxico Group, and Ben Riley's Monk Legacy Septet. Escoffery has attributed his success to the influence of

the jazz legends who came before him, a few of whom served as mentors to Escoffery—most notably Jackie McLean, a saxophonist and composer who rose to fame during the heydays of bebop and hard bop. *Veneration: Live at Smoke* (2007), Escoffery's first live album, pays tribute to McLean, who died in 2006. McLean, whose own work was steeped in the blues, instilled in Escoffery an appreciation for the blues sound. "One of McLean's stylistic hallmarks was his warm, dramatically expressive sound . . . expressing emotions from ecstatic joy to blues-drenched melancholy. Like his mentor, Escoffery also maintains a visceral, earthy edge in his playing no matter how intellectually complex or technically demanding his music gets," Owen McNally wrote for the *Hartford (Connecticut) Courant* (August 30, 2007). McNally wrote for the same newspaper (August 5, 2008), "Graced with a robust tone and fluent phrasing crackling with invention and daring . . . Wayne Escoffery believes in creating accessible music—a form of heresy for the elite jazz priesthood that venerates the abstruse and arcane."

Of West Indian descent, Wayne Escoffery was born in London, England, on February 23, 1975. He grew up without his father; in 1983 he and his mother left London, living briefly in Montreal, Canada; Florida; and Atlanta, Georgia, before settling in New Haven, Connecticut, in 1986. New Haven, home of Yale University, provided Escoffery with a plethora of opportunities to explore his creative interests. At 11 he joined the prestigious New Haven Trinity Boys Choir and toured with them internationally. "I got exposed to a lot of great classical choral music," Escoffery told Jason Crane for *All About Jazz* (October 1, 2007, on-line), adding that his experience in the choir "was a great beginning for me to get my ear together and get an understanding of the basics of music." Escoffery picked up the saxophone as an elementary-school student, introduced to the instrument by a traveling musician who visited his school. "He could play every instrument," Escoffery told Crane. "So he came and did a performance and played the saxophone, trumpet, violin." Escoffery described his first foray into the jazz world to Bill Carbone for the *New Haven Advocate* (June 2, 2010, on-line). "I have family in Jamaica, so I went for the summer and I went to a music store in Kingston and said, 'I want to learn jazz, give me the recording of the best jazz saxophone player,'" Escoffery said. Referring to a commercially successful but often critically reviled jazz musician, he added, "So they gave me a Kenny G recording. And they're like, 'This is the best dude, learn this.' So I pretty much learned everything on the recording. I didn't know any better." Soon after that, Escoffery discovered recordings by the celebrated pianist, composer, and big-band leader Duke Ellington and embarked on a full-fledged study of jazz.

As a teenager Escoffery attended the Neighborhood Music School, one of the nation's 10 largest community arts schools, which provides advanced training on more than 30 instruments and, according to its Web site, boasts one of the largest ensemble programs in the U.S. Escoffery also attended the Educational Center for the Arts, where he took music classes every afternoon during high school. In about 1991 Escoffery began attending Jazzmobile, in the Harlem section of New York City, on Saturdays. Founded by the jazz pianist, composer, and educator Billy Taylor, Jazzmobile is a nonprofit organization that presents jazz festivals and offers jazz workshops and clinics to young people under the guidance of top-tier musicians. Jazzmobile afforded Escoffery his first brush with real jazz musicians and with the New York City jazz scene, whose atmosphere he found exciting and inspiring.

In 1992, during his senior year of high school, Escoffery was introduced to the mentor who would enrich his musicianship and propel his career. While participating in a jam session in New Haven, Escoffery became friends with Jimmy Greene, a fellow saxophonist; Greene told Escoffery that he had been working with the legendary saxophonist Jackie McLean through an organization called the Artists Collective in Hartford, Connecticut, and invited Escoffery to join. McLean and his wife, Dollie, had founded the collective in 1970, after several African-American students complained to McLean that they had been exposed to very little art relating to their culture. The collective offers programs in dance, theater, music, and visual arts. Escoffery joined the collective's big band, which was run by the members of McLean's band, including the pianist Alan Palmer, the bassist Nat Reeves, and the trombonist Steve Davis. Impressed by Escoffery's talent, in 1993 McLean offered him a full scholarship to the Hartt School, a music and performing-arts conservatory at the University of Hartford, where McLean headed the jazz department. Escoffery described McLean to Crane as a "father figure" to his class, encouraging yet tough. "J-Mac didn't hold his words," Escoffery said, recalling an instance at the Hartt School when McLean told a student, "The stuff you're playing is baby talk. We need to be making sentences here, using real words."

While at the Hartt School Escoffery and Greene both received private lessons from McLean. (At the school the two were nicknamed "the twin towers" because of their standout talent.) Escoffery and Greene lived with their fellow saxophonists and classmates Julius Tolentino and Chris Allen. "There was a very healthy amount of competition there," Escoffery told Crane. "We were all pushing each other, much like a family." While at the Hartt School, Escoffery continued to play a Tuesday-night gig that he had kept up since high school, at an old New Haven haunt called Rudy's, even though he had to attend McLean's master class the following morning. (He faithfully played the gig for six years.) Escoffery would make the 35-minute drive every week, sometimes not returning to Hartford until 2:00 a.m. "I would still get up Wednes-

day morning to do my long tones [an exercise in which a saxophonist holds one note for an extended period, focusing on reaching perfect tone] an hour before class, because . . . I knew that Jimmy was going to sound great, and I knew Julius was going to sound good, and so-and-so was going to sound good."

Escoffery graduated summa cum laude from the Hartt School in 1997 with a bachelor's degree in jazz performance and immediately entered the Thelonious Monk Institute of Jazz (named for the celebrated pianist and composer) at the New England Conservatory, in Boston, Massachusetts. During his time at the institute (1997–99), Escoffery met and played with some of the biggest names in jazz, including the hard-bop saxophonist George Coleman, the bassist Ron Carter, and the be-bop pianist and composer Barry Harris. One summer Escoffery and an ensemble of Monk Institute students spent two weeks touring with the pianist Herbie Hancock. In 1999 Escoffery graduated from the Monk Institute, earned a master's degree from the New England Conservatory, and moved to New York City. His connections from the Monk Institute landed him a gig with the pianist Eric Reed, who had been a visiting artist there. Reed invited Escoffery to play with his septet at the Village Vanguard, a famous New York club that has hosted such luminaries as Monk, Miles Davis, and Sonny Rollins. Escoffery also played on Reed's 2001 album *Happiness*. Escoffery's performance impressed executives at Reed's record label, Nagel-Heyer, and the saxophonist signed with the label in 2001, releasing his debut solo album, *Times Change*, the same year. The record was well-received; Bill Milkowski noted for *Jazz Times* (May 2002, on-line) that it distinguished Escoffery as "an exciting new talent to watch." *Times Change* featured Carl Allen (on drums), Aaron Goldberg (piano), and Joel Forbes (bass). That year Escoffery also became a member of the Mingus Big Band, which specializes in music by the bassist and composer Charles Mingus and consists of a revolving ensemble of players selected by the composer's widow, Sue Mingus. In 2002 Escoffery recorded *Tonight at Noon* with the Mingus Big Band. He also contributed to the trombonist David Gibson's 2002 album *Maya* as well as the bassist Lonnie Plaxico's 2003 record *Rhythm and Soul*. "When you have your own group you are under your own terms. You do what you want to do and you are aware of what your limits are. It is up to you whether or not you want to push those limits," Escoffery explained to Joe Montague in an interview for *Jazz Review* (July 2007, on-line). "When you are a sideman, you are going to be asked to do things that maybe you haven't thought about before, or perhaps that you might not have thought that you would like to do. You keep developing skills [as a sideman] that you are going to need to become a better musician."

In 2004 Escoffery was selected by the Grammy Award–winning producer, arranger, and trumpeter Don Sickler (whom Escoffery had met at the

Monk Institute) to join the Ben Riley Monk Legacy Septet. The septet, as described by Escoffery's Web site, is an "innovative piano-less group dedicated to carrying on the legacy of jazz great [pianist] Thelonious Monk." At that time Escoffery was the member of two other groups that paid homage to the legends of jazz. He was handpicked by the trumpeter Wynton Marsalis, the artistic director of Jazz at Lincoln Center, to play with two groups— the Music of Dexter Gordon and the Music of Miles Davis—as part of Jazz at Lincoln Center's Music of the Masters tour.

Also in 2004 Escoffery recorded his second solo album, *Intuition*, through Nagel-Heyer. That recording included performances by Jeremy Pelt on trumpet, Rick Germanson on piano, Gerald Cannon on bass, and Ralph Peterson on drums. An accomplished jazz singer, Carolyn Leonhart, whom Escoffery had begun dating in 2002, contributed vocals to the song "I Should Care" on *Intuition*. (The couple were married in a ceremony at Poets House in New York City in January 2004.) The album garnered both positive and lukewarm reviews. For *Jazz Times* (July/August 2004, on-line), Chris Kelsey wrote that Escoffery sounded "more or less like any of a zillion other super-fast and clean 1960s postbop revivalists," while Ray Cominsky, writing for the *Irish Times* (November 19, 2004), praised Escoffery's "panache, skill and considerable imagination." In 2005 Escoffery lent his talents to four albums, among them David Gibson's *The Path to Delphi*; *I Am Three*, by the Mingus Big Band; *Twin Song*, by the Israeli guitarist Avi Rothbard; and Leonhart's *New 8th Day*.

The next year Escoffery was invited to join the trumpeter Tom Harrell's quintet, an opportunity Escoffery's Web site calls "one of the most coveted gigs in jazz." Escoffery told Montague that Harrell's arrangements require him to stretch himself musically. "His compositions sound simple but when you play them, the harmonies are so complex. With every song of his that I learn, I have to take it home and study it to really understand the harmonies that he is using. . . . It changes my playing. I play in a different way when I play with Tom." In 2006 Escoffery recorded *Live in Tokyo at the Blue Note* with the Mingus Big Band and *Memories of T* with the Ben Riley Monk Legacy Septet. On June 2 and 3 Escoffery and his band Veneration (which includes Hans Glawisching on bass, Lewis Nash on drums, and the saxophonist's close friend Joe Locke on vibraphone) recorded their performances at the Smoke jazz club in New York. The recording, released through Savant Records in 2007 as *Veneration: Live at Smoke*, was dedicated to Jackie McLean, who died in March 2006. (It features Escoffery's take on McLean's "Melody for Melonae," which was named for the late saxophonist's daughter, from the 1962 album *Let Freedom Ring*.) *Veneration* won much praise from critics, who noted the musical prowess Escoffery displayed on numbers such as the Billy Strayhorn/Duke Ellington classic "Isfahan," Booker Lit-

tle's "Bee Vamp," and "Melody for Melonae." Escoffery next recorded *Hopes and Dreams* (2008, also released by Savant Records), with the Veneration band plus Jonathan Blake on drums. Recent recordings for which Escoffery served as sideman or group member include *G-Rays* (2008), by David Gibson; *Force of Four* (2008), by Joe Locke; *The Brother Thelonious Quintet* (2009), by the group of the same name; Harrell's *Light On* (2007), *Prana Dance* (2009), and *Roman Nights* (2010); and *Playdate* (2009), by the group of the same name, whose members are Escoffery, the pianist Noah Baerman, the drummer Vinnie Sperrazza, and the bassist Henry Lugo. Escoffery collaborated on an album with Leonhart in 2007 (*If Dreams Come True*) and another in 2010, *Tides of Yesterday*. McNally described Leonhart and Escoffery as "one of the jazz world's most glamorous and gifted, young power couples." Of *Tides of Yesterday*, Christopher Loudon wrote for *Jazz Times* (May 2010, on-line), "That Carolyn Leonhart can hold her own as a superlative vocalist is undeniable. . . . But Leonhart's vocal prowess is, as has been the case on two previous albums, exponentially increased when she is paired with her equally gifted saxophonist husband." Talking with Montague, Escoffery said about working with his wife, "A lot of time when I compose stuff, she is at my side, and I will ask her questions. . . . We really guide each other in a great way."

Escoffery has both a musical ear and a sartorial eye: the dapper musician has worked as a model, and in 2007 he played one of his compositions in a TV commercial for Grey Goose vodka, which proclaimed Escoffery—in keeping with the brand's ad campaign—to have "discerning taste." Escoffery is currently on the faculty at the New York Jazz Academy. He has also taught at Artists Collective and the Litchfield Jazz Festival Summer School, and he has participated in the Thelonious Monk Institute's Jazz Ambassador program in the United States, South America, and Jamaica. Escoffery makes himself available whenever possible to teach private and ensemble music lessons in the tradition, he has said, of his mentors. In 2010 Leonhart gave birth to the couple's first child, Vaughn Jalen. Escoffery and his family live in Harlem.

—M.M.H.

Suggested Reading: *All About Jazz* (on-line) Oct. 1, 2007; escofferymusic.com; *Hartford (Connecticut) Courant* B p5 Dec. 10, 2006, p20 Aug. 30, 2007; *Jazz Review* (on-line) July 2007; *New Haven Advocate* (on-line) June 2, 2010

Selected Recordings: *Times Change*, 2001; *Intuition*, 2004; *Uptown*, 2009; with Carolyn Leonhart—*If Dreams Come True*, 2007; *Tides of Yesterday*, 2010; with Veneration—*Veneration: Live at Smoke*, 2007; *Hopes and Dreams*, 2008

Selected Recordings (as contributor): with the Brother Thelonious Quintet—*The Brother Thelonious Quintet*, 2009; with David Gibson—*Maya*, 2002; *The Path to Delphi*, 2005; *G–Rays*, 2008; with Tom Harrell—*Light On*, 2007; *Prana Dance*, 2009; *Roman Nights*, 2010; with Carolyn Leonhart—*New 8th Day*, 2005; with Joe Locke—*Force of Four*, 2008; with the Mingus Big Band—*Tonight at Noon*, 2002; *I Am Three*, 2005; *Live in Tokyo at the Blue Note*, 2006; with Lonnie Plaxico—*Rhythm and Soul*, 2003; with Ben Riley's Monk Legacy Septet—*Memories of T*, 2006; with Eric Reed—*Happiness*, 2001; with Avi Rothbard—*Twin Song*, 2005

Frazer Harrison/Getty Images for CineVegas

Everson, Kevin Jerome

Feb. 1, 1965– Artist; filmmaker; educator

Address: McIntire Dept. of Art, University of Virginia, P.O. Box 400872, Charlottesville, VA 22904-4130

The art films of Kevin Jerome Everson have been recognized around the world for their compelling depictions of the midwestern African-American working class. Born in the Rust Belt, Everson has drawn inspiration from, and featured in many of his films, members of his own family. His oeuvre comprises five feature films and more than 70 shorts—seen at prestigious galleries, museums, and film festivals around the globe—that blur the line between fiction and documentary, containing both archival footage and scripted scenes with actors. Everson is also well-known as a photogra-

pher, sculptor, and painter; as an artist, he has said, he is interested in the performative aspect of everyday labor. "Because America's full of bigots and stuff, we always ask somebody what they do for a living," Everson told Colin Dabkowski for the *Buffalo (New York) News* (June 11, 2010). "I think that's maybe our first or second question, so we're always defined by work. But if you go to Trinidad or Italy or the Congo, Brazzaville, places I've been to, people never talk about what they do for a living. They talk about their family and stuff like that, and how they feel. But in America, work is on your mind all the time. In my films, I like to kind of emphasize that." For example, Everson's short *Second Shift* (1999) accentuates the hand motions of a guard at a correctional facility (played by Everson) as he performs his daily routine—carrying his lunch pail to work or putting his keys in a bin to be inspected. *A Week in the Hole* (2001) depicts a paint-factory worker learning new skills during his first day on the job. For a scene in his critically acclaimed 2010 feature, *Erie*, Everson focused his camera on workers sorting and sterilizing medical equipment. While some might consider Everson's films tedious in their examination of the mundane, Ed Salter argued in *Artforum International* (May 1, 2010) that as a whole, Everson's abstracted view of working-class reality captures "the resonance between the art of workers and the work of artists."

Kevin Jerome Everson was born on February 1, 1965 and grew up in a predominantly African-American, working-class neighborhood in Mansfield, Ohio; 80 miles from Cleveland, Mansfield became a booming manufacturing town in the decades after its founding, in 1808, and was, along with Cleveland, a destination for many southern blacks during the Great Migration of the 20th century. Everson's father was a mechanic, and his mother was a bank teller. In an interview for *C-ville: Charlottesville (Virginia) News & Arts* (online), Everson said that when he was growing up, "I think my cousins and brothers and I worked on a comic book or something like that. But I wasn't very good at it. Mostly it was stuff like *Spider-Man*, copying artists like Gil Kane. But I didn't really do anything with art until I got to college. I was kind of a jock." Everson studied art in college and graduate school, working in different mediums, including sculpture. He told Emma Rathbone for *UVA Today* (April 26, 2011, on-line), a University of Virginia publication, "I started doing films because I thought it was another way to explain the sculpture I was doing. I needed a time-based medium, and I wanted to explore how long things last." He received a B.F.A. degree from the University of Akron, in Ohio, in 1987, and an M.F.A. degree from Ohio University, in Athens, in 1990.

Everson's art first began attracting attention in the early 1990s, when he participated in an exhibition called Natural Selections at the Longwood Art Gallery (now located at Hostos Community College) in the Bronx, a borough of New York City. Impressed by Everson's work, Thelma Golden included one of his installations in Black Male: Represen-tations of Masculinity in Contemporary American Art (1994), a controversial show she was curating at New York's Whitney Museum of American Art. Everson's installation included a small, handmade end table meant to represent a piece of mass-produced furniture that was in Everson's home when he was growing up. Everson then collaborat-ed with the William Busta Gallery, in Cleveland, to produce for the Whitney an installation and ac-companying film called Adult Material. Critics were unimpressed by the interactive portion of the exhibit, which invited viewers to reenact the ac-tion of the film, in which a young boy discovers what seems at first to be pornographic material in his parents' bedroom—but which actually consists of family photos and pictures of a black couple kissing. The short film, however, went on to win the Georgia Mae Campbell Award at the 1996 Cleveland Film Festival. That same year Everson was awarded a grant for photography from the prestigious John Simon Guggenheim Memorial Foundation. He was so surprised that after receiv-ing a call of congratulations from the foundation's representatives, he called them back to make sure that he had really won the award. Then he called his mother. "She didn't know what it meant," he told Steven Litt for the Cleveland Plain Dealer (April 20, 1996). "I told her it was like the Heisman Trophy for photography."

Meanwhile, Everson had begun teaching art, with stints at the University of Akron; Oberlin Col-lege, in Ohio; and, beginning in the late 1990s, the University of Tennessee at Knoxville, where he be-came an assistant professor. "It's rewarding," he told Litt of teaching. "It's fun and it's honest work. I just like being around that debate circle, talking about art." In 1997 he completed a short film, Elev-en Eighty Two, which elaborated on a theme Ever-son had explored in a sculpture called Corrections 1996, exhibited at the Cleveland Museum of Art. While a prison guard speaks in a voiceover, the film shows images of uniforms. The title refers to a guard's starting hourly wage at the time—$11.82. (When other work dried up in Mansfield, Ever-son's hometown, many residents found jobs at a nearby correctional facility.)

Everson made his first full-length film, Spice-bush, in 2005. (The name is derived from Missis-sippi's state butterfly, the spicebush swallowtail.) Originally envisioning the project as a series of shorts, Everson instead decided to present the ex-perimental vignettes as a 70-minute feature. Spice-bush incorporates several media, including 16mm film, still photography, and video, to portray docu-mentary-style scenes, scripted scenes, found news footage, and—an Everson signature—new footage doctored to look like archival film. "The result," Laila Lalami wrote for the film magazine the Inde-pendent (January 1, 2005, on-line), "is a collage representing the African American landscape from the mid-20th century to early 21st century, a stun-ning overview of black experience in this country,

from segregation to desegregation to resegrega-tion." The 17-segment, fragmented narrative fol-lows the transporting of furniture from a manufac-turer in Ohio to a grade school in Mississippi. The film creates the effect, Robert Koehler wrote for Va-riety (July 18, 2005), of "thumbing through an ex-tended family photo album. . . . But the full emo-tional effect of Spicebush comes after it's over, as an observant viewer puts together the full picture." Everson, he added, is like "an anthropologist with a touch of the poet." Everson released his second feature, Cinnamon, the following year. That proj-ect, a departure for the artist, examines the world of African-Americans in drag racing. Again, Ever-son used both scripted material and found footage in the film. The characters in Cinnamon are a bank teller and a mechanic who find joy in competing in drag-racing events on weekends. "Mixing docu-mentary and performance art with only the faintest whiff of narrative, Everson captures the arbitrary rhythms of average lives with such an absence of significance that it's tempting to conclude that nothing happens in his films . . . ," Tim Grierson wrote for LA Weekly (April 5, 2007). "Everson goes beyond fetishizing or ennobling mundane labor; rather, he nonchalantly observes how the escapist pleasure of a personal passion brings meaning and balance to a person's otherwise humdrum life. . . . Cinnamon speaks to the unknowable in-ner lives of the anonymous people around us all."

The Golden Age of Fish (2008) is an experimen-tal feature of interwoven narratives, tracing the his-tory of Cleveland to prehistoric times. The title re-fers to the Cleveland Shale of the Devonian age, hundreds of millions of years ago—a period noted for the appearance of many new species of fish. In 2010 Everson released Erie, a feature consisting of a series of single-take shots filmed in and around the Lake Erie region. The first sequence in the film finds two workers putting up a billboard poster that shows a black man wearing a beret and leaning against a Volkswagen Beetle. The sign reads: "There's a bit of cool in every bug." Not revealed in the film is that the ad is a fake for which Everson commissioned the poster, using a photograph of his uncle. Other scenes include a young girl (Ever-son's daughter) watching a candle slowly burn to its base, young performers singing and krump dancing, and two women wearing ponchos on a boat approaching Niagara Falls. "When people are doing their tasks, I try to respect their task and pay homage to their task and try to frame it up as hand-somely as I can," Everson told Dabkowski. "I just want to present it as form." His latest feature film, Quality Control (2011), examines workers in an Al-abama dry-cleaning shop. "Work is arduous and repetitive," Koehler wrote for Variety (April 27, 2011), "yet Everson's unobtrusive camera ob-serves—as his films often do—people who can joke while doing tasks many would find humorless."

"The short film is like an art object," Everson told a reporter for the Buffalo (New York) News (July 10, 2009). "I can experiment with form, and time, and cadence, and texture, and stuff like that more so than with a feature. Features I do as well, but I have to keep the audience in mind with longer films because you're asking them to invest more time, so the short form I like 'cause then I can play with content a little bit more." Everson has made several short films—some no longer than two minutes—that have received considerable attention from art galleries and film festivals. For his 2007 film *Something Else*, Everson appropriated 1970s news footage in which a white journalist interviews the newly crowned Miss Black Roanoke of Virginia. He asks her, "Do you prefer to be in a segregated pageant?" She responds: "Well, I don't think it's a matter of preference. I think it's a matter of whether I was to win or lose, you understand. Because in the other pageant—I call it the regular pageant—the black girl doesn't have much of a chance of winning. I hate to say it, but it's kind of true. It's not that it's segregated, but it's necessary to segregate, in order to give black girls a chance to feel . . . 'up.'"

According To . . . (2007) frames old TV-news clips (about a black man drowning in Virginia and an elderly black woman dying of burn-related injuries) with an interview of an old man who speaks lucidly at first but then has trouble remembering his past. As the film progresses, and updates of the news stories are shown, we learn that the deaths were not accidents. "Everson's careful framing of these stories . . . ," Cora Fisher wrote in the *Brooklyn (New York) Rail* (June 2011), "indicts the film image as a medium that purports to objectively capture life while it hides the salient facts." *Playing Dead* (2008) also makes use of disturbing archival footage. In it, a white journalist interviews a black man who was beaten by a gang of whites in his driveway the night before; the victim's brother was killed, and the interviewee survived the attack by pretending to be dead. *Emergency Needs* (2007) deconstructs its subject—a news conference held by Carl B. Stokes of Cleveland, the first African-American mayor of a large city, during the riots of 1968—through a split screen, as an actress reenacts Stokes's gestures.

Everson's interest in mid-century found footage is driven partly by how difficult it is to find. "Nobody aimed a camera at black folks back then," Everson told Lalami. Lalami paraphrased him as saying, "Most of what's available from that period doesn't represent the diversity of black experience, but instead it focuses on the serious, newsworthy events from the civil rights era, like school desegregation in the South or African Americans hard at work in factories." She added, "In other words, Everson says, African Americans were documented only insofar as 'they fit within the white culture.'"

Discussing his approach to creating films, Everson told the *C-ville* interviewer that instead of coming up with an idea and then devising the means to express it, he carries that process out in reverse: "Every year I come up with a formal issue I want

to exercise—color, time, sound and footage, aggressive editing or no editing, and I go from there." Quoting Everson as saying that his first duty is not to document African-American experience but to make art, Lalami observed that Everson "always looks for the art object first, regardless of how it fits within the larger discourse." Everson told Lalami, "As for righting the wrongs of the Western image-making machine, I just don't have the cash for that."

In addition to the grant from the Guggenheim Foundation, Everson has been awarded a National Endowment for the Arts fellowship, two National Endowment for the Humanities fellowships, and residencies at the well-known Yaddo and Mac-Dowell artists' colonies. His films have been shown at numerous festivals, including the Sundance Film Festival, the Rotterdam International Film Festival, the Berlin International Film Festival European Film Market, the LA Film Festival, and the New York Underground Film Festival, at which he won the award for best documentary for *Spicebush* in 2005.

Everson's films and other work have been exhibited at New York's Museum of Modern Art. The Whitney Museum of American Art included a collection of his work called More Than That: Films by Kevin Jerome Everson in its 2008 biennial.

Everson is currently a film professor at the University of Virginia in Charlottesville, which has been his home for the past 10 years. One of his former students there, Han West, told a reporter for the university's publication *Arts and Sciences* (online), "With Kevin, and this sounds cliché, but the world is literally our classroom. He takes students to New York each year to look at film and art, and he is always around for us. . . . There are really no bounds to how he acts as a teacher, a mentor and a friend to a lot of us." Everson has a daughter from a past relationship; his son, DeCarrio Antwan Couley, was killed at the age of 25 in 2010. Everson's retrospective at the Whitney, More Than That, was dedicated to his son's memory.

—M.M.H.

Suggested Reading: *Artforum* p228 May 1, 2010; *Brooklyn (New York) Rail* (on-line) June 2011; *Buffalo (New York) News* G p2 July 10, 2009, G p16 June 11, 2010; (Cleveland) *Plain Dealer* E p8 Apr. 20, 1996; *Independent* (on-line) Jan. 1, 2005; *LA Weekly* (on-line) Apr. 5, 2007; people.virginia.edu; *Variety* p39 July 18, 2005, (on-line) Apr. 27, 2011

Selected Films: features—*Spicebush*, 2005; *Cinnamon*, 2006; *The Golden Age of Fish*, 2008; *Erie*, 2010; *Quality Control*, 2011; shorts—*Eleven Eighty-Two*, 1997; *Six Positions*, 1998; *Imported*, 1999; *Merger*, 1999; *Second Shift*, 1999; *Thermostat*, 2000; *Avenues*, 2000; *Room Temperature*, 2001; *The Daily Number*, 2001; *Pick Six*, 2001; *A Week in the Hole*, 2001; *72*, 2002; *Special Man*, 2002; *Fumble*, 2002; *Un Euro*

Venti Due, 2002; *Vanessa*, 2002; *Sportello Quattro*, 2002; *Pictures from Dorothy*, 2003; *Aquarius*, 2003; *Chemistry*, 2003; *From Pompei to Xenia*, 2003; *Fifeville*, 2005; *Blind Huber*, 2005; *Two-Week Vacation*, 2005; *Memoir*, 2005; *Twenty Minutes*, 2005; *The Virginia Line Up*, 2007; *The Picnic*, 2007; *Next to You*, 2007; *The Principles*, 2007; *Nectar*, 2007; *Something Else*, 2007; *According to...*, 2007; *The Reverend E. Randall T. Osborn, First Cousin*, 2007; *North*, 2007; *Emergency Needs*, 2007; *O.T.*, 2008; *Broad Day*, 2008; *140 Over 90*, 2008; *Ike*, 2008; *The Wilbur*, 2008; *Wolf Ticket*, 2008; *Ring*, 2008; *Key to the Cities*, 2008; *Playing Dead*, 2008; *Home*, 2008; *Ninety-Three*, 2008; *Undefeated*, 2008; *Second and Lee*, 2008; *The Simple Antennae*, 2009; *The Citizens*, 2009; *Lead*, 2009; *Honorable Mention*, 2009; *Around Oak Grove*, 2009; *Telethon*, 2009; *The Camps*, 2009; *Watchworks*, 2009; *753 McPherson Street*, 2009; *Old Cat*, 2009; *Company Line*, 2009; *Act Three: Finale*, 2010; *Act Two: Stop Drop Roll*, 2010; *Act One: Betty*, 2010; *American Motor Company*, 2010; *Fillmore*, 2010; *House in the North Country*, 2010; *BZV*, 2010; *Corn and Cotton*, 2011; *Fifteen an Hour*, 2011; *Half On, Half Off*, 2011; *The Pritchard*, 2011; *The Equestrians*, 2011

Chip Somodevilla/Getty Images

Fallin, Mary

Dec. 9, 1954– Governor of Oklahoma (Republican)

Address: State Capitol, 2300 N. Lincoln Blvd., Rm. 212, Oklahoma City, OK 73105

The political career of the Republican Mary Fallin has been a series of "firsts" for the state of Oklahoma. After two terms in the Oklahoma State House of Representatives, Fallin became the first woman and the first Republican to serve as the state's lieutenant governor, upon taking office in 1995. She remained in that position until 2007, when she became the first woman since 1920 elected to represent Oklahoma in the U.S. Congress. Most recently Fallin defeated the Democrat Jari Askins in the gubernatorial election of November 2010, and she be-

came the state's first female governor when she was sworn into office, on January 10, 2011. A fiscal conservative, Fallin aims to cut wasteful spending from Oklahoma's state budget, lower taxes for families and small businesses, and fight government-run health care in favor of what she calls a more affordable private-insurance market.

Fallin was born Mary Newt Copeland on December 9, 1954 at the Whiteman Air Force Base in Warrensburg, Missouri, where her father, Joseph Newton "Newt" Copeland, was serving in the U.S. Air Force. She is the older of two children, with a brother six years her junior. Fallin moved several times with her family in Oklahoma; when she was five they settled in Tecumseh. She attended Tecumseh High School, where she played basketball, volleyball, and softball; she was selected to play shortstop for the all-county team. Fallin became interested in politics when, as a high-school senior, she served as a page in the State House of Representatives. In an interview with Ken Raymond for the *Oklahoman* (September 26, 2010, on-line), Fallin described her teenage self as a "very clean cut girl" who "didn't even drink or party." The daughter of two Democrats, Fallin said that she registered as a Democrat when she came of age because her "mother and father said that's what everyone did."

Fallin attended Oklahoma Baptist University, in Shawnee, from 1973 to 1975. She then transferred to Oklahoma State University (OSU), in Stillwater, from which she received a B.S. degree in human environmental sciences, with a focus on family relations and child development, in 1977. It was shortly after graduating from OSU that Fallin became aware of the similarity between the Republican Party's stances on certain issues and her own views. In an interview for the Women of Oklahoma Legislature Oral History Project (October 7, 2008, on-line), sponsored by OSU, Fallin told Tanya Finchum, "A friend of mine invited me to the Young Republicans meeting and actually they showed me the platform between the Democrat[ic] Party and the Republican Party. And I actually read it! And determined I was really a conservative Republican. I liked fiscal discipline in spending, and

I was conservative on social issues and believed in limited government. So I actually switched by the time I was about 21 or so to be a Republican." She told Finchum about breaking the news to her parents, "I can still remember going home and telling my father . . . that I was going to become a Republican instead of a Democrat and he said, 'Well if you want to do something that stupid, then you go right ahead.' And unfortunately he didn't live long enough to see me ever become elected to office." Fallin's new political affiliation was further complicated by her having recently helped her father in his successful second campaign to become mayor of Tecumseh. His first attempt had failed, Fallin told Finchum, because he had not campaigned extensively enough. Fallin has said that her involvement in her father's campaigns taught her a great deal about the importance of meeting voters face to face. After Fallin's father's death, in 1983, Fallin's mother, Mary Jo Copeland, became the first female mayor of Tecumseh when she agreed to serve in her husband's place.

After her graduation from OSU, Fallin spent more than a dozen years in a variety of positions, many of them connected to the travel and tourism industry. From 1981 to 1982, for example, she served as the state travel coordinator for the Oklahoma Department of Tourism; from 1983 to 1984 she was the marketing director at Brian Head (Utah) Hotel & Ski Resort; from 1984 to 1987 she was the director of sales at a Residence Inn Hotel; and from 1988 to 1990 she served as district manager of Lexington Hotel Suites. Fallin explained to Finchum that those experiences in the business world contributed to her decision to run for the Oklahoma State House of Representatives in 1990: "As the seat [in the Oklahoma legislature] came open, I was listening to all these different issues around the state dealing with business, because at that time I was running a business. I was always dealing with workers comp and health care insurance and education and trying to find a quality work force. . . . So I was really paying attention to issues at the Capitol."

Starting in January 1990 Fallin set aside a couple of thousand dollars of her own money, assembled a small team of volunteers, and began running a campaign out of the dining room of the home she shared with her then-husband, an Oklahoma City dentist, Joseph P. Fallin. Early on in her campaign, Fallin, who was already the mother of a three-year-old daughter, discovered that she was pregnant with her second child. Determined to stay in the race, Fallin enlisted her mother to assist in the care of her daughter. Increasingly unable to go door-to-door to introduce herself to potential voters as her pregnancy progressed, she set up a phone bank and started making calls instead. Despite Fallin's confidence that she could handle the stress of being pregnant and running for office at the same time, some of her critics were quick to question her decision to continue with the campaign. "To even run as a young pregnant mom in my 30's was quite the

thing back in 1990," Fallin recalled in her interview with Finchum. "It was not the norm to do that and I did take some criticism from those who said, 'What about your children? Aren't you thinking about your children?' And of course I was and that was hurtful for people to say that." Fallin has said that in retrospect she feels she made the right decision. "Now my children are [grown] and I know my daughter would actually like to run for office and follow in my footsteps. . . . Both of them have turned out quite well and have done very well in school and we've all made it through very well."

Fallin's son was born between the time of her win in the Republican primary, in August 1990, and her general-election victory in November. She told Ginnie Graham for *Tulsa World* (August 8, 2010, on-line), "There are times when people wonder if Mary Fallin . . . can handle the hard rigors of politics. I say, 'You have a baby between the primary and general elections, then tell me how tough I am.'" Four years later, after serving two terms in the Oklahoma State House, Fallin was elected as the state's lieutenant governor, a position she held through 2007. She was the first Republican and the first woman in Oklahoma history ever to be elected to that post. Among other acts, as lieutenant governor Fallin sat on 10 boards and commissions, among them the Tourism and Recreation Commission. She worked to support economic development and small businesses, opposing government regulation. Also during her tenure she formed a task force to rebuild a children's day-care center destroyed in 1995 in the Oklahoma City bombing. In addition, she worked at the local level to oppose the national health-care reform then proposed by the administration of President Bill Clinton and spearheaded by First Lady Hillary Rodham Clinton. In 2000 Fallin used her authority as president of the state Senate to force the vote that passed the Right to Work statute. The Right to Work statutes, currently enforced in more than 20 (mostly southern and western) U.S. states, guarantee each resident the right to work without joining a union.

In 1998 Fallin endured a messy public divorce, with her husband accusing her of having an affair with a state trooper who was acting as her bodyguard. A private detective hired by her husband reportedly saw Mary Fallin and the state trooper kissing and holding hands. Although Fallin and the trooper initially denied any impropriety, the trooper eventually admitted to "unprofessional conduct" and resigned.

In 2006, while serving her third term as lieutenant governor, Fallin made a run for the seat in the U.S. House representing Oklahoma's Fifth Congressional District. Fallin defeated the Democrat David Hunter in the general election with 60 percent of the vote, making her the first woman to be elected to represent the state in Congress since 1920, when Alice Mary Robertson won the office. Fallin easily retained the seat in the 2008 election. In Congress Fallin served on the Transportation and Infrastructure, Armed Services, and Small

Business Committees. She was a member of the executive committee of the National Republican Congressional Committee and served as small-business chair of the Republican Policy Committee, co-chair of the Congressional Caucus on Women's Issues, and communications chair of the Republican Study Committee. In nearly all of her votes as a congresswoman, Fallin sided with her party. She supported the $700 billion bank-bailout measure of Republican president George W. Bush but opposed the $787 billion economic-stimulus plan introduced by President Barack Obama, a Democrat. Fallin also expressed opposition to the health-care reform bill passed under Obama's administration. In four years she sponsored a relatively modest number of bills—16—most of which addressed local concerns, such as a measure that sought to prevent any prisoners at the Guantánamo Bay facility from being moved to prisons in Oklahoma.

Because of the term limits written into the Oklahoma State Constitution, the Democrat Brad Henry, who had served as governor of Oklahoma since 2003, was ineligible to run for a third consecutive term in 2010. In September 2009 Fallin announced her intention to run in the 2010 gubernatorial election. In addition to Fallin, five other prominent Oklahomans ran for governor: on the Republican side, the businessmen Roger L. Jackson and Robert Hubbard and State Senator Randy Brogdon, and on the Democratic side, Attorney General Drew Edmondson and Fallin's successor as lieutenant governor, Jari Askins. Fallin took the Republican primary with nearly 55 percent of the vote (Brogdon followed with 39 percent). Askins's narrow Democratic-primary win guaranteed that the "Sooner State" would see its first-ever female governor.

In the months leading up to the general election, Fallin and Askins engaged in two debates and went head-to-head on many of the key issues affecting Oklahomans, including wasteful government spending and reform of the state's prison system. Both candidates supported efforts to reduce Oklahoma's incarceration rate, which is one of the highest in the nation, but where Fallin suggested programs such as a drug court, an alternative to incarceration in which nonviolent drug offenders would receive mental-health and substance-abuse counseling, Askins's emphasis was on targeting substance abuse and mental illness through community-based early intervention. While both candidates agreed that budget shortfalls would require that Oklahoma find new ways to run its state programs, Askins proposed the creation of a task force that would evaluate every state agency and find ways to consolidate and eliminate waste, while Fallin made more general promises to downsize government. Both candidates supported Oklahoma's right to opt out of coverage under the federal health-care law and opposed State Question 744, a proposal designed to raise to the regional average the amount of money Oklahoma spends per student. As quoted by Grant Slater in the *Oklahoma*

Gazette (October 13, 2010, on-line), Fallin said that if elected governor, "my biggest priority would be to get our economy back on track and to focus on jobs. That means keeping our tax burden low. It means reforming areas of business like workers' comp insurance, looking at more lawsuit reform"—to guard against what are often called "frivolous" lawsuits with the potential to clog the court system and waste taxpayer funds. "Also, education," she added. "Creating a stronger educated workforce so we can be more attractive to jobs." On Election Day Fallin, who received an endorsement from former Alaska governor and 2008 vice-presidential candidate Sarah Palin, was victorious, with 60 percent of the vote.

A fervent conservative, Fallin opposes same-sex marriage, abortion rights, and a progressive tax system (in which higher tax rates are levied against wealthier individuals). She supports teacher-led prayer in public schools and absolute gun rights, or the absence of restrictions on gun ownership. As models that she looks to in her capacity as governor, Fallin has cited the tort-reform work of Mississippi governor Haley Barbour, former governor Jeb Bush's efforts to improve school test scores in Florida, and the fiscal conservatism practiced by Governor Mitch Daniels of Indiana.

Fallin married the attorney and farmer D. Wade Christensen in November 2009. Christensen has four grown children from his previous marriages. Fallin's daughter, Christina, is a registered State Capitol lobbyist, and her son, Price, is a student at Oklahoma University. Fallin and Christensen share a 4,000-square-foot home in the city of Edmond.

In her interview with Finchum, Fallin likened the "rewarding" experience of holding public office to being in college again: "You learn so much about so many different issues. And you have the opportunity to actually make a difference." Her wish, she told Finchum, is to be regarded by future generations as "a woman who truly cared about her state and worked very hard on her state's behalf."

—H.R.W.

Suggested Reading: *Oklahoma Gazette* (on-line) Oct. 13, 2010; *Oklahoman* (on-line) Sep. 26, 2010; *Tulsa World* (on-line) Feb. 28, 2009, Aug. 8, 2010; Women of Oklahoma Legislature Oral History Project (on-line) Oct. 7, 2008

Frazer Harrison/Getty Images

Fieri, Guy

(fee-ER-ee)

Jan. 22, 1968– Chef; restaurateur; television personality; cookbook writer

Address: Johnny Garlic's, 8988 Brooks Rd., Windsor, CA 95492

The chef, restaurateur, television personality, and cookbook writer Guy Fieri "has brought a new element of rowdy, mass-market culture to American food television," Julia Moskin wrote for the *New York Times* (August 10, 2010, on-line). Fieri, she continued, is "the rare reality-show winner who has translated a small-screen victory into a national fan base, and the rare chef who has transcended the food-TV genre." That victory occurred when Fieri was voted the winner on the 2006 television cooking-contest series *The Next Food Network Star* and became the host of his own cooking show, *Guy's Big Bite*, which is now in its ninth season; the transcendance refers to his outside-the-box shows *Diners, Drive-Ins and Dives* and *Tailgate Warriors* and his hosting of the NBC game show *Minute to Win It*. Known for his spiky bleached-blond hair, retro-style bowling shirts, flashy jewelry, and catchphrases, Fieri has attracted large television and concert-hall audiences—including a high proportion of men—with his joviality, enthusiasm, charm, and unpretentious approach to cooking. John Devore, writing for the blog *Slashfood* (November 20, 2009), described him as "a loud, garish frat man who shills a cuisine based on five simple tastes: salty, crunchy, meaty, spicy and chocolatey" and creates dishes that "explode with brash flavors and fill the belly." In the decade before he gained popularity virtually overnight as a television chef, Fieri established two successful restaurant chains—Johnny Garlic's and Tex Wasabi's—in northern California. He told Moskin that his chef-cum-rock-star persona "reflects his real passions: food, family, music, fast cars, sports and generally having an excellent time."

The older of the two children of James and Penelope Ferry ("Jim" and "Penny" to family and friends), Guy Ramsay Ferry was born on January 22, 1968 in Columbus, Ohio. He adopted his ancestral surname in 1995, after he got married, in honor of his great-grandfather Giuseppe Fieri, whose name was Americanized when he arrived in the U.S. from his native Italy. Guy Fieri grew up with his younger sister, Morgan, in Ferndale, California, a village in the northeastern part of the state, near the Pacific coast and the border with Oregon. His parents, both hippies when they married, opened a shop there named Abraxas (after a 1970 Santana album), selling candles and leather goods. The couple maintained a strict macrobiotic diet, with staples including tofu, bulgur (a form of whole wheat), steamed fish, and other relatively bland foods. Eager for tastier fare, young Fieri cooked a meal for his family one night: rib-eye steaks, pasta, and bottled spaghetti sauce. He recalled to David Hochman for *Playboy* (January 1, 2010), "I remember my dad. He took one bite, put down his fork and glared at me. It's as clear today as it was 30 years ago. 'You know, Guy?' he said. 'This might be the best steak I've ever had.' Total relief! And on top of that, my sister had to do the dishes. I was hooked."

Earlier, at the age of 10, Fieri had become an enthusiastic fan of soft pretzels, after discovering them during one of his family's annual trips to Squaw Valley, a California ski resort. Dismayed by how much money he was spending on that snack, his father suggested that he "get out of the lemonade business and get into the pretzel business," as Fieri recalled to Donna Tam for the *Eureka (California) Times Standard* (August 15, 2009). Fieri learned how to bake the pretzels and, dubbing his business the Awesome Pretzel, began selling them at fairs and other local events, using a cart that he had made, with his father's help, from a large tricycle. Thanks to his savings from his business and dishwashing jobs and to a monetary gift from his parents, he spent his junior year of high school as an exchange student in Chantilly, France. That experience "really opened my eyes to great cooking," he told David Hochman.

Upon returning to the U.S., at 17, Fieri earned a General Equivalency Diploma (GED) instead of returning to high school. Concurrently, he got a job at a Red Lion Inn in Eureka, where he worked his way up from bus boy to flambé cook. Fieri then enrolled at the University of Nevada at Las Vegas (UNLV), where he took courses in hospitality management and earned a B.S. degree in hotel administration in 1990. He then joined the Stouffer Corp., serving as manager of Stouffer's flagship restaurant in Long Beach, in Los Angeles County, California, for three years before becoming district manager of the restaurant chain Louise's Trattoria; with Louise's, he oversaw six restaurants and guided recruiting and training efforts. In 1996 Fieri, who by that time had married, moved farther north, to Sonoma County, California. While he was working as a waiter in Santa Rosa, Fieri and Steve Gruber, his business partner, made plans to open a chain of Italian bistros in that county. The first, called Johnny Garlic's, opened its doors in Santa Rosa that same year. The second Johnny Garlic's opened in Windsor in 1998, and the third in Roseville in 2008. Earlier, the success of Johnny Garlic's had inspired Fieri and Gruber to develop a second chain, Tex Wasabi's, whose menu combines American-style sushi (with neither seafood nor seaweed) and southern-barbeque-style cooking. The first Tex Wasabi opened in Santa Rosa in 2003, and the second in Sacramento, in Sacramento County, in 2007.

In 2006, after much prodding from friends, Fieri made a last-minute decision to audition for *The Next Food Network Star*. His audition videotape—one of more than 10,000 sent to the network—was among "the last ones we reviewed, and when we popped it in, we sat back with our mouths open," Bob Tuschman, a Food Network executive, recalled to Cynthia Hubert for the *Sacramento Bee* (April 11, 2007). "Guy is someone who leaps off the screen and into your living room. We said, 'He's got what it takes.'" Fieri and the other seven finalists appeared in each of the eight installments of the show's second season, demonstrating how they prepared their specialties—in Fieri's case, his self-described "off the hook" California dishes. The Food Network star and restaurateur Bobby Flay, who served as one of the judges, and other Food Network personalities and chefs including Rachael Ray and Emeril Lagasse offered comments and advice to each contestant. For the last installment, which aired in April 2006, Fieri organized a viewing party that included four of the other competitors and helped raise $38,000 for Valley of the Moon, a Sonoma County shelter for abused and neglected children. Viewers who selected Fieri as the overall winner of the competition included the many Santa Rosans reached by the billboard and media campaign mounted on his behalf by his friends. As his prize, Fieri won the opportunity to present a six-installment cooking show on the Food Network.

Guy's Big Bite, as the show was named, premiered on June 25, 2006. "It's as unpretentious as I could make it," Fieri told Gail Pennington for the *St Louis (Missouri) Post-Dispatch* (June 21, 2006). Now in its ninth season, it features recipes for dishes ranging from mojito chicken to pepperoni lasagna to Bloody Mary flank steak. "I don't think we anticipated what a huge star Guy would instantaneously become," Bob Tuschman told Cynthia Hubert after the show's second season. "Viewers of all ages embraced him. They thought he was charming, adorable, fun and personable, and they loved his food. From the moment those first shows aired, ratings started improving in that time slot, and the show continues to find a new audience."

The success of *Guy's Big Bite* led to Fieri's second Food Network show, *Diners, Drive-Ins and Dives*, in which he travels around the U.S. in search of funky eateries that serve classic dishes. Introduced as a one-hour special in November 2006, the series began airing once a week in April 2007. Each installment shows Fieri sampling food at a series of three restaurants. He is seen arriving at the usually unassuming eaterie in a 1967 Camaro Super Sport convertible while dressed in his trademark bowling shirts, flip flops, and sunglasses. After taking a bite or two of any dish, he usually proclaims that it is "off the hook," "Thai's money!," or "on like Donkey Kong" (the last phrase, trademarked by Nintendo, referring to a video game). According to Julia Moskin, *Diners, Drives-Ins and Dives*—which Fieri refers to as "Triple D"—"isn't a cooking show as much as a carefully engineered reality show. Mr. Fieri descends on a casual restaurant that may well serve only chili dogs, or it may be a Chinese-Jamaican place in a Florida strip mall or a family-owned taqueria in Chicago that pickles its own chipotles. . . . Avoiding the reverent tone that many food shows take on as soon as the camera enters the kitchen, Mr. Fieri goes in looking for what's interesting and funny. He has Rachael Ray's friendliness but avoids her unstoppable cutesiness, and fans say that his honest opinions come across. (Among the dishes he has barely managed to taste on camera: pigs' tails; liver; and . . . a sludgy brown soup made from fresh snapping turtle, a Pennsylvania tradition.)" "Fieri has been called many things (restaurateur, cook, author, TV personality), but, truth be told, he's mostly a professional taste tester, all gusto and mouth-watering adjectives," Shelley Fralic wrote for the Montreal, Canada, *Gazette* (May 9, 2010). Recipes for some of the foods Fieri has enjoyed during his journeys appear in his cookbooks *Diners, Drive-Ins and Dives: An All-American Road Trip . . . with Recipes!* (2008) and *More Diners, Drive-Ins and Dives: A Drop-Top Culinary Cruise Through America's Finest and Funkiest Joints* (2009). The food writer and former Food Network producer Ann Volkwein co-authored both books.

Since February 2008 has Fieri hosted (or co-hosted, during the first season) the weekly series *Ultimate Recipe Showdown*, in which home cooks compete for a $25,000 prize and a chance to have one of their dishes included on the menu of the restaurant chain T.G.I. Friday's. A panel of judges considers original recipes in six categories: comfort food, party food, hot and spicy dishes, burgers, cakes and desserts, and hometown favorites. Also since 2008 Fieri has hosted the series *Guy Off the Hook*, in which he prepares California-cuisine-style dishes before a studio audience. He hosted a one-hour special, *Guy's Family Feast*, for Thanksgiving 2008 and has appeared on Food Network programs including *Dinner: Impossible, Ace of Cakes,* and *The Best Thing I Ever Ate.*

In November and December 2009 Fieri offered demonstrations of his cooking techniques during the *Guy Fieri Roadshow,* a 21-city tour that began in Lowell, Massachusetts, and ended in Las Vegas, Nevada. Dubbed "a culinary rock show" by Jennifer Hernandez, writing for the *Boise (Idaho) Weekly* (December 15, 2009), it took place in venues seating as many as 5,000 people; at each loction a 16-member staff assembled a $150,000 demonstration kitchen. The show included live music, provided by the Los Angeles–based DJ Cobra, drinks made by the Australian "flair bartender" Hayden "Woody" Wood, audience participation, and Fieri's collaborations with local chefs and culinary students. "Mr. Fieri's cheerful embrace of taste at the expense of tradition is an example of what makes him so popular," Julia Moskin wrote, "and of why other chefs tend to dismiss him. He'd rather have the loud love of the guys in the audience at Caesars than awards from the James Beard Foundation."

For two seasons beginning in March 2010, Fieri hosted a prime-time game show on NBC called *Minute to Win It,* in which contestants had to complete unusual tasks using household items—for example, unrolling a roll of toilet paper as fast as possible. In the fall of 2010, he began hosting the Food Network series *Tailgate Warriors,* a collaborative project with the National Football League whose focus is sports fans' tailgate picnics; its fourth installment aired on January 29, 2011. Commenting on his myriad projects, Fieri told John Kiesewetter for the *Cincinnati Enquirer* (March 24, 2010), "I am living the American dream. . . . I'm going a million miles an hour, but I have really good people around me. It's a very concerted collective effort of a lot of people." Remarking on his hectic schedule, he told Moskin, "Look, the fame rocket is only on the upward trajectory for a limited time."

Fieri has served as a spokesperson for T.G.I. Friday's, and he appeared in a TV commercial for the insurance company Aflac in 2010. He and his wife, Lori, live in Santa Rosa, California. His parents' house, which he had built for them, is next door. The Fieris have two sons—Hunter, age 14, and Ryder, five. "There's nothing I love more than cooking for my family," Fieri told BariNan Cohen for *Good Housekeeping* (April 2010). He and his family enjoy camping and dirt-biking. He told Dutch Mandel for *AutoWeek* (May 4, 2009), "I only have a couple of vices. I don't smoke. I don't do drugs. I do like cars." In 2008 he owned a half-dozen sports cars, a pickup truck, and a recreational vehicle, all of them either yellow or black.

—C.C.

Suggested Reading: *Buffalo (New York) News* F p3 Aug. 16, 2009; *Eureka (California) Times Standard* Local News Aug. 15, 2009; Food Network Web site; *Monterey (California) County*

Herald Food May 19, 2010; (Montreal, Canada) *Gazette* A p21 May 9, 2010; *New York Times* (on-line) Aug. 10, 2010; *Sacramento (California) Bee* F p1+ Apr. 11, 2007; *San Francisco Chronicle* (on-line) May 2, 2006

Selected Books: with Ann Vollwein—*Diners, Drive-Ins and Dives: An All-American Road Trip . . . with Recipes!,* 2008; *More Diners, Drive-Ins and Dives: A Drop-Top Culinary Cruise Through America's Finest and Funkiest Joints,* 2009

Courtesy of Devin Zida Liao

Fiore, Mark

(fee-OR-ee)

1969– Cartoonist; animator

Address: c/o San Francisco Chronicle, 901 Mission St., San Francisco, CA 94103

Since 2001 Mark Fiore has been making short, animated, self-syndicated political cartoons that are posted on the Web sites of the *San Francisco Chronicle,* the *Village Voice, Salon,* and *Mother Jones* and elsewhere on the Internet, including Fiore's personal site (markfiore.com). In 2010 he received the Pulitzer Prize for editorial cartooning, in recognition of his "biting wit, extensive research and ability to distill complex issues," according to the Pulitzer Web site, which stated that he had "set a high standard for an emerging form of commentary." The award—given for "a distinguished cartoon or portfolio of cartoons characterized by originality, editorial effectiveness, quality of drawing and pictorial effect, in print or on-line or both"—was notable for several reasons: it was the first Pulitzer to honor work that appears exclusively online, the first solely for animated video, and the first for a self-syndicated editorial cartoonist. Prior to devoting himself full-time to creating animated editorial cartoons, Fiore had a brief stint, in 2001, as a staff cartoonist at the *San Jose (California) Mercury News*. Before that he had worked as a freelancer; his hand-drawn cartoons appeared in the *San Francisco Chronicle*, the *Los Angeles Times*, and many other newspapers.

The initial steps for creating an animated cartoon are similar to those for printed political cartoons. After some reading, research, and brainstorming, Fiore makes a drawing on paper using ink and brushes. After scanning those images into his computer, he starts on the labor-intensive task of adding detail, color, and animation; later, he adds music, speech, and voice-overs (provided by actors). Fiore considers his animated cartoons, which generally run from 45 seconds to two minutes, to be a type of journalism. "I'm not completely making this stuff up," he told Rob Rogers for the *Marin (California) Independent Journal* (April 14, 2010). "Everything I do is based in fact, based in research. People forget sometimes that this is still journalism. It starts with news events." Fiore has recently addressed such issues as Arizona's new immigration law, the catastrophic BP oil spill in the Gulf of Mexico, the Catholic Church's child-molestation scandals, relief efforts in Haiti after the powerful earthquake there, California's ban on same-sex marriage, and the populist-conservative Tea Party movement. In the cartoon "Trust Me" (June 9, 2010), which included a 1950s-style newsreel voiceover, Fiore satirized those who support voluntary self-regulation by the food, coal, oil, and financial industries; he showed such people trumpeting the slogan "Trust me, what could possibly go wrong?" until crises hit each of the above-mentioned industries, at which point they demand swift government action. In "Police State Pete" (April 28, 2010), which had a mock deep-voiced cowboy voiceover, Fiore took on Arizona's new immigration law: an overly excited sheriff arrests people whom he "reasonably" suspects of being in the U.S. illegally; those arrested, including a Mexican-American with deep roots in Arizona and an Italian-American visiting from New York, turn out to be citizens who "look foreign." Some of Fiore's cartoons are a part of his "Do Something" series, which conclude with a way viewers can help. For example, his cartoon "Aid Quake," about the earthquake in Haiti, ends with a "Click Here to Help" link, which takes readers to a Google site dedicated to disaster relief for Haitians.

Mark Fiore was born in 1969 and grew up in California—in the San Francisco Bay Area and Los Angeles—and Idaho. From a young age he loved to draw, and he told Rogers that he "wanted to be a political cartoonist from the first time I heard the job existed." After receiving a bachelor's degree in political science from Colorado College, in Colorado Springs, in 1991, Fiore embarked on a career as a freelance editorial cartoonist. His work was published first in small Colorado newspapers and then in such papers as the *Los Angeles Times*, the *Washington Post*, and Bay Area papers including the *San Francisco Chronicle* and the *Oakland Tribune*. In the late 1990s, he told Shawn Moynihan for *Editor & Publisher* (May 2010), he concentrated on regional and local California concerns rather than national issues and news and won a new market with the *San Francisco Examiner* as well as the *Chronicle*. "There was such a glut of [national] stuff coming in that I was able to make my way in the door," he told Moynihan.

Toward the end of the 1990s, after teaching himself to use the video/animation software program Flash, Fiore tried his hand at animating his cartoons. He put those experiments on hold in early 2001, after he was hired as a full-time editorial cartoonist for the *San Jose Mercury News*, which had published some of his cartoons in the past. At the time it seemed to him to be an ideal job and a dream come true, as it provided a steady paycheck and a regular outlet for his work. The previous editorial cartoonist, Scott Willis, had left a year earlier, and the newspaper's editors appeared to be grateful and enthusiastic to have Fiore on board. In a *Mercury News* (February 18, 2001) editorial that appeared on Fiore's first day, the editors called Fiore an "emerging star" and concluded, "Mark's cartoons are hard-hitting and fun. He has a keen news sense, he knows California, and he's quickly getting acquainted with San Jose, whose mayor and council may have been puzzled during a recent meeting to see a young man in the audience sketching them. He'll be back." After a few months on the job, however, Fiore felt his creativity being stifled, both by the physical environment (his office had no windows) and the management, which, he recalled to Dave Astor for *Editor & Publisher* (June 11, 2005), told him to "go easy" on President George W. Bush. Accounts differ as to whether Fiore quit his job or was fired.

On his Web site Fiore later recalled that he "happily fled the print world" to devote his energy to animation. After leaving the paper he spent a few months improving his expertise with Flash software, then created a few sample animated cartoons. "There were hardly any people doing it, and you can count on one hand the amount of people who are still doing it," he told Shawn Moynihan. "I loved it immediately and I knew it was a good business move at the time, but it still was a shot in the dark. But back in those days, it was amazing. You'd call an editor, and they'd be [watching simple animations] and flipping out, saying, 'It's moving! And it's on the Web!!' It was an easy in to at least wow editors—they were freaking out over eye blinks." The samples he submitted to the editors at *sfgate.com*, the *San Francisco Chronicle*'s Web site, reached Vlae Kershner. "I didn't really know how to make heads or tails out of what he was doing. It was pretty novel stuff," Kershner told Rogers. "Then Sept. 11 happened, and he gave us this incredibly powerful animated cartoon. It was called 'Find The Terrorist,' and in it you had to click on different people to figure out if they were terrorists or not. And that's when I knew we had something." Fiore's work, which was self-syndicated, began to appear regularly on the *San Francisco Chronicle* site and other Web sites. By the middle of 2002, Fiore had stopped producing printed cartoons and began focusing solely on creating animation. With his new medium, he felt, he could make a more powerful impact than he could with printed cartoons. He told Matthew Mirapaul for the *New York Times* (March 17, 2003), "I can play on people's eyeballs and emotions more than I could on the page."

In December 2009 Fiore submitted an iPhone app (application) to Apple Inc. The app, which Fiore called NewsToons, would allow iPhone users to view Fiore's animated political cartoons on their mobile devices. Apple rejected the app. Laura McGann, writing for the Nieman Journalism Lab Web site (April 15, 2010), quoted from the e-mail message that Fiore received from Apple, which read in part, "We've reviewed NewsToons and determined that we cannot post this version of your iPhone application to the App Store because it contains content that ridicules public figures and is in violation of Section 3.3.14 from the iPhone Developer Program License Agreement." That particular section, according to the message, states that an app can be rejected if Apple finds any of its content "obscene, pornographic, or defamatory." In his column for *Slate.com* (April 15, 2010), Jack Shafer argued that, in part, Apple was creating "a prudish atmosphere guaranteed to offend nobody." Then, after Fiore won the Pulitzer Prize, Apple invited him to resubmit his app. While he was waiting for Apple to reply, Fiore told Brian Stelter for the *New York Times* (April 17, 2010), "Sure, mine might get approved, but what about someone who hasn't won a Pulitzer and who is maybe making a better political app than mine? Do you need some media frenzy to get an app approved that has political material?" Apple approved Fiore's app, but for Fiore, along with many other political cartoonists, the free-speech issue remained unresolved. The Association of American Editorial Cartoonists, of which Fiore is a member, sent a letter to Apple charging that Apple's ban on ridiculing public figures essentially shuts out satirists and political cartoonists from the iPhone and the iPad, both of which are becoming increasingly popular.

The Pulitzer Prize jury that honored Fiore for his work in April 2010 included Lucy Shelton Caswell, the curator of the Ohio State University Cartoon Research Library and Museum; two newspaper editorial-page editors and one vice president; and an editorial cartoonist. Fiore has been honored twice by the National Cartoonists Society (in 2001 and 2002) and twice by the Online News Association (in 2002 and 2008). He earned the Robert F.

Kennedy Journalism Award, from the Robert F. Kennedy Center for Justice & Human Rights, in 2004 and the James Madison Freedom of Information Award, from the Society of Professional Journalists, in 2006.

Fiore and his wife, Chelsea Donovan, a management consultant, live in Fairfax, California, 15 miles north of San Francisco.

—D.K.

Suggested Reading: *Editor & Publisher* p29 Oct. 27, 2003, p19 May 2010; markfiore.com; pulitzer.org; *San Francisco Chronicle* A p1 Apr. 13, 2010; *Slate.com* Apr. 15, 2010

Selected Cartoons (all 2010): "Whose Marriage Is It?"; "Aid Quake"; "Deficit Destruction"; "Bipartisan Brawlathon"; "Un-Gay"; "Hierarchy Complicitus"; "Police State Pete"; "Inky Al-Jihadi"; "Trust Me"

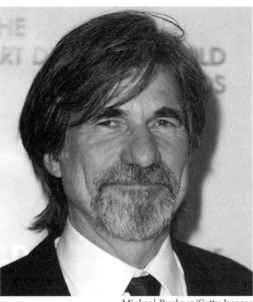

Michael Buckner/Getty Images

Fisk, Jack

Dec. 19, 1945– Film production designer

Address: c/o Gersh Agency, 9465 Wilshire Blvd., Sixth Fl., Beverly Hills, CA 90212

According to Dennis Lim, writing for the *New York Times* (January 6, 2008), Jack Fisk—a production designer and onetime film director—is "one of the most fascinating unsung figures in American movies." Unlike some production designers/art directors, who have worked on hundreds of features, Fisk has lent his hand to only two dozen films;

many of those, however, have come to be seen as consummate works of art. He has been the production designer for each of the five films by the legendary auteur Terrence Malick: *Badlands* (1973), *Days of Heaven* (1978), *The Thin Red Line* (1998), *The New World* (2005), and *The Tree of Life* (2011). He has created futuristic environments (in *Phantom of the Paradise*, 1974) and apocalyptic landscapes (in *Carrie*, 1976) for the noted visual stylist Brian De Palma; and he has fashioned psychologically menacing backdrops for the idiosyncratic director (and Fisk's longtime friend) David Lynch, in movies including *Mulholland Drive* (2001). Fisk collaborated with the five-time Academy Award–nominated filmmaker Paul Thomas Anderson on the critically praised saga *There Will Be Blood* (2007), which was loosely based on the Upton Sinclair novel *Oil!* (1927) and starred Daniel Day-Lewis. For that film, described by Richard Schickel for *Time* (December 24, 2007) as "one of the most wholly original American movies ever made," Fisk garnered his first Oscar nomination, for best art direction, which he shared with Jim Erickson. As with Day-Lewis, whose meticulous preparation for roles has become Hollywood legend, Fisk's "method" approach to that film's sparse production design is representative of his work: he typically immerses himself in the cultures or historical periods of the films to which he is assigned, then re-creates the buildings of those cultures or periods, using materials that contribute to an unusually authentic look. Fisk also tends toward a more hands-on approach to set building than other production designers. "In a more literal sense than cinematographers, production designers are responsible for the look of a film—they create its physical reality—and Mr. Fisk's projects tend to be more physically demanding and more rooted in reality than most," Lim wrote. "I'm the luckiest designer I know," Fisk said to Lim. "I have an association with . . . great artists where I don't really question them, and they give me a lot of freedom. I get to hang out with friends and I get to build stuff." Anderson noted for the same article, "Jack likes to hit nails into wood. And he likes a good adventure."

Jack Fisk was born on December 19, 1945 in Canton, Illinois, and grew up in Alexandria, Virginia. As a high-school student there, he enjoyed painting and sculpting. During his freshman year he befriended a fellow student, David Lynch, who would later become an acclaimed filmmaker. (Lynch was married to Fisk's sister, Mary, from 1977 to 1987.) "In the whole high school we were basically the only artists," Lynch recalled to Lim. "In this conservative world all we wanted to do was paint and live the art life." After high school the two enrolled at the Pennsylvania Academy of the Fine Arts, in Philadelphia. Fisk created sculptures for Lynch's first short film, *Six Men Getting Sick* (1966). Lynch next helped Fisk land his first job on a feature film: making plaster objects that resembled gold bricks for a Western that was being shot in Utah. In 1971 Fisk served as the art director

for a Roger Corman–produced film about motorcycle culture, *Angels Hard as They Come*. (During that time production designers were more commonly referred to as art directors.) "I was so scared of not doing what I was supposed to do that I did everything," Fisk said to Lim. He was the art director for similarly low-budget films such as *Cool Breeze* (1972), a black-exploitation or "blaxploitation" remake of John Huston's *The Asphalt Jungle* (1950), and *The Slams* (1973), a blaxploitation heist movie starring Jim Brown.

Fisk's big break came in 1973, when the then-unknown filmmaker Terrence Malick hired him as the art director for his debut feature, *Badlands*. Starring Martin Sheen and the newcomer Sissy Spacek, and based on the real-life 1957 murder spree of Charles Starkweather and his girlfriend, Caril Anne Fugate, *Badlands* was universally hailed as a masterpiece. Fisk adopted a minimalist approach to the film's production design; he re-created 1950s-era housing without romanticizing its look, which had the effect of emphasizing Malick's visual preoccupation with nature—a mainstay in his films. For a sequence in the woods, he made a tree house—the lead characters' hideaway—from raw woodland materials. Fisk's barebones layout added to the film's dreamlike aura, which was highlighted by sweeping shots of the South Dakota plains and Montana's badlands. Fisk has credited Malick, a classmate of Lynch's at the American Film Institute, for permanently changing his outlook toward film. He explained to Lim, "That's the first time I realized film could be a fine art, equal to painting or sculpture." Also during the shooting of the film, he became romantically involved with Spacek, whom he married on April 12, 1974.

Fisk next collaborated on two features directed by Brian De Palma: the rock opera *Phantom of the Paradise* (1974) and the horror masterpiece *Carrie* (1976), which starred Spacek. For the former, about an aspiring songwriter whose music is stolen by a diabolical record producer, Fisk designed a futuristic environment that echoed the androgynous 1970s glam-rock scene. For *Carrie* he created a Gothic cathedral–style house, furnished with gaudy items that reflected the maniacal religious fervor of the title character's mother, portrayed by Piper Laurie. Fisk recalled for the 2001 documentary *Visualizing "Carrie,"* "I went all over Los Angeles to the Spanish areas where they have a lot of religious shops looking for interesting artifacts to put in the house." Considered by many to be the greatest achievement of De Palma's career, *Carrie* employed several innovative camera techniques, among them the use of split-screen cinematography, split diopter lenses, minutes-long slow-motion sequences, and long, continuous crane shots. Fisk adapted to the director's complex visual style by using what he has called a "liquid" set in certain scenes, which allowed his production crew to move the set freely without loss of continuity—both to keep up with and stay out of the way of De Palma's ever-moving camera. Other structures created for the film included a full-size high-school gymnasium, where the teen loner Carrie has been invited as a joke to the prom, and a half-scale replica of the Gothic-style house (built in order to be burned to the ground). Additionally, Fisk came up with a credible substitute for the pig's blood poured on Carrie in the climactic scene, by combining Karo syrup with food coloring.

In 1977 Fisk had a cameo as the Man in the Planet in David Lynch's surreal horror cult classic *Eraserhead.* The following year he teamed up again with Malick for *Days of Heaven* (1978), a Depression-era drama about transient laborers (played by Richard Gere and Brooke Adams) who have come to the Texas panhandle to harvest crops on a farm. After they conspire to take advantage of the farmer who hired them (played by Sam Shepard), the laborers end up in a dangerous love triangle. Shot at the hours of dusk and dawn and featuring panoramic representations of the Texas prairie (actually filmed in Alberta, Canada), *Days of Heaven* was described by Michael Atkinson for the *Village Voice* (March 24, 1999) as "almost incontestably . . . the most gorgeously photographed film ever made," an opinion shared by many other critics. (Néstor Almendros, the film's director of photography, won an Oscar for best cinematography.) For the film Fisk was given the daunting task of building a fully furnished Victorian mansion from the ground up in less than a month. Modeling the house after the famous Edward Hopper painting *House by the Railroad* (1925), he built it with plywood, material he used to make other parts of the set as well; those included a farmer's house and a massive wheat-processing plant. Constant production halts due to the malfunctioning of the farming machinery made the movie's 100-plus-day shoot the most difficult and demanding assignment of Fisk's career; it was also his last collaboration with Malick until 1998, when the director made his next film.

After *Days of Heaven* Fisk stopped designing for a time to make movies of his own. In 1981 he made his directorial debut, with *Raggedy Man*, a World War II–era melodrama about a small-town switchboard operator (played by Spacek) who falls in love with a sailor (Eric Roberts) on leave. The film received generally favorable reviews, though most critics felt it could have done without its enigmatic title character, the center of a violent climax to an otherwise poignant story. Vincent Canby wrote in a review for the *New York Times* (September 18, 1981), "*Raggedy Man* is something like a country-and-western ballad that relates a supposedly sad, melodramatic story but whose simple, repetitive, upbeat rhythms effectively deny the awfulness of the events being sung about." He concluded that *Raggedy Man* "is not a great movie, but it has some of the considerable appeal of something heard late at night, after a number of beers, on a jukebox, in a roadhouse far from anywhere."

Fisk followed *Raggedy Man* with *Violets Are Blue* (1986), a film about a famous photographer (Spacek) who returns after a 15-year absence to her hometown of Ocean City, Maryland. There, she re-encounters her high-school sweetheart (played by Kevin Kline), who has since married and had a child. Although the movie received mixed reviews, Fisk was lauded for his careful direction of pivotal sequences, including a dinner-table scene in which Spacek's character is bombarded by awkward questions from the Kline character's son. Vincent Canby wrote for the *New York Times* (April 11, 1986), "*Violets Are Blue* looks less like the romantic movie it means to be than like a failed concept for a romantic movie, played by a top-notch cast of bankable actors. The only thing missing is a screenplay of any real interest or coherence. The writing credit goes to Naomi Foner, but from what we see on the screen, it's a screenplay to which too many people have made contributions. . . . Considering how well he did with *Raggedy Man*, Jack Fisk . . . cannot be blamed as the director. *Violets Are Blue* seems more like a corporate mistake." Fisk went on to direct one more feature, a black comedy titled *Daddy's Dyin' . . . Who's Got the Will?* (1990). In the 1990s Fisk also ventured briefly into television, directing the courtroom drama *Final Verdict* (1991) and helming two episodes of the short-lived, David Lynch–produced comedy series *On the Air* (1992).

Fisk reunited with Malick on the poetic war epic *The Thin Red Line* (1998). (Before then Malick had been all but unreachable for 20 years; his absence from the movie scene in the wake of his acclaimed earlier work, and the speculation about its cause, had attained the status of myth.) Fisk had heard at a party about Malick's return to filmmaking, recalling to Clyde H. Farnsworth for the *New York Times* (October 5, 1997), "I suddenly got kind of jealous to think of anyone else working with Terry Malick. I sent him a fax saying that I'd finally recovered from *Days of Heaven* and that I'd love to work with him again." The film, adapted from James Jones's novel of the same name about U.S. forces in the Battle of Guadalcanal in World War II, featured dozens of noted performers, among them Sean Penn, Adrien Brody, James Caviezel, George Clooney, John Cusack, Woody Harrelson, Elias Koteas, Nick Nolte, John C. Reilly, and John Travolta. Fisk was responsible for building World War II–era fighter jets and for re-creating a village on the Solomon Islands, in the Pacific. For months he scouted locations in search of a mountain that would serve as the physical centerpiece of the film—the shooting location for a scene in which a company of U.S. soldiers charges up a hill to overcome Japanese forces. Settling on a mountain in Queensland, Australia, Fisk and his crew carved a path through the rainforest-like foliage to allow the actors passage to the top. The meditative tone of the film, achieved in part through eight different voiceover narrators and shots of men in combat juxtaposed with images of windblown blades of grass, lush foliage, and exotic fauna, was enhanced by Fisk's art direction: he flew to Australia during the winter before the start of filming to seed the hill with special grass. In an interview with *Playboy* (April 1, 1999), Nolte explained, "[Malick] had arranged soldiers in that grass so they were only revealed when the grass moved a certain way. It was stunning! I turned to Jack Fisk . . . and I said, 'Jesus, that grass is fantastic.'" One challenge Fisk encountered was that on several occasions nearby cattle ate grass and other parts of the set. He noted to Fiona Hudson for the Sydney, Australia, *Daily Telegraph* (February 18, 1999), "We learned some great tricks to make [the grass] last as long as possible." *The Thin Red Line* received seven Oscar nominations and has come to be regarded as one of the best of modern war films.

Fisk next collaborated on two films directed by Lynch, with whom he had remained close over the years. The first, *The Straight Story* (1999), based on real events and starring Richard Farnsworth and Spacek, is about an aged man's journey on a lawnmower across Iowa and Wisconsin to reunite with his estranged brother; it is considered the most mainstream and accessible of all of Lynch's films. The second, *Mulholland Drive* (2001), is a critically acclaimed mystery-thriller centering initially on the relationship of an aspiring actress (played by Naomi Watts) with an amnesiac (Laura Harring) who turns up in the Los Angeles apartment the actress is borrowing from her aunt; later, Watts and Harring appear as different characters, whose relationship has parallels with that of the actress and the amnesiac. For that film Fisk used dark color schemes to create the brooding set pieces that matched the film's psychologically shadowy tone. (Lynch won his fourth best-director Oscar nomination for the film.)

Over the next four years, Malick asked Fisk to accompany him on several scouting excursions in preparation for his next major undertaking: a retelling of the storied 1600s Jamestown-settlement romance between John Smith and Pocahontas. "He was telling me how beautiful the Chickahominy River in Virginia was," Fisk told Rachel Wimberly for *Daily Variety* (January 11, 2006). "The first day I went down that river, I found the location for the fort and Indian village." The film, titled *The New World* (2005), starred Colin Farrell as Smith and the newcomer Q'orianka Kilcher as Pocahontas. Like the reclusive director's three previous efforts, the film was critically praised. For the film, Fisk replicated the log fort and mud buildings of Jamestown by using local materials that the settlers would most likely have used in the 17th century. He also spent months researching seeds for corn, tobacco, melons, and other crops, in preparation for the planting of a three-acre field. He explained to Scott Bowles for *USA Today* (December 16, 2005), "We were going for authenticity with everything we did. We were going to build real villages. We were going to film in the woods with a camera and as few people as possible. Nature has always

played a big part of Terry's movies, but I'd never worked on anything like this." He said in the 2006 documentary *Making "The New World,"* "Terry likes things more real and it was much more fun to build this real."

In 2007 Fisk was the production designer/art director for Paul Thomas Anderson's epic *There Will Be Blood*, which starred Daniel Day-Lewis and was very loosely based on Upton Sinclair's muckraking 1927 novel, *Oil!* For the film he and Anderson scouted locations all over the western United States for months before settling on Marfa, Texas, which provided them with the starkly beautiful landscapes they were looking for. (Marfa has been used as a shooting location in other films, including the 1956 George Stevens movie, *Giant*, and, more recently, the Coen brothers' critically acclaimed 2007 thriller, *No Country for Old Men*.) Fisk built a massive wooden oil derrick and an oil-rich town (called Little Boston) on a 60,000-acre ranch, modeling the town after another Hopper painting, *Early Sunday Morning* (1930), which shows storefronts shortly after sunrise. He created the derrick with the help of a 1916 blueprint; the completed structure was used in the film's most visually stirring sequence, when oil erupts through the derrick, which soon burns to the ground. To create a believable replacement for oil, Fisk and his art crew combined food coloring with a food additive called methylcellulose (also used in a McDonald's restaurant item, the McFlurry). To build the town Fisk used salvage lumber, explaining to Lim, "I got together about five carpenters. I didn't have any plans, and I told them not to bring levels. We just marked the space and started laying the foundation. I figured that's the way they would have done it then." Fisk was also responsible for finding the mansion that served as the home of Day-Lewis's obsessive oil-prospector character, Daniel Plainview. After looking at mansions all over New Mexico and Texas, he chose the Greystone Mansion, in Beverly Hills, California, which—fittingly—had been a gift from the oil tycoon Edward Doheny to his son. Greystone was chosen in part for the film's violent conclusion, which takes place in the mansion's bowling alley. The scene required Fisk and his production crew to reconstruct the badly damaged alley. Fisk won his first Oscar nomination, for best art direction, for his work on the film, an honor he shared with Jim Erickson. (*There Will Be Blood* received eight Oscar nominations in total and won for best actor and best cinematography.) Driven by Day-Lewis's powerhouse performance, the film was universally hailed as a masterpiece and has drawn comparisons to some of the greatest films ever made, including Orson Welles's *Citizen Kane* (1941).

Fisk teamed up with Malick a fifth time, for *The Tree of Life* (2011). Malick had reportedly been working on that highly ambitious project "for 35 years that I know of," as Fisk noted to an interviewer for the *Charlottesville (Virginia) News & Arts Weekly* (April 26, 2010, on-line). The film, which stars Brad Pitt and Sean Penn, has been described as everything from a small 1950s period drama to an epic story about the evolution of mankind; cutting-edge technology helped create its sweeping images of nature, the cosmos, and prehistoric Earth (including dinosaurs). In true Mallickian fashion, other details of the plot have—as of early May 2011—been largely kept under wraps from the public. Filmed in various locations throughout Texas, including Smithsville, Houston, Matagorda, Bastrop, and Austin, *The Tree of Life* was originally slated for a 2009 release, but production delays and distribution issues pushed the date back. The film received its world premiere in the main competition of the 2011 Cannes Film Festival, in May.

During *Tree of Life*'s many delays, Fisk collaborated with the director Francis Lawrence on *Water for Elephants*, the 2011 film adaptation of Sara Gruen's popular historical novel of the same name. For the Depression-era film, about a veterinary student who goes to work for a traveling circus after his parents are killed, Fisk was charged with creating circus wagons and a train as well as a massive, canvas big top. Starring Robert Pattinson, Reese Witherspoon, and Christoph Waltz, *Water for Elephants* received mixed reviews, but many made note of its stunning visual and production elements. Claudia Puig, in a review for *USA Today* (April 22, 2011), called the film's production design "one of its greatest assets. Fisk re-creates life in 1931 in vivid fashion. So detailed are the sets that you can almost smell the piles of dung and bales of hay," while Mal Vincent wrote for the Norfolk *Virginian-Pilot* (April 23, 2011) that Fisk "has done a masterful job of turning the Depression into a world of moonlit, silhouetted trains crossing the slums." Roger Ebert wrote for the *Chicago Sun-Times* (April 22, 2011), "[Fisk] has created a believable circus here, and even the train itself has a personality." Fisk has since completed work on Malick's sixth feature, a yet-to-be-titled romance starring Rachel McAdams, Javier Bardem, and Ben Affleck. The film, reportedly a companion piece to *The Tree of Life*, is expected to be released in 2012.

Fisk lives with Spacek in Charlottesville, Virginia. The couple have two daughters: Schuyler Elizabeth Fisk and Virginia Madison Fisk.

—C.C.

Suggested Reading:imdb.com; *Los Angeles Times* F p1 Dec. 27, 2007; *New York Times* Arts and Leisure p14+ Jan. 6, 2008; *USA Today* E p1 Dec. 16, 2005

Selected Films: as production designer—*Angels Hard As They Come*, 1971; *Badlands*, 1973; *Phantom of the Paradise*, 1974; *Carrie*, 1976; *Days of Heaven*, 1978; *The Thin Red Line*, 1998; *The Straight Story*, 1999; *Mulholland Drive*, 2001; *The New World*, 2005; *There Will Be Blood*, 2007; *The Invasion*, 2007; *Water for Elephants*, 2011; *The Tree of Life*, 2011; as director—*Raggedy Man*, 1981; *Violets Are Blue*, 1986; *Daddy's Dyin' . . . Who's Got the Will?*, 1990; as actor—*Eraserhead*, 1977

Franco, James

Apr. 19, 1978– Actor; artist; writer; filmmaker

Address: James/Levy/Jacobson, 3500 W. Olive Ave., Suite 1470, Burbank, CA 91505

In the late 1990s, when the director, writer, and producer Judd Apatow met the actor James Franco, "he thought the 20-year-old was funny, strange, skinny and very greasy. He couldn't understand why women found him so attractive," Amy Raphael wrote for the London *Guardian* (January 24, 2009, on-line). "Still, the producer cast the intense young actor in *Freaks and Geeks*"—an acclaimed television show about high-school students that brought Franco his big break. Today, Franco is considered one of Hollywood's top leading men—a Method actor who has won critical acclaim for his riveting performances and who boasts a legion of fans attracted to his good looks and onscreen charisma. Although *Freaks and Geeks* lasted for only one season, from 1999 to 2000, Franco parlayed his exposure on the show into starring roles, turning in a near-perfect portrayal of the 1950s movie icon James Dean in the 2001 television movie about the actor; playing the troubled best friend of Peter Parker, the title character's alter ego, in the three *Spider-Man* movies; and performing as a bumbling drug dealer in the Judd Apatow–produced comedy *Pineapple Express* (2008). Franco received praise in 2008 for his work in the biographical film *Milk* and in 2010 for his portrayals of the poet Allen Ginsberg in *Howl* and the trapped mountain climber Aron Ralston in *127 Hours*, the last performance earning him an Academy Award nomination for best actor.

In addition to his career as an actor, Franco has been a film director, screenwriter, author, painter, and mixed-media artist, prompting some to deride him as egotistical and overexposed while others call him a polymath. As James Mottram pointed out for the London *Independent* (December 31, 2010, on-line), "For an actor who has always shied away from the spotlight, James Franco is in danger of becoming ubiquitous."

James Edward Franco was born on April 19, 1978 in Palo Alto, California, the eldest of the three sons of Betsy (Verne) Franco and Douglas Eugene Franco. His mother is a successful author of children's books, and his father runs a shipping-container company and manages a nonprofit orga-

Slaven Vlasic/Getty Images

James Franco

nization that helps women and children in Third World countries. Betsy Franco's mother, Mitzi Verne, is the owner of a respected art gallery in Cleveland, Ohio.

Pushed by his parents to do well in school, Franco got good marks, including excellent SAT scores. Perhaps as a result, however, he also had a rebellious phase, drinking alcohol, shoplifting, and skipping classes, among other acts. "It was teen angst," he told Raphael. "I was uncomfortable in my own skin." He improved his behavior during his junior and senior years at Palo Alto High School and was soon taking advanced-placement classes. "I was a loner, and pretty quiet," he recalled to Christina Hu for an article posted on the *Paly Voice* Web site (January 3, 2006), run by students in Palo Alto High School's Web journalism class. "I think I was just going through a lot of changes; I studied a lot, wrote a lot, and read a lot. I was a little unhappy, but it was probably just teenage angst, like everyone else." Like his father, Franco was gifted in mathematics, and he held an internship with Lockheed Martin, a technology company, for a brief period. He also developed an interest in art, taking after-school classes in life drawing. In addition, during his senior year, feeling shy but encouraged by his drama teacher, he appeared as the lead in a number of school plays—experiences that inspired him to pursue acting.

Franco graduated from high school in 1996 and attended the University of California, Los Angeles (UCLA), with the intention of studying English. Much to his parents' chagrin, he dropped out after his freshman year to study acting. His friends also questioned his decision. "All my friends looked at me with pity thinking I made a pretty poor move,"

he told Cindy Pearlman for the *Chicago Sun-Times* (January 22, 2006). "But after you take the leap, you know in your heart if you made the right move or not." Franco began to take lessons with the respected drama coach Robert Carnegie at Playhouse West, in North Hollywood. Within a year he had an agent and began auditioning for roles. His first filmed acting appearance was in an episode of the TV police drama *Pacific Blue*, in 1997, little more than a year after he graduated from high school. He then had roles in the television films *1973* (1998) and *To Serve and Protect* (1999) and in an episode of the crime drama *Profiler* (1999). Franco had his feature-film debut in a small role in *Never Been Kissed* (1999), a romantic comedy starring Drew Barrymore and David Arquette. His first starring role was in the romantic comedy *Whatever It Takes* (2000), in which he and another up-and-coming young actor, Shane West, played students from different social circles who come together to help each other win their dream girls. The film, a modern adaptation of the play *Cyrano de Bergerac*, was poorly received by critics.

It was Franco's turn as a wayward teen in the hit series *Freaks and Geeks* (1999–2000) that first put the spotlight on him. In the series, set in a suburban Michigan high school in the early 1980s, Franco played Daniel Desario, a "freak" and rebel who often got into trouble and struggled to get his rock band off the ground. The show centered on Lindsay Weir (played by Linda Cardellini), an "A" student and "geek" who was eager to hang out with the more rebellious crowd, led by Daniel and his friends. Critics hailed *Freaks and Geeks* as a groundbreaking series, one that addressed typical adolescent issues in a fresh light, with well-developed characters and intelligent humor. Reviewers found that Franco played Daniel with nuance, occasionally revealing his seemingly distant character's softer, less-rebellious side in serious situations. David Weigand observed for the *San Francisco Chronicle* (July 29, 2001), "As Daniel Desario, Franco was rarely at the center of the show's weekly story arc, but anyone who noticed him couldn't help thinking that if Hollywood ever made a James Dean biopic, Franco was a natural for the title role." *Freaks and Geeks*, created by Paul Feig and produced by Judd Apatow, also featured the comedic actor Seth Rogen as one of Daniel's friends. Canceled after one season, the show has remained something of a cult hit on DVD.

On the strength of his work as the sensitive "bad boy" Daniel, Franco secured the title role in the 2001 TNT film *James Dean*. The movie follows the short career of the iconic real-life actor, who won praise for his performances in *Rebel Without a Cause* and *East of Eden* (both 1955) and *Giant* (1956) before his untimely death in a car crash. To prepare for the role, Franco started smoking and spent time away from his friends—contributing to a sense of alienation similar to that Dean is remembered for portraying. Most critics appreciated the film and Franco's performance, with some noting a striking physical resemblance between Franco and Dean. For his performance Franco won a Golden Globe Award for the best actor in a miniseries or television film and received Emmy Award and Screen Actors Guild Award nominations.

In 2002 Franco appeared in the first film of the blockbuster *Spider-Man* series, based on the adventures of the Marvel Comics superhero. *Spider-Man*, directed by Sam Raimi, starred Tobey Maguire as the awkward Peter Parker, a high-school student who develops arachnid-like powers after a genetically altered spider bites him. The film also starred Willem Dafoe as the villain Green Goblin; Kirsten Dunst as Parker's love interest, Mary Jane; and Franco as Parker's friend Harry Osborn, who—not knowing that Peter is Spider-Man—vows to kill the superhero to avenge the death of the Green Goblin, who was Harry's father. Franco told *Entertainment Weekly* (April 18, 2008, on-line), "I was auditioning for Peter Parker. But it wasn't like the role of a lifetime for me. I was never a big comic-book fan. And the part I got had a lot more psychological push and pull than you would normally expect. So it worked out really well in the end." The film became a major commercial success and earned critical acclaim for Raimi's directing, the special effects, and the acting.

Also in 2002 Franco appeared in a small role in the action film *Deuces Wild* and the dramas *Mother Ghost* and *Sonny*. The last-named film, which was the actor Nicolas Cage's directorial debut, focuses on the titular character (Franco), who becomes a male prostitute in 1980s New Orleans, Louisiana. The film received negative reviews for its uninspired plot and acting. Franco also appeared that year in *City by the Sea*, a crime/mystery starring Robert De Niro and Frances McDormand. That film concerned a New York policeman (De Niro) who must save his son (Franco) after he is caught up in a drug-related killing. The film garnered mixed reviews, with some critics praising Franco. Owen Gleiberman wrote for *Entertainment Weekly* (September 4, 2002, on-line) that Franco "speaks here with the soft, barely articulate wail of a wounded young boy, and he turns his face into a road map of desolation. He's never less than transfixing." In 2003 Franco played the character Josh in the director Robert Altman's *The Company*, an ensemble drama about a group of ballet dancers, which also starred Neve Campbell and Malcolm McDowell. The next year he reprised his role as Harry Osborn in *Spider-Man 2*, which met with as much enthusiasm as the first film and depicts the friendship between Parker and Osborn as it begins to unravel.

Franco next starred in the offbeat comedy *The Ape* (2005). That was followed by the role of Captain Prince in the World War II film *The Great Raid*, which fared poorly at the box office. In 2006 Franco acted in three films that were regarded as flops—*Annapolis, Flyboys,* and *Tristan + Isolde.* His work in those mediocre movies led Franco, according to Anderson, to "a crisis of faith" and the feeling that he was "funneling all his effort into glossy, big-budget entertainment over which he had no control, and of which he wasn't proud." As a result he decided to return to UCLA, where he took literature and creative-writing courses. Anderson wrote that Franco "threw himself back into his education with crazy abandon," talking his advisers into letting him exceed the normal course load and asking classmates to record the lectures he missed while on film sets. Franco graduated within two years, in 2008, with an above-3.5 grade-point average and an undergraduate degree in English.

Meanwhile, Franco co-starred in *In the Valley of Elah* (2007), which featured Tommy Lee Jones as a father looking for his missing son in war-torn Iraq, and appeared alongside Sienna Miller in the drama *Camille* (2008). He also acted in *Spider-Man 3* (2007), this time taking the villainous role hinted at in the prior films—that of the new Green Goblin. In her appraisal of the film, Stephanie Zacharek wrote for *Salon.com* (May 4, 2007), "Of all the actors here . . . Franco is the one who has improved with each successive picture: As a young man battling his own dark side, he brings smudgy layers of depth to a character that might otherwise be a cartoon. In one sequence, a verbal face-off with Peter, his left eye droops in a sinister, lazy appraisal of his sometime best friend; the moment suggests that Franco might have more to show us than most of his roles have required of him."

Franco made his directorial debut in 2007 with *Good Time Max.* He also wrote and starred in the film, which is about two gifted siblings, one of whom finds success as a surgeon while the other turns to drugs. The next year he acted in the popular "stoner" comedy *Pineapple Express,* produced by Judd Apatow and also starring Seth Rogen. The film centers on Dale (Rogen) and Saul (Franco), two pot-smoking friends who get caught up with a gang of drug dealers. For his performance Franco received a Golden Globe Award nomination for best actor in a musical or comedy.

In 2008 Franco had a supporting role in Gus Van Sant's *Milk,* about the real-life gay politician and activist Harvey Milk, who was assassinated by a political rival in 1978. In that highly praised film, Milk was played by Sean Penn; Franco, as Milk's lover, Scott Smith, won a 2008 Independent Spirit Award for best supporting actor. In his review of the film for the *Los Angeles Times* (November 26, 2008, on-line), Kenneth Turan wrote that Franco "is a nice match for . . . [Penn] as the lover who finally has enough of political life."

In 2010 Franco played Allen Ginsberg in the well-received experimental film *Howl;* most critics appreciated Franco's portrayal of the influential Beat poet. That year Franco also starred in the independent film *William Vincent,* about a pickpocket who begins working for a drug dealer. Eric Eisenberg wrote for cinemablend.com (April 25, 2010), "Certainly surprising the audience is the performance by Franco, who, whether you know him as Harry Osborn from the *Spider-Man* films or as drug-dealer Saul in *Pineapple Express*, is playing a whole new breed of character here. Walking through life with what can only be described as ataxia, he shows the occasional smirk in conversation as though he knows everything before it's said. Where the performance really shines is when he is at work for the boss—whose name is never given—and you see what the character is truly capable of, giving us the slightest of insight to his past life."

Franco's other 2010 roles included one in the romantic drama *Eat, Pray, Love*, which starred Julia Roberts, and that of the real-life mountain climber Aron Ralston in *127 Hours*. Ralston was trapped by a boulder for more than five days in 2003 before amputating his own arm with a small, dull-edged knife in order to survive. The film, based on Ralston's autobiography, won acclaim for Franco's performance, and Franco was nominated for an Academy Award for best actor. Mike Scott wrote for the New Orleans *Times-Picayune* (November 24, 2010, on-line), "The key to it all is Franco, playing Ralston in a high-wire act of a performance that has him taking audiences through a range of emotions, even though for the majority of the film he has no co-stars to lean on, no sets to explore. Just a backpack full of props and a ton of acting ability."

Since he received his undergraduate degree, Franco has continued to pursue his education, earning an M.F.A. degree in creative writing from Columbia University, in New York City, in 2010. He is currently a Ph.D. student at Yale University, in New Haven, Connecticut, and he has also taken film classes at New York University's Tisch School of the Arts and writing classes at Brooklyn College.

When he is not acting or studying, Franco paints and writes. He has exhibited his paintings and mixed-media art at galleries, and his short stories have been published in *Esquire* and *McSweeney's*. In 2010 he published a book of short stories, *Palo Alto*. The collection, about aimless and nihilistic youth in Franco's hometown, received generally mixed reviews, with some critics describing Franco's character development as weak. Mary McNamara wrote for the *Los Angeles Times* (October 17, 2010, on-line), "Franco seems to grasp the literal meaning of 'God is in the details'—virtually every character has his or her gene pool racially dissected and locations are rendered with GPS precision—but not the spirit. None of the characters come to life because none of them are allowed to be more than a sum of what they see and do." In his review for the *New York Times* (October 22, 2010, on-line), Joshua Mohr observed, "As a writer, Franco needs to harness the skills he's cultivated as an actor, mainly the ability to inhabit a consciousness independent of his own."

In 2010 the Clocktower Gallery in New York City hosted Franco's exhibition The Dangerous Book Four Boys, a multimedia installation of experimental films, sculptures, photographs, and drawings that touched on the themes of childhood, sexuality, and destruction. Although some critics thought that the exhibit lacked depth and a sense of purpose, others found that it showed promise. Roberta Smith wrote for the *New York Times* (August 19, 2010), "Some people would probably feel better to read that Mr. Franco's Clocktower effort can be dismissed as bad beyond redemption, an outsider's naïve dalliance in things he doesn't really understand. I initially inclined toward that conclusion, although in the end it turned out to be more interesting and complicated than that."

Franco has also dabbled in performance art. According to Anderson, Franco's recurring role on the television soap opera *General Hospital*, in which he played the character Franco, an artist and serial killer, was intended as an art piece. In an article he wrote for the *Wall Street Journal* (December 4, 2009, on-line) about his appearance on the show, Franco, a fan of performance art, explained, "I disrupted the audience's suspension of disbelief, because no matter how far I got into the character, I was going to be perceived as something that doesn't belong to the incredibly stylized world of soap operas. Everyone watching would see an actor they recognized, a real person in a made-up world. In performance art, the outcome is uncertain—and this was no exception. My hope was for people to ask themselves if soap operas are really that far from entertainment that is considered critically legitimate. Whether they did was out of my hands." Anderson wrote, "This fit nicely into a constellation of ideas Franco had already been thinking about: the difference between high art and mass art, the space between performance and real life, the vagaries of taste. So Franco called *General Hospital,* one of TV's most popular and longest-running soap operas. The result is a small, double-edged pop-culture masterpiece—a black hole of publicity in which everything works both within the frame of the show and as a commentary on Franco's career."

In other forays into the self-referential, Franco played himself in an episode of the sitcom *30 Rock*, and in January 2011 it was announced that he would be teaching a class at Columbia College Hollywood in which students use footage of the actor to create a documentary about him. The course is called "Master Class: Editing James Franco . . . with James Franco."

Franco is scheduled to appear in the upcoming films "Your Highness," "Rise of the Apes," "Maladies," "The Broken Tower," "Lovelace," and "The Iceman." On February 27, 2011 he and the actress Anne Hathaway hosted the 83rd Academy Awards. Franco is currently in a relationship with the actress Ahna O'Reilly.

In an essay for *Time* (December 15, 2010, on-line), Joel Stein dubbed Franco the "coolest person of the year." He wrote that Franco "is the man who risked looking like an idiot over and over and yet never did. The man who was a movie star, a novelist, a soap-opera actor, a director, a visual artist, a Yale Ph.D. student in English, a Funny or Die video poster, a drag model on the cover of a magazine for transsexuals and a choice to co-host the next Oscars." Commenting on his acting career, his art projects, and the increasingly vague line between the two, Franco told Kyle Buchanan for movieline.com (January 22, 2010), "It's not like I'm trying to cultivate some image of myself. It's more like I'm allowed to do certain things and I'm given certain opportunities—like being on *General Hospital* and having this whole crazy character sculpted for me—because of that. I mean, I'm trained as an actor so I could play different characters, but for now, there's something about how playing myself mixes the imaginary world that I'm entering with my outside life. It brings them together in an interesting way. For these projects I'm doing that for, it's a very interesting intersection."

—W.D.

Suggested Reading: All Movie Guide Web site; (London) *Guardian* (on-line) Jan. 24, 2009; (London) *Independent* (on-line) Dec. 31, 2010; movieline.com Jan. 22, 2010; *New York* (on-line) July 25, 2010; Paly Voice Web site Jan. 3, 2006

Selected Films: as actor—*Never Been Kissed*, 1999; *Whatever It Takes*, 2000; *James Dean*, 2001; *Spider-Man*, 2002; *Deuces Wild*, 2002; *Mother Ghost*, 2002; *Sonny*, 2002; *City By the Sea*, 2002; *The Company*, 2003; *Spider-Man 2*, 2004; *The Ape*, 2005; *The Great Raid*, 2005; *Annapolis*, 2006; *Flyboys*, 2006; *Tristan + Isolde*, 2006; *In the Valley of Elah*, 2007; *Spider-Man 3*, 2007; *Pineapple Express*, 2008; *Camille*, 2008; *Milk*, 2008; *Howl*, 2010; *William Vincent*, 2010; *127 Hours*, 2010; as writer, actor, and director—*Good Time Max*, 2007

Selected Television Shows: *Freaks and Geeks*, 1999–2000; *General Hospital*, 2009–11

Selected Books: *Palo Alto*, 2010

Courtesy of The Rockefeller University

Fuchs, Elaine

(fyooks)

May 5, 1950– Molecular and cellular biologist; educator

Address: The Rockefeller University, 1230 York Ave., New York, NY 10065

At a White House ceremony hosted by President Barack Obama on October 7, 2009, the molecular biologist Elaine Fuchs received the National Medal of Science—the country's highest scientific honor—for her far-reaching contributions to medical science. The focus of Fuchs's research is the body's largest organ, the skin: its diverse cells, the proteins that build those cells, and the 54 genes that guide the production of keratins, the most prevalent of those proteins. Fuchs has furthered medical science by greatly increasing what is known about those genes and proteins. By means of a technique known as reverse genetics, she has discovered the genetic bases for some 90 skin disorders and cancers and has begun to elucidate the biological mechanisms that enable skin stem cells to "develop tissue that can become outer skin or hair follicles or sweat glands," as she told Claudia Dreifus for the *New York Times* (June 21, 2010). "I'd like to know how one stem cell can create tissues so different from one another." Fuchs and many other scientists are confident that increased knowledge about skin stem cells will lead to methods of inducing the growth of new skin in burn victims, to cite one major potential benefit of Fuchs's research. As an educator at the University of Chicago for more than two decades and, since 2002, at Rockefeller University, in New York City, Fuchs has also furthered medical science as mentor to more than 100 other scientists—among them many women—who are now teaching and conducting research at dozens of facilities in the U.S. and elsewhere. Fuchs heads the Laboratory of Mammalian Cell Biology and Development at Rockefeller. She has received funding as a Howard Hughes Medical Institute investigator since 1988. In 2010 she was elected president of the International Society for Stem Cell Research. Her many awards include the 2004 Dickson Prize in Medicine from the University of Pittsburgh, which recognized her for achievements that "place her in the top cadre of the most creative scientists worldwide."

Elaine Fuchs was born just outside Chicago on May 5, 1950, four years after her only sibling. She grew up in nearby Downers Grove. Her mother, a homemaker and gardener, played the piano and painted in oils; her father was a geochemist at the Argonne National Laboratory. Her father's sister, who lived next door, was a biologist (also at Argonne) and a fervent feminist; her own sister, Jannon Fuchs, is a research neuroscientist at the University of North Texas. When Fuchs and her sister were young, their mother made butterfly nets for them, using broomsticks, coat hangers, and kitchen netting, and the girls would spend hours chasing butterflies in neighborhood fields. Fuchs also liked to hunt small creatures in local ponds and creeks. Her father used to take the girls to visit Chicago's Museum of Science and Industry, and Fuchs has recalled asking for science books for Christmas. "Growing up in such a family," and with a semi-wild environment at her doorstep, "I developed a deep interest in science that has carried me through my professional life," Fuchs told Fiona Watt for *Journal of Cell Science* (September 29, 2004, on-line). "If I think back to the family influences that shaped my choice of career, I remember that my Dad strongly advocated my being an elementary school teacher. My aunt . . . was denied admission to medical school and she encouraged me to go into medicine. My mom told me that she thought I was a good cook and therefore I should become a chemist. My older sis was my idol, although I found her intelligence intimidating. She thought I should become an anthropologist. . . . I was strongly encouraged by my family to go to college and do something with my life."

Fuchs attended the University of Illinois at Urbana-Champaign, where she majored in chemistry, earning a B.S. degree with highest distinction in 1972. Her undergraduate thesis described an experiment in physical chemistry in which molecules of nickel passed through quartz in the presence of an electric field.

After her graduation Fuchs applied to the Peace Corps, in hopes of working in Chile; when she learned, after taking courses in Spanish and Latin American history, that she had been assigned to Uganda, she decided against serving in the corps, because the brutal dictator Idi Amin controlled Uganda then. Instead, she entered the graduate program in biochemistry at Princeton University, in Princeton, New Jersey. She conducted research on bacteria in the laboratory of the molecular biologist Charles Gilvarg, who, she told Watt, was "quite open about his views that women should not be in science." Although she worked extremely diligently, Gilvarg sometimes compared her unfavorably with one of his male graduate students (in part, she has suggested, because she was not singlemindedly focused on science: during her five years at Princeton, she traveled widely, visiting Mexico and nine countries in Asia, South America, and Europe). Nevertheless, Fuchs has said that she will always feel grateful to Gilvarg for teaching her the proper way to conduct well-controlled experiments—that is, by setting up controls so as "to be able to interpret an unexpected finding," she told Monya Baker for *Nature Reports Stem Cells* (May 14, 2009, on-line). Fuchs earned a Ph.D. degree in biochemistry in 1977. Her doctoral dissertation discussed physiological and biochemical changes in Bacillus Megatorium, a large soil bacterium, during a process called sporulation.

Fuchs next embarked on postdoctoral studies in the laboratory of Howard Green, a professor of cell biology at the Massachusetts Institute of Technology (MIT), in Cambridge. Green, a pioneer in mammalian stem-cell biology, had discovered a way to grow stem cells from human skin in the laboratory. (The cells were harvested from the circumcised foreskins of newborn males.) It was that breakthrough that had attracted Fuchs to his lab, because she wanted to study human cells rather than bacteria and thereby, she hoped, contribute more directly to medical science. In particular, she told Watt, she "wanted to study the biochemical mechanisms underlying the balance between growth and differentiation in normal human cells." Moreover, she told Baker, "if I wanted to understand what was abnormal, I had to first understand what was normal." "I learned cell culture from a master," she told Robin Marantz Henig for the *HHMI Bulletin* (May 2010). "Howard really paid attention to the kind of detail that, even now, very few people have the capacity to do." "My experience at MIT had a powerful impact on my career . . . ," she recalled to Watt. "Nearly every lab at MIT was humming with brilliant postdocs, and I rapidly got hooked on the excitement of the science around me." Although she had long doubted her abilities, at MIT she "began to think that perhaps a scientific career might even be a possible goal for me," she told Watt. At MIT Fuchs was a co-author with Green of three major papers regarding keratin genes and their expression—that is, the process by which keratin proteins and skin cells develop. The expertise in cell biology and epidermal cell culture that she gained in his lab underlie all the research she has conducted since her time at MIT.

In 1980 Fuchs was hired as an assistant professor in the University of Chicago's Biochemistry Department. As the first woman in that 15-member department, she did not always feel welcome among her male colleagues, but she gained support from women in other departments, among them the cytogeneticist Janet Rowley and the molecular biologist Susan Lindquist, who became one of Fuchs's closest friends. Later, as a tenured faculty member, Fuchs discovered that her salary was lower than that of starting male assistant professors, and she successfully lobbied for a pay increase. In 1985 the university reorganized the biological-science departments, and Fuchs became an associate professor in the Department of Biochemistry and Molecular Biology. She retained a joint appointment in that department, which was home to many of her original university colleagues; she was promoted to full professor in 1989 and in 1993 was named the Amgen professor of basic sciences. Concurrently, in 1988 she became a Howard Hughes Medical Institute (HHMI) investigator—a position that allowed her to continue to conduct her research in Chicago. (The institute's headquarters are in Chevy Chase, Maryland.)

Continuing research she had begun as a postdoctoral student in Green's lab, at the University of Chicago Fuchs focused on skin, the organ that serves as a barrier between the body and its environment and helps to maintain its internal temperature. Skin originates as a single layer of undifferentiated epithelial cell that in the mouse surrounds an embryo in the second week of life. On average, a human adult has about 20 square feet of skin. It is made up of an outer layer, the epidermis (which itself consists of several layers), and, directly underneath, the dermis, which contains blood and lymph vessels, nerve endings, and fat tissue. Notable appendages of the epidermis are sweat glands, hair follicles, and associated oil glands. Those epithelial appendages extend into the dermis, but the skin epithelium and dermis are separated by a basement membrane, rich in extracellular matrix proteins and growth factors. Present within the skin epithelium are stem cells, which continually regenerate epidermis, hair follicles, and glands during normal wear and tear and in response to injury. Skin stem cells and epithelial cells are among the few kinds of mammalian cells that, after their removal from a living animal, can flourish in the laboratory, where they are grown in special dishes in nutritional mediums.

Fuchs's primary subjects are mice—in particular, transgenic mice, which were developed in 1980. Transgenic mice grow from fertilized eggs that have been genetically altered and then implanted in the uteruses of surrogate mouse mothers. Fuchs had been studying the major structural proteins of the skin epithelium and begun to realize that those proteins, called keratins, were essential for the mechanical strength and integrity of the skin tissue. To discover what skin disorders of keratins might look like, Fuchs and her graduate student Robert Vassar genetically altered the so-called keratin 14 (K14) gene, which is responsible for the production of the keratins found in the innermost layer of the skin epidermis. Soon thereafter, they did the same for keratin 10 (K10), found in the superficial layers of the epidermis.

For some time Fuchs and her co-workers detected no abnormalities in the transgenic baby mice born in her lab. Then one day Fuchs's lab manager, Linda Degenstein, noticed in the cage of one surrogate-mother mouse a partially eaten infant whose skin looked abnormal. Round-the-clock observation of surrogate mothers due to give birth revealed that almost immediately after an infant with abnormal skin was born, its mother would eat it— "nature's way," in Fuchs's words, of dealing with severely affected baby mice. Examinations of such infants rescued before they were devoured indicat-

ed that during the rigors of birth, their skin had blistered badly, leaving them unable or unlikely to survive. Analyzing the pathology of the mutant mice led Fuchs and her team to two human skin diseases that closely resembled the two types of disorders in their transgenic mice: epidermolysis bullosa simplex (EBS) and epidermolytic hyperkeratosis (EH). "Within a year," Robin Marantz Henig wrote, Fuchs, Vassar, and others in Fuchs's lab "had worked out the genetic basis for both EBS and EH, building on a discovery Fuchs had made [at MIT], that as epidermal stem cells differentiate, they switch off two keratin genes, K5 and K14, and switch on two others, K1 and K10."

Fuchs's landmark discovery was described in a paper entitled "Mutant Keratin Expression in Transgenic Mice Causes Marked Abnormalities Resembling a Human Skin Disease," published in *Cell* (January 25, 1991). "This is really just a beautiful piece of work," the dermatologist Thomas S. Kupper, then with the Washington University School of Medicine, told Natalie Angier for the *New York Times* (October 1, 1991). "It shows there are more ways to find a disease gene than to simply apply the standard gene-mapping approaches." According to Angier, "Physicians emphasized that the discovery would have no immediate use for people who suffer from the skin disease, but said that knowledge of how skin replenishes itself from the underlying dermal layer upward to the outer epidermis could result in new therapies for skin disorders and to accelerate wound healing." "I think it has widespread applicability, and you're going to see these kinds of approaches become more and more common in the future," Fuchs said to Angier. "If you have protein, and you're interested in knowing what its function is, one of the best ways to investigate it is to create these mutations." Reverse genetics is particularly useful in the study of diseases that do not appear to be inherited.

Another mystery that Fuchs is steadily unraveling is how a skin stem cell develops into skin or hair. "Hair is so structurally different from the epidermis that it seems extraordinary that you can generate both structures from one cell type," Fuchs told an *HHMI Bulletin* (June 1999) reporter. "So we asked two questions: How does this happen, and what signals dictate this decision?" In seeking answers, Fuchs began by exploring how hair keratin genes are regulated and how that process differs from that of epidermal keratin genes. She uncovered a key regulatory factor that had also been studied by immunologists. That hair-cell factor, called lymphoid enhancer-binding factor-1 (LEF-1), is a transcription factor—a "protein that can combine with other proteins and then bind to specific sites on DNA, turning genes either on or off." Fuchs's team was baffled as to how LEF-1 switched the hair keratin genes on until another scientist, in Germany, discovered that LEF-1 needed a co-factor, called beta-catenin, in order to perform the switch. Beta-catenin was interesting to the scientists because it was already known to be a "key player in what is known as the 'Wnt signaling pathway,' a major biochemical route that determines the developmental fate of cells," as the *HHMI Bulletin* writer put it. Fuchs created another transgenic mouse to determine whether excessive amounts of beta-catenin would influence hair-follicle growth. An extra dose of beta-catenin caused mature skin cells to behave "as if they were embryonic skin cells, or . . . stem cells," Fuchs explained to the *HHMI Bulletin* reporter. In the words of Robin Marantz Henig, "For a stem cell to become a hair follicle, at the right moment, the pathway known as Wnt must be turned on, and another, known as BMP, must be switched off. In the absence of these opposing signals, the stem cell becomes skin." The mice developed a superabundance of hair follicles and thus became "super-furry" (although no hair grew where normally it would never grow—for example, on the pads of the rodents' feet). In addition, the mice developed benign tumors in many of their hair follicles—an abnormality that has helped to shed light on the causes of common noncancerous human skin lesions. Fuchs's findings, described in the November 25, 1998 issue of *Cell*, may someday lead to treatments for hair loss in humans.

In 2002 Fuchs joined the Rockefeller University, in New York City, as the head of the Laboratory of Mammalian Cell Biology and Development and as the Rebecca C. Lancefield professor. In 2004 Fuchs and her co-workers developed a general method to mark different types of stem cells of the body with a green fluorescent marker. While they used the method to isolate and monitor the stem cells of the hair follicle, the method has since been used to isolate and track other types of stem cells, including those of the hematopoietic system. That technology has led to greater understanding of the movement of skin stem cells and the changes they undergo as they move (described in *Science*, January 16, 2004) and the roles of the transcription factors Lhx2 and Tcf3 in the behavior of skin stem cells (*Science*, June 30, 2006 and *Cell*, October 6, 2006, respectively). In the February 20, 2007 issue of the *Proceedings of the National Academy of Sciences*, Fuchs reported a successful experiment in which skin stem cells from adult mice were used to create mouse clones. "While only a few percent of the clones survived to become healthy mice," Robin Marantz Henig wrote, "the experiment demonstrated that skin stem cells can be successfully reprogrammed . . . to generate all 220 different cell types in the body." Fuchs has since published several dozen reports of her research, in publications including *Cancer Cell*, *Nature*, the *Journal of Cell Biology*, *Genes and Development*, *Cell Cycle*, *Methods in Molecular Biology*, *Cell Stem Cell*, and the *Journal of Clinical Investigation*, among others.

When Ben Short, an interviewer for the *Journal of Cell Biology* (December 28, 2009, on-line), asked Fuchs about her research goals, she said, "We've identified lots of new genes that change their expression patterns as stem cells make epidermis and hair follicles. But we can't use classical genetics to figure out what all these changes mean. . . . We're developing new strategies to make functional analyses of mouse skin development a more tractable process. There are many signaling pathways that must converge to build and maintain tissues during normal development and wound repair, and a lot of pathways go awry to generate the myriad of human skin disorders, including cancers. We know a little bit here and there, yet we still have a lot of pieces to fill in. But I love the puzzle!"

In 1988 Fuchs married David T. Hansen, currently a professor of philosophy and education at the Teachers College of Columbia University. She and her husband live in New York City. In their leisure time they enjoy visiting art museums.

—W.D.

Suggested Reading: *HHMI Bulletin* p6+ June 1999, p17+ May 2010; hhmi.org; *Journal of Cell Biology* p938+ Dec. 28, 2009; *Journal of Cell Science* (on-line) Sep. 29, 2004; lab.rockefeller.edu/fuchs; *New York Times* C p3 Oct. 1, 1991, (on-line) June 21, 2010; Rockefeller University Web site; searlescholars.net

Selected Books: as co-author and co-editor (with W. James Nelson)—*Cell-Cell Junctions*, 2010

Gammons, Peter

Apr. 9, 1945– Sportswriter; television journalist

Address: MLB Network, 40 Hartz Way, Suite 10, Secaucus, NJ 07094

"Modern baseball writing began with Peter Gammons," Bob Ryan wrote for the *Boston Globe* (August 1, 2005) the day after the Baseball Writers Association of America recognized Gammons with its highest honor, the J. G. Taylor Spink Award, for his outstanding work as a baseball writer. Gammons's career as a sportswriter began in June 1968, during his college years, when he served as a summer intern with the *Boston Globe*. He became a full-time *Globe* sportswriter in February 1969, and—except for two breaks totaling about six years in the 1970s and 1980s, when he wrote for *Sports Illustrated*—he remained with the *Globe* until the end of 1999. During those three decades he wrote some 6,300 articles and Sunday columns for the *Globe*, and the National Sportscasters and Sportswriters Association named him the Sportswriter of the Year three times (in 1989, 1990, and 1993). A baseball aficionado and passionate fan of the Boston Red Sox since childhood, Gammons is known as the quintessential baseball insider. His general knowledge, encyclopedic store of baseball history, lore, and statistics, thousands of personal contacts, sense of humor, and humanistic values all enrich his writings. "People interest me, maybe even more than

Peter Gammons

the game: why people do things, why people succeed, why people fail. I love talking to these guys," Gammons told Marty Dobrow for *Sport* (May 1, 1999). Dan Shaughnessy, who like Ryan was a colleague of his at the *Globe*, wrote for the July 30, 2005 edition of that paper, "There was plenty of substance to accompany the unique and much-copied style" of Gammons's Sunday columns. "No one worked the trenches harder than Gammons. He was first at the ballpark, last to leave, and . . . got everything firsthand. It's easy and lazy for writers to repeat stuff they hear from other writers. We've all done it. But Gammons got (and continues to get) his information from the players, coaches, managers, general managers, and owners." Gammons served as an ESPN Major League Baseball (MLB) analyst for more than 20 years, beginning in 1988, and for most of that time, he also wrote for ESPN.com and ESPN's print magazine. In 2009 he left ESPN to become an analyst for the MLB television network and columnist for MLB.com. He is the author of one book, co-author of two others, and editor of the anthology *The Best American Sports Writing* (2010).

One of the four children of Edward Babson Gammons and the former Betty Allen, Peter Warren Gammons was born on April 9, 1945 in Boston, Massachusetts. One of his mother's ancestors was Ethan Allen, an American Revolutionary War hero. Gammons and his siblings grew up on the campus of the Groton School, an elite college-preparatory boarding school where his father, an organ designer, taught music. He has recalled listening, at age three, as Groton's assistant headmaster—his godfather—teased his mother after the Boston Red Sox lost the American League play-offs to the Cleve-

land Indians. Early on his mother imbued him with a love for baseball and the Red Sox. She even allowed him to leave class before the school day ended in order to attend Red Sox opening games at their home stadium, Fenway Park. "I grew up in a house where when I got home from school my mother greeted me with, 'Can you believe they traded Jim Piersall for Vic Wertz and Gary Geiger?,'" Gammons said during his acceptance speech at the Spink Award ceremony. He also said that his older brother, Edward Jr., called Ned (now an Episcopal minister), "weaned me on respect and reverence for the history and texture of the game."

As a youth Gammons picked apples to earn money for train fare and tickets to games at Fenway Park. At the Groton School, where he completed eighth through 12 grades, he played on the student baseball and basketball teams, served as president of the glee club, and, during his free time, organized and played guitar with two bands. After he graduated from Groton, in 1963, he entered the University of North Carolina (UNC) at Chapel Hill. At the suggestion of an upperclassman, Curry Kirkpatrick, an editor with the *Daily Tar Heel*, the campus newspaper (who later wrote for *Sports Illustrated*), Gammons joined its staff. After two or three years, he dropped out of college and formed a band in Boston. Unable to make a go of it in music, he returned to UNC. In 1968 he won a summer internship with the *Boston Globe*. He was assigned to cover political news at the *Globe*, but on his first day, June 10, 1968, a managing editor recruited him for the sports department. His first article appeared in the *Globe* the next day. "It was fast evident that he was doing what he was born to do," Dan Shaughnessy wrote in his book *At Fenway: Dispatches from the Red Sox Nation* (1997). Between June 11 and August 19, 1968, 40 *Globe* articles carried Gammons's byline.

Gammons left UNC again after the fall 1968 term, having accepted the offer of a full-time job with the *Globe*. Later, by means of correspondence courses, he earned a B.A. degree from UNC. Gammons wrote full-time for the *Globe* from February 11, 1969 through September 2, 1976; from February 26, 1978 to April 4, 1986; and, as a special correspondent, from September 3, 1990 through December 4, 1999. Between July 24, 2000 and May 16, 2003, a dozen of his articles appeared in the *Globe*.

During his first three years or so as a *Globe* sportswriter, Gammons wrote about high-school and college competitions. In 1972 he became the *Globe*'s beat reporter for the Red Sox. He soon developed a reputation as a tireless worker and innovative writer. According to many baseball writers and others, Gammons's Sunday columns changed the way newspaper reporters wrote about sports. "Gammons was the inventor of the endless notes column, in which no player, no statistic, no anecdote, no observation was too obscure," Mark Whicker wrote for the *Orange County (California) Register* (July 6, 2004). "He worked the clubhouse—both clubhouses—to staggering effect." "I think he understands the strengths and weaknesses of all teams much better than a lot of general managers do," the *New York Times*'s Yankees beat writer Buster Olney told Marty Dobrow. Gammons's ability to get stories before they become available to others stems in large part from the vast network of reliable sources—players, coaches, general managers, and owners—he has developed. Much of that has involved the telephone. Bill Griffith wrote for the *Globe* (December 15, 2004) that once, during the 1970s, the *Globe*'s communications coordinator noticed a staggeringly high figure on that month's phone records: "Never to be forgotten is the sight of her running into sports editor Dave Smith's office, waving a handful of bills, and shrieking, '[Gammons's] monthly phone bill is higher than his salary!'"

Gammons's style also reflected his wide knowledge of pop culture, especially rock music, his interest in the humanities, and his sensitive awareness of human nature and the natural world. "Instead of writing play-by-play and boozing with the manager, Gammons connected with young players and wrote about the way games smelled and sounded," Whicker wrote. Gammons's writing strengths also included remarkable speed. After the Red Sox defeated the Cincinnati Reds, 7–6, in Game Six of the 1975 World Series, for example, he typed eight pages of copy in 15 minutes, employing several Telecopiers (fax machines) because he was writing faster than the machines could transmit. His write-up (October 22, 1975) began with a now-classic description of Carleton Fisk's game-winning home run: "And all of a sudden the ball was there, like the Mystic River Bridge, suspended out in the black of morning." After the Red Sox were defeated in Game Seven, Gammons wrote for the *Globe* (October 23, 1975), "She is in retreat this morning, Olde Fenway, resting. Her affair with Kismet fell through at the very last, and while it was good, it was not to be this time." For the October 26, 1975 edition, in an article headlined "Sox Realized All But Elusive Dream," his concluding words referred to the center fielder Fred Lynn, the pitcher Luis Tiant, the owner of the Red Sox since 1933, and the number of years since the team had last won the World Series, in 1918: "We have postponed autumn long enough now. There are storm windows to put in, wood to chop for the whistling months ahead. The floorboards are getting awfully cold in the morning, the cider sweet. Where Lynn dove and El Tiante stood will be frozen soon, and while it is now 43 years for Thomas A. Yawkey and 57 for New England, the fugue that was the 1975 baseball season will play in our heads until next we meet at the Fens again."

Gammons's book *Beyond the Sixth Game: What's Happened to Baseball Since the Greatest Game in World Series History* (1985) opened with a description of the 1975 series and offered a "a game-by-game recitation of Boston's past nine seasons, spiced up with brief profiles of various actors in the never-ending Red Sox melodrama," Jonathan Yardley wrote for the *Washington Post* (April 10, 1985). It also discussed the demise of the so-called reserve clause in baseball players' contracts (which made players, in effect, the property of their teams' owners, analogous to indentured servants in past centuries) and a federal court's ruling in favor of free agency, in 1976. While Yardley found *Beyond the Sixth Game* tedious, the book struck Robert L. Rice, the *Library Journal* (March 15, 1985) reviewer, as a "marvelous saga." Gammons, Rice wrote, "is widely regarded as baseball's best and most prolific daily chronicler. And with this superb work he should reach an audience that goes beyond the confines of sports fans. . . . Gammons combines a beat reporter's obsession with facts, a novelist's narrative skill, and a humorist's ear for the truly hilarious to give us an unforgettable portrait of baseball's most turbulent decade."

During his first, year-and-a-half absence from the *Globe* (1976–78) and second, four-and-a-half-year absence (1986–90), Gammons served as a senior writer for *Sports Illustrated* (*SI*). "I couldn't pass up an opportunity to transfer what I was doing to a forum the size of *SI*," he told Donald J. Barr for *Sports Illustrated* (April 14, 1986). Barr wrote that "around the batting cages this spring, he was one of the most talked-about acquisitions of the off-season." During his first *SI* stint, Gammons reported mostly on ice-hockey games. During the second he covered many of MLB's most important events and wrote a column, called "Inside Baseball," which provided readers with material similar in nature to what he had written for the *Globe*. While with *Sports Illustrated* Gammons co-authored, with the Cy Young Award–winning pitcher Roger Clemens (who was then in his mid-20s and playing for the Red Sox), the book *Rocket Man: The Roger Clemens Story* (1987).

In 1988 Gammons joined ESPN as a part-time analyst. *Sports Illustrated*'s managing editor, Mark Mulvoy, expressed unhappiness that Gammons was sharing his knowledge and stories with ESPN, leading Gammons in 1990 to give up his full-time position with *Sports Illustrated* and instead to write for *SI* on a freelance basis. In the same year he became a full-time writer for *ESPN The Magazine* and ESPN.com. Gammons has said that he struggled a bit during his transformation from print journalist to television commentator. "I didn't do very well at first," he told Dan Quinn for the *Sporting News* (November 12, 1990), "but I had a lot of help." He pointed out that he was the first writer to broadcast for ESPN, "so I think they were more patient with me than they would usually be. Before I was in the electronic media, I thought it was easy." Gammons appeared regularly on ESPN's *Baseball Tonight*, *SportsCenter*, and news programs before his departure from that network, in 2009.

With Jack Sands, a sports agent, Gammons co-wrote *Coming Apart at the Seams: How Baseball Owners, Players, and Television Executives Have*

Led Our National Pastime to the Brink of Disaster (1993). The book's thesis is that the greed of owners, players, and television executives was damaging baseball as a national sport and alienating fans. Charles Stein, in a review for the *Boston Globe* (April 12, 1993), called the volume "a classic 1980's tale of greed" as well as "a depressing book, in part because its characters are so unlikable and unsympathetic." Stein continued that the book offers some revealing points, but "there is more inside baseball here than most fans will want to slog through." James DiGiacomo, a reviewer for *America* (April 17, 1993), wrote, "This is a book for the fans who really care about the game, who wonder how we got where we are and are looking for constructive criticism." On April 6, 1993 Gammons and Sands appeared as "talking heads" on "The Trouble with Baseball," an installment of the Public Broadcasting System series *Frontline*. Many of the issues about which Gammons and Sand had written in *Coming Apart at the Seams* became the subjects of discussion the following year, when a dispute between team owners and players resulted in a 232-day strike (August 12, 1994–April 2, 1995), during which more than 900 games were cancelled, including the 1994 World Series.

Gammons has sometimes been criticized for speculating at excessive length about possible changes in team personnel or other events that never materialize and for relying too much on hearsay. He has dismissed such complaints, explaining to Marty Dobrow that he is willing to write about anything "as long as I know that somebody's seriously discussing it." More deals are discussed than are consummated, he said, and his primary goal is to serve as "the eyes and ears of the fans."

In 2000 Gammons helped organize a concert in Boston called Hot Stove, Cool Music. The concert featured Boston-area bands and performers, among them Gammons and members of the Red Sox. Proceeds from the concert and a concurrent auction of baseball memorabilia were donated to the Jimmy Fund, a charity devoted to the fight against cancer. "Most guys I know host charity golf tournaments . . . ," Gammons explained, as quoted on the Web site hotstovecoolmusic.org. "I don't golf, so this is my version of that. It's the best way I know to bring together my two greatest passions, baseball and rock music, while raising money for a great cause." Currently, Gammons and Theo Epstein, the Red Sox executive vice president/general manager, host the twice-yearly Hot Stove, Cool Music events. The last concert, held in January 2011, included a baseball roundtable discussion; it raised $300,000 for the charity founded by Epstein and his twin brother, Paul, which is called the Foundation to Be Named Later and supports nine nonprofit groups that help homeless children and others in the Boston area.

In 2006 Gammons recorded the album *Never Slow Down, Never Grow Old*; a compilation of bluesy rock covers with one original song, "She Fell from Heaven," it was released on the Rounder label. Gammons played guitar and sang, with backing by professional musicians (including George Thorogood and Juliana Hatfield) and former and current Red Sox players. "We'd advise Gammons not to give up his day job only because he's so good at it," Sarah Rodman wrote for the *Boston Globe* (July 4, 2006), "but . . . Gammons makes a pretty good rocker." Proceeds from sales of the album have gone to the Foundation to Be Named Later.

In 2004 Gammons received the J. G. Taylor Spink Award (named for the longtime publisher of the *Sporting News*), which the Baseball Writers Association of America presents annually to a sportswriter for "meritorious contributions to baseball writing." In 2006 Gammons suffered a brain aneurysm; he spent a month in the hospital and returned to work after another two months. He and his wife, the former Gloria Fay Trowbridge, who have been married since 1968, live in Brookline, Massachusetts, a suburb of Boston.

—N.W.M.

Suggested Reading: Associated Press (on-line) July 7, 2006; *Boston Globe* D p14+ July 23, 2000, C p1 July 30, 2005, D p8 Aug. 1, 2005; *Cincinnati Enquirer* C p2 May 30, 1999; ESPN.com Aug. 1, 2005; MLB.com; *Orange County (California) Resister* July 6, 2006; *Sports Illustrated* p30 Apr. 14, 1986; *USA Today* C p3 Aug. 25, 1992; Shaughnessy, Dan. *At Fenway: Dispatches from the Red Sox Nation*, 1997

Selected Books: *Beyond the Sixth Game: What's Happened to Baseball Since the Greatest Game in World Series History*, 1985; *Rocket Man: The Roger Clemens Story* (with Roger Clemens), 1987; *Coming Apart at the Seams: How Baseball Owners, Players, and Television Executives Have Led Our National Pastime to the Brink of Disaster* (with Jack Sands), 1993

Gasol, Pau

(gah-SOHL, pow)

July 6, 1980– Basketball player

Address: Los Angeles Lakers, 555 N. Nash St., El Segundo, CA 90245

The Los Angeles Lakers' power forward Pau Gasol, Ramona Shelburne wrote for the *Daily News of Los Angeles* (April 20, 2008), "is a superstar who is content with the corner locker." Since he was traded to the Lakers, midway through the 2007–08 season, Gasol has been widely regarded as one of the best complementary players in the National Basketball Association (NBA); he has been referred to, as Lee Jenkins noted for *Sports Illustrated* (March 29, 2010), as the "perfect Robin for [Kobe Bryant's] Batman." Taking much of the leadership burden

Harry How/Getty Images

Pau Gasol

from Bryant, Gasol was a pivotal figure in the Lakers' winning consecutive NBA championships in 2009 and 2010. "It's hard to think of a player in the last few years who came and changed a team as much as he has," the Lakers' starting point guard Derek Fisher told Mark Whicker for the *Orange County (California) Register* (June 18, 2010). Prior to joining the Lakers, Gasol spent six and a half seasons with the Memphis Grizzlies, where he set franchise records for career games played (476), minutes played (16,904), field goals made (3,324) and attempted (6,533), free throws made (2,301) and attempted (3,152), total rebounds (4,096), blocks (877), and points (8,966). In his first season with the Grizzlies, the Spanish-born Gasol won the NBA's Rookie of the Year Award, becoming the first and, to date, only European player to win that honor. He is also the first Spaniard and first Grizzlies player to be named to the NBA All-Star team (2006); he was named to his second and third All-Star teams as a member of the Lakers, in 2009 and 2010. He earned a silver medal with the Spanish National Team at the 2008 Summer Olympics, in Beijing, China, and won a gold medal with Spain at the 2006 International Basketball Federation (FIBA) World Championships. Gasol is known for his cerebral style of play and has been described as "a terrific shooter for a big man, an excellent passer and a smart player with or without the ball," David Leon Moore wrote for *USA Today* (May 7, 2008). Sekou Smith noted for the *Indianapolis Star* (August 28, 2002), "He's a silky-smooth 7-footer with a point guard's ballhandling skills. He has the size . . . and heart to bang and block shots in the paint, yet he's versatile enough to work away from the basket and hit jumpers with ease." For a while during his years in the NBA, some questioned Gasol's toughness and competitiveness, for his perceived aversion to a more physical style of play; he put the "soft" label to rest in 2008, by adding more muscle to his naturally lanky frame, which has increased his strength and allowed him to play more aggressively. Aito Garcia Reneses, the head coach of the Spanish National Team, told Jenkins about the finesse with which Gasol plays, "There are other players who can do the same things as Pau. But for some reason it's just not as nice to look at."

The oldest of three brothers, Pau Gasol was born on July 6, 1980 in Barcelona, Spain, to Agusti and Marisa Gasol. (The name "Pau" was was inspired by the place where he was born, Hospital de Sant Pau.) He grew up in the Catalonian town of Sant Boi de Llobregat, a Barcelona suburb, in an upper-middle-class family that stressed the importance of education, hard work, and discipline. His father was a nurse before he became a hospital administrator; his mother was a doctor of internal medicine. Gasol's interest in basketball was partly shaped by his parents, who both stand over six feet tall—his father at six-foot-three and his mother at six-foot-one—and played basketball in organized leagues. Gasol's younger brothers, Marc and Adria, also took up basketball: Marc has since joined his brother in the NBA, as a center for the Memphis Grizzlies, and Adria plays high-school basketball for Lausanne Collegiate School in Memphis, Tennessee. (Gasol's parents now live in Germantown, a Memphis suburb; his father works for the Los Angeles, California–based health-care company Grifols, and his mother serves as a volunteer at St. Jude Children's Research Hospital.)

Beginning when he was six, Gasol attended Escola Llor, an exclusive, private elementary school less than a five-minute walk from his home. He took up basketball there at the age of nine. Precocious and mature beyond his years, Gasol worked hard to develop his basketball skills but placed an even greater emphasis on his schoolwork. "I'm very competitive and that translated to my studies," he told Ronald Tillery for the Memphis *Commercial Appeal* (October 10, 2003). "I always wanted the best grades. I always wanted to be the best at whatever I did." Ricard Farres, the athletic director of Escola Llor, said to Chuck Culpepper for the *Los Angeles Times* (February 10, 2008), "While he was an introverted guy, we could see he was more mature than the rest of the students. The way he spoke. He seemed like an older boy. His reasoning. Not totally his words, but his reasoning." Gasol also played piano well.

As a boy Gasol aspired to become a doctor. He developed that desire at the age of 11, after he heard the news that the Los Angeles Lakers superstar Magic Johnson—whom he admired—was HIV positive. "I was deep in thought," Gasol recalled to Lee Jenkins. "I was trying to figure out what it meant and what I should do. It was one of those moments that sticks in your mind and stays there your whole life." Johnson further inspired Gasol's love for basketball during the 1992 Summer Olympics, held in Barcelona, as a member of the United States' gold-medal-winning "Dream Team"—which also included the NBA luminaries Michael Jordan, Larry Bird, Charles Barkley, Scottie Pippen, and David Robinson and is remembered as one of the greatest assemblages of talent in sports history. Gasol told Ramona Shelburne, "That group of guys was amazing. I think it sent a message to the rest of the world that, that's how you're supposed to play, that's how the great players play. . . . It definitely left a mark on me and motivated me." Not long after the Olympics, Gasol's room became a kind of shrine to many of the NBA stars he had seen play that summer.

In his teens Gasol was forced to give up one of his passions, the piano, in order to focus more on basketball and academics. Standing out on the basketball court for his height—he was six-foot-four as a 15-year-old—he initially played guard because of his agility and ability to direct offenses. Ricard Farres told Chuck Culpepper, "In spite of being a very tall player, he wasn't clumsy at all. He was very agile. He was given more respect, more possibilities [by his coaches]." Gasol played for a team in the neighboring town of Cornella for three seasons before moving on to FC Barcelona's junior national team in 1997, at the age of 16. Describing his versatility, his coach Joan Montes recalled to Culpepper, "He was very intelligent and very smart. He just showed he could do everything. . . . He was very, very open, paying attention to everything. . . . He had a lot of personality, and he loved to give ideas about strategy and everything." Gasol played just one season on FC Barcelona's junior team before rising to its top-level club during the 1998–99 season. He played three seasons there, during which he caught the attention of numerous NBA scouts. During the 2000-01 season Gasol averaged 11.3 points and 5.2 rebounds per game and helped lead FC Barcelona to the Spanish national title; he was named the title game's Most Valuable Player (MVP). While playing for Barcelona Gasol also enrolled in medical school; he left after a year due to the demands of his basketball schedule. Agusti Gasol told Ronald Tillery, "In our country there is a moment in the life of a player to decide whether to study or play basketball. You continue school or pursue professional career. Pau made the decision."

Gasol continued to hone his game on European basketball courts in the three months leading up to the 2001 NBA draft. After entering his name for consideration just three days before draft day, on June 28, 2001 he was selected in the first round, as the third overall pick, by the Atlanta Hawks; he was then traded to the Memphis Grizzlies. (Gasol was the highest-drafted European player in NBA history at the time; the Houston Rockets' center Yao Ming gained that distinction during the 2002 NBA draft, when he was selected as the first overall pick.) On November 1, 2001 Gasol made his NBA debut, in a game against the Detroit Pistons, scoring four points, with four rebounds, one assist, and one block in 17 minutes. The Grizzlies lost the game, 90–80. After receiving limited playing time in his next two contests, Gasol made his first career start in the fourth game of the season, against the Phoenix Suns, breaking out with 27 points on 11-of-17 shooting, three rebounds, four assists, three blocks, and one steal in 39 minutes. (He had won the starting job after the Grizzlies' power forward Stromile Swift suffered an ankle injury.) Gasol, recalling the game, said to Sekou Smith, "During the first three games I was real nervous and not playing my game. I wasn't very comfortable. That game [against Phoenix] made me realize I could play here." Gasol went on to start the remaining 78 games of the season for the Grizzlies and blossomed, ranking at or near the top of nearly every statistical category for rookies. He led all rookies in per-game averages for points (17.6), rebounds (8.9), blocks (2.1), and field-goal percentage (0.518), while finishing second in average number of minutes played (36.6) and eighth in assists per game (2.7). Gasol was named the Western Conference Rookie of the Month for November, January, and March and was named the NBA Rookie of the Year at the end of the season, receiving 117 of a possible 126 votes. He was also named to the NBA's All-Rookie First Team. The Grizzlies, though, finished in last place in their division, with a 23–59 record, leading to a series of personnel shifts that offseason, including the hiring of the former Los Angeles Laker and Hall of Famer Jerry West as general manager. In spite of the Grizzlies' disappointing season, then–Head Coach Sidney Lowe told Smith, "In all my years [as an NBA player and coach] I've never been around a rookie who had such an impact on a ballclub." (After a 0–8 start to the 2002–03 season, Lowe was fired as head coach and replaced by Hubie Brown.)

Gasol had another impressive season in 2002–03, starting all 82 games and averaging 19 points per game. He was the Grizzlies' leading scorer in 45 games and led the team in points per game, rebounds per game (8.8), field-goal percentage (.510), blocks per game (1.8), minutes per game (36.0), and double-doubles, or double digits in both points and rebounds (32). He also finished ninth in the NBA in field-goal percentage and 10th in double-doubles. The Grizzlies, meanwhile, finished with a 28–54 record, the third-worst in the Western Conference. Gasol continued to be the Grizzlies' most reliable player during the 2003–04 season. He started each of the 78 games in which he appeared and led the team in averages of points per game (17.7), rebounds per game (7.7), and blocks per game (1.69). He scored in double figures in 76 of 78 games, recording 20 or more points 27 times and 30 points twice. The Grizzlies enjoyed a dramatic turnaround and made the play-offs for the first time in franchise history, after posting a franchise-record 50 wins. In the opening round of the play-offs, the team lost to the San Antonio Spurs in four games. In the series Gasol averaged 18.5 points, 5.0 rebounds, 2.5 assists, and 1.50 blocks per game.

In the summer of 2004, Gasol joined the Spanish National Team for the Olympics in Athens, Greece. After cruising to a 5–0 record in their pool, Spain lost to the U.S. in the quarterfinals and finished sixth overall. Nonetheless, Gasol led the tournament in scoring (an average of 22.4 points per game) and blocks. That summer he signed a six-year, $86 million deal with the Grizzlies. During the 2004–05 season, Gasol appeared in only 56 games, missing 26 due to injury. He was the Grizzlies' high scorer in 26 of those contests and averaged 17.8 points, 7.3 rebounds, 2.4 assists, and 1.7 blocks per game. The Grizzlies made the play-offs for the second consecutive season but were again swept in the first round, losing to the Phoenix Suns in four games. At the urging of Head Coach Mike Fratello, who took over the team following Hubie Brown's resignation two months into the 2004–05 season, Gasol approached the 2005–06 campaign with a greater leadership role in mind. During the regular season he put up career-high numbers in averages of points per game (20.4), assists per game (4.6), and minutes per game (39.2) while tying a career high in rebounds per game (8.9). He was subsequently named to his first All-Star team, becoming the first player in franchise history to earn the honor; as a reserve for the Western Conference, he pulled down a game-high 12 rebounds. After leading the Grizzlies to a 49–33 regular-season record, Gasol was a pivotal figure in preparing Memphis for the postseason, in which they were eliminated in the first round by the Dallas Mavericks, losing again in four games. (The Grizzlies' 12-game play-off losing streak is the longest in NBA history.)

During the summer of 2006, Gasol returned to the Spanish National Team for the FIBA World Championships, held in Japan. Spain won all nine of their games in the tournament and defeated Greece in the championship final, 70–47, to take home the gold medal and their first world title. Gasol missed the championship game after fracturing his left foot near the end of Spain's semifinal win over Argentina. He was still named the MVP of the tournament, after averaging 21.3 points in eight games. As a result of his injury, Gasol missed the first 23 games of the 2006–07 NBA season. He returned to put up career-high numbers in the 59 games in which he appeared, with averages of points per game (20.8) and rebounds per game (9.8), while tying a career high in blocks per game (2.1). That season, in a game against the Toronto Raptors, Gasol surpassed the former Grizzly Shareef Abdur-Rahim as the franchise's all-time leading scorer. He also eclipsed Abdur-Rahim's franchise record for most free-throw attempts and became the all-time franchise leader in minutes played and field goals made. The Grizzlies, however, finished with a league-worst 22–60 record, leading to West's resignation as general manager at the end of the season. That off-season Marc Iavaroni, a highly touted assistant coach from the Phoenix Suns, was brought on as head coach.

Gasol split the 2007–08 season between the Grizzlies and the Los Angeles Lakers. In 39 games with the Grizzlies, he averaged 18.9 points, 8.8 rebounds, 3.0 assists, and 1.4 blocks per game. On February 1, 2008 Gasol was involved in a trade that sent him and a 2010 second-round draft pick to the Lakers. (In return, in addition to other players, the Grizzlies got the rights to Marc Gasol, Pau's younger brother.) With the Lakers Gasol quickly picked up Head Coach Phil Jackson's celebrated triangle offense and established an instant chemistry with the team's superstar guard Kobe Bryant. "Since the first time he stepped on the floor, we automatically had a great relationship and understanding of where we like to operate on the floor," Bryant told David Leon Moore. Together with Bryant, Gasol was an integral part of the Lakers' NBA-championship run. In the 2008 NBA Finals, the Lakers lost to the Boston Celtics in six games. Despite averaging 16.9 points, 9.3 rebounds, and 4.0 assists in the Finals, Gasol was physically outmatched in the series by the Celtics center Kendrick Perkins and power forward Kevin Garnett, leading some to blame him for the loss as well as question his toughness. As a result, Gasol devoted himself during the following off-season to an intensive weight-training regimen to add more muscle to his frame. Later that summer he led Spain to the silver medal at the Olympics in Beijing.

Over the last two seasons, Gasol has emerged as one of the best number-two options in the NBA. During the 2008–09 season he averaged 18.9 points, 9.6 rebounds, 3.5 assists, and one block per game, while earning his second career All-Star selection. That season Gasol won his first NBA championship, when the Lakers defeated the Orlando Magic in the NBA Finals. He earned his third career All-Star selection during the 2009–10 season, when he averaged 18.3 points, 11.3 rebounds, 3.4 assists, and 1.7 blocks. Gasol then helped lead the Lakers to their second consecutive NBA championship, as they defeated the Boston Celtics in seven games in the 2010 NBA Finals. Gasol and the Lakers entered the 2010–11 season with hopes of attaining a third consecutive NBA championship, sometimes called a three-peat. As of early February 2011, Gasol was averaging 18.4 points, 10.6 rebounds, and 3.7 assists, and the Lakers were ranked second in the Western Conference with a 34–15 record.

Gasol lives in Redondo Beach, California. He is fluent in Spanish, English, Italian, and Catalan (the language spoken in his native Spanish province of Catalonia). He enjoys reading and listening to music in his spare time. Gasol is an official partner with Children's Hospital and St. Jude Children's Research Hospital in Memphis and is a Spanish ambassador to UNICEF, a role in which he participates in programs that support children with AIDS. "I wasn't able to become a doctor like I planned," Gasol told Lee Jenkins. "So I try to make an impact in other ways."

—C.C.

Suggested Reading: *Daily News of Los Angeles* C p1 Apr. 20, 2008; *Indianapolis Star* H p20 Aug. 28, 2002; *Los Angeles Times* D p1+ Feb. 10, 2008; (Memphis, Tennessee) *Commercial Appeal* D p5 Oct. 10, 2003; *Sports Illustrated* (on-line) Mar. 29, 2010; *USA Today* C p1 May 7, 2008

Ghesquière, Nicolas

(jess-kee-AIR)

1971– Fashion designer

Address: Balenciaga, 10 Ave. George V, 75008 Paris, France

"If he isn't the most important designer of his generation, it's hard to think who would be," the fashion critic Cathy Horyn wrote of Nicolas Ghesquière for the *New York Times* (October 4, 2006), declaring that he was "one of a handful of young visionaries trying to look at the future of fashion in a believable way." In 1997, at the age of 26, Ghesquière—a native of France who has no academic training in fashion design—was named the creative director, or head designer, of Balenciaga, a celebrated fashion house based in Paris, France, whose fortunes had declined steadily in the previous decade. His association with Balenciaga began the year before, when he was hired to design mourning clothes, golf apparel, and uniforms for the Asian market—a job glaringly lacking in prestige. Previously, as a teenager, he apprenticed with the designers Agnès B and Corinne Cobson; he then worked for less than two years (in 1991 and 1992) with Jean-Paul Gaultier, the so-called enfant terrible of the French fashion scene, and for the next several years as a freelance knitwear designer. Since Ghesquière's arrival at Balenciaga, the label has regained much of its earlier cachet, and its earnings have greatly increased, in what David Livingstone, writing for the *Toronto (Canada) Star* (January 28, 2010), described as "one of the great revitalizations in fashion history"; *WMagazine.com* (October 2007) reported that in 2007, after years in the red, the firm broke even. Currently, Balenciaga's couture collections and other apparel and accessories are sold in boutiques in three dozen cities worldwide—ranging from New York and Paris to St. Petersburg, Russia, Hangzhou, China, and Ho Chi Minh City, Vietnam—as well as in upscale department stores and on-line. According to a brief profile of him posted on the *New York Times* Web site in late 2010, Ghesquière's influence in recent years "has been enormous—the armies of young women in shrunken blazers, hipless trousers and blocky orthopedic-friendly footwear have been his doing." He is also known for his slim-cut trousers and handbags, and he has introduced a fragrance and a line of menswear. In August 2007 Ghesquière was the subject of Kate Betts's cover

story for a special style and design issue of *Time*. "Every season," Betts wrote, "his runway shows provide direction and ideas to each level of the fashion business, from the designer market right down to the mass market."

The second of two brothers of a Belgian father and a French mother, Nicolas Ghesquière was born in 1971 in Comines, France, along the border with Belgium. His father, a former swimming coach, manages a golf course. Ghesquière was raised in Loudun, a village in the Poitou-Charentes area of France that dates from the medieval era. As a seven-year-old, he knitted a sweater. Later he enjoyed reading science-fiction novels, watching films, fencing, swimming, and horseback riding, but not playing golf, because, by his own account, his brother always beat him at it. His favorite pastimes included transforming his mother's curtains into dresses and crafting earrings from parts of chandeliers. Most of his friends were girls, he told Tom Ford for *Interview* (January 21, 2010, on-line), and he delighted in "commenting on the way they were dressed." When, at 15, he announced to his parents his intention of becoming a fashion designer, his father helped him to write letters to a few designers, asking for a summer job. One of them, Agnès B (born Agnès Troublé), hired him for a month as a gofer at her Paris studio. On weekends during the next school year and the following summer, he assisted Corinne Cobson, a knitwear designer.

Much to his parents' dismay, at 16 Ghesquière quit school to work full-time with Cobson. After a year and a half, having decided that "fashion was too hard," as he recalled to Sally Singer for *Vogue* (March 2001), he returned to Loudun to finish high school. Then, at 18, he had another change of heart; disregarding the fierce opposition of his father, who wanted him to become a physical-education teacher, and the tearful pleading from his mother, he moved to Paris to pursue a career in fashion. While rooming with a friend he supported himself for a while by selling African statues on Paris's Left Bank. Then, in 1991, he met Myriam Schaefer, a top assistant to the highly unorthodox French designer Jean-Paul Gaultier, and "on the spot," Cathy Horyn wrote for the *New York Times* (August 28, 2005), Schaefer hired him to work with her. "He was absolutely charming . . . ," Schaefer told Horyn. "He was intelligent, and he knew what he wanted to do." While holding that job Ghesquière became acquainted with Gaultier's designer Lionel Vermeil, who introduced him to designers who would later work with him—Marie-Amélie Sauvé and Nathalie Marrec.

Although Ghesquière gained valuable insights and experience while with Gaultier, the putdowns and overt animosity of many of Gaultier's employees, he told Horyn, led him to leave the firm, in 1992. For the next four years or so, he designed knitwear as a freelancer. His work entailed traveling to factories in eastern France, where, according to Horyn, "he learned to deal with the blunt demands of provincial buyers ('Stretch doesn't sell!' 'No black!')."

Stephen Lovekin/Getty Images

Nicolas Ghesquière (r.) with the actress Jennifer Connelly

In 1996, in what Horyn called a "step down," Ghesquière joined Balenciaga. That Paris fashion house was established in France in 1937 by Cristóbal Balenciaga (1895–1972), after he fled his native land during the Spanish Civil War (1936–39). Balenciaga's elegant designs for European celebrities, royalty, and members of the aristocracy—and, later, Americans including First Lady Jacqueline Kennedy—strongly influenced haute couture and, to a lesser degree, popular fashion trends for more than a quarter-century. Balenciaga's protégés included Oscar de la Renta, André Courrèges, Emanuel Ungaro, and Hubert de Givenchy. In 1968 he closed his shop and, except for rare commissions, retired. In 1986 the French fragrance company Jacques Bogart bought the rights to the Balenciaga name; beginning in 1992, with the Dutch-born Josephus Thimister as creative director, Balenciaga again offered a line of haute-couture fashions.

Ghesquière first assisted in Balenciaga's licensing department and then designed mainly uniforms, golf outfits, and funeral and mourning apparel for Asian buyers. The next year Thimister resigned (or, according to some sources, was fired). When Helmut Lang turned down an offer from Balenciaga's owner, Jacques Konckier, to take Thimister's job, Balenciaga tapped Ghesquière to replace him. Before long Ghesquière was reportedly ousted, then quickly rehired in the face of rave reviews of his debut show. In a representative assessment, Constance C. R. White, a *New York Times* (October 21, 1997) style reporter, described his designs as "a dissertation on architectural cut. Exclusively in black and white, the collection was deliberately and successfully severe. Wool dresses

floated downward as if held by invisible threads. Trousers fell so sharply and precisely they made an uninterrupted line from waist to ankle. A pagoda-sleeved coat with an obi-type sash was so impeccably cut that it appeared able to make any woman magically posture perfect." The originality of Ghesquière's designs attracted other fashion insiders as well. In particular, his slim-cut trousers, which seemed to lengthen women's legs, earned high praise and quickly became one of his signature pieces. In 1998 Ghesquière won the Vogue/VH1 Avant Garde Designer of the Year Award. Within two years of his appointment as head designer, Balenciaga's sales had doubled, though it remained in the red.

In 2001, for the first time, the Balenciaga collection included a handbag—the Lariat, a rectangular, logo-free bag made of artificially aged goat leather. Sales of the bag languished until Ghesquière came up with the idea of giving bags, just before New York City's Fashion Week, free of charge to 30 women well known in the industry, including the model Kate Moss, the actresses Charlotte Gainsbourg and Chloë Sevigny, and the newly appointed editor of French *Vogue*, Carine Roitfeld. The bag became immensely popular, with many shops reporting long waiting lists of women eager to buy it. Touted as the "it" bag of 2001, the Lariat is still considered a classic, "must-own" accessory in some circles. Internet posts about the Lariat and other Balenciaga bags in 2010 showed photos of the actress and fashion icon Mary-Kate Olsen carrying a Lariat bag and the actresses Katie Holmes, Gwyneth Paltrow, and Jennifer Connelly and the singer Christina Aguilera holding others in Balenciaga's line of bags. (Prices of the bags usually start at above $1,000.) To this day Balenciaga salespeople reportedly inform Ghesquière when noteworthy individuals appear at his stores; then he proposes that they collaborate with him: he will give them Balenciaga clothes or accessories in return for their being seen in public wearing or carrying them.

In 2001, one month after Ghesquière won the International Designer of the Year Award from the Council of Fashion Designers of America, Balenciaga was acquired by the Gucci Group (a subsidiary of PPR, which currently owns labels including Yves Saint Laurent, Alexander McQueen, and Puma). The financial and other support provided by Gucci's chief executive officer, Domenico De Sole, and the expertise of Gucci's creative director, Tom Ford, were supposed to help ensure Balenciaga's success. After 9/11, however, sales plummeted, and De Sole and Ford focused on developing Gucci, the group's most commercial label. In negotiations aimed at cutting costs, they agreed to keep Ghesquière's Paris atelier open, rather than transferring its operations to a less expensive site outside France, but refused to fund a spring-fashions runway show. Balenciaga's smaller show, held at the Gagosian Gallery, in New York City, "wowed" attendees, according to a *Los Angeles Times* (February 15, 2002) writer.

That year a brief controversy surrounded Ghesquière, after a patchwork vest from his spring ready-to-wear collection was revealed to be virtually identical to a vest designed in 1973 by Kaisik Wong, a relatively unknown California designer, who died in 1990. Ghesquière readily admitted that, mistakenly thinking that the vest was a "theatrical costume," as he told Cathy Horyn for the *New York Times* (April 9, 2002), he had copied it from a photo in the book *Native Funk & Flash* (1974), by Alexandra Jacopetti. "This is how I work," he explained. "I've always said I'm looking at vintage clothes." Noting that "copying is part of the history of fashion," Cathy Horyn suggested that the flap regarding Ghesquière's "plagiarism" simply reflected his fame and Wong's obscurity and was also driven by recent, troubling or unresolved cases of plagiarism, sampling, and ownership in the worlds of publishing, music, and art. Lawrence Lessig, a Stanford University law professor, told Horyn, "We borrow and change—that's the creative process." In an about-face during an interview with Daisy Garnett for *New York.com* (2003), Ghesquière said of the copied vest, "Absolutely I made a mistake."

In February 2003 Ghesquière exhibited his fall collection at the Dia Center, steps away from Balenciaga's newly opened boutique in the Chelsea district of New York City. According to Belinda Luscombe, writing for *Time.com* (February 24, 2003), the collection "presented difficult but fascinating ensembles, some resembling sea anemones in high boots." Assessing the same show, Janet Ozzard wrote for *InStyle.com* (February 13, 2003), "Ghesquière excels at pushing his medium to its limit. . . . But he's also a master of the classics who can toss off a perfectly cut black blazer." When Daisy Garnett visited the New York store that month, it was "full of tiny minidresses, scuba-inspired tops, and the jersey pants and cycle shorts that insiders [had] been trying to get their hands on since October," she wrote for *New York* (February 17, 2003). Ghesquière's next collection featured apparel with a "sculptured, futuristic/militaristic silhouette," Sarah Mower wrote for *InStyle.com* (October 8, 2003)—"things that give power to femininity," the designer said to her. His March 2004 collection included urban streetwear, such as aviator jackets and short coat-dresses, and his version of Cristóbal Balenciaga's balloon skirt; in October 2004 he showed flounced cocktail dresses—updates of Balenciaga's 1958 original design—and beaded jackets and coats.

In 2004 John Ray replaced Tom Ford as Gucci's creative director, and the next year Robert Polet replaced Domenico De Sole as the firm's chief executive. Ghesquière reportedly welcomed those changes, in part because of increasing artistic differences he had been experiencing with Ford and De Sole and also because under Ray and Polet, his contacts with Gucci and PPR executives increased significantly. After viewing Balenciaga's spring 2006 collection, Cathy Horyn wrote for the *New York Times* (October 5, 2005), "Street and couture, rebel outrage and high-haute sophistication—that was the balancing act pulled off by Mr. Ghesquière. . . . [He] has had nearly ten years to work out Balenciaga in his mind, and this collection represents the maturing of those ideas—the skinny pants, the patchwork dresses, the layered historicism. He was once considered a risk. He is now an example in the luxury-goods world of why it's worth the wait."

In June 2006 the actress Nicole Kidman wore a Ghesquière-designed dress at her wedding to the country singer Keith Urban. The next month an exhibition of some of Ghesquière's work was mounted at the Louvre's Museum of Fashion and Textiles, in Paris. That winter Ghesquière helped to organize an exhibit at the Museum of Decorative Arts, also in Paris, called The Past Is the Future, about Cristóbal Balenciaga and the resurrection of his couture house after his death. Along with his friend Dominique Gonzalez-Foerster, an artist, he designed a two-floor exhibit with projections of runways on its walls and dummies wearing vintage and contemporary Balenciaga apparel. A review in *Fashion FM* (April 24, 2007) described the show as "an excellent mix of past and present, avant-garde and classic, showing that Nicolas Ghesquière is more than a genius designer, his creative talent goes further[,] into modern art."

An item from Ghesquière's spring 2007 show that inspired many on-line comments was a pair of gold leggings evocative of the limbs of the *Star Wars* character C3PO; according to various sources, their cost was anywhere from $100,000 to $159,000. A widely discussed ensemble from his fall 2007 show consisted of white jodhpurs, a sporty blazer with contrasting piping, and a fringed scarf (the last of which was priced at $5,595). As an alternative to those high-end riding breeches, the Gap began selling its version of jodhpurs; their popularity led other labels to follow suit. Another item that sparked much talk was the $1,400 Sportiletto heel, a multicolored stiletto-heeled sandal with complicated bindings reminiscent of those on snowboarders' footware. The fall collection struck Elizabeth McKeekan, who reviewed it for the Glasgow, Scotland, *Herald* (October 17, 2007), as "some of the most inspiring and eclectic clothes that fashion fans have ever seen."

A Ghesquière-designed floral dress with puffy sleeves and short bouffant skirt made a splash when the actress Jennifer Connelly wore it to the premiere of the film *Reservation Road*, in October 2007. In 2008 Connelly was featured in Balenciaga's apparel ads, and Charlotte Gainsbourg appeared in ads for Balenciaga's new fragrance. A woman who serves as the "face" of Balenciaga in ads, photographed by the Dutch team of Inez van Lamsweerde and Vinoodh Matadin, must look "quite elegant and skinny with a nervous face" and not "overtly sexual," van Lamsweerde told Sally Singer for saovany.onfinite.com (November 16, 2004).

Unlike his competitors, Ghesquière has access to the extensive Balenciaga archive, a firsthand source of inspiration and guidance. In his description of his fall 2008 collection, he referred to Cristóbal Balenciaga's influence: "austere, but with a bit of Spanish drama," as Sarah Mower quoted him as saying in *InStyle.com* (February 26, 2008). "It's quite cinematographic, an idea of film noir . . . but it's really me exploring the DNA of the house, with my sci-fi things going on with the plastics and latex." The result, according to Mower, was "an extraordinary synthesis of rigorous line and shiny, high-tech surfaces." "The genius of Ghesquière's Balenciaga is that he can extrude something so smoothly modern from so many layered references," she noted. In her *InStyle.com* (September 30, 2008) review of his spring 2009 collection, she extolled the designer's "complex, futuristic synthesis of line, cut, and glinting surfaces," and she again referred to "the genius" of Ghesquière's Balenciaga, calling it his "projection of couture techniques into the world of new technology." Two Ghesquière designs—a choker and a pair of pointy shoes—appeared on a list of "30 best accessories" in the September 2008 issue of *Harper's Bazaar*. The April 2009 cover of *Vogue* showed the singer Beyoncé wearing a Ghesquière-designed off-the-shoulder gown.

In a glowing review of his latest couture collection, unveiled during Paris Fashion Week in the fall of 2010, Susannah Frankel wrote for the London *Independent* (October 1, 2010, on-line), "Ghesquière's signatures—retro-futurism, a strange mix of hard-to-identify fabrics and a respect for tradition directed into ever more uncharted territory—continue to ring out loud and clear."

Citing his "relentless sense of innovation," in 2006 *Time*'s editors included Ghesquière among the world's 100 most influential people. In 2008 Ghesquière was made a Chevalier of Arts and Letters, the French government's highest arts honor, and the Accessories Council, a nonprofit U.S. trade organization, hailed him as the Designer of the Year. In 2010 Ghesquière won the Fashion Group International's Superstar Award and was nominated for a Global Fashion Award (a new honor) in the category "most influential designer." According to Daisy Garnett in 2003, Ghesquière "is tiny and fine-boned, and he looks like a boy, but his enthusiasm is infectious." She also wrote, "His friendly and unassuming demeanor is legendary: He is modest and thoughtful, without a single hard or defensive edge." The openly gay Ghesquière has an apartment in Paris.

—T.O.

Suggested Reading: balenciaga.com; *BusinessWeek* (on-line) Oct. 17, 2005; InStyle.com; *Interview* p62+ Feb. 2010; *New York* p110+ Feb. 17, 2003; *New York Times* p8 Oct. 4, 2006, G p4 Oct. 18, 2007, (on-line) Feb. 20, 2002; *New York Times Magazine* p53+ Apr. 14, 2002; *New Yorker* p56+ July 3, 2006; *Vogue* p476+ Mar. 2001

Courtesy of Keith Gilyard

Gilyard, Keith

Feb. 24, 1952– Sociolinguist; writer; poet; educator

Address: Pennsylvania State University, Dept. of English, 20 Burrowes Bldg., University Park, PA 16802

Keith Gilyard, a professor at Pennsylvania State University (usually referred to as Penn State), is an expert in the field of sociolinguistics, the study of language as affected by social and cultural factors. He is perhaps best known for his views on African American Vernacular English (AAVE), sometimes called Ebonics. (The latter term was coined by the psychologist Robert L. Williams in 1973.) "Linguistics educators generally agree that . . . AAVE is a legitimate language variety in its own right," Gilyard explained in an article for *Insight on the News* (March 31, 1997). Referring to the public battles waged about whether AAVE should be considered a valid mode of communication in schools and other such settings, Gilyard added, "In other words, linguists do not regard AAVE the same way as the pundits and politicians who have garnered most of the media spotlight."

In addition to writing such sociolinguistic volumes as *Voices of the Self: A Study of Language Competence* (1991), which won an American Book Award; *Let's Flip the Script: An African American Discourse on Language, Literature, and Learning* (1996); and *True to the Language Game: African American Discourse, Cultural Politics, and Pedagogy* (2011), Gilyard, an accomplished poet, is the author of *American 40: Poems* (1993), *Poemographies* (2001), and *How I Figure: Poems* (2003).

An expert on the works of John Oliver Killens, the founding chair of the Harlem Writers Guild, Gilyard has also penned two books on that influential novelist, essayist, and teacher: *Liberation Memories: The Rhetoric and Poetics of John Oliver Killens* (2003) and *John Oliver Killens: A Life of Black Literary Activism* (2010).

Raymond Keith Gilyard was born in the Harlem section of New York City on February 24, 1952. Called Keith by his family, he moved with his parents and three sisters to the borough of Queens at the age of six. Entering elementary school at P.S. 149, Gilyard was one of only two black children in his class. Initially uncomfortable in his new, predominantly Jewish neighborhood, he decided to construct a separate persona when dealing with whites, and he asked his teacher and fellow students to address him only as Raymond. "They cannot meet Keith now," Gilyard told himself, as he recalled in *Voices of the Self.* "I will put someone else together for them and he will be their classmate until further notice. That will be the first step in this particular survival plan." Later, as Gilyard wrote for *Insight on the News*, "I learned how to juggle standard and vernacular [language] to my communicative benefit, a juggling that linguists call code-switching. I juggled several sub-identities into one big, complicated, code-switching identity. Even while running the streets—and running them pretty well from a street point of view—I always wanted to be a player in the public arena, in respectable forums."

As a boy Gilyard was riveted by current events. "I had my eye on the civil rights and black power movements," he wrote for *Insight on the News*, explaining that he was in grade school when the prominent Mississippi civil rights activist Medgar Evers was killed, in 1963, in junior high at the time Malcolm X was fatally shot, in 1965, and in high school when Martin Luther King Jr. was assassinated, in 1968. "I always wanted to voice opinions about the American social order and knew I had to acquire as much language power as I could to do so effectively," Gilyard wrote for *Insight on the News*. "Along the way, and because of my goals, I excelled at reading and writing. The trip was not the smoothest one and in psychic terms it was expensive. But I paid." Gilyard developed an interest in poetry as a teenager. He read extensively and has called Haki Madhubuti's *We Walk the Way of the World* an enormous influence on him. (Madhubuti, born Don Luther Lee, was a member of the Black Arts movement, the aesthetic branch of the Black Power movement.)

Gilyard earned a bachelor's degree from the City University of New York (CUNY), an M.F.A. degree from Columbia University, in New York, and a doctoral degree in education from New York University. In 1980, soon after earning his master's degree, he began teaching in Long Island City, New York, at LaGuardia Community College, one of the two-year schools in the CUNY system, and the following year he joined the faculty of CUNY's Med-gar Evers College, in the borough of Brooklyn. There, Gilyard met John Oliver Killens, who was then a Medgar Evers faculty member. In an interview with Rudy Lewis for *Chicken Bones*, a literary journal, after the 2003 publication of *Liberation Memories*, Gilyard recalled reading *The Cotillion*, Killens's satirical novel about black class divisions, when it was published, in 1971. "Back then I wasn't that serious a student of African American literature," he admitted. "I was getting up on the poetry but hadn't done much in reading the novels. I was scribbling a little prose as well as poetry, but my reading of fiction was lagging way behind my composing efforts even though my reading should have been way out in front. I think John's book came into the Langston Hughes Library in Queens . . . and since I hung around the library all the time I just bumped into it." He continued, "I got through almost all of the novel in one sitting, just read on through the night. I was drawn in by the language, the political and cultural issues addressed, and the characters." Killens co-founded the Harlem Writers Guild in the 1950s, inspired such authors as Maya Angelou, and was twice nominated for the Pulitzer Prize—for *And Then We Heard the Thunder* (1962) and *The Cotillion*—but by the late 1970s, his work was receiving little attention from the general public. Gilyard, who went on to teach at Syracuse University in 1994 and at Penn State in 1999, told Don Schanche for the *Macon (Georgia) Telegraph* (February 6, 2005) about Killens, "He's been neglected. [I've been] trying to get him back on the agenda for this generation of literary scholars."

Gilyard published *Liberation Memories: The Rhetoric and Poetics of John Oliver Killens* in 2003 and was widely praised for bringing Killens back into the spotlight. "Though [Killens] no longer has a significant readership, he played a large part in the postwar development of African American literature, a point that is made convincingly in [Gilyard's] new study . . . ," Jonathan Yardley wrote for the *Washington Post* (July 24, 2003). "Gilyard argues that Killens's influence on younger black writers, both as exemplar and as mentor, was substantial." In 2010 Gilyard published the biography *John Oliver Killens: A Life of Black Literary Activism*. "Gilyard's affection and admiration for his subject shine through his words without falling into hero worship," J. G. Stinson wrote for the *Fore-Word Review* (June 16, 2010). Herb Boyd wrote for the *New World Review* (Vol. 3, No. 11, on-line), "The book is a fantastic testament to a writer and activist who was as unstinting in his literary pursuits as he was uncompromising in his political stances. . . . Gilyard has performed an admirable service and it's hard to believe anyone will be more definitive in capturing the wide arc that Killens cut through the literary firmament."

By the time his books on Killens were published, Gilyard had already made a name for himself in the field of sociolinguistics. *Voices of the Self: A Study of Language Competence*, which had originated as his 1985 doctoral thesis, was published for a general audience in 1991. "*Voices of the Self* alternates chapters about Gilyard's own life and education with chapters examining scholarship on language acquisition and linguistic development," a description on the Annenberg Learner Web site states. "One of the key ideas underlying both sections is Gilyard's belief that the language and experiences of children must have a legitimate place in the classroom. He writes: 'A pedagogy is successful only if it makes knowledge or skills achievable while at the same time allowing students to maintain their own sense of identity.' As his own story illustrates, young African American boys can feel that there is no way to truly be themselves and also succeed in school. Gilyard writes that 'a failure to learn Standard English is more accurately termed an act of resistance: Black students affirming, through Black English, their sense of self in the face of a school system and society that deny the same.'" *Voices of the Self*, which was widely adopted as a college text, garnered an American Book Award from the Before Columbus Foundation. In 1996 Gilyard published *Let's Flip the Script: An African American Discourse on Language, Literature and Learning*. On the Web site of Wayne State University Press, Geneva Smitherman, a linguist and professor of black studies, wrote: "This latest book by Keith Gilyard is a brilliant, inspiring collection of personal essays about freedom and literacy, and the life force that can empower us in our quest to 'flip the script'"—or turn a challenging situation to one's advantage. "There are profound truths in this visionary work from a major voice in the field. Written in an engaging style by a homeboy scholar, the book is a must-read for those of us engaged in the educational enterprise."

Although the term Ebonics (a combination of the words "ebony" and "phonics") was coined in 1973, it was rarely used by either linguists or the general public. In late 1996, however, it began appearing in headlines across the country when the Oakland, California, school board passed a resolution recognizing Ebonics as the legitimate, primary language of most of its African-American pupils. The resolution contained provisions calling for "standardized tests and grade scores [to] be remedied by application of a program with teachers and aides who are certified in the methodology of featuring African Language Systems principles in instructing African American children both in their primary language and in English," and for "earmark[ing] District general and special funding" to "devise and implement the best possible academic program for imparting instruction to African American students in their primary language for the combined purposes of maintaining the legitimacy and richness of such language . . . and to facilitate their acquisition and mastery of English language skills."

A firestorm of controversy was ignited, and the board quickly reworded the resolution, explaining, as Frank Rich wrote for the *New York Times* (January 8, 1997, on-line), "that its incendiary separatist manifesto was misinterpreted and that its only intention was to recognize that black English can be a tool for teaching standard English to chronically failing students." In an article for the Linguistic Society of America's Web site, the Stanford University linguist John R. Rickford asserted, "At least some of the overwhelmingly negative reaction to the Oakland resolutions arose because the resolutions were misinterpreted as proposals to teach Ebonics itself, or to teach in Ebonics, rather than as proposals to respect and take it into account while teaching standard English." Rickford pointed out that an established method of studying language known as contrastive analysis "involves drawing students' attention to similarities and differences between Ebonics and Standard English. Since the 1960s, it has been used successfully to boost Ebonics speakers' reading and writing performance in Standard English, most recently in public schools in Dekalb County, Georgia, and Los Angeles, California."

Once Ebonics had become a topic for public discourse, however, the controversy raged on. Referring to the racist overtones of some of the discussion, Rich wrote, "Since it became clear two days after the story broke that no Oakland school (or other American public school, for that matter) is going to teach black English as a language, or accept it as an end in itself in lieu of standard English, you have to wonder if the open-and-shut yet interminable ebonics debate is carrying water for something else." He concluded, "Rather than confront the tough question of how we as a nation might actually mobilize against the meltdown of education (and everything else) in the inner city, it's far more entertaining to get sidetracked into an escapist, no-brainer debate about ebonics instead."

Gilyard gained attention when he weighed in on the debate, writing, for example, in his article for *Insight on the News*, that Ebonics "is not a broken version of any other verbal system and has the same standing among linguists as any other variety of language, be it an English version or otherwise. Like spoken languages worldwide, AAVE is fully conceptual, composed of 10 to 70 meaningful sounds; has consonants and the requisite number of vowels; has noun and verb elements; has rules of syntax; and contains statements, commands, questions and exclamations. No contemporary linguist would talk about AAVE as slang, substandard, incorrect, deficient or jive talk."

In 1997, when he was still teaching at Syracuse University, Gilyard was chosen to edit Syracuse University Press's *Spirit & Flame: An Anthology of Contemporary African American Poetry*. In the introduction to that volume, he wrote, "Whenever we poets gathered to chart our course in the lean years, that is, the period (1975 or so until now) when corporate publishers pulled the plug on the

Electric Black Poetic, we knew we had serious literary work to do beyond merely writing poems. Wishing to maintain an aesthetic fervor to help propel progressive political struggle, some of us founded journals and magazines; others began small presses and/or published our own manuscripts. Despite such vital movement, of which I was a part, I still harbored the desire, because anthologies are a key vehicle of dissemination, to edit a compendium that would hold up to a big, bad, promising, encompassing, Black, revolutionary, lyrically strutting ideal." He continued, "I haven't totally fulfilled that urge yet, but *Spirit & Flame: An Anthology of Contemporary African American Poetry* takes much of the edge off." Gilyard's own poetry has been published in the collections *American 40: Poems* (1993), *Poemographies* (2001), and *How I Figure: Poems* (2003). A review of *Poemographies* posted on the Annenberg Learner Web site states, "Gilyard's poems are nostalgic 'word pictures' of home, family, and the complications of being African American in America. Though his subjects range from New Zealand and Amadou Diallo to his grandmother's death and his lifelong attachment to fellow poet Lorenzo Thomas, Gilyard evokes the music and speech of an urban environment and sensibility in the details and rhythm of each." Gilyard explained to the Annenberg writer, "I just always felt that, as a poet, in some sense I was not just representing myself, but I was trying to speak for an experience that was shared by others who don't have the power of the word."

Gilyard's most recent book, *True to the Language Game: African American Discourse, Cultural Politics, and Pedagogy* (2011), is a collection of new and previously published scholarly essays. In addition to his own writing on sociolinguistics, Gilyard has co-edited such volumes as *Race, Rhetoric, and Composition* (1999) and *Rhetoric and Ethnicity* (2004).

Gilyard is also the editor of the textbook *African American Literature* (2004) and the author of *Composition and Cornel West: Notes Toward a Deeper Democracy* (2008). Since 2005, the same year he was inducted into the International Literary Hall of Fame for Writers of African Descent, he has held the title of distinguished professor at Penn State. Among his accolades are the Penn State Class of 1933 Medal of Distinction in the Humanities (2005) and the Faculty Scholar Medal for Outstanding Achievement in the Arts and Humanities (2006). A past chair of the Conference on College Composition and Communication, he currently serves as the president of the National Council of Teachers of English (NCTE).

—M.M.H.

Suggested Reading: *Ebony* p22 July 2003; *ForeWord Review* (on-line) June 16, 2010; *Insight on the News* p24 Mar. 31, 1997; *Macon (Georgia) Telegraph* A p1 Feb. 6, 2005; *Washington Post* C p1 July 24, 2003

Selected Books: *Voices of the Self: A Study of Language Competence*, 1991; *American 40: Poems*, 1993; *Let's Flip the Script: An African American Discourse on Language, Literature, and Learning*, 1996; *Poemographies*, 2001; *Liberation Memories: The Rhetoric And Poetics of John Oliver Killens*, 2003; *How I Figure: Poems*, 2003; *Composition and Cornel West: Notes Toward a Deeper Democracy*, 2008; *John Oliver Killens: A Life of Black Literary Activism*, 2010; *True to the Language Game: African American Discourse, Cultural Politics, and Pedagogy*, 2011

Christian Petersen/Getty Images

Ginobili, Manu

(jih-NOB-blee, MAN-u)

July 28, 1977– Basketball player

Address: San Antonio Spurs, 1 AT&T Center, San Antonio, TX 78219

The San Antonio Spurs shooting guard Manu Ginobili is "a human maraca, best when in motion, most noticeable when thumping against something solid," Sean Deveney wrote for the *Sporting News* (June 17, 2005). Since he joined the Spurs, a National Basketball League (NBA) team, in 2002, the six-foot six-inch Ginobili has established himself as one of professional basketball's most electrifying players. Known for his fearless style of play and unbridled passion and energy, he has proven to be one of the Spurs' most valuable players over the last decade, playing an integral role in their winning NBA championships in 2003, 2005, and

2007. "If future Hall of Fame forward Tim Duncan is the Spurs' soul, Ginobili is the heart, fearless, energetic and reliable," Jeff Zillgitt wrote for *USA Today* (April 29, 2010). "He is the unique star who is flashy and scrappy." With his all-around shooting and defensive skills, Ginobili won an NBA All-Star selection in 2005, and in 2008 he was named the NBA's Sixth Man of the Year (the sixth man being the team's principal substitute) and earned All-NBA Third Team honors. He is the first native of South America and first sixth man in history to receive All-NBA honors. Ginobili has also been a member of the Argentine national basketball team since 1998; he helped lead Argentina to the gold medal at the 2004 Summer Olympics, in Athens, Greece, the bronze medal at the 2008 Summer Olympics, in Beijing, China, and the silver medal at the 2002 International Basketball Federation (FIBA) World Championships. Ginobili has been widely credited with popularizing basketball in Argentina and is currently one of only two players (along with Bill Bradley) in NBA history to have won an Olympic gold medal, an NBA championship, and a Euroleague championship. Guillermo Vecchio, a former head coach of Argentina's national team, told Johnny Ludden for the *San Antonio (Texas) Express-News* (August 7, 2005), "Manu has brought Argentina to the world and the world to Argentina's doorstep." He added, "Who has done more in basketball?"

The youngest of the three sons of Jorge and Raquel Ginobili, Emanuel David "Manu" Ginobili was born on July 28, 1977 in Bahia Blanca, a port city in the Patagonia region of Argentina, about 400 miles southwest of Buenos Aires. Widely regarded as the capital of Argentine basketball, Bahia Blanca is one of the few cities in Argentina where basketball is as popular as soccer, the country's national sport. Ginobili's father, who worked in a cigar factory, played basketball in a club league and later served as president of Club Bahiense del Norte, in Bahia Blanca. His older brothers, Leandro and Sebastian, played basketball professionally, in Argentina and Spain, respectively. Ginobili's father started giving him ball-handling lessons when Manu was two. As a child Ginobili followed the lead of his brothers and tried to emulate his hero, the Chicago Bulls superstar Michael Jordan.

As a boy Ginobili watched NBA broadcasts on TV, and starting at age seven, he improved his basketball skills for hours every night at Club Bahiense del Norte. He dedicated an equal amount of time to his studies and excelled in subjects including math and geography. One of his youth-league coaches, Oscar Huevo Sanchez, noticed his talent early on. "From 10 to 15 years old, he was always the one-on-one champ, the 3-point champ," he told Ludden for the *San Antonio Express News* (September 2, 2002). Nevertheless, his small size sometimes kept Ginobili off youth teams. "People saw him so little and thin, they didn't think he could play," Sanchez told Ludden. "But he would always win them over with his style"—a fearless, hard-nosed style mirroring that of another of Ginobili's heroes, the soccer standout Diego Maradona. Another of his former coaches, Gabriel Colamarino, told Lucy Hood for the *San Antonio Express-News* (January 17, 2003) that Ginobili was "a shooter. He didn't defend anyone, so I taught him to play more with the team, to defend the basket."

Ginobili attended public schools and studied English at a language academy. He has said that if he had remained short, he might have become an accountant or worked in the tourism industry. Thanks go a growth spurt at 16, Ginobili turned professional at 18, as his brothers had, and signed with the Argentine team Andino La Rioja, which Sanchez coached. In his first game with Andino, he scored nine points in four minutes. "He had something at every age level that was a common trend in his basketball game: He wasn't inhibited; he wasn't shy," Sanchez told Ludden (September 2, 2002). After one season with Andino, Ginobili moved with Sanchez to Club Estudiantes de Bahia Blanca, in the Ligua Nacional de Baquet (National Basketball League), the top level in the Argentine league system. In the second of his two seasons with that team, he averaged 24.9 points per game. During that time he caught the attention of European clubs and NBA scouts, including the San Antonio Spurs' president, R. C. Buford (who became the team's general manager in 2002).

In 1998 Ginobili moved to Europe and signed with Basket Viola Reggio Calabria, an Italian professional team. During the 1998–99 season, he averaged 16.9 points, 2.8 rebounds, and 1.5 assists in 29 games. Although he appeared to be "little more than a sinewy bundle of potential," Fran Blinebury wrote for the *Houston Chronicle*, those numbers led the Spurs to select him in the second round of the 1999 NBA draft, as the 57th overall pick—later regarded as one of the greatest draft steals of all time. Gregg Popovich, the Spurs' head coach, told Ludden (September 2, 2002), "We didn't know how he would develop but we had already seen he could perform well in a competitive environment." Instead of signing with the Spurs, Ginobili spent one more season with Reggio Calabria, then joined Italy's Kinder Bologna in the summer of 2000.

In his first season with Kinder Bologna, Ginobili blossomed. He improved his game under the guidance of Ettore Messina, a leading European coach, and in 2001 he helped lead Kinder Bologna to win the Triple Crown: the Italian League championship, the Euroleague championship, and the Italian Cup. He was named the Italian League Most Valuable Player (MVP) and the Euroleague Finals MVP for the 2000–01 season. During the 2001–02 season, Ginobili averaged 19.9 points, 4.3 rebounds, 2.2 assists, and 4.3 steals per game and was again named the Italian League MVP. In Euroleague play that year, he averaged 15.2 points, 3.6 rebounds, and 3.1 assists in 22 games. During the summer of 2002, Ginobili joined the Argentine national team for the FIBA World Championships, in Indianapolis, Indiana. Argentina upset the U.S. in the semifinals, becoming the first country in history to beat a U.S. team made up of NBA players. The Argentinians then lost to Yugoslavia in the championship final on a disputed call and took home the silver medal. Ginobili was subsequently named to the all-tournament team, despite suffering a sprained right ankle in the tournament.

Following his breakthrough performance at the 2002 World Championships, in which he averaged 14.1 points despite playing for limited minutes, Ginobili took advantage of an opt-out clause in his Kinder Bologna contract and signed a two-year, $2.94 million deal with the Spurs. During his rookie season Ginobili was used mainly in a reserve role and played backup to the veteran shooting guard Steve Smith. Because of injuries he missed 11 games during the first half of that season; in March 2003, during the second half, he was named the Western Conference Rookie of the Month. In 2002–03 he appeared in 69 regular-season games and averaged 7.6 points, 2.3 rebounds, 2.0 assists, and 1.4 steals in 20.7 minutes per game. He was also named to the NBA's All-Rookie Second Team and was an integral part of the Spurs' championship run. The Spurs, who had a 60–22 regular-season record, defeated the Phoenix Suns, the defending champion Los Angeles Lakers, and the Dallas Mavericks, successively, in the first three rounds of the play-offs, before overcoming the New Jersey Nets in the 2003 NBA Finals to win their second NBA championship. After that victory Ginobili was named Argentina's Sportsman of the Year and met Argentina's president, Nestor Kirchner. A gym in Bahia Blanca was named in his honor.

Ginobili enjoyed a bigger role in 2003–04, making 38 starts in 77 games and averaging 29.4 minutes per game. He increased his numbers in all major categories, averaging 12.8 points, 4.5 rebounds, 3.8 assists, and 1.8 steals per game. He finished seventh in the NBA in steals and was the Spurs' leading scorer in 14 games, second only to Tim Duncan. He scored in double figures in 54 of 77 games, recording 20 or more points 11 times and 30 points once. The Spurs finished third in the Western Conference with a 57–25 record but lost the chance to defend their title after losing to the Los Angeles Lakers in the second round of the play-offs. In the 2003–04 postseason, Ginobili averaged 13.0 points, 5.3 rebounds, 3.1 assists, and 1.7 steals in 10 games.

In the summer of 2004, Ginobili returned to the Argentine national team for the Olympics, held in Athens. After posting a 3–2 record in their pool, Argentina upset the U.S. in the semifinals and then defeated Italy in the final to win their first-ever gold medal. Ginobili was named the tournament's MVP after leading the team in both scoring (16.7 points per game) and assists (3.3 per game). The landmark victory sparked a basketball craze in Argentina, and members of the gold medal–winning squad were greeted as heroes. One of Ginobili's teammates, Luis Scola, now a power forward with the NBA's Houston Rockets, recalled to Johnny

Ludden for the *San Antonio Express-News* (August 10, 2005), "It was like a revolution. Basketball was the second sport in the country, but always so far, far away from soccer. For one week, it changed. Basketball was what everybody was focused on. People in restaurants, bars, nightclubs [were] looking at us." Ginobili's huge following forced him to travel around Argentina with a phalanx of guards. That summer he signed a six-year, $48 million deal with the Spurs. Shortly afterward Argentine police foiled a kidnapping plot in which one of his brothers was the target.

During the 2004–05 season, Ginobili started each of the 74 games in which he appeared. He achieved career-high numbers in points (16.0), assists (3.9), and minutes per game (29.6) and finished with a team-leading average of 1.6 steals per game, good for 11th in the league. He also scored in double figures in 62 games, scoring 20 or more points 18 times and 30 points four times. In January 2005 Ginobili recorded a career-high 48 points and a team-high six assists in a single game—an overtime victory (128–123) over the Phoenix Suns. The next month he was named to his first NBA All-Star team, as a reserve for the Western Conference. Alongside the center Tim Duncan and the point guard Tony Parker, Ginobili helped lead the Spurs to the Southwest Division title, with a 59–23 record. Dubbed the Spurs' "Big Three"—and rivaling other "Big Threes" in the NBA, including the Boston Celtics' Ray Allen, Paul Pierce, and Kevin Garnett and the Miami Heat's LeBron James, Dwyane Wade, and Chris Bosh—they extended their momentum into the 2004–05 play-offs, in which the Spurs defeated the Denver Nuggets, the Seattle Supersonics, and the Phoenix Suns, in the first round, Western Conference semifinals, and Western Conference finals, respectively. Then, in the 2005 NBA Finals, the Spurs defeated the Detroit Pistons in seven games to win their third NBA championship. Ginobili averaged career-high postseason numbers in scoring (20.8 points per game) and rebounds (5.8 rebounds per game) and finished one vote shy of sharing the NBA Finals MVP Award with Duncan.

Ginobili appeared in 65 games and missed 16 because of foot and ankle injuries during the 2005–06 season. He experienced a drop in numbers, averaging 15.1 points, 3.6 assists, 3.5 rebounds, and 1.6 steals per game. The Spurs advanced to the postseason for the ninth consecutive year, then lost to the Dallas Mavericks in seven games in the second round of the play-offs. In the postseason Ginobili averaged 18.4 points, 4.5 rebounds, 3.0 assists, and 1.5 steals in 13 contests. During the summer of 2006, he returned to the Argentine national team for the FIBA World Championships, held in Japan. Argentina cruised to a 5–0 record in their pool before losing to the eventual gold-medal winner, Spain, in the semifinals, 75–74. Ginobili subsequently helped the Spurs win their fourth NBA championship, in 2006–07, when they swept the Cleveland Cavaliers in four games. That season he was used more as a spark plug off the bench, starting in only 36 of the 75 games in which he appeared and averaging 27.5 minutes, 16.5 points, 4.4. rebounds, 3.5 assists, and 1.5 steals per game. Ginobili was the only player in the league that season to average more than 15 points per game while playing an average of fewer than 30 minutes per contest. Commenting on his style of play, Gregg Popovich told Jeff Zillgitt, "He's angular and almost looks helter-skelter, but it's helter-skelter with a purpose and a plan. He combines some incredible ball skills with great desire, great passion and an unbelievable will to win, and that's what makes him special."

During the 2007–08 season, Ginobili was the Spurs' main contributor off the bench; he posted career highs in the 74 games in which he appeared, in average number of points (19.5), rebounds (4.8), assists per game (4.5), and three-point field-goal percentage (0.401). That year he was named the NBA's Sixth Man of the Year and was selected for the All-NBA Third Team. Ginobili thus became the first South American and first sixth man in history to earn All-NBA honors. The Spurs, meanwhile, finished third in the Western Conference, with a 56–26 record, then lost to the Los Angeles Lakers in the Western Conference Finals in five games. Despite suffering an ankle injury in the first round of the play-offs, in a series against the Phoenix Suns, Ginobili succeeded in putting up solid numbers, averaging 17.8 points, 3.8 rebounds, and 3.9 assists in 17 postseason games. Later that summer he was cleared to play at the 2008 Olympics, in Beijing, where he led Argentina to the bronze medal.

After aggravating his ankle injury in Argentina's Olympic semifinal loss to the U.S., Ginobili underwent successful arthroscopic surgery on that ankle. While he recuperated he missed the first 12 games of the 2008–09 season. Ginobili appeared in only 44 games that season because of other injuries and missed the entire postseason after he suffered a stress fracture to his right fibula. The Spurs lost to the Dallas Mavericks in five games in the first round of the play-offs, marking their first round-one exit since 2000. Ginobili returned to form during the 2009–10 season, when he averaged 16. 5 points, 3.8 rebounds, a career-high 4.9 assists, and 1.4 steals per game. He helped the Spurs advance to the Western Conference semifinals, where they were swept by the Phoenix Suns in four games. In April 2010 Ginobili signed a three-year, $39 million contract extension with the Spurs. He returned as a full-time starter for the Spurs during the 2010–11 season.

Ginobili has been married to the former Marianela Orono since July 2004. On May 16, 2010 the couple welcomed the birth of twins, Dante and Nicola. Ginobili is fluent in Italian and English as well as Spanish. He enjoys watching movies and listening to music in his leisure time. He is an Argentine ambassador to UNICEF and has been an active participant in the NBA-FIBA program Basket-

ball Without Borders, whose goal is to increase global goodwill through basketball.

—C.C.

Suggested Reading: *Houston (Texas) Chronicle* Sports p1+ July 17, 2005; NBA.com; *Oregonian Sports* D p1 Feb. 18, 2003; *San Antonio (Texas) Express-News* C p1+ Sep. 2, 2002, C p1 Jan. 17, 2003, C p1+ Aug. 7, 2005, C p1+ Aug. 10, 2005; San Antonio Spurs Official Web site; *Sporting News* NBA Finals p10+ June 17, 2005; *USA Today* C p1+ Apr. 29, 2010

Courtesy of Addeo Music International

Glasper, Robert

Apr. 6, 1978– Jazz pianist

Address: c/o Blue Note Records, 150 Fifth Ave., New York, NY 10011

The worlds of jazz and hip-hop are usually separate, but some musicians—such as the pianist Robert Glasper—are deeply involved and highly respected in both. On the one hand, Glasper has toured with the soul singer Maxwell and the hip-hop artists Q-Tip and Mos Def. On the other, he has played with such jazz luminaries as the trumpeter Roy Hargrove and the bassist Christian McBride. Glasper had been playing on the New York City jazz scene since the late 1990s and had already released an album on an independent label when, in 2005, he made headlines as the latest artist signed by the influential and respected jazz label Blue Note Records. His latest record for the label, *Double Booked* (2009), is divided into two sections: the first is his take on the straight-ahead jazz trio, and the second combines jazz, funk, soul, and hip-hop. "I think what I'm doing is right in line with where it's supposed to be," Glasper told Scott Frampton for *Esquire* (November 19, 2009). "I'm playing what's fresh, what's now. It's not even of the future; it's now, but because jazz is so caught up with the past, now seems far ahead." *Double Booked* has been very well received by music critics, and a song from the album, "All Matter," was nominated for a Grammy Award for best urban/alternative performance. Mike Flynn wrote for *Time Out* (August 27, 2009), "Glasper's kinetic keyboard skills dazzle throughout this album. . . . While hip hoppers have long since made a virtue of 'borrowing' jazz samples, Glasper's genius is to produce and amalgamate these elements live and direct." That amalgamation might have inspired Nate Chinen's take on Glasper's music; Chinen wrote for the *New York Times* (November 3, 2005), "The chief attraction of Mr. Glasper's aesthetic is a sound that is instantly accessible, but with a light touch of the opaque." Glasper's other records on Blue Note are *Canvas* (2005) and *In My Element* (2007).

Robert Glasper was born on April 6, 1978 in Missouri City, Texas, about 20 miles southwest of Houston. His first musical influence was his mother, Kim Yvette, a celebrated jazz, blues, and gospel singer in Houston. She would often bring her son to nightclubs so he could hear her sing. There was a piano in Glasper's home, and from the age of seven, he would "bang around" on it, he told *Current Biography* (the source of quotes in this article unless otherwise noted); within a few years he could play by ear songs he had heard on the radio. Until the age of 12, Glasper concentrated mainly on playing sports, particularly running track, but starting in junior high school, he became more and more absorbed in music. Around that time he began playing piano in church, where he honed his skills as a performer. By the age of 16, he was performing at three churches several times a week; one of them had a congregation of 5,000. His mother's jazz band routinely rehearsed at her house, and the band's pianist occasionally taught Glasper jazz chords, chord changes, and songs. At that age Glasper mostly knew how to play gospel music, but he was eager to learn jazz: "There are certain ways you can voice certain chords that can suggest a style of music, so [the pianist] kind of taught me hip, cool voicings to play, 'cause sometimes I would play things in a very old-fashioned grandmother way and he'd be like, 'That's old. This is the hip way to play it.' I'd play [a chord] in the root position, a very vanilla, boring kind of way, and he'd say, 'Don't start with that note. Lead with this note, play that note second, this note third. . . .' That's where I got the first real taste of jazz right in front of me."

In the mid-1990s Glasper attended the High School for the Performing and Visual Arts in Houston. Although he never received any formal piano training (even at school), his life involved almost nonstop music. On weekdays at his high school, he played in a jazz combo and a jazz big band, learned harmony, and studied song charts; on weekends he played gospel music at church. The latter proved to be an enduring influence. "Growing up in church gave me my way of hearing harmony," Glasper told Ted Panken in an interview for jazz.com (August 28, 2009). "I would take church and gospel harmonies and mix them with the jazz harmonies I know. That's not too normal in jazz. . . . I would write gospel tunes all the time, and people would say about my gospel tunes, 'They sound a little jazzy.' But then, when I played jazz, they say, 'I hear gospel.' I try not to ignore any part of my background or what I hear." Glasper elaborated on what playing in church taught him about touching people's emotions: "[At] church, that's when you develop being spiritual in music, being able to touch someone with a song. When you play in church, the audience, the congregation, the choir, are all reacting to you as well. Everything you play, the singers are reacting to you, the audience is reacting to that, and it's all very spiritual. I think that's another part of music that I take from church as well—not playing for the sake of playing but for the spiritual aspect, the emotion, the realness of it, the organic honesty of the whole thing."

After graduating from high school, in 1997, Glasper moved to New York City, where he attended the New School's jazz and contemporary-music program on a full scholarship. Within a few years Glasper's taste in music had begun to expand. He had broadened his jazz palate, listening to the work of such idiosyncratic jazz pianists as Thelonious Monk, and crossed the border into socially conscious hip-hop (songs by Q-Tip, Mos Def, and the Roots, among others) and neo-soul (the work of singers including D'Angelo, Maxwell, and Erykah Badu). While still at the New School, from which he graduated in 2001, Glasper began performing on the road with the saxophonist Kenny Garrett and the trumpeter Roy Hargrove; playing as a sideman for the bassist Christian McBride and the guitarist Russell Malone; touring with the live hip-hop bands of Q-Tip and Mos Def; and playing with the jazz/neo-soul singer Bilal, whom he had met at the New School. Also, perhaps most important for his development as a bandleader, he had a weekly gig at the Up Over Jazz Café, which was around the corner from his apartment, in the borough of Brooklyn. Every Thursday Glasper led a jazz trio, which gave him a chance to write songs, try them out on audiences, experiment, and improvise, all on a new Yamaha grand piano. (Over time the trio included different drummers and bass players.) That experience helped him to find his sound. "Sometimes," he recalled, "there was only the bartender there. And sometimes, there were 60, 70 people there." In a review of one of Glasper's performances at the café in 2003, when he had been playing there for four years, Ben Ratliff wrote for the *New York Times* (April 14, 2003), "Mr. Glasper was exploding songs into fantasias. There is a little [of the pianist] Keith Jarrett in him, not only because he ignores any boundaries that may lie between traditional postwar jazz piano and freer, more gestural playing, but also because he gets wrapped up in the music, continually changing its mood, its tempo, its overall hue." His performance, Ratliff concluded, was "impressively articulated."

That year Glasper released *Mood* (2003), his first album as bandleader, which consisted mostly of songs performed with his trios and included other tracks with guitar, tenor sax, and vocals by Bilal. Glasper wrote six of the nine tracks, and even the covers had noticeably original arrangements. His versions of Herbie Hancock's "Maiden Voyage," with Bilal on vocals, was inspired by the alternative rock group Radiohead's "Everything in Its Right Place," a song from their experimental album *Kid A* (2000); and Irving Berlin's "Blue Skies" was reharmonized in a way that left Glasper's fingerprints on the melody. Glasper's own compositions on the album included the hard-bop "L.N.K. Blues," the waltz "In Passing," and the hip-hop influenced "Interlude." Although *Mood* was well-received by many jazz critics, the record—released on the independent Spanish label Fresh Sound New Talent—received little to no coverage in mainstream magazines and newspapers. "Robert Glasper, as the main melodic voice, excels in providing crisp melodic statements," Gerard Cox wrote for allaboutjazz.com (April 21, 2003). "His soloing is not yet terribly distinctive but there are compensations in the form of a nice, lighter touch and in restraining his considerable chops in the service of space." One major exception to the lack of mainstream press coverage was Ben Ratliff's consistently laudatory reviews of Glasper's live performances. In the *New York Times* (July 5, 2004), Ratliff observed that Glasper's "first set at the Fat Cat [jazz club the previous week] suggested that his trio—with Brandon Owens on bass and Damion Reid on drums—deserves comparison with the best of the newer piano trios, those led by Jason Moran, Bill Charlap and Brad Mehldau." The following month Glasper got his first headlining gig at one of New York City's marquee jazz clubs, the Blue Note. In attendance that evening was the Blue Note Records president and CEO, Bruce Lundvall, who, having heard *Mood*, wanted to see Glasper perform live. Lundvall liked what he heard, and the label asked Glasper to record five songs as a further test of his skills. Again Lundvall was favorably impressed. (His professional success aside, 2004 was an extraordinarily trying year for Glasper; in April his mother, age 43, and her husband were found murdered in their Texas home.)

Glasper was signed by Blue Note in April 2005. The music press made much of his being the first up-and-coming instrumentalist signed by the label in five years. *Canvas* (2005), his first album with the label, got a good deal of attention and led to more gigs at marquee New York jazz clubs, such as a weeklong residence at the Village Vanguard. The history and prestige of Blue Note Records almost guaranteed that *Canvas* would have a bigger audience than Glasper's previous release, and the pianist felt the pressure of the expectations placed on the new record. "Blue Note, in its rich history, has all my favorite pianists on it," Glasper said. "So here I come now. I'm the new guy. A lot of cats have been trying to get signed and they didn't get signed, so it's a proving-yourself kind of deal." (Among the dozens of great jazz artists who recorded with the label in the past are Miles Davis, John Coltrane, and the pianists Horace Silver, Herbie Hancock, Bud Powell, and Monk.) Having played on the trumpeter Terence Blanchard's album *Bounce* (2003), Glasper had learned a "recording trick" for easing pressure in the studio: having a few drinks. The idea was to create a jazz-club atmosphere; while no one got drunk during the recordings, Glasper found that drinking two or three glasses of wine and choosing the right recording time—afternoon or evening rather than morning—could make a positive difference in the quality of the record. Glasper had his drummer, Damion Reid, and bassist, Vincente Archer, accompany him on most of the album, on such tracks as the melodic, complex "Rise and Shine" and his take on Herbie Hancock's "Riot," the only cover song on the album. Glasper saw the album as a vehicle to showcase his strengths as a composer. "A lot of cats, when they come out, they'll do a lot of standards or blueses, because that's what people are used to—to prove themselves as a good piano player, like check out how fast I can play. . . . I didn't want to do that," he said. Citing Stevie Wonder as one whose music has the power to inspire and even heal the listener, Glasper said, "That's the kind of album I was trying to make." In a review for the *Washington Post* (November 4, 2005), Geoffrey Himes found that Glasper's technical prowess still outweighed his originality: "Glasper runs through chords and arpeggios in both hands as briskly and fluidly as some pianists handle single notes in the right hand, and the thickened harmonies he accumulates along the way often make his piano trio sound like a quartet. . . . But Glasper's compositions and solos still lack definition, and his waves of notes often sound more decorative than momentous."

As suggested by the title of his next album, *In My Element* (2007), Glasper was becoming more comfortable with the attention he had been receiving and loosening up musically. Whereas his previous album had included guest musicians, his new work focused exclusively on the trio. Because the trio had been on tour with the material for some time and had been playing together for four years, in the studio they recorded most of the songs in one take. "It didn't just sound like three cats getting together," Glasper said. "It sounded like a group." The consensus regarding *In My Element* was that Glasper had, to a greater extent than before, developed his own voice; Glasper agreed with that assessment, saying, "I think this is my classic record." With the instrumentation limited to bass, drums, and piano, Glasper's piano voice could be heard more clearly. In a review for *New York* (April 9, 2007), Martin Johnson observed, "The music is direct, forceful, inventive, and accessible without pandering."

Glasper's most ambitious and critically acclaimed record to date is *Double Booked* (2009). The title is a reference to Glasper's involvement in both the jazz and the soul/hip-hip worlds, which sometimes leads to his being booked in two different venues in one night. Stylistically the album is divided in two: the first half, the Robert Glasper Trio, with Chris Dave on drums and Vincente Archer on bass, is Glasper's take on the acoustic jazz trio, which includes the improvisatory, post-bop "No Worries," the joyful, carefree "Yes I'm Country (And That's OK)," and the only cover on the album's first half, Monk's "Think of One." The second half, the Robert Glasper Experiment, combines jazz, funk, hip-hop, and soul. With Dave on drums, the Experiment also features Derrick Hodge on electric bass, Casey Benjamin on saxophone and vocoder, Jahi Sundance on turntables, and Bilal and Mos Def on vocals. Although the Trio and the Experiment are quite different, Ratliff wrote for the *New York Times* (August 30, 2009), "both halves use slow-rolling grooves, excitable solo passages that gather up stride piano in [their] reach, and intricate rhythm-section arrangements as sharp and stylized as Thelonious Monk's."

Years before his solo debut, Glasper had begun to appear as a sideman—on Bilal's *1st Born Second* (2001), Jeremy Pelt's *Profile* (2002), Robert Hurst's *Unrehurst* (2002), Terence Blanchard's *Bounce* (2003), and others. Glasper has continued to contribute his talents to a variety of records, both jazz and hip-hop, among them Jaleel Shaw's *Perspective* (2005) and *Optimism* (2008), Marcus Strickland's *Twi-Life* (2006), Kanye West's *Late Registration* (2005), Meshell Ndegeocello's *The World Has Made Me the Man of My Dreams* (2007), and Q-Tip's *The Renaissance* (2008). Glasper plans to start recording his new album in April 2011. Set for an August release, it will be devoted entirely to his hip-hop/soul Experiment project, which will include guest musicians such as Common, Meshell Ndegeocello, Mos Def, and Erykah Badu. Glasper will also continue to work with his jazz trio. "That," he said, "is my first love."

—D.K.

Suggested Reading: allmusic.com; *Boston Globe* E p16 Jan. 13, 2006; jazz.com Aug 28, 2009; *New York* p82+ Apr. 9, 2007; *New York Times* E p6 July 5, 2004, E p 24 Apr. 15, 2005, Arts and Leisure p16 Aug. 30, 2009

Selected Recordings: *Mood*, 2003; *Canvas*, 2005; *In My Element*, 2007; *Double Booked*, 2009

Gleick, James

(glik)

Aug. 1, 1954– Science writer

Address: c/o Pantheon Books, 212 E. 50th St., New York, NY 10022

James Gleick writes dense yet highly readable books on science and technology. In his first book, *Chaos: Making a New Science* (1987), he set out to illuminate the increasingly significant role of chaos theory in our lives and in academia. (Chaos theory is the study of dynamic systems, such as the economy or the weather, in which very small differences in initial conditions may have significant consequences.) *Chaos* became a best-seller as well as a finalist for the National Book Award and the Pulitzer Prize. Gleick's most recent work, *The Information: A History, a Theory, a Flood* (2011), combines history, logic, science, linguistics, original research, and illuminating anecdotes from the worlds of science and technology to trace the evolution of human methods of communicating information—from the development of alphabets to the age of computers. That book, Janet Maslin wrote in her review for the *New York Times* (March 7, 2011), "is so ambitious, illuminating and sexily

theoretical that it will amount to aspirational reading for many of those who have the mettle to tackle it. Don't make the mistake of reading it quickly. Imagine luxuriating on a Wi-Fi-equipped desert island with Mr. Gleick's book, a search engine and no distractions. *The Information* is to the nature, history and significance of data what the beach is to sand." Gleick's best-selling biographies of the scientists Richard Feynman and Isaac Newton were each short-listed for the Pulitzer Prize. His books have been translated into 25 languages.

James Gleick was born in New York City on August 1, 1954. His father, Donen, worked as a lawyer in Manhattan; his mother, Beth, was a newsletter editor. Beth Gleick was also the author of *Time Is When* (1960), an illustrated children's book about the concept of time. From a very young age, Gleick was found to be highly intelligent. His younger sister, Elizabeth (called Betsy), recalled in an interview with David Diamond for *Wired* (August 1999), "The talk was always about how brilliant he was, how brilliant and incredibly focused." (Gleick also has a younger brother, Peter.) At Riverdale Country School, in the New York City borough of the Bronx, Gleick earned very good grades in math and science. In 1972 he enrolled at Harvard College, in Cambridge, Massachusetts, where, after deciding that he was not equipped to become a mathematician, he majored in English and linguistics.

Phyllis Rose, courtesy of Random House

James Gleick

He also began writing for the Harvard Crimson, the campus daily newspaper. After graduating, in 1976, Gleick moved to Minneapolis, Minnesota, where he helped found *Metropolis*, an alternative weekly paper; he served as the paper's managing editor until it folded, the following year. One of his employees at *Metropolis* was a recent college graduate, Cynthia Crossen. The two began a romantic relationship and married two years later.

In 1977 Gleick joined the writing staff of the *New York Times*, where his science reporting planted the seeds of his first book. After working in a series of positions at the *Times*, including assistant Metro editor, Gleick became one of the paper's more prominent science reporters. His first article for the *New York Times Magazine* (August 21, 1983) was a cover story about the mathematician/linguist Douglas Hofstadter. Not long afterward Gleick began writing for the weekly Science Times section. In his reporting, Diamond wrote, "Gleick detected a common theme running through many of his subjects: a search for patterns in seemingly random events and structures that was at the theoretical core of chaos theory. The more he learned about chaos, the more interested he became." Speaking to Diamond, Gleick elaborated: "The basic lessons of science were not necessarily connected to stuff that we care about, but it struck me that that wasn't true of chaos [theory]. Chaos was a science that was uniting all kinds of disciplines." As a result of his science writing for the *New York Times*, Gleick was sought out by book publishers and signed a contract to write a book about chaos theory.

In *Chaos: Making a New Science* (1987), Gleick set out to introduce the public to chaos theory and to the often eccentric scientists and researchers who were making the greatest impact on the field. Gleick began the book with the story of a key event in the development of chaos theory: In 1961 the meteorologist Edward Lorenz used a set of computerized mathematical equations to simulate and study weather systems, taking into account the interactions of many factors (such as wind, atmospheric pressure, and humidity) to make a forecast. He then reran part of the computer operation, entering what he thought was the same data; he was unaware that he was entering numbers up to only three decimal places instead of six, as he had the first time. He marveled when he got a different result. He then realized that he had input less-precise numbers and came to a conclusion that would launch chaos theory: seemingly small differences in a dynamic system (such as Earth's atmosphere) could yield significantly different and unexpected results. A decade later those insights led Lorenz to originate the term "butterfly effect." (In his 1972 paper "Predictability: Does the Flap of a Butterfly's Wings in Brazil Set Off a Tornado in Texas?" Lorenz argued that the seemingly infinite interconnectedness of nature makes initial factors—however small—significant in ways that are hard to understand.) By the 1980s physicists, mathematicians, biologists, and other researchers who were studying chaos theory—in their quest for finding "a regular irregularity," as Gleick puts it—were no longer on the fringes of the scientific establishment. (Eventually other dynamic systems, such as the economy, would be examined through the lens of chaos theory.) Gleick spent the remainder of the book acquainting the reader with the lives and research of modern chaos theorists, such as Benoit Mandelbrot, Mitchell Feigenbaum, and J. Doyne Farmer. Their goal is to understand and predict the behavior of seemingly unpredictable systems.

Chaos had a considerable effect on those whose work it discussed. Doyne Farmer told Diamond, "Gleick's book changed the whole field. People started to take themselves too seriously. Those who were left out [of the book] got pissed off at those who weren't. Things got ugly." The Nobel Prize–winning physicist Murray Gell-Mann, in an interview with Diamond, complained that Gleick's book "exaggerated the importance" of chaos theory. That view, however, was not the consensus in the scientific community. *Chaos: Making a New Science* received generally excellent reviews, became a best-seller, and was a finalist for both the National Book Award and the Pulitzer Prize. "Mr. Gleick is a skilled science reporter and his writing is always clear and sometimes brilliant," Frank Kendig wrote for the *New York Times* (October 15, 1987), "but he takes us through difficult, often mindboggling territory. . . . Unlike relativity and quantum mechanics, chaos is a science of everyday things—of art and economics, of biological rhythms and traffic jams, of waterfalls and weather. Curiously, the very familiarity of these phenomena makes the new discoveries more difficult to comprehend and absorb. Almost every one of Mr. Gleick's paragraphs contains a jolt, and the urge to reread them is strong. The questions they instill in the reader do not arise from lack of understanding or clarity; rather, they spring from the revolutionary nature of the material—can I believe what I just read? Can this really be true?"

The success of *Chaos* led to a seven-figure, two-book deal for Gleick, who now had the financial freedom to write books full-time. (He left the *Times* in 1988; he would later return as a columnist.) Gleick's next book was *Genius: The Life and Science of Richard Feynman* (1992), a biography of the brilliant, eccentric Nobel Prize–winning physicist. Early in his career Feynman took part in the Manhattan Project—the United States' ultimately successful quest to build an atomic bomb during World War II—and emerged as one of the most revered physicists of the second half of the 20th century. He became known to the general public in 1985, with the publication of his best-selling autobiographical book *Surely You're Joking, Mr. Feynman!* The following year he gained even more popularity by helping to investigate the explosion of the space shuttle *Challenger*. Feynman's demonstration of the cause of the disaster, for which he used a model of the shuttle, a C clamp, a rubber O-ring, and a glass of cold water, was seen by 250 million people on prime-time television. Gleick also covered the physicist's private life, including his three marriages, his love of pranks, and his bongo-playing. A review of *Genius* for the *Economist* (January 30, 1993) stated: "Understanding theories and understanding people are different experiences and skills; in this admirable life of [a] theorist, Mr Gleick helps his readers to do both at the same time, and thus to learn something about how great ideas are born." *Genius* became a best-seller and was short-listed for the Pulitzer Prize.

In 1993 Gleick, along with a friend who was a programmer, founded the Pipeline, a successful Internet-service company. Gleick served as the Pipeline's chairman and chief executive officer until 1995, when it was bought in a multimillion-dollar deal by PSINet, an Internet-service provider. Also in the mid-1990s, Gleick wrote a column, "Fast Forward," for the *New York Times Magazine*. During its four-year run, the column, as Diamond put it, "critically evaluated the limitations and frustrations of technology, and the scramble to define its future." One of Gleick's most important pieces was a 1995 cover story about the U.S. government's antitrust action against Microsoft, in which he argued that Microsoft was indeed seeking to establish monopolies.

On a personal level, the 1990s brought tragedy for Gleick. He had started taking flying lessons in the late 1980s, drawn to the challenge and adventure that flying offered. In the summer of 1997, he purchased a small airplane, an 11-year-old, two-seat, rear-engine Long-EZ. On the morning of December 20, 1997, Gleick flew the plane with his adopted eight-year-old son and only child, Harry, sitting in the passenger seat; Harry had flown with his father many times before. This time, however, the plane landed short of the runway, crashing into an embankment. Gleick and his son were trapped for half an hour before help arrived, and Harry was pronounced dead at the scene. Gleick, badly injured, was taken to a hospital. As a result of the crash, he lost his left leg (he soon got a prosthesis) and spent five months at a rehabilitation center, recovering and learning to walk again. Even after his release from the hospital, Gleick continued with physical therapy for many months.

While recovering, Gleick returned to writing—working first on the "Fast Forward" column, then on his third book. Compared with the very positive reception of Gleick's first two books, the critical response to his next one was lukewarm. *Faster: The Acceleration of Just About Everything* (1999) presented the case that the key feature of modern life is people's ever-changing relationship with time. Everything—such as technology, communication, and popular entertainment—is getting faster, Gleick contended. In 37 short chapters Gleick provided facts and examples to illustrate that point, asking such questions as whether the human brain and body will be able to keep up with the increasing pace of modern technology, work, and travel. Many critics felt that the book itself moved too quickly, providing a wealth of facts but without a context in which to consider them or a coherent thesis. The writer and sociologist Todd Gitlin, in a review for the *Los Angeles Times* (September 12, 1999), called the book "engaging but breathless," writing that although "Gleick's examples are sometimes surprising and fun, they tend to pile up rather than accumulate into an argument." Gleick's next book, *What Just Happened: A Chronicle from the Information Frontier* (2002), was better received. That book comprises essays, published in the *New York Times* between 1992 and 2001, on various technology-related topics and issues and their social and cultural significance; the subjects include on-line advertising and battles over Web domain names. In a book review for the *New Scientist* (July 13, 2002), Wendy M. Grossman observed that the essays "have held up remarkably well."

For *Isaac Newton* (2003) Gleick used original documents and a great number and variety of scholarly texts to recount the life and work of one of the most famous figures in the history of science, known for discovering the three laws of motion and the law of universal gravitation, among other contributions. In a review for the *Los Angeles Times* (July 20, 2003), Timothy Ferris found the book to be "an elegantly written, insightful work that brings Newton to life and does him justice. Its brevity, which may or may not have been premeditated, seems to have resulted from a rare and relentless insistence on saying solely what can be said confidently and afresh." In addition to his subject's work and theories, Gleick touched upon the man's disposition—Newton was known as a mean person and a loner—and Newton's awareness of the shortcomings of his theories and speculation about future discoveries, such as that of a force that exists between microscopic objects at the shortest distances from one another, which we now know as nuclear force. The first 14 "gracefully composed chapters," Ferris wrote, make for an "exemplary" biography; he called the 15th chapter, in which Gleick examined Newton's place in history, "a small masterpiece." *Isaac Newton* was shortlisted for the Pulitzer Prize.

Gleick spent the next seven years working on his latest book, *The Information: A History, a Theory, a Flood* (2011). He told Kevin Kelly for *Wired* (March 2011), "I've been thinking of this book my whole career. When I was working on *Chaos*, [scientists] would try to explain Claude Shannon's invention of information theory to me. I didn't understand it at the time. Investigating Shannon's ideas became the fulcrum of this book." The definite article of the book's title ("the"), often used for unitary concepts such as "the" Internet or "the" universe, is not an arbitrary choice. Gleick argued that practically everything is information, from DNA to the contents of e-mail messages, and that the history of humanity can best be told in terms of how we have communicated information. *The Information*, Tim Wu wrote for *Slate.com* (March 27, 2011), is "a highly ambitious and generally brilliant effort to tie together centuries of disparate scientific efforts to understand information as a meaningful concept. For a society that believes itself to live in an information age, the subject could hardly be more important." Gleick provided a history of information technology, starting with the development of alphabets and moving on to the telegraph, the telephone, the fax machine, and the computer, all while making the case that those innovations are all part of a continuum, a whole in which one technology evolves from its predecessor(s). As Gleick had done many times in previous works, he included in his book tales of odd, interesting figures, the most important in *The Information* being Claude Shannon, a Bell Labs engineer/mathematician whose 1948 technical-journal paper "A Mathematical Theory of Communication" is considered the founding document of information theory. (Also, Shannon's master's thesis, written in the late 1930s, provided the framework for digital computers—the manipulation of two symbols, 1 and 0—that is still used today.) In the 1948 paper Shannon famously argued that communication technology has to be concerned only with transmitting messages, not with the meanings, if any, of the messages. Gleick's "mind-bending exploration of theory," as Wu put it, also considers, for example, "Richard Dawkins' idea that humans might be best described as little more than information carriers. This follows if we believe Dawkins' idea that our bodies are containers for DNA, which itself is just a code and a storage format, from an informational point of view." Discussion of the "flood," mentioned in the book's subtitle, refers to our current state of information overload. The flood, Gleick argued, is not entirely bad; it has allowed for everything from Wikipedia to scientific databases in chemistry and ecology.

From 1989 to 1990 Gleick was the McGraw Distinguished Lecturer at Princeton University, in New Jersey. He contributed text to Eliot Porter's book of photos *Nature's Chaos* (1991). In 2000 he served as the first editor of the Best American Science Writing book series.

—D.K.

Suggested Reading: around.com; *Economist* p86 Jan. 30, 1993; *New York Times* C p28 Oct. 15, 1987, E p7 Sep. 2, 1999, C p1 Mar. 7, 2011; *Slate.com* Mar. 27, 2011; *Wired* Aug. 1999, Mar. 2011

Selected Books: *Chaos: Making a New Science*, 1987; *Genius: The Life and Science of Richard Feynman*, 1992; *Faster: The Acceleration of Just About Everything*, 1999; *What Just Happened: A Chronicle from the Electronic Frontier*, 2002; *Isaac Newton*, 2003; *The Information: A History, a Theory, a Flood*, 2011

Gonzalez, Tony

Feb. 27, 1976– Football player

Address: Atlanta Falcons, 4400 Falcon Pkwy., Flowery Branch, GA 30542

Tony Gonzalez of the Atlanta Falcons is considered by some to be the best tight end in the history of the National Football League (NFL). He currently holds NFL records for receptions (1,053 as of early December 2010), receiving yards (12,344), and touchdowns by a tight end (86) as well as records for most 100-yard receiving games (27), receptions in a single season (102 in the 2004 season), and most seasons with 1,000 or more receiving yards by a tight end (four). He also ranks second among active players in receptions and is expected to become just the seventh position player in NFL history to reach the 1,000-reception plateau. Known for his speed and unrivaled work ethic, the six-foot five-inch, 250-pound Gonzalez helped transform the tight-end position in the late 1990s into a dynamic offensive weapon, bringing an unusual pass-catching ability and athleticism to a position traditionally reserved for blocking. Joe Posnanski explained for the *Kansas City Star* (April 24, 2009), "Gonzalez is a glamour tight end. He invented that position. Tight end had been for gritty men too rough to be pompous-and-fabulous wide receivers, but also too mobile to be offensive linemen. Tight ends were bloodied and muddied and fierce." The Kansas City Chiefs' former head coach

Dimitrios Kambouris/Getty Images for Playboy

Tony Gonzalez

Marty Schottenheimer said to Randy Covitz for the *Kansas City Star* (April 24, 2009) about Gonzalez, "He's almost like a wide receiver in a tight end's body. You were never reluctant to throw the ball up in the air [to Gonzalez] even if he was covered, because he was going to win the size battle [against the opposing team's defense] all the way. There was a reason he caught a lot of those balls, beyond the fact he had great hands. He created a lot of his own space because of his size against defensive backs."

Gonzalez was selected by the Kansas City Chiefs in the first round of the 1997 NFL Draft and spent 12 seasons with that organization before being traded to the Falcons in 2009. As a member of the Chiefs, he was named to the Associated Press First-Team All-Pro team five times, in 1999, 2000, 2001, 2003, and 2008, and was named to the American Football Conference (AFC) Pro Bowl team 10 times, from 1999 to 2008. He was also named to the *Sporting News* and *Sports Illustrated* NFL All-Decade teams for the 2000s. In his first season with the Falcons, Gonzalez caught 83 passes for 867 yards and scored six touchdowns, setting a franchise record for most receptions in a single season by a tight end. "Tony makes it pretty easy for a quarterback," the Atlanta Falcons' quarterback Matt Ryan told Paul Newberry for the Associated Press (September 16, 2009). "I just try to put the ball in a spot where he can make a play on it, and he always seems to do that."

In several ways Gonzalez stands apart from others off the field, too: unlike many of his peers in football, who feast on copious amounts of red meat, Gonzalez adheres to a strict vegetarian diet, which he wrote about in his 2009 book, *The All-*

Pro Diet. He is also an avid reader who has studied religion and spirituality extensively.

Anthony David Gonzalez was born on February 27, 1976 in Huntington Beach, California. When he was a child, his mother, Judy, divorced his biological father, Joseph, and married Michael Saltzman, a hospital administrator; Saltzman stepped in as a father figure for Tony Gonzalez and his older brother, Chris. Gonzalez's varied racial and ethnic heritage has been covered extensively in the media: his paternal grandfather was a native of Cape Verde, a then-Portuguese-held group of islands off the coast of Africa, and his paternal grandmother hailed from Jamaica; his maternal grandparents are of African, American Indian (Apache and Sioux), Irish, and Polish descent. (Gonzalez's original family surname, "Goncals," was changed to "Gonzalez" by immigration officials when his paternal grandfather arrived in the U.S.; as a result many people assume that Gonzalez is primarily Hispanic.) Gonzalez told Randy Covitz for the *Kansas City Star* (August 24, 1997), "When I fill out an application, I put 'Other.' I might put 'Hispanic.' It's confusing when you're growing up, especially because Huntington Beach is all white. . . . I take pride in it. I enjoy being eclectic. It helped me grow."

During his childhood Gonzalez enjoyed surfing and skateboarding before being introduced to team sports by his brother, who played in organized football leagues from a young age. As a result of his brother's influence, at 11 he started playing—albeit reluctantly—in the Pop Warner league, the largest and oldest youth-football organization in the U.S. "I had to rattle and push him to go to practice," Chris Gonzalez recalled to Steve Hummer for the *Atlanta Journal-Constitution*, as posted on Gonzalez's official Web site. "Plenty of time, I wanted to go outside and throw some passes and he didn't want to do it. So I would literally start a fight with him just to get him [angry] and get him up. Then, once he was already up, he'd say, 'OK, let's go outside and play.'" Despite receiving a lot of encouragement from his brother, Gonzalez's early years of playing football were difficult; he was sometimes unwilling to participate in the six plays per game he was guaranteed by the Pop Warner rules. "I got kicked all over the place," he told Covitz. "I was terrible. I would ride to practice, and get halfway there, and say, 'I don't want to go to practice' and I didn't go." Another difficulty for Gonzalez involved a bully who harassed him throughout most of his time in middle school, leading him to rush home each day. It was not until his middle-school graduation that he confronted the bully. Gonzalez's stepfather told Hummer, "That bully changed his life forever. After that, he was afraid of nothing."

During the summer after his middle-school graduation, Gonzalez began playing youth-league basketball. (Gonzalez took up the sport at the urging of a friend's father, who recognized his potential.) He proved to be a natural on the basketball court and scored 18 points in his first game. Judy

Gonzalez noted to Covitz, "He liked basketball more than football, because that's something you can practice on, hour after hour." Gonzalez attended Huntington Beach High School, where he excelled in both basketball and football. As a junior he averaged 17.1 points and 9.1 rebounds per basketball game and was named an All-USA Honorable Mention by *USA Today*. Also during his junior year, Gonzalez came into his own as a football player. On defense he recorded 68 tackles and six sacks as a middle linebacker; on offense he caught 38 passes for 800 yards and seven touchdowns as a tight end. He posted even more impressive numbers as a senior, when he caught 62 passes for 945 yards and made 13 touchdowns. He subsequently earned first-team All-American honors as a tight end and linebacker. Meanwhile, Gonzalez was racking up achievements in basketball, averaging 22 points per game as a senior and breaking Huntington High's career-scoring record. In the spring of 1994, he was named Orange County's High School Athlete of the Year. (The Los Angeles County winner of that award that year was the golf prodigy Tiger Woods.) Gonzalez was heavily recruited by colleges for both football and basketball. He chose to remain in his home state, deciding on the University of California (UC) at Berkeley, where he excelled at both sports, particularly football.

Gonzalez decided to forgo his senior year at UC and declare himself eligible for the 1997 NFL Draft. Standing six feet five inches and weighing 250 pounds, with a 36-inch vertical leap, Gonzalez—as was widely expected—was taken in the first round, by the Kansas City Chiefs, who selected him as the 13th overall pick. Gonzalez has said that he would have been able to pursue a professional basketball career had he been three inches taller. "I would be in the NBA. It's true," he told D. Orlando Ledbetter for the *Atlanta Journal-Constitution* (December 24, 2009). "But the thing is, I didn't have enough time to practice. Just my approach to football, if I took that approach to basketball, I'd been getting 1,000 shots a day and working on my [ball-handling]. I would have spent five to six hours a day in the gym."

During his rookie year Gonzalez played in 16 games and made 33 receptions for 368 yards (11.2 on average) and two touchdowns. He scored his first career touchdown in a week-six contest against the Miami Dolphins, in which he made a diving 21-yard catch in the end zone. He was also a contributor on special teams and blocked a punt in a week-14 game against the San Francisco 49ers. The Chiefs finished the regular season with an AFC-best 13–3 record but lost against the Denver Broncos in the AFC Divisional play-off round, 14–10. In that game Gonzalez scored the Chiefs' only touchdown, on a 12-yard pass from the quarterback Elvis Grbac. During that off-season the Chiefs added several notable players to their roster, including the defensive linemen Leslie O'Neal and Chester McGlockton and the receiver Derrick Alexander, in hopes of making a run at the Super Bowl.

Gonzalez became a vital part of the Chiefs' offense, starting all 16 games during the 1998 campaign. Despite facing double coverage in most of those games, he recorded 59 receptions for 621 yards (10.5 on average) and two touchdowns. The Chiefs, however, finished with a disappointing 7–9 record. The head coach, Marty Schottenheimer, resigned that off-season and was replaced by the Chiefs' defensive coordinator, Gunther Cunningham.

The 1999 season brought a breakthrough for Gonzalez. After missing the season opener, against the Chicago Bears, due to sprained ligaments in his right knee, he returned to start the remaining 15 games and recorded a team-high 76 receptions for 849 yards (11.2 on average) and 11 touchdowns. Gonzalez's touchdown total marked the second-highest in team history and was good for second (behind the Indianapolis Colts' Marvin Harrison) among all AFC pass-catchers. At the end of the season, he became the first Chiefs tight end to earn a Pro Bowl selection and was a consensus first-team All-Pro selection. The Chiefs missed out on the play-offs for the second consecutive year, with a 9–7 record. The team was dealt a major blow on February 8, 2000, when their perennial All-Pro linebacker and defensive anchor Derrick Thomas died following a car accident. The dispirited Chiefs finished the 2000 season with a 7–9 record, missing out on the play-offs again. Gonzalez, meanwhile, established himself as a bona fide superstar, starting all 16 games and recording 93 receptions for 1,203 yards (12.9 on average) with nine touchdowns. His 93 catches were the fourth-highest by a tight end in NFL history, and his 1,203 receiving yards were the fifth-highest single-season total for a tight end in league history. He led all NFL tight ends in receptions, yards, and touchdowns and became the first tight end in history to record four consecutive 100-yard receiving games. He also teamed up with Derrick Alexander to set franchise records for most catches (171) and receiving yards (2,594) for a Chiefs' receiving tandem. Gonzalez earned his second Pro Bowl selection and was again a consensus first-team All-Pro selection.

At the start of the 2001 season, Cunningham was replaced by Dick Vermeil. While his role was slightly diminished under Vermeil's new offensive schemes, Gonzalez continued to put up solid numbers during the 2001 campaign, starting all 16 games and catching 73 passes for 917 yards (12.6 on average) and six touchdowns. He was selected as a starter in his third straight Pro Bowl and was voted first-team All-Pro for the third year in a row. While the Chiefs displayed flashes of potential throughout the season, they finished with a 6–10 record. Tired of losing and dismayed over his contract situation, Gonzalez—as a negotiating ploy—played with the Miami Heat's rookie team in the National Basketball Association (NBA) summer league that year. After missing the entire 2002 NFL preseason, Gonzalez was signed to a seven-year deal worth $31 million; the deal included a signing bonus of $10 million.

During the 2002 season Gonzalez started 16 games and recorded 63 catches for 773 yards (12.3 on average) and seven touchdowns, the last figure tying for the most by a tight end in the NFL that year. While his numbers dropped from previous years, his peers selected him to his fourth Pro Bowl. Fueled by a powerhouse offense but held back by a below-par defense, the Chiefs finished with a mediocre 8–8 record. Gonzalez helped steer the Chiefs back to the play-offs in 2003, when he led all NFL tight ends in receptions (71), receiving yards (916), and touchdowns (10). The Chiefs finished with a 13–3 record and captured the AFC West division crown. After receiving a first-round bye in the play-offs, they lost to the Indianapolis Colts in the AFC divisional round, 38–31. In that game Gonzalez caught four passes for 55 yards. At the end of the season, he was named to his fifth consecutive Pro Bowl and selected to his fourth All-Pro team.

The Chiefs' hopes of returning to the play-offs in 2004 faded after the running back Priest Holmes suffered an injury midway through the season. Most of the offensive burden was placed on Gonzalez, who often found himself blanketed in coverage by opposing defenses. Undaunted, Gonzalez recorded an NFL-high 102 receptions for 1,258 yards and seven touchdowns in 16 starts. His reception total was the highest for a tight end in NFL history and marked the first time since 1986 that a tight end had won the league's receiving title. Meanwhile, his 1,258 receiving yards were the second-highest total by a tight end in league history, falling just 32 yards short of Kellen Winslow's record of 1,290 yards in 1980. Unable to overcome the loss of their star running back, among other factors, the Chiefs finished with a 7–9 record.

During the 2005 season Gonzalez continued to confirm his status as the best tight end in the NFL. That year he recorded a team-high 78 receptions for 905 yards (11.6 on average) and two touchdowns. In September of that year, in a game against the Oakland Raiders, he became the fourth tight end in league history to pass the 7,000-yard mark. Then, in a November contest against the Houston Texans, he became the first tight end in history to record eight consecutive seasons with 50 or more catches. The Chiefs finished with an impressive 10–6 record and placed second in their division but missed out on the play-offs. That off-season Vermeil retired and was replaced by Herm Edwards. The Chiefs rallied under Edwards's fiery leadership and compiled a 9–7 record during the 2006 season, which helped them earn a wild-card play-off berth. In the wild-card round the Chiefs lost to the Indianapolis Colts, 23–8. During the regular season Gonzalez started 15 games and recorded 73 receptions for a team-high 900 yards (12.3 on average) and five touchdowns. That season he broke the wide receiver Otis Taylor's franchise marks for receiving yards and touchdown re-

ceptions and surpassed Holmes's franchise record for most yards from scrimmage. Gonzalez earned his eighth straight Pro Bowl selection and was a second-team Associated Press All-Pro selection.

In contrast to an underachieving Chiefs' offense, Gonzalez remained as productive as ever in 2007, reaching a number of career milestones. He led the team and all NFL tight ends in receptions (99) and receiving yards (1,172 yards) and was named to his ninth consecutive Pro Bowl. In an October contest against the Cincinnati Bengals, he broke Shannon Sharpe's record for the most receiving touchdowns by a tight end. Then, in a December game against the New York Jets, he broke Sharpe's record for most catches by a tight end in league history. Also that month he recorded his third season with 1,000 receiving yards, tying him with Sharpe, Winslow, and Todd Christensen for most ever by a tight end. In week four of the 2008 season, Gonzalez broke Sharpe's record for most receiving yards by a tight end, ranking first among NFL tight ends in receptions (96), receiving yards (1,058), and touchdowns (10). That season he became the first tight end to record four career 1,000-yard seasons. He also earned his 10th consecutive Pro Bowl selection, the most by a tight end. The Chiefs, however, ranked among the worst teams in the NFL, with disastrous 4–12 and 2–14 records in 2007 and 2008, respectively.

During the 2008 off-season Gonzalez was traded to the Atlanta Falcons in exchange for a second-round pick in the 2010 NFL Draft. The trade was a result of his unhappiness with the direction of the Chiefs' organization, which was being rebuilt under Head Coach Todd Haley, who had replaced Edwards following the 2008 season. The Falcons, under second-year head coach Mike Smith, the reigning NFL Coach of the Year, and franchise quarterback Matt Ryan, were seen as a team on the rise and as a good fit for Gonzalez, who explained to Steve Hummer, "I wanted to go to a team that had a good quarterback and had a good shot at the playoffs. There were about three teams I was looking at. . . . In the end, knowing what I know now, this is the best place I could have been. I got lucky. It really is a dream offense." In his first season with the Falcons, Gonzalez finished second on the team in receiving yards (867) and receptions (83), while making six touchdowns. His receptions set a Falcons record for most by a tight end in a single season, topping Alge Crumpler's mark of 65, set in 2005. While the Falcons had hoped to build on their 11–5 record from the previous season, they failed to make the play-offs for a second consecutive year, after amassing a 9–7 record. Throughout the season the team had been hampered by injuries of several key players, including Ryan and the Pro Bowl running back Michael Turner. The Falcons' 2010 season has been much more successful; as of early December 2010, the team had posted an NFL-best 10–2 record.

In spite of his advancing age, the 34-year-old Gonzalez has said that he wants to play for several more seasons, in hopes of contributing to a Super Bowl title. He explained to Covitz for the *Kansas City Star* (August 12, 2010), "Physically, I feel like I can play another three, four years at a pretty good level. Right now, everybody knows what I'm playing for. It's no secret. I'm playing for a Super Bowl. . . . That's what all my energy is for, that [Super Bowl] ring." Commenting on the same topic, Head Coach Mike Smith said to D. Orlando Ledbetter about Gonzalez, "I see a guy that's got the body of a 25-year-old. I think he could play seven or eight more years. He's got the genetic makeup to play for a long, long time."

On July 20, 2007 Gonzalez and his longtime girlfriend, October, held a commitment ceremony in Huntington Beach. The couple have a daughter, Malia, who is three. Gonzalez also has a son, Nikko, nine, from a previous relationship, with the entertainment reporter Lauren Sanchez. In 1998 the athlete established the Tony Gonzalez Foundation, which supports the Boys & Girls Clubs of America and Shadow Buddies, a program that provides racially diverse male and female dolls to ill children. Gonzalez collaborated with the nutritionist Mitzi Dulan to write the book *The All-Pro Diet* (2009), which chronicles Gonzalez's path to becoming a vegetarian. In conjunction with the publication of the book, he began endorsing a line of nutritional supplements under the brand name All-Pro Science. Gonzalez is also the co-founder of Xtreme Clean 88, a commercial cleaning service based in Kansas City.

—C.C.

Suggested Reading: Associated Press Sep. 26, 2008, Apr. 24, 2009, Sep. 16, 2009; *Atlanta Falcons* Web site; *Atlanta Journal-Constitution* C p1 May 9, 2009, C p1 Dec. 24, 2009; *Kansas City Star* K p19+ Aug. 24, 1997, p123+ Aug. 26, 2001, B p8 Apr. 24, 2009; *Tony Gonzalez* Web site

Selected Books: *The All-Pro Diet* (with Mitzi Dulan), 2009

Gordon, Jaimy

July 4, 1944– Writer

Address: c/o Random House Inc., 1745 Broadway, New York, NY 10019

The novelist, poet, and short-story writer Jaimy Gordon was happy just to be nominated when she attended the National Book Award ceremony in December 2010, wearing an old red dress and having prepared no speech. As Gordon, her publisher, and nearly everyone in the literary establishment saw it, she had three strikes against her as a nominee: she was not very well known, the novel for which she had been nominated—*Lord of Misrule*—was published by a very small press, and its subject is horseracing, not one that most people associate with award-winning literary fiction. Moreover, in addition to Gordon, the five nominees included better-known writers, such as Nicole Krauss (for *Great House*) and Lionel Shriver (*So Much for That*). Still, the reviews of Gordon's book, and of her previous work, had been excellent. "In her novels, stories and poetry, Gordon has pushed the limits of style—explored the empty places in her articulate characters and works—so that language drags meaning behind it like a fur coat trailing blood," Susan Salter Reynolds wrote for the *Los Angeles Times* (December 6, 2010). "Her language is so textured that her pages seem three-dimensional." Such praise notwithstanding, many were surprised when Gordon—the clear underdog—won.

Gordon's first novel, *Shamp of the City-Solo* (1974), became a minor cult classic; her next two novels—*She Drove Without Stopping* (1990) and

Peter Blickle, courtesy of Random House

Bogeywoman (1999)—received a bit more mainstream recognition, both for their descriptive language and eccentric characters. As a result of the National Book Award nomination, Vintage, a subsidiary of Random House, acquired the paperback rights to *Lord of Misrule*; Random House will publish Gordon's next novel. On the subject of winning the award, Gordon told Chris Fusciardi for the *Kalamazoo (Michigan) Gazette* (November 14, 2010), "Certainly, for the last 10 years, I felt like I was going to end my career admired by other writers, but without much of a public reputation. I'm getting up there in years, so I was really beginning to think, 'This is a career that is not ending with a big bang.' And I was just getting used to that idea. And all of a sudden, there was a big bang."

One of five siblings, Jaimy Gordon was born on July 4, 1944 in Baltimore, Maryland, where she grew up in an upper-middle-class section of the Upper Park Heights neighborhood. Her father, David, was an attorney; her mother, Sonia, was a potter. Her home was a short distance from the Pimlico racetrack; she told Charles McGrath for the *New York Times* (December 16, 2010) that she came from "a long line of horseplayers." After high school she attended Antioch College, in Yellow Springs, Ohio, where she received a B.A. degree in English, with honors, in 1966. She spent the next few years writing and working odd jobs. Following a brief period in California, she returned to Maryland, where she worked at a jail and then wrote articles on food for a newspaper, the *Frederick News-Post*. She then fell in love with a man who trained horses at a racetrack, which is how she began working as a groom—one who takes care of horses—at the Charles Town track, in West Virginia, and then at the Green Mountain Park track, in Vermont. Speaking of her initial reaction to the track, Gordon told Andrew Beyer for the *Washington Post* (November 12, 2010), "It was love. I loved being around horses and had no fear of them. I liked the racetrack people—plenty of them are generous souls, they're not crybabies, they're not too moralistic, which suited me fine. The raffishness of life there appealed to me at that age"—her mid-20s. Those she encountered, she said, also included "bad people who exploited horses ruthlessly" and "old grooms who worked till they couldn't work anymore—their lot was kind of tragic." After three years of working as a groom and hot walker (one who walks horses after races and workouts so they can cool down), Gordon decided to return to academia. By all accounts, her choosing to attend Brown University, in Providence, Rhode Island—as opposed to the University of Iowa's Writing Workshop, the country's best-known program of its kind—was due to Brown's proximity to a Rhode Island racetrack.

"I came to Brown direct from three years of working on half-mile racetracks, hardly a literary milieu," Gordon told Gretchen Johnsen and Richard Peabody in an interview for *Gargoyle Magazine* ("circa 1983," according to the magazine's Web site). "I was too used to a solitary writing habit by that time to be a model member of a writers' workshop, but the great thing about that M.A. program, that English department, and indeed the Providence literary climate, is the extent to which diversity and eccentricity are permissible. Providence is an old and pleasant city with a harbor and a quite spectral literary past that includes figures like [the fiction writer and poet Edgar Allan] Poe, [the fiction writer H. P.] Lovecraft, and [the poet and critic] S. Foster Damon. Robert Coover, another writer whose work I value, moved there in 1980 with only the slenderest connection to Brown. He and his family simply chose to make their home in Providence. I thought that significant." Gordon received a master's degree in English, with a concentration in creative writing, in 1972 and earned a doctor of arts degree in creative writing in 1975.

Meanwhile, McPherson & Co.—a small press run by Bruce McPherson, whom Gordon had met at Brown—had published Gordon's first novel, *Shamp of the City-Solo* (1974). The novel, set in a parallel universe, tells the story of a man whose obsession with fame leads him to a city known as the Big Yolk—modeled on New York, the "Big Apple"—to participate in a kind of competition of rhetoric. "*Shamp* is [an] infantile novel in many ways, and I don't mean that as any aspersion upon its literary merit," Gordon told the *Gargoyle Magazine* interviewers. "Its protagonist Hughbury Shamp's obsessive idea is that, if you don't get famous, life is a mistake, an enactment of doom start to finish, and that was my preoccupation when I was eight years old, no later. The sexuality in *Shamp* is largely pre-genital, that is, infantile. The hero boldly quits his parents in true picaresque style, but then speedily attaches himself to three masters with all the anxious fervor of a parentless waif. Even the choice of a male protagonist is infantile. Hughbury Shamp is not really male; he's an hysterical neuter with a flair for ornate sophistry and a strong instinct of self-preservation. That's a version of me in my inchoate state." The novel became a minor cult classic. Still, within a year it had gone out of print, and although it was reissued in 1980—and would be again in the 1990s—it received no mainstream media coverage. In the interview with *Gargoyle*, Gordon offered her take on the reprinting: "[*Shamp*] was one of the first small press novels, during a burst of small press activity; therefore it was a small press phenom, in a year when there could be such a thing. The second time around the timing was not as good. I knew it wouldn't be, but Bruce is an unflagging optimist; that's why he's the editor of a small press and I'm not. *Shamp* should not have been allowed to lapse from print in the first place . . . but a reprint was financially impracticable at the time."

Around the time of the publication of her second novel, *She Drove Without Stopping* (1990), Gordon was still mostly unknown to the general public, although she was beginning to gain attention from the mainstream press. "Long, ambitious, sad, macabre, *She Drove Without Stopping* asks a hundred unanswerable questions," Carolyn See wrote for the *Los Angeles Times* (June 25, 1990). "The first and most important is: Why in the world is it that some parents hate their children? The second, and at least as important: How can the child heal himself or herself, find a place in the world and stop being so dopily *brokenhearted* about it? The author does some amazing things with this by now familiar tale." Set in the 1950s and '60s, the novel focuses on Jane Turner, whose father beats and sexually molests her during her childhood. As a young woman Jane leaves college to live with her boyfriend, Jimmy, in an abandoned farmhouse in the Midwest, where they make friends with a haphazard crew of artists and Beatniks, and where Jane feels at home until she is raped—one of a series of misfortunes she experiences. Jane also, in See's words, "finds lovers, adventures, sexuality, fun."

Another troubled young woman is the hero of Gordon's third novel, *Bogeywoman* (1999), which critics lauded for its author's humor, wit, and gift for language and dialogue. Ursula Koderer, the novel's heroine, has been referred to disparagingly as "Bogeywoman" since the age of seven by her peers, who suspect that she is a lesbian. She is also Jewish, which adds to her sense of being an outsider. At the age of 16, when Ursula is at sleepaway camp, she reluctantly acknowledges to herself that she feels a powerful attraction to girls. After a fling with a fellow female camper goes wrong, Ursula cuts her forearm with a razor blade and as a result is sent to an exclusive, private sanitarium, where she later has an affair with a beautiful, middle-aged doctor, Madame Zuk; the two eventually run away together. "In this funny, tender, ambitious novel . . . Jaimy Gordon takes the well-worn coming-of-age/coming out genre and, as if to get our attention, flips it inside out," Deborah Picker wrote for *LA Weekly* (December 10, 1999). In her review of *Bogeywoman* for the *Los Angeles Times* (January 2, 2000), Judith Dunford called it a "wildly inventive new novel" and noted the "magnitude of Gordon's accomplishment." Dunford wrote, "While it is specific and descriptive, the language—ornate, slangy, full of private puns—is also itself clearly meant to stand as a metaphor for Ursie's perceived 'otherness.' Still, if language is *Bogeywoman*'s greatest pleasure, it paradoxically also is the book's major weakness. Gordon can't seem to stop; there are times when the three-ring word circus gets unpleasantly self-conscious, as though Gordon were more interested in making you read the language than the book and as though she prefers whiz-bang verbal flashiness to the plodding demands of character development." The *Los Angeles Times* (December 3, 2000) selected *Bogeywoman* as one of the best books of 2000.

Around that time Gordon began working on *Lord of Misrule* (2010). The novel started as an expansion of Gordon's short story "A Night's Work," which had been included in *Best American Short Stories* in 1995. The novel paints an elaborate picture of the people and horses inhabiting the unsavory world of a dingy, half-mile racetrack in West Virginia. The initial inspiration for writing the book, Gordon told Christopher Walton for the *Detroit Free Press* (December 5, 2010), was her love of horses. She added: "Horse racing is thrilling, and I sensed that the world of cheap horse racing—violent, brutal, cynical, scary—is, to a certain kind of American romantic, of great interest." After years in which she submitted the book unsuccessfully to publishing houses, Gordon set it aside. Later, her friend and publisher Bruce McPherson encouraged her to revise it, and with support from McPherson and others, Gordon rewrote the novel's beginning and altered its structure, creating four parts—one for each race described, with each part narrated by a different character. Many strange characters populate the book, including Medicine Ed, a 72-year-old groom who has been working with horses since the age of eight; Two-Tie, a suave loan shark with a hand in all the track's activities; Tommy Hansel, a tall, handsome trainer; and 25-year-old Maggie, who is—in an autobiographical twist by Gordon—in love with Tommy. A critic wrote for the *New Yorker* (January 3, 2011), "Gordon's characters—despite caricaturish names like Suitcase Smithers and Medicine Ed—are complex and finely drawn, and she successfully steers clear of most horse-racing clichés, while unspooling a plot of corruption and intrigue. Gordon saves her best writing for the horses, describing castrations, accidents, beatings, and deaths with painful intimacy. She also excels at drawing out short races into several pages while retaining all their pace and excitement."

Gordon is also the author of the masque *The Rose of the West* (1976); the novellas *Private T. Pigeon's Tale* (1979) and *Circumspections from an Equestrian Statue* (1979); and the narrative poem *The Bend, The Lip, The Kid* (1978), the story of a prison inmate named McMagus. In writing that work, which is heavy with slang, Gordon drew from her experience of teaching creative writing at a Rhode Island state prison, from 1971 to 1973. From the German she has translated Maria Beig's *Lost Weddings* (1990) and *Hermine, an Animal Life* (2005). She has received three literature fellowships from the National Endowment for the Arts, the last in 1991; that year she also received an award from the American Academy and Institute of Arts and Letters. Her short stories, poems, essays, and translations have appeared in the *Colorado Review*, *Missouri Review*, *Ploughshares*, *Antioch Review*, *Michigan Quarterly Review*, *Poetry International*, and other publications.

Gordon "has a huge corona of springy, tightly curled hair that suggests prolonged exposure to a light socket, and a personality to match: forthright, disarming, uncensored," McGrath wrote. "She is a wiser, chastened version of the reckless young female character who turns up in many of her books and never misses a chance to endanger herself." Gordon joined the English Department faculty at Western Michigan University, in Kalamazoo, as an assistant professor in 1981. She received tenure in 1987 and attained the post of full professor in 1992. In 1988 she married Peter Blickle, who teaches German at Western Michigan University. The couple live in Kalamazoo in separate, nearby houses.

—D.K.

Suggested Reading: gargoylemagazine.com; *Kalamazoo (Michigan) Gazette* A p2 Nov. 14, 2010; *Los Angeles Times* E p8 June 25, 1990; *Los Angeles Times Book Review* p2 Jan. 2, 2000, D p6 Dec. 6, 2010; *New York Times* C p1 Dec. 16, 2010

Selected Books: *Shamp of the City-Solo*, 1974; *She Drove Without Stopping*, 1990; *Bogeywoman*, 1999; *Lord of Misrule*, 2010

Alberto E. Rodriguez/Getty Images

Gordon-Levitt, Joseph

Feb. 17, 1981– Actor; founder of hitRECord.org

Address: c/o Creative Artists Agency, 162 Fifth Ave., Suite 6, New York, NY 10010-6047

In 1985, at the age of four, Joseph Gordon-Levitt was cast in the role of a happy consumer in several television commercials, and except for the two years or so that he spent as an undergraduate, he has worked in TV and/or film almost continuously ever since. At 15 he won the part of an alien masquerading as an American teenager on the sitcom *3rd Rock from the Sun* and became something of a heartthrob among young girls. When he entered college, after *3rd Rock*'s sixth and last season, he felt ready for something new. The lure of the screen proved to be stronger than the appeal of academia, but by his own account, his college-classroom experiences helped him to figure out what he wanted to achieve in his vocation. He has since appeared in independent films including *Brick, Mysterious Skin, Shadowboxer*, and *(500) Days of Summer*

and Hollywood movies including *The Lookout* and *Inception*. The actor Jeff Daniels, who co-starred with Gordon-Levitt in *The Lookout*, told Franz Lidz for the *New York Times* (March 25, 2007), "There's a mystery and a privacy to what goes on in Joe's head. We can see him work through his thoughts. We can almost hear him. Of the actors I've worked with under 30, Joe was the least interested in anything other than what happened in between 'action' and 'cut.' He had no entourage, and I never saw him on a cell [phone] discussing his career with a publicist. If he wasn't acting the character, he was thinking about him."

In 2006 Gordon-Levitt launched hitRECord.org, which he has described as "a professional open collaborative production company." Through the Creative Artists Agency's speakers division, he has visited colleges nationwide to demonstrate how hitRECord.org operates. "On one hand, it is a kind of an anarchistic, democratic, chaotic, collective thing," he said during an appearance at the University of Maryland, as quoted by Molly Marcot for the campus newspaper, the *Diamondback* (April 27, 2011, on-line). "On the other hand, it's very much directed by one individual, that being me." Currently hitRECord.org has more than 40,000 registered members. Some of the work developed on hitRECord.org has been screened at the Sundance and South by Southwest film festivals. Any profits are split between the company and the contributing artists. "The Hollywood industry is crumbling," Gordon-Levitt told the University of Maryland students who attended his workshop. "And you're just as likely to be a successful artist by making your art, making good art, connecting with your audience through the Internet, through live shows, through whatever it is. . . . You don't need to wait around for some Hollywood producer to hire you."

The second of the two sons of Jane Gordon and Dennis Levitt, Joseph Leonard Gordon-Levitt was born on February 17, 1981 in Los Angeles, California. He had a close friendship with his brother, Daniel, a performer whose specialties included fire dancing; in 2010 Daniel died of an apparent drug overdose, at age 36. Gordon-Levitt's maternal grandfather, the late Michael Gordon, was a theater and film director; his credits included the 1950 motion-picture version of *Cyrano de Bergerac*, for which José Ferrer, in the title role, won an Oscar, and the hit comedy *Pillow Talk* (1959), with Rock Hudson and Doris Day. While blacklisted in Hollywood in the 1950s for alleged Communist ties, he worked in New York City as a stage director. Gordon-Levitt's parents are both social activists. They met while working at the left-leaning radio station KPFK-FM, in North Hollywood, where his father was the news director and his mother was involved with programming. Jane Gordon ran for Congress in California in the 1970s as a member of the Peace and Freedom Party. She and her husband are founding members of the Progressive Jewish Alliance, whose goals include social and economic justice. "My dad never blew anything up, but he probably had friends who did. He and my mom have always preached that the pen is mightier than a Molotov cocktail," Gordon-Levitt told Franz Lidz, after recalling that as a child he used to "riffle through the anarchist literature of his father's youth," in Lidz's words.

Gordon-Levitt grew up in the Sherman Oaks district of Los Angeles. At age four he played the scarecrow in a preschool production of *The Wizard of Oz* attended by a talent agent who represented two of his classmates. Impressed by his performance, the agent suggested to Jane Gordon that young Joe could get acting jobs in commercials. The idea pleased the boy, and he was soon hired for ads for Sunny Jim peanut butter, Pop-Tarts, Kinney Shoes, and Cocoa Puffs. At age six he portrayed the son of Tommy Lee Jones's character in the made-for-television Western *Stranger on My Land* (1988). Later that year he was cast as the son of a policewoman (Jaclyn Smith) in the TV movie *Settle the Score* and appeared in two episodes of the sitcom *Family Ties*. By the early 1990s Gordon-Levitt had won recurring roles on the revival of the Gothic soap opera *Dark Shadows* and on Norman Lear's short-lived political comedy *The Powers That Be*. He also had small roles on TV shows including *Murder, She Wrote* and *Quantum Leap*.

Gordon-Levitt made the transition to the big screen in 1992, as the young Norman Maclean (portrayed as an adult by Craig Sheffer) in *A River Runs Through It*, based on Maclean's semiautobiographical novella of the same name and directed and narrated by Robert Redford. His performance earned him a Young Artist Award nomination from the Young Artist Foundation. In 1994 Gordon-Levitt landed his first starring role, that of a foster child who secures divine assistance for his favorite baseball team, in the Disney film *Angels in the Outfield*. He appeared in four episodes of the TV sitcom *Roseanne* and was cast as the son of Demi Moore's character in the crime film *The Juror* (1996), co-starring Alec Baldwin.

More notably in 1996, at age 15, Gordon-Levitt was chosen for the role of Tommy Solomon, an adult alien inhabiting the body of a suburban American teenager, on the USA network's sitcom *3rd Rock from the Sun*. The show's premise was that four aliens were sent to Earth (the third planet in orbit around the sun) from another galaxy to impersonate an American family in order to study human behavior. Much of what the aliens learned came from television and movies rather than real life and proved to be misinformation, the source of many of the show's comical situations. For the next five years, Gordon-Levitt spent most of his time on the *3rd Rock* set with his cast mates—John Lithgow, Kristen Johnston, Jane Curtin, and French Stewart. As a major character in a top-rated, Emmy Award–winning series, Gordon-Levitt found himself featured in such magazines as *'Teen* and *Sassy*, and he attracted a great deal of attention whenever he was in public. "When I was a teenager, if anyone recognized me for anything I did, it would ruin my day," Gordon-Levitt told Neva Chonin for the *San Francisco Chronicle* (March 25, 2007, on-line). "I couldn't handle it. It was some sort of neurotic phobia. I guess I was paranoid that people would treat me differently, or in an unfair way, because of my job. Even back then, I really didn't like the whole idolatry that goes on with actors and found the celebrity thing distasteful. I still do."

Concurrently while working on in *3rd Rock*, Gordon-Levitt portrayed a terminally ill teen in Joe Gayton's little-noticed independent drama *Sweet Jane* (1998), with Samantha Mathis in the title role, and was seen alongside Heath Ledger and Julia Stiles in Gil Junger's high-school comedy *10 Things I Hate About You* (1999), which earned him a second nomination for a Young Artist Award. In his only appearance in the sitcom *That '70s Show*, in a 1998 episode, Gordon-Levitt's character shared a kiss with the character played by the actor Topher Grace. Their kiss was reportedly the first between males to be broadcast on North American prime-time TV. "I was totally proud of that, and I still am," Gordon-Levitt told Brandon Voss for the *Advocate* (August 2010, on-line). "It was a great bit, and it got a great reaction."

In 2001, eager to grapple with a new challenge, Gordon-Levitt moved to New York City and enrolled at Columbia University, where he majored in French. By his own account, although he dropped out after about two years, his experience at Columbia benefited him greatly. "I realized it doesn't matter what classes you're taking. It only matters who the teachers are," he told Lidz. "They made me see I wasn't just alive to have fun. I started to care about the world, and I wanted to somehow connect with it." He told Chonin, "I grew to care more about my place in the world. New York will do funny things to a person, being around that many people. And moving out of the city I grew up in was probably the smartest thing I've ever done. . . . I grew to care about my connection to everybody else on this planet, and in searching for how I could make that connection more meaningful, I landed back in acting. Now I'm delighted when something I've done means something to someone. What else is there in being alive in this world other than engaging with other people here?" While in New York Gordon-Levitt made his stage debut Off-Broadway, at the Soho Playhouse, in a production of Austin Pendleton's drama *Uncle Bob*.

Two films in which Gordon-Levitt next worked—Rian Johnson's *Brick* and Gregg Araki's *Mysterious Skin*—premiered at the 2005 Sundance Film Festival. In *Brick* he portrayed Brendan, a high-school student trying to find the connection between the murder of his estranged ex-girlfriend and a local drug ring. Brendan wears a sweatshirt and not the trench coat and fedora associated with Dashiell Hammett's fictional detective Sam Spade—and with Humphrey Bogart, who played Spade in the film *The Maltese Falcon*; nonetheless, Gordon-Levitt struck several reviewers of *Brick* as a teenage Spade/Bogart stand-in.

In *Mysterious Skin* Gordon-Levitt's character, Neil, is a gay street hustler who during childhood was sexually abused by an athletic coach. "It was definitely the first time I'd been cast in the sort of sexualized, sex object role," the actor told Brandon Voss. "I didn't really think of myself like that before." He also told Voss that he was not concerned about the possibility that filmgoers might confuse his sexual orientation with that of any character he plays: "Public perception is something you can't worry about because it's a loser's game. There's nothing positive that can come from paying attention to that kind of thing—not just wondering whether or not someone thinks you're gay but also worrying what people will think of who you're dating or what you drive. I just do my best to ignore all that." Gordon-Levitt was recognized with a top acting honor at the Seattle International Film Festival and a nomination for a Gotham Breakthrough Award for his performance in *Mysterious Skin*. In a review of the film for *Salon.com* (June 17, 2005), Stephanie Zacharek wrote, "Gordon-Levitt's performance is remarkable: There are moments when his face looks so blank and closed off we can barely see a person there. But little by little, he gives us more and more. . . . [When,] for the first time, Neil recognizes what it's like to connect sensually and emotionally with another human being, . . . this newfound awareness registers on his face with barely a flicker. But it's enough."

Gordon-Levitt had supporting roles in Barbara Kopple's film *Havoc* and Lee Daniels's *Shadowboxer*, both released in 2005. He received considerable acclaim for his lead performance in *The Lookout* (2007), written and directed by Scott Frank and co-starring Jeff Daniels and Matthew Goode. Gordon-Levitt played Chris, a star high-school athlete who suffers a serious brain injury in a car accident that leaves two of his friends dead and his girlfriend maimed. After he takes a job as a bank janitor, an ex-boyfriend of his sister's recruits him to serve as a lookout in a robbery of the bank. "It's a classic heist that just has an interesting character at the center," Gordon-Levitt told Chonin. "I tried not to play it like, 'Here's the head-injury man.' I wanted to play an individual who's a whole person. He's a guy whose brain just works a certain way that's different from the way most people's brains work." He told Larry Ratliff for the *San Antonio (Texas) Express-News* (April 8, 2007, online), "The really interesting thing about Chris to me is that he woke up a new person after his accident, but he still remembers who he was. There's still that guy in him." To prepare for the role, Gordon-Levitt hung out with three brain-damaged young men. "Chris is such a sad, dark character that if Joe had made him angry, he would have gotten on the audience's nerves real fast," Scott Frank said to Lidz. "Instead, Joe downplayed the disability by projecting a kind of childish honesty, a direct quality that kids have." In a review of *The Lookout*, David Edelstein wrote for *New York* (March 23, 2007, online), "Gordon-Levitt is a major tabula rasa actor. It's simpler to say what he doesn't do wrong—anything—than what he does right. As in *Mysterious Skin* and *Brick*, he's a minimalist; no fuss, no placards, no Method sense-memory exercises. You don't catch him 'playing' brain-damaged. You know his Chris is in chaos by the way he doesn't seize the space, by what he takes away from the character. His feelings run deepest when the rubber face goes slack."

Alongside Ryan Phillipe and Channing Tatum, Gordon-Levitt played a veteran of the Iraq war in Kimberly Peirce's *Stop-Loss* (2008). In Marc Webb's *(500) Days of Summer* (2009), he starred as Tom, an architect turned writer for a greeting-card company, who falls in love at first sight of his new co-worker, Summer (played by Zooey Deschanel). Summer informs him early on that she does not believe in love or marriage, but Tom refuses to believe that she will not change her mind. The film earned mostly positive reviews. Among its admirers was Stephanie Zacharek, who wrote for Salon.com (July 17, 2009), "Everything that's wrong, on the surface, with *(500) Days of Summer* pales in light of everything that's going on *beneath* its surface. . . . If the movie . . . is at times overly calculated, in the end it manages to hit the core of what it means to have every romantic hope dashed." Describing Gordon-Levitt as a "terrific, understated actor," she concluded that he "may be the real key to what makes *(500) Days of Summer* work." *(500) Days of Summer* premiered at the 2009 Sundance Film Festival, where it got a standing ovation. Gordon-Levitt's work in the film brought him nominations for an Independent Spirit Award and a Golden Globe Award.

In the fall of 2009, Gordon-Levitt appeared in Sebastian Gutierrez's ensemble comedy *Women in Trouble*; he reprised his role in the film's sequel, *Electra Luxx* (2010). Also in 2010 Gordon-Levitt co-starred with Leonardo DiCaprio and Ellen Page in Christopher Nolan's unusually complex science-fiction thriller *Inception*, about a corporate thief (DiCaprio) who extracts his booty from people's dreams and now must attempt the reverse task—that of planting ideas within a businessman's dreams. He hires Gordon-Levitt's character to help him. Speaking of Gordon-Levitt's attitude during shooting, Nolan told Jeff Gordinier for *Details* (August 2010, on-line), "He never loses his sense of enthusiasm—truly boyish *enthusiasm* for the fun thing we're doing. When you work on big movies, everybody gets jaded, myself included, and you have to remind yourself: If we were 10 years old, this would be pretty damn exciting. Joe never seems to forget that." The actor will next be seen with Seth Rogen in a film about a man who is diagnosed with cancer and resolves to fight the disease in part through humor.

"Get Joe rolling and it's only a matter of minutes before the conversation is ping-ponging between Buddhism and Fellini, French poets and Russian clowns," Gordinier wrote. "But his brightness is so shiny and childlike, as he swivels around in an er-

gonomic chair at his house in the Los Angeles hipster playground of Silver Lake, that even his eyelids seem to grin." Gordon-Levitt also maintains an apartment on the Lower East Side of New York City. He told Lilibet Snelling for *Anthem* (February 28, 2007, on-line), "The point of acting [is] to affect people. When I hear that I've done something that made someone laugh or made someone cry or made someone *think*, that's what inspires me to continue doing what I'm doing." He continued, referring to his company, hitRECord.org, "And it's not just artists who can do that—it's everybody. Every single person in the world can apply their time and effort and power toward what they believe in. Everyone with a computer and an Internet connection can get their voice heard. Isn't that exciting?"
—H.R.W.

Suggested Reading: *Anthem* (on-line) Feb. 28, 2007; *Details* (on-line) Aug. 2010; hitRECord.org; *Houston Chronicle* p8 July 23, 2009; *New York* (on-line) June 29, 2009; *New York Times* (on-line) Mar. 25, 2007; *San Francisco Chronicle* (on-line) Mar. 25, 2007; *USA Today* D p3 Jan. 22, 2010

Selected Television Shows: *3rd Rock from the Sun*, 1996–2001

Selected Films: *A River Runs Through It*, 1992; *Angels in the Outfield*, 1994; *The Juror*, 1996; *Sweet Jane*, 1998; *10 Things I Hate About You*, 1999; *Brick*, 2005; *Mysterious Skin*, 2005; *The Lookout*, 2007; *Stop-Loss*, 2008; *(500) Days of Summer*, 2009; *Inception*, 2010

Thos Robinson/Getty Images

Graff, Laurence

June 13, 1938– Diamond and jewelry merchant; philanthropist

Address: Graff USA, 46 E. 61st St., New York, NY 10065

The British jeweler Laurence Graff is known as the "king of diamonds." Like the previous holder of that unofficial title, Harry Winston (1896–1978), an American, Graff buys and sells gems and jewelry. But unlike Winston, who helped out in his father's jewelry store starting in early childhood, Graff learned the trade during his teens as an ap-

prentice and built his business—Graff Diamonds International—on his own. The world's most prominent broker of diamonds, he is the first individual in the international diamond industry to establish a vertically integrated enterprise; he thus oversees everything from diamond exploration and excavation to cutting, polishing, design, setting, and wholesale and retail sales. Graff owns a controlling stake in the South African Diamond Corp. (Safdico), a diamond wholesaler and manufacturer based in Johannesburg, South Africa, and, since 2008, a large stake in Gem Diamonds, a publicly traded mining company. Graff Diamonds generates nearly $1 billion in annual worldwide sales; its inventories are valued at hundreds of millions of dollars, and Graff's personal fortune is estimated to total $2.5 billion. His clients include members of royal families, tycoons, and megawatt celebrities of many stripes. Meredith Etherington-Smith, the editor in chief of *Christie's Magazine* (published by the London-based auction house Christie's), who chronicled Graff's rags-to-riches story in her book *The Most Fabulous Jewels in the World* (2007), told Samantha Conti for *Women's Wear Daily* (*WWD*, October 22, 2007) that Graff "has a psychic relationship with diamonds. From his very early life, he's had a remarkable sense of observation, of places, of details." She added, "He has a remarkable consistency of vision not only for his designs, but for the advertising, the stores, his longstanding clients and the preservation of the brand." The proceeds from sales of *The Most Fabulous Jewels in the World*, which Graff self-published, support Nelson Mandela's Children's Fund. Graff also aids children in Africa through the Graff Diamonds Foundation and his organization FACET (For Africa's Children Every Time).

Laurence Graff was born into a religiously observant Jewish family on June 13, 1938 in London, England. His father, Harry Graff, immigrated to Great Britain from Russia, and his mother, the former Rebecca Segal, was a native of Romania. His brother,

Raymond, who was born in 1947, supervises Graff Diamonds craftspeople at the company's Mayfair, London, site. Graff was raised in the East End of London, a down-at-the-heels area in which many immigrants had settled during the late 19th and early 20th centuries. During his first seven years, his family lived in a single room adjacent to the confectionary shop that his father had opened prior to enlisting in the British military in World War II. His mother ran the shop while his father "made suits off the Commercial Road," Godfrey Barker wrote for the British Web site This Is Money (August 5, 2008), referring to a major artery that connects the East End to central London.

Graff has traced his fascination with precious stones and jewelry ("jewellery," in Great Britain) to an early age. As a youth he sometimes witnessed the sale of diamonds in Hatton Garden, the historic hub of London's diamond trade, which was near his home. His extremely poor marks in school led his parents to urge him to join the workforce. He quit school at 14 and at 15 became an apprentice to a jeweler in Hatton Garden. He performed such menial chores as scrubbing toilets and washing floors. After three months—"for some unknown reason," he told Peter M. Brant for *Interview* (December 2008/January 2009)—he was fired. He soon landed a job with another jeweler, who taught him how to make small pieces of jewelry and to repair and remodel rings and other items. "I learned all the ways to make something look new again," he told Brant. Several years later, after that business folded, Graff joined with another jeweler and started a new venture, with Graff as the salesman and his partner as the craftsman. Repair contracts and sales of inexpensive new pieces of jewelry proved to be insufficient to keep their business in the black. When Graff was 18 he became its sole owner and assumed all its debts. Meanwhile he had begun to buy small diamonds on credit and have them made into rings. "And very, very slowly, I started to build up," he told Brant.

By the time Graff was in his early twenties, he was selling jewelry of his own design to buyers all over Great Britain. "I can't draw. I can't paint," he told Brant. "But what I can do is tell somebody else what to do. I'm a creator. . . . I have the eye, so I can move things around. I can put stones together. I can match them." At 22 he launched his eponymous diamond-jewelry brand. At 24 he opened two small jewelry shops in London. He then began traveling abroad to gain additional clients. A turning point for Graff came when he visited a jewelry exhibition in Singapore in the 1960s. While there he secured a space for a jewelry display at a Singapore department store and met the then–prince of Brunei, Hassanal Bolkiah, and his wife, Saleha Mohamed Alam. (The couple, now the sultan and queen consort of Brunei, are still his clients.) Graf soon landed other wealthy clients. He recalled to Susan Adams for *Forbes* (August 13, 2007), "All of a sudden I was selling $10,000, $20,000 worth of diamonds at a time." Graff also caught the attention

of Hollywood insiders and helped create some of the costume jewelry that Elizabeth Taylor wore in the film *Cleopatra* (1963).

Through his connection to the Brunei royal family, Graff came into contact with many Arabs who had gotten rich during the 1970s oil boom. Those clients led Graff to open his first major retail store, in the exclusive Knightsbridge district of London, in 1973 (not 1974, as some sources state). Also that year Graff (who had closed his other two shops) became the first jeweler to be honored with the Queen's Award for Enterprise. During the following years "I went everywhere," he told Geraldine Fabrikant for the *New York Times* (June 19, 2011). "I was the first real Westerner who came into that market as a wholesaler: a man carrying a case of jewels."

When oil money began to dry up in the late 1980s and early 1990s, Graff began to invest in commercial London real estate. In 1993 he moved his London store to its current location, on New Bond Street, in the city's posh Mayfair district. In 1998 he purchased a 51 percent stake in Safdico, a wholesale diamond manufacturer that is among 93 corporate entities (known in the diamond trade as sightholders) authorized to purchase rough diamonds from the Diamond Trading Co. (DTC), the arm of the De Beers Group that, according to the DTC Web site, "sorts, values and sells just over 40% of the world's rough diamonds by value." (The number of sightholders changes every three years.) That controlling stake facilitated Graff's move toward vertical integration. He now purchases roughly half of his company's stock of uncut diamonds from Safdico. The diamonds are cut and polished in the plants Graff maintains in Johannesburg; Botswana; Antwerp, Belgium; and New York. All his original jewelry designs are created in his London and New York corporate offices; he also maintains corporate offices in Geneva, Switzerland; Tokyo, Japan; and Hong Kong, China. Graff's retail chain currently includes 32 stores in the U.S., Europe, the Middle East, and Asia, and since 2001 Graff boutiques have operated in Saks Fifth Avenue department stores.

Graff has acquired, and in some cases sold, some of the world's rarest and most precious gems. Among them are the Magnificence, a 244-carat white diamond; the Maharajah, a 78-carat yellow diamond; the Idol's Eye, a 70.21-carat blue-white diamond; the Hope of Africa, a 115.91-carat diamond; the Emperor Maximilian, a 42-carat diamond; the Graff Dream, a 100.09-carat yellow diamond that took Nino Branco, a master cutter, nine months to complete; the Graff Constellation, a 102.79-carat round diamond cut from the $18.4 million, 478-carat Light of Letseng; and the Lesotho Promise, a 603-carat rough diamond unearthed in the Letseng Mine in Lesotho, Africa, in 2006. Graff paid $12.4 million for the Lesotho Promise; the 26 varied polished diamonds cut from that stone were set in a single necklace whose value in mid-2011 exceeded $60 million.

One of the most treasured gemstones in Graff's collection is the Wittelsbach-Graff Diamond, a blue diamond that he bought at a Christie's auction in London in 2008 for the then-record sum of $24 million. That gem, which King Philip IV of Spain gave to his daughter Margarita Teresa when she became engaged to Emperor Leopold I of Austria in 1664, has been compared to the Hope Diamond—with the two seen as the most flawless blue diamonds in existence. Graff was criticized for his decision to recut the diamond, from 35.52 carats to 31.06 carats, to remove imperfections, but even his critics have conceded that the diamond is now close to perfection. In 2010 the Smithsonian's National Museum of Natural History, in Washington, D.C., displayed both the Wittelsbach-Graff Diamond and the Hope Diamond, the latter of which had not been exhibited in public since the 1958 World's Fair, in Brussels, Belgium. In November 2010, at a Sotheby's auction in Geneva, Graff eclipsed his own record with a winning, phoned-in bid of $45.6 million for a 24.78-carat pink diamond. He named the gem the Graff Pink and described it as "the most fabulous diamond I've seen in my career," according to Scott Reyburn, writing for Bloomsburg News (November 16, 2010, on-line).

In the wake of the global economic crisis, Graff has turned his attention to China's rapidly growing diamond market. "We make more sales to newer money than to older money," he told Geraldine Fabrikant. "Americans are not attracted in the same way in spending money on jewelry as in the Far East." Graff, who plans to open retail stores in mainland China and Taiwan, remains optimistic about the international market for precious diamonds. He explained to Garry White for the London Sunday Telegraph (January 4, 2009), "The mass market has been hit, but there will always be a market for quality gems. In the part of the market in which we operate, clients are rare, but so are the diamonds. There are more clients than diamonds." He told Fabrikant, "Billionaires everywhere in the world like to keep some of their wealth in something easily transportable."

In 2007 Susan Adams described Graff as "charming and outrageously self-promoting, blunt and full of braggadocio, obsessed with superlatives" and as "trim" and "nattily attired." His world-class collection of contemporary art contains works by Picasso, Francis Bacon, Andy Warhol, William Kentridge, Anton Smit, and Jean-Michel Basquiat. Graff is a member of the International Director's Council of the Guggenheim Museum, in New York, the International Council of the Tate Modern, in London, and the boards of the Berggruen Museum, in Berlin, Germany, and the Museum of Contemporary Art in Los Angeles, California. He won a second Queen's Award for Excellence in 2006; in 1977 and 1994 he won the Queen's Award for Export Achievement.

Graff and his wife, the former Anne-Marie Bessière, a native of France, married in 1962. They have two sons, François, a Graff Diamond executive, and Stephane, an artist, and a daughter, Kristelle. Graff's wife instituted divorce proceedings in 2009, after she (and the public) learned that Graff had fathered a daughter with Josephine Daniel, one of his former employees; the couple later reconciled. Graff owns homes in London, New York, Gstaad, in Switzerland, and Cap Ferrat, in southern France; he also owns a 150-foot yacht, a private plane, and a vineyard, called Delaire, in South Africa.

—C.C.

Suggested Reading: Forbes p84 Aug. 13, 2007; Graff Diamonds International Web site; Interview p198+ Dec. 2008/Jan. 2009; (London) Sunday Telegraph p6 Jan. 4, 2009; New York Times p1 June 19, 2011; PrivatAir Magazine p42+ Autumn 2010 (on-line); W p146+ Dec. 1, 2006; Etherington-Smith, Meredith. The Most Fabulous Jewels in the World, 2007

Frazer Harrison/Getty Images for Overture

Gray, F. Gary

July 17, 1969– Film and music-video director

Address: c/o William Morris Agency, 151 El Camino Dr., Beverly Hills, CA 90212

"If Spike Lee is the king of black filmmakers, F. Gary Gray is the prince," Zach Dionne wrote for GQ (January 20, 2010, on-line). "The tireless, underrated, pure-entertainer prince." As Dionne observed, Gray—from his earliest work, as a music-video director, to his most recent feature film—has always sought to entertain on a grand scale. When he was in his early 20s, he began to win awards for his high-concept, cinematic music videos for R&B and hip-hop artists including TLC, Coolio, Ice Cube, Queen Latifah, and Dr. Dre. Those ground-breaking videos—among them the iconic video for TLC's 1995 hit "Waterfalls"—brought Gray the opportunity to direct his first feature film, the stoner comedy *Friday* (1995), which became an unexpected hit. Gray scored another hit with his next movie, the heist drama *Set It Off* (1996), which led to his first big-budget project: directing the thriller *The Negotiator* (1998), starring Samuel L. Jackson and Kevin Spacey. Since then he has helmed major Hollywood films in several genres, including the action films *The Italian Job* (2003) and *A Man Apart* (2003), the crime comedy *Be Cool* (2005), and the taut thriller *Law Abiding Citizen* (2009). Although initially seen as a filmmaker rooted in hip-hop, Gray has proven to be a director capable of tackling many genres. "With all respect to hip-hop, I really don't want to restrict myself, labeling my films hip-hop films, just like I wouldn't want to restrict them as just black films," he told Donnell Alexander for *Salon.com* (November 1996). "My plans . . . will always be to make good stories. If it takes place in the 'hood, if it takes place in outer space, if it takes place in Canada . . . or in the Grand Canyon, that's where I'm going to shoot it."

Felix Gary Gray was born on July 17, 1969 in New York City. His parents divorced when he was young, and he was raised by his mother, a secretary, in the tough South Central neighborhood of Los Angeles, California. His father lived in Chicago, Illinois, and worked at an army base. When, at the invitation of his uncle, the actor Phil Lewis, Gray attended a play called *The African-American*, the experience proved eye-opening. Gray told Bernard Weinraub for the *New York Times* (July 26, 1998, on-line), "He was like, 'You need to see this play with your little brother,' and I'm like, 'Tough guys don't see plays.' I finally decided to go, and I was blown away. I knew then and there that there was something there for me."

When Gray was a teen, his parents decided he would live with his father and attend Highland Park High School, a prestigious public school in an affluent Chicago suburb. There, Gray worked at a local cable-access station, where he learned how to direct and edit videos. After high school he returned to the West Coast to take classes at Los Angeles City College and pursue his newfound passion for filmmaking.

Gray attended college for a year before dropping out, at age 20, to work as a cameraman at BET, Fox Television, CNN, E!, and other cable stations. When he was 23 he used borrowed equipment and his savings to make a short film about street gangs, *Divided We Fall*. While he never finished the film, he used a trailer for it to persuade industry contacts to give him a shot at creating music videos. As a

video director Gray preferred to shoot in 35mm film (the standard gauge for motion pictures) and often introduced narratives into his videos. He believed so firmly in using 35mm that on occasion he accepted lower fees in order to have more money in the budget for the expensive film stock. "Most of [my] music videos *were* short films—they had dialogue, action sequences," he told Dionne. "I shot with cranes and helicopters. I wanted to create cinema-like moments."

Some of Gray's earliest music videos, from 1993, include two for the rap group Cypress Hill as well as Ice Cube's "It Was a Good Day." The latter video, which follows the West Coast rapper through what appears to be an ideal day in his life, was later ranked by *Rolling Stone* as one of the top 100 videos of all time. In 1994 Gray directed the videos for Outkast's "Southernplayalisticadillacmuzik," Queen Latifah's "Black Hand Side," and Coolio's "Fantastic Voyage." The last-named video, which depicts the rapper Coolio in a vivid dream about going to the beach, earned Gray the 1995 *Billboard* Music Video Award for best rap video.

In 1995 Gray also won the video-of-the-year honor at the MTV Video Music Awards ceremony for "Waterfalls," based on a song by the R&B trio TLC. The video, which also won three other MTV honors and an NAACP Image Award, comprises vignettes reflecting the social ills explored in the song's lyrics and computer-generated imagery of the three singers changing form, from water to flesh and back again. Commenting on that big-budget production, Gray told Dionne, "I was paid like $50,000 more than I was paid to direct *Friday*." At the 1995 MTV ceremony, Gray also won the prize for best rap video for Dr. Dre's "Keep Their Heads Ringin'," part of the soundtrack of Gray's debut film, *Friday*.

Gray's foray into directing feature films came about when Ice Cube—who had become a Hollywood actor with his acclaimed performance in the 1991 urban drama *Boyz n the Hood*—was looking for a director for a screenplay he had written with his musical collaborator, DJ Pooh. The action in *Friday*, made with a relatively small budget of $3 million provided by New Line Cinema, takes place over the course of a day, in which two out-of-work friends (played by Ice Cube and the then-unknown comedian Chris Tucker) must repay money to a drug dealer by 10 p.m. Most of the story takes place in the front yard of a house in South Central Los Angeles, where the two friends interact with eccentric neighborhood characters. The film received mixed reviews but earned $30 million at the box office and eventually became a cult hit. (It also spawned two sequels, neither directed by Gray.) Alexander wrote that the film, "a funny, low-budget . . . meditation on marijuana and downtime in the hood," is "likely to remain a cult hit as long as renting videos and smoking pot go hand in hand." Mal Vincent, in a review of the film for the Norfolk *Virginian-Pilot* (May 8, 1995), wrote, "Although it is crudely produced and has an el-cheapo budget, it is impossible to easily dismiss this infectious laugh-getter. Set entirely in one day . . . the film is little more than a group of stereotyped characters in a drug-oriented culture— something like 'Cheech and Chong Go to the 'Hood.' The language is often scatological and the casual treatment of drugs is regrettable. But if you can get beyond all that, the mood is actually one of innocence and child-like confusion."

Commenting on the surprise success of *Friday*, Gray told Dionne, "We filmed it in 20 days on the block I grew up on in South Central L.A. After watching it the first time, I thought my career was over—I wasn't sure if the movie worked. We had no idea it would be so successful." He told Limara Salt for the film magazine *Little White Lies* (April 22, 2010, on-line) that much of *Friday's* success can be attributed to the film's comedians, especially Tucker, who became a star after the film's release. He recalled, alluding in part to the inexperience of the cast and crew, "In terms of the type of control you have with a classically trained actor or someone who understands the filmmaking, it was a tough process. It worked out and we were surprised." In the same interview, commenting on *Friday's* cult success and crossover appeal, he said, "I'm happy that I can go to Russia and a person can barely speak English yet they'll quote *Friday*. It's crazy."

After the success of *Friday*, Gray was offered the opportunity to direct similar comedies, but he turned them down in favor of the drama *Set It Off*. He explained to Dionne, "I always wanted to surf the genres. *Set It Off* wasn't a formulaic film or story—you had [the female stars] doing things you would ordinarily see men doing. It was the antithesis of a Hollywood movie. Queen Latifah gave the performance of a lifetime and I got a chance to show what I could do dramatically and in the action realm." The film, which focuses on four struggling Los Angeles women who rob a bank, starred Jada Pinkett (now known as Jada Pinkett Smith), Vivica A. Fox, Kimberly Elise, and the rapper/actress Queen Latifah. Thematically darker than *Friday*, *Set It Off* offered Gray, who was also executive producer, a bigger budget ($6 million) and the opportunity to direct action sequences and develop complex characters. The film received mixed reviews but was hailed for its unusual premise and for the riveting performances of its four leading actresses. It also proved to be another major box-office hit for New Line Cinema. Alexander observed, "*Set It Off* is not the kind of escapist fare that leaves the mind once the harsh light of the multiplex lobby hits the eye. It's a stylish tale about a quartet of poor black women . . . who take to robbing banks when clean living can't pay the rent. Their ill-fated mission, paradoxically, puts them on the path to self-actualization. Though some viewers will be unsettled by its message, others will recognize *Set It Off* as this year's zeitgeist film."

For his next feature, Gray, then only 28, made a bona fide Hollywood blockbuster with *The Negotiator* (1998), whose budget ($50 million) was the largest ever afforded an African-American filmmaker. The thriller stars Samuel L. Jackson as Danny Roman, a top police hostage negotiator falsely accused of crimes. After other means have failed to clear his name, Roman resorts to taking his own hostages at the police office he believes set him up. Kevin Spacey played Chris Sabian, the hostage negotiator called in to handle the situation. In seeking to create sympathy for Jackson's character, Gray took cues from the acclaimed 1975 bank-robbery film *Dog Day Afternoon*; he told Weinraub, "That was a great hostage movie. And that film must have been an amazing challenge. How do you manage to feel totally sympathetic to the Al Pacino character, a bank robber who's trying to get money for a sex-change operation for his gay lover? They did it."

The Negotiator got a mixed critical response. In a representative review, Owen Gleiberman wrote for *Entertainment Weekly* (July 31, 1998, on-line), "*The Negotiator* is a clever B-movie synthesis of *The Fugitive*, *Dog Day Afternoon*, and *Die Hard*. I call it a B movie because the characters don't have much texture; they're all but defined by the pressure-cooker situation in which they find themselves. Watching Danny rattle and improvise, we never feel, as we did with Al Pacino's Sonny in *Dog Day Afternoon*, that we're witnessing the fraught climax to an already messy and tangled existence. Nevertheless, *The Negotiator*, once it gets going . . . is a satisfyingly tense and booby-trapped thriller about the meeting of two relentless minds."

After *The Negotiator* Gray tried his hand at television, with the Fox network drama series *Ryan Caulfield: Year One*. The show, about the titular rookie police officer, played by Sean Maher, was canceled after only two episodes. Gray then returned to the big screen with the thriller *A Man Apart* (2003), starring Vin Diesel, known for his work in action movies. The film is about an undercover Drug Enforcement Agency operative, Sean Vetter (Diesel), out for vengeance against the drug lord who murdered his wife. To prepare for the film, Gray conducted research and interviewed a real drug dealer. The film was generally panned by critics, who found it riddled with clichés and lacking in entertainment value. It also failed to generate the box-office earnings of prior Diesel vehicles. Gray told Dionne about the film, which he also executive-produced, "I have mixed feelings about it; I didn't direct the last 10 minutes because I was working on *The Italian Job* and had to split my time between the two. I didn't get a chance to put all my energies into *A Man Apart* in the way I wanted to. I'm still proud of the movie, but I wish I had given it the attention it deserved."

Gray's other 2003 film, *The Italian Job*, fared much better than *A Man Apart*. Inspired by the 1969 British film of the same name, *The Italian Job* starred Mark Wahlberg, Charlize Theron, Edward Norton, Jason Statham, Seth Green, the rapper and actor Mos Def, and Donald Sutherland. It follows a team of thieves as they seek revenge, in the form of a heist, against a former accomplice. The film includes riveting chase sequences through the narrow canals of Venice, Italy, and the congested streets of Los Angeles. Gray described the movie to Alberlynne Harris for blackfilm.com (March 2003) as being more homage than remake, explaining, "It's a different story, a different plot. It was really important for us to leave the original alone." Critics described the film as a smart, entertaining action picture and lauded the chase scenes as original and engaging. Robert Koehler wrote for *Variety* (May 26, 2003, on-line), "Proponents of the studios' recent penchant for remakes of beloved pics have strong defense in *The Italian Job*. Not only is this new 'Job' a generally better movie than the satisfying 1969 caper starring Michael Caine and Noel Coward, it moves through the paces with a light, confident grace very much its own. Director F. Gary Gray's production, and writing team Donna and Wayne Powers' script, succeed with a complete overhaul of the original from the chassis up." *The Italian Job* earned $106 million during its theater run and, through its chase sequences, helped popularize the Mini Cooper, the tiny car made by the British Motor Corp. that was used in the original film. Gray recalled to Dionne about the experience of creating the film, "I remember standing in the Italian Alps with 500 technicians from eight different countries shooting an action sequence. Here I am, this young black kid in the middle of it all, and it's like heaven. It was my first time shooting a movie out of the country, and I know for a fact they'll never let anyone shoot another boat chase in Venice after us. If you enjoyed that, savor it, because it'll never happen again."

Gray's next feature film, which he also produced, was *Be Cool* (2005), based on the 1999 crime novel by Elmore Leonard, a sequel to Leonard's 1990 novel, *Get Shorty* (which was made into a hit film in 1995 by Barry Sonnenfeld). The film centers on the mobster Chili Palmer, the main character in *Get Shorty* (played in both films by John Travolta), as he tries to break into the music industry. *Be Cool* was released to lukewarm reviews.

Law Abiding Citizen, Gray's 2009 feature, starred Gerard Butler as Clyde Shelton, who takes the law into his own hands after the man who helped murder his family escapes the death penalty by testifying against his accomplice. Shelton's vengeance is aimed not only at the killer but at those who, in Shelton's view, failed to see justice done—including the chief prosecutor, Nick Rice (Jamie Foxx), and other public officials in Philadelphia, Pennsylvania, where the film is set. Confounding investigators, Shelton appears to be committing murders, or at least orchestrating them, while in prison. The film received mixed reviews, with some critics pointing to the chemistry between Foxx and Butler as a high point. "Foxx and Butler make a well-matched pair in their grim determination," Roger Ebert observed for the *Chicago Sun-Times* (October 14, 2009), in a review available on rogerebert.suntimes.com. He noted that the film "is one of those movies you like more at the time than in retrospect. I mean, *come on,* you're thinking. Still, there's something to be said for a movie you like well enough at the time." Gleiberman, in his *Entertainment Weekly* review (October 14, 2009, on-line), found the film's premise to be preposterous, writing, "Clyde is meant to be nuts, but too often it's *Law Abiding Citizen* that checks rationality at the door."

Although Gray has focused primarily on feature films since the release of *Friday*, he has continued to direct music videos. "Directors don't get an opportunity to play," he told Alexander. "Actors have workshops. Musicians have bands. Directors, who are in the same kind of creative medium, don't have an opportunity to play or to test certain things. And video is a playground for me." Gray's works in the genre include, in addition to those mentioned earlier, those for Whitney Houston's "I Believe in You and Me" (1996), R. Kelly's "If I Could Turn Back the Hands of Time" (1999), Outkast's "Ms. Jackson" (2000), Jay-Z's "Show Me What You Got" (2006), and Rick Ross's "Super High" (2010). He is said to be in the running to direct "Kane & Lynch," a movie based on the video game *Kane & Lynch: Dead Men*. Since at least 2008 he has also been planning a biographical film about the soul singer Marvin Gaye, tentatively titled "Marvin."

Commenting on his success as a genre-hopping filmmaker, Gray told Dionne, "You really can't say the guy who made *Friday* made *Law Abiding Citizen*; it's a different style, a truly different genre, a psychological thriller. You get penalized in this industry for being *too* different—people like to peg you and say, 'This is the action guy,' 'This is the comedy guy.' I've been lucky to take risks."

—W.D.

Suggested Reading: All Movie Guide Web site; *GQ* (on-line) Jan. 20, 2010; imdb.com; *Little White Lies* (on-line) Apr. 22, 2010; *New York Times* (on-line) July 26, 1998; *Salon.com* Nov. 1996; Donalson, Melvin. *Black Directors in Hollywood*, 2003

Selected Films: *Friday*, 1995; *Set It Off*, 1996; *The Negotiator*, 1998; *The Italian Job*, 2003; *A Man Apart*, 2003; *Be Cool*, 2005; *Law Abiding Citizen*, 2009

Selected Music Videos: "It Was a Good Day," 1993; "Black Hand Side," 1994; "Fantastic Voyage," 1994; "Waterfalls," 1995; "I Believe in You and Me," 1996; "If I Could Turn Back the Hands of Time," 1999; "Ms. Jackson," 2000; "Show Me What You Got," 2006; "Super High," 2010

Frazer Harrison/Getty Images

Gray, Jim

1959– Sportscaster

Address: Westwood One Main Office, 1166 Sixth Ave., 10th Fl., New York, NY 10036

The veteran sportscaster Jim Gray is widely recognized as a "probing, well-connected, occasionally aggravating reporter . . . , an international player, a familiar figure throughout sports broadcasting and, at times, a controversial one," Ailene Voisin wrote for the *Sacramento (California) Bee* (May 23, 2010). Since he began his career in broadcast journalism, as an undergraduate in the late 1970s, Gray has reported on thousands of athletic competitions, among them eight Olympic Games; two dozen National Football League (NFL) Super Bowls; Major League Baseball (MLB) games including nine World Series; 18 National Basketball Association (NBA) Finals; and 14 National Collegiate Athletic Association (NCAA) championship games. He has also covered more than 20 Masters Golf Tournaments, more than 400 world-championship boxing matches, and the Rose, Cotton, Orange, and Sugar Bowls—college-football championship games. At various times Gray has worked for ESPN, NBC, CBS, and ABC; currently, he is heard on the Westwood One radio network, and on television he is seen on Showtime and the Golf Channel and provides play-by-play reporting for the Sacramento Kings basketball team. He also covers athletic events as a freelancer.

Gray "always found a way to get to the center of a story, whoever that turned out to be," Ted Shaker, the executive producer of CBS Sports between 1986 and 1992, told Richard Sandomir for the *New York Times* (August 17, 2010, on-line). The sports commentator Mike Breen said of Gray to Sandomir, "He's a bulldog. He's not simply trying to report stories, he's trying to break news, and he does it with an unbelievable Rolodex"—that is, he has myriad contacts in the sports world and elsewhere. Gray's résumé also includes seven years as a national feature reporter for NBC's *Today Show*. In addition, he has interviewed eight U.S. presidents or presidents-elect (beginning with Richard Nixon) as well as leaders of other governments, celebrities, and a huge number of athletes. Gray himself has occasionally become the subject of news stories, notably for interviews he conducted with the heavyweight boxer Mike Tyson in 1997, the baseball player Pete Rose in 1999, and the basketball player LeBron James in 2010. He has earned four Sports Emmy Awards, and in 1998 and 1999 the American Sportscasters Association named him Sports Reporter of the Year. In 2005 Gray was awarded a star on the Hollywood Walk of Fame. *USA Today* has honored him as Sports Reporter of the Year several times, and in 2005 it named him the nation's best sports reporter of the previous quarter-century.

One of three brothers, Jim Gray was born in 1959 in Denver, Colorado, to Lorna (Sadie) Gray and Jerry Gray, a business executive of eastern European descent. According to the *Denver (Colorado) Post* (May 24, 2001), his father was a longtime partner in the real-estate firm of Miller, Klutznick, Davis, and Gray. At Thomas Jefferson High School in Denver, Jim Gray was an All-State tennis player. After he graduated, in 1977, he applied for a summer job at the TV station KBTV (now KUSA). He failed in that attempt, but after he enrolled at the University of Colorado (CU) at Boulder, Cecil L. Walker, a KBTV executive who was visiting the school, noticed him by chance and remembered him. Walker told him that the station had an opening for an intern, and Gray landed the position. At KBTV he gained a hands-on education in many facets of television sports reporting under the guidance of the veteran Denver sportscaster Mike Nolan. Nolan, Gray told Joe Findley, who interviewed him for the CU School of Journalism and Mass Communication Web site (Fall 1997), was "patient and wonderful," and he inspired Gray to change his career goal from advertising to sportscasting.

After he earned a bachelor's degree, in 1981, Gray joined PRISM (Philadelphia Regional In-Home Sports and Movies), a cable channel in Pennsylvania's biggest city. He served as a play-by-play announcer for Philadelphia 76ers basketball games, alongside the renowned basketball coach-turned-sportscaster Chuck Daly, and as a sports anchor and host for Philadelphia Phillies baseball games. He left PRISM in 1983, when he was hired as an associate producer for *16 Days of Glory* (1986), the director Bud Greenspan's documentary about the 1984 Olympics, in Los Angeles, California. In 1984, in his next job, Gray was the West Coast bureau chief for the then five-year-old ESPN (the Entertainment and Sports Programming Network). In those days, he told Dusty Saunders for the *Rocky Mountain News* (June 30, 2003), "I'd tape an interview with Tommy Lasorda following a Dodgers game in Los Angeles on Thursday night, rush to the airport and put it on a plane for Hartford"—near Bristol, Connecticut, where ESPN was headquartered. "Someone would drive over from Bristol and pick it up. . . . The tape would be processed and ready for SportsCenter on Friday." Noting how antiquated that time-consuming procedure now seems, Gray added, "Times have really changed." With ESPN Gray covered NBA games and such events as the America's Cup (yacht racing) and the Super Bowl. In October 1987, scooping all other journalists, he revealed that the Los Angeles (now St. Louis) Rams' running back Eric Dickerson had been traded to the Indianapolis Colts.

In 1988 Gray left ESPN to report for *NFL Live*, NBC's National Football League pregame show, and for that year's Summer Olympics, in Seoul, South Korea. In April 1989 the network chose O. J. Simpson to replace him on *NFL Live*, and he left NBC. The next year CBS hired Gray for its pregame pro-football series, *The NFL Today*. At CBS he also covered the World Series, NCAA basketball tournaments, the Masters Golf Tournaments, and the Winter Olympics, in Albertville, France. He returned to NBC in February 1994, after CBS lost its coverage of NFL games. Gray broadcast commentary for NBC's NFL and NBA broadcasts, covering such events as the Super Bowl, the NBA All-Star Game, and the NBA Finals. He also covered the World Series, the Masters Golf Tournaments, golf's Ryder Cup and Presidents Cup matches, and the 1996 and 2000 Summer Olympic Games, in Atlanta, Georgia, and Sydney, Australia, respectively. He was praised for his reporting on the bombing that occurred at Centennial Olympic Park, in Atlanta, during the 1996 Games. He left NBC when his contract expired, in the fall of 2002.

Earlier, while with NBC, Gray began to cover championship boxing matches for the Showtime Network. In addition, in 2001 Gray joined Westwood One as host of that radio network's Monday Night Football pregame and halftime shows. On the Westwood program he conducts interviews, recaps the outcomes of the previous Sunday's NFL games, offers other league news, and previews the upcoming Monday Night Football match. Also for Westwood One he covers the NCAA men's basketball tournament. From 2002 to 2008 he served a second stint with ESPN, covering football and basketball telecasts. He rejoined NBC for the 2008 Summer Olympics, in Beijing, China. The next year he started working for the Golf Channel, as a reporter for *Golf in America* and "Live From" telecasts. In 2010 Gray began broadcasting for select Sacramento Kings games.

Gray won the National Sportscasters and Sportswriters Association's Broadcast of the Year Award for his brief interview with Tyson on June 28, 1997,

in Las Vegas, Nevada, immediately after the aborted second fight between Tyson and Evander Holyfield. As Showtime's ringside reporter during that match, Gray witnessed Tyson bite off a piece of Holyfield's right ear and then bite his left ear, leading the referee to disqualify Tyson and end the fight with seconds left in round three. In the midst of the ensuing melee, involving furious spectators and others, Gray—alone among the journalists present—secured the permission of the fight's promoter, Don King, to enter Tyson's dressing room, where he asked Tyson to explain why he had acted as he had. Tyson referred to his own battered and bleeding face but did not say anything directly about Holyfield. "I was just trying to listen to his side of the story, to be fair and to be objective," Gray told Leonard Shapiro for the *Washington Post* (July 2, 1997).

Gray was widely vilified by members of the public and the media in 1999 for his interview with Pete Rose, who during his career as a player set many Major League Baseball records that remain unbroken. In August 1989, during his sixth season as manager of the Cincinnati Reds, Rose accepted his banishment from all MLB activities because of evidence indicating that he had bet on games. He accepted that ban—or, in MLB parlance, agreed to be placed on the league's "ineligible" list—in exchange for a promise that he would not be formally charged with gambling on games, which MLB regulations prohibit. Then, in 1999, MLB officials decided to honor an election in which fans chose Rose for the All-Century Team; in conjunction with his selection, the officials allowed Gray, as NBC's field reporter, to interview Rose following a public celebration of the All-Century Team on October 24, 1999, the day Game Two of that year's World Series was held. During the interview Gray suggested to Rose that the American public was "very forgiving" and that the present moment offered an opportunity for Rose to admit to and apologize for gambling on games. Although Rose insisted that he was "not going to admit to something that didn't happen," according to a transcript on the *Sports Illustrated* Web site (August 6, 2005), Gray repeatedly advised him to "acknowledg[e] what seems to be overwhelming evidence" regarding the gambling or otherwise admit his guilt. After Gray's fourth attempt Rose declared, "I'm surprised you're bombarding me like this . . . on a great night, a great occasion. . . . This is a prosecutor's brief, not an interview, and I'm very surprised at you." "This ended up becoming an indictment on the American media as much as anything, because Gray was ridiculed by the public and the press alike for having the gall to try to bring journalistic credibility to a prefabricated, shiny, happy, people event," *Sports Illustrated* noted in a postscript to the transcript. After the interview Gray received a lot of hate mail and even death threats. "I don't apologize for it. I stand by it, and I think it was absolutely a proper line of questioning," he told Sean Keeler for the *Cincinnati (Ohio)*

Post (October 26, 1999, on-line). "I was just doing my job," he maintained in a conversation with Dusty Saunders for the Denver, Colorado, *Rocky Mountain News* (January 12, 2004), a few days after the publication of Rose's memoir *My Prison Without Bars* (written with Rick Hill), in which Rose admitted that he had engaged in gambling on games.

Another of Gray's much-publicized interviews was one with the Los Angeles Lakers basketball player Kobe Bryant. That conversation aired on ESPN on October 28, 2003, during an ongoing feud between Bryant and another Lakers star, Shaquille O'Neal, that had become public; the interview also came a few days after a Colorado judge announced that Bryant would stand trial on charges of raping a 19-year-old hotel worker. Earlier, on July 18, 2003, after Bryant had stated at a news conference that he was guilty of adultery but was innocent of rape, Gray had spoken highly of Bryant during an interview with Nancy Grace for CNN; after noting that he had interviewed Bryant "countless" times, he declared, "I have never seen this guy in any way, shape or form have a bad public or private moment." During Gray and Bryant's October 28 conversation, Bryant spoke disparagingly of O'Neal, intimating that O'Neal had come to the Lakers' training camp "fat and out of shape," had blamed others for Lakers' defeats, and had faulted Lakers' publicists for not attributing his problems to injuries, so as to cover up his poor physical condition. When Gray asked Bryant, "Do you feel Shaq has been supportive in regards to your legal situation?," Bryant answered, "He is not my quote unquote big brother. A big brother would have called to lend his support this summer. I heard absolutely nothing from him." (In July 2004 O'Neal was traded to the Miami Heat, and the following September the criminal charges against Bryant were dismissed, because his accuser refused to testify in court against him.)

In 2006 and 2007 Gray secured exclusive interviews with the baseball player Barry Bonds, an outfielder for the Pittsburgh Pirates (1986–92) and the San Francisco Giants (1993–2007). Like Rose, Bonds holds many MLB records, among them the greatest number of home runs hit during regular seasons—762, a total he reached in 2007, surpassing by seven the record set by Hank Aaron in 1974. Questions regarding Bonds's suspected use of performance-enhancing drugs, known as anabolic steroids, had surfaced as early as 2003. In grand-jury testimony in late December 2003, which was illegally leaked to the public, Bonds denied using any MLB-banned substances, insisting that his increased power and significantly bulked physique came from bodybuilding exercises, an improved diet, and approved supplements or creams—flaxseed oil and arthritis balm—given to him by his trainer. In both interviews, the latter of which aired on MSNBC's *Countdown with Keith Olbermann* on November 1, 2007, Gray asked Bonds how he would respond to accusations that he had used anabolic steroids, and Bonds maintained that such al-

legations were false. Two weeks later, based on accumulating evidence, a federal grand jury indicted Bonds on charges of perjury and obstruction of justice in his 2003 testimony; he is scheduled to stand trial in March 2011.

More recently, in 2010, Gray used his clout with LeBron James's management team, called LRMR, to arrange an exclusive interview with the basketball star. In that one-hour, live interview special, which aired during prime-time on ESPN, James revealed after weeks of intense media and public speculation that he would leave the Cleveland Cavaliers and join the Miami Heat. Nearly 10 million viewers watched the interview, which was held at a Boys & Girls Club in Greenwich, Connecticut on July 8, 2010. Afterward Gray was strongly criticized in many quarters for dragging out the interview by asking LeBron more than a dozen questions before the all-important one—which team's contract James intended to sign—which came nearly a half-hour after the special's start. Some sources, among them the *New York Post* (July 9, 2010, on-line), accused Gray of receiving payment from LRMR for his role in the special. Gray vehemently denied that charge, telling Howard Kurtz for the *Washington Post* (July 10, 2010, on-line), "I didn't take a penny from LeBron or any entity connected to him." "I would never take a nickel from somebody I'm interviewing," he declared. According to Kurtz, "Gray said he essentially agreed to work for free, minus expenses, because James was donating the advertising proceeds—$2.5 million, as it turned out—to the Boys & Girls Clubs of America."

Gray became a subject of news reports again on August 11, 2010. During a press conference held that day at the site of the Professional Golfers Association (PGA) Championship in Haven, Wisconsin, Corey Pavin, the captain of the Ryder Cup team, denied telling Gray—as reported the day before on the Golf Channel—that Tiger Woods would be chosen for that year's team. "His interpretation of what I said is incorrect," Pavin said at the press conference, as transcribed for asapsports.com (August 11, 2010). "There's nobody that's promised any picks right now. It would be disrespectful to everybody that's trying to make the team." Immediately after the press conference ended, according to Steve Elling, a reporter for CBSSports.com (August 11, 2010), Gray confronted Pavin. With the tip of his index finger pressed to Pavin's chest, Gray "called him a liar and barked, 'You're going down.'" Pavin's wife never made public the recording she claimed to have made of Gray's accusation and threat.

"You are what you are," Gray told Ailene Voisin in May 2010. "I don't want to change who I am." He added that he had told Joe and Gavin Maloof, members of the family that owns the Sacramento Kings, "Look, let's be honest. I don't set out to aggravate people, but if a question needs to be asked, I'll ask it. If that upsets people, so be it." Voisin described Gray as "a youthful-looking 50, with a slender build, sharp features and medium brown hair that seldom slips out of place." Gray and his wife, Frann, live in Santa Monica, California. The couple established the Jim Gray Scholarship Fund, for students at the School of Journalism and Communications at the University of Colorado. Gray has also been a major supporter of the Boys and Girls Clubs of America, the Special Olympics, the Multiple Sclerosis Society, and other charitable organizations.

—C.C.

Suggested Reading: *Atlanta (Georgia) Journal-Constitution* E p12 Oct. 28, 1999; (Denver, Colorado) *Rocky Mountain News* F p18 Feb. 27, 1995, C p2 June 30, 2003; *Miami (Florida) Herald* D p5 June 11, 2004; *New York Times* (on-line) Aug. 17, 2010; *Pittsburgh (Pennsylvania) Post-Gazette* D p2 Oct. 31, 1999; *Sacramento (California) Bee* C p1 May 23, 2010

Grizzly Bear

Music group

Rossen, Daniel
1982– Singer; songwriter; guitarist

Bear, Chris
1982– Drummer; arranger; recording engineer

Droste, Ed
Oct. 22, 1978– Guitarist; singer

Taylor, Chris
1981– Bassist; singer

Address: c/o Warp Records, 285 W. Broadway # 550, New York, NY 10013-0465

Grizzly Bear makes music that offers layered, complicated arrangements with a pop sensibility and that incorporates elements of doo-wop, 1960s pop, choir, and psychedelia with vocal harmonies reminiscent of the Beatles, the Beach Boys, the Band, and Simon and Garfunkel. Their songs build slowly and unfold in multiple directions. The band began as a solo project in the bedroom of its singer/songwriter Ed Droste, in 2003; with the addition of the drummer, arranger, and recording engineer Chris Bear, the bassist and reed player Chris Taylor, and the singer, songwriter and guitarist Daniel Rossen, Grizzly Bear became the ensemble it is today. Both *Yellow House* (2006), their first album as a four-man band, and *Veckatimest* (2009), their second full-length album, received a great deal of critical attention and praise. In 2009 *Veckatimest* peaked at number eight on the *Billboard* 200 chart. Nate Chinen, a *New York Times* (December 20, 2009) critic, placed that album at number five on

his top-10 list for the year, and the influential music Web site *Pitchfork.com* (October 1, 2009) included it among the top 200 albums of the new millennium. Grizzly Bear has toured with Feist, TV on the Radio, and Radiohead and have performed live with Paul Simon, the Brooklyn Philharmonic, and the London Symphony Orchestra. During Grizzly Bear's tour with Radiohead in 2008, the latter's keyboardist/guitarist Jonny Greenwood told the audience that Grizzly Bear is his "favorite band in the world." In several interviews the rapper Jay-Z, a self-described Grizzly Bear fan, said that he hoped hip-hop artists—whom he saw as working in a generally stagnant musical climate—would find inspiration in the band's novel composing and songwriting.

The founding member of Grizzly Bear, the singer/songwriter Edward F. Droste, was born on October 22, 1978. He and his brother grew up in Watertown, Massachusetts, a Boston suburb, in the yellow house where Grizzly Bear later recorded their album of that name. His mother, Diane "Di" Droste, was a music teacher who enjoyed playing the autoharp and maracas, and one of his aunts was a classically trained, professional cellist. His maternal grandfather chaired the Music Department at Harvard University, in Cambridge, Massachusetts, for a while; his grandfather's interests were classical and choral music and "classic vocal jazz," Droste told Rick Moody for *Bomb* (Summer 2010). "My grandfather was very into us gathering around a piano and singing. Before dinner, after dinner, gather 'round!," he recalled to Moody. His parents had eclectic tastes; they liked to listen to 19th-century Scottish folk songs, classical and choral music, and even "Crystal Gayle–like stuff," Droste told Moody. Droste, too, liked popular music. "My first stage was the stadium bands: Madonna and Tom Petty and Aerosmith," he told Joan Anderman for the *Boston Globe* (August 12, 2008). "Then U2 and REM. Then I found Pavement and Liz Phair." He told Moody that he "must have listened to" the first Phair album "5,000 times." "I think it's the only band or artist I've ever obsessed over," he added. Droste played guitar in high school and took some lessons; he gave up the instrument after graduation. At that time he had no intention of becoming a musician.

After he completed high school, Droste spent a year abroad. He studied art in Italy and Greece and did volunteer work in a community in Zimbabwe while he lived with a local family. Back in the U.S., he entered Hampshire College, in Amherst, Massachusetts, where he became extremely depressed. "It felt like a small, irritating environment" as well as "remote and isolating," he told Moody. He also said, "I was dealing with some personal stuff, like coming out of the closet, so it was a transitional period." He left Hampshire and enrolled in writing classes at the Gallatin School of Individualized Study, a division of New York University (NYU). At NYU he became friendly with the drummer Christopher Bear (born in 1982). (Droste had named his future band before meeting Bear.)

Tom Hines, courtesy of Press Here Publicity
Grizzly Bear: top: Chris Bear (left), Ed Droste; bottom: Chris Taylor (left), Daniel Rossen

The end of a long-term romantic relationship left Droste feeling very low, and in 2003 he started recording songs in his bedroom. In just over a year, he recorded 35. Bear, who had expertise in recording technology, helped him arrange and engineer the songs and also added drums to a few tracks. The result was *Horn of Plenty* (2004), a 14-song debut album, which identified the artist as Grizzly Bear and was released on the independent, recently founded label Kanine Records, based in the New York City borough of Brooklyn. In an interview with Lizzy Goodman for *New York* (May 11, 2009), Droste said, "That album is this weird faded Polaroid of my past. . . . The songs felt fully realized at the time because I didn't really know what I was doing." *Horn of Plenty*'s layered vocals, effects, samples, organs, reed instruments, and acoustic guitars led some critics to classify it as psychedelic folk music. "Songs like the opening 'Deep Sea Diver' and the mesmerizing 'Shift' crawl along at an almost funereal pace, the latter featuring what sounds like a scratchy Gramophone recording of a piano augmented only by echoing whistles, clapping, trippy found sounds, and weirdly hypnotic multi-tracked vocals," Bret Love wrote for allmusic.com. "As a whole, the album produces a murky sound that unfolds like a narcotic dream you can't quite shake upon waking. This is the kind of album you'll want to listen to late at night, perhaps a few sheets to the wind, with the lights off and headphones on to allow these creepy, quiet little tunes to worm their way into your subconscious." Droste's album earned plaudits from the music press (notably *Pitchfork.com*) and other musicians. In 2005 *Horn of Plenty* was reissued as a double al-

bum, with the second disc containing 17 remixes of Grizzly Bear songs by electronic artists including Final Fantasy (born Owen Pallett), Dntel (James Scott Tamborello), and DJ Simon Bookish (Leo Chadburn).

In 2005 Grizzly Bear became a four-member band—or, rather, as Droste had intended, a collective of collaborators, not merely backup musicians, to help Droste overcome his unease about performing live and to broaden his musical horizons. Chris Bear introduced Droste to Chris Taylor (born in 1981), a bassist and reed player. The trio played a handful of live shows, but Droste felt there was something missing. Bear then introduced Droste to the singer, songwriter, and guitarist Daniel Rossen (born in 1982), who joined the band as a vocalist and songwriter. All of them knew one another from NYU, but unlike Droste, the other three were musically trained, particularly in jazz.

In the summer of 2005, all four band members brought their instruments and studio equipment from their Brooklyn apartments to the yellow house in Watertown. During a month when his mother was elsewhere on vacation, Droste and his bandmates set up a studio in the living room, which contained a Steinway piano formerly owned by one of Droste's great-grandmothers. "We realized that if we were going to do a record, we needed to get out of [New York] because there are just too many friends here, too many distractions," Droste told Grayson Curring for *Pitchfork.com* (October 9, 2006). He added, "We didn't have money for a studio. This was the perfect place. We were able to record at all times of night or whenever we wanted to. We were able to set up and leave everything set up and just have this big Victorian house just sort of letting us live in it and record whatever we wanted." Droste and Rossen wrote most of the songs and arrangements; in every other way the recording was a collaboration among all four band members. Taylor served as the band's sound engineer, a position he still occupies. He also sang and played bass and occasionally a reed instrument; for example, for one track, he created a bass tone by playing a clarinet through a pitch shifter. Postproduction continued for about seven months.

Yellow House (2006), released by the independent British label Warp Records, was Grizzly Bear's first album as a four-piece band. It is more ambitious, grand, layered, and powerful than *Horn of Plenty*—all without losing the latter's intimacy. "Easier," the opening track, features wind and brass instruments, banjo, acoustic guitar, some electronic elements, and smooth vocals. "Marla," a slow waltz, has a mellow acoustic guitar, melancholic vocal harmonies, and piano lines. (The song is an adaptation of a tune written by one of Droste's great-aunts in the 1930s.) "Colorado," the last track, starts slowly with vocal harmonies that are as comforting as they are ominous and then, toward the end, builds to a drum-driven beat with hypnotic vocal harmonies, with the band slowly singing the line "What now? What now? What now?" Other songs, such as "Little Brother" and "On a Neck, On a Spit," exhibit subtle country-music elements in the vocal phrasing and the banjo and guitar playing. *Yellow House* received a good deal of praise both from critics and fellow musicians. In a profile of Grizzly Bear for the *New Yorker* (May 11, 2009), Sasha Frere-Jones wrote, "The songs on *Yellow House* are interconnected and full of audible air. They seem to glow from within, as though the electricity had gone out and the house were lit only by candles. It was my default album for 2006, never polite and never annoying, even when the songs are roughened up with clatter and howls. That's the Grizzly Bear trick: despite the complexity of its arrangements, none of what the band does feels precious or forced." With regard to "Knife," the album's best-known song, Frere-Jones wrote, "Droste's singing is warm and sleepy, as if nothing could go wrong, while the lyrics describe a situation where nothing goes right: 'I want you to know, when I look in your eyes, with every blow comes another lie.' The singing could be the original vocal take from a Phil Spector B-side, but slowed way down; the band surrounds it with a stream of high noises—the feedback of guitars, voices straining, synthesizers droning—that fight the sweetness of the vocal. . . . When Droste plays three fuzzy sustained chords and sings the chorus—'Can't you feel the knife?'—several woodwinds play in unison with the guitar and bass notes, making a familiar sound soft and unfamiliar. All of a sudden, the backing vocals are bleeding in from above, like the tub upstairs overflowing." Daniel Rossen, Frere-Jones continued, "described *Yellow House* to me as an 'anxious cloud,' and that description fits 'Knife' well, though the song is as blissful as it is disorienting." Jeff Tweedy, the frontman of the band Wilco, wrote for the *New York Times* (July 22, 2007) that Grizzly Bear makes "really beautiful, evocative music that has a gauzy fuzziness to it; you can't accurately pinpoint their place in time. Their music is like a painting by Monet. . . . I like records that have their own internal logic, their own universe. [*Yellow House*] feels like a fully formed world, a real place that I'm not a part of but I get to visit."

In 2007 Grizzly Bear released *Friend*, an 11-track EP that consists of remixes, alternate takes, and covers of Grizzly Bear songs and cameos by other musicians. Band of Horses covers "Plans," and Atlas Sound covers "Knife"; Beirut and the Dirty Projectors contribute vocals to "Alligator (Choir Version)"; and Grizzly Bear performs a version of "He Hit Me (And It Felt Like a Kiss)" by the 1960s female vocal group the Crystals. The EP attracted less attention than *Yellow House* but received positive reviews.

The band's next full-length album, *Veckatimest* (2009), was recorded in upstate New York and at Droste's grandmother's old cottage on Cape Cod, Massachusetts. (Its name is that of a tiny island near Cape Cod.) The record is more pop-oriented than *Yellow House* and at times less layered but re-

tains Grizzly Bear's signature sound. *Veckatimest* contains a variety of textures and musical styles. In a conversation with Chris Martins for the Austin, Texas, A.V. Club section of the *Onion* (June 16, 2009, on-line), Rossen said, "We have such a tendency to layer and layer, to put every idea on every track, so we made an effort to strip things down a bit—to have bare vocal performances and purely instrumental parts. We also pushed ourselves toward songs with more of a steady beat. A pop approach is tough for us because we're very improvisatory. We tried to temper that with a little bit of simplicity." "Simplicity" characterizes *Veckatimest* only to a point. The record is full of lush, intense, and interwoven vocal harmonies and intricate details; it includes several string and choral arrangements by the young contemporary classical composer Nico Muhly and backup vocals (on a few tracks) by the Brooklyn Youth Chorus. The release of the album brought the band a new level of recognition. Their fame continued to grow during an international tour, a series of performances at music festivals (among them South by Southwest and the Pitchfork Music Festival), and appearances on *Late Show with David Letterman* and *Late Night with Conan O'Brien*.

In a review of *Veckatimest* for *Pitchfork.com* (May 26, 2009), Paul Thompson, who gave the album a 9/10 rating, wrote, "Yeah, *Veckatimest* sounds worked-over, but in the best of ways; carefully embellished, stripped bare when applicable, full of the joy of sounds colliding with other sounds. Grizzly Bear was once Ed Droste's band, but no longer; it's a family affair, and only four guys so completely serious about music-making could come together to make an album this labor-intensive sound so airy, so natural." Frere-Jones wrote of *Veckatimest*, "If *Yellow House* was a respite, a quiet, single-story structure, the band's new album . . . is a sprawling water park, sending you through different sluices and dropping you from pools down into slides that give onto small lakes." The album's 12 tracks include "Two Weeks," a cheerful number with a bouncy keyboard beat and 1960s-style, pop-influenced vocal melodies. The '60s influence is also apparent in "Cheerleader," which lays dreamy, teen-pop vocal harmonies (and the voices of the youth choir in the background) on top of a steady drumbeat and bright, reverb-soaked guitars. The vocals and chugging rhythm of the melancholic "Ready, Able" build until, halfway through the song, the drums begin beating and Droste and Rossen hypnotically repeat the lines "They go, we go / I want you to know what I did I did." The delicacy of the singing contrasts with the messages of lines such as "All your useless pretensions are weighing on my time," from the track "While You Wait for the Others," and instances when the entire band sings long "ohhh's" and "ahhh's" come across as a paradoxical blend of power and fragility.

Grizzly Bear's music has been used in several films, notably Philip Seymour Hoffman's directorial debut, *Jack Goes Boating* (2010), and the entire soundtrack for the romantic drama *Blue Valentine* (2010), directed by Derek Cianferance and starring Ryan Gosling and Michelle Williams.

The band began work on its next album in May 2011.

All four Grizzly Bear members live in Brooklyn, within walking distance of one another.

—D.K.

Suggested Reading: allmusic.com; *Bomb* (on-line) Summer 2010; brooklynvegan.com Sep. 8, 2006; grizzly-bear.net; *New York* p44+ May 11, 2009; *New Yorker* p110+ May 11, 2009; *Pitchfork.com* Oct. 9, 2006

Selected Recordings: *Horn of Plenty*, 2004; *Yellow House*, 2006; *Veckatimest*, 2009

Frederick M. Brown/Getty Images

Grylls, Bear

June 7, 1974– Adventurer; writer; television personality

Address: c/o The Rights House, Drury House, 34-43 Russell St., London WC2B 5HA, England

The British adventurer, writer, and television host Bear Grylls is currently the Discovery Channel's "premier ambassador of outdoor danger," Scott Collins wrote for the *Los Angeles Times* (June 22, 2008). A former member of the Special Forces Reserve of England's Territorial Army, Grylls first made a name for himself with a number of record-breaking feats, among them reaching the summit of Mount Everest, in 1998, thereby becoming, at age 23, the youngest Briton to do so. He rose to fame internationally as the host of the Discovery Channel's popular television series *Man vs. Wild*, which debuted in 2006 and is now in its seventh season. He has since impressed tens of millions of viewers worldwide with his daring and his survival skills: in each installment of the series, Grylls parachutes into a region of Earth that is extremely inhospitable to humans (except, in some cases, those living there) and then demonstrates the often ingenious means by which he makes his way back to "civilization." Writing for *Outside* magazine (May 2010, on-line), Hampton Sides described Grylls as having "an infectiously affable persona that's part Tarzan, part MacGyver, and part Austin Powers" and added, "While many of his survival tips seem of dubious practical value—when lost in the Serengeti, is it really a good idea to hand-squeeze your drinking water from a fresh elephant turd?—his antics are addictively watchable." Grylls's antics include his eating worms, insects, raw flesh, carrion, and other things usually thought of as inedible. Although he has been labeled a showman, Grylls has maintained that his goal is to awaken people to the power and beauty of nature. "We live in an amazing world, and we're charged with living boldly," he told Collins. "It's a shame to lose these skills that allow us to live in nature. So much of our brain is absorbed with moneymaking and computers. The most fulfilled people I know are absorbed with nature. We have, deep within us, a love for the outdoors. There's more to the world than your boss and trying to impress your girlfriend with a big car."

Edward Michael Grylls was born on June 7, 1974 in Bembridge, a village on Great Britain's Isle of Wight, in the English Channel. His sister, Lara, is eight years his senior. Grylls's sister began calling him Teddy early on; his current legal first name, Bear, evolved from that nickname. "I was a bossy big sister, and he was my toy," Lara Grylls recalled to Hampton Sides. "I was always getting him to do things. When he was seven years old, I bribed him to eat an entire package of bacon, raw!" Grylls willingly accepted his sister's challenges, and "thus was born a habit of regarding questionable gastronomy as a rewarding form of shock entertainment," Sides wrote. His parents, Sir Michael Grylls (who died in 2001), a Conservative Party politician and former Royal Marine, and his mother, Lady Sally Grylls (née Ford), helped nurture his adventurous spirit. When Grylls was four, his father started teaching him how to sail and climb. "He instilled in me two things: follow your dreams and look after your friends," Grylls told Patricia Cohen for the *New York Times* (June 15, 2007). His mother reportedly influenced his habit of eating foul-tasting proteins; Grylls recalled to more than one reporter that she once served him spoiled pork chops retrieved from the family garbage bin.

When Grylls was eight years old, he joined the Cub Scouts; his association with the British Boy Scouts Association has continued ever since. Also when he was eight, his father gave him a picture of Mount Everest; the world's tallest peak, it rises 29,029 feet (8,848 meters) in the Himalaya Mountains along the border of Nepal and Tibet. The picture "captivated" him, as Grylls wrote in his book *The Kid Who Climbed Everest* (2001). "I would sit there trying to work out the scale of the huge ice fields I saw in the foreground, and to judge how steep those summit slopes would really be. My mind would begin to wander, and soon I would actually be on those slopes—feeling the wind whip across my face. From these times, the dream [of climbing Everest] was being born within me." Grylls spent his summer and winter holidays climbing with his father on the chalk cliffs near their home on the Isle of Wight; the two vowed to climb Everest together someday.

Grylls was educated at boarding schools, including, starting at age 13, Eton College (usually referred to simply as Eton); one of England's most prestigious private preparatory schools, it counts among its alumni members of the British royal family and people of great distinction in many fields. While there Grylls became known as "the kid who could climb the highest flagpole and hang somebody's underpants up in the middle of the night," he told Amanda Hooton for the Sydney, Australia, *Morning Herald* (September 11, 2010). He added, "I think, with a place like Eton, you bury yourself in the things you're good at; you find an identity there. So it's no surprise I do these things now." Along with his friend Mick Crosthwaite, Grylls launched Eton's first mountaineering club and led fellow students on climbing expeditions in Scotland and Wales. Also as a teenager he learned to skydive and earned a second-degree black belt in Shotokan karate.

After graduating from Eton, in 1992, Grylls and a friend spent several months hiking in the Himalayas in India. He thought about joining the Indian Army; instead, he returned to England to attend the University of London. Concurrently, he enlisted in the United Kingdom Special Forces Reserve; he was among a select few to be chosen for the elite Special Air Services (SAS) of the British Territorial Army. During his three years of service as a saber soldier in the 21 SAS Regiment, he received training in desert and winter warfare, unarmed combat, combat survival, signaling, parachuting, the use of explosives, and the handling of medical emergencies. (He had left college to serve in the military; he later attended the University of London part-time and earned a degree in Hispanic studies in 2002.)

Grylls's service in the SAS ended prematurely, in late 1996, after a parachuting accident in Zambia, in Africa: his parachute ripped upon opening at 16,000 feet, causing him to plummet to the ground at twice the normal speed; he landed on his back, with only his empty parachute pack to cushion his fall, and suffered three partially crushed vertebrae. A doctor later told him that he had come "within a whisker of severing my spinal cord, and paralyzing myself for life," he recalled in *The Kid Who Climbed Everest.* Grylls underwent eight months of treatment and therapy in army medical and rehabilitation centers in Africa and England, and his back healed completely.

"This long road to recovery . . . taught me that life was precious," Grylls wrote in *The Kid Who Climbed Everest.* "I had learnt this the hard way. I had come within an inch of losing all my movement and, by the grace of God, still lived to tell the tale. I had learnt so much, but above all I had gained an understanding of the cards that I had been playing with. This scared me." It also led him to act upon his vow of climbing Mount Everest (though not with his father). He signed onto a British expedition team headed by his friend Neil Laughton, a former Royal Marine, and spent about a year acclimating his body for climbing at extremely high altitudes. His preparations included climbing the 22,329-foot (nearly 6,806-meter) Mount Ama Dablam, in the Himalayas of eastern Nepal, in October 1997; at 23 he was the youngest Briton to reach its summit. That achievement notwithstanding, in the months leading up to the start of the Everest expedition, Grylls tried in vain to find sponsors to cover his anticipated costs—$25,000. (In 2011 the average cost for climbers on commercially organized expeditions to Everest was approximately $65,000.) He ultimately won sponsorship from the Soldiers, Sailors, Airmen, and Families Association, Forces Help, and the construction consultancy firm Davis, Langdon and Everest (now Davis Langdon LLP).

Grylls spent three months on Everest. For some of that time, he further acclimatized his body by climbing up and coming down repeatedly at levels beneath the peak. For much of the year, weather conditions are too harsh for climbers to attempt reaching the summit; most climbers try in May. Grylls and his expedition mates began their ascent in May 1998. At 19,000 feet Grylls fell into a crevasse—a fearsome accident that failed to discourage him from continuing. He also persisted despite the altitude sickness that he suffered nearly every day. On May 26, 1998 Grylls, at 23, entered the *Guinness Book of World Records* as the youngest Briton to reach the summit of Mount Everest. He and Laughton were the only members of their team to accomplish their goal. Recalling the four climbers from other teams who died on the mountain that month (one in a fall, two from exhaustion, and one from exhaustion and oxygen deprivation), Grylls described his conquest of Everest to Patricia Cohen as "kind of a hollow victory." (In 2006 Rob Gauntlett of Great Britain reached Everest's summit at age 19; in January 2009 Gauntlett suffered a fatal accident while climbing in the French Alps.) Grylls's account of his Everest experience, called *Facing Up* in the United Kingdom and *The Kid Who Climbed Everest* in the U.S., earned favorable reviews and became a best-seller in Britain when it was published, in 2001.

Earlier, in 2000, Grylls led the first team to circumnavigate the U.K. on a Jet Ski, which took roughly 30 days and raised money for the Royal National Lifeboat Institution. Later that year he rowed naked for 22 miles along the River Thames in a homemade bathtub to raise funds for a friend who had lost his legs in a mountaineering accident. Then, in 2003, he led the first team to cross the North Atlantic part of the Arctic Ocean unassisted in an open, rigid inflatable boat, an event filmed for a television documentary; proceeds were contributed to the Prince's Trust, the U.K.'s largest youth-focused charity. That journey is described in Grylls's second book, *Facing the Frozen Ocean* (2004), which was short-listed for the British Sports Book of the Year.

In 2005 Grylls and two others, wearing tuxedos and oxygen masks, broke the record for the highest open-air formal dinner party; theirs took place at 25,000 feet in the basket of a hot-air balloon. That stunt honored the 50th anniversary of the Duke of Edinburgh's Award, a charitable organization that, according to its Web site, offers young people activities that develop "the whole person—mind, body and soul—in an environment of social interaction and teamworking." Later in 2005 Grylls led the first attempted paramotoring expedition over Venezuela's Angel Falls, the world's highest waterfall. (Paramotoring is powered paragliding.) In 2007 Grylls flew a paramotor over the Himalayas, reaching the altitude of Everest's summit. The next year he and a colleague broke the world record for the longest continuous indoor freefall, at the Airkix indoor skydiving facility in Milton Keynes, Great Britain. Also in 2008 he led the first team to climb what were considered to be the most remote peaks in the world, in Antarctica. (Some of the mountains had no names.) That expedition was sponsored by a company called Ethanol Ventures and was "designed to test how well vehicles powered by bioethanol worked in extreme conditions," according to Steven Morris, writing for the London *Guardian* (December 8, 2008, on-line). Morris also reported that Grylls had broken his shoulder in a fall and was to be airlifted to a hospital in South Africa. In 2010 Grylls led a team in a 2,500-mile journey across the Northwest Passage in an ice-breaking, rigid inflatable. Their aim was to raise awareness about the effects of global warming and attract donations to the children's charity Global Angels.

Earlier, in 2002, Grylls had made his television debut: in a scenario inspired by his Everest climb, he appeared in a commercial for the deodorant Sure for Men that aired in Great Britain. In 2004 he appeared in a four-part British prime-time TV documentary series, *Escape to the Legion*, about the lives and activities of members of the French Foreign Legion. That series drew the attention of Discovery Channel executives, who offered him the chance to host a new show called *Man vs. Wild*. He was initially reluctant to take the job, he explained to Julie Jacobson for the Wellington, New Zealand,

Dominion Post (June 16, 2009), because "I just didn't want to be a smiley TV presenter. The more I said that, the more [the producer] said, 'Well, we don't want a smiley TV presenter. We want the good, the bad, the ugly, the raw, the mess.' I feel really lucky and pleased that I did say yes in the end." *Man vs. Wild* debuted on the Discovery Channel on March 10, 2006, with a pilot titled "The Rockies," which followed Grylls as he parachuted into a grizzly-populated area of the Rocky Mountains, in British Columbia, Canada, and then found his way back to a road. In others among the 14 installments of the show's first season, Grylls parachuted into a Costa Rican rainforest, a savannah in northern Kenya, and the Florida Everglades. The hour-long show was an immediate success and went on to become one of the highest-rated cable programs in the U.S. It was soon syndicated to many other countries, with the title *Man vs. Wild* in Australia, New Zealand, and Canada; *Born Survivor: Bear Grylls* in England; and *Ultimate Survival* elsewhere in Europe and in Asia and Africa. *Man vs. Wild*, whose seventh season began in July 2011, now reaches upwards of one billion cable-television or satellite-TV subscribers in 170 countries, making it one of the most popular shows in the world. As of midsummer 2011 Grylls and his team had filmed nearly 80 installments.

According to Hampton Sides, *Man vs. Wild* "may be the only hit series in the history of television that features exactly . . . one person. There is no dialogue on his show—only soliloquies. For a whole hour, [Grylls] gamely treks across the deserts or jungles or steppes or savannas of our perilous world, gleefully ad-libbing, flexing his survival skills—the life of his own marooned party." In an interview with James Wigney for the Melbourne, Australia, *Sunday Herald Sun* (June 12, 2011), Grylls attributed much of the show's success to his four-man crew, which includes a cameraman, a soundman, a director, and a safety consultant. "They are unsung heroes," he said. "They work incredibly hard carrying the heavy gear and a huge part of my motivation for doing the show is that I get to hang out with them and go to some incredible places." Viewers of *Man vs. Wild* have seen Grylls scaling cliffs, jumping from the tops of waterfalls, swimming in shark-infested waters, and, in every installment, devising highly unusual ways to surmount difficult and dangerous conditions. He has used skin from a sheep carcass as a sleeping bag and zebra skin to make a canoe; wrapped a urine-drenched T-shirt around his head as protection from desert heat; and given himself an enema with fetid water to prevent dehydration. Grylls may be best known for his gastronomic inventiveness and adventuresomeness: in most installments he is shown eating something that most people would find too disgusting to ingest. Examples include frozen yak eyeballs, goat testicles, raw zebra meat, the larvae of a giant rhino beetle, camel intestinal fluid, and his own urine (to keep hydrated).

Man vs. Wild received criticism for misleading viewers with some of its earlier installments, in which some situations were staged and Grylls received more help than was revealed. The Discovery Channel responded by making the show more transparent; in addition, it airs a disclaimer at the beginning of each installment and after every commercial break, which reads, in part, "Bear Grylls and the crew receive support when they are in potentially threatening situations. . . . On some occasions, situations are presented to Bear so he can demonstrate survival techniques." In one example of such a situation, Grylls was seen eating a rabbit; in a voiceover he said that he had not succeeded in capturing any rabbits himself and was showing, with a rabbit from an outside source, that rabbits were a source of food in that area. Grylls, who performs all of his own stunts, told Sides, "Nobody likes personal criticism, especially when your job basically involves risking your life every day. But it goes with the territory. When you have a number-one cable show, you're going to get the odd Exocet missile sent your way."

Another TV series in which Grylls stars, called *Worst Case Scenario*, debuted on the Discovery Channel in May 2011. That show is based on a popular series of survival books, manuals, and merchandise produced under the same name. The show, which runs for a half-hour, is "a kind of urban, heavily staged variation on Man vs. Wild," in the words of Amanda Hooton.

Grylls's third book, *Man vs. Wild: Survival Techniques from the Most Dangerous Places on Earth* (2008), was published in Great Britain the previous year with the title *Born Survivor*. Grylls has also written an outdoor guidebook, *Great Outdoor Adventures* (2009), a children's adventure series called *Mission Survival*, and another memoir, *Blood, Sweat, and Tears* (2011). Grylls has made guest appearances on TV shows including *The Tonight Show with Jay Leno*, *The Late Show with David Letterman*, *Jimmy Kimmel Live!*, *The Oprah Winfrey Show*, and, on British TV, *Friday Night with Jonathan Ross*; he has also appeared in TV ads for Old Spice deodorant. He has given motivational speeches worldwide. Under the umbrella of the British outdoor-clothing company Cragshoppers, he started his own clothing line, and his name is associated with a brand of survival knives and other equipment sold by the Portland, Oregon–based company Gerber.

Grylls lives in a houseboat on the Thames in London with his wife, Shara, and their three sons: Jesse, Marmaduke, and Huckleberry. The Gryllses also own St. Tudwal's Island West, off the coast of northern Wales, where they spend part of each summer. In 2009 Grylls, at age 35, became the youngest man ever to be named the Chief Scout of the British Boy Scout Association (founded in 1907). "I've got a dream job," he told Hampton Sides. "I take a lot of physical risks, and the reality is that I'm cold, wet, and scared a lot of the time. But I feel really privileged. I'm completely unemployable in anything else. The truth is, I feel like I've been doing this since I was five years old. If someone had told me then, when I was climbing trees and caked in mud, that one day I'll have a job doing the same exact thing, I would have thought it was heaven." He added, "I have aspired to many things. Growing up is not one of them."

—C.C.

Suggested Reading: Bear Grylls Web site; *Los Angeles Times* E p1 June 22, 2008, D p18 July 17, 2011; (Melbourne, Australia) *Sunday Herald Sun* p19 June 12, 2011; *New York Times* E p18 June 15, 2007, E p1 May 16, 2008; *Outside* (online) May 2010; (Sydney, Australia) *Morning Herald* p14+ Sep. 11, 2010; (Wellington, New Zealand) *Dominion Post* p4 June 16, 2009

Selected Television Programs: *Man vs. Wild*, 2006– ; *Worst Case Scenario*, 2011–

Selected Books: *The Kid Who Climbed Everest*, 2001; *Facing the Frozen Ocean*, 2004; *Great Outdoor Adventures*, 2009; *Blood, Sweat, and Tears*, 2011

Haley, Nikki

Jan. 20, 1972– Governor of South Carolina (Republican)

Address: The Governor's Mansion, 800 Richland St., Columbia, SC 29201

In January 2011 the Republican Nikki Haley was sworn in as South Carolina's governor. Her election represented two firsts: she is the state's first female governor, and as an Indian-American, she is the first nonwhite person to hold that office in South Carolina. Further, she is only the second Indian-American governor in United States history (after Bobby Jindal of Louisiana, elected in 2008). Haley won the backing of the conservative Tea Party movement with her calls for smaller government and fiscal reform, and she has been compared to the movement's matriarch, former Alaska governor Sarah Palin, whose support played a crucial role in Haley's victory. "[Haley] has what people had hoped Sarah Palin had had," Kendra Stewart, a political scientist at College of Charleston, told Jim Davenport for the Associated Press (June 17, 2010). "I think people felt like Sarah Palin was lacking the substance but Nikki Haley actually has that substance."

Haley was born Nimrata Nikki Randhawa on January 20, 1972 in Bamberg, South Carolina. Her parents, who came from Punjab, India, immigrated to the United States and settled in the late 1960s in Bamberg, becoming that small town's only Indian residents. Haley's father, Ajit S. Randhawa, was a

Nikki Haley

Chip Somodevilla/Getty Images

professor at Voorhees College, in Denmark, South Carolina, and her mother, Raj, taught in the public-school system in Bamberg. Haley has shared stories illustrating the difficulties she faced while growing up in a town whose residents viewed one another, literally, in black and white terms. When Haley was about five, her parents entered her and her sister, Simran, in the Little Miss Bamberg pageant. The judges, who had always selected one black queen and one white queen, disqualified Haley and her sister because they were unsure of which category to place them in. (The judges still allowed Haley to sing a song, "This Land Is Your Land.") The Randhawas raised their children in the Sikh religion, which combines elements of Hinduism and Sufi Islam. According to tradition, Sikh men wear turbans and are not supposed to cut their hair—though Haley's brother had his cut after suffering relentless teasing at school. "It's survival mode," Haley explained to Shaila Dewan and Robbie Brown for the *New York Times* (June 13, 2010, on-line). "You learn to try and show people how you're more alike than you are different." Haley never let her background interfere with her political aspirations, which began early. Her seventh-grade social-studies teacher, Harriet Coker, recalled to Robert Behre for the Charleston, South Carolina, *Post and Courier* (September 12, 2010), "Raj [Haley's mother] told me that when Nikki was 5, she said, 'I want to be mayor of Bamberg.'"

As Haley entered her teen years, her family opened a gift shop and women's-clothing store called Exotica International. The business operated out of the family's home at first, and then, as it prospered, grew to become a chain of stores. At 13 Haley began working for the store and took over the

bookkeeping. She attended Clemson University, in South Carolina, receiving a degree in accounting in 1994. She then worked as an accounting supervisor for the Charlotte, North Carolina–based recycling corporation FCR Inc. After leaving FCR Haley returned to her family's clothing firm, helping it become a multimillion-dollar business. Despite Exotica's success, Haley was frustrated by how government policies were affecting business. She has cited that frustration as the catalyst for her involvement in politics. "I'm an accountant and small business person who saw how hard it was to make a dollar and how easy it was for the government to take it," she often said on the gubernatorial campaign trail, as quoted by Arian Campo-Flores for *Newsweek* (July 12, 2010).

In 2004, upon learning that State Representative Larry Koon, a Republican from South Carolina's 87th District, in Lexington County, was retiring, Haley entered the race to succeed him. After Koon—who had served the 87th District for over 30 years—recanted his decision and announced that he would seek another term, Haley remained in the race. The contrast between the two Republican candidates (no Democrat ran) was striking. Dewan and Brown noted that Lexington County was undergoing a major transition from rural community to wealthy suburban town filled with new and more diverse residents; Haley, most sources recalled, represented the changing face of Lexington County in both appearance and campaign style. Campo-Flores wrote, describing Haley's tenacity in the race, "She knocked on doors. She plunked herself down at the entrance to subdivisions and handed out coffee and doughnuts. She marched into smoke-filled redneck bars and wooed the blue-collar clientele inside." Koon, meanwhile, Campo–Flores wrote, "was the epitome of old rural South Carolina."

In an article for *Time* magazine (June 9, 2010), Michael Scherer wrote, "Dirty politics has a rich history in South Carolina, where trickery is regularly embraced as innovation." Terry Sullivan, an aide to the Haley supporter and former Massachusetts governor Mitt Romney, told Scherer that politics "is a little different" in South Carolina. "It's kind of a knife fight." Indeed, as Haley's poll numbers surged, the race took an ugly turn. In an effort to tap into the conservative electorate's perceived prejudices, Koon's campaign ran a newspaper ad using Haley's full name, Nimrata Randhawa Haley, and claiming that she was not a "REAL Republican." According to Scherer, unsigned e-mail messages circulated claiming that Haley was a Buddhist, while "passing drivers shouted things about Hindu cow worship at her volunteers." (Haley converted to Christianity before marrying Michael Haley, a Methodist, in 1996.) Koon's attacks on Haley's origins did not help him. Haley took Koon's seat in an impressive upset and was reelected in 2006 and 2008.

As a state representative Haley became an ally of Republican governor Mark Sanford. The two joined forces to reduce government spending and to lower taxes. Haley took on the issue of legislative transparency, introducing a bill that would require lawmakers to cast their votes publicly through roll call rather than through secret ballot. (South Carolina is one of the few states that allow legislators to vote secretly.) Haley believed that South Carolina legislators abused the secret-ballot system to approve generous retirement benefits for themselves. "I was disgusted," Haley told Philip Rucker for the *Washington Post* (June 12, 2010). "That was an arrogance that I just wasn't going to stand for. It was an embarrassing moment for the Republican Party. And I knew I had to fix it." Her actions won her few friends in the state legislature; fellow legislators accused her of "grandstanding," and she was removed from a powerful subcommittee of which she had hoped to become chairwoman. She won public support, however. (The bill that Haley introduced, the Spending Accountability Act, was passed by the South Carolina House of Representatives on March 25, 2010. It awaits state Senate approval.)

Haley's bid for governor, in 2010, was presented by her campaign as representing the choice of fiscal reform over politics as usual. Haley also attacked what she referred to as South Carolina's "good ol' boy network." (South Carolina ranked 50th in the U.S. in the number of women elected to public office, as Lisa Miller reported for *Newsweek* [September 27, 2010].) Her candidacy received a significant boost in May, when Sarah Palin—the former Alaska governor and 2008 Republican vice-presidential nominee—endorsed Haley, dubbing her a representative of the "emerging, conservative, feminist identity," as quoted by Robert Costa for National Public Radio (June 9, 2010). Palin's support catapulted Haley to national attention, landing the state representative on the cover of *Newsweek* magazine twice during the campaign—once alone and once with Palin and the other "Mama Grizzlies," the name Palin gave the conservative female candidates she endorsed. "Sarah Palin has energized the conservative movement like few others in our generation," Haley stated, as quoted by Andy Barr for politico.com (May 13, 2010). "I am extremely proud that she has offered her support to my candidacy." Another endorsement came from Governor Sanford's ex-wife, Jenny Sanford. (Governor Sanford, whom Barr described as "politically radioactive," created a scandal that drew national attention in 2009 when he admitted to using state travel funds to visit his mistress in Argentina.) Both Sanfords had supported Haley, but thanks in part to the public sympathy the governor's wife received in the midst of her husband's scandal, Jenny Sanford's endorsement boosted Haley's poll numbers even further.

Soon after the endorsement from Palin, a political blogger named Will Folks—formerly Governor Sanford's volatile press secretary and later a politi-

cal consultant for Haley—wrote on his popular Web site, FITSNews, that he and Haley had once had an "inappropriate physical relationship." Folks promised to provide unassailable evidence to support his claim, but none ever materialized. Haley vehemently denied the story, promising that if she were elected governor and evidence of the alleged affair were ever produced, she would resign. A week and a half later, Larry Marchant, a campaign consultant for one of Haley's opponents in the primary, Lieutenant Governor Andre Bauer, alleged that he and Haley had had a brief sexual encounter in 2008. After Haley denied the second accusation, Bauer challenged her to take a polygraph test to prove her version of events. She refused to do so, and the public, perhaps seeing Haley as a victim of dirty politics, rallied around her.

Meanwhile, others attempted to turn Haley's ethnicity and religion into issues in the race. In early June the Lexington Republican state senator Jake Knotts appeared on an Internet political talk show saying of Haley: "We already got one raghead [a reference to President Barack Obama] in the White House. We don't need another in the Governor's Mansion." (That ethnic slur typically targets Arabs or other ethnic or religious groups whose members wear turbans; rumors had persisted that Obama was a Muslim.) Knotts later half-heartedly apologized, insisting that he had been joking, but his comments had already made national headlines. As Amy Gardner reported for the *Washington Post* (June 21, 2010), some prominent South Carolina figures publicly questioned the legitimacy of Haley's Christian faith—noting, for example, that the reference to "God Almighty" on her campaign Web site was changed to "Christ" only after Haley became a front-runner in the primary. Addressing that issue, Haley wrote for her Web site, "My faith in Christ has a profound impact on my daily life and I look to Him for guidance with every decision I make. . . . Being a Christian is not about words, but about living for Christ every day." When questioned about how she viewed the possibility of becoming the country's only female Indian-American governor after a bruising campaign, Haley responded, as quoted by Dewan and Brown, "I love that people think it's a good story, but I don't understand how it's different. I feel like I'm just an accountant and businessperson who wants to be a part of state government."

On June 8, 2010, the day of the Republican primary, Haley topped the field with 49 percent of the vote. Because she did not receive a majority, a runoff election with the second-place finisher, Representative J. Gresham Barrett, was required. In that contest, held on June 22, Haley won with 233,332 votes to Barrett's 125,408, as noted by George Joseph, writing for *India Abroad* (July 2, 2010), which ran Haley's photo on its front page with the headline "The Future Is Here." Joseph noted that Haley's win had brought "a proud night for the Sikh community" and observed that while Haley "looked very American" as she made her victory speech, she "had gold bangles and a silver kada (one of the tenets of Sikhism) on her hand." Ultimately, it was Haley's plainspoken conservative message that resonated with voters. Jim Davenport, writing for the Associated Press (June 17, 2010), quoted a retired businessman as saying that he supported Haley because she stood for "less taxes, less government and more freedom. It's very simple."

In the general election Haley faced the Democrat Vincent Sheehan, a state senator. This time attacks against Haley focused on her professed standard of transparency and her ability to handle money. She came under fire in particular for her history of late tax payments. Addressing the issue, she stated, according to Yvonne Wenger and Robert Behre for the *Post and Courier* (October 22, 2010), "This is political silliness. . . . The fact is that Michael and I, we were in our young 30s. We went through an income cycle of him joining the military, me starting to serve in the House and him closing a business. We saw income ups and downs. We filed extensions. When we filed extensions, we had to pay penalties and we had to pay interest, and we did that." Sheehan's campaign attempted to turn Haley's newfound national celebrity against her. A facetious press release on September 18, 2010, titled "Sheehan Concedes Texas" (a reference to Haley's speaking at the national Republican convention in Austin, Texas), accused Haley of "ignoring South Carolina . . . as she runs for governor of the United States." Haley, meanwhile, used the electorate's seeming displeasure with the national government to her advantage. She talked about her opposition to the health-care legislation championed by President Obama (which she referred to as "Obamacare") and painted Sheehan as one of its biggest supporters.

On Election Day Haley captured 51 percent of the vote. Her victory was attributed in part to her success at sticking closely to key economic talking points. For example, in a Q & A with Haley and Sheehan published by the *Post and Courier* (October 18, 2010), the candidates were asked, "Is it time for state hate-crime legislation?" Sheehan responded, "What the state needs to do is enforce the laws that we have and make sure that regardless of why a crime is committed that they are fully prosecuted. I don't think the key is changing the law. I think the key is enforcing the law." Haley, by contrast, answered, "No. It's time for jobs." Trey Walker, who worked on Haley's general-election campaign, told John O'Connor for the South Carolina *State* (November 7, 2010), "She's a gifted retail politician. She's very engaging. She was able to synthesize her message better than anybody." Many saw widespread disapproval of the president's job performance as being responsible for the wave of Republican victories across the country on Election Day 2010. "To be a Republican running statewide in South Carolina in the year of anti-Obama is to be virtually elected," the University of Virginia political scientist Larry Sabato told O'Connor.

As early as mid-November 2010, Haley had assembled a financial team to help her assess the state's budget and identify excesses in government spending to help reduce South Carolina's budget deficit; the state faced a reported $1 billion shortfall. "I don't want to wait until January to deal with [the budget]," Haley told Behre for the *Post and Courier* (November 17, 2010) in her first one-on-one interview after the election. "We want to get in front of this crisis and not behind it." Haley also assembled a 14-member transition team comprised of business leaders and her husband, Michael Haley, an officer in the South Carolina National Guard. The team was to help select the heads of the 14 state agencies, who would make up Haley's cabinet.

Haley and her husband have two children: a daughter, Rena, who is 12, and a son, Nalin, who is nine.

—M.M.H.

Suggested Reading: (Charleston, South Carolina) *Post and Courier* A p1 Sep. 12, 2010, (on-line) Oct. 18, 2010, Nov. 17, 2010; National Public Radio (on-line) June 9, 2010; (New York) *India Abroad* A p6 July 2, 2010; *New York Times* p24 June 10, 2010, (on-line) June 13, 2010; *Newsweek* p32+ July 12, 2010, (on-line) Sep. 27, 2010; NikkiHaley.com; (South Carolina) *State* (on-line) Nov. 7, 2010; *Spartanburg (South Carolina) Herald Journal* (on-line) Oct. 21, 2010; *Time* (on-line) June 9, 2010; *Washington Post* A p1 June 12, 2010, A p1 June 21, 2010

Hamels, Cole

Dec. 27, 1983– Baseball player

Address: Philadelphia Phillies, Citizens Bank Park, One Citizens Bank Way, Philadelphia, PA 19148

While many Major League Baseball (MLB) pitchers have relied on blistering fastballs and bewildering curveballs to retire opposing batters, the Philadelphia Phillies' left-hander Cole Hamels has built his career around throwing a devastating changeup—a pitch that normally travels 10 miles per hour (mph) slower than a fastball and is used primarily to disrupt batters' timing. Hamels, who also throws a curveball and two types of fastballs (a four-seamer and a cutter), is known for throwing a variation of the changeup called the circle change. "The pitcher spreads his last three fingers around the ball," Pat Jordan wrote for the *New York Times* (April 3, 2011), "then forms a little circle with his forefinger and thumb on the side of the ball. Then he just throws a fastball and his grip prevents it from going fast. The best circle changes, like the one thrown by Hamels, either seem to die at the plate or fade

Jim McIsaac/Getty Images

Cole Hamels

for business with the San Diego school district, and his mother is a part-time teacher. Hamels started pitching at an early age; as a Little Leaguer he received pitching lessons from Fred Westfall, a former semiprofessional baseball player who pitched in the New York Mets' minor-league system in the 1970s. "Cole was a skinny kid who had a Ron Guidry-like release, that whip action," Westfall recalled to Kevin Kernan for the *New York Post* (May 21, 2006), referring to a former New York Yankees pitcher. "He always took direction well and was just a great kid." In middle school Hamels began harboring dreams of becoming a major-league pitcher. He worked daily on his arm mechanics and on mastering different pitching grips. "He was so accurate," his mother told Jim Salisbury for the *Philadelphia Inquirer* (October 3, 2007). "He could pick out something at any distance and nail it."

Hamels attended Rancho Bernardo High School in San Diego. With its nationally renowned baseball program, the school has been dubbed "the Factory" for the high number of major-league prospects whose skills were developed there. Hamels, who stood around five feet eight inches tall and weighed 140 pounds in ninth grade, pitched for Rancho Bernardo's freshman team; at the time his fastball clocked in at 82 to 83 miles per hour. "You had seniors who could hit 95 mph," he told Jeremy Cothran. "I wasn't throwing anything close to that, so it was like batting practice to them. My coach said if I could develop something slower, something that would fool them, then I might be more successful." Around that time Hamels began developing a changeup under the guidance of a pitching coach, Mark Furtak. (Changeups do not put as much strain on a developing pitcher's arm as other pitches, such as curveballs and sliders.) He was inspired to do so by having grown up watching the San Diego Padres' closer and MLB saves leader Trevor Hoffman, who routinely baffled hitters with his trademark changeup—nicknamed the "Bugs Bunny pitch" for its deceptive nature. (Hoffman's record of 601 saves was broken in September 2011 by Mariano Rivera of the Yankees.) Under Furtak, Hamels learned to throw a traditional circle changeup. That pitch requires gripping the baseball's horseshoe-shaped seam with the index finger and thumb—which settle into "OK"-gesture position—then releasing the ball from the middle and ring fingers and pinkie. Though changeups are thrown like fastballs, the unusual grip creates a downward spin that gives the illusion that the airborne ball is being pulled backward just before reaching the batter. "What makes Hamels' changeup so nasty is the downward plane that it follows," Cothran wrote. "His delivery is more over the top—followed with a high-leg finish—than most pitchers', which gives the pitch the impression that it is falling off a cliff."

away from a right-handed batter like a soft cutter. It's a deceptive pitch, easier to master than to hit." Jeremy Cothran wrote for the Newark, New Jersey, *Star-Ledger* (April 18, 2008) that Hamels's changeup "[dips] like a screwball before it opens a trapdoor and vanishes." Hamels joined the Phillies straight out of high school, in 2002, and enjoyed a highly successful albeit injury-riddled minor-league career before making his major-league debut, in May 2006. After earning his first All-Star selection, in 2007, Hamels achieved his breakthrough in the 2008 postseason, when he was named Most Valuable Player (MVP) of both the National League Championship Series (NLCS) and the World Series; he posted a 4–0 record in the play-offs to help the Phillies capture their sixth NL pennant and second-ever World Series title. He went on to play pivotal roles in the Phillies' 2009 return to the World Series (which they lost to the New York Yankees) and in their fifth consecutive NL East title, in 2011. Entering the 2011 season, Hamels rounded out a remarkable Phillies' pitching rotation that included the reigning NL Cy Young Award–winner and perennial All-Star Roy Halladay, the 2008 AL Cy Young Award–winner Cliff Lee, and the three-time All-Star Roy Oswalt. Comparing Hamels with another talented southpaw, the Hall of Famer and former Baltimore Orioles pitcher Jim Palmer told Jordan, "Hamels is a [Tom] Glavine but with a better fastball and less control."

The oldest of the three children of Gary and Amanda Hamels, Colbert Michael "Cole" Hamels was born on December 27, 1983 in San Diego, California. He has a sister, Jillian, and a brother, Mitchell. Hamels's father is an assistant superintendent

Armed with the changeup, Hamels made Rancho Bernardo's varsity baseball team as a sophomore and went undefeated on a team that included the future first-round MLB draft picks Matt Wheatland and Scott Heard. At that point he was already using the changeup as his primary "out," or strikeout pitch. "It wouldn't be over the plate," Hamels noted to Mike Sielski for the *Bucks County Courier Times* (May 8, 2007), "but I could always get guys to fish." During those years Hamels also liked to play street football with his friends. In one game he rammed his shoulder into a parked car; the accident did not seem to have harmed him until, in the middle of a pitch in a summer-league baseball game before his junior year, his arm broke. Talking to Scott Lauber for the Wilmington, Delaware, *News-Journal* (July 10, 2007), Hamels described the sound as being like that of "a tree branch breaking." The injury forced him to miss his entire junior season and put his future baseball prospects in jeopardy. He soon met with Jan Fronek, an orthopedic surgeon who is the San Diego Padres' team physician, who inserted thin metal rods into the marrow of his humerus and ordered him to stay off the pitcher's mound for eight months. After completing his medical rehabilitation, Hamels trained at the facilities of the National Pitching Association, a pitching camp and performance laboratory based in San Diego. Under the direction of the former major-league pitcher and pitching coach Tom House, the laboratory's co-founder, he began an intensive strength-and-conditioning program. Then, during the summer of 2001, Hamels started pitching again, despite his fear that he would again break his arm. "You decide this is your only shot," Hamels told Lauber. "I didn't want to do anything else, so I had to get over that fear. When you love something so much, you have to do whatever you can. I just told myself, if my arm breaks again, so be it. But I had to at least try it."

By the time Hamels entered his senior year at Rancho Bernardo, his fastball was consistently in the mid-90-mph range, thanks largely to a growth spurt and muscle development; he now stood six feet three inches tall and weighed 175 pounds. All doubts about his future pitching were put to rest in his first start following his injury, when he struck out the first three batters he faced on the minimum nine pitches. Through five innings Hamels retired every batter he faced, before being removed due to a predetermined 50-pitch limit. His high-school coach, Sam Blalock, recalled to Todd Zolecki for the *Philadelphia Inquirer* (September 21, 2006), "It was unbelievable. He had the poise back then. He never faltered in high school. He just dominated. We've had some good pitchers in San Diego. David Wells. Mark Prior. There have been quite a few, but he's the best pitcher I've ever seen in high school." That performance was the start of a senior season that saw him post a perfect 10–0 record with an even more remarkable 0.39 earned-run average (ERA). Those numbers caught the attention of major-league scouts all over the country and prompted Hamels to forego college (he had been offered a scholarship by the University of Southern California) to enter the 2002 MLB amateur draft. The Phil-

adelphia Phillies drafted him 17th overall in the first round and awarded him a signing bonus of $2 million.

Hamels spent three seasons in the Phillies' farm system, which were exceptionally successful for him despite several injuries. In 2003, his first full season in the minors, he pitched for the Phillies' single-A affiliate, the Lakewood Blueclaws, in Lakewood Township, New Jersey, where he went 6–1 with a 0.84 ERA in 13 games. Later that year he moved up to the organization's advanced single-A affiliate in Clearwater, Florida, the Clearwater Phillies (now the Clearwater Threshers), for which he recorded 32 strikeouts in 26.1 innings. Hamels entered the 2004 season rated by *Baseball America* as the Phillies' best prospect. He showcased his talent when, as a non-roster invitee to the Phillies' annual spring-training camp, he pitched two scoreless innings and struck out the MLB stars Derek Jeter and Alex Rodriguez during an exhibition game against the New York Yankees. His progress was slowed, however, by left-elbow tendinitis, and he made just four starts with the Clearwater Phillies before being sidelined for the remainder of the year. Hamels's physical troubles continued into 2005, when he broke his pitching hand in a bar fight several weeks before spring training. The injury, which required surgery, delayed his return until June of that year. Despite pitching well on his return, Hamels, who made three starts for Clearwater before being promoted to the Phillies' double-A squad in Reading, Pennsylvania, lasted only a month before back spasms forced the Phillies to bench him for the second consecutive year.

Hamels opened the 2006 season with the Blueclaws before moving to the Clearwater Phillies. After four starts with that club, he was promoted to the Phillies' triple-A affiliate, the Scranton/Wilkes-Barre Red Barons, for which he recorded 36 strikeouts and allowed just one run and one walk in three starts. While some questioned Hamels's durability, the Phillies felt he had seen enough of the minor leagues—he had posted a career record of 14–4 with a 1.43 ERA and 276 strikeouts—and decided it was time to call him up to the majors. Hamels made his major-league debut on May 12, 2006, in a game against the Cincinnati Reds. He pitched nearly five shutout innings, striking out seven batters and allowing one hit and five walks, and earned a no-decision in an 8–4 win for Philadelphia. Two of Hamels's strikeouts (the first and the last) came against the future Hall of Famer Ken Griffey Jr. Hamels pitched another five scoreless innings in his second career MLB start, against the Milwaukee Brewers, but allowed four runs in 6 1/3 innings in a 5–4 Phillies loss. After missing his third scheduled start with a shoulder injury, he returned to pick up his first major-league win, 10–1, on June 6, 2006, in a game against the Arizona Diamondbacks. Despite encountering typical first-year struggles, Hamels finished his rookie campaign with a respectable 9–8 record and 4.08 ERA in 23 starts. He also finished with 145 strikeouts, good for third among NL rookies. The Phillies, meanwhile, barely missed out on a wild-card play-off spot after finishing second in the NL East with a record of 85–77.

During the 2007 season Hamels went 15–5 with a 3.39 ERA while striking out 177 batters and walking just 43 in 183.1 innings, earning his first career All-Star selection; that year he led the Phillies in wins, ERA, and strikeouts. He also pitched his first complete game and recorded a career-high 15 strikeouts, in an April game against the Cincinnati Reds. He flirted with a perfect game in a May contest with the Brewers, in which he struck out 11 and allowed just two runs in a 6–2 Phillies victory. Hamels's solid pitching down the stretch helped the Phillies squeak by the New York Mets for the NL East Division title; the team finished with an 89–73 regular-season record to earn the franchise's first play-off berth since 1993. In the NL Division Series (NLDS), the Phillies were swept by the Colorado Rockies in three games. Hamels lost Game One of the series, allowing three hits, three runs, and four walks in 6.2 innings.

In 2008 Hamels had a breakout year, compiling a 14–10 record and setting career highs in starts (33), innings pitched (227.1), and strikeouts (196). He also recorded his first two shutouts, recording both at home and before the All-Star break, making him the first Phillies pitcher to accomplish that feat since Curt Schilling in 1993; in addition, he pitched two complete games. Hamels delivered on offense as well, with a career-high 17 hits, the highest total for a Phillies pitcher since 1991. The Phillies successfully defended their NL East Division crown, with a record of 92–70, and advanced to the play-offs for the second consecutive year. Hamels started Game One of the NLDS against the Brewers, in which he struck out nine and allowed just two hits and one walk over eight innings to earn his first career play-off win. After defeating the Brewers in four games, the Phillies faced the Los Angeles Dodgers in the National League Championship Series. The Phillies won the series in five games to earn their first NL pennant and first World Series berth since 1993. Hamels was named NLCS MVP after winning Game One and Game Five of the series, posting a stellar 1.93 ERA with 13 strikeouts. He was then named MVP of the World Series, after going 1–0 with a 2.77 ERA in two starts against the Tampa Bay Rays, whom the Phillies defeated in five games for the franchise's second-ever championship. In the process Hamels became only the fifth player in baseball history to win two postseason MVP awards in the same year; the others are Willie Stargell (1979), Darrell Porter (1982), Orel Hershiser (1988), and Liván Hernández (1997). Prior to the 2009 season, Hamels signed a three-year, $20.5 million contract extension with the Phillies.

Over the next two seasons, Hamels posted records of 10–11 and 12–11, respectively, with the Phillies returning to the play-offs and defending their NL East crown in each of those years. In 2009 the Phillies, who had finished with a 93–69 regular-season record, returned to the World Series but lost to the New York Yankees in six games. Hamels pitched Game Three of the series but struggled, allowing five earned runs over 4.1 innings in an 8–5 Phillies loss. In December 2009 the Phillies acquired the starting pitcher and Cy Young Award–winner Roy Halladay—arguably the game's best pitcher and the prized free agent of the 2010 MLB off-season—from the Toronto Blue Jays for four minor-league prospects. With that acquisition Hamels was immediately relegated to number two in the rotation. The one-two punch of Halladay and Hamels helped the Phillies win their fourth consecutive NL East title in 2010, as they finished with an MLB-best 97–65 record. Prior to the 2010 trade deadline, in July, the team had added even more firepower to its rotation, with the acquisition of the starting pitcher Roy Oswalt, a three-time All-Star, from the Houston Astros. Nonetheless, the Phillies were unable for a third straight year to return to the World Series, losing to the San Francisco Giants in the NLCS in six games.

During the 2011 off-season the Phillies acquired still another prize starting pitcher, the 2008 Cy Young Award–winner Cliff Lee, from the Texas Rangers. (Lee had been a member of the Phillies earlier, during the second half of the 2009 season.) That acquisition immediately led sports analysts and pundits to pick the Phillies as the favorites to win the 2011 World Series. Meanwhile, they hailed the team's four-man rotation of Halladay, Lee, Oswalt, and Hamels—dubbed the Big Four—as the best 1-2-3-4 combination in the game and began comparing them to other legendary pitching staffs, the most recent being the Atlanta Braves' rotation of the 1990s, which included the Cy Young Award–winners Greg Maddux, John Smoltz, and Tom Glavine and the All-Star and 1991 NLCS MVP Steve Avery.

Extremely high expectations surrounded the Phillies' talent-heavy quartet. Hamels, now the number-four man in the rotation, held up his end of the bargain: in July 2011 he was named to his second career All-Star team, after going into the 2011 midseason break with a record of 11–4 and a stellar 2.32 ERA. He finished the 2011 season with a record of 14–9 and career-best 2.79 ERA, while pitching a career-high three complete games. Along with Halladay and Lee, Hamels emerged as a candidate for the NL Cy Young Award after finishing among the league leaders in several categories, ranking second in walks plus hits per innings pitched (0.99), fifth in complete games, sixth in ERA, and ninth in wins. Thanks to their dominant pitching rotation, the Phillies finished with the best record in baseball for the second consecutive year, with a franchise-best 102 wins and 60 losses, and won their fifth consecutive NL East title. In the 2011 postseason Hamels earned the win in Game Three of the NLDS against the St. Louis Cardinals, after striking out nine and allowing five hits and three walks over six innings. The Phillies won the game, 3–2, but failed to advance past the NLDS, losing to the underdog Cardinals in five games.

With "flowing black hair" and a "tall, skinny frame," Scott Lauber wrote, Hamels looks "more like a California surfer than a major-league pitcher." Those striking features helped him become a mini-celebrity following the 2008 World Series: he and his wife, Heidi Strobel, a former *Playboy* cover model and contestant on the sixth season of the popular reality show *Survivor*, made the rounds on the talk-show circuit, appearing together on *Late Show with David Letterman* and *The Ellen DeGeneres Show*. Hamels and Strobel, who married on December 31, 2006, live in Glen Mills, Pennsylvania. Their son, Caleb Michael, was born in October 2009. That year the couple founded the Hamels Foundation, which helps raise funds for inner-city schools in Philadelphia and awards scholarships to high-school students seeking higher education. The foundation also owns and operates a school in the African country of Malawi.

—C.C.

Suggested Reading: (Bucks County, Pennsylvania) *Courier Times* D p1+ May 8, 2007; *New York Post* p87 May 21, 2006; *New York Times* MM p24+ Apr. 3, 2011; (Newark, New Jersey) *Star-Ledger* p39 Apr. 18, 2008; *Philadelphia Inquirer* Sep. 21, 2006, E p1 Oct. 3, 2007; *USA Today* C p1 Oct. 9, 2008; (Wilmington, Delaware) *News Journal* C p1 July 10, 2007

Stephen Dunn/Getty Images

Hamilton, Josh

May 21, 1981– Baseball player

Address: Texas Rangers, 1000 Ballpark Way, Arlington, TX 76011

The Texas Rangers' outfielder Josh Hamilton has earned the nickname "the Natural" for his prodigious power and uncanny athletic ability. Mark Emmons, writing for the *Contra Costa (California) Times* (October 29, 2010), called him "that rarest of gems—a five-tool player who combines speed, power, and skill on a 6-foot-4, 240-pound frame," while Tom Verducci proclaimed for *Sports Illustrated* (August 17, 2010, on-line), "There is nobody like him in baseball, and possibly nobody this good, this big, this fast and this unique . . . since

Mickey Mantle in his prime." Like the mythic character Roy Hobbs in the Bernard Malamud novel and Barry Levinson film *The Natural*, Hamilton traveled a long road to baseball superstardom: he was the number-one overall pick in the 1999 Major League Baseball (MLB) draft, signing with the Tampa Bay Rays, and was considered a "can't miss" prospect, until injuries and well-chronicled drug and alcohol addictions kept him out of baseball for three seasons, from 2003 through 2005. Reinstated by the league in 2006 after getting sober and rediscovering his Christian faith, Hamilton was picked up by the Cincinnati Reds in that year's Rule 5 draft, which protects gifted minor-league players from languishing in farm systems. He made his long-awaited MLB debut with the Reds in 2007 and enjoyed a productive, albeit injury-riddled, rookie campaign. After spending one season with the Reds, Hamilton was traded to the Texas Rangers, where he has since emerged as one of baseball's finest all-around players. After an injury-plagued 2009 season, which saw Hamilton's much-publicized relapse with alcohol, he returned in 2010 to lead the majors in several statistical categories, despite missing 29 games due to injury, and earn his third consecutive All-Star selection; he was also named the 2010 AL Most Valuable Player (MVP). In the 2010 postseason Hamilton was named MVP of the American League Championship Series (ALCS) and helped lead the Rangers to their first-ever World Series. (The Rangers lost to the San Francisco Giants in the series, four games to one.) The Rangers' president, the Hall of Fame pitcher Nolan Ryan, told Marc Topkin for the *St. Petersburg (Florida) Times* (October 26, 2010) about Hamilton, "He's the most gifted athlete I've seen since [former Astros All-Star] Cesar Cedeno. And as far as natural talent, he rates up there with Mickey Mantle and Willie Mays and those kinds of guys." Discussing Hamilton's stature among current MLB players, the Rangers' general manager, Jon Daniels, said to the same writer, "I don't know if he's the most talented guy in the game but he's certainly in the discussion."

The younger of the two sons of Tony and Linda Hamilton, Joshua Holt Hamilton was born on May 21, 1981 in Raleigh, North Carolina. His father played baseball and football in high school, and his mother was a competitive amateur softball player; his brother, Jason, was a star baseball player at Athens Drive High School, in Raleigh. Hamilton began playing baseball at the age of five, fostering dreams of becoming a professional player. Both of his parents recognized his talent early on and played a major role in his athletic development. They taught him the importance of hard work and discipline and signed him up for baseball leagues year-round. During his youth, his father, who worked as a shop foreman at a Ditch Witch factory (which manufactured products for underground construction), often pitched to him to help develop his batting skills. As Hamilton got older he excelled in other sports, such as football, basketball, soccer, and track, before honing in on baseball. (Hamilton, whose shoe size has been given variously as 16 and 19, reportedly stopped competing in track after his feet outgrew manufactured running shoes.)

Hamilton attended Athens Drive High School, where he played center field and pitched on the varsity baseball team. With his above-average speed and power, he quickly stood out among his peers. "When he was barely 15," Evan Grant wrote for the *Dallas Morning News* (January 27, 2008), "Hamilton was already a North Carolina sports legend. He was that rarest of finds, a true five-tool player"—one who is able to hit for both average and power and has excellent base-running skills, speed, and throwing and fielding abilities. "Left-handed, he was so gifted that he occasionally played shortstop and even hoped to be a catcher. But coaches were too protective of his arm because when he pitched, he hit 95-96 mph. When he played the outfield, nobody ran on him. When he hit, everybody gasped at the power." In addition to being able to pitch in the mid-90-mph range consistently, Hamilton, who was discovered to have 20-10 vision, ran the 60-yard dash in 6.7 seconds and had a batting speed of 110 mph. A former scout, Jax Robertson, now an executive with MLB's Pittsburgh Pirates, told Grant, "I've seen some really special amateur players—Kirk Gibson and Bo Jackson—but Josh is the most talented kid I've ever seen. Every skill was above average; some were off the charts. He had instincts, athleticism, passion, and compassion."

Hamilton caught the attention of major-league scouts during his junior year at Athens Drive, when he batted an astonishing .636 with 12 home runs and 56 RBIs and was named North Carolina High School Gatorade Player of the Year. During his senior season he hit .529, with a school-record 13 home runs, 35 RBIs, and 20 stolen bases. As a pitcher during his junior and senior seasons, Hamilton posted an 18–3 record with 230 strikeouts in 143 innings. After being named North Carolina High School Gatorade Player of the Year for the second consecutive year, as well as *USA Baseball*'s

Amateur Player of the Year and *Baseball America*'s High School Player of the Year, he chose to forgo college to enter the 1999 MLB Draft. The Tampa Bay Rays selected Hamilton first overall in the draft's first round and awarded him a contract that included a then-record signing bonus of $3.96 million; he was the first high-school position player to be the number-one overall pick in the draft since Alex Rodriguez in 1993. Upon signing with the Rays, Hamilton boldly predicted, as noted by Dave Sheinin for the *Washington Post* (February 13, 2007), "I'm thinking three years in the minors, then maybe 15 years in the majors. Then I'll have to wait five years to get into the Hall of Fame."

When Hamilton entered the Rays' farm system, his parents quit their jobs to travel with him. He got off to a very promising start: in the summer of 1999, he joined the Rays' Rookie League team in Princeton, West Virginia, where he batted .347 with 10 home runs, 48 RBIs, and 17 steals, before moving up to the organization's short-season class-A affiliate, the Hudson Valley Renegades, in Fishkill, New York. Hamilton then spent the 2000 season with the class-A Charleston River Dogs of the South Atlantic League, where he batted .302 with 13 home runs, 61 RBIs, and 14 stolen bases and was selected to the All-Star team. Despite season-ending surgery on his right knee, he was named the league's co-MVP and was voted Minor League Player of the Year by *USA Today*.

Entering the 2001 season rated by *Baseball America* as the game's best prospect, Hamilton seemed destined for a rapid ascent to the majors. Then, on February 28, 2001, he and his parents were involved in a traffic accident in Bradenton, Florida, when a dump truck ran a red light and struck their pickup truck. Hamilton suffered a back injury that kept him out of spring training, and his mother sustained injuries that required her to move back to Raleigh with her husband for medical care. Hamilton began the 2001 season with the Rays' class-AA affiliate in Orlando, Florida, where he played in just 23 games before injuring his back again. After coming off the disabled list, he was reassigned to the class-A club in Charleston, but his season was cut short by other injuries. Frustrated and idle because of his injuries, and away from his parents for the first time, Hamilton began frequenting a tattoo parlor in Bradenton, whose patrons introduced him to drugs and alcohol. He recalled to Dave Sheinin, "My first drink—my first drink ever—was at a strip club down there, with the tattoo guys. Pretty soon, I started using [cocaine]. First the powder. Then crack. I was 20."

In 2002 Hamilton played for the Bakersfield, California, Blaze, the Rays' advanced class-A affiliate, where he hit .303 with nine home runs and 44 RBIs in 56 games. That July his season was cut short prematurely for the third straight year, when he was forced to undergo season-ending elbow and shoulder surgeries. Afterward, Hamilton drifted further into drug use. Over the next four years, his life would be characterized by "failed drug tests, suspensions from baseball, trips to jail and countless 'Where the hell did I sleep?' morning mysteries," Richie Whitt wrote for the *Dallas Observer* (June 12, 2008). During that period Hamilton added 26 tattoos to his body, failed at least four MLB-sanctioned drug tests, made eight trips to rehab, and squandered most of his signing bonus. He was granted a leave of absence by the Rays for the entire 2003 season to deal with his off-the-field issues and was then suspended by MLB for the 2004 season after failing several drug tests; subsequent failed drug tests and suspensions kept him out of baseball in 2005. Hamilton, who sometimes had hallucinations and admitted to attempting suicide on several occasions, told Sheinin, "With what I was going through, I wasn't thinking about anything but using. Baseball, life in general, it wasn't a priority. It was basically getting high. I'd go six, seven, eight months without even swinging a bat. I honestly thought I might never play baseball again."

During his exile from baseball, Hamilton met and befriended Michael Chadwick, a North Carolina homebuilder and faith-based motivational speaker who had overcome drug addiction. Chadwick gave him a job with his house-building company and began guiding him toward recovery. During that time Hamilton began dating Chadwick's daughter, Katie; the two married in November 2004 and moved into a modest home in North Carolina shortly afterward. (They had attended Athens Drive High School together and had dated briefly in 2002.) Six months after they were married, the couple separated due to Hamilton's continuing cocaine use and the acts to which it drove him: he pawned his wife's wedding ring for crack and spent $100,000 on drugs in six weeks. Hamilton missed the birth of his first daughter, Sierra, in August 2005, due to drugs. It was not until he was kicked out of his house and moved in with his grandmother, Mary Holt, that he realized the magnitude of his problem. At her urging, Hamilton, who had dropped to 185 pounds, decided to give up drugs and alcohol for good.

In June 2006, sober for eight months, Hamilton was reinstated by MLB and allowed to participate in extended spring training with the Rays. Sent back to class-A ball, he played in 15 games for the Hudson Valley Renegades. During that summer he also trained at the Winning Inning, a baseball academy in Clearwater, Florida, for developing players. In December 2006 Hamilton was acquired by the Cincinnati Reds in the Rule 5 draft. (The annual Rule 5 draft is meant to prevent talent-heavy baseball organizations from keeping major league–caliber players in their minor-league systems; players picked in the draft must be kept on their new teams' 25-man active rosters all season rather than on the 40-man rosters.)

After batting a stellar .403 in spring training, Hamilton made his long-awaited major-league debut, on April 2, 2007, in an opening-day game against the Chicago Cubs. He appeared as a pinch hitter in the game, held at the Reds' Great American Ballpark, and lined out in his only at-bat. On April 10 Hamilton made his first career start, in a contest against the Arizona Diamondbacks, in which he collected his first career hit—a two-run home run off the pitcher Edgar Gonzalez. Hamilton finished the season with solid numbers, batting .292 with 19 home runs and 47 RBIs in 90 games, despite making two separate trips to the disabled list, due to gastroenteritis and wrist and hamstring injuries. To ensure that he remained on the straight and narrow that year, the Reds placed him under the guidance of one of his former youth-basketball coaches, Johnny Narron, a former MLB first baseman and minor-league hitting coach who began serving as both his baseball mentor and minder. (Narron was suggested for the job by his older brother, Jerry, the Reds' manager at the time.)

In December 2007 Hamilton was traded to the Texas Rangers for the pitchers Edinson Volquez and Danny Herrera. Narron followed him there, keeping an eye on Hamilton while serving as an assistant hitting coach. Hamilton quickly rewarded the Rangers' faith in him. During 2008 spring training, he batted .556 with 13 RBIs in just 14 games and easily clinched the Rangers' starting centerfielder spot. He carried that momentum into the regular season, when he batted .330 with six home runs and a major-league-leading 32 RBIs for the month of April, when he was named the American League Player of the Month. He was then named Player of the Month for May, after batting .322 with eight home runs and 29 RBIs, making him the first AL player in baseball history to start the season with consecutive Player of the Month awards. Hamilton was selected by fans as one of the starting outfielders for the AL at the 2008 All-Star Game, at Yankee Stadium, and was also chosen to participate in the 2008 MLB Home Run Derby. At the derby, held the day before the All-Star Game, he hit a record 28 home runs in the first round, breaking Bobby Abreu's single-round record of 24, set in 2005; he hit 13 home runs in a row, three of them more than 500 feet (his longest was 518 feet). Despite losing in the final round of the derby to the Minnesota Twins slugger Justin Morneau, he finished the contest with a total of 35 home runs, the second-highest total in the history of the contest (to Abreu's 41). Hamilton cooled off during the second half of the season but still finished the year with impressive numbers, hitting .304 with 32 home runs, an AL-leading 130 RBIs, and 35 doubles; he also finished in a tie for first place in the AL in total bases, with 331. The Rangers finished second in the AL West Division, with a 79–83 record.

Hamilton's 2009 season was hampered by injuries, which led to a significant drop in his numbers. That year he batted .268 with 10 home runs, 19 doubles, and 54 RBIs in 89 games. Those below-average totals notwithstanding, Hamilton was selected for the AL All-Star team for the second consecutive year. His injury-plagued season was further tarnished by a widely reported misstep with alcohol: in August 2009 the sports blog Deadspin.com posted photos from the previous January showing him shirtless and cavorting with three women in a bar in Tempe, Arizona. When reports about his actions became public, Hamilton revealed that he had told his wife, the Texas Rangers, and MLB officials about the incident the day after it occurred, and he said, as quoted by Gil LeBreton in the *Fort Worth Star-Telegram* (August 9, 2009), "I hate [that] this happened. But it is what it is. You deal with it. And I realize that, obviously, I'm not perfect, and that it's an ongoing struggle, a battle, that is very real. A lot of people don't understand how real it is." (Hamilton has reportedly not drunk alcohol since that incident.)

Hamilton bounced back in 2010 to put up one of the best offensive campaigns in Rangers history. He achieved a major-league-leading and franchise-record .359 batting average, capturing his first batting title, and recorded 32 home runs, 40 doubles, and 100 RBIs. He became the first AL player to hit .359, with at least 40 doubles, 30 home runs, and 100 RBIs, since the New York Yankees' Lou Gehrig in 1934. He also led the majors in slugging percentage (.633), topped MLB in on-base percentage plus slugging percentage, or OPS (1.044), and was selected for his third straight All-Star team. He was named AL Player of the Month for June after batting .454 with nine home runs and 10 doubles; he also recorded 49 hits, breaking a Rangers franchise record for most hits in a month. Despite missing 25 of the Rangers' final 30 games due to two fractured ribs, and 29 games in total due to injury, Hamilton was named the 2010 AL MVP, receiving 22 of 28 first-place votes from the Baseball Writers Association of America; he became only the fourth player in baseball history to win his league's MVP award after playing in 133 or fewer regular-season games (the others are Hall of Famers Mickey Mantle and George Brett, in 1962 and 1980, respectively, and Barry Bonds, in 2003). The Rangers, meanwhile, won the AL West with a 90–72 record and advanced to the play-offs for the first time since 1999.

Facing the defending-champion New York Yankees in the American League Championship Series (ALCS), Hamilton helped lead the Rangers to their first AL pennant and first World Series berth. He was named ALCS MVP after recording four home runs and seven RBIs and drawing an ALCS-record five intentional walks in the six-game series. In the World Series the Rangers lost to the San Francisco Giants in five games. Prior to the 2011 season, Hamilton signed a two-year, $24 million contract extension with the Rangers.

In October 2008 Hamilton wrote (with the sportswriter Tim McKeown) the memoir *Beyond Belief: Finding the Strength to Come Back.* The book chronicles his comeback in baseball and traces his journey from drug addict to spiritually reawakened Christian husband and father. Hamilton and his wife, Katie, have three daughters, Julia (Katie's daughter from a previous relationship), Sierra, and Michaela. Hamilton speaks frequently at

baseball stadiums and other venues about the ways in which his religious faith helped him to overcome his addictions. He told Joey Johnston for the *Tampa Tribune* (October 5, 2010), "Growing up, all I ever wanted to do was play baseball. But I think [with] what has happened in my life, my ultimate calling might be sharing my story."

—C.C.

Suggested Reading: *Charleston (South Carolina) Post and Courier* A p1+ Mar. 18, 2007; *Chicago Sun-Times* p71 July 15, 2008; *Dallas (Texas) Morning News* Jan. 27, 2008; ESPN.com July 5, 2007; *Los Angeles Times* D p8+ Feb. 20, 2007; *Sports Illustrated* p30+ June 2, 2008; *St. Petersburg (Florida) Times* (on-line) Oct. 24, 1999; *USA Today* C p1+ June 7, 2006; *Washington Post* E p1+ Feb. 13, 2007

Gregory Shamus/Getty Images

Harrison, James

May 4, 1978– Football player

Address: Pittsburgh Steelers, 3400 S. Water St., Pittsburgh, PA 15203

Known as one of the hardest-hitting and most versatile linebackers in the National Football League (NFL), James Harrison of the Pittsburgh Steelers has routinely instilled fear in his opponents with his ferocious play. "Whether rushing the passer, playing the run with his punishing tackles or dropping into coverage," Bob Glauber wrote for *Newsday* (January 16, 2009), "Harrison is as complete a linebacker as you could ever want." Harrison's on-field relentlessness has a parallel in his long journey to NFL stardom: he signed with the Steelers as an undrafted rookie out of Kent State University in 2002, then was cut three times by the team in a span of 13 months, leading him to sign with the Pittsburgh rival Baltimore Ravens, who sent him to play with Germany's Rhein Fire of the now-defunct NFL Europe. Returning to the Ravens after a brief stint with the Fire, Harrison was cut from that team, too, and spent several weeks contemplating retirement before being picked up by the Steelers a fourth time, during training camp in 2004. He earned a roster spot with the Steelers as a special-teams player and backup linebacker, playing in those roles until 2007, when he was named the team's starting right outside linebacker. Since then Harrison has served as the linchpin of the Steelers' defense, which consistently ranks among the best in the league. He has earned four consecutive Associated Presss (AP) All-Pro selections (2007–10) and made four straight Pro Bowl teams (2007–10), and in 2008 he became the first undrafted player and fifth Steeler ever to win the NFL's Defensive Player of the Year Award. That same year he helped lead the Steelers to their record sixth championship, when they defeated the Arizona Cardinals, 27–23, in Super Bowl XLIII; in that game he broke the record for the longest play in Super Bowl history, making a 100-yard interception return for a touchdown on a pass thrown by the Cardinals quarterback Kurt Warner at the end of the first half.

In his remarkable rise from obscure practice-squad player to one of the league's best defensive players, Harrison has often been perceived by peers, coaches, and pundits as a "dirty player" for his punishing hits and all-out aggressiveness on the field. Describing his "seek-and-destroy mentality," Jarrett Bell wrote for *USA Today* (February 3, 2011) that Harrison is "prone to hit with such a fury that, in the eyes of NFL officials seeking to better protect defenseless players, he sometimes has crossed the line of legality." That "fury" had repercussions during the 2010 season, when Harrison became the unwilling face of the NFL's crackdown on illegal hits after receiving a league-high four fines totaling $100,000. Nonetheless, he helped the Steelers that year to make their second Super Bowl appearance in three seasons. Commenting on his style of play, Harrison said to Ralph N. Paulk for the *Pittsburgh Tribune Review* (September 11, 2011), "If I see a chance to stretch somebody out without crippling them, I'm going to do it. That's what I'm paid to do." He added, "I want to punish the guy that's across from me. When I step inside those [white] lines, I'm out there to prove something."

The youngest of the 14 children of James Harrison Sr. and Mildred Harrison, James Harrison Jr. was born on May 4, 1978 in Akron, Ohio. Along with his many siblings and step-siblings, the combined offspring of his parents' previous marriages (he is their only child together), in addition to cousins, he grew up in a five-bedroom home in Akron and was raised in a strict household. Harrison's father worked at Portage Broom & Brush before retiring from the Cuyahoga Valley National Park Association; his mother, who also reared her murdered sister's six children, worked mostly in the retail industry. Harrison was seven years younger than his closest sibling. "There was always a competition, whether it was who's faster, who can jump higher, who can scream louder," he told Joe Bendel for the Greensburg, Pennsylvania, *Tribune-Review* (November 27, 2005). "And we'd fight, too. Even though I was so much younger, I'd still be in some fights. But the next day, it was squashed. It was all love."

Growing up 40 miles from Cleveland Municipal Stadium (now known as Cleveland Browns Stadium), Harrison developed an interest in football as a boy and rooted for the Cleveland Browns. He started playing youth-league football at the age of eight, after his best friend, David Walker, persuaded Harrison's mother to sign him up. "I didn't want my son getting hurt running around on that field," Mildred Harrison told Sean D. Hamill for the *New York Times* (January 6, 2009). "And I didn't want him wasting time hoping for a pro career. As everyone tells me now, I was wrong." On the gridiron Harrison's natural athletic ability was immediately evident, but his poor work ethic and lackluster attitude toward practice threatened to end his football career before it started. He changed his ways after receiving advice from his father. Harrison recalled to Hamill, "[My father] told me . . . 'I don't care if you're in a game or in practice—when you're inside them lines, you play everybody as if they're playing against you, hit everybody as if they're talking about your momma.'" Harrison's father told Paulk about his son's pro career, "The hitting he's doing now is nothing new to him. . . . He wakes up in the morning wanting to hit somebody."

Harrison attended Archbishop Hoban High School, a Catholic school in Akron, where he played on the football squad under the renowned coach Mo Tipton. Midway through his freshman year, he transferred to Coventry High School, in nearby Coventry Township, after Tipton was hired at that school to overhaul its football program. Under Tipton Harrison excelled on offense, defense, and special teams, as a running back, linebacker, and punter, respectively. His success on the field, however, did not carry over to the classroom, and his parents repeatedly threatened to pull him from the team due to his poor grades. "I still didn't want him to play football, but I thought it was a good weapon to use against him," Harrison's mother recalled to Chuck Finder for the *Pittsburgh Post-Gazette* (January 11, 2009). "I drove up [to practice] and said, 'Get in this van, we're going home.' He said, 'Mom, I'll bring [my grades] up.' And he made Dean's List. I thought, 'This football came in pretty handy.'" Tipton described Harrison to Marla Ridenour for the *Akron Beacon Journal* (April 2, 2004) as "a heck of an athlete who had to focus on his grades, which he did." During his time at Coventry, Harrison, one of only a handful of African-Americans at a predominantly white school, was frequently subjected to racial taunts. "This was not an African-American community here by any means, and people were rough on him," Coventry's offensive coordinator Gary Hutt told Finder. "I don't know if I would have taken all the stuff James took."

By his senior year at Coventry, Harrison's anger at that situation had started to boil over, and he was suspended twice. He missed two games for challenging an assistant coach to a fight, and on another occasion he was suspended for one game for making lewd gestures to an opposing team's fans, in response to their hurling racial slurs at him. Later in his senior year, Harrison found himself in court, having gotten caught up—along with several other players and a coach—in an incident that involved a BB gun and resulted in injuries to two teammates. Originally charged with assault, he pleaded guilty to disorderly conduct and was forced to pay a fine. (Harrison's coach received a stiffer penalty.)

Harrison was a standout football player throughout his high-school career, but his off-the-field transgressions cost him potential scholarship offers from schools that had considered him, including the football powerhouses Ohio State University, the University of Notre Dame, and the University of Nebraska. As a result he enrolled at Kent State University, in Kent, Ohio, where he was a walk-on football player. His parents agreed to pay his tuition for his first two years at the school; Harrison constantly jeopardized his eligibility for a scholarship there with his poor grades. Though still bitter about losing the interest of big-name football programs, he turned around his performance in the classroom thanks to the "coaches' table," a weeknight study hall for players with sub-par grades, implemented by the head football coach, Dean Pees. Under Pees's guidance Harrison earned the required 3.0 grade-point average and soon developed into a standout football player for the Golden Flashes. During his junior season (2001), he was elected a team captain and established himself as one of the best defensive players in the Mid-American Conference (MAC). That year he recorded 98 tackles, three interceptions, five passes defensed, three forced fumbles, and one fumble recovery, led the MAC with 15 sacks, and finished second in the conference with 20 tackles for losses. Harrison was selected to the All-MAC First Team at outside linebacker, finished third in the voting for the conference's Defensive Player of the Year Award, and was named the Golden Flashes' Outstanding Defensive Player for the second straight year. Pees, who developed a close relationship with Harrison, told Marla Ridenour, "I've coached for 32 years and I don't know if I've ever seen a young man change his life more than James Harrison did." While attending Kent State, Harrison, who majored in general studies, worked at a nurs-

ing home and developed close relationships with patients there. He opted to forego his senior year and enter the NFL draft.

Standing an even six feet and weighing 240 pounds, Harrison was considered by professional scouts to be undersized for the position of linebacker or defensive lineman in the NFL. Consequently, he was passed over in the 2002 NFL draft, despite receiving training-camp invitations from several teams. The Pittsburgh Steelers eventually signed Harrison as an undrafted rookie free agent, reportedly after his then-agent persuaded the team to take him along with another player as part of a package deal. Harrison was soon released from the Steelers, due largely to his trouble in learning the team's complicated defensive schemes. (Harrison was reportedly so confused during those early practices that he would often stop in the middle of plays and ask the coaches to take him off the field.) Two days after his release, Harrison signed with the Steelers' practice squad. He remained there until midway through the last month of the 2002 regular season, when he was made an active member of the team's 53-man roster, after the running back Vernon Hayes was placed on injured reserve. Harrison made his professional debut in the Steelers' final regular-season game, in a Week 17 matchup against the Baltimore Ravens. In the game, which the Steelers won, 34–31, Harrison did not accumulate any statistics.

Harrison participated in the Steelers' training camp the following season but was again released and signed to the practice squad. He remained on that squad for only three weeks before being released from the team a third time. By then Harrison had developed a reputation as an uncoachable player with a bad attitude. Mike Archer, then the Steelers' linebacker coach and now the defensive coordinator at North Carolina State University, said to Sean D. Hamill that Harrison "liked football. But he did not like, in my opinion, the structure of football." Shortly after the conclusion of the 2003 regular season, Harrison was signed by the Baltimore Ravens, who immediately sent him to develop overseas with Germany's Rhein Fire of the NFL Europe league. (NFL Europe operated from 1991 until 2007; during those years NFL teams often sent younger prospects to the league to receive more hands-on coaching and game experience.) In June 2004, after a brief stint with the Fire, whose 10-game season ran during the spring, Harrison returned to the Ravens. Just 10 days later he was cut from the team, which instead signed one of his Rhein Fire teammates, the tight end Daniel Wilcox. Harrison "was a wild buck trying to make the team," the Ravens' then-coach, Brian Billick, recalled to Judy Battista for the *New York Times* (October 31, 2010). "He was more about the physical than the mental."

After getting cut from the Ravens, Harrison returned to Akron for six weeks and got his commercial-driver's license. "I almost quit to become a bus driver," he recalled to Randy Covitz for the *Kansas*

City Star (January 31, 2009). "I was going to get a regular job like everyone else." Still determined to join an NFL team if he had the chance, Harrison got a break in late July 2004, when the Steelers called him for a fourth tryout with the team, after their starting linebacker Clark Haggans broke fingers on his right hand while lifting weights. "There was something about Harrison the Steelers liked," Covitz wrote. "He had a mean streak that fit the tradition of nasty, surly, hard-hitting Steelers linebackers." Taking a more professional approach to football and showing a better grasp of the Steelers' defense, Harrison earned a roster spot out of training camp as a special-teams player and backup linebacker. Commenting on his transformation, Harrison explained to Covitz, "The difference is maturity. . . . You're young and you're stubborn and you just want to do your things your own way. That's just not the way it's going to work."

During the 2004–06 seasons, Harrison served primarily as a special-teams player and backup linebacker while occasionally playing defensive end. In 2004 he made his first NFL start at linebacker for the Steelers in a Week 10 matchup against the division rival Cleveland Browns. Starting in place of the Pro Bowl linebacker Joey Porter, who had been ejected from the game for fighting, Harrison performed solidly in a 24–10 Steelers victory, finishing with six tackles, a sack, one quarterback hurry, and one pass defensed. That year he earned three more starts at linebacker due to another injury to Clark Haggans and scored his first touchdown on a fumble recovery in the final regular-season game, against the Buffalo Bills. Meanwhile, he finished the year with a career-high 25 special-teams tackles and emerged as a standout on the squad. The Steelers ended the season with a league-best 15–1 record but lost to the eventual Super Bowl champion New England Patriots in the AFC Championship Game, 41–27.

Harrison filled in for Haggans as a starter on three more occasions (again due to injury) during the 2005 season but spent the bulk of the year on special teams. He finished with 36 tackles and three sacks and also pulled down the first interception of his career, in a Week Five game against the San Diego Chargers. That season Harrison won attention and popularity around the league during a Week 16 game against the Cleveland Browns, when he body-slammed a drunken Browns fan who had run onto the field. The incident later became known as "the Slam." Harrison also played in two of the Steelers' four postseason games, most notably Super Bowl XL, in which the Steelers defeated the Seattle Seahawks, 21–10, to tie a league record with their fifth Super Bowl title; in the game he recorded a team-high three special-teams tackles.

In 2006 Harrison signed a four-year, $6.5 million-plus contract with the Steelers. That year he appeared in only 11 games, missing five due to an injured ankle, and made his lone start of the season in the regular-season finale, against the

Cincinnati Bengals. He finished the season with eight tackles on defense and 15 special-teams tackles. The Steelers failed to defend their title and missed out on the play-offs after finishing third in the AFC North, with a record of 8–8. At the end of the season, the Steelers' longtime head coach Bill Cowher resigned after 15 years. He was replaced by the Minnesota Vikings' defensive coordinator Mike Tomlin.

With the controversial release of Joey Porter (for reasons related to the salary cap) during the 2007 off-season, Harrison was named the Steelers' starting right outside linebacker. In his first season as a starter, he enjoyed a breakthrough year, starting all 16 games and setting career highs in nearly every statistical category. Harrison finished with 98 combined tackles and led the Steelers with 8.5 sacks and seven forced fumbles. He also made two fumble recoveries and an interception and tied for second on the team with 12 special-teams tackles. The highlight of Harrison's season was a Week Nine performance on *Monday Night Football* against the Baltimore Ravens, in which he recorded eight tackles, 3.5 sacks, three forced fumbles, one interception, and a fumble recovery. He was named GMC Defensive Player of the Week for that performance and was then named the AFC Defensive Player of the Month for November after standout defensive work in games against the Cleveland Browns, New York Jets, and Miami Dolphins. Harrison was subsequently named the Steelers' Most Valuable Player (MVP) for the 2007 season and was selected to his first Pro Bowl as a starting linebacker for the AFC squad. He was also named to the AP All-Pro Second Team. The Steelers won the AFC North Division with a record of 10–6 and advanced to the postseason; they were defeated by the Jacksonville Jaguars in the wild-card play-off round, 31–29.

During the 2008 season Harrison established himself as one of the NFL's best defensive players, serving as one of the anchors of a Steelers defense that led the league in fewest points (13.9) and yards allowed per game (237.2), on average. He set a Steelers' franchise record with 16 sacks, surpassing Mike Merriweather's single-season mark of 15 in 1984; he also led the league and matched a career high with seven forced fumbles and recorded a career-high 101 combined tackles in 15 games. Harrison was voted team MVP for the second consecutive year and earned his second straight Pro Bowl selection; he was also named to the AP All-Pro First Team for the first time. Despite missing the final game of the regular season because of a hip injury, Harrison won the AP NFL Defensive Player of the Year Award, receiving 22 first-place votes to 13 for the second-place finisher, DeMarcus Ware of the Dallas Cowboys. In the process he became the fifth Steelers and first undrafted player to receive the honor; the other Steelers were the Hall of Famers Joe Greene (1972, 1974), Mel Blount (1975), Jack Lambert (1976), and Rod Woodson (1993). (In 2010 the Steelers' All-Pro safety Troy Polamalu received the honor.)

With strong play by Harrison and the rest of the team's dominating defense, the Steelers successfully defended their AFC North Division title, with a record of 12–4, and returned to the Super Bowl. They overcame the San Diego Chargers and Baltimore Ravens, in the AFC Divisional play-off round and AFC Championship Game, respectively, before facing the NFC-champion Arizona Cardinals in Super Bowl XLIII, which was held at Raymond James Stadium in Tampa, Florida, on February 1, 2009. The Steelers defeated the Cardinals, 27–23, to earn the franchise's NFL-record sixth Super Bowl title. In the dramatic game, which was decided in the final seconds on a six-yard touchdown reception by the wide receiver Santonio Holmes (who was named Super Bowl MVP), Harrison made three tackles and a Super Bowl–record, momentum-changing 100-yard interception return for a touchdown on the final play of the first half. The Steelers' legendary defensive coordinator Dick LeBeau described Harrison's feat to Ed Bouchette for the *Pittsburgh Post-Gazette* (November 1, 2009) as "the greatest single defensive play in Super Bowl history."

The Steelers signaled their faith in Harrison during the 2009 off-season, when they signed him to a six-year, $51 million contract extension. (The contract was then the largest ever given to a Steelers defensive player.) Harrison carried his dominant play from the previous year into 2009, finishing with 79 combined tackles, 10 sacks, and five forced fumbles. He was named a Pro Bowl starter for the third straight year and earned his second career selection to the AP All-Pro Second Team. Pittsburgh, however, failed to defend its title and missed out on the play-offs with a record of 9–7.

The Steelers bounced back and reestablished themselves as an AFC powerhouse in 2010, when they finished with a 12–4 record to win their third AFC North title in four seasons. Harrison again played a major role in the team's regular-season success, recording 100 combined tackles, 10.5 sacks, six forced fumbles, two interceptions, and one fumble recovery; he earned his fourth consecutive All-Pro selection (Second Team) and made his fourth straight Pro Bowl team. His superb season was largely overshadowed by a series of fines the league levied against him for violent hits. Harrison received a league-high four fines totaling $100,000. Jarrett Bell paraphrased Harrison as saying that he had been a "victim of selective enforcement." The athlete told Bell, "In other situations, guys go in there and do the same thing I did week in and week out and they don't get a flag, nor a fine. They had to have somebody to be the poster boy." That matter notwithstanding, Harrison finished third in the voting for the 2010 AP NFL Defensive Player of the Year Award (losing to his teammate Troy Polamalu) and helped the Steelers return to the Super Bowl for the second time in three seasons. The team lost to the Green Bay Packers in Super Bowl XLV, 31–25.

Harrison has been known to deflect attention from himself, instead crediting the team as a whole for accomplishments. He said to Bob Glauder in 2009, "The defense is built to play with 11 guys, and if all 11 guys are on the same page, playing the same defense on the same play, there's nothing that can go wrong and that's just how we feel about it."

The next year, though, Harrison found himself at the center of controversy for vitriolic remarks he had made about his teammates, several other NFL players, and the football commissioner for a July 2011 *Men's Journal* article titled "James Harrison: Confessions of an NFL Hitman." He later issued an apology for his comments, while claiming that some of them had been taken out of context. After undergoing two operations on his back during the off-season, Harrison entered the 2011 season in hopes of returning to full health. Those hopes were dampened when, during a Week Four contest with the Houston Texans, he suffered a fracture in the orbit of his right eye in a helmet-to-helmet collision with the Texans' tackle Duane Brown. The injury required surgery, and as of the first week of October, the length of his recovery was unknown. Before the injury, in four games Harrison had recorded 23 combined tackles, two sacks, and one forced fumble.

Harrison has earned the nickname "Deebo" from his teammates after the character of the same name (portrayed by Tom Lister Jr.) in the *Friday* movies, starring Ice Cube. He has two sons, James III (born in 2007) and Henry (born in 2009), with his longtime girlfriend, Beth Tibbott. Harrison was the subject of a 2009 book, *Never Give Up*, written by Bill Moushey and Bill Parise. He has been involved in charitable activities and recently established the James Harrison Family Foundation, to assist needy families. The foundation has pledged money to match the total of his fines.

—C.C.

Suggested Reading: (Akron, Ohio) *Beacon Journal* Feb. 8, 2009; (Cleveland) *Plain Dealer* D p1 Nov. 9, 2007; (Greensburg, Pennsylvania) *Tribune-Review* Nov. 27, 2005; *Kansas City Star* D p1 Jan. 31, 2009; *New York Times* B p10 Jan. 6, 2009, Sports p1 Oct. 31, 2010; *Pittsburgh Post-Gazette* A p1 Jan. 11, 2009, D p9 Nov. 1, 2009; *Pittsburgh Tribune Review* Sep. 11, 2011; *USA Today* C p1 Feb. 3, 2011; Moushey, Bill and Bill Parise. *Never Give Up*, 2009

Jonathan Stark, courtesy of Big Hassle Media

Hatfield, Juliana

July 27, 1967– Singer; songwriter

Address: Ye Olde Records, P.O. Box 398110, Cambridge, MA 02139

For a brief period in the early 1990s, the singer, songwriter, and indie-rock-band frontwoman Juliana Hatfield was part of alternative rock's crossover into the mainstream. Her 1992 debut solo album, *Hey Babe*, and its commercially successful follow-up, *Become What You Are*, offered confessional and confrontational songs that merged Hatfield's penchant for pop melody with punk-rock guitar playing and quirky, bittersweet vocal delivery. While alternative or "grunge" rock bands such as Nirvana and Pearl Jam topped the charts during that era, Hatfield came to represent—along with other alternative-rock icons including Liz Phair and PJ Harvey—a "90's wave of smart female rockers . . . speaking up about love, sex, power, and ambition," as Jon Pareles wrote for the *New York Times* (October 2, 1994). Though she was lumped in with that burgeoning group of female artists, Hatfield's singing stood out; Renee Graham wrote for the *Boston Globe* (July 30, 1993) that her "fragile chirp of a voice is what distinguishes her from all the screamers and screechers of the alternative scene. Hatfield describes her voices as 'young-sounding,' a stark contrast to the adult laments she writes and sings about." Those "laments"—songs expressing anger and self-doubt—led some in the media to paint her as a bitter or depressed artist, an image she has never quite escaped.

Hatfield first achieved recognition with the Boston, Massachusetts–based band the Blake Babies, in the late 1980s. The Blake Babies became college-radio favorites before disbanding in 1991, leaving Hatfield to focus on solo material. Her early radio and Music Television (MTV) hits, including "My Sister" and "Spin the Bottle," put her on the pop charts and in the pages of mainstream magazines, and her ambiguous relationship with the Lemonheads' frontman and teen heartthrob Evan Dando added to her visibility. That period in the spotlight was brief, and by the mid-1990s, when interest in alternative music had waned, she was back to being a cult icon. She has remained one for over a decade, while releasing albums independently to mostly positive reviews. Julia Askenase wrote for *Paste Magazine* (July 28, 2008, on-line) about Hatfield, "Since her grunge-rock heyday, she's oscillated between raw alt-rock and manicured pop on album after album, though always maintaining her signature confessional lyrics and eternally girlish voice." In 2010 she released the self-produced album *Peace & Love* and began a fund-raising project in which fans could pay her for personalized songs. Hatfield also reunited that year with Dando to perform a series of sold-out shows, which extended into 2011. Joan Anderman wrote for the *Boston Globe* (August 24, 2008), "As a cultural artifact, Hatfield hovers in the celebrity purgatory reserved for artists who aren't hot commodities but still matter. You don't hear her songs on the radio anymore, even though they keep getting better."

Juliana Hatfield was born on July 27, 1967 in Wiscasset, Maine, to Philip M. Hatfield, a radiologist, and Julie Hatfield, a *Boston Globe* fashion writer. She was raised in the affluent Boston suburb of Duxbury, Massachusetts, the only girl, and middle child, among three siblings. Music was an integral part of her upbringing; both of her parents were amateur pianists, and they signed her up for lessons. Her mother was a member of a local church choir, in which Hatfield had her first public singing experiences. When she was 11 her parents divorced. "I remember being completely shocked and freaked out by it. I couldn't believe it was happening," she told Renee Graham. "Then I sort of blocked it out of my mind, and convinced myself that it had no effect on me. Lately, I've realized it was really hard."

Hatfield was still studying classical piano when, in her early teens, she became interested in rock and pop. Early on, her record collection consisted of lighter pop fare, such as the work of Olivia Newton-John and the Carpenters, as well as albums by the British new-wave group the Police. In high school she joined a band, the Squids, that played covers of songs by the Police and other groups. Then, at 15, she was introduced to punk rock by her older brother's girlfriend (or, according to some sources, a babysitter or live-in nanny). She took to the music immediately and was especially intrigued by the abrasive singing of Exene Cervenka of the Los Angeles, California, band X. "All the women singers I knew were these pop divas—which I really appreciate, I really like that stuff. But Exene was someone who wasn't the greatest singer technically, but she was singing from the gut," Hatfield recalled to Renee Graham. "It was really raw. And it was cool." Hearing punk led Hatfield to pick up the electric guitar and dig deeper into the world of alternative rock music; she eventually discovered the work of such pioneering groups as the Velvet Underground, R.E.M., and the Replacements.

At Duxbury High School Hatfield felt alienated from most of her peers and struggled to find classmates with similar musical tastes. For a semester after high school, she attended Boston University; it was not until she transferred to the prestigious Berklee College of Music, in Boston, where she received vocal training and graduated with a major in songwriting, that she found like-minded peers. Among them were John Strohm and Freda Love Smith (born Freda Boner), who were dating each other; they had played in bands while growing up in the Bloomington, Indiana, area. While walking around the Berklee campus, Strohm and Smith frequently noticed Hatfield, who stood out because, as Smith put it to Joan Anderman, "She wore the same thing every day: a leather biker jacket, jeans and a white T-shirt, and clunky shoes, with her hair in a ponytail. Juliana didn't look like anyone else at Berklee. There was an aura about her, and I was drawn to her air of mystery." The couple introduced themselves to Hatfield, and the three discovered their shared love of X and several 1980s alternative-rock bands.

The new trio dubbed themselves the Blake Babies—the name that the famed Beat poet Allen Ginsberg suggested when Strohm and Smith asked him at a lecture they attended to name their band. (The work of the 18th/19th-century British poet and artist William Blake had influenced Ginsberg's writings.) Hatfield initially played lead guitar, then switched to bass guitar and vocal duties, while Strohm took over on lead guitar and Smith played drums. The three moved into a residence owned by Hatfield's mother in the city's Allston neighborhood, a part of Boston known for its thriving independent-music scene. There, they lived and practiced songs—for a brief period—with Evan Dando, a Boston native and friend of Hatfield's who later achieved widespread fame with his pop-rock band the Lemonheads. The Blake Babies released an EP, the self-financed *Nicely, Nicely*, in 1987, and the band's infectious, "jangle-pop" sound quickly caught on in Boston. Like the band's Boston-based contemporaries, the Blake Babies soon became a college-radio favorite and achieved sufficient underground recognition to warrant music videos, national and international tours, and minor commercial radio play. During its brief existence, in addition to numerous EPs, the band recorded two critically lauded full-length albums, *Earwig* (1989) and *Sunburn* (1990).

The Blake Babies merged melodic and sonic guitar elements with bittersweet, pop-friendly male/female vocals and Hatfield's often-acerbic lyrics. Her soft vocal delivery came to characterize the Blake Babies; Mike Boehm wrote for the *Los Angeles Times* (February 14, 1991), "The Blake Babies aren't afraid to lead with the sweetness in Hatfield's voice, nor are they against crafting melodies that display an unabashed fondness for pure pop. At the same time, the effort to 'fight,' or 'counteract' that sweetness, as Hatfield puts it, is evident, and the resulting tension brings a pretty-but-tough duality to the band's sound." In a review of *Sunburn*, considered by some critics to be the band's best effort, Stewart Mason wrote for allmusic.com, "*Sunburn* is primarily the album on which Juliana Hatfield's songwriting prowess first flourishes, and it's possibly her finest collection of songs." In 1991, after a tour of Europe, Hatfield, Strohm, and Smith agreed to break up the Blake Babies. Hatfield told Greg Kot for the *Chicago Tribune* (July 16, 1992), "We just grew out of the Blake Babies, or I did, anyway. I was so unsatisfied musically, not because of any one person's fault, but because of how we worked together as a band." Strohm and Smith returned to Indiana and formed the band Antenna, which achieved minor acclaim in the independent-rock community, and Hatfield became a solo artist. The Blake Babies' compilation *Innocence and Experience* came out in 1993, and the band regrouped in 2001 to release *God Bless the Blake Babies*.

After contributing lyrics to the former Bangles singer Susanna Hoffs's 1991 debut album, *When You're a Boy*, Hatfield began to record original songs with several other artists, including Dando, the fIREHOSE bassist Mike Watt, and the singer-songwriter John Wesley Harding. That material made up her 1992 solo debut, *Hey Babe*, which was a minor commercial hit and received good reviews in major publications including *Rolling Stone*, *Interview*, *Esquire*, and the *New Yorker*; *Entertainment Weekly* voted it one of the top 10 records of 1992, and it received an added boost by the commercial breakthrough that year of the Lemonheads' *It's A Shame About Ray*, to which Hatfield had contributed bass lines and backing vocals. Although still rooted in pop, the songs on *Hey Babe* were darker than those she had recorded with the Blake Babies; their lyrics focused on themes of failed romance, disillusionment, and self-doubt. While praising the album, members of the press interpreted its lyrics as clues about Hatfield's life and personality. Subtle barbs such as the line, "I see a long-lost home in his eyes; he sees a nice hotel in mine," from the song "Forever Baby," gave some journalists the impression that Hatfield was depressed and bitter—a notion with which she did not agree. She told Steve Morse for the *Boston Globe* (January 15, 1993), "It bothers me to be stereotyped, but everybody that makes music gets stereotyped. I just try not to listen to it too much."

In 1992 and 1993 Hatfield's life was further complicated by fervent media interest in her relationship with Dando. Although the two have claimed that they never had a romantic relationship, their frequent collaborations (including the Lemonheads' 1993 album, *Come on Feel the Lemonheads*, which includes a song about Hatfield) and Dando's status as a heartthrob led the alternative-music press to speculate. Then, for a 1992 article in *Interview* magazine, Hatfield admitted to being—at the age of 25—a virgin. That revelation stirred up another wave of unwelcome attention from the press. "I said that a year ago, and I was naive . . . ," Hatfield later told Mike Boehm for the *Los Angeles Times* (September 8, 1993). "I just thought it was an interesting thing for a person my age to say. I thought it would make people think. I tell journalists to get off it. It just shows you where people's minds are: In the gutter. I've learned a lot." She told Darel Jevens for the *Chicago Sun-Times* (October 4, 1992), "I just made a decision to not do it until I know 100 percent that I want to, and that's never happened. . . . I wanted to see if I could make it to 25. And I have." In 1992 Hatfield's burgeoning popularity as an alternative-rock icon led to her appearances in a fashion spread in *Vogue*; on the cover of *Sassy*; and in features and photo shoots for *GQ*, *Details*, and *Elle*. Hatfield said she did not change her look to suit those glossy magazines. "I'm not really fashion conscious, I just wear what I wear," she told Julie Romandetta for the *Boston Herald* (August 2, 1993). "I don't go after these things, I don't know why they want me."

Thanks to the success of *Hey Babe*, Hatfield signed a contract with Atlantic Records. In 1993 she released her second solo album, *Become What You Are*. To record the album, she had formed the Juliana Hatfield Three with the bassist Dean Fisher and the drummer Todd Phillips. Hatfield has been quoted as saying that she was happier with *Become What You Are* than with its predecessor, and the new album was a bigger commercial success than *Hey Babe*, selling more than 100,000 copies within a month of its release. (*Hey Babe* had sold only about 60,000 by 1993.) It also boasted the hit radio single and frequent MTV video "My Sister" as well as "Spin the Bottle," which was later made into a music video and included on the soundtrack of the 1993 film *Reality Bites*, directed by Ben Stiller. Compared with *Hey Babe*, *Become What You Are* received praise for its tighter musicianship and Hatfield's quirky songwriting. In contrast to the confessional nature of *Hey Babe*, Hatfield's new songs took on a narrative bent, with observational lyrics. She confronted a rapist in "A Dame with a Rod," mocked notions of romance on "Spin the Bottle," and paid homage to her home state in "Feelin' Massachusetts." Although she does not have a sister, she created a fictional one for "My Sister" in order to examine family and romantic quarrels.

Hatfield's next record, *Only Everything*, was released in 1995, when alternative rock had begun its decline in popularity. Only one single, "Universal Heartbeat," found its way to MTV and commercial radio, and the album did not last long on the charts. It received mixed reviews; Howard Cohen wrote for the *Miami Herald* (April 19, 1995), "Blandly simplistic guitar-playing based on repetitive chords doesn't help Hatfield's efforts. *Only Everything* is like listening to Barbie front a less-accomplished Nirvana. Not the desired effect, we're sure." Some critics, however, heard artistic growth in the songwriting; Christopher John Farley wrote for *Time* (April 3, 1995), "While her meanings have grown more elusive, Hatfield's melodies—as well as her light, birdlike voice—have grown more assertive. . . . Hatfield's earlier CDs showed promise but didn't fully deliver. The enjoyably ambiguous *Only Everything* sends a clear message that she's a true talent."

In 1996 Hatfield left Atlantic out of frustration after the label's executives refused to release her album "God's Foot," which they felt lacked the commercial potential of her previous efforts. In 1997 Hatfield released the EP *Please Do Not Disturb* on an independent label and performed at that year's Lilith Fair, a festival comprising female musical artists. Hatfield has been outspoken about the tendency of the media and other musicians to highlight female performers' gender, arguing that to refer to those musicians as "women in rock" is to reduce them to novelty status. In an interview with Moira McCormick for the *Rolling Stone* Web site (December 5, 1997), she responded to female critics who accused her of failing to support a feminist agenda: "Do they realize that by what they do, they're knocking down everything they're probably trying to achieve? They're backpedaling, making it impossible to make changes in the way things are perceived."

Hatfield released the full-length *Bed* in 1998 on the Zoe label (an imprint of Rounder Records). In 2000 Zoe released two of her albums simultaneously—*Beautiful Creature* and *Total System Failure*. *Beautiful Creature* showcased Hatfield at her most intimate yet, with soft acoustic-guitar work that stood in stark contrast to the angry, distorted rock of *Total System Failure*, which she recorded with a one-off band, Juliana's Pony. In 2001 Hatfield rejoined the Blake Babies for the album *God Bless the Blake Babies* and a reunion tour. *God Bless the Blake Babies* received positive reviews.

After the Blake Babies reunion, Hatfield and Smith continued to work together, forming a three-piece band with Heidi Gluck, of the group the Pieces, called Some Girls—named after a Rolling Stones album. The group released two albums, *Feel It* (2003) and *Crushing Love* (2006). Meanwhile, Hatfield had returned to her solo material, releasing *In Exile Deo* (2004), an album the *New York Times* music critic Jon Pareles named one of the year's 10 best. She started her own record label, Ye Olde Records, to release *Made in China* (2005) and her 2008 album *How to Walk Away*, which both received mixed reviews. Produced by Andy Chase of the indie-pop band Ivy, *How to Walk Away* found Hatfield singing in a lower register than usual. Nate Chinen wrote for the *New York Times* (August 17, 2008), "The record pairs Ms. Hatfield's compact songs with an unabashedly commercial sound, a strategy that works about half the time. Songs like 'Remember November' and 'Such a Beautiful Girl' end up sounding overworked, undeserving of the special treatment. But when Ms. Hatfield presents herself as a wronged partner ('The Fact Remains'), or simply the wrong partner ('Just Lust'), she can be gripping." Also in 2008 Wiley & Sons published *When I Grow Up*, Hatfield's candid memoir of her struggles with depression, anxiety, and anorexia. The book chronicled her life on the road, her recurring thoughts of suicide, and her often-stressful relationships with pop and rock stars.

Hatfield's next solo album, *Peace & Love*, was released on her label in 2010. That work represented the first time Hatfield had been involved in every aspect of an album's creation—from writing and performing to recording, engineering, producing, and playing all the instrumental parts. Consisting of low-key acoustic songs with layered vocals, *Peace & Love* stood in marked contrast to her previous album. Reviews of the record ranged from favorable to negative, with some finding that the stripped-down sound accentuated Hatfield's strengths while others reached the opposite conclusion.

In May 2010 Hatfield offered to write personalized songs for fans willing and able to pay $1,000 each; the money was to be used to fund her new projects and bring out her previously unreleased material. After sending payment, fans were asked to e-mail Hatfield information about their hobbies, interests, and other aspects of themselves that would inspire lyrics. Within three months each paying fan would receive a unique disk containing a recording of an original song (in a numbered, hand-painted cardboard sleeve) in the acoustic style of the material on *Peace & Love*. Hatfield asked that the recipients of the songs agree not to try to profit from them, as she would own the copyrights to the songs. She also offered, for those who could not spend $1,000, to enter their names for $10 each into a lottery, with the winner receiving a personalized song. She initially planned to write a total of 20 such songs but stopped after taking 11 orders. Later in the year, after finding the project rewarding, she began a second wave of personalized songs. She wrote for her Web site, "I worried, when I first announced I was going to do this, that it would be hard for me, a grind, a slog, a plodding exercise in whoring myself out for money. How would I write about and care about people I didn't know? BUT I have been really blindsided by how much I have enjoyed the process and how it has brought me closer, in an enlightening and wonderful way, to humanity in general and to the unique

subset of personalities that is my superfanbase. Before I embarked on this challenging project/experiment, I was totally burned-out on songwriting, burned-out on singing about myself, and now I am completely re-energized and inspired again."

From August 2010 through early 2011, Hatfield and Dando mounted a series of successful acoustic shows in New York City; Boston; Philadelphia, Pennsylvania; and other East Coast locations. They performed as a duet, with one backing the other on their respective songs.

Hatfield lives in Cambridge, Massachusetts.

—W.D.

Suggested Reading: All Music Guide Web site; *Boston Globe* p55 Jan. 15, 1993, p25 July 30, 1993, N p1 Aug. 24, 2008; *Los Angeles Times* F p2 Sep. 8, 1993; *New York Times* (on-line) Sep. 3, 2008; *Santa Fe New Mexican* P p38 June 25, 2004

Selected Recordings: with the Blake Babies—*Earwig*, 1989; *Sunburn*, 1990; *Innocence and Experience*, 1993; *God Bless the Blake Babies*, 2001; with Some Girls—*Feel It*, 2003; *Crushing Love*, 2006; as solo artist—*Hey Babe*, 1992; *Become What You Are*, 1993; *Only Everything*, 1995; *Bed*, 1998; *Beautiful Creature*, 2000; *Total System Failure*, 2000; *In Exile Deo*, 2004; *Made in China*, 2005; *How to Walk Away*, 2008; *Peace & Love*, 2010

Selected Books: *When I Grow Up*, 2008

Hayes, Terrance

Nov. 18, 1971– Poet; educator

Address: Dept. of English, Carnegie Mellon University, Baker Hall 259, 5000 Forbes Ave., Pittsburgh, PA 15213-3890

Having loved to draw and paint since childhood, Terrance Hayes majored in visual arts in college, but in graduate school, in the mid-1990s, he studied poetry. "I never did a painting and started weeping. But I would do that with poems. So I thought clearly, this is what my calling is," he told Bill O'Driscoll for the *Pittsburgh (Pennsylvania) City Paper* (April 27, 2006, on-line). Since 2001 Hayes has taught courses in poetry at Carnegie Mellon University, in Pittsburgh, where he is now a full professor of creative writing. In 2010 he won a National Book Award for *Lighthead*, his fourth collection of poems. His earlier volumes are *Muscular Music* (1999), an expansion of his master's-degree thesis; *Hip Logic* (2002); and *Wind in a Box* (2006). "Terrance Hayes is, I think, one of the two or three most exciting young African-American po-

Yona Harvey, courtesy of Penguin Books
Terrance Hayes

ets of his generation, and one of the four or five most exciting poets period," Keith Tuma, a professor of English at Miami University in Ohio, told O'Driscoll. Tuma, who included poems by Hayes in his anthology *Rainbow Darkness* (2005), also said that Hayes is "really taking chances with pushing poems in surprising, twisting, serpentine directions. The whole poem can turn itself upside down in the blink of an eye."

"I'm not really that interested in style," Hayes told Margaret Quamme for the *Columbus (Ohio) Dispatch* (April 27, 2005). "I don't want to be a 'new formalist'; I don't want to be a 'confessional poet'; I don't want to be an 'African American poet'; I don't want to be like 'the young hip-hop poet.' But I'm interested in all those segments of a personality or an aesthetic." Hayes's poems address a wide range of subjects and issues and reflect the evolution of his thinking and feelings about them. "What it means to be male, and what it means to be African American, . . . are some of the things that come up in my work often," he told Erin Keane for the Louisville, Kentucky, *Courier-Journal* (November 11, 2009). "Those things . . . are not fixed, they're always becoming." Hayes told John Mark Eberhart for the *Kansas City (Missouri) Star* (December 1, 2004), "Surprise is at the root of why I write poetry. Intellectual surprises, emotional surprises . . . that result not necessarily in spontaneous free writes, but in rigorous revisions and excavations." He also told Eberhart, "Sometimes writing is like searching for the light switch in a pitch black room. Some poets know going in how to find it. . . . But working to be continuously surprised, I can engage politics and autobiography without being limited by them. I don't

mind knocking around in the dark for a little while. There is a frustration and anxiety at being lost, of course, but there is also faith that the search will result in a lovely blast of light." In addition to the National Book Award, Hayes's honors include a Whiting Writers Award and fellowships from the National Endowment for the Arts and the John Simon Guggenheim Memorial Foundation. In a review of *Lighthead*, John Freeman wrote for the Cleveland, Ohio, *Plain Dealer* (November 29, 2010), "Poetry has two kinds of music. There is the sound it makes when read aloud, and then it has an inner composition, too—that strange, occult rhythm verses make when your mind, not your lips, mouths the words. Terrance Hayes is one of the rare poets who can braid these two sounds into a kind of harmony."

Terrance Hayes was born on November 18, 1971 in Columbia, South Carolina. He was raised there by his mother, Ethel Hayes, who worked as a guard at a state prison, and her husband, James Hayes, a U.S. Army professional who spent much of Hayes's childhood away from home. During his teens Hayes began to doubt that James Hayes was his biological father. "I'm just very different than everybody in my family," he told O'Driscoll. In addition, he wondered why his younger brother, and not he, was named James Hayes II. When, at 18, Hayes confronted his mother with his suspicions, she told him, "You're right," as he recalled to O'Driscoll. "But that was it, she wasn't going to say anything else." In 1997, after a sporadic years-long search, Hayes learned the name of his biological father, Butch Tyler; another seven years passed before he located Tyler and the two met. He has acknowledged that for many years, questions about his parentage sometimes occupied him to the point of obsession and strongly influenced his poetry.

Hayes's mother has recalled that Terrance, her first child, spent much time reading or drawing. As a high-school student, his tastes in music differed from those of his peers, she told O'Driscoll: he listened to recordings by the jazz saxophonist John Coltrane, the vocalist Sarah Vaughn, and the gospel singer Mahalia Jackson. Hayes began writing poetry in middle school but few people, if any, knew about it. "I never thought that caring about poems and books meant anything," he told O'Driscoll. "It's like liking food—it doesn't necessarily mean you're going to have it as a career." As a student at Spring Valley High School, in Columbia, in the late 1980s, Hayes earned recognition through sports. Already towering above his classmates—he later reached the height of six feet five inches—he excelled on the basketball court, playing on the varsity team for three years; in addition, he ran track. He was also interested in painting and spent a summer studying visual art at the Governor's School for the Arts in Greenville, South Carolina.

The first member of his family to attend college, Hayes received a full basketball scholarship to Coker College, a small liberal-arts school in Hartville,

South Carolina. At Coker he majored in visual arts, with an emphasis on painting, and also studied philosophy, English, and theater; in addition, he was named an Academic All-American in basketball. "College may be the only time a student has so many avenues to knowledge before him or her," he said in an interview for the Coker College Web site in late 2010. "I say, let a foot touch as many avenues as possible before settling on a path." During his undergraduate years only an occasional girlfriend or English professor ever read his poems. The latter included Lois Rauch Gibson. "Terrance was already a poet when he was a student at Coker," Gibson wrote for the Coker College Web site. "His work has become more and more impressive over time." Gibson set Hayes on the path to graduate school. "It wouldn't be an overstatement to say that Dr. Gibson influenced my life tremendously as a teacher, advocate, and a friend," Hayes is quoted as saying on the Web site. "In the most literal and essential sense, I would not be [at Carnegie Mellon] were it not for Dr. Gibson."

After he earned a B.A. degree, in 1994, Hayes entered the graduate program in English at the University of Pittsburgh. He decided to concentrate on poetry—"the most unlikely thing" that his family and friends might have imagined he would choose, he told O'Driscoll. His teachers included the poets Ed Ochester, Lynn Emmanuel, and Toi Derricotte. "I thought it was great to see . . . these three very different aspects of what a poet can be, and just take stuff from all of them," Hayes told O'Driscoll. He told Pat Berman for the Columbia, South Carolina, *State* (November 30, 2003) that he did not feel intimidated by graduate students who had extensive backgrounds in poetry. It was partly their presence that led him to scan or read virtually every poetry book in the university library, earning him the nickname "Library Guy." "I wanted to participate in the discussions. I wasn't going to be complacent," he told O'Driscoll. While Hayes was at the University of Pittsburgh, Derricotte co-founded (with Cornelius Eady) the Cave Canem Foundation, whose mission is to foster the development and careers of African-American poets, through workshops, readings, an annual poetry retreat, prizes, and publications. Hayes earned an M.F.A. degree from the University of Pittsburgh in 1997.

Also in 1997 Hayes married Yona Harvey, a poet who had earned a master's degree in library and information science at the University of Pittsburgh. After their marriage the couple moved to Japan, where Hayes and Harvey taught briefly. The couple then lived for about two years in Columbus, Ohio, and for another two years in New Orleans, Louisiana, where Hayes taught English at Xavier University. In 2001 they returned to Pittsburgh, where both Hayes and Harvey joined the Department of English at Carnegie Mellon University.

Hayes's first book of poems, *Muscular Music*, was published as part of Carnegie Mellon's Classic Contemporaries Series in 1999, during his residence in Columbus. The poems, most of which came from his master's thesis, included personal and family stories and reflected his thoughts about black identity and culture, masculinity, and Pittsburgh and its hip-hop artists. In an interview years later with Ray Suarez for the TV program *NewsHour with Jim Lehrer* (April 24, 2008), Hayes recalled, "Since I took my first poetry classes in Pittsburgh and I realized my first community of poets in Pittsburgh, this became initially the . . . locus for a lot of my poems. So that when I think about what sort of poet I am or what sort of landscape it is that interests me, for a long time it has been the landscape of concrete, and the landscape of rivers, and the landscape of the sorts of people that I'd meet riding the buses or walking through some of the neighborhoods." In a review of *Muscular Music* for *Callaloo* (Spring 2002), as quoted by William W. Starr in the Columbia, South Carolina, *State* (March 5, 2000), Shara McCallum wrote, "These poems are hard-hitting, honest, sincere and yet suffused with tenderness." Tyrone Williams, who assessed *Muscular Music* for *African American Review* (Fall 2000), was less impressed, writing, "The collection seems to be less the heralding of a new 'voice' or sensibility than a kind of summing up of past and current trends." *Muscular Music* won the Kate Tufts Discovery Award, bestowed by Claremont Graduate University, in California, and the Whiting Writers Award.

In 2001 the National Poetry Series, a literary awards program, received from Cornelius Eady the manuscript for Hayes's next collection, *Hip Logic*, and chose to sponsor its publication. (Each year the program's judges select five manuscripts for that honor.) Published by Penguin Books in 2002, the book was a finalist for the *Los Angeles Times* Book Award for poetry and a runner-up for the James Laughlin Award, from the Academy of American Poets. Eady wrote for a blurb that appears on the back cover of *Hip Logic*, "Terrance Hayes is one elegant poet. First you'll marvel at his skill, his near-perfect pitch, his disarming humor, his brilliant turns of phrase. Then you'll notice the grace, the tenderness, the unblinking truth-telling just beneath his lines, the open and generous way he takes in our world." In another back-cover comment, Toi Derricotte wrote, "There is always a spiritual question driving the poetry of Terrance Hayes. What does it mean to be a black man? What does it mean to be an artist? He dances at the crossroads. Here is a brilliant and compassionate poet inventing new doorways for the heart." In an assessment of *Hip Logic* for *Black Issues Book Review* (September/October 2002), Tonya Maria Matthews wrote, "With incredible sensitivity, Hayes takes his readers through the soul of a black man seeking truth, while learning to walk the walk."

Hayes received a National Endowment for the Arts Fellowship in 2005. The next year he published *Wind in a Box*. One poem in that collection, "Woofer (When I Consider the African-American)," begins, "When I consider the much discussed dilemma / of the African-American, I think not of the diasporic / middle passing, unchained, juke, jock, and jiving / sons and daughters of what sleek dashikied poets / and tether fisted Nationalists commonly call Mother / Africa, but of an ex-girlfriend," the daughter of a black mother and white father, whose family basement became the site of their trysts. The poem ends, "I think of a string of people connected one to another / and including the two of us there in the basement / linked by a hyphen filled with blood; / linked by a blood filled baton in one great historical relay." In a review for the *Pittsburgh Post-Gazette* (April 23, 2006), Peter Blair wrote, "Opening Terrance Hayes' new book of poetry is like being drawn into whirling tornadoes of emotions, words and poetic styles, revealing a poet not afraid to take chances or take on any subject, no matter how fraught with cultural land mines." *Publishers Weekly* named *Wind in a Box* one of the best 100 books of 2006.

In 2009 Hayes was named a John Simon Guggenheim Memorial Foundation fellow. He used the fellowship money to travel to Japan to study pecha kucha—a Japanese term, loosely meaning "chit-chat," that refers to an event in which each participant must present 20 slides depicting his or her work and talk about each image for 20 seconds, for a total of precisely six minutes and 40 seconds. According to the Web site of the organization Charleston Creative Parliament, pecha kucha is "a mix of show-and-tell, open-mike night and happy hour that has become a forum for ideas on design, architecture and other forms of creativity. Devised in 2003 in Tokyo, Pecha Kucha Night has spread virally to over 135 cities around the world as an informal forum for creative people to meet, network and show their work in public." Hayes had already participated in such an event: the 2008 Carnegie Mellon School of Architecture graduation ceremony, in which people from various fields presented slides of their work. "I loved the result of putting together intense and powerful pieces of separate poems and creating a new and unique poem," he told a States News Service (July 9, 2009) reporter.

Hayes created the cover illustration for *Lighthead* (2010), as he had for its three predecessors. Included in *Lighthead* are four pecha kucha–like poems, each section of which is four or five lines. The pecha kucha–like poems are "For Brothers of the Dragon," "Twenty Measures of Chitchat," "Arbor for Butch, a pecha kucha after Martin Puryear" (a contemporary African-American sculptor), and "Coffin for Head of State, a pecha kucha after Fela Kuti" (the Nigerian "king of Afrobeat," a singer, songwriter, multi-instrumentalist, and social activist who died of AIDS-related causes in 1997). In the "Poetry Chronicle" section of the *New York Times Book Review* (April 22, 2010), Stephen Burt wrote that *Lighthead* "puts invincibly restless wordplay at the service of strong emotions." "Hayes makes good use of his prodigious imagination (the 'light' in his 'head'), and he knows that all storytellers make some things up," Burt continued. Yet Hayes "wants to keep faith with tough facts, especially

with black life in the rural South. . . . All his poems tell three (or more) stories at once." "Hayes's work is terrific, and characteristic of a certain strain in contemporary poetry," Gregory Cowles wrote for the *New York Times* (November 18, 2010, on-line) on the day the poet won the National Book Award for *Lighthead*: "it's grounded in narrative even as it's linguistically dense and playful, with allusions to formal verse traditions and to pop culture new and old. There's an appealing restlessness and reach and witty musicality" in Hayes's poems, "with meanings that can explode in a thousand directions in every line."

Hayes was named the poet laureate of Coker College in 2010. His poems have been published in many periodicals, among them *American Poetry Review*, *Antioch Review*, *Black Renaissance Noir*, *Black Warrior Review*, the *Bloomsbury Review*, *Callaloo*, *Columbia Poetry Review*, *Harvard Review*, *Indiana Review*, *McSweeney's Literary Journal*, *Ploughshares*, *Poetry*, the *New Yorker*, and the *Southern Review*. His poems have appeared in many anthologies as well. Hayes can be heard reading some of his poems on the Web site poets.org.

Known for his warmth and charisma, Hayes lives with his wife, their daughter, Ua, and son, Aaron, in Pittsburgh. When Mark Eberhart asked him what activities he engaged in when he is "not writing poetry," he responded, "These days when I'm not being a husband, father and teacher, I'm trying to find time to paint and exercise a minor piano hobby. But I'm never 'not writing poetry.' If you are as foolish as I am, you believe every word dreams of becoming a poem."

—M.M.H.

Suggested Reading: (Cleveland, Ohio) *Plain Dealer* (on-line) Nov. 29, 2010; (Columbia, South Carolina) *State* F p1 Mar. 5, 2000, E p1 Nov. 30, 2003; *Columbus (Ohio) Dispatch* B p4 Apr. 27, 2005; *Kansas City (Missouri) Star* (on-line) Dec. 1, 2004; (Louisville, Kentucky) *Courier-Journal* V p36 Nov. 11, 2009; *NewsHour with Jim Lehrer* (on-line) Apr. 24, 2008; *Pittsburgh (Pennsylvania) City Paper* p24 Apr. 26, 2006; *Pittsburgh (Pennsylvania) Post-Gazette* H p6 Apr. 23, 2006; *Publishers Weekly* p53 Mar. 22, 2010; States News Service (on-line) July 9, 2009

Selected Books: *Muscular Music*, 1999; *Hip Logic*, 2002; *Wind in a Box*, 2006; *Lighthead*, 2010

Smartset Photography 2010

Henderson, Fergus

July 31, 1963– Chef; restaurateur

Address: St. John Bar and Restaurant, 26 St. John St., London EC1M 4AY, England

Rachel Cooke wrote for the London *Guardian* (September 12, 2004, on-line), "For the uninitiated . . . there is something scary about Fergus Henderson's cooking. 'Eew!' they say, when you tell them that, for lunch, you ate pig's cap with dandelion, or blood cakes with fried eggs. 'No! You DIDN'T!' they squeal, when you admit that, for dinner, you scoffed tripe and onions, or giblet stew." Henderson, who presides over the renowned London, England, restaurant St. John, has been lauded for his philosophy of "nose to tail eating," which calls for making use of the entire animal—including such parts as trotters (pigs' feet) and entrails. Michael Bateman wrote for the London *Independent* (September 6, 1998, on-line), "Having turned against the tide of Modern British Cooking (with its bits and bobs from Thailand and Tuscany tossed into the melting-pot)," Henderson "has built up a sturdy menu of items from British butchers which are seldom seen on the supermarket shelf: offal of all sorts, and not just livers, hearts, kidneys, but tongue, spleen, bones, tripe, tails, ears." A writer for *Art Culinaire* (March 22, 2010) observed that since its opening, in 1994, St. John has "provide[d] comfort to traditionalists through the reassuring embrace of recipes that have sated the nation's citizens for centuries. By merging the contemporary world with the past, St. John inhabits its own universe. The restaurant transcends a label and lets the food, as Henderson says, 'speak for itself.'"

In the introduction to Henderson's cookbook *The Whole Beast: Nose to Tail Eating* (2004)—which had been published originally, in 1999, as *Nose to Tail Eating: A Kind of British Cooking*—the chef and television personality Anthony Bourdain wrote of his early encounters with Henderson's food: "I saw his simple, honest, traditional English country fare as a thumb in the eye to the Establishment, an outrageously timed head-butt to the growing hordes of politically correct, the [animal rights activists], the European Union, the practitioners of arch, ironic fusion cuisine and all those chefs who were fussing about with tall, overly sculpted entrees of little substance and less soul."

Fergus Henderson was born on July 31, 1963 to Brian and Elizabeth (Evans) Henderson, both of whom were architects; he was raised in North London. (Brian Henderson was a partner in the commercial firm YRM, which designed London's Gatwick Airport.) In his contribution to the book *Home: 50 Tastemakers Describe What It Is, Where It Is, What It Means* (2007), by Stafford Cliff, Henderson wrote, "My mom cooked very well and my dad was a big eater and we travelled and ate very well in restaurants. They were a big feature in our lives. The theory is that our family was held together so well and for so long by a white tablecloth." Henderson told the writer for *Art Culinaire* that his childhood meals often consisted of traditional British fare. His mother, he recalled, "cooked boiled ham parcels. Boiled beef. Everything was boiled. There was a lot of boiled meat. Steamed pudding. Tripe and onions. Cooked perfectly. She was a good cook and I feel I have a lot to answer for, but here I am." In *Home* Henderson related one of his "most telling" childhood memories: "coming downstairs in the morning and finding the paisley tablecloth still there from dinner the night before, and a delicious smell of old cigar smoke and undrunk wine and coffee and so forth. I remember, as a young kid, sensing that something good had been going on and that I was missing out."

Henderson received his early education at King Alfred's School, in Hampstead, in London. He went on to attend the Chelsea School of Art, where he remained for a year. Thinking that he would follow in his parents' footsteps, he then began studying at the Architectural Association School of Architecture, in London. Still, he has recalled, food was almost always on his mind—even when he was designing buildings. "When I was at architecture school I started cooking at a place called Smiths in Covent Garden with a few chums," he told an interviewer for *Fork* magazine (August 30, 2009, on-line). "We would be cooking things like cassoulet and pot au feu for a few people on Sundays. When I finished at architecture school, I went to Smiths and asked if I could change the menu and I sort of fell into [a job]." Henderson has suggested to interviewers that he was unsuited for a desk job. He told Rachel Cooke, "I worked in a few offices. The office lunch was a fairly earth-shattering moment, sitting eating at the drawing board. Lunch should be joy unbounding." After leaving the restaurant in Covent Garden, Henderson cooked at the Globe, a club in Notting Hill.

In 1992 Henderson and the New Zealand–born chef Margot Clayton, whom he would marry the following year, opened a restaurant above the French House, an old pub located in London's fashionable Soho area. Known as the French House Dining Room, the venue offered traditional British and French cuisine served in a quiet, rustic atmosphere. "I used to drink there rather frequently, so I knew the landlord," Henderson recalled to Cooke. "The good thing about it was that it involved as small a financial risk as possible. It was just the two of us and a kitchen porter. . . . So, you see, I've always had my own kitchen, and that's given me a kind of natural momentum. I've been allowed to follow my own pursuits. I should have sat at the feet of some wiser, older chef but, as it turned out, I didn't. I don't think it's done me too much harm."

Particularly inspired by a meal of deep-fried trotters that he had eaten in Paris, France, on his wedding night, Henderson began serving dishes at his new venue containing often-ignored parts of animals. "The menu at the French House was just common sense," he told Jay Rayner for the London *Observer* (March 22, 2009, on-line). "We'd always enjoyed the extremities. After all, once you've knocked an animal on the head you might as well use it all."

Under Henderson and Clayton, the French House Dining Room received largely favorable reviews from food critics. Fay Maschler wrote for the London *Evening Standard* (October 12, 1993), for example, "What joy when two instinctively good chefs marry one another and run a restaurant. . . . Theirs is robust food with potent flavours served in quantities that stop you in your tracks. The short menu changes daily and nearly always includes something unexpected, for example sea urchins or a particularly creative way with offal."

In October 1994 the couple and a business partner, Trevor Gulliver, opened St. John, not far from London's Smithfield Meat Market. The restaurant—located in what Cooke described as "half Georgian townhouse and half old smokehouse, the last smoking having taken place in 1967"—specializes in the traditional British cuisine repopularized by Henderson. Rayner wrote for the London *Observer* (October 14, 2007, on-line), however, "A lot has been made about the overt Britishness of Henderson's cookery, and there's no doubt that, with his interest in ox tongue and brown shrimps and tripe, this is indeed a British restaurant. But it is also inspired, I think, by a sensibility found on the other side of the Channel. That impeccable veal chop, butchered thick and with a fine char and a ballast of fat, alongside the leaves of well-dressed chicory, looked in its simplicity distinctly Italian. Other dishes, like a boozy hare broth—essentially an unclarified consommé—loaded with mushrooms, strike me as being the British equivalent of French paysanne [peasant] food." Reviews were almost universally laudatory. (Henderson has told interviewers that he was surprised at the number that contained bad puns, such as "ofally good" and "bone appetit.")

Henderson's best-known dish—and the only permanent menu item at St. John—is the roasted bone marrow with parsley salad. The meal, a favorite of critics and regulars alike, consists of a few pieces of beef bone, roasted until the marrow is soft, accompanied by sourdough toast and parsley salad. Describing the dish for the London *Guardian*'s Word of Mouth blog (November 13, 2009), Rayner wrote, "Apart from the fact that it's a huge pleasure to eat—the softness of the marrow, the crunch of the toast and salt, the slap of the salad—the whole aesthetic of the plate came to sum up the restaurant itself: this was a place that was all about the essentials, and didn't resist an eating opportunity just because it didn't look exactly pretty."

Henderson was instrumental in designing St. John. Michael Bateman observed, "Henderson trained as an architect, not a chef. So his restaurant (no surprise) is an architectural space. He has created an environment in which there is no distraction from the food—he has no truck with interior design, no fancy decor, mirrors, lights, drapes, blinds, carpets, paintings, flowers. Nothing to distract the eye, nor even the ear, for there is no background music. . . . The only embellishment is a row of 150 wooden coat-hooks above head height. The plain wooden floor is battleship grey. There are two air-conditioning units high on the ceiling. That's it. No restaurant in the country is as unadorned as this."

In 1996 Henderson was diagnosed with Parkinson's disease, a neurological disorder that affects speech and motor skills. "Your arms start flying around everywhere," he recalled to Jamie Merrill for the London *Independent* (September 18, 2007). "It rather got in the way of lunch." Henderson began to cook less and less. "Eventually I had to step down and hand [tasks] over to my head chef, which was a bit sad," he told Merrill. In 2005 Henderson underwent a new surgical procedure known as Deep Brain Stimulation (DBS), in which a specialized pacemaker is implanted in the brain in an attempt to control the patient's tremors and erratic movements. His condition improved significantly. "The way I look at it is that they drilled into my skull and now I can cook again," he told Merrill. Henderson has since helped raise funds so that others can undergo DBS.

In 2003 St. John Bread & Wine—a less-formal "sister" restaurant, bakery, and wine shop—opened in Spitalfields, an area of London's East End. "Bread & Wine is a plain room: Jane Eyre sort of plain," the notoriously prickly restaurant critic A. A. Gill wrote for the London *Times* (October 5, 2003, on-line). "The menu is a list of convivial, hospitable combinations that you won't have seen out together before. Brown shrimp and white cabbage, lentils and goat curd, duck leg and carrots and brawn with pickled red cabbage were all exemplary, intelligent, exciting dishes that held your attention. There were others, though, that suffered from that English belief that hardship itself is a virtue. Such as duck neck, chicory and watercress. Eating duck's necks is like eating soggy dog breath. . . . But none of this is really the point. What makes customers loyal to St John is that this, at last, is food that speaks their language and says decent, kind and quietly flattering things about them and their families. This is the restaurant that we might have got if George Orwell had married Elizabeth David. It's that winning home-grown combination of casual austerity with flashes of spectacular opulence, like an old tweed jacket with a paisley silk lining."

St. John was designated Restaurant of the Year at the 2001 London Restaurant Awards ceremony, and in 2009 it received a coveted Michelin star. Since its opening it has made regular appearances on *Restaurant* magazine's list of the 50 best restaurants in the world. (In 2010 it ranked at number 43.) In 2005 Henderson was named a Member of the Order of the British Empire (MBE) for his services to gastronomy.

In recent years Henderson's philosophy of "nose to tail eating" has been adopted by numerous other cooks. Rayner noted in his *Observer* article of March 22, 2009: "Britain is [now] littered with gastro pubs and restaurants doing a roaring trade in pig's head galettes and glistening jewels of bone marrow, in pigs' trotters and roast beef served cold and pink on bread fried off in dripping. The St John menu writing style—terse to the point of monosyllabic, bereft of adjective or verb—has become the gastro-pub default. And his impact has not merely been restricted to the restaurant table. Last September [the grocery chain] Waitrose announced that it was going to start selling pigs' cheeks and trotters for the first time. That simply would not have happened were it not for Henderson. When supermarkets begin changing their stock, something serious is going on."

In addition to *The Whole Beast: Nose to Tail Eating*, Henderson is the author of *Beyond Nose to Tail: More Omnivorous Recipes for the Adventurous Cook* (2007). His latest venture, the St. John Hotel, is scheduled to open at One Leicester Street, in London, in 2011. When asked by an interviewer for the Web site FindEatDrink.com (June 17, 2010) if he would ever open a restaurant that offered something other than traditional British food, Henderson replied, "No, not that I'm jingoistic, just I'm a British man cooking in Britain, using British ingredients, and that makes sense to me."

Henderson and his wife have three children: Hector, Owen, and Francis. They live in the Seven Dials section of Covent Garden.

—W.D.

Suggested Reading: *Art Culinaire* p34 Mar. 22, 2010; *Fork* (on-line) Aug. 30, 2009; (London) *Evening Standard* p32+ Oct. 12, 1993; (London) *Guardian* (on-line) Sep. 12, 2004; (London) *Independent* Extra p8 Sep. 18, 2007, (on-line) Sep. 6, 1998; (London) *Observer* (on-line) Oct. 14, 2007, Mar. 22, 2009; (London) *Times* (on-line) Oct. 5, 2003

Selected Books: *The Whole Beast: Nose to Tail Eating*, 2004; *Beyond Nose to Tail: More Omnivorous Recipes for the Adventurous Cook*, 2007

Chip Somodevilla/Getty Images

Herbert, Gary

May 7, 1947– Governor of Utah (Republican)

Address: Utah State Capitol Complex, 350 N. State St., Suite 200, P.O. Box 142220, Salt Lake City, UT 84114

After Utah governor Jon Huntsman Jr. resigned to become the U.S. ambassador to China, in 2009, his lieutenant governor, Gary Herbert, stepped into the post. The following year Herbert won a special election to fill the seat for the remainder of Huntsman's term, which will expire in 2012. Since he took office Herbert has received particular attention from the media for his focus on states' rights. In a recent speech, as quoted by Robert Gehrke in the *Salt Lake Tribune* (January 27, 2011, on-line), he asserted, "I firmly believe if we, as a state, fail to vigorously fight to protect and defend our rights under the Constitution, those rights will invariably be seized and usurped by the federal government. I remind Washington: We are a state, not a colony, and I assure you, on my watch Utah will not stand idly by." Among other initiatives, he has signed a series of bills designed to give Utah sweeping power to curb illegal immigration, and he has fought for exemptions from the 2010 federal health-care-reform law in order to allow Utah's state-run, free-market health-exchange program to grow with minimal federal regulation.

Herbert, a fiscal and social conservative, has demonstrated his willingness to compromise when necessary. His immigration-reform legislation, for example, contains language allowing for a future guest-worker program in Utah—a provision condemned by some of his fellow Republicans. In an endorsement of Herbert, an editorial writer for the *Salt Lake Tribune* (October 4, 2010, on-line) observed, "By any objective measure, Herbert is a bona fide conservative on both financial and social issues. But in Utah, where the Republican-dominated Legislature is pulling further to the right every day, dancing happily with tea party enthusiasts, Herbert has emerged as a moderating force, a voice of reason."

Gary Richard Herbert was born on May 7, 1947 in American Fork, Utah, to Paul and Carol (Boley) Peters. When he was young his parents divorced, and his mother married Duane Barlow Herbert, who later adopted Gary. Duane, who died in January 2010, was a devout Mormon as well as an active businessman and community leader. Among other pursuits, he worked as a dairy manager and real-estate broker, owned and ran a construction company, and founded and managed the Timp Missionary Bookstore. He also headed the Orem Chamber of Commerce and the Orem Council PTA and served multiple missions for the Church of Jesus Christ of Latter-day Saints.

Carol and Duane raised their seven children (Gary, Brent, Connie, Linda, Susan, Tom, and Holly) in Orem, about 45 miles south of Salt Lake City. The future governor, then nicknamed "Herbie," attended Orem High School, where he played as a third baseman and pitcher on the baseball team, served as a quarterback on the football team, and proved to be a skilled point guard on the basketball team. He told Lisa Riley Roche for the Salt Lake City *Deseret News* (August 2, 2009, on-line), "Sports were a big part of my life growing up. I'd probably still be in my cocoon without sports." In addition to showing athletic prowess, Herbert earned good grades and developed an intense interest in history.

After graduating from high school, Herbert served for two years in Washington, D.C., on a mission for the Church of Jesus Christ of Latter-day Saints. He then studied engineering and accounting at Brigham Young University (BYU), a Mormon-affiliated school in Provo, Utah. While there he met and married Jeanette Snelson, a bank teller and former Miss Springville beauty-pageant winner. (Jeanette has told journalists that she agreed to their first date, an outing to see the film *Butch Cassidy and the Sundance Kid*, mainly because Herbert drove a new Pontiac GTO.)

Herbert left BYU without graduating, in order to join the Utah National Guard and start a career in real estate. He served as a staff sergeant for six years and also worked alongside Duane at Herbert & Associates Realtors, in Orem. In 1985, as mortgage rates rose and the real-estate business suffered, he and Jeanette, who by then had three sons and three daughters, opened a child-care service called the Kids Connection, which they ran for over two decades.

When he was 40 Herbert, increasingly dismayed by the poor condition of the real-estate market and the economy in general, decided to make a bid for public office. "I felt like government was a lot to blame," he told Roche. "That's what really prompted me to run for office. It was more out of anger and frustration and [a need for] self-defense in the real estate business." Herbert vied for a seat on the Orem City Council but lost by 32 votes. In 1990 he was appointed to the Utah County Commission after Commissioner Brent Morris left his post to run for a seat in the U.S. Congress. Herbert was later elected to the commission and served a total of 14 years. During that time he was also the president of the Utah Association of Counties and the Utah Association of Realtors, as well as a board member of the Provo-Orem Chamber of Commerce and the Utah Water Conservancy District.

Rebecca Walsh wrote for the *Salt Lake Tribune* (February 5, 2007, on-line) that during his time on the county commission, Herbert "distinguished himself as an affable advocate for transportation and smart growth." Others have questioned whether Herbert distinguished himself in any way. Sheena McFarland wrote for the *Salt Lake Tribune* (July 12, 2009, on-line), for example, "During his 14 years on the Utah County Commission, Herbert didn't rock the boat. With a few standout exceptions, he often agreed with his colleagues on matters ranging from approving a bond for building a new $4 million baseball stadium to opposing removing the sales tax on groceries because it would hurt local budgets." Herbert said to Robert Gehrke for the *Salt Lake Tribune* (October 23, 2010, on-line) that he has always focused on reaching consensus rather than pushing his own viewpoint. "I'm not afraid to have people around me that disagree with me," he said. "I'm very comfortable with my principles that I espouse. I'm comfortable with what my goals and objectives are, and I feel that chances are enhanced for reaching those goals and objectives if I build coalitions."

Herbert joined a crowded field of Republican hopefuls in Utah's 2004 gubernatorial race. He dropped out of the race before the Republican State Convention when a front-running opponent, Jon Huntsman Jr., scion of a powerful Utah family, asked him to join his ticket as the candidate for lieutenant governor. Rebecca Walsh observed that his "decision to bow out [of the governor's race] is proof of Herbert's political savvy. He knew he was an underdog—both in name recognition and resources. Lieutenant governor is a more solid stepping stone to governor than the Utah County Commission."

Huntsman added Herbert to his ticket because of the valuable connections to local leaders he had formed as a county commissioner, his popularity with conservatives, and his understanding of rural citizens of Utah. "I know where my limitations are. I knew where I needed fortifications," Huntsman told Walsh. "I thought between the two of us, there wasn't an issue that one of us didn't have some experience in. From my standpoint, it was a pretty pragmatic choice."

The Huntsman-Herbert ticket was successful; Huntsman defeated the incumbent Republican governor, Olene Walker, in the primary before triumphing over the Democratic nominee, Scott Matheson Jr.—whose running mate was Karen Hale—with 57 percent of the vote. In 2008 Huntsman and Herbert won reelection with a resounding 77 percent of the vote.

As lieutenant governor, Herbert took a more active role than many who had held the post before him. Not content to undertake a "ceremonial, shoved-on-the-shelf, ribbon-cutting" job, as he told Walsh, he was put in charge of public lands, transportation, and homeland security, among other areas. He and Huntsman, although very different, reportedly enjoyed a good working relationship. "Huntsman supports civil unions for gay couples, while Herbert does not. Huntsman is quite moderate on environmental issues. . . . Herbert attends meetings with traditional energy developers and expresses strong support for carbon-based energy sources," Frank Pignanelli and LaVarr Webb wrote for the *Deseret News* (April 26, 2009, on-line). "In interviews with the national news media, Huntsman criticizes congressional conservatives in Washington as out-of-touch. Herbert is much more respectful of party elders, and he attends and speaks at most county Republican conventions, where he tosses out conservative red meat to the delegates. . . . They understand they are playing different roles, but they view them as complementary. They didn't plan it out this way, but the relationship has evolved into something that actually works quite well for both of them."

In 2009 Huntsman was tapped by the Barack Obama administration to become the ambassador to China, and Herbert assumed the governorship. The following year, in a special election against the Democrat Peter Corroon, the mayor of Salt Lake County, he won by a wide margin, with 64 percent of the vote, despite coming under some fire for accepting campaign contributions from state contractors. (He pointed out that while he enjoyed the support of the business community, his opponent was accepting large contributions from organized labor.)

When he succeeded Huntsman Herbert took the reins of a state suffering the throes of an economic recession. Since then he has worked to attract new business to his state, and many pundits, including some attached to the Washington, D.C.–based

Brookings Institution, have noted that Utah is emerging from the crisis in relatively good condition. The metro areas of Salt Lake City and Ogden, in particular, "have experienced some of the swiftest recoveries in the nation," according to a report posted on the institute's Web site (March 14, 2011). According to Herbert's own Web site, in 2010 "corporate recruitment incentive offers from the Governor's Office of Economic Development . . . resulted in the creation of 3,386 new jobs, nearly $3 billion in new state wages, some $250 million in capital investment and $260 million in new state revenue over the life of the incentives." Herbert is especially ardent in his opposition to raising taxes in an attempt to bridge budget gaps. "I borrow the phrase from Ronald Reagan that it's not that taxes are too low, it's that spending is too high," he told McFarland. "The economy will grow if we don't have government oppressing the free market."

In 2009 Herbert, more socially conservative than Huntsman, drew the ire of gay-rights groups for arguing that discrimination based on sexual orientation need not be banned through legislation. (It is currently legal in Utah to fire someone because he or she is gay or transgender.) He said at a press conference, as reported by the Associated Press (April 28, 2009, on-line), "We don't have to have a rule for everybody to do the right thing. We ought to just do the right thing." Herbert has also raised the concern of those in favor of abortion rights. In March 2010 he signed a bill, sponsored by the Republican state representative Carl Wimmer, that would lead to charges of criminal homicide being brought against women who obtain abortions outside legal channels. (He signed the bill only after language listing "reckless behavior" as a punishable offense was removed, citing a concern that a woman could be held responsible for an accidental miscarriage.) He is expected to sign into law other Wimmer-sponsored bills, including one that calls for surprise inspections of abortion clinics and one that would bar clinics from firing personnel based solely on their refusal to perform abortions.

Herbert has received a great deal of press attention—and mixed responses—for his views on illegal immigration. In March 2011 he signed a series of bills, collectively dubbed the "Utah Solution," that gave police broad power to enforce immigration law but also called for a state guest-worker program, among other provisions. Seen as a compromise, the measure was praised by the Obama administration, Democrats, and centrist Republicans for its moderation. By contrast, Herbert has been criticized by far-right conservatives, including members of the Tea Party movement, for seeking to grant "amnesty" to illegal immigrants through the guest-worker program and another program allowing for a migrant-worker partnership with Mexico. Those provisions would require a waiver from the federal government to be implemented, because the U.S. Constitution holds that immigration law and policy do not come under the purview of the states. Herbert hopes to receive the waivers and position Utah as a model of immigration reform for the rest of the country.

Herbert is opposed to the health-care-reform legislation enacted by Congress and the Obama administration in 2010, and he supports Utah's fledgling free-market health-exchange program, which was initiated in August 2009. (Only Utah and Massachusetts have statewide health-exchange programs, which offer purchasers of insurance a variety of plans from different insurance companies, with different benefits and pricing.) Herbert has expressed concerns that federal regulations will eventually hurt his state's program. "We're a private-sector state, and we don't know that they're going to allow a private-sector approach to solving health care costs," he told Sarah Kliff for Politico.com (February 16, 2011).

Herbert currently chairs the Economic Development and Commerce Committee of the National Governors Association. He has also sat on the association's Healthcare Reform Task Force and its Special Committee on Homeland Security and Public Safety. He will be up for reelection in 2012 and is expected to face primary challenges from several more-conservative Republicans. (Congressman Jason Chaffetz, a Tea Party favorite, is often mentioned as a possible contender.)

While Huntsman is often reported to be exploring a presidential bid, Herbert has said that he has no political aspirations higher than the Utah governor's office. He told McFarland, "My strength happens to be that I've lived here all my life. We all have strengths, and I certainly have plenty of weaknesses, but one of my strengths is going to be that I do know Utah."

Herbert and his wife have six children and more than a dozen grandchildren. Their daughter Kimberli is married to BYU football coach and former pro player Ben Cahoon, and their son Brad is married to the country singer and former *American Idol* contestant Carmen Rasmusen.

—W.D.

Suggested Reading: Associated Press (on-line) Apr. 28, 2009; Politico.com Feb. 6, 2011; (Salt Lake City) *Deseret News* (on-line) Apr. 26, 2009, Aug. 2, 2009; *Salt Lake Tribune* (on-line) Feb. 5, 2007, July 12, 2009, Oct. 4, 2010, Jan. 27, 2011

Hertzberg, Hendrik

July 23, 1943– Journalist

Address: New Yorker *Magazine, 4 Times Sq., New York, NY 10036-6561*

The longtime *New Yorker* columnist Hendrik Hertzberg possesses one of the more measured and graceful voices in American political journalism. For eight years beginning in 1969, Hertzberg wrote for the *New Yorker*'s Talk of the Town section before becoming a speechwriter for President Jimmy Carter. In the 1980s he brought his political insights to the *New Republic*, which under his editorship received three National Magazine Awards. He returned to the *New Yorker* in the early 1990s as the executive editor under the magazine's newly appointed and controversial editor in chief Tina Brown; later in that decade Brown's successor, David Remnick—the *New Yorker*'s current editor—made Hertzberg the principal writer of the Talk of the Town's Comment section, the magazine's political column. In the introduction to Hertzberg's *Politics: Observations & Arguments, 1966–2004* (2004), a 650-page collection of his writing, Remnick wrote: "Hendrik Hertzberg has been the principal political voice of The New Yorker. But the voice has always been his own. It is a remarkable voice: at once courteous and ferocious, seductive and caustic, tender and urbane. As an analyst of American public life Hertzberg is logical, humane, and morally acute; as a writer he has tone control the way [the jazz singer] Billie Holiday had tone control."

Photo by Dmitry Kiper

Hertzberg, who proudly calls himself a liberal, laments that others on the political left have shied away from the term. In an interview with *Current Biography*, the source of quotes for this article unless otherwise noted, Hertzberg said: "It's a wonderful label, better than 'progressive.' It's based on the word 'liberty.' Liberty is something I'm in favor of. . . . I'm not for progress for its own sake. But

I am for liberty for its own sake. And it's a better name than 'conservative' too. What's so great about just conserving?" Hertzberg believes *New Yorker* readers to be liberal (in the sense of open-minded) and rational people who do not subscribe to fanatical thinking on either side of the political spectrum and who, even if they might disagree with him on certain topics, share a sensibility he can speak to. In 2009 *Forbes* magazine included Hertzberg on its list of the 25 most influential liberals in the U.S. media.

Hendrik Hertzberg, known to his friends as Rick, was born on July 23, 1943 in New York City. Six years later the family—Hertzberg, his sister, Katrina, and their parents—moved to a farmhouse in Rockland County, north of New York City. Raised by a Jewish father and a Christian mother, Hertzberg grew up in a secular home where justice and morality were discussed as they applied to domestic and international politics. His parents were democratic socialists who strongly opposed communism and totalitarianism. His father, Sidney Hertzberg, was a political activist and occasional journalist; his mother, Hazel Whitman, a great-grandniece of the poet Walt Whitman, was a teacher and historian. At the age of nine, Hertzberg got his first taste of politics, helping his mother hand out buttons and leaflets for the Democrat Adlai Stevenson's 1952 presidential campaign. The next year, during a car trip with his parents and sister from New York to Colorado, Hertzberg read and collected the newspapers of every town where the family stopped. Before his teens he was already reading the *New York Times* every day, and he recalled feeling angry when, in 1956, at the age of 13, he read about the Soviet Union's crushing the anti-Communist revolution in Hungary. During his years at Suffern High School, Hertzberg was an exchange student in Toulouse, France, and he became fluent in French.

At Harvard University, in Cambridge, Massachusetts, Hertzberg was so busy at the *Crimson*, the campus daily newspaper of which he became managing editor, that at one point during his last two years—which coincided with the assassination of President John F. Kennedy, in November 1963—he was placed on academic probation for a semester. For the *Crimson* he wrote about local and national politics, including the 1964 presidential election. (He voted for the Democratic incumbent, Lyndon Johnson, and has voted for every Democratic presidential nominee since.) Late one morning Hertzberg got a phone call from a man who identified himself as William Shawn, the editor of the *New Yorker*. "Yes," Hertzberg replied before hanging up, thinking that his friends were playing a prank on him, "and this is Marie of Romania." Then the phone rang again, and the caller insisted, "No, this really *is* William Shawn." Shawn had found out about Hertzberg after one of the magazine's writers, Lillian Ross, saw Hertzberg interviewed on a television documentary about members of his generation; also, Hertzberg was in the same class at Har-

vard as one of Shawn's sons, the playwright, actor, and memoirist Wallace Shawn. William Shawn was interested in having Hertzberg write for the *New Yorker*, but Hertzberg, feeling inexperienced as well as concerned about being drafted into the military to fight in Vietnam, declined Shawn's offer to join the magazine. Instead, after graduating with an A.B. degree, in 1965, he worked as editorial director of the National Student Association, the nation's largest student organization, which had the goal of promoting civil rights in the South and democracy abroad; the position brought a draft deferment.

Less than a year later, in the summer of 1966, the 23-year-old Hertzberg moved to San Francisco, California, where he worked as a reporter for *Newsweek*; he covered Ronald Reagan's campaign for governor, the beginnings of hippie culture, and figures in the San Francisco music scene, most notably the Grateful Dead and Jefferson Airplane. "It was very exhilarating," he recalled, "to go from flying around the state with Reagan to a community meeting of hippies in the Haight/Asbury to a long night with the Grateful Dead at the Fillmore." While he was enjoying himself, he felt that it was only a matter of time before he would be drafted. Around that time it was revealed that the CIA, in order to have a presence in student activity, had been secretly financing the National Student Association; that revelation, Hertzberg said, disillusioned and radicalized him, at least to a degree, as it did many other young people. The combination of those factors led him—even though he opposed the war—to enlist in the U.S. Navy, which he thought would give him more options than those he would face after being drafted into the army. Though he requested shore duty in Saigon, South Vietnam, he was posted to New York City, where he occasionally wrote speeches for navy officials defending U.S. dealings with the United Nations. At the time he was also—against navy rules—volunteering for the presidential campaign of U.S. senator Robert F. Kennedy, until the candidate was assassinated, in June 1968. With his antiwar feelings growing stronger, Hertzberg felt that he could no longer serve in the navy, and after a protracted process—following his unsuccessful application for conscientious-objector status—he was discharged, in 1969.

With William Shawn's offer still standing, Hertzberg went to work for the *New Yorker*, where he wrote mostly short, light pieces for the magazine's Talk of the Town section. Although he occasionally covered antiwar demonstrations or other political events, Hertzberg wrote mostly about rock concerts and various odd characters and curious goings-on around town, such as the recent arrival of John Lennon and Yoko Ono, who had moved to New York's Greenwich Village neighborhood.

In the mid-1970s, feeling restless, Hertzberg took a few months off to write speeches for New York governor Hugh Carey. Upon his return to the *New Yorker*, at the end of 1976, he got a call from

James Fallows, the head speechwriter for President-elect Jimmy Carter and a former *Crimson* president, offering him a position on Carter's speechwriting staff. Hertzberg enthusiastically accepted. After Fallows left his post, in 1979, Hertzberg became Carter's chief speechwriter. During his four years on the White House staff, by far "the highest point" for Hertzberg came in March 1979: after the 1978 Camp David Accords between Israel and Egypt began to fall apart, President Carter flew to Egypt, where he addressed the Parliament, and then to Israel, where he addressed the Knesset, that country's legislative body. Hertzberg, accompanying the president on short notice, worked on both speeches. On the flight back from the Middle East, knowing that the signing of the 1979 Egypt–Israel Peace Treaty was virtually assured, Hertzberg felt a sense of accomplishment. In addition to the addresses to the Knesset and the Egyptian Parliament, Hertzberg wrote Carter's address to the Indian Parliament, his "Energy and National Goals" speech to the American people (known as the "malaise" speech, for what some claimed was its scolding tone toward Americans), his address at the opening of the John F. Kennedy Library, and his farewell address, following his defeat by the Republican Ronald Reagan in 1980. (While Hertzberg had a key role in writing speeches, he was often one of dozens who wrote, rewrote, and edited them.) During his years in the White House, Hertzberg got a close behind-the-scenes look at how national and international politics work. With that knowledge, he returned to journalism.

In 1981 Hertzberg became the editor of the *New Republic*, a Washington, D.C.–based weekly magazine that was considered a "must-read" among those on the left seeking to be well-informed. The magazine, for which Hertzberg edited the political section, was owned by Hertzberg's former political-science tutor at Harvard, Martin Peretz, who was politically to the right of Hertzberg. "Generally," Hertzberg said, "his way of running the magazine was to hire an editor [who] was to his left, who would restrain him—but not completely. In the end, he was the boss. But he wanted to have somebody fighting him." For the most part Hertzberg and Peretz were in agreement about opposing Ronald Reagan's staunchly conservative domestic policies, which cut social services; favored industry over the concerns of environmentalists; and endorsed the "trickle-down" theory, or the idea that tax cuts for the rich would benefit the rest of the population. Hertzberg was troubled, though, by the *New Republic*'s editorial support of Reagan's international policies—in particular, the administration's aid to the Nicaraguan Contras (guerrillas), who were fighting that country's Sandinista government. (In the first half of the 1980s, the United States, in what would later become known as the Iran-Contra affair, sold weapons to Iran and used the profits to help support the Contras.) After four years at the magazine, Hertzberg decided it was time to leave.

Hertzberg next joined the John F. Kennedy School of Government at Harvard University, first as a fellow of its Institute of Politics, then as a senior associate at its Joan Shorenstein Barone Center on the Press, Politics and Public Policy. While teaching seminars and counseling students, he continued to contribute political essays to the *New Republic*, and in 1988 he covered the presidential race for the magazine. The following year he returned to the magazine, first as editor, then as a senior editor. This time Hertzberg burned out more quickly. As the internal fights among the writers and editors—about story ideas, policies, and politics—got "nastier," Hertzberg decided it was time to move on. Despite the infighting, the magazine's recognition and prestige grew: during Hertzberg's second stint as editor, from 1989 to 1991, the *New Republic* won three National Magazine Awards— one for reporting and two for general excellence.

In 1992, after nine years at *Vanity Fair*, Tina Brown became editor of the *New Yorker*. One of her first moves was to hire Hertzberg as her principal deputy. "She hired me," Hertzberg said, "partly as an act of reassurance to the staff, because I had been there and I was kind of popular there. Also, I was very sympathetic to her and of the need to revolutionize the magazine, to bring the magazine into the present." Among other changes, Brown and Hertzberg put in the *New Yorker*'s table of contents descriptions of articles and reviews (instead of simply categories, such as "A Reporter at Large" or "The Current Cinema"); included by-lines in Talk of the Town pieces; brought a new focus on news-related stories and celebrities; and, for the first time in the magazine's history, published photographs and full-page illustrations. Brown, in yet another controversial move, also fired 79 people and brought on board 50 new writers, including Malcolm Gladwell, Anthony Lane, Jane Mayer, Jeffrey Toobin, and David Remnick.

In 1998 Remnick replaced Brown as editor and made Hertzberg the default writer of Talk of the Town's Comment section. One of Hertzberg's most-talked-about Comment pieces appeared shortly after the 9/11 terrorist attacks, in the September 24, 2001 issue of the *New Yorker*, in which he argued that calling the terrorist group Al Qaeda's attacks "acts of war" was a "category mistake." According to him, the matter was not simply one of semantics. "The metaphor of war—and it is more metaphor than description—ascribes to the perpetrators a dignity they do not merit, a status they cannot claim, and a strength they do not possess," Hertzberg wrote. "Worse, it points toward a set of responses that could prove futile or counterproductive." Because the terrorists "do not constitute or control a state," he argued, the terrorist attacks should be deemed a "crime." In retrospect Hertzberg said that the label "crime" did not "really summon up the importance of the event and its political intent." The attacks, he said, "were more than a crime but less than a war. But I thought the war metaphor lent itself to making certain kinds of mistakes, which sure enough are the mistakes that have been made [in both the Iraq and Afghanistan wars]. If you're a hammer, everything looks like a nail. And if you're at war, you look around to have a war in a familiar way." Had the 9/11 terrorist attacks been designated as a new kind of crime, Hertzberg said, it might have been clear that the way to deal with the perpetrators was to concentrate on police methods—to pursue the terrorists in a discriminate way. When, soon after 9/11, the George W. Bush administration began pushing for the invasion of Iraq and the overthrow of its leader, Saddam Hussein, Hertzberg was skeptical about the rationale for the war and its projected outcome. A week before the start of the war with Iraq—which the administration claimed had so-called weapons of mass destruction—Hertzberg wrote for the *New Yorker* (March 17, 2003), "Both among those who, on balance, support the coming war and among those who, on balance, oppose it are a great many who hold their views in fear and trembling, haunted by the suspicion that the other side might be right after all. . . . The divisions are profound, and the most agonizing are not between people but within them." Later in the piece he observed that the Bush administration had "undermined the power of the convincing reasons for confronting Saddam (such as his consistent failure to disclose and dispose of his weapons of mass destruction) by mixing them with unconvincing ones (such as his alleged cooperation with Al Qaeda)." Hertzberg was ultimately opposed to the war—51 percent against it, as he said—while David Remnick was 51 percent in favor of it. "Our views were fairly close," Hertzberg recalled. "It just so happened that the line—yes or no—fell between our views." When it turned out that there were no weapons of mass destruction in Iraq—and that the claims that such weapons existed were the result of either faulty U.S. intelligence, deliberate deceit on behalf of the Bush administration, or both—Remnick, Hertzberg said, was the angrier of the two, because he felt he had been misled.

In 2008, when the Democratic presidential candidate Barack Obama was continually and incorrectly labeled a "socialist" by various Republican politicians and conservatives, Hertzberg wrote for the *New Yorker* (November 3, 2008), "When Barry Goldwater and Ronald Reagan accused John F. Kennedy and Lyndon Johnson of socialism for advocating guaranteed health care for the aged and the poor, the implication was that Medicare and Medicaid would presage a Soviet America. . . . The Republican argument of the moment seems to be that the difference between capitalism and socialism corresponds to the difference between a top marginal income-tax rate of 35 per cent and a top marginal income-tax rate of 39.6 per cent. The latter is what it would be under Obama's proposal, what it was under President Clinton, and, for that matter, what it will be after 2010 if President Bush's tax cuts expire on schedule."

After more than 40 years in journalism, the issue Hertzberg still finds most fascinating, urgent, and relevant, and one that subtly permeates his political writing, is "the relation between the structure of the American government and the political outcomes." Hertzberg would like, ideally, to abolish the separation of powers between the executive and legislative branches. In the U.S. there are three arms of national government elected independently from one another: the Senate, the House of Representatives, and the presidency. Hertzberg would prefer a unitary system, like those in many European democracies, in which the nation's president would be chosen by a lower legislative house. Such a system, he believes, would produce a more coherent, nimble, and accountable government. The legislative branch of the U.S. government, Hertzberg told *Current Biography*, is often slow and unproductive because in the Senate a majority is usually not enough to pass legislation: a super majority (60 out of 100 senators) is often needed to override the threat of a filibuster. Furthermore, he said, the Senate itself is "a mistake": "Having two senators per state regardless of the population of the state does not make sense. And the reason we have it is because of a dirty deal back in the Constitutional Convention between Rhode Island and South Carolina." Hertzberg noted that he sees current political battles and most attempts to pass and negotiate bills through the lens of those systemic shortcomings. Although he admits that little can be done to alter the basic structure of the U.S. government, he believes that another idea he supports, the so-called National Popular Vote plan for presidential elections, could lead to change. Under the current practice, a presidential nominee receives 100 percent of a state's electoral votes by winning a simple majority, or even just a plurality, of the popular votes in that state. Because the margin of victory does not matter, one consequence is that a candidate can win the presidency even though his or her opponent has won a majority of the votes cast in the nation, as happened in 1876 and 2000. More important, Hertzberg argued, is that because the election outcome in most states is a foregone conclusion—with, for example, Texas predictably voting Republican and California predictably voting Democratic—those states (and thus the concerns of their voters) get ignored by the nominees of both parties during election campaigns. Worse still, Hertzberg believes, is that except in a dozen or so "battleground states," there is little or no point in get-out-the-vote efforts or other forms of grassroots organizing. Under the National Popular Vote plan—devised by the Stanford University professor John R. Koza—the president would be elected based simply on the majority or a plurality of the total number of ballots cast throughout the nation, regardless of state boundaries. The plan would not require any changes in the Constitution. Instead, each state legislature would pass a law, entitled "Agreement Among the States to Elect the President by National Popular Vote," under which the state would pledge to cast its electoral votes for the nationwide winner, regardless of whether that candidate had carried the state. The plan would not go into effect until agreed upon by enough states to account for at least 270 of the nation's 538 electoral votes—a majority. As of January 2011, six states and the District of Columbia, possessing 74 electoral votes among them, had enacted the law. Hertzberg said that some politicians of both parties (particularly incumbents comfortable with the status quo) oppose the plan because they do not want more people "they never heard of"—especially young voters—turning up at the polls. Civic groups such as Common Cause, the League of Women Voters, and FairVote, an electoral-reform organization of which Hertzberg is a board member, support the plan. "What's great about it," Hertzberg said, "is every vote will be equally worth casting, no matter where you live." Hertzberg argued that if those "systematic flaws" in our political system are not addressed, the United States will be less capable of dealing with its relative decline as an economically and politically dominant world power, as well as with the threat of global warming.

Hertzberg is also the author of *¡Obamanos! The Birth of a New Political Era* (2009), a collection of his *New Yorker* writing about Barack Obama from 2004 to 2009, and *One Million* (1970), a graphic representation of the title quantity, via 200 pages of dots, with 5,000 per page.

Hertzberg and his wife, Virginia Cannon, have been married since 1998. They have a son, Wolf. The couple met in 1992 at the *New Yorker*, where Cannon is now a senior editor. They divide their time between their homes in Manhattan and nearby Nyack, New York. Aside from a great deal of research, Hertzberg's writing process for the *New Yorker* columns involves, he said, no specific method "other than to suffer for a few days and worry that I'll never be able to do this and will have to commit suicide or move out of the country."

—D.K.

Suggested Reading: *Harvard Magazine* Jan./Feb. 2003; *Los Angeles Times* R p3 Aug. 1, 2004; *New York Times* A p18 Dec. 15, 1980; *New York Times Book Review* p7 July 4, 2004; newyorker.com; *Washington Post* T p4 July 18, 2004

Selected Books: *One Million*, 1970 ; *Politics: Observations & Arguments, 1966-2004*, 2004; *¡Obamanos! The Birth of a New Political Era*, 2009

Hoagland, Tony

Nov. 19, 1953– Poet; educator

Address: University of Houston, 223D Roy Cullen Bldg., 4800 Calhoun Rd., Houston, TX 77004

"I never liked the smell of high culture," the poet Tony Hoagland told Fritz Lanham for the *Houston Chronicle* (February 15, 2004). A dedicated populist, Hoagland concluded three decades ago, while in graduate school, that he wanted his poems to offer "clarity, accessibility, entertainment, irreverence, and the idea of the poet as guide," as he recalled to Jennifer Grotz for *Ploughshares* (Winter 2009/10). Judging by reviews of his four poetry books—among them *Sweet Ruin* and *What Narcissism Means to Me*—and citations accompanying his many honors, his work embodies all those characteristics. In addition, according to Lanham, Hoagland's poetry is "both sociable—a lot of different people and voices figure in—and social, in that it's concerned with material culture and popular culture and the way those impact the life of the spirit." Hoagland's poems are also "seriously funny, despite their often not-so-funny subject matter," the former U.S. poet laureate Charles Simic wrote for the *New York Review of Books* (June 24, 2010). Indeed, in 2005 Hoagland won the Poetry Foundation's Mark Twain Poetry Award, which recognizes "a poet's contribution to humor in American poetry," according to the group's Web

Kenna Bonner, courtesy of Blue Flower Arts

site. "There is nothing escapist or diversionary about Tony Hoagland's poetry," Stephen Young, the foundation's program director, wrote for that site. "Here's misery, death, envy, hypocrisy, and vanity. But the still sad music of humanity is played with such a light touch on an instrument so sympathetically tuned that one can't help but laugh. Wit and morality rarely consort these days; it's good to see them happily, often hilariously reunited in the winner's poetry." Writing for the *Washington Post* (November 13, 2005), another former U.S. poet laureate, Robert Pinsky, noted that Hoagland belongs to the tradition of Twain, whose comedy "cuts to what is complacent, unexamined and blandly corrupt in American life." Hoagland's work, Pinsky continued, "is not the mild, dismissive chuckle of standard 'comic poetry,' reassuring its audience that everything is either okay or can't be helped. Like Twain, Hoagland prefers the outrageous."

Hoagland's early work dealt primarily with his preoccupations with family matters, issues connected with masculinity, and "the sufferings of romantic love," as the poet told Grotz. "Much later, when I woke from the stupor of autobiography," he said, "I discovered that identity was composed of a lot of other things besides familial trauma; it included race and money and being American and technology and historical currents. Eventually it turned out that these things were more interesting to me than my first person insights and testimonies." He also said, "Now, I would say that I am deeply engaged in at least two kinds of poetry: one is the sensibility of realism, the appetite for seeing and seeing through. The other is poetry which can achieve through its plenitude of voice and energy and imagination a kind of authentic self-generated joy which . . . testif[ies] to our spiritual resourcefulness, our innate ability to transcend our circumstances, whatever they are." "It is the job of the poet to give pleasure, to amaze and exhort as well as to testify to the real; to demonstrate the capabilities of human genius and joy . . . ," Hoagland wrote in his book *Real Sofistikashun: Essays on Poetry and Craft* (2006). "How else will we remember anything is possible?" In an interview with Miriam Sagan for the Tres Chicas Books Web site (2003), Hoagland said, "To me, a good poem threatens the reader a little, crosses over some line of the social contract, or the poetic contract, which sets off alarms. A really good poem is the poem which . . . reminds the reader that reading or listening is not a safe, living-room-[La-Z-Boy]-museum-tea-party experience, but that poetry is about open heart surgery, being woken up, or taken somewhere unexpected and dangerous."

Reading Hoagland's latest poetry collection, *Unincorporated Persons in the Late Honda Dynasty* (2010), spurred Charles Simic to write that Hoagland "is a poet aware of the hard lives most Americans lead to a degree rarely encountered in contemporary poetry. This is his subject. And so is his sense that something has gone deeply wrong. . . . He laments that it had taken him a long time to get the world into his poems. He doesn't have to worry anymore. It's all there." In a review of the same book, Dwight Garner wrote for the *New York Times* (February 5, 2010), "There are 15 or 20 better poets in America than Tony Hoagland, but few deliver more pure pleasure. His erudite comic poems are backloaded with heartache and longing, and they function, emotionally, like improvised explosive devices: the pain comes at you from the cruelest angles, on the sunniest of days." Garner concluded, "This plain, unincorporated, free-range American poet is one you'll want to know about."

Hoagland has taught at many schools; currently, he is a professor at the University of Houston, in Texas, and a faculty member of Warren Wilson College, in Asheville, North Carolina. In 2005 he won the O. B. Hardison Prize from the Folger Shakespeare Library, in Washington, D.C., which celebrates excellence in both poetry and teaching.

Along with his twin brother, William, Anthony Dey Hoagland was born on November 19, 1953 in Fort Bragg, North Carolina, where his father, a U.S. Army physician and paratrooper, was stationed then. He has an older sister. Until Hoagland entered seventh grade, his family moved often. They lived in places including El Paso, Texas; Oahu, Hawaii; Birmingham, Alabama; and Asmara, in the highlands of Ethiopia, in what is now Eritrea. While in Asmara Hoagland's mother was diagnosed with breast cancer. After she underwent surgery his father ended his military career. The family moved back to the U.S., where his mother continued to receive medical treatment. The Hoaglands soon settled in southeastern Louisiana, near Bayou Lafourche. As a student in South Lafourche High School, in Galliano, Hoagland excelled in science, worked on the school yearbook, and was popular among his peers. Nevertheless, he described himself to Fritz Lanham as "a screwed-up teenager." During his high-school years, his brother died after inhaling a cooking spray to get high. At about the same time, his mother's cancer recurred. An anthology called *New Voices in American Poetry*, which a friend gave him, provided some solace during that difficult period. "When something has knocked you for a loop—that's when people go to poems," Hoagland remarked to Lanham.

Hoagland attended Williams College, in Williamstown, Massachusetts, until his sophomore year, in 1973; he then learned that his mother's illness had become life-threatening, and he returned to Louisiana. As he had during summers while in high school, he worked on boats that traveled between oil rigs in the Gulf of Mexico. When his mother's health deteriorated further, he and his father became her primary caregivers. Hoagland's labors of love included bathing her—an act described in his poem "Lucky," which begins, "If you are lucky in this life, / you will get to help your enemy / the way I got to help my mother / when she was weakened past the point of saying no." In his conversation with Brian Brodeur for the blog How a Poem Happens (November 5, 2009), Hoagland described in detail the process of composing "Lucky."

Hoagland's mother died in 1973. After her death Hoagland hitchhiked to the western U.S., where he lived briefly with members of the Rainbow Family, a leaderless group dedicated to peaceful coexistence worldwide. He next joined a school-bus-load of fruit pickers, who followed the harvest in Utah, Idaho, and Washington State. After that year's harvest Hoagland experienced communal living in San Francisco and nearby Berkeley, California. In 1974, having grown "tired of all the togetherness," as he told Current Biography, he returned to Louisiana. He worked there until summer's end in 1975, when he hitchhiked to Iowa City, Iowa, and enrolled in classes at the University of Iowa (UI) as a walk-in student. UI hosts the Iowa Writers' Workshop, and though Hoagland was not in the program, he interacted with some of its participants. He became friends with a group of aspiring poets and began to write poetry himself.

During the summer of 1976, Hoagland took courses at the Jack Kerouac School of Disembodied Poetics, founded in 1974 by the poets Allen Ginsberg and Anne Waldman and others at the Naropa Institute (now Naropa University), in Boulder, Colorado. He studied Buddhism and poetry with Ginsberg and attended lectures by the poets Ted Berrigan, Robert Creeley, and Michael McClure. At Naropa Hoagland was introduced to literature associated with the Beat Generation, a term coined by Jack Kerouac, the author of On the Road—a book that, along with Ginsberg's long poem "Howl," is among the most famous of the Beats' works. Hoagland was struck by differences between Beat poetry and poems produced by more traditional contemporary poets, such as Marvin Bell, Louise Glück, Philip Levine, and James Tate.

By 1977 Hoagland had accumulated enough credits to earn a B.G.S. (bachelor of general studies) degree from the University of Iowa. Eager to live in a place where nobody knew him, he moved to Ithaca, New York, and found work as an attendant at Truman State Forest and as a janitor for Cornell University Press. While working in press offices at night, he would often stop to read manuscripts he happened to notice. During his two years in Ithaca, he wrote a lot of what he later judged to be bad poetry. "I was incredibly untalented," he told Don Lee for Ploughshares (Winter 1994/95). "It took a long, long time for me just to get competent. When you're a student of poetry, you're lucky if you don't realize how untalented and ignorant you are until you get a little better. Otherwise, you would just stop."

In 1978 Hoagland won acceptance to the graduate program in creative writing at the University of Arizona (UA) at Tucson. His professors and mentors there included the poets Jon Anderson, Tess Gallagher, and Steve Orlen. As a graduate student he sometimes taught classes. He earned an M.F.A. degree in 1983. He remained in Tucson to pursue a doctoral degree at UA, but after a year or so, he dropped out. He remained in Tucson to work in the writers-in-the-schools program run by the UA Po-etry Center. During the next several years, he taught at a series of schools, including Arizona Western College, in Yuma. In 1985 he wrote in Provincetown, Massachusetts, where, having won a fellowship, he participated in the six-month residency program run by the Fine Arts Work Center. That year marked the publication of Hoagland's first chapbook (typically, such books have fewer than 50 pages), A Change in Plans. His second chapbook, Talking to Stay Warm, appeared in 1986. In 1987 he won the first of his two National Endowment for the Arts fellowships (the second coming in 1994).

In 1988 Hoagland moved to Berkeley and taught at nearby schools: the College of the Holy Names (now Holy Names University), in Oakland (1989–90), and St. Mary's College of California, in Moraga (1990–91). During the summer of 1991, he was a writer-in-residence at Kalamazoo College, in Michigan. That fall his companion, Betty Sasaki, joined the faculty of Colby College, in Waterville, Maine, and Hoagland moved to Waterville with her. He taught at the University of Maine at Farmington in 1992 and the next year became an instructor at Colby. Also in 1993 he joined the faculty of the low-residency master's-degree writing program at Warren Wilson College, in Asheville, North Carolina, where he was required to teach for only two weeks per semester.

Earlier, in 1990, Hoagland's third chapbook, History of Desire, appeared. His first full-length collection of poems, Sweet Ruin, earned the 1992 Brittingham Prize in Poetry from the University of Wisconsin (UW); the UW press published it as a book that year. The poet Donald Justice, who chose Sweet Ruin for the Brittingham award, wrote of the work, as quoted on the UW press Web site, "There is a fine strong sense in these poems of real lives being lived in a real world. This is something I greatly prize. And it is all colored, sometimes brightly, by the poet's own highly romantic vision of things, so that what we may think we already know ends up seeming rich and strange." Sweet Ruin won the 1993 Great Lakes Colleges Association New Writers Award, and in 1994 it earned the John C. Zacharis First Book Award, from Emerson College, in Boston, Massachusetts.

Beginning in about 1990 Hoagland had suffered from an immune-system disorder and often felt unwell. In around 1996 a treatment for his malady was discovered, and he regained his health. The year 1998 saw the publication of Hoagland's second book, Donkey Gospel, which was lauded for its humor, straightforward language, and solid ties to everyday experience. Donkey Gospel won the James Laughlin Award, with which the Academy of American Poets recognizes an outstanding second book. The poet William Matthews, who served on the Laughlin Award jury, wrote of Donkey Gospel, as quoted on the Academy of American Poets' site Poets.org, "There's an underlying sweetness to these poems, and a gratitude for having survived so much human fecklessness (including, of course, one's own), and these complicate the poems' anger and puzzlement and rumple their severe surfaces. The resulting mixture has much of the complexity of a personality that willingly weathers its own perplexities and experience, rather than striking a pose of competence and trying to ride out the storm."

Around that time Hoagland accepted a position as a visiting professor at New Mexico State University at Las Cruces. He later became a full-time faculty member. In 2000 he won both a Guggenheim Foundation fellowship and a Jenny McKean Moore fellowship; with the latter, bestowed by George Washington University, in Washington, D.C., he taught a writing workshop for college students and another, free workshop for adult residents of the metropolitan Washington area. Later in that decade he taught at the University of Pittsburgh, in Pennsylvania.

Hoagland's third book of poetry, *What Narcissism Means to Me*, was published in 2003. Hoagland told Miriam Sagan that though the title "is obviously ironic, it's intended to have multiple playful and serious dimensions. . . . The dilemma I want to represent is the dilemma I feel: the dilemma of the self, to recognize that self-centeredness is often a kind of confinement in a small space, a blindness. . . . There is so much space in the world, so much to know and learn, one wants to move outwards and to relate to it and to celebrate and explore it. So the title refers to growing out." In a departure from his previous work, Hoagland wrote some of the poems in the book in the voices of friends of his. He told Sagan, "Having multiple speakers in a poem makes the poems less dominated by a single voice, and that felt like a relief to me. It meant that one person didn't have to 'solve' the issues presented by the poem, and maybe that nobody has to solve anything—that the poem could become more of an exploration than an experience of crisis and resolution. Less like therapy and more like a salon of interesting talkers."

In a representative, enthusiastic review for the on-line literary journal *Blackbird* (Spring 2004), the poet Christian Horlick described *What Narcissism Means to Me* as Hoagland's "most realized volume of poetry." He continued, "It succeeds in its dance of changing tones and shifting perceptions—despite the fact that one of the themes of the book is the struggle against change, the poems are in constant flux. . . . These poems are temperamental; they often wake up on the wrong side of the bed and demand things. In the end, they are candid—and triumphant—witnesses to Hoagland's passion for all that it means to live." *What Narcissism Means to Me* was a finalist for a National Book Critics Circle Award.

In 2003 Hoagland accepted the post of associate professor of English at the University of Houston. Three years later he was promoted to full professor. In 2008 he won the second annual Jackson Poetry Prize from Poets & Writers. According to that organization's Web site, "The $50,000 prize honors an American poet of exceptional talent who has published at least one book of recognized literary merit but has not yet received major national acclaim. The award is designed to provide what all poets need—time and the encouragement to write."

In a brief interview posted on the Web site of Emerson College, which publishes *Ploughshares* (February 18, 2010), Hoagland told *Ploughshares*'s editor, John Skoyles, that he is currently writing a book "that describes the rules, stages, degrees, and styles of association and disassociation in contemporary poetry." "Writing essays is a way, for me, of figuring things out in plain terms," he said, "and I guess I think that—counter-intuitively—as American poetry has become more and more abstract, . . . stylized, and jargonized than ever, our poetry needs someone not afraid to be Dumb, to try to figure it out for us civilians."

Hoagland and Betty Sasaki married in 1995 and divorced a few years later. The poet currently lives in Houston with the travel and fiction writer Kathleen Lee; they also own a house in Wellfleet, Massachusetts.

—F.C., M.H.

Suggested Reading: *American Poetry Review* p19+ Sep./Oct. 2010; How a Poem Happens (on-line) Nov. 5, 2009; *New York Review of Books* p50+ June 24, 2010; *Ploughshares* p220+ Winter 1994/95, p7+, p185+ Winter 2009/10; *Santa Fe New Mexican* F p2 Dec. 21, 2003; Tres Chicas Books Web site, 2003

Selected Books: poetry—*Sweet Ruin*, 1992; *Donkey Gospel*, 1998; *What Narcissism Means to Me*, 2003; *Unincorporated Persons in the Late Honda Dynasty*, 2010; essays—*Real Sofistikashun: Essays on Poetry and Craft*, 2006

Selected Chapbooks: *A Change in Plans*, 1985; *Talking to Stay Warm*, 1986; *History of Desire*, 1990; *Hard Rain*, 2005; *Little Oceans*, 2009

Horne, Gerald

Jan. 3, 1949– Historian; writer; educator

Address: Dept. of History, University of Houston, 4800 Calhoun Rd., Houston, TX 77004

Gerald Horne, a scholar of African-American history, has written more than 20 books. The major recurring themes of his work include the status and struggles of blacks in the United States, America's relationship to political and civil rights movements in such countries as Zimbabwe, Kenya, Mexico, Jamaica, and India, and the connection between the experiences of African-Americans and the struggles of people elsewhere—for example, the influence of the Indian leader Mahatma Gandhi

Courtesy of the College of Liberal Arts and Social Sciences, University of Houston

Gerald Horne

on the thinking of the U.S. civil rights leader Martin Luther King Jr. A Marxist thinker, Horne has also published prolifically on the overlapping histories of race and class issues in the U.S. Several of his books have focused on the U.S. government's fierce pursuit of real and alleged communists in the 1940s and '50s—particularly in the film industry—and the harmful effects of that campaign on labor unions and the public perception of workers' rights to unionize; that impact, in turn, Horne has argued, weakened progressive movements as a whole, with disastrous consequences for the economic underclass and people of color. Some of Horne's better-known books include *Fire This Time: The Watts Uprising and the 1960s* (1995), *Race Woman: The Lives of Shirley Graham Du Bois* (2000), *Class Struggle in Hollywood, 1930–1950: Moguls, Mobsters, Stars, Reds & Trade Unionists* (2001), and *The Color of Fascism: Lawrence Dennis, Racial Passing, and the Rise of Right-Wing Extremism in the United States* (2006). Horne is a professor in the Department of History at the University of Houston, in Texas.

One of six children, Gerald Horne was born on January 3, 1949 in St. Louis, Missouri, to Jerry Charles and Flora Dell (Armstead) Horne. His father worked as a truck driver; his mother was a homemaker who occasionally worked as a maid. As a boy Horne became a passionate reader, thanks to the examples set by his three older sisters, and got his library card at the age of eight. Two years later Horne and his family were forced to move to another poor neighborhood, but this time one that was integrated. He believes that his current political perspective took root during the next period of his youth. He wrote in an e-mail message to *Current Biography*, "Growing up in Jim Crow St. Louis in poverty, subjected to almost casual acts of bigotry and racism, is sufficient to make anyone a radical—the wonder is that more are not."

Horne received a B.A. degree from the Woodrow Wilson School of Public and International Affairs at Princeton University, in Princeton, New Jersey, in 1970. During his college years he met and befriended many students from Africa and became interested in that continent's history and political issues; he protested South Africa's legally enforced system of racial segregation, known as apartheid. Horne received a law degree from the University of California at Berkeley, in 1973, and a master's degree (1978) and Ph.D. (1982) in history from Columbia University, in New York City.

After receiving his doctorate Horne taught at Sarah Lawrence College, in Bronxville, New York, from 1982 to 1988. Starting in the mid-1980s Horne also worked as a labor lawyer. From 1985 to 1986 he was the executive director of the National Conference of Black Lawyers (NCBL). During that time he served by invitation as one of the mediators of the civil war in Sudan, a very poor country in northeastern Africa, which began in 1983 and has continued despite a 2005 peace agreement; his efforts led him to travel frequently to New York City, London, England, and Khartoum, Sudan's capital. As the executive director of the NCBL, Horne was also involved with issues of national importance, such as the fight against racism and anti-Semitism. For example, under his leadership, in 1985 the NCBL formed a privately based police-review panel in San Diego, California, to investigate allegations that that city's police force had abused minorities and had connections to the Ku Klux Klan. After leaving the NCBL, in 1986, Horne worked for two years as a special counsel for a large local union of health-care workers, Local 1199 Health and Hospital Workers Union, a division of the AFL-CIO headquartered in New York City.

In 1988 Horne left the East Coast to become a professor at the University of California at Santa Barbara, where he taught history and black studies and later served for one year as the head of the Black Studies Department. In 1992 he ran unsuccessfully as a member of the Peace and Freedom Party for a seat in the U.S. Senate. While he understood that his chances of victory were extremely slim, he believed his candidacy had a purpose: to raise awareness of particular issues, including what he saw as the need to defend affirmative action, raise taxes on the wealthy, and cut military spending significantly. In an interview with Tracy Wilkinson for the *Los Angeles Times* (October 30, 1992), Horne said, "The historical function of certain third parties . . . is to raise cutting-edge ideas that are not now on the immediate horizon." (The Democrat Dianne Feinstein, who won the election, continues to serve in the Senate.) In November 1995 Horne accepted an offer to join the University of North Carolina at Chapel Hill as a tenured professor in two departments: communication studies and African and Afro-American studies.

In addition to the professorship, Horne agreed to become director of the university's Sonja Haynes Stone Black Cultural Center, which required $7.5 million for a new campus facility (nearly $2 million had been raised by the time Horne took on the role of director). Aside from fund-raising, Horne had to take on the role of in-house diplomat. There was a perception on campus and in the community, especially from the center's critics, that the cultural center was a place of black separatism and radical politics. In an interview with Ben Stocking for the Raleigh, North Carolina, *News and Observer* (February 19, 1996), Horne labeled as a misconception the notion that the center was for African-Americans exclusively. In 2000, while abroad in Hong Kong, China, as a Fulbright scholar (he had traveled to Zimbabwe in 1995 in the same capacity), Horne submitted his resignation as the director of the Black Cultural Center so that he could focus on his research. The following year he returned to the University of North Carolina, where he resumed his professorial duties. Later, in 2003, he joined the Department of History at the University of Houston as the John J. and Rebecca Moores chair of history and African-American studies.

Horne's first book to receive significant notice in the mainstream press was *Fire This Time: The Watts Uprising and the 1960s*. In the Watts section of Los Angeles, California, in the 1960s, African-Americans suffered from poor schools, a lack of job opportunities, substandard housing, and police brutality, among other societal ills. Against that backdrop, in August 1965 highway patrol officers stopped Marquette Frye, a 21-year-old black man, who was suspected of drunken driving. Though the officers were prepared to let Frye off with a warning, more officers soon arrived on the scene, after which the young man was beaten with batons. A crowd of onlookers grew from dozens to hundreds and started throwing bottles and rocks at the officers, who responded with more violence. The resulting Watts riots lasted seven days and resulted in the deaths of 34 people, injuries to thousands, and the arrests of 4,000. Approximately 35,000 people were said to have taken active roles in the riots, which caused an estimated $100 million to $200 million in property damage.

Given the dire situation of African-Americans in Los Angeles, Horne argued in *Fire This Time*, the riots should not have come as a surprise; he termed the events of August 1965 a "food riot," in which stores were looted for food and other goods by blacks who felt they had been denied access to the American dream. Horne also made the case—in the process making his Marxist perspective clear—that one of the reasons for the desperate situation of so many Los Angeles blacks was the weakening of the trade unions and other progressive groups due to the "Red scare," the hunt for and persecution of real and alleged communists by the American government in the 1940s and '50s. In addition, Horne wrote that the unchecked brutality of the Los Ange-les Police Department resulted in the 1991 beating of Rodney King, a black man, by white officers—whose acquittal after a highly publicized trial the following year led to more riots. In a review of *Fire This Time* for the *Boston Globe* (August 21, 1995), Michael Kinney wrote, "While his suggestion that a contributing factor was the destruction of a viable political left during the red scare of the 1950s may find few supporters, Horne offers solid evidence of the social and economic conflicts that found their expression in violence."

With *Race Woman: The Lives of Shirley Graham Du Bois* (2000), Horne provided the first full-length biography of the woman known today mainly as the second wife of the African-American scholar and activist W.E.B Du Bois. When Shirley Graham married W.E.B. Du Bois, in 1951, she was in her 50s, while he was in his 80s. At the time she was already one of the best-known black women in America, and Horne asserted that the most interesting and historically significant events of her life occurred before 1951. "Drawing on Graham Du Bois's personal papers and extensive interviews with family and friends," a reviewer wrote for *Publishers Weekly* (August 7, 2000), "Horne's book may not completely unravel the enigma of Shirley Graham Du Bois, but it gets closer to her heart and soul than any previous attempt." Shirley Graham Du Bois was born in 1896 and raised in a strictly religious home in Indianapolis, Indiana. Early on she understood the significance of education and the potential it offered. She married young and had two sons. She then divorced her husband, left her children with her parents, earned a master's degree from Oberlin College, and moved to Paris, France, where she studied at the Sorbonne. After she returned to the United States, she produced the all-black opera *Tom-Tom* (1932) and other shows. In the 1940s she published several best-selling biographies of famous African-Americans, including Frederick Douglass. She was also a committed advocate of civil rights, women's rights, and anti-colonialism. In 1961, after a decade of marriage, Shirley and W.E.B. Du Bois renounced their American citizenship—as committed communists, they found it difficult to continue living in the United States—and moved to the African nation of Ghana, where Shirley Du Bois worked as the director of Ghana TV. In a review of *Race Woman* for the *Village Voice* (December 12, 2000), Julia Leigh found that Horne "has brought to light an extraordinary career many mainstream historians find it more comfortable to overlook."

Horne's *Class Struggle in Hollywood, 1930–1950: Moguls, Mobsters, Stars, Reds & Trade Unionists* (2001) also got a good deal of attention in the mainstream press, especially in Los Angeles. In the book, which focuses on union movements and class politics, Horne told the story of the Hollywood movie industry of the 1930s and '40s, a time during which the organized-labor movement in the movie-making industry rose in importance and then, for various reasons, collapsed. For seven months starting in March 1945, when Horne began the story, the Conference of Studio Unions (CSU)—which included unions of carpenters, office employees, set decorators, painters, screen publicists, and story analysts, who wanted better pay and more reasonable work schedules—went on strike over a dispute with the International Alliance of Theatrical Stage Employees (IATSE), a union with mob connections (it previously had leaders installed by the gangster Al Capone). In October 1945, when police and mob-hired thugs went on the attack against picketing members of the CSU near the Warner Bros. studios, a riot broke out, putting an end to CSU's strike. A year later the union was "crushed by the studios because it was not sufficiently docile and, therefore, clashed with the dominant ethos of the U.S.—and Hollywood—elite," Horne told *Current Biography*. "The issue of 'communist' was a typical red herring designed to distract attention from this bitter reality. Arguably, Hollywood labor has yet to recover from this epochal setback." When movie studios began in 1947 to blacklist screenwriters, actors, and directors they perceived to be communist, the absence of a strong union, Horne argued, made it that much easier for them to do so. *Class Struggle in Hollywood* is divided into chapters that provide the perspectives of "Reds," "moguls," and "mobsters and stars," sometimes with overlapping narratives of the same incidents. In the book Horne offered the theory that although there was a Communist Party presence in California (it had about 10,000 members), the party was not involved in the CSU strike—but that, nonetheless, the perception and charges of Communist involvement led to CSU's demise. Sheri Linden wrote in a review for *Variety* (May 7–13, 2001): "Horne's labor-oriented view of the film biz provides images not often seen in Hollywood chronicles: glimpses of the stars who crossed picket lines and those who honored them; tactical discussions at Screen Actors Guild meetings; the Los Angeles Police Department's Red Squad conducting tireless surveillance of local Communists; the Culver City cops being put on the MGM payroll. Hardly ancient history, *Class Struggle in Hollywood* is a thought-provoking look at the rise and fall of a progressive force in the movie-making industry."

In *The Final Victim of the Blacklist: John Howard Lawson, Dean of the Hollywood Ten* (2006), Horne revisited the U.S. government's determined pursuit of "reds" working in the Hollywood movie industry. Aware of the enormous power of movies to shape people's perceptions and beliefs, the U.S. government was determined to eradicate supposedly communist messages in major motion pictures. John Howard Lawson started out as a playwright in New York City in the 1920s and by the following decade had switched to screenwriting. By that time he was also a passionate supporter of communism. He reached the peak of his success as a screenwriter during the early 1940s, writing such pictures as *Sahara* (1943), a World War II film starring Humphrey Bogart. In an interview with Farai Chideya for National Public Radio (August 14, 2006), Horne mentioned a "scene in that movie that was a breakthrough in terms of the cinematic depiction of African-Americans. You see this black man chase down a Nazi in the desert and strangle him. . . . And this strangling was symbolic and metaphorically depicting the strangling of white supremacy that was coming out of World War II. And it's this kind of cinematic dynamite that, of course, caused John Howard Lawson to be hauled before congressional committees." In 1947, while testifying before the House Un-American Activities Committee, Lawson refused to answer questions about his affiliation with the Communist Party; as the questioning—led in part by Republican congressman Richard Nixon—grew heated, Lawson was escorted away from the microphone. He was charged with contempt of Congress and sent to prison. Later he continued to write screenplays—such as the antiapartheid drama *Cry, the Beloved Country* (1952), starring Sidney Poitier—under a pseudonym, because he had been blacklisted. Lawson, along with nine other screenwriters and directors, were placed on the famous Hollywood Ten blacklist.

In a largely negative review of *The Final Victim of the Blacklist* for the *Los Angeles Times* (December 3, 2006), the film critic Richard Schickel criticized Horne for rarely quoting from Lawson's scripts or offering film summaries—perhaps, Schickel wrote, because Horne was "afraid detailed descriptions of this work will expose Lawson to ridicule." Schickel also took issue with other facts Horne left out: for example, that Lawson tried to get the producer Adrian Scott and the director Edward Dmytryk, both of whom were also part of the Hollywood Ten, to restore to the film *Cornered* (1945) parts of the script they had deemed too propagandistic. "Since all these incidents are discussed in other sources, one suspects the author of a selectivity that is, to borrow a phrase, unfortunate and tragic," Schickel wrote. "This, one is also bound to say, is how history was once written in the Soviet Union—with all the inconvenient parts left out. But poor as Horne's performance is, his book has a curious fascination. For Lawson was a not unfamiliar type: a writer whose skills did not match his intellectual ambitions, but who found a different kind of satisfaction in ideological bullying. Such people compel our mystified attention. How do they discipline their human waywardness? What makes them subsume themselves in dubious causes? What, in short, makes them so coldly and mechanically tick?"

Horne's recent books include *The Color of Fascism: Lawrence Dennis, Racial Passing, and the Rise of Right-Wing Extremism in the United States* (2006), *The End of Empires: African Americans and India* (2008), and *W.E.B. Du Bois: A Biography* (2010). In *The Color of Fascism*, Horne told the story of Lawrence Dennis, one of the most prominent leaders of the American fascism movement. Born in Atlanta, Georgia, in 1893, Dennis was the child of a black mother and a father whose race is unknown. Relatively light-skinned, and an admirer of the Nazis, Dennis decided to pass as a white man. In a review of *The End of Empires*—a book that examined connections between African-Americans and the people of India—a staff writer for *Publishers Weekly* (June 23, 2008) wrote: "Horne presents a variety of examples of cultural cross-pollination—African-Americans reading Gandhi and writing on colonialism while Indians were writing on the race problem in the United States, and more. Readers interested in African-American history, race relations and anticolonialist movements will find Horne's book overstuffed and somewhat rambling, but still an informative and useful exploration of fresh territory."

In an interview for *Political Affairs* (December 6, 2010, on-line), Horne was asked why he had written a biography of W.E.B. Du Bois when, as the interviewer pointed out, David Levering Lewis had won two Pulitzer Prizes (in 1994 and 2001) for his "monumental, definitive" two-volume work on the same subject. Horne responded, "I wanted to be more forthright about some of his political ties and more forthright about his evolution than perhaps previous writers have been, and I wanted to write it, hopefully, in a style that was more acceptable to the lay reader, the non-professorial, non-history-graduate-student reader." He added, "I think the value of my biography, and a good deal of my work on Du Bois in general, has been the stressing of his later years as a key to graphing the true greatness of Du Bois, insofar as his voice was critical. It is very interesting what happens during that particular moment."

Horne is also the author of *Black and Red: W.E.B. Du Bois and the Afro-American Response to the Cold War, 1944–1963* (1986), *Communist Front? The Civil Rights Congress, 1946–1956* (1988), *Studies in Black: Progressive Views and Reviews of the African American Experience* (1991), *Reversing Discrimination: The Case for Affirmative Action* (1992), *Black Liberation/Red Scare: Ben Davis and the Communist Party* (1993), *Race for the Planet: The U.S. and the New World Order* (1994), *Powell v. Alabama: The Scottsboro Boys and American Justice* (1997), *From the Barrel of a Gun: The United States and the War Against Zimbabwe, 1965–1980* (2001), *Race War: White Supremacy and the Japanese Attack on the British Empire* (2004), *Red Seas: Ferdinand Smith and Radical Black Sailors in the United States and Jamaica* (2005), *Cold War in a Hot Zone: The United States Confronts Labor and Independence Struggles in the British West Indies* (2007), *The Deepest South: The United States, Brazil, and the African Slave Trade* (2007), *White Pacific: U.S. Imperialism and Black Slavery in the South Seas after the Civil War* (2007), *Blows Against the Empire: U.S. Imperialism in Crisis* (2008), and *Mau Mau in Harlem? The U.S. and the Liberation of Kenya* (2009). Horne is also the co-editor, with Mary Young, of

the books *Testaments of Courage: Selections from Men's Slave Narratives* (1995) and *W.E.B. Du Bois: An Encyclopedia* (2001).

In his 2010 interview for *Political Affairs*, Horne was asked why so much of his work "centered on African Americans in an international context." He responded, "There are many reasons. One is trying to break free from the manacles of so-called 'American exceptionalism,' which tends to see the United States as an island unto itself and totally unique and doesn't take into account the global currents that have shaped this nation inevitably and inexorably. . . . I shudder to think where we people of African descent would be without our allies in the international community. It's been our everything, quite frankly." In an earlier interview for the same publication (December 10, 2009, on-line), Horne had given an example of such an alliance: he mentioned the labor leader Tom Mboya, a member of the Luo ethnic group in the African nation of Kenya. Mboya, a frequent visitor to the U.S, met in the 1960s with President John F. Kennedy, and, in Horne's words, "they cooked up a scheme to bring more African students to the United States to study. This was in direct response to [the Soviet Union's] attempt to do the same thing. . . . Mr. Mboya, being Luo, of course sought to bring his Luo compatriots to these shores, and there you see how Barack Obama, Sr. wound up at the University of Hawaii two years after statehood, where he meets Stanley Ann Dunham and they fall in love, and the product of that union is the current U.S. president, Barack H. Obama."

Horne lives alone in Houston. He is a fan of international films and documentaries. He also is a lover of music, particularly jazz. He told *Current Biography* that he believes in "sound personal habits," such as exercise and abstaining from the use of tobacco and alcohol. He has a daughter, Flora.
—D.K.

Suggested Reading: *Boston Globe* p30 Aug. 21, 1995; (London) *Guardian* p10 Apr. 4, 2007; *Los Angeles Times* E p1 Aug. 11, 1995, R p4 Dec. 3, 2006; National Public Radio (on-line) Aug. 14, 2006; *Variety* p75 May 7–13, 2001; *Village Voice* p97 Dec. 12, 2000

Selected Books: *Black and Red: W.E.B. Du Bois and the Afro-American Response to the Cold War, 1944–1963*, 1986; *Communist Front? The Civil Rights Congress, 1946–1956*, 1988; *Studies in Black: Progressive Views and Reviews of the African American Experience*, 1992; *Reversing Discrimination: The Case for Affirmative Action*, 1992; *Black Liberation/Red Scare: Ben Davis and the Communist Party*, 1993; *Race for the Planet: The U.S. and the New World Order*, 1994; *Fire This Time: The Watts Uprising and the 1960s*, 1995; *Powell v. Alabama: The Scottsboro Boys and American Justice*, 1997; *Race Woman: The Lives of Shirley Graham Du Bois*, 2000; *Class Struggle in Hollywood, 1930–1950: Moguls,*

Mobsters, Stars, Reds & Trade Unionists, 2001; From the Barrel of a Gun: The United States and the War Against Zimbabwe, 1965-1980, 2001; Race War: White Supremacy and the Japanese Attack on the British Empire, 2004; Black and Brown: African Americans and the Mexican Revolution, 1910–1920, 2005; Red Seas: Ferdinand Smith and Radical Black Sailors in the United States and Jamaica, 2005; The Final Victim of the Blacklist: John Howard Lawson, Dean of the Hollywood Ten, 2006; The Color of Fascism: Lawrence Dennis, Racial Passing, and the Rise of Right-Wing Extremism in the United States, 2006; Cold War in a Hot Zone: The United States Confronts Labor and Independence Struggles in the British West Indies, 2007; The Deepest South: The United States, Brazil, and the African Slave Trade, 2007; White Pacific: U.S. Imperialism and Black Slavery in the South Seas after the Civil War, 2007; The End of Empires: African Americans and India, 2008; Blows Against the Empire: U.S. Imperialism in Crisis, 2008; Mau Mau in Harlem? The U.S. and the Liberation of Kenya, 2009; W.E.B. Du Bois: A Biography, 2010; as co-editor (with Mary Young)—Testaments of Courage: Selections from Men's Slave Narratives, 1995; W.E.B. Du Bois: An Encyclopedia, 2001

Stephanie Mitchell, courtesy of Harvard University

Huybers, Peter

(HY-bers)

1974– Climate scientist

Address: Harvard University, Dept. of Earth and Planetary Sciences, 20 Oxford St., Cambridge, MA 02138

The climate scientist Peter Huybers, a veteran of the U.S. Army, has been an assistant professor in the Department of Earth and Planetary Sciences at Harvard University since 2007. A recipient of a 2009 John D. and Catherine T. MacArthur Foundation award—often called the "genius grant"—Huybers is known for studying global climate change starting with the Pleistocene era, which began about 1.8 million years ago and lasted until the end of the most recent ice age, around 12,000 years ago. He has collaborated on extensive research concerning ice ages and their relationships to volcanic activity and the tilt of Earth's axis in relation to its orbital path. Huybers has also studied what he calls the skewing of the seasons, which has, within the past 50 years, caused the hottest and coldest days of the year to arrive nearly two days earlier than before, on average. Huybers "combines a deep appreciation for geologic and geochemical problems, along with a sophisticated understanding of the physics of the climate system, wrapped together with a sharp and insightful ability to take disparate data sets and interpret them in a statistically rigorous manner," Daniel P. Schrag of Harvard said, as quoted on the American Geophysical Union (AGU) Web site; the occasion was the December 16, 2009 ceremony at which Huybers received the AGU's James B. Macelwane Medal. Schrag added that Huybers "is also a gentle and kind spirit, engaging students and colleagues in a way that makes collaborations blossom, even with scientists from vastly different disciplines—quite unexpected from a former tank commander." Huybers's work examines worldwide annual temperature changes and looks at the history of the planet's ice sheets and glaciers. His research, for which there is limited evidence, has allowed him to develop significant theories that may help scientists better understand global climate change.

One of the two children of Peter and Noreen Huybers, Peter J. Huybers was born in 1974. Before deciding to pursue a career in science, he considered becoming a Jesuit priest. "I don't regret my choice," he was quoted as saying on the AGU Web site. In 1996 Huybers graduated with a B.S. degree in physics from the United States Military Academy, at West Point, New York. For the next two years he served in the U.S. Army as a tank-platoon leader in Germany and Bosnia. From 1998 to 1999 he was a member of the National Guard in Louisiana; during that time he also taught physics at Isidore Newman High School, in New Orleans. In 1999 Huybers began a five-year stint as a research assistant in the Department of Earth, Atmospheric, and Planetary Sciences at the Massachusetts Institute of Technology (MIT), in Cambridge, where he also served in the National Guard until 2003.

Huybers earned his Ph.D. in climate physics and chemistry from MIT in 2004. His doctoral thesis, entitled "On the Origins of Ice Ages: Insolation Forcing, Age Models, and Nonlinear Climate Change," was awarded the school's Carl-Gustaf Rossby Prize as the best thesis of the year in MIT's Program in Atmospheres, Oceans, and Climate Change. During the following two years, Huybers completed a National Oceanic and Atmospheric Administration postdoctoral fellowship in climate and global change in the Geology and Geophysics Department at the Woods Hole Oceanographic Institution, in Woods Hole, Massachusetts. He also served in the U.S. Army Reserves at that time. In 2006 Huybers became an environmental fellow in the Department of Earth and Planetary Sciences at Harvard University, in Cambridge. The following year he became an assistant professor of earth and planetary sciences at Harvard.

In 2005 Huybers taught a course at MIT on abrupt climate change. That same year he and Carl Wunsch, his mentor at MIT, carried out a study that correlated the timing of the last seven ice ages with the variations in the tilt of Earth's rotation axis. The tilt, also referred to as obliquity, amounts to an average difference of 23.5 degrees between the axis and Earth's orbital path; the obliquity is responsible for the four seasons. Huybers and Wunsch's research found that the end of the ice ages, known as glacial terminations, seem to have occurred at times when our planet was experiencing its largest obliquity. "The apparent reason for this is that the annual average of sunlight in the higher latitudes is greater when the tilt is at maximum," Huybers said to Michael Schirber for LiveScience.com (March 20, 2005). Huybers and Wunsch arrived at that conclusion by studying the fossils of small organisms, called foraminifera, found on the bottom of the ocean. The foraminifera make shells with the oxygen in the ocean; their fossils helped Huybers and Wunsch to determine the ratio of heavy to light oxygen in the ocean, which corresponds to the amount of ice on Earth. (Light oxygen has one or two fewer neutrons than heavy oxygen. The less light oxygen, the more ice.) The scientists also concluded that our planet does not necessarily "thaw out" every time it reaches maximum tilt. "The Earth is skipping obliquity beats," Huybers told Schirber.

Huybers later worked with Alexander R. Stine, a graduate student in the Department of Earth and Planetary Science at the University of California at Berkeley, and Inez Fung, a planetary-science professor and co-director of the Berkeley Institute of the Environment. Their study, published in the January 22, 2009 issue of *Nature*, maintained that the hottest day of the year has been coming approximately 1.7 days earlier than it did prior to 1954, and that the difference between winter and summer temperatures on Earth has decreased over the past half-century, with winter temperatures warming more than summer temperatures. Huybers and his colleagues used information from a publicly available database of global surface (land and ocean) temperature measurements from 1850 to 2007, which was provided by the University of East Anglia's Climate Research Unit in the United Kingdom. The researchers concluded—as have the overwhelming majority of scientists studying global warming—that human activity has contributed to the change in climate.

In 2009 Huybers conducted a study with the Harvard scientist Charles Langmuir that examined the role of volcanoes at the end of the last ice age. "We were trying to understand, how has volcanic activity on a global scale changed over the last 40 thousand years," Huybers said in an interview for EarthSky.org (January 11, 2010). "And what we did was, we took as many different radio carbon dates [as] we could find of individual volcanic eruptions, and using statistical models, attempted to reconstruct what the frequency of volcanic events were, through time." According to Huybers, "The major finding was that there was a dramatic uptick in volcanic activity during the last deglaciation." That means it is possible that volcanic eruptions around the world caused planetary warming and melting of ice; the melting may have taken weight off rock beneath the ice, which may in turn have caused more volcanic activity. Eruptions send carbon dioxide, or CO_2, a greenhouse gas, into Earth's atmosphere, contributing to the heating of the planet, which, Huybers theorized, helped—along with obliquity—to trigger the end of the last ice age. "I think ice ages are really the outstanding mystery in Earth sciences," Huybers told EarthSky.org.

The MacArthur Foundation awarded Huybers a $500,000 "genius grant" in 2009. A citation on the foundation's official Web site reads, "Through his imaginative yet simple interpretations of fundamental questions in climatology, geology, and oceanography, Huybers is advancing our understanding of both past and ongoing climate change." As quoted by Alvin Powell and Steve Bradt in the *Harvard Gazette* (September 22, 2009), Huybers said, "I imagine [the MacArthur award] will help in my work, research, and teaching—all of which are closely connected—in two ways. First, I would like to use some portion of it to directly support novel climate research, something that would not usually be funded." He added that the money would also help him, his wife, Downing Lu, a military physician, and their young son, Pax, "to spend more time together."

Huybers's work was a beneficiary of the American Recovery and Reinvestment Act (ARRA), better known as the 2009 economic-stimulus package, signed into law by President Barack Obama. According to a Targeted News Service article (October 15, 2009), the funding given to Huybers was meant to "finance a project to apply a new algorithm for examining the relationship between precipitation and temperature using proxy records of climate, such as from tree rings, in conjunction with instrumental records." In addition, Huybers received the James B. Macelwane Medal at a 2009 ceremony in San Francisco, California.

Huybers is a member of the National Research Council committee reviewing the U.S. Antarctic Program. He has also been a member of the Environmental Science and Public Policy Committee; the Harvard University Center for the Environment; the Harvard Oceanography Committee; the Energy, Climate, and Global Change Faculty Working Group; and the Cambridge Climate Advisory Committee, among other groups. His articles have been published in journals including *Nature*, *Geophysical Research Letters*, *Quaternary Science Reviews*, *Paleoceanography*, and the *Journal of Physical Oceanography*.

—J.P.

Suggested Reading: *Boston Globe* Metro p1 Sep. 22, 2009; EarthSky.org Jan. 11, 2010; *Harvard Gazette* (on-line) Sep. 22, 2009; LiveScience.com Mar. 30, 2005

Jaroussky, Philippe

(jah-ROOS-kee, fil-LEEP)

Feb. 13, 1978– Opera and ensemble singer; solo countertenor

Address: c/o EMI Classics, 304 Park Ave. S., New York, NY 10010

When the French sopranist countertenor Philippe Jaroussky made his stage debut, in 1999, "he was fortunate in his timing," Fernanda Eberstadt wrote for the *New York Times* (November 21, 2010). "In the last few decades, much of the Baroque repertory—the operas and sacred music of composers like Monteverdi, Purcell and Gluck, as well as that of lesser-known masters—has enjoyed a widespread revival. And with it, that most startling of voices, the countertenor—a grown man who sings like a turbo-charged choirboy, performing the roles of heroes or saints that were originally written for a castrato and that are often sung by a female mezzo-soprano." Thanks to that newly reborn interest, Jaroussky has become one of the most critically acclaimed countertenors in the world, as well as an artist with an enthusiastic following among concertgoers. He appears in Baroque-era operas, performs with his own ensemble, Artaserse, and also sings as a soloist, and he has given many concerts in Asia and North America as well as Europe. Jaroussky—who is also a baritone—has made many recordings, too. The Italian mezzo-soprano Cecilia Bartoli told Eberstadt, "When I heard Philippe Jaroussky for the first time, I was struck by his musicality and sensibility. There is a beauty in his phrasing and a delicacy, if not fragility in his soul, that touches the listener profoundly." The English countertenor James Bowman, referring to Johann Sebastian Bach (1685–1750), who is recognized as one of the greatest composers of all time, told Eberstadt, "Jaroussky sounds like the boy Bach would have loved to write for."

Countertenors sing in the highest register of the male voice, seeking to emulate castrati—male singers living in the 17th and 18th centuries who were castrated before puberty in order to keep their voices childlike, in the soprano range. The castrati singers were musical stars of their day, performing both male and female roles in operas. Prepubescent castration was discontinued completely by the end of the 19th century; in the 20th century countertenors began to fill the roles originally written for and performed by castrati. Through the use of falsetto (in which the voice is raised to a higher register than in ordinary singing), countertenors seek to sound as similar as possible to castrati, although, as Eberstadt noted, "today most countertenors regard castrati as a gold standard that cannot be matched." Some commentators use the labels "sopranist" and "countertenor" indiscriminately, while others consider the former to be a subcategory of the latter. "It's true that there is something potentially ridiculous about this voice coming out of a man's body," Jaroussky told Eberstadt. "People talk about the countertenor being a third sex, or something quasi female, but I think for me it's more a way of staying a child."

Philippe Jaroussky was born on February 13, 1978 in the upper-middle-class Paris suburb of Maisons-Laffitte. His surname is that of his Russian-born paternal grandfather, who fled Russia during the Bolshevik Revolution. His father, Daniel, works as a commercial agent, and his mother, Jacqueline, as a lighting designer. His brother, Didier, who is 10 years older, is a computer salesman. Jaroussky's family was not musical, but his mother loved to listen to recordings of the opera singer Maria Callas. When Jaroussky was young he painted copies of pictures by Pablo Picasso and Vincent van Gogh, leading his parents to believe he would become a professional artist. As part of a French national requirement that children take music lessons, Jaroussky began playing violin when he was 11; he later won first prize at a performance at the Conservatory of Versailles, where he studied music. When he was 15 he also started playing the piano. Talented on both instruments, he was told (erroneously, as the success of a number of others attests) that he had begun playing too late to make a career with either one.

When he was 18 Jaroussky attended a concert given by the Martinique-born sopranist countertenor Fabrice di Falco. "I was shocked by the disjunction between his physique and that high crystalline voice," he recalled to Eberstadt. "He had this beautifully androgynous face, and a voice like Barbara Hendricks. As soon as I heard him, I had the strangest feeling that I could do that, too. I

Simon Fowler, courtesy of Seldy Cramer Artists
Philippe Jaroussky

knew right away that this was what I wanted to do with my life."

In 1996 Jaroussky sought out di Falco's coach, Nicole Fallien. "Philippe came to me and asked me to teach him how to sing," Fallien told Eberstadt. "He had a lovely voice, but tiny. I said, 'Maybe you should stick with the violin.' He said: 'I want to sing. And what's more, I want to sing in a head voice'"—a reference to falsetto—"which means even smaller. I said, 'I'm not sure you'll succeed.' He said, 'Don't worry; I'm sure'—not to be arrogant, but to encourage me. Well, he wasn't wrong." Jaroussky studied with Fallien for more than two years. "I was quite unhappy with instruments because everybody was saying to me all the time I was too old, you know?" he told Steve Dow for the Sydney, Australia, *Sun-Herald* (February 7, 2010). "Finally when I started to sing everybody was saying to me, 'Oh, you're very young.'" Jaroussky told Cree Carrico for ClevelandClassical.com (January 25, 2010), "When I was a violinist or a pianist I could hide myself behind the instrument. You cannot do that with the voice. It's so direct. It's a direct reflection of your personality and that's why people like singers. It's just your voice. You cannot lie. When I started to sing I had this feeling of being completely naked."

In 1999 Jaroussky received a diploma as a violinist from the Early Music Faculty of the Conservatoire de Paris. Following Fallien's advice, that same year he enrolled in a vocal course taught by the acclaimed French countertenor Gérard Lesne. Later in 1999 Jaroussky made his professional debut, at the Royaumont and Ambronay Festivals, in France, singing in Alessandro Scarlatti's oratorio *Sedecia: Re Di Gerusalemme* ("Sedicia: King of Je-

rusalem"), with Il Seminario Musicale ("Instrumental Ensemble"), which Lesne had founded with the goal of introducing 17th- and 18th-century Italian and French Baroque music to a wider audience. Jaroussky won praise from music critics for his performance. (A recording of one of the concerts was released by Virgin Classics in 2001.) In 2000—at the behest of the French conductor Jean-Claude Malgoire, and with the French ensemble La Grande Écurie et la Chambre du Roy—Jaroussky sang in a performance of the trilogy *L'Orfeo* ("Orpheus"), *Il ritorno d'Ulisse in patria* ("The Return of Ulysses"), and *L'incoronazione di Poppea* ("The Coronation of Poppea"), by one of the originators of opera, Claudio Monteverdi. He told Eberstadt, "Now when I hear recordings from that period, my voice sounds so tight and childish, and yet there was something touching about it too."

By 2001 Jaroussky's career was flourishing. "Everything went very fast for me . . . ," he told Cree Carrico. "I'm quite a lucky guy, everything was so easy for me." In a review of one of his early albums, *Vivaldi—Catone in Utica*, which Malgoire and his ensemble recorded for the Italian label Dynamic, John W. Barker wrote for *American Record Guide* (November 1, 2002), "Jaroussky fills the comparatively minor role of Arbace with a luscious sound that would easily win him identification as a female contralto in a blindfold test." Both Jaroussky and the Polish tenor/sopranist Jacek Laszczkowski, in the role of Caesar, Barker continued, "renew impressions that, though they can never approximate the unique vocal colors and power of top-flight castratos, the latest crop of countertenors can hold their own dramatically and can at least match the fullness of corresponding female voices."

In 2002 Jaroussky formed an instrumental ensemble, Artaserse, to back him. ("Artaserse" is the Italian form of the name of a Persian king, Artaxerxes I, who ruled during the fourth century B.C. and was a subject of more than a dozen early Italian operas, all of which used the same text.) The ensemble performs music by lesser-known Baroque-era composers and little-known music by well-known Baroque composers. Jaroussky told Eberstadt, "There's a sly side to it too: when you are the first to record a song, you aren't under the same pressure as if you were performing Bach's *Magnificat*. It's virgin territory." The musicians—two violinists, a violist, a guitarist, a theorbist (a theorbo being similar to a lute), and an organist who also serves as a harpsichordist—use instruments made during the Baroque period or made to resemble period instruments. Jaroussky's recordings with Artaserse include a selection of music by Benedetto Ferrari (2003), an album of Vivaldi cantatas (2005), *Beata Virgine* (2006), and *Sances: Stabat Mater: Motets to the Virgin Mary* (2010).

The last-named album contains motets by various composers and the Stabat Mater (a 13th-century Latin hymn concerning Mary at the crucifixion of Christ) composed in the late 1600s by Giovanni Felice Sances. In a review for the All Music Guide Web site, James Manheim wrote, "Jaroussky has sung Baroque opera, but his modest-sized voice is really ideal in chamber music like that heard on this disc. . . . Almost everything here is extremely low-key, with Jaroussky's exquisitely controlled voice floating serenely, largely without vibrato, above murmuring accompaniment from his own group, the Ensemble Artaserse. . . . The whole disc is a sterling example of how an almost completely neglected repertory can be brought to life anew by a performer who enters into it with the desire and talent to express its essence."

Among Jaroussky's other albums are *Un Concert pour Mazarin* (2006), with Jean Tubéry and the Ensemble La Fenice; *Vivaldi Heroes* (2007), recorded with Jean-Christophe Spinosi conducting the Ensemble Matheus; *Carestini: The Story of a Castrato* (2007), which offers music by Gluck, Handel, and others, with Emmanuelle Haïm conducting Le Concert d'Astrée; *Lamenti: Italian Baroque Operas* (2008), with Haïm and Le Concert d'Astrée; and *Un'Opera Immaginaria* (2009), an imaginary opera comprising music assembled from Handel's works by the French musicologist Ivan A. Alexandre, in which Jaroussky was joined by a half-dozen other singers. "I like very much to do CDs because I know the CD will survive me," Jaroussky told Dow. "I think you become an artist also because you want to fight with your own death, you know? Of course that's impossible, but it's not something sad. I think it's a very optimistic energy . . . you can really enjoy each moment, you know?"

Jaroussky recorded *J. C. Bach: La Dolce Fiamma: Forgotten Castrati Arias* (2010) with the instrumental ensemble Le Cercle de L'Harmonie, conducted by Jérémie Rhorer. The arias were written by Johann Christian Bach, the 11th son of Johann Sebastian Bach. Jaroussky told Dow that because they were intended to be sung by castrati, who "were like super-singers and had quite superhuman capacities," the album "was the most difficult CD to record; there are so many long phrases, but I like this type of challenge." The record went gold in France, although it received mixed reviews. In an assessment for *Opera News* (February 2010, online), Roger Pines wrote, "Jaroussky deserves praise for bringing this repertoire to light, and for his interpretive intelligence throughout a demanding program, but the vocalism proves wildly variable. His impressive breath control and flexibility, the latter on display in the *Orfeo* aria and in Arbace's *aria di tempesta* from *Artaserse* (1760), merit bravos. Chest notes—seemingly belonging to another voice altogether—are problematic, however, as is the lack of a real trill. Singing in an exceptionally high tessitura"—that is, the range of the notes and their arrangement—"Jaroussky can float piano tones above the staff, but that area of the voice consistently turns shallow and thin in any more heroically scaled passage. The loveliest portion of the instrument is its lower octave; this listener there-

fore hopes that, in a still-young career, the undeniably gifted Jaroussky will focus on alto repertoire exclusively. Music sitting as high as what we hear on this disc is better left to the numerous flexible-voiced female mezzo-sopranos working today who can do it complete justice."

In 2010 Jaroussky appeared in concert in Sydney and Melbourne, Australia, with the Australian Brandenburg Orchestra, with whom he had performed three years earlier. Peter McCallum, the reviewer for the *Sydney Morning Herald* (February 22, 2010, on-line), wrote, "Jaroussky's intonation is immaculate and the tone, though small, is always unforced. He has some wonderfully sweet notes, particularly at the top of his range, and there is a fresh purity to the sound, particularly in the upper range. As with many countertenors, the challenge is to establish evenness over the range, and notes in the low register, just before the breakout of falsetto, are less effective and tend to need special treatment. Jaroussky articulates the language very well, which gives a natural sense of phrase to his lines, and he has the capacity to draw out the cadence most elegantly."

In December 2010 Jaroussky released *Caldara in Vienna: Forgotten Castrato Arias* (with Emmanuelle Haïm conducting Concerto Köln), a collection of operatic arias by the Baroque composer Antonio Caldara. On January 13, 2011 he made his Carnegie Hall debut, in that venerable New York City site's Weill Recital Hall. The pianist Jérôme Ducros served as his accompanist. The program consisted of two dozen songs (most of them about three to four minutes long) by 10 French composers from the 19th–20th centuries, among them Camille Saint-Saëns, César Franck, Ernest Chausson, and Cécile Chaminade—the same selections that Jaroussky recorded with Ducros in 2009 for his album *Opium: Mélodies françaises*. Vivian Schweitzer, who reviewed the concert for the *New York Times* (January 16, 2010, on-line), thought that the "pure, boyishly radiant voice and admirable coloratura technique" that Jaroussky displayed in his performance of Baroque scores sometimes sounded "too virginal for the dark passion" of the more contemporary French lyrics. But, she added, "he often performed expressively and with finesse, floating his top notes with delicate pianissimos." She wrote that in one of his encores—a reprise of Chaminade's "Sombrero"—Jaroussky switched "with amusing facility between baritone and countertenor."

In March and April 2011, Jaroussky was scheduled to perform in Budapest, Hungary; London; Nice, France; and Krakow, Poland.

"I can live without singing, but I can't live without music," Jaroussky told Dow. "I've seen some older singers who find it very difficult to stop and I understand that because you have dedicated your life to it." He said he probably would not perform in public after the age of 60 but would instead teach master classes and continue to conduct ensembles. In his leisure time he enjoys searching for undiscovered or little-known scores in museums and libraries. Jaroussky's partner, he told Dow, is "not in music but he's supporting me of course, a lot."

—W.D.

Suggested Reading: All Music Guide (on-line); ClevelandClassical.com Jan. 25, 2010; EMI Classics (on-line); *New York Times Magazine* p38+ Nov. 21, 2010; *Opera News* p66 Mar. 2008; *Sydney (Australia) Morning Herald* Extra p8 Feb. 7, 2010, News & Features p10 Feb. 16, 2010

Selected Recordings: with Artaserse—*Benedetto Ferarri: Musiche Varie*, 2003; *Vivaldi: Virtuoso Cantatas*, 2005; *Beata Virgine*, 2006; *Sances:*

Stabat Mater: Motet to the Virgin Mary, 2010; *Un Concert pour Mazarin* (with Jean Tubéry and the Ensemble La Fenice), 2006; *Vivaldi Heroes* (with Jean-Christophe Spinosi conducting the Ensemble Matheus), 2007; *Lamenti; Italian Baroque Operas*, 2008; *Un'Opera Immaginaria* (with Ivan A. Alexandre and various artists), 2009; *J.C. Bach: La Dolce Fiamma: Forgotten Castrati Arias* (with Jérémie Rhorer conducting La Cercle de L'Harmonie), 2010; *Caldara in Vienna: Forgotten Castrato Arias* (with Emmanuelle Haïm conducting Concerto Köln), 2010;

Rick Diamond/Getty Images

Johnson, Jamey

July 14, 1975– Country singer/songwriter

Address: c/o Fitzgerald Hartley Co., 1908 Wedgewood Blvd., Nashville, TN 37212

"Jamey Johnson has the appearance and the style of a classic country music outsider," Wayne Bledsoe wrote for the *Knoxville (Tennessee) News-Sentinel* (March 18, 2010). "He writes story songs. He sounds like an old-fashioned honky-tonker and looks like a fella who might whallop you upside the head in a bar fight." Johnson's three major-label albums—*The Dollar* (2006), *That Lonesome Song* (2008), and *The Guitar Song* (2010)—have been praised for their straightforwardness and sincerity.

"Some people bleed words and he's one of those guys," Dean Dillon, a fellow country artist, told Sarah Rodman for the *Boston Globe* (May 8, 2009). "He can wear his heart on a piece of paper pretty well." Johnson appears to be just as straightforward and sincere away from the stage or recording studio. "There's no separation between his music and him," the actor Matthew McConaughey, a friend of Johnson's, told Randy Lewis for the *Los Angeles Times* (September 28, 2010). "Jamey doesn't perform, he's just who he is." In an interview for the *Washington Post* (September 15, 2010), Johnson told Chris Richards, "I write songs. I write music. And I put music on my albums and I deliver that to people. And I go out there every night to play my music to people who come to see our shows. And if they enjoy it, we got a good deal worked out."

Jamey Johnson was born into a conservative Christian family on July 14, 1975 in Enterprise, Alabama. He was raised in a rural area outside Montgomery, the state capital. At about the age of 10, he learned to play the guitar from his uncle, and as a teenager he saved enough money to buy an Epiphone guitar that he named Old Maple. In addition to gospel music, which he performed with his father in church, Johnson enjoyed listening to southern rock and heavy metal. He had a particular love for country tunes. "We lived in a trailer off in the wilderness," Johnson recalled to Richards. "Metallica don't sound right when it echoes off the trees. But [the country music of] Don Williams does quite well out there."

One of Johnson's biggest musical influences was the iconic country star Hank Williams Sr. Johnson and his friends sometimes visited the grave of the music legend, who died in 1953 at the age of 29 and was buried in Montgomery. "There ain't a whole lot to do around Montgomery if you ain't old enough to drink," Johnson told Bledsoe. "But we could always score a bottle of whiskey and go up there and break out some Hank songs or some good old country songs. That's one of my favorite places to go." (Johnson has since performed with Williams's son, the popular country artist Hank Williams Jr.)

Johnson, who soon began to play in local clubs, attended Jacksonville State University on a music scholarship. "I whizzed through music theory," he told Jon Caramanica for the *New York Times* (September 23, 2010). After two years of college, he dropped out and joined the U.S. Marine Corps Reserves. "It was a good time," Johnson told Aaron Beck for the *Columbus (Ohio) Dispatch* (January 29, 2009). "After one of my corporals in the unit heard me sing, I had to carry a guitar out to wherever we were going. We'd go to the Mojave Desert for a few weeks, and I'd end up getting passed around from Hummer to Hummer with a guitar." After eight years Johnson was honorably discharged—the same week that the others in his unit were told that they were being sent to Iraq.

In 2000 Johnson moved to Nashville, Tennessee, often referred to as the home of country music. "I don't know that I had any particular expectations," he told Ray Waddell for *Billboard* (September 15, 2010, on-line). "I knew that I wanted to write songs and go around and sing my songs for the people. I'm not sure exactly where that desire comes from, or where the ability comes from, but I would assume they both come from the same source." Arriving in Nashville with his dogs in the back of his Dodge pickup truck and little money in his pocket, Johnson found work with a sign company and an industrial pumping outfit. From 2001 to 2004 he ran his own construction firm, restoring buildings that had been damaged by fires, hurricanes, and tornadoes. Concurrently, he began performing in Nashville clubs, where he met other songwriters and helped record demo tapes for them; among his first was a duet with the then-unknown singer Gretchen Wilson.

In 2002 Johnson self-released the album *They Call Me Country*, and he soon signed a songwriting deal with EMI. It took longer to win a recording contract. "[Record executives] said no, but they didn't say never. When they passed, they never said they didn't like my voice," he told a reporter for the *Palm Beach (Florida) Post* (February 10, 2006). "It doesn't mean [I had] a bad product. The market just wasn't right for it." Then, in 2005, after repeated auditions, Johnson landed a recording contract with the BNA label. "When I got that record deal, that was my party," Johnson told Chris Welch for the *Huntsville (Alabama) Times* (November 19, 2009). "Me and my friends would go take over a bar. We were just as wild as hell and having the time of our lives." In 2006 he released the album *The Dollar*, whose title single was described in the *Palm Beach (Florida) Post* article as "a tearjerker about a boy who asks his mother how much money it would take to pay his daddy to take him fishing or play catch." The single peaked at the number-14 spot on *Billboard*'s hot-country-songs chart; the album sold a comparatively modest 77,000 copies.

Johnson was subsequently dropped from the label. "I was a little stunned and a little mad, a little frustrated and a little hurt," he admitted to Ken Tucker for *Billboard* (July 19, 2008, on-line). "I've never been fired from anything in my life." At the time Johnson was going through a divorce from his wife, Amy. Depressed, he secluded himself. "I wouldn't talk to anybody," he told Tucker. "I wouldn't go out to clubs. I didn't want to be at any party. I quit drinking for more than a year. I rented a basement in a friend's house and stayed there, coming up with songs and ideas." In an interview with Randy Lewis for the *Los Angeles Times* (January 3, 2009), Johnson said, "I had tremendous highs and tremendous lows at the same time, and if that ain't the formula for a tornado, I don't know what is. It was a lot to deal with, so I did what I always do: I tried to get the noise out of my head and get down to music." He recorded the resulting album, *That Lonesome Song*, with the Kent Harley Playboys. "It was just a bunch of friends making a garage-band-type record," he explained to Aaron Beck.

The album, which Johnson had initially self-released, caught the attention of Universal Music Group Nashville chairman Luke Lewis, who offered him a contract with the subsidiary Mercury Nashville Records. "I had released [*That Lonesome Song*] on the Internet," Johnson told Ray Waddell. "I had already turned down two record labels. Both of them said they wanted me to make records for them, but neither one of them said they wanted that record. . . . I sat down and talked with Luke Lewis, and one of the first things he said about it was 'I don't know what you guys are doin' in that studio, I don't care. Just don't mess with that sound.' . . . That's how we started off our relationship."

In August 2008 Mercury released *That Lonesome Song* nationwide, and within a few months it had sold more than 500,000 copies. "The critical cliché would be 'They don't write albums like *That Lonesome Song* any more,' which is at least partially true," a reviewer wrote for the All Music Guide Web site. "The raw emotion and barely controlled heartache that Johnson brings to his singing and songwriting on the album aren't exactly in style in 2008's country market, but lovers of old-fashioned hardcore country and honky tonk music will be stunned by its emotional depth and strong melodies." Johnson was invited to appear on the *Late Show* with David Letterman and the *Tonight Show* with Jay Leno, and the album went on to receive multiple Grammy nominations. The track "In Color" made the *Billboard* country-single top 10 and was named song of the year by both the Country Music Association (CMA) and the Academy of Country Music (ACM). (In 2007 "Give It Away," co-written by Johnson and recorded by George Strait, had won the same CMA and ACM honors.)

In September 2010 Johnson released *The Guitar Song*, a 25-track double album. On his Web site he described the recording as "a tale" and added,

"The first part of it is a very dark and sordid story. And then everything after that is progressively more positive, reassuring and redemptive." In a review for the *St. Petersburg (Florida) Times* (September 16, 2010), Luke Preston wrote, "*The Guitar Song* is one of the most powerful albums released in the past decade and it will place Jamey Johnson in the same league as the country music heroes whose signatures cover his guitar." Similarly impressed, Ann Powers wrote for the *Los Angeles Times* (September 14, 2010, on-line), "Jamey Johnson's music is hard, like a metal slide on a pedal steel guitar; it's real, like the kernel of truth within the tall tales swapped by studio musicians after much Jack Daniel's has been consumed. It's a consummate blend of artifice and self-revelation, an intricately crafted container for elemental stuff—the dirt of work, the sweat of love, the tears of a particularly bad hangover." *The Guitar Song* has been nominated for a Grammy Award as best country album, and Johnson is in contention for a Grammy in the category of best male vocal performance for the track "Macon." (The awards show will air on February 13, 2011.)

Johnson is sometimes chided for co-writing the 2005 novelty hit "Honky Tonk Badonkadonk" for the country artist Trace Adkins. Writing for the *Tennessean* (February 17, 2006), Peter Cooper described the song as an "up-tempo celebration of a woman's ample posterior," and in a *New York Times* (January 30, 2006) article, Ben Ratliff called it a "hyper-pumped, sports-bar anthem about looking at women from the back, strained with torrid metaphors and a bit of hip-hop slang." Johnson defended the song to the *Palm Beach (Florida) Post* reporter, saying, "Sometimes you just write a stupid ditty. . . . Hell, we weren't out to save the world. But there are so many people out there who are so stressed out, if it takes a dumb . . . song to bring them out of their rut, why not let 'em have what they want?"

In March 2010 Johnson, who has a daughter, Kylee, with his ex-wife, received the Rising Star Award from the Alabama Music Hall of Fame. He is said to be producing an album for the Blind Boys of Alabama, a venerable gospel group with whom he performed at the Hall of Fame ceremony.

—J.P.

Suggested Reading: *Billboard* (on-line) July 19, 2008; *Los Angeles Times* E p1 Jan. 3, 2009; *New York Times* (on-line) Sep. 23, 2010; *Palm Beach (Florida) Post* TGIF p51 Feb. 10, 2006; *Washington Post* C p1 Sep. 15, 2010

Selected Recordings: *The Dollar*, 2006; *That Lonesome Song*, 2008; *The Guitar Song*, 2010

Kan, Naoto

Oct. 10, 1946– Prime minister of Japan

Address: Kantei, 1-6-1 Nagata-chō, Chiyoda-ku, Tokyo 100-8968, Japan

In June 2010 Naoto Kan, the leader of the Democratic Party of Japan (DPJ), won election as his country's prime minister, becoming its sixth leader in four years and the first in over a decade who was not born into a family of politicians. Previously, Kan had served as Japan's deputy prime minister as well as its minister of finance, among other posts. In the mid-1990s, as minister of health and welfare, he rose to prominence and gained a reputation for integrity when he exposed governmental negligence that had resulted in the spread of HIV through contaminated blood products. In 1996 Kan co-founded the DPJ, which was the country's main opposition party until 2009, when it replaced the Liberal Democratic Party (LDP) as the ruling body in the Japanese legislature. Prior to the devastating earthquake and tsunami that struck Japan in March 2011, Kan's government was not expected to survive for very long, due to perceived missteps in handling Japan's economic woes. Although the crisis provided a temporary reprieve from his political problems, Kan is once again struggling to hold on to his position as the leader of Japan.

Saul Loeb/AFP/Getty Images

"I grew up in a typical Japanese salaryman's family," Naoto Kan said during his candidacy for prime minister, as quoted in a profile on the BBC News Web site (September 13, 2010). "I've had no special connections." He was born on October 10, 1946 in Yamaguchi, Japan. His father was a supervisor at a glass company. In 1970 Kan received a degree in applied physics from the Tokyo Institute of Technology. That year he began working for a patent-law office, and in 1971 he passed the exam to become a patent lawyer. Around that time Kan, having developed a fondness for the Chinese game mahjong, invented and sought a patent for a machine to calculate the game's scores. In 1974 he opened his own patent-law office. Also in the 1970s he became a civil activist, concentrating mostly on environmental and feminist issues. During that decade he served on the campaign staff of a women's-rights activist, Fusae Ichikawa, during her successful run for a seat in the House of Councillors, the upper house of the Diet, Japan's legislature. In 1980 Kan himself, following three failed attempts, joined Japan's House of Representatives, the lower house of the Diet; he was a member of the now-defunct Social Democratic Federation. In 1993 Kan became chairman of the Committee on Foreign Affairs in the lower house. Beginning three years later he served as Japan's minister of health and welfare under Prime Minister Ryutaro Hashimoto, of the conservative LDP, which ruled Japan almost continuously from the mid-1950s until 2009.

As minister of health and welfare, Kan gained popularity with Japanese citizens after uncovering a practice that had begun in the early 1980s, when the Health Ministry failed to ban the use of unsterilized blood products despite the possibility that some of the blood was infected with HIV (human immunodeficiency virus, which causes AIDS). As a result of that failure, thousands of blood-product recipients contracted HIV, and hundreds, many of them hemophiliacs, died. (The ministry did not institute the use of sterilized blood products until 1985.) Kan exposed the matter by pressuring reluctant ministry bureaucrats to reveal documents proving that the government had failed to prevent the use of tainted blood products. Kan told Sheryl WuDunn for the New York Times (October 11, 1996), "Until I started the project and issued orders on exactly how to find [the documents], they were looking for them with their eyes closed." Kan also publicly apologized to the victims and their families and approved a plan for them to receive financial compensation. "Until Kan's tenure," Miyamoto Masao, a former Health Ministry official, told Hilary E. MacGregor for the Los Angeles Times (July 19, 1996), "politically appointed ministers did not have any control over the system." A Japanese political reporter told MacGregor, "We have waited 30 years for a politician like Kan."

In 1996 Kan co-founded the liberal Democratic Party of Japan, which became the leading opposition to the LDP. Two years later he became the DPJ's president, a post he held until 1999, when charges that he was dictatorial led to his replacement by the party co-founder Yukio Hatoyama. That year Kan served as chairman of DPJ's Policy Research Council, and in 2000 he became secretary general of the DPJ. In 2002 Kan once again became president of the DPJ; he led the party until 2004, when he resigned after admitting that as health minister he had failed through an oversight to make 10 months' worth of state pension payments. Seeking redemption, Kan shaved his head, wore traditional Buddhist clothing, and made a pilgrimage to dozens of temples. In 2006 he became vice president of the DPJ. Two years later he took the post of lead director of the House of Representatives' Committee on Budget.

In 2003, as the DPJ's leader, Kan had spearheaded a merger with the Liberal Party (LP), led by Ichiro Ozawa, in a successful attempt to weaken the LDP's hold on power. In September 2009 the DPJ gained control of the Diet, and Yukio Hatoyama became the prime minister of Japan. Kan was named deputy prime minister, a position he held until June 2010. During that time he served as the minister of state for national policy, economic and fiscal policy, and science and technology policy. In January 2010 he also began serving as Japan's minister of finance; in that position he led the National Strategy Bureau, a new agency that aimed to give Japanese elected officials rather than nonelected bureaucrats control over policy and budgets. In June 2010 Hatoyama suddenly announced his resignation as prime minister of Japan, due to his failure to fulfill his campaign promise to have a U.S. military base removed from the Japanese island of Okinawa. As a candidate to replace Hatoyama, Kan promised that he would work to rein in the national debt and improve Japan's relations with China and the United States. On June 4 he was chosen by the DPJ to become the 94th prime minister of Japan since 1885, winning 291 votes against 129 for Shinji Tarutoko, a little-known legislator. After taking office with a 60 percent approval rating, Kan warned citizens about the country's massive debt and suggested that tax hikes would be necessary. He introduced a plan that would double the sales tax to 10 percent, an idea that proved highly unpopular among Japanese citizens. As a result his approval rating began to decrease.

A month after Kan became prime minister, the DPJ performed poorly in Japan's parliamentary elections and lost its majority in the House of Councillors. Also in July 2010, in a highly unusual development, Kan's wife, Nobuko Kan, published a book titled What on Earth Will Change Now That You Are Prime Minister?, which appeared to question her husband's ability to lead the nation. "If the Japanese public had any doubts about the man who took the top job barely a month ago," Anita Singh wrote for the London Telegraph (July 22, 2010), "the first lady's comments are unlikely to reassure them." As quoted by Singh, Nobuko Kan wrote, "I believe [Kan] is best suited to giving directions on the spot in support of somebody else." Nobuko Kan also offered negative opinions of her husband's fashion sense, cooking skills, and public-speaking ability. Naoto Kan has referred to his wife as his political "opposition in the home" and once told reporters the he was afraid to read her book. "What she tells me all the time is that she is a primary voter, meaning that when I talk to our voters about my ideas, she says if she does not get convinced with what I say, no voters would buy my argument," Kan said in an interview with CNN.com (November 16, 2010). "She tells me to try to convince her first with my argument. For me, she is the most challenging voter." CNN referred to the "playfully adversarial relationship" between the prime minister and his wife; the *Wall Street Journal* (January 12, 2011, on-line) noted, "While Mrs. Kan has been a vocal commentator, and even critic, of her husband's performance, she has also been one of his hardest campaigners."

In September 2010 Ichiro Ozawa made an unsuccessful attempt to replace Kan as prime minister. Before the election Kan—who garnered 721 points to Ozawa's 491—campaigned in support of job creation, greater fiscal austerity, and a potential consumption-tax increase; Ozawa campaigned for aggressive government spending. "Kan's prevailing wasn't a big surprise," Kensuke Takayasu, a political scientist at Seikei University, told John M. Glionna and Yuriko Nagano for the *Los Angeles Times* (September 15, 2010). At the time Takayasu felt that there was no "legitimate reason for [Kan] to leave his position."

On March 11, 2011 parts of eastern Japan were devastated by a 9.0-magnitude earthquake—the most powerful in the country's recorded history—which led to massive tsunami waves, causing even greater destruction; hundreds of aftershocks have followed the earthquake. More than 15,300 people died, and others are still missing. As a result of the disaster, several nuclear-power-plant cooling systems were destroyed, leading to multiple explosions and dangerous levels of radiation leakage. Faced with what has been called Japan's worst crisis since World War II, Kan accepted foreign aid and introduced an emergency-spending package. He also urged Japanese citizens to remain calm and work together to overcome the tragedy. In the first few weeks after the disaster, Kan's political fortunes seemed to be on the rise. Soon, however, the government came under criticism; Kan in particular was criticized for his slow response to the disaster and for the way he handled the nuclear crisis. In addition, Kan was accused of violating local laws by accepting political donations from a foreigner. (He maintained that he had not known the donor was foreign.) In April 2011 the head of the LDP called for Kan to step down as prime minister. In a poll taken by the *Nikkei* business newspaper, nearly 70 percent of those asked also felt that Kan should be replaced.

Not everyone believed that Kan's resignation would benefit the nation. "Even if Kan were replaced, it's not like the situation would change completely," the DPJ lawmaker Masaharu Nakagawa told Sachiko Sakamaki and Takashi Hirokawa for Bloomberg.com (April 21, 2011).

"What's important is that the current government improve its direction and come up with an appropriate vision for reconstruction." "It is impossible to change prime ministers at a time like this," Hajime Ishii, a DPJ upper-house member, said to Justin McCurry for the London *Guardian* (April 18, 2011, on-line). "Other countries would view that as abnormal. At a time when we must work on rebuilding after the earthquake, it is not possible to have a DPJ leadership vote or a general election." In April 2011 the DPJ performed poorly in nationwide municipal elections. In June Kan said that he would step down after the country had had more time to recover from the earthquake and tsunami.

Sometimes referred to as "Kan the Irritable" or "Ira-Kan," the Japanese prime minister is known for having a short temper, though he has been said to have mellowed in recent years. "Kan is not your typical Japanese politician," Hilary E. MacGregor wrote. "He favors a tan suit, not a politician's gray. He gestures with his hands, reaching out to his audience, rather than holding his arms stiffly at his sides. He fields questions from reporters, straying from texts prepared by bureaucrats. He is passionate and committed."

Since 1971 Kan, a Buddhist, has been married to Nobuko, who, according to multiple sources, is also his cousin. The couple have two sons, Gentaro and Shinjiro.

—J.P.

Suggested Reading: CNN World (on-line) Nov. 16, 2010; *Japan Times* (on-line) June 5, 2010; *Los Angeles Times* A p8 Sep. 15, 2010; *New York Times* A p12 Oct. 11, 1996; (Singapore) *Straits Times* Sunday Review p6 July 7, 1996

Kane, Patrick

Nov. 19, 1988– Hockey player

Address: Chicago Blackhawks, United Center, 1901 West Madison St., Chicago, IL 60612

Widely considered to be among the best right wings in the National Hockey League (NHL), the Chicago Blackhawks' Patrick Kane is a "playmaker," as Eric Duhatschek wrote for the Toronto, Canada, *Globe and Mail* (May 21, 2010), "the one who moves fluidly through every zone, effortlessly finding open ice where none exists." Selected first overall by the Blackhawks in the 2007 draft, at the age of 18, Kane went on to win the NHL's Calder Memorial Trophy, honoring the league's best rookie, after leading his team and all NHL rookies with 72 points—21 goals and 51 assists—in the 2007–08 season. In his sophomore season Kane was named to the All-Star team, after achieving the team's second-highest point total (70, comprising 25 goals and 45 assists). In the 2009–10 season Kane posted

Patrick Kane

Jason Merritt/Getty Images

played home games until 1996. They moved that year into a new stadium, the HSBC Arena, a few blocks away; when construction on the HSBC Arena was near completion, an aunt of Kane's, a city councilwoman, arranged for him to sign his name on one of the stadium's steel beams. Kane learned how to skate at the age of six and began playing ice hockey competitively the next year. He also began playing roller hockey with neighborhood children, a group that included the future NHL star Tim Kennedy. Kane's mother recalled to Melissa Isaacson for the *Chicago Tribune* (November 11, 2007), "At 6, Patrick would go out to the street with a hockey net and his rollerblades, and if the kids weren't serious about playing, he would come back inside. I'd say, 'Pat, go back out. They're just kids. They're just playing.'" Kane played two seasons in the mite division (for children ages eight and younger) of the Cazenovia Park Youth Hockey Association, in Cazenovia, a suburb of Syracuse, where he learned the intricacies of skating and stick handling.

Kane's development as a hockey player was fostered by his father, a longtime hockey fan, who ran a car dealership before selling it in order to devote his full attention to developing his son's natural hockey skills. Tiki Kane would drive his son to as many as four games a day, seven days a week. Also, in order to expose his son to higher levels of play, he often paid for him to attend tryouts for upper-level leagues, with no intention of allowing him to play in them. "Sometimes I didn't want to skate," Patrick Kane recalled to Tim Graham for the *Buffalo (New York) News* (February 11, 2007). "My dad would push me so hard to get better. I remember one day I had already played three games and I was on my way to the fourth. I said, 'Dad, what team am I playing for right now?' I didn't even know." By the third grade Kane was considered too good to play with his peers. While competing in a summer league in Wheatfield, a town in Niagara County, Kane scored so many goals that parents of other players petitioned for him to be removed from the league. From then on Kane played in leagues for older players.

After moving up from the mite division, Kane played for a squirt (ages nine and 10) travel team out of West Seneca, New York, in which he recorded more than 100 goals and 100 assists in one season. He then moved on to the peewee (ages 11 and 12) and bantam (ages 13 and 14) levels, playing for the Buffalo Regals and Depew Saints, respectively. Unlike most of his peers, Kane played hockey year-round. "One of the things that helped me was when the season was over, I'd play the whole summer, and people playing winter hockey would take off and play baseball," Kane told Isaacson. "When I'd come back for the regular hockey season, I was so ahead of everyone." Although he dominated the competition at each level as a youth, Kane's short physical stature led many to doubt his ability to withstand the physical demands of higher-level hockey, which included "checking," a defensive technique in which a play-

the best numbers of his young career, leading the Hawks in scoring and finishing ninth in the league with 88 points (30 goals and 58 assists). On June 9, 2010 he scored the series-winning goal in the overtime portion of Game Six in the best-of-seven Stanley Cup finals. The win, over the Philadelphia Flyers, marked the Blackhawks' first Stanley Cup title in 49 years. In the same year Kane was the youngest member of the U.S. national team that won the silver medal at the 2010 Winter Olympics, in Vancouver, British Columbia, Canada. One of the main factors contributing to a renewed enthusiasm for hockey in Chicago—one of the biggest sports cities in the U.S.—Kane has enjoyed a rising celebrity in recent years. "On the current landscape of Chicago superstars . . . there is Kane and there is everybody else," David Haugh wrote for the *Chicago Tribune* (January 7, 2010). "In every way, Kane has progressed slightly more in his development and plays on a better team than Derrick Rose of the Bulls [basketball team]. He has delivered on promise in a way Jay Cutler of the Bears [football team] didn't. And with apologies to [the baseball players] Carlos Zambrano and Mark Buehrle, neither the Cubs nor the Sox has a product they can sell to the masses as reliable or marketable as No. 88."

The first of the four children of Patrick Kane Sr. (known as "Tiki") and Madonna "Donna" Kane, Patrick Kane was born on November 19, 1988 in Buffalo, New York. His three younger sisters are Erica, Jessica, and Jacqueline. Kane and his family were fans of Buffalo's NHL team, the Sabres, and Kane was captivated as a child by such Sabres stars as the goalie Dominik Hasek and the center Pat LaFontaine. The family's home was just a few miles from Memorial Auditorium, where the Sabres er uses his body or stick to gain control of the puck. Tiki Kane told Graham, "The word was, 'As soon as checking becomes involved in the game, Kane's not going to be able to score and move in and out of the play.' But I knew when he was 8 he was getting roughed up even when it wasn't allowed. He was being checked, shadowed, bumped every chance. I knew when checking did become involved he was going to be readier than anyone else out there. As soon [as] checking became involved, it wasn't a factor at all. It was really fun to see that happen."

At the age of 14, seeking tougher competition, Kane relocated to Detroit, Michigan, to play for Honeybaked, the city's triple-A hockey club in the Tier I Midwest Elite Hockey League. Residing with the family of his assistant coach, the former NHL player and Stanley Cup winner Pat Verbeek, Kane attended the first two years of high school in Detroit. The move was initially difficult for Kane, who called his mother in tears after his family dropped him off. "He needed to go away from home," Verbeek explained to Graham. "That first couple months was tough. But near the end of the year he started to understand. He didn't like it, but he knew he had to do it." Under the guidance of both Verbeek, who at five feet nine inches was also considered small for an NHL player, and the team's head coach, Donnie Harkins, who used a tough-love approach to push Kane to his full potential, Kane further developed his skills.

During the 2003–04 season with Honeybaked, Kane played in 70 games and recorded 160 points (83 goals and 77 assists), helping the team advance to the national midget finals, where they were defeated by the Depew Saints, Kane's former team. Kane's stellar performance with Honeybaked won him an invitation to attend the U.S. National Development Program, in Ann Arbor; in two seasons playing with U.S. junior national teams, Kane posted 172 points (84 goals and 88 assists) in 121 games. His point total in the 2005–06 season (102) broke the under-18 scoring record held by Phil Kessel (98). At the 2006 International Ice Hockey Federation (IIHF) World Under-18 Championships, in Sweden, Kane led the tournament in goals (seven) and points (12), contributing to the United States' 3–1 victory over Finland to win the gold medal. Kane was also named to the Tournament All-Star team. In 2007 he helped the U.S. under-20 squad capture a bronze medal at the World Junior Championships. He finished fourth in tournament scoring in the seven-game series, posting five goals and four assists.

Meanwhile, as a freshman and sophomore in high school, Kane turned down scholarship offers from several colleges with strong hockey programs, such as the University of Michigan and Boston College, and instead entered the 2006 draft of the Ontario Hockey League (OHL), a major junior league in Canada for players ages 15 to 20. Kane thought that the OHL, in which teams play twice the number of games as teams in the National Collegiate

Athletic Association (NCAA), would better prepare him for a career in the NHL. Kane was selected first overall by the London Knights, under Coach Dale Hunter. During the 2006–07 season he played in 58 games and led the league in points with 145 (62 goals and 83 assists), capturing the OHL scoring title. He also won the Emms Family Award, honoring the OHL's best first-year player, and was a runner-up for the Red Tilson Trophy, for most valuable player.

Kane's performance both in Canada and on the international circuit led many observers to predict he would be a number-one pick in the 2007 NHL draft, though some continued to express doubts about him because of his size (he stood five feet 10 inches and weighed 166 pounds). Kane silenced his detractors when he was indeed the draft's first-overall pick, by the Chicago Blackhawks. Kane was the Blackhawks' first-ever number-one pick and the highest pick ever to come out of Buffalo. Kane later told Graham, "I think I kind of proved a lot of people wrong and proved to myself I can play this game in this body." Kane was welcomed with great fanfare when he arrived in Chicago. On June 25, 2007 he threw the ceremonial first pitch at Wrigley Field baseball stadium and sang "Take Me Out to the Ball Game" with the Blackhawks' head coach, Denis Savard. Along with the young center Jonathan Toews (who was drafted in 2006 but made his NHL debut with Kane in 2007), Kane became one of the new faces of the franchise. Chicagoans viewed the addition of Kane to the team as a key part of a major rebuilding effort by the Blackhawks, which had not had a winning season or qualified for the play-offs since 2002. Kane signed a three-year contract with the Blackhawks in July 2007. In the off-season he prepared for training camp by overhauling his diet in an effort to add muscle to his wiry frame.

Kane made his NHL debut on October 4, 2007, in a game against the Minnesota Wild. Two days later he recorded his first assist and scored his first shootout goal—a game-winner against Dominik Hasek, his boyhood idol—in a contest with the Detroit Red Wings. On October 19 Kane scored his first career regulation goal and posted two assists, in a game against the Colorado Avalanche. He was named NHL Rookie of the Month for October, after recording 16 points (five goals and 11 assists). By the end of the 2007–08 season, Kane led the team and all NHL rookies with 72 points (21 goals and 51 assists). His assist total set a franchise record for the most by a rookie and was both the highest assist total on the team and the second-highest in the league. Additionally, Kane led both the team and NHL rookies with 28 power-play points (points scored when the opposing team is shorthanded by one or two players because of penalties) and was tied for the league's highest shootout-goal total, with seven on nine attempts, for a 77.8 percent season average. In June 2008 Kane beat out his teammate Toews and the Washington Capitals' center Nicklas Backstrom for the Calder Memorial Trophy, awarded annually to the NHL's Rookie of the Year. He was also named to the NHL All-Rookie Team. The Blackhawks, meanwhile, finished the season with more wins than losses for the first time in six years, with a record of 40–34–8, just a few wins shy of a berth in the Western Conference play-offs. Also that year Kane played for the U.S. team in the 2008 World Hockey Championships, held in Halifax, Nova Scotia, and Quebec City, Quebec. He posted 10 points (three goals and seven assists) in the seven-game series, in which the United States placed sixth.

Four games into the 2008–09 season, Coach Savard was fired and replaced with Joel Quenneville, who had most recently helmed the Colorado Avalanche. Quenneville implemented a more disciplined, puck control–oriented team philosophy, which immediately paid off for a Blackhawks team whose focus had long been on speed and skating skills. Kane finished the 2008–09 regular season with 70 points in 80 games, placing second on the team in assists (45) and fourth in goals (25). He also led the team in power-play goals (13). On January 1, 2009 Kane played in the second annual NHL Winter Classic—an event in which two NHL teams play a regular-season game outdoors—at Wrigley Field, where the Blackhawks lost to the Detroit Red Wings, 6–4. Kane helped the Blackhawks finish the regular season with a record of 46–24–12, good for second place in the Central Division, behind the Red Wings, and fourth place in the Western Conference. In his Stanley Cup play-offs debut, Kane led the Blackhawks with nine goals and finished second on the team in points, with 14 in 16 games. In Game Six of the Western Conference semifinals, against the Vancouver Canucks, Kane recorded his first career hat trick (at least three goals in a single game) in the 7–5 series-clinching win. Upon defeating the Canucks, the Blackhawks advanced to the Western Conference finals for the first time since 1995. They lost the series to the Red Wings, 4–1. That season Kane was the lead vote-getter for the Western Conference All-Star team, and along with Toews he competed in the 2009 All-Star Game, held in Montreal, Canada.

By the 2009–10 off-season, Kane had become one of the highest-profile players in the NHL. He became the youngest player to appear on the cover of an NHL video game, on EA Sports' NHL 10, released in September 2009. His meteoric rise to the top of the hockey world, however, was temporarily halted on August 9, 2009, when he and a cousin, James Kane, were arrested in Buffalo after allegedly assaulting a cab driver during a dispute over a fare. According to the driver, Patrick and James Kane punched him when he was unable to provide 20 cents in change for the $15.00 the two had paid on a $13.80 fare; they then took the money back and ran off. Without ever addressing the specifics of the incident, both Kane and his lawyer, Paul J. Cambria, asserted that the media had made too much of the matter and that Kane had not committed a crime. The charges were ultimately reduced

to noncriminal disorderly conduct, to which Patrick and James Kane pleaded guilty. They were ordered to write apologies to the cab driver and received no penalties on the condition that they stay out of trouble for one year. Commenting on the much-publicized incident, Patrick Kane told Leonor Vivanco for the Chicago Tribune (November 11, 2009), "It's one of those things where it might be better if it happened sooner rather than later because you realize who your true friends are, who's going to be there for you throughout your whole life. Maybe it humbled me even more." He continued, "I'm not mad about what happened. I'm not mad that it got blown out of . . . proportion in the media. . . . But at the same time, I think I'm looking to move forward and just try to be a regular kid."

On December 3, 2009 the team expressed their faith in Kane by signing him to a five-year contract extension worth $31.5 million. Kane played well during the 2009–10 season, averaging one point per game and leading the team in scoring with 88 points (30 goals and 58 assists). In February 2010 Kane and other NHL stars traveled to Vancouver, British Columbia, to compete in the 2010 Winter Olympics. (Since 1998 the NHL has allowed its players to compete in the Winter Olympics, during which the NHL season is suspended.) The youngest member of the U.S. team, Kane posted five points (three goals and two assists) in six games, contributing to the United States' silver-medal finish; the team lost to Canada, 3–2, in a thrilling overtime final. When the NHL season resumed, in early March, the Blackhawks quickly distinguished themselves from the other teams in the Central Division and finished with a division-best record of 52–22–8. In the first two rounds of the play-offs, the Hawks defeated the Nashville Predators and the Vancouver Canucks, respectively, before facing the San Jose Sharks in the Western Conference finals. The Hawks swept the Sharks in four games and advanced to their first Stanley Cup finals since 1992. Facing the Philadelphia Flyers, who had notched several historic upset victories in earlier play-off rounds, the Blackhawks took the series in six games, clinching their first Stanley Cup title in 49 years. Kane scored the series-winning goal in overtime and began celebrating before referees had even confirmed the goal. "The coolest feeling in the world," Kane said, describing his state of mind after the game, as quoted by Dan McGrath in the New York Times (June 11, 2010, on-line). "To score the winning goal in the Stanley Cup finals is something you dream about as a kid. It's unbelievable." Kane scored a total of 28 points during the play-offs (10 goals and 18 assists).

During the 2010–11 off-season, the Blackhawks traded away several core players in return for other players and draft picks, in an effort to meet salary-cap requirements. As of early January 2011, the Blackhawks were ranked ninth in the Western Conference and third in the Central Division, with a record of 21–17–3. By that time Kane had posted

11 goals and 18 assists in 32 games. In December 2010 he missed eight games due to an ankle injury.

Kane, who is nicknamed "Kaner," is very close to his three sisters and enjoys spending his free time with them, as well as with other family members and friends. Bucky Gleason, writing for the *Buffalo (New York) News* (December 14, 2007), described Kane as having "a confident but quiet demeanor. Pull off his helmet, take away his ungodly hands and [Wayne] Gretzky–like hockey sense, and he's no different from the kid bagging your groceries."

—C.C.

Suggested Reading: *Buffalo (New York) News* D p1 Feb. 11, 2007, A p1 Dec. 14, 2007, D p1+ Feb. 11, 2007, A p1+ Dec. 14, 2007, D p2 Apr. 30, 2008, D p1+ May 19, 2009, B p1+ Dec. 11, 2009; Chicago Blackhawks Official Web site; *Chicago Reader* p16+ June 17, 2010; *Chicago Tribune* C p11+ Nov. 11, 2007, p12 Nov. 11, 2009, C p1 Jan. 7, 2010; *New York Times* (on-line) June 11, 2010; (Toronto, Canada) *Globe and Mail* S p3 May 21, 2010

Kaufman, Moises

(MOY-zez)

Nov. 21, 1963– Playwright; theater director

Address: Tectonic Theater Project, 520 Eighth Ave., Suite 313, New York, NY 10018

"The purpose of my life's work has been to question how theater speaks—trying to figure out how this art form speaks at a time of film, television, radio, and the Internet," the playwright and director Moises Kaufman told *Current Biography* (the source of quotes for this article unless otherwise noted). "This bombardment [of information] has made us desensitized to narratives but also opened an opportunity, so that when we go to the theater we crave a certain kind of human contact. So then the question is: How do you make the stage speak and construct narratives in a way that is so uniquely theatrical that it forces you to look at narratives in a different way?" Playing with audiences' expectations and notions of narrative is the essence of Kaufman's approach to directing and writing plays. Some of his best-known plays are based on fact and incorporate his reflections on the very concepts of writing and research; that meta element, however, functions not as an extraneous gimmick but as a seamlessly integrated aspect of the plays' themes and plots. For *The Laramie Project* (2000), Kaufman and his theater company, the Tectonic Theater Project, spent over a year interviewing locals in the small town of Laramie, Wyoming, after the brutal 1998 murder there of Matthew Shepard, a gay college student. Kaufman

thought the town had been portrayed in the media simply and stereotypically—as being full of hicks and rednecks—and wanted to understand what Laramie's residents thought and felt about the tragedy. The play told their story as well as that of Kaufman's and his troupe's experiences in Laramie. After its Off-Broadway premiere, which received glowing reviews, *The Laramie Project* was performed at hundreds of theaters around the world. In 2002 Kaufman directed (for HBO) a film version of the play, which starred Laura Linney, Peter Fonda, and Christina Ricci.

Kaufman first gained acclaim in 1997, at the age of 33, for *Gross Indecency*. Written and directed by Kaufman, that drama concerns the court trials of Oscar Wilde, during which his writing—overtly satirizing Victorian morality—became an issue along with the homosexual acts of which he stood accused. Kaufman made his Broadway debut as a director in 2003, with *I Am My Own Wife*, the story of another controversial historical figure: a transvestite who ran a secret gay club in Berlin, Germany, during the Nazi era and, later, under Communist rule. Six years later Kaufman returned to Broadway, as both writer and director, with *33 Variations*; that play, about Beethoven's music, starred Jane Fonda. Kaufman's latest Broadway credit is his direction of Rajiv Joseph's Pulitzer Prize–nominated comedy–drama *Bengal Tiger at the Baghdad Zoo*, which stars Robin Williams as a gruff, philosophical tiger who ponders aloud questions about war, human nature, and his animal self. Charles Isherwood of the *New York Times* (April 1, 2011) praised Kaufman for directing the play with "gorgeous finesse."

Moises Kaufman was born on November 21, 1963 in Caracas, Venezuela, into an Orthodox Jewish family with Eastern European roots. He has two younger siblings, a brother and a sister. Kaufman's father, a Ukrainian-born Holocaust survivor, immigrated to Venezuela; Kaufman's mother was born in Venezuela, to parents also from Ukraine. At age nine Kaufman discovered that he was gay, which was "very traumatic," as he told Barbara Isenberg for the *Los Angeles Times* (July 29, 2001). "In an Orthodox Jewish community, it's a horrendous thing to have happen. And in a Catholic, macho country, it's the worst thing you can be. But the Jewish community had taught me that being different was not something to be looked down upon and had already given me the tools to deal with it." As a boy Kaufman attended a yeshiva, a religious Jewish school. On family trips to New York City, he was exposed to art and culture. When he was 14 he attended an international theater festival in Caracas, where he was entranced by the avant-garde works of such theater luminaries as Peter Brook, Pina Bausch, and Tadeusz Kantor. "In the yeshiva, there was no theater education at all," Kaufman recalled to *Current Biography*; as a consequence, during those years he did not think of theater, which he loved, as a world he could enter. "Just like I knew there were homosexuals," he added,

Bryan Bedder/Getty Images

Moises Kaufman

smiling, "but I never knew *I* could be one." In college, while studying business (he received a B.A. degree in that subject in 1985), Kaufman joined an experimental theater company, with which he toured Europe and Latin America. He spent five years with the company, becoming one of its lead actors; by the end of that time, he realized he wanted to direct.

In 1987 Kaufman left Venezuela to attend the Tisch School of the Arts at New York University (NYU), in New York City, where he studied directing in the Experimental Theater Wing. Once he entered the New York theater world, where being gay or Jewish is fairly common, he was often labeled "Latino." Kaufman, a proud New Yorker, has expressed a distaste for being labeled according to any single aspect of his identity.

At NYU Kaufman began to develop the ideas about theater that would inform his work. Anton Chekhov's 1896 play *The Seagull*, Kaufman said, is a fine theatrical example of realism; by way of comparison, he noted that other artistic movements of that era, such as Post-Impressionism (the works of Henri Matisse and Henri de Toulouse-Lautrec, for instance), had been superseded by newer movements—such as Cubism, Expressionism, Abstract Expressionism, and Pop Art—which have themselves since faded. Just as one should not expect to see a Matisse painting at a contemporary-art museum, Kaufman said, one should not necessarily expect to see Chekhovian-style realism at the theater today. Accordingly, during his three years at NYU—which he left without a degree—Kaufman sought to discover what he calls "new theatrical vocabularies." He decided that his work would be about "exploring what can happen on the stage."

Spurred by his love of experimental theater, Kaufman co-founded—along with his romantic partner, Jeffrey LaHoste—the Tectonic Theater Project. "Tectonic refers to the art and science of structure," according to the company's Web site, "and [the name] was chosen to emphasize the company's interest in construction—how things are made, and how they might be made differently." In 1991, as the company's artistic director, Kaufman—at 27—staged *Women in Beckett*. A series of short plays by Samuel Beckett, the work received lukewarm reviews. Three years later his production of Franz Xaver Kroetz's *The Nest* earned him an Obie Award nomination.

Kaufman remained relatively unknown to New York's theater audiences until 1997, when the city's most influential theater critic wrote a glowing review of his Off-Off-Broadway play about the trials of Oscar Wilde. In 1895 the Irish-born novelist and dramatist Wilde, whose plays *The Importance of Being Earnest* and *An Ideal Husband* had received rave reviews in his adopted home of London, England, sued a man who had accused him publicly of being a "sodomite"—specifically, of having had sexual relations with the accuser's son. Wilde then withdrew the suit after suggesting during the trial, with his customary and—in this case—reckless wit, that although he had not had homosexual relations with that particular young man, he might have done so had the young man been better-looking. In the conservative, sexually repressed climate of Victorian England, Wilde endured two additional trials and was ultimately convicted of "gross indecency with male persons." (While some of his homosexual countrymen fled to France to escape possible trials and public humiliation, Wilde chose to stay and face the charges. After being convicted, he spent two years in prison.) *Gross Indecency: The Three Trials of Oscar Wilde*, which Kaufman wrote and directed, made use of biographical information, newspaper accounts, and trial transcripts. Ben Brantley of the *New York Times* (March 19, 1997) called the play "a sharply intelligent, dramatically fresh take" on a subject that had been covered many times; he added that *Gross Indecency* was written and directed "with a scintillating style of its own" and was a "must-see" event. The play made the case that Wilde, ostensibly on trial for homosexual acts, was actually tried for his "immoral" writings. At one point in one of the trials, a lawyer asked him to comment on the morality of the views expressed by the main character of his novel *The Picture of Dorian Gray*. Brantley noted that Kaufman "has created what is as much a multilevel study in public perceptions of class, art and sexuality as a portrait of one man's downfall, while retaining the pull of the old-fashioned courtroom drama." Kaufman recalled thinking after reading Brantley's review, "My life is about to change." He was right: theatergoers and critics flocked to see the play, and *Gross Indecency* moved to the Minetta Lane Theatre, Off-Broadway, where it ran for more than 600 performances. Soon

Kaufman started receiving offers from all over the country to direct the play. Since then *Gross Indecency* has been staged in more than 40 theaters around the world. The work won a Lucille Lortel Award for outstanding play in 1998.

In October 1998 Kaufman, along with most of the nation, first heard the name Matthew Shepard. One night in his hometown of Laramie, Wyoming, the 21-year-old Shepard was savagely beaten with a handgun by two local men who had found out that he was gay. Shepard was left unconscious and tied to a fence until he was discovered and taken to a hospital, where he died. (Two men later confessed to the murder.) The national media soon flooded to Laramie, a previously little-known, working-class town with a population of 27,000. Kaufman decided to explore the effects that the horrific event had had on the town and would have during the coming year. "What hit me more than the crime itself," Kaufman said, "was that in the next few days you couldn't open a newspaper without seeing something about Matthew Shepard. And to me, that was shocking, because there are a thousand antigay crimes committed in the United States, but for some reason this one resonated." Along with members of the Tectonic Theater Project, Kaufman made several visits to Laramie. Over the course of a year, the group conducted tape-recorded interviews with 200 locals, in bars, churches, stores, diners, and homes. Along with a group of other writers, Kaufman chose about 60 of those interviews, which, in conjunction with court transcripts, media reports, and journal entries that Tectonic company actors wrote during their time in Laramie, became the text of the play. Two years after the murder, *The Laramie Project*, directed by Kaufman, premiered in Denver, Colorado, about two hours by car from where Shepard had been beaten. A few months later the play moved Off-Broadway, to the Union Square Theatre, where it was very well received. Writing for the *New York Times* (May 19, 2000), Ben Brantley called it an "enormously good-willed, very earnest and often deeply moving work of theatrical journalism."

The Laramie Project did not include a reenactment of the murder. Instead, the play focused on the lives of Laramie residents after the crime: their take on what had happened, their relationships to one another, their views about their town, and their opinions about a New York theater troupe's coming to ask questions. In the play eight actors portrayed a total of 60 characters, including themselves, Kaufman, bartenders, shop owners, clergy, police officers, the cyclist who discovered the critically injured Shepard, and many others. "The way the media portrayed Laramie was very biased," Kaufman said in an interview with Jose Orozco for *Morphizm* (March 21, 2005, on-line). "They portrayed it as a town full of hillbillies, rednecks, and cowboys. So, of course, a crime of this nature could happen in a town like that, but it wouldn't happen anywhere else in the country. Well, what we found was rather the opposite. Laramie was special not because it was so different, but because it was so similar to so many other towns in America." Ten years after Shepard's murder, Kaufman and his company returned to Laramie to conduct more interviews. The following year, in October 2009, 150 theaters in cities around the globe—including New York; Los Angeles, California; Orlando, Florida; Hong Kong, China; and Madrid, Spain—staged readings of *The Laramie Project: 10 Years Later*.

Kaufman's next play, *I Am My Own Wife: Studies for a Play About Charlotte von Mahlsdorf*, was staged on Broadway after a successful Off-Broadway run. The play earned its author, Doug Wright, a Pulitzer Prize. Kaufman considers Wright to be "one of the best writers in America." *I Am My Own Wife* tells the story of a German transvestite and homosexual who lived in Berlin under two of the most cruel and oppressive regimes of the last century—Nazi Germany and Communist East Berlin. Lothar Berfelde began cross-dressing as a teenager and later changed his name to Charlotte von Mahlsdorf. At age 15 he killed his abusive father, who had been a Nazi. Mahlsdorf was convicted but went free after a Russian bomb struck the prison where he was incarcerated. Against great odds, during World War II Mahlsdorf—who referred to himself as a female—successfully ran a secret gay club in Berlin. (During the 1920s Berlin had a thriving gay scene, which was crushed after the Nazis came to power.) Later, for three decades, while East Berlin was under Soviet control, Mahlsdorf ran an antique furniture museum that was also a gay hangout. How, Wright wondered, was Mahlsdorf able to survive and do what he did? At one point in the play, the character based on Wright tells Mahlsdorf: "It seems to me you're an impossibility. You shouldn't even exist." That line is an example of one of Kaufman's approaches to drama: one in which the craft of constructing the play is itself incorporated into the work. (Wright had interviewed von Mahlsdorf many times.) As the play reveals, Mahlsdorf's survival had much to do with a fact he had kept secret: while living in East Berlin, he served as an informant for the Communist secret police. When Wright discovered that, he began to feel ambivalent about the man he had long admired, and with Kaufman's encouragement, he incorporated that ambivalence into the play's theme and dialogue. *I Am My Own Wife* was a one-man show starring Jefferson Mays, who played Mahlsdorf, Wright, and more than 30 other characters. The play, for which Kaufman received a Tony Award nomination for best director, received excellent reviews. In addition to winning the 2004 Tony Award for best play, *I Am My Own Wife* won the Drama Desk Award for outstanding new play.

Kaufman next directed several plays outside New York, including a Chicago staging of Tennessee Williams's *One Arm*, about a disfigured former boxer who becomes a prostitute and then a murderer, and Oscar Wilde's *Lady Windermere's Fan*, a satirical comedy about Victorian morals, mounted at the Williamstown Theatre Festival, in Massachusetts. He then returned to New York, where in 2006 he directed *Macbeth* at the outdoor Delacorte Theater, as part of the city's annual Shakespeare in the Park festival. Liev Schreiber, considered to be one of the country's best Shakespearean actors, played the title role, and Jennifer Ehle, a respected stage actress, was cast as Lady Macbeth. In that production, set in the early 20th century, Kaufman examined through the relationship between Macbeth and his wife the complex interconnectedness of gender and personal and political power.

Kaufman returned to Broadway in 2009 with *33 Variations*. The play, which he both wrote and directed, starred Jane Fonda, who was making her first Broadway appearance in 46 years. In a generally favorable review, John Lahr wrote for the *New Yorker* (March 23, 2009) that the play was "a musicology lecture disguised as an intellectual detective story within an emotional melodrama." In 1819 Beethoven was asked to write a variation on a simple waltz composed by his publisher, Anton Diabelli. Four years later Beethoven had created not one but 33 variations, which are commonly known as the *Diabelli Variations* and are considered to be some of the greatest classical-piano pieces ever written. In Kaufman's play the 71-year-old Fonda played Katherine Brandt, a musicologist who is suffering from the early stages of a motor-neuron disease and is determined to figure out why Beethoven spent four years working on those variations. The play alternates between the stories of Brandt and Beethoven, each of whom experiences a physical decline while in the grip of an obsessive pursuit. *33 Variations* ran on Broadway for three months and then received a Tony Award nomination for best play.

In 2010, in a collaboration between his theater company and the Gotham Chamber Opera, Kaufman directed the Spanish composer Xavier Montsalvatge's 1947 opera *El Gato Con Botas (Puss in Boots)*. The opera is based on a 17th-century French fairy tale in which a cat, through ingenuity and trickery, wins for his destitute master a princess and a kingdom. The mezzo-soprano Ginger Costa-Jackson sang for the cat—a skinny, funny-looking creature controlled by three puppeteers present on stage. "When I started working with puppets," Kaufman told Rob Weinert-Kendt for the *New York Times* (October 1, 2010), "some of my actor friends joked, 'Oh, now you can just get your actors to do what you want.' But actually, with the cat you have three puppeteers and a singer. So the problem is multiplied by four. You have to direct every gesture, every look, every emotion." The opera received enthusiastic reviews.

The following year Rajiv Joseph's *Bengal Tiger at the Baghdad Zoo*, under Kaufman's direction, premiered on Broadway. Directing the play, Kaufman said, was "a delicious joy." *Bengal Tiger* starred Robin Williams, who was making his Broadway debut as an actor. "The great thing about Robin Williams," Kaufman said, "is not only his talent and his humor and his craft, but also his generosity and his humility. He comes into the rehearsal room and he's very, very humble. He's an actor rolling up his sleeves and getting to work. He was able to create a character that made people forget that he is Robin Williams." Played by Williams without an animal costume (only tattered clothes, a natural beard, and unkempt hair suggested the nature of his character), the tiger serves as the narrator. The play's action takes place in Baghdad, Iraq, during the early days of the U.S. invasion of that country, in March 2003. The Baghdad Zoo has been decimated, and two American soldiers guard its lone tiger. The tiger paces in his cage and makes humorous, existentialist observations. When one of the soldiers tries to feed him, the tiger bites off his hand and, as a result, is shot and killed by the other soldier. The tiger then wanders the streets of war-torn Baghdad as a ghost, haunting the soldier who shot him, asking the audience and himself questions about the nature of violence, and witnessing the American soldiers' obsession with a golden handgun—the very same one used to shoot him—which the Americans had stolen during a raid of the Iraqi leader Saddam Hussein's mansion. The golden gun, a symbol of both violence and wealth, is one of the play's many metaphors; others include ghosts (each character who dies becomes one), which haunt the men who have taken lives and represent the soldiers' inability to escape the consequences of their actions. The play received many good reviews, although the praise was not unanimous. John Lahr of the *New Yorker* (April 11, 2011), in a mostly negative review, called Kaufman's direction "sluggish," whereas a reviewer for *Variety* (April 11, 2011) wrote that Kaufman had made a "wonderful production that honors the terrible mystery of being human."

Kaufman's latest project is his direction of Tennessee Williams's *One Arm*, which opened in June 2011 at the Acorn Theater, in New York, to mostly positive reviews.

Kaufman lives in Manhattan.

—D.K.

Suggested Reading: ibdb.com; lortel.org; *New York Times* C p13 Mar. 19, 1997, E p1 May 19, 2000, E p1 May 28, 2003; *New Yorker* p78 Mar. 23, 2009; tectonictheaterproject.org

Selected Plays: as director—*Women in Beckett*, 1991; *The Nest*, 1994; *I Am My Own Wife: Studies for a Play About Charlotte von Mahlsdorf*, 2003; *Macbeth*, 2006; *Bengal Tiger at the Baghdad Zoo*, 2011; as playwright and director—*Gross Indecency: The Three Trials of Oscar Wilde*, 1997; *The Laramie Project*, 2000; *33 Variations*, 2009

Selected Films: as writer and director—*The Laramie Project*, 2002

Stephen Lovekin/Getty Images for IMG

Kotb, Hoda

(KAHT-bee, HOH-dah)

Aug. 9, 1964– Broadcast journalist

Address: NBC News, 30 Rockefeller Plaza, New York, NY 10112

In a career in broadcast journalism that spans 25 years, Hoda Kotb has become expert in reporting both hard news and soft news. In an interview with Leslie Gray Streeter for the *Palm Beach (Florida) Post* (November 27, 2010), Kotb said that for a long time, she had been "under the mind-set that you had to wear just one hat. But then I thought about it, and it doesn't have to be that way. After all, I do like to read the *New York Times* and *US Weekly*. You can still be respected and put a clown nose on. Matt Lauer does it on the *Today* show. I think that once people know your hard side, it's fun to see the softer side, too." For six years after she graduated from college, in 1986, Kotb worked for a series of network-affiliated television stations in towns in Mississippi, Illinois, and Florida; then, for another six years, she was a reporter and anchor for WWL-TV, a CBS affiliate in New Orleans, Louisiana. As a correspondent for the weekly TV news magazine *Dateline NBC* since 1998, she has handled assignments connected with the current wars in Iraq and Afghanistan; the Israeli-Palestinian conflict; the Indian Ocean tsunami of 2004; and Hurricane Katrina. In 2000 she succeeded in interviewing Aung San Suu Kyi, the most prominent pro-democracy activist in Burma, who, until her release in November 2010, spent a total of 15 of the last 21 years under house arrest and had rarely talked to any journalists. From 2004 to 2008 Kotb also served as host of the weekly syndicated series *Your Total Health*, and since 2007 she has co-hosted the fourth hour of NBC's morning news program *Today*, most recently with Kathie Lee Gifford. Kotb's honors include a 2002 Edward R. Murrow Award, from the Radio and Television News Directors Association; Gracie Awards, in 2003 and 2008, from the Alliance for Women in Media; and a 2008 Peabody Award, from the Grady College of Journalism and Mass Communication at the University of Georgia. Her memoir, *Hoda: How I Survived War Zones, Bad Hair, Cancer, and Kathie Lee*, written with Jane Lorenzini, was published in 2010.

Hoda Kotb was born on August 9, 1964 in Norman, Oklahoma, to Abdel and Sameha Kotb, who immigrated to the U.S. from Cairo, Egypt, in 1959. Her father was a petroleum and mining engineer, and her mother has worked at the Library of Congress for many years. The Kotb family, who included Hoda's older sister, Hala, and younger brother, Adel, moved to Morgantown, West Virginia, before Hoda Kotb entered a local public kindergarten. In her memoir (the source of quotes in this article unless otherwise noted) Kotb wrote, "My parents were so proud to be American citizens. They dressed in the current styles and demanded we speak English as our first language. They wanted us to be red, white, and blue. We were United States citizens and were taught to never consider ourselves different." Before Kotb entered the fourth grade, her father accepted a job that required the family to spend two years abroad, first in Egypt, then in Nigeria. Kotb was unhappy to leave Morgantown, but she now believes that living abroad helped her to become a well-adjusted adult. After they returned to the U.S., the family lived briefly in West Virginia before moving to a diverse neighborhood in Alexandria, Virginia, where their neighbors included Greeks and Chinese. During summers the family visited relatives in Egypt, and Kotb learned that "Hoda Kotb is actually the Jane Smith of the Nile. If you walk down the streets of Cairo and yell, 'Hi, Hoda!' a dozen girls will turn. Over there, I am every girl. Here, I'm unique. And I like that."

After graduating from Fort Hunt High School, in Alexandria, in 1982, Kotb enrolled at Virginia Polytechnic Institute (Virginia Tech), in Blacksburg, to study broadcast journalism. At college she joined the Delta Delta Delta sorority. During her junior year her father died suddenly of a heart attack. Despite her intense grief Kotb forced herself to stay focused on her schoolwork, as she knew her father would have wanted. She earned a B.A. degree in 1986 and then went to Cairo, where she lived with a paternal uncle and aunt while she looked for work with the CBS, NBC, and ABC news bureaus in that city. After a prolonged effort Kotb was hired by the CBS bureau chief, Penny Rogg, to fill an entry-level position. About a year later Kotb returned to the U.S. and embarked on another search for a job. According to Audrey Fischer, writing for the *Library of Congress Information Bulletin* (April 2010), she received 27 rejections during two weeks of crisscrossing the South in her mother's car. Her quest ended when Stan Sandroni, the news director of WXVT, a CBS-affiliated TV station in Greenville, Mississippi, hired her as a reporter. In a question-and-answer (Q&A) session posted on the *Inside Dateline* Web site (October 18, 2007), Kotb said that if the WXVT job had been the first one offered to her, "I might not have taken it, because it was such a small market, you had to shoot your own stuff, and you got paid government cheese money. But after everyone else telling me no no no, it was great."

One day when Kotb was at the WXVT studio, Sandroni hurried into the newsroom and asked agitatedly, "Who's got a blazer?" When Kotb said that she did, Sandroni told her that she would have to substitute for a regular evening-news anchor who had called in sick. "That's the beauty of small-market television," Kotb wrote. "The litmus test for who would anchor the evening news was whoever had a blazer!" Although Kotb made the mistake of starting that newscast by saying, "Good morning, I'm Hoda Kotb!," she was later chosen to be WXVT's five-o'clock news anchor.

After eight months in Greenville, Kotb moved to Moline, Illinois, where she spent two years as a morning anchor and general-assignment reporter at WQAD-TV, the local ABC affiliate. She next worked for two and a half years at WINK-TV in Fort Myers, Florida, as a weekend anchor and reporter. She remained for six years (1992–98) with WWL-TV, the CBS affiliate in New Orleans, Louisiana, serving as a reporter and anchor for the 10 o'clock evening news.

Kotb was negotiating with WWL-TV for a new contract when, in September 1997, Elena Nachmanoff, an NBC News vice president, invited her to interview for a position with *Dateline NBC* in New York City. In the on-line Q&A, Kotb called the "knock from NBC News" a milestone for her: "Your whole life you dream of the network! Who doesn't dream of the network?" After the interview Kotb returned to New Orleans, where, during the next week, she heard nothing from NBC while WWL-TV executives pressured her to sign the new contract. When Nachmanoff finally called, she said that *Dateline NBC* executives questioned whether Kotb—who at WWL-TV rarely spoke on air for more than a minute or two at a time—was equipped to handle assignments that would require her to report on air for at least 15 minutes and possibly much longer. Nachmanoff said that NBC was willing to test her readiness by flying her back to New York, where she would be given a producer, two crews, a lead, and 24 hours to put a story together. Kotb was midway through the assignment when the world learned that the Roman Catholic nun and celebrated humanitarian Mother Teresa had died, in India. To cover that news story, NBC sent to India the crews working with Kotb.

Kotb returned to New Orleans, where she completed the assignment with WWL crews. Later she was summoned to New York again, to screen her report for NBC executives. A few days later the network offered her a job. She agreed to remain with WWL-TV through the end of the February 1998 ratings season.

As a *Dateline NBC* correspondent, Kotb has covered a wide range of events in the U.S. and overseas, some of which she described in *Hoda*. In 2000 she interviewed the Nobel Peace Prize winner and leading Burmese political dissident Aung San Suu Kyi, who was under house arrest and had not been interviewed by an American television news reporter in 11 years. In December 2001 Kotb traveled to the Gaza Strip and the West Bank to work on a series about how Americans are perceived in those parts of the Middle East. After the U.S. and its allies launched the war in Iraq in March 2003, Kotb was among the NBC correspondents chosen to report from the war zone. Before she left the States, Kotb participated in a three-day training camp in Virginia to prepare her for situations she might encounter in Iraq. In one exercise, a staged kidnapping, Kotb tried to retain awareness of her surroundings while a canvas bag covered her head—a maneuver that later helped her keep her bearings during a sand blackout in the desert. Kotb then flew to southern Turkey, where she witnessed U.S. troops leaving Incirlik Air Base for Iraq.

On April 6, 2003 the NBC journalist David Bloom died suddenly of a heart attack in Iraq, and NBC asked Kotb if she wanted to take Bloom's place; he had been embedded with the U.S. Army's Third Infantry Division and had been reporting from a tank fitted with live television and satellite equipment. After serious consideration Kotb decided that the risk was too great and declined. Soon afterward, while she and her photographer were at a fruit stand in an open-air market in a predominantly Shi'a Muslim area of Baghdad, Iraq's capital, preparing for a so-called stand-up shoot (for local "color"), a group of men started shouting angrily and running toward them. She and the photographer succeeded in getting into their crew's car and leaving the scene before the men reached them. Kotb later learned that that market was in a neighborhood considered particularly unsafe for Americans, and she had incurred the men's wrath because the shirt she was wearing had three-quarter-length sleeves, thus leaving the lower part of her forearms bare. "It was a dangerous lesson learned," she wrote.

In 2004, with David Corvo, Ellen Mason, and Olive Talley, Kotb earned a National Headliners Award, from the Press Club of Atlantic City, for their *Dateline NBC* report *Saving Dane—Adoptees Rage*. With the *Dateline* producer Tim Uehlinger, Kotb reported on the aftermath of Hurricane Katrina in New Orleans soon after the disaster, in August 2005, and a year later.

In 2006, in the series *The Education of Ms. Groves*, Kotb followed a new college graduate, 21-year-old Monica Groves, during her difficult first year of teaching at the Jean Childs Young Middle School, an inner-city school in Atlanta, Georgia. In college Groves had studied English and Spanish but had taken no education courses; as a member of the Teach for America corps, she received only five weeks of teacher training. Groves embarked on her teaching stint with high hopes, enthusiasm, and lofty goals for her students, but often, for much of the school year, she found herself unable to keep their attention or prevent them from misbehaving. "I didn't expect for it to feel like such a fight, such a struggle," she was seen telling Kotb. "Either you attack the day or it attacks you. And it beats you down." Groves also offered her thoughts in a video "diary," and Kotb visited the homes of three of the sixth-graders and spoke to their caregivers—in one case, a grandmother who had sole responsibility for Kotb's student and his two brothers. "It's not what I had planned at all," the grandmother, who said she was "over 75," told Kotb of her second tour of duty in child-rearing. "And it's not what I would choose to do, but if this is what I need to do, I just feel like I just get up and do it the best I can." With help from the principal, Groves began to take control in the classroom and to inspire many of her students to perform at a far higher level than they had until then. At the end of the school year, she told Kotb, "This whole experience from beginning to end has been like a mirror up to my face. And I've seen how flawed I am. I've seen how much work I need. . . . I was just humbled by it all. Because it's difficult and I wasn't able to be what I know I hope to be someday. But I'm working on it." *The Education of Ms. Groves* brought NBC News a 2008 Alfred I. DuPont–Columbia University Award and earned Kotb, and a dozen others involved in its production, a 2008 Peabody Award. "The troubling plight of urban schools is well documented, but rarely are the root causes behind the failures explored," the Peabody citation noted. "*The Education of Ms. Groves* provides an enlightening window on this world. . . . Putting human faces to the stories of students and teachers in struggling schools," the series "serv[ed] as a sobering reminder of work yet to be completed."

When, in September 2007, NBC expanded its popular morning news program *Today* to include a fourth hour (10:00–11:00 a.m., Eastern Standard Time), Kotb campaigned successfully to win the job of co-host. Along with Natalie Morales and Ann Curry, she shared anchoring duties for the new segment, which was designed to have a lighter tone than the other three hours. In April 2008 Kathie Lee Gifford, best known as the foil to Regis Philbin on ABC's *Morning Show* (1985–88) and *Live with Regis and Kathie Lee* (1988–2000), replaced Morales and Curry as Kotb's co-host. Kotb plays the straight woman to Gifford, whom Felicia R. Lee, writing for the *New York Times* (April 17, 2008, on-line), described as "jazzing up the fourth hour,

. . . injecting a blend of humor and candor that manages to be both self-deprecating and celebratory." "Her verbal Ping-Pong with Ms. Kotb felt immediately comfortable," Lee reported after interviewing Gifford.

The 600th installment of the fourth hour aired in July 2010. Regular segments include the "Joy Fit Club," with the nutrition and weight-loss expert Joy Bauer; "Ambush Makeover," in which women, chosen at random while standing in the plaza outside NBC's New York studios, are newly made up and attired; "Everybody Has a Story"; "Fan of the Week"; Bobbie Thomas's "Beauty Buzz"; and "Kathie Lee and Hoda's Favorite Things." Despite the conscious effort to end *Today* on a high note, the fourth hour occasionally includes serious subjects. On one installment, in November 2007, Kotb talked about being diagnosed with breast cancer earlier that year and the mastectomy and reconstructive surgery she underwent.

In 2008 Kotb delivered the commencement address at the Virginia Tech graduation ceremony. In 2010 she presented the keynote address, titled "My Journey," at that year's Library of Congress celebration of Women's History Month.

Kotb lives in New York City. In the mid-2000s she was briefly married to the tennis coach Burzis Kanga. Five feet nine inches in height, she exercises regularly. She has run in the Susan G. Kome Race for the Cure and in 2009 completed a triathlon (consisting of running, bike riding, and swimming) on the New Jersey shore.

—H.R.W.

Suggested Reading: American Program Bureau Web site; *Broadcasting and Cable* p3 Aug. 20, 2007; Everything New Orleans Web site Oct. 16, 2010; Greater Talent Network Web site; *Inside Dateline* Q&A at today.msnbc.msn.com Oct. 18, 2007; *New Orleans Times-Picayune* (on-line) Oct. 16, 2010; *USA Today* B p8 July 26, 2010; Kotb, Hoda. *Hoda: How I Survived War Zones, Bad Hair, Cancer, and Kathie Lee* (with Jane Lorenzini), 2010

Selected Books: *Hoda: How I Survived War Zones, Bad Hair, Cancer, and Kathie Lee* (with Jane Lorenzini), 2010

Selected Television Shows: *Dateline NBC*, 1998–; *Your Total Health*, 2004–08; *Today*, 2007–

Courtesy of DuPont

Kullman, Ellen J.

Jan. 22, 1956– Businesswoman

Address: E. I. DuPont de Nemours & Co., 1 Righter Pkwy., #3200, Wilmington, DE 19803-1510

Since January 2009 Ellen Kullman has been the chief executive officer (CEO) of the global firm E.I. DuPont de Nemours & Co. The Wilmington, Delaware–based chemical company, best known simply as DuPont, is involved in product manufacturing and innovation in the fields of nutrition, electronics, agriculture, safety and protection, and transportation, among others. Kullman joined DuPont in 1988, as a marketing manager, and moved up the company's ranks to positions including vice president and general manager of DuPont's mineral-products division, executive vice president in charge of DuPont Safety and Protection, and company president; at the end of 2009, while retaining the title of CEO, she became chair of DuPont's board. Kullman is the first female CEO in the company's 200-year history and one of the few women to head a *Fortune* 500 company. While nearly every financial journalist made sure to mention those facts in the stories announcing her promotion to CEO, Kullman steered discussions toward her skills and vision as a leader. In an interview with *Chemical Week* (November 22, 2010), Kullman said that her approach to management is based on "a belief in setting clear goals and objectives, and then giving my colleagues the resources and support to achieve them. As a leader, I also encourage all my colleagues to focus on what we can control; to be willing to accept change and adjust;

to communicate clearly and often; and to always maintain pride around our work. I value transparency and accountability. I emphasize the importance of an external focus, always aware of how we're doing opposite the competition, and of understanding the immediate realities and future opportunities in the markets in which we operate. I expect all this to be accomplished while advancing the core values that are the foundation of our company." In advancing those values, Kullman told the *Chemical Week* interviewer, "my focus is on growth through market-driven science that responds to the megatrends we've identified where DuPont innovation will make a difference in the lives of people around the world." Those "megatrends" are the increasingly urgent needs to supply food to the world's growing population, end the nation's reliance on fossil fuels, ensure the health of the environment, and explore growing markets, particularly in developing countries.

Taking over as CEO amid the recent global economic recession, Kullman moved to cut DuPont's costs by eliminating thousands of staff and contract jobs and reducing the number of layers in the management hierarchy. At the same time she was careful to continue funding research and development. Her approach appears to have succeeded: after reporting a sharp reduction in earnings in 2009, the company rebounded in 2010, with revenues up 21 percent. Kullman has received many honors from the financial press, being included on *Forbes* magazine's list of the World's 100 most powerful women, the *Wall Street Journal* roundup of 50 women to watch, and *Fortune* magazine's list of the 50 most powerful women in business.

The youngest of four siblings in an Irish-American family, Kullman was born Ellen Jamison on January 22, 1956 in Wilmington. Her father, Joseph, founded and ran a landscaping-contracting business, Brandywine Nurseries, where her mother, Margaret, was in charge of the bookkeeping and office operations. Kullman's brother Brien, who currently operates the company with another sibling, Joseph Jr., said about his sister to Andrew Eder and Eric Ruth for the Wilmington *News Journal* (September 24, 2008), "I always tell everybody I always thought she was the smartest one of the four of us. Whenever she ever put her mind to anything, she always carried it through 100 percent."

Kullman attended St. Mary Magdalen School and then the Tower Hill School, a college-prep institution in Wilmington, where among other activities she played lacrosse and basketball. Standing five feet nine inches, Kullman "could out-jump the six-footers" in basketball, she told Bob Yearick for *Delaware Today* (June 2009, on-line). Her coach, Patty Marshall, recalled to Yearick, "She was an aggressive player, a good rebounder. She was smart and knew how to box out, get good position. She got beat up pretty good at times, but she could give as well as she got." Kullman's history teacher, Ed Hughes, saw how interested she was in math and science and encouraged her to apply to a college with a good engineering program. "Hughes really helped me understand that my interest and love for science and math weren't a bad thing," she told Richard Sine for the Wilmington *News Journal* (October 26, 2004).

Kullman attended Tufts University, in Medford, Massachusetts, where she received a B.S. degree in mechanical engineering in 1978. After graduating she worked in technical service and sales at the Westinghouse Electric Co. In 1983 Kullman earned an M.B.A. degree from Northwestern University, in Illinois. That year she joined the General Electric Co. (GE), where she held business-development, marketing, and sales jobs.

In 1988 Kullman was hired as a marketing manager by the medical-imaging division of DuPont. DuPont was founded in 1802 as a company that manufactured gunpowder. Early in the next century, the company's focus shifted to chemicals, materials such as synthetic rubber, and energy. Today DuPont operates in approximately 90 countries and employs 60,000 people. In 1990 Kullman was promoted to the position of business director of DuPont's X-ray-film division. Two years later she became its global business director for electronic imaging and printing. In 1994, by which point she had married Michael Kullman and given birth to a daughter and twin sons, Kullman was promoted to the position of global business director of the white-pigment and mineral-products division. The following year she assumed the posts of vice president and general manager of that unit, becoming the first woman in DuPont's history to hold the position of vice president. Kullman often worked 12-hour days and spent about 40 percent of her job-related time on the road. The company allowed her to work from home several days per week so she could spend more time with her children. Kullman stayed on as vice president and general manager as she moved through various DuPont divisions: safety resources (1998–99), which she launched; bio-based materials (1999–2000); and DuPont Flooring Systems & DuPont Surfaces (2001–02).

For four years starting in 2002, Kullman served as the group vice president of DuPont Safety & Protection, a division of the company that offers safety consulting to businesses and government agencies and oversees the development of safety products for those in high-risk professions, such as firefighters and police officers. In that position she increased her department's sales from $3.5 billion to $5.5 billion. Summarizing a speech Kullman gave on the importance of worker safety, David Elbert wrote for the *Des Moines (Iowa) Register* (September 6, 2003): "While DuPont products like flexible Kevlar gloves help protect workers from workplace injuries, the key to workplace safety is persuading top managers that safety pays. . . . Safe workplaces add to corporate profits by reducing downtime resulting from equipment shutdowns and from having to train new workers to replace injured employees. . . . Safety also boosts worker morale, which also increases productivity. . . .

One management technique DuPont uses to reduce on-the-job injuries is peer groups for enforcement of workplace rules. . . . The company found that peer groups are more effective, and often harsher in handing out punishment, than managers were. Peer groups . . . are 'closer to the problem' and are potential victims of a co-worker's lapse of judgment. The group's personal stake makes them effective enforcers of safety rules."

In 2005 DuPont established a Consumer Products group, which under Kullman's direction made products for the consumer market with a focus on three areas: outdoor activities (items such as pool-cleaning products), surfaces (products for car surfaces and floors), and home and safety (water filters, oven mitts, and other such products). DuPont was well-known for manufacturing items crucial to the functioning of other companies' products—for example, its Teflon is used by other companies for nonstick coatings—but the company also sought to use its brand name to sell its own line of consumer products. In 2006 Kullman was promoted to executive vice president for DuPont Safety & Protection, DuPont Coatings and Color Technology, corporate marketing and sales, and safety and sustainability.

From October 1 to December 31, 2008, Kullman served as DuPont's president, and on January 1, 2009 she became the company's CEO. At the end of that year, in addition to the CEO position, Kullman became the company's chairman. She succeeded the outgoing CEO, Charles Holliday, who had held that post since 1998. Much was made of the fact that Kullman was the first woman to lead DuPont. Kullman, for her part, downplayed the significance of gender. "I'm not sure being a woman adds or detracts from it," she told Robert Westervelt for *Chemical Week* (September 29, 2008). "My management style is my own."

Kullman began her tenure as DuPont's president only months after the beginning of the worldwide economic crisis. The tough economic climate led to some tough choices. In December 2008 the company announced that it would lay off about 2,500 employees (about 4 percent of its workforce) as well as 4,000 contract workers. The cuts focused largely on the declining construction and automotive industries. In May 2009, with Kullman as CEO, DuPont announced that it would lay off 2,000 more employees; by that point the company had also cut a total of 10,000 contract workers. Kullman's efforts to reduce costs were not limited to terminating lower-level employees. In June 2009, after discussing with her senior executives possible reductions in management posts, Kullman eliminated DuPont's vice-president positions and gave oversight powers to three top leaders; she also consolidated the company's 23 businesses into 13. In July the company announced that its year-to-date cost reductions had reached about $600 million, more than half of its projected goal.

In an interview with Andrew Eder for the Wilmington *News Journal* (December 6, 2009), Kullman said, "You always question yourself, are you doing enough? Are you doing too much? Where are you drawing that line? And what position are you in when the recovery starts to respond?" Some critics believed that Kullman was cutting too many jobs. In an interview with Eder, Kenneth Henley, general counsel for the International Brotherhood of DuPont Workers, which represents company employees in five states, said, "There was a dire situation, but the reaction to it was shortsighted and counterproductive." Henley pointed out that at the time of the article's publication, as business had begun to improve, DuPont was paying 30 percent overtime to workers and was giving severance pay to those who were cut, which led him to conclude that the company's costs were higher than they would have been had Kullman not made so many cuts. He added, "I really feel there was a short-term perspective, and an effort to satisfy investors and the financial community." Many analysts and investors, however, praised Kullman's initiatives, particularly as DuPont emerged in 2010 as a company with one of the highest-performing stocks and remained so in 2011.

In addition to shedding jobs and lowering expenses in other ways, Kullman focused on the four "megatrends" of the world's economy, which Eder summarized as "the increasing demand for food, the need to protect people and the environment, the desire to lessen dependence on fossil fuels and the growth of emerging markets." With the first goal in mind, Kullman led DuPont in a months-long acquisition negotiation with the Danish food-ingredients maker Danisco. In January 2010 DuPont offered to purchase the company for $5.8 billion, an offer Danisco's shareholders rejected. In April Kullman upped the offer to $6.3 billion. Once that offer was accepted, in May, DuPont started the process of integrating the company. Kullman received praise for her handling of the Danisco deal, DuPont's first major purchase under her leadership—and the largest since the company's acquisition of the agricultural-seed marketer Pioneer Hi-Bred, in 1999. In April 2011 DuPont announced that its first-quarter earnings were higher than expected: DuPont earned $1.43 billion, $1.36 per share higher than analysts had predicted. The company's Latin American sales increased by 30 percent; agricultural sales, thanks in part to farmers' buying DuPont's genetically modified seeds, went up 18 percent; and chemical sales, due in part to paint makers' purchases of titanium dioxide (a paint ingredient), went up 27 percent. Speaking with Bob Yearick, Kullman, looking ahead to taking on the role of CEO, had said: "I think we have a strong foundation in science. Now the challenge is to build on top of that—to build out the businesses in our applied bioscience area, to build out the businesses further in agriculture, and to really see how that foundation in science can add tremendous opportunities for top-line growth and real differentiation." That indeed appears to be the direction in which she is leading the company.

Richard Sine reported that Kullman "credits her outgoing personality in helping her assert herself in male-dominated worlds." Kullman said to Sine that she "never viewed [herself] as different" in those worlds. "I think that helps because you're not looking for [signs of gender prejudice], you're saying, 'Hey, let it go.' And if I'm comfortable, everybody else is comfortable." She added, "I'm not shy, that helps as well." Kullman's husband, Michael, is the head of global marketing at DuPont. The couple live in Wilmington. They have three children: Maggie, Stephen, and David. Kullman's children have all, like their mother, participated in team sports. "I tell my kids," Kullman said to Yearick, "you don't always get to choose who you work with or play with, but you get to choose how you interact with them and work with them. So I think [that as a team player] you learn a lot about working with people and understanding different people's skills and strengths and weaknesses and how then you can work together to create a better outcome."

—D.K.

Suggested Reading: *Chemical Week* p8 Sep. 29, 2008, p32 Nov. 22, 2010; *Des Moines (Iowa) Register* D p1 Sep. 6, 2003; dupont.com; (Wilmington, Delaware) *News Journal* Dec. 6, 2009

Kurtz, Howard

Aug. 1, 1953– Journalist; writer

Address: Reliable Sources, CNN, One CNN Center, Atlanta, GA 30303

Howard Kurtz is "probably the most important media reporter in America, and with good reason," Franklin Foer wrote for the *New Republic* (May 15, 2000), where Foer was then senior editor. "He's not only tireless," Foer continued; "he's an unusually gifted newshound." Similarly, Alex Jones, a Pulitzer Prize–winning journalist and Harvard University educator, told Garrett M. Graff for the *Washingtonian* (July 2005) that Kurtz is the country's "most influential media reporter." "I don't think anyone does what Howard Kurtz does, certainly not with the energy, zest, and passion," he added. The *New Yorker* writer Steve Coll, a colleague of Kurtz's when both men worked for the *Washington Post*, told Graff, "Howard works more efficiently and energetically than any other reporter I've ever worked with. It's almost weird. What he demonstrates is that all of the rest of us, without ever being aware of it, waste a lot of time over the course of the day."

For two years early in his career (1976–78), Kurtz did legwork for the muckraking investigative reporter Jack Anderson, arguably the journalist

Brendan Hoffman/Getty Images

Howard Kurtz

most feared by Washington, D.C., movers and shakers and the most popular political columnist of his time. Kurtz spent three years with the *Washington Star* before joining the *Washington Post*, in 1981, when the *Star* folded. He began writing the *Post*'s "Media Notes" column in 1990. During his 29 years with the *Post*, he wrote thousands of columns and news articles and, on his own time, five books. Starting in 2000 Kurtz also participated in a weekly hourlong on-line chat with *Post* readers and wrote a five-day-a-week blog for the newspaper.

Kurtz's last *Washington Post* article, published on October 18, 2010 as a "Media Notes Extra," was headed "Bloggers Are Scooping Sleaze into the Mainstream News World." In it Kurtz announced that he was leaving the world of print journalism to become the Washington, D.C., bureau chief of the two-year-old Web site the *Daily Beast*—"an evolutionary move, not a revolutionary one, as we all grasp for ways to sustain and reinvent journalism," he wrote. In his new job he monitors the *Daily Beast*'s coverage of government and politics and writes about "the intersection of politics and the media," according to a CNN.com profile of him. Since 1998 Kurtz has hosted CNN's one-hour Sunday-morning interview program *Reliable Sources*, which casts a critical eye on the American media.

Although on occasion Kurtz faulted the *Washington Post*'s coverage of newsworthy events, and at times he has questioned the rightness of CNN's offerings and operations, he has long been accused of conflicts of interest in his role of media watchdog. And although he has refused to reveal publicly his ideological preferences, he has sometimes been charged with having a right-wing bias. Such

accusations intensified after his marriage, in 2003, to Sheri Annis, his second wife, a Republican media consultant and political commentator. Those criticisms notwithstanding, in 2004 Kurtz won the Mongerson Prize for Investigative Reporting from the Medill School of Journalism at Northwestern University.

The son of Leonard and Marcia (Turetzky) Kurtz, Howard Alan Kurtz was born on August 1, 1953 in the New York City borough of Brooklyn. His father worked in the clothing business; his mother was a homemaker. His parents still live in the Brooklyn apartment in which he grew up with his younger sister, Barbara; his grandmothers lived nearby, and he visited them regularly. As a fourth grader, according to Garrett M. Graff, he starred in a play he wrote himself. He loved *X-Men*, *Spider-Man*, and other comic-book series and created some of his own, with unflattering depictions of classmates and teachers. He earned excellent grades but irritated his teachers with his excessive talking. During his high-school years, Kurtz played electric organ in a rock band and pickup basketball games and held odd jobs. In his senior year his classmates voted him "most likely to succeed," after he campaigned for that designation with signs showing a shapely young woman saying, "Boys! If you vote for Howie Kurtz, I'll want to thank each and every one of you personally."

In 1970 Kurtz enrolled at the State University of New York (SUNY)–Buffalo, where he earned a B.A. degree in English in 1974. As a freshman he joined the staff of the thrice-weekly campus newspaper, the *Spectrum*, and as a senior he served as its editor. He wrote editorials fiercely critical of the school's administrators and of the policies of U.S. president Richard Nixon. On October 10, 1973 Kurtz ordered the printing of an extra issue of the *Spectrum*, to report the resignation of Vice President Spiro Agnew. The Pulitzer Prize–winning investigative journalist Gary Cohn, whose *Spectrum* career coincided with Kurtz's, told Graff that Kurtz "had high standards. He wanted the paper to be good and fair. I never saw anyone who could write so many stories, and good stories. I've worked with a lot of people who were fast and never seen anything like it since." "My four years on the *Spectrum* is what got me into journalism," Kurtz told Graff. During his senior year Kurtz attended a talk given at SUNY–Buffalo by the newspaper columnist Jack Anderson, who won a Pulitzer Prize in 1972 for national reporting. Impressed by Kurtz's pointed questions, Anderson arranged for Kurtz to have an unpaid summer internship with him in Washington, D.C. The Watergate scandal was then big news, and Kurtz was working for Anderson when the scandel led President Nixon to resign, on August 8, 1974.

In 1975 Kurtz earned a master's degree at the Columbia University School of Journalism. Soon afterward he landed a job at the *Record* (often referred to as the *Bergen Record*), a daily newspaper for residents of Bergen County, a densely populated part of northern New Jersey. He was assigned to the night shift, from 5:00 p.m. to 1:00 a.m., and reported on happenings in two small towns. The *Washington Post* staff writer Marc Kaufman, a colleague of Kurtz's at the *Record*, recalled to Graff, "Howie was among the most talented and aggressive reporters to come through there." Kurtz left the *Record* in 1976 to accept a full-time job, for less pay, with Anderson and the senior investigative reporter Leslie Whitten; the column co-written by Anderson and Whitten, "Washington Merry-Go-Round," was syndicated to some 700 newspapers with 45 million readers. Anderson and Whitten's assistants at that time included such budding journalists as Brit Hume, Jon Lee Anderson, Gary Cohn, and Michael Kranish, all of whom, like Kurtz, conducted interviews and researched back-up material for the column. According to Graff, "Even in an ambitious group, Kurtz stood out," for his tenacity, productivity, and knack for getting scoops.

Eager to see his own byline in print, Kurtz left Anderson and Whitten in 1978 to become a reporter for the *Washington Star*, the capital city's once-great afternoon daily, which had been sold to Time Inc. earlier that year after a steady decline in ad sales and readership. The *Star*'s well-regarded writers at that time included Jonathan Yardley, Michael Isikoff, Jack Germond, Mary McGrory, Fred Hiatt, and Jules Witcover and such up-and-comers as Maureen Dowd and Jane Mayer. In mid-1981 the *Washington Star* went bankrupt and ended publication, after 130 years. Immediately afterward, along with a half-dozen other unemployed *Star* reporters, Kurtz joined the *Washington Post*, at the invitation of the *Post*'s then–metropolitan editor, Bob Woodward (who, with his *Post* colleague Carl Bernstein, had made a name for himself as an investigative reporter during the Watergate scandal). Kurtz's first *Post* promotion brought him to the paper's national desk, where he covered Capitol Hill and the Justice Department. In 1982 and 1986 he earned a Front Page Award from the Washington-Baltimore Newspaper Guild. In 1987 he was named the *Post*'s New York City bureau chief. His three years in that job, Kurtz told Graff, "may have been the most fun I've ever had in this business. . . . New York has this larger-than-life quality, where it contains all of the country's problems writ large with an extra layer of weirdness. I felt that I was in a unique position to understand New York because I'd grown up there, but I had to push myself journalistically to peel back the layers of this municipal onion."

When, in 1990, the *Post*'s first-ever media correspondent, Eleanor Randolph, moved to another *Post* job, Kurtz succeeded her as the newspaper's media reporter. At that time few newspapers or magazines besides the *Post*, the *New York Times* and the *Los Angeles Times* had journalists on staff devoted solely to media news and assessments of the media's performance and influence. Decades earlier, in 1927, the writer Robert Benchley had

launched a column called "The Wayward Press" in the *New Yorker* magazine, but it had appeared only sporadically. Then, for 18 years beginning in 1946, the *New Yorker* published 83 "Wayward Press" columns written by A. J. Liebling, whose critiques of the daily press were noted for their wit and literary polish. In assuming Randolph's mantle, Kurtz broadened his purview over the years to include Internet posts as well as the content of the print media and television, on subjects ranging from celebrity scandals to newly published books to political campaigns. Commenting to Graff on Kurtz's writing style and productivity, Jack Shafer, who writes the column "Press Box" for *Slate.com*, referred to the famous *New Yorker* writer Roger Angell: "Of course Kurtz is no A. J. Liebling in the same way that the beat reporter is not Roger Angell writing on baseball. Roger Angell gets to write about the World Series four months after it happened, and Liebling got to pick his stories and write at length about them. Kurtz is in the trenches, like an ink-stained wretch—writing every other day, breaking stories, and adding string to stories"—that is, tying up loose ends.

On October 5, 2010 Ned Martel, Marcus Brauchli, and Liz Spayd, the *Washington Post*'s style editor, executive editor, and managing editor, respectively, sent a memo to the newspaper's staff announcing that Kurtz was leaving the *Post* to join the *Daily Beast*. In their memo the editors wrote that as the *Post*'s media specialist, Kurtz had "covered not just journalists but the folks in the political sphere who try to steer the conversation—White House press secretaries, campaign strategists, gossip bloggers, late-night talk-show hosts," and that he had "marshall[ed] fresh evidence not just daily but hourly about the powerhouses, personalities and opinion-shapers of the media world." They also wrote, "He has become known as a straight-shooter by every anchor and editor and reporter who has been on the other end of his inquiries. He bravely covered the very organization he has called home and won the respect and independence that can only come with consistently solid and fair reporting."

Others have complained that as the host of a show on CNN, the *Post* media-reporter Kurtz could not avoid a conflict of interest, and some have questioned his neutrality as an interviewer. Prominent among Kurtz's critics is the journalist Eric Alterman, whose column, "The Liberal Media," has appeared in the *Nation* since 1995. In his book *What Liberal Media?* (2003), Alterman declared, "Whatever his personal ideology may be, it is hard to avoid the conclusion, based on an examination of his work, that Kurtz loves conservatives but has little time for liberals." In a passage from *What Liberal Media?* published earlier in the *Nation* (February 24, 2001), Alterman offered examples of that alleged bias in interviews in which Kurtz discussed actions of President Bill Clinton and President George W. Bush. Regarding the former, Alterman wrote, "Kurtz even went so far as to give credence to the ludicrous, [Rush] Limbaugh-like insistence that somehow Bill Clinton caused the corporate meltdown of the summer of 2002." Regarding Bush, Alterman wrote, Kurtz "demanded of his guests, 'Why is the press resurrecting, like that 7-million-year-old human skull, this thirteen-year-old incident, in which Bush sold some stock in his company Harken Energy?'"

In what was presented as an example of Kurtz's conflict of interest, Jacques Steinberg penned an article for the *New York Times* (May 29, 2008) headlined "CNN Reporter's Interview Raises Ethical Questions." In it Steinberg wrote that Kurtz had not been a "disinterested interviewer" four days earlier when he talked with Kimberly Dozier on *Reliable Sources*. Kurtz's interview with Dozier focused on his guest's memoir, *Breathing the Fire*, which recounted the incident in which Dozier, as a CBS journalist, was critically wounded while on assignment in Iraq: "Mr. Kurtz's wife, Sheri Annis, had been paid to serve as a publicist for Ms. Dozier's memoir," Steinberg reported—a fact that Kurtz had not mentioned until the end of the interview. In another incident that raised questions about Kurtz's journalistic neutrality, the anonymous reporter who maintains the Web site *Inside Cable News* (*ICN*) complained on July 11, 2010 about Kurtz's omissions on *Reliable Sources* that morning. Kurtz had briefly mentioned but had failed to discuss CNN's July 7 firing of Octavia Nasr, an Arabic-speaking Lebanese journalist, who had served for two decades as CNN's senior editor for Middle East news. CNN ousted her three days after she had written on Twitter that she was "sad to hear of the passing of Sayyed Mohammad Hussein Fadlallah. One of Hezbollah's giants I respect a lot." (The U.S. government considers Hezbollah a terrorist group, and Fadlallah had openly praised Arab murderers of Israelis; he had also called for equal rights for Arab women.) Kurtz offered "no analysis or commentary," the *ICN* reporter complained. "This would not appear to be so galling if Kurtz hadn't devoted an entire segment to Levi Johnston apologizing to Sarah Palin and another to Rush Limbaugh talking about how Barack Obama would have been a tour guide in Hawaii instead of President if he weren't black. The Nasr story was tailor made for *Reliable Sources* to cover. . . . Would the story have been treated differently if the subject wasn't a former CNN employee?"

Kurtz's first piece for the *Daily Beast*, posted on October 24, 2010, described the mood among President Barack Obama's White House staff in the days preceding the year's midterm elections. On the night of the election (November 2), Kurtz participated in a live *Daily Beast* chat. Later that month for the *Daily Beast*, Kurtz conducted a two-part interview with the former Republican political consultant Roger Ailes, who is currently the chairman and chief executive officer of Fox News and the chairman of Fox Television Stations. On the November 28, 2010 installment of *Reliable Sources*, Kurtz discussed the recent on-line deluge of seemingly trivial news. His guests for that installment were Paul Steinhauser, CNN's deputy political director, who writes for the "CNN Political Ticker"; Ana Marie Cox, a *GQ* columnist; and Michael Shear, the lead writer for the *New York Times* "Caucus Blog."

Kurtz's first book, *Media Circus: The Trouble with America's Newspaper*s (1993), became required reading in many college journalism classes. For his second book, *Hot Air: All Talk, All the Time* (1996), Kurtz interviewed many U.S. television and radio talk-show hosts. In a representative assessment of *Hot Air*, Mark Hertsgaard wrote for the *New York Times Book Review* (March 3, 1996), "A wealth of anecdotes, personality sketches and behind-the-cameras eavesdropping makes his book smooth and undemanding reading. What is lacking, unfortunately, is depth and rigor." The title of Kurtz's third book, *Spin Cycle: How the White House and the Media Manipulate the News*, was changed to *Spin Cycle: Inside the Clinton Propaganda Machine* soon after its publication, in 1998. It reached bookstores only a few days after public revelations about President Bill Clinton's intimate relations with Monica Lewinsky during the latter's stint as a White House intern, and it became a bestseller. Kurtz's next book was *The Fortune Tellers: Inside Wall Street's Game of Money, Media, and Manipulation* (2000). To research it he spent 18 months "at the elbows of the new breed of cable and Internet Wall Street journalists and, equally important, the 'analysts' who pop up on screen and push their products, often without disclosing their own financial interests," James Boylan wrote for the *Columbia Journalism Review* (September/October 2000). A reviewer for the *Economist* (October 28, 2000) recommended *The Fortune Tellers* as "essential reading for anyone who gets their share tips off the telly—or who worries about the consequences of the rise of the individual investor." Kurtz's most recent book, *Reality Show: Inside the Last Great Television News War* (2007), is about the rivalries among CBS, NBC, and ABC television-news anchors.

Kurtz and his second wife, Sheri Annis, live in Chevy Chase, Maryland, with their daughter, Abby, who was born in 2004. Annis is the president of Fourth Estate Strategies; according to the company's Web site, she previously served as "the spokeswoman for California's Proposition 227, the successful measure to eliminate California's failed bilingual education programs" and "played a major role in California's Proposition 209 campaign, which eliminated race and gender-based preferences in government hiring, contracting and education." From his marriage in 1979 to Mary Tallmer, a social worker, which ended in divorce, Kurtz has two daughters, Judy and Bonnie.

—C.C.

Suggested Reading: *American Journalism Review* p31+ Mar. 1994; CNN.com/CNN/anchors; *New Republic* p26+ May 15, 2000; *New York Times* C

p1+ Nov. 2, 2005; *UBToday* (on-line)
Spring/Summer 1998; *Washingtonian* p44+ July
2005

Selected Books: *Media Circus: The Trouble with
America's Newspapers*, 1993; *Hot Air: All Talk,
All the Time*, 1996; *Spin Cycle: How the White
House and the Media Manipulate the News* (also
published as *Spin Cycle: Inside the Clinton
Propaganda Machine*), 1998; *The Fortune
Tellers: Inside Wall Street's Game of Money,
Media, and Manipulation*, 2000; *Reality Show:
Inside the Last Great Television News War*, 2007

Lady Antebellum

Country-music group

Haywood, Dave
*July 5, 1982– Singer; songwriter; multi-
instrumentalist*

Kelley, Charles
Sep. 11, 1981– Singer; songwriter

Scott, Hillary
Apr. 1, 1986– Singer; songwriter

*Address: c/o Capitol Records Nashville, 3322 W.
End Ave. #11, Nashville, TN 37203*

Despite being firmly grounded in country music,
Lady Antebellum has cultivated a style that incorporates elements from the pop, rock, R&B, and soul
genres, which has helped the group achieve wide
appeal. Consisting of co-lead vocalists Charles Kelley and Hillary Scott and backup vocalist and multi-instrumentalist Dave Haywood, Lady Antebellum—known to fans simply as "Lady A"—has
enjoyed a meteoric rise to the top of the music
world since its formation in Nashville, Tennessee,
in 2006. The group made its recording debut in
2007, as backup vocalists on the pop pianist Jim
Brickman's hit single "Never Alone," before winning a contract with Capitol Records Nashville and
releasing the debut single "Love Don't Live Here"
later that year. In April 2008, after months of eager
anticipation in the country-music world, Lady
Antebellum released its self-titled first album,
which debuted at number one on the *Billboard*
country-albums chart, marking the first time a new
group or duo had achieved that milestone in 45
years. The record quickly went platinum, spawn-
ing the group's first number-one hit single, "I Run
to You," which achieved crossover status. Lady
Antebellum's second studio album, *Need You Now*
(2010), topped the *Billboard* 200 and country-
album charts. Propelled by the success of its lead
single, the title track, *Need You Now* became the
second-best-selling album of 2010 (behind

Eminem's *Recovery*) and has been certified triple-
platinum by the Recording Industry Association of
America (RIAA). Lady Antebellum's rapid rise in
popularity culminated in its appearance at the 53d
Annual Grammy Awards ceremony, on February
13, 2011, where the trio performed a medley of
songs and took home the Grammy for album of the
year, as well as four prizes for the single "Need You
Now."

Known for their songwriting prowess, the members of the trio wrote or co-wrote most of the songs
on their studio albums. Haywood, considered the
group's musical anchor, explained to Brandy Mc-
Donnell for the Oklahoma City *Oklahoman* (June
11, 2010), "I think at the core of everything we do
is our songwriting. I think that's where our chemistry starts, and our friendship has grown out of
that." He continued, "I think people just like good
music, and all we want to do is just try to write music that we feel like is great and hopefully people
respond to it. The one thing that's remained true
across the history of country—if you look at it from
the '30s and '40s of Roy Acuff and Bill Monroe, all
the way to now—it's songs about real life. And a lot
of pop music doesn't hit on that."

The first of the three children of Van Haywood,
a dentist and dentistry professor, and Angie Haywood, a schoolteacher, Dave Haywood was born
on July 5, 1982 in Augusta, Georgia. He spent the
first decade of his life in Chapel Hill, North Carolina, where his father taught at the University of
North Carolina's School of Dentistry. Haywood's
father was a pioneer in the development of teeth-
whitening procedures in the 1980s and is credited
with inventing the now widely used night-guard
teeth-whitening method. In an interview with
Mary Colurso for the *Birmingham (Alabama) News*
(May 8, 2009), Dave Haywood described his father,
who now teaches at the School of Dentistry of the
Medical College of Georgia, as a "rock star" of dentistry, "the Bruce Springsteen of the dental world."
Haywood's family, which includes his younger sister, Lisa, and his younger brother, Michael, is also
musical. His mother taught him to play the piano
when he was in elementary school, and his father
taught him guitar in middle school; around that
time he also started playing the clarinet. Haywood
often harmonized with his parents and siblings on
long car trips and also sang in the youth choir at
Trinity-on-the-Hill United Methodist Church, in
Augusta. As a child he was a fan of such country-
inflected rock acts as the Allman Brothers Band
and the Eagles, both known for songs with multi-
vocal harmonies.

Haywood moved back to Augusta with his family in 1993. At Riverside Middle School in Evans,
Georgia, an affluent Augusta suburb, he met and
befriended his future bandmate Charles Kelley.
The son of Gayle and John W. Kelley, a cardiologist, Charles Kelley was born on September 11,
1981. His interest in music was sparked when he
was very young by his older brothers, John and
Josh, who exposed him to a wide range of musical

Jason Kempin/Getty Images

Lady Antebellum (l. to r.): Dave Haywood, Hillary Scott, Charles Kelley

styles. As teenagers Charles and Josh Kelley formed a southern-rock outfit called Inside Blue with two local musicians, Pat Blanchard Jr. and Adam Hatfield; Charles served as the group's lead vocalist and drummer, while Josh played the electric guitar. The group performed at local venues and recorded a five-song CD that caught the attention of the legendary soul singer James Brown, who wanted to sign them to a record deal. "He loved our songs, but they wanted to change everything, so my dad and brother said 'no deal,'" Josh Kelley recalled, in a biography posted on his official Web site. "I'm glad they did that because it afforded both me and Charles the opportunity to grow up and see the world and really have things to write about."

Haywood and Kelley attended Lakeside High School, in Evans. Haywood was a member of the tennis team and played in a jazz band with Josh Kelley, while Charles Kelley was a member of the golf team. As seniors Haywood was voted "most talented" and Charles Kelley "best all-around" by their classmates. Upon graduating from Lakeside High, in 2000, Haywood and Kelley both attended the University of Georgia (UGA) at Athens, where they began their musical partnership. Haywood recalled to Erin Zureick for the *Augusta Chronicle* (November 14, 2010), "When we were in college, I was roommates with his best friend, so I literally saw him every day at the house. He would come over, and I would just be playing guitar. I remember one day our senior year he came over and said, 'What was that chord progression that you were playing?' I said it was just a little something, and he said, 'Play it again,' and started humming some-

thing. . . . We ended up writing our first song senior year together." Haywood and Kelley both graduated from UGA in 2004, earning degrees in management systems and finance, respectively.

After graduating Haywood landed a computer-security position in Atlanta, and Kelley worked in construction with his brother John in Winston-Salem, North Carolina. Those nonmusical pursuits were short-lived, however. "I was miserable," Haywood told Doug Pullen for the *El Paso (Texas) Times* (March 20, 2009). In mid-2005 Kelley left his construction job and moved to Nashville to pursue a music career. In 2006 he invited Haywood to join him there. Staying at the home of Kelley's brother Josh, who had already launched a successful pop-music career (he is known for such hit singles as "Amazing" and "Only You"), the duo began writing songs and performing at local venues. In May of that year, Kelley was approached by Hillary Scott, an aspiring singer and songwriter, who recognized him at a popular Nashville music bar called 12th & Porter. Recalling their meeting, Scott told Janis Fontaine for the *Palm Beach (Florida) Post* (January 27, 2009), "I was working on a solo career. Then I discovered . . . Josh Kelley on My-Space Music . . . and that led me to listen to Charles' stuff. He had something that caught not just my eye, but my ear. One night out in Nashville I recognized him and told him I really like his music."

The elder daughter of two veterans of country music, the singers Linda Davis and Lang Scott, Hillary Dawn Scott was born on April 1, 1986. Her sister, Rylee Jean, was born in 2000. Scott grew up in Nashville, where she enjoyed a rich musical upbringing. Her mother enjoyed mild success as one-half of the country act Skip & Linda before touring as a backup singer for Reba McEntire in the 1980s and '90s. Linda Davis is perhaps best known for her 1993 number-one country duet with McEntire, "Does He Love You," which won a Grammy Award for best country vocal collaboration. Lang Scott also performed with McEntire, spending eight years as a backup vocalist and guitarist in her touring band. Hillary Scott told Martin Bandyke for the *Detroit (Michigan) Free Press* (August 20, 2009) that as a child she wanted "to do everything but be a musician. I wanted to be a nurse, I wanted to be a chef. It probably changed weekly." Music, though, was always an integral part of her life. "It's ingrained in me, like another arm," she told David Menconi for the Raleigh, North Carolina, *News & Observer* (September 23, 2010). She began to develop her voice in high school, and after performing alongside her parents for three years in the Linda Davis Family Christmas Show, an annual event in Nashville, she decided to pursue music as a career. After graduating from Nashville's Donelson Christian Academy, in 2004, she enrolled at Middle Tennessee State University (MTSU), in Murfreesboro, where she studied music business and management. Concurrently, Scott pursued a solo career in Nashville. She caught the attention of several music labels after working with the country-music singer Victoria Shaw. She also auditioned for the reality television series *American Idol* twice but failed both times to advance past the first round. When Scott met Kelley, in 2006, she had just completed her sophomore year at MTSU and had recently failed to land what would have been her first major record deal. She later explained, in a biography posted on Lady Antebellum's official Web site, "Being a solo artist wasn't for me. I wasn't cut out for it. I didn't handle the pressure at all."

Scott, Kelley, and Haywood began as a songwriting team, but a desire to perform together led them to form Lady Antebellum. "It didn't take but one show and we knew that this was what we needed to do," Kelley told Brian Mansfield for *USA Today* (August 1, 2008). Scott told Menconi: "The timing of everything has been pretty amazing. . . . It's not like anyone approached us and said, 'You need to meet this person; your voices would sound great together.' It was very much a natural progression into becoming a band, and we've always respected that aspect of how it all happened. It's been kind of amazing. Like something bigger than us has been running the ship." The trio settled on its name after being photographed in front of a majestic, southern-style antebellum home on a publicity shoot. Lady Antebellum began making the rounds on the Nashville club circuit, and before long the group was noticed by Gary Borman, a manager who has worked with Keith Urban and James Taylor, among other major artists. Borman signed Lady Antebellum as a client before the group had even obtained a record deal, impressed by the trio's "vitality, commitment to songwriting and the quality of the songs they were coming [up] with," as he told Ken Tucker for *Billboard* (January 9, 2010, on-line). He added, "It was different than anything I'd heard."

Lady Antebellum's recording debut as guest vocalists came on Jim Brickman's "Never Alone," which was released as a single in 2007 and was included on the next year's reissue of his 2002 record *Valentine.* The song reached number 14 on the *Billboard* adult-contemporary chart. In June of that year, the group signed a recording contract with Capitol Records Nashville. In October Lady Antebellum released its first single, "Love Don't Live Here," which reached number three on the *Billboard* country-singles chart. A self-titled debut album followed in April 2008. Co-produced by Paul Worley and Victoria Shaw, the album entered *Billboard*'s country-albums chart at number one and the *Billboard* 200 chart at number four. The album received mostly favorable reviews, with many critics complimenting the unique vocal interplay between Kelley and Scott. In a review for the All Music Guide Web site, William Ruhlmann wrote, "Kelley has a sturdy country baritone, but he sometimes sounds a bit too pleased with his own rich tone and comes off mannered. Scott, by contrast, seems to know that her voice can't match Kelley's for distinctiveness, so she works harder at coming up with striking phrasing and emotional force. The contrast gives their duets a chemistry that is the band's strongest element."

Just a month after the release of its debut, Lady Antebellum won the prize for best new duo or group at the Academy of Country Music (ACM) Awards ceremony. The trio went on to be named, collectively, best new artist at the Country Music Association (CMA) Awards ceremony and earned Grammy nominations for best new artist and best country performance by a duo or group, for the song "Love Don't Live Here." Haywood acknowledged to Brandy McDonnell, in another article for the *Oklahoman* (July 10, 2009), "We definitely were in the right place at the right time; I mean there's no doubt about it. There's a lot of talented people out there, and why we worked and other people didn't, I don't know. I think in the country industry, there was just maybe a need for a group sound at that point of time when we were coming out, and it just kind of clicked, and it kind of worked. There's no doubt in my mind that it was meant to be because of the way that's worked out. There's definitely a higher power looking over us."

The album *Lady Antebellum* spawned two more Top 20 country singles, "Lookin' for a Good Time" and "I Run to You." The former, released in June 2008, peaked at number 11 on the *Billboard* country-singles chart; the latter was released in January 2009 and became the group's first single to become a number-one hit. It earned the top spot on the country-singles chart in July 2009 and achieved crossover status, peaking at number 31 on the *Billboard* Hot 100 chart. The love ballad includes the lyrics, "This world keeps spinning faster / Into a new disaster / so I run to you / I run to you baby / And when it all starts coming undone / Baby you're the only one I run to / I run to you." Scott told Ken Tucker, "Our fans grasped who we were with 'I Run to You.' The message and that song is so much about what we're about. It was like two puzzle pieces fitting together. Now you know us and we know you." At the 43d Annual CMA Awards ceremony, in November 2009, the song won the prize for single of the year, and the trio won best-vocal-group honors. In the latter category the band bested Rascal Flatts, who had won the award in each of the last six years. By the end of 2009, the album *Lady Antebellum* had been certified platinum by the RIAA.

The group released its highly anticipated second album, *Need You Now*, on January 26, 2010. The success of the first album had allowed Lady Antebellum to work with some of Nashville's most respected writers, such as Craig Wiseman, Josh Kear, Monty Powell, and Michael Busbee. The title track, about longing for companionship in the middle of the night, was released in August 2009 and had already become an enormous hit by the time of the album's release. After spending five consecutive weeks in late 2009 atop the *Billboard* country-songs chart, the song "Need You Now" achieved crossover status, reaching number two on the *Billboard* Hot 100 chart. Stemming from the success of that single, which was certified quadruple-platinum by the RIAA after four weeks, *Need You Now* debuted at number one on the *Billboard* 200 and the *Billboard* country-albums charts and reportedly sold 480,922 copies in its first week of release. A little over a month later, the album had sold 1.2 million copies, and it has since sold more than three million copies in the U.S.

Need You Now also produced the hit singles "American Honey" and "Our Kind of Love," both of which reached number one on the *Billboard* hot country-songs chart, as well as the Top 10 country hit "Hello World." The album was a major critical success. In his review for the All Music Guide Web site, Thom Jurek noted that Scott, Kelley, and Haywood "stick very close to the formula of their debut: a slew of mid- and uptempo love songs, a sad ballad, and a couple of rocked-up good-time tunes, all self-written with some help from some of Nashville's most respected writers." He added that "the band's seamless, polished, and savvy brand of contemporary country is even more consistent than it was on their debut; it's virtually flawless in its songwriting, production, and performance." Crystal Bell, in a review for *Billboard* (January 29, 2010, on-line), wrote that the album "showcases the group's ability to combine its own contemporary country sound and folk-rock flair with a familiar formula, making it a refreshing addition to the ever-expanding country genre." Paul Worley, who co-produced the record, told Ken Tucker, "There's a convergence of talent and energy with the three of them. Dave is the brains, Hillary's the heart, and Charles is the drive. They are all creative people, but they don't overlap. The combination is powerful."

Less than a week after the release of its sophomore album, Lady Antebellum performed the title track at the 52d Annual Grammy Awards ceremony, held at the Staples Center in Los Angeles, California. There, the trio won the prize for best country vocal performance by a duo or group, for "I Run to You." That song was also nominated for a Grammy in the category of best country song, but lost to Taylor Swift's "White Horse." Lady Antebellum was nominated for five ACM Awards and, at the ceremony in April 2010, won for top vocal group; "Need You Now" won for song of the year and single record of the year. That summer "I Run to You" won Lady Antebellum a Country Music Television (CMT) Award for best group video, and the group also won a Teen Choice Award and an American Music Award (AMA) in the category of best country group. At the 44th CMA Awards ceremony, in November 2010, the group won the prizes for best group and single of the year, for "Need You Now."

At the 53d Grammy Awards ceremony, in February 2011, Lady Antebellum performed a medley of songs that included "If You Don't Know Me by Now," "American Honey," and "Need You Now." By the end of the night, the group had won the Grammy for best country album as well as four

prizes for the song "Need You Now," in the categories of song of the year, record of the year, best country song, and best country vocal performance by a duo or group. "Need You Now" was only the second country song in history to win, at the same ceremony, Grammys both for song of the year—which honors the writer of the song apart from the particular recording—and record of the year, which honors the particular recording of a song. The song has so far seen more than four million paid Internet downloads; during the first week of April 2011, it became the most-downloaded country song of all time.

In the fall of 2010, Lady Antebellum—who had opened for such major country artists as Martina McBride, Tim McGraw, and Kenny Chesney—launched its first headlining tour, which saw the group perform 35 concerts in cities across the U.S. Also in 2010 the band released a six-song Christmas EP, called *A Merry Little Christmas*, which reached number one on the *Billboard* top holiday-albums chart. The band is currently working on its third studio album, which is expected to be released in 2011.

Kelley is the only member of the trio who is married. He wed the publicist Cassie McConnell in June 2009. Kelley is brother-in-law to the actress Katherine Heigl (best known for her role on ABC's *Grey's Anatomy*), who is married to his brother Josh. All the members of the band reside in the Nashville area.

—C.C.

Suggested Reading: All Music Guide Web site; *Augusta (Georgia) Chronicle* A p1 Nov. 14, 2010; *Billboard* (on-line) Jan. 9, 2010, Jan. 29, 2010, Feb. 20, 2010; *Birmingham (Alabama) News* G p12 May 8, 2009; *Detroit (Michigan) Free Press* Z p13 Aug. 20, 2009; *El Paso (Texas) Times* (on-line) Mar. 20, 2009; (Minneapolis, Minnesota) *Star Tribune* E p1 Oct. 22, 2010; *New York Times* C p1 June 12, 2010; (Oklahoma City) *Oklahoman* D p3 July 10, 2009, D p6 June 11, 2010; *Palm Beach (Florida) Post* D p1 Jan. 27, 2009

Selected Recordings: *Lady Antebellum*, 2008; *Need You Now*, 2010

Lampley, Jim

Apr. 8, 1949– Sportscaster; film and television producer

Address: HBO Sports, 1100 Ave. of the Americas, New York, NY 10036

The sportscaster Jim Lampley "has distinguished himself among his peers for his uniquely cerebral and probing take on sports, his passion, and his

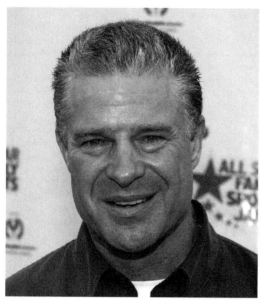

Jim Lampley

Vince Bucci/Getty Images

courage to speak his mind and to call something as he sees it," Salvatore Difalco wrote for the Canadian magazine *Toro* (January 27, 2009, on-line). Lampley launched his career in network television in 1974, when he was in his mid-20s. That year ABC Sports chose him and one other candidate from among more than 400 applicants for the newly created position of sideline reporter for televised college-football games. As one of ABC's first sideline correspondents, Lampley was instrumental in shaping the evolution of sports journalism. He later held jobs with NBC, CBS, HBO (Home Box Office), the USA and Turner Sports networks, and the radio stations WFAN, in New York City, and KMPC (now KSPN), in Los Angeles, California. He worked as a news anchor for KCBS in Los Angeles from 1987 to 1992. Lampley is probably best known for the blow-by-blow commentary he has provided since 1988 for upwards of 400 prize fights for *HBO World Championship Boxing*, HBO pay-per-view boxing productions, and, since its debut, in 1996, *HBO Boxing After Dark*; he has become "the 'voice' of boxing," in Difalco's words, and one of the sport's most prominent enthusiasts. Also for HBO he has covered what is formally known as the Championships and popularly known as Wimbledon—the world's oldest tennis tournament, held annually in England. Having reported on location during 14 Olympic Games—more than any other sportscaster to date—he became the "face" of the Olympics for many television viewers.

Along with statistics and other standard fare, Lampley has routinely broadened his commentary to include social aspects of sports and wideranging, thought-provoking discussions touching on other matters. In 2005 and early 2006, he wrote a blog for the news and opinion Web site the *Huffington Post*. In 1995 he co-founded the company Crystal Spring Productions, whose few films include *Welcome to Hollywood* (2000). He himself has appeared in the role of a sportscaster in several movies, and his voice has been heard in others; the latter include David O. Russell's *The Fighter* (2010), whose soundtrack contains a recording of Lampley's commentary during the May 18, 2002 boxing match between "Irish" Micky Ward (portrayed by Mark Wahlberg in the film) and Arturo Gatti, which was broadcast on HBO.

In an assessment of ABC's coverage of the 1982 New York City marathon, Tony Schwartz wrote for the *New York Times* (October 26, 1982, on-line), "Jim Lampley is one of the few television sports reporters who can conduct a brief, efficient and effective live interview without resorting to predictable sports cliches." Another *New York Times* (March 4, 1987) sportswriter, Richard Sandomir, characterized him as a "smart [and] descriptive announcer," and a third, Gerald Eskenazi, in an article for the March 4, 1988 edition, described Lampley as "sometimes acerbic, sometimes whimsical but always knowledgeable." According to Ben Grossman, writing for *Broadcasting & Cable* (February 13, 2006), Lampley "has earned a reputation offcamera for diligence and outspokenness."

James Clifford Lampley was born on April 8, 1949 and grew up in Henderson, North Carolina, and Miami, Florida. When he was five years old, his father died; afterward, he was raised primarily by his mother. To compensate for the absence of a father, as Leroy Cleveland wrote for fightsaga.com (February 28, 2011), his mother nurtured his avid interest in sports and saw to it that he played sports with his peers. Lampley has said that beginning when he was very young, his mother also made him conscious of social injustices. As an 11-yearold, he watched TV broadcasts of the 1960 Summer Olympics, during which he saw the Ethiopian Adebe Bikila win the marathon while running barefoot. Near the finish line Bikila passed the Obelisk of Axum, a monument that Italian troops had taken from Ethiopia in 1939. "From that moment . . . ," Lampley told Bill Fleischman for the *Philadelphia Daily News* (February 10, 2006), "I understood the special importance of the synthesis between sports and society that the Olympics represent." At Southwest Miami High School, Lampley was the star of the golf team. Following his highschool graduation, in 1966, Lampley enrolled at the University of North Carolina (UNC) at Chapel Hill. Although he was talented enough to play golf for the university, academically he failed to qualify for a varsity team. He earned a B.A. degree in English in 1971, then began working toward a master's degree in mass communications, also at UNC–Chapel Hill. While in graduate school he covered sports events in or near Chapel Hill for local TV and radio stations. He also worked as a golf caddy.

In 1974, along with more than 400 others nationwide, Lampley applied for the newly created job of "college-age reporter" for ABC Sports. The two people to be hired for that position were to cover college football games from the sidelines and talk about other aspects of undergraduate life. They would be expected to differentiate college football from National Football League (NFL) games and to awaken TV viewers to the entertainment value and spirit of college football. Lampley performed poorly during his first interview, coming across as "arrogant, antagonistic, alienating and abrasive," according to Ben Grossman. Nevertheless, as one of the few applicants with on-air reporting experience, he earned an on-camera audition in which he had to interview the quarterback George Mira. Unbeknownst to ABC, Mira had become one of Lampley's heroes in the early 1960s, when Mira played for the University of Miami football team, and Lampley had continued to follow him during Mira's eight seasons with the NFL. "I had the guy's jersey in my closet," Lampley recalled to Ben Grossman. "I knew more about this guy than anyone alive." Lampley aced the audition and secured the job; when he was hired he left graduate school without completing his degree. Don Tollefson, then a Stanford University student, won the second sideline-reporter position.

At first ABC charged Lampley and Tollefson with providing public-interest stories involving fans, mascots, cheerleaders, and family members of players. "The original intent was that we weren't going to be football news reporters," Lampley told Pierce W. Huff for the New Orleans, Louisiana, *Times-Picayune* (January 4, 2004). But "by the third or fourth week that's pretty much all we did during a game"—"provide injury reports or anything else newsy that might emerge from what was happening on the sideline with the team." Lampley found that his expanded role sometimes placed him at odds with sportswriters for daily papers: some of them resented Lampley for "scooping" them, since he was reporting the news live. Lampley told Huff that a group of sportswriters led by Blackie Sherrod of the *Dallas (Texas) Times Herald* banded together to try to persuade coaches to ban Lampley and Tollefson from the sidelines. Lampley and Tollefson had won favor with a few influential coaches, however, and the disgruntled print journalists failed. "From that point forward pretty much every major college football telecast and eventually NFL games wound up having a sideline reporter," Lampley told Huff.

A longer-lasting problem for Lampley stemmed from the request by colleges and National Collegiate Athletic Association (NCAA) officials that he refrain from saying anything that might reflect badly on the schools, players, or coaches involved in the games. "When I came out of the University of North Carolina, I saw myself as a journalist and so I was going to approach my job on a no-holds-barred basis and be as independent and free as any journalist could be," Lampley told Paul Attner for the *Washington Post* (October 3, 1977). NCAA officials, however, saw "the college football package as a forum for promoting the college game," Lampley explained to Attner. "I've felt it was an opportunity to tell the story of college football from all sides. If it isn't positive for the game, they don't want it on." After Lampley prepared a report about three University of Notre Dame football players who had been suspended earlier for three years for violating dormitory rules, Notre Dame representatives lodged a complaint against him. Lampley "did a piece on [the three players] anyway, but he admits [that] the fact he couldn't talk to them hindered the quality of the report," Attner wrote. In another instance, Lampley's account of beer drinking among students at two colleges led administrators to protest to the NCAA. One dean of students "said I gave an unfair portrayal of college life," Lampley told Attner. "That's ridiculous. They are scared to death to see anything that demonstrates that college students are real humans who drink beer and yell like other people." "It got to the point that if I didn't hear from the NCAA for a few weeks, I thought I wasn't doing my job," he added. Nevertheless, Lampley had to accept "institutional restraints that we have no control over," he acknowledged to Attner. "I have found it's impossible to examine a story and tell it freely. . . . Do we tell the whole truth? Not always, because there is too much money on the line. I can tell a story to the degree it doesn't harm the relationship between the TV network and the promoter or sports organization involved. We have limitations which we have to recognize and live within."

Lampley covered college football for three years before taking on other assignments for ABC Sports. For *Wide World of Sports*, he provided play-by-play coverage for an array of athletic events, including such little-publicized pursuits as wrist wrestling and demolition derbies. He later provided play-by-play for *Monday Night Football* and *College Football Scoreboard*. In 1982 and 1983 Lampley covered *Race Across America*, a transcontinental bike race. He made his Olympic Games debut in 1984, at Sarajevo, in what was then Yugoslavia, in February and in Los Angeles during the summer; his real-time commentary for the men's swimming contests, one of the Games' most-watched television events, impressed observers. (Sources differ as to the year in which he first served as an Olympic Games reporter.) In 1985 he provided roadside reporting for the first televised Indianapolis 500, the 500-mile automobile race held annually in Speedway, Indiana, and he served in the same role the following year.

While Lampley secured high-profile assignments with ABC, his relationship with network executives was contentious at times. One reason was his outspoken disapproval of network executives' preferences for sports programs that earned the most advertising dollars. "The image of *Wide World of Sports* was built through 20 years of realizing that while it's important to make money, it's also crucial to create a sense in the viewer's mind that this is meaningful and entertaining and relevant to my life right now," Lampley told Steve Weinstein for the *Los Angeles Times* (November 21, 1987). "That attitude has been completely lost at ABC Sports, and that was a large part of what I couldn't agree with." His differences with the then-new ABC Sports chief Dennis Swanson led Swanson to "demote" Lampley in 1986 by shifting him almost solely to coverage of boxing—which Swanson did not know had been a favorite spectator sport of Lampley's since childhood. ABC also assigned Lampley to report on-location at the 1988 Winter Olympics, at Calgary, Alberta, Canada.

In 1987 Lampley joined CBS as a sports anchor for KCBS-TV in Los Angeles; the job included sports correspondence for CBS-TV. He now worked every day, which had not been the case at ABC. After less than two years, Lampley became a full-time KCBS-TV news anchor. Concurrently, HBO hired Lampley to report on tennis events at Wimbledon and ringside at boxing matches. During that period he also hosted shows on the 24-hour sports-radio stations WFAN, in New York, and KMPC, in Los Angeles. In 1992 KCBS-TV ended his stint as a news anchor—a move that left him feeling relieved. "It's an extremely intense occupation in the sense that you are constantly treated like a guinea pig," Lampley told Weinstein. "You're the subject of daily [market] research of all kinds—people grabbing people in shopping centers and pulling them over and showing them your picture and saying, 'Do you like him? What don't you like?' And, let's face it, after a while sitting in front of a camera— where the most important thing is cosmetics and presentation, and you're reading someone else's words off the prompter—it can get to be a grinding routine. And then, what's really perverse about it is that, after a while, you recognize that the time you have the most fun is when something terrible happens. The only time you get a chance to go on the air and deal extemporaneously with information and use what I call real broadcasting talents is when dozens of people have died in a plane crash or the entire community is threatened by an earthquake or a guy with a gun is holding a school yard hostage."

Lampley reported for CBS from Albertville, France, at the 1992 Winter Olympics. That year he went to work for NBC, which assigned him to cover football and golf. He came to believe that his experience as a news anchor had made him a better sportscaster. "It's true I always wanted to err more toward Howard Cosell than the host of play-by-play men who would rather slam their hand in a car door than have to deal with a serious issue," Lampley told Steve Weinstein for the *Los Angeles Times* (November 2, 1992). "But to a certain degree, having spent four years as a newscaster has given me more freedom to go ahead and mine the vicarious thrill-fantasy-world value of sport and participate in people's desire to feel that part of it and to escape. I feel looser now as a sportscaster,

more spontaneous, and I'm not nearly as self-conscious about demonstrating my own personal relationship with serious content." For NBC Lampley covered the 1994 Winter Olympic Games, held in Lillehammer, Norway. He also continued working for HBO, where his duties had expanded to include contributions to the television magazine *Real Sports with Bryant Gumbel.*

During his coverage of the 1996 Summer Olympics, in Atlanta, Georgia, Lampley decided that he was juggling too many jobs. In the previous decade he had had a virtually uninterrupted series of assignments (some of them simultaneously) with different networks, and he concluded that wearing so many hats had made specialization—and promotion—difficult. "I was trying to do too much and my performance suffered," he told Rudy Martzke for *USA Today* (July 22, 1998). "I missed my first NBC golf tournament. Five times I did HBO fights on the East Coast and showed up for NBC NFL games the next day with no sleep. I realized I had made a lot of money [reportedly nearly $2 million a year], but while I had willingly become a hired gun, I suffered from a lack of concrete identity." NBC had already dropped him from *NFL Live* and weekend golf coverage, so he cut most of his ties with NBC in order to concentrate on his responsibilities with HBO. However, he covered Olympic Games for NBC in 1998, 2000, 2002, 2004, 2006, and 2008. Richard Sandomir wrote for the *New York Times* (February 15, 1998, on-line) that at the 1998 Winter Games, in Nagano, Japan, Lampley gave broadcasts in freezing temperatures and developed laryngitis. But "despite the weather and his scratchy voice, his style is intact, complete with verbal edge, savvy writing and sharp ad-libbing."

As a specialist in boxing for HBO, Lampley has become one of the sport's top commentators. Lampley has announced more than 400 fights, beginning with the Mike Tyson–Tony Tubbs match in Tokyo, Japan, in 1988. He currently serves as one of the blow-by-blow announcers on *HBO World Championship Boxing*, HBO pay-per-view boxing productions, and *HBO Boxing After Dark*. His colleagues at HBO, one or more of whom report alongside him, include Larry Merchant, Emanuel Steward, and, since 2005, Max Kellerman. In 1992 Lampley was honored with the Sam Taub Award for excellence in broadcast journalism, presented by the Boxing Writers of America Association, and he has been inducted into the World Boxing Hall of Fame. He hosted the 2003 12-part HBO boxing-documentary series *Legendary Nights*, which won an Emmy Award in the category of "outstanding edited sports series." "What makes boxing so exciting is the depth of the psychological confrontation each fight produces," he told an interviewer for HBO's Web site (April 21, 2006). By his own account, boxing commentary suits him because he enjoys the flexibility and editorializing the job makes possible. "The whole process of calling boxing matches is so subjective, so challenging, so complex . . . ," Lampley told Bob Raissman for the New York *Daily News* (May 5, 1996). "Working a fight isn't like going out and calling football games or baseball or basketball where there is a continuing statistical line, a scoreboard and obvious empirical evidence of what's going on. Calling a fight is a challenge to your vision, your security and your willingness to change what you're saying if what happens in the ring changes." Lampley told Salvatore Difalco, "Most sports start out from a platform of perceived legitimacy. They tried to fend off accusations of illegitimacy. In boxing you sort of start at the level of corruption and try to go up from there. So, you're in a freer landscape to begin with. I mean, there's no outrage. What could you possibly see that you haven't seen before? And the truth is always stranger than fiction. And so that presents a palette where if you can think in a provocative way, like Larry Merchant, you can scare up really interesting angles for stories, as he does. And the other thing is of course we're on a premium-pay cable network, and therefore there are no advertisers. And as a sportscaster I can absolutely tell you that your level of freedom is dramatically affected by the fact that there are no advertisers who are invested in the broadcast. You know, if we make a risky joke or an extreme observation, you don't have to worry that Procter & Gamble is going to call the salesman on Monday and say, 'We don't like that.' And that's a big help."

In January 2007 Lampley was arrested following allegations by his former girlfriend Candice Sanders (Miss California of 2003) that he had thrown her against a wall on New Year's Eve while he was under the influence of drugs and alcohol. In February 2007 Lampley was charged with violating the terms of a previous restraining order; although he maintained that he was innocent of Sanders's charges, he pleaded no contest and was sentenced to three years of probation and mandatory participation in a domestic-violence recovery program. Those events marked the end of Lampley's occasional appearances as the guest host of *The Jim Rome Show*, a weekday-morning radio talk show.

Lampley's three marriages ended in divorce. His first wife (1970–77) was Linda Sharon Lee. From his second marriage, to the former Joanne Faith Mallis (1979–90), he has two daughters—Brooke, a specialist with the auction house Christie's, and Victoria, a photographer. With his third wife, Bree Walker-Lampley (1990–99), he has one son, Aaron, and one stepdaughter, Andrea. He and Walker-Lampley co-founded Crystal Spring Productions, which is based in Beverly Hills, California; the two reportedly remain close. Jim Lampley lives in Southern California.

—N.W.M.

Suggested Reading: *Broadcasting and Cable* p22 Feb. 13, 2006; HBO Web site; (New Orleans) *Times-Picayune* p8 Jan. 4, 2004; (New York) *Daily News* p69 May 5, 1996; *Philadelphia Daily News* p123 Feb. 10, 2006; *Toro Magazine* (online) Jan. 27, 2009; *USA Today* C p3 June 23, 1989, C p2 July 22, 1998, C p3 Apr. 6, 2007; *Washington Post* D p1 Oct. 3, 1977

Lee, Sandra

July 3, 1966– Television cooking-show host; cookbook writer; philanthropist

Address: Sandra Lee Semi-Homemade, 1453A 14th St., Suite 126, Santa Monica, CA 90404

The television cook and writer Sandra Lee is nationally known for her "semi-homemade" recipes and the mantra that accompanies them: "Seventy percent store-bought, ready-made plus 30 percent fresh allows you to take 100 percent of the credit." Indeed, Lee has trademarked the phrase "semi-homemade" and has turned it into a multimillion-dollar brand name. "Sandra Lee didn't invent convenience cuisine . . .," Teresa J. Farney noted for the Colorado Springs, Colorado, *Gazette* (March 5, 2003). "But with her classy blond good looks, down-home techniques and savvy marketing skills, she's become the high-profile ambassador for it." While attending a culinary academy for a few weeks in 1998, Lee realized that she had no interest in spending a lot of time in the kitchen, so—convinced that many working women shared that sentiment—she started to simplify the process of preparing homemade meals. In a February 22, 2011 interview for *Vogue*, she told Gully Wells, "I learned how to break down these complicated recipes—it was like a science project—and create quicker, easier versions that ordinary women could relate to."

Some food writers and others have complained about Lee's shortcuts to cooking, not least because her recipes rely on many already prepared ingredients that are high in sugar, saturated fats, and salt. Such criticism notwithstanding, Lee's approach has brought her great success. She is the publisher and editor in chief of her own magazine, *Sandra Lee Semi-Homemade*, which as of mid-2011 reportedly had a circulation of 300,000, and she has published two dozen cookbooks, with titles including *Semi-Homemade Fast-Fix Family Favorites* and *Semi-Homemade Money Saving Slow Cooking*. Her memoir, *Made from Scratch*, came out in 2007. A workaholic who has been described as fiercely ambitious and as having a missionary zeal for her work, Lee also hosts two popular television cooking shows on the Food Network— *Semi-Homemade Cooking with Sandra Lee* and *Sandra's Money Saving Meals*—and has served as

Stephen Lovekin/Getty Images

Sandra Lee

a guest food expert on national TV shows including *Good Morning America*, *Today*, *Ellen*, and *Tyra*. Lee told Kathleen Purvis for the *Charlotte (North Carolina) Observer* (September 8, 2010) that the strong reactions, both pro and con, to her approach to cooking surprised her. "I think it was one of those brands that got both ends of the spectrum," she said. "And that's how you know it's meaningful, when you get a reaction." Lee has said that criticism of her methods no longer troubles her. "When the press takes a shot at me and *Semi-Homemade*, they take a shot at every single woman in America trying to get a meal on the table and make it special," she told Cristina Kinon for the New York *Daily News* (May 3, 2008). "What my job is is to facilitate her. It's not my place to judge her, and quite frankly, it's not anyone else's place either." Lee is a major supporter of food banks in New York State and has inspired large contributions of foods from companies such as Tyson.

Lee was born Sandra Lee Waldroop on July 3, 1966 in Santa Monica, California. (She changed her surname legally to Lee in 1997.) Her father, Wayne Waldroop, and mother, the former Victoria Svitak (called Vicky), were high-school sweethearts who married in their teens, right before her birth; they divorced soon after the birth of her younger sister, Cindy. When Lee was around two years old, her mother left her and her sister with their paternal grandmother—Lorraine Waldroop—whom Lee came to think of as her mother; according to Benjamin Wallace, writing for *New York* (April 4, 2011), Lee has credited her grandmother with being "an early role model—a coupon-clipping cafeteria worker who created a joyful, loving home filled with the comforting smell of bak-

ing"; her grandmother, who lived in Santa Monica, ran a food pantry there. When Lee was about six, Vicky returned for her daughters and took them to live with her and her second husband, Richard Christiansen, in Marina del Rey, California. The family later moved to Washington State, after Richard, a computer programmer, found a job there.

By Lee's own account, her mother and stepfather abused her both verbally and physically. After the births of Lee's half-sister and two half-brothers—Kimmy, Richie, and Johnny—Lee's stepfather abandoned the family. Lee, who was then about 13 years old, found herself responsible for much of the care of her four younger siblings; her mother, who suffered from migraine headaches and was dependent on prescription pain killers, spent a great deal of time "lying on the couch, taking pills and screaming at us," Lee wrote in her memoir. Household chores such as cooking, cleaning, and paying the bills also fell to Lee. She would deposit the family's welfare checks in the bank and use food stamps to buy groceries; the baking mix Bisquick became a staple. "I was so glad Grandma had taught me how to cook and be frugal, because there was no other way for us to make it through," Lee wrote in her autobiography. "I daydreamed of being a normal kid, but that wasn't the reality I lived in."

Shortly before she turned 16, Lee left home, following many altercations with her mother and some sort of sexual advances from her stepfather, who had rejoined the family—"the memoir leaves vague" precisely what he did to her, Wallace wrote. After living with a boyfriend's family for a while, she moved in with her biological father, who lived in west-central Wisconsin. She attended Onalaska High School, in La Crosse County. During that period Wayne Waldroop was found guilty of sexually assaulting his girlfriend and received a one-year prison sentence. "Through all this," Wallace wrote, Lee "found ways to feel better about her life," in part by reading novels by Danielle Steel, listening to the music of the singer/songwriter Stevie Nicks, and serving as a school cheerleader.

After her high-school graduation, Lee attended the University of Wisconsin at La Crosse. "Going to college was like starting over again," she wrote in her memoir. "I discovered I had a knack for putting together business outlines and marketing plans and decided to pursue a business degree." As an undergraduate Lee held several part-time waitressing jobs. During her junior year she dropped out of school and moved to Los Angeles, California, where she worked for an import-export company. According to Wallace, she represented the firm at home-and-garden shows, where she demonstrated O-Mega stun guns (used for personal protection) and Black & Decker security systems. While renting a room in nearby Malibu, she fashioned her own window treatments, by draping large pieces of fabric around bent wire hangers. An aunt and uncle praised her decorative draperies and encouraged her to find ways to profit from her inventiveness. Heeding their advice, Lee rented a booth at the Los Angeles County Fair and began to sell the hardware for her creations, which she called Kraft Kurtains.

In the 1990s Lee established Sandra Lee Simply Living, her own line of do-it-yourself decorating products. After she traded in her 1972 Dodge Charger for a van, she and her half-sister, Kimmy, traveled to county fairs, where they pitched her products. "Starting a business is like climbing Mt. Everest," Lee wrote in *Made from Scratch*. "You either prepare and train for the journey or you fail. There were months of heavy cash flow and months of being completely strapped waiting for customers to pay. I always rolled my profits back into the company so it would continue to grow." After a while Lee earned enough money to make her own infomercial, and she began to sell her wares on the home-shopping TV channel QVC. In addition, major retail chains such as Wal-Mart and Target began to carry her products. Within a year and a half, she had sold over $20 million worth of merchandise. She had also had to grapple with several lawsuits, brought by manufacturers who claimed that some of her wares infringed on their own patented products. According to Wallace, Lee responded with countersuits and won two patents herself. She also diversified her line, expanding it to upwards of 150 products with such items as wall-stencil kits and ready-to-grow plants (containers filled with soil, seeds, and fertilizer).

Toward the end of the 1990s, financial difficulties forced Lee to shut down her company. She decided to pursue a career in cooking, and in 1998 she enrolled for a short course at the Ottawa, Canada, branch of the Cordon Bleu Institute, an internationally known culinary school. She was surprised by the complexity of the recipes in the curriculum and how time-consuming they were. "After spending a week stripping tendons from veal chops, I decided I'm too busy for this and I think others are, too," she said in the interview with Teresa J. Farney. "Why not find other ways to make flavorful food in half the time?" That idea led Lee to develop her semi-homemade cooking concept. "Semi-homemade means that the recipe is 70 percent store-bought and 30 percent fresh ingredients and creativity," she told Janice Okun for the *Buffalo (New York) News* (February 5, 2003). "But you take 100 percent of the credit."

In 2002 Miramax Books published Lee's first cookbook, *Semi-Homemade Cooking*, which she dedicated to her grandmother, who had died a few years earlier. *Semi-Homemade Cooking*, which reached one of the specialized best-seller lists compiled by the *New York Times*, is subtitled *Quick Marvelous Meals and Nothing Is Made from Scratch* and contains 100 recipes. In it Lee wrote, "The Semi-Homemade cooking approach is easily done by combining several prepackaged foods, a few fresh ingredients, and a 'pinch of this with a hint of that' to make new, easy, gourmet-tasting, inexpensive meals in minutes." "What makes Lee's

cookbook stand apart," Rebecca Sodergren wrote in a positive review for the *Pittsburgh (Pennsylvania) Post-Gazette* (March 11, 2004), "is her attempt to be all things to all people. The other cookbooks typically emphasize only speed; Lee wants to have it all: fast, easy, low-cost, flavorful, gourmet. Finish a full day's work, then serve up a delicious, gorgeous meal without breaking the bank and still have time to put on some music, sip a glass of wine and dine at leisure." In a negative review for the *Seattle Post-Intelligencer* (October 23, 2002), Hsiao-Ching Chou wrote, "I think there are good intentions buried somewhere in the Sandra Lee package. She wants to make lives easier. There is nothing inherently wrong with creating time-saving tricks in the kitchen. But if you're so busy that you don't even have time to shred a cup of carrots, then why bother 'cooking' at all?"

According to Benjamin Wallace, Lee, "like many of today's familiar lifestyle personalities," helped to fill the "domestic-diva power vacuum" that occurred when the homemaking guru Martha Stewart became "distracted" by the charges of insider trading that led to her imprisonment in 2004. A former colleague of Lee's told Wallace, "Sandra always said she was going to be the next Martha Stewart." In spite of criticism of her cooking methods, Lee's concept struck a chord, and the Food Network recruited her to host a televised cooking program. One of the highest-rated new shows on the channel, *Semi-Homemade Cooking with Sandra Lee* premiered in 2003. For a while Lee was not always comfortable in front of the camera. "Every time they yelled 'Cut!' I would cry," she admitted to Elisa Ung for the Bergen County, New Jersey, *Record* (February 26, 2008). "I had to get waterproof mascara because I didn't know what I was doing." Each installment of *Semi-Homemade Cooking with Sandra Lee*—which has been nominated for multiple daytime Emmy Awards—offers a different "tablescape" based on the theme of the featured meal and cocktail. "There's inspiration everywhere," Lee said to Patti Martin for the *Asbury Park (New Jersey) Press* (February 27, 2008). "I can find a plate or a piece of fabric and work off that."

After publishing several additional cookbooks, Lee released a memoir, *Made from Scratch*, in 2007. She later became the editor in chief of her own bimonthly magazine, *Sandra Lee Semi-Homemade*, which made its debut in 2009. "This is her name, face and brand, so she is very involved," Alyce Head, the magazine's editor, said of Lee in an interview with Mary Constantine for the *Knoxville (Tennessee) News-Sentinel* (March 11, 2010). "The team will start out with a skeleton outline that we give to Sandra. It includes topics, recipes and photography, and sometimes she will come back with suggestions on those ideas. After we incorporate her ideas, it goes to layout, then Sandra sees it again for approval before it's printed."

Also in 2007, Lee recalled to Beth D'Addono for the *Philadelphia Daily News* (May 14, 2009, on-line), she had approached Food Network decision makers "and pitched the idea of a series about cooking on a budget, and everybody said no—that it wasn't a relevant idea that was meaningful to a broad group of people." The network later reconsidered that conclusion, and in 2009 *Sandra's Money Saving Meals* made its debut. According to the Food Network's Web site, the show "guarantees viewers an average savings of 39%–50% on every grocery store bill."

Lee is the national spokesperson for two programs run by the organization Share Our Strength: the Great American Bake Sale and Operation Frontline, both of which aim to end hunger among children in the United States. She is also an active supporter of God's Love We Deliver and Project Angel Food, which provide food for sick people who are homebound. She is a founding member of the Los Angeles chapter of the U.S. Fund for UNICEF (United Nations Children's Fund), which aids mothers and children in developing countries. She has lectured at Yale University's School of Management and has participated in Harvard Business School's annual Woman's Entrepreneurial Conference.

Writing for the now-defunct magazine *Gourmet* (September 2003), Margy Rochlin described the five-foot nine-inch Lee as "model-pretty" and as talking "faster than a carnival barker." Caryl M. Stern, the head of the U.S. Fund for UNICEF, told Wallace that Lee is "unbelievably resourceful and quick on her feet." Lee's marriage in 2001 to Bruce Karatz, a real-estate developer and corporate executive, ended in divorce in 2005. In 2006 she began dating Andrew Cuomo, the son of former New York State governor Mario Cuomo; Andrew Cuomo, who was the U.S. secretary of housing and urban development during the second term of President Bill Clinton and later served as the New York State attorney general, was elected governor of New York in 2010. Lee and Cuomo share a home in Westchester County as well as the governor's mansion, in Albany. Cuomo shares custody of his daughters—Mariah and Cara, who are twins, and Michaela—with his former wife, Kerry Kennedy (a daughter of U.S. senator and attorney general Robert F. Kennedy), from whom he is divorced. Lee, who has referred to Cuomo's daughters as her "semi-homemade" children, "thinks of Andrew's girls as if they were her own biological kids," Colleen Schmidt, a longtime friend of Lee's, said to Michael Barbaro for the *New York Times* (May 15, 2010). "In 2010 I made a very conscious effort to get ahead of my work," Lee said in her interview with Gully Wells. "I cleared the decks and reorganized the company so that I would have more time to devote to Andrew. I've always seen my job as making life easier for my audience, and now my job is to make life easier for him. I need to understand this new landscape and figure out how I can best contribute in a meaningful way. But we have this great opportunity to make a difference for people in need."

—J.P.

Suggested Reading: (Bergen County, New Jersey) *Record* F p5 Feb. 26, 2008; (Colorado Springs, Colorado) *Gazette* Food p1 Mar. 5, 2003; *New York* p30+ Apr. 4, 2011; *New York Times* A p1+ May 15, 2010; *Philadelphia Daily News* Features p41 May 14, 2009; semihomemade.com; *Vogue* (on-line) Feb. 22, 2011; Lee, Sandra. *Made from Scratch: A Memoir*, 2007

Selected Books: *Semi-Homemade Cooking*, 2002; *Semi-Homemade Desserts*, 2003; *Semi-Homemade Cool Kids' Cooking*, 2006; *Semi-Homemade Gatherings*, 2006; *Semi-Homemade Cooking Made Light*, 2006; *Semi-Homemade Grilling*, 2006; *Semi-Homemade Slow Cooker Recipes*, 2006; *Made from Scratch: A Memoir*, 2007; *Semi-Homemade Fast-Fix Family Favorites*, 2008; *Semi-Homemade Comfort Food*, 2010

Selected Television Shows: *Semi-Homemade Cooking with Sandra Lee*, 2003– ; *Sandra's Money Saving Meals*, 2009–

Lieberman, Daniel E.

June 3, 1964– Anthropologist; biologist; educator; writer

Address: Human Evolutionary Biology Dept., Harvard University, 11 Divinity Ave., Cambridge, MA 02138

Daniel E. Lieberman, a professor of human evolutionary biology at Harvard University, has spent most of his career studying heads and feet. His book *The Evolution of the Human Head* (2011), which draws upon 15 years of his research, examines the development (prenatal to adult), evolution, and functions of the human head. Illustrated with many charts, drawings, and photos, the book was written not only for scientists but also for informed laypeople, and it has been lauded for its breadth and multidisciplinary approach. "If a single word describes this book, it is integrative," Chris McManus, a professor of psychology and medical education at University College London, wrote for the London *Times Higher Education* (February 17, 2011). "The author integrates material from anatomy, physiology, physics, biomechanics, molecular and developmental biology, but brings all under the umbrella of evolutionary theory." On Lieberman's Harvard Web site, he poses the question: Why does the human body look the way it does? "I think this is an important question to tackle from an evolutionary perspective not

Courtesy of Harvard University Press

Daniel E. Lieberman

lack our ability to sweat profusely, and they cannot gallop and pant at the same time, human hunters can pursue their prey in the midday sun until the animals collapse from heat exhaustion. This kind of persistence hunting is rare today, but was probably an important way to hunt before the comparatively recent invention of the bow and arrow within the last 100,000 years."

A son of Philip Lieberman and the former Marcia Rubinstein, Daniel Eric Lieberman was born on June 3, 1964, while his father was serving as a lieutenant in the U.S. Air Force. Philip Lieberman, the Fred M. Seed professor of cognitive and linguistic sciences at Brown University, in Providence, Rhode Island, has studied and written extensively about the evolution of human vocal anatomy and linguistic and cognitive abilities; his current research deals with the neural pathways connected with speech and cognition. He is also an accomplished photographer whose work has been exhibited extensively in group and solo shows and appears in many publications. Photos of his illustrate Marcia R. Lieberman's books about walking in Switzerland and alpine regions of France and Italy.

Daniel Lieberman earned an A.B. degree in anthropology, summa cum laude, from Harvard College, in Cambridge, Massachusetts, in 1986. He received master's degrees in biological anthropology from Cambridge University, in England, in 1987 and in anthropology from Harvard University in 1990. Three years later he earned a Ph.D. in anthropology from Harvard. From 1993 to 1996 Lieberman was a junior fellow at Harvard, where he conducted research in human evolution and paleoanthropology, the latter being a multidisciplinary study of human ancestors that combines paleontology and physical anthropology. That fellowship overlapped with his time as an assistant professor (1995 to 1998) at Rutgers University, the state university of New Jersey. He spent the next three years as an associate professor at George Washington University, in Washington, D.C., before joining the Harvard faculty as a professor of biological anthropology, in 2001. Since that year he has also headed the Department of Human Evolutionary Biology (known before 2009 as the Biological Anthropology Program of the Department of Anthropology).

Paleoanthropologists theorize that hominins— all species that are more closely related to humans than to apes—have inhabited Earth for millions of years. (Scientists are currently debating the precise definitions of "hominins" and "hominids.") The main feature all hominins have in common is bipedalism, the ability to walk on hind limbs (or legs, as with people). During the course of evolution, many significant variations among hominin species emerged, with each transformation setting the stage for the next. Scientists have so far discovered more than 20 species of hominins. The oldest known hominin species is *Salhelanthropus tchadensis*, which is believed to have lived between 7.6 million and six million years ago. A cranium, jaw fragments, and teeth of the skull of an individ-

only to understand better why humans are the way they are, but also because the evolutionary bases of human anatomy and physiology provide insights on how to prevent many kinds of illnesses and injuries," he wrote. He then elaborated on his field of interest: "Much of my research focuses on the unusual nature of the human head. Unlike other mammals, we have very large brains, nearly balanced heads with short vertical necks that attach near the center of the skull's base, no snouts, external noses, small teeth, short round tongues, a descended larynx, and tiny faces that are tucked almost beneath the frontal lobes. How, when, and why did these features evolve? And what do they tell us about the selective forces that acted during human evolution?"

While researching the head Lieberman also developed a fascination with running, particularly its role in human evolution. In an op-ed piece for the *Boston Globe* (April 15, 2007), he wrote: "Millions of years of evolution shaped the human body into a remarkable running machine. Most of today's marathoners run because it makes them feel good both physically and mentally. But, for our ancestors, running was a means of bringing home the bacon. About 2 million years ago, our ancestor, Homo erectus, hunted big animals armed with nothing more than a sharp untipped spear (stone spearheads were invented only about 200,000 to 300,000 years ago). Killing a big animal like a kudu or a wildebeest with a sharp stick isn't easy, because one must get very close to the animal to spear it. One kick from the prey's legs or a blow from its horns can kill a hunter. Running changed all that. Human hunters can run for miles at speeds that require most mammals to gallop. Since quadrupeds

ual of that species were found in 2001 in the Djurab Desert, in Chad, in north-central Africa, by a team led by the French paleontologist Michel Brunet (which nicknamed the skull Toumaï, meaning "hope of life" in a local tribal language). Because it is so old, the skull's mix of hominin and apelike features surprised paleoanthropologists the world over. On July 11, 2002 an image of the partial skull appeared on the cover of the British journal *Nature*. "It is a monumental discovery," Lieberman told Ann Gibbons for *Science* (July 12, 2002). "It is unquestionably one of the great paleontological discoveries of the past 100 years."

Species from the genus *Australopithecus* appeared on Earth approximately four million years ago. (A genus is a classification for related species. For example, the genus *Homo* includes nine species, among them *Homo neanderthalens*, commonly called Neanderthals, and *Homo sapiens*— people, or contemporary humans. All *Homo* species except *Homo sapiens* are extinct.) One of the world's best-known fossils, a 3.2-million-year-old, nearly 40-percent-complete skeleton found in Ethiopia in 1974 (commonly referred to as Lucy), belongs to the genus *Australopithecus*, which consists of several bipedal species that exhibited a mixture of ape and human features. The next evolutionarily significant hominins were early species of the genus *Homo*, which, among other attributes, are considered to be the first stone-tool makers and the first runners. One such species, *Homo erectus*, lived from 1.8 million years ago until as recently as 50,000 years ago. *Homo erectus*, so-called for its upright posture, had relatively small teeth, an external nose (as opposed to a snout), and a brain twice the size of nearly all its ancestors'. *Homo erectus* fossils have been found in Indonesia, China, Kenya, and the country Georgia, in Eurasia. *Homo heidelbergensis*, which lived between 500,000 and 200,000 years ago, was a big-brained, skilled hunter and is considered to be a probable ancestor of humans and Neanderthals, the latter of which appeared around 200,000 years ago in Europe and Asia. Neanderthals had rugged physiques, hunted, used relatively sophisticated tools (such as sharpened tips on tree-branch spears), and apparently died out around 30,000 years ago. *Homo sapiens* appeared nearly as long ago as Neanderthals: the oldest-known human fossil dates back approximately 195,000 years. Human fossils have been found on every continent except Antarctica.

In a paper published in *Nature* (May 14, 1998) titled "Sphenoid Shortening and the Evolution of Modern Human Cranial Shape," Lieberman compared the skulls of modern humans ("modern" meaning *Homo sapiens*) and those of other hominins. The two most important features of modern human skulls that distinguish them from the skulls of other hominins, he wrote, are (1) the roundish (rather than ovoid) shape of our braincases and (2) the positions of our relatively small faces, which are tucked under (rather than in front

of) the braincase. Prior to the publication of that paper, Lieberman had been studying the process of bone growth in humans and their ancestors for approximately six years. He used a portable X-ray machine to record images of the skulls of hominins and humans. About a year before the publication of the *Nature* paper, Lieberman had computerized hundreds of X-rays and other images of skulls and discovered the crucial importance of the sphenoid bone, a butterfly-shaped bone that touches 17 of the 21 other bones in the human skull. (There are eight bones in the cranium, which surrounds the brain, and 14 in the face.) In an interview with Matthew Reilly for the New Jersey *Star-Ledger* (May 14, 1998), Lieberman called the sphenoid bone "the cornerstone of the skull." He added: "Just change the shape of one bone and it has all kinds of effects on how much the face projects in front of the brain case. In turn, facial projection affects all sorts of aspects of our overall cranial shape, such as how large our brow ridge is and how steep our forehead is. What I was able to show is that a very simple change in the way the skull grows creates this difference in facial projection. That's the most important thing that makes humans different from other hominids. It has so many effects on other aspects of skull shape."

In 2002 Lieberman co-authored a paper in Volume 99 of the *Proceedings of the National Academy of Sciences* titled "The Evolution and Development of Craniofacial Form in *Homo sapiens*." In it he argued that the two primary distinguishing features of the modern human skull came about as a result of small, relatively quick changes over the course of evolution. Evidence to support that theory came from measurements made by Lieberman and his colleagues of various characteristics of many skulls: those of 100 recent *Homo sapiens*, 10 older modern humans, five Neanderthals, four *Homo heidelbergensis*, and many skulls of modern children and chimpanzees during various stages of their development. In an essay for *Science* (February 15, 2002) about the study, Michael Balter observed, "The growth patterns of humans and chimpanzees showed that these uniquely human features stem from early developmental shifts in the bones making up the cranial base. For example, the anterior (forward) segment of the cranial base is 15% to 20% longer relative to cranial size in modern humans than in either extinct species [Neanderthal and Heidelberg Man], and the base is bent at a much sharper angle in moderns. That flexing allows the face to grow tucked under the braincase rather than jutting forward, explains Lieberman. . . . The fact that these traits arise almost entirely during prenatal and infant development is important, he says: This kind of early alteration in growth pattern, rather than later developmental tinkering, can create major changes in body form." Balter cited a recent study—one that strengthened Lieberman's argument—by the University of Zurich anthropologist Marcia Ponce de Leon, who found that crucial differences between Neanderthals and modern humans emerge very early in the lives of individuals, probably before birth. Furthermore, Lieberman asserted that what set off the change in the shape of the skull of the modern human was an expansion of the brain's frontal and temporal lobes, which are connected with such functions as speech, planning, creative thinking, artistic expression, and memory. Lieberman's conclusion—that during evolution the expansion of the brain caused the skull to change shape—may seem counterintuitive, but when he spoke with Balter, Lieberman pointed out that studies of brain deformations in living infants show that "the shape of the brain changes the shape of the braincase and not vice versa." Various researchers, Balter noted, disagreed with some of Lieberman's methods and assumptions. The paleoanthropologist Christopher Stringer, for example, observed that because Lieberman studied mostly complete faces and skulls, he may not have taken into account incomplete (and possibly transitional) skulls that might have indicated slower evolutionary transitions than Lieberman suggested. The paleoanthropologist Ian Tattersall took issue with Lieberman's focus on the two main traits; independent features such as reduced brow ridges, Tattersall told Balter, are also important. However, Tattersall said that he agreed with Lieberman's overall conclusion: "I would be very surprised if the distinctions between Homo sapiens and its closest relatives were not due to a relatively small genetic change with major developmental consequences."

While conducting research on the head along with the University of Utah biologist Dennis Bramble, Lieberman developed an interest in running. Although many animals can outrun humans over short distances, very few can run continuously for more than 15 minutes, as humans can. No animal can compare to humans when it comes to endurance running. But how did this curious phenomenon come about? Lieberman and Bramble published a paper in Nature (November 18, 2004) titled "Endurance Running and the Evolution of Homo," in which they proposed that several characteristics in humans are uniquely adapted for running: a ligament attached to the back of the skull stabilizes the head during running, long tendons in the legs act as springs, relatively large buttocks stabilize the body as it moves very quickly, and millions of sweat glands prevent the body from overheating. The consensus among anthropologists when the Nature paper appeared was that the long legs and relatively short arms of early Homo species were adaptations for better walking. Lieberman and Bramble, however, argued that running is physically very different from walking—even fast walking. Furthermore, Lieberman speculated that because running (while hunting) led to a diet richer in protein and fat than would previously have been necessary, it could have led to the evolution of bigger brains (in humans), which require a large amount of energy. The paper received a good deal of attention in the mainstream press.

In a paper for Nature (January 28, 2010) that he co-authored, Lieberman asserted that running shoes cause the very injuries they are supposed to prevent. Although advocates of running barefoot (or as close to barefoot as possible) had made similar claims for some years, Lieberman gave the idea scientific legitimacy by conducting experiments on the biomechanics of running. In his laboratory Lieberman has used a treadmill that calculates the force of impact a runner's foot makes as it hits the ground and infrared video cameras that measure that force of impact on joints. The invention of modern running shoes in the 1970s changed how humans run. People who grow up running barefoot—some Kenyans, for example—land mostly on the front, or ball, of the foot when they first touch the ground, while those who have always run while wearing shoes land heel first. The force of impact when one lands on the front of the foot is significantly less than the force when landing on the heel, which, according to Lieberman, is like getting hit on the heel with a hammer. When runners who had grown up running barefoot wore shoes, they still landed on the balls of their feet because doing so had become a habit. Lieberman warned that runners used to wearing shoes should not abruptly and exclusively switch to running barefoot or to footwear that simulates barefoot running; rather, they should incorporate the switch gradually. Lieberman disclosed that Vibram—the company that makes FiveFingers shoes, which simulate barefootedness—partly funded his research but did not design or influence his study.

In 2011 Harvard University Press published Lieberman's exhaustively researched, 700-plus-page book The Evolution of the Human Head, which offers answers to the question, Why does the human head look the way it does? Because the head is made up of so many neighboring, interconnected parts—bones, teeth, flesh, muscles, tongue, eyes, glands, nerves, and sensory organs—it is often difficult to say precisely what during the course of evolution was cause and what was effect. Humans, unlike our distant evolutionary ancestors, have external noses as opposed to snouts; one advantage of such an arrangement is that it helps us regulate the moisture in the air after we inhale it, but was that an evolutionary adaptation or a consequence of another change?

The human head has many other distinct characteristics: whereas most animals have long, rectangular tongues, we have short, rounded ones; no other animal can choke on its food, but because humans have a common pathway for food and air, we can choke—but that arrangement also gives us the ability to talk; although, compared to other animals, our sense of smell is very poor, we have a remarkable ability to "smell" for flavor through our throats; and, because of the invention of cooking and other ways to process our food, which makes food soft, individuals' jaws do not grow to be as big as they would if they ate tougher foods regularly, which results in the crowding of teeth—an aspect of development that may have evolutionary implications as well. The last-named characteristic is related to chewing, the subject of an entire chapter in the book. Lieberman studied the effects that chewing hard food rather than soft food would have on the development of the skull. In an experiment he fed hard food to one group of pigs and soft food to another; after some time the jaws of the pigs eating hard food were significantly larger than those in the soft-food group. In another experiment Lieberman connected electrodes to people's jaws to measure how they use their chewing muscles while eating raw goat meat as opposed to cooked goat meat.

In his review for *Times Higher Education*, Chris McManus called *The Evolution of the Human Head* "wonderful and inspiring," and in an assessment for *American Scientist* (March/April 2011), Brian T. Shea wrote, "The book is quite unusual in that it includes a comprehensive review of the soft tissues associated with cranial features and discusses them within the context of evolutionary morphology and the fossil record of the human skull. I can think of no other volume that packages the anatomy of the human head in this fashion."

Lieberman has received many grants from the National Science Foundation, as well as the American Federation for Aging Research, the Busch Biomedical Research Foundation, and George Washington University's Research Enhancement Fund. In addition to the above-cited journals, Lieberman has published his work in periodicals including the *American Journal of Physical Anthropology*, the *Journal of Human Evolution*, the *Journal of Neurotrauma*, and *Integrative and Comparative Biology*. He has co-edited two books—*Interpreting the Past: Essays on Human, Primate and Mammal Evolution* (2005) and *Transitions in Prehistory: Essays in Honor of Ofer Bar-Yosef* (2009). (The Israeli-born Bar-Yosef is a professor of prehistoric archaeology at Harvard University and the curator of paleolithic archaeology at Harvard's Peabody Museum of Archaeology and Ethnology.) In 2009 Lieberman and two of his colleagues won an Ig Nobel Prize, which, according to the Web site Improbable Research, honors "achievements that first make people laugh, then make them think." They earned the prize in the physics category, for "analytically determining why pregnant women don't tip over," according to the Web site; their explanation appeared in the paper "Fetal Load and the Evolution of Lumbar Lordosis in Bipedal Hominins" (*Nature*, December 13, 2007).

Lieberman and Antonia Courthope Prescott married in 1993; they live in Cambridge, Massachusetts. Their daughter, Eleanor, is in ninth grade.

—D.K.

Suggested Reading: Associated Press (on-line) Jan. 27, 2010; *Boston Globe* (on-line) Jan. 30, 2011; fas.harvard.edu; *Harvard Magazine* (on-line) Jan./Feb. 2011; (London) *Times Higher Education* p52 Feb. 17, 2011; *Science* (on-line) Feb. 15, 2002, July 12, 2002

Selected Books: *The Evolution of the Human Head*, 2011; as co-editor—*Interpreting the Past: Essays on Human, Primate and Mammal Evolution*, 2005; *Transitions in Prehistory: Essays in Honor of Ofer Bar-Yosef*, 2009

Stephen Lovekin/Getty Images

Lipton, James

Sep. 19, 1926– Television host; producer; writer; actor; educator

Address: James Lipton Productions, 159 E. 80th St., New York, NY 10075-0535

When James Lipton arrived as dean of the Actors Studio Drama School at the New School, in New York City, in 1993, he came armed with years of formal training and experience in acting, dance, writing, and production. Lipton had a role on *The Lone Ranger*, as the nephew of the title character, in the early 1940s, when he was a teenager and that show aired only on radio; he also had a recurring role on the soap opera *The Guiding Light* for several years beginning in the 1950s, first on radio and then on television. In that decade and the next, he wrote scripts for *The Guiding Light* (for some years as head writer) and two other soap operas. In the 1960s, in addition to other work, he wrote the book and lyrics for two Broadway musicals and formed his own production company. During the 1970s and 1980s, among many other projects, he produced a dozen television specials for the comedian

Bob Hope, including one that was shot in mainland China, and he organized the first televised inauguration-eve concert for an American president-elect (Jimmy Carter), held at the Kennedy Center, in Washington, D.C.

Since 1994 Lipton has served as the creator, executive producer, writer, and host of the TV show *Inside the Actors Studio*, which airs in the U.S. on the Bravo network and in 125 other nations and attracts upwards of 94 million viewers. The one-hour program shows portions of seminars in the three-year master's-degree program offered by the Actors Studio Drama School, which moved from the New School to Pace University's Lower Manhattan campus in 2006. (Lipton stepped down as dean that year.) In most segments of the series, which is currently in its 17th season, Lipton interviews a well-known actor or actress, often an Academy Award winner who trained at the Actors Studio; his guests have also included award-winning directors, producers, writers, and musicians and occasionally the entire casts of films or Broadway shows. To date, some 250 professionals have appeared on the show, responding to questions posed by Lipton and the students. Although questions address the guests' work, not their private lives or gossip about them, discussions of craft inevitably include reminiscences or other disclosures of a personal nature. "The show is, in the end, about the interior life of those who love the art form, about the struggle that leaves them lonely, introspective, unsure," Chris Hedges wrote for the *New York Times* (March 1, 2001). "Mr. Lipton's encyclopedic knowledge and unconditional acceptance—he lets his guests edit things they do not like from the tape—combine to create intimate and often moving portraits of lives in progress." "In an age that often seems to disdain content," Hedges wrote, *Inside the Actors Studio* is "a show about ideas." The actor Kevin Kline told Hedges that Lipton "has a lifelong commitment to the art or craft of acting. He never makes light of it. He never turns it into a sound bite. He reviews your entire career." Lipton included reflections on his own life and work in his book *Inside "Inside"* (2007), a history of the program. One of his other books, the best-selling *An Exaltation of Larks* (1968), which is about collective nouns both old and new, has never been out of print; an expanded edition was published in 1993.

Of Jewish descent, James Lipton was born on September 19, 1926 in Detroit, Michigan, where he grew up. He was the only child of the widowed Lawrence Lipton and his second wife, the former Betty Weinberg. His mother was a teacher and librarian. His father, a native of Poland, came to the U.S. as a young child. Seldom steadily employed, Lawrence Lipton was a journalist, columnist, fiction and nonfiction writer, poet, and educator. In Chicago, Illinois, in the early 1920s, he socialized with such literary notables as Carl Sandburg, Edgar Lee Masters, Sherwood Anderson, and Ben Hecht; in Southern California three decades later, he be-

friended Allen Ginsberg, Kenneth Rexroth, Lawrence Ferlinghetti, and other Beat poets and writers. His memoir cum chronicle *The Holy Barbarians*, which Harry T. Moore assessed on the front page of the *New York Times Book Review* (May 24, 1959), discusses the Beat community, in which Lawrence Lipton played a central role as a sort of "father confessor," according to Moore. For several years in the 1950s, Lawrence Lipton ran "jazz canto" workshops and the annual West Coast Poetry and Jazz Festivals. With his third wife, Georgiana Randolph, he published two dozen mystery novels under the pseudonym Craig Rice. He later divorced Randolph and married Nettie Brooks (who, in 1983, as Nettie Lipton, wrote the *Dictionary of Literary Biography* entry about him). In his book *The Erotic Revolution* (1965), Lawrence Lipton focused on what he called "the new morality." His correspondence and other material are preserved in the rare books and manuscripts collection of the University of Southern California.

James Lipton learned about his father's activities and career secondhand, because when he was six, his father left the family; afterward, Lipton lived with his mother (for some years in his maternal grandparents' house). During the next four decades, he saw his father no more than a dozen times, and neither he nor his mother ever received any financial support from him. Lipton's parents divorced sometime in the 1930s. "Year after year," Lipton wrote in *Inside "Inside"*, his father "was as far from my thoughts as from my presence." By his own account, Lipton found out about his father's death, in 1975, through a newspaper obituary.

Earlier, by the time Lipton had reached three years of age, he had learned to read, and by age 12 he had written three novels, none of which was published. During his years at Central High School, a Detroit public school, he wrote for the student newspaper; worked as a copyboy for the *Detroit Times*, a theater usher, and a glassware cleaner in a factory; and occasionally acted in productions mounted at the Catholic Theater, in Detroit. In 1942 he was cast as Dan Reid, the young nephew of the Lone Ranger, the title character of a show broadcast three nights a week on the Detroit radio station WXYZ. For a while after high school, he attended Wayne State University, in Detroit. Shortly before World War II ended, he enlisted in the military, undergoing training as a pilot. After his discharge he lived for a while in Paris, France, supporting himself as a "mec"—someone whom prostitutes hire to guide tourists to them. Then, with the intention of studying law, Lipton settled in New York City (as did his mother, who found work in the rare-books and -manuscripts section of an upscale department store).

Lipton told Murray Dubin for the *Philadelphia Inquirer* (October 13, 2002) that for some time he resisted considering a career in the arts, because "my father was so bizarre . . . and I was afraid I'd end up like him." Nevertheless, for the next decade, while he took classes in academic subjects and film and theater production at New York colleges, he also studied with revered figures in the performing arts. He spent two years with the famed acting coach Stella Adler, who had studied under the Russian theater director and actor Constantin Stanislavski (also spelled "Stanislavsky"); with Lee Strasberg, Adler had adapted Stanislavski's acting principles for Americans. Lipton then trained in acting for four years with Adler's second husband, the director Harold Clurman, who in 1931 had co-founded the Group Theatre; next, he studied for two years with Robert Lewis, a member of the Group Theatre and a co-founder of the Actors Studio. He took classes with Hanya Holm, a modern-dance pioneer, the choreographer Alwin Nikolais, and the ballet teachers Ella Daganova and Benjamin Harkarvy, and he studied voice with the mezzo-soprano Eva Gauthier and the holistic vocal coach Arthur Lessac. To help pay the bills and supplement his mother's meager income, Lipton took whatever acting jobs he could land. He had the leading role in an obscure independent film called *The Big Break* (1951) and parts in plays broadcast on the CBS-TV program *The Silver Theatre* and the NBC-TV show *Armstrong Circle Theatre.*

In 1951 Lipton appeared in his first Broadway play: *The Autumn Garden*, by Lillian Hellman. Directed by Harold Clurman until a week before it opened, when Hellman insisted on taking over, and starring the renowned actors Fredric March and Florence Eldredge, the drama ran for three months. At about that time, Lipton was cast as Dick Grant, a physician, on the radio soap opera *The Guiding Light*; when the show began airing on television, in 1952, he continued to portray the character. In addition to performing the role of Grant, which remained his until 1962, Lipton helped to write the program's scripts and was eventually named head writer. Concurrently, in 1956 he became a scriptwriter for a second soap opera, *The Edge of Night*, and in the 1960s for a third—*Another World.*

Teaming up with the composer Sol Berkowitz, who had arranged the music for the Broadway musical *The Unsinkable Molly Brown* (1960), Lipton wrote the book and lyrics for a musical called *Nowhere to Go but Up.* Set in the early years of the Prohibition Era (1920–33), it focused on two real-life federal agents who, often in disguise, closed down an extraordinary number of bootlegging operations and speakeasies. Collaborators on *Nowhere to Go but Up* included such theater luminaries as Sidney Lumet, who staged it; Kermit Bloomgarten, who co-produced it; and Tharon Musser, who designed the lighting. Co-starring Tom Bosley, Martin Balsam, and Dorothy Loudon, the musical opened at the Winter Garden Theatre, on Broadway, in November 1962. It earned scathing reviews and closed after one week.

Lipton's next musical, *Sherry!*, was created with the composer Laurence Rosenthal (who had written scores for films including *A Raisin in the Sun*, *The Miracle Worker*, and *Becket*) and was based on George S. Kaufman and Moss Hart's comedy *The Man Who Came to Dinner* (1939). Mounted at Broadway's Alvin Theatre (later renamed the Neil Simon Theatre), *Sherry!* closed in May 1967 after 14 previews and 72 regular performances. More than three decades later, the music producer Robert Sher, who specializes in Broadway cast albums, approached Lipton about making a recording of *Sherry!* Lipton rearranged the score (the only copies of which had been discovered by Sher in a trunk stored in the Library of Congress) with the help of his wife and Rosenthal. In 2004 Angel Records released a studio album of *Sherry!*, made with two European orchestras and performers including Tommy Tune, Bernadette Peters, Phyllis Newman, Nathan Lane, Carol Burnett, Mike Myers, and Lillias White as well as Lipton and Rosenthal. On the Web site musicals101.com, the musical-theater historian John Kenrick wrote of the CD, "Musical theatre buffs will not be able to resist this star-studded recreation of the 1967 adaptation of *The Man Who Came to Dinner.* Nathan Lane is delicious as the petulant Whiteside, Bernadette Peters is perfect as his long-suffering secretary, and Carol Burnett sings the hell out of the show-stopping title tune. . . . Three cheers to . . . Sher for pulling together this dream recording." In an album review for *sfgate.com* (February 15, 2004), Robert Hurwitt wrote, "*Sherry!* is a somewhat diluted version of the original, and some of the best songs owe too obvious a debt to [the librettist and lyricist Alan Jay] Lerner and [the composer Frederick] Loewe. But there's a delightful verve to the whole proceedings."

Lipton's television work in the 1970s included writing the scripts for the TV soap opera *The Best of Everything*, which was based on a novel by Rona Jaffe and aired from March 30 to September 25, 1970. With Gail Kobe, he wrote the scripts for the daytime series *Return to Peyton Place* (April 1972–January 1974), a spin-off of the primetime series *Peyton Place* (which was based on a best-selling 1959 novel by Grace Metalious). Also in the 1970s (and early 1980s) Lipton produced, executive-produced, and/or directed a dozen Bob Hope specials, which served as celebrations of the actor's birthdays. Lipton coordinated "The Star Spangled Gala," a four-and-a-half-hour event held at New York City's Metropolitan Opera House on May 9, 1976 as a fund-raiser for the Performing Arts Research Center of the New York Public Library at Lincoln Center; among the participants were such stars of film, theater, dance, and music as Elizabeth Taylor, Chita Rivera, Gwen Verdon, Shirley Verrett, Jean-Pierre Rampal, Paul Simon, Judith Jamison, Mikhail Baryshnikov, and Natalia Makarova, the last two of whom performed in the premiere of Jerome Robbins's *Other Dances.* Lipton also organized the concert that was broadcast live from the Kennedy Center, in Washington, D.C., on January 19, 1977, on the eve of the inauguration of Jimmy Carter as president of the U.S. Writing for the *New York Times* (July 20, 1977), Clive Barnes described that concert as "fast-moving and well-paced" and as "truly democratic," with a mixture of black, white, and Hispanic performers who addressed "concerns regarding women, equality, old age, peace and religion." For NBC, Lipton produced the three-hour TV special *Bob Hope on the Road to China* (1979), which was filmed in Beijing, China; in addition to Hope, performers included Baryshnikov, Crystal Gayle, and Caroll Spinney, who has provided the voices of Big Bird and Oscar the Grouch on *Sesame Street.* On Broadway, Lipton produced the play *The Mighty Gents*, which closed after nine performances in 1978 but earned its leading man, Morgan Freeman, several award nominations, and he produced a cabaret-style show starring the comedy duo John Monteith and Suzanne Rand, which ran for 79 performances in 1979.

Lipton was the head writer for the daytime TV soap opera *Capitol* (March 29, 1982–March 20, 1987), which was set in a fictional suburb of Washington, D.C. He wrote the scripts for two made-for-TV movies that aired in 1985: *Copacabana*, created for the popular singer/songwriter Barry Manilow, whose character bore some resemblance to Manilow himself, and *Mirrors*, based on a novel Lipton published in 1981, about a ballerina who struggles to find work in New York City. Alvin Klein, paraphrasing Lipton for the *New York Times* (May 17, 1981), wrote that *Mirrors* is about dancers "who share the spotlight and never possess the limelight." "I'm not that fond of everything that's been written or filmed about dance," Lipton explained to Klein. "They're essentially variations on *42d Street.* The star is hurt, the understudy goes on and a new star is born. More interesting to me are all those dancers to whom that never happens."

In the early 1990s Lipton was granted membership in the Actors Studio (a rare privilege, since he had never studied there) and was soon named to its board of directors. Serving mainly aspiring actors but also would-be directors and playwrights, the Actors Studio was set up in New York City in 1947 by Elia Kazan, Robert Lewis, and Cheryl Crawford, with the goal of giving students an "opportunity to explore and improve their craft in a safe, laboratory environment with colleagues with whom they share the same process of work," according to the studio's Web site. Lee Strasberg was the studio's artistic director from 1951 until his death, in 1982; currently, Ellen Burstyn holds that position as well as that of co-president, along with Harvey Keitel and Al Pacino. In 1966 a West Coast branch opened. Those admitted to the Actors Studio, through a notoriously selective process of auditions, pay nothing and become lifelong members, with the right to return at any time to brush up on their skills. Until the early 1990s contributions from wealthy donors (successful alumni) kept the studio afloat; when Lipton joined its board, bankruptcy loomed. The idea for a graduate-level Actors Studio Drama School came to Lipton as a way to rescue the Actors Studio: funds would come from tuition and fees paid by students in the master's-degree drama program and monies from its associated university. (The tuition for the 2010–11 academic year was $32,983; scholarships and financial aid were available.)

The Actors Studio Drama School opened in the fall of 1993. Lipton wrote in *Inside "Inside"* that in his role as dean (analogous to director or chair), he wanted the faculty to emphasize a "fundamental lesson of theater," which is that the script of a play "*is not the play*, but the *text* of the play. . . . The casting, the rehearsals, the costuming and makeup, the director's imagination, the life experiences and training of the actors who must take the playwright's characters off the printed page and deliver them, via their own bodies and minds and understanding and attitudes and strengths and weaknesses, to the stage in three dimensions and recognizable life—all that, *plus* the writer's text, is 'the play.'" "The second pillar of our program . . . ," he wrote, "decreed that, while our writers and directors [as well as actors] would receive intensive specialized training in their crafts, in the first year of our drama school, all three disciplines would study the actor's craft side by side in the same classroom." Lipton's current title is vice president of the Actors Studio and dean emeritus of the Actors Studio Drama School's M.F.A. program.

The drama school's noncredit class/seminar "Inside the Actors Studio" debuted with the same title on television on April 26, 1995, with Paul Newman (the Actors Studio president from 1982 to 1994) as Lipton's first guest. Nearly all of Hollywood's A-list actors and actresses have since appeared on the show. On March 14, 2011 Bradley Cooper, who earned a master of fine arts degree from the Actors Studio Drama School in 2000, became the first graduate of the school to become an *Inside the Actors Studio* interviewee. Lipton has said that to prepare for each of his interviews, he devotes two weeks to learning as much as possible about his guest's life and career; during the seminar he refers not to a Teleprompter but to the hundreds of large blue index cards on which he has jotted his notes. According to Chris Hedges, as an interviewer Lipton "uses a combination of abject fawning over his guests, a pomposity that even he acknowledges, and astute and diligent research to achieve what most talk show hosts never attain: a serious and studied look at the craft of filmmaking and acting. . . . No one is interrupted. Criticism is nonexistent. Dud projects are ignored. No one is ambushed." "It is not journalism," Lipton said to Hedges. "It is meant as an antidote to what is normally done with these people. I want to create an environment where people are willing to talk about the craft, not about themselves as people but as artists." "It almost always works," Hedges commented.

Several decades earlier, in 1968, the first edition of Lipton's book *An Exaltation of Larks* was published. It had two double entendres in its subtitle, which read *Or the Venereal Game.* Lipton undoubtedly chose the word "venereal" to attract browsers, since they would automatically assume that the word referred to sexually transmitted diseases. "Venereal" has another meaning as well, however, as it is also derived from the archaic word "venery," meaning the practice of hunting or the animals that are hunted—that is, game. The main sources for the traditional collective nouns included in Lipton's book date from the 15th century: one, known as the Egerton manuscript #3307 and preserved in the British Library, in London, contains liturgical texts and songs; the other, *The Book of St. Albans*, has sections on hunting, hawking (hunting by means of trained hawks), and heraldry and is believed to be the first published work to offer a compilation of collective nouns. In *Inside "Inside"* Lipton wrote, "*The Book of St. Albans* yielded up the definitive list that included not only the anticipated *gaggle of geese* and *pride of lions* but such unexpected flights of literary imagination as *an unkindness of ravens, a murmuration of starlings, a rag of colts, a skulk of foxes, a leap of leopards, a tidings of magpies, a charm of finches, a shrewdness of apes, a knot of toads, a parliament of owls* and *an exaltation of larks*, which gave me, the instant I happened on it, the title of my book."

In *An Exaltation of Larks*, Lipton wrote, "It may surprise you, as it did me, to discover that, of the 164 terms in *The Book of St. Albans*, 70 of them refer not to animals, but to people and life in the fifteenth century, and every one of these social terms makes the same kind of affectionate or mordant comment that the hunting terms do. By 1486"—the year *The Book of St. Albans* was published—"the terms were already a game, capable of codifications; and if you think the social terms were casually intended and soon forgotten, be advised that the ninth term in the *St. Albans* list is the perennial *bevy of ladies*, and the seventeenth term in the list is none other than a *congregation of people*."

One morning in late November 1968, Lipton talked about *An Exaltation of Larks* on TV, on the *Today Show*, which was then co-hosted by Barbara Walters, Hugh Downs, and Joe Garagiola. By the end of that day, all 5,000 copies of the first printing had been sold out, and within a week another 200,000 copies had been ordered, printed, and shipped. Expanded editions published since, among them one subtitled *The Ultimate Edition* (1993), which contains more than 1,000 terms, offer such modern coinages as "a chisel of repairmen," "a rash of dermatologists," "a slouch of models," and "an unction of undertakers."

Lipton has been awarded three honorary doctorates, and in 2001 the French minister of culture named him a chevalier (analogous to a knight) of the Order of Arts and Letters. In 2007 he received a Lifetime Achievement Award from the National Academy of Television Arts and Sciences. Lipton is an amateur pilot, and as an equestrian he has won a number of show-jumping championships. He is fairly fluent in both French and Latin. His

marriage to the actress Nina Foch, in 1954, ended in divorce in 1959. Since 1970 he has been married to Kedakai Turner Lipton, a former model who is currently a vice president with the Corcoran Real Estate Group. The Liptons own a townhouse on Manhattan's East Side and a house in Southampton, on Long Island, New York.

—F.C.

Suggested Reading: Bravo Web site; emmyonline.org; filmreference.com; imdb.com; *New York Times* p2 Mar. 1, 2001; *Philadelphia Inquirer* H p1 Oct. 13, 2002; *Washington Post* U p8 Apr. 23, 1995; Lipton, James. *Inside "Inside"*, 2007

Selected Books: *An Exaltation of Larks*, 1968; *Mirrors*, 1981; *An Exaltation of Larks: The Ultimate Edition*, 1993; *An Exaltation of Home and Family*, 1993; *An Exaltation of Business and Finance*, 1993; *An Exaltation of Romance and Revelry*, 1994; *Inside "Inside"*, 2007

Selected Television Shows: as producer, writer, and host—*Inside the Actors Studio*, 1994–

Selected Musicals: *Nowhere to Go but Up* (book and lyrics), 1962; *Sherry!* (book and lyrics), 1967

Logan, John

Sep. 24, 1961– Screenwriter; playwright

Address: c/o Creative Artists Agency, 9830 Wilshire Blvd., Beverly Hills, CA 90212

John Logan has built a resoundingly successful career as both a playwright and a screenwriter. His earliest dramas—*Never the Sinner*, staged in Chicago, Illinois, in 1985, shortly before his 24th birthday, and *Hauptmann*, produced a year later in the same city—received highly admiring reviews. Self-described as "very bookish," Logan did a great deal of research for *Never the Sinner* and *Hauptmann*, each of which is based on events surrounding a murder—one in 1924 and the other in 1932—that the media dubbed "the crime of the century." He also conducted extensive research for his most recent play, *Red*, whose protagonist is the 20th-century Abstract Expressionist artist Mark Rothko. *Red*, which opened in London in 2009 and on Broadway in 2010, struck many critics as "something rare in modern drama: a totally convincing portrait of the artist as a working visionary," in the words of Michael Billington, writing for the London *Guardian* (December 9, 2009). *Red* earned six Tony Awards, including the prize for best play, along with the Drama Desk and Outer Critics Circle Awards for outstanding play.

Stephen Shugerman/Getty Images

John Logan

Terentius Afer, known as Terence), "I am human, so nothing human is alien to me." He told Smith, "I think I exorcise my demons in my work."

John D. Logan was born in the U.S. on September 24, 1961 to immigrants from Northern Ireland. His father's job, as a U.S. Navy architect, led the family—which included his older brother and sister—to move repeatedly, to San Diego, California; Seattle, Washington; and coastal cities in New Jersey. When Logan was around seven, his father persuaded him to watch *Hamlet* (1948), Laurence Olivier's film adaptation of Shakespeare's tragedy. The experience awakened him to the power of acting and storytelling. While growing up in New Jersey, Logan would sometimes take the train into Manhattan on weekends to see Broadway shows.

When he enrolled at Northwestern University, in Evanston, Illinois, Logan intended to pursue acting; he later decided to concentrate on writing. David Downs, one of Logan's theater teachers at Northwestern, told Sid Smith, "He realized he'd never be a great actor and that his imagination really flourished in writing." In college Logan's voracious reading included all of Shakespeare's three dozen plays. For a yearlong playwriting course, Logan wrote a play about two brilliant, wealthy, homosexual Chicago residents, Nathan Leopold and Richard Loeb; in 1924, at ages 19 and 18, respectively, Leopold and Loeb murdered their 14-year-old neighbor Bobby Franks to prove to themselves that they were supermen who could commit the perfect crime. The murder—dubbed "the crime of the century"—and the trial that followed had fascinated Logan since his early teens. (The crime was the subject of many books, films, and plays.) Unlike most of the students in the class, Logan did not turn in a series of scene scripts. Instead, for nine months he researched the murder case, using court transcripts and newspaper articles, and then wrote his play—*Never the Sinner*—in two weeks. By the time he graduated from Northwestern, in 1983, with a B.F.A. degree in theater, he had become determined to make playwriting his career. To supplement his meager income in that field, he worked for over a decade in the Northwestern University Law School.

Two years after Logan completed college, *Never the Sinner* premiered at Chicago's Stormfield Theatre, with Bryan Stillman and Denis O'Hare playing the killers. The drama focused on the murderers' intellectual and emotional relationship and moral environment; it included excerpts of statements made to the trial judge by their attorney—the renowned Clarence Darrow—and the prosecutor. (Because Leopold and Loeb had pleaded guilty, there was no jury.) Most critics greeted *Never the Sinner* with praise. In a review for the *New York Times* (December 2, 1997) of the Off-Broadway mounting of Logan's significantly revised script of *Never the Sinner* a dozen years later, D. J. R. Bruckner called the play "remarkable" and wrote, "The secret of its power . . . is a rejection of sensationalism in presenting one of the most

Logan's dozen Hollywood credits include the screenplays for *Gladiator, The Aviator* (both of which brought him Academy Award nominations), and *Sweeney Todd: The Demon Barber of Fleet Street*. He also came up with the story lines for the films *Any Given Sunday, Star Trek: Nemesis*, and *The Last Samarai*, and he conceived the way the aircraft manufacturer, motion-picture producer, and record-setting pilot Howard Hughes was depicted in *The Aviator*. Martin Scorsese, *The Aviator*'s director, was "immediately engrossed" by Logan's approach to that film, as he wrote in his introduction to the published version of the screenplay (Miramax Books, 2004). "I was fascinated by the drama of this young man. . . . This is rare, to take a real historical figure . . . and get the audience involved in the drama of his life from page one. . . . John had written a wonderfully complex character, rather than a Famous Man, a story rather than a historical pageant."

The Chicago-based theater director and screenwriter Frank Galati told Sid Smith for the *Chicago Tribune* (December 12, 2004) that Logan was "a natural for the screen-play form, drawn to the epic, the historical and the sweeping narrative even as a playwright." In choosing his subjects, Logan has also been drawn to people widely regarded as thoroughly evil (such as the convicted murderer Bruno Richard Hauptmann and the fictional killer Sweeney Todd), impossibly egomaniacal (the filmmaker and actor Orson Welles and the publisher William Randolph Hearst), or creepily eccentric (Howard Hughes). Rejecting the idea that any person can be totally one-sided and unworthy of redemption, Logan has said of himself (quoting the second-century B.C. Roman dramatist Publius sensational crimes of the 1920's. The wild response is clearly noted . . . but the focus is constantly screwed tighter on just the two killers until an unspoken conclusion seems forced on the audience." *Never the Sinner* won the Outer Critics Circle Award for outstanding Off-Broadway play in 1998.

The year 1986 saw the premiere of Logan's drama *Hauptmann*, at the Victory Gardens Theater, in Chicago. The play's title character, Bruno Richard Hauptmann, a German immigrant, was executed in 1936 for the kidnapping and murder four years earlier of the 20-month-old son of the iconic American aviator Charles Lindbergh. After a great deal of research on that case—also called "the crime of the century" by the media at the time—Logan came to believe (as have some others) that Hauptmann was innocent. "The play makes use of recent evidence suppressed at the time of Hauptmann's conviction; but it also celebrates the killer himself, allowing him to be part victim and part vaudevillian," Sid Smith wrote in a review of *Hauptmann* for the *Chicago Tribune* (November 16, 1986). "In one harrowing segment, [Hauptmann] even describes how he would have stolen the child had he been the real kidnaper. That lets Logan have it both ways. However much we become convinced by the facts that Hauptmann the man was innocently executed, we still get a spine-tingling sense of Hauptmann the legend, the 'lone wolf' and grubby-looking 'child killer' of contemporaneous headlines." A year after its Chicago premiere, *Hauptmann* won the prestigious Fringe First Award at the Edinburgh International Arts Festival, in Scotland. (It was one of six entries so honored from among nearly 400 others.) *Hauptmann* was presented in New York at the Off-Broadway Cherry Lane Theatre in 1992, with Denis O'Hare in the title role.

Logan's *Snow*, a 17-actor drama about the Russian Revolution and the fall of the Romanovs, Russia's last imperial dynasty, premiered at the Stormfield Theatre in 1987. It was followed by *Speaking in Tongues*, about the possibly politically motivated killing of the Italian film director and writer Pier Paolo Pasolini, in 1975; it debuted at the New Playwrights' Theater in Washington, D.C., in 1988. *Music from a Locked Room* (1989), set in an upper-class home in pre–World War II England, first ran at the Victory Gardens Theater, as did *Scorched Earth* (1991), which focused on the electoral campaign of a handsome but spineless and valueless politician and the anti-death-penalty crusade of an idealistic lawyer who was once the politician's lover. Writing for the *Chicago Tribune* (May 31, 1991), Richard Christiansen called *Scorched Earth* "a short, keen, intelligent piece that probes relationships through a series of confrontations that are deeply personal and highly political." By contrast, Albert Williams, writing for the *Chicago Reader* (June 6, 1991, on-line), judged the play to be "two-dimensional" and declared that its "naivete and woolly-headedness" made *Scorched Earth* "tedious theatergoing." Logan's next works for the-

ater were *Riverview: A Melodrama with Music* (1992), about Chicago's landmark amusement park; *Showbiz* (1993), a play-within-a-play about the tumultuous lives of stage actors; and *The View from Golgotha* (1996), which premiered in Australia.

"Working in the theater is great, but nobody makes any money, so it was a natural [segue] into movies," Logan told Patrick J. Sauer for *Inc* magazine (December 1, 2004), noting that he had written 14 plays in his first 10 years "in the theater trenches." The first of Logan's filmscripts was for *Tornado!* (1996), a made-for-television romance cum thriller. In Hollywood Logan met with a talent agent to whom he pitched 10 movie ideas. The agent liked one of them—"King Lear in the NFL" (the National Football League)—and Logan devoted the next 12 months to writing the script that became *Any Given Sunday* (1999). "I always wanted to write something about football and it really wouldn't work as a play, so I wrote a screenplay instead," he told Patrick J. Sauer. Logan wrote the final script (which incorporated ideas contributed by Daniel Pyne) with Oliver Stone. Directed by Stone, *Any Given Sunday* starred Al Pacino, Cameron Diaz, and Jamie Foxx. It received mixed reviews. Logan's second made-for-TV movie, *RKO 281*, aired on HBO in 1999. Based on the 1988 documentary *The Battle Over Citizen Kane* (made for the public-television series *The American Experience*) along with a lot of other material, *RKO 281* is about the making of Orson Welles's classic film *Citizen Kane*. The publisher William Randolph Hearst, whose immense ego rivaled Welles's, was the model for the newspaper tycoon Charles Foster Kane, and he made a furious effort to prevent the production and release of the film. Directed by Benjamin Ross and executive-produced by Tony and Ridley Scott, *RKO 281* starred Liev Schreiber as Welles and James Cromwell as Hearst.

Logan and two others—David Franzoni and William Nicholson—were the writers of the filmscript for *Gladiator* (2000). Directed by Ridley Scott, the two-and-a-half-hour epic was set in the second century and starred Russell Crowe as Maximus, a former Roman general who is captured by slave traders and, as a slave, made to fight in the Colosseum. *Gladiator* was a box-office success and earned Logan an Academy Award nomination (and Crowe an Oscar), but reviews were generally mixed. Writing for the *New York Times* (May 5, 2000), the critic Elvis Mitchell dismissed the film as "grandiose and silly," while Desson Howe, in an assessment for the *Washington Post* (April 28, 2000), wrote, "If you enjoy visceral (and I mean visceral) action, crowd-whooping heroics and stirring acts of resistance against tyranny, if the aphorism 'hack or be hacked' rings true, then *Gladiator* is one extended guilty pleasure." Logan's next two works for Hollywood—*Star Trek: Nemesis* (2002), starring Patrick Stewart, and *The Last Samurai* (2003), starring Tom Cruise—also failed to impress reviewers.

The critical and commercial success of Martin Scorsese's *The Aviator* (2004) significantly boosted Logan's status in the film world. Logan worked on its script for five years, during which he read many biographies, aviation histories, Senate transcripts, and other relevant materials. "I wrote 15 drafts, which is highly unusual," he told Smith. "I wanted to keep hacking away until I made it the best it could be." To try to change the widely held image of its main character, Howard Hughes, as an unkempt, deranged old man, Logan said, "it was vitally important . . . to show the dynamic, powerful, even visionary person he was, as well as one steeped in incredible glamour." "At its heart," he said, *The Aviator* is "the examination of one man's soul." On the *Charlie Rose Show* (December 16, 2004), Martin Scorsese, who directed *The Aviator*, spoke about another aspect of the script that interested him: its revelations about the U.S. and "the whole idea of aviation, the whole idea of the last frontier. . . . [Americans] had gone as far west as you can, at the end of the 19th century. At the beginning of the 20th century, . . . the American dream continues, only it's Hollywood and in the air." Starring Leonardo DiCaprio (as Hughes) and Cate Blanchett (as Katharine Hepburn, one of Hughes's many romantic interests), *The Aviator* covered the making of Hughes's multimillion-dollar directorial debut, *Hell's Angels* (1930), about World War I fighter pilots; his obsessions with planes and women; his confidence and charm; and his growing mental instability. Many critics observed that despite its length, the film maintained a seamless momentum. The film received a total of 11 Oscar nominations, including one for best original screenplay, and won five.

Logan next concentrated on a screenplay based on the Tony Award–winning 1979 Broadway musical *Sweeney Todd: The Demon Barber of Fleet Street*, with music and lyrics by Stephen Sondheim and libretto by Hugh Wheeler. Loosely based on an apocryphal tale that hatched in Great Britain in the early 19th century, *Sweeney Todd* has as its title character a barber who was banished to Australia by a cruel judge who coveted Todd's wife, Lucie. After he returns to England and learns from Mrs. Lovett, who owns a nearby bakery, that Lucie poisoned herself after the judge raped her, Todd vows revenge, first on the judge and then on mankind in general. The flesh of those he kills winds up in Mrs. Lovett's meat pies. As a teenager Logan had attended the original production three times. "I'd never seen anything that bloody but at the same time so ravishingly beautiful and emotionally harrowing," he told David Benedict for the London *Observer* (December 23, 2007). Logan feared—unnecessarily, as it turned out— that Sondheim, one of his idols, would react negatively when he learned that his three-hour musical would have to be cut substantially for the big screen. "Steve's a real man of the cinema . . . ," Logan said on the National Public Radio program *Morning Edition* (December 21, 2007). "He didn't want a film re-

cording of the stage play; he wanted a movie." Sondheim and Logan worked together for several years to turn the theatrical *Sweeney Todd* into a motion picture. The screenplay, however, was written solely by Logan, who also served as the movie's producer. Directed by Tim Burton and starring Johnny Depp as Todd and Helena Bonham Carter as Mrs. Lovett, the film won nearly unanimous critical praise. In a review for the *New York Times* (December 21, 2007), A. O. Scott wrote that *Sweeney Todd* was "as dark and terrifying as any motion picture in recent memory. . . . Indeed, *Sweeney* is as much a horror film as a musical: It is cruel in its effects and radical in its misanthropy, expressing a breathtakingly, rigorously pessimistic view of human nature. It is also something close to a masterpiece." "It may seem strange that I am praising a work of such unremitting savagery," Scott continued. "I confess that I'm a little startled myself, but it's been a long time since a movie gave me nightmares. And the unsettling power of *Sweeney Todd* comes above all from its bracing refusal of any sentimental consolation."

In 2009, after an absence of more than a decade, Logan returned to the stage with *Red*, set in the New York City studio of the Abstract Expressionist painter Mark Rothko in the years 1958 to 1960, when he was in his mid-50s and famous worldwide. (He later committed suicide, in 1970, at age 66.) The play has only two characters—the gloomy, arrogant, passionate, sardonic, philosophical, and always serious Rothko and his young assistant, Ken, an aspiring painter, with whom he shares—at times in angry outbursts—his artistic principles, insights, frustrations, and anxieties. Rothko wants to be understood; he cares nothing for being liked or admired. The play is as much about art and creativity in general as it is about Rothko's painting in particular. In both the London production and *Red*'s mounting in New York, in 2010, Alfred Molina played Rothko and Eddie Redmayne his assistant. "As much as any stage work I can think of, *Red* captures the dynamic relationship between an artist and his creations," Ben Brantley wrote for the *New York Times* (April 2, 1010). In a review for the *New Yorker* (April 12, 2010), John Lahr wrote, "In teaching Ken how to look at his art, Rothko indirectly teaches us. It's an exciting education. Logan's dialogue is a sleight of hand; behind its wallop is a lot of learning."

Logan wrote the screenplays for several films scheduled for release in 2011, including an adaptation for the screen of Shakespeare's *Coriolanus*, directed by Ralph Fiennes; *Rango*, an animated film directed by Gore Verbinski whose hero is a chameleon voiced by Johnny Depp; and Scorsese's *Hugo*, based on Brian Selznick's Caldecott Award–winning illustrated novel. (The novel's inspiration was the highly inventive French animator Georges Méliès, who began making films in the late 1800s.)

Logan is reputed to be extraordinarily hardworking and unusually amiable as a collaborator. Openly gay, he avoids discussions of his private life. His house in Malibu, California, contains original works of art and first editions of books by Sinclair Lewis, Thomas Wolfe, and others of his favorite authors.

—D.K.

Suggested Reading: charlierose.com; *Chicago Tribune* C p8 Sep. 11, 1985, C p1 Dec. 12, 2004; ibdb.com; imdb.com; lortel.org; *New York Times* C p3 May 29, 1992, E p5 Dec. 2, 1997, II p1 Jan. 9, 2005

Selected Plays: *Never the Sinner*, 1985; *Hauptmann*, 1986; *Snow*, 1987; *Speaking in Tongues*, 1988; *Scorched Earth*, 1991; *Riverview: A Melodrama with Music*, 1992; *Showbiz*, 1993; *The View from Golgotha*, 1996; *Red*, 2009

Selected Films: *Tornado!*, 1996; *Bats*, 1999; *RKO 281*, 1999; *Any Given Sunday*, 1999; *Gladiator*, 2000; *The Time Machine*, 2002; *Star Trek: Nemesis*, 2002; *Sinbad: Legend of the Seven Seas*, 2003; *The Last Samurai*, 2003; *The Aviator*, 2004; *Sweeney Todd: The Demon Barber of Fleet Street*, 2007; *Rango*, 2011

Michael Buckner/Getty Images

Lubezki, Emmanuel

1964– Cinematographer

Address: c/o Jacob & Kole Agency, 6715 Hollywood Blvd., Suite 216, Los Angeles, CA 90028

During a breathtaking action sequence in the film *Children of Men*, a dystopian science-fiction thriller released in 2006, a character played by Clive Owen is shown running through a labyrinth of dilapidated apartment buildings and war-ravaged streets amidst grenade explosions, a fusillade of machine-gun fire, and sweeping chaos. The seven-and-a-half-minute scene, which was shot entirely with a hand-held camera in natural light, is widely regarded as one of the most dazzling single-shot action sequences ever committed to film. While the sequence was largely the brainchild of the film's

director, Alfonso Cuarón, the man responsible for realizing it was Cuarón's cinematographer, Emmanuel Lubezki, who received his fourth Oscar nomination for his efforts.

Described by Stephanie Zacharek for the on-line magazine *Salon* (December 25, 2006) as "one of the finest cinematographers working," Lubezki has made a career of wowing filmgoers with bravura visual passages that seemingly defy cinematographic limitations. Many of those passages have come in films directed by Cuarón; in addition to *Children of Men*, their collaborations include *Solo con tu pareja* (1991), whose title can be translated as "Only with Your Partner," although it was released internationally as *Love in the Time of Hysteria*; *A Little Princess* (1995); *Great Expectations* (1998); and *Y tu mamá también* (2001), whose title translates as "And Your Mother Too."

Lubezki has also been highly sought after by other acclaimed directors, including Mike Nichols (*The Birdcage*, 1996), Tim Burton (*Sleepy Hollow*, 1999), Michael Mann (*Ali*, 2001), Joel and Ethan Coen (*Burn After Reading*, 2008), and Terrence Malick (*The New World*, 2005, and *The Tree of Life*, 2011). "I think what keeps me interested in what I do is that I can go from one thing to another and try not to repeat myself," Lubezki explained to Jim Hanas for *Creativity* (October 1, 2008). "One of the things that I enjoy doing is going from one style to another without imposing something onto an idea. . . . The less people know about cinematography, the better I feel. When I read a review of a movie and nobody talks about me, I think I have succeeded."

Emmanuel Lubezki Morgenstern, who is of Jewish descent, was born in 1964 in Mexico City, Mexico. He has two siblings. Lubezki was given the nickname "Chivo," which means "goat," at the age of five, reportedly for his mischievousness; some still call him that. His paternal grandmother was born in Russia and fled to China with her family during the Bolshevik Revolution; after living for a time in Shanghai, her family tried to immigrate to the United States. Because of restrictions on the number of refugees the U.S. would accept, they were forced to settle in Mexico. There, Lubezki's grandmother met and married his grandfather, and the two became part of a troupe of stage actors who performed in the Yiddish-language theater.

Lubezki's father, Muni, an actor, and his mother, Raquel, often took him to movies when he was a child. "I remember watching Italian movies and films from America without reading the subtitles," Lubezki noted in an interview posted on Kodak.com. "I was always interested in watching the images even if I didn't understand the words." Captivated by the indelible images in films made by such European masters as Federico Fellini and Pier Paolo Pasolini, as well as by such Hollywood auteurs as Martin Scorsese and Francis Ford Coppola, Lubezki took up still photography. "I took pictures of everything from my family to rusted pieces of abandoned trains and railroad tracks and buildings in the city," he recalled in the Kodak.com interview.

In high school Lubezki used a Super-8 camera to shoot a student documentary about sugarcane workers in the Mexican state of Vera Cruz. In the early 1980s he enrolled at the Universidad Nacional Autónoma de México (National Autonomous University of Mexico, or UNAM), in Mexico City, where he studied history before switching to film. At the university's film institute, the Centro Universitario de Estudios Cinematográficos (CUEC), he befriended Cuarón, a fellow student. Lubezki did not immediately feel comfortable at the elite school. "They only wanted to hear that I loved Russian films and obscure Polish films," he told Lisa L. Blake for Daily Variety (January 10, 2003). "The administrators absolutely did not want to know that I love Scorsese or [Steven] Spielberg. All of us entering film school knew this was the drill—you had to lie about who you really loved if you wanted to get in." Both Lubezki and Cuarón were eventually expelled from the school for refusing to adhere to the strict requirements of their film program.

After leaving school Lubezki began working on various Mexican television productions and shorts while trying to break into feature films. For aspiring young filmmakers in Mexico in the 1980s, jobs were few and far between. "At that time," Lubezki explained to the Kodak.com interviewer, "it was practically impossible for a young person to find work on movies. The industry was very small and the unions were completely closed to new people. There was a rule that only allowed seven cinematographers in the union, so you had to wait for somebody to die or retire before you became an operator, and then you waited for another cinematographer to die or retire." Along with Cuarón and his fellow director Guillermo del Toro (who would go on to direct the Oscar-nominated film Pan's Labyrinth and the Hellboy film franchise), Lubezki got his professional start by working on the cult horror and science-fiction-themed television series La Hora Marcada, which was reminiscent of Rod Sterling's The Twilight Zone and ran on Mexican television from 1986 to 1990. Lubezki shot several episodes of the series in 1989 and 1990, and in 1991

he shot his first feature film, Bandidos ("Bandits"), which told the story of three children searching for their parents during the Mexican Revolution.

In 1991 Lubezki collaborated with Cuarón on Solo con tu pareja, about a womanizer who becomes suicidal after one of his jilted conquests bamboozles him into believing he is HIV-positive. The film, Cuarón's feature debut, became a major hit in Mexico and earned Lubezki a nomination for the 1992 Ariel Award for best cinematography. (Ariel Awards are Mexico's equivalent of the Oscars.) At the same ceremony, Lubezki won his first Ariel, for his work on Alfonso Arau's Like Water for Chocolate (1992), an adaptation of Laura Esquivel's best-selling 1989 novel of the same name. Starring Marco Leonardi and Lumi Cavazos as star-crossed lovers during the Mexican Revolution, the film became the highest-grossing Spanish-language film ever released in the U.S., and it took home almost a dozen Ariel Awards, including one for best picture. Gary Arnold wrote for the Washington Times (March 5, 1993) that Arau and Lubezki "evoke the period [of the film] in frequently breathtaking sepia imagery, splendidly tinted and filtered to suggest a glamorous storybook heritage, teeming with empassioned ghosts and supernatural-inspirational resonance."

Lubezki's work on Like Water for Chocolate brought him to the attention of Hollywood. He quickly found work on the thriller The Harvest (1992) and the ensemble drama Twenty Bucks (1993). Later in 1993 Lubezki shot two episodes of Fallen Angels, a noir crime series executive-produced by Sydney Pollack, which aired on the Showtime network. The episodes, "The Quiet Room" and "Murder, Obliquely," were directed by Steven Soderbergh and Cuarón, respectively. Lubezki was then hired to work on Ben Stiller's directorial debut, Reality Bites (1994), about the post-college challenges faced by a group of young people living in Houston, Texas. Lubezki also continued to work on Mexican productions and won two more Ariel Awards, for his work on the films Miroslava (1993), about the tragic life of the 1950s Mexican film actress Miroslava Stern, and Ámbar (1994), the story of a hunter who embarks on a life-changing expedition to an imaginary land.

Lubezki next worked with Cuarón as the cinematographer for A Little Princess (1995), a remake of the 1939 Shirley Temple movie of the same name. A Little Princess, loosely based on the classic novel by Frances Hodgson Burnett, tells the story of an imaginative 10-year-old British girl, Sara Crewe, who is sent to a boarding school when her father leaves to serve in World War I. After her father goes missing in action and is presumed dead, Crewe is tormented by the school's authoritarian headmistress, Miss Minchin, who strips her of all privileges and possessions and forces her to perform menial chores in exchange for her keep. The remake received widespread praise from critics despite poor box-office returns. In a review for Variety (April 30, 1995, on-line), Todd McCarthy called it "that rarest of creations, a children's film that plays equally well to kids and adults" and lauded its "visual style," which "fully expresses all of the story's thematic potential without ever going overboard into show-offy excess for its own sake." His work on the film earned Lubezki his first Academy Award nomination; he was the first Mexican cinematographer to be recognized by the Academy of Motion Picture Arts and Sciences since Gabriel Figueroa won a nomination for his work on John Huston's *Night of the Iguana*, in 1964.

Following *A Little Princess*, Lubezki worked on Arau's first English-language film, *A Walk in the Clouds* (1995), which tells the story of a married World War II veteran (Keanu Reeves) who falls in love with the daughter (Aitana Sanchez-Gijon) of a staunchly traditional vineyard owner. Though the film as a whole received mostly tepid reviews, Lubezki's sumptuous cinematography, which created a storybook look, was singled out for praise. "Drenching the screen with burnished amber light and moody shadow," Joe Brown wrote for the *Washington Post* (August 11, 1995), "cinematographer Emmanuel Lubezki gives the movie a hand-tinted look. He films the Napa vineyard as if it were Heaven, and the kitchen and dining room scenes have the sensual radiance that was so enchanting in *Like Water for Chocolate*."

Lubezki next shot Mike Nichols's comedy *The Birdcage* (1996), which starred Robin Williams and Nathan Lane, using rich, vibrant colors to reflect their characters' lavish and flamboyant lifestyle. After working on Cuarón's *Great Expectations* (1998), an adaptation of Charles Dickens's classic novel, and Martin Brest's *Meet Joe Black* (1998), a poorly received romantic drama starring Brad Pitt and Anthony Hopkins, Lubezki was hired as the director of photography for Tim Burton's gothic horror film *Sleepy Hollow* (1999). Based on the Washington Irving short story "The Legend of Sleepy Hollow," the film starred Johnny Depp as the eccentric police constable Ichabod Crane, who travels to the village of Sleepy Hollow to investigate a series of gruesome murders allegedly committed by the mysterious Headless Horseman (Christopher Walken). In order to realize Burton's fantastical vision, Lubezki used the iconic Hammer horror films of the 1950s and 1960s as models, creating a high-contrast look with muted colors. "I didn't want to make the movie even more baroque, more packed with elements," he told John Calhoun for *Lighting Dimensions* (November 1999). "And I didn't want to light with hard light. I wanted the light to be almost invisible, though not naturalistic—more pictorial, like an old book of illustrations." Lubezki used lights mounted on 120-foot-tall cranes to shoot the re-created village of Sleepy Hollow, which was constructed on a private parcel of land north of London, England (causing local residents to report UFO sightings); there was an abundance of smoke used as well. He explained to Calhoun, "There is not really night and not really day in the movie. There are scenes that are darker and scenes that are lighter, but everything takes place in dusk." *Sleepy Hollow* received mostly favorable reviews from critics, most of whom made note of its stunning visual elements; the film took home an Academy Award for best art and set direction, and Lubezki earned both his second Oscar nomination for best cinematography and his first American Society of Cinematographers (ASC) Award nomination. (The acclaimed cinematographer Conrad Hall reportedly did second-unit work on *Sleepy Hollow* simply for a chance to work with Lubezki.)

In 2001 Lubezki made another film with Cuarón, *Y tu mamá también*, a coming-of-age Spanish-language film about two teenage boys (Diego Luna and Gael Garcia Bernal) who embark on a road trip with an attractive older woman (Maribel Verdú). Lubezki used natural lighting and hand-held cameras to enhance the sexually explicit and voyeuristic nature of the film. Evoking the style of the French Nouvelle Vague (New Wave) films of the late 1950s and 1960s, *Y tu mamá también* was a major critical and commercial success, earning an Oscar nomination for best original screenplay and taking in more than $33 million in worldwide box-office receipts.

For *Ali* (2001), a biographical film about the iconic heavyweight-boxing champion Muhammad Ali (with Will Smith in the title role), Lubezki once again shot predominantly with hand-held cameras, aiming for a documentary-like immediacy. He told the Kodak.com interviewer, "Ninety-nine percent of *Ali* was either handheld or shot with a Steadicam, because we wanted that tactile energy." Lubezki explained to John Calhoun for *Lighting Dimensions* (January 2002), "[The director, Michael Mann,] wanted the movie to feel very current, very immediate. Many things in the movie are historic events, and are very fresh; people who were there are still alive. All those things needed a certain realism, to be recreated in a way that would feel real."

Lubezki next directed the photography for two children's films: Bo Welch's *The Cat in the Hat* (2003), based on the Dr. Seuss book and starring Mike Myers, and Brad Silberling's *Lemony Snicket's A Series of Unfortunate Events* (2004), which starred Jim Carrey. In 2004 Lubezki also worked on *The Assassination of Richard Nixon*, Niels Mueller's independent drama about a failed 1974 attempt on President Nixon's life.

The following year Lubezki teamed up with the legendary director Terrence Malick for *The New World* (2005), which tells of the founding of the Jamestown settlement in 1607 and centers on the love between Pocahontas (Q'orianka Kilcher) and John Smith (Colin Farrell). For his work on the film, which was shot almost entirely in natural light, Lubezki earned his third Oscar nomination for best cinematography.

The centerpiece of Lubezki's cinematographic oeuvre is arguably the postapocalyptic science-fiction film *Children of Men* (2006), for which he won his fourth Oscar nomination for best cinematography and his first ASC and British Academy of Film and Television Arts (BAFTA) awards. "I didn't want to light the movie, or at least I didn't want it to feel lit," he told a reporter for *American Cinematographer* (December 2006). "I want the viewer to feel as though the action is happening for real. I didn't want to make anything pretty or beautiful unnecessarily." Cuarón and Lubezki devised several lengthy, innovative single-shot action sequences, which, in addition to the now-famous seven-and-a-half-minute battlefield scene, included an unbroken six-minute shot inside a car that made use of a specially designed camera rig called the Two Axis Dolly; that device allowed the camera to move fluidly in, out of, and around the vehicle.

Critics were impressed. Stephanie Zacharek wrote, for example, "Even in a picture where the smallest gears all work perfectly and harmoniously, Emmanuel Lubezki's cinematography is a unifying and galvanizing force. . . . Even though he's working in a muted, sober palette, the colors still look vital and not simply tired. Even his graphite and smoke-silver futuristic London, certainly not a place where you'd want to take a vacation, has a wary, beaten-down beauty, as if the city itself were haunted by memories of what it used to be." In an assessment for the *Los Angeles Times* (December 22, 2006, on-line), Kenneth Turan wrote that despite "an undeniably pulpy premise . . . two things elevate *Children of Men*: One is the sheer forcefulness of the storytelling, the other the film's brilliant visual look and style." Turan concluded, "Most remarkable of all is what Cuarón's longtime director of photography Emmanuel Lubezki has accomplished by shooting entirely hand-held with few lights, greatly increasing the film's verisimilitude. Although everyone will notice the bravura work of camera operator George Richmond during one continuous seven-minute-plus battle scene, the skill of the cinematography team carries the film from the beginning to the end." In addition to his ASC and BAFTA awards, Lubezki won best-cinematography prizes from the Austin Film Critics Association, the Chicago Film Critics Association, the Las Vegas Society of Film Critics, the Los Angeles Film Critics Association, and the National Society of Film Critics, among other groups.

Lubezki's most recent work includes Martin Scorsese's *Shine a Light* (2008), a concert documentary about the legendary English rock band the Rolling Stones, for which he worked as a camera operator under head cinematographer Robert Richardson; the Coen brothers' *Burn After Reading* (2008), a dark comedy starring George Clooney, Frances McDormand, John Malkovich, Tilda Swinton, and Brad Pitt; and Terrence Malick's *The Tree of Life* (2011), a highly ambitious film starring Brad Pitt and Sean Penn. Of the last-named work, which features grand images of nature and the cosmos as well as human drama, Lubezki explained to Steven Zeitchik for the *Los Angeles Times* (January 16,

2011, on-line), "Photography is not used to illustrate dialogue or a performance. We're using it to capture emotion so that the movie is very experiential. It's meant to trigger tons of memories, like a scent or a perfume, or like when you go into a house and it smells maybe like chocolate, and it takes you to your past. . . . The movie is like great music. It doesn't move you the way a normal movie does. It moves you from a very primordial place in your brain."

Lubezki's upcoming projects include an untitled romance directed by Malick and "Gravity," a science-fiction thriller directed by Cuarón. Both are scheduled for release in 2012.

Lubezki often supplements his film work with commercials and has shot ads for such major companies as American Express and Nike. He told the Kodak.com interviewer that commercial assignments were "the best workshop to keep you from rusting, and for trying new equipment and experimenting."

Lubezki lives in Los Angeles, California. His brother, Alejandro, is a screenwriter and director.
—C.C.

Suggested Reading: *American Cinematographer* p60+ Dec. 2006, p54+ Oct. 2008; *Creativity* p58 Oct. 1, 2008; *Daily Variety* A p20 Jan. 10, 2003; Kodak.com; *Lighting Dimensions* Nov. 1999, Jan. 2002; *Los Angeles Times* (on-line) Dec. 22, 2006, Jan. 16, 2011

Selected Films: *Solo con tu pareja*, 1991; *Like Water for Chocolate*, 1992; *The Harvest*, 1992; *Twenty Bucks*, 1993; *Miroslava*, 1993; *Reality Bites*, 1994; *Ámbar*, 1994; *A Little Princess*, 1995; *A Walk in the Clouds*, 1995; *The Birdcage*, 1996; *Great Expectations*, 1998; *Meet Joe Black*, 1998; *Sleepy Hollow*, 1999; *Y tu mamá también*, 2001; *Ali*, 2001; *The Cat in the Hat*, 2003; *The Assassination of Richard Nixon*, 2004; *Lemony Snicket's A Series of Unfortunate Events*, 2004; *The New World*, 2005; *Children of Men*, 2006; *Burn After Reading*, 2008; *The Tree of Life*, 2011

Machado Ventura, José Ramón

Oct. 26, 1930– First vice president of the Cuban government; second secretary of the Communist Party of Cuba

Address: c/o Cuba Interests Section, 2630 and 2639 16th St., N.W., Washington, DC 20009

In February 2008, when the ailing Fidel Castro stepped down from his post as president of Cuba—an island nation that lies about 90 miles south of Key West, Florida—he chose his younger brother Raúl to take his place. Raúl, in turn, chose José Ramón Machado Ventura as the first vice president of

Pedro Rey/AFP/Getty Images
José Ramón Machado Ventura

the Cuban government. Machado Ventura, a Communist Party stalwart and former minister of health, had long been Raúl Castro's right-hand man; thus, his appointment to the number-two spot came as little surprise to government insiders. The news was greeted, however, with some disappointment on the part of the public; although both Fidel and Raul Castro had admitted that Cuba was in need of younger, reform-minded leaders, Machado Ventura was then 77 and considered one of his nation's "historicos," a member of the generation that had fought alongside the Castro brothers during the 1959 Cuban revolution. Brian Latell, a political analyst and scholar, told Pablo Bachelet for the *Miami Herald* (February 25, 2008) that the situation reminded him of that in the Soviet Union during the early 1980s, when Leonid Brezhnev died and was succeeded by Yuri Andropov and then Konstantin Chernenko."Old men were replacing very old men," Latell said. "This is a gerontocracy."

In early 2011 Fidel Castro gave up leadership of the Cuban Communist Party, marking the first time that his name had not appeared at the top of the party roster. Still, the status quo was, for the most part, maintained. Raúl became party head, and Machado Ventura, at age 80, was given the number-two spot. According to an Associated Press report (April 19, 2011, on-line), Raúl explained at the Sixth Party Congress, "We have kept various veterans of the historic generation, and that is logical due to the consequences of the mistakes that have been made in this area. These have robbed us of a back bench of mature substitutes with enough experience to take on the country's top positions." Pledging an eventual "rejuvenation" of the party,

he called for a limit of two consecutive five-year terms to be set in place. Machado Ventura will thus be forced to step down as vice president in 2018, when he is in his late 80s.

José Ramón Machado Ventura was born in San Antonio de las Vueltas, a town in central Cuba, on October 26, 1930. He attended medical school at the University of Havana, in the nation's capital, where he was active in a militant student group whose members were opposed to the dictatorship of Fulgencio Batista, who had overthrown the government of President Carlos Prío Socarrás in a coup on March 10, 1952.

Machado Ventura graduated from medical school in 1953 and subsequently became an early member of Cuba's 26th of July Movement, a revolutionary organization led by Fidel Castro and dedicated to Batista's ouster. The movement derived its name from the failed attack on the Moncada Barracks, an army facility in the city of Santiago de Cuba, that had taken place on that date in 1953; the Castro brothers had been imprisoned in the wake of the incident and released in 1955.

On December 2, 1956, sailing from Veracruz on the yacht *Granma*, the Castros and 80 compatriots, including Machado Ventura and another young physician, Ernesto "Che" Guevara, landed on the north coast of Oriente Province in Cuba. The rebels were quickly attacked by the Cuban Air Force and were easily defeated, with only 12 men remaining of the original 82. Nevertheless, that handful of survivors gained a foothold in the Sierra Maestra, where they waged a fierce guerrilla fight against the Batista government with a growing force of volunteers. (The Sierra Maestra is the largest mountain range in the country, extending some 150 miles along the southeastern coast and reaching an elevation of 6,476 feet at Turquino Peak. The mountains have attained an almost mythic status among Cuba's citizens, not only as the base of Castro's revolution but as a refuge for Cuban rebels dating back to the early 16th century.)

When Guevara was hit in the foot by a bullet during one battle in the mountains, Machado Ventura performed crude surgery to remove it, using a razor blade. In 1958, as the guerrilla war intensified, Machado Ventura was promoted to the rank of captain and selected to be part of a team that left the mountains to establish a second front in Oriente Province. Later reaching the rank of major, he was assigned to organize a network of hospitals and clinics.

By late December 1958 Batista's forces were weakening, and on New Year's Day 1959, he went into exile in the Dominican Republic. The following day Castro's forces marched triumphantly into Havana. Most Cubans initially celebrated Castro's victory over the tyrannical Batista, but the new regime quickly proved to be dismayingly brutal, conducting mass executions of suspected Batista supporters with no attempt to hold fair trials.

Fidel Castro was sworn in as the premier of Cuba on February 16, 1959, and Raúl became commander of the armed forces. Machado Ventura was named minister of health, serving in that post until the late 1960s. In 1965 he became a member of the central committee of the newly formed *Partido Comunista de Cuba* (PCC), the Communist Party of Cuba, which remains the country's only recognized political party. (Other parties exist but are forbidden to campaign or conduct any other activities that might be considered counterrevolutionary.) In 1965 Machado Ventura also traveled to central Africa to consult with Guevara, who was leading a clandestine effort to launch a Marxist guerrilla movement there.

Machado Ventura made international headlines in 1967, when he was the only Cuban statesman to attend the 50th anniversary celebration of the Bolshevik Revolution of 1917, at the Kremlin, in Moscow, Russia. Although the Soviets had lent Cuba significant financial support, relations between the two countries had cooled somewhat after the Cuban Missile Crisis (known in Cuba as the October Crisis) in 1962. The tense, weeks-long affair had ensued after U.S. president John F. Kennedy revealed that according to intelligence reports the Soviet Union was building bases in Cuba for long-range ballistic missiles. The two world powers were brought to the brink of nuclear war. Fidel Castro, who was not a party to the negotiations between Kennedy and Soviet premier Nikita Khrushchev that ended the crisis, criticized the latter for not obtaining greater concessions for Cuba. Castro declared in January 1963 that the Soviet–American agreement was not binding upon Cuba, and he stubbornly boycotted the 1967 festivities, sending Machado Ventura in his stead. "Well-informed observers have no doubt that the entire Cuban performance is a conscious attempt to belittle the great Soviet occasion," Henry Kamm wrote for the *New York Times* (November 5, 1967). "The Russians seem to share the feeling."

Despite such occasional appearances in the international news, Machado Ventura was not widely recognized outside Cuba, where he served quietly—and relatively uneventfully—as an apparatchik for decades. In early 1968, however, according to some sources, he entered into a series of personal squabbles with Fidel Castro, and he was ousted as health minister. His political career was reportedly in limbo for several months, before he was sent as a delegate to the Matanzas Province, home to one of Cuba's most profitable industries, the harvesting and processing of sugar cane, because the party bureaucrats in charge there were failing to meet production goals. Under Machado Ventura's leadership, sugar production increased several-fold. His organizational acumen recognized, he dedicated himself to troubleshooting for the party, staying in Fidel's good graces thanks to Raúl's advocacy.

English-language sources vary as to the exact trajectory of Machado Ventura's career, but most state that in the early 1970s, he became first secretary of the PCC provincial committee in Havana and that at the First Party Congress, held in 1975, a decade after the PCC's founding, he became a member of the politburo, the party's principal policy-making committee. Shortly thereafter he was elected to the PCC's central committee secretariat.

In 1976, after the ratification of a Cuban constitution, a unicameral *Asamblea Nacional del Poder Popular*, or National Assembly of People's Power, was formed. The assembly, which meets twice a year, has about 600 members, half of whom are nominated by municipal committees and half by such public groups as trade unions and student organizations. The assembly has the power to pass, amend, and repeal laws; control the national budget; and set foreign policy. It is also responsible for electing a 31-member Council of State, which has the authority to exercise most powers between sessions of the assembly. The president, secretary, first vice president, and five secondary vice presidents of the Council of State are also members of Cuba's Council of Ministers. (Ministries include those related to the economy, labor, science, metallurgy, foreign investment, and tourism.) After the formation of the National Assembly, Machado Ventura became a member of the Council of State and a representative for the town of Guantánamo.

After the restructuring of the PCC's central committee in 1990, Machado Ventura remained a member of the secretariat and a valued member of Raúl Castro's inner circle. A key organizer of the Fourth Party Congress, he was given broad-ranging responsibility in such areas as staff policy, basic industry, and government services.

The era of *Perestroika*, during the late 1980s, when economic and political reforms were introduced in the Soviet Union, marked the start of a difficult period in Cuba. Machado Ventura was vehemently opposed to any such reforms, saying, as quoted by Juan O. Tamayo in the *Miami Herald* (January 17, 1996), that the Cuban Communist Party must "form an ideological trench, impenetrable and indomitable, from which Marxist ideology . . . can be defended and from which diversionist ideology can be countered." With the fall of the Soviet Union, in 1991, Cuba lost billions of dollars in aid per year, and Fidel Castro was forced to make concessions to keep the nation solvent, encouraging some Western investment and attempting to revitalize Cuba's tourist industry. In 1992 the National Assembly voted to reform the 1976 constitution, and soon self-employment was legalized and free farmers' markets sprang up. Amid those and other changes, Machado Ventura cautioned, according to Tamayo, "These are times that require the maximum ideological firmness, because we're forced into maximum flexibility."

When Fidel Castro fell seriously ill in 2006 and was forced to delegate many of his traditional duties and titles, he made Machado Ventura the leader of all national and international education projects. Raúl Castro began with increasing frequency to fulfill his brother's presidential duties. Two years later, when Fidel officially left the presidency, he appointed Raúl as his successor. Despite admitting the need for younger politicians to revitalize the country, Raúl turned to Machado Ventura as his second in command, passing over Carlos Lage, a vice president of the Council of State and committed reformer whom many Cubans hoped he would pick.

Machado Ventura, widely described in the media as a hard-line communist and staunch Raúl Castro loyalist, was seen as a disappointing and unexciting choice. "There aren't too many people in Cuba who can be outshined by Raúl Castro. Machado Ventura might be one of them," Daniel Erikson, a member of a Washington, D.C., think tank specializing in Latin America, told Oscar Avila for the *Chicago Tribune* (February 26, 2008). "One of Fidel Castro's secrets to political success was having a loyal No. 2 who he could easily overshadow, that being Raúl Castro. I feel like Raúl Castro might be taking a page from Fidel's playbook in picking a No. 2 who has his back."

Little changed in Cuba during the early days of the new regime. In 2010, however, Raúl Castro and Machado Ventura began implementing limited reforms in hopes of resuscitating the nation's struggling economy, which had been particularly hard hit by a series of hurricanes two years before. By the end of 2010, for example, the government had awarded 75,000 new licenses to fledgling private-sector entrepreneurs, according to *Granma*, the Communist Party's official newspaper. Other measures were promised, such as the legalization of privately owned real estate.

In April 2011, at the Sixth Party Congress, Fidel Castro stepped down as the head of the PCC, and Raúl was elected first party secretary; Machado Ventura assumed the number-two spot on the party's leadership roster. In response, the *Miami Herald* (like many other newspapers) published a scathing op-ed piece (April 19, 2011). "We aren't ageist," the piece asserted. "America has its own obsession with youth, and wisdom certainly is sorely lacking in many of our politicians today, regardless of age and political leanings. The problem we have with the Cuban regime's 'new' cadre of leadership is that they're still partying like it's 1959, when they were the revolutionary *comandantes* who toppled another dictator with promises of democracy. Fifty-two years later, Cuba has been ravaged by one failed communist policy after another, and despite Raúl Castro's promises of 'reforms' nothing really changes because Cuba's rulers in a one-party state control the press, the labor unions, and every aspect of people's lives." The piece concluded, "Term limits remain Cubans' latest hope—and so does the biological clock." Carlos Alberto Montaner, an exiled Cuban journalist, quipped in a column for the same paper (April 4, 2011, on-line), "The greatest danger facing the rul-

ing circle is not yankee imperialism but an enlarged prostate."

Little information about Machado Ventura's personal life has been published in readily available English-language sources. He is sometimes referred to in Cuba as "Machadito," because of his short stature.

—M.M.H.

Suggested Reading: Associated Press (on-line) Feb. 25, 2008; BBC News (on-line) Apr. 19, 2011; *Chicago Tribune* C p8 Feb. 26, 2008, C p13 July 27, 2010; *Miami Herald* A p12 Jan. 17, 1996, A p1 Feb. 25, 2008; *New York Times* (on-line) Nov. 5, 1967, Aug. 1, 2006, Feb. 24, 2008, Feb. 25, 2008, July 27, 2011

Michael Lionstar, courtesy of Random House

Madrick, Jeff

July 15, 1947– Economist; writer; journalist; educator

Address: Challenge: The Magazine of Economic Affairs, *80 Business Park Dr., Armonk, NY 10504*

"The typical male worker today in the middle of the pack, the median, makes less today, less discounted for inflation, than the typical median worker made in 1969. . . . That people make the same or less today than they made 40 years ago is a stunning historical fact." The economist, journalist, and writer Jeff Madrick made those remarks to Guy Raz on July 10, 2011, during the National Public Radio program *Weekend Edition Sunday*. Madrick linked such "stagnation of wages," as he phrased it, to what he called the "assault on government oversight and regulation" that began in the 1970s and, promoted by members of Congress and unelected government officials as well as Wall Street power brokers and lobbyists, continued in the following years. One consequence of diminishing oversight and weaker regulations of the financial industry, Madrick said, was that many members of the financial community became greedy; indeed, greed became "something to be proud of." "But greed implies something else," he added. "Greed implies making so much money you're willing to violate the rules. And that begins to undermine the economy, undermine prosperity and, most important, undermine the potential for economic growth."

Madrick has closely monitored the nation's economic conditions for more than four decades. He has done so since his time as a graduate student at the Harvard Business School; while working for *Money Management*, *Business Week*, and the *New York Times*; as editor, since 1995, of *Challenge: The Magazine of Economic Affairs*; as a reporter and commentator for NBC News; as a professor at the Cooper Union and the New School; as a consultant to U.S. senator Edward M. Kennedy of Massachusetts and others; as a regular contributor to the *New York Review of Books* and, on-line, the *Huffington Post*; as a frequent contributor to the *Washington Post*, *Institutional Investor*, the *Nation*, and other popular periodicals and professional journals; and as the author of five books.

The titles and subtitles of Madrick's books indicate his standpoints to some degree: *Taking America: How We Got from the First Hostile Takeover to Megamergers, Corporate Raiding, and Scandal* (1987); *The End of Affluence: The Causes and Consequences of America's Economic Dilemma* (1995); *Why Economies Grow: The Forces that Shape Prosperity and How We Can Get Them Working Again* (2002); *The Case for Big Government* (2009); and *Age of Greed: The Triumph of Finance and the Decline of America, 1970 to the Present* (2011). Madrick is also the author of "The Business Media and the New Economy," a research paper he wrote in 2001 as a fellow at the Shorenstein Center on the Press, Politics and Public Policy, an arm of Harvard University's Kennedy School of Government.

A brief article that Madrick wrote for the June 2011 issue of the *Harvard Business School Alumni Bulletin* summarizes some of his observations about recent economic history. During his time at Harvard (fall 1969 to spring 1971), he wrote, "a famous futurist of the day was predicting that U.S. productivity would grow at 4 percent annually from that point on. In fact, stocks on average did not rise at all in the 1970s. Productivity grew more slowly in the ensuing thirty years than it had for any prolonged period since the 1800s. My class's first decade out from HBS was marked by economic and financial pain, high inflation and high unemployment, widespread anger, and shifting ide-

ologies. Then, in 1982, the bull market in stocks began. It changed the way companies were managed. CEOs focused on getting the stock price up. There was a takeover movement, then junk bonds, and then leveraged buyouts, which emphasized short-term profit gains. Wall Street firms became securities-trading companies more than money-raising companies. Meanwhile, an ideological war was developing in the country between those who believed government was largely the cause of the economic problems that bedeviled the nation and those who believed unbridled business was the culprit."

Madrick continued, "As a journalist and writer, I had a front-row seat for much of this. I got to know many of the key players and interviewed and closely observed others. . . . What I didn't know was the damage—not *always* damage, but on balance, plenty of it—that some would do over time. In the name of profits, the workings of a free market, pure self-interest, and outright greed, the American financial system stopped doing what it was supposed to do. . . . For decades, America's capital went into bad real estate, inflated LBOs [leveraged buyouts], securitization, high-tech fantasies, and inflated housing prices. For lack of productive investment, private and public (infrastructure, education), the foundation of the U.S. economy has been gravely weakened. Finance was not working because it was not adequately regulated. In the end, it is not a story of economics but of people."

Jeffrey G. Madrick was born in the New York City borough of the Bronx on July 15, 1947. His father, Milton Madrick, was the son of Russian-Jewish immigrants. As a U.S. Army officer during World War II, Milton Madrick was stationed in the Philippines when American forces, led by General Douglas MacArthur, liberated that nation from its Japanese occupiers. While there he met his future wife, Corazon Arego, the daughter of a Spanish couple living in Manila, the Philippines' capital. As a child Madrick moved with his family to Seaford, a town on Long Island, New York. Like other Seaford youngsters, he attended public schools in nearby Levittown. He graduated from General Douglas MacArthur High School in 1965. He then attended the School of Commerce (now the Stern School of Business) at New York University, where he earned a B.S. degree in economics in 1969 and was the class salutatorian. Two years later he received an M.B.A. degree from the Harvard Business School (HBS), in Cambridge, Massachusetts. After he completed his formal education, he returned to New York City, where, for the most part, he has remained ever since.

From 1972 to 1975 Madrick was a writer and columnist for *Money Management*, a magazine associated with the London *Financial Times*. In the latter year he moved to *Business Week*, where until 1978 he served as a financial editor and wrote a column, called "Inside Wall Street"; the excellence of his writing earned him a Page One Award from the Newspaper Guild in 1979. In that year and the next, Madrick served as the executive assistant to the president of Columbia Pictures. From 1980 to 1985 he worked for ESPN, first as a writer and consultant and then for ESPN's ACE Award–winning *Business Times*, which aired from 1983 to mid-1985, as a TV correspondent and commentator. From 1985 to 1993 Madrick served as an economic reporter and commentator for NBC-TV News. He also produced the NBC show *Strictly Business*, which won an Emmy Award in 1987.

In the course of his work, Madrick interviewed many economists, financial experts, and people at the highest levels in industry and government. They included the Nobel Prize–winning University of Chicago economics professor Milton Friedman; the financial and options-pricing theorist Fischer Black; Robert E. Rubin, a longtime Goldman Sachs executive and, later, U.S. treasury secretary; Walter Wriston, the chief executive officer (CEO) of Citicorp (now called Citigroup), whom Madrick has labeled "a pioneer in the effort to deregulate financial markets"; Jack Welch, the chairman and CEO of General Electric; the lawyer Joseph H. Flom, who played a major role in many corporate takeovers beginning in the 1970s; Alan Greenspan, the chairman of the Federal Reserve; the financier Michael Milken, known as the "junk-bond king," who caused the bankruptcy of his employer, the investment-banking firm Drexel Burnham Lambert, and served a prison sentence in the 1990s for securities-law violations; and Ivan F. Boesky, a prominent speculator and arbitrager who made a fortune from stock-market trades connected with acquisitions, mergers, and hostile takeovers. Madrick, who served as a consultant to Boesky for a while, edited Boesky's book, *Merger Mania: Arbitrage: Wall Street's Best Kept Money-Making Secret* (1985). The year after its publication, the U.S. Securities and Exchange Commission fined Boesky $100 million after finding him guilty on civil charges of insider trading. His image as a symbol of Wall Street corruption and greed was reinforced when, in November 1987, after a criminal trial, he received a three-year prison sentence for securities fraud.

Madrick's first book—*Taking America: How We Got from the First Hostile Takeover to Megamergers, Corporate Raiding, and Scandal*—had been published earlier that year. (In Great Britain its title was *Marrying for Money*.) In an assessment for the *New York Times Book Review* (May 20, 1987), Myron Kandel noted among his few criticisms of *Taking America* that Madrick had "deal[t] very tenderly" with Boesky in it. As a whole, Kandel felt, the book "is a readable and well-paced narrative of some of the biggest deals in recent business history." *Taking America*, he wrote, "suggests that the takeover movement developed a momentum of its own, with corporate chief executives moving companies around as if they were pieces of a board game and managing—and discarding—businesses as if they were mere portfolios of stocks instead of living organizations with employees, traditions,

products, customers and suppliers. It became cheaper to buy companies than to build them, and then it often became necessary to sell off or eliminate some of the pieces to pay for the purchase. In addition, Mr. Madrick says, the investment bankers and lawyers were playing Iago to the C.E.O.'s Othello." "There are a number of worthwhile books on one or more recent takeover contests . . . ," Kandel noted. "But Mr. Madrick makes a special contribution by offering a wide-ranging overview of the takeover mania and its impact on the way big business is controlled and operated. Particularly valuable are his nutshell descriptions of the principal behind-the-scenes players who have guided the decisions made in the executive suites." *Business Week* chose *Taking America* as one of the year's 10 best books, and the *New York Times* included it on its list of the year's notable books.

Madrick published his next book, *The End of Affluence: The Causes and Consequences of America's Economic Dilemma*, in 1995. In it he argued that the U.S. had enjoyed an unprecedented average yearly growth rate of about 3.4 percent since the Civil War (the Great Depression being a temporary setback). For over a century, he explained, America's growth had been propelled by worker productivity, which rose an average of 2 percent annually, with a corresponding growth in real wages: the wages of members of the middle class doubled every 35 years, and their standard of living rose accordingly. "Spreading prosperity, growing incomes, rising home ownership, expanding leisure time, increasing access to a good education, more secure retirements, the steady climb towards the middle class by more and more Americans, and an economy whose bounty has consistently exceeded expectations defines the golden age" and exemplifies the American dream, Madrick wrote. Then, around 1973, economic growth began to slow, falling to an average of 2.3 percent annually. That decrease prevented the creation of about $12 trillion worth of goods and services and led to stagnation in real wages. The multiple causes of that change included the entrance into the workforce of baby boomers and a growing number of immigrants and women, the financial burdens on the federal government of Great Society programs, inflation, and greatly increased competition from other countries. "The resulting loss of markets meant fewer jobs and lower wages for American workers, the abandonment of some industries, idle capacity in many others and reduced capital investment overall," Madrick wrote.

In general, the economists who reviewed *The End of Affluence* found much to praise but questioned aspects of Madrick's analysis—not surprisingly, since most of them differed to some extent with Madrick and with one another regarding the causes of America's changed economic landscape and possible ways to inject new life into it. The Harvard University economist Robert Z. Lawrence, who assessed the book for *Foreign Affairs* (January/February 1996), wrote, "Madrick is stronger in describing the problem than in prescribing solutions. Yet in criticizing Madrick humility is in order because no one has yet solved the productivity slowdown mystery. It is something like the economists' version of cancer. We know there is a disease with very complex causes. We know the things you can do to increase your chances of a cure, but we cannot be certain of all the causes or the solutions. Madrick is right to warn us about misplaced optimism and the snake oil of quick fixes. But he is wrong when he discounts the potential contribution of measures such as improved education and training, better technology, higher savings and investment, and trade with emerging economies. . . . We do not know the cure for the slow growth in living standards but can be pretty sure that" all those measures "are likely to help." Louis Uchitelle, who covers economic issues for the *New York Times* (October 1, 1995), praised *The End of Affluence* and Madrick for making "sophisticated economics easy reading," then wrote, "There are weak spots in his book, the most glaring being his vague suggestions for improving the national lot, although the whole point of his book is that there is no way for America's economy to regain its old, singular status. His various suggestions appear in the final chapter, and they can be ignored. The history definitely should not be ignored. Nothing is more striking in this book than the author's account of economic growth since the Civil War." *The End of Affluence* spent two weeks on the *New York Times* best-seller list.

Madrick edited the book *Unconventional Wisdom: Alternative Perspectives on the New Economy* (2000). Its 14 essays include "Capitalism and the Erosion of Care," by Paula England and Nancy Folbre; "Why Stocks Won't Save the Middle Class," by Edward N. Wolff; "Russia, the West, and the Failure of the Free Market," by Ngaire Woods; and "The Case for International Capital Controls," by James Crotty.

In 2001, the year he was a Shorenstein fellow at Harvard, Madrick started working as a consultant for the Democratic U.S. senator Edward M. Kennedy of Massachusetts. Madrick helped to write the senator's speeches and his book *America: Back on Track* (2006), which described seven challenges facing the U.S.—among them "reclaiming our constitutional democracy," "protecting our national security," and "guaranteeing health care for every American"—and ways to address them. Harold Meyerson, writing for the *American Prospect* (November 2006), called the book "a clear statement of the liberal world view at a moment when such statements are desperately needed." Madrick and Kennedy remained close friends until Kennedy's death, in 2009. "He was wonderful to work with, very caring and idealistic," Madrick told *Current Biography*. "Kennedy gave me confidence in my own ideas. We did not agree on everything . . . but he liked in particular my attitudes towards the importance of government. He had to temper his views for political reasons, I'd say."

In *Why Economies Grow: The Forces that Shape Prosperity and How We Can Get Them Working Again* (2002), Madrick discussed the "new economy" rhetoric that dominated the media in the 1990s and noted that that "new economy" had not been accompanied by the creation of new institutions—the expansion of children's day care, for example. In a review of *Why Economies Grow* for the *Washington Monthly* (December 2002), Robert J. Shapiro wrote that Madrick's analysis lacked proof. "But Madrick's point is not to provide data or evidence," he acknowledged, "but to shift our economic thinking away from factors like innovation and skilled labor, and back to the demand side of the economy. That provides the basis for his own agenda for prosperity: To keep domestic market demand growing, we need ongoing budget deficits to finance public investment, a higher minimum wage, expanded job programs, pensions and healthcare for all workers, more income support and training for the unemployed and so on, and on"—all of which require a large, activist federal government.

That is the subject of Madrick's next book, *The Case for Big Government* (2009). In it Madrick argued that President Ronald Reagan was wrong when he declared, in 1981, in his first inaugural address, that "government is not the solution to our problem; government is the problem." "There really is no example of small government among rich nations," Madrick observed. Historically, he pointed out, activist American federal governments were responsible for the Louisiana Purchase, the Homestead Acts, the Morrill Acts (which led to the founding of land-grant colleges), the construction of highways and other public works, the maintenance of police and fire departments, and the preservation of wilderness (overcoming persistent laissez-faire arguments to do all of that). "Even now, there are devotees of the anti-public sector stripe trying to make the case that it was big government that brought us the current great recession . . . ," Max Neiman wrote for the *Political Science Quarterly* (Spring 2010). "*The Case for Big Government* contributes a counterweight to the apologists for private sector failure and misconduct. [Madrick's] book critically examines the anti-government theology that has dominated policy discussions for the past four decades." Madrick's "goal here is not to persuade conservative commentators such as George Will or the disciples of Milton Friedman," Richard Parker wrote for the *New York Review of Books* (March 12, 2009), "but rather journalists, academics, policy intellectuals, and politicians who have embraced the earlier 'public marketeering' consensus—as well as members of a younger generation who may be unfamiliar with past achievements of government and the potential of the public sector." *The Case for Big Government* was one of two finalists for the 2009 PEN/John Kenneth Galbraith Award for Nonfiction.

Madrick's most recent book is *Age of Greed: The Triumph of Finance and the Decline of America, 1970 to the Present* (2011). "Madrick's subtitle gets it right . . . ," the Nobel Prize–winning economist Paul Krugman and his wife and sometime collaborator, the economist Robin Wells, wrote for the *New York Review of Books* (July 14, 2011). "Despite what some academics (primarily in business schools) claimed, the vast sums of money channeled through Wall Street did not improve America's productive capacity by 'efficiently allocating capital to its best use.' Instead, it diminished the country's productivity by directing capital on the basis of financial chicanery, outrageous compensation packages, and bubble-infected stock price valuations." Krugman and Wells concluded, "*Age of Greed* is a fascinating and deeply disturbing tale of hypocrisy, corruption, and insatiable greed. But more than that, it's a much-needed reminder of just how we got into the mess we're in—a reminder that is greatly needed when we are still being told that greed is good." Madrick's inclusion of many biographical sketches in *Age of Greed*, Margaret Quamme wrote for the *Columbus (Ohio) Dispatch* (May 29, 2011), enabled him "to give a human face to what might otherwise be an overwhelming welter of information about complicated hedge-fund strategies, petrodollar recycling, junk bonds and subprime mortgages."

In a conversation with Lynn Parramore about *Age of Greed* for the *Huffington Post* (May 31, 2011, on-line), Madrick said, "I think greed always exists. It rises and falls with the times. But when it's unchecked by government, which has been happening since the 1970s, it festers on itself. It becomes outsized and it badly distorts the economy. That is to say, self-interest rises to a level of greed that overwhelms the economic invisible hand. When self-interest turns into greed, people start using the power of business to undermine the way markets should work. . . . They didn't just take more risk. They were not deluded. Many of them took more risks than they should and merely did it because they made a buck. So greed really drove this decade: money and self-interest in the extreme drove very bad decision-making on Wall Street, which in turn, it's important to emphasize, deeply harmed the American economy." He also said, "Greed would have remained checked had government been doing what it should be doing. And that's a tragedy of the age."

Madrick is a senior fellow at the Roosevelt Institute, in New York. From his first marriage (1969–75), to Gloria Jean Adrian, which ended in divorce, Madrick has an adult daughter, Matina. His second wife, Kim Baker, is the co-founder and creative director of Gouda, which specializes in educational gifts for museums, and the owner of Kim Baker Design, a luxury-furniture company. Madrick and his wife live in the Greenwich Village section of New York City.

—M.M.H.

Suggested Reading: CNN (transcript) Nov. 23, 1995; *Columbia Journalism Review* p21+ May/June 2008; *Foreign Affairs* p146 Jan./Feb. 1996; *Fortune* (on-line) Dec. 8, 1986; *Harvard Business School Alumni Bulletin* (on-line) June 2011; Jeff Madrick Web site; *Los Angeles Times* (on-line) Oct. 20, 1985; Schwartz Center for Economic Policy Analysis, the New School (on-line)

Selected Books: *Taking America: How We Got from the First Hostile Takeover to Megamergers, Corporate Raiding, and Scandal*, 1987; *The End of Affluence: The Causes and Consequences of America's Economic Dilemma*, 1995; *Why Economies Grow: The Forces that Shape Prosperity and How We Can Get Them Working Again*, 2002; *The Case for Big Government*, 2009; *Age of Greed: The Triumph of Finance and the Decline of America, 1970 to the Present*, 2011; as editor—*Unconventional Wisdom: Alternative Perspectives on the New Economy*, 2000

Ellen Wallenstein, courtesy of the Living Theatre

Malina, Judith

June 4, 1926– Actress; theater director

Address: The Living Theatre, 21 Clinton St., New York, NY 10002

The actress, writer, and theater director Judith Malina co-founded the Living Theatre—the oldest experimental theater in the United States—with her first husband, the late Julian Beck, in 1947. The Living Theatre was part of the larger renewal of

New York City's downtown theater scene that took place in the mid–20th century, partly as a backlash against the bland offerings of post–World War II Broadway. Influenced by the subversive ideas that inspired theater movements in Europe, the Living Theatre and other experimental troupes in the United States began to address contemporary political issues through provocative—sometimes shocking—performances. One source of those ideas was France's Antonin Artaud, known as the father of the Theatre of Cruelty, a movement whose adherents strove to shatter the audience's false reality, or the "fourth wall" separating them from the players, by awakening their senses with music, movement, and spectacle. Artaud's influence on the Living Theatre was evident early on in many of its productions, including, notably, *The Connection* (1959), which placed the audience among a group of drug addicts who talked, played jazz, and waited for their "fix." Another major influence on Malina and Beck was the German-born playwright Bertolt Brecht, who championed the notion of epic theater, the idea that theater should be a forum for political ideas. Brecht's influence can be seen in the Living Theatre's promotion of an anarchist-pacifist vision of world peace, which Malina and Beck termed the "Beautiful Non-violent Anarchist Revolution." Malina explained to Robert Nott for the *Santa Fe New Mexican* (May 16, 2003), "I think that poets, theater artists, and intellectuals have always asked the question: Is there a better way to run the world? I think theater has always been part of trying to make this a better world. Theater artists think it's possible to create a world of love and peace, and everyone wants to live in that world of love and peace. Poets give hope to the idea that what we want is really possible. That's our motive; I think it spurs on art and always has." The Living Theatre continues to attract young artists to its stage.

Judith Malina was born in Kiel, Germany, on June 4, 1926 to a rabbi, Max Malina, and his wife, the former Rosel Zamora. In 1928 the family immigrated to New York City, where Max Malina founded a largely German-Jewish congregation. First settling in the Manhattan neighborhood of Yorkville, the family soon moved—after the area became "too anti-Semitic," Malina told Jerry Tallmer for *Thrive* magazine (May 2007, on-line)—to the Broadway Central Hotel, where Malina spent most of her childhood. Rosel Malina, who had long harbored dreams of becoming an actress, gave her daughter lessons in elocution, singing, and movement. Judith Malina also participated in recitals at her school and synagogue. In 1932, when Malina was six years old, she joined her parents on a trip back to Germany, which was then coming under Nazi influence. Upon their return to the States, the Malinas worked to spread the news about the cruelty they had witnessed, handing out pamphlets whose cover read, "Do You Know What Has Happened to Your Jewish Neighbors?" At a mass rally to save European Jews, held at Madison Square Garden in 1933, Judith Malina recited a poem about a Jewish child who is driven out of a Berlin playground by adults screaming, "Jude! Jude!" (meaning "Jew" in German). Her performance "brought down the house," Lehman Weichselbaum noted for *Jewish Week* (February 14, 2011, on-line).

At the age of 12, Malina returned home from school one day and announced—to the displeasure of her father—that she was a pacifist. She has identified herself as such ever since and has even asserted that Adolf Hitler could have been disarmed by the power of love. Malina dropped out of high school after the death of her father, in 1940. With her mother's encouragement she began studying acting under the renowned German theater director Erwin Piscator at the New School for Social Research's Dramatic Workshop, where her classmates included the actors Marlon Brando and Elaine Stritch and the playwright Tennessee Williams. There, she became acquainted with the epic theater philosophy, espoused by Piscator and, most famously, Brecht, that would later influence much of her work with the Living Theatre.

Malina met Julian Beck, a young abstract-expressionist painter who had recently dropped out of Yale University, when she was 17. The two soon became inseparable, and Malina introduced him to her ideas about the theater. Beck soon developed his own ideas about the art form. "What he taught me was very simple," Malina told Weichselbaum. "Make it personal and make it true to yourself." Married in 1948, the couple incorporated their unconventional views on sexuality into their work. Malina and Beck—the latter of whom had once been diagnosed by a psychiatrist as having "homosexual tendencies" and advised to date women as a form of treatment—practiced an open marriage, occasionally sharing lovers, including the Living Theatre company member Hanon Reznikov. (Malina and Reznikov, who was 25 years her junior, married in 1988, several years after Beck's death.)

Malina and Beck founded the Living Theatre in 1947 in their West End Avenue apartment. At a time when Off-Broadway and Off-Off-Broadway theaters did not yet exist, their intention was to build a "citadel of emotionally direct expression," as Weichselbaum put it, through which they could communicate their anarchist-pacifist politics. In 1951 Malina and Beck began producing shows at the Cherry Lane Theatre on Commerce Street, in Greenwich Village. Some of the earliest performances included *Ubu Roi* ("King Ubu"), Alfred Jarry's absurdist retelling of Shakespeare's *Macbeth*; Gertrude Stein's *Doctor Faustus Lights the Lights*; and the poet John Ashbery's *The Heroes*. In the 1950s they also staged work by the poet T. S. Eliot, the artist Pablo Picasso, the experimental composers John Cage and David Tudor, and the poet Dylan Thomas. In 1953 the Cherry Lane Theatre was closed after Beck's paper sets were declared a fire hazard. The Living Theatre then moved to a loft on

Manhattan's Upper West Side, before finding a home in a defunct department store on Sixth Avenue and 14th Street. By the mid-1950s Malina and Beck had established themselves as members of the upper echelon of New York's bohemian avant-garde arts scene.

In about 1958 Jack Gelber, then a 26-year-old aspiring playwright from Chicago, Illinois, approached Beck and Malina on the doorstep of their New York apartment and thrust a script into their hands. "Julian looked at it, read a bit of it, then came running to me in the bedroom," Malina recalled to Tallmer for the *Downtown Express* (January 23–29, 2009, on-line). "He said: 'This is the play we want to do.'" The play was *The Connection*, a "jazz play"—as it was referred to at the time, because it featured a live jazz band—that would catapult the Living Theatre into the national spotlight. Directed by Malina, the play focused on a group of heroin addicts waiting for a character named Cowboy to arrive with their fix; the Freddie Redd Quartet and the young saxophonist Jackie McLean provided the music. The play opened to mixed reviews. As Tallmer noted in 2009, one reviewer from the *New York Times* (Louis Calta, in the July 16, 1959 edition) dismissed the play a "farrago of dirt." Tallmer himself—at the time a young theater reviewer who had recently helped found the *Village Voice*—was among those who led the charge in the play's favor. In his 1959 *Voice* review, as quoted in the *Downtown Express*, Tallmer wrote, "This is the first production of any sort (not just theatre) in which I have seen (heard?) modern jazz used organically and dynamically to further the dramatic action rather than merely decorate or sabotage it." *The Connection*, also noted for breaking down the "fourth wall" between performers and audience, ran for 700 performances, toured Europe, and won Malina and the Living Theatre an Obie Award. A film version, with the original cast and directed by Shirley Clarke, was released in 1962.

During the 1960s the Living Theatre continued to present stage readings of plays and poetry by such notable literary figures as William Carlos Williams, Allen Ginsberg, Gregory Corso, and Paul Goodman. The next play that received significant attention at the theater was *The Brig* (1963). Written by Kenneth Brown, a former U.S. marine, and directed by Malina, *The Brig* was an autobiographical piece about Brown's time in a military prison. "The play shows how it's possible for nice young people from Wisconsin to commit atrocities," Malina told Trav S. D. for the *Village Voice* (April 3, 2007, on-line) during the play's 2007 revival. "They receive all this obedience training and do all this drilling, and it becomes irresistible for them to obey rather than think or feel." Indeed, the play shocked audiences of 1963. During its run the Living Theatre was shut down by the Internal Revenue Service—on charges of tax evasion, later dropped—and for the final showing of *The Brig*, the company, audience, and press had to enter the

performance space through the roof, using rope ladders. Later, when Malina and Beck appeared in court to address the tax charges, they took the opportunity to stage an impromptu political performance for the judge and lawyers—and were thrown in jail for contempt of court. (Malina has been arrested more than a dozen times in several countries for acts of civil disobedience related to work with the Living Theatre.)

After *The Brig* the Living Theatre's members became interested in collective creation—a theater movement aimed at democratizing the creative process by devising plays through group writing. In the mid-1960s the company began performing works created that way at various locales around New York. One piece, *Mysteries . . . And Smaller Pieces* (1964), was virtually wordless and lacked a plot, characters, scenery, and costumes, instead relying on nonverbal sounds and improvisation. The Living Theatre Web site describes the composition as "pure communication between performers and audience" that "[offers] the audience the opportunity of assisting in a series of rituals meant to liberate the actor's deepest resources." The theater's nonverbal interpretation of Mary Shelley's *Frankenstein* (1965) was presented in much the same way. Clive Barnes wrote for the *New York Times* (October 3, 1968, on-line) that the Living Theatre's innovations represented the "development of the theater as a place of wonderment and miracles, a circus-like home of rituals to be celebrated by a generation that has lost the time and the place for ritual."

The concepts of ritual and spiritual exercise informed much of the Living Theatre's work throughout the late 1960s, which the company spent mostly in Europe. One of their most famous and controversial pieces, *Paradise Now*, premiered in 1968 at the Festival d'Avignon, in France. Intended to be an expression of the ensemble's belief that the Beautiful Non-violent Anarchist Revolution could be achieved only after the sexual revolution had taken place, and that all violent energy could be transformed by an acceptance of free love, the piece included chanting, song, dance, nudity, and simulated—and, sometimes, actual—sex. Audience members were encouraged to participate and often did. A particularly memorable performance of *Paradise Now*, at Yale University, also in 1968, culminated with a parade en masse onto New Haven's York Street, where 10 performers, including Malina, and several audience members were arrested for indecent exposure. "The audience participates with us in trying to see how close we can—in that theater—get to feel revolutionary actions and how many changes we can make," Malina said, explaining the collaborative aspect of the piece, as quoted by Baobao Zhang in the *Yale Daily News* (September 15, 2009, on-line). "At some places it was greater and at some places it's less. At Yale, it was very lively and full of imaginary activity."

During the mid-1970s the Living Theatre traveled the world staging a cycle of plays, collectively called The Legacy of Cain, in such nontraditional venues as a prison in Brazil (where Beck, Malina, and other company members served time for inciting political upheaval, among other charges); in steel mills in Pittsburgh, Pennsylvania; and in front of banks, government buildings, and housing projects. During those years—often in Rome, Italy, and Paris, France—the troupe performed numerous free "street theater" shows before large audiences.

When the Living Theatre returned to New York, in the early 1980s, having found tremendous success with audiences abroad—particularly in Italy, where Living Theatre Europa, a facet of the group, thrives today—Malina and Beck were disappointed by the cold reception of American audiences to their work. Indeed, in the Living Theatre's absence, avant-garde theater in New York City had evolved; the physical style of performance typical of the Living Theatre could be seen on Broadway in Andrew Lloyd Webber's musical *Cats*, and there was nudity in the commercially successful *Hair*. In short, the Living Theatre was no longer shocking, and its message was viewed as passé. In 1984 the company performed a cycle of four plays at the Joyce Theatre: an abstract revival of Brecht's version of *Antigone*; a version of Ernst Toller's *Masse Mensch* (1921), called *The One and the Many*; and original plays by Beck and Reznikov, titled *The Archeology of Sleep* and *The Yellow Methuselah*, respectively. The works were received poorly. Frank Rich wrote for the *New York Times* (January 19, 1984), "The Living Theatre is now a straggly collection of indistinguishable riffraff; the troupe could be a defrocked Moonie ashram, or maybe a seedy bus-and-truck company of *Godspell* at the end of a 15-year tour."

Beck was both a major artistic contributor to the Living Theatre and its administrative head, and after his death from stomach cancer, in 1985, Malina struggled to keep the group going. The company moved into a new space on Third Street in Manhattan. Malina, along with Reznikov, who became her new co-director, produced a range of works in the late 1980s. One such work was *Poland/1931* (1988), Reznikov's adaptation of poems in Jerome Rothenberg's 1974 book of the same name. The piece was notably quieter than the theater's previous work, but it was still labeled "vintage" and found to have a "'60s air" by a *New York Times* critic, D. J. R. Bruckner (April 28, 1988, on-line). *The Tablets* (1989), adapted by Reznikov and based on poetry by Armand Schwerner, fared slightly better with critics. Bruckner called the performance, in his review for the *New York Times* (June 11, 1989, on-line), "often eloquent and sometimes amusing." Malina and Reznikov followed *The Tablets* with *The Zero Method* (1992), the well-received *Anarchia* (1993), and *Capital Changes* (1998), based on Fernand Braudel's 1992 work, *Civilization and Capitalism: 15th–18th Century*.

In 2001 the Living Theatre members traveled to southern Lebanon to collaborate with a group of college students on a three-week theater project, at the site of the infamous Khiam prison, where, during Israel's 18-year occupation of southern Lebanon, thousands were detained without trial and tortured; the site is now a museum of torture run by the Islamic military group Hezbollah. (The prison was run by the South Lebanese Army as well as Israeli forces.) With the students—many of whom had lost family members during the occupation—the company members rehearsed their 1997 anti-death-penalty piece, *Not in My Name*. They then performed the piece with the students in Tripoli, Libya, and in Beirut, Lebanon, as part of anti-death-penalty protests there. The troupe also worked with the students to develop a site-specific play about Khiam. "Hearing Judith Malina say there must always be some people in the world offering a utopian message of nonviolence, even among people defending against occupation, even if it sounds naive, has helped me see my purpose exactly," one student participant in the project told Alisa Solomon for the *Village Voice* (July 17, 2001, on-line). Malina told Solomon that her Jewish ancestry "never came up" among the students.

Also in 2001 the Living Theatre presented a piece called *Resistance!*, drawn from recollections of members of the resistance movements against the Nazis and Benito Mussolini's regime in Italy. The play had been conceived and first performed in 1999, in Italy, under the title *Restenza!* In 2007, for the first time in over a decade, the Living Theatre found a home in New York City, in a small space on Clinton Street on Manhattan's Lower East Side. For the space's inaugural performance, Malina chose a revival of *The Brig*. "My first impulse was to open with some collective work, because we like to do that," Malina told Tallmer for *Thrive*. "But you know, the politics of our time—abuses of prisoners—torture—well, *The Brig* became the thing to do."

That same year Malina appeared in the Living Theatre's production of *Maudie and Jane*, based on Doris Lessing's 1938 novel *The Diary of a Good Neighbour*. The play and the book follow a self-absorbed magazine editor who befriends an odd, foul-smelling elderly woman. Taking on the latter role, Malina demonstrated to critics and audience members that at age 81, she was "still dancing around the stage, taking off her clothes, doing her best to shake up the world," as Caryn James wrote for the *New York Times* (December 13, 2007). The next year the company performed the site-specific work *No Sir!* in New York City's Times Square. The piece was a direct response to the seven-minute commercial that had been playing on a loop in front of the military recruiting station in the square. The year 2008 also saw the death of Reznikov at age 57, from complications of a stroke; his death left Malina, for the first time, virtually alone in running the Living Theatre. Despite the company's modest successes and its historic importance in the avant-garde theater world, money was a constant worry.

To honor Reznikov, Malina completed and produced the play he had been working on at the time of his death. Called *Eureka!*, the piece, performed in 2008, was inspired by Edgar Allan Poe's last book, which has the same name. In 2009 the Living Theatre presented a revival of *The Connection*. The company's most recent production, *Korach* (2010), directed by Malina, told the story of the biblical figure Korach, who opposed Moses as the leader of the Israelites.

Numerous books and documentary films have chronicled the history of the Living Theatre. Malina, who begins each day by writing in her journal, has published her journal entries in *The Enormous Despair: The Diary of Judith Malina, August 1968 to April 1969* (1972) and *The Diaries of Judith Malina (1947–1957)* (1984). She has also published a poetry collection, *Poems of a Wandering Jewess* (1982).

Malina has appeared in a handful of films, including *Dog Day Afternoon* (1975), in which she played the mother of Sonny Wortzik (Al Pacino); *The Addams Family* (1991), as Grandmama Addams; and the 2010 romantic comedy *When in Rome.* (She has said that her earnings for her role in *The Addams Family* funded the Living Theatre for three years.) Malina has also had several television roles, perhaps most notably playing Aunt Dottie in the HBO series *The Sopranos* in 2006.

Malina has won many honors for her work, among them eight Obie Awards. She was named Humanist of the Year by the New York Humanist Church in 1984, and, along with the late Julian Beck, she was inducted into the American Theatre Hall of Fame in 2003.

From her marriage to Beck, Malina has a son, Garrick "Gary" Beck, and a daughter, Isha Beck Appell. She maintains a residence above the Living Theatre, in Manhattan.

—M.M.H.

Suggested Reading: *Downtown Express* (on-line) Jan. 23–27, 2009; *Fifth Estate* p13 Fall 2008; *Jewish Week* (on-line) Feb. 14, 2011; (Montreal, Canada) *Gazette* E p5 May 9, 2009; *New York Times* p70 Oct. 12, 1986, E p6 Dec. 13, 2007, (on-line) Oct. 3, 1968, Apr. 28, 1988, June 11, 1989; *Thrive* magazine (on-line) May 2007; *Village Voice* (on-line) July 17, 2001, Apr. 3, 2007; *Yale Daily News* (on-line) Sep. 15, 2009; Kotynek, Roy, and John Cohassey. *American Cultural Rebels: Avant Garde and Bohemian Artists, Writers and Musicians from the 1850s through the 1960s*, 2008; Tytell, John. *The Living Theatre: Art, Exile, and Outrage*, 1995

Selected Plays: *Ubu Roi*, 1951; *Doctor Fautus Lights the Lights*, 1951; *The Heroes*, 1952; *The Connection*, 1959; *The Brig*, 1963; *Mysteries . . . And Smaller Pieces*, 1964; *Frankenstein*, 1965; *Antigone*, 1967; *Paradise Now*, 1968; *Seven*

Meditations on Political Sado-Masochism, 1973; *The Destruction of the Money Tower*, 1975; *Six Public Acts*, 1975; *The Yellow Methusaleh*, 1984; *The Archeology of Sleep*, 1984; *Poland/1931*, 1988; *The Tablets*, 1989; *The Zero Method*, 1992; *Anarchia*, 1993; *Not in My Name*, 1997; *Capital Changes*, 1998; *Resistance!*, 2001; *The Brig* (revival), 2007; *Maudie and Jane*, 2007; *No Sir!*, 2008; *Eureka!*, 2008; *The Connection* (revival) 2009; *Korach*, 2010

Selected Films: *Dog Day Afternoon*, 1975; *The Addams Family*, 1991; *When in Rome*, 2010

Selected Books: *Paradise Now: Collective Creation of The Living Theatre*, 1971; *The Enormous Despair: The Diary of Judith Malina, August 1968 to April 1969*, 1972; *Poems of a Wandering Jewess*, 1982; *The Diaries of Judith Malina (1947–1957)*, 1984

Saul Loeb/AFP/Getty Images

Malloy, Dan

July 21, 1955– Governor of Connecticut (Democrat)

Address: State Capitol, 210 Capitol Ave., Hartford, CT 06106

In January 2011 Dan Malloy, a Democrat, became the 88th governor of Connecticut. Prior to winning the governorship, he was the longest-serving mayor of Stamford, Connecticut, a post he held from 1995 until 2009. During his youth it would have seemed unlikely to most that Malloy—who is dyslexic—would one day hold his state's highest office. "Realistically, if you asked people about me from my childhood, they would not have predicted the level of success that I've been able to accomplish," he said to Susan Haigh in an interview for the Associated Press, as quoted in the Danbury, Connecticut, *News-Times* (May 20, 2006, on-line). "If you can't read, you can't do math and you can't spell, then how is anyone going to assume that you can be successful?" Despite his disorder Malloy was determined to perform well in school, a goal he reached in part by listening to books on tape and mastering his ability to communicate verbally. "I was an oral learner," he said to Haigh. "I have very good recall. It was a good way to learn, to learn the language, to learn skills, skills that you might use to convince people of your point, your argument, that sort of thing." After earning a law degree, he served as an assistant district attorney in New York City and then as a partner at a Connecticut-based law firm before deciding to enter politics. During his tenure as mayor of Stamford, Malloy helped to create jobs and lower crime rates. He also improved the city's parks, schools, and public housing. In addition, he introduced a program that provides universal access to prekindergarten. His success aside, "you can't separate me from my upbringing as a child overcoming learning disabilities and having to make my way through that . . . ," he told David M. Halbfinger for the *New York Times* (February 15, 2011, on-line). "It's a miracle that I'm here."

The youngest of eight children, Dannel Patrick Malloy was born on July 21, 1955 in Stamford. His mother, Agnes, was a school nurse, and his father, Bill, worked as an insurance salesman. His parents (who are now deceased) could not agree on whether to name their son Daniel; then, one day, they passed a street named Dannell Drive. "My mother looked at the sign and said, 'You know, if we drop one l, we can pronounce it Dannel,'" Malloy told Christopher Keating for the *Hartford (Connecticut) Courant* (March 11, 2010). "And that's how I got my name." During his childhood Malloy's teachers began to notice that he had difficulties with reading, spelling, math, and motor coordination. "I was diagnosed as mentally retarded as late as the fourth grade," he recalled to Raymond Hernandez for the *New York Times* (August 11, 2010, on-line). "My mother knew it wasn't true." It was later discovered that Malloy was suffering from dyslexia, a learning disability that makes it difficult for a person to recognize and understand written words and symbols. At the time of his diagnosis, there was little known about the disorder. To offset his inability to read and write well, Malloy developed a sharp memory and good speaking skills. When he was 10 his mother gave him a ring to wear on his right hand, so he would always know right from left; she also gave him a radio to hone his listening skills. "You could sense that things were starting to happen, things were becoming easier," he recalled to Susan Haigh. "I was really developing the compensatory skills." Reading and writing still do not come easily to Malloy; prior to making speeches he plans mentally what he is going to say and avoids using notes.

In 1972, during his junior year of high school, Malloy suffered compressed vertebrae while playing football. He was given painkillers, causing him to develop undetected ulcers that led to rapid and drastic weight loss and pancreatic failure. His doctors at St. Joseph's Hospital in Stamford, who did not know how to treat him, sent him home for Christmas, thinking he would not live long. The ulcers were eventually discovered with the use of a more advanced X-ray machine at Stamford Hospital, enabling doctors there to treat Malloy, who later recovered completely. After graduating from Westhill High School, he went on to earn a B.A. degree, magna cum laude, from Boston College, in Massachusetts, in 1977. During his freshman year he met his future wife, Cathy, then a student at Newton College of the Sacred Heart. She helped Malloy prepare his college papers. "He would just sort of speak the paper. He would talk and I would transcribe it on a yellow pad, read it back to him and type it up," Cathy Malloy recalled to Haigh.

In 1980 Malloy received a law degree from Boston College and passed an oral bar exam. That year he relocated to Brooklyn, New York, where he worked as an assistant district attorney until 1984. In that post he won 22 convictions out of 23 felony cases. In 1985 Malloy became a partner at Abate & Fox, a law firm in Stamford. Around that time he also began serving in a series of posts in city government, including member of the board of finance and member of the board of education. He left Abate & Fox in 1995, when he became the mayor of Stamford, following a landslide victory over the two-term Republican mayor, Stanley Esposito. During his 14-year tenure as mayor, the longest in the city's history, Malloy helped to create new office buildings and attract more business and visitors to Stamford, resulting in thousands of new jobs. He also implemented the first citywide preschool program, which guarantees that all four-year-old children can attend prekindergarten regardless of their parents' or guardians' income levels. For that act he received an Outstanding Achievement Award from the U.S. Conference of Mayors in 2003.

According to his official Web site, as mayor Malloy helped to lower the city's crime rate by 63 percent. While he was in office, Stamford was named by the Federal Bureau of Investigation (FBI) as one of the safest cities in the country. Malloy was also involved in the renovation of public housing and the expansion of Stamford's parks and schools. "Dan left a significant legacy of school building projects," the former board of education president Richard Freeman told Magdalene Perez for the Bridgeport *Connecticut Post* (November 28, 2009). In addition, Malloy contributed to the development of the Urban Transitway, which, when completed, will reduce traffic in downtown Stamford.

"He helped establish Stamford as a place where quality projects could be approved quickly and built on time," Kip Bergstrom, the head of Stamford's Urban Redevelopment Commission, said in an interview with Perez. "[Malloy] was very aggressive in promoting his agenda," the former Stamford board of representatives president Carmen Domonkos told Perez. "There were some tensions when the legislative side and the mayor's side didn't see eye to eye." Malloy's critics claimed that he spent tax dollars on unnecessary projects. He was also accused of giving city contracts to companies that had done work on his home; those allegations were later dismissed for lack of evidence.

In 2004 Malloy launched a campaign for governor, becoming the first registered candidate for the 2006 gubernatorial election. He announced his candidacy early so that he could start raising money and introducing himself to voters outside Stamford. "To put the decision off any longer would've probably eliminated me from consideration," he explained to Jeff Holtz for the *New York Times* (February 8, 2004). Malloy "established himself as a very knowledgeable and credible candidate," Gary Rose, chairman of the Department of Government and Politics at Sacred Heart University, said of Malloy to Magdalene Perez for the *Stamford Advocate* (November 30, 2008). After receiving the Democratic Party endorsement at the state convention and spending nearly $4 million on his campaign, Malloy lost by a few percentage points to John DeStefano, the New Haven, Connecticut, mayor, in the primary election. (DeStefano was defeated by the Republican Jodi Rell in the general election.) Roy Occhiogrosso, Malloy's friend and political adviser, said in an interview with Raymond Hernandez, "On primary night in 2006, it was like he was thinking about how long it had taken to get to that point and how long it would take to get back to that point if he chose to run again. I'm sure he wondered that night if it might be over."

After serving four terms as mayor of Stamford, Malloy decided against seeking reelection in 2011. Instead he launched a second gubernatorial campaign, after learning that Richard Blumenthal, Connecticut's highly popular incumbent attorney general, was not going to enter the race for governor. Malloy officially announced his candidacy in March 2010; two months later he won the Democratic nomination. In the primary election he defeated Ned Lamont, a Greenwich, Connecticut, businessman, with 58 percent of the vote. Lamont had spent nearly $9 million of his own money on his campaign; Malloy had spent only $2.5 million, provided by Connecticut's public-financing program. He became the first candidate to win a gubernatorial nomination using the state's funding.

During his campaign for governor, Malloy received endorsements from organizations including the Connecticut Police and Fire Union, the Connecticut Council of Police Unions, and the Connecticut Working Families Party. In the 2010 general election Malloy was victorious over the Republican Thomas C. Foley, a Connecticut businessman and a former U.S. ambassador to Ireland. (Like Lamont, Foley had spent millions of his own money on his campaign.) Although initially there was confusion over the results of the race, it was ultimately determined that Malloy had defeated Foley by approximately 6,000 votes. Shortly after he was elected, he attended the National Governors Association's Seminar for New Governors, held in Colorado, to hear advice from the top executives of other states.

Malloy was sworn in as Connecticut's 88th governor at the State Armory in Hartford on January 5, 2011. Succeeding Jodi Rell, who did not seek reelection, he became the state's first Democratic governor since 1991. Malloy is socially liberal; he approves of gay marriage and opposes the death penalty. He was an advocate of the health-care-reform legislation passed by Congress in 2010 and signed into law by President Barack Obama (although he does not consider it to be flawless), and he supports alternative-energy sources. He has said that two of his primary focuses as governor will be creating jobs and establishing economic stability for the residents of Connecticut.

Financially conservative, Malloy—one of the few gubernatorial candidates who did not promise tax cuts—has proposed raising Connecticut's income and sales taxes by $1.5 billion. For residents who earn more than $50,000 annually, he wants to increase the personal-income tax from 5 to 5.5 percent; for residents making more than $500,000 per year, he seeks to raise the figure from 6.5 to 6.7 percent. Malloy's proposed budget also includes an increase in general sales taxes, from 6 to 6.35 percent. He feels that the tax hikes are necessary due to Connecticut's expected budget deficit of $3.5 billion in 2012. "It's what's right for my state," he explained in the interview with David M. Halbfinger. "Connecticut would not be Connecticut if we cut $3.5 billion out of the budget. We are a strong, generous, hopeful people. We'd be taking $800 million out of education. You can't do that in this state. You'd have to gouge the Medicaid system. You'd have to close 25 percent of the nursing homes. What do you do with people?" A *New York Times* (March 10, 2011) editorial stated in praise of Malloy, "In comparison to New York's $88 billion budget or New Jersey's of $29 billion, Gov. Dannel Malloy's budget in Connecticut is a mere $19.7 billion. Yet Governor Malloy has managed to create a better, fairer budget than both of his colleagues. And he is doing it without bombast, without YouTube, without making hard enemies or playing favorites. . . . Beyond his balance of cuts and taxes, and unlike New York and many other states, Mr. Malloy has proposed adopting generally accepted accounting principles, or GAAP. This is a particularly daring thing for a governor to do. GAAP does not allow the usual budget antics—like pushing expenses forward to next year and pulling revenues back into this year to make the budget appear to be balanced. Mr. Malloy has acknowledged that this kind of open accounting would add $73 million to the deficit in the upcoming budget and $48 million the year after. It is too bad that his colleagues in most other states aren't brave enough to do that."

Malloy has lectured at the University of Connecticut. He has served as a member of the Mayors Against Illegal Guns coalition and is a former trustee of the U.S. Conference of Mayors, a former president of the Connecticut Council of Municipalities, and a former member of the Stamford Cultural Development Organization.

Malloy and his wife, Cathy, have been married since 1982. Cathy Malloy works as the director of a sexual-assault and rape-crisis center. The couple live in Hartford and have three sons: Benjamin, Dannel, and Samuel.

—J.P.

Suggested Reading: (Bridgeport) *Connecticut Post* (on-line) Nov. 28, 2009; (Danbury, Connecticut) *News-Times* (on-line) May 30, 2006; *Hartford (Connecticut) Courant* B p1 Mar. 11, 2010; *New York Times* (on-line) Aug. 11, 2010; *Stamford (Connecticut) Advocate* State and Regional News Nov. 30, 2008

Chip Somodevilla/Getty Images

Markell, Jack

Nov. 26, 1960– Governor of Delaware (Democrat)

Address: Carvel State Office Bldg., 820 N. French St., 12th Fl., Wilmington, DE 19801

In 2008 the Democrat Jack Markell, then a three-term state treasurer, was elected governor of Delaware. Markell made a fortune in the 1990s as one of the founding members and top executives of the telecommunications giant Nextel, and he has brought his financial and technological savvy to his political posts. Citing job creation and education reform among his priorities as governor, he has traveled abroad to meet with business leaders and bring jobs and investment to Delaware, and he has worked to ensure that the state's public-school system is better funded and its achievements better

measured than before, with new and improved testing. As a gubernatorial candidate in 2008, Markell outlined his positions on those and other issues in his 80-page "Blueprint for a Better Delaware." In March 2010 Markell signed into law four renewable-energy bills that comprise the Clean Energy Jobs package. "This was designed to put people to work in clean energy jobs that can help grow our economy now and support the health of our environment long-term," Markell was quoted as saying in a press release posted on his Web site (July 28, 2010). Delaware's secretary of the environment and energy, Collin O'Mara, added, "These green energy bills will help the state transition at a faster rate to renewable energy. We can dramatically reduce our reliance on fossil fuels in the next 15 years and move closer to the healthy environment and green economy we want in Delaware. The bills also provide an opportunity for all Delaware citizens to participate in buying clean power, using clean power and being a part of the clean technology transition." In 2011 Markell signed into law legislation that made same-sex civil unions legal in Delaware—the eighth state to pass such a measure.

The youngest of three children, Jack A. Markell was born on November 26, 1960 in Newark, Delaware, to William "Bill" Markell and Elaine "Leni" Markell. He and his brother, David, and sister, Judy, grew up in the Newark neighborhood of Windy Hills. Markell's mother, a social worker in public health, was an active volunteer with the United Way and with Temple Beth El, the synagogue the family attended. Bill Markell, who died in 2009, was a Fulbright scholar and World War II veteran; he chaired the Department of Business Administration and later the Accounting Department at the University of Delaware, from which he retired with the title Arthur Anderson professor of accounting. He also served on the audit committee of Delaware's state pension fund and with many charitable organizations; for a while he was the principal of Temple Beth El's Hebrew school. "We lived pretty simply," Markell's brother, now a professor specializing in environmental law at Florida State University College of Law, told Beth Miller for the Wilmington, Delaware, *News Journal* (September 6, 2008). "The emphasis was not on living it up but on living simply and giving back. I think that has shaped [Jack's] career." The Markells frequently opened their home to those in need and hosted several foreign-exchange students. "Three nights a week we had people over for dinner—people with no family, no friends," Jack Markell recalled to Miller. "This is what you did."

One day when Markell was 10, he walked out to the family's backyard to find a patch of grass burned in the shape of a swastika. Leni Markell sent a letter to members of the community, informing them of what had happened and eliciting their sympathy and support. "People of all types came together to say, 'You're not alone,'" Jack Markell told Miller. "And when you're 10 years old and you see in the eyes of your 10-year-old friends penetrating sympathy, 'I'm with you buddy,' . . . it represents the best of what communities are about."

The young Markell was a state-champion ping-pong player. Popular in his class, he ran successfully for student office in middle school. Just after he was elected president of his senior class at Newark High School, his father offered him a special opportunity: Bill Markell, who was to spend a year-long sabbatical teaching in Manchester, England, and New Zealand, proposed that his son come along and attend school in each location. (During his working years Bill Markell also taught in France, Bulgaria, and Slovakia.) The two traveled extensively during that year. Markell was horrified by the poverty he encountered in New Delhi, India; the experience would help propel him into public service. "When we got off the bus [in New Delhi]," Markell recalled to Miller, "there was a group of Indians—hands outstretched, eyes and mouths pleading. I remember seeing business Indians stepping over homeless Indians and thinking, 'This could never happen where I'm from.'" After Markell returned from his year abroad, he gave an address at his class's high-school graduation, in 1978. Titled "Our Good Fortune," the speech focused on the privileges enjoyed by Americans; Markell encouraged his class, Miller wrote, to "give back."

Markell attended Brown University, in Providence, Rhode Island, graduating with a B.A. degree in economics and Third World studies in 1982. He then considered joining the Peace Corps but decided to take a different path. "I reached the conclusion that if you really want to change things, you had to speak the language of business," he told Miller. "People who control the purse strings call a lot of the shots." Markell pursued an M.B.A. degree at the University of Chicago, in Illinois. While in graduate school he worked for the First National Bank of Chicago, spent six months in Chile, volunteered in a Chicago homeless shelter, and taught English to Vietnamese refugees. He also spent a year at the London School of Economics. He completed his studies in 1985 and began working the

next year as a consultant for the well-known McKinsey & Co. management consulting firm in Washington, D.C. There, he met Delaware's former lieutenant governor S. B. Woo, who was planning to run for a seat in the U.S. Senate. Markell took eight months off from his job in 1988 to serve as Woo's deputy campaign manager.

After Woo lost the race, Markell joined the business of a friend, one of the founders of Fleet Call—which would be renamed Nextel. He spent a year traveling the country to purchase smaller companies and thus assemble a "network capable of supporting a large telecommunications system," Nancy Charron wrote for the Wilmington *News Journal* (January 5, 1999). Markell and his partners created the network with an eye toward supporting static-free digital-telephone technology; Nextel was one of the first companies to offer digital service. During that time Markell raised millions of dollars for the new company, and he is credited with giving Nextel its name. "In the early years, almost every month we worried about whether we would make it," Markell told Charron. Based in Rutherford, New Jersey, Nextel grew to employ more than 8,000 workers by 1995, the year Markell left his post as the company's senior vice president for corporate development. During that time the value of Nextel's stocks rose and fell, and at one point Markell and other Nextel executives were the defendants in a class-action lawsuit accusing them of insider trading and of inflating stock prices with claims of technology the company did not possess. The suit was later dismissed.

By the time Markell left Nextel, he had become interested in public service. In explaining what led him to change his professional goals, he has often cited a conversation with his grandmother Mollie Dworetzky, which took place a year or so after he had started working at Nextel. Visiting her Brooklyn, New York, apartment, he told her stories about fax machines, cell phones, and the new technologies his company was exploring. She replied, as Markell recalled to Miller, "So what? You can send a piece of paper through the air. But there are babies having babies. There are people killing people. There are people who are so cruel to each other." In 1997, soon after he joined the Comcast Corp. as vice president for development, commuting from his home in Delaware to his office in Philadelphia, Pennsylvania, Markell began to feel restless. "At the end of my life, the question is: What contribution did you make?" he said to Charron. "I really felt . . . this was the time to do it." He told his colleagues at Comcast he was leaving to run for Delaware state treasurer. "We were floored," the Comcast board chairman, Ralph J. Roberts, told Charron. "Here's a guy that had a very major role [in the company]. . . . I think it's quite wonderful—the very thing we should admire in people."

Markell sought out the advice of nearly 50 people involved in politics. He told Charron that the best advice he received was to "first get the support of [my] employer and family and to make sure [I] had a fire in the belly. Also, before I went out and start[ed] talking to people about my candidacy, I needed to know why I was running." On Election Day in 1998, eight months after quitting his job, Markell unseated the four-term Republican incumbent Janet Rzewnicki with 58 percent of the vote. In his position (in which he took an enormous pay cut), Markell was credited with using effectively the fiscal principles he had learned in the private sector and with pushing for technological innovation in government. In 2000, due to Markell's expressed interest in putting the Web to use in government, then-Governor Tom Carper appointed Markell the head of the state's e-government task force. Markell told Patrick Jackson for the Wilmington News Journal (June 19, 2000) that while the Internet could never replace in-person communication, it could allow officials to "set things up so you can do basic things over the Internet" and thus "[free] up people to help citizens with more complicated problems." Markell was reelected in 2002 and 2006, claiming an overwhelming 70 percent of the vote in the latter year. During his tenure as state treasurer, Markell earned two Innovation Awards from the Council of State Governments. The first was for his role in the creation of a program called Health Rewards, meant to "improve the health care of state employees and reduce costs through comprehensive physical exams," according to his Web site. The second Innovation Award was for a program called the Delaware Money School, created to "increase financial literacy through classes on topics such as saving for college and retirement planning."

In June 2007 Markell announced his bid for governor. (Due to term limits, Governor Ruth Ann Minner, a Democrat, was vacating her seat.) In a Democratic primary that saw a record-breaking $5 million spent, Markell ran against the Democratic Party favorite and two-term lieutenant governor, John Carney Jr. Carney had his party's official endorsement and those of more than a dozen unions and 40 elected officials; moreover, as lieutenant governor, Beth Miller wrote for the Wilmington News Journal (August 31, 2008), he was already only "a step away from the top office." The Carney campaign tried to paint Markell as a disgruntled outsider, while Markell's camp said that Carney was a conservative problem-solver, lacking a bold vision to lead the floundering state. "He has had eight years to get things done," Markell told Miller, referring to Carney's position as lieutenant governor, "and things haven't changed." "Change" was the operative word in election races across the country in 2008, including that for the presidency, as voters faced economic hardship and other challenges. Dewey Beach, Delaware, mayor Bob Fredrick told Miller: "I'm backing Markell, and it has been the most difficult decision of my life. The thing that swayed me is the exact same thing that is going on at the national level—the climate of change. At a crossroads like this, I can't be a wimp and sit it out. It's time for a change." "Some have

said it's not my turn," Markell told voters, as reported by Miller. "To them I say, 'It may not be my turn, but it's my time.' . . . I'm in the right place at the right time. Delaware is ready for a message of change." Markell, who released a financial-policy report called "Blueprint for a Better Delaware," won an upset victory in the primary and asked in his victory speech that voters give him "a mandate for progress," Randall Chase reported for the Associated Press (September 10, 2008).

In the general election, facing the Republican Bill Lee, a retired judge, Markell claimed victory with 67.5 percent of the almost 400,000 votes cast. The euphoria of Markell's win did not last long in the face of the serious problems plaguing the state. When Markell entered office, according to Bob Yearick, writing for Delaware Today (December 14, 2009), he faced a $750 million budget deficit, the near-collapse of two of the state's largest industries (banking and automobile manufacturing), and burgeoning unemployment. Two months after his inauguration, Markell presented a budget aimed at closing the deficit by cutting $331 million in spending and, among other initiatives, reestablishing a sports-betting lottery in the state—a plan thwarted by the U.S. Court of Appeals. After months of political haggling, Markell signed the $3.091 billion budget in July 2009. Yearick wrote of the outcome: "Despite a few failed proposals, which Markell blamed on the GOP, the governor can point to a state operating budget that is 8.1 percent smaller than the previous one. Criticism focuses mostly on the failure to significantly cut payroll, which is 46 percent of the state's operating costs."

In 2009 the U.S. Census Bureau estimated the population of Delaware to be 885,100. With 23,600 jobs lost in Delaware between August 2008 and August 2009, jobs remain Markell's central focus, followed by "shrinking the expense of government," he told Yearick. For Markell the two are related; he believes that companies are drawn to locations with efficient government. "So as we shrink the expense of running government," Markell said to Yearick, "I think we send a signal to businesses that this is the kind of place they want to be." Markell's third priority is education. He pleased many constituents when he appointed Lillian Lowry from Delaware's Christina School District as the state's secretary of education. Together Markell and Lowry replaced the much-criticized Student Testing Program, which tracked students' learning relative to statewide standards, with a testing program that measures individual students' progress during the course of the school year. In 2010 Delaware won the federal grant competition "Race to the Top" for innovative improvements to the state's public schools. "Normally, winning a race means you get a chance to stop and celebrate," Markell said in his weekly message on March 25, 2011, as recorded on his Web site, "but it feels like we are still racing forward together with good reason." Reforms implemented and planned include a more precise measurement of teacher performance, evaluations for new teachers, and the ability to enforce dramatic changes in underperforming schools.

In 2010 Markell embarked on a trade mission to Taiwan and mainland China in an attempt to expand Delaware's export markets and attract new manufacturers and investors to the state. "Many Asian companies are exploring opportunities to set up manufacturing operations in North America," he told a reporter for the Targeted News Service (November 4, 2010). "We want them to decide that Delaware is the best place to start and grow their business." During his trip Markell met with President Ma Ying-jeou of Taiwan and visited the headquarters of Motech Industries, in Taipei. That year Motech invested in a Newark, Delaware, facility that manufactures solar modules. That investment saved 75 local jobs, and the facility has expanded to add 75 more jobs to its operations. Earlier that year Markell had traveled to Europe, visiting business leaders in Germany and England, on a similar mission.

In 2011 Markell introduced a balanced-budget proposal that focused on job creation and education. He said in a press release (January 27, 2011) published by the Targeted News Service that allocating money for public schools was "the greatest investment we can make in our future." He added: "Last year, more than 30 states balanced their budgets by anticipating that the federal government might provide additional funds to states to pay for schools and Medicaid costs; but Delaware balances its budget with the money it had, not the money it hoped to get. Because the federal government did provide those resources later in the summer, Delaware began preparations for the Fiscal Year 2012 budget better able to meet its challenges."

In 2010 Markell declared February Teen Dating Violence Awareness and Prevention Month. "As the father of two teenagers, I know how critical it is to talk directly and openly with our kids and let them know to never stand for abuse of any kind," he said, according to a reporter for the States News Service (February 4, 2010).

In 2004 Markell was chosen for the prestigious Henry Crown Fellowship, sponsored by the Aspen Institute. Henry Crown Fellowships are presented to candidates ages 30 to 45 who, as stated on the Aspen Institute Web site, "have achieved significant success in their respective fields" and "have reached an inflection point in their careers and are looking to give back to society in a broader, more substantive manner." The program involves four seminars in the U.S. and abroad over the course of two years. In 2006 Markell was invited to be a Rodel Fellow in Public Leadership at the Aspen Institute, an honor extended to young political leaders; the two-year program includes three weekend seminars in Aspen, Colorado.

Markell is a devoted cyclist who participates in the annual Tour de Delaware bike ride, a 50-mile event. He met his wife, Carla, when both were in kindergarten. The couple married in 1990 and have two children, Molly and Michael. Markell and his family live in Wilmington.

—M.M.H.

Suggested Reading: Aspen Institute Web site; Associated Press (on-line) Sep. 10, 2008; *Delaware Today* (on-line) Dec. 14, 2009; Jack Markell Web site; States News Service (on-line) Feb. 4, 2010; Targeted News Service (on-line) Nov. 4, 2010, Jan. 27, 2011; (Wilmington, Delaware) *News Journal* A p1 Jan. 5, 1999, B p1 June 19, 2000, A p1 Aug. 31, 2008, B p1 Sep. 6, 2008

Michael Loccisano/Getty Images

Marling, Brit

1983(?)– Actress; screenwriter; producer; director

Address: c/o United Talent Agency, 9560 Wilshire Blvd., Beverly Hills, CA 90212

In a remarkable coup for a film-industry neophyte, two motion pictures that Brit Marling co-wrote, co-produced, and starred in gained acceptance to the 2011 Sundance Film Festival, an annual event widely regarded as the most important showcase for independent cinema in the United States. The first of her films, *Another Earth*, was co-written and directed by Mike Cahill; the second, *Sound of My Voice*, was co-written and directed by Zal Batmanglij. Marling met Cahill and Batmanglij in the early 2000s, when all three were undergraduates at Georgetown University, where Marling was studying economics and the men had started to make short films together. Close friends and, for some years, roommates, the trio have worked together or in pairs nearly nonstop ever since. With Cahill, Marling made the documentary *Boxers and Ballerinas* (2004), which focused on two children growing up in Cuba and two Cuban-American youngsters living in Miami, Florida. With that work she gained experience in screenwriting, cinematography, and editing. Afterward, in Los Angeles, California, Marling attempted to launch a career as an actress, but the only roles offered to her failed to portray "strong, powerful, sexy, entitled women" or to offer "representations of how to be a girl or woman in the world," she told Maria Elena Fernandez for the *Daily Beast* (July 18, 2011, on-line). Frustrated and disillusioned, she stopped auditioning for parts and instead devoted the next few years to learning the art and craft of screenwriting, as a means of creating roles for herself. (Cahill and Batmanglij also polished their screenwriting skills, with the goal of directing their own films.) *Another Earth* and *Sound of My Voice* were the first feature films that she, Cahill, and Batmanglij made (on shoestring budgets) using their own screenplays. Ann Hornaday, who attended the Sundance festival held in January 2011, wrote for the *Washington Post* (February 27, 2011) that both films "proved bracingly ambitious, forward-thinking alternatives in a festival lineup that is still often dominated by derivative, dysfunctional family dramas and teen angst."

"To say that . . . *Another Earth* stole the show at this year's Sundance Film Festival would be a gross understatement," Kee Chang wrote for *Anthem Magazine* (July 18, 2011, on-line). Marling told Chang, "The response after the screening was overwhelming. People just leapt to their feet and started applauding." A committee of scientists and film professionals awarded *Another Earth* the festival's $20,000 Alfred P. Sloan Prize, "for its original use of subtly rendered scientific concept—the sudden appearance of an alternate Earth where everyone may be living parallel lives and destinies—to explore the themes of remorse and forgiveness," according to a Sundance Institute press release (January 28, 2011, on-line). It also earned a Special Jury Prize in Sundance's U.S. dramatic competition, which pitted 16 films chosen from among 1,102 submissions. Fox Searchlight Pictures, a division of 20th Century Fox, bought the rights to both that film and *Sound of My Voice*. *Another Earth* opened in theaters nationwide in July 2011; the latter was scheduled to be released later in the year. Marling, who has expressed the desire to develop further as an actress, will appear in 2012 in Nicholas Jarecki's film "Arbitrage," along with Tim Roth, Richard Gere, and Susan Sarandon, and in Robert Redford's "The Company You Keep," starring Redford, Sarandon, Shia LaBeouf, and Nick Nolte.

Alexandra Brittany Marling was born in Chicago, Illinois, in about 1983. Her parents, John H. Marling and the former Heidi Johnson, are real-

estate developers. Marling told Maria Elena Fernandez that during her childhood her family moved often. Wherever she lived she would cast neighborhood children in little dance-heavy plays that she wrote and directed. She would charge $20 for tickets to their Saturday-night performances. "And just because we were so bold, my parents' friends would actually pay to come see these ridiculous Janet Jackson–inspired plays," she told Fernandez. The family was living in Winter Park, Florida, when Marling attended Dr. Phillips High School, in nearby Orlando. As a student in the school's performing-arts program, she appeared in various plays.

After her high-school graduation, Marling enrolled at Georgetown University, in Washington, D.C. Her fear of the financial uncertainties that mark many people's careers in acting, and the example set by her mother, who has an M.B.A. degree in finance, led her to major in economics; she also took courses in studio art. During her freshman year she attended a student film festival, where she watched the screening of a movie by made two Georgetown upperclassmen, Mike Cahill and Zal Batmanglij. "I remember it won first place and I just popped up and led the standing ovation for the film," she said in an interview with Jen Yamato for *Movieline.com* (March 21, 2011). "The filmmakers came onstage to get the award . . . and I saw them and I was like, 'Okay. I have to be friends with these people.'" She soon introduced herself to them, and the three began to collaborate on short-film projects.

Following her junior year at Georgetown, Marling secured a summer internship in New York City with the global investment-banking and securities firm Goldman Sachs. The job required long hours and gave her an indelible taste of the world of finance. "I had this sense when I was working at the bank that I could measure out my life in coffee spoons," she told Daniel Holloway for *Backstage.com* (January 28, 2011). "I knew exactly where I was going to be in two years, three years, what would happen, how my salary would change—and it wasn't me." Moreover, whereas earlier as she had taken "the 'starving artist' phrase very literally . . . ," as she told Amy Longsdorf for the Pottstown, Pennsylvania, *Mercury* (July 31, 2011, on-line), "later on, I decided that if you didn't do what you wanted with your life, you'd starve in another way. It would be an emotional starvation and the light in you would be snuffed out." Her reservations about finance became stronger after Cahill and Batmanglij persuaded her to join them in a contest for which they had to complete a film in 48 hours. During those two days, she told Fernandez, she realized that "you can be a workaholic doing something you feel passionate about or you can be a workaholic doing something you don't feel passionate about. After that, I didn't want to go back to school."

At the end of the summer, Marling turned down Goldman Sachs's offer of a full-time position upon completion of her degree. She also took a leave of absence from Georgetown in order to travel with Cahill to Cuba to make a film. "I wasn't the radical girl at school wearing the dark eye makeup and smoking cigarettes who never goes to class and says, 'I'm running off to Paris,'" Marling told David Walters for *Details* (June 2011, on-line). "This was the opposite of that: [I was] the girl who spent every night studying in the library, getting perfect grades, suddenly saying, 'I'm dropping out. I'm going to Cuba. I'm going to be an artist.' You can imagine the shock."

The seed for Marling and Cahill's Cuba film was planted in 2003, when, as Marling told Isabel C. Gonzalez for the *Washington Post* (April 17, 2005), "a friend showed us these striking photos of kids in Cuba with tiny bodies and baby-fat faces wearing huge boxing gloves and looking into the camera with all this bravado. At this young age, these kids were completely aware that if they worked hard and became successful boxers they might be able to leave the country. Then we thought it was important to find the feminine side of the equation. In terms of artistic endeavors in Cuba, that meant following a ballerina." Over the course of a year and a half, Marling and Cahill traveled several times to Cuba and to Miami, Florida, to make a documentary about aspiring ballerinas and boxers. They then had to choose from some 350 hours of video footage the most effective 90 minutes. "Learning to use the camera is the easiest part," Marling told Gonzalez. "The hardest part is figuring out what you have to say that is unique."

Boxers and Ballerinas (2004), co-written and co-directed by Marling and Cahill, follows a young boxer and a young ballerina in Cuba and a similarly focused boy and girl in Miami. "The differences between the repressive, limited life of Castro's Cuba and the spoiled-by-endless-opportunities world of modern Miami have never been more beautifully contrasted than in *Boxers and Ballerinas*, a lyrical documentary on the lives of athletes and dancers on both sides of the Florida Strait," Roger Moore wrote in a review for the *Orlando (Florida) Sentinel* (April 8, 2005). By contrast, the Cleveland, Ohio, *Plain Dealer* (March 16, 2005) critic, Wilma Salisbury, complained, "*Boxers and Ballerinas*, an unconventional documentary, raises more questions than it answers about options open to talented young Cubans and Cuban-Americans. . . . The pace is dizzying, the locale of some scenes ambiguous, and the English subtitles are difficult to read." The documentary won a "Best of the Fest" honor at the 2005 Breckenridge Festival of Film, in Colorado, and, for Marling and Cahill, a 2005 Director's Award from the Cinequest San Jose Film Festival, in California. Meanwhile, at her parents' urging, Marling had returned to Georgetown University, and in 2005 she graduated as the valedictorian of her class.

After completing *Boxers and Ballerinas*, Marling moved to Los Angeles, where she, Cahill, and Batmanglij shared a house in the Silver Lake section. She then began seeking work as an actress. "As an actor I found it really hard to navigate the space of being a young ingenue type without totally losing my morality," she declared in an interview with Nigel M. Smith for *IndieWire.com* (January 28, 2011)—"morality" referring to her principles regarding worthwhile parts. "What people ask of you is that you do bad movies that don't matter, and if you wade through that swamp you eventually get to be part of stories that mean something," she said to Vanessa Lawrence for *W Magazine* (April 2011, on-line). "Nobody says to a surgeon, 'Part of paying your dues is to remove kidneys illegally and sell them on the black market.' I can't think of another profession where losing your morality is part of the job." "I didn't want to play these roles where women are constantly in these submissive positions or being sexually abused or harassed or just sexual objects," she told Jen Yamato. Marling decided that she herself would have to write screenplays, she continued, as "a way to get to act in things that I thought were meaningful, and hopefully write stronger roles for other women." "So I found I had to learn how to write. I started to teach myself by reading screenplays." Her learning process took several years. During that time Marling began to write one script with Cahill and another with Batmanglij (both of whom aimed to direct). "I basically had no life for a long time," she told Smith. "But we were just doing them to do them and maybe to prove to ourselves that we could make them."

The script that Marling wrote with Cahill became *Another Earth*, which Cahill, in an interview with Euan Kerr for Minnesota Public Radio (August 4, 2011, on-line), categorized as "a minimalist science fiction romantic dramatic thriller"—which Marling declared to Kerr was the "best" description she had heard. Marling and Cahill told Kerr that space had interested them for a long time, and that they had often amused themselves by weaving stories about "space factoids," in Kerr's words. Generally, Marling and Cahill felt, films in the science-fiction genre had impressive special effects but lacked characters and storylines that were emotionally engaging; on the other hand, when "you go to a smaller indie drama . . . you're given what you need emotionally, but you miss the breadth of a concept," Marling commented to Vanessa Lawrence. The heroine of *Another Earth* is Rhoda (played by Marling), who is poised to enter the Massachusetts Institute of Technology to study astrophysics. While driving home from a high-school-graduation party one night, she stares at a planet identical to Earth (and supposedly supporting duplicates of all Earth's inhabitants) that has just appeared in the solar system. Highly distracted—and inebriated as well—she crashes into another car, killing a mother and her young son. At the end of a four-year jail sentence, full of remorse and wanting to make amends, she seeks out the husband and father of her victims (played by William Mapother), a musician named John who has barely functioned since the tragedy. While Rhoda and John (who is unaware of her true identity) slowly reach out to each other, Rhoda ponders the idea that her counterpart on Earth Two has avoided the disaster that changed the course of her own life and John's.

According to the Sundance Institute press release, "*Another Earth* is a beautiful example of how filmmakers can take complex scientific ideas such as the multiverse and create unforgettable and moving human stories that appeal to a wide audience." Tasha Robinson, the reviewer for the A.V. Club (July 21, 2011, on-line), judged the "raw visual aesthetic" of *Another Earth* to be "in keeping with its low budget, but just as suitable to its raw feelings of loss, regret, and longing. It's all indie to a fault, from the handheld HD camera to the achy Fall On Your Sword score, but Cahill makes the most of his budget limitations by suggesting things he doesn't reveal. In fact, the movie is more suggestive than direct throughout: Most of the philosophical questions are raised not by the characters . . . but by overheard snatches of reportage and media commentary. The approach not only lets the leads steep in their restrained, deeply felt performances, it opens up the world into a wider setting where everyone seems to be experiencing the same unease, confusion, and loneliness. It's an ambitious premise and a risky approach, but Cahill and his cast execute it beautifully." James Verniere, a *Boston Herald* (July 29, 2011) critic, was less enthusiastic, writing, "I found Marling recessive to a fault, making me wonder often if Rhoda was just plain stupid."

The script that Marling co-wrote with Batmanglij and co-produced became *Sound of My Voice*. Directed by Batmanglij, it is set in contemporary Los Angeles and stars Christopher Denham and Nicole Vicius as Peter and Lorna, who, with the intention of making a documentary, infiltrate a mysterious cult led by a Maggie (Marling), who claims to have traveled back in time from the year 2054. Ann Hornaday described the film as "a taut, superbly crafted drama," while Todd Gilchrist, writing for *Box Office Magazine* (August 19, 2011, on-line), expressed admiration for the film's "brilliant manipulations"—"the sorts of flourishes that distinguish this film from the landscape of debuts that, by comparison, feel as telegraphed and cliched as a studio tentpole." "Although there are snippets of backstory and a full-fledged mythic tale of creation for Maggie, what's most interesting about *Sound of My Voice* is how spartan the film is with its details—that terseness creates a lot of intrigue . . . ," Gilchrist wrote. "Meanwhile, the film's emotional core is not merely cemented together with great, measured writing, but with performances equal to that writing's ambiguity and intensity."

Thanks to her newfound fame in the filmmaking industry, Marling has gained "access to scripts and projects that are really meaningful, and that's really exciting," Marling told David Walters. Universally described as beautiful, personable, and funny, Marling currently lives in Los Feliz, in a house overlooking downtown Los Angeles.

—J.P.

Suggested Reading: *Anthem Magazine* (on-line) July 18, 2011; *Backstage.com* (on-line) Jan. 28, 2011; britmarling.net; CBSNews.com Aug. 14, 2011; *Daily Beast* (on-line) July 18, 2011; *Details* (on-line) June 2011; *Los Angeles Times* D p5 Feb. 6, 2011; *New York Times Magazine* p42 June 26, 2011; *Orlando (Florida) Sentinel* (on-line) Aug. 11, 2011; (Pottstown, Pennsylvania) *Mercury* (on-line) July 31, 2011; *Washington Post* C p1 Jan. 27, 2011; *WMagazine.com* Apr. 2011

Selected Films: as co-writer and co-director—*Boxers and Ballerinas*, 2004; as actress—*Political Disasters*, 2009; as actress, writer, and producer—*Sound of My Voice*, 2011; *Another Earth*, 2011

Maron, Marc

Sep. 27, 1963– Comedian; radio host; podcast interviewer; writer

Address: WTF, P.O. Box 50753, Los Angeles, CA 90050

Since the age of 11, "all that I ever wanted was to be a comedian with a point of view," Marc Maron told Christie Chisholm for *Alibi* (December 23–29, 2010, on-line), an Albuquerque, New Mexico, alternative weekly. Now 48, Maron launched his career as a stand-up comic over a quarter-century ago, when he was in college. "There was never any other option for me . . . ," he told Chisholm. "It was never like, Ah, that's it, I'm going to law school, time to get a job. I would rather have no money living on a friend's couch." Maron has pursued his dream with varying degrees of success, beginning with what became known as alternative comedy—the form he has practiced ever since. He has hosted a show on the television network Comedy Central, starred in an HBO comedy special, contributed his voice to an animated TV cartoon, released four comedy CDs, written a book, co-hosted several radio programs, and appeared on the TV series *Late Night with Conan O'Brien* 44 times, a record number for a comedian on any late-night talk show. His greatest success has come recently, with his podcast, called *WTF with Marc Maron*; recorded twice weekly in his garage, it consists of interviews that Maron conducts, primarily with other comedians. Soon after its debut, in September

Ben Gabbe/Getty Images

Marc Maron

2009, it became the number-one downloaded comedy podcast; averaging upwards of 230,000 downloads a week, it has consistently been among the top-10 podcasts downloaded on iTunes.

On October 26, 2010, the day after Maron's first *WTF* interview of Ira Glass, the host of the National Public Radio series *This American Life*, Glass wrote for his *This American Life* blog, "Being interviewed by Maron reminded me of an old axiom about interviewing: that an interview is a party you're throwing and your guest will mirror your behavior. Marc is an insanely intense guy, and stares into you as you talk—it really feels like his eyes are piercing inside you—and then when he speaks he reaches inside himself and talks in the most heartfelt way possible. In a room with that, you'd have to be made of stone not to respond in the most soulful way you can summon up. He's emotionally present and he makes you emotionally present. I don't think that's any kind of calculated move, it's who he is when he's performing. And of course it gets amazing results."

During an interview for the National Public Radio program *All Things Considered* (April 2, 2011), Guy Raz said to Maron, "It sounds almost like you're kind of a therapist, in a way, for some of these people." Maron responded, "And for myself. . . . I've been thinking a lot about that assessment of what I'm doing. And what I think, honestly, is that one of the things that has been lost in this culture is the ability for people to sit and talk for real—you know, for an hour. I mean, really, when was the last time you just sat and talked to someone for an hour? . . . Is that therapy, or is it just some sort of human pastime that has become lost? . . . But I think that what's happened to me personally,

from listening and talking to my peers, I feel like I'm living more in the present. . . . I have more humility about myself and my problems, in terms of finding that they're not unusual. So if it's been therapy for anybody, it's probably for me." Maron told Christie Chisholm, "With me, the struggle really, as it turns out, was always to sort of become myself in some respect. . . . What's happened over the year, in me talking to my peers, and talking and expressing myself on the mic, is that I've started to get through that, and kind of [talk] about a lot of the obstacles that I was in the middle of when I started and also just professionally and many other ways." "It's always been sort of a personal evolution," he noted.

The first child of "standard, middle-class Jews," as the comedian described his parents to Ellen Umansky for the *Forward* (June 4, 1999), Marc Maron was born on September 27, 1963 in Jersey City, New Jersey. His father, Barry R. Maron, practices orthopedic surgery in Albuquerque, New Mexico; his mother, Toby Maron, sells real estate in Florida. His younger brother, Craig, has a business called Vision Coaching. Maron spent his early childhood in Pompton Lakes, New Jersey, with his parents and grandparents, while his father finished medical school. When he was seven his family moved to Anchorage, Alaska, where his father served two years in the U.S. Air Force. The Marons moved to Albuquerque when Marc was in third grade.

By his own account, at 11 Maron realized he wanted to become a stand-up comedian. "I actually thought it was a noble profession," he wrote for his Web site. "I remember being a kid and watching [Don] Rickles and [Buddy] Hackett on the tube, reading the My Favorite Jokes column at the back of *Parade* magazine every Sunday, listening to [George] Carlin, [Richard] Pryor, Cheech and Chong records with my little brother, going to Woody Allen movies, and staying up late on Saturdays to see the first season [in 1975] of *SNL* [*Saturday Night Live*]. To me being a comic meant to be autonomous, angry, truthful, and funny. It meant being alive and present in the moment. It meant having the freedom to figure out and then be who I am in the purest way and to do it shamelessly in front of people, impose it on them and try to blow some minds in the process. It meant avoiding the soul death of the day job." Maron has cited Richard Pryor as an especially powerful influence on him. "Pryor's first comedy special served as a template to me for emotional honesty in stand-up," Maron told Bill Brownstein for the Montreal, Canada, *Gazette* (July 21, 2009). "This is something I've been working toward my entire career. Comedy is usually rooted in some sort of fear or sadness. It is entertainment, but at the same time, it's good to disarm people when performing. I like the laughter that could be the crying a few seconds later."

Maron graduated from Highland High School, in Albuquerque. As an undergraduate at Boston University, in Massachusetts, he studied English and film and occasionally performed stand-up routines at local venues. After he earned a bachelor's degree, he settled in Los Angeles, California, where, beginning in 1986, he did stand-up for several years at the Comedy Store and other venues. (He also worked as a Comedy Store doorman.) While in Los Angeles Maron became a heavy smoker and abuser of cocaine, marijuana, and alcohol. He also became fascinated with the Beat movement of the 1950s. Maron later acknowledged that during that time, he alienated some fellow comics and squandered several professional opportunities.

Maron returned to Boston briefly, then lived in San Francisco, California, for two years. He moved to New York City in 1993. All the while he was performing stand-up in small clubs. He also hosted some programs on the Comedy Central network, among them *Short Attention Span Theatre*, which ran from 1989 to 1994. Alone or with Janeane Garofalo, he performed at the now-defunct Luna Lounge, in New York, which offered humor that was dubbed alternative comedy; rejecting traditional punch lines, such comedy might feature "aspects of sketch comedy, improvisation, performance art or monologue," according to comedian.about.com; moreover, "most alternative comedy is intellectual on some level, either in its content (the jokes require an educated audience) or in its form (the audience has to understand how the approach being taken satirizes something traditional, for example)." With his angry, neurotic, and deeply personal brand of humor, which focused on his Jewish identity and painful events in his life, Maron reportedly became a Luna Lounge favorite. "He really was the real deal," the comedian Dave Attell told Dan Saltzstein for the *New York Times* (January 6, 2011, on-line). "He truly did hate himself. . . . He turned it into gold. Nobody does angry and bitter better than him." In 1995 Maron's photo appeared in a spread in *New York* magazine along with images of Attell and the comedians Louis C.K. and Sarah Silverman. That year his performance at the Filmore in San Francisco aired as a half-hour special on HBO. Around that time he auditioned unsuccessfully for *Saturday Night Live.* He has said that he failed to be hired because he was high on drugs when he met with the show's producer, Lorne Michaels. Later in the 1990s Maron stopped using drugs and alcohol.

In 1998 Maron traveled to Israel with his second wife, the writer and comedian Mishna Wolff, to visit a friend. Maron brought a camcorder and became "obsessed with taping everything," he told Umansky. "You know, in case God decided to talk to me, in case I'm given instructions." He incorporated his experiences in Jerusalem, Israel's capital, in a comic monologue, *Jerusalem Syndrome and Other 'Narcissistic Delusions.'* The title refers to an actual condition identified by psychiatrists, which Maron described as a temporary psychological state that affects some visitors to Jerusalem: "All of a sudden, they begin thinking of themselves like biblical characters, like they're a part of some larger universal story, a grand unfolding," he told Umansky. Maron said in his act that he realized he had been suffering from the syndrome his whole life. He went on to recall that after he lost his religious faith, at a young age, he replaced it with fervent brand loyalty, leading him to take "pilgrimages" to Hollywood, a Coca-Cola museum, and a Philip Morris cigarette factory. *The Jerusalem Syndrome* had an extended run Off-Broadway in 2000 and 2001 and earned many positive reviews. Maron's book based on the act, *Jerusalem Syndrome: My Life as a Reluctant Messiah*, was published in 2001.

Also in the late 1990s and early 2000s, on television, Maron contributed his voice to the animated Comedy Central show *Dr. Katz, Professional Therapist* and was a guest on *Late Night with David Letterman* four times and *Late Night with Conan O'Brien* 44 times. In 2000 Maron had a small part as an angry concert promoter in the film *Almost Famous.* All the while he continued to perform stand-up. "I garnered a lot of respect from fellow comics," he told James Sullivan for the *Boston Globe* (May 29, 2011), "but I never really built an audience on the road with any consistency."

In April 2004 Maron landed a job as a co-host of *Morning Sedition*, which aired weekdays from 6:00 to 9:00 a.m. on Air America Radio (AAR), a newly launched, politically liberal talk network. *Morning Sedition* featured fast-paced banter between Maron and the journalist Mark Riley—known as "Marc and Mark"—with Riley serving as the straight man. One segment was called "Marc Maron and the Temple of Doom," a takeoff on 1940s and '50s radio serials. Maron told a *PR Week* (October 18, 2004) interviewer that he had long been interested in the medium of radio. "I thought AAR was a good cause . . . ," he said. "And I like to talk and learn and improvise." Conflicts between Maron and the producer, Danny Goldberg, led to Maron's departure from the show in December 2005, when his contract expired.

Maron's small legion of fans clamored for him to return to radio. He did so in February 2006, on the Los Angeles station KTLK, as a co-host, with the comedian Jim Earl, of *The Marc Maron Show.* The program was available through AAR's subscription package and offered interviews, comedic skits, and chat. It was often delayed because of coverage of Los Angeles Dodgers games and was later prerecorded. AAR procrastinated for so long in renewing the show for syndication that it was canceled, in July 2006. In September 2007 Maron returned to the network to co-host, with the comedian Sam Seder, the weekday Webcast *Breakroom Live with Maron & Seder.* "I had been fired from [Air America] two or three times," Maron recalled to an interviewer for *Backstage.com* (June 1, 2011). "I didn't want to have anything to do with them, but I was in the middle of a divorce, and I was about to lose everything. That job really just got me out of my divorce without losing my house." The show moved from the Web to radio in January

2009; it was canceled that July. AAR filed for bankruptcy in January 2010.

Meanwhile, in May 2008 Maron had toured with Andy Kindler and Eugene Mirman in a show called *Stand Uppity: Comedy That Makes You Feel Better About Yourself and Superior to Others*. That year and the next, Maron performed in a stand-up act called *Scorching the Earth*. The show was a brutally honest account of the end of his marriage to Wolff, who had left him in 2007. Brownstein wrote of *Scorching the Earth*, "Maron is tough on his ex, but he is even tougher on himself. Yet for all its angst, the show not only touches a nerve but also has moments of high humour—albeit of the darkish variety."

By that time Maron had grown frustrated with his lack of mainstream success. Many of his peers from New York's alternative-comedy scene had attained fame—starring in their own television shows, building film careers, or securing major stand-up gigs—and Maron struggled to understand why he had not. One reason, he concluded, was that his foray into liberal talk radio had hurt his image as a comic. "I didn't think I was being true to what a comic's supposed to do, which is not be partisan necessarily, but to try to speak a language that anyone can understand, and get at the truth that way," he told the *Backstage.com* interviewer. For whatever reason, though he was often referred to as "a comedy legend," Maron found himself "unbookable," as he put it. "I couldn't get any road work," he told *Backstage.com*. "I was washed up, . . . and I had no real plan. I thought, 'I built it, and they're not coming. So what the f— do I do now?'"

In September 2009 Maron began sneaking into the AAR studios in the evenings to record his own podcast, with the help of Brendan McDonald, who served as his producer. Called *WTF with Marc Maron*, the show consisted of a 10-minute introduction by Maron followed by an interview with a friend or acquaintance of his, often a fellow comedian he had lost touch with or alienated over the years. After the first 20 or so installments, Maron moved from his apartment in the New York City borough of Queens to a house in the Highland Park section of Los Angeles. He has since recorded most of his podcasts in a modest studio he set up in his garage. Maron relates to his guests personally and professionally, and he takes pride in holding honest conversations with them, in which they discuss their childhoods, their vices and insecurities, and their experiences as comedians. "Most of them live difficult lives," Maron told Saltzstein. "So that was always more in the forefront than 'Let's talk about the business of comedy.'"

The podcast quickly gained a cult following among fans of Maron and other comics. One of Maron's best-known interviews was with Robin Williams, in which the actor and comedian talked about his struggles with drug addiction and depression. Referring to the dark side of comedy, Williams said, as quoted by Saltzstein, "I guess it's that fear that they'll recognize—as you know—how insecure are we really? How desperately insecure that made us do this for a living?" In another notable interview, Maron asked the Latino comedian Carlos Mencia about rumors that he had stolen jokes. Mencia denied the rumors, but afterward Maron learned from several other Latino comedians that Mencia had dissembled during their discussion. When Maron interviewed Mencia again, Mencia admitted to stealing jokes. "Had it been anyone else, I would have said, 'I answered that question a million times,'" Mencia told Saltzstein. "But [Maron]'s a comedian, he's a friend. . . . He's got power, man." Still another memorable *WTF* interview was with Louis C.K., the creator and star of the critically acclaimed TV series *Louie*. In the two-part discussion, Maron admitted that their friendship had ended mainly because of his jealousy of Louis's success, and the two seemed to reestablish their friendship on the air. Maron's other guests have included Sarah Silverman, Janeane Garofalo, Jonathan Winters, Adam Corolla, Andy Dick, Margaret Cho, Ray Romano, Judd Apatow, Stephen Tobolowsky, Bobcat Goldthwait, Garry Shandling, Ben Stiller, Conan O'Brien, Amy Poehler, Richard Lewis, Jimmy Fallon, Demetri Martin, Sandra Bernhard, Ira Glass, and Barry Maron, Maron's father. The 200th interview was recorded in August 2011.

WTF soon began to attract more than 230,000 downloads a week, making it one of the most popular downloaded comedy podcasts on iTunes and elsewhere. As of June 8, 2011, according to Right on PR (on-line), *WTF* had been downloaded 20 million times; Maron himself told Guy Raz that in the first half of March 2011, there had been a million downloads. According to many sources, *Vanity Fair*, the *New York Times*, and others have named *WTF* a "must-listen" podcast. Despite its success, the podcast generates only modest revenues, from listener donations, show sponsors, and, beginning recently, charges for access to "premium" installments. In May 2011 Maron edited a 10-installment package of *WTF* podcasts for the nonprofit Public Radio Exchange, which licenses and distributes radio programs. Some local public-radio stations, among them WNYC, WBEZ in Chicago, and KCRW in Los Angeles, have picked up the package.

WTF has led to increasing interest in Maron as a stand-up comic. In August 2010 he performed a stand-up act called *This Has to Be Funny* at Union Hall in Brooklyn, New York. The show was recorded and released in 2011 as a comedy CD. Maron's earlier CDs are *Not Sold Out* (2005), *Tickets Still Available* (2006), and *Final Engagement* (2009).

In June 2011 Maron shot a "mini-pilot" for a sitcom for Fox TV; co-written by Duncan Birmingham, it is about a comedian (played by Maron) who records a podcast in his garage in which he interviews comedians. Ed Asner plays Maron's father in the pilot. Maron has also secured a book deal and is currently working on a second memoir.

Like his second marriage, Maron's first marriage, to Kimberley Reiss, ended in divorce. He lives in Los Angeles with several cats.

—M.R.M.

Suggested Reading: *Alibi* (on-line) Dec. 23–29, 2010; *All Things Considered* (transcript) Apr. 2, 2011; *Backstage.com* June 1, 2011; *Forward* p18 June 4, 1999; *Fresh Air* (transcript) Sep. 21, 2000; *LAist* (on-line) June 15, 2011; (Montreal, Canada) *Gazette* D p1 July 21, 2009; *New York Times* (online) Jan. 6, 2011; *PR Week* Media p12 Oct. 18, 2004; wtfpod.com; Maron, Marc. *Jerusalem Syndrome: My Life as a Reluctant Messiah*, 2001

Selected Recordings: *Not Sold Out*, 2005; *Tickets Still Available*, 2006; *Final Engagement*, 2009; *This Has to Be Funny*, 2011

Selected Radio Shows: *Morning Sedition*, 2004–05; *The Marc Maron Show*, 2006; *Breakroom Live with Maron & Seder*, 2007–09

Selected Podcasts: *WTF with Marc Maron*, 2009–

Selected Books: *Jerusalem Syndrome: My Life as a Reluctant Messiah*, 2001

Larry Busacca/Getty Images for the Recording Academy

Mars, Bruno

Oct. 8, 1985– Singer; songwriter; music producer

Address: c/o Atlantic Records Group, 1290 Ave. of the Americas, New York, NY 10104

In 2010 Bruno Mars burst from obscurity to become a pop-music phenomenon with *Doo-Wops & Hooligans*, his first full-length album. Mars garnered a total of seven Grammy Award nominations in 2011, taking home the coveted award for best male pop-vocal performance for his hit single "Just the Way You Are," which reached number one on the *Billboard* music charts. He was also a featured artist on "Nothin' on You," a song he wrote for the rapper B.o.B, and "Forget You," which he penned for Cee Lo Green—both of which were nominated for record of the year. The notion that Mars is an "overnight sensation" belies the impressive résumé of the 25-year-old vocalist, who began performing at the age of four and at 19 became a member of the hit-making songwriting team the Smeezingtons.

Mars has been compared to artists in genres as diverse as the hip-hop of the 2000s and the doo-wop of the 1950s and '60s—the doo-wop comparison highlighted during his performance at the 2011 Grammy Awards ceremony, where the vintage-attired singer was broadcast in black and white. "Bruno is poised to be one of the next generation's greats," Green told Matt Diehl for the *Los Angeles Times* (February 6, 2011), while another collaborator, Travie McCoy, told Jason Lipshutz for *Billboard* magazine (October 9, 2010) that listening to Mars "belt" was like "hearing Michael Jackson for the first time." Mars, a Hawaii native, has been touted for blending aspects of hip-hop, pop, reggae, soul, and rock, a mix that he says comes easily to him. "Hawaii is basically in the middle of the world, so you're exposed to every type of music . . . ," he said, as quoted on his Web site. "It's hard to put myself in a box. I just write songs that I strongly believe in and that are coming from inside. There's no tricks. It's just honesty with big melodies."

One of six children, Bruno Mars was born Peter Gene Hernandez on October 8, 1985 in Honolulu, Hawaii. His mother, Bernadette "Bernie" Hernandez, a former professional singer, is Filipino; his father, Pete Hernandez, a percussionist and singer, is of Puerto Rican heritage and came from Brooklyn, New York. Pete Hernandez, whose stage name was Dr. Doo-Wop, performed regularly with his doo-wop revival group, the Love Notes. Mars was nicknamed Bruno as a toddler because his father thought he resembled a chubby wrestler, Bruno Sammartino. (The surname Mars came much later, chosen after the singer joked that he was "out of this world.") Mars's mother has recalled that from a very early age, her son was interested in, even obsessed with, performing songs. "He was a natural," she told John Berger for the *Honolulu Star-Advertiser* (February, 13, 2011). "At age 2 he would lock himself in the room and do his thing over and over and over. He would come out and show us. . . . Even if he couldn't pronounce the words, he would sing the beat and he was on pitch." Mars emulated the legendary Elvis Presley, after learning to find his favorite Presley songs on VHS recordings of the singer's movies. His father has recalled waking up in the middle of the night to find the toddler in front of the television, practicing his moves.

Mars got his first break at the age of four, when the Love Notes were performing at the opening of a Sheraton Hotel in Japan. Mars begged his father to let him go onstage, and when his father relented, Mars showed off the Presley imitation he had perfected in front of the TV. "I pulled him up on stage, and he started shaking his legs and the people went wild," his father told Berger. Mars reprised his act in Waikiki, Honolulu's resort area, and soon became an integral part of his father's show—as well as the youngest Elvis impersonator in Hawaii. (When the Hernandezes had to appear in Family Court to prove that Mars was not being forced to perform, Mars got up on a table and sang and danced for the judge.) At six Mars made a cameo appearance in the 1992 film *Honeymoon in Vegas*, starring Nicolas Cage, singing Presley's "Can't Help Falling in Love."

As a teenager Mars gave performances for the Waikiki revue based on the music of Michael Jackson. (With a strong voice and dance moves, Mars has drawn many comparisons to Michael Jackson. Today he is well known for performing a mix of Nirvana's "Smells Like Teen Spirit" and Jackson's "Billie Jean" during concerts.) Mars attended President Theodore Roosevelt High School in Honolulu, where he directed a school play, organized a Love Notes spin-off group with his friends, and choreographed pep rallies; meanwhile, he maintained his goal of becoming a successful performer and musician. "I'd rarely see him carrying books, but he always had a guitar or ukulele or something," Mars's father told Berger of his son's high-school days.

After graduating, in 2003, at the age of 17, Mars moved to Los Angeles, California. In 2004 he signed with Motown Records, but the partnership fizzled after disappointing results in the studio. Mars has blamed his own inexperience for that outcome, though he told Lipshutz that another cause was his was frustration with "bouncing around from producer to producer." Race was an issue for Mars, whose heritage is not instantly identifiable—which record executives saw as a drawback in terms of marketing. "Sadly, maybe that's the way you've got to look at it," he told Jon Caramanica for the *New York Times* (October 6, 2010). "I guess if I'm a product, either you're chocolate, you're vanilla, or you're butterscotch. You can't be all three." The failed Motown deal yielded one positive result: through it Mars met the songwriter Phillip Lawrence. "He was clearly talented," Lawrence told Lipshutz of Mars, "but there was no control as

to where he was going." The two began creating their own music—Mars was a gifted, self-taught guitarist, bassist, pianist, and percussionist—and producing songs for others. They called themselves the Smeezingtons, a name that grew out of "smeeze," their variation on the word "smash," and were soon joined by the sound engineer Ari Levine. The Smeezingtons worked out of Levine's LevCon Studios, which Diehl called a "ramshackle cottage" on a "seedy Hollywood side street," collaborating on music with which they hoped to attract record companies. Levine described their sound to Diehl as "that weird middle ground, where there's live instruments but it's still rhythmic and pop." The Smeezingtons' style was a far-reaching blend of vintage doo-wop, rock, pop, and, occasionally, reggae. Mars also crossed genres on his own, earning money by performing in a by-request cover band called Sex Panther. When a record label contacted the Smeezingtons, it was to ask to use one of the group's songs for another artist. At first Mars said no, but when the label increased the offer, he agreed. "It was either that, or I was going back to Hawaii," Mars told Lipshutz. "After we sold the first track, it opened our eyes."

In 2008 the Smeezingtons wrote the song "Long Distance" for the R&B singer Brandy, and their collaboration with the Hasidic Jewish reggae rapper Matisyahu in 2009 yielded the song "One Day," which was used as a theme song of the 2010 Winter Olympics. But it was working with the Somali-born hip-hop artist K'naan in 2008, Mars told Lipshutz, that established the definitive Smeezington sound, which includes "live instrumentation and programmed drums, but with a classic, vintage feel." K'naan recorded "Wavin' Flag" with the Smeezingtons, which became the anthem of the 2010 FIFA World Cup. Around that time a writing credit on Flo Rida's song "Right Round" captured the attention of Atlantic Records' artist-and-repertoire director, Aaron Bay-Schuck, who set up a meeting for Mars and Lawrence with Elektra Records. During the meeting Mars played five songs, including "Nothin' on You" and "Billionaire," the latter of which he had written in London, England; he and Levine had been given the equivalent of about $500 to write and produce for an artist there, not knowing that, with the dollar-pound exchange rate, the money was barely enough to live on during their 11-day stay. "We thought we were broke in California . . . ," Mars recalled to Lipshutz. "So we've got no money, and I'm walking the streets and came up with, 'I wanna be a billionaire, so frickin' bad.'" Elektra's co-presidents, Janick and Mike Caren, liked what they heard. "Every song sounded like a smash," Janick told Lipshutz. "As soon as they walked out of the meeting, I said, 'We have to sign these guys.'"

Two of the songs that had so impressed the Elektra executives paved the way for Mars as a solo artist. "Nothin' on You" was recorded by the rapper B.o.B, and "Billionaire" went to the former Gym Class Heroes frontman, Travie McCoy. Neither artist intended at first to include Mars on his track, but in the end, each did. "There was one other prospect for the hook," McCoy told Lipshutz, "but . . . after [Mars] went in and laid down the final vocals it was a no-brainer. We had to keep him on the record." Both songs broke the *Billboard* Top 10 in 2010; "Nothin' on You" reached number one, while "Billionaire" peaked at number four. Released on the Internet in the fall of 2010, Mars's collaboration with Cee Lo Green—subversively titled "F**k You!"—became a viral hit. The song was later edited for radio and re-titled "Forget You." It peaked at number two on the *Billboard* Hot 100 after being performed at the Grammy Awards ceremony in February 2011.

In May 2010 Mars released a digital EP called *It's Better If You Don't Understand*. His official debut album, *Doo-Wops & Hooligans*, was released the following October. His first single, a ballad called "Just the Way Your Are," came out in July and topped the charts in both the U.S. and the U.K. Mars's second single, "Grenade," achieved the same feat, nabbing number-one spots in Ireland, Australia, Canada, and New Zealand as well. Reviewers have been mostly kind to Mars. Though Alexis Petridis, writing for the London *Guardian* (January 21, 2011), criticized the simplicity of Mars's lyrics and dismissed his music as too "saccharine," Caramanica wrote, "Mr. Mars is a true rarity. His debut album . . . is an effortless, fantastically polyglot record that shows him to be a careful study across a range of pop songcraft. 'Grenade' is a hybrid of ethereal 1980s pop with modern-day Kanye Westesque drums. On the jumpy, salacious 'Runaway Baby,' he channels Little Richard. 'The Lazy Song' and 'Liquor Store Blues' borrow heavily from roots reggae, and on 'Our First Time' Mr. Mars approximates the slinkiness of Sade." Mars, who long ago perfected the seemingly effortless dance moves of Michael Jackson, is known for imitating the "King of Pop" at his own shows. Neil McCormick wrote for the London *Telegraph* (January 26, 2011) that Mars was "ludicrously entertaining" in performance, engaging his audience with "the pizzazz of a veteran showman." McCormick wrote, "Bounding energetically on stage in a sharp, black suit and tie, flashing his choppers like a dental model and swinging a Stratocaster [guitar], Bruno Mars is clearly not short of confidence."

After his successful night at the 2011 Grammy Awards ceremony, Mars completed a largely sold-out European tour. He planned to return to the U.S. in May. His meteoric rise was marred by an arrest in Las Vegas, Nevada, in the fall of 2010 for possession of a small bag of cocaine. Mars reportedly told the arresting police officer that he had never used drugs before. When Mars appeared in court, in February 2011, he pleaded guilty to a charge of possession; he received a year's probation and had to pay a $2,000 fine and perform 200 hours of community service.

Mars lives in Los Angeles.

—M.M.H.

Suggested Reading: *Billboard* (on-line) Oct. 9, 2010; *Honolulu Star-Advertiser* (on-line) Feb. 13, 2011; (London) *Guardian* p13 Jan. 21, 2011; (London) *Telegraph* (on-line) Jan. 26, 2011; *Los Angeles Times* E p1 Feb. 6, 2011; *New York Times* C p1 Oct. 6, 2010

Selected Recordings: *It's Better if You Don't Understand*, 2010; *Doo-Wops & Hooligans*, 2010

Scott Halleran/Getty Images

Matthews, Clay III

May 14, 1986– Football player

Address: Green Bay Packers, P.O. Box 10628, Green Bay, WI 54307-0628

"I always thought I was going to play in the NFL," the Green Bay Packers linebacker Clay Matthews III told Tom Pedulla for *USA Today* (February 2, 2011, on-line). "It was probably naïve to think that, given the percentages, but I put blinders on and it worked out." By "percentages," Matthews was probably referring to the slim chance that any individual will be picked in a National Football League draft, and to his slow start as a college player. In his case, however, many observers would have given him far better than usual odds, because his paternal grandfather, his father, and a paternal uncle all played professional football, and one of his older brothers was a member of the University of Southern California (USC) football team in 2003, when the Trojans won both the Associated Press and the Football Writers Association of America national championships. Matthews played with the Trojans, too, after a year as a walk-on and then as a redshirt. He entered his third year at USC with a scholarship and enjoyed great success on the playing field that season and the next two; indeed, he won Co-Special Teams Player of the Year honors in 2006, 2007, and 2008. In the summer of 2008, after his graduation from USC, he was drafted by the Green Bay Packers in an unusual trade and signed a five-year contract worth $9.3 million. He set several records during his rookie year and finished third in the voting for the Associated Press 2009 Defensive Rookie of the Year Award. "He's always on his feet," the Packers' general manager, Ted Thompson, told Todd Rosiak for the *Milwaukee (Wisconsin) Journal Sentinel* (April 26, 2009). "He has great hips and balance. He can use his hands effectively against offensive linemen and running backs. He can run; he can move in space. He can do the things that anybody looks for in a defensive player." During the 2010 season Matthews firmly established himself as one of the most talented and versatile pass-rushers in the league.

The fourth of the five children of William Clay Matthews Jr. and Leslie Matthews, William Clay Matthews III was born on May 14, 1986 in Northridge, California. His grandfather Clay Matthews Sr. was a standout lineman at Georgia Tech and was selected in the 25th round of the 1949 NFL Draft by the Los Angeles Rams before being traded to the San Francisco 49ers. He played defensive end for the 49ers in 1950 and then, after he served in the Korean War, from 1953 to 1955. Clay Matthews Sr.'s sons Clay Jr. (born in 1956) and Bruce (born in 1961) were both All-American football stars at USC and were first-round NFL draft picks. Clay Jr. played for the Cleveland Browns for the first 16 of his 19 seasons in the NFL, during which he earned four Pro Bowl selections and established himself as one of the best linebackers in the league. He is the Browns' franchise leader in games played (232) and career sacks (76.5) and also holds the distinction of being the oldest player in the NFL, at 40 years and 282 days, to record a sack. He spent the last three years of his career with the Atlanta Falcons and retired after the 1996 season, having played in 278 career games, most among linebackers in NFL history. Bruce Matthews, meanwhile, spent his entire 19-year NFL career with the Houston Oilers/Tennessee Titans franchise. Considered one of the best offensive linemen in NFL history, he earned 14 consecutive Pro Bowl selections (1988–01), tying an NFL record, and was named to the NFL's All-Decade Team for the 1990s. He was elected to the Pro Football Hall of Fame in 2007, his first year of eligibility. Clay Matthews III's eldest brother, Kyle, played safety for USC from 2000 to 2003 and was a member of the Trojans' 2003 national championship team.

Clay III started playing football at the age of nine, when he joined a youth league in Lilburn, Georgia. (He was supposed to have joined a soccer team, but his mother missed the signup deadline for it.) The year that Clay Matthews Jr. retired from the NFL, he moved his family to the Los Angeles suburb of Agoura Hills. Clay III attended Agoura High School, where his father served as the varsity football squad's defensive coordinator. As a freshman Clay stood five feet five inches tall and weighed 125 pounds. He did not become big enough to join the football team until his senior year, when his height reached six feet two inches and his weight climbed to 210 pounds. His famous name notwithstanding, he garnered little attention from schools in the National Collegiate Athletic Association (NCAA) Football Bowl Subdivision (FBS), the highest level of college football (formerly known as Division I-A). (Division I-A and Division I-AA football schools were renamed Football Bowl Subdivision and Football Championship Subdivision [FCS] in 2006; Division I-AAA schools do not have football programs but are Division I in all other sports.) "I wasn't the biggest guy, I wasn't the fastest, I wasn't the best football player in high school," Matthews noted to Michael Lev for the *Orange County (California) Register* (November 27, 2008). "Rightfully so, I didn't get the interest from major Division I universities."

After receiving one scholarship offer from an FBS school, the University of Idaho, and offers from several FCS schools and junior colleges, Matthews enrolled at USC in the fall of 2004 as a walk-on football player. (Walk-ons have not received scholarships, but they must participate in all workout and practice sessions and also maintain acceptable grades.) Matthews's parents reacted to that decision with some skepticism. His father recalled to Lev, "I said, 'If that's where you want to go, fine. Don't go there because you think you should, because I went there and your uncle went there.' He had a concept of what he could do. And he never seemed to waver from that." At that time the Trojans, a perennial nationally ranked football powerhouse, had an abundance of talented players and had won (along with the Louisiana State University Tigers) the 2003 NCAA national championship. While redshirting during his freshman season, in 2004, Matthews added bulk to his body and maintained his four years of athletic eligibility. That year the Trojans won their second consecutive NCAA football title, after compiling an 11–0 record and then overwhelming the Oklahoma Sooners, 55–19, in the 2005 Orange Bowl. Throughout the season USC's head coach, Pete Carroll (now the head coach of the NFL's Seattle Seahawks), had offered Matthews opportunities to play in several of what turned into blowout wins, but he declined each time in order to keep his redshirt status (and thus extending his eligibility for the team to a fifth year). "I knew that I was capable of so much more," Matthews told Gary Klein for the *Los Angeles Times* (September 23, 2008, on-line).

In 2005 the Trojans' assets increased with the arrival of the freshmen linebackers Brian Cushing, Rey Maualuga, and Kaluka Maiava (all of whom were later drafted into the NFL). Their presence did not benefit Matthews, however, who received limited playing time on defense during his first three years of athletic eligibility. Nevertheless, he participated in 12 of 13 games as a reserve linebacker and special-teams player and impressed coaches with his work ethic and skills. In the fall of 2006, he won a scholarship. Matthews subsequently became a special-teams standout and was honored with the Trojans' Co-Special Teams Player of the Year Award in 2006 and 2007. He earned a starting spot during his senior season, in 2008, in which he was moved into the stand-up "elephant" position, which is a hybrid linebacker/defensive end, somewhat equivalent to an outside linebacker in a 3-4 NFL defensive scheme (a defensive alignment comprised of three down linemen and four linebackers). Matthews, who now stood six feet three inches and weighed upwards of 240 pounds, started 10 of 13 games and finished with 56 tackles (nine for losses), 4.5 sacks, two forced fumbles, two fumble recoveries, and a blocked field goal. He also shined on special teams and earned a third consecutive Co-Special Teams Player of the Year Award, becoming the only USC player ever to win that honor in three consecutive years. Matthews finished his career at USC with 96 tackles, including 13 for losses, and 5.5 sacks in 50 games played.

By the end of his senior season, Matthews's draft stock had risen considerably. He increased his stock even more with strong performances at the 2009 Senior Bowl and 2009 NFL Scouting Combine, annual invitation-only events at which top college players are evaluated. At the Scouting Combine Matthews completed the 40-yard dash in 4.62 seconds, one of the fastest times among linebacker prospects, and he performed well in other tests, posting a 35.5-inch vertical jump and recording 23 repetitions in the 225-pound bench press. Kevin Greene, a former All-Pro linebacker and now the Packers' outside linebackers coach, told Tom Pedulla, "I saw heart. I saw a motor. I saw passion. I saw a kid who, with a little polish here or there, could be a stone-cold diamond." Greene's lobbying led the Packers to trade three draft picks (one second-rounder and two third-rounders) to the New England Patriots in order to reacquire their first-round pick (as well as gain a fifth-round pick) and draft Matthews with the 26th overall selection in the 2009 NFL Draft. That transaction marked the first time that Ted Thompson, the Packers' general manager since 2005, had ever traded up into the first round to select a player. Matthews graduated from USC in 2009, with a degree in international relations, and that July he signed a five-year, $9.93 million contract with the Packers. Commenting on his meteoric rise, he told John Romano for the *St. Petersburg (Florida) Times* (February 2, 2011), "I know it sounds cliché, but my success is based on the fact I've had to scratch and claw for everything to get to where I'm at. . . . I'll never feel like I've arrived. There's always something to accomplish."

Matthews missed the Packers' first three preseason games because of a hamstring injury. He recovered in time for the Packers' season opener, against the Chicago Bears on September 13, 2009. In his professional debut he recorded one tackle for loss in a 21–15 Packers' victory. His appearance in that game helped the Matthews clan become only the second family in history with members of three generations in the NFL. (The first was the Pyne family—George Pyne Jr., George Pyne III, and Jim Pyne. Clay III's cousin Kevin Matthews, a son of Bruce Matthews, made his debut as a center for the Tennessee Titans in 2010, so there are now three families with three generations of NFL players.) The following week Matthews posted the first sack of his professional career, in a contest with the Cincinnati Bengals. In week four of the season, he made his first career start as the Packers' right outside linebacker, during a contest against the Minnesota Vikings that was broadcast on TV on *Monday Night Football*. In that game, which the Packers lost, 30–23, Matthews had a breakout performance, making five tackles and scoring his first career touchdown on a 42-yard fumble return after taking the ball from the Vikings running back Adrian Peterson. He was the Packers' starting right outside linebacker the following week, in a contest with the Detroit Lions, in which he made five tackles and posted a then career-high two sacks. The Packers shut out the Lions, 26–0, and Matthews was named Pepsi NFL Rookie of the Week. He continued to impress throughout his rookie season, starting 13 of 16 games and finishing with a team-leading and franchise rookie record 10 sacks, the most by a Packers rookie since the statistic became official, in 1982. He added 58 tackles (42 solo), a forced fumble, six passes defensed, and a team-leading 35 quarterback hits. Matthews also led the Packers and all NFL rookies with three fumble recoveries, and his 10 sacks placed him second among league rookies (behind the Washington Redskins linebacker Brian Orakpo, who had 11).

Bolstered by the league's second-ranked defense and the emergence of the Pro Bowl quarterback Aaron Rodgers, the Packers finished second to the Minnesota Vikings in the National Football Conference (NFC) North Division, with a record of 11–5. They advanced to the postseason, where they lost to the Arizona Cardinals in the NFC wildcard playoff round, 51–45, in an overtime shootout; the game set NFL postseason records for combined points (96), touchdowns (13), and first downs (62). Matthews himself made history by becoming the first rookie ever to record a sack, a forced fumble, and a defensive fumble recovery in a postseason game. Following the 2009–10 NFL play-offs, he was added to the NFC Pro Bowl squad, as a replacement for the injured Chicago Bears linebacker Lance Briggs. He became the first Packers rookie to be selected for the Pro Bowl since the receiver James Lofton in 1978. Matthews was also named to the Pro Football Weekly and Professional Football Writers of America (PFWA) All-Rookie teams.

Matthews was named the NFL Defensive Player of the Month for September 2010 after recording six sacks in his first two games (a league high for the first two games), against the Philadelphia Eagles and the Buffalo Bills, respectively. He missed a week-six game against the Miami Dolphins due to a hamstring injury but ended the season with a career-high 13.5 sacks while adding 54 tackles, two forced fumbles, and one interception for 62 yards and a touchdown in 15 games. He served as a major catalyst for the Packers' defense, which ranked sixth overall in the league, allowing an average of only 15 points and 309.1 yards per game. The Packers again finished second in the NFC North, with a record of 10 wins and six losses, and entered the play-offs as the NFC's sixth seed. Matthews recorded 13 tackles and 3.5 sacks in three play-off games, with the Philadelphia Eagles, the Atlanta Falcons, and the Chicago Bears, which the Packers won, 21–16, 48–21, and 21–14, respectively. In Super Bowl XLV, in which the Packers faced the Pittsburgh Steelers, Matthews made three tackles—one of them, in which he took down the Steelers running back Rashard Mendenhall in the fourth quarter, resulting in a pivotal, momentum-changing forced fumble. The Packers defeated the Steelers, 31–25, to secure their fourth Super Bowl title and a record 13th NFL championship. At the end of the season, Matthews was named to the Pro Bowl team and also earned his first Associated Press All-Pro First Team selection. He was barely edged out in the voting for that year's Associated Press NFL Defensive Player of the Year Award, earning 15 first-place votes to 17 for the Steelers safety Troy Polamalu. Matthews was recognized as the NFC Defensive Player of the Year and was honored with the Professional Butkus Award as the league's top linebacker.

On July 26, 2011 Matthews revealed publicly that he had played the second half of the 2010 season with a stress fracture in his shin. He reported to the Packers training camp several pounds lighter than the 258 pounds he had weighed during the 2010 season, having devoted much of the off-season to improving his cardiovascular endurance.

With his long, flowing blond hair and Herculean build, Matthews has drawn comparisons to Thor, the mythical Norse god of thunder. He recently signed a one-year endorsement deal with the shampoo brand Suave for Men; he has also been seen on television as a spokesman for the Pittsburgh, Pennsylvania–based retailer Dick's Sporting Goods. He has appeared on television programs including *The Tonight Show with Jay Leno*, *The Ellen DeGeneres Show*, and *WWE SmackDown*, and he served as a presenter at the 53rd Annual Grammy Awards. Matthews lives in Agoura Hills. In his spare time he enjoys watching movies, hunting, and hanging out with friends and family. His younger brother, Casey, was a standout linebacker at the University of Oregon and was drafted by the Philadelphia Eagles in the fourth round of the 2011 NFL Draft. His cousin Kevin's younger brother, Jake, is

an offensive lineman for Texas A&M University.
—C.C.

Suggested Reading: (Akron, Ohio) *Beacon Journal* Apr. 5, 2009; *Los Angeles Times* (on-line) Sep. 23, 2008; (Milwaukee, Wisconsin) *Journal Sentinel* C p5 Apr. 26, 2009, (on-line) Nov. 7, 2010; *New York Times* D p1+ Jan. 15, 2011; (St. Petersburg, Florida) *Times* C p1 Feb. 2, 2011; *USA Today* (on-line) Feb. 2, 2011; *Wisconsin State Journal* E p1 Oct. 25, 2009

Michael Loccisano/Getty Images

Maxwell

May 23, 1973– R&B singer; songwriter; producer

Address: c/o Columbia Records, 550 Madison Ave., New York, NY 10022

Along with such artists as D'Angelo and Erykah Badu, the musician known as Maxwell as been widely credited for the emergence of neo-soul music in the mid-1990s. Maxwell "knows the difference between the overt, sexually obnoxious R&B music so prevalent in the mainstream, and the classic, steamy yet romantic type perfected by genre icons such as Marvin Gaye, Barry White and Teddy Pendergrass," Mario Tarradell wrote for the *Dallas Morning News* (June 7, 2010). In a profile for the All Music Guide Web site, Steve Huey agreed, noting approvingly that Maxwell's relatively old-fashioned themes "set him apart from the vast majority of his bump 'n' grind lover-man contemporaries."

Maxwell's *Urban Hang Suite*, his debut recording, was released in 1996 to enthusiastic reviews. In a retrospective for BBC.com (January 28, 2009), Daryl Easlea described it as "a heartfelt, soulful album that praises monogamous love" and went on to explain, "Released at the height of hip-hop's popularity, it was a novel idea, and one that slowly and surely caught on. Although the name of the genre was coined a couple of years later, the album can be seen as the birth of Neo-Soul."

After releasing the follow-up albums *Embrya* (1998) and *Now* (2001), Maxwell took a long hiatus from the music industry. He told Dan Aquilante for the *New York Post* (September 22, 2009), "Being away from it all allowed me to refocus my creative energies." He returned to the spotlight with *BLACKsummers'night* (2009), which earned him two Grammy Awards. Although the album attracted praise from critics, some felt that Maxwell's reentry into the business had been timed poorly. Allison Stewart, for example, wrote for the *Washington Post* (July 7, 2009), "Neo-soul was less a revolution than a spectacular retreat, a return to the warmth and the stateliness of classic R&B with a few contemporary flourishes. Maxwell did the old thing well, at a time when nobody else was doing it at all. These days, everyone's doing it. . . . *BLACKsummers'night* has the peculiar misfortune of being a respectable, often charming retro-soul record at a time when respectable, often charming retro-soul records are not uncommon." Despite such naysayers, Maxwell, who also produces albums under the name Musze, intends *BLACKsummers'night* to be the first in a trilogy of conceptually related albums.

The musician was born Gerald Maxwell Rivera on May 23, 1973 in the New York City borough of Brooklyn. An only child, he is of Haitian and Puerto Rican descent. When Maxwell was three years old, his father, Maximilliano, was killed in a plane crash while visiting relatives. His grieving mother became exceptionally protective. As a result, Maxwell spent most of his childhood indoors, rather than playing outside. "There was a whole universe inside my room with my books and TV," he told Cheo Hodari Coker for the *Los Angeles Times* (July 14, 1996). "I didn't get out that much, but in my imagination, I played basketball and baseball with the best of them."

A devout youth, Maxwell sang in the choir of his Baptist church. Although his talent was obvious, he remained shy and reserved. "In high school, nobody paid any attention to me," he told Lonnae O'Neal Parker for the *Washington Post* (September 6, 1999). "I was the nerd. I was like the weird kid walking around in the hallway." When he was 17 Maxwell borrowed an old Casio keyboard from a friend and spent hours at a time playing the instrument. "Music was like an epiphany," he told Coker. "It was what gave me this voice and a bridge to human people, 'cause when I was younger, I didn't really feel human."

During his late teens Maxwell worked as a waiter by day and played music in small New York City venues by night. Too shy to date, he instead spent his free time writing hundreds of songs. He later began to record demo tapes, which he circulated to his friends.

In 1994 Maxwell landed a contract with Columbia Records. The label's executives had little faith in the commercial appeal of his debut recording, *Urban Hang Suite*, and shelved the album until 1996. Before its release Maxwell also tangled with Columbia's marketers, who insisted that a photo of him should appear on the cover. "I wanted people to come to the music and not base any opinion on the image," Maxwell explained to Jean A. Williams and Mary Houlihan-Skilton for the *Chicago Sun-Times* (October 11, 1996). A compromise was struck: when the album reached stores, the front cover depicted a pair of women's high heels, seemingly shed in haste onto the floor of a hotel room, and only the back showed a photo of the artist.

Maxwell's *Urban Hang Suite* greatly exceeded the expectations of Columbia executives, selling a million copies shortly after its release, earning a Grammy Award nomination for best R&B album of the year, and ultimately reaching double-platinum status. "Ascension (Don't Ever Wonder)," one track from the album, received significant radio airplay on both urban and Top 40 stations and reached the Top 10 of *Billboard*'s hot dance music and hot R&B/hip-hop singles charts. Critics were impressed. "Richly atmospheric—it kicks off with the sound of a stylus dropping on vinyl—the album is an ambitious song cycle that follows an adult romance from first encounter to dramatic conclusion," Richard Harrington wrote for the *Washington Post* (October 16, 1996). "Along the way it examines the complex tangle of emotions produced by love, the joy of sex and the push and pull of commitment, even the spiritual yearning at the roots of it all." Calling it "a sophisticated and stylized take on late-'60s and early '70s-soul," Stephen Cook wrote for the All Music Guide Web site that *Urban Hang Suite* "is destined to become a classic contemporary R&B disc."

In 1997 Maxwell appeared on the popular show *MTV Unplugged* and released an EP of his performance titled *Maxwell Unplugged*. "The very fact that Maxwell performed on *MTV Unplugged* indicates that he is more ambitious than the average urban soulster," Stephen Thomas Erlewine wrote for the All Music Guide Web site. "[The resulting EP] illustrates that he is a skilled, subtle vocalist capable of more nuance than the majority of his contemporaries. . . . With its soaring vocals and sexy, sinewy rhythms, [it] only whets the appetite for his second full-length album."

That sophomore recording, *Embrya*, was released in 1998 to mixed notices. In one representative review, Rebecca Little wrote for the *Chicago Sun-Times* (July 12, 1998, on-line), "*Urban Hang Suite* garnered attention in part because its music and lyrics strayed from R&B's lust- and sex-littered

Kevin Winter/Getty Images

Maxwell

beaten path. Instead, Maxwell delivered messages of love, romance and relationships, on top of sensual '70s-style grooves. With . . . *Embrya*, he continues that trend, but unfortunately loses the momentum and excitement he created with *Hang*. Nevertheless, *Embrya* is a nice collection of love songs, all earthy, not terribly exciting, but adequate for setting the mood." The album sold well, however, peaking at number three on the *Billboard* Hot 200 chart, and like its predecessor, it received a Grammy nomination for best R&B album of the year.

In 1999 Maxwell sang on the soundtrack of the movie *Life*, which starred Eddie Murphy and Martin Lawrence as prisoners who forge a bond during their years of incarceration. Maxwell's track, "Fortunate," which had been written by R. Kelly, landed at number one on *Billboard*'s hot R&B/hip-hop songs chart.

Two years later Maxwell released *Now*, his third full-length album, which reached the number-one spot on both the *Billboard* R&B albums and Top 200 charts. "As mellowed-out as much of *Now* is, it's definitely not aural wallpaper, but a cohesive effort that rewards repeated listenings," Tom Sinclair wrote for *Entertainment Weekly* (August 20, 2001). "His angelic falsetto conjures an image of a man in a state of perpetual grace. Even on the relatively up-tempo tracks . . . Maxwell sounds as if he's singing from a hot tub in heaven." In a review for the *Boston Herald* (August 31, 2001), Sarah Rodman quipped, "[The popular recording artist] Prince doesn't make truly terrific Prince albums anymore. Don't despair. Maxwell is doing it for him." Rodman continued, "Maxwell continues to distinguish himself from the current glut of over-

wrought and under-erotic R&B lotharios with his retro, almost absurdly soulful ways. Organic funk, steamy slow jams and spiritually searching ballads all benefit from the Brooklyn native's achingly sexy voice, which slides from bedroom growl to feathery falsetto in a note's time. . . . 'Now' would be a good time to get this album."

Following the release of *Now*, Maxwell took a hiatus from recording. "I needed a break," he told Jon Pareles for the *New York Times* (June 28, 2009). "The guys who really become famous become quite robotic in their ways. . . . Everything is based on them achieving, being No. 1, trumping the next person that they're competing with on some level, and I just didn't want to be that monster." Maxwell focused instead on his spiritual and personal life. "I just wanted to be a guy," he told Joy Sewing for the *Houston Chronicle* (November 6, 2008). "I needed to really establish my own sense of self worth apart from the music."

Maxwell spent much of his time in his native Brooklyn, where he maintained a low profile and dated women who had never heard his music. While out of the public eye, he also cut off his signature halo of fluffy hair. "It wasn't symbolic," he said to Sewing. "I didn't go to a mountain somewhere and have the priest come and say a prayer, light candles and cut my hair. No, I literally got my own scissors and did my thing."

Maxwell made his long-awaited comeback in 2008, with a surprise performance at that year's Black Entertainment Television (BET) Awards. His rendition of the legendary soul singer Al Green's hit "Simply Beautiful" was greeted with enthusiasm by the audience. "Most times, when you go away for six years and you try to come back, it's a wrap," he told Sewing. "But that didn't happen [to me]. It sends a great message to all musicians out there that you can pace yourself, live your life, and if you do music that comes from your heart, people will be around."

In 2009 Maxwell released *BLACKsummers'night*, his first album in nearly a decade. Debuting in the number-one spot on the *Billboard* Top 200 albums chart, it produced such hit singles as "Pretty Wings," "Bad Habits," and "Fistful of Tears." Ken Capobianco wrote for the *Boston Globe* (July 6, 2009, on-line), "Men, are you ready? That satisfied sigh you're going to hear tomorrow is the sound of America's women once they get a listen to Maxwell's first record in eight years. . . . *BLACKsummers'night* reminds you why Maxwell is the premier R&B vocalist of his generation and how much has gone wrong in his absence. Even at his nastiest (meant in the good sense), Maxwell is still tender, and these tracks, filled with devotion, heartbreak, and a little bit of social conscience, are sung with remarkable grace and subtlety." In a review for the New York *Daily News* (July 7, 2009), Jim Farber wrote, "*BLACKsummers'night* offers that rarest of balances: It's both embraceable and unbound."

BLACKsummers'night garnered a Grammy Award as best R&B album of the year, and the single "Pretty Wings" earned Maxwell the Grammy for best male R&B vocal performance. He has announced that he will release two related albums— "blackSUMMERS'night" and "blacksummers'NIGHT"—within the next few years.

Maxwell is currently unmarried. His female fans have been known to fling flowers and underwear onto the stage during his live performances. He told Mario Tarradell, "It's always been about the crowd. The middle man will change every day of the week, from vinyl to cassettes to CDs to record labels to the Internet, but the audience is always the audience."

—J.P.

Suggested Reading: *Chicago Sun-Times* SE p22 July 28, 1996, (on-line) July 12, 1998; *Dallas Morning News* C p5 July 3, 1997, E p1 June 7, 2010; *Detroit News* M p12 May 20, 2010; *Houston Chronicle* Preview p10 Nov. 6, 2008; *New York Times* Arts & Leisure p18 June 28, 2009; *St. Petersburg (Florida) Times* W p16 June 10, 2010; *Washington Post* B p7 Oct. 16, 1996, C p1 Sep. 6, 1999, C p5 July 7, 2009

Selected Recordings: *Maxwell's Urban Hang Suite*, 1996; *Embrya*, 1998; *Now*, 2001; *BLACKsummers'night*, 2009

Courtesy of National Geographic Society

Mayor, Mireya

(MAY-or, mir-AYE-uh)

1974(?)– Anthropologist; television personality

Address: National Geographic Society, 1145 17th St., N.W., Washington, DC 20036-4688

The explorer, anthropologist, and former National Football League (NFL) cheerleader Mireya Mayor earned two Emmy Award nominations for her work as a correspondent for the National Geographic series *Ultimate Explorer*, which took her around the world to observe gorillas, sharks, squids, leopards, and other wildlife. While Mayor is best-known as a television personality, she holds a doctorate in physical anthropology and has docu-

mented many rare primates, discovered several previously unknown species, and fought for the conservation of natural habitats. As quoted on the Web site for her memoir, *Pink Boots and a Machete: My Journey from NFL Cheerleader to National Geographic Explorer* (2011), she explained that she appears on television in part because that medium "has the power to help people know and connect with these animals and habitats that are disappearing. We may be facing the largest mass extinction of our time, so awareness is crucial. If we don't act now it will be too late." In 2010 Mayor hosted two animal-themed television shows on the National Geographic channel, *Wild Nights with Mireya Mayor* and *Mystery Gorillas*.

As one of only a handful of well-known female explorers and anthropologists, Mayor has been nicknamed "the female Indiana Jones" and "the female Steve Irwin." She told A. Pawlowski for CNN.com (March 31, 2011), "I think that it's pretty clear by [those nicknames] that there aren't a lot of women who do what I do. People need an image they can relate to and everyone knows Indiana Jones and Steve Irwin, and so I think by just attaching the word female in front of them, it lets people get an instant connection to what I do."

An only child, Mayor was born in about 1974 in Miami, Florida. She was raised, as she recalled in her memoir, "by not one but three very opinionated and headstrong women: my mother, whom I call Mami; my aunt Ica; and my grandmother, forever remembered as Mima." Her mother, a medical student in her native Cuba, fled that country for the U.S. as a 20-year-old in the 1960s, after refusing to pledge allegiance to the regime of Fidel Castro. Mayor does not recall ever meeting her father, a native of Spain, who met her mother while he was as an exchange student at the University of Miami. She wrote in her memoir, "My mom was both mother and father to me, and I observed the strength and integrity with which she handled both those roles." In Miami her mother worked as a secretary to an oncologist before becoming a nurse. Mayor learned to speak English at the age of five; although she later came to embrace her Cuban roots, she often wished, as a young girl, for a more "American"-sounding name.

"A tight-knit family with little means," Mayor wrote in her book, "we never ventured very far. Miami was my universe, and New Jersey, where most of my cousins lived, was as foreign and exotic as it got." She noted, however, that "in my mom's efforts to show me the world beyond my driveway, we took frequent trips to the zoo, where I was mesmerized by the variety of creatures and re-creations of their jungle environments. I pictured myself living in mocked-up rainforests, and that, I truly believe, is where my love affair with nature began."

Despite her interest in nature, Mayor was made to focus on ballet and piano lessons, because in her mother's eyes, as Mayor wrote, "joining the Girl Scouts would no doubt lead to camping, and that . . . was far too dangerous." She described her upbringing, in which she wore homemade dresses and was given dolls to play with, as being "fit for a princess, a Cuban princess." Nonetheless, she spent more time exploring the outdoors in shorts and T-shirts than she did playing with dolls. She was also allowed to keep a host of pets, including dogs, cats, birds, fish, rabbits, hamsters, and a chicken named Maggie. As a girl Mayor excelled at basketball. In high school she had a major role in a student theatrical production, and afterward she appeared in musicals at the local Actors' Playhouse theater.

After completing high school Mayor found a talent agent and got work as an extra in movies. At one point she was a "bikini-clad model," as she recalled in her memoir, on the Spanish-language TV show Sabado Gigante. After discovering the need to supplement her income with office jobs, work that she found depressing, Mayor decided to seek a college degree. Following two years at a community college, she enrolled at the University of Miami, where she pursued a double major in English and philosophy. Meanwhile, missing her work as a performer, on the advice of a friend she tried out to be a cheerleader for the Miami Dolphins of the NFL. One of only 32 to make the cut, she spent the next four years as both a student and a cheerleader.

In 1996, in order to fulfill a university science requirement, Mayor randomly chose an anthropology course. The course proved to be inspiring. "My anthropology professor talked about her experiences chasing monkeys in the jungle, and that fascinated me," Mayor told Melissa Farenish for the Daily Item (January 28, 2010, on-line). She soon began to read about the work of the influential female primatologists Jane Goodall and Dian Fossey and decided that she wanted to conduct research on primates in the wild. Goodall and Fossey "were my role models," Mayor told Farenish of those pioneering women.

After graduating from the University of Miami, Mayor was eager to study primates. She applied successfully for a Fulbright scholarship to participate in the Smithsonian Institution's Guyana proj-ect in South America, which involved observing the rare white-faced saki (a species of monkey). On her decision to leave the cheerleading squad and study in the jungle, she told Darlene Cavalier for Scientific American (March 1, 2011, on-line), "The cheerleaders reacted to my decision, the same way everybody else does! They thought I was nuts, and with some good reason. . . . At 22, never having been camping I set out to a remote and virtually unexplored jungle in South America with nothing more than pink boots, a hammock and a backpack. I left all 'civilization' behind, where there is no electricity or hot showers, or even a way to call home. They reacted to my news pretty much the same way my family did initially. And like my family, they are now my biggest cheerleaders, always supportive of my endeavors."

Mayor accompanied the Smithsonian team on two expeditions in the summer of 1996. In her book she recalled that during those expeditions, in which she experienced sweltering heat, encountered countless biting insects, and overcame a life-threatening blood infection, she "evolved from naïve cheerleader to daring explorer," one who "never stopped dreaming of my next adventure." Mayor co-authored several papers about her research in Guyana, including, with Shawn M. Lehman, the director of the Smithsonian's Guyana project, "Survey of the Distribution and Diversity of Primates in NW Guyana," published in the American Journal of Primatology (1999).

With another grant Mayor headed to the African island nation of Madagascar in 1997 to study sifakas. There are nine species of sifakas, which are members of a family of primates known collectively as lemurs. Lemurs are indigenous only to Madagascar—that is, in the wild they live nowhere else. As of 2010 scientists had identified 101 distinct species, many of which are considered in danger of extinction to a greater or lesser degree. Sifakas are so rare that in the late 1990s some experts believed they no longer existed, and for two weeks Mayor and her research assistants failed to find them. Then they happened upon villagers who led them to an isolated location where Mayor and her team observed an impressive number of silky sifakas, whose fur is all white, and Perrier's sifakas, which are all black. Mayor is the co-author of several articles about the sifakas, published in such journals as the American Journal of Physical Anthropology, Neotropical Primates, and Lemur News. For her Ph.D. dissertation for the State University of New York at Stony Brook, Mayor discussed how forest fragmentation and other human activities in Madagascar are endangering primates, using the sifakas as a case study. Mayor earned a doctorate in physical anthropology in 2008.

In 2000, while studying the sifakas, Mayor and a colleague, Edward Louis of the Henry Doorly Zoo, in Omaha, Nebraska, discovered what they believed to be a previously unknown species of mouse lemur when one of the creatures got caught in one of their traps. DNA testing later confirmed that it was, indeed, a new species of *microcebus* (mouse lemur), believed to be the smallest primate in the world. (Some mouse lemurs weigh less than two ounces.) The discovery (one of a dozen new mouse-lemur species identified since 2000) elevated Mayor's status as an anthropologist and primatologist. She later lobbied for the protection of the species, and the prime minister of Madagascar agreed to designate the lemur's habitat as a national park. As quoted in the biography of Mayor on the National Geographic Web site, she said that her discovery was "one of those things you never thought could happen in the 21st century." She also recalled the difficulty of identifying the species and protecting its habitat. Her efforts were documented in an installment of the National Geographic TV channel's *Ultimate Explorer* series, "King Kong in My Pocket," which aired in 2003. Mayor has continued to visit Madagascar for research and observation; in the past she has spent between three and 10 months at a time there, according to her Web site.

Mayor's association with the National Geographic Society began in 1999, when, for an installment of the series *Out There*, she was tapped to discuss lemurs and the catlike, carnivorous fossa, one of their main predators. Shortly afterward she debuted in the *Ultimate Explorer* series, in "Lemur Rescue," which focused on sifakas. In 2001, impressed by the young primatologist, the National Geographic Society offered her a staff position as an on-air correspondent. In her book she recalled, "I had spent years studying primates in remote jungles. . . . I had gotten a taste of exploration and adventure, but I wanted more. Don't get me wrong, I'm not an adrenaline junkie. But as a correspondent for National Geographic, I would go places and work with animals I'd never seen before."

One of Mayor's first appearances as a correspondent on the *Ultimate Explorer* series was in "Gorilla Wild." In that 2003 documentary she is seen meeting an Italian conservationist, Chloe Cipolletta, who was observing western lowland gorillas at the World Wildlife Fund's Gorilla Habituation Project in the Dzanga-Sangha protected area of the Central African Republic (CAR). The project's goal was to habituate the gorillas—that is, accustom them to the nearby presence of humans—for ecotourism purposes. During her visit to the CAR, Mayor had an unsettling encounter with one of the gorillas. "The first time I was charged by one of these gorillas, even though I knew that it was likely a bluff, it was terrifying," she told Brian Handwerk for the National Geographic Web site (August 15, 2003). "I'd be lying if I didn't say that. They are letting you know who is the boss. But I already knew who was the boss; it was very clear from their sheer size and power."

Other *Ultimate Explorer* installments in which Mayor has appeared include "Devils of the Deep" (2003), in which she traveled to Guaymas, Mexico, to observe the aggressive Humboldt squid in the Sea of Cortez; "Love Those Dogs" (2004), in which she accompanied police dogs on their beat; and "Into the Lost World" (2004). On the last-named expedition, Mayor and her colleagues climbed several mountains in Guyana and came across two never-before-discovered species of frog.

In one of her most grueling expeditions, Mayor and three others—the writer and filmmaker Benedict Allen; a geophysicist, Pasquale Scatturo; and a journalist, Kevin Sites—attempted to retrace the journey made by the Welsh journalist and explorer Henry Morton Stanley in 1871 to find the seemingly lost Scottish explorer David Livingstone in Africa. The latter-day journey was filmed for *Expedition Africa*, a series produced by the reality-television specialist Mark Burnett, which aired on the History Channel in 2009. Mayor and her companions traveled 970 miles through Tanzania, struggling to find food and avoid dangerous animals in the difficult-to-navigate terrain. In a review for *Variety* (May 28, 2009, on-line), Brian Lowry noted that the team spent as much time arguing as they did exploring, thus giving the show the appearance of reality television rather than educational programming. Mayor, for her part, found the experience rewarding, writing in her book that not until completing the trek could she "look back and take in the full scope of the expedition. Our journey had begun more than four weeks before, 20 miles off the coast of eastern Africa. We four modern-day explorers had sailed toward the unknown, into the deep interior of Tanzania. We had travelled through the most stunning, epic, and unforgiving African terrain, fraught with danger. We had argued incessantly and laughed till it hurt. Now, as we approached a mango tree–lined avenue, it looked like the Garden of Eden, little changed from Livingstone's and Stanley's day. . . . The immense hardships and dangers of the trip and the pain of missing my children seemed small prices to pay for the pride and joy I felt at that moment."

In 2010 Mayor hosted the National Geographic TV series *Wild Nights with Mireya Mayor*. For that series she searched for animals that inhabit urban areas. For example, she traveled to New Orleans, Louisiana, to find feral hogs, to Rio de Janeiro, Brazil, to see large rodents and crocodiles, and to Miami to observe the local wildlife, including a Burmese python, a native of the Indian subcontinent and one of the world's largest snakes. (The one Mayor saw had escaped or been released from captivity.) She also hosted *Mystery Gorillas*, in which she investigated western lowland gorillas in the Congo.

Mayor earned two Emmy Award nominations in 2005 for her work on *Ultimate Explorer*. In 2007 the National Geographic Society named her an Emerging Explorer and awarded her a $10,000 research grant. Mayor wrote the introduction for and contributed to the National Geographic *Complete Survival Manual* (2009), which details emergency-preparedness and survival techniques. She has also written articles for the National Geographic children's magazines *Explorer* and *Extreme Ex-*

plorer. She has made appearances on television news and talk shows including *Today* and *Despierta America* and has given lectures at various schools and universities.

Mayor lives in Miami with her husband, Roland, and their four daughters. Of all the places she has visited, Mayor has expressed a particular connection to Madagascar. As quoted on the National Geographic Web site, she said, "This phenomenal natural laboratory could vanish in our lifetime—becoming the stuff of history books, not science books. Until I can walk away in good conscience, knowing it's going to be okay, I just can't leave."

—W.D.

Suggested Reading: CNN.com Mar. 31, 2011; *Daily Item* (on-line) Jan. 28, 2010; mireyamayor.com; nationalgeographic.com; *Scientific American* (on-line) Mar. 1, 2011

Selected Television Shows: *Expedition Africa*, 2009; *Wild Nights with Mireya Mayor*, 2010; *Mystery Gorillas*, 2010

Selected Books: *Pink Boots and a Machete: My Journey from NFL Cheerleader to National Geographic Explorer*, 2011

Alex Wong/Getty Images

McDonnell, Bob

June 15, 1954– Governor of Virginia (Republican)

Address: Office of the Governor, Patrick Henry Bldg., Third Fl., 1111 E. Broad St., Richmond, VA 23219

Since he won the 2009 race for governor of Virginia, Bob McDonnell has been viewed as a rising star of the Republican Party. Following President Barack Obama's State of the Union address in January 2010, McDonnell—only 11 days after being sworn in as the 71st governor of Virginia—delivered the Republican response to the president's speech, offering the GOP's perspective on several issues, such as job creation and economic growth. During his campaign for governor, McDonnell emphasized job creation and made an attempt

to appeal to moderate and independent voters by sidestepping divisive social issues, such as same-sex marriage and abortion—both of which he had strongly opposed in the past. As governor McDonnell has cut billions of dollars from the state budget without raising taxes and committed significant funding to infrastructure. Prior to taking office McDonnell, a lawyer by training, served as the state's attorney general, from 2006 to 2009; during his tenure he focused particularly on increasing penalties for child molesters and drug dealers. From 1992 to 2006 he served as a member of Virginia's lower legislative house. A year after McDonnell's address to the nation, an article by Alexander Burns in *Politico.com* (February 8, 2011) described the Virginia governor as being one of several 2012 Republican vice-presidential prospects over whom "the GOP is buzzing."

The oldest of five children in a Catholic family, Robert Francis McDonnell was born on June 15, 1954 in Philadelphia, Pennsylvania. The following year the family moved to Fairfax County, in northern Virginia. McDonnell spent the rest of his childhood there, with the exception of a brief period when the family lived in Germany, where McDonnell's father, John, a lieutenant colonel in the U.S. Air Force, had been stationed. After retiring from the air force, in 1964, his father worked for the Naval Investigative Service. His mother, Emma, worked for Olin Teague, a Democratic U.S. congressman from Texas. McDonnell attended the Bishop Ireton High School, in Alexandria, Virginia, where he played football. After graduation he attended the University of Notre Dame, in South Bend, Indiana, on a full army Reserve Officers' Training Corps (ROTC) scholarship. In 1976 McDonnell married Maureen Gardner (with whom he now has five children), received a B.B.A. degree in management, and, in the fall, went on active duty in the U.S. Army. He was a platoon leader and ran an army medical clinic in West Germany until 1979, when he went to Fort Eustis, in Newport News, Virginia, to serve as a medical-supply officer. During those years he took correspondence classes at Boston University, in Massachusetts, from which he received a master's degree in business administration, in 1980. After leaving active duty, in 1981, McDonnell served as a member of the army reserves until 1997, retiring as a lieutenant colonel.

Meanwhile, for four years starting in 1981, McDonnell worked in various positions (ultimately as a manager) for the American Hospital Supply Corp. in several locations, primarily in the suburbs of Chicago, Illinois, and in Kansas City, Missouri. Deciding to further his education, McDonnell enrolled with funding from the G.I. Bill at Regent University, in Virginia Beach, Virginia, whose motto was "Christian leadership to change the world." Founded by the televangelist and media mogul Pat Robertson, the school was then called CBN University, after Robertson's Christian Broadcasting Network. McDonnell received both a law degree and a master's degree in public policy in 1989.

McDonnell had his first taste of politics the year before his graduation from Regent University. In 1988 he worked as an intern for the House Republican Policy Committee, where he got a chance to interact with various politicians, most notably the Republican congressman Jerry Lewis of California, the committee's chair. The year following his graduation, McDonnell worked as an assistant prosecutor in Virginia Beach. In a profile for the *Washington Post* (October 27, 2005), Maria Glod reported that McDonnell, in his capacity as assistant prosecutor, helped a young woman on the witness stand tell a jury about her years of sexual abuse at the hands of her stepfather. Speaking to Glod almost 15 years after the trial, McDonnell said, "I can't remember her name, but I can see her face. She was very dysfunctional . . . and all the doctors told us it was the result of sustained sexual abuse. That woman was never going to be the same because of what that child molester did." According to Glod, McDonnell did not feel that as a prosecutor he could make the kinds of changes—with regard to victims' rights—that he wanted to make. So he decided to seek political office.

In 1991 McDonnell won the race for a seat in the Virginia House of Delegates, the 100-member lower house of the Virginia General Assembly. During his 14 years in Richmond, Virginia, representing his state's 84th District, he eventually became the assistant majority leader and the chairman of the House Courts of Justice Committee. He played a key role in introducing and passing many bills, including those aimed at cracking down on gangs, sex predators, and drunk drivers; he also succeeded in reforming the system for reappointing judges and in passing a law to improve the private/public partnership on transportation. In addition, McDonnell sponsored or co-sponsored bills to limit access to abortion, such as a required 24-hour waiting period for those seeking the procedure, and four bills (all unsuccessful) to establish in Virginia so-called covenant marriage, which would, among other stipulations, make divorces

more difficult to obtain. During his time in the lower house, McDonnell gained recognition in Virginia and received many honors. He was named the National Child Support Enforcement Association National Legislator of the Year (1998) and the Virginia Sheriffs' Association Legislator of the Year (2005); he also received a good deal of support from Christian conservatives, such as being named Legislator of the Year (1998 and 2001) by the Family Foundation of Virginia, which, for example, opposes abortion rights and same-sex marriage.

His reputation for having Christian values and being tough on crime helped win McDonnell the Republican nomination for state attorney general, in June 2005. In her profile of McDonnell, which was published a week before the November election, Glod observed that McDonnell had "made reform of sexual predator laws a centerpiece of his campaign, saying he would push for 25-year mandatory sentences for people convicted of sexually assaulting children. A second offense would bring a life sentence. He thinks sex offenders who aren't in prison should be monitored using Global Positioning System tracking and wants the state to consider random checks to see whether sex offenders are sending updated information to Virginia's online registry." McDonnell's critics expressed concern about his socially conservative beliefs, such as his strong opposition to abortion rights and same-sex marriage. In an interview with Glod, the Democratic delegate Brian J. Moran said, "I respect Bob's legislative ability. I respect his sharp mind. But he's going to use the attorney general's office to advance a right-wing political agenda." During the campaign McDonnell also had to face a challenge from his conservative supporters: in 1993, during his first years as a delegate, he had supported a one-handgun-a-month law, which was intended to make it harder for criminals to buy guns in large quantities. That vote so displeased the National Rifle Association (NRA) that the gun-rights group, which nearly always endorses Republicans, supported McDonnell's Democratic opponent for attorney general, R. Creigh Deeds. McDonnell won the November election, but only by about 360 votes—making it the closest statewide race in Virginia history.

McDonnell's time as Virginia's attorney general was defined by his pursuit of a socially and fiscally conservative agenda, his political rivalry with the state's Democratic governor, Timothy Kaine, and a series of initiatives to increase penalties for criminals—particularly child molesters, drug dealers, and gang members. At the same time, in a case that went before the U.S. Supreme Court, McDonnell's office supported the successful challenge to the Washington, D.C., ban on handguns. He favored offshore drilling for oil and gas and opposed a ban on smoking in bars and restaurants. In 2006 he criticized Governor Kaine's executive order making it illegal for the state to discriminate against homosexuals in hiring, employment, and promotion; McDonnell argued that the governor had overstepped his constitutional authority, and the governor, in turn, accused McDonnell of favoring discrimination in the workplace. On several occasions, however, the two worked together. Following the Virginia Tech massacre, in 2007 (in which a student previously diagnosed as mentally ill shot and killed 32 people and wounded 25 others), the attorney general's office, with support from the governor, worked on improving mental-health laws related to purchasing guns. However, McDonnell's opponents, mostly Democrats, argued that he ran the attorney general's office in a highly partisan manner. McDonnell, in an interview with Tyler Whitley and Jim Nolan for the *Richmond (Virginia) Times-Dispatch* (March 9, 2009), disagreed with that assessment: "We wanted a professional office that served its clients well. It was not a partisan office. It was a law firm." As quoted in the same article, C. Richard Cranwell, chairman of the Democratic Party of Virginia, disagreed: "Just like his time in the legislature, Bob McDonnell's service as attorney general has been marked by a dogged pursuit of his own ideological agenda, instead of solving real problems for real Virginians." Those who worked under McDonnell during his tenure as attorney general told Whitley and Nolan that morale in the office was high. McDonnell "was not a micro-manager," Rusty McGuire, an assistant attorney general from 2003 to early 2008, said. "He gave you his vision and let you carry out that vision."

In February 2009 McDonnell resigned his post as Virginia's attorney general to focus on his campaign for governor. With his conservative credentials well established, McDonnell ran unopposed in the Republican primary. In the general election he again faced R. Creigh Deeds. Most political observers noticed a less conservative, more moderate McDonnell during the months of campaigning prior to the November election. In March, for example, he announced that he would like to preserve 400,000 acres of land in Virginia. The *Washington Post* (May 14, 2009) story that carried the announcement had a headline that read: "McDonnell Goes Green in a Move for the Middle." McDonnell's strategy appeared to focus on job creation and de-emphasize socially divisive issues. During his last debate with Deeds before the election, McDonnell, who was leading in the polls, was asked whether there are any instances in which he thinks abortion should be allowed, such as when the life of the mother is in danger or in cases of rape or incest. His answer, as it appeared in the *Washington Post* (October 21, 2009), was, "I was raised in a middle-class Catholic family in Northern Virginia. My parents taught me about protecting innocent life, about protecting the family. And those are my personal views." During the campaign McDonnell also relied heavily on his reputation for being tough on crime. He issued several extensive proposals for fighting crime, including lifetime monitoring of sexual predators via GPS systems and other technologies, longer mandatory minimum sentences for repeat drug offenders, and trying as adults those juveniles who repeatedly commit violent crimes. Democratic legislators, in turn, criticized McDonnell for opposing federal stimulus funds that included money for law enforcement.

At the end of the summer of the campaign season, McDonnell's attempt to present himself as a moderate hit a snag. It was revealed that in 1989, at the age of 34, McDonnell had submitted a master's thesis at Regent that advocated the teaching of traditional Judeo-Christian values in public schools, criticized the legalization of contraceptives for unmarried couples, argued that the government should favor married couples over "cohabitators, homosexuals or fornicators," and sought to make the case that working women and feminists were "detrimental" to the family. After the story broke McDonnell denied that he still held those beliefs and said, as quoted by Amy Gardner in the *Washington Post* (August 30, 2009), that the thesis "was simply an academic exercise and clearly does not reflect my views."

McDonnell and Deeds occasionally agreed on issues; for example, they both supported reform of Virginia's highly partisan redistricting system. Deeds had long been a proponent of such reforms, whereas McDonnell, who had long opposed it, came to endorse the creation of a bipartisan committee that would redraw the districts. "Whatever the reasons for Mr. McDonnell's election-year conversion, it is a welcome development and a sign of at least modest hope," read an op-ed article in the *Washington Post* (October 5, 2009). "And none too soon. In the last state legislative elections, in 2007, just 17 of the 140 seats in Virginia's General Assembly were seriously contested."

In November 2009 McDonnell won the governorship, and for the first time in 12 years, Republicans swept all statewide offices in Virginia. During his first month in office, beginning in January 2010, McDonnell laid out a series of proposals to stimulate the state's economy. The plan called for increasing tourism funding, opening more charter schools, graduating 100,000 more college students in the next 15 years, drilling for oil and natural gas offshore, and making it easier, by eliminating levels of bureaucracy, for people and companies to open and run new businesses in Virginia. McDonnell said he opposed raising taxes and instead suggested that the state make the following cuts, summarized by Anita Kumar and Rosalind S. Helderman in the *Washington Post* (January 26, 2010): "McDonnell proposes saving $500,000 by eliminating a maintenance reserve fund, $4 million by not filling vacant positions at the Department of Correctional Education, $1.2 million by deferring equipment purchases at the Department of Corrections and $5 million from an additional federal grant for a food stamp program. He also recommends spending $21 million collected through last year's tax amnesty program and collecting an additional $25 million through reducing the state's contribution to the retirement system." Because the state was facing a $4.2 billion budget shortfall over the next two years, those measures would not have been nearly enough. Thus in September the governor proposed a 4 percent tax on sales in bars and restaurants, and in December he outlined a transportation plan to fix the state's roads and bridges; to pay for it, the transportation secretary proposed issuing bonds, whereas Democrats, reluctant to take on more debt, proposed raising taxes, which McDonnell said was out of the question. In January of the following year, McDonnell got five leading Democrats in the Virginia state Senate to co-sponsor his multibillion-dollar transportation package. Those Democrats found McDonnell's argument—that the state should borrow money because of low interest rates and construction prices—to be persuasive.

During his first year in office, McDonnell cut about $4 billion from the state budget, secured $2.9 billion in bonds for transportation and $100 million for colleges, and did not raise taxes. He had legislative failures as well—namely, the defeat of his proposals to reform Virginia's pension system and to privatize the state's liquor stores. During the first year of his term as well as the beginning of the second, he made several political moves that were controversial, surprising, or both. During his campaign McDonnell had expressed his support for redistricting reform, but in April 2011, in a battle that remains unresolved, he vetoed a redistricting bill, saying that its proposed changes would be illegal and would divide too many cities and towns; Democrats accused him of engaging in political theater. In March 2010 McDonnell issued an executive directive—an order that is not legally binding—informing state employees that they can be disciplined or fired for discrimination based on sexual orientation. Although some gay-rights advocates accepted that development as good news, others argued that the directive was an empty gesture, since it cannot be legally enforced. The move also displeased some social conservatives. In April of the following year, McDonnell expressed his opposition to proposed regulations that would make it illegal for private adoption agencies to discriminate against prospective parents based on sexual orientation. In 2010, to celebrate Virginia's heritage, McDonnell declared April to be Confederate History Month. He was criticized in the press and among academics for failing to acknowledge that slavery was the chief source of the conflict that led to the Civil War and that not all Virginians (especially not the state's 500,000 African-American slaves) had supported the Confederacy. "I find it obnoxious, but it's extremely typical," the prominent Civil War scholar James McPherson was quoted as saying in the *Washington Post* (April 7, 2010). "The people that emphasize Confederate heritage and the legacy, and the importance of understanding Confederate history, want to deny that Confederate history was ultimately bound up with slavery." McDonnell promptly apologized, and in the following year he declared April to be Civil War

History in Virginia Month, issuing a new proclamation that denounced slavery and acknowledged its role in the Civil War. Also that year McDonnell lifted a ban on carrying guns openly in state parks and added an amendment to a health-insurance bill that would restrict access to abortion for women taking part in a state-sponsored health-insurance pool, except in cases of rape, incest, or endangerment of the woman's life. In March 2011, while delivering the Republican weekly radio address to the nation, McDonnell said that he had cut $6 billion from Virginia's budget—a claim he has made many times. In their investigation of the claim, the nonpartisan Web site politifact.com judged that statement to be "barely true": a plan to cut $2.5 billion had already been in place a year and a half before McDonnell took office; furthermore, it is not true that all the money cut from the budget was balanced with spending cuts, as McDonnell had claimed. (Spending cuts accounted for $2.34 billion.)

McDonnell and his wife, Maureen, have five adult children: Jeanine, Cailin, Rachel, Robert, and Sean. Jeanine is a veteran of the Iraq war.

—D.K.

Suggested Reading: bobmcdonnell.com; politifact.com; *Richmond (Virginia) Times-Dispatch* Mar. 9, 2009; *Slate.com* Apr. 7, 2010; *Washington Post* Oct. 27, 2005, Aug. 30, 2009, B p1 Mar. 1, 2011

McIlroy, Rory

(MAK-il-roy)

May 4, 1989– Golfer

Address: PGA European Tour, European Tour Bldg., Wentworth Dr., Surrey GU25 4LX, England

On June 19, 2011 the Northern Ireland–born golfer Rory McIlroy won the 111th U.S. Open Championship, held at the Congressional Country Club in Bethesda, Maryland, to capture his first major title. At 22 years and 46 days old, McIlroy became the youngest winner of that event since Bobby Jones, in 1923, and the second-youngest player to win a major since World War II (behind Tiger Woods, in 1997). In total McIlroy set 12 U.S. Open records, including those for lowest four-round total (268) and lowest score in relation to par (16-under). McIlroy's victory solidified his status as the "next big thing" in golf, with many touting him as the most likely heir to Woods, his boyhood idol, whose career has largely fallen into decline since his highly publicized 2009 sex scandal. McIlroy's fellow countryman Graeme McDowell, who won the 2010 U.S. Open, called the young golfer "the best player I've ever seen," according to Larry Dorman, writing for the *New York Times* (June 20, 2011). "He's great

Rory McIlroy

Sam Greenwood/Getty Images

for golf. He's a breath of fresh air for the game, and perhaps we're ready for golf's next superstar, and maybe Rory is it." With his Open victory—his third win as a professional—McIlroy also put to rest any doubts that he could successfully close major tournaments; his triumph followed a series of near-misses at other majors, including an epic collapse at the 2011 U.S. Masters Tournament, in Augusta, Georgia, two months earlier, when he became the first player in history to blow a four-shot advantage after leading during the previous three rounds. With a faultlessly fluid swing, excellent hand-eye coordination, and formidable power, as well as a carefree and self-effacing demeanor, the five-foot nine-inch, 160-pound McIlroy is believed to have all the tools to win multiple major championships and is already considered a viable candidate to challenge the golfing legend Jack Nicklaus's record of 18 major victories. "The thing about these major championships is the history and the prestige," McIlroy said to Dorman. "Just being able to add your name to a list like Ben Hogan, Jack Nicklaus, Tom Watson and Arnold Palmer—that is the most satisfying thing about it."

The only child of Gerry and Rosemary McIlroy, Rory McIlroy was born on May 4, 1989 in Holywood, a suburb of Northern Ireland's capital, Belfast. His paternal grandfather, who worked in the Belfast shipyards where the *Titanic* was built, was a golfing enthusiast, and Rory McIlroy's father, who was raised in public housing 200 hundred yards from the Holywood Golf Club, took up the sport as well. McIlroy was introduced to golf by his father, a scratch player (one who golfs without a handicap), who began taking him to the driving range when he was an infant. When he was around

two years old, he received his first plastic golf club, and within a couple of years, he was reportedly able to drive real golf balls 40 yards. It was not long before McIlroy became obsessed with the sport. As a youngster he would chip balls along the halls of the family's house and into the washing machine. His parents fed his obsession by buying him an instructional video made by the six-time major champion Nick Faldo, titled *Nick Faldo's Masterclass*, which he watched so often that he started calling himself "Rory Nick Faldo McIlroy." He also became a diehard fan of Tiger Woods, after watching a telecast of Woods winning the 1996 U.S. Amateur Championship.

When McIlroy was seven years old, he became the youngest member of the Holywood Golf Club. Since the club did not normally accept members that young, he underwent an interview in which he promised to behave well and follow all club rules. "At that time his bag was as big as he was," his father recalled to John Huggan for *Golf World* (March 9, 2009). "He was small growing up. We had to stuff newspapers down the bag so that his clubs would stick out enough that he could reach them. At one stage his mother had to put a cushion down there." McIlroy began training under Michael Bannon, the club's head golf professional. Under Bannon, his coach and mentor, he developed his golf swing and quickly rose through the junior ranks. "Rory has always been different from the others," Bannon noted to Huggan. "He was always beyond his years. He has always been able to hit shots any shape or height. . . . His strengths are mental. He has the spark you only see in a few people. He'll never be happy with where he is. He always wants to get to the next stage."

McIlroy first drew the public's attention at the age of nine, when he won the 1998 Publix Junior Under-10 Championship, in Doral, Florida, by five strokes—defeating a field of 80 competitors from two dozen countries. (At nine McIlroy also reportedly made his first career hole in one.) Afterward, McIlroy's parents took on extra jobs to support his career: his father tended bar and cleaned the locker rooms at a local rugby and cricket club during the day and worked at the Holywood Golf Club at night; his mother worked night shifts at a local 3M factory. The money they earned went toward traveling expenses for junior tournaments in which McIlroy competed; they also saved up enough money to install a lighted putting green in the yard of their home. McIlroy has credited his parents not only for his success as a golfer but also for keeping him grounded and humble. "They never pushed me [into golf] at all," he noted to Juliet Macur for the *New York Times* (June 20, 2011). "I wanted to do these things, and they were very supportive." McIlroy's career was also aided by John Stevenson, his principal at Sullivan Upper School in Holywood. Stevenson, who retired in 2010, allowed him to skip classes and exams so he could travel to golf events and hid his absences from education authorities. McIlroy took only one General Certificate of Secondary Education (GCSE) exam, instead of the five previously agreed upon, scoring an "A" in physical education. Stevenson told the *Irish Examiner* (June 21, 2011), "I was determined that the school was not going to get in his way."

McIlroy wasted little time in fulfilling his promise as a golfer. He won four consecutive Ulster Boys Championships, from 2001 to 2004, and was a member of the winning European Junior Ryder Cup team in 2004. Also that year he won the Irish Boys Championship and Irish Youth Championship, was honored with the Tom Montgomery Award for best under-18 player in Ireland, and participated in his first European Tour event, playing as an amateur at the British Masters. In 2005 McIlroy became, at 16, the youngest-ever winner of the West of Ireland Championship and of the Irish Close Championship. Then, in July of that year, he dazzled spectators at an event held at the notoriously difficult Dunluce Links of the Royal Portrush Golf Club, in County Antrim, Northern Ireland, when he set a new course record with a score of 61. In 2006 he successfully defended his West of Ireland and Irish Close titles and captured the European Amateur Championship.

In 2007 McIlroy made the cut on the European Tour for the first time, at that year's Dubai Desert Classic, in Dubai, United Arab Emirates, and won the Sherry Cup, which helped him achieve the number-one spot in the world amateur golf rankings. That July he entered his first major championship, as an amateur at the British Open, held at the Carnoustie Golf Links in Carnoustie, Scotland, and won worldwide attention after being the only player in the field to shoot a bogey-free opening round. He finished the event with the lowest amateur score (+5, tied for 42d place) and was awarded the silver medal. One of his competitors at the event, Scott Verplank, said about McIlroy to the *Irish Independent* (July 23, 2007), "He looks like a 14-year-old but plays like a man of 28." McIlroy was part of the British and Irish team at the 2007 Walker Cup, held that September at the Royal County Down Golf Club in Newcastle, Northern Ireland, posting a record of 1-2-1 in the match-play event, which the U.S. won. After that event McIlroy turned professional and signed a contract with International Sports Management (ISM), an agency based in Cheshire, England.

After making the cut in his first professional event at the 2007 British Masters, McIlroy notched third- and fourth-place finishes at the 2007 Alfred Dunhill Links Championship and 2007 Madrid Open, respectively, to secure his European Tour card for the 2008 season. He performed well in his first year on the tour, collecting one second-place finish, six top-10 finishes, and 10 top-25 finishes. He finished the season ranked 36th on the European Tour money list (known until 2009 as the Order of Merit), which helped him break into the top 100 of the official world golf rankings for the first time. McIlroy started the 2009 season auspiciously, when he finished second in the UBS Hong Kong Open. That performance landed him in the top 50 of the world golf rankings and guaranteed him a coveted spot at that year's Masters Tournament in Augusta, Georgia.

On February 1, 2009 McIlroy won his first professional tour event, at the Dubai Desert Classic. That victory elevated him to number 16 in the world rankings. Later that month he competed in his first U.S. event as a professional, the WGC-Accenture Match Play Championship, in which he lost to the Australian golfer Geoff Ogilvy in the quarterfinals. McIlroy's performance in that tournament prompted Ogilvy to call him "by far the best young player I've ever played with," according to John Huggan. He added, "He hits the ball well, chips and putts well and his demeanor is fantastic." McIlroy competed in several other PGA Tour events leading up to that April's Masters Tournament, including the Honda Classic, the WGC-CA Championship, and the Shell Houston Open, in which he tied for 13th, tied for 20th, and tied for 19th place, respectively. Then, at the Masters Tournament, his major championship debut as a professional, he tied for 20th place. McIlroy's 2009 season was highlighted by his performances at the U.S. Open, in which he placed 10th, and the PGA Championship, in which he placed tied for third. He finished the year ranked second on the European Tour earnings list, with $3,610,020, and cracked the top 10 of the world golf rankings for the first time, moving up to number nine.

The 2010 season saw McIlroy record his second victory as a professional, and first win on the PGA Tour, at the Quail Hollow Championship (now known as the Wells Fargo Championship), held at the Quail Hollow Club in Charlotte, North Carolina. On the final day of the tournament, he shot a course-record 62 to beat Phil Mickelson by four strokes. With that win McIlroy became the first player since Tiger Woods to win a PGA Tour event before his 21st birthday. He showed even greater flashes of his potential at that July's British Open Championship, held at the historic Old Course at St. Andrews, in Fife, Scotland, when he shot a nine-under-par 63 in the opening round; that marked the lowest-ever first-round score in the Open Championship's 150-year history and tied the record in a major tournament for lowest single-round score. McIlroy finished in a tie for third at the British Open, which moved him up to a world ranking of seven. That August he finished tied for third at the PGA Championship, which was played at the Whistling Straits Course in Haven, Wisconsin. That performance marked his third top-three finish in a major.

After helping Europe defeat the U.S. in the 2010 Ryder Cup, McIlroy announced that he would play full-time on the European Tour while competing in 10 or 11 events in the U.S. per year; he explained that he wanted to be closer to family and friends. It was in the U.S., however, that McIlroy joined the elite ranks of golf. Following solid performances at the Abu Dhabi HSBC Golf Championship, Omega

Dubai Desert Classic, and WGC–Cadillac Championship, in which he placed second, tied for 10th, and tied for 10th place, respectively, McIlroy competed in his third career Masters Tournament, in April 2011. In the first round he shot a bogey-free seven-under-par 65, which not only led the field but helped him become, at 21, the youngest player ever to lead the Masters at the close of the first day. He continued to tear up the field in the second and third rounds and entered the fourth round with a comfortable four-shot lead. Nonetheless, on the fourth day of the tournament, McIlroy's play unraveled, and he shot a disastrous round of 80 to finish tied for 15th place and four-under for the tournament, which was won by the South African golfer Charl Schwartzel. Ollie Brown, writing for the London *Daily Telegraph* (April 11, 2011), described McIlroy's fourth-round Masters collapse as "the most spectacular—and surely the most affecting—Augusta implosion anyone could remember." (McIlroy's fourth-round score of 80 is the worst ever by a professional golfer who has led the Masters after three rounds.)

Following his disappointment at the Masters, McIlroy regrouped and sought advice on closing tournaments from the golf legend and all-time majors leader Jack Nicklaus. The two conferred while McIlroy was playing in Nicklaus's annual invitational, the Memorial Tournament, held in Dublin, Ohio, a week before the 2011 U.S. Open. (McIlroy placed fifth in that event.) Nicklaus said to McIlroy, as quoted by Sally Jenkins for the *Washington Post* (June 19, 2011), "Pressure is what you live for. You want to have pressure on you. You don't want to come down to the last hole needing to make par to finish 20th. You want to come down to the last hole with pressure on you to win. Everyone is going to put pressure on you. That's going to happen in life. If you are going to be successful, you're going to have pressure." McIlroy faced pressure head-on at the U.S. Open at the Congressional Country Club, in Bethesda, and delivered one of the most remarkable performances in golf history. As he had at the Masters, McIlroy led for the first three rounds of the tournament, but this time he finished with a record 16-under-par 268 to win the event—as well as his first career major—by eight strokes. He became the youngest U.S. Open champion since Bobby Jones in 1923 and the first player to win the U.S. Open with all four rounds in the 60s (65-66-68-69). He broke 12 U.S. Open records altogether, including lowest 36-hole total (131, 11-under-par), lowest 54-hole total (199), lowest 72-hole total (268), and shots under par (16), and his play drew immediate comparisons to Tiger Woods's historic showing at the 2000 U.S. Open at Pebble Beach, when he shot 12-under-par and won by 15 strokes. "I was very honest with myself, and I knew what I needed to do differently," McIlroy, who dedicated his victory to his parents, told Steve DiMeglio for *USA Today* (June 20, 2011). "I had a clear picture in my mind of what I needed to do and where my focus needed to be when I got myself in that position again. And luckily enough for me, I was able to get in that position. To be able to finish it off the way I did, it just tells me that I learned from it and I've moved on and now I've got this, I can go ahead and concentrate on getting some more."

After his U.S. Open triumph, McIlroy took a three-week break from tournament golf before making his return, at the 2011 British Open. He failed to contend at the Open Championship, owing partly to harsh weather conditions, and finished tied for 25th. He also struggled at that year's PGA Championship, held at the Highlands Course of the Atlantic Athletic Club in Johns Creek, Georgia, where he finished tied for 64th. McIlroy, who has earned more than $10 million in prize money, is currently the third-ranked golfer in the world.

"For all the suddenness of his elevation to golf's aristocracy, there is still an endearing touch of the tearaway about McIlroy," according to Ollie Brown. "His resemblance to Dennis the Menace is so striking you half-expect him to have packed a pea-shooter alongside his seven-iron." A writer for the *Irish Times* (November 13, 2010) noted that McIlroy has a "slouchy, skateboarder's athleticism"; finding McIlroy to be more accessible than Tiger Woods, the same writer observed that "unlike Woods, who let nothing or no one in, McIlroy's way seems to be to keep his life as open as possible." McIlroy told Huggan about his idol, "I'll never be able to do what Tiger has done. He has brought so many people into the game, those who would never have played but for him. . . . If I'm able to do half of the things he's done, I'll be more than happy." McIlroy, who is an ambassador for UNICEF, lives just outside Belfast in a house whose grounds are equipped with a wide variety of putting greens and practice areas made to resemble those he encounters at tournaments. An avid collector of automobiles, he is said to own more than a dozen luxury sports vehicles. He is also a fan of the Manchester United Football Club.

—C.C.

Suggested Reading: Associated Press June 10, 2011; *Dallas Morning News* C p2 Apr. 7, 2009; *Golf World* p36+ Mar. 9, 2009; *Irish Times* p23 Aug. 21, 2007, p12 Nov. 13, 2010; (London) *Independent* p52 Jan. 21, 2010; *New York Times* D p1 Apr. 9, 2011, A p1 June 20, 2011; *USA Today* C p1 Mar. 10, 2009, C p1 June 20, 2011; *Washington Post* A p1 June 19, 2011

Francois Durand/Getty Images

McShane, Ian

Sep. 29, 1942– Actor

Address: c/o International Creative Management, 10250 Constellation Blvd., Los Angeles, CA 90067-6207

Distinguished by his deep, wolfish voice, jet-black hair, and ability to portray a remarkably wide range of emotions and characters, the actor Ian McShane made his debut in film, television, and theater in his native Great Britain the year he turned 20, nearly a half-century ago. He has since appeared in well over 150 television series, stage productions, and films for the big and small screens and has lent his voice to a handful of animated features. Despite many troubled years marked by heavy drinking, drug use, excessive partying, and tumultuous personal relationships, McShane has rarely lacked work, and his performances have nearly always received high praise. Among the general public he is probably best known for his starring roles in such television series or miniseries as *Jesus of Nazareth*, *Lovejoy* (which he also produced), *Deadwood*, and *Kings* and his work in the films *Sexy Beast*, *Scoop*, *44 Inch Chest*, and *Pirates of the Caribbean: On Stranger Tide*. He provided the voices of characters in the recent films *Shrek the Third*, *The Golden Compass*, *Kung Fu Panda*, and *Coraline*.

The power of the actor's portrayal of Lovejoy, an immensely knowledgeable, charming, somewhat unscrupulous antiques dealer, led Marvin Kitman, a *New York Newsday* (January 5, 1987) critic, to misidentify the color of McShane's bluish-gray eyes. "What a joy it is to see McShane, who played the prime minister in *Disraeli*" on British televi-sion, Kitman wrote. "At last, he is not a villain. In American shows such as the mini-series *Bare Essence*, he's always the bad guy. McShane, with those glowing black eyes like pieces of coal, is magnificent as Lovejoy, a man who spends his life flirting with danger, and customers, in a profession that is not normally thought to be dangerous to life and limb. . . . McShane as Lovejoy will soon be a major cult figure on TV" among members of "the above-average audience. And he deserves the adulation. He captures one of the most complex characters in a TV series in years." In an article for *Time* (February 28, 2005) about *Deadwood*, in which McShane played a highly complex saloonkeeper named Al Swearengen, James Poniewozik wrote, "Many actors might play such a character with wicked intensity. McShane excels at bringing out Swearengen's contradictions, not just with bluster but also with 'the slightest gesture and simple stare,'" in the words of his fellow *Deadwood* actor Timothy Olyphant. Writing for the *Massachusetts Review* (Autumn 2008), Normand Berlin described McShane's portrayal of Max in a Broadway production of Harold Pinter's play *The Homecoming* as "exceptional." Offering examples of the actor's impressive versatility, Berlin wrote, "Max, on stage more than any other character, begins and ends the play, and McShane nicely negotiates the many changes in his character's moods and behavior. Blustering and cursing, an ineffectual Big Daddy, viciously cruel in his treatment of his brother Sam, violent in his verbal attack on Lenny . . . paternal in his advice to Joey, self-pitying in his recollection of the past with Jessie . . . proud of his 'instinctive understanding of animals,' always able to 'smell' a good horse . . . clever in his business negotiations with Ruth, pitiful in his sobbing words to Ruth at play's end, McShane's Max dominates the stage."

"Everything you do should teach you a lot," McShane told Jenelle Riley for *BackStage.com* (August 3, 2006). "I've been doing this a long time, but you're tested every year. When someone says, 'I've been an actor for 40 years,' I wonder, 'Well, is that one year multiplied by 40?' Because most people just amble along and do the same old crap. Or you can do something intriguing and take challenges as they come along. Otherwise you never grow. And you're only as good as the last thing you did."

Ian David McShane was born on September 29, 1942 in Blackburn, England, and grew up in nearby Manchester. His mother, the former Irene Cowley, was a homemaker; his Scottish-born father, Harry, played professional soccer for the Blackburn Rovers and Manchester United before becoming an announcer for the latter team. As a boy McShane played soccer but quit after he realized that he would never be as good as his father. One of his prized possessions was a cowboy outfit his father brought back after a visit to the U.S. A class trip to see Shakespeare's *Coriolanus* in Stratford-upon-Avon awakened his interest in theater. Encouraged by a teacher who had noticed his talent, McShane began performing in plays as a student at Stretford

Grammar School, a middle/secondary school near Manchester; notably, he won the title role of *Cyrano de Bergerac*. The same teacher suggested that he pursue an acting career. McShane gained admission to the prestigious Royal Academy of Dramatic Arts (RADA), in London, England, where he roomed with John Hurt and where Anthony Hopkins was among his classmates. After 18 months at RADA, McShane won the part of Harry, a heavy-drinking troublemaker who butts heads with his college professors, in the film *The Wild and the Willing* (1962; released in the U.S. as *Young and Willing*). With his first film role under his belt, McShane dropped out of school to devote himself to building his career.

McShane made his professional stage debut in 1962, in the role of Charley in Fred Watson's *Infanticide in the House of Fred Ginger*, one of several experimental plays that the Royal Shakespeare Company mounted at the Arts Theatre in London's West End. In other stage work in London, he portrayed the title character in Philip King's *How Are You, Johnnie?* at the Vaudeville Theatre in 1963; Ralph in *The Easter Man*, by Evan Hunter (also known as Ed McBain), at the Globe Theatre in 1964; and Tom in Tennessee Williams's *The Glass Menagerie*, at the Haymarket Theatre in 1965. In 1967 he co-starred with Ian McKellen and Judi Dench in Aleksei Arbuzov's *The Promise*, at the Playhouse in Oxford, England. *The Promise* depicts members of a romantic triangle in the Soviet Union in 1942, during the siege of Leningrad by German Army forces; again in 1946, after World War II; and finally in 1959, during the regime of Nikita Khrushchev. On its opening the play earned ecstatic reviews; it soon moved to the Fortune Theatre, in London, and then to the Henry Miller's Theater, on Broadway (with Eileen Atkins replacing Dench). In an assessment of the New York production, which marked McShane's Broadway debut, Clive Barnes wrote for the *New York Times* (November 15, 1967), "Ian McShane as Marik, blustering, desperately proud and easily hurt, left a remarkable impression (he made the character exist and grow in the mind even when he was off-stage)."

Meanwhile, McShane had made his TV debut as well in 1962, appearing in a play by Robert Muller—*Thank You and Goodnight*, an installment of *Armchair Theatre*, a British ITV-network drama series that aired from 1956 to 1974. His other television work in the 1960s included roles in episodes of the British series *First Night* (1963); *Z Cars* (1964); *Redcap* (1965); *You Can't Win* (1966); the miniseries *Wuthering Heights* (1967), in which he portrayed Heathcliff; and several dramas presented for *ITV Play of the Week*. On the silver screen he was seen in *The Pleasure Girls* (1965); *Gypsy Girl* (1966); alongside Michael Caine, Trevor Howard, and Harry Andrews in the World War II epic *The Battle of Britain* (1969); and opposite Suzanne Pleshette in the featherweight comedy *If It's Tuesday, This Must Be Belgium* (1969). In a *New York Times* (April 25, 1969) review, Vincent Canby panned the last-named film but wrote that McShane was "particularly good as the indefatigable tour guide."

In the last years of the 1960s, McShane became an increasingly heavy user of alcohol and recreational drugs. "I had about a 20-year party," he told Joan Anderman for the *Boston Globe* (June 6, 2004, on-line). "I took everything lightly and everything came quite easily. I just wanted to have a good time and make some money to fuel my social life. I did a lot of work and wouldn't call any of it memorable." In 1971 McShane was cast in the film *Villain* as Wolfe, a petty thief and the lover of Vic, a gang leader, played by Richard Burton. A notorious alcoholic, Burton was then "at the height of his drinking powers," McShane told Maureen Paton for the London *Evening Standard* (July 12, 2000). Each morning McShane would visit Burton's trailer to review their lines over grapefruit-juice-and-vodka cocktails; at lunchtime they would have a few beers at a bar. An anecdote McShane has often recounted relates to a kiss Wolfe and Vic shared in a scene from *Villain*. Burton "said to me one night, . . . 'You know, I'm very glad you're playing this part,'" McShane told John Hiscock for the London *Daily Mirror* (September 1, 2004). "I said, 'Really, that's nice, Richard.' He said, 'Well, you remind me of Elizabeth'"—the actress Elizabeth Taylor, Burton's wife at that time.

McShane's first role in a big-budget Hollywood film came with Herbert Ross's *The Last of Sheila* (1973), about six movie-industry figures who engage in what turns into a deadly parlor game while on a pleasure cruise. He portrayed the boyfriend and manager of an actress (played by Raquel Welch). McShane also appeared in such high-profile television miniseries as *Roots* (1977) and *Jesus of Nazareth* (1977), in the latter of which he played Judas Iscariot. He was cast as Ali Ben Yousef in the televised historical drama *Marco Polo* (1982) and as Rainier III of Monaco in the TV biography *Grace Kelly* (1983), about the actress who gave up her Hollywood career, in 1955, to marry the prince. Also in 1983 McShane was seen as a Greek tycoon in 11 episodes of the soap opera *Bare Essence*. In 1985 McShane had roles in NBC's three-part miniseries *Evergreen*, adapted from a Belva Plain novel, and in the miniseries *A.D.*, about Jesus's followers and the emperors of Rome in the years following Christ's crucifixion. He played villains on such prime-time shows as *Dallas*, *Magnum P.I.*, and *Miami Vice*. In 1988 he appeared in the TV movie *The Great Escape II: The Untold Story*, and in 1988–89 he was seen in eight of the 12 episodes of *War and Remembrance*.

Speaking of the 1970s and 1980s, McShane told Stephan Phelan, who interviewed him for Scotland's *Sunday Herald* (September 19, 2004), "There are some jobs that I don't even remember doing, in the blizzard of alcohol and drugs." In 1975 McShane moved from London to Los Angeles, California, to be near his second wife, Ruth

Post, a model, and their two children. Despite his many roles during the previous dozen years, he was not well known in Hollywood. Struggling to find challenging work, he turned increasingly to alcohol to dull his frustration and disappointment. He developed a reputation as a party boy and joined a group of hard-drinking young men—others included the screen and TV writers Dick Clement and his partner Ian La Frenais—who called themselves "the Bang Club," for their practice of pulling imaginary guns on one another in crowded places. "Yes, I do remember: if you didn't fall down, you had to buy another drink," McShane recalled, years later, to a reporter for the Hamilton, New Zealand, *Waikato Times* (March 5, 2005). "My God, how stupid, but how funny." During the shooting of *The Fifth Musketeer*, in Vienna, Austria, in the mid-1970s, McShane left his wife for the Dutch-born soft-core-pornography actress Sylvia Kristel, who had starred in the sexually explicit film *Emmanuelle*. Fueled by drinking and drug use, the couple's quarrels often turned ugly. Their tumultuous relationship ended after three or four years. In 1979, while filming *Cheaper to Keep Her*, McShane met the American actress Gwen Humble, who became his third wife, in 1980. His drinking continued until 1988, when he joined Alcoholics Anonymous; he has been sober ever since. "I'd had 25 years of boozing and using other recreational substances and I woke up one morning and decided I'd had enough," he told Hiscock. "I never liked the taste of alcohol anyway." He told the same interviewer, "I've had my wild times. I don't regret them, but they're in the past."

By the mid-1980s McShane had grown weary of small roles. "That stuff was fun," he told Stephan Phelan. "But there comes a point where you think, yeah, I'm rather good at this, in a way. So I decided to do a series for myself." He formed Witzend Productions with the goal of creating his own TV show. The idea for *Lovejoy* came from a fan, who had given him a script to read and offhandedly suggested that he read the Lovejoy novels, by John Grant (the pseudonym of Jonathan Gash). "I didn't want to do the play," McShane told Kay Gardella for the Kitchener-Waterloo, Ontario, *Record* (January 29, 1994), "so I ignored it and read the novels instead and was impressed. When I arrived in England I bought the rights." McShane starred in and wrote and directed some of the episodes of *Lovejoy*, a comedy-adventure series about a roguish antiques dealer, based in East Anglia, who is known only by his surname. Lovejoy is a "divvie," meaning that his intuition enables him to distinguish a real antique from a fake. In each episode he "spends as much time chasing villains and helping victims recover their property as he does making money," Diane Joy Moca wrote for the St. Louis, Missouri, *Post-Dispatch* (September 21, 1991). The show premiered in 1986 on England's BBC1 and on A&E in the U.S. a year later and was a hit with critics and audiences. After one season, however, McShane and his co-producers failed to strike a re-

newal deal with the networks, and the show was canceled. In 1991, after differences between the producers and the network were resolved, *Lovejoy* returned to the air in England; it resumed in the U.S. in 1993. By the time the series ended (in 1994 in England and 1996 in the U.S.), McShane had become a household name in England and had established a solid reputation in the U.S. as well.

Also on TV in the 1990s, McShane starred in the short-lived program *Madson*, as a man who, after serving time in prison for his wife's murder, seeks revenge on the police officer who framed him. From time to time he appeared as a guest star on such shows as *Columbo* (1990) and *The Naked Truth* (1997). In 1996, in a West End theater, he played the devil in a musical version of the 1987 film *The Witches of Eastwick* (which was based on a John Updike novel). That experience "taught me a good lesson," he told Phelan: "never do a musical. When in doubt, they just put in another song. Instead of working on that bit between the songs, which is called acting."

McShane's career got a boost in 2000, thanks to Jonathan Glazer's critically acclaimed crime thriller *Sexy Beast*, about a retired, self-exiled gangster (Ray Winstone) whose former boss (Ben Kingsley) recruits him for another job. McShane played Teddy Bass, "a merciless gangster, whose evil demeanor permeates the atmosphere of the entire film," Jenny Jeltes wrote for *University Wire* (July 3, 2001). A number of reviewers overlooked McShane's stellar performance, in light of those of Winstone and Kingsley, but McShane told Terry Lawson for the *Detroit (Michigan) Free Press* (July 8, 2001): "It doesn't bother me a bit. I think it was Milton Berle who said he'd rather be sh*t in a hit than a hit in sh*t. I'm all right with that." McShane appeared opposite Frankie Muniz in the children's spy comedy *Agent Cody Banks* (2003) and on episodes of the television shows *In Deep* (2002) and *The Twilight Zone* (2003).

McShane was awaiting a new assignment in 2002 when he was invited to submit an audition tape for the upcoming HBO series *Deadwood*. "My 60th birthday was coming and I wasn't going to do it, not at my age," McShane told Joan Anderman. Then, when he learned that *Deadwood*'s creator was David Milch, the producer and head writer of the acclaimed series *NYPD Blue* and *Hill Street Blues*, McShane sent in a tape. After he met with Milch, McShane was cast as the series' star, Ellis Alfred Swearengen, the owner of the Gem Saloon in Deadwood, South Dakota, a real town that flourished during a 19th-century gold rush. Like the real Swearengen (1845–1904), McShane's character peddles prostitutes, whiskey, and drugs and controls gambling. Other historical figures portrayed in Deadwood, whose 36 episodes aired from March 21, 2004 to August 27, 2006, included Wild Bill Hickock, Calamity Jane, E. B. Farnham, and Seth Bullock. "The script sinks the myth of the Wild West, and the foundations of modern America, deep into a pit of mud, blood, horse manure and moral chaos—Deadwood was built out of greed for gold, over the territory and the graves of native Sioux tribes," Stephan Phelan wrote. *Deadwood* became known for its colorful, extremely profane language as well as its frequent graphic violence. McShane's portrayal of a ruthless opportunist who retains grains of humanity earned him the 2005 Golden Globe Award for best actor in a television drama and nominations for Emmy and Screen Actors Guild Awards, also in 2005. Despite the show's success, HBO canceled it after two seasons, reportedly so that Milch could launch another series.

In Woody Allen's film comedy *Scoop* (2006), McShane had a small part as the ghost of a hard-boiled reporter who helps an aspiring journalist (Scarlett Johansson) expose a serial killer. In the same year he played a grieving father in Joseph McGinty Nichols's *We Are Marshall*, about the aftermath of the 1970 chartered-plane crash that killed nearly all the members of the Marshall University football team as well as seven coaches and trainers and everyone else on board. In the over-the-top comedy *Hot Rod* (2007), McShane played the stepfather of Rod (Andy Samberg), an Evel Knievel wannabe. By his own account, McShane enjoyed wrestling with Samberg for several scenes. "I hadn't done any physical comedy, so you learn a lot," he told Gene Triplett for the *Oklahoman* (August 3, 2007). McShane's portrayal of Max in the 40th anniversary revival of Harold Pinter's *The Homecoming* earned him rave reviews.

McShane played the charismatic but wicked King Silas Benjamin in NBC's short-lived series *Kings* (2009). Set in modern times and advertised as a retelling of the biblical David and Goliath story, *Kings* was canceled after a dozen episodes. "The show sparkles with imagination," Kyle Smith wrote for the *New York Post* (March 13, 2009), and he noted McShane's "titanic presence." By contrast, Mark Dawidziak described *Kings* for the *Cleveland (Ohio) Plain Dealer* (March 14, 2009) as "clunky," "drearily paced," and "thematically heavy-handed," but he also wrote, "Only the ever-dependable McShane adds some badly needed life to these ponderous proceedings, and the producers don't even have the sense to turn him loose on a regular basis." In the eight-part 2010 miniseries *The Pillars of the Earth*, which was based on a Ken Follett novel and is set during a period in 12th-century Britain known as "the Anarchy," McShane depicted a cruel bishop. In films in 2009 he appeared opposite Renee Zellweger in the widely panned psychological thriller *Case 39* and in *44 Inch Chest*, a "very strange, often terrible affair that is nevertheless mesmerizing, in a limited way," according to David Denby, a *New Yorker* (February 1, 2010) critic. Denby also wrote, "McShane, stealing the movie, is slyly superior as a man who has never felt love." In the critically drubbed, Rob Marshall–directed fourth installment of *Pirates of the Caribbean* (2011), subtitled *On Stranger Tides*, McShane was cast as Bluebeard—and the father of Pe-

nelope Cruz's character, Angelica, a former lover of Captain Jack Sparrow (Johnny Depp). In the *Los Angeles Times* (May 20, 2011), Betsy Sharkey described McShane as Bluebeard as "doing his witty wicked thing," while A. O. Scott, the *New York Times* (May 19, 2011) reviewer, wrote that the actor "brings a floridly sinister death-metal-meets-*Deadwood* vibe" to his role. McShane is starring in Bryan Singer's next movie, "Jack the Giant Killer," which is scheduled for a 2012 release.

While McShane's hair remains black, his beard is threaded with gray. His first marriage (1965–68), to the actress Suzan (or Suzanne) Farmer, ended in divorce, as did his marriage to Ruth Post (1970–77). His daughter, Kate, is the mother of his two grandchildren; his son, Morgan, is a musician. He and his third wife, Gwen Humble, live in the Venice Beach section of Los Angeles.

—M.R.M.

Suggested Reading: *Boston Globe* N p1 June 6, 2004; *Esquire* p25 May 2009; (Hamilton, New Zealand) *Waikato Times* Features p1 Mar. 5, 2005; imdb.com; (Kitchener-Waterloo, Ontario, Canada) *Record* E p7 Jan. 29, 1994; (London) *Evening Standard* p36 July 13, 2000; *Los Angeles Magazine* p23+ May 2005; (New York) *Daily News* Sunday Now p27 June 25, 2006; *New York Post* p99 Aug. 3, 2007; (Scotland) *Sunday Herald* p4 Sep. 19, 2004

Selected Films: *The Wild and the Willing*, 1962; *The Pleasure Girls*, 1965; *If It's Tuesday, This Must Be Belgium*, 1969; *The Battle of Britain*, 1969; *Villain*, 1971; *The Last of Sheila*, 1973; *Ransom*, 1975; *Code Name: Diamond Head*, 1977; *The Pirate*, 1978; *The Great Bank Robbery*, 1979; *The Fifth Musketeer*, 1979; *Yesterday's Hero*, 1979; *Cheaper to Keep Her*, 1981; *The Letter*, 1982; *Exposed*, 1983; *Ordeal by Innocence*, 1984; *Too Scared to Scream*, 1985; *The Murders in the Rue Morgue*, 1986; *Chain Letter*, 1988; *White Goods*, 1994; *Sexy Beast*, 2000; *Man and Boy*, 2002; *Agent Cody Banks*, 2003; *Nine Lives*, 2005; *Scoop*, 2006; *We Are Marshall*, 2006; *Shrek the Third*, 2007; *Hot Rod*, 2007; *The Seeker: The Dark is Rising*, 2007; *The Golden Compass*, 2007; *Kung Fu Panda*, 2008; *Death Race*, 2008; *Coraline*, 2009; *44 Inch Chest*, 2009; *Case 39*, 2009; *Pirates of the Caribbean: On Stranger Tides*, 2011

Selected Television Shows: *Z Cars*, 1964; *You Can't Win*, 1966; *Wuthering Heights*, 1967; *Roots*, 1977; *Jesus of Nazareth*, 1977; *Life of Shakespeare*, 1978; *Disraeli*, 1978; *Marco Polo*, 1982; *Bare Essence*, 1983; *Evergreen*, 1985; *Lovejoy*, 1986–96; *Miami Vice*,1987–89; *War and Remembrance*, 1988–89; *Young Charlie Chaplin*, 1989; *Dallas*, 1989; *Madson*, 1996; *In Deep*, 2002; *Trust*, 2003; *The Twilight Zone*, 2003; *Deadwood*, 2004–06; *Kings*, 2009

Meacham began his career in journalism right out of college, first with the *Chattanooga (Tennessee) Times* and then as a writer for the *Washington Monthly*. While he was serving as *Newsweek*'s co–managing editor and then as editor, the magazine won four National Magazine Awards and was a finalist for 20 others. For about five years beginning in 2006, Meacham co-wrote and co-edited, with Sally Quinn, the *Washington Post* blog and column "On Faith," and he co-hosted the PBS Friday-night television program and on-line series *Need to Know*. In January 2011 he joined Random House as an executive vice president and editor, with responsibility for acquisitions as well.

An only child, Jonathan Ellis Meacham was born on May 20, 1969 in Chattanooga, where he grew up. His father, Jere Ellis Meacham, who died in 2008, was a corporate and trade-association executive and labor-relations negotiator. Meacham's parents divorced when he was very young; afterward he spent much of his time with his paternal grandparents—Jean Austin Meacham, a University of Tennessee assistant dean, and Ellis K. Meacham, a well-known Chattanooga attorney and city judge who wrote a trilogy of well-regarded historical novels about an officer in the naval division of the British East India Co. Judge Meacham had politically minded friends and was an acquaintance of several Tennessee governors and the three-term U.S. senator Al Gore Sr., and Meacham has credited him with sparking his interest in history and politics. He told Alex Kuczynski for the *New York Times* (May 24, 1999) that his "earliest memories are talk of politics and personalities" among his grandfather and others. The talk ranged from "what was going on in Watergate"—a reference to the scandal that led to President Richard Nixon's resignation, in 1974—to "who was going to become the new county lawyer," he told Kuczynski. He added that he started reading newsweeklies at an early age, and that Tuesdays, when *Time* and *Newsweek* would arrive in the mailbox, "were a big day in my house."

Meacham was raised in the Episcopal faith. On the "On Faith" Web site, he described himself as "a believing, middle-of-the-road American Protestant"; he also wrote, "I believe strongly—totally—in religious liberty and freedom of conscience," and "I am fascinated by the ways in which faith—and its absence and its abuses—has shaped the world in which we live." Meacham completed the elementary grades at the St. Nicholas School, an Episcopal institution, and then attended the McCallie School, a private, nonsectarian college-preparatory school with a Christian tradition; he graduated from McCallie in 1987. He next entered Sewanee: the University of the South (known universally as Sewanee), in Tennessee, which is owned and governed by the 28 southeastern dioceses of the national Episcopal Church. As an undergraduate he was a member of a fraternity, a drinking club called the Wellingtons, and an upperclassmen's social group, the Red Ribbons; he

Brendan Smialowski/Getty Images for *Meet the Press*

Meacham, Jon

May 20, 1969– Book-publishing executive; journalist; writer; former editor of Newsweek

Address: Random House, 1745 Broadway, New York, NY 10019

In 1995, at the age of 26, only five months after he had joined *Newsweek* as a national-affairs writer, Jon Meacham was named editor of the magazine's national-affairs department. In 1998 he advanced to *Newsweek*'s number-two position, that of managing editor (a post he shared with Ann McDaniel). Eight years later, at age 37, he was promoted to editor in chief. He left *Newsweek* in 2010, after the Washington Post Co. sold the financially troubled magazine. Meacham is widely recognized not only for his expertise in American history and politics but also for his knowledge of Christianity and the history of religion in the U.S., and he has "written extensively . . . on the tension between faith and reason in American life," Max Byrd wrote for the *Wilson Quarterly* (Winter 2009). During his dozen years with *Newsweek*, Meacham published approximately 170 articles (including a few for other periodicals), edited an anthology about the American civil rights movement, and wrote three best-selling books: *Franklin and Winston*, about the friendship of President Franklin Delano Roosevelt and British prime minister Winston Churchill; *American Gospel*, subtitled *God, the Founding Fathers, and the Making of a Nation*; and *American Lion*, about Andrew Jackson and his presidency, which won the Pulitzer Prize for biography in 2009.

also served as editor of the *Sewanee Purple*, the campus newspaper, and was elected to the honor society Phi Beta Kappa. He earned a B.A. degree in English, summa cum laude, in 1991 and was his class salutatorian. According to Kathryn Williams, writing for *Sewanee Magazine* (Winter 2005), he was a finalist for a Rhodes scholarship. Professors of his whom Williams interviewed all remembered Meacham as academically outstanding; one of them said that he was the only student who ever earned a grade of A+ in his course.

After college Meacham returned to his hometown and worked for a year as a reporter for the *Chattanooga Times*. He then became a staff writer for the *Washington Monthly*, which focuses on "ideas and characters that animate America's government," according to its Web site. Charles Peters, the magazine's founder and editor in chief at that time, served as a mentor to him. Meacham told Kuczynski that he regarded his experience with the *Washington Monthly* as "journalism boot camp." His first article for the magazine (June 1992) was a review of the book *The Vital South: How Presidents Are Elected*, by Earl Black and Merle Black. His subsequent articles included one about the entrepreneur Christopher Whittle's Edison Project, a multibillion-dollar plan to build a network of for-profit schools (October 1992); "Voting Wrongs," about recent congressional redistricting, which Meacham charged was tantamount to gerrymandering along racial lines (March 1993); the April 1994 cover story, "What the Religious Right Can Teach the New Democrats"; the September 1994 cover story, "The GOP's Master Strategist," about William Kristol, the founder and editor of the conservative newsmagazine the *Weekly Standard*; and the January/February 1995 cover story, "The Truth About Twentysomethings."

Meacham's work for the *Washington Monthly* impressed *Newsweek*'s then-editor, Maynard Parker, and in January 1995 Parker hired him as a national-affairs writer. His first article for *Newsweek* (January 16, 1995) was entitled "A Defiant South Secedes Again," which charged that Congress's "southern suburban politicians" were giving short shrift to vital government services in their quest for federal budget cuts. Five months later Meacham was promoted to national-affairs editor. In October 1998 Parker died; the next month his successor, Mark Whitaker, promoted the 29-year-old Meacham to managing editor (a post shared with Ann McDaniel, *Newsweek*'s longtime Washington bureau chief). Various observers attributed Meacham's extraordinarily rapid rise at *Newsweek* to his editorial and managerial skills, broad knowledge of history, attention to detail, and youth, the last of which *Newsweek* executives hoped would draw a greater number of younger readers (and thereby more advertisers).

In one of his earliest assignments in his new job, Meacham edited *Newsweek*'s award-winning coverage of the scandal involving President Bill Clinton and the former White House intern Monica Lewinsky and Clinton's impeachment (in December 1998) and acquittal (in February 1999). Between January 1999 and August 2010, Meacham wrote upwards of 140 *Newsweek* pieces, among them journalistic essays on political, social, and religious matters; book reviews; obituaries of individuals including former President Ronald Reagan, U.S. senator Ted Kennedy, the historian Arthur Schlesinger, and the journalist and author David Halberstam; interviews with people including former president George H. W. Bush, President George W. Bush, former president Clinton, U.S. senator and Republican presidential candidate John S. McCain, President Barack Obama, Secretary of State Hillary Clinton, Wayne LaPierre (the head of the National Rifle Association), the evangelical Christian minister and author Rick Warren, and the neuroscientist and critic of religion Sam Harris. During that time he also edited one book and wrote three, and his by-line accompanied articles in the *Washington Monthly* and the *New York Times Book Review*.

Earlier, in October 2006, Meacham had been named editor of *Newsweek*. (Whitaker became the vice president and editor in chief of new ventures at Washingtonpost.Newsweek Interactive.) Meacham's responsibilities included overseeing all editorial operations at the magazine and determining long-term editorial direction and strategy, at a time when increasing numbers of readers were turning to the Internet for news. Shortly before his promotion was announced, Meacham told Howard Kurtz for the *Washington Post* (September 6, 2006), "The idea that you can be either entirely analysis or entirely scoop-driven is a false choice. We have to earn people's attention. Reporting is at the heart of the enterprise. We have to break news like a Web site, tell it like a monthly and do it every week." "What's happening now is that headlines are delivered by the Web," he told Rachel Smolkin for the *American Journalism Review* (April/May 2007). "That has pushed newspapers to become more like the newsmagazines were in '82, and it's pushed the newsmagazines to produce a monthly-quality product on a weekly basis, and it's pushed the monthlies into the place of the great quarterlies, and now the quarterlies have become books." He also declared to Smolkin that in an era of 24/7 news, newsweeklies still have an important role to play: "In an ocean of information, there have to be lighthouses. Could people survive without *Time* or *Newsweek*? Sure. I think their lives would be the poorer for it."

For some years *Newsweek*'s earnings from advertising, subscriptions, and newsstand sales had been dropping, and by 2008 the magazine had fallen into the red. According to James Robinson, writing for the London *Observer* (March 1, 2009), Meacham and other decision makers, including executives at the Washington Post Co., *Newsweek*'s owner, tried to attract greater numbers of higher-income readers and advertisers of products that might appeal to such readers. The plan involved changing *Newsweek*'s focus from on-location news coverage to less-expensive but high-quality articles offering opinion and analysis. In essence, Robinson wrote, the decision makers had concluded that *Newsweek*'s "future lies in interpreting the world, rather than reporting on it"—a mission closely associated with that of the London, England–based weekly the *Economist*, which offers news summaries as well. John Koblin reported for the *New York Observer* (February 8, 2008, on-line) that during a talk for graduate students at the Columbia School of Journalism in February 2008, when Meacham asked whether anyone in the audience read *Newsweek* or *Time*, no one responded—except for one man who shouted "No!" When questioned, the man said that he read the *Economist*. After noting to the audience that *Newsweek* journalists were reporting from 13 countries overseas and that some of them were "risking their lives right now," Meacham said, "How to communicate that we have things to say that are both factually new and analytically new and to get you under the tent is a fact that scares me. . . . How to get . . . past this image that we're just middlebrow, you know, a magazine that your grandparents get, or something, that's the challenge. And I just don't know how to do it, so if you've got any ideas, tell me."

In addition to the radical change in content and a redesign, in 2009 *Newsweek*'s staff was reduced to fewer than 200, almost half its size in the late 1990s; its newsstand price was raised from $4.95 to $5.95; and the price to subscribers was doubled, to about 90 cents. Indeed, in a move that Meacham described to Howard Kurtz for the *Washington Post* (May 18, 2009, on-line) as "hugely counterintuitive," subscription renewals were discouraged, and their number was expected to drop by some 50 percent, to 1.5 million. "If we can't convince a million and a half people we're worth less than a dollar a week, the market will have spoken," Meacham said. By the end of 2009, *Newsweek*'s losses totaled more than they had the year before. On May 5, 2010 Donald E. Graham, the chief executive officer and chairman of the Washington Post Co., announced that *Newsweek* was for sale. Three months later the public learned that Sidney Harman, an inventor of audio equipment and an enormously successful businessman, had acquired *Newsweek* for $1, along with responsibility for its $47 million in debts. The press release that announced the sale also revealed that Meacham was stepping down as editor. (In November 2010 *Newsweek* merged with the e-zine the *Daily Beast*; Tina Brown, the latter's editor in chief and cofounder, currently edits both.)

In March 2011, about two months after he assumed his current post as a Random House executive vice president and editor, Meacham announced that his first acquisition was a book being written by former vice president Al Gore, who won an Academy Award for his documentary about global warming, *An Inconvenient Truth* (2006). The new book is about "the drivers of global change," in Gore's words, according to Dave Itzkoff, writing for the *New York Times* (March 15, 2011, on-line).

During the decade that ended with his departure from *Newsweek*, Meacham published four books. The first, *Voices in Our Blood: America's Best on the Civil Rights Movement* (2001), is an anthology of essays written between the 1940s and the end of the the 20th century by activists and/or writers including Benjamin Mays, John Lewis, Malcolm X, Richard Wright, Henry Louis Gates Jr., Eudora Welty, James Baldwin, William Faulkner, John Steinbeck, E. B. White, Maya Angelou, Alice Walker, Ralph Ellison, Ellis Cose, Stanley Crouch, William Styron, Tom Wolfe, and Howell Raines. "That most of the selections were not written as retrospectives or histories, but were prepared in the heat of the civil rights struggle, is one of the great virtues of this anthology," James Ralph wrote for the *Chicago Tribune* (March 25, 2001). "They stand as documents of an earlier era, ready to unveil the emotions and assumptions of another time."

Meacham's second book, *Franklin and Winston: An Intimate Portrait of an Epic Friendship* (2003), offers a detailed picture of the relationship between Roosevelt and Churchill, who met for the first time in 1941, a few months before the U.S. entered World War II. "With nearly ninety pages of notes and bibliography, some new archival research, oral histories and author interviews, [Meacham] has also written a compellingly readable account," John Kentleton wrote for *History* (October 2006). In a review for *Time* (December 22, 2003), Lance Morrow described the book as "a close-focus historical tracking shot of the two men, very human, heroic and imperfect, moving along through—and making—great history." "Most of the anecdotes have been told a thousand times, but Meacham manages to align the two giants in a way that makes the stories seem fresh . . . ," Morrow wrote. "Meacham's version contains no revisionism or lèse majesté. On the contrary, it is written with a sort of intelligent reverence."

In the April 25, 2011 edition of *Time* (on-line), Richard Stengel, *Time*'s editor, called Meacham "one of America's foremost thinkers on the role of religion in public life." One product of his thinking on that topic is his book *American Gospel: God, the Founding Fathers, and the Making of a Nation* (2006). In *American Gospel* Meacham wrote, "The intensity with which the religious right attempts to conscript the Founders into their cause indicates the importance the movement ascribes to historical benediction by association with the origins of the Republic. . . . [If they] can convince enough people that America was a Christian nation that has lost its way, the more legitimate their efforts in the political arena seem. The problem with their reading of history is that it is wrong. There is no doubt . . . that the Founders lived in and consciously bequeathed a culture shaped and sustained by public religion, one that was not Christian or Jewish or Muslim or Buddhist but was simply transcendent, with reverence for the 'Creator' and for 'Nature's God.'" Reviews of *American Gospel* ran the gamut from enthusiastic to mixed to derisive. George Westerlund, writing for *Library Journal* (May 1, 2006), "highly recommended" it as "a balanced account"; in the *Christian Century* (July 11, 2006), Gerald L. Sittser wondered if Meacham "truly grasps the complex relationship between Christian faith (still dominant in America) and public religion," while Garrett Ward Sheldon, the reviewer for the *Journal of Church and State* (Winter 2008), dismissed *American Gospel* as "ideological political journalism at its worst."

In on-line questions and answers about his most recent book, *American Lion: Andrew Jackson in the White House* (2008), for the *Washington Post* (December 16, 2008), Meacham explained, "My book tries very hard to paint Jackson and all his sins, which are enormous. He was an unrepentant slaveholder who thwarted the forces of abolition, and . . . he was the mastermind of Indian removal, a tragedy that, like slavery, stands at the heart of the American experience. I chose to call my book *American Lion* not to lionize Jackson but to capture the contradictions at his core. . . . I wanted to write it because I believe Jackson represents the best of us and the worst of us. . . . To understand Jackson is to understand how America has long raised political and cultural cognitive dissonance to an art form. We are capable of living with enormous inequality and injustice while convincing ourselves that we are in fact moving toward what Churchill called the 'broad, sun-lit uplands.'" In honoring *American Lion* with the 2009 Pulitzer Prize for biography, the award committee described the book on pulitzer.org as "an unflinching portrait of a not always admirable democrat but a pivotal president, written with an agile prose that brings the Jackson saga to life." According to Max Byrd, the *Wilson Quarterly* reviewer, "Little here is new, but everything is so carefully and brilliantly set out for the general reader that Meacham's book should now become the biography of choice." "*American Lion* is enormously entertaining, especially in the deft descriptions of Jackson's personality and domestic life in his White House," Andrew Cayton wrote for the *New York Times Book Review* (November 14, 2008). "But Meacham has missed an opportunity to reflect on the nature of American populism as personified by Jackson. What does it mean to have a president who believes that the people are a unified whole whose essence can be distilled into the pronouncements of one man? Populist resentment is to democracies as air is to fire. But republics may endure best when leaders remain uncertain . . . as to whether the people can be entirely trusted with their own government. . . . Should we assume that what is best for the United States (as defined by men like Jackson) is best for us all?"

Meacham's article "What If There's No Hell?" was the cover story of the April 25, 2011 issue of *Time*. Meacham is a member of the Council on For-

eign Relations, the board of regents of Sewanee: the University of the South, the vestry of Trinity Church Wall Street, the leadership council of the Harvard Divinity School, and the national advisory group of Washington National Cathedral. He and his wife, the former Margaret Keith Smythe (known as Keith), live in New York City with their three children: Samuel Ellis, Mary Austin, and Margaret Randolph. Keith Meacham is a contributing editor for *Elle Decor*.

—M.M.

Suggested Reading: *American Journalism Review* (on-line) Apr./May 2007; Jon Meacham Web site; (London) *Observer* p9 Mar. 1, 2009; *Los Angeles Times E* p1+ Apr. 5, 2006; *Media Matters for America* (on-line) Apr. 23, 2007; *New York Times C* p12 May 24, 1999; *Newsweek* (on-line) June 14, 2004, Oct. 27, 2008; *Sewanee Magazine* p16+ Winter 2005

Selected Books: *Franklin and Winston: An Intimate Portrait of an Epic Friendship*, 2003; *American Gospel: God, the Founding Fathers, and the Making of a Nation*, 2006; *American Lion: Andrew Jackson in the White House*, 2008; as editor—*Voices in Our Blood: America's Best on the Civil Rights Movement*, 2001

Meyrowitz, Carol M.

Feb. 28, 1954– Businesswoman

Address: TJX Companies, 770 Cochituate Rd., Framingham, MA 01701

As the chief executive officer (CEO) and president of the TJX Companies, Carol Meyrowitz oversees more than 160,000 employees and 2,850 off-price retail stores—stores that charge significantly less for high-quality brand-name apparel and home merchandise than most other retail outlets. In September 2011 TJX owned 963 T. J. Maxx, 875 Marshalls, and 366 HomeGoods stores in the U.S.; 213 Winners, 82 HomeSense, five Marshalls, and three StyleSense stores in Canada; and 322 T. K. Maxx and 24 HomeSense stores in four European nations (England, Ireland, Germany, and Poland), making it the largest off-price retailer for clothing and home products in the world. Except for one 10-month period, when she served as an independent adviser for TJX, Meyrowitz has been a TJX employee since 1983, when she was hired as a buyer for one of its chains; she was named president of TJX in October 2005 and CEO in January 2007. "Meyrowitz's leadership has sustained consumer confidence in her company," a writer for *Chain Store Age* (December 31, 2007, on-line) declared nearly a year after the latter promotion was announced. In addition, the writer continued, she "has reinvigo-

Courtesy of TJX Companies

Carol M. Meyrowitz

rated TJX's merchandise offerings with more fashion-forward goods, and tested designer departments. The results of her efforts, and her steadfastness, are seen in the chain's performance. At a time when many retailers are struggling, TJX remains on the upswing." Although the worldwide recession that began in December 2007 hurt TJX's business to some extent, three years later Marianne Wilson and Connie Robbins Gentry wrote for *Chain Store Age* (December 17, 2010, on-line) that Meyrowitz had "proved herself to be totally in sync with her customers and their needs." In 2010 TJX ranked 119th on the *Fortune* 500 list, with revenues of $21.9 billion, 8 percent more than in 2009. *Fortune* has listed Meyrowitz herself among the world's 50 most powerful women in business every year from 2006 to 2010 (its most recent such ranking).

Based in Framingham, Massachusetts, TJX grew out of the New England Trading Co., a wholesale women's-undergarment supplier founded in 1919 in Boston, Massachusetts, by two brothers, Max and Morris Feldberg, who had immigrated to the U.S. from Russia. Ten years later the Feldbergs moved into retail sales, with a store that sold women's hosiery—the first of the Bell Hosiery Shops. In 1956 Max's son, Stanley Feldberg, and Sumner Feldberg, Morris's son, opened a discount department store called Zayre; it, too, expanded into a chain, and the company went public in 1962. The Zayre Corp. purchased Hit or Miss, a chain that carried off-price women's-specialty apparel, in 1969. In 1976—spurred by the burgeoning successes of such chains as Walmart—the Feldbergs hired a Marshalls executive, Benjamin "Ben" Cammarata, to launch a new line of off-price stores selling upscale apparel and home products. Thus was

born T. J. Maxx, which began with two stores in 1977; by 1994, when Howard Rudnitsky profiled Cammarata for *Forbes* (January 31, 1994), there were 514 T. J. Maxx outlets in the U.S. According to the T. J. Maxx Web site in mid-2011, "Our buyers are on the hunt over 40 weeks a year for the hottest items of the season. So when a designer overproduces and department stores overbuy, we swoop in, negotiate the lowest possible price, and pass the savings on. . . . Unlike department stores that buy seasonally, we have thousands of fresh items delivered to our stores every week. So, the best shopping strategy is to pop in often."

Zayre introduced the catalogue retailer Chadwick's of Boston in 1983, BJ's Wholesale Club in 1984, and HomeClub (a big-box store specializing in materials for building contractors and do-it-yourself homeowners) in 1986. In 1988, spurred by shrinking profits, the Zayre Corp. sold its 392 Zayre discount stores to Ames Department Stores for $800 million and became the TJX Companies, the umbrella for T. J. Maxx, Hit or Miss, Chadwick's, HomeClub, and BJ's. (TJX spun off HomeClub in 1989 and BJ's in 1997; neither is now associated with TJX.) In 1991 TJX purchased the Winners chain in Canada. The year 1992 marked the debut of the HomeGoods chain, and 1994 that of T. K. Maxx in England. In 1995 TJX acquired Marshalls, whose motto is "Never pay full price for fabulous" and which was then the nation's second-largest off-price retail chain; the Marmaxx Group came into being soon afterward. The next year TJX sold Chadwick's, and in 1998 it launched A. J. Wright, an off-price chain whose merchandise was less costly than that sold at T. J. Maxx or Marshalls. Winners introduced HomeSense, a chain similar to HomeGoods. TJX bought the Bob's Stores chain in 2003. Since 2007, when she became TJX's CEO, all major TJX actions and transactions have had Meyrowitz's stamp of approval.

The daughter of Sidney Meyrowitz and Helen (Schoenberger) Meyrowitz, Carol M. Meyrowitz was born in New York City on February 28, 1954. Her father (who died in 2009) was a furrier who owned his own business. Her mother is an accomplished artist; she has exhibited widely, and her work is in the permanent collections of several museums. Meyrowitz's older brother, Andrew, is a real-estate broker and developer. No readily available print or Internet publications mention Meyrowitz's childhood, the schools she attended, or her activities until 1983, the year she began her career with TJX (then known as the Zayre Corp.). Her first job was buyer for Hit or Miss. She started to rise through the ranks early on: from 1987 to 1989 she served as Hit or Miss's vice president and merchandising manager. (In 1995 TJX closed 69 Hit or Miss stores and sold the chain's 399 remaining stores because of "problems in the women's discount apparel industry," in the words of a *New York Times* [August 16, 1995] reporter, which had led to plummeting sales.)

In 1989 Meyrowitz was promoted to vice president and senior merchandise manager of Chadwick's of Boston. In 1990 she became Chadwick's general merchandise manager. From 1991 to 1996 she served as the chain's senior vice president of merchandising. Meyrowitz then became Chadwick's executive vice president of merchandising, a position she held until 1999, when she became the senior vice president of merchandising for the Marmaxx Group, the umbrella for the TJX brands Marshalls and T.J. Maxx. (TJX sold Chadwick's in 1996.) Meyrowitz's next Marmaxx titles were executive vice president of merchandising (2000–01) and president. Concurrently, in 2001 she took on the position of executive vice president of TJX. In 2003, according to Wolfgang Saxon's obituary of Stanley Feldberg for the *New York Times* (May 16, 2004), TJX's annual revenue equaled about $12 billion and its workforce totaled about 100,000 employees. In 2004 Meyrowitz served as TJX's senior executive vice president.

At the beginning of 2005, Meyrowitz left TJX to seek "new opportunities and challenges," as she put it, according to Jessica Pallay, writing for the Harrisonburg, Virginia, *Daily News-Record* (November 15, 2004). Ernie Herrman, who had been the Marmaxx Group's chief operating officer, was named TJX's president. For 10 months in 2005, Meyrowitz served as an adviser to the TJX Companies and a consultant for Berkshire Partners, a Boston-based private-equity firm (not connected with Berkshire Hathaway, Warren Buffett's company).

In October 2005 Meyrowitz returned to TJX to assume the post of president. (Herrman was given the titles of senior executive vice president and group president.) "In Carol, we have an extremely creative merchant with great strategic vision, leadership ability, and operational experience, as well as extensive off-price expertise and knowledge of TJX," Ben Cammarata, TJX's CEO at that time, was quoted as saying in *Business Wire* (October 6, 2005). In 2006 Meyrowitz joined Cammarata as one of TJX's two directors. (TJX also has a half-dozen independent directors, who are not TJX employees.) "Carol has been responsible for some of [TJX's] most successful initiatives," Cammarata was quoted as saying in an article for *Just-Style* (September 8, 2006, on-line). "She is a visionary leader and great generator of ideas."

In 2007 Meyrowitz succeeded Cammarata as CEO. (He retained and still holds the position of chairman of the board.) At around that time a widespread security breach of the company's computer system occurred, giving hackers access to the credit and debit cards of TJX customers who had bought merchandise at company stores. The company announced that the stolen information affected millions of customers who made purchases at TJX stores between May 2006 and January 2007; TJX later revealed that people who had bought merchandise at any TJX store from January 2003 to June 2004 were also at risk due to suspected computer hacking in 2005. According to the December 31, 2007 *Chain Store Age* article, Meyrowitz handled the crisis in an exemplary fashion. "If there were an award for grace under pressure, Carol Meyrowitz . . . would deserve it," the reporter wrote. "The fact that the largest payment-card data breach to date occurred on her watch may always be a chapter in her memoirs, but it is not the whole story. What's more telling is how Meyrowitz confronted the crisis, assumed control of security risks within her company, and encouraged cooperative action between banks, payment-card companies and merchants industrywide."

In 2008 TJX sold the Bob's Stores chain to two private-equity firms. Because of the worldwide recession and "unfavorable exchange rates," as an Associated Press (AP) writer put it (November 12, 2008, on-line), TJX's profits declined by 6 percent that year. "Given the challenging times, we believe our results speak to our ability to hold our own in tough business cycles," Meyrowitz said, according to the AP reporter. "We are extremely focused on buying right and running with leaner-than-usual inventory levels, which has led to faster inventory turns and strong merchandise margins."

In 2009 Meyrowitz signed a new contract with TJX that had an expiration date of January 29, 2011; the contract guaranteed an annual base salary of at least $1.47 million. That same year Meyrowitz earned $17.4 million in total compensation. In 2007 and 2009 TJX opened T. K. Maxx stores in Germany and Poland, respectively. In 2010 the company announced plans to open more than 1,000 new stores and to introduce "smaller concept" stores. That year TJX shut 71 of its A. J. Wright stores and converted 91 others to T. J. Maxx, Marshalls, or HomeGoods outlets, and closed two distribution centers; in the process 4,400 employees were laid off. In a company press release (December 10, 2010, on-line), Meyrowitz stated, "While I believe this move makes us a much stronger company and will benefit TJX in both the near-term and long-term, it was not an easy decision as many positions will be eliminated and it will be difficult for our affected associates. As a company, however, it will allow us to focus our financial and managerial resources on our highest return businesses, all of which have significant growth opportunities, as well as to significantly improve the economic prospects of our business." Meyrowitz's words were quoted in nearly 700 on-line publications, ranging from *CNN Money* and *Daily Finance* to the *Forest Park (Illinois) Review*, the last of which reported that the A. J. Wright store in the Forest Park Mall was scheduled to close at the end of February 2011.

Meyrowitz's total compensation in 2010, $23.1 million, included $1.6 million in salary. In February 2011 she signed a new employment contract with TJX, according to which she would continue to serve as CEO for the next two years and would remain a director. "The re-signing is clearly an endorsement of the accomplishments and the good work that she and the organization have done under her regime," Michael Tesler, a partner with the consulting firm Retail Concepts, told Thomas Grillo for the *Boston Herald* (February 2, 2011). In fiscal year 2011 Meyrowitz received more than $23 million in total compensation, and TJX's net sales grew by 8 percent. In *Retail Merchandiser* (June 1, 2011, on-line), Meyrowitz was quoted as saying that in 2010 "our bottom line grew substantially." "This speaks to the extraordinary flexibility of our off-price business model . . . ," she said. "We are running our business with lean, fast-turning inventories, which, in 2010, again led to even stronger merchandise margins. This, combined with our continued cost reduction initiatives, helped drive large increases in profitability."

The TJX Foundation, which the Feldman family set up in 1966 (as the Zayre Foundation), aided about 2,000 nonprofit organizations in the U.S., Canada, and Europe in 2010. According to its Web site, the foundation "focuses its charitable giving on programs that provide basic-need services to disadvantaged women, children and families in communities where we do business." In 2004 Mey-

rowitz won the Woman of the Year Award from the Needlers Foundation, which, like the TJX Foundation, contributes money to various charities. The award came with a cash prize of more than $700,000, which Meyrowitz contributed to the Joslin Diabetes Center. Meyrowitz is a member of the center's board of overseers. She has also served on the boards of directors of Amscan Holdings Inc., the Yankee Candle Co., Staples Inc., and Party City Holdings.

Meyrowitz is married to John deBairos, who owns a real-estate firm. The couple live in Newton, Massachusetts, and have two adult daughters—Ariel and Danielle. In her spare time Meyrowitz enjoys traveling, working out, and reading.

—J.P.

Suggested Reading: *Boston Globe* Business p7 Apr. 30, 2010; *Boston Herald* Business p23 Feb. 2, 2011; *Chain Store Age* (on-line) Dec. 31, 2007; (Harrisburg, Virginia) *Daily News Record* p28 Nov. 15, 2004; tjx.com; *USA Today* Money B p3 Dec. 30, 2009

Michele, Chrisette

Dec. 8, 1982– R&B singer

Address: c/o Def Jam Records, Worldwide Plaza, 825 Eighth Ave., 28th Fl., New York, NY 10019

"I describe my sound like this," the singer/songwriter Chrisette Michele told Frances Moffett for *Jet* (July 16, 2007): "A scientist took all of the elements of music and put them together to see if they would explode." Trained in jazz, Michele studied the music of such great singers as Ella Fitzgerald, Billie Holiday, and Sarah Vaughn. Now, she is being compared to them. Michele's breakout performance on the rapper Jay-Z's 2006 single "Lost One," followed by her vocals on "Can't Forget About You," by the rapper Nas, signaled the arrival of a major, eclectic new talent; Melanie Sims wrote for the Associated Press (June 18, 2007) that Michele's "jazzy vibrato endowed those tracks with the element most rappers try to capture by sampling old-school tracks."

Michele is "equally comfortable scatting sassy jazz notes around a melody or nailing that melody straight-on with her pure, flawless voice," Michael Hamersly wrote for the *Miami (Florida) Herald* (March 14, 2008). Perhaps her confidence comes from her training and her control over her music: Michele writes most of her own songs. She wrote all of the tracks on her 2007 debut album, *I Am*, including the hit single "Be OK," which won Michele a Grammy Award in 2009. That same year her second album, *Epiphany*, debuted in the number-one spot on the *Billboard* music charts.

LG Mobile Phones via Getty Images

Never one to generate tabloid headlines, Michele is known instead for devoting time to causes including Curls4TheCure, which offers custom-made wigs for those who have lost their hair during chemotherapy, and the Grammy Foundation, which supports high-school music programs. On her latest album, *Let Freedom Reign* (2010), and in her philanthropic work, social issues figure prominently, and she sees being a role model as one of her most important contributions. "Mentorship is one of my favorite things to do," she told Tammy La Gorce for the *New York Times* (July 29, 2007). "People need someone to look up to. People need to see someone else make it."

The first of three children, the singer was born Chrisette Michele Payne on December 8, 1982 on Long Island, New York, and grew up in the Long Island town of Patchogue. Her father, Lemuel Payne, was a high-school English teacher and a deacon in the Upper Room Christian World Center church in Dix Hills, near Patchogue, where Michele performed her first solo, at age four. "I remember the coat I had on," she told Hamersly, "the hairstyle, the shoes—everything. And I sang real low. I had a really deep voice when I was little. My mom said I should sing higher." Michele's mother was a gospel-choir singer and church worker. Michele recalled to Bob Mehr for the Memphis, Tennessee, *Commercial Appeal* (July 2, 2010) that church music was an early and strong influence on her. "I grew up in the church, and gospel was my foundation. Traveling across the country as a really young girl, 5 and 6 years old, with my mom and her choir was a great part of me growing up." Hearing the music of the gospel singer Hezekiah Walker and the gospel and R&B singers BeBe and CeCe Winans "was big," she said. "Music was gospel for me, and gospel was music."

Michele has described her childhood as very busy. "My parents had me in girl scouts, tap class, and piano lessons," she recalled to Audrey J. Bernard for the *New York Beacon* (July 5, 2007). "It wasn't like I was cut off from the world, but there just wasn't a lot of media influence in my life during those early years." As a result, she told Hamersly, "I never wanted to be a superstar. . . . I just knew I wanted to sing all my life." She has admitted that as a child and teenager she would get upset when faced with a subject or activity at which she did not excel. Kathy Chaney, writing for the *Chicago Defender* (September 3, 2008), chronicled Michele's visit to South Central Community Center in Chicago, Illinois, and the stories she shared there about her teen years; the singer told her audience that she knew she wanted to be a singer and needed to learn how to play the piano, but was frustrated because she "sucked" at it. Instead of lamenting her inadequacy, Michele practiced tirelessly. "Make a list of the things you are weak at and work hard each day to strengthen them," Michele suggested.

Michele's parents and extended family instilled in her a generosity and compassion for others that would inspire her philanthropic efforts of later years. She told Bernard that when she was growing up, her house was always full of people. "If my mother saw a homeless pregnant woman on the street, chances are they would soon be staying with us," she said. "I learned so much about the world listening to these folks' stories, and to this day their experiences can be heard in my material."

In high school Michele was a member of the student government, choir, step team, pep squad, and African-American Club. She also broadened her musical horizons. "I fell in love with alternative music—someone like Erykah Badu, even though she was neo-soul, it was different," she told Mehr. "Different than what was on the radio. Definitely not pop. After that, it was jazz." Michele traces her discovery of jazz to when she was 17 and her high-school music director introduced her to "The Girl from Ipanema," recorded by the Brazilian jazz artist Astrud Gilberto. She then began absorbing the catalogues of such vocal-jazz greats as Fitzgerald, Holiday, Vaughn, and Nat King Cole. "I love the chords and the chord progressions—they just wake up a song," she told Hamersly. "I try to simplify it, though."

Michele enrolled at Five Towns College, in Dix Hills, graduating with a degree in jazz vocal performance. She has cited her teachers there as a strong influence on her career. "Although I did have talent, often that is not enough," she conceded to Bernard. "My professors taught me how to be a professional and to be serious about my music. They taught me how to put the music that I dream about at night on paper in the morning." She told Clayton Perry in an interview for Blogcritics.com (June 12, 2009) that she listened to recordings by artists such as Holiday and the contemporary singer Lauryn Hill through her headphones "over and over again." She said, "Every single riff, every single word, every single lick, I would play until I could emulate it as my own. That's the way I studied. Some people studied Bach in front of the piano. Some people studied different opera singers, whoever. Jazz was my first love, so those are the people I love the most."

Throughout college Michele performed at open-mic nights around New York City to hone her skills. On one such night, in 2005, Michele caught the attention of the neo-soul singer India.Arie. "India saw me singing at the Village Underground in New York City," Michele told Bernard. "She came backstage that first night and graciously offered me a gig as her opening act." Michele began opening for India.Arie and other artists, including Angie Stone and Kern, while hoping that the company she kept would not pigeonhole her. "My whole thing was, I hope they don't think I'm limited to being a neo-soul artist," she explained to Laura Checkoway for *Vibe* magazine (May 2007). "I love Celine Dion. I love Whitney Houston. I love adult contemporary pop music."

At 24 Michele signed with the major record label Island Def Jam Music Group. She had auditioned for Def Jam's chairman, Antonio "L.A." Reid, who reportedly told Michele that he got "goose bumps" when she began to sing; Reid signed her on the spot. "When Chrisette Michele enters a room," he later told Bernard, "the room becomes a better place."

Michele would be given a chance to be seen in a different—and very public—light in her collaborations with the rappers Jay-Z and Nas. Michele added an unusual flavor to singles for both artists, drawing on the influence of Billie Holiday, and gained national attention.

Though she was a rising star, 2006 was a difficult year for Michele. She and her mother (who is also her manager) were sued by a smaller record company, Four Kings, which had worked with Michele in the past, for a breach of contract for signing with Def Jam. Also, shortly after she wrote the song "Your Joy," about the love between a father and child, her father was diagnosed with prostate cancer. (He later recovered.) Acknowledging that that was a tough time for her family, Michele wrote a dedication to her father, a "humble hero," in the liner notes of her debut album.

That album, I Am (2007), featured collaborations with the 10-time Grammy Award winner Babyface, will.i.am, John Legend, and Salaam Remi. The album was heavily influenced by jazz, which set Michele apart from her pop and R&B contemporaries. "I've been creating songs since I was twelve," she told Bernard, "so I knew I needed the right musical blend in order to stand out." Michele also told Bernard that it was her goal to create a "seamless" album that nonetheless sampled several musical styles. "I don't feel as though I was the typical deacon's kid, because I was taught early on to speak my mind and not be afraid to think," she told Bernard. "To me, that is one of the things that helped keep me focused as an artist who is trying to do something different in music."

Several other factors set Michele apart from her fellow female recording artists. After the release of I Am, she began to field questions about her weight, as she told La Gorce. "I never knew I was fat until Def Jam signed me," Michele said bluntly. "But then I started doing interviews, and people would ask, 'How's it been dealing with your weight all these years?'" Michele took such questions in stride, explaining that she was raised with a healthy sense of self-esteem. "Every day since I was little my mom would say, 'You're beautiful, you're amazing.'" Also distinguishing Michele from many of her music contemporaries was her wholesome image, boosted by songs such as "Good Girl," from I Am, in which Michele sang, "I'm a good girl / Ain't too many good girls." "I've been asked to shake it up, spin around, drop it like it's hot—but I just say, 'Sorry, I can't do that,'" she told La Gorce, referring to suggestive dance moves. Michele also became known for her philanthropy. Disgusted by the practice of celebrities' being paid large sums of money to attend and be seen at corporate or otherwise high-profile parties, Michele proposed a new way to "party," making appearances at fundraising events—often in her hometown—for charities. "It's amazing; people say you get all this money when you walk through a party," she said to Renee Michelle Harris for the South Florida Times (July 31–August 6, 2009). "I said, 'How about we don't do any more parties and walk through some charity organizations, and walk through some tough neighborhoods, walk through some streets and let that be our party. Let the homeless guy be our celebrity.'" (Michele is currently producing and directing a documentary, "Project Awareness," that highlights social issues across the U.S.)

In early 2009 Michele won a Grammy Award for best urban/alternative performance for her single "Be OK." Later that year she released her second album, Epiphany. "There's definitely more vulnerability on this record," she told Christina Fuoco-Karasinski for the Flint (Michigan) Journal (June 11, 2009). "It's a break-up album in so many ways." Michele never commented on any personal break-up that inspired the album, saying only, "I knew there would be a lot of people who had been through break-ups that might look for answers in the songs that I wrote and sing. I wanted to make sure that I gave both sides of the story." Michele also relinquished some control on Epiphany, recording several songs written by others. She told Glenn Gamboa for Newsday (May 3, 2009) that she had previously turned down a song, "Irreplaceable," written by Ne-Yo and the Norwegian production team Stargate, which went on to become one of the biggest hits of the decade when it was recorded by Beyoncé. Learning a lesson, she began working with the producer Ne-Yo on Epiphany, which, she said, was a humbling process. "And so, I learned something about myself," she told Gamboa. "What I learned was that it takes a village to raise a child. No man is an island. I'm not here by myself. Somebody else besides me has a great idea. And that was part of my epiphany . . . recognizing that there are amazing people all around me who don't want anything more than to lend themselves to who I am, to give to me who they are and allow me to experience life through their eyes. And that's what Ne-Yo was able to give to me, he was able to give me a beautiful perception of my own life." Epiphany debuted at number one on the Billboard charts, dominating record sales the week of its release.

Michele's most recent record, Let Freedom Reign, was released in 2010. "I've always been somebody who's really interested in what's going on in the world and society," she told Mehr of the album. "So this is gonna be a moment where there are a lot of songs that talk about what it's like growing up in America. The album is a more conceptual piece, with interludes that tie everything together." The album features "I'm a Star," which celebrates female empowerment, and the title track, a collaboration with Talib Kweli and Black Thought, which comments on religion as it is represented by politicians. Michele said that she was inspired by Marvin Gaye's groundbreaking 1971 album, What's Going On, which, she told Mehr, is a "beautiful album out of ugly situations and issues. . . . You listen to the words, and you think maybe I can do something, maybe I can help what's happening in the world. It's about listening and being moved to action."

Michele was recently named a spokesperson for Saving Our Daughters, a national book club for teen girls that aims to bring attention to the issue of domestic violence. She allowed her new single, "I'm a Star," to be used as an anthem by the group.

Michele has appeared as herself on the television shows *Lincoln Heights* (2007) and *Girlfriends* (2008). When asked what she would like to do if she were not a singer, Michele told Hamersly: "I'd be a lawyer. I like to argue and get my point across."

—M.M.H.

Suggested Reading: Associated Press (on-line) June 18, 2007; Blogcritics.com June 12, 2009; *Chicago Defender* p38 Sep. 3, 2008; *Jet* p40 July 16, 2007; (Memphis, Tennessee) *Commercial Appeal* G p4 July 2, 2010; *Miami Herald* G p6 Mar. 14, 2008; *New York Beacon* p24 July 5, 2007; *New York Times* LI p8 July 29, 2007; *South Florida Times* A p1 July 31, 2009; *Vibe* (on-line) May 2007

Selected Recordings: *I Am*, 2007; *Epiphany*, 2009; *Let Freedom Reign*, 2010

Pascal Le Segretain/Getty Images

Millepied, Benjamin

(MEEL-pee-yeh)

1977– Ballet dancer; choreographer

Address: New York City Ballet, 70 W. 63d St., New York, NY 10023

Years before he gained a new level of international acclaim for choreographing the ballet performances in Darren Aronofsky's feature film *Black Swan* (2010), a psychological drama in which he also danced alongside the actress Natalie Portman, Benjamin Millepied had already established himself as a prominent ballet dancer, choreographer, and impresario. The French-born Millepied joined the New York City Ballet (NYCB) in 1995, at the age of 17. He became a soloist three years later and was

promoted to principal dancer in 2002. During his teens he was mentored by the legendary American choreographer Jerome Robbins and danced in ballets created by Robbins as well as other renowned choreographers, including George Balanchine, Peter Martins, and Helgi Tomasson. After 2003 Millepied began to focus more on creating his own ballets, which has led to a great deal of collaboration. In 2006, for example, he created a solo dance piece for the Russian-born ballet superstar Mikhail Baryshnikov, and the following year he collaborated with the modern classical composer and Philip Glass protégé Nico Muhly. The past two years have seen the debuts of his ballets *Quasi Una Fantasia* and *Plainspoken*, among other works. In 2010 *Crain's New York Business* placed Millepied on its "40 Under 40" list of New York's rising stars.

Benjamin Millepied—whose last name translates loosely as "thousand-footed"—was born in 1977 in Bordeaux, France. When he was an infant, his family (which included his two older brothers) moved to Dakar, Senegal, in West Africa, where his father, a decathlete, trained track-and-field athletes; his mother, a modern-dance teacher and former ballerina, studied and taught African dance. The family's neighbors would often play drums, and Millepied, who developed a fascination with music at an early age, began playing the instrument. (He gave up drums around the age of 12.) Millepied returned to Bordeaux when he was five years old, and by age eight he was taking modern-dance lessons, with instruction and encouragement from his mother. After he saw Mikhail Baryshnikov dance in the film *White Nights* (1985), Millepied knew he wanted to learn ballet, and at 12 he switched to that form exclusively. He studied at the Bordeaux Opera House with Vladimir Skouratoff and at age 13 went on to the Conservatoire National, in Lyon, France, where for three years he studied with Michel Rahn. When Rahn suggested that he attend the School of American Ballet (SAB), the young man agreed. (SAB is the official training academy of the New York City Ballet, which was founded in 1948 with the Russian-born George Balanchine as its artistic director and

Jerome Robbins, who joined the following year, as its associate artistic director. The ballet company, under Balanchine, sought to use elements of classical dance to create uniquely modern American ballets.) Millepied spent the summer of 1992 at the school, and the following year, when he was 16 years old, he returned to SAB as a full-time student, with a scholarship from the French Ministry of Foreign Affairs.

In 1994 Millepied made two great career leaps: he won the prestigious Prix de Lausanne in an international competition for young dancers; and he performed a solo in *2 & 3 Part Inventions*, a ballet (with music by Bach) Robbins had created especially for advanced SAB students. Robbins's selection of Millepied was a strong indication—to the school, to the ballet world, and to the arts and culture press—that the great choreographer had immense confidence in the young man's abilities. In a review for the *New York Times* (June 6, 1994), Anna Kisselgoff called the ballet "infinitely fresh and wonderful" and described Millepied's solo as "brilliant." Following that triumph, Robbins often took the young man to dinner or the ballet and introduced him to his friends and colleagues, some of whom would support Millepied's work later in his career. During the following year, his last with the ballet school, Millepied performed in Balanchine's *La Source*. Jack Anderson, reflecting the opinion of several dance critics at the time, wrote for the *New York Times* (June 5, 1995), "Mr. Millepied dances as if he loves the joy of motion, yet he should guard against moments of technical untidiness." That year the dancer also won the ballet school's Mae L. Wien Award for Outstanding Promise.

Upon completing his training at SAB, Millepied was invited to join the New York City Ballet. In the fall of 1995, at the age of 17, he became a member of NYCB's corps de ballet—dancers who perform as a group, generally behind soloists. In 1997 Millepied debuted in the solo male role in Balanchine's one-act version of the ballet *Swan Lake*. Millepied, Kisselgoff wrote for the *New York Times* (January 20, 1997), "has the nobility that makes up for occasional technical glitches and some awkwardness in his partnering. His solo had a stylish joyousness." In the summer of that year, in the pages of the *New York Times* (June 30, 1997), Kisselgoff sang Millepied's praises for his performance as Oberon, a male-lead role, in Balanchine's take on Shakespeare's *A Midsummer Night's Dream*: Millepied and his dancing partner, she wrote, were "so exciting and polished that they seemed born to the ballet." Kisselgoff later added: "Mr. Millepied enhanced his characterization from the start with startling assurance. Some of his leaps were odd, as in a scissor jump that became a split in the air. But few could top the corruscating brilliance of his leg beats or the dazzle of his overall performance." The following year Millepied danced as the Faun, also a male-lead role, in the Robbins-choreographed *The Four Seasons*; during

that performance one of his leaps set a new elevation record at the ballet company. Also in 1998 Millepied was promoted to soloist by the company, and he was singled out by *Dance Magazine* (November 1, 1998) as one of "five outstanding young City Ballet male dancers" who had a "bright future with the company."

In 2001 Millepied had major roles in Balanchine's *La Source*, Helgi Tomasson's *Prism*, Peter Martins's *Zakouski*, and Balanchine's *Divertimento from 'Le Baiser de la Fée,'* with music by Igor Stravinsky. *Prism*, set to Beethoven's First Piano Concerto, is a modern departure from, as well as an embrace of, ballet's classical forms. Writing for the *New York Times* (January 13, 2001), Kisselgoff enthusiastically pointed out: "By the time Benjamin Millepied opens the third section, exploding into a bravura split turn in the air, the basic steps are no longer basic. *Prism* is all serious uplift, and there is nothing more fitting than its close. Like a heavenly conductor, Mr. Millepied turns his back to the audience and raises his arms to the ensemble, which springs up before him. Let there be music, let there be dance, is his message, and joy to the world." The following year Millepied appeared in Robbins's *Dances at a Gathering*, Balanchine's *Symphony in C*, Martins's *Hallelujah Junction*, with music by John Adams, Melissa Barak's *If by Chance*, and the Italian choreographer Mauro Bigonzetti's *Vespro*, with music by Bruno Moretti. All were fairly well received. Perhaps the most unusual of the lot, *Vespro*, used aspects of Futurism to suggest a link between man and machine—Millepied and the grand piano onstage—and Dadaism, with its elements of chaos and absurdity. In the beginning of the dance, Millepied threw himself on the keyboard of the grand piano, with every bang bringing more dancers onstage. Throughout the performance, he played a mixture of group leader, troublemaker, and seducer. In 2003 he appeared in Robbins's comedic *Fancy Free*, Christopher Wheeldon's *Carousel (a Dance)*, Balanchine and Alexandra Danilova's *Coppelia*, Balanchine's *A Midsummer Night's Dream*, and Robbins's *Piano Pieces*. The last, a ballet for 21 dancers with piano accompaniment, was notable for Millepied's high, energetic jumps, for which he had developed a reputation.

When Millepied was promoted by NYCB to principal dancer—the highest rank a dancer can achieve at a ballet company—in the spring of 2002, he had recently begun his career as a choreographer. Following the premiere of *Passages* (2001) at the Conservatoire National, Millepied started presenting his own productions under the name Danses Concertantes, which featured his choreography and dancers from prestigious companies, especially NYCB and American Ballet Theatre. Some of his early pieces—*Triple Duet* (2002), with music by Bach; *Circular Motion* (2004), with music by Daniel Ott and Steve Reich; *Double Aria* (2004), with music by Ott; and *On the Other Side* (2004), with music by Philip Glass—were performed in

London, England (at the Sadler's Wells Theatre) or on Long Island, New York, and later in New York City. In 2003 Millepied was approached by wealthy patrons asking him to help establish a dance presence in the Hamptons, an affluent section of Long Island. So, in addition to his dancing for NYCB and managing/choreographing for Danses Concertantes, Millepied became the creative director of Morriss Center Dance, a branch of a private school in Bridgehampton, Long Island. As creative director he taught schoolchildren, did fund-raising, and organized ballet performances.

For Millepied 2006 was an especially busy year. In March, at an event called "Benjamin Millepied & Company" at the Joyce Theater, one of Manhattan's premier modern-dance venues, Danses Concertanes premiered four ballets. Among them were Andonis Foniadakis's *Phrases, Now*, a modern ballet for five in which Millepied danced, and *Closer*, a romantic ballet for two choreographed by Millepied, accompanied by a live piano performance of Philip Glass's "Mad Rush." *Closer* was originally created for the American Ballet Theatre dancers (and real-life couple) Gillian Murphy and Ethan Stiefel, but after Stiefel was injured, Millepied took his place. The ballet examines the relationship between the dancing couple; after their solos the dancers reunite, embracing. Speaking to Claudia La Rocco for the *New York Times* (March 14, 2006), Millepied said, "The piece needs classical technique but a modern sensibility, or fluidity. There's a lot of ballet dancers who want to be flashy. I wanted a certain simplicity, Robbins-esque, the way I enjoy moving. It was the safest choice to put myself in." The summer of that year also saw the premiere of Millepied's *Years Later* at the University of Buffalo at Amherst, New York. *Years Later* was performed by the legendary Baryshnikov, one of Millepied's inspirations. The 58-year-old Baryshnikov danced alongside a black-and-white training video (in the background) of his younger self, with music by Meredith Monk, Erik Satie, and Philip Glass. The following year, after performances in Europe, *Years Later* had its Manhattan premiere at the Baryshnikov Arts Center, where Millepied was a resident artist. The performance not only displayed Baryshnikov's enduring talent and passion but also served as a kind of rumination on the aging process. As a result of the collaboration, Millepied and Baryshnikov became friends. In an interview with La Rocco for the *New York Times* (May 17, 2009), Millepied said that he admires not only Baryshnikov's talent and abilities but also his curiosity.

Another 2006 collaboration would prove significant and lasting. After the young composer Nico Muhly conducted Millepied's ballet *Amoveo* at the Paris Opera Ballet, the two stayed in touch. Just as Millepied had worked with Jerome Robbins during his teens, so Muhly, then only 24, had worked with Philip Glass a few years earlier. Set to re-orchestrated excerpts from Glass's opera *Einstein on the Beach*, *Amoveo* was re-choreographed for 12 dancers when it returned to the Paris Opera Ballet in 2009. In 2007 the American Ballet Theatre staged Millepied's ballet *From Here on Out*, which was set to an orchestral score by Muhly. *From Here on Out* featured six male-female couples, with dancers sometimes switching partners or dancing in threes or sixes. In a review for the *New York Times* (October 29, 2007), Alastair Macaulay wrote, "Mr. Muhly's score has, as the overture alone shows, a striking range of sonority and structure, and Mr. Millepied's ballet has craft, discipline and a welcome energy." The following year the two collaborated again. The Millepied-choreographed ballet *Triade*, with an original score by Muhly, premiered at the Paris Opera Ballet in the fall of 2008. The ballet featured four dancers on a bare stage with a black curtain as its main decoration. Millepied was praised by critics for having created a uniquely modern ballet about love, seduction, and attraction. Millepied wrapped up the year with a Danses Concertantes presentation of his ballet *Without*, set to music by Chopin. Around that time *New York* magazine (December 15, 2008) called Millepied the year's best choreographer: "*Without*, with its air of intrigue and simplicity of movement, cements Millepied as someone with a unique vision worth seeing—especially in the spring, when he'll deliver a new ballet at the start of City Ballet's season."

Indeed, in the spring of 2009, Millepied's *Quasi Una Fantasia*, with music by Henryk Gorecki, premiered at the City Ballet's spring gala. *Quasi Una Fantasia*, a ballet for 20 dancers, was the choreographer's first major commission by the company of which he is a principal dancer. Praise for the ballet, as it had often been with Millepied's work, was qualified. "Mr. Millepied uses this score like film music: just a couple of long, quiet chords are enough to prompt lifts that travel in changing diagonal paths across the stage," Macaulay wrote for the *New York Times* (May 15, 2009). "The choreography . . . abounds in visually striking groupings, tableaus, lines and shapes, organized with fluency. This is by far the most accomplished work I have seen by Mr. Millepied in terms of technique. Some of this skill carries through into the more intimate sections, which feature some striking shapes." Although Macaulay praised the choreography's organization, he took aim at its lack of expression, drama, and poetry. By contrast, Rebecca Milzoff, writing for *New York* (May 18, 2009), called the ballet a "movingly unified work." Speaking to Milzoff, Millepied said, "I feel like now I'm a choreographer for the first time." Also that year Millepied presented his 24-dancer ballet *Everything Doesn't Happen at Once* at Avery Fisher Hall, a renowned music venue at New York City's Lincoln Center, with music by David Lang.

The following year Millepied had two NYCB premieres—those of *Why Am I Not Where You Are*, in the spring, and *Plainspoken*, in the fall—that left reviewers more impressed with the choreography than with what it conveyed. *Plainspoken*—a ballet for four men and four women, all NYCB principal dancers, with an original score by David Lang—explores the neurotic nature of romantic relationships. Writing for the *Wall Street Journal* (October 14, 2010), Robert Greskovic observed that the ballet "unfolded as a busy sampler of pointlessly playful or dramatic moods." Like many reviewers, Macaulay of the *New York Times* (October 8, 2010) acknowledged Millepied's talent, but he offered this critique: "I still can't see why, for all his skill, Mr. Millepied . . . became a choreographer in the first place. Where artists have inspiration, he has accomplishment. Though I often wish several real choreographers had more of his resources, I certainly wish he had even a little of the expressive singularity, the creative peculiarity, that characterizes those choreographers we think of as artists."

When it came to creating the choreography for the film *Black Swan,* Millepied had to deal with two main challenges: making the actress Natalie Portman, who is not a professional dancer, look believable as a ballerina; and putting a new twist on a ballet classic. Although the reception of the film in the ballet world was mixed, *Black Swan* received many positive reviews and won Portman the Oscar for best actress. In December 2010 Millepied and Portman announced that they are having a child together and are engaged to be married.

—D.K.

Suggested Reading:*New York* Sep. 3, 2007, Dec. 15, 2008; *New York Observer* Sep. 30, 2009; *New York Times* E p1 Apr. 5, 2005, E p3 Mar. 14, 2006, Arts and Leisure p8 Dec. 7, 2008; nycballet.com

Selected Ballets: as dancer—*2 & 3 Part Inventions*, 1994; *Napoli: Pas de Six*, 1995; *La Source*, 1995; *Swan Lake*, 1997; *Midsummer Night's Dream*, 1997; *The Four Seasons*, 1998; *Prism*, 2001; *Zakouski*, 2001; *Dances at a Gathering*, 2002; *Symphony in C*, 2002; *Hallelujah Junction*, 2002; *If by Chance*, 2002; *Vespro*, 2002; *Fancy Free*, 2003; *Carousel (a Dance)*, 2003; *Coppelia*, 2003; *Piano Pieces*, 2003; as choreographer—*Passages*, 2001; *Triple Duet*, 2002; *Circular Motion*, 2004; *Double Aria*, 2004; *On the Other Side*, 2004; *28 Variations on a Theme by Paganini*, 2005; *Casse–Noisette*, 2005; *Closer*, 2006; *Capriccio*, 2006; *Years Later*, 2006; *Amoveo*, 2006; *From Here on Out*, 2007; *Petrouchka*, 2007; *Triade*, 2008; *Without*, 2008; *Quasi Una Fantasia*, 2009; *Everything Doesn't Happen at Once*, 2009; *Sarabande*, 2009; *Anima*, 2009; *Why Am I Not Where You Are*, 2010; *Plainspoken*, 2010

Milnor, John

Feb. 20, 1931– Mathematician; educator; writer

Address: Mathematics Dept., State University of New York, Stony Brook, NY 11794-3651

"There are many mathematicians with extraordinary achievements to their names. . . . But even in this illustrious company, John Milnor stands out as quite exceptional," the British mathematician William Timothy Gowers told R. Ramachandran for the Indian magazine *Frontline* (April 23, 2011). "It is not just that he has proved several famous theorems: it is also that he has made fundamental contributions to many areas of mathematics, apparently very different from each other, and that he is renowned as a quite exceptionally gifted expositor"—that is, he is known for writing clearly and compellingly about his field. "As a result," Gowers added, "his influence can be felt all over mathematics." Milnor has been an innovator in math since his years as a student at Princeton University, in the late 1940s and early 1950s. In his freshman year he came up with what was soon dubbed the Fáry-Milnor theory, which proved a hypothesis concerning knots that had long seemed to be resistant to confirmation. (The Hungarian mathematician István Fáry came up with a proof independently.) In 1956, at the age of 26—in what many regard as possibly his greatest achievement—Milnor

Courtesy of Institute for Mathematical Sciences, SUNY–Stony Brook

discovered "that in seven dimensions there exist smooth objects that can be converted into the seven-dimensional equivalent of spheres"—a particular kind of spheres that became known as Milnor exotic spheres—"only via intermediates with sharp kinks," Philip Ball wrote for *Nature* (March 23, 2011, on-line). Davide Castelvecchi and John Matson, writing for *Scientific American* (March 24, 2011, on-line), noted that "from the point of view of calculus," Milnor's exotic seven-dimensional sphere and an "ordinary" seven-dimensional sphere "were different animals." Later, working on his own and then with the French mathematician Michel Kervaire, Milnor proved that in seven dimensions there exist 28 different exotic spheres.

Those feats, according to the on-line MacTutor History of Mathematics, "opened up the new field of differential topology" and led the International Congress of Mathematicians in 1962 to award Milnor the Fields Medal; the most prestigious honor in mathematics at that time for those under 40 years of age, the medal is presented every four years. Milnor won the National Medal of Science in 1967 and the Wolf Prize in 1989, and he has received three Leroy P. Steele Prizes from the American Mathematical Society (AMS). The first came in 1982, for his 1956 *Annals of Mathematics* paper on exotic spheres, and the second in 2004, for his "expository contributions ranging across a wide spectrum of disciplines including topology, symmetric bilinear forms, characteristic classes, Morse theory, game theory, algebraic K-theory, iterated rational maps . . . and the list goes on," according to the AMS Web site. The 2004 Steele Prize citation stated, "The phrase sublime elegance is rarely associated with mathematical exposition, but it applies to all of Milnor's writings. Reading his books, one is struck with the ease with which the subject is unfolding and it only becomes apparent after reflection that this ease is the mark of a master." Milnor was given a third Steele Prize in 2011, for "his overall achievements and his influence on mathematics in general, both through his work and through his excellent books," the AMS stated. Earlier in 2011 Milnor earned an honor arguably even more lofty than the Fields Medal: the $1 million Abel Prize, introduced by the Norwegian Academy of Science and Letters in 2002 to honor mathematicians of all ages and to rectify the lack of a Nobel Prize (awarded by the Royal Swedish Academy of Sciences) for mathematicians. The Abel Prize committee noted (on-line) that "all of Milnor's works display marks of great research: profound insights, vivid imagination, elements of surprise, and supreme beauty."

To help laypeople gain a glimmer of understanding of Milnor's achievements, the Abel Web site explained that topology is "a major area of mathematics concerned with shapes, such as curves, surfaces, solids, etc. In topology one studies properties of the shapes that are preserved through continuous deformations, twisting, and stretching of objects" without tearing or gluing. (Topology is sometimes referred to as "rubber-band geometry.") A donut and a coffee mug with one handle are considered "topologically equivalent" because theoretically they can be "molded" to form the same shape without tearing or gluing. If a mug were to be "stretched" to form a donut, or a donut is transformed into a mug, its topology remains the same, but the geometry of its surface is changed, because the distance between two given points has changed. Similarly, a cube can theoretically be made into a sphere—the simplest topological shape. Some of Milnor's work also refers to more than three dimensions and thus involves "worlds" fundamentally different from the three-dimensional world in which we live. Entities having four or more dimensions can be described mathematically, but only a minuscule number of people can mentally picture such worlds. As James Gleick wrote for the *New York Times* (August 12, 1986), "One dimension is a line. The second dimension comes when you add a second line at right angles to the first, so that now you have east-west and north-south"—that is, a flat surface, like a piece of paper. "The third dimension requires a new line at right angles to the others, so you must leave the flat plain and draw one up-down"—thus forming a cube. "To imagine a fourth dimension, it is necessary to imagine a fourth line at right angles to all the others, and this most mortals cannot do."

It is possible that Milnor is able to imagine what most people cannot. At the 1986 International Congress of Mathematicians, Gleick wrote, "some kind of inner vision" led Milnor "to start gesturing with his hands" when he was talking about work involving four-dimensional as well as two-dimensional entities: "His hands formed loops and handles in the air, as though he were describing some new kind of suitcase." Milnor told Ed Regis, the author of *Who Got Einstein's Office?* (1986), "If I can give an abstract proof of something, I'm reasonably happy. But if I can get a concrete, computational proof and actually produce numbers I'm much happier. I'm rather an addict of doing things on the computer, because that gives you an explicit criterion of what's going on. I have a visual way of thinking, and I'm happy if I can see a picture of what I'm working with."

Milnor began teaching at Princeton in 1953, the year before he earned a doctorate there, and in 1960, at age 28, he was promoted to full professor. Other than the year he taught at Oxford University, in England (1957–58), the year he worked at the University of California at Los Angeles (1967–68), and the two years he worked at the Massachusetts Institute of Technology (1968–70), he spent the next 18 years at the Institute for Advanced Study, which is on the campus of Princeton University but is not formally affiliated with that school. In 1989 he joined the faculty of the State University of New York (SUNY) at Stony Brook. He is the co-director of the school's Institute for Mathematical Sciences.

In "Growing Up in Old Fine Hall," a talk given at Princeton in 1996 (its title refers to the building that housed Princeton's Mathematics Department until 1970), Milnor said, "What I love most about the study of mathematics is its anarchy! There is no mathematical czar who tells us which direction we must work in, what we must be doing. . . . I like to picture the frontier of mathematics as a great ragged wall, with the unknown, the unsolved problems, to one side, and with thousands of mathematicians on the other side, each trying to nibble away at different parts of the problem using different approaches. Perhaps most of them don't get very far, but every now and then one of them breaks through and opens a new area of understanding. Then perhaps another one makes another breakthrough and opens another new area. Sometimes these breakthroughs come together, so that we have different parts of mathematics merging, giving us wide new perspectives."

John Willard "Jack" Milnor was born on February 20, 1931 in Orange, New Jersey, to Joseph Willard Milnor and Emily (Cox) Milnor. He grew up with an older brother, Robert, in Maplewood, New Jersey. Milnor's father earned a bachelor's degree in mathematics and became an engineer; as a Western Union Telegraph Co. employee, he invented a half-dozen patented devices. He died at age 59 in 1949. While growing up young Jack read the math books in his father's collection. In 1948, at age 17, he enrolled at Princeton University, in Princeton, New Jersey. During a freshman poetry class, his professor read aloud a poem Milnor had written and told the class, "This is exactly what not to do," Milnor recalled to Bart Jones for *Newsday* (April 10, 2011). "It made me realize whatever talents I had were elsewhere."

During Milnor's undergraduate years at Princeton, the mathematician and game theorist John Nash was pursuing a doctorate there. (Later, in 1994, Nash won the Nobel Prize in economics for the work he described in his dissertation; he was immortalized in the biography *A Beautiful Mind*, by Sylvia Nasar, and the 2001 film of the same name.) In "Growing Up in Old Fine Hall," Milnor reminisced about his experiences as an undergraduate: "Fine Hall was in a real sense my home for many years," he said. "I was young and shy, and had no talent for dealing with people. Fine Hall was a wonderful new world for me. There was a common room where one could make oneself at home, and a marvelous library. Among the graduate students I particularly remember . . . John Nash. I had never really heard much or reacted much to classical music before I came to Princeton. I first learned about Bach by listening to Nash wandering around the halls whistling. I also learned about Game Theory, and Nash Equilibrium Theory. (Since I was very young, I assumed that it was the most natural thing in the world for a graduate student to develop a mathematical theory which changed the way we think about social sciences.)" (In 2002 Milnor won a Lilly Reintegration Award, from the pharmaceutical company Eli Lilly, for his role in helping Nash to reenter the Princeton community during his years of struggle with schizophrenia.)

During his freshman year Milnor took mostly graduate-level math courses. One was a course in differential geometry (which uses algebra and calculus to tackle problems in geometry) taught by the Canadian-born mathematician Albert Tucker. According to Princeton legend, one day Milnor noticed a notoriously difficult, unproved conjecture written on the blackboard. Known as the Borsuk conjecture (for the Polish mathematician Karol Borsuk), it concerned "the total curvature of a knotted curve in space," Virginia Chaplin wrote for the *Princeton Alumni Weekly* (May 9, 1958). There are thousands of kinds of knots, each of which is "a closed curve in space" without "open ends," according to the Abel Prize Web site; the theory of knots, the Web site explained, "is a subfield of mathematics aiming to describe all knots." "Two knots are said to be equivalent if we can transform one into the other by pulling and pushing branches of the rope, but not cutting or gluing. The simplest of all knots is the circle. It is often called an unknot since it is mathematically a knot, but not normally viewed as a knot." Milnor mistakenly assumed that the problem on the blackboard was a homework assignment, and in a few days he came up with a proof. He then handed the proof to Tucker, saying, according to an article in the on-line archives of the *Daily Princetonian*, "Would you be good enough to point out the flaw in this attempt? I'm sure there is one but I can't find it." Neither Tucker nor other professors in the Mathematics Department could find any errors. Tucker encouraged Milnor to submit his proof to the Princeton publication *Annals of Mathematics*. "A few months later," Sylvia Nasar wrote in *A Beautiful Mind*, "Milnor turned in an exquisitely crafted paper with a full theory of the curvature of knotted curves in which the proof of the Borsuk conjecture was a mere by-product." The paper was published in 1950 in Volume 50 of the *Annals of Mathematics*, and was "more substantial than most doctoral dissertations," Nasar wrote. Nasar also noted that while still a teenager, Milnor had become the Mathematics Department's "golden boy." Also in 1950, as he had the year before, Milnor earned a Putnam fellowship for his outstanding performance during the William Lowell Putnam Mathematical Competition, held annually for U.S. and Canadian college students.

Milnor completed his undergraduate studies in three years, earning an A.B. degree in mathematics in 1951. That year marked the publication of the first of several papers he wrote about game theory for the Rand Corp., a nonprofit think tank. The theory of games originated mainly with the Princeton mathematician John von Neumann, who co-wrote, with the economist Oskar Morgenstern, *Theory of Games and Economic Behavior* (1944). During the summer of 1952, while Milnor was pursuing his doctorate at Princeton under the supervision of the mathematician Ralph Fox, he worked on game theory at the Rand Corp. in Santa Monica, California. As a graduate student, having won a Procter fellowship from Princeton, he also studied at the Federal Institute of Technology in Zurich, Switzerland. In 1953 Milnor joined Princeton's mathematics faculty, as a Eugene Higgins lecturer; the next year he completed his dissertation, titled "Isotopy of Links," and earned a Ph.D. degree. (In topology, "links" are groups of knots that do not intersect; the definition of "isotopy" requires knowledge of additional, highly technical mathematical concepts.) For four years beginning in 1955, Milnor was an Alfred P. Sloan fellow. He rose to assistant professor in 1956 and was promoted to associate professor in 1958. In January 1960 he became the youngest Princeton faculty member in 50 years to be promoted to full professor. Within two years he had been named Henry Putnam university professor (an endowed chair that recognizes a scholar of extraordinary ability).

Milnor has often said that, above all else, he considers himself to be a problem solver. His inquisitory nature has led him to study many areas of mathematics. In its announcement (January 6, 2011, on-line) that Milnor had won that year's Leroy P. Steele Prize for Lifetime Achievement, the AMA stated, "Milnor opened up several fields: singularity theory, algebraic K-theory, and the theory of quadratic forms. Although he did not invent these subjects, his work gave them completely new points of view. For instance, his work on isolated singularities of complex hypersurfaces presented a great new topological framework for studying singularities, and at the same time provided a rich new source of examples of manifolds with different extra structures. The concepts of Milnor fibers and Milnor number are today among the most important notions in the study of complex singularities." Milnor accepted the Abel Prize from King Harald V of Norway in a ceremony in Oslo held on May 24, 2011.

The Rand Corp. published Milnor's books *Games Against Nature* (1952), *Reasonable Outcomes for N-Person Games* (1953), *On Games of Survival* (1955), and (with Lloyd S. Shapley) *Values of Large Games II: Oceanic Games* (1960). His other books include *Morse Theory* (1963); *Topology from the Differentiable Viewpoint* (1965, 1997); *Singular Points of Complex Hypersurfaces* (1968); *Introduction to Algebraic K-Theory* (1971); *Symmetric Bilinear Forms* (with Dale Husemöller, 1973); *Characteristic Classes* (with James D Stasheff, 1974), about so-called smooth manifolds and vector bundles; *Dynamics in One Complex Variable* (2006); and *Differential Topology* (2007). From 1994 to 2010 the AMS published *Collected Papers of John Milnor*, a five-volume set.

Colleagues of the six-foot three-inch Milnor have described him as unusually amiable. From his marriage to the Swiss-born Brigitte Weber, in 1954, Milnor has three children: Steven, Daniel, and Gabrielle. That marriage ended in divorce, as did his brief, second marriage, in 1968, to the mathematician Tilla Weinstein. In the early 1980s he married the mathematician Dusa McDuff; their son, Thomas, born in 1984, is currently a graduate

student in mathematics at the University of British Columbia, Canada. McDuff, a native of England and a longtime member of the SUNY–Stony Brook faculty, is currently the Helen Lyttle Kimmel professor of mathematics at Barnard College, in New York City. She has one daughter, Anna, from her first marriage. Milnor and McDuff live in Setauket, on Long Island, New York.

—M.M.H.

Suggested Reading: Abel Prize Web site; American Mathematical Society (on-line) Apr. 2004, Jan. 6, 2011; *Daily Princetonian* (on-line) Jan. 15, 1960; *Frontline* (on-line) Apr. 23, 2011; *Nature* (on-line) Mar. 23, 2011; *New York Times* (on-line) Aug. 12, 1986; *Newsday* A p17 Apr. 10, 2011; *Princeton Alumni Weekly* (on-line) May 9, 1958; *Scientific American* (on-line) Mar. 24, 2011; Nasar, Sylvia. *A Beautiful Mind*, 2001; Rossi, Hugo, ed. *Prospects in Mathematics*, 1999

Selected Books: *Morse Theory*, 1963; *Topology from the Differential Viewpoint*, 1965; *Lectures on the H-Cobordism Theorem*, 1965; *Singular Points of Complex Hypersurfaces*, 1969; *Introduction to Algebraic K-Theory*, 1971; *Symmetric Bilinear Forms* (with Dale Husemöller), 1973; *Characteristic Classes* (with James Stasheff), 1974; *Dynamics in One Complex Variable*, 1999

Ming, Jenny

1955– Business executive

Address: Charlotte Russe, 4645 Morena Blvd., San Diego, CA 92117

Since 2009 Jenny Ming has been the CEO of the women's-clothing chain Charlotte Russe. Originally a purveyor of trendy, affordable clothing and accessories for teenage girls, Charlotte Russe began to fall behind its larger competitors when the girls who made up its market base graduated to more "adult" retailers, while younger teen girls—the most fickle market—were wooed by newer stores including Hollister Col, owned by Abercrombie & Fitch. Since she took the reins at Charlotte Russe, Ming has begun to revive the company, implementing creative and often unexpected marketing strategies aimed at changing the company's image and broadening the age range of its clientele. Advertising new, high-end basics, such as well-made T-shirts available in a variety of colors and a selection of office-appropriate styles, Ming aims to appeal to teens and working women alike.

Ming was interviewed by the teen magazine *CosmoGIRL!* in March 2005, while she was still at the helm of the retail giant Old Navy. The interview was part of the magazine's Project 2024,

Courtesy of Alison Brod Public Relations

Jenny Ming

aimed at putting a woman in the Oval Office by the year 2024; as the project involved showcasing successful women, Ming was an excellent candidate, having parlayed her interest in clothing into a lucrative business career. She began at the bottom of the corporate retail ladder, working her way to *Fortune* magazine's 2003 list of the "50 Most Powerful Women in Business" and becoming a symbol of success for women and Asian-Americans alike. In the interview with *CosmoGIRL!*, Ming credited her successes to hard work and a positive attitude. "Instead of thinking that everything is difficult . . . I'm very optimistic. I see the glass half-full," she said, going on to impart what she felt any mother would want her teenage daughter to know when trying to start a career. Fittingly, *CosmoGIRL!* chose Kameron Ming, Ming's then-19-year-old daughter, to interview her. Kameron wrote in the introduction to the article, "The most important thing my mom has told me about success is to find out for myself what I'm passionate about and not just do what other people expect of me. Otherwise, she says, I'll never be satisfied."

One of five children, Jenny Ming was born in 1955 in Canton, in the province of Guangdong, China. By 1949 that country's Communist leader, Mao Zedong, had established the People's Republic of China and begun taking control of China's provinces. When Ming was three months old, her family fled on foot and by boat to the nearby Portuguese island colony of Macau, near Hong Kong, after their property was seized by the government. The family remained in Macau for almost a decade before moving to the North Beach neighborhood of San Francisco, California. There, Ming's father worked as a printer, and her mother had a job in a factory. Ming's mother had "never had a job before. But she worked . . . and went to school to learn English," Ming told *CosmoGIRL!* "So I learned to have her energy." Ming's mother dreamed that Ming would become a pharmacist. "She had no idea that I was really bad at chemistry," Ming told Jenny Strasburg for the *San Francisco Chronicle* (February 29, 2004).

When the family arrived in the United States, in 1964, Ming was nine and did not speak any English. "Only my 13-year-old sister, the eldest . . . spoke English, and she took me to school," Ming wrote with Amy Zipkin for a *New York Times* (October 27, 2002) article. "I was in the fourth grade. The teacher sat me next to another Chinese girl. I didn't understand her because we spoke different dialects. . . . She did a lot of finger-pointing, telling me what to do. I learned English in E.S.L. [English as a second language] class and by watching T.V. I wanted to be American so badly."

During high school Ming took odd jobs. She learned to sew and worked as a seamstress from her home on weekends. At San Jose State University, in California, she initially studied home economics. Her college boyfriend, Mitchell Ming, who is now her husband, said to her, "'You love clothes, you should be a retail buyer. You should take some business classes,'" Ming recalled to her daughter Kameron. "I thought, Why not? Thinking back, that was a really big turning point." Ming changed her major to clothing merchandising and graduated in 1978.

In an interview with Adam Bryant for the *New York Times* (October 17, 2010), Ming described her first retail job, with the now-defunct California-based department-store chain Mervyn's: "I was just out of college . . . and I was a department manager in domestics—linens, towels, those kinds of things. The salespeople tended to be housewives. And one month into my job, my boss called me in and said: 'You know, Jenny, you're not going to make it in the business. You're just too nice, and you let everybody walk all over you.' Of course, you can imagine if it's your first month on the job and someone's telling you that. It's pretty devastating. So the next day I went back to work, and I told all the sales associates . . . exactly what [my boss had] said because I just had to tell them the truth. And they were really surprised. I said: 'You know, I let you guys talk all the time. I'm probably going to get fired, and then you are going to get a new boss, and they are going to probably be much, much harder on you than I am.'" Ming reached a compromise with her employees, allowing them to schedule breaks to talk with their friends in exchange for a more professional working atmosphere. The women appreciated Ming's honesty and because of it, she said, were willing to help her. Ming has cited that experience as an important lesson in leadership. "I learned . . . to communicate, to set expectations, and not be afraid to tell the truth," she told Bryant.

Ming later became a buyer for Mervyn's. Then, in 1986, she joined Gap Inc. When it was founded, in 1969, Gap primarily sold blue jeans; the business expanded rapidly from its first store, in San Francisco, becoming one of the most popular retail chains in the world. While specializing in jeans, it soon became known for its clean-cut basics and "All-American" style. It would later house brands such as Banana Republic, which Gap acquired in 1983. In 1989 Ming became a Gap division vice president for men's merchandising, and in 1994 she was hand-picked by Gap's CEO, Millard ("Mickey") Drexler, to help launch a new Gap brand called Old Navy. For four years Ming ran Old Navy's merchandising department, assuming responsibility for store design, visual merchandising, planning, and distribution. In 1998 she was selected by Gap to become the brand's president. Old Navy aimed to provide basics such as T-shirts and jeans at prices lower than those at Gap. "What we wanted to do was capture some of the customers that bought Gap at markdown [but] who couldn't really buy at full price," Ming told Jenny Strasburg. "There [are] a lot of people who can't buy at full price who say, 'OK, if it's at markdown, then I could afford it.'" The first Old Navy store opened in Colma, California, and bore the brand name Gap on its sign. The Gap logo soon disappeared, as more stores opened and Old Navy became successful in its own right. Insiders have said that it was Old Navy's (and Ming's) eye for trends that set it apart from other bargain-retail merchandisers, including Target and Wal-Mart. The chain succeeded in part because it managed to attract several different kinds of customers, from men to teenage girls. "Teens can embrace you in a second, but they can drop you just as fast," Marshall Cohen, president of NPDFashionworld, a division of the consulting firm NPD Group Inc., told Strasburg. Ming, however, was confident that her strategies—including the selling of low-waist jeans, handbags, and pajama pants—would attract the teen market without alienating other shoppers. "Teens are a part of the family, because we're a family brand," Ming told Strasburg. "But is it all about the teen? No."

Ming was careful in selecting items for Old Navy. She drew inspiration from her observations and expected her employees to do the same. She told Bryant about the workers she sought to hire, "I look for someone who is very diverse, someone who has an incredible sense of curiosity, who knows what's going on in pop culture. You have to be aware because clothing is about being of the moment. So if you're not aware of what's going on around you in pop culture, music, food, clothes—they all kind of blend together—then you might not be right for an apparel retailer." Sharing an example of what inspired her retail innovations, she confided to *CosmoGIRL!* that the "bottoms-only" pajama-pants craze originated with her older daughter, Kristin. When Ming dropped Kristin off at junior high school on "Pajama Day," she noticed that Kristin and her friends wore pajama pants

paired with tank tops instead of matching pajama shirts. Old Navy then began producing pajama pants in varying patterns, and a teen trend was born—or at least heavily supported by the successful marketing campaign conducted by Old Navy. Ming was perceptive when it came to her customers. When Strasburg asked Ming how she brought the "average guy" (who is seen as seldom purchasing clothing) to the store, Ming replied, "Actually, socks—because they have to replenish that." She added that once in the store, men would perhaps be drawn to Old Navy's array of men's apparel, including the successful painter pants. ("Our painter-pant campaign was the first campaign to really focus on men, and we saw a great improvement in men coming into the store," Ming told T.R. Nothum for the on-line magazine *Future* in the spring of 2003.) While traveling abroad Ming noticed teens in London, England, wearing dark blue jeans. "So I thought, 'Let's darken our stonewash a little,'" she told reporters for *Bloomberg BusinessWeek* (January 10, 2000, on-line). "Now, we have a whole section of dark denim." Under Ming Old Navy became a national retail giant, earning more than $6 billion per year in more than 900 stores.

Beginning in 2004, however, Old Navy's sales began to slip, as the chain lost business to competitors. In 2006, the same year Ming announced her departure from Old Navy, the brand reported sales to be down 7 percent, against 6 percent in 2005, according to Emili Vesilind, writing for *Women's Wear Daily* (October 17, 2006). "I left Old Navy and Gap after 20 years determined to take some time off, to travel just for pleasure," Ming stated in an interview for the Web site of Advent International, the private equity firm for which she next worked. "Then during my travels, particularly in Asia, which was a real inspiration, I started getting creative again. Sometimes, when you're in the midst of running a business, it's hard to see what's going on around you—you're under a lot of pressure to deliver. When you step away, you can start to imagine more possibilities. I got excited about retail again. I was refreshed and I realized how much I loved the business." In 2008 Ming signed on with Advent as an operating partner, assigned to explore investment opportunities in retail. When David Moin, writing for *Women's Wear Daily* (September 9, 2008), asked if she would consider running a retail company bought by Advent International, Ming responded, "It's possible, if it's fun and attractive enough, but I'm not ready to say that for sure."

A year later Ming came across the "fun and attractive" company for which she had been searching. "I don't think that Advent would have considered buying Charlotte Russe until I looked at it and explained what I thought the opportunity was. Then they recognized that there might be something there," Ming stated for the Advent Web site. Charlotte Russe, a 35-year-old retail company specializing in inexpensive trendy fashions for girls and young women, was facing hard times. Ming saw the brand as being "stuck in the 1990s," as she told Max Padilla for the *Los Angeles Times* (August 8, 2010). "The store and selection had become too focused on the teenage customer," Padilla wrote, "who shopped the store for inexpensive accessories and prom dresses but graduated from Charlotte Russe as soon as she graduated from high school." According to the Charlotte Russe Web site, in 2007 the company's board of directors had determined that "significant changes were necessary to improve operational performance and build greater value for stockholders." To support those efforts, the company sought a buyer.

In August 2009 Advent International bought Charlotte Russe for about $380 million, and Ming assumed the post of CEO of the company, whose central offices were in San Diego. Ming's first order of business was to expand the firm's headquarters to the more cosmopolitan San Francisco. "Our decision to locate our creative hub in San Francisco will better position us in a key market place that will allow for a greater source of creative talent," Ming said in a February 2010 press release. "Maintaining a presence in both San Francisco and San Diego will help us build our organization and reposition our brand later this year for the benefit of the customers." The repositioning efforts began almost immediately. Ming employed a team of designers and dispatched them across the globe. "[The design team] will shop quite a bit, not only in San Diego, but [Los Angeles], London, New York, Japan, and they'll look at a lot of trend services and online to help edit the trends," Ming told Lori Weisberg for the *San Diego Union Tribune* (April 4, 2010, on-line). By "editing," Ming meant that designers would pick only the best of the many trends they observed. Editing was an important component of the Charlotte Russe makeover; it was designers' ability to filter the multitude of global trends that set Charlotte Russe apart. Ming not only pared down the trends, she also offered basics and created a more navigable store. The result was more minimalist and, Ming told Padilla, "more elevated. It's better-edited fashion with incredible pricing."

In another notable brand-rebuilding effort, Charlotte Russe capitalized on its connection to the celebrity stylist Eric Daman, who helped to dress the female casts of the successful TV shows *Sex and the City* and *Gossip Girl.* Daman brought star power and exclusivity to Charlotte Russe. When he held a private dinner for fashion insiders to showcase the store's 2009 fall wardrobe, Emili Vesilind wrote for the *Los Angeles Times* (September 23, 2009), "Even the most 'over it' style writers found themselves cooing over the [1980s television show] *Dynasty*-worthy earrings, long, messy strands of pearls, chunky, silver-toned chains, studded leather-like cuffs and over-the-top cocktail rings. 'The jewelry is ridiculous,' noted Daman, 'and the price is, like, two-for-$8. No zeros in it.'"

Ming has implemented creative and often unexpected marketing strategies to broaden the age range of Charlotte Russe's clientele, from teens to working women in their late 20s. Recently, Ming invited a group of popular fashion bloggers (females age 14 and up) to participate in Project Mannequin. "We were trying to figure out how to reach out to those customers who do not know about Charlotte Russe," Ming told Lisa Marsh for *StyleList* (July 21, 2010, on-line). "It's all about what her interests are, and she reads blogs more than anything." The bloggers were given full access to Charlotte's Closet, a New York City loft housing all of Charlotte Russe's current wares, and were challenged to assemble outfits for specific occasions ("dinner with parents, Sunday brunch, etc.," Marsh explained) in under 20 minutes. Afterward, shoppers were encouraged to vote on-line for their favorite outfits. "We want the people who know about her [the potential Charlotte Russe customer] and are hands-on to interact with us," Ming continued. "We have never really engaged bloggers on this level. I think this is the future." She told Bryant. "I think we have to have the mentality of a start-up. I think it makes you hungry."

Ming has spoken with candor about her professional journey. In January 2006 she told Sheree Curry for allbusiness.com that when the Gap CEO, Mickey Dressler, first asked her if she was interested in becoming the head of Old Navy, she said no. "Another person in my place would not have done that," she told Curry. "As Asians and women, we tend to underestimate ourselves. We were taught to be humble, instead of tooting our own horns, to stay more in the shadow." However, Ming soon realized that she was not living up to her full potential. "As an immigrant . . . I think you set limits and I was just happy to be here and get a good education and be an everyday citizen," she explained to John Gittelsohn for the *Orange County Register* (June 27, 2006). "I think . . . we hold that kind of ceiling to ourselves. . . . One lesson I learned is to really seize the opportunity and step up to more than I ever imagined."

In 2000 Ming was named one of the top 25 managers in the country by *BusinessWeek*. She serves as a board member of the Committee of 100, which, according to its Web site, is "a national non-profit non-partisan organization that brings a Chinese American perspective to issues concerning Asian Americans and U.S. relations with China." She also sits on the board of the Merage Foundation for the American Dream and the advisory board of Cornell University's College of Human Ecology.

Ming, her husband, and their three children own Korbin Kameron Vineyards (named for Ming's twin son and daughter) in Sonoma Valley, California. Mitchell Ming's title is "proprietor," and Korbin Ming serves as the vineyard's head of sales and marketing.

—M.M.H.

Suggested Reading: Advent International Web site; *CosmoGIRL!* Mar. 2005; Charlotte Russe Web site; *Los Angeles Times* (on-line) Sep. 23, 2009, Aug. 8, 2010; *New York Times* (on-line) Oct. 27, 2002, Business p2 Oct. 17, 2010; *Orange County (California) Register* (on-line) June 27, 2006; *San Diego Tribune* (on-line) Apr. 4, 2010; *San Francisco Chronicle* p11 Feb. 29, 2004; *StyleList* (on-line) July, 21, 2010; *Women's Wear Daily* p2 Oct. 17, 2006, p5 Sep. 9, 2008

Paul Stuart, courtesy of Random House

Mitchell, David

Jan. 12, 1969– Writer

Address: c/o Random House Inc., 1745 Broadway, New York, NY 10019

"Lavishly talented as both a storyteller and a prose stylist," the English writer David Mitchell "is notable for his skill and his fertility," the novelist and literary critic James Wood wrote for the *New Yorker* (July 5, 2010). "Without annoying zaniness or exaggeration, he is nevertheless an artist of surplus: he seems to have more stories than he quite knows what to do with, and he ranges across a remarkable variety of genres—conventional historical fiction, dystopian [science fiction], literary farce." In positive and negative reviews alike, Mitchell's novels—for which he was won several prestigious literary honors—have been described as difficult and ambitious, and his writing has been compared to that of such heavyweights as Tolstoy, Dostoyevsky, Thomas Pynchon, Vladimir Nabokov, James Joyce, Mark Twain, J.D. Salinger, and

Haruki Murakami. The range of genres in his fiction is sometimes evident within a single work, and his experimentation has extended to structure, in novels that employ nonlinear narrative and multiple levels of reality. Having established a reputation with his first published novel, *Ghostwritten* (1999), which features nine narrators spread around the globe, Mitchell gained a new level of acclaim with *Cloud Atlas* (2004), his third novel, which sold approximately one million copies worldwide. That book encompasses six separate, interconnected narratives set in widespread locales, over a span of hundreds of years. Mitchell's most recent novel is *The Thousand Autumns of Jacob de Zoet* (2010). His work has been translated into 19 languages. In 2007 *Time* magazine named him one of the world's most influential novelists.

David Stephen Mitchell was born on January 12, 1969 in the village of Ainsdale, on the west coast of England. He and his older brother were raised in rural Worcestershire, in the central part of the country. Mitchell did not speak until the age of five; two years later he developed a stammer. (Unlike stutterers, who repeat certain sounds, stammerers often pause involuntarily after certain consonants.) When Mitchell was a boy, the threat of nuclear war frightened him; feeding his fear was his reading of John Wyndham's postapocalyptic novels. He also read fantasy novels, such as the Lord of the Rings series, by J. R.R. Tolkien, and drew elaborate maps based on those books. As a teenager he collected postcards and wrote poetry, pursuits he kept from his schoolmates for fear of being teased or worse. Mitchell's parents were visual artists, and from them he learned "from a fairly young age," as he told Malcolm Jones for *Newsweek* (March 25, 2002), "that you could make a living from the creative contents of your own mind." Mitchell explained to Ian Hocking for the Web site magicrealism.co.uk that because his parents are artists, "people think I grew up in some big bohemian house in Hampstead or somewhere like that, whereas in fact I had one of the straightest middle-class upbringings . . . that I know of."

After high school, in what he has called his first true adventure, Mitchell traveled with his girlfriend through India and Nepal for two months. Then, in 1987, he began his studies in English and American literature at the University of Kent, in Canterbury, England. Mitchell told Wyatt Mason for the *New York Times* (June 25, 2010, on-line) that he was not a particularly good student or extremely interested in books—that he occasionally wrote short stories but was primarily interested in going out with women. However, Jan Montefiore, a literature professor of his, recalled matters differently, telling Mason that Mitchell was a good student and a capable, creative writer. "People with great abilities are often arrogant," Montefiore said. "And he never was. . . . I don't think he fully realized his own talent."

After earning a B.A. degree and an M.A. degree in comparative literature, also from Kent, Mitchell taught English as a second language in England, Italy, and, later, Hiroshima, Japan. (His then-girlfriend was from Hiroshima.) By that point he was writing a great deal. After finishing his first novel, he sent its first few chapters to nearly 20 literary agents and publishers. One agent, Mike Shaw, expressed interest. "I could see the talent," Shaw told Mason. "David could write, but the book was out of control and over the top. No structure, many characters. I'd never seen anything so extreme as that first typescript from David. So godawful in one sense and so promising in another." After some encouragement from Shaw, Mitchell abandoned his first novel and began work on a new one. After completing the first half of what would become *Ghostwritten* (1999), Mitchell sent Shaw the manuscript. "How he learned so quickly how to structure and stay in control I have no idea," Shaw told Mason. "All I can say is that he worked—and works—very, very hard." Around that time Mitchell met a woman named Keiko Yoshida, who would become his wife.

The publication of *Ghostwritten* in the United Kingdom made an impression on critics that was rare for a first novel. Mitchell told the stories of nine characters—a shady British trader in Hong Kong, China; the elderly female proprietor of a tea shack near a sacred mountain in China; a terrorist in Okinawa, Japan; a record-store employee in Tokyo, Japan; a ghost-like spirit that invades the minds of others in Mongolia; a drummer in London, England; an art thief in St. Petersburg, Russia; a female physicist hiding in Ireland from the CIA; and a radio deejay in New York City—all unaware of how their paths converge. Although the laudatory reviews were not unqualified, they clearly pointed to Mitchell's talent and potential. Citing James Joyce and Samuel Beckett as other writers whose first full-length works of fiction were episodic or made up of connected stories, Nicholas Blincoe wrote for the London *Guardian* (August 21, 1999), "Mitchell may only be starting out, but he is in fine company, perhaps the best the 20th century has to offer." While some of the chapters—each focusing on a different character—are "outstanding pieces of prose," Blincoe wrote, others "fall flat," including, in his view, those about the drummer and the art thief. Writing for the *New York Times* (September 12, 2000), Michiko Kakutani pointed to the chapter concerning the ghost-like spirit: "The addition of another voice, meant to represent that of a disembodied spirit who can move from host to host, century to century, continent to continent, glosses the entire story with a pompous, New Agey tone. Instead of lending credibility to the novel's apocalyptic ending, this voice undermines it." But Kakutani also cited the author's strengths: "When Mr. Mitchell stays away from the philosophical mumbo jumbo and sticks more closely to the here and now, he is decidedly more successful." *Ghostwritten* won the John Lle-

wellyn Rhys Prize (awarded to writers under 35) and was shortlisted for the *Guardian* First Book Award.

Mitchell's next novel, *Number9Dream* (2001), was just as ambitious as its predecessor and perhaps even more polarizing. In *Number9Dream*, a young man, Eiji Miyake, goes to Tokyo—a very modern, high-tech metropolis—from a small village in rural Japan in search of his father, who has abandoned him. Eiji, who is prone to daydreaming, is soon embroiled in a variety of dangerous encounters: a violent altercation with his father's lawyer, a disturbing encounter with the Yakuza (the Japanese mafia), and a near-death experience in a storm—some of those events being either nightmares or fantasies. The name of the book is a reference to the Beatles' song "Revolution 9," whose only lyrics are repetitions of "number nine." Kakutani of the *New York Times* (March 15, 2002) gave Mitchell's book a wholly negative review: "As in *Ghostwritten*, which recounted the intersecting stories of a dozen people connected by six (or fewer) degrees of separation, Mr. Mitchell shows his dexterity as a writer in this volume by shifting gears among a wide variety of styles. This time, however, a Murakami-like air of detachment hovers over the proceedings, distancing the reader from Eiji's experiences and emphasizing that many of the passages Mr. Mitchell has concocted in this volume are contrived—and superfluous—in the extreme." While several reviewers echoed Kakutani's complaints, others viewed the work positively. Writing for *Newsweek*, Jones observed: "Funny, tenderhearted and horrifying, often all at once, [*Number9Dream*] refashions the rudiments of the coming-of-age novel into something completely original." The novel was shortlisted for the Man Booker Prize for Fiction.

Cloud Atlas (2004), Mitchell's most ambitious and difficult work to date, quickly won him a new level of critical acceptance and admiration. "Reader beware: *Cloud Atlas* will likely be among the most exasperating books you will ever read," Jenny Barchfield wrote for *Newsweek* (August 30, 2004). "But swallow your frustration (and your urges to hurtle the book out the nearest window), and stick with author David Mitchell. You're in for a wild, wonderful ride." The book incorporated several literary styles and genres—including travel journalism, traditional fictional narrative, and the epistolary form—to tell the story of six characters whose connection to one another spans several continents and hundreds of years. The story begins with Adam Ewing, an American traveling in the 1850s to the Chatham Islands, in the South Pacific. Ewing records his adventures in a journal, which comes to an abrupt end. The reader is then transported to 1930s Belgium and the life of a would-be composer, Robert Frobisher; then to California in the 1970s, where a journalist, Luisa Rey, works to uncover an industrial conspiracy; then to present-day London, where a book editor inadvertently finds himself in a home for the elderly; then to a Korea of the near future; and, finally, to Hawaii of the distant future, where a man witnesses the annihilation of humanity. The English newspaper *Sunday Telegraph* raised eyebrows when it refused to review the book, with a critic for the paper calling it "unreadable." Most reviewers, however, praised the novel, albeit with occasional reservations. For the *New York Times* (August 29, 2004), Tom Bissell wrote: "Let it be said that Mitchell is, clearly, a genius. He writes as though at the helm of some perpetual dream machine, can evidently do anything, and his ambition is written in magma across this novel's every page. But *Cloud Atlas* is the sort of book that makes ambition seem slightly suspect. . . . If Mitchell's virtuosity too often seems android, one suspects this says less about his achievement and more about the literature of formal innovation. This is a book that might very well move things forward. It is also a book that makes one wonder to what end things are being moved." By contrast, Melissa Denes wrote for the London *Guardian* (February 21, 2004), "What saves [Mitchell's] books from being just brilliant formal experiments is the heart with which he writes, the humour, and the absolute conviction with which he draws his characters." *Cloud Atlas* received several honors, including the British Book Awards Literary Fiction Award. A film version of *Cloud Atlas* is slated for a 2011 release.

Mitchell's next book, *Black Swan Green* (2006), took both fans and literary critics by surprise. The novel is a loosely autobiographical portrait of a 13-year-old boy, Jason, growing up in Worcestershire in 1982. The boy, as Mitchell did, stammers and (secretly) writes poetry; he feels out of place and misunderstood and occasionally makes thoughtful, mature observations. Around him the Cold War is raging; under Prime Minister Margaret Thatcher, England is engaged in a far-off war in the Falklands; Gypsies are camping in the woods near his home, which is causing a hysterical reaction in the town; and Jason, meanwhile, experiences his first kiss, smokes his first cigarette, and hears his first Duran Duran record. Some, including the reviewer for the *Economist* (April 8, 2006), dismissed the novel as run-of-the-mill, with "stock discoveries about sex or yearning speculations about the future [that sound] all too painfully familiar." Many reviewers, however, disagreed with that assessment. "By settling into a single narrative voice, and skipping the pyrotechnics," Daniel Zalewski wrote for the *New Yorker* (April 17, 2006), "Mitchell has come by something that eluded him before: a sense of earned emotion." The book was shortlisted for several honors, including the Quill Book Award.

Mitchell's fifth and latest novel, *The Thousand Autumns of Jacob de Zoet* (2010), is set in 1799 on a man-made island near Nagasaki, Japan. Though the Japanese have effectively isolated themselves from the West, they allow the Dutch to trade and live on that island. The novel's hero, Jacob de Zoet, is a young, uptight clerk employed by the Dutch East India Co. Jacob does his best to juggle two difficult, nearly impossible tasks: ridding the company of corruption and winning the love of a Japanese midwife named Orito. After Orito unexpectedly disappears, Jacob attempts to penetrate the nightmarish, prison-like temple to which she was "sold" by her family. In his review of the novel, Wood pointed to "Mitchell's immense natural gifts: a vast range of characters, each touched with difference; fabulously fluent and intelligent dialogue; scenes that are dramatically shaped but lack obtrusive manipulation; above all, an apparently effortless inhabiting of the Japanese context." Less impressed with the novel was Louisa Thomas, who wrote for *Newsweek* (July 19, 2010), "What seems at first to be such fertility, an overabundance of life, turns out to be weirdly sterile. . . . It is almost as if Mitchell were a brilliant magician who can't help but wave his hands and admit the whole thing is fake." On a more positive note, the novelist and memoirist Dave Eggers, in his review of the book for the *New York Times* (July 4, 2010), concluded, "Its pacing can be challenging, and its idiosyncrasies are many. But it offers innumerable rewards for the patient reader and confirms Mitchell as one of the more fascinating and fearless writers alive."

Mitchell lives with his wife, Keiko, and their two children in West Cork, Ireland. In his profile Mason described him as a "tall, gracious, high-spirited man." Mitchell is currently working on his next novel.

—D.K.

Suggested Reading: magicrealism.co.uk; *New York Times* E p8 Sep. 12, 2000; *New York Times Magazine* p22 June 25, 2010; *New York Times Book Review* p1 July 4, 2010; *New Yorker* Apr. 17, 2006, July 5, 2010; theparisreview.org; thousandautumns.com

Selected Books: *Ghostwritten*, 1999; *Number9Dream*, 2001; *Cloud Atlas*, 2004; *Black Swan Green*, 2006; *The Thousand Autumns of Jacob de Zoet*, 2010

Moffett, Mark W.

Jan. 7, 1958– Ecologist; writer; photographer

Address: National Museum of Natural History, Smithsonian Institution, P.O. Box 37012, Washington, DC 20013

In the last 25 years, the explorer, ecologist, insect expert, photographer, and writer Mark W. Moffett has had close encounters with some of the world's most dangerous and fascinating animals, including deadly frogs, poisonous snakes, carnivorous insects, crocodiles, elephants, tigers, and bears; his adventures have earned him a variety of sobri-

Courtesy of University of California Press

Mark W. Moffett

quets, such as "Dr. Bugs," "the Indiana Jones of Etymology," and, after the primatologist who studied chimpanzees in the wild, "the Jane Goodall of ants." In an interview with *Current Biography*, the source of quotes for this article unless otherwise noted, Moffett conceded with a laugh, "The 19th-century-explorer ideal is kind of outside the norm nowadays. So it's pretty amazing that I'm continuing to do it."

In the mid-1980s, while he was still in graduate school at Harvard University and studying under the Pulitzer Prize–winning biologist Edward O. Wilson, *National Geographic* first published Moffett's stories and photos, which featured extremely close-up shots of ant life. Moffett quickly developed a reputation for his ability to photograph those tiny creatures. He has since contributed many articles and hundreds of photos to *National Geographic*, focusing on rainforest plants, frogs, snakes, spiders, and various insects, especially ants. "For me, life is about telling stories," Moffett, who tends to speak with a youthful excitement about his work, said. "I'm known for my photography, but I could take or leave photography. It's just one means of telling a story. Too much of conservation is presented as dry statistics, and it turns people off. It's not passion, it's not relating to people's emotions. I'm more into figuring out ways of using the arts to tell stories."

Moffett's two major books do just that. *The High Frontier: Exploring the Tropical Rainforest Canopy* (1994) focuses on plant and animal life in the canopy—the continuous, uppermost layer of the forest, made up of treetops—in the rainforests of Africa, Asia, and Latin America. For that book Moffett, along with other scientists, climbed trees, ascend-

ed man-made metal towers, hung on ropes from branches, and took a great many photos of plants and animals. His latest book, *Adventures Among Ants: A Global Safari with a Cast of Trillions* (2010), contains extraordinary stories and photos of ants engaging in such human-like behavior as warfare, hunting, farming, and even the acquisition of slaves. For the *New York Times Book Review* (June 13, 2010), Richard B. Woodward observed that Moffett "writes with an entertainer's instinct for hooking a restless audience. Luckily, our voyeurism about the gory, pitiless world of insects is also his." In a blurb that appears on the back of the book, Jane Goodall wrote, "It is so well written and captures his excitement so wonderfully that it will bring this wealth of information to a far wider audience." Thanks to his multiple appearances on National Public Radio programs, guest spots on the TV shows *Late Night with Conan O'Brien* and *The Colbert Report*, and a recent performance as a headliner for the New York–based public-storytelling group the Moth, Moffett's work is reaching a wide range of people. Toward the end of Moffett's first appearance on *Late Night with Conan O'Brien* (May 23, 2007), a smiling Conan O'Brien told Moffett, "Who the hell are you? . . . You have to come back, because I have to find out more about you. You intrigue me, sir."

Mark W. Moffett was born on January 7, 1958 in Salida, a small town in central Colorado. When he was about seven, he and his family moved to a small town in Michigan, and soon afterward they went to live in Ohio. His mother, Millie, was a homemaker, and his father, Don, was a Presbyterian minister who, upon leaving the church, became a career adviser. Moffett's parents remember their son observing ants while he was still in diapers. A few years later Moffett gave breadcrumbs to an ant colony in his backyard and watched the frenzy that ensued. (That is his first memory.) The ants' social interactions, he recalled, reminded him of how people act, whether fighting or working together. Moffett was in awe of the natural world in general; he loved plants and animals and recalls chasing snakes, frogs, lizards, insects, and rabbits, the last of which he fed to his pet python. He climbed all sorts of trees, including the red maple in his family's backyard, with "the speed and grace of a monkey making its rounds," he recalled. When he was about 12, the family moved to yet another small town: Beloit, Wisconsin. Moffett soon joined the Wisconsin Herpetological Society, a group (otherwise made up of adults) that met once a month to discuss reptiles and amphibians. For the society's newsletter he wrote a paper about his experience of raising three-horned Kenyan lizards. One evening at dinnertime Moffett, who was then 14, got a long-distance call from a zookeeper in South Africa seeking advice on raising that species of lizard. The zookeeper, who had read Moffett's paper, assumed Moffett was a scientist. As he enthusiastically dispensed advice, Moffett felt "awesome." A socially awkward boy, he felt thrilled at having a long conversation with an adult on a subject that was important to him.

Moffett read a lot as a young man. One of the books he found most fascinating was *The Insect Societies* (1971), by the renowned biologist and ant specialist Edward O. Wilson, with whom Moffett would later work as a graduate student at Harvard University, in Cambridge, Massachusetts. Moffett also immersed himself in the adventure stories of such naturalist thinkers and explorers as Charles Darwin, Mary Kingsley, and Henry Walter Bates. He read books by contemporary field scientists, such as Jane Goodall's work on chimpanzees in Tanzania (*My Friends, the Wild Chimpanzees*; *In the Shadow of Man*) and George Schaller's work on lions and gorillas in Africa (*Serengeti: A Kingdom of Predators*; *The Year of the Gorilla*). Growing up in a small town, Moffett fantasized about immersing himself in the study of an animal population in a far-distant country. Despite being well-read and insatiably curious, Moffett did not do well in high school. He eventually dropped out. "I was not interested in school," Moffett recalled. "I was off doing my own thing."

A year after dropping out, Moffett enrolled at Beloit College, a progressive school in Wisconsin, where he studied biology. Excused from many classes when tests showed that he had already mastered their subject matter, he was able to focus on research and exploration. During his freshman year Moffett—bright, curious, and "good at catching things"—was asked by a scientist to join him on a two-month expedition to study venomous snakes in Costa Rica. During that trip Moffett helped catch snakes and crocodiles and also "kept chasing down ants on the sly." In the introduction to his book *Adventures Among Ants*, Moffett wrote: "One day as I wandered alone in the rainforest, lizards squirming in the sack hooked over my belt, I heard a barely audible sound that was subtly different from that made by any creature I had met so far. . . . Looking around, I spied a flow across the ground in front of me—a thick column of quickly moving orange-red ants carrying pieces of scorpions and centipedes, flanked by the pale-headed soldiers equipped with recurved black mandibles [jaws] that were almost impossible to remove after a bite. These were workers of the New World's most famous army ant, *Eciton burchellii*. Later that same day, I would be awestruck by an even more massive highway of ants, several inches wide, formed by the New World's most proficient vegetarians—leafcutter ants hauling foliage home like a long parade of flag-bearers." As an undergraduate Moffett later returned to Costa Rica to study butterflies and went to the Andes Mountains in Peru to study beetles. But he really wanted to study ants. So upon his return from Peru, Moffett wrote a letter to Edward O. Wilson. To his surprise, Wilson wrote back, inviting Moffett to visit his Harvard office. (Wilson had by that point won the first of his Pulitzer Prizes, for his book *On Human Nature* [1979]; he would receive a second in 1991,

for *The Ants*, co-written with Bert Hölldobler.) Moffett eventually did drop by, and after talking with his hero for an hour—they talked like excited children about ants, he recalled—he left with a renewed sense of wonder.

In 1981 Moffett began graduate studies under Wilson at Harvard, which, at its Museum of Comparative Zoology, houses the world's largest collection of preserved ants. One day Moffett was looking through the collection and came across dried specimens of *Pheidologeton*, a species he would come to call the marauder ant. What amazed Moffett most about those ants was how different many were from one another in size and appearance: the smallest workers (minors) were thin and smooth, the medium-sized ones (medians) were somewhat bigger, and the large workers (majors) were, relatively speaking, huge, weighing up to 500 times more than the minors. In *Adventures Among Ants*, Moffett recalled: "I left the collection that day certain I had found something special: few ants display anything close to the extreme polymorphism of *Pheidologeton*." He finished his coursework in a year (rather than the usual two years); then, after receiving a grant from the National Geographic Society, the nonprofit scientific/educational institution that publishes *National Geographic*, Moffett left for Asia.

Moffett spent the next two and a half years traveling through India, Sri Lanka, Nepal, New Guinea, Hong Kong, Singapore, Malaysia, Thailand, Indonesia, and the Philippines. His first grant was small, so he watched his money carefully; during his first six months in India, he spent a total of $100. He was chronically hungry and thin, and he dressed in local attire—usually a lungi (or sarong), a long cloth wrapped around the waist and worn like a skirt. When he encountered problems or had questions relating to his work, he would write letters to Wilson, but because two months would pass before he got replies, he invariably came up with solutions himself—which he came to consider "the ideal education." Because, at that point, Asia's ants had been studied very little, Moffett found a great variety of previously unobserved and "bizarre" ant species. Prior to leaving Harvard he had taught himself to take photos "so people would believe my stories. Otherwise they might think I was dreaming things up while smoking something with a guru." After taking six rolls of film in his first half-year abroad, Moffett sent them undeveloped to *National Geographic*, his sponsor, which, when his film was developed, flew a writer to India to talk to him about publishing the photographs. How did Moffett succeed in getting such a renowned magazine interested in him so early on? "Photography came naturally to me, without practice or effort," Moffett said. "The fact is, I've been looking at ants since I was a kid, so I have this intuition about ants. I was never interested in the camera itself. It's a microscope—it allows me to see the ants—so all I have to do is press a button when my intuition says something important is happening."

Several years elapsed, however, before the magazine published Moffett's work. Prior to seeing his photos, the magazine's editors had assumed that such close-up photos of ants were impossible, so they had committed to working with an artist, who painted close-up images of ants. After his two-and-a-half-year stint in Asia, Moffett returned to the U.S., met with a *National Geographic* photo editor, Mary G. Smith, and, after looking for the first time at the photos he had taken, told her he could do better. He went back to Asia to take more photographs.

Those photographs and Moffett's writing were first published in *National Geographic* in August 1986, when he was still a graduate student. Titled "Marauders of the Jungle Floor," his first, photo-filled story provided extensive details of the life and diversity of marauder ants in South Asia. During that time Moffett grew weary of academia, which he found to be full of "chaos, meetings, and red tape." And as he continued to produce work for *National Geographic*, "it became more and more obvious to me that I was having more fun and able to do more of what I wanted to do by using photography and writing to pay my rent and fund my research." In 1987, after finishing a dissertation on marauder ants, Moffett received a Ph.D. degree in ecology and evolutionary biology.

What began as another story for *National Geographic* became Moffett's first book, *The High Frontier: Exploring the Tropical Rainforest Canopy* (1993). At the time of the book's publication, many media reports featured statistics on the decline of the world's rainforests, detailing numbers of acres and species being lost to development. Finding those reports to be dry, Moffett made it his mission to inform the public about the wonder and majesty of the rainforest and how all of its species live together; if the nature stories in his book could engage people on an emotional level, he reasoned, they would care more about what was at stake. In the foreword to *The High Frontier*, Edward O. Wilson wrote: "The richest habitats on earth are the tropical rainforests. Although they cover only six percent of the land surface, they contain more than half the species of plants and animals on earth. They are also, together with the deep sea floor, the least examined of the biotically rich environments."

Conditions at the tops of trees are very different from those on the rainforest's ground level: there is less humidity, more sunlight, and many microorganisms, insects, and other animals unique to the canopy. Moffett introduced each chapter with a paragraph-length adventure story, with more such tales in the pages that followed. He prefaced the chapter titled "Insects on a Rampage," for example, with this anecdote: As he was climbing a tree in a Peru rainforest, his rope suddenly shifted several inches, causing him to sway and dirt and plant bits to rain down, temporarily blinding him; because at that moment his hands were holding gear, he wrapped his legs around a branch, unwit-

tingly crushing an ant nest. "Ant workers descended my leg and fell like kamikazes on the rest of my body. . . . [They] gashed at my skin with their mandibles and sprayed formic acid into my wounds. I had found my first ant garden the hard way." In addition to insects, the canopy is home to birds, reptiles, and mammals, both big and small. The chapter "Furred and Feathered" includes photos showing creatures in each category in trees: a macaque hanging upside-down, a sloth sitting contentedly, a green viper presumably using its infrared vision, and a spectacled bear standing on a thick branch. The spectacled bear, which can weigh up to 400 pounds, is the most arboreal (tree-dwelling) of all bears; it can even construct a treetop bed made of broken branches. One day, from a tree in a Colombian rainforest, Moffett watched a mother bear climb an adjacent tree in search of bromeliads, the flowing plant that is its main source of food. As the mother bear climbed, her cub watched. "Suddenly," Moffett wrote in the book, "my tree began to shake: the cub was climbing up to check me out. He was larger than I had estimated. As I anxiously shook my foot in his direction, [the] mother let out a roar. I looked around. How can a person in a tree run or hide from an angry canopy bear? Fortunately the cub was as alarmed by the roar as I. He shimmied down my tree and bounded off with his mother into the forest." Moffett's book received some notice in the national press, limited mostly to paragraph-length but uniformly positive reviews. Anne Raver wrote for the *New York Times* (June 5, 1994) that *The High Frontier* was a "cross between an adventure story . . . and poetic biology."

Life as a modern explorer-naturalist has not always been easy for Moffett, who usually puts most of his income back into his work. Following the publication of *The High Frontier*, he experienced a particularly "tough slog," financially and professionally, which lasted over a decade. His attempts to get various projects off the ground—such as further exploration of the tepui mountains and sinkholes of Venezuela—went nowhere. During that time, however, Moffett continued to write and take photos for *National Geographic*. For example, the July 1995 issue featured his report on leafcutter ants of Latin America. He told that story with the aid of his photos—including a full two-page spread of an ant shown 50 times larger than life-size—and an illustration of the ants' city-like underground colonies. For the January 1997 issue, Moffett revisited the subject of forest canopies, this time in the American Northwest, particularly Oregon and Washington, where he took photos from a 250-foot-high gondola and from the top of a 2,000-year-old sequoia. He also set a Guinness world record, climbing and measuring a 365.5-foot coastal redwood with the biologist Steve Sillett. In articles published in three issues at the end of the millennium—February and May 1999 and May 2000—Moffett examined the relationship between ants and plants. Although most aspects of such relationships are neutral, with ants neither harming nor helping the plants, others are mutually beneficial. While plants provide ants with food and shelter, ants attack intruding insects, such as beetles and caterpillars; provide fertilizer after digesting the food they bring back; and rip apart vines that would otherwise weigh trees down or block vital sunlight.

Moffett spent six years working on the book *Adventures Among Ants: A Global Safari with a Cast of Trillions* (2010), which examines ants as individuals and as members of societies. In the book, before getting into details, Moffett gave "a brief primer on ants": their vision is generally poor, but their antennae allow for good senses of touch and smell; they use their mandibles to manipulate objects; each of their feet is flexible and can cling to surfaces with the aid of two claws and soft, adhesive pads; the size of an ant colony can range from four ants to tens of millions; "any ant recognized as an ant is female; males do exist, but they are socially useless [they die soon after mating] and resemble wasps rather than ants," which is why, throughout the book, Moffett refers to the ant as "she"; an ant hatches from its egg as a larva, grows, becomes a pupa, and then emerges as an adult, ready to take on a role, such as worker, soldier, or queen (the size, and therefore role, an ant will take on is predetermined by the amount of food it receives as a larva, as well as the temperature of its immediate environment and its genetic makeup); and ants are global, present on every continent except Antarctica. Combining his scientific expertise with his many adventure stories, Moffett described marauder ants' swarming strategy and intricate highway systems; African army ants' knife-blade-like mandibles, which are capable of piercing flesh; weaver ants' excellent nest-building skills; Amazon ants' use of other ants as slaves; leafcutter ants' farming techniques (they grow edible fungi on pieces of leaves); and Argentine ants' enormous underground colonies—some 1,000 miles long—along the coasts of California, Italy, Spain, and other areas. In his assessment for the *New York Times Book Review*, Richard B. Woodward wrote: "Along with honoring the interdependence of life forms and offering provocative thoughts on the meaning of individuality within a rigid but highly intelligent mass-minded hierarchy, the author heightens awareness of the mundane, deadly struggles for survival that go on every day beneath our feet."

In addition to *National Geographic*, Moffett has written and taken photos for *Natural History* and *International Wildlife* magazines. He is also the author of *Face to Face with Frogs* (2008), in which his large, colorful photos of some of the world's most fascinating frogs accompany his text. That book, unlike his other works, was written for both children and adults. To promote the book Moffett appeared on *The Colbert Report* (February 7, 2008), where Stephen Colbert exclaimed, "This book is so gorgeous, I wish I was in it."

Moffett has received many honors, most notably the 2006 Lowell Thomas Medal for Exploration, from the Explorers Club, and the 2008 Roy Chapman Andrews Society's Distinguished Explorer Award. Since 1998 he has been a research associate in entomology at the Smithsonian Institution. During his time at Harvard's Museum of Comparative Zoology, he served as the associate curator of entomology (1988–91) and as a research associate in entomology (1991–97). At the University of California, Berkeley, he served as a visiting scholar at the Museum of Vertebrate Zoology (1998–2006) and as an associate curator at the Essig Museum (2001–07).

Moffett's wife, Melissa Wells, works as a healthcare consultant when not traveling with her husband in nations including Namibia, Botswana, Zimbabwe, Yemen, Honduras, and Argentina. Her videography of Moffett's research abroad has appeared on the *National Geographic* Web site and in Moffett's 2009 exhibit at the Smithsonian Institution, titled "Farmers, Warriors, Builders: The Hidden Life of Ants," which is currently touring the U.S. Moffett and Wells were married on January 2008, during a research expedition on Easter Island, in the South Pacific. They wore beaten-bark clothes in a traditional Easter Island ceremony held on a volcano rim, a video of which is now archived in the Smithsonian's Anthropology Department. The couple live in the New York City borough of Brooklyn.

—D.K.

Suggested Reading: doctorbugs.com; *Harvard Magazine* (on-line) Jan. 2007; nationalgeographic.com; National Public Radio *Fresh Air* June 17, 2010; *New York Times* Travel p4 June 13, 2010; *Washington Post* C p12 June 10, 2009

Selected Books: *The High Frontier: Exploring the Tropical Rainforest Canopy*, 1994; *Face to Face with Frogs*, 2008; *Adventures Among Ants: A Global Safari with a Cast of Trillions*, 2010

Morneau, Justin

(MORE-no)

May 15, 1981– Baseball player

Address: Minnesota Twins Target Field, 550 Third Ave. N., Minneapolis, MN 55403

Justin Morneau of the Minnesota Twins is "without a doubt one of the best first basemen in baseball and one of the great hitters in the game," Sid Hartman wrote for the Minneapolis, Minnesota, *Star Tribune* (August 15, 2010). Standing at six feet four inches and weighing 235 pounds, the Canadian-born Morneau, who bats left-handed and throws

Hannah Foslien/Getty Images

Justin Morneau

The younger of the two sons of George and Audra Morneau, Justin Ernest George Morneau was born on May 15, 1981 in New Westminster, a city in the Lower Mainland region of British Columbia, Canada. His father, a former child-care worker, owned and ran a sporting-goods store and later worked in a warehouse, and his mother was an elementary-school teacher. His parents had also been athletes: his father played hockey for the Brandon Wheat Kings, an elite junior team in Canada's Western Hockey League (WHL), before being drafted by the now-defunct Minnesota North Stars of the National Hockey League (NHL), and his mother had played competitive fast-pitch softball. (They divorced when Morneau was seven years old.) Also drawn to sports by his older brother, Geordie, Morneau first swung a bat at the age of two. He later played T-ball in New Westminster and, like many other Canadian youths, took up hockey, playing goalie. His favorite sports teams growing up were the Boston Bruins and the Vancouver Canucks, in the NHL, and the Toronto Blue Jays of Major League Baseball (MLB). Morneau's father coached a number of youth baseball teams, including several of Morneau's teams. His father also contributed to Morneau's athletic development by critiquing his swing—which he continued to do well into Morneau's professional years.

Morneau's baseball talent was evident early on, and as a result, he often competed against children in older age divisions. When he was 13 years old, he hit an astonishing 13 home runs in 14 at-bats in a baseball tournament otherwise comprised of 15- and 16-year-olds. At 14 he awed a crowd of spectators at another tournament by hitting a 500-foot home run. Morneau played catcher on New Westminster Secondary School's varsity baseball team and goalie on the varsity hockey team; he also played basketball. Throughout high school Morneau worked hard to perfect his batting mechanics, trying to model his swing after that of John Olerud—then a member of the Blue Jays—who was known for his smooth left-handed stroke. "In high school, he'd go to the batting cage as soon as the lunch bell went and hit 500 balls and then come back for his last class in the afternoon," Morneau's father recalled to John Intini for *Maclean's* (October 16, 2006). "He hit about 300 days a year."

As a junior at New Westminster, Morneau was forced to choose between baseball and hockey. Despite being recruited to play goalie for the WHL's Portland Winterhawks, he decided to focus on baseball. Morneau led New Westminster's varsity baseball team to the national championships in 1997 and 1998. After being named the school's Athlete of the Year during his senior season, Morneau, who also played catcher for Canada's national junior team, decided to forgo college to enter the 1999 MLB draft. By that time most scouts considered him to be among Canada's best hitting and catching prospects. The Minnesota Twins selected Morneau in the third round of that draft (89th overall) and awarded him a contract that included a

right-handed, is able to hit for both average and power, while using discipline and patience at the plate to draw walks consistently and work pitching counts to his advantage. Ron Gardenhire, the Twins' manager since 2002, described Morneau to Jim Mandelaro for the *Rochester (New York) Democrat and Chronicle* (March 22, 2003) as a "pure hitter," and Scott Pitoniak wrote for the same publication (May 8, 2004) that he possesses "a viciously fluid left-handed swing reminiscent of Darryl Strawberry and John Olerud in their primes." After spending several seasons playing in the minor leagues, Morneau made his major-league debut with the Twins in 2003 and has since emerged as one of the team's most potent offensive threats, playing a major role in the team's winning American League (AL) Central Division titles in 2003, 2004, 2006, 2009, and 2010. He had a breakout year in 2006, when he became only the second Canadian in history to win the AL Most Valuable Player (MVP) award, after recording a career-high batting average (.321) and career-high totals in home runs (34) and runs batted in, or RBIs (130). He has since been named to four consecutive All-Star teams (2007–10) and consistently ranks among the AL leaders in most offensive categories. Following a successful 2010 season, which was cut short due to a concussion, Morneau returned to the Twins' lineup in 2011. Commenting on his long recovery, he explained at a press conference, as quoted by Shi Davidi for the Canadian Press (February 21, 2011, on-line), "There's very few things in life that I like more than hitting a baseball. It's a long road and each person goes through it differently. Hopefully we took the right amount of time and everything reacts well."

signing bonus of almost $300,000. Shortly after being signed Morneau produced a flurry of home runs during a ceremonial batting practice in front of Twins executives at Minneapolis's Metrodome. The Twins executive Rob Anthony later described the performance as "the most amazing batting practice display he'd ever seen from a draft pick," as Joe Christensen noted for the *Star Tribune* (April 2, 2005).

Upon entering the Twins' farm system, Morneau was moved from catcher to outfield, where he played only briefly before being assigned to first base. The new position allowed him to hit in every game, while avoiding the physical demands of playing catcher. In the summer of 1999, Morneau joined the Twins' Gulf Coast League team in Fort Myers, Florida, where he batted .302 with nine RBIs in 17 games. He opened the 2000 season there, before playing with the Elizabethton Twins in the Appalachian League. Morneau split the 2001 season among the single-A Quad City River Bandits of the Midwest League, the single-A Fort Myers Miracle of the Florida State League, and the Twins' double-A affiliate in New Britain, Connecticut, notching a cumulative average of .314, along with 97 RBIs and 16 home runs in 127 games. Also in 2001 Morneau played with the Canadian national team at that year's Baseball World Cup.

While Morneau's relatively unimpressive defensive skills remained a topic of debate among observers, his superior offensive talents all but guaranteed his rapid ascent to the majors. As quoted by Peg Hill in the *Vancouver (British Columbia) Sun* (July 23, 2003), a scouting report in the publication *Baseball Yearbook* read: "Morneau won't provide a Gold Glove, but he will bring the best bat in the system." After attending the Twins' annual spring-training camp, Morneau spent the entire 2002 season in New Britain. That summer he was selected for the MLB All-Star Futures Game. In September 2002 Morneau earned a postseason call-up to the triple-A Edmonton Trappers and helped the team win the Pacific Coast League championship.

Morneau entered the 2003 season rated by *Baseball America* as the game's best first-base prospect. That spring he was invited back to the Twins' spring training camp, where he divided his time between first base and designated hitter. In eight games he hit a stellar .429, with three home runs and 10 RBIs. (Morneau had been forced to miss the first week and a half of training camp after fracturing a toe.) Despite those impressive numbers Morneau was sent back to the minors to make room for the Twins' Gold Glove–winning first baseman Doug Mientkiewicz. After 20 games with New Britain, Morneau was promoted to the triple-A Rochester Red Wings of the International League. He played in 37 games with the Red Wings before making his major-league debut, on June 10, 2003, in a game against the Colorado Rockies, in which he collected two hits in four at-bats while serving as the Twins' designated hitter in that 5–0 loss. Morneau picked up four more hits in his next two

major-league contests, and on June 17 he hit his first home run in the majors. Opposing pitchers soon picked up on Morneau's weaknesses at the plate, which included a tendency to swing at—and miss—changeup pitches. In 40 games with the Twins that year, he hit just .226 in 106 at-bats, with four home runs and 16 RBIs. That September Morneau was again sent back to the minors, closing out the year with the Red Wings.

After 37 games with the Red Wings in 2004, during which he displayed more patience and maturity at the plate, Morneau was called back up to the major-league squad in May of that year. He became the Twins' starting first baseman that July, after the team traded Mientkiewicz to the Boston Red Sox. (Mientkiewicz had spent most of July on the disabled list with a wrist injury.) Morneau immediately made an impact as the fourth batter in the lineup, hitting for a .271 average with 19 home runs and 58 RBIs in 74 games. Thanks to Morneau's power output—along with the Cy Young–caliber pitching of the rookie Johan Santana—the Twins won the AL Central Division for the third year in a row, with a 92–70 record. They were knocked out of the play-offs in the first round, losing the series 3–1 to the New York Yankees.

Morneau hoped to build on his solid sophomore campaign in 2005, but an off-season that "could have been dedicated to medical science," as Joe Christensen put it, complicated matters. The 2004–05 winter saw Morneau suffer and recover from appendicitis, chicken pox, pleurisy, and pneumonia, and in March he underwent minor surgery to have a lymph node removed. He had largely regained his health by the start of the regular season; then, after two weeks, he sustained a concussion after being struck in the head by a wild pitch, thrown by the Seattle Mariners' Ron Villone, and missed 13 games. Upon returning to the Twins' lineup later that April, Morneau enjoyed a brief period of success at the plate, before lingering elbow problems and the after-effects of his many illnesses caught up with him, resulting in a slump that saw his batting average dip below .250. Morneau finished the year with a .239 batting average in 141 games, along with career highs in most other offensive categories, including home runs (22), RBIs (79), and total bases (214). His RBI total was also the team's highest. The Twins, meanwhile, finished with a 83–79 record, which placed them third in their division and left them out of the play-offs for the first time since 2001.

After representing Canada in the inaugural World Baseball Classic, held in March 2006, Morneau opened that season in disappointing fashion. By June he was hitting .235, leading members of the Twins organization to question "whether he would ever become a competent hitter," Souhan noted for the *Star Tribune* (November 22, 2006). A turning point in Morneau's season and career came on June 7, when Gardenhire called him in for a meeting during a series against the Seattle Mariners, in which he was performing poorly.

"That was a bit of a wake-up call," Morneau, who had been spending many of his nights partying with friends, recalled to Souhan. "There was a lot of stuff going on off the field that didn't need to be. My focus wasn't what it needed to be. They [Twins officials] opened my eyes. They said, 'You can be this good.'" The heart-to-heart talk with Gardenhire paid immediate dividends, and Morneau began to develop a routine to help improve his focus. From June 8 to the end of the season, he led the majors with a .362 batting average, topping .400 in July, and consistently ranked near the top in the AL in most offensive categories. Morneau and his teammate Joe Mauer—who preceded Morneau in the batting lineup and who was also experiencing a breakout season—became known as the "New M&M Boys," after the original pair with that nickname, Roger Maris and Mickey Mantle. Morneau finished the season with career-highs in batting average (.321), home runs (34), doubles (37), RBIs (130), total bases (331), and slugging percentage (.559). His RBI total ranked second in the AL; it also tied Larry Walker's 1997 record for the most RBIs in a season by a Canadian player and placed him second among the Twins' all-time single-season RBI leaders (behind Harmon Killebrew's 140 in 1969). Morneau's onslaught on offense helped propel the Twins to a 96–66 record and the AL Central Division title—their fourth in five years. Though the Twins were swept in the first round of the play-offs by the Oakland Athletics, Morneau's undeniable impact on the club did not go unnoticed, and he was named the 2006 AL MVP, receiving 15 of 28 first-place votes from the Baseball Writers Association of America. He became the first Canadian to win the AL MVP award and only the second Canadian to be named Most Valuable Player in either league (after Larry Walker, who won the National League MVP award in 1997). Morneau was also the first member of the Twins in 29 years to be presented with that honor (after Rod Carew in 1977). His other end-of-season accolades included the Calvin R. Griffith Award, honoring the Most Valuable Twin, and the 2006 AL Louisville Slugger Silver Slugger Award.

The 2007 season saw Morneau carry his momentum over from the previous year. He was named the AL Player of the Month for May, after batting .314 with 10 home runs and 29 RBIs, and was then selected for his first All-Star Game. In July of that year, Morneau recorded the first three-homer game of his career, in a contest against the Chicago White Sox, becoming only the fourth Twins player to accomplish that feat. Morneau finished the season with a .271 average, 31 home runs, and 111 RBIs. The Twins, however, failed to defend their AL Central title, finishing third in their division with a 79–83 record. In January 2008 Morneau signed a six-year, $80 million contract extension with the Twins, including a $6 million signing bonus. The contract was the most lucrative in Twins history.

During the 2008 season Morneau played in a major league–leading 163 games and batted .300, with 23 home runs and 129 RBIs. That year he matched a career-high total in runs scored (97) and set new career highs with 47 doubles and 76 walks; his doubles total also set a new Twins single-season record. He made his second All-Star Game appearance, as a reserve player for the AL squad, and participated in the 2008 MLB Home Run Derby. While much of the attention at that year's derby was given to the slugger Josh Hamilton, a recovering drug addict with an inspirational story—he hit an astonishing 28 home runs in the first round, the highest total in a single round in the history of the event—Morneau overcame Hamilton in the finals, becoming the first Canadian to win the competition. Following the event Morneau told Christensen for the *Star Tribune* (July 15, 2008): "I think everyone will remember Josh Hamilton's 28 home runs, more than they'll remember that I won the thing. But I'm just glad I was a part of it." The Twins finished the 2008 season tied for first place in the AL Central with an 88–74 record. To determine the division winner, the Twins engaged in a single play-off game with the Chicago White Sox (who had finished with the same record), which they lost, 1–0. Morneau finished the season second in the balloting for the MVP award, losing to the Boston Red Sox's Dustin Pedroia. He won his second Calvin R. Griffith Award and was awarded the Lionel Conacher Award, honoring the Canadian Press Male Athlete of the Year.

Over the next two seasons, Morneau continued to solidify his place among baseball's best first basemen. In 2009 he batted .274 with 30 home runs, 31 doubles, and 100 RBIs, while earning his third All-Star selection. That year Morneau played in 135 games before being placed on injured reserve, the result of a stress fracture in his lower back, which forced him to miss most of September as well as all of the play-offs. The Twins overcame his absence to win the AL Central crown (after defeating the Detroit Tigers in a one-game play-off) but again were ousted in the first round of the postseason.

Morneau returned in 2010 to put up blistering numbers in the season's first half, helping him earn his fourth consecutive All-Star selection. For the first time fans selected him as the AL's starting first baseman. He missed the midseason classic after sustaining a concussion on July 7, when he was accidentally kneed in the head by the Toronto Blue Jays' John McDonald while sliding into second base. Originally placed on the 15-day disabled list, Morneau—who had suffered two past concussions—missed the Twins' final 78 games due to post-concussion syndrome. At the time of his injury, he ranked first in the AL in on-base percentage (.437), second in on-base plus slugging percentage (1.055), third in both batting average (.345) and slugging percentage (.618), seventh in home runs (18), and 10th in RBIs (56). The Twins went on to repeat as AL Central champions, with a 94–68 record, but were again swept in the first round of the play-offs, by the Yankees. Morneau's injury has helped raise awareness of the severity of baseball-related concussions, and in April 2011 the MLB instituted a seven-day disabled list specifically for players who have suffered blows to the head.

Morneau is known among his teammates for his elaborate pregame rituals. He has been married to the former Krista Martin since January 2009. The couple's first child, a daughter named Evelyn, was born in September 2010. That year Morneau was named the Twins' finalist for the Roberto Clemente Award for his many humanitarian efforts.

—C.C.

Suggested Reading: Canadian Press (on-line) Feb. 21, 2011; *Halifax (Nova Scotia) Daily News* Sports p36 July 10, 2007; *Maclean's* p63 Oct. 16, 2006; (Minneapolis, Minnesota) *Star Tribune* C p3 May 25, 2004, S p8+ Apr. 2, 2005, C p1 Nov. 22, 2006, C p1 Apr. 17, 2007, C p1 July 15, 2008, C p3 Aug. 15, 2010; *New York Times* VIII p5 Sep. 24, 2006, B p16 Sep. 30, 2010; *Rochester (New York) Democrat and Chronicle* D p5 Mar. 22, 2003, D p1 May 8, 2004; *Vancouver (British Columbia) Sun* G p5 July 23, 2003, C p7 Apr. 14, 2011

Peter Knutson, courtesy of HarperCollins

Nesbø, Jo

(NESS-buh, yew)

Mar. 29, 1960– Writer; musician

Address: c/o Salomonsson Agency, Svartensgatan 4 116 20, Stockholm, Sweden

"I like that readers know what they are getting with a crime novel," the Norwegian writer Jo Nesbø told Vit Wagner for the *Toronto (Canada) Star* (May 15, 2011). "They know that the writer is going to do something with his right hand that you can see, while doing a trick with his left hand that you can't. I like that game." Nesbø is the creator of the fictional Norwegian detective Harry Hole (pronounced "HOO-leh"), who made his literary-world debut in 1997 and is the hero—or antihero—in a

series that now numbers nine books. In Norway, whose population is not quite five million, some 1.5 million copies of the Harry Hole novels have been purchased; in many other countries including the U.S—where six of the nine books were available in English as of midsummer 2011—the Hole books have been best-sellers, and total sales have topped nine million. Although Nesbø has insisted that his Harry Hole novels have little in common with mysteries or police procedurals by other Scandinavian authors, the Hole novels have garnered comparisons to an array of popular Norwegian, Swedish, Danish, and Finnish crime series. Most prominent among them is the so-called Millennium Trilogy, written by the Swedish journalist and social activist Stieg Larsson, who died in 2004. Laura Wilson wrote for the London *Guardian* (January 22, 2011, on-line) that since the first of Larsson's books, *The Girl with the Dragon Tattoo*, was published (in Sweden in 2005, in the U.S. in 2008), "there's been something of a Nordic noir bonanza . . . with every new Scandinavian crime novel, whether good, bad or indifferent, being engulfed in a blizzard of hyperbole, and every author trailed as 'the next Stieg Larsson'. While this label is neither intelligent nor helpful, it is probably fair to say that, in terms of both critical and commercial success, . . . Nesbø is the writer to whom it is the most applicable."

Nesbø's crime writing has been categorized as "Nordic noir"—"that moody, intricate and emotion-tangled style of crime writing made famous in North America by such writers as Henning Mankell and . . . Larsson," Angela Hickman wrote for Canada's *National Post* (May 30, 2011). Hickman added, "Nesbø brings his own flavour to the genre, starting with his own hard-boiled detective." The novels in the Harry Hole series follow their main character as he pursues killers and other wrongdoers as well as corrupt colleagues, sometimes in the process getting caught in webs of international crime. A troubled, irritable loner, Hole struggles with a drinking problem and his relationships with women. Hole is "a character of contradiction," Nesbø told Scott Timberg for the *Los Angeles*

Times (May 22, 2011). "He's devoted his life to his job—catching killers and putting them behind bars. But at the same time he doesn't really believe this solves any problems—for himself, for the victims, or for society. He likes the hunt—he's not really interested in the catching. He's like some of the serial killers he's been hunting, for whom the actual killing is an anticlimax." Hole, Nesbø told Mary Ann Gwinn for the *Seattle Times* (March 14, 2010, on-line), "doesn't give in easily to his alcoholism. It's not like the traditional hard-boiled detective who wakes up each morning and has a hangover. . . . This is a man whose alcoholism is his Achilles' heel." According to Laura Wilson, "All the characters, both heroes and villains, are toting phenomenal amounts of personal baggage, none more so than Hole himself. He has a full checklist of the character requirements of the noir hero—being melancholic, alcoholic, intuitive, uncompromising, anti-authority and, although often unsanitary, astonishingly attractive to women. . . . He also has the requisite backstory, in the form of a lost love and a dying father with whom he has unfinished emotional business. Apart from this, he has near-superhuman powers of recovery, whether from a mammoth hangover, an avalanche, or the attentions of a frenzied psychopath. And boy, does he need them." Nesbø told Vit Wagner, "Harry Hole is not going to have eternal life, so yes there will be an end to the series. I know how many books there are. And I'm not telling anyone."

"Character is important and largely credible in the Nesbø books, and that is part of what makes them consistently appealing," Wendy Lesser wrote for *Slate.com* (May 11, 2011). "But it is their plots—brilliantly conceived, carefully worked out, and complicatedly satisfying—that finally make them un-put-downable." Barry Forshaw wrote for the London *Independent* (March 5, 2010), "If . . . your taste is for tough and gritty narratives with a relentlessly page-turning quality, well . . . Jo Nesbø is . . . your man. That he is able to combine the urgency of the best storytellers with a keen and intelligent engagement with social issues may well be the reason why Nesbø is shaping up to be the next big name in Scandinavian crime fiction."

Earlier in his career Nesbø earned his living as a stockbroker and a member of a highly successful band called Di Derre. He told an interviewer for the blog Irresistible Targets (June 9, 2010), "I still play 50–60 gigs a year. Just me and a bass player, except in summer when the full band gets together to play festivals. It's a hobby now, I do it for fun." Nesbø has also written a theatrical musical, several children's books, short stories, and the novel *Headhunters*, in which Harry Hole is not a character.

Jo Nesbø was born on March 29, 1960 in Oslo, Norway, and raised in the coastal city of Molde, near the Norwegian Sea. His mother was a librarian; his father, a businessman, "grew up in Brooklyn and he and my grandparents told me all these stories about the Bay Ridge area, it was almost like I grew up there too," Nesbø told Blake Wilson for

the *New York Times* (March 12, 2010, on-line). Nesbø's brother, Knut, whose birth followed his by one year, is a sports reporter for the Norwegian Broadcasting Corp. The brothers grew up surrounded by books; in a question-and-answer section on his Web site, Jo Nesbø wrote, "My father used to spend every afternoon reading in the sitting room. He told stories too, long, familiar narratives told so well that we wanted to hear them again and again." The first novel Nesbø has recalled hearing his father read out loud was William Golding's 1954 classic, *Lord of the Flies*. "My father wasn't too sure if the Nobel Prize–winning author was suitable for a boy aged just seven, but I insisted. Why? Because of the cover: a blood-dripping pig's head on a stake." He also wrote, "As I listened to my father read, I knew I wanted to try and write myself. I was already impressing kids my own age, even slightly older ones, with my gruesome ghost stories."

Nesbø's main boyhood passion was soccer. As a teenager he played for Molde Fotballklubb, a professional soccer team. (His brother played for Molde FK as well.) He dreamed of joining Tottenham Hotspur, a London-based English Premier League club, but injuries to the ligaments in his knees thwarted that desire. Because he had devoted little time to his schoolwork and had poor grades, Nesbø realized that he had few career options. To remedy that situation he signed up for military service. During his three years with the army, he attended high-school-level classes, became self-disciplined, and began reading literary classics. "When I finally held my high school diploma in my hands . . . , with top-notch grades, I experienced a deep, heartfelt satisfaction I had never felt before, and perhaps not since either," he wrote in the autobiographical sketch posted on his Web site (the source of quotes in this article unless otherwise stated). "Now I could get into pretty much any school or any program I wanted."

In 1982 Nesbø enrolled in a program in economics and business administration at the prestigious Norwegian School of Economics and Business Administration, in Bergen; he took courses for three years at the undergraduate level and during the final, fourth year, at the master's-degree level. He earned a Norwegian *Siviløkonom* degree in 1986. (Literally, *siviløkonom* means "civil economist" and is considered a professional title.) Nesbø then began working as a stockbroker in Oslo. (According to various sources, before he became a novelist he also worked as a taxi driver and a freelance journalist.) At one point he was tapped to work in the options division of what was then known as DnB NOR ASA (the Norwegian Bank Co.), the largest financial-services group in Norway. Concurrently, with friends, he formed a band, De Tusen Hjem ("The Thousand Homes"), which played "the kind of industrial noise rock you get when you're really bad at playing, have plenty of electricity, big amps and practice in a basement," he wrote. He also wrote pop songs, and in 1992 he formed a new band, Di Derre ("That There"), with himself on guitar and vocals; his brother, Knut, on vocals and guitar; Sverre Beyer on drums (later replaced by Espen Stenhammer); and Magnus Larsen on bass guitar. Di Derre, which performs pop-rock music, initially served as the house band at Café Felix, in Oslo. After signing a contract with the Sonet label, the band toured the country and released four albums—*Den Derre med Di derre* ("The Derre with the Derre," 1993), *Jenter og Sånn* ("Girls and Stuff," 1994), *Gym* (1996), and *Slå Meg Pa!* ("Turn Me On!," 1998). Thanks to the single "Jenter" ("Girls"), on the second album—a song that Norwegian radio stations still air—Di Derre became a huge success in Norway; the single reached the European pop charts, and Nesbø and his bandmates became national pop stars.

After a year in which he spent days at his workstation and nights at gigs, Nesbø became exhausted. "I was so burned out that I hated everything and everyone I worked with, including myself," he wrote. He arranged a six-month leave of absence from his day job and performance and traveled with his laptop to Australia, with plans to write a book about his band. Instead, he completed a crime novel—the first in the Harry Hole series. Among his inspirations were crime novels by the American writer Jim Thompson (1906–77), whose more than 30 books include *The Killer Inside Me*, *Savage Night*, *The Grifters*, and *Pop. 1280*. Nesbø told Scott Timberg, "I wasn't that into crime novels at all, but a friend introduced me to the work of Jim Thompson—I loved all his books. When I read [Raymond] Chandler, it was a bit comic, these romantic, melancholy monologues. To me, Thompson was braver, more extreme." Other American authors whom Nesbø admires include Mark Twain, Ernest Hemingway, Charles Bukowski, Philip Roth, Don DeLillo, and Cormac McCarthy.

After Nesbø returned to Norway, he sent his manuscript to various publishers under a pseudonym, because he did not want any of them to be "tempted to publish a crap book by a pop-star-turned-writer," he wrote. He also resigned from his stockbroker's job in order to devote himself to writing. "My father had died two years before: the very same year he had retired and was going to start writing the book he had been planning about his experiences during the Second World War. But his time ran out. And I wasn't going to let the same thing happen to me." Within three weeks Nesbø had acquired a publisher. His first novel, *Flaggermusmannen* ("The Bat Man," 1997), whose cover identifies him by his real name, introduced Harry Hole, an incorruptible detective with the Oslo Crime Squad who often takes actions without the permission of his superiors. Nesbø told Malin Rising for the Associated Press, as posted on Military.com (May 11, 2011), that "Hole" was the name of a policeman he met during his childhood and also refers to the two main characters in the British film noir *The Third Man* (1949)—Harry Lime (played by Orson Welles) and Holly Martins (por-

trayed by Joseph Cotten). In *Flaggermusmannen* Hole must help Australian police find the person who killed a minor Norwegian celebrity in Australia. During the course of the investigation, Hole falls in love with the murdered woman's best friend and finds himself entangled in a seedy criminal underworld. "With a mix of elation and terror I waited for the reviews to deal with that pop music guy who dared to write crime fiction!" Nesbø wrote. "But the reviews were on topic, serious and focused on the book, not on me as a person. And, best of all, they were positive." A best-seller in Norway, *Flaggermusmannen* won the 1997 Riverton Prize for best Norwegian crime novel and the Glass Key Award from the group Crime Writers of Scandinavia.

The next novel in the series, *Kakerlakkene* ("The Cockroaches," 1998), follows Hole in Bangkok, Thailand, as he attempts to identify the killer of the Norwegian ambassador to that Southeast Asian nation. The third book, *Rødstrupe* (2000), was the first Hole book to be translated into English, with the title *The Redbreast*, and became available in the U.S. in 2006. (Although Nesbø is fluent in English, all the English versions of the Hole books have been translated by Don Bartlett, a native of Great Britain.) In *The Redbreast*, while trying to ensure that a dangerous neo-Nazi winds up in prison, Hole stumbles across an assassination plot against Norway's crown prince. Linked to the main story is a historical subplot about Norway's struggle against Hitler's invading forces during World War II. "It was the story my father had wanted to tell, about Norwegians on both sides of Nazism during the Second World War," Nesbø explained. "About the mythical self-image of the Norwegian people and a nation actively resisting Hitler. About why people make the choices they do and the victor's privilege of writing history. If writing the first two books was like playing a solo on an acoustic guitar, this was like directing an orchestra. When it was finished I knew that if the critics slaughtered the book or if it failed commercially, I would have to give up writing and find something new. Because *The Redbreast* was simply the best I had to offer."

In a representative enthusiastic assessment of *The Redbreast*, Marilyn Stasio wrote for the *New York Times Book Review* (December 23, 2007) that early in the story "an old man who has just received a death sentence from his doctor goes into the palace gardens in Oslo and kills an ancient oak tree. 'Yes!' you think. 'What a terrible act, but what wonderful symbolism!' And you'll be amazed when, hundreds of pages later, the real reason for the aboricide is revealed, along with the answers to other seemingly minor mysteries (including the significance of the title) that figure in the novel's ingenious design. The engineering of the interlocking plot pieces is intricate because it has to support Nesbø's complicated ideas—and dire thoughts—about Norwegian nationalism, past and present. While giving his ambitious book the form of a police procedural, featuring Harry Hole, an attractive if familiarly flawed loose cannon of a cop, the author expands his street-level subplots into a narrative that reaches all the way back to World War II, when Norway was under German occupation." In a review for *USA Today* (January 16, 2008, online), Dennis Moore wrote that Nesbø's "scenes are so vivid that you can imagine them playing across the big screen. The pacing is swift. The plot is precise and intricate. The characters are intriguing. And the novel combines two of the best cinematic genres: war sagas and crime thrillers." *Rødstrupe* won the 2000 Norwegian Booksellers' Prize for best novel of the year. In 2004 members of Norwegian book clubs chose *Rødstrupe* as the best Norwegian crime novel ever written.

Subsequent books in the Hole series are *Sorgenfri* (2002; published in the U.S. as *Nemesis* in 2008); *Marekors* (2003; *The Devil's Star*, 2005); *Frelseren* (2005; *The Redeemer*, 2009); *Snømannen* (2007; *The Snowman*, 2011); and *Panserhjerte* (2009; *The Leopard*, 2011). As *The Leopard* begins, Hole has quit his job in Norway and has traveled to an opium den in Hong Kong, China. A ruse involving his ailing father brings him back to Oslo, where Hole is drawn into the search for a serial killer. "*The Leopard* is about more than catching a serial killer," Hickman wrote. "The politics of the Oslo police are ever-present and the plot swirls through motives of international business ventures and the ongoing war in the Congo. Nesbø also fills out his characters with nuanced pop-culture interests and families who remain an active presence in their lives." Echoing a complaint of a few other critics, Hickman also wrote, "His characters' lives, though, are exhausting, and perhaps none moreso than Hole's. His history of substance abuse wears on him throughout the story, and with Nesbø so closely tied to his hero, their eight-novel relationship might be starting to show its age." Nesbø told Hickman, "The novels are getting darker and darker, and Harry is drifting toward the dark side. I like the guy, so it's depressing that he can't seem to pull himself together and get a life."

The ninth Hole novel, *Gjenferd* ("Phantom"), went on sale in Norway in June 2011. Excerpts (in English translation) from a half-dozen reviews of *Gjenferd* for Norwegian periodicals, posted on the Web site of Nesbø's literary agency, Salomonsson, extolled that latest installment of the series as "great, somber summer reading," "masterfully done," "a crime novel that pleases on every level,"and "possibly the best in the series."

Nesbø's other published books include the short-story collection *Karusellmusikk* (2001) and the stand-alone book *Headhunters* (2008), which was scheduled to go on sale in the U.S. in September 2011. An adaptation of *Headhunters* for the big screen, produced by the Swedish company Yellow Bird, was slated to open in Europe in August 2011; another film based on *Headhunters* will be produced by Americans. Nesbø has also written three books for children about a daft inventor. The two

available in English are *Doctor Proctor's Fart Powder* (2010) and *Bubble in the Bathtub* (2011). Nesbø told Monica Hesse for the *Washington Post* (May 3, 2011, on-line) that the Doctor Proctor books grew out of his daughter's requests and suggestions for stories. "When you're an established name, you know that a children's book will have a pretty good chance of getting picked up," he said to Hesse. "Like Madonna," who has published five children's books. "It's not that I had this great idea."

The worst criminal attacks in Norway since World War II were committed on July 22, 2011 by Anders Behring Breivik, a Norwegian Christian fundamentalist and right-wing extremist; Breivik killed at least 77 people by means of a car bomb in Oslo and shootings at a youth camp on Utøya, a nearby island. In response, Nesbø published an op-ed piece in the *New York Times* (July 26, 2011, online). "For many years, it seemed as if nothing changed in Norway," he wrote. "You could leave the country for three months, travel the world, through coups d'état, assassinations, famines, massacres and tsunamis, and come home to find that the only new thing in the newspapers was the crossword puzzle. It was a country where everyone's material needs were provided for. . . . Until Friday, we thought of our country as a virgin—unsullied by the ills of society. An exaggeration, of course. And yet." He concluded, "If there is no road back to how things used to be, to the naïve fearlessness of what was untouched, there is a road forward. To be brave. To keep on as before. To turn the other cheek as we ask: Is that all you've got? To refuse to let fear change the way we build our society."

Nesbø's honors include the William Nygaard Bursary Award (2002), for *Nemesis*; a Special Commendation from the Finnish Academy of Crime Writers (2007), for *The Devil's Star*; and the Norwegian Booksellers' Prize (2007) and Norwegian Book Club Prize (2008), for *The Snowman*. The British Crime Writers Association shortlisted *The Redbreast* for the Duncan Lawrie International Dagger in 2007, and the Mystery Writers of America nominated *Nemesis* for a 2010 Edgar Award.

Nesbø's only child, a daughter, is 11 years old. Nesbø is not married to the girl's mother. He lives in Oslo, in an apartment in which he installed a rock-climbing wall.

—W.D.

Suggested Reading: (Canada) *National Post* B p9 May 30, 2011; Jo Nesbø Web site; *Living Scotsman* (on-line) June 27, 2011; (London) *Guardian* (on-line) Jan. 22, 2011; *Los Angeles Times* E p6 May 22, 2011; *New York Times* (on-line) Mar. 12, 2010; *Slate.com* May 11, 2011; *Toronto (Ontario, Canda) Star* E p1 May 15, 2011; *Wall Street Journal* (on-line) May 11, 2011; *Washington Post* (on-line) May 3, 2011

Selected Books in English Translation: Harry Hole series—*The Devil's Star*, 2005; *The Redbreast*, 2006; *Nemesis*, 2008; *The Redeemer*, 2009; *The Snowman*, 2011; *The Leopard*, 2011

Courtesy of Marco Borggreve

Nézet-Séguin, Yannick

(nay-ZAY say-GHEN, YAH-nik)

1975– Orchestra conductor

Address: Philadelphia Orchestra, 260 S. Broad St., Suite 1600, Philadelphia, PA 19102

"Though a diminutive figure," the music maestro Yannick Nézet-Séguin "exudes charisma on the podium," Anthony Tommasini wrote for the *New York Times* (August 6, 2009). "He has striking musical ideas and communicates with his players through gestures that blend kinetic animation with elegant precision." Since June 2010 Nézet-Séguin—a Canadian-born conductor of symphonic repertoire and opera—has been the music director designate of the Philadelphia Orchestra, whose previous leaders have included the luminaries Eugene Ormandy, Riccardo Muti, and Leopold Stokowski. He also serves as music director of the Rotterdam Philharmonic, of the Netherlands; artistic director and principal conductor of the Orchestre Métropolitain in Montreal, Canada; and principal guest conductor of the London Philharmonic Orchestra, in England.

Since he was a child, Nézet-Séguin—perhaps the most celebrated conductor to have emerged from Canada—has wanted to lead orchestras. "The

funny thing is that when you're that young, you dream of something without really knowing what it implies," he told Tom Service for the London *Guardian* (October 15, 2009). "But, on my way to becoming a conductor, I haven't had many surprises. I had a dream, and that dream has come true, and there is something normal about it, in a way." Nézet-Séguin formed a close relationship with the legendary maestro Carlo Maria Giulini, attending by invitation all of the older man's rehearsals and concerts in 1997 and 1998, before assuming the Montreal Métropolitain's leadership in 2000, at age 25. He made his European conducting debut four years later. He has guest-conducted orchestras around the world, including the Toronto Symphony; the philharmonic orchestras of Berlin, Germany, Vienna, Austria, and Stockholm, Sweden; the Mozarteum Orchestra of Salzburg, in Austria; the Vancouver Symphony, in Canada; the Orchestre National de France; and the Chamber Orchestra of Europe. In the United States he has conducted in Boston, Massachusetts; New York; Washington, D.C.; and Los Angeles, California, among other cities. "When I'm on the podium, it feels natural, like I belong there," Nézet-Séguin said to Steven Mazey for the *Ottawa (Canada) Citizen* (February 20, 2010). "But off the podium, I of course have this fear that it could all end tomorrow. . . . I am always reminding myself how lucky I am to be here."

Yannick Nézet-Séguin was born in Montreal, Canada, in 1975. His last name combines the maiden name of his mother, Claudine Nézet, and the surname of his father, Serge Séguin. His parents both taught education at the Université du Québec à Montréal; he has two sisters, Sylviane and Isabelle, who are also teachers. When he was five years old, Nézet-Séguin began to take piano lessons with Jeanne-d'Arc Lebrun-Lussier, and by the age of 10, he had decided that he wanted to become a conductor. He was inspired after attending concerts by the Swiss conductor Charles Dutoit, who was maestro of l'Orchestre Symphonique de Montréal at the time. "I became fascinated by it and began to wave a stick with recordings," he recalled to Steve Smith for *Time Out New York* (September 9, 2010). "Dutoit would introduce pieces and be very accessible, and that had a big impact on me as a little boy," he told Robert Everett-Green for the Toronto, Canada, *Globe and Mail* (February 4, 2008). "If it had not been for this, I would maybe never have been a conductor."

During his youth Nézet-Séguin attended the Conservatoire de Musique du Québec, in Montreal, where he studied piano, composition, chamber music, and conducting. "My main conducting teacher was actually my piano teacher"—Anisia Campos—"because a conductor is also an interpreter," he recalled to Everett-Green. "She was a very old-school teacher, very strict and demanding. She wouldn't allow any compromise in my piano study just because I wanted to be a conductor. I remember some years, I was really angry with her, because she wanted to develop some aspect of my playing that I considered very superficial. But I'm so grateful now. I couldn't have wished for a better teacher." He learned from her, as he was quoted as saying by the *Australian* (January 25, 2001, online), that "the best way to develop as a conductor is to become a better musician." For two summers when he was a teenager, Nézet-Séguin also studied choral conducting at Westminster Choir College, in Princeton, New Jersey. "I learned early in Princeton that everything you do has an impact on the sound," he explained to Matthew Gurewitsch for the *New York Times* (August 2, 2009). "I do move a lot. But I try never to be calculating or self-conscious about what I do. Maybe I just conduct big because of my small stature." When he was 19 years old, he became music director of the Choeur Polyphonique de Montréal, for which he had been singing since he was a child.

In the 1990s Nézet-Séguin furthered his education through master classes with figures including the preeminent Italian conductor Carlo Maria Giulini, who died in 2005. "[Giulini] remains completely special for me," Nézet-Séguin said in the interview with Tom Service. "He used to say that conductors were 'luggage and transit.' That was their function: the composers need their masterpieces to be carried and brought to people, so that's what we're doing. It's about not taking yourself too seriously." "Young as I was, he treated me almost as a colleague," he told Matthew Gurewitsch, "always putting my questions back into my own hands. Giulini always said that gesture must be the extension of your thought. When something goes wrong, it's because you don't have a clear idea. When the idea is simply the extension of your thought, the gestures will be clear and immediate."

Nézet-Séguin was named chorus master and assistant conductor of the Opéra de Montréal in 1998. Two years later, when he was 25, he received the Virginia-Parker Award, given annually to a Canadian classical musician or conductor under the age of 32. That honor brought him a great deal of attention, and in the same year the Orchestre Métropolitain appointed him as its principal conductor and artistic director. In 2004 Nézet-Séguin made his European conducting debut, with the Orchestre National du Capitole de Toulouse, based in France. Around the same time he began a five-year tenure as the principal guest conductor of the Victoria Symphony, in Canada. From 2005 to 2007 he served as a guest conductor of the Rotterdam Philharmonic Orchestra, and in 2008 he replaced Valery Gergiev as its principal conductor. "I never imagined I was a real candidate," he admitted to Everett-Green. "Maybe that's what got me the job, because I didn't act like someone who wanted the job. I just worked the way I always do." Also in 2008 Nézet-Séguin was appointed as principal guest conductor of the London Philharmonic and led the Philadelphia Orchestra for the first time, conducting Tchaikovsky's Symphony no. 6 and Rachmaninoff's Piano Concerto no. 2, with André Watts as soloist.

In 2009 Nézet-Séguin made his well-received New York Metropolitan Opera debut, with Richard Eyre's revival of Georges Bizet's *Carmen*. Anthony Tommasini wrote in a review of the performance for the *New York Times* (January 2, 2010), "The singers benefited immensely from the work of the rising 34-year-old Canadian conductor Yannick Nézet-Séguin . . . who led a bracing, fleet and fresh account of the score, although he started the rousing prelude at a breakneck, frenetic tempo." The following year Nézet-Séguin conducted Nicholas Hytner's production of Giuseppe Verdi's *Don Carlo*. "Few Verdi singers know how to shape a recitative so eloquently—palpably aided by Nézet-Séguin . . . ," the music critic David Patrick Stearns wrote for the *Philadelphia Inquirer* (November 24, 2010). "He found inner voices in the orchestra that propel the action; blends brought new coloristic dimensions to even the most familiar passages; climaxes were masterfully built but never forced."

In June 2010 Nézet-Séguin, at 35, was selected as the eighth music director of the Philadelphia Orchestra; he signed a seven-year contract and will officially assume the position in the 2012–13 season. Nézet-Séguin has said that he felt a connection with the orchestra right away. "In every orchestra it's an average of very dedicated people and some who are worn down by the years," he explained to Marcia Adair for the *Los Angeles Times* (August 1, 2010). "In this orchestra I felt that it was so easy to get roughly everyone involved. It's my role to awaken the fire and joy of music making. Maybe for some people it's strange; for me that's why it clicked." Blair Bollinger, the bass trombone player who headed the orchestra's Conductor Search Committee, said to Adair, "Right from the first rehearsal the orchestra really responded to him. He has a fantastically clear technique, which makes it very comfortable." The choral conductor and tuba player Alain Cazes said to Robert Everett-Green for the *Globe and Mail* (October 30, 2010), "[Nézet-Séguin] has the ability to transfer his passion to the orchestra. . . . He's a great communicator. His requirements become our requirements. And he's always polite and respectful." Everett-Green wrote that Nézet-Séguin "describes himself as a risk-taker, willing to follow the impulse of the moment in performance even if it means colouring over the lines a little." After his appointment was announced, Nézet-Séguin attended a Philadelphia Phillies baseball game at Citizens Bank Park, where he conducted tens of thousands of fans in a seventh-inning-stretch rendition of the song "Take Me Out to the Ball Game."

Nézet-Séguin has said that the offer to lead the Philadelphia Orchestra came much sooner than he thought it would. "I was expecting to have to meet the orchestra for a third, fourth or fifth visit," he said in the October 30, 2010 interview with Everett-Green. "I was expecting that one of the big five American orchestras would be somewhat cold, or playing their usual stuff very professionally. . . .

But there was something extremely available about those musicians, and I responded very strongly to that." While the Philadelphia Orchestra has been struggling financially, many hope that Nézet-Séguin will help reverse the company's fortunes. Toward that end the conductor has added a week of performances to the three weeks he had already scheduled for the 2011–12 season in Philadelphia, where his appearances have proven to be highly popular.

In addition to his upcoming post with the Philadelphia Orchestra, Nézet-Séguin continues to serve as music director of the Rotterdam Philharmonic and principal guest conductor of the London Philharmonic. He also plans to maintain his post as artistic director and principal conductor of Montreal's Orchestre Métropolitain. "As I'm going on with this career, I realize every day that I need my place in Montreal, my hometown, because I love the city," he said in the interview with Steven Mazey. "It helps me settle down. Whenever I get back to the Orchestre Métropolitain, I feel it is rewarding musically, and I think we are still growing together. If that were not the case, I would say that it's time to move on." He added, "To do five or six concerts a season with this orchestra in which I have been growing for the past 10 years is not a lot to ask."

Nézet-Séguin has received numerous honors, including a Royal Philharmonic Society Award (2009) and a National Arts Centre Award (2010), the latter of which was presented as part of the Governor-General's Performing Arts Awards and included a commemorative medallion and $25,000. In April 2011 he was granted an "Honoris causa Doctorate" by the Université du Québec à Montréal, "to acknowledge his radiating international musical career and for his relentless endeavour towards promoting classical music." He has made a series of critically acclaimed live recordings, notable among them a 2007 CD of Bruckner's Seventh Symphony and a 2011 disc of Berlioz's *Symphonie Fantastique*.

In 2012 Nézet-Séguin will conduct for the first time at the Royal Opera House in London's Covent Garden; he will also officially become the new musical director of the Philadelphia Orchestra. His contract with the London Philharmonic Orchestra extends to 2014, and his contracts with the Orchestre Métropolitain and the Rotterdam Philharmonic will be in effect until 2015. "For me it's a question of enjoying as much as possible whatever I'm doing, wherever I am," Nézet-Séguin told Steve Smith, after being asked about his professional goals. "I'm privileged that my career is now leading to the main cities and the most wonderful opera houses and orchestras. But I've decided not to project myself and say, 'Okay, after this I would like to be there.'" Nézet-Séguin has said that in the future he will cut back on his appearances as a guest conductor. His primary goal, he told Smith, is "to remain as happy as I am—and for the rest, I'll trust life."

—J.P.

Suggested Reading: *Los Angeles Times* E p10 Aug. 1, 2010; *New York Times* (on-line) Aug. 2, 2009; *Ottawa (Canada) Citizen* G p1 Feb. 20, 2010; *Philadelphia Inquirer* D p1 July 19, 2010; (Toronto, Canada) *Globe and Mail* R p1 Feb. 4, 2008

Selected Recordings: *Nino Rota*, 2003; *Conversations for Trombone and Piano*, 2003; *Mahler: Symphony no. 4*, 2004; *Kurt Weill*, 2005; *Mozart: Lieder*, 2006; *Debussy: La Mer, Prélude à l'aprés-midi d'un faune, Britten: Four Sea Interludes, Mercure: Kaleidoscope*, 2007; *Bruckner: Symphony no. 7*, 2007; *Bruckner: Symphony no. 8*, 2009; *Beethoven, Korngold: Violin Concertos*, 2009; *Fantasy: A Night at the Opera*, 2010; *Ravel: La Valse, Daphnis et Chloe Suite no. 2*, 2010; *Brahms: German Requiem*, 2010; *Richard Strauss: Ein Heldenleben/Four Last Songs*, 2011; *Schmitt: La Tragédie de Salomé, Franck: Symphonie en Ré*, 2011; *Berlioz: Symphonie fantastique, Cléopatre*, 2011

Fred R. Conrad/*The New York Times*, courtesy of the Penguin Group

Nocera, Joe

May 6, 1952– Journalist

Address: New York Times, *620 Eighth Ave., New York, NY 10018*

In the spring of 2011, Joe Nocera became a columnist for the op-ed page of the *New York Times*, which Ted Nesi—interviewing Nocera for Public Radio International (April 11, 2011, on-line)—

called "the most valuable real estate in American journalism." Nocera began writing for the *New York Times* and the weekly *New York Times Magazine* in 2005, contributing the "Talking Business" column to the daily paper and longer articles to the Sunday edition. From 1995 to 2005 he worked at *Fortune* in a variety of positions, including editorial director, and prior to that he cut his teeth as a business writer through columns for *Esquire* and *GQ* and various positions as a writer and editor for *Washington Monthly*, *Texas Monthly*, and *New England Monthly*, among other publications. Nocera is known for his literary approach to business and financial journalism; he often mixes narratives, anecdotes, and informed observations with the requisite facts and figures. His reporting and commentary have run the gamut of business writing, covering Wall Street and its power players, elected officials and government policy, and the business side of sports, entertainment, art, and more; in the past few years, he has also written extensively about the recession that began in 2007. He is the co-author of the book *All the Devils Are Here: The Hidden History of the Financial Crisis* (2010), which chronicles the events that led to the recession, and the sole author of *A Piece of the Action: How the Middle Class Joined the Money Class* (1994) and *Good Guys and Bad Guys: Behind the Scenes with the Saints and Scoundrels of American Business (and Everything in Between)* (2008), a collection of articles.

Jack Shafer wrote for *Slate.com* (June 12, 2006), "Nocera demystifies the world of business with original thinking, brainy reporting, and the ability to see around corners. Although opinionated, he's not really a pundit who tells you what he thinks about executive pay or stock options or antitrust as much as what he's learned from his reporting." Shafer also observed, "Not every Nocera column comes equipped with a solution to that week's business-world problem. But when Nocera reaches a conclusion, he's not shy."

Of Irish and Italian ancestry, Joseph Nocera was born on May 6, 1952 and grew up in Providence, Rhode Island. He attended Classical High School in Providence, where he had what he described to Nesi as "memorable teachers" and a "wonderful education" that was "based around writing." While there he played on the basketball team. At the time he graduated, in 1970, he planned to study math in college. "I realized when I got to college," Nocera told Nesi, "that I was never going to be good enough in that," so he switched his major to journalism, earning a B.S. degree from Boston University, in Massachusetts, in 1974. He told Nesi that he was inspired to pursue journalism after reading the influential magazine articles of that time. He explained that he "didn't have the sort of investigative" proclivities of the *Washington Post* reporters Bob Woodward and Carl Bernstein, who uncovered the Watergate political scandal, but added, "What was also happening, not just because of Watergate but also because of [the Vietnam War]

and all that stuff, was the magazines in America at that time—it was like a golden age. *Esquire* was publishing Norman Mailer. *Rolling Stone* was publishing Tom Wolfe. *Harper's* was publishing what was edited by Willie Morris. The *Atlantic* was fabulous. So you're in college and you're reading these wonderful stories, and you're thinking—man, that's what I'd really like to do."

After graduating Nocera worked as a freelance writer in Boston before joining the Capitol Hill News Service, in Washington, D.C., for which he covered stories in Pennsylvania and served as bureau chief. For two years beginning in 1978, he was an editor at *Washington Monthly*, and from 1982 to 1986 he was a senior writer with *Texas Monthly*. During the 1980s he also served as a contributing editor at *Newsweek* and as executive editor of *New England Monthly*. One of his stories for the *Texas Monthly*, published in October 1982 and available on texasmonthly.com, focused on the financier and "corporate raider" T. Boone Pickens Jr. as he led his oil company, Mesa Petroleum, in major acquisitions. At the beginning of the article, Nocera, demonstrating his ability to reveal the "big picture" by focusing on a smaller scenario, discussed a minor business convention in order to shed light on the high-stakes world of Wall Street mergers. He wrote that for the very busy Pickens, "if there were good reasons for ducking the convention, there was a better one for attending: it was the best way to keep America's oil analysts from knowing what he was up to. His concern was easy to understand. Because what analysts do is largely predictive in nature—their ultimate goal is to forecast for the investment houses that employ them whether a stock will go up or down—they are always on that minute scrap of information that will give them an edge in predicting stock prices. As a result, analysts are, both by nature and by training, gossip-mongers. And had Boone Pickens canceled his appearance at their convention, the rumors that had swirled around him for over a year would have gathered and swelled like a tornado. Every oil analyst in America would have had the same thought at the same moment: if Boone Pickens is so busy that he has to cancel his speech here, he must be planning something . . . he must be getting close to making a deal . . . he must be preparing to [attempt a takeover of] Cities Service Company! Which, of course, was exactly what Pickens was doing." Nocera also wrote articles for *Texas Monthly* that were unrelated to finance. In an article from the November 1986 issue, for example, he demonstrated the failings of the Texas mental-health system by portraying the struggles of a schizophrenic man trapped within it.

From 1988 to 1990 Nocera worked at *Esquire*, writing the "Profit Motive" column; he wrote the same column for *GQ* from 1990 to 1995. In the latter year he began a decade-long stint at *Fortune*, holding the successive posts of contributing writer, editor-at-large, executive editor, and, finally, editorial director. Meanwhile his 1994 book, *A Piece* of the Action: How the Middle Class Joined the Money Class, won the New York Public Library's Helen Bernstein Award for best nonfiction book of the year. In the book Nocera observed that money managers' successful efforts to circumvent governmental regulations limiting interest rates, combined with the willingness of middle-class citizens to take on credit cards, adjustable-rate mortgages, stocks, mutual funds, and more, led to a "money revolution." The book also includes profiles of finance-industry pioneers such as Charles Schwab and Charles Merrill. In an assessment for the *New York Times Book Review* (October 23, 1994), Lawrence S. Ritter wrote, "Mr. Nocera sets out to demonstrate 'how the middle class joined the money class' and he does just that: credit cards and mutual funds have indeed, for better or worse, transformed the spending and saving habits of millions of middle-income Americans. . . . How it all happened is a story worth telling, and Mr. Nocera narrates it admirably, with rare insight and considerable flair." Kevin Phillips found some fault with Nocera's approach, however, writing for the *Washington Post* (November 13, 1994) that "three-quarters of . . . Nocera's book is a well-researched, detailed yet easy to read chronicle of the emergence of the U.S. financial-services industry over the last 40 years—from the pioneering roles of the Bank of America and Merrill Lynch to the latter-day mutual fund, discount broker and credit card industries. The other quarter is P.R.-flavored hype about how these new products and services have helped the middle class, lucky folks, to join the money class. Unfortunately, the two components come in the same binding, so the discriminating reader faces a conundrum."

In 2005 Nocera left *Fortune* and joined the New York Times Co. as a staff writer for the *New York Times Magazine* and as a business columnist for the daily paper. That column, "Talking Business," which appeared each Saturday, focused on a wide variety of financial topics and related stories. Some of Nocera's pieces from 2006, for example, include one about Apple Inc.'s controversial policies regarding malfunctioning iPods, another about the tendency of some financial analysts to spend more time courting companies than analyzing them, and others about growing companies such as Home Depot and Whole Foods. Some stories used personal anecdotes as jumping-off points for larger business commentary. In his piece about Apple's iPod policy, "Good Luck with that Broken iPod" (February 4, 2006, on-line), Nocera related his own frustration over the company's tedious customer-service process while observing that many other tech companies, too, offer only limited product support, which they regard as unprofitable, particularly when the items they sell are relatively inexpensive. He wrote, "Consumers, though, don't really understand this. As much as they like being able to buy computers for less than $1,000, they don't realize that one of the trade-offs is minimal tech support. Nor do the companies spell this out; in-

stead, they pretend that their service is terrific. Thus, there is a gap between what customers expect from companies that sell them complicated digital machines, and what companies feel they need [to] do to ensure that those machines make money. . . . It seems to me that Apple is on a dangerous course. Yes, it has strong incentives to minimize tech support, but to say 'Not Our Problem' whenever an iPod dies is to run the serious risk of losing its customers' loyalty."

With the worldwide economic recession that emerged in 2007, Nocera began to focus on the consequences of Wall Street's downturn and on the conclusions that leading figures in the political and financial realms drew from them. He also analyzed the reasons for the recession and offered his views on how to better regulate the financial system. He often looked to history to help explain the present; in "A System Overdue for Reform" (March 29, 2008, on-line), writing about the need to reform the U.S. financial system, he explained, "The main concern in the wake of the [Great] Depression was the banking system—so banks wound up heavily regulated. Investment banks, by contrast, were far less important to the overall financial system, so they wound up with a very different kind of regulation; in general, they can take all the risk they want with their balance sheets without the government saying boo. Yet over the last few decades, and especially since the abolition of the Glass-Steagall Act, the Depression-era law that separated investment banks from commercial banks, the two kinds of institutions have come to perform many of the same functions. All kinds of banklike institutions have sprung up that are largely unregulated. . . . Indeed, thanks to securitization, banks don't have anywhere near the assets or power they used to have—while investment banks are a far larger and more powerful part of the financial system."

Nocera's pieces for the *New York Times Magazine* were generally related to business. Among his articles were one about the financial workings of the Dia:Beacon museum, in Beacon, New York, and another about self-made philanthropists. He also wrote pieces for *Play*, a *New York Times* weekly e-mail newsletter that focuses on sports; his articles often covered the business side of sports and included, for example, a story about American financiers' buying stakes in English soccer teams.

In April 2011 Nocera became a regular columnist for the op-ed section of the *New York Times*. His column appears twice a week. In it Nocera has critiqued the financial industry and its key players; he has also discussed his views on political events and world affairs. In one piece, "You Call That Tough?" (May 6, 2011, on-line), he took federal prosecutors to task for failing to bring charges against financial executives who may have been complicit in the financial crisis, arguing, "So long as prosecutors resist bringing criminal cases against financial executives, they are sending a message. Crime pays."

Good Guys and Bad Guys: Behind the Scenes with the Saints and Scoundrels of American Business (and Everything in Between), a collection of Nocera's business profiles, was published in 2008. Michael Hirsh wrote for the *New York Times* (June 18, 2008, on-line), "Business writers, like painters, follow different schools and approaches. Nocera specializes in portraying the human drama behind the economic trends; he is the Hieronymus Bosch of the financial world, and Wall Street is his *Garden of Earthly Delights*, teeming with strange, sometimes horrifying and occasionally wonderful characters. As with Bosch, on Nocera's canvas it's the 'evil' ones we are irresistibly drawn to, financial bad boys like the junk-bond financier Michael Milken and Henry Blodget, the disgraced Merrill Lynch analyst. Yet even as Nocera feeds our fascination for these characters, he often finds good things to say about them, and occasionally faults his colleagues in the press for simplistically dismissing them as criminals or confidence men."

With Bethany McLean, Nocera co-authored the book *All the Devils Are Here: The Hidden History of the Financial Crisis* (2010), which chronicles the events that led to the recent recession and discusses the parts that top executives, policy makers, and institutions played in it. Some of the figures the authors describe as "devils"—those who had a hand in bringing on the financial crisis—include the former Countrywide Financial chief executive officer (CEO) Angelo Mozilo; the former Merrill Lynch CEO Stanley O'Neal; the former Federal National Mortgage Association (Fannie Mae) CEO Franklin Raines; and Alan Greenspan, the former chairman of the Federal Reserve. Daniel Gross wrote for the *Washington Post* (December 30, 2010, on-line), "Unlike many of the quickie books on the crisis, *All the Devils Are Here* is tightly written, methodical and unsensationalistic. But its revelations are just as shocking as those in most of its less-well-aged predecessors."

Nocera has written articles on business and other topics on a freelance basis for the *Wall Street Journal*, *Newsweek*, and *Washington Monthly*. He also serves as a business commentator for the National Public Radio program *Weekend Edition with Scott Simon*. In 1997 he was the anchor of the PBS *Frontline* documentary "Betting on the Market." In 2007 he was a finalist for the Pulitzer Prize for commentary. He is the recipient of two Gerald Loeb Awards and three John Hancock Awards; both are given for excellence in business and financial journalism. For the publishing house Portfolio, he edited *The Smartest Guys in the Room* (2003), a bestselling book about the downfall of the Enron energy corporation, written by McLean and Peter Elkind.

Nocera, discussing the differences between journalism today and when he was starting out, told Nesi, "There's actually a lot more ways to follow your vision than there used to be, where you had to go to a newspaper, learn your craft the way they wanted you to learn it. Now you can be first-person, you can be opinionated, you can be writing about some obscure thing that you could never get a newspaper interested in—because the Internet exists. So I think journalism has a fabulous future." He has a daughter, Kate Nocera, who writes for *Politico*.

—W.D.

Suggested Reading: *nytimes.com*; *Slate.com* June 12, 2006; WPRI.com Apr. 11, 2011

Selected Books: *A Piece of the Action: How the Middle Class Joined the Money Class*, 1994; *All the Devils Are Here: The Hidden History of the Financial Crisis* (with Bethany McLean), 2010

Palast, Greg

(PAL-ast)

June 26, 1952– Investigative journalist

Address: c/o American Program Bureau, 313 Washington St., Suite 225, Newton, MA 02458; c/o Dutton Publicity, 375 Hudson St., New York, NY 10014

"I don't see myself as an investigative reporter," the journalist, writer, and documentary filmmaker Greg Palast told Thai Jones for the Albany, New York, *Times Union* (June 18, 2006). "I see myself as a reporting investigator." Palast has also labeled himself a "forensic economist," and he has compared himself to Sam Spade, the dogged, hard-boiled fictional private detective created by Dashiell Hammett and portrayed by Humphrey Bogart in the film *The Maltese Falcon*. Palast began his career in the 1970s as a consultant for state governments, mainly concerning utilities, and an investigator for labor unions and other noncorporate groups. He turned to journalism to alert a greater number of people to wrongdoings that he believed were being perpetrated by companies, politicians, lobbyists, and governments—activities that, in his view, the mainstream media in the U.S. has ignored or downplayed intentionally or through ignorance. His column, "Inside Corporate America," appears in the London *Guardian* and its sister newspaper, the Sunday *Observer*; he is also on the staff of the British TV program *Newsnight*, on which he is seen in the field wearing his signature raincoat and old gray fedora. According to Palast, the profit-driven American media cannot afford to publish what he writes, because his words are likely to antagonize the corporations that generate advertising revenue. (Only a few articles by Palast have appeared in U.S. print publications, among them the *Nation*, *Harper's*, *In These Times*, the *Progressive*, the *Washington Post*, and *Rolling Stone*.) "I don't like being in journalistic exile," he told a *PR Week* (May 22, 2006) interviewer. "I don't

Daragh McDonagh, courtesy of Greg Palast

Greg Palast

like my words trying to swim across the Atlantic. They could drown—and that usually happens. But it's nearly impossible for raw, original investigative journalism to really make it into U.S. papers."

Palast has investigated the *Exxon Valdez* oil spill in Prince William Sound, Alaska, in 1989; the influence of corporate lobbyists on government policy in Great Britain in the late 1990s; the controversial ballot counting in Florida after the 2000 presidential election, after which the U.S. Supreme Court declared the Republican candidate, George W. Bush, the winner; the Enron Corp.'s role in the energy crisis that affected millions of Californians in 2001–02; former president George H. W. Bush's ties to the Saudi Arabian royal family and Saudi millionaires (in particular, members of the bin Laden family) and his success in quashing official scrutiny of their connections to terrorists; ways in which the International Monetary Fund, the World Bank, the World Trade Organization, and the U.S. Treasury Department harm rather than help developing nations; and current plans to build two dozen nuclear power plants in the U.S.—two to be built by the company that owns the plant in Fukushima, Japan, that was damaged by the earthquake and tsunami of March 2011. Some of those matters and others are the subjects of Palast's books *The Best Democracy Money Can Buy* (2002), which earned the U.S. National Press Club's Arthur Rowse Award for Press Criticism, and the collection *Armed Madhouse* (2006), whose original subtitle called it "dispatches from the front lines of the class war." Both books were *New York Times* best-sellers, and each has been updated and expanded.

Palast's investigative reporting on the televangelist Pat Robertson's business empire earned him the 1998 David Thomas Prize from the London *Financial Times* and a nomination for the 2000 Business Writer of the Year award from the Press Association, a British group. Palast co-directed, co-produced, co-wrote, and appeared as himself in the documentary *Bush Family Fortunes*; the film was shown in 2005 at the now-defunct Freedom Cinema Festival, where it won the George Orwell Courage in Journalism Award. Through his Web site Palast sells DVDs of that documentary and his other films: *The Assassination of Hugo Chávez* (2006), about the president of Venezuela; *Big Easy to Big Empty: The Untold Story of the Drowning of New Orleans* (2007); *The Election Files* (2008), about the last three U.S. presidential elections; and, most recently, *Palast Investigates* (2009), a compilation of reports that aired on *Newsnight*.

Writing for the *Columbus (Ohio) Dispatch* (June 19, 2006), Bill Eichenberger characterized Palast as "a righteous crusader for truth and justice"; Anne Simpson, a Glasgow, Scotland, *Herald* (April 1, 2002) reporter, described him as a "swashbuckling subversive ever on the alert" and as "among the last of that old-fashioned journalistic breed, the outraged pamphleteer, a tireless investigative reporter striving to expose the gross and tiny tyrannies of life." Palast declared to Eichenberger, "Most of the pinheads in America who consider themselves journalists aren't reporters; they're repeaters. They go to press conferences and raise their hands politely, hoping to ask the president's official prevaricators what they should say. They rewrite press releases and pen bootlicking profiles of corporate CEOs who poison kids, then take away health insurance. These reporters are not scum. That would be unfair. It's their editors who are scum—news murderers, every one of them. . . . So they call me a 'muckraker'—a person who digs through the mud and glop of government and corporate files. Well, that's exactly what I am. I shovel up the dirt and garbage of our American democracy and show it to you." In an interview with Alexander Greenwood for SoonerThought.com (May 11, 2006), Palast said, "I want to make enemies. I don't want anyone from either [political] party to like Greg Palast; I want them to know that I'm going to get the truth out."

Palast's work has been praised by the environmental lawyer Robert F. Kennedy Jr.; Joseph E. Stiglitz, the winner of the 2001 Nobel Prize in economics; the documentary filmmaker Michael Moore; and the cognitive scientist and activist Noam Chomsky. His detractors include Kathleen Harris, Florida's secretary of state in 2000, who, as widely quoted on the Web, has described him as "twisted" and "maniacal," and people who, believing that the U.S.'s so-called war on terror was designed to indulge Israel and American Jewish organizations, have accused Palast of being an apologist for Israel and Zionism. Palast's articles about influence peddling among members of British prime minister Tony Blair's cabinet led the British tabloid the *Daily Mirror* one day in 1998 to publish Palast's portrait on its front page under the headline "The Liar." In May 2007 Markos Moulitsas, the founder of the blog dailykos.com, criticized Palast for repeatedly referring to "500 Karl Rove emails"; in Palast's view the emails were evidence that Rove—a Republican strategist and George W. Bush adviser—had helped remove thousands of African-Americans and others from voter-registration rolls in Florida in 2000, but Moulitsas charged that the label "Rove emails" was inaccurate and that there was virtually nothing incriminating in the messages. He also labeled Palast "dangerous," for claiming that Democrats knew about Rove's role in suppressing black votes but refused to do anything about it because they might someday want to resort to Rove's tactics.

Palast gives lectures through the American Program Bureau. On his Web site he solicits contributions to the Palast Investigative Fund, a charitable trust, to help him continue his work. He told *Current Biography*, "Until all the dragons are slain, I'm not resting."

The only son of Gilbert L. and Gladys (Kaufman) Palast, Gregory Allyn Palast was born on June 26, 1952 in Los Angeles, California. He has one sister, Geri Palast, a lawyer, who served as assistant secretary of labor for congressional and intergovernmental affairs during the presidency of Bill Clinton; currently, she is the executive director of the Campaign for Fiscal Equity, which focuses on funding of New York State public schools. Greg Palast dedicated his first book to his mother, who held a school-cafeteria job, and his father, a World War II veteran and furniture salesperson who "hated every minute" of his working life, in Palast's words; Gil Palast also co-founded the La Mesa-Foothills Democratic Club, in California. Greg Palast wrote in his first book that he grew up in "the scum end" of Los Angeles, "between the power plant and the garbage dump." During his youth he developed "a great anger and dislike" for the privileged, he told Simpson. He attended Fernangeles Elementary School and Richard E. Byrd Middle School, Los Angeles County public schools. At 13 he began attending civil rights demonstrations; during a Vietnam War protest in 1970, he was arrested.

Earlier, Palast attended John H. Francis Polytechnic High School, in Los Angeles. He told *Current Biography* that he left the school before his senior year. "Basically they were melting my brain, and I had to save myself," he said. "Before I finished high school, I talked my way into college. Before I finished college, I talked my way into graduate school." After a brief stint at San Fernando Valley State College (now California State University at Northridge), Palast transferred to the University of California (UC) at Los Angeles and then UC–Berkeley. At Berkeley Palast met a member of the radical political group the Weathermen, who encouraged him to familiarize himself with right-

wing politics and learn about the "ruling elite" from "the inside." Spurred by that advice, Palast applied successfully to the University of Chicago, in Illinois, where he studied economics; one of his professors was Milton Friedman, who won the Nobel Prize in economics in 1977 and later served as an adviser to President Ronald Reagan. Palast earned an A.B. degree from the university in 1974 and an M.B.A. in 1976.

During the next decade Palast worked as an investigator for blue-collar organizations including the United Steelworkers of America, the United Electrical Workers Union, and the Enron workers' coalition in Latin America. "I didn't want to take some pig job," he told *Current Biography*. "So I decided I wanted to do something interesting, and use some skills for the working class." One case in which he was heavily involved for years concerned the Long Island Lighting Co. (Lilco) and its construction from 1973 to 1984 of the Shoreham Nuclear Power Plant (which operated for a total of only 48 hours before it was permanently shut down, in 1989). The government of Sussex County, in Long Island, New York, a Lilco customer, armed with evidence Palast had unearthed, successfully sued Lilco for deceiving the public regarding the costs of construction in order to justify rate increases. Leonard Buder wrote for the *New York Times* (December 6, 1988) that Palast (known as Gregory Palast then), in his capacity as an economist and utilities specialist, testified in behalf of Sussex County at the Lilco trial held in 1988. In 1998, after a series of legal appeals, Lilco was converted into a public-private hybrid, with the Long Island Power Authority, a government agency, gaining ownership of parts of the utility—the outcome that Palast had hoped for all along, he told *Current Biography*. In John Rather's *New York Times* (May 3, 1998) account of that conversion, which led to significant reductions in customers' utility rates, Palast was identified as a "utility regulation analyst." By his own account, he served as a consultant to 19 U.S. state governments.

Palast became involved in another long, drawn-out case shortly after the oil tanker *Exxon Valdez* suffered rips in its hull when it ran aground on Bligh Reef in Prince William Sound, off the southern coast of Alaska, on March 24, 1989. An estimated 11 million gallons of crude oil (or far more, according to some sources) gushed from the damaged ship, ultimately covering about 11,000 square miles of the sea and more than 1,000 miles of shoreline. The oil coated and killed hundreds of thousands of seabirds and mammals along with their food supplies: countless salmon and other fish, which died not only from contact with the oil but also because of the destruction of the vast populations of plankton and other organisms that made up their diets. The deaths of the fish, in turn, destroyed the livelihoods of thousands of Native American fishermen. In its public pronouncements the Exxon Corp. called the environmental disaster an accident and blamed it on one man—

Joseph Hazelwood, the tanker's captain. Members of the Chugash Alaska Corp., which represents the fishermen and other native Alaskans who live along the southern coast, recruited Palast to look into the causes of the spill and possible recourse for those who had lost their means of support because of it.

After extensive research Palast concluded that the spill was an accident that had been waiting to happen. When the tanker struck Bligh Reef, Captain Hazelwood was below decks, having fallen asleep after getting drunk. His replacement as lookout, the third mate, had no way of getting a warning from the device (a radar reflector) planted near Bligh Reef, because for over a year the ship's radar had been broken; the tanker's owner, the Exxon Shipping Co., had refused to allocate funds to have it fixed. In addition, from information contained in corporate documents, Palast discovered that executives of Exxon and the five other companies that own the Alaska pipeline knew that, contrary to legal requirements, the equipment in place to contain spills within Prince William Sound was grossly inadequate, but that they had voted against the expensive measures necessary to improve it. Moreover, an Exxon technician revealed to Palast that samples of contaminated seawater collected months and years earlier had alerted Exxon managers that smaller oil spills had already occurred, but that the managers had ordered the worker to "dump out oily water and refill test tubes from a bucket of cleansed sea water," Palast wrote in *The Best Democracy Money Can Buy*. In another piece of evidence (the whole of which, according to Palast, filled four volumes), one former commander of the Port of Valdez (the *Exxon Valdez*'s point of departure in Alaska) told Palast that when he showed his supervisor a report to be filed with government agents regarding an earlier oil spill, he was told, "You made a mistake. This was not an oil spill." In 1994 a jury awarded $5 billion in punitive damages to the Native American fishermen and other injured parties, but for years afterward, through legal maneuvers undertaken at a cost of hundreds of millions of dollars, Exxon avoided making any payments. In 2008—by which time about a fifth of the 32,000 original plaintiffs had died—the U.S. Supreme Court ruled that Exxon's punitive damages could not exceed $507.5 million.

In an article for Truthout.org (May 4, 2010), Palast wrote that "the party most to blame" for the *Exxon Valdez* oil spill was not Exxon but BP (formerly British Petroleum). BP Pipelines (Alaska) Inc. is another of the companies that own the Alaska oil pipeline. On April 20, 2010 an offshore rig leased to BP that was drilling for oil in the Gulf of Mexico off the coast of Louisiana exploded, killing 11 crew members and, during the next several months, spilling at least 185 million gallons of oil (or as much as 227 million gallons, some sources maintain). The oil spread over thousands of miles of seawater, polluted hundreds of miles of shore-

line, and killed huge numbers of fish, shrimp, seabirds, and other animals. "In the end, this is bigger than BP and its policy of cheaping-out and skiving the rules," Palast wrote for Truthout.org. "This is about the anti-regulatory mania which has infected the American body politic. While the 'tea baggers' are simply its extreme expression, US politicians of all stripes love to attack 'the little bureaucrat with the fat rule book.' . . . Americans want government off our backs . . . that is, until a folding crib crushes the skull of our baby; Toyota accelerators speed us to our death; banks blow our savings on gambling sprees; and crude oil smothers the Mississippi. Then, suddenly, it's, 'where the hell was the Government!'"

Earlier, in 1995, Palast's frustration over what he saw as journalists' complicity with, or obliviousness to, a massive Prince William Sound cover-up led him to become a reporter himself. He secured a job with the center-left London *Observer* and the London *Guardian*. (The former is published on Sundays; since 1993 it has been owned by the latter, which comes out Mondays through Saturdays.) At that time both newspapers were owned by the Scott Trust, which had been set up in 1936 to ensure that the *Guardian* remained editorially independent; the trustees were forbidden to benefit personally from the publication of the newspapers, and all profits were returned to the *Guardian*. In 2008 the trust was converted to a limited company; like its predecessor, the Scott Trust Ltd. does not pay dividends, and all profits from the *Guardian* and the *Observer* are plowed back for their operating expenses.

In one of his earliest investigations in Great Britain, Palast went undercover, pretending to represent Texas oil shippers and power-plant builders and intimating that he himself was on the take, as a means of looking into corporate lobbyists' dealings with British cabinet officials and members of Parliament. "Investigative reporting requires massive amounts of time, money and resources, and most news outlets aren't willing to make that commitment," Palast told a reporter for the *Oregonian* (April 4, 2003). "And most investigative reporters in America aren't really trained as investigators. They're promoted from within because they've done a good job elsewhere in the paper, but they don't really know how to investigate." The so-called cash-for-access scandal was dubbed Lobbygate and became front-page news in Great Britain in 1998, about a year after Tony Blair became prime minister. Mark Johnson reported for *PR Week* (April 18, 2003, on-line) that thanks to recommendations by the British governmental Committee on Standards in Public Life and the British trade group the Association of Professional Political Consultants, "lobbyists now work as strategists for their clients, offering advice on which ministers to meet on each issue, how to build a case to government, as well as arranging meetings. But no personal introductions." In the first edition of *The Best Democracy Money Can Buy*, Palast wrote that "the real story" was not about lobbyists but about "Tony Blair and his inner circle" and "New Labour's obsessional pursuit of the affection of the captains of industry and the media."

The controversy surrounding the counting of ballots in Florida in the 2000 U.S. presidential election led Palast to investigate the problems that had beset many of the state's polling places and thousands of voters on Election Day, particularly in several southern Florida counties that were heavily Democratic and African-American. (According to the later-released federal tally, in Florida, where 5,851,785 votes were officially recognized in the presidential contest, the total number of votes for the Republican nominee, George W. Bush, surpassed the number cast for the Democratic nominee, Al Gore, by 637, or .0001 percent.) There was much turmoil connected with the recount of the ballots, which continued until December 12, 2000, when the U.S. Supreme Court ruled that the recount must end; during that process the U.S. news media repeatedly discussed problems with paper ballots as well as computer-voting-machine malfunctions and breakdowns in the southern counties. Palast learned that some 180,000 ballots that had been cast were not counted because they had been "spoiled" in some way; of those, according to U.S. Civil Rights Commission demographers, an estimated 54 percent had been cast by African-Americans. Palast also discovered that before Election Day, with the approval of Jeb Bush, Florida's Republican governor and a brother of George W. Bush, Florida's Republican secretary of state, Katherine Harris, had removed the names of 57,700 Floridians (a figure Palast later revised upwards, to 94,000) from voting rolls on the grounds that they had previously been convicted of felonies and were thus prohibited from voting in Florida. But, as Palast later wrote for *Harper's* (November 2004), "only 3 percent" of the 94,000 "could later be verified as former convicts." Many of those who were turned away at the polls had been found guilty only of misdemeanors, and in thousands of other cases, their names were identical or merely similar to those of convicted criminals. When Palast returned to Florida in 2004, he found that only about 1,000 of those purged from the voting rolls in 2000 had been reinstated. "Those who attempt to get back their vote," he wrote, "have been required, depending on the county, to seek clemency from Jeb Bush for crimes committed by others, or to provide fingerprints for investigation, or to undergo ad-hoc court-like proceedings to prove they are themselves and not some convict with a similar name." In the October 14, 2004 issue of the *New York Times*, the columnist Paul Krugman cited Palast's 2000 and 2004 investigations in Florida and wrote that the abuses by state officials were not "aberrations." Rather, Krugman declared, "they're the inevitable result of a Republican Party culture in which dirty tricks that distort the vote are rewarded, not punished."

Palast wrote about the events in Florida for the *Observer*. In *The Best Democracy Money Can Buy*, they are described in a chapter called "Jim Crow in Cyberspace," which begins, "In the days following the presidential election, there were so many stories of African Americans erased from voter rolls you might think they were targeted by some kind of racial computer program. They were." The 2002, 2003, and 2004 editions of that book are all subtitled *An Investigative Reporter Exposes the Truth About Globalization, Corporate Cons, and High-Finance Fraudsters*. The first, 2006 edition of *Armed Madhouse* was subtitled *Who's Afraid of Osama Wolf?, China Floats, Bush Sinks the Scheme to Steal '08, No Child's Behind Left, and Other Dispatches from the Front Lines of the Class War*; the 2007 edition is subtitled *From Baghdad to New Orleans: Sordid Secrets & Strange Tales of a White House Gone Wild*.

Palast is currently investigating plans for the construction of some two dozen new nuclear power plants in the U.S., for which, he wrote in a report for Truthout.org and BuzzFlash.org (March 14, 2011), the administration of President Barack Obama may provide as much as $56 billion in loans. In the same report he identified one such proposal as the South Texas Project, which calls for the building of two such plants on the Gulf Coast of Texas. According to Palast, the principal builder under consideration is the Tokyo Electric Power Co., the owner of the nuclear power plant in Fukushima, Japan, that was damaged by the earthquake and tsunami that struck Japan on March 11, 2011. Another possible participant is a division of the company Shaw Construction, which, Palast charged, faked safety tests connected with the Shoreham nuclear power plant in the 1970s.

Palast is the co-author, with Jerrold Oppenheim and Theo MacGregor, of *Democracy and Regulation: How the Public Can Govern Essential Services* (2003), which was written for and published by the United Nations International Labour Organisation. Parts of it were based on lectures Palast had given at Cambridge University, in England, and the University of São Paulo, in Brazil. The book explains how water, gas, electricity, and telephone services are supplied and regulated in the United States and how, by emulating aspects of the U.S. systems, other nations could reduce the costs of providing such services. *Democracy and Regulation* won the 2004 Upton Sinclair Freedom of Expression Award from the American Civil Liberties Union.

Palast lives in the U.S. with his wife and occasional collaborator, Linda Levy, and their teenage twins, a son and a daughter.

—C.S.

Suggested Reading: (Albany, New York) *Times Union* J p1 June 18, 2006; (Glasgow, Scotland) *Herald* p9 Apr. 1, 2002; gregpalast.com; *Los Angeles Times* Calendar p1 May 19, 2003

Selected Books: *The Best Democracy Money Can Buy*, 2002; *Democracy and Regulation: How the Public Can Govern Essential Services* (with Jerrold Oppenheim and Theo MacGregor), 2003; *Armed Madhouse*, 2006

Selected Films: *Bush Family Fortunes*, 2005; *The Assassination of Hugo Chávez*, 2006; *Big Easy to Big Empty: The Untold Story of the Drowning of New Orleans*, 2007; *The Election Files*, 2008; *Palast Investigates*, 2009

Jonathan Sachs, courtesy of Lookout Books

Pearlman, Edith

June 26, 1936– Writer

Address: c/o Lookout Books, Dept. of Creative Writing, University of North Carolina–Wilmington, 601 S. College Rd., Wilmington, NC 28403

For over four decades beginning in the late 1960s, Edith Pearlman's insightful, touching, crisply crafted short stories appeared in various magazines, literary journals, and newspapers but remained under the radar of most critics and members of the reading public—despite the fact that she earned many literary honors, including on three occasions one of America's most prestigious awards for short fiction, the O. Henry Prize. During that time she also published three books—*Vaquita and Other Stories* (1996), *Love Among the Greats and Other Stories* (2002), and *How to Fall* (2005)—and saw her work included in prominent anthologies, among them *Best American Short Stories*

(1998, 2000, 2006). Pearlman's relative obscurity ended after Lookout Books published *Binocular Vision: New & Selected Stories*, in January 2011. In a single day the book received glowing notices in the pages of the *New York Times* and the *Los Angeles Times*, with both critics starting their reviews by admitting that they had never heard of the 74-year-old Pearlman. "You know, I've known all along that I had a rather small following, so I wasn't surprised they hadn't heard of me," Pearlman said in an interview with *Current Biography*, the source of quotes for this article unless otherwise noted. In his review for the *Los Angeles Times* (January 16, 2011), David L. Ulin wrote that it was *because* he had never heard of Pearlman that he got to experience "the great joy of discovering her, the thrill of coming upon a writer with an eye, and a command of language, so acute." Roxana Robinson, in her assessment for the *New York Times Book Review* (January 16, 2011), described the writing in *Binocular Vision* as "intelligent, perceptive, funny and quite beautiful." The following week the *New York Times* included the book on its "Editors' Choice" list.

In her stories Pearlman explores identity and human relationships through the lens of such universal or common conditions as heartbreak, love, jealousy, fear, death, guilt, loneliness, immigration, and assimilation. Her settings are as diverse as her themes: Israel, Europe, Latin America, and the United States, particularly Godolphin, a fictitious town based on Brookline, Massachusetts, where Pearlman has lived for decades with her husband. Her stories are greatly admired for, among other characteristics, their carefully constructed sentences and overall structure. Pearlman subscribes to the shorter-is-better approach. "Careful revision and boiling down make for stories in which each word needs to be the right one," Ellen Steinbaum wrote for the *Boston Globe* (September 7, 2003) about Pearlman's work. Over the decades her writing process has not changed at all. "I write on a typewriter," Pearlman told *Current Biography*. "I revise and revise, also on a typewriter. The story doesn't get into the computer until the last several drafts." In an interview with Steinbaum, Pearlman elaborated on her writing process: "I revise by retyping the entire page. I know the computer makes it easier to revise, but not easier to revise well. The longer you work at a piece, the better it gets. And the shorter it gets. I want to inspire would-be writers to become passionate about parts of speech. The mechanics of writing are important to master in order to do justice to the content."

Pearlman was born Edith Grossman on June 26, 1936 in Providence, Rhode Island. She and her younger sister, Betty, were raised by their father, a physician, and mother, a homemaker. Her parents always had books in the house, and her aunt, a high-school English teacher who lived with the family, read literary works to the young Pearlman, particularly the writings of Shakespeare. Pearlman attended Radcliffe College, in Cambridge, Massachusetts, and received a B.A. degree in English in 1957. (At that time Radcliffe was a women's liberal-arts college affiliated with Harvard University, also in Cambridge. The two schools officially merged in 1999.) In college she read fiction by F. Scott Fitzgerald, William Faulkner, Ernest Hemingway, and other modern American authors. After graduation Pearlman worked for 10 years as a computer programmer for IBM and then General Electric. The computers she worked with, she recalled, "were as big as a building. . . . They looked nothing like your desktop computer." After getting married, in 1967, Pearlman left her programming career behind and began to write fiction. By 1968 her stories were being published in *Seventeen* and *Redbook*, female-oriented magazines that no longer publish fiction. Within a year Pearlman had moved on to literary magazines, such as *Ascent*, the *Antioch Review*, and the *Iowa Review*. In an interview with Ben Steelman for the Wilmington, North Carolina, *Star-News* (March 5, 2011), she said that "in the old-fashioned way, my husband supported me in return for raising the kids, keeping house and planning the social life. I rather liked it. I felt I had a patron." Even though she became a highly prolific writer, Pearlman never made much money from her short stories.

Pearlman's first book, *Vaquita and Other Stories*, was published nearly three decades after she had begun her literary career. The timing was not her choice. Pearlman had tried many times to put out a collection but was unable to interest a publisher. She used to joke, she recalled, that she "would publish her first book in time to be buried with it." On a more serious note, Pearlman said that she found her inability to find a book publisher "odd," since she was winning prize after prize for her short stories. "Nobody wanted my collections until 1996—and now," Pearlman added with a high-pitched, amused laugh, "they all want it." Her predicament, she acknowledged, was not unique, as many good writers struggle to find publishers. For *Vaquita*, Pearlman selected 15 of her previously published stories, some with overlapping themes, characters, and settings. "Donna's Heart" and "Dorothea" are both set in a soup kitchen called the Ladle, which caters to homeless women. The latter story centers on an overflowing toilet, which the volunteers have difficulty keeping the homeless women from using until they put a clothed dummy on it, to make the toilet look as if it is occupied. The volunteers enjoy the novelty of the situation, which in turn makes them feel guilty. "Pearlman doesn't stop where you think she might, with the women gaining new understanding about the distance between themselves and the women they serve," Jane McCafferty wrote for the *Pittsburgh Post-Gazette* (November 24, 1996). "What happens in this story is both surprising and inevitable." McCafferty called the book as a whole "remarkable for its scope, vision and craft. Each story is so well imagined, I kept suspecting Pearl-

man of having actually lived the lives of her characters, who are as varied as they are interesting." (Pearlman had volunteered in a soup kitchen for 10 years.) In the story "Donna's Heart," Pearlman shows the simultaneously lovely and disorderly atmosphere of that soup kitchen—and how many people in the town, with various moral and political views, question the motivations and actions of Donna, who runs the kitchen. "Vaquita," the title story, features Señora Perera, an elderly Polish-Jewish woman who survived World War II by hiding from the Nazis for a year in a barn with a cow by her side. The story is set in a Latin American country, years later, during the early days of a revolution. Despite the chaos, Perera, the country's health minister, continues to do her job during her last days in office, visiting needy families across the country. In "Stranger in the House," a French-born Israeli man is insanely jealous over his American wife, who works with refugees in Jerusalem. "Like so many of these stories, the private torments of the heart take place inside of, and despite of, greater political realities," McCafferty wrote. "People are often depicted as well-meaning, but often lonely and at the mercy of their own passions." In 1996 the author received the Drue Heinz Literature Prize, presented by the University of Pittsburgh Press to honor short fiction. Rosellen Brown, a judge for that year's Heinz Prize, said in an interview with Michael Gelbwasser for the *Jewish Advocate* (June 27, 1996), "What a pleasure it is to see the characters of *Vaquita* living their rich lives in the tumultuous and difficult world. These characters are experienced but not cynical, sophisticated and wry and hopeful in spite of every terrible thing they've seen, and Edith Pearlman's generous intelligence keeps them from looking foolish for their commitment."

Pearlman's next two short-story collections—*Love Among the Greats* (2002) and *How to Fall* (2005)—received mostly positive, enthusiastic reviews, albeit not much attention in the mainstream press. *Love Among the Greats* includes stand-alone stories as well as interconnected ones. The latter include the tale of Michal, told over the course of four stories. Michal, a woman with a Jewish father and a non-Jewish mother, marries Bellamy, her best friend from college, who turns out to be gay and a philanderer. She then marries Malachi, a pediatrician, who truly loves her. In "The Big Fish," Michal and Malachi, a former Baptist, are in Israel, where each has a different religious experience, which underscores their differences. Among the book's stand-alone stories is "The Jigsaw Table," in which a family—mother, father, and three children—work on a jigsaw puzzle together, an act symbolizing the family's unity; their togetherness gets disrupted when a friend comes to visit and works on the puzzle with them. In "Allog," set in Jerusalem, a Southeast Asian aide cares for an elderly, incapacitated man and, over time, develops a personal relationship with nearly everyone in the elderly man's apartment building. In a review for the *Seattle Times* (February 2, 2003), Mary Ann Gwinn, the paper's book editor, wrote that although she was "not a big short-story fan," she was deeply impressed with Pearlman's book: "She tells wonderfully well-drawn stories about people who live uneventfully, but with great richness and contentment." The book won the Spokane Annual Fiction Prize.

Pearlman's third collection, *How to Fall*, followed three years later. The title story describes a meeting between a television comedian of the 1950s and the club-footed teenage girl who has been writing him love letters. "Trifle" is set in a Godolphin restaurant where a teenage girl, who has run away from home, listens to the conversations of those nearby. Most of the book's other stories also feature female characters: obese, alcoholic women in "The Large Lady," a struggling Belgian-Jewish refugee living in Israel in "Madame Guralnik," and an American woman who has an affair during her trip to Jerusalem in "The Message." In his review for *Salon.com* (February 23, 2005), Andrew O'Hehir wrote, "In another writer, I might find Pearlman's subject matter too cloying or too claustrophobic. . . . But Pearlman's perceptions are so sharp and so fair-minded that I can't resist her; she neither wants to attack the lives her characters lead nor defend them, only to capture them as honestly as she can." In a mixed review for the *Forward* (March 25, 2005), Susan Comninos complained that despite Pearlman's record of originality, *How to Fall* lacks that quality, owing much to the work of several Jewish writers—namely Cynthia Ozick, Nathan Englander, and the Israeli author Yehudit Hendel. *How to Fall* won the Mary McCarthy Prize for Short Fiction. Aside from the *Salon.com* notice and a positive, paragraph-length *New York Times* review, the book received little mainstream press; Pearlman was still largely unknown in the literary world.

That changed with the publication of *Binocular Vision: New & Selected Stories* (2011). The book, with an introduction by the fiction writer Ann Patchett, comprises 34 stories, more than half of them—including "Vaquita," "ToyFolk," and "Allog"—from the author's previous collections. "Patchett compares Pearlman to John Updike and Alice Munro," David L. Ulin wrote, "but a more accurate analogue, I think, is Deborah Eisenberg. Like Eisenberg, Pearlman crafts densely wrought, at times elliptical, narratives that avoid easy epiphanies; like Eisenberg also, she is comfortable with Europe or Latin America as a setting. Often, her stories revolve around a subtle dislocation, in which her characters can't help but be surprised by the world." Pearlman was asked by several interviewers whether a particular theme unites the stories. "All I can say," she said, deadpan, "is that they were all written by the same woman." In "The Coat," a married Jewish couple, former directors of a displaced-persons camp in Germany in 1947, are living in New York City. When the wife finds a stylish man's coat and starts wearing it, she begins to ponder the meaning of immigration and identity. In "Fidelity," a travel writer, out of revenge for his editor's affair with the writer's wife, pens wonderful descriptions of cities that do not exist; the editor, knowing the descriptions are of fictitious places, guiltily publishes them anyway. In "Binocular Vision" a girl uses her father's binoculars to spy on her next-door neighbors, about whom, she comes to realize, she knew very little. That story is a meditation on what we assume about people we barely know. "In such a large collection," Clea Simon wrote for the *Boston Globe* (February 4, 2011), "drawn from four decades, there are bound to be some misses. On the whole, these occur in the older works. . . . Pearlman is a master of the form, and the majority of these stories are note-perfect. But by gathering some earlier pieces along with her newest work, this volume shows an artist who has never stopped developing." Speaking to *Current Biography*, Pearlman admitted as much: "I think my stories are more ambitious now than they used to be. A slightly more complicated plot, perhaps. Or a slightly more interesting protagonist. But some of my early stories, I think, were also ambitious and had deep characters. So I don't think there has been a dramatic change, but I probably write more of the ambitious stories now than I used to."

Pearlman loves the works of many writers, including John Updike and Emile Zola as well as less-well-known writers, such as Sylvia Townsend Warner and Penelope Fitzgerald, each a 20th-century English poet and novelist. Charles Dickens, she said, is her "all-time favorite."

Pearlman is often asked whether she will ever write a novel, the assumption being that—as often happens—a novel would naturally follow a short-story collection. "I fooled them three times, and I think I'll fool them again," she said. "I don't have any wish to write a novel and I love writing short stories. And I think I would miss the kind of concentration that one has to bring to a short story. . . . I love waking up in the morning and thinking first thing about the story I'm writing."

Pearlman lives in Brookline with her husband, Chester. They have two grown children and a grandson. According to Pearlman's official Web site, her hobbies include "reading, walking, and matchmaking."

—D.K.

Suggested Reading: edithpearlman.com; *Jewish Advocate* p22 June 27, 1996; *Los Angeles Times* E p9 Jan. 16, 2011; *New York Times Book Review* p1 Jan. 16, 2011; Salon.com Feb. 23, 2005; *Seattle Times* K p9 Feb. 2, 2003

Selected Books: *Vaquita and Other Stories*, 1996; *Love Among the Greats and Other Stories*, 2002; *How to Fall*, 2005; *Binocular Vision: New & Selected Stories*, 2011

Will Ragozzino/Getty Images

Pelley, Scott

July 28, 1957– Broadcast journalist; television news anchor

Address: CBS Evening News, 524 W. 57th St., New York, NY 10019

The multiple Emmy and Peabody Award–winning broadcast journalist Scott Pelley "harkens back to a day when CBS was the gold standard in television news," David Bauder wrote for the Associated Press (April 28, 2011, on-line). Bauder made that declaration shortly before Pelley replaced Katie Couric as the anchor and managing editor of the *CBS Evening News*, on June 6, 2011. Pelley is known for his commanding on-air presence and interviewing skills, and his appointment is viewed as CBS's attempt to return to its hard-news roots, in the tradition of the earlier *Evening News* anchors Walter Cronkite and Dan Rather, one of Pelley's mentors. According to Phil Rosenthal, writing for the *Chicago Tribune* (May 4, 2011), Pelley "is the anti-Couric" and represents "staid and modest journalistic tradition. The bigger the stories he covers, the more he seems to slip into their background. But he is as good as anyone at bringing them into the spotlight." Dan Rather described Pelley to Bauder as being "relentless as a reporter" and "relentless in his drive to do good journalism. He's a rock-solid believer in the tradition, history, legends and myths of CBS News." Pelley has spent over two decades with CBS, serving as a general-assignment reporter and a White House correspondent before joining *60 Minutes*'s stable of journalists in 2004. Jeff Fager, the chairman of CBS News and the executive producer of *60 Minutes*, told Me-

lissa Maerz for the *Los Angeles Times* (May 4, 2011) that Pelley has "covered every type of story imaginable, more than any other reporter in his generation. He's been everywhere, and to me, that results in credibility." Pelley has also conducted interviews with many high-profile national and international figures.

Pelley, whose promotion led to a reduction in his role with *60 Minutes*, hopes to bring that newsmagazine's sensibility to the *Evening News*, by focusing on "original reporting, unique insights, and fairness to everyone involved in the story," as he told Maerz, and by offering the sorts of in-depth investigations he has conducted for *60 Minutes*. He told David Zurawik for the *Baltimore Sun* (May 22, 2011), "The anchoring at the end of the day is the least important part of my day. It's an opportunity to speak to the audience, which I'm most grateful for. But the most important part of the day is the 10 hours before that when you go in as managing editor and you sit with the senior staff and figure out what you're going to cover and how you're going to cover it." Pelley told Brian Stelter for the *New York Times* (May 4, 2011), "We've got enormous strength. What the broadcast needs is a little bit of leadership. The correspondents and producers need to understand that we're going to be about original reporting and about bringing unique insight into the news, so that we add value for the viewers."

The younger son of John Pelley and the former Wanda Graves, Scott Cameron Pelley was born on July 28, 1957 in San Antonio, Texas. When Pelley was three years old, his family moved to Lubbock, Texas, where he and his brother, John, grew up. In Lubbock his father sold used cars and ran several small nightclubs, and his mother worked as a real-estate agent. As a boy Pelley hoped to become a photographer for *National Geographic*, and by the age of 12, he was processing his own pictures in a makeshift photo lab in his bedroom. His fascination with photography led him at 15 to take a job as a copyboy at the *Lubbock Avalanche-Journal*. Since the job required applicants to be at least 16, Pelley had lied about his age; to disguise the fact that he was not legally allowed to drive, his mother would drop him off several blocks from the newspaper's offices. As a copyboy Pelley worked in the wire room, where he took pride in being one of the first to learn about the day's news. Pelley told Richard Huff for the New York *Daily News* (May 4, 2011), "I loved this business early on."

Pelley attended Coronado High School in Lubbock, where he impressed teachers with his confidence, maturity, and industriousness. Meanwhile, at the *Lubbock Avalanche-Journal*, he quickly rose from copyboy to reporter, after helping on a breaking news story at the behest of Dave Knapp, then the paper's executive editor. In an interview with Chris Hodenfield for the *New Canaan–Darien Magazine* (January 2010, on-line), he recalled that Knapp "picked me out of the wire room, took me into the city room, sat me in front of the typewriter, and that was the end of my photography career and the beginning of my reporting career."

After he graduated from high school, in 1975, Pelley attended the journalism school at Texas Tech University, in Lubbock. Concurrently, he landed a job as a news reporter at KSEL-TV (now KMAC-TV), an ABC affiliate based in Lubbock. Pelley's experiences at the station proved to be invaluable. "This was a little wood-burning TV station, literally out in the middle of a cotton field," he told Hodenfield. "We had to do everything. We went out and shot the stories, we brought the film back and processed it ourselves. We were shooting car wrecks and ribbon cuttings. I would write the ten o'clock news for the anchorman." Pelley remained at KSEL-TV for three years, then quit college to take a job with WBAP-TV (now KXAS-TV), an NBC affiliate based in the Dallas–Fort Worth area. He thus transferred from the 137th-largest market in the country to the 10th.

Pelley worked at WBAP-TV until 1981, when he was fired following a disagreement with a news director. He told Michael Granberry for the *Dallas Morning News* (June 21, 1998), "You've got to have that firing on your resume to have any character. I think insubordination is a sign of character, and for a reporter, it's absolutely essential." Pelley then spent nine months at the PBS affiliate KERA-TV, in Dallas, where he worked on a business show that later folded due to inadequate funding. By that time he had interviewed several times, without success, for a reporter position at WFAA-TV in Dallas, an ABC affiliate and one of the largest stations in the country. Pelley maintained his campaign for a job there after KERA-TV shut down, and in 1982 the station's then–news director, Marty Haag, offered him a Saturday job. Pelley accepted, then showed up not only on Saturdays but every weekday as well. Haag told Granberry, "Scott knew exactly what he wanted. He wasn't overly arrogant or ambitious, but he was always there. He volunteered to be the first one out the door on every breaking story." After several weeks Pelley secured a full-time reporter's job with the station.

During his seven-year tenure at WFAA-TV, Pelley covered important events, including the 1985 Mexico City earthquake and the space-shuttle *Challenger* disaster, in 1986. He became known for his outstanding work ethic, doggedness, and well-coiffed appearance. Usually the first WFAA reporter to be assigned to breaking news stories, Pelley asked tough questions in a manner that seemed to put his interview subjects at ease. Bert Shipp, then the WFAA-TV assignments editor, told Granberry, "Pelley did everything for us but change in a phone booth." After two years or so with WFAA, Pelley actively sought work at CBS, and he reportedly contacted various CBS executives every six months for five years before he won a job offer. "You'll get 30 no's for every one yes," he told students during a lecture at Texas Tech University, as quoted by Logan G. Carver in the *Mass Communicator* (Summer 2006, on-line), Texas Tech's College of Mass Communications alumni magazine. "Dogged persistence is what gets people hired."

In 1989 Pelley joined CBS News as a correspondent based in New York. In 1990 he was sent to Dhahran, Saudi Arabia, to cover the Persian Gulf War. During his year there he covered events including the Iraqi missile strikes on Saudi Arabia and the ousting of Iraqi troops from Kuwait by the U.S. and its allies. After he returned to Dallas, he reported on national affairs, including the 1992 presidential campaigns of Bill Clinton and Ross Perot, the 1993 bombing of the World Trade Center, the Los Angeles, California, earthquake of 1994, the Oklahoma City bombing, in 1995, and the trial of the Oklahoma City bomber Timothy McVeigh, in 1997. He won an Emmy Award for his coverage of the FBI's 50-day siege of the Branch Davidian complex, near Waco, Texas, in 1994, and another for his investigations into the TWA Flight 800 disaster, in 1996, in which 230 people died when the plane exploded shortly after takeoff from New York and crashed into the Atlantic Ocean.

In September 1997 Pelley began a two-year stint as CBS's chief White House correspondent. He helped break several stories connected to President Bill Clinton's intimate relations with the onetime White House intern Monica Lewinsky and the subsequent impeachment of the president. Pelley was the first to report that Lewinsky had agreed to serve the Office of the Independent Counsel as a cooperating witness, and he broke the news that President Clinton had been subpoenaed to testify before a grand jury. In his interview with Chris Hodenfield, Pelley described events surrounding Clinton's impeachment as "dangerous," adding, "People were gunning for the President of the United States, and you couldn't be wrong. You had all these entities that weren't supposed to be talking, but were. The Office of the Independent Counsel, the President's lawyers, the Justice Department, the FBI, all leaking information. Which was illegal. The whole thing was tremendously dangerous because there was a lot of bad information—terrible lies being told to reporters to spin the story one way or another. We developed a lot of sources and broke a lot of news, and I'm glad to say were not wrong in anything." Pelley also covered Clinton's visits to South America, Africa, China, and Europe.

In June 1999 Pelley left the White House to become a correspondent for CBS's *60 Minutes II*, a weekday expansion of the network's flagship Sunday-night newsmagazine. The hour-long show, which had debuted six months earlier, aired on Wednesday nights and later on Friday nights. During the show's run, which ended in 2005, Pelley won an award from the organization Investigative Reporters and Editors for his 1999 exposé of child slavery in India (which led the U.S. Customs Service to ban the importation of products made by children in forced-labor facilities in India). He also collected an Emmy Award in 2001 for his report about a new sign language created by deaf children in Nicaragua. Pelley was among the first to report from ground zero, in Lower Manhattan, New York City, on the morning of the 9/11 terrorist attacks. In 2002 he received an American Women in Radio and Television Gracie Allen Award for his report on youngsters whose parents had died in the World Trade Center attacks. Pelley also became a favored interviewer of President George W. Bush; he was the first to interview Bush after the controversial 2000 presidential election and was the only reporter to land an interview with him on the first anniversary of 9/11. In 2003 Pelley began filing reports for *60 Minutes*'s Sunday edition. He was the first CBS correspondent to report from Baghdad, the capital of Iraq, at the start of the Iraq war, in 2003.

In 2004 Pelley officially joined the Sunday edition of *60 Minutes*. He traveled extensively all over the world to focus on timely subjects and issues and frequently returned to the Middle East to cover the wars in Iraq and Afghanistan. "I am looking for epic stories of human struggle," he told Peter Johnson for *USA Today* (March 29, 2007), "big issues that I can get my arms around—especially in places that are difficult to get to and which most people don't see." In 2005 Pelley led an Emmy Award–winning investigation into the CIA practice of "rendition," in which suspected terrorists are brought overseas to prisons for questioning and possible torture. In 2006 he traveled to the North Pole for a two-part story on global warming, which offered evidence that the Bush administration had spread false accounts of research reports by climate scientists, in order to block legislation aimed at controlling emissions of greenhouse gases. In 2007 Pelley reported on the effects of global warming in Antarctica. Pelley traveled to the Darfur region of Sudan in 2006 to provide information on the genocide occurring there, and in 2008 he visited China to reveal the black-market dismantling of "e-waste," or electronic waste (discarded electronic products such as computers and televisions), brought there from the U.S. The e-waste investigation was highly acclaimed and won an Emmy Award, a George Polk Award (from Long Island University, in New York), a Gerald Loeb Award (from the University of California–Los Angeles School of Management), the Radio Television Digital News Association's Edward R. Murrow Award, a Sigma Delta Chi Award (from the Society of Professional Journalists), and an Investigative Reporters and Editors Award.

Also as a *60 Minutes* correspondent, Pelley interviewed President Bush at Camp David, Maryland, in 2007; later that year he talked with the Iranian president Mahmoud Ahmadinejad in Tehran, Iran. Pelley's hard-hitting style was particularly evident during the latter interview, when, following a series of questions regarding Iran's alleged acquisition of nuclear weapons, Ahmadinejad accused him of being a CIA agent. "The interviews that are somewhat contentious, those are tremendously fun," Pelley told Chris Hodenfield. "The more evasive the subject is, the more fun it is, the

thrusting and parrying, trying to corner them into the answer that they're so desperate not to give you." He added, "As we know now, [Ahmadinejad] lied all the way through that interview, because we were talking principally about nuclear weapons." Also in 2007 Pelley won an Emmy Award for his interview of the former CIA director George Tenet, who discussed the agency's mishandling of pre-9/11 intelligence. In 2008 Pelley became the first journalist in at least two decades to interview an incumbent Federal Reserve chairman—Ben Bernanke, with whom he spoke about the global economic crisis. He earned another Emmy Award for that broadcast, which he followed up with a series of accounts of people and businesses affected by the recession.

In 2010 Pelley interviewed the U.S. Supreme Court justice John Paul Stevens, shortly before Stevens's retirement after 35 years on the court—a span that made him the third-longest-serving justice in U.S. history, after William O. Douglas and Stephen Johnson Field. In September of that year, Pelley talked with Mike Williams, the chief electronics technician of the Deepwater Horizon, the leased, BP-operated offshore oil-drilling rig that exploded on April 20, 2010 in the Gulf of Mexico, killing 11 crewmen and triggering the worst oil spill in history. Williams was on duty on the rig when it blew up; unable to reach a lifeboat, he was forced to jump into the gulf from a height of 10 stories to escape the flames. In an apparent attempt to control witnesses' accounts of the disaster to news media, BP insisted shortly after the disaster that Williams and the other survivors sign "statements of fact" regarding what had happened. Pelley has called his conversation with Williams, which earned an Alfred I. duPont–Columbia University Award, his "best interview ever."

In May 2011 CBS announced that Pelley would succeed Katie Couric as the anchor and managing editor of the *CBS Evening News*. CBS executives expressed the hope that Pelley will make the *Evening News* more competitive with NBC's *Nightly News* and ABC's *World News*, which have consistently held the top two spots in the Nielsen ratings since the 1980s. Media observers have also perceived Pelley's appointment as an indication that CBS News intended to shift its content more toward hard news, with fewer human-interest features. In a CBS News press release announcing Pelley's appointment, Jeff Fager stated, as quoted by Phil Rosenthal, "We like to think of CBS News as the 'reporter's network,' and I can't think of anybody in this business better suited for the anchor chair than Scott."

On June 6, 2011 Pelley made his official debut as anchor of the *CBS Evening News*. In a review of his inaugural broadcast for the *New York Times* (June 6, 2011, on-line), Alessandra Stanley observed, "No anchor is likely to recapture Mr. Cronkite's cachet and unquestioned authority. What Mr. Pelley really offers is a return to a glamour-free newscast; he is earnest and solemn, dependable and not too dashing. On Monday he showed none of Ms. Couric's pizzazz or Dan Rather's emotion. In style and temperament, Mr. Pelley is closer to Bob Schieffer and Harry Smith, CBS veterans who have filled in as evening anchor with affable aplomb." Stanley added, "The fact that Mr. Pelley's first broadcast wasn't flashy or particularly dramatic at least reminded viewers of one thing they liked about him on *60 Minutes*, namely that he is a serious journalist who does big stories without showy gimmicks."

Pelley serves on the board of directors of the International Rescue Committee and is the co-chair of the committee's board of overseers. In 2006 he was inducted into the Texas Tech University alumni Hall of Fame; he currently serves on the board of the university's School of Mass Communications.

After visiting Pelley at home, Chris Hodenfield described as "beguiling" the journalist's "booming hello, his hale and hearty manner, his flashing eyes, his swift interest in you." In 1983 Pelley married the former Jane Boone, a onetime broadcast journalist. For some years the couple were residents of McLean, Virginia; since 2008 they have lived with their son, Reece, and daughter, Blair, in Darien, Connecticut. Both Reece and Blair have written for the Darien High School student newspaper.

—C.C.

Suggested Reading: Associated Press (on-line) Apr. 28, 2011; *Baltimore Sun* E p1 May 22, 2011; CBS News Web site; *Chicago Tribune* C p21 May 4, 2011; *Los Angeles Times* D p1 May 4, 2011; *New Canaan–Darien Magazine* (on-line) Jan. 2010; *New York Times* B p1 Apr. 12, 2011, B p3 May 4, 2011

Selected Television Shows: as correspondent— *60 Minutes*, 2004– ; as anchor—*CBS Evening News*, 2011–

Pennebaker, James W.

(PEN-ee-bayk-ur)

Mar. 2, 1950– Social psychologist; educator; writer

Address: Dept. of Psychology, University of Texas, 1 University Station A8000, Austin, TX 78712

In the 1970s, three years into his marriage, as the social psychologist James W. Pennebaker told Joann Ellison Rodgers for *Psychology Today* (September/October 1993), he and his wife "went through what all people do who question the nature of a relationship and its future." "She was in law school, I was in grad school, and it was a horrible time," he recalled. Feeling isolated and depressed, Pennebaker began writing to sort out his thoughts and feelings about his marriage. (His wife talked to friends.) Over the course of several days, his writing led him not only to insights about his marriage but also to conclusions regarding his parents, career, sexuality, and other matters. After about a week of such self-exploration, Pennebaker felt his depression lifting and was able to understand and view more clearly and calmly his relationship with his wife. "Each day after writing, I felt fatigued and yet freer . . . ," Pennebaker told Claudia Smith Brinson for the Columbia, South Carolina, *Slate* (July 22, 2007). "Writing helped me to let go and address a number of personal issues that I was too proud to admit to anyone."

That experience sparked Pennebaker's interest in the effects of disclosure, in the form of speaking or writing, on psychological and physical health. A pioneer in the field of therapeutic writing, Pennebaker has conducted many studies that confirm that writing about personal trauma has many benefits, notable among them a strengthened immune system. Pennebaker has published his findings on therapeutic writing in dozens of journal articles and in his book *Opening Up: The Healing Power of Confiding in Others* (1990). Currently the chair of the Department of Psychology at the University of Texas at Austin, he is also known for having helped to create the word-counting and -analysis software Linguistic Inquiry and Word Count (LIWC), which is used to illuminate how people's word choices in spoken or written language reflect their personalities and social milieu. Pennebaker has used LIWC to analyze language used by individuals including poets, politicians and other public figures, and victims of trauma. His book *The Secret Life of Pronouns: How Our Words Reflect Who We Are* was scheduled for publication in August 2011.

The son of William Fendall Pennebaker and the former Elizabeth Whiting, James Whiting Pennebaker was born on March 2, 1950 in Midland, Texas. He told Rodgers that his childhood was "very enjoyable." He attended the University of Arizona for two years and then earned a B.A. degree from Eckerd College, in St. Petersburg, Florida, in 1972. In college, he told Rodgers, he was "something of a thrill seeker and got into psychology after music and eight other majors. Psychology seemed the most fun. I wasn't trying to 'work through' anything. It was Allen Funt on [the TV show] *Candid Camera* who inspired me the most. He watched from behind curtains and that's what psychologists did and I liked that." Pennebaker earned a Ph.D. degree in psychology from the University of Texas at Austin in 1977.

Marsha Miller, courtesy of the Office of Public Affairs, University of Texas at Austin

James W. Pennebaker

After completing his doctorate Pennebaker taught at the University of Virginia at Charlottesville until 1983. His failure to gain tenure there was "a major blow" to his self-esteem, he told Rodgers. "Short of thinking about bombing the place, I wrote and plotted revenge. Seriously, I wrote to help get an understanding of what had happened. I realized finally that my hope that my record would prevail was naive." He added, "Ten years later, it still grates on me, but significantly less. I'm amazed 10 years later how much bitterness and anger I still feel. Just talking to you about it is stressful. So I'll stop." From 1982 to 1983 (while still at the University of Virginia), Pennebaker worked for the Federal Bureau of Investigation (FBI) as a polygraph-unit instructor, training people who administered lie-detector tests. He became an associate professor at Southern Methodist University (SMU), in University Park, a section of Dallas, Texas, in 1983. In 1987 he was promoted to full professor. From 1995 to 1997 he served as the chair of SMU's Psychology Department. Since 1997 he has been a professor of psychology at the University of Texas at Austin; he has chaired the Psychology Department there since 2005. Also since that year he has held the post of International Professor of Psychology at the three-campus University of Central Lancashire, in England.

Earlier, in the late 1970s, at the FBI's request, Pennebaker delivered a series of talks to polygraph instructors. All the instructors reported what seemed to him a surprising observation. Whereas virtually all suspects—whether guilty or not—had markedly nervous reactions when they underwent polygraph tests, suspects who were coaxed into confessions by their testers showed no signs of ner-

vousness the next time they were hooked up to the device. "[The suspect's] heart rate is low, his skin conductance is low, his blood pressure is low," Pennebaker told Henry Dreher for *East West Natural Health* (July 1, 1992). "Just before the handcuffs are put on and he's carted off, every polygraph instructor I've talked to has said that the suspect will get up, warmly shake his hand, and thank him. Many polygraphers get Christmas cards from people in jail."

Soon afterward, in a survey Pennebaker conducted of 700 female college students, 10 percent reported that they had suffered a traumatic sexual experience before the age of 17. A follow-up survey conducted in collaboration with the publication *Psychology Today* (*PT*) revealed that out of 24,000 *PT* readers, 22 percent of women and 10 percent of men reported that they had experienced a sexual trauma before age 17. The vast majority of the victims had never discussed the incidents with anyone, and those silent sufferers were more likely to develop stomach ulcers, infections, heart problems, and other illnesses later in life than those who revealed what had happened to them. Intrigued by the apparent links between the withholding of traumatic memories and physiological stress on the one hand, and between confession and physiological relaxation on the other, Pennebaker wondered if the same effects could be observed in the long term: that is, whether repression might lead to poor long-term health and whether disclosure might foster good health and a sense of well-being.

Later, along with the psychologist Janice Kiecolt-Glaser and the immunologist Ronald Glaser, Pennebaker studied the physical effects of confession on the immune system. Using as subjects the college students from his first study, he required each to sit in a quiet cubicle and write about a traumatic experience for 20 minutes a day, four days in a row. Pennebaker and his collaborators collected blood samples from the participants before and after each writing session and then again six weeks later, measuring the activity of each person's T-cells—cells that help protect against infectious diseases and attack certain tumors. Compared with those of people in a control group, who did not write about their traumas, the T-cells of those who took part in the exercise were notably more active. The students who wrote about traumas that they had never before confided to others showed the greatest increase in T-cell activity. The exercise also appeared to affect the students' immune systems over the longer term: over the next six months, the participating students' visits to healthcare providers dropped significantly. Because the physical benefits from writing tended to dwindle as time passed, Pennebaker suggested that the subjects repeat the writing exercise whenever they were troubled by past traumas.

In 1982 Pennebaker published his findings in a textbook, *Psychology of Physical Symptoms*. At the annual meeting of the American Psychological Association in 1986, Pennebaker presented his finding that healthy physiological changes are more common among students who "talked or wrote about the most traumatic experience in their lives," as quoted by Robert Locke in the *San Diego Union-Tribune* (May 28, 1986). Many people, Pennebaker said, "are every day thinking about these horrible things in their lives, but they've never told anyone about it." In contrast to the findings of some other psychologists, which showed that normal mental health is predicated on a small degree of self-deception, Pennebaker said, "Our hypothesis is, if you maintain the deception, you increase the effort and the risk of disease (such as ulcers, cancer, and hypertension). If you don't talk about it, are you more prone to disease? We have a great deal of evidence suggesting the answer is yes."

Pennebaker studied about 360 residents of San Francisco, California, who were directly affected by the Loma Prieta earthquake, which occurred on October 17, 1989. He interviewed each person eight times over the course of 50 weeks following the earthquake, as well as a similar number of residents of unaffected cities. Pennebaker observed that in the first three to four weeks after the earthquake, the victims talked about their experiences without hesitation. After six weeks he found that although those affected thought about the event as often as they had earlier, they spoke about it much less often and were much less willing to listen to others talk about it. During that period, which Pennebaker dubbed the "inhibition phase," victims maintained a "subtle conspiracy of silence," he told Carin Rubenstein for the *New York Times* (August 18, 1993). They also suffered declining health: three to 12 weeks after the earthquake, about half of the San Francisco subjects reported feeling sick at least once a week. In later years Pennebaker and other researchers identified a similar inhibition phase in groups who had experienced trauma as a result of the Persian Gulf War, the death of Princess Diana, and the September 11, 2001 terrorist attacks. Pennebaker recommended that victims of natural disasters or other traumatic events talk or write about their experiences and emotions not only initially but also after the first few weeks, to avoid the declining health associated with the inhibition phase.

In a study of 60 engineering executives in their 50s who had recently been laid off from the Dallas-based technology company Texas Instruments, Pennebaker, along with Eric D. Buhrfeind and Stefanie P. Spera of Southern Methodist University, measured the effects of therapeutic writing after loss of a job. Twenty of the executives spent 20 minutes a day, for five consecutive days, writing about their thoughts and feelings. Another 20 kept an hour-by-hour record of their job-seeking activities, and the remaining 20 wrote about trivial subjects for 20 minutes a day for five days. After four months the differences among the groups were obvious. Thirty-five percent of those who had written about their feelings had found jobs, whereas only

5 percent of the third group had succeeded and none of those who had kept time-management journals had done so. Because those in the first group did not devote more time to their job searches or have more interviews than those in the other two groups, Pennebaker concluded that they had performed better at job interviews because they "had worked through their anger and bitterness and developed a balanced perspective," he told Henry Dreher. Pennebaker speculated that those in the second group had performed poorly because the time-management exercise encouraged obsessive worrying, anxiety, and self-destructive thought processes. The findings were published in the *Academy of Management Journal* (Volume 37, 1994).

Pennebaker's book *Opening Up: The Healing Power of Confiding in Others* (1990) offers information about his research, an account of his personal experience in using writing during the difficult period of his marriage, and step-by-step instructions for using therapeutic writing exercises on one's own. Pennebaker recommended writing at a time and place free of disturbances at the end of a workday or before bed. He also suggested that people write continuously, without worrying about spelling or grammar. "[Writing] really is different from talking," Pennebaker noted to Marina Pisano for the *San Antonio (Texas) Express-News* (May 30, 2004). "For one thing, it slows things down. You stand back. You're forced to organize things in ways you haven't done before." A revised edition of *Opening Up* was published in 1997 with the subtitle *The Healing Power of Expressing Emotions.* That edition has been translated into German, Spanish, Korean, Japanese, Hungarian, Polish, and Indonesian.

Pennebaker's research on the benefits of writing and talk therapy for coming to grips with traumatic events led him to wonder what could be learned from analyzing every single word people use when they speak or write. In 2001, along with Roger J. Booth and Martha E. Francis, Pennebaker created the software program Linguistic Inquiry and Word Count. LIWC (pronounced "luke") notes how many times each word in a given text was used and, by means of its vast dictionary, assigns each word to one or more categories; for instance, the words "talk" and "they" are assigned to the category "social words," while "cheek," "hands," and "split" are considered biological words. Pennebaker first used the program to analyze a series of texts written by people as they recovered from serious illnesses or other forms of trauma. He found that as people's health improved, their use of first-person pronouns decreased while their use of causal words, such as "because," "cause," and "effect," increased. Pennebaker concluded that people whose health was improving were not "simply ruminating" about the traumatic experiences, but instead "were changing the way they were thinking about things," as he explained to Jessica Wapner for the *New York Times* (October 14, 2008). According to Pennebaker's University of Texas home page, LIWC can also help to identify a writer's or speaker's gender, approximate age, and social class. (For instance, women tend to use more pronouns whereas men tend to use more articles, prepositions, and big words.) In addition, Pennebaker noted on his Web site that word use can also indicate whether a person is telling the truth, whether a speaker is dominant in a conversation, and a person's relative level of testosterone.

In 2001 Pennebaker used LIWC technology to analyze the texts of poets—a group that tends to have a much higher rate of suicide than the general population—to determine if a poet's word choices could predict his or her suicidal tendencies. In the study researchers analyzed 300 works written by nine well-known poets who had committed suicide—among them John Berryman, Anne Sexton, and Sylvia Plath—and nine notable poets who had not. The LIWC analysis showed that the group of poets who had committed suicide used the pronoun "I" much more often than other poets and made fewer references to other people. They also had fewer references to "us," "we," and "our" than the other poets at similar stages in their careers. In the late stages of their careers, they used fewer "communication words," such as "talk," "share," or "listen." Pennebaker concluded that the suicidal poets' word choices reflected a declining interest in social relationships. "Beforehand, I would have predicted that the suicidal poets would have been more dark and depressing and used more negative emotion words and fewer positive emotion words," Pennebaker told William Hageman for the *Chicago Tribune* (August 31, 2001). Instead, he found that the suicidal poets expressed more positive emotion than the nonsuicidal poets and about the same degree of negative emotion. Pennebaker thought that that finding might be connected with symptoms of bipolar disorder, a form of mental illness, characterized by alternating extremes of exuberance and despair, that can lead to suicide. In the paper "Word Use in the Poetry of Suicidal and Non-Suicidal Poets," written with S. W. Stirman and published in *Psychosomatic Medicine* (Volume 63, 2001), Pennebaker noted that although certain words appeared to be markers for suicide, the study was incomplete and the issue should be further researched.

Pennebaker has also used LIWC to analyze the speaking style of public figures. His analysis in 2002 of speech patterns of Rudolph Giuliani during Giuliani's eight years as mayor of New York City focused on his spontaneous responses to questions from the press. Pennebaker found that in his first term (1994–98), during which he implemented tough crime-fighting programs and gained a reputation for irascibility, the mayor used more big words, more articles ("a," "an," and "the"), and fewer pronouns than he did during his second term (1998–2002). The pronouns he used during his first term, Pennebaker noted, often referred to "a vague group of crime-fighters." During his second

term, in the wake of his being diagnosed with prostate cancer in the spring of 2000 and the September 11, 2001 terrorist attacks, Giuliani's word choices changed dramatically. He used many more inclusive pronouns to refer to all New Yorkers and far fewer "anger" words, such as "hate." While Giuliani had often been described as "sarcastic, irritable, and defensive," as Erica Goode wrote for the *New York Times* (February 6, 2002), Pennebaker concluded that "in the face of a crisis, Giuliani's mask dissolved."

In 2008, at the request of the FBI, Pennebaker analyzed the word choices of the radical terrorist group Al Qaeda in videotapes, interviews, and letters. One of Pennebaker's conclusions was that, while the Al Qaeda leader Osama bin Laden's use of first-person pronouns had remained relatively consistent for several years, his second-in-command, Ayman al-Zawahri, had recently begun to use first-person pronouns much more frequently. In his report, published in the *Content Analysis Reader* (July 2008) and quoted by Wapner, Pennebaker concluded, "This dramatic increase suggests greater insecurity, feelings of threat, and perhaps a shift in his relationship with bin Laden."

During the 2008 presidential-election campaign, Pennebaker and his colleagues used LIWC to analyze the word choices of the candidates and members of the media who covered the races. He regularly posted his observations on a Web site, Wordwatchers.wordpress.com. In an October 12, 2008 post, Pennebaker noted that throughout the campaign, the Democratic nominee, U.S. senator Barack Obama of Illinois, used verbs at a remarkably higher rate than the Republican nominee, U.S. senator John McCain of Arizona. McCain used articles much more often than Obama did. "These patterns suggest that McCain's natural way of understanding the world is to first label the problem and find a way to put it into a pre-existing category," Pennebaker noted. "Obama is more likely to define the world as ongoing actions or processes." LIWC has been translated into several languages and is available for purchase on-line.

Currently Pennebaker and his research team are involved in a project "that explores people's relationships with others when they are harboring a big secret," according to his Web site. Their research material consists of e-mail messages sent and received on the gmail accounts of volunteers 18 years of age or older who have saved most of their incoming and outgoing mail for the past year and who have kept big secrets for the past year or two. The participants will not have to reveal their secrets.

Pennebaker's therapeutic-writing techniques are now used widely by physicians, psychiatrists, and others, and their beneficial effects have been confirmed in many studies. He told Joann Ellison Rodgers that laypeople should "never take any finding too seriously," in Rodgers's paraphrase. "Be your own researcher; learn what works for you. What works for others may not help you at all. Borrow an idea, apply it to yourself, and it if works take it. If not, move on." Pennebaker's research has been funded by the National Science Foundation, the National Institutes of Health, and the Department of Defense. His many honors include an honorary doctoral degree from the University of Louvain, in Belgium; the Pavlov Award from the Pavlov Society; and the President's Associates University Teaching Award from the University of Texas. He lives in Austin with his wife, Ruth Burney Pennebaker, who has published several novels for young adults, one novel for adults, and a memoir; she also maintains a blog called geezersisters.com. The couple have two adult children—a daughter, Teal, and a son, Nicholas.

—M.R.M.

Suggested Reading: *Chicago Tribune* C p1 Aug. 31, 2001; (Columbia, South Carolina) *Slate* p9 July 22, 2007; *East West Natural Health* p74+ July 1, 1992; *New York Times* Science Desk p11 Aug. 18, 1993, p5 Oct. 14, 2008; *Psychology Today* p56+ Sep./Oct. 1993; *San Antonio (Texas) Express-News* K p1 May 30, 2004; *San Diego Union-Tribune* A p1 May 28, 1986; wordwatchers.-wordpress.com;

Selected Books: *Psychology of Physical Symptoms*, 1982; *Opening Up: The Healing Power of Confiding in Others*, 1990; *The Secret Life of Pronouns: How Our Words Reflect Who We Are*, 2011; as editor—*Collective Memory of Political Events*, 1997

Astrid Stawiarz/Getty Images

Pinsky, Drew

Sep. 4, 1958– Physician; radio talk-show host; television host; writer

Address: c/o Lapides/Lear Entertainment, 14724 Ventura Blvd., Penthouse, Sherman Oaks, CA 91403

"I have a pretty keen ethical compass, that's why I can walk this line," Drew Pinsky told Kara Jesella for the *New York Times* (February 3, 2008). Pinsky was referring to the line that separates his work as a practicing physician and psychotherapist—he is board-certified in both internal medicine and addiction medicine—from his activities as the cele-

brated radio and television personality known as Dr. Drew. As Dr. Drew, Pinsky has offered health-, sex-, and addiction-related advice on radio since the early 1980s, when he began co-hosting a segment of the show *Loveline*; he has remained with *Loveline* as host or co-host ever since. On television Pinsky has imparted words of wisdom in the same subjects since the mid-1990s, as co-host of the TV version of *Loveline*, which aired from 1996 to 2000; as a medical expert for news and talk shows; and as the host of *Strictly Sex with Dr. Drew*, *Strictly Dr. Drew*, *Sex . . . with Mom and Dad*, *Celebrity Rehab with Dr. Drew*, *Sex Rehab with Dr. Drew*, and *Sober House*. In a piece about *Celebrity Rehab* for the *New York Times Magazine* (January 3, 2010), Chris Norris described Pinsky as the "face of addiction medicine" and the "surgeon general of youth culture." Pinsky, Norris continued, "commands an unusual blend of medical credentials and pop-culture savvy—he is fluent in textese, neuroscience, nitrous hits and psychodynamics, which he combines with a cool, eloquent charisma honed over 25 years in the media." "My goal was always to be part of pop culture and relevant to young people, to interact with the people they hold in high esteem," Pinsky told Jesella.

Pinsky has extended his reach to youths as well as to older people in other ways as well: through his Web site, drdrew.com; lectures at colleges and elsewhere; newspaper articles; and several books. Now 52, Pinsky has maintained a private medical practice for many years, and he is a staff member of Huntington Memorial Hospital, in Pasadena, California. He is also an assistant clinical professor of psychology at the Keck School of Medicine of the University of Southern California, in Los Angeles. For two decades he served as the medical director or co–medical director of the Department of Chemical Dependency Services of Aurora Las Encinas Hospital, in Pasadena. He has been honored by the Planned Parenthood Association of America (in 1998); the Henry J. Kaiser Foundation (also in 1998); the National Council on Sexual Addiction and Compulsivity (1999), for his contributions to public education; and the Entertainment Industries Council (2008), for his accurate portrayals of addiction and mental health in his shows.

David Drew Pinsky was born on September 4, 1958 in Pasadena. His younger sister, Dana, born in 1964, is a paralegal. His mother, born Eleanor Stansbury, appeared in a half-dozen films (under the name Helene Stanton) before devoting herself to full-time homemaking; his father, Morton, was a physician. As a boy Pinsky sometimes accompanied his father on house calls, and from early on he aspired to pursue a career in medicine. As a student in the high-school division of Polytechnic School, a private institution in Pasadena, he played on the football team, acted in student theatrical productions, and was elected class president. He attended Amherst College, in Amherst, Massachusetts, where he studied psychology as part of his premed curriculum. After he earned a B.S. degree, in biology, in 1980, he entered the University of Southern California School of Medicine (known as the Keck School of Medicine since 1999). He graduated with an M.D. degree in 1984. After serving a residency (1984–88) at Huntington Memorial Hospital, he began working at Aurora Las Encinas Hospital, where he became the medical director of the Department of Chemical Dependency Services in 1989 and later co–medical director. His book *Cracked: Putting Broken Lives Together Again* (2003) was inspired in part by his experiences at the hospital, where he worked until early 2010. Also in the late 1980s Pinsky set up a private practice in Pasadena.

Earlier, while Pinsky was in his fourth year of medical school, a friend working at the Los Angeles rock radio station KROQ suggested that Pinsky join the staff of its late-Sunday-night call-in show, *Loveline*. The program's creators, the disk jockeys Jim "Poorman" Trenton and Egil Aalvik ("Swedish Egil"), wanted someone to respond to questions of a medical nature that they were not equipped to handle. Although he had not yet earned a medical degree, Pinsky was brought on board, as a volunteer, to host a segment called "Ask a Surgeon." (He worked without pay for the next seven years.) While listening to *Loveline* the weekend before he started in the job, he heard one of the disk jockeys announce that a "real doctor" would soon be answering inquiries about sexually transmitted diseases. "I was wondering what I'd gotten myself into," he recalled to Bram Teitelman for *Billboard Radio Monitor* (January 21, 2005). In any event, the need for informed advice was obvious to him. "I was overwhelmed at the ignorance and need for education, and the desperateness of the listening community out there," he told Craig Rosen for the *Los Angeles Times* (January 27, 1985). "Let's say, Lisa, a 14-year-old . . . , calls and says that she was molested by her stepfather five months ago, and now she found out he has gonorrhea. She'll want to know whether or not she should have herself checked out."

After about a half-year, Pinsky, Trenton, and "Spacin'" Scott Mason, KROQ's operations manager, launched a new segment, "On Call with Dr. Drew," which soon became very popular. "On Call" started with 15 minutes of similarly themed songs (often about sex), after which the three men took callers' questions. Trenton provided comic relief and Pinsky offered practical advice, while Mason contributed suggestions that had elements of both. Renee Tawa, writing for the *Los Angeles Times* (August 22, 1993), described "On Call with Dr. Drew" as a "live-wire mixture of bawdy guests, in-studio antics, crude sexual banter and, when Pinsky [could] slip in a word edgewise, sound medical advice to scared young callers who ask[ed] about AIDS, sex, suicide and drugs." In 1992 *Loveline* began broadcasting for two hours every night from Sunday through Thursday. By the next year *Loveline* had begun reaching additional cities along the West Coast and had become the top-rated radio show in its time slot. Also in 1993 Riki Rachtman, the host of the MTV heavy-metal show *Headbanger's Ball*, replaced Trenton. The change in personnel pleased Pinsky, who told Jon Matsumoto for the *Los Angeles Times* (May 23, 1994) that with Trenton, "we constantly verged on the edge of being exploitative and harming people." With the more-subdued Rachtman, he said, "I feel proud and comfortable, and I feel like we're doing some good work here and there."

In 1995 *Loveline* became syndicated nationally through the radio network Westwood One, and the comedian Adam Carolla joined it as an additional co-host. Clashes between Carolla and Rachtman led the latter to leave in 1996; he was not replaced. According to Andi Geloo, writing for the *Washington Times* (October 26, 1996), Pinsky's "medical expertise intermingles with Mr. Carolla's unrestrained and hilarious stream-of-personal-life tidbits to create a lighthearted atmosphere in which teen-agers can seek valid advice by exposing dangerous details with impunity." *The Drew and Adam Book: A Survival Guide to Life and Love* (1998), which Pinsky and Carolla wrote with Marshall Shine, covers much of the same ground as the shows.

For nearly a year after Carolla's departure, in 2005, Pinsky hosted *Loveline* by himself. The KROQ disk jockey known as Stryker (Ted Stryker, born Gary Sandorf) served as co-host for nearly three years, beginning in 2006. Since early 2010 Pinsky's co-host has been another KROQ personality, Michael "Psycho Mike" Catherwood. *Loveline* currently airs live from 10:00 p.m. to midnight, Pacific Standard Time, Thursday through Sunday, on KROQ. It is syndicated nationwide to many other stations (usually, ones devoted to rock or alternative music or talk) and can be heard internationally on-line, through Web sites of affiliate stations.

In late 1996 *Loveline* began airing not only on radio but also as an hour-long show broadcast every weeknight on MTV with a studio audience present. Except for the addition of celebrity guests, its format resembled that of the radio version; viewers could ask for advice via phone, fax, e-mail, prerecorded videos, or live video conference. "Here are young adults willing to stand up, with a microphone, and ask on national television whether they should tell their boyfriend/girlfriend that they've been sleeping with their best friend . . . ," L. Kelly wrote for the *Wichita (Kansas) Eagle* (March 12, 1997), adding that the show's "real star" was "the very frank—and often very funny—discussion about sex and relationships." With its hosts "dispensing advice on everything from addiction to impotency," Karla Peterson wrote for the *San Diego Union-Tribune* (May 22, 1997), *Loveline* "is frank, funny and fascinating. . . . It is also totally addictive, so don't tune in unless you plan on getting hooked." By 1998 the TV version of *Loveline* was attracting some 500,000 viewers, and the radio show about three million listeners. Although Pinsky told Jae-Ha Kim for the *Chicago Sun-Times* (November 24, 1996) that he and Carolla enjoyed the "anonymity" afforded by radio, they "couldn't pass up the opportunity to reach another audience" via TV. "It breaks my heart to hear the terrible things that have happened to some of the people who call us," he said. "They don't know of any other outlet to straighten out their lives so they come to us. The way we look at it, we're not there to treat them so much as we are to educate them, and the TV show gives us another forum to do this."

Some parents and others, Don Mayhew reported for the *Fresno (California) Bee* (November 9, 1997), disapproved of *Loveline*'s "candid language and willingness to explore outrageous behavior with a decidedly tolerant tone." Carolla acknowledged to Neal Justin for the Minneapolis, Minnesota, *Star Tribune* (February 23, 1997) that "there's a fair amount of locker-room talk, a fair amount of innuendo—and sometimes not even innuendo," but he insisted that "if we don't create that environment, then we're never going to reach the people we want to talk to. You put two doctors on here talking about abstinence for two hours a night [on radio], you're not going to get a 13-year-old to tune in. He's got to hear a rock star. He's got to hear a fart joke." Pinsky felt similarly; as he had told Geloo, "My willingness to crawl into [teen] culture and take some of the abuse and just go along with them makes me OK in their eyes. The reason they choose to talk with me is that I am not judgmental. I acknowledge that this is their culture, and I am just an honored visitor." The televised *Loveline* went off the air in 2000.

In 1999 Pinsky unveiled drdrew.com, which offers health and lifestyle advice in the form of articles and streamed video segments. In 2000 he served as a "health and human-relations expert" on the first season of the reality-television series *Big Brother*. Since then he has appeared as a guest on TV shows hosted by Larry King, Tyra Banks, Ellen DeGeneres, Conan O'Brien, and Chelsea Handler, among others, and he is a regular contributor

on the *Today Show*. He has also served as a medical expert on news programs on CNN, MSNBC, and other networks. He voiced characters on the TV cartoon *Family Guy* and the Carolla-produced prank-phone-call puppet show *Crank Yankers* and appeared as himself in an episode of the teen drama *Dawson's Creek*. He played a doctor in the film *New York Minute* (2004), starring Mary-Kate and Ashley Olsen. The year 2004 also saw the publication of Pinsky's book *When Painkillers Become Dangerous: What Everyone Needs to Know About OxyContin and Other Prescription Drugs*, co-written with four others.

Pinsky hosted his own sex-themed talk show, *Strictly Sex with Dr. Drew*, on the Discovery Health Network in 2005. The show was dropped after 10 installments and was followed in 2006 by a similar series, *Strictly Dr. Drew*, which ran for a year on the same network. Pinsky launched a new radio talk show, *Dr. Drew*, in November 2007, with KGIL in Los Angeles as the flagship station. The show, which was similar to *Loveline*, was canceled in 2008.

Celebrity Rehab with Dr. Drew has aired on the Video Hits One (VH-1) network since January 2008. Each season consists of eight or nine installments, during which the camera follows Pinsky and rehab-center staff members as they assist patients through talk therapy and medical interventions. The program does not hide some of the unpleasantness that may accompany treatment: patients have been filmed while suffering severe physical withdrawal symptoms or behaving belligerently or violently. Those undergoing treatment—newsmakers, not all of them entertainers, who are addicted to alcohol and/or drugs—have included Brigitte Nielsen, Jeff Conaway, Daniel Baldwin, Jaimee Foxworth, Steven Adler, Rodney King, Gary Busey, Mackenzie Phillips, Tom Sizemore, Heidi Fleiss, Rachel Uchitel, and Dennis Rodman. Each celebrity patient is paid to participate in the program, which is filmed at the Pasadena Recovery Center. The idea for *Celebrity Rehab* came from Pinsky, its executive producer, who, according to Norris, was "alarmed by the tabloids' portrayal of addiction as yet another indulgence of the rich and famous" and wanted to reveal some of the hazards of addiction while helping victims well-known to many TV viewers. "For me, addiction exposes all of the brain mechanism under the influence of a profoundly distorted primary motivation," Pinsky told Norris. "It's such a window into how we function as human beings." He also wanted to target drug and alcohol abuse as a symptom of what he believes is a "toxic new form of narcissism, stoked by the media," as Norris put it—an "emerging strain of supernarcissism" marked by "histrionics, aggression, hypersexuality, [and] drug abuse," often associated with people who successfully audition for reality shows such as *Big Brother*. (That cultural phenomenon is the subject of Pinsky's 2009 book, *Mirror Effect: How Celebrity Narcissism Is Seducing America*.) Michael

Hirschorn, a VH-1 executive from 2001 to 2008, told Norris, "Dr. Drew is one of a relatively small number of psychiatric professionals who is both credible and 100 percent TV-friendly. And he was willing to take all of the risks on himself, to say, 'I'm gonna guarantee that this will be a legitimate and nonexploitative process.'"

In response to the accusation of some critics that Pinsky has indeed exploited addicted celebrities, Pinsky told Jesella that the people who participate in *Celebrity Rehab* "'know exactly what they're getting into and have allowed [us] to resolve the problem, to help others." Other critics of *Celebrity Rehab* have cautioned that the presence of cameras at the treatment center "may create a set of false circumstances that may unduly change the subjects' behavior," as John Kelly, the associate director of the Center for Addiction Medicine at Massachusetts General Hospital, told Tenley Woodman for the *Boston Herald* (January 10, 2008). Jeffrey Foote, a clinical psychologist who treats substance abusers and is the executive director of the Center for Motivation and Change, in New York, complained to Norris, "The velvet-glove confrontational stuff Pinsky does is what works for TV, but it's not what works for patients," and he warned, "The dramatic confrontations seen on the show are actually more likely to drive less-severe substance abusers, who are by far the majority, away from seeking treatment." John J. Mariani, the director of the Substance Treatment and Research Service at Columbia University, told Norris, "The problem here is that Dr. Drew benefits from their participation, which must have some powerful effects on his way of relating to them. He also has a vested interest in the outcome of their treatment being interesting to viewers, which is also not in their best interest. Treatment with conflicts of interest isn't treatment." Pinsky has maintained that "nearly all" former participants "credit *Rehab* with helping them," according to Norris, who also wrote, "Many physicians who treat addiction salute [the show's] efforts, and a large number of recovering addicts praise its portrayal of addiction as a disease." Pinsky also told Norris, "The people that need what we have are watching VH1. Not the people watching educational TV, the NPR crowd. You gotta give 'em what they want so you can give 'em what they need." "The problem with my peers is that they don't understand television," he remarked. His shows *Sex Rehab with Dr. Drew* and *Sober House* both debuted in 2009; *Sex . . . with Mom and Dad*, aimed at encouraging teens to talk with their parents about sex, debuted the previous year. Pinsky is slated to host a talk show on the TV channel HLN that will debut in 2011.

With his closely cropped silver hair, perennial tan, "gym-buff torso," and stylish clothing and eyeglasses, Pinsky reminded Norris of Superman's alter ego, Clark Kent; widely described as self-effacing, he admitted to Norris that in some ways he is a "closet narcissist." "I was struck by Pinsky's disarming conversation style, which involved fre-

quent nods, appreciative laughs, affect mirroring and gentle knee pats," Norris wrote. A self-described workaholic, Pinsky typically runs five miles at least three days a week and regularly lifts weights. He likes to listen to opera and is a trained baritone. He and his wife, the former Susan Sailer, married in 1991. The couple live in Pasadena with their triplets—two sons, Douglas and Jordan, and a daughter, Paulina, who were born in 1992.

—W.D.

Suggested Reading: *Billboard Radio Monitor* Jan. 21, 2005; Keppler Associates Web site; *Los Angeles Times* J p8 Aug. 22, 1993; *New York Times* (on-line) Feb. 3, 2008, Feb. 8, 2009; *New York Times Magazine* p26+ Jan. 3, 2010; *Newsweek* p62 June 15, 1998; *People* p65 Feb. 11, 2008; *Washington Times* B p1+ Oct. 26, 1995

Selected Books: *The Drew and Adam Book: A Survival Guide to Life and Love* (with Adam Carrolla), 1998; *Cracked: Putting Broken Lives Together Again,* 2003; *When Painkillers Become Dangerous: What Everyone Needs to Know About OxyContin and Other Prescription Drugs* (with Stephanie Brown, Robert J. Meyers, William White, Marvin D. Seppala), 2004; *Mirror Effect: How Celebrity Narcissism Is Seducing America* (with S. Mark Young and Jill Stern), 2009

Selected Radio Shows: *Loveline,* 1984– ; *Dr. Drew,* 2007–08

Selected Television Shows: *Loveline,* 1996–2000; *Strictly Sex with Dr. Drew,* 2005; *Strictly Dr. Drew,* 2006–07; *Celebrity Rehab with Dr. Drew,* 2008– ; *Sex . . . with Mom and Dad,* 2008– ; *Sex Rehab with Dr. Drew,* 2009– ; *Celebrity Rehab Presents Sober House,* 2009–

Pressman, Edward R.

Apr. 11, 1943– Film producer

Address: Edward R. Pressman Film Corp., 47 Murray St., New York, NY 10007

In the past four decades, Edward R. Pressman has produced or executive-produced nearly 80 films, many of them by independent filmmakers. His reputation rests in part on his ability to recognize and nurture outstanding talent and his eagerness to go out on a limb for projects that he regards as original and worthwhile. Pressman was 26 when his first feature film debuted, in 1969; called *Out of It,* the movie was directed by Paul Williams, his business partner at that time. Pressman's credits since then include Brian De Palma's *Sisters,* Wolfgang Pedersen's *Das Boot,* Terrence Malick's *Badlands,* John Milius's *Conan the Barbarian,* Oliver Stone's two

David Livingston/Getty Images

Edward R. Pressman

Wall Street pictures, Barbet Schroeder's *Reversal of Fortune*, Kathryn Bigelow's *Blue Steel*, Danny DeVito's *Hoffa*, David Byrne's *True Stories*, Harold Becker's *City Hall*, and Mary Harron's *American Psycho*. "I think I went into film for the same reason I went into philosophy," Pressman, who studied philosophy at Stanford University and the London School of Economics and Politics (LSE) in the 1960s, told Lawrence Van Gelder for the *New York Times* (August 2, 1985). "It seemed the most comprehensive field. It combined elements of art and academics with business and economics. I think film is the most encompassing form of enterprise in the modern world—from painting to music to theater to dance. Business and all the wide range of our culture—that's what appealed to me." He told Robert Epstein for the *Los Angeles Times* (February 11, 1993) that the films he had chosen to produce fell into "three broad groups": "pop fantasy," such as De Palma's *Paradise Lost*, Alex Proyas's *The Crow*, and Danny Cannon's *Judge Dredd*; "sophisticated, urban films," such as *Wall Street* and *Hoffa*; and totally independent films, in which no major studio is involved in any way, among them Abel Ferrara's *Bad Lieutenant* and Stone's *Talk Radio*. (Many independently made films are supported to some extent by Metro-Goldwyn-Mayer, Warner Bros., or other major studios.)

Pressman's work has earned him retrospectives at the Museum of Modern Art (MoMA), in 1988, and the Brooklyn Academy of Music (BAM), in New York City, in 2001. "It's rare for us to do a retrospective of a producer's work," Adrienne Mancia, a longtime MoMA film curator, told Joseph Gelmis for New York *Newsday* (January 8, 1988). "And certainly we haven't done anyone in mid-

career, which is where Ed Pressman is." But Pressman, Mancia declared, "is the very model of the kind of independent film maker this country needs. He takes risks with his own money, backing new talent. He's loyal to young filmmakers, very sensitive to the needs and demands of artists." In 1989 Pressman was named the "producer of the decade" in a poll of 54 U.S. film critics conducted by *American Film* magazine, and that same year he was named a Chevalier des Arts et Lettres of France; in 2003 the Independent Feature Project, an organization of independent filmmakers, honored him with the Gotham Award for lifetime achievement. "Finding a serious appreciation of a producer in the American press is not a common experience," the film critic David Thomson wrote for the *New York Times* (February 4, 2001). "The impresarios of theater, the museum world, or opera and popular music have their place. But in film the producer is almost invariably cast as the heavy in the story of art versus commerce—whereas any number of encounters in Hollywood will confirm that there are few people as money-minded as some of our directors, and that few are as devoted to making good, different pictures as Edward R. Pressman."

Somewhat analogous to project managers in other industries, producers oversee the entire filmmaking process. They select scripts for development, secure financing, approve the choice of (and sometimes hire) directors, principal actors, and production staff, and ensure that movies are completed according to schedule and within their budgets. Because of difficulties in funding or in gaining all required rights, changes in scripts, the firing or quitting of directors or actors, location problems, or myriad other stumbling blocks, many years may pass between the conception of a film and the picture's release. "I establish the context for the film maker to realize his vision," Pressman explained to Charles Champlin for the *Los Angeles Times* (January 7, 1988). "Sometimes I have to introduce a new film maker to the whole process, help him find a cinematographer and so on. Other times the focus is just on the script. As a producer I function differently on different projects. The hardest thing to learn is how *not* to be something the film maker doesn't need. The ideal is the partnership of the producer and the film maker." Pressman added, "Mine is a vicarious role, I suppose. I live through the visions of others. But I love it, helping people who want to work." The responsibilities of an executive producer usually lie in financial, legal, or other corporate realms rather than in creative aspects of the making of a film. Pressman talked about the sorts of vagaries and complexities connected with filmmaking in his interview with Robert Epstein and in a conversation posted (June 2006) on the Web site of M. J. Simpson, a writer whose expertise includes science-fiction and horror movies. The Edward R. Pressman Film Corp. has offices in Los Angeles, California, and New York. With John Schmidt Pressman founded the production and distribution company ContentFilm in 2001. With Terrence Malick he established the firm Sunflower Productions in 2004.

Edward Rambach Pressman—"Ed" to friends and associates—was born on April 11, 1943 in New York City to Jack and Lynn (Rambach) Pressman. He has a younger brother, James, and an older half-sister, Ann, from his mother's first marriage. His father founded a toy company in 1922, after serving in World War I. Now called the Pressman Toy Corp., it has enjoyed great success since the late 1920s, when Jack Pressman acquired the rights to a German game and marketed it in the U.S. as Hop Ching Checkers, later known as Chinese Checkers. After Jack Pressman's death, in 1959, Lynn Pressman ran the company, and Ed Pressman helped her. Lynn Pressman married and was widowed twice more. James Pressman has served as the toy company's CEO since 1977.

The Pressman family lived on New York City's West Side. The filmmaker James Toback, a neighbor and classmate of Ed Pressman's, told David Thomson that Pressman was a "quiet, shy, bookish" boy who "always had the best toys, and he'd share them." Pressman has traced his love of business to the activities of his energetic and creative parents, and his love of films to his youth, when he worked at one or another of the concession stands in three movie theaters owned by an uncle of his; he was allowed to watch up to four movies on those days. He attended New York City private schools run by the Ethical Culture Society: through sixth grade, the Ethical Culture School, in Manhattan, and for the next six years, the Fieldston School, in the Riverdale section of the Bronx. The teenage Pressman was deeply impressed by M, The Blue Angel, and From Caligari to Hitler and other films his teacher of modern history included in the curriculum.

Pressman earned a B.A. degree in philosophy, with honors, from Stanford University, in California, in 1965 and then enrolled at LSE, in England. Eager to be in a filmmaking environment, he took a nonpaying job at the Columbia Pictures office in London. During that period he became a fan of French New Wave films. At a party he met Paul Williams, a Harvard University alumnus and Cambridge University graduate student. "We talked about film half the night. He'd made a documentary at Harvard and had an idea for a short film," Pressman told Champlin. Pressman told Thomson that he pictured Williams as the brilliant actor and director Orson Welles and himself as the notoriously bad-tempered studio head Louis B. Mayer; he has never wanted to direct films himself. "With Paul, at the beginning, I totally loved getting behind his vision," he recalled to Thomson. Pressman's wife, the actress Annie McEnroe, told Thomson, "Eddie once said, 'You have to be a very quick thinker to be a director.' And he likes to take his time. . . . But once he makes up his mind—the perseverance!"

In England Pressman and Williams formed a production company and made a short film, Girl, inspired by the same-titled Beatles song. (The film was shown at the MoMA retrospective, in 1988.) After they returned to the U.S., the partners opened an office in New York. The office soon became a popular gathering place for New York University film-school graduates, including Martin Scorsese and Brian De Palma. Thanks to the creditworthiness of his parents' business, Pressman secured $225,000 to finance his and Williams's first feature film, Out of It. Written and directed by Williams and produced by Pressman, Out of It featured Jon Voight as a suburban high-school football star. United Artists (UA) bought the movie and contracted Pressman and Williams for two more pictures. Capitalizing on the popularity of Midnight Cowboy, which propelled Voight to stardom in 1969, UA released Out of It at the end of that year. It was screened at the 1970 Berlin International Film Festival.

Pressman and Williams next made the drama The Revolutionary (1970), "a masterful piece of social observation," according to an undated Time Out Film Guide review; the movie starred Voight, Robert Duvall, and Seymour Cassel. Their third feature film, Dealing: Or the Berkeley-to-Boston Forty-Brick Lost-Bag Blues (1972), based on a novel by Michael Crichton and his brother, Douglas, starred Robert F. Lyons, John Lithgow, and Barbara Hershey. At one point around that time, as Pressman recalled to Champlin, he "had a choice of three projects"—"a George Lucas script called 'Cruising,' which later became American Graffiti; a Scorsese script called 'Gaga,' which in a changed form became Mean Streets, and Brian's 'Sisters.' I did Sisters"—a psychological thriller, released in 1973. By that time Williams had parted ways with Pressman, to pursue other interests.

Pressman next served as executive producer for Terrence Malick's debut film, Badlands (1973), which won a huge amount of critical acclaim. Badlands—written by Malick as well—starred Martin Sheen and Sissy Spacek in a dramatization of Charles Starkweather and Caril-Ann Fugate's real-life killing spree, in 1958. In 1993 Badlands was added to the National Film Registry, which recognizes "culturally, historically, or aesthetically significant" motion pictures.

Along with Girl, The Revolutionary, Out of It, and Sisters, Badlands was among the 11 films MoMA chose for its retrospective of Pressman's work, held in 1988. The others included Phantom of the Paradise (1974), a satirical rock-and-roll musical directed by De Palma; Despair (1978), the first English-language film by the renowned German director Rainer Werner Fassbinder; John Byrum's Heart Beat (1980), a fictionalized, fact-based glimpse into the lives of the writer Jack Kerouac, his buddy Neal Cassady, and Cassady's wife (played by John Heard, Nick Nolte, and Sissy Spacek, respectively); and Das Boot, released in Germany in 1981 and in the U.S., with the actors' voices dubbed in English, in 1982. Based on an internationally best-selling book by Lothar-Günther Buchheim, *Das Boot* is about a World War II patrol mission conducted by a German U-boat crew. It was the first feature film by the German director Wolfgang Petersen to receive worldwide acclaim and won six Academy Award nominations.

Also included in the MoMA retrospective was *Conan the Barbarian* (1982), with Arnold Schwarzenegger in the title role. After seeing the then–professional bodybuilder in the documentary *Pumping Iron* (1977), Pressman began looking for a project in which to cast him. He decided on a fantasy series by Robert E. Howard, set thousands of years ago. Oliver Stone and John Milius loosely based the script on Howard's tales, and Milius directed the film, with Schwarzenegger in the title role and James Earl Jones as Conan's nemesis. Made for an estimated $20 million, *Conan the Barbarian* grossed nearly $40 million domestically and $29 million overseas. Pressman sold the rights to its sequel, the less successful *Conan the Destroyer* (1984), to finance other projects. The 11th film in the MoMA retrospective was *True Stories* (1986), directed by David Byrne of the musical group the Talking Heads; the filmscript was by Byrne, the Pulitzer Prize–winning playwright Beth Henley, and the actor Stephen Tobolowsky. Pressman executive-produced *True Stories*; its cast included Byrne (as narrator), John Goodman, Swoosie Kurtz, Spalding Gray, and Annie McEnroe.

Seven of the films in the MoMA retrospective appeared in the 25-film Pressman retrospective at BAM in 2001. The others included Fred Schepisi's *Plenty* (1985), with Sir John Gielgud, Meryl Streep, Sam Neill, and Sting; Oliver Stone's *Talk Radio* (1988), starring Eric Bogosian, based on the same-named Pulitzer Prize–nominated one-man play (1987) by Bogosian and Ted Savinar; David Hare's *Paris by Night* (1988), with Michael Gambon and Charlotte Rampling; and Kathryn Bigelow's *Blue Steel*, with Jamie Lee Curtis and Ron Silver—the last-named being one of five Pressman-produced films that premiered in 1990. BAM also screened two of the others: Barbet Schroeder's *Reversal of Fortune*, starring Jeremy Irons, who won an Oscar for his portrayal of the real-life Claus von Bülow; and *To Sleep with Anger*, which Charles Burnett directed from his own screenplay. *To Sleep with Anger* starred Danny Glover as a mysterious drifter whose prolonged visit to the home of an old acquaintance (played by Paul Butler) and his wife (Mary Alice) leads to serious troubles within their family. For his direction and screenwriting, Burnett won the Special Jury Award and Grand Jury Prize at the Sundance Film Festival as well as two Independent Spirit Awards and a prize from the National Society of Film Critics.

Pressman himself earned an Independent Spirit Award nomination as the co-producer, with Michael Hausman, of David Mamet's *Homicide* (1991). With Mary Kane, he earned another nomination, for Abel Ferrara's *Bad Lieutenant* (1992).

Both films were BAM selections. BAM also honored *Hoffa* (1992), directed by Danny DeVito from a script by David Mamet, about the enormously powerful, controversial head (1958–71) of the International Brotherhood of Teamsters. Jack Nicholson was cast as Jimmy Hoffa, while DeVito played a fictional sidekick of the union boss and Armand Assante portrayed one of Hoffa's Mafia associates. Additional BAM selections included *Wall Street* (1987); *Good Morning, Babylon* (1987), an English-language film by the Italian directors Paolo and Vittorio Taviani; Harold Becker's *City Hall* (1996); and James Toback's *Two Girls and a Guy* (1997). Two other BAM choices had received a great deal of media coverage even before their releases: Alex Proyas's *The Crow* (1994), whose star, Brandon Lee (the son of the martial-arts expert Bruce Lee), was accidentally killed a few days before the completion of shooting, and Mary Harron's *American Psycho* (2000), based on an exceedingly controversial, graphically violent novel by Bret Easton Ellis, whose narrator, a narcissistic Wall Street investment banker, is a psychopathic serial killer. Harron and her co-screenwriter, Guinevere Turner—the last of a long series of writers and/or directors whom Pressman considered for those jobs—kept most of the violence off-screen, and *American Psycho*, which starred Christian Bale, won a Special Recognition for Excellence in Filmmaking Award from the National Board of Review of the U.S. in 2000.

In 2000 Pressman executive-produced George Butler's documentary *The Endurance*, about the British explorer Ernest Shackleton's attempt to cross Antarctica (1914–17), and the Chinese director Zhang Yimou's bittersweet comedy *Happy Times*. He was one of three executive producers of Jim Simpson's *The Guys* (2002), adapted by Simpson and Anne Nelson from Nelson's play about a fire captain preparing a eulogy for the men he lost on 9/11. Pressman's other credits from the 2000s include the Norwegian director Hans Petter Moland's *The Beautiful Country* (2004); Michael Apted's *Amazing Grace* (2006); Simon Hunter's *Mutant Chronicles* (2008); and Oliver Stone's *Wall Street: Money Never Sleeps* (2010).

Pressman and his wife, Annie McEnroe, who married in 1983, live in New York City. Their son, Sam, is a senior at Stanford University.

—M.A.S.

Suggested Reading: *Business Times Singapore* Raffles Conversation Feb. 9, 2008; *Los Angeles Times* VI p1 Jan. 7, 1988; *New York Times* C p8 Aug. 2, 1985, II p25 Sep. 13, 1992, II p26 Feb. 4, 2001; pressman.com

Selected Films: as producer or co-producer—*Out of It*, 1969; *The Revolutionary*, 1970; *Dealing: Or the Berkeley-to-Boston Forty-Brick Lost-Bag Blues*, 1972; *Sisters*, 1973; *Phantom of the Paradise*, 1974; *Heart Beat*, 1980; *The Hand*, 1981; *Conan the Destroyer*, 1984; *Plenty*, 1985;

Wall Street, 1987; *Talk Radio*, 1988; *Blue Steel*, 1990; *Reversal of Fortune*, 1990; *Waiting for the Light*, 1990; *Homicide*, 1991; *Year of the Gun*, 1991; *Bad Lieutenant*, 1992; *Hoffa*, 1992; *The Crow*, 1994; *Street Fighter*, 1994; *City Hall*, 1996; *The Crow: City of Angels*, 1996; *Two Girls and a Guy*, 1997; *Legionnaire*, 1998; *American Psycho*, 2000; *The Crow: Salvation*, 2000; *The Beautiful Country*, 2004; *The Crow: Wicked Player*, 2005; *Amazing Grace*, 2006; *Mutant Chronicles*, 2008; *The Bad Lieutenant: Port of Call—New Orleans*, 2009; *Wall Street: Money Never Sleeps*, 2010; as executive producer or co-executive producer—

Badlands, 1973; *Despair*, 1978; *Paradise Alley*, 1978; *Das Boot*, 1981; *Conan the Barbarian*, 1982; *The Pirates of Penzance*, 1983; *Crimewave*, 1985; *True Stories*, 1986; *Masters of the Universe*, 1987; *Good Morning, Babylon*, 1987; *Walker*, 1987; *Paris by Night*, 1988; *To Sleep with Anger*, 1990; *Dream Lover*, 1994; *Judge Dredd*, 1995; *The Endurance*, 2000; *Happy Times*, 2000; *The Guys*, 2002; *The Cooler*, 2003; *Party Monster*, 2003; *The Hebrew Hammer*, 2003; *The King*, 2005; *Thank You for Smoking*, 2005; *Driving Lessons*, 2006; *Fur: An Imaginary Portrait of Diane Arbus*, 2006

Rick Diamond/Getty Images

Price, Lisa

May 18, 1962– Entrepreneur

Address: Carol's Daughter, 99 Hudson St., New York, NY 10013

Lisa Price is the founder of Carol's Daughter, a brand of all-natural beauty products aimed at African-American consumers. Price began making her wares as a hobby in about 1990, mixing up small batches of Mango Body Butter and Honey Pudding skin lotion in her home kitchen; her business has since grown into a multi-million-dollar enterprise, with endorsements from such celebrity spokespeople as Jada Pinkett Smith and Mary J. Blige and products in numerous retail outlets, including Macy's and Sephora. "Carol's Daughter has made other people in the beauty business look at African American consumers in a different way," Price,

who named her enterprise in honor of her mother, wrote for *Newsweek* (October 4, 2008, on-line). "When I first started to do this, the black products were always at the back of the drugstore on the lower shelves. They were always dusty, dirty and sticky; they looked like nobody ever touched them. That's changing. . . . It's great to be part of that shift."

Lisa Price was born to Carol and Robert Hairston on May 18, 1962 in the New York City borough of Brooklyn. She grew up in the Bedford-Stuyvesant section of the borough, part of a large, extended family of Trinidadian descent that included some 20 cousins, all of whom lived nearby. At the time of her birth, her father worked for a youth organization; he later attended law school and became a professor of business law. Her mother worked for the phone company. Price had one biological brother, Philip. Her parents divorced when she was 10 years old, and both remarried when she was in high school. Her mother, whose new married name was Hutson, subsequently adopted six more children. As a result, some journalists have stated that Price is one of two siblings, while others assert that she is the oldest of eight. In her memoir, *Success Never Smelled So Sweet: How I Followed My Nose and Found My Passion* (2004), Price wrote, "I know my mother wouldn't want me to make a distinction between her biological and adopted children, because to Mommy we were *all* her babies; however, I feel I must because [the adoptions] show how big her heart was."

Price loved perfume and cologne even as a child. Once, while serving as a flower girl at an aunt's wedding, she refused to scatter handfuls of rose petals as directed, because she wanted to take them home with her. Self-conscious about her weight, she wore fragrances to make her feel attractive. "When I was a preteen and got an allowance, I headed to the drugstore where I bought perfumes like Heaven Scent, Love's Baby Soft and some kind of green apple bath set that smelled so tart that I just had to have the bath oil, the lotion, the powder and the cologne," she wrote in her memoir. "Fragrances were my friends. They made me feel pretty and made bad times seem not so bad."

Although she was a bright and curious student, Price did not enjoy school. "It felt like a job," she wrote. "The environment was strict and emphasized discipline. And while I strived to get high marks to make the adults around me happy, doing so alienated me from my peers." Things improved somewhat when, thanks to her singing voice, she gained admission to the High School of Music & Art, a public school located in the New York City neighborhood of Harlem. (It has since merged with the School of Performing Arts to become the Fiorello H. LaGuardia High School of Music & Art and Performing Arts. The 1980 movie *Fame* and its 2009 remake were set there.) Although younger than the other students, because she had finished middle school early, Price thrived in the bohemian, creative atmosphere.

Price's father was unenthusiastic about her dreams of a singing career, and after Price graduated from high school, he encouraged her to attend the City College of New York's legal-studies program, where she could have received a law degree at the age of 22. Although she complied, she left the program after less than a year.

Price subsequently became involved in Ausar Auset, a Pan-African religion that draws from the culture of ancient Egypt. (Many sources refer to Ausar Auset as a cult.) She took on the name Khoret Amen Tera, and at 20 she was married in a group wedding with several other couples. The union was an unhappy one and was quickly dissolved.

After leaving her first husband, Manuel, Price found a job in the mail room of the United Nations. She also adopted the stage name Topaz and became a member of an all-female singing group, Fedora, which performed in local nightclubs. Her transition to a more secular life was a rocky one. "The worlds of American popular culture and Ausar Auset were as different as night and day and [as] incompatible as oil and water," she wrote in *Success Never Smelled So Sweet*. "At first I didn't want to admit how deep this conflict was, because I was close to so many people in the [Ausar Auset] community and believed in many of the teachings. I also felt like I had messed up again because the huge life-change I thought was so right for me was turning out to be so wrong."

After late-night gigs with Fedora, Price frequently called in sick at her U.N. job, and in 1987, when she was discovered to have forged several doctors' notes, she was forced to resign. As she distanced herself from Ausar Auset, Price began dating, and in 1988 she made the agonizing decision to terminate an unwanted pregnancy. She also began using credit cards to purchase the accoutrements of her new lifestyle and got so deeply into debt that, despite finding an administrative job, she declared bankruptcy.

In the fall of 1989, things began to look up for Price. Through a friend she found work as a writer's assistant on the phenomenally popular sitcom *The Cosby Show*, of which she had long been a fan.

"While at *Cosby* I learned that it is possible to love your job. I discovered the joy and satisfaction that comes from working at what you feel passionate about. And I found that it could be okay to work hard and not get paid a lot. If you love what you do, you figure all that other stuff out," she wrote in her memoir. "I didn't realize it at the time, but I was also learning the work ethic and commitment that was required to be an entrepreneur."

Price's personal life was also on an upswing. On December 28, 1991 she married Gordon Price, who later joined her on the *Cosby* set as a driver. During that period Price started to experiment with crafting scented creams, lotions, and bath products in her kitchen—mixing her ingredients with the handheld beater that she and her grandmother had used for baking when she was a child. She gave the items to co-workers and friends as gifts, and soon people began asking to purchase her homemade wares.

In 1992 *The Cosby Show* went off the air, and Price and her husband found a series of other TV-production jobs. She also continued to make her beauty products, packing them in old baby-food jars and making labels by hand. She found that the items were popular at flea markets and craft fairs, but she still considered the pursuit a mere hobby. One day in 1993, while sitting on her bed filling jars with body cream, she saw an installment of *The Oprah Winfrey Show* that changed her way of thinking. "She had women on her show that had started businesses with little or no money," Price recalled to Tony Cox for National Public Radio (May 31, 2004, on-line). "Listening to the women go through their checklist on how they knew they had a good business, whether or not they knew their repeat customer, if they loved what they were doing, I realized I was answering 'yes' to all these questions, so this light bulb kind of went off that said, 'You know what? This isn't a hobby. This could actually be a business.'"

"When I was starting my business and looking for a name, I made two lists," Price told Caroline V. Clarke for *Black Enterprise* (July 2003). "One had all the things I was, and the other had all the things I wanted to be. One of the things I was was Carol's daughter. When I read it out loud I got goose bumps. It just seemed right, and it stuck." Initially, Price devoted a section of her Brooklyn apartment to Carol's Daughter; as word spread about the quality of her hair and skin products, customers, including a growing number of local celebrities such as Erykah Badu, flocked there to shop. She and Gordon realized that their landlord would eventually tire of the situation, and in 1999 the first free-standing Carol's Daughter boutique opened, in the gentrifying Fort Greene section of Brooklyn. "I was nervous," Price confessed to Melissa Stark in an interview for NBC's *Today Show* (June 16, 2004, on-line). "Are people going to come in? You know, am I going to be able to pay the rent? Is it going to be popular? And the first day there was a line outside the door for people to come in."

"The products at this Fort Greene beauty shop are so fresh that they have expiration dates and some must be refrigerated after opening," Marie Redding wrote for the New York *Daily News* (August 20, 2000). "With names like butter, milk, jam, and jelly, you'll be tempted to sample everything."

Soon Carol's Daughter was being written up in such national publications as *Essence* and *B. Smith Style*, and Price was featured on high-profile TV shows including *The View* and *The Oprah Winfrey Show*. The influential Winfrey, who had been introduced to Carol's Daughter when the actress Halle Berry sent her a gift basket of its products, expressed a particular fondness for one of Price's foot creams, sending sales skyrocketing.

On February 14, 2003 Price's mother died of a heart attack. For most of her adult life, Carol had been battling a debilitating neuromuscular disease, but she rarely complained and had always been a positive and stabilizing presence in her daughter's life. "I just keep reminding myself what she would say, what she would do, what she would want and I've been praying a lot. She'd always remind me to pray and reassure me that God would not give me more than I could handle. That keeps me going," Price told Caroline V. Clarke a few months after her mother's death. "Somebody told me at the funeral that I should never feel sad thinking that my mother didn't know how much I loved her because I showed her while she was alive. I honored her by naming something for her while she was here. I'll never forget how I felt the first time I read the words Carol's Daughter. It's who I'll always be."

In 2004 Price published *Success Never Smelled So Sweet*, which she co-authored with Hilary Beard. "For someone so successful," Lisa J. Curtis wrote for the Black Entrepreneur's Hall of Fame Web site (January 5, 2006, on-line), "Price's book, surprisingly, often focuses on the slumps in her life—obesity, abortion, bankruptcy, miscarriage, and the death of her mother . . . rather than her triumphs." "I feel like I made myself less vulnerable because I didn't hide anything," Price told Curtis. "I told it, and I told it the way I wanted to tell it: So many different events contribute to the person that I am now. . . . I'm hoping other people that go through traumatic experiences or can't seem to get over an event will say, 'If she can get over that, then I can get over this thing that happened to me.'"

In 2005 Price formed a partnership with Steve Stoute, a record executive and public-relations maven. "I knew that I'd done all that I could on my own," she told Terry Pristin for the *New York Times* (October 25, 2006). "It was more important for the brand to become what it can become than for me to have control of it." That year Stoute helped raise $10 million with an investment team that included the hip-hop star Jay-Z, the actors Jada Pinkett Smith and Will Smith, and the producer Tommy Mottolo. "I've never been in the beauty business," Stoute told Pristin. "All I knew was this woman had a great story. And I knew as a business-man that she had an undervalued asset." Jada Pinkett Smith, long a user of the products, became a spokesperson for Carol's Daughter.

Price soon opened a large flagship boutique and spa in Harlem, as well as dedicated stores in several malls. Carol's Daughter grossed $10 million in sales in 2006, the year the company partnered with Sephora, a popular national cosmetics chain. A partnership with Macy's soon followed, and in 2008 the brand began to sell on the Home Shopping Network, becoming one of the network's top beauty lines. That year sales reached $25 million. In 2009 the company created a licensed line of products for children, coinciding with the release of the animated film *The Princess and the Frog*, which featured Disney's first African-American princess. In 2010 the singer Mary J. Blige helped create Carol's Daughter's first celebrity fragrance. Called My Life, the perfume sold more than 60,000 units in six hours the day it was introduced on the Home Shopping Network.

Price's honors include an Entrepreneur of the Year Award from the National Black MBA Association and an Entrepreneurial Excellence Award from *Working Women* magazine. She lives in Brooklyn with her husband and their three children: Forrest, Ennis, and Becca.

—J.P.

Suggested Reading: *Black Enterprise* p96 July 2003; (New York) *Daily News* Your Money p6 Apr. 30, 2007; *New York Times* C p9 Oct. 25, 2006; *Newsweek* p70 Oct. 13, 2008; *Tampa (Florida) Tribune* Business p1 Oct. 26, 2006; Price, Lisa and Hilary Beard. *Success Never Smelled So Sweet: How I Followed My Nose and Found My Passion*, 2004

Selected Books: *Success Never Smelled So Sweet: How I Followed My Nose and Found My Passion* (with Hilary Beard), 2004

Rapp, Adam

June 15, 1968– Playwright; novelist; filmmaker; musician

Address: c/o Gersh Agency, 41 Madison Ave., 33d Fl., New York, NY 10010

"The world is designed to destroy you," Adam Rapp told the playwright Marsha Norman when she interviewed him for *Bomb* magazine (Spring 2006, on-line). That idea permeates the books that Rapp has published and the many plays he has written, 20 of which have been produced Off-Broadway, by regional theaters, by theaters overseas, and, once, on Broadway, when Rapp's *Jack on Film* was included in a charitable event called "The 24 Hour Plays 2006." Self-described as "a

Courtesy of Steve Freeman

Adam Rapp

gay man who is dying of cancer. Hulick predicted that fans of Rapp's novels "will be eager to read [*Punkzilla*]—and with good reason: Rapp's quirky idiomatic expressions, striking word choices, and stream-of-consciousness prose style are ample evidence that his facility with language remains as impressive as ever." Rapp's other young-adult novels are *Missing the Piano*; *The Buffalo Tree*; *The Copper Elephant*; *Little Chicago*; *33 Snowfish*; *Under the Wolf, Under the Dog*; and the graphic novel *Ball Peen Hammer*. His novel for adults is *The Year of Endless Sorrows* (2006).

"The novel, for me, is very meditative, something that I know and feel I have a kind of authority with," Rapp told Carolyn Clay for the *Boston Phoenix* (October 12–19, 2000, on-line). "It seems like something that takes months or a year or two years. But the playwriting is this fever thing. The plays kind of burst out of me, and I don't know why. The stuff I write about in plays tends to be the stuff that keeps me up at night, and the stuff I write about in novels tends to be the things I think about during the day. So there's kind of a nocturnal haunting to my playwriting." In a review of Rapp's play *The Metal Children* for the *New York Times* (May 20, 2010, on-line), Charles Isherwood described what he thought might be "the single funniest scene Mr. Rapp has written," then added, "But those who prize this prolific playwright for his pitch-dark sensibility need not fear that he's taken a turn for the lighthearted, or for that matter the moralistic."

The second of the three children of Mary Lee (Baird) Rapp and Douglas C. Rapp, Adam M. Rapp was born on June 15, 1968 in Joliet, Illinois, near Chicago. He was raised in the Roman Catholic faith with his older sister, Anne, and younger brother, Anthony, mostly in Joliet. Catholicism, he told Celia Wren for *American Theatre* (February 2004), "definitely haunts my theatre work." Rapp's father was a computer scientist with the U.S. Department of Veterans Affairs. His mother, who suffered from the inherited disease neurofibromatosis, was a nurse; her employers included Joliet's maximum-security prison. When Rapp was in his late teens, Mary Lee Rapp became the foster mother to her youngest sister's baby daughter. His mother's long battle with cancer, from which she died, in 1997, is described in his brother's book, *Without You: A Memoir of Love, Loss, and the Musical Rent* (2006). Rapp's parents divorced in 1974, leaving his mother with primary responsibility for him and his siblings.

In about 1977 Rapp's brother got his first acting job. Because Anthony's income soon exceeded his mother's and Mary Lee wanted to keep the family together, Anthony's subsequent jobs, in regional theater, led to a series of moves, with disruptions in the children's schooling. They also led to Rapp's increasing rage and occasional rebelliousness. He spent half of fifth grade in a reformatory, the Glenwood School for Boys, near Chicago. In 1981, when he was in eighth grade, Anthony Rapp was cast as the title character in a musical that was produced

jock who discovered he was an artist," as David Ng reported for *American Theatre* (October 2007), Rapp has also written and directed two adaptations of his plays for cinema, *Winter Passing* (2005) and *Blackbird* (2007), and has performed with two bands. His play *Red Light Winter* won an Obie Award special citation and was nominated for the Pulitzer Prize for Drama in 2006, and the music that he wrote for his play *Essential Self-Defense* was nominated for a Drama Desk Award in 2007. He has also won a bevy of other honors, among them the Roger L. Stevens Award from the Kennedy Center Fund for New American Plays, in 2000. Despite Rapp's success, his plays are "uncompromising in their bleak worldview," Ng wrote, though not necessarily without humor. His novels—eight for young adults and one for adults—are similarly cheerless, ending without resolution or, at best, with only a faint chance of a better future for their characters. "I don't know if I have the ability to write an ending like *My Fair Lady*'s, when everyone gets what they want after a few minor conflicts," Rapp told Norman. "If I tried to write that it would just be false. Or I'd have someone enter with a machine gun."

"Nobody writes about the disposable, marginalized youth of America with the same sense of uncomfortable, voyeuristic fascination as Adam Rapp, though his novels . . . can feel gratuitously brutal," Jeannette Hulick wrote for the *Horn Book* (May/June 2009) in a review of *Punkzilla*, one of Rapp's books for young adults. *Punkzilla*'s hero, at 14, lives on the streets after his escape from a military academy; he engages in illegal activities, including experimentation with drugs, before journeying across the U.S. to visit his older brother, a for Broadway, and Rapp's mother moved with her three children to New York City. The show folded in January 1982, after 10 preview performances, but several months passed before his mother had sufficient funds to return to Joliet. Rapp fiercely resented his forced absence from school. "I was gonna be the starting point guard for the school basketball team," he told Bruce Miller for *American Drama* (Winter 2005), "and just as the season is about to begin, my whole life is just yanked away." Soon afterward Rapp moved to the home of his father and his first stepmother, in Chicago, but he felt no happier there and began to behave badly. Consequently, he spent his high-school years at a military academy, St. John's Northwestern, in Delafield, Wisconsin, a two-to-three-hour drive north of Chicago. Recalling his separations from his family during fifth grade and high school, he told Ann Angel for the *ALAN Review* (Fall 2000, on-line), published by the Assembly on Literature for Adolescents, an arm of the National Council of Teachers of English, "I'm sure this has [had] an enormous effect on my work."

Although at St. John's Northwestern Rapp held his own as a member of the varsity basketball team, he felt painfully self-conscious, because, he told Angel, he "didn't go through puberty until much later" than his peers. Feeling socially isolated and inept, he turned to fiction for consolation and came to regard some fictional characters as his friends. He especially liked J. D. Salinger's novel *The Catcher in the Rye* (1951), whose protagonist, Holden Caulfield, exhibits stereotypical teenage angst and alienation. "I feel I know Holden Caulfield better than many of the guys I played basketball with in college," he told Angel.

After he graduated from St. John's, Rapp enrolled at Clarke College, a Roman Catholic institution in Dubuque, Iowa, on a basketball scholarship. He considered becoming a doctor until he took a course in poetry. "I thought [being a doctor] would be heroic . . . ," he told Marsha Norman. "Then I thought about the years of medical school, and the misery. At least if I write I can control the content of that space that's being taken up in my mind." Rapp majored in fiction writing and psychology and earned a bachelor's degree from Clarke in 1991.

Rapp then moved to New York City, with the goal of pursuing a career as a writer. For several years he held jobs with book publishers; feeling like "this dorky, naïve guy from Illinois," as he recalled to David Ng, he kept mostly to himself. ("The theater, where you have to be more articulate, has forced me to open up more," he remarked to Ng.) Rapp's brother, meanwhile, who had had roles in three feature films, was appearing in the premiere staging of John Guare's play *Six Degrees of Separation*, on Broadway. Within a short time the years-long estrangement between the brothers ended, when each agreed to read the other's writings.

Sura, the 12-year-old hero of *The Buffalo Tree*, Rapp's debut young-adult novel, which was published by Boyds Mills Press in 1993, has been sentenced to eight months in a juvenile-detention center for stealing automobile-hood ornaments. He is the only white boy at the facility, whose staff and inmates are, with few exceptions, sadistic and violent. "Although the brutality is unremitting, the book is hard to put down," Nancy Vasilakis wrote for *Horn Book Magazine* (July/August 1997), after the book was reissued by Front Street, a division of Boyds Mills. "The action plays out under Sura's watchful, cagey eyes, and his tone of bravado relieves the harshness without resorting to sentimentality. Mostly though, it is his toughness of spirit that inspires and makes the reading of this novel a transcendent experience." *School Library Journal* listed *The Buffalo Tree* among the best books for young adults of 1997.

Rapp's next novel, *Missing the Piano*, was published in 1994. Its hero, 15-year-old Mike, becomes a boarding student at a military academy, his mother having chosen to accompany his sister, an actress, on a road show and his stepmother having refused to house him. "Rapp portrays the school as an extremely bleak place where abuse and bigotry are constants," Tom S. Hurlburt wrote for *School Library Journal* (June 1994). "Mike is continually badgered, bullied, and bloodied, even on the basketball court, the one place he hoped to find refuge. . . . The ending offers a glimmer of hope but doesn't dismiss any of Mike's ongoing problems. Rapp produces an above-average read, showing a knack for sustaining the tense mood of the story." The American Library Association (ALA) named *Missing the Piano* the best book for young adults and best book for reluctant readers in 1995.

In Rapp's dystopian third novel, *The Copper Elephant* (1995), children toil as slaves in mines, while aboveground, constant acidic rain blisters skin. *Little Chicago* (1998), Rapp's next book, according to Deborah Stevenson, the editor of the *Bulletin of the Center for Children's Books* (June 2002), is "a vivid exploration of the life of a kid with little to lose"—11-year-old Blacky, who is sexually abused by his mother's boyfriend, often goes hungry, and lives in an environment of seemingly "irreversible entropy," in Stevenson's words. The main characters in *33 Snowfish* (2003) are a teenager who has murdered his parents, a prostitute addicted to drugs, and a boy "who has recently escaped from sexual bondage with an abusive pedophile . . . ," Joel Shoemaker wrote for *School Library Journal* (April 2003). "Depraved and depressing? Oh yeah, and the shocks just keep on coming. The fearsome elements escape the pages like nightmares loosed into daylight." Shoemaker concluded, "Spare descriptions and stellar characterization reel readers into the dark and violent world of these dispossessed and abused young people. . . . For those readers who are ready to be challenged by a serious work of shockingly realistic fiction, it invites both an emotional and intellectual response, and begs to be discussed."

In *Under the Wolf, Under the Dog* (2004), the 17-year-old narrator recalls what led to his residence in a home for suicidal or drug-addicted teenagers: the destructive behavior that followed his mother's death from cancer, his brother's suicide soon afterward, and his father's inability to cope with those events. *Punkzilla* (2009) was among the five 2009 Michael L. Prinze Honor Books, chosen by the Young Adult Library Services Association, an arm of the ALA. Rapp's most recent book for young adults, *Ball Peen Hammer* (2009), is a graphic novel, illustrated by George O'Connor, whose four main characters are government slaves in an environmentally poisoned world.

Meanwhile, nearly two decades earlier, Rapp had entered the world of theater peripherally, while assisting his brother during the latter's occasional forays into directing plays Off-Broadway. The wondrous possibilities of live drama struck him suddenly when he was about 23, when he attended a performance of *Six Degrees of Separation*, in which his brother played the character Ben. Seeing Guare's drama "was a watershed experience," he recalled to Helen Shaw for *Time Out New York* (September 23, 2008, on-line). "It was theatrical and scary, and New York functioned like a character. John Guare became a hero for me." Rapp began to read plays by many writers. He was particularly drawn to works by Sarah Kane, which are marked by graphic depictions of horrific violence, and by Sam Shepard, many of whose plays focus on severely dysfunctional families. Rapp soon began to experiment with the form himself. "I fell in love with playwriting because it's a magical space that stories could happen in," he told David Ng. He recalled to Carolyn Clay, "I was really excited by the prospect of doing something live, three-dimensional, where people were doing things to each other on stage. Part of it, too, was just that when you have a play in rehearsal, you have a family. The novelist part of me has always felt solitary and secluded. I'm not very good at parties, at doing normal social things. . . . Theater became a great excuse to talk to people." By 1997 Rapp had written four plays. Three of them—*Ghosts in the Cottonwoods*, *Trueblinka*, and *Gompers*—debuted in 1996, 1997, and 2003, respectively, at the Eugene O'Neill Theater Center, in Waterford, Connecticut, which is dedicated to introducing works by up-and-coming writers.

The script for *Ghosts in the Cottonwoods* accompanied the application Rapp sent to the Playwrights Program at the Juilliard School, in New York City, in the late 1990s. Marsha Norman, the program's co-director (with Christopher Durang) since 1994, discerned the drama's quality immediately. "After you read thousands of plays by young writers, you can pretty much tell in 10 pages whether the playwright is going to get you," she wrote for *Bomb*. "The voice is either clear or not, the dramatic sensibility is either there or it isn't, and the writer either knows or doesn't know what his personal 'content' is, the stuff he will draw on

for a lifetime of writing. But it didn't even take 10 pages with Adam Rapp. . . . I knew in a single sentence that Adam was a writer the world was going to listen to for as long as he felt like writing." Rapp won a fellowship and participated in the Playwrights Program in 1998 and 1999.

For many months afterward Rapp tried in vain to find a producer for his plays. "I had almost given up," he told Shaw. "I was broke, subletting my apartment because I couldn't afford it and crashing on my ex-girlfriend's couch. I was having a hard time, drinking and doing drugs." Then, in 2000, the American Repertory Theater (ART), in Cambridge, Massachusetts, mounted Rapp's one-actor play *Nocturne*. Named for a somber piano piece by Edvard Grieg, *Nocturne* is narrated by a native midwesterner and former piano prodigy who has moved to New York City's East Village. It opens with the words, "Fifteen years ago I killed my sister"—a reference to the accident that occurred when the sister, a very small girl, darted in front of the car her brother was driving one day when he was 17. The man's parents have never recovered from the tragedy; the accident has kept him, too, gripped in agonizing sorrow that is only beginning to lose its hold, in part through the literature he comes across while working in a bookstore. *Nocturne* won the Boston Theater Critics Association Elliot Norton Award for outstanding new script and was named best new play by the Independent Reviewers of New England.

Nocturne's success at ART "made other people think they could take a risk on me," Rapp told Shaw. In 2000 Rapp won a so-called suite residency with the New York avant-garde theater company Mabou Mines, giving him access to rehearsal space and artistic and technical assistance. In 2001 *Nocturne* was presented at the New York Theater Workshop, with actors depicting, in addition to the brother, the parents, sister, and the brother's new love interest, though they remain mostly silent. In a review for the *New York Times* (May 21, 2001), Ben Brantley described the brother's narration, which fills two and a quarter hours, as "the sound of someone drowning his sorrows in metaphors" and concluded, "Although the power of *Nocturne* lies in its hypnotic accumulation of words, it's hard to avoid wishing that its narrator had more original, and certainly more succinct, means of self-expression." The Associated Press theater critic Michael Kuchwara, as quoted on the Web site of Broadway Play Publishing Inc., described *Nocturne* as "a startling, unnerving work of art that fiercely pushes the boundaries of theater. The play . . . is dense, almost novelistic, in its approach to a personal horror story. *Nocturne* is also intensely lyrical, musical in its sounds and in its silences. Make no mistake. Rapp is an original—a distinctive voice unafraid to be too descriptive." In 2001 the New York Community Trust recognized Rapp's potential with a Helen Merrill Playwriting Award.

The year 2001 also saw the first presentation, at ART, of Rapp's *Animals and Plants*. The play's protagonists, Burris and Dantly, have become unlikely buddies in their decade as a drug seller's flunkies. A blizzard has stranded the men in a dingy motel, where they await the arrival of a delivery; soon, betrayal threatens to end their friendship. *Finer Noble Gases*, which premiered at the 2002 Humana Festival, in Louisville, Kentucky, is set in the slovenly East Village apartment of the four spaced-out members of a has-been rock band. The play struck Bruce Weber, writing for the *New York Times* (April 10, 2002), as "a brashly vulgar and cacophonous work that is basically a lament for society's lonely and alienated," while a reviewer for the theater database doollee.com described it as a "freakishly funny and vividly-imagined absurdist nightmare" in which events move "from the hilarious to the disturbingly existential." Later in 2002 the Off-Broadway Rattlestick Theater mounted the first production of Rapp's *Faster*, an apocalyptic tale in which two uneducated lowlifes plan to sell a kidnapped girl, leading to a confrontation with Satan.

The inspiration for *Stone Cold Dead Serious*, Rapp told Kyle Brenton for ART.org (February 1, 2002), was "the most bizarre, life-and-death sales pitch I've ever heard," in an advertisement that aired on a home-shopping TV channel. The ad "became a door for me to walk through into this world in which a video game championship is a legitimate way for a son to try and save his family." The championship depicted in the play ends with a real-life beheading carried out by its hero, a 16-year-old midwestern video-game genius. The mounting on the extremely wide Loeb stage at ART led Rapp to regard the play as possibly allegorical, he told Brenton. In his review of a production presented by the Edge Theatre Company at the Off-Broadway Chashama Theater, Bruce Weber—who noticed Rapp tending the theater's bar—wrote for the *New York Times* (April 18, 2003, on-line) that while flawed, *Stone Cold Dead Serious* is "brave, compassionate, and, at times . . . breathtakingly moving. It is the work of a playwright who is forging a real voice."

Rapp was nominated for a Pulitzer Prize for *Red Light Winter*, which he directed for its premiere, at the Steppenwolf Theatre, in Chicago. Described by Charles Isherwood for the *New York Times* (February 10, 2006, on-line) as "a frank, graphic story of erotic fixation and the havoc it can wreak on sensitive souls," *Red Light Winter* depicts the poisonous friendship of Matt, a good-natured but painfully awkward playwright, and Davis, a friend from college who has become a smooth-talking, hotshot editor. Davis, who earlier stole Matt's girlfriend, hatches a plan to cure his friend's loneliness by bringing him a prostitute from the Red Light District of Amsterdam, the Netherlands, where the pair are on holiday.

Rapp's plays *Essential Self Defense* and *Kindness* debuted at Playwrights Horizon, in New York City, in 2006 and 2007, respectively. For his next drama, *The Metal Children* (2009), Rapp fictionalized the controversy that erupted in 2005 when the Reading, Pennsylvania, school board learned about the contents of *The Buffalo Tree* and banned it from all curricula and school libraries. At a meeting held by Reading residents a year later, Rapp himself spoke about the book. In recalling that experience for *Broadway.com* (May 18, 2010), he wrote, "I told the audience I really was interested in writing about survival and mercy and loyalty; that it was a violent world I was dealing with, but none more violent than the stuff we see in the streets, on TV, on the Internet." He also wrote, "In some ways, the play *The Metal Children* is a fantasy of what I was expecting in Reading. It is part nightmare, part old-fashioned wish, and my attempt to meditate on both sides of an issue that means a lot to me: kids reading books. I've always believed that kids are much wiser than we think they are, and to deprive them of complex expressions of art because of violence or sexual content is to condescend to them." When he reread *The Buffalo Tree* in 2006, he wrote, "I honestly couldn't decide whether it was appropriate for all kids who are 14 and up, as it says on the back of the book. I don't have kids. I think in some ways, I have never grown up and therefore I consider myself good source material, but the closest I have come to parenting has been raising my three-year-old dog, Cesar. . . . But if I had a little girl or a boy, perhaps I would find the content in *The Buffalo Tree* salacious and unnecessarily violent. Therefore it was important to me to discuss both sides of this issue, to not easily dismiss those who are against the novel (*The Metal Children*) within the play. And as the play *The Metal Children* has developed, I have done my best to honor this."

A workshop production of *The Metal Children* was mounted at the Vineyard Theater, in New York, in 2008; it opened officially on May 19, 2010 at the same location, with Billy Crudup in the role of the author. In a review for the *New York Times* (May 20, 2010, on-line), Charles Isherwood wrote, "*The Metal Children* at first might appear to be a predictable story of the culture wars, in which the forces of good—meaning liberal-minded, culturally sophisticated New Yorkers and their sympathetic brethren in Middle America—do battle with the armies of the Christian right, self-righteous and closed-minded. To his credit, Rapp indulges only mildly in such schematic pigeon-holing. Instead he presents a more murky, ambiguous tale of the dangerous ideological uses to which literature can be put, by its champions and its detractors alike."

Rapp has served as a guest instructor at the Yale School of Drama. He lives with his brother and his dog in the East Village. Anthony Rapp's acting credits in theater include the part of Mark in the original mounting of the musical *Rent* and the title role in a Broadway revival of the musical *You're a*

Good Man, Charlie Brown. In 2001 he starred in a production of *Nocturne* at the Berkeley Repertory Theatre, in California. He has also appeared in two dozen films, including *Six Degrees of Separation, Rent, A Beautiful Mind, Blackbird,* and *Winter Passing,* and on TV shows, among them *The X-Files.*

—H.R.W.

Suggested Reading: *ALAN Review* (on-line) Fall 2000; *American Drama* p110+ Winter 2005; *American Theatre* p36+ Feb. 2004, p38+ Oct. 2007; *Bomb* (on-line) Spring 2006; *Boston Phoenix* (on-line) Oct. 12–19, 2000; *Broadway.com* May 18, 2010; dollee.com; edgetheater.org; *Time Out New York* (on-line) Sep. 25–Oct. 1, 2008

Selected Books: *The Buffalo Tree,* 1993; *Missing the Piano,* 1994; *The Copper Elephant,* 1995; *Little Chicago,* 1998; *33 Snowfish,* 2003; *Under the Wolf, Under the Dog,* 2004; *The Year of Endless Sorrows,* 2006; *Punkzilla,* 2009; *Ball Peen Hammer,* 2009

Selected Plays: *Ghosts in the Cottonwoods,* 1996; *Trueblinka,* 1997, *Nocturne,* 2000; *Animals and Plants,* 2001; *Finer Noble Gases,* 2002; *Gompers,* 2003; *Essential Self Defense,* 2006; *Kindness,* 2007; *The Metal Children,* 2009

Frederick M. Brown/Getty Images

Rice, Constance L.

Apr. 5, 1956– Civil rights lawyer; activist

Address: The Advancement Project, 1541 Wilshire Blvd., Suite 508, Los Angeles, CA 90017

The civil rights lawyer and activist Constance "Connie" Rice does not hesitate to tell people that in her job, she walks a tightrope. As the co-founder of the public-advocacy and legal-action group Advancement Project, the former litigator serves as a mediator between some of the poorest communities in Los Angeles, California, and the city's power structure—and between violent gangs and police officers who have sometimes been too willing to use force against them. "It may blow up in my face," she said about her work to Diane Lefer for the Chapel Hill, North Carolina–based publication the *Sun* (April 2008), "but I'm trying to clear a place where new ideas can be vetted and tested. We have to create some safe zones for innovative people in both camps." She said to Lefer, "I always begin with the question, 'Who has the power to change this?' Sometimes it's the voters. When it comes to police reform, it's the police. I need to ally myself with the people who can solve the problem." Rice works tirelessly to end street violence, which she calls a "disease," through strategies that counter the forceful tactics used by police. She told Lefer, "My strategy is to figure out what people need in order to create change themselves." The last 20 years have seen "an epidemic of youth gang homicide," Rice told students at the University of California at Los Angeles in 2010, "which means that our kids are killing each other at such a high rate that epidemiologists are classifying it as an epidemic. . . . We can't arrest our way out of this problem." Instead, Rice called for a "24/7 effort to build up the community so that they are inoculated against the virus that is violence." Most recently, Rice was enlisted by the U.S. Department of Defense to share innovative strategies for dealing with insurgencies in Iraq and Afghanistan, which have similarities to gang activity in the U.S.

At the height of the gang violence, in 2007, the number of gangs in Los Angeles County was estimated at more than 714, with upwards of 80,000 members, according to Peter Landesman, writing for *LA Weekly* (December 13, 2007). Many of the gangs formed in the 1960s from communities of African-Americans, Hispanics, Asians, and other racial and ethnic groups. Crimes committed by those gangs were comparatively minor, including petty theft and fistfights between rivals. In the 1980s drug trafficking was introduced into the gang culture, giving members a stronger reason to protect their home turf as they competed for customers. Drugs alone, however, do not account for the current state of affairs in Los Angeles, the country's epicenter of gang violence, with 70 percent of all homicides in the city attributed to street gangs.

Landesman interviewed Father Gregory Boyle, a Jesuit priest and founder of Homeboy Industries, which helps reform gang members in the mostly Hispanic East L.A. neighborhood; Landesman wrote, "[Boyle] tells me that gang behavior is changing, and the change is chilling. Everywhere he sees signs of the erosion of known and protected codes of conduct, such as methods of assassination that used to protect the innocent, and territorial respect—which he says reflect an accelerating sense of desolation among poor urban youth. Gangs today are less about neighborhoods and rivalries. They've become repositories for hopelessness." Rice's experiences have mirrored those of Father Boyle. She talked to one gang member, she told Lefer, asking him where he saw himself in 10 years; "I don't," he replied.

The *Los Angeles Times* has called Rice one of "the most experienced, civic-minded, and thoughtful people on the subject of Los Angeles," and the publication *California Law Business* placed her on the list of the 10 most influential lawyers in the state. Rice has expressed an unwavering faith in the voices of individuals and the power of community and grassroots activism, because, as she told Lefer, "power concedes nothing without a demand." In her work during the 1990s for the Legal Defense Fund of the National Association for the Advancement of Colored People (NAACP), the nation's oldest and largest civil rights group, she is credited with winning $1.6 billion in awards in civil rights and class-action lawsuits; those include a landmark 1996 civil rights case against the Metropolitan Transit Authority (MTA) of Los Angeles, in which she won a decision in favor of the Bus Riders Union that allocated substantial funding to improve bus service in poorer neighborhoods. In 2000 she won a lawsuit that brought $750 million from the city for construction of new schools.

Despite her victories, Rice began to question the value of litigation as a means to effect change. "I always thought of litigation as the battering ram," she explained to Lefer. "You use it to break open the front door and make room for people to enter. Law is easy if you're in it only to win cases. But if I win a case against the police department and then send my clients back to a neighborhood where they dodge bullets and their kids aren't getting educated and their medical benefits have been cut off because they lost their second job, how much of a victory is that? Litigation," she concluded, "can't do the delicate work of creating the political will to solve problems." Rice has dedicated the past 12 years to such "delicate work," devoting her time and energy to engage with gangs in Los Angeles and staunch their proliferation.

Rice's supporters and enemies alike call her fearless; she has sued the Los Angeles Police Department (LAPD), the Los Angeles Housing Authority, and the Department of Water and Power (of which she was briefly president). "Many of my friends are in office. I've been suing my friends for

20 years . . . ," Rice told Lefer. "Even when you know the people in power, you still have to be a burr under their saddle and demand change."

A second cousin of former U.S. secretary of state Condoleezza Rice (their fathers were first cousins), Constance LaMay Rice was born on April 5, 1956 in Washington, D.C. She has two younger brothers. Her mother, Anna L. (Barnes) Rice, was a science teacher, and her father, Phillip Leon Rice, was a colonel in the U.S. Air Force. Because of her father's career, the family moved often, and most of Rice's childhood was spent on military bases around the U.S. and abroad. Writing for the *Daily Beast* (October 18, 2010, on-line), Christine Pelisek described Rice as a "precocious and strong-willed" child. "At the age of 5," Pelisek wrote, "Connie was a budding champion of underdogs who, at the Cleveland Zoo, tried to coerce her brother into helping her free a lion." Education was very important to the Rice family. Genethia Hayes, a close friend of Rice's, told Pelisek that Rice's parents impressed upon their daughter the "obligation to do something credible and courageous and meaningful with your life." Rice attended Town and Country School in London, England, and graduated from Universal City High School, in Texas, in 1974. At 18, during her senior year, Rice offered to do all of the family ironing so that she could stay home from school and watch television coverage of the U.S. Senate hearings on the Watergate scandal. (The scandal involved the break-in at Democratic National Committee headquarters at the Watergate complex, in Washington, D.C., by Republican operatives and the subsequent coverup by members of President Richard M. Nixon's administration.) In July, when the House Judiciary Committee considered articles of impeachment against Nixon, Rice became entranced by the committee member and Democratic representative Barbara Jordan of Texas, who called for the impeachment of the president. (Nixon resigned and was pardoned by his successor, Gerald R. Ford.) Jordan was the first African-American congresswoman to be elected from the Deep South; her participation in the hearings made her a national figure. Inspired by Jordan, Rice decided to study law.

Rice attended Harvard University, in Cambridge, Massachusetts, where she received a B.A. degree in government in 1978. Her time there—shortly after the school became co-ed and during a particularly nasty desegregation battle—was difficult. "When I was at Harvard, I never felt blacker in my life," Rice told Scott Shibuya Brown for the *Los Angeles Times* (November 27, 1994). "It was never an issue until I went there. It was a hostile environment in which to learn. Everything about you was under siege." During her first year, she was badly beaten by a classmate she had refused to date. Resolving to never again find herself defenseless, she studied the Korean martial art Tae Kwon Do, and by the time she graduated from Harvard, she was a national champion in the sport. In 1980 Rice was awarded both a first degree black belt and the Root Tilden Public Interest Scholarship to attend the New York University School of Law. She earned her J.D. degree in 1984.

During law school Rice served as a clerk for the State of New York Department of Law in 1982 and was mentored by Lani Guinier, then with the NAACP Legal Defense Fund, in 1983. After graduation she clerked for Judge Damon J. Keith of the U.S. Court of Appeals for the Sixth Circuit in Detroit, Michigan, from 1984 to 1986. As a clerk, Rice—who told Lefer that she views capital punishment as an "obscenity"—filed petitions on behalf of death-row prisoners, among them a white supremacist. While her efforts failed in his case, the prisoner sent Rice a thank-you note before his execution. Also during those years Rice became involved with the case of a death-row inmate, Billy Moore, a young black man accused of killing a friend's uncle after a drunken altercation. Thanks to her work on his behalf, Moore was released in 1989. During her time as a law clerk, some of her male colleagues tried to limit her work to menial tasks and exclude her from important discussions, going so far as to make decisions in the men's room; when Rice and another female clerk discovered that practice, they began following the men inside.

Rice worked as an associate for the firm of Morrison and Foster, in San Francisco, California, from 1986 to 1987. In the latter year she served as special assistant to the associate vice chancellor of the University of California, Los Angeles, and in 1990 she joined the NAACP Legal Defense and Educational Fund in Los Angeles as western regional counsel; she eventually became co-director of the office. She also became president of the Los Angeles Department of Water and Power, a post she held from 1990 to 1995.

In 1992 the acquittal in the first Rodney King trial—in which four white police officers were tried for beating King, a black man, in an event captured on videotape—spawned riots in Los Angeles. In the wake of the violence, Rice was credited with fostering the truce between the city's infamous Bloods and Crips gangs. The gang leaders had decided that retribution killings—often for trivial offenses—had to stop. They modeled their truce on the Camp David Peace Accords between the Israelis and the Egyptians, with Rice supplying the gangs with copies of documents relating to the accords. She joked to Lefer, "I was like their research assistant." The truce, though no longer in effect, led to a significant drop in street violence. For Rice the truce proved that change could be enacted from within the community.

In 1993 gang leaders called upon Rice, whom they had come to see as a neutral, trustworthy figure, a second time. The occasion was Easter weekend (a time of many outdoor festivities), just before the verdict was to be announced in the civil trial of the officers accused of beating King; the city was on edge, with police, expecting the worst, preparing to don riot gear. As Rice recalled to Lefer, a gang member called her and said, "You need to call the police chief and tell him there are going to be some dead cops." Rice telephoned a police captain, Bruce Haggerty, and urged him to have officers in his division set aside their riot gear and enlist gang-intervention workers instead. The plan worked, and the weekend proceeded peacefully (perhaps aided by the verdict: two officers were convicted of violating King's civil rights). Those events marked the beginning of Rice's consistent role as mediator between the gangs and the LAPD.

Rice had brought many abuse-of-force lawsuits against the LAPD. "We won all of them," she told Lefer, "but we hadn't made a dent in the problem." Rice admitted, "I had fun suing them. . . . They were so awful to our clients, and so racist and sexist and brutal." A canine-unit case in 1992 changed Rice's approach to her work. The case involved the high number of incidents in which police dogs, handled by brutal officers, bit suspects, usually gang members or juvenile delinquents. Rice presented the statistics to the judge: the dogs had an 80 percent bite rate, and victims had a 47 percent hospitalization rate. When the judge suggested that the LAPD settle the case, the department asked the city for money to fix the problem themselves. "I recognized their sincerity," Rice told Lefer, "so we told the city to give them the money." Within six months the bite rate was 5 percent; the canine unit had fired some officers and hired replacements. That case led Rice to think of other ways to end what she called the "mentality of brutality" among officers. "Of course, one of the first lessons I learned was that they don't call it 'brutality.' They call it 'good policing,'" she told Lefer. "My language shut down the debate. I wasn't communicating. I was still fighting them."

From 1997 to 2001 the LAPD was embroiled in the Rampart corruption scandal, so named for the area of Los Angeles in which many police officers were accused of illegal activities that included stealing drugs from evidence rooms and killing or beating suspects and then framing them to hide the officers' abuses. In one such case Javier Ovando, an unarmed gang member, was shot and left paralyzed by Officer Rafael Perez and his partner. The officers then framed Ovando and testified against him in court. As the scandal and the subsequent trials ensued, the LAPD was accused of minimizing the scandal and failing to address the depth of corruption within the department. The city was the target of more than 200 lawsuits, resulting in the overturning of 156 felony convictions (including Ovando's), the prosecution of nine officers and the firing or suspension of 23, and the awarding of $70 million in legal settlements. In 2003 Rice was asked to author a report on whether the city had adequately addressed the causes of the police misconduct and, if not, what needed to be done.

Rice spent two years talking to various groups of officers in the LAPD. She asked about the practice of shielding corrupt officers and, as Melanie Mack wrote for the Los Angeles Sentinel (July 13, 2006), looked for ways to alleviate "the rampant mistrust and open hostility between poor underclass communities" and the police. She found that the LAPD was woefully understaffed and, as a result, had taken to overreaction and use of excessive force in many situations. "When you have too few officers," Rice told Lefer, "they puff themselves up like porcupines to look more fierce than they are." She encouraged the police to reward officers for improving communities rather than simply making arrests, because, she told Lefer, "if no one gets promoted for making sure a kid *doesn't* get arrested, why should anyone do it?" Of her research, she told Lefer, "I brought together police, gang intervention workers, sociologists, educators, demographers, and epidemiologists who study violence as a disease—a real dream team of experts on gangs. And that team told the city and the county what they had to do to end a youth-gang homicide epidemic that their policies had helped create." Rice summed up her findings and recommendations in the landmark 2007 report "A Call to Action: The Case for Comprehensive Solutions to Los Angeles' Gang Epidemic." The report, which has been called "the Marshall Plan for gangs," called for programs balancing law enforcement with crime prevention. Rice currently co-chairs a commission to reform the LAPD's training and incentive programs.

Rice's report found that despite a decline in crime in the nation as a whole, crime in Los Angeles was surging; she also found that factions of larger gangs were spreading to other cities. Rice has been an outspoken critic of the methods employed by the LAPD in addressing gang violence, especially a policy called "containment suppression," which, Rice told Lefer, "actually guarantees high levels of violence in poor areas" by making sure it does not spread to other areas in the city. The LAPD, she argued, is "not there to provide public safety" but "to make sure the violence doesn't spread." The result, Rice reported, is bleak. "I started looking at some of the conditions in the communities where the violence was," Rice told Lefer. "The levels of post-traumatic stress disorder among children in hot spots for gang activity are the same as in [the war-torn Iraqi cities of] Mosul and Baghdad."(The most recent official statistic, according to Landesman, is 47 percent.) Those alarming levels of violence have not escaped the attention of the federal government; the U.S. military, according to Landesman, sends medics to train in local Los Angeles trauma units because the conditions there so closely resemble those of warfare.

In the summer of 2008, Rice teamed up with the city of Los Angeles to implement a program called "Summer Night Lights," which for the past three years has offered recreational activities, mentoring and counseling programs, meals, and other services at parks and housing complexes four days a week until midnight—safe activities during the times when most violent crimes occur. By 2010 the program was operating at 24 sites, feeding an average of 10,929 people free meals each night. In places where people were once afraid to turn on their lights at night for fear of drive-by shootings, the results were striking: "Overall, serious gang-related crime has fallen 40.4% in the Summer Night Lights neighborhoods when compared with the summer of 2007," Scott Gold reported for the *Los Angeles Times* (October 31, 2010). "These neighborhoods are capable of transforming themselves away from violence," Deputy Mayor Guillermo Cespedes, who runs City Hall's Office of Gang Reduction and Youth Development, told Gold. "They will choose this over body bags. . . . The city cannot afford to not do this program. It doesn't solve all of the problems we need to solve. But it is a wise strategy."

In 1998 Rice left the Legal Defense Fund when she, Stephen R. English, and Molly Munger founded the nonprofit group Advancement Project, of which Rice is a co-director. The firm of English, Munger, & Rice handles the legal aspects of the Advancement Project's work, while the organization focuses on alternatives to litigation in its efforts to "dismantle structural barriers to inclusion, secure racial equity, and expand opportunity for all," as its Web site states. According to the site, the group's mission is "to develop, encourage, and widely disseminate innovative ideas, and pioneer models that inspire and mobilize a broad national racial justice movement to achieve universal opportunity and a just democracy." The group was instrumental in raising $25 billion for new school facilities throughout the state of California, including $5 billion to relieve overcrowding in urban schools.

When contacted by the Defense Department to help quell insurgencies in Iraq and Afghanistan, Rice at first thought the department had confused her—as others have—with her famous second cousin, Condoleezza Rice. (The two met as adults, and while they do not share political views, they have formed a close friendship.) After it was established that it was Constance Rice the Defense Department sought, Rice began applying the experience and expertise she has gained in her work with Los Angeles gangs to anti-insurgency strategies in the two war-torn countries.

Among dozens of other awards, Rice received an honorary doctorate from Occidental College in 2003, and in 2004 she was given the Women Lawyers of Los Angeles Ernestine Stahlhut Award. She is an occasional commentator for both National Public Radio and the *Huffington Post* and has appeared on *Nightline*, the *Oprah Winfrey Show*, and other TV programs. She is currently working on a book, tentatively titled "Power Concedes Nothing."

Rice lives in Los Angeles.

—M.M.H.

Suggested Reading: advancementproject.org; (Chapel Hill, North Carolina) *Sun* p4 Apr. 2008; *Daily Beast* (on-line) Oct. 18, 2010; *Journal of Blacks in Higher Education* p36 Oct. 31, 2004; *Los Angeles Daily News* (on-line) Sep. 26, 2004; *LA Weekly* (on-line) Dec. 13, 2007; *(Los Angeles) Sentinel* A p1 July 13, 2006, A p7 Aug. 3, 2006; *Los Angeles Times* (on-line) Oct. 31, 2010

Frazer Harrison/Getty Images

Rice, Linda Johnson

Mar. 22, 1958– Chairman of Johnson Publishing Co.

Address: Johnson Publishing Co., 820 S. Michigan Ave., Chicago, IL 60605

Linda Johnson Rice is the chairman of Johnson Publishing Co., the largest African-American-owned-and-operated publishing firm in the U.S. Founded by her father, John H. Johnson, in 1942, Johnson Publishing Co. is headquartered in Chicago, Illinois, and has offices in New York City; London, England; Paris, France; and Washington, D.C. The company is synonymous in the public mind with its publications *Ebony*, a general-interest magazine, and *Jet*, a weekly newsmagazine; it also owns and manages Fashion Fair, a cosmetics line, and ran the *Ebony* Fashion Fair, a touring fashion show that was overseen by Rice's mother until 2009. The Johnson Publishing Co. brands cater to African-American consumers. "I think of what a terrific entrepreneur and pioneer my father was," Rice said in an interview with Ed Gordon for the National Public Radio program *News & Notes* (July

4, 2005), "and how he realized 60 years ago that there was no real voice for African-Americans to really see themselves in a very positive and successful light, in a light of achievement."

As a child Rice often accompanied her parents to the Johnson offices. "They sort of developed her for the business," William Berry, a former editor at *Ebony*, told Shashank Bengali for the University of Southern California (USC) publication *Trojan Family Magazine* (Winter 2002). "Early on she got exposure to all aspects of the business. I've watched her career over the years, and she's retained the availability of an ordinary person who has extraordinary access to power and capital." After graduating from college, in 1980, Rice began to work full-time for Johnson Publishing Co. She later attended night classes and earned a master's degree in business administration. In 2002 Rice was named chief executive officer (CEO), a title she held until 2010. That title "wasn't something that was handed to me on a silver platter," she told Adrienne Murrill for Northwestern University's alumni magazine, *Kellogg World* (Summer 2007), adding, "I worked for it throughout my whole adult life."

Linda Johnson Rice was born on March 22, 1958 in Chicago. She was adopted by John H. Johnson and Eunice W. Johnson, the latter of whom served as the Johnson Publishing Co.'s secretary and treasurer. (John Johnson died in 2005, Eunice five years later.) The couple also had an adopted son, John Jr., who suffered from sickle-cell anemia and died in 1981. After taking out a $500 loan with his mother's help, John H. Johnson, the grandson of slaves, created a magazine for African-Americans, *Negro Digest*, in the early 1940s. The publication's circulation reached 50,000 within a year. (It was discontinued in 1976.) In 1945 he began publication of a monthly magazine entitled *Ebony*, whose name was suggested by his wife; he created *Jet* in 1951. Over the following decades those publications became staples in African-American homes. Johnson established Fashion Fair Cosmetics in 1973.

Before the age of 10, Rice had begun spending time at Johnson Publishing Co.'s headquarters. "It was a giant babysitter," she said in the interview with Bengali. William Berry told Bengali, "She was always asking you questions, trying to figure out what you were doing. She had that great innocence and candor of a younger person." Rice would sometimes attend editorial meetings at the *Ebony* offices, where she would occasionally give advice about which image to use on the cover of the magazine. "We'd struggle over different pictures, and then Linda would say something like, 'Well, so-and-so's not frowning in that picture. I like that one better,'" Berry recalled to Bengali. "And sometimes you thought, 'You know, she's right.'" As a child she would also travel with her mother to Paris, France, and Italy, where they would shop for the *Ebony* Fashion Fair. Also in her youth Rice enjoyed horseback riding; she has won a number of equestrian awards.

Rice wanted to attend college in Southern California, having grown attached to that region after her parents purchased a vacation home there when she was 14 years old. After visiting the USC campus, she decided that the school was a good fit for her. "It just felt so comfortable," she recalled to Bengali. "I liked the atmosphere. And I could tell there was a fascinating mix of people." In 1980 Rice received a B.A. degree in journalism from USC's Annenberg School for Communication. "There was nothing pretentious about Linda at all," Tanya Turner, a former USC student who knew Rice, said to Bengali. "Everybody knew who she was, she was very popular, but she was a regular student, just there to get an education like we all were." During the summers of her college years, Rice was a gofer at the family's company; after receiving her undergraduate degree, she served as the vice president and fashion coordinator of *Ebony* magazine until 1985, when she became her father's executive assistant. "I had her sit in on all the meetings," John H. Johnson recalled to Bengali. "She was copied on all the important correspondence that came to me, plus she got my answers. She was right there with me at all times."

While working as vice president and executive assistant to the publisher, Rice attended classes at the J. L. Kellogg Graduate School of Management at Northwestern University, in Evanston, Illinois. During that time she also traveled to Europe to help choose models for the *Ebony* Fashion Fair. "Going to school part-time and working is never easy . . . ," she said in an interview with *Ebony* (November 1992). "But going to Northwestern was very interesting. I went part-time at night, and it was interesting to get the perspective of other people going to school at night. You learn a lot from them, especially from study groups." Rice has said that her graduate education helped prepare her for her role as head of Johnson Publishing Co. "We did a lot of case study work [at Northwestern], which is really the Harvard Business School method also," she explained in the *Ebony* interview. "And it really taught you how to think through a problem. How to recognize what the problem is. How to come up with different strategies to solve the problem. How to look at the competition and the barriers to entry, as they call it. And then how to come up with a conclusion for it. And I think that was very important."

In 1987 Rice received an M.B.A. degree. Two days after her graduation, she became Johnson Publishing Co.'s president and chief operating officer (COO), positions she held until 2002, when her father appointed her as CEO. Prior to the announcement of her promotion, John H. Johnson had been away from the company for nearly a year due to health problems, and Rice had taken on his responsibilities. "The way it happened was so poignant," she told Caroline V. Clarke for *Black Enterprise* (June 30, 2002). "We had just finished our regular editorial meeting for *Ebony*, and after every meeting I [would] stay and talk to my dad about the issues of the day. Once everyone left, he hands me this formal letter on his stationery and the first paragraph says, 'Thanks for all you've done while I was out. You've done a wonderful job.'" She continued, "So, I just thought this was a congratulations letter, and I said, 'Dad, this is so sweet.' Then I kept reading, and the second paragraph says, 'In light of all that you've done, I want you to have the title of CEO.' At first I was totally speechless, then I looked at him and said, 'I've been working toward this my whole life.' He was silent for a moment, then he said, 'Well, you'd better leave before both of us start crying.'"

As CEO Rice was responsible for overseeing the company's domestic and international business operations. She created new packaging, advertising, and product launches for Fashion Fair Cosmetics. She also launched the Web site Ebony-Jet.com and helped to redesign the print magazines, making them more trendy and sleek. In addition, she approved an agreement with the Associated Press to digitize and sell photos from the company's archives. In 2005 Rice announced plans to license merchandise that would advertise the *Ebony* brand on products such as clothing, personal technology, and home goods. The company signed a deal with TurnerPatterson, a marketing and licensing company that targets minority consumers. "We have built up the brand name of *Ebony* over the last 60 years, and it's a name that's very well recognized," Rice told Eric Herman for the *Chicago Sun-Times* (June 20, 2005). "I thought this would be a growth opportunity for the company, and a great way to brand the name in other areas." She told Herman that her father approved of her decision: "He thought it was a great idea. He told me, 'You're the CEO. You're in charge.'"

In addition to her post as CEO, Rice became chairman (the title she prefers) of the Johnson Publishing Co. in 2008—three years after her father died. Also in 2008 she authorized a revenue-sharing agreement with Google, which made past issues of the magazines available on-line. In early 2010 Earvin "Magic" Johnson, a famous retired National Basketball Association player, expressed interest in purchasing *Ebony* and *Jet* magazines but was unable to negotiate a deal with the company. Later that year, after the death of her mother, Rice stepped down from her position as CEO. She was replaced by her friend Desirée Rogers, a former White House social secretary, who had recently become a corporate strategy consultant for Johnson Publishing Co. Although she no longer controls the day-to-day operations of the company, Rice continues to hold the title of chairman.

Rice has served on the boards of the United Negro College Fund, Kimberly-Clark Corp., Omnicom Group Inc., Magazine Publishers Association, and Northwestern Memorial Corp., among other organizations. She is a member of the Economic Club of Chicago, the Commercial Club of Chicago, the Executive Club of Chicago, and After School Matters. Her honors include the Women of Power

Award from the National Urban League, the Trumpet Award from Turner Broadcasting, and the Alumni Merit Award from the University of Southern California. She has been named one of Chicago's 100 Most Powerful Women by the *Chicago Sun-Times* and has been included on *Crain's Chicago Business*'s lists of 40 Under 40 and the 100 Most Influential Women.

In 2011 Rice sold her four-bedroom, 5,393-square-foot condominium at the Carlyle, a lakefront building in Chicago, which she had purchased in 1987. According to an April 12, 2010 article on the Chicago Real Estate Forum Web site, Rice, who also owns a home in Palm Springs, California, was going to move into her parents' condo, which is also located at the Carlyle. From 1984 to

1994 Rice was married to André Rice, a stockbroker who later founded two private investment companies. She and her former husband are the parents of a daughter, Alexa Christina. In 2004 Rice married Mel Farr Sr., a former National Football League player who currently owns automobile dealerships in Michigan.

—J.P.

Suggested Reading: *Advertising Age* PeopleWorks p40 Aug. 10, 1987; *Black Enterprise* p136 June 30, 2002; *Chicago Tribune* Woman News p7 July 28, 1999; *Ebony* p208+ Nov. 1992; (University of Southern California) *Trojan Family Magazine* (on-line) Winter 2002

David Paul Morris, courtesy of W.W. Norton

Roach, Mary

Mar. 20, 1959– Journalist; writer

Address: c/o W. W. Norton,. 500 Fifth Ave., New York, NY 10110

"My books are all about the human body in unusual circumstances, whether it's dead or in a sex lab or in zero gravity," Mary Roach told *Current Biography*. "I write about science," she said, "but I don't write about it in the kind of depth that most science writers do." For that reason, Roach explained, she prefers to call herself a "science goober" ("goober" being another word for "goofball") rather than a science writer, as others usually identify her. Roach's career in science journalism began

in the 1980s, when, while working in the public-relations department of the San Francisco Zoo, she began publishing articles in *Vogue, Health,* and other national magazines. Inquisitive and adventurous by nature, she became known for her engaging, unorthodox first-person narrative style, her interviewing skills, and her readiness to serve as a test subject. For her third book, *Bonk: The Curious Coupling of Science and Sex* (2008), for example, she and her husband had sex in an ultrasound machine while a scientist looked on; for the fourth, *Packing for Mars: The Curious Science of Life in the Void* (2010), she experienced weightlessness in a military jet. *Bonk* and *Packing for Mars,* like Roach's first and second books—*Stiff* (2003), about human cadavers, and *Spook* (2005), about quests to find evidence for an afterlife—earned enthusiastic reviews and became best-sellers. "The true subject of Roach's two books about death"—*Stiff* and *Spook*—"is human life, the quirky ways people confront the unknown, the mysterious, the terrifying," Floyd Skloot wrote for the *Chicago Tribune* (October 9, 2005). "She has a huge heart, a strong sense of empathy for the oddball, and she's willing to go to great lengths to find and report stories from the hinterlands of understanding."

Mary Roach was born on March 20, 1959 in Hanover, New Hampshire. Her mother, Clare, was 44 when she was born; her father, Wally, was 65. Earlier, her mother had worked as a secretary at Dartmouth College, in Hanover; her father had been a professor of speech and had also directed student theatrical productions there. "What stands out about my father are not the things he couldn't do but the things he did," Roach wrote in an essay for the *New York Times* (June 15, 1997). "That most of them were done from a sitting position hardly seems to matter. My father was an artist, a storyteller, a character. When I was 11, he painted a life-size elephant on the basement floor because elephants were my favorite animal. He taught me to draw, marking a squiggle on a sheet of paper and challenging me to finish the picture. He framed my finger paintings and hung them on the living room wall, and when guests commented, he'd make up the name of 'a noted abstract artist' and wink at me. My father, in short, was a very cool dad." Roach's parents raised her and her older brother, Rip, in Etna, a town in rural New Hampshire. Roach often played outdoors with neighborhood children. By her own account, she was a curious child and a straight-A student through high school, but neither her classes nor extracurricular activities at school appealed to her much. At home she watched a lot of TV shows, indiscriminately.

Roach's father never went to church; her mother, however, insisted that her children attend cate-chism classes and church services. "As a kid, I found it incredibly boring," Roach told *Current Biography* (the source of quotes in this article unless otherwise noted). "I hated church. My brother and I would just zone out." Roach's mother also read Bible stories to her before bedtime. In the introduction to *Spook*, Roach recalled that she rejected the Bible's accounts of Jesus's walking on water and re-storing the dead Lazarus to life. "I could not be-lieve these things had happened," Roach wrote, "because another god, the god who wore lab glass-es and knew how to use a slide rule, wanted to know how, scientifically speaking, these things could be possible. Faith did not take, because sci-ence kept putting it on the spot."

After high school Roach enrolled at Wesleyan University, in Middletown, Connecticut. She ma-jored in psychology, because she thought that do-ing so would allow her to study in Europe during her junior year. She spent that year in London, En-gland, and also traveled to other countries, most memorably Greece and Morocco. Through her trav-els, she said, she realized that there are "a whole lot of other ways to live in this world." After she earned a B.A. degree, in 1981, Roach and a few friends drove to San Francisco, California, where she settled.

After working for several years as a freelance copy editor, Roach found a part-time public-relations job with the San Francisco Zoo. She wrote press releases and answered inquiries from journalists, such as one regarding a false rumor that the zoo's cheetahs had been "sucked dry" by fleas. She has recalled wondering, "Wow! How many fleas would that take? And how much blood is in an average flea? How much blood is in a cheetah? . . . Rather than denying a story or doing damage control, which is what a good PR person would do, I could relate more to the journalist calling. I was always very incautious and impulsive in terms of what I would say." During that period, as a free-lancer, she also wrote for the Sunday magazine published jointly by the *San Francisco Chronicle* and the *San Francisco Examiner*. She soon started writing regularly for national magazines including *People, Vogue, Esquire, In Health* (later renamed *Health*), *Gentlemen's Quarterly* (now *GQ*), *Discover-er, International Wildlife*, and, by the late 1990s, *Salon.com*. She wrote on a wide range of subjects,

among them meteorite hunters, armpit odor, spray-on sex pheromones, an Amazonian tribe with an extraordinarily high murder rate, and paruresis—a phobic inability to urinate in public restrooms. During the course of her research, Roach learned that she has "a high tolerance for unusual situa-tions."

When her literary agent asked Roach if she might be interested in writing a book, Roach looked at how many hits her *Salon.com* stories had received. The most frequently visited of her stories turned out to be two about cadavers, so she chose them as the subject of her first book, *Stiff: The Curi-ous Lives of Human Cadavers* (2003). The book is not about death, dying, or the loss of loved ones, as Roach noted in her introduction; rather, it is about bodies that are studied or otherwise handled after death and (with very rare exceptions) are re-garded as anonymous. As early as around 300 B.C., she reported, King Ptolemy I of Egypt allowed phy-sicians to cut open the dead to figure out how the body works. For more than 2,000 years thereafter, legal and cultural restrictions made all cadavers except those of executed murderers off-limits to would-be dissectors, although some, in secret, paid grave robbers to disinter bodies recently buried. In Europe in the 18th and 19th centuries, the fear of being buried alive or burying someone alive be-came so widespread that doctors devised tests to confirm that a person was dead (one French physi-cian recommended three hours of tongue pulling), and mechanisms were built into coffins to enable a person buried in error to signal to those above-ground. During the 18th century Frenchmen re-peatedly tried to determine how long conscious-ness could be detected in a guillotined head. In *Stiff* Roach also described plastic surgeons honing their skills on severed heads of cadavers at a medi-cal-school anatomy lab and an operating-room scene in which surgeons removed the heart, kid-neys, and liver of a brain-dead patient in an organ-transplant procedure. Nearly every reviewer de-scribed *Stiff* as not only fascinating but surprising-ly funny. *Stiff* was named the best book of 2003 by the *San Francisco Chronicle, Entertainment Week-ly*, and National Public Radio's *Science Friday* seg-ment and has been translated into many languages, among them French, Greek, Italian, German, Chi-nese, and Japanese.

In the chapter "How to Know If You're Dead" in *Stiff*, Roach discussed "beating-heart cadavers"—people who legally and neurologically are dead be-cause their brains have died but whose bodies are kept alive by respirators so that they can become tissue and organ donors. The changing definition of what it means to be clinically dead led to Roach's brief historical overview of the "scientific search for the soul." Roach expanded on that topic in her next book, *Spook: Science Tackles the After-life* (2005), which describes efforts of physicians, scientists, sheep ranchers, and others to find out what happens to the intangible soul, spirit, or mind when people die. In the first chapter, "You Again:

A Visit to the Reincarnation Nation," Roach recounted her talks in India with a man investigating supposed instances of reincarnation. She later cited a scientist who in 1907 reported the weight loss of a recently deceased person as being 21 grams (a finding that has since been debunked). Roach also discussed some of the countless misguided attempts people have made to contact the dead—and thus prove the existence of an afterlife—via Ouija boards, crystal balls, telephones, voice recorders, computers, and electromagnetic fields. Like *Stiff*, *Spook* was a best-seller and received much critical praise.

One day, while browsing in a medical-school library, Roach stumbled upon a 1983 report of a sex-research experiment. "It had never really occurred to me, before that moment, that sex has been studied in labs, just like sleep or digestion or exfoliation or any other pocket of human physiology," Roach wrote in "Foreplay," the foreword to her next book, *Bonk: The Curious Coupling of Science and Sex* (2008). The clinical study of sexual physiology, she discovered, "did not get rolling in earnest until the 1970s," but, as she pointed out in *Bonk*, there were a few notable exceptions. Starting in 1890 Robert Latou Dickinson, a multitalented obstetrician and gynecologist, would take his patients' detailed sexual histories as part of their physical examinations. Although at the time, Roach noted, asking such questions was considered to be "unthinkable," Dickinson's patients gave him detailed accounts of their experiences of sex and masturbation. Dickinson, in Roach's words, "ushered the clitoris into the spotlight." During the 1940s and 1950s, the biologist Alfred Kinsey and his colleagues, in an effort to "document the full spectrum of human sexuality," as Roach put it, interviewed some 18,000 American men and women about their sex lives and published their detailed findings in two highly controversial, best-selling volumes. In the attic of his home, with the goal of understanding the physiology of sex, Kinsey observed and photographed, with video cameras, dozens of gay and straight people performing sexual acts. (Such research conducted in a public university would probably have had undesirable repercussions.) Starting in the mid-1950s, the psychologists William Masters and Virginia Johnson conducted research on the physiology of sex by observing sexual acts in the laboratory. Their groundbreaking books *Human Sexual Response* (1966) and *Human Sexual Inadequacy* (1970) presented convincing evidence that many widely held beliefs regarding human sexuality were wrong.

Roach and her husband, Ed Rachles, furthered the cause of scientific understanding by engaging in sex in the Diagnostic Testing Unit of London's Heart Hospital while inside a machine that captures three-dimensional moving-picture ultrasound images. Their activity was monitored by Jing Deng, a scientist who, Roach wrote, was "the first to gather moving images of internal sexual anatomy." In her account of their experience in *Bonk*, Roach wrote that as Ed kept up "an idle, disaffected rhythm," he and Deng talked about their children and she kept notes. During the men's chat, her husband said to Deng, "You look so young to have a fifteen-year-old. How old are you?" "I'm forty-five in August," Deng replied. "And the little one?" Ed asked. "How old?" "Just two and a half. You can ejaculate now."

Bonk received many positive reviews. "Is the book all bells and whistles? Mostly," Deborah Blum wrote for *New Scientist* (April 26, 2008). "But I'm a big admirer of 'subversive education' in science writing—the ability of a writer to seduce the reader into a really good story, one that's so entertaining that you don't realise you're actually learning a lot about science. Roach does that very well." In the *New York Times Book Review* (March 30, 2008), Pamela Paul commended Roach for being a "bold, tenacious and insatiable reporter," although she wondered if Roach's many humorous footnotes and other attempts at humor might be counterproductive. In a minority view among critics, Janet Maslin, the weekday *New York Times* (April 7, 2008) reviewer, complained that *Bonk* was too jokey and not especially informative. A best-seller, *Bonk* was chosen as one of the best books of the year by the *San Francisco Chronicle*, the *Boston Globe*, and *Seed* magazine.

In her latest book, *Packing for Mars: The Curious Science of Life in the Void* (2010), Roach's focus is again on the human body. Because aspects of moving, eating, eliminating bodily wastes, and maintaining hygiene are so different in the zero-gravity environment of space from the way they are on Earth, astronauts must learn how to accomplish those activities in simulated zero-gravity environments. In an account of her own experience of weightlessness, during the flight of a C-9 military transport jet, Roach described the sensation as resembling "a physical euphoria. You suddenly are free of the weight of your organs inside you and your arms hanging off your shoulders. It's different than being in a swimming pool [where] you can feel the resistance of the water. It isn't like anything you've ever experienced. It's like you don't have a body." *Packing for Mars*, M. G. Lord wrote for the *New York Times Book Review* (August 8, 2010), "is an often hilarious, sometimes queasy-making catalog of the strange stuff devised to permit people to survive in an environment for which their bodies are stupendously unsuited."

Roach has contributed personal essays and many book reviews to the *New York Times*. Her next book, also about "unusual things related to the human body," is scheduled for publication in 2012.

Roach and her husband, Ed Rachles, live in Oakland. For many years Rachles worked for the *San Francisco Chronicle* as a designer and graphic artist. He has two adult children from a previous marriage.

—D.K.

Suggested Reading: *Chicago Tribune* C p3 Apr. 5, 2008; maryroach.net; *New Scientist* p46 Apr. 26, 2008; *New York Times* E p9 Oct. 6, 2005; *San Francisco Chronicle* F p1 July 4, 2004

Selected Books: *Stiff: The Curious Lives of Human Cadavers*, 2003; *Spook: Science Tackles the Afterlife*, 2005; *Bonk: The Curious Coupling of Science and Sex*, 2008; *Packing for Mars: The Curious Science of Life in the Void*, 2010

Stephen Lovekin/Getty Images

Rogers, Desirée

June 16, 1959– Publishing executive

Address: Johnson Publishing Co. Inc., 820 S. Michigan Ave., Chicago, IL 60605

Desirée Rogers, who in June 2010 was named CEO of the Johnson Publishing Co.—the home of *Ebony* and *Jet* magazines—is no stranger to positions of power. The former White House social secretary has also served as the executive director of the Illinois Lottery and as an executive with Peoples Energy Corp. of Chicago, Illinois. Rogers was included on *Crain's Chicago Business*'s lists of the Top 25 Women to Watch and 40 Under 40 Business Leaders, and she has been recognized by *Black Enterprise* as one of the Top 50 Most Powerful African American Business Women and the Top 75 Most Powerful Blacks in Corporate America. While Rogers carried out her duties at the White House with both style and businesslike precision (she was the first social-secretary appointee to have an M.B.A. degree), her longtime devotion to fashion and well-

publicized, expensive lifestyle did not sit well with a public in the throes of economic hardship; she was also criticized for referring to the president of the United States as a "brand"—a term that pointed to her efforts to have the White House reflect the tastes and priorities of President Barack Obama. A security breach at an otherwise successful state dinner in late 2009 led to Rogers's resignation. Currently, Rogers is overseeing what Richard Prince described for the *Root* (March 5, 2011) as a "top-to-bottom redesign" at *Ebony* magazine. From new Web content to an update of the 65-year-old logo, Rogers is seeking to deliver *Ebony* to "a new generation of readers," Prince wrote. The fruits of her labors were available on newsstands in April 2011.

Rogers was born Desirée Glapion on June 16, 1959 in New Orleans, Louisiana. According to Amy Chozick, writing for the *Wall Street Journal* (April 30, 2009, on-line), she is a descendant of a Creole voodoo priestess, Marie Laveau Glapion. Her father, Roy Glapion Jr., was a public-school teacher and sports coach who later became athletic director of New Orleans schools, finance chairman of the Zulu Social Aid and Pleasure Club, and a member of the city council; Chozick reported that Roy Glapion "used to ask little Desirée to serve drinks or gumbo and help entertain when company arrived." Her mother, Joyce, founded three day-care centers with Rogers's maternal grandmother, Marie. Rogers and her younger brother, Roy, were raised in a privileged home, but Rogers was determined to succeed in her own right. "I never had to say, 'Go do your homework,'" her mother recalled to DeNeen L. Brown for the *Richmond (Virginia) Times Dispatch* (February 22, 2009). Growing up in New Orleans's Seventh Ward, Rogers attended high school at the Catholic, all-girls Academy of the Sacred Heart, from which she graduated in 1977. She then enrolled at Wellesley College, in Wellesley, Massachusetts. Rogers earned a B.A. degree in political science in 1981. While in college she participated in an exchange program, traveling to Switzerland to study international politics and business. During her time abroad she was inspired to obtain a graduate degree in business administration. "Since I was a child I wanted to run a business," she told Barbara Rose for the *Chicago Tribune* (September 12, 2004). "I love to see people achieve excellence, their own excellence."

Rogers spent two years in the workforce before attending business school. She worked in sales for the Xerox Corp. and as a supervisor for AT&T. "It was part of my game plan," she told Genevieve Buck for the *Chicago Tribune* (July 3, 1991). "I knew I never wanted to be a salesperson, but I wanted to understand the skill. And I wanted an introduction to managing people as a way to influence their work." Rogers earned an M.B.A. degree from Harvard University, in Cambridge, Massachusetts, in 1985, then moved to Chicago to work again for AT&T—this time in operations. In 1987 she moved briefly to the AT&T headquarters, in

New Jersey. Three weeks later her boyfriend, John Rogers Jr., the founder of the investment firm Ariel Capital Management, proposed to her; Rogers accepted and moved back to Chicago, where she took a job with the Levy Organization, which oversees real-estate and food businesses. The couple married in 1988 and had a daughter, Victoria, two years later.

John Rogers, a Chicago native, was well-connected and introduced his wife to the city's leaders in business and politics. Young and highly successful, the couple quickly became the toast of the city. Outside of their work, they became philanthropists, and Desirée Rogers served on the boards of the Children's Memorial Hospital and the Chicago Children's Museum and the women's board of the Museum of Contemporary Art, among other institutions. Larry Levy, head of the Levy Organization, told Buck, "She was a star, but . . . she wanted to run her own company." After leaving the Levy Organization, Rogers founded Museum Operations Consulting Associates. The firm specialized in "operating and providing consulting services to museum retail stores," Buck wrote.

When the Republican Jim Edgar was elected governor of Illinois, in 1990, members of his transition team suggested that Rogers apply for a state job. (A Republican during those years, Rogers was a delegate at the 1992 GOP national convention.) "John and I had discussed such a possibility—that one of us, probably me, would at some point become involved with a not-for-profit organization or with the city or state government," Rogers told Buck. She submitted her application and was appointed soon afterward to run the Illinois Lottery, where she headed a staff of 330. Her job primarily involved managing costs and increasing sales, tasks she approached with enthusiasm. She made changes to the managerial structure and evaluated the advertising firm affiliated with the agency, which had not been done since the lottery's inception, in 1974. Rogers impressed her employers from the start; Governor Edgar's executive assistant for economic and policy concerns, Mike Belletire, told Buck that Rogers was a "breath of fresh air." Rogers and her team reversed the decline of the lottery with innovative marketing techniques. They came up with a new slogan, "Somebody's gonna Lotto . . . it might as well be you," and implemented a 1-800 number and credit-card payment options. By 1995 the lottery had increased its revenue by 7 percent. Rogers gained celebrity in Chicago by appearing on the lottery's television segment. Later, in a conversation with William Norwich for *Vogue* (February 2009), she compared her experience with the Illinois Lottery to her job as White House social secretary, as she "met a true cross-section of people" while heading the lottery. "The common thread among them never was just getting rich, but being able to do something wonderful—like adding a room to the house for an elderly mother, or paying for the grandkids' tuition. If I can re-create that kind of enthusiasm at the White House, then I'm doing my job."

Rogers left the lottery in 1997 and was hired at Peoples Energy gas company as vice president of corporate communications, ushering her, Genma Stringer Holmes wrote for the *Tennessee Tribune* (March 11, 2010), into the "gentleman's club of regulated utilities." In an interview with Jeff Share for *Pipeline & Gas Journal* (November 1, 2005), when asked how her background helped prepare her for working in the energy industry, she responded: "In 1997, the utility industry was starting to change as residential deregulation began in Illinois. I thought my skill set might be helpful, given I was coming from the outside and might have a different point of view. It has been very exciting to combine the disciplines of marketing and operations." Rogers oversaw customer operations, marketing, sales, media relations, and community and government affairs. She led the company in what she referred to as a "branding campaign," she told Marcia Froelke Coburn for *Chicago Magazine* (August 2000), to improve Peoples Energy's public image. "We are a 150-year-old company," she said. "But, really, energy is not something you think about. You expect it to work; you get your bill, you pay it." She added, "It's a matter of thinking about how my product touches people's lives and how can I make people aware of that." In 2000 Rogers was named chief marketing officer, and in 2004 she was elected president of Peoples Energy's subsidiaries, Peoples Gas and North Shore Gas.

In 2008 Rogers was appointed president of social networking for the Allstate Financial insurance company. She was charged with the task of developing an on-line network through which customers could connect with one another regarding retirement and financial services. "The idea of the [social network] would be to have a forum where people can talk about these things among themselves and, at the same time, [Allstate would] provide them with factual information about financial products and retirement," she told Nathan Conz for *Insurance & Technology* (August 11, 2008).

Meanwhile, after getting married, Rogers had become close friends with Valerie Jarrett, then deputy chief of staff under Chicago mayor Richard M. Daley, and Linda Johnson Rice, chairwoman of the Johnson Publishing Co. Jarrett, currently a top presidential adviser, reportedly took the young Obamas under her wing after she hired Michelle Obama for a job in the mayor's office in the early 1990s. In addition, John Rogers had played basketball at Princeton University with Michelle Obama's brother. Thus, Rogers's relationship with the future president and First Lady began even before Barack Obama's political career. Published sources are not clear as to when or whether Rogers changed her party affiliation, but she was a major fundraiser during the 2008 presidential campaign of Barack Obama, a Democrat.

In November 2008, when Rogers had been with Allstate for only a few months, Obama was elected president. Shortly afterward he appointed Rogers as White House social secretary, making her the first African-American to hold the post. With encouragement from the Obamas, Rogers was determined to redefine the position, in which she would be responsible for coordinating all events at the White House, from state dinners to the annual Easter egg rolls on the White House lawn; she saw her mission as both making the White House more open to the public and making it reflect the "Obama brand." She began by ruffling a few feathers. "It is a tradition among former White House social secretaries that whenever a new person is named to that position her immediate predecessor hosts a lunch to welcome her into what they call their sisterhood," Bob Colacell wrote for *Vanity Fair* (June 2010); Rogers's welcome lunch was hosted by Amy Zantzinger, a social secretary during the George W. Bush administration, and attended by other women who had held the position in the past, including the group's "doyenne," Letitia "Tish" Baldrige, who served during the John F. Kennedy administration. Colacell was told by a "Washington insider": "Tish gave [Rogers] some advice, and Desirée said she didn't care about tablecloths and china and flowers—that was not what she was there to do. For her, a woman like Tish is a dinosaur. She's not interested in what she has to say."

"Above all," Chozick wrote, "Rogers is a world-class networker—the ultimate social engineer, not just planning White House dinner parties as well as her own intimate soirees but also connecting powerful people in her orbit." Rogers said to Brown, "Partly for me as a businessperson, it was important this not be a job that I would be picking flowers all day—even thought I think that is fun. That is not what I want to do for my job. I don't think that is where I would add the most value."

Rogers and First Lady Michelle Obama endeavored to make the White House more accessible, or, as Chozick wrote, to make it the "people's house." In an effort to celebrate American culture, Rogers scheduled nightly events including poetry jams, music concerts, and dance and theater performances, involving such celebrities as the filmmaker Spike Lee, the jazz musician Esperanza Spalding, the Irish-American poet Paul Muldoon, and the popular group Earth, Wind and Fire. "Our goal really is to bring the house alive," Rogers told Rachel L. Swarns for the *New York Times* (May 12, 2009) about that diverse assemblage. "We're all American, but all of us come from different backgrounds. We want to expose Americans to other Americans that are doing brilliant work." Rogers was also credited with revamping traditional White House events, such as the Easter egg roll, which, for the first time, families across the country could attend via an on-line ticket lottery.

A force in both business and high society, Rogers became the most highly publicized social secretary in recent memory, if not ever. Though by all accounts she performed her job with impressive efficiency (and often to sparkling praise), her glamorous lifestyle away from the job became the subject of public scrutiny; during a time of high unemployment and economic turmoil, some observers found her appearances at fashion shows and in expensive clothing on magazine covers to be insensitive. Her undoing, however, was a security gaffe during the Obamas' first state dinner, in honor of visiting Indian prime minister Manmohan Singh, in November 2009. During an otherwise "elegant evening, a logistically complicated affair for 300-plus guests," Jocelyn Noveck wrote for the Associated Press (December 4, 2009), a couple—the Salahis—entered uninvited. The next day the "crashers," as they became known, posted on-line photos of themselves mingling with the president and other high-ranking officials. Though it was acknowledged that the Secret Service should have checked for the Salahis' names on its list of invited guests, lawmakers and noted journalists, including Maureen Dowd of the *New York Times*, blamed Rogers for not checking each guest in herself. Adding fuel to the fire, Rogers had seated herself among the guests. Noveck wrote that some accused Rogers of "putting her own aggrandizement over her job." Tish Baldrige came to Rogers's defense, telling Noveck, "I have sat at state dinners and so have many other social secretaries. Of course, you're constantly getting up. But I don't begrudge her at all for seating herself at the dinner." John Rogers—who had divorced Desirée Rogers amicably in 2000 and who had attended the state dinner—said to Noveck, "It's extraordinary to see someone's life's work mischaracterized in this way. I just don't understand it. She's working 12–15 hours a day, just trying to do a great job. Desirée has brought excellence to everything she's done in her life." Desirée Rogers and members of the Secret Service were asked to appear before Congress for hearings, on the grounds that the security breach had endangered the lives of the first family. The director of the Secret Service testified, but Rogers did not. In February 2010 she resigned.

Four months later Rogers accepted a position as the new CEO of Johnson Publishing Co., which owns both *Ebony* and *Jet* magazines. Those publications, aimed at an African-American readership, were established in 1945 (*Ebony*) and 1951 (*Jet*). Rogers hopes to draw new advertisers and improve Web content for the iconic magazines. According to a reporter for the *Jacksonville (Florida) Free Press* (October 14, 2010), the average monthly circulation for *Ebony* had fallen 14 percent from 2009 to 2010; that of *Jet*, a weekly magazine, had declined by 12 percent. "I'm not trying to be a hero here," Rogers told the *Jacksonville Free Press* of her efforts to boost revenue. "I'm trying to take my time and really make certain that we do what we need to do to be solid." Rogers spearheaded a major redesign of *Ebony* that debuted in April 2011. She told Phil Rosenthal for the *Chicago Tribune* (March 6, 2011, on-line) that she referred to the new look as "*Vanity Fair* plus *O* (the Oprah Winfrey magazine) plus soul," and that with it she hoped to attract "the next generation of *Ebony* readers."

Chozick wrote about the five-foot 10-inch, photogenic Rogers, "Her voice is a smooth unaccented soprano with a hint of a playful Louisiana drawl that she uses to add an extra kick to a story every now and then." Linda Johnson Rice said to Coburn, "I think people often find Desirée cold, even to the point of frosty at first. But that's an initial reaction. Underneath, she is a warm and funny person." Rogers was named one of the seven co-chairs in charge of organizing Chicago mayor-elect Rahm Emanual's inauguration, scheduled for May 16, 2011. In 2003 she was diagnosed with early-stage breast cancer; she is now cancer-free and has become an advocate for women's health. Her daughter, Victoria, currently attends Yale University.

Rogers is single and lives in Chicago.

—M.M.H.

Suggested Reading: Associated Press (on-line) Dec. 4, 2009; *Chicago Magazine* (on-line) Aug. 2000; *Chicago Sun-Times* p1 Dec. 12, 1993; *Chicago Tribune* p5 July 3, 1991, C p1 Sep. 12, 2004, (on-line) Mar. 6, 2011; *Insurance & Technology* (on-line) Aug. 11, 2008; *Jacksonville (Florida) Free Press* p7 Oct. 14, 2010; *New York Times* (on-line) May 12, 2009; *Pipeline & Gas Journal* p12 Nov. 1, 2005; *Richmond (Virginia) Times Dispatch* J p8 Feb. 22, 2009; *Tennessee Tribune* A p4 Mar. 11, 2010; *Vanity Fair* p162 June 2010; *Vogue* p180 Feb. 2009; *Wall Street Journal* (on-line) Apr. 30, 2009

Doug Benc/Getty Images

Rosenhaus, Drew

Oct. 29, 1966– Sports agent

Address: Rosenhaus Sports Representation, 6400 Allison Rd., Miami Beach, FL 33141

In the July 27, 2005 edition of the *Milwaukee Journal*, the sports agent Drew Rosenhaus was quoted as having said a decade earlier, "Ideally, I would like to be in a position where I represent 100 guys in the NFL [National Football League], to be in a position where I could control whether some teams win or lose." The agent, who established Rosenhaus Sports Representation in the late 1980s, has achieved at least part of his goal: his client list totals more than 100 members of the NFL, more than any other sports agent, and he has represented players on every team in the league. Rosenhaus is as hated by other agents—many of whom have accused him of stealing clients—as he is beloved by his clients, for whom he has won some of the most lucrative contracts in the history of pro football. He has admitted that he is not above bending the truth when it comes to serving his clients' monetary interests. Still, he said in an interview with Jake Trotter for the *Oklahoman* (May 4, 2008), "I think there's a misperception out there about me. People look at agents and they think that they're just out there to make money for their clients. I can't speak for other agents, but as for myself, I care about my clients like they're my own family. . . . I'm out to help these young men grow and have a better life after football and during football to be the best that they can be because I'm in the business of helping people have better lives."

Drew Rosenhaus was born on October 29, 1966 in South Orange, New Jersey. His father, Robert, worked in real estate and manufactured boats. In 1970 Rosenhaus moved with his family to Miami, Florida, where he and his younger brother, Jason, became avid fans of the Miami Dolphins football team; their father became friends with some of the players, inviting them to his home, where Drew and Jason got to ask them questions about football. For a time Drew Rosenhaus aspired to play the sport professionally, but he came to realize that he had less talent for football than for academics. He did, however, take up the martial art of tae kwon do, later receiving a black belt.

After graduating in 1984 from the Jewish High School of South Florida (since renamed the Hillel Community Jewish High School), Rosenhaus enrolled at the University of Miami, where he studied history and broadcast journalism and earned a degree in three years. He intended to become a sportscaster; while tutoring University of Miami football players, however, he discovered that he would prefer to be a sports agent. With that in mind he applied successfully to Duke University School of

Law, in Durham, North Carolina, and received a J.D. degree in 1990. Following his first year of law school, Rosenhaus worked for the sports agent Mel Levine (who would later serve over two years in prison for bank-loan fraud). Levine was impressed by Rosenhaus's occasional circumvention of the truth, such as when he telephoned the Syracuse University football office to recruit the player Tommy Kane and obtained Kane's contact information by pretending to be his tutor. "I impressed Levine," Rosenhaus told Michael Bamberger and Don Yaeger for *Sports Illustrated* (July 15, 1996). "But I soon found out that I was teaching him, he wasn't teaching me." In 1989, during his second year of law school, Rosenhaus took on his first client, Robert Massey of North Carolina Central University. After Massey was drafted by the New Orleans Saints, Rosenhaus, in an early indication of his desire for visibility, invited ESPN to cover his negotiations with the Saints' general manager, Jim Finks.

Around the time that he became Massey's agent, Rosenhaus established Rosenhaus Sports Representation. Although he now focuses on football representation exclusively, Rosenhaus acted as an agent for the Major League Baseball player Chuck Carr in 1994. Carr, who was the National League's stolen-base champion, was seeking a three-year, $4 million contract with the Florida Marlins; at the time the team was offering him only a one-year contract worth $230,000. Rosenhaus lowered the salary requirement to $2 million over two years, then $490,000 per year, offers the team rejected. In an attempt to drive up the Marlins' offer, Carr walked out of training camp for three days. That hardball tactic was not effective, and Carr settled for $230,000 per year, but the holdout tactic would be used frequently by Rosenhaus in the future.

In 1994 Rosenhaus began negotiations with the Pittsburgh Steelers over the tight end Eric Green. Green, who had led the Steelers with 63 receptions for 942 yards the previous season, had scored 20 touchdowns in four years, more than any other tight end in Steelers history. Although Green's contract had run out, the Steelers named Green its franchise player and initially offered him a one-year contract, worth $1.4 million, which would prohibit him from joining another team without that team's sacrificing two first-round draft picks. The Steelers next offered Green a contract worth $1.8 million annually for four years, still $1 million less per year than he had sought. After the team failed to respond to Green's salary demands, Green played anyway, beginning with a game against the Dallas Cowboys. It seemed to many that Green had relinquished hopes of signing a more lucrative contract. Rosenhaus proved them wrong, however, by orchestrating a six-team bidding war, which resulted in Green's being signed to the Dolphins in 1995 for six years and $12 million and becoming the highest-paid NFL tight end in history up to that time. Two days before the contract was signed, Rosenhaus had told each of the six teams—the Washington Redskins,

the Green Bay Packers, the Los Angeles Raiders, the Steelers, the Cleveland Browns, and the Dolphins—that their offers were not high enough, thus giving each team time to re-bid. Unaware that their offer had been the highest made, the Dolphins re-bid, raising Green's signing bonus by $200,000 and his average annual salary from $1.88 million to $2 million. Rosenhaus later sought to justify his tactic, telling the *Miami Herald* (March 19, 1995): "It's not lying. It's negotiating. Everybody lies when they negotiate. It's like playing poker. It's no different from keeping a straight face when you know you're going to lose. I was just doing what I could do to put my client in the best position possible. I bluffed. I was never the type of guy who said check out our offer. I was never specific. I worked in generalities. Everything I said, I was doing for my client's best interest. Did I lie to the media? At that time, maybe I did. It depends on what you consider a lie. Really, I was manipulating for the sake of my client." (One year later Green's contract was rescinded following a knee injury, which had prevented him from attending 39 practices during the 1995–96 season.)

Also in 1995 Rosenhaus dealt with two prominent public-relations matters. One of his clients, the University of Miami defensive tackle Warren Sapp, had failed an NFL drug test, and the *New York Times* reported that Sapp had tested positive for marijuana and cocaine. Although the NFL denied the cocaine allegations, the drug controversy proved detrimental to Sapp's draft value. Previously, he had been considered the best defensive tackle in the NFL draft and was the projected number-two draft pick, but after the story ran, he was drafted 12th by the Tampa Bay Buccaneers. Rosenhaus claimed that the story had cost Sapp $1 million in signing bonuses and an additional $1 million in salary; the four-year deal was worth $4.4 million with a $2.3 million bonus. Two years later Sapp was pulled over on the road by police and charged with marijuana possession. The case was dismissed on the grounds that the traffic stop had been illegal, since there had been no evidence demonstrating that Sapp was carrying drugs. That episode did not stop the Buccaneers from offering Sapp a contract extension in 1998, which, at over $36 million, made him the highest-paid defensive player in the NFL. Rosenhaus again needed to perform damage control when the Seattle Seahawks wide receiver Brian Blades was charged with manslaughter for the accidental shooting of his cousin, Charles. After Blades posted bond, on July 19, 1995, Rosenhaus told Amy Driscoll for the *Miami Herald*, "Brian has been through hell. He has lost his best friend and a loved one." In June 1996 Blades was convicted of manslaughter, a decision overturned three days later. Although the case was appealed, the acquittal was upheld. Rosenhaus remained at his clients' sides during their respective ordeals, often defending them before the media. Another of his clients, Louis Oliver of the Dolphins, said about him to Randell Mell for the *Fort*

Lauderdale (Florida) Sun-Sentinel (July 30, 1995), "You know Drew's going to be there and do his best for you. You call Drew, and you know he's going to be there."

Rosenhaus acted as an adviser for *Jerry Maguire,* a 1996 film about a young sports agent (the title character, played by Tom Cruise); in the film one of Maguire's clients fires him in favor of a slick, heartless agent played by Jay Mohr, widely reported to be modeled on Rosenhaus. Rosenhaus had a cameo in that movie as well as in another football-themed film, *Any Given Sunday.* In 1996 Rosenhaus became the first sports agent to appear on the cover of *Sports Illustrated* (July 15, 1996). Accompanying his image were the caption "The most hated man in pro football" and a quote he had given in the interview: "I am a ruthless warrior. I am a hit man. I will move in for the kill and use everything within my power to succeed for my clients." The profile detailed his ambition, drive, and estrangement from other sports agents, many of whom have accused him of actively stealing their clients—a charge he has denied. "He will not only lie," Bamberger and Yaeger wrote for the article, "he will also scream, cajole, threaten, and whine to defend his clients' interests. For Rosenhaus, clients' needs come before the needs of a team, the league, and even Rosenhaus himself. Which is why he is the hottest young agent in the NFL. . . . Other agents despise Rosenhaus, and some team executives are loath to do business with him. He has been described as slithering and blindly ambitious." On the subject of stealing clients, Rosenhaus told the reporters, "If a guy [player] is unhappy, if a guy wants to leave his agent, if a guy is in the process of changing agents, I will strike, and I will go right for the jugular. But I will not call a guy up and say, 'Hey, you ought to dump your agent.'" Another agent, David Ware, expressed a different view, telling Bamberger and Yaeger, "Drew tells a player that he's worth more money, that his agent is not doing enough for him, that he's better than the guy starting in front of him. Now the player is not only mad at his agent, he's mad at the team management. He sees the guy starting in front of him as a co-conspirator. . . . If the only thing players are concerned about is their next deal, it's not going to produce winning football."

One of Rosenhaus's less successful negotiations involved a holdout by Errict Rhett, in 1996. Rhett, a running back for the Tampa Bay Buccaneers, was entering the third year of his contract, for which he would be paid $336,000. He and Rosenhaus considered that to be gross underpayment; Rhett had completed an outstanding 1,000 yards in each of his two seasons with the team, and many NFL starting backs at the time were earning substantially more. The Buccaneers, however, stated clearly that they would not renegotiate the contract; underscoring their stance, they charged Rhett $5,000 for each day he sat out. After 94 days Rhett returned and accepted half of his original salary, claiming to do so because of his love of football and

his wish to become a free agent the next season, which would have been impossible if he had continued to hold out. In 1997 Rhett fired Rosenhaus, telling the *Tampa (Florida) Tribune* (June 3, 1997), "Since he started representing me, nothing . . . was happening really positive."

Rosenhaus followed up those negotiations with two successful holdouts in 1998, one involving the Miami Dolphins defensive tackle Tim Bowens and the other the Baltimore Ravens cornerback Duane Starks. Bowens, who sat out for four weeks, returned when the Dolphins acquiesced to his request to receive his $2.88 million salary up-front. Starks, the Ravens' number-one draft pick, returned after only 16 days, signing a four-year contract worth approximately $7 million. Starks told Mike Preston for the *Baltimore Sun* (August 6, 1998), "The holdout was not something I wanted to do. I wanted to be here, and this is something that could have been done a while ago. But I left a lot of things in his [Rosenhaus's] hands."

One of Rosenhaus's greatest successes was the much-discussed deception involving the running back Willis McGahee. McGahee, who helped bring the University of Miami football team a Division I national championship in 2001, was a finalist for the Heisman Trophy, an award given to the country's top college football player. He broke University of Miami records, completing 10 100-yard performances and carrying the ball 1,753 yards in 2002. Still, McGahee was a risky choice for NFL teams because of his injury in the 2003 Fiesta Bowl, in which he tore three ligaments in his knee. Rosenhaus assuaged the NFL's doubts by exaggerating the speed of McGahee's recovery, telling the media—which quickly repeated his claims—that McGahee would be a first-round draft pick and that the New England Patriots' coach, Bill Belichick, had visited Miami in April 2003 in order to watch McGahee work out; in reality Belichick had gone there to see not only McGahee but five other Miami players as well. When Rosenhaus announced a McGahee workout before the draft, nine teams attended. In an even more elaborate charade, Rosenhaus called McGahee's cell phone during the ESPN draft telecast to make it appear that the running back was being telephoned by teams hoping to draft him. Rosenhaus said when he called McGahee, as quoted in the *Buffalo (New York) News* (April 29, 2003), "Pretend I'm an NFL team calling you. Look happy. Maybe we can get some team that's watching to think we're talking to other teams." McGahee was drafted by the Buffalo Bills in the first round, making him the 23d overall pick.

In 2005 Rosenhaus became the sports agent with the most clients in the NFL, representing more than 90 players. Also that year Rosenhaus came under much scrutiny for his management of the notoriously demanding and spiteful Philadelphia Eagles star wide receiver Terrell Owens. The previous year Owens had caught 77 passes totaling 1,200 yards and 14 touchdowns before sustaining an injury, then recovered and played in the Super

Bowl, making nine catches for 122 yards. Because of his strong performance, Owens believed he deserved compensation beyond the seven-year, $49 million deal he had signed only one year earlier. Furthermore, because his previous agent had missed the deadline in filing paperwork to allow Owens to become a free agent, Owens had not been able to negotiate as one. The result, according to Rosenhaus, quoted in the *Pittsburgh Post-Gazette* (April 17, 2005), was that Owens "had to take a substandard deal because he had no leverage." Rosenhaus added that Owens had "outperformed" the deal and should be compensated for his stellar play. A Philadelphia city councilman took exception to Rosenhaus's tactics, calling for an investigation into the agent's business license and tax status and stating in a letter to the city's Department of Licensing and Inspections, "In a working class city, where the median salary is less than $30,000 per year. . . . it's insulting to watch a man do sit-ups in the driveway of his multi-million dollar house and complain about making $49 million over seven years."

While Rosenhaus received much criticism for the Owens holdout, many of his clients defended him, including the Eagles' Jerome McDougle, who told the *Philadelphia Inquirer* (May 1, 2005) about his agent, "He's a good guy who really works hard for his players. Some agents are out for themselves, and they're not trying to do what's best for the player all the time. Drew is always looking out for the player. The people who hate him are the guys in the front office who don't want to pay the players. Drew fights for his players, and his players love him." Clifton Brown wrote for the *New York Times* (May 24, 2005), "Rosenhaus says he knows that many fans will never understand players who are making millions asking for more money. But in a league in which contracts are not guaranteed and every game brings potential for serious injury, Rosenhaus sees himself as the underdog, negotiating against owners who have far more security than his clients."

On August 10, 2005 an argument between the Eagles' coach, Andy Reid, and Owens resulted in Owens's being barred from practice for a week. On November 3, 2005, in an interview with Graham Bensinger of ESPN, Owens made disparaging remarks about the Eagles organization and his teammates, saying that the Eagles showed a "lack of class" for not acknowledging his 100th touchdown catch and hinting that the team would be more effective if the quarterback Donovan McNabb were replaced by Brett Favre. In a development that created a media frenzy, Owens was suspended for four games and then cut from the team only one day before he was to receive his $5 million roster bonus. Rosenhaus called a press conference in the driveway of Owens's New Jersey home, where Owens apologized to the Eagles and Rosenhaus famously responded to most questions—including, "What have you done for your client besides get him kicked off the Eagles?"—by answering, "Next question."

The next season Rosenhaus was instrumental in Owens's signing with the Dallas Cowboys for three years and $25 million. Discussing that deal, Rosenhaus said, according to the *Fort Worth (Texas) Star-Telegram* (March 20, 2006), "I deliver for my clients. . . . That's why they hire me. I do appreciate Terrell's confidence in me. There were a lot of people who took shots at me publicly, and that's OK, because I can deal with that." That year Rosenhaus also negotiated a six-year contract for the Cincinnati Bengals wide receiver Chad Johnson (now known as Chad Ochocinco) worth $35.5 million, a deal that made him the highest-paid receiver in the NFL. In recent years other notable football players have signed on with Rosenhaus's agency, some leaving other agents in the process; the list includes DeSean Jackson and Chris Clemons (both 2009) and Ahmad Bradshaw and Carlos Dunlap (both 2011). Rosenhaus also represents Plaxico Burress, the NFL player released from prison in June 2011 after serving 20 months for firing a gun in a New York City nightclub.

Part of Rosenhaus's appeal for clients has been that he often charges them only 2 percent of the amounts of their contracts, rather than the standard industry fee of 3 to 4 percent. For years Rosenhaus's agency consisted of only himself and his brother, Jason; Rosenhaus said that he did not hire secretaries or assistants because he preferred having direct connections with his clients. Rosenhaus Sports Representation is currently made up of five agents.

Rosenhaus lives in Miami Beach, Florida. He has appeared as a commentator on television programs including *ABC Primetime Live*, the ESPN shows *Pardon the Interruption* and *Outside the Lines*, and the HBO shows *Real Sports* and *Inside the NFL*. He is the co-author of two books—*A Shark Never Sleeps: Wheeling and Dealing with the NFL's Most Ruthless Agent* (1997) and *Next Question: An NFL Super Agent's Proven Game Plan for Business Success* (2008).

—T.O.

Suggested Reading: *Chicago Sun-Times* F p24 Feb. 4, 2007; (Fort Lauderdale, Florida) *Sun-Sentinel* C p1 Apr. 27, 2003, Sports Apr. 7, 2011; *Miami Herald* D p1 Aug. 12, 2005; *Milwaukee Journal Sentinel* C p1 July 28, 2005; (Oklahoma City) *Oklahoman* B p2 May 4, 2008; *Sports Illustrated* July 15, 1996

Selected Books: *A Shark Never Sleeps: Wheeling and Dealing with the NFL's Most Ruthless Agent*, 1997; *Next Question: An NFL Super Agent's Proven Game Plan for Business Success*, 2008

Jason Kempin/Getty Images for Tribeca Film Festival

Rosenthal, Jane

Sep. 21, 1956– Film producer; co-founder and president of Tribeca Productions

Address: Tribeca Productions, 375 Greenwich St., Eighth Fl., New York, NY 10013

Jane Rosenthal had a decade of production experience under her belt—having helped make some 90 movies, mostly for television—when the actor Robert De Niro chose her to join him in a new filmmaking endeavor. "I spent a year looking for somebody," De Niro, the celebrated star of movies including *Mean Streets*, *Taxi Driver*, and *Raging Bull*, told Meryl Gordon for *New York* (April 29, 2002). "I interviewed around twenty people and re-interviewed them, and re- and re-interviewed them, and finally felt [Rosenthal] was the best person for it, and I wasn't wrong. She still is." In 1989, along with her husband, Craig Hatkoff, Rosenthal and De Niro set up Tribeca Productions, named for the neighborhood in the New York City borough of Manhattan where De Niro has lived for many years (an area within a **tri**angle **be**low **Ca**nal Street, also spelled "TriBeCa"). Working day-to-day with Rosenthal as his co-producer, De Niro directed his first film, the critically lauded *A Bronx Tale*, and he has gained younger generations of fans as a comic actor, parodying his earlier, tough-guy screen persona in Tribeca productions including *Analyze That*, *Analyze This*, *Meet the Parents*, and *Meet the Fockers*.

Tribeca Productions is located in a renovated factory now called the Tribeca Film Center—"the first commercial space in Tribeca dedicated to housing film, television, and entertainment companies," according to the company's Web site. The center helped to transform a previously down-and-out neighborhood into one of New York City's most desirable commercial and residential sections. The revival of the economy of Lower Manhattan after the terrorist attacks of September 11, 2001 was Rosenthal, De Niro, and Hatkoff's expressed goal when, in 2002, they launched the Tribeca Film Festival. According to the Web site of Tribeca Enterprises—the company that since 2003 has served as an umbrella for Tribeca Productions and the Tribeca Film Festival—the nine annual festivals held to date have attracted a total of more than 3.25 million attendees, generated some $660 million in business in Lower Manhattan, and introduced to the public more than 1,200 films from upwards of 80 countries. "More than ever," Stephen Holden wrote for the *New York Times* (April 18, 2008), "TriBeCa resembles a sprawling downtown answer to the New York Film Festival. While TriBeCa's older uptown cousin scoops up the best films from Cannes for their New York premieres in the fall, TriBeCa does the same for award-winning films from Berlin, Sundance, Toronto and other festivals." Holden also wrote that the Tribeca Film Festival "has become an indispensable bulwark against the isolationist mentality of the moviegoing public. Without it, many worthy international films might never be seen in New York. For some of those films the TriBeCa festival will be their only chance to be seen outside of specialized series organized by museums and film societies."

In addition to the festival, Tribeca Enterprises currently runs Tribeca Cinemas, which has two theaters and a reception space, and the nonprofit Tribeca Institute, which fosters the growth of independent cinema. In 2010, through a new arm called Tribeca Film, Tribeca Enterprises began releasing independent and foreign movies digitally as well as in theaters. In February 2011 the company announced that it will increase from 11 to 26 the number of films available on electronic devices and through video-on-demand in homes and motels. "There are hundreds of wonderful films that never have the chance to reach a wider audience, and we want to seize any possible opportunity to change that," Rosenthal told Brooks Barnes for the *New York Times* (February 27, 2011, on-line). She also said, "With the rapidly evolving landscape, we all have to be extremely fast on our feet."

The first of the three children of Martin and Ina Rosenthal, Jane Rosenthal was born on September 21, 1956 in Providence, Rhode Island, where she grew up. (According to some sources, her birthplace was Denver, Colorado.) Her father ran an import-export business with her mother, who sometimes acted in local amateur productions. Her parents divorced in 1985. Since the late 1990s her mother has appeared in bit parts in several Hollywood movies. Rosenthal told Meryl Gordon for *New York* (April 29, 2002) that as a child she "never fit in. I was always tall for my age. When I would walk down the street with my girlfriends, they'd walk on the sidewalk and I'd walk in the gutter to try to be the same size. I am really shy by nature, painfully shy." Her mother, however, told Gordon that early on her daughter exuded confidence. "Jane was not a straight-A student, she never wanted to go to school," she said. "It was too confining for her. She wanted to get out in the world." Her mother also remarked, "She always had to be at the top of the heap." In 1969, at 12, Rosenthal volunteered with the successful gubernatorial campaign of a Rhode Island judge, Frank Licht. At 16 her application to serve in the state House of Representatives as a page was rejected because the position was reserved for male college students. Unwilling to accept the status quo, she persuaded House staffers to hire her and thus became "the youngest person and the first girl to be a page," she told Gordon.

After her sophomore year of high school, Rosenthal entered an experimental program at Brown University, in Providence. In 1975 she transferred to the Tisch School of the Arts at New York University (NYU), where she earned a B.A. degree in 1977. While at NYU she worked part-time as a researcher for the CBS series *The NFL Today* and as an assistant for the Actors Workshop production of the musical *The Best Little Whorehouse in Texas*. After that show moved to Broadway, in 1978, she served briefly as an assistant to the directors Tommy Tune and Peter Masterson. One of her tasks was to secure tickets to the supposedly sold-out performances for West Coast TV executives recently arrived in New York for "pilot week," when they shopped for new scripts for the fall TV lineup. Her efficiency impressed CBS executives, and she was hired to work for CBS in Los Angeles, California.

Rosenthal held various positions with CBS until 1984; her last title there was associate director of motion pictures for television. In 1984 and 1985 she worked at Universal Studios as vice president for feature production. She next joined the Walt Disney Co. (1985–87) as the vice president for production. There, she worked with Martin Scorsese, the director of the Disney Studios' *The Color of Money* (1986). She next moved to Warner Bros. TV (1987–88), serving as the vice president for movies and miniseries. According to Gordon, during her television-production years her 90-odd projects included everything from "disease-of-the-week weepies to adaptations of books," the latter including the harrowing memoir *Haywire* (1977), by Brooke Hayward.

By the late 1980s, Rosenthal told Charles Lyons and Jonathan Bing for *Variety* (September 28, 2001), she had become "unhappy as a studio exec. I was much more interested in the process, in a more detailed way than you can be at a studio. So much of studio life revolves around politics." Through Scorsese she learned that Robert De Niro was seeking a partner with whom to form a production company; fearing that De Niro might be difficult to work with, she hesitated for months before meeting with him. In 1989 Rosenthal, her husband,

Craig Hatkoff, a banker and real-estate developer, and De Niro set up Tribeca Productions. De Niro lived in Tribeca, an area that most commercial enterprises had abandoned by the 1960s; in the 1970s visual artists began living and working there, but even into the 1980s, it retained an air of dereliction. Rosenthal became president of Tribeca Productions, whose offices are in a 60,000-square-foot former coffee factory on Greenwich Avenue. Dubbed the Tribeca Film Center, the site soon attracted members of the city's independent-cinema community. Those who rented space included Miramax Films, the producer and director Ron Howard, and many agents.

The producers of a film oversee its creation from start to finish, including selecting the script, securing financing, approving hirings of the director, principal actors, and many of the scores of other people necessary to make the film, and ensuring that the work is completed on schedule and within its budget. As De Niro's co-producer, Rosenthal is reportedly one of the few people in the film industry who can sway the notoriously recalcitrant actor. The producer Harvey Weinstein told Gordon, "Jane can make Bob do things the right way, the polite way, and Bob will listen to her in a way he'll never listen to Marty Scorsese and me. He has the ultimate respect for her." Asked how she and De Niro interact, Rosenthal told Lyons and Bing, "The key has always been a certain trust. He's always said, 'Here's what I want to do, go do it.'" De Niro told Gordon, "She will tell me what she feels, and she'll disagree with me and stuff. Sometimes I'll want to do it this way, and she'll say, 'Let's stop and think for a minute.'"

Tribeca Productions' first offering was Scorsese's thriller *Cape Fear* (1991), starring De Niro as an insane but intellectually sharp rapist who, upon his release from prison, seeks revenge on the public defender (played by Nick Nolte) who intentionally failed to win an acquittal for him. Rosenthal did not work directly on that film, which was a remake of a 1961 movie starring Robert Mitchum as the rapist and Gregory Peck as the lawyer. The first feature that Rosenthal and De Niro co-produced (with others) was the drama *Thunderheart* (1992); that film starred Val Kilmer as Ray, an FBI agent who gains respect for his long-rejected Native American heritage in the course of investigating a murder on an economically depressed, socially troubled Indian reservation that one character calls "a third world right here in America." Michael Apted, who directed *Thunderheart* from a script by John Fusco, had earlier made the documentary *Incident at Oglala*, about the American Indian activist Leonard Peltier. Janet Maslin, in an admiring review for the *New York Times* (April 3, 1992), wrote that while *Thunderheart* "has the shape of a thriller, it also has a documentary's attentiveness to detail. . . . A film this intent on authenticity might easily grow dull, but this one doesn't."

The year 1992 also saw the release of Tribeca Productions' *Night and the City*, which the writer Richard Price based loosely on Jules Dassin's 1950 film noir starring Richard Widmark. Directed by Irwin Winkler, the later version earned mixed reviews when it debuted, at the New York Film Festival. Critics responded enthusiastically to Tribeca Productions' next effort, *A Bronx Tale* (1993), De Niro's directorial debut. Written by and co-starring Chazz Palminteri, the quasi-autobiographical film shows a boy named Calogero at age nine (depicted by Francis Capra), in the 1960s, in the Italian section of the New York City borough of the Bronx, when Sonny (Palminteri), a member of the local Mafia, takes him under his wing. Seen next at 17, Calogero (Lillo Brancato) is torn between adopting the principles of Sonny or those of his father, Lorenzo (De Niro), an upstanding, blue-collar family man. In a four-star review for the *Chicago Sun-Times* (October 1, 1993), Roger Ebert wrote that *A Bronx Tale* "is a very funny movie sometimes, and very touching at other times. . . . What's important about the film is that it's about values."

An all-star cast—Diane Keaton, Meryl Streep, Leonardo DiCaprio, De Niro, Hume Cronyn, and Gwen Verdon—appeared in Tribeca Productions' *Marvin's Room* (1996). That film was adapted by Scott McPherson from his award-winning, same-titled play, which grew out of his observations of his ill grandfather and caregiving aunt and his experiences as the lover of a man dying of AIDS. (McPherson himself died of AIDS in 1992.) The silver-screen debut of its director, Jerry Zaks (a successful theatrical director), *Marvin's Room* won a nomination for a Screen Actors Guild Award for the entire cast; it also won a Christopher Award for Rosenthal, De Niro, their co-producer, Scott Rudin, their two executive producers, Zaks, and McPherson. *Wag the Dog* (1997) earned a bevy of award nominations and several prizes—including one for its director, Barry Levinson, at the Berlin International Film Festival. Outrageously cynical but enormously entertaining, in the opinion of most reviewers, *Wag the Dog* starred De Niro as a self-effacing political fixer and Dustin Hoffman as a brazenly conceited Hollywood producer; the two come up with a fictitious war in Albania as a way to distract the American public from charges concerning the U.S. president's sexual misconduct with an underage female, accusations that have surfaced shortly before Election Day and threaten the chief executive's reelection.

Tribeca Productions scored a huge box-office success with *Analyze This* (1999), in which Billy Crystal portrayed a fast-talking psychotherapist recruited by a panic-stricken mobster (De Niro) desperate to regain his former toughness. Directed by Harold Ramis from a screenplay that he co-wrote, *Analyze This* is "a fleet, unself-conscious, eminently enjoyable picture, where one-liners carom merrily like stray bullets," but it does not "work overtime to hit all the funny buttons," Stephanie Zacharek wrote for *Salon.com* (March 5, 1999). *Analyze This* won an American Comedy Award as the year's funniest picture and a Golden Globe nomination in the category of best comedy or musical. A sequel, *Analyze That* (2002), disappointed most critics.

A low point for Rosenthal and De Niro came in 2000, with the release of their critically panned, commercially unsuccessful attempt to re-create for the big screen the 1960s TV cartoon *The Adventures of Rocky and Bullwinkle*. The *New York Times* (June 30, 2000) film critic A. O. Scott dismissed the film as a "noisy, bloated mess," while Barry Paris, the reviewer for the *Pittsburgh Post-Gazette* (June 30, 2000), wrote that he had never seen "a movie I disliked more than this one." Rosenthal, who had gained rights to the Rocky and Bullwinkle characters only after years of effort, told Gordon, "The failure felt so personal. I'm always worried about my career, but this wasn't 'I'll never work again.' It was 'I don't know if I *can* work again.'" By contrast, Tribeca's next film, *Meet the Parents* (2000), which arrived in theaters only four months later, proved to be a resounding box-office success. Directed by Jay Roach (whose credits include the *Austin Powers* comedies), it starred De Niro as Jack Byrnes, a retired CIA operative and overbearing father, and Ben Stiller as Greg Focker, a nurse who hopes to win the hand of Byrnes's daughter, Pam. Its sequel, *Meet the Fockers* (2004), in which Greg introduces the Byrneses to his mother (portrayed by Barbra Streisand) and father (Dustin Hoffman), earned mediocre reviews but fared extremely well at the box office. Since then Tribeca Productions has released *Rent* (2005), *The Good Shepherd* (2006), *What Just Happened* (2008), and *Little Fockers* (2010). Tribeca has also produced several movies or miniseries for TV, including *Witness to the Mob* (1998), *Holiday Heart* (2000), and *Chicken Club* (2002).

Earlier, in the face of the severe drop in business in Lower Manhattan following the 9/11 terrorist attacks, Rosenthal, De Niro and Hatkoff came up with the idea for the Tribeca Film Festival. "Our neighborhood was completely devastated," Rosenthal told Matthew Ross for indiewire.com (May 8, 2002). "This [festival] was really designed as a way to stimulate the economy and do what we could to help to boost the morale of our community." She also said, "I'd like our community to feel that there are things to look forward to, that the neighborhood is blocked off for a festival and not by fire trucks." Thanks to Rosenthal's and De Niro's film-industry connections and New York City government contacts, Hatkoff's success in attracting sponsors (notably, American Express), and the help of more than 1,000 volunteers, the festival was organized in only four months. Held the second week of May 2002, it attracted more than 150,000 attendees and some 600 journalists to events including a series of restored classics; another series, called "Best of New York," curated by Scorsese; panel discussions; and guests speakers such as former U.S. president Bill Clinton and former South

African president Nelson Mandela. Feature films, documentaries, shorts, and children's films from more than a dozen countries premiered at nine sites (among them a local high school). The motion pictures included Calli Khouri's *Divine Secrets of the Ya-Ya Sisterhood*, George Lucas's *Star Wars: Episode II—Attack of the Clones*, Nicole Holofcener's *Lovely and Amazing*, Zhang Yimou's *Happy Times*, Vojko Anzeljc's *The Last Supper*, Dylan Kidd's *Roger Dodger*, and Tribeca Productions' *About a Boy*, directed by Chris Weitz and Paul Weitz and starring Hugh Grant, Nicholas Hoult, and Toni Colette.

The next year, in an opinion piece called "Appreciations," Verlyn Klinkenborg wrote for the *New York Times* (May 3, 2003) that the Tribeca Film Festival "has earned its aesthetic credentials in a tough industry. More important, it has turned the very idea of a film festival into something more public and more family-oriented than we usually imagine. In part, this is a way of recognizing the kind of neighborhood TriBeCa has become. But it is also a way of recognizing what the city itself needs, a way of connecting families and culture." Since 2003 the festival has been run by the media company Tribeca Enterprises, founded that year by Rosenthal, De Niro, and Hatkoff. In response to those who have faulted the festival for becoming a profitable enterprise, Rosenthal told a reporter for the Associated Press (April 26, 2008, on-line), "The not-for-profit model is broken. The festival runs better and we're able to get media and marketing dollars that we wouldn't be able to get if we were strictly a not-for-profit only getting foundation money."

Rosenthal is a member of the board of directors of the foundation that is building the September 11 memorial and museum in Lower Manhattan. Her leisure interests include yoga and searching for collectible items on-line. She and her husband live on New York's Upper West Side with their daughters, Juliana and Isabella. With Juliana, Isabella, or both as co-writers, Hatkoff—the founder of Turtle Pond Publications—has published several best-selling children's books, among them *Owen & Mzee: The True Story of a Remarkable Friendship* and its sequels and *Knut: The Baby Polar Bear*.

—W.D.

Suggested Reading: cityfile.com; *Entertainment Weekly* p25 May 24, 2002; *New York* (on-line) Apr. 29, 2002; *New York Times* (on-line) May 1, 2005, Mar. 2, 2010; *Premiere* p78+ Nov. 1992; Tribeca Enterprises Web site; *Variety* A p13 Sep. 28, 2001, A p7 Oct. 21–27 2002; *Vogue* p156+ Aug. 1993; *Who's Who in America* (on-line)

Selected Films: *Thunderheart*, 1992; *Night and the City*, 1992; *A Bronx Tale*, 1993; *Faithful*, 1996; *Marvin's Room*, 1996; *Wag the Dog*, 1997; *Analyze This*, 1999; *The Adventures of Rocky and Bullwinkle*, 2000; *Meet the Parents*, 2000; *About a Boy*, 2002; *Analyze That*, 2002; *Meet the Fockers*, 2004; *The Good Shepherd*, 2006; *What Just Happened?*, 2008; *Little Fockers*, 2010

Selected Television Shows: *Tribeca*, 1993; *Witness to the Mob*, 1998; *Holiday Heart*, 2000; *Chicken Club*, 2002

Rosenwinkel, Kurt

Oct. 28, 1970– Jazz guitarist; composer

Address: c/o Word of Mouth Music Inc., 235 E. 22d St., 9F, New York, NY 10010

Since the mid-1990s Kurt Rosenwinkel has been hailed as one of the world's top jazz guitarists, acclaimed for the complexity and melodicism of his playing as well as his fondness for experimentation. His unique sound—which he augments with effects-laden vocals that follow his guitar lines—has set him apart from others, and he has pushed the boundaries of contemporary jazz by incorporating elements of electronica into his material. A writer for allaboutjazz.com described Rosenwinkel as an "adventurous, searching artist whose playing is marked by a kind of kinetic melodicism, darkly delicate lyricism and cascading, horn-like lines" and one who has "established an instantly recognizable voice on the guitar—warm and fluid with a tinge of overdrive, a touch of sustain and echo with a penchant for dissonance. His singing quali-

ty on the instrument is all the more enhanced by the fact that he is often literally singing in unison." Commenting on Rosenwinkel's idiosyncratic guitar sound, the celebrated jazz tenor-sax player Joshua Redman told Andrew Gilbert for the *Boston Globe* (March 20, 2005), "He somehow manages to write music that is incredibly sophisticated and complex, but so excruciatingly beautiful. He's created his own harmonic world, which in and of itself is a huge accomplishment in jazz. He has this incredible sense of melodic clarity and lyricism. His sound is so personal."

Initially a sideman in the bands of the vibraphonist Gary Burton and the drummer Paul Motian, among others, Rosenwinkel first caught the attention of jazz critics with albums of standards. He then met with praise for his recordings of original music, including *The Enemies of Energy* (2000), *The Next Step* (2001), and *Heartcore* (2003), the last of which incorporated elements of hip-hop and electronica. Although not as progressive as his previous albums, Rosenwinkel's more recent releases—*Deep Song* (2005) and *Reflections* (2009), among others—have won the guitarist

Lourdes Delgado, courtesy of Word of Mouth Music
Kurt Rosenwinkel

praise and expanded his audience. In a review of *Deep Song* for the *New York Times* (March 7, 2005), Ben Ratliff observed, "Kurt Rosenwinkel has become one of the better guitarists in jazz, patient and serious, with a misty tone and a desire to pilot his lyricism through greater areas of harmony."

Kurt Rosenwinkel was born on October 28, 1970 in Philadelphia, Pennsylvania. He was raised in a musical family; his mother, who had trained as a concert pianist, and his father, an architect who enjoyed musical improvisation, played twin grand pianos. "Since I was a young kid, I felt like I had an internal impulse to make music," he recalled to Ted Panken for jazz.com (October 17, 2008). At nine Rosenwinkel began playing piano; at 12 he picked up the guitar, after hearing the Beatles' album *Sgt. Pepper's Lonely Hearts Club Band.*

Rosenwinkel was not exposed to jazz until he began to listen to it on the radio, during high school. From there, "I started getting into more advanced forms and more mature and deeper musics," he told Panken. "I developed a thirst for the more complicated music. I liked [the Canadian pop/rock group] Rush. I went from listening to hard rock, to progressive rock, to electric jazz and fusion, and then into acoustic jazz." As a sophomore he started playing with the regular jazz performers at the Blue Note club in Philadelphia; meanwhile, he studied the jazz standards in a volume of sheet music called *The Real Book*. At the club, he told Panken, "they'd welcome me up on the stage, and I'd call [the Victor Young jazz standard] 'Stella By Starlight' and they would launch into some intro that was all so new to me. I had no idea how they knew it. It wasn't in *The Real Book*.

It was a great education for me about what jazz really is. It's not what you learn on the page; it's this whole tradition. So I really got a good dose of that—the spirit, improvisation, connecting with people, lifting things off the ground. That's how I fell in love with jazz." In an interview with Franz A. Matzner for allaboutjazz.com (December 9, 2009), Rosenwinkel said, "I committed to playing music for my life when I was nine! Since then, it's never been a question. So, I never committed to a career in jazz. It's all just music to me. Whether it's this or that, I like it all—mostly. I became a jazz musician because so much of the music I love is called that, and it inspired me to learn and grow in that direction."

During his high-school years, Rosenwinkel took jazz-piano lessons with Jimmy Amadie; his aim, at least in part, was to decide which instrument he wanted to focus on. After graduating, and settling on guitar, he enrolled at the Berklee College of Music, in Boston, Massachusetts. There, he met the faculty member and jazz vibraphonist Gary Burton, who in the 1960s had pioneered a four-mallet playing style (vibraphones are traditionally played with two mallets). After three years Rosenwinkel dropped out of Berklee to tour with Burton's band as a sideman, from 1991 to 1992. He told John Kelman for allaboutjazz.com (June 20, 2005), "Gary's band was the first really professional sideman gig that I had—it was the first international touring experience, it was the first kind of high profile scenario, so I really felt that it was a big break. It was a great experience from a professional point of view in terms of gaining experience and an entry into the world of what it means to be a jazz musician, what life is like as a jazz musician. Gary's a master musician, so listening to him play his solo pieces every night was the most musically inspiring experience for me in that band. He's a true master of the vibraphone."

Rosenwinkel next moved to New York City and joined Paul Motian's Electric Bebop Band, in which he was able to hone his improvisational skills. "In Gary's band the parameters of the music were very specific, very specified, very controlled," he told Kelman. "In Paul's band *some* of them were set; there were some basic premises, like we're going to play bebop tunes, and this is going to be the arrangement. . . . But beyond that there wasn't any musical guidance. . . . The entire experience for me was about absorbing [Motian's] time feel and his feel for music." Around that time Rosenwinkel also performed with the saxophonist Joe Henderson's group and had regular gigs at Smalls Jazz Club, in the Greenwich Village section of Manhattan, in New York City.

In 1995 Rosenwinkel won a Composers Fellowship from the National Endowment for the Arts. He used the money to record his first solo album, *East Coast Love Affair* (1996), released on the Fresh Sound New Talent label. Recorded live at Smalls, the album featured the trio he had formed with the drummer Jorge Rossy and the bassist Avishai Cohen. "I wasn't even thinking about any kind of long term strategy, in terms of kinds of albums I wanted to make," Rosenwinkel recalled to Kelman. "At the time I was in New York, living hand to mouth and developing music with my friends. I happened to be doing a lot of sessions with Jorge Rossy—I've known him for years. We were doing a lot of jam sessions at each others' houses and in the New York scene." The record consists of jazz standards along with two original tunes—the title track and "B Blues." Rosenwinkel's next album, *Intuit* (1998), released on the Criss Cross label, also comprised standards, composed by Irving Berlin, Charlie Parker, and George Gershwin, among others. For that album Rosenwinkel played alongside Michael Kanan on piano, Joe Martin on bass, and Tim Pleasant on drums. In a review for allaboutjazz.com, C. Andrew Hovan wrote, "The tunes are familiar, but how they're transformed is something else all together! Rosenwinkel gets a clean, yet warm sound from his guitar and his improvisations are imbued with the kind of advanced melodic development that marks his writing. . . . One gets the sense that Rosenwinkel is at one with the music at hand and even his shorter statements speak volumes to anyone with an ear for standards or jazz guitar. His sidemen certainly do justice to the material and provide great support, but it's really Rosenwinkel who steals the show here. Taken on its own terms, this one comes highly endorsed. It's even further proof, as well, that Rosenwinkel knows his history and is likely to become a force to be reckoned with over the next several years." David R. Adler wrote for the All Music Guide Web site, "Rosenwinkel's sound throughout this straight-ahead excursion is fairly dry—a touch of reverb, no shimmering delay, no ethereal vocalizing, a bit less distinctive than usual. His highly modern approach to harmony often comes through, however, even on vehicles as traditional as 'Darn That Dream.' And, as always, he uses the physical properties of the guitar to alter the sonic dimensions of his lines, as when he plays a long string of 16th notes near the bridge during his solo on 'When Sunny Gets Blue.'" Adler also noted that the "way he interacts with these [other] straight-ahead players says a great deal about his breadth as a jazz musician. It also foreshadows his later attempts to blur the boundary between standard and original repertoire."

Of his penchant for playing standards, Rosenwinkel explained to Kelman, "I think, in terms of the feeling I want to get to, it's the same thing [as playing original material], but in terms of the actual music it's very different. I have an awareness of my own relationship to standards that has evolved over the years, and it's an important part of being a jazz musician. It's a good backdrop to really see how your playing is, it's almost this sort of neutral stylistic context where you can discover what kind of player you are, what the qualities of your playing are."

Rosenwinkel's first album of original material, *The Enemies of Energy*, released on the Verve label in 2000, included the work of the tenor saxophonist Mark Turner (a Berklee classmate of Rosenwinkel's and one of his frequent collaborators, both on recordings and in live performance), the keyboardist Scott Kinsey, the bassist Ben Street, and the drummer Jeff Ballard. In a review for the *Toronto Star* (January 15, 2000), Geoff Chapman wrote, "Achieving a singular sound on guitar these days is tough but Kurt Rosenwinkel, though a newcomer to band leadership, may have done it. His mix of jazz and its musical cousins produces tightly-woven fusion for thinking people that goes far beyond tinkling and tinkering with technique. With four sympathetic colleagues, notably tenor Mark Turner, Rosenwinkel colours a 10-tune session with clever writing, interesting execution and the ability to vary instrumental sonics. 'Grant' is just one excellent example of bringing disparate effects together in dense, sophisticated textures. Up-tempo tunes like 'Point Of View,' 'Number Ten,' and 'Synthetics' feature fascinating interplay." Other critics, too, were pleased with the record—though not all. Jules Epstein wrote for the *Philadelphia Tribune* (February 11, 2000) that *The Enemies of Energy* "confines itself to stereotypic settings, atop which the few interesting saxophone lines are inadequate to generate real interest. It is appropriate to note that one song is titled 'synthetics,' an apt description of this approach to jazz."

Rosenwinkel next signed with the Impulse! label, for which he recorded an album entitled "Under It All"; when Universal later took over Impulse!, the record was shelved, and it has yet to be released. Rosenwinkel followed the release of *The Enemies of Energy* with that of *The Next Step* (2001), a live album recorded with Ballard, Street, and Turner for the Verve label. The guitarist told Kelman that he had had to fight Verve for full creative control over the album: "While with *Enemies* and *Under It All*, the core of those records was my quartet, which was a working band, they were very compositionally-motivated records. *The Next Step* was a record where I really wanted to capture the sound of the band live, and so we're playing original tunes, and that's an important part of it; but the real thing of it is the live interaction of the band. In the beginning I had to fight a little bit more to get the go-ahead from Verve for *The Next Step*; they wanted me to do a different record. But . . . after the record came out and it got a lot of critical acclaim, I think that from that point on they kind of trusted my instincts." A review by Mike Zwerin for the *New York Times* (September 26, 2001, online) read, "Rosenwinkel teams up here with . . . Mark Turner; they are flavors of the day in New York. They are also fine, introspective players. They do represent a—if not the—next step. . . . Young and talented, they will certainly grow; they already deserve more than one good listen."

Lourdes Delgado, courtesy of Word of Mouth Music

Kurt Rosenwinkel

Rosenwinkel's next effort was *Heartcore* (2003), for which the guitarist composed all of the songs and recorded on studio equipment at his home in Brooklyn, New York. The record was a departure from Rosenwinkel's previous material; while it showcased more playing by Turner, Street, and Ballard, it also made use of electronic drums and synthesizers as well as digital sampling, and it included production work by the hip-hop artist Q-Tip of the group A Tribe Called Quest. Indeed, Rosenwinkel's inspiration for the album came from hip-hop; he explained for his Web site, "From record to record, I've always tried to make things more simple, more direct. . . . I wanted to have the same kind of immediacy that Q-Tip's music has. He was always the voice over my shoulder: 'Keep it simple. Keep it direct.'" Rosenwinkel also noted, "A lot of the harmonic moments in hip-hop remind me of what I hear in, say, [the Austrian-born composer Arnold] Schoenberg's music. He'll create a chord that is very much dependent on the dynamics of the performance—the strings are mezzo piano, the oboe is mezzo forte, and the piccolos are piano piano. Together they produce a harmony that might not work in jazz theory, but works perfectly in reality. You hear the same things in a hip-hop mix. It's all in the ear—something works because it sounds like it works." He added, "Those kind[s] of lessons are very important for the jazz musician. It's a great antidote for the pedagogical, theoretical school of jazz."

In a review of *Heartcore*, Richard S. Ginell wrote for the All Music Guide Web site, "With this recording, guitarist Kurt Rosenwinkel creates a unique sound world, blending elements of jazz and rock with electronica, occasional Third World strains, and other grooves in an absorbing, inward journey that defies classification. . . . In a way, this is 21st century expressionism of a sort, creating levels of ambiguity and uncertainty, leaving the listener out on a limb yet always intrigued. Give it a shot; you may not want to leave this twilight zone." Matt Merewitz opined for allaboutjazz.com (October 28, 2003), "If this isn't the future sound of jazz, then I can't imagine what is."

Rosenwinkel's next release was *Deep Song* (2005), a return to form for the guitarist. Lloyd Sachs wrote in a review of the album for Amazon.com, "Having made a compelling departure into trippy fusion on his last CD, *Heartcore*, . . . Rosenwinkel returns here to a more familiar postbop sound, but with no loss of nerve or verve. Joined by a pair of frequent cohorts . . . he effortlessly moves in and out of the mainstream pocket, thriving on bright unison lines and sighing lyrical constructions. Rosenwinkel is a cerebral player, but with his naturally warm, tangy tone, he readily converts ideas to emotion, adding celestial seasoning to songs including the standard, 'If I Should Lose You,' with his subtle wordless vocals." Kelman observed, "Following the more mainstream *The Next Step* and an '03 take on electronica, *Heartcore*, *Deep Song* feels like a consolidation and acknowledgement of everything Rosenwinkel has done to date. While the instrumentation is more straightforward . . . this is far from a mainstream record, with an energy and modernity that is equally strong testament to Rosenwinkel the writer as it is Rosenwinkel the guitarist." The record revisited some songs Rosenwinkel had recorded earlier; Kelman wrote for allaboutjazz.com (February 28, 2005), "What is immediately striking is a sense of *authority* and even stronger sense of adventure in Rosenwinkel's playing." In 2008 Rosenwinkel released the double album *The Remedy* on the ArtistShare label. He recorded the work live at the Village Vanguard, in Manhattan, with the Kurt Rosenwinkel Group, consisting of Turner, the pianist Aaron Goldberg, the bassist Joe Martin, and the drummer Eric Harland. The album comprises more than 120 minutes of material, with some tunes upwards of 20 minutes long. *The Remedy* was well-received, landing at number 38 on the *Village Voice* 2008 *Voice* Jazz Poll Winners list.

Rosenwinkel's most recent disk, *Reflections* (2009), recorded under the name Kurt Rosenwinkel Standard Trio, marks the guitarist's eighth album as a bandleader and features Harland and the bassist Eric Revis. The album represented a return to standards, with songs by Thelonious Monk and Wayne Shorter. Tom Moon, in a review posted on the National Public Radio Web site (December 15, 2009), observed, "Rosenwinkel has cultivated his following by bucking tradition, so I was a bit dismayed to learn about his latest project. It's a set of mostly familiar ballads and jazz standards—the kind of program expected of a tradition-minded jazz musician. It seemed Rosenwinkel was following the conventional path. Then I heard his version of 'Reflections.' Thelonious Monk's piece is usually treated as a kind of sacred text, but Rosenwinkel doesn't play it that way. There's a hint of restlessness in his approach, as if he's determined to find an entirely new language for it. . . . What I hear in this is someone thinking like a composer, shaping a musical narrative one carefully considered phrase at a time. It's a fundamentally different enterprise from the daredevil high-speed babble that usually happens when jazz musicians play standards. They're out to stun with genius technique. Rosenwinkel, a composer first and foremost, wants to illuminate the architectural 'soul' of the tunes instead."

Rosenwinkel's distinctive practice of singing wordlessly to accompany his guitar melodies has often been praised by jazz critics. Kelman noted, "Singing what he plays is, in fact, another key aspect of Rosenwinkel's sound. While other guitarists have used this as more of [a] novel effect, with Rosenwinkel it's a natural and integrated concept." "It's something that's always come naturally to me," Rosenwinkel explained to Kelman. "I've never worked on it . . . it just always came naturally to me; I was always able to sing anything I played. It's like I'll have an impulse to sing something, and then my fingers will just be coordinated with that impulse. And then sometimes, vice versa; if I have a visual idea, I'll know how that will feel to sing it as well, so whether the melody comes from the voice or whether the melody comes from some visual idea, I can always play what I want to sing, and sing what I want to play." To amplify his singing, Rosenwinkel performs with a Levalier microphone clipped to his shirt and plugged into an amp and effects-loop pedal. He began to recognize the importance of his singing when he started gigging at Smalls. "I sing quite loudly, so even before I discovered that microphone [the Levalier] it had become part of my sound," he told Kelman. "That's the way I discovered that the voice was part of my guitar sound, in fact. People would come up after shows and say, 'What kind of effect are you using?' I'd say I was using a delay and a reverb, and they'd say, 'No, there's some kind of chorus effect or harmonizer,' and I didn't realize what they were talking about. Then I realized that what they were talking about was the voice and that's how I discovered that it was a part of my sound." From January 4 to January 9, 2011, Rosenwinkel held a residency at the Village Vanguard in New York City, performing standards and original compositions with the pianist Aaron Parks, the bassist Ben Street, and the drummer Ted Poor.

Rosenwinkel has contributed guitar to the Q-Tip albums *The Renaissance* (2008) and *Kamaal/The Abstract* (2009). In 2003 he moved to Zurich, Switzerland, for a teaching job. He now lives in Berlin, Germany, where he is a professor of jazz guitar at the Jazz Institute of Berlin. He and his wife, Rebecca, a native of Switzerland, have two sons, Silas and Ezra. Despite the complexity of his playing style and his innovative compositions, Rosenwin-

kel believes his music is generally accessible. He told Kelman, "I've never been trying to write something that's complicated, that's not my purpose at all in discovering sounds and organizing them into compositions. For me what that's all about is containing some kind of fascination, or mood, or some kind of aesthetic quality that's pleasing to the ear. I'm only a conceptualist insofar as it translates to actual sound. So for me, the stuff under the hood is really meant to be under the hood; it has to be there in order for the melodies to come out, for the mood to be accessible. But at the end of the day I *want* my music to be accessible because I want to communicate."

—W.D.

Suggested Reading: allaboutjazz.com June 20, 2005, Dec. 9, 2009; *Boston Globe* Arts/Entertainment p9 Mar. 20, 2005; jazz.com Oct. 17, 2008; *Ottawa Citizen* Arts E p5 June 30, 2004

Selected Recordings: *East Coast Love Affair*, 1996; *Intuit*, 1998; *The Enemies of Energy*, 2000; *The Next Step*, 2001; *Heartcore*, 2003; *Deep Song*, 2005; *The Remedy*, 2008; *Reflections*, 2009

Rubio, Marco

May 28, 1971– U.S. senator from Florida (Republican)

Address: 402 S. Monroe St., 317 The Capitol, Tallahassee, FL 32399

In November 2010 the conservative Republican Marco Rubio, the son of Cuban exiles, was elected to the United States Senate from Florida, defeating the Democrat Kendrick Meek and Florida's Republican-turned-Independent governor Charles Crist, once the heavy favorite in the race. Prior to his campaign for the Senate seat, Rubio represented the 111th District in the Florida House of Representatives from 2000 to 2008, during which he held the positions of majority whip, majority leader, and, finally, speaker. Rubio's name has often been connected with the Tea Party, a political movement that emerged in the late 2000s with fiscal conservatism as its rallying cry. "I'm very proud of my association with the Tea Party, but I think people misunderstand what the Tea Party movement is in America," he said to Jim Acosta for the CNN television program *American Morning* (August 25, 2010). "It's not a centralized organization or a political party. It's the sentiment of everyday Americans who think that Washington has it wrong, [that] they're taking our country in the wrong direction. And they're looking for voices in American politics that will stand up to that and offer a clear alternative. And that's what we're doing."

Chip Somodevilla/Getty Images

Marco Rubio

Marco Rubio was born on May 28, 1971 in Miami, Florida. His parents were immigrants who had fled Cuba in 1959, after Fidel Castro's ascension to power there. Both of his parents were employed in the service industry; his father, Mario, who died in September 2010, spent most of his life working as a bartender, and his mother, Oria, held jobs as a hotel housekeeper and stock clerk at Kmart. Rubio has a brother, Mario, and two sisters, Barbara and Veronica. As a child he developed an interest in public service in part because his maternal grandfather, Pedro Victor Garcia, used to discuss politics and history—particularly the Cuban war for independence from Spain—with the young boy. "Most kids weren't interested in that stuff. They wanted to play," Rubio's sister Veronica told Alex Leary for the *St. Petersburg (Florida) Times* (March 4, 2007). "But my brother was fascinated with history." She also recalled that Rubio "liked to talk a lot" and that his third-grade teacher sent home a note suggesting that Rubio become a lawyer. Rubio said to Lesley Clark for the *Miami Herald* (March 9, 2003) that he was a Democrat "for two weeks" when he was nine years old; at that time the Democratic U.S. senator Edward "Ted" Kennedy of Massachusetts was challenging the incumbent Democratic president, Jimmy Carter, for the 1980 presidential nomination. Rubio was soon enchanted, however, by the Republican Ronald Reagan, who went on to defeat Carter in that year's general election. "Here was this cowboy," Rubio said to Clark. When he was eight years old, Rubio and his family left Miami for Las Vegas, Nevada. They returned to Miami in 1985, the year that Rubio's grandfather died.

Rubio attended South Miami High School, where, despite his comparatively small size, he played cornerback on the school's football team. "Marco Rubio was like [the New England Patriots quarterback] Tom Brady, characterwise," Rubio's former teammate Octavio Matamoros told Tim Elfrink for the *Miami New Times* (July 22, 2010). "You could always tell he understood the game from an intellectual standpoint even if he wasn't the fastest guy or the biggest guy out there." Rubio graduated from high school in 1989 and accepted a football scholarship to attend Tarkio College, in northwest Missouri. He attended that small school for one year before transferring to Santa Fe Community College, in Gainesville, Florida. He transferred once more, to the University of Florida, and in 1993 he received a B.S. degree in political science. He then enrolled at the University of Miami in pursuit of a law degree, which he earned in 1996.

During law school Rubio became politically active. He served as an intern for the Republican congresswoman Ileana Ros-Lehtinen and was a political coordinator for the Republican nominee Bob Dole's 1996 presidential campaign. (Dole lost in the general election to the Democratic incumbent, Bill Clinton.) During a meeting at Dole's headquarters, Rubio gave an impressive motivational speech. "It kind of took the thunder away from the elected officials," the Florida congressman David Rivera said to Alex Leary. "It was an indication of his potential charisma in public life." Rubio soon attracted the attention of Al Cardenas, who was co-chairman of the Dole campaign in Florida at the time. "He had good people skills and helped the volunteers keep their spirits up," Cardenas told Lesley Clark for *Naked Politics* (August 20, 2009). "That's when I first thought he might be going places." Cardenas gave Rubio a job as a clerk in his law firm and hired him full-time after he passed the state bar exam.

In 1998 Rubio won a seat on the West Miami City Commission, where he served for the next two years. At the turn of the century he made a bid for a seat in the Florida House of Representatives during a special election. With the help of family members, he generated support by walking around neighborhoods and knocking on doors. He also raised enough money for a few radio advertisements. "My lasting memory of that race," Rubio told Leslie Clark for the *Miami Herald* (March 9, 2003), "is my seven-months pregnant wife, Jeanette, who hates politicking, standing at a precinct in Hialeah, handing out pledge cards." Although he initially finished second in the Republican primary election, he won it by 64 votes following a runoff election and—in a district where the Republican nomination practically guaranteed victory in the general election—was soon serving in the state legislature.

Reelected to the post in 2002, 2004, and 2006—without opposition except in 2004—Rubio worked his way up to become the majority whip and then the majority leader. Occasionally his youthful appearance led to his being mistaken for an aide; once, while Rubio was serving as majority leader, the lieutenant governor told him to photocopy some documents. During his time in the House, Rubio began touring the Sunshine State and hosting meetings called "Idearaisers," at which he and other Floridians would discuss ways to improve life in the state. He later turned some of those ideas into a 224-page book, *100 Innovative Ideas for Florida's Future* (2006). He used those ideas as his political platform when he became the youngest-ever and first Hispanic Florida House speaker, in 2006. "Marco's genius was in actually listening to people around the state and compiling the list of ideas," Don Gaetz, a member of the Florida Senate, said to Aaron Sharockman for the *St. Petersburg Times* (February 28, 2010). "He branded those ideas and that's the sign of a smart politician." As mentioned on MarcoRubio.com, those ideas included "measures to crack down on gangs and sexual predators, promote energy efficient buildings, appliances and vehicles, and help small businesses obtain affordable health coverage." According to that site, 57 of the proposals were ultimately passed into law. (Sharockman's *St. Petersburg Times* article, however, suggests otherwise. "Based on our analysis, he has fallen short . . . ," Sharockman wrote. "Based on our findings, 24 of Rubio's 100 ideas became law. Ten others were partially enacted. . . . But 23 of the 57 ideas he claims were enacted either aren't law or could not be law.")

Term limits prevented Rubio from running in the 2008 election for a seat in the Florida House of Representatives. In 2009 Rubio announced his candidacy for the U.S. Senate from Florida. The post was being vacated by Mel Martinez, who had stepped down with a year and a half remaining in his first term; Martinez's interim replacement was George LeMieux. Rubio's chief opponent in the primary was Charles Crist, the governor of Florida, who was initially seen as a shoo-in for Senate seat. The beginning of Rubio's campaign found him far behind in the polls and struggling to compete at fund-raising with Crist, who at one point commanded more than 12 times as much money as his opponent. Several of Rubio's strategists and fund-raisers advised him to abandon his campaign for Senate and enter the race for attorney general. Staying in the race, he eventually received endorsements from former Arkansas governor and 2008 presidential candidate Mike Huckabee; U.S. senator Jim DeMint of South Carolina; Mike Pence of Indiana, the chairman of the House Republican Conference; and former Florida governor Jeb Bush. In addition, he received support from the former Alaska governor and 2008 vice-presidential nominee, Sarah Palin, a heavily influential favorite of the Tea Party, although the two had never met. (Crist's support of Democratic president Barack Obama's 2009 economic-stimulus package cost the governor crucial Republican support.)

As the campaign progressed, Rubio, who spoke frequently about tax reform, had greater success at fund-raising and surpassed Crist in the polls by a significant margin, leading Crist to drop out of the primary race and abandon the Republican Party so he could run as an Independent candidate against Rubio and Democratic congressman Kendrick Meek in the general election. "I always knew that I'd have to run against two people who support the Barack Obama agenda," Rubio said to Jeff Celeny for the *New York Times* (August 22, 2010). "I just didn't know I'd have to run against them at the same time." According to that article, while campaigning Rubio explained to a voter that he did not plan to be the "opposition to Barack Obama," but to instead "create an alternative." In the interview with Jim Acosta, Rubio said, "The reason why I got in this race . . . when nobody had thought we had the chance to win, was because I looked at the other people running and I realized none of them are going to stand up to the direction Washington is taking us and offer a clear alternative."

By October 2010 Rubio had accumulated $18.25 million, while Crist and Meek had raised only $13.38 million and $8.26 million, respectively. Rubio's largest contributions came from Club for Growth, a conservative political group; Elliott Management, a hedge fund run by Paul Singer; Senate Conservatives Fund, a political action committee; Flo Sun Inc., a sugar manufacturer; and Crow Holdings, an investment firm. He was also backed by members of the oil and gas, health-care, and real-estate industries. In addition, Rubio received $7 million in small donations from ordinary citizens. "I've always told people they buy into our agenda, we don't buy into theirs," he said to Alex Leary and Lesley Clark for the *St. Petersburg Times* (November 20, 2010). "We tell people where we stand on the issues, and if people want to help us get elected, with some exceptions, we're willing to accept their help." In the November 2010 general election, Rubio won with 86 percent of the Republican vote and 51 percent of the Independent vote.

As senator Rubio has promised to promote fiscal responsibility. Some have doubted his abilities in that area, however, due to his personal debt and the various accusations that he used Republican Party credit cards for personal spending—charges he has dismissed as inaccurate. Rubio also expressed hopes to revise the U.S. tax code, reducing taxes on businesses and wealthy individuals. In terms of education, he said he will strive to create additional scholarships for private schools, foreign-language curricula in elementary schools, more educational options for students and parents, and less federal control of education. Among other stances, Rubio opposes funding for stem-cell research and abortion, same-sex marriages, the open presence of homosexuals in the military, the replacement of coal and oil with alternative fuel, and restrictions on the right to bear arms. He is against Obama's stimulus package, supports a balanced-budget amendment to the Constitution, and voted to repeal the Obama administration's health-care legislation. He does not advocate a timetable for troop withdrawal from Afghanistan. He has criticized the controversial immigration legislation recently passed in Arizona, which calls for police officers to stop anyone they have reason to believe is an illegal alien and detain those who do not provide documentation of legal status. Rubio is a member of the Senate Commerce, Small Business, Foreign Relations, and Intelligence Committees. Currently, according to Carl Hulse, writing for the *New York Times* (February 26, 2011, on-line), "he eschews national political coverage and talks primarily to the state news media. He has passed up high-profile gatherings like a recent conservative conference in favor of events back home. . . . He did not join the Senate's new Tea Party Caucus." Hulse noted, "The thinking is that Mr. Rubio . . . needs to build credibility and establish himself as a serious senator if he is to take advantage of a promising future."

Rubio was named freshman legislator of the year by the Florida Petroleum Marketers Association. He has served on the board of the Miami Performing Arts Center, the Latin Builders Association, and Alafit International, a nonprofit organization that promotes global literacy. For four years beginning in 2005, he practiced with the law firm Broad and Cassel, and he served as a consultant for Jackson Memorial Hospital. He has worked as a political analyst for Univision, a Spanish-language television network, and he taught a course in state politics as a visiting professor at Florida International University. He has been the Florida chair of the Grand Old Party Action Committee (GOPAC). In 2003 he formed two political committees: Floridians for Conservative Leadership and Floridians for Conservative Leadership in Government.

When he took office, in January 2011, Rubio became Florida's second-ever Cuban-American senator; Mel Martinez was the first. There has been speculation that he may eventually run for president. "As a Hispanic representing the nation's largest battleground state," Beth Reinhard wrote for the *Miami Herald* (November 3, 2010), "Rubio immediately becomes a kingmaker in the 2012 presidential race, if not a potential contender." When asked if he has the desire to be on a Republican presidential ticket, Rubio told the host of the Fox program *Your World with Neil Cavuto* (November 2, 2010), "That is not in our future, I don't think. . . . I am just looking forward to serving in the Senate."

Since 1998 Rubio, a Roman Catholic, has been married to Jeanette Dousdebes, a Colombian-American and former Miami Dolphins cheerleader. The couple live in West Miami, Florida, with their four children: Amanda, Daniella, Anthony, and Dominic.

—J.P.

Suggested Reading: (Fort Lauderdale, Florida) *Sun-Sentinel* B p1 Sep. 11, 2005; *Miami (Florida) Herald* B p1 Mar. 9, 2003; *Miami (Florida) New Times* (on-line) July 22, 2010; *New York Times* (on-line) Aug. 22, 2010; *St. Petersburg (Florida) Times* A p1 Mar. 4, 2007

Selected Books: *100 Innovative Ideas for Florida's Future*, 2006

Michael Lionstar, courtesy of Knopf

Russell, Karen

July 10, 1981– Writer

Address: c/o Denise Shannon Literary Agency, 20 W. 22d St., Suite 1603, New York, NY 10010

"With her first novel, *Swamplandia!*," Karen Russell "has established herself as much more than a literary upstart with a quirky style," Scott Ditzler wrote for the *Kansas City Star* (February 6, 2011). "She is a talent deserving of her many accolades, a writer of strong wit and silencing pathos, and quite simply, a lot of fun to read." Russell's first book was the widely praised, award-winning short-story collection *St. Lucy's Home for Girls Raised by Wolves* (2006)—a "darkly witty book of fairy tale-ish stories," David Colman wrote for the *New York Times* (April 1, 2007). One of the stories in that volume, called "Ava Wrestles the Alligator," had been far longer in Russell's original version. "I was disturbed by the way the story had ended" when it was cut for inclusion in the book, Russell told Elizabeth Floyd Mair for the Albany, New York, *Times-Union* (February 6, 2011), "and

I really wanted to return to those two sisters. I had really enjoyed embroidering that world." "That world" comes alive in *Swamplandia!*, about Ava Bigtree and her family, who operate a theme park in the Florida Everglades that includes humans performing with alligators. "Russell's first novel is a wild ride of a performance," Brett Josef Grubisic wrote in a review for the *National Post* (February 4, 2011). "With explicit nods to *The Inferno* and *Through the Looking-Glass, Swamplandia!* tells of the meteoric descent of a larger-than-life family residing in a rickety self-made wonderland." "Vividly worded, exuberant in characterization," *Swamplandia!* "is a wild ride," Emma Donoghue wrote in a front-page assessment of *Swamplandia!* for the *New York Times Book Review* (February 3, 2011). "The plot . . . is nothing special—dysfunctional family pull apart, then pull together—but the execution is. This family, wrestling with their desires and demons, will neither succumb nor triumph, but survive in their scarred way, and will lodge in the memories of anyone lucky enough to read *Swamplandia!*"

Russell was 23 years old when one of her tales, "Haunting Olivia," was published in the *New Yorker*—a noteworthy achievement in the literary world and one that she shared with John O'Hara, J. D. Salinger, John Cheever, John Updike, Peter Taylor, Raymond Carver, and Ann Beattie, among other masters of the short story. In 2005 Russell was named to *New York* magazine's list of 27 impressive New Yorkers under the age of 26. In 2009 she received a 5 Under 35 Award from the National Book Foundation; the next year her story "The Dredgeman's Revelation" was published in the July 26, 2010 issue of the *New Yorker*, the whole of which was devoted to the magazine's "20 Under 40" up-and-coming writers. Her stories have also appeared in such publications as *Granta, Oxford American: The Southern Magazine of Good Writing*, and the annual anthology *The Best American Short Stories*. In 2011 she won the annual Fiction Prize from Bard College, in Annandale-on-Hudson, New York, an honor that included a $30,000 prize and a writer-in-residence position at the school.

Karen Russell was born on July 10, 1981 in Miami, Florida, where she grew up with her sister and brother. One of her grandfathers lived with her family or close by. Her parents are both native Floridians who felt strongly nostalgic for the Florida of the past and often reminisced about it at home. The Russells frequently took family trips to parts of the Everglades; they visited other areas of natural interest, too, as well as Indian reservations. One year Russell's class visited the Miccosukee Indian Village, in the Everglades near Miami, and watched a man wrestling an alligator. Her recollection of that event strengthened rather than faded as she grew older, she told an interviewer for Reading Group Guides (February 23, 2011, on-line), adding, "For reasons I can't perfectly explain, this day has become one of my favorite memories." Although

Russell was never a tomboy, she and her best friend enjoyed playing in the "swampy mangrove patch" in her family's backyard, she recalled to Alden Mudge for BookPage.com (February 2011). She said to Liane Hansen for National Public Radio (September 3, 2006), "I think if I had even an ounce of skill at like kickball or something, I would have been on the field with other kids, you know, getting picked first for teams and stuff. But because I'm sort of short and graceless, I just always felt more comfortable reading . . . it seemed safer." Russell loved to read fantasies; she has cited as especially powerful influences the science-fiction novel *The Day of the Triffids*, by the British writer John Wyndham; stories by Lewis Carroll and Madeleine L'Engle; L. Frank Baum's Oz books; and, as she told a Random House interviewer (July 20, 2010, on-line), "the Ohio/Mars fusion of Ray Bradbury's stories, the evil clown towns of Stephen King, . . . *Watership Down* with its psychic rabbits—the weirder the better, basically." She told the same interviewer, "My favorite books were always the ones where I felt like an alternate world had been created in some star cradle by the author and, in an amazing feat of compression, shrunken down into a 200-page book. . . . I think I wanted to create strange but familiar snow-globe worlds almost as soon as I started reading these books."

In September 1999 Russell enrolled at Northwestern University, in Evanston, Illinois. "I don't think I was exactly an 'overachiever' in college, but I was always achieving," she wrote for a *New York Times* (September 30, 2007) essay. "I really believed that A's were like magical talismans, charms for a safe and happy future. Even one moment spent away from studying felt wanton, stolen. I still don't know whom I thought I was stealing from." While in college Russell majored in Spanish, and she spent one year studying in Seville, Spain. Much to her distress, she found that little was expected of her in her classes, and because of the two-hour midday siesta, she found herself with too much leisure time. "I felt like the worst sort of fool then, a midday insomniac feeling nostalgia for homework," she wrote in her *Times* essay.

In 2003 Russell earned a B.A. degree from Northwestern. As a graduate student at Columbia University, in New York City, she wrote in the school's computer laboratory. In a significant achievement for a young author, two of her early stories, "Haunting Olivia" and "Accident Brief," appeared in the *New Yorker*, in the issues of June 13–20, 2005 and June 19, 2006, respectively. Russell completed an M.F.A. degree in 2006, the same year that "St. Lucy's Home for Girls Raised by Wolves" was included in the spring issue of *Granta* and the 10-story collection bearing the same title was published by Knopf. "St. Lucy's Home for Girls Raised by Wolves" is about young female offspring of werewolves who live in a convent, where the nuns attempt to civilize them. Its plot, Mark Budman wrote for the *American Book Review* (November/December 2006), "could be considered a metaphor of race relationships, punctuated with frequent use of the term 'brothers' and 'sisters' applied to werewolves' cubs. Or it's a metaphor for juvenile crime and societal punishment. Or it's a metaphor for immigration and xenophobia." Budman added, "The presence of metaphors, whatever they are, and the intricate language they are constructed with, give Russell's stories an edge over traditional genre." Irving Malin, a critic for *Review of Contemporary Fiction* (Spring 2007), wrote, "The growing pains, the victory over culture shock, are so suggestive that we don't know where our sympathies lie. Should we admire civilized existence or primitive warfare? Russell is such a fascinating writer because she continually *unbalances* us."

Similarly, the story "From Children's Reminiscences of the Westward Migration" illustrates what Éllís Ní Dhuibhne, writing for the *Irish Times* (May 26, 2007), characterized as Russell's "blurring of the boundaries between animals and people"; narrated by a boy, the tale follows his family as they travel across the U.S. in a wagon pulled by the boy's father, who is a minotaur. According to Ní Dhuibhne, "The complexity of the boy's relationship to his bull father is so delicately expressed that the story works as a universal coming-of-age tale." The book also includes "Haunting Olivia," about two brothers searching for their younger sister, who has drowned; that tale struck Ní Dhuibhne as "very funny, outrageously imaginative, and profoundly moving." The other stories include "Lady Yeti and the Palace of Artificial Snows," "Z.Z.'s Sleep-Away Camp for Disordered Dreamers," "The Star-Gazer's Log of Summer-Time Crime," "Accident Brief, Occurrence # 00/422," and "Ava Wrestles the Alligator." In the last story, originally published in *Zoetrope: All-Story* (Summer 2006), the mother of 12-year-old Ava and her older sister, Osceola (Ossie), has died, and their father has abandoned them in Swamplandia!, the theme park that once supported their family; now Ava is trying to rescue her sister from her entanglement with a ghost and prevent her from eloping with him.

When Russell first showed "Ava Wrestles the Alligator" to her editor, the story was far longer. "So we cut it and did an ice-cream scoop of what felt like the dramatic part of that material," she told Nicole Rudick for the *Paris Review* blog (February 3, 2011). "But I wanted it to be a longer thing." Russell told Rege Behe for the *Pittsburgh (Pennsylvania) Tribune-Review* (January 30, 2011) that she felt that all the other stories in *St. Lucy's Home for Girls Raised by Wolves* simply ended, "and I was content to say, 'check please,' and on to the next one. But 'Ava Wrestles the Alligator,' those characters and that place, I just couldn't shake them." The grip that the characters and place held on her resulted in her expanding the story into the full-length novel *Swamplandia!* (2011).

Swamplandia! is the name of a theme park operated in the 1980s by the Bigtree family on a small island off the southern coast of Florida that is reachable only by ferry. In addition to Ava and Ossie, the family includes the girls' older brother, Kiwi; their mother, Hilola; and their father, Chief Bigtree. "Bigtree" is not the father's real surname, and the parents are not descendants of Indians, though they claim to be as a way to draw customers. One of Swamplandia!'s attractions is a performance in which Hilola swims among alligators and wrestles with them. After Hilola dies, of ovarian cancer, the remaining Bigtrees experience hard times, not only because of Hilola's death but because of the opening on the mainland of a far more alluring new amusement park, called World of Darkness. The Bigtrees' income diminishes to zero, spurring Chief Bigtree to leave Swamplandia! to seek a way to revive his business and Kiwi to take a job as a janitor with World of Darkness. Ossie loses her grasp on reality and, convinced that she is romantically involved with a ghost, vanishes into the Everglades. Thirteen-year-old Ava sets out on a dangerous quest to find her. Ava narrates part of the book; the rest is narrated by Kiwi, who suffers many awful experiences at his job.

Janet Maslin, in an assessment for the weekday *New York Times* (February 17, 2011), wrote, "*Swamplandia!* stays rooted in the Bigtree family's emotional reality. Take away the wall-to-wall literary embellishments, and this is a recognizable story, if not a familiar one. But there's no need to take those embellishments away. They are an essential, immensely enjoyable part of this novel's strange allure, and they have been rendered with commanding expertise, right down to the most tangential details." *Swamplandia!* "is magical realism, American style; lush language, larger-than-life surrealism, a vertiginous line on every page between hopes, dreams, and reality, a disorienting mirage of a book," Susan Salter Reynolds wrote for the *Los Angeles Times* (February 13, 2011). "What holds it all together is the voice. Russell's writing is clear, rhythmic and dependable, even as her imagination runs wild." A dissenting view came from Alice Gregory, who wrote for the *New York Observer* (February 1, 2011), "Ms. Russell's verbal ground is loamy and fragrant, but like the tropical soil of her setting, it's nutrient-poor, leached of minerals by the neon flowers and superfoods that grow there. Her specificity is sometimes exhausting, her quirkiness (that exclamation point!) tiresome. The particulars she deals in are inconceivably weird, like those of an anime plot, but they come embedded in a matrix that lacks real characters with whom we might empathize. . . . For now, at least, Ms. Russell is better when writing short stories, where she can splash us with colorful language and dunk us in deranged dimensions, where we can enter the fun house and then get the hell out."

In response to a question from the *Paris Review* interviewer about moving from the constraints of short-story writing to the requirements of creating an entire novel, Russell said, "It was really tricky, because the way I write stories isn't really compatible with novel writing, and my favorite part of any kind of writing is always on the sentence level. I would end up writing sections that amounted to a lot of drafting, and I don't really outline, so I had only a rough idea of what I wanted. I ended up with a lot of material that didn't make the cut for the book, and it was very painful, because I had spent so much time on the sentences." She added, "There was also the endurance part of it, staying with these characters and letting them change over time, writing down blind alleys and then backing up again. I thought that was almost the scariest part, because oftentimes with a story I will get the ending first or early on, or just feel like I can put all the parts together; this wasn't like that."

The annual collection *The Best American Short Stories* included "St. Lucy's Home for Girls Raised by Wolves" in 2007, and another Russell tale, "The Seagull Army Descends on Strong Beach," in 2010. Russell's "Help Wanted" appeared in *The Best of Lady Churchill's Rosebud Wristlet* (2007) and "Vampires in the Lemon Grove" in *The Year's Best Fantasy and Horror: Twenty-First Annual Collection* (2008).

When asked about the use of her imagination during the writing process, Russell told Liane Hansen, "It's like dreaming on the page. It's like flying or something. That's a great space to be in." Russell is currently writing short stories and a novel set during the 1930s Dust Bowl. She lives in the Washington Heights section of Manhattan, in New York City.

—J.P.

Suggested Reading: BookPage.com Feb. 2011; *Irish Times* Weekend p13 May 26, 2007; *New York Times* (on-line) Sep. 30, 2007; *New Yorker* (on-line) June 14, 2010; *Paris Review* blog Feb. 3, 2011; *Pittsburgh (Pennsylvania) Tribune-Review* (on-line) Jan. 30, 2011; *Portland (Oregon) Mercury* (on-line) Feb. 17, 2011; Reading Group Guides Web site Feb. 23, 2011

Selected Books: *St. Lucy's Home for Girls Raised by Wolves*, 2006; *Swamplandia!*, 2011

Rylance, Mark

Jan. 18, 1960– Actor; playwright; former theater director

Address: c/o The Broadway League, 729 Seventh Ave., Fifth Fl., New York, NY 10019

Mark Rylance has earned critical acclaim in England and the United States since the 1980s for his portrayals of many of Shakespeare's immortal characters—most notably Hamlet. The actor Al Pacino, a great admirer of his work, has often been quoted as saying, "Mark Rylance makes acting Shakespeare look as though Shakespeare had written the play for him the night before." Rylance joined the Royal Shakespeare Company when he was 22. His portrayal of Hamlet seven years later led many critics to call him the greatest Shakespearean actor of his generation, the greatest Hamlet of the last 50 years, or simply the greatest contemporary English-speaking stage actor. In 1995, at age 35, Rylance was named artistic director of Shakespeare's Globe, a then-unfinished replica of the open-air theater in London, England, in which Shakespeare's plays were performed in the first half of the 17th century. During his 10-year stint in that position, the Globe staged about 40 productions—Rylance appeared in more than a dozen—that attracted in total upwards of two million people, while the theater became a highly respected performance space.

Rylance's appointment as the Globe's artistic director initially raised the hackles of many Shakespeare aficionados, because he doubts that Shakespeare was the author of all the plays attributed to

Ian Gavan/Getty Images

him. "The Shakespeare authorship question," as it is known, is central to Rylance's play, *I Am Shakespeare*, in which he starred when it premiered, in 2007. Rylance has since appeared in leading roles, on Broadway and in London theaters, in plays including Marc Camoletti's *Boeing-Boeing*, which earned him both a Tony Award and a Drama Desk Award for best actor; David Hirson's Molière-inspired *La Bête*; and Jez Butterworth's *Jerusalem*, for which he won another Tony Award. Rylance has had roles in 10 feature films, among them *Pros-*

pero's Books (1991), an adaptation of Shake-speare's The Tempest; Angels and Insects (1995); Intimacy (2001); and The Other Boleyn Girl (2008). He earned a BAFTA Award for best actor for his portrayal of David Kelly, the British Iraq-weapons inspector who committed suicide in 2003, in the made-for-TV BBC movie The Government Inspector (2005).

In a particularly ecstatic, representative appreci-ation of Rylance's skills, John Lahr wrote of the ac-tor's work in Jerusalem for the New Yorker (May 9, 2011), "Rylance's deep and daring performance . . . defies the tropes of critical language. It is un-precedented, really. You could position it some-where between acting and athletics; its mesmeriz-ing, sensual recklessness, however, has to be wit-nessed to be understood. Rylance makes you be-lieve not only that giants exist but that he is one of them. And he is."

The first of the three children of David Waters and his wife, Ann, David Mark Rylance Waters was born on January 18, 1960 in Ashford, Kent, En-gland. In 1962 the family moved to the U.S., after his father accepted an offer to teach English at the Choate School, in Connecticut. Until the age of about five, Rylance suffered from a serious speech impediment. "It seems that I didn't use conso-nants. I just used vowels," he told Paul Taylor for the London Independent (April 27, 2003). "My fa-ther says he remembers being embarrassed on trains with me rambling excitedly about things outside. Everyone would look. I think my thoughts were ahead of my ability to communicate them." Not long after he began to speak normally, Rylance started to put on plays at home, with his friends and his brother, Jonathan, as actors. (Jonathan is now a professional wine expert; Rylance's sister, Susannah, is a novelist.)

In 1969 Rylance's family moved to Milwaukee, Wisconsin. Both of his parents taught at the Uni-versity School, in Milwaukee, which Rylance at-tended through 12th grade. In high school he took part in all aspects of the school's drama program, including lighting design and set construction; he excelled at the latter. Along with his father, who played the Gravedigger, Rylance at 16 took on the title role in his school's production of Hamlet. The following year he auditioned successfully (in New York City) for the Royal Academy of Dramatic Art (RADA), a highly regarded school in London. After high school he moved to London, where he trained at RADA and took lessons with a vocal coach. His first role as a professional actor was in Shaun Law-ton's play Desperado Corner, mounted by the Glas-gow, Scotland–based Citizens Theatre, in 1981.

In 1982 Rylance, at 22, became a member of the Royal Shakespeare Company (RSC). Located in Shakespeare's birthplace, Stratford-upon-Avon, the RSC is one of the most famous classical-theater companies in the world. In his first year with the RSC, Rylance appeared in a production of The Tempest. In 1984 he starred in J. M. Barrie's Peter Pan, giving a performance that reportedly made many audience members weep. During the sum-mer of 1989, he gave eight performances a week—four as Romeo and four as Hamlet. The director Ron Daniels built his RSC production of Hamlet around the idea of Hamlet's being driven mad by his father's murder. Rylance "conveys both Ham-let's infinite solitude and desperation," Michael Billington wrote for the Manchester Guardian Weekly (May 14, 1989), "clutching his head with terrifying self-awareness on 'O, it hath made me mad' and even crying 'O, vengeance' from a curled-up position as if conscious of his own impo-tence. . . . What Mr Rylance gives us, as clearly as I have seen, is Hamlet's sheer spiritual isolation." Moments of dark humor rubbed some conservative critics the wrong way—when Hamlet cheerfully said "Goodnight" to his mother while dragging away the corpse of Polonius, for example, or when he spit in Ophelia's face to rub away her makeup. "What amazed many of us, though," Paul Taylor wrote later for the London Independent (October 5, 1994), "was the way this bonkers, alternative co-median of a Prince also managed—thanks to Ry-lance's haunted sweetness of countenance and that intense but wary rapport he can build up with an audience—to project Hamlet's infinite solitariness and injured spirituality better than any contender within memory."

Rylance believes in the therapeutic power of Shakespeare, for himself and others. Hamlet, he told Cynthia Zarin for the New Yorker (May 5, 2008), "did a lot of favors for me. He saved my life, in a way. He allowed me to express things I felt. He got me into the Royal Academy, and into the R.S.C.; he's always been a kind of gateway, and he's always insistent and unapologetic."

In 1990 the RSC's production of Hamlet toured the U.S., with Rylance in the title role; it generally earned glowing reviews. Also that year Rylance and the pianist and composer Claire van Kampen (whom he married in 1992) founded a small theater company, Phoebus Cart. With Rylance in the role of Prospero, they mounted a production of Shake-speare's The Tempest that was presented out-of-doors, without a stage, on the site where the origi-nal Globe Theatre once stood, in London, and else-where in the open air, during a U.K. tour that Ry-lance financed.

Rylance received acclaim as a comedic actor—and won an Olivier Award, England's equivalent of the Tony Award—for his depiction of Benedick in Shakespeare's comedy Much Ado About Noth-ing. The key to the show's success, Michael Bil-lington wrote for the London Guardian (July 8, 1993), was Rylance's "brilliant" performance, in which he illuminated the humorous and touching aspects of his character's transition from an I'll-never-get-married bachelor to a man truly in love. The next year Rylance appeared in an unconven-tional production of another Shakespeare comedy, As You Like It: the action took place in a casino cum wrestling arena in the American South. Ry-lance was singled out for his performance as

Touchstone, the jester. In a review of the New York City production, Wilborn Hampton wrote for the *New York Times* (January 26, 1994) that Rylance "pretty much steals the show." In 1995, back in England, Rylance directed a Phoebus Cart mounting of *Macbeth*, in which he portrayed Macbeth as the shaven-headed, power-mad leader of a sinister, New Age–style religious cult. The production, regarded as both ambitious and a missed opportunity, received mixed reviews.

The criticisms of Rylance's unconventional production of *Macbeth* were mild in comparison with the many fierce objections to his appointment in mid-1995 as artistic director of the new Globe Theatre. The opposition stemmed from disapproval not only of Rylance's eccentric interpretations of some of Shakespeare's works but also his long-held suspicion that Shakespeare did not write all of the plays attributed to him. Rylance believes that a small group of well-educated people, most likely headed by the writer, politician, and philosopher Francis Bacon, wrote much of the great body of work generally attributed to Shakespeare. Although most actors, directors, and scholars do not doubt Shakespeare's authorship, the scarcity of documents dating from the Bard's lifetime (1564–1616) and various perplexing questions continue to drive speculation. (There are no records of Shakespeare's having attended any college or other school, for example. No original copies of his plays survive, no letters written by him have ever been found, and although in his will he specified how he wanted his money and household effects, including his "second-best bed," to be distributed, there is no mention of books, suggesting that, strangely for a supposed literary genius, he may not have owned any.)

The original Globe Theatre, in London, where many of Shakespeare's plays were staged during his lifetime, opened in 1599. A circular, open-air arena with no lighting other than the sun, it had seating areas on three tiers of balconies and a pit near the stage for standees, known as groundlings, who paid a penny to get in. The Globe was demolished by Puritans in 1644. The American actor and director Sam Wanamaker began in 1949 to dream of rebuilding the Globe. In 1970 he set up the Shakespeare Globe Trust; by the time of his death, in 1993, he had acquired a site only a few hundred yards from that of the first Globe, and construction of the new theater had begun. Others raised sufficient funds to complete the building, which is similar to the original. An "artistic directorate" whom Wanamaker selected chose Rylance as the theater's artistic director. In that position he was expected to stage about 180 performances annually, from late spring to early fall, when the weather in London is more likely than at other times to be suitable for open-air events.

The new Globe opened to the public in the summer of 1997, with a production of Shakespeare's early comedy *The Two Gentlemen of Verona*. Queen Elizabeth II, who was present, saw Rylance

in the role of Proteus, one of the gentlemen. The next year Rylance brought the production to the New Victory Theater, in New York. Ben Brantley, in a review for the *New York Times* (January 13, 1997), called the show "vigorous" and described Rylance's portrayal of Proteus as "mournful, petulant, painfully confused, a bit like the anguished, mumbling James Dean in *Rebel Without a Cause*. Mr. Rylance achieves the remarkable feat of seeming inarticulate while speaking in high-flown blank verse." The Globe next presented *A Chaste Maid in Cheapside*, by Thomas Middleton (1580–1627), and *Henry V*, both in 1997; *The Merchant of Venice* and *The Honest Whore*, the latter by Middleton and his contemporary Thomas Dekker, the next year; and an all-male production of *Antony and Cleopatra*, in 1999. (During Shakespeare's lifetime all female roles were played by men or boys.)

The Globe's 2000 production of *Hamlet* that Ben Brantley attended led him to praise its "absorbing, fast-paced clarity" and Rylance's "compelling" lead performance, but in the same review, for the *New York Times* (August 17, 2000), he described the supporting performances as "generally pedestrian." Paul Taylor, who also saw Rylance's Hamlet at the Globe, wrote for the London *Independent* (June 12, 2000), "At a venue which tempts some actors into orgies of crowd-pleasing exaggeration, he is the one genius who can create both a magically intimate rapport with the audience and an infinitely subtle sense of the progress of his character's inner life."

In February 2002, 400 years after the original's premiere, Rylance starred in an all-male production of Shakespeare's comedy *Twelfth Night*, in which he cast himself as Olivia. British critics raved about the show, and Rylance won an Olivier Award for his portrayal. *Twelfth Night* earned similar plaudits during its U.S. tour, in 2003. The Globe's 2003 staging of *Richard II* was also aired on BBC-TV, as was its 2004 production of *Measure for Measure*. The last Globe productions in which Rylance appeared were *The Tempest*, in which he reprised his depiction of Prospero, and *The Storm*, a translation by Peter Oswald of Plautus's *Rudens*, written in about 200 B.C. In the London *Guardian* (August 16, 2005), Maddy Costa described Rylance's performance in *The Storm* as "a shameless, critic-baiting masterclass in orchestrating audience participation and eliciting huge cheers."

By the time Rylance relinquished his position, critics and other theatergoers who had feared in 1995 that the re-created Globe would become a Disneyland-like tourist trap acknowledged that Rylance had developed the theater into "one of London's liveliest cultural resources," according to the *Economist* (May 21, 2005). When Dominic Cavendish, interviewing him for the London *Telegraph* (July 14, 2009), asked Rylance if he missed the Globe, he responded, "It was a great grief to go, but also a relief. Eventually the job overwhelmed me. I had moments when I saw the success of it but mostly I couldn't. I left because I had disagreements with the board about the general direction of the centre but to be fair, . . . I got tired and I was starting to make mistakes. So it was a good thing I stepped down when I did."

Soon after he left the Globe, Rylance began writing the play *I Am Shakespeare*, a kind of introduction to "the Shakespeare authorship question." (The play's full title is *The BIG Secret Live!—I Am Shakespeare—Webcam Daytime Chatroom Show*.) The leading character, Frank Charlton, is an Internet broadcaster preoccupied with his conviction that Shakespeare's plays were written by others. The Bard comes to discuss and debate the issue with Frank, as do such plausible behind-the-scenes authors as Francis Bacon, Edward de Vere, and Mary Sidney. Rylance co-directed, with Matthew Warchus, and played Frank in a production that premiered at the Chichester Festival, in England, in 2007 and then toured the United Kingdom. In a review for the London *Evening Standard* (September 3, 2007), Kieron Quirke, referring to a teaching method based on theater, called *I Am Shakespeare* "the best acted, funniest and least patronising bit of Theatre in Education you'll ever see." "The great thing about the evening is that Rylance has done his research well and tosses academic savvy in the air like so many balls, juggling them in and out of this wonderful text like a carnival act," Richard Edmonds wrote for the *Stage* (September 11, 2007, on-line).

Rylance gave a Tony Award–winning performance as Robert in a revival of the 1960s French farce *Boeing-Boeing*, directed by Matthew Warchus, that opened at the Longacre Theater, in New York, in May 2008. Robert is the naive, provincial friend of Bernard, a businessman living in Paris, France, who is dating three stewardesses of different nationalities. Thanks to their precise schedules, the stewardesses are never in Paris at the same time. The arrangement begins to fall apart when the airlines' schedules change, and it comes further unstuck when Robert arrives on Bernard's doorstep. The performances of other members of the cast—Bradley Whitford, Christine Baranski, Gina Gershon, Kathryn Hahn, and Mary McCormack—earned positive reviews, but most critics agreed that Rylance stood out. Brantley wrote for the *New York Times* (May 5, 2008) that Rylance "exercises a supremely graceful clumsiness and hang-dog cheer that evokes the great Buster Keaton." Cynthia Zarin called his performance "manic, exuberant, and wryly introspective—Chaplin by way of Candide." In 2008 Rylance also portrayed the title character in a revival of Henrik Ibsen's *Peer Gynt* at the Guthrie Theater, in Minneapolis, Minnesota.

In 2009, at the Duchess Theatre, in London, Rylance appeared in a revival of Samuel Beckett's sad yet absurdly humorous *Endgame* as the old, blind, chair-bound Hamm. Rylance "pulls off a miracle here," Paul Taylor declared in the London *Independent* (October 16, 2009). "The performance feels extraordinarily free and full of spur-of-the-moment inspiration, yet it's also absolutely disciplined and true to Beckett's sense that life is a matter of trying to kill time with routines that bore you out of your mind with their repetitiveness."

Also in 2009 Rylance starred in the debut production of Jez Butterworth's *Jerusalem*, directed by Ian Rickson at the Royal Court Theatre, in London. Rylance played the ex-daredevil Johnny "Rooster" Byron, a boastful, charismatic anarchist with a strong appetite for drugs and alcohol, who lives in a messy trailer in rural England. Byron philosophizes, parties, and hangs out with and sells drugs to local teenagers. Rylance's performance, generally regarded as brilliant, earned him both an Olivier Award and a London *Evening Standard* Theater Award. Butterworth told Dominic Cavendish, "As far as I'm concerned you might as well burn this script after we've finished with it because I don't see how anyone else could do it as well as [Rylance] does. You need to feel the charisma of a genuine eccentric, someone who gives you goose-pimples when they walk on. Mark Rylance just has all that, naturally." Rylance and half of the British cast remained with *Jerusalem* when it came to the Music Box Theater, in New York, in April 2011. "Mr. Rylance's galvanizing physical performance gives full due to Johnny the loser, with his imbalanced walk and halting speech, testaments to a bone-breaking, brain-frying life . . . ," Ben Brantley wrote for the *New York Times* (April 21, 2011), after he saw the play in New York. "But Mr. Rylance also captures—to a degree I can imagine no other contemporary actor doing—Johnny's vast, vital, Falstaffian appetite for pleasure, for independence, for life itself. . . . His Johnny Byron is truly a performance for the ages." *Jerusalem* ended its run in New York in September 2011. Rylance gave the Tony Award he won for his work in *Jerusalem* to an elderly British-Romany builder named Mickey Lay, whose reminiscences during the hours the men spent together provided inspiration for Rylance's Johnny.

From October 14, 2010 to January 9, 2011, Rylance appeared opposite David Hyde Pierce in a production of David Hirson's *La Bête* at the Music Box Theater, in New York. When Frank Rich, writing for the *New York Times* (February 11, 1991), saw the New York debut of *La Bête*, in 1991, he labeled it "a mock-Molière comedy of manners and ideas as refracted through (or deconstructed by) a post-modern sensibility." In the revival Rylance was cast as Valère, a buffoonish writer and actor so unabashedly in love with his own vacuous words and ideas that he refuses to stop talking. "Valère is a fabulous creation, and Rylance . . . inhabits him to the limits of wonderful," John Lahr wrote for the *New Yorker* (October 25, 2010).

Rylance is known for his modesty, compassion, and strong sense of fairness and justice. He is an active supporter of the organizations Survival International and Peace Direct. Rylance's wife, Claire van Kampen, was the Globe's founding music director/composer in residence; she also wrote the music for the revivals of *Boeing-Boeing* and *La Bête*. Rylance and van Kampen have homes in New York and London. From her first marriage, van Kampen has two grown daughters, Natasha and Juliet. Juliet Rylance, as she is known professionally, played Mary Sidney in *I Am Shakespeare*. She won an Obie Award in 2010 for her portrayal of Rosalind in the Sam Mendes–directed production of Shakespeare's *As You Like It*, which was presented in New York and London.

—D.K.

Suggested Reading: ibdb.com; imdb.com; (London) *Independent* p21 Oct. 5, 1994, p9 Feb. 2, 2002, (on-line) Apr. 27, 2003; *New Statesman* (on-line) Sep. 12, 2011; *New York Times* C p11 Jan. 13, 1997, (on-line) Apr. 21, 2011; *New Yorker* p38 May 5, 2008, p92 Oct. 25, 2010, p80 May 9, 2011

Selected Plays: *Peter Pan*, 1984; *Much Ado About Nothing*, 1993; *As You Like It*, 1994; *Macbeth*, 1995; *Antony and Cleopatra*,1998; *Hamlet*, 2000; *Twelfth Night*, 2002; *Richard II*, 2003; *Measure for Measure*, 2004; *The Tempest*, 2005; *I Am Shakespeare*, 2007; *Boeing-Boeing*, 2008; *Endgame*, 2009; *Jerusalem*, 2009; *La Bête*, 2010

Selected Films: *Prospero's Books*, 1991; *Angels and Insects*, 1995; *Intimacy*, 2001; *Leonardo*, 2003; *Richard II*, 2003; *The Other Boleyn Girl*, 2008

Harry How/Getty Images

Sacramone, Alicia

(sah-krah-MOH-nee, ah-LEESH-ya)

Dec. 3, 1987– Gymnast

Address: 4 Hastings Rd., Winchester, MA 01890

On October 23, 2010 Alicia Sacramone won the gold medal in the vault competition at the World Artistic Gymnastics Championships, held in Rotterdam, the Netherlands. Sacramone's victory was especially notable because, at 22, she was older than nearly all of her competitors and because she had just emerged from a long hiatus from gymnastics competition, which began after her participa-

tion in the 2008 Summer Olympic Games, in Beijing, China, when she announced her retirement from the sport. The U.S. women's gymnastics team won a silver medal at those Games, but despite assurances to the contrary from her teammates and nearly all gymnastics aficionados, Sacramone blamed herself—specifically, for her mishaps in two events—for the team's failure to bring home the gold. "It took me time to realize that I literally did the best I could . . . ," she told an interviewer for USA Gymnastics (May 14, 2009, on-line), the national governing body for competitive gymnastics. "It may not have been my best competition ever but I couldn't have done any more than I did, I couldn't have trained any more than I did."

The International Federation of Gymnastics, which oversees all global competition, recognizes five varieties of gymnastics: artistic, rhythmic, aerobic, acrobatic, and trampoline. In women's artistic gymnatics competition, judges score performances in the vault, the uneven bars, and the balance beam; in the floor exercise (also called floor routine); and all-around execution. In team events the gymnasts perform individually, with cumulative scores deciding the winning team. Sacramone began training in gymnastics when she was eight years old, after studying dance for five years. "I always loved performing in front of a crowd," Sacramone told an *Inside Gymnastics* (July 22, 2007) interviewer. "In gymnastics we express ourselves through our routines, especially on the floor. I put everything I have into every routine. I get to show a little bit more of my personality during my floor routine because it is my own personal style that I'm displaying for the crowd to see. I love entertaining people, and I do that best when I'm having fun on the competition floor." Sacramone's victory in Rotterdam in 2010 brought her total first-, second-, and third-place wins in international competition to nine—a number achieved by only two other American gymnasts, Shannon Miller and Nastia Liukin. In U.S. national contests, she has won five gold medals in the vault, more than any other American woman. USA Gymnastics named her Sportswoman of the Year in 2005, 2006, and 2007. In the last of those years, in her role as captain of the U.S. women's team, Sacramone was acclaimed for the leadership and inspirational abilities that enabled that team to win the title at the World Championships. Serving in the same capacity at the 2008 Summer Olympics, she earned praise and gratitude from her teammates for her motherly support and encouragement. In college-level gymnastics Sacramone set Brown University records as a freshman there, in 2006–07, and she placed first in all five events at that year's Ivy League Classic. In an unusual move for a female gymnast, she trained full-time off-campus (with her longtime coach, Mihai Brestyan) during that academic year.

Alicia Marie Sacramone was born on December 3, 1987 in Boston, Massachusetts, and grew up in Winchester, a Boston suburb. Her parents are Frederick J. Sacramone Jr., an orthodontist, and Gail Sacramone, who owns and manages a beauty salon. Her brother, Jonathan, born in 1982, identifies himself on his Web site as an actor, comedian, and writer. At age three Sacramone began taking lessons in dance, a pursuit that includes training in balance, grace, flexibility, form, and other essentials associated with gymnastics. "From when she was a little girl, she needed to be busy," Sacramone's mother told an Associated Press reporter, as posted on sports.espn.go.com (August 28, 2007). Sacramone continued studying dance for five years. One day when Alicia was eight, her mother saw her performing cartwheels at a shopping mall. Soon afterward her mother enrolled her in gymnastics lessons with Mihai Brestyan, a former coach of the Romanian national team, and his wife, Silvia, at Gymnastics and More, a club in Woburn, Massachusetts. Sacramone later trained with the Brestyans at the American Gymnastics Club, a facility they opened in Ashland, Massachusetts. Brestyan has said that he knew immediately that Sacramone would be a champion, telling Andy Nesbitt for the *Boston Globe* (July 17, 2003), "You could see it right away because she has the personality to be seen. She's a very social kid, a very beautiful kid in the movements, a very talented kid. She already had all those ingredients. The only problem was how do we put this all together. So we started to work." That work included building Sacramone's physical strength as well as skills on the uneven parallel bars, the vault, and the balance beam and in the floor exercise. "She never was the champion all the time, but she was the only one 100 percent committed to do this," Brestyan told Nesbitt. When Sacramone attended Winchester High School, her mother told Vicki Michaelis for *USA Today* (October 14, 2010), "if she didn't get a good grade on a paper, the next day she'd say to the teacher, 'What can I do to make it up?' She was always that way." By that time Sacramone was training seven hours a day and attending school half-time. At age 15 she became the youngest member of the U.S. national

gymnastics team, after placing third in the floor routine, with a score of 9.350 out of 10, and fourth in the vault, with 9.375, to rank 14th overall in the 2003 National Championships, in Milwaukee, Wisconsin.

Sacramone's hopes of earning a berth on the 2004 U.S. Olympic team were crushed when she placed 19th at the U.S. Nationals, in June of that year. Soon afterward she suffered a back injury, forcing her to take time off from the sport. While her back healed she "did a lot of thinking about my future," she told the *Inside Gymnastics* (July 22, 2007) interviewer. "That summer my motivation was low. I came to the gym when I pleased because I was injured, but each day I wasn't there I felt like a part of me was missing. I missed gymnastics." On December 5, 2004, two days after her 17th birthday, Sacramone won gold medals in the vault and the floor exercise at the 2004 Pan American Gymnastics Union Individual Event Finals, in Maracaibo, Venezuela. Six days later she won another gold medal in the vault, with a score of 9.481 (thus surpassing the 2004 Olympic Games gold and bronze medalists), at the World Cup Final, in Birmingham, England—the most prestigious international event since that year's Olympic Games.

Sacramone placed first in the floor exercise and in the vault and third all-around and on the balance beam at the 2005 U.S. Classic, in Virginia Beach, Virginia. She came in first in the vault and in the floor exercise—in the latter, with a score of 9.9—and third on the balance beam at the 2005 Visa Championships, in Indianapolis, Indiana. Internationally in 2005, among other events, she won the gold in the vault and silver in the floor exercise at the American Cup, on Long Island, New York; gold in the vault at the World Cup, in Paris, France; and bronze in the vault and gold in the floor exercise (with a score of 9.612 in a routine that included a near-perfect triple twist) at the World Championships, in Melbourne, Australia. At the 2005 Pan American Championships, in Rio de Janeiro, Brazil, her team won the gold medal, and Sacramone placed first in the vault contest and the floor exercise.

Sacramone came in second in the vault at the World Cup, held in May 2006 in Ghent, Belgium, and second in the vault at the World Championships, in October 2006 in Aarhus, Denmark. She did not compete in the floor exercise in Aarhus because, during the qualifying round, she violated a newly instituted rule that required gymnasts to make at least two connected leaps during the dance passes; the quarter-turn Sacramone made between leaps led to a .50-point subtraction from her score and her elimination from that event. USA Gymnastics appealed that decision, without success. Because of that .50 deduction, Team USA came in second, behind China, rather than first at that year's World Championships.

Earlier in the fall of 2006, Sacramone had enrolled at Brown University, in Providence, Rhode Island, with the intention of majoring in sociology.

Brown is about 60 miles by car from the Brestyan gym—near enough for her to continue training three days a week, for four hours, with Brestyan. To the surprise of many, she joined the school's gymnastics team as well. (Although many male gymnasts attend college full-time and compete at the college level, very few women do.) During her freshman year Sacramone set Brown records in the vault, the floor exercise, and the all-around. She became the first Ivy League gymnast to finish first in every event and win the all-around at the Ivy Classic; she set a new Ivy Classic record in the all-around and tied the record for the vault. She was the Northeast Regional Floor Champion and was named the Eastern College Athletic Conference Rookie of the Year. Her grueling schedule proved to be extremely difficult. "I'm not going to lie, I thought balancing both elite and college gymnastics would be easier," she admitted to *Inside Gymnastics* (July 22, 2007). "It took a lot of hard work to keep everyone happy. I would drive home to train with Mihai almost every morning, drive back to Brown where I would go to class, then run to Brown's practice. . . . Looking back on the year now I realized how hard it really was." At the U.S. Classic, in Battle Creek, Michigan, in July 2007, she came in first in three events—vault, balance beam, and floor exercise. The next month, at the 2007 Visa Championships, in San Jose, California, she won the gold in the vault.

"When I was younger, I didn't like the vault," Sacramone told John Powers for the *Boston Globe Magazine* (October 7, 2007). "I was scared to run as fast as I could into a solid object. Now it's one of my specialties. . . . I'm looking straight at the horse when I take my ten running steps. You can definitely mess up the vault if you over-run it, so you have to find your speed. After I do the block, which is the two-handed push off the horse that gets me in the air, I've got to stay clean, with my arms and elbows tight. At some point, you're between fifteen and twenty feet in the air. You have to think about the little things, like pointing your toes, because a lot can go wrong up there. If something is wrong, I can tell. But there's a way you can still save the vault by knowing what to tweak. It's how much you're in touch with yourself. When I'm in the air, my eyes are open. I'm always looking for the mat to know where I am, to get ready for the landing."

Sacramone turned professional in September 2007, thereby ending her eligibility to compete in college gymnastics. At the 2007 World Championships, held that month in Stuttgart, Germany, she was a member of the first American women's gymnastics team to win that competition outside the U.S.; with her score of 15.325, she placed second in the floor exercise, thus tipping the cumulative team score in favor of the U.S., leaving the Chinese team—the favorites going into the competition—behind by .95. (A score of 15.325 represents the total of amounts for difficulty plus the amount for execution, the latter beginning at 10.0 with points

subtracted for poor execution or poor artistry.) "Sacramone's winning floor exercise was as clutch as any pass ever thrown by Peyton Manning or basket made by [Michael Jordan]," Eddie Pells wrote for the Associated Press (September 7, 2007, online). Speaking of her floor routine, Sacramone told *Sports Illustrated* (September 17, 2007), "I've never been so nervous. I was so relieved when I finished because I knew there was nothing more I could have done. That's the best I can do." Sacramone also excelled as the women's team captain. "Alicia is the ideal for that," Marta Karolyi, the U.S. gymnastics team coordinator, told the *Boston Globe* (September 27, 2007). "She is looked up to and she deserves that role. She has the personality and she cares about the young gymnasts and for the common goal of the team." Commenting on the U.S.'s upset over China, E. M. Swift wrote for *Sports Illustrated* (September 17, 2007), "The audacious Americans . . . displayed the sort of camaraderie, charisma, and guts that attracts the nation to this dangerous, beautiful sport once a quadrennium."

Sacramone did not attend college during the 2007–08 academic year; instead, she prepared for the 2008 Olympics. Her training included an arduous regimen of six-day-a-week strength-building exercises and cardiovascular workouts. To keep up her morale, she told Amy Van Deusen for *Women's Health* (June 2008, on-line), "I remind myself that I've been working for this so long, that it'd be silly to give it up after so many years of hard work. Also, that this tough part . . . is temporary." At the Friendship International Exchange, held in Huntsville, Texas, in May 2008, her first competition in eight months, Sacramone won the titles on both the balance beam, with a score of 15.600, and the floor exercise, with 15.500. One month later, at the the Visa Championships, in Boston, Sacramone, competing in three events, placed first in the vault, second in the floor exercise, and third on the balance beam.

At the Olympic trials, held in Philadelphia, Pennsylvania, on June 22, 2008, only Shawn Johnson and Nastia Liukin were chosen for the women's team. Sacramone was selected a month later, at the mini-camp run by Marta Karolyi at the Karolyis' ranch, near Houston, Texas. Chellsie Memmel, Samantha Peczek, and Bridget Sloan completed the team, for which Sacramone served as captain. At the 2008 Summer Olympic Games, in Beijing, the artistic-gymnastic events took place from August 9 to 19. In individual events Sacramone won no medals and placed no higher than fourth, in the vault. She also suffered two mishaps during the team finals—a fall from the balance beam and a fall during her floor exercise. Because of those falls, Sacramone blamed herself for the failure of the American women's team to win the gold medal, which went to China by a narrow margin. The U.S. team won the silver medal, and by all accounts their loss of first place to China could not be attributed to Sacramone's slips. Paul Ziert, writing for *International Gymnast* (August 13, 2008), demonstrated "with simple arithmetic" that Sacramone "did not cost the American team a gold medal." "It was not your fault, Alicia," he declared, echoing many others. A few months later Amy Van Deusen wrote for *Women's Health* (on-line), "Experts have debated whether the U.S. women could have won, even with a perfect meet." Nevertheless, by that time Sacramone had announced her retirement from competitive gymnastics.

During her absence from competition, Sacramone completed one or two more terms at Brown, serving as a volunteer coach for the women's gymnastic team. She also engaged in various corporate events, such as reporting on fashions before the 2009 Golden Globes ceremony for the cable-TV network E!, working as a representative for the Los Angeles, California–based men's sportswear company Tankfarm, and serving as a "spokesmodel" for the cosmetics company CoverGirl. In the summer of 2009, she decided to resume gymnastics training; after moving from Los Angeles to her parents' home, in Winchester, she began working with Brestyan again. She emerged from retirement officially in July 2010, when she competed in the CoverGirl Classic, in Chicago, Illinois, placing first in both the vault and the balance-beam events. "Mentally, it's like I never went away," she told David Barron for the *Houston (Texas) Chronicle* (August 11, 2010), the day after the start of the 2010 Visa Championships, held in Hartford, Connecticut. "Now, I'm pretty much back to everything I had at the Olympics, which is surprising. Building the strength was hard. It took a lot of weight work. But now I feel my running and power are back." Sacramone placed first in the vault and second in the balance-beam contest at the Visa Championships. Then, on October 23, 2010, at the World Championships, in Rotterdam, she won the gold medal in the vault. (The only other American woman to win the vault in that contest is Kayla Williams, who did so in 2009.) "I am glad to be back representing the U.S.," she said after her victory, Diane Pucin reported for the *Los Angeles Times* (October 23, 2010, on-line). "To walk away like I did after the Olympics . . . it's nice to set my mind to something, work hard and come back and get a big reward for all the work that I've done. It makes it worthwhile."

Sacramone has expressed a desire to attend Harvard University. She has been dating the Denver Broncos' quarterback Brady Quinn since mid-2010.

—T.O.

Suggested Reading: *Boston Globe* p10 July 17, 2003, E p1+ Sep. 27, 2007; *Boston Globe Magazine* p37 Oct. 7, 2007; *Brown Daily Herald* (on-line) Nov. 16, 2006; *Inside Gymnastics* (on-line) July 22, 2007; *Los Angeles Times* D p1 Aug. 20, 2007; *Sports Illustrated* p92 Sep. 17, 2007; sports.espn.go.com Aug. 28, 2007; *USA Gymnastics* Web site; *Women's Health* (on-line) June 2008

Courtesy of the MacArthur Foundation

Saez, Emmanuel

Nov. 26, 1972– Economist; educator; writer

Address: University of California–Berkeley, Dept. of Economics, 549 Evans Hall #3880, Berkeley, CA 94720

The French-born Emmanuel Saez views the shifts and policies in the area he studies—the economy—from both theoretical and empirical perspectives, basing conclusions on data measured in traditional ways while also studying real-world factors that theory does not normally take into account. For example, he has focused on such topics as retirement-plan decisions, tax policy, Social Security, and the distribution of income and wealth; his studies, many of which have been completed in collaboration with his fellow Frenchman Thomas Piketty, have helped to confirm that income inequality in the United States has been on the rise. Saez's work has revealed that the richest 1 percent of the American population currently claims nearly a quarter of the country's income, the highest percentage since the 1920s. "I think inherently the study of inequality is interesting precisely because regular people care about inequality," Saez told Kathleen Maclay and Sarah Yang for a University of California, Berkeley (UC–Berkeley), press release (September 28, 2010, on-line). "When they see statistics of income equality increasing, poverty statistics, they react strongly. It does have an impact on how they feel, and hence the decision they will take in the political arena." Saez, who has taught at UC-Berkeley since 2002, was the 2009 recipient of the John Bates Clark Medal from the American Economics Association, second in prestige in the field only to the Nobel Prize. In 2010 he received a John D. and Catherine T. MacArthur Foundation fellowship, often called the "genius grant."

"Nobody has done more to describe the broad changes in income distribution in the United States that have taken place during the last ninety years . . . ," David Warsh wrote of Saez for EconomicPrincipals.com (April 26, 2009). "He is emblematic of a new generation that takes public finance seriously, devising more explicit and efficient tax codes, and measuring behavioral responses to tax changes about which political activists and their think-tank acolytes previously have only argued." Saez currently serves as the director of UC–Berkeley's Center for Equitable Growth. He is also an associate editor of the publications *International Tax and Public Finance* and *Quantitative Economics*. His numerous papers have appeared in distinguished publications such as the *Quarterly Journal of Economics*, *American Economic Review*, *National Tax Journal*, and the *Journal of Economic Literature*, among many others.

Emmanuel Saez was born on November 26, 1972 in France. In 1994 he graduated with a B.A. degree in mathematics from the École Normale Supérieure, in Paris, France. Two years later he earned a master's degree in economics from the Department and Laboratory of Applied and Theoretical Economics (DELTA), also in Paris. Saez received a doctorate in economics from the Massachusetts Institute of Technology (MIT), in Cambridge, in 1999. He then served for three years as an assistant professor of economics at Harvard University, also in Cambridge. Also during that time he was a faculty research fellow in the Public Economics Program at the Cambridge-based National Bureau of Economic Research (NBER), a nonprofit research organization that disseminates unbiased reports among academics, public-policy makers, and business professionals; he went on to become a research associate of the NBER program beginning in 2003.

From July 2001 to June 2002 Saez was a visiting assistant professor at UC–Berkeley; during the next year he served as an assistant professor of economics at the school. He became an associate professor in mid-2003 and a full professor in 2005, and in 2010 he was named the E. Morris Cox professor of economics and director of Berkeley's Center for Equitable Growth. He is currently a research fellow at IZA (the Institute for the Study of Labor) and the CESifo Group, which is made up of the Center for Economic Studies (CES), the Ifo Institute for Economic Research, and other organizations. He also serves as co-director of the Public Policy Program at CEPR (the Center for Economic and Policy Research).

In the winter of 2007, the *Journal of Economic Perspectives* published a paper entitled "How Progressive Is the U.S. Federal Tax System? A Historical and International Perspective," co-written by Saez and Piketty. For the paper the two men conducted a study based on analyses of public microfile tax-return data; the purpose was to determine how all taxes affect Americans at various levels of income. "Most analyses of progressivity"—that is, increases in income-tax rates as income goes up— "look at the income, payroll, estate, and corporate taxes in isolation," Christopher Shea wrote for the *Boston Globe* (April 15, 2007), "but Piketty and Saez have assembled all of these into one picture." The pair also examined how tax burdens for those in the upper-income brackets have decreased over the past several years, and they wrote that "the progressivity of the U.S. federal tax system at the top of the income distribution has declined dramatically since the 1960s."

In their groundbreaking paper Saez and Piketty declared essentially that Americans who earned the most money in 2005 paid around 35 percent of their incomes in federal taxes, while in 1960 top-earning Americans had paid twice that percentage. They concluded that "the most dramatic changes in federal tax system progressivity almost always take place within the top 1 percent of income earners, with relatively small changes occurring below the top percentile." The MIT economist James Poterba said to Christopher Shea that Saez and Piketty's paper "does a very careful job of putting together 40-odd years of data, which goes well beyond what most people have done."

In 2009 the American Economic Association awarded Saez the John Bates Clark Medal, which is given to an American economist under the age of 40. (Saez has both French and American citizenship.) "This came as a surprise and the greatest honor I could get from the profession," he told Kathleen Maclay for a UC–Berkeley press release (April 29, 2009). "It is most rewarding and motivating to see that my work has generated interest and recognition among colleagues and students in economics." "Emmanuel is deeply deserving of the honor," since "his work on income inequality and taxation has helped to shape my own thinking on these matters, and it had no small influence on [President Barack Obama's] Budget," Peter Orszag, an economist who worked with Saez and headed the Office of Management and Budget (OMB) from January 20, 2009 to July 30, 2010, wrote in an OMB blog post (April 27, 2009). Orszag added, "Emmanuel's work on income inequality has helped to point the way for the Administration in its pledge to rebalance the tax code, with a tax cut going to 95 percent of working Americans while asking those at the very top to contribute more." (As it turned out, in 2010 President Obama granted tax cuts to those in lower income brackets while also striking a deal with congressional Republicans to extend for two years the tax cuts for the wealthy enacted under President George W. Bush—in exchange for extensions of unemployment benefits and other concessions by Republicans.)

In 2010 Saez was one of 23 individuals to receive the MacArthur Foundation's "genius grant," which brings each winner $500,000 over the course of five years. "After I found out, I only called my wife, because they tell you that you can only tell one person," he recalled to Lou Fancher for the *Contra Costa (California) Times* (May 12, 2011). The monetary award comes with no strings attached. When asked how he was going to spend the money, he told Fancher, "You know, I'm already paid to do what I do, so I will just continue. But now, I will be able to fund additional studies and hire students to assist me." In his September 28, 2010 interview with Kathleen Maclay and Sarah Yang, Saez said that the award offers "great encouragement to devote more time to help explain my work to the broader public, especially when the results can have an impact on current policy debates, such as the taxation of top incomes. . . . Not feeling like a genius, I see this award as recognition that my academic work on inequality and taxation has also been useful in the public debate beyond academia."

Saez's honors include the Alfred P. Sloan Doctoral Dissertation Fellowship (1998); the National Tax Association dissertation prize (1999); the CESifo prize in Public Economics for best paper by a young scholar (2002); the Best Graduate Teacher Award from UC–Berkeley's Economics Graduate Students Association (2002); an Alfred P. Sloan Research Fellowship (2003); the Purvis Memorial Prize of the Canadian Economic Association for best publication of the year on Canadian economic policy (2006); and an Elected Fellowship from the American Academy of Arts and Sciences (2010). In 2011 the American Economic Association named his article "Do Taxpayers Bunch at Kink Points?" the best paper published in the *American Economic Journal: Economic Policy* in 2010.

Justin Lanhart wrote for the *Wall Street Journal* (April 25, 2009, on-line) that Saez is "an easy going Frenchman who loves surfing." *Pour une révolution fiscale*, a book he co-co-wrote, in French, with Piketty and Camille Landais, was published in 2011.

—J.P.

Suggested Reading: *Boston Globe* D p1 Apr. 15, 2007; *Contra Costa (California) Times* My Town May 12, 2011; University of California–Berkeley, press release (on-line) Sep. 28, 2010; *Wall Street Journal* (on-line) Apr. 25, 2009

Selected Books: *Pour une révolution fiscale* (with Thomas Picketty and Camille Landais), 2011

Saks, Elyn R.

Oct. 3, 1955– Legal scholar; writer; educator; advocate for the mentally ill

Address: USC Gould School of Law, Rm. 418, 699 Exposition Blvd., Los Angeles, CA 90089

The position Elyn R. Saks has held since 1998 at the University of Southern California (USC) Gould School of Law—Orrin B. Evans professor of law, psychology and psychiatry and the behavioral sciences—indicates the recognition she has earned as a highly accomplished legal scholar and educator. But it does not reveal the breadth of her areas of expertise, which include criminal law, especially as it relates to the mentally ill, and the branch of family law that is devoted to the rights of children; nor does it suggest the extent of her contributions outside the classroom as an advocate for enlightened legal and medical policies regarding people with serious mental disorders. In addition, her title gives no hint of the unusual depth of her knowledge, gained through decades of agonizing, first-hand experience as a victim of schizophrenia. Fearful of the stigma associated with mental illness, for many years Saks succeeded in keeping her disorder a secret from all but a few friends, relatives, and mental-health professionals while she advanced in her career. She gained tenure at USC in 1994 and built a solid reputation in the legal and mental-health communities with dozens of journal articles and three books: *Jekyll on Trial: Multiple*

Will Vinet, courtesy of USC Gould School of Law

Personality Disorder and Criminal Law (1997, written with her close friend Stephen H. Behnke); *Interpreting Interpretation: The Limits of Hermeneutic Psychoanalysis* (1999); and *Refusing Care: Forced Treatment and the Rights of the Mentally Ill* (2002).

In 2007, despite a warning that she might become known as "the schizophrenic with a job," Saks published *The Center Cannot Hold: My Journey Through Madness*, a memoir in which she described in graphic detail her episodes of severe psychosis, her crippling delusions, her hospitalizations in England and the U.S., and her treatments with a series of psychoanalysts. The book tells of her acknowledgment, after many years of denial, that schizophrenia is an illness, not a manifestation of lack of will or effort, and that medication is vital to keep it under control. She also wrote about the crucial role that the support of family members, friends, professors, therapists, and her husband has played in her attaining happiness personally and professionally. Like her superior intellectual abilities and "a frequently unattractive stubborn streak that's worked in my favor as often as it has against me," that support network has made her "an exception to a lot of rules," in her words.

The decision to disclose her illness publicly, Saks wrote in *The Center Cannot Hold*, stemmed in part from her desire to explain the nature of schizophrenia and refute some of the myths surrounding it, such as the beliefs that victims display psychotic behavior nonstop and that schizophrenics are far more dangerous than those not afflicted with the disease. It also stemmed from Saks's knowledge that first-person accounts by schizophrenics are rare. "Comparatively few schizophrenics lead happy and productive lives," she wrote; "those who do aren't in any hurry to tell the world about themselves." "Ultimately, I decided that writing about myself could do more good than any academic article I'd ever pen," she wrote, and that "the benefits would be worth the risks." In 2007 *Time* included *The Center Cannot Hold* among its top 10 nonfiction books of the year, and the work was honored by the National Alliance on Mental Illness and several other organizations. In 2009, in announcing that Saks had won a MacArthur Foundation fellowship—a so-called genius grant—for her past and potential achievements, the foundation noted on its Web site that her memoir had "provided additional gravity to her contribution to scholarship, practice, and policy," and it predicted that the book would enhance her current research on high-functioning schizophrenics and "extend her impact on mental health law and disability rights policy."

Saks studied philosophy as an undergraduate at Vanderbilt University, in Nashville, Tennessee, and ancient philosophy at the graduate level at Oxford University, in England. She then earned a law degree from Yale University, in New Haven, Connecticut, in 1986. Before she joined the faculty of the Gould School of Law, in Los Angeles, in 1989, she represented indigent clients as a staff attorney with Connecticut Legal Services (1986–87) and taught at the University of Bridgeport School of Law (1987–89), also in Connecticut. She served as Gould's associate dean for research from 2005 to 2010. Saks has taught psychiatry at the School of Medicine of the University of California at San Diego since 2003 and is an instructor at the Institute of Psychiatry, Law, and Behavioral Science at USC's Keck School of Medicine. She is currently working toward a doctorate in psychoanalysis at the New Center for Psychoanalysis, in Los Angeles.

The first of three children, Elyn Ronna Saks was born on October 3, 1955 in Miami, Florida, to Herbert Saks (called Bert), a lawyer, and his wife, Barbara. She grew up with her brothers, Warren and Kevin, in suburban North Miami. When she was 13 her parents opened a shop selling antiques and collectibles. In an interview for *Behavioral Health Central* (May 30, 2009, on-line), Saks recalled her early years as being "very non-traumatic and benign. I had very caring, loving parents and younger brothers I was crazy about and had sibling rivalries with." Her parents, she wrote in her memoir, "gave me and taught me what I needed to make the most of my talents and strengths." Nevertheless, she continued, "there were certain signs that things were not well. By an early age, I developed phobias and obsessions and night terrors." Her first memory of what she referred to in her memoir as "disorganization" occurred when she was about eight. She was standing in the family's living room when, moments after her father chastised her for bothering him while he was working, "something odd" occurred: "My awareness (of myself, of him, of the room, of the physical reality around and beyond us) instantly grows fuzzy. Or wobbly. I think I am dissolving. I feel—my mind feels—like a sand castle with all the sand sliding away in the receding surf. *What's happening to me?*" Saks instinctively felt that she should not tell her parents or anyone else what had happened. "I didn't hear people talking about things like that," she told *Current Biography*. Despite warning signs, Saks believes that she would not have been diagnosable as schizophrenic at that time. "A lot of kids look like I did when I was a kid and they grow up to be fine," she pointed out to *Current Biography*.

During the summer following her sophomore year at North Miami Senior High School, Saks took an intensive course in Spanish language and culture in Mexico along with some of her classmates. While in Mexico she smoked marijuana for the first time. Shortly after she returned to Florida, at a friend's suggestion, she tried the psychedelic drug mescaline. The mescaline caused hallucinations, and she felt its effects for days afterward. Concerned that she had damaged her brain, Saks confessed to her parents having used marijuana (but not mescaline) but refused to promise that she would never again experiment with drugs. Her parents immediately enrolled her in an outpatient program for drug abusers, and for the next two years, she spent five hours every day after school at a rehabilitation center; during summers she remained at the center all day. Saks believes she benefited from being there, "because I'd adopted counterculture values—achievement doesn't matter, that kind of thing," she explained to Lee Randall for the *Scotsman* (October 6, 2007, on-line). "If I'd gone to college in that state of mind I wouldn't have studied, and getting good grades opened a lot of doors. But I kind of wish I'd been sent to a psychiatrist instead, because some of the craziness of the program was problematic." In particular, those running the program condemned the use of any drugs that altered the functioning of the brain, a stance that Saks embraced—to her later detriment, when it came to the antipsychotic medications that her doctors prescribed.

One morning during her teens, Saks experienced a psychotic episode of a kind common among schizophrenics. As she recalled in *The Center Cannot Hold*, she suddenly felt compelled to leave her class and walk the three miles to her home. "As I walked along, I began to notice that the colors and shapes of everything around me were becoming very intense. And at some point, I began to realize that the houses I was passing were sending messages to me: Look closely. You are special. You are especially bad. Look closely and ye shall find. There are many things you must see. See. See." Saks told her mother about the voices, but instead of consulting a physician, her parents took her to the rehabilitation center, where she had to convince the counselors that the episode had not been drug-induced. After a few days nobody mentioned the incident again.

Upon graduating from high school, Saks enrolled at Vanderbilt University, where (as is common among schizophrenics at that age) symptoms of her mental illness took the form of "gradual deterioration of basic common-sense hygiene—what the mental health community calls 'self-care skills' or 'activities of daily living,' " Saks wrote in her memoir. "Once away from my parents' watchful eyes, I grew inconsistent about asking myself the taken-for-granted questions. Or maybe I was muddled sometimes about what the right answers to those questions should be. Are showers really necessary? How often do I need to change clothes? Or wash them? Have I eaten anything yet today? Do I really need to sleep every night? Do I have to brush my teeth every day? . . . Taking care of myself meant doing more than reading a book or finishing a term paper, it meant strategizing, organizing, keeping track. And some days, there just wasn't enough room in my head to keep it all together."

Nevertheless, as she had in high school, Saks shone in the classroom; she earned A's not only in philosophy, her major, but in every subject. "At the same time my mind was starting to betray me, it was also becoming the source of enormous satisfaction," she said in delivering the Hoffman Memorial Lecture in Law and Psychiatry at the University of Virginia School of Law in 2009. "I discovered academia. Great ideas, high aspirations, and people whose own intellectual work is clearly one of the stalwarts of my recovery, and I was lucky to discover the pleasure of that kind of work early." "For me, my work is one of the last things to go,"

Saks told *Current Biography*, explaining that it "keeps me together." Saks was elected to the honor society Phi Beta Kappa in her junior year of college. She ranked first in her class when she graduated with a B.A. degree, summa cum laude, with high honors in philosophy, in 1977. She earned Vanderbilt's Founder's Medal for First Honors.

Saks won a Marshall scholarship to study ancient philosophy at Oxford University. Soon after her arrival in England, she fell into a deep depression and became overwhelmed by psychotic thoughts, believing herself to be an evil person who was responsible for thousands of deaths. Thoughts of setting herself on fire led to the first of her two hospitalizations during the four years that elapsed before she earned an M. Litt. (master of letters) degree from Oxford, in 1981. (The thesis she wrote struck the examining committee as being comparable in quality to a doctoral dissertation.) During the first hospitalization, which lasted four months, Saks burned herself with cigarettes, lighters, heaters, and boiling water, as commanded by voices she heard. The next year she began a daily course of therapy with a Mrs. Jones (the pseudonym Saks gave her in her memoir), a follower of the post-Freudian psychoanalyst Melanie Klein (1882–1960). Unlike Sigmund Freud (1856–1939) and many contemporary psychoanalysts, "Klein believed that people with psychosis could benefit from analysis . . . ," Saks wrote. "It was her theory that psychotic individuals are filled with (even driven by) great anxiety, and that the way to provide relief is to focus directly on the deepest sources of that anxiety." Adhering to Jones's only stated rule, Saks would "say everything that came to my mind, no matter how embarrassing, trivial, or inappropriate it might seem," in her words; Jones would then interpret what Saks had said as expressions of Saks's unconscious or unacknowledged fear, anger, envy, or other emotion. Jones—whose fee was a small fraction of what American therapists charged—was invariably tolerant, patient, understanding, and "both extremely empathic and rigorously honest," according to Saks. After Saks completed her studies at Oxford, she spent an extra year in England so as to continue her treatment with Jones. During that time she audited courses in psychology and volunteered at a mental hospital.

In late summer 1982 Saks enrolled at the Yale Law School, but that academic year she spent no more than a few weeks as a student, because shortly after she arrived in New Haven, her psychotic symptoms again became acute. One of her professors brought her to an emergency room; there, when she refused to relinquish a six-inch nail she had found on a school-building roof during a psychotic episode, she was immobilized with leather restraints and forced to swallow an antipsychotic drug. From there she was admitted to the Yale Psychiatric Institute. During her 15-hour stay there, workers pinned her arms and legs to her bed with leather straps and further restricted her movements by covering her with a tight net that extended from her neck to her ankles. "No single hallucination, no threat of demonic forces or impulses I couldn't control had ever held me hostage like this," Saks wrote in her memoir, recalling her terror and rage at being shackled and the considerable physical pain the straps caused. During the next three weeks, while at the Psychiatric Evaluation Unit of Yale–New Haven Hospital, she was repeatedly restrained in the same way. Saks has since publicly denounced the use of such restraints (which ended in Great Britain two centuries ago) as counterproductive as well as cruel. "Once the force ceases, the patient has no incentive not to return to the ways he or she never rejected for him- or herself," she noted to Robert A. Burt in a discussion transcribed for *American Imago* (Summer 2008), a journal co-founded by Freud. "Perhaps more important, the person is deterred from seeking future treatment, lest he or she be subjected to inhumane treatment again."

While in the Yale–New Haven Hospital, Saks, for the first time, received a specific diagnosis: "chronic paranoid schizophrenia with acute exacerbation"; her prospects for improvement, she learned, were slim. Before that point, although she had read an enormous amount about psychology and mental illness, she had held fast to the belief that other people also suffered from scrambled, violent, frightening, delusional thoughts but "were simply more adept than I at masking the craziness, and presenting a healthy, competent front to the world. . . . My problem was not that I was crazy; it was that I was weak." In "Some Thoughts on Denial of Mental Illness," published in the *American Journal of Psychiatry* (September 2009), Saks wrote that she had thought of herself as simply "socially maladroit." "The illness was not something happening to me, but something I was doing," she wrote. For that reason, although she knew that her delusions and hallucinations subsided when she took her prescribed pills, she would repeatedly cut the recommended dosage and then stop taking the medication altogether.

That self-destructive behavior ended in the late 1990s: as Saks recalled in "Some Thoughts on Denial of Mental Illness," one of her "rationalizations," "that I was choosing to think or do things that might happen to look like schizophrenia symptoms, fell apart when I noticed something about my behavior. A friend told me that a drug we were both on made her tap her toes. Well, I was constantly tapping my toes, too, but I totally resisted the idea that it was a side effect of the medicine. This was something I was choosing to do, not something that was 'happening' to me. I could stop it whenever I wanted. (I overlooked the fact that within a short time, I would be doing it again, unless I constantly attended and tried to stop.) One day I got on a new drug, and the toe-tapping stopped. It occurred to me that on some level, the toe-tapping was a side effect of the medication and not something I was choosing to do. It became ob-

vious to me that as much as I tried—and I tried very hard—when I got off medication, I would get symptoms. And I started to think that the delusional beliefs were like the toe-tapping—symptoms of an illness and not something I was choosing. With that belief came an acceptance that I indeed had a mental illness. (And with this acceptance, paradoxically, my illness came to define me much less.)"

By that time Saks had established herself as an outstanding legal scholar and educator. While in law school she had served as editor of the *Yale Law Journal* and won the Francis Wayland Prize, given to the student "showing greatest proficiency in preparing and presenting a case in negotiation, arbitration, and litigation," according to the school's Web site. She had gained tenure at USC and earned a named professorship at its law school; published two books; penned articles for journals including the *International Journal of Law and Psychiatry*, the *Journal of Contemporary Legal Issues*, *Psychiatric Quarterly*, and the *Public Affairs Quarterly*; and embarked on funded research into issues concerning mental capacity and the law. In addition, she had formed many precious friendships, among them one with the man she later married.

In the past decade Saks's research has focused on "ethical dimensions of psychiatric research and forced treatment of the mentally ill," according to weblaw.usc.edu, and coping mechanisms used by high-functioning schizophrenics. After serving for five years (2005–10) as the associate dean for research at USC's law school, Saks returned to the classroom, teaching courses in mental-health law, the links between that branch of law and the criminal-justice system, and aspects of family law.

In *The Center Cannot Hold: My Journey Through Madness* (written with the help of Larkin Warren), in addition to her struggles with mental illness and her experiences as a student and teacher, Saks described her hospitalization for a life-threatening brain bleed (whose symptoms were at first dismissed as manifestations of her psychosis) and her bouts with breast cancer and ovarian cancer. The side effects of antipsychotic medications can be extremely serious, and one or another of those that Saks took may have played a role in her having those cancers. It is possible that by avoiding medication for long periods, Saks was spared other injurious side effects. She has also maintained that her strongmindedness regarding her course of treatment helped her immeasurably in becoming a highly functioning person. "I hope that the book will remind readers that everyone has challenges and problems to overcome," Saks said to Lee Randall. "In that sense it's every person's story. It's not the story of one woman who, through the sheer force of will, defied the odds! A huge amount of resources were put into me: treatment for years and years, medication, friends who were supportive, family, my husband. If more resources were put into the mental health system a lot of people could live up to their personal potential."

With part of her MacArthur Foundation prize money, Saks plans to set up the Saks Institute for Mental Health Law, Policy, and Ethics at USC. According to weblaw.usc.edu, the institute "will spotlight one important mental health issue per academic year and is a collaborative effort that includes faculty from seven USC departments: law, psychiatry, psychology, social work, gerontology, philosophy and engineering."

Saks met her husband, Will Vinet, when he was working in the USC law library; his current vocations include carpentry. The couple live in a condominium apartment in the Westwood section of Los Angeles.

—H.R.W.

Suggested Reading: *American Imago* p309+ Summer 2008; *American Journal of Psychiatry* p972+ Sep. 2009; *Behavioral Health Central* (on-line) May 30, 2009; *Scotsman* p12+ Oct. 6, 2007; *Ventura County (California) Star* (on-line) May 17, 2008; *Washington Post* C p10 Sep. 22, 2009; weblaw.usc.edu; Saks, Elyn R. *The Center Cannot Hold: My Journey Through Madness*, 2007

Selected Books: *Jekyll on Trial: Multiple Personality Disorder and Criminal Law* (written with Stephen H. Behnke), 1997; *Interpreting Interpretation: The Limits of Hermeneutic Psychoanalysis*, 1999; *Refusing Care: Forced Treatment and the Rights of the Mentally Ill*, 2002; *The Center Cannot Hold: My Journey Through Madness*, 2007

Emmanuel Dunand/AFP/Getty Images

Santorum, Rick

(san-TORE-um)

May 10, 1958– Former U.S. senator from Pennsylvania (Republican); presidential candidate

Address: Santorum for President Iowa Headquarters, 11306 Aurora Ave., Urbandale, IA 50322

On June 6, 2011 former U.S senator Rick Santorum of Pennsylvania announced on the ABC program *Good Morning America* that he was entering the race for the 2012 Republican presidential nomination. Santorum is often referred to as a "culture warrior" for his fervently conservative views on family, religion, marriage, and abortion; a devout Catholic, Santorum was included on the *Time* magazine (February 7, 2005) list of the "25 Most Influential Evangelicals." "Never underestimate the power of social issues" among voters, he once said, as quoted in an editorial by George Will for the *Washington Post* (February 3, 2011); indeed, his stances on those issues have proved to be both a large factor in his political success and the chief source of ammunition for his critics. Santorum first gained attention as a brash, outspoken young U.S. congressman in the early 1990s, when he became a member of the House "Gang of Seven," who strongly criticized some of their colleagues' banking practices. In 1995, at the start of his first Senate term, he sponsored a bill to ban so-called partial-birth abortion; growing heated in debates, Santorum called any exception to the ban—including those to safeguard the health of the mother—"phony" and a "loophole" sought by those plagued by "selfishness" and "individual self-centeredness," as quoted by Marie Diamond in *ThinkProgress* (June 8, 2011). In 2003, during his second Senate term, Santorum made a statement regarding *Lawrence vs. Texas*, a U.S. Supreme Court case involving that state's sodomy law, in which he famously—or infamously—mentioned homosexual relations in the same sentence with bestiality. "I have no problem with homosexuality," he maintained, as quoted in *USA Today* (April 23, 2003, on-line). "I have a problem with homosexual acts." He took issue with the right to privacy, or the idea that "you can do whatever you want to do, as long as it's in the privacy of your own home," he told an Associated Press (April 7, 2003) reporter. "If the Supreme Court says that you have the right to [gay] consensual sex within your home," he said, as quoted by Geoff Earle in the *Hill*

(April 30, 2003), "then you have the right to biga-my, you have the right to polygamy, you have the right to incest, you have the right to adultery. You have the right to anything." Santorum's support for a constitutional amendment to ban same-sex mar-riage has drawn fury from the gay, lesbian, bisex-ual, and transgender (LGBT) community, and he recently told David Gregory on the NBC show *Meet the Press* (June 12, 2011) that he supported bring-ing criminal charges against doctors who perform abortions. While many argue that such views re-flect a dangerous moral fanaticism, supporters tout Santorum's rhetoric as brave. "He is not a pander-er," Mark McKinnon, a political strategist and for-mer critic of Santorum, wrote for the *Daily Beast* (June 6, 2011, on-line). "He believes what he be-lieves. And he is willing to take unpopular stands."

Though he is best known for his views on moral-ity, Santorum has been a champion of antipoverty legislation, working closely with Democrats with the aim of helping low-income families. Michael Sokolove noted in a profile of Santorum for the *New York Times Magazine* (May 22, 2005, on-line) that during his time in the Senate, Santorum re-spected Democratic colleagues who were "deter-mined, passionate liberals." Santorum said to Sokolove, "That's what political discourse is all about. You bring in your moral code, or worldview, and I bring in mine."

Richard John Santorum was born on May 10, 1958 in Winchester, Virginia, to Aldo Santorum, an Italian immigrant and clinical psychologist who died in 2011, and Catherine (Dughi) Santorum, a nurse. Both of Santorum's parents were employed by the Veterans Administration (VA), and he and his siblings (an older sister and a younger brother) spent much of their childhood, beginning when Santorum was seven, living on the grounds of a VA hospital in Butler, Pennsylvania, near Pittsburgh. Family life was defined more by a shared enthusi-asm for sports than by Catholicism, though the Santorums considered themselves religious and at-tended church every Sunday. "You had to basical-ly be dead not to go," Santorum told Michael Sokolove. "If you could watch television, if you could get up and walk, you could go." Prayers be-fore dinner and bedtime were a part of Santorum's upbringing; politics was not. "I didn't even know if my parents were Republicans or Democrats," Rick Santorum's brother, Dan, told Sokolove, "and I don't know if Rick knew either." The summer be-fore Santorum's senior year of high school, the family moved to the Chicago, Illinois, area. San-torum played basketball for Carmel High School, in Illinois, and served as the team manager. As a teenager he earned the nickname "Rooster" for his competitive spirit and a cowlick that stood straight up on the back of his head. "He would debate any-thing and everything with you, mostly sports," his high-school classmate Larry Goettler told Mike Newall for the *Philadelphia City Paper* (September 29, 2005). "He was like a rooster. He never backed down."

Santorum graduated from high school in 1976 and then enrolled at Pennsylvania State Universi-ty, where he was inspired to study political science after working on the U.S. Senate campaign of the Republican John Heinz to fulfill a class require-ment. Santorum became active and outspoken po-litically; by the time he was a senior, he had re-vived the Penn State Republican Club and become the state chairman of the College Republicans. He was also a member of the Tau Epsilon Phi fraterni-ty. Santorum earned a B.A. degree in 1980 and an M.B.A. degree from the University of Pittsburgh in 1981. While attending the Dickinson School of Law, in Carlisle, Pennsylvania, he worked as an ad-ministrative assistant for Doyle Corman, a moder-ate, pro-choice Republican Pennsylvania state sen-ator. "[Santorum] had an innate ability of under-standing politics," Corman told Newall, "and knew how to get business done." Santorum re-ceived a J.D. degree in 1986. In 1987 he became an associate at the law firm of Kirkpatrick & Lockhart, where his clients included World Wrestling Enter-tainment.

In 1990 Santorum ran for a U.S. House seat in Pennsylvania's 18th District against the seven-term Democratic incumbent, Doug Walgren. When he announced his intentions, friends and family were surprised by his ambition. "I figured he'd run for borough councilman or something like that first, but that's not Rick's style," Santorum's former roommate Ray Conlon told Newall. A win for San-torum was considered such a slight possibility that even the Republican National Committee refused to make a donation to his campaign. Santorum ap-pealed to the Christian right for support. "Having returned to my Church after a period of absence, I now understand the connection between a person-al, vibrant faith commitment and the moral fiber of our nation's need," he wrote in his campaign litera-ture, as quoted by Newall. (According to his friends and family members, Santorum became a strict Roman Catholic after meeting his future wife, Karen.) After reportedly knocking on more than 25,000 doors, Santorum (outspent by Walgren, $717,000 to $251,000) won the race with 51 per-cent of the vote. As a freshman congressman San-torum joined the feisty "Gang of Seven," which in-cluded his fellow first-term representatives John Boehner of Ohio, John Doolittle of California, Scott Klug of Wisconsin, Jim Nussle of Iowa, Frank Riggs of California, and Charles Taylor of North Carolina. The group helped expose congressional banking practices in which representatives were allowed to overdraw their House checking accounts without penalty. The Gang of Seven also criticized such congressional perks as the House-subsidized res-taurant and barber shop. Santorum was reelected in 1992 even though—due to redistricting de-signed for his defeat—his constituency had be-come largely Democratic. Also in 1992 he earned a seat on the House Ways and Means Committee, while also serving as the ranking minority member of the Subcommittee on Human Resources.

Almost immediately after his reelection, Santorum began his Senate campaign. In 1994 he faced the Democrat Harris Wofford, who had been appointed to the Senate in 1991, after the death of Senator John Heinz in a plane crash. During the heated campaign Santorum emphasized his support for medical savings accounts and his opposition to gun control. Meanwhile, Wofford, a former civil rights activist, talked about the need for government-sponsored health care (though the healthcare legislation proposed by President Bill Clinton had recently failed to pass) and his support of the 1994 crime bill, aimed at stricter gun control. Santorum won with a little over 49 percent of the vote to Wofford's 47 percent. Santorum called his victory, as quoted by Anick Jesdanun for the Associated Press (November 9, 1994), "a referendum against big government." Of the reputation he had made for himself in the House, Santorum added to Jesdanun, "I suspect I will be a rabble-rouser in the Senate as well." At the time, while Santorum was an outspoken advocate of smaller government and reduced taxes, his name was not yet synonymous in the public mind with the social conservatism that would distinguish him as one of the most right-wing members of the Republican Party. "Although conservative," Jesdanun wrote in 1994, "Santorum has not openly joined the family values campaign of the religious right. He said he considers himself an independent thinker and is not afraid to criticize colleagues or make unpopular proposals." After being sworn in Santorum was appointed to serve on the Armed Services and Agriculture Committees.

Santorum's first act as a "rabble-rouser" in the Senate came in 1995, when he took to the floor during budget meetings with a homemade sign that read "Where's Bill?"—a reference to what Santorum saw as a lack of leadership on President Clinton's part during budget negotiations. In 1996 Santorum was the Senate's floor manager in the creation of the Personal Responsibility and Work Opportunity Reconciliation Act, or the welfare-reform bill of 1996. Among the provisions of the legislation—which President Clinton signed into law on August 22, 1996—were a five-year limit on federal welfare benefits, a requirement for able-bodied recipients of aid to go to work after two years, and incentives for states to create jobs for people on welfare. President Clinton had vetoed two earlier versions of the bill that he thought provided too little protection for poor children. "I believe that if you play by the rules, you can provide for your family and live the American dream," Santorum told Sharon Brooks Hodge for *Headway* magazine (January 31, 1996). "Everyone wants to paint [welfare reform] as hurting children to save money. That's not what it's about." He added that he did not know the total amount of the cuts in funding. "It's not like we set out to cut $40 million," he said to Sharon Brooks Hodge. "Our vision was to try and make this system work for more Americans." President Clinton acknowl-

edged, as quoted by AllPolitics.com (August 22, 1996), that the legislation was not perfect but represented an important step in overcoming "the flaws of the welfare system for the people who are trapped in it." A decade later the *New York Times* columnist David Brooks called the reform (October 29, 2006) "the most successful piece of domestic legislation of the past 10 years." He added, "Almost every time a serious piece of antipoverty legislation surfaces in Congress, Rick Santorum is there playing a leadership role." During his time in the Senate, Santorum worked with Democrats to sponsor legislation including measures aimed at combating the global AIDS epidemic, providing Third World debt relief, establishing savings accounts for children of low-income families, instituting home-ownership tax credits, and rewarding saving by low-income families.

Personal tragedy struck Santorum and his family in 1996, while he was working on legislation that would ban what are often called partial-birth abortions (those performed after 4.5 months of pregnancy). When Santorum's wife, Karen, was in the early stages of pregnancy with the couple's fourth child, sonograms revealed that the fetus suffered from a fatal defect and would not be able to survive outside the womb for more than a short time. The family was devastated. Karen soon developed a life-threatening intrauterine infection; doctors told her that to save her life they needed to induce labor, a procedure the Santorums equated with abortion, since it would result in the unborn child's death. Then, after 20 weeks of pregnancy, Karen went into labor naturally. The Santorums named the baby—who lived for only two hours—Gabriel. "What happened after the death is a kind of snapshot of a cultural divide," Sokolove wrote. "Some would find it discomforting, strange, even ghoulish—others brave and deeply spiritual." Instead of allowing the corpse to be taken to a morgue immediately, Santorum and his wife spent the night in the hospital with Gabriel between them, then took him home to show his siblings. Karen wrote a book, *Letters to Gabriel: The True Story of Gabriel Michael Santorum* (1998), chronicling the family's experience. In it she referred to her husband's work in the Senate, writing: "When the partial-birth abortion vote comes to the floor of the U.S. Senate for the third time, your daddy needs to proclaim God's message for life with even more strength and devotion for the cause." (The Partial Birth Abortion Ban Act was signed into law by President George W. Bush in 2003. The U.S. Supreme Court upheld the constitutionality of the ban, 5–4, in 2007 in *Gonzales v. Carhart.*) Newall quoted Santorum as writing in his 2005 book *It Takes a Family*, "Life changes us all, but often nothing like death. . . . After Gabriel, being a husband, being a father was different, being a legislator was different. I was different."

In 2000 Santorum won his bid for reelection, defeating Ron Klink, a Democrat and four-term congressman from western Pennsylvania. Santorum became the chairman of the Senate Republican Conference, making him his party's third-highest-ranking member in the Senate. In the first years of his second term, Santorum focused on legislation to allow government grants for faith-based antipoverty organizations (similar to a provision in the 1996 welfare-reform law) and on an aggressive initiative, known as the K Street Project, to increase the number of Republicans among Washington, D.C., lobbyists. (The project was named for a Washington street on which many lobbying firms are headquartered.) The Senate Ethics Committee objected to the K Street Project after allegations that senators were using party affiliation to decide which lobbyists were granted access to them or their staffs. With Senator Joseph Lieberman, a then-Democrat from Connecticut, Santorum took a lead role in seeking tax deductions and credits for faith-based organizations under an executive order from President George W. Bush. The legislation stalled due to objections over granting federal funds to groups that might discriminate on the basis of religion or sexual orientation. Also during his second term, Santorum called for additional patrol agents at the U.S.'s northern and southern borders; sought to discourage international investment in Iran's energy sector, as a way of thwarting that country's nuclear ambitions; advocated the promotion of democracy in Iran; co-sponsored legislation to end dependence on foreign oil; and helped pass the Stem Cell Therapeutic and Research Act of 2005, which allowed for the storage of human-umbilical-cord-blood stem cells for research and treatment of disease.

In 2005 Santorum published the book *It Takes a Family: Conservatism and the Common Good*. The title is a jab at Hillary Clinton's 1996 book *It Takes a Village: And Other Lessons Children Teach Us*, which called for a society that viewed the welfare of children as a collective responsibility best carried out with the help of government. Santorum disputed that notion, likening the "village" to "big" government, whose involvement in child-rearing he viewed as a dangerous infringement upon the family unit—which he believes is the foundation of a stable society. In his view the advocates of a "top-down" approach to society— "bigs" or "village elders," as he referred to them disparagingly in his book—include "big news media, big entertainment, big universities and public schools, some big businesses and some big national labor unions, and, of course the biggest Big of all, the federal government." Among the controversial topics discussed in the book is the notion that radical feminism has led to a culture that does not respect stay-at-home mothers. Santorum also argued that there should be a stronger emphasis on personal responsibility when it comes to raising children. "We have a culture around us that elevates and celebrates freedom that is equivalent with license or simply choice instead of a freedom that says we have a responsibility to do what we ought to do, not to do simply what we want to do," Santorum wrote in response to a reader's question on the *Washington Post* Web site (July 25, 2005). "And that's where my definition of selfless freedom comes in. The place we learn about selflessness first is the family, from mom and dad, who sacrifice their wants and desires for the benefit of one another and their children, and where children are told that they must sacrifice for the benefit of the family. When the family breaks down, the lesson often is never taught or modeled." Santorum is also the author of *Rick Santorum: A Senator Speaks Out on Life, Freedom, and Responsibility* (2005).

Santorum faced reelection again in 2006. His challenger was Bob Casey, a Democrat and a son of former Pennsylvania governor Bob Casey Sr. The race proved to be extremely tough for Santorum, and for the first time, his controversial views appeared to repel more voters in his state than they attracted. "People want to go in a new direction," Casey said on the campaign trail, as quoted by Danielle Knight in *U.S. News & World Report* (August 28, 2006), referring to the deeply unpopular Bush administration. "Senator Santorum's record has been a 98 percent voting record with the president." Santorum's finances also came under scrutiny after he received over $70,000 from the Penn Hills public school district to offset tuition costs for "cyber-schooling" for his children (who were being home-schooled). Though the Santorums had once maintained a residence near Penn Hills, the family now lived in Virginia, making them ineligible to receive aid. It was also discovered that Santorum's charitable organization, the Operation Good Neighbor Foundation, had used only 40 percent of its $1.25 million expenditure between 2001 and 2004 for charity. (A spokesperson for the foundation said that nearly 37 percent of spending was on fund-raising events.) With slipping approval ratings, Santorum was considered one of the most vulnerable incumbents in the midterm election. In November 2006 he lost by a 17-point margin, which most attributed to his support of the war in Iraq and the president's proposed plan for privatizing Social Security. Following his defeat Santorum served for several years as a senior fellow at the Ethics and Public Policy Center, a think tank, and he has been a frequent contributor to Fox News. He also practiced law at the Washington, D.C., branch of the firm Eckert Seamans Cherin & Mellott, LLC. Santorum continued to air his views publicly, expressing skepticism, for example, over the human causes of global warming.

Currently, in seeking the 2012 Republican presidential nomination, Santorum is rallying his conservative base in early-primary states such as Iowa, New Hampshire, and South Carolina. He has assured listeners that he is "in it to win." He said of his record, as quoted by Colby Itkowitz in the *Allentown (Pennsylvania) Morning Call* (June 6, 2011), "If you look back at what I did and when I did it, people can say: You know what? He may have lost but he didn't flinch. He stood by what he believed in and he continued the fight through the end."

Santorum met his wife, Karen, who is trained as both a nurse and an attorney, in 1989. The couple have seven children: Elizabeth, John, Daniel, Sarah, Peter, Patrick, and Isabella, a toddler, who was diagnosed with the genetic disorder Trisomy 18, which is caused by a chromosome defect and affects both mental and physical development. Few victims survive beyond childhood. The family lives in Leesburg, Virginia.

—M.M.H.

Suggested Reading: *Allentown (Pennsylvania) Morning Call* (on-line) June 6, 2011; AllPolitics.com Aug. 22, 1996; Associated Press (on-line) Nov. 9, 1994; *Campaigns & Elections* p43 Oct./Nov. 2005; *Daily Beast* (on-line) June 6, 2011; *Headway* p10 Jan. 31, 1996; *Hill* p4 Apr. 30, 2003; *Meet the Press* (on-line) June 12, 2011; *New York Times* (on-line) May 22, 2005, Oct. 29, 2006; *Philadelphia City Paper* (on-line) Sep. 29, 2005; *Philadelphia Inquirer* (on-line) Oct. 22, 2010; *Pittsburgh City Paper* p19 May 7, 2003; *U.S. News & World Report* (on-line) Aug. 28, 2006; *Washington Post* (on-line) Feb. 3, 2011, July 25, 2005; Santorum, Karen. *Letters to Gabriel: The True Story of Gabriel Michael Santorum*, 1998

Selected Books: *Rick Santorum: A Senator Speaks Out on Life, Freedom, and Responsibility*, 2005; *It Takes a Family: Conservatism and the Common Good*, 2005

Quentin Huys, courtesy of Daniela Schiller

Schiller, Daniela

Oct. 26, 1972– Cognitive neuroscientist

Address: Mount Sinai Medical Center, Atran Berg Laboratory Bldg., Rm. 218, 1428 Madison Ave., New York, NY 10029

According to the Israeli-born cognitive neuroscientist Daniela Schiller, "These are really interesting times in science, because in the last 10 years there has been a change in the way we see memory." One of the most significant aspects of that change stems from the discovery that unlike, say, a diamond necklace, which remains the same every time it is retrieved from and then replaced in a safe deposit box, a memory is not set in stone after its formation in the brain, in a process called consolidation. Rather, it evolves: every time the memory is retrieved to become a conscious thought, it returns to its storage place in a chemically altered form—that is, it is updated or reconsolidated, with molecular changes at the cellular level. If the memory is associated with fear, the conscious feeling of fear that the memory induces changes as well each time it is recalled; often, that feeling becomes stronger. For her doctoral dissertation, earned at Tel Aviv University, in Israel, Schiller studied memory formation and retrieval in mice. Since 2004, when she arrived at New York University (NYU) as a postdoctoral student to conduct research under the neuroscientists Joseph LeDoux and Elizabeth Phelps, she has studied the same phenomena in humans. "That's exactly where the science is now," Schiller told *Current Biography* (the source of quotes in this article unless otherwise stated): "starting to translate everything to the human brain and the clinical population"—that is, people with psychological problems. In an article published in the journal *Nature* in January 2010, Schiller reported that in an experiment with humans that did not include the use of drugs, she and her team at NYU determined that in applying therapeutic techniques to eliminate fear associated with painful memories, the timing of those techniques appears to be crucial. "Our research suggests that during the lifetime of a memory there are windows of opportunity where it becomes susceptible to be permanently changed," Schiller said, according to an NYU press release (December 9, 2009, on-line). "By understanding the dynamics of memory we might, in the long run, open new avenues of treatment for disorders that involve abnormal emotional memories"—in particular, more-effective ways to help the many people who suffer from post-traumatic stress disorder (PTSD) as a result of having experienced such frightening events as earthquakes and other natural disasters, armed conflicts, rape, torture, terrorist attacks, and plane or car crashes. For her highly innovative work and its potential benefits to humanity, Schiller earned the Blavatnik Award for Young Scientists from the New York Academy of Sciences in 2010. Also that year the Mount Sinai Medical Center in New York City recruited Schiller to set up a research program in cognitive and affective neuroscience within its Department of Psychiatry.

The youngest of the four children of Zigmund Schiller and his wife, Daniela Schiller was born on October 26, 1972 in Rishon LeZion, Israel, near Tel Aviv. Her mother, a nurse, worked at night. In an instance of her childhood anxieties, Schiller remembers calling out for her mother on many nights even when she knew her mother was not home. Her father was a "very reserved" man, as she described him, and he steadfastly refused to talk about his experiences as a Holocaust survivor. But in Israel schoolchildren begin learning about the Holocaust from a young age, "and what I heard in school was very horrifying," Schiller said. On Holocaust Remembrance Day, an annual event in Israel, documentaries about the Holocaust air on TV, and when a siren sounds at 10:00 a.m., all activities in the country halt for two minutes, to honor the estimated six million Jews and millions of others killed by German Nazis during World War II. Early on Schiller absorbed the lesson that "everything that happens to you is nothing compared to the Holocaust," and "that's how you judge things." Among those "things" were a childhood skateboard accident, to which she forced herself to respond without tears, and the beatings she occasionally suffered at the hands of neighborhood children who thought she looked German.

Schiller met a German in person for the first time during her teens, when she spent a summer on a kibbutz—one of the approximately 250 settlements in Israel where up to a few hundred families live communally; volunteers from overseas often work in such communities for varying lengths of time. One evening Johann, a young volunteer from Berlin, Germany, began to read to her from a book of German poetry. Previously, Schiller had heard German spoken only in movies about the Holocaust, and the sound of the words "pouring" from Johann's lips terrified her. "I start to see images of Nazis pushing Jews into trailers, skeletal humans behind barbed wires, smoke coming out of gas chambers, until I scream, 'Stop!'" Unable to explain her reaction, she pretended to Johann that he had stepped on her toes.

In Israel, with a few exceptions, military service is required after high school for all non-Arab Israeli men (who must serve three years) and women (who must serve two years). Schiller wanted to serve in a combat unit, but in 1991, when she joined the army, such assignments were virtually nonexistent for women. The recommendation of a teacher who had seen her in a high-school play led to her recruitment as a producer by the army's entertainment and education division. She produced shows written, directed, and performed for active-duty soldiers by members of the Israeli army and

reservists. After she completed her military service, in 1993, she became a producer of concerts and lectures on science, history, and art for the general public. She also became the drummer for a band, called the Rebellion Movement, which played "original Hebrew rock influenced by American folk-rock," in her words.

Concurrently, Schiller attended Tel Aviv University. She earned a B.A. degree in psychology and philosophy in 1996 and a Ph.D. degree in cognitive neuroscience in 2004; in the interim she taught courses in psychology at Tel Aviv University and elsewhere. Her dissertation concerned a facet of emotional learning in schizophrenics: "the ability to acquire emotional responses to previously ignored stimuli, which is impaired in patients suffering from chronic schizophrenia," as she described it for the Web site psych.nyu.edu. The failure to react to stimuli is called persistent latent inhibition. Working in the laboratory of Ina Weiner, who studies the use of antipsychotic drugs in treating schizophrenia, Schiller developed a model for studying persistent latent inhibition in mice. (Injecting certain viruses in pregnant mice has been found to produce schizophrenia-like behavior in their offspring during what is equivalent to adolescence in humans.) Schiller then examined the neural circuitry associated with schizophrenia in the rodents' brains and investigated the benefits, if any, of antipsychotic drugs given to the mice. An article and abstracts about her research that she co-authored appeared in the journal *Neural Plasticity* in 2002 and the journals *European Neuropsychopharmacology* and *Biological Psychiatry* in 2003, respectively.

In experiments regarding memory formation and retrieval in rats or mice, scientists can observe the animals' behavior, measure their physiological responses (for example, changes in blood pressure and quantities of hormones circulating in the blood), and observe changes in brain scans. In Joseph LeDoux's experiments involving conditioned learning, rats would soon ignore a repeated, non-threatening sound; they would freeze and arch their backs and their hearts would beat faster when their feet were subjected to mild electric shocks accompanied by the same sound. After a sufficient number of repetitions of those two stimuli, the sound and the shock, they would freeze, and their heartbeats accelerate, upon hearing the sound alone, without the shock. LeDoux discovered that only one part of the brain—the amygdala—was necessary for such fear conditioning. Furthermore, every time the sound triggered the retrieval of the rats' "fear" memory, reconsolidation of that memory took place: particular neurons in the amygdala underwent molecular changes, including the synthesis of new proteins—changes that could be detected after the memory went back into storage.

Researchers can observe behavioral responses to stimuli in humans, too, and they can measure people's physiological responses and scan their brains; in addition, while with nonhuman animals "you don't have access to what they actually know," in Schiller's words, scientists can ask people to describe their memories and their feelings (though such descriptions can never be considered complete, since no person can know precisely what another person is thinking or feeling). But everyday memory formation and retrieval is far more complicated in humans than it is in mice or other animals, not least because of the role of language in those phenomena and the far more complex cultural and social environments in which people form their memories. "It's not at all clear that you can translate all the information acquired in animals to humans, especially to traumatic memories because we don't have a laboratory model for traumatic memories; [they are] just too intense, too complex to create," Schiller said.

Schiller devised her groundbreaking, three-day experiment with the aid of LeDoux and the psychologist Elizabeth Phelps after she came to NYU as a postdoctoral researcher, in 2004. Since memory research is still in its infancy, experiments involving humans rely on a simple, clearcut stimulus-response setup. Schiller's subjects, 65 men and women, faced a computer screen on which a blue square and yellow square would flash repeatedly, but not at the same time. Sometimes the flashing yellow square would be accompanied by a mild electric shock administered to the subjects' wrists. The shock caused the subjects to sweat (a classic fear response), which in turn reduced their skin's resistance to the conduction of electricity—a phenomenon known as galvanic skin response. (Galvanic skin response is the basis of lie-detector tests.) The next day Schiller divided the subjects into three groups. The people in each group experienced fear when the yellow squares flashed on the screen, though no shocks were administered. Then, between 10 minutes and six hours later, the first group received therapy known as "extinction training": the yellow squares were again flashed repeatedly without any shocks. The second group underwent extinction training more than six hours later. The third group (the control) received no extinction training. On the third day the subjects in the first group had no fear response when they saw the flashing yellow squares, but those in the second and control groups responded with increased sweating. Those results indicated that within six hours of the retrieval of a memory of a fearful experience, that memory can be replaced by a new one (through extinction training) that does not induce fear. When conducted after six hours, extinction training leads to the formation of a second, newly consolidated memory, and both the first and the second memories return to the brain's storage cells. When Schiller retested 19 of her subjects a year later, those from the first group, for whom extinction training had erased their fear, reacted with little fear (as measured by their galvanic skin response) to the combination of flashing yellow squares and shocks, while people in the other two groups responded as fearfully as they had a year earlier.

"The aim is not to erase the memory altogether; we just want to block the emotional aspect of it," Schiller said.

According to the December 9, 2009 NYU press release, Phelps said, "Previous attempts to disrupt fear memories have relied on pharmacological interventions"—that is, drugs. "Our results suggest such invasive techniques may not be necessary." Avoiding the use of drugs would avoid the side effects, ranging from mild to potentially life-threatening, that are associated with virtually every medication (though some individuals may not experience any). Moreover, the testing of drugs for use in humans is invariably a years-long, enormously expensive process that must start with extensive testing in nonhuman animals. Thus, "using a more natural intervention that captures the adaptive purpose of reconsolidation," in Phelps's words, would be both far less expensive and safer.

Currently, Schiller is using magnetic resonance imaging (MRI) to determine the neurological links between memory and fear. "That's the next big question," she said. "In animals, we know that in particular the amygdala is an area that is critical for the formation of such associations. If you target this particular region during reconsolidation you can permanently block emotional memories in animals. In humans I'm working on the same thing with MRI scanners—scan the brain while [people] form these memories and they reactivate them, while they are exposed to a new learning, and how it's incorporated—and how they express the memory later."

Schiller, whose recreational interests include sky diving, said, "I think I did my own independent investigation of fear in my personal life because the aim was always to overcome fear, so I was very attuned to what I feel, how to overcome it, what I feel after. . . . Fear is like a barrier and I was annoyed. I think it's the general relationship people have with their emotions. . . . Emotions can take over. They steer you in a certain way, they color the way you think, what you do, what you're willing to do, what you avoid, so they have a lot of power. I'm interested in that power because I think it's unjustified."

Schiller is the drummer for the Amygdaloids, a band whose songwriter, lead vocalist, and rhythm guitarist is Joseph LeDoux. Its other members are Tyler Volk (lead guitarist), an NYU professor of biology, and Nina Curley (bass guitarist), an NYU doctoral student in psychology. Songs on their debut recording, *Heavy Mental* (2007), bear such titles as "Mind Body Problem" and "An Emotional Brain." The country singer Roseanne Cash and the autism expert Simon Baron Cohen contributed to their second album, *Theory of My Mind* (2010), whose 13 tracks include "Mind Over Matter," "Brainstorm," "How Free Is Your Will," "Mists of Memory," and "Fearing." The band performed at NYU's graduation ceremony at Madison Square Garden, in New York City, in May 2007 and at the Kennedy Center, in Washington, D.C., in 2008.

Schiller has also participated in storytelling events and contests arranged by an organization called the Moth.

"You think that either you're an artist or that you're a scientist, but it's actually the same," Schiller said. "You heavily rely on your own creativity and your own ideas. . . . Science, I think more than we realize, relies upon hunch and intuition. It is very methodical, analytical, and logical—but your ideas and the way you think about things is very similar to the creative process. You have insights and unique associations—different feelings that give you a new perspective—like art." Schiller lives in New York City.

—M.M.H.

Suggested Reading: Amygdaloids Web site; *Discovery* (on-line) Dec. 28, 2009; Israel21c.org Dec. 10, 2009, Nov. 28, 2010; (London) *Guardian* (on-line) Dec. 9, 2009; National Institutes of Health (on-line) Dec. 9, 2009; New York Academy of Sciences (on-line) Oct. 21, 2010; *New York Times* (on-line) Mar. 6, 2007; *Scientific American* (on-line) Mar. 23, 2010, June 28, 2010, July 20, 2010; TheBeautifulBrain.com June 4, 2010

Selected Recordings with the Amygdaloids: *Heavy Mental*, 2007; *Theory of My Mind*, 2010

Courtesy of Schaefer & Company Communications

Schreiber, Ryan

Jan. 26, 1976– Founder and CEO of Pitchfork.com

Address: Pitchfork Media, *2035 W. Wabansia Ave., #2, Chicago, IL 60647*

In 1995, at the age of 19, having ruled out continuing his formal education past high school, Ryan Schreiber singlehandedly launched the Web site *PitchforkMedia.com* from a makeshift office in the basement of his parents' home. Although he had never counted writing among his strengths, Schreiber was determined to use the rapidly developing Internet to share with the outside world his preoccupation with indie rock and other underground music and parlay his passion into a career. Since

then, judging by its approximately 30 million page views per month, *Pitchfork.com*, as it is now known, has grown about 100,000 times more popular than it was at the end of its first year of publication. Among fans of indie music, music-store managers, music-label executives, and members of the music media, it has also grown immeasurably more influential. In an article for the *Columbia Journalism Review* (May/June 2006), Kiera Butler labeled *Pitchfork.com* "the first major Web-based tastemaker"; according to Jon Caramanica, writing for the *New York Times* (July 14, 2010, on-line), it is "now the most prominent brand in online music journalism" and is "widely believed to have the power to pluck a band from obscurity and thrust it into the indie consciousness, and to push it out just as quickly." Its dominance in the digital age has been compared to that of the twice-monthly music magazine *Rolling Stone* in the 1970s, and Schreiber himself to Jann Wenner, *Rolling Stone*'s founder and publisher. In 2006 Schreiber organized the first annual Pitchfork Music Festival, in Chicago, Illinois, where *Pitchfork* is headquartered; at the 2010 festival, which "sold out months in advance," as Claire Suddath reported for *Time.com* (August 15, 2010), 54,000 ticket buyers chose from 46 acts. Schreiber's music-video Web site, Pitchfork.tv, debuted in 2008. That year also saw the publication of the book *The Pitchfork 500: Our Guide to the Greatest Songs from Punk to Present*, edited by Schreiber and Scott Plagenhoef, *Pitchfork*'s editor in chief.

Pitchfork.com rates new albums on a scale of 0.0 to 10.0, in increments of 0.1. In 2004 Pitchfork gave a 9.7 rating to *Funeral*, the first album released by the then-unknown Canadian indie-rock band Arcade Fire. "That amazing review was really the band's first validation, saying: 'Everyone needs to pay attention to this,'" Martin Hall, the publicist for Merge Records, the band's label, told J. Freedom du Lac for the *Washington Post* (April 30, 2006). "Before that Arcade Fire had been below the radar. But the floodgates opened." The album became the fastest-selling title in the label's history and reached *Billboard*'s Top 200 album chart. Similarly, in 2005 *Pitchfork*'s 8.5 rating for *The Best Party Ever*, the debut recording of the band Boy Least Likely To, immediately boosted the album's wholesale orders many-fold. By contrast, *Pitchfork*'s 0.0 rating for *Travistan* (2004), a solo album by Travis Morrison, the band Dismemberment Plan's frontman, proved to be its death knell, and the previously well-regarded Morrison found himself in the music world's doghouse. "Up until the day of the review, I'd play a solo show, and people would be like 'That's our boy, our eccentric boy.' Literally, the view changed overnight," Morrison told du Lac.

Some industry insiders have complained that many *Pitchfork* reviewers are "mean-spirited," according to du Lac, and they decry the writers' "cooler-than-thou indie-elitist tone." Stephen Sowley, for example, the product manager of Reckless Records, an independent Chicago store, described *Pitchfork* reviews to du Lac as "smarmy," "not always about the music," and "not polite"; the writers, he charged, "embrace every sort of stereotypical, cynical faction of indie hipsterism." (Nevertheless, he admitted, he visited *Pitchfork.com* "all the time, because I need to know what people are going to come in and ask for. If they give a glowing review to a record, with a high number rating, it goes crazy.") Speaking with Kiera Butler, the longtime *Village Voice* music critic Robert Christgau faulted *Pitchfork* writers for practicing "opinion-wielding for its own sake," and he argued that many were too young or inexperienced to understand the art of criticism. If they "would like to leave their world, and especially go back in history, that's much harder," he said. "They just haven't heard enough music."

Others have lambasted the writers for striving too hard to differentiate their work from reviews in mainstream music publications. Rob Harvilla, for example, wrote for the Oakland, California, *East Bay Express* (March 19, 2004), "In attempting to avoid the colorless blurb graveyard, a *Pitchfork* review can swing the pendulum too far in the other direction: a dense, hugely overwritten, utterly incomprehensible brick of critical fruitcake." In *Pitchfork*'s defense, Schreiber told Lindsey Thomas for the Minneapolis/St. Paul, Minnesota, *City Paper* (June 14, 2006), "I trust the writers to their opinions and to their own style and presentation. The most important thing to me is they know what they're talking about and are insightful. The last thing that I would want to do is dumb it down. . . . More and more criticism is not about criticism; it's about making comparisons. If you like this band, you might like this. To me, that's not what criticism ever was." Schreiber told du Lac, "Honesty is such an important journalistic attribute. And you have to be completely honest in a review. If it gets . . . tempered at all for the sake of not offending somebody, then what we do sort of loses its value. . . . That's so the opposite of what criticism is supposed to be. . . . We're just really

honest, opinionated music fans. We might be completely over the top in our praise, or we might be cruel. But to anybody who reads the site, it's clear that we're not pulling any punches."

Ryan Schreiber was born on January 26, 1976, in Victoria, Minnesota, a suburb of Minneapolis. Even as a child, he told Butler, "I was so into music I was kind of weird. Music was all I ever really wanted to talk about." Schreiber attended Hopkins High School, in nearby Minnetonka, where, he told Lindsey Thomas, he did not strive to excel. "I don't want to say it was all I could do to graduate or that I barely scraped by, but I was not a high achiever by any stretch," he said. When he was a teenager, his musical tastes leaned predominantly toward indie rock; he listened to alternative and college radio stations to hear new bands, and he read fanzines that focused on that mostly unheralded music. "All my friends were doing Xeroxed zines, and some small local papers were able to get interviews with artists that I really liked," he recalled to Dave Itzkoff for *Wired* (September 2006). "I thought 'It can't really be that difficult if these guys are doing it. Why them and not me?'"

After his high-school graduation, Schreiber got a job as a clerk at Down in the Valley, a record store in Golden Valley, another nearby town. When a friend introduced him to the then-nascent Internet, he saw the potential for posting his opinions about underground music on a Web site. "I wanted there to be a resource on the Web that didn't exist at the time," he told Thomas. "Back in the day if you searched for [the art-punk band] Fugazi, you'd get virtually zero results." In 1995, using earnings from his sales of vinyl records—some of them on the then-new Web site eBay.com—Schreiber launched *PitchforkMedia.com*. The site's name was inspired by the pitchfork tattooed on a hand of the character Tony Montana (played by Al Pacino) in Brian De Palma's crime film *Scarface* (1983). "It just seemed concise and easy to say, and it had these evilish overtones," Schreiber told Itzkoff. Schreiber used a computer in his parents' basement and posted album reviews and band interviews monthly. His first published review on the Web site was of *Pacer*, by the Amps, a now-defunct Ohio indie-rock band. "I was just this kid with opinions, and writing was probably not really my forte," he told Lindsey Thomas for the St. Louis, Missouri, *Riverfront Times* (June 28, 2006, online). "But that was the avenue that made the most sense for me at the time. I struggled for a long time in the early years in terms of writing anything that most people would actually want to read." In addition, he confessed to J. Freedom du Lac, "when I started out, it was really about laying into people who really deserved it." In one review frequently cited as an example of *Pitchfork*'s early meanspiritedness, Schreiber wrote of the rock band Stone Temple Pilots and its lead vocalist, Scott Weiland, in a review of their album *Tiny Music . . . Songs from the Vatican Gift Shop* (1996), "There's nothing for sale at the Vatican Gift Shop but lousy, repetitive riffs, wimpy lyrics, and a drug-addled sonofab*tch that should have OD'ed a long time ago."

By the end of its first year, *PitchforkMedia.com* was averaging about 300 page views a day. To pay the freelance writers whose articles supplemented his own, Schreiber sold space on the site to advertisers. To support himself, he worked as a telemarketer. He later moved operations to the basement of his girlfriend's parents' house. (He and that girlfriend, Elizabeth, later married.) In 1999 he quit his telemarketing job and, with his savings and $2,000 accrued from selling some of his albums, moved to Chicago in hopes of turning *Pitchfork* into a full-time career. At one point he became destitute and, according to one source, had to live briefly outside Illinois, in a cabin owned by his parents. Readership was still modest when, in October 2000, an over-the-top paean to the band Radiohead's album *Kid A*, by the *Pitchfork* freelancer Brent DiCrescenzo, boosted readership virtually overnight. "The writing was so purple, so outrageous," Schreiber recalled to Claire Suddath. "People passed it around because it was funny."

Pitchfork's popularity increased further after Schreiber revamped the site, expanding *Pitchfork*'s content with music-related news, longer reviews, and reviews of more types of music. By 2003 the Web site was receiving about 500,000 visitors a month, and prices for ad space had risen to as much as $700. Schreiber moved the Web site's operations from his apartment in Chicago's Wicker Park neighborhood to an office on the city's north side, and he hired one of his freelance writers, Eric Carr, to sell ads. In the next several years, he hired six more full-time staff members and two part-time reporters; by 2006 his stable of freelancers had risen to about 50, and the site was getting about 4.5 million hits per month. Also by that year, according to Thomas, *Pitchfork* had become "the main arbiter of taste among independent music fans—a distinction once claimed by zines, college radio and mainstream music mags." By mid-December 2010 about 1.8 million individuals were viewing the site about 30 million times per month, and *Pitchfork* had a full-time staff of two dozen. His employees included Chris Kaskie, president; Scott Plagenhoef, editor in chief; managing, news, and associate editors; three staff writers; six people handling advertising and business strategy; a technical director, art director, and developer; and six Pitchfork.tv staff members. The site also listed 44 contributing writers. According to Damian Joseph, writing for *BusinessWeek Online* (April 23, 2008), Internet ad consultants estimated that at that time, *Pitchfork*'s ad revenues amounted to "at least $5 million a year." Kaskie, Joseph wrote, revealed to him "only that revenue [had] grown by . . . 70% each of the past four years."

While not quantifiable, the part that *Pitchfork*'s writers' literary and musical proclivities play in the site's success is undoubtedly large. Armed with their extensive knowledge of the indepen-

dent-music scene and their fiercely held judgments, they keep readers updated on music news and offer assessments of albums within a day or two of their releases. Enjoying an unusual amount of creative freedom, they have often produced highly idiosyncratic critiques. "*Pitchfork* is home to the kind of full-on-rant-think-piece-takedown that was once the specialty of long-and-strong journalism legends like Greil Marcus and Lester Bangs," David Carr wrote for the *New York Times* (April 29, 2005). Rob Mitchum, a *Pitchfork* contributor who is also a University of Chicago science writer, told Whet Moser for the *Chicago Tribune* (October 16, 2003) that as a University of Michigan undergraduate who hoped to see his music reviews published in the student newspaper, he "very quickly ran up against the wall of conventional review writing where you go track [by] track." With *Pitchfork*, he continued, "I realized I could write a freeform rant and just type." Moser noted that "like the independent scene *Pitchfork* covers, the magazine's reviews are not only challenging, they're stylistically diverse and sometimes completely unhinged." Greg Kot noted for the *Chicago Tribune* (April 3, 2005) that *Pitchfork* reviews reflected their authors' unbridled enthusiasm for music; their prose, he wrote, "remains wildly erratic, it is fervent; the most hostile reviews are written with the passion of a freshly jilted lover berating her ex." In the last few years, Schreiber and Plagenhoef have tried to improve the quality of *Pitchfork*'s writing; a posted article may represent the last of a series of drafts. They have also extended *Pitchfork*'s coverage to pop, jazz, and other musical genres.

Claire Suddath, who attended the 2010 Pitchfork Music Festival, a three-day event held in July in Union Park, Chicago, wrote for *Time.com*, "It's here at Union Park that the evolution of the term *indie* most clearly manifests itself. After nearly 20 years of changing tastes and label consolidation, *indie* has become a catchall that suggests less what the music sounds like than the type of people who listen to it. The music may be rock or dance or hip-hop, but it all appeals to Pitchfork's shaggy-haired, skinny-jeans-wearing crowd."

In 2007 Schreiber and his wife (but not *Pitchfork*'s offices) moved from Chicago to the New York City borough of Brooklyn. According to Leon Neyfakh, writing for the *New York Observer* (June 23, 2010, on-line), Schreiber attends four or five local shows every week.

—W.D.

Suggested Reading: *Chicago Tribune* C p1 Apr. 3, 2005; *Columbia Journalism Review* p53 May/June 2006; *Crain's Chicago Business* p72 Nov. 5, 2007; (Minneapolis, Minnesota) *Star Tribune* A p1 Sep. 10, 2006; *New York Sun* p13 July 17, 2007; *New York Times* (on-line) July 14, 2010; *Pitchfork.com*; *Slate.com* Nov. 28, 2006; (St. Louis, Missouri) *Riverfront Times* (on-line) June 28, 2006; *Washington Post* N p1+ Apr. 3, 2006

Selected Books: as co-editor—*The Pitchfork 500: Our Guide to the Greatest Songs from Punk to Present*, 2008

Michael Indresano, courtesy of BJ's Wholesale Club

Sen, Laura J.

July 7, 1956– President and CEO of BJ's Wholesale Club

Address: BJ's Wholesale Club Corporate Offices, 1 Mercer Rd., Natick, MA 01760

Since 2009 Laura J. Sen has been the chief executive officer (CEO) of BJ's Wholesale Club, which sells a wide variety of household items at discounted prices to customers who each pay an annual membership fee to shop at one of the company's almost 200 locations. Although smaller than such competitors as Sam's Club (which is owned by Walmart) and Costco, BJ's has earned a spot on the Fortune 500, appearing on the 2011 list at number 221, with reported annual profits of $95 million. Sen, one of the few female CEOs of a Fortune 500 firm, has been widely praised for her management style; she spends at least 20 percent of her time walking the aisles of BJ's clubs, talking to employees and shoppers. She told Catherine Elton for the *Boston Globe* (January 9, 2011): "I say to the team members [employees], 'If you had a magic wand, what would you do?' And then I pause and say, 'Because I have a magic wand.'" "That is why she is so successful," Burt Flickinger III, a retail consultant, told Elton. "Most of her competitors tend to spend their time behind their desks in corporate headquarters or spend excessive time with Wall

Street analysts, bankers, or investors. Laura is fully focused on the front lines."

Laura J. Sen was born on July 7, 1956 and raised with her two siblings in Wakefield, Massachusetts. Her mother, an Irish-American, and father, a Chinese-American, met while working for the Massachusetts Department of Transportation, she as a secretary and he as an engineer. Although her ethnic background made her somewhat unusual in her middle-class suburban neighborhood, Sen was a popular figure at Wakefield High School, where she was a cheerleader and competed in field hockey, gymnastics, and track.

After graduating from high school, Sen studied French at Boston College, in Massachusetts. Although she was proficient in working with numbers, she had little interest in business courses, finding them inconsistent with the liberal political views she then held. Sen spent her junior year in Paris, France, initially sharing an apartment with an elderly French woman who died soon after the start of the semester. Unwilling to return home, Sen set about finding new lodgings; she quickly found work as an au pair for a wealthy family. "I had never been around people who owned jets and skied in Gstaad and had clothing custom-made. It opened my eyes," Sen told Amy Zipkin for the *New York Times* (April 26, 2009).

Sen earned a B.A. degree in romance languages in 1978. She married her college sweetheart, Michael Egan, a fledgling microbiologist who later became the head of a biotechnology firm. Sen herself became an executive trainee with the New England–based department-store chain Jordan Marsh. Unhappy working in the firm's handbag department, where she had been assigned, she left after a year to join the Zayre Corp., a retail conglomerate based in Framingham, Massachusetts. Hired as a gofer, as she told Zipkin, within a few years Sen had been placed in charge of inventory management for the company's toy division. (During her tenure in that post, the wildly successful Cabbage Patch and E.T. dolls were introduced, sparking buying frenzies that posed particular challenges for the inventory system.)

Sen was promoted several times during her decade at Zayre and held titles including stationery buyer and children's-apparel buyer. She was serving as the divisional merchandise manager of lingerie when the corporation dissolved. She explained the complex machinations to Zipkin: "Zayre Discount Stores was sold to Ames Department Stores in 1989. BJ's and HomeBase, another former Zayre unit, [had been] spun off to form Waban Inc. One of my mentors was at BJ's and asked me to join it. But while the breakup was going on, we weren't allowed to transfer from one subsidiary to another. Management wanted to keep the talent intact to facilitate the transfer to Ames. Meanwhile, I got an offer from another chain. The mentor convinced Zayre's management that because I was going to leave anyway, they might as well make an exception and let me go to BJ's."

BJ's was started in 1984 and named in honor of a daughter (Barbara Jean) of one of the founders. It was still a relatively small concern when Sen joined. "I put together processes and systems for logistics, distribution and inventory control," she explained to Zipkin. "I didn't have a blueprint. I made it up as I went along. I designed cross-dock buildings to receive truckloads of merchandise and ship it on pallets to the stores." By 1994 Sen had been promoted to senior vice president of general merchandise.

In 1997 Waban dissolved, and BJ's and Home-Base each went public in separate offerings. From January 1997 to February 2003, Sen, who remained with BJ's, served as executive vice president of merchandise and logistics. In mid-2002 Sen had been a strong candidate for the post of CEO; she was passed over, however, in favor of Michael Wedge, then the executive vice president of club operations, who ascended to the top spot in September of that year. Sen admitted to Zipkin, "I tried working with [Wedge] but my impression was that our management styles were very different." After six months she was asked to leave the company. Rather than feeling angered or dismayed, she looked forward to spending more time with her family. "My daughter was 15 and my son was 13," she told Elton. "I thought, 'This is my big chance to be a mom.' I've never been home being a mom. But all they needed at that point was money and a ride."

Sen instead threw her energies into her own re-tail-consulting firm, advising such companies as Kroger, Harris Teeter, Meijer, and Fred Mayer on business development, merchandising, and logistics. She also become involved with several Boston-area nonprofit groups, relishing the chance to play a hands-on role in their operations. She became a member of the board at the Pine Street Inn, a local homeless shelter where she regularly served dinner and organized special events. She also completed a rigorous training program in order to volunteer as a tutor in Boston's Chinatown district, and when she joined the board of the Boston Ballet, she began taking classes at the group's studios.

In late 2006 Wedge, who had presided during a period of disappointing sales and slow growth, left BJ's. (He is now a director of the Federal Reserve Bank of Boston.) Herb Zarkin, a longtime BJ's exec-utive, took over as CEO. Thinking that Zarkin might be able to use her consulting services, Sen met him for lunch at a steakhouse in Framingham. Instead of hiring her as a consultant, Zarkin insist-ed she rejoin the company, telling her that he would not leave the restaurant until she agreed. Surprised, but happy, she did so. "The next day I called her," Zarkin recalled to Elton, "and I said, 'You know, Laura, we never talked about titles, stock options, or salaries.' And she said, 'Herb, I trust you. Whatever you do I know will be the right thing.' She isn't driven by money or the title, she is driven by doing her job, coming up with new ideas, making sure we give back to the community.

She is driven by all the right things." "It takes awhile to understand the club industry," he later told Christina Veiders for *Supermarket News* (February 18, 2008), "and her knowledge is a blessing for us. Laura is not a stranger. We don't have to do a dance for a long period of time in order to under-stand each other."

Sen told Elton that "other than the days my two children were born and the day I got married," the day she returned to BJ's as an executive vice presi-dent, in January 2007, "was one of the most amaz-ing days of my life." In January 2008 Sen was pro-moted to president and chief operating officer (COO), which placed her in charge of day-to-day operations. "Expertise and logistics and merchan-dising is viewed as a big asset when it comes to the club warehouse business, where efficient delivery of goods to the sales floor at the lowest possible cost is critical," Veiders wrote, explaining Sen's as-cension. "The core business hasn't changed since I started in 1989," Sen told Veiders. "It is just a matter of how we execute against that. We have a team not just at the executive level but throughout the organization that has a very deep background. They know how to do this."

Sen made an immediate practice of walking around stores and asking employees of all ranks for their suggestions. She found, as she later told Jenn Abelson for the *Boston Globe* (February 8, 2009), that "the merchandise had grown so much that it was difficult for members to find what they want-ed. We had strayed from wholesale club funda-mentals—value, merchandise excitement, and effi-ciency." Sen and Zarkin devised a plan to rid the club of slow-selling items, including private-label products of questionable quality, and to stabilize relationships with the company's vendors. By the third fiscal quarter of 2008, BJ's was reporting a large increase in net income that represented a strong turnaround from the lag in sales under Wedge.

Sen took over as CEO when Zarkin stepped down, in February 2009. While her career was thriving, her private life was taking a devastating turn. Her husband of almost three decades was bat-tling melanoma, and during the last weeks of his life, Sen moved into his hospital room. "When Mi-chael was dying, Laura was starting to develop some public notoriety as a female CEO," Ann Car-ter, a personal friend and fellow businesswoman, told Elton. "You couldn't help but feel the irony of Laura finally getting her due, but knowing she would trade it all for some kind of miracle where Michael was concerned." Egan died in April 2009. Sen returned to work a few weeks later, and in Au-gust of that year, she and BJ's donated $100,000 to the Beth Israel Deaconess Medical Center for the creation of the Michael Egan Memorial Research Laboratory.

Sen's grief did not seem to affect her job perfor-mance, and she remained a visible force in the business world. In 2010 she was named to the *For-bes* list of the 100 most powerful women in the world (at number 82), and during the first quarter of 2011, the net income of BJ's rose 19 percent, to $33.7 million, while sales rose 10 percent, to $2.77 billion. Most analysts credited the good overall performance to the company's focus on everyday food items and gasoline, rather than big-ticket electronics or other luxury items.

On June 29, 2011 BJ's reached a $2.8 billion buyout agreement with the private-equity firms Leonard Green & Partners and CVC Capital Partners. "BJ's will benefit from the continued execution of our business plan and the significant retail expertise of our new partners at LGP and CVC, as well as from continued investments in our clubs, our people, and technology, and the future of our business," Sen declared in a statement, as quoted by Abelson in the *Boston Globe* (June 30, 2011). Abel-

son reported that the move would allow BJ's to expand beyond its core markets in the Northeast and Southeast without having to worry about quarterly profits.

Sen, who lives in Brookline, Massachusetts, could reportedly make almost $15 million in a so-called "golden parachute" arrangement if she does not remain at BJ's after the deal is finalized. She has one daughter, Kathryn, and one son, Sean.

— M.M.H.

Suggested Reading: *Boston Globe* G p13 Feb. 8, 2009, (on-line) Jan. 9, 2011, June 30, 2011; *Boston Herald* p21 Dec. 13, 2008; *Forbes* (on-line) Oct. 13, 2010; *New York Times* (on-line) Apr. 26, 2009; *Supermarket News* p19 Feb. 18, 2008, p1 Nov. 24, 2008

Pornchai Kittiwongsakul/AFP/Getty Images

Shinawatra, Yingluck

(shin-ah-WAHT, yeeng-luck)

June 21, 1967– Prime minister of Thailand; former businesswoman

Address: House of Representatives, National Assembly, 2 Uthong Nai Rd., Dusit District, Bangkok 10300, Thailand

"It would be wrong to call Yingluck Shinawatra's rise to power rapid," Tania Branigan Surin wrote of that Thai businesswoman-turned-politician for the London *Guardian* (July 6, 2011). "It was rocket-fuelled." On July 3, 2011, after campaigning for

less than two months, the 44-year-old Yingluck—who had no prior hands-on political experience—won her bid for prime minister of Thailand when her party, Pheu Thai ("For Thai"), captured 265 of the 500 seats in the House of Representatives. (The House is the lower body of the Thai Parliament, also known as the National Assembly; the upper house, the Senate, has 150 members.) On August 5, 2011 31 representatives from four smaller parties joined the 265 Pheu Thai members of the House to elect her officially as the nation's first female prime minister. Thailand's king, Bhumibol Adulyadej, approved the legislators' choice of Yingluck three days later. That same week Yingluck introduced her 34-member cabinet to her fellow citizens.

Yingluck is the 28th prime minister of Thailand since the nation was transformed from an absolute monarchy to a constitutional monarchy, in 1932. She is following in the footsteps of her older brother Thaksin, who was elected prime minister in 2001 and reelected in 2005; he is the only person ever to have served a full four-year term as Thailand's head of government after a victory at the polls. In 2006 Thaksin was ousted in a bloodless military coup (one of 10 successful and eight foiled military takeovers in Thailand since 1933). During the next five years, the government changed hands five times. Massive protests by ordinary citizens against the nation's rulers occurred in 2008, 2009, and 2010. The violence that erupted in Bangkok, the Thai capital, during clashes of demonstrators and security forces in 2010 led to dozens of fatalities and more than 2,000 injuries—nearly all among ordinary citizens—as well as more than $1.5 billion in arson-related property damage and severe disruptions to daily life and business, including tourism, one of the country's main sources of revenue. A large proportion of the protestors, called Red Shirts, remained loyal to Thaksin, even though he fled to Dubai in 2008 to avoid imprisonment after being found guilty of corruption.

Although the Shinawatra family is among the richest in the nation, the majority of Thaksin's supporters are low-income Thais, most of whom live in rural areas, and others who feel that they have not benefited proportionally from Thailand's rapid advance toward first-world status. The latter include "emerging petty entrepreneurs and small business people who cannot see why they do not enjoy the privileges of the elite in Bangkok" and "people who have been described as 'having some high school education and . . . a pickup truck,'" Milton Osborne, a specialist in Southeast Asia, wrote for the *Lowy Interpreter* (July 12, 2011, online), published by the Lowy Institute for International Policy, based in Sydney, Australia. Thaksin's appeal stems from his image as a populist—for example, he worked with his hands while growing up, and he can speak a Thai dialect widely used in northern rural districts. In addition, as prime minister he pushed (successfully, to some degree) for price supports for agricultural products, extensive debt relief for farmers, and universally affordable medical care; moreover, during his time in office, income among the poor in both urban and rural areas increased significantly, although on average it is still one-third that of the average in Bangkok, Daniel Ten Kate reported for *Bloomberg News* (June 16, 2011, on-line). Yingluck, who has cited her brother as her business and political mentor, shares Thaksin's political, social, and economic views. He and Yingluck remain in very close contact, and despite Thaksin's absence from Thailand, he was highly influential during his sister's election campaign; some referred to him as her de facto campaign manager. (Her campaign slogan was "Thaksin thinks, Pheu Thai acts.") According to Mark MacKinnon, writing for the Toronto, Canada, *Globe and Mail* (July 4, 2011), when Yingluck was asked if she thought she won the election because of her brother, she replied, "Thai people selected first myself, second Pheu Thai policy, third my management team. People did not select me only because my last name is Shinawatra." While many of her opponents have warned that she will serve as Thaksin's puppet, Yingluck has maintained that as the government's leader, she will make decisions independently.

"Thailand's people remain split . . . ," Thanyarat Doksone wrote for the Associated Press (August 5, 2011, on-line). Yingluck, Thanyarat continued, "must navigate complex political terrain and find a delicate equilibrium between the coup-prone army and the elite establishment on one side, and the so-called Red Shirt movement on the other. The Red Shirts helped vote her into office and want to see justice meted out for the bloody military crackdown that ended the movement's protests in Bangkok last year." Echoing that analysis, Siripan Nogsuan Sawasdee, an associate professor of political science at Chulalongkorn University, in Bangkok, told Thanyarat, "To reinforce the stability of her government, Yingluck must find

a way to work in harmony with the military and the conservative powers without affecting what the Red Shirts have been fighting for"—which "won't be easy," Thanyarat wrote.

The youngest of 10 children (nine, according to some sources), Yingluck Shinawatra was born to Lert (also spelled "Loet") and Yindi (alternately written as "Yindee") Shinawatra on June 21, 1967 in San Kamphaeng, Chiang Mai Province, in northern Thailand. According to the book *The Shinawatra Family* (2011), by Thanawat Suppaiboon, as summarized in an article posted on the Web site of the Australian National University's College of Asia and the Pacific (August 8, 2011), Lert and his wife had two sons and eight daughters; three of the latter are deceased. Yingluck's family nicknamed her Pou, which means "crab" in Thai. (Among family and friends virtually all Thais are referred to by the nicknames bestowed on them as infants. More formally, Thai adults address one another by their given names, sometimes preceded by the honorific "Khun," which is equivalent to Mr., Mrs., or Miss.) Yingluck's father (who died in 1997) and several of her siblings served in the Thai Parliament; one of her nieces is currently a member. Somchai Wongasawat, the husband of her sister Yoawapa (called Dang), served as Thailand's prime minister for less than three months in 2008. "I've known about politics since I was a kid," Yingluck said at her first press conference, as quoted in a Xinhua General News Service (July 4, 2011) profile.

When Yingluck was in elementary school, her mother died, and Thaksin, who is 18 years her senior, took on the role of second father to her. A teacher at Yingluck's high school recently told a TV interviewer that "everyone remembered her because she was the beautiful one," according to Thanyarat Doksone. Yingluck graduated from the Faculty of Political Science and Public Administration of Chiang Mai University with a bachelor's degree in 1988. She received a master's degree in public administration from the historically black Kentucky State University, in Frankfort, in 1991. (Thaksin earned a master's degree in criminal justice from nearby Eastern Kentucky University in 1975.)

According to *The Shinawatra Family*, a great-grandfather of Yingluck's immigrated to Thailand from China in the mid-19th century and raised cattle for a living. One of his sons, Yingluck's paternal grandfather, became a silk trader. Under Lert the family's holdings grew to include fruit orchards, a coffee shop, a bus company, a car dealership, a gas station, and a movie theater, where as a young girl Yingluck sold tickets. Thaksin expanded the business exponentially when he launched companies involved in communications, the field in which Yingluck later came to specialize as a business-woman. After she completed her formal education, Yingluck returned to Thailand and began to work for Shinawatra Directories Co., a yellow-pages business. She served as manager of the company

(1991–94), then general manager (1995–96), then vice president (1997–98). In 1999 Yingluck assumed the post of executive vice president of service operations at the telecommunications firm Advanced Info Service, Thailand's largest mobile-phone company and another of her family's businesses; she became its senior executive vice president of wireless corporate planning in 2001 and president of wireless communications in 2002. In 2006 Yingluck began serving as the acting president and acting senior vice president of business development of SC Asset Corp. Public Co. Ltd., a real-estate-development firm under the Shinawatra umbrella. In 2006 she also became a director of that corporation. Next, until 2011, she held the titles of executive president, acting chief executive officer, and secretary of SC Asset Corp. In an interview with Daniel Ten Kate, Than Thienachariya, a former executive with one of Advanced Info Service's main rivals, said that as a businesswoman Yingluck was "honest, compromising and diplomatic" and that she did not use "the media to attack her competitors or anything like that. She avoided confrontation."

Meanwhile, in 2001, Yingluck's brother Thaksin had been elected prime minister of Thailand, as a member of the Thai Rak Thai Party (the Pheu Thai Party's precursor); he was reelected four years later. In 2006 Thaksin was overthrown in a military coup. Twelve days later General Surayud Chulanont became prime minister. Beginning in January 2008 a succession of four others led the government. The last of those four, and the only one to gain the post through the ballot, was Abhisit Vejjajiva, who took over as prime minister on December 17, 2008. In May 2011, less than two months before the scheduled July 3 national elections, Yingluck launched a campaign for prime minister. Her principal opponent was the incumbent, Abhisit, then-leader of Thailand's Democratic Party. During her campaign Yingluck promised to find solutions to Thailand's unemployment and other economic problems and to help lead conflicting groups toward reconciliation. She avoided making negative statements about her opponents.

"Yingluck is putting a fresh, attractive, feminised face on her brother's brand," Tania Branigan Surin wrote. According to Surin, she "sprinted through her tightly managed campaign with a permanent, dazzling smile on her lips, a relentlessly positive message and a string of ambitious spending pledges to improve rural life." The *China Post* (July 4, 2011) asserted, "With her telegenic looks, relaxed demeanor and carefully choreographed stage routines, Yingluck . . . has proven a hit on the campaign trail." The media often mentioned that Thaksin had once referred publicly to Yingluck as his "clone," planting in some people the fear that he was manipulating her so that he could eventually make a comeback. "[Thaksin and I] are alike in the sense that I have learned from him in business and I understand his vision, how he solves problems and the way he built everything

from the beginning," Yingluck told an Agence France Presse (AFP) reporter, as quoted in the *China Post*. She told Mark MacKinnon for the Toronto, Canada, *Globe and Mail* (July 6, 2011), "I am capable enough to make my own decisions."

More than 70 percent of eligible voters cast their ballots on Election Day, July 3, 2011. Yingluck's party won 265 of the 500 seats in the House of Representatives; Abhisit, who had formed a coalition supported by the military, wealthy businesspeople, high-level bureaucrats, and others, won 160. Those results led Abhisit to resign as leader of the Democratic Party. On August 5, 2011 Yingluck earned the Pheu Thai Party's 265 votes in the House, plus 31 votes of members of four small parties who had agreed to form a coalition with the Pheu Thai, to become Thailand's new prime minister. One hundred ninety-seven other legislators abstained from voting.

On August 8, 2011 Thailand's king endorsed the legislature's selection of Yingluck as prime minister. Now 83 years old, Bhumibol Adulyadej (pronounced, roughly, "POOM-ee-pohn ah-DOON-yadate") assumed the throne in June 1946 and is the world's longest-reigning monarch. Although he has rarely intervened during periods of civil unrest or political turmoil and did not do so in 2009 or 2010, he is considered a unifying and stabilizing force in Thailand, not least because he is highly revered and even beloved by the vast majority of Thais of all classes and groups. According to a profile posted on the BBC News Web site (September 22, 2009), three years after the military abruptly removed Thaksin from power, "the king's name and image" were being "invoked by factions both for and against Mr Thaksin." Those factions were still at odds two years later, and some political analysts predict that serious conflicts will remain among various segments of Thailand's approximately 64 million people for some time. (About 9.3 million people live in Bangkok, with upwards of two million more in surrounding communities.) "Despite leading her . . . party to a convincing majority," Mark MacKinnon wrote (July 4, 2011), "Yingluck Shinawatra will still have to tread carefully in months ahead if she wants to avoid a confrontation with Thailand's powerful military and its allies in the monarchy and bureaucracy." In addition, according to Thanyarat Doksone, "Yingluck must prove she is not her brother's puppet, as critics claim, and deal with the controversial issue of his possible return from self-imposed exile under a general amnesty, which would enrage his opponents and could destabilize Thailand."

In describing her priorities as prime minister, Yingluck told Zoe Daniel for ABC Asia and Pacific News (July 4, 2011, on-line), "The first thing we have to [do is] solve the . . . economic problem, especially on high living expense. So we need to fix that as fast as we can. . . . Plus we have to accelerate the government spending so that spending will generate higher income and household income. So I think we need to do two thing[s] at the same time." The Pheu Thai Party has offered a stimulus package that includes raising the minimum wage and guaranteeing minimum prices for rice growers—measures that some have called financially unsound. Yingluck has also said that she wants to build high-speed train lines, make tablet computers universally available to students, and promote national reconciliation. Boris Sullivan, writing for *Thailand Business News* (June 5, 2011, on-line), complained that the Pheu Thai Party's agenda "does not contain anything about reforming Thailand's antiquated system of primary and secondary education, the single greatest impediment to long-term economic progress in the country; anything about reforming the country's regressive tax system that favours the rich over the poor; or anything about raising the productivity of Thailand's masses of unskilled and semi-skilled workers."

"In her TV interviews," Lawrence Osborne wrote for the *Daily Beast* (July 11, 2011, on-line), Yingluck "comes across as a typical Thai female presence: deft, slightly steely, understated, her gestures measured and imperturbable, the charm calculatingly uncalculating." He also described her as "at once corporate and feminine, dynastic and individual" and as having "a smile that seems impossibly unrehearsed and yet exquisitely mannered." He added, "The natural Thai inclination toward conciliation might have found its proper symbolic incarnation at long last. It's something to do with that quiet demeanor and cunning air of deference."

Yingluck is married to Anusorn Amornchat, the managing director of M Link Asia Corp., a business founded by one of Yingluck's sisters. The couple have one son, Supasek.

—J.P.

Suggested Reading:Associated Press (on-line) Aug. 5, 2011; *Bangkok Post* (on-line) May 16, 2011; BBC News (on-line) July 3, 2011; *Bloomberg News* (on-line) June 16, 2011; *Daily Beast* (on-line) July 11, 2011; *Economist* p51+ June 25, 2011, p14+, p22+ July 9, 2011; (London) *Guardian* Features p6 July 6, 2011; (London) *Independent* World p34 July 7, 2011; *New York Times* (on-line) July 4, 2011

Shiner, Lewis

Dec. 30, 1950– Writer

Address: c/o Subterranean Press, P.O. Box 190106, Burton, MI 48519

"I have a powerful need to create narratives that make sense of the events of my life," the novelist and short-story writer Lewis Shiner explained in an autobiographical essay, "Life as We Know It," posted on his Web site; for that reason, he wrote, much of his work is "heavily autobiographical." In an interview with Gavin J. Grant for BookSense.com, as posted on IndieBound.org (2001), Shiner said that *Say Goodbye*, his fifth novel, about a female musician's futile quest for stardom, was "actually my most autobiographical." The impetus for *Say Goodbye*, he told Grant, came when his "freelance writing career collapsed," in the early 1990s: he could find no work that he "felt comfortable with" as a writer for comic books, his earnings from his short stories, novels, and nonfiction pieces could not support him, and his vision of making a living as a drummer in a band had never materialized. With *Say Goodbye*, he said, "I wanted to write a novel that attacked the common wisdom that if you try hard enough, you can always get anything you want." The "intersection between dreams and the real world," he told M. M. Hall for *Publishers Weekly* (November 5, 2001), is "a theme I never seem to tire of." Since his college graduation, in 1973, Shiner has held day jobs as a construction worker and a graphic artist as well as a comic-book writer, and in the computer-software industry, he has worked as a programmer, a mar-

Courtesy of Lewis Shiner

keting manager, and a technical writer. He has also published upwards of 70 short stories (in such periodicals as the *Magazine of Fantasy and Science Fiction*, *Isaac Asimov's Science Fiction Magazine*, *Galileo*, *Mike Shayne Mystery Magazine*, the *Twilight Zone*, *Black Clock*, *Omni*, and *New Pathways*), and he has written seven novels, the latest of which, *Dark Tangos*, is scheduled to appear in August 2011.

Shiner's debut novel, *Frontera* (1984), earned him a place alongside William Gibson, Rudy Rucker, and other prominent writers at the forefront of "cyberpunk fiction," which "mixed punk attitude with an interest in computer technology," Jim McClellan wrote for the *Calgary (Alberta, Canada) Herald* (April 24, 1994). A lot of Shiner's subsequent work has often been categorized as science fiction or fantasy, but "speculative fiction" may be a more accurate classification: according to the description of that genre offered by the weekly Web magazine *Strange Horizons*, "These stories make us think. They critique society. They offer alternatives. They give us a vision of the future—and warn us of the potential dangers therein. They help us understand our past. They are full of beauty, and terror, and delight." Shiner told Gavin J. Grant, "I don't think about genre much, just about the best way to deal with whatever story and characters I want to do. And if you look at my work, all my novels have more in common with each other than with other novels of a particular genre." Shiner's second novel, *Deserted Cities of the Heart*, deals with Mayan prophecies and the end of the world, while *Slam* was inspired by socially alienated skateboarders in Austin, Texas. In writing *Glimpses* Shiner indulged his love of rock and roll, imagining a protagonist with the ability to "hear" long-lost or never-released rock albums. Coral Press, which publishes "musical novels," placed *Glimpses* at the top of its list of the 40 best novels about rock and pop and ranked *Say Goodbye* 14th. The *Los Angeles Times* included Shiner's next novel, *Black & White*, among its "2008 crime fiction favorites."

In 2009 Subterranean Press reprinted 40 of Shiner's short stories as well as one new tale in *Collected Stories*. According to a starred review in *Publishers Weekly* (October 5, 2009), the "powerful stories" in the collection "cover Shiner's career across three decades and multiple genres, showcasing hard-edged, often political genre fiction at its finest. . . . Shiner never fails to astound, and this collection highlights everything that makes him one of today's best storytellers." In a review for *Strange Horizons* (October 22, 2010), Jason Erik Lundberg wrote that Shiner's stories offer "a thoughtful and erudite exploration of how and why human beings treat one another the way they do. Shiner's prose sparkles with humanity, with empathy, and with clarity. Taken as a whole, the collection is a gift of narrative, a multifaceted examination into what it means to be a human being in any universe." Shiner's short fiction has been published in many anthologies, including several editions of the annual *Year's Best Science Fiction*.

Since 2007 Shiner has posted his short stories, essays, and novels on his Web site Fiction Liberation Front. In a "manifesto" posted on the site, he wrote, "Whatever future the short story has, the Internet will be involved in it. The thing that's least clear is how—or whether—artists will be compensated for their efforts. There's been no living to be made from short stories in my lifetime. But short fiction endures because it provides a way of introducing writers to new readers, and because there are stories that need to be told at that length. . . . The dramatic title I've given this project—Fiction Liberation Front—is a blatant attempt to attract attention. The main reason I write these things, after all, is for people to read them."

An only child, Lewis Gordon Shiner was born on December 30, 1950 in Eugene, Oregon, to Joel Lewis Shiner and his wife, Maxine. By his own account, his relationships with his parents were almost always fraught. His father (who died in 1988) was an archaeologist/anthropologist; he wrote articles and books about his fieldwork in North America and Africa and served for a while as the editor of the *Bulletin of the Texas Archaeological Society*. Lewis Shiner spent much of his first year living with a neighbor, while his mother, who suffered from severe asthma, received medical treatment or was hospitalized in a nearby town. He has speculated that because of those early separations, he and his mother (who died in 2001) "never bonded properly," he told Tina Hall for thedamnedinterviews.com (January 2011). "She always seemed a bit uncomfortable with me," he added, "like 'What is this kid doing here? Did I ask for this?'" He has described his father as generally bitter; without objection from his mother, his father invariably treated him harshly, frequently criticizing him, sometimes abusing him physically, and never displaying any affection toward him. Shiner was four when his father earned a Ph.D. degree in anthropology at the University of Arizona at Tucson. Joel Shiner then took a job with the U.S. National Park Service, and the Shiners moved to Seaford, Virginia, then to Macon and St. Simons Island, Georgia. Young Lew felt happiest when his father was away on field trips, sometimes for months at a stretch. For three years starting when he was eight, the Shiners lived in Globe, Arizona—the longest he had spent in any one place—and during summers he and his mother visited his father in New Mexico, where he was working on a park project. "By age eight . . . I was in many ways a fully-formed miniature adult," Shiner wrote in "Life as We Know It." "My parents got lots of compliments on how grown-up and well-behaved I was, and that seemed to not only make them happy but to justify all the punishment, both mental and physical, that had shaped me to that end."

Shiner's parents taught him to read when he was three, so that they would no longer have to devote any time to reading to him. Shiner soon learned to write as well, by copying stories and then changing them to suit himself. He enjoyed reading his parents' collections of *Mad* magazines and *Pogo* comic books. Inspired by Jules Verne's science-fiction novel *Twenty Thousand Leagues Under the Sea* (1869), at age seven he wrote his first, unfinished novel, "The Deep Blue Sea," about an adventuresome scuba diver. He later attempted a second novel and began writing short stories starring "The

Planets," a team of superheroes modeled after the DC Comics characters the Challengers of the Unknown. In the third through fifth grades, he created his own slim comic books, selling the originals (he had no way to reproduce them) to classmates for 15 cents each. His mother also bought some, though she judged his drawings to be "crappy," he told Tina Hall. He also became an enthusiastic fan of rock music.

Right after Shiner completed sixth grade, his mother was diagnosed with breast cancer. His father quit his job, because his supervisor would not allow him to remain in Globe while his wife underwent surgery and radiation therapy. "The one credit I will give my parents is that they were good in a crisis," Shiner wrote for his Web site. "They'd always taught me that when there was real trouble you got through it first and worried about the repercussions later. There was a sense during the summer of my mother's cancer that we were all pulling together, and it may be as close as we ever were as a family." The cancer treatments were effective, and the Shiners moved to Santa Fe, New Mexico, where Shiner's father got a job with the Museum of New Mexico. One assignment brought him to Sudan, in Africa, where the family lived for six months after Shiner completed seventh grade. During that time Shiner did not attend school; he read whatever English-language books and magazines he could find. He also wrote part of a novel about "the sole survivor of a mission to a deserted planet in the Sirius system," as he described it on his Web reminiscence. But "this was still not quite isolated enough for me, so I topped it off by blowing up the Earth he'd left behind in a nuclear war." The Shiners traveled in Europe for a month both before and after their stay in Sudan.

Shiner's father next joined the faculty of Southern Methodist University (SMU), in Dallas, Texas, and Shiner entered St. Mark's School of Texas, an all-boys private school. In his freshman year of high school, he "formed an attachment" with the father of a school friend, he recalled in "Life as We Know It"; "John's father . . . not only listened to me as if I were an adult, but was the first father I'd ever seen who was physically affectionate to his children. I knew instantly that I'd been missing it." In 1965, as a high-school sophomore, he attended a Bob Dylan concert—an event he has claimed "literally changed my life." He took up the guitar but had to stop playing after he seriously injured a finger while building scenery for his school theater group. In his junior year he began playing drums. He also continued writing fiction, publishing stories in his school's literary magazine—"morbid and obvious pieces full of faux nobility and stifled longings," in his words. In addition, he joined the school's fencing team and, later, its tennis team, and he played with his band at school parties and other events. With his girlfriend he attended concerts by such well-known bands and artists as Jimi Hendrix, the Jefferson Airplane, the Doors, Country Joe and the Fish, Cream, and the Mothers. In his

senior year he won a story contest sponsored by a local teen magazine and the St. Mark's School's Creative Writing Cup.

After he completed high school, Shiner enrolled at Vanderbilt University, in Nashville, Tennessee. During his freshman year he won the Henrietta Hickman-Morgan Award for Freshman English for one of his short stories. As a sophomore he assembled a collection of stories and cartoons and sent copies to a few publishers, all of whom rejected them. In the spring of 1970, having lost interest in his studies, Shiner dropped out of school. He had hoped to go on tour with his rock band, but after his fellow musicians replaced him on drums, he moved to Austin, Texas, and wrote a novel, "And Then Palestrina," about "an alienated, overly-creative nineteen-year-old misfit whose girlfriend dumps him," in his words, and who becomes a mass killer. Shiner then left Austin and moved to Dallas, where he formed a new band, Southern Cross, and returned to college. Thanks to his father's position, he was granted free tuition to SMU. He earned a bachelor's degree in English in 1973. He played drums with another band before pursuing a career in writing. "Like so many others before and after me, I decided I would try the Harlan Ellison write-a-story-a-week-until-you're-famous plan," he wrote for his Web site, referring to a multi-award-winning, extremely prolific writer of speculative fiction.

For the next couple of years, Shiner tried in vain to sell his science-fiction and detective stories to literary magazines. In 1976 he took a job writing for a Dallas computer company, and weeks later he sold his story "Tinker's Damn" to *Galileo*, a Boston, Massachusetts–based science-fiction magazine. He next sold to *Mystery Monthly* his story "Deep Without Pity," whose protagonist, Dan Sloane, a detective and Vietnam veteran, he hoped to make the anchor of a series. For the first time Shiner "dared to think of myself as a real, honest-to-god writer," he wrote in his Web essay. His joy was short-lived, however: *Galileo*'s published version of "Tinker's Damn" was heavily edited, and *Mystery Monthly* went out of business just before "Deep Without Pity" was slated to go to press. Three years passed before Shiner next sold a story, and during that time he became dependent on alcohol.

In 1978 Shiner recommitted himself to writing. He spent a month in Mexico City, Mexico, working on a novel to be called "In Transit," and after he returned to the U.S., he found a literary agent willing to take on his manuscripts. His next success was the sale of his story "Stuff of Dreams" to *Fantasy and Science Fiction* magazine in 1981. Although he fired his agent and struggled to sell his mystery stories, during the next few years he sold roughly one science-fiction story per month to Isaac Asimov's magazine and others. He regularly attended science-fiction conventions, where he met Jim Blaylock, Karen Joy Fowler, John Kessel, and other writers who became close friends of his.

Feeling increasingly confident that he was well positioned to sell a science-fiction novel, Shiner transformed "Soldier, Sailor," a short story he had written years earlier, into *Frontera*. In 1983 he sold the novel to Baen Books, which published it the following year. Set in a future in which corporations have replaced governments and humans have colonized the moon, *Frontera* is regarded as one of the first cyberpunk novels. It was a finalist for the 1984 Science Fiction and Fantasy Writers of America Nebula Award for best novel and the Philip K. Dick Award for best original paperback. Thanks to the book's success, Shiner bought a house and began working on *Deserted Cities of the Heart*, which grew out of the aborted "In Transit" and drew on exhaustive research the author conducted regarding Mayans, New Age philosophy, Latin American politics, and U.S. military helicopters and weaponry. He worked on the novel for three years, and in 1988, after clashing with Bantam Books' new-fiction division over editorial changes that he viewed as unacceptable, he sold the book to Doubleday. *Deserted Cities of the Heart* is set in a Mexican jungle, where Eddie, a washed-up rock star, has gone to join a Mayan cult. When Eddie's anthropologist brother, Thomas, searches for him, he is exposed to earthquakes, revolutionary wars, and Mayan end-of-days prophecies. "It all sounds a bit breathless, and awfully implausible," Richard Grant wrote for the *Washington Post* (July 31, 1988). "But trust me: Shiner makes it work. His narrative never flinches." In a review for the Toronto, Canada, *Globe and Mail* (June 17, 1989), Douglas Hill wrote, "Underneath the book's surface of revolutionary politics is a moving account of interweaving cultures in a forbidding land," and he labeled the book "entertaining" and "hard to put down." *Deserted Cities of the Heart* was a finalist for both the 1989 Nebula Award for best novel and the International Association for the Fantastic in the Arts William L. Crawford Fantasy Award.

Shiner got the ideas for his next novel, *Slam* (1990), while watching young skateboarders, reading *Thrasher*, a publication devoted to the skateboarding subculture, and pondering the fate of savings and other assets bequeathed to pets. The story centers on Dave, a lazy middle-aged man who, after six months in jail for tax evasion, becomes the caretaker of a property that an elderly woman has willed to her two dozen cats. Complications ensue when a series of offbeat characters vie for the estate. A *Publishers Weekly* (June 6, 1990) reviewer declared *Slam* to be "an unqualified delight," and Paul Di Filippo, writing for the *Washington Post* (August 16, 1990), praised the novel's "melancholy humor" and "sharp-witted street talk" and compared Shiner to both Philip K. Dick and Elmore Leonard.

Ray Shackleford, a stereo repairman and the protagonist of *Glimpses* (1993), is able to go back in time and hear albums that were never completed, such as *Smile*, which the singer and songwriter Brian Wilson of the Beach Boys abandoned in the late 1960s (and released a dozen years after *Glimpses* was published). Writing for the *Review of Contemporary Fiction* (March 22, 1994), Lance Olsen described *Glimpses* as "at once sad and humorous, sweet and tough-minded, richly and rigorously researched and amazingly well-imagined" and as "a first rate work of historiographic fiction for people who genuinely—and sometimes too innocently—love rock 'n' roll." *Glimpses* won the 1993 Austin Writers' League's Violet Crown Award and the 1994 World Fantasy Award, both for best novel.

When *Glimpses* was published, Shiner had been living in San Antonio, Texas; for a couple of years, he had worked as a writer for DC Comics. Forced by his precarious finances to take a full-time job with a computer company, he stopped writing fiction. "It shouldn't have been a big deal; I'd gone long periods without writing before," he wrote in "Life as We Know It." "Only this time I wasn't drinking, and I wasn't playing in a band. And this time I'd been really close to making it, close enough to taste it. I began to fall apart. Eventually"—after about two years—"it became clear, even to me, that I had to start writing again. I had to write not to become famous, not to become rich, and not to make up for a loveless childhood. I had to write for its own sake, for whatever satisfaction I could get from the act itself."

Shiner's fifth novel, *Say Goodbye* (1999), is about a young woman who moves to Los Angeles with dreams of making it big in the music business. In one of several mixed assessments, Mark Athitakis wrote for the *New York Times Book Review* (October 10, 1999), "Though its story lines are tied up too neatly—it's a slick, radio-ready fade of an ending—Shiner has written a fine novel about rock 'n' roll by believing more in musicians' human nature than in their mythologies." Excerpts from his next book, *Black & White* (2008), appeared in the *Southwest Review*, *Black Clock*, and *Subterranean* magazine. Set in Durham and Raleigh, North Carolina, the novel is about 35-year-old Michael Cooper, who uncovers a murder in the course of researching his family's history and the history of Hayti, a prosperous black Durham neighborhood that was demolished to make way for a highway. "Shiner weaves [his characters'] stories into a stunning tapestry that captures the hopes, dreams, greed, bigotry, ambitions and betrayals that shaped their destinies and those of our country," a *Publishers Weekly* (March 31, 2008) reviewer wrote. "While the crime plot builds to a conventional resolution, Michael's poignant discovery of his parents' roots and the splendid depiction of Durham's changing social fabric more than compensate." "The always-talented Shiner has produced some of his finest work to date here," Rick Klaw wrote in a review of *Black & White* for the *Austin Chronicle* (July 4, 2008).

As of mid-June 2011, all of Shiner's novels except *Dark Tangos* were available in PDF (portable document format) files on his Web site Fiction Liberation Front. Among the dozens of his short stories posted on that site are nine that appear nowhere else, among them "The Long Denouement," a "Raymond Chandler spoof" about "hard-boiled scribes and editors," in Shiner's words; "You Never Know," Shiner's entry for a contest co-sponsored by the car company Volkswagen and the romance-novel publisher Harlequin, calling for "a 200-word romantic short story that involved a VW Beetle"; "Mark the Bunny," a tale for children; and "Fear Itself," about a homeless man on Christmas Eve. The nonfiction pieces posted on the Fiction Liberation Front site include Shiner's introduction to his anthology *When the Music's Over* (1991), whose stories, by Shiner and a half-dozen of his friends, focus on conflicts resolved without violence. (Shiner donated his share of the earnings from sales of *When the Music's Over* to the organization Greenpeace.) The site also contains two unpublished Shiner screenplays—"Glimpses," based on the same-titled novel, and "The Next," which he described as an "action picture about vampire lawyers"—and translations of four of Shiner's short stories: "Perfidia," in French and Russian, "Lizard Men of Los Angeles," in Russian, "Stuff of Dreams," in Italian, and "Americans," in Spanish.

Shiner's decade-long marriage to Edith "Edie" Beumer ended in divorce in the early 1990s. His second marriage, to Mary Alberts, also ended in divorce, in 2001. Shiner lives in Durham. He currently works as a contract technical writer for IBM and an analyst for Sapphire Technologies. He told *Current Biography* that he is "in the very early stages of a major new novel" and that in his leisure time he enjoys swing and salsa dancing with his girlfriend.

—K.J.P.

Suggested Reading: *Austin (Texas) American-Statesman* K p6 Oct. 3, 1999; *Black Clock* (on-line) July 19, 2010; isfdb.org; Lewis Shiner's Web site; *New York Times* (on-line) Jan. 7, 1991; (Raleigh, North Carolina) *Metro Magazine* Art & Literature (on-line) Jan. 11, 2009; Subterranean Press (on-line); thedamnedinterviews.com Jan. 2011

Selected Books: *Frontera*, 1984; *Deserted Cities of the Heart*, 1988; *Slam*, 1990; *Glimpses*, 1993; *Say Goodbye*, 1999; *Black & White*, 2008; *Dark Tangos*, 2011

Smigel, Robert

(SMY-gl)

Feb. 7, 1960– Actor; comedian; puppeteer; television and film scriptwriter and producer

Address: c/o Creative Artists Agency, 162 Fifth Ave., Suite 6, New York, NY 10010-6047

"I get a lot of pleasure out of writing things that maybe I couldn't have *written* when I was 10 years old, but which remind me of things that made me *laugh* when I was 10 years old," the television and film writer, actor, comedian, and puppeteer Robert Smigel told Frazier Moore for the Associated Press Online (December 5, 2000). "There's a part of my personality that's never been completely comfortable with adulthood, that's for sure," Smigel declared to Dave Itzkoff for the *New York Times* (April 23, 2006). "And when you get into a field like comedy, that's inherently childish, where you make your own rules and you dress like a pig, it kind of reinforces that." Smigel started out in show business as an actor and writer with a small sketch-comedy group in Chicago, Illinois, in the 1980s, right after he completed college. He soon parlayed his juvenile sensibilities into an eminently successful career as a comic writer and puppeteer for television, for shows including *Saturday Night Live* (*SNL*), with which he spent more than 20 years in total; *Late Night with Conan O'Brien*; and the short-lived *The Dana Carvey Show*. In the opinion of Rocco Castoro, writing for *Vice* maga-

Ethan Miller/Getty Images

zine (October 2010, on-line), Smigel "has been responsible for a large chunk of the best American comedic television of the past 25 years." "He's made a good living pouring salt in the wounds of popular culture," Castoro wrote, "and he's done it in ways that are simultaneously hilarious and innovative." "Robert's not as concerned with boundaries, or at least he's the only one who sees his own boundaries," Lorne Michaels, the creator and executive producer of *SNL* and the executive producer of *Late Night with Conan O'Brien*, said to Itzkoff. "In that sense, he's fearless." On April 29, 2006 *SNL* devoted an entire hour-and-a-half installment to Smigel's "TV Funhouse" animations, making Smigel the only *SNL* writer ever to be so honored. Smigel has also appeared in feature films and has written the screenplays for two motion pictures. One of them, *Jack and Jill*, starring Adam Sandler, was scheduled for release in November 2011.

The only son of Irwin Smigel, a dentist and entrepreneur, and Lucille Smigel (called Lucia), Robert M. Smigel was born on February 7, 1960 in New York City. He grew up on the city's Upper West Side with his older sister, Bellanca, now an attorney. His father is one of the earliest practitioners of cosmetic dentistry; he founded and is the president of the American Society for Dental Aesthetics. In around 1980 Irwin Smigel demonstrated the new technique of dental bonding on an installment of the television show *That's Incredible!* reportedly viewed by 50 million people. In 2000 the New York University School of Dentistry inaugurated the annual Irwin Smigel Prize in Aesthetic Dentistry. "My dad is way more important to dentistry than I'll ever be to comedy," Robert Smigel told Frank DiGiacomo for the *New York Observer* (October 20, 2003). He has also described his father as very funny. Now 87, Irwin Smigel still maintains a dental practice. In 1987 he and his wife started Supersmile, a company that sells oral-hygiene products; its Web site carries testimonials from celebrities including Danny Aiello, Sarah Silverman, Kelly Ripa, Jimmy Fallon, and Gloria Steinem. Lucia Smigel is Supersmile's president and chief executive officer; Bellanca Smigel-Rutter serves as company counsel.

Posts about Robert Smigel on many Web sites (about 780 of them on September 8, 2011) state that his parents, who are Jewish, raised him "with a strong Jewish identity, which included Jewish day school, travel to Israel, and Jewish summer camps." By his own account, some of Smigel's comedy reflects the many hours of Saturday cartoons and other television shows that he watched as a child. "I could not sit through anything on TV that took itself seriously," he told Rocco Castoro. His favorite programs included *The Magilla Gorilla Show* and other Hanna-Barbera cartoons, *Gilligan's Island*, and *Lassie*. "My sister and I would literally kiss the TV at the end of the *Lassie* credits," he recalled to Castoro. Another early influence was a book of Charles M. Schulz's *Peanuts* comic strips that his father gave him when he was seven. (He was thrilled that same year to receive a doll of the *Peanuts* character Linus.) "It was kids, but it didn't talk down to kids," he said of *Peanuts* to DiGiacomo. "Nobody ever wins in the cartoon, and everybody is perpetually troubled by something or other. And nobody ever accomplishes anything to alleviate their anxieties. . . . It made you feel less alone in a profound way." "What I really wanted

to do when I was a little kid was to be a cartoonist," he told Castoro. "I was very good at drawing popular cartoon characters, but it just seemed like a pipe dream." Smigel, who still loves *Peanuts*, wrote the introduction to *The Complete Peanuts 1975 to 1976* (2010).

Smigel attended private schools in New York City. He told DiGiacomo that he cultivated the role of class "comedy bully." In high school, he said, "I was drawing cartoons with my friends and doing impressions of teachers and students." During two summer vacations he worked in his father's dental office. After he graduated from high school, he entered the pre-dentistry program at Cornell University, in Ithaca, New York. His career choice, he told Castoro, "was a completely fear-based decision." "I didn't particularly want to be a dentist," he said. "But in my mind, I had no confidence that I could succeed in show business or writing. It seemed way out of my reach." His very low grades, particularly in science-related courses, led him to transfer to New York University (NYU) and major in communications—"a complete waste of time," he commented to Castoro, except for the times when he "was supposed to be the writer or the director or the performer" of a project, in which case he "would shine." "It reminded me that I wanted to be a performer," he added. According to some sources he attempted pre-dentistry a second time with similar, unsuccessful results.

Smigel was still enrolled at Cornell when, in 1981, he got the chance to perform at a stand-up comedy competition on the NYU campus; he was among the winners. "It changed everything," he told Castoro. "I was like, 'Wow, I made strangers laugh!'" After he won a second contest, he began to perform at the Comic Strip, a club in New York City. For his act he dressed as an Orthodox rabbi, wearing a cotton-candy beard and a glum expression. He would slowly and painstakingly turn the pages of a large religious text, "licking my finger each time I turned a page," as he had seen old men do in his synagogue. "I would do that until people started laughing and then I would eat some of my beard," he told Castoro; he would then alternate page turning with beard eating. During the summer of 1982, at the suggestion of Tim Kazurinsky, a new member of *SNL*, Smigel took an acting class in Chicago that turned out to be "pretty much the springboard for the rest of my career," he told Castoro. After he earned a bachelor's degree, in 1983, Smigel moved to Chicago, where he studied improvisational theater at a workshop sponsored by the Second City comedy troupe (with which many *SNL* cast members got their starts). He also joined the improvisation group All You Can Eat, which became quite popular. "We didn't do improv onstage, just sketches," Smigel told Mike Sacks for Sacks's book *And Here's the Kicker: Conversations with Top Humor Writers About Their Craft* (2009). Smigel's future wife, Michelle Saks, worked behind the scenes for All You Can Eat. "It was probably the happiest time of my life," Smigel told

Sacks. In 1985, after seeing him perform with All You Can Eat, *SNL*'s then–head writers, Al Franken (now a U.S. senator) and Tom Davis, invited Smigel to join *SNL* as an apprentice writer.

In an interview with Nathan Rabin for the *avclub.com* (August 4, 2004), Smigel said that he felt "incredibly scared" during his first year with *SNL* and "really didn't do that well." "The second year, I was much more successful," he said, and he stopped worrying about being fired. Smigel created a host of memorable sketches and characters for *SNL*, including a skit in which the *Star Trek* cast member William Shatner told a convention of "Trekkies" to "get a life"; a mock commercial in which two heterosexual losers, after popping open cans of "Schmitts Gay Beer," metamorphosed into popular, happy homosexuals surrounded by attractive men at a pool party; "Pumping Up with Hanz and Franz," a parody of Austrian body-builders modeled on Arnold Schwarzeneggar; "The McLaughlin Group," a takeoff on the same-named weekly public-affairs panel discussion; and "Smart Reagan," a sketch in which then–President Ronald Reagan, played by Phil Hartman, "dropped his fumbling façade the minute he got behind closed White House doors and became a focused, super smart leader who did not suffer fools," in DiGiacomo's words. The recurring *SNL* segment "Bill Swerski's Super Fans," in which Smigel played one of several passionate, beer-guzzling followers of the Chicago Bears and Chicago Bulls sports teams, grew out of a sketch created by Smigel and his fellow *SNL* writers Conan O'Brien and Bob Odenkirk. Smigel and his fellow *SNL* writers won an Emmy Award in 1989 for outstanding writing in a variety or music program.

Smigel joined O'Brien again in 1991 to write the pilot for an ABC sitcom called *Lookwell*, starring Adam West, which never ran. Two years later Smigel left *SNL* (temporarily, as it turned out) to become the head writer for *Late Night with Conan O'Brien*, when O'Brien took over NBC's late-night time slot following David Letterman's move to CBS. "For me, that was the most exciting, invigorating job I've ever had," Smigel told DiGiacomo. The sketches he wrote for O'Brien, in collaboration with writers including Louis C.K., Bob Odenkirk, Dino Samatopoulos, and Tommy Blacha, "evolved into playing with visual jokes because Conan and I bonded over our love of cartoony humor," he told Castoro. He also said to Castoro, "It was important to me that the show have a very specific feel that was different from everyone else's." In *Late Night*'s "Clutch Cargo" segments (the name is that of a 1959 animated TV series), images of notable individuals were superimposed on Smigel's face, with Smigel's mouth visible as he mimicked the speech of the person he was supposed to be; much of what he said was improvised. In imitating Arnold Schwarzenegger, DiGiacomo wrote, Smigel "capture[d] the California governor's action-hero . . . disregard for anything but himself." Smigel's over-the-top impression of President Bill Clinton grew progressively absurd. "After a while, just to make Conan laugh, I started throwing in a Southern gumbo of whatever I could loosely apply" to Clinton, Smigel told DiGiacomo. Referring to a Looney Tunes cartoon character, he added, "I turned [Clinton] into Foghorn Leghorn for a while, where, when he was explaining things, I'd just have him go, 'I say, I say, I say, I say—I didn't do nuthin!'"

Smigel's unremittingly foulmouthed hand puppet, Triumph, the Insult Comic Dog, made his debut on *Late Night with Conan O'Brien* in 1997, during a sketch poking fun at the Westminster Dog Show. Said to be a native of Hungary, Triumph is a Rottweiler whom Smigel has compared to the sharp-tongued taxi dispatcher played by Danny De Vito in the TV sitcom *Taxi* and to the master put-down artist Groucho Marx; others have likened Triumph to Don Rickles, who specializes in offensive stand-up comedy. With Smigel speaking in a gruff voice in heavily accented English, Triumph gleefully and lewdly disparaged O'Brien's celebrity guests. "I understand why people love Triumph," Smigel told DiGiacomo. "He's very cute and he's got crazy eyes, and there's something very lovable about how happy Triumph is when he's being an a**hole to somebody. He's completely remorseless . . . just completely uncontrolled id." Deborah Solomon interviewed Triumph for the *New York Times Magazine* (February 13, 2005), shortly after Smigel's CD, *Come Poop with Me*, was nominated for a Grammy Award in the category of best comedy album. In addition to Smigel as Triumph, contributors to *Come Poop with Me* included Conan O'Brien, Jack Black, Adam Sandler, Janeane Garofalo, and Maya Rudolph. Triumph has his own Web site and continues to make guest appearances on TV and elsewhere. Smigel stopped writing for *Late Night with Conan O'Brien* in 1997, but he continued to appear on the show as Triumph and in other roles.

Smigel wrote for, executive produced, and appeared in *The Dana Carvey Show*, which aired on ABC in March and April 1996. Smigel's co-writers included Carvey, Charlie Kaufman, Louis C.K., Jon Glaser, and Robert Carlock, and its cast included the then-little-known Steve Carrell and Stephen Colbert. In an article headlined "Comedy Ahead of Its Time (if That Time Ever Comes)," Dave Itzkoff described the show for the *New York Times* (May 10, 2009) as "an outlandish skit series that was prescient and provocative and canceled after seven episodes." "It was probably the most bizarre variety show in the history of American television," Carvey told Itzkoff. Many viewers found its contents objectionable or even repellent. In the first installment, to cite one notorious example, in a skit inspired by Bill Clinton's assertion that he was "caring" and "nurturing," the president was shown with his chest bared, nursing puppies and kittens as well as a human doll on multiple pairs of nipples. When Rex Doane asked Smigel for *Salon.com* (April 9, 2001) what his experience with the show had taught him, he said, referring to the sitcom that aired on ABC in the preceding time slot, "Don't follow *Home Improvement* with a lactating president. I also learned that you don't go to a network that has never done anything remotely like what you're doing."

"The Ambiguously Gay Duo," a very short animated film that Smigel and Carvey had written for *The Dana Carvey Show*, was picked up by *SNL* later in 1996 and became the first title in its "TV Funhouse" shorts. "The Ambituously Gay Duo" featured a pair of superheroes (voiced by Carrell and Colbert) reminiscent of Batman and Robin, whose appearance and behavior led villains to speculate about their sexual preferences. J. D. Sedelmaier executed the animations for that segment of "TV Funhouse" and others, among them "X Presidents," in which former U.S. presidents were depicted as law-enforcing superheroes, and "Fun with Real Audio," in which the recorded voices of real politicians and others accompanied outlandish animations. Smigel's "TV Funhouse" shorts won first prize at the World Animation Festival in 1997.

According to Frazier Moore, for many years Smigel "harbored dreams of partnering real and fake creatures for comedic effect." Smigel realized those dreams with his series *Comedy Central's TV Funhouse*, whose eight installments aired in December 2000 and January 2001. Opening with a disclaimer—"The following program contains puppets, superheroes and Chihuahuas in mature situations. Viewer discretion is advised"—*TV Funhouse* had a live human host (Doug Dale), who interacted with animal puppets dubbed the "Anipals." The Anipals would ignore Doug's suggestions for wholesome activities, choosing instead to visit brothels and casinos, among other outings. In one scene an unfaithful feline puppet gave birth to a litter containing a puppy as well as real kittens. *TV Funhouse* "reveled in its offensiveness," Frank DeCaro wrote for the *New York Times* (September 14, 2008, on-line), adding that it was "blasphemous, bawdy and often brilliant as it combined low-tech puppetry, animated pop-culture satire and puerile humor into half-hours of jaw-dropping bad taste."

Smigel's silver-screen acting credits include parts in the movies *Billy Madison* (1995), *Happy Gilmore* (1996), *The Wedding Singer* (1998), *Little Nicky* (voice only, 2000), and *Punch-Drunk Love* (2002), all of which starred Adam Sandler, and *You Don't Mess with the Zohan* (2008), which starred Sandler and John Turturro; Smigel co-wrote that film with Sandler and Judd Apatow and also executive-produced it. Smigel co-wrote the screenplay for *Jack and Jill*, which stars Sandler as both title characters and was scheduled to open in November 2011. He has been cast in an as-yet-untitled comedy written and directed by Apatow that will also star Annie Mumolo, Paul Rudd, Leslie Mann, and Melissa McCarthy.

According to Dave Itzkoff, Smigel "has grown up to become a man with wild Pigpen hair, a Shaggy goatee and a permanent layer of Fred Flintstone stubble" (referring to characters from *Peanuts* and the animated TV series *Scooby Doo* and *The Flintstones*, respectively). Smigel lives with his family in Allendale, New Jersey, a New York City suburb. He and his wife, Michelle Saks-Smigel, have three sons: Daniel, born in 1998, and twin boys, born in 2008. Daniel has severe autism. To raise money for educational programs and other initiatives that help victims of autism and their families, in 2006 Smigel mounted *Night of Too Many Stars*, a one-night theatrical show in which Jon Stewart, Tina Fey, and many other celebrities appeared; new versions of the show were staged in 2008 and 2010 and, like the first one, were broadcast on Comedy Central.

—M.B.

Suggested Reading: *avclub.com* Aug. 4, 2004, June 15, 2009; *New York Observer* p1+ Oct. 20, 2003; *New York Times* (on-line) Apr. 23, 2006; *Salon.com* Apr. 9, 2001; *Vice* magazine (on-line) Oct. 2010; Sacks, Mike. *And Here's the Kicker: Conversations with Top Humor Writers About Their Craft*, 2009

Selected Television Shows: *Saturday Night Live*,1985–92, 1996– ; *Late Night with Conan O'Brien*,1993– ; *The Dana Carvey Show*, 1996; *TV Funhouse*, 2000–01

Selected Films: *Billy Madison*, 1995; *Happy Gilmore*,1996; *The Wedding Singer*, 1998; *Punch-Drunk Love*, 2002; *You Don't Mess with the Zohan*, 2008; *Jack and Jill*, 2011

Smith, Charles

Mar. 7, 1955– Playwright; educator

Address: Professional Playwriting Program, Kantner Hall, Rm. 210, Ohio University, Athens, OH 45701

"In this country, when it comes to race, it doesn't matter what the reality is. We see what we believe," the playwright and educator Charles Smith told an Asheville, North Carolina, *Mountain Xpress* (January 22, 2002) interviewer. In dramas including *Cane*, *Free Man of Color*, *Knock Me a Kiss*, *The Gospel According to James*, and the Pulitzer Prize–nominated *Black Star Line*, Smith has addressed issues of race through the lens of history—his own and his family's as well as that of the United States and other parts of the world. His "ability to look deeply into . . . his own life and his family . . . has given him a very particular view of the world and particularly about race in America," Janet Allen, the artistic director of the Indiana Repertory Theatre (IRT), which has commissioned and mounted plays by Smith since the 1990s, told

Courtesy of Charles Smith

Charles Smith

Mary Reed for the Ohio University magazine *Perspectives* (Autumn/Winter 2010). "I think he's been amazingly astute at . . . how he has harnessed his own early sense of disenfranchisement and anger . . . to find a real way to harness some of what could be very negative and corrosive stuff into art." "It's my way of shouting as loudly as I can," Smith told John Liberty for the *Kalamazoo (Michigan) Gazette* (October 9, 2005). "It's my way of grabbing people by the lapels and shaking them without being arrested."

Of mixed race, Smith grew up in a working-class part of the South Side of Chicago, Illinois. A high-school dropout and U.S. Army veteran, he discovered his love for theater as a community-college student. The first production of his first play took place in 1984, the year he earned a master's degree from the Iowa Playwrights' Workshop. Called *Jelly Belly*, the play won three awards and nominations for two others. In addition to the IRT, Smith has received commissions from the Goodman Theatre, in Chicago; the Seattle Repertory Theatre, in Washington State; the Acting Company, in New York City; Ohio University, in Athens; and the Victory Gardens Theater, in Chicago, where he is a member of the Playwrights Ensemble and currently playwright in residence. His plays have also been mounted in many other locations in the U.S. and overseas. Smith has taught at Ohio University since 1995 and, concurrently, has headed its Professional Playwriting Program; in 2010 the university named him a distinguished professor. He earned the Ohio Arts Council Individual Excellence Award in 2008.

Charles Robert Smith was born on March 7, 1955 in Chicago. His father died in a car accident when Smith was seven years old. He and his six brothers and sisters were raised on Chicago's South Side by their mother and stepfather, a taxi driver and security guard. His father and stepfather were African-American. Smith responded skeptically when, at age seven, he was told that his mother was white, and he sought the opinions of his friends. "They knew my mother," Smith recalled to the *Mountain Xpress* reporter. "So we went to my house, watched her for 20 minutes, and when we left they said, 'She's not white,' And I said, 'You're right.'"

Although neither his mother nor his stepfather had completed high school or pursued any of the arts, Smith was an avid reader, and he sometimes wrote in his spare time. "Nobody ever mentioned it, ever said, 'You can be a writer,'" he told Julia Keller for the *Chicago Tribune* (February 22, 2004). "It was always, 'Well, what factory you going to work at?'" Some of his siblings developed addictions to drugs and alcohol—in the case of one brother, Smith believes, as a way to conquer his feelings of terror. Smith himself "can remember being terrified for a very long time," he told Keller, "and then realizing, 'Well, what's the worst thing that can happen?' You have to move forward in spite of terror." Others among his siblings succumbed to what Julia Keller described as "the usual disappointments and near-misses and if-onlys."

Smith's behavior during his freshman year of high school led to his expulsion. He spent the next school year at an "adjustment center," he told Cleora Hughes for the *St. Louis (Missouri) Post-Dispatch* (February 28, 1991). When he returned to high school, administrators—unsure where to place him—repeatedly moved him among different age groups and "special" classes, including one for physically handicapped students. "I got bounced around so much I dropped out," he recalled to Hughes. "But I continued to read and write." He took a job in a factory, where he enjoyed his work and the camaraderie of other employees. Encouraged by co-workers to explore other options, he joined the U.S. Army. While stationed in South Korea, he happened upon a copy of Homer's *Iliad* and developed an interest in classic literature. During his stint in the army, he earned a GED.

After his military discharge, at age 22, Smith moved back home. He enrolled at Harold Washington College, a public community college in Chicago, in the hope of taking a course devoted to Chaucer. The school offered no such course, so Smith took a class in theater instead. He soon became involved in a student production of Milan Stitt's *The Runner Stumbles* and, during performances, would sit in the wings, watching every scene. (He had a bit part, too.) "Until then, I thought maybe I'd write novels, but I began to realize what a great thing it was to have a community of people to tell your story," he told Hedy Weiss for the *Chicago Sun-Times* (February 13, 2000). "And I thought: I can do that. I can write a play." The draft of a play he completed in two days greatly impressed his English professor, Edward Homewood. Homewood later drove him to Iowa City to interview for admission to the Iowa Playwrights' Workshop, a graduate-level program at the University of Iowa. Smith won acceptance to the program, but before he could participate in it, he had to earn an undergraduate degree. After three terms at the university (January 1980 through May 1981), during which he majored in English, with a minor in communication and theater arts, he received a B.A. degree. Smith then entered the Iowa Playwrights' Workshop, which awarded him an M.F.A. degree in 1984. Afterward he returned to Chicago, where he joined the Playwrights Ensemble at the Victory Gardens Theater. For a while he taught playwriting at Northwestern University, in nearby Evanston.

Smith's first play, *Jelly Belly*, was mounted in a workshop production by the American Theater of Actors in New York City in 1984 and performed by three additional companies in the next three years; its world premiere took place at the Victory Gardens in 1989. *Jelly Belly*'s title character is a neighborhood drug kingpin and murderer who, upon returning from a brief stint in prison, strives to regain the services of his former drug runner, Kenny. Kenny must decide whether to resume his illegal activities or keep working lawfully alongside his friend Mike, who hopes to start his own construction company someday. After viewing a performance of *Jelly Belly* at the Off-Broadway New Federal Theatre in 1990, Stephen Holden wrote for the *New York Times* (November 22, 1990) that the play "offers an unremittingly bleak portrait of inner-city life and the enormous pressure on working-class black men to be gangsters." While the character Jelly Belly is portrayed as a "walking nightmare," Holden wrote, "his arguments against the straight-and-narrow life have a kernel of truth. The barriers of race and class to Mike's realization of his dream, the play suggests, are nearly insurmountable." *Jelly Belly* won the Cornerstone National Playwriting Award (1985), the Theodore Ward National Playwriting Award (1988), and the NBC New Voices Award (1990) and was nominated for the Audelco Award for New York (1990) and the Black Theater Alliance Award for New York (1996). It is included in the book *Seven Black Plays*, edited by the theater director Chuck Smith.

Smith returned to a similar setting for his teleplays *Pequito* (1986) and *Fast Break to Glory* (1988), both of which aired on the NBC affiliate WMAQ in Chicago and earned Chicago/Midwest Emmy Awards.

Takunda (1987) evolved from Smith's drama *Tales of South Africa*, commissioned by the Repertory Theatre of St. Louis's Imaginary Theatre Company. Set during the political oppression of 1973 Rhodesia (now Zimbabwe), the play portrays the coming of age of Takunda, a 16-year-old black girl who must fend for herself after her father is imprisoned and her mother flees the country. *Takunda*

"has the streamlined story telling and immediacy of a folk tale, plus the well-earned anger of such South African spectacles as *Asinamali!* and *Poppie Nongena . . .*," Lawrence Bommer wrote for the *Chicago Reader* (July 2, 1987, on-line). "But *Takunda* is more than just one more third-world tragedy. Smith's poetry ennobles every survivor and every fatality—Takunda's frightened mother and fable-spinning grandmother" as well as her "self-serving lover . . . and particularly her father."

Also premiering in 1987 was Smith's one-act play *The Golden Leaf Rag Time Blues*, about the unlikely friendship between an African-American boy and an old Jewish man. It received workshop productions from both the American Blues Theatre Company in Chicago and the HBO New Writers Workshop, while Smith was a member of it.

Smith's play *Cane* (1991) is an adaptation of Jean Toomer's same-named, 1923 novel, which is widely considered a landmark work of the Harlem Renaissance. A mixture of drama, song, and dance in which 10 actors portray more than 40 characters, *Cane* was written under the auspices of the Michael and Marianne O'Shaughnessy Playwright Development Program. The inspiration for Smith's next work, *Young Richard* (1991), was the hysteria surrounding the murders of two dozen children and several adults, all African-American, in Atlanta, Georgia, within two years beginning in 1979. In writing *Young Richard* Smith was strongly influenced by the series of essays about the murders written by the African-American novelist, poet, playwright, and activist James Baldwin, collected in Baldwin's book *The Evidence of Things Not Seen* (1985). In those essays, Smith said to Hughes, Baldwin asked the questions "What would happen if the murders turned out to be unrelated? What if they were just random acts of violence?" "It seemed to Baldwin that we, as Americans, are too quick to place fault for the world's ills on larger entities . . . ," Smith said. "We want to believe that someone else is responsible for the violence, that someone else is responsible for the homelessness, that someone else is responsible for the litter. When in actuality, we are all to blame." *Young Richard* is not about the Atlanta murders. The title character is an African-American writer who loses the support of his white, "politically correct" patron because of his refusal to focus on "black issues"; instead, Richard attacks corporations and powerful individuals for causing the widespread problems of humans of all races and ethnic groups. According to Smith's Web site, csplays.com, "Richard ultimately discovers something about himself and personal responsibility." *Young Richard* was produced by the St. Louis Black Repertory Company and presented during the 1991 National Black Theatre Festival, two years after an initial workshop production by the American Blues Theatre Company.

In 1991 the Seattle Repertory Theatre commissioned Smith to write a play for young audiences to commemorate the 500th anniversary of Christopher Columbus's first voyage to the New World. The dark side of his four voyages—the brutal treatment and enslavement of thousands of native Caribbean-Americans by Columbus and his crews—is not widely known in the U.S. Smith's play *City of Gold* (1991) offers various perspectives of Columbus's life and deeds, portraying the explorer as neither hero nor conqueror but as a complex human being.

In his next play, *Freefall*, Smith made Chicago the home town of two estranged brothers: Grant, a police officer, and Monk, who shows up on Grant's doorstep after his release from jail. Their fraught confrontation leads them to realize the meaning of family. *Freefall* received its world premiere at Victory Gardens Theater in 1993 and was produced Off-Broadway by the Weissberger Theater Group in 1994. The *New York Times* (March 8, 1994) drama critic Ben Brantley wrote that the play "often creaks in its structural and plot devices, and its reversals of character can feel jarringly abrupt," but he noted Smith's "sharp ear for idiomatic dialogue" and praised his expertise "in presenting crime as a seductive and understandable option in a world of battered expectations."

In *Black Star Line* (1996), a Goodman Theatre commission, Smith focused on the Jamaican-born Marcus Garvey, the leader of the 1920s Back-to-Africa movement. The title refers to the shipping company Garvey founded with the aim of transporting African-Americans to Liberia. Admirers of *Black Star Line* included Tom Valeo, who described it for the Chicago *Daily Herald* (January 26, 1996) as "an entertaining and illuminating blend of historical fact and gripping drama," and Richard Christiansen, who wrote for the *Chicago Tribune* (January 28, 1996) that *Black Star Line* "may be the most important play produced at the Goodman [that] season. It tells us a lot about our country's history, but in so doing, it also, disturbingly, tells us a lot about where we still are today." *Black Star Line*'s detractors included the playwright and theater professor Paul Carter Harrison, who, writing for the *African American Review* (December 22, 1997), dismissed the play as "overstuffed" and "untutored" and accused Smith of manufacturing lies about Garvey and "arbitrarily manipulating facts to reconstruct African American history into a disingenuous docu-drama." Carter argued that Smith was representative of a "national problem" in which "large foundations pay substantial funds for the production of acceptable portrayals of the black experience for a subscriber-base audience which is predominantly white, rather than for productions that depict authentic black experience."

"I've thought long and hard about this issue, and I think I've arrived at a healthy conclusion," Smith told Hedy Weiss after similar accusations were leveled at him regarding his play *Knock Me a Kiss* (2000), about the short-lived marriage of the poet, playwright, and novelist Countee Cullen to Yolande Du Bois, the daughter of the scholar, educator, and activist W. E. B. Du Bois. Smith acknowledged that *Black Star Line* and *Knock Me a Kiss* have fictional and speculative aspects but noted that historians, too, often have agendas: "90 percent of what passes for history . . . contains an element of the writer's fantasy," Smith said to Weiss. "Many of the historians I've read on Du Bois and [the Harlem Renaissance] had agendas of their own, including some, in the 1950's and 1960's, who wanted to refute Cullen's homosexuality because they needed to make ideal black role models." *Knock Me a Kiss*, which premiered at Victory Gardens Theater, depicts Yolande as a spoiled young woman who, eager to maintain her expensive life style and please her adored father, agrees to give up her romantic interest in a struggling jazz musician to marry Cullen, her father's choice for her. In Smith's portrayal W. E. B. Du Bois regards the well-being of his race as outweighing that of his family. "Taking [the characters] down to the human sphere makes them a lot more interesting," Smith told Kerry Lengel for the *Arizona Republic* (January 29, 2006). "History, if we learn nothing but dates and platitudes, we learn it by rote, and we don't understand anything profound that we can apply to our own lives." *Knock Me a Kiss* was included in the anthology *The Best New Plays of 2000* and was mounted Off-Broadway in 2010.

Smith's adaptation of Mark Twain's novel *Pudd'nhead Wilson* was commissioned by the Acting Company, which performed it in 22 U.S. cities in 2001–02. "As a writer, I knew I'd be matched up with Twain, which is pretty formidable," Smith told the *Mountain Xpress* interviewer, "but he was only flirting with the ideas of race and how we perceive it. . . . I had to read between the lines to uncover his point of view. . . . There was a dark underside [to the novel], the scent of another story that could have permeated the original writing." Twain's tale is about two sons of Percy Driscoll, a rich white southerner—one, Tom, born to Driscoll's wife, and the other, called Chambers, to Roxy, one of his slaves. Roxy is only 1/16th black, and thus Chambers only 1/32d, and the babies closely resemble each other. Driscoll's wife dies, and when Tom and Chambers are three months old, Roxy, fearing her imminent sale to another slave owner, switches them in their cribs. Tom, now a slave (and called Chambers), grows up to be a fine human being, while Chambers (now called Tom) becomes arrogant and selfish. Smith's version called for a dark-skinned African-American actor to be cast as Driscoll's white son and a white actor as the 1/32d-black son. When the *Mountain Xpress* interviewer questioned him about that directive, Smith cited his childhood confusion regarding his mother's race and asked rhetorically, "Is our racial identity, more than anything, a state of mind?"

In 2002 Smith adapted Theodore Dreiser's novel *Sister Carrie* for the Indiana Repertory Theatre (IRT). His next play, *Free Man of Color* (2004), was commissioned by Ohio University (OU) to celebrate the school's bicentennial; the only requirement was that the university figure in the play. "I told Charles I didn't want a pageant," the school's then-president, Robert Glidden, told Keller. "I didn't want '200 years of Ohio University history.' I trust his art." Smith focused on the school's first black student, John Newton Templeton, a slave who gained his freedom and then enrolled at OU; he earned an A.B. degree in 1828, long before slavery ended in the U.S. Smith knew only that Templeton had boarded with the school's president Robert Wilson, who advocated the return of black Americans to Africa, and that Templeton had given a speech, entitled "The Claims of Liberia," at his graduation ceremony. From those few facts Smith fashioned a tale about education and assimilation and what it means to be "first." *Free Man of Color* premiered at Victory Gardens in 2004 and moved to Ohio University's Blackburn-Templeton Auditorium for the bicentennial celebration. It was awarded the 2004 Joseph Jefferson Award for Outstanding New Work and a John W. Schmid Award. In 2009 it was mounted at the Independent Theatre in Adelaide, South Australia, and in 2010 was performed Off-Broadway (with the title *Freed*).

Smith's play *Denmark* (2004), about a slave rebellion allegedly organized by the freed slave Denmark Vesey in 1822, was commissioned by Victory Gardens. Hedy Weiss, writing for the *Chicago Sun-Times* (October 16, 2006), called the play "a skillfully constructed and superbly acted drama that poses questions about the exceedingly thorny issue of just who is the freedom fighter and who is the terrorist." Smith wrote the book, David Sherman the music, and Lois Walden the lyrics for *Shoot the Piano Player* (2010), a musical adaptation of David Goodis's novel *Down There* (1956). (François Truffaut's famous French New Wave film of 1960, *Shoot the Piano Player*, was also based on *Down There*.)

Smith's most recent work, *The Gospel According to James*, was commissioned by the IRT and financed in part by a $50,000 grant from the Joyce Foundation and funding from the National Endowment for the Arts. The title character is James Cameron, who on August 7, 1930, at age 16, was lynched along with two friends by a white mob in Marion, Indiana, after they were jailed on charges of murdering a white man during a robbery and raping his girlfriend. Cameron was saved, possibly because one or more people in the mob declared that he was innocent, as he had claimed; a widely disseminated photo (now posted on the Internet) shows his two friends hanging above the mob, which by then had grown to include thousands of other townspeople. Cameron, reportedly the only person known to have survived an intended lynching, later became a civil rights activist, wrote a memoir, and founded America's Black Holocaust Museum, in Milwaukee, Wisconsin. In 2005, a year before his death, Cameron was present when the U.S. Senate formally apologized to black Americans for the failure of Congress ever to pass legislation declaring lynchings unlawful. In Smith's play Cameron and Mary Ball, the woman who accused the black men of rape, try to reconstruct the events of that long-ago August day. Their recollections do not match, thus calling into question the natures of memory and perception. "We look for truth," Smith told Mary Reed, "but I don't think there is truth." *The Gospel According to James* premiered at the IRT in March 2011 and was scheduled to open at Victory Gardens in May.

Smith joined the faculty at Ohio University in 1995. He is an OU distinguished professor of playwrighting, an OU presidential research scholar in arts and humanities, and the head of OU's Professional Playwriting Program, which he has transformed into one of the most respected programs of its kind in the U.S. In most such programs, Smith told Reed, students write plays and then their professors "tell you what you did wrong." By contrast, he said, he believes that "form follows function. I believe that what we have to do is figure out what the purpose of the play will be and that will determine how the play will be written." During OU's three-year program, students must write one full-length play each year and produce a short play every week. "There are so many playwriting programs that are theoretical," Smith told Reed. "People write plays, and then the program may produce only one play a year, which I think is a crime."

Smith lives in Athens, Ohio, with his wife, Lisa Quinn, and their teenage daughter, Elyssa. He also has two adult children from previous relationships: Trinity Smith and Tendai Kachingwe.

—M.M.H.

Suggested Reading: *African American Review* p713 Dec. 22, 1997; *Arizona Republic* E p1 Jan. 29, 2006; (Asheville, North Carolina) *Mountain Xpress* p30 Jan. 22, 2002; *Chicago Sun-Times* NC p4 Feb. 13, 2000, p41 Oct. 16, 2006; *Chicago Tribune* C p8 June 19, 1987, C p1 Feb. 22, 2004; *Kalamazoo (Michigan) Gazette* (on-line) Oct. 9, 2005; *New York Times* p13 Nov. 22, 1990, C p15 Mar. 8, 1994; *Perspectives* (on-line) Autumn/Winter 2010; *St. Louis Post-Dispatch* F p8 Feb. 28, 1991

Selected Plays: *Jelly Belly*, 1984; *Takunda* (formerly: *Tales of South Africa*), 1987; *The Golden Leaf Rag Time Blues*, 1987; *Cane*, 1991; *Young Richard*, 1991; *City of Gold*, 1991; *Freefall*, 1993; *Black Star Line*, 1996; *The Sutherland*, 1997; *Les Trois Dumas*, 1998; *Knock Me a Kiss*, 2000; *Pudd'nhead Wilson*, 2001; *Sister Carrie*, 2002; *Free Man of Color* , 2004; *Denmark*, 2004; *Shoot the Piano Player*, 2010; *The Gospel According to James*, 2011

Selected Teleplays: *Pequito*, 1986; *Fast Break to Glory*, 1986

Mandel Ngan/AFP/Getty Images

Sperling, Gene

Dec. 24, 1958– Director of the National Economic Council

Address: The White House, 1600 Pennsylvania Ave., N.W., Washington, DC 20500

"One of the reasons I've selected Gene is he's done this before." President Barack Obama made that statement, as quoted by Lori Montgomery and Brady Dennis in the *Washington Post* (January 7, 2011, on-line), during a news conference announcing the appointment of Gene Sperling as director of the National Economic Council (NEC). Sperling, a lawyer and public-policy expert, served as director of the NEC from 1996 to 2001, during the second term of President Bill Clinton; during those years, according to Obama, he "helped formulate the policies that contributed to turning deficits to surpluses and a time of prosperity and progress for American families in a sustainable way." The appointment of Sperling, the successor to Lawrence Summers, came as the Obama administration sought to take on experts who would help navigate the economy as it emerged from a recession, and who are able to negotiate economic policy with Republicans, who won control of the House of Representatives in the 2010 midterm elections. Although not an economist by training, Sperling has a reputation as a progressive thinker with regard to economic policy and as a capable political strategist. "The N.E.C. director job is uniquely well-suited for Gene because this is a job which is about figuring out what the economic policy should be, building consensus among policy makers and making sure that the policies are going to have the right impact in

the real world," Sheryl Sandberg, the chief operating officer of Facebook.com and a Treasury Department official in the Clinton administration, told Jackie Calmes for the *New York Times* (January 20, 2011, on-line).

After earning a law degree and working on the Democrat Michael Dukakis's ill-fated 1988 presidential campaign, Sperling joined the Clinton campaign in 1992 as its chief economic adviser. After Clinton won the presidency, Sperling was appointed deputy director of the newly created NEC. In 1996 he was promoted to the director's post, in which he helped formulate key economic policies, many of which favored the poor, and contributed to bringing about a budget surplus. In a review for the *New York Times* (January 22, 2006, on-line) of Sperling's book *The Pro-Growth Progressive*, Noam Scheiber wrote, "If you were inclined to identify Clintonism with a single person other than the big man himself, that person might well be Gene Sperling . . . a tireless advocate of fiscal discipline during the first term; an inveterate policy wonk throughout all eight years of the administration." After the Clinton administration ended, Sperling held a number of jobs outside the White House, before returning in 2009 as an adviser to Treasury Secretary Timothy Geithner in the Obama administration. In that role he proved to be a valuable asset to the president, helping to broker an important deal with Republicans in December 2010: in exchange for extentions of tax cuts for the wealthy, the administration secured an extension of unemployment benefits and a reduction of the payroll tax. As a result, Sperling emerged as a top contender for his current position in the White House. "There's no one who marries politics and policy as well," Joshua Steiner, a former Clinton administration official, told Calmes. "So when Gene gets a seat at the table, over time he gets recognized." Sperling began his second tenure as NEC director on January 20, 2011.

Gene B. Sperling was born on December 24, 1958 in Ann Arbor, Michigan, one of the four children raised in the upper-middle-class home of Lawrence Sperling, an attorney, and Doris Sperling, a public-school teacher. Sperling's parents were progressive-minded and took the time to educate their children about racial injustice and economic disparities. Recalling family car trips through the struggling Rust Belt city of Detroit, Michigan, Sperling told the journalist Matt Miller for a profile posted on mattmiller.com (November 1999), "You would see kids your age living in such bad conditions, It always seemed extremely unfair to me."

Sperling was his high school's star tennis player, ranking in the top 10 in the state. "When Gene played tennis, there was no ball that was too far for him to get—or think he could get," his father told David Shepardson for the *Detroit News* (January 7, 2011). "He goes at everything full blast." Sperling attended the University of Minnesota at Minneapolis on an athletic scholarship and earned a B.A. degree in political science in 1981. He was the captain of the school's varsity tennis team. During those years, in the fall of 1980, he interned for U.S. senator Carl Levin, a Michigan Democrat. He then attended law school at Yale University, in New Haven, Connecticut, earning a J.D. degree in 1985 and serving as senior editor of the *Yale Law Journal.* Sperling became increasingly interested in public policy during his time at Yale. "He basically never left his library cubicle," Christian Merkling, a classmate of Sperling's, told David S. Hilzenrath and Steven Mufson for the *Washington Post* (May 9, 1993). "He was obsessed with policy to an extent that made it difficult for even those of us interested in policy to talk to him. He was so wound up in the maze of whatever he was involved with."

During his summer breaks from Yale, Sperling worked as an unpaid research assistant for the future Clinton administration labor secretary Robert Reich, then a lecturer at Harvard University. Sperling was drawn to Reich's liberal economic philosophies, as were many politicians; Sperling told Miller, "I was really fascinated by the way he was able to be relevant." After earning his law degree, Sperling worked briefly for the NAACP Legal Defense Fund (LDF) and the National Abortion Rights Action League, now known as NARAL Pro-Choice America.

Sperling next attended the Wharton Business School of the University of Pennsylvania, in Philadelphia, but left before earning his M.B.A. degree to join the 1988 presidential campaign of Massachusetts governor Michael Dukakis. Sperling initially worked for the campaign as an unpaid staffer, handling small legal matters; according to Miller's article, after he was allowed to sit in on an economic-policy meeting, Sperling spoke up, and his ideas were greeted with enthusiasm. Miller wrote, "Within days Sperling was one of the campaign's key economic staffers, doing nightly conference calls with Reich and then–Harvard professor Lawrence Summers, who were advising Dukakis. These calls became a crash course in presidential-level policy development for Sperling, forcing him to integrate Summers' rigorous but often abstract economic analysis with Reich's strength at framing issues in compelling, real-world terms."

Dukakis, the Democratic nominee, lost the November 1988 general election to George H.W. Bush. Despite the loss Sperling views his time with the campaign as an invaluable learning experience. He told Hilzenrath and Mufson, "Presidential campaigns are the ultimate political education. You learn more in two months than in 10 years on a policy job." Sperling then worked as a researcher for the Harvard law professor Laurence Tribe before joining the office of New York governor Mario Cuomo as an economic adviser. Cuomo, a Democrat, was widely expected to run for president, and Sperling hoped to work on his campaign. By all accounts, when the governor decided not to run, Sperling was deeply disappointed.

Then, in 1992, based on his growing reputation in Democratic circles, Sperling was invited to serve as economic-policy director for the Clinton campaign. In that post he was the chief adviser on economic matters for Clinton, whose platform was based primarily on improving the U.S. economy. On November 3, 1992 Clinton was elected as the 42d president of the U.S., defeating George H.W. Bush, and Sperling became deputy director of economic policy for the transition team. Once in the White House, Clinton created the NEC, appointing the Wall Street investor Robert E. Rubin as the council's first director and Sperling as deputy director. According to its Web site, the NEC was created "to coordinate the economic policy process among all cabinet agencies, with respect to both domestic and international economics issues." Sperling told Hilzenrath and Mufson that joining the NEC at age 33, following 12 years of the policies of the Republicans Bush and Reagan, "felt like some weird kind of mix between the first day of summer camp and the French Revolution."

Sperling was instrumental in the creation of a number of the Clinton administration's early economic initiatives, including the 1993 Deficit Reduction Act, the Direct Student Loan Program, the Community Development Financial Institutions Program, the Technology Literacy Initiative, and the America Reads initiative. He was also involved in efforts to increase the Earned Income Tax Credit (a provision of the Deficit Reduction Act), a credit, based on income, for individuals or couples with children. On several occasions Sperling, a major proponent of the tax credit, fought Republicans who were bent on shrinking or eliminating it. In a 2007 article for Bloomberg.com (August 31, 2007), Sperling wrote, "The impact of these battles was worth the fight: the Clinton expansion has now meant about $100 billion in additional funding for working poor families since 1993." In advocating additional extensions of the credit, he observed, "These expansions further what President Clinton used to describe as the fundamental belief that in the U.S. no parent working full time should have to raise their children in poverty."

In 1995 Rubin was named U.S. treasury secretary, with Laura Tyson succeeding him as NEC director. When Tyson left the post, in 1996, Sperling took over, serving as director until 2001. According to the NEC Web site, he was charged with "ensuring that economic policy is consistent with the President's long term goals of maintaining financial discipline, making key investments in the American people, and opening foreign markets for American workers, farmers and businesses." Upon taking the post he became, at age 38, a member of the presidential Cabinet. During that time Republicans held the majority in Congress, the result of the so-called Republican Revolution of 1994. Sperling was able to negotiate successfully with Republicans on budget issues. In 1997 he was one of the main negotiators of the Balanced Budget Agreement, persuading the Clinton administration to accept certain Republican demands, including lower capital-gains and estate taxes that favored the wealthy, in order to gain concessions on funding for expanded health-care coverage for children, scholarships for community colleges, and child tax credits for an additional 13 million low-income parents. Sperling was also tasked with ensuring that Clinton stuck to the economic promises made during his two campaigns. Hilzenrath and Mufson observed that after the 1992 election, Sperling was essentially "deputized to remind the president of his campaign promises," and noted that Rubin called his deputy "the keeper of the flame." Sperling continued to hold Clinton to his campaign pledges when he became NEC director. According to Lee Siew Hua, writing for the Singapore *Strait Times* (November 21, 1999), he was "crowned the keeper of Clintonomics—an agenda laden with priorities from balancing the Budget to increasing social spending on education and the environment."

When it later became apparent that the Clinton administration would be able to announce the first budget surplus since 1969, Sperling realized that Republicans would want to return the surplus to voters through tax cuts. He spearheaded the "Save Social Security First" proposal, in which the surplus would be used, at least initially, to bolster the Social Security program in the face of the looming, unprecedented number of retirees from the Baby Boomer generation. Sperling's solution was successful; Michael Waldman, then Clinton's chief speechwriter, told Miller that the plan was "substantively sound, politically brilliant, and didn't leak [to the press prematurely, which is] almost unheard of in Washington."

In an article he wrote for *Blueprint Magazine* (March 25, 2002), posted on DLC.org, Sperling observed, "If not for President Clinton's 1998 State of the Union challenge to Congress to save the surplus until we knew how much was needed to secure Social Security's long-term solvency, surpluses could have disappeared long ago. Clinton's call to 'save Social Security first' froze all sides, and led, for several years, to a bipartisan commitment to save surpluses to pay down the national debt and increase savings for the baby boomers' retirement. The nation's decision to forgo current consumption and restrain popular political initiatives to meet the costs of future Medicare and Social Security liabilities was a rare moment of fiscal discipline and foresight."

In 1999 Sperling, with U.S. trade representative Charlene Barshefsky, negotiated the entrance of China into the World Trade Organization (WTO). That year Sperling, along with then–Treasury Secretary Lawrence Summers, also negotiated the Financial Modernization Bill (also known as the Gramm-Leach-Bliley Act), which repealed portions of the Glass-Steagall Act and allowed commercial banks, securities firms, and insurance companies to merge. (The Glass-Steagall Act, officially called the Banking Act of 1933, was enacted during the Great Depression to separate investment

and commercial banking.) Today, many economists cite the repeal as a contributing factor to the financial crisis and recession that began in 2008.

After Clinton's second term ended, in 2001, and the Republican George W. Bush became president, Sperling took on a number of part-time jobs. He held a position as a visiting fellow with the Brookings Institution, a nonprofit public-policy organization; wrote a column for Bloomberg News; and worked for the Council on Foreign Relations as a senior fellow for economic policy and as the director of the Center for Universal Education. In his position with the council, Sperling produced policy studies related to education in the Third World, with a focus on the education of girls. He also co-authored (with Barbara Herz) *What Works in Girls' Education: Evidence and Policies from the Developing World* (2004), published by the Council on Foreign Relations Press. In addition, he worked for a year for the Wall Street firm Goldman Sachs, serving as an adviser to a charitable program, 10,000 Women, which provided over $100 million to educate women in poor nations in business and management. From 2001 to 2004 Sperling served as a consultant for the popular NBC White House drama series *The West Wing* (1999–2006).

Sperling's 2006 book, *The Pro-Growth Progressive: An Economic Strategy for Shared Prosperity*, clearly defined his views on economics. He argued that progressives can achieve their goals by utilizing market forces. In his review of the book, Scheiber wrote, "More than anything else, *The Pro-Growth Progressive* embodies the neoliberal idea that all problems are solvable if we just set aside ideology and focus on what works. Sperling notes at the outset that resolving trade-related issues requires 'deep, honest exploration that does not easily fit within any right-left, pro-globalization-anti-globalization perspective.' Later he writes that 'neither progressives nor conservatives have articulated a vision for retirement security' that guarantees a reasonable nest egg while also helping workers invest in equities. Much of the book employs this third-way tone. Yet while Sperling appears to chide both sides equally, his book functions primarily as a useful reproach to progressives who believe that ideological purity requires rejecting market-friendly means."

Sperling was the economic adviser for Hillary Rodham Clinton's 2008 presidential campaign. After Clinton lost the Democratic nomination to Barack Obama, Sperling joined the Obama campaign. Following Obama's inauguration Sperling joined the Obama administration as a counselor to Treasury Secretary Timothy Geithner. He was involved in negotiating several key policy decisions, including the bailouts of the floundering car companies General Motors and Chrysler. He also helped negotiate the temporary extension of President Bush's tax cuts for the wealthy, favored by Republicans, in return for Republican support for extending federal unemployment insurance and cutting the payroll tax.

In January 2011 Obama named Sperling to succeed the NEC director, Lawrence Summers, who was stepping down. A few months earlier, when Sperling was one of several candidates in the running for the NEC post, his background came under scrutiny. Aside from his involvement in repealing portions of the Glass-Steagall Act, his tenure with Goldman Sachs, for which he was paid almost $900,000, was called into question by some liberals. Explaining those concerns, Ezra Klein wrote for the *Washington Post* (December 30, 2010, on-line), "You tend not to get paid that much for offering guidance to charitable endeavors. It is very hard to believe that Goldman Sachs wasn't attempting to buy influence with a politically savvy economist who had good relations—and would later go to work for—the incoming Democratic administration." Supporters of Sperling argued that his economic views do not favor Wall Street, citing his push for financial institutions to pay fees for receiving Troubled Asset Relief Program (TARP) assistance from the federal government. (No such fee was imposed on the banks.) As quoted in a *Mother Jones* article (January 6, 2011, on-line), Dean Baker, of the Center for Economic and Policy Research, defended Sperling, explaining, "I don't think it's a question of outright corruption. It's a question of orientation. Most people hear you got almost a million dollars for a part-time job, and they think there's a problem there. But people on Wall Street say, a million bucks is chicken feed." The author of the *Mother Jones* article, David Corn, wrote, "Democratic and Republican administrations—including Obama's—do tend to be filled at the top with lawyers and corporate officials who have raked in millions of dollars annually for years in the private sector. Sperling is not on par with these folks." While conceding that "due to his past service as NEC chief, [Sperling] was able to pull in far more money than the average do-gooding Washington policy wonk," Corn added, referring to the ruthless financier played by Michael Douglas in the *Wall Street* films, that Sperling "was no Gordon Gekko."

Sperling faces daunting challenges in his second stint as NEC director. Montgomery and Dennis observed, "When Sperling and [White House budget director Jacob] Lew were last in their current posts, the economy was booming, and they had balanced the federal budget for the first time in nearly 40 years after cutting a deficit-reduction deal with a Republican Congress. They return to a sluggish, post-recession recovery marked by chronically high unemployment, a rising national debt and the biggest budget deficits—measured against the economy—since World War II. Republicans are once again ascendant on Capitol Hill. And after two years of policymaking aimed at averting an economic meltdown, the administration is retooling for a protracted political fight over fiscal and economic issues in the run-up to the 2012 presidential campaign."

Sperling has been praised by colleagues for his communication skills both in political negotiations and in front of news reporters. He has also been commended for his ability to shape the economic policies of those he serves in appropriate ways. The Democrat Charles Schumer, the senior U.S. senator from New York, told Montgomery and Dennis that Sperling has the right combination of economic expertise and political know-how to help the Obama administration. "In 2009, the complete thrust had to be economics. Now, politics is every bit as important, and he can do both," Schumer said. "He has a feel for what is politically possible on the economic side of things. He gets it." Sperling said, as quoted by the two reporters, that his goal "is to figure out how to work with Republicans while taking home important progressive wins, to find that bridge where you both preserve your values and get things done."

During the Clinton years Sperling developed a reputation for working long hours and for his unkempt appearance and messy office—results of his obsession with his work. He is now married to Allison Abner, a former writer for *The West Wing*, and has two children, a four-year-old daughter with Abner and a teenage stepson; he has reportedly found a balance between his work and personal life. Jake Siewert, a Treasury Department counselor and former White House press secretary, told Richard Wolf for *USA Today* (January 7, 2011, on-line), "If he's writing e-mails at 2 a.m. now, it's because he's been up with his kids."

—W.D.

Suggested Reading: *Detroit News* A p1 Jan. 7, 2011; mattmilleronline.com; *New York Times* (on-line) Jan. 22, 2006, Jan. 20, 2011; *USA Today* (on-line) Jan. 7, 2011; *Washington Post* H p1 May 9, 1993, (on-line) Jan. 7, 2011; whorunsgov.org

Selected Books: *What Works in Girls' Education: Evidence and Policies from the Developing World* (with Barbara Herz), 2004; *The Pro-Growth Progressive: An Economic Strategy for Shared Prosperity*, 2006

Stengel, Richard

May 2, 1955– Managing editor of Time; *writer; former organization official*

Address: Time Inc., 1271 Ave. of the Americas, New York, NY 10020

In 2006, when he was named managing editor of *Time* magazine, Richard Stengel declared, "*Time* has to become indispensable again. It has to have a voice that people care about. In this big, teeming media forest, there are some places that need to be a guide to separate what's important from unim-

Andy Kropa/Getty Images

Richard Stengel

portant. That's a role that we can and should have," as quoted by Stephanie D. Smith for *Mediaweek* (May 22, 2006). At a meeting the next year of the Time-Life Alumni Society, composed of former staff members of both *Time* and *Life*, Stengel said, "The ultimate mission about sustaining *Time* is about greatness," according to Joe Hagan, writing for *New York* (March 12, 2007). "One of the things we're doing in the future is trying to be selective, go for the best. . . . I believe that is what will make *Time* great again." "In his first year as *Time*'s managing editor, [Stengel] did the near-impossible: He made the magazine seem relevant," Jon Friedman wrote for *MarketWatch* (July 11, 2007), after suggesting that "if the media handed out awards for 2006–07, . . . Stengel would be a good bet to win Rookie of the Year honors." For most of the years since 1983, Stengel has worked for *Time*, starting as a staff writer. Before he assumed his current position, he served as *Time*'s associate editor (1984–86) and as *Time.com*'s managing editor (2000), and he has been a senior writer, essayist, and contributor since 1989. Like others in the magazine and newspaper industry, as *Time*'s managing editor Stengel has had to grapple with the huge competition presented by news sources on the Internet and cable-news networks; with fewer subscribers, advertisers, and newsstand sales than in past decades, he has had to institute major cost-cutting measures, including laying off staff. In July 2010, in an effort to boost subscriptions and newsstand sales, he decreased the amount of content from current print issues that would be posted on *Time*'s Web site.

Stengel has left *Time* on three occasions for other pursuits, the first two while on leaves of absence. Off and on beginning in 1993, he helped the great South African civil rights leader Nelson Mandela with his autobiography, *Long Walk to Freedom* (1995). He left *Time* in 1999 to aid Bill Bradley, a former basketball star and former U.S. senator from New Jersey, in Bradley's bid for the Democratic nomination for president; he was Bradley's senior adviser and chief speechwriter during that ultimately unsuccessful campaign. In 2004 Stengel resigned from *Time* to become the president and chief executive officer of the National Constitution Center, in Philadelphia, Pennsylvania. He has written hundreds of essays and articles for *Time* on a vast array of subjects, and his byline has also appeared in periodicals including the *New Yorker*, the *New Republic*, *Smithsonian*, and *Gentlemen's Quarterly* (now called *GQ*). In addition, he has written three books—*January Sun: One Day, Three Lives, a South African Town*; *You're Too Kind: A Brief History of Flattery*; and *Mandela's Way: Fifteen Lessons on Life, Love, and Courage*—and has edited or co-edited several books published by Time Inc. He taught a course in politics and the media at Princeton University in the late 1990s. In 2010 *Newsweek* listed him among the 50 highest-earning people of political influence in the U.S.

Widely known as Rick, Richard Stengel was born on May 2, 1955 in New York City. His father, Robert L. Stengel, served in World War II; the first person in his family to attend college, he worked in his family's business. As a boy Stengel idolized the New York Knicks basketball star Bill Bradley. He attended Scarsdale High School, in an upscale New York City suburb. In 1973 he entered Princeton University, in Princeton, New Jersey. His admiration for Bradley (a Princeton alumnus) grew after he heard Bradley speak at the college. Stengel took a course about the "literature of fact"—nonfiction—taught by John McPhee, an acclaimed *New Yorker* writer, and he has credited McPhee with inspiring him to pursue a career in journalism; in an interview with Nathalie Lagerfeld for the *Daily Princetonian* (May 19, 2006, on-line), he called McPhee the hero of Stengel's own life story. At Princeton Stengel befriended Jim Kelly, a fellow student, whom he later succeeded as *Time*'s managing editor. As an undergraduate Kelly read a profile of Bradley that Stengel had written. "It was so terrific, it was clear to me that he would be the best writer in the class . . . ," Kelly told Lagerfeld. "He talked about how Bill Bradley would run down the court looking like 'a French woman hurrying home with the morning baguette.'" Stengel played basketball for the Princeton squad, as Bradley had, and he was a reserve player on the 1975 team, which won the National Invitation Tournament (organized by the National Collegiate Athletic Association). He earned a B.A. degree, magna cum laude, in 1977, then continued his education as a Rhodes scholar at Christ Church College, Oxford University, in England. He completed his studies in England in 1981.

That year Kelly, who had joined *Time* in 1978, helped Stengel get a job as a *Time* staff writer. At that time *Time*'s team of nearly 100 field correspondents would send their reports to *Time*'s New York City office, where staff writers would turn them into finished pieces. Stengel found a friend and mentor in Walter Isaacson, a fellow Rhodes scholar who had studied at Oxford University and became a renowned historian and biographer and, in 1996, editor of *Time*. Stengel was promoted in 1984 to associate editor and, in 1989, to senior writer; he also earned the titles of essayist and contributor. The subjects of his hundreds of essays and longer articles for *Time* include the latest generation of homeless in the U.S. (published in 1986), Faye Wattleton, the president of Planned Parenthood Federation of America (1989), a museum exhibit devoted to designs of the Italian shoemaker Salvatore Ferragamo (1992), ways in which the Internal Revenue Service's antiquated computer systems aided tax fraud (1997), the daily activities of New York City public-school principals (1999), the comedian Jerry Seinfeld (2002), the power of the White House during wartime (2006), the effects of Hurricane Katrina two years after it struck (2007), the future of the green revolution (2009), and President Barack Obama and his wife's call for volunteerism and national service (2009).

Stengel's first book, *January Sun: One Day, Three Lives, a South African Town*, was published in 1990. *January Sun* offers day-to-day accounts of three people living under apartheid, the system of government-mandated racial segregation and repression that lasted from 1948 to 1994. Stengel had already written about the African nation for *Time* and *Rolling Stone*, and with *January Sun*, he told the stories of a white veterinarian, a black cab driver, and an Indian merchant. In a review for the *San Diego Union-Tribune* (May 20, 1990), Anne Marie Welsh wrote that Stengel's book "has the truth and reality of art" and "creates an unforgettable picture of the way things were."

On the strength of *January Sun*, Nelson Mandela chose Stengel to help him compose his autobiography, *Long Walk to Freedom*, and in 1993 Stengel took a leave of absence from *Time* to do so. Mandela, who led the African National Congress then, spent 27 years in prison for his efforts to end apartheid; he was released in 1990 and in 1994 became the first president of South Africa to be elected by people of all races, after apartheid ended. "Mr. Mandela has been well served by his collaborator, . . . who preserved the unmistakable voice of Mr. Mandela—polite, good-humored—while curbing his tendency to speak in the collective voice of the movement and to name every person who attended every meeting," Bill Keller, the *New York Times*'s Johannesburg, South Africa, bureau chief from 1989 to 1991, wrote for the *Times* (December 18, 1994, on-line). "The narrative is enlivened by intimate detail and introspection that must have been coaxed from Mr. Mandela, since he is usually loath to speak of such things in public." During the near-

ly three years between Stengel and Mandela's first meeting and the publication of *Long Walk to Freedom*, Stengel often accompanied Mandela on his customary four-hour early-morning walks and many other times, and he tape-recorded some 70 hours of conversations—far more than Mandela had originally thought would be necessary and far less than the total number of hours the two men spent together. He also interviewed more than 50 of Mandela's family members, friends, and colleagues. Stengel co-produced the film *Mandela* (1996), which earned an Academy Award nomination for best documentary feature. Stengel's book *Mandela's Way: Fifteen Lessons on Life, Love, and Courage* (2010), blends biography—and Stengel's own reminiscences—with discussions of Mandela's principles for action.

During the 1998–99 academic year, Stengel taught a course called "Politics and the Press" at Princeton as a Ferris professor of journalism. In 1999 he took another leave of absence from *Time*, to serve as a senior adviser and chief speechwriter for Bill Bradley, who was seeking the Democratic Party's presidential nomination. "I was a journalist taking a temporary hiatus in politics. It was really an act of the heart rather than a career move," he told Lori Robertson, Lori Silverstein, and Meredith Hooker for *American Journalism Review* (July/August 2000).

Stengel's book *You're Too Kind: A Brief History of Flattery* appeared in 2000, shortly before Stengel returned to *Time* as managing editor of its Web site. "The stuff now that is exciting in journalism is online," he told Robertson, Silverstein, and Hooker. "I want to make the site Webbier, more fun, visually arresting and more personal." In 2001 Kelly replaced Isaacson as *Time*'s managing editor, and John Huey, Time Inc.'s editorial director, suggested that Stengel be promoted to editor of *Time*'s "Nation" section. Although Kelly was reluctant, because he thought that Stengel "wasn't managerially organized enough to oversee a ferocious presidential-election season," in Hagan's words, he gave Stengel the job. He often rewrote Stengel's stories, however, thereby creating a rift between the two friends.

In 2004, eager to "run something," according to Hagan, Stengel moved to Philadelphia to become the president and chief executive officer of the National Constitution Center, a nonprofit think tank that aims to increase understanding of the U.S. Constitution and promote civic involvement. "I really want to make it a place that's involved in the great public debates," Stengel told Stephan Salisbury for the *Philadelphia Inquirer* (February 2, 2004), citing gay marriage and "putting together a constitution in Iraq" as the kinds of issues the center might address. "There's a problem in public discourse: We have shouting on the left and shouting on the right, with nobody reasonable in the center," he told Sasha Issenberg for *Philadelphia Magazine* (April 2004). "You can take anything on the front page of the *Inquirer* and the *Times*, and

I can tell you why it has something to do with the Constitution." Under Stengel's leadership the center expanded its programming and visibility, and in 2005 it nearly reached its goal: to draw a million visitors in one year. "He's taken us from being a neophyte institution to an established part of the Philadelphia firmament," John C. Bogle, the chairman of the center's board of trustees, told Larry Eichel for the *Philadelphia Inquirer* (May 18, 2006).

Meanwhile, John Huey, who had been promoted to editor in chief of Time Inc., named Jim Kelly to the newly created position of managing editor for Time Inc. Huey offered the position of *Time*'s managing editor to Daniel Okrent, who turned it down but agreed to help Huey find someone else for the job. Their list of possible candidates included Stengel, who, in subsequent conversations with Okrent and Huey, complained that Kelly had not done enough to make *Time* competitive with emerging on-line news rivals. In a seven-page memo titled "The Overarching Question and the Answer," Stengel wrote, according to Hagan, "In this teeming media forest, this buzzing, blooming confusion of modern media, there's a need for a single iconic publication." He added that while other sources dealt in "clutter" and "opinion," *Time* should represent "knowledge," "clarity," and "authority." In May 2006 Huey announced Stengel's appointment as managing editor. "Rick is a true multi-media editor who is approaching this new assignment with tons of ideas, energy, and just the right amount of confidence," he wrote for a Time Inc. press release, according to Gawker.com (May 17, 2006). "I find him an especially exciting new Managing Editor because he has both the outsider's perspective and the insider's appreciation and knowledge of who and what makes *Time* tick. His intellectual depth and breadth are long established, as are his leadership qualities and competitive spirit." While, by his own account, he had planned to remain with the National Constitution Center for far longer than two years, Stengel said he looked forward to guiding "one of the greatest brands in history," Larry Eichel reported.

As *Time*'s 16th managing editor, Stengel faced the challenge of keeping the 83-year-old magazine afloat in the digital age. Ad sales had fallen by double-digit percentages, and *Time*'s profits had declined from $95 million in 1999 to $50 million in 2006. To reassure advertisers who questioned the accuracy of the magazine's circulation numbers (which determine its rates for ads), Stengel reduced the so-called rate base from 4 million to 3.25 million, eliminating the numbers of subscriptions that might not reflect true readership, such as those for doctors' offices. The reduced circulation led to reduced ad rates, and to compensate for the decreased revenue, Stengel raised the newsstand price by $1 and—adding to layoffs instituted before his return—cut 50 people from the staff. He also changed the day of publication from Monday to Friday—a move he said would be more convenient for readers, who were often too busy to read

magazines during the week. Stengel said a Friday release would also help *Time* "set the news agenda," according to David Carr, writing for the *International Herald Tribune* (January 9, 2007), rather than follow the competition. "We've traditionally been a mirror, and to me, we more and more have to be a lamp," he told Julie Bosman for the *New York Times* (September 4, 2006), explaining his plan to publish more analytical and opinion pieces. "As a lamp, you're shining a light on something."

Stengel ended *Time*'s longstanding practice of having New York City staffers rewrite stories filed from abroad, and he hired a team of "star" columnists, including Isaacson, the political writer Michael Kinsey, and the *Weekly Standard* editor William Kristol. In an attempt to draw more visits to Time.com, Stengel hired the 34-year-old Josh Tyrangiel, who had written music reviews under Isaacson, as Time.com's editor. The site was expanded to include blogs such as "Swampland," which deals with national politics. "You take the DNA for the original *Time* and then you grow it up in a different Petri dish which is online, and it becomes something new yet still has the integrity of what we've always done," Stengel told Ian Burrell for *Independent Media Weekly* (November 12, 2007). "It doesn't bother me if somebody discovers Time.online and has never read the magazine."

While Stengel said in some interviews that he wanted the new *Time* to develop the sort of high-brow reputation enjoyed by the *Economist*, he said *Time* must also appeal to a broad readership. "We mirror the demographics of America as a whole," he told Hagan. "The *New York Times* talks to people who already agree with all the things in the *New York Times*. I would argue that the bar for us is higher because we have a diverse audience. We're not preaching to the converted." He told Carr, "I think it is a false choice to say that something that is mass has to be dumbed down. We want to be accessible, but we want our readers to know that we understand they are smart."

Following *Time*'s tradition since 1927 of choosing a "person of the year" for the cover article of its last issue in December, Stengel chose "You"—ordinary "citizens of the new digital democracy"—for its 2006 cover, Russian president Vladimir Putin in 2007, President-elect Barack Obama in 2008, and Ben Bernanke, the chairman of the Federal Reserve, in 2009. Topics to which *Time*, under Stengel, has devoted entire issues included volunteerism and national service (September 21, 2009); environmental conservation, in particular the "perils of plastic" (April 12, 2010); and the possible repercussions of the U.S. military's departure from Afghanistan (August 9, 2010).

Stengel's wife is the former Mary Pfaff, a South African photojournalist he met while working with Mandela. Stengel has said that Mandela himself urged the two to marry. The couple, who wed in 1994, live in New York City with their sons, Gabriel and Anton.

—K.J.P.

Suggested Reading: *Chronicle of Philanthropy* (on-line) Aug. 3, 2006; *Daily Princetonian* (on-line) May 19, 2006; *Independent Media Weekly* p12 Nov. 12, 2007; *MarketWatch* July 11, 2007; *Mediaweek* p26+ May 22, 2006; *New York* p46+ Mar. 12–19, 2007; *New York Times* C p1+ Sep. 4, 2006; *Who's Who in America*

Selected Books: *January Sun: One Day, Three Lives, a South African Town*, 1990; *Long Walk to Freedom* (with Nelson Mandela), 1995; *You're Too Kind: A Brief History of Flattery*, 2000; *Mandela's Way: Fifteen Lessons on Life, Love, and Courage*, 2010

Jesse Grant/Getty Images

Sykes, Wanda

Mar. 7, 1964– Comedian; actress; writer

Address: c/o William Morris Agency, One William Morris Pl., Beverly Hills, CA 90212

The comedian and actress Wanda Sykes personifies "the angry loudmouth, hilariously outraged at the injustices of the world," Ari Karpel wrote for the *Advocate.com* (March 2009). "Her trademark is her voice, which always rises as she spits out expletives to expertly cut through any bull that sparks her anger—whether it's directed at former president George W. Bush . . . or people who oppose marriage equality." One of the most successful female comedians in the entertainment industry, Sykes gained fame with her original brand of acerbic, brazen, profane, righteously angry, politically and socially aware comedy. She began her ca-

reer in stand-up comedy and has put her talents to use as a writer, actress, talk-show host, and producer. She served as a writer and performer with *The Chris Rock Show* from 1997 to 2002, winning (along with a dozen others) a 1999 Emmy Award for her work. She has since appeared on TV in short-lived series of her own—*Wanda at Large*, *Wanda Does It*, and *The Wanda Sykes Show*; three stand-up-comedy specials; and programs including *Crank Yankers* and *The New Adventures of Old Christine*.

In its March 19, 2004 issue, *Entertainment Weekly* ranked Sykes 14th on its list of the 25 funniest people in North America. "Wanda Sykes is one furious ball of comedic energy," the magazine's editors wrote. "Whether lambasting Larry David on *Curb Your Enthusiasm* or heckling football players on *Inside the NFL*, the comedian with the distinctive nasal twang rarely fails to deliver a verbal smackdown." Sykes's book of humorous essays and brief commentary, *Yeah, I Said It*, was published in 2004. Sykes won an American Comedy Award in 2001, in the category of funniest female stand-up comic, and a BET Comedy Award in 2005, as outstanding supporting actress in a theatrical film, for her work in *Monster-in-Law*—one of the dozen films in which she has acted or voiced characters. In 2009 she made headlines when she became the first African-American woman and the first openly gay person to present the featured monologue at the annual White House Correspondents' Dinner.

In late 2010 the name "Wanda Sykes" appeared in conjunction with the word "sassy" in more than 14,000 search results on google.com and more than 26,000 on bing.com. Sykes hates to be referred to as "sassy." She told Joel Stein for *Time* (November 8, 2004), "Sassy to me is a put-down. It's given to black women. No one calls Ellen DeGeneres sassy. No one calls Robin Williams sassy. . . . Sassy is all attitude and no content. And I've got something to say."

Wanda Sykes was born on March 7, 1964 in Portsmouth, Virginia. She was raised with her older brother in middle-class Gambrills, Anne Arundel County, Maryland, near Washington, D.C. Her father was a U.S. Army colonel stationed at the Pentagon; her mother worked in banks. Sykes told Lee Michael Kats for the *Washingtonian* (June 11, 2010, on-line), "I think people just assume"—wrongly—"I had to fight my way through the hard life and the streets to get to where I am and that's where my personality comes from." She added, "It's not like everything was great. There was still racism and all where we grew up." Starting when she was about seven, she recalled to Kats, she became "very outspoken, and it got to the point that whenever [my parents] . . . had guests over, they would send me off to my grandmother's because they had no idea what was going to come out of my mouth. Not necessarily anything nasty or mean—it was just truth or facts. If I heard them say something about someone, or if someone owed them money, I had no problems bringing it up to that person." Around that time Sykes began to watch comedians on television; her favorites were Joan Rivers, Johnny Carson, and Lucille Ball. At Anne Arundel High School, she was known for her sense of humor; praise for her jokes peppered her high-school yearbook.

In 1982 Sykes enrolled at Hampton University, a historically black college in Virginia. She earned a B.S. degree in marketing in 1986 and soon found work with the National Security Agency (NSA), a branch of the U.S. Defense Department. Her job, as a contract specialist for equipment purchases, "was pretty boring," she told Kats. "Every now and then you get a cool project to work on, but mainly it was 'Oh, okay, this guy has a bad back; he needs a special orthopedic chair. Well, I need a note from your doctor saying you need a special chair. Okay, now I can order you your special chair.' . . . After five years I was bored silly." She began to contemplate a career in comedy, and in 1987 she made her debut, at a Coors Light Super Talent Showcase in Washington, D.C. She did not win that contest but enjoyed the experience enough to continue performing at comedy clubs at night and on weekends.

In an interview with blackfilm.com (May 2005), Sykes explained that her act developed slowly. "My first three or four years was me doing an impression of what I thought a stand-up comic was supposed to be . . . ," she said. "It was never about my point of view; I hadn't created a stage persona yet. It was just always the jokes. I was really gifted at being able to construct a joke, but . . . they weren't even memorable, my first jokes, because they were so about nothing. You know, it was like, 'hey, you know those big things you put in your car window, the auto shades? Did you know they have instructions on the side of them? They tell you to please remove auto shade before starting your ignition. Who needs this information?' You know, jokes like that—'have you ever seen a car coming at you on the highway with the big sunglasses?' It was . . . jokes like that, more observational things. It wasn't until I became more confident . . . [that] I put myself forward instead of the jokes; at first it was put the jokes out there and I'm just behind the jokes."

In 1992 Sykes quit her NSA job and settled in New York City, with hopes of performing on the comedy circuit. She told Scotty Ballard for *Jet* (October 13, 2003), "I figured the worst that could happen would be that I was wrong. If I tried it and it didn't work out, at least I walk away saying, 'It was something I wanted to try and it didn't work out, but at least I tried.' The only thing you're going to be is wrong, so just move on. It's not the end of the world. Don't be scared to take a chance." Sykes did stand-up in clubs before landing a spot as the opener for Chris Rock at Carolines on Broadway, a comedy nightclub. In 1997 Rock recruited Sykes to write and perform on his HBO program, *The Chris Rock Show*, whose format combined talk, sketches, and stand-up comedy and included both commen-

tary regarding social and racial issues and sophomoric humor. "It was a lot of fun writing for Chris because I felt like I was being challenged . . . ," Sykes told Scotty Ballard. "I know it made me a better writer." She remained with the show until 2002, when it was cancelled.

Three years earlier Sykes had made her feature-film debut, in a small role in the comedian Louis C.K.'s film *Tomorrow Night*. The next year, thanks to her fellow *Chris Rock Show* writer Lance Crouther, she attended a party for the cast and crew of the HBO sports show *Inside the NFL* (which currently airs on Showtime). She told Ballard that at the party, "I'm just being me . . . I'm just ripping on everybody—it was just for fun, you know? So, everybody's laughing." A month later, she recalled to Ballard, an HBO executive producer telephoned her and said, "I don't know who you are, but you had me cracking up at the party, and I would love for you to bring that energy to the show. Would you be interested?" She responded, "Hell yeah! I love football." Sykes has served as an *Inside the NFL* correspondent since 2002, inserting humor in her reports on events and during interviews with athletes and sports officials.

Starting in 1999 Sykes appeared in several episodes of the HBO comedy series *Curb Your Enthusiasm*, which stars Larry David as a fictionalized version of himself. David (who also writes and produces the show) presents himself as someone who lacks social skills; Sykes, cast as an exaggerated version of herself, would point out the unintentional racism of his comments with barbed remarks of her own. In 2001 Sykes played the character Christine Watson, the love interest of Drew Carey, in three episodes of the ABC sitcom *The Drew Carey Show*. In 2002 she began doing voice-over work for the puppet Gladys Murphy in Comedy Central's prank-phone-call show, *Crank Yankers*. In the early 2000s Sykes also had a minor role in the movie *Nutty Professor II: The Klumps* (2000), starring Eddie Murphy, and she played Biggie Shorty, a romantic interest and friend to Pootie Tang, the title character of a 2001 Louis C.K. film, which was adapted from a *Chris Rock Show* sketch. (Rock also produced and acted in the film.) Sykes was also cast in *Down to Earth* (2001), a comedy about reincarnation starring Rock.

In 2003 Sykes starred in her own sitcom, *Wanda at Large* (she was also a co-writer, with Crouther and others, and a co-producer), which aired on the Fox network. It centered on Wanda Hawkins, a struggling comedian who becomes a correspondent on a Sunday-morning political talk show, where she often irks her uptight co-workers. Sykes told Judith S. Gillies for the *Washington Post* (March 23, 2003), "Wanda Hawkins is basically me. . . . We have the same attitude, the same point of view . . . pointing out hypocrisies in the way we see the world, but the difference is that I'm not always on." Writing for Popmatters.com (March 31, 2003), Terry Sawyer praised Sykes for taking risks he found "admirable" and for "making any political observations at all" when "so much of the sitcom landscape is riddled with shows that hinge on humor tied solely to the idiosyncratic chemistry of stock characters or the tired regurgitation of slightly dysfunctional family melodrama." *Wanda at Large* aired after the highly popular *American Idol* until the fall of 2004, when Fox switched it to Friday nights—"the valley of death on the broadcast networks," Edward Wyatt wrote for the *New York Times* (November 7, 2009). A steep drop in ratings soon led to its cancellation.

The hour-long Comedy Central stand-up special *Wanda Sykes: Tongue Untied* (2003) was recorded in front of an audience at the John Jay College of Criminal Justice, a division of the City University of New York. Reviewing the special, in which Sykes aimed her skewers at political figures, celebrities, organized religion, and corporations, Alan Sepinwall and Matt Zoller Seitz wrote for the Newark, New Jersey, *Star Ledger* (January 10, 2003) that Sykes had "deliver[ed] a brand of rude, honest, well-crafted, intensely political comedy that's rarely practiced these days by anyone not named George Carlin or Chris Rock" and that "whatever the response, *Tongue Untied* is a quantum leap forward for Sykes, who's spent the last few years as one of the better kept secrets in comedy." Sykes's later comedy specials, both for HBO, were *Wanda Sykes: Sick & Tired* (2006) and *Wanda Sykes: I'ma Be Me* (2009). *Sick & Tired* and *I'ma Be Me* were nominated for Emmy Awards, in the categories of outstanding variety, music, or comedy special (*Sick & Tired*) and outstanding writing for such a special (*I'ma Be Me*). All three specials are available as DVDs.

In 2004, sponsored by Comedy Central, Sykes completed a national, 31-city stand-up-comedy tour. She also appeared in a new TV series, *Wanda Does It*. In each episode of that show, Sykes tried her hand at a different job, among them pilot, basketball coach, repo woman, professional gambler, and photographer. Co-created with Lance Crouther, *Wanda Does It* was "a sitcom disguised as a reality show in which the dialogue is improvised from an outline," in Joel Stein's words. According to Stein, after the cancellation of *Wanda at Large*, Sykes had come to doubt that "a writers' room can create an entertaining show. Reality [shows], she believes, [have] made people realize how wooden sitcoms feel." In an episode of *Wanda Does It* set at Chicken Ranch, a legal brothel in Nevada, Sykes was shown being trained by one of the resident prostitutes. "Sykes' hooker performance [was] so strong . . . that the Chicken Ranch manager ask[ed] Sykes if she can put her picture on its website," Joel Stein wrote. The run of *Wanda Does It* ended after six episodes.

Sykes appeared alongside Jennifer Lopez and Jane Fonda in the director Robert Luketic's *Monster-In-Law* (2005), a romantic comedy about a woman (Fonda) who distrusts her son's fiancée (Lopez). Sykes's portrayal of the Fonda character's sarcastic assistant was the film's partially saving

grace, according to some reviewers. Sykes next appeared in a small role as an angry customer in *Clerks II* (2006), a sequel to *Clerks* (1994), the director Kevin Smith's cult hit about aimless youth employed at a convenience store. She also had a role in the comedy *My Super Ex-Girlfriend* (2006), which starred Uma Thurman. In 2007 Sykes was cast in the director Tom Shadyac's *Evan Almighty* (a spin-off of Shadyac's *Bruce Almighty*), a comedy about a congressman (played by Steve Carell) who builds an ark after God warns him about an impending flood. Sykes, as one of the congressman's assistants, improvised many of her lines, as she had in *Monster-In-Law*.

Sykes's career as a voice-over artist for animated children's films began with *The Adventures of Brer Rabbit* (2006), in which she spoke the lines of Sister Moon. She provided the voice of Stella, a skunk, in the computer-graphics movies *Over the Hedge* (2006) and its sequel, *Hammy's Boomerang Adventure*, which came out on DVD the same year. In 44 episodes that aired between 2007 and 2009, Sykes was the voice of Bessy, a sarcastic cow, in the Nickelodeon animated series *Back at the Barnyard*, about farm animals.

Sykes appeared regularly on the sitcom *The New Adventures of Old Christine*, which ran from 2006 to 2010 on CBS. She played Barb, a friend and business partner of the title character (portrayed by Julia Louis-Dreyfus). Sykes told Josh Wolk for *Entertainment Weekly* (July 7, 2006, on-line) that she enjoyed having only one responsibility on the set—that of a member of the cast. "I learned from my Fox sitcom *Wanda at Large* that it'll be a while before I try another of my own," she said. "It's too much work for the way it gets treated and how much of it is out of your control. Doing *The New Adventures of Old Christine* is a cakewalk for me. I love the people, and it's nice to walk in, do the show, and leave everything there. I'm not at home tossing and turning, 'What are we gonna do about this episode?'"

In 2009, with the comedian Keith Robinson as co-host, Sykes launched a late-night talk show, *The Wanda Sykes Show*, on the Fox network. The program fared poorly. Some critics complained that Sykes's frequent defense of the Barack Obama administration and her lampooning of Republicans were uninspired and tiresome. Barry Garron, the television critic for the *Hollywood Reporter* (November 8, 2009), expressed a different view: "Though it lacked some of the subtle wit and sophistication found on Jon Stewart's *Daily Show*, [*The Wanda Sykes Show*] nonetheless provided a worthwhile perspective on where America is today compared to where it was at the end of the Bush presidency." The show was canceled in 2010, after one season.

In 1991 Sykes married the hip-hop and R&B record producer David Hall. Although she had known since childhood that she was a lesbian, she "made the choice to be straight as a kid," she told Karpel. "Early on I knew [that being gay] wasn't gonna fly. No way. And from the teachers and church and all it was, *This is wrong! What's wrong with me?* And you pray and ask God to take it away, and you bury it and bury it, and you shut that part of yourself off. Then you try to live the life you're supposed to live." Sykes and Hall divorced in 1998, but not because of her homosexuality, she told Karpel: "It's just that when you bury a part of ourself, you can take those relationships only so far because you can't be totally open. Once we were divorced there was a defining, liberating moment of, 'OK, I'm free of this marriage, now what?' It's kind of like giving yourself permission. I guess that's when I started actively dating women."

Sykes came out publicly as a lesbian at a gay-rights rally in Las Vegas, Nevada, in 2008. She told Karpel she felt compelled to so do after the passage in California of Proposition 8, a ballot measure that banned same-sex marriage. "I wasn't in the closet," she told Karpel, "but I was just living my life. Everybody who knows me personally knows I'm gay. And that's the way people should be able to live their lives, really. We shouldn't have to be standing out here demanding something we automatically should have as citizens of this country." In 2010 GLAAD (the Gay & Lesbian Alliance Against Defamation) honored Sykes with its Stephen F. Kolzak Award, for her "strong commitment to educating the public about the lives of LGBT [lesbian, gay, bisexual, and transsexual] people," according to the organization's Web site.

Sykes and her wife, Alex, a native of France, married shortly before Proposition 8 passed. In April 2009 Alex Sykes gave birth to twins, Olivia Lou and Lucas Claude. In her stand-up routines Sykes has talked about her experiences as a mother.

—W.D.

Suggested Reading: *Advocate.com* Mar. 2009; *Chicago Sun-Times* p48 Oct. 14, 2004; *Detroit Free Press* June 6, 2010; imdb.com; *Jet* p58 Oct. 13, 2003; *New York Times* (on-line) Nov. 7, 2009; *Time* p76+ Nov. 8, 2004; Wanda Sykes Web site; *Washingtonian.com* June 11, 2010; Sykes, Wanda. *Yeah, I Said It*, 2004; *Who's Who in America*

Selected Films: *Tomorrow Night*, 1999; *Nutty Professor II: The Klumps*, 2000; *Pootie Tang*, 2001; *Down to Earth*, 2001; *Monster-In-Law*, 2005; *Clerks II*, 2006; *My Super Ex-Girlfriend*, 2006; *Over the Hedge*, 2006; *Evan Almighty*, 2007

Selected Television Shows: *The Chris Rock Show*, 1997–2002; *Inside the NFL*, 2002–; *Wanda at Large*, 2003–05; *Wanda Does It*, 2004; *Back at the Barnyard*, 2007–09; *The New Adventures of Old Christine*, 2006–10; *The Wanda Sykes Show*, 2009–10

Selected Television Specials: *Wanda Sykes: Tongue Untied*, 2003; *Wanda Sykes: Sick & Tired*, 2006; *Wanda Sykes: I'ma Be Me*, 2009

Selected Books: *Yeah, I Said It*, 2004

Taleb, Nassim Nicholas

(TAH-leb, nah-SEEM)

1960(?)– Financial mathematician; philosopher; writer; teacher; former derivatives trader

Address: Research Center for Risk Engineering, Polytechnic Institute of NYU, Six MetroTech Center, Brooklyn, NY 11201

"I wake up every morning knowing that I don't understand what's going on," Nassim Taleb told Will Self for *GQ* (May 2009). "My product line is coming up with a systematic and unified way to deal with what we don't know." A native of Lebanon, Taleb is a financial mathematician, an expert in applied statistics, and a highly successful derivatives trader-turned-writer, teacher, and self-proclaimed philosopher/psychologist. He is best known among statisticians, professional investors, and the general public for his Black Swan Theory, which deals with the occurrence of extremely rare events that powerfully affect humans and the reluctance of most people to face the inevitability of such events. The name of the theory stems from the sighting by Willem de Vlamingh, a Dutch explorer, of black swans in an Australian river in 1697. De Vlamingh's observation overturned the long-held assumption among Europeans that, since swans in Europe were invariably white, all swans on Earth must be white. The Europeans' faulty reasoning regarding swans is an example of what is known as Hume's Problem of Induction, named for the 18th-century Scottish philosopher David Hume. As Hume pointed out, no matter how many times we see particular objects that have certain characteristics (such as white swans), we can draw no blanket conclusions or be certain about the characteristics of all such objects, because there may always be an exception (such as the black swans in Australia); even a single exception (one black swan) will show that our assumptions are wrong.

In his Black Swan Theory, Taleb extended Hume's principle to include events as well as objects. The tsunami that struck northeastern Japan on March 11, 2011 is such an event. Taleb labels such exceptional occurrences "outliers": happenings that are extremely rare and unexpected and are thus exceedingly unlikely and unpredictable.

Courtesy of Sarah Josephine Taleb

Nassim Nicholas Taleb

According to his theory, outliers are bound to occur—one can predict with virtual certainty that they will occur but not precisely when—and such events have had and will have a huge impact on people's lives. Their consequences can be positive, as in the case of the publishing of J. K. Rowling's Harry Potter books, or negative, as in the case of the unforeseen stock-market crashes of 1929 and 1987. Other examples of black swans that Taleb has offered include World War I, the proliferation of the personal computer, the arrival of the Internet, and the passion for owning celebrated Impressionist paintings among wealthy Japanese businessmen. Taleb's theory also holds that our brains are wired to dismiss or reject the possibility of outliers—few people plan for such eventualities—and that the occurrences of outliers lead people to come up with after-the-fact explanations for them that are dubious and useless. Taleb discussed the disproportionately substantial effects of rare and hard-to-predict events on the course of history in his best-selling, widely discussed book *The Black Swan: The Impact of the Highly Improbable* (2007). "History and societies do not crawl," he wrote in the book. "They make jumps. . . . Yet we (and historians) like to believe in the predictable, small incremental progression."

Taleb has a master's degree in business and a doctoral degree in financial mathematics. In 1999, after working for 16 years for a series of financial institutions and acquiring great wealth, he cofounded Empirica Capital—a "trading/hedging/protection operation," in his words; he closed the company in 2004. In addition to *The Black Swan*, Taleb's books include *Dynamic Hedging: Managing Vanilla and Exotic Options*; *Fooled*

by Randomness: The Hidden Role of Chance in Life and in Markets; and *The Bed of Procrustes: Philosophical and Practical Aphorisms.*

Taleb has taught mathematics at New York University's Courant Institute of Mathematical Sciences (1999–2007) and aspects of the "sciences of uncertainty" at the Isenberg School of Management of the University of Massachusetts at Amherst (2005–07). He was a visiting research professor at the London Business School, in England (2007–09). He has been a professor of risk engineering at the Polytechnic Institute of New York University since 2008 and a distinguished research scholar at the Said Business School of Oxford University, in England, since 2009. Taleb is a certified legal expert in the fields of risk management and derivatives and has written for many professional journals.

A son of Nagib Taleb and his wife, Minerva Ghosn, Nassim Nicholas Taleb was born in 1960 (or on September 11, 1958, according to one authoritative source) in Amioun, a predominately Greek Orthodox town in northern Lebanon about 50 miles northeast of Beirut, the nation's capital. He has a brother, Ziad. His parents were citizens of France, and his first language was French. Taleb's father was a prominent oncologist and hematologist who earned a doctorate in anthropology. Ancestors on his mother's side were socially and politically prominent for more than a century during the period when the region that became Lebanon was part of the Ottoman Empire. Taleb's maternal great-grandfather Nicolas Ghosn and grandfather, Fouad Ghosn, each served as Lebanon's deputy prime minister, and his paternal grandfather was a Lebanese Supreme Court judge.

In 1975 civil war broke out in Lebanon. At first, like most Lebanese, the Talebs believed that the fighting would end quickly, but the war continued for 16 years, and the family's financial and other assets shrank significantly. Taleb told a *Derivatives Strategies* interviewer (2001, on-line), "Maybe because I saw war in Lebanon, maybe that made me inherently skeptical. You have to be an enduring skeptic not to rule out rare events." When the conflict began Taleb was a student at the Grand Lycée Franco-Libanais, an elite private school in Beirut. After damage from a bomb forced the lycée to close temporarily, the teenager spent much of his time reading in his family's basement. In *The Black Swan* he recalled that his ruminations about how a country as seemingly peaceful as Lebanon could so quickly become mired in civil war led him to study works by the world's most important thinkers, in particular "theoretical accounts of wars and conflicts," so as to "get into the guts of History, to get into the workings of that big machine that generates events." Drawn to the works of philosophers including Georg W. F. Hegel, Karl Marx, and Arnold Toynbee, he decided that he would become a philosopher himself.

After he graduated from the lycée, Taleb enrolled at the University of Paris, in France, where he earned B.S. and M.S. degrees. He next attended the Wharton School of Business at the University of Pennsylvania, in Philadelphia, which awarded him an M.B.A. degree in 1983. According to the *Derivatives Strategies* interviewer, at Wharton "he skipped as many classes as he attended" and devoted much of his time to reading "some 150 English novels in an effort to improve his language skills." "I hated the research coming out of academia," he told the *Derivatives Strategies* writer. "It did not mesh with my notion of clinical validity. It was about how the world should behave because someone said it should behave that way."

Taleb worked briefly as a trainee for the Bankers Trust Co. before joining the French bank Indosuez (now part of Crédit Agricole) in Paris. He told Will Self that in taking such jobs, he aimed to gain financial independence. "I wanted to be a philosopher, an essayist, but I looked around me at people who worked as journalists and so forth, and they weren't free," he said. At Indosuez Taleb worked as a currency-options trader. Currency options allow an investor to buy or sell a country's currency at a certain exchange rate during, or at the end of, a specified period, regardless of changes in the currency's worth. On September 22, 1985 West Germany, the United Kingdom, France, Japan, and the U.S. signed the Plaza Accord, an agreement to devalue the U.S. dollar in relation to the German mark and the Japanese yen in an effort to bolster the U.S.'s economy and trade balance. Thanks to the Plaza Accord, some of the options Taleb acquired for Indosuez suddenly increased in value enormously. "I had no clue what had happened to me," Taleb told Stephanie Baker-Said for *Bloomberg Markets* (May 2008). "We were lucky. We made a lot of money but it was an accident." By contrast, many other companies and traders suffered because of the Plaza Accord, which they had not anticipated, and many traders lost their jobs.

At that point Taleb became focused on buying so-called out-of-the-money options, for which the exchange rate specified in the agreement is considerably higher or lower than the going market value of the particular currency. In 1986 he took a new job, with First Boston Inc. (now the Credit Suisse Group), where he accumulated a large sum of out-of-the-money options on Eurodollars (U.S. dollars deposited in banks outside the U.S.). On October 19, 1987, now known as Black Monday, the Dow Jones Industrial Average fell by 22.5 percent, the biggest one-day drop in U.S. stock-market history. The crash led the U.S. Federal Reserve to lower interbank borrowing rates, and the value of First Boston's Eurodollar options surged. While he has refused to divulge his personal profit, Taleb has said that most of his fortune stems from that event. Demetrios Diakolios, a former colleague of Taleb's at First Boston, told Baker-Said, "We all knew that he did well, that he cleaned up on that and made $35 million–$40 million. The equities guys below

us thought, 'Why did some guy upstairs make all this money on a day when everybody got killed?'"

In 1991 Taleb left First Boston to take the position of chief options trader at the Union Bank of Switzerland (now UBS). After less than a year, he left that job, partly, he has said, because he could not abide the "endless meetings." For a change of pace, Taleb moved to Chicago, Illinois, where he became a pit (or floor) trader and market maker (a person who assists in the buying or selling of stock) at the Chicago Mercantile Exchange. Around that time he started working toward a doctoral degree in financial mathematics at the University of Paris–Dauphine under Hélyette Geman, who has master's degrees in both mathematics and atomic physics and doctorates in both finance and mathematics (specifically, probability theory). He earned his Ph.D. degree in 1998; according to *Derivatives Strategies*, the subject of his thesis was "the transaction costs of forecasting volatility." The previous year Wiley had published *Dynamic Hedging: Managing Vanilla and Exotic Options*, an adaptation of his dissertation for traders that became options traders' "bible," according to *Derivatives Strategies*.

Earlier, while living in Chicago, Taleb had begun to suffer from a sore throat, attributing it to his frequent shouting on the floor of the mercantile exchange. Although the soreness persisted, he did not consult a doctor until after he left the exchange, in 1994. That year he assumed the position of global head of financial-option arbitrage at CIBC-Wood Gundy, a New York City unit of the Toronto-based Canadian Imperial Bank of Commerce. Still plagued by his sore throat, he underwent tests that revealed that he had throat cancer. Except for a few cigarettes he had tried during his youth, Taleb had never smoked, and as a nonsmoker his chances of getting throat cancer were remote; thus, his illness served as another, powerful reminder of randomness in life. Two years of radiation treatment sent the cancer into remission.

Taleb next worked as an options trader at a New York office of BNP Paribas, one of France's biggest banks. In 1999 he began teaching an evening graduate-level course on model failure in quantitative finance at New York University (NYU). After class Taleb would relax at a nearby café, where he would discuss finance with students and others. "It became an unofficial meeting place for people interested in quantitative finance and trading," Aaron Brown, the author of *The Poker Face of Wall Street* (2006), told Baker-Said. Taleb soon had an informal following that included Mark Spitznagel, an NYU graduate student. Later in 1999 Taleb left BNP Paribas to set up an investment firm, Empirica Capital Limited Liability Co., with Spitznagel as his partner. Empirica offered hedge-fund clients protection against big losses by balancing some of their trades with options holdings, an approach known as tail hedging. For the majority of Taleb's clients, Empirica investments served as a sort of insurance policy; if most of their other investments (ones made through other firms) decreased in value, there was a more-than-even chance that those they had made through Empirica would go up. Because Empirica purchased their options relatively inexpensively by buying in bulk, Taleb and Spitznagel guaranteed that investors' losses would never total more than 13 percent a year—an amount that, for investors, could be likened to an insurance premium. In 2004 Taleb shuttered Empirica, to devote himself full-time to thinking, scholarship, writing, and teaching; he and Spitznagel returned about $380 million to investors.

Earlier, in 2001, Taleb's book *Fooled by Randomness: The Hidden Role of Chance in Life and in Markets* was published. In that volume Taleb offered his ideas about why people have so much difficulty dealing with unexpected events and accepting the fact that sooner or later they are bound to occur, as they have throughout history. In an essay for the book *What We Believe but Cannot Prove: Today's Leading Thinkers on Science in the Age of Certainty* (2006), edited by John Brockman, Taleb summed up some of the contents of *Fooled by Randomness*: "We are good at fitting explanations to the past, all the while living in the illusion that we understand the dynamics of history. I believe there is a severe overestimation of knowledge in . . . almost all of social science (economics, sociology, political science) and the humanities—everything that depends on the nonexperimental analysis of past data. I am convinced that these disciplines do not provide much understanding of the world—or even of their own subject matter. Mostly, they fit a narrative that satisfies our desire (if not need) for a story. The implications defy conventional wisdom: you do not gain much by reading the newspapers, history books, analysis, economic reports; all you get is misplaced confidence about what you know. . . . It is said that the 'wise see things coming.' To me, the wise are those who know they cannot see things coming."

Fooled by Randomness made a favorable impression on Michael Schrage, the reviewer for *Across the Board* (January/February 2002), who wrote, "This is a book that takes an unusually rigorous—and rigorously unusual—look at the role of randomness in everyday life. . . . Viewing choice, decision-making, and thinking through Taleb's prism of probability, we are forced to conclude that many of our most cherished assumptions about intelligence, wit, and success are grievously flawed. What Taleb does brilliantly is take what we think we understand about probability and risk and make it shockingly clear that we don't. . . . Taleb is superb at giving the reader a sense of the subjective nature of probability. His book offers a peek at the sociology of statistical interpretation even as he explores its science. . . . Taleb's take on the psychology of risk . . . is also very helpful."

According to Joseph Nocera, who read *Fooled by Randomness* when a revised, paperback edition of the book appeared, in 2005, the original version "became a word-of-mouth sensation on Wall Street," as he wrote for the *New York Times* (October 1, 2005); the book was translated into a dozen languages. Nocera was among those reviewers who found aspects of *Fooled by Randomness* objectionable. "Mr. Taleb is a complicated man with a sizeable ego and a mode of thinking that is anything but linear," he wrote. "He drops names, sneers at his lessers (especially journalists and economists), and revels in the notion that big-shot academics 'oppose' him. . . . For me, the issue isn't so much that Mr. Taleb is wrong in his analysis. The problem is his fundamental nihilism. Taken to its logical extreme—something Mr. Taleb is happy to do—his stance strongly implies that it's pointless to even try to forecast things like stock prices or economic trends. Nor, he seems to be saying, should we even bother attempting risk management, since we always miss the big thing that winds up really mattering. And on both points, I think he's dead wrong. Think about it: how would the markets work if people weren't trying to anticipate the future? On what basis would you buy or sell a stock? Predicting cash flow for the next 20 years might be 'moronic'—but it's the only way we can try to value a stock." Nocera concluded, "The only thing worse than ignoring Mr. Taleb is buying completely into his world view. 'I am a radical skeptic,' Mr. Taleb told me. The rest of us should be skeptical, all right. We should try not to be fooled by randomness. But we should not be as skeptical as the author of *Fooled by Randomness*. That way lies madness."

Taleb expanded his arguments in his next book, *The Black Swan*. In doing so he created two metaphorical worlds, Mediocristan and Extremistan. The features of Mediocristan can be described by bell-shaped curves and parametric statistics; that is, measurements of those features fall within clearly defined boundaries. Examples of such features are people's heights, weights, and intelligence quotients and the annual amounts of rainfall in a given region. For each of those variables, most of the amounts or numbers fall in a middle range, around an average, with very few at the extreme minimum and extreme maximum; no figures would be hundreds of times bigger or smaller than any other. In Extremistan features cannot be described by bell curves or parametric statistics, because the minimums and maximums are many times smaller or greater than the averages. One example might be the average household income of a cross-section of 10,000 residents of Washington State that includes Bill Gates, the founder of Microsoft. Since Gates's income is many thousands of times greater than that of the average Washingtonian, no graph could be big enough to accommodate it. (The horizontal axis of a bell-shaped curve long enough to do so would have to be thousands of feet long.) Another example might be a graph showing death rates in towns within the Miyagi and Fukushima Prefectures of northeastern Japan in March 2011. The thousands of deaths caused in some towns by the March 11 tsunami would make use of an ordinary bell curve impossible. In *The Black Swan* Taleb argued that although the history of significant stock-market crashes indicate that the market must be considered a feature of Extremistan, economists and financial experts almost invariably discuss and predict its behavior as it if were a feature of Mediocristan. Thus, they disregard the possibility of sudden, huge, widespread declines in stock values. Taleb dedicated *The Black Swan* to the unorthodox mathematician Benoît Mandelbrot, an occasional collaborator of his. Like its predecessor, the book drew enthusiastic reviews as well as complaints regarding Taleb's putdowns of various experts and his denunciations of statistical analyses and forecasting. An international best-seller, it has been translated into more than 30 languages, and the London *Times* named it "one of the 12 most influential books since World War II."

Taleb told Wesley Yang for *New York* (December 13, 2010) that he is currently working on a book tentatively titled "Anti-Fragility" and subtitled "How to Live in a World We Don't Understand and Enjoy It." The impetus for writing the book, he said, was his realization that he has "an obligation to give a coherent account of how things should be, of how we should make decisions in the face of uncertainty." The book will contain what he described as "a complete blueprint from what you should eat to what we should do about the nation-state." In an article for *New Statesmen* (July 5, 2010), Taleb wrote, "My dream is to have a true 'epistemocracy'; that is, a society robust against expert errors, forecasting errors and hubris, one that can be resistant to the incompetence of politicians, regulators, economists, central bankers, bankers, policy wonks and epidemiologists."

Taleb and his wife, the former Cynthia Anne Shelton, married in 1988; they have a son, Alexander, and a daughter, Sarah. The couple own homes in Westchester County, New York, and Amioun. Taleb often travels to Paris and London; by his own account, he wrote a lot of *The Black Swan* while sitting in terminals at Heathrow Airport, outside London. "I have a strict rule: If I have allocated a period of time to do a job, and I do that job quicker, then the rest of the time I will do nothing . . . ," he told Self; "it will help me think more clearly, deeply, about the problem." On his Web site, fooledbyrandomness.com, Taleb wrote that one of his hobbies is "teasing people who take themselves and the quality of their knowledge too seriously and those who don't have the courage to sometimes say: I don't know." He also enjoys studying classical languages.

—H.R.W.

Suggested Readng: *Bloomberg Markets* p40+ May 2008; fooledbyrandom-ness.com; *GQ* p186+ May 2009; *New Statesman* p29 July 5, 2010; *New Yorker* p162+ Apr. 22, 2002; *Philosophy Now* p26+ Sep./Oct. 2008; *Time* p10 Dec. 13, 2010

Selected Books: *Dynamic Hedging: Managing Vanilla and Exotic Options*, 1997; *Fooled by Randomness: The Hidden Role of Chance in Life and in the Markets*, 2001; *The Black Swan: The Impact of the Highly Improbable*, 2007; *The Bed of Procrustes: Philosophical and Practical Aphorisms*, 2010

Courtesy of Paul Kolnik

Taylor, Janie

Oct. 25, 1980– Dancer

Address: New York City Ballet, 20 Lincoln Center Plaza, New York, NY 10023

Janie Taylor, a principal dancer for the New York City Ballet (NYCB), has never wavered from her chosen career path. The 30-year-old prima ballerina has been dancing since before she can remember, and as a teenager she expressed a desire to perform with the very company she dances with today. Though her ambition has never been a secret, Taylor has attracted a wide audience with her reputation as an enigma. "One of the sweet paradoxes about Janie Taylor is that her dancing is both old and new," Wendy Perron wrote for *Dance Magazine* (July 1, 2009). "She has the whiff of mystery of a truly romantic ballerina as well as the physical fearlessness of a totally contemporary dancer." That amalgamation of classic and contemporary styles—paired with a gymnastic eagerness—makes her a perfect fit for the ballets of George Balanchine. Balanchine, a revered choreographer, the founder of the School of American Ballet (SAB), and the artistic director of the New York City Ballet until his death, in 1983, revolutionized American dance with his original works and adaptations of classical ballets. "I . . . watched the NYCB perform Balanchine's choreography every night while I was a student at SAB," Taylor told Paul Kolnik for *Ballet News* (May 6, 2010, on-line), "and seeing his work made me want to dance even more. It still makes me feel excited about dancing today." Taylor has been compared to Balanchine's famous muse, Suzanne Farrell, for her spontaneity and individual style. Taylor herself is widely considered the muse of the NYCB's former artistic director and choreographer Peter Martins, for whom she has originated many roles. "Janie is wonderfully malleable, and dances with such complete abandon," Martins told Astrida Woods for *Dance Magazine* (July 1, 2009). "She is a unique creature."

At the seeming height of her career, Taylor was afflicted with a rare blood disorder, whose diagnosis eluded doctors for months. Treatments for the disease exacted a toll on her body, and it took Taylor nearly three years to recover fully. Her return to the stage was triumphant: critics have pointed to a greater depth in her work since her recovery. Whether in classic ballets such as *La Valse* and *Serenade* or the contemporary work of the rising choreographer Benjamin Millepied, Taylor has been praised for her "smooth reconciliation of opposites," as Jennifer Dunning wrote for the *New York Times* (June 28, 2005), her "recklessness and serenity, bold incisiveness and dreaming amplitude." Dunning added, "Steps, gestures, and characterizations fall away before the immediacy of her dancing."

Janie Taylor was born on October 25, 1980 in Houston, Texas, to Pam and Jeff Taylor. She took her first ballet class at two. "Ridiculous," she told Woods about being in the studio at that age. "It really didn't mean anything." Within a couple of years, however, she had come to love dance. She studied ballet with Gilbert Rome in Houston beginning when she was four. Her parents first saw the extent of her ambition when Taylor broke her leg at the age of 10. "She just couldn't wait to get back to [dancing]," her mother recalled to Kadee Krieger for the New Orleans, Louisiana, *Times-Picayune* (August 29, 1996), "she missed it so much." When Taylor was 12 her family moved to New Orleans, where she continued her training with Richard Rholden and Joseph Giacobbe at the Giacobbe Academy of Dance, in the city's parish of Mandeville.

In New Orleans Taylor attended St. Scholastica Academy and was a member of the New Orleans Youth Ballet. In 1994 she was one of three young people chosen to dance the role of Clara in the Delta Festival Ballet's annual production of *The Nutcracker* alongside professional dancers from the Zurich Ballet and the National Ballet of Mexico. In 1995 and 1996 Taylor attended summer sessions at the prestigious School of American Ballet, in New York City. In the fall of 1996, she was selected from among hundreds of young dancers across the country to enroll at the school on a full-tuition scholarship. About to enter the rigorous program—in which students have classes and rehearsals six days and nights per week, with very little free time—the 15-year-old Taylor told Krieger, "I know what I want to do. I know what I am working for. I have had to concentrate and to give up a social life. But it is worth it to dance." While training at SAB Taylor attended the Professional Children's School in Manhattan. In 1998 Taylor received the coveted Mae L. Wien Award for promising students at the SAB Annual Workshop and was invited to dance with the New York City Ballet as an apprentice. She joined the company's corps de ballet after only a month. She soon gained recognition for challenging feature roles in Balanchine-choreographed shows such as *The Nutcracker* (in which she danced in the role of Dewdrop), and *La Valse*, in which she appeared as the woman in white. Dunning wrote for the *New York Times* (December 22, 1999) of Taylor's debut in the former, "Janie Taylor brought her usual endearing spunkiness to the demanding choreography of the Dewdrop role. Nerves did not diminish the beauty of her fully shaped dancing, held arabesques and controlled abandon."

Taylor was promoted to the rank of soloist in 2001, and she enjoyed the distinction of becoming Martins's muse. Woods wrote that Martins admired Taylor's "adventurous spirit" and her "dancing-without-a-net kind of daring." She reported that in Martins's ballet *Morgen*, "Taylor's fearless leap and backwards lunge across her partner's shoulder invariably produce a collective gasp from the audience." For Martins, Taylor originated featured roles in *Morgen, Eros Piano, The Infernal Machine, Guide to Strange Places, Burleske, Them Twos, Viva Verdi,* and *Harmonielehre.* As a soloist Taylor made her debut in the role of the Sugarplum Fairy in *The Nutcracker.* In 2003 Taylor's June performance of Balanchine's *Who Cares?,* with music by George Gershwin, was described by Dunning for the *New York Times* (December 28, 2003) as one of the most unforgettable performances of that year; Dunning wrote, "She rode the Gershwin song 'The Man I Love' like a surfer shrugging her way across the highest wave." That same year, in a departure from her usual work, Taylor—along with the NYCB dancers Maria Kowroski, Charles Askegard, Ellen Bar, Millepied, and Abi Stafford—helped Martins choreograph the film *Barbie in Swan Lake* (2003), in which an animated version of the Mattel doll Barbie dances in that classic work. Using advanced motion-capture imaging, animators tracked the movements of the dancers, who wore reflective Lycra body suits as they created the dance sequences. The data were recorded by 16 cameras in the rehearsal room. Each dancer portrayed a specific character; Taylor was Carlita the Skunk. The dancers were devoted to their task, Martins told Valerie Gladstone for the *New York Times* (September 28, 2003). He added, "These films have the potential of reaching millions of young girls. It will probably be the first time they see ballet, and it will be performed realistically."

While performing the Sugarplum Fairy again in 2003, Taylor sustained a sprained foot. That and a subsequent ankle injury forced her to relinquish two lead roles that season, in Susan Stroman's *Double Feature* and Martins's *Eros Piano*. (She later danced in both successfully.) Her recovery was unusually slow, and before the start of the 2004 spring season, Taylor saw a doctor who told her that her blood-platelet count was dangerously low. She was diagnosed with a rare blood disorder, idiopathic thrombocytopenic purpura (ITP), an autoimmune disease that destroys platelets in the spleen that are necessary for normal blood clotting. For treatment Taylor received steroids on four days every two months; she could dance only if her platelet count was sufficiently high. She told Woods about monitoring her illness while rehearsing with NYCB, "First thing, every three mornings, I would run to get my blood test, then run to class, then rehearse all day, and then I would anxiously wait for my phone call to see if my blood was OK." Taylor also said that the steroids made her weak. It was clear that her condition was deteriorating when, during rehearsal one day, her leg popped out of her hip socket. In 2005, the same year that Taylor was made a principal dancer for NYCB, she had her spleen removed. Though the procedure seemed to improve her condition, the earlier steroid treatments and forced inactivity following the operation left her body very frail and her muscles atrophied. But Taylor was determined to return to the stage. "I started back from below zero," she told Woods. She danced infrequently, as the steroids had slowed her recovery; a torn calf muscle and a pulled thigh muscle took nearly two years to heal. The healing process was a frustrating one for Taylor. "I would let myself have a day to be upset," she told Woods. "I'd say, 'This day I can just cry all day. But tomorrow I have to go back. I will not let this thing defeat me.'"

Taylor's few appearances between 2005 and 2008 were critically successful. One role, in 2005, was especially satisfying for Taylor: she told Kolnik that it was one of her most challenging to date. Of her performance, Dunning wrote for the *New York Times* (January 24, 2005), "Janie Taylor . . . stood out for the clarity and expansiveness of her role debut in Balanchine's *Square Dance*. . . . Playful and risky, her dancing gave a 21st-century spin to choreography that navigates the common ground Balanchine saw in the traditions of American folk dance and preclassical ballet." In 2006 Taylor appeared in "Purple," an excerpt from Martins's 1987 ballet *Ecstatic Orange*. Writing for the *New York Sun* (November 20, 2006), Erica Orden noted that the work called for a dancer of "uncommon agility and delicacy." She also wrote, "The choreography requires [Taylor] to fold herself into back-breaking gymnastic positions, but it calls for a relatively small amount of pointe work. At first, it seems an odd choice; Ms. Taylor is a dancer with

a vibrant sense of attack and quickness. But the near-acrobatic ballet was chosen as a means of getting this still-recovering dancer onstage again."

By 2008 Taylor was on the mend and steadily building her repertoire. That year she appeared in a celebration of the work of the legendary choreographer Jerome Robbins. The piece in which Taylor danced was *Dybbuk*, based on S. Ansky's play *The Dybbuk*, about a woman who seeks to reunite with her dead lover. Alastair Macaulay, writing for the *New York Times* (May 3, 2008), praised Taylor's portrayal of the grieving woman: "You felt her character's crying soul, her psychic need." In 2009 Taylor originated a role in *Quasi Una Fantasia*, a ballet choreographed by her fellow NYCB principal dancer Benjamin Millepied. She appeared in his subsequent works *Plainspoken* and *Why am I not where you are* in 2010. Though Gia Kourlas, writing for the *New York Times* (September 27, 2010), gave the former a lukewarm review, she wrote rhapsodically of Taylor: "With her creamy skin and delicate otherworldliness—there's a bit of Grace Kelly in her countenance—Ms. Taylor gave the ballet a hint of Hitchcock."

The 2011 season saw Taylor's return in full swing. To the music of Claude Debussy, she danced an audience favorite, Robbins's 1953 *Afternoon of a Faun*, about an encounter between two young dancers in an empty studio. "Janie Taylor brings a mesmerizing attention—at once feverish and meditative—to her roles," Apollinaire Scherr wrote for the *Financial Times* (May 19, 2011, online), "but never the same fever or thought, which is why you want to catch her in every performance. In *Faun*, she alternates soft indirection with straightforwardness—all heavy-lidded eyes when glancing sidelong in the mirror at herself and at the boy . . . and all animal impulse when diving into his arms." She also debuted in *La Sonnambula*, Balanchine's take on a 19th-century opera about a poet who encounters a mysterious sleepwalker—the woman of his dreams. Leigh Witchel observed for the *New York Post* (May 23, 2011) of Taylor's performance as the ghostly woman: "Taylor brings a wild urgency to the stage. Asleep, but moving restlessly in staccato motion, she can see the poet, but she can't sense him." Witchel also wrote, "Taylor . . . is such an inevitable choice as a sleepwalker that you don't just love her performance, you feel as if it were already familiar, a feat of déjà vu."

Earlier in her career Taylor's movements were sometimes categorized as cold or mechanical, but such descriptions rarely appear in reviews of her performances anymore; she is now subject to a much different kind of critique. In an assessment of the NYCB 2010 production of Balanchine's *The Nutcracker* for the *New York Times* (January 2, 2010), Alastair Macaulay compared different dancers in the roles of the Sugar Plum Fairy and the Dewdrop: "I also saw . . . Janie Taylor tackle both roles. She lacks the full technique for either, and yet how boldly she claims the music, and how imaginatively she finds character within the steps.

Do such performances count as artistic victories or technical defeats?" He added, "There is a tension involved in watching Ms. Taylor that never arises with, say, Ana Sofia Scheller, a soloist who danced both roles with not just more ease but also more joy, more of the radiance the Kingdom of Sweets is all about. And yet it's Ms. Taylor who is more memorable. With no overlay of acting manners, she shows so sure an idea of each role, so firm a sense of the score, that she proves herself—sometimes by the skin of her teeth—an artist of maturity all too rare in this company."

In addition to work with NYCB, Taylor modeled the 2011 spring collection for the French fashion house Chloe. She appeared briefly as a dancer in the film *Center Stage* (2000), and in 2002 she danced in the nationally televised *Live from Lincoln Center* broadcast "New York City Ballet's Diamond Project: Ten Years of New Choreography," on PBS.

Taylor's boyfriend, the French-born Sebastien Marcovici, is also a principal dancer with NYCB. The two have often been partnered onstage.

—M.M.H.

Suggested Reading: *Ballet News* (on-line) May 6, 2010; *Dance Magazine* p14, p30 July 1, 2009; *Financial Times* (on-line) May 19, 2011; (New Orleans, Louisiana) *Times-Picayune* H3 p21 Aug. 29, 1996; *New York Sun* p9 Nov. 20, 2006; *New York Times* E p1 June 23, 2000, E p31 June 28, 2005, p30 May 23, 2011, (on-line) Dec. 22, 1999, Sep. 28, 2003, Dec. 28, 2003, Jan. 24, 2005, May 23, 2008

Selected Films: *Center Stage*, 2000; *Barbie in Swan Lake*, 2003

Phil Walter/Getty Images

Thompson, Tina

Feb. 10, 1975– Basketball player

Address: Los Angeles Sparks, 888 S. Figueroa St., Suite 2010, Los Angeles, CA 90017

"My love is to play basketball," the Los Angeles Sparks forward Tina Thompson said to Melissa Rohlin for the *Los Angeles Times* (August 6, 2010). "I've been blessed to play it for a living. Not many people get to do something they love to do and get paid for it." Thompson was the very first selection in the inaugural draft of the Women's National Bas-

ketball Association (WNBA), and she is the only current player who has been in the league since its debut season, in 1997. For the first 12 years of her career, Thompson played for the Houston Comets, helping them win four consecutive WNBA championships. During that time she also participated in the 2004 and 2008 Olympic Games, bringing home gold medals both times. Thompson has been selected as an All-Star nine times, and in 2010 she became the WNBA's all-time leading scorer.

When the Comets were disbanded, in late 2008, Thompson signed a contract with the Sparks, the team she has played with ever since. "Tina is definitely one of the best players the WNBA has ever seen," Anne Donovan, head coach of the WNBA's New York Liberty, said to Mark Medina for the *Los Angeles Times* (June 27, 2009). She stood out, Donovan added, "as a rookie and a younger player . . . then developed her own game. She did it as an Olympian. Now that she's in L.A., she just continues to shine." Despite her accomplishments, Thompson does not always enjoy the attention she draws. "That isn't my personality . . . ," she explained to Rohlin. "I value being a role model and having an influence on young girls, but all the other things that come with it, I don't need it."

Like many professional athletes, Thompson is known for having certain game-day rituals, such as eating her lunch around the same time, taking a 45-minute nap, showering after shootaround, and putting on the parts of her uniform in a certain order. She also enforces a specific seating arrangement on the bench during games. "I'm a Christian, so I'm not superstitious at all," she said to Brian Heyman for the *New York Times* (August 4, 2010). "It's more ritualistic. You continue to do the same things a certain way to help you focus and get you mentally prepared for the game. But I'm not one of those people that if I step on a crack, I think the world is going to end." One of her other requirements before each game is applying her "lucky" red lipstick—a habit that began in college after she forgot to wipe off her lipstick before a game in which, it turned out, she played very well. "It became part of my uniform," she told Jayda Evans for the *Seattle Times* (August 28, 2010). "I was kind of like, 'Oh, it must be the lipstick' and it stuck."

Tina Marie Thompson was born on February 10, 1975 in Los Angeles, California. She is one of five children, with two brothers and two sisters. Beginning when she was nine years old, she would go to a nearby recreation center where her brother Tommy and his friends played basketball. Although they did not let her join their games, she started playing basketball outside the center. "Once they challenged me and said things like 'Girls play with dolls and they don't play sports, especially basketball,' that was a tad bit of motivation," Thompson recalled to Brian Heyman. After she improved her game, the boys invited her inside, where she began competing with the future National Basketball Association (NBA) players Chris Mills and Cedric Ceballos. She also played three-on-three games with Tommy and her father on the playground. By the time she was in sixth grade, Thompson stood only an inch under six feet. When she began attending Inglewood Morningside High School (which the WNBA star Lisa Leslie also attended), she had grown to six-foot-two, her current height. She joined that school's basketball team and became the California AAA Player of the Year in 1993. She also tried playing volleyball, which did not work out well because, as she joked to Mike Downey for the *Los Angeles Times* (January 29, 1997), she was always tempted to shoot the volleyball into the basketball hoops.

In 1993 Thompson enrolled at the University of Southern California (USC), where she joined the school's basketball team and was named Freshman of the Year by the Pacific-10 Conference (PAC-10). She graduated in 1997 with a B.A. degree in sociology and a minor in psychology. Thompson initially intended to go to law school with the aim of becoming a judge, but her plans changed when the Houston Comets selected her as the first overall draft pick in the WNBA, whose maiden season was in 1997. "I actually didn't want them to draft me," she said in the interview with Mark Medina. "Los Angeles had the No. 3 pick, so I was expecting to play at home. For [the Comets] to pick me was kind of like a nightmare. In retrospect, that was awesome. But then, I was kicking and screaming." Although she was not happy in her first season, she played extremely well and led her team in blocked shots and rebounds. She was also selected as the Naismith Player of the Year in 1997 and helped the Comets win the first-ever WNBA championship. Around that time the cereal company Kellogg's became the official sponsor of the WNBA, and after the Comets won the league championship, Thompson and two of her teammates—Cynthia Cooper and Sheryl Swoopes (collectively known as the "Big Three")—were featured on a box of Kellogg's Special K cereal.

In her second year as a professional basketball player, Thompson led her team to another championship victory. In 1999 she was voted a Western Conference team starter in the WNBA's first All-Star Game and also contributed to the Comets' third consecutive championship win. At the turn of the century, Houston was victorious once again. (The Comets remain the only team in the league to have four titles.) Also in 2000 Thompson was named Most Valuable Player (MVP) of the WNBA All-Star Game. In 2001 she was selected as Player of the Week, and two years later she was named MVP in the National Women's Basketball League (NWBL) Pro Cup. In 2004 Thompson played on the USA Basketball Women's World Championship Team in the Olympics, in Athens, Greece, helping to win a gold medal.

Thompson missed a portion of the 2005 WNBA season due to pregnancy. During her time off she decided to take a break from working out. "This was the first time in my life that I had a real excuse to not do anything, and I just took advantage of it," she said to Wendy Carpenter for the Tacoma, Washington, *News Tribune* (August 15, 2005). "That year before was tough, with the Olympics and the training and the traveling and things that we did leading up to the Olympics—it was a pretty grueling year. So for good reason, I was just going to take off anyway. And then I got a wonderful surprise, and I just continued to take off." Six weeks after giving birth to a baby boy, whom she named Dyllan, she was back on the court. "Being a first-time mother I didn't realize how tough it would be to go away [from Dyllan]," she told Wendy Carpenter. "In the beginning, I would feel guilty going to the grocery store, just small things like that that you don't even think about at all before you have kids. But I'm definitely a person of my word, and I said [that I would go back to the WNBA], and you do what you say you're going to do." She added, "A few years from now—maybe five or 10—[Dyllan will] appreciate the fact that his mom was a pretty tough gal, being able to have him . . . and [soon] go back to work and be able to contribute." The Comets' then–head coach, Van Chancellor, told Carpenter, "Some other people might not have returned but I never considered Tina Thompson not returning—that's the kind of person she is, the kind of competitor she is." Following Thompson's pregnancy, it took time for her to be able to play the way she had before. She told Carpenter, "I was shooting around and making every shot, and I was thinking 'Oh, that's great.' But when you combine running up and down the court, and then making those shots, and defense, that's when it's like 'Wow!'" She added, "It's difficult—I definitely have a lot of respect and admiration for single, working mothers. . . . But I'm very, very happy with the blessing I've received and I'm not going to take it for granted and complain about it at all." During that time Thompson's mother stayed in Houston to help her take care of Dyllan.

The 2007 season proved to be a difficult one for the Comets; on top of having new teammates, they also had a new coach, Karleen Thompson, and owner, Hilton Koch. Thompson did her part, averaging nearly 25 points per game in the first 10 games of the season and 18.8 points over the course of the year. "Those things are hard to be proud of when they aren't attached to wins," she explained to Jenny Dial for the *Houston Chronicle* (July 18, 2007). The following year Thompson was selected to play for the USA team in the 2008 Olympics, which took place in Beijing, China. One of the four premier players for the United States, along with Leslie, Candace Parker, and Sylvia Fowles, she won her second Olympic gold medal. "People wondered how all of us would all play together, but it just worked out so well," Thompson told Ramona Shelburne for the *Daily News of Los Angeles* (September 7, 2008). "The talent, the camaraderie, this was definitely the best team I've ever been a part of."

At the end of 2008, the WNBA shut down operations of the Houston Comets after 12 years, after Koch, who had decided to sell the team, was unable to find a buyer. Thompson, who had expected to finish her career in Houston, then had to decide which team to join. After considering teams in Texas, Washington State, California, and Connecticut, she signed a three-year contract as a free agent with the Los Angeles Sparks, with the option to decide after each season whether or not she would return. Several factors contributed to her picking the Sparks. "I love Houston," she said in the interview with Mark Medina. "I'm totally still a California girl, though." Los Angeles, where she was raised, is home to her mother and grandmother. In addition, she knew some of the Sparks players, including Leslie, who had played with Thompson in the 2004 and 2008 Olympics and had become her rival in the WNBA.

When Thompson began playing for the Sparks, she wore the number 32 on her jersey in honor of Magic Johnson, the retired NBA point guard whom she has greatly admired since she was a child. In her first season with the team, Thompson helped the Sparks make it to the play-offs. In August 2010 Thompson was fewer than 30 points away from breaking the career scoring record of 6,263 points held by Leslie, who retired after the 2009 season. Thompson downplayed the significance of her imminent accomplishment, since the Sparks were having a challenging season. "It is not rewarding when you score a lot of points and you lose basketball games," she said to Ellen J. Horrow for *USA Today* (August 4, 2010). "The objective of the game is to win. . . . You can't win without your whole team," Thompson said in the interview with Melissa Rohlin. "Nobody pays attention to a team that loses no matter how well an individual player is playing."

During a loss to San Antonio, Thompson broke Leslie's record and became the WNBA's all-time leading scorer. By the end of August 2010, Thompson had racked up 6,413 career points and been named the Western Conference Player of the Month. She helped her team secure the number-four spot in the play-offs, in which they were eliminated after losing the first two games to the Seattle Storm. "She really put us on her back and carried us to the playoffs," the Sparks point guard Ticha Penicheiro said, according to Jayda Evans. During the 2010 season Thompson had suffered several injuries—pulled muscles in her calves, a twisted ankle, and a sore Achilles tendon—but continued playing. "It was hard, it was painful, I was hurting," she told Melissa Rohlin for the *Los Angeles Times* (August 31, 2010). "I didn't show that on the court."

By the end of the 2010 season, Thompson was considering retirement—as she had been for the past few years—although there was still one more year left on her contract with the Sparks. "I'm not one of those players that you're going to have to throw out of the league," she said in the interview with Brian Heyman. "You know when your body is not . . . recovering in the same way or you're not playing at the level that you're used to playing. When I get to that point, I'll definitely hang them up. I'm close. I'm definitely feeling older." Thompson is considering becoming a sports commentator as well as going back to school when she retires.

In addition to the Comets, the Sparks, and the 2004 and 2008 Olympic teams, Thompson has played for several other basketball clubs. She was a member of Italy's Rovereto Basket in the Women's National Basketball League (2001–02), the Republic of Korea's Kumho Falcons in the Women's Korea Basketball League (2003), the U.S.'s Houston Stealth in the National Women's Basketball League (2003), the Spartak Moscow Region, in Russia (2006–07), and the MCM Târgovişte, in Romania (2010).

As of December 2010 Thompson had not announced publicly whether or not she would be staying in the WNBA for the 2011 season.

—J.P.

Suggested Reading: *Houston Chronicle* Sports p3 July 18, 2007; *Los Angeles Times* (on-line) June 27, 2009; *New York Times* B p12 Aug. 4, 2010; *Seattle Times* (on-line) Aug. 28, 2010; (Tacoma, Washington) *News Tribune* South Sound C p3 Aug. 15, 2005

Doug Pensinger/Getty Images

Tomlin, Mike

Mar. 15, 1972– Football coach

Address: Pittsburgh Steelers, 3400 S. Water St., Pittsburgh, PA 15203-2349

"In a realm of sideline screamers and an alphabet consisting mostly of X's and O's, Mike Tomlin is a man of, for and about words," Chuck Finder wrote for the *Pittsburgh Post-Gazette* (July 22, 2007) about the 39-year-old head coach of the Pittsburgh Steelers football team. Known for his superb communication skills and his cerebral and detail-oriented approach to the game, Tomlin—the 10th African-American head coach in the history of the National Football League (NFL)—has achieved several distinctions since he assumed his post, on January 22, 2007. Among others, in 2009, in just his second season, Tomlin became the youngest head coach in NFL history to win a championship, when Pittsburgh defeated the Arizona Cardinals, 27–23, in Super Bowl XLIII. On February 6, 2011 Tomlin led the Steelers to the Super Bowl for the second time in three years, becoming the first coach to make two championship appearances before the age of 40. Although Pittsburgh failed to garner what would have been a record seventh Lombardi Trophy, losing to the Green Bay Packers, 31–25, the season was a successful one for the Steelers, who began the year without their franchise starting quarterback, Ben Roethlisberger, and overcame injury-related absences of many of their star players. Much of that success was attributed to Tomlin, who helped the Steelers remain grounded in the face of adversity. One of Tomlin's mentors, the former NFL coach Tony Dungy, now an analyst

with NBC, spoke of Tomlin's demeanor to Alan Robinson for the Associated Press (November 8, 2008, on-line): "He has great confidence without coming across as cocky and he has a great way to relate to his players." The Steelers' receiver and captain Hines Ward told Dave Fairbank for the Newport News, Virginia, *Daily Press* (September 9, 2007): "[Tomlin is] a straight-shooter. He's not going to sugarcoat things or make excuses. He's a stand-up guy who wants stand-up answers. That's all you can ask for as a player." Tomlin explained to Gerry Dulac for the *Pittsburgh Post-Gazette* (January 18, 2007, on-line), "It's not necessarily what you do from an X's and O's standpoint, but how you do it, what playing winning football is all about, not just inside the white lines but outside the white lines. . . . Coaches, in a lot of ways, whether you're a head coach, a coordinator or a position coach, are somewhat of a life coach. You have to be prepared to do the things that come with the job. If you're going to instruct men inside the white lines, you have to understand what outside the white lines affects what they do."

The younger son of Ed Tomlin Sr. and Julia Tomlin, Michael Pettaway Tomlin was born on March 15, 1972 in Newport News, Virginia. When he was 10 months old, his parents divorced. Growing up, Tomlin had little contact with his biological father, who was a star football player for the Hampton University Pirates in the late 1960s. Ed Sr. was selected by the Baltimore Colts in the 10th round of the 1969 NFL draft and played for one season in the Canadian Football League as a fullback with the Montreal Alouettes. Mike Tomlin and his brother, Ed Jr., who is three and a half years his senior, were raised by their mother, a shipyard worker, in a one-story home in the Beechurst section of Denbigh, Virginia; they also spent much of their childhoods with their grandparents Edward and Catherine Pettaway. When Tomlin was six years old, his mother married Leslie Copeland. A former semiprofessional baseball player who worked for the U.S. Postal Service, Copeland stepped in as a father figure for Tomlin and his brother. After Tomlin started playing Little League baseball, Copeland adjusted his work schedule so he could coach his stepson's team. "He was awesome," Tomlin told Ed Bouchette for the *Pittsburgh Post-Gazette* (May 16, 2007). "I always had the best equipment. We probably couldn't afford it. I had a $200 glove—I had a Wilson A2000 in Little League; that's a legitimate glove. I had the Bike Air football helmets, you name it. Cleats." He said to Jarrett Bell for the *Crisis* (Spring 2009) about Copeland, "The sacrifices that this guy made, the way he loved on me is no different from how I love on my kids. And those are my kids. I'm in awe of the love that he was able to give me and my brother."

Tomlin started playing in youth-football leagues at the age of eight. During those years he began keeping detailed notes, in photo albums and Franklin Planner books, of his athletic achievements—a practice he would carry on into adulthood and into his coaching career. As a seventh-grader, determined, detail-oriented, precocious, and extremely competitive, Tomlin "begged his mother to give him the same trigonometry exams that she made to tutor his 11th-grade brother," Chuck Finder noted. "I was a know-it-all," Tomlin recalled to Bell. "If I read it in a book or heard it in school, it had to be true. Know what I mean? Nobody could tell me different. It always created situations where I was in disagreement with my mother, my stepfather or my brother. And I never, ever backed down, to the point where I'd get sent to bed or get in trouble."

Tomlin attended Denbigh High School, where he was both an academic and athletic standout. As a freshman he made the junior-varsity football squad. Only five feet three inches tall and weighing barely 100 pounds at the time, Tomlin compensated for his physical limitations with his intellect. "It was survival," he explained to Bell. "You can get hurt as a little guy. I needed to know what was going on with the X's and O's as a matter of personal safety." In Tomlin's view, survival also meant keeping his academic achievements a secret from his athletic peers. Invariably listed on the honor role, he routinely threw out "Proud Parent of an Honor Student" bumper stickers when they arrived in the mail. "He didn't want his teammates to think he was a nerd," Tomlin's mother recalled to Fairbank. "He just wanted to be Joe Average Football Player." Tomlin participated in an intellectual competition called Odyssey of the Mind as a junior and was voted "Most Likely to Succeed" by his classmates as a senior.

Tomlin did not accumulate many impressive statistics as a high-school football player, due to Denbigh High's mostly run-oriented offense. Nonetheless, Tomlin—who grew to six feet two inches and filled out to 205 pounds—was recruited by a number of Ivy League schools, which were impressed with his athleticism and exceptional academic record. He also received commissions to the U.S. Military Academy, in West Point, New York, and to the U.S. Naval Academy, in Annapolis, Maryland. He chose instead to remain close to home, enrolling at the College of William and Mary, in Williamsburg, Virginia, which has a prestigious Division I-AA football team. Tomlin quickly picked up Head Coach Jimmye Laycock's complicated, pro-style offensive system and emerged as one of the team's leading receivers. He finished his college career at William and Mary with 101 receptions for 2,054 yards and 20 touchdowns and set a school record with a career average of 20.2 yards per catch; he served as co-captain of the team as a senior. Laycock described Tomlin to John O'Connor for the *Richmond (Virginia) Times Dispatch* (January 23, 2007) as "a very good player, a very smart player who worked at it." During his time at William and Mary, Tomlin became involved in the Big Brothers and Sisters of America program, establishing weekly mentoring meetings with his Kappa Alpha Psi fraternity brothers. "I re-

alized I was blessed, put in a position to see some things that a lot of people like me weren't in a position to see," he told Bell. "I just wanted to do my part to give back." Tomlin graduated from William and Mary in May 1995, with a degree in sociology.

Running a 4.4-second 40-yard dash and boasting a 40-inch vertical leap, Tomlin received tryouts with several NFL teams, including the Cleveland Browns and the San Francisco 49ers. Instead of trying to make it as a player, however, he decided to turn to coaching. Tomlin's mother, who wanted him to become a lawyer, recalled to Dave Fairbank, "I went ballistic. I told him, 'We didn't send you to William and Mary to get into coaching. You need to get a real job.' I mean, it was coaching. How hard could it be? But all the time, he kept saying, 'Mom, I have a plan.'" Tomlin's coaching career began in the fall of 1995, when he was hired as a wide receivers' coach at the Virginia Military Institute (VMI), in Lexington; his stipend was $12,000 per year. He immediately made an impression on the head coach, Bill Stewart, with his sincerity and passion. Stewart, now the head coach at West Virginia University, told Chuck Finder for the *Pittsburgh Post-Gazette* (July 23, 2007), "He was like a 30-year-old then. He coached like he played: He coached with a passion. . . . He wanted them to be tenacious, physical. The kid was born to coach. Born to teach."

After a year at VMI, Tomlin spent one season as a graduate assistant at the University of Memphis, in Tennessee, where he worked with defensive backs and special-team units. He then spent two seasons at Arkansas State University, in Jonesboro, where he coached wide receivers in 1997 and defensive backs in 1998. During the 1999 season Tomlin was hired as a defensive-backs coach at the University of Cincinnati, in Ohio. In his first season there, he helped the Bearcats' secondary unit improve from a rank of 111th in the nation in pass defense to 61st. Under his direction in 2000, the Bearcats ranked eighth in the nation in interceptions and fourth in total turnovers. Tomlin secured his first NFL coaching job in 2001, when he was hired as the defensive-backs coach for the Tampa Bay Buccaneers, in Florida; he replaced Herm Edwards, who became the head coach of the New York Jets. During the interview process Tomlin beat out more than a dozen candidates, most of whom already had NFL coaching experience. Tony Dungy, then Tampa Bay's head coach, told Dave Fairbank, "The one thing that impressed me about Mike was when he got to Tampa, he was able to communicate with every player on our team. That included veterans, rookies, young guys, older guys, and communication is his biggest strength. He knows the game. He knows it in a way that's not cocky, and he doesn't come across as a know-it-all. He's very confident in what he can do and very knowledgeable." At the time of his hiring, Tomlin, at 29, was younger than many of the Buccaneers' players.

Under the guidance of Dungy; Dungy's successor, Jon Gruden, who coached the Buccaneers from 2002 to 2008; and the legendary defensive coordinator Monte Kiffin, Tomlin mastered the vaunted Tampa 2 defense—an aggressive strategy relying on players who are skilled at making interceptions. He guided one of the most successful defensive backfields in the NFL. In his five seasons as the Buccaneers' defensive-backs coach, the team ranked sixth, first, fifth, fifth, and first in total defense, in 2001, 2002, 2003, 2004, and 2005, respectively. With the number-one-ranked defense during the 2002 season, the Buccaneers allowed just 252.8 yards per game. That year the team advanced to Super Bowl XXXVII, in San Diego, California, where they crushed the Oakland Raiders, 48–21, to capture the franchise's first and, to date, only championship. In that game Tomlin's secondary unit made four of the team's five interceptions, including two that were returned for touchdowns. In 2005 Tomlin's unit helped the Buccaneers to finish sixth in the league in pass defense, allowing only 183.1 passing yards per game. During his tenure as the Buccaneers' defensive-backs coach, Tomlin was credited with fostering the developments of such perennial All-Pros as the free safety John Lynch and the cornerback Ronde Barber.

In 2006 Tomlin was hired by Head Coach Brad Childress to become defensive coordinator for the Minnesota Vikings. That season the Vikings' defense ranked eighth in the NFL, improving from 21st in the league at the end of the previous year; they allowed an average of only 300.2 yards per game. More remarkably, the defense improved from 19th to first in the league in rush defense, allowing only 985 total yards rushing, the second-lowest total in NFL history. (The 2000 Ravens' defense, widely considered to be the best ever, allowed 970 yards.) In addition, Tomlin's defense did not allow a 100-yard rusher the entire season; in a game in December of that year, the Vikings held the Detroit Lions to minus-three yards rushing, the lowest rushing total for an NFL team over the previous 45 years. Many Vikings' defensive players cited Tomlin's energy, passion, and signature bluntness as the keys to their success. The Vikings' Pro Bowl defensive tackle Pat Williams told Chuck Finder (July 23, 2007), "He was smooth and serious. That's why all the guys loved him. He would always tell you the truth about how you were playing, about what was going on."

On January 22, 2007 Tomlin was named the 16th head coach of the Pittsburgh Steelers, when he was hired to replace Bill Cowher. At 34 Tomlin became only the third Steelers coach since 1969, after the celebrated four-time Super Bowl–winning coach Chuck Noll (1969–91) and Cowher (1992–06), and the first African-American coach in the history of the franchise. The Steelers' team president and co-owner, Art Rooney II, the son of the Steelers' owner and chairman, Dan Rooney, was impressed with Tomlin's intellect and interpersonal skills. During his two lengthy interviews

with the Rooneys, Tomlin brought a half-dozen binders with detailed plans for running the Steelers' storied franchise, including a schedule for each day of his first season as coach. Art Rooney recalled to Dave Fairbank, "Certainly, one of the things that set him apart is his character, his personality. The more we talked with him, the more comfortable we got with him." He added, "He's an impressive guy. Get in a room and spend two or three hours with Mike—you come away feeling like this is a special person. The main thing you think about is 'When this guy is standing up in front of your team, is he going to get his message across?' That, more than any one thing, is what convinced us that this was the guy." Tomlin signed a four-year deal worth approximately $10 million.

In his first season with Pittsburgh, Tomlin led the Steelers to a 10–6 record and an American Football Conference (AFC) North Division title. Entering the season as the NFL's second-youngest coach, he became only the second coach in team history to have a winning record, lead his team to a division title, and secure a play-off berth in his first year at the helm. That year the Steelers finished first in the NFL in total defense, allowing only 266.4 yards per game, and third in the league in rushing, with an average of 135.5 yards per game; they also received Pro Bowl-caliber play from their young star quarterback Ben Roethlisberger, who set new team records for touchdown passes (32) and passer rating (104.1). In the first round of the play-offs, the Steelers lost to the Jacksonville Jaguars, 31–29.

In 2008 Tomlin guided the Steelers to a 12–4 record and a second consecutive AFC North Division title. He set a Steelers record with 22 regular-season wins in his first two seasons at the helm and became the first coach in franchise history to win at least 10 games and lead his team to a division crown in each of his first two seasons. Tomlin's .688 winning percentage over two years was also a Steelers' record. That year the Steelers were anchored by their strong defense, which led the league in a number of categories, including averages for total defense (237.2 yards per game), pass defense (156.9 yards per game), and points per game (13.9). After defeating the San Diego Chargers in the AFC Divisional play-offs, 35–24, the Steelers faced their AFC North nemeses, the Baltimore Ravens, in the AFC Championship game. They won the contest, 23–14, helping Tomlin, then 36, to become the youngest coach in NFL history to lead his team to the Super Bowl, as well as the third African-American (after Tony Dungy and Lovie Smith) to accomplish that feat. He then became the youngest coach to win the Super Bowl, when the Steelers defeated the Arizona Cardinals, 27–23, in Super Bowl XLIII, to pick up a record sixth Lombardi Trophy. Tomlin was subsequently named the 2008 Motorola NFL Coach of the Year.

After failing to qualify for the play-offs during the 2009 season, with a 9–7 record, Tomlin's Steelers reestablished themselves among the NFL's elite in 2010, when they won their third AFC North title in four seasons, with a 12–4 record. Despite playing the first four games of the season without their franchise quarterback Ben Roethlisberger, who served a four-game suspension for various off-the-field infractions, the Steelers posted a 3–1 record in those games. During the season they also compensated for the absences of many other star players, including the Pro Bowlers Troy Polamalu, Aaron Smith, LaMarr Woodley, and Flozell Adams. Under Tomlin's guidance the Steelers soldiered through and returned to the play-offs. After defeating the Baltimore Ravens and New York Jets in the AFC divisional play-off round and the AFC Championship game, respectively, they secured their second Super Bowl berth in three seasons. In the process Tomlin became the first coach in history to guide his team to two Super Bowls before the age of 40. Though the Steelers lost to the Green Bay Packers, 31–25, in Super Bowl XLV, the team's season was considered a major success, and Tomlin garnered coach-of-the-year consideration for his efforts. Commenting on his evolution as a coach, Tomlin said to Alan Robinson for the Associated Press (January 31, 2009), "I pull from all of it on a day-to-day basis lessons learned from leadership.

It's about people. It's about taking care of the troops [players]. It's about putting them first. I've learned that if you are going to lead, you try to lead with a servant's heart. I try to do that, try to take care of my men and give them what they need to be great."

Tomlin "accents his coaching attire with designer shades and keeps his thin sideburns trimmed" and "is considered extremely cool for an NFL coach," Jarrett Bell wrote for *USA Today* (January 30, 2009). He and his wife, Kiya, who was a gymnast at William and Mary, have two sons, Michael and Mason, and a daughter, Harlyn Quinn. Tomlin is a voracious reader of nonfiction books and cites James Bradley's 2000 best-selling volume *Flags of Our Fathers* as his favorite. In 2008 he was named by Victoria's Secret as the NFL's Sexiest Coach.

—C.C.

Suggested Reading: *Crisis* Spring 2009; *New York Times* D p1 Jan. 26, 2009; (Newport News, Virginia) *Daily Press* A p1+ Sep. 9, 2007; *Pittsburgh Post-Gazette* D p1 May 16, 2007, A p1 July 22, 2007, D p1+ July 23, 2007, (on-line) Jan. 18, 2007; Pittsburgh Steelers Web site; *Richmond (Virginia) Times Dispatch* D p1 Jan. 23, 2007; *USA Today* C p1 Jan. 30, 2009

Tonner, Robert

(TAH-ner)

July 14, 1952– Founder of the Robert Tonner Doll Co.; fashion designer

Address: P.O. Box 4410, Kingston, NY 12402

"There are a handful of names that stand out in the doll world, and Robert Tonner is certainly among them," Toni Fitzgerald wrote for *Doll Reader* (April 2011, on-line). "One of the most acclaimed, accomplished, and successful doll artists of the current era, Tonner has a knack for combining current trends with true artistry." A fashion designer by training, Tonner oversaw a line of clothing for the industry icon Bill Blass before indulging a lifelong passion and founding Robert Tonner Doll Design—later renamed the Robert Tonner Doll Co.—in 1992. His dolls have since received the highest acclaim, and his company has won commissions to design dolls based on such well-known characters as Harry Potter and Spider-Man. Although doll making and collecting are pursuits most often associated in the public mind with women, Tonner told Fitzgerald, "Men have been a driving force for decades." For instance, he explained, with the exception of the venerable company Madame Alexander, founded by Beatrice Alexander Behrman in 1923, "most early doll companies were run by men," and Bernard Lipfert, a freelance doll maker who sold his work to such companies as Horsman

Scott Gries/Getty Images

and Effanbee, "designed the look of dolls for decades." Tonner has been credited with introducing such innovations as the first plus-sized fashion doll and the first doll whose backstory states that he is gay.

Robert Tonner and his twin brother, David, were born on July 14, 1952 in Bluffton, Indiana. Their father, Mart, was a self-trained engineer, and their mother, Virginia, was a homemaker. Virginia Tonner suffered from a variety of illnesses, including cancer, epilepsy, and the neuromuscular disorder myasthenia gravis. Because of Virginia's poor health, the family, which included an older brother, John, and a younger sister, Mary, often found itself in financial difficulty. Tonner told Stephanie Finnegan for her book *The Robert Tonner Story: Dreams & Dolls* (2000), "We were poor. No, not just regular poor, but dirt poor." The family lived in a dilapidated Victorian home that they could not afford to repair or maintain. Tonner has recalled being too embarrassed to bring friends to the shabby structure.

Mart Tonner had been a high-school basketball star, but his sons—particularly Robert—were unathletic. "If any of us caused my father any doubts or worries, it was me," Robert Tonner told Finnegan. "I think I realized my father might be uncomfortable during 'The Revlon Christmas.'" He explained, referring to a glamorously coiffed and clad doll made by the Ideal Co., "It had to be about 1957 or 1958, and I was really pushing for a Revlon doll. That was really all I wanted. And when Christmas Day rolled around, [my sister] Mary got the Revlon doll, and I got a cheaper, knockoff version." Tonner interpreted that turn of events as a sign that his father did not want him to play with dolls. "I made up my mind I was going to make my father happy," he told Finnegan. "I would make both my parents proud. So when I was seven or eight, I asked for a fire truck. Believe me, I did not want a fire truck but that request made my dad so happy. We couldn't afford it, but he went out and got me the most beautiful, big red fire truck with working ladders and hoses. And I couldn't have cared less about it."

Tonner found solace in watching television and became an avid viewer of such shows as *Bonanza*, *Bewitched*, *The Mickey Mouse Club*, and *The Wonderful World of Disney*. He also enjoyed drawing, using the art supplies he had learned to ask his parents for, rather than the more feminine playthings he actually coveted. Often he created paper dolls in secret, so as not to risk his father's disapproval. Tonner later learned to sew from his mother, who reasoned that despite his gender, sewing was a useful skill for him to have.

Tonner's teen years were difficult. "Remember, I was into fashion and drawing beautiful girls in beautiful outfits," he explained to Finnegan. "And yet in my real life as a teenager, I was living in Indiana in the late 1960s. I had to repress [many] impulses." In an attempt to fit in, Tonner dressed in nondescript jeans and T-shirts and dated girls from his high school.

In college Tonner initially aspired to study medicine, an area of interest to him because of his mother's poor health. The need to work to pay his tuition, however, made excelling in his classes difficult, and he transferred from school to school, trying to find a milieu in which he could do better. He attended Indiana University, Southern Colorado State College, and the University of Louisville for brief periods; then, in the spring of 1973, during a trip to New York City, he discovered the Parsons School of Design. He quickly enrolled in a summer session and did so well that he was offered a partial scholarship to return in the fall.

In 1975 Tonner, who had waited tables and worked in a movie theater to help pay his tuition, graduated from Parsons with a B.F.A. degree. Answering a newspaper classified ad, he was soon hired as an assistant at a sportswear company called Gamut. The job was a disappointment. Tonner found that he was called upon mainly to fetch coffee and run the photocopier, and it took more than two years for his supervisor to grudgingly agree to produce one of his designs—for a jacket that became a top seller for the company.

In 1978, thanks to an introduction from a model with whom he had worked, Tonner was hired by the famed designer Bill Blass. "I felt a lot like Dorothy in *The Wizard of Oz* during this time," he recalled to Finnegan. "I was from a small Midwestern town and I suddenly found myself blown into this big, fabulous, glittery new world." He was later assigned to oversee Blassport, Blass's moderately priced "bridge" line, and he remained affiliated with the company for almost 20 years. During that time he also headed his own label, Robert Tonner for Tudor Square.

Away from Indiana and making an enviable salary, Tonner was able to indulge his love for dolls, and in 1979 he began amassing a collection of modern fashion dolls, mass-marketed dolls of the 1950s and '60s, and high-end, one-of-a-kind dolls. On one of his shopping trips he met Glenn Mandeville, a well-known doll expert, author, and dealer. Mandeville "really took me under his wing when it came to learning about the history and the value of dolls," Tonner told Finnegan. "I think I was [initially] trying to replace, or maybe reinvent, my childhood. . . . Glenn taught me how to look at what was a good investment, and what dolls would hold their value, and why dolls have value to begin with."

One day Mandeville began enthusing about a particular doll sculptor. "And I thought, 'What in the world does he mean? A person sculpted that doll?'" Tonner recalled to Finnegan. "And suddenly, it was like a floodgate opened, and I made the connection: People make dolls. Artists sculpt heads." In 1981 Tonner tried sculpting his own, papier-mâché doll, using peach-colored wall paint in an attempt to achieve a realistic skin tone. Within a few years he had moved well beyond that amateurish effort, and in 1985 he felt confident enough to enter a competition sponsored by the National Institute of American Doll Artists (NIADA). NIADA was founded in 1963 by a group of artisans who aimed to celebrate individually crafted high-end dolls. The group's Web site explains, "Collections of mass-produced dolls, originally made for children to play with, are everywhere. Far rarer and generally unknown to the public are the original dolls handmade by artists with the same creative approach [that] is used in painting and sculpture. . . . A NIADA doll conveys a message, usually some facet of culture, which mirrors life and can be a record for future generations."

Tonner was accepted as a member of the organization in 1988, and in 1991 he became the chair of the NIADA standards committee. That year, while still working with Bill Blass, he founded his own company, which he dubbed Robert Tonner Doll Design. (The name was changed to the Tonner Doll Co. in 1994.) "As a doll collector, sculptor, and designer, my dream was to have a job where I could do all three things—so doll making was just the thing!" he told Toni Fitzgerald.

Tonner first created a line of 16-and-a-half-inch porcelain figures, costing some $1,500 each and meant solely for adult collectors. He debuted his creations, which boasted leather-lined joints and painstakingly detailed fashions, at the 1992 American International Toy Fair, in New York City. (Held annually, the event is the toy industry's largest trade show.) In 1992 Tonner reached another milestone, when one of his pieces, the Little Girl in the Duffle Coat, was chosen for the collection at the Museum of Decorative Arts at the Louvre, in Paris, France. (In 1997 a second piece, a porcelain Superman, received the same honor.)

In 1994 Tonner debuted the American Model Collection, which was comprised of 19-inch vinyl dolls that were as detailed and sumptuously dressed as his porcelain figures but were, at about $300 each, much more affordable for the average collector. (In 2005 the line was reconfigured, and the new dolls now stand 22 inches tall.)

By 1994 Tonner's creations were winning such accolades as the Doll of the Year (DOTY) title, given by *Doll Reader* magazine, and the *Dolls* magazine Award of Excellence. His work began appearing frequently on the covers of those publications and others. In 1995 he began a two-year term as president of NIADA and also raised more than $25,000 for the American Foundation for AIDS Research (amFAR) by mounting an auction of American Model dolls, each dressed by a prominent fashion designer. (At a similar event the following year, he raised a total of $280,000, $50,000 of which came from the action-film star Bruce Willis, who purchased a doll dressed in a Dolce & Gabbana outfit for Demi Moore, the actress to whom he was then married.)

In 1996 Tonner won the rights to produce a version of Betsy McCall, a character that had debuted on the cover of the popular women's magazine *McCall's* in May 1951. The character was featured regularly in the periodical as a paper doll, and later in that decade, an eight-inch, hard-plastic doll was produced. Fueled in part by intense nostalgia, Tonner's new 14-inch vinyl Betsy became a massive hit and remains one of the company's most popular

lines. In 2000 he also began producing an eight-inch plastic version based closely on the original.

Tonner often drew inspiration from decades past, basing dolls not only on Betsy McCall but on characters from such films as *Gone With the Wind* and *The Wizard of Oz* (both 1939) and on bygone-era stars including Joan Crawford, Ava Gardner, and Bette Davis. In 1998 Tonner introduced a doll based on Kate Winslet's character, Rose, from the blockbuster movie *Titanic* (1997), and he has since created dolls based on such relatively recent film franchises as *Star Wars*, *Harry Potter*, *Pirates of the Caribbean*, and *Twilight*.

In 1999 Tonner debuted Tyler Wentworth, a 16-inch fashion doll with an elaborate backstory that established her as a successful clothing designer. Other dolls in the line include Tyler's friends: Sydney Chase and Angelina (who, like Tyler, are white); Esmé (an African-American doll); Tyler's boyfriend, Matt O'Neill (who is white); and a cosmetics mogul, Mei Li (an Asian doll). Tonner's company Web site describes the effort that goes into the design and manufacture of the line: "Tyler's leg sculpt includes unique features such as 90-degree posturing when seated and shoulder joints that are designed to conceal the swinging hinge. This hinge allows Tyler's arms to move back and forth, side to side, and combinations of both motions without the shoulder seam inhibiting the lines when wearing strapless fashions. For the styles that come with bending arms, collectors will delight in Tyler's full range [of] motion in bending arm capability. The bending arm features a different hand sculpt to create more variety in arm poses. The body torso, upper arms and lower arms are constructed of hard plastic; the lower limbs and head are made of high-quality vinyl. This combination provides durable quality at working joints without compromising a blended look. Joints are hand-sanded to minimize their appearance to the eye. . . . For the newest articulated Tyler bodies, the engineering is truly remarkable. A side-to-side bending mechanism allows for drop shoulder posing. The swivel waist turns from left to right. Finally, the rotational hip joints allow for legs to be crossed, as well as a full range of leg stances." The post goes on to describe Tyler's hair, make-up, and clothing at similar length.

"To call [Tyler Wentworth] a 'fashion doll' would be a disservice," Jane Sarasohn-Kahn wrote for *Miller's Fashion Doll Magazine* (May 1999, online). "She breaks the barrier of just 'Better than Barbie,' which is the barometer some adult collectors have used for the past few years." Sarasohn-Kahn continued, "There is nothing 'faux' in this line. . . . Tyler is the real deal. She wears 100 percent cashmere, 100 percent silk, 100 percent wool, and originally-designed jewelry." In 2000, the year after the line debuted, Tonner's alma mater, the Parsons School of Design, hosted a runway show featuring human models wearing replicas of Tyler Wentworth clothing. Although there are now several companies producing 16-inch fashion dolls with backstories of their own, Tonner's Tyler Wentworth collection remains one of the most popular and avidly collected. "I have been around a lot of artists who do beautiful work, and look down on commercial work," Krystyna Poray Goddu, the founding editor of *Dolls* magazine, once said, according to Finnegan. "But Robert was never like that, not even from the beginning. He always wanted to give his work to a lot of people, and not in cheap reproductions. He was able to take small, beautiful art and make it beautifully mass-produced. It's been amazing to see one person actually build a company, but that's really what Robert has done."

In 2002 Tonner acquired the iconic doll company Effanbee, which had been established in 1912 and become known for such beloved dolls as Patsy and Dy-Dee Baby. He has been applauded by collectors and industry insiders for rescuing the firm from bankruptcy. In 2002 Tonner also introduced Emme, a fashion doll based on the real-life plus-size model and TV personality of the same name, who agreed to license her image only on the condition that the proceeds from the doll benefit body-image and self-esteem groups. Emme is generally considered to be the first plus-size fashion doll ever manufactured, and the move was widely applauded by parents' groups and hobbyists.

Tonner broke new ground again in 2010, when he introduced Andy Mills, whose backstory establishes him as a young gay man, living and working in New York City. "For years, our company has developed storylines to go with our products [and] it's long overdue to have a storyline that embodies society in more of its entirety," Tonner told a reporter for *Dolls* magazine (December 1, 2010, online). That year the Tonner Doll Co. moved its headquarters to Kingston, New York, where Tonner had purchased a granite and stone bank building originally erected in the 1860s.

In recent years Tonner has also created well-received collections of clothing for flesh-and-blood women. He and his longtime partner, Harris Safier, a real-estate broker, live in Kripplebush, a picturesque hamlet in upstate New York. (The setting provided the inspiration for a line of retro dolls called the Kripplebush Kids.) Together, Tonner and Safier have raised a son, Larry.

—M.R.

Suggested Reading: *Doll Collector* (on-line) Apr./May 2011; *Doll Reader* (on-line) Apr. 2011; *Dolls* (on-line) Aug. 1, 2002, Sep. 1, 2004, Feb. 1, 2006, Aug. 1, 2008, Mar. 13, 2009, June 18, 2010, Dec. 1, 2010, Dec. 23, 2010, May 4, 2011; *Miller's Fashion Doll Magazine* (on-line) May 1999; NIADA Web site; Robert Tonner Doll Co. Web site

---

Tseng, Yani

(tseng, yah-nee)

Jan. 23, 1989– Golfer

Address: Lake Nona Golf & Country Club, 9801 Lake Nona Rd., Orlando, FL 32827

When she won the Australian Ladies Masters on February 14, 2011, less than a month after she celebrated her 22d birthday, the Taiwanese-born Yani Tseng displaced Jiyai Shin of South Korea to claim the top spot on the Women's World Golf Rankings. Moments after she achieved that feat—which came four years after she turned professional and marked her 13th first-place finish as a pro—Taiwan's president, Ma Ying-jeou, sent her a personal message of congratulations. The next milestone in Tseng's career came on June 26, 2011, when, with her record-tying, 10-stroke victory at the Wegmans Championship, she became the youngest woman ever to win four Ladies Professional Golf Association (LPGA) Tour major championship events. (During each golf-tournament season, which runs from February through December, the LPGA holds four such events, known as majors; in 2011 the organization's schedule also included 23 other competitions.) Five weeks later, on

July 31, 2011, Tseng triumphed at the British Women's Open Championship (as she had the year before), thus becoming the youngest golfer—male or female—ever to win a fifth major title. To put her achievement in perspective, Tiger Woods won a fifth major at 24, and the Swedish-born Annika Sorenstam, Tseng's idol and mentor, was 24 when she won a major for the first time and 32 when she won her fifth major.

Tseng's unusual abilities in golf—notably, her exceedingly powerful swing—were obvious virtually from her introduction to the sport, when she was six; her passion for the game took root early on, too. As an amateur Tseng accumulated 15 international wins and four in the U.S.; in Taiwan she was the top-ranked amateur in 2004, 2005, and 2006. Widely described as outgoing, friendly, and vivacious, she has distinguished herself with come-from-behind victories in the last moments of games. Tseng was named Louise Suggs Rolex Rookie of the Year in 2008. In 2009 she became the youngest player ever to pass the $2 million mark in career earnings, after winning the Corning Classic and leading the LPGA tour in birdies. In 2010 she was honored as Rolex Player of the Year. Tseng told Damon Hack for *SportsIllustrated.CNN.com* (April 12, 2010), "I just keep telling myself, Commit to the shot and keep your tempo right, and keep smiling all 18 holes." "What stands out, golf-wise,

Scott Halleran/Getty Images

Yani Tseng

is she just has the entire package," the Golf Channel analyst Kay Cockerill told Brian Heard for WomensGolfCenter.com (June 3, 2009). "She's physically gifted and has all the tools." As of August 3 in the 2011 season, Tseng had finished in first place in three games, in second place in one, in third place in one, and in the top 10 in eight, and her earnings for the year stood at $1,329,383. Her career earnings totaled $5,948,753.

The second of three children, Yani Tseng was born on January 23, 1989 in Taiwan. (Her name in her native land is Tseng Yani.) According to some sources, her place of birth was Taoyuan City, in the northern part of the island. Her mother, Yu-Yun Yang, is a caddie, and her father, Mao-Hsin Tseng, is a top amateur golfer. Neither her older brother nor her younger sister is a golfer. Tseng began playing golf at age six, when her parents took her to the driving range near their home in Taipei, Taiwan's capital. Her athleticism and love for golf immediately became apparent, and her parents hired Tony Kao to coach her at the Chinese Taipei Golf Assocation, which has its own course. (Kao is still one of her coaches.) She was soon practicing more than five hours a day. "Every time I finished school I was so excited to practice," Tseng recalled to Steve DiMeglio for *USA Today* (June 10, 2009). "Golf is like going up to heaven." From early on Tseng displayed a powerful leg drive, which, Mark Gaughan observed for the *Buffalo (New York) News* (June 23, 2011), allows her to "play an explosive game and hit it longer than most players." (The distance a golf ball travels is determined mostly by how fast and powerfully the golfer swings the club. Club speed is generated by the golfer's arms and upper body, but Tseng has exhaustively practiced driving

her legs slightly upward in her swing, thus increasing the distance of her shot and giving her an advantage over many of her competitors.) Tseng has attributed the efficiency of her swing to an adage she learned as a child: "Just hit [the ball] as hard as you can, don't care where the ball is," she recalled to Gaughan. In one of her first competitive events, at age nine, she cried when she found herself unable to hit her ball out of a bunker (a specially constructed sandy depression that is considered a "hazard" in golf).

According to Brian Heard, Tseng spent a large part of her teen years "at a small golf academy away from her home in Taiwan." "I think that's why I'm so mature," she told Heard. "I stayed by myself. I didn't live with my family. So I've been able to handle [things] very well." In 2001 Tseng began training with Ernie Huang and Kai Chang, the general manager of the Oak Valley Golf Club, in Beaumont, California. The two men guided Tseng to early successes in U.S. Asian Junior Golf Association and USGA events. "She was considered the best women's amateur in Asia," Chang told Michelle Flores for *Southland Golf Magazine* (April 2008). In 2003 Tseng won the Callaway Junior World Golf Championship, an annual international amateur tournament held in San Diego, California; she finished as the runner-up in 2004. She won the Asia Pacific Junior Championship in 2003, 2004, and 2005. In one of her best-known victories, Tseng defeated the 14-year-old Michelle Wie in the final of the 2004 U.S. Women's Amateur Public Links Championship. (Wie had made history when, at 13, she became the youngest competitor to qualify for an LPGA major.) Tseng defeated another future LPGA star—Morgan Pressel—at the 2005 Women's North & South Amateur Championship. In all, Tseng's amateur accomplishments totaled four wins in the United States and 15 international victories. She was the top-ranked amateur in Taiwan in 2004, 2005, and 2006. In 2007 Tseng qualified for the LPGA tour on her first attempt, finishing sixth in the final tournament in Daytona, Florida, to earn exempt status for the 2008 LPGA season (that is, she did not have to qualify for most events). After turning pro she won the DLF Women's Indian Open, on the Ladies Asian Golf Tour, and she tied for sixth place at the CN Canadian Women's Open, on the CN Canadian Women's Tour.

In June 2008, at 19, Tseng won her first major—the McDonald's LPGA Championship, in which she held off Sorenstam and then-number-one-ranked Lorena Ochoa to narrowly defeat Maria Hjorth in a four-hole, sudden-death play-off. She was the first rookie to win a major since Se Ri Pak of South Korea, who won the same tournament 10 years earlier. Tseng was also the second-youngest major winner since Morgan Pressel, who won the 2007 Kraft Nabisco Championship at 18. "This is my dream," Tseng told Don Markus for the *Baltimore Sun* (June 9, 2008) after the game. "I feel it comes very fast. I couldn't believe it." That year

Tseng led the LPGA Tour in birdies, with 388; won the LPGA Championship at the Bulle Rock Golf Course, in Havre de Grace, Maryland; turned in a second-place finish at the Ricoh British Women's Open, at the Sunningdale Golf Club, in Berkshire, England; and passed the $1 million mark in season (and career) earnings after a runner-up finish at the LPGA State Farm Classic, at the Panther Creek Country Club, in Springfield, Illinois, where the South Korean golfer Ji Young Oh beat her in a one-hole, sudden-death play-off. Tseng defeated the up-and-coming Na Yeon Choi to win the 2008 Louise Suggs Rolex Rookie of the Year Award.

On May 24, 2009 Tseng won the LPGA Corning Classic, achieving a career-low 62 in the third round; with her 21-under-par 267, she beat both Soo-Yun Kang of South Korea and the American Paula Creamer by one stroke. Also that season she had runner-up finishes at the MasterCard Classic, the Wegmans LPGA, and the Hana Bank–Kolon Championship. Top-10 finishes included a tie for fourth at the Navistar LPGA Classic; ties for fifth at the SBS Open at Turtle Bay and the Corona Championship; and a tie for sixth at the Jamie Farr Owens Corning Classic. All told, in the 27 tournaments in which she participated in 2009, she had 14 top-10 finishes. Despite Tseng's successes that year, for a while her "mental game" weakened and her confidence diminished. In June, July, and August she completed five tournaments without recording a top-20 finish, and she missed the cut at the U.S. Women's Open, held on July 12. "It [was] the first time in my life I've felt that golf was really challenging me . . . ," she said, as quoted on the Web site Ladies on Tour (February 18, 2010). "Every tournament I was crying. My tears probably dried out I was crying so hard. I was putting so much pressure on myself." Tseng ranked sixth in the world when she had a face-to-face talk with Sorenstam that year; she took to heart her mentor's advice about changing her approach to the game. Speaking of upcoming competitions, she said, as quoted on ladiesontour.com, "I don't have any expectations. I just really want to enjoy it. It's really easy to say, but hard to do. I want to relax and just go and have fun. Relaxed is when I play my best golf."

Tseng's second and third major wins occurred in 2010 at the Kraft Nabisco Championship and the Ricoh Women's British Open, respectively. She also recorded the fifth victory of her LPGA career, at the P&G (Procter & Gamble) NW Arkansas Championship. On the Ladies European Tour (LET), she won the Handa Australian Women's Open. She was also named Female Player of the Year by the Golf Writers Association of America. Tseng finished the 2010 season by becoming the first player from Taiwan—and, at 21, the second-youngest—to win the Rolex Player of the Year Award. At the award ceremony, held at the Grand Cypress Resort, in Orlando, Florida, in December, Tseng read from a five-page script written in both English and Mandarin (which she learned while growing up, along

with Taiwanese, her native tongue). "I was nervous," Tseng told Tim Rosaforte for Golf World (February 7, 2011). "English is not my main language, but I wish more people knew I could speak English. If they want to talk to me, the fans, the media, they can." She added, "A lot of people think I'm from Korea." Tseng told Steve DiMeglio that she learned English by "just talking a lot and then talking some more;" she also took a course in Orlando in English as a second language.

At the beginning of 2011, Tseng ranked fifth in the world among female golfers. That February she won the Australian Ladies Masters—officially, the ANZ RACV (Australia/New Zealand Royal Automobile Club of Victoria) Ladies Masters. She thereby attained the number-one world ranking, overtaking Jiyai Shin of South Korea to become the first Taiwanese to be ranked best in the world in any professional sport. "I knew I could become world No. 1 sooner or later," Tseng told Lilian Wu for the Central News Agency–Taiwan (February 14, 2011), "but I did not expect it to happen so soon." On June 26, 2011 she won the Wegmans LPGA Championship, held in Pittsford, New York, and, at 22 years, five months, and three days, became the youngest player to claim victories in four LPGA Tour majors. At that event she finished 19 under par, one stroke short of what would have been a record.

On July 31, 2011, in Carnoustie, Scotland, Tseng won the British Women's Open Championship for the second year in a row, this time with a 16-under-par 272, beating Brittany Lang, an American, by four strokes. When she entered the third round, she trailed Caroline Masson of Germany by two strokes; she then triumphed over Masson by shooting a three-under-par 69, while Masson closed with 78. With that victory Tseng became the youngest person (male or female) in history to win five majors.

Tseng represents a growing number of Asian women (the majority of them from South Korea) who compete on the LPGA tour. She hopes to increase golf's popularity in Taiwan, where baseball is regarded as the national sport. "Golf is becoming more popular now and many players are playing in foreign countries too, which keeps up the motivation . . . ," Tseng told a reporter for the Business Times Singapore (September 27, 2008). "It's a great tool to put the country's name out internationally, and we can prove that Asians can play too and not be underestimated."

Tseng's fellow golfers have said that her exuberance is contagious. "She likes to joke around," the golfer Amy Huang told DiMeglio, "and she's very friendly—she can make friends everywhere. . . . Even in the beginning, when she had the language barrier, she still made friends with everybody." Emily Kay, a sportswriter for examiner.com (June 26, 2011), wrote that Tseng has been "known to sing to herself on the golf course." According to an article posted on FocusTaiwan.tw (August 3, 2011), her charitable donations in 2011 will include (in U.S. dollars) $50 for every birdie and

$200 for every eagle she scores in LPGA tournaments. Earlier in 2011 she participated in an event organized by United Way of Taiwan to raise money for the physically and mentally disabled.

In 2009 Tseng bought Sorenstam's former home, on the grounds of the Lake Nona Golf & Country Club, in an Orlando suburb. "Before [Sorenstam] left she said, 'You have to fill all the trophy cases,'" Tseng told the *Rochester (New York) Democrat and Chronicle* (June 20, 2010). Sorenstam has won 72 tournaments, and her trophy cases are "huge," Tseng said.

—M.M.H.

Suggested Reading: *Baltimore Sun* Z p3 June 9, 2008; *Buffalo (New York) News* D p1 June 23, 2011; *Business Times Singapore* (on-line) Sep. 27, 2008; Central News Agency–Taiwan (on-line) Feb. 14, 2011; *Golf World* p36 Feb. 7, 2011; golf.about.com; LPGA.com; (Palm Springs, California) *Desert Sun* (on-line) Jan. 7, 2011; *Southland Golf Magazine* Apr. 2008; *SportsIllustrated.CNN.com* Apr. 12, 2010; supersport.com July 31, 2011; *USA Today* C p10 June 10, 2009; WomensGolfCenter.com; yanigolf.com

Michael Tullberg/Getty Images

Tyler, the Creator

Mar. 6, 1991– Rapper; producer

Address: XL Recordings/Beggars, Group USA, 625 Broadway, 12th Fl., New York, NY 10012

"You can't really ignore Odd Future Wolf Gang Kill Them All," Paul Lester wrote for the London *Guardian* (May 7, 2011) about the prolific Los Angeles, California–based hip-hop collective. "Well, you could, but you'd have to not use the internet and not read any press. They are everywhere. There's a good reason for the ubiquity: OFWGKTA are astonishing, both on record and live, where they approximate the combined imagined force of the Sex Pistols, Slipknot and NWA." The collective (usually referred to as "Odd Future"), consisting of 11 members, has a catalogue of more than a dozen self-produced albums, which first generated a following on-line. Since it gained recognition in the mainstream music press, in 2010, Odd Future has become one of the most talked-about new groups in hip-hop, praised for its brilliant production work, unique rapping, shocking lyrics, and ability to win over a legion of devoted fans through social-media promotion and free music downloads. Chris Richards described the collective for the *Washington Post* (May 15, 2011) as "the most hyped pop act of 2011, and the most complex: a handful of bratty, sometimes-brilliant rappers, singers and producers who have spent the past year enchanting bloggers while building a feverishly devout fan base. Their vulgar lyrics grabbed the pop world's attention, and their reckless charisma has managed to keep it." The founder and leader of Odd Future is the 20-year-old rapper and producer known as Tyler, the Creator (the comma is an official part of his stage name). Tyler has also become the collective's breakout star, with the success of his self-released solo debut, *Bastard* (2009), and major-label follow-up, *Goblin* (2011). Critics have compared his minimalist production and clever rhyming to those of pioneering 1990s underground rap artists as well as the work of the shock-rapper Eminem. He has also been reviled, due to his penchant for raunchy, violence-obsessed, misogynistic, and homophobic lyrics. Andrew Nosnitsky wrote for *Billboard* (March 11, 2011, on-line) that Tyler is "rap's most buzzed-about new star—and quite possibly an emerging threat to both decency-minded parent groups and the major-label infrastructure." Those who take Tyler and Odd Future's lyrics least seriously may be the members of the collective themselves. Before an Odd Future performance in Washington, D.C., Chris Richards wrote that the group "will rap about murder, rape, kidnapping, arson, torture and necrophilia. It'll also rap about absentee fathers, puppy love crushes and how none of its absurdly violent boasts is actually true."

The rapper was born Tyler Okonma on March 6, 1991 in Los Angeles. He has a younger sister. His mother was a social worker. His father, who is African, was absent from his life from early on, which deeply hurt and angered the rapper; that absence would later become a recurring subject in his lyrics. In an interview with Kelefa Sanneh for the *New Yorker* (May 23, 2011), Tyler said that his father is Nigerian (he added, "That's what my mom told me—but she also told me she loved me, the other day"); he has publicly divulged few other details about him.

When Tyler was 12 he began to make his own beats with the software program Reason, and at age 13 he taught himself to play piano. Some of his early hip-hop influences were staples of the genre, such as Dr. Dre's *The Chronic* (2001) and the work of the rock, funk, and hip-hop band N.E.R.D. He later became interested in jazz, punk rock, electronica, and ambient music. He told Lester that some aspects of his own music—specifically, what Lester called "the plaintive atmospheres and mournful violins"—were inspired by "a bunch of French jazz, old soundtracks, library music, [music] . . . with crazy chord progressions and changes in it."

Tyler's teen years were tumultuous; he was plagued with asthma (from which he still suffers) and took Ritalin for hyperactivity, until he found that it interfered with his asthma medication. He was often disruptive in school and as a result attended a series of public schools in Los Angeles and Sacramento before enrolling at Media Arts Academy, in Hawthorne, California. That charter school, Sanneh wrote, "was also known as Hip-Hop High," a place that "used music facilities to lure students from all over the city who might otherwise have dropped out, or already had." Media Arts Academy allowed Tyler to develop his creative side; there, he made use of the school's music equipment and became skilled at graphic design.

A skateboarder, Tyler often went to a skate park near Media Arts Academy, where he began to make friends from around the city. Tyler and his friends soon formed a collective they dubbed Odd Future Wolf Gang Kill Them All, with the intention—at least on Tyler's part—of producing a magazine. Soon, however, they decided to create music instead. While there are said to be members of the group involved in various other creative pursuits, only 11 make music. One of the first members of the collective was the producer known as Left Brain, who shared Tyler's musical tastes. The rapper Hodgy Beats was the next to join. The others now include the 17-year-old rapper known as Earl Sweatshirt, the youngest member (he has not appeared with the collective recently because his mother sent him to a reform school in Samoa, prompting the oft-heard "Free Earl" rallying cry at shows); the rapper Domo Genesis; the R&B singer Frank Ocean, the oldest member at 24; the producer Matt Martian; the rapper Mike G; Taco and Jasper, who contribute little of a musical nature to Odd Future, which is a running joke among the collective; and Syd the Kid (also written as Syd tha Kyd), the group's sound engineer, overall producer, live deejay, and sole female. Tyler, considered the founder of the group and its de facto leader,

creates Odd Future's art and videos. The collective began to assemble tracks at the home of Syd the Kid's parents, in Los Angeles, where she had her own recording studio.

Since its formation Odd Future has created more than a dozen albums or "mixtapes," many initially made available as free downloads on the collective's Web site. Some are solo works, others collaborations among several members, still others projects of the full collective. Tyler's *Goblin* is the first to have been released on a label (XL Recordings); *BlackenedWhite* by MellowHype (Hodgy Beats and Left Brain) and Frank Ocean's mixtape, *nostalgia,ULTRA*, were slated for July 2011 releases on the Fat Possum and Def Jam labels, respectively. Tyler has rapped on, and had a hand in the production of, almost every Odd Future release, including its two full-collective mixtapes *The Odd Future Tape* (2008) and *Radical* (2010). In 2011 the collective signed a deal with Sony/RED for the distribution rights to its albums; the label agreed to let Odd Future retain creative control.

Tyler initially drew attention by posting his solo music on-line. With the help of a viral video for his song "French," he and Odd Future became an Internet sensation. His debut solo album, *Bastard* (2009), showcased what would become his signature sound: raspy vocals accompanied by ambient textures, minimal piano, and, occasionally, heavy drums and bass. His lyrics tackled themes of alienation, his absent father, his frustration with the opposite sex, and more. Most critics found the album to be both refreshing and unsettling. Tom Breihan wrote for *Pitchfork.com*, "*Bastard* is a minor masterpiece of shock art and teenage spleen-vent, a spiritual cousin of some of the most misanthropic tantrums that the L.A. hardcore scene produced 30 years earlier. But it's also a beautifully put-together piece of work, one that lays out its position right away and then does everything it can to keep you uncomfortable. Tyler is smart enough to start things off with the title track, a soul-laid-bare rant about evil thoughts and absent fathers over still, eerie piano plinks. The track works great on its own, but it also creates a context for all the rape jokes and murder talk that follows; no matter how grisly things get, you still stay on this kid's side to at least some extent. And things really do get grisly."

In 2010, thanks to the popularity of *Bastard* and other Odd Future releases, as well as a flurry of articles about Odd Future in the music press, the collective enlisted the former Interscope executives Christian Clancy and David Airaudio as managers. Odd Future toured in the fall of that year and broke into the mainstream with a chaotic performance of Tyler's "Sandwitches" on the TV show *Late Night with Jimmy Fallon* in February 2011. A black-and-white video for the *Goblin* single "Yonkers," in which Tyler eats a live cockroach and then appears to hang himself, added to the buzz when it went viral on the Internet.

Goblin was produced by Tyler and Left Brain. It was generally well-received, although most critics found space in their reviews to condemn the rapper's apparent homophobia and rape fantasies. Jon Caramanica wrote for the *New York Times* (May 8, 2011), "*Goblin* is spiteful, internal, confident, vitriolic, vividly bruised stuff, a shocking—and shockingly good—album that bears little resemblance to contemporary hip-hop. It has more in common with the stark, thick-with-feelings independent rap of the mid-to-late-1990s and also the improbably rich-sounding minimalism of the Neptunes in the early 2000s. For every caustic rhyme about violence there's a pensive, unexpectedly gentle production choice to go with it. Unlike the maximalism of hip-hop radio, you can feel the air in these songs, the gasping for breath."

Not all critics were pleased, however. Eric Harvey wrote for the *Village Voice* (May 11, 2011, online), "*Goblin*'s highest points and most infuriating moments come from the fact that it's a vérité depiction of the worst aspects of American boy culture. You know, hating girls because they don't like you because you're a weirdo, hating any and all authority figures because they try to tell you how not to be such a weirdo. But most importantly (and scarily), there's the part that involves lashing out about being viewed as a weirdo, and being summarily rewarded—i.e. seen as normal—for doing so. . . . Nobody cares about Tyler the Creator being someone's role model in 2011. Which in a way, is the scariest thing about *Goblin*—too much of his scary fantasizing, for too many boys, is all too normal."

The critical reception generated by *Goblin* was overshadowed somewhat by the reaction to its lyrical content. Caramanica wrote, "With imagery depicting rampant drug use, systemic violence against women, and any number of other distasteful things, Odd Future has become the flashpoint for reigniting the culture wars in hip-hop for a generation that hasn't previously experienced them, that didn't realize culture wars were still a possibility. No act in recent memory has engendered so many think pieces about music, think pieces about critics and think pieces about think pieces. Are the group's lyrics reports of literal desires? The goofs of misguided kids? Does the difference matter?" In defense of his music, Tyler has argued that he is not homophobic or ignorant of the realities of sexual violence. In an interview with *NME*, as quoted by Alex Macpherson in the London *Guardian* (May 9, 2011, on-line), he explained that he uses certain taboo words or evokes violent scenarios simply to shock, and that a word such as "f**got"—often used in his rhymes—is meant as a general insult and not a put-down of the gay community. "I'm not homophobic," he said. "I just think 'f**got' hits and hurts people." In defense of her musical collaborator, Syd the Kid, who is openly lesbian, told Lester about Tyler, "He . . . isn't necessarily saying, 'I want to rape so-and-so'. They're just sick, twisted fantasies that he's had, based on girls that have hurt him in the past. A lot of people have sick, twisted fantasies, so why not give them something to relate to?" Chris Richards wrote, "As heinous as some of Odd Future's lyrics can be, they still possess an exaggerated, cartoonish quality. They don't feel like a true espousal of violence, misogyny or homophobia so much as a big joke you're not in on. It's just too bad it has to be such an ugly joke."

Odd Future is currently producing a pilot for a series on the cable-television cartoon network Adult Swim, and Tyler is expected to release a third album, *Wolf*, in 2012.

Caramanica described the six-foot two-inch, deep-voiced Tyler as "lanky and sinewy and irrepressibly goofy, with a vibrant antisocial streak." The rapper, he added, is "partial to flamboyantly patterned shirts, gym socks pulled up to the knee and dessicated Vans; loves bacon and doughnuts; says he doesn't drink or do drugs; and can barely get a sentence out without a curse." Tyler's goal, according to a post he made on his Formspring account, as quoted by Jeff Weiss in the *Los Angeles Times* (April 10, 2011, on-line), is to "make great music . . . be the leader for the kids who were picked on and called weird, and show the world that being yourself and doing what you want without caring what other people think, is the key to being happy."

—W.D.

Suggested Reading: (London) *Guardian* Guide p6 May 7, 2011; *New York Times* Arts and Leisure p1 May 8, 2011; *New Yorker* p58 May 23, 2011; oddfuture.com; *Washington Post* T p1 May 15, 2011

Selected Recordings: *Bastard*, 2009; *Goblin*, 2011

Underworld

Music group

Hyde, Karl
May 10, 1957(?)– Vocalist; guitarist; songwriter; producer; remixer

Smith, Rick
May 25, 1959(?)– Keyboardist; songwriter; producer; remixer

Address: Tomato, 14 Baltic St. E., Top Fl., London EC1Y 0UJ, England

"There are few production outfits more important to the development of modern electronic dance music than Underworld," Justin Kleinfeld wrote for *Remix* magazine (March 1, 2006) about that British electronic group. "The group's importance doesn't lie with the fact that it was able to break through to the mainstream or that it produced countless club hits. Rather, Underworld's stamp

Perou, courtesy of Cooking Vinyl
Underworld's founders: Rick Smith (left) and Karl Hyde

on the dance world is marked by its jaw-dropping live show and ability to bring out the beautiful sides of our emotions. There aren't many dance-music songs that make people weep the way the beginning of 'Born Slippy' does. While on the other end of the spectrum, there are very few songs that bring the same electricity as the dynamic ending of 'Cowgirl.' Those tracks are classics because they are true songs and not just dance tracks made for a specific setting or mood." Underworld's founders are Karl Hyde, a vocalist and guitarist, and Rick Smith, a keyboardist; both are also songwriters, producers, and remixers. Since 1990 six others have been members of Underworld and its fore-bears. Only one of the six is still with them: Darren Price, who has served as keyboard player, studio engineer, and assistant since 2005.

Hyde and Smith started Underworld as a rock-funk act in the mid-1980s. The pair released two unsuccessful albums before the deejay Darren Emerson joined them, in 1990. With Emerson, Hyde and Smith reinvented themselves as a techno outfit and made the groundbreaking recording *Dubno-basswithmyheadman* (1993). Underworld's Mercury Prize–nominated next album, *Second Toughest in the Infants* (1996), enjoyed commercial success thanks to the chart-topping single "Born Slippy .NUXX," which the filmmaker Danny Boyle included on the soundtrack to *Trainspotting* (1996). Underworld's other studio albums include *Beaucoup Fish*, *A Hundred Days Off*, *Oblivion with Bells*, and *Barking*. The band has released a live CD and DVD set, *Everything, Everything*; a greatest-hits compilation, *1992–2002*; and three download-only albums, collectively titled *The Riverrun Proj-*

ect. Hyde and Smith helped to score the soundtracks for Anthony Minghella's *Breaking and Entering* (2006) and Danny Boyle's *Sunshine* (2007). "I'm always surprised that people struggle for creative ideas," Hyde told Craig Mathieson for the *Sydney (Australia) Morning Herald* (June 4, 2010). "The problem I find is that there are too many. The hard work comes from sorting them out and figuring what is worth taking further." Hyde and Smith have remixed work for other artists, including Depeche Mode, Björk, St. Etienne, Sven Vath, Simply Red, and Leftfield. The men are also co-founders of Tomato, a self-described "collective of artists, designers, musicians and writers."

Karl Hyde was born on May 10 sometime between 1957 and 1961 in Worcester, a town in the West Midlands, England. His attraction to music began early in life. At 11 he started playing the guitar. As a preadolescent Hyde shared an affinity for pop music with his father. During his teens his musical tastes expanded to include film soundtracks, electronic music, and music with avant-garde elements. One of his greatest influences was the British deejay John Peel, whose BBC Radio 1 show was among the first in Great Britain to broadcast nonmainstream music. Peel played recordings by such artists as the British art-rock group Roxy Music and the pioneering German electronic-music band Kraftwerk. "John was a great catalyst, the way he would turn us on to all this great music and connected like-minded people, just because you were tuned into one place—his radio show . . . ," Hyde told Stuart Barrie for the Glasgow, Scotland, *Daily Record* (July 21, 2006). "He opened up dub, German electronica, hardcore metal, African music, and all sorts of strange sounds."

Hyde studied art at Cardiff Art College, in Wales, in the latter half of the 1970s. (It is now the Cardiff School of Art and Design, a division of the University of Wales Institute, Cardiff.) During that time he played in several bands, among them the Screen Gemz, a pop group that incorporated elements of German electronica and Jamaican reggae and had a lot of fans in Cardiff. Shortly after completing his art studies, Hyde met Rick Smith by chance when both were working in a Cardiff diner, one during the day and the other at night. (Some sources report that they met at the college.) Richard Smith was born on May 25, 1959 (or 1960) in Ammanford, in Carmarthenshire County, Wales, to a minister and his wife, a piano teacher. He worked in a bank in his hometown before he enrolled at the Cardiff division of the University of Wales, with the intention of pursuing a career as a synthesizer engineer. Smith played the piano and, like Hyde, admired Kraftwerk and enjoyed various experimental forms of music. At Hyde's urging Smith joined the Screen Gemz as their synthesizer player.

The difficulties of touring Great Britain in a crowded transit van led to Smith's departure from the Screen Gemz after a year. The band itself dissolved in 1981. Hyde next joined Smith and the bassist Alfie Thomas to form a New Wave band called Freur. In 1983, after recruiting the drummer Bryn Burrows (from the British New Wave band the Fabulous Poodles) and the keyboardist John Warwicker, Freur landed a recording contract with CBS Records. The title track of Freur's first album, *Doot Doot* (1983), reached number two on the U.K. singles chart. The group released a second album, *Get Us Out of Here* (1985), and scored the soundtrack to the Clive Barker–penned horror film *Underworld* (1985; released in the U.S. as *Transmutations*) before disbanding, in 1986.

Taking inspiration from the Barker film, Hyde, Smith, Thomas, Burrows, and the bassist Baz Allen formed a funk-rock group and named themselves Underworld; the band's earliest incarnation, it is commonly called Underworld Mark 1. After signing with Sire Records, they released the albums *Underneath the Radar* (1988) and *Change the Weather* (1989), neither of which received much attention. In 1989 the group landed the opening slot on the U.S. leg of the farewell tour of the Eurythmics, the British electro-pop duo made up of Annie Lennox and Dave Stewart. "I stood in front of like 30,000 people," Smith told Tamara Palmer for *URBMagazine* (November/December 1999, online), as quoted on enotes.com. "It was nice for five seconds, and after that it was awful." Soon afterward Sire Records dropped the group, which then dissolved.

By that time Hyde and Smith had become fed up with the music industry and dissatisfied with their own musical development. "We were obsessed with Kraftwerk and dub music, yet we were stuck, in the middle of a tour, with a style we realized wasn't something we were interested in anymore," Hyde recalled to Emma Forrest for the London *Independent* (August 23, 1996). "Re-inventing yourself in the music business is anathema to most people—apart from the real innovators like Miles Davis or Frank Zappa. Most musicians are encouraged to stay the way they are." Hyde told Mark Jenkins for the *Washington Post* (April 18, 1999), "There are some things more important than trying to knock out hits. In the 1980s, Rick and I learned that this wasn't in our nature. We felt that if we just carried on, we were in danger of being caught up in a wave that wasn't of our own making."

After the Eurythmics tour Hyde worked in the U.S. as a session guitarist. He later became friendly with Deborah "Debbie" Harry and toured with her band, Blondie. Smith, meanwhile, had moved back to England, settling in Romford, in Greater London, Essex County, where he set up a makeshift recording studio in his bedroom. Through his brother-in-law, he met Darren Emerson (born on April 30, 1971 in Hornchurch, Greater London), then a young futures trader on the London Stock Exchange and a much-in-demand part-time deejay. Emerson was already a fixture in British acid house (a subgenre of house music, a kind of dance music) when Smith suggested to him that they work together. With rave culture spreading throughout England, the two began recording tracks with a strong

dance-club sensibility, fusing elements from indie rock, techno, electronica, and even jazz. Hyde soon joined them, and the three named their group Lemon Interrupt. In 1992 they released the singles "Dirty" and "Minneapolis" on one disk and "Bigmouth" and "Eclipse" on another, both on the dance label Junior Boy's Own, a subsidiary of London Records. The next year they readopted the moniker Underworld for the singles "Mmm . . . Skyscraper I Love You" and "Rez."

Dubnobasswithmyheadman (1993), the first album released by the second incarnation of Underworld (sometimes referred to as Underworld Mark 2), is regarded as "a towering landmark in the techno genre," Graeme Virtue wrote for the London *Sunday Herald* (November 10, 2002); Michael Bodey wrote for the Sydney *Daily Telegraph* (January 9, 2003) that it is "rightfully considered one of electronica's finest moments." With songs including "Dark & Long (Dark Train)," "Mmm . . . Skyscraper I Love You," "Dirty Epic," and "Cowgirl," the album "blends acid house, techno, and dub into a refined, epic headrush," Sal Cinquemani wrote for *Slant.com* (November 2, 2002). In a review posted on Amazon.com, Matthew Corwine called the album "a long and seductive hypnosis session, a decadent *film noir* journey through dark impulses and impure thoughts." "Vocalist Karl Hyde provides a monotonous, stream-of-consciousness narrative which, when chopped and rearranged, reveals a quintessentially British reserve that keeps the album mysterious," he wrote. *Dubnobasswithmyheadman* showcased Hyde's unconventional lyrics, which typically include everything from fragmented musings to snippets from found material, such as overheard conversations and answering machine recordings. "It can appear to be just noises, just sounds, disparate words but they're not," Hyde told Graeme Virtue. "They're my particular way of writing my autobiography, the fragments of my day which make up an impression of my state of mind in a particular place. . . . I write about everything I see and hear and overhear. I go to the music with several notebooks in my hand and look through them and see what's on the page that corresponds to how I feel about the music." With *Dubnobasswithmyheadman*, Jason Bracelin wrote for the *Las Vegas (Nevada) Review-Journal* (July 31, 2009), "Underworld gradually began to establish itself as a gateway act for a new form of electronic music, a hybridization of sorts, one that fused techno trademarks with a rock 'n' roll style, big production live show, a jam band's flair for improvisation and a hint of conventional songwriting that harnessed the dance music of the day to a fine, bayonet-sharp point." He added, "It was a deliberately broad sound, impulsive and amorphous, with songs that drifted apart and came together like cloud formations."

For their next album, *Second Toughest in the Infants* (1996), Underworld broadened their progressive sound by including elements from such genres as ambient, breakbeat, jungle, house, and pop. The single "Pearl's Girl" reached number 22 on the U.K. charts; the album received widespread critical praise and was nominated for a Mercury Music Prize (now known as the Barclaycard Mercury Prize), awarded annually to the best album from the United Kingdom or Ireland. In a review for the All Music Guide (on-line), Stephen Thomas Erlewine wrote, "*Second Toughest in the Infants* carries the same knockout punch of their debut, *Dubnobasswithmyheadman*, but it's subtler and more varied, offering proof that the outfit is one of the leading dance collectives of the mid-90s."

Second Toughest enjoyed rare commercial success for a techno album, selling a respectable 87,000 copies in the U.S. alone. Its appeal was attributed largely to Danny Boyle's controversial but critically lauded film *Trainspotting*, which featured the song "Dark & Long (Dark Train)" as well as "Born Slippy .NUXX." The latter, originally released as a B-side and heard over the end credits of the film, has stream-of-consciousness lyrics shouted over a thumping bass line with the now-famous "lager, lager, lager" refrain, which was inspired by Hyde's struggles with alcohol addiction. (It was not included on the original British release of *Second Toughest in the Infants* but was added to other versions and reissues of the album.) "Born Slippy .NUXX" reached number two on the U.K. charts and became a worldwide hit, selling more than a million copies. It served as "a powerful madeleine"—that is, a memory jogger—"for a generation, marking the point in the mid-Nineties when club culture became mass culture," Kitty Empire wrote for the London *Observer* (November 10, 2002). Comparing the electronic opus to one of the rocker Bruce Springsteen's best-known anthems, Empire added, "In many ways it is Underworld's 'Born in the USA'—woefully misunderstood by air-punching men like the 'lager, lager, lager' bit, but a skin-prickling anthem all the same." "Born Slippy .NUXX" has been included on many compilations, mash-up records, and remixes and remains an exceedingly popular dance track.

In early 1999 Underworld released the much-anticipated *Beaucoup Fish*. Its singles included "Moaner," released earlier on the soundtrack to the 1997 Joel Shumacher film *Batman & Robin*; the house track "Shudder/King of Snake," which sampled the bassline from Donna Summer's disco hit "I Feel Love"; "Push Upstairs"; and "Jumbo." Danya Pincavage wrote for the *University Wire* (July 22, 1999) that *Beaucoup Fish* "is not only stunningly good, but also even more musically complex than some of [Underworld's] previous work," with songs that "are more consistently dark and more complex than their earlier works." John Bush, in a review for the All Music Guide (on-line), wrote, "While *Second Toughest in the Infants* showed Underworld were no mere novices at introducing super-tough breakbeats, here the focus is on throwback acid-house and trance [a dance-music genre]. The effect is that Underworld have refused to compromise their artistic vision to any-

one's view of commercialism; as such the few excesses on *Beaucoup Fish* can be forgiven." Such praise notwithstanding, the album was a commercial disappointment, due to the overall waning interest in electronica at the time.

Emerson left Underworld in 2000 to pursue a solo career as a deejay and producer. He had earlier performed at the show that was recorded for the live album and DVD set *Everything, Everything*, which went on sale later that year. Contrary to speculation that Emerson's departure would mark the end of Underworld, Hyde and Smith continued as a duo, often referred to as Underworld Mark 3. Their first effort without Emerson, *A Hundred Days Off* (2002), maintained the group's dance-oriented sound and was generally well received by critics and fans alike; it included the hit song "Two Months Off," which peaked at number 12 on the U.K. singles chart.

Underworld's two-disc anthology, *1992–2002* (2003), included some previously unreleased singles and B-sides. The keyboardist and studio engineer Darren Price joined the band around the time they started recording *The Riverrun Project*, three download-only albums available through their Web site, underworldlive.com. Its three parts were *Lovely Broken Thing* and *Pizza for Eggs* (both made available in 2005) and *I'm a Big Sister, and I'm a Girl, and I'm a Princess, and This Is My Horse* (2006). Hyde noted to Justin Kleinfeld that *The Riverrun Project* "was born out of a desire for change." "Around 2003, we were feeling content and at ease, and that's a lethal place to be for an artist," he added. Also in 2006 Underworld released five limited-edition 12-inch singles that contained remixes of various *Riverrun* tracks, and they collaborated with the Lebanese composer Gabriel Yared on the score for Anthony Minghella's film *Breaking and Entering*.

Underworld's soundtrack accompanied Danny Boyle's science-fiction film *Sunshine* (2007). That year marked the release of the band's seventh studio album, *Oblivion with Bells*, which contains dance and ambient tracks; one song, "To Heal," was used as the central theme in *Sunshine*. Underworld's latest album, *Barking* (2010), includes collaborations with the Welsh drum and bass artist High Contrast, Deep Dish's Dubfire, the Grammy Award–winning trance deejay and producer Paul Van Dyk, and the British house artists Mark Knight and D. Ramirez. The album's lead single, "Scribble," peaked at number 32 on the U.K. dance-singles chart. In 2010 Underworld toured Europe, Asia, Australia, and the U.S. to promote *Barking*. Hyde told an interviewer for guestlisted.blogspot.com (May 18, 2010) that when performing live he and Smith try never to repeat themselves. "The music is never fully stationary," he said. "It's already done as a recorded piece of music, so when we play it live, each time it can become something new. Whenever we play, I've already done the show over and over in my mind so that way, when it comes to the actual event, I feel

I can be open to exploring ways of deconstructing everything and rebuilding it as it's happening."

In 1991 Hyde, Smith, and John Warwicker launched the design collective Tomato, which has offices in London and Hollywood, California, and, currently, 10 people on staff. According to its Web site, Tomato "has involved itself with hosting workshops, publishing, exhibiting, live performances and public speaking as well as working with clients in the areas of advertising, architecture, fashion, public installations, music, television, film and graphic design." The firm has designed all of Underworld's album covers and has produced all the videos and graphics for the group's live performances. Its outside clients include Microsoft, Nike, Adidas, Chevrolet, Sony, and Pepsi. In the area of art, in 2008 a show called Beautiful Burnout Artjam: The Art of Underworld was held at the Jacobson-Howard Gallery, in New York City. In 2010 an exhibit of paintings and films by Hyde called What's Going On in Your Head When You're Dancing was mounted at the Laforet Museum, in Harajuku, Japan; Smith's new record label, Bungalow with Stairs, made the soundtrack that accompanied the show.

Hyde and Smith are both married and live in Romford. Each reportedly has one child.

—C.C.

Suggested Reading: *ABC Magazine* p4 Nov. 19, 2006; DrownedInSound.com Sep. 29, 2010; (Edinburgh, Scotland) *Scotsman* p16 Feb. 26, 1999; (Glasgow, Scotland) *Daily Record* p36 July 21, 2006; *Las Vegas (Nevada) Review-Journal* p24 July 31, 2009; (London) *Guardian* p14+ Feb. 26, 1999; (London) *Independent* p6 Aug. 23, 1996; *Remix* p29+ Mar. 1, 2006; *South China Morning Post* p3 Nov. 4, 2007; (Tokyo, Japan) *Daily Yomiuri* p12 Oct. 5, 2007; tomato.co.uk; *Washington Post* G p1+ Apr. 18, 1999

Selected Recordings: as Freur—*Doot Doot*, 1983; *Get Us Out of Here*, 1985; as Underworld— *Underneath the Radar*, 1988; *Change the Weather*, 1989; *Dubnobasswithmyheadman*, 1993; *Second Toughest in the Infants*, 1996; *Beacoup Fish*, 1999; *A Hundred Days Off*, 2002; *1992–2002*, 2003; *Oblivion with Bells*, 2007; *Barking*, 2010

Verghese, Abraham

(ver-GEESS)

May 30, 1955– Physician; writer; educator

Address: Stanford Dept. of Medicine, 300 Pasteur Dr., S102C MC 5109, Stanford, CA 94305

Abraham Verghese, an infectious-disease specialist born and raised in Ethiopia by Indian parents, worked at the front lines of the AIDS epidemic in the mid-1980s in a small Tennessee city. He treated and comforted AIDS patients and their families in an environment in which both homosexuality and AIDS were stigmatized and in an era when being diagnosed with the virus was a virtual death sentence. Verghese chronicled his experiences in his best-selling book *My Own Country: A Doctor's Story of a Town and Its People in the Age of AIDS* (1994). Verghese, who received an M.F.A. degree from the University of Iowa Writers' Workshop in 1991, has written two additional best-sellers: another memoir, *The Tennis Partner* (1998), about his friendship with a medical student who was struggling with drug addiction, and a novel, *Cutting for Stone* (2009), a saga about twin brothers who become surgeons.

Verghese has long advocated empathy and sensitivity in the doctor-patient relationship, elements that he believes are often suppressed in rigorous medical training. As the first director (2002–07) of the Center for Medical Humanities & Ethics at the University of Texas Health Science Center at San Antonio, Verghese used art and literature to

Michael Gottschalk/AFP/Getty Images

teach medical students to imagine patients' experiences during treatment. He emphasized the importance of the hands-on physical examination at a time when advanced technology often takes precedence. Verghese has taught what is known as "bedside medicine" as a senior associate chair of the theory and practice of medicine at Stanford University Medical School, in California, since 2007. The position at Stanford assures that he has time to write. Verghese has said that although medicine is his first calling, he uses writing to learn from his experiences. He told Perri Klass for the *New York Times* (August 28, 1994), "We're allowed into part of people's lives that they often don't share with their spouses or their preachers. I don't think there are enough physician-writers, frankly. Given how many of us are privy to so many of these stories, it's interesting that there aren't more of us mining this material."

The second of three sons, Abraham C. Verghese was born on May 30, 1955 in Addis Ababa, the capital of Ethiopia, where his mother, Mariam Abraham Verghese, and father, George Verghese, taught physics. Natives of Kerala, a state in southwest India, his parents were recruited to teach in Ethiopia by Haile Selassie, the nation's emperor; impressed with the educational system in Kerala during a visit there after World War II—or by the sight of throngs of uniform-wearing children walking to their Christian schools, according to Abraham Verghese, writing for the London *Observer* (April 10, 2010)—the emperor hired some 400 teachers from Kerala for the new schools he was building in Ethiopia. Verghese's parents met soon after they settled in Ethiopia, in 1951. Abraham Verghese was raised in Addis Ababa among a community of teachers. A quiet child, he enjoyed reading and playing tennis; he would often spend hours hitting a tennis ball against the side of a shed, and according to a writer for *Book Browse* (on-line), he became "a compulsive collector . . . of tennis lore and trivia, a compiler of notebooks on tennis heroes, ephemeral styles, and trendy strategies." Early on Verghese viewed journalism as an attractive profession, but his parents told him he must pursue a career in a more "respectable" field, such as the law or medicine. At age 12 Verghese read W. Somerset Maugham's novel *Of Human Bondage*, whose main character is a physician and, for a while, an aspiring painter. At 15 Verghese began to attend premedical classes in Madras, India, and two years later he was accepted into medical school at what was then called Haile Selassie the First University, in Addis Ababa.

In 1973 a documentary made by Jonathan Dimbleby for British television, called *The Unknown Famine*, revealed massive famine in Wollo Province, in northeastern Ethiopia. The film arrived in Ethiopia with scenes of the emperor's luxurious lifestyle interspersed with images of starving people. Verghese and millions of others had grown up respecting Haile Selassie, the country's leader since 1930, for his success in modernizing much of Ethiopia; the revelations of the widespread poverty and suffering in rural areas made the emperor appear inept and corrupt. It was not long before a military group, known as the Derg, took control of the country after isolating the emperor in his palace. Verghese's parents fled to the U.S., while Verghese, who was in his third year of medical school, stayed on. Selassie was soon jailed, and civil war broke out, sparked by the execution-style killing of 59 distinguished Ethiopians—including former prime ministers, ambassadors, generals, and royals—on November 23, 1974, a date that became known as "Bloody Saturday." Working in a casualty ward, Verghese treated many of those who were injured in the violence.

Haunted by the sight of a dead man, killed by a bullet to the head and abandoned on the street, his head resting on what looked like a pillow of blood, Verghese left Ethiopia in late 1974, after the university he attended was shut down due to the escalating violence. He moved in with his parents and younger brother in a small house in Westfield, New Jersey. Verghese's parents encouraged him to resume his medical studies in the U.S., but he thought that he would have to earn an undergraduate degree before applying to medical schools. Reluctant to start from scratch, he took night jobs as an orderly at a series of hospitals and nursing homes. The jobs enabled him to move out of his parents' house and buy his own car. "I could see my blue-collar life starting to unfold," Verghese told Denise Grady for the *New York Times* (October 12, 2010). "I'd marry a Jersey girl, we'd live in an apartment someplace and take vacations in the Poconos when we could afford it." One night Verghese came across a copy of *Harrison's Principles of Internal Medicine*, a textbook he had used in medical school in Ethiopia. After paging through it Verghese was inspired to resume his medical studies. Granted educational status as a refugee by the Indian government, he was admitted to medical school at the University of Madras in Chennai, India. While gaining clinical experience in treating infectious diseases, he came to admire the hands-on style of medicine practiced in India, which differed significantly from the British style he had learned in Ethiopia. While in India Verghese married his first wife, an account executive at an advertising agency.

After he earned his medical degree, in 1979, Verghese returned to the U.S., in part because he wanted to have access to the latest medical technology. Verghese served his internship and residency at East Tennessee University, in Johnson City, whose population was about 50,000. (He had discovered that like most graduates of overseas medical schools, he was offered positions only in high-needs but less-than-prestigious hospitals, mainly in rural areas and inner cities.) After three years at East Tennessee University, he served a two-year infectious-disease fellowship at the Boston University School of Medicine, in Massachusetts. At Boston City Hospital he treated some of the first victims of the burgeoning HIV epidemic. Verghese returned to Johnson City in 1985 to work at a Veterans Administration (VA) hospital. Though the HIV virus had been wreaking havoc on gay communities and others in such major cities as San Francisco, Los Angeles, and New York for several years, Verghese did not expect to be treating many such patients in the small rural city. To his surprise he soon found himself treating a huge caseload of 80 to 100 patients infected with HIV. The patients included many gay men, as well as both men and women who had contracted the virus through contaminated blood transfusions or other means. Many of Verghese's patients had been raised in the Johnson City area and were now returning from the East or West Coast to die near loved ones. Because of strong prejudices regarding AIDS and homosexuality, the families of some AIDS victims refused to care for them. The relatives of one man dying of AIDS asked Verghese to record the official diagnosis as cancer, so that when the man died, he would be remembered with respect.

As it became increasingly unlikely that a cure for AIDS would arrive soon, Verghese found himself behaving less like a physician—he was unable to reverse his patients' inevitable fate—and more like a friend and confidant. Verghese believes that many of his gay patients, who had long felt like outsiders, may have found him relatively easy to talk to, since he, too, as an Indian among mainly white doctors and nurses, was an outsider. He devoted so much attention to his patients that he often neglected to spend much time with his wife and two young sons, and his marriage began to suffer. Over time some of the hospital staff began to resent Verghese for drawing AIDS patients to rural Tennessee. "The last straw," Verghese told Jan Reid for *Texas Monthly* (December 2004), "was when an administrator called me in and asked me if I thought we were going to see an increase in these cases at our hospital. 'Absolutely,' I said, and began to tell him what I knew and believed. He cut me off and said, 'I wonder how many more we'd see if you weren't here.'"

Verghese had long nurtured a passion for writing, keeping a journal since his youth and, as an adult, writing short stories in his spare time. In 1989, physically and emotionally exhausted, he cashed in his 401K, left Johnson City with his family, and enrolled at the prestigious University of Iowa Writers' Workshop. He also took a part-time job in an AIDS clinic in Iowa City. "As I look back, I think it was a very selfish thing to put my family through," he told Arthur Pais for *India Abroad* (February 6, 2009). "But it was also an act of self preservation. Writing, particularly non-fiction, had fascinated me from my teen years. I had also felt . . . that I would implode if I did not take a break." Though he worried initially that he had not read enough literature to excel in the program—his classmates spoke of literary theories with which he was unfamiliar—Verghese wrote stories that stood out for the rawness of their subject matter, drawn from his experiences of treating patients in Tennessee. By the time Verghese had earned an M.F.A. degree from Iowa, in 1991, a literary agent had sold one of his stories, "Lilacs," about AIDS victims in Boston, to the *New Yorker*; it appeared in the October 14, 1991 issue.

After he completed his master's degree, Verghese moved with his family to El Paso, Texas, where he became a professor of medicine and chief of the Division of Infectious Diseases at the Texas Tech University Health Sciences Center and worked at a county hospital. Meanwhile, *New Yorker* editors had asked Verghese to write a long nonfiction piece about HIV and AIDS in rural Tennessee. After the magazine rejected his proposal, Verghese reworked it into a proposal for what became his first book, *My Own Country: A Doctor's Story of a Town and Its People in the Age of AIDS.* Published in 1994, the book became a best-seller and received much praise for the beauty of its prose and its revelations about AIDS. "The greatest strength of this eloquently written book is its ability to weave together all those separate strands," Perri Klass wrote in a representative review for the *New York Times.* "It is at once a previously untold story of AIDS in America, a story of the South, a story of the modern-day immigrant experience in America and a story of a personal journey within the medical profession. Dr. Verghese illumines a number of landscapes here, and does it with more than a touch of the poet. He writes, for example, about the life inside the hospital—but not just any hospital. His greatest affection is reserved for the patients and staff of the Veterans Administration Hospital, that perennial poor relation of the medical system; perhaps never has a V.A. hospital been written about with such glowing lyricism." *My Own Country* won a Lambda Literary Award and was named one of the five best books of the year by *Time* magazine; it was also a finalist for the National Book Critics Circle Award. A made-for-TV movie version of the book, starring Naveen Andrews as Verghese, aired on Showtime in 2000.

During his early years in El Paso, Verghese found solace from his marital problems while playing tennis with David Smith (not the man's real name), a fourth-year medical student and former tennis professional from Australia, with whom Verghese became very close. Verghese wrote about the disintegration of his marriage and his friendship with Smith in his second memoir, *The Tennis Partner: A Doctor's Story of Friendship and Loss* (1998). During their tennis games Verghese revealed to Smith details about his marriage; he was shocked when Smith disclosed that he was a recovering cocaine addict who had to submit to random drug tests in order to remain in medical school. As Verghese came to rely more and more on his friend, he watched helplessly as Smith resumed intravenous drug use and eventually committed suicide. Writing the book was a cathartic experience for Verghese. He told Reid, "*The Tennis Partner* delivered me from the guilt of a terrible experience in my life. People who are close to others who've committed suicide are always thinking, 'What could I have done? How could I have stopped it?' Writing that book, telling that story, enabled me to learn that the addiction was David's illness. It was his responsibility." *The Tennis Partner* became a best-seller and appeared on the *New York Times*'s list of notable books of the year.

His modest prominence gave Verghese opportunities to talk publicly about the prevalence of drug addiction and suicide in the medical profession; suicide is the number-one cause of premature death among doctors, and about half of those suicides are related to substance abuse. According to Verghese, the phenomenon stems from a culture that encourages physicians to repress stressful feelings and other emotions related to their work. Verghese told Anthony Broadman for the Tucson, Arizona, *Daily Star* (November 17, 2003), "When they get ill [medical students] deny their patienthood and they focus on the symptoms. A very characteristic feature of physician addiction is that they began by treating a symptom with a drug and found to their great surprise that the drug did more than relieve the symptom; it relieved the dysphoria of their existence."

In 2002 Steven Wartman, then the dean of the School of Medicine at the University of Texas at San Antonio, founded the Center for Medical Humanities & Ethics and recruited Verghese as its first director. The center, according to its Web site, works to "assure that students are knowledgeable about the principles of medical ethics related to their professional activities. They are expected to be able to identify, analyze and resolve moral conflicts that arise in the care of a patient. The program helps heighten students' sensitivity to the patient's experience and preserve their innate empathy." In an interview with Geeta Sharma-Jensen for the *Milwaukee (Wisconsin) Journal Sentinel* (December 3, 2006), Verghese called the program "an attempt to remind the student and keep the student aware of the patient's life experience. Too often in medical training, we get so narrowly focused on the disease that we sometimes lose the ability to manage fully the patient's suffering."

In 2007 Verghese accepted a tenured position as a senior associate chair of Theory and Practice of Medicine, a division of Stanford University Medical School's Department of Internal Medicine. In addition to teaching, the position enabled him to spend about 40 percent of his time working on writing projects in a private office. At Stanford Verghese teaches what is known as "bedside medicine," a personal form of treatment that has gone out of fashion in recent years, as physicians increasingly rely on medical technology. In Verghese's view one aspect of bedside medicine, the thorough physical exam, serves to establish an important human relationship with patients and can save time and money often wasted on unnecessary diagnostic tests. Verghese told Bill Kettler for the Medford, Oregon, *Mail Tribune* (February 1, 2010) that patients often feel disconnected from their doctors. "If you listen to what patients say it's compelling," he said. "They say things like, 'The doctor never touched me,' or 'He never asked me to take my shirt off.'" Verghese continued, "When you're skilled at the bedside in the hospital, and

taking time to listen to the patient's story, you're a day and a half ahead of the doctor who's waiting for results to come back from the laboratory. . . . I'm under no illusion my hand is as sensitive as a CAT scan, but a CAT scan can't feel tenderness"— that is, a feeling of tenderness in a body part. One technique taught by Verghese that few American doctors use is the art of percussing—listening to the sounds produced by tapping parts of a patient's abdomen, chest, and sternum. Verghese has said that he is somewhat embarrassed by the attention he has received for the very old techniques he is teaching, which he learned during his training in Ethiopia and India, where advanced equipment was not available.

In 2009 Verghese published a novel, *Cutting for Stone*, which begins with the birth of conjoined twin boys to a nun in an Ethiopian hospital. The nun dies during their birth, and their father, Thomas Stone, a renowned British surgeon, flees the hospital, called Missing Hospital, a mispronunciation of "Mission." Separated and raised by Indian doctors, the twins, Marion and Shiva, become surgeons themselves; afterward their lives take very different paths, until a personal medical crisis brings them together briefly. The book's title comes from a line in the Hippocratic Oath, which was written some 2,500 years ago and is still recited by newly graduated M.D.s: "I will not cut for stone, even for patients in whom the disease is manifest; I will leave this operation to be performed by practitioners, specialists in this art." "Basically, it means don't do surgery unless you are skilled, no matter how much the patient is suffering," Verghese told Lynn Carey for the *Contra Costa (California) Times* (April 4, 2010). "I just like the ring of the phrase. Every year the most moving part of my year is when my students graduate, and I hear them recite that oath. This line moves me to tears." In a review for the Baton Rouge, Louisiana, *Advocate* (March 8, 2009), Greg Langley wrote, "The one overriding thing about Verghese's work is his storytelling. He seems almost incapable of writing a dull sentence or one that is not relevant to the story. He is focused and talented. Every little detail is fascinating. . . . In fact, it's hard to find a weakness in this book—maybe too much reliance on coincidence in the plot. But it's a work of fiction after all, so why fret about that? Just enjoy." "Verghese strives for the empathy of Anne Tyler and the scope of [Charles] Dickens," Erica Wagner wrote for the *New York Times Book Review* (February 6, 2009). "If he doesn't quite manage either, he is to be admired for his ambition. . . . Verghese's weakness is the weakness of a writer with too much heart: it's clear he loves his characters and he just wants to cram in every last fact about them, somehow." A best-seller, *Cutting for Stone* won the American Booksellers Association 2010 Indies Choice Award for adult fiction and the Northern California Independent Booksellers Association award for fiction for books published in 2009.

In addition to the *New Yorker*, Verghese's essays and short stories have appeared in publications including the *New England Journal of Medicine*, the *North American Review*, *Granta*, the *New York Times*, the *New York Times Magazine*, the *New York Times Book Review*, *Texas Monthly*, *Newsweek*, the *Wall Street Journal*, *Good Housekeeping*, *Sports Illustrated*, the *Atlantic Monthly*, and *British Esquire*. He frequently lectures about bedside medicine and the importance of retaining humanism in medical education and practice.

From his first, 15-year marriage, to Rajani Chacko, which ended in divorce in 1995, Verghese has two sons, Steven and Jacob. He met his second wife, the former Sylvia Parra, at an AIDS clinic in El Paso, where he was on staff and she was a volunteer. Her cousin and the cousin's lover, whom Verghese treated at the clinic, both died of AIDS. Verghese and his second wife married in 1996; they have one son, Tristan, born in 1998.

—M.R.M.

Suggested Reading: Abraham Verghese Web site; *BookBrowse.com*; *Housecalls* p45+ Mar./Apr. 2009; *lassiwithlavina.com* June 6, 2009; (London) *Observer* (on-line) Apr. 10, 2010; (Medford, Oregon) *Mail Tribune* (on-line) Feb. 1, 2010; *Milwaukee (Wisconsin) Journal Sentinel* E p1 Dec. 3, 2006; *OutlookIndia.com* Oct. 26, 1998; Stanford University Medical School Web site; *Texas Monthly* p48+ June 1997, p163+ Dec. 2004; *Washington Post* C p1 Feb. 16, 2009

Selected Books: *My Own Country: A Doctor's Story of a Town and Its People in the Age of AIDS*, 1994; *The Tennis Partner: A Doctor's Story of Friendship and Loss*, 1998; *Cutting for Stone*, 2009

Volkow, Nora D.

(VOHL-kahf)

Mar. 27, 1956– Neuroscientist; federal-agency administrator; educator

Address: National Institute on Drug Abuse, 6001 Executive Blvd., Rm. 5213, Bethesda, MD 20892-9561

The neuroscientist Nora D. Volkow has spent most of her career conducting innovative research on drug addiction. In the 1980s, using positron emission tomography (PET), Volkow showed that cocaine abusers had the same kinds of brain damage that occur in cases of minor strokes. Throughout that decade and the next, Volkow demonstrated—in experiments and studies using PET scans and magnetic resonance imaging (MRI)—that although various potentially addictive drugs affect the brain differently, they all share a powerful ability to cause changes in the goals and preferences of the user, by influencing the release of dopamine, a neurotransmitter that plays a crucial role in desire and motivation.

From 1987 to 2003 Volkow held important positions at the Brookhaven National Laboratory, an arm of the Office of Science of the U.S. Department of Energy (DOE) in Upton, on Long Island, New York. In 2003 she was appointed director of the National Institute on Drug Abuse (NIDA), a federal agency that funds most of the world's research on drug abuse and addiction. Volkow has been recognized by the medical and research communities for her significant contributions to our understanding of addiction. "She knows how to look at data better than anyone I've ever seen," Joanna Fowler, a renowned Brookhaven chemist and a longtime collaborator of Volkow's, told Guy Gugliotta for the *Washington Post* (August 21, 2003). In 2000 Volkow was named Innovator of the Year by *U.S. News & World Report*, and in 2007 her name appeared on *Time* magazine's list of the world's 100 most influential people and *Newsweek*'s "Who's Next" list.

Volkow believes that although addiction is a brain disease, its presence does not absolve addicts from all responsibility for their behavior. She also emphasizes, however, that we need a subtle and serious reevaluation of long-held and widely accepted concepts of addiction. "A sick person is still responsible to seek treatment and sustain it for as long as needed, just as a patient with AIDS has to take responsibility for seeking and staying in treatment," Volkow wrote in an e-mail message to *Current Biography*. (That message and a *Current Biography* phone interview with Volkow are the sources of all quotes in this article unless otherwise indicated.) "There is an important nuance in the case of addiction, though, in which, like for some other psychiatric conditions, the very foundations of free will and sound decision making might be severely impaired, dramatically lowering the ability of these patients to recognize their condition and lay out a rational plan to deal with it—at least to begin with. This is why it is so important for society to walk away from the stigma, recognize addiction for what it is and devise and deploy rational and humane ways of dealing with this devastating disease."

Nora Dolores Volkow was born on March 27, 1956 in Mexico City, Mexico. Her father, Esteban Volkov, was a Russian-born chemist who worked in the pharmaceutical industry. Her mother, Palmira Fernández, was a fashion designer; a native of Spain, she fled to Mexico in the 1930s, during the Spanish Civil War. Volkow has an older sister, Verónica, a translator, poet, and essayist, and younger twin sisters: Patricia, a physician and AIDS specialist, and Natalia, an administrator at Mexico's

Mary Noble Ours, courtesy of National Institute on Drug Abuse (NIDA)

Nora D. Volkow

National Institute of Statistics. (All the siblings changed the last letter of their surname from "v" to "w.") Volkow and her sisters were raised in the very house where one of their great-grandfathers, the Russian revolutionary Leon Trotsky (1879–1940), was assassinated. Trotsky (born Lev Bronstein) settled in Mexico City in 1937, after the Soviet dictator Joseph Stalin sent him into exile. After he came to Mexico, Trotsky and Natalya, his second wife, shared a house with another couple—the artists Diego Rivera and Frida Kahlo. Conflict spurred by the suspicion that Trotsky was having an affair with Kahlo led the Trotskys to move to a house nearby, on Calle Viena.

Soon afterward, in 1939, Nora Volkow's father, then named Vsevolod Platonovich Volkov, the son of one of Trotsky's two daughters from his first marriage, came to Mexico City to live with his grandfather. Then about 13 years of age, he had no other living relative except a half-sister whom he did not meet until decades later; his mother had committed suicide, and every other member of his family had died in Stalin's purges or prison camps or under unexplained, suspicious circumstances. One day in August 1940, Volkov came home to learn that Trotsky had been severely wounded in his study by a Soviet agent wielding an ice axe; his grandfather died the next day. Volkov continued to live in the house on Calle Viena; years later, after changing his given name to Esteban, he brought his wife to live there. (According to some sources, he has also used the name Esteban Volkov Bronstein.)

As youngsters growing up in the house on Calle Viena (the building is now part of the Trotsky Museum), Volkow and her sisters would play with Trotsky's clothes and look through his books and papers. "My father didn't know about that," Volkow said. "He would have been very upset. But children are children." From a very early age, Volkow knew about her great-grandfather's assassination, largely through information imparted by people (most of them strangers to the Volkovs) who had been drawn to visit the house by their interest in Trotsky. "As little girls, whenever somebody rang the bell and asked us to guide them through the house, we did so, and that was a privilege," Natalia Volkow told Bill Snyder for the Vanderbilt University Medical Center magazine *Lens* (February 2006, on-line). "We usually took a long time talking to them—listening to them." But Volkow and her sisters did not discuss Trotsky with their father; his memories made talking about his grandfather too painful for him.

Volkow was a curious, perceptive child and an avid reader. She spent hours watching people interact on the streets of Mexico City. She was fascinated, she recalled, by the "diversity of behavioral responses in both animals and humans" and by how "the brain can generate fear, pain, love, language." What most interested her was how people relate to one another, everyone from a mother and her child or two strangers passing each other on the street. She also spent a lot of time observing the behavior of stray dogs and people's interactions with them and the ways in which members of ant colonies work together.

Volkow completed her secondary-school education at the private, English-language Modern American School in Mexico City. When she graduated, in 1974, she was fluent in French and German as well as Spanish and English. She then took undergraduate courses as well as medical instruction at the Universidad Nacional Autónoma de México (National Antonomous University of Mexico), in Mexico City. Volkow was particularly interested in cardiology and biochemistry—especially the latter's application to cancer research—but her fascination with human behavior remained: she knew that she would ultimately pursue psychology and neuroscience. "Clearly," she said, "when I went to medical school, I went with the brain in mind."

Volkow earned an M.D. degree in January 1981; she ranked first in her class of 2,000 at her graduation and won the the Premio Robins Award for best medical student of her generation. About a month later Volkow read an article in *Scientific American* (October 1980) about the three-dimensional brain-imaging technique known as positron emission tomography (PET), in which scientists used scanners to track radioactive chemicals, called tracers, injected into patients suffering from Alzheimer's disease, epilepsy, the effects of strokes, and drug addiction. Different tracers were used to illuminate the parts of the brain involved in different activities. The technique was significant because scientists could learn noninvasively (that is, without surgery) about the functioning of the brains of people and animals. Reading the article marked a turning point in Volkow's life: she felt so excited about the prospect of using the technology that she abandoned her plans to pursue a postgraduate degree at the Massachusetts Institute of Technology and resolved to gain acceptance to the residency program in psychiatry at New York University (NYU). As partners in a collaborative program with Brookhaven National Laboratory, NYU Psychiatry Department researchers had access to the laboratory's PET scanners. With that goal she traveled to New York and secured an interview with the Psychiatry Department's chairman, Robert Cancro. In a conversation with Guy Gugliotta, Cancro recalled meeting Volkow: "It was clear she was bright, anxious, enthusiastic and you could see the drive." While at NYU Volkow earned the Laughlin Fellowship Award as one of the 10 outstanding psychiatric residents in the U.S.

Volkow's first professional paper, about the use of brain-imaging equipment for detecting cancerous brain tumors, reflected her medical training in Mexico. She soon turned her interest to schizophrenia, a psychiatric disorder that fascinated her: "It intrigued me because [the disorder] produces disruptions across a wide variety of processes," among them perception and reasoning; many schizophrenics suffer from hallucinations and delusions over which they have no control.

Chance led Volkow to turn from studying schizophrenia to researching drug addiction. In 1984 she left New York to take the post of assistant professor at the University of Texas Health Science Center at Houston; she also served as an attending physician at the university-affiliated Memorial Hermann Hospital. Although the hospital had imaging equipment, the patient population did not include schizophrenics. But there were many cocaine addicts. Abuse of certain drugs, such as alcohol, cocaine, and methamphetamine, produces psychosis in some people; symptoms of psychosis, as in schizophrenia, often include audio or visual hallucinations and/or delusional thinking. For that reason drug abusers would be suitable subjects for research for Volkow, who wanted to "get inside the process of psychosis."

Volkow was one of the first people—possibly the first—to use PET scans to examine the brains of drug addicts. She was surprised by what she found: as indicated by impaired blood flow, there was clear damage in their brains, similar to the destruction caused by small strokes. That was an "eye opener," Volkow said; the prevailing belief was that cocaine was a relatively safe drug, but the brain-imaging data she had collected showed that it was not. Volkow had also used general neuropsychological tests to evaluate her subjects. The addicts had performed relatively well on those tests, which measured such cognitive functions as memory and reaction time. Volkow concluded that the tests were not capable of detecting the brain damage that the PET scans revealed; moreover, such tests overlooked such phenomena as social intelligence, emotional intelligence, and multitasking abilities. Volkow's evidence notwithstanding, the medical community initially rejected her findings, because neuropsychological testing was well-established, whereas PET was a new technology. "In the beginning, I had a lot of trouble getting that data published," Volkow recalled. She commented to Bill Snyder, "When you go against the current it takes time to change its course." Three years passed before an article describing her research was published; entitled "Cerebral Blood Flow in Chronic Cocaine Users: A Study with Positron Emission Tomography," it appeared in the *British Journal of Psychiatry* in May 1988. Its three co-authors included the physicist Stephen Adler, whom Volkow married during her time in Texas.

Earlier, in 1987, Volkow had joined the Brookhaven National Laboratory, in Upton, New York, as an associate scientist with the Department of Medicine. She remained at the laboratory for 16 years, conducting research as director of the nuclear-medicine division (1994–2003), director of the NIDA/DOE Imaging Center (1997–2003), and associate director of life sciences (1999–2003). In addition to cocaine, Volkow investigated addictions to alcohol, nicotine, heroin, and methamphetamine. All those addictions involve dopamine, a neurotransmitter in the brain that plays a crucial role in desire, decision making, and motivation. The two most significant factors with regard to one's susceptibility to addiction are genes and environment: those with naturally high levels of dopamine receptors are much less likely than others to exhibit compulsive behavior when exposed to potentially rewarding stimuli—that is, they are much less likely to become addicts. Environmental factors, such as the availability of drugs and approval of their use among members of a person's family and social circle, also play important roles. For those reasons some but not all people who use drugs become addicted.

Dopamine transmits information to brain cells via the synapses, which exist at either end of each cell; the cells absorb the new information by means of receptors. Volkow and her colleagues found that there are "common changes in the brains of people regardless of the drug that they take. . . . And we showed that [for people addicted to drugs cited above] there was a decrease in the levels of dopamine receptors in their brains." Furthermore, Volkow and her colleagues discovered that the abuse of such drugs leads to abnormalities in the orbitofrontal cortex—a region in the brain's frontal lobes that allows us to attribute values to actions, people, and things. Such abnormalities can lead to potentially devastating effects, such as the destructive decision to continue or even intensify drug abuse. Ordinarily, if a person is hungry, the orbitofrontal cortex of the brain will give food a higher "value"—make it a higher priority—than at other times; once the person is no longer hungry, the "value" that person attributes to the food becomes negligible or nil. Among drug abusers, Volkow's studies have shown, the orbitofrontal cortex is in effect hijacked, which leads the addicts to place an extraordinarily high value on consuming the desired drug. Moreover, damage to that brain region disrupts those people's ability to behave appropriately in social situations, which may lead to social isolation, continued drug abuse, and criminal activity.

Although the drugs mentioned above have many effects in common, they also have different effects, because the molecular composition of each is different from that of the others. Cocaine is especially harmful in that it kills brain cells, by interfering with blood circulation in the brain; the drug known as ecstasy (also called E) interferes with the workings of the neurotransmitter serotonin, which is very important in mood regulation; and methamphetamine has an especially devastating effect on processes involving dopamine.

In a study of effects on the brain of methamphetamine use that Volkow conducted with Joanna Fowler and nine others, their subjects consisted of two groups: one contained 15 methamphetamine addicts who had been using the drug for at least two years and who had stopped using it for at least two weeks prior to the experiment, and the other comprised 21 people who had never used the drug. When, using PET scans, Volkow and her colleagues compared levels of dopamine in the addicts and the nonaddicts, they found that the former subjects' dopamine levels were more than 20 percent lower than those in the other group in areas of the brain crucial for movement, concentration, and motivation. Volkow and her colleagues published those findings in the March 2001 issue of the *American Journal of Psychiatry*.

In the mid-1990s Volkow and her colleagues started using MRI in addition to PET scans in their research. PET scans and MRI complement each other: PET scans reveal molecular functions and activity and changes in function and activity at the cellular level; MRI shows the structure of parts of the body—their size and shape—but does not provide information about function. Volkow has used both techniques in another area of research: her investigations of the heavy use or abuse of prescription drugs, including medications, such as Ritalin, extensively used to treat attention deficit and hyperactivity disorder (ADHD). In one study Volkow compared the brains of subjects injected with Ritalin (whose chemical structure is similar to that of amphetamine) with those of subjects injected with cocaine. The results, as Volkow wrote in a paper published in the *Archives of General Psychiatry* (Volume 52, Number 6, 1995), showed that the distribution of Ritalin in the brain was almost "identical to that of cocaine." In addition, both Ritalin and cocaine peaked a few minutes after injection: that is, the effects of both reached their maximums after a few minutes (between four and 10 minutes with Ritalin, between two and eight minutes with cocaine). The only significant difference between the two drugs revealed in that particular study, Volkow wrote, was that Ritalin took more than four times as long—90 minutes—as cocaine to leave the body. Ritalin is commonly prescribed to children who have been diagnosed with ADHD. However, Volkow pointed out, children (and adults) take the drug orally in pill form, not by means of injections or by snorting it, and the chemicals in pills metabolize differently from those that are injected or snorted; therefore, similarities between Ritalin and cocaine should not necessarily be used to condemn Ritalin as unsuitable as a treatment for ADHD.

In 2003 Elias Zerhouni, the director of the National Institutes of Health (NIH), appointed Volkow to the post of director of the National Institute on Drug Abuse (NIDA). Volkow was initially apprehensive, concerned that her new post would leave her little time for research, but she decided that she could not pass up an opportunity to make an impact on policy as well as science. (She still conducts research at Brookhaven as an NIH intramural scientist, usually for several days each month.) Principal activities at NIDA, whose budget in 2011 was $1.09 billion, include using state-of-the-art technologies to further understanding of the anatomy and physiology of the brain, behavioral development, and addiction and its consequences; uncovering genetic and environmental factors that predict vulnerability to addiction and effectiveness of treatments; addressing health disparities and vulnerabilities among different populations (such as adolescents, members of minorities, and people in prison); applying knowledge gained from basic and cognitive neuroscience to develop improved prevention and treatment strategies; developing and testing new medications and behavioral therapies to treat addiction; and studying the links between addiction and other diseases, especially HIV/AIDS.

Since the 1990s, and now as director of NIDA, Volkow has warned that many children are misdiagnosed as having ADHD (and consequently receive drugs that they do not need), while other children who have ADHD, particularly in minority communities, are not diagnosed properly or at all, and as a result become more likely to abuse drugs. The solution, Volkow has said, is to improve diagnosis and treatment. Volkow has studied neurological phenomena associated not only with drugs but with obesity. Her research has produced evidence that compulsive eaters have low levels of dopamine receptors in their brains and that their orbital frontal cortexes show signs of damage. However, it is important to note, Volkow said, that what motivates the drive to eat is more complex than what motivates the drive to take drugs. We eat not only for pleasure but also for calories and nutrition; furthermore, she added, "food addiction" is not an officially recognized disorder, while compulsive eating is; the latter can lead to obesity and various health problems.

Society often looks down on and misunderstands people suffering from psychiatric disorders, such as schizophrenia and bipolar disorder. That is true to an even greater extent regarding drug addicts, who suffer from what Volkow calls "a disease of the brain that produces a loss of your ability to exert control." "By far, the biggest obstacle that I [have] had to contend with in my career in general and as the NIDA director in particular," Volkow wrote, "is the stigma that society attaches to drug abuse and addiction. This stigma permeates every social domain and has many negative effects, which include the suboptimal involvement of the healthcare system in the management of substance use disorders and the continuous reluctance on the part of the pharmaceutical industry to invest [in] the research necessary for the development of effective addiction medications. On a different level, we are challenged by the fragmentation of the substance abuse field, which has pitted those who favor biological approaches for the treatment of substance use disorders (SUDs) against those who oppose them; those who support legalization of drugs to help combat crime vs. those who are against such efforts for fear of increasing the magnitude of the drug problem, and those who support the notion of addiction as a brain disease against those who believe that addiction is squarely a moral failure of an individual. These obstacles have imped-

ed the dialog around substance abuse and addiction and prevented effective treatments from reaching those who need them."

Volkow served as associate professor in the Department of Psychiatry at the State University of New York (SUNY) at Stony Brook from 1991 to 2003 and as associate dean at the School of Medicine at SUNY-Stony Brook from 1997 to 2003.

Fowler told Bill Snyder that "people just glom onto [Volkow]. She's like pouring out ideas all day. . . . She can take a problem and very easily see through it; see relationships, simplify things." Volkow maintains a residence in Chevy Chase, Maryland. A former competitive swimmer, she runs several miles daily. She also paints, "to break my patterns of thinking," she told Guy Gugliotta.

—D.K.

Suggested Reading: National Public Radio *Talk of the Nation* June 16, 2006; *New York Times* F p5 Aug. 1, 2003, D p1 June 14, 2011; *Newsweek* p78 Dec. 25, 2006; nida.nih.gov; Vanderbilt Medical Center *Lens* (on-line) Feb. 2006; *Washington Post* C p1+ Aug. 21, 2003

Wakefield, Tim

Aug. 2, 1966– Baseball player

Address: Boston Red Sox, 4 Yawkey Way, Boston, MA 02215

Tim Wakefield of the Boston Red Sox belongs to one of most exclusive fraternities in all of Major League Baseball (MLB): knuckleball pitchers. Like some of its most famous practitioners—Hoyt Wilhelm, Phil Niekro, Wilbur Wood, and Charlie Hough—Wakefield has made a successful career of throwing a pitch that rarely exceeds 68 miles per hour (mph), roughly 25 to 30 mph slower than the average major-league fastball. When thrown properly (from a pitcher's fingertips or knuckles), the knuckleball, or knuckler, has virtually no spin—causing unpredictability in its movement and trajectory and presenting myriad challenges to opposing batters trying to hit it, catchers trying to grab it, and umpires trying to call it a ball or a strike. As quoted in Wakefield's 2011 autobiography, *Knuckler*, co-written with the Boston sportswriter Tony Massarotti, the Hall of Fame outfielder/first baseman Willie Stargell once likened the challenge of throwing strikes with a knuckleball to "throwing a butterfly with hiccups across the street into your neighbor's mailbox."

Like his fluttering pitches, Wakefield's road to and in the majors has had twists and turns: originally signed as a first baseman by the Pittsburgh Pirates in the 1988 MLB draft, he tried unsuccessfully to slug his way to the major leagues before rein-

Jim Rogash/Getty Images

venting himself as a knuckleball pitcher during his early years in the minors. Wakefield had an auspicious debut with the Pirates in 1992, being named the *Sporting News* National League (NL) Rookie Pitcher of the Year after posting an 8–1 record with a 2.15 earned-run average (ERA), but he lost command of his knuckleball the following year and spent the 1994 season in the minor leagues. Released by the Pirates in 1995, he was then signed by the Boston Red Sox, where he resurrected his career and established himself as one of the game's most dependable pitchers. Wakefield has since amassed nearly 200 career victories, had four seasons with at least 16 victories each, and collected more than 2,000 strikeouts, while serving in practically every pitching role, from starter to reliever to set-up man to closer. His unselfishness and willingness to take on different roles have helped him anchor the Red Sox pitching staff for much of the 2000s and played a pivotal role in Boston's World Series victories in 2004 and 2007. In 2009 he earned the first All-Star selection of his career. In addition to his on-the-field accomplishments, Wakefield has been lauded for his tireless charitable work, and in 2010 he was the recipient of MLB's prestigious Roberto Clemente Award, honoring sportsmanship and community involvement. Entering the 2011 season, Wakefield was one of only two active MLB players to have spent at least 15 seasons with the same team (the other was the New York Yankees closer Mariano Rivera), and he held franchise pitching records for starts (407) and innings, while ranking second in career strikeouts and third in wins for the Red Sox.

Timothy Stephen Wakefield was born on August 2, 1966 in Melbourne, Florida, to Steve and Judy Wakefield. He has a sister, Kelly. His father designed circuits for the Harris Corp., which manufactures television and radio products and equipment, and his mother worked for the same company as a purchaser and professional assistant. Wakefield's father was a high-school track star. Tim Wakefield started playing baseball at the age of five and quickly became enamored of the sport. "He played T-ball, and then he never stopped," his mother recalled for *Knuckler*. "I think he played every year after that. We could see in Little League [that he was advanced]. He just kept getting better." As a boy Wakefield also enjoyed fishing.

Wakefield was introduced to the knuckleball by his father, who often played catch with him, usually after an exhausting day at work. The pitcher recalled to Josh Robbins for the *Orlando (Florida) Sentinel* (May 19, 2002), "He'd get home . . . and it got to a point where he just got tired of playing catch with me." To tire his son out, Steve Wakefield threw knuckleballs, which were hard for the boy to catch and made him eager to end the sessions. Those experiences led Wakefield to view the knuckleball, as do many others, as a gimmick pitch—one that is rarely thrown other than for show; it would be years before he considered using it as the centerpiece of his pitching arsenal.

Wakefield attended Eau Gallie High School, in Melbourne, where he pitched and played first base on the varsity baseball team. There, he stood out among his peers not only for his talent but also for his character. Ken Campbell, his coach at Eau Gallie, told Doane Hulick for the *Providence (Rhode Island) Journal-Bulletin* (July 29, 1995), "He was the type of kid you would like your own son to grow up and be like." Campbell added, "He was very competitive. He played first base for me, and he pitched. He didn't throw the knuckleball back then. His main forte for me was as a hitter." After graduating from Eau Gallie, in 1984, Wakefield was generally overlooked by National Collegiate Athletic Association (NCAA) Division I-A schools because of his size (he stood six-foot-two but was very thin). He was offered a baseball scholarship by only one school, Brevard Community College (BCC), in Brevard County, Florida. He attended BCC, hoping to distinguish himself there and transfer to a school with a bigger baseball program. Those plans were squashed when he clashed with the BCC coach, Ernie Rousseau, who did not guarantee him a starting spot on the team. Disheartened, Wakefield quit the team and contemplated giving up baseball for good until he received a call from Les Hall, the head coach at the Florida Institute of Technology (better known as Florida Tech). Hall offered him a spot on Florida Tech's baseball squad and became his mentor. (Wakefield finished his freshman year at BCC.)

Wakefield entered Florida Tech in the fall of 1985 as a redshirt freshman, which allowed him to keep his four years of athletic eligibility. While with the Florida Tech Panthers, he rejuvenated his baseball career. By that time he had reached the peak of his physical development, having bulked up to a muscular 210 pounds. Wakefield, who continued to play first base, emerged as one of Florida's top young hitting prospects during his sophomore season, when he set Panthers' single-season marks in home runs (22) and RBIs (71). He was named the Panthers' Most Valuable Player (MVP) that season, as well as during his junior season, when he collected 13 more home runs, bringing his career total to a school-record 40 (which still stands). Wakefield's hitting prowess impressed professional scouts, and in June 1988 he was selected by the Pittsburgh Pirates in the eighth round—200th overall—of that year's MLB amateur players' draft. He signed a contract that included a $15,000 signing bonus.

Wakefield's early experiences in the minors were humbling. In the summer of 1988, he played for the Pirates' Rookie League team, in Bradenton, Florida, before being assigned to the organization's short-season class-A affiliate, the Watertown Pirates, in Watertown, New York. Despite hitting a home run in his first professional at-bat, Wakefield struggled to make the adjustment to minor-league pitching, as well as to wooden (rather than aluminum) bats. Making matters worse was the death of his paternal grandfather, Lester Wakefield, shortly into his stint at Watertown. Wakefield had been extremely close with his grandfather while growing up and was devastated by the loss. In 54 games at Watertown, he hit a dismal .189, with just nine extra-base hits. Wakefield failed to make the squads of any of the Pirates' minor-league affiliates the following spring and was kept in extended spring training at the lowest level of the minors, described in *Knuckler* as "a no man's-land that sends the large majority of aspiring professional baseball players off to lives filled with bar stools, beer taps, gas stations, mail rooms, public works, and office jobs."

A turning point in Wakefield's career came when Woody Huyke, the Pirates' Gulf Coast League manager, happened to see him tossing knuckleballs to a teammate before a game. Captivated by the ball's uncanny movement, Huyke instructed him to throw more knuckleballs during games. Shortly afterward Wakefield was promoted to the Pirates' class-A affiliate in Augusta, Georgia, and then sent back to the organization's short-season class-A affiliate in the New York–Penn League, which had moved from Watertown to Welland, Ontario. In Welland, he made his first professional appearance as a pitcher—albeit as a conventional one, throwing fastballs and curveballs. Later, during the fall of 1989, he went back to Bradenton, where he was assigned as a full-time pitcher. Wakefield's conversion to pitcher was largely orchestrated by Huyke, who had persuaded the Pirates to keep him on as a developing knuckleball pitcher instead of releasing him due to his lack of promise as a position player. Huyke told Jack Curry for the *New York Times* (July 12, 2009), "I told them, 'If you're going to release him, make sure you look at his knuckleball.' The ball had a lot of movement. You never knew where it was going to go." Wakefield, referring to his initial reluctance to throw the knuckleball in competition, noted to the same writer, "I had to do it or finish school and get a job."

Wakefield's transformation into a full-time knuckleball pitcher saved his career. He spent the 1990 season with the Pirates' advanced class-A affiliate, the Salem Buccaneers, in Salem, Virginia, where he notched 10 victories in 28 starts. The following year the Pirates sent him to play with the class-AA Carolina Mudcats, where he went 15–8 with a 2.90 ERA in 25 starts. Wakefield then opened the 1992 season with the Buffalo Bisons, in the class-AAA International League. In 20 starts with the club that year, he went 10–3 with a 3.06 ERA and recorded a league-high six complete games. The Pirates called Wakefield up to the majors later that summer, and on July 31, 1992, he made his major-league debut, in a home game against the St. Louis Cardinals. He pitched a complete game, striking out 10 batters while throwing 146 pitches, in a 3–2 Pirates victory. Wakefield continued to pitch well for the Pirates throughout his rookie season, finishing with a record of 8–1 and a 2.15 ERA in 13 starts. He then pitched two complete-game victories against the Atlanta Braves in that year's National League Championship Series (NLCS), which the Pirates lost in seven games. At season's end the *Sporting News* named Wakefield the NL Rookie Pitcher of the Year.

Wakefield enjoyed a propitious start to the 1993 season, notching a 9–4 victory over the San Diego Padres in the Pirates' season opener, in which he struck out nine batters and issued nine walks. He was relegated back to the minor leagues after opening the season 1–6. Wakefield was assigned to the class-AA Carolina Mudcats, where he continued to struggle, going 3–5 with a 6.99 ERA in nine starts. He returned to the Pirates that September, after rosters expanded. Wakefield ended the year on a strong note, pitching consecutive complete-game shutouts over the Chicago Cubs and Philadelphia Phillies, respectively, but still finished with a 6–11 record and 5.61 ERA. He spent the entire 1994 season in the minors, with the class-AAA Buffalo Bisons, in an attempt to regain command of his knuckleball. Those efforts, however, proved to be unsuccessful, as he posted a 5–15 record with a 5.84 ERA in 29 starts, while recording league highs in hits (197), runs (127), walks (98), and home runs (27).

During 1995 spring training the Pirates released Wakefield, a decision that the team's then-manager, Jim Leyland, now the manager of the Detroit Tigers, described in *Knuckler* as "very difficult. I kind of remember sitting there with Cam Bonifay [the Pirates general manager], and it was just a very difficult thing. I think we felt that if he was ever going to get it [the knuckleball] back, it wasn't going to be with us. That was such heartbreak. In the long run, that was probably good for him, because I think it did kind of resurrect and resuscitate him, but it was hard at the time." Six days after his release from the Pirates, Wakefield was picked up by the Boston Red Sox, who signed him to a minor-league free-agent contract. The Red Sox's then–general manager, Dan Duquette, who had been instrumental in bringing Wakefield to the team, later described the pickup to Adam Kilgore for the *Boston Globe* (July 13, 2009) as being "like a gift from God."

In efforts to help rebuild Wakefield's confidence, as well as to help him regain command of his knuckleball, Duquette sent him to Fort Myers, Florida, to work with the Hall of Fame pitcher Phil Niekro, widely considered to be the greatest knuckleball pitcher of all time (with 318 career victories), and his younger brother, Joe Niekro, a successful MLB knuckleball pitcher in his own right (with 221 career victories). Wakefield spent approximately 10 days working with the Niekros before being assigned to Boston's class-AAA affiliate, the Pawtucket Red Sox, in Pawtucket, Rhode Island. After four starts with the club, Wakefield was called up to the Red Sox, where he quickly regained the same dominating form that he had established three years earlier. That season he won 14 of his first 15 decisions and posted a record of 16–8 with a 2.95 ERA, while finishing among the American League (AL) leaders in a number of pitching categories and earning a third-place finish in the balloting for the AL Cy Young Award. Bolstered by Wakefield's strong regular-season pitching performance, the Red Sox won the AL East Division title with an 86–58 record (in an abbreviated, 144-game schedule) and advanced to the postseason for the first time since 1990. While the Cleveland Indians swept the Red Sox in the first round of the play-offs, Wakefield was recognized for his efforts and was named the *Sporting News*'s AL Comeback Player of the Year.

Wakefield would enjoy a "steady, then superlative, then stagnant, then steady, remarkably steady" career with the Red Sox over the next 15 seasons, as Jack Curry noted. He spent his time as either a starter or reliever during the 1996, 1997, and 1998 seasons, in which he recorded 14, 12, and a career-high 17 wins, respectively. Then, midway through the 1999 season, the Red Sox's then–manager, Jimy Williams, asked him to become the team's closer. Filling in for Boston's primary closer, Tom Gordon, who had suffered a season-ending arm injury, Wakefield recorded 15 saves (in 18 opportunities) and made a total of 25 relief appearances before returning to the starting rotation later that summer. He finished the year with a 6–11 record and 5.08 ERA. The Red Sox, meanwhile, finished second in the AL East, with a 94–68 record, and advanced to the postseason for the second consecutive season. Wakefield made two short relief appearances for Boston in the AL Division series, which saw them overcome the Cleveland Indians in five games, but he was then left off the play-off roster for the American League Championship Series (ALCS) against the New York Yankees. The omission was seen as a major slight to Wakefield, who had made numerous sacrifices for the team throughout the season and had proved to be effective in a variety of roles. Many later attributed the decision to Boston's then–pitching coach, Joe Kerrigan, who viewed the knuckleball with skepticism at best, and with whom Wakefield had a tenuous relationship. The Red Sox lost the series to the eventual World Series–champion Yankees in five games.

Over the next three seasons, Wakefield moved between the bullpen and the starting rotation, as the Red Sox missed the play-offs each year. In 2000 he appeared in 51 games and made 17 starts, and in the following year, he pitched in 45 games and again made 17 starts. Wakefield spent the beginning of the 2002 season almost exclusively in the bullpen, before injuries to Red Sox starters gave him the opportunity to return to the starting rotation midway through the year. He finished the season with a record of 11–5 and a 2.81 ERA. That impressive performance led the Red Sox to install him as a permanent back-of-the-rotation starter during the 2003 season, which saw him go 11–7 with a 4.09 ERA in 202.1 innings. The Red Sox returned to the play-offs that year, finishing second in the AL East with a 95–67 record, but again lost to the New York Yankees in the ALCS. In the emotionally charged series between the archrivals—remembered for a Game Three brawl that saw the Red Sox ace Pedro Martinez rough up the Yankees' 72-year-old bench coach, Don Zimmer—Wakefield won Game One and Game Four and was brought in as an emergency reliever in a dramatic, extra-

inning Game Seven, but he gave up a series-clinching home run to the Yankees' infielder Aaron Boone in the 11th inning. Following that defeat, Wakefield apologized to fans, despite the fact that he had played a pivotal role in Boston's advancing to the series and had pitched masterfully in his first two starts.

Entering the 2004 season the Red Sox hired Terry Francona to serve as the club's new manager, replacing Grady Little. Under Francona, a former MLB journeyman player who had managed the Philadelphia Phillies from 1997 to 2000, Wakefield became a permanent regular starter. In 2004 he made 30 starts and went 12–10 with a 4.87 ERA and helped the Red Sox overcome a 3–0 deficit to defeat the Yankees in the ALCS in seven games. In the 2004 World Series, the Red Sox swept the St. Louis Cardinals in four games to win their first championship in 86 years.

As a starter over the next five seasons, Wakefield compiled a record of 61–51. He pitched in a career-high 225.1 innings during the 2005 season and matched a career high in wins (17) in 2007. That year the Red Sox swept the Colorado Rockies in the World Series to win their second championship in four seasons. (Wakefield was left off the World Series roster due to an injured shoulder.) After pitching through more shoulder problems during the 2008 season, in which he went 10–11 with a 4.13 ERA, Wakefield returned in 2009 to post the best first-half-of-the-season numbers of his career and went into the All-Star break tied for the major-league lead in wins, with 11; he also made Red Sox history by surpassing Roger Clemens for the most starts (383) in franchise history. He was named to his first All-Star team that year, becoming, at 42, the second-oldest first-time All-Star in history (behind the African-American Hall of Famer Satchel Paige, who was a 46-year-old All Star in 1952, following the integration of MLB). He made only four starts after the break due to several injuries and finished the year with an 11–5 record and a 4.58 ERA.

In 2010 Wakefield, while splitting his time between starting and relieving, achieved several milestones. In a May game against the Seattle Mariners, he recorded his 2,000th career strikeout, and in a June game against the Cleveland Indians, he surpassed Roger Clemens for the most innings pitched by a Red Sox player, with 2,777. Less than a week after eclipsing that record, he became one of just three active pitchers to reach 3,000 career innings pitched and the 129th pitcher in MLB history to accomplish that feat. (The other two active pitchers, Jaime Moyer and Andy Pettitte, were both inactive entering the 2011 season—Moyer is currently a free agent, and Pettitte retired after the 2010 season.) In September 2010, in a victory over the Tampa Bay Rays, he became, at 44, the oldest Red Sox pitcher in history to record a win. Despite those accomplishments the 2010 season was generally a disappointing one for Wakefield, who finished with a 4–10 record and a relatively poor 5.34 ERA, numbers he has attributed to his inconsistent role with the team throughout the season. Referring to his sometime-function as a "mop-up guy," or a pitcher sent in when victory is out of reach, Wakefield explained to Peter Keratosis for *Florida Today* (January 23, 2011), "I want to help the team win. I don't mind doing any job. I just don't want to be the guy who comes in when we're losing 10–0."

As of early August 2011, Wakefield was one win away from the elite 200-win plateau, with 199 career victories. On July 24, in a game against the Seattle Mariners, he recorded his 2,000th career strikeout with the Red Sox, becoming just the second pitcher in franchise history to reach that milestone. He currently ranks third in all-time wins with the Sox, with 185, trailing only Cy Young and Roger Clemens (who both had 192), and ranks second among the franchise's all-time strikeout leaders (behind Clemens, who had 2,590).

Wakefield has long been known as a quiet and modest man and as one of baseball's most charitable figures. His former manager Jim Leyland described him to Howard Ulman for the Norfolk *Virginian-Pilot* (July 13, 2009) as "one of the great ambassadors for the game." In 2010 he won the prestigious Roberto Clemente Award, awarded annually to the MLB player who "best exemplifies the game of baseball, sportsmanship, community involvement and the individual's contribution to his team." Wakefield, who had been nominated for the award on seven previous occasions, described it to Keratosis as "the ultimate award in baseball, an award for what you do off the field, for the dedication and the sacrifice and the service you put in for others, and it's named after a guy who made the ultimate sacrifice, losing his life trying to help others." (On December 31, 1972 Roberto Clemente died in a plane crash while traveling to Nicaragua to aid earthquake victims. He had long been known for his humanitarian work in Puerto Rico and Latin American countries. Clemente was elected posthumously to the Baseball Hall of Fame in 1973.) The many institutions to which Wakefield has given time and money include the Jimmy Fund, New England's Pitching in for Kids organization, and his own Wakefield Warriors program, which helps raise funds for the Franciscan Hospital for Children in Boston.

Wakefield and his wife, Stacy, have two children, Trevor and Brianna. In April 2011 Wakefield published the memoir *Knuckler: My Life with Baseball's Most Confounding Pitch*. He makes his off-season home in Melbourne. "Melbourne's a very, very small town that's very quiet, but it's where I grew up and it's where my roots are, and that's why I continue to stay there," he said to Robbins. "My family's all from there. I try to give back to the community that I came from as much as possible."

—C.C.

Suggested Reading: *Boston Globe* p1+ July 13, 2009, p1 Oct. 29, 2010; (Brevard County, Florida) *Florida Today* p1+ June 23, 2001, p1 Oct. 15,

2003, C p1 Jan. 23, 2011; *New York Times* p1 July 12, 2009; (Norfolk, Virginia) *Virginian-Pilot* C p1 July 13, 2009; (Orlando, Florida) *Sentinel* C p1+ May 19, 2002; *Sporting News* p34 June 15, 1992; *USA Today* C p1 July 10, 2009; Wakefield, Tim, with Tony Massarotti. *Knuckler: My Life with Baseball's Most Confounding Pitch*, 2011

Frederick M. Brown/Getty Images

Wallace, Chris

Oct. 12, 1947– Broadcast journalist

Address: Fox News Channel Studios, 400 N. Capitol St., N.W., Suite 550, Washington, DC 20001

Chris Wallace, a son of the longtime broadcast journalist Mike Wallace, has been in the news industry for over three decades. The host of the Sunday-morning public-affairs program *Fox News Sunday* since 2003, he began his career in print journalism. He moved from print to TV for two reasons, as he told David Perry for the *Lowell (Massachusetts) Sun* (April 23, 2007, on-line): "One, it's probably in the blood. I remember growing up and doing fake newscasts. And I enjoy it. But I also remember in 1972, working at the [Boston] *Globe*, I was in the newsroom watching the Republican National Convention. We had people on the scene in Miami Beach, but here were people watching the convention on TV." Wallace continued, "I figured I'd just cut out the middle man." Wallace was hired as a reporter for New York City's WNBC-TV, NBC's flagship station, in 1975, and three years later he moved to Washington, D.C., where he served as the network's chief White House correspondent for seven years (1982–89). During that time he also served as an anchor for the *Today Show* (1981–82), *NBC Nightly News* (1982–84 and 1986–87), and *Meet the Press* (1987–88). He joined ABC in 1988 and became known for his groundbreaking investigative reports as a chief correspondent for *Primetime Live*. He also served as a substitute host for *Nightline* and a correspondent for *20/20*. Wallace joined the Fox Network in 2003. "*Fox News Sunday*'s major appeal to viewers, if not guests, is Wallace's smile-as-you-slip-in-blade interviewing style," Glenn Garvin wrote for the *Miami Herald* (May 16, 2005, on-line). "He's an equal-opportunity ravager. . . . Aggressive without being abrasive, he uses old video clips to corner his subject, then dissects them with surgical precision." Wallace told Garvin, "Part of what you're doing in an interview is trying to provoke people." He continued, "Things are so packaged now. All these politicians come on [the show], they're so rehearsed, they've got a carefully practiced set of talking points. Anything you can do to get them off the script and thinking and talking in real time, I consider a great achievement."

Christopher Wallace was born on October 12, 1947 in Chicago, Illinois, to Norma Kaplan and Mike Wallace, a correspondent for the CBS television newsmagazine *60 Minutes* from its debut, in 1968, to 2006, when he officially retired. (He made occasional appearances on the show until 2008.) Chris Wallace's parents divorced when he was a year old, and his mother later married the journalist William A. "Bill" Leonard, who served as president of CBS News from 1979 to 1982. Chris Wallace did not have much of a relationship with his father until 1961, when his older brother, Peter, died at the age of 19, after falling from a mountain in Greece. The family did not learn about Peter's death until, several weeks after the accident, Mike Wallace traveled to Greece and found his son's body. That traumatic event prompted Mike Wallace to draw closer to Chris, and the two began to spend more time together. "We both felt an interest in this other person in our lives that we didn't know much about," Chris Wallace told Ed Bark for the *Dallas Morning News* (November 5, 2005).

Despite his father's success as a journalist, it was his stepfather who influenced Chris to pursue a career in journalism. "I hoped that he would follow in my footsteps," Mike Wallace told Bark. "But his stepdad had more to do with teaching Chris than I did." During long car rides Chris Wallace and Bill Leonard would often pretend to report the news together. "If the car hit a milestone, say 20,000 miles, we would do a special report," Wallace told Marisa Guthrie for *Broadcasting & Cable* (April 13, 2009). "He would be the anchor, and I would be on the assembly line in Detroit with the guy who had made the car. And then I'd be the White House correspondent talking about what this meant for the balance-of-trade deficit because this was a terrific General Motors car." In 1964, while leading CBS

News's election-coverage team, Leonard secured Wallace a job as a gopher at the Republican National Convention. "I got Walter Cronkite's coffee and things like that," Wallace told Bark. "I thought, 'You mean people really pay [reporters] to do this?' That's when the bug really bit." Wallace studied history at Harvard University, in Cambridge, Massachusetts, where he also served as a reporter for WHRB, the student-operated radio station. He graduated with a B.A. degree in 1969.

Wallace spent the next four years as a reporter for the *Boston Globe*, working his way up to cover national politics and the 1972 elections. In 1973 he made the transition from print to television news, taking a job as a reporter for WBBM, the CBS-owned station in Chicago. In 1975 Wallace was hired as a reporter with WNBC-TV in New York City. (He had turned down a job at CBS News in Washington, D.C., in part because he did not want to continue working for the same station as his father.) At WNBC Wallace became a chief correspondent on *Primetime Sunday*, anchored by Tom Snyder, and contributed to his unit's winning Associated Press and Peabody Awards in 1977. Wallace also covered the 1980 presidential campaigns and the Republican and Democratic national conventions and was the first network correspondent to report the Republican presidential nominee Ronald Reagan's selection of George H. W. Bush as his running mate. That same year Wallace won an Emmy Award for his work on NBC's documentary special *1980 White Paper: The Migrants*, which exposed the squalid working conditions of migrant laborers in Florida. A year later Wallace became co-anchor of NBC's morning news and talk program, the *Today Show*, alongside Jane Pauley and Bryant Gumbel. In 1982 he became the anchor of the Sunday edition of *NBC Nightly News*—the network's daily evening news program—and NBC's chief White House correspondent. In the latter role Wallace accompanied Reagan on his 1983 trip to Europe and covered the president's meetings with such world leaders as French president François Mitterrand and Queen Elizabeth II. He also reported on the 1984 and 1988 Republican and Democratic National Conventions and presidential races, and in 1985 he hosted the television special *Nancy Reagan: Portrait of the First Lady*. Wallace left *NBC Nightly News* in 1987 to serve as the moderator of the Sunday-morning interview and news program *Meet the Press*, a position he held through the next year.

In 1989 Wallace left NBC for ABC, which had been trying to persuade him to join the network for years. "I came pretty close in 1985 to going with ABC," Wallace told John Carmody for the *Washington Post* (December 7, 1988). Regarding his decision to join the network, he told Carmody, "NBC made me a generous offer and very much wanted to keep me. The fact is, ABC was offering me a prime time program, with an opportunity to do longer stories, and some investigative reporting and profiles. It was a challenge and an opportunity." Wallace became a correspondent for *Primetime Live*, a newsmagazine that covered both hard news and human-interest stories and was filmed before a live audience. The show, which premiered in 1989 with hosts Diane Sawyer and Sam Donaldson, was described by Walter Goodman for the *New York Times* (August 4, 1989, on-line) as being "somewhere between *Good Morning America* and *Nightline*, with a list toward the former." (Later, in 2000, Wallace served as senior correspondent for *Primetime Thursday*, hosted by Sawyer and Charles Gibson, after two years during which "Primetime Live" had been a segment on the ABC newsmagazine *20/20*.)

As a correspondent, Wallace conducted in-depth investigations of such issues as gender bias in contemporary society, baggage theft by U.S. airline employees, and antibiotic-resistant bacteria. His assignments often took him abroad; for instance, he interviewed members of the Polish Solidarity Underground—the first independent trade union established in the Communist Soviet Bloc—and reported on secret assassination groups in South Africa. His 1991 profile of Thaddeus Lott, an unconventional Houston, Texas, elementary-school principal, whose underprivileged students consistently outperformed students attending schools in more affluent suburbs, was honored with a Cine Golden Eagle Award and an American Film and Video Award and nominated for an Emmy Award. Wallace also won a 1993 Alfred I. duPont-Columbia Award, from Columbia University, for his investigation of the predatory lending practices of the Ford Motor Co. During his tenure with ABC, Wallace also served as a substitute for Ted Koppel as the host of the late-night news program *Nightline*. In 1996 he turned down an offer from NBC to host *Dateline*—which would have put him in direct competition with *60 Minutes*, hosted by his father—and instead signed a four-year contract to stay at ABC. Two years later he became the chief correspondent for *20/20*.

In 2003 Wallace joined the Fox network, replacing Tony Snow as the anchor of its weekly public-affairs program, *Fox News Sunday*, which is produced by Fox's cable-news arm, Fox News. Based in Washington, D.C., *Fox News Sunday* consists of interviews with some of the week's major newsmakers, followed by a discussion of news stories by a panel of pundits. Though some observers considered the move from a major news network to a cable network a step down, Wallace was happy to join Fox News, which, launched in 1996, had recently surpassed CNN as television's most-watched cable-news channel. He told Roger Catlin for the *Hartford (Connecticut) Courant* (December 6, 2003), "My first love is politics and government. . . . To go back to hard news, interviewing top newsmakers in Washington, was an offer I couldn't refuse." Wallace told Catlin that he was first impressed with Fox News during its coverage of the beginning of the Iraq War, in 2003. He further noted, "I became intrigued with this place with

fewer resources doing such aggressive reporting and making news." Within Wallace's first week as host, *Fox News Sunday* increased its audience by 75 percent, and it soon began to compete with Sunday-morning shows on the three major networks.

During the 2004 election season, Wallace reported live on such major events as the New Hampshire primary, the Iowa caucuses, and the Republican and Democratic conventions; he also covered the presidential debates and election-night results. Over the years he has interviewed numerous public figures on *Fox News Sunday*, including John Kerry, George H. W. Bush, Dick Cheney, Condoleezza Rice, Hillary Rodham Clinton, Colin Powell, Nancy Pelosi, Joe Biden, John Edwards, and John McCain. Wallace had his first television interview with his father in 2005, when the elder Wallace appeared on *Fox News Sunday* to promote his book *Between You and Me*. Perhaps the most memorable of Chris Wallace's *Fox News Sunday* interviews was with Bill Clinton, who appeared on the show in 2006 to discuss his efforts to address global challenges through the Clinton Global Initiative. During that interview Wallace asked the former president why he had not done more to stop the Islamic terrorist group Al Qaeda during his time in the White House. The question enraged Clinton, who accused Wallace of inviting him on the show under false pretenses and doing a "conservative hit job" on him. "I was utterly astonished. . . . It's not often you have a former president of the U.S. erupt at you," Wallace recalled to Perry. "I thought it was a fair, balanced and not especially inflammatory question," Wallace told Howard Kurtz for the *Washington Post* (September 25, 2006). "I even said, 'I know hindsight is 20/20.' But he went off. And once he went off, there was no bringing him back."

Wallace has been more successful than previous hosts in attracting Democratic guests to appear on *Fox News Sunday*, which, like much of Fox News's programming, is widely thought to have a conservative slant—a claim that Fox has consistently denied. Wallace too has expressed his view that Fox is unbiased, telling a writer for *Daily Variety* (October 28, 2003), "As far as any bias, I'd have to say that if you watch the Fox News Channel across the day, from morning to night, its reporting is serious, it's aggressive, it's thorough and it's even-handed." In 2005 Wallace told the radio host Howie Carr for Boston's station WRKO, as quoted by Newsmax.com (October 16, 2005), that since joining Fox News, he had noted a left-leaning bias in the political coverage of other major networks. Moreover, in Wallace's view, it is the optimism and energy at Fox—not its supposed political leanings—that sets it apart from other networks. "For somebody who had been at NBC 11 years and at ABC for 15, I really was increasingly struck by the amount of time we spent—and this was a phrase that was being used—'managing the decline,'" he told Garvin. "There was an overwhelming sense, I think at all the broadcast networks, that their future was behind them, that their best days had passed and that there was an inevitable slide downward in terms of audience and therefore of resources and budgets. It didn't seem like a very hopeful place to be." He added, "Fox was the only television operation that seemed to be growing, where the future seemed to be ahead of it, not behind it."

Although Wallace is a registered Democrat, he has stated that his affiliation is primarily pragmatic, given that the vast majority of registered voters and local elected officials in Washington, D.C., are Democrats. "The reason I'm a registered Democrat is that in Washington, D.C., there is really only one party. If you want a say in who's going to be the next mayor or councilman, you have to vote in the Democratic primary," he explained to Amy Argetsinger and Roxanne Roberts for the *Washington Post* (October 11, 2006, on-line). He continued, "Some people think [journalists] shouldn't vote at all—I think that's a little silly. . . . However I vote personally, I think I'm professional enough that it doesn't have anything to do with the way I cover the news."

In 2007 Wallace served as a panel member for the "First in the South" Republican presidential debate, in South Carolina, broadcast by Fox News. Wallace made headlines in September 2009, when, after President Barack Obama declined an invitation to be interviewed on Fox News during his media blitz to promote his health-care reform proposal, Wallace referred to the Obama administration during an appearance on the *The O'Reilly Factor* as "the biggest bunch of crybabies I have dealt with in my 30 years in Washington." In September 2010 Wallace and the Fox News Network filed a lawsuit against the Democrat Robin Carnahan's Senate campaign, for using almost 30 seconds of footage from Wallace's 2006 interview with her Republican opponent, U.S. representative Roy Blunt, in a campaign advertisement. The lawsuit, filed in the U.S. District Court for the western district of Missouri by the law firm Lathrop & Gage, alleges copyright infringement and invasion of Wallace's privacy in the ad's use of the footage and contends that the ad makes it appear that Fox and Wallace are endorsing Carnahan's campaign.

In 2004 Wallace published *Character: Profiles in Presidential Courage*, a book that examines crucial decisions made by 25 American presidents. Wallace, who signed a multiyear contract with Fox in November 2010, told Michele Willer-Allred for the *Ventura County (California) Star* (June 18, 2008), "Fox News is the happiest place to work, and it's the happiest I've ever been."

With his first wife, Elizabeth Farrell, whom he married in 1973, Wallace has four children: Peter, Margaret, Andrew, and Catherine. His second wife, Lorraine Smothers, whom he married in 1997, has a daughter, Sara, and a son, Remick, from her previous marriage, to the comedian Dick Smothers. Wallace and Smothers reside in Washington, D.C.
—J.P.

Suggested Reading: *Broadcasting & Cable* p20 Apr. 13, 2009; *Daily Variety* p5 Oct. 28, 2003; *Dallas Morning News* G p1 Nov. 5, 2005; *Hartford (Connecticut) Courant* Life D p1 Dec. 6, 2003; *Los Angeles Times* E p41 Dec. 7, 2003; *Lowell (Massachusetts) Sun* (on-line) Apr. 23, 2007; *Miami Herald* (on-line) May 16, 2005; *Ventura County (California) Star* (on-line) June 18, 2008; *Washington Post* B p1 Dec. 7, 1988, (on-line) Sep. 25, 2006, Oct. 11, 2006

Selected Books: *Character: Profiles in Presidential Courage*, 2004

Selected Television Shows: *Today Show*, 1981– 82; *NBC Nightly News*, 1982–84, 1986–87; *Meet the Press*, 1987–88; *Fox News Sunday*, 2003–

Joern Pollex/Getty Images

Wambach, Abby

(WAHM-bok)

June 2, 1980– Soccer player

Address: c/o U.S. Soccer Federation, 1801 S. Prairie Ave., Chicago, IL 60616

"I play best when I'm physical," the soccer standout Abby Wambach told Jeré Longman for the *International Herald Tribune* (October 3, 2003). "If I don't come off with grass stains and mud, I find myself thinking: 'What did I do? I must have done nothing.'" Fiercely competitive, extremely powerful, and seemingly fearless on the field, the five-foot 11-inch, 30-year-old Wambach has been playing soccer for 26 years. "Abby sticks her head where most players won't. [She] has made heading an art in the women's game," Tony DiCicco, the head coach of the U.S. Women's National Team for five years in the 1990s, told Jeff Jacobs for the *Hartford (Connecticut) Courant* (July 14, 2007). Wambach herself told a WHTK-AM interviewer, according to the *Rochester (New York) Democrat and Chronicle* (September 23, 2007), "I'm one of the most deadly headers in the world. If you're not going to mark me, I'm going to take advantage of it." As a teenager Wambach was named High School Player of the Year by the National Soccer Coaches Association of America, and as a student at the University of Florida, she set five school records and twice won Southeast Conference Player of the Year honors. In her senior year (2001–02), she joined the U.S. Women's National Team, and she has played with them ever since. At the 2004 Summer Olympic Games, Wambach scored a goal in overtime that clinched the gold medal for the U.S. women's team. (The team won the gold again in 2008, but a broken leg prevented Wambach from participating.) In 2009 she scored her 100th goal in international play, an accomplishment she shares with only four other American women and four women from other countries. By the end of that year, she had scored 101 goals in 131 games, a goals-per-game ratio that surpassed that of any other player in the history of U.S. soccer. In 2010 the International Federation of Association Football, the worldwide soccer governing body, ranked the U.S. Women's National Team first in the world. Also in 2010, for the fourth time, U.S. Soccer, which governs soccer nationally, named Wambach the Female Athlete of the Year. In 2002 and 2003 Wambach played professionally with the Washington Freedom; she was named to the Women's United Soccer Association (WUSA) All-Star Team that year. During the 2009 and 2010 seasons with the Freedom, which are now part of Women's Professional Soccer (WPS), Wambach was named Player of the Week a total of five times.

The youngest of the seven children of Peter and Judy Wambach, Mary Abigail Wambach was born on June 2, 1980 in Pittsford, New York, a suburb of Rochester. Her parents owned and managed a garden-supply store. Her siblings are Beth, the oldest, who is 11 years her senior, Laura, Peter, Matthew, Patrick, and Andrew, her elder by about two years. "Being the youngest kid in a large family was a great proving ground for me," she told Scott Pitoniak for the *Rochester Democrat and Chronicle* (August 8, 2004). "It forced me to become super competitive and made me more aggressive." Wambach's four brothers often roughhoused with her, and sometimes they would dress her in hockey pads, stand her at a goalpost, and practice their slap shots. At the age of four, Wambach joined a local youth soccer league. "Until then, we really didn't have any way to gauge how good she was because we had just seen her compete in various sports against her older sisters and brothers," her

father told Pitoniak. "But when you put her in a situation with her peer group for that first time, you couldn't help but notice the difference." When she was six and playing with seven- and eight-year-old girls, her mother once asked her why she seldom passed the ball to her teammates. "Because they don't know what to do with it when I pass it to them," she responded, as her mother recalled to Jeff DiVeronica for the *Rochester Democrat and Chronicle* (September 20, 2003). At nine Wambach began playing with a boys' league. She competed with and against boys for the next four years. "You talk to members of the women's Olympic team and you'll find that that was a common experience," her mother told Pitoniak.

At Our Lady of Mercy High School, a Catholic all-girls school in Rochester, Wambach was a star in both soccer and basketball. During the soccer team's conference championship game in her sophomore year, her coach sent her to tend goal during a decisive penalty kick, though she had never played that position. Wambach, who had already scored two goals, made the crucial save, and her team won the title. Wambach scored a total of 142 goals in high school, 39 as a senior. She was twice named All-Greater Rochester Player of the Year, and she made All-American in 1996 and 1997. In 1997 she earned High School Player of the Year honors from the National Soccer Coaches Association of America. She remains disappointed that her team blew a three-goal lead to lose the 1997 state championship and never won any state championship when she was a Lady of Mercy student. "Rochester, in essence, never really leaves me because that in a lot of ways motivates me to continue being better because that's something I know that I didn't accomplish," she told Rachel George for the *Buffalo News* (July 11, 2005).

After graduating from high school, in 1998, Wambach attended the University of Florida on a soccer scholarship; she majored in leisure-services management. In her freshman year she helped Florida's soccer team, the Gators, win a national championship. She ultimately set five school records: 96 career goals, 49 assists, 241 points, 24 game-winning goals, and 10 hat tricks, or three-goal games. Wambach was twice named Southeast Conference Player of the Year, and she made the All-American team three times. In her senior year she was the top National Collegiate Athletic Association (NCAA) Division 1 scorer, tallying 31 goals and 13 assists and leading the Gators to a Final Four appearance. She was voted runner-up for the 2001 Hermann Trophy, which honors the nation's best player. In 2002 Wambach finished third in voting for that prize. She missed a handful of matches during her senior season, after she was selected to play on the U.S. women's national soccer team. She made her debut with that team in the 76th minute of the Nike U.S. Women's Cup, in a game against Germany, which Team USA won, 4–1. (She has not yet earned her college degree.)

In February 2002 Wambach was drafted by the Washington Freedom, one of eight teams in the Women's United Soccer Association, a professional league founded in 2000. She was the second overall pick in the league's draft, and observers pegged her to take over scoring responsibilities in the absence of her injured teammate Mia Hamm, then the biggest star in women's soccer. "I don't mind the expectations," Wambach told Pitoniak for the *Rochester Democrat and Chronicle* (April 13, 2002). "You can either rise to the expectations and become great or you can shy away from them and become mediocre. I've always set pretty high goals for myself." In her first season with the Freedom, Wambach lived up to the hype, leading her team with 10 goals and nine assists. The Freedom won or tied their final eight matches of the regular season, securing a spot in the play-offs. The team defeated the Philadelphia Charge in the semifinals before losing to the Carolina Courage in the title game. Wambach was named Rookie of the Year.

Wambach continued to play with the national team, scoring five goals in her first seven matches, but she did not make the roster for an April 2003 match against Canada. Instead, she played with the Freedom after the Team USA game in the second contest of a doubleheader at RFK Stadium, in Washington, D.C. and performed very poorly. Worried that she might not make the U.S. roster for the upcoming World Cup tournament, Wambach spoke to April Heinrichs, the Team USA coach, who had also coached her in an under-16 team in 1996. Heinrichs told Wambach that her playing lacked intensity and she had to show more commitment. "She knew I could handle the criticism . . . ," Wambach told DiVeronica for the *Rochester Democrat and Chronicle* (September 21, 2003). "April put it in black-and-white terms for me and that's all I needed to hear." Newly determined, Wambach developed an on-field chemistry with Hamm, and she and Hamm later tied for the WUSA regular-season scoring title. According to Wambach's Web site, while partnered with Hamm she "sharpened her ability to read the game" and "learned how to stay focused on the game while being targeted by opponents for whom the only way to stop her was to knock her down." The Freedom won the 2003 WUSA championship, with Wambach scoring both goals in a 2–1 victory over the Atlanta Beat. She was named the game's Most Valuable Player.

After that game Wambach learned that she had been selected for the World Cup roster. In her first World Cup match, on September 23, 2003, she helped Team USA score, passing the ball to Hamm before colliding with a Swedish opponent;. Hamm then passed to Kristine Lilly, who broke a scoreless tie with a 15-yard goal. Team USA won the match, 3–1. On September 25, 2003, in a 5–0 win against the famously aggressive Nigerian team, Wambach scored her first World Cup goal. She told Abby Haight for the *Sunday Oregonian* (September 28, 2003) that she likes playing against rough, physical

squads. "I salivate when I see a team like that," she said. Christine Brennan, who attended the World Cup, wrote for *USA Today* (Octoter 2, 2003) that Wambach "is a magnificent force on the soccer field. She is a one-woman wrecking crew, a linebacker in a soccer jersey." On October 5, 2003 Team USA lost its semifinal match with Germany. The defeat was particularly crushing, because the WUSA had suspended play a short time earlier, citing a need to reorganize its finances, and many observers thought that a World Cup title was needed to revive flagging interest in women's soccer. (The WUSA was never revived. A new league, Women's Professional Soccer, was launched in 2008; 2009 marked its inaugural season.)

Team USA played its next major tournament in August 2004, at that year's Summer Olympics, in Athens, Greece. The squad won its first two matches, against Greece and Brazil, thus securing a spot in the quarterfinals. Wambach received yellow cards (with which soccer referees denote penalties) in both contests, and under international rules she was forced to sit out the team's third game, with Australia, which ended in a 1–1 tie. After defeating Japan and Germany, both by 2–1, Team USA met Brazil for the final game. The score stood at 1–1 until the 22d minute of a 30-minute overtime, when Wambach headed the ball into the net from 12 yards out. Brazil failed to score in the final eight minutes, and the U.S. team earned the Olympic gold medal for the first time since 1996. That match was the last major outing for Hamm, Julie Foudy, and Joy Fawcett, three members of the "Fab Five," a group that helped Team USA win the inaugural women's World Cup, in 1991.

In March 2005, as Team USA prepared to compete in the Algarve Cup, its first major tournament since Hamm's departure, Wambach asserted that she was ready to accept a leadership role. "This is a fantastic opportunity for me and the team to do something no other team has done—and that's to win a world championship without Mia, Julie and Joy," she told Greg Boeck for *USA Today* (March 3, 2005). Despite dwindling interest in women's soccer, as well as Heinrichs's resignation a month earlier, Wambach said she and her teammates were determined to press on. "It's difficult, but I don't think we're taking a step back," she said. "Because we won't let it go back. It's the one thing the veterans taught us before they left. It's that you can make noise when you stick together." While Team USA won the Algarve Cup (held annually in Portugal) without giving up a single goal, the women drew only 3,215 fans to its first post-Hamm match in the U.S. "Everybody that follows the U.S. women's national team knew that at some point there was going to be a major transition," their new coach, Greg Ryan, told Joseph White for the State College, Pennsylvania, *Centre Daily Times* (July 7, 2005). "This is it."

In November 2006, thanks to two Wambach goals, Team USA defeated Mexico in the Confederation of North, Central American and Caribbean

Association Football Gold Cup semifinals, thereby earning a place in the 2007 World Cup. "I can't say enough about the stress that's involved in qualifying, especially when you're expected to," Wambach told Ken Peters for the Associated Press (November 23, 2006). "We've dedicated so much time, devoted so much effort." The win marked the team's 31st straight game without a defeat, its longest streak up to that date. By mid-August 2007, in their previous 43 games, the women had lost only one game, on penalty kicks, and tied in six.

Later that month, during a World Cup warm-up match, Wambach injured a toe on her right foot. Her foot remained sore on September 11, as Team USA battled North Korea to a 2–2 tie in the first round of the World Cup, held in China. During that game Wambach suffered a gash on the back of her head in a collision with a North Korean player. While doctors closed the wound with 11 stitches, Wambach heard the crowd cheer, and she knew that North Korea had just taken a 2–1 lead. "I really had to hurry up the process," she told Stephen Wade for the Associated Press Online (September 12, 2007). "I was yelling at the doctors to get it done quicker. I cursed some bad words and hurried up and got my jersey on and ran as fast as I could." Not long after Wambach returned to the field, her teammate Heather O'Reilly scored, preventing a loss. Three days later Wambach scored both goals in a 2–0 victory over Sweden. The second came during the 58th minute of the game, when Wambach, running into the penalty area, fielded a pass off her chest and booted a left-footed shot into the upper left corner of the net. "It's one of those goals as a forward you say, 'Yeah, I meant to do that, to put it exactly where it went,' but you know, in this situation, I just hit it as hard as I could and it went in," she told journalists in China, as DiVeronica reported for the *Rochester Democrat and Chronicle* (September 15, 2007). Even Sweden's coach, Thomas Dennerby, was impressed. "If you like football, you like to see a goal like Abby Wambach's goal today," he said.

Team USA advanced to the semifinals and on September 22 defeated England, 3–0; Wambach scored the first goal, heading the ball into the net following a teammate's corner kick. She remained scoreless in the next game of the semifinals, in which Brazil took a 2–0 lead after only 27 minutes and then triumphed, 4–0, while Team USA suffered its worst loss since its start, in 1985. "We are not where we were 10 years ago," U.S. Soccer Federation President Sunil Gulati told Steven Goff for the *Washington Post* (September 28, 2007). "It's not because we are not better; it's because everyone else is rapidly investing in the game." "Brazil has amazing individual soccer players and today they played like a team," Wambach said. Referring to Ryan's controversial decision to start Briana Scurry rather than the team's regular goaltender, Hope Solo, and Shannon Boxx's ejection before halftime after she received two yellow cards, Wambach also said, "I am not going to sit here and make excuses

because we could've come out stronger. But today was Brazil's day and I am heartbroken." On September 30, 2007 Wambach scored twice in the World Cup consolation game (a match held to determine the third-place winner), helping Team USA beat Norway, 4–0. In all she scored six goals in the tournament.

In the 22 games in which she played in 2008, Wambach compiled a record of 13 goals and 10 assists—the second-highest number of assists for any Team USA player in a calendar year. Then, on July 16, in the women's last game before the Olympics—an exhibition match against Brazil—the tibia and fibula in Wambach's left leg shattered when she crashed into the Brazilian defender Andreia Rosa. The injury, which was repaired surgically, with a titanium rod inserted in her leg, required several months of recuperation and rehabilitation and kept Wambach from playing in the 2008 Summer Olympics, in Beijing, China. Despite dire predictions about how the squad would perform in her absence, Team USA came home from the Games with the gold medal.

Wambach returned to play on March 25, 2009 and participated in three more Team USA games that year. On July 19, in a 1–0 victory over Canada in her hometown, she scored her 100th career goal in international competition. A sold-out crowd in the new Impuls Arena, in Augsburg, Germany, on October 29 witnessed her 101st, as the Americans defeated the German team, 1–0. Wambach scored in eight of the 18 games in which she and Team USA competed in 2010, bringing her career total to 115. Currently, she trails only two others—Mia Hamm (158) and Kristine Lilly (129)—in that category. In a game against Haiti on October 28, 2010, she made three goals. The team's loss to Mexico on November 5 jeopardized its chances of competing in the 2011 World Cup; their victory over Italy on November 27 enabled them to qualify. The World Cup will be held in Germany in June and July. According to Jeré Longman, writing for the *New York Times* (November 27, 2010, on-line), "The United States is certainly capable of winning the tournament. Its record is 52–2–6 since the end of 2007"— when the Swedish-born Pia Sundhage became head coach—"22–1–3 in the past two years. Yet, with the exception of forward Abby Wambach, . . . Hope Solo, . . . and Christie Rampone, the Americans lack the forceful personalities of their pioneering predecessors like Foudy, Mia Hamm, Michelle Akers and Tiffeny Milbrett." Moreover, Longman wrote, "while Wambach remains ravenous, she is 30 now"—a relatively advanced age in international soccer. In January 2011 a heel injury kept Wambach away from competition.

Earlier, in the 17 games she played with the Washington Freedom in 2009, Wambach scored three game-winning goals and five additional goals and was named the Women's Professional Soccer Player of the Week three times. During the WPS 2010 season, she netted 13 goals, including five that spelled victory for the Freedom, and was named the Player of the Week twice. The Freedom's win–loss–tie records in 2009 and 2010, in which the WPS comprised seven teams, were 8–7–5 and 8–9–7, respectively. Wambach plans to play during the 2011 season, which is scheduled to begin in April with six teams.

According to some sources, Wambach stands five feet 10, not five feet 11. "I have many scars on my body from the game . . . ," she told Sal Ruibal for *USA Today* (September 25, 2007). "We get concussions, sometimes we get our heads cut open and leave the field with bloody knees or bloody noses. . . . It's just part of your daily life."

—K.J.P.

Suggested Reading: Abby Wambach Web site; Associated Press Sports News Aug. 16, 2004; *International Herald Tribune* p21 Oct. 2, 2003; *Los Angeles Times* D p4 Aug. 11, 2007; *New York Times* Play p10 Aug. 19, 2007; *Rochester (New York) Democrat and Chronicle* D p1 Apr. 13, 2002, A p1 Aug. 8, 2004, A p10 Aug. 27, 2004, A p1 Sep. 14, 2006, D p1 Sep. 15, 2007, D p1 Sep. 23, 2007; soccer.teamusa.org; *USA Today* C p7 Mar. 3, 2005; U.S. Soccer Web site; usolympicteam.com

Justin Sullivan/Getty Images

Washington, Ron

Apr. 29, 1952– Baseball manager; former coach and player

Address: Texas Rangers, 1000 Ballpark Way, Arlington, TX 76011

The Texas Rangers' manager, Ron Washington, has often been described as a baseball lifer, and he, too, has placed himself in that category. "Washington is the guy this game is built upon," John Romano wrote for the *St. Petersburg (Florida) Times* (October 27, 2010). "The stars make the money, the showboats grab the headlines, but the lifers are the ones who have helped preserve the game's integrity from one decade to the next. The guys willing to play any position. Willing to keep getting on that minor-league bus traveling from one small town to

the next. The guys willing to give as much as they take." Washington's baseball career began in 1970, when he served as a minor-league shortstop in the Kansas City Royals farm system. He spent 10 seasons in the minors, with a series of three organizations, before he joined the Minnesota Twins of Major League Baseball (MLB), in 1981; after six seasons with the Twins, he played one season each for the Baltimore Orioles, the Cleveland Indians, and the Houston Astros. After he retired as a player, in 1990, Washington worked for the New York Mets for five years before being hired as the Oakland Athletics' first-base coach, in 1996. As the Athletics' third-base and infield coach from 1997 to 2006, he helped foster the defensive developments of players including Eric Chavez, Miguel Tejada, and Jason Giambi. Washington has served as the Rangers' manager since the 2007 season. Art Howe, the Rangers' bench coach in 2007 and 2008, told J. Brady McCollough for the *Kansas City (Missouri) Star* (October 31, 2010) that Washington is "an American League manager with a National League brand of ball. He likes to use the bunt and the hit and run, to move runners. He really preaches quality at-bats." In 2010 Washington finished second in the voting for the American League (AL) Manager of the Year Award, after leading the Rangers to their first World Series berth.

The eighth of the 10 children of Robert and Fannie Washington, Ronald "Ron" Washington was born on April 29, 1952 in New Orleans, Louisiana. (One sibling died at birth, another while serving during the Vietnam War.) He spent his first years in the Desire Housing Projects, in the city's crime-ridden Ninth Ward; later the family moved to the somewhat safer St. Bernard Housing Project, in the Gentilly area. Washington's father was a truck driver, his mother a full-time homemaker. In such a large family, "little things were important," he told Carl Steward for the *Contra Costa (California) Times* (October 26, 2010). "Everything was shared. You had to rely on each other. I've talked a lot about what little things mean in baseball, but they also work in life." At an early age Washington learned the value of resilience. He told Mike

DiGiovanna for the *Los Angeles Times* (October 5, 2010), "You have to survive, you have to keep your clothes on and keep your money in your pocket, because someone was always trying to get it. I learned how to fend for myself because you had no choice. You get used and abused or you show people you're not going to have it."

As a youngster Washington considered the baseball diamond his home away from home. "Baseball was always in my blood for as long as I can remember," he told Bob Fortus for the New Orleans, Louisiana, *Times-Picayune* (September 26, 2010). "I just had a great passion for it." Throughout his youth Washington spent countless hours after school honing his athletic skills, mostly with older boys. He attended John McDonough High School as a member of its first integrated class. Washington played quarterback on the school football team and later became the first black player on McDonough's varsity baseball team, in the position of catcher in his first year there. His skills in baseball impressed his coach, Steve Kahn, who helped him earn a spot on a prestigious American Legion summer-league team after he graduated. Washington's performance with that team landed him a tryout with the Kansas City Royals, which had debuted in 1969. The Royals organization had started a baseball academy in Florida, to develop athletes with raw skills; many of the youths lived in inner cities. Out of 156 teenagers who attended the Royals' tryout camp in New Orleans, Washington was the only one invited back for a second tryout; he subsequently beat out another catcher to make the academy's first class of eight prospects. On July 17, 1970 Washington was signed by the Royals as an undrafted free agent.

Washington played in the Royals farm system for five seasons before being traded to the Los Angeles Dodgers in November 1976. During that period his coaches persuaded him to switch from catcher to middle infielder, because they felt that at 155 pounds, he was too fragile to withstand collisions at home plate. In 1977 Washington played with two Dodgers' affiliates, class-AA and then class-AAA, in San Antonio, Texas, and Albuquerque, New Mexico, respectively. In 160 minor-league games that year, Washington achieved a batting average of .309, with 160 hits, 25 doubles, 12 triples, eight home runs, and 25 stolen bases. In September 1977 he earned his first call-up to the majors and hit .368 in 10 games; that year the Dodgers won the National League (NL) pennant and advanced to the World Series, where they lost to the New York Yankees in six games. (Washington did not play in the series.) Washington opened the 1978 season in class-AAA Albuquerque, where he played well until he suffered a season-ending knee injury. The next season he injured his other knee and underwent surgery for a second time. In March 1980 the Dodgers traded him to the Minnesota Twins. He played with the Twins' class-AAA affiliate until 1981, when he earned a call-up to the MLB Twins.

During the 1981 season Washington batted .226 in 28 Twins games. In the next five seasons (1982–86), he played in 119, 99, 88, 70, and 48 games, respectively, almost exclusively as a reserve utility player. Washington has credited Billy Gardner, the Twins' manager from 1981 to 1985, with teaching him the value of gaining a player's trust. He has also praised Gardner's successor, Tom Kelly, who managed the Twins from 1986 until 2001, for his strong emphasis on fundamentals. During spring training in 1987, after 14 games under Kelly, Washington was traded to the Baltimore Orioles; that year he played in 26 Orioles games. Next, in 1988, he played in 69 games with the Cleveland Indians, and in 1989, seven games with the Houston Astros. He ended his playing career with the Texas Rangers' class-AAA affiliate, in Oklahoma City, in 1990. In his 10-season major-league career, Washington played in 564 games and batted, on average, .261, with 20 home runs, 22 triples, 65 doubles, and 146 RBIs.

Immediately after his retirement as a player, Washington became a coach for the New York Mets, spending the next five seasons in the organization's minor-league system. He also gained his first managerial experience, as skipper of the Mets' class-A South Atlantic League team in 1993 and 1994. Washington returned to the majors in 1996, when the Oakland Athletics' manager, Art Howe, named him the team's first-base coach. Howe, who had coached Washington as a rookie manager with the Astros in 1989, recalled to Dave Sessions for the *Fort Worth (Texas) Star-Telegram* (March 18, 2007), "I got to know what he was all about as a player, the kind of effort he gave me, the desire he had, how much he loved the game. I always remembered that." He added that hiring Washington was "probably one of the best decisions I ever made."

After the 1996 season Washington became the Athletics' infield and third-base coach, positions he held for the next 10 years. He helped transform the Athletics' infield into one of the best defensive units in the AL; he also played a vital role in the development of the team's third baseman Eric Chavez, a below-average rookie fielder who became a six-time Gold Glove winner (2001–06). Speaking of Washington, Chavez told Dave Newhouse for the *Alameda (California) Times-Star* (June 15, 2003), "Everything I've been able to accomplish, he fast-forwarded. He's a workaholic, and he has a way of getting his point across. If you're around him, everything is positive. He's fantastic. You could go to every guy in here, every infielder, and they'll tell you the same thing. All he wants to do is practice. He's not here for any of his personal reasons. He's here for us." In 2004 Chavez gave Washington his third Gold Glove Award and inscribed it with the words "Wash, not without you."

During his tenure with the Athletics, Washington was also responsible for the defensive improvements of the first baseman Jason Giambi and the shortstop Miguel Tejada, both of whom won

AL Most Valuable Player Awards, in 2000 and 2002, respectively. The Athletics' shortstop Bobby Crosby also flourished under Washington, winning the 2004 AL Rookie of the Year Award. The Athletics, meanwhile, earned five trips to the playoffs (2000–03 and 2006); they lost in the AL Division Series (ALDS) four times (2000–03) and in the AL Championship Series (ALCS) in 2006. The success of the Athletics during that period, despite the team's relatively small payroll, attracted a lot of media attention, as did the innovative methods of the squad's general manager, Billy Beane; they also inspired Michael M. Lewis to write *Moneyball: The Art of Winning an Unfair Game* (2003), which became a best-seller. According to Brad Townsend, writing for the *Dallas Morning News* (October 27, 2010), Washington is briefly mentioned in the book; he is portrayed first as having "a gift for making players want to be better than they were" but later is described, Townsend wrote, as "an old-school curmudgeon while discussing Beane's disdain for stolen base attempts and other aggressive base-running." Washington told Townsend, "I've got a ton of respect for Billy Beane. Those guys gave me an opportunity to become a major league coach. I learned a lot over there. . . . There's a lot that went on over there that I agreed with—and there's a lot that maybe I didn't agree with—but I kept it to myself. But I worked for them and I was a pro." (Washington is portrayed by Brent Jennings in the film version of *Moneyball*, released in 2011.)

In 2003 Dave Newhouse described Washington as "the hardest-working, most-positive, most-encouraging managerial prospect out there." Nonetheless, although he interviewed three times for the Athletics' manager's job, he was repeatedly overlooked for head-coaching positions. Then, on November 6, 2006, the Texas Rangers hired him to succeed Buck Showalter, who had managed the team since 2003. The last of five candidates, he had instantly impressed the Rangers' general manager, Jon Daniels, and then-owner, Tom Hicks, with his confidence and enthusiasm. (On August 12, 2010 the Pittsburgh sports-industry lawyer Charles "Chuck" Greenberg and the former Ranger pitcher and current president, Nolan Ryan, as partners in Rangers Baseball Express, bought the Rangers, which had declared bankruptcy earlier that year. Greenberg stepped down as the Rangers' CEO and left the organization in March 2011.) Daniels told Carl Seward that Washington is "real, he's genuine. Nothing is manufactured. When he first interviewed with us, he said, 'Listen to the message, not how I say it' because I think he thought people might take it the wrong way because of his speech inflection or whatever. But I liked the way he said it. There was passion in his voice, energy, heart . . . he wasn't reading from a script. I think everybody recognized what kind of man he was right away." Daniels told Fred Robinson for the New Orleans *Times-Picayune* (July 10, 2007) that Washington is "a unique personality. He has the positive outlook and is able to relate to the players. It's pro-

vided immediate dividends. He comes to the park and delivers the same message every day."

The Rangers had long been known as a one-dimensional team that relied solely on hitting prowess to win games, often at the expense of quality pitching and defense; they had had only one winning record (89–73, in 2004, when they finished in third place in the AL West) in the previous seven seasons. "They just wanted to see how many balls they could hit out of the ballpark," Art Howe told J. Brady McCollough. Immediately upon assuming his new job, Washington introduced "small-ball," which is characterized by aggressive baserunning, bunting, walks, and sacrifice flies as ways of scoring runs. While the Rangers performed poorly during Washington's debut season with them—they finished last in the AL West Division, with a record of 75–87—their record in 2008 was 79–83, good for second in their division. (The addition of the star centerfielder Josh Hamilton and the hiring of Nolan Ryan as team president contributed to their improvement.)

In 2009 the Rangers emerged as serious play-off contenders, largely on the strength of a more balanced pitching and hitting attack. They led the AL West for much of the season, then lost the division title to the Los Angeles Angels. They finished with their best record since 2004: 87 wins and 75 losses. The Rangers' steady turnaround was attributed in part to the players' willingness to adapt to Washington's strategies. Washington told Mike DiGiovanna, "My first couple years here, we'd be down three or four runs in the seventh inning and I'm taking [a first strike]. They weren't used to that. They were used to banging their way back into a ballgame. Well, when I got here, we didn't have those bangers, so we had to learn how to adjust and do things a different way. We had to learn how to pitch, to catch the ball, to run the bases and execute."

On March 17, 2010 an article posted on the *Sports Illustrated* Web site revealed that Washington had tested positive for cocaine during the All-Star break in July 2009. (Managers, coaches, and minor-league players, but not MLB players, are tested for the presence of recreational drugs in their systems; MLB players are tested for performance-enhancing drugs.) Before the results of the test came in, Washington alerted the baseball commissioner and his immediate bosses about his use of the drug—once only, he said—and offered to resign, but Ryan and Daniels opted to keep him on. He then entered MLB's drug-treatment program, in which he underwent nine months of counseling and drug tests every few days; at his request, the tests continued after he completed the program. MLB policy forbids the disclosure of information about first-time offenders, and Washington's participation in the program remained confidential. When reports of his positive cocaine test nevertheless became public, he acknowledged in a face-to-face talk with his players what he called his "terrible mistake." (He had been advised by MLB officials to keep silent before then.) "He told his side of the story, and then, one by one, guys stood up and said how we supported him . . . ," the third baseman and team captain Michael Young told DiGiovanna, "I said, 'Wash is the manager, he's the guy we want leading the ship.' And that's the way it's been." The Rangers' left fielder Josh Hamilton, who missed nearly four years of baseball due to his addictions to cocaine and alcohol, said of Washington to Tyler Kepner for the *New York Times* (April 15, 2010), "He had that moment of weakness, and he regrets it. Since it came out, we've put it behind us. We told him we love him and support him and we've moved on from there." Hamilton later told Bob Nightengale for *USA Today* (October 27, 2010), "I was addicted to drugs. I didn't care who I hurt. He's not an addict. He just made a mistake."

In 2010 Washington helped lead the Rangers to a regular-season record of 90–72—good for both their first postseason appearance and first AL West Division title since 1999 (and only the third division title in franchise history). In an MLB best, players went from first base to third base on singles 122 times, and the team also led the majors with a .276 team batting average. With the acquisitions of the catcher Bengie Molina in June 2010 and the 2008 Cy Young Award–winning pitcher Cliff Lee in July, Washington helped guide the Rangers to their first postseason series victories: the team defeated the Tampa Bay Rays in the ALDS and the New York Yankees in the ALCS, thus clinching their first World Series berth in franchise history. In that series the Rangers fell to the San Francisco Giants, losing four games to one. Washington finished second in the voting for AL Manager of the Year, a title that went to the Minnesota Twins' Ron Gardenhire. In a sign of growing camaraderie during the regular season and the postseason, Rangers celebrated outstanding plays with a hand gesture that became known as the "Claw"—"sort of a long-distance high-five," Steve DiMeglio wrote for *USA Today* (October 17, 2010, on-line); another gesture, the "Antlers," or "a pair of spread-open hands on the back of the head," in DiMeglio's words, acknowledged unusual speed and agility.

In November 2010 Washington signed a two-year contract extension with the Rangers.

Washington has taken courses at Manatee Junior College, in Bradenton, Florida. He and his wife, Gerry, married in 1972. Their home in New Orleans was destroyed by Hurricane Katrina in 2005; Mike DiGiovanna reported that with the help of thousands of dollars contributed by players, it has since been rebuilt. Washington was inducted into John McDonough High School's Hall of Fame in February 2009. He told Tim Brown for Yahoo! Sports (September 26, 2010, on-line), "I'm at peace. No matter what happens from this point on, I'm at peace. I hope I'm able to have a place in the game of baseball until my brains don't work anymore or I can't function. I'm a lifer. This is what I have a great passion for and I will always have a

passion for it. I don't think I could survive without it."

—C.C.

Suggested Reading: *Alameda (California) Times-Star* Sports June 15, 2003; Associated Press State & Local Wire, Sports Apr. 8, 2004; *Contra Costa (California) Times* Oct. 26, 2010; *Dallas (Texas) Morning News* C p1 Apr. 15, 2007, A p1+ Oct. 27, 2010; *Kansas City (Missouri) Star* C p10+ Oct. 31, 2010; *Los Angeles Times* C p1+ Oct. 5, 2010; (New Orleans, Louisiana) *Times-Picayune* Sports p1+ July 10, 2007, C p1+ Sep. 26, 2010; *San Francisco Chronicle* D p1+ May 20, 2005; *USA Today* A p1+ Oct. 27, 2010; Yahoo! Sports (on-line) Sep. 26, 2010

Gareth Cattermole/Getty Images

Wenner, Kurt

Apr. 17, 1958– Artist

Address: Master Artist, LLC, 809 Lark Dr., Fernley, NV 89408

The art of street painting originated in the Middle Ages, when practitioners traveled across Europe painting images of religious figures on the surfaces of city streets. The artists—who became known as "Madonnari," a reference to one of their most frequent subjects—received payment from passersby, in the form of food or coins, for their often mesmerizing works, which imitated the styles of earlier masters. Although Madonnari existed, mainly in Italy, for hundreds of years, they were largely unknown to most of the world until the last few decades, when street painting began to gain an international audience. The art form's revival was spurred in part by the popularity of the American-born Kurt Wenner—who is perhaps the most celebrated Madonnari of the day. One of only a handful of artists in the world to hold the title of "Master Madonnaro," Wenner is best known for his seemingly three-dimensional works, which depict scenes that, when viewed from the correct angle, appear sunken into the ground or seem to be rising from it. Prior to taking up street painting, Wenner worked as a graphic designer and an illustrator for the National Aeronautics and Space Administration (NASA). He began experimenting with illusory painting while studying classical art in Rome, Italy, in the early 1980s and gained international attention after his street paintings were featured in the award-winning 1985 *National Geographic* documentary *Masterpieces in Chalk*. Since then Wenner has received hundreds of commissions for public and commercial works, ranging from a giant street mural for Pope John Paul II to a series of popular ads for Absolut Vodka, and he has won numerous awards in the U.S. and Europe. Though the vast majority of Wenner's works are actually permanent—and include murals, oil paintings, sculptures, and architecture—Wenner continues to be best known for his chalk street paintings, which last days or weeks before fading in the sun or being washed away in the rain. "I'm not disappointed when it washes away because street painting is performance art," Wenner said in an interview posted on his Web site. "It's very much like attending a symphony. When the music ends everyone leaves with a memory of the music. My work is the same except one is left with a visual impression."

Kurt Wenner was born on April 17, 1958 in Ann Arbor, Michigan, and grew up in Santa Barbara, California. One of Wenner's great-great-grandfathers and a great-uncle were artists; his father was the provost at the College of Creative Studies at the University of California at Santa Barbara, and his mother was a music teacher. He has a sister who was a professional musician prior to becoming a journalist. Wenner displayed a talent for art at an early age and gained inspiration from his picturesque surroundings. "Santa Barbara was a small, sleepy beach town when I grew up there," he explained to Claudia Parentela in an interview for the *Extra Finger Blog* (May 26, 2011, on-line). "It always had many examples of beautiful architecture and gracious villas, which influenced me very much. Creativity was very much encouraged, although in the 60's it had a very hippie flavor to it." Wenner was a freshman at Santa Barbara High School when he decided he wanted to be an artist, a vocational choice opposed by his parents, who wanted him to follow a more practical career path. At the age of 16, Wenner won his first large-scale commission, a mural for the Santa Barbara chain McConnell's Ice Cream; the mural depicted the owners' family "in a composition that was a cross between *The Last Supper* and *Alice in Wonder-*

land," as Wenner noted to Parentela. Wenner continued to produce smaller-scale works, and by age 17 he was generating substantial income as a graphic artist.

After graduating from Santa Barbara High School, Wenner enrolled at the Rhode Island School of Design (RISD), in Providence, to study with David Macaulay, the author and illustrator of the book *Cathedral: The Story of Its Construction* (1973), which had been a major influence on Wenner. (Macaulay has also written and illustrated such similarly themed books as *Castle*, *City*, *Mill*, *Mosque*, *Pyramid*, and *Underground*.) Wenner received little encouragement in his chosen field at RISD. "They told me I had no talent," he recalled to Claudia Feldman for the *Houston Chronicle* (June 9, 2003). "They said I was excellent in a lot of things, but not drawing." Wenner transferred to the Art Center College of Design in Pasadena, California, where he received instruction from the painter Harry Carmean in the principles of classical drawing. "My interest in Renaissance classicism started with the simple desire to draw well," Wenner wrote in his artist's statement, posted on his Web site. "I was struck by the vast difference between how students and teachers drew in the 20th Century and the way artists drew 500 years ago. It seemed to me that artists of the past had abilities far beyond those of today." Wenner also taught himself artist's geometry, which would later provide the foundation for his street paintings and architectural designs.

After one year at the Art Center College of Design, Wenner ran out of money for tuition. To secure an income he took a position as a scientific illustrator with the nearby NASA Jet Propulsion Laboratory. (He landed the job after impressing a physics professor and NASA scientist with his drawing of a complex piece of equipment.) Wenner worked at the lab for two years, creating hand renderings of future space projects using scientific data. While at the laboratory Wenner witnessed the emergence of computer-graphics imaging (CGI) and realized that his own hand-drawn techniques would soon become obsolete to scientists—and perhaps even to artists. "Because my own studies were rooted in the ancient tradition of sacred geometry rather than technical drawing, I was concerned about this development," he told Parentela. "It occurred to me that the tradition and significance of geometrical drawing and design would become lost with computer graphics in the same way that the tradition of classical drawing had collapsed with the invention of photography." In 1982 Wenner, who had been taking courses in classical drawing at night, decided to quit his job and move to Rome. He explained to Parentela, "Eventually the time came when the only way to further my studies was to go to Italy and work from the masterpieces."

Arriving in Rome in the spring of 1982, Wenner began studying firsthand the works of the great masters: Michelangelo, Leonardo da Vinci, Raphael, and others. For six months he spent about eight hours a day in museums, immersing himself in classical painting and sculpture. He created original drawings of the pieces and sold them—mainly to tourists and museum employees—for modest sums. Wenner took a particular interest in the Mannerist and Baroque styles, which emerged in Italy in the 16th and 17th centuries. While in Rome he first encountered street painting. "One day, I saw a street painting and asked the artist what he was doing," Wenner recalled in an interview on his Web site. "He explained the tradition of street painting in Europe to me, and after viewing my museum drawings asked if I'd like to paint the head of an angel while he went to lunch. Working with the chalks came very naturally, and from that point on I've been street painting." For his first original chalk drawing, made in front of a Rome train station, Wenner received $550 in tips. He soon found that the tips he received from his street art could bring him up to three times his NASA salary, income that allowed him to continue his study of classical art in Rome.

Wenner was inspired to begin creating so-called three-dimensional street paintings after studying a technique used by European masters called anamorphism, which makes paintings on chapel ceilings appear proportional and three-dimensional when viewed from below. While traveling around Europe, Wenner was able to observe such frescos up close after being invited to climb scaffolding during cathedral renovations. "I started creating my particular perspective geometry by adjusting the proportions of the painted forms to accommodate the viewpoints of the spectators standing at the base of the work," Wenner explained to Parentela. "Unlike traditional anamorphic compositions, such as church ceilings, the viewing angles were very wide, and I started to use a curvilinear fisheye lens to document the compositions." He added, "My objective in inventing the 3D street painting was to insert my original classical drawings into contemporary environments. I established the creation of the works as performances that allowed the public to view the process of classical drawing." Wenner has often pointed out that his version of perspective geometry—which "combines a logical use of linear perspective with a projection outward from the human eye"—has not been summarized in a written work and differs from the methods used by other artists.

Though he used commercial chalks and pastels for his early street paintings, Wenner soon found that he could create pastels—from pure paint pigments and binders of wax, glue, soap, and other materials—that were more vivid, more resistant to rain and sun, and less expensive than commercial products. "Commercial chalk pastels don't have the right properties for my work and I can use mine on paper as well as on the street," Wenner told Donald Miller for the *Pittsburgh Post-Gazette* (September 25, 1997). "Mine are not powdery." Wenner, whose preferred work surface is pavement,

usually spends about three to five days on a single street painting. However, the weather, especially rain, can set him back hours or days. The street paintings fade over time and are washed away by rain; they typically last from a few days to a few weeks, depending on the weather. "People feel vast dismay that the drawing will wash away in the first rain," he told Miller. "But it's not a problem for me. I'm constantly aware my work is not permanent, and to me it doesn't have the feeling of a finished work. I consider street drawing a performance." Wenner records his work by photographing it from the optimal viewing perspective. For his paintings' subject matter, Wenner typically relies on his knowledge of European classical art. "In Italy the themes of the street paintings were generally religious," he told Parentela. "In the USA my favorite subjects are from classical mythology. Naturally, even mythological paintings were religious 2000 years ago, but in our time people think of them as allegories."

In 1985 Wenner, along with some of his work in Italy and Switzerland, was featured in *Masterpieces in Chalk*, the *National Geographic* documentary about street painting in Europe. The film won the Blue Ribbon Award at the American Film and Video Festival, in New York City; the Chris Statuette Award at the Columbus International Film + Video Festival, in Ohio; and the Gold Award at the Intercom Film Festival, in Chicago, Illinois, among other prizes. The film's success helped catapult Wenner to fame, paving the way for such trompe-l'oeil artists as Julian Beever, Manfred Stader, and Edgar Muller. It also spawned the organization of new street-painting festivals all over the world. During the mid-1980s Wenner won three consecutive titles at the I Madonnari International Street Painting Festival in Grazie di Curtatone, Italy, earning him the rare title of Master Street Painter, or "Master Madonnaro." He soon began working as a consultant to festival organizers and artists, advising them on methods and materials.

It was not long before Wenner began receiving commissions for street paintings from museums, festivals, and corporations. One of Wenner's first and best-known commissions was for a 75-foot-by-15-foot street mural he completed in the Italian city of Mantua, in 1989, based on Michelangelo's *Last Judgment* in the Sistine Chapel, to celebrate a visit from Pope John Paul II. Wenner worked with 32 of Europe's best street painters to create the massive composition, which took 10 days to complete; the pope reportedly liked the work so much that he autographed it. Wenner has often said that his favorite street painting he has completed to date is *Dies Irae*—also one of his most praised and photographed works. Sharing the title of the 13th-century Latin hymn about Judgment Day (which is part of the Roman Catholic requiem Mass), the street painting depicts writhing nude figures struggling to climb from the soft, yellow depths of the earth. Another work highlighted on Wenner's Web site, *Muses*, depicts the three goddesses who in mythology are thought to inspire literature and the arts, lounging in a pool that appears to be sunken into the street. "I enjoy teasing my audience with a wealth of illusions historical, stylistic and perceptual," Wenner told Linda Parri for the Australia *Sunday Times* (October 24, 2010). "While some recognize and appreciate the content, others may admire the richly embellished surfaces or technical virtuosity."

In 1991 Wenner presented a one-man show of his work at the Kennedy Center in Washington, D.C., becoming the first visual artist to exhibit there. Some of his other venues have included the Allen Theater in Cleveland, Ohio; the Southern Theater in Columbus, Ohio; the Cherry Creek Arts Festival in Denver, Colorado; the Detroit Festival of the Arts in Michigan; Burgos Centro Historico and Salamanca Centro Historico in Spain; and the Huis Ten Bosch in Nagasaki, Japan. In 2004 Wenner created a three-dimensional painting as part of the week-long celebration of the 100th anniversary of Times Square, in New York City. That year he was the featured artist at the Calgary Stampede, a 10-day event in Calgary, Alberta, Canada, that includes a rodeo, an exhibition, and a festival. Wenner's finished piece for that event, called *Wild Rodeo*, depicted several frantic horses bucking their riders. "You can see my horses have more of a renaissance look to them instead of a western look," he told Maria Canton for the *Calgary Herald* (July 13, 2004).

Wenner has also produced work for corporate advertising and promotional campaigns. In 1996 he created a print ad for Absolut Vodka as part of its "famous artist" ad series, which also included works by Andy Warhol and Keith Haring. In 2005 Wenner completed a series of three street paintings in Milan, Italy, each representing a modern-day version of hell—*Gluttony, Ghetto*, and *The Office*—as part of an ad campaign for the sportswear company Champion. For Dunkin' Donuts's 2006 promotion of their new fruit-flavored smoothies, Wenner created paintings of tall Dunkin' smoothies that seemed to rise from the street in several U.S. cities; free samples of the new product were given out at those events. Wenner's paintings have also been used in ad campaigns for such companies as BMW, Cadillac, Lexus, Lincoln, Toyota, Knorr Soup, Kraft Foods, Microsoft, and the Washington Lottery, among many others.

Though he is best known for his street art, the majority of Wenner's works are permanent pieces and include drawings, paintings, murals, figurative sculptures, and architectural designs. He designed and painted some 3,000 square feet of oil paintings and decorative plaster work for a private residence known as the Villa Zeffiro, in Santa Barbara, which was later featured in the magazine *Architectural Digest*. Wenner also designed and painted the entire ceiling of the Church of Saint George, near Lake Cuomo, in Montano Lucino, Italy, a project for which he completed more than 20

murals covering some 6,000 square feet of space. Some of Wenner's other Renaissance-style murals can be found in other churches, cathedrals, museums, shopping centers, corporate and government buildings, and hotel lobbies. After creating many paintings and decorations for private homes, Wenner began to receive requests for original architectural designs. He now accepts commissions to design homes, villas, exteriors, and other architectural detailing—all inspired by classical architecture from the Roman Renaissance. "Architecture provides me with the ultimate means to combine my different areas of study," Wenner explained on his Web site. "When I design a residence I like to think of it as a unified vision. I want to express the optimism and exuberance that I try to achieve in my painting. The goal of my work has always been to alter and manipulate the environment. I want the work to 'encompass' the viewer rather than sit tentatively in a frame. I try to create spaces in which people can live within a work of art, becoming part of the rich cultural continuum that the classical tradition proposes."

Wenner has lectured and conducted workshops for the National Gallery of Art, the Smithsonian Institution, Disney, and Warner Bros. Studios. In 1990 he established a two-day residency program to teach art to children at the Music Center of Los Angeles County, in California.

After living in rural Italy for 28 years, Wenner returned to the U.S., where he now resides with his wife, Elizabeth, and son, Anders. He has received numerous honors and awards over the years, including the Golden Bacchus from Barolo, the Golden Giotto from Milan, and the Kennedy Center Medallion, recognizing his contributions to arts education. Wenner is currently developing a street painting method that uses stereoscopy to achieve three-dimensional effects. He is also putting the finishing touches on a book about the history of street painting.

—C.C.

Suggested Reading: (Australia) *Sunday Times* p 56 Oct. 24, 2010; *Boston Herald* Finance p20 May 27, 2006; *Calgary (Alberta, Canada) Herald* A p2 July 13, 2004; *Chicago Sun-Times* p11 Oct. 5, 1997; *Columbus Dispatch* B p1 Sep. 26, 1998; *Extra Finger Blog* May 26, 2011; *Houston Chronicle* p1 June 9, 2003; Kurt Wenner Web site; (Palm Springs, California) *Desert Sun* B p6 Mar. 13, 2003; *Pittsburgh Post-Gazette* D p8 Sep. 25, 1997; *Salt Lake (Utah) Tribune* B p1 June 27, 1997

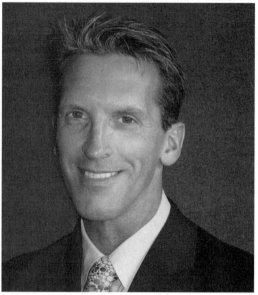

Courtesy of the Silverman Group

Wheater, Ashley C.

1958– Artistic director of the Joffrey Ballet

Address: Joffrey Ballet, 10 E. Randolph St., Chicago, IL 60601

Ashley C. Wheater, "a tall, elegant man with a charming knack for seeing both the beauty and the absurdity of life," Gia Kourlas wrote for the *New York Times* (October 14, 2007), "has made an impact in ballet over the years." The Scottish-born Wheater, who trained at the Royal Ballet School, in London, England, enjoyed an impressive performance career with companies in England, Australia, and the U.S. Forced to retire as a dancer in 1996 due to a neck injury that required surgery, he subsequently served as a ballet master and then assistant to the artistic director of the San Francisco Ballet. In 2007 Wheater was named the artistic director of the Chicago, Illinois–based Joffrey Ballet.

One of the nation's most prestigious dance companies, the Joffrey Ballet was founded in 1956 by Gerald Arpino and Robert Joffrey, both of whom are now deceased. Wheater was selected as the successor to Arpino, who had been leading the company since 1988. "I teach the company. I coach the company. I do all the hiring and firing," Wheater said in an interview with the *St. Louis Review* (December 4, 2010). "I make the decisions on all of the programming for the company, and that sometimes means hiring choreographers to create something for the company. I also do a fair amount of fundraising as well. I take care of the artistic side to the company." According to Susan Fulks, writing for the *Palm Beach (Florida) Daily News* (May 23, 2010), as artistic director Wheater "is maintaining the integrity of the mission set forth by Arpino and Joffrey in 1956 while infusing the company with a renewed energy and inspiration to move in new directions."

Ashley C. Wheater was born in 1958 in Cutler, Scotland. His mother was a mosaic and ceramic artist; his father, now deceased, was a part-time actor. When he was a small boy, his family moved to Delford, a town in England. Wheater became interested in dance after going with his mother to pick up his three sisters from ballet class. "I . . . heard the piano, saw the movement and decided that was what I wanted to do," he told Hedy Weiss for the *Chicago Sun-Times* (September 25, 2007). "I clearly remember thinking, 'How amazing that you can have music all day,'" he recalled to Jake Jarvi for *Sheridan Road* (October 19, 2010). "The music came first and the dancing came afterward." Wheater started dancing at age six; when he was nine he auditioned successfully for the Royal Ballet School, which he began to attend the following year. At 13 he was selected for a featured role in the Royal Ballet's premiere production of *A Death in Venice*, choreographed by Frederick Ashton.

Wheater progressed to the upper school of the Royal Ballet and later became a dancer with the company, performing at Covent Garden in such productions as *Swan Lake*, *Sleeping Beauty*, and *The Dream*. In 1977, at the suggestion of the celebrated Russian-born choreographer Rudolf Nureyev, one of his mentors, Wheater joined the London Festival Ballet, where he performed in contemporary and classical works and at 20 attained the position of principal dancer. Five years later he became a member of the Australian Ballet, for which he was also a principal dancer; he told Sid Smith for the *Chicago Tribune* (September 30, 2007) that when he asked Nureyev if he should join the Australian Ballet, his mentor replied, "Go, see the world." In the mid-1980s, after performing in *Suite Saint-Saëns* with that company, Wheater was invited by Gerald Arpino—who had staged the work—to join the Joffrey Ballet. For four years beginning in 1985, he served as a member of the Chicago-based ballet company, dancing in works by American choreographers including William Forsythe, Paul Taylor, Mark Morris, and Laura Dean. "When I was in the Joffrey, it was one of the best companies in America," Wheater said in the interview with Jake Jarvi. "They had extraordinarily talented dancers and a great repertoire of new and created works." In 1989 Wheater left his post at the Joffrey and relocated to California, where he became a soloist with the San Francisco Ballet; the following year he was promoted to principal dancer. As a member of the company, he performed in *Menuetto*, *Forevermore*, *The Four Temperaments*, and *In the Night*, among many other works, often in roles created for him.

In 1996, while with the San Francisco Ballet, Wheater was instructed by a choreographer to perform a move in which the full weight of his dancing partner, Evelyn Cisneros, was supported by his back and neck. After the pair completed the move, they were asked to try it again, but Wheater refused. "I realized the strain it was putting on my neck," he told Sam Whiting for the *San Francisco Chronicle* (May 5, 1996). The following day Wheater was unable to turn his head. After taking several weeks off from dancing, he performed with a partner, Muriel Maffre, at the San Francisco Ballet's annual summer smorgasbord, during which "I couldn't feel [Maffre's] hands or where my arms were," he said to Whiting. "It's amazing that Muriel and I got through it and I didn't let go of her." Wheater then underwent an MRI (magnetic resonance imaging) scan and learned that he had multiple ruptured discs in his neck that were putting pressure on his spine. In spite of that news, he performed in David Bintley's *The Dance House*, in a role created for him.

After experiencing a great deal of pain, in 1997 Wheater went to the spine center at St. Mary's Hospital in San Francisco to have a discogram—an X-ray examination of the intervertebral discs. "My doctors said: 'We don't have a lot of options here, but we need to operate. And if we operate, it's the end of your career,'" he recalled to Gia Kourlas. "I said: 'I just don't want to be in a wheelchair. If I can't dance, at least I want to be able to swim and teach and coach.'" He then underwent a cervical spondylosis, a surgical procedure that took four and a half hours and involved a bone graft from his hip. For three months after the operation, Wheater was required to wear a stiff torso-and-neck brace at all times. "It hit me after a month that I really was never going to dance again," Wheater said to Whiting. "I started to get really depressed. I am a very active person, but to be completely inactive and realize something I've done since I was 6 has come to an end is tough." No longer able to make a living as a dancer, Wheater was offered the position of ballet master with the San Francisco Ballet. While still wearing a halo brace, he began to coach dancers.

In 2002 Wheater became an assistant to the artistic director of the San Francisco Ballet, a post he held until 2007, when he replaced Gerald Arpino as the new artistic director of the Joffrey Ballet. His name had been suggested by the choreographer Lar Lubovitch to Jon H. Teeuwissen, a former executive director of the company, and he was unanimously voted in by the search committee. "I am so grateful to Lar for making that call," Teeuwissen told Gia Kourlas. "While other applicants had many strengths, there wasn't one who hit the ball out of the park. I don't mean to make him sound like a god or something, but Ashley really was the complete package: someone who had international experience, who had danced with the Joffrey and who had hands-on experience working with both founders." Wheater signed a five-year contract with the company. "This is probably the greatest thing that has ever happened to me. It feels right," he said in an interview with *Stay Thirsty* (November 2008, on-line). "It's a lot of work, but it's work that is so enjoyable even with all of the problems. . . . I believe in this company."

"My mother remembers when I was 12 years old, telling her that I wanted to have my own [dance] company," Wheater told Gerald M. Gay for the *Arizona Daily Star* (March 27, 2009). "I guess it has always been in the back of my mind." Wheater brought his own vision to the Joffrey Ballet. "When I came in, I looked at everything. I made a lot of big changes that dealt with structure and personnel," he said to Gay. He and the company's new executive director, Christopher Clinton Conway, Wheater added, "have really stripped the organization down to what we really need." One of the decisions he made in 2008 was not to renew the contract of Maia Wilkins, who had been a lead ballerina with the company. At the time Wilkins was 38 years old, and Wheater had decided to make more room for younger dancers. "We want to give people opportunities, and when I look around the company, I see a lot of talent," he told Sid Smith for the *Chicago Tribune* (April 13, 2008). "If you only give lead roles to the same few over and over, the whole flow of mentality becomes, 'Why should I work hard if I'm never going to get the chance?'" Wheater has also worked to expand the Joffrey's repertoire of performances to include newer full-length works, among them Ronald Hynd's *The Merry Widow* and Lar Lubovitch's *Othello*, and to diversify its dancers in terms of race. Wheater told Jake Jarvi, "Robert Joffrey was a great visionary. I think that he built his company on a blueprint of nurturing some of the greatest 19th and 20th century works, but also really pushing forward new creative work for the company. I want to do this for what Joffrey and Arpino started. They were truly mavericks of dance in America, and I feel there's a responsibility that goes with having this position." He said to Gay, "A lot of companies have focused so much on Europe. I'd like to re-establish Joffrey's vision, to build on American dancers and choreographers."

In addition to his responsibilities as artistic director, Wheater feels that it is important for him to continue to teach dancers. "That's how you imprint what you want," he explained to Gia Kourlas. "We make a choice in our lives to commit to something, and as I said to the dancers: 'Come to the studio and put in 110 percent. That's what I'm going to do.' Then you can spend the whole day getting somewhere. I would hope that every day I teach, I inspire people." Although Wheater spends a lot of time teaching, he does not choreograph. "I would sooner be the gardener," he told Kourlas, "than the landscape architect." He was quoted as saying in the *Stay Thirsty* article, "The strongest part of me is to teach and to coach, and I've always loved teaching whether it's a professional dancer, a principal dancer or a child in a ballet school. There is something about teaching that is such a fulfilling gift to be able to give back. . . . I love directing. I love deciding what the company should be dancing, how they should be dancing, and that all comes from teaching every day and coaching."

In 2008 the company spent more than $20 million on new headquarters in downtown Chicago, the Joffrey Tower, which includes a 140-seat black-box theater. The tower has glass walls so that people passing by can watch the dancers as they rehearse. The following year the company opened the Academy of Dance, Official School of the Joffrey Ballet, which is located in the Joffrey Tower and offers a wide variety of programs for dancers as young as three. "The school is such a passion for me," Wheater told Lynn Colburn Shapiro for *Dance Magazine* (August 1, 2009). "I would like to give back at least what was given to me." Addressing the attitude among some Americans that dance is not a manly pursuit, Wheater said in the interview with the *St. Louis Review*, "I think the misconception is that dancing is not a highly athletic art form, but it really is. If you put a really well trained male dancer against a football player, . . . there is no comparison. A male dancer is physically stronger in every way."

According to Hedy Weiss, the openly gay Wheater is "a tall, slender man with the golden coloring that evokes his surname." In 2010 he was chosen as a Lincoln Academy Laureate, the highest honor given by the state of Illinois.

—J.P.

Suggested Reading: *Chicago Sun-Times* Features p35 Sep. 25, 2007; *Chicago Tribune* C p4 Sep. 30, 2007; *New York Times* Arts and Leisure p28 Oct. 14, 2007; *San Francisco Chronicle* E p1 Sep. 26, 2007; *(Tuscon) Arizona Daily Star* C p8 Mar. 27, 2009;

Wendy Webb, courtesy of Penguin Group USA

White, Randy Wayne

June 9, 1950– Writer

Address: c/o Penguin Group USA, 375 Hudson St., New York, NY 10014-3672

Randy Wayne White, a writer of best-selling mystery novels, has often been compared to the late John D. MacDonald, another author of thrillers set in southwest Florida. White is best-known for the series that follows the adventures of Marion "Doc" Ford, a hard-nosed marine biologist and former intelligence operative, and Tomlinson, his eccentric hippie sidekick. White launched the Doc Ford series in 1990, with the publication of the critically acclaimed *Sanibel Flats*, which was selected by the American Independent Mystery Booksellers Association as one of its hundred favorite mysteries of the 20th century. To date he has written 18 Doc Ford novels, all set in and around Dinkins Bay, a fictional marina off Florida's Sanibel Island; the latest installment, *Night Vision*, was published in the spring of 2011. A resident of southwest Florida for nearly four decades, White began his writing career in the early 1970s, as a columnist for the *Fort Myers News-Press*; he later traveled the world as a monthly columnist and editor-at-large for *Outside* magazine, writing about natural history, archaeology, politics, and more. He spent years in between as a light-tackle fishing guide at Tarpon Bay Marina off Sanibel Island. For the Doc Ford series, White has drawn to a great extent on his memories of working as a fishing guide, and similarly colorful real-life experiences have informed his other works, which include a cookbook, several other nonfiction volumes, and two mystery series written under the respective pseudonyms Randy Striker and Carl Ramm.

Randy Wayne White was born on June 9, 1950 in Ashland, Ohio. He has a brother who is five years his senior and a sister who is five years his junior. White grew up on a farm just outside Pioneer, Ohio, and spent his summers in North Carolina, where his parents had come from. He later moved with his family to Davenport, Iowa. White developed a passion for books and reading at an early age. "I didn't see television until I was 12," he said to Jonathon King for the Fort Lauderdale, Florida, *Sun-Sentinel* (August 13, 2000). "We read when I was growing up on the farm, and there was a magic in books." He told Jay MacDonald for Bankrate.com (April 26, 2005), "I always thought if I could write a book, maybe I could be part of the magic I found in books. But I never really thought I was smart enough or capable of that."

White attended Davenport Central High School in Iowa, where he was "an amazingly poor student," as he told MacDonald, but a standout athlete in baseball, football, and springboard diving. After his parents left Davenport, White remained, living on his own and supporting himself financially while still in high school; among other jobs he worked for the Davenport Brass and Foundry and washed dishes at a bar. Following his high-school graduation, in 1968, White got a tryout with the Cincinnati Reds of Major League Baseball but was not signed. He then traveled the world before settling in southwest Florida, in 1972.

In Florida White began working as a columnist for the Fort Myers News-Press. At the time he had little reporting experience, having written only a few articles for local papers. Nonetheless, Bob Bentley, then the new editor in chief of the paper, told Thomas Becnel for the Sarasota (Florida) Herald-Tribune (November 29, 1998), "I could have gone with mediocre experienced people or the young hot ones. Randy was one of the young hot ones. There was something different about his style and his outlook on life. He worked hard, he worked cheap, and you could tell he was bright as the Dickens." White spent three years at the News Press, during which he worked to obtain a boat-captain's license. By that time he had worked numerous other jobs. As Glenn Miller noted for the Fort Myers News-Press (May 13, 2007), according to a 1974 ad in the paper, White had already "worked as an installer repairman and troubleshooter for a telephone company; shifted weights in an iron and brass foundry; worked as an oil rigger's roustabout in Colorado; played semi-pro baseball and industrial league football; taught swimming at a camp for mentally retarded; caught turkeys, baled hay and hoed corn out of soy beans in Ohio. Randy's painted garbage cans, taught springboard diving, janitored and written advertising copy." Miller added, "At the time, he was 24."

In 1974 White received his captain's licence and soon became a light-tackle fishing guide. He recalled to Jay MacDonald, "I was never passionate about fishing, but it was a way to make a living." White worked for 13 years as a guide out of Tarpon Bay Marina off Sanibel Island, spending more than 300 days of the year on the water; he guided more than 3,000 charter cruises in total. During that time he continued to pursue a writing career, contributing freelance articles to magazines. A break came in 1978, when Rolling Stone founded Outside magazine and published a piece he had written. White wrote many adventure stories for the publication. Jeff Klinkenberg noted for the St. Petersburg (Florida) Times (September 4, 2002) that in the course of traveling and writing for Outside, White "boxed with an old Hemingway sparring partner, swam naked in ice-filled water in the Arctic, tangled with a professional wrestler, learned to drive a car at a CIA anti-terrorist school, trained with Navy Seals and once, somehow, got stabbed on a city street in Peru." White was later named one of Outside's four editors-at-large.

While working as a fishing guide, White began writing novels. In the early 1980s he worked as a contract writer, turning out a series of Florida-based thrillers under the pen name Randy Striker: Key West Connection (1981), The Deep Six (1981), Cuban Death-lift (1981), The Deadlier Sex (1981), Assassin's Shadow (1981), Everglades Assault (1982), and Grand Canyon Slam (1982). The books White wrote as Carl Ramm include Atlanta Extreme (1986) and Denver Strike (1986). White became a full-time novelist in 1987, after the federal government closed the Tarpon Bay Marina to powerboat traffic. At the time White, who had married at 22, had two young sons to support. He told MacDonald, "Being absolutely unqualified to do anything else, I wrote a book." He said Sue Keller for the Fort Myers News-Press (February 17, 2011), "Losing my job was the best thing that ever happened to me."

In 1990, as part of a three-book deal, St. Martin's Press published White's first Doc Ford novel, Sanibel Flats. The book introduced readers to Dr. Marion Ford, a brooding marine biologist with a shady past, and his quirky sidekick, Tomlinson. Describing Ford as "one of those tough guys with a heart of gold," Jeff Klinkenberg compared the character—as have many others—to John D. MacDonald's fictional Travis McGee. Based in and around the fictional Dinkins Bay, off Sanibel Island, the series follows the two characters as they encounter villains and adventure in exotic places all over the world, from Nicaragua to Sumatra. Upon the publication of Sanibel Flats, White, who received a $5,000 advance for the book, was hailed by the Denver Post as "a major new talent who has produced a virtually perfect piece of work," as noted on the author's Web site. Sanibel Flats was later chosen by the American Independent Mystery Booksellers Association as one of its favorite mysteries of the 20th century.

White followed Sanibel Flats with two more novels from St. Martin's, The Heat Islands (1992) and The Man Who Invented Florida (1993). Dissatisfied with St. Martin's Press due to poor publicity and meager pay, White signed with G.P. Putnam's Sons for his fourth book in the Doc Ford series, Captiva (1996), for which he earned "a $70,000 or $80,000 advance," as he noted to MacDonald. Putnam has released every subsequent installment of the Ford series. White's other Doc Ford novels include North of Havana (1997), The Mangrove Coast (1998), Ten Thousand Islands (2000), Shark River (2001), Twelve Mile Limit (2002), Everglades (2003), Tampa Burn (2004), Dead of Night (2005), Dark Light (2006), Hunter's Moon (2007), Black Widow (2008), Dead Silence (2009), Deep Shadow (2010), and, most recently, Night Vision (2011). White has said that his earliest Ford books, published by St. Martin's, suffered from being virtually unedited. He told Jonathon King that he has "100 percent" trust in his editor at Putnam, who tells him to "cut this, this and this. And I cut that, that and that."

White has claimed to have traits similar to those of his two protagonists. He told J. T. Harris for the *Fort Pierce (Florida) Tribune* (June 22, 2003), "I like Ford because of his discipline, his work ethic. His analytical side is often at odds with his spiritual side. That's also true of me." He added, "I like Tomlinson because of his honesty and sense of humor. I don't like fakes, snobs." White has called the state of Florida the third most important character in his novels. He explained to Glenn Miller, "Florida is. . . . an amalgam of characters. People say that Florida is the north's southernmost state. That's true to a degree but Florida is also the Deep South in some locations. Florida is also Cuba. Florida is also the Bahamas. Florida is also Steubenville-by-the-sea. Florida is also Frog Island. And I love that aspect of Florida. It's a multiple character. Florida attracts predators. People come here from all over and they can come to be anything they choose and claim and people tend to believe because people tend to want to believe."

White's other works include the nonfiction books *Batfishing in the Rainforest* (1991), *The Sharks of Lake Nicaragua* (1999), *Last Flight Out* (2002), *An American Traveler* (2003), and *Gulf Coast Cookbook* (2006). His honors include the Conch Republic Award for Literature and the John D. MacDonald Award for Literary Excellence. In 2002 White won the Woods Hole Film Festival Best of Festival Award for his PBS documentary, *The Gift of the Game*, about his successful efforts to take baseball equipment to children in Cuba to revive a Little League program begun there by Ernest Hemingway. White has written many magazine articles, covering a wide array of topics, and has lectured all over the U.S.

Thomas Becnel described White as "a brawny guy with a broad face and bald pate. Not handsome, but with a grin that goes right up to his bright blue eyes. Charming, very good with people's first names." Jeff Klinkenberg added that he is "a tough-looking pug who shaves his head" and has "Paul Newman blue eyes and arms the size of a gumbo limbo trunk." White lives in Pineland, on Pine Island, 15 miles west of Cape Coral, on Florida's west coast. His house is situated on a Calusa Indian shell mound, thousands of years old, that is on Florida's list of historic places. His many interests include windsurfing, lifting weights, freemasonry, traveling, and collecting peppers and spices from all over the world, and he is part owner of Doc Ford's Sanibel Rum Bar & Grille. In 2010 White was one of 20 representatives who took part in a celebration honoring 150 years of freemasonry in Cuba. He has been married to the singer-songwriter Wendy Webb since 2007. He has two sons, Lee and Rogan, from his first marriage, to Debra Jane, and also has a teenage daughter.

—C.C.

Suggested Reading: Associated Press Jan. 3, 2005; Bankrate.com (on-line) Apr. 26, 2005; *Fort Myers (Florida) News-Press* E p8 June 8, 2003, A p1+ July 5, 2003, May 13, 2007; (Palm Beach, Florida) *Post* D p1 July 21, 1998; Randy Wayne White Official Web site; *Sarasota (Florida) Herald-Tribune* E p1 Nov. 29, 1998; *St. Petersburg (Florida) Times* D p1 Sep. 4, 2002

Selected Books: Doc Ford series—*Sanibel Flats*, 1990; *The Heat Islands*, 1992; *The Man Who Invented Florida*, 1993; *Captiva*, 1996; *North of Havana*, 1997; *The Mangrove Coast*, 1998; *Ten Thousand Islands*, 2000; *Shark River*, 2001; *Twelve Mile Limit*, 2002; *Everglades*, 2003; *Tampa Burn*, 2004; *Dead of Night*, 2005; *Dark Light*, 2006; *Hunter's Moon*, 2007; *Black Widow*, 2008; *Dead Silence*, 2009; *Deep Shadow*, 2010; *Night Vision*, 2011; as Randy Striker—*Key West Connection*, 1981; *The Deep Six*, 1981; *Everglades Assault*, 1982; *Grand Canyon Slam*, 1982; as Carl Ramm—*Atlanta Extreme*, 1986; *Denver Strike*, 1986; nonfiction—*Batfishing in the Rainforest*, 1991; *The Sharks of Lake Nicaragua*, 1999; *Last Flight Out*, 2002; *An American Traveler*, 2003; *Gulf Coast Cookbook*, 2006

Wilkerson, Isabel

1961– Journalist; nonfiction writer; educator

Address: Boston University, College of Communication, 640 Commonwealth Ave., Boston, MA 02215

For her work with the *New York Times*, for which she served as Chicago bureau chief, Isabel Wilkerson received the 1994 Pulitzer Prize for feature writing, becoming the first African-American woman to win the Pulitzer and the first black person to claim that award for individual reporting. In the mid-1990s Wilkerson began researching the migration of African-Americans, between 1915 and 1970, from the South to various cities in the North and West—a movement she has often called one of the greatest underreported stories of the 20th century; whereas in 1910 only 10 percent of African-Americans lived outside the South, by 1980 that figure was around 50 percent. After more than a decade of traveling, researching, reading, and interviewing some 1,200 people, Wilkerson published her first book, *The Warmth of Other Suns: The Epic Story of America's Great Migration* (2010), which quickly became a best-seller. Wilkerson focused on three people; through them she told the story of how millions of African-Americans left the horrendous work conditions and racial hatred of the South for—in the words of the novelist Richard Wright, himself a part of the Great Migration—"the warmth of other suns." The praise in the press for Wilkerson's book was unanimous. Janet Maslin of the *New York Times* (August 31, 2010) called it

Joe Henson, courtesy of Random House
Isabel Wilkerson

a "landmark piece of nonfiction" and commended Wilkerson for pulling off "an all but impossible feat." The African-American studies scholar Paula J. Giddings, in her review of *The Warmth of Other Suns* for the *Washington Post* (September 26, 2010), referred to the book as an "extraordinary and evocative work." In 2011 Wilkerson received the National Book Critics Circle Award for nonfiction.

Isabel Alexis Wilkerson was born in 1961 in Washington, D.C., to Alexander and Rubye Wilkerson. Her father, who had come to Washington from Virginia, was one of the celebrated Tuskegee airmen, African-American pilots who flew missions for the U.S. Army Air Corps in World War II; he and Wilkerson's mother, who came from Georgia, met in Washington while attending Howard University, a historically black school. As Wilkerson has pointed out, her parents met because they were participants in the Great Migration, to which Wilkerson owes her existence. Although Wilkerson's father, a civil engineer, was an avid newspaper reader—Wilkerson remembers him reading the *Washington Post* regularly—neither he nor Wilkerson's mother, a schoolteacher, encouraged their daughter to pursue journalism, a field no one in the family had ever entered; Wilkerson's father, as she told Zachary Fuhrer for the *Yale Daily News* (January 21, 2011, on-line), "would have been very happy if I had gone into engineering." Nonetheless, Wilkerson was good at writing from an early age, and she loved seeing her articles published in her high-school newspaper. "Oddly enough, the only other [profession] that I might have [entered] is architecture," Wilkerson told Fuhrer. "I briefly thought of that, and that might have not been a far

distance from writing, about the structure that has to go into the work of writing. Writing is not a stream of consciousness, whatever comes to mind and you write it down. There is structure and order required for good writing, as with architecture. So it's not that far of a leap."

Wilkerson enrolled at Howard University, the school she thought had the best college newspaper. She began writing for the paper, the *Hilltop*, during her freshman year and later became its editor in chief. During summers she interned at various daily newspapers, including the *St. Petersburg Times*, the *Atlanta Journal-Constitution*, the *Los Angeles Times*, and, most important to her, during the summer of 1982, the *Washington Post*. The following year she earned a B.A. degree and also won the Mark of Excellence Award—the so-called "student version of the Pulitzer Prize," sponsored by the Society of Professional Journalists—for feature writing for an article on a Washington office cleaner.

That story was noticed by the *New York Times* editor and op-ed columnist Anna Quindlen, and as a result, in 1985, Wilkerson began a career with the *Times*. For the first year or so, she wrote for the Metro section, after which she became a national correspondent; in that capacity she reported from many cities, including New York, Detroit, Michigan, and Chicago, Illinois, on topics such as politics, crime, health care, racial injustice, and education. In 1991 Wilkerson became the Chicago bureau chief of the *New York Times*, a position she held until 1995.

One of the many stories Wilkerson filed during her tenure as bureau chief was a profile of Nicholas, a boy living in a desperately poor neighborhood in Chicago. Nicholas, Wilkerson wrote for the *New York Times* (April 4, 1993), was a "gentle, brooding 10-year-old" who lived with his 26-year-old mother (a welfare recipient and former crack addict), his four younger half-siblings, and his mother's boyfriend. Wilkerson described the area—Englewood, a mostly black neighborhood on Chicago's South Side—as "a forlorn landscape of burned-out tenements and long-shuttered storefronts where drunk men hang out on the corner, where gang members command more respect than police officers and where every child can tell you where the crack houses are. . . . Living with fear is second nature to the children." It was in that environment that Nicholas shouldered the responsibilities of a grown man. "Of all the men in his family's life, Nicholas is perhaps the most dutiful," Wilkerson wrote. "When the television picture goes out again, when the 3-year-old scratches the 4-year-old, when their mother, Angela, needs ground beef from the store or the bathroom cleaned or can't find her switch to whip him or the other children, it is Nicholas's name that rings out to fix whatever is wrong. He is nanny, referee, housekeeper, handyman. Some nights he is up past midnight, mopping the floors, putting the children to bed and washing their school clothes in the bathtub. It is a nightly chore: the children have few clothes and wear the same thing every day." Twelve years later, in 2005, Wilkerson returned to talk to Nicholas's family as part of a *New York Times* series of articles about class in America. The articles, by Wilkerson and others, were later published in book form as *Class Matters* (2005).

Wilkerson traveled to such places as Des Moines, Iowa, and St. Louis, Missouri, to report on the 1993 flood in the Midwest, considered to be one of the most devastating natural disasters in American history. According to the National Weather Service Web site, because of the flood—in which hundreds of levees failed—50 people died, at least 10,000 homes were destroyed, at least 75 towns were fully under water, and damage totaled $15 billion. During the summer and fall of 1993, Wilkerson wrote nearly a dozen stories about the flood. On the one hand, Wilkerson told Fuhrer, "I found that disasters can actually bring out the best in humanity. The only beautiful thing about them is that they can strip away the barriers and [people] turn to people that they otherwise would never have spoken to. People are forced to make alliances with people they never would have thought they would need. . . . It's a spiritual challenge to rise to your higher self. And that's what I saw in the reporting that I did." On the other hand, she added, she found it challenging, in the middle of the catastrophe, to deal with so many people in need while focusing on her role as a journalist. "When you're a journalist covering that type of disaster, there are usually so many people who want to talk to you that you are actually forced to figure out how it whittles down. They all want help. They all want to show you pictures. They all want to know if you have access to FEMA [the Federal Emergency Management Agency]. As a journalist in the field, your task is to figure out how best to tell the story and not become the social worker that people might want you to be. Because you're not trained to be that. Generally speaking . . . there will always be people who try to take advantage." In 1994 Wilkerson won a Pulitzer Prize for feature writing.

Wilkerson began researching the Great Migration, she wrote on her Web site, "because I wanted to pull readers deep inside perhaps the greatest untold story of the Twentieth Century. . . . I wanted readers to imagine themselves in a hot, open field facing endless rows of cotton needing to be picked, having to bear the arcane laws of an arbitrary caste system and having to labor over the decision of their lives—whether to stay or whether to go. To capture the enormity of the phenomenon, I chose to trace the journeys of three different people who followed the three main streams of the Great Migration over the course of the decades it enfolded. To find them, I needed to reach as many as I could of this dwindling generation before it was too late." Wilkerson's search for members of that generation led her to meetings of the American Association of Retired Persons, union meetings, high-school reunions, Catholic churches in California, Baptist churches in South Carolina, and gatherings of various clubs and organizations in many other locations. In all, Wilkerson interviewed more than 1,200 people; she then conducted follow-up interviews with more than 30 people. She ultimately chose three people on whom to focus and conducted still more interviews with them. "One reason I ended up talking to over 1,200 people is because I got varying responses from wherever I went," Wilkerson said on the *Charlie Rose Show* (October 13, 2010). "One reason why the story hadn't been told . . . is because a lot of people didn't talk about it after they left. When they left they left for good, they didn't look back. . . . They put it behind them and didn't tell their children. Part of it is they didn't want their children to be burdened by what they had experienced, by the pain of it. Sometimes it was too difficult and heartbreaking to discuss."

In 1998 Wilkerson received a fellowship from the Guggenheim Foundation to advance her research. In addition to interviews and road trips, Wilkerson's research included another key component: analyzing newspaper articles, scholarly works, novels, and poems "to recount the motivations, circumstances and perceptions of the migration as it was in progress and to put the subjects' actions into historical context."

As *The Warmth of Others Suns* (2010) makes clear, there is no single archetypal story of the Great Migration, since it took place over nearly six decades and since the places where people ended up differed: because of train routes, where one had lived in the South often led to where one settled in the North or West. African-Americans living in Alabama, Mississippi, and Arkansas took trains to the Midwest, to cities such as Chicago, Cleveland, Ohio, and Detroit; those from Louisiana and Texas rode trains west to California, to places such as Los Angeles and the San Francisco Bay Area; and those living in Georgia, Florida, Virginia, and the Carolinas traveled by rail to Washington, D.C., Philadelphia, Pennsylvania, and New York City. With those three main migration patterns in mind (there were some exceptions), Wilkerson told the story of millions of people by focusing on three main people: one woman, Ida Mae Brandon Gladney, and two men, George Swanson Starling and Robert Joseph Pershing Foster.

Ida Mae Brandon Gladney lived in Mississippi with her three children and husband, a hardworking sharecropper. Tired of being cheated by the white landowner for whom he worked and afraid for his life after a relative was beaten nearly to death by whites for allegedly stealing turkeys, Gladney's husband decided to leave the South. In 1937 the family moved to Chicago, where, after a difficult search, Gladney found work at a hospital and her husband got a job at a Campbell's Soup factory. While Chicago was not free of racism, the level of racial intolerance there did not compare to that in Mississippi. Wilkerson's second subject, George Swanson Starling, worked in the fields in Florida, picking citrus fruits. Because of the low pay and terrible work conditions, he tried to organize a strike, which put him at odds with the growers. After a friend of Starling's warned him that the growers—with full knowledge and support from the local sheriff—were planning to lynch him, he went north. In 1945 he settled in the Harlem section of New York City, America's best-known black neighborhood. The third subject, Robert Joseph Pershing Foster, served as a surgeon in the Korean War. When he returned to his native Louisiana, he found that he was not allowed to practice medicine there. In 1951 he drove to California, a place that proved to be better in terms of race relations than his home state but one that was not without its problems: Foster, like many blacks during the Great Migration, had to endure prejudices from Northern-born African-Americans who had established themselves in the community.

The reviews for *The Warmth of Others Suns* were enthusiastic, though the praise was sometimes qualified when it came to Wilkerson's approach to her subject. "She tends to privilege the migrants' personal feelings over structural influences like the coming of the mechanical cotton picker, which pushed untold thousands of Southern blacks from the fields, or the intense demand for wartime factory labor, which pulled thousands more to manufacturing cities in the North," David Oshinsky wrote for the *New York Times Book Review* (September 5, 2010). "Wilkerson is well aware of these push-pull factors. She has simply chosen to treat them in a way that makes the most sense to her. What bound these migrants together, she explains, was both their need to escape the violent, humiliating confines of the segregationist South and their 'hopeful search for something better, any place but where they were. They did what human beings looking for freedom, throughout history, have often done. They left.'" A reviewer for the *Economist* (August 28, 2010) wrote: "Her account of [black migrants'] experiences lacks the objectivity and historical depth of Nicholas Lemann's classic: *The Promised Land* (1991). Her understanding of economics is shaky; her international perspective myopic. Hers instead is an oral history that lifts the spirits and warms the heart. . . . The Great Migration is over but its legacy is intact. Ms Wilkerson does not exaggerate when she claims that it changed American culture. The migrants brought the blues and gave birth to jazz, rock, rhythm and blues and hip-hop. They influenced the language, food, dance and dress of America. They helped create an influential black electorate and black middle class. Quite an achievement for a people once required to step off the pavement when a white person approached."

In addition to the above-mentioned awards, Wilkerson was the recipient of the George Polk Award in journalism in 1993 and the Journalist of the Year Award, from the National Association of Black Journalists, in 1994. Wilkerson taught journalism at Emory University, in Atlanta, Georgia, from 2006 to 2009. In 2009 she became a journalism professor and director of the narrative nonfic-

tion program at Boston University, in Massachusetts. Through the Random House Speakers Bureau, she has given many talks nationwide to promote her book. In 1989 she married Roderick Jeffrey Watts, a psychologist and college teacher.

—D.K.

Suggested Reading: bu.edu/com; *Charlie Rose Show* (on-line) Oct. 13, 2010; *Economist* Aug. 28, 2010; isabelwilkerson.com; *New York Times Book Review* p1 Sep. 5, 2010; *New Yorker* p76 Sep. 6, 2010;

Selected Books: *The Warmth of Other Suns: The Epic Story of America's Great Migration*, 2010

Frederick M. Brown/Getty Images

Williams, Saul

Feb. 29, 1972– Poet; writer; singer; actor; activist

Address: c/o Charlotte Gusay Literary Agency, 10532 Blythe Ave., Los Angeles, CA 90064

The poet, writer, actor, and activist Saul Williams is "the prototype synthesizer between poetry and hip-hop, stage and page, rap and prose, funk and mythology, slam and verse" and "one of spoken-word poetry's most charismatic performance poets," Mark Eleveld wrote for *Booklist* (February 1, 2006). Williams, who has been writing and performing since childhood, studied philosophy and acting in college and earned a master's degree in acting from New York University. His victory at a grand-championship slam—a competition in which contestants recite their own poetry—in New

York City in 1996 led to his appearance in the documentary *SlamNation* and his starring, award-winning role in the feature film *Slam*, which he also co-wrote. He has since appeared in other films for the big and small screens, served as an opening act for many performers, and released several EPs and four albums, the last two in collaboration with Trent Reznor, the frontman of the now-defunct band Nine Inch Nails. A fifth album, *Volcanic Sunlight*, is due in 2011. In a review of his third disk for the *New York Times* (November 4, 2007), Jon Pareles wrote, "If there ever was a clear border between hip-hop and activist poetry, Saul Williams crashes through it on his album *The Inevitable Rise and Liberation of Niggy Tardust!* . . . He declaims, chants, narrates and sings his visionary takes on the African-American condition and his own sense of purpose. Instead of slogans or polemics Mr. Williams slings hallucinatory images—'A rabid dog in heat on a dead end street'—while his producer . . . turns each track into a projectile. Thudding old-school drumbeats, looming synthesizers and sudden empty spaces give the songs clout, with verbal and nonverbal hooks." Williams has contributed to more than 20 albums by others. In addition, he has published four volumes of poetry. Through lectures, workshops, and performances in the U.S. and overseas, he has influenced thousands of schoolchildren, college students, and others of all ages who are interested in poetry and hip-hop. "Spoken word, like hip-hop, is a perfect reflection of what's going on in America, for better or worse," Williams said to Laura Bond for the Denver, Colorado, alternative newsweekly *Westword* (May 13, 2004). "If you want to know what's happening in your society, you've got to check out what's happening with your artists."

The last of three children and the only son of Saul Williams and his wife, Juanita Sealy-Williams, Saul Stacey Williams was born on February 29, 1972 in Newburgh, New York, where he grew up. His father was a Baptist minister who traveled a lot for his church; his mother was a grade-school teacher. He has told many interviewers that his mother was rushed from a James Brown concert directly to the hospital where he was born. Williams attended a magnet elementary school. As a child he began to write poetry, with leanings toward rap; he would search the dictionary for long words unfamiliar to him to make his raps unusual and complex. As he increased his vocabulary, he gained a growing awareness of the power of language. At his father's request he composed raps that were performed at church youth rallies. He was greatly influenced during his childhood and youth by T La Rock's single "It's Yours" (the first Def Jam Recordings release) and by the hip-hop records of Rakim, Boogie Down Productions (known as BDP), Big Daddy Kane, and Public Enemy, whose "Fight the Power" (1989) reportedly moved him to tears the first time he heard it.

Earlier, in the third grade, Williams had taken a class called "Shake Hands with Shakespeare," he recalled to Kimberly C. Roberts for the *Philadelphia Tribune* (October 23, 1998), and was cast as Marc Antony in a school production of an abridged version of *Julius Caesar*. "Literally, from that moment I was in every school play, and always knew that acting was what I wanted to do," he told Roberts. In the seventh grade Williams began to win speech and emceeing competitions. For his 13th birthday he received a gift of acting lessons. A former classmate of his has recalled Williams's performance as King Mongkut of Siam in a student rendition of the musical *The King and I*.

In an essay for *Essence* (June 2003), Williams wrote that for years he felt unhappy about his very dark complexion. One reason was that during his youth his peers called him Black Stacey (a name he gave to one of the songs on his eponymous, second album); another was that his father took "immense delight" in his "yellow daughter," who used to say, "I do not date dark-skinned men." Furthermore, people would advise him, "Make sure you marry a really light girl." His teenage addiction to a skin-lightening cream ended in part because of the dark-skinned African-born actor Djimon Hounsou's appearance in Janet Jackson's 1990 video for her song "Love Will Never Do (Without You)" and also because of the "new level of interest in me and my darker brothers" among female students that he noticed when he started college.

Williams attended the Newburgh Free Academy, a public high school. He spent a portion of the summer of 1989 as an exchange student in Brazil, gaining some proficiency in Portuguese. He also wrote part of a hip-hop opera. After his high-school graduation, in 1990, he enrolled at Morehouse College, a traditionally black, all-male school in Atlanta, Georgia. In a piece he wrote for an afropunk.com forum (December 2, 2009), Williams recalled that as a freshman, he tried to "express and explore all that I was on the verge of discovering . . . to question aspects of my upbringing, harness new disciplines, pursue my passions, and, quite simply, mature." "My first day at Morehouse," he wrote, "was the last day I combed my hair"—as his father had always insisted he do at home. Williams majored in philosophy and acting; since Morehouse did not have a drama department, he took acting classes at Morehouse's nearby sister school, the all-female Spelman College. At Spelman, he wrote for afropunk.com, "I acted, danced, recited poems, added formative layers to my creative process, and even received compliments on my hair." During his senior year Williams and several other Morehouse students launched a magazine, *Red Clay*, for which he wrote poetry and essays with social and political themes. He also wrote a play, *Yellow for Red*, about "the effects of misogyny in hip hop on a black brother and sister relationship," according to a Williams biographical timeline posted on the music Web site Giant Step. During the summer of 1994, after he earned a B.A. degree from Morehouse, he spent a month in Gambia, a small nation in West Africa where his mother had served as an exchange teacher. His experiences in Gambia led him to start keeping a journal.

In the fall of 1994, Williams enrolled in the master's-degree program in acting at the Tisch School of the Arts at New York University (NYU). Soon afterward, at a restaurant in the New York City borough of Manhattan, he attended a public poetry reading for the first time. "I saw someone on stage reciting what seemed like a monologue. I added up everything that I had done in my lifetime, and it seemed like a tailor-made art form for what I had been through," he told Kimberly C. Roberts. During his spring 1995 break, he went hiking on the outskirts of Seattle, Washington, and wrote and memorized the poem "Amethyst Rocks." Soon after he had returned to the city, while walking in the Fort Greene section of the New York borough of Brooklyn, he came upon the Brooklyn Moon Café while an open-microphone spoken-word event was taking place there. After watching for a while, he signed his name to the list of performers. In the audience were several people with connections in the arts, and that very night, after his recitation of "Amethyst Rocks," Williams was signed up for gigs as an opening act for the poet Allen Ginsberg at an NYU reading and for the rap/rock band the Roots. The Moon Café performance also led to his serving as an opener for the rapper KRS-One, the hip-hop band the Fugees, the Last Poets (widely regarded as forefathers of rap), the poet and musician Gil Scott-Heron, and the poet, writer, and activist Amiri Baraka.

Williams soon learned about the Nuyorican Poets Café, an eclectic performance and visual-arts exhibition space on the Lower East Side of Manhattan. ("Nuyorican" is a blend of "New Yorker" and "Puerto Rican.") At that café he participated in poetry slams, which, unlike ordinary poetry readings, are competitions, usually involving a weeding-out process. Typically, slam contestants must recite from memory and keep within a given time limit; they are judged (on a scale of one through 10) by previously chosen audience members. The performer with the highest combined score at the end of all the rounds is the winner. Slams became popular in the U.S. in the late 1980s and early 1990s, especially in large urban areas. In 1996 Williams won the grand championship slam at the Nuyorican Poets Café. He then competed with three other café winners on a team at that year's four-day National Poetry Slam, held in Portland, Oregon, in which teams from 27 cities participated. Williams did not win any events in Portland, but his performances received universal praise.

Paul Devlin filmed the 1996 National Poetry Slam for his documentary *SlamNation* (1998). In a review of the movie for the *Austin (Texas) Chronicle* (January 22, 1999, on-line), Russell Smith described *SlamNation* as "hugely entertaining" and wrote, "Slams are an audience-driven form, in which showmanship and raw charisma count at least as much as the absolute artistic merit of the poets' hyper-adrenal three-minute presentations. This leads to an obvious tension between the high-minded ideals of the movement's founder, Marc Smith, and the poets themselves, who've been forced to adapt their presentations to the ultra-competitive, maddeningly arbitrary judging format." Williams's style, Smith wrote, "is an intriguing fusion of hip-hop rhythms with Gil Scott-Heronesque lyrical sorties." Another *SlamNation* reviewer, the *New York Times* (July 17, 1998, on-line) critic Stephen Holden, described Williams as "one of the biggest stars of the [slam] movement" and as "a charismatic New Yorker whose poetry tends toward mind-twisting cosmic rumination with hallucinatory science-fiction scenarios that [he] delivers with an incantatory fervor." Holden declared that Williams's only "challenger as the unofficial king of the genre" was Taylor Mali, of Providence, Rhode Island. Williams later told Evelyn Nieves for the *New York Times* (September 27, 1998), "I was never really into slams. A lot of the poetry in these performances is all about performing, and not about poetry. To me, poetry has to work on the page. I did slams because of what I thought they could do for me. Once I won the [Nuyorican] grand slam, I stopped. I had nothing else to prove." However, during an interview with Vinnie BaggaDonuts (originally, Radicello) for tlchicken.com (September 2004), he said, "My favorite outlet, of everything I do, is performing."

In one notable result of his participation in slams, Williams's skills as a writer and performer caught the attention of the director and producer Marc Levin, who has made both documentaries and films that straddle fiction and nonfiction. Levin had written a partial script for a film about a petty drug dealer named Ray, who, while serving a brief prison sentence, finds redemption in poetry. Levin recruited Williams to help complete the screenplay and star as Ray. Set in Washington, D.C., Levin's *Slam* (1998) shows Ray at a prison poetry workshop run by Lauren (portrayed by Sonja Sohn, a real-life poetry slammer), who becomes Ray's love interest after his release. One scene was filmed in a real prison yard with actual inmates as well as actors. Levin, who expected 16 inmates to be there, ordered the film crew to "do establishing footage for the first 40 minutes, then do the poetry," Williams recalled to Henry Sheehan for the *Orange County (California) Register* (October 19, 1998). Levin instructed Williams to "just walk around and we'll get shots of our 16 guys looking intensely at you." But instead of 16 men there were about 150, who had been told only that cameras would be present in the yard. The inmates may have thought "it was *Hard Copy* or some news team documenting some stuff," Williams told Sheehan, and they apparently assumed that Williams was a new prisoner. "Someone said, 'How many guys did this guy have to snitch on in order to get this job?' So when it came down to the moment when the 16 guys were supposed to gather around me as if they were going to attack me, more than 16 came. They wanted a piece of me, too." In response, Williams immediately recited "Amethyst Rocks," and the men calmed down. "The poetry stopped them," he told Sheehan.

In a review of *Slam* headlined "Slam Is Poetry in Vibrant Motion" for the *San Francisco Chronicle* (October 23, 1998, on-line), Bob Graham labeled Williams a "genuine" actor and wrote that Williams's and Sohn's slamming—"where spoken poetry meets rap and jam session," in his words—"has the ring of truth. This is not mere recitation—it is personal expression of the most intense kind. Imagine the Romantic poets as jazz artists." In an *Entertainment Weekly* (October 23, 1998, on-line) review, Lisa Schwartzbaum wrote that the "blasts of verse" in *Slam* were "performed with such drama and passion that audiences may want to break into applause." After noting that the film had won the Grand Jury Prize and the Camera d'Or at the 1998 Sundance and Cannes Film Festivals, respectively, Schwartzbaum wrote, "Much of the cheering is directed toward the handsome, elegantly lanky Williams, himself a star on the spoken-word circuit, who makes Ray such an attractive convict—the kind of nonviolent, expressive, and reachable good fellow we hope, but don't expect, sits in every prison cell, waiting to turn his life around." Williams was nominated for an Independent Spirit Award in the category of best debut performance and earned a Gotham Award for his "breakthrough" performance in an independent film.

In other film work Williams had a bit part in Carl Franklin's *One True Thing* (1998) and a small role in Iain Softley's *K-PAX* (2001), and he starred in the mostly ignored *King of the Korner* (2000), directed by James Mathers. He has also appeared on television, in the recurring role of Sivad, the boyfriend of Lynn (played by Persia White), in the series *Girlfriends* in 2003 and in the made-for-TV version of Ruben Santiago-Hudson's drama *Lackawanna Blues*, directed by George C. Wolfe. He may also be heard in documentaries including *Underground Voices* (1996), *I'll Make Me a World* (1999), and *Coachella*, taped at the 2006 Coachella Valley Music and Arts Festival, held in Indio, California.

The year 1998 saw the publication of the slim volume *The Seventh Octave: The Early Writings of Saul Stacey Williams*—a blend of "Khalil Gibran and hip hop," according to its publisher—which contains poems dating as far back as Williams's high-school years. Williams's next book of poetry, *She*, was published 1999; the title appears on the cover with a square-root sign over the "he." That book, which bears the imprint MTV/Pocket Books, grew out of Williams's relationship with the performance artist Marcia Jones, the mother of his daughter, Saturn. His third volume, the epic poem *, Said the Shotgun to the Head* (2003; a comma appears before "Said"), from Atria/MTV Books, is "told from the view of a homeless man who is si-

multaneously searching for passion and bemoaning the decay of everything worth celebrating," Teresa Difalco wrote for *Willamette Week* (November 26, 2003, on-line). "It's a poetic kick to the head, infused with the wreckage of 9/11 and its trail of fear. . . . Like all of Williams' work, [it] is a controlled burn. That you can get right next to it makes it no less thrilling." In an assessment for *QBR: The Black Book Review* (December 31, 2003), Celeste Doaks described *Said* as "a symbolic countdown to death, or perhaps to life" that "sparkles with morsels of wisdom and faith along its journey to the end/beginning."

The Dead Emcee Scrolls: The Lost Teachings of Hip-Hop and Connected Writings (2006), Williams's most recent book, contains journal entries written in verse as well as raps composed during the previous dozen years. His self-proclaimed goal in compiling them was for readers "to be able to look at hip-hop lyricism" the way they "might look at scripture." "The most potentially controversial aspect of this association of hip hop with scripture may be Williams' writing of the word 'niggah' as 'NGH,' akin to the way the Hebrew word for God appears as 'YHWH' [Yahweh] in sacred texts," Mike Doherty wrote for the *National Post* (Toronto, Canada, edition, February 28, 2006). Williams told Doherty, "There's all this talk about the 'N-word.' I thought, 'Instead of trying to push it down, what would happen if we lifted it up?'" In *Booklist*, Mark Eleveld, who has edited several volumes about "the spoken-word revolution," as he calls it, judged *The Dead Emcee Scrolls* to be "unique in voice, daring in its trust to chance, and more concerned with wordplay than grandeur. It is strongly musical, uncorrupted, raw, and challenging" and "a must read" for any young-adult fan of hip-hop.

Since the late 1990s Williams has contributed to such multi-artist albums as *Eargasms—Crucialpoetics Vol. 1* (1997), *Black Whole Styles* (1998), and *The Unbound Project Vol. 1* (2000) and to albums by artists or groups including DJ Krust, Blackalicious, Coldcut, Nine Inch Nails, Nas, and Janelle Monáe. His first solo album, *Amethyst Rock Star*, was produced by Rick Rubin, the co-founder of the Def Jam label, and appeared in 2001. He has since made three additional albums—*Saul Williams* (2004) and two produced by Trent Reznor: *The Inevitable Rise and Liberation of Niggy Tardust!* (2007, "Niggy Tardust" being a Williams alter ego, as "Ziggy Stardust" was David Bowie's), and *Volcanic Sunlight*, which is scheduled for release in 2011. None of his albums has had mainstream success, but each has pleased various reviewers. "With *Amethyst Rock Star*," Andrew Parks wrote for the Syracuse University campus newspaper the *Daily Orange* (January 15, 2002), "Williams translates his poetry to music powerfully, but at times the listener may wonder what he is talking so passionately about. But that is the brilliance of this record. . . . It is meant to provoke thought." *Saul Williams*, Adam Greenberg wrote for AllMusicGuide.com, "like Williams in general, is difficult to categorize. However, that difficulty . . . is symptomatic of a wider variety of sound. Essentially all of the lyrical content is built upon Williams' poetry, largely sociocultural commentary and protest. What that poetry is laid over, however, is a wild variety of sound, from sparse to dense, droopingly slow to frantically fast." Greenberg concluded that the album "isn't going to be grabbing people from the radio. Once it gets a listen though, it's likely to seduce listeners and turn them into fans." Thom Jurek, another reviewer for AllMusicGuide.com, wrote of *The Inevitable Rise of Niggy Tardust!*, "From Reznor's textured ambience and scorched earth synths, Williams has crafted harder beats here than on anything he's done before." The result of their partnership, he continued, "feels like a new paradigm for hip-hop itself. Here, accepted and ignored notions of race and class are ripped to shreds leaving in their wake not a power structure but a different perception with rhythm as the soundtrack of that change." The final five tracks, Jurek wrote, "are a self and cultural analysis . . . a search and destroy mission for remaining ignorance. This is Williams' finest moment, and interestingly, one of Reznor's, too."

Williams lives in Paris, France. His daughter, Saturn, who was born in 1996, has sometimes performed alongside him. His son, Xuly Azaro, whose mother is the choreographer Fatima Robinson, was born in 2000. In 2008 Williams married Persia White; the two separated in 2009.

—F.C.

Suggested Reading: AfroPunk.com Dec. 21, 2009; *Black Book Review* p5 Dec. 31, 2003; Denver (Colorado) *Westword* (on-line) May 13, 2004; giantstep.net; Hip Hop Underground Web site; *New York Times* (on-line) Sep. 27, 1998; *Orange County (California) Register* (on-line) Oct. 19, 1998; *Philadelphia Tribune* E p7 Oct. 23, 1998; poets.org; Saul Williams Web site; *SplendidEzine.com*, 2003; (Syracuse University, New York) *Daily Orange* (on-line) Jan. 15, 2002

Selected Books: *The Seventh Octave: The Early Writings of Saul Stacey Williams*, 1998; , *Said the shotgun to the head*, 2003; *The Dead Emcee Scrolls: The Lost Teachings of Hip-Hop and Connected Writings*, 2006

Selected Recordings: *Amethyst Rock Star*, 2001; *Saul Williams*, 2004; *The Inevitable Rise and Liberation of Niggy Tardust!*, 2007; *Volcanic Sunlight*, 2011

Selected Films: *SlamNation*, 1998; *Slam*, 1998; *One True Thing*, 1998; *King of the Korner*, 2000; *K-PAX*, 2001

Wilson, Gretchen

June 26, 1973– Country-music singer

Address: c/o Club 27, Bubble Up, 160 Rains Ave., Nashville, TN 37203

"Unlike most women in country [music] in recent years," Randy Lewis wrote for the *Los Angeles Times* (May 22, 2004), the singer Gretchen Wilson "doesn't look like she just stepped off the cover of *Cosmo*, doesn't sing to soccer moms and doesn't pine for champagne and roses. In Wilson's world, a cold beer will do just fine." Wilson has refused to create an image of herself that does not accurately portray who she really is—a "redneck woman," to use the title of her breakout song. "To me, being a redneck woman means being a strong woman," she told Robert Hilburn for the *Los Angeles Times* (January 22, 2006). Acknowledging that the term "redneck" once had "other meanings," she added, "It's about holding your head up no matter what is happening." Wilson's disadvantaged upbringing is detailed in her 2006 memoir, *Redneck Woman: Stories from My Life*, which won a place on the *New York Times* best-seller list. Despite the hardships she faced, Wilson worked her way up from bartending high-school dropout to Grammy Award–winning country-music star. "I've just learned that throughout the years nothing out there

Jason Merritt/Getty Images

that's good really comes easy," she said in an interview for the CBS TV program the *Early Show* (March 31, 2010), "you have to work for everything." Critics and fans have celebrated not only

Wilson's rags-to-riches story but the quality of her voice—which has, in Hilburn's words, "the purity and power of Patsy Cline or Loretta Lynn"—and her faithfulness to country music's roots. Kyle Young, the director of the Country Music Hall of Fame and Museum, in Nashville, Tennessee, told Hilburn that Wilson "sings about her own life, which is what all great country artists have done."

After landing a major recording contract with Epic Records, in 2003, following years of struggle and rejection, Wilson released her debut album, *Here for the Party* (2004). The CD contained her hit single "Redneck Woman," which has been called the quickest-rising country single of all time and sold millions of copies. Since then Wilson has come out with three additional albums, to which she contributed much of the songwriting: *All Jacked Up* (2005), *One of the Boys* (2007), and, most recently, *I Got Your Country Right Here* (2010)—the last-named disk produced and distributed by Redneck Records, a label she established after leaving Epic Records, in 2009. "I hope I make enough of a mark in country music," she told Michael Rampa for *American Songwriter* (October 18, 2010, on-line). "I would like to be remembered as the redneck woman that came along just in time to tell the world to heck with everybody else. Be yourself."

Gretchen Frances Wilson was born on June 26, 1973 and raised in the very small town of Pocahontas, Illinois. Her mother, Christine, was 16 at the time of her daughter's birth. Wilson said about Pocahontas to Kevin C. Johnson for the *St. Louis (Missouri) Post-Dispatch* (May 9, 2004), "There's not a lot going on or a lot to do. Everybody is a little backward, but they're really good people. They look out for one another, stick up for one another. And everybody knows everybody's business." Her parents separated when she was a toddler, and her mother later married a man—10 years her senior—who became the father of Wilson's half-brother, Josh. Wilson's stepfather, a self-employed contractor, often cheated his clients by abandoning jobs after he was paid for materials; as a result, the family moved frequently, leaving rent unpaid as they relocated from one trailer to the next in different parts of Illinois, living among pig farms and cornfields. Sometimes the family lived in southern Florida. Wilson has said that during her youth she attended a series of approximately 20 schools. At the beginning of ninth grade, she dropped out of school and started cooking and serving drinks at a bar called Big O's, where her mother was employed. While working there she would go onstage and sing along to songs that were playing on CD. When she was 15 years old, Wilson began living on her own in Illinois. Over the next few years, she became a member of several musical groups, such as Sam A. Lama and the Ding Dongs, Midnight Flyer, and Baywolfe. Her performing was limited to singing and playing tambourine until, joining one band, she was called on to learn guitar—which she accomplished quickly.

In 1996, at 23, "with $500 and no clue about the music business," as Jon Bream wrote for the Minneapolis, Minnesota, *Star Tribune* (September 3, 2004), Wilson moved to Nashville, Tennessee, the center of the country-music world. There, while working at a bar called Printers Alley and singing on demo records, she met the singer-songwriter John Rich, who introduced her to other aspiring musicians; she soon became a member of Muzik Mafia, a group of singer-songwriters who performed in Nashville. During that time Wilson was living in a rented house with her then-boyfriend, Mike Penner, and their young daughter, while struggling to pay her bills. She attempted to land record deals with numerous Nashville labels, all of which turned her down. "I did showcase after showcase and the story was the same," she recalled to Robert Hilburn. "They thought my hair was too dated, that I was too heavy, too old." Then, in 2003, she won a recording contract with Epic Records, which is owned by Sony Music Entertainment, after performing for John Grady, a new executive at Sony—which had already turned Wilson down twice. "When John Grady said he wanted to sign me at Sony, I was shocked," Wilson told Hilburn. "I had given up. He was the first person I met at any label that I felt like he got it. I didn't even have to explain myself to him. I didn't have to change my ain'ts into isn'ts." Grady recalled being struck by the power of Wilson's voice. "She filled up the room," he said to Hilburn. "It was almost like my teeth were rattling. I identified with her right away because I know a lot of people like her. I grew up in a town in Nebraska as small as her hometown."

Early 2004 saw the release of Wilson's debut single, "Redneck Woman," which was the first song by a solo female singer to top the *Billboard* country-singles chart in over two years. Co-written by John Rich, "Redneck Woman" contains lyrics such as, "Cause I'm a redneck woman / And I ain't no high class broad / I'm just a product of my raisin' / And I say 'hey y'all' and 'Yee Haw' / And I keep my Christmas lights on, on my front porch all year long." Before coming up with the idea for the song, Wilson and Rich were brainstorming while watching Country Music Television. "We watched videos by two or three different females and I said, 'John, I don't know if I'm going to be able to do that,'" Wilson told Randy Lewis. "'Look at them—they're all so slick. That's not who I am.' And he asked me, 'Who are you?' And I said, 'I guess I'm just a redneck woman.' And that's what inspired it." The song topped the charts faster than any single in the previous decade and spent six weeks at the number-one spot. "When you hear 'Redneck Woman,' there's nothing up the middle about it," Dale Libby, a former senior vice president of sales for Sony Nashville, told Johnson. "Not only was 'Redneck Woman' a song we gravitated to, but when we first heard Gretchen and her vocal range and her command of the material, it was a real attraction." Due to the success of the song, Sony speeded up the release of Wilson's first album,

Here for the Party (2004), which entered the country-album chart at number one and went on to sell more than five million copies. As described by Robert Hilburn for the Los Angeles Times (September 25, 2005), "The album [has] some solid barroom tunes, both the rowdy kind that work best just when the bartender can't keep up with all the orders and the melancholy kind that serve as therapy when you're alone at closing time." With the release of Here for the Party, Wilson shot to fame.

Wilson's second album, All Jacked Up (2005), was also very successful, with singles including "All Jacked Up," "I Don't Feel Like Loving You Today," "Politically Uncorrect," and "California Girls." Around the same time she began working on her autobiography, Redneck Woman: Stories from My Life, which was co-authored by Allen Rucker and published in 2006. "In a song, you generalize so that listeners can put themselves into the story. But a book is just about you, so it's more detailed," Wilson told Alison Bonaguro for the Chicago Tribune (November 12, 2006). "I hope people will read parts and think, 'I know exactly how she felt. I can attach myself to that.'" According to Bonaguro, "Wilson's memoir has all the makings of a good read: disaster, dilemma and drama." In 2007 Wilson released her third album, One of the Boys, which is very personal and features more songs written by Wilson. "I'm a singer-songwriter and I write my experiences and the things that I've been through," she said to Ellen Mallernee in an interview for Gibson.com (October 18, 2007). "The best and the worst moments of my life are the things that I put on paper. This last record is my life as it was happening, and I'm really close to it. It's my diary set to music." One of the Boys did not sell as well as her previous albums.

In 2008 Wilson earned her GED. "This is something that I promised myself a long time ago that I would do," she told Julie Chen for the Early Show on CBS (May 6, 2008). "And I'm sure that having a little girl in school is a big part of it as well, you know, wanting to be able to be there for her and help her with her homework when the time comes."

In 2009 Wilson formed her own label, Redneck Records. "I have the ability to do whatever I want, to record what I want when I want," she said in the interview with Michael Rampa. "I don't have to ask anyone's opinion anymore. I don't need permission to do something on a creative piece of work from some suits that don't have a musical bone in their bodies." She added, "You don't stand over a painter's back when they're painting and say 'Oh! I wouldn't use that color, I'm not sure if it's safe.' A song is a piece of art. If you're not involved in the creation of the music you should just let the artist put it together and then the business people take it from there, but it doesn't work like that at a major label." Redneck Records produced the 2009 single "Work Hard, Play Harder," which Wilson co-wrote with John Rich and Vicky McGehee. The song is included on I Got Your Country Right Here, Wilson's fourth album, which went on sale in 2010. "This record is mainly upbeat, with only a few select tracks to slow down the pace," Jessie Aulis wrote for the Sherbrooke (Quebec) Record (April 16, 2010). "With the slower songs, Gretchen Wilson seems to show a different side of her personality. We get to see and hear a more vulnerable side of her on 'I'm Only Human' and 'I'd Like to Be Your Last.'" Described as a combination of country and southern rock, I Got Your Country Right Here debuted at number six on the Billboard country-albums chart.

Wilson's honors include a Horizon Award from the Country Music Association (2004), an American Music Award for favorite new artist (2004), a Grammy Award for best female country vocal performance (2005, for "Redneck Woman"), a Billboard Music Award for female country artist of the year (2005), an Academy of Country Music Award for top new artist (2005), a Country Music Television Award for female video of the year (2005, for "When I Think About Cheatin'"), and a Country Music Television Award for breakthrough video of the year (2005, for "Redneck Woman"). Also in 2005 she was named female vocalist of the year by the Country Music Association. After earning her GED, Wilson was given a 2009 National Coalition for Literacy Leadership Award by the Library of Congress. In 2010 her song "I'd Like to Be Your Last" received a Grammy Award nomination for best female country vocal performance.

Wilson purchased a farm near Nashville in 2004. Prior to her relationship with Mike Penner (which ended in 2005), she was married to Larry Rolens, a former bandmate; their union ended in divorce.

—J.P.

Suggested Reading: Chicago Tribune C p10 Nov. 12, 2006; (Fort Wayne, Indiana) Journal Gazette W p3 Feb. 24, 2006; Los Angeles Times E p1 Jan. 22, 2006; (Minneapolis, Minnesota) Star Tribune E p1 Sep. 3, 2004; St. Louis (Missouri) Post-Dispatch F p1 May 9, 2004; Wilson, Gretchen. Redneck Woman: Stories from My Life (with Allen Rucker), 2006

Selected Recordings: Here for the Party, 2004; All Jacked Up, 2005; One of the Boys, 2007; I Got Your Country Right Here, 2010

Courtesy of Brown University

Wood, Gordon S.

Nov. 27, 1933– Historian; writer; educator

*Address: History Dept., Box N, 79 Brown St.,
Brown University, Providence, RI 02912*

Many historians have enjoyed renown among those in their field, but rarely is one famous enough to surface in pop culture. An exception occurs in a scene in the acclaimed film *Good Will Hunting* (1997), in which several young people gathered in a bar try to best one another intellectually. One particularly smug participant baits the main character, a janitor played by Matt Damon, by saying, "I was just hoping you might give me some insight into the evolution of the market economy in the southern colonies. My contention is that prior to the Revolutionary War, the economic modalities, especially in the southern colonies, could most aptly be characterized as agrarian [and] pre-capitalist." Unbeknownst to him, the janitor, Will Hunting, has a photographic memory and a genius-level IQ, and he immediately replies, "Of course that's your contention. You're a first-year grad student. . . . That's gonna last until next year— you're gonna be in here regurgitating Gordon Wood, talkin' about, you know, the pre-Revolutionary utopia and the capital-forming effects of military mobilization."

Damon's character is referring to the Pulitzer Prize–winning historian and Brown University professor Gordon S. Wood, the author of such well-regarded volumes as *The Radicalism of the American Revolution* (1992), *Revolutionary Characters: What Made the Founders Different* (2006), *Empire of Liberty: A History of the Early Republic, 1789–*

1815 (2009), and *The Idea of America: Reflections on the Birth of the United States* (2011), among many other works on the history, meaning, and consequences of the American Revolution. In his assessment of *The Idea of America* for the *New York Times Book Review* (July 22, 2011, on-line), David Hackett Fischer wrote, "Gordon S. Wood is more than an American historian. He is almost an American institution. Of all the many teachers and writers of history in this Republic, few are held in such high esteem."

The son of Herbert G. Wood and Marion Wood, Gordon S. Wood was born on November 27, 1933 in Concord, Massachusetts, a town that figures largely in American history. (While the first shots of the Revolutionary War were fired in nearby Lexington, on April 19, 1775, later that day Minutemen from Concord repelled a large contingent of British Red Coats; the Battles of Lexington and Concord marked the first military engagements of the war.) Wood attended Tufts University, in Medford, Massachusetts, graduating summa cum laude with an A.B. degree in 1955. In order to fulfill a Reserve Officers' Training Corps (ROTC) obligation, Wood entered the U.S. Air Force. Although he initially aspired to a career in the Foreign Service and planned to return to Tufts upon his discharge to attend the Fletcher School of Diplomacy, his experiences in the military convinced him that he did not want to work for the government. (After several months of training to become an intelligence officer, he had instead been arbitrarily assigned as his squadron's personnel officer.) While still stationed in Japan, he applied to Harvard University, in Cambridge, Massachusetts, hoping to earn a graduate degree in history.

Wood told Jill O'Neill for the George Mason University History News Network (February 16, 2010, on-line), "Students should not apply to graduate school unless they feel history and scholarship as a calling, as something akin to a religious commitment. Otherwise they won't have the stamina to see them through. Doing history is a lonely business and not everyone has the stomach for it." Wood received an A.M. degree from Harvard in 1959. He then remained at the school, serving as a teaching fellow and earning a Ph.D. degree in 1964.

Upon completing his doctoral studies, Wood joined the faculty of the College of William and Mary, in Williamsburg, Virginia, as an assistant professor, remaining there until 1966. After brief stints back at Harvard (1966–67) and at the University of Michigan (1967–69), he was hired by Brown University, in Providence, Rhode Island, as an associate professor. Wood steadily ascended the ranks at Brown, becoming a full professor in 1971. He chaired the university's History Department from 1983 to 1986 and currently holds the titles of Alva O. Way university professor and professor of history emeritus. He has also held visiting professorships at Cambridge University and Northwestern University.

Wood told O'Neill of the importance of his field of study, "History is the queen of the humanities. It teaches wisdom and humility, and it tells us how things change through time. . . . [It] is the ultimate humanist discipline." Since the beginning of his career, Wood has focused on the American Revolution. "That one subject has occupied Wood for half a century—a concentration span that few can match. And after many years of labor in that field, he has transformed it," Fischer wrote. "Scholars before Wood had offered many interpretations of the Revolution, but none seemed quite right to him. He concentrated his work on the years from 1776 to 1828, an unusual choice. When he began, Wood remembers, this period had 'a reputation for dreariness and insignificance,' as 'the most boring part of American history to study and teach.'"

Wood, Fischer explained, "went deep into primary materials and made an open-minded effort to understand the language and thought of 18th-century Americans in their own terms." In such early books as *The Creation of the American Republic, 1776–1787* (1969) and *Representation in the American Revolution* (1969), Wood "demonstrated that Americans in those years invented 'not simply new forms of government, but an entirely new conception of politics,'" according to Fischer. "They rejected ancient and medieval ideas of a polity as a set of orders or estates. In their place they created a model of a state that existed to represent individual interests, and to protect individual rights." *The Creation of the American Republic* won the 1970 John H. Dunning Prize from the American Historical Association as well as Columbia University's 1970 Bancroft Prize, and it was nominated that year for a National Book Award in history and biography. Wood told Bonnie K. Goodman for the George Mason University History News Network (April 2, 2006, on-line), "Of my books, my favorite is my first, *The Creation of the American Republic, 1776–1787*, largely I suppose because it was the first and because it seems to have been the most influential, even though it has not sold the most copies. "

Wood proved to be a prolific writer, with essays appearing in such periodicals as the *Journal of the Early Republic*, the *Suffolk Law Review*, and the *National Forum*. He also contributed chapters to such books as *Freedom in America: A 200-Year Perspective* (1977), *New Directions in American Intellectual History* (1979), and *Beyond Confederation: Origins of the Constitution and American National Identity* (1987). Other laurels mounted. In 1981, for example, the New-York Historical Society awarded him the Kerr Prize for best article published that year in the quarterly journal *New York History*, and he was honored with a Daughters of Colonial Wars Award for an article that appeared in the *William and Mary Quarterly* in 1983. Wood told O'Neill that he strove to write for a broad audience. "It is no doubt difficult to write for two different readerships at the same time, both fellow historians and the general public," he asserted. "In at-tempting such writing one is apt to fall between the two groups of readers and reach neither. I think academic historians ought to try more often to write for a general public. Otherwise, they leave history writing for the educated public to the non-academic historians, whom they then often criticize for being too facile and simple." Of the importance of educating the general public about his area of specialty, he said, "The American Revolution is the most important event in American history, bar none. Not only did it legally create the United States, but it infused into our culture nearly all of our noblest ideals and highest aspirations. Our beliefs in liberty, equality, constitutionalism, and the well-being of ordinary people came out of the Revolution, as did the political institutions by which we still govern ourselves. The Revolution is what gives us our identity as Americans, and thus all Americans need to know about it."

In 1992 Wood published *The Radicalism of the American Revolution*, which won a Pulitzer Prize for history. Calling the volume "a provocative, highly accomplished examination of how American society was reshaped in the cauldron of revolution," a critic for *Kirkus Reviews* (November 15, 1991, on-line) wrote, "Perhaps, as is often noted, the American Revolution was not as convulsive or transforming as its French and Russian counterparts. Yet this sparkling analysis from Wood impressively argues that it was anything but conservative. Wood's contention that the Revolution was 'the most radical and far-reaching event in American history' may stretch the point (did it really have more of an impact than the Civil War?). But from now on it will be hard to argue that the rebellion was a genteel event that left fundamental institutions unscathed." In the *New York Times Book Review* (March 1, 1992, on-line), Pauline Maier deemed the work to be an "eloquent, learned, landmark book" and "the most important study of the Revolution to appear in over 20 years."

Wood next received widespread attention for *The American Revolution: A History*, published by the Modern Library in 2002. Critics were almost unanimous in their praise. In a review for the *Times Higher Education Supplement* (December 19, 2003, on-line), Peter Thompson wrote, "Wood's *The American Revolution* is that rare thing, a balanced survey that presents a powerful argument. It deserves to be widely read and discussed," and Barrett R. Richardson wrote for the *Virginian-Pilot* (May 26, 2002, on-line), "Wood's brilliant and succinct synthesis of . . . decades of scholarship on the American Revolution is a must-read for those wanting an introduction to the subject or a refresher course in this seminal period in our nation's history."

Wood followed that work with *The Americanization of Benjamin Franklin* (2004). In a review for *Cercles* (on-line), Robert Sayre wrote that Gordon's "first foray into biography seems to me highly successful. The portrait of Franklin that emerges from his study is a welcome corrective to the popular image and constitutes a substantial contribution to our understanding of the man."

Wood wrote about the personalities and lives of several other Founding Fathers, including Thomas Jefferson and John Adams, in his 2006 book, *Revolutionary Characters: What Made the Founders Different*. Most critics appreciated his fresh look at that iconic group. Fischer wrote, "Wood's purpose was not to celebrate or condemn these leaders, but to understand them. His results lead us beyond the hagiographers who celebrate the founders as demigods, and iconoclasts who revile them as racists and sexists, an approach Wood believes to be inaccurate and anachronistic." "Among historians in universities these days, essays often tilt toward sheer interpretation, leaving the substance of the past scanted. Gordon S. Wood's book bucks that trend, offering a good deal of empirical evidence—what was 'done'—in these absorbing essays from one of our leading scholars of the American Revolution," Robert Middlekauff opined for the *Washington Post* (May 28, 2006, on-line). "At several points in this volume, most notably the essays on [George] Washington and the epilogue, Wood argues that the founders contributed unwittingly to a democratic and egalitarian society that they never wanted." Wood, he added, "leaves us with an ironical appreciation of the founders' achievement."

The Purpose of the Past: Reflections on the Uses of History was published in 2008. In it Wood examined works by several of his fellow historians. "[He] finds disturbing recent trends in historiography that throw into question the historian's ability accurately to reconstruct the past," David Gordon wrote for the *Mises Review* (2008, on-line). "As if postmodernism were not enough, other types of thought also threaten the historian's effort to study the past for its own sake. Political theorists and ideologists of various stripes seek to subordinate history as it actually happened to their own ends. Wood's defense of objective history is salutary, and besides this, as one would expect from a historian of his eminence, he makes many illuminating remarks about concrete issues in American history."

Wood followed that book with *Empire of Liberty: A History of the Early Republic, 1789–1815* (2009). He told O'Neill, "The most meaningful insight I gained in writing *Empire of Liberty* was coming to realize the degree to which the Founders lived with illusions about the future, illusions involving the gradual disappearance of slavery, the saving of the native peoples, the nature of the economy, and so on. Of course, they did not know their future any better than we know ours, and we live with many illusions too, as future historians will surely point out. Good history gives us a tragic view of life, that is, not a pessimistic view, but a sense of the limitations of life, that not everything is possible, and few of us understand the situation we are in." In an enthusiastic notice for the *New York Times Book Review* (November 27, 2009, on-line), Jay Winik wrote, "Grand in scope and a landmark achievement of scholarship, *Empire of Liberty* is a tour de force, the culmination of a lifetime of brilliant thinking and writing."

Wood's most recent book, *The Idea of America: Reflections on the Birth of the United States* (2011)—a collection of 11 of his previously published essays, which have been substantially expanded and updated—has similarly been called the crowning achievement of his career. "What the book may sacrifice in overall unity it more than makes up for in the richness of its reflections on the character and import of the Founding. It is Mr. Wood's most 'personal' work, providing us, along with much fine history, glimpses into the thinker and the man," James W. Ceaser wrote for the *Wall Street Journal* (May 14, 2011, on-line). "The historian's role is the leitmotif that runs through this book. All history, Mr. Wood notes, is interpretation—indeed, how could it be anything else—if only because 'no single historian can know everything.' Yet the inevitable fact of interpretation does not provide a license, as postmoderns argue, to design 'narratives' as one likes, as if the past is the plaything for the writer to push an agenda or display his imagination. These creations, Mr. Wood is old-fashioned enough to remind us, are not as important or as interesting as real history itself. . . . In the end, as the corpus of Mr. Wood's works shows, 'the best apology is to tell the story exactly as it was.'"

Wood's other books include *Revolution and the Political Integration of the Enslaved and Disenfranchised* (1974), *Social Radicalism and Equality in the American Revolution* (1976), *The Making of the American Constitution* (1987), and *Monarchism and Republicanism in the Early United States* (2000). He has been the recipient of numerous fellowships from a variety of groups, including the Institute of Early American History, the National Endowment for the Humanities, the Guggenheim Foundation, and the Woodrow Wilson Center. Wood is a member of such prestigious organizations as the American Historical Society, the American Academy of Arts and Sciences, and the Society of American Historians. He sits on the board of advisers of the History Book Club and chairs the scholarly advisory committee of the National Constitution Center, among dozens of other such appointments.

Wood said to Bonnie K. Goodman, "Without a deep sense of history a person or a culture lacks perspective and wisdom. Despite the enormous number of history books that are published each year in the United States, most Americans do not seem to have a very deep sense of history. It might get in the way of our enthusiastic ebullience that we Americans can do anything." Wood struck a more serious note when he accepted the National Humanities Medal from President Barack Obama during a White House ceremony on March 2, 2011, saying, "After a half a century or more of studying history, I don't think there are any easy lessons that you come away with. I think it teaches one big lesson, which I would equate with wisdom—that things don't quite work out the way one intends, and that you have to be willing to accept the limitations of life." He added, "We don't teach history because we want to [create more] history teachers or history professors. We're teaching history because it enriches lives."

Wood and his wife, the former Louise Goss, who have been married since 1956, have three grown children: Christopher, Elizabeth, and Amy.

—M.R.

Suggested Reading: George Mason University History News Network (on-line) Apr. 2, 2006, Feb. 16, 2010; *Kirkus Reviews* (on-line) Nov. 15, 1991; *New York Times* (on-line) June 27, 2006, Mar. 1, 2010, July 22, 2011; *New York Times Book Review* (on-line) Mar. 1, 1992, Nov. 27, 2009; *Times Higher Education Supplement* (on-line) Dec. 19, 2003; *Virginian-Pilot* (on-line) May 26, 2002; *Washington Post* (on-line) June 6, 2004, May 28, 2006, Nov. 17, 2009

Selected Books: *Representation in the American Revolution*, 1969; *The Creation of the American Republic, 1776–1787*, 1969; *Revolution and the Political Integration of the Enslaved and Disfranchised*, 1974; *Social Radicalism and Equality in the American Revolution*, 1976; *The Making of the American Constitution*, 1987; *The Radicalism of the American Revolution*, 1992; *Monarchism and Republicanism in the Early United States*, 2000; *Revolutionary Characters: What Made the Founders Different*, 2006; *The Purpose of the Past: Reflections on the Uses of History*, 2008; *Empire of Liberty: A History of the Early Republic, 1789–1815*, 2009; *The Idea of America: Reflections on the Birth of the United States*, 2011

Marie Arana, courtesy of Jonathan Yardley

Yardley, Jonathan

Oct. 27, 1939– Literary critic; columnist; writer

Address: Home and office: 1500 Vermont Ave., N.W., #1, Washington, DC 20005

Since the summer of 1981, Jonathan Yardley has been a book critic for the *Washington Post Book World*. Though Yardley officially retired from the *Post* in 2006, he continues to write a weekly review for that newspaper. Among the most respected and widely read of book critics, Yardley is known for his scathing assessments of books he considers inferior or worse. In a 1998 critique, for example, Yardley described Kathryn Harrison's memoir *The Kiss*—which received favorable notices in the *New York Times* and the *Boston Globe*, among other publications—as "slimy, repellent, meretricious," and "cynical," adding, "The temptation to go on and on about this book, piling one abusive paragraph upon another, is extreme, but must be resisted. Space is short in this newspaper." Yardley has also denigrated works by such venerated authors as the Nobel Prize winner John Steinbeck, whom he once dismissed as a "plodding, graceless prose stylist." One of Yardley's pet peeves, he told Ken Adelman for the *Washingtonian* (January 2007), is "banal language [used] in bad ways—committing the twin sins of pretentiousness and wordiness. When you go to a concert and see someone sit down to play the piano, you assume he knows how to play. Likewise with someone who's written a book—you assume he knows how to write. Yet many don't." Some of Yardley's laudatory notices have been credited with boosting the careers of fledgling writers, among them Anne Tyler, Michael Chabon, and Edward P. Jones. "When Jonathan recommends a book with great enthusiasm, it's a rare event, and I often pick it up," Donald E. Graham, the Washington Post Co.'s head, told a *Washingtonian* (March 1998) reporter. Yardley has disputed the claim that his reviews lead people to seek out or avoid particular books. "I may influence a reader a bit, but I can't make anyone read a book," he told Ken Adelman. "I have an utterly unquantifiable degree of influence. It's probably pretty small. The bestseller list would look mighty different if I had anywhere near the influence people think I have."

Earlier in his career Yardley was a journalist and book reviewer for the *New York Times*; the Greensboro, North Carolina, *Daily News*; the *Miami (Florida) Herald*; and the *Washington Star*. In 1981 he won a Pulitzer Prize for his reviews. Yardley has written biographies of the writers Ring Lardner and Fred Exley, and he edited a posthumous professional memoir by H. L. Mencken. He has also published two collections of his columns—*Out of Step: Notes from a Purple Decade* (1991) and *Monday Morning Quarterback* (1998); *Our Kind of People: The Story of an American Family* (1989), about his parents; and a memoir, *States of Mind* (1993).

Yardley was born on October 27, 1939 in Pittsburgh, Pennsylvania, to William Woolsey Yardley and the former Helen Gregory. Ancestors of his settled in America in the 17th century. His father taught English and classics at private day schools before he became an Episcopal minister and, in 1971, the rector at Chatham Hall, a private secondary school for girls in Virginia. His mother was a member of Bennington College's first graduating class. As a child Yardley envisioned a career in hands-on journalism. He won a scholarship to the Groton School, a prestigious Massachusetts preparatory school, where he was often reprimanded for his defiant attitude. As an undergraduate at the University of North Carolina at Chapel Hill, he edited the school's newspaper, the *Daily Tar Heel*. He enjoyed that job greatly, and for about a year he wrote nearly all of the paper's editorials. He earned an A.B. degree in 1961.

That summer the newly married Yardley was a journalism intern in the *New York Times*'s Washington, D.C., bureau, under its chief, James Reston, who wrote a *Times* column as well. "As much as I admired and even venerated [Reston]," Yardley wrote, "I found that I wasn't cut out to emulate his reportorial example." Yardley was soon transferred to the *Times*'s New York City offices, where, among other assignments, he wrote news analyses for the paper's "News of the Week in Review" section. After three years, convinced that his career prospects at the *Times* were limited, he took a job as an editorial writer for the Greensboro, North Carolina, *Daily News* (now known as the *News & Record*). During the next 10 years, he also became the paper's book-review editor.

In 1968 Yardley was among 12 American journalists awarded Nieman Fellowships to attend Harvard University for one academic year. At Harvard he turned his attention to literature. After his return to Greensboro, in 1969, he began to devote a lot of time to writing book reviews; by the early 1970s his reviews had begun to appear in national publications. In 1974 he accepted a full-time position as the book-review editor at the *Miami Herald*. He edited the paper's weekly "Viewpoint" section as well as its book page.

During that time Yardley wrote his first book, *Ring: A Biography of Ring Lardner* (1977), about the tumultuous life of that sports columnist and short-story writer (1885–1933). In a review of *Ring*

for *Newsweek* (August 22, 1977), Raymond Sokolov criticized Yardley for praising Lardner's writing excessively, but he concluded, "On most occasions, . . . Yardley holds on to his senses and is admirably ready to call chaff chaff. The result is a useful record of a minor master's rapid rise . . . and of his equally rapid demise, wrecked by booze, struggling still to write for money, consumed by disease."

In 1978 Yardley left the *Miami Herald* to edit and write for the book-review section of the *Washington Star*, which Time Inc. had bought that February. In 1981 he won the Pulitzer Prize for his reviews of works of fiction and nonfiction, and he chaired the Pulitzer Prize jury that selected John Kennedy Toole's posthumously published novel *A Confederacy of Dunces* as that year's fiction winner.

Later in 1981, after publication of the *Star* ended, Yardley joined the staff of the *Washington Post Book World*, the *Washington Post*'s weekly standalone book-review section; he also became a weekly columnist for the *Post*'s "Style" section. Along with the *New York Times Book Review*, *Book World* was one of only a few such sections in American newspapers. While the *Post*'s other full-time book critic, Michael Dirda, viewed his job as "a form of literary entertainment," as Paul Starobin wrote for the *Washingtonian* (March 1998), Yardley declared that his "first obligation is to treat books as news. I've spent my life being a journalist, not a literary intellectual." Yardley quickly earned a reputation as a harsh critic. Indeed, he has expressed a preference for penning merciless judgments. "Some reviewers—of books, music, movies, whatever—write only positive notices; that undermines their credibility," he told Ken Adelman. "Yet attack seems more fun than praise. The very vocabulary of attack is more varied and interesting"—in other words, more entertaining. "'Wonderful,' 'extraordinary,' 'exceptional,' 'accomplished'—blah, blah, blah. You get bored fast. Readers don't get bored with adept attacks."

Yardley's book *Our Kind of People: The Story of an American Family* (1989) is an account of his parents' 50-year marriage. Yardley based the book on his father's voluminous correspondence and other family papers. He depicted his father as a "stickler for manners, a man immensely proud of his WASP heritage" and as "both admirable, pitiable, and laughable at times," according to Felicia Gressette's *Miami Herald* (March 12, 1989) review of the book. Although he devoted much less space to his mother, who had written far fewer letters than her husband, she came across "as the most real and lovable person in the book," Gressette wrote. Echoing some other critics, Gressette expressed the opinion that *Our Kind of People* "is most appealing to a non-Yardley in the passages that describe [the couple's] courtship and early days of marriage and assess their long relationship and reactions and capitulations to change. Alas, those finely drawn sections are sandwiched between long, dull pages of family history and minutiae."

Yardley edited a memoir by H. L. Mencken (1880–1956)—a writer and critic known for his elitism, satirical wit, and brutal honesty—from a huge manuscript that Mencken left unfinished when he died. Edited by Yardley to half its original length, it was published as *My Life as Author and Editor* (1993). Tom Wicker, a longtime *New York Times* political reporter and columnist and a novelist as well, wrote for the *Washington Monthly* (January 1, 1993), "*My Life as Author and Editor* is a memorable portrait of a time, several places, and many people—most particularly the brilliant writer, backyard bricklayer, consoling friend, ardent defender, lusty battler, frequent roisterer, perceptive editor, shrewd observer, and cranky soul that was H. L. Mencken." In an assessment for the *New York Times Book Review* (January 31, 1993), Terry Teachout wrote, "Yardley . . . has turned a massive document of interest mainly to scholars into a rich, absorbing memoir that anyone who cares about modern American literature will want to read." In his next book, *States of Mind: A Personal Journey Through the Mid-Atlantic* (1993), Yardley described his efforts to link his identity with the places where he had lived, most of them in the loosely delineated region known as the mid-Atlantic states.

Yardley's *Misfit: The Strange Life of Frederick Exley* (1997) is about the troubled mid-century American writer best known for his first book, *A Fan's Notes* (1968). Yardley first read *A Fan's Notes* when he was studying at Harvard. The novel traces the life of the narrator (a thinly disguised Exley) beginning with his childhood in Watertown, New York, where he grew up in the shadow of his athletically talented father; it describes his college years at the University of Southern California, his failed marriage, several periods spent in psychiatric institutions, his unsatisfying jobs, his drinking problem, and his obsession with the New York Giants football team. The book's title stemmed from Exley's realization that he was destined to be a spectator in life as well as sports. Like many others, Yardley loved the book, and he wrote a favorable review of the paperback edition. In 1974 he wrote a second glowing assessment, for the *New Republic*. Around that time Yardley received the first of many late-night phone calls from Exley, who usually sounded severely intoxicated. Though Yardley and Exley never met, they developed a friendship through phone calls and letters that lasted until Exley's death, in 1992. Yardley was one of many reviewers who tried to encourage Exley to stop drinking and focus on his writing. Exley's other novels, *Pages from a Cold Island* (1975) and *Last Notes from Home* (1988), drew far less admiration than *A Fan's Notes*.

Yardley told Bobby Maddex for *Gadfly Online* (May 1998), "I made some decisions about what I was going to do with that book—mainly keeping it short and almost impressionistic—which some

people just didn't like. They wanted a laundry list and I wasn't going to give them that." Marc Carnegie, who reviewed *Misfit* for the *American Spectator* (October 1997), found the book wanting: "For Yardley's obvious affection and admiration, . . . *Misfit* never gets at the essence of its immensely gifted and complicated subject. Instead he delivers an unsatisfying mix of incomplete research and some dubious literary criticism." By contrast, Jeff Turrentine, in a review for *Forbes* (September 22, 1997), described the book as "a respectful, very fine biography that fills in the many gaps in the story of Frederick Exley, the writer, and makes the story of Frederick Exley, the character, even more meaningful."

In 2002 the *Washington Post* stopped running Yardley's regular column of social, literary, and cultural commentary in its "Style" section. Subsequently, occasional pieces by him appeared in that section, in particular in the popular "Second Readings" series, in which Yardley reconsidered "notable or neglected" previously published books. He earned attention for several of them, including his harsh critique of J. D. Salinger's celebrated coming-of-age novel *The Catcher in the Rye* (1951). In his October 19, 2004 column, Yardley admitted that when he read the book as an adolescent, he considered Holden Caulfield, the book's 16-year-old narrator, to be a "kindred spirit." Rereading the book as an adult, however, "was almost literally a painful experience: The combination of Salinger's execrable prose and Caulfield's jeune narcissism produced effects comparable to mainlining castor oil." At the other end of the critical spectrum, in his January 2, 2007 reassessment of *The Great Gatsby* (1925), F. Scott Fitzgerald's classic critique of the American dream, Yardley called the book "the American masterwork, the finest work of fiction by any of this country's writers." A collection of Yardley's "Second Reading" columns is scheduled to be published in June 2011.

Yardley has named among his favorite writers William Faulkner, C. S. Forester, Peter Taylor, and Flannery O'Connor. *Invisible Man*, by Ralph Ellison, is among his favorite novels. He has cited T. Coraghessan Boyle, Richard Ford, and Annie Proulx as writers whom he considers to be overrated.

Since he retired from the *Post*, in 2006, Yardley has continued to contribute book reviews and other essays to the paper. His reviews from late 2010 include those for *A Voice from Old New York*, by Louis Auchincloss, and former president George W. Bush's memoir, *Decision Points*, which Yardley called "competent, readable, and flat." On February 15, 2009, after 38 years, the *Post* ended publication of *Book World*, shifting the book reviews to what is now called the "Style and Arts" section and another section, called "Outlook." *Book World* exists only on the paper's Web site, except for the rare occasions in which it appears in a separate print section.

Yardley's first marriage (1961–75), to Rosemary Roberts, ended in divorce. From it Yardley has two grown sons, James (called Jim) and William (called Bill), both of whom are journalists. Jim, the *New York Times*'s New Delhi, India, bureau chief, won a Pulitzer Prize for international reporting in 2006; he and his father are one of only two Pulitzer Prize–winning father-and-son pairs. (The other pair is Malcolm Johnson and his son, Haynes Johnson.) Bill is the *New York Times*'s Seattle, Washington, bureau chief. Yardley's second marriage (1975–98), to Susan L. Hartt, also ended in divorce. Since 1999 he has been married to Marie Arana, an award-winning former editor of the *Washington Post Book World* and currently a *Post* writer-at-large. Arana has written two novels and two works of nonfiction, including a memoir; she edited *The Writing Life: Writers on How They Think and Work: A Collection from the Washington Post Book World* (2003). Yardley and Arana live in the Logan Circle neighborhood of Washington and maintain an apartment in Lima, Peru, Arana's hometown.

Yardley has two stepchildren and several grandchildren.

—M.R.M.

Suggested Reading: *Forbes* Books p205 Sep. 22, 1997; *Gadfly Online* May 1998; *Miami Herald* C p7 Mar. 12, 1989; (Washington, D.C.) *American* p24+ Sep. 1, 2008; *Washington Monthly* p53+ Jan. 1, 1993; *Washington Post* (on-line) Oct. 19, 2004, Jan. 2, 2007; *Washingtonian* p64 Mar. 1998, p35+ Jan. 2007

Selected Books: *Ring: A Biography of Ring Lardner*, 1977; *Our Kind of People: The Story of an American Family*, 1989; *Out of Step: Notes from a Purple Decade*, 1991; *States of Mind: A Personal Journey Through the Mid-Atlantic*, 1993; *Misfit: The Strange Life of Frederick Exley*, 1997; *Monday Morning Quarterback*, 1998; as editor–Mencken, H. L. *My Life as Author and Editor*, 1993; Lardner, Ring. *Selected Stories*, 1997

Yates, David

1963– Film and television director

Address: c/o Casarotto Ramsay & Associates Ltd., Waverley House, 7–12 Noel St., London W1F 8GQ, England

When David Yates was first approached about directing *Harry Potter and the Order of the Phoenix* (2007), the fifth installment of the *Harry Potter* film series, he thought, as he wrote in an article for *Total Film* (August 2009), "Why would I want to do that? Somebody has already created that world." That world—a magical realm of teen wizards, dragons, and games played on airborne broomsticks—was created by J. K. Rowling, the uber-successful British author of the wildly popular book series. Despite having never read a word of the *Potter* books, and having only one feature film to his credit, *The Tichborne Claimant* (1998), Yates was handpicked by the *Harry Potter* producer David Heyman for his adeptness in directing young actors and for his critically acclaimed work for British television: projects including the 2003 BBC television miniseries *State of Play* and the 2004 BAFTA Award–winning two-part television drama *Sex Traffic*. Captivated by Rowling's characters and drawn to their world of wizardry, Yates ultimately decided to take on the career-changing assignment and made a smooth transition from television to the silver screen. Following in the tradition established by his predecessors in the series, Chris Columbus (who directed the first two installments), Alfonso Cuaron, and Mike Newell, Yates gave a distinctive style and look to *Harry Potter and the Order of the Phoenix*, which became a crit-

Stephen Lovekin/Getty Images

ical and commercial hit; grossing $938 million worldwide, it was the most successful major feature-film debut of all time. Yates has gone on to direct *Harry Potter and the Half-Blood Prince* (2009), *Harry Potter and the Deathly Hallows: Part 1* (2010), and *Harry Potter and the Deathly Hallows: Part 2*, which is scheduled to be released on July 15, 2011. He is the only filmmaker to helm more than two *Harry Potter* movies and is considered the preeminent director of the franchise, which has become the highest-grossing film series of all time, with more than $6 billion in worldwide box-office receipts. (The *Harry Potter* brand—books, films, and merchandise—has brought in an estimated $24 billion.) Yates, who spent six consecutive years working on the production of the four films, said of the *Harry Potter* franchise to Bob Thompson for the *Calgary (Canada) Herald* (November 19, 2010), "It's a bit like a national treasure now, and I am one of the curators."

David Yates was born in 1963 in St. Helens, a town in the Merseyside region of northwest England. He developed a passion for film at an early age and became fascinated with the works of such directors as David Lean, Ken Loach, Martin Scorsese, and Steven Spielberg. Yates has cited Spielberg's blockbuster film *Jaws* (1975) and Christian Nyby's science-fiction film *The Thing from Another World* (1951) as being two of his favorite movies while he was growing up. He reportedly saw *Jaws* 35 times, attempting to absorb its many elements and effects, from the story and characters to the reactions of the audience. At the age of 14, he started making films of his own with a camera his mother gave him; he often shot shorts with his brother, Andrew, in local parks.

Yates studied politics, English literature, and sociology at St. Helens College, in Merseyside. He also studied politics at the University of Essex and at Georgetown University, in Washington, D.C. While living in Swindon, a town in southwest England, in the late 1980s, Yates worked as a freelancer for the media-arts company Create Studios (usually written as Cre8 Studios), which helped him develop his first film project. In 1988 he produced, wrote, and directed the short film *When I Was a Girl*, which told the story of a young English girl coming of age after World War II. Shot in Swindon with a cast of local nonprofessionals and funded with a grant from Thamesdown Media Arts, the film was screened at festivals around the world. It won the award for best European short film at the Cork International Film Festival in Ireland and a Golden Gate Award at the San Francisco Film Festival. Those honors helped Yates win admittance to the National Film and Television School, in Beaconsfield, England, where he began studying in its directing program. While there he directed two shorts for British television: the 30-minute *The Weaver's Wife* (1991), about a young peasant girl living in rural Wiltshire in the late 16th century; and *Oranges and Lemons* (1991), a BBC drama about a Nigerian girl whose perceptions of England change after she takes a job at the Tower of London. Yates's graduation film, a 30-minute comedy titled *Good Looks* (1992), took home a Silver Hugo Award at the Chicago International Film Festival.

After graduating from the National Film and Television School, in 1992, Yates continued to work in British television. In 1994 he directed an installment of the award-winning documentary series *Moving Pictures*, which gave an in-depth look into the global film industry. The segment, "Low Budget," examined England's low-budget cinema

culture. Later that year Yates signed on for *The Bill*, a series that chronicled the lives of uniformed officers and detectives working in a London police precinct. He directed five episodes of the series, in 1994 and 1995. Yates then directed the three-part documentary series *Tale of Three Seaside Towns* (1995) and the 10-minute dramatic film *Punch* (1996) before making his feature-film debut, in 1998, with the independent drama *The Tichborne Claimant*. Shot on location in Merseyside and on the Isle of Man and based on a true story, the film starred Robert Pugh as the man who assumed the identity of a wealthy 19th-century English nobleman, Sir Roger Charles Tichborne, after the real Tichborne perished at sea. *The Tichborne Claimant* received an Emden Film Award nomination at the 1999 Emden International Film Festival, in Germany.

In 2000 Yates returned to television to direct three episodes of the seven-part BBC dramatic miniseries *The Sins*, about a reformed getaway-car driver (played by Pete Postlethwaite) tempted to commit the seven deadly sins. *The Sins* received British Academy of Film and Television Arts (BAFTA) Award nominations for best actor, best actress (Geraldine James), and best drama. Yates then helmed another BBC miniseries, *The Way We Live Now* (2001), a four-part adaptation of Anthony Trollope's 1875 novel of the same name. The miniseries starred David Suchet, Matthew Macfadyen, Shirley Henderson, and Cillian Murphy and captured the prize for best drama serial at the 2002 BAFTA Awards ceremony. Yates found himself back at the BAFTA ceremony the following year with a nomination for the 15-minute film *Rank* (2002), which investigated racial and cultural tensions in Scotland through the interactions between a street gang and a group of Somali refugees living in Glasgow.

In 2003 Yates directed BBC One's six-part miniseries *State of Play*, a political thriller, set in London, that centers on the downfall of a politician after a newspaper investigates a series of murders connected to him. Written by Paul Abbott and starring David Morrissey, John Simm, Kelly Macdonald, Polly Walker, Bill Nighy, and James McAvoy, the serial received widespread critical praise and won several honors, including a BAFTA nomination for best drama serial, the Broadcasting Press Guild Award, the Royal Television Society (RTS) Award, the Banff Television Festival's Rockie Award for best miniseries, and a Cologne Conference Award for best fiction program. It also marked a breakthrough for Yates, who was recognized for his taut direction and suspenseful pacing. He received a BAFTA Award nomination for directing and won the Directors Guild of Great Britain (DGGB) Award for outstanding directorial achievement. *State of Play* was later adapted by Hollywood for a 2009 political thriller of the same name, starring Russell Crowe, Ben Affleck, and Rachel McAdams.

The success of *State of Play* raised Yates's profile as a director and opened doors to other high-profile projects. After directing the made-for-television movie *The Young Visiters* (2003), adapted from Daisy Ashford's 1919 novella of the same name, he helmed the two-part British-Canadian television production *Sex Traffic* (2004). Starring Wendy Crewson, John Simm, and Anamaria Marinca, the film, in which two women are forced into prostitution in the Balkans, looks at the vast network of forces behind the vicious global sex trade. *Sex Traffic* was universally hailed by critics and won eight BAFTA Awards, including the honor for best drama serial. Yates was also recognized, winning a Gemini Award for best direction in a dramatic program or miniseries and earning his second DGGB Award nomination. "David is a fantastic actors' director," the producer David Heyman told Stuart Jeffries for the London *Guardian* (July 2, 2007), adding that he "has shown he can handle political subject matter in an entertaining way." Yates followed up *Sex Traffic* with the acclaimed 2005 made-for-television movie *The Girl in the Café*, a romantic comedy scripted by Richard Curtis and starring Bill Nighy and Kelly Macdonald. The film, about a civil servant (Nighy) who falls in love with a mysterious young woman (Macdonald) after meeting her in a London café, was broadcast simultaneously on the BBC in England and on the Home Box Office (HBO) network in the U.S. *The Girl in the Café* earned three Emmy Awards, including the prize for outstanding made-for-television movie. Yates earned an Emmy nomination for outstanding director of a miniseries. Asked by Jeffries why he had worked for the most part in television rather than film, Yates replied, "Because I get rubbish [film] scripts. Why would I want to direct rubbish films when I could work on a perfectly paced thriller . . . even if it is for telly?"

Mike Newell, who directed *Harry Potter and the Goblet of Fire*, the fourth installment in the series, decided not to take on any of the subsequent *Potter* films, due to the amount of work involved. Yates was among a handful of directors, who also included Jean-Pierre Jeunet (who directed the 2001 hit romantic comedy *Amélie*), Matthew Vaughn, and Mira Nair, considered to direct *Harry Potter and the Order of the Phoenix* (2007). Despite Yates's having no major feature-film credits to his name and having never read any of the *Harry Potter* books, the franchise's longtime producer, David Heyman, chose him. "You see a director with a real strong point of view," Heyman said of Yates, as quoted on the *Gryffindor Gazette* (April 11, 2007), a Harry Potter blog. "A really idiosyncratic sensibility. He is someone who . . . grounds things. He makes everything seem very real and authentic." He added that those directorial qualities were "very important" for *Harry Potter and the Order of the Phoenix*. Yates initially balked at the opportunity, but after making what he described in *Total Film* as the "worst pitch in history," he was offered and accepted the assignment, immersing himself in the *Potter* world. He explained to Harry Haun for *Film Journal International* (July 1, 2007), "I read the fifth book first, then I went back and read the others, and it was really interesting. I fell in love quite quickly because the characters are great." Referring to the premise of the *Potter* films, whose school-age main characters study wizardry, he added, "Education is a universal experience."

Filmed over a period of eight months on a budget of roughly $200 million, *Harry Potter and the Order of the Phoenix* was released on July 11, 2007. The film continues the escapades of Harry Potter (played by Daniel Radcliffe) and his two best friends, Ron Weasley (Rupert Grint) and Hermione Granger (Emma Watson), as they enter their fifth year at Hogwarts School of Witchcraft and Wizardry. The story centers on a warning issued by Harry about the return of the evil Lord Voldemort (Ralph Fiennes). Harry comes in contact with a secret society of wizards, known as the Order of the Phoenix, founded by Albus Dumbledore (Michael Gambon), the head of Hogwarts and Harry's confidant; the wizards reveal to Harry Voldemort's true intentions. Meanwhile, the authoritarian, abusive Dolores Umbridge (Imelda Staunton) is hired at Hogwarts by the Ministry of Magic to undermine Harry's power and influence. Though *Order of the Phoenix* is the series' longest book, at 896 pages, Yates made it into a 138-minute film, the shortest in the franchise. Like his *Potter* predecessors, he brought his own visual flair to the film—making careful use, for example, of light and dark to illustrate Harry's emotional transformation over the course of the story. Yates, who found inspiration in George Lucas's seminal 1973 coming-of-age film, *American Graffiti*, explained to Stuart Jeffries that *Order of the Phoenix* "is really a story about growing up into an adult world riven between good and evil" and is "about teenage rebellion."

While the comparative brevity of *Harry Potter and the Order of the Phoenix* initially generated a negative response from the series' fan base, the film was ultimately well received by critics. A. O. Scott, in a review for the *New York Times* (July 10, 2007), called the *Order of the Phoenix* "a tense and twisty political thriller, with clandestine meetings, bureaucratic skullduggery and intimations of conspiracy hanging in the air." Charles Frederick, making note of the film's dark qualities and political undertones, observed in a review for the London *Daily Telegraph* (June 29, 2007, on-line), "Harry is no longer just fighting off monsters in impressive set battles. He is fighting fear of failure and inner demons that wreck his peace of mind." Commenting on Yates's contribution to the film, the actor Daniel Radcliffe explained to Rob Carnevale, in an interview for indielondon.co.uk, "What David managed to do, which is fantastic, is that he took the charm of the films that Chris [Columbus] made and the visual flair of everything that Alfonso [Cuaron] did and the thoroughly British, bombastic nature of the film directed [by] Mike Newell and he's added his own sense of grit and realism to it that perhaps wasn't there so much before." Yates wrote for *Total Film* about his approach to directing, "It's about respecting and encouraging people; it's about the quality of the work. . . . Everything I've made has been run along this same ideology: to inspire work out of people rather than shout it out of them."

Like the *Potter* series' four previous film adaptations, *Harry Potter and the Order of the Phoenix* was a juggernaut at the box office, earning $333 million the week it opened and raking in $938 million in worldwide box-office receipts. (It is currently ranked 11th among the highest-grossing films of all time; the first five *Harry Potter* films together earned $4.5 billion at the box office.) Yates earned best-director honors at the 2008 Empire Awards, and the film won the People's Choice Award for best European film at the 2008 European Film Awards, presented by the European Film Academy. Yates said to Terry Lawson for the *Detroit Free Press* (July 8, 2007) about directing *Potter* films, "It is very hard work simply because there is so much going on in the stories and so many characters to be attended to. But once you do get involved, you are made confident by the fact that everyone else has been doing this for a long, long time and has gotten very good at it." Yates signed on to direct the final three *Harry Potter* films, making for an experience that he described to Bob Thompson as being "like running four marathons in a row." (From pre- to post-production, Yates spent a total of six consecutive years working on the four films.)

The series' sixth installment, *Harry Potter and the Half-Blood Prince*, was released in July 2009 and, like its predecessors, was a massive commercial success. The film, in which Harry discovers a book belonging to a mysterious entity known as the Half-Blood Prince, earned an Academy Award nomination for its cinematography (provided by the Frenchman Bruno Delbonnel, who served as *Amélie*'s cinematographer) and BAFTA Award nominations for best production design and best special visual effects. It also received positive reviews from critics, most of whom pointed out its dark themes and stunning visuals.

For the series' seventh and final installment, *Harry Potter and the Deathly Hallows*, Yates opted to split the story into two parts. Commenting on the decision, he explained to a writer for the *Toronto Star* (November 19, 2010), "We all sat down and agreed it was probably an interesting, cool thing to do. . . . I wanted to make two slightly different films: a kind of melancholy, haunting first film—like a chase through a road movie, something where you see these kids in their innocence breaking—and then I wanted to make the big old classic fantasy film with dragons." *Harry Potter and the Deathly Hallows: Part 1* was released on November 19, 2010 to both critical acclaim and commercial success; thus far, the film has brought in $947 million at the box office worldwide, making it the 10th-highest-grossing film of all time. *Harry Potter and the Deathly Hallows: Part 2* is scheduled to open in U.S. theaters on July 15, 2011 in 3D.

"Mild-mannered," "soft-spoken," "quiet," and "unassuming" are among the adjectives that have been used to describe Yates. He is married to Yvonne Walcott, an aunt of Theo Walcott, a professional soccer player for the Arsenal Football Club in the English Premier League. Yates is currently developing a historical war drama, "St. Nazaire," for David Heyman's production company, Heyday Films. The director said of the *Potter* series to a writer for the Ontario, Canada, *Carleton Place* (July 16, 2009), "These films are bigger than anyone— they're bigger than the producer, they're bigger than the writer. And I'm totally cool about that."

—C.C.

Suggested Reading: *Baltimore Sun* C p1 Apr. 30, 2009; *Detroit Free Press* p1 July 8, 2007; *Film Journal International* p14+ July 1, 2007; (London) *Guardian* p23 July 2, 2007; (London) *Observer* p24+ June 21, 2009; (London) *Sunday Times* p34+ Feb. 4, 2007; *Toronto (Canada) Star* E p4 Nov. 19, 2010; *Total Film* (on-line) Aug. 2009

Selected Films: *The Tichborne Claimant*, 1998; *Harry Potter and the Order of the Phoenix*, 2007; *Harry Potter and the Half-Blood Prince*, 2009; *Harry Potter and the Deathly Hallows: Part 1*, 2010; *Harry Potter and the Deathly Hallows: Part 2*, 2011

Selected Television Shows: *The Bill*, 1994–95; *The Sins*, 2000; *The Way We Live Now*, 2001; *State of Play*, 2003; *The Young Visiters*, 2003; *Sex Traffic*, 2004; *The Girl in the Cafe*, 2005

Obituaries

ALDREDGE, THEONI V. Aug. 22, 1922–Jan. 21, 2011 Costume designer. Theoni V. Aldredge created the costumes for more than 300 stage and film productions and won an Oscar for her lavish period costumes for the 1974 film *The Great Gatsby*. She also won three Tony Awards for costume design, for the Broadway plays *Annie* (1977), *Barnum* (1980), and *La Cage aux Folles* (1983). In 1984 more than 1,000 of Aldredge's designs appeared simultaneously on Broadway in five musical hits: *A Chorus Line*, *Dreamgirls*, *La Cage aux Folles*, *The Rink*, and *42nd Street*. She also served for more than 20 years as the principal designer for Joseph Papp and his New York Shakespeare Festival. Aldredge was born Theoni Athanasiou Vachliotis in Salonika, a seaport in Macedonia, in northeastern Greece. A year after her birth, she and her family moved to Athens. Her mother, Meropi (Gregoriades) Vachliotis, died when Theoni was a small child, and she and her three brothers were raised by their father, Athanasios V. Vachliotis, then the surgeon general of the Greek Army and a member of the nation's Parliament. During her childhood she learned to sew and embroider, and she especially enjoyed dressing her dolls. Aldredge attended the American School in Athens. Rejecting her father's suggestion that she remain in Greece for training in costume design and determined to continue her education in the U.S., in around 1949 she gained admittance to the Goodman School of Drama, then a division of the Art Institute of Chicago. In 1950 Aldredge made her debut as a costume designer when she created the apparel for the comedy *The Distaff Side* at the Goodman Theatre. She later served as a member of the theater's design staff and taught costume design at the theater's school. At Goodman she befriended the actress Geraldine Page, who, after being cast in the 1959 world premiere of the Tennessee Williams play *Sweet Bird of Youth*, persuaded the play's director, Elia Kazan, to hire Aldredge to design the wardrobe. That marked Aldredge's Broadway debut, and she soon found herself in great demand. In 1960 Aldredge designed costumes for Joseph Papp's adaptation of Shakespeare's *Measure for Measure*. Impressed with her work in that and other shows, Papp asked Aldredge to join his New York Shakespeare Festival. Aldredge became the company's head designer, creating costumes for some 80 productions over the next two decades. Among them were the musical comedy *I Can Get It for You Wholesale* (1962), which David Merrick produced and in which Barbra Streisand made her Broadway debut; Edward Albee's searing drama *Who's Afraid of Virginia Woolf?* (1962); *Luv* (1964), a comedy in which Mike Nichols directed Alan Arkin, Eli Wallach, and Anne Jackson; *Cactus Flower* (1965), a romantic comedy that starred Lauren Bacall and Barry Nelson; *A Delicate Balance* (1966), a Pulitzer Prize–winning drama by Edward Albee; and *Hair* (1968), a musical about the

hippie counterculture, which Papp produced at the Public Theater and which later moved to Broadway. Aldredge also designed the costumes for what was to become—at that time—the longest-running show in the history of Broadway: *A Chorus Line*, which premiered in 1975. Created and directed by Michael Bennett, *A Chorus Line* portrays an audition for a Broadway musical. For the show's exuberant closing number, in which the dancers perform in top hats and tuxedos, Aldredge convinced Bennett that fabric the color of champagne would better convey a feeling of celebration than would red fabric, which he had originally wanted. Aldredge won a Theatre World Award in 1976 for the play's costumes. In addition to *The Great Gatsby* (1974), for which Aldredge collaborated with Ralph Lauren to design hundreds of costumes in under 10 days, films in which her creations appear include *Network* (1977), *The Eyes of Laura Mars* (1978), *Ghostbusters* (1984), *Moonstruck* (1987), *Other People's Money* (1991), *Addams Family Values* (1993), *The Mirror Has Two Faces* (1996), and *The First Wives Club* (1996). Aldredge also designed costumes for ballet and opera, and in the 1980s she created a line of ready-to-wear clothing, commissioned by the actress Jane Fonda, called Jane Fonda Workouts. Her most recent work was designing the costumes for a 2006 revival of *A Chorus Line*. Aldredge died of cardiac arrest in Stamford, Connecticut. She is survived by her husband since 1953, Tom Aldredge, a successful stage actor who currently appears in the HBO series *Boardwalk Empire*. See *Current Biography* (1994). —W.D.

Obituary *New York Times* (on-line) Jan. 21, 2011

ALIA, RAMIZ Oct. 18, 1925–Oct. 7, 2011 Albanian politician. Ramiz Alia (rah-MEEZ uh-LEE-yah) made tentative strides toward democracy during his tenure as Albania's leader, which lasted from 1985, when he took over after the death of the Communist dictator Enver Hoxha, until 1992, when his government toppled in the wake of the collapse of Communism in the Soviet Union and Eastern Europe. Alia was born to a Muslim family of the Gheg ethnic group. Some sources list his birthplace as Shkoder, a city in northern Albania. He attended a French lycée in Tirana, and in 1939, when Italy occupied and annexed Albania, he joined the Albanian Fascist Youth League. During World War II he joined the Communist-led resistance, serving with the Seventh Shock Brigade of the National Liberation Army commanded by Hoxha, which harassed Nazi forces in Albania and Yugoslavia. By the time he was 19, Alia had risen to the rank of lieutenant colonel and political commissar of the army's Fifth Division. Consolidating his power in a Communist government closely allied with the Soviet Union, Hoxha proclaimed the founding of the People's Republic of Albania on January 11, 1946. Two years later Alia was elected to the Central Committee of the nation's Communist

Party and was appointed the leader of the Union of Working Youth. He also worked briefly on the party's propaganda staff. In 1955 Alia was appointed minister of education in the Hoxha government. Alia left the Education Ministry to join the ideological staff of the Central Committee in 1958, at a time when Albanian-Soviet relations were deteriorating. He took part in the deliberations that led in 1961 to the country's final rupture with the Soviet Union and a shift in allegiance to the People's Republic of China. In a purge of the pro-Soviet members of the Secretariat in 1960, Alia was named one of the national party secretaries under First Secretary Hoxha. In Hoxha's unrelievedly oppressive regime, Alia emerged as one of his most trusted advisers and aides. Robert D. McFadden wrote for the *New York Times* (October 7, 2011, on-line), "Alia had carried out many of the crackdowns, purges and executions ordered by Mr. Hoxha—resorting even to the Stalinist horrors of burying enemies alive—over decades of repression and Albanian isolation from the outside world." Alia was elected chairman of the Presidium of the People's Assembly, the official head of state, in November 1982. The following year he began filling in for the ailing Hoxha at official functions, and in the summer of 1984 he delivered a series of speeches around the country, a provincial tour that had been a Hoxha trademark. On April 13, 1985, two days after Hoxha's death, the 11th plenum of the Albanian Workers' Party Central Committee elected Alia to succeed him as first secretary. At first it appeared that Alia would faithfully adhere to Hoxha's policies. In a fervent eulogy to his mentor, Alia declared, as reported in the *Christian Science Monitor* (April 17, 1985), "The country and people swear to comrade Enver that they will always preserve and keep Albania as it is." It was not until the prodemocracy movement was well underway in Eastern Europe in 1989 that Alia began to call for concrete change, "granting amnesty to political prisoners, allowing multiparty elections and promising other democratic reforms—a complete about-face from his years as the provost of repression, censorship and internal controls," as McFadden wrote. Despite those halting steps, Albania's Communist regime, which was the last remaining in Europe, fell apart in 1991. Alia resigned as head of the coalition government the following year. In 1994 he was convicted of corruption and sentenced to several years in prison. He was released on appeal after only a year but was soon arrested once more, on the more serious charge of genocide. In 1997, while he was in prison awaiting trial, widespread political and economic unrest broke out in Albania, and in the ensuing chaos, Alia and his fellow prisoners were abandoned by their guards and escaped. (Later in the year the prosecutor general dropped genocide charges against him.) Reports surfaced that Alia was living in Greece or Sweden, but his actual whereabouts remained unknown. His death, at the age of 85, was announced by the Albanian government, but no other details were released. Alia was predeceased in 1986 by his wife of more than three decades, Semiramis Xhuvani. He is survived by his children: Xana, Besa, and Arben. See *Current Biography* (1991). —M.R.

Obituary *New York Times* (on-line) Oct. 7, 2011

ANDERSON, SPARKY Feb. 22, 1934–Nov. 4, 2010

Baseball manager. As manager of the Cincinnati Reds for several seasons in the 1970s, George "Sparky" Anderson led the team known as the "Big Red Machine" to four National League pennants and two World Series titles. He later managed the Detroit Tigers, leading them to a 1984 World Series title and becoming the first manager to win World Series championships in both the National and American Leagues. The son of a house painter, George Lee Anderson was born in Bridgewater, South Dakota. He grew up in Los Angeles, California, where his parents had moved to find jobs during the Great Depression. As a high-school basketball player, Anderson earned the nickname "Sparky" for his explosive temper. He was known to hurl basketballs at referees during games, and on one occasion he sent an opposing player crashing through two glass doors. While growing up, Anderson also played sandlot baseball and was a bat boy with the University of California team. In 1953, at the age of 19, he began his professional baseball career playing for minor-league teams in the Los Angeles Dodgers organization, establishing himself as a master of the double play at both shortstop and second base. Traded to the Philadelphia Phillies in 1958, Anderson played in that team's farm system until 1964, when he became the manager of the Phillies' minor-league affiliate in Toronto. After one successful year there, he went on to manage minor-league Phillies teams in Rock Hill, South Carolina; St. Petersburg, Florida; Modesto, California; and Asheville, North Carolina. While leading his teams to victory, Anderson learned to control his temper and developed an impressive rapport with his players. His success in the minor leagues caught the attention of major-league executives, and in 1969 he became the third-base coach for the San Diego Padres. In October 1969 Anderson accepted the invitation of the Cincinnati Reds' general manager, Bob Howsam, to become the Reds' field manager. At 35 Anderson was the youngest manager in the major leagues. He was also a relative unknown to most baseball fans; after he was selected a Cincinnati newspaper headline read: "Sparky Who?" Anderson inherited a young and talented club that included the All-Star catcher Johnny Bench, the slugging first baseman Tony Perez, and the perennial batting champion Pete Rose but lacked dedication, confidence, and good management-player relations. To establish and maintain rapport with his staff and players, Anderson relied on his pitching and batting coaches more than most managers dared, shrewdly capitalized on the aggressiveness of the fiery Pete Rose by appointing him team captain, and held regular meetings with Bench and the team's other superstars to receive their advice and solicit their cooperation. On the field he inspired confidence by exhibiting it, putting his players in tight situations, going for the big inning, and playing hunches, and he encouraged teamwork by ignoring individual achievement if the team performed poorly. In Anderson's first year as manager, the Reds won 102 games and captured the National League pennant—the team's first in nine years—before losing in the World Series to the Baltimore Orioles. Under Anderson the Reds went on to win three more pennants (1972, 1975, and 1976) and two World Series titles—a seven-game victory over the Boston Red Sox in 1975 and a sweep of the New York Yankees in 1976. The Reds' successful defense of the world championship was the first such feat by a National League team in half a century. After nine years with the Reds, Anderson was released in November 1978. Beginning in June 1979 he spent 16 and a half seasons managing the Detroit Tigers, leading the team to a World Series championship over the San Diego Padres, in 1984, and earning AL Manager of the Year honors twice. By the time he retired, in 1995, Anderson had won a total of 2,194 games. He gave much of the credit for his success to his players. During his induction ceremony into the Baseball Hall of Fame, in 2000, he said, in his characteristically imprecise speaking manner: "There's two kind of manager. One, it ain't very smart. He gets bad players, loses games and gets fired. There was somebody like me that I was a genius. I got good players, stayed out of the way, let 'em win a lot, and then just hung around for 26 years." Anderson died while in hospice care in Thousand Oaks, California. He is survived by his wife, Carol; his sons, Lee and Albert; his daughter, Shirlee; and several grandchildren. See *Current Biography* (1977). —M.M.H.

Obituary *New York Times* (on-line) Nov. 4, 2010

ARNESS, JAMES May 26, 1923–June 3, 2011 Actor. James Arness was best known for his portrayal of the iconic lawman Matt Dillon on the popular TV show *Gunsmoke*, which aired for two decades, from 1955 to 1975. Of Norwegian descent, he was born in Minneapolis, Minnesota, to Ruth (Duesler) and Rolf Aurness. (He later dropped the "u" from his surname.) Arness's younger brother also became an actor; he adopted the stage name Peter Graves and created another iconic character, that of Jim Phelps on the hit spy television series *Mission: Impossible*. Drafted into the U.S. Army during his freshman year (1942–43) at Beloit College, in Wisconsin, Arness, who stood six feet seven inches tall, was wounded in the leg at Anzio beachhead in 1944. After World War II he worked as a substitute radio announcer at station WLOL in Minneapolis for six months before drifting to Hollywood. While acting at the Bliss-Hayden Theatre in Beverly Hills, he was discovered by agent Leo Lance, who introduced him to a film producer, Dore Schary. Between his supporting roles in the Schary productions *The Farmer's Daughter* (1946) and *Battleground* (1949), Arness beachcombed in Mexico, worked at menial jobs, and collected veteran's benefits and unemployment insurance. He appeared in some 30 films before being cast as Matt Dillon in *Gunsmoke. Gunsmoke*, created on CBS radio by the director Norman Macdonnell and the writer John Meston in 1952, was adapted for TV three years later. The role of Dillon, which had been played by William Conrad on radio, was first offered to John Wayne, but Wayne recommended Arness in his stead. An instant hit, *Gunsmoke* ranked first in the Nielsen ratings in 1957 and remained among the top-10 shows annually thereafter, often occupying the number-one spot. Originally a half-hour presentation, it was expanded to a full hour in 1960 and soon became a cultural touchstone. Lawrence Laurent noted for the *Washington Post* (May 18, 1969): "The

great appeal of *Gunsmoke*, aside from the competence of the troupe, is its grimy, gritty version of the reality of frontier life. Matt Dillon, from the beginning, has dressed in plain work clothes, without the garish, flashy costumes that used to distinguish cowboy heroes. He has never professed any deep love or profound relationship with his horse." Writing for the *New York Times* (January 11, 1970), Robert Lasson asserted: "*Gunsmoke* is . . . mythic. . . . When Jim Arness rides furiously by in that opening credit, friends, that's not Marshal Matt Dillon. It's Odysseus and Theseus and Siegfried." The show was canceled in 1975, after more than 600 episodes. It remained the longest-running prime-time series in American TV history until 2009, when that record was broken by *The Simpsons*. Arness subsequently made dozens of television movies, including several *Gunsmoke*-related projects, and in 1977 he starred in the popular miniseries *How the West Was Won*. Arness died at the age of 88. He is survived by his second wife, the former Janet Surtees. His first union, to the former Virginia Chapman, ended in divorce in 1963. He had adopted Chapman's son, Craig, who predeceased him, in 2004. The couple also had two children together, Jenny and Rolf. Jenny died in 1975, reportedly committing suicide by overdosing on drugs. Arness is survived by Rolf, as well as by a stepson, Jim Surtees. See *Current Biography* (1973). —M.R.

Obituary *New York Times* (on-line) June 3, 2011

ASHFORD, NICKOLAS May 4, 1942(?)–Aug. 22, 2011 Singer and songwriter. Nick Ashford and Valerie Simpson comprised one of Motown's most prolific and successful songwriting teams in the 1960s and early 1970s and went on to become singing sensations themselves. Performing as Ashford & Simpson, they recorded such popular R&B albums as *Come As You Are* (1976), *So So Satisfied* (1977), *Send It* (1977), *Solid* (1984), and *Real Love* (1986). Nickolas Ashford was born in Fairfield, South Carolina, and grew up in Willow Run, Michigan. (There is some confusion about the year of his birth, with sources claiming either 1940, 1941, or 1942.) His father, Calvin, was a construction worker; his mother, Alice, was a homemaker. His musical education started in the Willow Run Baptist Church, where, as a teenager, he wrote gospel tunes for the junior choir. He spent a semester at Eastern Michigan College, in Ypsilanti, before dropping out and moving to New York, where he hoped to make it as a dancer. After several fruitless auditions, he ran out of money and was homeless for three months, sleeping on a bench in Bryant Park. In 1964 Ashford met Valerie Simpson at the White Rock Baptist Church, in Harlem. He had wandered into the church looking for a free meal and was immediately attracted to her, but when he found that Simpson was still in her teens, he quickly abandoned any romantic inclinations. Simpson, however, was looking for a songwriter for her gospel group, the Followers of Christ, and Ashford's talents quickly convinced all four women in the group to let him join. The group often sang at the Sweet Chariot, in Midtown Manhattan, an unusual nightclub where one could enjoy both gospel music and liquor. Pressure from church groups eventually forced the club to shut down, but not before the Followers of Christ gained some valuable exposure. Ashford and Simpson subsequently began writing secular songs together, selling their first love song, "I'll Find You," along with four others, for $75 to the Glover Record Co. While there were no hits in that batch, they persevered, and Simpson sang commercial jingles to supplement her income as the two struggled to make a name for themselves. They soon landed a job with Scepter Records, where they made $50 a week each, plus $20 for every song of theirs that the company accepted. The inspiration for their first hit song came after a long and unproductive day of work. In exasperation someone had yelled, "Let's go get stoned!" Simpson, sitting at her piano, made a chorus out of the phrase, and just 10 minutes later Ashford and Simpson completed the song. Recorded by Ray Charles in 1966, "Let's Go Get Stoned" became a national hit. The success of the song attracted the attention of the famous Motown label, and the two moved to Detroit to begin work as songwriters for the company. It took less than a year for Simpson and Ashford to write their first hit for Motown, "Ain't No Mountain High Enough," which was recorded by Marvin Gaye and Tammi Terrell and released in 1967. More hits followed, among them "You're All I Need to Get By," "Ain't Nothing Like the Real Thing," "Your Precious Love," and "Good Lovin' Ain't Easy to Come By," all recorded by Gaye and Terrell. Other hits included "Reach Out and Touch (Somebody's Hand)" and a remake of "Ain't No Mountain High Enough," both of which helped to establish the solo career of Diana Ross. Eventually, Motown allowed Ashford and Simpson to produce songs in addition to writing them. In 1973 their contract with Motown expired, and the pair signed a recording deal with Warner Bros. They married the following year. After recording several albums for the label, they moved on to Capitol Records, where they had the biggest hit of their career with the album *Solid*, whose title track, featuring Ashford's trademark falsetto, became a Top 20 hit. Even as they were recording their own albums, Ashford and Simpson continued to write songs for other performers. In 1973, the same year they signed with Warner Bros., they established their own music-publishing company, Nick-O-Val Music, and had trouble keeping up with the demand for their music. Their many songs for other artists included "I'm Every Woman," for Chaka Khan, and "Stuff Like That," for Quincy Jones. Their last album was *The Real Thing*, released in 2009. Ashford, who was being treated for throat cancer, died at a New York hospital. He is survived by Simpson and their two daughters, Nicole and Asia. See *Current Biography* (1997). —M.R.

Obituary *New York Times* (on-line) Aug. 22, 2011

BABBITT, MILTON May 10, 1916–Jan. 29, 2011
Composer; music educator. Milton Babbitt was known for his structurally rigid approach to musical composition, which applied notes of the 12-tone Western scale in particular rows or series. In a tribute published in the *New York Times* (January 29, 2011, on-line), Allan Kozinn praised Babbitt as "the standard-bearer of the ultrarational extreme in

American composition." Milton Byron Babbitt was born in Philadelphia, Pennsylvania, and grew up in Jackson, Mississippi. He began studying music at the age of four. Babbitt also developed an interest in mathematics early on through the influence of his father, Albert, an actuary, and later through his only brother, Albert E. Babbitt Jr., who worked as a mathematician for IBM. During his youth Babbitt studied the violin before switching to the clarinet and saxophone. Taking a particular liking to jazz and theater music, Babbitt started making his own musical arrangements at the age of seven. Upon graduating from high school, in 1931, at the age of 15, Babbitt enrolled at the University of Pennsylvania, where he intended to study mathematics like his father. He switched his focus to musical composition and theory, however, after discovering the music of Arnold Schoenberg, who originated the serial method of composition, and Anton von Webern. In 1933 Babbitt left the University of Pennsylvania and entered New York University, where he studied composition under Marion Bauer and Philip James. Shortly after graduating, in 1935, he began receiving private lessons from Roger Sessions, who was on the faculty of Princeton University. Babbitt, who considered Sessions an important mentor, went to Princeton to study and teach music in 1938. He received one of the university's first master of fine arts degrees in 1942. (In 1992 he was granted a long-delayed Ph.D. degree from the university; his thesis, which focused on the mathematical basis of Schoenberg's 12-tone row, was startlingly ahead of its time and had been rejected originally.) During World War II Babbitt taught mathematics at Princeton and did clandestine mathematical research in Washington, D.C. After the war he continued his affiliation with Princeton, succeeding Sessions as the university's William Shubael Conant Professor of Music in 1965 and becoming a professor emeritus in 1984. Babbitt also held teaching posts at New York City's Juilliard School, the Berkshire Music Center at Tanglewood, and the New England Conservatory in Boston, among other institutions. Among his notable former students are the music theorist David Lewin, the composer Paul Lansky, the theater legend Stephen Sondheim, and the jazz guitarist and composer Stanley Jordan. Aside from his academic career, Babbitt is widely recognized for his own compositions. His nonelectronic Three Compositions for Piano (1946–47) and Composition for Four Instruments (1947) were the first pieces to apply serial ordering to such elements as rhythm, register, instrumentation, dynamics, and timbre. Babbitt also had an interest in the composition of electronic music. In the 1950s he helped RCA develop its Mark II synthesizer, the world's first programmable electronic-music synthesizer, and in 1959 he became one of the first directors of the Columbia-Princeton Electronic Music Center, the first institution to be entirely devoted to the composition and study of electronically produced music. His earliest electronic pieces include Composition for Synthesizer (1961) and Ensembles for Synthesizer (1964). "The medium provides a kind of full satisfaction for the composer," he once said of electronic music, as quoted by Kozinn. "I love going to the studio with my work in my head, realizing it while I am there and walking out with the tape under my arm.

I can then send it anywhere in the world, knowing exactly how it will sound." Babbitt stopped composing electronic music in the mid-1970s but continued to compose nonelectronic pieces in subsequent decades. Some of his later works include *Beaten Paths for Marimba* (1988), *The Joy of More Sextets for Violin and Piano* (1988), *The Crowded Air for 11 Instruments* (1988), and *Consortini for Five Instruments* (1989). Babbitt—whose complex works sometimes required extra rehearsal time for even the most prestigious professional orchestras—received a number of awards for his contributions to the arts, including a special Pulitzer Prize citation for his life's work in 1982 and a MacArthur Foundation Fellowship in 1986. Babbitt died at the age of 94. His wife of more than 60 years, Sylvia, predeceased him, in 2005. He is survived by their daughter, Betty Anne Duggan, and two grandchildren, Julie and Adam. See *Current Biography* (1962). —C.C.

Obituary *New York Times* (on-line) Jan. 29, 2011

BALLESTEROS, SEVE Apr. 9, 1957–May 7, 2011
Golfer. Over the course of his colorful career, the self-taught Spanish golfer Severiano Ballesteros—known to sportswriters as "matador" or "conquistador"—won 45 events on the European Tour and four Professional Golfers' Association (PGA) Tour events, in addition to his five Major tournament wins: two at the Masters tournament and three at the British Open. He also competed on eight Ryder Cup teams, helping Europe rise to prominence in that event. In 1980, at age 23, he became the youngest player and the first European ever to win the Masters. (A 21-year-old Tiger Woods would become the youngest, in 1997.) Ballesteros's impressive ability to recover from his often erratic drives with creative mid-range shots and putts made him a particularly exciting player to watch. Severiano Ballesteros—widely known as "Seve"—was born in Pedrena, a fishing village on Spain's Bay of Biscay, on the country's north coast. He was the fifth son of Baldomero Ballesteros, a dairy farmer, and the former Carmen Sota. His oldest brother died in infancy, and the others, Baldomero Jr., Vicente, and Manuel, all became professional golfers. As a boy Severiano Ballesteros was a strong runner and soccer player. He learned to play golf from his maternal uncle, who was also a golf pro. At age nine he followed in the footsteps of his brothers and became a golf caddy. Because caddies were forbidden to play on the course, Ballesteros would move surreptitiously through the pine trees at twilight, trying all kinds of shots with an old iron that had been given to him. At age 10 he took part in his first competition, the annual caddies' championship; two years later he won the tournament with a score of 79. As a result he was given special permission to use the links in the evenings, and he once estimated that from the age of 12 until he was 17, he drove as many as 1,000 golf balls a day. He left school at 14 to concentrate entirely on golf. On his 17th birthday, in 1974, Ballesteros qualified for his first big event, the Portuguese Open at Estoril. The next year he failed by just three shots to qualify for the 1975 PGA Tour. (In later years he would often turn down the PGA Tour card in favor of playing in the European Tour.) In 1976 Ballesteros entered an astonishing 34 tournaments and finished some 120 rounds with only one missed cut, winning in the vicinity of $100,000. It was, however, his second-place tie with Jack Nicklaus, behind Johnny Miller, in the 1976 British Open at Royal Birkdale, that made him, at 19, an overnight sensation. After having led through two rounds, Ballesteros lost ground to Miller and Nicklaus in the third round. On the last hole he hit an impressive chip shot that landed between two bunkers, four feet from the hole; sinking that putt helped him secure the second-place tie. As Ben Wright noted for *Sports Illustrated* (August 8, 1977), Ballesteros's slashing swing, his reliance on "a magical short game to conjure his way out of trouble time and again," and his constant gleaming smile were "a refreshing change from the defensive, conservative British style." In October 1976 he became the youngest golfer, and only the fourth from overseas, to win the Harry Vardon Trophy for the lowest stroke average. Although he was a member of the Spanish Air Force from January 1977 until the spring of 1978, Ballesteros continued to rack up golf conquests during that period, winning numerous European Tour titles. In 1978 he was reported to be the highest-paid player on the European circuit, with winnings of about $800,000. He won his first U.S. title at the Greater Greensboro Open, in North Carolina, in April 1978. At the 108th British Open in July 1979, firing his long drives against 40-mile-per-hour winds, Ballesteros attained his first major championship. During that tournament he hit one of his most storied shots, on the 16th hole of the final round: using a sand wedge, he chipped his ball from the surface of the parking lot onto the green, where he made a 20-foot putt for birdie. At 22, he was the youngest golfer to win the British Open—the world's oldest golf crown—since 1868, and the first Continental European to do so since 1907. (He would capture the British Open title again in 1984 and 1988.) Ballesteros's achievements in 1979 earned him the Association of Golf Writers trophy, given to the player who had done the most for golf during the year, which had previously been presented only to residents of Great Britain and Ireland. Nine months after the British Open, he won his first Masters championship. In that event he entered the final round with a 13-under-par 275, just four strokes better than runners-up Jack Newton and Gibby Gilbert. After having established a 10-stroke lead at one point in the third round, he finished only four shots ahead of the second-place finisher, becoming the youngest player ever to win the Masters—three months younger than Jack Nicklaus had been when he won it in 1963. On April 27, 1980, two weeks after his Masters victory, Ballesteros won his first major title in his native Spain, the Madrid Open. He would go on to win his second Masters title in 1983. His last victory on the European Tour came in 1995, at the Spanish Open; after that, a chronic back problem limited his play. He was inducted into the World Golf Hall of Fame in 1999 and retired from the sport in 2007. In later years he ran a golf-course design business. Ballesteros, who died of brain cancer in his hometown of Pedrena, learned he had a tumor in 2008, after fainting at an airport. He is survived by two sons and a daughter from his marriage to Carmen Botin, which

ended in divorce in 2004. See *Current Biography* (1980). —M.R.M.

Obituary *New York Times* (on-line) May 7, 2011

BARRY, JOHN Nov. 3, 1933–Jan. 30, 2011 Composer; conductor. Probably best known for the theme that accompanies the pre-title sequences of the James Bond films, John Barry wrote music for more than 100 motion pictures and won five Oscars and four Grammy Awards. In an article for the Film Music Society Web site (February 2, 2011, on-line), John Burlingame wrote, "John Barry was one of a kind. He invented a new style of action-adventure music for the movies—that much is certain—but he was equally adept at quiet dramas, historical epics and contemporary thrillers. And what's more, he could write music appropriate to all of these kinds of movies and still sound like nobody else." John Barry Prendergast, one of three children, was born in York, England. His father, Jack, owned several local cinemas, and as a child Barry became an avid moviegoer. His early influences included the film composers Bernard Hermann, Alfred Newman, and Miklos Rozsa. He studied piano beginning at age nine, and in his mid-teens he received instruction in composition from Francis Jackson, a composer, conductor, and organist at York Minster, the largest Gothic cathedral in northern Europe. Drafted into military service in the 1950s, Barry played trumpet with dance bands and with a military band. In 1957, after resuming his civilian life in York, he played trumpet in his own jazz group, the John Barry Seven. The group, which remained together for four years, landed a recording contract with EMI Records, and several of their instrumental singles became hits, among them "Hit and Miss" and a cover version of the Ventures' surf-guitar classic "Walk Don't Run." Through such exposure Barry became an arranger for the popular British teen crooner Adam Faith, writing the score for Faith's movie *Beat Girl* (1960), released in the United States as *Wild for Kicks*. That same year he composed the music for the film *Never Let Go*, starring Peter Sellers. *Dr. No* (1962), the first James Bond film, was scored by Monty Norman, but Barry was tapped to arrange its theme. (The theme was credited as a Barry arrangement of a Norman piece, and controversy over the credits persisted for many years. In 2001 Norman won a libel suit against the London *Sunday Times* for crediting Barry as the song's composer.) Barry later wrote the complete scores for 11 James Bond films: *From Russia with Love* (1963), *Goldfinger* (1964), *Thunderball* (1965), *You Only Live Twice* (1967), *On Her Majesty's Secret Service* (1969), *Diamonds Are Forever* (1971), *The Man with the Golden Gun* (1974), *Moonraker* (1979), *Octopussy* (1983), *A View to Kill* (1985), and *The Living Daylights* (1987). (Many of the title songs used in the films became mainstream hits, including the single from *The Living Daylights*, which brought the pop group a-ha to international attention.) Other notable Barry scores from the 1960s include those for the films *Zulu* (1964), *Born Free* (1966), *The Lion in Winter* (1968), and *Midnight Cowboy* (1969). He won Oscars for his scores for *The Lion in Winter* and *Born Free* and received a second Oscar honoring his work on the theme song for *Born Free*, sung by Matt Monro

and co-written with Don Black. Barry won two more Oscars, for his scores for *Out of Africa* (1985) and *Dances with Wolves* (1990). He was nominated for Oscars for the scores to *Mary, Queen of Scots* (1971) and *Chaplin* (1992). Other films for which Barry composed include *The Tamarind Seed* (1974), *The Day of the Locust* (1975), *Robin and Marian* (1976), *The Deep* (1977), *The Cotton Club* (1984), *Jagged Edge* (1985), *Peggy Sue Got Married* (1986), *Howard the Duck* (1986), *Playing by Heart* (1998), and *Enigma* (2001). Barry also wrote music for a number of television shows and theater productions. In 1998 he was inducted into the Songwriters Hall of Fame. He won a British Academy of Film and Television Arts (BAFTA) Fellowship Award in 2005, and he was presented with a Max Steiner Lifetime Achievement Award, from the city of Vienna, in 2009. Barry nearly died in 1988 from a ruptured esophagus, reportedly caused by consuming a beverage that proved toxic; he underwent four major surgeries and took more than a year off from working. He died of a heart attack at his home in Oyster Bay, Long Island. He is survived by his fourth wife, Laurie; four children; and five grandchildren. See *Current Biography* (2000). —W.D.

Obituary *New York Times* (on-line) Jan. 31, 2011

BELL, DANIEL May 10, 1919–Jan. 25, 2011 Sociologist; writer; editor. During his long career Daniel Bell contributed numerous works to the study of post-industrialism, including, perhaps most notably, *The End of Ideology* (1960) and *Cultural Contradictions of Capitalism* (1978), both ranked among the 100 most influential books since World War II by the editors of the *Times Literary Supplement*. Bell was born Daniel Bolotsky in New York City. (The family adopted the last name "Bell" when he was 13.) His parents, Polish-Jewish immigrants, were employed as garment workers; his father died when Bell was eight months old. Until the age of six, when he began to learn English, Bell spoke only Yiddish. As an adolescent he was already reading the works of Karl Marx and John Stuart Mill, whose theories he tried to expound as a young soapbox orator for Norman Thomas, the leader of the Socialist Party. At 16 Bell began his studies at the City College of New York, at the time a hotbed of leftist ideology. His classmates included several students who would go on to achieve professional renown: the literary critic Irving Howe, the sociologists Nathan Glazer and Seymour M. Lipset, and the writer and editor Irving Kristol. Like them, Bell became part of the anti-Communist Left. Following his graduation from City College, with a B.S. degree in sociology, in 1938, Bell enrolled in graduate courses in the subject at Columbia University, in New York. While a student there he began to write for the *New Leader*, regularly contributing articles from 1939 to 1941. (He was exempt from World War II service for medical reasons.) In 1941 he was appointed managing editor of the magazine, a position he held until 1945, when he switched briefly to a job as managing editor of *Common Sense*. In the fall of that year, Bell became a social-sciences instructor at the University of Chicago. In 1948 he became labor editor at *Fortune* magazine, while maintaining his ties to academia as a part-time lecturer in sociology at Columbia, from 1952 to 1958. From 1957 to 1961 he was a member of the board of directors of the American Civil Liberties Union. He also served as a link between journalism and scholarly specialization by editing *The New American Right* (1955), a collection of essays he expanded and updated in 1963 under the title *The Radical Right*. At Columbia he became an associate professor of sociology in 1959 and received his Ph.D. degree in 1960. He was promoted to a full professorship in 1962. From 1959 to 1969 he also served as chair of the Department of Sociology at Columbia College. In 1960 Bell published *The End of Ideology: On the Exhaustion of Political Ideas in the Fifties*, the book that solidly established his reputation as an intellectual. It contained 16 of the many essays Bell had published over the previous decade. Most of them examined aspects of American life, such as the bureaucratization of capitalism, the decreased militancy of the labor movement, and the "cult of efficiency" in the workplace. In the last section of the book, which dealt with Marxism, the nature of Soviet behavior, and the failure of American socialism, Bell explored the impact of ideology on social behavior. The traditional systems of thought, he asserted, had been "exhausted" and lost their "power to persuade." The book was welcomed as a major contribution to the understanding of complex changes in contemporary society. In 1965 Bell published *The Reforming of General Education*, the results of a year-long study of undergraduate education. Also in 1965 Bell and Irving Kristol, his former classmate at City College, founded the quarterly magazine *Public Interest*, to promote the kind of dispassionate analysis of public issues that Bell had urged in *The End of Ideology*. Some of its more prestigious contributors included Daniel P. Moynihan, Robert A. Nisbet, Jacques Barzun, and Nathan Glazer. Both Bell and Kristol contributed articles on aspects of capitalism and modern life to a special issue of the *Public Interest*, published in the fall of 1970 and republished a year later as the book *Capitalism Today* (1971). Though never attaining wide readership, the *Public Interest* became a well-respected policy journal, later considered "one of the most intellectually formidable neoconservative publications," as Michael T. Kaufman put it in the *New York Times* (January 25, 2011, on-line). In 1973 Bell left the magazine, a move that was thought to be related to Kristol's increasingly conservative political stance, though Bell attributed the move to his own busy schedule. Throughout his career one of Bell's most consuming interests was the use of sociology for social prediction. In 1965 he became chair of the American Academy of Arts and Sciences' Commission on the Year 2000. In 1967 he predicted the rise of a "national information-computer-utility system, with tens of thousands of terminals in homes and offices 'hooked' into giant central computers providing library and information services, retail ordering and billing services, and the like," as Kaufman noted, and in his book *The Coming of Post-Industrial Society* (1973), he predicted the economic reliance on service-based economies and the decline of the dominance of manufacturing and agriculture. In 1980 Bell was appointed the Henry Ford II Professor of Social Sciences at Harvard University. Bell died at his home in Cambridge, Massachusetts. He is survived by his third wife, Pearl Kazin, whom he married in 1960; his daughter, Jordy; his son, David; four grandchildren; and one great-grandchild. See *Current Biography* (1973).—D.K.

Obituary *New York Times* (on-line) Jan. 25, 2011

BELL, DERRICK A. Nov. 6, 1930–Oct. 5, 2011 Lawyer; legal scholar; educator; social activist; writer. Derrick A. Bell will be remembered for his influential writings in critical race theory, a branch of scholarship that he pioneered; for being the first African-American to teach and gain tenure at the Harvard Law School; for his excellence as a teacher of law; and—perhaps even more widely and lastingly—for his efforts toward ending racial and gender discrimination and his refusal to compromise on his principles, even to his own detriment. "Courage is a decision you make to act in a way that works through your own fear for the greater good as opposed to pure self-interest. Courage means putting at risk your immediate self-interest for what you believe is right," he wrote in his memoir, *Ethical Ambition: Living a Life of Meaning and Worth* (2002). Another of his convictions was that "history is made through confrontation. Nothing gets done without pushing." "Taking action when you are treated unfairly has risks," he once said, "but remaining silent can also be costly." Derrick Albert Bell Jr. was born in Pittsburgh, Pennsylvania, to Derrick Albert Bell and Ada Elizabeth (Childress) Bell. His father, whose education ended with the sixth grade, owned a small trash-collection business; he often advised his son to distrust whites. Bell's mother taught him to reject compromise and capitulation when he was certain that he was in the right. Bell earned an A.B. degree in political science from Duquesne University in 1952. He spent the next two years in the U.S. Air Force; he served in Korea and rose to the rank of second lieutenant. In 1954 he enrolled at the University of Pittsburgh Law School. He ranked fourth in an otherwise all-white class when he graduated, with an LL.B. degree, in 1957. That year he was hired by the U.S. Department of Justice as an attorney in the conscientious-objector and civil rights divisions. When department officials informed him that to keep his job he would have to drop his membership in the National Association for the Advancement of Colored People (NAACP), because it presented a conflict of interest, he quit the job. He was employed briefly by the Pittsburgh branch of the NAACP before serving, from 1960 to 1966, on the staff of the NAACP's Legal Defense and Educational Fund; there, as a staff attorney, he worked with the future U.S. Supreme Court justice Thurgood Marshall. In that post he advised upwards of 300 legal teams handling school-desegregation lawsuits in Mississippi. He then returned to the federal government, to serve for two years as the deputy director of the Office of Civil Rights in the Department of Health, Education and Welfare (now the Department of Health and Human Services). He left in 1968 to take the post of executive director of the Western Center on Law and Poverty of the University of Southern California Law School. The next year he became the first black person to teach at the Harvard Law School and, in 1971, the school's first tenured black law professor. In 1980 he left Harvard and moved to Eugene, Oregon, where he served as the dean of the University of Oregon School of Law. The school's refusal to hire a female Asian-American lawyer he believed was qualified to fill a tenure-track position prompted him to resign in 1985. Bell returned to Harvard in 1986. In 1987 he conducted a several-day-long sit-in in his office to protest what he termed "an attack on ideological diversity": the school's denial of tenure to two white law teachers who supported a left-leaning movement called critical legal studies, which is based on the conviction that legal systems are designed to maintain unjust political systems. In the spring of 1990, Bell announced that he would take an unpaid leave of absence (thus forfeiting his $120,000 annual salary) until Harvard added to the faculty, for the first time, a tenured woman of color. He took that stand despite the strong disapproval of his first wife, who was then battling cancer. (Jewel Hairston Bell, his wife of 30 years, died of breast cancer later in 1990.) "I cannot continue to urge students to take risks for what they believe if I do not practice my own precepts," he explained at the time. In 1990 Bell joined the faculty of the New York University (NYU) School of Law as a full-time visiting professor of constitutional law, a position that he held at the time of his death. His legacy includes many articles for professional journals and popular periodicals, as well as such books as *Race, Racism, and American Law* (1973; sixth edition, 2008), which is required reading at many law schools; *Confronting Authority: Reflections of an Ardent Protestor* (1994); and *Silent Covenants: Brown v. Board of Education and the Unfulfilled Hopes for Racial Reform* (2004). Bell used fables and imaginary dialogues to discuss racism throughout American history in several volumes, including *Faces at the Bottom of the Well: The Permanence of Racism* (1992), which dismayed many blacks as well as whites with its bleak thesis. "Accepting racism as permanent is not putting up a white flag of surrender, but accepting the challenge of coming up with new ways to combat it," Bell told one reporter. Bell was also the author of *Gospel Choirs: Psalms of Survival for an Alien Land Called Home* (1996); at the NYU School of Law, he launched the Bell Annual Gospel Choir Concert. After meeting him for lunch one day, Susan Chira described the then-61-year-old Bell for the *New York Times* (October 28, 1992) as "surviv[ing] in a world that makes him angry all the time." "Yet, beneath the anger is pain," she added. Chira also wrote, "For an angry man, Derrick Bell is surprisingly good company. His smile is warm, his tone is mild, his gestures welcoming even as he talks of the unbridgeable gulf between blacks and whites. The same man who presents an unyielding front to his opponents quickly reveals his own vulnerabilities. He can be politically strident, yet personally charming. Racism and injustice obsess him, but he somehow avoids grimness and despair." Bell died of carcinoid cancer in New York City, where he lived with his second wife, Janet Dewart Bell, whom he married in 1992. From his first marriage, he had three sons—Derrick A. Bell III, Douglas Dubois Bell, and Carter Robeson Bell, who survive him. See *Current Biography* (1983). —M.H.

Obituary *New York Times* (on-line) Oct. 6, 2011

BLUMBERG, BARUCH July 28, 1925–Apr. 5, 2011 Virologist; Nobel laureate. Baruch Blumberg is credited with the discovery of the infectious hepatitis B virus, which can lead to cancer of the liver; he also developed a diagnostic test for the virus and helped to create a vaccine to prevent infection with it. For that research, which has saved millions of lives, he won the 1976 Nobel Prize in Physiology or Medicine. The second of three children, Baruch "Barry" Samuel Blumberg was born to Meyer and Ida Blumberg in New York City. He studied at Union College, in Schenectady, New York, interrupting his courses to serve in the U.S. Navy as a deck officer during World War II. In 1946 Blumberg received a B.S. degree from Union College, and in 1951 he earned his M.D. degree from Columbia University's College of Physicians and Surgeons. He also holds a Ph.D. degree in biochemistry, which he earned in 1957 from the University of Oxford's Balliol College. Upon completing his studies at Oxford, Blumberg moved back to the U.S. and served as head of the Geographic Medicine and Genetics Section of the National Institutes of Health, a post he held until 1964. During that time he conducted research in Africa, Japan, India, and Australia, among other locations, aiming to understand why people of differing ethnic, racial, and family backgrounds are either more resistant or more susceptible to certain diseases. For one study Blumberg and a fellow scientist, Anthony C. Allison, tested blood samples from patients with such blood diseases as hemophilia, anemia, and leukemia, which often require blood transfusions from dozens of different donors each year. Their goal was to determine whether antibodies in the blood would precipitate antigens from a variety of serums (the watery portion of blood that has clotted), representing blood samples from people of many different ethnic groups. Through those methods they were able to isolate variants of important serum proteins. In 1963 they made an unexpected discovery. From the blood of a hemophilic patient in New York they isolated antibodies that reacted against only one serum in the panel—a specimen from an Australian aborigine. Although Blumberg and his colleagues were not surprised that the Australian, who was a member of a distinctive and isolated race, differed from their other test subjects, they could not explain how a New York hemophiliac had encountered the so-called Australia antigen, which had been assumed to be unique to aborigines. After moving to the Institute for Cancer Research in Philadelphia in 1964, Blumberg continued his efforts to trace the distribution of the Australia antigen. He and his associates discovered that the occurrence of the antigen did not follow ethnic lines as closely as they had originally expected. If the Australia antigen was a polymorphism (or variant form) of a normal human protein, those who contracted it would retain it all their lives. Thus, when an antigen-negative patient at the institute became antigen-positive following an attack of liver disease, Blumberg realized he was dealing with a disease rather than a polymorphic protein. By 1967 Blumberg and his colleagues were sure that the Australia antigen was associated with the hepatitis B virus, which produces inflammation of the liver. Once Blumberg proved that the Australia antigen and hepatitis B were linked, programs were established to screen blood banks for the virus, thus reducing one of the major risks associated with blood transfusions. Preventing transfusion hepatitis was only the first important consequence of Blumberg's discovery, however, and he later helped develop a vaccine for the virus. For his work Blumberg was a co-recipient of the 1976 Nobel Prize in Physiology or Medicine. In 1989 he became a distinguished professor and senior adviser at the Fox Chase Cancer Center. Blumberg also taught at the University of Pennsylvania and served as a visiting professor at the University of Pittsburgh, Stanford University, and Oxford, among other schools. From 1999 to 2002 he led the Astrobiology Institute, a now-defunct branch of the National Aeronautics and Space Administration (NASA), where he and his colleagues investigated the origins of life, evolution, and the existence of microorganisms on other planets. In 2005 he was named president of the American Philosophical Society. Blumberg penned hundreds of scientific papers as well as several books, including *Hepatitis B: The Hunt for a Killer Virus* (2002). Blumberg died of a heart attack shortly after giving a keynote speech at a NASA conference. He is survived by his wife, the former Jean Liebesman, an artist, to whom he was married for over five decades. He is also survived by two daughters, Anne and Jane; two sons, George and Noah; and nine grandchildren. See *Current Biography* (1977). —J.P.

Obituary *New York Times* (on-line) Apr. 6, 2011

BONNER, ELENA Feb. 15, 1923–June 18, 2011 Activist. Elena Bonner and her husband, the Nobel Peace Prize winner and leading Soviet human-rights activist Andrei D. Sakharov, emerged unbowed from what has been termed "one of the most extraordinary struggles in history between a state and an individual—or, in this case, two individuals." Bonner, according to one *Newsweek* reporter, could "stare down any Soviet bureaucrat [and] outsmart any KGB thug." The future activist, whose first name is sometimes transliterated as Yelena, was born in Moscow, the older of the two children of Ruth Grigorievna Bonner and Gevork Alikhanov, both ardent members of the Communist Party of the Soviet Union (CPSU). Bonner was only 14 and had just finished the seventh grade when, in 1937, her mother and father were arrested in the great purge instigated by the Soviet dictator Joseph Stalin. Because of their father's execution and their mother's long imprisonment, she and her brother, Igor, went to Leningrad to live with relatives. Bonner finished school while working as a cleaning lady and, later, as a file clerk at a factory. In 1940 she enrolled in night courses at a teachers' institute and became involved with Communist Party youth groups. After the outbreak of war with Germany, she volunteered for the army, and while serving at the front on October 21, 1941, she sustained a concussion and other wounds that left her nearly blind. After her recovery she was assigned to a hospital train, and by the end of World War II, she had been promoted to the rank of lieutenant. For the next two years, Bonner was in and out of hospitals, as she struggled to retain her failing eyesight. When her condition stabilized, in 1947, she enrolled at the First Leningrad Medical Institute, where she

fell in love with a classmate, Ivan Vasilyevich Semyonov. They married and had two children. In 1953 Bonner graduated and began practicing pediatric and maternal medicine. Concurrently, she wrote for professional journals and edited several publications, including the collected poems of Vsevolod Bagritsky, a childhood sweetheart who had died fighting the Nazis. Despite her ongoing involvement as an organizer of the Communist youth group Komsomol, Bonner was not a member of the CPSU during those years, and it was only after the party denounced Stalinism that, in 1965, she joined. That same year Bonner and her husband separated. She continued to pursue her own career and political activities, and she soon began to chafe under the party's rigid dogmatism. When the Red Army invaded Czechoslovakia, in 1968, she felt confused and disillusioned. Her alienation from the party became final in 1970, when at the trial of a fellow dissident, she met Andrei D. Sakharov, a prominent leader of the nascent Soviet human-rights movement. Kindred spirits, they married in 1971, and in keeping with her convictions, she resigned from the CPSU the following year. In 1975 it was announced that Sakharov had been chosen as the recipient of the Nobel Peace Prize, the first Russian ever to be accorded that honor. When her husband was denied permission to travel to Oslo, Norway, for the awards ceremony on December 10, she went in his place and read a statement on his behalf. In the wake of the international recognition and acclaim, KGB surveillance of the Sakharovs intensified. Despite that, the couple and seven other prominent Moscow dissidents formed a "watchdog" group to monitor Soviet compliance with the 1975 Helsinki accords on human rights. Chagrined by their gestures of defiance, the KGB became increasingly impatient and frustrated by its inability to control the pair and to limit Sakharov's criticism of the Soviet invasion of Afghanistan. The agency moved unexpectedly on January 22, 1980, arresting Sakharov and sending him into internal exile in the city of Gorky, an industrial center then closed to Westerners. Since she was allowed to go with her husband and free to travel back and forth between Moscow and Gorky, Bonner became Sakharov's principal contact with the outside world. When she visited Gorky, Bonner endured persistent police searches in which her personal papers, and portions of a memoir her husband was writing, were regularly seized from her bags. Her routine was secretly filmed and her car vandalized repeatedly. The harassment did not abate during the times she returned to Moscow, and her health began to fail. She began to consider a move to the West, but Soviet authorities were adamant that her husband would not be allowed to accompany her if she left. The couple began a hunger strike in protest. The KGB fought back with a press campaign to vilify Bonner, who was attacked as an evil influence on her husband and as a Western agent. She was formally charged with eight counts of anti-Soviet activities, and on August 10, 1984, after a two-day secret trial, she was sentenced to five years in internal exile in Gorky. Those authorities who were responsible may have assumed that isolating the Sakharovs would end their effectiveness, but they soon discovered otherwise: Bonner and her husband repeatedly staged hunger strikes (which the KGB invariably ended by hospitalizing and force-feeding them) in a desperate bid to gain a pardon and issuance of a visa that would allow her to travel to the West for needed medical treatment. In October 1985 an exit visa was unexpectedly issued, and she flew to Italy on December 2 for an eye checkup and an audience with Pope John Paul II. During the trip she also met with British prime minister Margaret Thatcher and French president François Mitterrand; saw her mother and children, who had settled in Boston; was quietly received at the White House by John M. Poindexter, the national security adviser; and had surgeries to remove a tumor on her lip and to repair a heart defect. She also left behind a 70,000-word memoir. Entitled *Alone Together*, it had been written while she was recuperating from heart surgery. The book, which was excerpted in *Time* magazine, was published simultaneously in several Western countries in 1986. While some critics noted that the haste with which the book had been written was apparent, they were unanimous in praising the moral courage of the Sakharovs. The couple were stunned when just before Christmas of 1986, workers installed a telephone in their Gorky apartment. The following afternoon Sakharov received a personal telephone call from Soviet leader Mikhail Gorbachev informing him that both he and Bonner would be permitted to return to Moscow to live and work. Western observers viewed the move as a sign of Gorbachev's serious intent to pursue a policy of *glasnost*, or openness, in Soviet society. Sakharov died in 1989, but Bonner continued to be a strong voice for human rights. The apartment the couple shared in Gorky was turned into a museum, and for the last several years of her life, she resided in the U.S. Bonner, who is also the author of the 1992 memoir *Mothers and Daughters*, died of heart failure at the age of 88, in Boston. She is survived by her daughter, Tatiana; her son, Alexey; five grandchildren; and three great-grandchildren. See *Current Biography* (1987). —M.R.

Obituary *New York Times* (on-line) June 19, 2011

BORDABERRY, JUAN MARIA June 17, 1928–July 17, 2011 Former president of Uruguay. Juan Maria Bordaberry's "years as president, between 1971 and 1976, are remembered as perhaps the bleakest in Uruguay's history, marked by a wave of disappearances, torture and killings," Alexei Barrionuevo and Charles Newbery wrote for the *New York Times* (July 17, 2011, on-line). Of French-Basque descent, Bordaberry was born in Montevideo, the son of Domingo R. Bordaberry and Elisa Arocena de Bordaberry. His father, who owned one of the largest ranches in Uruguay, was also a lawyer and a member of the Senate. Juan Bordaberry received his early schooling in rural surroundings and then entered the University of Montevideo. After his father's death he dropped out of law school to manage the family ranch. Bordaberry's affiliation with the National (Blanco) Party—a conservative, rural-based group—as well as his expertise in agricultural economics, won him several official appointments. In 1959 he became chairman of the National Meat Board; in 1960 he served as a member of an honorary commission dealing with the

Agricultural Development Plan; and from 1960 to 1962 he was on the National Wool Board. Elected to the Senate on the Blanco ticket in 1962, Bordaberry served there until 1965. On October 3, 1969 he was named minister of agriculture and livestock by President Jorge Pacheco Areco. (After joining the Cabinet he switched affiliation to the mildly liberal Colorado Party.) During the late 1960s terrorist activity by the Tupamaros, an urban guerrilla group of Marxist students and workers who wanted to bring socialism to Uruguay by means of armed revolution, was escalating. To combat the violence Pacheco assumed an increasingly authoritarian stance, and he soon suspended certain basic civil rights. In the elections of November 1971, the two traditional parties were challenged by a leftist coalition, the Frente Amplio (Broad Front). Since the Tupamaros openly supported the Frente Amplio, the vote was viewed as a test of their popular following. The election also measured the popularity of President Pacheco in that it provided for a referendum on a constitutional amendment that would allow him to succeed himself. Bordaberry's name appeared on the ballot twice—as Pacheco's vice-presidential running mate and as his choice for president in the event that the amendment was rejected. During the bitterly fought campaign, the Colorados stressed their anti-Communism and pointed out the danger of radical change. Without any platform of his own, Bordaberry concentrated on backing Pacheco's reelection, echoing his demands for extraordinary presidential and police powers to defeat the Tupamaros as well as measures to eliminate Marxist influence from institutions of higher education. The constitutional amendment was roundly rejected on November 21, 1971, with less than 30 percent of the electorate voting for it, but although Pacheco was defeated in his bid for reelection, the presidential contest was so close that the result remained in dispute for some time. When the final results were announced, on February 15, 1972, Bordaberry was declared the winner by a narrow margin. Amid strong security precautions, he was sworn in for a five-year term as president on March 1, 1972. Soon after his inauguration, circumstances led Bordaberry to unleash repressive forces that far exceeded those Pacheco had employed. On April 14, 1972, in Montevideo, Tupamaros assassinated four officials of the Uruguayan government's anti-guerrilla campaign. On the following day Bordaberry proclaimed a "state of internal war" that ended most individual liberties and gave the government's armed forces a free hand. During the next three days, more than a dozen leftists were killed in gun battles. The military assault on the Tupamaros proved surprisingly successful. By June 1972 the guerrilla organization was in disarray, with hundreds of its members jailed, its hideouts discovered, and its weapons seized. But the experience of crushing the Tupamaros profoundly altered the armed forces: their long tradition of noninvolvement in Uruguayan internal affairs had been broken. From captured Tupamaro documents the military collected disturbing evidence of widespread official corruption. Furthermore, during the struggle many of the military officers had come to respect the Tupamaros and even to share some of their ideals. Therefore, with the guerrilla movement largely destroyed, the generals became the foremost critics of the status quo. In the fall of 1972, the armed forces began an investigation of "economic crimes" perpetrated by businessmen and politicians. By reorganizing his government, Bordaberry managed to smooth over a Cabinet crisis in October, provoked by the military arrest of Senator Jorge Batlle Ibanez, a prominent Colorado leader, but the new president's position was precarious. Hampered by waves of strikes, he made little headway against Uruguay's continuing economic decline. By early 1973 Uruguayans seemed to have lost all confidence in traditional politics. Meanwhile, the influence of the military on the government was steadily increasing. On February 7, 1973 Bordaberry appointed a new defense minister, Antonio Francese, who demanded the resignations of the army and air force commanders. In response, the armed forces occupied key positions in Montevideo. Although the offending minister resigned shortly thereafter, it was too late to stem the military tide. For several tense days Bordaberry negotiated with the army and air force officers, but he was ultimately forced to capitulate. An agreement ending the *golpe blando,* or "soft coup," was signed by Bordaberry and the armed forces commanders on February 13, 1973. The pact called for a military-dominated seven-member National Security Council that would be, in effect, a government behind the scenes. Having gained control of the executive branch, the officers next moved against the legislature, which, they felt, had been showing too much independence. On June 27, 1973 Bordaberry, under pressure from the military, ended 40 years of constitutional government in Uruguay by dissolving the Congress and all local legislative bodies. He remained president in name until 1976, when he was ousted altogether by military leaders. Bordaberry returned to his ranch to live as a private citizen. He was thrust into the public spotlight in 2006, however, when an investigation was launched into human-rights abuses that had occurred during his presidency. In 2010 he was sentenced to 30 years of confinement for his part in the coup and the military regime's crimes against humanity. (He had been found guilty of 14 murders and disappearances.) He served only a few months in prison before being released to house arrest because of his failing health. Bordaberry died in Montevideo and is survived by his wife, María Josefina Herrán Puig, and several children, including a son, Pedro, who now heads the Colorado Party. See *Current Biography* (1975). —M.R.

Obituary *New York Times* (on-line) July 17, 2011

BRODER, DAVID Sep. 11, 1929–Mar. 9, 2011 Journalist. David S. Broder was recognized as one of the top political reporters in the U.S., and during his career he was often referred to as the "dean" of the Washington press corps for his expertise and sharp news analysis. For more than four decades, he wrote for the *Washington Post,* winning a Pulitzer Prize in 1973 for his commentary. "He is the absolute antithesis of the hey-lookit-me ethos that—sadly—permeates our popular culture, and has crept into the effusions of some hot, hip, happening newsies," Brooks Peterson wrote for the *Corpus Christi (Texas) Caller-Times* (September 11, 2006). "Broder's copy

doesn't sizzle; neither does it pulsate with pizzazz. Where others foam and froth, Broder just gives us the goods—straight, no seltzer, no tiny paper umbrellas. What it all boils down to is: If Broder writes it, you can take it to the bank. Solid, solid, solid." The journalist was born in Chicago Heights, Illinois, to Albert Broder, a dentist, and his wife, the former Nina Salzer. As a boy David Broder loved athletics, but due to his thinness, poor eyesight, and lack of coordination, he was better at writing about sports than playing them. He attended the University of Chicago, where he earned both a B.A. degree (1947) and an M.A. degree (1951) in political science. As an undergraduate he wrote for the *Maroon,* the campus newspaper, and before long he worked his way up to editor. From 1951 to 1953 Broder served in the U.S. Army. After his discharge he moved to Bloomington, Illinois, where both he and his wife, the former Ann Creighton Collar, whom he had married in 1951, worked for the *Bloomington Pantagraph.* Broder spent two years reporting for the newspaper, developing a deep interest in covering politics in the process. In 1955 he moved to Washington, D.C., to begin writing for *Congressional Quarterly.* After five years with that publication, he became a political reporter for the *Washington Star,* where he remained until 1965, when he joined the staff of the *New York Times.* He worked in the newspaper's Washington, D.C., bureau, covering national politics, for 15 months. He left because of ongoing conflicts between his bureau and the paper's New York headquarters. He then took a job with the *Washington Post,* where he eventually became a senior writer with his own political-events column. Broder's column became nationally syndicated in 1970, published in some 300 newspapers. For a *Washington Post* (March 10, 2011, on-line) obituary of Broder, Ross K. Baker, a Rutgers University political-science professor, told Adam Bernstein, "I can't think of any columnist of a major newspaper who took academic political scientists more seriously than David Broder," adding that he could "reach beyond the dispensers of political wisdom in Washington and tap into a totally different plane than day-to-day commentators. . . . He could traffic in day-to-day gossip with the best of them, but his eyes were set a little higher, to look at broader trends." In the 1960s Broder began to appear on television as a pundit and panelist, and over the course of his career he was a regular guest on the PBS show *Washington Week in Review,* CNN's *Inside Politics,* and NBC's *Meet the Press.* He appeared on *Meet the Press* in excess of 400 times—more than any other journalist. Broder, who was widely praised for publishing an annual account of mistakes he had made in his reporting, covered every presidential election after 1956. He was also known for his coverage of state and local elections and for his massive list of contacts. He was the author or co-author of books including *The Party's Over: The Failure of Politics in America* (1972), *Changing of the Guard: Power and Leadership in America* (1980), *Behind the Front Page: A Candid Look at How the News Is Made* (1987), *The Man Who Would Be President: Dan Quayle* (1992), *The System: The American Way of Politics at the Breaking Point* (1996), and *Democracy Derailed: Initiative Campaigns and the Power of Money* (2000). In 2001 Broder joined the journalism faculty at the University of Maryland. He was a recipient of numerous honorary degrees, a National Society of Newspaper Columnists Lifetime Achievement Award (1997), and an Alumni Medal from the University of Chicago, among other such accolades. Broder died from complications of diabetes. He is survived by his wife; their four sons, George, Joshua, Matthew, and Michael; and seven grandchildren. See *Current Biography* (2010). —W.D.

Obituary *New York Times* (on-line) Mar. 9, 2011

CACOYANNIS, MICHAEL June 11, 1922–July 25, 2011 Film and theater director. Michael Cacoyannis was perhaps best known to the general public for his film *Zorba the Greek* (1964). He was born in Limassol, Cyprus, to Sir Panayotis Loizou and Angeliki (Efthyvoulos) Cacoyannis. Knighted by the British government in 1936, Panayotis achieved distinction both as an attorney and as a public servant. In 1939, after Michael Cacoyannis completed his secondary education at a Greek gymnasium, his father enrolled him at Gray's Inn in London, England, for the study of law. Although he earned a law degree and admission to the bar, he never worked as a lawyer. Instead he served, beginning in 1941, as head of the British Broadcasting Corp.'s program for occupied Greece and studied acting at the Central School of Dramatic Arts in London. Following World War II Cacoyannis remained with the BBC and made acting his vocation. His acting debut took place in London in 1947; he played Herod in Oscar Wilde's *Salome*. He became a familiar figure on the London stage during the next few years, acting leading roles in such productions as *Captain Brassbound's Conversion*, *The Fig Tree*, *Caligula*, and *Two Dozen Red Roses*. In 1950 he left the BBC to pursue writing and directing. In 1951, in his first adult literary effort, he wrote *Our Last Spring*, a screenplay based on the Greek novel of the same name. Hoping to produce the film himself, he made repeated—and fruitless—attempts to obtain financial backing. Cacoyannis moved from London to Athens, Greece, in 1953. There, he met the Greek star Ellie Lambeti and impressed her with his directorial acumen. With her and an actor friend's backing, he was selected both to direct her next screen vehicle and to write an original script for it. The movie, a comedy titled *Windfall in Athens* (1954), took nearly two years to make, partly because Cacoyannis had to master film techniques by trial and error. After its showing at the Edinburgh Film Festival, the film won international attention and soon became a top box-office hit. With his second film, *Stella* (1955), Cacoyannis substantially enhanced his own prestige and that of the Greek motion-picture industry. In the five years following the completion of *Stella*, Cacoyannis made four films: *A Girl in Black* (1957), which won a Golden Globe; *A Matter of Dignity* (1958), acclaimed by London critics as the best film of the year; *Our Last Spring* (1959); and *The Wastrel* (1960). During that time the director also staged, among other plays, Oscar Wilde's *A Woman of No Importance* and N. Richard Nash's *The Rainmaker* in Athens. Cacoyannis's next film, *Electra* (1961), won him a place among the world's great directors. Working from a script that he had adapted from the work by Euripides, on location

in Greece, and with an all-Greek cast, he fashioned the classic tragedy into a picture that received international acclaim. The film won a special prize at the Cannes Film Festival and some 20 additional international awards. Cacoyannis's next screen venture, *Zorba the Greek* (1964), starred Anthony Quinn. "[The picture] created a cultural phenomenon that transcended filmmaking," Paul Vitello wrote for the *New York Times* (July 25, 2011, on-line). "Quinn's barefooted, dancing, woman-loving Zorba became a symbol of Greek vitality that boosted Greek tourism for decades." The film earned an Oscar nod as best picture, and Cacoyannis was nominated as best director. (None of his later movies received that level of acclaim.) He subsequently directed numerous well-received plays, many by Euripides and Aristophanes, and several opera productions, including Puccini's *La Bohème* and Mozart's *La Clemenza di Tito*. Cacoyannis died in Athens and is survived by his sister, Giannoula. See *Current Biography* (1966). —D.K.

Obituary *New York Times* (on-line) July 25, 2011

CAREY, HUGH L. Apr. 11, 1919–Aug. 7, 2011 Former governor of New York. Hugh Carey served as the governor of New York from 1975 through 1982, and he was widely credited with averting one of the worst fiscal crises in the state's history. One of six brothers, Carey was born in the New York City borough of Brooklyn to Denis J. Carey, who founded a successful fuel-delivery company, and Margaret (Collins) Carey, a former secretary for the journalist Nellie Bly. After graduating from a Catholic high school in 1938, Carey entered St. John's College (now St. John's University), in Brooklyn, as a history major, but his studies were interrupted by World War II. Enlisting in the 101st Cavalry of the New York National Guard, he attended Officers Candidate School and was commissioned in the 104th Infantry Division. In combat in France, Belgium, Holland, and Germany, he rose to the rank of major and won the American Bronze Star and the French Croix de Guerre, among other honors. After his release from active duty, he attained the rank of lieutenant colonel in the Army Reserve. Carey subsequently entered St. John's Law School, earning his LL.B. degree in 1951. Joining the family concern, the Peerless Oil and Chemical Corp., he served first as sales manager and later as vice president. In 1960 Carey narrowly won a seat in the U.S. House of Representatives, beating the popular Republican incumbent, Francis Dorn, by some 1,000 votes. A relative liberal, he ultimately spent seven terms in Congress, serving on the House Education and Labor Committee and later on the influential Ways and Means Committee. In 1969 he ran for mayor of New York City, but when his teenage sons Hugh Jr. and Peter were killed in a car accident, he dropped out of the race. In 1974 Carey's wife, Helen, died of cancer. In November of that year, Carey, then a widower with several young children still at home, won New York's gubernatorial race, helped by a generous campaign chest provided by his brother Edward, the head of the New England Petroleum Corp. (While many observers were surprised that he ran, given his responsibilities at home, Carey claimed to need the distraction of an important job to help him cope with the recent loss of his wife.) Carey took the reins of a state facing one of the worst economic situations since the Depression. A previous governor, Nelson Rockefeller, who served from 1959 to 1973, when he stepped down to establish the bipartisan Commission on Critical Choices for Americans, had presided in an era of generous spending and escalating deficits. When he was inaugurated, in January 1975, Carey announced, "This government will begin today the painful, difficult, imperative process of learning to live within its means." With New York City close to bankruptcy at one point, and the entire state in dire financial straits, Carey took drastic action, persuading banks to refinance the city's debts and municipal unions to invest their pension funds in city bonds, creating the powerful Emergency Financial Control Board, and wrangling more than $2 billion in federal loan guarantees. He also ended free tuition at the City University of New York (CUNY), placed a freeze on welfare payments, raised public-transportation fares, and eliminated civil-service jobs. Such austerity measures, while effective, sometimes made him unpopular, and he was challenged in the 1978 primary by his own lieutenant governor, Mary Anne Krupsak. He eked out a victory over his Republican opponent, Perry B. Duryea, by only a slim margin that November. During his second gubernatorial term, Carey became known more for his personal life—marrying Evangeline Gouletas, a wealthy, thrice-divorced supporter, after a whirlwind courtship; dyeing his hair; and becoming a fixture on New York's black-tie circuit—than for his political agenda. At the end of his second term, in December 1982, he retired from politics, despite a long list of accomplishments that included reforming the state's nursing homes and attracting the 1976 and 1980 Democratic National Conventions to Madison Square Garden. He spent the ensuing years practicing law and later became an executive at the chemicals conglomerate W. R. Grace. Carey, who had divorced his second wife after less than a decade, died at his summer home on Shelter Island, New York, at the age of 92. In addition to the two sons he had lost in an auto accident, another son, Paul, predeceased him, in 2001. He is survived by his daughters, Alexandria, Susan, Marianne, Nancy, and Helen; his sons Christopher, Michael, Donald, Bryan, Kevin, and Thomas; and some 25 grandchildren. See *Current Biography* (1965). —M.R.

Obituary *New York Times* (on-line) Aug. 7, 2011

CHERNOMYRDIN, VIKTOR Apr. 9, 1938—Nov. 3, 2010 Former prime minister of Russia. Viktor Chernomyrdin served as Russia's prime minister from December 1992 to March 1998, during the tumultuous transition to a free-market economy that followed the fall of Communism. Gennadi E. Burbulis, a former parliamentarian, told Ellen Barry and Michael Schwirtz for the *New York Times* (November 4, 2010), "Chernomyrdin turned out to be the strongest, most effective and flexible bridge for the extraordinary work of our generation: raising and building a new Russia from the ruins of the totalitarian Soviet system." Chernomyrdin was born to a poor Cossack family in the Ural Mountains village of Cherny Ostrog, in Russia. In 1957 he began working

at the Orsk Oil Refinery as a metalworker and machinist, and eventually he became the chief of the refinery's technical unit. From 1973 to 1978 he served as the deputy chief engineer and director of the Orenberg Gas Refinery. Meanwhile, in 1963, Chernomyrdin became an instructor in the transportation department of the Orsk Region Communist Party; in time he became deputy head and then head of the department. Concurrently, he attended the Kuybishev Polytechnical Institute, from which he graduated in 1966, and in 1972, through a correspondence course, he earned an M.S. degree in technical sciences from the All-Union Polytechnical School. Chernomyrdin subsequently progressed steadily through the ranks of the Communist Party's Central Committee. In 1982 he was named deputy natural-gas minister, and in 1985 he was promoted to natural-gas minister. In that capacity, in 1989, he presided over the creation of Gazprom, a state-owned corporate complex that produced over 90 percent of Soviet natural gas. Chernomyrdin chaired Gazprom's board from 1989 until mid-1992, when he left to become deputy prime minister under Yegor Gaidar, who had just become acting prime minister. Concurrently, Chernomyrdin served as minister of fuel and energy. In December 1992 he was appointed by President Boris Yeltsin to replace Gaidar as prime minister. "While serving as prime minister, Mr. Chernomyrdin remained so closely associated with Gazprom that the political party he founded, Our Home is Russia, was jokingly referred to as 'Our Home is Gazprom,'" Barry and Schwirtz wrote. "His company was allowed to expand lavishly despite falling behind on tax payments. It also stepped in to assist the Kremlin at key moments, foreclosing on the media empire of Vladimir A. Gusinsky, who had turned into a sharp critic, and putting pressure on neighboring countries like Georgia and Ukraine when they fell behind on payments." Chernomyrdin's popularity arguably reached a peak in June 1995, when he effectively defused a hostage crisis connected with an armed conflict between Russian troops and Chechen rebels in the Republic of Chechnya. In 1998 Russia's already weak economy was severely affected by the fallout from the Asian financial crisis, as well as by declining prices for oil, one of its chief exports. Furthermore, back wages for millions of Russian workers continued to loom as a major problem. Against that backdrop of economic turmoil, Chernomyrdin was dismissed by Yeltsin, who replaced him with a young reformist, Sergei Kiriyenko. When Chernomyrdin's removal from office did little to quell the downward spiral of the economy, Yeltsin attempted to reinstate him as prime minister but was blocked from doing so by Parliament. When Vladimir Putin came to power, in 2000, he removed Chernomyrdin as chair of Gazprom, giving the post to Dmitri A. Medvedev. (In 2008 Medvedev succeeded Putin as president.) For the remainder of his career, Chernomyrdin served as an ambassador to Ukraine, and in that capacity he was an important participant in negotiations over natural-gas prices. (Ukraine's pipelines carry Russia's gas to Europe.) His tenure was marked by a bitterly contentious dispute in January 2009 that resulted in the blocking of Russian gas supplies to the European Union. Once listed as one of the wealthiest men in Russia thanks to his affiliation

with Gazprom, Chernomyrdin left his ambassador-
ship in June 2009 and died of undisclosed causes the
following year. He was predeceased by Valentina,
his wife of five decades, and survived by their two
sons. His funeral was broadcast live on Russian television. See *Current Biography* (1998). —H.R.W.

Obituary *New York Times* A p20 Nov. 4, 2010

CHILUBA, FREDERICK Apr. 30, 1943–June 18, 2011
Former president of Zambia. In 1991, when he became the first democratically elected president of
Zambia, Frederick Chiluba seemed to be ushering in
a new era in Zambian politics. His 11-year tenure,
however, was tarnished by corruption and efforts to
silence his opposition. The son of Jacob Titus Chiluba Nkonde and his wife, Diana Kaimba, Frederick Jacob Titus Chiluba was born in Kitwe, a major urban
center in what was then the Protectorate of Northern
Rhodesia. Chiluba's father worked in the region's
British-run copper mines. Still a child when his father died, Chiluba was reared mainly by his grandmother. He was forced to drop out of high school because of financial troubles at home, and he went to
work as a personnel clerk on a sisal plantation in
neighboring Tanzania, where he became interested
in the country's nascent labor movement. Already
resentful of the British colonialists, Chiluba became
a supporter of the anti-Western nationalist fervor
then sweeping Africa, and as a young man he became convinced that the Soviet Union and its Communist neighbors were his country's natural allies—a sentiment not uncommon among Africans at
that time. In 1966, back in Zambia, Chiluba became
an accounts assistant at a Swedish mining-
equipment company. About a year later he joined the
National Union of Building, Engineering, and General Workers, and in 1971 he was elected its chairman,
a post he retained until 1987. During Chiluba's reign
as the trade-union boss, his unwavering opposition
to the economic program of Kenneth D. Kaunda—the
ruler of the southern African nation since it gained
independence from Great Britain, in 1964—
occasionally got him into trouble with the government. Other labor leaders soon joined Chiluba in his
criticism of Kaunda's increasingly authoritarian
rule. The last straw came in 1972, when Kaunda declared his United National Independence Party
(UNIP) the country's sole legal political party. In
1974 Chiluba was elected leader of the Zambia Congress of Trade Unions (ZCTU), an umbrella organization comprising 18 affiliated unions; by that point he
believed that Zambia's most serious problems were
economic and that they could be solved only by li-
beralizing the economy and cooperating with the
West. In 1980 Chiluba, as head of the ZCTU, threatened to call a strike, and in January 1981 he and 16
other labor leaders were expelled by Kaunda from
the UNIP, effectively removing them from the leadership of their respective trade unions. Outraged workers staged sporadic strikes over the next several
months, resulting in a major domestic crisis. Later
that year Chiluba and three union leaders were arrested for plotting to overthrow Kaunda. Chiluba
was released three months later, after the imprisonment was ruled unconstitutional. Though there was
no evidence that he had conspired to remove Kaun-

da from the presidency, he was certainly promoting
himself as a viable alternative to the Zambian dictator. Chiluba gained support from various tribes and
groups in Zambia during the 1980s, but the demo-
cratic-revolution movement was largely dormant until 1989, when pro-democracy groups began to overthrow Communist regimes in Eastern Europe. Chiluba joined a coalition of business leaders, academics,
church leaders, and dissident politicians to form the
Movement for Multiparty Democracy (MMD). In December 1990 Kaunda—wearied by recent strikes—
lifted the ban on political activity, and the MMD immediately registered as a political party. At its first
national convention, held in February and March
1991, the MMD elected Chiluba as its president. His
elevation to the post also made him the MMD's presidential candidate in the elections scheduled for October 1991—the first multiparty elections since
1968. With his fiery oratory and impassioned calls
for economic reform and improved human rights, he
regularly drew large and enthusiastic crowds at his
campaign rallies. He appealed to citizens' desire to
take active roles in rebuilding their nation, which
had been ravaged by decades of corruption and economic mismanagement. Identifying the government's quasi-socialist policies as the source of Zambia's economic woes, he promised to rebuild the
country by restructuring the economy according to
free-market principles. On October 31, 1991 Chiluba
was elected president with 81 percent of the vote,
and the MMD won 90 percent of the vote in the legislative balloting for the National Assembly. Nicknamed "Mr. Fourfoot" because he stood less than
five feet tall, Chiluba initially appeared to be steering
the country toward greater openness and free-market
policies. He began to deregulate the price of maize,
the country's staple food, and took steps to rid the
government of bureaucrats who had few, if any,
qualifications beyond a devotion to Kaunda. However, over the course of his tenure as president, Chiluba
failed to end the country's dependence on foreign
aid or substantially affect its high poverty rate. His
government also became known for corruption. In
1996 he barred Kaunda from running against him by
altering the constitution to preclude candidates born
outside Zambia, and in 2001 he tried to rewrite the
law to allow him to serve a third term. When church
and civic groups protested, he appointed Levy
Mwanawasa, his former vice president, as his successor. Rather than concealing his predecessor's secrets, Mwanawasa publicly revealed the extent of
Chiluba's corruption. Charged with stealing half a
million dollars of public funds, Chiluba was sued by
Zambia's attorney general. At the trial, which took
place in Great Britain—where Chiluba was said to
have laundered millions of dollars—testimony revealed Chiluba's extravagant collection of clothing,
which included 349 shirts, 206 suits, and 72 pairs of
shoes. In 2007 a high court demanded that he return
$57 million to Zambia, a ruling Chiluba termed "rac-
ist" and "obscene." In the six-year-long criminal trial, Chiluba claimed that he had received millions of
gifts from corporations and other "well-wishers" but
did not reveal their identities. In 2009 he was acquit-
ted by a magistrate in a Zambian criminal court.
Chiluba, who had long suffered from chronic heart
problems, died in Lusaka. He is survived by his wife,

Regina, and, reportedly, 10 children. See *Current Biography* (1992). —M.R.M.

Obituary *New York Times* (on-line) June 19, 2011

CHRISTOPHER, WARREN Oct. 27, 1925–Mar. 18, 2011 Former U.S. secretary of state. As deputy secretary of state under President Jimmy Carter from 1977 to 1981, Warren Christopher served both as the congressional point man for securing the passage of the Panama Canal treaties, which provided for the return of control of the canal to the government of Panama, and as the chief American negotiator for the release of the 52 Americans taken hostage by Iranian students in the aftermath of the revolution that ended the repressive reign of Shah Mohammad Reza Pahlavi. He also served as secretary of state to President Bill Clinton from 1993 to 1997. Christopher, the fourth of the five children of Ernest Christopher, a banker, and the former Anna Lemen, a homemaker, was born in Scranton, North Dakota. Ernest suffered a stroke in 1937, following the collapse of his bank, and he died two years later; Anna subsequently worked as a sales clerk to support the family, which she moved to California. After graduating from Hollywood High School, Christopher attended the University of Redlands before transferring to the University of Southern California, in Los Angeles. He earned a bachelor's degree in 1945. On completing three years of service in the naval reserve, in 1946, he entered Stanford University Law School, where he was the founding editor of the *Stanford Law Review* and a member of the Order of the Coif, an honor society. Equipped with his law degree, which he received in 1949, he clerked for a year in Washington, D.C., for Justice William O. Douglas of the United States Supreme Court. Upon his return to Los Angeles in 1950, Christopher joined the prestigious and politically influential law firm O'Melveny & Myers, of which he was made a partner in 1958. In 1959 he worked as special counsel to California governor Edmund G. ("Pat") Brown, a Democrat. Perhaps Christopher's most prominent position in the California phase of his public-service career came in 1965, when he was appointed by Brown to the position of vice chairman of the McCone Commission, chaired by former CIA director John McCone, which was established to look into the causes of urban rioting that year in the Watts section of Los Angeles. Christopher's work on that commission brought him to the attention of President Lyndon B. Johnson, who appointed him to serve as deputy attorney general under Ramsey Clark. While serving in that role, from 1967 to 1969, Christopher worked to quell violence and ease racial tensions in Detroit and Washington. He then returned to O'Melveny & Myers, where he sat out the administrations of Presidents Richard Nixon and Gerald R. Ford. He was summoned back to Washington in 1976, when President Jimmy Carter appointed him to serve as his deputy secretary of state under Cyrus Vance. In carrying out Carter's foreign policy, which was marked by an emphasis on human rights—in rhetoric if not always in deed—Vance and Christopher accumulated a mixed record. In 1978 Christopher denounced the Khmer Rouge's actions in Cambodia, where that group of Commu-

nist revolutionaries led by Pol Pot had been conducting a ruralization campaign that had resulted in hundreds of thousands of deaths since 1975. But he was silent on the issue of violations of human rights in neighboring East Timor, which had lost an estimated one-fifth of its population after being invaded and occupied by Indonesia in 1975. In 1979 Christopher denounced the Nicaraguan dictator Anastasio Somoza, from whose regime the United States withdrew its support at that time. But evidently Christopher did not publicly criticize Philippine leader Ferdinand Marcos, who had placed his country under martial law in 1972 (not to be lifted until 1981) and who continued to receive American support. Christopher was more successful in the role of mediator and negotiator. Of particular concern during the Carter administration was the passage of the Panama Canal treaties, whereby the United States would honor its nearly century-old commitment to return control of the canal zone, and eventually of the canal itself, to the government of Panama. When the treaties, which had become a topic of intense public debate in 1977, ran into trouble in Congress in 1978, Christopher successfully defended the pacts, which were ratified by the Senate in March and April of that year. Another area in which Christopher was particularly effective was in alleviating tensions between the United States and its allies. In 1978 he promised to end the arms embargo against Turkey, which had threatened to withdraw from NATO, and in 1979 he was dispatched to Taiwan to work out a framework of economic cooperation and security arrangements for the island nation after Carter's official recognition of the People's Republic of China, on December 31, 1978, had made state-to-state relations with Taiwan impossible. Christopher also became a key administration spokesman against the 1979 Soviet invasion of Afghanistan, and he defended to Congress the administration's decision to boycott the 1980 Summer Olympic Games in Moscow. The most prominent role played by Christopher during the Carter administration came in its final year, when he emerged as chief negotiator in the Iranian hostage crisis, which began in November 1979 with the seizure by Iranian students of the American Embassy, and its 52 officials and staffers, in Tehran. A botched helicopter rescue attempt in April 1980 led to Vance's resignation; Christopher's hopes of succeeding his mentor were dashed when Carter selected Senator Edmund S. Muskie of Maine. Christopher considered resigning because of the snub, but he stayed on to continue to work for the release of the hostages. He became the primary American negotiator in September 1980, when a high Iranian official made conciliatory remarks and spelled out conditions for the release of the hostages. After Ronald Reagan was elected president two months later, Carter put pressure on Christopher to hurry the negotiations along, so that the hostages could be freed while he occupied the White House. On January 7, 1981 Christopher flew to Algeria for a final round of talks, which continued until a few minutes after Reagan was sworn into office, on January 20. Christopher was on hand in the Algerian capital of Algiers later that day to greet the planeload of former hostages on the first leg of their journey back to the United States. During Reagan's presidency, Christopher returned to

O'Melveny & Myers, where he played a prominent role in increasing the already nationally renowned firm's stature and scope. In 1991 Christopher was called on by Los Angeles mayor Tom Bradley to head a commission charged with investigating the allegations of brutality and racism in the Los Angeles Police Department, in the wake of the infamous Rodney King beating. Christopher returned to the national political scene in 1992, when he was selected to serve as head of the Democratic presidential nominee Bill Clinton's vice-presidential search committee. Christopher went on to serve as the manager of President Clinton's transition team before being appointed secretary of state. During his one-term tenure as Clinton's secretary of state, from 1993 to 1997, Christopher worked to expand NATO and broker peace in the Middle East, among other tasks. Exceptionally reserved and self-effacing, Christopher took the brunt of the criticism for the Clinton administration's failure to intercede quickly enough in the events leading up to the Rwandan genocide and inability to persuade China to improve its human-rights record. After stepping down as secretary of state, Christopher again returned to O'Melveny & Myers. In 2000 he directed the search for Al Gore's vice-presidential running mate and was later sent to supervise the Florida recount following that year's contested presidential election. Christopher died at his home in Los Angeles from kidney and bladder cancer. He is survived by his wife of over five decades, the former Marie Wyllis; their three children, Scott, Thomas, and Kristen; a daughter, Lynn, from his first, short-lived marriage, to Joan Southgate Workman; and five grandchildren. See *Current Biography* (1995). —C.C.

Obituary *New York Times* (on-line) Mar. 19, 2011

CLAYBURGH, JILL Apr. 30, 1944–Nov. 5, 2010 Actress. During her decades-long career, Jill Clayburgh was known for her portrayals of strong, independent women in a number of films, and she was nominated for Academy Awards for her roles in *An Unmarried Woman* (1978) and *Starting Over* (1979). Matt Schudel wrote for the *Washington Post* (November 6, 2010, on-line), "Clayburgh was part of the generation of female actors, including Sally Field, Faye Dunaway and Marsha Mason, who came of age during the feminist revolution of the 1960s [and] she brought an unflinching honesty to her roles." The actress was born in New York City to Albert Henry and Julia (Door) Clayburgh. Julia had been the producer David Merrick's secretary before her marriage, and Albert was the vice president of two successful companies. Clayburgh's paternal grandmother, Alma, was a celebrated opera singer and socialite. Clayburgh attended Sarah Lawrence College, in Bronxville, New York. While still in college she co-starred with her friend Robert De Niro in her first film, *The Wedding Party*, an independently financed production that another friend, Brian De Palma, helped to direct. After she had obtained her B.A. degree in theater from Sarah Lawrence, in 1966, she studied acting in Manhattan with Uta Hagen and joined the Charles Playhouse in Boston, where she worked in both the children's and adult companies. In 1968

Clayburgh made her Broadway debut, in *The Sudden & Accidental Re-Education of Horse Johnson*, which starred Jack Klugman and ran for five performances. Her other Broadway productions of that era included the musicals *The Rothschilds* (1970) and *Pippin* (1972). A turning point in Clayburgh's career came when she was cast as a prostitute in the made-for-television movie *Hustling* (1975) and was nominated for an Emmy Award for the role. Among Clayburgh's most iconic roles was that of Erica Benton in the 1978 film *An Unmarried Woman*; Benton is a recently divorced New York woman who—freed during the height of the 1970s sexual revolution from her marriage of 16 years—begins to explore her options. With few exceptions, critics agreed that Clayburgh had given a virtually flawless performance. In his evaluation for the *National Review* (April 14, 1978), John Simon found her Benton to be "a woman rendered in all the complex interplay of antithetical impulses, ranging from subservience and vulnerability to angry or hopeful resilience." Clayburgh's creation of the character brought her an Oscar nomination for best actress, the best-actress award (shared with Isabelle Huppert) at the Cannes Film Festival, and New York's Golden Apple for best film actress. The following year Clayburgh appeared as a single teacher pursuing a divorced man (played by Burt Reynolds) in *Starting Over*, which was a box-office success and earned Clayburgh her second Academy Award nomination. Some of Clayburgh's other noteworthy films include *It's My Turn* (1980), *First Monday in October* (1981), and *I'm Dancing as Fast as I Can* (1982). She frequently appeared on the small screen, in numerous TV movies and, later in her career, on such series as *Ally McBeal*, *Dirty Sexy Money*, *The Practice*, *Nip/Tuck*, and *Law & Order*. Clayburgh died after a 21-year battle with chronic lymphocytic leukemia. Her final film, the hit comedy *Bridesmaids*, opened in May 2011, months after her death. She is survived by her husband, the playwright David Rabe, to whom she had been married since 1978; her daughter, the actress Lily Rabe; her son, Michael; and her stepson, Jason. See *Current Biography* (1979). —W.D.

Obituary *New York Times* (on-line) Nov. 5, 2010

CORWIN, NORMAN May 3, 1910–Oct. 18, 2011 Radio pioneer. During the years that are widely considered the "golden age" of American radio—roughly the mid-1930s to the late 1940s—Norman Corwin, a dramatist and producer, brought to the medium a new degree of verbal facility and seriousness of purpose. Among his most-loved broadcasts—which included children's stories, satires, adaptations of poetry, and historical re-creations—were *They Fly Through the Air with the Greatest of Ease*, a powerful imagining of the thoughts of a Fascist bomber crew, which aired in February 1939; *We Hold These Truths*, a docudrama produced for the 150th anniversary of the Bill of Rights that was heard simultaneously on four American networks about a week after the attack on Pearl Harbor; and *On a Note of Triumph*, a poetic celebration of the Allied victory in Europe that was broadcast on May 8, 1945. Corwin was born in Boston, Massachusetts, the third son of the former Rose Ober and Samuel Corwin, a printer who had emigrated from England. "The interests of my boyhood vacillated between the Boston Symphony, the Boston Braves, and the Boston Public Library," Corwin wrote for the volume *World Authors 1900–1950* (1996). Misrepresenting himself as older, Corwin was hired as a cub reporter by the Greenfield, Massachusetts, *Daily Recorder* at the age of 17. He later moved to the *Springfield Republican*. "[For a decade] I covered everything from politics through crime to music, and was at various times a sports writer, movie critic and radio editor," he wrote for *World Authors*. "In 1936 I first let myself into the mixmaster of New York City, and after some skidding and churning I landed, more or less upright, in the program department of the Columbia Broadcasting System [CBS]." Corwin remained at CBS, producing such popular series as *26 by Corwin* and *Columbia Presents Corwin*, until 1949, when he quit in a dispute over the subsidiary rights to his radio writing. That year he joined the United Nations as chief of special radio projects, and in that capacity he produced several documentaries that were aired internationally. Despite the fulfillment provided by such efforts, Corwin gradually became disillusioned by the increasing commercialization of radio. Like many other political liberals in the early 1950s, he was blacklisted for alleged Communist leanings, and many of his projects went unrealized. He abandoned the medium entirely in 1955. However, that same decade he began to have some success as a screenwriter, and in 1956 his script for the film *Lust for Life*, about the artist Vincent Van Gogh, was nominated for an Academy Award. During the following decades Corwin worked as an occasional playwright (his 1959 drama, *The Rivalry*, about Abraham Lincoln and Stephen Douglas, ran on Broadway for 81 performances) and as a teacher of creative writing at various universities. He wrote several books, including the essay collection *Holes in a Stained Glass Window* (1978) and *Trivializing America* (1983), a volume of social criticism. He returned to radio in 1999, producing the half-hour public-radio broadcast *Memos to a New Millennium*, which was narrated by Walter Cronkite. A documentary film, *A Note of Triumph: The Golden Age of Norman Corwin* (2005), directed by Eric Simonson, garnered an Academy Award for best short documentary. Corwin, a 1993 inductee into the Radio Hall of Fame and two-time winner of the Peabody Award, died at his home in Los Angeles at the age of 101. He was predeceased, in 1995, by his wife of almost five decades, the actress Katherine Locke, and survived by their children, Anthony and Diane. See *Current Biography* (1940). —M.R.

Obituary *New York Times* (on-line) Oct. 19, 2011

DAVIS, AL July 4, 1929–Oct. 8, 2011 Owner of the Oakland Raiders football team. "Before there were sports franchise owners like George Steinbrenner, Jerry Jones or Mark Cuban, there was Al Davis, outspoken and brash, who was a central figure in the merger of the upstart American Football League with the established N.F.L., paved the way for the extravaganza known as the Super Bowl, and managed to win championships while irritating the rest of pro football," Bruce Weber wrote for the *New York*

Times (October 8, 2011, on-line). Davis was born in Brockton, Massachusetts, to Rose (Kirschenbaum) Davis and Louis Davis, the well-to-do proprietor of a clothing store and other enterprises. When he was five his family moved to the New York City borough of Brooklyn, where he attended P.S. 189, Winthrop Junior High, and Erasmus Hall High School. His sports idols were men in positions of power such as George Weiss, a general manager of the Yankees, and Branch Rickey, an owner of the Brooklyn Dodgers. Davis earned a bachelor's degree in English from Syracuse University in 1950. Sidestepping a career in the family business, that fall he fast-talked his way into a job as a football offensive-line coach at Adelphi College in Garden City, Long Island; in addition, he doubled as head baseball coach, the youngest ever hired by an American college. When he was drafted into the U.S. Army, in 1952, and assigned to special services at Fort Belvoir, Virginia, Davis became the first private ever to serve as the head coach of a military team. His allegedly underhanded methods for securing pro-football players and college stars who had been drafted into military service nearly triggered a congressional investigation. Nevertheless, after Davis's discharge, in 1954, his recruiting abilities helped him to land a job as a scout for the Baltimore Colts, and in 1955 he was hired as a line coach and chief recruiter for the Citadel. Several of his best recruits left the Citadel with Davis when, in 1957, he accepted a post as line coach for the University of Southern California (USC). Davis signed on as offensive end coach for the Los Angeles Chargers in 1960, the first year of play for the new American Football League (AFL), which had been founded in 1959. Although the AFL recruiters faced stiff competition for talent from the established National Football League (NFL), "baby-sitting" promising college stars who were also sought after by the NFL proved to be Davis's strength. His reputation for abrasive aggressiveness led to his appointment, on January 15, 1963, as both head coach and general manager of the AFL Oakland Raiders, a virtually stillborn franchise that had lost 33 of its first 42 games. Davis, the youngest person ever to be the head coach and general manager of a professional football team, worked hard to transform the Raiders' image. He changed the team colors to black and silver, assigned it the motto "Pride and Poise," and chose as its logo a helmeted pirate with a patch over one eye and crossed swords behind him. An avid reader of military history, Davis ran his training camp in paramilitary fashion and took elaborate security precautions to prevent opposing teams from discovering his stratagems. After earning only a .214 winning percentage under three different coaches in their first three seasons, under Davis's guidance the Raiders posted 10 wins against only four losses in 1963 and lost the Western Division championship by only one game. Davis was named Coach of the Year by the Associated Press, United Press International, *Sports Illustrated*, the *Sporting News*, and his fellow coaches. While the Raiders were maturing into a team to be reckoned with, the fledgling AFL was in the midst of a cutthroat bidding war for college recruits with the 47-year-old NFL and its commissioner, Pete Rozelle. Unhappy with the performance of Joe Foss, their own commissioner, the AFL owners hired Al Davis to replace him on April 8, 1966. Putting his recruiting talents to the test once again, the new commissioner set out to weaken the NFL clubs by signing their disgruntled star quarterbacks. Within only eight weeks NFL owners had acceded to a merger. After being passed over for the post of commissioner of the unified league in favor of Rozelle, a disgruntled Davis returned to the Oakland Raiders as the managing general partner with a 10 percent share of the club. Although Davis earned the loyalty of most of his players, many of whom had been undervalued by their former teams, his detractors maintained that he relied on such dirty tricks as watering the field before home games to slow opponents and bugging visiting teams' locker rooms to get an inside edge for his squad. According to Al Stump in *Los Angeles* magazine (November 1984), his "reputation as a spook, a shadowy saboteur who'd do anything to win . . . spread throughout the league to the point of paranoia." Davis also gained a reputation for feuding with football officials, suing the NFL several times and tarring the league as an "unlawful cartel" for forbidding him to move his franchise from Oakland to Los Angeles. (In 1982 the Raiders began playing at the Los Angeles Coliseum, but Davis changed his mind and in 1995 moved the team back to Oakland.) No less prickly with his own employees, Davis, who became the team's principal owner in 2005, saw several head coaches come and go during his tenure. During his reign the Raiders played in five Super Bowls and won three, in 1977, 1981 and 1984. They also became the first franchise in recent history to hire, according to Weber, "a Latino head coach (Tom Flores), a black head coach (Art Shell) and a female chief executive (Amy Trask)." Davis, a 1992 inductee into the Pro Football Hall of Fame, died at his home in Oakland. He is survived by his wife, Carol, and son, Mark. The Raiders released a statement upon his death that read, in part, "Al Davis was unique, a maverick, a giant among giants, a true legend among legends, the brightest star among stars, a hero, a mentor, a friend." Most other posthumous tributes to Davis described him as "irascible," "controversial," and "rebellious," among other such terms. "I don't want to be the most respected team in the league," Davis once said. "I want to be the most feared." See *Current Biography* (1985). —M.R.

Obituary *New York Times* (on-line) Oct. 8, 2011

DE LAURENTIIS, DINO Aug. 8, 1919–Nov. 10, 2010
Film producer. One of the giants of Italian cinema, Dino De Laurentiis played a vital role in reviving his country's film industry after World War II and produced hundreds of movies over a career that spanned over six decades. A larger-than-life personality and a fearless self-promoter, he was known as much for his blockbuster successes as for his colossal failures. Born in the town of Torre Annunziata on the Bay of Naples, in Italy, Agostino De Laurentiis was the third of seven children. His father, a prosperous mill owner and pasta manufacturer, groomed him to take over the business, and at the age of 15, De Laurentiis dropped out of school and began traveling around Italy selling his family's products. Struck by the magic of the cinema and dissatisfied with the career path planned for him, he fled to

Rome in 1937 to enroll in acting classes at the Centro Sperimentale di Cinematografia. His father, angered by the defection, cut off his allowance, but De Laurentiis found work as an extra to support himself while continuing his studies at the school. He soon discovered that he was more interested in creating films than in acting in them, and he subsequently took a series of motion-picture jobs, including prop man, assistant director, and unit-production manager, en route to becoming a producer. In 1941, after boldly convincing a financial backer of his credibility, De Laurentiis launched his own production company, Real Cine, in Turin, then the center of the Italian film industry. The following year he became executive producer of Lux Film. World War II, however, delayed De Laurentiis's progress. According to an article by Arthur L. Mayer in the *New York Herald Tribune* (June 3, 1956), during the war he "deserted from the Italian Army and hid out on the Isle of Capri to wait for the arrival of Allied troops whom he could join." The only books available to him for many months were Homer's *Odyssey* and Leo Tolstoy's *War and Peace*. He reread them often and became determined to film both classics someday. De Laurentiis was among the first to produce neorealistic films as part of the postwar reaction in Italy against the celluloid fantasies of Hollywood. His early movies included *La Miserie del Signor Travet* (1945), *Il Bandito* (1946), *La Figlia del Capitano* (1947), and *Il Brigante Musolino* (1950). One of his most successful postwar films was the story of migrant workers in the Po Valley rice fields, *Riso Amaro* (*Bitter Rice*), which was released in the United States in 1950. The film was notable for introducing to American audiences the Italian star Silvana Mangano, whom De Laurentiis married while making the picture. In 1950 De Laurentiis and a colleague, Carlo Ponti (who married the Italian actress Sophia Loren several years later), left Lux to form their own production company, Ponti-De Laurentiis Cinematografica. They soon produced Federico Fellini's masterpiece *La Strada*. Besides winning top honors in Europe, including the Grand Prize of the Venice International Film Festival in 1954, *La Strada*, which was released in New York City in 1956, won an Academy Award as the best foreign-language picture. In sharp contrast with *La Strada*, a low-budget picture with only three principal characters, was *War and Peace* (1956), one of many extravaganzas that De Laurentiis produced with an eye to capturing a wider audience. For that project he assembled an international roster of top stars, headed by Audrey Hepburn, Henry Fonda, and Mel Ferrer, to take the leading roles and signed King Vidor as director. (De Laurentiis is often credited as being among the first to realize the marketability of large, international co-productions.) Despite its mixed reception as a work of dramatic art, few critics denied that *War and Peace* was a stunning spectacle. Vista Vision and other new techniques made possible the depiction of such events as the Battle of Austerlitz on a scale never seen before. Technical experts supervised every detail of background and costumes to assure authenticity, and the Italian government provided 15,000 soldiers for the battle scenes. *War and Peace* marked the end of the Ponti-De Laurentiis partnership. The two had produced some 80 pictures together over the course of six years. After splitting with Ponti De Laurentiis worked as an independent producer, backing another Fellini Oscar winner, *Nights of Cabiria* (1957). During the 1960s De Laurentiis built a massive studio complex on the outskirts of Rome, dubbed Dinocitta, or "Dino City." There, he helped pioneer the now widely used practice of financing films by pre-selling the distribution rights in foreign countries and produced such films as Richard Fleischer's *Barabbas* (1961), John Huston's blockbuster *The Bible* (1966), Roger Vadim's *Barbarella* (1968), and Franco Zeffirelli's *Romeo and Juliet* (1968), among others. In 1972 De Laurentiis—facing financial troubles and onerous new regulations put into place by Italy's socialist government—was forced to close Dinocitta. He then moved to the U.S. and went on to produce a number of other well-known and critically acclaimed films, including *The Valachi Papers* (1972), *Serpico* (1973), *Death Wish* (1974), *Three Days of the Condor* (1975), *The Shootist* (1976), *Ragtime* (1981), *Conan the Barbarian* (1982), and *Blue Velvet* (1986). Those successes were accompanied by several high-profile failures, including the 1976 remake of *King Kong*, the killer-whale film *Orca* (1977), the disaster movie *Hurricane* (1979), and the David Lynch sci-fi adaptation *Dune* (1984). Although he was plagued by periodic financial difficulties, De Laurentiis continued to produce films until 2007; some of his later hits include the thrillers *Hannibal* (2001), *Red Dragon* (2002), and *Hannibal Rising* (2007). He also enjoyed a good relationship with the writer Stephen King and produced several film adaptations of King's work, including *The Dead Zone* (1983), *Cat's Eye* (1985), *Silver Bullet* (1985), *Maximum Overdrive* (1986), and *Sometimes They Come Back* (1991). For his lasting contributions to cinema, De Laurentiis won the prestigious Irving G. Thalberg Memorial Award (2001) from the Motion Picture Arts and Sciences board of governors and the David O. Selznick Award (2004) from the Producers Guild of America. He died at his home in Beverly Hills, California. He was predeceased in 1989 by his first wife. (The two had filed for divorce the year before her death.) He was also predeceased by a son, Federico, from his union with Mangano, who perished in a plane crash in 1981. De Laurentiis is survived by his second wife, the American-born producer Martha Schumacher; three daughters from his first marriage, Veronica, Raffaella, and Francesca, and two daughters from his second marriage, Carolyna and Dina; five grandchildren, one of whom is the popular Food Network personality Giada De Laurentiis; and two great-grandchildren. See *Current Biography* (1965). —C.C.

Obituary *New York Times* B p17 Nov. 12, 2010

DUTTON, DENIS Feb. 9, 1944–Dec. 28, 2010 Philosopher; writer; editor; digital-media guru. Denis Dutton was best known to the general public as the founder and editor of the Web site Arts & Letters Daily, which provides links to articles and essays on a wide range of subjects, including art, literature, philosophy, psychology, history, economics, and politics. A prominent figure in many of those fields, Dutton served as a professor of philosophy at the Uni-

versity of Canterbury, in New Zealand, from 1984 until his death. Denis Laurence Dutton was born in Los Angeles, California. His parents, William and Thelma, met while working at Paramount Pictures in the 1930s and later opened Dutton's Books, which became one of the best-known independent bookstores in Los Angeles. Denis Dutton grew up, along with two brothers and a sister, in the city's North Hollywood district. An avid reader, he also enjoyed conducting his own chemistry experiments. During his high-school years, his main interests were building telescopes, photographing the stars, and visiting observatories with friends. The order and beauty he found in astronomy filled him with philosophical wonderment. At the dinner table the family often discussed questions of value, existence, art, culture, science, and philosophy. Dutton entered the University of California at Santa Barbara (UCSB) as a chemistry major, but, finding himself drawn to the philosophy of art and aesthetics, he switched his major to philosophy after his first year. Like most thinkers at the time, he regarded aesthetic pleasure and values as being determined by one's culture, but he also suspected that there was something innate and natural in people's aesthetic preferences. After graduating from college, in 1966, Dutton joined the Peace Corps and spent two years in India. When he returned to the States, he spent a year studying at New York University and then returned to UCSB, where he pursued his doctoral degree. His thesis focused on the relationship between art and anthropology, particularly the perceived problems of cross-cultural understanding. After graduating, in 1973, he accepted a teaching position at the University of Michigan at Dearborn. During his time in Michigan, he founded the journal *Philosophy and Literature*, which is now published by Johns Hopkins University Press. In 1984 Dutton accepted a position at the University of Canterbury at Christchurch, New Zealand, teaching both graduate and undergraduate courses in the philosophy of art. In 1995, after encountering during three decades in academia much academic writing that he thought lacked depth and coherence, Dutton founded the Bad Writing Contest, for which readers were asked to submit to *Philosophy and Literature* academic writing they thought to be stylistically terrible and intellectually lacking. One well-known "winner" of the annual contest was the philosopher Judith Butler. (Feeling he had proved his point, Dutton ended the contest in 1999.) In October 1998 Dutton created Arts & Letters Daily, a Web site that would soon be included in what a great number of people—academics, philosophers, psychologists, scientists, businesspeople, university students, politicians, artists, and many others—read on-line. When the site was only three months old, the London *Observer*, in a widely quoted comment, called it the best Web site in the world. In 2002, when the site was receiving 1.5 million hits per month, Dutton was awarded the "People's Voice" Webby Award at a ceremony in San Francisco, California, and by 2009 the site was receiving three million hits every month. Also in 2009, on the 200th anniversary of the birth of Charles Darwin, the 19th-century English naturalist who developed the theory of natural selection, Dutton published *The Art Instinct: Beauty, Pleasure, & Human Evolution*. In that influential book Dutton attempted to present a coherent theory regarding human artistic practices and preferences from an evolutionary standpoint—a project that had occupied him for 15 years. During his lifetime Dutton contributed essays to many books, including *Literature and the Question of Philosophy* (1987), *Encyclopedia of Hoaxes* (1994), *The Encyclopedia of Aesthetics* (1998), *The Dictionary of Art* (1998), *The Literary Animal* (2005), and *The Encyclopedia of American Art* (2009). He also co-edited the books *The Concept of Creativity in Science and Art* (1981) and *The Forger's Art: Forgery and the Philosophy of Art* (1983). Dutton died of prostate cancer and is survived by his wife, Margit; his daughter, Sonia; and his son, Benjamin. See *Current Biography* (2009).—D.K.

Obituary *New York Times* (on-line) Dec. 31, 2010

EAGLEBURGER, LAWRENCE Aug. 1, 1930–June 4, 2011 Government official. Lawrence Eagleburger spent more than four decades as a diplomat and foreign-policy adviser; his tenure in government also included a short stint as secretary of state under President George H. W. Bush. Eagleburger was born in Milwaukee, Wisconsin, to Leon Sidney Eagleburger, a physician, and Helen (Van Ornum) Eagleburger, a teacher. Both parents were staunchly conservative Republicans, but Eagleburger allied himself with the party's more moderate wing. In 1948, for example, he supported Earl Warren, then the governor of California, for the Republican presidential nomination. As a member of the executive committee of the Wisconsin Young Republicans from 1949 to 1951 and as its vice chairman for his congressional district from 1950 to 1951, he was among the minority in his party to speak out against the state's controversial senator, Joseph R. McCarthy, for his reckless charges of Communist infiltration of the federal government. Meanwhile, after completing two years of study at Central State College at Stevens Point in 1950, Eagleburger transferred to the University of Wisconsin at Madison, where he received a B.S. degree two years later. From 1952 to 1954 he served in the U.S. Army, rising in rank to first lieutenant. He then returned to the University of Wisconsin to work toward a master's degree in political science, which he received in 1957. Because Eagleburger found his experience as a teaching assistant during his final year of graduate study to be unsatisfying and was bored by the prospect of a career in education, he took an immediate interest in a sign on a campus bulletin board that announced a forthcoming examination for the foreign service. From 1957 to 1959 Eagleburger served as third secretary at the American Embassy in Honduras. He was then reassigned to the State Department's Intelligence Research Bureau, where he worked as a political analyst for the next two years. After taking intensive language training in Serbo-Croatian for a year, he was posted to Yugoslavia as second secretary in the American Embassy's economics section in 1962. In the wake of the calamitous earthquake in Skopje, the capital of the Macedonian republic, in 1963, Eagleburger directed a massive relief effort, almost single-handedly arranging for the construction of an army field hospital in the

stricken area. As a result, he became something of a hero to the local people, who dubbed him Lawrence of Macedonia. Rotated back home in 1965, Eagleburger was named special assistant to the former secretary of state Dean Acheson. The following year he joined the staff of Walt W. Rostow, the head of the National Security Council, as an expert on European affairs. From 1967 to 1969 he was a special assistant to Undersecretary of State Nicholas deB. Katzenbach. Meanwhile, in 1968, Eagleburger became acquainted with Henry A. Kissinger while the two men were working on the transition team of President-elect Richard Nixon. When Kissinger was appointed national security adviser, he in turn chose Eagleburger as his executive assistant. Exhausted by the demands of his new post, one afternoon in June 1969 Eagleburger collapsed in his office and was rushed to the hospital. Following a period of bed rest, he was reassigned as chief of the political section of the U.S. mission to NATO in Belgium. In 1971 he received a call from his mother's longtime friend Melvin Laird, then the secretary of defense, who persuaded him to join the Defense Department—first as deputy assistant secretary and then as acting assistant secretary for international security affairs. When President Nixon appointed Kissinger secretary of state, in 1973, Kissinger hired Eagleburger as his executive assistant and deputy undersecretary of state for management, administrative posts in which he was responsible for coordinating Kissinger's frenetic daily schedule and managing his staff. Appointed ambassador to Yugoslavia by President Jimmy Carter in May 1977, Eagleburger was given a hero's welcome when he returned to Belgrade, where his contribution to earthquake relief in the previous decade was still remembered. In 1981 Eagleburger was named assistant secretary for European affairs by Secretary of State Alexander M. Haig Jr. (That appointment nettled hard-line conservatives in the new administration of President Ronald Reagan because of Eagleburger's longstanding ties with Henry Kissinger, who was considered by many right-wingers to be too accommodating toward the Soviet Union and China.) In January 1982 Eagleburger was promoted to undersecretary for political affairs, a post generally regarded as the pinnacle for career foreign-service officers. In April 1984 Eagleburger resigned from government service, partly because he felt that he was succumbing to burnout and partly because he wanted to earn more money for his labors. He became the president of the international consulting firm of his former mentor, Kissinger Associates, whose list of clients included such corporate giants as Coca-Cola, L. M. Ericcson of Sweden, Daewoo Group of South Korea, and the Volvo and Fiat automobile companies. But because his heart remained in foreign policy, he did not hesitate to accept an invitation from the new administration of President George H. W. Bush to return to the State Department as deputy to Secretary James A. Baker 3d in 1989. In that capacity he was sent to Israel in 1991, at the start of the Persian Gulf War, in order to persuade Prime Minister Yitzhak Shamir to stay out of the conflict. Other assignments took him to China and Panama. On August 23, 1992 Baker somewhat reluctantly answered the call of the Republican Party and became White House chief of staff and de facto manager of the flagging Bush reelection campaign. When Baker officially took on that duty, Bush, rather than naming a successor who would be subject to confirmation by the Democratic-controlled Senate in the middle of an election year, left Eagleburger in place to serve as acting secretary. After Bush lost the election to Bill Clinton, Eagleburger was officially named secretary of state, a post he held until January 20, 1993, when he was succeeded by Clinton's appointee, Warren Christopher. Later in life Eagleburger led the International Commission on Holocaust Era Insurance Claims and took part in the Iraq Study Group, which was headed by James Baker and called for, among other measures, a withdrawal of U.S. combat troops from Iraq by early 2008. Eagleburger, who had long suffered from poor health, died from pneumonia, a week after being treated for a heart attack. He was predeceased, in 2010, by his second wife, Marlene Ann Heinemann, to whom he had been married since 1966. (A short first marriage had ended in divorce in 1963.) He is survived by one son from his first marriage and two from his second. The sons, who all use their middle names to avoid confusion, are Lawrence Scott Eagleburger, Lawrence Andrew Eagleburger, and Lawrence Jason Eagleburger. See *Current Biography* (1992). —M.R.

Obituary *New York Times* (on-line) June 4, 2011

EDWARDS, BLAKE July 26, 1922–Dec. 15, 2010 Filmmaker. Blake Edwards, famed for such pictures as *Breakfast at Tiffany's* (1961), *The Pink Panther* (1963), and *10* (1979), was given an honorary award by the Academy of Motion Picture Arts and Sciences in 2004 for his body of work, which ranged from madcap comedies to satires to dark, psychological dramas. Edwards was born William Blake Crump in Tulsa, Oklahoma. His name was changed to Blake McEdwards after his mother, Lillian, married Jack McEdwards, an assistant director and movie-production manager. Edwards attended grammar and high school in Los Angeles, California, and then joined the U.S. Coast Guard. During his service he sustained a severe back injury diving into a shallow swimming pool after a night of partying. Edwards began working in Hollywood as an actor during World War II and appeared in two dozen movies between 1942 and 1948. "I worked with the best directors— Ford, Wyler, Preminger—and learned a lot from them," he once said, "but I wasn't a very cooperative actor. I was a spunky, smart-assed kid. Maybe even then I was indicating that I wanted to give, not take, direction." After he collaborated with his friend John Champion on the scripts for the low-budget Westerns *Panhandle* (1948) and *Stampede* (1949), the movies were released by the cut-rate production company Monogram Pictures, with Edwards and Champion as co-producers. Edwards then tried his hand at radio, writing for such programs as *Yours Truly, Johnny Dollar*; *The Lineup*; and *Richard Diamond, Private Detective*. He joined the B-movie unit of Columbia Pictures in 1952 as a scenarist and went on to co-script several films. Edwards made his directorial debut at Columbia with the 1955 Frankie Laine vehicles *Bring Your Smile Along* and *He Laughed Last* before moving on to Universal Pictures. His first big-budget movie was the navy comedy *Operation Petticoat* (1959), starring Tony Curtis and Cary Grant. The film turned out to be the greatest box-office success of the decade for Universal, setting Edwards on the path to success. Perhaps Edwards's most memorable film was *Breakfast at Tiffany's* (1961), adapted by George Axelrod from Truman Capote's novella and starring Audrey Hepburn. The cost of self-deluding escapism touched on in *Breakfast at Tiffany's* was explored in much darker terms in *Days of Wine and Roses* (1962), which followed the descent of a married couple from amiable party boozing to the lower depths of alcoholism. *Days of Wine and Roses*, despite its dark themes, was one of Edwards's most successful films; his direction of it won him a Golden Globe nomination and led to a reassessment of his reputation as a mere entertainer. Edwards scored another tremendous hit with the comedy *The Pink Panther* (1963), starring Peter Sellers as the astonishingly incompetent French detective Inspector Clouseau. That film was followed by a second Clouseau movie, *A Shot in the Dark* (1964). Edwards's second wife, Julie Andrews, first appeared in one of her husband's films when she played a dancer and singer who becomes a double agent in World War I in *Darling Lili* (1969), a volatile mixture of romance, farce, music, and aerial derring-do. *Darling Lili*, a wildly expensive film, was poorly received by audiences and critics and put Edwards in bad standing with the studio. After the subsequent flops *Wild Rovers* (1971) and *The Carey Treatment* (1972), the disappointed Edwards fled to Europe with his wife. "I determined in my own mind that I would never direct another film," he recalled. "I intended to keep on writing and knew I could make a good living from that alone. I didn't see where it was worth it to fight so much viciousness and irrationality to make pictures I believed in. I was escaping, and it was necessary that I do so." During his exile he wrote scripts for what would become some of his most memorable films, *10* (1979), about a successful songwriter (Dudley Moore) who has a midlife crisis and falls for a young blond newlywed (Bo Derrick), and *S.O.B.* (1980), a partly autobiographical, satirical attack on Hollywood. Edwards returned to the U.S. to direct the successful film *The Return of the Pink Panther* (1975), followed by *The Pink Panther Strikes Again* (1976), which fared even better, and *Revenge of the Pink Panther* (1978). Edwards received an Oscar nomination for his screenplay for *Victor/Victoria* (1982), which was based on the 1933 German film *Viktor und Viktoria* and tells the story of a starving singer (Julie Andrews) who moonlights as a man dressing as a woman. Edwards then resurrected the Pink Panther series (despite the death of Peter Sellers, in 1980) with two less-than-successful features: *Trail of the Pink Panther* (1982), which used archive footage of the actor, and *Curse of the Pink Panther* (1983), with Roger Moore in the part of Clouseau. Though audiences and critics did not embrace Edwards's later films, which included *That's Life* (1986) and *Sunset* (1988), he scored a hit by adapting and directing the stage version of *Victor/Victoria*, which opened on Broadway in 1995, with Andrews reprising her starring role. Edwards, who struggled with depression for much of his life, once told an interviewer, "My entire life has been a search for a funny side to that very tough life out there. I developed a kind of eye for scenes that made me laugh to take the pain away." Edwards died from complications of pneumonia in Santa Monica, California. He is survived by Julie Andrews, whom he married in 1969; a son, Geoffrey, and daughter, Jennifer, from his first marriage, to actress Patricia Walker; two daughters, Amy and Joanna, whom he adopted from Vietnam with Andrews; a stepdaughter, Emma, from Andrews's first marriage; and several grandchildren. See *Current Biography* (1996). —M.M.H.

Obituary *New York Times* (on-line) Dec. 16, 2010

EDWARDS, CHARLES C. Sep. 16, 1923–Aug. 7, 2011 Former U.S. government official; physician. Charles Cornell Edwards served as head of the Food and Drug Administration (FDA) from 1969 to 1973, a time of sweeping changes in the nation's regulation of prescription and over-the-counter drugs and food labeling. He then held a post as assistant secretary of health in the Department of Health, Education and Welfare; in that capacity he supervised the Public Health Service, the surgeon general's office, the National Institutes of Health (NIH), and the FDA. Edwards was born in Overton, Nebraska, to Charles Busby Edwards, a doctor, and Lillian (Arendt) Edwards. In 1941 he entered Princeton University, and two years later he transferred to the University of Colorado, where he earned a B.A. degree in 1945 and an M.D. degree in 1948. His surgical fellowship was interrupted by the Korean War, and as a member of the U.S. Naval Reserve, he served as a medical officer from 1950 to 1952. Continuing his studies after his discharge, Edwards obtained his M.S. degree in surgery from the University of Minnesota in 1956. Edwards spent the next several years running a private surgical practice, teaching, and working as the assistant director for medical education and hospitals for the American Medical Association. In late 1969 he was appointed commissioner of the FDA by President Richard M. Nixon. Edwards subsequently oversaw a review of hundreds of thousands of drugs, and in one of his most controversial and well-known actions, he ordered that a statement be included with every packet of birth-control pills, warning about such possible side effects as blood clots and breast cancer. Under his stewardship the FDA rapidly issued directives banning unsafe or ineffective antibiotics, nasal sprays, cyclamate sweeteners, and other products; removing mercury-tainted swordfish and tuna from the market; ordering more effective labeling on such items as pesticides, household cleansers, and juice drinks; limiting the use of amphetamine drugs; and urging the use of shatterproof lenses in all eyeglasses. In March 1973 Edwards was promoted to assistant secretary for health in the Department of Health, Education and Welfare, and he retained that post under Gerald R. Ford, following Nixon's resignation. In 1975, however, he quit in protest over the Ford administration's cuts to health programs for the poor. After leaving government service Edwards worked for various private companies and later became the head of the renowned Scripps Clinic and Research Foundation, later renamed the Scripps Institutions of Medicine and Science. After retiring from Scripps, in 1993, he spent the next two years as head of the California Healthcare Institute, a research and advocacy group. Edwards died at the age of 87, after a long illness. He is survived by his wife of over six decades, Sue; his children, Timothy, Charles Jr., David, and Nancy; and several grandchildren. See *Current Biography* (1973). —M.R.

Obituary *New York Times* (on-line) Aug. 28, 2011

EISNER, THOMAS June 25, 1929–Mar. 25, 2011 Biologist. Thomas Eisner was one of the fathers of the field known as chemical ecology. Along with the chemist Jerrold Meinwald, his longtime colleague at Cornell University, Eisner was responsible for numerous groundbreaking discoveries about the important role chemicals play in the lives of insects. Eisner was born in Berlin, Germany. His father, Hans, was a chemist, and his mother, the former Margarete Heil, was an artist. Eisner, who had an older sister, moved with his family to Barcelona, Spain, in 1933, a few weeks after Adolf Hitler came to power. After the outbreak of the Spanish Civil War, Eisner's family fled to France. In 1937 they abandoned Europe for South America and set up residence in Montevideo, Uruguay, where Eisner's father found work in the pharmaceutical industry. When Eisner's family moved to the U.S., in 1947, he enrolled at Champlain College, in Plattsburgh, New York. Two years later, after developing a good grasp of English, Eisner, who was already fluent in German and Spanish, transferred to Harvard University, in Cambridge, Massachusetts. There, he took his first course in entomology and realized that his fascination with insects could be the basis of a career. After earning a bachelor's degree from Harvard, in 1951, Eisner entered the university's graduate program in entomology, where he met fellow student E. O. Wilson, who would later become a leading expert on ants. Eisner and Wilson became close friends, and during the summer of 1952, the two took a long field trip, collecting insects from around the country for study. After receiving his Ph.D. degree from Harvard in 1955, Eisner did research in insect physiology at the university for two years before accepting a position as an assistant professor at Cornell University, in Ithaca, New York. (He considered the appointment ironic, given that Cornell had rejected him as an undergraduate.) Eisner remained at Cornell for the rest of his career and was named the Jacob Gould Schurman Professor of Biology in 1976. He directed the Cornell Institute for Research in Chemical Ecology from 1993 to 2006. At Cornell Eisner was best known for his work with Meinwald, a member of the university's Chemistry Department. The two spent over five decades uncovering the secrets of insect mating strategies, defense mechanisms, and modes of communication. Among other such discoveries, they found out how male bella moths use plant toxins to attract mates and how the bombardier beetle creates a chemical reaction within its body to shoot a boiling hot liquid from its abdomen as protection against predators. Eisner, who wrote several scholarly books about his field, was also a passionate nature photographer, as well as an accomplished pianist. An active conservationist, he served on the boards of the National Audubon Society, the National Scientific Council of the Nature Conservancy, the Union of Concerned Scientists, and the World Resources Institute Council. Among his numerous accolades, in 1994 he received the National Medal of Science, considered the highest scientific honor in the U.S. Eisner, who suffered from Parkinson's disease, died at his home in Ithaca. He is survived by his wife of 58 years, Maria; his three daughters, Yvonne, Vivian, and Christina; and six grandchildren. See *Current Biography* (1993). —C.C.

Obituary *New York Times* (on-line) Mar. 30, 2011

FALK, PETER Sep. 16, 1927–June 23, 2011 Actor. In a tribute published in the *New York Times* (June 24, 2011, on-line), Bruce Weber described Peter Falk's ability to marshal "actorly tics, prop room appurtenances and his own physical idiosyncrasies to personify Columbo, one of the most famous and beloved fictional detectives in television history." Falk's disarmingly shambling police detective debuted in the NBC series *Columbo* in 1971, and Falk went on to play the role off and on until 2003. Many noted that the famous character and Falk were indistinguishable in their eccentric wit and charm; Falk famously pulled the ratty trench coat—Columbo's trademark—from his own closet. Falk was born in New York City and raised in Ossining, New York, where his parents, Michael and Madeline (Hauser) Falk, ran a small clothing store. Surgeons removed his right eye, along with a malignant tumor, when he was three years old, and he was given a glass eye. At Ossining High School Falk was a three-letter athlete, president of his class, and an A-minus student. After graduating, in 1945, Falk served as a cook in the merchant marine for 18 months; studied at Hamilton College, in Clinton, New York, for two years; completed his work for a B.A. degree in political science at the New School for Social Research, in 1951; and earned an M.A. degree in public administration at Syracuse University, in 1953. After applying unsuccessfully for a job with the Central Intelligence Agency (CIA), he became a management analyst with the Connecticut State Budget Bureau, in Hartford. In his spare time Falk began acting with a local theater troupe. For the first time he began to consider the possibility of becoming a professional actor. In his late 20s he quit his job in Hartford and moved to New York City to try his luck in the theater. Falk made his professional debut Off-Broadway, as Sagnarelle in Molière's *Don Juan* at the Fourth Street Theatre on January 3, 1956. The following season he portrayed the bartender in the Circle in the Square's highly successful revival of *The Iceman Cometh*. A theatrical agent advised Falk not to expect much work in motion pictures, because of his glass eye, but the actor confounded those expectations by winning a series of bit parts. Falk made his film debut in the small role of the writer in *Wind Across the Everglades* (1958). His first gangster part was the minor character Nico in *The Bloody Brood* (1959), and so successful was his portrayal that he had to guard against being typecast. The movie that established Falk's reputation and brought him his first Academy Award nomination was *Murder, Inc.* (1960), a retelling of

the story of the infamous Brooklyn crime syndicate, in which he played Abe Reles, the gang's vicious chief assassin. In Frank Capra's comedy-melodrama *Pocketful of Miracles* (1961), Falk outshone Bette Davis, Glenn Ford, and a host of other luminaries and garnered his second Oscar nomination with his deftly comic portrayal of a gangster's bodyguard. Subsequent films included *Pressure Point* (1962); *The Balcony* (1963); *It's a Mad, Mad, Mad, Mad World* (1963); *Robin and the Seven Hoods* (1964); and *The Great Race* (1965). Falk also found himself in great demand for such TV programs as *Studio One*, *Robert Montgomery Presents*, and *Omnibus*. Among the made-for-TV movies in which Falk starred during that period were *Prescription: Murder* (1968) and *Ransom for a Dead Man* (1971), which marked the first programs in which he appeared as the deceptively scatterbrained Lieutenant Columbo, who looks dumber than his criminal prey—until he pounces. In September 1971 *Columbo* became one of three alternating 90-minute shows filling *The NBC Mystery Movie* slot. Kay Gardella observed for the New York *Daily News* (February 7, 1972): "There isn't a detective on television who can touch him, either in style or ratings." The following May the Academy of Television Arts and Sciences presented Falk with its award for best actor in a dramatic series for his performance in *Columbo*. He played the character on and off until 2003. Weber wrote of the iconic detective: "A lieutenant in the Los Angeles Police Department, Columbo was a comic variation on the traditional fictional detective. With the keen mind of Sherlock Holmes and Philip Marlowe, he was cast in the mold of neither—not a gentleman scholar, not a tough guy. He was instead a mass of quirks and peculiarities, a seemingly distracted figure in a rumpled raincoat, perpetually patting his pockets for a light for his signature stogie." After his last appearance as Columbo, Falk still acted occasionally; his final role came in the indie comedy *American Cowslip* (2009). Falk's other notable work included performances in the John Cassavetes films *Husbands* (1970) and *A Woman Under the Influence* (1974); he is also fondly remembered for starring in the movies *Mikey and Nicky* (1976), *The In-Laws* (1979), and *Wings of Desire* (1987). When not acting, Falk took great pleasure in making charcoal drawings and watercolors, and his work was exhibited in several galleries. He published an autobiography, *Just One More Thing: Stories from My Life*, in 2006. (The title was derived from a line Columbo said to each prime suspect, signaling to the audience that the detective was carefully setting a trap.) Falk, who had been suffering from Alzheimer's disease, died at his Beverly Hills home. He is survived by his second wife, Shera, and his daughters, Catherine and Jackie, from his first marriage. —M.M.H.

Obituary *New York Times* (on-line) June 24, 2011

FELLER, BOB Nov. 3, 1918–Dec. 15, 2010 Baseball player. In the 1940s and 1950s, Bob Feller of the Cleveland Indians was arguably the top pitcher in Major League Baseball (MLB). Soon after joining the Indians, at age 17, Feller became famed for his fastball, which earned him the nickname "The Heater from Van Meter." He retired from the Indians in 1956, after a career that spanned 18 seasons and included 2,581 strikeouts, three no-hitters (including one on Opening Day), 12 one-hitters, and an overall record of 266–162. During his career Feller led the American League (AL) in strikeouts in seven seasons, and he was the first pitcher to win 20 games before turning 21. His fastball was measured at 98.6 miles per hour; he once said he could throw up to 104 mph. Born Robert Andrew William Feller in Van Meter, Iowa, to William A. Feller and Lena (Forret) Feller, he was raised on his family's farm. As a youth Feller often helped his parents on the farm by milking cows, picking corn, and baling hay—tasks that he later said gave his right arm the strength needed for his pitches. His father, who had played baseball when he was young, encouraged his son, buying him needed equipment and helping him develop his skills. Together father and son listened to live baseball broadcasts, and when Bob Feller was 11, his father built a ballpark on the farm and formed a local team so that his son could compete against older players. Feller became a sensation on both his high-school and American Legion teams, and at just 17 he was spotted by a scout from the Cleveland Indians and added to the major-league roster without playing a single game in the minors. During his debut as a starter in 1936—two months before he turned 18—Feller struck out 15 St. Louis Browns batters. Three weeks later he tied the AL record by striking out 17 batters in a game against the Philadelphia Athletics. He became famous after that first season, and his picture appeared on the cover of *Time* magazine. In 1938 he broke the AL record he had tied two years earlier, by recording 18 strikeouts in a game against the Detroit Tigers. He made history again when he pitched baseball's only Opening Day no-hitter, on April 16, 1940, in a game against the Chicago White Sox. After Japan's bombing of Pearl Harbor, on December 7, 1941, Feller enlisted in the U.S. Navy and served as a gun captain on the USS *Alabama*, earning a number of medals during his time in the service. Feller sparked controversy in 1945 when, after pitching to the newly signed Jackie Robinson during an exhibition tour of California, he opined that Robinson would not have been considered for the major leagues if he had been white. (Feller later acknowledged that he had made a mistake.) In 1946, Feller's first full season of baseball after his return from the war, he gave what many consider the best performance of his career, going 26–15 with a 2.18 ERA and pitching 36 complete games and 10 shutouts. In 1948 Feller helped the Indians win their first American League pennant in 28 years. In that year's World Series, the Indians faced the Boston Braves and defeated them, 4–2. Feller led the AL in victories six times during his career, and he remains the franchise leader in innings pitched, complete games, wins, and strikeouts. During the 1950s Feller served as the first president of the Major League Baseball Players Association and helped to create a new pension plan for players. Feller, whose play noticeably declined after he suffered a shoulder injury in 1947, was the team's fourth starter during the Indians' record-breaking 111-win 1954 season and did not pitch in the team's four-game loss to the New York Giants in the World Series. He retired from baseball in 1956

and subsequently found work in the insurance industry. He was inducted into the Baseball Hall of Fame in 1962, in the same class as Jackie Robinson. In 1981 he returned to the Indians organization to work as a pitching coach during spring training. Over the years he continued to work in the team's public-relations office and make special appearances. Later in life he could often be seen in the press box at Progressive Field, where, outside the stadium, the Indians erected a statue of him winding up for a pitch. Feller, who died of leukemia, is survived by his second wife, Anne; three sons from his first marriage—Bruce, Steve, and Martin; two stepchildren—John and Rachel; and a grandson. See *Current Biography* (1941). —W.D.

Obituary *New York Times* (on-line) Dec. 15, 2010

FERMOR, PATRICK LEIGH Feb. 11, 1915–June 10, 2011 Writer; adventurer. Patrick Leigh Fermor—who was once described by the BBC as "a cross between Indiana Jones, James Bond and Graham Greene"—published numerous accounts of his adventures in Europe and the Caribbean that are now considered classic travel literature. Leigh Fermor was born in London, England, to Sir Lewis Leigh Fermor and Eileen (Ambler) Leigh Fermor. Lewis Leigh Fermor, a geologist who became the first president of the Indian National Science Academy, was a fellow of the Royal Society and distinguished by the Order of the British Empire. Shortly after Leigh Fermor's birth, his mother joined her husband on the Indian subcontinent, leaving her infant son to be raised by the family of a farmer in Northamptonshire. Young Leigh Fermor was educated at King's School, Canterbury, and spent the years prior to World War II traveling through continental Europe and the Greek archipelago. Describing Leigh Fermor's journey in the *New York Times* (June 11, 2011, on-line), Richard B. Woodward wrote: "On foot and on horseback, by train and automobile, Mr. Leigh Fermor found hospitality among people alien to most English speakers of the time: Orthodox Jewish woodcutters in Transylvania, Hungarian Gypsies, White Russian exiles, German barons, French-speaking monks in Austria, and Romanian shepherds along the Danube. At one point he strayed by mistake into a Munich beer hall crowded with Nazis." Leigh Fermor's experiences fostered his lasting interest in the history of language and traditional life in remote areas. Upon the outbreak of World War II, he enlisted in the Irish Guards and became liaison officer to the Greek Headquarters in Albania. Leigh Fermor fought in the battles of Greece and Crete, and after the fall of Crete, he returned there to organize the resistance movement and to command guerrilla operations on the island between 1942 and 1944. During the two and a half years he spent on the island disguised as a shepherd, he led a perilous expedition to capture and deliver to British authorities in Cairo a Nazi officer, Major General Karl Kreipe, who commanded the 22,000 German troops on Crete. Leigh Fermor completed his war service in North Germany as a team commander in the Special Allied Airborne Reconnaissance Force. After the war he spent a year as deputy director of the British Institute in Athens before resuming his travels, which took him to the Caribbean in 1947 and 1948. His first book, *The Traveller's Tree* (1950), which described his journeys through the Caribbean Islands, won that year's Heinemann Foundation Prize for literature and the Kemsley Prize in 1951. The London *Sunday Times* described the book as the work "of a born writer," noting that Leigh Fermor was "the ideal traveller, inquisitive, humorous, interested in everything." A *New York Herald Tribune* reviewer remarked that he covered his material in a "literate and polished style," while the *Christian Science Monitor* praised the "verve and enthusiasm" with which Leigh Fermor addressed himself to his subject. His debut was followed in 1953 by *A Time to Keep Silence*, a collection of Leigh Fermor's "meditations" on the value that he, as an unbeliever, found in occasional monastic retreats, and a novel, *The Violins of Saint-Jacques*, about a remote and feudal Caribbean island. The latter book was praised for its evocative power but thought more successful as a splendid spectacle than as a work of fiction; it nevertheless provided the basis for Malcolm Williamson's successful opera of the same name. Leigh Fermor's travel books *Mani: Travels in the Southern Peloponnese* (1958) and *Roumeli, Travels in Northern Greece* (1966), both about regions seldom visited and scarcely known, together confirmed his skill at comprehending—and recording in superbly vivid prose—the history, myth, and folklore of disparate places. Leigh Fermor was perhaps best known for his two autobiographical works, *A Time of Gifts* (1977) and *Between the Woods and the Water* (1986), both of which recounted his journey across prewar Europe as a teenager in the 1930s. After turning down a knighthood in 1991, he accepted that honor in 2004, after which he was known as Sir Patrick. Leigh Fermor and his wife since 1968, the former Joan Eyres Monsell, a photographer, maintained homes in southern Peloponnese, in Greece, and Worcestershire, England, where they were sought-after as dinner companions by both celebrities and locals. A fellow of the Royal Geographical Society and the Royal Society of Literature, Leigh Fermor worked well into advanced age and died in Worcestershire at 96. His wife had predeceased him, in 2003. See *Current Biography* (1955). —M.R.M.

Obituary *New York Times* (on-line) June 11, 2011

FERRARO, GERALDINE Aug. 26, 1935–Mar. 26, 2011 Politician. As the Democratic vice-presidential nominee and running mate of Walter Mondale in 1984, Geraldine Ferraro, an attorney and U.S. representative from New York, was the first woman ever nominated for national office by a major political party. Geraldine Anne Ferraro was born in Newburgh, New York, the fourth child and only daughter of Dominick Ferraro, an Italian immigrant who owned a lucrative restaurant and a five-and-dime store, and Antonetta L. (Corrieri) Ferraro. Of her siblings, only one, Carl, survived into adulthood. His twin brother died at birth, and Gerard, a younger brother (and Ferraro's namesake), was killed in an automobile accident at three years of age. When Ferraro was eight years old, her father died of a heart attack. Ferraro would later learn that her father had

been arrested for running a gambling ring and was scheduled to appear in court the day he died. Ferraro's mother, strapped for money, sold her husband's businesses and moved with her children to the South Bronx. Despite her financial troubles, she managed to earn enough—in part by beading wedding dresses—to send her daughter to Catholic girls' schools and then to Marymount College in Manhattan, on a scholarship. At Marymount Ferraro edited the school paper and was a competitive athlete; she graduated with a B.A. degree in English, in 1956. She then taught grade school in the New York City public-school system for four years while taking night classes at Fordham University Law School, where she received a J.D. degree, in 1960. The same year, a few days after she passed the bar exam, Ferraro married the real-estate developer John Zaccaro; she chose to retain her maiden name to honor her mother. Over the next 14 years, Ferraro devoted herself to caring for her three children, while occasionally working part-time as a civil lawyer for her husband's real-estate business and doing pro-bono work for women in New York Family Court. She also became increasingly involved in local politics. In 1974, after her cousin was elected Queens district attorney, Ferraro applied for and was accepted to a full-time position as an assistant district attorney in the Investigations Bureau. The following year she was assigned to the new Special Victims Bureau, handling cases of child abuse, domestic violence, and rape, and two years later she became the bureau's head. Ferraro gained a reputation as a tough prosecutor, and over time her growing conviction that factors such as poverty and social injustice were at the root of many crimes transformed her from a conservative into a liberal. In 1978, after the Democrat James J. Delaney stepped down from his seat representing New York's Ninth Congressional District in the U.S. House of Representatives, Ferraro ran to replace him. After winning a majority in a three-way Democratic primary, she went on to defeat the Republican Alfred A. DelliBovi. She was reelected in both 1980 and 1982. Thomas "Tip" O'Neill, the influential Speaker of the House, took an immediate liking to Ferraro because of her ingratiating manner, her diligence, and her support for organized labor. She opposed cuts in funding for social programs and favored aid to Israel. She also supported federal funding for abortions, especially in cases of rape or incest, though she stated that, as a Catholic, she personally opposed abortion. On issues of importance to her constituents, however, Ferraro did not hesitate to cross party lines, voting against mandatory busing and in favor of tax credits for parents of children attending private and parochial schools. In 1981 she co-sponsored the bipartisan Economic Equity Act. Her pragmatism, closeness to the Democratic leadership, and reputation among her male colleagues as "one of the boys" quickly brought her political rewards. With O'Neill's backing, in 1980 she was elected secretary of the Democratic caucus, a post that entitled her to sit on the important House Steering and Policy Committee, which controls committee assignments; she was reelected to that post in 1982. In 1981 Ferraro served as a House representative on the Hunt Commission, which was charged with rewriting the delegate-selection rules for the 1984 Democratic National

Convention. Ferraro's superior performance on that commission helped her get appointed, in 1983, to a post on the powerful Budget Committee. But it was her appointment as chair of the 1984 Democratic platform committee that won her almost instant party prominence, as the first woman to hold the post. Despite receiving criticism from a variety of groups, the platform that Ferraro's committee submitted for ratification at the Democratic convention pleased most party members, and Ferraro emerged as an even brighter political star. Her nomination as the running mate of Democratic presidential nominee Walter Mondale was endorsed by O'Neill, along with a number of other influential party members and such groups as the National Organization of Women. Although Ferraro freely acknowledged that she would not have been considered for the vice presidency if she were not a woman, she insisted that her selection was based on her qualifications for the position, not on political strategy. Nevertheless, critics of Ferraro's rapid rise to national leadership lost no time in pointing out her deficiencies, citing her limited experience in foreign affairs and military matters, which she had tried to address by taking fact-finding trips in 1983 and 1984 to Central America, the Middle East, Cyprus, and East Asia. Others judged her legislative experience as too meager for someone who would be second in line for the presidency. The campaign was also muddied by accusations of Ferraro's financial improprieties. She was pressured to release her financial information, after which the public learned about her husband's failure to pay owed taxes and evidence she had accepted contributions from organized crime. In the general election the incumbent, Republican president Ronald Reagan, won in a landslide. Although, in the view of many, Ferraro did not hurt the Democrats' chances of capturing the White House, she also did not attract as many votes from women, over half of whom voted for Reagan, as had been expected. Nevertheless, she and many others considered her candidacy important because it opened new opportunities for women and encouraged them to be more politically active. (Twenty-four years would pass before another woman was nominated for vice president by a major political party—when Republican U.S. senator John McCain selected then-Governor Sarah Palin of Alaska as his running mate in 2008.) During the Bill Clinton administration, Ferraro served as ambassador to the United Nations Human Rights Commission. She also co-hosted the CNN program *Crossfire* from 1996 to 1998, wrote books and articles, and served as a business consultant. In 1998 she was diagnosed with multiple myeloma, a bone-marrow cancer that suppresses the immune system. She died of complications from the disease at Massachusetts General Hospital. Ferraro is survived by her husband, John Zaccaro; their children, Donna, John Jr., and Laura; and eight grandchildren. See *Current Biography* (1984).
—D.K.

Obituary *New York Times* (on-line) Mar. 26, 2011

FITZGERALD, GARRET Feb. 9, 1926–May 19, 2011
Former prime minister of Ireland. Under the leadership of Prime Minister Garret FitzGerald, who served

for much of the 1980s, the government of the Republic of Ireland began to make progress in an Anglo-Irish dialogue and helped pave the way for peace in Northern Ireland. FitzGerald was born in Dublin to the nationalist poet and statesman Desmond Fitz-Gerald, a Catholic, and Mabel (McConnell) FitzGerald, a Presbyterian from Ulster. Raised in the Catholicism of his father, FitzGerald grew up in Bray, County Wicklow, where he received his elementary education at St. Brigid's School; in Dungarvan, County Waterford, where he began his secondary education at Colaiste na Rinne (Ring College), an Irish-language boarding school; and in Dublin, where he completed his secondary education at another boarding school, Belvedere College. Majoring in education and economics, he attended University College, Dublin, a constituent college of the National University of Ireland, where he earned a Ph.D. degree. In addition, he received a law degree from King's Inn, Dublin, and was called to the bar in 1946. Choosing not to practice law, FitzGerald worked as a research and schedules manager for Aer Lingus (Irish Air Lines) from 1947 to 1958. At University College, Dublin, he was a Rockefeller research assistant in 1958–59 and a lecturer in political economy from 1959 to 1973. For many years, beginning in 1954, he also worked in journalism, as a correspondent for BBC radio and for such print publications as the *Economist*, the *Financial Times*, and the *Irish Times*. FitzGerald, a member of Fine Gael, a business-oriented party, entered politics in 1965, when he joined the Seanad, a chamber of Ireland's bicameral legislature whose members are nominated by the prime minister, the universities, and several vocational panels, and voted in by an electoral college. He remained there until 1969, when he was elected to the other chamber, the Dail, whose members are directly elected by proportional adult suffrage. In the parliamentary election of February 1973, Fianna Fail, Ireland's Republican party, which had been in power for 16 years, failed to retain its absolute majority, and Liam Cosgrave, the leader of Fine Gael, formed a government in coalition with the Labour Party. FitzGerald was appointed minister for foreign affairs in the Cosgrave government, serving with that portfolio until Fianna Fail returned to power four years later. Following the electoral defeat of 1977, FitzGerald replaced Cosgrave as the leader of Fine Gael, and with his characteristic energy and drive, proceeded to rebuild the party. Under his leadership Fine Gael, once solidly conservative, became more liberal in social policy without abandoning its economic orthodoxy, and in four years it increased its parliamentary representation from 43 seats to 65, the total with which it emerged from the election of June 1981. Fianna Fail held 78 seats coming out of that election, but FitzGerald, who called for what he termed a "genuine republic," outwitted Charles Haughey, the incumbent Fianna Fail prime minister, in the race to form a new government, joining a coalition with Labour. That new government proposed a 30 percent increase in taxes, however, and following the defeat of the budget by one vote, Parliament was dissolved on January 27, 1982. In the ensuing election campaign, FitzGerald went to voters with virtually the same budget that had brought his government down. The only important change was the deletion of the politically sensitive value-added tax on children's clothing and shoes. It was a savvy move, and the Fine Gael–Labour coalition regained power later in the year. FitzGerald's second term as prime minister was substantially longer than his first. During that tenure, which lasted until 1987, he became known for his cooperation with British prime minister Margaret Thatcher, and he was instrumental in the signing of the Anglo-Irish Agreement of 1985, which gave the Irish Republic a formal advisory role in the affairs of Northern Ireland. It was considered a major step in the peace process, setting the stage for the 1998 Good Friday accord between Catholics and Protestants in Northern Ireland. FitzGerald retired from politics in 1992 but remained in the public eye as an *Irish Times* columnist and frequent TV and radio guest. The author of such books as *Towards a New Ireland* (1972), *All in a Life* (1991), *Reflections on the Irish State: Ireland Since Independence* (2003), *Ireland in the World: Further Reflections* (2005), and *Just Garret: Tales from the Political Front Line* (2011), he died shortly after the last-named memoir was published. His wife of over five decades, Joan, predeceased him, in 1999. He is survived by a daughter, Mary, and two sons, John and Mark. See *Current Biography* (1984). —M.R.

Obituary *New York Times* (on-line) May 19, 2011

FODOR, EUGENE Mar. 5, 1950–Feb. 26, 2011 Violinist. In 1974 Eugene Fodor (not to be confused with the travel-guide publisher of the same name) became the first American violinist ever to share top honors at the prestigious Tchaikovsky Competition in Moscow, Russia. Fodor was born in Denver, Colorado, to Eugene Fodor Sr. and the former Antoinette Pastore, both of whom played the violin. (Fodor's great-great-grandfather had founded the Fodor Conservatory of Music in Hungary.) Fodor has an older brother, John, who became a leading violinist with the Denver Symphony Orchestra; their sister, Deborah, was the only one in the family who did not play the violin. The family lived on an 80-acre ranch in the foothills of the Rocky Mountains, about 30 miles west of Denver. Fodor began to take violin lessons at the age of five with Harold Wippler, the concertmaster of the Denver Symphony Orchestra. At the age of nine, he made his first formal appearance (before a convent audience of 300 nuns) and made his debut as a soloist with the Denver Symphony at the age of 11. Before they entered their teens, both Fodor brothers were giving duo recitals throughout the West. After graduating from high school, in 1967, Fodor obtained a full scholarship to the Juilliard School, in New York City, where he studied with Ivan Galamian. He later took two semesters of master classes with Jascha Heifetz at the University of Southern California, followed by advanced studies at the University of Indiana in Bloomington. In 1972 he won the formidable Paganini Competition, held in Genoa, Italy, becoming the first violinist ever to win the award by unanimous decision of the judges. One of them, a Russian, invited him to enter the next Tchaikovsky Competition, scheduled for 1974. The demanding Russian music contest was a three-week ordeal that few Western contestants dared to enter. Of

the 19 judges on the 1974 violin jury, 11 were from the Soviet Union. After surviving the initial rounds, Fodor and a dozen other contestants passed on to the finals, which went on for six evenings. The enthusiastic audience response to Fodor's starting performance, when he played the unaccompanied Bach G minor sonata, continued with his interpretation of a movement from a Mozart concerto and had turned into rhythmic handclapping by the time he completed the two most difficult of Paganini's Caprices, Opus 1, numbers 17 and 24. The audience went on applauding even after a piano accompanist sat down to perform the Tchaikovsky Valse-Scherzo with Fodor. During the final rounds, while Fodor, the last contestant, performed the violin concertos of Tchaikovsky and Sibelius, the listeners remained in their seats, although they risked missing the last train of the Moscow subway. Despite the fact that the audience obviously preferred Fodor, the members of the jury awarded no gold medal on the grounds that none of the finalists had performed consistently well at all stages of the competition. Instead, they bestowed second-prize silver medals on Fodor and two Soviet violinists who happened to be students of jury members. Still, Fodor was the first American violinist to garner a top prize in the vaunted competition, and when he returned home from Russia, the governor of Colorado declared August 24th to be "Eugene Fodor Day." Fodor made his formal New York City debut at Avery Fisher Hall in Lincoln Center in November 1974, and many reviewers likened him to a young Heifetz. He subsequently signed a recording contract with RCA, performed at the White House, and became a frequent guest on the *Tonight Show* with Johnny Carson. One of the few classical musicians of his time recognized by the general public, during his heyday Fodor was celebrated as much for his youthful good looks—he was sometimes posed shirtless in publicity photos—as for his musical talents. His public image was altered in 1989, when he was arrested for breaking into a motel room and for possessing heroin and cocaine with intent to distribute. (He attempted to use his Guarnerius violin as surety; while the judge refused, he did release Fodor on his own recognizance.) Fodor was ultimately sentenced to mandatory drug treatment and probation, and although he made frequent attempts at sobriety, he periodically struggled with heroin, cocaine, and alcohol addiction for the remainder of his life. He continued to perform despite such difficulties, "but not always with the finest orchestras or in the most prestigious halls," as Margalit Fox wrote for the *New York Times* (March 2, 2011, on-line). In 2010, despondent over the course his life and career had taken, he stopped playing the violin entirely. Fodor died at his home in Arlington, Virginia. He is survived by his wife, Susan Davis; their three children, Daniella, Lindsay, and Dylan; his brother, John; his sister, Deborah; and two grandchildren. See *Current Biography* (1976). —J.P.

Obituary *New York Times* (on-line) Mar. 2, 2011

FORD, BETTY Apr. 8, 1918–July 8, 2011 Former First Lady; social activist. Elizabeth Ann Bloomer Ford, better known as Betty Ford, was the wife of U.S. president Gerald Ford, who served from 1974 to

1977. During her time in the White House, she became known for her candor, and she earned a reputation as a passionate advocate of women's rights, among other issues. Ford, a breast-cancer survivor, was noted for her work in raising awareness about the illness, and after overcoming her addictions to alcohol and prescription drugs, she helped found one of the most prominent rehabilitation centers in the U.S. A native of Chicago, Illinois, she was the youngest child and only girl born to William Stephenson and Hortense (Neahr) Bloomer. When Ford was a few years old, she moved with her parents and two older brothers to Grand Rapids, Michigan. Her father, a traveling salesman for firms dealing in industrial supplies, settled the family in a fashionable section of the city. Meanwhile, Ford's mother, who had wealthy relatives in Grand Rapids, was a socialite and became active in civic affairs. A spirited child, Ford enjoyed a privileged upbringing. A veteran of several years of dance training, during her teens she modeled clothes for a local department store and also worked as a dance instructor. Tragedy struck Ford's life in 1934, when her father died of carbon-monoxide poisoning while working on the family car. After graduating from Grand Rapids's Central High School, in 1936, Ford attended the Bennington School of Dance, in Vermont, for two summers. Her study there with Martha Graham, Charles Weidman, and Doris Humphrey increased her determination to become a professional dancer. In 1939 she broke free from her overly protective mother and left Grand Rapids for New York City, where she joined the Martha Graham Concert Troupe. While dancing under Graham, she also took a job as a model with the John Powers Agency and appeared in several fashion shows. Ford remained in New York until 1941, when she returned to Grand Rapids to become a fashion coordinator for the same department store that had employed her as a teenage model. In 1942 she married her first husband, William C. Warren, a local furniture dealer. The marriage ended five years later in divorce, on the grounds of incompatibility, and Ford did not ask for alimony. Shortly thereafter she began dating the former football star Gerald R. Ford, then a lawyer with lofty political ambitions, and following a whirlwind romance, the two married in October 1948. That same year Gerald Ford won election to the U.S. House, as the representative for Michigan's Fifth Congressional District, and the Fords relocated to Washington, D.C. After a brief stay in the nation's capital, they moved to the Virginia suburbs and settled in Alexandria, where they started a family and lived for nearly three decades. During his 13 consecutive congressional terms, Gerald Ford rose through the Republican ranks, becoming minority leader of the U.S. House in 1965. In addition to her routine household tasks, Betty Ford had to take on increased responsibility in rearing their children. The pressures of parenthood, together with the strain of her role as the civic-minded wife of an ambitious political leader, aggravated the pain of a pinched neck nerve, an injury she had incurred in the mid-1960s when she reached to raise a window. The injury remained a nagging problem, and her discomfort was one of the factors leading her husband to promise not to campaign for political office after 1974. However, his intention to leave the government for private law practice changed drastically after unprecedented political developments. On October 12, 1973 President Richard Nixon named Gerald Ford to succeed Spiro T. Agnew, who had resigned, as vice president of the United States. In early August 1974, while still preparing to move from her Alexandria home into the Admiral's House at the United States Naval Observatory in Washington, Ford learned that her new address was to be not the official vice-presidential residence, but the White House: shortly after the departure of Richard Nixon, forced to resign by the Watergate scandal, Gerald R. Ford took the oath of office as president. His wife, who held the Bible for the swearing-in ceremony, later remarked, "I really felt like I was taking that oath too." She responded to her new role with quiet competence and something of a flair for public service. She quickly developed a reputation for frankness, and as the nation's First Lady, she unreservedly offered her views on a number of controversial issues. Ford talked openly about sex (once famously stating that she shared a bed with her husband in the White House) and caused a stir with her endorsement of legalized abortion. She was applauded for her tireless support of the Equal Rights Amendment (ERA), and she emerged as a major force in the women's rights movement. In September 1974, shortly after moving into the White House, she was forced to undergo a radical mastectomy when doctors discovered cancer in her right breast, and she is widely credited with raising awareness of the disease, which was not often publicly discussed before then. After Gerald Ford's defeat by Jimmy Carter in the 1976 presidential election, the family left the White House. In 1978, after being confronted by her husband and children, Ford acknowledged her addiction to alcohol and to the painkillers she had been prescribed for her pinched nerve. She checked herself into the Long Beach Naval Hospital, where she spent a month receiving treatment. Ford's triumph over her drug and alcohol addiction led her to establish the nonprofit Betty Ford Center, in Rancho Mirage, California, with her neighbor the tire magnate Leonard Firestone. Opened in October 1982, the Betty Ford Center is now one of the most prestigious such facilities in the world. The center has treated more than 75,000 people, including such celebrities as Elizabeth Taylor, Liza Minnelli, Mary Tyler Moore, Johnny Cash, Mickey Mantle, and Darryl Strawberry. Ford served as chair of the center's board of directors until 2005, when her daughter, Susan, assumed the post. Ford was awarded the Presidential Medal of Freedom in 1991 and was a recipient of the Congressional Gold Medal in 1998. Her autobiography, *The Times of My Life*, was published in 1978, and a memoir about her drug and alcohol treatment, *Betty: A Glad Awakening*, appeared in 1987. She published *Healing and Hope: Six Women from the Betty Ford Center Share Their Powerful Journeys of Addiction and Recovery*, in 2003. Ford died of natural causes at the Eisenhower Medical Center in Rancho Mirage. She was predeceased by her husband, in December 2006. In addition to her daughter, Ford is survived by her sons, Michael, John, and Steven; seven grandchildren; and several great-grandchildren. See *Current Biography* (1975). —C.C.

Obituary *New York Times* A p1 July 9, 2011

FREUD, LUCIAN Dec. 8, 1922–July 20, 2011 Artist. Lucian Freud was known for his uncompromising, unflattering, coldly objective, and often unsettling portraits. Born in Berlin, Germany, the second of three sons, he moved with his family in 1933 to England, his home base for the rest of his life. His father, Ernst, the youngest son of the psychoanalysis pioneer Sigmund Freud, was an architect; his mother, Lucie, was a wealthy heiress. After his arrival in England, Freud was sent to a series of progressive schools, but his art classes proved to be unsatisfactory to him, and he was reportedly expelled at least once for rebellious behavior. He subsequently entered the Central School of Arts and Crafts in London, studying there for a year (1938–39). In 1939, the year in which he became a naturalized British citizen, he transferred to the smaller, atelier-like East Anglian School of Painting and Drawing in Dedham, Essex, which was run by the painter Cedric Morris. Even though Freud's habit of smoking at night started a fire that destroyed the school, Morris kept him on in his own home as a special student. (Some observers have called the story of the fire apocryphal.) When Freud was only 17, he sketched a self-portrait that was accepted for reproduction in Cyril Connolly's new magazine, *Horizon*. Other Freud drawings followed in *Horizon*, including ones of Connolly himself and of the magazine's editor, the poet Stephen Spender. Recognized in London art circles as a boy wonder, Freud led an independent, rather bohemian life, and he had a studio of his own in Maida Vale. In 1941 he joined the Merchant Navy, hoping to make it to New York City. Within months, however, he had received a medical discharge because of tonsillitis. He subsequently embarked on a year of drawing lessons at Goldsmiths' College, London. A painting trip abroad, which lasted for almost two years, took Freud first, in 1946, to Paris and later to Greece. After his return to England, he began work on the first well-defined group of his oeuvre, the so-called Kitty paintings, a series of portraits of his first wife, Kathleen Garman. Those paintings included *Girl with Roses* (1947–48), *Girl with a Kitten* (1947), and *Girl with a White Dog* (1950–51). Throughout the 1960s and 1970s, the tactile richness that had replaced the controlled linearity of Freud's earlier work became more pronounced. Along with his new technique came an expansion in the size of his compositions and a freeing-up of the relative positioning of painter and subject. Thus, in *Sleeping Head* (1962), the face, half obscured by the shoulder, is caught at an angle and seems to recede from the viewer. Soon after that Freud reversed the process and began what he called his "naked portraits," with the expression conveyed by the body, of which the head was merely another limb. For the next decade his work was devoted mainly to figures of women and men lying on rumpled beds or tatty couches, often asleep or in somnolent reverie, their nakedness fully revealed. Freud's self-portraits were, on the whole, very different from his direct, confrontational studies of other people. His sad, even hostile expression is blurred in *Small Interior* (1968–72), with its tiny mirrored glimpse of the artist at work, and in *Reflection with Two Children (Self-Portrait)* of 1965. In many respects *Large Interior, W.II (After Watteau)*, a portrait of four people huddled together on a cot in one of his nondescript studio rooms, painted in 1981–83, summed up Freud's motifs and mannerisms. As with most of Freud's works, there was no clue to any purpose or theme beyond that of recording faces that were meaningful to him but here "posed" in an attempt to rework Watteau's *Pierrot Content*. Their attitudes and expressions seemed only to register the fatigue of their long hours of sitting. Among the more controversial works of his later years was a 1995 portrait of Sue Tilley, an extremely obese JobCentre supervisor who had posed for him in the early 1990s; it was described by the auction house Christie's, as quoted by the BBC (May 14, 2008), as a "bold and imposing example of the stark power of Freud's realism" and was sold to the Russian oligarch Roman Abramovich for a record $33.6 million. Another was Freud's unflinching portrait of Queen Elizabeth II, which he painted during several sittings between May 2000 and December 2001 and which divided critics and audiences alike; many observers called it "extremely unflattering," while others deemed it realistic, honest, and brave. Although most of his paintings and drawings are owned by individuals, examples of his work can be found in a number of public collections in England, including the Tate and the National Portrait Gallery, at New York City's Metropolitan Museum of Art, and at the Hirshhorn Museum and Sculpture Garden in Washington, D.C., among other venues. Freud died after a brief illness at his home in London. He had once told John Walsh for the London *Independent* (May 30, 2002), "I'd like, ideally, to die in the studio, brush in hand." So intensely private was Freud during his later years that some called him a hermit and others labeled him a misanthrope. His marriage to Garman—which produced two daughters—ended in divorce, as did his second marriage, to Lady Caroline Blackwood. He was rumored to have some three dozen other children from affairs with younger women, although that figure is thought by some sources to be exaggerated. See *Current Biography* (1988). —D.K.

Obituary *New York Times* (on-line) July 21, 2011

FRYE, DAVID June 1934–Jan. 24, 2011 Impressionist; comedian. David Frye was best known for his impressions of public personalities and political figures, most notably Richard Nixon, which helped propel him to fame in the 1960s and 1970s. Frye was born David Shapiro in the New York City borough of Brooklyn, where his father, Irving, owned the Anchor Office Cleaning Co. He discovered his talent for mimicry as a teenager, when he would give dead-on impressions of people he encountered in his daily life. After graduating from James Madison High School in Brooklyn, Frye attended the University of Miami, where he began doing impressions of such film stars as James Cagney, Jimmy Stewart, and Cary Grant in campus productions; he also honed his craft at Miami strip clubs. Frye entertained his fellow servicemen while stationed with a U.S. Army Special Services unit in France. Upon receiving his discharge, in 1959, Frye returned to Brooklyn, where he worked days as a salesman for his father's office-cleaning business and spent his nights performing in local talent shows. In the 1960s Frye started making a name for himself on the New York City nightclub circuit, and he eventually quit his job as a salesman for his father's company in order to focus all of his energies on his comedy career. A turning point for Frye came in 1965, when he added a Robert F. Kennedy impression to his act, and he soon added other political figures to his routine, starting with Lyndon B. Johnson. In 1966 Frye caught the attention of talent scouts while filling in for a comedian at a prestigious Greenwich Village nightclub called the Village Gate. Impressed by his act, they booked him on the *Merv Griffin Show*, which led to appearances on other talk and variety shows, including the *Leslie Uggams Show*, the *Smothers Brothers Comedy Hour*, the *Dean Martin Show*, and the *Ed Sullivan Show*. During the 1968 presidential campaigns, he demonstrated his flair for mimicking Hubert Humphrey, George Wallace, William F. Buckley Jr., Nelson A. Rockefeller, and Everett M. Dirksen. Frye's career, however, was largely defined by the winner of that year's November election, Richard M. Nixon. His impression of the later-disgraced politician initially proved to be difficult. "It took me a long time to get Nixon—but it took the *country* a long time to get Nixon," Frye once told *Esquire*, as quoted by Wiliam Grimes in the *New York Times* (January 29, 2011, online). "Nixon has these brooding eyes that look like my eyes. That helped a lot. But the voice is still the main thing. He has a radio announcer's evenness of speech, very well modulated, and you can't pick out any highs and lows. If I hadn't had to do him, I wouldn't have tried." Frye used Nixon as the inspiration for his first comedy album, *I Am the President*, which was released in 1969 and sold 250,000 copies—then an extraordinarily high figure for a humor record. Nixon served as the centerpiece of his next three comedy albums, *Radio Free Nixon* (1971), *Richard Nixon Superstar* (1971), and *Richard Nixon: A Fantasy* (1973), the last of which drew on the Watergate scandal and featured a sketch that had a guilty Nixon asking Marlon Brando's lisping Godfather for help. Though many radio stations refused to play material from *Richard Nixon: A Fantasy*, stemming from its over-the-top content, Frye won a Grammy nomination for the album. Frye's fame dwindled following Nixon's resignation, in August 1974, but he continued to perform and add new impressions to his act in subsequent decades, including Jimmy Carter, Anwar El Sadat, Menachem Begin, Bill Clinton, and Al Gore, among others. His other comedy albums include *David Frye Presents the Great Debate* (1980), *Frye Is Nixon* (1996), and *Clinton: An Oral History* (1998). Frye, who never married, died of cardiopulmonary arrest at his home in Las Vegas, Nevada. He is survived by his sister, Ruth. See *Current Biography* (1975). —C.C.

Obituary *New York Times* (on-line) Jan. 29, 2011

GALVIN, ROBERT W. Oct. 9, 1922–Oct. 11, 2011 Businessman. Robert Galvin "took the reins of Motorola from his father and built a family-run business that pioneered Depression-era car radios and wartime walkie-talkies into a global maker of color television sets, cellphones and other ubiquities of the electronic age," according to Robert McFadden, writing for the *New York Times* (October 12, 2011, online). The only child of Paul Vincent and Lillian (Guinan) Galvin, Robert William Galvin was born in Marshfield, Wisconsin. He received most of his grammar-school education in Chicago, Illinois, where in 1928 his father and his uncle Joseph Galvin established the small battery-eliminator business that developed into Motorola. (A battery eliminator, as the name implies, allowed a consumer to plug a battery-powered radio into an electrical system.) Looking for a new market during the Depression, Paul Galvin next turned his attention to developing an automobile radio, which he began marketing under the name Motorola. The firm then extended its production to mobile communications. For some time it manufactured special receiving sets for police departments and gradually developed a revolutionary mobile radio transmitter. At the Wisconsin National Guard maneuvers in 1939, the transmitter attracted the notice of the Army Signal Corps. As a result the company began making a portable unit called the Handie-Talkie for the army, and it later developed the SCR300 FM Walkie-Talkie, which it supplied in mass quantities for use in World War II. (By 1944, the year Joseph Galvin died, the firm was producing more than $80 million worth of military equipment a year.) Robert Galvin briefly attended both Notre Dame and the University of Chicago before quitting at the age of 18 to work in the stockroom of the family's growing company. After serving in the Army Signal Corps during the war, he returned to the enterprise, and in 1945 he was made a director. In 1947 the company, which had gone public four years before, officially adopted the name Motorola Inc. In 1949 Galvin was promoted to executive vice president. After the Korean War broke out, in 1950, the company's government business boomed again, and sales that year shot up to $177 million. Early in 1952 Motorola, then manufacturing more mobile radio equipment than RCA, General Electric, and Westinghouse combined, established a separate national-defense division headquarters in Chicago. When he was elected president of Motorola Inc., on November 15, 1956, Galvin took over day-to-day direction of the corporation's enterprises from his father, who moved up to chairman of the board and continued as CEO until his death, in November 1959. (Lillian Galvin had been killed by burglars in 1942; the inheritance taxes due after her death had precipitated the decision to take the company public.) After his father's death Galvin became chairman and CEO, and under his direction Motorola began manufacturing a plethora of new products, including, in 1973, the first handheld mobile phone. Galvin stepped down as chairman in 1990 but continued to be a force on the company's board of directors. He retired from the board in 2001 and died of natural causes a decade later, at the age of 89. He was survived by his wife of 67 years, Mary; his daughters, Gail and Dawn; his sons, Christopher and Michael; 13 grandchildren; and 10 great-grandchildren. The Robert W. Galvin Center for Electricity Innovation at the Illinois Institute of Technology is named in his honor. See *Current Biography* (1960). —M.R.

Obituary *New York Times* (on-line) Oct. 12, 2011

GORECKI, HENRYK Dec. 6, 1933–Nov. 12, 2010 Composer. Henryk Gorecki became an important figure in classical-music circles in the late 1950s, when he joined Krzysztof Penderecki and Witold Lutoslawski in spearheading Poland's burgeoning avant-garde movement, but international renown did not come to him until the early 1990s, with the release of the Elektra Nonesuch recording of his Symphony no. 3. Subtitled "Symphony of Sorrowful Songs," the hypnotic, quasi-religious, three-movement work for orchestra and soprano became a huge transatlantic hit, climbing to the top of the classical charts in both the United States and Great Britain and achieving surprising crossover success on the British pop charts as well. The work's unexpected popularity stunned the music world and made Gorecki the first living classical composer to edge into the pop market. The son of Roman and Otylia, Henryk Mikolaj Gorecki was born in Czernica, a small town in Poland. His mother, a pianist, died when he was two, and several other family members perished in Nazi concentration camps during World War II. After graduating from high school, Gorecki worked as a teacher of young children, and when he was in his early 20s, he began his formal music training at a school in Rybnik, near his hometown. In 1955 he enrolled at the Higher School of Music in Katowice, where he studied for five years under the influential Polish composer Boleslaw Szabelski. Gorecki began making a name for himself as a composer while he was still a music student. He was fascinated by the postwar developments in musical techniques, and his earliest efforts were all avant-garde. After the Silesian Philharmonic Orchestra devoted an entire concert to Gorecki's works, in 1958, the conductor Andrzej Markowski commissioned the young composer to write a piece for the 1958 Warsaw Autumn Festival. Gorecki's contribution to the program was *Epitafium*, a miniature cantata for mixed choir and instrumental ensemble. Set to a text by Julian Tuwim, a contemporary Polish poet, the work was typical of Gorecki's youthful compositional style, which tended to be highly modernist and experimental, often juxtaposing meticulously organized sounds with colorful, pointillistic gestures. For the next few years, the Warsaw festival was an annual showcase for Gorecki, reinforcing his reputation as one of Poland's foremost young modernist composers. In 1960 Gorecki's groundbreaking and turbulent orchestral work *Scontri Collisions* had its debut, causing a sensation among listeners and critics alike. After graduating from the conservatory, in 1960, Gorecki studied in Paris, where he entered a new phase in his compositional evolution and began developing a leaner, more reflective style that was less musically complex and marked by an engaging directness of expression. *Three Pieces in the Olden Style* (1963), for string orchestra, heralded a move toward the tonal and modal language that characterized Gorecki's work for decades thereafter. The most noticeable sign of Gorecki's altered musical thinking was that trilogy's apparent simplicity and preoccupation with Polish folk music. (The role of folk music in Gorecki's compositions became increasingly apparent from the mid-1960s onward.) In 1968 Gorecki joined the faculty of the music academy in Katowice; he was promoted to the post of rector seven years later.

During his tenure there he composed Symphony no. 3, which later became his best-known work; it nonetheless met with a chilly reception at its world premiere, at an avant-garde music festival in France in 1977, in some part because of a droning, seemingly eternal repetition of an A-major triad at its conclusion. Gorecki's next major work, *Beatus Vir*, was also the subject of considerable controversy. A devout Catholic, Gorecki had been commissioned by Karol Cardinal Wojtyla, then the archbishop of Krakow, to write a piece commemorating the 900th anniversary of the martyrdom of St. Stanislaw. Shortly after commissioning the work, Cardinal Wojtyla was elected pope (and chose the name John Paul II), and it was during his first papal visit to his homeland, in June 1979, that *Beatus Vir* premiered. Local miners, goaded by Communist Party officials, took to the streets to protest the pope's visit and Gorecki's contribution to it. After his house was vandalized, the composer responded by resigning from all his official posts in Katowice, including that of rector of the conservatory. His resignation allowed him to devote more time to composing in the 1980s. Among the wide variety of works dating from that period are *Miserere* (1981), an ambitious choral piece; *Lerchenmusik* (1984–86), for clarinet, cello, and piano; *Totus Tuus* (1987), a liturgical choral work; and *Already It Is Dusk* (1988), his first string quartet, which he wrote for and dedicated to the Kronos Quartet. Meanwhile, European orchestras were beginning to program Gorecki's Symphony no. 3, and the French filmmaker Maurice Pialat used it as part of the soundtrack for his 1985 film, *Police*. After hearing a performance of the piece by the London Sinfonietta in 1989, Robert Hurwitz, a senior vice president of the Elektra Nonesuch record label, decided to record it with Dawn Upshaw as soprano soloist and David Zinman conducting the London Sinfonietta. (The symphony had been recorded twice already, but those versions had gone largely unnoticed.) Gorecki himself attended the recording sessions for the Nonesuch disk, which was released in April 1992 and quickly struck a resonant chord among music listeners worldwide. The symphony affected listeners so dramatically that one public radio station in California reported receiving calls from captivated motorists who had pulled off the road to listen. The symphony was later used on the soundtracks to the films *Fearless* (1993) and *Basquiat* (1996). Gorecki—whose many honors include first prize in the Warsaw Young Composers' Competition (1960) and the Prize of the Union of Polish Composers (1970)—died after being hospitalized for a lung infection. He is survived by his wife, Jadwiga; his son, Mikolaj; and his daughter, Anna. See *Current Biography* (1994). —D.K.

Obituary *New York Times* (on-line) Nov. 12, 2010

HANDLIN, OSCAR Sep. 29, 1915–Sep. 20, 2011 Historian. The Pulitzer Prize–winning historian Oscar Handlin is widely credited with changing public discourse on the topic of immigration. "He reoriented the whole picture of the American story, from the view that America was built on the spirit of the Wild West, to the idea that we are a nation of immigrants," James Grossman, the executive director of the American Historical Association, told Paul Vitello for the *New York Times* (September 23, 2011, on-line). Handlin, the oldest of four children, was born in the New York City borough of Brooklyn to Joseph and Ida (Yanowitz) Handlin, immigrants from Russia who owned a small grocery store. Despite their humble means, they stressed the importance of education to Handlin and his siblings. As a boy Handlin made deliveries to customers, often balancing a book on top of his cart so that he could read as he worked. He earned a B.A. degree from Brooklyn College in 1934, winning the Union League Award for history. He then entered Harvard University, where one of his most important mentors was the historian Arthur M. Schlesinger Sr., a pioneer in the area of immigration studies. Handlin received a master's degree in 1935. Schlesinger had suggested to Handlin the subject of his doctoral dissertation, which was published in 1941 under the title *Boston's Immigrants, 1790–1865: A Study in Acculturation*. The volume garnered the prestigious Dunning Prize from the American Historical Association. Handlin joined the faculty of Harvard as a history instructor in 1939, the year before being awarded his Ph.D. degree. He remained at the university until his retirement, in 1984. (In 1954 he became one of the first Jewish academics to achieve the rank of full professor at Harvard.) During his tenure there he also served as the director of the Harvard University Library (1979–84). Handlin, who wrote and edited dozens of books, including the multivolume *American Immigration Collection* (1969), is best known for *The Uprooted: The Epic Story of the Great Migrations That Made the American People* (1951), which won the 1952 Pulitzer Prize for history. "Dispensing with footnotes and writing in a lyrical style, Dr. Handlin emphasized the common threads in the experiences of the 30 million immigrants who poured into American cities between 1820 and the turn of the century," Vitello wrote. "Regardless of nationality, religion, race or ethnicity, [Handlin] wrote, the common experience was wrenching hardship, alienation and a gradual Americanization that changed America as much as it changed the newcomers. The book used a form of historical scholarship considered unorthodox at the the time, employing newspaper accounts, personal letters and diaries as well as archives. The *New York Times* described it [upon its publication] as 'history with a difference—the difference being its concern with hearts and souls.'" The book thrust Handlin into the spotlight as one of the country's foremost experts on immigration, and in the mid-1960s he was called upon to advise Congress on a piece of legislation that would abolish a longstanding quota system that discriminated against various ethnic groups. (The legislation ultimately passed.) Handlin died at his home in Cambridge, Massachusetts, at the age of 95. He was predeceased, in 1976, by his wife of four decades, Mary Flug Handlin, a historian with whom he often collaborated. He is survived by their children—David, Joanna, and Ruth—as well as by his second wife, Lilian Bombach Handlin, whom he married in 1977 and with whom he also co-wrote books. Most obituary tributes to Handlin quoted the opening line from *Uprooted*, which seemed to sum up his oeuvre: "Once I thought to write a history of the immigrants in America. Then I discovered that the immigrants were American history." See *Current Biography* (1952). —M.R.

Obituary *New York Times* (on-line) Sep. 23, 2011

HANNAN, PHILIP M. May 20, 1913–Sep. 29, 2011 Roman Catholic prelate. Philip M. Hannan, once the archbishop of New Orleans and a confidant and adviser to President John F. Kennedy, was an eloquent, liberal churchman who pressed for racial justice, ecumenism, religious liberty, and liturgical reform. Hannan was born in Washington, D.C., to Patrick Francis Hannan, an Irish immigrant plumbing contractor, and Lillian Louise (Keefe) Hannan. He studied for the priesthood at the Sulpician Seminary of the Catholic University of America and also attended the North American College in Rome, Italy, where he received a licentiate in theology in 1939. He was ordained in Rome on December 8, 1939. Hannon's first assignment after ordination was as an assistant pastor at St. Thomas Aquinas Church in Baltimore, Maryland. From 1942 to 1946 he was a chaplain to the paratroopers of the 82d Airborne Division of the U.S. Army. After leaving military service he studied for a doctorate in canon law at the Catholic University of America while serving as assistant pastor of St. Mary's Church in Washington. Upon receiving his doctoral degree from Catholic University, in 1948, Hannan was appointed vice-chancellor of the Archdiocese of Washington by Archbishop Patrick A. O'Boyle. While holding that office he met John F. Kennedy, then a young congressman. The two men began a long friendship, and throughout his political career, when Kennedy had a question about Church teachings, he called Hannan. The relationship was not general knowledge. "For it to be known that Kennedy was consulting at all with a Catholic bishop would have been politically harmful," Peter Finney Jr., the editor of the *Clarion Herald*, a church newspaper, told Dennis Hevesi for the *New York Times* (September 30, 2011, on-line). On November 25, 1963, three days after Kennedy's assassination, Hannan, who had become vicar general of the Archdiocese of Washington in 1960, delivered the eulogy at the president's funeral Mass. (He later delivered eulogies for Senator Robert F. Kennedy and for Jacqueline Kennedy Onassis.) From 1965 to 1988 Hannan served as the archbishop of New Orleans, fighting segregation, establishing programs for disadvantaged children, gaining federal support for affordable housing, advocating for AIDS patients, and creating one of the largest food banks in the nation. He died at the age of 98, at a hospice in New Orleans, and is survived by his brother, Jerry. See *Current Biography* (1968). —M.R.

Obituary *New York Times* (on-line) Sep. 30, 2011

HAREWOOD, GEORGE HENRY HUBERT LASCELLES Feb. 7, 1923–July 11, 2011 Member of the British royal family; opera expert. George Henry Hubert Lascelles, the seventh Earl of Harewood, was, according to a tribute by Tom Sutcliffe in the London *Guardian* (July 11, 2011, on-line), "unusual for a member of the royal family in deserving a substantial obituary on account of what he did rather than who he was." Harewood, the eldest grandchild of King George V and a cousin to Queen Elizabeth II, was one of his nation's foremost authorities on opera. He was born in London. His father, the sixth Earl of Harewood, was a wealthy landowner who held various public offices and was a former aide-de-camp to King George V. His mother was Princess Victoria Alexandra Alice Mary, generally known as Princess Mary, the only daughter of King George V and Queen Mary. As a child, growing up in London and at Harewood House in Yorkshire with his younger brother, Gerald, Harewood developed an intense interest in classical music, particularly opera, that grew even stronger during his years at Eton. While at Eton he was summoned to be a page at the coronation of George VI. Harewood, who also loved cricket and horse-racing, left Eton in 1941, and in 1942 he enlisted as a private in his father's regiment, the Grenadier Guards. While in Italy in June 1944, Harewood, then a captain, arrived too early at a rendezvous near Perugia. Trapped by the Germans, he was wounded, captured, and shipped to Colditz, the infamous prisoner-of-war camp in Germany. During the year he spent in Colditz, Harewood began to read through the volumes of *Grove's Dictionary of Music and Musicians*, and had reached the letter S (some sources state T) when the war drew to a close. In May 1945 a commandant handed him over to the Swiss unharmed. Harewood spent the year after the war in Canada, as an aide-de-camp to his great-uncle, the Earl of Athlone, who was serving as governor general. In 1946 he entered King's College, Cambridge University, and in May 1947, upon the death of his father, he succeeded him as seventh Earl of Harewood. Harewood received his B.A. degree in 1948, and after his graduation he worked for a time as an opera critic. In 1950 he founded the magazine *Opera*, the first British periodical in many years devoted exclusively to the subject. The following year Harewood became a board member of the Royal Opera House, Covent Garden, and in 1953 he left the magazine to devote himself full-time to Covent Garden as a casting manager, a post he retained until 1960. In 1972 he began serving as managing director of Sadler's Wells Opera, and when the company, a populist rival of the Royal Opera, was renamed in 1974 as the English National Opera (ENO), he remained. Harewood was the ENO's managing director until 1985 and then its chairman until 1986. "The competition between the Wells and Sir Georg Solti's [Covent] Garden, which faintly echoed the royal operatic rows involving Lord Harewood's Hanoverian forebears in Handel's day, was good for opera in Britain generally," Sutcliffe wrote. In addition to his duties with the ENO, Harewood was the artistic director of the Edinburgh Festival (1961–65), the Leeds Festival (1958–74), and the Adelaide Festival (1988) and an editor of *Kobbé's Complete Opera Book*, a well-regarded reference work that he revised and updated periodically. From 1949 to 1967 Harewood was married to the concert pianist Maria Donata Nanetta Paulina Gustava Erwina Wilhelmine Stein, who was known as Marion. Shortly after their divorce he married his second wife, the violinist and fashion model Patricia Elizabeth Tuckwell. (The divorce and remarriage required the permission of Queen Elizabeth II.) Harewood, who published an autobiography,

The Tongs and the Bones, in 1981, died at the age of 88. He is survived by Patricia; three sons from his first marriage: David Henry George (now the eighth Earl of Harewood), James Edward, and Robert Jeremy Hugh; a son, Mark Hubert, from his union with Patricia; a stepson, the writer Michael Shmith (the co-editor of *The New Kobbé's Opera Book*); and numerous grandchildren and great-grandchildren. See *Current Biography* (1965). —M.R.

Obituary *New York Times* (on-line) July 26, 2011

HARRIS, CYRIL June 20, 1917–Jan. 4, 2011 Acoustician. Cyril Harris, a noted architectural and acoustical consultant for concert halls, theaters, and opera houses, was influenced by the superb acoustics of such 19th-century concert halls as the Concertgebouw in Amsterdam, Conservatory Hall in Moscow, and Boston's Symphony Hall—all of which in turn had been patterned after the Neues Gewandhaus in Leipzig, Germany. Harris, who eschewed contemporary artificial sound-absorbing materials and techniques in favor of the traditional methods for achieving near-perfect sound, once explained, "The old concert halls in Europe, the great halls, were built without acoustical consultants but they worked well and the reason they worked well was the style of architecture used." Harris was responsible for renovations to the Metropolitan Opera in 1966 and the theaters of the John F. Kennedy Center for the Performing Arts in Washington, D.C., in 1971. His professional counsel also provided the basis for the radical reconstruction of Avery Fisher Hall at Lincoln Center, in New York; the Powell Symphony Hall in St. Louis, Missouri; the Great Hall at the Krannert Center for the Performing Arts in Urbana, Illinois; the Orchestra Hall in Minneapolis; Symphony Hall (now Abravanel Hall) in Salt Lake City; and the Benatoya Hall in Seattle, among others. Harris was born in Detroit, Michigan, the only child of Bernard O. Harris, a general practitioner, and Ida (Moss) Harris, a schoolteacher. Three years after her husband died in the influenza epidemic of 1918, Ida Harris moved with her young son to Hollywood, where Harris attended school. When his part-time after-school jobs as a messenger or delivery boy called for him to make a stop at Warner Bros., the film studio that pioneered the development of talking pictures, he purchased inexpensive used batteries from the studio to set up his own amateur broadcasting station, with the call letters W6IJE. Harris enrolled at the University of California at Los Angeles (UCLA); though he intended to study medicine, his aversion to chemistry prompted him to switch his major to mathematics, with a minor in physics. It was not until he reached his senior year that Harris discovered acoustics. His curiosity kindled by theoretical acoustical research, he read everything he could find on the subject and, after earning his B.A. degree, in 1938, pursued advanced degrees in physics. He received his M.A. degree in the subject from UCLA in 1940, and later that same year he transferred to the Massachusetts Institute of Technology (MIT) to study under the physicist Philip McCord Morse. After obtaining his Ph.D. degree from MIT, in 1945, Harris was offered a job by Harvey Fletcher, an acoustics expert and the director of physical research at the Bell Telephone Laboratories in Murray Hill, New Jersey. During his six years at Bell, Harris co-invented a talking typewriter. Harris left Bell Labs in 1951 and sailed to England for an extended "working vacation." For the next 18 months he worked, successively, as a consultant to the London branch of the U.S. Office of Naval Research and as a Fulbright exchange program lecturer in acoustics at the Delft University of Technology in the Netherlands. In 1952 he returned to the United States to accept a post as associate professor of electrical engineering at Columbia University, in New York City. By the late 1950s Harris had obtained enough work to keep eight engineers and four technicians busy. Over the course of his career, Harris designed the acoustics for more than 100 concert halls. His renovation of Avery Fisher Hall at Lincoln Center, in the 1970s, was among his best-known projects. Known as the Philharmonic Hall when it opened, in 1962, the hall had long been criticized for its acoustical problems. Harris's renovations included replacing the concrete floors with wood, thickening the ceiling plaster, and dispensing with the curved side balconies and back wall. His work was credited with transforming the hall into one of the world's important acoustic installations. (The hall was, however, re-renovated in 1992, after years of complaints about its effect on the sound of certain instruments.) From 1974 to 1984 Harris chaired the division of architectural technology in the Graduate School of Architecture, Planning, and Preservation at Columbia. He published several books on the science of acoustics and its application, including *Acoustical Designing in Architecture* (1980), which he co-wrote with Vern O. Knudson. Harris died at his home in Manhattan and is survived by his wife, Ann Schakne, a book editor, whom he married in 1949; his son and daughter; and three grandchildren. See *Current Biography* (1977). —M.M.H.

Obituary *New York Times* (on-line) Jan. 8, 2011

HATFIELD, MARK O. July 12, 1922–Aug. 7, 2011 Former governor of Oregon and U.S. senator. Mark O. Hatfield, a Republican, was frequently at odds with his party during his decades-long political career, particularly regarding the Vietnam War, military spending, health care, and conservation. Mark Odom Hatfield was born in the small town of Dallas, Oregon, the only child of Charles Dolen Hatfield, a railroad construction blacksmith, and Dovie (Odom) Hatfield, a schoolteacher. In the early 1930s the family moved to nearby Salem, the state capital. Introduced to politics as early as 1932 by his mother, a staunch Republican, he made the rounds of his neighborhood, distributing handbills calling for the reelection of President Herbert Hoover. By the time he was in high school, he was taking part in local Republican political campaigns, either as a full-time volunteer or as a paid employee. Hatfield studied political science at Willamette University, a Methodist-affiliated college in Salem. Shortly after obtaining his B.A. degree, in 1943, he joined the U.S. Navy. Assigned to a landing craft in the Pacific, he took part in the battles at Iwo Jima and Okinawa, and he was among the first Americans to see firsthand the devastation caused by the atomic bombing of Hiroshima.

He was discharged from military service in 1945 with the rank of lieutenant and received an M.A. degree in political science from Stanford University three years later. Hatfield joined the faculty of Willamette University as a political-science instructor in 1949. Within a year he had been promoted to associate professor and appointed dean of students, positions that he held until 1956. Meanwhile, he plunged into politics, quickly becoming state chairman of the Young Republican Policy Committee. In 1950 he easily won a seat in the Oregon legislature. Hatfield served as a state representative from 1950 to 1954 and as a state senator from 1954 to 1956. Upon his election in 1956 to the post of secretary of state, the second-ranking elective office in the executive branch of Oregon's government, he resigned from the Willamette faculty. Two years later Hatfield ran successfully for governor, becoming the youngest to win that office in the history of Oregon. He was reelected to a second term in 1962. Fulfilling a campaign pledge to revitalize his state's moribund economy, Hatfield launched an aggressive promotional campaign to encourage exports, expand trade with the Far East, and lure new industry to the state. His charm and demonstrable success made him a popular figure with Republican leaders, who tapped him to nominate Richard Nixon for president at the party's national convention in 1960 and to deliver the keynote address in 1964. Yet unlike many Republicans, he staunchly supported civil rights and opposed the war in Vietnam. The latter became a key issue in his 1966 campaign for the U.S. Senate, which he won. During his first term in that office, he supported or submitted many "end-the-war" bills. His outspoken opposition to the war cost him the support of Republican hard-liners and earned him a place on President Nixon's infamous "enemies list." Hatfield regularly voted against increases in military appropriations earmarked by the Pentagon, and he opposed the military draft. When the Republicans won control of the Senate in the 1980 election, Hatfield found himself in a position of some power, as the new chairman of the Appropriations Committee. He initially went along with President Ronald Reagan's budget- and tax-cutting proposals, but by 1982 he had modified his stance to retain needed social programs and to fund a public-works jobs bill. That year he and Senator William Proxmire joined forces to orchestrate an override of Reagan's veto of a $14.1 billion appropriations bill, handing the president his first major legislative defeat. Determined to apply the same fiscal scrutiny to military-spending proposals as the White House applied to social programs, Hatfield prodded the Pentagon to find ways to use funds more efficiently and supported a freeze on the testing and development of more nuclear weapons. Until he retired from the Senate, in 1997, and even afterward, as a private citizen, he also continued to emphasize the need for the federal government to increase its spending on health and medical research. Hatfield was the author of the memoirs *Not Quite So Simple* (1968) and *Against the Grain: Reflections of a Rebel Republican* (2000). He also wrote *Conflict and Conscience* (1971) and *Between a Rock and a Hard Place* (1976), about his evangelical faith and its relationship to his political life. Hatfield is survived by his wife, Antoinette, and their four children: Elizabeth, Mark, Theresa, and Charles. See *Current Biography* (1984). —D.K.

Obituary *New York Times* (on-line) Aug. 8, 2011

HEALY, BERNADINE P. Aug. 2, 1944–Aug. 6, 2011 Cardiologist; public-health official. Bernadine Healy was the first woman to direct the National Institutes of Health (NIH), and she also served for a time as the head of the American Red Cross (ARC). Healy was born in New York City, the second of the four daughters of second-generation Irish-Americans. She grew up in Long Island City, Queens, New York, where her parents, Michael and Violet, ran a small perfume business from their basement. In 1962 Healy entered Vassar College, in Poughkeepsie, New York, on a scholarship, majoring in chemistry with a minor in philosophy and graduating summa cum laude in three years. At Harvard University Medical School, from which she graduated cum laude with an M.D. degree in 1970, she was one of only 10 women in a class of 120. After completing her internship and residency at Baltimore's Johns Hopkins Hospital, in 1972, Healy spent two years as a fellow in pathology at the NIH's National Heart, Lung, and Blood Institute in Bethesda, Maryland. Upon her return to Johns Hopkins, in 1974, she became a fellow in the cardiovascular division of the School of Medicine, where she was a professor from 1976 to 1984. As the director of the Coronary Care Unit from 1977 to 1984 and the school's first female assistant dean for postdoctoral programs and faculty development for most of that period, she juggled teaching, cardiovascular research, writing, and clinical responsibilities. Appointed deputy director of the White House Office of Science and Technology Policy by President Ronald Reagan in February 1984, Healy was confirmed in the post that June. In November 1985 she was hired by the Cleveland Clinic Foundation to chair its research institute. In March 1991 Healy was confirmed by the George H. W. Bush administration as director of the NIH, the first woman ever to hold that high-level post. During her tenure there, she "cracked the whip on bureaucrats, recruited new talent, expanded the Human Genome Project and reversed policies that, like the medical establishment, had focused largely on men's health and virtually excluded women from clinical trials," according to Robert D. Mc-Fadden, writing for the *New York Times* (August 8, 2011, on-line). One of her most noteworthy accomplishments was the launch of the Women's Health Initiative, a sweeping study of cardiovascular disease, osteoporosis, and cancer in women. After President Bill Clinton failed to reappoint her in 1993, she entered, unsuccessfully, the 1994 Republican U.S. Senate primary in Ohio. The following year she became the dean of Ohio State University's College of Medicine and Public Health. In 1999 Healy stepped into another high-visibility position, as head of the ARC. Her time at the organization was troubled. McFadden explained, "While it was widely seen as an icon of humanitarian work, the organization was an unwieldy behemoth with 1,000 chapters, 1.2 million volunteers, 3,000 staff members and a $3 billion budget. It was also a house divided, with nonprofit disaster-relief on one side and, on the other, a blood business run like a corporation." Healy's

attempts at reform were met with great resistance, and she found herself in a firestorm of bad press in the wake of the terrorist attacks of 9/11. In particular, the ARC was denounced on the floor of Congress and elsewhere for allegedly deceiving the public by setting aside for other, future uses nearly half of the $564 million pledged to its Liberty Fund, created to help the families of victims of the attacks. It was also criticized for mounting a huge blood-collection drive after the attacks and continuing the drive even after it became clear that little blood would be needed for those injured—and that, with far too little storage space available for the amount of blood that was donated, most of that blood would have to be discarded. Forced out of the organization in late 2001, Healy subsequently became a commentator on health issues for CBS News and PBS-TV and began writing a regular column for *U.S. News & World Report*. Healy waged a long battle with cancer—she was diagnosed with a brain tumor in 1999 and was in the midst of chemotherapy when she accepted the presidency of the ARC—and she wrote a book about the topic, *Living Time: Faith and Facts to Transform Your Cancer Journey*, in 2007. She succumbed to the disease at the age of 67, at her home in Gates Mills, Ohio. She is survived by her second husband, Floyd D. Loop, a cardiac surgeon who once headed the Cleveland Clinic Foundation; their daughter, Marie; and another daughter, Bartlett, from her first marriage, to George Bulkley, a surgeon she had met while in medical school. See *Current Biography* (1992). —M.R.

Obituary *New York Times* (on-line) Aug. 8, 2011

HOIBY, LEE Feb. 17, 1926–Mar. 28, 2011 Composer; pianist. Lee Hoiby enjoyed remarkable success in writing in a conservative, tonal idiom that rejected the dissonant revolution in 20th-century music. Although Hoiby wrote many critically praised works for solo piano, chamber ensemble, and orchestra, he is perhaps best known for his operas—including *Summer and Smoke* (1971), based on the Tennessee Williams play, and a musical version of Shakespeare's *The Tempest* (1986)—as well as for his more than 100 songs set to famous texts and poems. He was also a virtuoso pianist who enjoyed a second career on the concert stage. Hoiby was born in Madison, Wisconsin, to parents who were amateur musicians. He began his piano studies at the age of five and made his debut as a composer at the age of six with a piano work he called "The Storm." Hoiby earned a bachelor of music degree from the University of Wisconsin in 1947 and went on to study at Mills College, in Oakland, California, where he received a master's degree in 1952. Unlike many fledgling composers, Hoiby had quick success in getting his works performed. Thomas Schippers and the NBC Symphony introduced Hoiby's *Nocturne* for orchestra in New York City in October 1950, and Erich Leinsdorf and the Rochester Symphony performed his ballet *Hearts, Meadows, and Flags* in November 1952. His accessible style undoubtedly helped to find an audience for those and his other early works, for in rejecting the atonality that held sway over many American composers in the early 1950s, Hoiby favored a deeply melodic idiom with lush orchestrations in the manner of late-19th-century romanticism. In the spring of 1958, Hoiby introduced his first one-act opera, *The Scarf*, at Gian Carlo Menotti's Festival of Two Worlds in Spoleto, Italy, and then brought the work to the New York City Opera the following year. Although he devoted most of his attention to opera in the late 1950s and early 1960s, Hoiby also composed many nonoperatic vocal works during that period, including the oratorio *A Hymn of the Nativity* (1960) and the symphonic song *Tides of Sleep* (1961). In 1964 Tennessee Williams invited Hoiby to choose one of his plays to make into an opera. After exhaustively studying the Williams canon, Hoiby selected the three-act drama *Summer and Smoke* (1948). The playwright Lanford Wilson served as his librettist, and *Summer and Smoke* was given its premiere at the St. Paul Opera on June 19, 1971 with highly acclaimed performances by Mary Beth Peil and John Reardon, who went on to star in the New York City Opera's production the following year. In 1982 Hoiby accepted a commission from the Des Moines Metro Opera to write an operatic version of Shakespeare's *The Tempest*. He said of that project, "I have never before found a project so affecting to me in an existential way." Among Hoiby's later works are the one-act chamber opera *This Is Rill Speaking* (1992); an unperformed opera based on *Romeo and Juliet*; and the choral work *Last Letter Home*, set to a note a soldier wrote before his death in Iraq. Hoiby, who lived near the banks of the Delaware River in Long Eddy, New York, died of metastatic melanoma at the age of 85. At the time of his death, he was reportedly working on a choral composition using lines from Ralph Waldo Emerson's essay "Nature." He is survived by his partner and longtime collaborator, Mark Shulgasser. See *Current Biography* (1987). —M.M.H.

Obituary *New York Times* (on-line) Mar. 29, 2011

HOLBROOKE, RICHARD C. Apr. 24, 1941–Dec. 13, 2010 Diplomat; investment banker. Richard C. Holbrooke was a foreign-policy guru who, beginning in the 1960s, held important diplomatic positions in every Democratic presidential administration. Holbrooke, whose early accomplishments included work in Vietnam during the war there and the successful restoration of full diplomatic relations with China, in 1979, was perhaps best known for overseeing the negotiations that resulted in the signing of the 1995 Dayton Peace Accords, which ended the war in Bosnia. In addition to his career in international diplomacy, he was a best-selling author and a successful investment banker. Holbrooke was born in New York City to Dan Holbrooke, a physician, and the former Trudi Moos, a potter. Holbrooke's father was originally from Poland, and his mother had emigrated from Germany, by way of Switzerland and Argentina. Of Jewish descent, both were atheists, and Holbrooke was not raised in the Jewish faith. He attended Scarsdale High School, in a suburb of New York, where he befriended David Rusk, a son of Dean Rusk, the future secretary of state under Presidents John F. Kennedy and Lyndon B. Johnson. Holbrooke developed a close relationship with the Rusk family after his father died of cancer, when Holbrooke was

15. In keeping with his father's wish, Holbrooke attended Brown University, in Providence, Rhode Island, on a full-tuition scholarship. He majored in math and physics before switching to history, and he served as editor of the school newspaper, the *Brown Daily Herald*. Upon graduating from Brown, in 1962, he joined the U.S. State Department as a foreign-service officer. After receiving language training, Holbrooke was sent to Vietnam, where he spent the next three years working in the U.S. Embassy and the Mekong Delta. He returned to the States in 1966 and joined the Vietnam staff of the Johnson White House. Holbrooke was a junior member of the U.S. delegation to the Vietnam peace talks in Paris, France, in 1968 and 1969, an experience that taught him much about the art of negotiation. Also during that period he wrote one of the volumes of the Pentagon Papers, the top-secret documentation of U.S. involvement in Vietnam dating back to the 1940s (brought to public light by the *New York Times* in 1971). In 1970, following a one-year fellowship at Princeton University, in New Jersey, Holbrooke was named director of the Peace Corps in Morocco. Two years later he became the managing editor of the quarterly journal *Foreign Policy*, a position he held for the next five years. During his tenure at *Foreign Policy*, he was also a contributing editor for *Newsweek* and a consultant to a presidential commission on foreign policy. In 1976 Holbrooke worked as a coordinator of national-security affairs on the successful presidential campaign of Jimmy Carter. He was then appointed by Carter to serve as assistant secretary of state for East Asian and Pacific affairs. In that position, which he held for the duration of Carter's presidency (1977–81), he led successful efforts to establish full diplomatic relations with China, capitalizing on President Richard M. Nixon's historic visit to that country in 1972. When Ronald Reagan succeeded Carter in the White House, in 1981, Holbrooke left government to work on Wall Street, founding the consulting firm Public Strategies with James A. Johnson, a future CEO of Fannie Mae. In 1985 he and Johnson sold the company to the investment-banking firm Lehman Bros., where both became managing directors. After earning millions of dollars in the private sector, Holbrooke returned to government service in 1993, when President Bill Clinton appointed him ambassador to Germany. He served in that role until September 1994, when he became assistant secretary of state for European and Canadian affairs. As a private citizen Holbrooke had been working with the International Rescue Committee in Bosnia and Herzegovina during the outbreak of fighting there, which had been precipitated by the secession from Yugoslavia of Croatia, Slovenia, Macedonia, and Bosnia. Holbrooke had become an outspoken critic of the West's response to the conflict, which involved a campaign of massacres, mass rapes, and other atrocities against Muslim populations in the region. Holbrooke made the conflict in Bosnia one of his main priorities. In August 1995, not long after the Srebrenica massacre, in which thousands of Bosnians in the city of Srebrenica were murdered or made refugees, Holbrooke was sent to the Balkans in a last-ditch effort to broker a peace deal among the warring parties. His mission led to the September 14, 1995 signing of an agreement by

the Serbian leader Slobodan Milosevic and the Bosnian Serb leaders Radovan Karadžić and Ratko Mladić to end the siege of the city of Sarajevo. A month later the warring parties agreed to a ceasefire. In November Holbrooke oversaw the final stages of negotiations, at Wright-Patterson Air Force Base near Dayton, Ohio, among Milosevic, President Franjo Tudjman of Croatia, and President Alija Izetbegović of Bosnia. The agreement, which came to be known as the Dayton Peace Accords and was formally signed in Paris, France, in December 1995, ended the three-year-long war. The deal involved a framework for dividing Bosnia into a Bosnian republic and a Bosnian-Croatian federation. After the signing of the peace agreement, Holbrooke returned to investment banking, published the best-selling memoir *To End a War* (1998), and occasionally served as an adviser to the U.S. State Department. (Holbrooke also co-authored, with former presidential adviser Clark Clifford, the best-selling 1991 memoir *Counsel to the President.*) He was summoned back to full-time government service in 1998, when Clinton named him the U.S. ambassador to the United Nations, a position he held for 17 months. Holbrooke then worked on the unsuccessful presidential campaigns of U.S. senators John Kerry, in 2004, and Hillary Rodham Clinton, in 2008, before being appointed by President Barack Obama to serve as a special adviser for Afghanistan and Pakistan in 2009. In that role, as Robert D. McFadden wrote for the *New York Times* (December 13, 2010, on-line), Holbrooke was wrestling with "how to bring stability to the region while fighting a resurgent Taliban and coping with corrupt governments, rigged elections, fragile economies, a rampant narcotics trade, nuclear weapons in Pakistan, and the presence of Al Qaeda, and presumably Osama bin Laden, in the wild tribal borderlands." Along with Secretary of State Hillary Clinton, Holbrooke played a key role in persuading Obama to send additional troops to Afghanistan and to increase aid and development projects in the region. Holbrooke died after two operations to repair a tear in his aorta. He is survived by his third wife, the writer Kati Marton; two sons, David and Anthony, from his first marriage, to the lawyer Larrine Sullivan; his brother, Andrew; and two stepchildren, Christopher and Elizabeth Jennings. See *Current Biography* (1998). —C.C.

Obituary *New York Times* (on-line) Dec. 13, 2010

HONDROS, CHRIS Mar. 14, 1970–Apr. 20, 2011 Photojournalist. Chris Hondros, a staff photographer for Getty Images, captured scenes of suffering and brutality in nearly a dozen war-torn countries. His poignant and graphic photographs appeared in the *New York Times*, the *Washington Post*, the *Los Angeles Times*, the *Economist*, *Newsweek*, and *Time*, among other major publications. "The task is to draw people in," Hondros told *Current Biography* in 2004, "and you do that by creating work with a certain amount of beauty. And beauty in the face of terror, in the face of pain, is nothing new." A first-generation American, Christopher E. Hondros was born in New York to a Greek father and German mother. His family moved to Fayetteville, North Car-

olina, when Hondros was a toddler. He earned a bachelor's degree in English literature from North Carolina State University in 1993 and moved to Troy, Ohio, where he took his first journalism job, as a photographer for the *Troy Daily News*. Hondros left Troy in 1994 and enrolled in the graduate program in photojournalism at Ohio University's School of Visual Communications. He completed the two-year program in 1996 and quickly found work as a staff photographer for the *Fayetteville Observer*. In 1998 he moved back to New York to become a photo editor for the Associated Press, and the following year he was awarded a $25,000 grant from the United States Agency for International Development (USAID) to take photos in Kosovo, a province in southern Serbia, which was then wracked by ethnic violence between Serbs and the province's ethnic Albanians. During that trip Hondros photographed grieving family members who had lost relatives in the fighting, ethnic Albanian soldiers, and some of the hundreds of thousands of refugees the conflict had created. In the fall of 1999, Hondros traveled on his own to Angola, in West Africa. There, he captured in pictures the hardships endured by starving, infirm, and displaced Angolan civilians in the town of Malanje, which was surrounded by rebels. In December of that year, Hondros took a job as a staff photographer for Getty Images. In that capacity he traveled to Sierra Leone, Afghanistan, Pakistan, Israel, Iraq, and Liberia, among other locales. For his 2003 photos from Liberia—where he found himself in the midst of the fighting as rebel groups struggled to wrest control of Monrovia, the nation's capital, from armed militias loyal to the Liberian government—Hondros was named a finalist for a Pulitzer Prize, and he received the Overseas Press Club's John Faber Award. He also earned honors in an annual photojournalism contest run by the National Press Photographers Association (NPPA). The photograph that captured the NPPA's first-place prize shows a young, shirtless Liberian militia leader in a celebratory half leap with both arms raised, his rocket-propelled grenade launcher clutched in one hand. Behind him, smoke rises; debris and spent shell casings are scattered on the bridge from which he has been shooting. He seems almost to be enjoying the frenzy of battle. The photograph was seen on the front pages of newspapers around the globe and became the haunting, iconic image of the long conflict. Hondros knowingly put himself in the line of fire for every assignment. "One of the ongoing themes in my work, I hope, and one of the things I believe in, is a sense of human nature, a sense of shared humanity above the cultural things we put on ourselves," he told *Current Biography*. "Clearly we are all quite similar. We put all these layers of ethnicity and culture on ourselves and it really doesn't mean that much compared to the human experience." In April 2011, while working in Libya, Hondros was fatally wounded in an attack by government forces on Misrata, a city held by rebels. He is survived by his mother; his brother, Dean; and his fiancée, Christina Piaia, a former photo editor, whom he was to marry in August 2011. See *Current Biography* (2004). —M.M.H.

Obituary *New York Times* (on-line) Apr. 20, 2011

HUSAIN, MAQBUL FIDA Sep. 17, 1915–June 9, 2011 Artist. Routinely compared to the 20th-century Spanish master Pablo Picasso, the Indian painter and filmmaker Maqbul Fida Husain shared with Picasso an astounding productivity—he claimed to have created some 60,000 works—and a dramatic influence over the art of his time. While Picasso's ties to his native Spain seem in some ways less important than his ties to France, where he lived for much of his life, Husain allied himself closely with Indian culture, the source of his strongest influences and most frequent subjects. Maqbul Fida Husain (often abbreviated M. F. and spelled Hussain; his first name was occasionally written Maqbool) was born in Pandharpur, in the Indian state of Maharashtra. English-language sources—even those coming from Husain himself—give contradictory accounts of his early life, but all agree that he lost his mother, Zunaib, when he was a toddler. His father, Fida, an accountant who was supportive of Husain's art, remarried, and the family moved north to the much larger city of Indore, in Madhya Pradesh, where Fida worked in a textile mill. In his youth Husain was sent to Sidhpur, in Gujarat, where he attended a madrasa (a Muslim religious school) for about two years. Unsuccessful as a student, even after changing schools, Husain was apprenticed to a tailor so that he would have some practical means of making a living. In about 1936 Husain moved to Mumbai, then known as Bombay. The city was the home of India's thriving movie industry, and Husain began working with a friend who hand-painted movie billboards, known as hoardings. Husain painted backgrounds and blended paints, earning barely enough to survive. Eventually he struck out on his own, and though the pay was better, it still amounted to only a few rupees—or even to nothing at all if a movie failed or the producers turned out to be unreliable. In the early 1940s, at about the time of his marriage, Husain gave up painting hoardings, and in order to earn a steadier income, he started working for a furniture company. Initially assigned to paint decorations on children's furniture, he successfully pushed the company to use more Indian motifs in its products and quickly moved up through the ranks to become a designer. In 1947, the year India gained independence from the British, Husain quit his job at the furniture manufacturer and had his first major exposure as an artist, when he participated in the annual show of the Bombay Art Society. His work soon brought him to the attention of members of the Progressive Artists Group, which had been founded in a rudimentary form during the previous decade by Syed Haider Raza and Francis Newton Souza but is generally described as not having come together as a coherent group until about the time Husain joined—making him one of the founding members. Over the next few years, Husain showed his work all over India in connection with the group, which advocated modernism and rejected traditional painting styles, and in 1950 he mounted his first one-person show. When buyers snapped up all his paintings, he started working as an artist full-time, and in 1955 his painting *Zameen* took the top prize at the country's first National Art Exhibition. In 1956 Husain created another important painting, *Between the Spider and the Lamp*. More than 28 square feet in size, the painting shows five women standing in a row, with a brightly lit lamp above one woman's head and a spider at the bottom. With a meaningless—but antique-seeming—script in the background, the painting resists easy interpretation; still, it remains one of Husain's most recognizable images and was used on an Indian postage stamp in 1982. The Progressive Artists Group fell apart in 1956, just as Husain was gaining an international reputation. Over the next three decades, Husain remained one of India's most visible painters, participating in group exhibitions or one-person shows in cities around the world, including Rome, Frankfurt, Baghdad, Kabul, and New York City. At home, Husain had shows in some of his country's most important galleries. In 1969 he had his first retrospective, called 21 Years of Painting. In 1971 Husain joined Picasso at the 11th São Paulo Biennial exhibition in Brazil. Other retrospectives of Husain's work during that period included exhibitions in Calcutta and New Delhi. Husain's reputation in India in the 1980s was augmented by occasional forays into performance art or high-profile celebratory works. His most famous paintings during that time took as their subject the missionary nun known as Mother Teresa. (His other muse and frequent subject was the actress Madhuri Dixit, whom he also directed in the 2000 film *Gaja Gamini*, made with $2 million of his own money.) As Husain's reputation grew, the prices he demanded for his paintings steadily increased. In June 1995, 10 works by Husain received the 10 highest amounts for bids for the more than 200 pieces sold in New York City by the auction house Sotheby's, which was holding its first-ever sale of contemporary Indian painting. The success of the sale, which brought in $1.2 million overall, announced to the world of high-end art collectors the arrival of Husain and his contemporaries. (In 2005 a private collector paid $2 million for his painting *The Last Supper*.) Husain's fame was frequently accompanied by controversy. Some Hindus took exception, for example, to his depiction of female Hindu deities, including Durga, Lakshmi, and Saraswati, in the nude. Conservative groups filed lawsuits against the artist, and members of the far-right Hindu group Bajrang Dal invaded his home and gallery and vandalized dozens of paintings. In 2006 the attacks reached a new intensity. In February of that year, an advertisement for an art auction that was going to be held to raise money for victims of the October 2005 earthquake that struck Kashmir featured a nude woman whose outline resembled the map of India. Taken to be the figure of Bharatmata, or Mother India, the image was considered offensive by some Hindus, including leaders of one of the country's political opposition parties, the Bharatiya Janata Party. With demands for Husain's arrest quickly escalating to calls for his beheading, galleries showing Husain's work began to be pressured into closing the exhibits, and some complied. Most notoriously, three men entered the Asia House gallery, in London, and defaced Husain's works with black spray paint. Despite the controversy he often fomented, Husain won three of the top civilian honors given by the Indian government: the Padma Shri (or Padmashri), the Padma Bhushan, and the Padma Vibhushan. Between 1986 and 1992, in recognition of his contributions to the arts, he was appointed to serve in the upper house of the Indian

Parliament. (He was known for sketching his fellow members rather than speaking.) Husain, who founded four museums to showcase his art, divided his time in later years between Dubai and England. He died of a heart attack while in London. He was predeceased by his wife, Fazila, in 1998, and is survived by six children. See *Current Biography International Yearbook* (2006). —M.R.

Obituary *New York Times* (on-line) June 9, 2011

JOBS, STEVEN Feb. 24, 1955–Oct. 5, 2011 Technology-industry innovator; entrepreneur. As co-founder of Apple, Steve Jobs was the major force behind the creation of such signature products as the Macintosh computer, the iPod, the iPhone, and the iPad. As head of Pixar Animation Studios, he oversaw the production of *Toy Story* (1995), *Finding Nemo* (2003), *Cars* (2006), and several other films that are among the most popular animated motion pictures in Hollywood history. Within hours of his death, spontaneous public memorials had occurred around the globe, from Cupertino, California, where Apple is headquartered, to London, Frankfurt, Sydney, Tokyo, Seoul, New Delhi, and Beijing. "There may be no greater tribute to Steve's success than the fact that much of the world learned of his passing on a device he invented," President Barack Obama noted in a statement issued by the White House. Obama ranked Jobs "among the greatest of American innovators—brave enough to think differently, bold enough to believe he could change the world, and talented enough to do it." "He exemplified the spirit of American ingenuity," the president said. "He transformed our lives, redefined entire industries, and achieved one of the rarest feats in human history: he changed the way each of us saw the world." Steven Paul Jobs was born in San Francisco, California, to Abdulfattah Jandali, a native of Syria, and Joanne Carol Schieble, two unmarried graduate students who gave him up as a newborn. He was adopted by Paul Jobs, a machinist, and Clara Jobs, an accountant. The couple also adopted a daughter, Patti, three years after adopting Jobs. (Jandali and Schieble later married and had a daughter together. Jobs met his stepsister after a successful search for his biological parents when he was in his late 20s and subsequently developed a warm relationship with her; she is the critically acclaimed novelist Mona Simpson.) During his high-school years, Jobs landed a summer job at Hewlett-Packard (HP), where he befriended a fellow employee, Stephen Wozniak. Jobs subsequently completed a single term at Reed College before dropping out. He remained on campus for several months, however, sleeping in friends' dorm rooms, auditing courses, and experimenting with psychedelic drugs. In 1974 he worked briefly for the computer-game maker Atari, then backpacked in India. Once back in California, he met up with Wozniak again through the Homebrew Computer Club, a local hobbyist group, and persuaded him to leave HP and become his business partner. Jobs and Wozniak began building rudimentary computers in Jobs's parents' garage. "Coming on the scene just as computing began to move beyond the walls of research laboratories and corporations in the 1970s, Mr. Jobs saw that computing was becoming personal—that it could do more

than crunch numbers and solve scientific and business problems—and that it could even be a force for social and economic change," John Markoff wrote for the *New York Times* (October 5, 2011, on-line). With an infusion of cash from a venture capitalist, their company, Apple Computers, soon moved to its own building, and on December 12, 1980 it went public. By the end of trading that day, Jobs had became a multimillionaire. During the next five years, Apple experienced both setbacks—the commercial failure of its next-generation computer, the Lisa, and an array of problems with the Macintosh, which debuted in January 1984—and achievements, notably the healthy sales of an improved Mac and Apple's entry into the Fortune 500. Jobs, though, had become mired in conflicts with John Scully, a former Pepsi executive whom Jobs had recruited in 1983 to be CEO of Apple. In May 1985 the board of directors, siding with Scully, stripped Jobs of all managerial and decision-making power. While away from Apple, Jobs founded NeXT Inc., which sold an operating system that was later used by Tim Berners-Lee to develop an early version of the World Wide Web, and acquired Pixar, then a small enterprise that, under his direction, positioned itself at the forefront of computer animation. In 1996 Apple acquired NeXT for a reported $430 million, and the following year Jobs was hired as an adviser. In 2000 he returned to the post of CEO. Back in the top spot, he continued to expand Apple's product lines, introducing, for example, iTunes and the iPod, an MP3 player. In 2007 Apple began selling the iPhone, which featured an innovative touch-screen interface, and by 2010 the company had sold some 90 million phones. That year the company brought out the iPad, a thin, lightweight tablet computer that sold 15 million units in the first few months of its introduction alone. Amid the media frenzy and public excitement that accompanied each of Apple's product launches, there was underlying concern about Jobs's health. Suffering from pancreatic cancer, he had a tumor removed in 2004, underwent a liver transplant in 2009, and took multiple leaves of absence from Apple before stepping down permanently in August 2011. "As the gravity of his illness became known, and particularly after he announced he was stepping down, he was increasingly hailed for his genius and true achievement: his ability to blend product design and business market innovation by integrating consumer-oriented software, microelectronic components, industrial design and new business strategies in a way that has not been matched," Markoff wrote. Jobs, who died at the age of 56 with an estimated fortune of more than $8 billion, is survived by his wife, Laurene Powell Jobs; their children, Eve, Erin, and Reed; a daughter, Lisa, from a previous relationship; his biological sister, Mona Simpson; and his adoptive sister, Patti Jobs. See *Current Biography* (1983). —M.H./M.R.

Obituary *New York Times* (on-line) Oct. 5, 2011

KAHN, ALFRED E. Oct. 17, 1917–Dec. 27, 2010 Economist; government official. Alfred E. Kahn, a longtime economics professor at Cornell University, was a leading regulatory scholar and was known for his stint as chair of the Civil Aeronautics Board in the late 1970s, during which he oversaw the deregulation of the nation's airline industry. Alfred Edward Kahn was born in Paterson, New Jersey, one of three children of Russian-Jewish immigrants. His father, Jacob, worked in a silk mill and later ran a mill of his own. After graduating from Evander Childs High School, in New York City, Kahn studied economics at New York University (NYU). An academic standout, he was elected to Phi Beta Kappa and graduated summa cum laude with a bachelor's degree in economics in 1936, at the age of 18. Kahn earned a master's degree from NYU in 1937 and then did postgraduate work at the University of Missouri before earning a Ph.D. degree from Yale University, in 1942, with a thesis that focused on Great Britain's role in the world economy. While writing his thesis Kahn worked in Washington, D.C., as a research economist for the Brookings Institution, the Justice Department's antitrust division, and the international economics unit of the Department of Commerce. That work was followed by a brief stint in the U.S. Army, in 1943. Kahn completed basic training but was soon discharged due to poor eyesight. Afterward, he returned to New York City to work as an economist for the Commission on Palestine Surveys. In 1945 Kahn relocated to Ripon, Wisconsin, to become an assistant professor and chair of the Economics Department at Ripon College. After teaching there for two years, he joined the faculty of Cornell University, in Ithaca, New York, where he spent the bulk of his academic career. He became a full professor at Cornell in 1955 and served as a member of its board of trustees, from 1964 to 1969, and as the dean of its College of Arts and Sciences, beginning in 1969. In 1970 Kahn published his landmark, two-volume work, *The Economics of Regulation*, which became the standard textbook on government regulation of business and industry. His expertise in regulatory and antitrust policies caught the attention of public officials, and in 1974 he took a six-year leave from Cornell to accept an appointment as chair of the New York State Public Service Commission, which oversees regulation of the state's utilities. During Kahn's tenure he overhauled the utilities' rate structures and introduced a new pricing system that offered lower electric rates to customers during off-peak hours. He also allowed customers to hook up their own equipment to the New York Telephone Co.'s system and required the telephone company to charge customers for directory assistance and credit the accounts of those who did not make such calls. In 1977, impressed with his work in public utilities deregulation, President Jimmy Carter appointed Kahn to succeed John Robson as chair of the Civil Aeronautics Board (CAB). At the time of his appointment, few industries were as tightly regulated as the airlines. Since its creation, in 1938, the CAB had not certified a single new domestic carrier. Moreover, it closely controlled air routes, kept fares high, and consistently discouraged applications for special rates or fare reductions. As head of the CAB, Kahn, in an effort to foster greater efficiency, worked to deregulate the airlines. He allowed airlines to sell seats at deep discounts without approval of the CAB, let airlines choose their own routes, reopened smaller airports to commercial traffic, and authorized international airlines to carry domestic passengers be-

tween points in the United States on international flights, among other reforms. His efforts culminated in the enactment of the Airline Deregulation Act of 1978. Those deregulatory measures helped to spur competition among airlines, led to lower rates and more affordable air travel, and paved the way for the rise of such lower-cost airlines as People Express, JetBlue, and Southwest Airlines. They also helped spur deregulation movements in other industries. (Decades later the measures championed by Kahn would contribute to the airline industry's severe financial troubles, resulting in mergers and bankruptcies.) In 1978 Kahn left the CAB to become Carter's inflation "czar" and to serve as chair of the Council on Wage and Price Stability—parts of a larger effort by the administration to curb inflation. Kahn's efforts in that role proved to be fruitless in the face of high oil prices and an overall poor economy, and in 1979 he resigned. In 1980 Kahn returned to Cornell, where he became the Robert Julius Thorne Professor Emeritus of Political Economy. During the course of his career, Kahn testified before U.S. House and Senate committees some 70 times and wrote more than 130 academic papers and several books. Some of his later works include *Letting Go: Deregulating the Process of Deregulation* (1998) and *Whom the Gods Would Destroy, or How Not to Deregulate* (2001). Known throughout his career for his deep aversion to euphemisms and bureaucratic language, Kahn served on the usage panel of the *American Heritage Dictionary* for more than 25 years. He died of cancer at his home in Ithaca, New York, and is survived by his wife, Mary Simmons Kahn; two daughters, Rachel Kahn-Fogel and Hannah Kahn; a son, Joel; a nephew, Peter S. Boone, for whom he and his wife were legal guardians; eight grandchildren; and two great-grandchildren. See *Current Biography* (1979). —C.C.

Obituary *New York Times* (on-line) Dec. 28, 2010

KEVORKIAN, JACK May 26, 1928–June 3, 2011 Pathologist; writer; inventor. The zeal with which Jack Kevorkian pursued his crusade to legalize physician-assisted suicide—an activity that landed him in jail on more than one occasion—captured the imagination of many people, while alarming and angering other segments of the public. Kevorkian believed that individuals with terminal illnesses or incurable conditions that cause intense suffering should have the right to die not only at a time of their own choosing but painlessly, with dignity, and with professional assistance. His long struggle to break through certain taboos surrounding death originated decades before he began putting his belief into practice. Kevorkian was born in Pontiac, Michigan, the only son of Levon Kevorkian, a former auto-factory worker who operated an excavating company, and his wife, a homemaker. He had two sisters, Margo and Flora. Kevorkian's parents were Armenian refugees whose relatives were among the estimated 1.5 million victims of atrocities committed by Turks during World War I. As a high-school student during World War II, Kevorkian taught himself German and Japanese; his knowledge of the former language would come in handy when he began to research the history of medical experimentation. After graduating from Pontiac High School with honors, in 1945, Kevorkian enrolled at the University of Michigan, from whose medical school he graduated in 1952. He then embarked upon an internship in pathology (the study of diseases and their effects on bodily tissues and fluids) at Henry Ford Hospital, in Detroit, where he experienced an epiphany. Confronted with a middle-aged woman with terminal cancer, who appeared "as though she was pleading for help and death at the same time," as Kevorkian recalled in his book *Prescription Medicide: The Goodness of Planned Death* (1991), he decided then and there that "doctor-assisted euthanasia and suicide are and always were ethical, no matter what anyone says or thinks." In 1953, the year in which he obtained a medical license in Michigan, Kevorkian began a stint as a U.S. Army medical officer during the Korean War. Following his discharge from the army, Kevorkian completed residencies at Pontiac General Hospital, Detroit Receiving Hospital, and the University of Michigan Medical Center. While he was a resident at Detroit Receiving Hospital, in 1956, Kevorkian was dubbed Doctor Death, a sobriquet he earned for photographing the retinas of patients at the moment of death in an attempt to study the blood vessels in the cornea. Kevorkian's name first appeared in newspapers in 1958, when he presented a paper entitled "Capital Punishment or Capital Gain" to a criminology-section meeting of the American Association for the Advancement of Science in Washington, D.C. In it he suggested that consenting death-row inmates be anesthetized before their executions so that their living bodies could be used for scientific experiments, after which their deaths would be finalized with a lethal overdose of the anesthetic. Thus, Kevorkian reasoned, the prisoners would benefit from a painless style of execution and society would benefit from the fruits of medical research. Believing that the publicity Kevorkian's views were attracting would harm the University of Michigan's credibility, his employers presented him with an ultimatum: cease and desist pursuing his unorthodox crusade or find work elsewhere. Kevorkian opted to return, as an associate pathologist, to Pontiac General Hospital, where he studied the possibility of transfusing blood to live recipients from cadavers of previously healthy people who had died suddenly of such causes as heart attacks, drowning, suffocation, or accidents. After leaving Pontiac sometime in the 1960s because of a dispute with a new chief pathologist, Kevorkian spent several years moving around the country to accept various pathology jobs. From 1982 to 1986 he devoted himself full-time to his writing and research, publishing numerous articles in an obscure German journal called *Medicine and Law*, the only publication that would print the results of his controversial research. Kevorkian found gainful employment as hard to come by as an editor who was willing to publish his work. "My curriculum vitae scares the hell out of people," he once said. He continued, however, to devote his energies to winning acceptance of his ideas. In 1989 David Rivlin, a quadriplegic who had made a public appeal for help to end his life, chose to have his respirator turned off, partly because, according to Kevorkian, no simpler, less painful method for ending his life existed. When Kevorkian heard about Rivlin's wishes, he went to work on a device that would allow Rivlin, and others like him, to turn off their life-support apparatuses. Although another doctor eventually disconnected Rivlin from his respirator, Kevorkian soon devised a working model of a machine, which he variously called the "Mercitron" or the "Thanatron," that could be operated at the touch of a button by people who were too disabled to kill themselves by other means. When his attempts to advertise the equipment were stymied, he found himself the beneficiary of free publicity via the news media. As a result of that publicity, Janet Adkins, a 54-year-old Oregon woman with Alzheimer's disease, contacted Kevorkian, in 1989. After several complications were overcome, she became the first person to commit suicide with Kevorkian's assistance. On June 4, 1990, in the back of his van, Adkins triggered the mechanism that released the solutions from three vials into her veins: the first was a saline solution; the second was sodium pentothal, an anesthetic; and the third was potassium chloride, which was intended to stop her heart. Four days later Kevorkian was prohibited from using his machine. Despite the prohibition he assisted in some 130 suicides over the next several years, with patients from all over the country seeking his help. (Afterward the machine was displayed in the museum of the Armed Forces Institute of Pathology, at the institute's request.) Kevorkian's subsequent cases generated heated controversy, and in 1999, after being convicted of second-degree murder in the death of one patient, Thomas Youk, who was suffering from amyotrophic lateral sclerosis, he was sentenced to 10 to 25 years in a maximum-security prison. (Kevorkian had taped Youk's death and sent the video to the popular program *60 Minutes*, which broadcast it.) Kevorkian was released from prison after eight years, promising that he would not conduct another assisted suicide. In 2010 he was portrayed by Al Pacino in the award-winning HBO biographical film *You Don't Know Jack.* In mid-2011, ill with kidney and respiratory problems, Kevorkian reportedly told those who visited him in the hospital that he would have liked the option of ending his own life. He died, instead, of a naturally occurring pulmonary thrombosis. He was survived by his sister Flora. Keith Schneider wrote for the *New York Times* (June 3, 2011, on-line): "His critics were as impassioned as his supporters, but all generally agreed that his stubborn and often intemperate advocacy of assisted suicide helped spur the growth of hospice care in the United States and made many doctors more sympathetic to those in severe pain and more willing to prescribe medication to relieve it." See *Current Biography* (1994). —M.R.

Obituary *New York Times* (on-line) June 3, 2011

KHEEL, THEODORE W. May 9, 1914–Nov. 12, 2010 Lawyer; labor arbitrator. Theodore Kheel resolved thousands of labor disputes involving workers ranging from bus drivers to football players and helped to end or avoid numerous potentially crippling strikes during his three-decade career as an arbitrator. Steven Greenhouse wrote for the *New York Times* (November 15, 2010, on-line), "Mr. Kheel, who played a pivotal role in ending newspaper, teacher and subway strikes in New York, was the go-to guy for mayors, labor leaders and business executives during the post-World War II era, when unions were far more powerful than they are now and a savvy, respected ringmaster was often needed to pressure and cajole all sides to reach a settlement." Theodore Woodrow Kheel (who was named after Theodore Roosevelt and Woodrow Wilson) was born in the New York City borough of Brooklyn to Samuel Kheel, the owner of a real-estate company, and his wife, the former Kate Herzenstein. He attended DeWitt Clinton High School, in the Bronx, and in 1935 received his B.A. degree from Cornell University, in Ithaca, New York. Two years later he graduated from the university's law school and passed the New York State bar exam. The day after taking the test, he married Ann Sunstein, a journalist and civic leader whom he had met in a literature class at Cornell. Kheel began his career in 1938 as a member of the National Labor Relations Board's legal staff, serving in Washington, D.C.; New York City; and Philadelphia, Pennsylvania. In early 1942 he joined the War Labor Board, which had been set up to rule in labor disputes and to control wage rates during World War II. In November 1942 Kheel was named director of the board's second regional district, which encompassed New York and northern New Jersey, and two years later he became the executive director of the National War Labor Board in Washington, D.C., serving at the same time as chair of the Steel Commission, an arm of the board. In 1946 he returned to New York City, at the request of Mayor William O'Dwyer, to become deputy director of the newly formed Division of Labor Relations, an agency that later became the city's labor department, and the following year he became the director. During his time at the Division of Labor Relations, Kheel befriended Michael Quill, who, as founder and head of the Transport Workers' Union, helped Kheel establish a good reputation among some of the city's top labor leaders. Kheel entered private practice as a mediator and arbitrator in 1948. In May 1949 Mayor O'Dwyer appointed him chair of the city's private transit system, a position that involved the settling of issues and disputes arising from the application of contracts between the Transport Workers' Union and seven private bus lines. In August 1956 Kheel assumed the additional post of arbitrator for New York's public Transit Authority and the Transport Workers' Union. He thus became, in effect, the peacekeeper for virtually all public transportation within New York City. His jurisdiction extended over approximately 8,200 employees of the private bus lines and over some 32,000 employees of the city's publicly owned rapid transit and bus lines, for whom the Transport Workers' Union had been recognized as the sole bargaining agent. Kheel also played a major role in mediating New York City's 114-day newspaper strike, which ended in March 1963. (His role in the negotiations was to draft the recommendations that served as a basis for a final settlement between the publishers and the printers' union and other unions involved.) Among his other noteworthy accomplishments, as the first permanent arbitrator for the seagoing segment of the American maritime industry on the Atlantic and Gulf Coasts, Kheel settled a strike aboard the nuclear-powered vessel Savan-

nah in August 1962. Kheel was summoned to Washington by President Lyndon B. Johnson in 1964 to help mediate negotiations to avoid a nationwide rail walkout. In 1978 Kheel helped settle a second newspaper strike, after an 88-day walkout against the New York Times, the New York Daily News, and the Washington Post. By the 1980s Kheel's labor contacts had been replaced by a new generation, and he lost much of his influence. During that time he also butted heads with New York mayor Ed Koch, who argued that Kheel's willingness to sign generous contracts with transit workers had contributed to the city's financial problems. Kheel resigned as transit arbitrator in 1983. In addition to his reputation as a skilled arbitrator, Kheel was widely known as a champion of civil rights. He served as president of the National Urban League from 1956 to 1960 and acted as a special consultant to the Committee on Equal Employment Opportunity under President John F. Kennedy. He was also a successful businessman and investor. Known for his fine taste in clothes and food, Kheel once owned a stake in Manhattan's high-end French restaurant Le Pavillon and was quoted in the Washington Post (November 15, 2010, on-line) as saying, "The best place to negotiate is where you can get the best food." After his retirement Kheel continued to practice law, with the firm Paul, Hastings, Janofsky & Walker, and he also worked as an environmental activist, founding the organizations Earth Pledge and the Nurture Nature Foundation. Kheel, whose wife died in 2003, is survived by six children, 11 grandchildren, and six great-grandchildren. See Current Biography (1964). —H.R.W.

Obituary New York Times A p27 Nov. 15, 2010

KILLEBREW, HARMON June 29, 1936–May 17, 2011 Baseball player. With 573 home runs in 22 seasons in the major leagues, Harmon Killebrew became a centerpiece of the Minnesota Twins organization in the 1960s and set an American League (AL) record for right-handed batters that lasted for 30 years. The youngest of four children, Harmon Clayton Killebrew Jr. was born in Payette, Idaho, a small town near the Oregon border, to H. C. and Katherine Pearl May Killebrew. His father, a former college football player and professional wrestler who worked as a house painter and sheriff, introduced him to sports. Killebrew developed his strength by lifting 10-gallon milk cans while working on dairy farms. As a freshman at Payette High School, he joined the baseball, basketball, and football varsity teams. In recognition of his exceptional all-around athletic performance, the school retired the number 12, which had adorned all of his uniforms, when he graduated. Killebrew had planned to accept a football scholarship to the University of Oregon, before a scout from Major League Baseball's Washington Senators, impressed by his dominant performance in the semi-pro Idaho-Oregon Border League, signed him to a $30,000 contract. Making his debut just days before his 18th birthday, Killebrew had a slow start, struggling defensively and demonstrating less-than-stellar speed. He spent most of 1954 on the bench, notching just four hits in his 13 times at bat, none of which was a home run. In 1955 he was at bat 80 times and had 16 hits, along with a fielding average of .936. During the next three years Killebrew shuttled between the Senators and the team's minor-league farm clubs, before being sent to the starting lineup, at third base, in 1960. He hit a home run on opening day and went on to become the slugging sensation of the AL that year, as attendance at Griffith Stadium was swelled by fans who came to watch him in action. Though he experienced a late-season slump, his home-run total for the season (42) was nevertheless enough to tie for the league's home-run championship. Killebrew remained with the franchise when it traveled to Minneapolis–St. Paul, Minnesota, and became the Twins. He went on to lead the AL in home runs in three consecutive seasons, from 1962 to 1964, and again in 1967. His strong performance contributed to the Twins' AL pennant win in 1965 (the team lost to the Los Angeles Dodgers in the World Series), as well as West division titles in 1969 and 1970. Killebrew was named to 13 All-Star teams during his career and won the AL Most Valuable Player title in 1969, after a season that saw him lead the league with 49 home runs and a career-best 140 RBIs. Killebrew played with the Kansas City Royals in 1975, his last major-league season before he retired. At that point only Babe Ruth had hit more home runs than Killebrew in the AL. His home-run record for right-handed batters lasted for three decades, before it was broken by Alex Rodriguez of the New York Yankees, who hit his 574th home run in 2009. Killebrew's hit total was 2,086, and his RBI total was 1,584. After his retirement from baseball, he worked in sports broadcasting with the Oakland Athletics, the Angels, and the Twins. He also ran an insurance company and an auto dealership. He was inducted into the Baseball Hall of Fame in 1984. A bronze statue of Killebrew in mid-swing stands outside the Twins' Target Field. In December 2010 Killebrew announced that he had esophageal cancer. He spent his final days at home in Scottsdale, Arizona. Killebrew's marriage to his first wife, Elaine, ended in divorce. He is survived by his second wife, Nita, and nine children. See *Current Biography* (1966). —M.R.M.

Obituary *New York Times* (on-line) May 17, 2011

KIRCH, LEO Oct. 21, 1926–July 14, 2011 Broadcasting executive. Once one of the leading media magnates in Europe, the German entrepreneur Leo Kirch saw his empire dissolve in 2002, when he was forced to declare bankruptcy. The bankruptcy, which involved billions of dollars in debt, was the largest in Germany since World War II. The son of a winemaker, Kirch was born in the city of Wurzburg. After earning a doctoral degree in business administration, he became an assistant professor of economics at Munich University. In the early 1950s Kirch left academia, opting for a career as a businessman. His introduction to the world of media and entertainment was as something of a peddler. In 1956 he borrowed about $58,000 from his wife's family and bought the German rights for a few Italian films, including Federico Fellini's critically acclaimed *La Strada* (1954). Kirch then traveled throughout the German countryside and rented the film, at a sub-stantial markup, to local movie houses. Kirch's shoe-string budget did not always allow for lodging, and as he traveled around Europe, seeking other films to import, he sometimes slept in his car. But he pressed on, and by 1958 he was purchasing the rights to several Italian films each year. Although German television was still in its infancy in the 1950s, Kirch traveled to the U.S. with the hope of importing American television shows and movies and selling them to German stations. The German broadcasting companies (then owned by the government) that made up his customer base were not willing to spend more than $900,000 on the films, but the United Artists and Warner Bros. studios, whose representatives he met in the U.S., refused to sell less than $2.7 million worth of film rights. Fearful that he would lose the Hollywood bid, Kirch obtained a loan and bought the entire rights package offered. Over the next decade he amassed a film library of 15,000 titles, the largest outside Hollywood in the 1950s and '60s. Between 1960 and 1980 Kirch continued to build his foreign-rights empire. Along the way he befriended powerful people in German politics, including Chancellor Helmut Kohl and Prime Minister Edmund Stoiber. In 1984 the German government gave up its monopoly on the television industry and opened the market to private investors. Kirch was among the first to invest, and that year he co-founded Sat1, Germany's first private, commercial broadcasting company. (In 1992 Sat1 acquired the exclusive rights to broadcast German soccer matches.) In the early 1990s Kirch purchased shares of Italy's pay-per-view television company, Telepiu, as well as Telecinco, one of Spain's most profitable broadcasting stations. He also began buying shares of Axel Springer Verlag, a print-publishing conglomerate. At its height Kirch's enterprise was the second-largest media company in Germany, after Bertelsmann. In 1996 Kirch hedged his bets on digital television, which he viewed as the next logical step in television technology. That year KirchMedia, as the conglomerate was named, launched Germany's first digital cable company, Premiere World, to deliver high-resolution images and interactive programming to customers. But in its first year, Kirch's digital TV enterprise, which counted the media mogul Rupert Murdoch as an investor, attracted only 100,000 customers. By 2001 there were only 2.4 million customers subscribing to Premiere World, the main channel for KirchPayTV, though he had hoped for at least four million. His investment in the technology, some economic analysts surmised, marked the advent of Kirch's downfall. By 2002 banks were unwilling to lend funds to Premiere World and other faltering Kirch units. Foundering under a debt of $5.7 billion, KirchMedia was forced to file for bankruptcy in April 2002. Kirch spent the last years of his life engaged in court battles with the former Deutsche Bank CEO Rolf Breuer, who, Kirch alleged, had made public comments that contributed to the Kirch group's collapse. Kirch, who had suffered from diabetes and near-blindness for years, died at the age of 84. He is survived by his wife, Ruth, and his son, Thomas. See *Current Biography International Yearbook* (2002). —M.M.H.

Obituary *New York Times* (on-line) July 14, 2011

KIRK, CLAUDE R. JR. Jan. 7, 1926–Sep. 27, 2011 Former governor of Florida. Claude R. Kirk Jr. "was one of the most fascinating characters in Florida in a state that is full of fascinating characters," James M. Denham, the director of the Lawton M. Chiles Jr. Center for Florida History at Florida Southern College, told Lizette Alvarez for the *New York Times* (September 28, 2011, on-line). "He was a maverick, an extremely independent person and outrageous." When Kirk was elected governor of Florida, in 1966, he became the first Republican to hold that office since Reconstruction. Kirk was born in San Bernardino, California, where his parents, Claude Roy Kirk Sr. and Sarah (McClure) Kirk, both worked as railroad clerks. The family moved from time to time, and Kirk spent portions of his youth in Illinois, where Kirk Sr. sold mobile homes for a living, and Alabama, where he manufactured vending machines. In 1943, after graduating from Lanier High School in Montgomery, Kirk enlisted in the Marine Corps Reserve. Discharged as a second lieutenant in 1946, he enrolled at Emory University, in Atlanta, Georgia, later transferring to Duke University, in Durham, North Carolina, where he earned a B.S. degree. He then attended the College of Law at the University of Alabama, graduating in 1949. To help meet his expenses as a student, Kirk had sold insurance and taught jujitsu to members of the Alabama highway patrol. Soon after finishing law school, Kirk was called back into active service with the Marines for combat duty in the Korean War. With only $408 to his name at the time of his discharge, in 1952, Kirk returned to selling insurance. In about 1956 he helped found the American Heritage Life Insurance Co., which soon became one of the most successful in the industry. Kirk had been a Democrat until 1960, when he switched to the Republican Party and campaigned for Richard M. Nixon for the presidency. In 1964 he challenged the Democratic incumbent, Spessard L. Holland of Florida, for his seat in the U.S. Senate. Running on an ultraconservative platform, Kirk made a respectable showing in the election but failed to defeat Holland. After that first foray into politics, Kirk returned to the world of business. Aware that Brazil was ripe for economic development, he formed the Kirk Investment Co., an unincorporated, unregistered firm, and opened a small office near the U.S. Embassy in Rio de Janeiro. His hopes that he might make a fortune through investments in South American industries failed to materialize, however, and he returned to Florida. Trying his luck in politics once more, he entered the May 1966 state primary and won the nomination as Republican candidate for the governorship. Although registered Democrats in Florida outnumbered Republicans by almost five to one, Kirk surprised observers by triumphing over his opponent, Robert King High, by a wide margin. He thus became the first Republican since 1872 to be elected governor of Florida. "Though Mr. Kirk served only one term, his decisions still reverberate. He was an early and strong proponent of environmental conservation in Florida, in one instance stopping the construction of an airport in the Everglades," Alvarez wrote. "He also signed off on a deal, known then as the Florida Project, with Roy Disney to build a theme park on vast tracts of land in sleepy Central Florida." During his first year in office alone, Kirk vetoed 48 bills, and reporters began calling him "Claudius Maximus." Among his most newsworthy stunts were riding a horse into a press conference and planting a state flag on the ocean floor to bring attention to the issue of Florida's territorial rights. One journalist of the day opined that Kirk was "playing Governor the way Errol Flynn used to play Captain Blood—charming, daring, somewhat arrogant, seldom going by the rules." Kirk lost the 1970 gubernatorial race to the Democrat Reubin Askew. Although he subsequently returned to the business world, he did not leave the political arena altogether, making occasional quixotic bids for the U.S. Senate, the U.S. presidency, and the Florida governorship again. Kirk's personal life was as colorful as his political career. In 1947 he had married Sarah Stokes, the daughter of an Alabama automobile dealer. They divorced in 1950, after their two daughters, Sarah and Katherine, were born. They remarried the following year and had twin sons, Franklin and William. Their second marriage ended in divorce in 1966. Kirk's second wife was the former Erika Mattfeld, a German-born model and actress he met while in Brazil. Kirk had surprised his friends and associates when he escorted Mattfeld to his inaugural ball, introducing her as "Madame X." They were married in early 1967, shortly after he took office. He was a stepfather to her daughter, Adriana, and together they had two more children, Claudia and Erik. Kirk died at his home in West Palm Beach at the age of 85. He was survived by Mattfeld, all of his children, 14 grandchildren, and five great-grandchildren. See *Current Biography* (1967). —M.R.

Obituary *New York Times* (on-line) Sep. 28, 2011

KNAUER, VIRGINIA Mar. 28, 1915–Oct. 16, 2011 Former government official; consumer advocate. Virginia H. Knauer (pronounced NOW-er) served as the director of the Office of Consumer Affairs under presidents Richard M. Nixon, Gerald R. Ford, and Ronald Reagan. Although the office had no statutory authority, she pushed rigorously for such reforms as unit pricing, which made it easier for consumers to compare the costs of similar products, and more concise product labeling. She was born Virginia Harrington Wright in Philadelphia, Pennsylvania. In 1937 she graduated from the University of Pennsylvania with a B.F.A. degree and later completed a year of postgraduate work at the Royal Academy of Fine Arts in Florence, Italy. In 1940 she married Wilhelm F. Knauer, a corporate lawyer. Her early years of married life were occupied with raising her two children, Wilhelm Jr., and Valerie, and with her cultural pursuits, which included portrait painting, collecting American antiques, and the restoration of colonial homes. Wilhelm Knauer had long been active in Pennsylvania Republican politics, and in 1952 his wife launched her political career by joining the organization Citizens for Eisenhower and Nixon. In 1956 she founded the Northeast Council for Republican Women and served as its president for several years. She was also active on the Philadelphia County Republican Committee, the Philadelphia Congress of Republican Councils, and the Pennsylvania Council of Republican Women. In 1959 Knauer became the first Republican woman ever elected to the Philadelphia city council. She remained on the seven-member council for two four-year terms. In February 1968 Governor Raymond P. Shafer, a Republican, appointed her head of the Pennsylvania Bureau of Consumer Protection, an arm of the state Justice Department. During her 14 months in office, she carried out an aggressive public-information campaign, making speeches, holding conferences, and supervising the production of what she called "the best consumer protection brochures in the country." On April 9, 1969 Nixon appointed her director of the Office of Consumer Affairs and his special assistant for consumer affairs. The office had no powers of enforcement or investigation, causing some critics, including Ralph Nader, then a prominent consumer advocate, to dismiss it as a mere "bully pulpit." Still, Knauer made effective use of the pulpit, testifying before Congress and various federal agencies, giving speeches around the country, and lobbying manufacturers and retailers on behalf of American consumers. She was also instrumental in establishing the Federal Consumer Information Center (now called the Federal Citizen Information Center), which distributes free or inexpensive consumer publications upon request. Knauer continued to hold the consumer-affairs position in the Ford administration; when the Democrat Jimmy Carter won the presidency, she left government service to found a consulting business, Virginia Knauer & Associates. In 1981 Reagan returned her to her old post, in which she served until 1988. Knauer died at the age of 96. She was predeceased, in 1982, by her husband, who had served for a time as deputy attorney general of Pennsylvania; in 1987 her son, a Philadelphia Common Pleas Court judge, died of cancer at the age of 45. Knauer is survived by her daughter, Valerie; three granddaughters, Virginia, Frances, and Nancy; and a great-grandson. See *Current Biography* (1970). —M.R.

Obituary *New York Times* (on-line) Oct. 27, 2011

KY, NGUYEN CAO Sep. 8, 1930–July 23, 2011 South Vietnamese leader. Nguyen Cao Ky was known as the flamboyant and outspoken young premier who ruled South Vietnam for two years during the Vietnam War. Ky was born in Son Tay, French Indochina, just outside Hanoi. An only son, he grew up with his two older sisters in a conservative atmosphere. His father was a schoolteacher. In 1948 Ky was admitted to the Nam Dinh Reserve Officers' School, a French military academy in the northern part of Vietnam. After completing his studies there, in 1952, he attended aviation schools in France and North Africa, and in mid-1954 he became a transport pilot with the French Air Force. In December 1954 Ky returned to his homeland, which had in the meantime become independent under the Geneva agreement, and assumed command of the Tan Son Nhut Air Force Base and the First Transport Group of the South Vietnamese Air Force. (France's withdrawal had divided Vietnam into the Communist North and the non-Communist South.) In 1956 Ky traveled to the U.S. to receive training at the Air Command and Staff College at Maxwell Field in Alabama. He was

named operations director of the Vietnamese Air Force high command in 1958 and served in that post until 1959, when, as a major, he was appointed commander of South Vietnam's 43d Air Transport Group. During that period Ky acquired a reputation as a hard-living playboy. Wearing a tailored black flying suit and lavender ascot, with a pearl-handled, chrome-plated revolver strapped to his side, Ky was often seen in Saigon nightclubs with a series of beautiful women on his arm. Although Ky did not play a major part in the 1963 military coup in which President Ngo Dinh Diem was assassinated, on December 17, 1963 the new premier, General Duong Van Minh, made him a one-star general and appointed him commander of the air force in a reorganization of the South Vietnamese military. As the country's ace pilot, he was idolized by South Vietnam's young women and accorded frequent press coverage. To celebrate his impending marriage, in 1964, he reportedly led a squadron of 20 Skyraiders in a low sweep over Saigon, followed by a bombing raid on a patch of jungle suspected to be a Vietcong stronghold. On January 30, 1964 Major General Nguyen Khanh, who had taken part in the overthrow of Diem and who was then favored by the U.S., seized control of the South Vietnamese government in a bloodless coup. As one of a group of politically minded young generals sympathetic to Khanh, Ky was named among the new premier's top aides. When in September 1964 a group of infantry generals tried to overthrow General Khanh's regime, Khanh fled to Ky's headquarters on the outskirts of Saigon. Ky's pilots flew their bomb-laden planes low over the rebellious troops, and the dissident generals soon capitulated. Shortly thereafter Khanh awarded Ky his second star, giving him a rank equivalent to that of a brigadier general. Ky also assumed the title of air vice-marshal at that time. On February 8, 1965, a day after the U.S. began bombing strategic North Vietnamese military targets, Ky led the first flight of South Vietnamese Air Force planes in a bombing mission over North Vietnam. On June 19, 1965 Ky was designated chairman of a 17-member Central Executive Council or War Cabinet, a position equivalent to that of premier, making him the ninth to hold such a position of power since Diem's assassination, in 1963. The appointment of Ky, who became the youngest premier in the history of the country, was at first opposed by the U.S. government and by Buddhist leaders. (He had stated in a press interview shortly before taking office that he admired Hitler but later insisted that his remarks had been taken out of context.) Still, in early 1966 Ky met with U.S. president Lyndon B. Johnson, and the two leaders agreed that social and economic reform and the establishment of a democratic government in South Vietnam were key factors in winning the war against the Communists. Johnson pledged at the meeting that the Americans and the South Vietnamese would carry on the war as "brothers in arms" while continuing to work toward a "just and honorable peace." During South Vietnam's 1967 presidential elections, Ky ceded power to his rival, General Nguyen Van Thieu. He served as Thieu's vice president until 1971. Thieu's government fell to North Vietnamese troops in 1975, and Ky fled to the U.S., settling in California, where for years he lived quietly out of the public eye. In 2002 he published a memoir, *Buddha's Child: My Fight to Save Vietnam*, and in 2004 he returned to his native land, where he made headlines by calling for reconciliation with the Communists. Ky died at a hospital in Kuala Lumpur, where he was being treated for respiratory problems. Ky, who was married three times, is survived by his six children (one of whom is Nguyen Cao Ky Duyen, a well-known entertainer) and several grandchildren. See *Current Biography* (1966)—M.M.H.

Obituary *New York Times* (on-line) July 22, 2011

LALANNE, JACK Sep. 26, 1914–Jan. 23, 2011 Fitness expert. Jack LaLanne became interested in nutrition and exercise as a teenager and went on to become a founder of the modern-day physical-fitness movement. Credited with establishing the country's first fitness club, LaLanne penned numerous books on the subject of fitness, hosted several exercise videos and shows, and sponsored a number of fitness and nutrition products. François Henri LaLanne, the son of French immigrants, was born in San Francisco, California. His father held down two jobs, one at the telephone company and one as a dance instructor, and his mother, a staunch Seventh-Day Adventist, worked as a maid. LaLanne spent much of his early childhood in Bakersfield, where his parents tried to make a living as sheep farmers. When disease wiped out their investment, the LaLannes went bankrupt and moved to Oakland. After his father died of a heart attack, during Jack's adolescence, he was brought up by his mother, who showered him with sugary junk food as a reward for good behavior. His poor eating habits came to affect every aspect of his life negatively: he had an uncontrollable temper, received failing grades in school, and was depressed and physically weak. At one point his family physician went so far as to recommend that LaLanne be removed from school for six months in order to regain his strength. After attending a lecture given by the nutritionist Paul C. Bragg, LaLanne was inspired to change his eating habits and become physically fit. He began eating healthy foods and lifting weights at a local YMCA. He became an athlete, competing in football, baseball, swimming, track, and wrestling. Upon graduating from high school, he turned down athletic scholarships to three different universities and instead went into business selling healthy foods prepared by his mother. He also set up his own gym in his home, where he trained aspiring firefighters and police officers. In 1936, at the age of 22, LaLanne opened Jack LaLanne's Physical Culture Studio in an old office building in Oakland. In addition to exercise equipment and weights, the fitness studio included a juice bar and health-food store. "People thought I was a charlatan and a nut," LaLanne once recalled, as quoted by Richard Goldstein in the *New York Times* (January 23, 2011, on-line). "The doctors were against me—they said that working out with weights would give people heart attacks and they would lose their sex drive." His business struggled at first, and he began to give massages to supplement his income. He had more success after he began marketing his services to skinny and overweight high-school boys, showing them how exercise could help turn their lives around. His success with those boys led their fathers to follow suit, and before long his health studio began to make money, enabling him to open several more. Over time LaLanne opened dozens of fitness studios, which were eventually licensed to the large chain Bally Total Fitness. In 1951 LaLanne became the host of his own exercise program, the *Jack LaLanne Show*, on a local San Francisco station; it became a nationwide show later that decade. Although his show stopped taping in the mid-1980s, it has continued to run on the channel ESPN Classic, and from 1981 to 1983 LaLanne also hosted another popular show, *Jack LaLanne and You*. LaLanne performed a number of stunts to promote fitness. In 1954, at the age of 40, he swam the length of the Golden Gate Bridge underwater, equipped with two air tanks. When he was 60 years old, he swam one-and-a-half miles while shackled, handcuffed, and pulling a 1,000-pound boat. A decade later he performed a similar feat, towing 70 boats carrying a total of 70 people. LaLanne was given a star on the Hollywood Walk of Fame in 2002 and was inducted into the California Hall of Fame in 2008. In addition to producing television shows and workout videos, LaLanne authored several books, including *The Jack LaLanne Way to Vibrant Good Health* (1960), *Foods for Glamour* (1961), *For Men Only, with a Thirty-Day Guide to Looking Better and Feeling Younger* (1973), *Revitalize Your Life After 50* (1995), and *Live Young Forever: 12 Steps to Optimum Health, Fitness and Longevity* (2009). LaLanne also designed exercise machines that became standards in the fitness industry and marketed lines of supplements, health food, and juicers. He worked out well into his 90s and followed a strict two-meal-per-day diet that consisted of such foods as hard-boiled egg whites, fruit, vegetables, oatmeal, soy milk, and fish. He died at his home in Morro Bay, California, as a result of respiratory failure from pneumonia. He is survived by his second wife, Elaine; their son, Jon; a daughter, Yvonne, from a former marriage; and his stepson, Dan. See *Current Biography* (1994). —J.P.

Obituary *New York Times* (on-line) Jan. 23, 2011

LANGHAM, MICHAEL Aug. 22, 1919–Jan. 15, 2011 Theater director. As the artistic head of such organizations as Canada's Stratford Shakespeare Festival and the Guthrie Theater in Minneapolis, Minnesota, Michael Langham became renowned for his productions of works by William Shakespeare, Anton Chekhov, Molière, and George Bernard Shaw. Among the actors whom he directed during his long career were John Gielgud, Peter O'Toole, and Christopher Plummer. Plummer long attributed his professional success to his breakout performance in Langham's 1956 production of *Richard V*. "I really owe my whole career to Michael," the actor told Bruce Weber for the *New York Times* (January 20, 2011). Langham was born in Somerset, England, to Seymour Langham and Muriel Andrews (Speed) Langham. He never met his father, a jute broker working in India who died shortly after his son was born. Langham spent some of his youth in Scotland, after his mother remarried, and he later attended Radley College, in Abingdon, Berkshire. After graduating, in 1937, he enrolled as a law student at the University of London; often, instead of studying, he acted under an assumed name at the Everyman Theatre in Hampstead and the London Arts Theatre. (His only success related to the field of law was reportedly as an opening batsman for the Law Society Cricket Club.) Upon the outbreak of World War II, in September 1939, Langham left the university to join the Gordon Highlanders and was commissioned as a second lieutenant. He was captured in France in 1940 and spent the next five years in prisoner-of-war camps in Germany. During his confinement he directed fellow prisoners in classic plays. Langham was liberated at the end of the war and discharged in 1946 with the rank of lieutenant. Upon returning to England he was engaged as assistant director for the Midland Theatre Company in Coventry, where his first production, in May 1946, was *Twelfth Night*. He soon took over the directorship of the theater. Early in his career he also directed at Birmingham Repertory Theatre, the Memorial Theatre in Stratford-on-Avon, and the Old Vic. By 1955 Langham was one of England's best-known directors. Langham first became associated with Canada's Shakespeare Festival in 1955, when he was invited to Stratford, Ontario, to direct *Julius Caesar*. The production was well received by critics: Walter Kerr of the *New York Herald Tribune* (June 29, 1955) called it "a series of richly lighted, eternally restless paintings" and added that Langham had "somehow found the secret of drawing the onlooker into the paintings." Appointed artistic director of the Stratford Shakespeare Festival in September 1955, Langham began his duties there with the 1956 season and remained until 1967. In 1960 Brooks Atkinson of the *New York Times* (July 30, 1960) described the company at Stratford under Langham's leadership as "the finest group of classical actors in North America." Langham served as the artistic director of the Guthrie Theater from 1971 until 1977, returning the financially ailing institution to solvency, in part by lengthening its season and expanding its touring component. He subsequently became the director of the drama division of the Juilliard School, in New York City, a post he held from from 1979 to 1992. He later worked as an adviser to the National Actors Theatre, a well-regarded company that had been founded by Tony Randall. Langham died from a lingering chest infection at his home in Kent, England. He is survived by his wife of more than 60 years, the actress Helen Burns; their son, Chris; and five grandchildren. See *Current Biography* (1965). —M.M.H.

Obituary *New York Times* (on-line) Jan. 20, 2011

LAURENTS, ARTHUR July 14, 1917–May 5, 2011
Playwright; screenwriter; director. Arthur Laurents's many projects included the librettos for two of Broadway's musical classics, *West Side Story* and *Gypsy*, the screenplays for such popular films as *The Way We Were* and *The Turning Point*, and the direction of the acclaimed premiere Broadway productions of *I Can Get It For You Wholesale* and *La Cage Aux Folles*. Laurents was born in the New York City borough of Brooklyn, to Irving Laurents, a lawyer, and Ada (Robbins) Laurents, a teacher. Raised in the Flatbush section of the borough, he got his first taste of the theater at summer camp, where he was picked for a part in the play *The Crow's Nest*, an experience that left him stagestruck. Laurents attended Cornell University, in Ithaca, New York, where he majored

in English. After receiving a B.A. degree, in 1937, he performed for a time in a satirical nightclub revue that he had put together with several friends, then devoted himself to writing radio plays, including episodes of the popular series *Hollywood Playhouse*, *Dr. Christian*, and *The Thin Man*. When the U.S. entered World War II, in 1941, he immediately enlisted in the army. Initially assigned to a paratroop unit at Fort Benning, Georgia, he ended up working on military training films. He also wrote the scripts for the radio programs *The Man Behind the Gun*, *Army Service Forces Present*, and *Assignment Home*. Developed to educate the public about the problems of returning servicemen, *Assignment Home* won a 1945 Variety Radio Award. Laurents soon began working on a psychological drama about a battle-scarred ex-soldier. In that play, *Home of the Brave*, an army psychiatrist discovers the cause of a young Jewish veteran's amnesia and partial paralysis to be subconscious guilt over the death of his gentile buddy. *Home of the Brave* opened to mixed reviews at the Belasco Theatre on Broadway in December 1945 and closed after only 69 performances; it was belatedly recognized by the majority of New York critics as a bold and important contribution to the postwar American theater. The play won for Laurents a grant from the American Academy of Arts and Letters and a share in the annual Sidney Howard Memorial Award for new playwriting talent. (A film version, rewritten by Carl Foreman as a story of racial rather than religious prejudice, was released in 1949.) After his next dramatic effort, *Heartsong*, failed to win over either critics or audiences during its pre-Broadway trial in 1947, Laurents reluctantly left New York for Hollywood, where he hoped to find a high-paying screenwriting job. In short order he turned out the screenplay for Alfred Hitchcock's technically innovative chiller *Rope* (1948), the final version of the script for *The Snake Pit* (1948), and the scenario for the contrived tearjerker *Caught* (1949). In the late 1940s Laurents's Hollywood assignments slowed to a trickle when he was falsely accused of harboring Communist sympathies and blacklisted. He returned to Broadway in February 1950 with *The Bird Cage*, a lackluster melodrama detailing the backstage troubles of a tyrannical cabaret owner, which ran for just three weeks. He fared better with *The Time of the Cuckoo*, a rueful comedy that became one of the unquestioned hits of the 1952–53 Broadway season. By the mid-1950s, with the blacklist behind him, Laurents was dividing his time between New York and Hollywood, where he earned a reputation for his skillful adaptations of plays and novels. His screen credits for those years include *Anastasia* (1956), which won an Academy Award for a young Ingrid Bergman, and *Bonjour Tristesse* (1958). During that period Laurents also began working on a contemporary musical version of *Romeo and Juliet*, with the feuds of rival New York City street gangs replacing the conflict between the Capulets and the Montagues. The concept originated with the choreographer Jerome Robbins, who first suggested it to Laurents and Leonard Bernstein, the composer, in 1949. The trio eventually brought in Stephen Sondheim to write the lyrics. When *West Side Story* opened at the Winter Garden on September 26, 1957, its raw vitality electrified audiences. While Bernstein's score and Robbins's high-voltage choreography and innovative staging were given much of the credit for that smash hit, Laurents's book also came in for its share of the praise, and the production is now considered a classic. Assured further Broadway assignments by the spectacular success of *West Side Story*, Laurents went on to collaborate with Sondheim and Jule Styne on *Gypsy*, a musical based on the memoirs of the stripper Gypsy Rose Lee, which opened in May 1959 to critical acclaim. Like *West Side Story*, *Gypsy* remains a perennial and oft-revived favorite. In the mid-1970s Laurents achieved his greatest commercial success to that date with the release of two motion pictures. The first, based on a novel he had written the previous year, was *The Way We Were* (1973), which starred Barbra Streisand as a left-wing Jewish intellectual and Robert Redford as the ambitious WASP novelist who becomes romantically involved with her. Next came *The Turning Point* (1977), which starred Anne Bancroft and Shirley MacLaine as middle-aged women confronting the choices they have made in life. That film marked Laurents's last Hollywood project. He returned to Broadway in 1983, directing the hit Jerry Herman/Harvey Fierstein musical *La Cage aux Folles*. His later works included the Broadway flop *Nick and Nora*, which ran for just days in 1991, and the Off-Broadway productions *The Radical Mystique* (1995), *Attacks on the Heart* (2003), *New Year's Eve* (2009), and *Come Back, Come Back, Wherever You Are* (2009). Laurents is the author of the memoirs *Original Story By: A Memoir of Broadway and Hollywood* (2000) and *Mainly on Directing: Gypsy, West Side Story, and Other Musicals* (2009). Nominated multiple times for Tony Awards, he won that honor as the author of the book for *Hallelujah, Baby!* in 1968 and best director of a musical for *La Cage aux Folles* in 1984. Laurents died at his home in New York City at the age of 93, from complications of pneumonia. His partner of over five decades, Tom Hatcher, predeceased him, in 2006. See *Current Biography* (1984). —M.R.

Obituary *New York Times* (on-line) May 5, 2011

LEVINE, JACK Jan. 3, 1915–Nov. 8, 2010 Artist. Jack Levine's realist paintings often skewered organized religion, militarism, big business, racism, and political corruption. The youngest of eight children, Levine was born in the South End slums of Boston, Massachusetts, to Samuel Levine, a Jewish immigrant from Lithuania who worked as a shoemaker, and the former Mary Grinker. At the age of eight, Levine moved with his family to the Boston suburb of Roxbury, where he took his first children's art classes. His drawings later caught the eye of Denman Ross, an art professor at Harvard University. From 1929 to 1931 Levine served as an apprentice to Ross, who introduced the developing artist to European tradition and the great paintings of the past. In 1935 Levine joined the Works Progress Administration (WPA) Federal Art Project. With a growing interest in social realism, he began creating paintings that depicted urban poverty and satirized social hypocrisy and government corruption. After some of his paintings were displayed at a 1936 exhibition of WPA art in New York City, he gained a degree of recognition

in the art world; he drew even more attention with his 1937 painting *The Feast of Pure Reason*, which depicted a capitalist, a politician, and a police officer—each with a bloated face and malevolent expression—smoking and drinking. In 1942 Levine was drafted into the U.S. Army. During his stint in the military, he served in the Medical Corps and the Corps of Engineers, and at one point he was assigned to paint portraits of officers. After his military discharge, in 1945, Levine settled in New York City and received a Guggenheim Fellowship. His first important postwar picture, *Welcome Home* (1946), was a bitterly satiric study of a solemn ceremonial dinner for a pompous, medal-bedecked general. Later that painting was to draw the ire of the House Committee on Un-American Activities (HUAC). Levine's insistence on shunning abstract expressionism and subsequent artistic movements resulted in his gradual marginalization in the art world. Still, he produced several more noteworthy paintings, including *The Royal Family* (1948), *Gangster Funeral* (1952–53), *Election Night* (1954), *The Prisoner* (1963), and *Panethnikon* (1979). Levine, a secular Jew, also created several paintings with biblical themes, including *Cain and Abel* (1961) and *David and Saul* (1989). His work has been featured in New York City's Museum of Modern Art and Metropolitan Museum of Art; the DeYoung Museum, in San Francisco; and the Brooklyn Museum, among other such venues. He was the subject of a 1985 documentary, *Jack Levine: Feast of Pure Reason*, directed and produced by David Sutherland. Levine was married to the former Ruth Gikow from 1946 until her death, in 1982. He is survived by his daughter, Susanna Levine Fisher, and two grandchildren. See *Current Biography* (1956). —J.P.

Obituary *New York Times* (on-line) Nov. 9, 2010

LUMET, SIDNEY June 25, 1924–Apr. 9, 2011 Filmmaker. Sidney Lumet, a towering figure in American film, directed more than 40 movies. He is known for taking on a diverse array of projects, and his films have long been noted for the complexity they uncover in their examination of ethical issues and human behavior. Lumet asserted that he always tried to keep his stories even-handed. "I'm not a propagandist," he told Frazier Moore for the Associated Press (January 10, 2001). "To me, it's important that I find something out about people. And if the story tells you a little bit about that person, then it's gonna tell you about that time and its issues, almost automatically. You don't have to reach." Lumet was born in Philadelphia, Pennsylvania, the only son of Eugenia (Wermus) Lumet and Baruch Lumet, an actor who enjoyed a long and varied career on stage and in radio, television, and film. In 1926 the family moved to New York City, where Baruch Lumet joined Maurice Schwartz's troupe at the Yiddish Art Theatre. Young Sidney made his acting debut alongside his father in the cast of a Yiddish Art Theatre production when he was four years old. He went on to appear in several Broadway shows as a child and attended the Professional Children's School in New York. Lumet served from 1942 to 1946 as a radar repairman with the U.S. Army. He then returned to New York, where he began directing Off-Broadway and summer-stock productions. In the 1950s he directed several television series and more than 200 plays for CBS's *Playhouse 90*, NBC's *Kraft Television Theatre* and *Studio One*, and other such dramatic programs. Lumet received an Emmy Award for his TV production of Eugene O'Neill's *The Iceman Cometh* (1960). He made his debut as a stage director with a revival of George Bernard Shaw's *The Doctor's Dilemma* at New York's Phoenix Theater in 1955. Lumet's first motion picture, *Twelve Angry Men* (1957), an adaptation of a play by Reginald Rose that Lumet had first directed on television, is the story of a murder-trial jury that is impeded in its rush to condemnation by a lone dissenter, a thoughtful man of conscience—played in the film by Henry Fonda—who steers the other 11 jurors, one by one, to a judgment of not guilty. Critics were unanimous in their praise of *Twelve Angry Men*, which is now considered a classic. Another of Lumet's notable early pictures was an adaptation of Eugene O'Neill's brooding and autobiographical family drama *Long Day's Journey into Night* (1962), which won Lumet a 1963 Directors Guild of America Award. The most controversial of the director's films of that period was *The Pawnbroker*, based on Edwin Lewis Wallant's novel about Sol Nazerman, the operator of a pawnshop in Spanish Harlem that is a front for a black racketeer. The year 1973 saw the beginning of Lumet's most successful string of films. *Serpico*, a thriller based on a true story of an honest policeman (played by Al Pacino) surrounded by crooked ones, was the first of Lumet's celebrated studies of police corruption in New York City. His adaptation of the Agatha Christie mystery *Murder on the Orient Express* (1974) was also successful, with critics noting not only the performances of the all-star cast but also the beautiful photography, an area in which Lumet's films had not previously been praised. Next came the hit *Dog Day Afternoon* (1975), about a bank robbery in New York City, featuring Pacino in another standout performance, as a man seeking money for his lover's sex-change operation. Lumet is perhaps best known for his follow-up movie, *Network* (1976), a satire of the network-news industry that starred Faye Dunaway, William Holden, and Peter Finch and spawned the famous line "I'm mad as hell, and I'm not going to take it anymore!" *Network* earned 10 Academy Award nominations and brought Lumet a Golden Globe Award for his direction. Lumet next directed two adaptations of Broadway plays, *Equus* (1977) and *The Wiz* (1978), the latter of which envisioned *The Wizard of Oz* with an African-American cast. The early 1980s saw Lumet helm *Prince of the City* (1981), an adaptation of Robert Daley's book about a whistle-blowing New York City cop that won Lumet a New York Film Critics Circle Award, and the compelling courtroom drama *The Verdict* (1982), starring Paul Newman, James Mason, Jack Warden, and Charlotte Rampling, with a script by David Mamet. After a string of relatively forgettable films, Lumet helmed *Running on Empty* (1988), the tale of a family on the run from the FBI, because the parents had participated in a bomb attack on a napalm lab in 1971 as a protest against the war in Vietnam. For the 1997 crime drama *Night Falls on Manhattan*, Lumet received praise for crafting morally complex characters whose actions often fell in the gray area between right and wrong. In 2001

Lumet returned to television after 40 years, directing and producing the weekly courtroom drama *100 Centre Street* for the A&E cable network. The show, which took its title from the address of Manhattan's Criminal Courts Building, ended its run in 2002. In 2006 he directed Vin Diesel in the movie *Find Me Guilty*, based on the criminal trial of the mobster Giacomo "Fat Jack" DiNorscio. His last feature film was the critically acclaimed *Before the Devil Knows You're Dead* (2007), about two brothers (Philip Seymour Hoffman and Ethan Hawke) who decide to rob their parents' jewelry store. In total Lumet's films received more than 50 Academy Award nominations, including four nominations for Lumet as best director (for *Twelve Angry Men*, *Dog Day Afternoon*, *Network*, and *The Verdict*); he also received seven Directors Guild of America Award nominations. In 2005 the Academy of Motion Picture Arts and Sciences presented Lumet with an award for lifetime achievement. Among his many other honors was the Directors Guild's prestigious D. W. Griffith Award, given for an unusually distinguished body of work. Lumet was unusual as an American director because he never made a picture in Hollywood, choosing to set many of his films in New York. "Locations are characters in my movies," he once wrote, as quoted in the *New York Times* (April 9, 2011, on-line). "The city is capable of portraying the mood a scene requires." Lumet, who reportedly died from lymphoma, was divorced three times: from the actress Rita Gam, the heiress and designer Gloria Vanderbilt, and Gail Jones (the daughter of the actress and singer Lena Horne). In 1980 he married his fourth wife, Mary Gimbel. She survives him, along with his stepdaughter, Leslie Gimbel; a stepson, Bailey Gimbel; two daughters, Amy and Jenny, from his marriage to Jones; nine grandchildren; and a great-granddaughter. See *Current Biography* (2005). —M.R.M.

Obituary *New York Times* (on-line) Apr. 9, 2011

MAATHAI, WANGARI Apr. 1, 1940–Sep. 25, 2011 Environmentalist; social activist; Nobel laureate. Wagnari Maathai won the 2004 Nobel Peace Prize "for her contribution to sustainable development, democracy and peace," according to the citation issued by the Norwegian Nobel Committee. Maathai was the first African woman—and only the 12th woman overall since 1901—to win the prestigious peace prize. Maathai was born in Nyeri, Kenya, and was raised in a farming community in the White Highlands. Her parents were subsistence farmers who belonged to the Kikuyu tribe. The oldest daughter in a family of six children, Maathai would normally have been expected to assume responsibility at an early age for many of the household chores, in accordance with tradition in rural Kenya, but her parents were relatively progressive and agreed that she should receive a good education. Her teachers at the Loreto Limuru Girls High School recognized her academic talent and helped her to obtain a scholarship to Mount St. Scholastica College, in Atchison, Kansas. After earning a B.S. degree in biology there, in 1964, she entered the University of Pittsburgh, in Pennsylvania. When Maathai received her M.S. degree in biological sciences, in 1966, she became one of the first women in all of eastern and central Africa to earn an advanced degree at a foreign institute of higher learning. In 1971, upon earning her Ph.D. degree in anatomy from the University of Nairobi, she became the first woman in central or eastern Africa to hold a doctorate. In 1976 she was appointed chairperson of the University of Nairobi's Department of Veterinary Anatomy and Physiology, and the following year she became an associate professor. In both cases she was the first woman in the region to hold such a position. In another rare distinction for an African woman, between 1973 and 1980 Maathai served as overall director of the Red Cross in Kenya. When her husband, Mwangi, a businessman, ran for a seat in the Kenyan Parliament in the early 1970s, Maathai lent her support to his campaign, and in doing so she exposed herself to the problems facing Kenya's urban poor. Following her husband's victory in the election, Maathai established a small employment agency through which she helped to give poor Kenyans jobs planting trees and shrubs. She centered her agency's efforts on planting trees because in some regions in Kenya, a lack of fuelwood for cooking was leading to malnutrition. In addition, she recognized that planting trees would help to stem desertification and soil erosion and would promote beautification. Although her agency struggled to stay afloat, Maathai remained committed to finding a way to encourage Kenyans to take active roles in preserving their environment, and in 1977 she succeeded in persuading the National Council of Women of Kenya (NCWK) to embrace her cause. As a result, Maathai's foundering enterprise was transformed into a national organization that became known as the Green Belt Movement (GBM). Maathai began touring internationally to speak out against environmental damage and its ties to poverty, and she often raised the ire of Kenyan president Daniel arap Moi, who deemed the Green Belt Movement "subversive." She was also undergoing personal travails; her husband, threatened by her growing power and independence, spuriously charged that she had committed adultery and forced her through an acrimonious three-week divorce trial that riveted the nation. (When she criticized the judge during the proceedings, she was thrown in jail.) Still, by the early 1990s approximately 80,000 GBM members had planted 10 million trees in more than 1,000 GBM nurseries in Kenya. In addition, the GBM's program had been replicated in nearly a dozen other sub-Saharan African countries and had gained the support of the United Nations. Maathai's desire to improve the quality of life of ordinary Kenyans led her to take a more active role in her country's political life. For example, she became a member of the Forum for the Restoration of Democracy, the most formidable of the political parties established after a ban on political activity was lifted by Moi's administration in December 1991. Her growing political stature, in turn, added to the government's antipathy for her. On several occasions she was detained, interrogated, or jailed by the police as part of the government's campaign to discredit prominent figures associated with the country's pro-democracy movement. In 1997 she ran for president of Kenya, but, unable to spread her message through the state-run media, she garnered few votes. Her situation improved after Moi left office, in 2002,

and in that year's parliamentary elections she won 98 percent of the vote in the Tetu Constituency. In January 2003 she was appointed assistant minister of the environment, natural resources, and wildlife by President Mwai Kibaki. In 2004, a year in which the number of trees planted by the GBM totaled 30 million, Maathai was awarded the Nobel Peace Prize. Despite that honor—only one of dozens that she received over the course of her career—she fell out of favor with the Kibaki administration and subsequently lost in the 2007 parliamentary elections. Maathai, who wrote several books, including the 2006 memoir *Unbowed*, fought ovarian cancer for the last year of her life. She died at a Nairobi hospital at the age of 71. She is survived by her three children: Waweru, Wanjira, and Muta. See *Current Biography* (1993). —M.R.

Obituary *New York Times* (on-line) Sep. 26, 2011

MACNEIL, CORNELL Sep. 24, 1922–July 15, 2011 Opera singer. "Cornell MacNeil was a giant in an age of giants, an artist whose vast, sumptuous baritone and muscular performing style helped establish a new golden age of Verdi singing at the Metropolitan Opera and other theaters of the first rank," F. Paul Driscoll wrote for *Opera News* (August 2011, online). The youngest of three sons, MacNeil was born in Minneapolis, Minnesota, to Walter MacNeil, a dentist, and Harriet MacNeil, a singer. Encouraged by his success in winning an Apollo Club Award as best male vocalist during his senior year in high school, MacNeil followed up graduation with a year devoted to voice study but decided that college was not for him. To learn a practical trade that would enable him to earn a living, he enrolled in a government training school, where he studied to be a machinist. He kept his artistic ambitions alive by occasionally performing with local theatrical groups and in radio plays. A scholarship to the Julius Hartt School of Music in Hartford, Connecticut, enabled him to return to his singing career, and in 1945 he became a member of the glee club at Radio City Music Hall, in New York City. MacNeil had his first major opportunity to sing opera when the composer Gian Carlo Menotti selected him for the baritone lead role of John Sorel in his new opera *The Consul*, which opened on Broadway in 1950 and ran for 269 performances. The opera earned Menotti a Pulitzer Prize; it also brought MacNeil recognition and praise. For the next few years, MacNeil studied voice during the day and supported the needs of his growing family by working as a night foreman at a plant. When, in 1953, he felt that the time was right, he quit his job and made a successful debut as Germont in Verdi's *La Traviata* at the New York City Opera. For the next several years, he remained with that company, singing a variety of roles. MacNeil made his debut performance at La Scala, in Milan, Italy, as Charles V in the Verdi opera *Ernani*, in 1959. That year he also made his debut at New York's Metropolitan Opera, in Verdi's *Rigoletto*, and was placed under contract by the company. (He ultimately performed in that opera more than 100 times.) His other signature roles at the Met included Renato in Verdi's *Ballo in Maschera*, Scarpia in Giacomo Puccini's *Tosca*, and Guido di

Monforte in Verdi's *I Vespri Siciliani*. MacNeil was featured in numerous telecasts from the Met, including performances of *Otello*, *Rigoletto*, *Tosca*, and other such popular works. In all he sang in more than 600 productions over the course of his career at the Met. MacNeil also sang at such storied venues as the Opera de Paris, Wiener Staatsoper, and Covent Garden. As president of the American Guild of Musical Artists, a post he held for much of the 1970s, MacNeil represented the onstage performers of the Metropolitan Opera and other leading companies in contract negotiations with management. Soon after singing in a 1987 production of *Tosca*, MacNeil, by then suffering from heart problems, retired from the Metropolitan Opera. He died at an assisted-living facility in Charlottesville, Virginia. He is survived by his second wife, Tania, as well as by five children—Walter, Mary, Dennis, Susan, and Katherine—from his first marriage. See *Current Biography* (1976). —D.K.

Obituary *New York Times* (on-line) July 17, 2011

MCDUFFIE, DWAYNE Feb. 20, 1962–Feb. 21, 2011 Comic-book writer; writer and producer of animated cartoons. Dwayne McDuffie was a co-founder of the now-defunct Milestone Media, which introduced a more culturally diverse group of superheroes to the comic-book industry. He was born in Detroit, Michigan, and attended the Roeper School for gifted and talented children, in Bloomfield Hills, a wealthy area northwest of Detroit. With the emergence of the civil rights and black-pride movements of the 1960s, black characters were increasingly being featured in the comics that McDuffie, an African-American, read as a youth. Without exception, however, the characters—including the Black Panther, an African king with the speed and strength of his animal namesake; Infantryman Gabe Jones of Marvel Comics' *Sgt. Fury and His Howling Commandos*; and Joe Robertson, a newspaper editor who appeared regularly in *Spider-Man*—were written and drawn by white men. In an interview with the *New York Times* (August 4, 1993), McDuffie said: "You only had two types of characters available for children. You had the stupid angry brute and the he's-smart-but-he's-black characters. And they were all colored either this Hershey-bar shade of brown, a sickly looking gray or purple. I've never seen anyone that's gray or purple before in my life. There was no diversity and almost no accuracy among the characters of color at all." Always creative, McDuffie began making rudimentary comic books in elementary school. He attended the University of Michigan, where he received a B.A. degree in literature, followed by an M.S. degree in physics, another area of intense interest for him. He then moved to New York City to attend New York University's Tisch School of the Arts, where he studied filmmaking. McDuffie ran out of money for tuition, however, and did not graduate from the program. In 1987, after a brief stint as a copy editor at a financial publication, McDuffie was hired as a special-projects editor at Marvel Comics, the venerable outfit responsible for such iconic characters as Spider-Man, the Fantastic Four, and Captain America. There, he wrote for several comic series and helped develop the first line of Marvel superhero trading cards. He also came up with the idea for a miniseries about a company, called Damage Control, that cleans up after the battles between superheroes and villains. In 1990 McDuffie left Marvel to work as a freelance writer. He soon teamed with Derek T. Dingle (a business journalist with considerable financial savvy), Denys Cowan (a fellow artist with whom McDuffie had worked at Marvel), and Michael Davis (another veteran artist) to co-found Milestone Media. Milestone specialized in books featuring such minority characters as Xombi, a Korean-American superhero; the Blood Syndicate, a group of Latino, Asian, and African-American crimefighters; and the black superheroes Icon, Hardware, and Static. Static, an inner-city high-school student who is sprayed with an experimental chemical during a gang war and subsequently exhibits electromagnetic powers, inspired the creation of *Static Shock* (2000–04), an animated series that aired on the WB television network. Milestone's business model resembled that of an independent record company under the umbrella of a major label: Milestone retained artistic and managerial independence, hiring its own artists and writers and creating its own stories and graphics, while DC Comics handled printing, marketing, and distribution. Despite the popularity of Milestone's characters and storylines, which often dealt with such social issues as teen pregnancy and racism, the company folded in 1997, as the comic-book industry as a whole began to suffer declining sales. In 2002 McDuffie joined the creative staff of *Justice League* (also known as *Justice League of America* or *JLA* and in later seasons called *Justice League Unlimited*), a Cartoon Network series featuring several notable DC Comics characters, including Batman and Superman. The program, which he began producing as well as writing in 2003, was a big hit with fans and aired until 2006. McDuffie also wrote the story for an associated video game, *Justice League Heroes*. He returned to Marvel in 2007 to work on the *Fantastic Four* series, and from 2008 to 2010, he was involved in the award-winning animated TV show *Ben 10: Alien Force*. McDuffie's many professional honors include a 2003 Humanitas Prize for an episode of *Static Shock* that dealt with the issue of gun violence, a 2009 Comic-Con International Inkpot Award, and more than 10 Parents Choice Awards. He died the day after his 49th birthday, due to complications from heart surgery. He is survived by his second wife, the comic-book writer Charlotte Fullerton, and his mother, Edna McDuffie Gardner. See *Current Biography* (2010). –J.P.

Obituary *New York Times* (on-line) Feb. 23, 2011

NYROP, DONALD Apr. 1, 1912–Nov. 16, 2010 Airline executive; former U.S. government official. After working as a federal airline regulator in the early 1950s, Donald Nyrop served as CEO of Northwest Airlines (1954–78), helping it to become one of the most profitable and safest companies in the industry. Nyrop was born in Elgin, Nebraska, the son of William A. and Nellie (Wylie) Nyrop. He graduated from Doane College, in Nebraska, in 1934, with a B.A. degree in history, and then attended George Washington University Law School, in Washington, D.C., supporting himself by working as an auditor for the General Accounting Office. After receiving a law degree, in 1939, Nyrop came across a newspaper ad about an opening for an attorney at the Civil Aeronautics Authority, which, established in 1938, was charged with regulating airline fares and determining routes, among other responsibilities. Nyrop's daughter Kathryn told the *New York Times* (November 27, 2010) that Nyrop referred to the money he paid for the newspaper containing the ad as "the best nickel he ever spent." Nyrop became an attorney in the general counsel's office of the Civil Aeronautics Authority and the Civil Aeronautics Board. In January 1942 he became executive officer to the board chair. Later that year Nyrop joined the U.S. Air Force as an executive operations officer in the Air Transport Command. He served in World War II for just over three years and was released from active military duty with the rank of lieutenant colonel in January 1946, receiving the Legion of Merit Medal. Nyrop then served as a specialist in international policy matters for the Air Transportation Association. In 1946 and again in 1947, he was a member of the official U.S. delegation for the International Civil Aviation Organization Assembly. In August 1948 Nyrop became the deputy administrator in charge of operations for the Civil Aeronautics Administration, which acted under the supervision of the Department of Commerce. He was promoted to administrator in September 1950. About six months later President Harry S. Truman nominated him to the post of chair of the Civil Aeronautics Board, an appointment confirmed by the U.S. Senate on April 17, 1951. He was reappointed to that post in December 1951. In his new role Nyrop was responsible for the regulation of economic aspects of air-carrier operations, including the fixing of rates for passenger and air-mail service, the promulgation of safety standards and civil air regulations, and the investigation of aircraft accidents. Nyrop resigned the chairmanship in 1952 to practice law. In 1954 he accepted the positions of CEO and chair of Northwest Airlines, thus becoming the industry's youngest chief executive. Nyrop was "famous for being frugal," as Brent Baskfield, a retired Northwest executive, told the *New York Times*. For example, in order to save both money and weight, Nyrop removed almost all paint from the outside of the company's planes, using only what was needed to identify the airline. A shrewd businessman, he had several run-ins with the pilots' and machinists' unions, resulting in strikes during his tenure. By the time he retired, in 1978, Northwest Airlines had one of the best safety records in the industry and was one of the most consistently profitable. Nyrop remained a member of the Northwest board until 1984. (Northwest was acquired by Delta Air Lines in 2008.) Nyrop, who died at his home in Edina, Minnesota, was married to Grace Cary, a former flight attendant and registered nurse, whom he met on a flight from Washington to New York in 1941. His wife died in 1993. His son, Bill, a professional hockey player, died in 1995. Nyrop is survived by three daughters (Kathryn, Nancy, and Karyn) and eight grandchildren. See *Current Biography* (1952). —M.M.H.

Obituary *New York Times* (on-line) Nov. 27, 2010

OHGA, NORIO Jan. 29, 1930–Apr. 23, 2011 Businessman. As head of the Sony Corp. in the 1990s, Norio Ohga was the architect behind some of the company's most influential products, including the compact disc (CD), the high-definition television (HDTV), and the digital video disc (DVD). The son of Shoichi Ohga, a wealthy lumber trader, and his wife, Toshi Mizuno, Norio Ohga was born in the town of Numazu, in the Shizuoka Prefecture of Japan. An adolescent when Japan entered World War II, he was exempted from working at a nearby military factory because he suffered from pleurisy. He thus had time to study science, mostly on his own, and to indulge his passion for music. He spent a substantial part of the war years practicing the piano and taking singing lessons. By the time he was 18, he knew he wanted to become a professional vocalist. After the war ended Ohga enrolled at the Tokyo National University of Fine Arts and Music, in the nation's capital. He was a student there when, in the late 1940s, a Japanese company, Tokyo Tsushin Kogyo (Tokyo Telecommunications Engineering Corp.), began to market Japan's first reel-to-reel magnetic tape recorder. Ohga, a baritone, found the tape machine wanting, and he wrote a letter to the company pointing out its deficiencies and suggesting ways to overcome them. The letter caught the attention of the company's cofounder Akio Morita, and in 1953 Morita hired Ohga as a part-time consultant. After completing his studies at Tokyo National University, in 1953, Ohga entered the Hochschule für Musik, a respected music and performing-arts school in Berlin, in what was then West Germany. After three years of voice training, he embarked on a singing career, performing in both Europe and Japan. Meanwhile, Morita's company—which was renamed Sony in 1958—had begun to grow into a major manufacturer of electronic goods. Morita eventually persuaded Ohga, who had over the years continued to work as a consultant for the company, to abandon his plans for a career as an opera singer and work for Sony full-time. After settling again in Japan, Ohga began working as the general manager of Sony's professional tape-recorder division. Before long he was promoted to director of Sony's entire tape-recorder business. In 1961 he became the head of Sony's design center, which handled the design of all Sony products. "Ohga made sure . . . that the company would be presenting a single face to the world," David E. Sanger wrote for the *New York Times Magazine* (February 18, 1990). "From the design center came Sony's cool black finishes and the European styling that immediately distinguished its products from other Japanese makes." In 1969 Morita chose Ohga to head the CBS/Sony Group, one of Japan's first joint ventures with an American company. In the 1970s Ohga worked with engineers at Sony and Philips to develop the compact disc; he reportedly requested that the device have a 75-minute recording capacity so that listeners could enjoy the entirety of Beethoven's Ninth Symphony. Ohga was named president and chief operating officer of Sony in 1982, the same year the company introduced the compact disc to the world. During the next decade Sony grew fourfold. Ohga helped launch many new consumer products in the late 1980s and early '90s, among them the digital audio tape (DAT), digital mini-disc (DMD), HDTV, and

DVD. He became chief executive in 1989. Around that time Sony purchased CBS Records for $2 billion and Columbia Pictures for $3.4 billion, confirmiing both Sony's prominence and Japan's emergence as a major economic power. (Sony's foray into the film business ultimately proved disastrous, however; mismanagement of Sony Pictures Entertainment later led to billions of dollars in losses.) Ohga spearheaded the development of the Sony PlayStation video-game player, which was introduced in 1994. In April 1995 Ohga—who had recently become chairman of the company—chose his successor: Nobuyuki Idei, a marketing expert who had worked for Sony for 35 years. Idei, whose selection surprised many business leaders because he was several tiers below other Sony executives, became chief executive in 1999. Ohga stayed on as chairman until 2000. Sony struggled under Idei, and he was replaced in 2005 by Howard Stringer, the current chief executive. Ohga, who occasionally professed a desire to quit business and return to music, had opportunities to serve as a guest conductor of various symphony orchestras. He died of multiple organ failure and is survived by his wife since 1957, Midori Matsubara. See *Current Biography* (1998). —M.R.M.

Obituary *New York Times* (on-line) Apr. 24, 2011

OLSEN, KENNETH H. Feb. 20, 1926–Feb. 6, 2011
Businessman. Kenneth Harry Olsen was the founder of the Digital Equipment Corp. (DEC). At its peak, in the 1980s, DEC was the second-largest computer company in the world. During his decades-long tenure as the firm's CEO and guiding force, Olsen oversaw the development of numerous innovations that helped reshape the computer industry. In 1986 Olsen was famously proclaimed by *Fortune* magazine to be "arguably the most successful entrepreneur in the history of American business." Born in Bridgeport, Connecticut, Olsen was the second of four children born to Oswald Olsen, a designer of machine tools, and the former Elizabeth Svea Nordling, both stern, religious people of Norwegian heritage. While growing up in the working-class Connecticut town of Stratford, Olsen spent much of his time in the basement of his home, inventing gadgets and repairing broken radios. He served in the U.S. Navy during World War II, and during that time he obtained his first formal training in electrical engineering. After leaving the navy, in 1946, Olsen enrolled at the Massachusetts Institute of Technology (MIT), in Cambridge. He received bachelor's and master's degrees in electrical engineering from MIT, in 1950 and 1952, respectively. While studying at MIT Olsen began working in the university's new Lincoln Laboratory. There, he helped develop air-defense technologies for the Office of Naval Research and the U.S. Air Force. Olsen worked on the development of a computerized flight simulator known as the Whirlwind and was also involved in the development of the Semi-Automatic Ground Environment (SAGE) early-warning system for tracking enemy aircraft. For the latter project he was sent to work as a liaison with International Business Machines (IBM), which had won the contract for the actual manufacturing of the system. After returning to MIT, Olsen applied what

he had learned at IBM to the building of the first transistorized research computer. He realized that the breakthroughs he and his colleagues were making and writing papers about had little impact outside academia, and he longed to have some practical effect on the rest of the world. He knew that such relatively simple computing jobs as tracking a scientific experiment or maintaining an inventory list did not require the expensive, room-sized mainframes produced by IBM. With an MIT associate, Harlan Anderson, he began to look for backing for his idea for a small general-purpose computer. In 1957 they attracted a $70,000 investment from Georges F. Doriot of the American Research and Development Corp. Doriot advised them to make something other than computers, however, because he felt that it would be too difficult for a fledgling enterprise to compete with IBM, Burroughs, and RCA—companies that had already entered the relatively new and precarious computer business. Opening DEC in one corner of a woolen mill dating back to the Civil War era, Olsen and Anderson, who were joined by Olsen's brother Stan, took Doriot's advice and began producing the printed-circuit logic modules used by engineers to test equipment. DEC's circuit modules, as Olsen had always intended, became the building blocks of the company's first computer. That was marketed in 1960 and equipped for interactive computing with a cathode-ray-tube terminal similar to that of a television screen. Olsen called it the Programmed Data Processor or PDP-1, to help customers suspend their disbelief in a computer that sold for $120,000 instead of the then-standard $1 million, that was relatively small (the size of a compact refrigerator), and that could be installed anywhere. The device was well received by the engineers, scientists, and technicians at whom it was aimed. It was accepted as standard equipment after the International Telephone & Telegraph Corp. began buying it in great quantities for message-switching. DEC's PDP-8 computer, introduced in 1965, ultimately revolutionized the way in which industries conducted business, making it economical and practical for a technician to perform a computing job on the spot, instead of having to wait for a turn on the company mainframe. Considered the first true minicomputer, the PDP-8 sold for an astonishingly low basic price of $18,000 and opened up entirely new markets for DEC. (IBM, by comparison, did not enter the minicomputer market in earnest until late 1976.) While Digital ranked among the most profitable companies in the nation during its peak in the 1980s, Olsen's reluctance to embrace new trends—particularly the personal computer—ultimately resulted in the company's downfall. In 1992, after several executive departures, layoffs, and financial setbacks, Olsen was forced by his board of directors to resign; six years later DEC was acquired by Compaq, which would later merge with Hewlett-Packard. After leaving Digital Olsen founded a new company, Advanced Modular Solutions, but it ultimately failed. He retired in 2000. During his career he received many honors, including the Franklin Institute's Vermilye Medal in 1980, the first Institute of Electrical and Electronic Engineers (IEEE) Leadership Award, and the first IEEE Computer Society Award. Olsen died at the age of 84. His wife of 59 years, the former Eeva-Liisa

Aulikki Valve, predeceased him, as did one of their sons, Glenn. He is survived by a daughter, Ava; a son, James; his brother Stan; and five grandchildren. See *Leaders of the Information Age* (2003). —C.C.

Obituary *New York Times* (on-line) Feb. 7, 2011

OTTO OF AUSTRIA, ARCHDUKE

OTTO OF AUSTRIA, ARCHDUKE Nov. 20, 1912– July 4, 2011 Member of the European Parliment; heir to the Austro-Hungarian throne. Franz Joseph Otto Robert Maria Anton Karl Maximilian Heinrich Sixtus Xavier Renatus Ludwig Gaetan Pius Ignatius von Hapsburg-Lorraine, more commonly known as Otto von Hapsburg (or Habsburg), was an heir to the imperial throne of Austria-Hungary. If World War I had not taken place, he might have become the emperor of Austria and king of Hungary as well as Bohemia, Dalmatia, Slavonia, Galicia, Illyria, and other places that today exist as independent states only on 1918 maps. Instead, he employed his patriotism and dream of a unified Europe to build a fruitful career in politics. Otto's mother, Zita de Bourbon-Parma, a cousin of Alfonso XIII of Spain, married Archduke Karl, the great-nephew of Emperor Franz Josef, in 1911. Otto was born in Reichenau the following year. In 1916, when the elderly Franz Josef died, Karl ascended to the throne as Charles IV. However, at the end of World War I, the empire was dissolved, and in 1919 the monarch was deposed and exiled to live in relative poverty along with his family. Charles IV died on the Portuguese island of Madeira, on April 1, 1922; on that date Otto, still a child, became the official head of the dynasty. After living for several years in Spain, where Otto was addressed as "Your Majesty" and attended high school, the family moved to Belgium, where he studied political science and economics at the Catholic University of Louvain. He earned a doctoral degree in 1935. After the Anschluss (the occupation and annexation of Austria by Nazi Germany) in March 1938, Otto's Austrian estates, which had been briefly restored, were taken away by the Nazis; a price was placed on his head throughout the Reich; and Hungary, his last hope, joined the Axis. Otto and his family took refuge in Portugal and then the U.S., and after the war he lived in exile in France and Spain. In 1954 he settled in the Bavarian town of Pocking, and he subsequently became a member of the conservative Christian Social Union. Officially renouncing his claim to the throne in 1961, Otto served as a member of the European Parliament from 1979 to 1999. Possessed of a fervent desire to see the continent reunited, he served for a time as the president of the Pan-European League, and in 1989 he helped organize a peace protest called the Pan-European Picnic, on the border of Austria and Hungary, which included a symbolic opening of the border. During that event almost 700 East Germans living under oppressive Communist rule managed to flee to the West. "This momentary piercing of the Iron Curtain became one the events that hastened the fall of the Berlin Wall and the unification of cold war Europe," Nicholas Kulish wrote for the *New York Times* (July 4, 2011). Otto died in his sleep at the age of 98 at his home in Pocking. He was predeceased by his wife of almost six decades, Regina von Sachsen-Meiningen, in 2010. Otto is survived by his younger brother, Felix;

seven children; and 22 grandchildren. See *Current Biography* (1941). —M.M.H.

Obituary *New York Times* (on-line) July 4, 2011

PERCY, CHARLES

PERCY, CHARLES Sep. 27, 1919–Sep. 17, 2011 Businessman; former U.S. senator. Charles Percy spent several years at the helm of the Bell & Howell Co. before being elected to represent Illinois in the U.S. Senate, where he served from 1966 to 1984. Of British descent (one of his ancestors, George Percy, was a governor of the Jamestown colony), Charles Harting Percy was born in Pensacola, Florida, to Edward H. Percy, a bank clerk, and his wife, the former Elizabeth Harting, a concert violinist. Percy's father lost his job and the family's life savings in the stock-market crash of 1929. The younger Percy took on a series of odd jobs, including selling magazines door-to-door, to help make ends meet. One day he asked his Sunday-school teacher, Joseph McNabb, the president of Bell & Howell, if there was a job opening for his father at the then-small camera company. McNabb hired Edward Percy as an office manager and, at the same time, offered Charles Percy a summer job in customer relations. Following his graduation from New Trier High School in Winnetka, Illinois, Percy enrolled at the University of Chicago on a half-tuition scholarship. To make up the difference and earn pocket money, he worked part-time in the dormitory cafeterias and in the college library. Later, he took over the cooperative agency that sold food, linen, coal, and appliances to dormitories and fraternity houses. By adopting large-volume purchasing methods, he turned the cooperative into a money-making operation that grossed upwards of $150,000 a year. After earning a bachelor's degree in economics, in 1941, Percy joined Bell & Howell as the manager of the company's new war-coordinating department, which manufactured electrical and optical equipment for the armed forces. The following year he was promoted to assistant corporate secretary and named to the board of directors. In 1943 Percy enlisted in the U.S. Navy as an apprentice seaman. After leaving the service, in 1945, with the rank of lieutenant, he returned to Bell & Howell as corporate secretary for industrial relations and foreign manufacturing programs. As Joseph McNabb's hand-picked successor, he was elected president of Bell & Howell after the older man's death, in 1949. Then 29, Percy was the youngest chief executive of a major corporation in the nation. Under his direction the company took major steps into the consumer-electronics market; revenues were $13 million a year when he took over, and by 1963, when he stepped down, they were more than $160 million. A moderate Republican, he ran for governor of Illinois in 1964 but narrowly lost to Otto Kerner Jr. He fared better politically in 1966, when he won an upset victory over Paul H. Douglas, a respected three-term Democratic incumbent, for a seat in the U.S. Senate. (His personal life, however, was marred by tragedy during the '66 campaign; one of his 21-year-old twin daughters, Valerie, was bludgeoned to death in the family home. The murderer was never found.) Percy's outspokenness on such issues as the Vietnam War and poverty thrust him into the national spotlight, and for a relatively unknown freshman senator, he received an extraordinary amount of national press coverage, most of it favorable. Because of his impeccable credentials and his Kennedyesque style, many observers viewed him as a possible compromise presidential candidate in 1968. He declined to run, however, choosing instead to endorse Governor Nelson Rockefeller of New York, who was similarly moderate. During his 18-year tenure in the Senate, Percy worked well with Democrats and often scored highly with liberal voters. He "averaged a 52 percent rating from the liberal Americans for Democratic Action and only 30 percent from the American Conservative Union," Adam Clymer wrote for the *New York Times* (September 17, 2011, on-line). "With the party having moved steadily to the right since then, it was a rating few if any Republicans would receive today." In the 1984 Senate race, Percy, by then chairman of the Foreign Relations Committee, was defeated by his Democratic opponent, Paul M. Simon. He remained in Washington, where he ran a business-consulting firm. Percy, who had been suffering from Alzheimer's disease for several years, died at the age of 91. He was survived by his second wife, Loraine Diane Guyer, whom he married in 1950. (His first wife, Jeanne Valerie Dickerson, died in 1947, after only four years of marriage.) He was also survived by two children, Roger and Sharon (Valerie's twin), from his first marriage; two children, Gail and Mark, from his second marriage; nine grandchildren; and six great-grandchildren. See *Current Biography* (1977). —M.R.

Obituary *New York Times* (on-line) Sep. 17, 2011

PEREZ, CARLOS ANDRES Oct. 27, 1922–Dec. 25, 2010 Former president of Venezuela. Carlos Andrés Pérez, who served two terms as Venezuela's president (1974–79 and 1989–93), is best known for nationalizing his country's iron-ore and oil industries during his first stint in office. He was born Carlos Andrés Pérez Rodriguez, the 11th of 12 children, in the Andean town of Rubio. His father was a prominent merchant and coffee grower. Pérez obtained his primary education in Rubio, at the Colegio María Immaculada, run by the Dominican fathers. At 15 he became involved in politics as a member of the clandestine Partido Democrático Nacional, which later formed the nucleus of Acción Democrática. In 1939 Pérez moved with his family to Caracas, Venezuela's capital. There, he completed his secondary education at the Liceo Andrés Bello, where he served as president of the student center and obtained his bachillerato in 1943. From 1944 to 1947 he studied law at the Universidad Central de Venezuela, but he never obtained a law degree. After the formation of the non-Communist, leftist Acción Democrática (AD), in 1941, Pérez spent several years working as a youth party leader in Caracas and Táchira. In 1943 he founded the Association of Venezuelan Youth, which brought together groups sympathetic to AD. In 1945 he took part in a successful revolution against the conservative government of General Isaías Medina Angarita. Rómulo Betancourt, who became president of the revolutionary junta, named Pérez his personal secretary. In 1946 Pérez won election to the Táchira legislative assembly and to the

Chamber of Deputies of the National Congress and was also named secretary to the Council of Ministers. He remained in those posts for two years, while the AD government enacted a series of liberal reforms. But in November 1948—the year he married his first cousin Blanca, with whom he would eventually have six children—a right-wing counter-revolution occurred. Colonel Márcos Pérez Jimenez and other officers staged a coup, and many of the AD leaders were jailed. Pérez spent a year in a Caracas prison before being expelled from the country. The peripatetic life of a political exile—spent in Colombia, Cuba, and Costa Rica—was Pérez's lot until 1958. After the overthrow of the Pérez Jimenez dictatorship, in 1958, Carlos Andrés Pérez returned to Venezuela to help reconstruct the AD. Later that year he was elected to the Chamber of Deputies from Táchira, and in 1960–61 he served as director general of the Ministry of the Interior; in 1962 he was named interior minister. Pérez was assigned the job of crushing a group of leftist guerrillas, which he did, albeit with questionable methods. Pérez headed his party's congressional delegation from 1964 to 1967. Although the AD suffered a defeat in the December 1968 election, Pérez was elected for the fourth time to the Chamber of Deputies. From 1969 to 1974 he again led the AD congressional delegation, this time in opposition to the administration. Throughout the 1973 presidential campaign, Pérez employed the theme "Neither weakness nor tyranny" to soften the image he had gained as interior minister. Pérez won the presidency in December of that year and took office in March 1974. The most important issue in Venezuela after the election concerned the fate of the country's oil industry. Because of the worldwide energy shortage, the Arab oil embargo, and the quadrupling of petroleum prices in 1973, nations with large oil reserves had almost overnight gained great wealth and power. Pérez moved quickly to establish national control over the economy. During his first term he nationalized the iron-ore, steel, and oil industries. He left office in 1979 but was elected once again in 1989. He quickly announced a series of spending cuts as well as higher gas prices, news that was greeted by rioting in the streets. He responded to the unrest by ordering a security crackdown that resulted in the loss of hundreds of lives. In 1992 Pérez faced two coup attempts, one led by the future president Hugo Chavez. In 1993 Pérez was removed from office on corruption charges and placed under house arrest for two years. After Chavez was elected president, in 1998, Pérez went into exile. He lived for a time in the Dominican Republic, where he faced accusations of conspiring to oust Chavez. In 2003 he settled in the U.S. with his mistress, Cecilia, with whom he had two daughters. He remained there, in Florida, until his death at age 88, despite facing extradition in connection with his brutal suppression of the 1989 riots. See *Current Biography* (1976). —D.K.

Obituary *New York Times* (on-line) Dec. 26, 2010

PETIT, ROLAND Jan. 13, 1924–July 10, 2011 Dancer; choreographer. Roland Petit was alternately celebrated and dismissed over the course of his long career. Known for his innovative ballets, which pushed the boundaries of traditional dance with overt eroticism, he also worked on several crowd-pleasing Hollywood movies. He was born in the Paris suburb of Villemomble, to a French father and Italian mother. Petit's father owned a small bistro in the market district of Paris, and his mother founded the dancewear company Repetto. As a boy Petit was fond of performing for patrons of his father's café, and by the age of 10, he had entered the ballet school of the Paris Opera. There, he studied under Gustave Ricaux and later worked with Serge Lifar, the chief choreographer, maître de ballet, and danseur étoile of the Opera Ballet. At age 16 Petit was accepted into the corps of the troupe, and in 1943 he was promoted to the rank of premier sujet in Lifar's production of Manuel de Falla's *L'Amour Sorcier*. Meanwhile, beginning in 1941 and throughout the Nazi occupation of Paris during World War II, Petit gave annual recitals in Paris. Shortly after the city's liberation, at the end of the summer of 1944, Petit left the Opera Ballet to launch a solo career. Several months later he teamed up with the ballet critic Irene Lidova and the impresario Claude Giraud to choreograph a series of recitals exhibiting the talents of the younger generation of French dancers who had grown up during the occupation. The success of those performances led Petit and Lidova to establish Les Ballets des Champs-Élysées with Serge Diaghilev's collaborator and secretary, Boris Kochno, in 1945. Over the next two years, the company toured all over Europe, winning acclaim for such masterful ballets as *Les Amours de Jupiter* and *Le Jeune Homme et la Mort*. By 1948 Petit had left Les Ballets des Champs-Élysées to organize Les Ballets de Paris de Roland Petit. Featuring the work of some of France's foremost writers, composers, and painters, and comprised of 15 young soloists, the troupe immediately won over critics and audiences with its daring ballets, the most notable of which was arguably a freely adapted version of Georges Bizet's *Carmen* in 1949. Starring his future wife, Renée (later Zizi) Jeanmaire, as a tunic-clad seductress, the ballet became a succès de scandale in London and New York for its frank sexuality. Petit, who married Jeanmaire in 1954, was not immune to the lures of Hollywood, and during the 1950s he choreographed such American films as *Hans Christian Andersen* (1952), *Daddy Long Legs* (1955), *The Glass Slipper* (1955), and *Anything Goes* (1956). After returning to Paris he choreographed many ballets and music-hall revues and also served as director of the Paris Opera Ballet for a short time in the early 1970s. He subsequently moved to Marseille, and in 1972 he founded the Ballet National de Marseille, which he directed for the next 26 years. Petit choreographed more than 150 ballets, working with such stars as Margot Fonteyn, Rudolf Nureyev, Maya Plisetskaya, Mikhail Baryshnikov, and Natalia Makarova. Petit, who penned a 1993 memoir, *J'ai dansé sur les flots* ("I Have Danced on the Waves"), died of leukemia in Geneva, Switzerland. He is survived by Zizi Jeanmaire and their daughter, Valentine, a dancer and actress. See *Current Biography* (1952). —C.C.

Obituary *New York Times* (on-line) July 10, 2011

PRICE, MARGARET Apr. 13, 1941–Jan. 28, 2011
Opera singer. Margaret Price was known for her rich voice and her roles in such operas as *Le nozze di Figaro* and *Don Carlo*; at one point she was widely considered the world's foremost living Mozart soprano, and she also became closely associated with the works of Verdi. Price was born in Blackwood, South Wales. Her father was a teacher, and her mother worked long hours as a nurse. Having to assume many of her mother's household responsibilities, Price had no time for normal childhood play. She looked after her developmentally disabled younger brother, and on Fridays she was excused from school so that she could go to town to pay the family's bills and do their shopping for the weekend. Both of Price's parents played piano and encouraged her to do so as well, but she preferred singing. Although her parents let her take singing lessons at the age of nine, they did not encourage her to consider a career in the arts, steering her instead toward a job in teaching. Still, she auditioned for the Trinity College of Music in London and won a scholarship at age 15. After leaving Trinity, at 19, Price performed for almost two years with the Ambrosian Singers, a well-known professional chorus. Early in 1962 she auditioned successfully for the role of Cherubino in a Welsh National Opera production of *Le nozze di Figaro*. Partly because she did not then know Italian, that first experience on the opera stage was so bad that she almost resolved never to have another. She recovered, however, and after an audition with the Royal Opera Company, she was signed as Teresa Berganza's cover (not understudy) for Cherubino at Covent Garden in London in the spring of 1962. The conductor and impresario James Lockwood spent long hours teaching her Italian and coaching her, and when Berganza became ill, and an understudy could not be found in time, Price went on and had a succès fou with both audience and critics. Price's work with Lockwood on Cherubino was the beginning of a long relationship. Lockwood taught her five languages, formed a duo with her, and became what she has called her "second set of ears." He convinced her that she was not a mezzo-soprano, as she had originally believed, but a soprano. With Lockwood as her accompanist, Price signed with the BBC and regularly performed lieder and chamber-music compositions on television in the middle and late 1960s. She made her American operatic debut as Pamina in Mozart's *Die* Zauberflöte with the San Francisco Opera in 1969, and she sang Fiordiligi in the same composer's *Così fan tutte* with the Lyric Opera of Chicago in 1972. She returned periodically to sing with both companies in the following years. In her appearances in major European opera houses and festivals, she became closely identified with such Mozart roles as the Countess in *Le nozze di Figaro*, Doña Anna in *Don Giovanni*, and Constanze in *Entführung aus dem Serail*. Feeling her way into the Verdi repertory, Price undertook Desdemona in *Otello* at the Paris Opera in 1976. Later that year she reprised that role with the Paris company on a visit to the Metropolitan Opera, in New York City. In 1978, at the height of her fame, she gave a solo recital to a packed house at Carnegie Hall, in New York. During the 1980s Price added to her repertoire the title roles in Cilea's *Adriana Lecouvreur* and Richard Strauss's

Ariadne auf Naxos, among other parts. In 1982 she sang the female lead on a recording of Wagner's *Tristan und Isolde*; although the recording was beloved by opera fans, she never attempted to perform the part onstage. In 1993 Price was made a dame of the British Empire, and six years later she retired to the coast of Wales, where she led a quiet life, teaching an occasional voice student and raising golden retrievers. She died of heart failure at her home near the Irish Sea, leaving no immediate survivors. See *Current Biography* (1986). —D.K.

Obituary *New York Times* (on-line) Feb. 1, 2011

PRICE, REYNOLDS Feb. 1, 1933–Jan. 20, 2011 Writer. Reynolds Price was best known for such novels as *A Long and Happy Life* (1962) and *Kate Vaiden* (1986), which established him as a major southern writer on a par with such luminaries as Eudora Welty and William Faulkner. In an autobiographical sketch he prepared for *World Authors 1950–1970*, Price described Macon, North Carolina, where he was born Edward Reynolds Price to William Solomon Price and Elizabeth (Rodwell) Price, as "a town of 227 cotton and tobacco farmers nailed to the flat red land at the pit of the Great Depression." His father sold insurance and electrical appliances in the series of semirural North Carolina towns where Price was raised after the family lost their original home. Price's writing ability helped to win him an Angier Duke scholarship to Duke University, in Durham, North Carolina, in 1951. At Duke he wrote two of the short stories that would later appear in his collection *Names and Faces of Heroes* (1963). He met the writer he claims as his greatest influence, Eudora Welty, when she came to speak at Duke in 1955, during his senior year. Their meeting marked the beginning of an informal apprenticeship and a lifelong friendship. After graduating from Duke in 1955, with a B.A. degree, Price went to England for three years to study at Merton College, Oxford University, on a Rhodes scholarship. There, he continued to receive encouragement for his work from such notables as Stephen Spender and W. H. Auden. While at Oxford he wrote a thesis on the role of the chorus in John Milton's *Samson Agonistes* and continued to produce short stories, some of which Stephen Spender published in the magazine *Encounter*. In 1958 Price returned to Duke University and joined the faculty of its English Department. Except for his visiting professorships elsewhere and his few trips abroad, he remained there until his death, teaching creative writing and courses on the work of Milton as well as on the Gospels. He was named the James B. Duke Professor of English in 1977. According to one of his star students, the novelist Anne Tyler, who wrote a reminiscent article about him for *Vanity Fair* (July 1986), he was something of a romantic figure on campus, wearing "a long black cape with a scarlet lining" and making an impact as a teacher that made him seem "older than God." His first novel, *A Long and Happy Life* (1962), earned Price widespread critical acclaim and an unwanted reputation as the "new Faulkner." Set among the folk and fauna of eastern North Carolina, it tells the story of a spunky and naïve young heroine, Rosacoke Mustian, who becomes pregnant after a sexual encounter with a young man, Wesley Beavers, whom she has loved for years but who is so indifferent to her that he fails to recall her name correctly immediately after their tryst. Their marriage is brought about not by love, as she had hoped, but by the pregnancy. The protagonist of Price's second novel, *A Generous Man* (1966), is Rosacoke's brother, Milo. (The family is revisited in *Good Hearts*, which appeared in 1988.) In 1975 Price published *The Surface of the Earth*, which he called the book that he was "born to write." The novel contains a visionary chronicle of 41 years in the lives of two families intertwined through marriage, the Mayfields and the Kendals. That book was the first in an ambitious trilogy that also included *The Source of Light* (1981) and *The Promise of Rest* (1995). In 1984 doctors discovered a malignant tumor on Price's spine. After undergoing several operations and radiation treatments, he was left paralyzed from the waist down and confined to a wheelchair for the rest of his life. He continued to write, and one of his most acclaimed novels, *Kate Vaiden*, was published in 1986. In the book the title character's father inexplicably kills her mother and then himself, leaving the 11-year-old orphan in the care of an aunt and uncle. Years later, when Kate's young lover dies, she begins to shun any deep commitment to other human beings, even abandoning her own son for decades. Critical response to *Kate Vaiden* was overwhelmingly positive. Michiko Kakutani, in her review for the *New York Times* (June 24, 1986), called it a "fierce validation" of Price's original promise as a writer and a novel that "glows with the fine, burnished fire of mature ambition." The book won the 1986 National Book Critics Circle Award for fiction. Among Price's other acclaimed books are the memoir *Clear Pictures: First Loves, First Guides* (1989); the novel *Blue Calhoun* (1992); a second memoir, *A Whole New Life* (1994), about his struggle with cancer and paralysis; and his final book, *Ardent Spirits: Leaving Home, Coming Back* (2009), about his studies at Oxford and his early experiences as a teacher at Duke. (In the last-named book, Price revealed that he was gay.) The Christian themes evident in Price's earlier novels became even more pronounced in *Roxanna Slade* (1998) and *The Good Priest's Son* (2005). Additionally, he published two books of biblical scholarship, *A Palpable God* (1978) and *The Three Gospels* (1996). Price, who also wrote several volumes of poetry, was a member of the American Academy of Arts and Letters and a recipient of the John Tyler Caldwell Award for the Humanities from the North Carolina Humanities Council. He was a recipient of the University Medal for Distinguished Meritorious Service at Duke, and in 2008 a professorship in his name was established. Price died of a heart attack and is survived by his brother, Will. See *Current Biography* (1987). —W.D.

Obituary *New York Times* (on-line) Jan. 20, 2011

QADDAFI, MUAMMAR AL 1942–Oct. 20, 2011 Libyan dictator. Muammar Qaddafi, who ruled Libya for 42 years, from 1969 until his death at the hands of revolutionary forces, was the longest-serving head of state in the modern-day Arab world. He possessed, as Alyssa Fetini wrote for *Time* magazine (February 3, 2009, on-line), "a reputation that [ran] the gamut from eccentric revolutionary to international pariah over his long career." Qaddafi was the only son and the youngest of the four children of Mohammed Abdul Salam bin Hamed bin Mohammed, an illiterate Bedouin herder of camels and goats, and his wife, Aisha. He was born, according to most sources, in a tent in the Libyan desert, about 20 miles inland from the coastal town of Sirte. (As transliterated from the Arabic, the family name also appears in such forms as Gaddafi, Qhadafi, and Khadafi.) While Qaddafi believed that he had been born in the Islamic month of Muharram, which corresponded at the time to March in the Gregorian calendar, there is widespread dispute about the exact date of his birth, with various sources stating either January 7 or June 7. Qaddafi's family enjoyed few, in any, of the modern conveniences of Western civilization, living much as their forebears had lived for centuries, and he was the first family member to gain a formal education. By the time he entered secondary school, in 1956, he was a devout admirer of Egypt's Gamal Abdel Nasser, a Pan-Arabist and the preeminent leader of the independence movement in the Arab world. After graduating, in 1963, Qaddafi enrolled at the Royal Libyan Military Academy, in Benghazi, with the ambition of gaining a following within the ranks of the army and overthrowing Libya's pro-Western monarch, King Idris. On September 1, 1969, while Idris was out of the country for medical treatment, Qaddafi led several fellow officers in seizing the government. They dissolved Parliament and established a Revolutionary Command Council to rule the newly named Libyan Arab Republic. Qaddafi declared himself the commander in chief of the armed forces, a position that made him the de facto head of state, and at 27 he became one of the youngest leaders in the Middle East and North Africa. Qaddafi's Islamic fundamentalist and quasi-socialistic conception of society eventually became known as the "Third Universal Theory," aspects of which he discussed in the *Green Book*, a three-volume work published in the late 1970s. "Qaddafi declared that his political system of permanent revolution would sweep away capitalism and socialism. But he hedged his bets by financing and arming a cornucopia of violent organizations, including the Irish Republican Army and African guerrilla groups, and he became an international pariah after his government was linked to terrorist attacks, particularly the 1988 bombing of a Pan Am jet over Lockerbie, Scotland, which killed 270 people," Neil MacFarquhar wrote for the *New York Times* (October 20, 2011, on-line). "By the time he was done, Libya had no parliament, no unified military command, no political parties, no unions, no civil society and no nongovernmental organizations. His ministries were hollow, with the notable exception of the state oil company." Qaddafi also periodically brutalized his own people, televising public trials and executions and bombing entire Libyan towns that he suspected of being opposition strongholds. Still, relations with the West normalized somewhat in the wake of 9/11, when Libya shared its intelligence on Al Qaeda with the U.S. and condemned the terrorist attacks on American soil. After Libya accepted responsibility for the Lockerbie bombing and agreed in 2003 to pay restitution to the families of victims, relations stabilized even further, and Great

Britain and the U.S. established diplomatic ties. Despite Qaddafi's somewhat increased credibility, MacFarquhar wrote, "the West and the rest of the Arab world tended to treat him as comic opera," thanks in some part to his flamboyant wardrobe of heavily decorated military uniforms and African robes as well as his cadre of high-heeled female bodyguards. In 2009 Qaddafi was appointed to a one-year term as head of the African Union. That year he made his first-ever speech at the United Nations General Assembly, alternately amusing and angering onlookers with a rambling, 90-minute discourse denigrating the Security Council, reiterating his long-held belief that Israel and Palestine should be united as a single state called Isratine, calling for renewed investigations into the assassinations of John F. Kennedy and Martin Luther King Jr., advocating that U.N. headquarters be moved to Libya, and theorizing that swine flu had been developed as a biological weapon, among other statements and demands. In a prescient blog entry for the *Daily Beast* (January 28, 2011), Philip Shenon cast doubts about Qaddafi's future, writing, "With Libya's immediate neighbors convulsed by public protests over the brutality and kleptocracy of their ruling families, a newly leaked cable from the U.S. Embassy in Libya suggests that strongman Muammar Qaddafi has created a decadent, money-hungry family dynasty that could find itself the target of the next Arab revolution in the streets." In February 2011 a riot broke out in Benghazi following the arrest of the human-rights activist Fethi Tarbel, and by the end of the month, rebel militias had taken control of the city of Misrata. In March the rebel National Transitional Council (NTC) declared itself Libya's sole representative. After months of relentless fighting, in August rebel forces entered Tripoli and destroyed Qaddafi's compound. In September an interim government was installed, and world leaders called for Qaddafi's rapidly dwindling loyalist forces to surrender. On October 20 NTC fighters captured Qaddafi in Sirte—dragging him from his hiding place in a large concrete pipe, beating him, and shooting him in the head. (The capture and beating were recorded on video, but the actual shooting is not seen on-screen; rebel forces have maintained that he was killed in a crossfire, but most international observers discount that version of events.) Qaddafi's son Mutassim was also killed, and the two corpses were put on public display for several days before being buried in an undisclosed location. Qaddafi had six other sons and a daughter. Of those sons, two have reportedly fled to Algeria and one to Niger, one is unaccounted for, and two were killed earlier in the conflict. In addition to the offspring still alive, Qaddafi is survived by his second wife, Safia Farkash. See *Current Biography* (1992). —M.R.

Obituary *New York Times* (on-line) Oct. 20, 2011

RITCHIE, DENNIS Sep. 9, 1941–Oct. 12, 2011 Computer programmer. Dennis Ritchie made enormous contributions to computer science by designing the widely used C programming language and co-developing the Unix operating system. "The tools that Dennis built—and their direct descendants—run pretty much everything today," Brian Kernighan, a Princeton University computer scientist, told Steve Lohr for the *New York Times* (October 13, 2011, on-line). Ritchie was born in Bronxville, New York, and moved with his family to Summit, New Jersey, as a child. His father, Alistair, worked as an engineer at nearby Bell Labs, and his mother, Jean, was a homemaker. In 1963 Ritchie graduated from Harvard University with a bachelor's degree in physics and remained to pursue a Ph.D. degree in applied mathematics. As a graduate student he worked at the computer center at the Massachusetts Institute of Technology (MIT) and became deeply interested in computing. In 1967, while still working toward his doctoral degree, he joined Bell Labs. (Bored by his classes, Ritchie never handed in his thesis.) At Bell Labs he began working with Kenneth Thompson on the Multics project, a multiorganizational effort that included Bell, MIT, and General Electric (GE). Multics, which is short for "multiplexed information and computing services," was intended to be a panacea for the growing pains of the emerging community of computer users. Early mainframes could accommodate only one user at a time, a wasteful and frustrating process when many researchers were competing for the opportunity to run their programs. During the 1960s time-sharing operating systems that allowed for multiple simultaneous users were created. The organizations behind the development of Multics hoped to build an even more ambitious operating system, one that could accommodate up to 300 users simultaneously. The costs of the project and the labor necessary to complete it grew unmanageable, and Bell Labs withdrew in 1969. Ritchie and Thompson were frustrated by the cancellation of the project and resolved to continue working on such a system. The result was Unix. Ritchie subsequently developed the C programming language, which made the Unix operating system portable, allowing its implementation on almost any computer system with a minimum of code changes. "The C language and Unix reflected a point of view, a different philosophy of computing than what had come before," Lohr wrote. "In the late '60s and early '70s, minicomputers were moving into companies and universities—smaller and at a fraction of the price of hulking mainframes. Minicomputers represented a step in the democratization of computing, and Unix and C were designed to open up computing to more people and collaborative working styles. Mr. Ritchie, Mr. Thompson and their Bell Labs colleagues were making not merely software but, as Mr. Ritchie once put it, 'a system around which fellowship can form.'" Ritchie wrote a seminal text, *The C Programming Language* (1978; updated in 1988), which sold millions of copies and was translated into more than two dozen languages. He remained at Bell Labs until his retirement, in 2007. For the last few years of his life, he suffered from poor health, battling prostate cancer and heart disease. He died at his home in Berkeley Heights, New Jersey, at the age of 70. He was survived by his brothers, Bill and John, and his sister, Lynn. In a tribute posted on the Bell Labs Web site, the three wrote, "Dennis was an unfailingly kind, sweet, unassuming, and generous brother—and of course a complete geek. He had a hilariously dry sense of humor, and a keen appreciation for life's absurdities—though his world view was entirely de-

void of cynicism or mean-spiritedness. We are terribly sad to have lost him, but touched beyond words to realize what a mark he made on the world." See *Current Biography* (1999). —M.R.

Obituary *New York Times* (on-line) Oct. 13, 2011

ROBERTSON, CLIFF Sep. 9, 1923–Sep. 10, 2011 Actor. Although Cliff Robertson once told a reporter, "Nobody made more mediocre films than I did," the actor nonetheless enjoyed a long and largely successful career that included such hit pictures as *Picnic* (1955); *PT 109* (1963), in which he portrayed John F. Kennedy; *Charly* (1968), for which he won an Oscar; and *Spider-Man* (2002). An only child, Clifford Parker Robertson 3d was born in La Jolla, California, to Clifford Robertson, the heir to a ranching fortune, and Andree Robertson. His parents were divorced when he was one, and his mother died when he was two. He had little contact with his father and was raised by his maternal grandmother and an aunt. At La Jolla High School, Robertson acted in school plays, mainly, as he told reporters, to get out of classes. After serving for a time in the Merchant Marine, Robertson, who was exempt from military conscription during World War II due to a weak left eye, spent a year at Antioch College, in Yellow Springs, Ohio, where he studied journalism and did field reporting for the *Springfield (Ohio) News*. Leaving Antioch without earning a degree, he settled in New York City and supported himself with menial jobs while studying at the Actors Studio and looking for stage roles. In the summer of 1947, he toured the Catskills in a production of *Three Men on a Horse*, and later the same year he almost reached Broadway in an important supporting role in *The Lady and the Tiger*. (The production closed after a disappointing tryout in Clifton, New Jersey.) From 1948 to 1950 Robertson was in the national company of the hit show *Mister Roberts*, and he made his New York City debut as Matthew Anderson in *Late Love* at the National Theatre on October 13, 1953. In February 1955 he portrayed Peter Whitfield in a New York City Center production of *The Wisteria Trees*, directed by Joshua Logan, and when Logan was casting for the film *Picnic*, he selected Robertson to play Alan, the suitor displaced by the lustful vagrant (William Holden). On the strength of his performance in *Picnic*, Columbia Pictures signed Robertson to a long-term contract. His Columbia films, few of which earned praise from critics, included *Autumn Leaves* (1956), *Gidget* (1959), *Battle of the Coral Sea* (1959), *Underworld U.S.A.* (1961), and *The Interns* (1962). (Later, in 1977, Robertson's fortunes became tangled with Columbia's once more, when he blew the whistle on David Begelman, the studio's president, upon discovering that Begelman had forged his name to a $10,000 check. Begelman, suspected of embezzling tens of thousands of dollars from the studio, pleaded no contest to charges of grand theft, was sentenced to three years of probation, and was fired.) At other studios in the late 1950s and early 1960s, Robertson made such films as *The Girl Most Likely* (1957), *The Naked and the Dead* (1958), *The Big Show* (1961), and *My Six Loves* (1963). His big break came when Warner Bros. chose him to play John F. Kennedy in *PT-109* (1963), the story of the future president's exploits as the commander of a motor torpedo boat in the Solomon Islands during World War II. Despite the added leverage he gained from *PT-109*, Robertson continued to be cast in more than his fair share of middling roles, in such uneven pictures as *633 Squadron* (1964), *Love Has Many Faces* (1965), *Masquerade* (1965), *Up from the Beach* (1965), and *The Devil's Brigade* (1968). He fared somewhat better on television, which tended to provide him with meatier roles than Hollywood. He starred in *Days of Wine and Roses* in its original, TV version, and he won an Emmy Award for his performance in *The Game*, shown on NBC's *Chrysler Theatre* during the 1965–66 season. His only Oscar-winning performance was in a role that Robertson himself had created on television. During the 1960–61 season he had played the title character in a network presentation of *The Two Worlds of Charly Gordon*, based on Daniel Keyes's book *Flowers for Algernon*, a poignant tale about a developmentally disabled man who undergoes brain surgery and blossoms into a genius only to regress gradually to his former state. Robertson was taken with the role, bought the movie rights to it, and finally, after years of trying at various studios, persuaded Selmur Productions, a subsidiary of ABC, to make the picture with him in the role of Charly and Claire Bloom in the part of the therapist with whom Charly falls in love. Released in 1968, *Charly* won Robertson best-actor honors at the 1969 Academy Awards ceremony. Although he never again attained that level of acclaim, Robertson remained busy, appearing in a wide variety of TV movies and miniseries, including *The Man Without a Country* (1973), *A Tree Grows in Brooklyn* (1974), *The Yanks Are Coming* (1974), *My Father's House* (1975), *Return to Earth* (1976), *Obsession* (1976), *Washington: Behind Closed Doors* (1977), *Two of a Kind* (1982), *Dreams of Gold: The Mel Fisher Story* (1986), and *Ford: The Man and the Machine* (1987). He was also familiar to TV viewers with his recurring role as Dr. Michael Ranson on the series *Falcon Crest*, on which he appeared in 1983 and 1984, and for his many commercials for AT&T, a company he represented for a decade. In 2002 Robertson acted in the blockbuster film *Spider-Man*, playing the superhero's uncle. While his character was killed in the first movie, he was seen in flashbacks in the 2004 and 2007 sequels, the latter of which marked his final screen credit. Robertson's marriage to the actress Cynthia Stone lasted from 1957 to 1960 and produced one daughter, Stephanie. It ended in divorce, as did his second marriage, to the actress Dina Merrill. That union, which lasted from 1966 to 1986, produced a daughter, Heather, who died of cancer in 2007. Robertson, a devoted amateur pilot, died of natural causes a day after his 88th birthday. He is survived by Stephanie and one grandchild. See *Current Biography* (1969). —M.R.

Obituary *New York Times* (on-line) Sep. 10, 2011

ROSS, ROBERT Dec. 26, 1918–Mar. 19, 2011 Entrepreneur. Robert Ross spent most of his career running an import-export business, selling such items as fertilizer, grain, pantyhose, and anti-snoring medicine, before founding the Ross University School of Medicine, a for-profit medical school in the Caribbean. The youngest of the six children of Nathan Rosen, a paint contractor, and Minnie Rosen, Robert Rosen, who later changed his surname to Ross, grew up in Detroit, Michigan. His father died when he was eight years old, and to help support his family, Ross took a job delivering newspapers. By the time he was 15, his route—which included morning and afternoon deliveries—had become one of the biggest in Detroit, and although the Great Depression was raging, he was netting over $100 a week—four times the average weekly salary in the U.S. in 1933. After his graduation from high school, in about 1936, Ross continued to deliver papers until he joined a brother-in-law of his in the wholesale-pharmaceuticals business. Dissatisfied with his salary—$15 a week—Ross supplemented his pay by selling over-the-counter drugs and other items to grocery stores, which few salesmen had done before then. After concluding that there was little future for him in wholesale drugs, Ross quit his job and enrolled in a business course at the University of Michigan at Ann Arbor. He later abandoned the course to engage in various entrepreneurial pursuits. By age 25 Ross had married and become a father. In 1944, toward the end of World War II, he was drafted into the U.S. Army and sent to serve in Europe. While overseas he earned money by buying 20 Mickey Mouse watches from a Frenchman at five dollars each and then selling them individually to Russian soldiers for $100. Successfully avoiding an army assignment to a bomb-disposal group after the war in Europe ended, he used his experience in buying and selling to obtain a job as the manager of a post exchange (known as a PX, a retail store on an army base that caters to soldiers). He also worked at the Coca-Cola bottling plant, in Stuttgart, Germany, which made it possible for him to trade soft drinks for food for his supply-short unit. Returning to Detroit, he became a distributor of television sets, selling them to bars in anticipation of sports broadcasting. Ross's actions eventually attracted the interest of the local Mafia, headed by the nephew of Al Capone, who was worried that Ross was hurting his jukebox business. Ross responded by making Capone's nephew a business partner. Ross moved to New York City in 1948 and began supplying electron tubes to such manufacturers as RCA, General Electric, and Sylvania. He also opened his own transistor factory. Expanding overseas, he created Eastern Europe Inc. and began importing, exporting, and trading in lumber, plastics, grain, crude oil, textiles, electronics, and aluminum and other metals. In 1973 Eastern Europe Inc. was among 150 U.S. companies invited to Communist China, after U.S. president Richard Nixon and Mao Zedong, the leader of the Communist Chinese government, agreed to normalize relations between the two nations. In 1976, upon learning that a staff member's son had been rejected by every U.S. medical school to which he had applied, Ross resolved to establish a medical school outside the U.S. Set up with the help of various consultants, the Ross University School of Medicine opened in 1979 on the island nation of Dominica, with about a dozen students. Classes were held in a motel in Roseau, Dominica's capital city, until the building's destruction by Hurricane David later that year. Afterward, Ross built a new facility on the 46-acre campus of a defunct college. The medical school attracted retired faculty from U.S.-based schools who were interested in earning an income in the Caribbean. Because the school required students to pass the same exams as students in American schools, it was approved by the U.S. government as a recipient of federal funds, in the form of guaranteed student loans. Ross allowed qualified overseas students who lacked the money for tuition to be admitted if they could secure barter agreements whereby—usually in return for the student's promise to provide medical services in his or her home country after earning an M.D. degree—their governments would provide some commodity, such as a quantity of steel, in exchange for free tuition. The school proved successful; about 95 percent of its graduates were accepted to residencies at U.S. hospitals, often in hard-to-fill positions in urban neighborhoods. In 2000 Ross sold the school—which by then also included a veterinary school and boasted 1,700 medical and 1,000 veterinary students—for $135 million to a private-equity firm. That same year Ross tried to open a for-profit medical school in Casper, Wyoming, but the proposal failed after it was opposed by the Wyoming Medical Society. Ross went on to open a nursing school, in 2005, and a medical school, in 2008, on St. Kitts, an island in the West Indies. Later Ross became involved in the field of remote learning, in which American universities offer courses through the Internet. Ross is the recipient of an honorary doctoral degree from the Southern School of Optometry, in Memphis, Tennessee, and he also bought the title Lord of the Manor of Halton Lea, Northumberland, at a London auction. As a result, he was able to print business cards that read, "Dr. Robert Ross, Lord of the Manor of Halton Lea, Northumberland." Ross, who died from cancer of the urethra, is survived by his wife, Anne; his sons, Warren and Bryan; his daughters, Nancy Ross and Carole Walker; two stepdaughters; 13 grandchildren; and six great-grandchildren. See *Current Biography* (2002). —W.D.

Obituary *New York Times* (on-line) Mar. 21, 2011

ROSZAK, THEODORE Nov. 15, 1933–July 5, 2011 Social critic; writer; educator. Theodore Roszak was the author of *The Making of a Counter Culture: Reflections on the Technocratic Society and Its Youthful Opposition* (1969), which examined the youth revolution of the day and popularized the term "counterculture." Roszak was born in Chicago, Illinois. His father, Anton, was a carpenter. Roszak earned a B.A. degree from the University of California, Los Angeles, in 1955, and a Ph.D. degree from Princeton University, in New Jersey, in 1958. From 1959 to 1963 he taught history at Stanford University, in California. He then worked in London, England, editing *Peace News*, a pacifist journal, and later became a professor of history at what is now California State University, East Bay, retiring from that post in 1998. A prolific writer, Roszak began in 1966 to write regularly for the *Nation* and then went on to contribute to the *Atlantic, Harper's*, the *New York Times*, and many other publications. In 1969, the

same year as the Woodstock Festival, Roszak's book *The Making of a Counter Culture* attempted to explain what seemed to be widespread but unrelated outbursts of student dissent. The book was both a study of the youth movement's origins and a critique of the society that had produced that movement. Roszak's principal thesis was that contemporary technocratic society, dominated by "the myth of objective consciousness" and the pursuit of science, had alienated young people, who sought alternatives in magical or visionary approaches to experience, such as Eastern religions, psychedelic drugs, and nontraditional, communitarian relationships. The volume, which was nominated for a National Book Award, became a minor classic as a sourcebook for the young; and even critics who found his view of science to be uninformed and misguided agreed that the book offered sociological insight into the foundations of the youth movement. Another of his significant books was *Where the Wasteland Ends: Politics and Transcendence in Post-Industrial Society* (1972). In the book's introduction Roszak explained: "My purpose is to discover how . . . the essential religious impulse was exiled from our culture, what effect this has had on the quality of our life and course of our politics, and what part the energies of transcendence must now play in saving urban-industrial society from self-annihilation." The book was also nominated for a National Book Award. As the 1970s neared their end, Roszak offered a cultural history of the decade in *Person/Planet: The Creative Disintegration of Industrial Society* (1978). Disagreeing with those who saw the period as simply a conservative reaction to the radicalism of the 1960s, Roszak pointed to many signs that people still yearned for religious transcendence and "authentic personhood." Roszak's later nonfiction books include *The Cult of Information: A Neo-Luddite Treatise on High-Tech, Artificial Intelligence, and the True Art of Thinking* (first published in 1985 and updated several times), *The Voice of the Earth: An Exploration of Ecopsychology* (1992), *America the Wise: Longevity, Revolution and the True Wealth of Nations* (1998), *The Gendered Atom: Reflections on the Sexual Psychology of Science* (1999), *World, Beware!: American Triumphalism in an Age of Terror* (2005), and *The Making of an Elder Culture: Reflections on the Future of America's Most Audacious Generation* (2009). In a tribute published in the *New York Times* (July 12, 2011, on-line), Douglas Martin quipped, "Roszak chronicled a generation's journey from hippies to hip replacement." Roszak also wrote several novels, including *Bugs* (1981), *Flicker* (1991), *The Memoirs of Elizabeth Frankenstein* (1995), and *The Devil and Daniel Silverman* (2003). He died at his home, in Berkeley, California, after being treated for liver cancer. He is survived by his wife, Betty; daughter, Kathryn; and a granddaughter. See *Current Biography* (1982). —D.K.

Obituary *New York Times* (on-line) July 12, 2011

RUBOTTOM, R. RICHARD Feb. 13, 1912–Dec. 6, 2010 Diplomat; university administrator. R. Richard Rubottom greatly helped to influence U.S. relations with Latin America. He is particularly known for serving as a high-level government strategist on

American policy toward Cuba in the 1950s. Roy Richard Rubottom Jr. was born in Brownwood, Texas, to Jennie Eleanor (Watkins) Rubottom and Roy Richard Rubottom Sr., who ran a boardinghouse. After attending public schools in Brownwood, Rubottom enrolled as a scholarship student at Southern Methodist University, in Dallas, Texas, in 1928. Editor of the school newspaper, he was also a member of the Lambda Chi Alpha and Sigma Delta fraternities. In 1932 Rubottom received a bachelor's degree in journalism from Southern Methodist, where he also earned a master's degree in international relations. (Various sources list either 1933 or 1935 as the year he was awarded the master's degree.) He subsequently pursued a doctoral degree in Latin American affairs at the University of Texas at Austin, but he never completed the requirements of the program because of his work obligations. To earn a living Rubottom took on jobs as a traveling secretary for Lambda Chi Alpha, a kitchen-equipment salesman with the Century Metalcraft Corp. in Chicago, a salesman of oil-field equipment with the Guyberson Corp. in Dallas, Texas, and an assistant dean of student life at the University of Texas. During World War II he served in the U.S. Navy and was stationed in Mexico and Paraguay, among other places. In 1946, following his discharge, Rubottom was hired as a vice president of the State National Bank in Corsicana, Texas. During that time he took a special exam for war veterans with experience in international affairs, and in 1947 he was appointed to the Foreign Service. After being posted to such locales as Colombia and Spain, Rubottom was recalled to Washington in 1956 and appointed deputy assistant secretary of state for inter-American affairs. The following year he was appointed assistant secretary of state. In that post his specific duties included supervising U.S. embassies in Latin America, maintaining relations with Latin American representatives in Washington, initiating and coordinating policy with regard to the Inter-American system for money and banking, and carrying out policies concerning Puerto Rico. When Rubottom accompanied then–Vice President Richard M. Nixon on his tour of eight South American countries, in 1958, he witnessed anti-American rioting in Peru and Venezuela. The participants in those violent demonstrations attributed the deplorable economic conditions in their countries to U.S. policies and voiced their dissatisfaction with America's perceived cordiality to Latin American dictators. Rubottom, who reportedly earned Nixon's ire during the trip, maintained that the protests obscured the warmth with which the majority of Latin Americans received the mission. He was subsequently removed from his position as assistant secretary of state, and in 1960, under President John F. Kennedy, he became the ambassador to Argentina. In later years he held the post of vice president of Southern Methodist University, where he also taught political science. In addition, he served for a time as the president of the University of the Americas in Puebla, Mexico. Rubottom, 98 years old at the time of his death, was predeceased in 2008 by his wife of almost seven decades, the former Billy Ruth Young. He is survived by his two sons, John and Frank; his daughter, Eleanor;

four grandchildren; and one great-grandchild. See *Current Biography* (1959). —J.P.

Obituary *New York Times* (on-line) Dec. 19, 2010

SABATO, ERNESTO June 24, 1911–Apr. 30, 2011
Writer; activist. With the awarding in 1985 of the Miguel de Cervantes Prize—considered the equivalent of the Nobel in Hispanic letters—the Spanish government paid homage to the Argentine writer Ernesto Sabato's decades of literary endeavor. His novels and essays, which have been translated into several languages, have moved readers the world over with their unsparing examination of the human condition and their concern for the survival of moral values in the modern world. Sabato's fame as a writer was enhanced by his role as a champion of social justice, which received international attention when he presided over the commission investigating the cases of those persons who disappeared during Argentina's military dictatorships. Sabato was born in Rojas, a small town in Buenos Aires Province, 160 miles west of Argentina's capital. He was the 10th of 11 sons of Francisco Sabato and Juana Maria Ferrari de Sabato, Italian immigrants who settled in Argentina at the end of the 19th century and established the town's flour mill. He attended the Colegio Nacional in La Plata, completing his high-school education in 1928. He enrolled the following year in the Instituto de Fisica at La Plata's Universidad Nacional, but, swept up by the political currents of the day, he was distracted from his studies for several years by his involvement in anarchist and Communist movements. Although he was appointed to the post of secretary general of Argentina's Communist Youth organization in 1933, he suffered a crisis of faith in communism while attending a party congress in Brussels and fled to Paris rather than go to the Soviet Union for an indoctrination course. In Paris he stole a volume of mathematical analysis from a bookstore and, as he described it, found "inner peace" in the order and logic of scientific thought. He subsequently returned home to Argentina and his university studies, completing work on his doctoral degree in 1937. In 1938 Sabato received a fellowship from the Asociación Argentina para el Progreso de las Ciencias to study atomic radiation at the prestigious Joliot-Curie Laboratory in Paris. Once back in France, he was irresistibly drawn to the world of art and became involved with the surrealist group living there, particularly with André Breton. He began writing a never-finished novel, *La fuente muda* ("The Silent Fountain"), and at the same time continued his scientific research. In 1939 he moved to the U.S. because his fellowship had been transferred to the Massachusetts Institute of Technology (MIT), in Cambridge. After returning to Argentina, Sabato accepted professorships in quantum theory and the theory of relativity at the Universidad Nacional in La Plata and in physics at the Instituto del Profesorado in Buenos Aires. He held those appointments from 1940 to 1945, when he was dismissed because of his opposition to Juan Domingo Peron's government. While teaching, Sabato continued to write. In 1941 he became a regular contributor to *Sur*, Argentina's leading literary magazine. In 1943 he took a leave of ab-

sence from teaching, retreating to the hills of Córdoba Province to write. He decided not to return to academia. In 1945 he published the book he had worked on during his sabbatical, *Uno y el universo* ("One and the Universe"), which presented Sabato's condemnation of the moral neutrality of scientific thought, as well as his scrutiny of a variety of philosophical and literary issues. The book was well received in Buenos Aires, where it won both the Municipal Prose Prize and the Sociedad Argentina de Escritores' Sash of Honor. Because he still did not have enough money to live on, despite that literary recognition, in 1947 Sabato accepted an appointment with the United Nations Educational, Scientific, and Cultural Organization (UNESCO) in Paris, but finding himself unable to cope with the bureaucratic nature of the work, he left after only two months. On his way back to Buenos Aires, he began writing his novel *El tunel* (*The Tunnel*). After several publishing houses in Buenos Aires rejected the finished manuscript, Sabato's friends at *Sur* had it printed in 1948. An immediate best-seller, *El tunel* gained international recognition. Among his subsequent works are the 1961 novel widely considered to be his masterpiece, *Sobre heroes y tumbas* (*On Heroes and Tombs*); the 1963 essay collection *El escritor y sus fantasmas* ("The Writer's Ghosts"); the 1969 essay collection *La convulsion politica y social de nuestro tiempo* ("The Political and Social Convulsion of Our Time"); the 1973 essay collection *La cultura en la encrucijada nacional* ("Culture at the National Crossroads"); the 1974 novel *Abaddon el Exterminador* (*Angel of Darkness*); and the 1981 essay collection *La robotizacion del hombre* ("The Robotization of Man"). During the military regimes with which Argentina was burdened from 1976 to 1983, Sabato was a bold and outspoken critic of repression and violations of human rights, despite the repeated threats that were made against his life. Those threats continued after Raúl Alfonsin, the democratically elected president, named him in 1983 to head the 12-member National Commission on the Disappearance of Persons, which spent nine months investigating the kidnapping and torture of alleged opponents of the military governments. Presented to the government in September 1984, the completed report, known as "El Informe Sabato," was a damning 50,000-page collection of evidence documenting the disappearance of 8,961 people at the hands of the armed forces. That revelation was later condensed into a 500-page book entitled *Nunca Mas* ("Never Again"). As a consequence of the work of the commission, several former heads of military governments faced public trial to establish their responsibility for the disappearances. Sabato died at the age of 99 from complications of bronchitis. Matilde Kusminsky Richter, his wife of over six decades, died in 1998. He is survived by Elvira Gonzalez Fraga, his longtime friend and collaborator; a son, Mario; and several grandchildren and great-grandchildren. See *Current Biography* (1985). —M.R.

Obituary *New York Times* (on-line) May 1, 2011

SANDAGE, ALLAN June 18, 1926–Nov. 13, 2010 Astronomer. For decades Allan Sandage, who began his career as an assistant to the influential astronomer Edwin Hubble, was involved in one of the most ambitious of human endeavors: determining the size and age of the entire universe by making careful observations with powerful telescopes. Keith Cooper wrote for *Astronomy Now* (November 16, 2010, online), "As Hubble's protege, Sandage never came close to achieving his mentor's celebrity status, nor did he try to, but while Hubble set the ball rolling, it was Sandage who corrected his mistakes and introduced unprecedented accuracy into the measurements of the Universe, continuing the tradition of showing how what we think we know is merely the tip of the iceberg." An only child, Sandage was born in Iowa City, Iowa, and raised in Ohio. His father was a professor of business, and his mother was a homemaker. Sandage became interested in astronomy in his youth, after looking through a friend's telescope. His father later bought him his own, and he began watching the skies both night and day; for one four-year period in his teens, he kept a record of the number of sunspots he observed. Sandage attended Miami University, in Oxford, Ohio—where his father taught—and studied physics and philosophy. After two years of study, he was drafted into the U.S. Navy; he served for 18 months during World War II as an electronics specialist in Gulfport, Louisiana, and at Treasure Island, in San Francisco, California. By the time he left the military, his father had started teaching at the University of Illinois, in Urbana, so he enrolled there. Sandage gained practical experience in astronomy by working as a volunteer in the university's observatory. In 1948 he earned a bachelor's degree in physics. When Sandage graduated from Urbana, the grand 200-inch Hale mirror telescope—the biggest telescope in the world at the time—was being constructed, at the Palomar Observatory, in Southern California. Eager to work at the observatory, he entered the newly created astronomy program at the California Institute of Technology (Caltech), in Pasadena, which was then running the Palomar Observatory in collaboration with Carnegie Observatories. While there, Sandage got opportunities to work with some of the best-known astronomers of the day, among them Hubble. After Hubble suffered a heart attack and sought a graduate student to help him, Sandage took on that duty. He began making regular trips to Palomar, which was about two hours southeast of Pasadena, to serve as Hubble's surrogate observer. Sandage earned a Ph.D. degree from Caltech in 1953, and when Hubble died that year, Sandage took over his research. As data poured in and errors were discovered in Hubble's work (the result of the weaker telescopes the elder scientist had been using), Sandage gradually revised Hubble's estimate of the age of the universe and corrected other errors. By 1958 Sandage had announced that the universe was actually seven to 13 billion years old—much older than Hubble had estimated. Cooper wrote, "Literally overnight Sandage had expanded the Universe to unimaginable scales, just as Hubble had done before him, and this resulted in a more accurate assessment of Hubble's Constant, which is the measure of the expansion of the Universe." (In 2001 NASA scientists, with access to increasingly sophisticated instruments, including the orbiting telescope that bears Hubble's name, announced that the universe was about 12 billion years old.) In his later years Sandage continued to make important observations about the ages of stars, the formation of galaxies, and the existence of quasars, among other areas. In addition to the comprehensive *Hubble Atlas of Galaxies* (1961), he wrote more than 500 papers. Although he retired from the Carnegie Observatories in 1997 as a staff member emeritus, he was active up until almost the time of his death, publishing a paper in the *Astrophysical Journal* in June 2010. Sandage, known for his moody nature and tendency to argue with his fellow scientists, was the recipient of numerous awards, including the prestigious National Medal of Science and the lucrative Crafoord Prize of the Swedish Royal Academy of Sciences. Sandage died of pancreatic cancer at his home in San Gabriel, California. He is survived by his wife, Mary, and his two sons, David and John. See *Current Biography* (1999). —W.D.

Obituary *New York Times* (on-line) Nov. 17, 2010

SCHAEFER, WILLIAM DONALD Nov. 2, 1921–Apr. 18, 2011 Former Baltimore politician. "New York had its Fiorella H. La Guardia. Chicago had its Daleys," Robert D. McFadden wrote for the *New York Times* (April 18, 2011, on-line), "and Baltimore had William Donald Schaefer: the name on park benches, garbage trucks, office buildings, construction sites, horse races at Pimlico—and on the psyche of Baltimoreans in the 1970s and '80s." As mayor of Baltimore, Maryland, for 16 years, Schaefer was credited with transforming the city from the dilapidated port known as "Mobtown" or "Survival City" in the early 1970s into a modern tourist center, complete with upscale waterfront businesses and restaurants and a new National Aquarium. Critics called Schaefer impulsive, impatient, and a bully, but admirers praised his action-oriented and decisive manner. After serving as mayor of Baltimore, Schaefer was elected in 1986 as the 58th governor of Maryland by the greatest margin of victory in the state's gubernatorial history. After two terms as governor, he served two terms as state comptroller before being ousted in his 2006 reelection bid—his first defeat in over half a century. William Donald Schaefer was born in West Baltimore, the son of William Henry and Tululu Irene (Skipper) Schaefer. He was educated in Baltimore public schools and graduated from Baltimore City College in 1939. After obtaining an LL.B. degree from the University of Baltimore law school, in 1942, he entered the U.S. Army, earning officer rank and supervising military hospitals in Europe. After his return to the U.S., Schaefer practiced real-estate law while working toward an LL.M. degree from the University of Baltimore, which he received in 1951. Concerned with housing and city planning in Baltimore, Schaefer joined citizen associations, eventually assuming leadership roles. After two failed bids for a city-council seat in the 1950s, he received his needed break in 1955, when, with backing from a local Democratic activist, Irv Kovens, he won his third bid. In 1967 he became city-council president. Over the next few years, Thomas J. D'Alesandro Jr., who

was then the mayor of Baltimore, assigned more and more responsibility to Schaefer. In 1971, after D'Alesandro decided not to seek reelection, Schaefer entered the contest for the Democratic nomination, the winner of which was virtually assured the mayor's post in a city where registered Democrats outnumbered Republicans five to one. Running on his record in the city council, Schaefer received 56 percent of the vote in the Democratic primary and easily won the general election. Early in his administration he created special city agencies that reported directly to him as a means of combating inefficiency and bureaucratic red tape at City Hall. During his tenure he also helped the city obtain a new subway system, convention center, science museum, outdoor concert pavilion, and new offices and hotels. Schaefer's most lasting mark on Baltimore was the redevelopment of a 3.2-acre waterfront site known as Harborplace. The complex, which included a network of shops and restaurants developed by the urban planner James W. Rouse, adjoined by the $21.3 million National Aquarium, opened in 1981. Harborplace became the symbol of the "new Baltimore," a shining city for tourists to visit rather than a decrepit urban byway between New York City and Washington, D.C. Critics had scoffed when Schaefer promised to turn Baltimore into a tourist center, but Harborplace, in its first year of operation, 1980–81 (before the opening of the aquarium), attracted 18 million visitors, more than Florida's Walt Disney World. It also created thousands of jobs. Reelected three times, by 1983 Schaefer was so closely identified with the city that he adopted the campaign slogan "Vote for Baltimore"; that year he won reelection by the largest margin he ever received, sweeping every ward. He was known for his unorthodox methods; for example, he once sold 500 abandoned lots for one dollar apiece to urban homesteaders and commercial shells for $100 to businessmen. He also made a habit of visiting city neighborhoods on weekends, looking for potholes, broken street lamps, littered parks, or missing bus shelters, and then, on Monday mornings, dispatching "action memos" in which he mandated that the problems be taken care of immediately. He regularly used his influence to push forward development projects and lure new businesses, and he promoted himself and the city through flamboyant means. For instance, when the new National Aquarium was not ready to open by its July 4, 1981 deadline, he donned a striped Victorian swimsuit and plunged into the seal pool. In the spring of 1986, Schaefer, who had been singled out as a strong contender for the Maryland State House since 1981, entered the campaign for the Democratic nomination for the governorship. In September 1986 he won the Democratic gubernatorial primary, defeating the runner-up, the liberal Democrat Stephen H. Sachs, with 62 percent of the vote. Then, in November, he was elected governor with an overwhelming 82 percent of the vote. To the surprise of some of his critics—who feared he would become little more than the "governor of Baltimore"—Schaefer traveled widely in the state, visiting regions long neglected before his tenure and dispensing state aid to resolve local problems. He overhauled the state legal code and was credited with improving social programs, education, transportation, and pollution-cleanup efforts. He also oversaw the completion of the publicly financed Oriole Park, at Camden Yards, in 1992. After leaving office due to term limits, in 1995, Schaefer joined a Baltimore law firm. He also held a chair named after him at the University of Maryland. In 1998 he won the state comptroller's job and served two relatively un-noteworthy terms, occasionally gaining attention for his feuds with Democratic governor Parris N. Glendening. He lost his reelection bid in 2006. Schaefer never married; he lived for much of his life with his mother (who died in 1983) in the row house in which he grew up. After he became governor, his childhood friend Hilda Mae Snoops, a divorcée, served as his official hostess in the governor's mansion. She died in 1999. Schaefer died at a retirement home in Catonsville, Maryland. See *Current Biography* (1988). —M.R.M.

Obituary *New York Times* (on-line) Apr. 18, 2011

SHALIKASHVILI, JOHN M. June 27, 1936–July 23, 2011 Military leader. Four-star general John Shalikashvili, a native of Poland, was the first foreign-born chairman of the U.S. Joint Chiefs of Staff. Shalikashvili was born in Warsaw, the second of the three children of Dmitri Shalikashvili, who hailed from the Soviet republic of Georgia, and Maria Shalikashvili, a Pole of half-German, half-Russian ancestry. His father was separated from the rest of the family after Germany invaded Poland in September 1939. During the invasion Dmitri Shalikashvili defended his adopted land as a member of the cavalry, which surrendered to the Nazis after a few weeks. Briefly imprisoned, he was released with the help of his wife, who had relatives in Germany. In 1942, hoping to fight for Georgia's independence, he became a liaison officer for the German-organized Georgian Legion, which was instead sent to help repel the Allied invasion of Normandy in June 1944. Following the Allied liberation of France, he was transferred to a Georgian battalion in Italy under the command of the Waffen SS, Hitler's elite shock troops. (John Shalikashvili did not learn about this part of his father's life until his Senate confirmation hearings, nearly 50 years later.) Meanwhile, since 1942 the Shalikashvilis had been living in an elegant six-room apartment in Warsaw. In August 1944 the Polish Resistance waged a full-scale rebellion against the German occupiers, who crushed the 63-day uprising with artillery shelling and bombing. With the Resistance forces fighting in the barricaded streets, Maria Shalikashvili moved her family into the basement. After surviving for a time with no water, no electricity, and virtually no food, Maria Shalikashvili and her children were transported by cattle car to a transit camp in eastern Germany. From there they traveled to Pappenheim, a Bavarian village, where they lived in a castle on the estate of wealthy relatives. The family was reunited when Dmitri Shalikashvili, who had been captured by the British in 1945, was released in 1946. Sponsored by a branch of the Episcopal church and by relatives who were willing to conceal the Nazi connection, John Shalikashvili and his family immigrated to the United States in 1952 and settled in Peoria, Illinois. His father got a job in the accounting department of the local utilities company, and his mother went to work as a bank clerk. Enrolling as a junior at Peoria Central High School, Shalikashvili took a full course load, and after school he improved his English-language skills by watching John Wayne movies. It did not take him long to become assimilated. He joined the German and soccer clubs, played tennis, and competed in track, cross-country, and table tennis. A good student, he received a scholarship to Bradley University in Peoria, where he studied mechanical engineering. He joined the Young Republicans and pledged a fraternity. He graduated with a B.S. degree in mechanical engineering in June 1958, a month after becoming a United States citizen and a month before he was drafted into the army. After serving the first six months of his hitch in Missouri and Arkansas as a private, Shalikashvili was selected for officer candidate school at Fort Sill, Oklahoma, in 1959. Later that year he was commissioned as a second lieutenant of artillery. His first field command, over a mortar platoon in Alaska from 1959 to 1960, proved to be so enjoyable that he decided to make the military his career. It was not until 1968, after stints in Texas and West Germany, that he first experienced combat. By then he had attained the rank of major and had been assigned as a senior district adviser to South Vietnamese forces in Trieu Phong, an area rife with Vietcong soldiers, just south of the North Vietnamese border. He earned a Bronze Star for leading an attack on two enemy-held islands. His responsibilities there went beyond fighting; he also helped supervise rice production, advised and trained the local militia, organized elections, and took part in various other political activities. In 1970 Shalikashvili earned a master's degree in international affairs from George Washington University, in Washington, D.C., and in 1971 he attained his first staff position, that of operations officer in South Korea. In 1975 he assumed command of an artillery battalion in Fort Lewis, Washington, and four years later he became a division artillery commander in Germany. In 1981 he began honing his diplomatic skills as chief of the Politico-Military Division, Office of the Deputy Chief of Staff for Operations and Plans at the Pentagon's Department of the Army. Promoted to brigadier general a few years later, he became deputy director of strategy, plans, and policy for the same department, later advancing to the position of director as a major general. In April 1991 Shalikashvili assumed command of Operation Provide Comfort, one of the largest humanitarian-relief efforts ever undertaken. Involving a total of about 23,000 troops from the U.S., Britain, France, Italy, Spain, and the Netherlands, it provided food, clothing, and relocation services to hundreds of thousands of Kurdish refugees who had fled the troops of the Iraqi dictator, Saddam Hussein, in the wake of the war in the Persian Gulf. Shalikashvili credited Operation Provide Comfort with expanding his view of the role the military could play in the world. "That was the first time that I saw firsthand what an enormous capacity the armed forces have for doing good," he once said. From August 1991 to June 1992, Shalikashvili served as assistant to Joint Chiefs of Staff chairman Colin Powell. He then earned his fourth star as a general and became supreme allied commander of U.S. forces in Europe and of NATO. Shalikashvili assumed the post of chairman of the Joint Chiefs of Staff in October 1993, succeeding Powell and becoming the first foreign-born soldier ever to hold that post. In his new capacity he advised President Bill Clinton on crises in Haiti, the Balkans, and other locales. Shalikashvili was in office during the implementation of the military's controversial "Don't Ask, Don't Tell" policy on gay soldiers, and while he initially supported the measure, he later came to advocate for gays' and lesbians' being allowed to serve openly. Shalikashvili retired in 1997 and became a visiting professor at Stanford's Center for International Security and Cooperation. In 2004 he suffered a stroke that left him partially paralyzed; his death was caused by a second stroke. Shalikashvili's first wife, Gunhild, died in 1965. He is survived by his second wife, Joan, and their son, Brant. See *Current Biography* (1995). —M.M.H.

Obituary *New York Times* (on-line) July 23, 2011

SHEARING, GEORGE Aug. 13, 1919–Feb. 14, 2011 Jazz musician; composer. George Shearing was a talented pianist who composed some 300 songs, including the jazz standard "Lullaby of Birdland." Shearing, the youngest of nine children, was born in London, England, to James Phillip Shearing, a coalman, and the former Ellen Amelia Brightner, who cleaned railway cars at night. Born blind, Shearing began studying music at the age of five. He was encouraged in his musical ambitions by a teacher at the Linden Lodge School for the Blind, in London, and during his late teens he decided to become a jazz pianist. He landed his first job as a piano player in a local pub in 1936. (Although he had been offered a college scholarship, his family desperately needed the small salary that he earned at the pub.) Shearing later became a member of the Frank Weir Quartet and the Claude Bampton All-Blind Band. In time he was named Britain's most popular jazz pianist—seven years in a row—by the editors of *Melody Maker* magazine and earned his own 15-minute BBC radio show. When the American jazz musicians Glenn Miller, Mel Powell, and Fats Waller heard Shearing perform in London, they suggested that he come to the United States. World War II delayed that trip. During the war Shearing toured England with the Ambrose Octet and entertained the troops. He moved to the U.S. in 1947, determined to find his own sound rather than merely imitating his American counterparts, and he eventually began working as an intermission pianist at the Three Deuces, a New York City nightclub. He also made guest appearances on such radio programs as the *Arthur Godfrey Show* and the *Piano Playhouse*. He began to collaborate with the vibraphonist Margie Hyams, the guitarist Chuck Wayne, the bassist John Levy, and the drummer Denzil Best, and in 1949 the quintet recorded the popular single "September in the Rain," which sold close to one million copies. In 1952 Shearing composed "Lullaby of Birdland," as the theme song for a radio show broadcast from New York City's famed Birdland nightclub. The tune, whose lyrics were written by George Weiss, went on to be covered by numerous artists, including Sarah Vaughan. Shearing spent most of the next three decades playing gigs with a quintet. Though its mem-

bers changed frequently, he molded the group into a fine-tuned machine that performed complex pieces with a suave and sophisticated style. During the 1950s and 1960s, the "Shearing sound" became widely known in jazz clubs across two continents. As a bandleader Shearing helped to popularize both bebop and classical music, making them more accessible for the general listener. To an extent the George Shearing Quintet became a prisoner of its own success. While always in demand, selling out rooms in both the United States and Europe, the group was restricted to playing the same tunes that had made it famous, a frustrating situation for Shearing. Starting in the late 1970s, he began working in duos, first with the bassist Brian Torff and later with the bassist, pianist, and composer Don Thompson. Shearing's work with Thompson, who was an excellent sight reader of music, gave him the freedom to be more spontaneous and creative in concert. In the early 1980s Shearing and Thompson also began working with the singer-composer Mel Torme. Joined also by Torme's drummer, Donny Osborne, they formed a quartet to be reckoned with. Of his 50th anniversary in music, which he celebrated in 1986, the pianist told John S. Wilson for the *New York Times* (February 23, 1986): "I wish it could go on forever. It's good in the 50th year of your career to find that you can still find the same degree of excitement about playing as you did in your first." Shearing, who had recorded with such singers as Peggy Lee, Nancy Wilson, and Nat King Cole, retired from the stage in 2004, after requiring hospitalization due to a fall. That same year he published an autobiography, *Lullaby of Birdland*. Shearing died of congestive heart failure at his home in New York City. He is survived by his second wife, Eleanor Geffert, and his daughter, Wendy Ann, from his first marriage, to Beatrice Bayes, which ended in divorce. (Shearing and Bayes, who met in an air-raid shelter during World War II, also had a son, who died in infancy.) Shearing performed for three U.S. presidents (Gerald R. Ford, Jimmy Carter, and Ronald Reagan) as well as for Queen Elizabeth II of England, who knighted him in 2007. See *Current Biography* (1998). —J.P.

Obituary *New York Times* (on-line) Feb. 14, 2011

SHEED, WILFRID Dec. 27, 1930–Jan. 19, 2011 Writer. The best-selling writer Wilfred Sheed drew on his bicultural experience as a British-born American to develop one of the most distinctive, polished, and urbane prose styles on either side of the Atlantic. "Mr. Sheed's characters are almost invariably stricken with an agonized sense of self-awareness, exacerbated by their Roman Catholicism," Christopher Lehmann-Haupt wrote for the *New York Times* (January 19, 2011, on-line) about Sheed's fiction. "They all but die of hyperconsciousness, laughing as they go to their fates." The second child of Francis "Frank" Sheed and Mary "Maisie" Ward, who co-founded the avant-garde Catholic publishing house Sheed & Ward, Wilfrid John Joseph Sheed was born in London, England. Because of the work of his eccentric parents, who as Anglican converts to Roman Catholicism were prominent in England's Oxford Movement, Sheed and his older sister, Rosemary, grew up surrounded by religious intellectuals and thinkers. (Sheen was the godson of the prolific English writer G. K. Chesterton.) When Sheed was three years old, his parents moved to New York to open the American branch of Sheed & Ward. He spent his early years attending schools in England and America, and as a result he viewed himself as an outsider at an early age. In 1940 he settled with his family in Torresdale, a suburb of Philadelphia, Pennsylvania. At the age of 14, Sheed was stricken with polio, and for the rest of his life, he walked with the aid of a leg brace and a cane. His dreams of becoming a professional baseball player dashed, he quickly turned to books, reading works by such authors as Ernest Hemingway, Ring Lardner, James Thurber, E. M. Forster, and P. G. Wodehouse—each of whom influenced Sheed's later writing style. He returned to England to study history at Lincoln College, part of the University of Oxford, earning a bachelor's degree in 1954 and a master's degree in 1957. Upon completing his studies Sheed briefly lived in Australia before settling in New York, where he took a job writing movie and book reviews for the Catholic magazine *Jubilee*. He served as an associate editor there from 1959 to 1966. In the 1960s Sheed also wrote drama criticism and served as a book-review editor for the liberal Catholic journal *Commonweal*, and in the 1970s he wrote a column called "The Good Word" for the *New York Times Book Review*. During that time Sheed began writing fiction. His debut novel, *A Middle Class Education* (1960), offers a satirical account of the Oxford education of a Rhodes scholar. Sheed's second novel, *The Hack* (1963), tells the story of Bert Flax, a writer of inspirational pieces for a Catholic publication. He followed that with *Square's Progress* (1965), about a marriage temporarily broken by boredom, and *Office Politics* (1966), which chronicles the rise and fall of staff members at a small liberal journal. The latter book was nominated for a National Book Award and received widespread critical praise. Sheed's other novels include *The Blacking Factory* (1968), *Max Jamison* (1970), *People Will Always Be Kind* (1973), *Transatlantic Blues* (1978), and *The Boys of Winter* (1987). Sheed also produced a steady stream of nonfiction. Among his notable nonfiction works were *Muhammad Ali* (1975), a portrait of the heavyweight boxing champion; *Clare Boothe Luce* (1982), an in-depth look into the life of the famed playwright, editor, and journalist; *Frank and Maisie: A Memoir with Parents* (1985), a comprehensive family history; *My Life as a Fan* (1993), an account of Sheed's lifelong passion for baseball; and *In Love with Daylight: A Memory of Recovery* (1995), a memoir in which Sheed recounted his recovery from major illnesses: polio, addiction to drugs and alcohol, depression, and cancer. For many years Sheed contributed to the *New Yorker* and other publications as a book reviewer and an essayist. Collections of his reviews and essays include *The Morning After* (1971), *The Good Word and Other Words* (1978), and *Essays in Disguise* (1990). Sheed's last published work, *The House That George Built: With a Little from Irving, Cole, and a Crew of About Fifty* (2007), a history of American popular music, became a bestseller. In 1987 he won a Grammy Award for best album-liner notes for the 1986 Frank Sinatra compilation album, *The Voice: Frank Sinatra, the Columbia*

Years (1943–1952). Sheed, who was a judge for the Book of the Month Club from 1972 to 1988, died of complications from a bacterial infection at a nursing home in Great Barrington, Massachusetts. He is survived by his second wife, Miriam Ungerer Sheed; his sister, Rosemary; three children—Francis, Elizabeth, and Marion—from his first marriage, which ended in divorce; two stepdaughters; and four grandchildren. See *Current Biography* (1981).—C.C.

Obituary *New York Times* (on-line) Jan. 19, 2011

SHRIVER, R. SARGENT Nov. 9, 1915–Jan. 18, 2011 Social activist; former government official. R. Sargent Shriver, a brother-in-law of President John F. Kennedy, was appointed in 1961 as the founding director of the Peace Corps, a volunteer organization that sends young Americans to work and teach in developing countries. Later, under President Lyndon B. Johnson, Shriver headed a new antipoverty agency, and he subsequently served as an ambassador to France. Throughout his life he remained devoted to volunteerism and the fight against poverty. Robert Sargent Shriver Jr. was born in Westminster, Maryland. His father was a banker with financial interests in Maryland and New York. (The Shrivers, a Roman Catholic family, had arrived in Maryland in 1693, and one ancestor, David Shriver, was a member of the first Congress, which added the Bill of Rights to the Constitution; another, Robert Owings, received an original land grant from Lord Baltimore.) Shriver studied at Yale University, where he was active on the *Yale Daily News* and founded the America First club at the university. He graduated cum laude in 1938 and three years later earned an LL.B. degree from Yale Law School. Shriver was employed briefly with the New York law firm Winthrop, Stimson, Putnam & Roberts before he enlisted in the U.S. Navy as an apprentice seaman. He received an ensign's commission in 1941 and served aboard battleships and submarines in the Atlantic and Pacific. Richly decorated, he was returned to inactive duty as a lieutenant commander in 1945. After his discharge Shriver pursued journalism instead of law and took a position as an assistant editor at *Newsweek*. In 1946 he was approached by Joseph P. Kennedy, a former U.S. ambassador to England and the chairman of the Securities Exchange Commission during the 1930s. Kennedy gave Shriver the assignment of editing the letters of his son Joseph P. Kennedy Jr., who had been killed on a mission over the English Channel during World War II. Subsequently, Kennedy took Shriver into his business organization and gave him other assignments. In 1947 Kennedy asked Shriver to go to Washington, D.C., to help his daughter Eunice Mary Kennedy in setting up a national conference on juvenile delinquency, under the authority of the attorney general. Settling in Chicago the following year, Shriver became active in the political and social life of Illinois. He and Eunice Kennedy were married in 1953. From 1955 to 1960 he sat on the Chicago board of education, serving as president of the organization for much of that time. He resigned to serve as an adviser to his brother-in-law Senator John F. Kennedy in his successful campaign for the U.S. presidency. In April 1961 Shriver became the director of the newly established Peace Corps. In

1964, the year after John F. Kennedy was assassinated, President Lyndon B. Johnson appointed Shriver director of the new Office of Economic Opportunity, a sprawling antipoverty agency that oversaw such programs as Head Start and the Job Corps. In 1967 Shriver founded the National Clearinghouse for Legal Services, later renamed the Sargent Shriver National Center on Poverty Law. In 1968 Johnson appointed Shriver ambassador to France, where he remained for two years before returning to the U.S. to explore other political possibilities. In 1972 he appeared on the Democratic ticket with presidential hopeful George McGovern; the two lost in a landslide to the Republican incumbents, Richard Nixon and Spiro Agnew. Undaunted, Shriver vied for the Democratic presidential nomination four years later. Knocked out of the crowded primary race by Jimmy Carter, who went on to victory in the general election, Shriver decided to leave the political arena. During his later years he practiced law and took on leadership roles with the Special Olympics, which had been founded by his wife in the late 1960s. Shriver, who was awarded the Presidential Medal of Freedom in 1994, is the subject of a 2004 biography by Scott Stossel, *Sarge: The Life and Times of Sargent Shriver*, as well as a 2008 PBS documentary, *American Idealist: The Story of Sargent Shriver*. He died at the age of 95, after suffering from Alzheimer's disease for several years. Predeceased, in 2009, by his wife, Shriver is survived by his sons, Robert, Timothy, Mark, and Anthony; his daughter, Maria, a broadcast journalist and a former first lady of California; and 19 grandchildren. See *Current Biography* (1961). —D.K.

Obituary *New York Times* (on-line) Jan. 18, 2011

SILBERMAN, CHARLES E. Jan. 31, 1925—Feb. 5, 2011 Writer. Charles E. Silberman combined the talents of an investigative journalist with those of a perceptive social analyst to produce important books on the most pressing domestic problems of the 20th century. Such volumes as *Crisis in Black and White* (1964), *Crisis in the Classroom: The Remaking of American Education* (1970), and *Criminal Violence, Criminal Justice* (1978)—each the result of years of painstaking research supported generously by a major foundation—won wide critical acclaim. Silberman was born in Des Moines, Iowa, and raised in New York City. In 1941 he graduated from DeWitt Clinton High School and enrolled in the liberal-arts program at Columbia University. From June 1943 to June 1946, he served with the U.S. Naval Reserve. In October 1946 he earned a B.A. degree from Columbia, where he subsequently remained for three years of graduate work in economics. In 1949 Silberman joined Columbia's faculty as an instructor and lecturer in economics. Four years later, when his wife became seriously ill and her medical bills outstripped his salary, he switched to a more lucrative writing career. Hired in 1953 by *Fortune* magazine, he wrote about economics and business, governmental economic policy, automation, corporate finance, consumer behavior, and, eventually, social problems. His first book, *Crisis in Black and White*, was the outgrowth of an article about urban problems that had been featured in the March 1962 issue of

Fortune. After the piece, which was titled "The City and the Negro," appeared, the public-affairs division of the Ford Foundation made a grant of $23,000 to Columbia on Silberman's behalf, enabling him to take a leave of absence from *Fortune* to research and write the full-length book, which was published at the height of the civil rights struggle. Speaking with the frankness that was to become the hallmark of his work, he admitted that he had deliberately set out to "offend and anger" both blacks and whites because the truth about American race relations was, in his words, "too terrible" not to offend them. *Crisis in Black and White* won the Four Freedoms Literary Award and the National Conference of Christians and Jews Superior Merit Award. His next book, *The Myths of Automation* (1966), is a collection of articles on technology and the labor market that had previously appeared, in slightly different forms, in *Fortune*. The year that book was published, Silberman took another leave of absence from *Fortune*, to direct a $300,000 educational-research project commissioned and funded by the Carnegie Corp. of New York. After more than three years of research and writing, including visits to 250 schools by Silberman and his staff, he published *Crisis in the Classroom*, a book that went far beyond its original goal of examining teacher education to analyze what was wrong with American schools at all levels, from the elementary school to the university, and to suggest ways to improve them. In 1972 Silberman was hired by the Ford Foundation to head its Study of Law and Justice, a $537,000 research project that culminated in *Criminal Violence, Criminal Justice*, which contained the assertion that "most of what is believed about crime and about the criminal justice system is false or irrelevant." "My goal is not simply to correct errors and clear up misunderstandings," Silberman wrote in his foreword. "It is to change the way Americans think about criminals and crime and about the operation of our system of criminal justice." Silberman was also the author of *A Certain People: American Jews and Their Lives Today* (1985). Active in such Jewish organizations as the now-defunct Synagogue Council of America, he described *A Certain People* as his most personal book. Silberman's wife, Arlene, to whom he had been married since 1948, died in 2010. He died of a heart attack the following year at his home in Sarasota, Florida, and is survived by his four sons (David, Richard, Jeffrey, and Steven) and six grandchildren. See *Current Biography* (1979). —M.M.H.

Obituary *New York Times* (on-line) Feb. 13, 2011

SNIDER, DUKE Sep. 19, 1926–Feb. 27, 2011 Baseball player. The Hall of Fame center fielder Duke Snider was an integral part of the Brooklyn Dodgers during that team's heyday, in the 1950s. "The Duke," as he was fondly known, led the Dodgers to six National League pennants and two World Series titles. In a feat matched by only a handful of other players, he hit 40 or more home runs in five consecutive seasons. In 1964 Snider ended his 18-season career—which included five seasons with the Dodgers after they moved to Los Angeles and stints with the New York Mets and the San Francisco Giants—with a

.295 batting average, 2,116 hits, and 407 home runs; among those was, in 1957, the last home run ever made at Ebbets Field, the Dodgers' Brooklyn stadium, which was demolished in 1960. Edwin Donald Snider was born in Los Angeles, California, and grew up in nearby Compton. His father, Ward Snider, a naval shipyard worker and semiprofessional baseball player, gave Snider the nickname "Duke" after he saw his five-year-old son confidently strutting home from his first day at school. Snider played baseball, basketball, and football at Compton High School and won 16 letters. His size, speed, and high-powered throwing arm aroused interest among Major League Baseball (MLB) scouts, and in March 1944 he signed a contract with the Brooklyn Dodgers organization, for a bonus of $750 and a salary of $275 a month. Snider made his professional debut as a pinch hitter on the Dodgers' farm team based in Montreal, in the International League, during the 1944 season. From December 1944 to May 1946, Snider was on active duty in the U.S. Navy; he served in the Pacific for 11 months as a fireman second class aboard the submarine tender *Sperry*. After he returned to civilian life, he remained on farm teams until 1947, when, after impressing the Dodgers coach Clyde Sukeforth by hitting four home runs in six games for the farm team in Fort Worth, Texas, he was brought up to play with the major-league squad as a pinch hitter; he had his first major-league hit on the same day Jackie Robinson broke the league's color barrier. Snider had his first full season in the majors in 1949. In the middle of that year, after the Dodgers manager Burt Shotton taunted Snider for his reluctance to face left-handed pitchers, he had a batting surge that lifted his average to .292 and his home-run total to 23. That season Brooklyn won the National League pennant but lost the World Series to the New York Yankees. The Dodgers won the National League pennant and faced the Yankees in the World Series again in 1952, 1953, 1955, and 1956; they won in 1955, in a seven-game series. Becoming known for his strong defensive play in the outfield and his frequent home runs, Snider led the National League in numerous statistical categories over the years, including runs scored in 1953, 1954, and 1955; RBIs (136) in 1955; and home runs (43) in 1956. In 1957 Snider followed the Dodgers to their new home in Los Angeles, where he spent the next five years. Before the 1963 season he was sold to the struggling New York Mets organization, and the following year he played for the San Francisco Giants. He retired from baseball at age 38; he went on to manage teams in the Dodgers and San Diego Padres farm systems and later served as a broadcaster for both the Padres and the Montreal Expos. He was inducted into the Baseball Hall of Fame in 1980. In the 1990s Snider served two years of probation and was fined $5,000 after pleading guilty to tax fraud for failing to report thousands of dollars he had earned from selling autographs and sports memorabilia. Snider died of natural causes in Escondido, California. He is survived by his wife, Beverly; two sons, Kevin and Kurt; and two daughters, Pam and Dawna. See *Current Biography* (1956).—M.M.H.

Obituary *New York Times* (on-line) Feb. 27, 2011

SOLARZ, STEPHEN J. Sep. 12, 1940–Nov. 29, 2010 U.S. representative from New York. During his 18 years (1975–93) in the U.S. House as New York's 13th Congressional District representative, the Democrat Stephen J. Solarz was one of Congress's leading voices on foreign affairs. He was born in New York City to Sanford Solarz, a lawyer, and the former Ruth Fertig, who divorced not long after his birth. Solarz was initially raised by his father and stepmother and then by a widowed aunt in Brooklyn, after his father divorced again. He was elected president of the student body at his high school and later attended Brandeis University, in Waltham, Massachusetts, where he edited the school paper. Upon earning a B.A. degree from Brandeis, in 1962, Solarz enrolled at the Columbia University School of Law. Having already decided on a career in politics and government, and finding the work in law school "uninteresting," he soon transferred to Columbia's Department of Public Law and Government, earning a master's degree in 1967. During his time at Columbia, Solarz joined the ranks of the Brooklyn reform Democrats. At 25 he entered the political fray as the campaign manager for Melvin Dubin, an anti–Vietnam War activist, in his bid for New York's 13th Congressional District seat in the House. Dubin lost the election to the Republican Betram Podell, who became Solarz's opponent when Solarz ran for the seat years later. After teaching political science for a short time at Brooklyn College and New York Community College, in 1968 Solarz was elected to the New York State Assembly, representing Brooklyn's 45th District. He served three terms in the Assembly, from 1969 to 1975, championing such liberal causes as gay rights and prison reform. As a member of the Assembly's minority party, however, Solarz became increasingly frustrated with his ineffectuality, and in 1973 he made an unsuccessful bid for the Democratic nomination in the race for Brooklyn borough president. The following year he won the Democratic primary for New York's 13th Congressional District, and, without the support of the Brooklyn Democratic Party organization, he defeated the incumbent, Podell, with 82 percent of the vote. As a freshman House lawmaker, Solarz secured an appointment to the influential Foreign Affairs Committee. He went on to use that position to appeal to his large Jewish constituency, championing such causes as American aid to Israel. Solarz soon established a reputation as one of the leading congressional authorities on international affairs. During his nine terms in Congress, he visited more than 100 countries (earning him the nickname "the Marco Polo of Congress") and met with numerous world leaders. Named chair of the House Foreign Affairs Subcommittee on Africa in 1979, Solarz became a strong supporter of African nationalist movements and led successful efforts to prevent House conservatives from lifting sanctions against the white-minority regime of Bishop Abel Muzorewa in Rhodesia (now Zimbabwe). In 1980 he became the first American congressman in three decades to visit North Korea, and the following year he left his post on the Subcommittee on Africa to take on the chairmanship of the House Foreign Affairs Subcommittee on Asian and Pacific Affairs. In that role he helped develop a peace plan to end genocide in Cambodia and led an investigation into the misuse of foreign aid by the outgoing Philippine president, Ferdinand Marcos, and his wife, Imelda—whose 3,000 pairs of shoes, uncovered in the investigation, came to represent the regime's extreme excesses. Solarz's efforts also helped shape the policies of President Ronald Reagan's administration regarding such places as Central America, Lebanon, Pakistan, and South Africa. In 1991 Solarz found himself at odds with members of his own party after co-sponsoring a resolution supporting President George H. W. Bush's efforts in the Persian Gulf War. By 1992, as a result of the 1990 U.S. Census, New York State's congressional delegation had shrunk from 34 to 31, and Solarz's district was divided. He opted to run for a seat in New York's 12th Congressional District, which included parts of Queens, Manhattan, and Brooklyn and had been drawn to engineer a win by a candidate of Hispanic origin. As predicted, Solarz was defeated in the primary by Nydia M. Velazquez, who remains the district's representative. Solarz's campaign had also suffered mightily from a House ethics investigation that found that he and his wife had written hundreds of bad checks from their account at the U.S. House bank. Although Solarz avoided criminal charges, his wife, the former Nina Koldin, pleaded guilty in 1995 to two criminal counts and was sentenced to probation. After leaving Congress Solarz served as a consultant and volunteer for several nonprofit international organizations and helped form the International Crisis Group, an independent nonprofit agency dedicated to resolving deadly conflicts. Solarz died of esophageal cancer at a Washington hospital. He is survived by his wife; his mother, Ruth Robin; two half-brothers, Avrom and Seth Robin; his stepson, Randy Glantz; his stepdaughter, Lisa Prickett; and four grandchildren. Solarz's book *Journeys to War and Peace: A Congressional Memoir* was published in June 2011. See *Current Biography* (1986). —C.C.

Obituary *New York Times* (on-line) Nov. 29, 2010

SORENSEN, THEODORE C. May 8, 1928–Oct. 31, 2010 Presidential adviser; lawyer; writer. Theodore C. Sorensen was best known for his service as President John F. Kennedy's special counsel and speechwriter. "Amply endowed with the qualities required for an intimate adviser at the highest levels, Mr. Sorensen was regarded as a man of ideas and ideals, keen intellect and a passion for public service," Martin Weil and Emma Brown wrote for the *Washington Post* (November 1, 2010, on-line). "From Mr. Sorensen—or from his close and fruitful collaboration with his president—came the words by which Kennedy called on the nation to achieve such goals as placing a man on the moon and providing civil rights to all Americans." Sorensen was born in Lincoln, Nebraska, to Christian Abraham and Annis (Chaikin) Sorensen. His father, a lawyer of Danish descent, served as the state attorney general of Nebraska from 1929 until 1933. His mother, of Russian-Jewish descent, was a social worker, pacifist, and feminist. In 1945 Sorensen graduated from Lincoln High School and went on to attend the University of Nebraska as a Regents Scholar. There, he chaired the campus constitutional convention and the mock United Na-

tions; became a member of the school's debate team, drama club, and band; and served as president of the university YMCA. In 1949 Sorensen enrolled at the University of Nebraska's College of Law. The editor in chief of the *Nebraska Law Review*, he was admitted into the Order of Coif, an honor society for those in the field of law. In 1951 Sorensen received an LL.B degree, graduating at the top of his class. He subsequently moved to Washington, D.C., where he became an attorney for the Federal Security Agency and then for the Department of Health, Education, and Welfare. Concurrently, Sorensen worked as a staff researcher for the joint congressional subcommittee on railroad retirement. Impressed by Sorensen's work, Senator Paul Douglas of Illinois recommended him for a job as an administrative assistant to John F. Kennedy, the newly elected U.S. senator from Massachusetts. While Kennedy was recovering from a back injury in 1955, Sorensen did the research for Kennedy's Pulitzer Prize–winning *Profiles in Courage* (1956), a collection of biographical sketches about American legislators who exercised independent judgment in the face of pressures from their constituents. (Some political observers assumed that Sorensen was the volume's ghostwriter, but the documentary evidence of Sorensen's research notes and Kennedy's handwritten drafts suggested otherwise.) On January 2, 1960 Kennedy announced that he was a candidate for the Democratic presidential nomination. What followed has been described as one of the most successful political campaigns ever waged in the U.S. Sorensen, serving in the capacity of chief political strategist and speechwriter, traveled with the candidate through every state, courting politicians, determining the most likely real sources of power, and lining up delegates. Kennedy won the Democratic nomination, and in 1961 he became the 35th president of the United States. Sorensen famously contributed to Kennedy's inaugural address, which included the much-quoted line, "Ask not what your country can do for you, ask what you can do for your country." When Kennedy was assassinated, in 1963, Sorensen was bereft. Seven years later he ran unsuccessfully for the U.S. Senate seat once held by Robert Kennedy. In 1976 President-elect Jimmy Carter asked Sorensen to become the director of central intelligence. Wary of the CIA's activities, yet eager to be a part of the government, Sorensen somewhat reluctantly accepted the position. The offer was withdrawn, however, after it discovered that as a teenager, Sorensen had registered with the draft board as a conscientious objector. In the decades that followed, he advised such world leaders as Nelson Mandela and Anwar Sadat and resumed practicing law, working for many years at the New York City–based firm Paul, Weiss, Rifkind, Wharton & Garrison. In 2001 Sorensen suffered a stroke that caused partial loss of his eyesight, which did not stop him from writing, mentoring younger lawyers, and making speeches. Sorensen, whose first two marriages—to Camilla Palmer and Sara Elbery—ended in divorce, was the author of several books, including the best-selling biography *Kennedy* (1965) and a memoir, *Counselor: A Life at the Edge of History* (2008). He suffered a second stroke a week before his death and is survived by his third wife, Gillian Martin, a former U.N. official;

their daughter, Juliet; three sons from his first marriage, Eric, Stephen, and Philip; and several grandchildren. See *Current Biography* (1961).—J.P.

Obituary *New York Times* (on-line) Oct. 31, 2010

STAATS, ELMER June 6, 1914–July 23, 2011 Former U.S. comptroller general. Elmer Staats was appointed comptroller general by President Lyndon B. Johnson in 1966 and subsequently served in the post under Richard M. Nixon, Gerald R. Ford, and Jimmy Carter as well. He was born to Wesley Staats, a farmer, and Maude (Goodall) Staats in Richfield, Kansas. In 1931 he entered McPherson College, in the central part of his home state, to prepare for a career in public service. (He had seven siblings but was the only one in his immediate family to attend college.) He majored in government, and in addition to joining the interscholastic debating and forensic teams, he served as editor of the college newspaper, as a board member of the yearbook, as president of the International Relations Club, and as president of the senior class. Also a leader of his class scholastically, he gave the valedictory address when he graduated, with a B.A. degree, in 1935. During the following year Staats served a fellowship at the University of Kansas, where he again specialized in government, writing his master's thesis on the subject of state supervision of local government in Kansas. In 1936 he was elected to Phi Beta Kappa and Pi Sigma Alpha (the honorary political-science fraternity) and was awarded an M.A. degree. He spent the summer of 1936 in Topeka as a research assistant with the Kansas Legislative Council and then enrolled at the University of Minnesota. A teaching assistantship enabled him to meet his expenses while working on his doctoral dissertation, "Personnel Standards in the Federal Social Security Program," and while completing other requirements for his Ph.D. degree, which was conferred in 1939. That year Staats joined the division of administrative management of the Bureau of the Budget (now known as the Office of Management and Budget), where he was occupied until 1943 with management analysis and survey work for several federal agencies. He was deferred from military service during World War II so that he could help in setting up civilian agencies handling defense-related problems. Transferred in 1943 to the war agencies section of the bureau, he shared in the organization and budgetary-review responsibility for the War Production Board, Office of Price Administration, Office of Civilian Defense, and other departments. From 1945 to 1947 he held the title of chief of the war-agencies section, followed by a brief stint, in late 1947, as chief administrative officer of the bureau. By the end of the year, he had moved to the office of assistant director in charge of legislative reference, which had the tasks, among others, of coordinating legislative proposals from federal agencies. His appointment to the post of deputy director of the Bureau of the Budget in 1950 was the culmination of more than a decade of steady advancement for Staats. In 1953 he left government service to become research director for Marshall Field & Co. in Chicago. He returned to Washington a year later and joined the administration of Dwight D. Eisenhower as executive officer of the newly established operations co-

ordinating board of the National Security Council, where he remained for four years, after which he rejoined the Bureau of the Budget. With his appointment by Johnson in early 1966 to head the General Accounting Office (GAO), which had responsibility for investigating government expenditures and maintaining accounting standards, Staats moved from the executive branch to the legislative branch of the federal government. A long term of office, 15 years, protected the nonpartisan character of the post, allowing Staats to make criticisms and recommendations to Congress independently of any political consideration under Johnson and, later, Nixon, Ford, and Carter. Despite the nonpolitical nature of the position, "G.A.O. reports during Mr. Staats's term [sometimes] bore political consequences," according to Dennis Hevesi, writing for the *New York Times* (August 5, 2011, on-line). "A 1972 audit of President Richard M. Nixon's re-election committee, for example, showed that campaign contributions had been used to finance the Watergate break-in." Prohibited from being reappointed after his term ended, Staats stepped down in 1981. According to GAO estimates, he had saved taxpayers some $20 billion during his tenure. Since 2004 the General Accounting Office has been called the Government Accountability Office (retaining its acronym), and thanks in some part to Staats, it has expanded its focus to evaluating such government programs as Social Security and military procurement. It now employs thousands of lawyers, engineers, and IT specialists in addition to the accountants who comprised the bulk of its workforce in the 1960s. Staats died at the age of 97. He was predeceased, in 1992, by his wife of more than 50 years, Margaret Shaw Rich. He is survived by a son, David, and two daughters, Deborah and Catharine. See *Current Biography* (1967). —M.R.

Obituary *New York Times* (on-line) Aug. 5, 2011

STERNE, HEDDA Aug. 4, 1910–Apr. 8, 2011 Artist. Hedda Sterne belonged to a group of influential European-born artists living in New York City during the middle of the 20th century. Her association with the Abstract Expressionists and other avant-garde artists was cemented in 1950, when she signed an open letter to the director of the Metropolitan Museum of Art, accusing the institution of hostility to progressive art. A photograph of Sterne and 14 of the other 17 artists who signed the letter—among them Mark Rothko, Jackson Pollock, and Willem de Kooning, who collectively became known as the "Irascible 18"—was published in *Life* magazine and ultimately achieved legendary status. Despite her association with those artists, Sterne shared few of their artistic and philosophical concerns, and her own work, which encompassed many stylistic changes over the course of her lifetime, never achieved the same prominence. Sterne was born Hedda Lindenberg in Bucharest, Romania, the daughter of Simon and Eugenie (Wexler) Lindenberg. She came from a highly cultivated, well-traveled, art-loving family that gave her numerous art books when she was a girl, and she would industriously copy paintings by Holbein, Titian, Picasso, and others. She studied art in Paris and at the Kunsthistorisches Museum, in Vienna; she also studied philosophy at the University of Bucharest. She married Fritz Stern in 1932; when they divorced, soon afterward, she kept the surname but added an "e." Working in Europe in the 1930s, Sterne took a great interest in collage, sculpture, and abstract art in general, and her own output during that time was determinedly avant-garde and abstract. She exhibited Surrealist collages in Paris and London in the late 1930s, before escaping a roundup and murder of Jews in Bucharest in 1941 and traveling to New York City, where she became involved with the avant-garde and Surrealist art movements. In 1943 she had her first solo show in the U.S. at the Wakefield Gallery in New York. Her early paintings had a romantic and nostalgic air, evoking childhood and European family life, and were often described as "whimsical." She exhibited regularly through the 1940s and '50s, including multiple shows at the Betty Parsons Gallery in New York. (Parsons subsequently became her longtime dealer.) She also exhibited at the Galleria dell'Obelisco in Rome, Italy; the Museu de Arte Moderna in São Paulo, Brazil; the Smithsonian Institution in Washington, D.C.; and the Rhode Island School of Design, among other venues. It was through Parsons that Sterne befriended many Abstract Expressionist artists. Parsons also introduced her to her second husband, a fellow Romanian, the artist and cartoonist Saul Steinberg, to whom she was married from 1944 to 1960. After a trip to Vermont with Steinberg, she became interested in farm machinery and began painting images of machines combined with human forms. In the mid-1950s she began to paint airports, skyscrapers, and bridges. A reviewer for *Arts* (November 1, 1954) noted that in those paintings, the city itself was depicted as "a city-jungle as secret and frightening as the black night, where space looms like a monstrous and monumental beast." In the 1960s Sterne produced a series of vertical canvases striped with horizontal bands of color and made ink drawings of various organic forms. She often painted portraits of her friends, and in 1970 she displayed dozens of them in an installation called Hedda Sterne Shows Everyone, mounted at the Betty Parsons Gallery. Retrospective exhibitions of Sterne's work were held at the Montclair Art Museum in New Jersey, in 1977, and the Krannert Art Museum at the University of Illinois, in Champaign-Urbana, in 2006. "Hedda was always searching, never satisfied," Parsons said, as quoted in the *New York Times* (April 11, 2011, on-line). "She had many ways; most artists just have one way to go." Sterne died at her home in Manhattan at the age of 100. She had no immediate surviving relatives. See *Current Biography* (1957). —M.R.M.

Obituary *New York Times* (on-line) Apr. 11, 2011

STEWART, ELLEN Nov. 7, 1919–Jan. 13, 2011 Theatrical producer. Ellen Stewart was the founder and director of La MaMa Experimental Theater Club in New York City, an Off-Off-Broadway performance space that was an integral part of the downtown drama scene for almost five decades. Many important writers and actors passed through the theater; according to an obituary of Stewart by Robert Simonson on the *Playbill* Web site (January 13, 2011),

"Over the years, the company nurtured aborning talents such as the playwrights Sam Shepard, Tom Eyen, William Hoffman, Lanford Wilson, Adrienne Kennedy, Rochelle Owens, Jeff Weiss, Harvey Fierstein, and Jean Claude Van Itallie; the directors Robert Wilson, Julie Bovasso, Tom O'Horgan, Richard Foreman, Wilford Leach, and Meredith Monk; performance artists including John Kelly and Blue Man Group; and the actors Al Pacino, Robert De Niro, and Harvey Keitel." In their obituary of Stewart for the *New York Times* (January 13, 2011, on-line), Mel Gussow and Bruce Weber wrote, "Few producers could match her energy, perseverance and fortitude. In the decades after World War II her influence on American theater was comparable to that of Joseph Papp, founder of the New York Shakespeare Festival, though the two approached the stage from different wings. Papp straddled the commercial and noncommercial worlds, while Ms. Stewart's terrain was international and decidedly noncommercial." Unless the conversation concerned a beloved theatrical project, Stewart never cared to discuss her personal background. Some reporters asserted that her cultural origins were Creole, and the French-like cadence of her speech, as well as her upbringing in Alexandria, Louisiana, seemed to support that assertion, but according to most reports she was descended from Geechees, the slaves who settled along the Ogeechee River in Georgia. (In the Geechee dialect, English is sprinkled with Africanisms.) She studied at Arkansas State College to be a teacher, and during World War II she worked as a riveter at a defense plant in Chicago. She moved to New York City in 1950, hoping to attend a fashion-design school, but ended up working a string of jobs to support herself, including a stint as an elevator operater at Saks Fifth Avenue. Fortuitously, her original clothing designs, which she wore while operating the elevator, attracted interest, and Saks hired her to work as a designer. (Two of the gowns worn at the coronation of Queen Elizabeth II in 1953 were Stewart originals.) In 1962 Stewart rented a small basement in New York's East Village neighborhood in order to help her foster brother, Frederick Lights, a playwright struggling to find a venue for his work. The minuscule space was initially called Cafe La MaMa, and later La MaMa E.T.C. (Experimental Theater Club). The theater, which did not charge admission but collected donations, soon began to put on plays on a regular basis. The plays ran the gamut from classics to contemporary drama, performance art, dance, and more, and they were generally mounted with a minimal budget and a taste for bucking conventional theater. The first play produced at Cafe La Mama was an adaptation of Tennessee Williams's story *One Arm*, presented in July 1962. "Now you must understand," Stewart told John Gruen for *New York* (July 22, 1968), "this was a tiny place which held only about twenty-five people, and the playing area was about the size of a single bed. In fact, the only prop we had was a single bed. All the plays we did concerned a single bed. . . . We also had a lot of ketchup because we put on a lot of gory murder plays." Michael Locasio's *In a Corner of the Morning* was the first original play produced at La Mama, in August 1962, and the first production of a play by Harold Pinter in New York was La Mama's staging of *The Room*, in November of that year. Success came slowly, and at one point neighbors phoned the authorities, fearing that Stewart was running a brothel. Eventually the theater gained recognition as one of several emerging Off-Off-Broadway playhouses, which were forming as Off-Broadway venues became more mainstream. The theater found a permanent home in 1969, at a former meatpacking plant on East Fourth Street. There, Stewart was able to configure two larger theaters and office space, and in 1974 she opened the Annex, a 295-seat theater down the street. (That theater was renamed the Ellen Stewart Theater in a gala celebration in 2009.) During the ensuing decades Stewart became a major force in the theater world. Her accolades include a MacArthur Foundation Fellowship (1985), a Tony Honor for Excellence in Theatre (2006), and a Praemium Imperiale from the Japan Art Association (2007). Stewart was married at least once and had a son, Larry Hovell, who died in 1998. She also has an adopted son, Duk Hyung Yoo, and eight grandchildren, all of whom survive her. See *Current Biography* (1973). —W.D.

Obituary *New York Times* (on-line) Jan. 13, 2011

STOTT, JOHN Apr. 27, 1921–July 27, 2011 Evangelical clergyman. One of the most influential evangelical preachers of the last half-century, John Stott authored dozens of books that were published in more than 70 languages, and his writings and preaching paved the way for two generations of evangelicals and evangelists. Stott is best known for being one of the principal framers of the Lausanne Covenant, a highly influential evangelist manifesto that was drafted in Switzerland in 1974. The youngest of three children, Stott was born in London, England. His father, Sir Arnold W. Stott, was a well-known physician and an agnostic, and his mother, Lady Emily Stott, came from a Lutheran family. As a child Stott attended services and Sunday school with his mother and two sisters at All Souls Church, an Anglican parish on Langham Place, near Oxford Circus, in London. Those experiences inspired Stott to pursue a religious vocation, and after graduating from the Rugby School, in 1939, he enrolled at Trinity College, a division of Cambridge University, in England. Stott graduated from Trinity with a degree in French and theology in 1943 and then transferred to Ridley Hall Theological College, also at Cambridge, in order to be ordained as an Anglican cleric. He was ordained a minister in the Church of England in 1945, at which point he began serving as an assistant curate at All Souls Church. Two years later he earned a master's degree at Cambridge, and in 1950, at the age of 29, he became the rector of All Souls. He held that post for the next 25 years, during which he gained significant influence in the church as a preacher, evangelist, and author. He earned particular renown for his 1958 work, *Basic Christianity*, which sold more than 2.5 million copies worldwide. Stott wrote dozens of other books aimed at both laymen and members of the clergy, and he used much of the royalties from his books to help the poor in developing countries. In 1971 Stott founded Langham Partnership International, an evangelical organization dedicated to teaching pastors in impoverished countries effective ways to preach. The partnership

grew to include five national and 10 regional nondenominational movements. Stott was one of the major architects of the landmark Lausanne Covenant, which was signed by more than 2,300 evangelicals from 150 nations at the 1974 International Congress on World Evangelization, held in Lausanne, Switzerland. The covenant declared the core principles of world evangelism. Upon stepping down as rector of All Souls, in 1975, Stott took on the title of rector emeritus. In his later years he remained active with the Langham Partnership and continued to be a prolific author. His last book, *The Radical Disciple: Some Neglected Aspects of Our Calling*, was published in 2010. Stott was named one of the world's 100 most influential people by *Time* magazine in 2005 and was named a Commander of the Order of the British Empire by the British government in 2006. (He served as a chaplain to Queen Elizabeth II from 1959 to 1991.) Stott retired from the ministry in 2007 and was the subject of an authorized two-volume biography by Timothy Dudley-Smith: *The Making of a Leader: John Stott: A Biography of the Early Years* (1999) and *A Global Ministry: John Stott: A Biography of the Later Years* (2001). Stott died of natural causes at the College of St. Barnabas facility for retired clergy, in Lingfield, Surrey. A lifelong celibate, he left no immediate survivors. See *Current Biography* (2005). —C.C.

Obituary *New York Times* (on-line) July 27, 2011

TAYLOR, BILLY July 24, 1921–Dec. 28, 2010 Jazz musician. Billy Taylor, one of jazz music's most eloquent spokesmen for nearly 50 years, "was a living refutation of the stereotype of jazz musicians as unschooled, unsophisticated, and inarticulate," as Peter Keepnews wrote for the *New York Times* (December 29, 2010, on-line). Though renowned for his technical skill as a musician, Taylor is better known for his many efforts to disseminate jazz to those other than musicians and aficionados. He won particular esteem for initiating the Jazzmobile program, which brought free music programs to disadvantaged inner-city youth. Taylor was born in Greenville, North Carolina, to William Taylor, a dentist, and Antoinette Taylor, a schoolteacher. Soon afterward he moved with his family to Washington, D.C. By the time he was seven, he was studying saxophone, guitar, and drums; he settled on the piano when he discovered that pretty girls often joined him on the piano bench when he was playing. By age 12 Taylor was playing in local jazz clubs. At Washington's Dunbar High School, Taylor played in the school band and studied classical music with Henry Grant, who had also taught Duke Ellington. By the time Taylor entered the predominantly black Virginia State College, in 1938, he was playing professionally. He graduated with a B.S. degree in music in 1943, and after being rejected for military service for health reasons, he worked briefly at a government job in Washington while performing during the evenings at nightclubs. In August 1943 he moved to New York City, where two days after his arrival, he was invited to join Ben Webster's Quartet at the Three Deuces Club on West 52d Street. By the mid-1940s Taylor's musical career as a sideman and a recording artist was well under way, thanks to his work with such jazz artists as Stuff

Smith, Quincy Jones, Clark Terry, Roy Eldridge, Coleman Hawkins, and Herbie Mann. A landmark in his career was his appearance, during 1950–51, as the house pianist at Birdland, Broadway's top jazz room. In residence there for almost two years, he performed with some of the great modernists of his time, including Eldridge, Dizzy Gillespie, Charlie ("Bird") Parker, Miles Davis, Lee Konitz, Art Blakey, Milt Jackson, Lester Young, and Stan Getz. He formed his own trio in 1951, with the bassist Charles Mingus and the drummer Marquis Foster, and worked at clubs in Chicago, Boston, and New York. In 1953 *Down Beat* magazine's international jazz critics' poll designated Taylor "best new star pianist." In addition to performing, Taylor composed material especially for Ethel Smith, Tito Puente, Edmundo Ros, and Slim Gaillard, among others; in total he wrote more than 300 songs, including "I Wish I Knew How It Would Feel to Be Free," often sung by civil rights activists, and the ambitious 1983 piece "Suite for Jazz Piano and Orchestra." Taylor became well known to those outside jazz's inner circles with his many television and radio jobs. In 1959 he joined the staff of the Harlem-based radio station WLIB-FM as a disc jockey, and within three years he had a five-hour-a-day, six-day-a-week program. When he changed over to a jazz program on WNEW in September 1962, he became the first black host of a daily show on a major New York City radio station. He returned to WLIB in 1964 and remained there until 1969. He later helped found Inner City Broadcasting, which bought WLIB in 1971. "When I was at WLIB I was doing the kind of show that had not been done before in New York," he told Barbara Campbell for the *New York Times* (January 3, 1971). "I was conditioning people's tastes for all kinds of jazz from very far in to very far out. I also interviewed jazzmen and for the first time people found out that a lot of them had something special to say. . . . When Dr. [Martin Luther] King was killed, I opened up my radio show so people could call in and let off some of the frustration instead of setting things on fire out of desperation, and it worked." When the British television personality David Frost began his syndicated CBS-TV talk-show series, the *David Frost Show*, Taylor was hired as its musical director. From its very first program, in July 1969, until its last one, in June 1972, Frost's "O.K. Billy!" was the phrase that introduced some of the most exciting music on the air. Taylor also served as host and pianist on the National Public Radio series *Jazz Alive!* and, more recently, *Billy Taylor's Jazz at the Kennedy Center*, which debuted in 1994 and ran through 2002. Later he was a cultural correspondent on the CBS News program *Sunday Morning*. In 1968 New York City mayor John V. Lindsay appointed Taylor to the New York Cultural Council, and in 1970 Governor Nelson A. Rockefeller named him to the New York State Temporary Commission on Cultural Resources. He held other, similar positions over the years, including a seat on an advisory panel that called for greater support for jazz from the National Endowment for the Arts (NEA), in 1980. Taylor first performed at the White House in April 1969, at a birthday party for Duke Ellington. In 1988 Taylor received the $20,000 Jazz Master's Award from the NEA, and in 1992 he was presented with the National Medal of Arts. Taylor,

who received a doctorate in music education from the University of Massachusetts, Amherst, in 1975, preferred to be called "Dr. Taylor." He served as a Yale Fellow at Calhoun College and taught at the C. W. Post College of Long Island University and the Manhattan School of Music. Taylor lived in the Riverdale section of the Bronx, in New York City. He died of heart failure and is survived by his wife, Theodora, and his daughter, Kim Taylor-Thompson. His son, Duane, died in 1988. See *Current Biography* (1980). —M.M.H.

Obituary *New York Times* (on-line) Dec. 29, 2010

TAYLOR, ELIZABETH Feb. 27, 1932–Mar. 23, 2011 Actress; philanthropist. One of the most famous iconic stars in Hollywood history, Elizabeth Taylor captivated audiences all over the world with her violet-eyed beauty and glamour. She appeared in more than 50 films, including such classics as *National Velvet* (1944), *A Place in the Sun* (1951), *Giant* (1956), *Cat on a Hot Tin Roof* (1958), and *Cleopatra* (1963), and won two best-actress Oscars, for her performances in *Butterfield 8* (1960) and *Who's Afraid of Virginia Woolf?* (1966). Equally known for her eight marriages (including two to the actor Richard Burton), sumptuous jewels (including the 33.19-carat Krupp Diamond and a 69.42-carat, pear-shaped gem that came to be called the Taylor-Burton Diamond), and numerous health scares, Taylor was the subject of near-constant tabloid coverage, which often overshadowed her exceptional on-screen career. In her later years Taylor dedicated much of her time to humanitarian work and social activism, and she emerged as a major figure in the fight against AIDS in the 1980s and 1990s. The film critic Vincent Canby once wrote of Taylor, as quoted in a tribute to the actress in the *New York Times* (March 23, 2011, on-line), "More than anyone else I can think of, Elizabeth Taylor represents the complete movie phenomenon—what movies are as an art and an industry, and what they have meant to those of us who have grown up watching them in the dark." Taylor was born in London, England, to American parents. Her father, Francis, was an art dealer who had relocated to London from New York, and her mother, the former Sara Warmbrodt, was a stage actress who had performed as Sara Sothern prior to her marriage. Taylor, who had an older brother, Howard, spent her early childhood in England before moving to the U.S. with her family just before the outbreak of World War II. Settling in Pasadena, California, and later in Beverly Hills, Taylor possessed a natural beauty and charm that soon brought her to the attention of film executives. Spurred into acting by her mother, she obtained a contract with Universal Pictures in 1941 and made her silver-screen debut the following year in *There's One Born Every Minute* (1942). Soon afterward the producer Sam Marx, who at the time served as an air-raid warden alongside Francis Taylor, was seeking a girl to play the granddaughter of an English lord in *Lassie Come Home* (1943), and he arranged a screen test for Elizabeth Taylor that immediately won her a contract with MGM. Her next pictures included *Jane Eyre* (1944) and *The White Cliffs of Dover* (1944). She made a major breakthrough with her starring turn in the equestrienne drama *National Velvet* (1944), in which she gave what was generally considered to be one of the all-time greatest performances by a child actress. Unlike many other child stars, Taylor made a smooth transition to more mature roles. As an invalid in *Cynthia* (1947), she received a much-publicized "first screen kiss" from Jimmy Lydon, and in quick succession she appeared in *A Date with Judy* (1948), *Julia Misbehaves* (1948), and *Little Women* (1949). Taylor had her first full-fledged adult role, that of the wife of a Soviet spy (played by Robert Taylor), in *Conspirator* (1950), before appearing in Vincente Minnelli's popular comedy *Father of the Bride* (1950), which co-starred Spencer Tracy. (Off-screen, she married her first husband, the hotel heir Conrad Hilton Jr., that year. The union lasted only nine months, after which she married her second husband, the actor Michael Wilding.) Taylor told Richard Meryman for *Life* (December 18, 1964) that the first film in which she was "asked to do any acting" was *A Place in the Sun* (1951), George Stevens's adaptation of Theodore Dreiser's novel *An American Tragedy*. She received widespread critical praise for her portrayal of the beautiful Angela Vickers in that film, which co-starred Montgomery Clift and Shelley Winters. In 1956 Taylor played the wife of Rock Hudson's character in George Stevens's *Giant*, a multigenerational saga about a Texas cattle rancher, his family, and his associates. Based on Edna Ferber's epic novel of the same name, it is noted for being the last of James Dean's three films. Taylor next starred in the Civil War epic *Raintree County* (1957), which reunited her with Montgomery Clift, who became a close friend. Though the film was panned by critics, it earned Taylor the first of four consecutive Academy Award nominations. After winning nominations for her compelling performances in *Cat on a Hot Tin Roof* (1958), which co-starred Paul Newman, and Joseph L. Mankiewicz's *Suddenly, Last Summer* (1959), which co-starred Clift and Katharine Hepburn, Taylor took home the coveted statuette for her portrayal of a New York call girl in Daniel Mann's *Butterfield 8* (1960). Taylor famously demanded (and won) a million-dollar salary for her next film, Joseph Mankiewicz's *Cleopatra* (1963), making her the highest-paid star in Hollywood. Though the costly, much-delayed historical epic received a mixed reaction from critics, it was partly responsible for sparking one of Hollywood's most legendary romances—that of Taylor and the still-married Richard Burton, who co-starred in the role of Mark Antony. Drawing the insatiable attention of tabloids all over the world, Burton divorced his wife and in 1964 married Taylor. The pair starred in a number of other pictures together, including *The Sandpiper* (1965); *Who's Afraid of Virginia Woolf?* (1966), for which Taylor won her second Academy Award; *The Taming of the Shrew* (1967); *Doctor Faustus* (1967); *The Comedians* (1967); *Boom!* (1968); *Under Milk Wood* (1971); and *Hammersmith Is Out* (1972). Taylor and Burton divorced in 1974 and then remarried 16 months later, before divorcing a second and final time in 1976. (Burton died of a brain hemorrhage in Switzerland in 1984.) During the 1980s and 1990s, Taylor appeared only sporadically in films, while making several forays into television, portraying the

famed gossip columnist Louella Parsons in *Malice in Wonderland* (1985), for example, and the aging actress Alexandra Del Lago in Tennessee Williams's *Sweet Bird of Youth* (1989). She also appeared on a number of television series, including the popular daytime soap operas *General Hospital* and *All My Children*. Taylor's final appearance in a feature film came in 1994, when she portrayed Fred Flintstone's mother-in-law in the live-action comedy *The Flintstones*. In 2001 she had a small part as a crusty Hollywood agent in the Carrie Fisher–penned television film *These Old Broads*, which starred Fisher's mother, Debbie Reynolds; Shirley MacLaine; and Joan Collins. Taylor's relationship with Debbie Reynolds was reportedly amicable, despite the fact that after Taylor's third husband, the impresario Mike Todd, died in a plane crash, in 1958, she took up with Reynolds's husband, Eddie Fisher. Fisher left Reynolds to become Taylor's fourth husband, sparking a frenzy of media stories depicting Taylor as a ruthless homewrecker. When Taylor later left Fisher for Burton, few professed surprise. Taylor devoted much of her later life to humanitarian work and to her many business endeavors. Following the death of her longtime friend and former co-star Rock Hudson of AIDS, in 1985, Taylor co-founded the American Foundation for AIDS Research and raised more than $200 million for the cause. At the 1993 Academy Awards ceremony, Taylor was honored with the Jean Hersholt Humanitarian Award for her activism, and in 2001 she received a Presidential Citizens Medal. Taylor, who converted to Judaism in 1959, also dedicated herself to various Jewish and Israeli causes. In addition to her marriages to Hilton, Wilding, Todd, Fisher, and Burton, Taylor was married to the Republican politician John Warner from 1976 to 1982 and to the construction worker Larry Fortensky, whom she had met while receiving treatment for drug and alcohol addiction at the Betty Ford Clinic, from 1991 to 1996. Taylor was the subject of dozens of books and penned a handful herself, including *Elizabeth Takes Off: On Weight Gain, Weight Loss, Self-Image & Self-Esteem* (1988) and *My Love Affair with Jewelry* (2002). She died of congestive heart failure at Cedars-Sinai Medical Center in Los Angeles. At the time of her death, Taylor left behind a jewelry collection said to be valued at $150 million and a total estate estimated to be worth between $600 million and $1 billion, thanks in some part to her lucrative fragrance line, which includes the perennially popular perfume White Diamonds. She is survived by her sons Michael and Christopher Wilding; her daughter, Liza Todd, and adopted daughter, Maria Burton; 10 grandchildren; and four great-grandchildren. See *Current Biography* (1985). —C.C.

Obituary *New York Times* (on-line) Mar. 23, 2011

THOMPSON, SADA Sep. 27, 1929–May 4, 2011 Actress. Sada Thompson was perhaps best known to the general public for her role as Kate Lawrence in the groundbreaking TV show *Family*, which aired from 1976 to 1980 and traced the story of a middle-class California clan as they dealt with such issues as drug addiction, homosexuality, and adultery. Long before then, however, she had established a stellar reputation on the stage, and the *New York Times* critic Walter Kerr had called her "one of the American theater's finest actresses." No matter the medium, she won wide praise, as Bruce Weber wrote for the *New York Times* (May 5, 2011, on-line), "for her portrayals of archetypal mothers, from the loving family caretaker and the world-weary, had-it-with-the-kids older woman to the brutalizing harridan and mythical adulteress and murderess." Thompson was born in Des Moines, Iowa, the oldest of the three children of Hugh Woodruff and Corlyss Elizabeth (Gibson) Thompson. Her unusual given name was acquired from her maternal grandmother, a redoubtable Irishwoman who had driven to Nebraska in a covered wagon. When Thompson was about five, the family moved to New Jersey, where her father became an editor of a string of poultry magazines. Her childhood, though happy, was rather uneventful until her parents took her to see Cole Porter's Broadway musical *Red, Hot and Blue*, a hit of the 1936–37 season. Enchanted, she became determined to pursue an acting career. She attended the Carnegie Institute of Technology Drama School, and while still a student, she began appearing in professional productions at the Pittsburgh Playhouse; at the Playhouse in Erie, Pennsylvania; and in the summer-stock productions of the Henrietta Hayloft Theatre in Rochester, New York. She graduated from the Carnegie Institute with a B.F.A. degree in 1949. Settling in New York, she found work as a speech teacher at the 92nd Street Y, where she met Dylan Thomas, who asked her to participate in a reading of *Under Milk Wood*, a radio play in verse form that he was writing. On May 14, 1953 Thompson made her New York City debut at the Y, reading several of the 63 parts in *Under Milk Wood*. She subsequently found herself in great demand for Off-Broadway productions of such works as Molière's *The Misanthrope*, Chekhov's *Ivanov*, and Charles Morgan's *The River Line*. In the summer of 1957, she joined the newly formed American Shakespeare Festival at Stratford, Connecticut, beginning a long association with that prestigious company. In what has been described as a career-making performance, she opened Off-Broadway in 1970 in Paul Zindel's *The Effect of Gamma Rays on Man-in-the-Moon Marigolds*, in which she played a slovenly mother trapped in a love-hate relationship with her two daughters. For her work in the production, she earned an Obie Award, a Drama Desk Award, and the Variety Poll of New York Critics Citation. Thompson also appeared occasionally on Broadway, and she won a Tony Award in 1972 for her work in George Furth's four-vignette drama, *Twigs*. In that show she took on four roles, those of a mother and her three daughters. Although she had read for the part of only one of the girls, the director, Michael Bennett, decided to take advantage of her enormous range and cast her to play all four parts. Audiences and critics were unanimous and vociferous in their praise for her accomplishment, and she won both a Drama Desk Award and a Tony Award for her performance. Among Thompson's film credits are the made-for-television movies *The Pursuit of Happiness* (1971), *Desperate Characters* (1971), *The Entertainer* (1976), *Our Town* (1977), *Princess Daisy* (1983), *The Adventures of Huckleberry Finn* (1985), *My Two Loves* (1986), *Fear Stalk* (1989), *Andre's*

Mother (1990), *Any Mother's Son* (1997), and *The Patron Saint of Liars* (1998), and the major motion picture *Pollock* (2000). She also made occasional guest appearances on such popular TV shows as *The Love Boat* and *Cheers*. She became best known to a wide general audience for portraying Kate Lawrence, the caring matriarch on the landmark series *Family* (1976–80), which was developed by Mike Nichols and Aaron Spelling. "I get bugged by little bitsy scenes where I just have to stand around looking maternal," she once said, as quoted by T. Rees Shapiro in the *Washington Post* (May 7, 2011, on-line). During the show's run she was nominated four times for an Emmy Award, winning once, in 1978. Thompson died of lung cancer at a Connecticut hospital at the age of 83. She is survived by her husband, Donald Stewart, a former airline executive to whom she had been married since 1949, and her daughter, Liza Stewart, a costume designer. See *Current Biography* (1973). —M.R.

Obituary *New York Times* (on-line) May 5, 2011

TOOKER, GEORGE Aug. 5, 1920–Mar. 27, 2011 Artist. George Tooker addressed such themes as love, sex, death, alienation, grief, and bureaucracy in his paintings. Many critics have referred to him as an American Surrealist, but in an interview with Selden Rodman for the volume *Conversations with Artists* (1961), Tooker denied the connection. "It is the novelty and shock value of the surrealists that disturbs me. I am after reality—painting impressed on the mind so hard that it recurs as a dream, but I am not after painting dreams as such, or fantasy." He continued, "Painting, to be really convincing, has to come from a strong emotion, as it seems to in the work of [Edward] Hopper, whom I admire greatly." Notwithstanding the bizarreness of their imagery, Tooker's paintings are only a step from the realism of Hopper, making plain the social and psychological fears that Hopper only implies. Tooker was born in the New York City borough of Brooklyn and spent most of his boyhood on Long Island. He attended the exclusive Phillips Academy, in Andover, Massachusetts, and then received a bachelor's degree from Harvard University in 1942. After serving briefly with the U.S. Marines, he gravitated to New York City, where he studied at the Art Students League from 1943 to 1945. In 1946 Tooker studied privately with Paul Cadmus, whose detailed tempera technique and Surrealist-tinged subjects greatly influenced him. The Surrealist painter Jared French also figured prominently as Tooker's guide and friend. By 1947 Tooker was exhibiting his work at the Whitney Museum, in New York City, which later purchased *The Subway*, a painting depicting apparently angst-ridden and harried people in a low-ceilinged subway station. The first one-man show of Tooker's work was held in 1951 at the Edwin Hewitt Gallery, in New York City. Although he would not become as well known as the Abstract Expressionists of his era, Tooker, who earned extra income at one point in his career by making custom furniture, was held in high regard by fellow artists and critics, and his work was shown at such venues as the Museum of Modern Art (MoMA), in New York; the Institute of Contemporary Art, in London; the Art Institute of Chicago; and the

Corcoran Gallery of Art, in Washington, D.C. In addition to *The Subway*, his most celebrated works include *Government Bureau* (1956), a painting of a group of civil servants (all with the same features) and hapless citizens inspired by the artist's experience in dealing with the New York City Department of Buildings; *Waiting Room* (1959), which Tooker described as depicting "a kind of purgatory"; and *Teller* (1968), a variation on *Government Bureau* in a fiduciary setting. After his longtime romantic partner, the artist William Christopher, died at their winter home in Spain, in 1973, Tooker embraced Roman Catholicism—a move that was reflected in some of his later work. In 1973 he was honored with a major show organized by the Fine Arts Museums of San Francisco that later traveled to Chicago and New York, among other places, and in 2008 a Tooker retrospective was mounted at the National Academy Museum, in New York. In his later years Tooker came to be considered "one of the most distinctive and mysterious American painters of the 20th century," as William Grimes wrote for the *New York Times* (March 29, 2011, on-line). At the age of 90, Tooker died of kidney failure at his home in Hartland, Vermont. He is survived by his sister, Mary. See *Current Biography* (1958). —D.K.

Obituary *New York Times* (on-line) Mar. 29, 2011

TOZZI, GIORGIO Jan. 8, 1923–May 30, 2011 Opera singer. The celebrated bass Giorgio Tozzi sang with New York City's venerable Metropolitan Opera more than 500 times. Tozzi was born in Chicago, Illinois, the only child of Enrico Tozzi, an Italian immigrant laborer, and Anna (Bontempi) Tozzi. On the family's home phonograph, popular tunes alternated with Caruso and Tetrazzini records. Tozzi was educated in Roman Catholic parochial schools, and at the age of 13, he took his first singing lessons. At 17 he made his first public appearance as a singer, with a Chicago amateur group in a performance of a Neapolitan operetta called *Scugnizza*. Tozzi attended De Paul University, where he majored in biology. In 1943, while in his junior year, he was drafted into the U.S. Army. Upon his discharge, three and a half years later, Tozzi returned to Chicago and began using his musical gifts to help support his family, in financial need as a result of his father's ill health. Then a baritone, he sang in nightclubs and in the chorus of the Chicago Theater of the Air, which was broadcast on local radio. Concurrently, he embarked on a serious course of vocal study. Leaving Chicago for New York, Tozzi appeared in the American premiere of Benjamin Britten's opera *The Rape of Lucretia*, which opened to mixed reviews and a short run at the Ziegfeld Theatre on December 29, 1948. Moving to England in 1949, for five months Tozzi played the prizefighter in love with a princess in Sir Charles B. Cochran's production of the musical comedy *Tough at the Top* at the Adelphi Theatre in London. After that show closed, Tozzi traveled to Milan, Italy, where he enrolled at the Conservatorio Giuseppe Verdi and the Scuola Musicale di Milano. He became convinced that he would sing better as a basso tessitura than as a baritone and began to familiarize himself with the basso repertoire. While waiting for delayed financial aid from the U.S. government under the G.I. Bill, Tozzi became destitute. He pawned his possessions and, in the midst of his vocal studies, was forced into what he considered a premature debut as an operatic basso. That debut took place in the summer of 1950 at Milan's small Teatro Nuovo, where the Associazione Lirica e Concertistica, a government-funded organization set up for the development and placement of young operatic talent, was holding its first showcase. Tozzi was signed up for four appearances as Count Rodolfo in Bellini's *La Sonnambula*. His appearances at the Teatro Nuovo led to engagements at the Royal Opera in Cairo (where he was singing when the 1952 Egyptian revolution broke out), provincial Italian opera houses, and houses elsewhere in Europe. He sang at La Fenice (Venice), Il Massimo (Palermo), San Carlo (Lisbon), Municipal Opera (Nice), and the state opera houses of Wiesbaden, Munich, and Stuttgart, among other places. In December 1953, on the opening night of the season, Tozzi made his debut at La Scala in Milan in a new production of Catalani's *La Wally*, earning widespread recognition and praise. He was approached in 1954 by the Metropolitan Opera Association, and on March 9, 1955 he made his first appearance at the Metropolitan Opera House in New York City in the important role of Alvise in Ponchielli's *La Gioconda*. During the next two decades, Tozzi entrenched himself as a principal bass of the Metropolitan Opera, appearing in productions of *Aïda*, *Rigoletto*, *Die Meistersinger*, *The Marriage of Figaro*, *Lucia di Lammermoor*, *Eugene Onegin*, *Don Giovanni*, *The Barber of Seville*, *The Magic Flute*, and *Tristan and Isolde*, among many others. He occasionally performed lighter fare, as in 1957, when he appeared as Emile de Becque opposite Mary Martin in a West Coast revival of the Rodgers and Hammerstein musical *South Pacific*. He was heard on the soundtrack (singing for Rossano Brazzi) in the film version of that musical in 1958. He assumed a speaking role in the motion picture *Shamus* (1973), a part he won when the producer of that motion picture happened to see a television commercial Tozzi had made for Fiat in which he spoke in a light Italian accent. In 1975 Tozzi gave his last performance with the Met, singing the role of Colline in *La Bohème*. He continued to sing in other venues, and in 1979 he garnered a Tony Award nomination for his work in a Broadway revival of Frank Loesser's musical comedy *The Most Happy Fella*. (He had previously won three Grammy Awards—for a 1959 recording of *Figaro*, a 1960 recording of *Turandot*, and a 1962 recording of *Aïda*.) Tozzi went on to make guest appearances on such popular TV series as *The Odd Couple*, *Baretta*, and *Kojak*. He also taught at such institutions as the Juilliard School, in New York City, and Indiana University's renowned Jacobs School of Music. At the time of his death, from a heart attack, at the age of 88, Tozzi was a distinguished professor emeritus at the Jacobs School. He was predeceased by his first wife, the singer Catherine Dieringer, in 1963. He is survived by his second wife, Monte Amundsen, a singer whom he married in 1967; their children, Eric and Jennifer; and three grandchildren. See *Current Biography* (1961). —M.R.

Obituary *New York Times* (on-line) June 2, 2011

TWOMBLY, CY Apr. 25, 1928–July 5, 2011 Artist. According to a tribute by Randy Kennedy for the *New York Times* (July 5, 2011, on-line), Cy Twombly's career "slyly subverted Abstract Expressionism, toyed briefly with Minimalism, seemed barely to acknowledge Pop art and anticipated some of the concerns of Conceptualism." Born Edwin Parker Twombly Jr. in Lexington, Virginia, the artist always used his father's nickname, given to Twombly senior when he was a major-league baseball player in the 1920s. The son, who had begun to paint in his early teens, enrolled at the Boston Museum School of Fine Arts in the late 1940s, but soon returned south to study at Washington and Lee University with the help of a Virginia Museum of Fine Arts scholarship. He took classes at the Art Students League in New York in 1950 and 1951, when his first solo exhibitions were held in New York and Chicago. At the league he met the painter Robert Rauschenberg. At Rauschenberg's suggestion he attended the avant-garde Black Mountain College, in North Carolina, where his mentors included the abstract painters Robert Motherwell and Franz Kline and the social realist Ben Shahn. He then left for a year abroad, living and working with Rauschenberg in Rome, Italy, and Morocco. After he returned from Rome, in 1953, a joint showing of Twombly's abstractions and Rauschenberg's work was held at the Stable Gallery, in New York. Although the show was attacked by both fellow artists and critics, two years later the Stable Gallery granted Twombly another showing, this time of his wall-scale, graffiti-covered canvases. In the early 1950s Twombly served for about a year in the U.S. Army. After receiving a medical discharge, he returned to New York, and he later took a short-lived post as the head of the art department at a small college in Virginia. In 1957 he moved to Rome, where he spent the rest of his life. In Italy he met Tatiana Franchetti, a portrait painter, whom he married in 1959. (She died in 2010). At first Twombly's works—for the most part untitled—were "named" for words or names seemingly present in the deceptively childlike scrawls of which they consisted: the names of Italian cities, his own signature and, occasionally, other half-obscured words. Later, male and female genitalia, numerals, and marks suggestive of actual architectural features or alluding to works of the old masters were added to his repertoire. Reverberations of the classical past mixed with mocking parody in paintings such as *The Second Part of the Return from Parnassus* (1961). In the early 1960s Twombly's "rapturous scribbling" (so termed by the *Time* critic Robert Hughes) became more agitated and was combined with blobs and streaks of oil colors often applied directly from the tube. A firming-up, a move from "a notation of passion to a notation of rationality"—as the 1983 Stephen Mazoh Gallery exhibition catalogue put it—came with the so-called gray paintings of 1967 to 1970. After 1971 the artist began to introduce collage more frequently into his work. The 1972 *Captive Island Collage*, for example, consists of a postcard picture of Florida veiled with crayon marks. *Narcissus* (1976) comprises pictures of the flower collaged on sheets of drawing paper and almost obliterated by the artist's scrawls. In 1977–78 he completed one of his most ambitious compositions, *Fifty Days at Iliam*, which was executed in oil paint, crayon, and pencil on canvas and measures 85 feet wide by 10 feet high. Twombly's way of painting often involved a direct physical handling of the medium: digging into paint with a pencil, crayon, palette knife, or the end of a brush and even drawing on a paint-covered surface with his fingernails. In 1994 the Museum of Modern Art (MoMA) in New York City mounted a career retrospective that met with great success, and early the following year the Menil Collection, a museum in Houston, Texas, opened the Cy Twombly Gallery to house an extensive permanent collection of the artist's work. Twombly remained productive even into the new millennium. At the 2001 Venice Biennale, he exhibited a piece called *Lepanto*, consisting of 12 panels of paintings inspired by the famous 16th-century sea battle of combined European forces against an Ottoman fleet. The following year he presented his first major exhibition in the United Kingdom in more than two decades. In 2005 a major retrospective of Twombly's art, titled *Cy Twombly: 50 Years of Works on Paper*, opened at the Menil Collection; it included 90 of Twombly's paintings and sculptures. In a review for the *Houston Chronicle* (May 29, 2005), Patricia Johnson observed that the retrospective seemed to highlight an ongoing debate over the merits of Twombly's work: "After awhile, Twombly comes to seem like a Rorschach test. One critic wrote that a careful reading of Twombly's images 'permits the viewer to penetrate an apparent chaos to arrive at inner silence.' Another called the pictures 'silly scribblings.'" In another example of an extreme reaction to Twombly's work, in 2007 a woman was so moved by his painting *Phaedrus*, which was displayed at France's Collection Lambert, that she kissed it, leaving a lipstick mark. Another major Twombly retrospective, *Cycles and Seasons*, opened at London's Tate Modern in 2008 and featured works from the previous 50 years. In 2009 Twombly was asked by the curators at the Louvre, in Paris, France, to paint a mural to be placed on the ceiling of one of the galleries there, making him the first American to receive such an honor. The 3,750-square-foot work, in the museum's Salle des Bronzes, was unveiled in 2010. Twombly died at his home in Rome after a long battle with cancer. He is survived by his son, Cyrus Alessandro (who is also an artist) and two grandchildren. See *Current Biography* (1988). —D.K.

Obituary *New York Times* (on-line) July 5, 2011

VERRETT, SHIRLEY May 31, 1931–Nov. 5, 2010 Opera singer. Shirley Verrett was sometimes referred to in the opera world as the "black Maria Callas." Her success is all the more impressive when one considers that throughout her career, which began at a time when racial relations in the United States were anything but harmonious, she was forced to deal with the inescapable reality of being an African-American performer in the almost exclusively white world of classical singing. She was born in New Orleans, Louisiana, to Leon Solomon Verrett, a building contractor, and Elvira (Harris) Verrett, both strict Seventh Day Adventists. All members of the family—including a sister and four brothers—were talented at singing or playing musical instruments, and some of their ancestors and relatives were New Orleans jazz musicians. Verrett had no formal voice training in childhood, but her father was a constant guide to her, and she sang in the church choirs that he directed. When Verrett was five years old, the family moved to Oxnard, California. At the urging of her father, who felt that her singing would be best pursued as a leisure-time adjunct to a less precarious livelihood, she studied business administration at Ventura College. After receiving an associate's degree, in 1951, she obtained a realtor's license and opened a real-estate office in Los Angeles. At the end of a year, her business was prospering, but she longed to pursue a music career. Verrett began voice training under Anna Fitziu, a former Metropolitan Opera soprano, and soon turned her full attention toward a singing career. In 1955, through contacts made by Fitziu, Verrett made an appearance on *Arthur Godfrey's Talent Scouts*, a network television show. Her singing caught the attention of Marian Szekely-Freschl, a noted voice teacher on the faculty of the Juilliard School of Music, in New York City. Verrett became a student of Szekely-Freschl and, with the help of scholarships and awards, remained at Juilliard for six years, receiving her diploma in voice in 1961. (Among her major patrons during her years of study was the musical-comedy composer Richard Rodgers.) During her first two years at Juilliard, Verrett's singing was confined to student recitals, opera workshops, and other amateur performances. Her first professional engagement was at the Antioch College Shakespearean Festival, in Yellow Springs, Ohio, in the summer of 1957, when she sang featured roles in Benjamin Britten's *The Rape of Lucretia* and Kurt Weill's *Lost in the Stars*. She sang in the Weill work in her New York professional operatic debut, with the New York City Opera at City Center in 1958. In 1960, when Leopold Stokowski returned to the podium of the Philadelphia Orchestra after an absence of 19 years, he chose Verrett as a soloist for the occasion. Her first appearance in the title role in *Carmen* was in a Gian Carlo Menotti production of the Bizet opera at the Festival of Two Worlds in Italy in 1962. The following year she toured the Soviet Union, where she received enthusiastic praise. After her return to the U.S., she made her American television debut, singing the "Habanera" from *Carmen* on the *Ed Sullivan Show*, a popular program to which she returned several times. Verrett made her Metropolitan Opera debut, as Carmen, in September 1968. She quickly grew disenchanted with that company and was reportedly often at odds with its general manager. Feeling that she was not being treated properly and that her talent was not being nurtured, she left the Metropolitan Opera after a single season. After performing with such companies as the Paris Opera and the San Francisco Opera, Verrett agreed to return to the Met in 1973 to appear in the five-and-a-half-hour, uncut version of Berlioz's *Les Troyens*. Before opening night the other female lead fell ill, and Verrett volunteered to play both roles—that of Cassandra in Part I and Dido in Part II—"a tour de force that entered Met annals," Anthony Tommasini wrote for the *New York Times* (November 6, 2010, on-line). When the La Scala company visited the U.S. in commemoration of the American Bicentennial, in September 1976, Verrett assumed the soprano

part in a performance of Verdi's *Requiem* at New York's Carnegie Hall. Soon afterward, in Boston, during a Met tour, she took over the soprano role of Norma (having previously sung the mezzo-soprano part of Adalgisa in that Bellini opera), becoming the first singer in the 20th century and only the third in opera history to have sung both roles and ranges. Verrett's albums include the hymn collection *How Great Thou Art, Precious Lord* (1964), *Seven Popular Spanish Songs* (1965), the folk/protest album *Singin' in the Storm* (1966), and numerous operas, including Gluck's *Orfeo ed Euridice*, Donizetti's *Maria Stuarda*, and Verdi's *Luisa Miller*. In 1994, having retired from opera, she made her Broadway debut, in Rodgers and Hammerstein's *Carousel*. In 2003 she published her autobiography, *I've Never Walked Alone*, taking the title from a lyric in *Carousel*. Verrett, who suffered from allergies that occasionally affected her singing, died of heart failure at her home in Ann Arbor, Michigan, after being ill for several months. She is survived by her husband, the artist Lou LoMonaco; her adopted daughter, Francesca; and a granddaughter. See *Current Biography* (1967). —D.K.

Obituary *New York Times* (on-line) Nov. 6, 2010

WAITZ, GRETE Oct. 1, 1953–Apr. 19, 2011 Runner. Grete Waitz is considered the preeminent female distance runner in the sport's history. Though she set world records for 3,000-meter (three-kilometer), eight-kilometer, 10-kilometer, 15-kilometer, and 10-mile races, she is best known for her astonishing marathon performances. She won nine New York City Marathons—setting three world records—along with two London Marathons, the Stockholm Marathon, and the world championship marathon. She was born Grete Andersen in Oslo, Norway, the youngest of the three children of John Andersen, a pharmacist, and Reidun Andersen, a grocery-store clerk. Growing up in an athletic family, Waitz became involved in sports early, starting with handball and moving on to gymnastics and track. Her potential as a runner was noticed by a neighbor, the Olympic javelin champion Terje Pedersen, who recruited her for his track team when she was 11. Running only sprints at first, Grete soon graduated to 400 meters. She quickly realized that her strong point was distance. In 1972 Waitz emerged without a medal from her first Olympic competition, the 1,500 meters, then the longest women's Olympic run. (Women had for years been excluded from competing in distance events; they were excluded from the Boston Marathon until Katharine Switzer participated in that event disguised as a man in 1967. Though women were not excluded from the New York City Marathon when it was inaugurated, in 1970, none finished the event until 1972.) In the 1974 European championships, Waitz placed third in the 1,500 meters, and the following year she set a record with her time in the 3,000 meters (three kilometers). She was eliminated in the semifinals of the 1,500 meters in the Olympics in Montreal in 1976. In 1977 she won the World Cup at 3,000 meters, and in 1978 she finished fifth in the 1,500 meters in the European championships, with a time of 4:00.6, just 0.6 seconds away from the bronze medal. When she was not running, Waitz worked as a teacher in Oslo public schools.

She was the oldest member of the Norwegian track team in 1978, when she was invited by the New York Road Runners Club to run in the New York Marathon. Waitz, who had never run more than 13 miles in training, looked at the race as something of a lark. Her strategy was to try to conserve her strength in the beginning while keeping up with the race's favorite, Germany's Christa Vahlensieck, and to hope for the best in the final miles. She followed Vahlensieck for the first nine miles before pulling out in front, completing the unfamilar course among a swarm of male competitors. Her time of 2:32:30, which put her in 88th place overall, was a new women's world record by over two minutes. Waitz returned to her teaching job in Norway but soon decided that the time and attention she devoted to running would shortchange her students. She quit teaching, with the intention of returning to it in the future, and focused on competing in distance races. She set numerous world records before returning to New York to run in the 1979 marathon, in which she broke her own record, with a time of 2:27:33, finishing 69th overall. Waitz did not compete in the 1980 Moscow Olympic Games (the Norwegian Athletic Federation had joined the U.S. in boycotting the events in protest of the Soviet invasion of Afghanistan), but she won the women's international cross-country championship for the third straight year; set new world records for five miles, 10 miles, 15,000 meters, and 20,000 meters; bettered her 10,000-meter mark by 15 seconds; and again finished first among women in the New York Marathon, with an improvement of two minutes and 25 seconds in her time. Her clocking in the 1980 marathon would have beaten all the men who finished in the 1970 marathon, including the winner, Gary Muhrcke, and all male Olympic marathon gold medalists before 1952. Waitz went on to win the race six more times, in the years 1982–86 and 1988. She ran her last marathon in 1992 with her friend Fred Lebow, the founder of the New York Marathon, who had been diagnosed with brain cancer; they crossed the finish line with clasped hands, with a time of 5:32:35. Waitz's accomplishments had a tremendous effect on the participation of women in distance running: in 1978, the year of her first marathon victory, 938 of 8,937 participants in the New York Marathon were women, and by 2010 there were 16,253 women out of 45,350 entrants. The women's marathon became an Olympic event in 1984, the year Waitz took home the silver medal. After retiring from serious competitive running, Waitz, who had become a national hero, lived a mostly quiet life. She did some coaching and took part in various charity events. She also established a five-kilometer race in Oslo, and in 2005, after being diagnosed with cancer, she started a foundation to sponsor runners and to support cancer hospitals and patients. Waitz died from the disease in Oslo; she is survived by her brothers and her husband, Jack. See Current Biography (1981). —M.R.M.

Obituary New York Times (on-line) Apr. 19, 2011

WILLIAMS, DICK May 7, 1929–July 7, 2011 Baseball player and manager. Dick Williams competed in the major leagues as a utility player for 13 seasons (every year from 1951 through 1964 except 1955) before making his mark as a Hall of Fame manager. Known for his hard-nosed demeanor and old-school approach to the game, Williams was one of only two managers in history to lead three franchises to the World Series and one of only seven managers to win pennants in both leagues. He won consecutive World Series titles with the Oakland Athletics in 1972 and 1973 and guided the Boston Red Sox and the San Diego Padres to the American League (AL) and National League (NL) pennants, in 1967 and 1984, respectively. Williams was born in St. Louis, Missouri, where his father, Harvey, worked as a plant protection manager. Williams and his older brother, Ellery (who played professional football briefly with the New York Giants), were avid baseball fans who attended big-league games regularly. At the age of 13, Williams moved with his family to California. Settling in Pasadena, Williams attended the high-school division of Pasadena Junior College, where he was a standout football, basketball, and baseball player. Forced to drop out of football due to a knee injury, he began focusing most of his energies on baseball, and during his senior season, he won a spot on the All-Southern California high-school baseball team. Williams signed his first professional contract, with the Brooklyn Dodgers, directly after his high-school graduation, in June 1947, and then honed his skills at Dodgertown, the organization's famed Florida-based training facility. He made his major-league debut with the Dodgers in 1951 but played only sparingly in his five seasons with the club (1951–54, 1956). Williams initially appeared as an outfielder, but a debilitating shoulder injury early in his career forced him to learn other positions, including first, second, and third base. As a result he was used mostly in a utility role during his subsequent major-league stints with the Baltimore Orioles (1956–57, 1961–62), Cleveland Indians (1957), Kansas City Athletics (1959–60), and Boston Red Sox (1963–64). During his 13-year playing career, Williams hit 70 home runs and posted a career batting average of .260 in 1,023 games. After retiring as a player, he immediately went into management and spent three seasons helming clubs in the Red Sox farm system before signing on to manage the organization's major-league club in 1967. That year Williams unexpectedly led the Red Sox, who had posted eight consecutive losing seasons, to the AL pennant, in large part by instilling a culture of hard work and dedication that stressed the importance of fundamentals. While the Red Sox lost to the heavily favored St. Louis Cardinals in seven games in the 1967 World Series, that season (now often referred to as "the impossible dream") was considered a major success for the team. Williams led the Red Sox to a fourth-place finish in the AL in 1968 and was en route to guiding them to a third-place finish the following year before being fired with nine games left in the 1969 season. After spending 1970 as the third-base coach for the Montreal Expos, he was hired to manage the Oakland Athletics. Working under the Athletics' colorfully eccentric owner, Charlie Finley, who had assembled a team of such talented superstars as Reggie Jackson, Bert Campaneris, Sal Bando, Catfish Hunter, Vida Blue, and Rollie Fingers, Williams guided the Athletics to consecutive World Series titles in 1972 and 1973; the team thus became baseball's first repeat champion since the 1961–62 New York Yankees. Williams resigned, however, after the 1973 World Series, in retaliation for Finley's seemingly frivolous meddling. Afterward, Williams was immediately signed by another famously meddlesome owner, George Steinbrenner, to manage the New York Yankees, but the deal was quashed when Finley insisted on receiving two leading Yankees' prospects as compensation. After a managing stint with the California Angels, now the Los Angeles Angels of Anaheim (1974–76), Williams moved to the NL to manage the Montreal Expos. He managed the Expos for five seasons, helping to lead them to the play-offs for the only time in their 36-year history in Montreal, during the 1981 strike-shortened season. Williams then managed the San Diego Padres for four seasons (1982–85), during which he transformed the team from perennial losers into NL pennant winners in 1984. In the 1984 World Series, the Padres lost to the Detroit Tigers in five games. Nonetheless, Williams joined the Hall of Fame manager Bill McKechnie as the only managers ever to take three franchises to the World Series. Williams's last managerial stint came with another chronic loser, the Seattle Mariners, a team he managed for three seasons, from 1986 to 1988. He finished his 21-season managerial career with a record of 1,571 wins and 1,451 losses and is among only seven managers to have won pennants in both leagues. After retiring, Williams served as an adviser and scout with the New York Yankees organization in the 1990s and 2000s. In 2008 he was inducted into the Baseball Hall of Fame as a manager. Williams, who penned the 1990 autobiography *No More Mister Nice Guy*, died at a hospital near his home in Henderson, Nevada, of an aneurysm. He is survived by his wife, Norma; three children; and five grandchildren. See *Current Biography* (1973). —C.C.

Obituary *New York Times* (on-line) July 7, 2011

WILSON, LANFORD Apr. 13, 1937–Mar. 24, 2011
Playwright. In a tribute to the Pulitzer prize–winning playwright Lanford Wilson published in the *New York Times* (March 24, 2011, on-line), Margalit Fox described his work as "earthy, realist, greatly admired, widely performed [and] centered on the sheer ordinariness of marginality." Lanford Wilson was born to Ralph Eugene Wilson and the former Violetta Careybelle Tate in Lebanon, Missouri. When he was five years old, his parents divorced. His mother later remarried, and Wilson moved with her to Ozark, Missouri, where his stepfather farmed for a living. After high school Wilson attended Southwest Missouri State College for one year. In order to live closer to his father, he then moved to San Diego, California, where he worked in an aircraft plant and studied at San Diego State University from 1956 to 1957. Relocating to Chicago next, he worked in the art department of an advertising agency and took classes at the University of Chicago. During that time he attempted unsuccessfully to sell short stories he had written, and he also became involved in theater acting and playwriting. In 1962 Wilson moved to New York City, where his one-act play *So Long at the Fair* was produced Off-Off-Broadway at Caffe Cino

in 1963. *The Madness of Lady Bright* premiered at that venue the following year, and its title character, an aging gay man, is often cited as a landmark in the theater world. (Wilson, who was gay, was widely credited with being among the first mainstream American playwrights to feature openly homosexual characters in their work.) *Balm in Gilead*, Wilson's first full-length play, was staged at La MaMa in 1965. It was a sensational success, with dozens of would-be ticket buyers turned away every night and the fire marshal threatening to close down the venue because of overcrowding. The play is set in a seedy all-night café in New York and concerns the interaction among the whores, pimps, junkies, and pushers of all races and sexual orientations who frequent the place. *The Rimers of Eldritch* (1966), about the physical and moral decline of a small midwestern town, was less of a popular success but won Wilson his first major critical prize, the Vernon Rice–Drama Desk Award for best Off-Broadway play of the year. In 1969 Wilson made his Broadway debut, with *The Gingham Dog*, which closed after only a handful of performances. That same year he co-founded the Manhattan-based Circle Theater Company, a collaborative effort of directors, actors, and playwrights. (It later became known as the Circle Repertory Company and was shut down in the mid-1990s.) *Lemon Sky*—Wilson's semiautobiographical play about his troubled relationship with his father—made its Off-Broadway debut in 1970 at the Studio Arena Theater in Buffalo, New York. "A memory play in content and form, *Lemon Sky* reminds us that Mr. Wilson is our primary heir to Tennessee Williams," Frank Rich wrote for the *New York Times* (December 12, 1985, on-line), in a review of a Broadway revival of the work. (The play later inspired a 1988 television movie of the same name, starring Kevin Bacon.) In 1973 *The Hot l Baltimore* appeared Off-Broadway, where it ran for nearly three years, won New York Drama Critics Circle and Obie Awards for best play, and even inspired a short-lived TV sitcom. In 1980 Wilson received a Pulitzer Prize for the 1979 play *Talley's Folly*. That drama was an installment of the Talley Cycle, Wilson's three-part saga of a Missouri clan, which touched upon the loss of idealism and the complexity of modern life. The trilogy also includes the works *Talley & Son* and *Fifth of July*, the latter of which opened on Broadway in 1980 with Christopher Reeve playing a gay paraplegic Vietnam veteran living in his childhood home. Other important plays written by Wilson include *Burn This* (1987), *Angels Fall* (1983), *Redwood Curtain* (1993), and *Rain Dance* (2002). Wilson is survived by his stepsister, Judy, and his two half-brothers, John and Jim. See *Current Biography* (1979). —J.P.

Obituary *New York Times* (on-line) Mar. 24, 2011

WINEHOUSE, AMY Sep. 14, 1983–July 23, 2011
Singer. Amy Winehouse was one of the leading young vocalists to emerge from Great Britain in recent years. Equally adept at singing soul, jazz, and R&B music, she was often compared to such legendary greats as Billie Holiday. Her lyrics (which include graphic descriptions of sex, love, abuse, and loss) made plain, however, the influence of hip-hop

on her largely retro style. Some listeners considered Winehouse—as pilloried in the tabloid press for her hard-drinking lifestyle as she was beloved by critics—the harbinger of a revival in British popular music. Winehouse was born in London and grew up in Southgate, a middle-class neighborhood a few miles north of Charing Cross. Her father, Mitch, was a cab driver, and her mother, Janis, a pharmacist. They divorced before she reached her teens. Though her parents were not musical, Winehouse had numerous musical influences while growing up: her mother's brothers were jazz musicians, and her paternal grandmother was reportedly involved in a relationship with the British jazz great Ronnie Scott. She was thus introduced at an early age to the songs of Ella Fitzgerald, Dinah Washington, and Sarah Vaughan, among others. Winehouse also became a fan of such hip-hop acts as Salt-n-Pepa and Nas. As a teen she attended the Sylvia Young Theatre School, in London, but she was expelled after only a year, reportedly for piercing her nose. She got a break when the British singer Tyler James, who had been a classmate, gave her demo tape to executives at his record label, Island/Universal Music. Shortly thereafter she was signed to a recording contract and received professional management. Winehouse's debut album, *Frank*, was released in the U.K. in 2003. That collection of songs, several of which she cowrote, reflected her interest in popular standards, jazz, soul, and hip-hop. British music fans embraced *Frank*, sending it to the upper reaches of the U.K. music charts. The album, which earned multiplatinum sales status in Great Britain, went on to be nominated for several honors, including two Brit Awards (comparable to the Grammy Awards in the U.S.) and the 2004 Nationwide Mercury Prize. That same year Winehouse's debut single, "Stronger than Me," won the Ivor Novello Award, given by the British Academy of Composers and Songwriters, for best contemporary song. While music critics were praising her debut album, other journalists (and music Web sites) were paying more attention to her rambunctious, alcohol-fueled public appearances. When representatives from her management company suggested she enter a rehabilitation facility, she refused and later parted ways with the company. "Rehab," a track on her sophomore release, *Back to Black* (2006), recalled that period of her life. (An oft-quoted line in "Rehab" is "They tried to make me go to rehab / I said, 'No, no, no.'") Inspired by the sounds of the "girl groups" of the 1950s and early 1960s, such as the Ronettes, *Back to Black* evoked the beehive hairdos and tail-finned cars of the era—while at the same time including a touch of modern R&B and soul. (Winehouse's physical appearance was also a mix of retro and modern: she was known for her towering beehive of dark hair, her heavy black eyeliner, and her many tattoos.) Following the release of *Back to Black* in the U.S., in March 2007, Winehouse received many positive reviews from American critics. In 2007 she married Blake Fielder-Civil, a fellow musician. Later that year her drug and alcohol problems led to a hospital stay, after which she canceled a string of tour dates, including a pair of concerts she was slated to open for the Rolling Stones. Despite such troubles, the following year she won five Grammy Awards, including one for best new artist. Wine-house divorced her husband in 2009, after a string of widely reported brawls and allegations of infidelity. She died in her London apartment at the age of 27, putting her in the so-called "27 Club." (Several other drug-addicted musicians, including Jimi Hendrix and Janis Joplin, also died at that age.) Much to the surprise of many journalists, her autopsy showed no illegal drugs in her system; rather, the level of alcohol in her blood was enough to kill her. She is survived by her father, mother, and brother. See *Current Biography International Yearbook* (2007). —D.K.

Obituary *New York Times* (on-line) July 23, 2011

WOOD, JOHN July 5, 1930–Aug. 6, 2011 Actor. John Wood, known for his precisely articulated delivery and perfect timing, was highly praised for his performances in such modern plays as *Rosencrantz and Guildenstern Are Dead* and *Travesties* and in such Shakespearean fare as *King Lear* and *The Tempest*. Wood was born in Derbyshire, England, to parents who were interested in the arts, especially music, and as a boy he spent much of his spare time hanging around local theaters and music halls. His father saved enough money to send him to a prestigious public school in Bedfordshire. A rebellious student, Wood ignored school regulations and often failed to show up for rugby practice, an infraction for which he was, by his own account, regularly beaten by the head boy—the future novelist John Fowles. After graduating, in the late 1940s, Wood was conscripted and sent to Officers Cadet School. Assigned to the Royal Horse Artillery, he advanced to the rank of lieutenant before he was granted a medical discharge following two almost-fatal freak accidents (one in an auto and one involving a gunshot). Returning to civilian life, he enrolled at Oxford University as a law student, but he was more interested in his extracurricular theatrical activities. His critically acclaimed performance in the title role of *Richard III* during his last year at Oxford brought him contract offers from several major repertory companies, including the Old Vic, which he joined in 1954; he left the company two years later. In 1957 he made his West End debut, as Don Quixote in Tennessee Williams's *Camino Real*. Largely because he refused to compromise his artistic standards, Wood's only stage credits over the next decade were the Wali in *Brouhaha*, in 1958, and Henry Albertson in *The Fantasticks*, in 1961. He supported himself by accepting a number of television roles that included Sydney Carton in *A Tale of Two Cities*, the title character in *Barnaby Rudge*, and leading parts in dramas by Anton Chekhov, George Bernard Shaw, and Arthur Schnitzler. When his career hit "rock bottom," to use his term, Wood met the idiosyncratic playwright Tom Stoppard, who was then just beginning to make his mark. Wood played leading roles in BBC-TV productions of Stoppard's short plays *A Separate Peace*, *Teeth*, and *Another Moon Called Earth*. He then tackled the part of Guildenstern in the Broadway production of *Rosencrantz and Guildenstern Are Dead*, in 1967, earning a Tony Award nomination for his efforts. He subsequently appeared in two Jerry Lewis film comedies, *One More Time* (1970) and *Which Way to the Front?* (1970). Back on the stage in England, he played Frederick the Great in Romulus Linney's historical drama

The Sorrows of Frederick and Richard Rowan in Harold Pinter's staging of *Exiles*, James Joyce's psychological study of friendship and marital fidelity. Wood reprised the role of Richard Rowan during his first season with the Royal Shakespeare Company (RSC), which he joined in 1971. His other first-year assignments were Yakov Bardin in Maxim Gorky's *Enemies*, the eponymous hero in the Restoration comedy *The Man of Mode, or Sir Fopling Flutter*, and Mark in Jean Genet's *The Balcony*. At Stratford-upon-Avon in the spring of 1972, he essayed his first Shakespearean roles since leaving the Old Vic. His portrayals of a slack-witted Antipholus of Syracuse in *The Comedy of Errors* and a demented Saturninus in *Titus Andronicus* delighted critics, but it was his electrifying characterization of Brutus in Trevor Nunn's staging of *Julius Caesar* that established his reputation as a classical actor. He assumed the title role in *Sherlock Holmes*, at the Aldwych Theatre in London in January 1974. Building on A. Conan Doyle's sketchy descriptions of Holmes, the actor created a character who was at once superior and vulnerable. His impersonation of a world-weary genius trapped by his own intellect contributed to the play's popularity in London and, later in the year, on Broadway. Critics on both sides of the Atlantic agreed that he was Holmes incarnate, and his portrayal garnered him another Tony nomination. While playing Holmes in repertory at the Aldwych, Wood began rehearsing one of the most complex and difficult roles of his career: that of Henry Carr, the senile poseur whose time-warped recollections provide the narrative of *Travesties*, Tom Stoppard's kaleidoscopic comedy about the relevance of art to society. When the play opened on Broadway, in 1975, critics highly praised Wood's performance, and he won a Tony Award for the role, which Stoppard had written specifically for him. Returning to London in 1976 for the RSC's new season, Wood performed in George Bernard Shaw's *The Devil's Disciple*, and the following year he starred in *Every Good Boy Deserves Favour*, Stoppard's look at the erosion of personal liberty under Communism, with music by Andre Previn. Having been granted resident-alien status by the U.S. government, Wood returned to New York in September 1977 to head an American cast in a production of Molière's comedy *Tartuffe*. On Broadway the following year, he originated the role of Sidney Bruhl in Ira Levin's comedic mystery *Deathtrap*, which ran for almost four years. Well before the show closed, having wearied of the tedium of a long commercial run, Wood returned to repertory in the National Theatre's 1979 productions of *Undiscovered Country* and *Richard III*. (He was replaced in *Deathtrap* by a series of actors who included Robert Reed and Farley Granger.) Late in 1981 Wood succeeded Ian McKellen as the composer Antonio Salieri (1750–1825) in the New York cast of Peter Shaffer's Tony Award–winning *Amadeus*. Wood returned to the RSC in the late 1980s and starred over the next few years in numerous plays, including Shakespeare's *The Tempest* and *King Lear* and Ibsen's *The Master Builder*. Wood also appeared in an occasional film, including Woody Allen's *The Purple Rose of Cairo* (1985) and Franco Zeffirelli's *Jane Eyre* (1996). His last stage role came in 2006, in Arthur Miller's *Resurrection Blues*, directed by Robert

Altman at the Old Vic. He was made a Commander of the Order of the British Empire the following year. Wood died in his sleep at the age of 81 and is survived by his second wife, Sylvia, and their three children: Rufus, Ghislaine, and Sibylla. He is also survived by a son, Sebastian, from his first marriage, to the opera singer Gillian Neason. See *Current Biography* (1983). —D.K.

Obituary *New York Times* (on-line) Aug. 6, 2011

YALOW, ROSALYN S. July 19, 1921–May 30, 2011 Biophysicist; Nobel laureate. In 1977 Rosalyn S. Yalow became only the second woman ever to win the Nobel Prize in Medicine. She was honored for her development (with Solomon A. Berson, who died in 1972) of radioimmunoassay (RIA), an ingenious application of nuclear physics in clinical medicine that makes it possible for scientists to use radioisotopic tracers to measure the concentration of pharmacologic and biologic substances in the blood and other fluids of the human body and in other animals and plants. Yalow and Berson invented the technique in 1959 to measure the amount of insulin in the blood of adult diabetics, and it was subsequently applied to scores of other medical problems. Yalow was born Rosalyn Sussman in New York City to Simon Sussman, the owner of a small paper and twine business, and the former Clara Zipper, neither of whom had finished high school. She obtained her early education in Bronx public schools and then entered Hunter College (now part of the City University of New York) in 1937, at a time when recent developments in nuclear physics had aroused great interest. In January 1941, when she obtained a B.A. degree with honors, she became the first woman to graduate from Hunter with a degree in physics. The following month she was accepted as a teaching assistant and graduate student in the College of Engineering at the University of Illinois, where she was the only woman in a class of 400 students. (It had not been easy for her to gain acceptance into a graduate program; a Purdue University administrator had reportedly written on her application, "She is from New York. She is Jewish. She is a woman.") She married Aaron Yalow, a fellow student, in 1943. While engaged in the research leading to her doctoral dissertation, she became highly adept at assembling apparatuses for the measurement of radioactive substances, a skill that she put to good use later as a medical physicist. She was awarded a Ph.D. degree in physics from the University of Illinois College of Engineering in January 1945. That year she returned to New York City, worked briefly in a research laboratory, and then taught physics to pre-engineering students at Hunter. In 1947 she obtained a position as a consultant to the Radiotherapy Service at the Bronx Veterans Administration (VA) Hospital. In that capacity she established and equipped one of the first radioisotope laboratories in the U.S. (Radioisotopes are tracer molecules, labeled or tagged with radioactive atoms.) In 1950 she left her teaching position at Hunter to devote her time to her work at the Bronx VA Hospital. That year Yalow had begun to work with Solomon A. Berson, who had just completed his residency in internal medicine at the Bronx VA Hospital. Utilizing Berson's training in clinical medicine, physiology, and anatomy and Yalow's background in mathematics and physics, the two researchers began a collaborative effort that lasted over two decades. They used radioisotopes to measure blood volume, assess the distribution of serum proteins in bodily tissues, and diagnose thyroid disease. They soon became interested in diabetes, and in the course of their investigations of the disease, they developed radioimmunoassay, a method that uses radioactive substances to measure minute substances—such as insulin—in blood plasma and other bodily tissues. Their work met with initial resistance because it challenged conventional wisdom, and scientific journals at first refused to publish their findings. Despite such skepticism, Yalow and her colleagues went on to use RIA to measure such substances as vitamin B12 and the hepatitis B virus, among many others. RIA, as Denise Gellene wrote for the *New York Times* (June 1, 2011, on-line), "invigorated the field of endocrinology, making possible major advances in diabetes research and in diagnosing and treating hormonal problems related to growth, thyroid function and fertility." In 1977 Yalow became the second woman to win a Nobel Prize in Medicine. (The first was Gerty Theresa Cori, who shared the prize with her husband, Carl, three decades earlier for their studies of human metabolism.) Berson had died in 1972, making him unable to share in the prize, which is not awarded posthumously. In addition to the Nobel, Yalow was the recipient of many other prizes, including a 1976 Albert Lasker Medical Research Award. A member of the National Academy of Sciences, she was, at the time of her death, a senior medical investigator emeritus at the Bronx VA Hospital and the Solomon A. Berson distinguished professor-at-large at New York's Mount Sinai School of Medicine. Yalow was predeceased by her husband, Aaron, in 1992. She is survived by her children, Benjamin and Elanna, and two grandchildren. See *Current Biography* (1978). —M.R.

Obituary *New York Times* (on-line) June 1, 2011

ZISKIN, LAURA Mar. 3, 1950–June 12, 2011 Film producer. As president of Fox 2000 from 1994 to 1999, Laura Ziskin was responsible for choosing stories and scripts and overseeing the production of up to a dozen films each year, including such successes as *No Way Out*, *Pretty Woman*, *What About Bob?*, and *As Good as It Gets*. She made a foray into the special-effects film genre in 2002, when she produced the first of the three movies in the *Spider-Man* series. Ziskin was born in California and has described her younger self as "a Jewish girl from the Valley." After graduating from the School of Cinema at the University of Southern California, in Los Angeles, in 1973, she began working in television, first as a scriptwriter for the series *The Dating Game* and then as a development executive. She subsequently entered the film industry, working as a production assistant on the films *A Star Is Born* (1976), starring Barbra Streisand, and as an associate producer for *The Eyes of Laura Mars* (1978). When she was about 27, Ziskin gave up her job to marry the writer Julian Barry. The couple moved to Connecticut, where, for the next few years, Ziskin helped raise Barry's three children from a previous marriage. By 1980 the couple had returned to Los Angeles, and soon afterward a producer hired Ziskin to evaluate potential scripts. In 1984 Ziskin formed a production company, Fogwood Films, in partnership with the actress Sally Field. The studio's first feature film was *Murphy's Romance* (1985). That was followed by several big successes, including *No Way Out* (1987), one of the first thrillers to combine sex and suspense, in which Ziskin cast the then relatively unknown actor Kevin Costner. The director Garry Marshall recruited Ziskin to be the executive producer for what was to become one of her most beloved films: *Pretty Woman*—the story of a prostitute (Julia Roberts) and a businessman (Richard Gere) who fall in love—which Marshall had been hired to direct. While fine-tuning the script for *Pretty Woman* with Marshall, Ziskin was responsible for a significant change in the last lines of dialogue that, in her view, kept the film from being patronizing to women. Early in the film Roberts's character tells the businessman that when she was young, she dreamed that a knight in shining armor would rescue her. In the scene that concludes the film, the Gere character climbs a fire escape to the woman's apartment. Ziskin recalled the scene, and the added line, to *People* (Spring 1991): "Richard says, 'So what happened when he climbed the tower to rescue her?' Julia says, 'She rescued him right back!' I didn't want a movie whose message would be that some nice guy will come along and give you nice clothes and lots of money and make you happy." Ziskin continued, "Those words at the end said these people changed each other." *Pretty Woman* became the second-highest-grossing film of 1990 and something of a classic romantic comedy. Ziskin conceived the stories for two of her projects— *What About Bob?* (1991) and *Hero* (1992)—in collaboration with the Academy Award–winning screenwriter Alvin Sargent. In 1994 she made her directorial debut, with a romantic-comedy short entitled *Oh, What a Day! 1914*, which was screened at the highly competitive Sundance Film Festival that year. Around that time Ziskin accepted the offer of Peter Chernin, the chairman of Twentieth Century Fox, to head Fox 2000, a newly created division. Fox 2000's first release was the Gulf War story *Courage Under Fire* (1996), starring Meg Ryan and Denzel Washington, which won both good reviews and solid box-office earnings. During the rest of Ziskin's tenure at Fox 2000, the studio produced a diverse array of films, including *One Fine Day* (1997), *Volcano* (1997), *To Die For* (1995), *As Good as It Gets* (1997), *The Thin Red Line* (1998), and *Fight Club* (1999). When Ziskin left Fox 2000, she joined Columbia Pictures. Soon afterward, although she had never before undertaken a special-effects-based movie, she produced *Spider-Man* (2002), starring Tobey Maguire as the Marvel Comics superhero. She later helped produce the two sequels to the blockbuster hit—as well as a third, "The Amazing Spider-Man," which is set for a 2012 release. Ziskin served as the producer of the annual Academy Awards ceremony in 2002 and 2007. After being diagnosed with breast cancer, in 2004, she became a strong advocate for cancer research and fund-raising. In 2008 she produced an hour-long telethon that raised some $100 million for the cause. Ziskin died at her home in Santa Clara,

California, from complications of the disease. She is survived by her second husband, Alvin Sargent, and her daughter, Julia Barry, from her first marriage. See *Current Biography* (1997). —M.R.M.

Obituary *New York Times* (on-line) June 13, 2011

CLASSIFICATION BY PROFESSION—2011

ACTIVISM
Ai Weiwei
Aronson, Jane
Assange, Julian
Badinter, Elisabeth
Banerjee, Mamata
Chan, Paul
Crenshaw, Kimberlé
  Williams
Drooker, Eric
Kan, Naoto
Rice, Constance L.
Smigel, Robert

ANTHROPOLOGY
Lieberman, Daniel E.
Mayor, Mireya

ARCHITECTURE
Ai Weiwei
Wenner, Kurt

ART
Ai Weiwei
Chan, Paul
Drooker, Eric
Everson, Kevin Jerome
Fiore, Mark
Franco, James
Tonner, Robert
Underworld
Wenner, Kurt

ASTRONOMY
Chang Díaz, Franklin

BUSINESS
Abagnale, Frank
Achatz, Grant
Bastianich, Joseph
Batali, Mario
Blankfein, Lloyd
Brûlé, Tyler
Braly, Angela F.
Buckley, George W.
Cain, Herman
Cam'ron
Carroll, Cynthia

Chang Díaz, Franklin
Cora, Cat
Denton, Nick
Dudley, Bob
Elsenhans, Lynn
Enders, Thomas
Fallin, Mary
Fieri, Guy
Gonzalez, Tony
Graff, Laurence
Haley, Nikki
Henderson, Fergus
Kullman, Ellen J.
Lampley, Jim
Lee, Sandra
Markell, Jack
McDonnell, Bob
Meyrowitz, Carol M.
Ming, Jenny
Pressman, Edward R.
Price, Lisa
Rice, Linda Johnson
Rogers, Desirée
Rosenhaus, Drew
Rosenthal, Jane
Schreiber, Ryan
Sen, Laura J.
Shinawatra, Yingluck
Taleb, Nassim Nicholas
Tonner, Robert

COMEDY
Brand, Russell
Maron, Marc
Smigel, Robert
Sykes, Wanda

CONSERVATION
Mayor, Mireya

DANCE
Millepied, Benjamin
Taylor, Janie
Wheater, Ashley C.

ECONOMICS
Duflo, Esther
Madrick, Jeff

Saez, Emmanuel
Sperling, Gene

EDUCATION
Abagnale, Frank
Abramson, Jill
Arnett, Jeffrey Jensen
Aronson, Jane
Badinter, Elisabeth
Barfield, Tanya
Brannaman, Buck
Breazeal, Cynthia
Chan, Paul
Crenshaw, Kimberlé
  Williams
Crossan, John Dominic
Doerr, Anthony
Dolan, Timothy
Duflo, Esther
Escoffery, Wayne
Everson, Kevin Jerome
Fuchs, Elaine
Gilyard, Keith
Gordon, Jaimy
Hayes, Terrance
Hertzberg, Hendrik
Hoagland, Tony
Horne, Gerald
Huybers, Peter
Lieberman, Daniel E.
Lipton, James
Madrick, Jeff
Malloy, Dan
Millepied, Benjamin
Milnor, John
Pennebaker, James W.
Pinsky, Drew
Rapp, Adam
Rosenwinkel, Kurt
Rubio, Marco
Saez, Emmanuel
Saks, Elyn R.
Schiller, Daniela
Smith, Charles
Verghese, Abraham
Volkow, Nora D.
Wenner, Kurt

Wilkerson, Isabel
Wood, Gordon S.

FASHION
Ghesquière, Nicolas
Tonner, Robert

FILM
Amalric, Mathieu
Ball, Alan
Brand, Russell
Cam'ron
Chan, Paul
Dardenne, Jean-Pierre and
   Luc
Desplat, Alexandre
Diggs, Taye
Drooker, Eric
Everson, Kevin Jerome
Fisk, Jack
Franco, James
Gordon-Levitt, Joseph
Gray, F. Gary
Lampley, Jim
Lipton, James
Logan, John
Lubezki, Emmanuel
Marling, Brit
McShane, Ian
Palast, Greg
Pressman, Edward R.
Rapp, Adam
Rosenthal, Jane
Rylance, Mark
Smigel, Robert
Sykes, Wanda
White, Randy Wayne
Williams, Saul
Yates, David

FINANCE
Blankfein, Lloyd
Nesbø, Jo
Taleb, Nassim Nicholas

GASTRONOMY
Achatz, Grant
Bastianich, Joseph
Batali, Mario
Cora, Cat
Fieri, Guy
Henderson, Fergus
Lee, Sandra

GOVERNMENT AND POLITICS, FOREIGN
Banerjee, Mamata
Enders, Thomas
Kan, Naoto
Machado Ventura, José
   Ramón
Shinawatra, Yingluck

GOVERNMENT AND POLITICS, U.S.
Bernard, Michelle
Brewer, Jan
Cain, Herman
Fallin, Mary
Haley, Nikki
Herbert, Gary
Hertzberg, Hendrik
Malloy, Dan
Markell, Jack
McDonnell, Bob
Rogers, Desirée
Rubio, Marco
Santorum, Rick
Sperling, Gene

HISTORY
Crossan, John Dominic
Doig, Ivan
Horne, Gerald
Meacham, Jon
Wilkerson, Isabel
Wood, Gordon S.

JOURNALISM
Abramson, Jill
Assange, Julian
Bernard, Michelle
Brûlé, Tyler
Brantley, Ben
Crowley, Candy
Cunningham, Bill
Denton, Nick
Doig, Ivan
Fiore, Mark
Gammons, Peter
Gleick, James
Gordon, Jaimy
Gray, Jim
Hertzberg, Hendrik
Kotb, Hoda
Kurtz, Howard
Madrick, Jeff
Meacham, Jon

Nocera, Joe
Palast, Greg
Pelley, Scott
Rice, Linda Johnson
Roach, Mary
Schreiber, Ryan
Stengel, Richard
Wallace, Chris
White, Randy Wayne
Wilkerson, Isabel
Yardley, Jonathan

LAW
Bernard, Michelle
Blankfein, Lloyd
Braly, Angela F.
Crenshaw, Kimberlé
   Williams
Horne, Gerald
Kan, Naoto
Malloy, Dan
McDonnell, Bob
Rice, Constance L.
Rosenhaus, Drew
Rubio, Marco
Saks, Elyn R.
Santorum, Rick
Sperling, Gene

LITERATURE
Banerjee, Mamata
Barfield, Tanya
Doerr, Anthony
Doig, Ivan
Drooker, Eric
Franco, James
Gilyard, Keith
Gordon, Jaimy
Hayes, Terrance
Hoagland, Tony
Kaufman, Moises
Lipton, James
Logan, John
Mitchell, David
Nesbø, Jo
Pearlman, Edith
Rapp, Adam
Russell, Karen
Shiner, Lewis
Smith, Charles
Verghese, Abraham
White, Randy Wayne
Williams, Saul
Yardley, Jonathan

Crowley, Candy
Gray, Jim
Lampley, Jim
Maron, Marc
Pinsky, Drew

RELIGION
Cain, Herman
Crossan, John Dominic
Dolan, Timothy

ROYALTY
Catherine, Duchess of
Cambridge

SCIENCE
Breazeal, Cynthia
Carroll, Cynthia
Chang Díaz, Franklin
Fuchs, Elaine
Gleick, James
Huybers, Peter
Kullman, Ellen J.
Lieberman, Daniel E.
Mayor, Mireya
Moffett, Mark W.
Roach, Mary
Schiller, Daniela
Volkow, Nora D.

SOCIAL SCIENCES
Arnett, Jeffrey Jensen
Gilyard, Keith
Horne, Gerald
Saez, Emmanuel
Saks, Elyn R.
Wood, Gordon S.

SPORTS
Barbosa, Leandro
Bautista, Jose
Beckett, Josh
Billups, Chauncey
Boxx, Shannon
Brannaman, Buck
Calhoun, Jim

Creamer, Paula
Drogba, Didier
Gammons, Peter
Gasol, Pau
Ginobili, Manu
Gonzalez, Tony
Gray, Jim
Grylls, Bear
Hamels, Cole
Hamilton, Josh
Harrison, James
Kane, Patrick
Lampley, Jim
Matthews, Clay III
McIlroy, Rory
Morneau, Justin
Rosenhaus, Drew
Sacramone, Alicia
Thompson, Tina
Tomlin, Mike
Tseng, Yani
Wakefield, Tim
Wambach, Abby
Washington, Ron

TECHNOLOGY
Assange, Julian
Breazeal, Cynthia
Chang Díaz, Franklin
Denton, Nick
Gleick, James
Markell, Jack

TELEVISION
Amalric, Mathieu
Ball, Alan
Bastianich, Joseph
Batali, Mario
Brûlé, Tyler
Brand, Russell
Cora, Cat
Crowley, Candy
Diggs, Taye
Fieri, Guy
Fisk, Jack

Franco, James
Gammons, Peter
Gordon-Levitt, Joseph
Gray, F. Gary
Gray, Jim
Grylls, Bear
Kaufman, Moises
Kotb, Hoda
Kurtz, Howard
Lampley, Jim
Lee, Sandra
Lipton, James
Logan, John
Lubezki, Emmanuel
Maron, Marc
Mayor, Mireya
McShane, Ian
Pelley, Scott
Pinsky, Drew
Price, Lisa
Rosenthal, Jane
Rylance, Mark
Smigel, Robert
Sykes, Wanda
Wallace, Chris
Williams, Saul
Yates, David

THEATER
Ball, Alan
Barfield, Tanya
Brantley, Ben
Chan, Paul
Cromer, David
Diggs, Taye
Gordon-Levitt, Joseph
Kaufman, Moises
Lipton, James
Logan, John
Malina, Judith
McShane, Ian
Rapp, Adam
Rylance, Mark
Smith, Charles

2011 INDEX

This is the index to the January 2011–November 2011 issues. It also lists obituaries that appear only in Current Biography Yearbook 2011. For the index to the 1940–2005 biographies, see Current Biography Cumulated Index 1940–2005.

Gasol, Pau Mar 2011
Ghesquière, Nicolas Jan 2011
Giles, Cameron *see* Cam'ron
Gilyard, Keith Oct 2011
Ginobili, Manu Apr 2011
Glasper, Robert Mar 2011
Gleick, James Jul 2011
Gonzalez, Tony Jan 2011
Gordon, Jaimy Jul 2011
Gordon-Levitt, Joseph Jun 2011
Gorecki, Henryk obit Yrbk 2011
Graff, Laurence Sep 2011
Gray, F. Gary Mar 2011
Gray, Felix Gary *see* Gray, F. Gary
Gray, Jim Jan 2011
Grizzly Bear Sep 2011
Grylls, Bear Oct 2011

Haley, Nikki Feb 2011
Hamels, Cole Nov 2011
Hamilton, Josh Apr 2011
Handlin, Oscar obit Yrbk 2011
Hannan, Philip M. obit Yrbk 2011
Harewood, George Henry Hubert Lascelles obit Yrbk 2011
Harris, Cyril obit Yrbk 2011
Harrison, James Nov 2011
Hatfield, Juliana Aug 2011
Hatfield, Mark O. obit Yrbk 2011
Hayes, Terrance Apr 2011
Haywood, Dave *see* Lady Antebellum
Healy, Bernadine P. obit Yrbk 2011
Henderson, Fergus Feb 2011
Herbert, Gary May 2011
Hernandez, Peter Gene *see* Mars, Bruno
Hertzberg, Hendrik Mar 2011
Hoagland, Tony May 2011
Hoiby, Lee obit Yrbk 2011
Holbrooke, Richard C. obit Yrbk 2011
Hondros, Chris obit Yrbk 2011
Horne, Gerald Sep 2011
Husain, Maqbul Fida obit Yrbk 2011
Huybers, Peter Apr 2011
Hyde, Karl *see* Underworld

Iverson, Ethan *see* Bad Plus

Jaroussky, Philippe Mar 2011
Jobs, Steven obit Yrbk 2011

Johnson, Jamey Feb 2011

Kahn, Alfred E. obit Yrbk 2011
Kan, Naoto Jul 2011
Kane, Patrick Feb 2011
Kaufman, Moises Aug 2011
Kelley, Charles *see* Lady Antebellum
Kevorkian, Jack obit Yrbk 2011
Kheel, Theodore W. obit Yrbk 2011
Killebrew, Harmon obit Yrbk 2011
King, David *see* Bad Plus
Kirch, Leo obit Yrbk 2011
Kirk, Claude R. Jr. obit Yrbk 2011
Knauer, Virginia obit Yrbk 2011
Kotb, Hoda Apr 2011
Kullman, Ellen J. Nov 2011
Kurtz, Howard Jan 2011
Ky, Nguyen Cao obit Yrbk 2011

Lady Antebellum Jul 2011
LaLanne, Jack obit Yrbk 2011
Lampley, Jim Oct 2011
Langham, Michael obit Yrbk 2011
Laurents, Arthur obit Yrbk 2011
Lee, Sandra Aug 2011
Levine, Jack obit Yrbk 2011
Lieberman, Daniel E. May 2011
Lipton, James Jul 2011
Logan, John Feb 2011
Lubezki, Emmanuel Jul 2011
Lumet, Sidney obit Yrbk 2011

Maathai, Wangari obit Yrbk 2011
Machado Ventura, José Ramón Sep 2011
MacNeil, Cornell obit Yrbk 2011
Madrick, Jeff Nov 2011
Malina, Judith Jun 2011
Malloy, Dan Jun 2011
Markell, Jack Jul 2011
Marling, Brit Oct 2011
Maron, Marc Nov 2011
Mars, Bruno May 2011
Matthews, Clay III Oct 2011
Maxwell Jul 2011
Mayor, Mireya Sep 2011
McDonnell, Bob Sep 2011
McDonnell, Robert F. *see* McDonnell, Bob

McDuffie, Dwayne obit Yrbk 2011
McIlroy, Rory Nov 2011
McShane, Ian Jul 2011
Meacham, Jon Jun 2011
Meyrowitz, Carol M. Nov 2011
Michele, Chrisette Apr 2011
Middleton, Catherine *see* Catherine, Duchess of Cambridge
Millepied, Benjamin Apr 2011
Milnor, John Jul 2011
Ming, Jenny Jan 2011
Mitchell, David Jan 2011
Moffett, Mark W. Oct 2011
Morgenstern, Emmanuel Lubezki *see* Lubezki, Emmanuel
Morneau, Justin Jun 2011

Nesbø, Jo Sep 2011
Nézet-Séguin, Yannick Nov 2011
Nocera, Joe Oct 2011
Nyrop, Donald obit Yrbk 2011

Ohga, Norio obit Yrbk 2011
Okonma, Tyler *see* Tyler, the Creator
Olsen, Kenneth H. obit Yrbk 2011
Otto of Austria, Archduke obit Yrbk 2011

Palast, Greg Jun 2011
Palast, Gregory *see* Palast, Greg
Payne, Chrisette Michele *see* Michele, Chrisette
Pearlman, Edith Jun 2011
Pelley, Scott Aug 2011
Pennebaker, James W. Aug 2011
Percy, Charles obit Yrbk 2011
Perez, Carlos Andres obit Yrbk 2011
Petit, Roland obit Yrbk 2011
Pinsky, Drew Feb 2011
Prendergast, John Barry *see* Barry, John
Pressman, Edward R. Feb 2011
Price, Lisa Feb 2011
Price, Margaret obit Yrbk 2011
Price, Reynolds obit Yrbk 2011

Qaddafi, Muammar Al obit
Yrbk 2011

Ramm, Carl *see* White,
Randy Wayne
Rapp, Adam Mar 2011
Rice, Constance L. Apr 2011
Rice, Linda Johnson Jul 2011
Ritchie, Dennis obit Yrbk
2011
Rivera, Gerald Maxwell *see*
Maxwell
Roach, Mary Jan 2011
Robertson, Cliff obit Yrbk
2011
Rogers, Desirée Jun 2011
Rosenhaus, Drew Jul 2011
Rosenthal, Jane Apr 2011
Rosenwinkel, Kurt Jul 2011
Ross, Robert obit Yrbk 2011
Rossen, Daniel *see* Grizzly
Bear
Roszak, Theodore obit Yrbk
2011
Rubio, Marco Apr 2011
Rubottom, R. Richard obit
Yrbk 2011
Russell, Karen May 2011
Rylance, Mark Nov 2011

Sabato, Ernesto obit Yrbk
2011
Sacramone, Alicia Mar 2011
Saez, Emmanuel Sep 2011
Saks, Elyn R. Feb 2011
Sandage, Allan obit Yrbk
2011
Santorum, Rick Aug 2011
Schaefer, William Donald obit
Yrbk 2011
Schiller, Daniela Mar 2011
Schreiber, Ryan Feb 2011

Scott, Hillary *see* Lady
Antebellum
Sen, Laura J. Oct 2011
Shalikashvili, John M. obit
Yrbk 2011
Shearing, George obit Yrbk
2011
Sheed, Wilfrid obit Yrbk 2011
Shinawatra, Yingluck Oct
2011
Shiner, Lewis Jul 2011
Shriver, R. Sargent obit Yrbk
2011
Silberman, Charles E. obit
Yrbk 2011
Smigel, Robert Nov 2011
Smith, Charles May 2011
Smith, Rick *see* Underworld
Snider, Duke obit Yrbk 2011
Solarz, Stephen J. obit Yrbk
2011
Sorensen, Theodore C. obit
Yrbk 2011
Sperling, Gene Apr 2011
Staats, Elmer obit Yrbk 2011
Stengel, Richard Jan 2011
Sterne, Hedda obit Yrbk 2011
Stewart, Ellen obit Yrbk 2011
Stott, John obit Yrbk 2011
Sykes, Wanda Jan 2011

Taleb, Nassim Nicholas May
2011
Taylor, Billy obit Yrbk 2011
Taylor, Chris *see* Grizzly Bear
Taylor, Elizabeth obit Yrbk
2011
Taylor, Janie Aug 2011
Thompson, Sada obit Yrbk
2011
Thompson, Tina Jan 2011
Tomlin, Mike Aug 2011
Tonner, Robert Oct 2011

Tooker, George obit Yrbk
2011
Tozzi, Giorgio obit Yrbk 2011
Tseng, Yani Sep 2011
Twombly, Cy obit Yrbk 2011
Tyler, the Creator Aug 2011

Underworld Nov 2011

Verghese, Abraham Nov 2011
Verrett, Shirley obit Yrbk
2011
Volkow, Nora D. Oct 2011

Waitz, Grete obit Yrbk 2011
Wakefield, Tim Sep 2011
Wallace, Chris Feb 2011
Wambach, Abby Mar 2011
Washington, Ron May 2011
Wenner, Kurt Sep 2011
Wheater, Ashley C. May 2011
White, Randy Wayne Nov
2011
Wilkerson, Isabel Oct 2011
Williams, Dick obit Yrbk
2011
Williams, Saul Jun 2011
Wilson, Gretchen Apr 2011
Wilson, Lanford obit Yrbk
2011
Winehouse, Amy obit Yrbk
2011
Wood, Gordon S. Oct 2011
Wood, John obit Yrbk 2011

Yalow, Rosalyn S. obit Yrbk
2011
Yardley, Jonathan Jan 2011
Yates, David Apr 2011

Ziskin, Laura obit Yrbk 2011